BUSINESS LAW
PRINCIPLES, CASES, AND POLICY

Second Edition

BUSINESS LAW
PRINCIPLES, CASES, AND POLICY

Second Edition

Mark E. Roszkowski
University of Illinois at Urbana-Champaign

Scott, Foresman and Company
Glenview, Illinois   London, England

To My Parents,
Stanley and Catherine Roszkowski

Library of Congress Cataloging-in-Publication Data

Roszkowski, Mark E.
  Business law: principles, cases, and policy / Mark E.
Roszkowski.—2nd ed.
    p.   cm.
  Includes index.
  ISBN 0-673-39927-3
  1. Commercial law—United States.   I. Title.
KF889.R68   1989
346.73'07—dc19   88-32130
[347.3067]   CIP

Credits
Figure 1–1 (from the *Federal Reporter*), Figures 21–1,
21–2, 22–1, 22–2 (adapted from *West's Legal Forms,*
Vol. 13, 2d ed.), Figures 31–1, 31–2 (adapted from
West's Legal Forms, Vol. 14, 2d ed.), Table 49–2
(adapted from Thomas L. Hazen, *The Law of Securities
Regulation*): Copyright © 1985 by West Publishing
Company. Reprinted by Permission.

Supplement to Appendix F: Reprinted from the *Model
Business Corporation Act Annotated (Third Edition)*
with the permission of Prentice Hall Law & Business
Copyright © 1988 by the American Bar Foundation. All
rights reserved.

Table 2–1: (adapted from Goldberg, Green, and Sander,
Dispute Resolution.) Copyright © 1985. Reprinted with
permission of Little, Brown and Company.

  2 3 4 5 6-RRC-94 93 92 91 90 89

Preface

The jurist Roscoe Pound once noted, "Law must be stable and yet it cannot stand still . . . . [The legal order] must be overhauled continually and refitted continually to the changes in the actual life which it is to govern."* This peculiar dichotomy of law—the need for stability and the need for change—poses special problems for the author of a business law textbook who desires not only to inform students of what the law is but also to assist them in anticipating what the law will be. Since publication of the first edition of *Business Law; Principles, Cases, and Policy,* courts, legislatures, and attorneys have continued the process of overhauling and refitting the law to accommodate rapidly changing business practices and commercial needs. This second edition of the text incorporates significant changes in the area of business law while retaining coverage of the basic rules and principles that provide the stability necessary for business planning and policy. Specifically, this edition retains the overall organization, chapter format, pedagogical features, and ancillary package of the first edition, and incorporates a number of important revisions and additions:

1. New cases—Forty-three new cases have been added to this edition to improve and update the case coverage of the first edition. Three-quarters of the new cases were decided since 1984, and over one-half of the new decisions were rendered in 1987 or 1988.

2. New discussion questions—To provide more complete coverage, almost seventy new chap-

ter-ending questions and problems have been added to this edition. These questions are based primarily upon recently decided appellate court cases.

3. Viewpoint essays—Most of the part-ending viewpoint essays are new or revised. These essays, which are authored by leading legal commentators, examine current and emerging legal issues.

4. New topic coverage and substantive law update—The entire text has been updated to reflect changes in the law since the first edition was written. In many instances, discussions have been expanded, rewritten, or reorganized to improve clarity or comprehensiveness. In addition, a number of important new topics have been added. Major changes or additions appear in the following chapters.

▪ Chapter 1. *Law and Courts* Expanded coverage of law and ethics.

▪ Chapter 2. *Civil Dispute Resolution* Greatly expanded coverage of alternative dispute resolution techniques.

▪ Chapter 4. *The Constitution and Business Regulation* Expanded treatment of the powers and role of administrative agencies in business regulation.

▪ Chapter 5. *Tort Law* Expanded coverage, including discussion of multiple defendants in tort actions, and additional coverage of important business-related torts such as false imprisonment and intentional interference with business relations.

▪ Chapter 9. *Contract Formation—Consideration* Updated coverage of the continuing controversy among the states regarding whether UCC §1-207 displaces the common law of accord and satisfaction.

---

*Pound, *Interpretations of Legal History 1* (1923).

■ Chapter 16. *The Sales Contract—Basic Obligations* An introduction to new UCC Article 2A, governing personal property leasing. The official text of Article 2A is included as part of the Uniform Commercial Code in Appendix B.

■ Chapter 20. *Products Liability* Substantially revised, including increased coverage of breach of warranty as a products liability theory, an update on the effect of comparative fault principles in strict products liability actions, and a new section on current trends in products liability.

■ Chapter 27. *Bank Deposits and Collections; Credit Cards and Electronic Fund Transfers* Substantially revised to include coverage of the Expedited Funds Availability Act and Federal Reserve Regulation CC.

■ Chapter 29. *Creditors' Remedies* Increased coverage of the now widely adopted Uniform Fraudulent Transfer Act, which is designed to replace the Uniform Fraudulent Conveyance Act.

■ Chapter 30. *Bankruptcy* Coverage of new Chapter 12 of the Bankruptcy Code, "Adjustment of Debts of a Family Farmer with Regular Annual Income," and adequate protection of secured creditors in reorganization proceedings.

■ Chapter 32. *Secured Transactions—Priorities* Coverage of repeal by federal law of the "farm products" exception contained in UCC §9-307(1).

■ Chapter 35. *Bailments, Documents of Title, and Letters of Credit* Expanded letters of credit coverage, which includes an explanation of the "standby" letter of credit.

■ Chapter 40. *Introduction to Agency* Expanded textual and case treatment of the employment at will doctrine and its many exceptions.

■ Chapter 49. *Securities Regulation* Revised and expanded to include additional coverage of state tender offer regulation and insider trading.

■ Chapter 51. *The Sherman Act* A new section discussing the controversial law governing termination by a manufacturer of one retail or wholesale dealer at the request of another or others.

■ Chapter 53. *Employment and Labor Law* Expanded treatment of the Social Security Act and Age Discrimination in Employment Act; Coverage of the Employee Polygraph Protection Act and the Worker Adjustment and Retraining Notification Act, both enacted in 1988.

■ Chapter 54. *Environmental Law* Coverage of the 1987 amendments to the Clean Water Act.

Ancillaries

Instructor's Manual (prepared by the author and Christie L. Roszkowski). The instructor's manual contains detailed teaching outlines, briefs of cases included in the book, and discussions of the questions and problems appearing at the end of each chapter. The manual is packaged in loose-leaf binder to facilitate its use in the classroom, and to allow the teacher to add materials.

Test Bank. The test bank contains over 3,200 items, and is available both in printed form and on disk for IBM PC.

Student Study Guide. The study guide includes multiple choice and true-false questions for individualized study and self testing. It assists the student in learning legal terminology, and reinforces the main points of each chapter.

Transparency Masters. The transparency masters include figures and tables adapted from the text and brief lecture outlines.

Acknowledgments

As with the first edition, I have been assisted in this revision by Christie L. Roszkowski, who selected and edited most of the cases and drafted discussion questions and text discussions. I also would like to thank the staff of Scott, Foresman Higher Education/Professional Division, and the following professors: Carey H. Kirk, University of Northern Iowa; John D. McBride, Wichita State University; W. Alfred Mukatis, Oregon State University; James L. Porter, University of New Mexico; John Thomas, State University of New York at Buffalo.

I further would like to acknowledge the contribution of the following professors who wrote or revised the part ending essays (viewpoints) for this edition: John C. Coffee, Jr., Columbia University; Thomas Donaldson, Loyola University; Richard A. Epstein, University of Chicago; Thomas H. Jackson, University of Virginia; James E. Krier, University of Michigan; Edward Rubin, University of California at Berkeley; and Gary T. Schwartz, University of California at Los Angeles.

Finally, I would like to thank Carol Halliday, who expertly typed all drafts of the revised manuscript.

Mark Edward Roszkowski

From the Preface to the First Edition

Business Law: Principles, Cases, and Policy is a comprehensive introduction to the legal principles governing business, the legal system within which business operates, and the role of the government in regulating business conduct. It is designed to provide comprehensive substantive business law coverage, coupled with the flexibility to adapt to the needs of many different educational institutions, their teachers, and students.

I decided to write this text because I perceived a need for a business law text that, standing alone, could teach difficult and complex topics in a clear and organized manner. The need for such a text is particularly acute in business law. Like other business law professors, I have inadequate class time to cover the numerous topics comprising modern business law and the legal environment. Accordingly, an ideal text must not only be able to reinforce and supplement principles developed in the classroom, but also must be written and organized so that teachers with limited lecture or class discussion time may cover topics through readings assigned from the text. An effective business law text also must be comprehensive, allowing the teacher to pick and choose among a variety of topics, to design a course or courses tailored to a particular curriculum and the needs of the particular students.

These goals and the following basic principles guided my approach to each topic:

1. The organization leads the reader logically through each subject by starting with basic definitions, concepts, and principles and then moving to more advanced applications and variation of the principles. This approach minimizes confusion, allows the teacher to choose the level of coverage, and permits efficient coverage of detailed topics.

2. The book carefully defines and explains the language of the law. Key terms are boldfaced where defined in the text and compiled in a list at the end of each chapter.

3. To enhance student understanding of complex topics, hypothetical examples and textual discussion of actual cases are used throughout the text to illustrate legal principles. In this manner, the student studies legal rules in the context of the fact situations in which they are applied.

4. The text explains not only the substance and derivation of legal rules, but also the rationale for, or policy behind, them. This approach, coupled with the liberal use of hypothetical examples, promotes student understanding and retention of the legal concepts and principles.

General Organization and Content

The text, which may be used in both traditional business law and legal environment of business courses, contains fifty-seven chapters organized into nine parts:

I Introduction to Law and the Legal System

II Contracts

III Sales

IV Commercial Paper

V Debtor-Creditor Relations
VI Property
VII Business Organizations
VIII Government Regulation of Business
IX Special Topics

Statutory appendices, a glossary, subject index, table of cases, and table of statutes are included at the end of the text.

Some of the unique or distinctive features of this text's coverage include the following:

1. Viewpoints at the end of each part written by scholars who comment upon selected emerging and current legal issues pertaining to that part of the text.
2. An introductory chapter explaining the constitutional framework of government regulation of business. This chapter provides the background for the detailed coverage of securities regulation, antitrust law, employment and labor law, and environmental law contained in Part VIII.
3. An introductory chapter briefly introducing property and the Uniform Commercial Code, topics important to a complete understanding of the following contracts, sales, commercial paper, and debtor-creditor chapters.
4. Careful integration of UCC contract material into the basic contracts chapters. This approach avoids needless duplication in coverage, and compares and contrasts Code and common law contracts principles on a topic-by-topic basis.
5. Detailed coverage of commercial paper including a separate chapter on liability of parties for forgery and alteration, and coverage of credit cards and electronic fund transfers.
6. Four separate chapters focusing on tort law: Chapter 5 (Tort Law), Chapter 20 (Products Liability), Chapter 41 (Agency and Torts), and Chapter 55 (Accountants' Liability). The products liability chapter explains the major theories of recovery, the development of the strict liability in tort doctrine, and its relationship to the law of warranty.

7. Comprehensive coverage of debtor-creditor law including government regulation of credit, creditors' remedies (including fraudulent conveyances and bulk transfers), bankruptcy, and the law of security (mortgages, secured transactions, and suretyship).
8. Extensive consumer protection coverage, including unconscionability and contracts of adhesion, fraud, warranty (including the Magnuson-Moss Warranty Act), Federal Trade Commission holder in due course rule, Consumer Credit Protection Act, consumer bankruptcy under Chapters 7 and 13 of the Bankruptcy Code, warranty of habitability in residential leases, and consumer protection under the Federal Trade Commission Act.
9. Comprehensive property law coverage discussing traditional real and personal property issues, intellectual property, land use regulation, and decedents' estates and trusts.
10. Extensive business organizations coverage including discussions of "at will" termination of employment, workers' compensation, and special problems of closely-held corporations.
11. Coverage of all topics tested on the Uniform Certified Public Accountants Examination, including accountants' liability, insurance law, and principal and income allocation.
12. A chapter devoted to international legal problems.

Chapter Organization

Each chapter begins with a listing of major topics and concludes with a summary of the principles covered in the chapter. Legal case excerpts are integrated into the chapters and questions and problems follow each chapter.

Cases

The cases are chosen to illustrate and reinforce important legal concepts discussed in the text. Some cases supplement textual material by explaining or developing the history or rationale for a legal principle. The cases are edited to retain the court's reasoning and policy, and the court's application of its holding to the facts of the case. The facts are summarized by the author in sufficient detail to give the reader a clear understanding of the events underlying the controversy. These features should facilitate using the cases for class discussion and promote student understanding. The cases represent a mix of classic and recent cases, and are drawn from both the state and federal court systems. Three-quarters of the excerpted cases were decided since 1975, and almost one-third of the decisions were rendered between 1982 and 1986. Appendix A contains a guide to reading the cases excerpted in the text.

Questions and Problems

Following each chapter are a series of questions and problems. Some of the questions review the basic concepts discussed in the text, whereas others expand the focus to address related subjects or issues not covered in the text. In many instances, the questions are based on actual court cases. Frequently, to facilitate discussion, events occurring in a number of actual decided cases are combined into a hypothetical fact situation. A question or series of questions then follows the statement of facts. These questions often ask the reader to change or add facts and consider the legal implications of the change or addition. As in the case excerpts, the facts are stated in sufficient detail to provide a basis for discussion and analysis.

Acknowledgments

I would like to thank the following professors, who reviewed portions of the manuscript. Their comments were very helpful and many of their suggestions have been incorporated into the text.

Don B. Allen, University of Rochester
E. Elizabeth Arnold, University of San Diego
Stanley R. Berkowitz, Northeastern University
Harvey Boller, Loyola University
Mark A. Buchanan, St. Cloud State University
Frank Chong, Southeast Missouri State University

Robert R. Criss, Auburn University
William H. Daughtrey, Virginia Commonwealth University
Vincent DiLorenzo, St. John's University School of Law
Debra Dobray, Southern Methodist University
Susan Gardner, California State University, Chico
Marjorie Girth, State University of New York at Buffalo
Leonard D. Goldberg, University of Washington
Jan Greenberg, University of Texas at Arlington
Vance S. Gruetzmacher, University of Wisconsin, Stevens Point
Ilse S. Hawkins, University of Cincinnati
Janine Hiller, Virginia Polytechnic Institute and State University
June A. Horrigan, California State University, Sacramento
Michael E. Howard, University of Iowa
Dugald W. Hudson, Georgia State University
Dan E. Huss, Miami University (Ohio)
Timothy W. Ihloff, North Texas State University
James M. Jackman, Oklahoma State University
Carey H. Kirk, University of Northern Iowa
Duane Lambert, California State University, Hayward
Paul Lansing, University of Iowa
Martin H. Malin, Illinois Institute of Technology
Gene A. Marsh, University of Alabama
David Minars, Brooklyn College
Leo C. Moersen, George Washington University
Donald W. Paule, Washington University
Mark Phelps, University of Oregon
Robert A. Prentice, University of Texas at Austin
Jordan B. Ray, University of Florida
Luis Rodriguez, Arkansas State University
Robert A. Schlifke, Indiana University, South Bend
Arthur Stelley, Indiana University, Bloomington
William S. Stewart, University of North Carolina, Chapel Hill
John M. Thomas, State University of New York at Buffalo
Joel S. Welber, Eastern Michigan University

Mark Edward Roszkowski

Contents

Chapter 9
Contract Formation—Consideration
191

Chapter 10
Capacity and Legality   215

Part Three
SALES   361

Chapter 16
The Sales Contract—Basic Obligations   363

Chapter 17
The Sales Contract—Title and Risk of Loss   380

Chapter 18
The Sales Contract—Remedies   395

Part Four
COMMERCIAL PAPER   *463*

Chapter 33
Suretyship 678

Part Six
PROPERTY 699

Chapter 34
Intellectual Property; Personal Property Ownership and Transfer 701

Chapter 35
Bailments, Documents of Title, and Letters of Credit   722

Chapter 36
Real Property Ownership   742

Guide to Reading Legal Case Excerpts

Case Format

Edited opinions of actual cases are reprinted throughout this text to illustrate how rules of law are applied to factual situations. The following information will help you understand the format of each edited opinion.

Name of Case

The formal name of the case is printed at the beginning of the case; for example, *Smith v. Jones, California v. Brown, Acme Corporation v. Motor Company*. Only the listed first party on each side is shown in the case name. For example, if Johnson and Green sued Banks, Inc., the case name would be *Johnson v. Banks, Inc.*

Sometimes the case name may include a procedural phrase. For example, ex rel. (meaning "on the relation of" or "on behalf of")may be used as follows: *California ex rel. Washington v. ABC Co.* This phrase indicates the state of California is acting on behalf of the party named Washington in a suit against ABC Co. Another frequently used phrase is *In re* which generally means "in the matter of." A case entitled *In re Will of Garcia* concerns a legal proceeding involving the will of Garcia. Bankruptcy cases also are prefaced with the term *In re*.

Citation to Legal Reporter (including court of decision and date)

Decisions of court cases are published in volumes known as reporters. West Publishing Company has developed a national reporter system of state and federal court opinions. Table 1 provides a list of the reporters (including the courts covered by each reporter).

All citations are listed in the same format: volume, abbreviated name of reporter, first page of opinion. Thus, for example, 377 P.2d 897 indicated the case is printed in Volume 377 of the Pacific Reporter, Second Series at page 897.

Following the citation, the court of decision and the date of the decision are listed in parentheses. For state court opinions, only the name of the state is shown if the decision was written by the state's highest court. If, however, the decision was rendered by an intermediate appellate court the abbreviation "App." (meaning Appellate Court) follows the state name. To illustrate, (Mich. 1986) indicates that the decision was rendered by the Supreme Court of Michigan in 1986. (Fla. App. 1975) indicates an opinion rendered by an intermediate appellate court of Florida in 1975.

For federal court cases, the name of the federal appellate court or district is listed with the date of decision in parentheses following the citation. United States Supreme Court cases show only the date in parentheses. For example, (2d Cir. 1982) indicates the decision was rendered by the federal Second Circuit Court of Appeals in 1982. (S.D.N.Y. 1964) means the decision was written by the federal district court for the Southern District of New York in 1964. Decisions rendered by a federal bankruptcy court list "Bkrtcy" and the federal district: (Bkrtcy., N.D. Ill. 1986) indicates an opinion written by the Bankruptcy Court for the Northern District of Illinois in 1986.

Summary of Facts and Prior Legal Proceedings

Following the citation, the facts underlying the dispute and a history of the proceedings in the lower court or courts are presented. This summary has been written by the author and includes the facts pertinent to the reprinted portion of the opinion.

Edited Court Opinion

The name of the judge who wrote the decision precedes the opinion. An ellipse (. . .) indicates that part of the decision or a citation to legal authority has been edited

| Table 1 | Coverage of National Reporter System | |

State Cases

Abbreviation	Reporter	Coverage
A. A.2d	Atlantic Reporter Atlantic Reporter, Second Series	Conn., Del., Me., Md., N.H., N.J., Pa., R.I., Vt., and D.C.
N.E. N.E.2d	North Eastern Reporter North Eastern Reporter, Second Series	Ill., Ind., Mass., N.Y., and Ohio
N.W. N.W.2d	North Western Reporter North Western Reporter, Second Series	Iowa, Mich., Minn., Neb., N.D., S.D., and Wis.
P. P.2d	Pacific Reporter Pacific Reporter, Second Series	Alaska, Ariz., Cal., Colo., Hawaii, Idaho, Kan., Mont., Nev., N.M.,Okla., Or., Utah, Wash., and Wyo.
S.E. S.E.2d	South Eastern Reporter South Eastern Reporter, Second Series	Ga., N.C., S.C., Va., and W.Va.
S.W. S.W.2d	South Western Reporter South Western Reporter, Second Series	Ark., Ky., Mo., Tenn., and Tex.
So. So.2d	Southern Reporter Southern Reporter, Second Series	Ala., Fla., La., and Miss.
Cal. Rptr.	California Reporter	California Supreme Court and Intermediate Appellate Courts
N.Y.S. N.Y.S.2d	New York Supplement New York Supplement, Second Series	All New York state courts

or deleted. Brackets ([]) indicate material inserted by the author.

Disposition

At the conclusion of the opinion, the court's disposition of the case usually is stated in brackets. "Affirmed" means the court has upheld the decision of the lower court. "Reversed" indicates that the lower court's decision was voided. "Remanded" means the case was sent back to a lower court.

Studying a Case

Analyze each case to ensure that you understand its ruling. Every student develops a method of analyzing a case but that analysis at least should include consideration of the following factors.

1. What is the legal issue presented to the court? The facts present a question of law to the court and you should identify this issue.

2. What is the holding of the case? In other words, what is the court's conclusion of law that resolves the issue? The court's holding determines the legal effect of the facts of the case.

3. What is the court's reasoning? Most of the edited opinions include the court's explanation of the reasons for reaching its holding. In some cases the judge will comment on some rule of law that is not necessarily involved in, or essential to the determination of, the case under consideration. Or, the court may enunciate a legal

Table 1   (continued)

Federal Cases

Abbreviation	*Reporter*	*Coverage*
S.Ct.	Supreme Court Reporter	U.S. Supreme Court
F. F.2d	Federal Reporter Federal Reporter, Second Series	U.S. Circuit Courts of Appeals*
F.Supp.	Federal Supplement	U.S. District Courts*
B.R.	Bankruptcy Reporter	Bankruptcy cases from U.S. Bankruptcy Courts and other federal courts
F.R.D.	Federal Rules Decisions	U.S. District Courts
Cl.Ct.	Claims Court Reporter	U.S. Claims Court and other federal courts reviewing claims court decisions
M.J.	Military Justice Reporter	United States Court of Military Appeals; courts of military review

*Reporter also covers other federal courts but no cases from these courts are reprinted in the text.

principle or rule for purposes of illustration, analogy, or argument. These comments are known as *dicta* (from the Latin *obiter dictum* meaning "a remark by the way"). Although *dicta* is not part of the court's holding, it may provide insight into the court's reasoning.

4. What is the effect of the court's holding on the factual controversy under review? Consider how the rule of law resolves the factual dispute and determine which party won the case.

Read the following case. At the conclusion, the case is analyzed in the manner suggested above.

E. I. duPont deNemours & Company, Inc. v. Christopher
431 F.2d 1012 (5th Cir. 1970)

Plaintiff E. I. duPont deNemours & Company, Inc. (DuPont) was constructing a plant for production of meth-

anol in Beaumont, Texas. After DuPont employees noticed an airplane circling over the construction site, DuPont investigated and discovered that defendants Rolfe and Gary Christopher were taking aerial photographs of the site. The Christophers told DuPont that they had been hired to take the photographs but refused to disclose their client's name.

DuPont sued the Christophers alleging that they had wrongfully appropriated DuPont's trade secrets by taking the photographs. DuPont claimed that it had developed a secret process for producing methanol and that photographs of the construction site would enable a skilled person to deduce the secret process. The Christophers alleged that under Texas law, photographing the construction site did not constitute wrongful appropriation of trade secrets based on the facts alleged by DuPont. Prior to holding a trial or further proceedings, the trial court allowed the Christophers to appeal the ruling.

Goldberg, Circuit Judge

. . . The question . . . is whether aerial photography of plant construction is an improper means of obtaining another's trade secret. We conclude that it is and that the Texas courts would so hold. . . .

We think . . . that the Texas rule is clear. One may use his competitor's secret process if he discovers the process by reverse engineering applied to the finished product; one may use a competitor's process if he discovers it by his own independent research; but one may not avoid these labors by taking the process from the discoverer without his permission at a time when he is taking reasonable precautions to maintain its secrecy. To obtain knowledge of a process without spending the time and money to discover it independently is *improper* unless the holder voluntarily discloses it or fails to take reasonable precautions to ensure its secrecy.

In the instant case the Christophers deliberately flew over the DuPont plant to get pictures of a process which DuPont had attempted to keep secret. The Christophers delivered their pictures to a third party who was certainly aware of the means by which they had been acquired and who may be planning to use the information contained therein to manufacture methanol by the DuPont process. The third party has a right to use this process only if he obtains this knowledge through his own research efforts, but thus far all information indicates that the third party has gained this knowledge solely by taking it from DuPont at a time when DuPont was making reasonable efforts to preserve its secrecy. In such a situation DuPont has a valid cause of action to prohibit the Christophers from improperly discovering its trade secret and to prohibit the undisclosed third party from using the improperly obtained information. . . .

In taking this position we realize that industrial espionage of the sort here perpetrated has become a popular sport in some segments of our industrial community. However, our devotion to free wheeling industrial competition must not force us into accepting the law of the jungle as the standard of morality expected in our commercial relations. Our tolerance of the espionage game must cease when the protections required to prevent another's spying cost so much that the spirit of inventiveness is dampened. Commercial privacy must be protected from espionage which could not have been reasonably anticipated or prevented. We do not mean to imply, however, that everything not in plain view is within the protected vale, nor that all information obtained through every extra optical extension is forbidden. Indeed, for our industrial competition to remain healthy there must be breathing room for observing a competing industrialist. A competitor can and must shop his competition for pricing and examine his products for quality, components, and methods of manufacture. Perhaps ordinary fences and roofs must be built to shut out incursive eyes, but we need not require the discoverer of a trade secret to guard against the unanticipated, the undetectable, or the unpreventable methods of espionage now available.

In the instant case DuPont was in the midst of constructing a plant. Although after construction the finished plant would have protected much of the process from view, during the period of construction the trade secret was exposed to view from the air. To require DuPont to put a roof over the unfinished plant to guard its secret would impose an enormous expense to prevent nothing more than a school boy's trick. We introduce here no new or radical ethic since our ethos has never given moral sanction to piracy. The market place must not deviate far from our mores. We should not require a person or corporation to take unreasonable precautions to prevent another from doing that which he ought not do in the first place. Reasonable precautions against predatory eyes we may require, but an impenetrable fortress is an unreasonable requirement, and we are not disposed to burden industrial inventors with such a duty in order to protect the fruits of their efforts. "Improper" will always be a word for many nuances, determined by time, place, and circumstances. We therefore need not proclaim a catalogue of commercial improprieties. Clearly, however, one of its commandments does say "thou shall not appropriate a trade secret through deviousness under circumstances in which countervailing defenses are not reasonably available." . . .

[T]he espionage was an improper means of discovering DuPont's trade secret.

[Judgment affirmed and remanded for further proceedings.]

---

1. Issue: Whether aerial photography of a plant under construction is an improper means of obtaining trade secrets.

2. Holding: Aerial photography of a plant under construction is an improper means of obtaining trade secrets.

3. Reasoning: Trade secrets properly may be obtained by reverse engineering or independent research. Other methods of obtaining trade secrets are improper unless the holder voluntarily discloses the secrets or fails to take reasonable precautions to ensure secrecy. To protect the spirit of inventiveness, holders of trade secrets must be protected from industrial espionage not reasonably anticipated or prevented.

4. Effect: Judgment for plaintiff DuPont affirmed. DuPont took reasonable efforts to preserve the secrecy of its methanol production method; therefore, third parties were not entitled to take aerial photographs of the site. DuPont may prohibit the defendants Rolfe and Gary Christopher from taking photographs of its plant and from disclosing the information to third parties.

Part One

INTRODUCTION TO LAW AND THE LEGAL SYSTEM

News stories about business and the law frequently appear in magazines, newspapers, and on television. Billion dollar mergers of multinational corporations, criminal investigations of insider trading in the securities industry, bribery of business and government officials to secure important contracts, million dollar judgments awarded to parties injured by defective manufactured goods, and industry-wide work stoppages caused by striking employees have captured headlines and the public interest in recent years. Unfortunately, many people conceive of business law only in terms of such extraordinary cases. Although controversial or newsworthy court actions do raise complex and interesting issues, they also contribute to a conception of business law as a discipline largely removed from the everyday lives of individuals. In fact, however, business laws shape every stage of commercial enterprise

and every relationship between commercial actors. Whether involved in marketing, accounting, finance, or administration, business managers rely every day upon the intricate framework of the law. The study of that intricate framework initially requires an understanding of the nature and sources of law and the workings of the court system.

Introduction to Law and Business Law

In its most basic sense, **law** is the body of rules and principles of conduct that are enforceable through sanctions. Within every society, rules of conduct have evolved to maintain harmony and order. In more primitive societies these rules consist only of customs and norms that are enforceable through informal social sanctions. As societies increase in size and complexity, however, rules of conduct become formalized, usually through a government that adopts and enforces the rules for the society. The law of the United States, for example, consists of rules and principles of conduct that are enacted or adopted by the government, and are embodied in constitutions, statutes, and judicial decisions.

Although law preserves peace and stability, thus allowing members of society to pursue economic and social activities, it is ineffectual unless the society also develops a **legal system**—institutions and processes for enforcing the law. In the United States, the legal system consists primarily of the courts, which are a part of the government. The courts serve two important functions: they provide a forum and process by which those who fail to conform to the law are punished by the government and they provide a system to resolve disputes among private individuals who cannot agree upon proper rules of conduct. In performing these functions, the courts apply rules of law previously established by the government or, in the absence of such rules, develop new legal principles to maintain order. Once a court renders a decision it has the power, with the backing of the government, to force compliance. Courts thus impose sanctions against those who fail to follow legal rules. The threat of these sanctions usually is sufficient to induce compliance with the law.

Law and Business

In the United States, the law governs the conduct of all persons including **artificial persons** (such as corporations) as well as **natural persons** (human beings). Because businesses are considered persons and, thus, members of society, many of the legal rules and principles affecting business are merely general laws that affect all persons. For example, the rights and duties of a property owner are established by general property law whether the property is a factory owned by a business or a private residence owned by an individual. The principles of contract law enable both individuals and businesses to rely upon agreements—for example, to purchase a home or raw material for manufacturing—by providing a private legal remedy to persons injured by another's failure to perform an agreement. Other legal rules have been established specifically to govern the conduct of businesses and business relationships. The securities laws regulate the sale and trading of the stocks and bonds issued only by businesses. Antitrust laws enacted to protect competition affect only those in business.

Law both restricts and facilitates business operations. Some laws, such as those prohibiting price fixing or requiring a safe workplace, clearly limit business practices. In contrast, other legal rules are designed to facilitate or encourage business activities. Few businesses, for example, could operate without reliable and enforceable principles of contract law that allow the sale, purchase, and exchange of goods and services. Businesses would

not invest in plant and equipment without the assurance that their property rights in these items will be protected by law. Moreover, legal principles of corporate law and agency have enabled businesses to expand and achieve efficiencies of scale.

Although American law clearly affects the operation of businesses, business also influences the development of the law. For instance, the law of negligence developed initially to provide compensation for injuries resulting indirectly from the emergence of a modern, industrialized society. Entire new areas of law—such as antitrust, securities regulation, and environmental law—have been created in response to changing business activities. As businesses increased production of goods, the law of products liability developed to determine whether manufacturers and distributors should be responsible for injuries caused by their products. In short, business and law engage in a dynamic process, each shaping and influencing the development of the other.

Law and Ethics

Despite the law's importance of a source of rules of conduct, few societies could function effectively if they depended solely on law as a basis for social conduct. The morals—principles of right, good, and fairness—of individual members of a society provide a more informal and pervasive basis for standards of conduct. From norms, beliefs, and values, individuals develop ethics, systems of moral standards and beliefs, that address the most fundamental issues of social conduct such as honesty, loyalty, fair treatment of others, and respect for human life and dignity. Like law, ethics provide standards of conduct for individuals. Unlike law, however, ethics are not imposed or enforced by an external authority such as the government. Rather, ethical standards derive from an individual's internalized moral principles and are applied by the individual. Thus, through law society imposes and enforces legal standards of conduct applicable to all of its members while through ethics an individual develops and applies his or her own moral standards of conduct. The purpose of law then is to govern the conduct of all members of society while ethics provide guidance for individual conduct.

Although law and ethics derive from different

authorities and for different purposes, they often are related, especially in a democratic society like the United States in which the people are the source of power. Law generally reflects basic moral principles shared by members of its society because people will not long comply with a body of rules that they consider wrong or evil. Thus, a law prohibiting murder not only preserves order but also reflects a widely held ethical belief that human life should be protected. In other cases, however, legal rules are morally neutral—for example, the law's requirement that all vehicles be driven on the right side of the road. In still other cases, the law may partially reflect moral principles but may not fully incorporate an ethical standard as the legal standard. Most people would agree, for example, that lying is immoral but under American law, lying is illegal only in limited circumstances, such as when it constitutes perjury or fraud. Similarly, most individuals believe that it is unethical to break promises, but American law enforces only those promises that meet the requirements of a legal contract. In the following excerpt,[1] Oliver Wendell Holmes, Jr., noted legal philosopher, and Associate Justice of the United States Supreme Court from 1902–1932, articulates his view of the distinction between law and morals.

> The first thing for a business-like understanding of the [law] is to understand its limits, and therefore I think it desirable at once to point out and dispel a confusion between morality and law. . . . You can see very plainly that a bad man has as much reason as a good one for wishing to avoid an encounter with the public force, and therefore you can see the practical importance of the distinction between morality and law. A man who cares nothing for an ethical rule which is believed and practised by his neighbors is likely nevertheless to care a good deal to avoid being made to pay money, and will want to keep out of jail if he can.
>
> I take it for granted that no hearer of mine will misinterpret what I have to say as the language of cynicism. The law is the witness and external

deposit of our moral life. Its history is the history of the moral development of the race. The practice of it, in spite of popular jests, tends to make good citizens and good men. When I emphasize the difference between law and morals I do so with reference to a single end, that of learning and understanding the law. . . .

> If you want to know the law and nothing else, you must look at it as a bad man, who cares only for the material consequences which such knowledge enables him to predict, not as a good one, who finds his reasons for conduct, whether inside the law or outside of it, in the vaguer sanctions of conscience. . . . The law is full of phraseology drawn from morals, and by the mere force of language continually invites us to pass from one domain to the other without perceiving it, as we are sure to do unless we have the boundary constantly before our minds. The law talks about rights, and duties, and malice, and intent, and negligence, and so forth, and nothing is easier, or I may say, more common in legal reasoning, than to take these words in their moral sense, at some stage of the argument, and so to drop into fallacy. For instance, when we speak of the rights of man in a moral sense, we mean to mark the limits of interference with individual freedom which we think are prescribed by conscience, or by our ideal, however reached. Yet it is certain that many laws have been enforced in the past, and it is likely that some are enforced now, which are condemned by the most enlightened opinion of the time, or which at all events pass the limit of interference as many consciences would draw it. Manifestly, therefore, nothing but confusion of thought can result from assuming that the rights of man in a moral sense are equally rights in the sense of the Constitution and the law. No doubt simple and extreme cases can be put of imaginable laws which the statute-making power would not dare to enact, even in the absence of written constitutional prohibitions, because the community would rise in rebellion and fight; and this gives some plausibility to the proposition that the law, if not a part of morality, is limited by it. But this limit of power is not coextensive with any system of morals. For the most part it falls far within the lines of any such system, and in some cases may extend beyond them,

---

1. Holmes, The Path of the Law, 10 Harv. L. Rev. 457, 459–460 (1897).

for reasons drawn from the habits of a particular people at a particular time. . . .

The distinction between law and morals is especially important in studying business law because historically businesses often have used legal standards as the sole basis for determining appropriate social conduct. This perspective is reflected in the following statement by the chief executive of a company accused of using a cheap—and possibly harmful—form of alcohol in manufacturing mouthwash:

> We broke no law. We're in a highly competitive industry. If we're going to stay in business, we have to look for profit wherever the law permits. We don't make the laws. We obey them. Then why do we have to put up with this "holier than thou" talk about ethics? It's sheer hypocrisy. We're not in business to promote ethics. Look at the cigarette companies, for God's sake! If the ethics aren't embodied in the laws by the men who made them, you can't expect businessmen to fill the lack. Why, a sudden submission to Christian ethics by businessmen would bring about the greatest economic upheaval in history![2]

As suggested by this quotation, many businesspeople believe that establishing ethical standards is the responsibility not of businesses but of the government through its power to make laws. Others believe ethical matters are beyond the scope of business decisions, arguing instead that the common good is best served by strict adherence to the free market theory of competition. This viewpoint was expressed by economist Milton Friedman as follows:

> The view has been gaining widespread acceptance that corporate officials and labor leaders have a "social responsibility" that goes beyond serving the interest of their stockholders or their members. This view shows a fundamental misconception of the character and nature of a free economy. In such an economy, there is one and only one social responsibility of business—to use its resources and engage in activities designed to increase its profits so long as it stays within the rules of the game, which is to say, engages in open and free competition, without deception or fraud. . . . Few trends could so thoroughly undermine the very foundations of our free society as the acceptance by corporate officials of a social responsibility other than to make as much money for their stockholders as possible.[3]

More recently, however, as businesses have grown in both size and influence, many people recognize that businesses are social as well as economic entities. This dual economic and social aspect of business is especially evident in large corporations whose conduct affects not only shareholders but also suppliers, customers, consumers, employees and sometimes even entire communities. In contrast to the position articulated by Milton Friedman, many people now suggest that businesses, which operate as distinct, but artificial persons, have the same obligations as natural persons to develop and apply ethical standards. Professors Kenneth E. Goodpaster and John B. Matthews, Jr., of the Harvard Business School summarize this point of view as follows:

> A corporation can and should have a conscience. The language of ethics does have a place in the vocabulary of an organization. . . . Organizational agents such as corporations should be no more and no less morally responsible (rational, self-interested, altruistic) than ordinary persons. . . . Legal systems of rules and incentives are insufficient, even though they may be necessary, as frameworks for corporate responsibility. Taking conceptual cues from the features of moral responsibility normally expected of the person in our opinion deserves practicing managers' serious consideration.[4]

---

2. Carr, "Is Business Bluffing Ethical?", *Harv. Bus. Rev.*, 143, 148, January/February 1968.

3. Friedman, *Capitalism and Freedom* 133 (1962).

4. Goodpaster and Matthews, "Can a Corporation Have a Conscience?", *Harv. Bus. Rev.* 132, 133, 138, January/February 1982.

In the wake of several well-publicized business scandals during the 1980s, businesspeople increasingly have considered not only the legal but also the moral responsibilities of businesses but no clear consensus on the issue has emerged.

Even businesses that acknowledge an obligation to act ethically or morally have had difficulty in developing and implementing procedures to meet this obligation. Part of the difficulty stems from a growing realization that moral issues can arise from all aspects of business operations. Traditionally, discussion of business ethics was restricted to topics such as deceptive advertising, honesty in contract negotiations, and bribery. Today, however, issues relating to the moral responsibilities of business extend from marketing decisions—such as the ethics of selling dangerous products—to personnel matters—including the fairness of hiring and firing practices and conditions in the workplace—to financial affairs—such as ethical issues arising from mergers and acquisitions—to the firm's relationship to the community in which it operates—including damage to the environment or the disruptions created by plant closings or relocation of operations. In short, almost all business decisions, but especially those with uncertain and extended consequences that affect many individuals, other organizations and even government operations, can present significant ethical questions.

To determine appropriate business conduct for decisions not guided by a legal standard, some persons have advocated the adoption of a business code of ethics, similar to those used by professionals, such as attorneys, physicians, and engineers. Although no ethical code has been developed to cover all businesses, many industries and trade associations have adopted codes applicable to their members. Similarly, corporations increasingly are developing formal codes of ethics or conduct to help guide employees in considering ethical issues during the decision-making process.

Although legal standards cannot be equated with moral standards for purposes of ethical inquiry, the principles of business law discussed in this text provide an opportunity to examine both ethical issues and legal issues. In many cases, for example, the rule of law provides an ethical minimum to which a business should at least adhere. Knowl-edge of the rule of law can help frame issues and establish basic premises. Further, many of the laws discussed in this text are based on moral judgments and, therefore, are subject to ethical analysis as to validity. Finally, because business ethics is an area of applied ethics, the factual situations presented in the legal cases reprinted throughout the text provide a concrete basis for ethical inquiry.

Classifications of Law

Legal study encompasses a wide variety of subjects. Before examining specific topics, it is helpful to examine the broad general characteristics of legal rules and principles. These characteristics, common to many legal systems, provide a basis for classifying or categorizing the various areas of law. The following sections discuss traditional methods of classifying law.

Substantive and Procedural Law. Law may be classified as either substantive or procedural. **Substantive law** defines the rights to which a person is entitled and the duties a person is obligated to perform. Rights and duties are correlative: for each right there exists a corresponding duty. A person's right to freedom of speech, for example, imposes a corresponding duty on the government not to restrain that freedom. The rules of substantive law compose what most people consider the law. This text primarily concerns the substantive legal rules that govern business transactions including property, contracts, commercial paper, debtor-creditor relations, business organizations, and government regulation of business.

Procedural law establishes the mechanisms to enforce the rights and duties created by substantive law. Because the courts are the primary forum for applying and enforcing the law, much procedural law concerns the process by which rights and duties may be enforced in courts. Procedural law includes the rules for initiating a lawsuit, making motions, conducting a trial, and appealing a judgment.

The relationship between substantive and procedural law is illustrated in the following example. The rules of substantive property law grant a landowner the right to exclude others from entering on his land; all persons have a duty not to enter on land that is owned by others. Violation of this duty is known as "trespass." Assume that Doaks and Jones are adjoining landowners and recently Jones has driven her car over Doaks's land as a shortcut to her own property. Despite Doaks's request that Jones stay off his land, she has refused.

Procedural law provides a method by which Doaks may enforce his right and Jones's duty. Doaks may file a lawsuit against Jones in the local court and may request a judge to order Jones to stay off his land and to pay for any damages that Jones has caused. If the judge finds that Jones committed trespass, the judge may order her to cease entering on Doaks's land and to pay for damage to the land. If Jones refuses to comply with the judge's orders, the judge after further procedures may impose sanctions to force compliance.

Thus, substantive and procedural law are complementary. Without the enforcement mechanisms of the procedural law, substantive rights and duties are illusory. Without the substantive law, however, procedural law is unnecessary because there are no rights and duties to enforce.

Criminal and Civil Law. Both the substantive and procedural law of the United States may be further classified as either criminal or civil law. **Criminal law** consists of principles and rules that protect society as a whole by establishing certain minimum standards of acceptable conduct and punishing those who fail to meet those standards. Criminal law thus creates duties owed to the community or public at large and is penal in nature. Substantive criminal law defines the classes of conduct deemed particularly injurious to the public welfare—such as murder, robbery, or assault—and establishes a penalty—such as a fine, prison term, or even capital punishment—for those who are found guilty of committing the acts. Criminal laws are enforced by legal proceedings (prosecutions) in which the government brings alleged wrongdoers before the court for a determination of guilt or innocence in accordance with rules of criminal procedure. In criminal proceedings, the government acts on behalf of society and the penalty paid by the convicted wrongdoer benefits society as a whole.

In contrast to criminal law, which vindicates violations of duties owed to the public and is penal

in nature, **civil law** concerns relations between individuals and is remedial in nature. Although both criminal and civil law establish standards of conduct, civil law is enforced not by the government but by particular individuals who are injured by persons who violate civil law standards. The injured party brings the dispute to court, seeking a personal remedy from the alleged wrongdoer. If a court finds that the person violated the rules of civil law, the wrongdoer is held liable—or responsible—for the resulting injuries. The injured party may then obtain a judicial remedy, usually the payment of money, to compensate for the injury.

Certain conduct may violate both civil and criminal law. Criminal law, for example, requires an automobile driver who exceeds the maximum speed limit to pay a penalty. The government may prosecute the driver, who must pay a fine if found guilty. If the driver also caused an accident while driving over the speed limit, he may have violated a civil law that prohibits negligent (careless) conduct. A person injured in the accident might sue the driver who, if a court finds negligence, may be held liable for the negligently caused injuries. In this situation, the criminal law serves to protect society: a maximum speed limit reduces the likelihood of an automobile accident that would interfere with safe and peaceful travel on thoroughfares. The civil law protects the individual by creating a source of compensation to someone injured by another's carelessness.

Public and Private Law. Legal subjects often are designated as either public or private. **Public law** consists of principles and rules that involve the government in its capacity of representing society. In public law, the government or an agency of the government participates and acts on behalf of society. For example, in criminal law, which is one area of public law, the government as a representative of society brings the wrongdoer to court. Other areas of public law include constitutional and administrative law.[5]

---

5. Criminal law is discussed on page 6 and in Chapter 3. Constitutional law issues are discussed throughout the introductory chapters, particularly Chapters 3 and 4. Administrative law is discussed in Chapter 4.

Private law consists of rules and principles that involve persons (whether artificial or natural) as private individuals. Much of civil law is private law. Private law cases may involve the government but in its capacity as a member of society rather than as a representative of society. Traditionally, private law has encompassed three areas of law: torts, property, and contracts, all of which are discussed later in the text.[6]

Derivation of American Law

The general classifications and functions of law described above provided a basis for establishing a legal system in the United States at the time the colonies won their independence from England. At that time, two general legal systems existed in Western Europe: common law (in England) and civil law (in most other countries). The civil law system, which evolved from Roman law, establishes all basic principles of law in a code, a collection of statutes adopted by a parliamentary body. The American founders, however, decided to establish a common law system in the United States.

Under the common law system, the basic principles of law are set forth in case law, decisions written by judges to resolve specific cases. The common law historically is based on custom. When resolving disputes, the judges of the court refer to prior cases to ascertain how similar disputes were resolved and apply the customary law derived from the preceding cases to resolve the current dispute. In England, the common law developed in three royal courts—Exchequer, King's (or Queen's) Bench, and Common Pleas—that served as the only centralized legal system in England.

Specialized courts—such as ecclesiastical courts, local manorial courts, and a variety of commercial courts—existed apart from the royal courts. Despite attempts by English lords to restrict the powers of the royal courts, they eventually absorbed most of the more limited courts. By the eighteenth century, common law royal courts were the predominant legal system in England.

Many familiar elements of law originated in the English common law courts. The use of a jury in both criminal and civil cases was a common law practice. The adversarial system in which each party to a dispute presents its case to the court was characteristic of the common law courts. These courts also employed the remedy of awarding money damages to injured parties in civil cases.

Although most of the English courts had merged into the common law courts by the time of American independence, one independent system still existed: the **courts of equity,** also known as the **courts of chancery.** Courts of equity developed as a result of the static, rigid, and inflexible nature of the common law courts, and provided relief when no satisfactory remedy was available in those courts. Appropriate legal relief was often unavailable in the common law courts because a party wishing to try a case before a court of law had to obtain a *writ,* a written document authorizing the initiation of the lawsuit. Each type of case had its own writ, and if no writ specifically fit the factual situation of a new type of case, a person generally was not allowed to bring suit. Prior to the late thirteenth century, English kings used an informal procedure to refer cases not covered by the common law writs to the chancellor, a clergyman who served as a minister to the king.

For example, the common law courts were authorized to award money damages as the only remedy, but money damages were sometimes an inadequate remedy. If, for instance, Jones repeatedly trespassed on Smith's land, a common law court could award Smith money damages for any injury caused by Jones, but lacked the power to prevent Jones from trespassing in the future. The king began to refer these special types of cases to the chancellor, whose duty was to provide a fair and equitable resolution of the problem without the restrictions that bound the common law courts. One remedy developed by the chancellor for cases such as Smith's was the *injunction:* an order to refrain from doing an act. Failure to comply with an injunction could be punished by imprisoning the wrongdoer.

This informal referral system developed into a formal system in the late thirteenth century after the English lords, in an effort to curb the growth of a centralized court system, enacted a law restricting

---

6. Tort law is introduced in Chapter 5. Property law is introduced in Chapter 6 and is discussed in Part VI. Contract law is discussed in Parts II and III.

the powers of the common law courts. For many years thereafter, the common law courts could only provide limited relief in legal disputes. The king, therefore, referred an increasing number of cases to the chancellor, who established the courts of equity to handle them.

The courts of equity did not use the prior case law as the basis of resolving cases. Instead, they attempted to provide fair and equitable resolution of disputes based on broad, general rules summarized in maxims such as "Equity does not suffer a wrong to go without a remedy," "He who comes into equity must come with clean hands," and "Equity regards substance rather than form." The courts of equity operated without a jury and provided remedies unavailable in the common law. In addition to the injunction, these remedies included *rescission* (an order voiding contracts obtained unfairly) and *specific performance* (an order requiring a party to perform contractual obligations). When the Americans established a common law system, they also adopted many of the principles and procedures of the complementary system of equity. Even today, the historical distinctions between the two systems affect the operation of American law.

The Role of an Attorney

An **attorney** (attorney at law, lawyer, counselor at law) is a person who has been authorized by one or more states to practice law on behalf of clients. The attorney plays an important role in the American legal system. The American Bar Association has summarized the general functions of the attorney as follows:

> As advisor, a lawyer provides a client with an informed understanding of the client's legal rights and obligations and explains their practical implications. As advocate, a lawyer zealously asserts the client's position under the rules of the adversary system. As negotiator, a lawyer seeks a result advantageous to the client but consistent with requirements of honest dealing with others. As intermediary between clients, a lawyer seeks to reconcile their divergent interests as an advisor and, to a limited extent, as a spokesperson for each client. A lawyer acts as evaluator by examining a client's legal affairs and reporting about them to the client or to others.[7]

The specific functions of an attorney depend on the wants and needs of the individual client. Lawyers representing business clients frequently draft documents (such as contracts, trusts, partnership agreements, corporate charters and bylaws) as well as act as advisor, advocate, or negotiator. Some business clients routinely seek an attorney's advice prior to making major business decisions; others consult an attorney only if they recognize that a question of law or a legal dispute has arisen. Large businesses increasingly have employed "in house counsel"—lawyers who work solely for the business—to participate in day-to-day business operations and provide legal advice.

American law requires attorneys to comply with a variety of ethical and professional duties and responsibilities. Although the specific duties may vary from state to state, attorneys are required to maintain the highest standard of ethics and conduct in relation to a client. A lawyer is required to exercise independent professional judgment on behalf of a client and to represent a client competently and zealously within the bounds of the law. An attorney also must preserve the confidence and secrets revealed by a client while seeking legal advice.

To encourage complete and open communications between lawyer and client, all states recognize an attorney-client privilege that prevents an attorney from disclosing communications made with a client while seeking legal advice. A client may, however, waive the privilege and consent to the disclosure. Although the privilege covers a client's admission of previous criminal acts, it does not extend to a client's proposed criminal or fraudulent acts. In general, an attorney is required to discourage a client from committing criminal or fraudulent acts and, if unsuccessful, may be required to reveal the proposed unlawful conduct to the proper authorities.

The American Bar Association and many states maintain committees that render confidential opin-

---

7. Model Rules of Professional Conduct, Preamble: A Lawyer's Responsibilities, American Bar Association (1983).

ions to attorneys who are uncertain of their ethical duties in a specific situation. If a client believes an attorney has breached his or her ethical duties, most states—through the judiciary, bar association, or licensing authority—provide a procedure to review alleged misconduct. An attorney who has violated ethical or professional duties is subject to discipline, including loss of the privilege to practice law, by state authorities.

Sources of Law in the United States

Under the democratic form of government in the United States, the people are considered the sovereign and thus are the source of all powers including the power to establish law. The American people have adopted a republican form of government in which elected representatives exercise these powers. In general, therefore, the government in its representative capacity is the source of law in the United States.

The United States operates under a system of federalism with two levels of government. At the national level, the federal government adopts and enforces laws that are binding on the citizens of all states. Additionally, each of the fifty states that compose the United States enacts laws that are effective within that state. The governments at both the state and federal levels are organized in accordance with the doctrine of separation of powers so that governmental powers are divided among the three branches of government, each possessing checks upon the powers of the others. The legislative branch adopts written laws called "statutes," which are executed by the executive branch of the government. The judicial branch of government enforces the law in specific cases and controversies presented to the courts. The laws applied by the judiciary derive from three principal sources: constitutions, statutes, and the common law.

Constitutions

A **constitution** establishes the basic principles, governmental structure, and law of a state or nation. Each of the United States has adopted its own written constitution and all of the states have ratified the federal Constitution and have agreed to comply with its provisions.

United States Constitution. The United States Constitution is the written agreement that binds the states together as a federation. It consists of seven articles adopted in 1787 and twenty-six amendments adopted between 1791 and 1971. The Constitution serves three important functions: (1) it limits the powers of the states and their governments, (2) it enumerates the powers that the states have delegated to the federal government, and (3) it guarantees certain rights to the people of the United States.

Limitation on States' Powers. Because each state is a sovereign entity, it has the inherent power to enact its own laws. The federal Constitution, however, restricts this power by making state law subordinate to federal law. The **Supremacy Clause** of Article VI of the Constitution provides:

> This Constitution, and the Laws of the United States which shall be made in Pursuance thereof; and all Treaties made, or which shall be made, under the Authority of the United States shall be the supreme Law of the Land; and the Judges in every State shall be bound thereby, any Thing in the Constitution or Laws of any State to the Contrary notwithstanding.

The Supremacy Clause requires a court to invalidate and refuse to enforce any state law that conflicts with the federal Constitution, federal statutes, or federal treaties. The Supremacy Clause provides a general limitation on state powers, but other provisions of the Constitution more specifically restrict state powers. These provisions, for example, prohibit the states from entering into treaties with foreign nations, taxing imports and exports, impairing contractual obligations, and coining money.

Enumeration of Federal Powers. Unlike the states, the federal government has no inherent powers but possesses only those powers that the states have delegated to it. The Constitution enumerates those delegated powers; the states have retained all other powers. Article I of the Constitution establishes Congress (consisting of the House of Representatives and the Senate) as the legislative branch of government and sets forth the congressional powers. Congress is empowered, for example, to impose taxes, to regulate interstate commerce and commerce with foreign countries, to issue currency, to appropriate money, to reduce or expand the number of courts, and to provide for the national defense. Congress exercises its powers by enacting federal statutes. The House of Representatives also has the power, in appropriate cases, to impeach judicial and executive officers, and the Senate has the power to try all impeachments.

The Constitution vests the executive powers of the federal government in the president, who appoints executive officers, including a cabinet, to assist in performing executive duties. In addition to executing federal laws, the president serves as commander-in-chief of the armed forces. As a check on the legislative power, the president has the power to veto acts of Congress, which Congress may override only by a two-thirds vote of both houses. The president also has the power, with the advice and consent of the Senate, to make treaties with foreign nations and to appoint ambassadors and judges of the Supreme Court.

The Constitution delegates federal judicial power to the United States Supreme Court and other federal courts established by Congress. The federal courts can hear only limited types of cases, which are discussed in detail later in this chapter. Under the **doctrine of judicial review,** federal courts have the power to determine whether the acts of the legislative and executive branches of government comply with the Constitution and to refuse to enforce those acts that violate it. Although this doctrine, which imposes a significant limitation on the powers of the other branches, is not explicitly stated in the Constitution, the United States Supreme Court asserted its existence in the following landmark case.

Marbury v. Madison

5 U.S. (1 Cranch) 137 (1803)

In the election of 1800, Thomas Jefferson, a Republican, defeated the incumbent president John Adams, a Federalist. Following the election, President Adams appointed Federalists to fill forty-two vacancies as federal justices of the peace and initiated the formal appointment procedure that required the secretary of state to deliver sealed commissions

to the appointees. All of the commissions, however, were not delivered prior to the inauguration of Jefferson, and the new secretary of state, James Madison, refused to deliver the remaining commissions. William Marbury, an appointee who had not received his commission, filed suit in the Supreme Court requesting a writ of mandamus[8] ordering Madison to deliver the commissions. Marbury asserted his right to bring his suit in the Supreme Court based on the Judiciary Act of 1789, a federal statute that authorized the Supreme Court "to issue writs of mandamus . . . to persons holding office under the authority of the United States."

Although the case was fraught with political issues, the Supreme Court focused on a narrow issue: whether the provisions of the Judiciary Act of 1789 violated the Constitution. The Constitution enumerates the types of cases that may be brought to the Supreme Court and these cases do not include disputes seeking a writ of mandamus to federal officials. The Supreme Court concluded that Congress's attempt to expand the types of cases that the Court may hear to include those cases not listed in the Constitution was "repugnant" to the Constitution. The Court then considered whether it should follow the law established by the Judiciary Act of 1789.

Chief Justice Marshall

. . . The question, whether an act, repugnant to the constitution can become the law of the land, is a question deeply interesting to the United States. . . .

The powers of the legislature are defined and limited; and that those limits may not be mistaken, or forgotten, the constitution is written. To what purpose are powers limited, and to what purpose is that limitation committed to writing, if these limits may, at any time, be passed by those intended to be restrained? . . . .

The constitution is either a superior paramount law, unchangeable by ordinary means, or it is on a level with ordinary legislative acts, and, like other acts, is alterable when the legislative shall please to alter it.

If the former part of the alternative be true, then a legislative act contrary to the constitution is not

---

8. A writ of mandamus is an order issued by a court commanding a public official to perform a specific act or duty.

law: if the latter part be true, then written constitutions are absurd attempts, on the part of the people, to limit a power in its own nature illimitable.

Certainly all those who have framed written constitutions contemplate them as forming the fundamental and paramount law of the nation, and, consequently, the theory of every such government must be, that an act of the legislature, repugnant to the constitution, is void. . . .

If an act of the legislature, repugnant to the constitution, is void, does it, notwithstanding its invalidity, bind the courts, and oblige them to give it effect? Or, in other words, though it be not law, does it constitute a rule as operative as if it was a law? . . .

It is emphatically the province and duty of the judicial department to say what the law is. Those who apply the rule to particular cases, must of necessity expound and interpret that rule. If two laws conflict with each other, the courts must decide on the operation of each.

So if a law be in opposition to the constitution; if both the law and the constitution apply to a particular case, so that the court must either decide that case conformably to the law, disregarding the constitution; or conformably to the constitution, disregarding the law; the court must determine which of these conflicting rules governs the case. This is of the very essence of judicial duty.

If, then, the courts are to regard the constitution, and the constitution is superior to any ordinary act of the legislature, the constitution, and not such ordinary act, must govern the case to which they both apply. . . .

The judicial power of the United States is extended to all cases arising under the constitution.

Could it be the intention of those who gave this power, to say that in using it the constitution should not be looked into? That a case arising under the constitution should be decided without examining the instrument under which it arises?

This is too extravagant to be maintained.

In some cases, then, the constitution must be looked into by the judges. And if they can open it at all, what part of it are they forbidden to read or to obey? . . .

. . . [T]he framers of the constitution contemplated that instrument as a rule for the government of courts, as well as of the legislature. . . .

It is also not entirely unworthy of observation, that in declaring what shall be the supreme law of the land, the constitution itself is first mentioned; and not the laws of the United States generally, but those only which shall be made in pursuance of the constitution, have that rank.

Thus, the particular phraseology of the constitution of the United States confirms and strengthens the principle, supposed to be essential to all written constitutions, that a law repugnant to the constitution is void; and that courts, as well as other departments, are bound by that instrument.

The rule must be discharged.

Guarantee of Individual Rights. In addition to limiting the powers of the states and enumerating the powers of the three branches of the federal government, the Constitution delineates certain rights that are guaranteed to United States citizens. Most of these rights are set forth in the Bill of Rights, the first ten amendments to the Constitution. Included in the Bill of Rights are the people's rights to freedom of speech and religion, to freedom from unreasonable searches and seizures, to a speedy and public trial by an impartial jury in criminal prosecutions, and to due process of law. The Constitution imposes a duty on the government not to infringe on these rights of individuals.

State Constitutions. In addition to the federal Constitution, each state has adopted its own constitution. Although the provisions of these constitutions vary, each generally outlines the principles and organization of the state's government and the rights guaranteed to citizens of the state, and divides the state powers among executive, legislative, and judicial branches of government. All state constitutions establish multilevel state judicial systems with trial courts for resolution of disputes and controversies and one or more appellate courts to review the decisions rendered by the trial courts. State court systems are discussed in more detail later in this chapter.

Statutes

Statutes—written laws enacted by the legislature—are the second source of law in the United States. Congress adopts federal statutes and the legislative body of each state enacts state statutes. Federal and state statutes must comply with the federal Constitution. A state's statutes also must be consistent with its constitution. Many states also authorize other governmental units, such as counties or cities, to enact statutes, usually called "ordinances," which are effective within the local units. Both federal and state legislatures may authorize administrative agencies to issue rules and regulations that clarify or explain statutes. These administrative rules and regulations, though not equivalent to statutes, are generally interpreted and applied by the courts in a manner similar to statutes.

Federal and State Codes. Statutes are compiled in official codes. All federal statutes are codified in the **United States Code** (U.S.C.), which is divided into various "titles." For example, federal bankruptcy law is codified in Title 11 of the U.S.C. Title 15, "Commerce and Trade," contains the antitrust laws and a number of other important statutes affecting business. The states maintain their own official codes, which are published under a variety of names such as "Illinois Revised Statutes," "Michigan Compiled Laws," "Code of Georgia," "Massachusetts General Laws Annotated." Rules and regulations issued by administrative agencies are usually compiled in volumes separate from the official codes. For example, federal regulations are compiled in the **Code of Federal Regulations** (C.F.R.).

Uniform State Laws and Model Acts. Subject only to the constraints of the United States Constitution and limitations of the state constitution, each state legislature has the power to enact statutes that it deems appropriate for the welfare of its citizens. As a result, the substance of state statutes varies widely. As long as state statutes concern issues of only local interest, inconsistencies among the statutes of different states are of little practical importance.

With the development of nationwide communication and transportation systems in the 1800s, however, both businesses and individuals began to engage in interstate activities that were hindered by inconsistent state laws. In 1892, in an effort to facilitate interstate activities, seven states organized

the Conference of State Boards of Commissioners on Promoting Uniformity of Law in the United States and in 1915 the Conference reorganized as the National Conference of Commissioners on Uniform State Laws. Today, each state, the District of Columbia, and Puerto Rico appoint at least one commissioner to the organization. The commissioners consider the areas of law requiring uniformity, draft legislation known as **uniform codes, acts,** or **laws,** and encourage their adoption by each of the states. The individual state legislatures consider a uniform act as they do any other legislative bill. If a uniform act is passed by the legislature, it becomes a part of the state's statutes.

The National Conference has drafted more than 250 uniform acts, many of which address areas of business law. The Uniform Commercial Code (UCC), which is discussed in detail throughout this book, has been adopted by all states except Louisiana, which has adopted only part of it. Other uniform laws that will be discussed later in the book include the Uniform Partnership Act, the Uniform Limited Partnership Act, the Uniform Fraudulent Conveyance Act, the Uniform Principal and Income Act, and the Uniform Probate Code.

The National Conference, as well as other organizations, also drafts **model acts** that serve as guidelines to state legislatures in drafting other types of legislation. Although model acts do not necessarily concern subjects requiring uniformity among the states, the expertise of the commissioners, especially in complex areas of the law, facilitates enactment of well-drafted legislation. As with uniform laws, model acts that are adopted by a state become a part of the state statutes.

The Common Law

The third source of law in the United States is the **common law**—rules and principles of law embodied in cases previously decided by the courts. When an issue is presented to a court for resolution, it looks first to constitutions and statutes to ascertain whether they provide a rule of law to resolve the issue. If neither provides such a rule, the court will apply the rules of the common law. Thus, the three major sources of law stand in an hierarchical relationship. Statutes must comply with any relevant constitutional provision, and the common law is subordinate both to constitutions and statutes. Areas of law discussed in this text that are based largely upon common law principles include torts, contracts, restitution, suretyship, property, trusts, and agency.

Precedent and the Doctrine of Stare Decisis. Use of the common law as a source of law is based on the **doctrine of *stare decisis,*** which derives its name from the Latin phrase *stare decisis et non quieta movere* meaning "to adhere to precedents and not to unsettle things established." The doctrine of *stare decisis* provides that courts will adhere to and apply principles of law decided in prior cases to later cases involving substantially the same facts. The **holding,** or rule of law that resolved the issues, of the prior case serves as authority or **precedent** for resolution of the issues of subsequent cases that involve the same or similar facts. A court, therefore, applies one rule of law to all cases involving the same or similar facts and issues.

To illustrate the doctrine of *stare decisis,* assume Andrews promised to make a gift of $500 to the Cancer Society of America. Andrews later refused to fulfill his promise and the Cancer Society sued him alleging breach of promise. The court ruled in favor of Andrews holding that a promise to make a gift is not legally enforceable. Ten years later, the Heart Disease Institute sues Baker alleging that she had breached her promise to give $1,000 to the Institute. The two cases are substantially the same: each involves breach of a promise to make a gift. The court in the second case would use the precedent of the first case to hold that Baker's promise is not legally enforceable.

The doctrine of *stare decisis* and its use of precedent facilitate consistency, fairness, and predictability in the application of the law. William O. Douglas, Associate Justice of the Supreme Court from 1939 to 1975, summarized the purposes of the doctrine as follows:

> The law is not properly susceptible to whim or caprice. It must have the sturdy qualities required of every framework that is designed for substantial structures. Moreover, it must have uniformity when applied to the daily affairs of men.

Uniformity and continuity in law are necessary to many activities. If they are not present, the integrity of contracts, wills, conveyances and securities is impaired. . . . *Stare decisis* serves to take the capricious element out of law and to give stability to a society. It is a strong tie which the future has to the past.[9]

Methods of Creating and Changing Precedent. Despite the need for consistency and predictability, sometimes the use of precedent is not appropriate. In some cases, no applicable rule of law has been announced in the common law. In such cases, the court considers the issue to be one of *first impression* and reaches a holding that serves as a new rule of law under the common law.

Cases involving completely new factual situations are rare. Prior cases usually involve similar but not identical facts. If a court is convinced that the facts of the current case significantly differ from those of prior cases, the court may distinguish the case on its facts and issue a new rule of law. As a result, the common law retains its vitality and flexibility to accommodate changing times.

Sometimes the facts of a new case may not be distinguishable from those of a prior case, yet the rule of law of the earlier case may no longer be valid because of changed social conditions. In such circumstances, a court may overrule the precedent, declaring the pre-existing rule of law to be invalid, and issue a new rule. Overruling precedent is a drastic measure that courts try to avoid because it creates uncertainty and unpredictability.

An alternative way of changing common law precedent is by legislative act. The legislature can invalidate common law principles by adopting statutes that create a different rule of law. A statute that repeals or abolishes a common law principle is said to be in "derogation" of the common law. In the following case, the court considers the importance of precedent and the methods of overruling a common law rule.

---

9. The Eighth Annual Benjamin N. Cardozo Lecture delivered before the Association of the Bar of the City of New York on April 12, 1949.

Molitor v. Kaneland Community Unit District No. 302

163 N.E.2d 89 (Ill. 1959)

Plaintiff Thomas Molitor, a student, was injured when the school bus in which he was riding drove off the road and exploded. Molitor sued defendant Kaneland Community Unit District No. 302, alleging that the school bus driver, an employee of the school district, negligently caused Molitor's injuries. The trial court dismissed his lawsuit on the grounds that the common law of the State of Illinois provided that the state and its subdivisions, including school districts, could not be held liable for negligently caused injuries under the doctrine of sovereign immunity. The appellate court affirmed. In the following opinion, the Illinois Supreme Court overruled application of the doctrine of sovereign immunity to school districts.

Klingbiel, Justice

. . . It appears that while adhering to the old immunity rule, this court has not reconsidered and reevaluated the doctrine of immunity of school districts for over fifty years. . . .

[I]n 1898 . . . the Illinois court extended the immunity rule to school districts in the leading case of *Kinnare v. City of Chicago,* . . . 49 N.E. 536. . . . That opinion reasoned that since the State is not subject to suit nor liable for the torts or negligence of its agents, likewise a school district, as a governmental agency of the State, is also "exempted from the obligation to respond in damages, as master, for negligent acts of its servants to the same extent as is the State itself." Later decisions following the Kinnare doctrine have sought to advance additional explanations such as the protection of public funds and public property, and to prevent the diversion of tax moneys to the payment of damage claims. . . .

Surveying the whole picture of governmental tort law as it stands in Illinois today, the following broad outlines may be observed. The General Assembly has frequently indicated its dissatisfaction with the doctrine of sovereign immunity upon which the Kinnare case was based. Governmental units, including school districts, are now subject to

liability under the Workmen's Compensation and Occupational Disease Acts. . . .

Coming down to the precise issue at hand, it is clear that if the above rules and precedents are strictly applied to the instant case, plaintiff's complaint . . . was properly dismissed. . . .

It is a basic concept underlying the whole law of torts today that liability follows negligence, and that individuals and corporations are responsible for the negligence of their agents and employees acting in the course of their employment. The doctrine of governmental immunity runs directly counter to that basic concept. What reasons, then, are so impelling as to allow a school district, as a quasi-municipal corporation, to commit wrongdoing without any responsibility to its victims, while any individual or private corporation would be called to task in court for such tortious conduct?

The original basis of the immunity rule has been called a "survival of the medieval idea that the sovereign can do no wrong," or that "the King can do no wrong." . . .

We are of the opinion that school district immunity cannot be justified on this theory. . . .

We do not believe that in this present day and age, when public education constitutes one of the biggest businesses in the country, that school immunity can be justified on the protection-of-public-funds theory. . . .

Neither are we impressed with defendant's plea that the abolition of immunity would create grave and unpredictable problems of school finance and administration. . . .

We are of the opinion that none of the reasons advanced in support of school district immunity have any true validity today. Further we believe that abolition of such immunity may tend to decrease the frequency of school bus accidents by coupling the power to transport pupils with the responsibility of exercising care in the selection and supervision of the drivers. . . .

We conclude that the rule of school district tort immunity is unjust, unsupported by any valid reason, and has no rightful place in modern day society.

Defendant strongly urges that if said immunity is to be abolished, it should be done by the legislature, not by this court. With this contention we must disagree. The doctrine of school district immunity was created by this court alone. Having found that doctrine to be unsound and unjust under present conditions, we consider that we have not only the power, but the duty, to abolish that immunity. . . .

We have repeatedly held that the doctrine of *stare decisis* is not an inflexible rule requiring this court to blindly follow precedents and adhere to prior decisions, and that when it appears that public policy and social needs require a departure from prior decisions, it is our duty as a court of last resort to overrule those decisions and establish a rule consonant with our present day concepts of right and justice. . . .

[Judgment reversed and remanded.]

Interpretation of Statutes. The common law is a source of precedent for rules and principles of law not set out in a statute or constitution. Prior case law also provides precedent for the interpretation of a constitution or statute. That is, a body of case law has developed under most constitutional provisions and statutes interpreting what their language (which is often general) means as applied to specific fact situations. For example, §1 of the Sherman Act, the major federal antitrust statute, declares illegal "every contract, combination, . . . or conspiracy, in restraint of trade. . . ." The specific business conduct that violates this prohibition is found not in the Sherman Act, but in the voluminous body of cases decided under the Act since it was enacted in 1890. Thus, even in areas of law based upon a statute or constitutional provision, prior court decisions often are an important, and often the major, source of legal rules. The case law interpreting statutes and constitutions develops through the doctrine of *stare decisis* in much the same manner as the common law.

Application of a statute necessarily requires that a court determine the meaning of the statute. Through case law, courts have adopted rules and techniques to assist them in interpreting statutes in cases of first impression.

Plain Meaning Rule. Courts usually first apply the "plain meaning" rule, under which a statute is interpreted by considering the literal meaning of the words. Using this rule the court examines only the statute as written, without reviewing any other sources. Although the plain meaning rule is appealing in its simplicity and minimizes "judicial legislation," most courts do not rely solely on this rule to interpret a statute. Often a legislature adopts a statute without considering all ramifications, so that use of the plain meaning rule can lead to absurd results if the law is applied literally. Moreover, the inherent nature of language creates ambiguity due to various definitions and connotations of words. Supreme Court Justice Oliver Wendell Holmes summarized these problems by stating:

> A word is not a crystal, transparent and unchanged, it is the skin of a living thought and may vary greatly in color and content according to the circumstances and the time in which it is used.[10]

As a result courts have developed other methods of determining the meaning of a statute.

Legislative History. One method of ascertaining the meaning of a statute is to examine its legislative history, including previous drafts of the statute, committee reports, or transcripts of floor debate. Examining these sources helps determine the purpose of the statute or the intent of the legislators. Although the legislative history sometimes provides the necessary clarification, often it does not resolve the ambiguity. As a result, through the common law, the courts have adopted rules of construction to facilitate statutory interpretation.

Rules of Construction. Rules of construction are maxims that simplify the analysis of statutory language. One rule, known as *noscitur a sociis*, provides that words take meaning from those with which they are associated. In short, the meaning of the words should be determined from the context in which they are used. A special form of this rule is known as *ejusdem generis:* the meaning of a general term following a set of specific terms should be limited to items of the same class as the specific terms. Consider a federal statute that prohibits transporting across state lines a stolen "au-

---

10. *Towne v. Eisner*, 38 S. Ct. 158, 159 (1918).

tomobile, automobile truck, automobile wagon, motorcycle or any other self-propelled vehicle not designed for running on rails.'' In *McBoyle v. United States* (1931),[11] the Supreme Court considered whether this statute could be interpreted as prohibiting taking a stolen airplane across state lines. Application of the rule of *ejusdem generis* would have required the court to determine the meaning of the general term (''self-propelled vehicle not designed for running on rails'') from the list of specific terms (automobile, automobile truck, etc.). Although the Court based its holding on other grounds, it probably would have determined that the rule of *ejusdem generis* would not allow application of the statute to an airplane because as Justice Holmes noted ''a vehicle running on land is the theme.''

Two other rules of construction frequently invoked by courts state ''penal statutes should be strictly construed'' and ''statutes in derogation of the common law should be strictly construed.'' In other words, these types of statutes should be narrowly interpreted. In penal statutes the purpose of the rule is clear: a person should not be subject to criminal penalties unless the statute clearly states that his conduct is illegal. In the *McBoyle* case, the Court used this rule to set aside the conviction of the person who had transported the airplane across state lines.

The purpose of the strict construction of statutes in derogation of the common law is less clear. Generally, the rule reduces the unpredictability that may result when a statute changes a well-established common law rule. By interpreting the statute narrowly, the courts seek to prevent its application to situations not clearly within the statute, thus decreasing the likelihood of application to persons who could not foresee that the rule was applicable to them.

Rules of construction are simply tools used by the courts to interpret statutes. Although the rules provide some consistency in statutory interpretation, their use is not mandatory.

State and Federal Common Law. Each state has its own body of case law comprised of decisions of its courts, including substantive rules of law in areas not covered by statute or constitution, and the court's interpretations of statutes and constitutions. Generally, the precedents of one state are not binding on the courts of other states. Nevertheless, a state court may look to decisions in other states for guidance when adopting a new principle of law in a case of first impression or in a case overruling an outmoded rule of law.

The federal courts also have a body of case law that includes the decisions of all federal courts. Federal case law, however, includes rules of law interpreting only federal statutes and the Constitution. There is no body of federal substantive common law that is applied in the absence of a federal statute or constitutional provision. Rather, in such cases, the federal courts generally use the common law of the state in which the court is located. These topics will be further discussed later in this chapter.

Restatement of the Law. When considering an issue of first impression or outdated precedent, a court also may consult legal treatises and scholarly works for guidance to determine the appropriate rule of law to adopt. A major civil law treatise, widely used by the courts, is the **Restatement of the Law** (often simply called ''the Restatement''), which is published by a national organization of attorneys, law professors, and judges known as the American Law Institute. The Restatement provides a unique perspective on the law because its purpose is to state ''the law as it would be decided today by the great majority of courts.''[12] Therefore, the Restatement does not necessarily reflect the rules of the common law as they have been adopted by the courts. Rather, it contains the principles of common law that the American Law Institute believes would be adopted if all courts reexamined their common law rules.

Although the entire work is called the *''Restatement of the Law,''* it is usually referred to by its individual topics (for example, *''Restatement of Torts,'' ''Restatement of Contracts''*). Those parts of the *Restatement* that have been revised since their initial adoption are referred to by addition of

11. 51 S. Ct. 340 (1931).

12. Restatement in the Courts, Permanent Edition 12 (1945).

Table 1–1	**Restatement of the Law and Dates of Adoption**

Restatement Topic	Year of Adoption
Restatement of Contracts	1932
Restatement (Second) of Contracts	1979
Restatement of Agency	1933
Restatement (Second) of Agency	1958
Restatement of Torts	1934
Restatement (Second) of Torts	1965
Restatement of Conflict of Laws	1934
Restatement (Second) of Conflict of Laws	1969
Restatement of Trusts	1935
Restatement (Second) of Trusts	1959
Restatement of Property	1936
Restatement (Second) of Property (Landlord and Tenant)	1976
Restatement (Second) of Property (Donative Transfers)	1983
Restatement of Restitution	1936
Restatement of Security	1941
Restatement of Judgments	1942
Restatement (Second) of Judgments	1982
Restatement of Foreign Relations Law of the United States	1965

the word "Second" to the title—for example, The *Restatement (Second) of Contracts*. Table 1–1 presents a list of the various parts of the Restatement and their dates of adoption.

When a court must decide an issue of first impression, it frequently adopts the rule of law of the Restatement. The Restatement also has been instrumental in providing a basis for overruling outmoded principles of the common law. As a result, many of the cases reprinted in this book cite the Restatement for rules of common law and the text discusses the rules of the Restatement as examples of common law principles. The Restatement itself is not a part of the common law, but if a court adopts a rule promulgated by the Restatement, that rule becomes a part of the state's common law.

American Court Systems

The judicial branch of government is responsible for applying and interpreting the law. The courts that compose the judicial branch, therefore, serve a crucial function in maintaining law and order in the United States. They provide a forum for the peaceful resolution of civil disputes and serve as a tribunal for the impartial enforcement of criminal laws in a fair and consistent manner. A court cannot initiate judicial action. Private individuals, businesses, or other branches of the government must present a case or controversy to the court before it can interpret and apply the law. Legal cases are initiated by a party known as the **plaintiff** who seeks some form of judicial relief from another known as the **defendant**.

Jurisdiction

A court also is restricted to hearing cases that lie within its jurisdiction. **Jurisdiction** is the power and authority to render a binding decision of law. The jurisdiction of a court is established in the statute or constitution that created the court. Unless a legal case is within a court's jurisdiction, the court lacks the legal authority to resolve the case.

Original and Appellate Jurisdiction. Courts may possess original or appellate jurisdiction. A court of **original jurisdiction** has the power to render the initial decision in a case. In other words, the court is the proper forum in which the parties commence the lawsuit and first obtain a legal ruling resolving the case. In the court of original jurisdiction, a trial is held, evidence is presented, and the judge enters an order determining a party's liability in a civil case or guilt or innocence in a criminal case.

Courts of **appellate jurisdiction** are empowered to review cases that have been tried by a court of original jurisdiction. The courts of appellate jurisdiction correct and revise legal errors that were made in the prior proceedings. Trials are not conducted in these courts. Instead, courts of appellate jurisdiction merely review the trial that was held in the court of original jurisdiction. Some courts have both original and appellate jurisdiction. The United States Supreme Court, for example, has original jurisdiction over cases between two or more states but also has appellate jurisdiction over other types of cases.

Subject Matter Jurisdiction. The statute or constitution that creates a court also establishes its **subject matter jurisdiction**. A court of general subject matter jurisdiction is empowered to hear all types of disputes including civil and criminal cases and cases at law and at equity. In contrast, a court of limited subject matter jurisdiction has the power to hear only certain categories of disputes. The federal bankruptcy courts, for example, are courts of limited subject matter jurisdiction; they have the power only to resolve cases concerning federal bankruptcy law.

State Court Systems

Every state in the United States has established its own court system. Although the structures of these systems differ, most states have created inferior courts, trial courts, and appellate courts.

State Inferior Courts. Some states have established courts of original and limited subject matter jurisdiction to handle cases of a specialized nature. These courts include probate courts (sometimes called "surrogate" or "orphans" courts) for cases involving wills and distribution of a deceased person's property, traffic courts for prosecution of violations of traffic laws, and municipal courts for minor criminal cases in larger cities.

Additionally, many states have established small claims courts, which are courts of original jurisdiction that are restricted to hearing civil cases involving a limited dollar amount, usually less than $2,500. Small claims courts provide simple and quick resolution of minor civil cases and relieve the trial courts of substantial workload. Many of these courts operate on weekends or during evening hours, use informal rules of procedure, or allow the parties to represent themselves rather than employ an attorney.

State Trial Courts. For the majority of cases, a state trial court is the court of original jurisdiction. Most state trial courts are courts of general subject matter jurisdiction and are empowered to hear all civil and criminal cases. Depending on the state, the trial courts may be called "circuit courts,"

"courts of common pleas," or "district courts." Trial courts usually are located in larger cities within the state or in the county seats.

As suggested by its name, the trial court is the forum in which the trial occurs to establish the facts underlying the case. A judge presides over the trial to make rulings of law and a jury may be employed to make factual determinations. Trials are discussed more fully in Chapters 2 and 3.

State Appellate Courts. All states have established appellate courts with appellate jurisdiction to review the decisions of the inferior and trial courts. Due process of law entitles a party to a lawsuit to one appeal of right. By following procedures established by state law, a person dissatisfied with the ruling made by the court of original jurisdiction may obtain review by an appellate court. Some states have only one appellate court, usually called "the supreme court," while other states have an intermediate appellate court, usually called "the court of appeals" or "appellate court," and a supreme court.

Intermediate Appellate Courts. In states with an intermediate appellate court, a party's appeal of right generally is to that court. To facilitate the appellate process, some of the more populous states have subdivided the state into districts and have established an intermediate appellate court in each district. The district serves a number of counties or circuits and, therefore, hears intermediate appeals only from trial courts within those counties or circuits.

State Supreme Courts. In states without an intermediate appellate court, appeals of right are taken to the state supreme court. In states with an intermediate appellate court, the state supreme court provides another review of cases already reviewed by the court of appeals. In those states, the supreme court usually has the power to select the cases it wants to review from petitions filed by parties following the intermediate appeal. For most cases tried within the state court system, the state supreme court is the court of last resort. The United States Supreme Court, however, may provide further review of some cases as discussed later in this chapter.

Function of Appellate Courts. The function of the appellate courts is to review inferior trial court decisions to determine whether reversible error has occurred. In contrast to the trial court, where only one judge presides over a case, appellate cases usually are reviewed by a panel of three or more judges who reach a decision by majority vote. The appellate court does not retry a case; it merely reviews the record of the trial, the briefs provided by the parties, and oral arguments made by the attorneys of the parties. Generally, appellate courts are restricted to reviewing issues of law; the appellate court ordinarily accepts the facts as found by the trial court unless they are clearly erroneous. If an appellate court determines that reversible error occurred in the lower court, it will reverse the case and correct the error or send the case back to the lower court for further proceedings.

Federal Court System

Article III, Section 1 of the Constitution provides:

> The judicial Power of the United States, shall be vested in one supreme Court, and in such inferior Courts as the Congress may from time to time ordain and establish.

Thus, the only constitutionally mandated federal court is the Supreme Court, but Congress has established a federal court system composed of three main tiers: the United States District Courts, the United States Courts of Appeals, and the United States Supreme Court. In addition, Congress has established several other courts to hear special cases.

Specialized Federal Courts. For some cases, the court of original federal jurisdiction is a specialized court with limited subject matter jurisdiction. These specialized courts include, for example, the United States Claims Court, which has jurisdiction over cases involving claims against the United States arising from government contracts, and the Court of International Trade, which has jurisdiction over cases involving import transactions.

United States District Courts. The United States District Courts, the trial courts of the federal judicial system, are the courts of original jurisdiction

for most federal cases. Under federal statute, the country is divided into ninety-six districts, each of which has a district court. Every state has at least one district; those states with larger populations have more than one district within their boundaries. Federal district court judges are appointed for life by the president with the advice and consent of the Senate.

Unlike most state trial courts, federal district courts are courts of limited subject matter jurisdiction. The majority of the district court cases are based on federal question jurisdiction and diversity of citizenship jurisdiction. **Federal question jurisdiction** applies to cases arising under the Constitution, federal statutes, and treaties of the United States. For example, a federal district court has the power to hear cases involving the constitutionality of actions of both state and federal government, as well as those applying federal statutes.

About thirty percent of cases filed in the federal district courts arise under **diversity jurisdiction.**[13] Generally, diversity cases are those in which the plaintiff and defendant are citizens of different states. For diversity purposes, a corporation is a citizen both of the state in which it is incorporated and of the state in which its principal place of business is located. Federal statute limits the jurisdiction of federal district courts to diversity cases in which the amount in controversy exceeds $10,000.

The purpose of diversity jurisdiction is to allow parties a forum that will be free from bias that might occur in a state trial court. If, for example, a citizen of Illinois sued a citizen of Ohio in an Illinois state court, the judge's or the jury's prejudice against the out-of-state citizen could deny him a fair trial in the state court. The federal court provides an alternative forum that may be free of local bias. Because of the heavy caseload of the federal district courts, many jurists have suggested that federal diversity jurisdiction be eliminated or that the jurisdictional amount of $10,000 be increased.

United States Courts of Appeals. While the United States district courts serve as the trial courts of the federal judicial system, the courts of appeals

---

13. According to the Administrative Office of the United States Courts, 67,071 of the 238,982 cases filed in federal courts in 1987 were diversity cases.

are the intermediate courts with appellate jurisdiction. A party to a federal lawsuit generally is entitled to one appeal of right to the appropriate court of appeals. Federal law divides the country into twelve judicial circuits, each encompassing several districts. The court of appeals for each circuit has the power to review district court decisions only from districts within the circuit. For example, the Second Circuit encompasses New York, Connecticut, and Vermont. The Second Circuit Court of Appeals can review decisions only from federal district courts within those three states. Additionally, a thirteenth federal appellate court, called the United States Court of Appeals for the Federal Circuit, has appellate jurisdiction over: cases from the United States Patent and Trademark Office, the United States Claims Court, and the Court of International Trade; some decisions of federal agencies; and patent cases decided in the various federal district courts. Figure 1–1 indicates the states and territories within each of the federal judicial circuits.

The justices of the courts of appeals are appointed by the president with the advice and consent of the Senate. Most cases are reviewed by a panel of three justices who issue a written decision representing the ruling of a majority of the panel. In certain cases, usually involving very important issues, all justices for the circuit review the case, a procedure called *en banc* review. Again, a written decision is rendered representing the majority opinion. As in the state appellate courts, the federal courts of appeals generally review only the law and do not retry the facts as found by the district court. Attorneys for the parties may submit legal briefs and present oral arguments to the court of appeals.

| *Figure 1–1* | **The Thirteen Federal Judicial Circuits** |

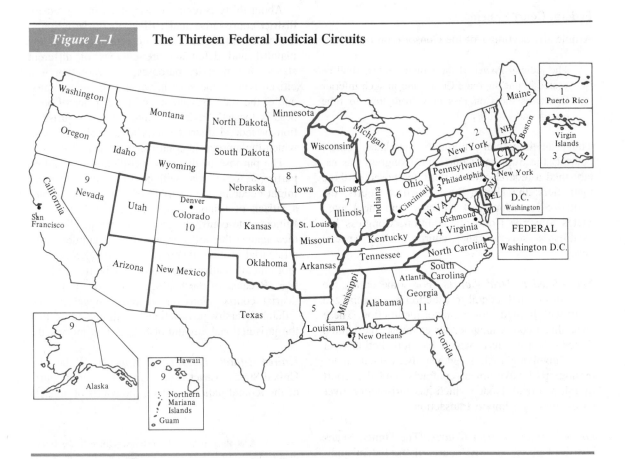

United States Supreme Court. The court of last resort in this country is the United States Supreme Court, a court composed of a chief justice and eight associate justices, all of whom are appointed by the president with the advice and consent of the Senate. The Supreme Court is primarily a court of appellate jurisdiction with the power to review cases from both the federal courts of appeals and the state supreme courts. Generally, the Supreme Court retains discretion whether to accept a case for review. A party seeking Supreme Court review must file a petition summarizing the issues of the case. If the Supreme Court justices exercise their discretion to review the case, the Court will issue a **writ of certiorari** granting the petitioning party the right to Supreme Court review. According to the Court's rules, ''a review on writ of certiorari is not a matter of right, but of judicial discretion, and will be granted only when there are special and important reasons therefor.''[14] As a result the Court grants a writ of certiorari only in a few cases although thousands of petitions are filed each year.

The Supreme Court also is a court of original jurisdiction for a very few types of cases. If a lawsuit is between two or more states, the Supreme Court not only is the court of original jurisdiction but is also the exclusive forum for resolution of the dispute. Additionally, the Supreme Court is a court of original but not exclusive jurisdiction for: cases in which a foreign ambassador, public minister (an upper-level diplomatic representative), or consul is a party; cases between the United States and a state; and cases in which a state sues citizens of another state or aliens. Because federal district courts also have original jurisdiction over these types of cases, the Supreme Court rarely exercises original jurisdiction.

Relationship Between State and Federal Courts

Each state court system and the federal court system are independent of one another. Generally, once a suit is begun in a court of original jurisdiction in one system, the case and subsequent appeals remain within that system. A case filed in a California trial court, for example, must be appealed through the California appellate courts, rather than through the appellate courts of another state or of the federal government. One exception to the independent functioning of state and federal courts is the United States Supreme Court's power to review a few types of appeals from the highest state courts.

For many civil cases, a number of courts will have subject matter jurisdiction over the case. The plaintiff is entitled to select the court of original jurisdiction in which to file the claim; the defendant usually has no voice in selecting the court.[15] If, however, a plaintiff sues a defendant in a state trial court, but the case could have been filed in a federal district court, the defendant may have the case transferred to the federal district court for the district and division in which the state court is located. The federal court's power to transfer the case is known as ''removal jurisdiction.'' For example, if Garcia, a resident of Ohio, wishes to sue Evans, a resident of Kentucky, for damages for breach of contract in excess of $10,000, the case could be brought in a state trial court with general subject matter jurisdiction or in a federal district court on the basis of diversity jurisdiction. If Garcia chose to file the suit in an Ohio trial court, Evans could request that the case be transferred to a federal district court. The defendant, however, does not have the option of having the case transferred to another state court; removal may be made only to federal court. This rule allows a defendant the opportunity to avoid possible prejudice in the state court through removal to federal court. Figure 1–2 indicates the general organization of the federal and state court systems.

Applicable Law

The function of a court is to apply the appropriate law to cases presented to it for resolution. A court, therefore, must determine what substantive law is applicable to each case. Regardless of the source of substantive law, a court always applies its own procedural law.

---

14. U.S. Sup. Ct. Rule 17, 28 U.S.C.

15. As a practical matter, the plaintiff's choice may be restricted by the court's jurisdiction over the defendant which will be discussed in Chapter 2.

| Figure 1–2 | **The Federal and State Court Systems** |

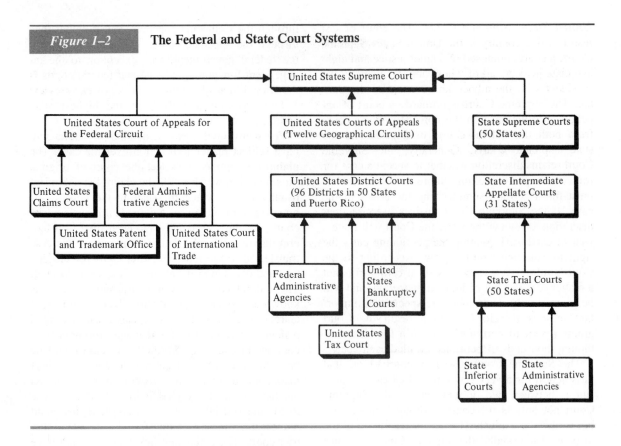

State Courts. In general, a state court applies the law of its own state. In civil cases, not governed by constitution or statute, the state's common law is the appropriate source of law. If a case in the state court involves a federal statute or the federal Constitution, the Supremacy Clause of the Constitution requires the judge to apply these federal laws, following the principles of the federal common law.

Conflict of Laws in State Courts. Because state courts usually operate independently of one another, the law of one state generally is inapplicable in the courts of other states. If, however, the events giving rise to a lawsuit occur in a state other than the state in which the lawsuit is brought, the court may be required to apply the law of that state. Each state has adopted rules of law to determine when and how a court will apply another state's law, an area of law known as **conflict of laws.**

Consider, for example, that an automobile accident occurs in New York City between driver A and driver B, both residents of New Jersey. A sues B for negligence in the state court of New Jersey. Should the New Jersey court apply New Jersey negligence law or New York negligence law? To resolve this question, the judge of the case must look to New Jersey's conflicts of law. The judge uses the conflicts of law rules of the state in which the court is sitting. In an effort to maintain consistent and predictable law, most states' rules of conflicts of law require the court to apply the law of the state in which the events underlying the dispute occurred. Thus, New Jersey's conflicts of law would require that the New Jersey court apply the rules of negligence of the state in which the accident occurred—that is, New York negligence law. The rules of conflicts of law are especially important when the states have different laws that may affect the outcome of the case. One purpose served by the law of conflicts of law is to prevent the plaintiff from *forum shopping*—choosing to sue in a particular state because its laws are more advantageous.

Federal Courts. As previously noted, two types of cases are brought in federal courts: cases involving federal law and cases involving diversity of the parties. In cases involving federal statutes or the Constitution, the federal courts apply federal law, including federal case law interpretations of the statutes and Constitution.

In cases involving diversity jurisdiction, however, the federal courts apply the substantive law of the state in which the court is sitting. For example, a federal district court located in Illinois hearing a case based upon diversity of citizenship applies Illinois law. Therefore, the federal court must follow local substantive constitutional, statutory, and common law in diversity jurisdiction cases. Although federal courts always applied state constitutional law and statutes when appropriate, for many years the federal courts developed their own body of substantive common law for diversity cases. In 1938, the United States Supreme Court overruled the holdings of prior cases that had allowed the federal courts to ignore state common law and held that federal courts exercising diversity jurisdiction were also required to apply the substantive common law of the local state.

Erie Railroad Co. v. Tompkins

58 S. Ct. 817 (1938)

While walking along a pathway next to defendant Erie Railroad Co.'s railroad tracks in Pennsylvania, plaintiff Tompkins was struck and injured by a train owned by Erie. Tompkins, a citizen of Pennsylvania, sued Erie, a New York corporation, for damages in a federal district court located in New York. Pennsylvania common law provided that persons using pathways along a railroad right of way were trespassers and that railroad companies were liable to trespassers only if the railroad had acted wantonly or willfully. Erie argued that the Pennsylvania common law rule should be applied. Tompkins argued that the federal court should disregard the Pennsyl-

vania law and adopt a rule holding the railroad company liable if it had acted negligently. The trial court held that the Pennsylvania common law was inapplicable and Tompkins was awarded $30,000 in damages; the Second Circuit Court of Appeals affirmed. Erie was granted a petition of certiorari to the United States Supreme Court.

Justice Brandeis

. . . The question for decision is whether the oft-challenged doctrine of *Swift v. Tyson* shall now be disapproved. . . .

First. Swift v. Tyson, [41 U.S. (16 Pet.) 1 (1842)] held that federal courts exercising jurisdiction on the ground of diversity of citizenship need not, in matters of general jurisprudence, apply the unwritten law of the State as declared by its highest court; that they are free to exercise an independent judgment as to what the common law of the State is—or should be. . . .

Second. Experience in applying the doctrine of *Swift v. Tyson* had revealed its defects, political and social; and the benefits expected to flow from the rule did not accrue. Persistence of state courts in their own opinions on questions of common law prevented uniformity; and the impossibility of discovering a satisfactory line of demarcation between the province of general law and that of local law developed a new well of uncertainties.

On the other hand, the mischievous results of the doctrine had become apparent. Diversity of citizenship jurisdiction was conferred in order to prevent apprehended discrimination in state courts against those not citizens of the State. *Swift v. Tyson* introduced grave discrimination by non-citizens against citizens. It made rights enjoyed under the unwritten "general law" vary according to whether enforcement was sought in the state or in the federal court; and the privilege of selecting the court in which the right should be determined was conferred upon the non-citizen. Thus, the doctrine rendered impossible equal protection of the law. In attempting to promote uniformity of law throughout the United States, the doctrine had prevented uniformity in the administration of the law of the State. . . .

The injustice and confusion incident to the doctrine of *Swift v. Tyson* have been repeatedly urged as reasons for abolishing or limiting diversity of citizenship jurisdiction. Other legislative relief has been proposed. If only a question of statutory construction were involved, we should not be prepared to abandon a doctrine so widely applied throughout nearly a century. But the unconstitutionality of the course pursued has now been made clear and compels us to do so.

Third. Except in matters governed by the Federal Constitution or by Acts of Congress, the law to be applied in any case is the law of the State. And whether the law of the State shall be declared by its Legislature in a statute or by its highest court in a decision is not a matter of federal concern. There is no federal general common law. Congress has no power to declare substantive rules of common law applicable in a State whether they be local in their nature or "general," be they commercial law or a part of the law of torts. And no clause in the Constitution purports to confer such a power upon the federal courts. . . .

The fallacy underlying the rule declared in *Swift v. Tyson* is made clear by Mr. Justice Holmes. The doctrine rests upon the assumption that there is "a transcendental body of law outside of any particular State but obligatory within it unless and until changed by statute," that federal courts have the power to use their judgment as to what the rules of common law are; and that in the federal courts "the parties are entitled to an independent judgment on matters of general law":

> "But law in the sense in which courts speak of it today does not exist without some definite authority behind it. . . . the authority and only authority is the State, and if that be so, the voice adopted by the State as its own [whether it be of its Legislature or of its Supreme Court] should utter the last word." [*Black & White Taxicab & Transfer Co. v. Brown & Yellow Taxicab & Transfer Co.*, 48 S. Ct. 404, 409 (1928).]

Thus the doctrine of *Swift v. Tyson* is, as Mr. Justice Holmes said, "an unconstitutional assumption of powers by courts of the United States which no lapse of time or respectable array of opinion should make us hesitate to correct." [*Black & White Taxicab & Transfer Co. v. Brown & Yellow Taxicab & Transfer Co.*, 48 S. Ct. 404, 408 (1928).]. . .

The Circuit Court of Appeals ruled that the question of liability is one of general law; and on that ground declined to decide the issue of state law. As we hold this was error, the judgment is reversed and the case remanded to it for further proceedings in conformity with our opinion.

Since the *Erie* decision the federal courts in exercising diversity jurisdiction apply the substantive common law of the state in which the court is located. In later decisions, the Court held that the substantive common law includes the rules of conflicts of law. As a result, in diversity cases the federal courts apply the same law that would have governed had the case been tried in the state courts.

Sometimes the federal courts must decide a case presenting an issue not previously resolved by the state courts. In these cases, the federal court may review related state law and decide the issue as it believes the state court would if it had had the opportunity to establish a rule of law. Nevertheless, the federal court may follow the "abstention" doctrine by which the court allows the state courts to rule on the issues prior to deciding the federal case. Because the abstention doctrine often results in protracted litigation, some states have adopted a procedure known as "certification of issues of law" that allows the federal court to obtain a ruling on the appropriate law from the state supreme court and then apply that law to the case before it.

Statutes of Limitation

Even if a court has jurisdiction over a particular case, the operation of a statute of limitations may prevent the court from exercising that jurisdiction. A **statute of limitation** requires the plaintiff to file a lawsuit within a specified period of time after the legal claim arises. A plaintiff who fails to file suit within the statute of limitation loses the right to recover on the claim. The typical statutory period runs from the date the legal claim arises to the date the suit is filed. How long it takes to ultimately dispose of the suit after filing is irrelevant. The purpose of a statute of limitation is to protect a defendant's rights by preventing persons from filing "stale claims," those that are so old that witnesses may have forgotten the relevant facts, may have died or moved out of the jurisdiction, or may have lost or destroyed relevant documents.

Statutes of limitation have been enacted by both

the federal and state legislatures for most civil and criminal cases. The UCC provides a four-year statute of limitations for claims involving contracts for the sale of goods.[16] States commonly provide a twenty-year statute of limitation on actions to recover possession of land. Cases seeking recovery for personal injury, sustained in an automobile accident for example, are commonly governed by a two-year statute of limitations. At both the state and federal level, criminal actions for very serious crimes such as murder may generally be commenced at any time without limitation.[17] Limitation periods for other criminal offenses vary. For example, prosecution of most federal crimes must be commenced within five years after the offense was committed.[18]

In cases within a court's equity jurisdiction, the doctrine of "laches" serves a purpose similar to that of a statute of limitations. Laches allows the court to deny recovery to a plaintiff who unreasonably delays in presenting an equitable claim to the court.

SUMMARY

1. In the United States, law is the body of principles and rules applied and enforced by the courts. Substantive law defines the rights and duties of members of society while procedural law establishes the mechanisms for enforcing rights and duties. Criminal law protects society as a whole by imposing penalties on those who violate minimum standards of socially acceptable conduct, whereas civil law protects individuals by providing remedies to those injured by the unlawful conduct of others. Public law involves the government in its capacity as a representative for all of society, while private law concerns persons in their individual capacities.

2. In the United States, both the individual state and the federal governments create law, and are organized under the doctrine of separation of powers by which governmental powers are divided among the legislative, executive and judicial branches. The three primary sources of law in the United States are constitutions, statutes, and the common law. A written constitution is a document that establishes the basic principles, governmental structure, and law of a state or nation. Statutes are written laws enacted by the federal or state legislatures. The common law consists of the body of cases previously decided by the courts.

3. The United States Constitution serves three important functions: (1) it limits the powers of the states; (2) it enumerates the powers the states have delegated to the federal government; and (3) it guarantees certain rights of the people of the United States. The doctrine of judicial review, first articulated in *Marbury v. Madison,* empowers the courts to review the acts of the executive and legislative branches of government and to refuse to enforce acts of those branches that violate the Constitution.

4. Under the doctrine of *stare decisis,* the courts follow the precedent found in the common law to resolve cases involving the same or similar facts. Precedent may be changed by a court's overruling the prior case or by the legislature's enacting statutes in derogation of the common law.

5. Courts interpret statutes in accordance with previous interpretations found in the case law. To assist in interpreting statutes in cases of first impression, the courts look to legislative history and may apply rules of construction.

6. A court is empowered to render binding decisions of law only in cases within the court's jurisdiction. Courts of original jurisdiction have the power to render the initial decision in the case. Courts of appellate jurisdiction are authorized only to review cases that have been tried in a court of original jurisdiction. Courts of general subject matter jurisdiction are empowered to hear all types of cases while courts of limited subject matter jurisdiction have authority to hear only specific types of cases.

7. State court systems generally include inferior courts, trial courts, and appellate courts. State trial courts usually are courts of general subject matter jurisdiction.

8. The federal court system consists of specialized inferior courts, United States district courts, courts of appeals, and the Supreme Court. Federal district courts, which are courts of limited subject matter jurisdiction, predominantly hear cases based on federal law and on

---

16. UCC §2-725. See discussion in Chapter 18.

17. See, for example, 18 U.S.C. §3281.
18. 18 U.S.C. §3282.

diversity of citizenship of the parties. The Supreme Court is the ultimate appellate court in the United States and reviews cases from both the state and federal court systems.

9. Generally, state courts apply the law of their own state. Federal courts apply federal law in cases based on federal question jurisdiction and the law of the state in which the court is sitting in cases based on diversity jurisdiction. The rules of conflicts of law establish the applicable law in both state and federal court cases in which state law from different states is involved.

10. To prevent persons from filing "stale" claims, state and federal statutes of limitation require the plaintiff to file a suit within a specified period of time after occurrence of the facts entitling the plaintiff to recover.

KEY TERMS

law	uniform codes, acts, or
legal system	laws
artificial persons	model acts
natural persons	common law
attorney	doctrine of *stare decisis*
substantive law	holding
procedural law	precedent
criminal law	Restatement of the Law
civil law	plaintiff
public law	defendant
private law	jurisdiction
courts of equity (courts of	original jurisdiction
chancery)	appellate jurisdiction
constitution	subject matter jurisdiction
Supremacy Clause	federal question
doctrine of judicial review	jurisdiction
statute	diversity jurisdiction
United States Code	writ of certiorari
Code of Federal	conflict of laws
Regulations	statute of limitation

QUESTIONS AND PROBLEMS

1-1 Define the words "justice" and "morals," using a dictionary if necessary. Explain the differences and similarities among the meanings of law, justice, and morals.

1-2 The legislature of the state of Illinois enacted an antitrust statute which included the following provision: "When the language of this Act is the same or similar to the language of federal antitrust law, the courts of this state in construing this Act shall follow the construction given to the federal law by the federal courts." In a lawsuit based on the state law, a party raised the issue that this provision violated the doctrine of separation of powers. Do you agree? Explain.

1-3 Under the common law, judges "make law." Is the use of the common law system in the United States consistent with the republican form of government and the doctrine of separation of powers? Explain.

1-4 Professor Karl Llewellyn, in discussing the common law and *stare decisis* stated:

In the large, disregarding for the moment peculiarities of our law and legal doctrine—in the large precedent consists in an official doing over again under similar circumstances substantially what has been done by him or his predecessor before. The foundation, then, of precedent is the official analogue of what, in society at large, we know as folkways, or as institutions, and of what in the individual, we know as habit. And the things which make for precedent in this broad sense are the same which make for habit and for institutions. It takes time and effort to solve problems. Once you have solved one it seems foolish to reopen it. Indeed you are likely to be quite impatient with the notion of reopening it. Both inertia and convenience speak for building further on what you have already built; for incorporating the decision once made, *the solution once worked out,* into your operating technique *without reexamination* of what *earlier went into* reaching your solution. [Llewellyn, *The Bramble Bush* 64–65 (1951)]

In the preceding quotation, is Professor Llewellyn indicating the advantages or the disadvantages of the doctrine of *stare decisis* and the use of precedent? Explain.

1-5 Reconsider the example on page 15 of the text in which the court held that a promise to make a gift is not legally enforceable.
(a) Assume in the example that Andrews orally promised to make a gift but in the subsequent case Baker's promise to make a gift was in writing. Should the court follow the holding of the Andrews case? Explain.
(b) Assume that a third case arises in which Chang promises to make a gift of $1,000,000 to the Metropolitan Art Museum on April 1. Relying on that promise, the museum enters into a contract to purchase a Van Gogh painting for $1,000,000. The museum must pay the seller of the painting on April 15 and intends to use Chang's gift for

that purpose. On April 1, Chang notifies the museum that he will not make the gift and the museum sues Chang for breach of promise. Should the court follow the precedent of the Andrews case? Why or why not?

1-6 In 1983, Willie was riding a horse on a Louisiana state highway when he was involved in an accident with an automobile. A blood test revealed that Willie was under the influence of alcohol at the time the accident occurred. Louisiana authorities filed criminal charges against Willie for operating a vehicle while intoxicated. The Louisiana criminal statutes include the following definition:

> The crime of operating a vehicle while intoxicated is the operating of any motor vehicle, aircraft, vessel or other means of conveyance while under the influence of alcoholic beverages, narcotic drugs, central nervous system stimulants, hallucinogenic drugs or barbiturates. . . .

Willie was found guilty, fined $350, and sentenced to thirty days in jail. Willie has appealed the case. Should the appellate court hold that the quoted statute is applicable to Willie's conduct? Explain by applying the appropriate rules of statutory construction.

1-7 Federal law provides that federal judges are appointed to their positions for life although they may be removed from office for misconduct. Suggest reasons why this law was adopted. Many state judges are elected by the general electorate and, therefore, must run for re-election on a periodic basis. Suggest reasons for these state laws. Do you think appointment or election of judges is a better policy? Explain.

1-8 XYZ Corporation breached a contract to manufacture and deliver certain machinery to Fred, a resident of California. Fred sued XYZ in a trial court of the state of California, a court of general subject matter jurisdiction. XYZ is a Delaware corporation with its principal place of business located in Arizona.

(a) Does the trial court have subject matter jurisdiction over this case? Why or why not? Do other state trial courts in the United States have subject matter jurisdiction? Explain.

(b) XYZ would prefer to have this case tried in a federal court. Would a federal district court have subject matter jurisdiction over the case? Explain. Could XYZ have the case transferred to a federal district court? Explain.

Major Topics

- the methods of resolving civil disputes
- the stages of a civil lawsuit from pretrial proceedings through appellate review
- the process of a civil trial, including the roles of the judge and jury
- the purpose and procedure of appellate review
- the legal effect of obtaining a judgment

Almost all the day-to-day activities of a business create potential for a civil dispute: a supplier may fail to deliver goods under a contract; a customer may refuse to pay a bill; one of the business's products may injure a consumer; an employee may be injured in a manufacturing plant; a marketing plan may involve restraint of trade. Although good business managers attempt to minimize the potential for dispute through careful planning, even the best-run businesses cannot avoid them.

A business that becomes engaged in a legal dispute may resort to **litigation,** contesting the claim in court, to resolve it. Because litigation has become increasingly time-consuming and costly, however, it often is not the best method for resolving a business dispute. The formal procedures of litigation, which are discussed later in this chapter, can require a business and its employees to devote valuable time to collecting and reviewing evidence, meeting with attorneys, and attending court hearings. Further costs are incurred to retain attorneys

who must draft documents, attend court hearings, review evidence and legal precedent, interview witnesses, and otherwise plan for trial. Additionally, litigation rarely resolves a dispute quickly. Because of pretrial proceedings and the volume of cases in the courts, most lawsuits do not come to trial until one to two years after they have been initiated[1] and complicated cases involving multiple parties or complex issues may not come to trial for many years. Complex business issues may further protract proceedings because the judge or jury is not familiar with economic, scientific, or other specialized information. Even after trial, the case may be prolonged by appeal. Litigation also often creates hostility between the parties, a result that is especially detrimental if the parties must maintain a business relationship such as a long-term contract or employer-employee relationship. Moreover, because court proceedings and documents generally are open to the public, a litigated case may produce adverse publicity for a business or the opportunity for its competitors to obtain valuable information. In addition, a successful plaintiff does not have the benefit of the damage award until the case is resolved and the judgment collected. Finally, even a strong case can be lost, and uncertainty regarding

---

1. In 1982, the median disposition for a federal case that went to trial was 19 months. State court cases generally take longer. ''The Trauma and Tedium of a Lawsuit,'' *U.S. News & World Report* 51, 52, Nov. 1, 1982.

the outcome of a case often adversely affects both parties' ability to plan operations.

Alternative Dispute Resolution

Because of the expense, delay, and uncertainty of litigation, most civil disputes involving businesses are resolved using alternative dispute resolution (ADR), processes. ADR encompasses a variety of procedures including time-tested techniques such as negotiation, mediation, and arbitration, as well as recent innovations such as minitrials and private trials. Although ADR is available to resolve any legal controversy, many ADR techniques are particularly suitable for resolving business disputes.

Almost all ADR techniques emphasize quick resolution of disputes using informal procedures and allow the parties to avoid crowded court dockets and the protracted appellate process. As a result, the delays associated with litigation generally are eliminated. Expedited or abbreviated ADR procedures often reduce the time parties and attorneys must devote to a dispute, thereby minimizing expenses. Further time and expense can be avoided by using ADR methods that employ experts as decision makers or facilitators to resolve complex business problems not readily understood by judges or juries. The informal procedures of ADR, as well as its emphasis on quick resolution, tend to minimize the hostility and frustration that can arise during a dispute so ADR is especially suitable for resolving disputes between businesses that must maintain long-term relationships. Most ADR processes also are conducted in private, free from scrutiny by competitors or the public.

Various methods of alternative dispute resolution are discussed in the following sections. The appropriate method for resolving a specific dispute depends on a number of factors including the nature of the dispute and the relationship of the parties.

Negotiation

The vast majority of business disputes are resolved through negotiation, a process by which two parties with differing demands reach an agreement generally through compromise and concession. Whether negotiation is informal (for instance, one or more telephone conversations between two business people), or formally structured (such as a meeting or meetings scheduled solely to resolve the dispute), the negotiation process generally follows a similar format. After defining their positions and communicating them to one another, the parties usually engage in a period of discussion, oral or in writing, in which they analyze the strengths and weaknesses of the other. Finally, one or both of the parties propose solutions usually requiring concessions by each. If the parties can mutually agree on appropriate concessions, the dispute will be resolved. Without agreement, the parties eventually become deadlocked, and resort to more formal dispute resolution techniques.

Negotiation is the simplest and most efficient method of dispute resolution, provided the parties truly desire to resolve their differences. Negotiation is such a common practice in business relationships that the parties often do not consciously realize that they are engaging in a dispute resolution technique. Although effective negotiating skills and strategies can be learned in business schools and other programs, negotiating parties also should be knowledgeable about the legal principles underlying their dispute. Many businesses, therefore, either consult with their attorneys throughout the negotiation process or refer the matter to their attorneys who then negotiate the dispute on behalf of their clients.

Mediation

If disputing parties reach a deadlock, they may seek the assistance of a third party to resolve the controversy. **Mediation** is a relatively informal process in which a neutral third party, the mediator, helps resolve a dispute. A mediator generally has no power to impose a resolution. In many respects, therefore, mediation can be considered as structured negotiation in which the mediator facilitates the process. Although mediators use different techniques and strategies, the mediator usually initiates the process by meeting with the disputing parties, either individually or jointly, to explain the mediation process and to gather information about the parties and their dispute. The mediator then attempts to define the issues, establish an agenda for mediation, and preserve an atmosphere conducive to communication. Through meetings with the parties, the mediator assists them in generating options for settlement and assessing the options. Finally, the mediator helps the parties reach concessions and compromises that will lead to a final settlement. If a resolution is reached, the mediator may help reduce the agreement to writing and work with the parties to implement the agreement.

Mediation, like negotiation, rarely is successful unless both parties truly desire to resolve their differences. Parties usually voluntarily agree to retain a mediator after a dispute has arisen, but some contractual agreements (such as a collective bargaining agreement between a business and a union) may require mediation of any disputes arising under the contract. Mediation long has been a popular technique for resolving labor-management conflicts and international business disputes, particularly those involving businesses and business people from Far Eastern countries. More recently, mediation has been used successfully to settle relatively minor consumer claims and landlord-tenant disputes, family matters relating to divorce and child custody, and environmental law problems involving numerous parties. Many courts now offer mediation services to help parties settle lawsuits prior to trial.

Mediation can resolve business disputes quickly and inexpensively because good faith negotiation often improves with the presence of a neutral third party. A good mediator also knows strategies and techniques to facilitate communication, minimize distrust and help develop alternatives when the parties are unable to achieve these goals without guidance. If the mediator also has expertise in the subject area of the dispute, the mediation process can expedite a fair resolution. The primary disadvantage of mediation is the mediator's lack of power to impose a binding resolution. Therefore, time and effort may be devoted to mediation without reaching a solution. To protect the legal interests of their clients, many attorneys now participate in mediation, if only to review the final agreement reached through the process.

Arbitration

Like mediation, **arbitration** uses a neutral third party to resolve a dispute. Unlike the mediator, however, an arbitrator generally is empowered to impose a binding decision that resolves the dispute

and that may be enforced by a court if the parties fail to comply. Unlike the court, which is a branch of government, the arbitrator derives its power to impose a binding decision from an express contract, the arbitration agreement, between the parties. Most frequently, parties to a contract include a provision requiring any disputes arising under the contract to be resolved through arbitration. Alternatively, parties may enter into an arbitration agreement, sometimes called an *Ad Hoc* agreement, after a dispute arises. Many arbitration agreements provide for a panel of three arbitrators, who reach a decision by majority vote.

The arbitration contract may establish all of the rules for the arbitration process, including selection of the arbitrator, designation of the site for the arbitration, procedures for presentation of evidence, and deadlines for hearings and the decision. Rather than develop these rules for each agreement, parties may simply incorporate rules previously developed by existing arbitration organizations, such as the American Arbitration Association, the International Chamber of Commerce, or the United Nations Commission on International Trade Law. The American Arbitration Association, a not-for-profit organization specializing in arbitration and other ADR methods since 1926, suggests the following standard clause for insertion in commercial contracts:

> Any controversy or claim arising out of or relating to this contract, or the breach thereof, shall be settled by arbitration in accordance with the Commercial Arbitration Rules of the American Arbitration Association, and* judgment on the award rendered by the arbitrator(s) may be entered in any court having jurisdiction thereof.[2]

Although the exact process depends on the agreement, arbitration typically follows a standard procedure. The following discussion is based on the Commercial Arbitration Rules of the American Arbitration Association.

To initiate the process, one or both parties notify the arbitrator or arbitration association that the dis-

---

2. American Arbitration Association, *Commercial Arbitration Rules* 2 to (1988).

pute is being submitted to arbitration. If the agreement does not specify the arbitrator, selection often is made from a panel of arbitrators. The American Arbitration Association, for example, maintains a panel of 60,000 arbitrators, many of whom have expertise or specialize in certain types of disputes. After appointment, the arbitrator generally assumes responsibility for the arbitration process and schedules a hearing with notice to the parties. The arbitrator also may schedule an administrative conference or preliminary hearing with the parties to arrange the production and exchange of pertinent evidence or to discuss any matters that could expedite the proceedings. At the arbitration hearing, each party presents its claims, evidence and witnesses subject to the arbitrator's determination of relevancy and materiality. Generally, legal rules of evidence do not apply. Following the hearing, the arbitrator may allow the parties to submit written briefs. The arbitrator then renders a written decision, known as an "award," that resolves the dispute and grants any remedy deemed just by the arbitrator. Although the award may explain the reasons for the decision, a formal opinion is not required and the award usually need not follow legal precedent.

If the arbiration is binding, the parties must comply with the award. To ensure enforcement, most arbitration agreements provide for entry of a judgment on the award in a court where it then may be enforced in the same manner as a judgment rendered by the court. At the request of one or both of the parties, the court may provide a limited review of the award generally restricted to a determination that the arbitration proceedings were fair and unbiased. The court, however, will not review the merits of the case. In the following decision, the Supreme Court considers the appropriate scope of review of an arbitration award in a labor relations case.

United Paperworkers International Union, AFL-CIO v. Misco, Inc.

108 S.Ct. 364 (1987)

> Isiah Cooper worked at a paper converting plant owned by Misco, Inc. where he operated a hazardous machine used to cut coils of paper. Following a police search of Cooper's home where substantial amounts of marijuana were found, Cooper was arrested and charged with possession of marijuana. At the time of his arrest, Cooper was sitting in the backseat of a white Cutlass automobile located on Misco's parking lot; a lighted marijuana cigarette was in the frontseat ashtray. Although Cooper was alone at the time, two other men recently had left the automobile. The police later searched Cooper's own car and found marijuana gleanings. Cooper notified Misco that he had been arrested for possession of marijuana. Several days later, after Misco learned that Cooper had been arrested on its parking lot in a car containing a lighted marijuana cigarette, Misco discharged Cooper asserting that his presence in the Cutlass violated company rule II.1 prohibiting use or possession of controlled substances on company property.
>
> Misco's employees were represented by the United Paperworkers International Union, AFL-CIO and worked under a collective bargaining agreement that required binding arbitration of any grievance arising from interpretation or application of the contract. Cooper filed a grievance protesting his discharge and the matter was referred to an arbitrator for resolution of the issue whether Misco had "just cause to discharge [Cooper] under Rule II.1." The arbitrator ruled in favor of Cooper finding that the evidence was insufficient to prove that he had used or possessed marijuana on company property. The arbitrator ordered Cooper reinstated and Misco filed suit in federal district court requesting that the award be set aside. The district court ordered the award to be set aside on the ground that it violated public policy. After the court of appeals affirmed, the Supreme Court granted the union's petition for review.

Justice White

. . . Collective-bargaining agreements commonly provide grievance procedures to settle disputes between union and employer with respect to the interpretation and application of the agreement and require binding arbitration for unsettled grievances. In such cases, and this is such a case, the Court made clear almost 30 years ago that the courts play only a limited role when asked to review the decision of an arbitrator. The courts are not authorized to reconsider the merits of an award even though the parties may allege that the award rests on errors of fact or on misinterpretation of the contract. . . .

Because the parties have contracted to have disputes settled by an arbitrator chosen by them rather than by a judge, it is the arbitrator's view of the facts and of the meaning of the contract that they have agreed to accept. Courts thus do not sit to hear claims of factual or legal error by an arbitrator as an appellate court does in reviewing decisions of lower courts. To resolve disputes about the application of a collective-bargaining agreement, an arbitrator must find facts and a court may not reject those findings simply because it disagrees with them. The same is true of the arbitrator's interpretation of the contract. The arbitrator may not ignore the plain language of the contract; but the parties having authorized the arbitrator to give meaning to the language of the agreement, a court should not reject an award on the ground that the arbitrator misread the contract. . . . So, too, where it is contemplated that the arbitrator will determine remedies for contract violations that he finds, courts have no authority to disagree with his honest judgment in that respect. If the courts were free to intervene on these grounds, the speedy resolution of grievances by private mechanisms would be greatly undermined. . . . Of course, decisions procured by the parties through fraud or through the arbitrator's dishonesty need not be enforced. But there is nothing of that sort involved in this case.

The Company's position, simply put, is that the arbitrator committed grievous error in finding that the evidence was insufficient to prove that Cooper had possessed or used marijuana on company property. But the Court of Appeals, although it took a distinctly jaundiced view of the arbitrator's decision in this regard, was not free to refuse enforcement because it considered Cooper's presence in the white Cutlass, in the circumstances, to be ample proof that Rule II.1 was violated. No dishonesty is alleged; only improvident, even silly, fact-finding is claimed. This is hardly sufficient basis for disregarding what the agent appointed by the parties determined to be the historical facts. . . .

The Court of Appeals . . . held that the evidence of marijuana in Cooper's car required that the award be set aside because to reinstate a person who had brought drugs onto the property was contrary to the public policy "against the operation of dangerous machinery by persons under the influence of drugs or alcohol." 768 F.2d, at 743. We cannot affirm that judgment.

A court's refusal to enforce an arbitrator's award under a collective-bargaining agreement because it is contrary to public policy is a specific application of the more general doctrine, rooted in the common law, that a court may refuse to enforce contracts that violate law or public policy. . . . [A] court's refusal to enforce an arbitrator's *interpretation* of such contracts is limited to situations where the contract as interpreted would violate "some explicit public policy" that is "well defined and dominant, and is to be ascertained 'by reference to the laws and legal precedents and not from general considerations of supposed public interests.' " [*W. R. Grace & Co. v. Rubber Workers*, 103 S.Ct. 2177 (1983), quoting *Muschany v. United States*, 65 S.Ct. 442 (1945).] . . .

As we see it, the formulation of public policy set out by the Court of Appeals did not comply with the statement that such a policy must be "ascertained 'by reference to the laws and legal precedents and not from general considerations of supposed public interests.' " . . . The Court of Appeals made no attempt to review existing laws and legal precedents in order to demonstrate that they establish a "well defined and dominant" policy against the operation of dangerous machinery while under the influence of drugs. Although certainly such a judgment is firmly rooted in common sense, we explicitly held in *W. R. Grace* that a formulation of public policy based only on "general considerations of supposed public interests" is not the sort that permits a court to set aside an arbitration award that was entered in accordance with a valid collective-bargaining agreement.

Even if the Court of Appeals' formulation of public policy is to be accepted, no violation of that policy was clearly shown in this case. . . .

To conclude from the fact that marijuana had been found in Cooper's car that Cooper had ever been or would be under the influence of marijuana while he was on the job and operating dangerous machinery is an exercise in fact-finding about Cooper's use of drugs and his amenability to discipline, a task that exceeds the authority of a court asked to overturn an arbitration award. The parties did not bargain for the facts to be found by a court, but by an arbitrator chosen by them who had more opportunity to observe Cooper and to be familiar with the plant and its problems. Nor does the fact that it is inquiring into a possible violation of public policy excuse a court for doing the arbitrator's task. . . .

[Judgment reversed.]

———————————————————————

Arbitration can be an excellent method for resolving business disputes, especially those involving contractual matters, because the parties obtain a definite resolution of the controversy usually within a reasonable period of time. Warren E. Burger, then Chief Justice of the United States Supreme Court, summarized the advantages of arbitration by stating: "My own experience persuades me that in terms of cost, time, and human wear and tear, arbitration is vastly better than conventional litigation for many kinds of cases. . . . I cannot emphasize too strongly to those in business and industry—and especially to lawyers—that every private contract of real consequence to the parties ought to be treated as a 'candidate' for binding private arbitration.[3]"

The success of private arbitration had led many states and some federal courts to authorize the use of court annexed arbitration. Under these programs, trial courts may require non-binding arbitration of certain civil suits but either party may request litigation of the suit if dissatisfied with the arbitration proceedings. Those jurisdictions using court annexed arbitration report a reduction in both court congestion and court costs.

Other ADR Methods

In recent years, new ADR methods have been devised to meet special problems. Two recently developed forms of dispute resolution are of special interest to business: mini-trials and private trials.

The mini-trial, which was first used in 1977 to resolve a patent dispute, is a form of structured negotiation designed specifically for businesses. At a mini-trial, the attorneys present a summary of the evidence and law underlying the dispute to the parties' upper level management executives who have the authority to settle the dispute. Generally, a neutral adviser or moderator presides over the proceedings but the adviser has no power to resolve the dispute. The attorneys usually present factual information informally without witnesses, but expert witnesses often are employed to support the parties' assertions. At the conclusion of the presentation, the executives meet in private—without attorneys or support staff—and try to reach an agreed settlement based on the evidence presented during the mini-trial. In some cases the adviser may provide some assistance, serving as a sort of mediator, to help the executives reach agreement.

Private trials, sometimes described as "rent-a-judge," are a special form of litigation in which the parties agree to have their case resolved by a retired judge authorized to try cases under state law. The decision of the retired judge then is entered as the judgment of the court in which the case was filed. A private trial, therefore, must follow all of the procedural rules that apply to court trials and the decision is subject to appeal (see discussion of litigation that follows). Private trials, which were first developed in California, currently are available only in about one-fifth of the states as authorized by state statute. The primary advantage of a private trial is the speed with which the dispute can be resolved because the retired judge is not encumbered with a heavy workload. Private trials also enable the parties to select a judge who has expertise in the subject matter of the dispute so that the trial may be expedited and the likelihood of legal error minimized.

Alternative dispute resolution processes are likely to continue to grow in the future. They have proved important in saving time and money, in providing more flexible, and often private, methods of resolving disputes, and in relieving court congestion. Yet, alternative dispute resolution will not replace the judicial system because litigation serves important purposes that cannot be achieved by private means. Table 2–1 briefly compares the various methods of civil dispute resolution.

———————————————————————

3. Burger, *Using Arbitration to Achieve Justice*, Remarks before the American Arbitration Association and the Minnesota State Bar Association (August 21, 1985), reprinted in *The Arbitration Journal* 4, 6 (December, 1985).

Table 2–1	Comparison of Methods of Civil Dispute Resolution*			
	Litigation	*Arbitration*	*Mediation*	*Negotiation*
Private/Public	Public	Private	Private	Private
Third Party Involvement	Judge: neutral decisionmaker imposed on parties; generally no expertise in subject of dispute.	Arbitrator: neutral decisionmaker usually selected by parties; generally has expertise in subject of dispute.	Mediator: facilitator selected by parties; generally has expertise in subject of dispute.	None
Procedural Characteristics	Very formal; applies procedural and substantive rules set by law.	Formal; procedural and substantive rules may be set by parties.	Usually informal; unstructured.	Usually informal; unstructured.
Presentation of Evidence	Each party may present evidence and arguments, generally limited by rules of relevance.	Each party may present evidence and arguments, generally limited by rules of relevance.	Each party may present evidence and arguments, usually without limitations.	Each party may present evidence and arguments, usually without limitations.
Final Outcome	Judgment, supported by opinion.	Award, sometimes supported by opinion.	Parties seek mutually acceptable agreement.	Parties seek mutually acceptable agreement.
Enforceability	Binding, subject to appellate review.	Generally binding, subject to limited judicial review.	If agreement reached, may be enforced as contract.	If agreement reached, may be enforced as contract.
Variations	Private judging (parties allowed to select judge).	Court-annexed arbitration (non-binding arbitration required in conjunction with litigation).	Mini-trial (upper level management participates; limits on presentation of evidence and arguments).	

*This table is adapted from Goldberg, Green, and Sander, *Dispute Resolution* 8–9 (1985).

Litigation—Pretrial Proceedings

In litigation, a dispute is resolved in a court of law by a neutral judge who applies principles of law set forth in constitutions, statutes, and the common law. Courts generally apply law in a consistent manner using the doctrine of *stare decisis*. The court system also provides parties the opportunity to litigate new issues of law in order to develop rules that can be used for guidance in determining future conduct. Perhaps the most important advantage of litigation is that the parties are guaranteed due process of law. The Fifth and Fourteenth Amendments to the Constitution prohibit the federal and state governments from depriving a person

of life, liberty or property without due process of law. Because the courts, as one branch of the government, are empowered in civil cases to deprive a person of property—for example, by granting a remedy requiring one party to pay money damages to the other—they must comply with the constitutional due process mandate in resolving civil disputes.[4]

Due process of law (specifically "procedural due process") entitles a party to a civil lawsuit to

---

4. Criminal proceedings must also comply with the requirements of due process (see Chapter 3).

receive notice of the alleged violation of law and a hearing in which the party may defend its actions. To implement this guarantee, courts have adopted rules of civil procedure to be followed in lawsuits. Each state, as well as the federal government, has its own rules of civil procedure; yet, they generally are very similar. Thus, all lawsuits proceed in three broad stages: the pleadings stage, the discovery stage, and the trial. Some cases include a fourth stage—the appeal. At any time during this process, the parties may agree to settle their case, and at certain points the court may terminate the case as a matter of law. As a result, fewer than ten percent of civil lawsuits actually reach trial.[5]

Pleadings Stage

Pleadings are written documents that summarize the facts and establish the legal issues of a lawsuit. These documents are filed with the court and are served on the parties to the lawsuit. The pleadings include the complaint, the answer, counterclaims, crossclaims, third-party complaints and answers to the counterclaims, crossclaims, and third-party complaints.

The Complaint. A lawsuit begins when the plaintiff files a **complaint** against a defendant.[6] The complaint includes a statement of the basis for the court's jurisdiction, allegations of fact, and a prayer or demand for relief. The allegations of fact are the plaintiff's statement of the facts underlying the dispute and must present a **cause of action:** facts that, if proven, entitle the plaintiff to judicial relief. Statutory law and the common law establish the elements of a cause of action. A cause of action for breach of contract, for example, requires that the facts establish the following elements: the existence of a contract, the defendant's duty to perform some act under the contract, the defendant's failure to perform, and an injury to the plaintiff resulting from the defendant's failure to perform. If

the plaintiff bases a claim on more than one cause of action, the facts supporting each cause of action are listed in separate counts within the complaint.

Following the allegations in each count, the plaintiff requests the court to provide a remedy for the alleged wrong in a statement called the **prayer for relief.** Usually, the plaintiff requests **damages,** a monetary award.[7] Damages are known as the "legal remedy" or "remedy at law" because a monetary award was the traditional remedy available in courts of law. Because most courts of law and equity have been merged in the United States, the prayer for relief can include a request for an equitable remedy such as an injunction or specific performance of a contract.

Many lawsuits involve only two parties, but in other cases, multiple parties may be involved. If two or more persons join together to bring a lawsuit, they are called "co-plaintiffs." Similarly, the plaintiff or plaintiffs may sue more than two or more persons who become "co-defendants."

State and federal statutory law have created a special type of lawsuit known as a **class action** for cases involving numerous plaintiffs. In a class action one or more persons may file a lawsuit on their own behalf and on behalf of all persons (the class) having claims based on common issues of fact and law. Under federal law, all members of the class must be notified of the lawsuit. Those who agree to become a part of the class then are bound by a court decision resolving the dispute. A class action might be appropriate, for example, if a large group of consumers purchased a defective product from a manufacturer. The class action serves to prevent multiple suits that might result in inconsistent judgments and facilitates litigation of matters in which

---

5. See, for example, Administrative Office of the U.S. Courts, *Annual Report of the Director.*

6. In some states or in certain types of cases, the initial pleading is called a petition; the party filing the suit is called the petitioner; and the party being sued is called the respondent.

---

7. Damages are of various types. For example, general damages (also called "actual" or "compensatory" damages) are designed to compensate the plaintiff for the direct and immediate losses suffered because of the defendant's conduct. Special or consequential damages, on the other hand, may be requested for injuries peculiar to the plaintiff which would not normally occur to other plaintiffs under similar conditions. Consequential damages are discussed in detail in Chapter 15 and Chapter 19. A third form of damages is known as punitive damages (or exemplary damages) which consist of a monetary award in excess of plaintiff's actual losses designed to punish the defendant for aggravated misconduct. Punitive damages are discussed further in Chapter 15.

no individual plaintiff has a claim large enough to justify the expenses of litigation.

Service of Process. After the plaintiff files the complaint, the defendant must be provided notice of the suit by **service of process**—formal delivery of the complaint and a summons to the defendant. The **summons** orders the defendant to appear in court on a certain date or to answer the complaint within a specified number of days. The proper method of service of process varies from state to state but, generally, requires the sheriff to personally serve the defendant with the summons and complaint. In some cases, service of process may be made by mailing or delivering the complaint and summons to the defendant's residence. The sheriff usually provides a written record of service of process to the court.

Personal Jurisdiction. Service of process is effective only if the court has personal jurisdiction over the defendant. **Personal jurisdiction** is a court's power and authority to issue a judgment that is binding on the parties.[8] The plaintiff, by filing the lawsuit with the court, voluntarily submits to its jurisdiction thereby agreeing to be bound by the court's judgment of the case.

Personal jurisdiction over the defendant, however, depends on the relationship of the defendant to the state in which the court is located. A state court has personal jurisdiction over all persons who are domiciled within the state and who are properly served with the summons and complaint. A defendant who is not a resident of the state is subject to a state court's personal jurisdiction if the defendant, while present in the state, is properly served with the summons and complaint. A nonresident may also consent to the court's personal jurisdiction thereby waiving the right to challenge the authority of the court to issue a judgment binding on him.

If, however, an out-of-state resident does not consent or is not served within the state, a state court has personal jurisdiction only over a defendant who has had *minimum contacts* with the state. In other words, a nonresident defendant who has certain contacts, ties, or relations with the state may be subject to the personal jurisdiction of that state's courts. To determine whether an out-of-state defendant has had minimum contacts with the state, the court examines the nature and extent of the activities that the defendant has conducted within the state. The court determines whether the defendant has in some way enjoyed the protection and benefits of the state's laws so that he or she should be obligated to submit to the state court's jurisdiction.

The concept of minimum contacts is especially important in determining when businesses or corporations that distribute goods or services in various states should be required to defend lawsuits filed against them in those states. In the landmark case of *International Shoe Co. v. State of Washington,*[9] the United States Supreme Court first examined the minimum contacts that subject an out-of-state corporation to the personal jurisdiction of a state court. International Shoe Co., a corporation with its principal place of business in Missouri, employed salespeople who lived in the state of Washington and solicited orders there. The corporation had no offices in Washington and all merchandise was shipped from St. Louis. The state of Washington sued International Shoe Co. in a Washington court for failure to pay unemployment taxes for several of its salespeople who worked in the state. Service of process was made by delivering the notice of assessment to a salesman in Washington and mailing a copy by registered mail to International Shoe's offices in St. Louis. In holding that the Washington state court had personal jurisdiction over International Shoe Co., the Supreme Court noted that

> [the Due Process Clause] does not contemplate that a state may make binding a judgment *in personam* against an individual or corporate defendant with which the state has no contacts, ties, or relations. . . . But to the extent that a corporation exercises the privilege of conducting activities within a state, it enjoys the benefits and pro-

---

8. Personal jurisdiction should not be confused with a court's subject matter jurisdiction—the statutory or constitutional grant of power to a court authorizing it to resolve certain types of cases. A court's personal jurisdiction over the parties is determined on a case-by-case basis.

---

9. 66 S. Ct. 154 (1945).

tection of the laws of that state. The exercise of that privilege may give rise to obligations, and, so far as those obligations arise out of or are connected with the activities within the state, a procedure which requires the corporation to respond to a suit brought to enforce them can, in most instances, hardly be said to be undue. . . .

Applying these standards, the activities carried on in behalf of appellant in the State of Washington were neither irregular nor casual. They were systematic and continuous throughout the years in question. They resulted in a large volume of interstate business, in the course of which appellant received the benefits and protection of the laws of the state, including the right to resort to the courts for the enforcement of its rights. The obligation which is here sued upon arose out of those very activities. It is evident that these operations establish sufficient contacts or ties with the state of the forum to make it reasonable and just, according to our traditional conception of fair play and substantial justice, to permit the state to enforce the obligations which appellant has incurred there. Hence we cannot say that the maintenance of the present suit in the State of Washington involves an unreasonable or undue procedure. . . .[10]

Long Arm Statutes. Since the Supreme Court's holding in *International Shoe Co.*, most states have enacted **long arm statutes** to codify the minimum contacts that subject a nonresident defendant to a state court's jurisdiction. Generally, these statutes provide that a court has personal jurisdiction over a defendant in cases arising from:

1. The defendant's transacting business in the state;
2. The defendant's contracting to supply goods or services in the state, or to insure any person, property, or risk located in the state;
3. The defendant's committing a tort in the state or causing injury as a result of business transacted or solicited in the state; or

4. The defendant's owning, using, or possessing real property interests in the state.

Note that when jurisdiction over a defendant is based solely upon a long arm statute, only causes of action arising from acts enumerated in the statute may be asserted against the defendant. That is, by coming into the state to defend a suit based upon long arm jurisdiction, the defendant is not thereby subjected to the general personal jurisdiction of the state's courts.

Although long arm statutes give a court personal jurisdiction over a nonresident defendant, service of process still must be made. Usually, the long arm statutes require that the summons and complaint be delivered to the out-of-state defendant or to an agent of the defendant located within the state. States generally require a corporation to appoint an in-state agent upon whom service of process may be made as a condition of doing business within the state.

At issue in the following case was whether a defendant should be subjected to personal jurisdiction under a long arm statute.

Rostad v. On-Deck, Inc.
372 N.W.2d 717 (Minn. 1985)

While umpiring a softball game in Minnesota, plaintiff Dean Rostad was injured by a bat weight, a doughnut-shaped metal ring that is slipped over a baseball bat while a batter is taking warm-up swings. During the softball game, the bat weight slipped off a bat and hit Rostad in the head. Rostad and his wife sued defendant On-Deck, Inc., a New Jersey corporation that had manufactured the bat weight, in a Minnesota trial court. On-Deck requested dismissal of the case alleging that the court lacked personal jurisdiction over On-Deck.

On-Deck had no offices, property, or employees in Minnesota. On-Deck formerly had employed a national distributor to market the bat weights and later sold them directly to retailers such as Sears and K-Mart. The bat weight that injured Rostad had been found by a softball player at a ballfield located in Minnesota. Rostad offered evidence establishing that bat weights were sold by local stores but could

---

10. 66 S. Ct. at 160.

not establish that the one causing his injury had been purchased in Minnesota.

The trial court dismissed the suit but the court of appeals held that the court had personal jurisdiction over On-Deck because of On-Deck Inc.'s contacts with the state of Minnesota. On-Deck appealed to the Minnesota Supreme Court.

Yetka, Justice

. . . The issue in this case is whether Minnesota can exercise jurisdiction over a foreign corporation which sells products in Minnesota through distributors under a "stream of commerce" theory and when the plaintiffs cannot show how the particular product arrived in the state.

The plaintiffs seek personal jurisdiction over On-Deck, Inc., a New Jersey corporation, by Minnesota's long arm statute. It allows jurisdiction over a defendant if that defendant "[c]ommits any act outside Minnesota causing injury or property damage in Minnesota." Minn. Stat. § 543.-19, subd. 1(d) (1984). . . .

Due process requires that a defendant have minimum contacts with a jurisdiction before being required to defend against a lawsuit in that jurisdiction. . . . To have minimum contacts, the defendant must have purposefully availed itself of the privilege of conducting activities within the jurisdiction. . . . In Minnesota, a five-factor test . . . is used to determine if minimum contacts exist. It requires the court to evaluate:

1. The quantity of contacts with the forum state,
2. The nature and quality of contacts,
3. The source and connection of the cause of action with these contacts,
4. The interest of the state providing a forum,
5. The convenience of the parties.

. . . The first three factors are the most important. . . .

1. *The Quantity of the Contacts*

Despite having sold thousands of its bat weights here, On-Deck claims it has no contacts with Minnesota. On-Deck points out that it has never had an office, sales outlet, place of business, or agent for service of process here. It claims it has never had a direct contact with Minnesota. This may be true, but it fails to account for On-Deck's numerous indirect contacts with Minnesota.

On-Deck ignores its indirect contacts with Minnesota because it believes that, after the United States Supreme Court's decision in *World-Wide Volkswagen Corp. v. Woodson* [100 S. Ct. 559 (1980)], "purposeful contacts" must be direct contacts. . . .

The *World-Wide Volkswagen* case dealt with a [New York] regional distributor and a retail dealer of cars at the end of the distribution chain who were being hailed into court in a jurisdiction [Oklahoma] far from their areas of distribution simply because the plaintiff had driven the car to that jurisdiction. . . . Jurisdiction over the automobile's manufacturer and importer was assumed, though not at issue. . . . Regional distributors and retail dealers cannot, according to the Supreme Court, be forced to defend lawsuits in jurisdictions far from their area of business just because a plaintiff brought the product to the jurisdiction. . . .

Far different, however, is the situation of a manufacturer or a primary distributor. . . . A manufacturer who places its product in the stream of commerce in an effort to serve, directly or indirectly, markets in a jurisdiction is subject to suit in that jurisdiction under *World-Wide Volkswagen*.

Although On-Deck does not have any direct contacts with Minnesota that can be proven in this case, it has a plethora of indirect contacts. It entered into contracts with others to distribute its products throughout North America, Hawaii and the Caribbean, a market which specifically includes Minnesota. The On-Deck trademark and Elston Howard's picture are on the packaging of every weight. Both Frank Hamilton, the owner of On-Deck, and Elston Howard, the president of On-Deck, have traveled the United States extensively marketing their product. On-Deck's distributors have, in fact, attempted to and been quite successful at marketing the product in Minnesota, and On-Deck has profited as a result. Frank Hamilton's claim that he never knew his products were marketed in Minnesota, aside from its incredulity, is irrelevant. On-Deck's distribution contracts and marketing efforts were calculated attempts to create a national market for his product, a market which specifically includes Minnesota. The bat weights arrived here not by some fortuitous happenstance of a plaintiff bringing the product to the jurisdiction as in *World-Wide Volkswagen,* but by the purposeful marketing efforts of On-Deck and On-Deck's distributors. On-Deck, having attempted and succeeded in penetrating the market in Minnesota for bat weights, albeit through distributors, has had numerous contacts with Minnesota.

2. The Nature and Quality of the Contacts

The appellant argues that because this bat weight was found on a field and there is no way of discovering how the weight came to this state, On-Deck's contacts with Minnesota are not of a quality sufficient to support jurisdiction. This argument ignores the fact that often there is no way that a plaintiff can know how a defective product actually weaved its way through commerce's labyrinth. The fact that the manufacturer's goods came to the jurisdiction by an unknown and thereby a possibly circuitous route does not change the fact that the product injured someone in a jurisdiction where the manufacturer can expect to be sued. . . .

The nature of On-Deck's contacts have been, for the most part, sales. It has profited by sale of thousands of its bat weights in Minnesota. In a commercial operation, sales are the most tangible contact with a jurisdiction. Although through intermediaries, these sales were accomplished under the marketing contracts for the benefit of On-Deck. Additionally, there was marketing on On-Deck's part. It specifically required that its trademark be placed prominently on the packages of its product. Elston Howard, the president of the company, was pictured on every package. It can be assumed that its distributors also marketed the product in this state. On-Deck thrust its corporate image into the jurisdiction, both by its own packaging requirements and the actions of its distributors, and profited by it. The nature and quality of On-Deck's contacts weigh in favor of jurisdiction.

3. The Source of the Contacts

The source of the contacts is, in the first instance, from On-Deck itself. It wanted a national market, a market including Minnesota, so it contracted with others to achieve its distribution goals. Through

savvy marketing, the bat weight became a desirable item, desirable enough that somebody purchased this bat weight and desirable enough that, when found, it was put to use at its intended purpose. On-Deck will not now be allowed to hide behind the structuring of its distribution system when On-Deck's intent was to enter the market here and profit thereby. . . .

[Judgment affirmed.]

Personal Jurisdiction in Federal Courts. The federal government has adopted rules similar to those of the states to govern service of process for cases brought in federal district courts.[11] If the defendant is an individual or corporation, federal law also allows service of the summons and complaint to be made according to the rules of the state in which the federal court is located. A federal district court has personal jurisdiction over a defendant who is properly served and a resident of the state, or who is served within the state, or who is subject to the state's long arm statute. In certain cases involving multiple parties, a federal district court may also obtain personal jurisdiction over a defendant properly served who resides within 100 miles of the court, even in another state. In addition, specific federal statutes often permit service of federal court process beyond the territorial limits of the state in cases brought under those statutes. In the federal courts, service of process generally is made by a United States marshall.

Answer to the Complaint. After service of process has been made, a defendant who intends to contest the lawsuit files an answer to the complaint or a motion to dismiss the complaint within the time period specified in the summons. If the defendant does not file an answer or motion, the court may enter a **default judgment**—a ruling in favor of the plaintiff granting the relief requested in the complaint. To contest the lawsuit on its merits, the defendant files an **answer** to the complaint within the time specified in the summons. In the answer, the defendant must reply to each allegation of the

---

11. Fed. R. Civ. P. Rule 4, 28 U.S.C.

complaint by admitting or denying the truth of the allegation. If the defendant does not know whether the allegation is true or false, and so states, the statement has the same effect as a denial. The complaint and answer establish the issues of the case. Every allegation of the complaint not admitted in the answer must be proved by the plaintiff; all facts admitted are accepted as established when the trial occurs.

The answer also must list any affirmative defenses that the defendant intends to prove at trial. An **affirmative defense** is an allegation of facts that the law recognizes as a bar to the plaintiff's claim. Affirmative defenses are discussed further in later chapters but include matters such as expiration of the statute of limitations, discharge of the claim by bankruptcy, or prior adjudication of the claim.

Counterclaims, Crossclaims, and Third-Party Complaints.

At the same time the defendant answers the complaint, she also may file counterclaims against the plaintiff. A **counterclaim** is a complaint filed by the defendant against the plaintiff.[12] The defendant also may file appropriate **crossclaims**—complaints against other parties listed as defendants in the lawsuit. Crossclaims generally must arise from the same occurrence underlying the original complaint. The defendant named in the original complaint also may sue other persons not named as parties in the original suit by filing a pleading called a **third-party complaint.**

Assume that an automobile accident occurs involving separate cars driven by Alfred, Betty, and Charlie. Alfred as plaintiff files a complaint naming Betty and Charlie as defendants and alleging that each of them negligently caused the accident. Betty, who believes that the accident was caused by Alfred and Charlie, could file a counterclaim for negligence against Alfred and a crossclaim for negligence against Charlie. Assume further that Betty

believes the accident also was caused in part by Donna, a bicyclist who rode into the street in front of the cars. Betty could file a third-party complaint against Donna.

Counterclaims, crossclaims, and third-party complaints are treated procedurally as complaints. That is, the counterdefendant, crossdefendant, or third-party defendant must be served with the counterclaim, crossclaim, or third-party complaint. Each party then has the opportunity to answer and assert other claims against the named parties or third parties. In a complicated lawsuit, the filing of pleadings may continue for several months until all appropriate persons are brought into the lawsuit.

Motions.

A **motion** is an application to the court to issue an order on a matter of law. Motions—either written or oral—are made during pretrial proceedings and throughout a trial. After a party makes a motion, the judge generally allows oral or written arguments in support of or in opposition to the motion. The judge rules either by granting or by denying the motion. During the pleadings stage, the parties may file various types of motions including a motion to dismiss the complaint, a motion for judgment on the pleadings, and a motion for change of venue or "place of trial."

Motion to Dismiss the Complaint.

A **motion to dismiss the complaint** is filed by the defendant, usually in lieu of answering the complaint. The motion may request the court to dismiss the lawsuit on the grounds that the court does not have the power or authority to hear the case or to provide the remedy requested by the plaintiff. For example, the defendant may file a motion to dismiss on the grounds that the court lacks subject matter jurisdiction over the case or lacks personal jurisdiction over the defendant. Another basis for a motion to dismiss is that the complaint fails to state a claim for which judicial relief may be granted (sometimes called a "general demurrer"). This motion basically asserts that even if the plaintiff could prove all of the allegations of fact, the facts do not establish a legally recognized cause of action entitling the plaintiff to a judicial remedy.

If the judge grants a motion to dismiss, the case is dismissed, effectively ending the lawsuit. If, however, the judge denies the motion, the defen-

---

12. Counterclaims are either compulsory or permissive. In most jurisdictions, the law requires the defendant to file all compulsory counterclaims: legal claims arising from the same facts alleged in the original complaint. A defendant who fails to do so may be barred from suing on the claim in the future. Permissive counterclaims are any that the defendant is not required to file. Permissive counterclaims usually concern facts not related to the plaintiff's cause of action.

dant then must answer the complaint and the pleadings process continues.

Motion for Judgment on the Pleadings. After all pleadings have been filed, one or both of the parties may file another motion called a **motion for judgment on the pleadings,** which is similar to a general demurrer and allows the court to rule as a matter of law that one of the parties is entitled to judgment. Because the pleadings generally reveal many disputed facts, this motion is granted infrequently.

Motion for Change of Venue. Another motion that may be made by the defendant is a motion for change of venue, or "place of trial." Venue is sometimes confused with jurisdiction so that the distinction between the two should be carefully noted. **Venue** rules determine which particular court among those having subject matter and personal jurisdiction *should* hear the case.

In state cases, proper venue varies with the circumstances. Generally, cases should be brought in the county where any defendant resides or in the county where the transaction causing the dispute occurred. If all defendants are nonresidents, the case may be tried in any county. If title to real estate is in dispute, proper venue is the county where the land is situated.

A defendant who believes the case has been brought in an improper venue may make a motion for change of venue. In some cases, a motion for change of venue is filed to move a case to another court if a fair trial cannot be obtained (due, for example, to adverse pretrial publicity) in the original venue. Generally, the defendant must make a motion for change of venue prior to commencement of the trial. If the court grants the motion, the court simply transfers the case to the proper venue. If not, the case proceeds as usual and the judgment entered by the court is binding on the parties. Thus, improper venue does not affect the court's jurisdiction.

In federal civil cases, venue depends upon whether a federal question or diversity of citizenship case is involved. In federal question cases, proper venue is the judicial district in which either all defendants reside, or the claim arose. In diversity cases, the case may be tried in the judicial district where all plaintiffs reside, all defendants reside, or where the claim arose.[13]

Discovery Stage

After all pleadings have been filed, the judge fixes a period of time during which the parties are entitled to engage in **discovery** to ascertain the evidence pertinent to the lawsuit. Discovery is a relatively recent innovation in litigation that enables the parties to discover all relevant facts prior to trial and encourages full disclosure of the facts at the trial. Discovery helps assure that a case is decided on its merits rather than on the investigative or rhetorical skills of the parties or their attorneys. The discovery methods help elicit the facts of the case in a relatively inexpensive manner thereby minimizing the advantage that wealthier litigants might otherwise have. Discovery substantially reduces the number of cases that require a trial for resolution. As facts become evident during the discovery stage, the parties often settle the case as the strengths and weaknesses of their positions are disclosed. Despite these laudable purposes, abuse of discovery procedures, including unnecessary or excessive discovery, is often cited as the major cause of unreasonable delays in resolving civil lawsuits.

Failure to comply with discovery procedures may result in serious penalties, including fines or even imprisonment for contempt of court. The court may dismiss the case or enter a judgment for one party if the other party fails to provide information requested during discovery.

Five general discovery tools are available: (1) depositions, (2) interrogatories, (3) request for production of documents and things, (4) physical and mental examinations, and (5) requests for admission.

Depositions. A **deposition** is the testimony under oath of a person (the deponent) who is examined (deposed) out of court by a party to the lawsuit. The party requesting a deposition must notify all other parties of the time and place of the deposition. If the deponent is not a party to the lawsuit and will not voluntarily attend the deposition, the

---

13. 28 U.S.C. §1391.

court will issue a **subpoena,** a court order commanding the person to appear and present his or her testimony. The party who requested the deposition asks the deponent questions that he or she must answer. Following this examination, the other parties also may ask questions of the deponent. The proceedings are recorded, generally by a stenographer, and a transcript is available for a fee to the parties who request it. Although depositions usually are made orally, most jurisdictions allow written depositions. In a written deposition written questions are submitted by the deposing party and cross-examination questions are submitted by the other parties to which the deponent responds under oath in writing. Oral depositions generally are more effective in eliciting pertinent information; however, written depositions may be necessary if the deponent resides at a great distance from the parties.

Interrogatories. **Interrogatories** are written questions submitted to a party by another party. The party who receives the interrogatories must submit written answers under oath. Although interrogatories may be useful in ascertaining information directly relevant to the case, they are often used to obtain the names of witnesses and the location of documents or other evidence that will be examined further by using the other discovery methods.

Request for Production. A third discovery tool is the request for production of documents and things. To use this device, a party provides a written request to another party to produce specified materials in his possession or control for examination and copying. Generally, the items must be described with some specificity. If the items are immovable or difficult to transport, the party may request entry to property to allow inspection of the items.

Physical and Mental Examinations. If the physical or mental condition of a party is at issue in a lawsuit, the judge may order the person to submit to a physical or mental examination by a physician. The judge makes such an order only if requested by one of the parties and the judge deems that cause has been shown for an examination—for example, when one party has claimed physical or mental injury by an opposing party.

Request for Admission. The final tool available during the discovery stage is the request for admission, a written request from either party asking the other party to admit certain facts or opinions of facts or the genuineness of specified documents. Admissions, which are made under oath, are considered to be established, thereby eliminating the necessity of proving the matter at trial.

Scope of Discovery. Under the Federal Rules of Civil Procedure, the scope of discovery is broad: ''Parties may obtain discovery regarding any matter, not privileged, which is relevant to the subject matter involved in the pending action. . . . It is not ground for objection that the information sought will be inadmissible at the trial if the information sought appears reasonably calculated to lead to the discovery of admissible evidence.''[14] The scope of discovery under state law varies but is similar to the federal rule. Excluded from discovery are materials that are the work product of the attorneys representing the parties and privileged information; for example, information protected by the attorney-client, doctor-patient, or priest-penitent privilege. A party who is required to submit to a mental or physical examination, however, must waive the doctor-patient privilege for the examination.

The following case discusses application of the work product doctrine and attorney-client privilege to discovery of materials held by a corporate defendant.

Simon v. G. D. Searle & Co.
816 F.2d 397 (8th Cir. 1987)

Plaintiff Debra Simon sued Defendant G. D. Searle & Co. for damages resulting from her use of the ''Cu-7,'' an intrauterine contraceptive device manufactured by Searle. In response to a request for production of documents, Searle produced approximately 500,000 documents from its files relating to the Cu-7 but refused to produce other documents from its risk management department. The district

---

14. Fed. R. Civ. P. Rule 26(b)(1), 28 U.S.C.

court, relying on a report by a special master appointed by the court, ordered Searle to produce all risk management documents except those containing "specific litigation strategy or mental impressions of attorneys in evaluating cases, or setting a[n insurance] reserve for a specific case." Searle objected to producing documents prepared by its corporate officials because they included information derived from reports of the company's attorneys. The district court stayed its discovery order pending Searle's appeal of the order to the Eighth Circuit Court of Appeals.

Wollman, Circuit Judge

. . . Searle's first argument is that its risk management documents are protected from discovery by the work product doctrine. That doctrine was established in *Hickman v. Taylor* [67 S.Ct. 385 (1947)], and is now expressed in Rule 26(b)(3) of the Federal Rules of Civil Procedure, which provides that "a party may obtain discovery of documents and tangible things * * * prepared in anticipation of litigation or for trial by or for another party or by or for that other party's representative * * * only upon a showing that the party seeking discovery has substantial need of the materials." . . . The work product doctrine was designed to prevent "unwarranted inquiries into the files and mental impressions of an attorney," *Hickman*, . . . 67 S.Ct. at 393, and recognizes that it is "essential that a lawyer work with a certain degree of privacy, free from unnecessary intrusion by opposing parties and their counsel." . . . 67 S.Ct. at 393.

. . . [T]he risk management documents at issue were generated in an attempt to keep track of, control, and anticipate the costs of Searle's products liability litigation. . . . When Searle receives notice of a claim or suit, a Searle attorney sets a case reserve for the matter. Case reserves embody the attorney's estimate of anticipated legal expenses, settlement value, length of time to resolve the litigation, geographic considerations, and other factors. . . . The individual case reserves set by the legal department are then used by the risk management department for a variety of reserve analysis functions, which the special master found were motivated by business planning purposes including budget, profit, and insurance considerations. The work product doctrine will not protect these

documents from discovery unless they were prepared in anticipation of litigation. . . . [W]e do not believe it can be said that the risk management documents were prepared for purposes of litigation. . . . The risk management department was not involved in giving legal advice or in mapping litigation strategy in any individual case. The aggregate reserve information in the risk management documents serves numerous business planning functions, but we cannot see how it enhances the defense of any particular lawsuit. Searle vigorously argues that its business is health care, not litigation, but that is not the point. Searle's business involves litigation, just as it involves accounting, marketing, advertising, sales, and many other things. A business corporation may engage in business planning on many fronts, among them litigation.

Although the risk management documents were not themselves prepared in anticipation of litigation, they may be protected from discovery to the extent that they disclose the individual case reserves calculated by Searle's attorneys. The individual case reserve figures reveal the mental impressions, thoughts, and conclusions of an attorney in evaluating a legal claim. By their very nature they are prepared in anticipation of litigation and, consequently, they are protected from discovery as opinion work product. . . . We do not believe, however, that the aggregate reserve information reveals the individual case reserve figures to a degree that brings the aggregates within the protection of the work product doctrine. The individual figures lose their identity when combined to create the aggregate information. . . . The purpose of the work product doctrine—that of preventing discovery of a lawyer's mental impressions—is not violated by allowing discovery of documents that incorporate a lawyer's thoughts in, at best, such an indirect and diluted manner. Accordingly, we hold that the work product doctrine does not block discovery of Searle's risk management documents or the aggregate case reserve information contained therein. . . .

Searle also argues that its risk management documents are protected by the attorney-client privilege. . . .

The risk management documents reflect attorney-client communications running in two directions. First, the aggregate reserve information contained in the documents incorporates the individual case reserve figures communicated by the legal department to the risk management department—an attorney-to-client communication. Second, the record indicates that some of the risk management documents themselves were delivered to Searle attorneys—a client-to-attorney communication.

Assuming *arguendo* that the attorney-client privilege attaches to the individual case reserve figures communicated by the legal department to the risk management department, we do not believe the privilege in turn attaches to the risk management documents simply because they include aggregate information based on the individual case reserve figures. For the reasons that we have already stated in relation to the work product doctrine, we do not believe that the aggregate information discloses the privileged communications, which we are assuming the individual reserve figures represent, to a degree that makes the aggregate information privileged. The attorney-to-client communications reflected in the risk management documents are therefore not protected by the attorney-client privilege.

Although the aggregate reserve information does not confer attorney-client privilege protection to the risk management documents, those documents that were given to Searle attorneys may still be privileged client-to-attorney communications. The special master . . . stated: "A business document is not made privileged by providing a copy to counsel. * * * Thus, those documents from one corporate officer to another with a copy sent to an attorney do not qualify as attorney client communications." . . . We perceive no error in this statement of the law, which appears to have been carefully applied by the special master to the point of redacting sections of privileged material from within individual documents.

Minnesota adheres to [the] classic statement of the attorney-client privilege, which requires that an attorney-client communication relate to the purpose of obtaining legal advice before it is protected. . . . Moreover, a number of courts have determined that the attorney-client privilege does not protect client communications that relate only business or technical data. . . . Just as the minutes of business meetings attended by attorneys are not automatically privileged, . . . business documents sent to corporate officers and employees, as well as the corporation's attorneys, do not become privileged automatically. . . . Client communications intended to keep the attorney apprised of business matters may be privileged if they embody "an implied request for legal advice based thereon." *Jack Winter, Inc. v. Koratron Co.,* 54 F.R.D. 44, 46 (N.D.Cal.1971). . . .

[Judgment affirmed.]

Motion for Summary Judgment. During the discovery stage many cases are settled and others are disposed of through a **motion for summary judgment.** The party who makes such a motion must establish that no relevant facts are in dispute, thereby allowing the judge to decide the case as a matter of law. Unlike the motion for judgment on the pleadings, the summary judgment motion must be supported by statements under oath that prove the lack of factual controversy. Frequently, information obtained by deposition, interrogatories, mental or physical examination, or request for admissions is used to establish these facts.

Trial

If a case proceeds beyond the pleadings or discovery stage, the judge sets it for **trial,** a formal proceeding in court in which the issues established in the pleadings are resolved. Two types of trials are available, jury trial or bench trial.

Jury Trials and Bench Trials

In a jury trial, a **petit jury** (or simply a jury)—a body of disinterested persons—is selected to determine all issues of fact. After hearing factual evidence offered by the parties, the jury decides what actually happened. The judge advises the jury of the pertinent law in the case and the jury then applies the law to the facts to determine which party wins the case. In other words, in a jury trial, the judge decides issues of law and the jury determines issues of fact.

The Seventh Amendment of the United States Constitution guarantees a right to a jury trial in common law cases in the federal courts and most state constitutions create a similar right in state courts. In cases based on a statutory cause of action, the parties are entitled to a jury trial only if the statute so provides. The parties do not have the right to a jury trial in equity cases.

Even if the right to jury trial is guaranteed, federal and state law generally require that a party take some affirmative step to assert that right. For example, in federal courts a party must demand a jury trial in writing during the pleadings stage. Similar rules have been adopted by the states. A party who fails to assert the right to a jury trial may lose it.

Traditionally, a jury was composed of twelve men selected from the citizens of the community in which the court was located. Today, juries include both men and women and statutes allow fewer than twelve jurors. Although many states still employ twelve-person juries, the Supreme Court has upheld the constitutionality of a jury in civil cases with as few as six persons.[15]

The alternative to a jury trial is a bench trial, which is used if the parties waive their right to a jury trial or in cases for which there is no right to a jury trial. In a bench trial, the judge determines all issues of fact and decides all issues of law.

Burden of Proof

The function of the trial is to allow the trier of fact—the jury in a jury trial, the judge in a bench trial—to resolve the issues of the case. The parties to the lawsuit present the facts of the case through **evidence**—legally admissible testimony of witnesses, and documents or other pertinent tangible items offered to prove the facts alleged in the pleadings.

The pleadings and the substantive law establish which party bears the **burden of proof**—the duty or obligation to prove the disputed fact or facts constituting a cause of action or affirmative defense. Generally, the plaintiff bears the burden of proving the facts of the complaint that have not been admitted by the defendant. At a minimum, the plaintiff must establish a "prima facie" case— some evidence supporting each allegation of the complaint that, unless contradicted or rebutted by other evidence, would entitle the plaintiff to re-

cover. In other words, the defendant automatically prevails without producing any evidence, unless the plaintiff proves a prima facie case. Once the plaintiff establishes a prima facie case, the defendant then bears the burden of proving the facts alleged in any affirmative defenses. In addition, the defendant has the opportunity to present pertinent evidence rebutting the plaintiff's evidence. Similarly, the plaintiff may rebut the evidence offered by the defendant to prove the affirmative defenses.

The duty of the party bearing the burden of proof in most civil cases is to establish by a preponderance of the evidence (it is more probable or likely than not) that his allegations are true. In other words, the party bearing the burden of proof must provide evidence that is more persuasive or convincing than that provided by the opposing party. After considering all evidence presented by the parties, the trier of fact determines which allegations of fact are true based on the credibility of the witnesses and the quality of the evidence.

The Trial Process

Courts follow statutory rules of procedure that facilitate the organized presentation of evidence at the trial. Most trials therefore follow a similar order of proceeding: selection of the jury, opening statements, presentation of evidence, closing arguments, and instructions to the jury.

Jury Selection. A jury trial begins with the selection of the jury through **voir dire examination,** a procedure by which the potential jurors are questioned under oath to determine whether they are suitable to serve on the jury for the particular case. The judge requests a group of persons selected randomly from a pool of potential jurors to appear in the courtroom to answer a series of questions designed to elicit potential jurors' bias or prejudice against any of the parties. To dismiss a potential juror, a party exercises a challenge that excuses an individual from serving on the jury. Generally, each party is entitled to an unlimited number of *challenges for cause*—disqualification of the potential juror because of business or personal ties to a party or attorney or because of demonstrated bias concerning the merits of the case—and to a limited number of *peremptory challenges*—disqualification

---

15. *Colgrove v. Battin*, 93 S. Ct. 2448 (1973).

of the potential juror for which the party need not state a reason. The voir dire examination continues until the appropriate number of jurors has been selected.

Opening Statements. At the beginning of the trial, each party may make an opening statement, a general explanation of the case and of the facts that the party will try to prove. Opening statements are not evidence; they serve to clarify the case and to provide a framework so that the jury will better understand the evidence presented later in the trial.

Presentation of Evidence. Following the opening statements, the plaintiff presents evidence usually through the testimony of witnesses who are under oath. A witness who is called by the plaintiff is first subject to **direct examination** by which the plaintiff asks questions that are answered by the witness. Thereafter, the defendant is entitled to **cross-examination** of the witness, further questions concerning the testimony elicited on direct examination. Evidence also may be presented through tangible items such as documents, records, charts, or other items relevant to the case. Tangible items are admitted as evidence only if a witness attests that they are genuine and establishes the relevancy of the items to the issues of the case. The items then are labeled as **exhibits** and become a part of the evidence. After the plaintiff has called all witnesses and entered all exhibits that she believes meet the burden of proving the allegations of the complaint, the plaintiff rests her case.

Generally, the defendant then will make a **motion for directed verdict** requesting the court to rule as a matter of law that the defendant is entitled to judgment in his favor. The judge will grant the motion only if the plaintiff has failed to meet her burden of proof, that is, if the plaintiff has not presented a prima facie case. If the motion is granted, the judge rules in favor of the defendant and the trial ends. Usually, however, the motion is denied and the defendant has the opportunity to present evidence.

The procedure followed by the defendant is similar to that of the plaintiff. The defendant generally provides evidence to rebut the plaintiff's evidence. In addition, the defendant must prove the facts of any affirmative defenses that were pled. After presenting all of his evidence, the defendant rests his case.

The plaintiff then has the opportunity to offer rebuttal evidence in response to evidence provided by the defendant. Rebuttal evidence is limited to matters raised by the defendant's evidence; the plaintiff cannot use rebuttal to introduce new matters that should have been raised during plaintiff's case. Following rebuttal, the defendant may offer evidence in rejoinder to rebut facts presented by plaintiff's rebuttal evidence.

During the presentation of evidence, the parties are limited by rules of evidence that ensure a fair and orderly trial by admitting only evidence that is relevant, probative, and not unduly prejudicial. A party who believes that certain evidence will violate the rules of evidence objects to its admission. If the objection is sustained, the evidence is excluded; if the objection is overruled, the evidence is allowed.

One well-known rule is that hearsay evidence is inadmissible. *Hearsay* is testimony of a statement made out of court by a person who is not a witness. Although some hearsay evidence is admissible, it is usually excluded to prevent admission of evidence from persons who cannot be cross-examined in court.

Another rule of evidence prevents certain persons from testifying about privileged information disclosed in specific, socially important relationships. For example, as discussed in Chapter 1, an attorney generally cannot testify about matters disclosed by a client. Communications made in other relationships, such as physician-patient, priest-penitent, and husband-wife also are privileged. By excluding privileged information in these cases, the law encourages full communication to an attorney, physician, priest, or spouse by ensuring that confidentiality will not be breached without the consent of the client, patient, penitent, or other spouse.

Following the presentation of the evidence both parties generally make a motion for directed verdict. This motion requests the court to rule as a matter of law that the moving party is entitled to judgment in his favor. Because granting the motion removes the fact-finding from the jury, such motions are seldom granted.

Closing Arguments. After all evidence has been presented, each party is entitled to make closing arguments, statements to assist the trier of fact—especially in a jury trial—to analyze the evidence of the case. Like the opening statement, the closing argument is not evidence and the parties may analyze only the presented evidence; no arguments may be made concerning information that was not presented in evidence.

Jury Instructions. At the close of a jury trial, the judge provides **jury instructions** or **charges** to the jury. These instructions explain the rules of law pertinent to the case, including an explanation of the burden of proof, definitions of preponderance of the evidence, and a summary of the elements of the cause of action. Using these instructions, the jury must determine the facts of the case and apply the rules of law to them to resolve the dispute.

The Verdict. After receiving the jury instructions, the jury retires to the jury room and elects a foreman. After a period of discussion and analysis, the jurors usually reach a **verdict,** a formal decision of the issues of the case. Although at common law the verdict was the unanimous decision of the jurors, the laws of some states now allow verdicts that are not unanimous. If the jury cannot reach a verdict, it is called a "hung jury" and upon request of one or both of the parties, a new trial will be held with another jury.

Usually, the judge requests a "general" verdict in which the jury makes a general finding for the plaintiff or the defendant and assesses the amount of damages. In some cases, however, the judge may request a "special" verdict in which the jury merely makes a finding of fact on each issue of the case. The judge then applies the law to these facts to resolve the dispute. If a special verdict is used, the jury instructions usually are limited to defining the necessary legal terms without full explanation of the law applicable to the case. Special verdicts simplify the jury's role and reduce the possibility of error. Nevertheless, most cases are still resolved by general verdicts.

After announcement of the verdict, the losing party usually files a motion for **judgment notwithstanding the verdict** (or judgment *non obstante*

veredicto or judgment *n.o.v.*) requesting the court to find as a matter of law that the jury's verdict was incorrect and to enter judgment in favor of the moving party. If granted, the court enters judgment for the plaintiff even though the jury has returned a verdict for the defendant, or vice-versa. The motion is similar to the motion for directed verdict and the judge will grant the motion only if the evidence was insufficient to support the jury's verdict.

In bench trials, of course, the judge decides both issues of fact and of law. As a result, no jury instructions are prepared. Following closing arguments, the judge makes findings of fact and conclusions of law and determines the appropriate remedy.

Entry of Judgment. At the conclusion of the case, the judge pronounces the decision of the case that is entered into the court's records. Because the case may be terminated at any time during the litigation process, entry of judgment does not necessarily occur only after the trial. If, for example, the defendant fails to answer the complaint, judgment by default will be entered. In addition, judgment is entered in favor of the moving party if the court grants a motion for judgment on the pleadings, a motion for summary judgment, a motion for directed verdict, or a motion for judgment notwithstanding the verdict. In some cases, even if the parties voluntarily settle the case during the litigation process, they may agree to a judgment by consent, which will be entered in the court's records.

Post-trial Proceedings

Further legal proceedings sometimes follow entry of judgment. A party dissatisfied with the judgment may seek review of the case by an appellate court. Or, further assistance of the trial court may be needed to secure enforcement of a judgment.

Appellate Review

After judgment is entered by the trial court, the parties have the right to appeal the case to the appropriate appellate court. Generally, appeal may be taken only after final judgment, but occasionally a court order that does not terminate the case may be grounds for an appeal. The appellate process commences when one of the parties (usually, but not necessarily, the party who lost at trial) files a *notice of appeal* with the trial court. The notice, which is served on all parties, must be filed within a time period set by statute or the right to appeal is waived. Enforcement of judgment may be postponed pending appellate review if the party seeking the appeal posts a bond.

The appealing party, known as the **appellant,** then prepares a **brief,** a written document summarizing the legal errors that the appellant alleges occurred at trial and for which he requests review by the appellate court. The brief also includes citations to precedent and to statutory and constitutional law to support the appellant's contentions of legal error. The brief then is served on the opposing party who is called the **appellee.** The appellee may file a reply brief, a written document containing arguments and legal citations in opposition to those in the appellant's brief. The trial court also sends the appellate court a copy of the record, which includes pleadings, discovery documents, and a written transcript of the trial.

Upon receipt of these documents, the appellate court may schedule oral arguments and both the appellant and the appellee may make oral presentations before a panel of judges of the appellate court. During the oral arguments, the appellate judges ask questions of the attorneys for clarification and elucidation of points presented in the briefs. After review of the record, briefs, and oral arguments, the appellate court publishes a written opinion in which it decides the issues raised on appeal.

The appellate court reviews the proceedings to determine whether the trial court committed *prejudicial error,* a legal error that substantially affected the parties' right to a fair trial. An appellate court may find that a trial court committed *harmless error,* an error that did not affect the fairness of the trial. If the appellate court determines that no prejudicial error occurred, it **affirms** the trial court's judgment. If, however, the trial court committed prejudicial error, the appellate court **reverses** or sets aside the judgment entered by the trial court. When the appellate court reverses a judgment, the court also **remands**—sends back—the case to the trial court. If the record provides sufficient evidence to determine how the case should have been decided, the appellate court orders the trial court to enter the correct judgment on remand. If, however, the record does not provide a basis for determining the correct outcome, the appellate court orders a new trial or other legal proceedings on remand.

As discussed in Chapter 1, a party may be able to obtain further appellate review by a higher state appellate court or by the Supreme Court. Ultimately, however, after all appellate review, the case terminates and a final judgment is entered in the trial court's records. Each appellate court usually writes an opinion to explain the legal reasoning underlying its decision that is published and becomes a part of the common law of the jurisdiction.

Effect of Judgment

Due process entitles a party to litigate a legal dispute. This right is, however, limited by the doctrine of *res judicata* and the Full Faith and Credit Clause of the United States Constitution.

Res Judicata **and** *Collateral Estoppel.* The common law doctrine of **res judicata** (''the thing has been decided'') provides that final judgment by a court of competent jurisdiction is conclusive on the parties and prevents relitigation of the cause of action. The doctrine is designed to prevent a party who was unsuccessful in the lawsuit from beginning a new lawsuit to try to obtain a more favorable ruling on the same dispute. Thus, after the appellate process has been completed (or the time to file an appeal has expired), the parties may not relitigate the case. If a party does file a subsequent lawsuit on the same cause of action, the defendant asserts res judicata as an affirmative defense and the second suit will be dismissed during the pleadings stage.

Closely related to res judicata is the doctrine of **collateral estoppel.** It provides that issues actually decided in one lawsuit are conclusively determined for later lawsuits between the same parties involving different causes of action. Collateral estoppel usually is invoked when an issue that is critical to the second suit was litigated in a previous suit. If the issue was fully litigated and necessary to the outcome of the prior decision, the adversely affected party is estopped or precluded from relitigating the issue. Thus, whereas res judicata prevents successive suits based on the same claim, collateral estoppel prevents relitigation of issues common to two or more claims between the parties.

Full Faith and Credit. Article IV, Section 1, of the United States Constitution provides that: "Full Faith and Credit shall be given in each State to the . . . judicial Proceedings of every other State." The **Full Faith and Credit Clause** prevents relitigation of cases previously decided in other states. Once a court of competent jurisdiction enters judgment on a cause of action in one state, other states must recognize the judicial proceedings and apply the doctrine of res judicata.

The Full Faith and Credit Clause also enables a plaintiff to obtain enforcement of a judgment in other states. Thus, for example, if a court of California enters judgment against a defendant who lives in Oregon, the plaintiff may enforce the judgment in Oregon where the defendant is likely to maintain assets. Generally, the plaintiff first must register the judgment in the state where he seeks enforcement. As a part of the registration process, the state may require one of its trial courts to re-

view out-of-state judicial proceedings to determine that the court rendering the judgment had subject matter jurisdiction over the case and personal jurisdiction over the defendant. If the court finds that the out-of-state court did have jurisdiction, the judgment will be registered in the court's records and may be enforced like any other judgment.

Enforcement of Judgment

A final judgment awarding damages becomes a debt of the defendant. Every state provides a number of judicial remedies to assist creditors in collecting debts from unwilling debtors. These remedies aid a creditor, usually after obtaining a judgment, in locating and seizing the debtor's assets and applying them to the unpaid debt. These remedies are designed to reach assets held by the debtor and by third parties, such as banks and employers, indebted to the debtor. They also reach assets transferred by the debtor to third parties with the intent to hinder, delay, or defraud creditors. State debt collection remedies are discussed in more detail in Chapter 29.

Because a judgment is effective only for a lim-

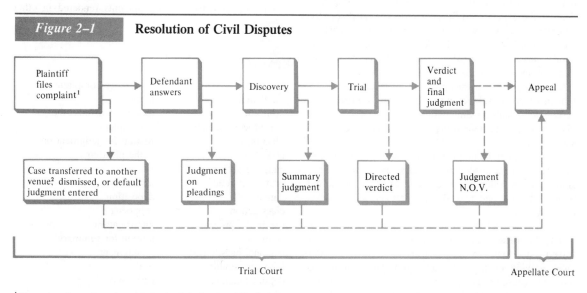

| *Figure 2–1* | **Resolution of Civil Disputes** |

[1] At any stage, the parties may agree to resolve their dispute outside of court.
[2] Depending upon the jurisdiction, a motion for change of venue may be made until the time of trial.

ited amount of time, usually five to ten years depending on state law, a plaintiff who fails to secure prompt payment of the judgment may later be prohibited from collecting it. Nevertheless, a court has the discretion to renew the judgment if the plaintiff can establish a legitimate reason for failing to collect the damages.

Figure 2–1 summarizes the principles of civil dispute resolution discussed in this chapter.

SUMMARY

1. Civil disputes are common among both businesses and individuals. Although most disputes are resolved by compromise, mediation, or arbitration, many disputes are litigated, or resolved in court. A lawsuit consists of three general parts: the pleadings stage, the discovery stage, and the trial.

2. A lawsuit begins with the filing of pleadings that establish the disputed issues of a case. Pleadings consist of the complaint, the answer, counterclaims, crossclaims, third-party complaints, and answers to counterclaims, crossclaims, and third-party complaints.

3. To satisfy the constitutional requirements of due process, a defendant must be notified of the lawsuit through service of process that can be made properly only if a court has personal jurisdiction over the defendant. A state court obtains personal jurisdiction over the defendant in four instances: (1) the defendant is a resident of the state in which the court is located; (2) the defendant is served while present in the state in which the court is located; (3) the defendant consents to the court's jurisdiction; or (4) the defendant has had "minimum contacts" with the state in which the court is located. A federal court has personal jurisdiction over defendants who are subject to the state court's jurisdiction, certain defendants residing within 100 miles of the federal district court, and defendants subject to specific federal statutes.

4. The parties to a lawsuit gather evidence prior to trial by using the discovery methods that include depositions, interrogatories, production of documents and things, physical and mental examinations, and requests for admission.

5. The trial is a formal proceeding in court in which the issues established in the pleadings are resolved. At a trial, the party bearing the burden of proof must provide evidence by testimony and exhibits to prove the cause of action by a preponderance of the evidence. In a jury trial, the jury determines issues of fact and applies the facts to the law, and the judge determines issues of law. In a bench trial, the judge resolves issues of both fact and law.

6. Prior to or during the trial, the parties to a lawsuit obtain rulings on questions of law by filing motions. Common motions include the motions to dismiss the complaint, for judgment on the pleadings, for change of venue, for summary judgment, for directed verdict, and for judgment notwithstanding the verdict.

7. At the conclusion of the trial, a party who is dissatisfied with the trial court's judgment may obtain review of the case by the appellate court. The appellate courts review trial proceedings to determine whether prejudicial error occurred. Appellate courts issue written opinions that become a part of the common law of the jurisdiction.

8. Following entry of final judgment, the doctrine of *res judicata* precludes relitigation of a cause of action and the doctrine of collateral estoppel prevents litigation of the same issues in other lawsuits. Further, the Full Faith and Credit Clause of the Constitution requires state courts to recognize valid judgments rendered in other states.

KEY TERMS

litigation	third-party complaint
mediation	motion
arbitration	motion to dismiss the
due process of law	complaint
pleadings	motion for judgment on
complaint	the pleadings
cause of action	venue
prayer for relief	discovery
damages	deposition
class action	subpoena
service of process	interrogatories
summons	motion for summary
personal jurisdiction	judgment
long arm statute	trial
default judgment	petit jury
answer	evidence
affirmative defense	voir dire examination
counterclaim	burden of proof
crossclaims	direct examination

cross-examination
exhibits
motion for directed verdict
jury instructions or charges
verdict
judgment notwithstanding
the verdict
appellant

brief
appellee
affirm
reverse
remand
res judicata
collateral estoppel
Full Faith and Credit Clause

QUESTIONS AND PROBLEMS

2-1 A recent study comparing litigation to arbitration found that 95% of the court cases were settled prior to a full trial while fewer than 50% of the cases submitted to arbitration were settled prior to resolution by the arbitrator. Suggest reasons for this disparity.

2-2 Neither mediation nor arbitration generally requires adherence to rules of substantive law. Thus, precedent may be ignored. Discuss the effect of this policy on society, giving consideration to the reasons that courts use precedent.

2-3 In each of the following cases, the employer and union have entered into a collective bargaining agreement, similar to the one described in *Misco* (see page 33), requiring arbitration of employee grievances. The federal court has been asked to refuse enforcement of the arbitration awards. How should the court rule?

(a) The employer, a trucking and shipping company, fired the employee, a truck driver, who was involved in an accident while driving a company truck. A police officer called to the scene of the accident issued the employee a traffic citation for drinking intoxicating liquors while on duty after the driver admitted having had a drink at the previous rest stop. The Federal Motor Carrier Safety Regulations prohibit truck drivers from consuming intoxicating liquor while on duty. The arbitrator ordered the employer to reinstate the employee after finding that the employer had failed to thoroughly investigate the cause of the accident which the driver claimed had been caused by mechanical failure.

(b) The employer operates a nuclear power plant where the employee works as a machinist. The employee works in an area known as a secondary containment area which serves as a pressurized buffer zone to prevent the spread of any radiation that might escape from the primary containment area at the core of the nuclear reactor. To prevent radiation leakage, a mechanical locking system allows only one exit door in the area to be opened at any time. The employee, who was authorized to leave for lunch, was unable to exit because a truck was unloading at another door. In violation of company policy and federal nuclear regulations, the employee requested a plant engineer to deactivate the locking mechanism on a second door and the engineer complied. Although the employee's actions caused no injury and did not jeopardize public safety, the employer terminated his employment. The arbitrator ordered the employer to reinstate the employee on the ground that termination was too severe. Federal law requires strict adherence to nuclear regulations to protect the public safety. The arbitrator found that the employee had not realized the gravity of the violation although he had received training about safety regulations.

2-4 Suggest reasons why a person or business involved in a civil dispute would prefer to litigate the case rather than to resolve it by alternative means.

2-5 Major Motor Co., an automobile manufacturer, has determined that because producing engines for its cars is too expensive, it will purchase engines from Common Engine, Inc. The two companies will enter into a multimillion dollar contract extending over five years. Major Motor would like to include a provision requiring arbitration if any problems arise during the course of the contract, but prefers not to use the rules or clauses developed by the AAA. Draft the arbitration clause. Would you include some method for selecting an arbitrator? Why or why not? Include a provision that describes the method for choosing the arbitrator.

2-6 Consider whether the trial court has personal jurisdiction over the defendant in each of the following cases:

(a) Plaintiff sues defendant in a California trial court. Defendant resides in California but is attending college in Arizona where service of process is made on the defendant.

(b) Plaintiff sues defendant, a resident of Tennessee, in the federal district court of Arkansas. Defendant has not had minimum contacts with the state of Arkansas. A federal marshall serves the summons and complaint on defendant on an airplane flight from Memphis to Dallas while the plane is flying directly over Arkansas.

(c) Asahi, a Japanese manufacturer, sells tire valves to Cheng Co., a Taiwanese manufacturer, which incorporates the valves into tires sold worldwide. Mortimer was injured in a motorcycle accident in California allegedly caused by a defect in a tire manufactured by Cheng. Mortimer sues both Asahi and Cheng. Asahi argues that California lacks personal jurisdiction over it because Asahi has never conducted business in California. Mortimer claims that Asahi's intentional act of placing its products in the stream of commerce—by selling them to Cheng—coupled with Asahi's knowledge that some of the components would find their way to California proved a sufficient basis for personal jurisdiction under the Due Process Clause.

(d) Jewel, a resident of Alaska, took a vacation in Mexico where she rented a car from Avis-Mexico. While in Mexico, Jewel was injured in an accident allegedly caused by Avis-Mexico. After returning home, she sued Avis-Mexico and Avis-U.S. in an Alaska state court. Both defendants argued that they were not subject to jurisdiction of the Alaskan courts. Affidavits filed by the parties showed that Avis-U.S., a Delaware corporation, grants Avis car rental franchises throughout the United States. The franchise allows the franchisee to use the Avis name in exchange for payment to Avis-U.S. Avis-U.S. maintains a toll-free telephone number available nationwide (including Alaska) by which reservations can be made to rent cars anywhere in the world. Avis-U.S. also advertises in national and international publications that reach Alaska residents. Although Avis-U.S. has no employees, property or bank accounts in Alaska, it has entered into several franchise agreements with car rental agencies in Alaska that use the Avis name. One of the Alaska franchisees paid Avis-U.S. $11,000 during the preceding year. Avis-U.S. is not involved in the operation of the Avis-Mexico franchise because it operates outside the United States. Avis-Mexico has no employees, property or bank accounts in Alaska. The record shows that the only contact Avis-

Mexico has had with Alaska is the car rental agreement with Jewel.

2-7 Parties to contracts often include a provision called a choice of forum clause that specifies the jurisdiction in which any case or controversy arising under the contract will be litigated.

(a) Why would parties to a contract want to include a choice of forum clause?

(b) Should courts enforce choice of forum clauses? Why or why not?

2-8 In 1984, a disastrous industrial accident occurred in Bhopal, India when lethal gas released from a chemical plant operated by Union Carbide India Limited killed over 2,000 people and injured at least 200,000 almost all of whom were Indian citizens. Most of the material witnesses reside in India. Union Carbide India Limited is an Indian corporation but is a subsidiary of the American Union Carbide Corporation (UCC). UCC provided the original design for the plant but it was constructed under supervision of Indian engineers who made substantial design changes. Some of the original design records are maintained at UCC's office. Preliminary studies suggest that the accident occurred as a result of design defects in the plant. Both the courts of India and the federal courts of the United States have subject matter jurisdiction over cases arising from the accident, but the Indian courts do not have personal jurisdiction over UCC. About 145 Indian plaintiffs filed class action suits in the United States against UCC. UCC has filed a motion for change of venue requesting the case be moved to India. How should the court rule?

2-9 Explain the purposes of the pretrial stages (pleading and discovery) of litigation. What are the advantages and disadvantages of these stages? Some people, including many lawyers and judges, believe that the pleading and discovery stages unduly complicate and prolong a trial. Suggest ways that these stages could be improved and made more efficient.

2-10 Plaintiff was injured by an explosion that occurred at a power plant operated by Central Gas and Electric Co. Plaintiff is uncertain as to the exact cause of the explosion or the source of his injuries. An expert has suggested that the explosion could have been caused by a faulty generator, improper installation of the generator, poor installation of power or gas lines, faulty design of the plant, or improper construction of the plant. The expert suggests that plaintiff must obtain the design and construction plans for the plant and must talk with the various people who constructed the plant and installed the equipment. Plaintiff has learned from a friend that at least three architects designed the plant, several contractors supervised construction, and at least fifteen companies performed installation as subcontractors. Plaintiff has sued Central Gas and Electric. Explain in some detail how the discovery tools could be used to obtain the information necessary to prove his case.

2-11 Johnny Plaintiff, a child, was injured when the pajamas he was wearing caught fire and rapidly burned. Plaintiff sued the manufacturer, Seabuck Co., alleging that the pajamas were unreasonably dangerous. Plaintiff filed a request that Seabuck produce a record of all complaints and communications concerning injuries or deaths allegedly caused by the burning of children's nightwear manufactured by Seabuck. Seabuck objected to the request arguing that obtaining the information was an impossible task because the company filed all of its claims alphabetically by name of claimant rather than by type of claim. Seabuck offered to allow the plaintiff's attorney to visit its home office in Chicago where she could try to locate the documents.

(a) Are the documents sought by Plaintiff subject to discovery?

(b) How should the court rule on Seabuck's objection?

2-12 In mediation and arbitration hearings, witnesses often explain their evidence in narrative form rather than by the question and answer technique used in courts. Suggest reasons for the use of direct and cross-examination in court. What problems might arise if witnesses simply told their story? Are there any types of cases for which such a technique might be appropriate? Explain.

2-13 In recent complex business litigation, several parties have raised the argument that a jury might not be capable of understanding the issues. These parties have suggested that use of a jury in such cases constitutes a denial of due process of law and, therefore, the cases should be tried without a jury. Opposing parties have argued that because the right to a jury trial is constitutionally guaranteed, even complex cases must be tried by a jury if at least one party requests a jury trial. These issues were raised in the recent case, *In re Japanese Electronic Products Antitrust Litigation,* 631 F.2d 1069 (3d Cir. 1980). The case was brought by two American manufacturers of electronic equipment who sued sixteen Japanese companies for violation of the antitrust laws. The plaintiffs requested a jury trial; the defendants requested the case to be tried without a jury on the grounds that the case was too complex for a jury. After noting that the discovery stage had lasted 9 years and had produced millions of documents (including over 100,000 pages of depositions), the defendants suggested the following issues would be too difficult for the jurors to reach reasonable findings:

(a) The case would require the jury to compare prices only on identical items sold in Japan and the United States necessitating the jury to understand and distinguish the technical features of thousands of types of electronic equipment.

(b) The jury would need to understand international trade over a 30-year period, including business practices and market conditions in Japan.

(c) The jury would be required to determine whether differential pricing occurred and, therefore, would need to understand foreign currency fluctuations and complex rebate schemes.

(d) The jury would have to understand complex marketing, accounting, and economic concepts including relevant product market, relevant geographic market, and market share.

The court also noted that the trial was expected to last over one year. Should the court try the case without a jury? Explain.

2-14 Why do appellate courts usually accept the facts as determined in the trial court rather than reviewing issues of fact?

Major Topics

- the definition and classification of crimes and the sources of criminal law
- the elements of a crime and an introduction to criminal offenses and responsibility
- an introduction to business crimes, including principles of corporate criminal liability
- the law of criminal procedure, including an introduction to the constitutional limitations on criminal procedure, and an explanation of the various stages in the criminal process

Unlike civil law, which is primarily designed to resolve disputes and provide compensation, criminal law is designed to protect society from harm by preventing certain undesirable conduct by both individuals and business entities. That is, criminal law attempts to conform conduct to socially accepted norms by punishing or threatening to punish those who violate the minimum standards of acceptable behavior outlined in the criminal law.

Criminal law is a broad subject encompassing primarily two major fields of study: substantive criminal law and criminal procedure. **Substantive criminal law** defines those acts and omissions that are crimes and describes the punishment to be imposed for that conduct. It also prescribes the various defenses or qualifications that may relieve a person from liability for an otherwise criminal act. **Criminal procedure** is the law governing the var-

ious steps of a criminal proceeding from preliminary investigation to arrest to trial through termination of punishment. This chapter reviews the basic elements of substantive criminal law and criminal procedure, with special emphasis on crimes relevant to business.

Substantive Criminal Law

A **crime** is an act or failure to act, which is injurious to the public welfare, that violates a law prohibiting or commanding the act, and subjects the offender to punishment prescribed by law. Punishment for criminal conduct may include one or a combination of the following sanctions: death, imprisonment, fine, removal from office, or disqualification to hold a given office. Crimes were first defined in the English common law in an effort to protect individuals or their property and to deter conduct disruptive of social order. In the United States each state has enacted a statute, a criminal or penal "code" defining and punishing criminal conduct within the state. Many of these statutes are patterned after the Model Penal Code, drafted by the American Law Institute and published in 1962. Although many states still recognize some common law crimes, most substantive criminal law is statutory. In addition to state criminal codes, the federal government has also enacted criminal statutes, codified in Title 18 of the United States Code entitled "Crimes and Criminal Procedure." Federal law does not recognize common law crimes. Because both the state and federal governments have enacted criminal statutes, the same conduct in some cases may constitute more than one crime. For example, bank robbery is a violation of both state and federal criminal law and the offender may be prosecuted and punished by both sovereigns.

Crimes generally are classified into three categories: treason, felonies, and misdemeanors. **Treason** involves attempting by overt acts to overthrow the government of the sovereign to which the offender owes allegiance, or betraying the sovereign into the hands of a foreign power.[1]

Treason, of course, represents only a small percentage of criminal prosecutions. Most criminal law involves felonies and misdemeanors, commonly known as **offenses. Felonies,** which are the more serious offenses, are under most definitions crimes punishable by death or imprisonment in the state penitentiary. Other crimes, such as those punishable only by fine or imprisonment in a local jail or both, are **misdemeanors.** Some criminal statutes distinguish felony and misdemeanor according to the length rather than, or in addition to, the place of imprisonment. For example, any offense punishable by death or imprisonment for a term exceeding one year is a felony; any other offense is a misdemeanor.

Elements of a Crime

The definition of most crimes includes two elements: a criminal act (the *actus reus,* guilty act, or deed of crime) and the state of mind that accompanies or concurs with the act or omission (the *mens rea* or guilty mind, that is, the criminal intent). A few crimes, known as strict liability crimes, consist only of a criminal act; no criminal intent is necessary.

The Criminal Act. The criminal act may be one of commission—a voluntary bodily movement—or may be an act of omission—a failure to perform an act required by law. Most crimes, such as murder, are perpetrated by acts of commission. Other crimes are specifically defined in terms of failure to act; that is, the criminal statute imposes a duty to

act and makes breach of that duty a crime. Federal and state statutes, for example, make it a crime for a taxpayer to fail to file a tax return, or for a person to fail to register for the military draft.[2] Note that possession is treated in criminal law as a voluntary act if the offender knowingly procured or received the thing possessed or was aware of his or her control of the thing for a time sufficient to terminate possession. Thus, possession is the criminal act in such common crimes as possession of illegal drugs or stolen property.

State of Mind. The second element of most crimes defines the state of mind that must accompany the criminal act. Whereas the physical elements vary widely among crimes, crimes are classified according to their mental element or state of mind as either crimes requiring that the defendant be at *fault* (subjectively or objectively) or crimes imposing liability without fault.

Subjective Fault. Criminal law characterizes three types of mental culpability as subjective fault: (1) intention, (2) knowledge, and (3) recklessness. These states of mind are known as "subjective" because they describe the actual state of mind of the criminal. He or she must have a "bad" or "guilty" mind.

Consider, for example, the following definition of larceny:

> A person steals property and commits larceny when, with intent to deprive another of property . . . , he wrongfully takes, obtains or withholds such property from an owner thereof.[3]

The criminal act described in this statute is taking, obtaining, or withholding another person's property. A person commits the crime of larceny, however, only if this act is accompanied by subjective fault: "with *intent* to deprive another of property." Subjective fault is also required in a statute impos-

---

1. Black, *Law Dictionary* (5th ed. 1979).

2. Many crimes may be committed either by affirmative act or failure to act. A parent who fails to provide medical care for his sick child who dies as a result, may be found guilty of criminal homicide.

3. This illustration is based upon New York Penal Law §155.05.

ing liability upon a person receiving stolen property *"knowing* it to be stolen." Similarly, subjective fault is required for conviction of reckless homicide, for example, killing an individual through *reckless* driving of a motor vehicle.

Objective Fault. Some crimes define the criminal state of mind objectively, requiring, for example, that the defendant act "negligently," "carelessly," or "with reason to know." In these crimes, the mental element focuses on the state of mind of a reasonable person in the defendant's position, not the defendant's actual state of mind. Objective fault, for example, is required under a statute imposing criminal liability upon a person who receives property "having reason to know" that it had been stolen. That is, in this case criminal responsibility results if a reasonable person would have known the property was stolen, whether or not the defendant, *in fact,* knew it was stolen.

Strict Liability Crimes. Crimes imposing liability without any requirement of fault are commonly known as "strict liability" or "absolute liability" crimes. Criminal responsibility requires only the act; no concurrent mental state is required. That is, a strict liability crime is one imposing criminal penalties upon "whoever does or omits to do . . . ." rather than upon "whoever (intentionally, knowingly, recklessly, or negligently) does or omits to do. . . . " Usually, strict liability crimes are misdemeanors carrying relatively light penalties. Strict criminal liability is commonly imposed for violations of pure food and drug laws, illegal sales of intoxicating liquor, sales of misbranded articles, and minor violations of traffic and motor vehicle laws.

Offenses and Responsibility

Categories of Offenses. The Model Penal Code recognizes five basic categories of substantive criminal offenses:

1. Offenses involving danger to the person. These offenses include criminal homicide (murder, manslaughter, and negligent homicide), assault, kidnapping, false arrest, and sex offenses such as rape.

2. Offenses against property. This category includes arson, burglary, robbery, theft (larceny), forgery, and fraudulent business practices.
3. Offenses against the family. These include incest, bigamy, and sexual abuse of children by family members.
4. Offenses against public administration. Examples of such offenses are bribery, perjury, obstruction of justice, resisting arrest, and escape.
5. Offenses against public order and decency. In this category are disorderly conduct, public drunkenness, loitering, and prostitution.

In addition, both the states and the federal government regulate the possession, use, manufacture, and distribution of commodities such as dangerous drugs and firearms. Violations of these statutes are often serious criminal offenses.

Inchoate Crimes. An important class of criminal offenses are the **inchoate crimes,** so named because the conduct they prohibit is designed to culminate in the commission of another crime but has failed to do so. The major inchoate offenses are attempt, solicitation, and conspiracy to commit crimes.

The crime of **attempt** is committed if a person, with the intent to commit some other crime, performs an act or acts constituting a substantial step (going beyond mere preparation) toward the commission of that crime. In many attempts, the defendant does all acts necessary to commit the substantive crime but is unsuccessful because of an extraneous or fortuitous circumstance. For example, a person who, with intent to kill, fires a gun at the intended victim and misses (or pulls the trigger and the firing mechanism malfunctions) is guilty of attempted murder. Note, however, that an act constituting criminal attempt need not be the last or ultimate step toward commission of the substantive crime.

A person commits **solicitation** when, with intent that a crime be committed, he or she asks, orders, or otherwise encourages another to commit that crime. Note that the crime solicited need never be committed. For example, assume A desires to kill B. A therefore approaches C, and requests that C kill B. A is guilty of solicitation, whether or not C consents or ever attempts to kill B.

The crime of **conspiracy** requires that a person, with the intent that a crime be committed, agree with another or others to the commission of that offense. Thus, agreement is the essence of a criminal conspiracy. Conspiracy statutes are among the most potent and frequently used weapons in criminal law enforcement. Under the general federal conspiracy statute, codified in §371 of Title 18 of the United States Code, criminal liability may be imposed for conspiracies to defraud the United States or its agencies and conspiracies to commit any offense against the United States. Criminal conspiracy under federal law requires an agreement between two or more persons to achieve an illegal objective, coupled with one or more overt acts in furtherance of the conspiracy. Violators may be fined up to $10,000 or imprisoned up to five years, or both. If, however, the offense that is the object of the conspiracy is only a misdemeanor, punishment may not exceed that prescribed for such misdemeanor.

All inchoate offenses involve conduct that is preliminary to the commission of some criminal act. Inchoate offenses serve several important functions in criminal law: (1) they permit timely intervention by law enforcement officials to prevent commission of completed offenses, (2) they allow arrest and punishment of those who have indicated a clear disposition toward criminal conduct, and (3) they allow punishment of persons who are unable to achieve their criminal objectives due solely to circumstances beyond their control. The law of conspiracy serves an additional function: it protects the public against the grave and continuing danger inherent in group criminal activity.

Defenses. A defendant who has committed a crime may escape liability by proving one of the various defenses recognized by the criminal law. These defenses involve unusual or extraordinary circumstances in which the purposes of the criminal law would not be served by convicting the defendant. For example, a defendant charged with homicide may be excused if he can prove that he killed the victim in self-defense. A person charged with sell-ing illegal drugs may escape liability if he can prove entrapment—that a law enforcement official or agent, in order to obtain evidence to prosecute the defendant, incited or induced the defendant to commit a crime that he was not, absent the inducement, predisposed to commit. Persons who have not achieved a minimum age (generally thirteen) also may not be held criminally responsible. Another defense, perhaps the most well known and controversial that may be raised by the defendant, is the so-called "insanity defense." Unlike other defenses, which if proven result in acquittal and release of the defendant, a defendant found not guilty by reason of insanity is ordinarily committed to a mental institution.

Criminal Liability. A person is responsible for his own criminal acts and, under some circumstances, may be responsible for criminal acts committed by others. For example, as previously noted, conspiracy is itself a substantive crime. Co-conspirators may also be held liable for foreseeable crimes committed by others in furtherance of the conspiracy.

In addition to conspiracy, the Model Penal Code and many state statutes hold a person accountable for another's conduct if he is an accomplice of the other person in the commission of the offense. Generally, an **accomplice** is a person who, with the purpose of promoting or facilitating commission of a crime, solicits another to commit it, or aids or agrees or attempts to aid the other in planning or committing it. An accomplice may be convicted upon proof of commission of an offense and his complicity, even if the person claimed to have committed the offense has not been prosecuted or convicted, has been convicted of a different offense, or has been acquitted.[4]

For federal crimes, §2(a) of Title 18 of the United States Code imposes criminal liability on a person who directly commits an offense and upon one who "aids, abets, counsels, commands, induces or procures its commission." The following case illustrates an additional basis recognized under federal law for imposing criminal liability on one person for acts of another.

---

4. Model Penal Code §2.06.

United States v. Heyman
794 F.2d 788 (2d Cir. 1986)

Defendant Alan Heyman, an account executive with Merrill Lynch, Pierce, Fenner & Smith, Inc. (Merrill Lynch), was responsible for a joint customer account held by Sam and Evelyn Silber. In February 1982, the Silbers wanted to deposit a large amount of cash into this account, but they did not want the transaction reported to the Internal Revenue Service because the Silbers had not declared the cash as income for tax purposes. Under federal law, however, Merrill Lynch was required to file a Currency Transaction Report (CTR) with the IRS for cash transactions of more than $10,000. To circumvent the CTR requirement, Heyman and another Merrill Lynch account executive opened three new individual accounts; one in the name of Sam Silber, one in the name of Evelyn Silber, and the third in the name of the Silbers' daughter, Pearl Schmutter. On February 16, 1982, Heyman deposited $9,900 into each of the four accounts maintained for the Silbers. Although a total of $39,600 cash was deposited, Merrill Lynch did not file a CTR because each transaction involved less than $10,000. Heyman divided a deposit of $17,000 between two of the Silber accounts in May. On July 26, 1982, Sam Silber gave Heyman a suitcase containing $70,000 in cash for deposit. Heyman opened six new joint and individual accounts in the names of the Silbers and their relatives and deposited $7,000 in each of the ten Merrill Lynch accounts. Merrill Lynch did not file CTRs for the transactions that occurred in May and July.

The following year, the federal government indicted Heyman for conspiracy and for causing a financial institution to fail to file CTRs for transactions involving more than $100,000 during a twelve month period in violation of 31 U.S.C. §§ 5313 and 5322. After a jury convicted him of the charges, Heyman appealed.

Irving R. Kaufman, Circuit Judge

We are asked to determine whether a statute proscribing certain conduct by financial institutions was properly applied in prosecuting an employee who caused his brokerage firm to unwittingly violate the statute. . . .

Concerned that the nation's financial institutions were serving a larger and increasingly important role in the laundering of unreported income or illegally obtained funds, Congress enacted the Bank Secrecy Act in 1971. The Act provides for "certain reports or records where they have a high degree of usefulness in criminal, tax, or regulatory investigations or proceedings." The Secretary of the Treasury is authorized to prescribe by regulation specific recordkeeping and reporting requirements for financial institutions. . . . Pursuant to that authority, the Secretary implemented [regulations] requiring all financial institutions to file a report for every currency transaction over $10,000.

On appeal, Heyman contends that 31 U.S.C. § 5313 and the regulations promulgated thereunder proscribe only certain conduct by financial institutions, and that an individual cannot be convicted of violating the terms of the Act. The Government counters that Heyman's conviction is firmly supported by 18 U.S.C. §2(b), which provides that one who willfully causes another to commit a crime is punishable as a principal.

In weighing the merits of these arguments, we acknowledge, and the Government concedes, that Heyman did not have a legal duty to file CTRs in his capacity as an account executive at Merrill Lynch. The cashier's department carried that responsibility. We agree with the Government, however, that criminal liability may attach to Heyman's actions through the operation of 18 U.S.C. §2(b), which provides:

> Whoever willfully causes an act to be done which if directly performed by him or another would be an offense against the United States, is punishable as a principal. . . .

[A] 1951 amendment of §2(b) . . . broadened the scope of criminal liability. . . . to impute criminal liability to anyone who "willfully causes an act to be done which if directly performed by him *or another* would be an offense against the United States." (emphasis added). [Prior decisions of this court have] held that the addition of the words "or another" reflected a desire by Congress to hold criminally liable those who cause others to commit crimes, without regard to the guilt or innocence of the intermediary or the legal capacity of the defendant to commit the crime.

The application of this principle is dispositive in this case. Heyman himself had no legal responsibility to file CTRs. By structuring his customers' deposits so that no single transaction involved an amount greater than $10,000, however, Heyman willfully caused Merrill Lynch to fail to file the appropriate CTRs. Had Merrill Lynch, a financial institution, structured the transaction as Heyman did, it would have violated federal law. Because §2(b) holds liable as a principal any person who willfully causes an act to be done which if directly performed by another (here, Merrill Lynch) would be a federal offense, Heyman is criminally liable for violation 31 U.S.C. §§ 5313 and 5322. . . .

Finally, the requirement of §2(b) that a defendant's acts be "willful" provides adequate protection for individuals who might unwittingly stumble into a violation of federal law. . . . We believe this lends persuasive support to the large number of cases holding that any individual, including a customer, may be held criminally liable for willfully causing a financial institution to fail to file CTRs. . . .

[Judgment affirmed.]

Business Crimes

Types of Offenses. Although violent crimes such as murder, rape, and armed robbery remain serious concerns of the criminal justice system, an increasing amount of crime is committed by individuals or corporations in the conduct of business operations. Such "white collar" or business crime includes bribery (including illegal rebates, kickbacks, and bribery of foreign officials), criminal fraud, illegal political contributions, income tax evasion, criminal antitrust violations (primarily price fixing and bid rigging), and criminal violation of other regulatory statutes such as federal securities law or food and drug laws. Of course, traditional crimes such as forgery, embezzlement, and theft also occur in business. In addition to these offenses and viola-

tions of the federal conspiracy statute, other federal criminal statutes of particular importance to business include the Racketeer Influenced and Corrupt Organizations Act (RICO)[5] and the federal mail and wire fraud statutes.[6]

RICO was enacted by Congress primarily to prevent and punish financial infiltration and corrupt operation of legitimate business operations through patterns of racketeering activity. For example, the Act prohibits using racketeering income to acquire an interest in a business enterprise or to establish or operate an enterprise.[7] Though its primary purpose was to eradicate organized crime and corruption, RICO is not limited to persons connected with traditional organized crime or to activities commonly considered racketeering, such as extortion, gambling, property theft rings, drug trafficking, and loan sharking. Rather, the Act defines "racketeering activity" expansively to include also securities fraud; mail and wire fraud; bankruptcy fraud; embezzlement of pension, welfare, or union funds; obstruction of justice; and violations of currency transaction reporting laws.[8] Accordingly, many white collar crimes committed by legitimate business enterprises are potential RICO violations. Penalties are severe including fines of up to $25,000, imprisonment of up to twenty years, or both, and forfeiture of property derived from racketeering activity.

Federal law also imposes criminal liability for mail and wire fraud. Conviction generally requires proof that the defendant devised a scheme to defraud and used the mails, telephone, radio, or television to further or execute the scheme. The fraudulent scheme need not itself constitute a crime or a violation of federal law. Violators may be fined up to $1,000 or imprisoned up to five years, or both. The mail and wire fraud statutes have been used to reach a wide variety of deceptive schemes, including mail order frauds and schemes involving kickbacks or bribes paid to corporate employees or public officials.

---

5. 18 U.S.C. §§1961–1968.
6. 18 U.S.C. §§1341, 1343.
7. 18 U.S.C. §1962(a).
8. 18 U.S.C. §1961(1).

Corporate Criminal Liability. The corporation is the dominant form of business organization in the United States. As discussed in Chapter 45, a corporation is a legal entity, an "artificial" person created by compliance with state laws authorizing corporate existence. Though it is a legal entity, the corporation acts only through its agents—its officers and employees. If crimes are committed in the corporate setting, the law must address two important issues: (1) the liability of the corporation for the crimes of its agents and (2) the liability of an individual corporate agent for crimes committed by the agent or others during the course of the agent's employment.

Liability of the Corporation. A corporation is generally responsible for crimes committed by any agent who acts within the scope of employment and with intent to benefit the corporation.[9] The following case illustrates the application of this rule.

United States v. Hilton Hotels Corporation

467 F.2d 1000 (9th Cir. 1972)

The operators of various hotels, restaurants, and other businesses in Portland, Oregon, formed an association to attract conventions to the city. To finance the association, each member contributed specified amounts of money. Companies that sold supplies to hotels were asked to contribute 1% of the amount of their sales to hotel members. Hotel members agreed to boycott or curtail purchases from suppliers who refused to contribute.

The Hilton Hotel in Portland was a member of the association. According to corporate policy, hotels in the Hilton Hotel Corporation chain were not supposed to boycott suppliers as prescribed by the association. On two occasions, the manager and assistant manager of the Portland Hilton Hotel told the hotel's purchasing agent not to participate in the boycott and to follow the policy of purchasing supplies on the basis of price, quality, and service.

---

9. Note, Developments in the Law—Corporate Crime: Regulating Corporate Behavior Through Criminal Sanctions, 92 Harv. L. Rev., 1227, 1247 (1979).

Despite these instructions, the purchasing agent threatened a supplier with loss of the hotel's business unless the supplier contributed to the association. The purchasing agent admitted that he made the threat because of personal anger toward the supplier's representative.

Under the federal Sherman Act, an agreement among competitors to refuse to deal with a supplier or to threaten to refuse to deal with a supplier may be a criminal violation of the antitrust laws. The federal government charged the appellant Hilton Hotels Corporation with violation of the Sherman Act and the jury returned a guilty verdict. Hilton Hotel Corporation appealed, arguing that it could not be held guilty for the acts of its employees that were contrary to corporate policy and to the corporation's instructions to the employees.

Browning, Circuit Judge

. . . Congress may constitutionally impose criminal liability upon a business entity for acts or omissions of its agents within the scope of their employment. . . . Such liability may attach without proof that the conduct was within the agent's actual authority, and even though it may have been contrary to express instructions. . . .

The intention to impose such liability is sometimes express . . . but it may also be implied. The text of the Sherman Act does not expressly resolve the issue. For the reasons that follow, however, we think the construction of the Act that best achieves its purpose is that a corporation is liable for acts of its agents within the scope of their authority even when done against company orders. . . .

Because of the nature of Sherman Act offenses and the context in which they normally occur, the factors that militate against allowing a corporation to disown the criminal acts of its agents apply with special force to Sherman Act violations.

Sherman Act violations are commercial offenses. They are usually motivated by a desire to enhance profits. They commonly involve large, complex, and highly decentralized corporate business enterprises, and intricate business processes, practices, and arrangements. More often than not they also involve basic policy decisions, and must be implemented over an extended period of time.

Complex business structures, characterized by decentralization and delegation of authority, commonly adopted by corporations for business purposes, make it difficult to identify the particular corporate agents responsible for Sherman Act violations. At the same time, it is generally true that high management officials, for whose conduct the corporate directors and stockholders are the most clearly responsible, are likely to have participated in the policy decisions underlying Sherman Act violations, or at least to have become aware of them.

Violations of the Sherman Act are a likely consequence of the pressure to maximize profits that is commonly imposed by corporate owners upon managing agents and, in turn, upon lesser employees. In the face of that pressure, generalized directions to obey the Sherman Act, with the probable effect of foregoing profits, are the least likely to be taken seriously. And if a violation of the Sherman Act occurs, the corporation, and not the individual agents, will have realized the profits from the illegal activity.

In sum, identification of the particular agents responsible for a Sherman Act violation is especially difficult, and their conviction and punishment is peculiarly ineffective as a deterrent. At the same time, conviction and punishment of the business entity itself is likely to be both appropriate and effective.

For these reasons we conclude that as a general rule a corporation is liable under the Sherman Act for the acts of its agents in the scope of their employment, even though contrary to general corporate policy and express instructions to the agent.

Thus the general policy statements of appellant's president were no defense. Nor was it enough that appellant's manager told the purchasing agent that he was not to participate in the boycott. The purchasing agent was authorized to buy all of the appellant's supplies. Purchases were made on the basis of specifications, but the purchasing agent exercised complete authority as to source. He was in a unique position to add the corporation's buying power to the force of the boycott. Appellant could not gain exculpation by issuing general instructions without undertaking to enforce those instructions by means commensurate with the obvious risks. . . .

[Judgment affirmed.]

Liability of Corporate Agents. In addition to corporate liability, criminal responsibility may also be imposed upon individual corporate agents for employment-related criminal acts. First, individuals are liable for their own criminal conduct, whether or not committed in a corporate capacity. Thus, corporate agents are not insulated from criminal liability simply because their acts were committed in the name of or on behalf of the business organization. Second, a corporate official may be liable as an accomplice by directing, authorizing, participating in, or acquiescing in the criminal activity of others. Third, responsible corporate managers who violate a statutory duty to discover and correct criminal violations within the corporation committed by subordinates, may themselves be criminally responsible. This *responsible share standard* of liability has been used to convict high corporate officials for violating strict liability criminal statutes including the Federal Hazardous Substances Act, the Occupational Safety and Health Act, the Federal Water Pollution Control Act, and most notably, as the following case illustrates, the Federal Food, Drug, and Cosmetic Act.

United States v. Park
95 S. Ct. 1903 (1975)

Respondent John Park was chief executive officer of Acme Markets, Inc., a retail food chain with 36,000 employees, 874 retail outlets, and 16 warehouses. The federal government charged both Park and Acme with violations of the Federal Food, Drug, and Cosmetic Act. Acme pleaded guilty but Park pleaded innocent.

The evidence at trial established that food held in Acme's warehouses had been contaminated by rodent infestation and other unsanitary conditions. Following an inspection of the warehouse the Food and Drug Administration (FDA) had notified respondent of the conditions in a detailed letter. Following a second inspection, the charges had been filed against Acme and Park. Park testified that as chief executive officer he had referred the problems to individuals responsible for sanitation who were "dependable subordinates." The jury instructions provided in part:

> The statute makes individuals, as well as corporations, liable for violations. An individual is liable if it is clear, beyond a reasonable doubt, that the elements of the adulteration of the food as to travel in interstate commerce are present. As I have instructed you in this case, they are, and that the individual had a responsible relation to the situation, even though he may not have participated personally.
>
> The individual is or could be liable under the statute, even if he did not consciously do wrong. However, the fact that the Defendant is [president] and is a chief executive officer of the Acme Markets does not require a finding of guilt. Though he need not have personally participated in the situation, he must have had a responsible relationship to the issue. The issue is, in this case, whether the Defendant, John R. Park, by virtue of his position in the company, had a position of authority and responsibility in the situation out of which these charges arose.

The jury found Park guilty of the charges. He appealed. The Court of Appeals reversed on the grounds that the jury instructions were improper. The United States Supreme Court granted a writ of certiorari.

Chief Justice Burger

. . . The question presented by the Government's petition . . . was whether "the manager of a corporation, as well as the corporation itself, may be prosecuted under the Federal Food, Drug, and Cosmetic Act of 1938 for the introduction of misbranded and adulterated articles into interstate commerce." . . .

The rule that corporate employees who have "a responsible share in the furtherance of the transaction which the statute outlaws" are subject to the criminal provisions of the Act was not formulated in a vacuum. . . . Cases under the Federal Food and Drugs Act of 1906 reflected the view both that knowledge or intent were not required to be proved in prosecutions under its criminal provisions, and that . . . a corporate agent, through whose act, default, or omission the corporation committed a crime, was himself guilty individually of that crime. The principle had been applied whether or not the crime required "consciousness of wrongdoing," and it had been applied not only to those corporate agents who themselves committed the criminal act, but also to those who by virtue of their managerial positions or other similar relation to the actor could be deemed responsible for its commission.

In the latter class of cases, the liability of managerial officers did not depend on their knowledge of, or personal participation in, the act made criminal by the statute. Rather . . . [i]t was enough in such cases that, by virtue of the relationship he bore to the corporation, the agent had the power to prevent the act complained of. . . .

. . . [I]n providing sanctions which reach and touch the individuals who execute the corporate mission—and this is by no means necessarily confined to a single corporate agent or employee—the Act imposes not only a positive duty to seek out and remedy violations when they occur but also, and primarily, a duty to implement measures that will insure that violations will not occur. The requirements of foresight and vigilance imposed on responsible corporate agents are beyond question demanding, and perhaps onerous, but they are no more stringent than the public has a right to expect of those who voluntarily assume positions of authority in business enterprises whose services and products affect the health and well-being of the public that supports them. . . .

[T]he Government establishes a prima facie case when it introduces evidence sufficient to warrant a finding by the trier of the facts that the defendant had, by reason of his position in the corporation, responsibility and authority either to prevent in the first instance, or promptly to correct, the violation complained of, and that he failed to do so. . . .

Reading the entire charge satisfies us that the jury's attention was adequately focused on the issue of respondent's authority with respect to the conditions that formed the basis of the alleged violations. Viewed as a whole, the charge did not permit the jury to find guilt solely on the basis of respondent's position in the corporation; rather . . . the jury could not have failed to be aware that the main issue for determination was [Park's] accountability, because of the responsibility and authority of his position, for the conditions which gave rise to the charges against him. . . .

[Judgment reversed.]

Criminal Procedure

Although the legislature enacts statutes to define substantive criminal laws and the penalties for violating them, the executive branch of government is responsible for enforcing the criminal law by investigating crimes, arresting and charging persons suspected of committing crimes, and prosecuting those suspects in courts of law. A legal proceeding that determines the guilt or innocence of a person charged with a crime is known as a **prosecution.** Because criminal law is designed to protect society generally, criminal prosecutions are maintained by public officials on behalf of the people of a state or the United States. Therefore, the plaintiffs in criminal prosecutions are, for example, the "People of the State of _____," or the "State of _____," or the "United States." The defendant in a criminal case is, of course, the person charged with a violation of substantive criminal law. Every state and the federal government have adopted rules of criminal procedure that establish the process by which executive officers bring an accused person to court for a determination of guilt or innocence.

Enforcement of Criminal Law

A variety of state law enforcement agencies investigate alleged violations of the criminal law including local police departments, state police, and state bureaus of investigation. In addition, in some states specialized agencies investigate specific types of crime (for example, drugs, organized crime, and child abuse). After the investigation, the offender may be prosecuted in court. Attorneys known as "state's attorneys" or "district attorneys" are responsible for presenting the state's case to the court. In most states, these "prosecutors" are supervised by the state attorney general.[10]

At the federal level, approximately fifty federal agencies, including the Federal Bureau of Investigation, are responsible for investigating violations of federal criminal statutes. United States attorneys, who are appointed by the president, prosecute federal criminal cases. The attorney general supervises the prosecutors and the Justice Department may provide additional support to the United States attorneys.

Cases involving violations of state law are prosecuted in state courts, either in the trial courts or in specialized felony courts, misdemeanor courts, or traffic courts. Federal criminal cases generally are tried in the federal district courts. The judiciary of both the federal and state courts employ officers known as "magistrates" or "commissioners" to perform judicial functions such as issuing warrants and setting bail.

Criminal Jurisdiction and Venue

As in civil cases, in criminal prosecutions the court must have jurisdiction both over the subject matter and the person. Generally, state trial courts have subject matter jurisdiction over state offenses committed either wholly or partly within the state. In state cases, the proper venue (place of trial) is usually the county in which the offense was committed. The federal district courts have original jurisdiction, to the exclusion of any state court, to try all federal criminal offenses.[11] Proper venue for federal cases is generally the federal district (for example, Northern District of Illinois or Eastern District of New York) in which the offense was committed.[12]

Jurisdiction over the person (the defendant) in criminal cases is obtained by arrest. If the arrest is made in a state other than the one in which the offense was committed, extradition of the defendant is required. **Extradition** is the surrender by one state (or country) of an individual accused of a crime to another state or country having jurisdiction to try the offender. The duty of one state to extradite criminals sought in other states is contained in Article IV, Section 2, Clause 2 of the Constitution, which provides:

> A Person charged in any State with Treason, Felony, or other Crime, who shall flee from Justice, and be found in another State, shall on de-

---

10. In many states, prosecutors are elected officials who serve an entire county. In larger cities, the state's attorney may prosecute only felonies while a city attorney handles misdemeanor cases.

11. 18 U.S.C. §3231.

12. Fed. R. Crim. P. Rule 18, 18 U.S.C. The court may grant a change of venue if local prejudice or pretrial publicity prevent the defendant from receiving a fair trial in the original venue.

Table 3–1	**Bill of Rights Provisions Relating to Criminal Procedure**

Amendments	Provisions
Fourth	Prohibition against unreasonable searches and seizures
Fifth	Right to prosecution by grand jury indictment for infamous crimes
	Prohibition against double jeopardy
	Privilege against self-incrimination
	Requirement of due process
Sixth	Right to assistance of counsel
	Right to speedy trial
	Right to jury trial
	Right to confront opposing witnesses
	Right to compulsory process for obtaining witnesses
	Right to public trial
	Right to be informed of the nature and cause of the accusation
Eighth	Prohibition against excessive bail
	Prohibition of cruel and unusual punishment

mand of the executive Authority of the State from which he fled, be delivered up, to be removed to the State having Jurisdiction of the Crime.

The legal machinery to execute the Extradition Clause is contained in both federal statutes[13] and in the Uniform Criminal Extradition Act, which has been enacted in forty-eight states. The Supreme Court has held that the Extradition Clause creates a mandatory duty to deliver up fugitives on a proper demand, and that the federal courts have authority under the Constitution to compel state officials to perform this ministerial duty of delivery.[14] In addition to extradition among the various states, the United States has entered into bilateral treaties of extradition with over ninety countries.

The Constitution and Criminal Procedure

The Bill of Rights guarantees a number of specific rights to a person accused of a crime. In fact, over half of the separate rights contained in these amendments concern criminal procedure. Some of these rights apply to the trial stage of the criminal process. Others safeguard the rights of a suspect prior to the trial and affect the methods by which police investigate criminal activity, collect evidence, and treat a suspect prior to trial. Because criminal procedure is essentially a branch of constitutional law, the United States Supreme Court, which interprets the Constitution, plays a pivotal role in developing and applying principles of criminal procedure. The various Bill of Rights provisions relating to criminal procedure are shown in Table 3–1.

The Due Process Clause. The Fifth Amendment (applicable to the federal government) and Fourteenth Amendment (applicable to the states) prohibit both federal and state governments from depriving a person of "life, liberty, or property, without due process of law." As noted in Chapter 2, this provision has long been interpreted to require "procedural" due process—notice and hearing—before life, liberty, or property are taken. The various stages of the criminal process discussed later in this chapter are designed to provide procedural due process in criminal prosecutions.

13. 18 U.S.C. §3181 et seq.
14. *Puerto Rico v. Branstad*, 107 S. Ct. 2802 (1987).

In addition, the Due Process Clause of the Fourteenth Amendment plays an important role in determining the specific constitutional guarantees available to the accused in a *state* prosecution. The Bill of Rights was enacted solely to limit the power of the federal government. Accordingly, the specific rights guaranteed to the criminally accused, by the terms of the Bill of Rights, apply only in *federal* prosecutions. The Supreme Court has, however, held that the Due Process Clause of the Fourteenth Amendment, which is applicable to the states, guarantees all rights that are fundamental principles of liberty and justice. If the court determines that a given Bill of Rights guarantee is fundamental, it is then incorporated and applied to the states through the Due Process Clause of the Fourteenth Amendment. Through this process of "selective incorporation," occurring in a series of cases decided primarily since 1961, the Supreme Court has held fundamental, and therefore applicable to the states, most of the Bill of Rights criminal procedure provisions.[15]

The following material discusses constitutional guarantees important in the early stages of the criminal process: the right to be secure from unreasonable searches and seizures, the privilege against self-incrimination, and the right to the assistance of counsel. Other guarantees applicable in the trial stage and beyond are discussed later in the chapter.

Right to Be Secure from Unreasonable Searches and Seizures. The Fourth Amendment provides:

> The right of the people to be secure in their persons, houses, papers, and effects, against unreasonable searches and seizures, shall not be violated, and no Warrants shall issue, but upon probable cause, supported by Oath or affirmation, and particularly describing the place to be searched, and the persons or things to be seized.

This amendment serves as limitation on the powers of the government in arresting (seizing) a person

suspected of committing a crime and in obtaining evidence (search and seizure of things) to be used in criminal trials.

The Supreme Court has indicated that to comply with the Fourth Amendment the police should obtain an arrest warrant prior to arresting a suspect. An **arrest warrant** is a writ issued by a magistrate or other appropriate official authorizing the police to take a specified person into custody. To obtain an arrest warrant, the police must provide to the magistrate a sworn statement of facts. If the magistrate determines that the statement establishes probable cause—that is, a substantial probability—that a criminal offense has been committed and that the person to be arrested committed the offense, he will issue a warrant for the suspect's arrest.

Despite the preference for an arrest warrant, the courts have recognized that an arrest without a warrant sometimes may be lawful. Generally, arrest without a warrant is legal if the police officer has reasonable grounds to believe that the arrestee has committed a felony, or if the arrestee commits a misdemeanor or felony in the officer's presence. The arrested person subsequently may challenge the legality of the arrest, whether made with or without a warrant, and require that a court determine that probable cause for the arrest existed at the time the arrest was made.

Although the Fourth Amendment appears to protect only "persons, houses, papers, and effects," the Supreme Court has liberally construed the scope of the amendment's protection. Recognizing that the purpose of the amendment is to protect people, the Court has held that anything that a person justifiably seeks to preserve as private is protected from unreasonable searches. Thus, a person's home, as well as his office, hotel room, and automobile may not be subjected to unreasonable searches.

Because the Fourth Amendment prohibits only "unreasonable searches," many cases have attempted to define under what conditions a search is reasonable. Generally, a search by a police officer is reasonable if it is made pursuant to a proper search warrant or with proper consent.

Prior to conducting a search, a police officer may obtain a **search warrant** from a magistrate or other appropriate official by providing a sworn statement of the facts that justify the request to search a spec-

---

15. The Eighth Amendment prohibition against excessive bail and the Fifth Amendment requirement that infamous crimes be prosecuted by grand jury indictment have not been incorporated and applied to the states.

ified place to obtain specified items. The statement must establish probable cause—substantial evidence that the items are located in the place to be searched and that the items are connected with illegal activities. If the magistrate determines that the officer's statement establishes probable cause, the magistrate will issue a warrant describing the place to be searched and the items to be seized. Although the magistrate initially determines that probable cause has been established, that determination may later be challenged.

A search also is considered reasonable if proper consent is obtained. Whether consent is proper generally depends on two issues: whether the person consenting to the search has the authority to do so and whether the consent was made voluntarily. The authority to grant consent may be in issue if the place to be searched is under the custody of more than one person: for example, a house shared by more than one person, an apartment owned by one person and occupied by another, an office of an employee located on the premises of the employer. If an authorized person consents to a search, the consent must be made voluntarily. Thus, if the police coerce a person into consenting to the search, it will be considered illegal. The police, however, generally are not required to advise the person that he or she may refuse to consent to a search.

Even if a police officer conducts a search without a proper warrant or consent, the search and seizure of property may be lawful if it is reasonable. For example, a search made incident to a lawful arrest may be reasonable. Generally, such a search is limited to the person of the arrestee and to the area of his immediate control, for the purpose of locating a weapon or to prevent the destruction of evidence. Police seizure of items "in plain view" is also reasonable if a police officer is lawfully present in a place and observes an item he or she knows to be related to criminal activity.

Privilege Against Self-Incrimination. The Fifth Amendment provides that no person shall be "compelled in any criminal case to be a witness against himself." Thus, a defendant cannot be required to testify, and a person cannot be required to provide self-incriminating evidence at the trial of

another person. To compel testimony from a witness who might refuse to testify because of self-incrimination, the government may grant immunity from prosecution to the witness.

The privilege against self-incrimination also limits the power of the police in obtaining confessions or other information from a person accused of a crime. As discussed later in this chapter, such statements are considered to have been lawfully obtained only if certain procedural safeguards have been provided.

Right to Counsel. The Sixth Amendment provides that "In all criminal prosecutions, the accused shall enjoy the right . . . to have the Assistance of Counsel for his defence." Many of the cases interpreting the Sixth Amendment concern the right of an indigent defendant to have legal counsel appointed to represent him at government expense. Generally, an indigent defendant is entitled to representation in all felony cases and in misdemeanor cases punishable by a prison sentence[16] at any "critical stage" following the initiation of adversary judicial proceedings. A stage in the criminal proceedings is critical if potential substantial prejudice to the defendant's rights is inherent in the particular confrontation and counsel may be able to help avoid that prejudice.[17] The summary of the criminal process that follows indicates the critical stages at which legal counsel should be made available.

Exclusionary Rule. Although the Bill of Rights guarantees the right to be secure from unreasonable searches and seizures, the privilege against self-incrimination, and the right to counsel, the Constitution does not specify how these rights are to be enforced. To help safeguard these rights, the Supreme Court has adopted the **exclusionary rule,** which provides that evidence obtained in violation of the Fourth Amendment, the Fifth Amendment

---

16. If a court fails to provide counsel in a misdemeanor case, no prison sentence may be imposed. Although the Supreme Court has not established that counsel in such cases is constitutionally mandated, some states have extended the right to counsel to all criminal cases.

17. *Coleman v. Alabama,* 90 S. Ct. 1999 (1970).

self-incrimination privilege, and the Sixth Amendment right to counsel must be excluded in a criminal prosecution of the person whose rights were violated. Because the excluded evidence frequently is crucial to establishing guilt, application of the exclusionary rule may lead to the acquittal or other discharge of a criminal defendant who clearly is guilty of a crime. As a result, many advocate abolition or less stringent application of the rule. Proponents of the exclusionary rule, however, argue that it is the only effective method of deterring the police from unlawful violation of the Constitution. At issue in the following case was whether the defendant's Fourth and Fifth Amendment rights had been violated.

Andresen v. Maryland
96 S. Ct. 2737 (1976)

The State of Maryland arrested and charged Peter Andresen, an attorney, with criminal fraud in conjunction with the sale of a piece of real estate known as "Lot 13T" in Potomac Woods, Maryland. During the investigation and prior to Andresen's arrest, a court had issued a search warrant to the police authorizing the search of Andresen's law office and the office of a corporation operated by Andresen. The warrants listed specific items pertaining to Lot 13T to be seized "together with other fruits, instrumentalities and evidence of crime at this [time] unknown." The police conducted the searches during the daytime and Andresen was present during the search of the law office.

Following the filing of formal charges, the trial court conducted a suppression hearing to determine the admissibility of the documents obtained during the searches. The court held that only one item, a file marked "Potomac Woods General," was admissible among the fifty-two items seized from the corporation office. Seventeen of twenty-eight items seized from the law office were held to be admissible.

At trial, the State introduced some of the seized items into evidence. Andresen was found guilty. Andresen appealed, asserting that admission of his business records into evidence effectively compelled

him to testify against himself in violation of the Fifth Amendment. Andresen also argued that the search violated his Fourth Amendment rights because the search warrant had not properly described the items to be seized. The appellate court affirmed the trial court's holdings on these issues. Andresen was granted a writ of certiorari by the Supreme Court.

Justice Blackmun

. . . There is no question that the records seized from petitioner's offices and introduced against him were incriminating. Moreover, it is undisputed that some of these business records contain statements made by petitioner. . . . The question, therefore, is whether the seizure of these business records, and their admission into evidence at his trial, compelled petitioner to testify against himself in violation of the Fifth Amendment. . . .

Petitioner contends that "the Fifth Amendment prohibition against compulsory self-incrimination applies as well to personal business papers seized from his offices as it does to the same papers being required to be produced under a subpoena." . . . Compulsion of the accused was . . . absent in *Couch v. United States,* [93 S. Ct. 611 (1973)], where the Court held that a summons served on a taxpayer's accountant requiring him to produce the taxpayer's personal business records in his possession did not violate the taxpayer's Fifth Amendment rights.

Similarly, in this case, petitioner was not asked to say or to do anything. The records seized contained statements that petitioner had voluntarily committed to writing. The search for and seizure of these records were conducted by law enforcement personnel. Finally, when these records were introduced at trial, they were authenticated by a handwriting expert, not by petitioner. Any compulsion of petitioner to speak, other than the inherent psychological pressure to respond at trial to unfavorable evidence, was not present. . . .

[A]lthough the Fifth Amendment may protect an individual from complying with a subpoena for the production of his personal records in his possession because the very act of production may constitute a compulsory authentication of incriminating information, . . . a seizure of the same materials by law enforcement officers differs in a crucial respect—the individual against whom the search is directed is not required to aid in the discovery, production, or authentication of incriminating evidence.

A contrary determination that the seizure of a person's business records and their introduction into evidence at a criminal trial violates the Fifth Amendment . . . would prohibit the admission of evidence traditionally used in criminal cases and traditionally admissible despite the Fifth Amendment. For example, it would bar the admission of an accused's gambling records in a prosecution for gambling; a note given temporarily to a bank teller during a robbery and subsequently seized in the accused's automobile or home in a prosecution for bank robbery; and incriminating notes prepared, but not sent, by an accused in a kidnapping or blackmail prosecution. . . .

Accordingly, we hold that the search of an individual's office for business records, their seizure, and subsequent introduction into evidence do not offend the Fifth Amendment. . . .

We turn next to petitioner's contention that rights guaranteed him by the Fourth Amendment were violated because the descriptive terms of the search warrants were so broad as to make them impermissible "general" warrants. . . .

Although petitioner concedes that the warrants for the most part were models of particularity . . . he contends that they were rendered fatally "general" by the addition, in each warrant, to the exhaustive list of particularly described documents, of the phrase "together with other fruits, instrumentalities and evidence of crime at this [time] unknown." . . . The quoted language, it is argued, must be read in isolation and without reference to the rest of the long sentence at the end of which it appears. When read "properly," petitioner contends, it permits the search for and seizure of any evidence of any crime.

General warrants of course, are prohibited by the Fourth Amendment. "[T]he problem [posed by the general warrant] is not that of intrusion *per se*, but of a general, exploratory rummaging in a person's belongings. . . . [The Fourth Amendment addresses the problem] by requiring a 'particular description' of the things to be seized." [*Coolidge*

v. New Hampshire, 91 S. Ct. 2022, 2038 (1971)]. . . .

In this case we agree with the determination of the Court of Special Appeals of Maryland that the challenged phrase must be read as authorizing only the search for and seizure of evidence relating to "the crime of false pretenses with respect to Lot 13T." . . . The challenged phrase is not a separate sentence. Instead, it appears in each warrant at the end of a sentence containing a lengthy list of specified and particular items to be seized, all pertaining to Lot 13T. We think it clear from the context that the term "crime" in the warrants refers only to the crime of false pretenses with respect to the sale of Lot 13T. The "other fruits" clause is one of a series that follows the colon after the word "Maryland." All clauses in the series are limited by what precedes that colon, namely, "items pertaining to . . . lot 13, block T." The warrants, accordingly, did not authorize the executing officers to conduct a search for evidence of other crimes but only to search for and seize evidence relevant to the crime of false pretenses and Lot 13T. . . .

[Judgment affirmed.]

Stages in the Criminal Process

The individual states and the federal government have enacted rules of criminal procedure. Procedures vary somewhat among the various jurisdictions and also may differ depending on the nature of the crime. Offenses committed by persons under a minimum age (for example, seventeen years) generally are handled through the juvenile court system rather than the criminal justice system applicable to adult offenders.[18] Juvenile courts are designed to provide protection, guidance, care, custody, and guardianship of delinquent minors (those

---

18. State laws may authorize the juvenile court, after investigation and a hearing, to permit certain juveniles to be prosecuted as an adult under the criminal law. In addition, the age of adult criminal responsibility may be lowered (for example, to fifteen years) for certain serious crimes such as murder, rape, and armed robbery.

who perform acts which would be crimes or other violations of law if committed by an adult), minors otherwise in need of supervision or authoritative intervention (such as truants, runaways, or drug addicts), minors who are neglected or abused, and those who are abandoned or otherwise without a parent, guardian, or legal custodian. Figure 3–1[19] illustrates how cases move through the criminal justice system. The text that follows provides a general description of the criminal process applicable to adult offenders.

Arrest. Most criminal cases begin when the police arrest a suspect—take him into custody for the purpose of charging him with a crime. The suspect then is taken to the police station for **booking**, an administrative procedure during which the suspect's name, time of arrest, and alleged crime are recorded in the police records, and the defendant may be photographed or fingerprinted. A suspect who is taken into custody or otherwise deprived of freedom in any significant way must be given the "Miranda warning" before any interrogation. The warnings are required by the classic United States Supreme Court case, *Miranda v. Arizona,* decided in 1966.[20] In that case, the court held:

> [W]hen an individual is taken into custody or otherwise deprived of his freedom by the authorities in any significant way and is subjected to questioning, the privilege against self-incrimination is jeopardized. Procedural safeguards must be employed to protect the privilege, and unless other fully effective means are adopted to notify the person of his right of silence and to assure that the exercise of the right will be scrupulously honored, the following measures are required. He must be warned prior to any questioning that he has the right to remain silent, that anything he says can be used against him in a court of law, that he has the right to the presence of an attorney, and that if he cannot afford an attorney one will be appointed for him prior to any questioning

if he so desires. Opportunity to exercise these rights must be afforded to him throughout the interrogation. After such warnings have been given, and such opportunity afforded him, the individual may knowingly and intelligently waive these rights and agree to answer questions or make a statement. But unless and until such warnings and waiver are demonstrated by the prosecution at trial, no evidence obtained as a result of interrogation can be used against him.[21]

Initial Appearance. Following an arrest, the prosecutor generally determines whether to charge the suspect with an offense. If charges are filed, the prosecutor prepares a complaint listing the offenses allegedly committed and the complaint is signed either by the police officer or a complaining witness. The police then must take the accused without unreasonable delay for the initial appearance before the magistrate, who notifies the accused of the charges of the complaint and of his constitutional rights. If the case involves a minor misdemeanor and the accused pleads guilty, the magistrate may have the authority to try the case and impose the sentence immediately. Other misdemeanor cases are set for trial. In misdemeanor cases punishable by imprisonment, the initial appearance is considered a critical stage entitling the accused to legal counsel if the accused is required to enter a plea.

If the charge is a felony, however, the magistrate sets the matter for a preliminary hearing and may set bail. **Bail** is a security or obligation given by the accused or another to obtain the accused's release from custody. The purpose of bail is to ensure that the accused will appear at the scheduled court proceedings. A person who posts bail is released, but forfeits the bail if he or she fails to appear at the subsequent proceedings.

Preliminary Hearing. The **preliminary hearing** is a proceeding held before the magistrate to protect the accused from unwarranted prosecution. At the hearing, the prosecutor presents evidence through witnesses who are subject to cross-examination by the accused's counsel. The prosecution generally

---

19. Taken from the *President's Commission on Law Enforcement and the Administration of Justice: The Challenge of Crime in a Free Society* 8–9 (1967).

20. 86 S. Ct. 1602 (1966).

21. 86 S. Ct. at 1630.

Figure 3–1   A General View of the Criminal Justice System

This chart seeks to present a simple yet comprehensive view of the movement of cases through the criminal justice system. Procedures in individual jurisdictions may vary from the pattern shown here. The differing thicknesses of line indicate the relative volumes of cases disposed of at various points in the system, but this is only suggestive since no nationwide data of this sort exist.

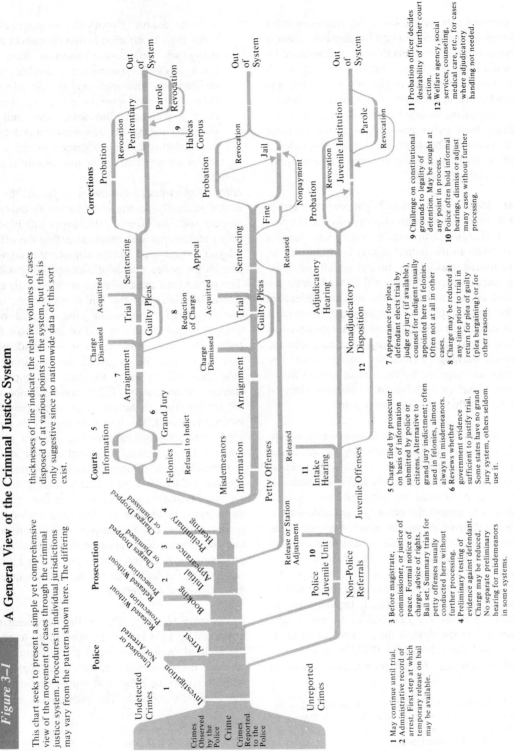

1 May continue until trial.

2 Administrative record of arrest. First step at which temporary release on bail may be available.

3 Before magistrate, commissioner, or justice of peace. Formal notice of charge, advice of rights. Bail set. Summary trials for petty offenses usually conducted here without further processing.

4 Preliminary testing of evidence against defendant. Charge may be reduced. No separate preliminary hearing for misdemeanors in some systems.

5 Charge filed by prosecutor on basis of information submitted by police or citizens. Alternative to grand jury indictment; often used in felonies, almost always in misdemeanors.

6 Reviews whether government evidence sufficient to justify trial. Some states have no grand jury system, others seldom use it.

7 Appearance for plea; defendant elects trial by judge or jury (if available), counsel for indigent usually appointed here in felonies. Often not at all in other cases.

8 Charge may be reduced at any time prior to trial in return for plea of guilty (plea bargaining) or for other reasons.

9 Challenge on constitutional grounds to legality of detention. May be sought at any point in process.

10 Police often hold informal hearings, dismiss or adjust many cases without further processing.

11 Probation officer decides desirability of further court action.

12 Welfare agency, social services, counseling, medical care, etc., for cases where adjudicatory handling not needed.

must introduce evidence sufficient to establish that there is probable cause to believe that a felony has been committed, and that the accused committed it. If the magistrate determines that probable cause exists, the magistrate "binds over" the accused for prosecution. If the magistrate determines that probable cause has not been established, the accused is discharged. Generally, the preliminary hearing is a critical stage giving rise to the right to legal counsel.

Formal Charge. The next step in the criminal process is to file formal charges against the accused by either an indictment issued by a grand jury or an information filed by the prosecutor without the intervention of a grand jury. A **grand jury** is a group of citizens whose function is to consider evidence of criminal conduct presented by the prosecutor and to determine whether the accused should be required to stand trial for a criminal offense. Unlike the petit jury, whose function is to decide facts, the grand jury is an accusatory and investigatory body that determines probable cause—whether sufficient evidence exists that an offense has been committed and the accused committed it. Although the size varies according to state or federal law, grand juries traditionally are composed of twenty-three persons with the affirmative vote of a majority (twelve) required for indictment (a "true bill"). If the grand jury finds no probable cause it returns a "no bill." If the grand jury does find probable cause, the prosecutor prepares an **indictment:** a written accusation setting forth the facts and charging the accused of violation of specific statutes. The indictment is signed by the foreman of the grand jury and then is filed with the court.

The Fifth Amendment provides: "No person shall be held to answer for a capital, or otherwise infamous crime, unless on a presentment or indictment of a Grand Jury." Under this provision and the federal rules of criminal procedure, prosecution of *federal* offenses punishable by death or imprisonment for a term exceeding one year must be prosecuted by grand jury indictment. Any other federal offense may be prosecuted either by indictment or information.[22] An **information,** a written

accusation setting forth the facts and charging violation of the criminal statutes, is prepared and signed by the prosecutor and then filed with the court.

The Supreme Court has held that commencing prosecution by grand jury indictment is not fundamental, and is therefore not binding on the states through the Fourteenth Amendment Due Process Clause.[23] Accordingly, only about one-half of the states require that felony prosecutions be initiated by grand jury indictment. The remaining states permit the prosecutor to proceed either by information or indictment. In these states, information is the almost exclusive method of initiating prosecution. Note that misdemeanor prosecutions are almost always commenced by information.

Traditionally, the grand jury was designed to provide a buffer between the prosecutor and the accused, exercising independent judgment concerning whether or not to prosecute. Because only prosecution evidence is presented, however, the grand jury is often criticized as merely a rubber stamp wielded by the prosecutor. As one commentator noted: "[T]he prosecutor . . . if he is candid, will concede that he can indict anybody, at any time, for almost anything, before any grand jury."[24] Despite its criticisms, the grand jury is a very useful tool for investigating major criminal activity such as organized crime or public corruption because its proceedings are conducted in secret. Further, the grand jury has subpoena power allowing it to compel testimony and obtain evidence.

Filing the information or indictment starts the formal court proceedings in a criminal case just as the filing of the complaint commences the court proceedings in a civil suit. The procedural steps preceding the information or indictment serve to protect the rights of the accused prior to the involvement of the judiciary.

Arraignment. Following the formal filing of charges the case is set for **arraignment,** a hearing before the court at which the indictment or information is read to the defendant. The arraignment

---

22. Fed. R. Crim. P. Rule 7(a), 18 U.S.C.

23. *Hurtado v. California,* 4 S. Ct. 111 (1884).
24. Campbell, Eliminate the Grand Jury, 64 J. Crim. L. & Criminology 174 (1973).

serves to fulfill the constitutional requirement that the accused "be informed of the nature and cause of the accusation." The arraignment is a critical stage entitling the defendant to legal counsel if desired.

The defendant may file motions objecting to the charges on procedural grounds, seeking suppression of evidence obtained in violation of his constitutional rights, or alleging a bar to the proceeding such as a statute of limitations. The defendant also may move for a change of venue, especially if the case has received substantial publicity. Finally, the defendant may file a *bill of particulars,* a request for detailed information explaining the facts or the charges. Because there is very little pretrial discovery in criminal cases, the bill of particulars serves as a tool to discover the evidence of the prosecution.

If the judge does not dismiss the case as a result of the motions, the defendant is required to answer the charges by entering a *plea* of not guilty, guilty, or *nolo contendere* (no contest). If the defendant pleads not guilty, the case is set for trial. If the defendant pleads guilty, the judge may sentence the defendant or set a later hearing for sentencing.

In the federal courts and in some state courts the defendant may enter a plea of **nolo contendere** rather than pleading guilty or not guilty. The legal effect of a plea of nolo contendere is the same as that of a guilty plea: the defendant may be sentenced as if he had been found guilty. The plea of nolo contendere, however, may not be used as an admission of guilt in other court proceedings. This result is especially important in certain cases, such as antitrust law, where the defendant's conduct could result in civil liability. Acceptance of a nolo contendere plea is discretionary with the judge.

The defendant usually enters a plea of guilty or nolo contendere as a result of *plea bargaining,* negotiations with the prosecutor in which the defendant agrees to enter a plea in exchange for the prosecutor's promise to drop or reduce some of the charges or to recommend a particular sentence. The judge, though not bound by any promises made by the prosecutor, usually follows the prosecutor's recommendations. Plea bargaining reduces the case load of the trial courts and allows prosecutors to devote more time to major cases. It is appealing to a defendant who will receive a predictable and limited sentence rather than face the uncertain result of a trial.

Trial. The Sixth Amendment entitles the defendant to a speedy and public trial by an impartial jury. If the government unduly delays the trial, the court may dismiss the case. The federal government and most states have adopted statutes prescribing the time limits within which a case must be brought to trial.

Right to Jury Trial. The Sixth Amendment explicitly guarantees the right to a jury[25] trial in "all criminal prosecutions." The Supreme Court has, however, held that this right does not apply to trials for "petty offenses," generally those punishable by less than 6 months imprisonment. In federal prosecutions, juries are composed of twelve persons and verdicts must be by unanimous vote of the jurors.[26] To ensure that the jury trial is fair, the Supreme Court has established that a jury must be selected from a cross section of the community.

The right to jury trial in *state* criminal cases is usually guaranteed by state constitutions and has also been applied to the states through the Fourteenth Amendment Due Process Clause.[27] In *state* cases, however, the Supreme Court has upheld less than twelve-person juries and less than unanimous verdicts.

In general, a defendant may waive the right to trial by jury, although some states prohibit waiver or allow waiver only if the prosecution agrees. Similarly, in federal prosecutions, the defendant may waive the right to jury trial only with approval of the court and consent of the government.[28] If the right is waived, a bench trial is held.

Conduct of Trial. A criminal trial is similar to a civil trial. If the defendant has not waived the right to a jury trial, jurors are selected by voir dire

---

25. The jury referred to in the Constitution is the petit jury that determines issues of fact and should not be confused with the grand jury.

26. Fed. R. Crim. P. Rules 23, 31, 18 U.S.C.

27. See, *Duncan v. Louisiana,* 88 S. Ct. 1444 (1968).

28. Fed. R. Crim. P. Rule 23(a), 18 U.S.C.

examination.[29] The attorneys make opening statements and the prosecution presents its case through the testimony of witnesses and tangible evidence. Witnesses are subject to cross-examination by the defendant's attorney, which satisfies the Sixth Amendment provision entitling the defendant to confront witnesses against him.

In a criminal trial, the prosecution bears the burden of proving beyond a "reasonable doubt" that the defendant committed all elements of the crime. The prosecution bears a greater burden of proof in a criminal case than a civil plaintiff, who generally need only prove his case by a "preponderance of the evidence." The defendant is not required to present evidence, is not required to testify, and bears no burden of proof in criminal proceedings. Nevertheless, the defendant may offer evidence through his own witnesses who are subject to cross-examination by the prosecutor. At the conclusion of the evidence, closing arguments are presented and instructions are read to the jury.

As in a civil trial, the jury retires to the jury room to deliberate and reach a verdict. If the jury cannot reach a verdict—a "hung jury"—the court will dismiss the jury and order a new trial. If the jury returns a verdict of not guilty, the defendant is acquitted: the court enters judgment in favor of the defendant who then is released.

If the jury returns a verdict of guilty, the judge usually enters judgment in accordance with the jury's findings. Prior to judgment, however, the defendant may make posttrial motions requesting judgment n.o.v. or a new trial. A motion for judgment n.o.v. is granted only if the judge determines that the jury could not reach a verdict of guilty beyond a reasonable doubt in light of the evidence. The judge will grant a motion for a new trial if he or she determines that a material error prejudicial to the defendant occurred during the proceedings. If the court denies the defendant's motions, the

judge will sentence the defendant, sometimes at a later hearing.

Appellate Review. Following entry of judgment, a convicted defendant is entitled to one appeal of right, usually to the intermediate appellate court or, in states with only one appellate court, the state supreme court, to that court. In some cases (for example, those in which the defendant has been sentenced to death), state law often provides for direct appeal to the state supreme court bypassing the intermediate court. In criminal cases the state is not entitled to appeal a judgment of acquittal. The Supreme Court has held that the Sixth Amendment right to counsel applies to the defendant's appeal of right.

The procedure for appellate review is similar to that in civil cases. Depending on the issues raised in the appeal of right, the defendant may in some cases obtain further appellate review by the state supreme court or the United States Supreme Court either by appeal or by writ of certiorari.

Post-conviction Remedies. In addition to the direct attack of a judgment through the *appellate* courts, the defendant also may attempt a "collateral" attack by filing a petition in the *trial* courts. The best-known form of collateral attack is an application for **writ of habeas corpus**. The writ is a judicial order that directs a government official (for example, the warden) to produce the prisoner in order to test the legality of the imprisonment. The availability of the writ is guaranteed by Article 1, Section 9, Clause 2 of the United States Constitution and by state constitutions.

Usually, applications for writs of *habeas corpus* are directed to the federal courts by persons in state custody. Under federal law, the defendant must allege that the imprisonment violates the Constitution, federal law, or treaties, and must first exhaust state remedies.[30] The federal court reviews the state court proceedings, and may discharge the defendant or order a new trial if federal law has been violated. The large majority of habeas corpus proceedings are unsuccessful. Following the federal

---

29. Frequently, the scope of voir dire examination is broader than that in a civil trial. Both the prosecution and the defense are entitled to unlimited challenges for cause. The defendant usually is entitled to more peremptory challenges than in a civil trial. The number of peremptory challenges also may increase for more severe crimes.

---

30. 28 U.S.C. §2254.

district court's ruling, the defendant may appeal the judgment.

If a prisoner is held by federal officials, federal law provides a statutory remedy similar to that provided for those in state custody.[31] The scope of review of a federal case may be narrower because the court does not have to review alleged constitutional violations previously raised at trial or on appeal.

Finally, most states provide a statutory basis for collateral attack to persons imprisoned by state officials. These statutory remedies provide an opportunity for a state court to review the basis for imprisonment and to determine whether the prisoner's constitutional rights have been violated.

Double Jeopardy. The Fifth Amendment provides that no person shall "be subject for the same offence to be twice put in jeopardy of life or limb." This provision, frequently referred to as prohibiting **double jeopardy,** has been interpreted to mean that a person cannot be subjected to a second trial for the same offense (1) after a conviction, (2) after an acquittal, or (3) after "jeopardy attaches." In a criminal case heard by a jury, jeopardy attaches when the jury is impaneled and sworn. In a bench trial, jeopardy attaches when evidence is introduced. The Double Jeopardy Clause also prohibits prosecution appeals if the defendant would have to be retried if the prosecution wins the appeal.

Retrial is, however, permitted with the defendant's consent or for a "legally sufficient reason." For example, a defendant may be retried if a mistrial is granted on the defendant's motion, or if an appellate court orders a new trial as a result of the defendant's appeal of a guilty verdict. In these cases, the subsequent trials are deemed to be with the defendant's consent. Retrials are also permitted for legally sufficient reasons such as death of a judge or juror, a hung jury, or other conditions making a fair trial impossible.

The Double Jeopardy Clause does not prohibit successive prosecutions by the state and federal governments for the same conduct. For example, bank robbery is both a state and federal crime and the defendant can be tried and punished separately by each sovereign. The Double Jeopardy Clause merely prohibits multiple prosecutions by the same sovereign.

SUMMARY

1. Criminal law is designed to protect society by setting minimum standards of socially acceptable conduct and punishing those who violate those standards. A crime is an act or failure to act in violation of a law prohibiting or commanding the act, which is injurious to the public welfare and subjects the offender to punishment prescribed by law. Substantive criminal law defines, generally by statute, which acts or omissions are crimes and prescribes the punishment to be imposed. Crimes generally are classified into three categories: treason, felonies, and misdemeanors.

2. Most crimes require two elements: a criminal act and a state of mind concurrent with the act. Although the criminal act varies widely among crimes, crimes are classified according to state of mind as either requiring that the defendant be at fault or imposing liability without fault. Four types of mental culpability are recognized for crimes requiring fault: intention, knowledge, recklessness, and negligence. In crimes imposing liability without fault, so-called strict liability crimes, criminal responsibility requires only the act; no concurrent mental state is required.

3. A number of specific criminal offenses are recognized under state and federal law, including "inchoate" crimes (such as attempt, solicitation, and conspiracy), so named because the conduct they prohibit is designed to culminate in commission of another crime but has failed to do so. A person who commits a crime may escape liability if he or she is able to prove one of the various extraordinary defenses, such as insanity, to criminal responsibility. Under principles of accomplice and conspiracy liability, a person may be convicted of criminal acts committed by others.

4. Although traditional violent crimes, such as murder, rape, and armed robbery, remain serious concerns of the criminal justice system, an increasing amount of crime is committed by individuals or corpo-

---

31. 28 U.S.C. §2255.

rations in the conduct of business operations. In such business or "white collar" crime, the law must frequently determine when a corporation should be held liable for crimes of its agents, and when corporate agents should be held liable for crimes committed during the course of their employment.

    5. Although the legislature enacts substantive criminal statutes, the executive branch is responsible for enforcing them. Various state and federal law enforcement agencies are responsible for investigating alleged violations of the criminal law. Criminal proceedings, known as "prosecutions," are maintained by public officials on behalf of the people of a state or the United States. Criminal jurisdiction and venue are determined by principles much simpler than those applied to civil cases. The law of criminal procedure governs the various steps of a criminal proceeding from preliminary investigation through termination of punishment.

    6. The United States Constitution guarantees a number of specific rights to persons accused of a crime. These rights are contained in the Fourth, Fifth, Sixth, and Eighth Amendments. Rules of criminal procedure, both state and federal, must therefore conform with interpretations of these provisions by the United States Supreme Court.

    7. The usual stages of a criminal proceeding include arrest, the defendant's initial appearance, the preliminary hearing, formal charge (either by grand jury indictment or by information prepared by the prosecutor), arraignment, trial, appellate review, and, in some cases, postconviction remedies. The defendant is entitled to trial by jury in most criminal prosecutions. Further, under the "double jeopardy" provision of the Fifth Amendment, a defendant generally may not be subjected to a second trial for the same offense.

KEY TERMS

substantive criminal law	arrest warrant
criminal procedure	search warrant
crime	exclusionary rule
treason	booking
offense	bail
felony	preliminary hearing
misdemeanor	grand jury
inchoate crimes	indictment
attempt	information
solicitation	arraignment
conspiracy	nolo contendere plea
accomplice	writ of habeas corpus
prosecution	double jeopardy
extradition	

QUESTIONS AND PROBLEMS

3-1   Why have statutes almost totally supplanted the common law as the source of substantive criminal law? Why are strict liability crimes usually limited to relatively minor offenses? Why does the law punish inchoate crimes?

3-2   The Model Penal Code defines theft as follows:

> A person is guilty of theft if he [or she] takes, or exercises unlawful control over, movable property of another with purpose to deprive him [or her] thereof.

(a) What is the criminal act described in this statute?

(b) What is the state of mind necessary to commit the crime of theft?

3-3   The Model Penal Code also defines the crime of theft by deception which includes the following:

> A person is guilty of theft if he [or she] obtains property of another by deception. A person deceives if he [or she] purposely:

(a) creates or reinforces a false impression, including false impressions as to law, value, intention or other state of mind; . . . or

(b) prevents another from acquiring information which would affect his [or her] judgment of a transaction. . . .

Marilyn owns and operates Marilyn's Luxury Automobiles, a retailer of fine cars. Consider whether Marilyn has committed the crime of theft by deception in each of the following cases:

(a) Ronald, a devoted fan of the famous, but now deceased, celebrity Rock Star, purchased a pre-owned Rolls Royce from Marilyn for $75,000. During the sales negotiations, she tells him that Rock Star previously owned the car. Marilyn had purchased the car from Rock Star's personal agent who told her that the car had been Rock Star's favorite possession. In truth, the automobile formerly belonged to the agent's mother and Rock Star had never used it.

(b) Marilyn sells an Italian sports car to Mario for $60,000. She describes the car upholstery as "Italian Butterleather," which, as Marilyn knows, is a trade name for a new type of plastic upholstery that looks exactly like leather. Just prior to showing the car to Mario, Marilyn sprayed the interior with "Leather Scent," a commercial spray that smells like leather. As Marilyn opened the door for Mario, she sniffed the air and stated "Don't you just love the smell of real leather?'' In fact, leather seats are an option on the automobile and cost an additional $8,000.

3-4   While his wife was out of town, Staples, a mathematician, rented an office under an assumed name located directly over a bank. He brought drilling tools, a blow torch, and other equipment to the office and began to drill through the office floor. He failed to pay rent after one month but left the equipment in the office. The landlord discovered the equipment and notified the police who arrested Staples. Staples made the following statement:

> Saturday, the 14th . . . I drilled some small holes in the floor of the room. Because of tiredness, fear, and the implications of what I was doing, I stopped and went to sleep.
>
> At this point I think my motives began to change. The actual commencement of my plan made me begin to realize that even if I were to succeed, a fugitive life of living off of stolen money would not give the enjoyment of the life of a mathematician however humble a job I might have.
>
> I still had not given up my plan however. I felt I had made a certain investment of time, money, effort, and a certain psychological commitment to the concept.
>
> I came back several times thinking I might store the tools in the closet and slowly drill down covering the hole with a rug of linoleum square. As time went on (after two weeks or so), my wife came back and my life as bank robber seemed more and more absurd.

At trial, Staples argued that he had abandoned his plan to rob the bank. The trial court nevertheless found him guilty of attempted burglary. Is the court correct?

3-5   Mary, an ambitious employee of BFC Co., offered an illegal bribe to a government official to obtain preferential treatment for BFC. The government charged both Mary and BFC with violation of a criminal statute prohibiting bribery. Explain under what circumstances you believe BFC could be held guilty for the criminal acts committed by Mary.

3-6   For many years the courts and legislatures have struggled to find an appropriate penalty for corporate crimes. The problem is especially difficult when employees commit ''white collar crimes'' not for their own enrichment but for the benefit of the corporation. Traditionally, the courts have fined the corporation and the employee, or both, for such criminal activities. Suggest alternatives that might be more effective both as a deterrent to corporate crime and as punishment for those committing unlawful activities. Discuss the advantages and disadvantages of these alternatives.

3-7   Historically, defendants guilty of crimes committed in the business setting such as tax evasion, embezzlement, bribery, or fraud have received lighter sentences than those convicted of ''street'' crimes such as burglary or theft even if the business crimes involved larger sums of money. Suggest reasons for this disparity in sentencing. Do you believe that in general a person guilty of business crime should receive a lighter sentence than someone guilty of a crime like burglary? Explain.

3-8   In the last few years, increased attention has been paid to a variety of white collar crimes that have been committed by employees of corporations. In some cases, the employees commit the crime for the benefit of the corporation although the employee also may benefit incidentally. If, for example, a salesperson illegally bribes an official to receive preferential treatment for purchases of the corporation's products, the corporation may benefit by increased sales but the salesperson also may benefit by receiving higher commissions or favorable job reviews leading to promotion. In other cases, an employee may use opportunities arising within the course of his or her employment to commit criminal acts that benefit the employee with little or no benefit to the corporation. A stockbroker, for example, may illegally use inside information obtained through her employment to purchase stocks for her own account and to personally profit from the transaction.

(a) Does a corporation have a legal or ethical obligation to prevent employees from engaging in illegal practices for the benefit of the corporation?

(b) Does a corporation have a legal or ethical obligation to prevent employees from engaging in illegal conduct for their own benefit?

(c) What, if anything, should a corporation do to prevent criminal wrongdoing by its employees? Why?

3-9   Jones, an employee of Film Recovery Systems, Inc., a film processing company, died of cyanide poisoning as a result of working with cyanide on a daily basis in his job at the processing plant. Subsequently, an investigation established that conditions in the plant were totally unsafe and in violation of state and federal occupational health and safety laws. The corporation's president was well aware of the dangers of working with cyanide and admitted that he knew that other workers had become ill before Jones died of acute cyanide poisoning resulting from an on-the-job exposure.

The state criminal code provides:

A person who kills an individual without lawful justification commits murder if, in performing the acts which cause the death:

(1) He either intends to kill or do great bodily harm to that individual or another, or knows that such acts will cause death to that individual or another; or

(2) He knows that such acts create a strong probability of death or great bodily harm to that individual or another. . . .

A person who unintentionally kills an individual without lawful justification commits involuntary manslaughter if his acts whether lawful or unlawful which cause the death are such as are likely to cause death or great bodily harm to some individual, and he performs them recklessly. . . .

A person who causes bodily harm to or endangers the bodily safety of an individual by any means, commits reckless conduct if he performs recklessly the acts which cause the harm or endanger safety, whether they otherwise are lawful or unlawful. . . .

A person is reckless or acts recklessly, when he consciously disregards a substantial and unjustifiable risk that circumstances exist or that a result will follow, described by the statute defining the offense; and such disregard constitutes a gross deviation from the standard of care which a reasonable person would exercise in the situation.

Of what crime or crimes, if any, should the corporation's president be convicted?

3-10 Joe Friendly, a police officer, has been investigating Marvin for possible criminal drug trafficking. In each of the following situations, determine whether Joe is required to advise Marvin of his rights as provided in *Miranda.*

(a) Joe asks Marvin to have a drink at a local bar. While sitting in a booth, Joe begins to question Marvin about his activities.

(b) Joe visits Marvin at his home and begins questioning him about his activities.

(c) While performing patrol duty on a very cold night, Joe stops Marvin and asks him to sit in the patrol car where Joe begins to ask questions.

(d) Joe and his partner Fred stop Marvin on an isolated street late at night and begin asking him questions.

3-11 The exclusionary rule has been strongly criticized for many years by judges, lawyers, police officers, politicians, and the public.

(a) Discuss the purposes of the exclusionary rule and the disadvantages of its use.

(b) Suggest other methods of achieving the purposes of the rule that would minimize its disadvantages.

3-12 In criminal cases the extensive discovery procedures used in civil cases are not employed. Why?

3-13 Discuss the advantages and disadvantages of the grand jury system.

3-14 The double jeopardy clause prohibits a retrial after conviction of the defendant. Why would the prosecutor want to retry an already convicted offender?

Chapter 4

The Constitution and Business Regulation

- the sources and scope of federal and state power to regulate business and commerce
- constitutional limitations on federal and state powers to regulate business and commerce
- the nature and scope of administrative agencies' powers to regulate business

The proper relationship between government and business has been debated throughout American history. The economic and political issues underlying this controversy have yet to be resolved. Those who favor the *laissez-faire* theory argue that any government regulation of business creates undesirable interference with the free market and competition. Others assert that complete regulation of business is necessary to prevent monopolization, to allocate scarce resources, and to protect the public safety and health. The laws of the United States generally have reflected a compromise between these two extreme viewpoints. Since the founding of the United States, businesses have been subject to some, but not total, regulation by both federal and state government.

This chapter examines the sources of governmental powers to enact laws that regulate business and constitutional restrictions on those powers. The chapter concludes with a discussion of administrative agencies created by the government to implement and enforce regulatory laws.

Governmental Power to Regulate Business and Commerce

Both state and federal governments regulate business. State control of business activity is achieved through the exercise of two inherent powers: the state police power and the power to tax. The federal government regulates business by exercising specific powers delegated to it by the states in the Constitution. Most important among these is the power to regulate interstate commerce.

State Powers to Regulate Business

Police Power. A state's **police power** is its inherent authority to establish laws for the protection of the health, safety, morals, and general welfare of its citizens. Prior to 1850, state statutory law was fairly limited, but as industrialization increased during the latter part of the century, many states began to use the police power to protect their citizens from social and economic problems created by rapidly growing businesses and corporations. Today, state and local governments have enacted legislation that regulates a broad spectrum of business activities. The police power is the source, for example, of laws that set statutory requirements for construction of buildings; impose fire and health standards for restaurant, retail, and manufacturing operations; and establish conditions of employment in businesses. In some cases, the states have used the police power to limit certain business activities regionally or statewide. Zoning laws, for example, usually allow manufacturing operations only in specified areas of a city or county. Despite the broad general authority created by the state police power, it is subject to constitutional limitations discussed later in this chapter.

Power to Tax. A second inherent power of the states is the **power to tax**: the authority to require financial contributions to state government. Although the primary purpose of taxation is to provide revenues to support the operations of government such as fire and police protection, taxation is also a form of indirect regulation due to its economic impact on business activities. Most states impose income and property taxes on businesses as well as individuals. Other taxes, such as corporate franchise taxes and license taxes, are paid solely by business.

A business that is organized as a corporation must pay an initial franchise tax to obtain a corporate charter from the state and an annual franchise tax to maintain its corporate status. Some states require a license to engage in a specific type of business and require payment of a license tax to secure and maintain the license. A license often is required, for example, to operate a retail store or restaurant or to practice medicine or law. License taxes often provide a regulatory effect. The amount of the license tax, for example, often effectively limits the number of businesses that are engaged in the licensed activity.

Many other forms of taxation are used by the states, including sales taxes, death taxes, use taxes, and excise taxes on specified goods or services. Like the police power, the power to tax is subject to constitutional restrictions.

Federal Power to Regulate Business: The Commerce Clause

Under the Articles of Confederation, which governed the federal union prior to adoption of the Constitution, the federal government had no authority to control business activities among the states. During this period the individual states established trade barriers and taxes that severely limited interstate trade. States with major ports, for example, imposed taxes on goods from foreign na-

tions. These trade restrictions created a national economic crisis due to the shortage of necessary goods and the lack of markets for goods produced in the states. One of the objectives of the Constitutional Convention in 1787 was to improve commercial relations among the states.

The **Commerce Clause** of the Constitution was adopted in an effort to resolve these problems and today it is the primary source of the federal government's power to regulate business. The Commerce Clause provides:

> The Congress shall have Power . . . to regulate Commerce with foreign Nations, and among the several States, and with the Indian Tribes.[1]

Of the three subjects covered by the Commerce Clause—international commerce, interstate commerce, and commerce with the Indian tribes—interstate commerce has produced the most significant legal and political problems. One difficult issue has been to define the scope of Congress's authority under the Commerce Clause; in other words, what types of business activities could be considered interstate commerce subject to regulation by the federal government.

This issue did not become important until the period of business growth and industrialization that began after the Civil War during which Congress increasingly exercised its power to regulate interstate commerce by adopting statutes designed to control a variety of business activities. Businesses challenged these statutes alleging that Congress was exceeding its authority and impinging on activities better regulated by the states. During this period, the Supreme Court tended to uphold the constitutionality of federal statutes that regulated commercial activities directly related to trade between the states, but tended to strike down laws that controlled activities that were more local in nature even if they affected interstate commerce. Thus, the Court held that the Commerce Clause enabled Congress to regulate railroad rates because railroads were used for interstate transportation.[2] In contrast, the Supreme Court held that a federal law

---

1. U.S. Const. art. I, §8, cl. 3.
2. *Shreveport Rate Cases,* 34 S. Ct. 833 (1914).

prohibiting the interstate shipment of goods manufactured in factories employing children was unconstitutional.[3] The Court perceived manufacturing and employer-employee relations to be matters for state and local regulation and beyond the scope of federal regulation. The Court also struck down statutes that appeared to reflect a Congressional intent to regulate public health, morals, or welfare, subjects more appropriately regulated by the states under their police powers. In general, then, the Supreme Court initially narrowly construed the federal power to regulate interstate commerce and, as a result, federal regulation of business was limited.

The Court's interpretation of the scope of federal power to regulate interstate commerce underwent a dramatic change during the 1930s. Following the election of 1932, President Franklin D. Roosevelt perceived a public mandate that the federal government resolve the nationwide economic and social problems of the Great Depression. Beginning in 1933, Congress, pursuant to its powers under the Commerce Clause, enacted many of Roosevelt's "New Deal" programs designed to end the Depression. During Roosevelt's first term, the Supreme Court, using a variety of theories, consistently held the legislation to be unconstitutional and beyond the scope of Congress's Commerce Clause powers. In 1937, however, the Court reversed itself and began to uphold the constitutionality of federal statutes regulating economic conditions. During the years that followed, the Court increasingly held that the federal government's powers under the Commerce Clause were broad and not narrowly restricted to regulating actual trade between states.

The Supreme Court has adhered to a broad construction of Congress's Commerce Clause power. Today, Congress has virtually unlimited power to regulate interstate commerce. As long as Congress can establish that a business activity affects interstate commerce, Congress may enact legislation regulating it. This power extends even to intrastate business activities—those that occur in only one state—if the business activity has a substantial effect on interstate commerce or if the activity in combination with other similar activities might have a cumulative effect on interstate commerce.

In modern Commerce Clause cases, the courts generally defer to Congress's judgment regarding the policy and purposes of legislation. Once the relationship between the regulation and interstate commerce has been established, the courts do not even require that the legislation have a commercial purpose. The federal Civil Rights Act of 1964, for example, prohibits racial discrimination in public accommodation (for example, hotels, restaurants, gasoline stations) if the operation of the establishment "affects commerce." Clearly, at least one purpose of this statute is to prevent racial discrimination, a moral consideration generally within the purview of the police power of the states. Nevertheless, the Supreme Court upheld the validity of the Civil Rights Act.[4]

In the case that follows, the Supreme Court considers the scope of federal authority under the Commerce Clause.

McLain v. Real Estate Board of New Orleans, Inc.
100 S. Ct. 502 (1980)

The petitioner James McLain, on behalf of persons who had employed real estate brokers in New Orleans, filed suit against the respondent Real Estate Board of New Orleans, Inc. and other respondents including a real estate trade association and six real estate firms. Petitioner alleged that the respondents had engaged in a price-fixing conspiracy to control real estate broker commissions, a violation of the federal Sherman Act adopted by Congress pursuant to its Commerce Clause power to regulate interstate commerce. The petitioner alleged that the respondents' activities were "within the flow of interstate commerce and have an effect upon that commerce."

The trial court dismissed petitioner's complaint on the ground that "brokerage activities are wholly intrastate in nature and . . . they neither occur in nor substantially affect interstate commerce." The

---

3. *Hammer v. Dagenhart*, 38 S. Ct. 529 (1918).

4. *Heart of Atlanta Motel, Inc. v. United States,* 85 S. Ct. 348 (1964).

court of appeals affirmed and the petitioner was granted a writ of certiorari by the Supreme Court.

Chief Justice Burger

. . . The broad authority of Congress under the Commerce Clause has, of course, long been interpreted to extend beyond activities actually *in* interstate commerce to reach other activities, while wholly local in nature, nevertheless substantially *affect* interstate commerce. . . . This Court has often noted the correspondingly broad reach of the Sherman Act. . . .

It can no longer be doubted . . . that the jurisdictional requirement of the Sherman Act may be satisfied under either the "in commerce" or the "effect on commerce" theory. . . .

Although the cases demonstrate the breadth of Sherman Act prohibitions, jurisdiction may not be invoked under that statute unless the relevant aspect of interstate commerce is identified; it is not sufficient merely to rely on identification of a relevant local activity and to presume an interrelationship with some unspecified aspect of interstate commerce. . . .

To establish the jurisdictional element of a Sherman Act violation it would be sufficient for petitioners to demonstrate a substantial effect on interstate commerce generated by respondents' brokerage activities. Petitioners need not make the more particularized showing of an effect on interstate commerce caused by the alleged conspiracy to fix commission rates, or by those other aspects of respondents' activity that are alleged to be unlawful. . . .

[I]t cannot be said that there is an insufficient basis for petitioners to proceed at trial to establish Sherman Act jurisdiction. It is clear that an appreciable amount of commerce is involved in the financing of residential property in the Greater New Orleans area and in the insuring of titles to such property. The presidents of two of the many lending institutions in the area stated in their deposition testimony that those institutions committed hundreds of millions of dollars to residential financing during the period covered by the complaint. The testimony further demonstrates that this appreciable commercial activity has occurred in interstate commerce. Funds were raised from out-of-state investors and from interbank loans obtained

from interstate financial institutions. Multistate lending institutions took mortgages insured under federal programs which entailed interstate transfers of premiums and settlements. Mortgage obligations physically and constructively were traded as financial instruments in the interstate secondary mortgage market. Before making a mortgage loan in the Greater New Orleans area, lending institutions usually, if not always, required title insurance, which was furnished by interstate corporations. Reading the pleadings, as supplemented, most favorably to petitioners, for present purposes we take these facts as established.

At trial, respondents will have the opportunity, if they so choose, to make their own case contradicting this factual showing. On the other hand, it may be possible for petitioners to establish that, apart from the commerce in title insurance and real estate financing, an appreciable amount of interstate commerce is involved with the local residential real estate market arising out of the interstate movement of people, or otherwise.

To establish federal jurisdiction in this case, there remains only the requirement that respondents' activities which allegedly have been infected by a price-fixing conspiracy be shown "as a matter of practical economics" to have a not insubstantial effect on the interstate commerce involved. . . . It is clear, as the record shows, that the function of respondent real estate brokers is to bring the buyer and seller together on agreeable terms. For this service the broker charges a fee generally calculated as a percentage of the sale price. Brokerage activities necessarily affect both the frequency and the terms of residential sales transactions. Ultimately, whatever stimulates or retards the volume of residential sales, or has an impact on the purchase price, affects the demand for financing and title insurance, those two commercial activities that on this record are shown to have occurred in interstate commerce. Where, as here, the services of respondent real estate brokers are often employed in transactions in the relevant market, petitioners at trial may be able to show that respondents' activities have a not insubstantial effect on interstate commerce. . . .

[Judgment vacated and remanded.]

Constitutional Limitations on Federal and State Regulation of Business

Although state police and taxing powers and the federal Commerce Clause powers are broad, they are subject to limitations imposed by the Constitution. The following sections discuss constitutional restrictions on state and federal powers to regulate business activities.

Limitations on the State Police and Taxing Powers

The Commerce Clause. The Commerce Clause of the Constitution not only authorizes Congress to regulate interstate commerce but also restricts the states' powers to adopt legislation that may affect interstate commerce. Because of the Commerce Clause, states cannot directly regulate interstate commerce. Thus, for example, a state statute prohibiting the sale of candy bars manufactured out of state would be considered unconstitutional.

Under the Commerce Clause, however, state legislation that incidentally affects interstate commerce sometimes is permissible. Consider, for instance, a New York statute that requires all candy bars manufactured or sold within the state to include a list of ingredients on the wrapper. This statute would control purely intrastate candy bar products—those manufactured and sold in New York—and also would affect some interstate candy production—candy bars manufactured in New York for sale in other states as well as candy bars made out of state for sale in New York. In determining whether such indirect state regulation of interstate commerce is constitutional, the courts consider whether the state legislation has been preempted by federal law and whether the state law unduly burdens or unfairly discriminates against interstate commerce.

Federal Preemption. If Congress enacts legislation under its Commerce Clause power, federal law sometimes preempts (overrides) state regulation of that activity. Federal preemption occurs if Congress evidences an intent to exclude all state legislation on a subject. Congress may explicitly state its intent in the statute or the courts may infer congressional intent from the legislative history or statutory scheme. In a few cases, the Supreme Court has inferred preemption if federal regulation is so detailed and comprehensive that state regulation would be likely to interfere with federal law. The Court also has suggested that in some subject areas requiring national uniformity, states are preempted from regulation even in the absence of a federal statute.

Even if Congress does not intend to exclude all state legislation in some field of interstate commerce, state regulation is preempted to the extent that a state law conflicts with a federal statute or impedes the purposes and objectives of Congress. For example, a California statute required that at the time of sale, packaged food products must weigh at least as much as the weight shown on the package. Federal law allows the weight of a packaged food product to vary within a specified range because of loss of moisture in shipping. The Court held that the federal law preempted state regulation of the shipping weight of packaged food and invalidated the California statute.[5] In such cases, the state statute is invalidated because the Supremacy Clause provides that the federal statute overrides a conflicting state statute.

State Regulatory Statutes Affecting Interstate Commerce. In most areas of business regulation, federal law does not preempt state regulation so the states may enact laws that incidentally affect interstate commerce. The courts apply the following standard in determining the validity of state statutes that affect interstate commerce:

> Where the statute regulates evenhandedly to effectuate a legitimate local public interest, and its effects on interstate commerce are only incidental, it will be upheld unless the burden imposed on such commerce is clearly excessive in relation to the putative local benefits.[6]

This standard requires a legitimate purpose for the state statute: for example, a need to protect the health, safety, or welfare of local citizens. The statute also must apply evenhandedly to both in-

---

5. *Jones v. Rath Packing Company,* 97 S. Ct. 1305 (1977).

6. *Pike v. Bruce Church, Inc.,* 90 S. Ct. 844, 847 (1970).

trastate and interstate commerce. Statutes that attempt to protect local industry from out-of-state competition through trade barriers that discriminate against interstate commerce are illegal.

Finally, in applying this standard, the court weighs the benefits of the regulation to the state against the burdens on interstate commerce. If the benefits outweigh the burdens, the state legislation usually is upheld unless the court determines that the benefits could be achieved through other forms of regulation less burdensome on interstate commerce. The following case illustrates application of the Commerce Clause limitations on state legislation.

Kassel v. Consolidated Freightways Corporation of Delaware
101 S. Ct. 1309 (1981)

An Iowa statute prohibited the use of 65-foot double-trailer trucks within the state but allowed the use of 55-foot single-trailer and 60-foot double-trailer trucks. Appellee Consolidated Freightways Corporation of Delaware, a national trucking company, sued appellant Raymond Kassel, the Director of the Iowa Department of Transportation, and other Iowa officials alleging that the Iowa statute violated the Commerce Clause. Despite Iowa's defense that the statute was a reasonable safety measure adopted under its police power, the trial court held that the statute was unconstitutional because it substantially burdened interstate commerce. The court of appeals affirmed and the Iowa officials appealed to the Supreme Court.

Justice Powell
. . . The [Commerce] Clause requires that some aspects of trade generally must remain free from interference by the States. When a State ventures excessively into the regulation of these aspects of commerce, it "trespasses upon national interests," [*Great A & P Tea Co. v. Cottrell,* 96 S. Ct. 923, 928 (1976)] and the courts will hold the state regulation invalid under the Clause alone.

The Commerce Clause does not, of course, invalidate all state restrictions on commerce. . . . The extent of permissible state regulation is not al-

ways easy to measure. It may be said with confidence, however, that a State's power to regulate commerce is never greater than in matters traditionally of local concern. . . . For example, regulations that touch upon safety—especially highway safety—are those that "the Court has been most reluctant to invalidate." [*Raymond Motor Transport, Inc. v. Rice,* 98 S. Ct. 787 (1978)]. . . .

But the incantation of a purpose to promote the public health or safety does not insulate a state law from Commerce Clause attack. Regulations designed for that salutary purpose nevertheless may further the purpose so marginally, and interfere with commerce so substantially, as to be invalid under the Commerce Clause. . . .

Applying these general principles, we conclude that the Iowa truck-length limitations unconstitutionally burden interstate commerce. . . .

Here . . . the State failed to present any persuasive evidence that 65-foot doubles are less safe than 55-foot singles. Moreover, Iowa's law is now out of step with the laws of all other Midwestern and Western States. Iowa thus substantially burdens the interstate flow of goods by truck. In the absence of congressional action to set uniform standards, some burdens associated with state safety regulations must be tolerated. But where, as here, the State's safety interest has been found to be illusory, and its regulations impair significantly the federal interest in efficient and safe interstate transportation, the state law cannot be harmonized with the Commerce Clause. . . .

Statistical studies supported the view that 65-foot doubles are at least as safe overall as 55-foot singles and 60-foot doubles. . . . Iowa concedes that it can produce no study that establishes a statistically significant difference in safety between the 65-foot double and the kinds of vehicles the State permits. . . .

Consolidated, meanwhile, demonstrated that Iowa's law substantially burdens interstate commerce. Trucking companies that wish to continue to use 65-foot doubles must route them around Iowa or detach the trailers of the doubles and ship them through separately. Alternatively, trucking companies must use the smaller 55-foot singles or 60-foot doubles permitted under Iowa law. Each of these options engenders inefficiency and added expense. The record shows that Iowa's law added about $12.6 million each year to the costs of trucking companies. Consolidated alone incurred about $2 million per year in increased costs. . . .

Perhaps recognizing the weakness of the evidence supporting its safety argument, and the substantial burden on commerce that its regulations create, Iowa urges the Court simply to "defer" to the safety judgment of the State. . . .

The Court normally does accord "special deference" to state highway safety regulations. . . . Less deference to the legislative judgment is due, however, where the local regulation bears disproportionately on out-of-state residents and businesses. Such a disproportionate burden is apparent here. Iowa's scheme, although generally banning large doubles from the State, nevertheless has several exemptions that secure to Iowans many of the benefits of large trucks while shunting to neighboring States many of the costs associated with their use.

At the time of trial there were two particularly significant exemptions. First, singles hauling livestock or farm vehicles were permitted to be as long as 60 feet. . . . As the Court of Appeals noted, this provision undoubtedly was helpful to local interests. . . . Second, cities abutting other States were permitted to enact local ordinances adopting the larger length limitation of the neighboring State. . . . This exemption offered the benefits of longer trucks to individuals and businesses in important border cities without burdening Iowa's highways with interstate through traffic. . . .

It is thus far from clear that Iowa was motivated primarily by a judgment that 65-foot doubles are less safe than 55-foot singles. Rather, Iowa seems to have hoped to limit the use of its highways by deflecting some through traffic. . . . The Court of Appeals correctly concluded that a State cannot constitutionally promote its own parochial interests by requiring safe vehicles to detour around it. . . .

Because Iowa has imposed this burden without any significant countervailing safety interest, its statute violates the Commerce Clause. . . .

[Judgment affirmed.]

State Taxation Statutes Affecting Interstate Commerce. Just as states may use the police power to regulate some activities that affect interstate commerce, states also may impose taxes that affect interstate commerce. Direct state taxation of goods in interstate commerce is illegal, but incidental taxation of interstate commerce or of businesses engaged in interstate commerce is generally permissible if the state can establish some nexus (connection) between the tax and the state. This connection may be established for property taxes if there is a taxable situs in the state—that is, if the property is located within the state. Income taxes may be imposed on businesses if there is a nexus between the business transactions conducted in the state and the tax. For example, the states may impose income taxes on businesses domiciled within the state or engaged in commercial activities within the state. Nevertheless, income taxes must be apportioned in a manner that bears a reasonable relationship to the business activities conducted within the state. Taxes that are based on an actual nexus to the state and are properly apportioned generally do not violate the Commerce Clause.

Import-Export Clause. State taxation of goods in international commerce is limited by the **Import-Export Clause** of the Constitution, which states:

> No State shall, without the Consent of the Congress, lay any Imposts or Duties on Imports or Exports, except what may be absolutely necessary for executing its inspection Laws. . . .[7]

This provision prohibits a state from imposing a direct tax on imports or exports solely because the goods have been received from or are bound for a foreign country. The provision, however, does not prohibit assessment of a nondiscriminatory tax before or after the goods are in transit.

In *Michelin Tire Corporation v. Wages*, the Supreme Court considered the validity of a Georgia tax imposed on all personal property in the state. Michelin challenged assessment of the tax on its inventory of goods made in France and held in a Georgia warehouse for distribution in the United

---

7. U.S. Const. art. I, §10, cl. 2.

States. The Court upheld the tax assessment against Michelin and stated:

> . . . [S]uch property taxes are taxes by which a State apportions the cost of such services as police and fire protection among the beneficiaries according to their respective wealth; there is no reason why an importer should not bear his share of these costs along with his competitors handling only domestic goods. The Import-Export Clause clearly prohibits state taxation based on the foreign origin of imported goods, but it cannot be read to accord imported goods preferential treatment that permits escape from uniform taxes imposed without regard to foreign origin for services which the State supplies. . . .[8]

A similar rule applies to incidental taxation of exports. Until domestic goods bound for foreign countries are placed in transit or begin their "physical entry into the stream of exportation,"[9] they may be subject to nondiscriminatory taxation by the states.

The Import-Export Clause applies only to state taxation of imports and exports. The Constitution also prohibits the federal government from taxing exports but allows direct federal taxation of imports.

Privileges and Immunities Clause. The Constitution places further restrictions on the states' police and taxing powers by the **Privileges and Immunities Clause,** which provides:

> The Citizens of each State shall be entitled to all Privileges and Immunities of Citizens in the several States.[10]

This provision prohibits states from unreasonable discrimination against out-of-state citizens, including out-of-state businesses. As explained by the Supreme Court, "one of the privileges which the clause guarantees to citizens of State A is that of doing business in State B on terms of substantial equality with the citizens of that State."[11]

The Court, for example, has held unconstitutional a state statute requiring state residents to pay $25 for a commercial fishing license and nonresidents to pay $2,500 for the same license.[12] Similarly, the Privileges and Immunities Clause prohibits unreasonable discriminatory income taxation. For instance, a New York income tax that allowed exemptions for resident taxpayers and their dependents but allowed no exemptions for out-of-state residents was held to violate the Privileges and Immunities Clause.[13]

The Contract Clause. The Constitution prohibits the states from passing any "Law impairing the Obligation of Contracts."[14] The original purpose of this provision, known as the **Contract Clause,** was to prevent states from enacting debtor relief laws, a practice that had occurred in several states following the American Revolution. To encourage credit arrangements necessary for economic growth, the drafters of the Constitution provided creditors some assurance that their existing contracts would not be adversely modified by state law. Under the Clause the states may impose statutory obligations on parties to contracts made *after* the statute is enacted.

Despite its original purpose, the Contract Clause was interpreted expansively during the nineteenth century to protect established property and business interests against excessive state regulation. The Contract Clause, however, fell into disuse during the late nineteenth and early twentieth centuries, as the Supreme Court began to use the Due Process Clause (under principles of "substantive" due pro-

---

8. *Michelin Tire Corporation v. Wages*, 96 S. Ct. 535, 541 (1976).

9. *Kosydar v. National Cash Register Co.*, 94 S. Ct. 2108, 2114 (1974).

10. U.S. Const. art. IV, §2, cl. 1. The Fourteenth Amendment contains a provision prohibiting the states from abridging "the privilege and immunities of citizens of the United States." Courts have interpreted this clause to protect the rights accruing to a citizen of the United States—for example, the right to vote in federal elections or to interstate travel. The clause has not been used to protect rights of state citizenship.

---

11. *Toomer v. Witsell*, 68 S. Ct. 1156, 1162 (1948).

12. *Id.*

13. *Travis v. Yale & Towne Mfg. Co.*, 40 S. Ct. 228 (1920).

14. U.S. Const. art. I, §10, cl. 1.

cess) to test state economic regulation and strike down statutes that were inconsistent with the free market theory of economics. Substantive due process itself fell from vogue in the mid 1930s and since that time the Supreme Court has usually deferred to the judgment of the legislature in determining appropriate economic policy.

Despite this trend toward judicial restraint, the Supreme Court has recently held that the Contract Clause remains a device for judicial review of state economic legislation that restrospectively affects private contracts. As noted by the Court in *Allied Structural Steel Company v. Spannaus* (1978): "If the Contract Clause is to retain any meaning at all . . . it must be understood to impose *some* limits upon the power of a State to abridge existing contractual relationships, even in the exercise of its otherwise legitimate police power."[15]

In general, a state may adopt a statute that substantially modifies existing contracts only if the legislation is necessary to meet an important and widespread social problem. The statute is more likely to be held constitutional if it only temporarily alters the contractual relationship, or affects a field that the state has previously regulated. For example, the Supreme Court held that a state statute placing a moratorium on mortgage foreclosures during the Depression did not violate the Contract Clause.[16] Although the statute modified existing mortgage contracts, the Court found that the need to protect homeowners from loss of their homes justified the the moratorium. In contrast, in a more recent case, the Court held that a state statute that permanently modified private contractual pension plans violated the Contract Clause.[17] The Court noted that the statute, designed to protect the interest of employees who participated in certain private pension plans, was not directed at a broad societal interest and severely and permanently changed the private contractual arrangements. In short, modern Contract Clause interpretations represent "only a refusal to abdicate the judicial role in the enforcement of the Contract Clause, rather than a return to

the pre-1937 model of judicial protection of economic interests."[18]

Bill of Rights and Fourteenth Amendment Limitations

Although the Bill of Rights and the Fourteenth Amendment guarantee certain rights to individuals, some of the constitutional amendments also protect the rights of businesses to be free from government interference. The following sections briefly discuss the limitations that the First, Fourth, Fifth, and Fourteenth Amendments impose on both state and federal regulation of business.

Freedom of Speech. The First Amendment prohibits federal and state governments from adopting laws abridging freedom of speech. The Supreme Court has interpreted **freedom of speech** broadly to include freedom of expression in oral and written communications as well as nonverbal actions with symbolic value (for example, saluting a flag, wearing an armband).

Under the First Amendment, the government generally cannot restrain someone from engaging in free expression or punish a person for having engaged in free expression if the restraint or punishment is based on the content of the speech. For example, if the federal government refused to allow any public speech on the subject of nuclear war, the government's action would violate the First Amendment because the basis for restraining the speech is its content, that is, the subject of nuclear war.

Freedom of expression, however, is not absolute. Defamatory speech and obscenity, for example, are considered to be unprotected speech subject to regulation and punishment by the government. The government also may impose reasonable time, place, and manner regulations on expression. The government, for example, may prohibit all demonstrations or parades unless the participants first obtain a governmental license or permit. If, however, the state required a permit only if the demonstration or speech concerned a specific topic (for example, nuclear war), the reg-

---

15. 98 S. Ct. 2716, 2721 (1978).

16. *Home Building & Loan Assn. v. Blaisdell,* 54 S. Ct. 231 (1934).

17. *Allied Structural Steel Company v. Spannaus,* 98 S. Ct. 2716 (1978).

18. Nowak, Rotunda & Young, *Constitutional Law* 471 (2d ed. 1983).

ulation would be illegal because the content of the speech was the basis for the regulation.

If a type of communication is subject to First Amendment protection, then the expression is protected whether its source is an individual or a business such as a corporation.[19] For many years, the courts considered **commercial speech** (such as advertisements for products or services) to be unprotected. More recently, however, the Supreme Court has held that although commercial speech is subject to regulation (for example, truth in advertising), it is entitled to some protection from governmental regulation. The following case explains the rationale for First Amendment protection of commercial speech.

Virginia State Board of Pharmacy v. Virginia Citizens Consumer Council, Inc.
96 S. Ct. 1817 (1976)

Under a Virginia statute, a pharmacist who published or advertised the price of prescription drugs was guilty of unprofessional conduct and subject to a monetary fine or suspension of his license to practice pharmacy. Appellee the Virginia Citizens Consumer Council, Inc., a consumer group, filed suit in federal district court alleging that the statute effectively prohibited the advertising of prescription drug prices in violation of the First Amendment guarantee of free speech. The District Court held the Virginia statute unconstitutional and appellant, the Virginia State Board of Pharmacy, a regulatory state agency, appealed to the United States Supreme Court.

Justice Blackmun
. . . The appellants contend that the advertisement of prescription drug prices is outside the protection of the First Amendment because it is "commercial speech." There can be no question that in past decisions the Court has given some indication that commercial speech is unprotected. . . .

Here, . . . the question whether there is a First Amendment exception for "commercial speech" is squarely before us. Our pharmacist does not wish to editorialize on any subject, cultural, philosophical, or political. He does not wish to report any particularly newsworthy fact, or to make generalized observations even about commercial matters. The "idea" he wishes to communicate is simply this: "I will sell you the X prescription drug at the Y price." Our question, then, is whether this communication is wholly outside the protection of the First Amendment. . . .

[W]e may assume that the advertiser's interest is a purely economic one. That hardly disqualifies him from protection under the First Amendment. . . .

As to the particular consumer's interest in the free flow of commercial information, that interest may be as keen, if not keener by far, than his interest in the day's most urgent political debate. Appellees' case in this respect is a convincing one. Those whom the suppression of prescription drug price information hits the hardest are the poor, the sick, and particularly the aged. A disproportionate amount of their income tends to be spent on prescription drugs; yet they are the least able to learn, by shopping from pharmacist to pharmacist, where their scarce dollars are best spent. When drug prices vary as strikingly as they do, information as to who is charging what becomes more than a convenience. It could mean the alleviation of physical pain or the enjoyment of basic necessities.

Generalizing, society also may have a strong interest in the free flow of commercial information. Even an individual advertisement, though entirely "commercial," may be of general public interest. . . . Obviously, not all commercial messages contain the same or even a very great public interest element. There are few to which such an element, however, could not be added. Our pharmacist, for example, could cast himself as a commentator on store-to-store disparities in drug prices, giving his own and those of a competitor as proof. We see little point in requiring him to do so, and little difference if he does not.

Moreover, there is another consideration that suggests that no line between publicly "interesting" or "important" commercial advertising and the opposite kind could ever be drawn. Advertis-

19. *First National Bank of Boston v. Bellotti*, 98 S. Ct. 1407 (1978).

ing, however tasteless and excessive it sometimes may seem, is nonetheless dissemination of information as to who is producing and selling what product, for what reason, and at what price. So long as we preserve a predominantly free enterprise economy, the allocation of our resources in large measure will be made through numerous private economic decisions. It is a matter of public interest that those decisions, in the aggregate, be intelligent and well informed. To this end, the free flow of commercial information is indispensable. . . . And if it is indispensable to the proper allocation of resources in a free enterprise system, it is also indispensable to the formation of intelligent opinions as to how that system ought to be regulated or altered. Therefore, even if the First Amendment were thought to be primarily an instrument to enlighten public decisionmaking in a democracy, we could not say that the free flow of information does not serve that goal.

Arrayed against these substantial individual and societal interests are a number of justifications for the advertising ban. These have to do principally with maintaining a high degree of professionalism on the part of licensed pharmacists. . . .

It appears to be feared that if the pharmacist who wishes to provide low cost, and assertedly low quality, services is permitted to advertise, he will be taken up on his offer by too many unwitting customers. They will choose the low-cost, low-quality service and drive the "professional" pharmacist out of business. They will respond only to costly and excessive advertising, and end up paying the price. They will go from one pharmacist to another, following the discount, and destroy the pharmacist-customer relationship. They will lose respect for the profession because it advertises. All this is not in their best interests, and all this can be avoided if they are not permitted to know who is charging what.

There is, of course, an alternative to this highly paternalistic approach. That alternative is to assume that this information is not in itself harmful, that people will perceive their own best interests if only they are well enough informed, and that the best means to that end is to open the channels of communication rather than to close them. If they are truly open, nothing prevents the "professional" pharmacist from marketing his own assertedly su-

perior product, and contrasting it with that of the low-cost, high-volume prescription drug retailer. But the choice among these alternative approaches is not ours to make or the Virginia General Assembly's. It is precisely this kind of choice, between the dangers of suppressing information, and the dangers of its misuse if it is freely available, that the First Amendment makes for us. Virginia is free to require whatever professional standards it wishes of its pharmacists; it may subsidize them or protect them from competition in other ways. . . . But it may not do so by keeping the public in ignorance of the entirely lawful terms that competing pharmacists are offering. In this sense, the justifications Virginia has offered for suppressing the flow of prescription drug price information, far from persuading us that the flow is not protected by the First Amendment, have reinforced our view that it is. We so hold.

[Judgment affirmed.]

Guarantee of Due Process. The Fifth and Fourteenth Amendments prohibit the federal and state governments from depriving a person of life, liberty, or property without due process of law. For purposes of the Due Process Clauses, "persons" include both natural persons and corporations. As applied to business regulation, procedural due process generally requires that the government must engage in a fair decision-making process prior to depriving a business of property. Most regulatory statutes establish certain standards with which a business must comply. Failure to comply with those standards may subject the business to criminal penalties or to civil liability. If the statutes are enforceable through the judicial system, a business is entitled to the procedural due process available in court proceedings—notice by a complaint, indictment, or information and the right to a trial in which the business may defend itself.[20]

Some business regulations, however, are enforceable in hearings conducted by an administra-

---

20. See the discussion of procedural due process in Chapters 2 and 3.

tive agency.[21] If a business may suffer loss of property through the administrative hearing, the business is entitled to procedural due process: notice of the alleged violation and the right to defend itself at the hearing.

Guarantee of Equal Protection. The Fourteenth Amendment provides in part that "No State shall . . . deny to any person within its jurisdiction the equal protection of the laws."[22] This provision, known as the **Equal Protection Clause,** explicitly limits the powers of the states, and the Supreme Court's interpretation of the Due Process Clauses requires that the federal government also provide equal protection. The guarantee of equal protection extends to both individuals and businesses.

Equal protection limits the way the government may classify persons for purposes of regulation. Laws generally establish classifications. Liquor laws, for example, classify individuals based on age: most states prohibit individuals under the age of twenty-one from purchasing alcoholic beverages, while those over age twenty-one legally can purchase alcohol. Under the Equal Protection Clause, the government can establish classifications, but they must relate to a proper governmental purpose. In determining whether a governmental classification complies with the equal protection guarantee, the courts examine the purpose of the statute and then consider whether the method of classification bears a sufficient relationship to that purpose. If the governmental classification is not properly related to an appropriate purpose or if the classification is arbitrary or based on impermissible criteria, the classification violates equal protection.

Under equal protection analysis, the courts essentially prohibit certain types of classifications, most notably those made on the basis of race. During the last 35 years, every statute that the Supreme Court has reviewed involving a governmental racial classification has been invalidated as a violation of equal protection. Other types of classifications also are closely examined by the courts. Laws that classify persons on the basis of sex, for example, are invalidated unless the government can prove that the classification is substantially related to an important governmental objective.[23] This burden of proof is difficult but less strict than that required with racial classifications.

Legislation adopted for economic or social purposes generally is upheld by the courts so long as the law is rationally related to a legitimate governmental purpose. Because economic or social purposes are the basis for most laws regulating business, these laws usually comply with the constitutional guarantee of equal protection.[24] The following case illustrates the judicial review of a regulatory statute challenged on equal protection grounds.

Minnesota v. Clover Leaf Creamery Company
101 S. Ct. 715 (1981)

The Minnesota legislature enacted a statute prohibiting the retail sale of milk products in plastic, nonreturnable, nonrefillable containers. The stated purpose of the statute was to conserve energy, conserve natural resources, and ease solid waste disposal problems. The statute permitted the sale of milk products in other nonreturnable, nonrefillable containers such as paperboard cartons. The respondent Clover Leaf Creamery Company, a producer of milk products, sued the petitioner, the state of Minnesota, alleging that the statute violated the Equal Protection Clause of the Constitution. Clover Leaf argued that the statute would not achieve its stated objectives but instead would deplete energy and natural resources and increase solid waste.

The trial court held that the statute violated the Equal Protection Clause and the Minnesota Supreme Court affirmed. The State of Minnesota petitioned for review of the United States Supreme Court.

21. These hearings will be discussed in greater detail later in this chapter.

22. U.S. Const. amend. XIV, §1.

23. See, for example, *Craig v. Boren,* 97 S. Ct. 451 (1976).

24. For an extended introduction to the Equal Protection Clause see Nowak, Rotunda & Young, *Constitutional Law* 585–611 (2d ed. 1983).

Justice Brennan

. . . The parties agree that the standard of review applicable to this case under the Equal Protection Clause is the familiar "rational basis" test. . . . Moreover, they agree that the purposes of the Act cited by the legislature—promoting resource conservation, easing solid waste disposal problems, and conserving energy—are legitimate state purposes. Thus, the controversy in this case centers on the narrow issue whether the legislative classification between plastic and nonplastic nonreturnable milk containers is rationally related to achievement of the statutory purposes.

Respondents apparently have not challenged the *theoretical* connection between a ban on plastic nonreturnables and the purposes articulated by the legislature; instead, they have argued that there is no *empirical* connection between the two. They produced impressive supporting evidence at trial to prove that the probable consequences of the ban on plastic nonreturnable milk containers will be to deplete natural resources, exacerbate solid waste disposal problems, and waste energy, because consumers unable to purchase milk in plastic containers will turn to paperboard milk cartons, allegedly a more environmentally harmful product.

But States are not required to convince the courts of the correctness of their legislative judgments. Rather, "those challenging the legislative judgment must convince the court that the legislative facts on which the classification is apparently based could not reasonably be conceived to be true by the governmental decisionmaker." *Vance v. Bradley* [99 S. Ct. 939, 950 (1979)]. . . .

Although parties challenging legislation under the Equal Protection Clause may introduce evidence supporting their claim that it is irrational, . . . they cannot prevail so long as "it is evident from all the considerations presented to [the legislature], and those of which we may take judicial notice, that the question is at least debatable." [*United States v. Carolene Products Co.,* 58 S. Ct. 778, 784 (1938)]. Where there was evidence before the legislature reasonably supporting the classification, litigants may not procure invalidation of the legislation merely by tendering evidence in court that the legislature was mistaken. . . .

The State identifies four reasons why the classification between plastic and nonplastic nonreturnables is rationally related to the articulated statutory purposes. If any one of the four substantiates the State's claim, we must reverse the Minnesota Supreme Court and sustain the Act.

First, the State argues that elimination of the popular plastic milk jug will encourage the use of environmentally superior containers. There is no serious doubt that the plastic containers consume energy resources and require solid waste disposal, nor that refillable bottles and plastic pouches are environmentally superior. Citing evidence that the plastic jug is the most popular, and the gallon paperboard carton the most cumbersome and least well regarded package in the industry, the State argues that the ban on plastic nonreturnables will buy time during which environmentally preferable alternatives may be further developed and promoted. . . .

We find the State's approach fully supportable under our precedents. . . . The Equal Protection Clause does not deny the State of Minnesota the authority to ban one type of milk container conceded to cause environmental problems, merely because another type, already established in the market, is permitted to continue in use. Whether *in fact* the Act will promote more environmentally desirable milk packaging is not the question: the Equal Protection Clause is satisfied by our conclusion that the Minnesota Legislature *could rationally have decided* that its ban on plastic nonreturnable milk jugs might foster greater use of environmentally desirable alternatives.

Second, the State argues that its ban on plastic nonreturnable milk containers will reduce the economic dislocation foreseen from the movement toward greater use of environmentally superior containers. The State notes that plastic nonreturnables have only recently been introduced on a wide scale in Minnesota, and that, at the time the legislature was considering the Act, many Minnesota dairies were preparing to invest large amounts of capital in plastic container production. . . .

Moreover, the State explains, to ban both the plastic and the paperboard nonreturnable milk container at once would cause an enormous disruption in the milk industry because few dairies are now able to package their products in refillable bottles or plastic pouches. Thus, by banning the plastic container while continuing to permit the paperboard container, the State was able to prevent the industry from becoming reliant on the new container, while avoiding severe economic dislocation. . . .

The state legislature concluded that nonreturnable, nonrefillable milk containers pose environmental hazards, and decided to ban the most recent entry into the field. The fact that the legislature in effect "grandfathered" paperboard containers, at least temporarily, does not make the Act's ban on plastic nonreturnables arbitrary or irrational.

Third, the State argues that the Act will help to conserve energy. It points out that plastic milk jugs are made from plastic resin, an oil and natural gas derivative, whereas paperboard milk cartons are primarily composed of pulpwood, which is a renewable resource. . . .

The Minnesota Supreme Court held, in effect, that the legislature misunderstood the facts. The court admitted that the results of a reliable study support the legislature's conclusion that less energy is consumed in the production of paperboard containers than in the production of plastic nonreturnables, but, after crediting the contrary testimony of respondents' expert witness and altering certain factual assumptions, the court concluded that "production of plastic nonrefillables requires less energy than production of paper containers." 289 N.W.2d, at 85.

The Minnesota Supreme Court may be correct that the Act is not a sensible means of conserving energy. But we reiterate that "it is up to legislatures, not courts, to decide on the wisdom and utility of legislation." *Ferguson v. Skrupa* [83 S. Ct. 1028, 1030, (1963)] . . . [T]he Minnesota Supreme Court erred in substituting its judgment for that of the legislature.

Fourth, the State argues that the Act will ease the State's solid waste disposal problem. Most solid consumer wastes in Minnesota are disposed of in landfills. A reputable study before the Minnesota Legislature indicated that plastic milk jugs occupy a greater volume in landfills than other nonreturnable milk containers. This was one of the legislature's major concerns. . . .

The Minnesota Supreme Court found that plastic milk jugs in fact take up less space in landfills and present fewer solid waste disposal problems than do paperboard containers. . . . But its ruling on this point must be rejected for the same reason we

rejected its ruling concerning energy conservation: it is not the function of the courts to substitute their evaluation of legislative facts for that of the legislature.

We therefore conclude that the ban on plastic nonreturnable milk containers bears a rational relation to the State's objectives, and must be sustained under the Equal Protection Clause. . . .

[Judgment reversed.]

Administrative Agencies

As the regulation of business has increased, state and federal administrative agencies have assumed primary responsibility for implementing and enforcing the myriad statutes enacted by the legislatures. Today hundreds of agencies are involved in the regulation of business and industry, including the major federal administrative agencies summarized in Table 4–1. The remainder of this chapter provides an introduction to federal administrative agencies. Most of the general principles that govern federal agencies also apply to state agencies.

The term "administrative agency" refers in general to a unit of government that is responsible for executing and enforcing statutes. Two types of administrative agencies operate at the federal level: independent agencies and executive agencies. Independent agencies, which are designed to minimize political influence and pressure on agency action, are created by Congress and are governed by a commission or board appointed by the president, subject to Senate confirmation. These commissioners or board members serve fixed terms in office and cannot be removed except for cause. Almost all independent agencies are free-standing governmental units that exist organizationally outside the three branches of government—that is, they are not a part of the legislative, executive or judicial branch—so they sometimes are described as the "fourth branch" of government. Independent agencies, such as the Federal Trade Commission and the Securities and Exchange Commission, include some of the largest and most influential agencies that regulate business and the economy.

In contrast, executive agencies are units within the executive branch of government and the heads

Table 4–1	**Major Federal Administrative Agencies Involved in Business Regulation**
Agency	*Area of Regulation*
Commodity Futures Trading Commission (CFTC)	Trading of futures and commodity options, gold and silver leverage contracts
Consumer Product Safety Commission (CPSC)	Safety of consumer products
Environmental Protection Agency (EPA)	Pollution control
Equal Employment Opportunity Commission (EEOC)	Employment discrimination
Federal Communications Commission (FCC)	Interstate and foreign communications (radio, television, telegraph, telephone, satellites)
Federal Deposit Insurance Corporation (FDIC)	Insurance of bank deposits
Federal Energy Regulatory Commission (FERC)	Production and sale of natural gas, sale of electricity, oil pipeline companies
Federal Reserve Board	National credit and monetary affairs
Federal Trade Commission (FTC)	Antitrust, corporate mergers, unfair trade practices, and unfair methods of competition
Food and Drug Administration (FDA)	Safety of food, drugs, cosmetics, and medicinal devices
Internal Revenue Service (IRS)	Federal tax laws
International Trade Commission (ITC)	International trade activities
Interstate Commerce Commission (ICC)	Interstate surface transportation
National Labor Relations Board (NLRB)	Labor relations
Nuclear Regulatory Commission (NRC)	Operation and use of nuclear reactors, nuclear materials
Occupational Safety and Health Administration (OSHA)	Safety and health in the workplace
Patent and Trademark Office	Patents and trademarks
Pension Benefit Guaranty Corporation	Private pension plans
Securities and Exchange Commission (SEC)	Securities law
Social Security Administration (SSA)	Social Security contributions and benefits programs

of these agencies generally are appointed by the president. Although some of the appointments require Senate approval, the head of an executive agency usually is subject to removal by the president. Most executive agencies are located within Cabinet departments; for example, the National Highway Traffic Safety Administration is located within the Department of Transportation and the Food and Drug Administration is part of the Department of Health and Human Services. Executive agencies generally have more restricted powers than independent agencies and the scope of their authority often is narrower or limited to one industry. Yet, some executive agencies, such as the Internal Revenue Service and the Social Security Administration, are very powerful and play a major

role in business regulation. Since its creation in 1970, the Environmental Protection Agency, the only executive agency not located within a Cabinet department, has become one of the largest federal agencies and its regulatory authority affects almost all industries. Although most executive agencies were not created by Congress, federal statutes adopted by Congress may impose duties and responsibilities on executive agencies or their administrators.

Powers of Administrative Agencies

Congress has delegated a variety of powers to administrative agencies. In general, these powers are analogous to those exercised by the three branches of government. Like the executive branch, some agencies are authorized to investigate and prosecute violations of federal law. Other agencies have the power to engage in rule-making, a process of adopting rules and regulations that are enforced like statutes enacted by the legislature. Some administrative agencies also are responsible for adjudicating individual cases involving issues of fact and law through administrative hearings that resemble court cases tried by the judiciary. Individual federal statutes that create an agency or that establish the activities subject to the agency's regulation also define the powers—investigative, prosecutorial, rule-making, or adjudicative—granted to the agency. Additionally, Congress has adopted the **Administrative Procedure Act**[25], a comprehensive statute that sets forth the procedures agencies must follow when engaging in rule-making or adjudication and that regulates dissemination of information gathered by agencies.

Investigation and Prosecution. Many administrative agencies possess the power to investigate and prosecute—functions traditionally exercised by the executive branch of government. Some administrative agencies are authorized to engage in investigation of specific individuals or businesses suspected of violating the law. If authorized by statute, such agencies may compel disclosure of information. The Federal Trade Commission, for example, has the following powers:

> . . . the [Federal Trade] Commission, or its duly authorized agent or agents, shall at all reasonable times have access to, for the purpose of examination, and the right to copy any documentary evidence of any person, partnership, or corporation being investigated or proceeded against; and the Commission shall have power to require by subpoena the attendance and testimony of witnesses and the production of all such documentary evidence relating to any matter under investigation.[26]

An administrative agency may demand only information relevant to legitimate investigations within the scope of the agency's authority. Further, requests for information generally must be reasonable, that is, not unduly vague or oppressive, and may not include privileged information. If a business subpoenaed by an agency wishes to contest the request, the business may seek a judicial order to quash the subpoena, but if the business merely fails to comply with the request, the agency may seek a judicial order including a penalty for contempt. In either case, judicial review minimizes the possibility of agency abuse of its investigative powers.

Some administrative agencies with investigatory powers also are authorized to prosecute violations of federal law. If an agency seeks criminal penalties, the case must be prosecuted in federal court generally with the assistance of the federal Department of Justice. In other cases involving only civil laws or regulations, Congress has authorized some agencies to try the matter within the agency through an administrative hearing.[27]

Administrative Searches. Some statutes authorize administrative agencies to conduct inspections of a business as a method of investigating compliance with regulations. The Supreme Court has held that such inspections, even when conducted only in conjunction with civil violations, constitute "searches" and are subject to the Fourth Amendment's prohibition against unreasonable searches and seizures. These **administrative searches** are a practical means to enforce laws relating to safety and health such as food and drug preparation and handling, pollution controls, and building and workplace safety and fire codes. The owner or manager of the premises may consent to an administrative search but if consent is refused, an administrative search is valid only if the government obtains a warrant by demonstrating probable cause either that conditions on the premises violate the law or that the search is made pursuant to reasonable legislative or administrative standards.[28] These standards, for example, might provide that the sites are selected for inspection on a random or periodic basis. The Supreme Court has, however, recognized a limited exception to the warrant require-

---

25. 5 U.S.C. §§551–559, 701–706.
26. 15 U.S.C. §49.

27. Administrative hearings are discussed at page 99.
28. *Marshall v. Barlow's, Inc.,* 98 S.Ct. 1816, 1824–1825 (1978).

ment for "pervasively regulated business[es]."[29], and for "closely regulated" industries "long subject to close supervision and inspection."[30] These industries, such as liquor and firearms, have such a history of government regulation and oversight that proprietors enjoy no reasonable expectation of privacy.

Information Gathering. Most investigations conducted by agencies are for the purpose of prosecution. Administrative agencies, however, also engage in a broad spectrum of information gathering activities for other purposes. An agency may gather and analyze data to provide information for public and private policy making. The Commerce Department, for example, collects a variety of economic and business information that is made available to other governmental units, to businesses, and to the general public. Much of this information is acquired from public sources or is disclosed voluntarily by businesses and individuals. Other information collected by agencies is provided by businesses or individuals in compliance with federal law. Sometimes a business provides data to secure a governmental benefit such as a government contract, a license to operate, or approval to market a product. Regulations of the Food and Drug Administration, for example, require a manufacturer who proposes to market a new drug to submit information about its composition, method of manufacture, recommended labeling, as well as test data demonstrating its safety and effectiveness. Other federal laws require businesses to gather and keep specified information and records. The Occupational Safety and Health Act, for example, requires businesses to maintain records of employee accidents and illnesses and exposure to hazardous substances. Agencies generally may mandate specified record keeping or submission of reports on matters relating to the agency's area of regulation if authorized by statute.

Freedom of Information Act. Administrative agencies possess vast amounts of information and data that have been accumulated through their investigative and information gathering powers. In 1966, in response to claims that government information was inaccessible, Congress amended the Administrative Procedure Act by enacting the **Freedom of Information Act (FOIA)**.[31] The FOIA requires federal agencies to make agency records available for examination or copying to any person who requests the records. Under the FOIA, the requesting party need not provide a reason for access, but some records are exempt from disclosure. The Act establishes nine categories of exempt documents, including certain national defense and foreign policy secrets, internal personnel matters, items exempted from disclosure by other statutes, and certain inter-agency and intra-agency memoranda. Exemption 4 of the FOIA provides that the Act "does not apply to matters that are . . . trade secrets and commercial or financial information obtained from a person and privileged or confidential."[32] This exemption has been especially important to businesses that have provided information to the government but desire to prevent competitors from gaining access to the information. When an FOIA request is made for data submitted by a business, most agencies notify the business and may allow it to comment on whether exemption 4 should apply. The following case, which interprets this exemption, is known as a "reverse-FOIA" claim, because the plaintiff is attempting to prevent disclosure of information that it provided to the government.

CNA Financial Corporation v. Donovan
830 F.2d 1132 (D.C. Cir. 1987)

CNA Financial Corporation is an insurance company that does business with the federal government. As a condition of receiving federal contracts, CNA must submit to the government various reports demonstrating its employment practices involving women and minorities and its affirmative action goals for the future. Pursuant to the FOIA, a group called Women Employed requested copies of some

---

29. *United States v. Biswell,* 92 S.Ct. 1593, 1596 (1972).
30. *Colonnade Catering Corp. v. United States,* 90 S.Ct. 774, 777 (1970).

---

31. 5 U.S.C. §552.
32. 5 U.S.C. §552(b)(4).

of the CNA employment and affirmative action reports. After the federal government notified CNA of the request, the Office of Federal Contract Compliance Programs (OFCCP) of the Department of Labor decided over CNA's objections to release the information. CNA brought suit against Raymond Donovan, Secretary of Labor, requesting the court to apply exemption 4 of the FOIA and order OFCCP not to disclose the information. The district court affirmed OFCCP's decision and CNA appealed.

Spottswood W. Robinson, III, Circuit Judge

. . . We next consider CNA's contention that OFCCP erred in its interpretation and application of the legal standard summoned by FOIA Exemption 4. The controlling test in this circuit was articulated more than a decade ago in *National Parks & Conservation Association v. Morton*, [498 F.2d 765 (D.C. Cir. 1974)], and has since been consistently followed. In pertinent part, it states that commercial or financial information is "confidential" under Exemption 4 if disclosure of the information "is likely to . . . cause substantial harm to the competitive position of the person from whom the information was obtained." [*Id.* at 770.] This criterion has been interpreted to require both a showing of actual competition and a likelihood of substantial competitive injury. Because OFCCP explicitly stated the proper standard to be applied, our review of the agency decision is confined to the question whether OFCCP correctly applied that standard to the facts of this case.

As an initial matter, we note that the scope of review of OFCCP's decision is governed by the Administrative Procedure Act. . . . OFCCP's action may be set aside only on one or more of a limited number of bases, of which the relevant one is that it is "arbitrary, capricious [or] an abuse of discretion." [*Worthington Compressors, Inc. v. Costle*, 662 F.2d 45, 50 (D.C. Cir. 1981).] Our inquiry must be "searching and careful," but "[a] court is not empowered to substitute its judgment for that of the agency." [*Citizens to Preserve Overton Park v. Volpe*, 91 S.Ct. 814, 824 (1971).]

CNA and OFCCP disagree on what material is within the purview of Exemption 4. The data that OFCCP proposes to release can be grouped into three principal types: statistics on the racial and sexual composition of the workforce within various CNA departments; goals developed for equal employment purposes; and "applicant flow information" showing the percentage, by race and sex, of applicants hired from without and employees promoted from within.

CNA's objections and the responses thereto by OFCCP may also be arranged in three occasionally overlapping categories. First, OFCCP says that much of the information sought by CNA to be confined is already publicly available, and this assertion has not been contested before this court. To the extent that any data requested under FOIA are in the public domain, the submitter is unable to make any claim to confidentiality—a *sine qua non* of Exemption 4. . . .

Second, several of CNA's claims with respect to other information relate not to alleged competitive harm but rather to anticipated displeasure of its employees or to adverse public reaction. CNA has protested, for example, that release of information on the number of women and minorities hired might result in unfavorable publicity. It also fears that its employees may become "demoralized" following disclosure of data showing the percentage of individuals promoted. We have previously found such complaints unrelated to the policy behind Exemption 4 of protecting submitters from external injury. These proffered objections simply do not amount to "harm flowing from the affirmative use of proprietary information by competitors." [*Public Citizens Health Research Group v. FDA*, 704 F.2d 1280, 1291 (D.C. Cir. 1983).]

The remaining disagreements between CNA and OFCCP concern the long-range consequences of the release of the data at issue. CNA submitted affidavits predicting a number of harmful effects; OFCCP, while offering no independent evidence, has answered these contentions with its own predictions of the repercussions of disclosure. One noteworthy objection by CNA to revelation of application flow data is that it would enable competitors more easily to direct their recruiting efforts to the best sources of potential employees. OFCCP counters with the logical rejoinder that these data will not be of any particular help to competitors since the employee-source and employee-position categories are broad, and the applicant pool is a function of the labor market and beyond an individual competitor's control.

These and other similar contentions presented no more than two contradictory views of what likely would ensue upon release of information that CNA sought to protect. In each case, OFCCP retorted with reasonable and thorough prognoses of its own. We thus are confronted by the type of judgments and forecasts courts traditionally leave largely to agency expertise, with judicial review limited by the narrow standard sanctioned. After careful consideration of OFCCP's decision, we are satisfied that it cannot in any way be characterized as arbitrary, capricious, or an abuse of discretion. CNA's objections were answered fully, and OFCCP's explanations of anticipated effects were certainly no less plausible than those advanced by CNA. Each of OFCCP's explanations is well reasoned, logical and consistent, and predictive judgments are not capable of exact proof. We find OFCCP's application of Exemption 4 entirely rational, and therefore legally permissible. . . .

[Judgment affirmed.]

Rule-Making. Many federal agencies possess rule-making power, the authority to adopt rules and regulations to carry out the provisions of statutes enforced by the agency. Rule-making enables an agency to clarify its policies, procedures and interpretation of statutes subject to the agency's regulation. When authorized by statute, the agency also can adopt legislative or substantive rules that fill in the gaps or add details to federal statutes. For example, the federal Clean Water Act, which regulates water pollution, delegates to the Environmental Protection Agency (EPA) the authority to set specific standards for each type of pollutant that may be discharged into navigable waters. Thus, the legislative rules of the EPA, rather than the provisions of the Clean Water Act, actually regulate pollution control. Legislative rules cannot contradict the provisions of a statute and generally are enforced like statutes.

Because of the prospective binding effect of legislative rules, agencies must comply with established procedures when adopting such rules. The Administrative Procedure Act recognizes two types of rule-making procedures: formal rule-making and informal rule-making. An agency initiates formal rule-making by providing notice of its proposed rule in the Federal Register and then must allow all interested parties to submit written responses. The agency, members of its governing board, or an administrative law judge must conduct a formal hearing at which evidence is presented, subject to cross-examination and rebuttal, in support of the rule. A full record of the hearing must be maintained and the final rule must be based exclusively on information presented in the record. Formal rule-making, which in many ways resembles a trial, can be time-consuming, expensive, and inefficient and is required by only a few federal statutes.

Most legislative rules, therefore, are adopted pursuant to informal rule-making procedures which also begin with Federal Register publication of a notice of the proposed rule. After an opportunity for interested parties to submit written data and arguments, the agency may adopt a final rule with a "concise general statement of [its] basis and purpose."[33] Although most agencies prepare a record in support of the rule, the contents of the record are not prescribed by law so often all data received by the agency is not included. Informal rule-making allows an agency greater flexibility to adapt the rule-making process to its own needs. Some agencies, for example, will hold public hearings or will solicit information from certain parties, such as the regulated industries, even if not required by law. Nevertheless, the informal rule-making process has been criticized for allowing agencies to disregard options or to ignore conflicting information.

Agencies maintain even broader discretion in adopting regulations that are not considered to be legislative or substantive. The Administrative Procedure Act establishes no procedure for interpretive rules, policy statements or rules of agency procedure. Interpretive rules, which explain an agency's construction of statutory language, and policy statements are important because, although they do not have the legal force of a statute, courts generally defer to an agency's expertise in interpreting statutes.

The authority to adopt rules is one of the most

---

33. 5 U.S.C. §553(c).

important powers delegated to administrative agencies. Rule-making relieves Congress from having to enact detailed statutes that are sufficiently comprehensive to cover all aspects of a subject. Because each agency develops expertise in its area of regulation, agency adoption of rules and standards often provides effective and practical regulation that accomplishes the goals of Congress.

Adjudication. Some administrative agencies possess powers, similar to those of the judiciary, to apply and enforce statutes, rules, and regulations in administrative hearings. These proceedings are conducted by an administrative law judge to determine factual matters, to obtain compliance with specified laws or regulations, to resolve claims of private individuals or businesses, and to determine whether the government will issue a license.

Administrative hearings, which must meet the requirement of procedural due process, follow procedures similar to those of a trial. The proceeding usually is initiated by filing a complaint that is answered by the respondent. Most complaints are filed by the agency itself although private businesses or individuals sometimes may initiate the proceeding. Following a period for discovery, evidence is presented, witnesses are examined and cross-examined, rulings are made on motions, and an order is issued by the administrative law judges.

The **administrative order,** like a judgment in a court trial, terminates the hearings. If the administrative law judge finds that a party violated the law, the judge may issue a **cease and desist order** that commands the wrongdoer to stop the illegal practice. Most agencies do not have the power to enforce the orders of administrative law judges. Rather, if a party fails to comply with a cease and desist order, the agency must bring a suit in federal court to obtain judicial enforcement.

As in court trials, a dispute may be settled prior to completion of an administrative hearing. The administrative law judge may issue a **consent order** in which the party, without admitting guilt, agrees to stop the allegedly illegal practice. Consent orders usually require public notice prior to becoming effective. A consent order may be enforced like a cease and desist order.

Administrative hearings resemble bench trials in the courts. The administrative law judge makes findings of both fact and law. Generally, procedure in an agency hearing is less formal than at a trial; for example, complaints may be served by mail and rules of evidence may not apply. Although the parties usually have the right to counsel, many parties do not retain attorneys. Moreover, an administrative law judge does not have the power to impose criminal penalties or to award civil damages.

Administrative hearings reduce the caseload of federal courts and generally save parties time and money. Due to the specialization and expertise of an administrative law judge, adjudication by an agency often is more efficient and may result in a more pragmatic approach than judicial resolution.

Government Control of Administrative Agencies

Despite the broad powers that have been delegated to administrative agencies, they remain subject to control by all three branches of the government. These controls help to minimize abuse of power by an agency.

Executive Control. Generally, the president has the power to appoint and remove the heads of executive administrative agencies. Although the president also appoints the commissioners who head independent agencies, statutes restrict the presidential power. Commissioners usually are appointed to staggered terms for an established number of years, and the president must await expiration of a commissioner's term before appointing a new commissioner. Federal law also requires that some commissions be politically balanced. For example, no more than three of the five commissioners of the SEC may belong to the same political party. The authority to appoint officers and commissioners allows the president to staff administrative agencies with people who support and implement his policies.

Critics of independent agencies assert that if the president has no authority to remove agency heads before their terms expire, or if Congress reserves a power to remove, the agencies violate the constitutional separation of powers doctrine. The critics argue that the executive powers delegated to independent agencies may be constitutionally exercised only by officials subject to the continuing supervisory control of the president, and who cannot be removed by Congress. Although the Supreme Court has upheld statutes restricting the president's removal power, it is likely to reexamine its position in the near future.

The executive exercises further control of agencies through the budget process. Prior to submitting budgets to the Congress, appropriations for administrative agencies are reviewed and revised by the Office of Management and Budget (OMB), which is under the president's control. Although Congress is not required to adopt OMB's budget, it does influence congressional allocations. The scope of an administrative agency's activities, of course, depends on the amount of funding it receives.

Legislative Control. Congress creates administrative agencies and retains the power to terminate them. Congress rarely exercises this power because of political pressures from interested parties and most agencies virtually become permanent. The legislature, however, still retains important controls. For example, it can expand or restrict the powers of an administrative agency. If Congress does not approve of an agency rule, it can change the rule by statute. Through the budgetary process, Congress can limit financial appropriations and effectively diminish the agency's powers. Finally, the legislature retains some control over personnel by requiring Senate approval of the appointment of some agency heads and commissioners.

Judicial Control. Judicial review of the actions of administrative agencies provides a third form of control. Although the courts may review both an agency's rule-making and administrative orders, they generally limit review to procedural aspects of these decisions.

Prior to reviewing an administrative agency decision, the court requires the complaining party to establish that it has *standing to sue*. Standing exists if the party has been injured in fact by an agency decision and is "arguably within the zone of interests to be protected or regulated by the statute or constitutional guarantee in question."[34] The stand-

ing requirement ensures that a legitimate controversy exists and prevents suits by persons who disagree with agency decisions merely on political or philosophical grounds.

The courts also require a party who seeks judicial review of an agency decision to exhaust all administrative remedies prior to undertaking a court case. In other words, the party must use remedies offered by an agency before going to the courts. The purpose of this requirement is to limit court review only to those issues that have been thoroughly considered by the agency and to decisions that clearly represent a final position of the agency.

Under Securities and Exchange Commission (SEC) procedures, for example, a party dissatisfied with an administrative order issued by an administrative law judge can request the SEC commissioners to review the decision. If, however, the party instead files suit in court seeking reversal of the order, the court will dismiss the suit and order the party to exhaust his administrative remedies— that is, obtain review by the commissioners. The commissioners might reverse or change the order, thereby eliminating the need for judicial review or restructuring the issues that ultimately may be reviewed by the court.

Judicial Review of Agency Rule-making. Even if a party establishes standing and exhausts his administrative remedies, a court usually provides only limited review of an agency's rule-making. When a party challenges a rule promulgated by an administrative agency the court traditionally considers two issues: (1) whether the agency has acted within the scope of authority validly delegated by the legislature and (2) whether the agency rule-making process provided due process of law.

If an agency adopts a rule that exceeds the authority that Congress has granted to the agency, the rule is said to be *ultra vires* (beyond one's power) and is invalid. Because Congress has delegated such broad authority to administrative agencies, a court rarely holds a rule to be *ultra vires*. Most judicial review of agency rule-making therefore concerns due process of law. If, for example, an agency has failed to follow the appropriate procedure (notice and a hearing) or has acted arbitrarily or capriciously, the court can invalidate the rule. In recent years, some agencies have revoked or re-

---

34. *Association of Data Processing Service Organizations, Inc. v. Camp,* 90 S.Ct. 827, 830 (1970).

vised previously adopted rules. In the case that follows, the court considers the procedure that an agency must follow prior to revoking a rule.

Motor Vehicle Manufacturers Association v. State Farm Mutual Automobile Insurance Company

103 S. Ct. 2856 (1983)

In 1966, Congress enacted the National Traffic and Motor Vehicle Act, which directed the secretary of the Department of Transportation (DOT) to issue standards to "meet the need for motor vehicle safety." In 1977, DOT issued Standard 208, a regulation requiring automobile manufacturers to install "passive occupant restraint systems"—devices, such as automatic seatbelts or airbags, that restrained an automobile occupant without any action by the occupant. Although automobile manufacturers were free to choose the type of passive restraint, almost all manufacturers began plans to install automatic safety belts. In 1981 the National Highway Traffic Safety Administration (NHTSA), an agency within DOT, rescinded Standard 208.

State Farm brought suit against DOT on the ground that the rescission of Standard 208 was improper. The court of appeals (the court of original jurisdiction) held that the rescission was arbitrary and capricious. The Supreme Court accepted the case for review.

Justice White

. . . The [National Traffic and Motor Vehicle Safety] Act . . . authorizes judicial review under the provisions of the Administrative Procedure Act (APA) . . . of all "orders establishing, amending, or revoking a Federal motor vehicle safety standard," 15 U.S.C. §1392(b). Under this authority, we review today whether NHTSA acted arbitrarily and capriciously in revoking the requirement in Motor Vehicle Safety Standard 208 that new motor vehicles produced after September 1982 be equipped with passive restraints to protect the safety of the occupants of the vehicle in the event of a collision. Briefly summarized, we hold that the agency failed to present an adequate basis and explanation for rescinding the passive restraint re-

quirement and that the agency must either consider the matter further or adhere to or amend Standard 208 along lines which its analysis supports.

The regulation whose rescission is at issue bears a complex and convoluted history. Over the course of approximately 60 rulemaking notices, the requirement has been imposed, amended, rescinded, reimposed, and now rescinded again. . . .

In February 1981 . . . Secretary of Transportation Andrew Lewis reopened the rulemaking due to changed economic circumstances and, in particular, the difficulties of the automobile industry. . . . After receiving written comments and holding public hearings, NHTSA issued a final rule . . . that rescinded the passive restraint requirement contained in Modified Standard 208.

In a statement explaining the rescission, NHTSA maintained that it was no longer able to find, as it had in 1977, that the automatic restraint requirement would produce significant safety benefits. . . . This judgment reflected not a change of opinion on the effectiveness of the technology, but a change in plans by the automobile industry. . . . By 1981 it became apparent that automobile manufacturers planned to install the automatic seatbelts in approximately 99% of the new cars. For this reason, the life-saving potential of airbags would not be realized. Moreover, it now appeared that the overwhelming majority of passive belts planned to be installed by manufacturers could be detached easily and left that way permanently. . . . For this reason, the agency concluded that there was no longer a basis for reliably predicting that the standard would lead to any significant increased usage of restraints at all.

In view of the possibly minimal safety benefits, the automatic restraint requirement no longer was reasonable or practicable in the agency's view. The requirement would require approximately $1 billion to implement and the agency did not believe it would be reasonable to impose such substantial costs on manufacturers and consumers without more adequate assurance that sufficient safety benefits would accrue. . . .

The agency's action in promulgating . . . standards . . . may be set aside if found to be "arbitrary, capricious, an abuse of discretion, or otherwise not in accordance with law." 5 U.S.C. §706(2)(A). . . . We believe that the rescission or modification of an occupant protection standard is subject to the same test. . . .

The scope of review under the "arbitrary and capricious" standard is narrow and a court is not to substitute its judgment for that of the agency. Nevertheless, the agency must examine the relevant data and articulate a satisfactory explanation for its action. . . . Normally, an agency rule would be arbitrary and capricious if the agency has relied on factors which Congress has not intended it to consider, entirely failed to consider an important aspect of the problem, offered an explanation for its decision that runs counter to the evidence before the agency, or is so implausible that it could not be ascribed to a difference in view or the product of agency expertise. . . .

The ultimate question before us is whether NHTSA's rescission of the passive restraint requirement of Standard 208 was arbitrary and capricious. We conclude, as did the Court of Appeals, that it was. . . .

The first and most obvious reason for finding the rescission arbitrary and capricious is that NHTSA apparently gave no consideration whatever to modifying the Standard to require that airbag technology be utilized. Standard 208 sought to achieve automatic crash protection by requiring automobile manufacturers to install either of two passive restraint devices: airbags or automatic seatbelts. There was no suggestion in the long rulemaking process that led to Standard 208 that if only one of these options were feasible, no passive restraint standard should be promulgated. . . .

The agency has now determined that the detachable automatic belts will not attain anticipated safety benefits because so many individuals will detach the mechanism. Even if this conclusion were acceptable in its entirety . . . standing alone it would not justify any more than an amendment of Standard 208 to disallow compliance by means of the one technology which will not provide effective passenger protection. It does not cast doubt on the need for a passive restraint standard or upon the efficacy of airbag technology. . . . Given the effectiveness ascribed to airbag technology by the agency, the mandate of the Safety Act to achieve traffic safety would suggest that the logical response to the faults of detachable seatbelts would be to require the installation of airbags. At the very least this alternative way of achieving the objec-

tives of the Act should have been addressed and adequate reasons given for its abandonment. But the agency not only did not require compliance through airbags, it did not even consider the possibility in its 1981 rulemaking. Not one sentence of its rulemaking statement discusses the airbags-only option. . . . We have frequently reiterated that an agency must cogently explain why it has exercised its discretion in a given manner . . . and we reaffirm this principle again today. . . .

[Judgment vacated and remanded for further proceedings.]

Judicial Review of Administrative Hearings. In reviewing decisions of administrative law judges or other hearing officers, the courts generally perform appellate-type review, determining only whether any errors of law occurred. For example, the court may review whether the agency acted within the scope of its statutory authority, whether the hearing procedure complied with procedural due process, and whether the decision violated any constitutional provisions. A few statutes, however, do allow the court to obtain further evidence if the judge deems it appropriate.

In most cases, the court will accept the administrative law judge's findings of fact if they are supported by substantial evidence: "such relevant evidence as a reasonable mind might accept as adequate to support a conclusion."[35] In determining whether the record of the hearing provides substantial evidence to support the administrative law judge's findings, the court must consider both evidence supporting and contradictory to the findings.[36] Thus, the record as a whole must provide substantial evidence.

Administrative Agencies—Problems and Reforms

Administrative agencies are an integral part of federal government regulation. They perform important tasks that would be difficult for the executive,

---

35. *Consolidated Edison Co. v. National Labor Relations Board*, 59 S. Ct. 206, 217 (1938).

36. *Universal Camera Corp. v. National Labor Relations Board*, 71 S. Ct. 456 (1951).

legislative and judicial branches of government to undertake in a systematic manner. As the size and number of agencies have grown in the last 50 years, so too have their functions. Although most of the older agencies, such as the Interstate Commerce Commission and the Federal Trade Commission, were developed to handle financial and commercial affairs, the newer agencies, such as the Environmental Protection Agency, the Equal Employment Opportunity Commission, and the Occupational Safety and Health Administration, are responsible for health, safety and social matters. Although no new agencies have been created in over ten years, their continued growth, combined with economic problems, has generated much criticism from the public, government officials, and particularly the business community. Yet, even the strongest supporters recognize that agencies could operate more efficiently.

Some of the harshest criticism has concerned the proliferation of rules and regulations issued by administrative agencies. Many businesses argue that compliance with agency rules is too expensive and hampers competition, especially in international markets.[37] In the late 1970s, following years of steadily increasing numbers of regulations, the executive branch of government implemented programs to curb the growth of rules. This reform continued during the Reagan administration through an executive order granting the Office of Management and Budget (OMB) significant authority to review proposed agency regulations and to require data documenting their need. Despite these reform efforts, however, agencies continue to issue volumes of rules.

Another recurring criticism of agencies questions the relationship between agencies and businesses they regulate. Frequently, the president will select administrators who have worked in the field subject to the agency's regulation. Although such an arrangement ensures some familiarity and expertise in that field, critics suggest that it may undermine the independence of the agency. Similarly, after terminating their employment with the government, officials often find employment in the industry they formerly regulated. To minimize potential conflicts of interest, Congress enacted the Ethics in Government Act[38], which restricts some former upper level government officials from lobbying their former agencies after leaving office.

Reforms of government agencies are likely to continue in the future as the executive and legislative branches try to find effective but efficient ways to regulate business. Yet, despite strong criticism, administrative agencies will continue to play a central role in the regulation of business because of the crucial functions they perform.

SUMMARY

1. States regulate business activities through the exercise of two inherent powers: the state police power and the power to tax. Federal regulation is based upon specific powers enumerated in the United States Constitution, most notably the Commerce Clause. Although the Supreme Court formerly adopted a narrow construction of federal powers under the Commerce Clause, today Congress may regulate virtually any activity that has an effect on interstate commerce.

2. Under the Commerce Clause and the Supremacy Clause, the federal government may preempt state legislation in a specific area of commerce either explicitly or implicitly through comprehensive regulation. Absent federal preemption, state regulation of business that has an incidental effect on interstate commerce is permissible if the regulation serves a legitimate state purpose and the benefit of the regulation outweighs the burden on interstate commerce.

3. In addition to the Commerce Clause, other constitutional provisions impose limitations on state police and taxing power. For example, the Import-Export Clause prohibits state taxation of imports and exports in the stream of commerce. The Privileges and Immunities Clause prohibits the states from unreasonably discriminating against out-of-state residents. The Contract Clause

---

37. The costs associated with environmental, health, and safety regulation have been especially high. The problems associated with compliance are discussed in detail in Chapter 54.

38. 18 U.S.C. §207.

limits the power of the states to abridge existing contractual relationships.

4. The Constitution imposes various limitations upon both federal and state powers to regulate business. The First Amendment restricts government from prohibiting commercial speech but allows limited regulation of commercial speech. The Fourth Amendment limits state and federal governments' powers to conduct administrative searches. The Fifth and Fourteenth Amendments provide the guarantees of due process and equal protection.

5. The federal and state governments create administrative agencies to implement and enforce regulatory laws governing specified industries or areas of commerce. Administrative agencies perform various functions including investigation and prosecution, rulemaking, and adjudication by administrative hearing.

6. The three branches of government exercise control over administrative agencies. The executive branch has the power to appoint heads of the agencies and to influence budget appropriations. The legislative branch has the power to create and terminate agencies, and to expand and restrict their powers or budgets. The judicial branch has the power to review agency rule-making and adjudication to determine whether the agency has complied with statutory and constitutional law.

KEY TERMS

state police power	Equal Protection Clause
state power to tax	Administrative Procedure
Commerce Clause	Act
Import-Export Clause	administrative search
Privileges and Immunities	Freedom of Information
Clause	Act
Contract Clause	administrative order
freedom of speech	cease and desist order
commercial speech	consent order

QUESTIONS AND PROBLEMS

4-1 Compare and contrast the state police power and the federal government's power to regulate interstate commerce as currently interpreted by the Supreme Court.

4-2 A New York statute provides that packaged alcoholic beverages may be sold only in stores operated by the state. A recent amendment to the statute allows retail grocery stores to sell packaged "wine coolers"—a mixture of wine and fruit juice—so long as the beverage contains less than 6% alcohol.

(a) Does the New York state statute, as amended, violate the Commerce Clause? Explain.

(b) Assume that the amendment allows retail grocery stores to sell wine coolers only if the beverage contains less than 6% alcohol and it is made only from wine produced within the state of New York. Six other states produce wine for marketing in interstate commerce. Does this amendment violate the Commerce Clause? Explain.

4-3 An ordinance of the city of Madison, Wisconsin, prohibited the sale of milk unless it had been processed and bottled in a licensed plant within a five-mile radius of the city. The legislative history of the ordinance shows that it was adopted to protect the health of local citizens. Because the city of Madison could control the production standards of milk from nearby plants by inspection of the plants, the ordinance served to protect citizens from contaminated milk. A milk producer from Illinois who operates a milk plant outside the 5-mile radius sues the city of Madison alleging that the ordinance discriminates against interstate commerce. How should the court rule? Explain.

4-4 The city of Burbank, California, adopted an ordinance prohibiting jets from taking off or landing at the local airport between the hours of 11:00 P.M. and 7:00 A.M. The Federal Aviation Administration previously had granted Pacific Southwest Airlines the right to operate a flight that landed at 11:30 P.M. Pacific Southwest sues the city of Burbank.

(a) What grounds might Pacific Southwest allege to establish that the local ordinance is invalid?

(b) How should the court rule?

4-5 The state of North Carolina imposes a property tax on all tobacco present in the state on January 1 of each year. The RJRT Company objected to the state's applying this tax to tobacco imported from foreign countries that RJRT was storing in North Carolina warehouses on January 1. Assuming that RJRT intended to use this tobacco in cigarettes that primarily would be consumed in the United States, would application of the tax to the foreign goods be unconstitutional? What if RJRT intended to ship the tobacco to France where it would be made into cigars?

4-6 The state of Montana requires hunters to obtain a license to hunt elk and other game in the state. The fee charged to out-of-state residents is $225 while in-state residents paid a fee of only $30.

Does the statute comply with the Constitution? Explain.

4-7 Massachusetts enacted a statute prohibiting corporations from making contributions or expenditures "for the purpose of . . . influencing or affecting the vote on any question submitted to the voters, other than one materially affecting any of the property, business or assets of the corporation." The statute explicitly states that income tax matters do not materially affect corporations.

(a) What purpose would this statute serve?

(b) Assume you are employed by a corporation that wishes to publicize its views on a public referendum to increase income taxes. Suggest reasons why the statute may be unconstitutional.

4-8 The state of Alaska has adopted a statute that requires all companies to grant preference to Alaska residents when hiring new employees. To qualify as a resident, a person must reside in the state for at least 1 year. Is the statute constitutional? Explain.

4-9 A common complaint of the business community is that the government (federal and state) imposes too many regulations on business.

(a) Explain why businesses generally oppose regulation.

(b) Are there any instances in which a business would favor regulation by the government? Explain.

(c) Assuming that either the state or federal government will regulate businesses, is a Fortune 500 corporation more likely to prefer regulation by the state or federal government? What type of regulation would a small business operating only in one locality prefer? Explain.

4-10 In *Ferguson v. Skrupa,* 83 S. Ct. 1028, 1030-1031 (1963), Justice Hugo Black stated:

Under the system of government created by our Constitution, it is up to legislatures, not courts, to decide on the wisdom and utility of legislation. . . . [C]ourts do not substitute their social and economic beliefs for the judgment of legislative bodies, who are elected to pass laws.

(a) Consider the standards used by the courts in cases challenging federal statutes for alleged violations of the Commerce Clause. Do those standards contradict or support Justice Black's statement? Explain.

(b) Assume that a business opposes the economic purposes of a federal statute. If courts refrain from invalidating such statutes, what recourse does a business have? Explain.

4-11 Justice Benjamin Cardozo stated that the Constitution "was framed upon the theory that the peoples of the several states must sink or swim together, and that in the long run prosperity and salvation are in union and not division" (*Baldwin v. G. A. F. Seelig, Inc.,* 55 S. Ct. 497, 500 (1935)).

(a) Explain the meaning of this statement.

(b) Explain how the Commerce Clause, the Privileges and Immunities Clause, and the Import-Export Clause, as interpreted by the Supreme Court, effectuate the theory referred to by Justice Cardozo.

4-12 A New York statute requires businesses that dismantle automobiles to obtain a license, to maintain records recording the acquisition and disposition of each motor vehicle and its parts and to make those records and any inventory available for inspection by state officials. One purpose of the statute is to reduce or eliminate auto theft in New York. At the time the statute was enacted, the governor noted that motor vehicle theft in New York was a multimillion dollar industry (in 1976, over 130,000 vehicles valued at $225 million had been stolen); that the high theft rate had significantly raised insurance premiums; and that stolen vehicles frequently were used in the commission of other crimes.

Ace Parts & Metal, a New York business subject to regulation under the statute, purchases old automobiles, dismantles them and sells the salvaged parts to other businesses and individuals. Two state inspectors visited Ace and asked to inspect the premises and records. When the manager stated that he maintained no records, the inspectors, over the manager's objections, inspected the premises, noting the registration numbers of various automobiles. Subsequent investigation revealed that several of the automobiles had been stolen.

(a) Assume that the purpose of the inspection was to determine whether the business was in compliance with the statute but that no criminal penalties were available for failure to comply. Should the state inspectors be required to obtain a warrant to conduct the inspection?

(b) Assume the purpose of the investigation is to uncover evidence of criminal activities. Would a warrantless search be lawful? If the state of New York attempted to prosecute

Ace or its manager for criminal possession of stolen property, should the evidence obtained during the investigation be admissible?

4-13 The Federal Reserve Board is a federal agency with rule-making powers. In accordance with proper procedures, the Board issued Regulation Z which consists of legislative rules for administering the Truth-In-Lending Act. Subsequently, the Board issued an interpretation of the word "finance charge" as used in the Truth-In-Lending Act and Regulation Z. The regulation was issued without following informal rule-making procedures.

(a) Did the Federal Reserve Board properly adopt the rule interpreting "finance charge"?

(b) What is the legal effect of the rule?

4-14 From time to time, politicans, businesspersons, and others have suggested that administrative agencies should be abolished. What effect would such an action have on the three branches of government?

4-15 The Federal Trade Commission (FTC) is authorized to conduct administrative hearings if it has reason to believe that a business or individual "has been or is using any unfair method of competition or unfair or deceptive act or practice in or affecting commerce." The Federal Trade Commission Act and the Administrative Procedure Act require the FTC to issue a complaint setting forth the alleged misconduct, to hold a hearing before an administrative law judge where the charged party may present evidence and testimony and to have the administrative law judge render a decision on the matter. Either party may appeal an adverse decision to the full Federal Trade Commission and if the decision of the Commission is unsatisfactory, either party may obtain judicial review.

In 1973, following a nationwide oil shortage, the FTC issued a complaint against Socal and seven other major oil companies alleging that they had engaged in unfair methods of competition. At the time the FTC issued the complaint, it had not examined any of Socal's employees or records. After Socal filed a motion to dismiss the complaint, which was denied by the FTC, Socal filed a complaint in the federal district court requesting that the court order the FTC to withdraw the complaint on the ground that the FTC did not have "reason to believe" that Socal had acted illegally. How should the court rule?

The law of torts is a pervasive area of law imposing liability for intentional and unintentional conduct, and affecting individuals, businesses, and governmental bodies. Tort law imposes liability for injuries caused by automobile accidents and airline crashes, by dangerous conditions on land, by fraud or defamation, by defective products, or by medical or other professional malpractice. Potential tort liability is a fundamental consideration in prudent personal and business planning and is a major reason for insurance. Indeed, the perceived risk of tort liability often determines what goods or services businesses provide, the form those goods or services take, and the design and maintenance of buildings and equipment used in manufacturing, wholesaling, retailing, and service operations.

Introduction to Tort Law

A **tort** (Latin *tortus:* "twisted") is "a private or civil wrong or injury, other than breach of contract, for which the court will provide a remedy in the form of an action for damages."[1] Whereas contract law is designed to compensate one person for injuries caused by another's failure to perform a special form of promise, a contract, tort law provides compensation for legal wrongs committed against a person or her property arising independently of any contract between the parties. A person who commits a tort is known as a **tort-feasor,** and acts or omissions constituting torts are said to be "tortious."

Torts and Crimes Distinguished

The nature of a tort can be clarified somewhat by comparing it to another form of wrong, a crime, discussed in Chapter 3. A crime is an offense or wrong committed against the public generally, for which the public vindicates its rights through a criminal prosecution. A criminal prosecution is maintained by the sovereign (state or federal government) and punishes the defendant's conduct by imposing a fine, prison term, or both. Criminal law is contained in statutes, both state and federal, that

---

1. Black, *Law Dictionary* (5th ed. 1979); Prosser and Keeton, *The Law of Torts* 2 (5th ed. 1984).

define the prohibited conduct and outline the penalties imposed. Criminal law is not generally designed to compensate individuals injured by criminal conduct.

In contrast, tort actions are maintained by the injured individual seeking compensation from the defendant for the injury caused by the defendant's conduct. Tort law is derived from state common law, developed by the courts on a case-by-case basis. Thus, tort and criminal actions differ in three important respects: (1) the identity of the plaintiff (the public generally versus an injured individual), (2) the nature of the relief sought (punishment versus compensation), and (3) the source of the law (statute versus common law).

Assume A punches B, breaking B's nose. In this case, the state may take criminal action under its criminal code against A for assault and battery, leading to a fine or prison sentence. In addition, B may file a tort action against A using common law tort principles to recover damages to compensate for the injuries.

As indicated above, although the same conduct may be both a crime and a tort, most torts are not crimes. Torts are simply those wrongs, other than breach of contract, for which the law provides compensation through a civil action.

Grounds of Tort Liability

Tort actions, like other civil actions, begin when a person injured by another's act or omission files a complaint in an appropriate court alleging that the defendant has committed a tort and requesting damages. All tort actions require the plaintiff to prove (1) the existence of a legal duty owed by the defendant to the plaintiff, (2) breach of that duty, and (3) injury or damage as a proximate result of the defendant's breach.

Tort liability is imposed on three basic grounds: intent, negligence, and strict liability. In intentional torts, the tort-feasor acts deliberately with the desire to harm the plaintiff. The *Restatement (Second) of Torts* finds a person's conduct **intentional** if he either "desires to cause the consequences of his act, or . . . believes that the consequences are substantially certain to result from it."[2] As the

probability that the harmful consequences will follow decreases to less than substantial *certainty,* the conduct is no longer intentional, but becomes reckless, or ultimately merely negligent, conduct that increases the *risk* of harm.

Thus, in intentional and negligent torts, the law imposes liability because of the defendant's "fault" in causing the plaintiff's harm. Intent and negligence simply represent differing degrees of fault. In strict liability torts, on the other hand, the defendant is held liable in the absence of either negligence or an intent to interfere with the plaintiff's legally protected interests. That is, the defendant is held strictly liable—liable without fault.

Tort law recognizes certain defenses that extinguish or reduce the defendant's liability. That is, even if a plaintiff establishes all the elements of a tort, a defendant who proves facts constituting a legitimate defense may prevent or limit the plaintiff's recovery. A number of important defenses to tort actions are discussed later in this chapter.

Damages in Tort Actions

Tort law enables an injured party to recover damages for injuries caused by the defendant's tortious conduct. Generally, the plaintiff is entitled to compensatory damages, a monetary award designed to compensate the plaintiff for the injuries caused by the defendant. Compensatory damages include, for example, payment for medical bills, property damage, loss of income, total or partial disability, and in some cases "pain and suffering."

In some cases, the defendant also may be assessed **punitive** or **exemplary damages,** a monetary award designed to punish the defendant and to deter similar conduct by the defendant or others in the future. Through punitive damage awards, tort law uses a criminal law concept—punishment—to supplement the basic compensatory purpose of tort actions. Punitive damages are awarded only in cases involving a defendant's intentional and deliberate disregard for others' rights. Punitive damages may be awarded for many of the intentional torts discussed in this chapter and for fraud, an aggravated intentional tort committed in conjunction with a contract, discussed in Chapter 11.

The amount of damages, like the issue of liability, usually is determined by the trier of fact, normally the jury. Compensatory damage awards must

---

2. *Restatement (Second) of Torts* §8A.

be supported by evidence. Punitive damage awards, however, need bear no relation to the actual compensatory damages and often greatly exceed them. In the last few years, as a part of "tort reform" legislation, many states have placed "caps" on damages, limiting the amounts that may be awarded for pain and suffering and as punitive damages.

Multiple Defendants in Tort Actions

Frequently, a plaintiff's injury is caused by tortious conduct of more than one person. In such cases, the plaintiff generally sues all persons whose conduct was a factor in causing the injury. If the defendants acted in concert, they are considered to be joint tort-feasors and are held jointly and severally liable for damages: all defendants together are responsible to pay the damages (joint liability) and each defendant individually is responsible to pay the full amount of damages (several liability). So, for example, if Punch and Judy, acting in concert, commit the tort of battery and a jury awards damages of $1,000, the plaintiff may collect a total of $1,000 from Punch and Judy or $1,000 from either Punch or Judy. The plaintiff's recovery is limited, however, to the total damage award so she could not recover $1,000 from Punch and $1,000 from Judy. Generally, joint tort-feasors who act in concert are not entitled to receive contribution from the other defendants. Thus, for example, if Punch paid the full $1,000, he would have no right to obtain partial or full repayment from Judy.

In many cases, multiple defendants do not act in concert but each independently commits an act that contributes to the plaintiff's injuries. In an automobile accident, for example, two drivers may commit separate negligent acts that combine to injure the plaintiff. If a distinct injury is caused by each defendant, or if the injuries reasonably can be apportioned among the defendants, damages will be assessed against each defendant individually. If, however, no reasonable basis exists for apportioning damages, states traditionally have imposed joint and several liability on all defendants. When joint and several liability is imposed, each defendant is responsible for all damages even if his or her conduct alone might not have caused the entire injury.

Imposing joint and several liability on multiple defendants is based on the policy that an innocent plaintiff should not be denied recovery from defendants who partially caused the injury merely because the plaintiff cannot prove the extent of injury caused by each defendant. Generally, a defendant subject to joint and several liability who pays the judgment is entitled to obtain contribution from the other tort-feasors if they did not act in concert. Nevertheless, for many years defendants have criticized joint and several liability because some defendants—such as large corporations or parties carrying insurance—often are forced to pay the full amount of the judgment and are unable to obtain contribution from poorer or uninsured defendants. In some cases defendants whose conduct only minimally contributed to a plaintiff's injuries have been required to pay for all damages. Recognizing the basic unfairness of such results and the financial burden they create for certain defendants (such as corporations and governmental bodies) and their insurers, many states have enacted statues to change the laws applicable to multiple tort defendants. Texas, for example, recently revised its laws to impose joint and several liability only on defendants who are at least 20% responsible for the plaintiff's injuries. Other states, like Montana and South Dakota, require at least 50% responsibility before a defendant may be subjected to joint and several liability. Several states recently have abolished joint and several liability unless the defendants act in concert.

Intentional Torts

Intentional torts may be classified according to the interest protected. A person may be held liable in tort for intentionally interfering with another's person, property, or business relations.

Intentional Interference with the Person

Various tort actions are designed to protect a person's physical or emotional well-being against intentional interference. Tort law protects a person against harmful or offensive bodily contacts (and apprehension of such contacts), and confinement. It also protects intangible emotional interests such as a person's peace of mind, reputation, or right to be left alone. The torts safeguarding these interests include battery, assault, false imprisonment, intentional infliction of emotional distress, defamation, invasion of privacy, and misuse of legal proceedings.

Assault and Battery.

The related torts of assault and battery protect a person against intentionally inflicted harmful bodily contact and threat of such contact. A **battery** is a harmful or offensive *contact* with a person which is intended by the actor to cause such a contact. A battery may be committed by a direct use of force, such as a punch, or indirectly, such as by placing a tripwire across a path used by the plaintiff. Note that liability for battery may be imposed whether or not the contact causes physical injury.

In contrast, an **assault** occurs if a person, intending to cause a harmful or offensive contact, acts in a manner that places another in imminent *apprehension* of such a contact. That is, an assault amounts to a threat to use force, which would convince a reasonable person of the actor's ability and opportunity to carry it out. Although both assault and battery are often present in the same case, not all batteries require a prior assault. For example, it is battery but not assault to strike a person from behind. A person injured by an assault or battery is entitled to recover damages to compensate for the mental disturbance and physical illness or injury sustained. In addition, punitive damages are often appropriate because assault and battery usually involve an intent to injure. Assault and battery are also crimes, subjecting the defendant to punishment under state criminal law in addition to tort liability.

A defendant in an assault or battery case may avoid liability by proving that she acted reasonably in self-defense or in the defense of others. The defendant may use force likely to cause death or serious injury, however, only if she reasonably believes that such force is necessary to prevent death or serious injury to herself or another, or to prevent the commission of a forcible felony. Similarly, although one may use reasonable force in the protection of property, there is no privilege to use deadly force unless there is also a threat to the property owner's personal safety that would justify the use of such force in self-defense. This rule applies even if the plaintiff is a trespasser. Finally, the plaintiff's consent to the assault or battery is a complete defense.

False Imprisonment.

Tort law safeguards an individual's freedom of movement by imposing liability for **false imprisonment** (or **false arrest**). A person who intentionally confines another within fixed boundaries has committed false imprisonment. Although the "confinement" must be total and complete, offering no reasonable means of escape, actual incarceration or imprisonment is not required. Thus, a person may be confined not only by physical barriers (for example, by being locked in a room), but also by physical force, threat of physical force, or other forms of duress.

Many false imprisonment cases involve improper arrests by police officers or other officials. In the business setting, a retailer's detention of a suspected shoplifter may give rise to a false imprisonment claim. In recognition of the serious problems posed by shoplifting, most states have adopted statutes (sometimes called merchant protection legislation or shopkeeper's privilege statutes) that relieve a merchant from liability for false imprisonment if the merchant acts reasonably in detaining and confining suspected shoplifters. Compliance with such a statute is a complete defense to a claim of false imprisonment. The following case illustrates a false imprisonment suit brought by a suspected shoplifter.

Adams v. Zayre Corporation
499 N.E.2d 678 (Ill. App. 1986)

Plaintiff Mary Adams sued defendant Zayre Corporation for false imprisonment as a result of events that occurred at a retail store operated by Zayre. After shopping in various departments for about 30 minutes, Adams purchased two blankets for which she paid cash at a check-out counter near the front of the store. As Adams and her daughter exited the store, they were detained by two members of Zayre's security staff who escorted the women to a security room in the store. According to testimony from Adams and her daughter, the security officers grabbed them and held each by the arm as they returned to the store. The security officers testified that they had asked Adams and her daughter to return to the store and that the women had done so voluntarily. The security manager further testified that she had seen Adams place a radio in her purse while she was shopping, but the radio was not found in Adams's or her daughter's possession in the security room. After being detained for approximately 30 minutes, Adams and her daughter were allowed to leave.

Following a trial, the jury found Zayre liable for false imprisonment and awarded Adams compensatory damages of $2,500 and punitive damages of $30,000. Zayre appealed.

Strouse, Justice

. . . False imprisonment consists of the unlawful restraint, against a person's will, of that individual's personal liberty or freedom of locomotion. . . . Defendant is, however, afforded protection by sections 16A-5 and 16A-6 of the [Illinois] Criminal Code. . . . The statute empowers a merchant who has reasonable grounds to believe that a person has committed retail theft to detain such person in a reasonable manner for a reasonable length of time. . . .

A review of the record reveals that plaintiff's case in chief presents a case of false imprisonment. She testified that the security guard grabbed her by the arm after she exited the store. A minor struggle ensued, after which she was forcibly led back into the store and ushered to a security area. Four witnesses testified that she was under their forcible control.

Defendant had the burden of proving that it fell within the scope of sections 16A-5 and 16A-6, *i.e.*, that the actions of its security force were reasonable. This factual determination was for the jury. . . .

The record reflects that the jury could have found defendant's actions to be unreasonable—both in manner of execution and time of detention. "The use of unnecessary force on suspected shoplifters by store personnel, as well as rudeness and harassment of the suspects, have been factors upon which the courts have determined either that the manner of detention was not reasonable as intended by the statute or that a finding to that effect was supportable." (Annot., 47 A.L.R.3d 998, 1020 (1973).) There was also corroborated testimony that defendant detained plaintiff for one-half hour—15 minutes of which was after they had concluded their search and investigation and determined that there

were no grounds to continue holding the plaintiff. Further, based on the disputed testimony, the jury could have found that no reasonable grounds existed for holding the plaintiff. We therefore cannot say that the jury's verdict as to general damages was against the manifest weight of the evidence.

We last address defendant's contention that punitive damages are inappropriate. Punitive damages are permitted where an arrest is effected recklessly, oppressively, insultingly or willfully, with a design to oppress and injure. . . . The manner of plaintiff's apprehension has already been described. This apprehension was conducted in violation of the store's own guidelines as to the manner in which a suspect is observed and detained. These guidelines provide that a store security officer making an arrest must have continual and unbroken surveillance of a subject after the alleged taking, up to the actual apprehension of the subject. The officer must follow the suspect in such a manner as to have "both the subject and the merchandise under observation *at all times. If the subject gets out of sight even for a moment the apprehension cannot be made unless another theft act is witnessed.*" Since the security officers thoroughly searched the plaintiff and found no radio, it can only be concluded that even if plaintiff had taken a radio, it was not in her possession at the time she left the store and she should not have been detained.

Also, the store guidelines for approaching suspected shoplifters were violated. The store policy as to approaching suspects is as follows:

> "Again, when the suspect reaches the sidewalk (outside the store) and the officer is sure of his case, this approach is suggested: 'Excuse me, my name is Sandy Smith, Store Security (showing I.D.). May I examine your cash register receipt for (describe the article or articles concealed). When identification of the article has been established and examination of the receipt shows no ringup, ask the suspect to return to the store to privately discuss the incident. If at all possible avoid touching the suspect. There are circumstances where this is necessary, sometimes the person needs to be coached along with the hand placed under an arm for direction and guidance through the store, BUT ROUGH TACTICS MUST BE AVOIDED."

The testimony of plaintiff and others was that this apprehension was conducted in a reckless, oppressive, insulting, and willful manner. . . . Here, the jury found a factual basis for the punitive award and we cannot say that the jury's award of punitive damages was against the manifest weight of the evidence. . . .

[Judgment affirmed.]

Intentional Infliction of Emotional Distress. Mental pain and anxiety have long been recognized as an element of damages in other personal torts such as assault, battery, and false imprisonment. Perhaps because of the difficulty of proof and fear of false or trivial claims, tort law was slow to recognize intentional infliction of mental injury as a separate tort theory. Modern courts, however, allow compensation in tort for intentionally imposed severe emotional distress and the resulting bodily injury if the defendant's conduct is "extreme and outrageous." To recover, the plaintiff must prove (1) outrageous conduct by the defendant, (2) the defendant's intent to cause (or reckless disregard of the probability of causing) emotional distress, and (3) the plaintiff's suffering extreme and severe emotional distress caused by the defendant's conduct.

Clearly, this test is imprecise and does not permit recovery for most insults, threats, annoyances, bad manners, rudeness, or other realities of modern life. Its application depends upon the particular circumstances of each case. Courts have allowed recovery for (1) spreading a false rumor that the plaintiff's spouse or child had been seriously injured or committed suicide, (2) threatening to lynch or beat up the plaintiff unless he left town or signed an agreement, (3) invitations to illicit intercourse accompanied by repeated badgering and hounding, (4) abusive tactics by debt collectors such as harassing phone calls, threats, or abusive language,[3] (5) bullying tactics by insurance adjusters seeking to force a settlement, (6) threats or verbal abuse of particularly susceptible persons such as invalids,

children, or pregnant women, and (7) mishandling or mutilation of dead bodies by funeral directors, hospitals, and others.

Defamation. The law has long protected, through a tort action for **defamation,** a person's interest in his or her reputation and good name. To recover for defamation, the plaintiff must prove that a false and defamatory statement was made and communicated or "published"[4] to a third party, and that the defendant was at fault in disseminating the defamatory statement. As defined by the *Restatement (Second) of Torts,* a communication is defamatory if it "tends so to harm the reputation of another as to lower him in the estimation of the community or to deter third persons from associating or dealing with him."[5] Liability for defamation requires the statements to be *false* and defamatory. Truth is an absolute defense to a defamation action, even if the statement is inspired solely by ill will toward the plaintiff and for the purpose of injuring or destroying his reputation.

A defamatory communication may be a statement of fact: Betty says to Carol, "Andy is a liar, a drunk, an adulterer, and a thief." Or it may be a statement of opinion, if the comment creates the impression that the opinion is based upon undisclosed defamatory facts: Bob says to Carol, "I think my next door neighbor, Alice, is involved in an auto theft ring." The jury might find that this is not a mere expression of opinion, but implies that Bob knows undisclosed facts which justify the opinion. In this case, Bob's opinion is defamatory.

Defamatory statements can be directed against a particular living individual, a group, or a class. An individual member of a group may recover if the group is small enough so that the statement can be reasonably interpreted as referring to a particular member, or if the circumstances clearly indicate that the statement refers to that particular member. Assume Robert, at a party, states "all doctors are

---

3. Abusive debt collection practices are now regulated by federal law—see discussion in Chapter 29.

4. An action for defamation protects reputation, a "relational" interest involving the opinion others in the community hold regarding the plaintiff. Accordingly, defamation requires that the defamatory statement be communicated by the defendant to a person other than the one defamed.

5. *Restatement (Second) of Torts* §559.

incompetent and dishonest.'' Charles, one of 100 local doctors, has not been defamed. If, however, Charles was at the party and the only doctor present, persons present might reasonably believe Robert was specifically referring to Charles. A corporation or partnership may also be defamed if the statement discredits the way it does business or deters others from dealing with it. Though a corporation or partnership has no reputation in a personal sense, it has a business reputation that is entitled to protection. Thus, defamatory statements concerning a business's credit, honesty, or efficiency are actionable.

Libel and Slander Distinguished. The law recognizes two forms of action for defamatory publications, libel and slander. **Libel** involves the publication of a defamatory statement by written or printed words (as in a newspaper, book, or magazine), by its embodiment in other physical form, (as in a picture or statue), or by radio or television communication. **Slander,** on the other hand, involves communication of the defamatory statement by spoken words or gestures, such as the nod of the head, a wink, or hand gesture.

The importance of the distinction between libel and slander lies in the requirements for proving damages. If a defamatory statement constitutes libel, injury is presumed and the plaintiff may recover without any proof that his or her reputation has been impaired or any other injury has resulted. The jury is allowed to estimate and assess damages for injury to the plaintiff's reputation without actual proof of harm.

If, on the other hand, the defamatory statements are merely slanderous, recovery is allowed without proof of actual damage in only four situations. These include slanderous statements that the plaintiff (1) has committed a crime punishable by imprisonment or that is regarded as involving ''moral turpitude,'' (2) has contracted a ''loathsome'' (venereal) disease, (3) has engaged in conduct that adversely affects his fitness to perform his business, trade, or profession, or (4) has been guilty of serious sexual misconduct, such as adultery. A slanderous statement relating to conduct other than that outlined above is actionable only if the plaintiff is able to prove ''special harm''—the loss of something having monetary or economic value. Thus, a

person slandering another by calling him a ''bastard'' or ''liar'' is not liable in the absence of proof of specific injury resulting from the statement—for example, if a person overhearing the statement withdraws a job offer previously extended to the plaintiff.

Fault in Defamation Actions. The law of defamation essentially entered a new era in 1964 when the Supreme Court held that defamation actions are limited by the First Amendment, which prohibits laws abridging freedom of speech and the press. In *New York Times Company v. Sullivan,*[6] the Supreme Court held that a public official, such as an elected official or government employee, is prohibited ''from recovering damages for a defamatory falsehood relating to his official conduct unless he proves that the statement was made with 'actual malice'—that is, with knowledge that it was false or with reckless disregard of whether it was false or not.''[7] Under this test, the defendant is not liable for negligently or inadvertently publishing a defamatory statement (such as by failing to adequately check sources). Actual knowledge of falsity or reckless disregard of the truth is required. Subsequent Supreme Court decisions have extended this ''knowledge-reckless disregard'' rule to candidates for public office and public figures. ''Public figures'' include both persons who have achieved pervasive fame or notoriety (who are public figures for all purposes in all contexts) and those who voluntarily inject themselves into a particular public controversy (who become public figures for a limited range of issues).

This rule is designed to prevent use of defamation actions to deter free discussion and criticism of public issues and persons by the press. As noted by the Court in the *New York Times* case,

> [W]e consider this case against the background of a profound national commitment to the principle that debate on public issues should be uninhibited, robust, and wide-open, and that it may well include vehement, caustic, and sometimes un-

---

6. 84 S. Ct. 710 (1964).
7. 84 S. Ct. at 726; *Restatement (Second) of Torts* §580A.

pleasantly sharp attacks on government and public officials.[8]

Liability for defamation is expanded if the defamatory statement relates to a private person or to a public figure or official concerning a purely private matter. Like public officials and public figures, private individuals may recover for statements made with knowledge of falsity or reckless disregard of the truth. Private plaintiffs, however, may also recover for false and defamatory statements published merely as a result of the defendant's negligence.[9] Thus, the press is insulated from defamation actions for nonnegligent mistakes reporting newsworthy events concerning private individuals.

At issue in the following case was whether the plaintiff was a public figure.

Waldbaum v. Fairchild Publications, Inc.
627 F.2d 1287 (D.C. Cir. 1980)

Greenbelt Consumer Services, Inc. (Greenbelt) is a diversified consumer cooperative that owns retail supermarkets, furniture and gift stores, and automobile service stations. Plaintiff Eric Waldbaum was president and chief executive officer of Greenbelt from January, 1971, to March, 1976. When Greenbelt dismissed Waldbaum, *Supermarket News,* a trade publication owned by defendant Fairchild Publications, Inc. (Fairchild), published an article stating in part that Greenbelt had "been losing money the last year and retrenching."

Waldbaum sued Fairchild for libel alleging that this statement was false and had damaged his reputation as a businessman. Fairchild argued that Waldbaum was a public figure and should be denied recovery because the alleged misstatement had not been made with actual malice. Waldbaum asserted that he was not a public figure and, therefore, should be entitled to damages if he could prove that

---

8. 84 S. Ct. at 721.
9. *Gertz v. Robert Welch, Inc.,* 94 S. Ct. 2997, 3010-3011 (1974); *Restatement (Second) of Torts* §580B; Discussion of negligence law begins later in this chapter.

---

the false statement had been made negligently. The trial court held that Waldbaum was a public figure and granted summary judgment for Fairchild. Waldbaum appealed.

Tamm, Circuit Judge
. . . In [*Gertz v. Robert Welch, Inc.,* 94 S. Ct. 2997 (1974)] the Court focused on the public or private status of the plaintiff in determining how to protect simultaneously individual reputation, freedom of the press, and public debate. It found that a private individual has little means of redressing a defamatory statement except by legal action. . . . It therefore held that a state may allow a private person to recover for defamation under any standard, as long as that standard does not impose liability without fault. . . .

This balance shifts, however, when one turns from private persons to public officials or figures. First, those who enter the public spotlight have greater access to the media to correct misstatements about them, as shown by their preexisting media exposure. . . . More important . . . public figures "invite attention and comment," . . . 94 S. Ct. at 3009. They thus accept the risk that the press, in fulfilling its role of reporting, analyzing, and commenting on well-known persons and public controversies, will focus on them and, perhaps, cast them in an unfavorable light. . . . Although these generalities may not fit every situation exactly, they draw a relatively clear line for the press to follow. . . .

With this background, we turn to the standards themselves for determining when a person is a public figure. A court first must ask whether the plaintiff is a public figure for all purposes. . . . [A] general public figure is a well-known "celebrity," his name a "household word." The public recognizes him and follows his words and deeds, either because it regards his ideas, conduct, or judgment as worthy of its attention or because he actively pursues that consideration.

As a general rule, a person who meets this test has access to the media if defamed. . . . In general, too, the person has assumed the risk that public exposure might lead to misstatements about him . . . the media serve as a check on the power of the famous, and that check must be strongest when the subject's influence is strongest. . . .

Few people, of course, attain the general notoriety that would make them public figures for all purposes. Nevertheless, many persons "have thrust themselves to the forefront of particular public controversies in order to influence the resolution of the issues involved." *Gertz v. Robert Welch, Inc.,* . . . 94 S. Ct. at 3009. . . .

As the first step in its inquiry, the court must isolate the public controversy. A public controversy is not simply a matter of interest to the public; it must be a real dispute, the outcome of which affects the general public or some segment of it in an appreciable way. The Supreme Court has made clear that essentially private concerns or disagreements do not become public controversies simply because they attract attention. . . . Rather, a public controversy is a dispute that in fact has received public attention because its ramifications will be felt by persons who are not direct participants. . . .

Once the court has defined the controversy, it must analyze the plaintiff's role in it. Trivial or tangential participation is not enough. . . . The plaintiff either must have been purposely trying to influence the outcome or could realistically have been expected, because of his position in the controversy, to have an impact on its resolution. In undertaking this analysis, a court can look to the plaintiff's past conduct, the extent of press coverage, and the public reaction to his conduct and statements. . . .

With the foregoing analysis in mind, we now must determine whether Judge Corcoran correctly concluded that Waldbaum was a public figure. . . . Fairchild concedes that he was not a general-purpose public figure. . . .

Evidence submitted with Fairchild's motion for summary judgment indicates clearly that Greenbelt was an innovative company often the subject of news reports. As the second largest cooperative in the nation it attracted attention, and its pathbreaking marketing policies—e.g., unit pricing, open dating, and highly competitive advertising—became the subject of public debate within the supermarket industry and beyond. . . .

[Waldbaum] has admitted that as president and chief executive officer, he pursued these policies and other consumer-oriented activities. . . . He felt that educating the community at large was one function of a cooperative such as Greenbelt. . . .

Being an executive within a prominent and influential company does not by itself make one a public figure. In many cases, a corporate official is simply a conduit for announcing and administering company policies made by others. Similarly, many executives who do make corporate policy do not thereby take stands in public controversies. These descriptions, however, do not fit Eric Waldbaum at Greenbelt. His own deposition indicates that he was the mover and shaper of many of the cooperative's controversial actions. . . . In short, as Judge Corcoran so aptly put it, "he did not become merely a boardroom president whose vision was limited to the balance sheet. He became an activist, projecting his own image and that of the cooperative far beyond the dollars and cents aspects of marketing." . . . Given Greenbelt's prominence, his activities certainly extended beyond those of a profit-maximizing manager of a single firm.

Thus, it would appear to a reasonable person that Waldbaum had thrust himself into the public controversies concerning unit pricing, open dating, the cooperative form of business, and other issues. He did so in an attempt to influence the policies of firms in the supermarket industry and merchandising generally. In the process, he assumed the risk that comment in the press might turn to the successfulness or profitability of enterprises under his management, for the commercial success or failure of the actions he was advocating certainly is strong evidence in the public debate over whether other firms should adopt them. Furthermore, Waldbaum had prior dealings with the media. . . . Although he personally was not frequently the subject of articles, he was somewhat familiar with press operations and had held press conferences to discuss Greenbelt's policies and operations. Looking at the overall picture we conclude that Waldbaum was a public figure for the limited purpose of comment on Greenbelt's—and his own—innovation policies and that the article giving rise to this action was within the protected sphere of reporting. Because Fairchild concededly did not act with "actual malice," it was entitled to summary judgment. . . .

[Judgment affirmed.]

Invasion of Privacy. In the early twentieth century,[10] courts began to recognize invasions of privacy as compensable in a tort action. The **right to privacy** is generally defined as simply the right to be left alone. For example, an invasion of privacy action may provide compensation for the following types of interference:

1. Intentional intrusions, highly offensive to a reasonable person, into a person's solitude or private affairs. For example, a person may recover for another's spying through windows, tapping telephone wires, or making harassing phone calls or visits.

2. Wrongful appropriation of another's name or likeness. For example, a person may be held liable for using another's name or picture to promote the defendant's product, business, or other commercial venture.

3. Publicity portraying a person in an objectionably false light if the defendant knows the portrayal is false or that it recklessly disregards the truth. If the false publicity given to the plaintiff is also defamatory, an invasion of privacy action provides an additional or alternative remedy.

Misuse of Legal Proceedings. The law generally allows free access to the courts to resolve civil disputes. In certain cases private individuals may also institute criminal proceedings. Despite this general policy favoring use of legal proceedings, tort law protects individuals against unjustifiable criminal and civil litigation commenced by other private individuals.

Malicious Prosecution. The only proper purpose of a criminal proceeding is to bring an offender to justice, thereby aiding in enforcement of the criminal law. A private person who commences a criminal case against another for any other purpose is therefore liable for **malicious prosecution** if he or she initiates the case without reason to believe that the accused has committed a crime, and the case is ultimately terminated in favor of the accused.[11] Improper purposes include ill will or animosity toward the accused, or a desire to gain a private advantage, such as to force payment of a debt. Even if the case is commenced for an improper purpose, however, no recovery is allowed if the plaintiff is proven guilty.

Wrongful Use of Civil Proceedings. Liability may be imposed upon a person who files a civil lawsuit known to be based upon manufactured or perjured testimony, or solely because of animosity or ill will, or to force a settlement not related to the merits of the claim (a "nuisance" suit). Liability also may be imposed upon a defendant who files a spurious counterclaim solely to delay prompt consideration of the plaintiff's original claim.

Abuse of Process. An **abuse of process,** which often accompanies misuse of civil or criminal proceedings, occurs when a person uses a legal process to accomplish a purpose for which it was neither designed nor intended. For example, both malicious prosecution and an abuse of process occur when a person files a false criminal complaint against another in order to extort payment of a debt. Or, assume Alan institutes proceedings against his father, Bob, to have him committed to a mental institution. Bob is not incompetent and Alan's sole purpose in filing the case is to obtain control of Bob's assets after he is committed. Alan is liable in tort to Bob for an abuse of process.

Intentional Interference with Property

Interests in property are classified as either real or personal (see Chapter 6). Real property includes interests in land, and personal property includes anything else that can be owned. Personal property with tangible physical existence, such as automobiles, clothing, and appliances, is commonly known as a "chattel." Tort law protects against

---

10. *Pavesich v. New England Life Ins. Co.,* 50 S.E. 68 (Ga. 1905).

11. Most criminal cases are commenced by public prosecutors, such as district attorneys and United States attorneys. A public prosecutor is absolutely privileged to initiate criminal cases. Accordingly, malicious prosecution cases are maintained only against private individuals who initiate criminal cases.

interference with an owner's right to possess and use real property through an action for trespass and nuisance. The right to use and possess personal property is protected through actions for conversion and trespass to chattels.

Trespass. A person is liable for **trespass** if he or she intentionally interferes with another's right to exclusive possession of real property. Trespass occurs if, without permission or legal privilege, a person intentionally (1) enters land possessed by another, (2) causes anything or anyone to enter onto the land, (3) remains on the land, or (4) fails to remove from the land a thing which he is under a duty to remove. Liability for trespass may be imposed even though the trespasser's presence causes no harm to the land, its possessor, or other thing or person on the land. Thus, an intentional intrusion upon land in possession of another is a trespass even if the actor is mistaken concerning the right or privilege to enter. Assume Beth reasonably mistakes the location of the property line between her property and her neighbor, Ann. As a result, Beth occupies a six-foot strip of Ann's land. Beth is liable to Ann for trespass.

Nuisance. The legal term **nuisance** refers to a human activity conducted on land or a physical condition of land that is harmful or annoying to neighboring landowners or members of the public generally. Under some circumstances, a person responsible for creating or maintaining a nuisance on his property may be subject to criminal sanctions. In other cases, the person responsible for a nuisance may be liable in tort for injuries caused by the nuisance. The nature and extent of the liability depends on whether a ''public'' (or ''common'') nuisance or ''private'' nuisance is involved.

Public Nuisance. A **public nuisance** involves invasion of public rights, those common to all members of the public. It is essentially a catch-all minor *criminal* offense encompassing a wide range of miscellaneous conduct offensive to public health, safety, morals, peace, and comfort. All states have statutes declaring certain specified conduct or conditions to be public nuisances. Examples include houses of prostitution; buildings used

in commission of other criminal offenses (such as storage of contraband); obstruction of or encroachment upon public highways, streets, and navigable waterways; storage or manufacture of explosives in the midst of a city; maintenance of diseased animals or other conditions injurious to public health (such as a pond breeding mosquitoes); pollution of air by odors, dust, or smoke; excessively loud or continuous noises; and pollution of streams, lakes, or other bodies of water. In addition to criminal sanctions, an incidental private tort damage remedy has also been developed to compensate those members of the public who suffer particular harm, distinct from that suffered by members of the public in general.

Private Nuisance. Unlike the public nuisance, a **private nuisance** is a strictly private *tort* remedy, closely related to the tort of trespass. Private nuisance is designed to protect against invasions of the private interest in the *use and enjoyment of land,* whereas trespass protects against wrongful interference with *possession of land.* Private ''use and enjoyment'' refers to that use of land a person is privileged to make as an individual, not as a member of the general public. The law protects not only the ''interest'' in present use and enjoyment for residential, agricultural, commercial, industrial, or other purposes, but also the pleasure, comfort, and enjoyment normally derived from occupancy of land.

The types of conduct constituting a private nuisance are infinitely variable. The activity involved may interfere with the physical condition of the land itself, such as vibration due to blasting or manufacturing, destruction of trees or crops, flooding, or polluting water. It may affect the possessor's comfort or enjoyment by the intrusion of loud noises (for example, due to barking dogs or a manufacturing process), excessive smoke, gas, light, heat, fumes, or odors. Or, it may simply affect the possessor's peace of mind or threaten future injury (such as a neighbor keeping a vicious dog or storing explosives or other dangerous materials). Most nuisances are intentional only in the sense that the defendant has created or continued a condition with knowledge that an interference with plaintiff's interest will occur or has occurred.

Not all intentional interference with the private use and enjoyment of land is actionable. The law of nuisance represents an attempt to balance the conflicting interests of landowners. These interests are, on one hand, the general principle that a person should be able to use his property as he sees fit, and, on the other, the opposing principle that a person is bound to use his property in such a manner as not to unreasonably interfere with the use and enjoyment of neighboring property. The court must, therefore, make a comparative evaluation of these competing interests to determine whether or not tort liability should be imposed.

This comparative evaluation is made by testing the "reasonableness" of the defendant's conduct. In other words, an intentional interference with the use and enjoyment of another's land is actionable as a private nuisance only if the invasion is both substantial and *unreasonable*. An intentional interference is unreasonable if the gravity (seriousness) of the harm outweighs the utility (meritoriousness) of the actor's conduct.[12]

Conversion and Trespass to Chattels. Unreasonable interference with use and possession of tangible personal property is compensable in tort through an action for conversion or, for less severe intrusions, trespass to chattels. **Conversion** occurs when one person intentionally exercises control over a chattel belonging to another, which so seriously interferes with the owner's right to control it that the possessor "may justly be required to pay the other the full value of the chattel."[13] In other words, a person who has "converted" another's goods to his own use is effectively forced to buy the property from the owner.

Conversion occurs in various ways including dispossessing the owner—taking the chattel from his possession without his consent or through fraud or duress, destroying or altering the property, or using it in a manner that seriously interferes with the owner's right of use. Whether the interference is serious enough to constitute conversion is a matter of degree, dependent upon the circumstances of the particular case. Assume Ted entrusts his car to Bill, a used car dealer, to be sold. Bill drives the car once for ten miles on a personal errand. Bill has not converted the car. If, however, he drives the car 5,000 miles, a conversion occurs, requiring him to pay Ted the value of the car. The same result occurs if Bill substantially alters the car, destroys it, or refuses to return it at Ted's request.

Although conversion is always an *intentional* exercise of control over another's property, the converter merely must intend to exercise control over the chattel; no intent to interfere with another's rights is required. Thus, a defendant who mistakenly believes that she has the right to possession or consent of the owner is not relieved of liability. For example, a person who innocently buys stolen goods is liable to their owner for conversion.

Sometimes, a person interferes with possession or use of another's property or impairs its physical condition, quality, or value without actually converting the property. In this case, the owner may recover for any loss sustained through an action for **trespass to chattels.** Generally speaking, a mere technical trespass is insufficient to establish liability; actual injury must be shown. For example, if Ann pets Pat's dog, no liability for trespass to chattels results. Ann would, however, be liable for kicking and injuring Pat's dog. A possessor is nevertheless privileged to use reasonable force against others to prevent even harmless interference with possession of her chattels.

Intentional Interference with Business Relations

A contract is a legally enforceable promise or set of promises. Contract law, which forms the basis of many business relationships, is a distinct and well-developed area of law that is discussed in detail in Chapters 7 through 19 of this text. Tort law extends protection to contracts by imposing liability for intentional interference with the performance of contracts, a tort now recognized by almost all states. Under §766 of the *Restatement (Second) of Torts,* a person who "intentionally and improperly

---

12. Some of the factors considered in weighing the *gravity of the harm* are (1) the extent of the harm, (2) the character of the harm, and (3) the social value of the type of use or enjoyment invaded. Factors relevant in ascertaining the *utility* of the conduct include (1) the social value of the conduct attacked as a nuisance, (2) the suitability of the conduct to the character of the locality, and (3) the impracticability of preventing or avoiding the invasion.

13. *Restatement (Second) of Torts* §222A(1).

interferes with the performance of a contract'' between two other persons ''by inducing or otherwise causing'' one of them not to perform is liable in tort for damages to the other party to the broken contract. Some states also extend protection to advantageous business relationships or expectancies not amounting to contracts through the tort of intentional interference with prospective contractual relations.

To establish a claim for intentional interference with the performance of a contract, the plaintiff must prove that the defendant knew that the plaintiff had entered into a contract with another party and that the defendant improperly or unjustifiably caused that party to breach (not to perform) the contract. A defendant who induces the breach through illegal or otherwise tortious conduct clearly acts improperly. Assume, for example, that Chris contracts to deliver goods to Barbara and that Fred, with knowledge of this contract, intentionally destroys the goods. Fred would be liable to Barbara for intentional interference with contract. Many cases, however, involve conduct that is not so clearly wrongful, requiring courts to apply a balancing test that considers the nature of the defendant's conduct and motive, the nature of the contract, and the interests and relations of the parties. Since the classic English case *Lumley v. Gye* (1853),[14] courts have allowed recovery even if the means to induce the breach were not illegal or tortious. Thus, for example, if ABC Co. knowingly induces Robin to breach her employment contract with XYZ, Inc. by offering her a higher salary, ABC Co. may be held liable to XYZ, Inc. for intentional interference with contract.

The tort of intentional interference with prospective contractual relation is not as clearly defined in the case law. Section 766B of *Restatement (Second) of Torts* provides that a defendant intentionally and improperly interferes with the plaintiff's prospective contractual relation by inducing or otherwise causing another not to enter into or continue the prospective relation, or by preventing another from acquiring or continuing the prospective relation. If, for example, Arnold and Juanita are negotiating a contract and Leonard unjustifiably tells Juanita that he will sue her if she enters into the contract, Leonard may be held liable to either Arnold or Juanita for interference with the prospective contractual relation. As in intentional interference with contract, many cases involve a defendant who engages in tortious or illegal conduct, such as defamation or antitrust law violations, to prevent others from entering into a contract. In such cases, courts usually hold the defendant liable for intentional interference with prospective contractual relation. In other cases, courts use the same balancing test described above to evaluate the defendant's conduct. Additionally, several defenses are available to the defendant including, most importantly, competition. Generally, if a competitor interferes with a prospective contract, the competitor is not liable if the competitor is acting in its own interest and does not act tortiously or illegally. So, for example, if Robin is negotiating an employment contract with ABC Co. and XYZ, Inc., a competitor, offers her a higher salary which Robin accepts, XYZ would not be liable for interference with the prospective contract. If, however, XYZ acted wrongfully, for instance by slandering Robin causing ABC to discontinue negotiations, XYZ may be liable.

The following case illustrates the principles of intentional interference with contract. Note that the case is complicated by the fact that the contract is terminable at will; that is, either party is entitled to terminate the contract at any time. As a result, the case in many ways resembles an action for intentional interference with prospective contractual relation.

Williams v. Chittenden Trust Company
484 A.2d 911 (Vt. 1984)

The plaintiff Robert Williams, an architect, contracted with the owner of land in Fayston, Vermont to design a 64-unit condominium project. After completion of 28 units, the owner encountered financial difficulties and considered abandoning the project. Instead, the owner contacted the defendant Schleicher-Soper Architects, an architectural firm, seeking information about the possibility of improving the marketability of the condominium project

---

14. 2 El. & Bl. 216, 118 Eng. Rep. 749 (Q.B. 1853).

and reducing its construction costs. Using plans and drawings prepared by Williams, Schleicher-Soper recommended changes that it incorporated into the plans at the owner's request. After authorizing Schleicher-Soper to prepare more detailed plans, the owner notified Williams that the project had been abandoned and cancelled the contract with Williams. The owner then contracted with Schleicher-Soper to serve as architect and completed the condominium project.

Williams sued Schleicher-Soper alleging that the architectural firm had committed the tort of intentional interference with contractual relations. A jury found in favor of Williams and Schleicher-Soper appealed.

Hill, Justice

. . . This Court [has] recognized the existence of the tort of interference with contractual relations. . . . The elements of this tort are . . . set forth in §766 of the *Restatement (Second) of Torts*. . . . [To] be liable for interference with a contractual relationship [under the *Restatement* test], the defendant must have intentionally and improperly induced or caused the owner not to perform under its contract with the plaintiff. A review of the record in this case convinces us that the plaintiff presented sufficient evidence of intentional and improper inducement.

Intent to interfere with a contractual relationship exists if "the actor acts for the primary purpose of interfering with the performance of the contract, and also if he [or she] desires to interfere, even though he [or she] acts for some other purpose in addition." *Restatement (Second) of Torts* § 766 comment j (1979). Intent also exists if the actor does not act with the desire to interfere with the contract but knows that interference will be substantially certain to occur as a result of his or her action. . . .

At the first meeting between the defendant and the owner in this case, the defendant was told that the plaintiff was the designer of the project. The defendant was also given copies of the plaintiff's drawings before the defendant began its own drawings. Thus, the evidence showed that, before it began its drawings, the defendant either knew or had reason to know of the existence of the contract between the plaintiff and the owner. Knowledge of

the existence of the contract is a prerequisite to being found liable for interfering with that contract. . . . Knowledge of the existence of the contract is not automatically the equivalent of intent to interfere with the contract. However, from the evidence produced in this case, a reasonable jury could conclude that the defendant knew its actions would interfere with the plaintiff's contract, since by preparing detailed plans and drawings, the defendant was providing the same services as those the plaintiff was to provide under the contract. The jury could also find intent from the fact that the defendant knew the project was experiencing financial difficulties, and the defendant's services were being offered at a cheaper cost than the plaintiff's services were to be provided under the terms of the contract.

The plaintiff also presented sufficient evidence for the jury to find that the defendant "induced or otherwise caused" the owner not to perform under its contract with the plaintiff. Although it was the owner and not the defendant who initiated their first contact, the owner had not yet decided, at that time, to terminate its contract with the plaintiff. The defendant then offered to perform architectural services for the owner at a price substantially below that charged by the plaintiff, and at a time when the owner's project was suffering from serious financial difficulties. The inducement required for the tort of interference with a contract need not rise to the level of coercion, threats, or compulsion. . . . The jury may find that inducement exists if the defendant's acts caused the owner not to perform its contract with the plaintiff. . . .

Finally, we think the plaintiff presented sufficient evidence to convince the jury that the defendant's actions were "improper." The defendant argues that the contract between the owner and the plaintiff was terminable at will, and that . . . the defendant's interference with the contract was allowed competition and not improper interference. This Court has held, however, that "[p]rotection is appropriate against unjustified interference with reasonable expectancies of profit though the contract is terminable at will or unenforceable against the promiser in an adversary proceeding. [In addition,] there is no legal right . . . knowingly [to] invade the contract relation of others solely to promote the intervenor's financial interest." *Mit-*

chell v. Aldrich [163 A.2d 833, 836, 837 (Vt. 1960)]. . . .

[Judgment affirmed.]

Negligence

"Negligence" Defined

Most tort liability is not based upon conduct intended to cause injury; rather, it is imposed for negligence—conduct which creates an unreasonable *risk* of injury. As noted in the *Restatement (Second) of Torts,* **negligence** is "conduct which falls below the standard established by law for the protection of others against unreasonable risk of harm."[15] The standard of conduct "established by law" to which a person must conform to avoid being negligent is that of a "reasonable" person under like circumstances. That is, negligence is "the omission to do something which a reasonable man, guided upon those considerations which ordinarily regulate the conduct of human affairs, would do, or doing something which a prudent and reasonable man would not do."[16]

Negligence alone, however, does not subject a person to tort liability. To recover in a cause of action based upon negligence, the plaintiff must prove

1. that the defendant owed the plaintiff a legal duty not to be negligent,
2. that the defendant breached that duty by failing to act as a reasonable person would act under the circumstances,
3. that the defendant's negligence was the "proximate" or "legal" cause of an injury suffered by the plaintiff, and
4. that the plaintiff suffered actual loss, damage, or injury as a result of the defendant's conduct.

The law of negligence is of fairly recent origin, recognized as a separate tort only during the early part of the nineteenth century. It grew dramatically in importance when it was used to compensate for injuries caused by the industrial revolution and early railroads. Today, the law of negligence is the dominant legal theory to provide compensation for accidental injury.

Standard of Conduct—The "Reasonable Person"

To avoid liability for negligence, a person must conform his or her conduct to that of a "reasonable person" under similar circumstances. The **reasonable person** is a hypothetical, fictitious person who possesses characteristics of attentiveness, knowledge, intelligence, and judgment required by society for the protection of others. The reasonable person is therefore a personification of the community ideal of reasonable behavior, possessing only those human weaknesses or frailties that the community will tolerate under the circumstances. Against this objective of external standard—the conduct of a reasonable person under the circumstances—the defendant's conduct is compared to determine whether negligence liability should be imposed.

Although the reasonable person generally represents a uniform standard, certain persons are judged by more lenient standards. For example, although a person's insanity or other mental illness does not relieve him from liability for conduct unbecoming a reasonable person, physical disability may. That is, a person who is ill or otherwise physically disabled must conform his conduct to that of a reasonable person under a similar disability. To avoid liability for negligence, children, as well, need only conform their conduct to that of a reasonable person of similar age, intelligence, and experience under the circumstances. On the other hand, persons with superior skill or competence, such as doctors, attorneys, architects, engineers, or accountants, avoid negligence liability only by exercising the amount of care that is reasonable in light of their superior learning, experience, or ability.

The standard of conduct of a reasonable person may be determined in various ways. Initially, a statute or administrative regulation may establish a minimum level of conduct and provide that a violation is negligence. Even in the absence of express

---

15. *Restatement (Second) of Torts* §282.
16. *Blyth v. Birmingham Waterworks Co.,* 11 Ex. 781, 784, 156 Eng. Rep. 1047, 1049 (Ex. 1856).

provision for tort liability, courts often adopt the requirements of a statute or regulation as defining negligence.[17] In this case, an unexcused violation of the statute or regulation is negligent in itself (negligent "per se"); no further evidence of negligence is required. Courts have used this approach, for example, to impose liability upon defendants for injuries to employees, hotel guests, restaurant patrons, and members of the public caused by violations of fire codes, pure food laws, laws requiring safety devices on machinery, and other statutes designed for the protection of others.

If no legislative enactment provides an obligatory standard of conduct, a decision or line of decisions rendered by the jurisdiction's appellate courts often define the reasonable person standard applicable to a wide variety of fact situations. For example, judicial decisions in most states define the standard of care required of a locomotive engineer approaching a highway crossing and a motor vehicle driver approaching the same crossing to determine liability for the many accidents occurring at railroad grade crossings.

In the absence of statute or judicial decision governing the particular facts of the case, the court (judge) may determine on its own whether the defendant was negligent. Usually, the court will instruct the jury in the law of negligence, and let the jury compare the defendant's conduct to that of a reasonable person under the circumstances. The reasonable person standard provides flexibility allowing the jury to consider the particular circumstances and individuals of the case, while furnishing, as far as possible, a uniform standard of conduct.

Proximate Cause

To recover in an action for negligence, the plaintiff must prove some reasonable connection between the defendant's conduct and the injury sustained by

the plaintiff. In legal terms, courts state that the defendant's conduct must be the "proximate" or "legal" cause of the injury. The concept of **proximate cause** comprises a number of legal issues that collectively limit the defendant's liability for the consequences of his or her negligent acts. In resolving proximate causation issues, two basic questions are commonly presented: (1) Did the defendant's conduct *in fact* cause the injury? That is, did the defendant's negligent act or omission trigger a sequence of events that ultimately resulted in the plaintiff's injury? (2) Assuming a causal connection can be established between the negligence and the injury, did the defendant owe a duty to the particular injured plaintiff to protect him or her against the event that in fact caused the injury? These two questions are discussed below.

Causation in Fact. At its most basic level, proximate causation requires proof that the defendant's negligent conduct (either an act or failure to act) in fact caused the plaintiff's injury. The issue is generally a matter for the trier of fact, usually the jury, to decide. Courts have developed two basic rules to determine causation in fact.

"But-for" or "Sine Qua Non" Test. Under this test, the defendant's conduct is the proximate cause of the injury if the injury would not have occurred *but for* that conduct. If the event would have occurred whether or not the defendant had been negligent, the defendant's negligence is not the proximate cause of the harm. For example, assume Don owns a car in need of brake repair. Despite the long stopping distances required, he continues to drive the car, a negligent act. While Don is driving the car slowly in a residential neighborhood, Phillip, a child, darts from behind a parked car and is hit and seriously injured by Don's car. Evidence at trial proves that even if the brakes had been in the best of condition, Don could not have stopped in time to avoid hitting Phillip. Don's negligence is not the proximate cause of Phillip's injury.

"Substantial-Factor" Test. The "but-for" test resolves most causation questions but proves inadequate when two or more acts of negligence bring about the injury. To resolve this case, many

---

17. To guide the court, §286 of the *Restatement (Second) of Torts* provides that the court should find negligence in violations of statutes or regulations whose purpose is: (1) to protect the class of persons including the person or persons injured, (2) to protect the particular interest invaded by the violation, and (3) to protect that interest against the kind of harm that has resulted and the particular hazard causing the harm.

courts use the *substantial factor* test. Under this test, when separate acts of negligence combine to produce a single injury, each tort-feasor is responsible for the entire result even if his or her act alone might not have caused it. That is, a defendant's negligence need not be the only cause, or the last or nearest cause. Liability is imposed upon any defendant whose negligence is a substantial factor in causing the plaintiff's injury.[18]

Foreseeability of Harm. Tort liability is not necessarily imposed simply by showing that the defendant's negligent conduct was a substantial factor in producing the plaintiff's injury. Negligent conduct may injure one or thousands of people in various ways and trigger a chain of events causing injuries far removed in time and place from the original negligent act. The difficult question the law must answer is whether the defendant should be liable to all potential plaintiffs for all consequences of his negligent conduct or whether some limitation on the extent of liability should be recognized.

The classic case addressing this issue is *Palsgraf v. Long Island Railroad Company* (1928).[19] In this case, a passenger carrying a package was attempting to board a train operated by defendant Long Island Railroad as the train left the station. The defendant's employees, in attempting to assist the passenger to board the train, negligently knocked the package from the passenger's arms and it landed on the track. The package contained fireworks, which exploded. Either the explosion or the stampede of frightened passengers knocked over some heavy scales at the other end of the platform, which struck Palsgraf causing injuries for which she sued.

On these facts, Judge Benjamin Cardozo, speaking for the majority, found the railroad not liable because there had been no negligence toward the plaintiff. In his opinion negligence was based upon the relation between the parties, and therefore must be grounded upon the foreseeability of harm to the person in fact injured. Thus, although the employees had been negligent toward the holder of the package, they had not been negligent to the plaintiff, standing far away, outside the zone of apparent danger. As noted by Judge Cardozo: "The plaintiff sues in her own right for a wrong personal to her, and not as the vicarious beneficiary of a breach of duty to another."[20]

The rule of *Palsgraf*—that there is no liability for negligence to the unforeseeable plaintiff—has been widely cited and probably represents the majority rule on the issue. Yet it has been frequently and harshly criticized by many courts and commentators, including three dissenting judges in *Palsgraf* itself. As noted by Judge Andrews in dissent:

> Due care is a duty imposed on each one of us to protect society from unnecessary danger, not to protect A, B, or C alone. . . .
>
> The proposition is this: Every one owes to the world at large the duty of refraining from those acts that may unreasonably threaten the safety of others. Such an act occurs. Not only is he wronged to whom harm might reasonably be expected to result, but he also who is in fact injured, even if he be outside what would generally be thought the danger zone.[21]

Despite the *Palsgraf* "foreseeability" limitation, few cases actually restrict liability short of holding the defendant liable for all injury of which his negligence is a substantial cause. The fact that the negligent defendant "neither foresaw nor should have foreseen the extent of the harm or the manner in which it occurred does not prevent him from being liable."[22] Further, the foreseeability is a matter of hindsight, measured from the court's point of view looking back upon events which in fact occurred, not from what the defendant should have foreseen at the time of the accident. Under this test, the defendant is relieved of liability only if "looking

---

18. In determining whether a given defendant's negligence is a substantial factor in causing injury, the following circumstances are considered: (1) the number of other factors contributing to the injury, (2) whether the defendant's conduct has created a force (or series of forces) in active and continuous operation up to the time of injury or has created a harmless situation unless acted upon by forces beyond his control, and (3) lapse of time. *Restatement (Second) of Torts* §433.

19. 162 N.E. 99 (N.Y. 1928).

20. 162 N.E. at 100.

21. 162 N.E. at 102–103.

22. *Restatement (Second) of Torts* §435(1).

back from the harm to the actor's negligent conduct, it appears to the court *highly extraordinary* that it should have brought about the harm.''[23] This test appears extremely difficult for a negligent defendant to meet. For example, in one case, a person negligently driving his car crashed into and knocked over a power line pole; the downed power line shut off power to a traffic control box at a remote intersection causing traffic signals to stop functioning; as a result two cars collided at the uncontrolled intersection. On these facts, the accident was held to be a foreseeable consequence of the defendant's negligence.[24] The cases involving what consequences are or are not foreseeable are impossible to reconcile. This confusion results from the difficulty in articulating and applying a standard of foreseeable harm.

Intervening Causes. Although the defendant is negligent, the ultimate injury may occur as a result of a *later* independent cause for which the defendant is not responsible—an intervening cause or force. If the later event is judged a ''supervening'' or ''superceding'' cause, the defendant is relieved of liability for negligence. In determining whether an intervening force is a supervening cause, various factors are considered. These include whether the injury is different in kind from that which would otherwise have resulted from the defendant's negligence, whether the intervening force operates independently of the original negligence or is a normal result of that negligence, and whether the intervening force is due to the act of a third party and the character (negligent, intentional, or criminal) of that act. In short, the test is similar to that previously discussed: the defendant is liable if the intervening cause is ''foreseeable''; if not, the defendant's liability is ''superceded'' by the subsequent event. Most intervening causes including the later negligence of a third party meet this foreseeability requirement. For example, a person who negligently breaks another's leg is also liable for the subsequent negligent treatment of the leg by a doctor. If, however, the injury is caused by a subsequent *intentionally tortious or criminal* act of a third party, which is not within the scope of risk created by the original negligence, the defendant is relieved of liability. Assume Gene, a contractor, digs a trench near a public sidewalk to run a gas pipe. Gene negligently fails to erect a barrier next to the trench. Donna, passing Louise on the sidewalk, negligently bumps into her causing Louise to fall into the trench. Gene is liable to Louise. Had Donna intentionally pushed Louise into the trench, Gene would be relieved of liability.

The following case illustrates basic principles of proximate causation in a negligence case.

Hairston v. Alexander Tank and Equipment Co.
311 S.E.2d 559 (N.C. 1984)

John Hairston purchased a new automobile from Haygood Lincoln-Mercury, Inc. (Haygood). After installing new wheels, Haygood delivered the car to Hairston. As Hairston was approaching a bridge on Interstate 85 approximately 3½ miles from the dealership, the left rear wheel came off the car. Because there was no shoulder on the road, he stopped the car in the far right lane. A passing motorist driving a van stopped his vehicle about 20 feet behind Hairston's car, set the hand brake, turned on his emergency flashers, and telephoned for assistance on his mobile telephone. Traffic continued to pass on the road using the left lane to avoid the stopped vehicles. A flatbed truck owned by Alexander Tank and Equipment Co. (Alexander Tank) and driven by Robert Alexander, struck the van knocking it into the rear of the Hairston automobile. Hairston, who had been standing between his car and the van, was killed.

Plaintiff Bettye Hairston sued both Haygood and Alexander Tank and Equipment Co. for damages alleging that their negligence had caused her husband's death. The evidence established that Haygood had failed to tighten the lug nuts on the wheels thereby causing the wheel to fall off Hairston's car. The evidence also showed that Alexander's negligence caused him to collide with the van that struck and killed Hairston. The jury found both Haygood

---

23. *Restatement (Second) of Torts* §435(2). Emphasis added.

24. *Ferroggiaro v. Bowline,* 315 P.2d 446 (Cal. App. 1957).

and Alexander Tank had acted negligently. The trial court, however, granted Haygood's motion for judgment n.o.v. and held that Alexander's negligence had been the proximate cause of Hairston's death. Upon the appeal of Bettye Hairston and Alexander Tank, the court of appeals affirmed. The North Carolina Supreme Court granted certiorari.

Martin, Justice

. . . In order to establish actionable negligence, plaintiff must show (1) that there has been a failure to exercise proper care in the performance of some legal duty which defendant owed to plaintiff under the circumstances in which they were placed; and (2) that such negligent breach of duty was a proximate cause of the injury. . . .

We agree with the Court of Appeals that the record clearly reveals sufficient evidence from which a jury could find the first requisite of liability, negligence. That Haygood violated a legal duty to this plaintiff in failing to tighten the lug bolts on the left rear wheel and in failing to check the new car before delivery is self-evident.

For reasons which follow, however, it is also our opinion that from the evidence presented at trial the jury could reasonably infer that defendant's negligence was a proximate cause of Hairston's death. The jury could further infer from the facts in this case that while the subsequent negligence of defendant Alexander Tank joined with Haygood's original negligence in proximately causing the death of Hairston, it did not supercede the negligent acts of Haygood and thereby relieve Haygood of liability.

Proximate cause is a cause which in natural and continuous sequence, unbroken by any new and independent cause, produced the plaintiff's injuries, and without which the injuries would not have occurred, and one from which a person of ordinary prudence could have reasonably foreseen that such a result, or consequences of a generally injurious nature, was probable under all the facts as they existed. . . . Foreseeability is thus a requisite of proximate cause, which is, in turn, a requisite for actionable negligence. . . .

It is well settled that the test of foreseeability as an element of proximate cause does not require that defendant should have been able to foresee the injury in the precise form in which it actually occurred. . . .

The law requires only reasonable prevision. A defendant is not required to foresee events which are merely possible but only those which are reasonably foreseeable. . . .

There may be more than one proximate cause of an injury. When two or more proximate causes join and concur in producing the result complained of, the author of each cause may be held for the injuries inflicted. The defendants are jointly and severally liable. . . .

Applying the foregoing to the facts of this case to determine whether the negligence of defendant Haygood was a proximate cause of decedent's death, the decisive question is one of foreseeability. Under the circumstances here disclosed, we believe a jury could find that a reasonably prudent person should have foreseen that Haygood's negligence in failing to tighten the lugs on the wheel of the new automobile could cause the car to be disabled on the highway and struck by another vehicle, causing harm to the driver. Absent Haygood's original negligence, the tragic series of events on I-85 would not have occurred; the danger was foreseeable. Proximate causation is thus established and, with it, defendant's liability.

We turn now to the question whether the evidence in this case is susceptible of the single inference by the jury that Haygood's negligence ceased to be the proximate cause of decedent's death and that it was superseded and insulated by the subsequent negligence of defendant Alexander Tank.

The Court of Appeals found that Alexander was negligent in failing to keep a proper lookout for vehicles stopped on the highway and in failing to keep his vehicle under proper control. "These negligent acts of Alexander—new and independent of any negligent acts of Haygood—constitute the proximate cause of injury and the death of plaintiff's intestate, and the negligence of Haygood was shielded by the subsequent acts of negligence by Alexander." [299 S.E.2d at 795.]

We do not agree with the conclusion of the Court of Appeals. Under the applicable law summarized above, the negligent acts of Alexander quite properly may be found to be a proximate cause of the injury and death in this case: Without Alexander's negligence, the collision would not have occurred; the injury was clearly foreseeable, given the failure to keep a proper lookout. It is also true, of course, that Alexander's unfortunate lack of attention to the road acted independently of Haygood's earlier carelessness. These facts, however, do not of themselves absolve defendant Haygood from his liability.

Insulating negligence means something more than a concurrent and contributing cause. It is not to be invoked as determinative merely upon proof of negligent conduct on the part of each of two persons, acting independently, whose acts unite to cause a single injury. . . . Contributing negligence signifies contribution rather than independent or sole proximate case. . . .

We hold that on the facts of this case a jury might readily find that defendant Haygood could have reasonably foreseen the subsequent acts of Alexander and the resultant harm to Hairston that occurred on I-85, barely six minutes and 3.5 miles away from the Haygood dealership. Alexander's negligence in driving was, as the Court of Appeals noted, inexcusable. It was not, however, so highly improbable and extraordinary an occurrence in this series of events as to bear no reasonable connection to the harm threatened by Haygood's original negligence. . . . The area of risk created by the negligence of Haygood included the subsequent events and wrongful death of John Hairston. . . .

[Reversed and remanded for entry of judgment in accordance with the jury's verdict.]

Defenses

Even after the plaintiff has proven negligence, the defendant may raise one or more defenses, based on the plaintiff's conduct, that can reduce or extinguish liability. These include contributory negligence, assumption of the risk, and comparative negligence.

Contributory Negligence. **Contributory negligence** is negligence on the plaintiff's part which, combining with the defendant's negligence, causes the plaintiff harm. Traditionally, the plaintiff's contributory negligence was a complete bar to recovery against a defendant who would otherwise be liable to the plaintiff for negligence. This harsh ''all-or-nothing'' rule has been severely criticized

for many years. It causes great injustice by denying any recovery to a slightly negligent plaintiff against a substantially more culpable defendant. In addition, though the rule theoretically promotes caution by making the plaintiff responsible for his own conduct, it may in fact promote negligence by giving the defendant a means to escape liability for his wrong.

Judicial hostility to the harsh contributory negligence defense led to development of the **last clear chance doctrine,** which allowed a plaintiff to recover despite his or her own negligence. Under this doctrine, the plaintiff is allowed to recover if (1) the plaintiff's negligence places her in a helpless position (or a perilous position to which she is inattentive), and (2) the defendant discovers the plaintiff's perilous position, and (3) then, with the means and time to avoid the accident, the defendant negligently fails to do so. The doctrine applies only when the plaintiff's prior negligence becomes remote in the chain of causation, giving the defendant an opportunity to avoid the injury despite the plaintiff's conduct. Because the doctrine requires that the defendant have sufficient time to think and act, it is not used in accidents which happen quickly. The doctrine is most commonly applied to railroad employees and automobile drivers who discover persons, animals, or vehicles stranded on the roadway or track, but then negligently fail to stop in time to avoid collision.

Assumption of Risk. **Assumption of the risk** is an additional defense available to the defendant in negligence actions. In general, a plaintiff who voluntarily assumes the risk of harm caused by the defendant's negligent conduct may not thereafter recover for that harm. Thus, assumption of the risk rests upon the plaintiff's consent (express or implied) to encounter a known unreasonable danger created by the defendant's conduct. By voluntarily proceeding in the face of a known danger, the plaintiff may be acting reasonably or unreasonably. If he or she is acting unreasonably, the conduct also constitutes contributory negligence. Thus, the two defenses will often overlap and the plaintiff may be denied recovery on either basis. The great majority of cases involving assumption of risk are of this type. Assume Pat continues to drive a car after she discovers its brakes are dangerously defective because they were negligently repaired by Joe's Brake Service. Pat is subsequently injured when the brakes fail. When sued by her for negligence, Joe may defend himself on the basis that Pat was either contributorily negligent or had assumed the risk.

Note that assumption of the risk is determined according to a subjective standard; that is, did *this* plaintiff know, understand, and appreciate the risk. In contrast, contributory negligence is determined according to an objective standard; that is, did the plaintiff fail to use the amount of care a *reasonable person* would exercise for his own safety under similar circumstances.

Comparative Negligence. The last clear chance doctrine represents a judicial attempt to relieve negligent plaintiffs from the harsh effects of the contributory negligence doctrine. It suffers, however, from the same weakness as the contributory negligence doctrine, placing a loss caused by the negligence of both parties solely upon one of them. For this reason, the contributory negligence doctrine has been supplanted in most American jurisdictions by a rule of **comparative negligence,** in which the negligent plaintiff, instead of being denied recovery altogether, is awarded damages reduced in proportion to his fault (negligence) in causing the injury. This change, which has been accomplished both by statute (applicable to negligence actions generally or invoked in limited situations) and judicial decision, is a recent development, occurring primarily since 1969. In the following case, the California Supreme Court rejected the contributory negligence doctrine and substituted a system of comparative negligence. Note the form of comparative negligence which the court adopts, and its effect on the doctrines of last clear chance and assumption of risk.

Li v. Yellow Cab Company of California

532 P.2d 1226 (Cal. 1975)

Plaintiff, Nga Li, was injured when her car was struck broadside by a taxi cab driven by Robert Phillips, an employee of Yellow Cab. The accident occurred while she was attempting to make a left turn across three lanes of traffic into the driveway of a service station. The court found that Phillips had been negligent for driving at an unsafe speed at the time of the accident. It also found, however, that Li's left turn "was made at a time when a vehicle was approaching from the opposite direction so close as to constitute an immediate hazard." Accordingly, the court found Li contributorily negligent and denied her any recovery. She appealed.

Sullivan, Justice

. . . It is unnecessary for us to catalogue the enormous amount of critical comment that has been directed over the years against the "all-or-nothing" approach of the doctrine of contributory negligence. The essence of that criticism has been constant and clear: the doctrine is inequitable in its operation because it fails to distribute responsibility in proportion to fault. . . .

Furthermore, practical experience with the application by juries of the doctrine of contributory negligence has added its weight to analyses of its inherent shortcomings: "Every trial lawyer is well aware that juries often do in fact allow recovery in cases of contributory negligence, and that the compromise in the jury room does result in some diminution of the damages because of the plaintiff's fault. But the process is at best a haphazard and most unsatisfactory one." [Prosser, Comparative Negligence, 41 Calif. L. Rev. 1, 3-4 (1953)]. . . .

We are . . . persuaded that logic, practical experience, and fundamental justice counsel against the retention of the doctrine rendering contributory negligence a complete bar to recovery—and that it should be replaced in this state by a system under which liability for damage will be borne by those whose negligence caused it in direct proportion to their respective fault. . . .

Although several states which apply comparative negligence concepts retain the last clear chance doctrine . . . the better reasoned position seems to be that when true comparative negligence is adopted, the need for last clear chance as a palliative of the hardships of the "all-or-nothing" rule disappears and its retention results only in a windfall to the plaintiff in direct contravention of the principle of liability in proportion to fault. . . . As for assumption of risk, . . . [w]e think it clear that the adoption of a system of comparative negligence should entail the merger of the defense of assumption of risk into the general scheme of assessment of liability in proportion to fault in those particular cases in which the form of assumption of risk involved is no more than a variant of contributory negligence. . . .

It remains to identify the precise form of comparative negligence which we now adopt for application in this state. Although there are many variants, only the two basic forms need be considered here. The first of these, the so-called "pure" form of comparative negligence, apportions liability in direct proportion to fault in all cases. This . . . is the form favored by most scholars and commentators. . . . The second basic form of comparative negligence, of which there are several variants, applies apportionment based on fault *up to the point* at which the plaintiff's negligence is equal to or greater than that of the defendant—when that point is reached, plaintiff is barred from recovery. . . . The principal argument advanced in its favor is moral in nature: that it is not morally right to permit one more at fault in an accident to recover from one less at fault. Other arguments assert the probability of increased insurance, administrative, and judicial costs if a "pure" rather than a "50 percent" system is adopted, but this has been seriously questioned. . . .

We have concluded that the "pure" form of comparative negligence is that which should be adopted in this state. In our view the "50 percent" system simply shifts the lottery aspect of the contributory negligence rule to a different ground. As Dean Prosser has noted, under such a system "[i]t is obvious that a slight difference in the proportionate fault may permit a recovery; and there has been much justified criticism of a rule under which a plaintiff who is charged with 49 percent of a total negligence recovers 51 percent of his damages, while one who is charged with 50 percent recovers nothing at all." [Prosser, Comparative Negligence, 41 Calif. L. Rev. 1, 25 (1953)] In effect " . . . The partial rule simply lowers, but does not eliminate, the bar of contributory negligence." [Juenger, Brief for Negligence Law Section of the State Bar of Michigan in Support of Comparative Negligence as Amicus Curiae, Parsonson v. Construction Equipment Company, 18 Wayne L. Rev. 3, 50 (1972)]. . .

We also consider significant the experience of the State of Wisconsin, which until recently was considered the leading exponent of the "50 percent" system. There that system led to numerous appeals on the narrow but crucial issue whether plaintiff's negligence was equal to defendant's. . . .

For all of the foregoing reasons we conclude that the "all-or-nothing" rule of contributory negligence as it presently exists in this state should be and is herewith superseded by a system of "pure" comparative negligence, the fundamental purpose of which shall be to assign responsibility and liability for damage in direct proportion to the amount of negligence of each of the parties. Therefore, in all actions for negligence resulting in injury to person or property, the contributory negligence of the person injured in person or property shall not bar recovery, but the damages awarded shall be diminished in proportion to the amount of negligence attributable to the person recovering. The doctrine of last clear chance is abolished, and the defense of assumption of risk is also abolished to the extent that it is merely a variant of the former doctrine of contributory negligence; both of these are to be subsumed under the general process of assessing liability in proportion to negligence. . . .

[Judgment reversed.]

Owners and Occupiers of Land

In modern times, automobile accidents, industrial accidents, and product-related injuries form the bulk of negligence litigation. Another area of negligence that has generated a huge body of case law is the liability of owners and occupiers (such as tenants) of land for injuries occurring on their property.

Under the traditional common law rule, the liability of possessors of land to persons on the land is based upon the duty owed to the person injured. Generally, the duty owed depends upon the *status* of the injured person as a trespasser, licensee, or invitee. A **trespasser** is a person who enters or remains upon another's land without a privilege to do so created by the possessor's consent or otherwise. A **licensee** is a person privileged to enter or remain upon the land only by virtue of the possessor's consent. Licensees include members of the possessor's household, social guests, and those present on the land solely for their own purposes and to whom the privilege of entering was extended as a mere personal favor. An **invitee** is one of two types: a public invitee or a business invitee. A **public invitee** is a member of the public invited to enter or remain on the land for a purpose for which the land is held open to the public (such as a person entering a museum or library to examine the exhibits or read a book). A **business invitee** is a person invited to enter or remain on the land for purposes connected with business dealings with the possessor of the land (a patron of an appliance store or grocery store).

Liability to Trespassers. Generally a possessor of land is not liable to trespassers for physical injury caused by her negligent failure to put the land in a reasonably safe condition for their reception, or to conduct activities on the land in a manner that will not endanger them. This rule is subject to a number of exceptions that significantly limit its availability as a defense to actions by the trespasser.

Although most of these exceptions, if applicable, merely impose a duty upon the possessor to warn or to exercise reasonable care to avoid injury to the trespasser, a special exception, applicable when trespassers are *children,* may impose additional duties. Under §339 of the *Restatement (Second) of Torts,* if a possessor (1) maintains an artificial condition upon the land around which he or she knows or should know children are likely to trespass, and (2) the condition poses an unreasonable risk of death or injury to such children who, because of their youth, are unable to discover the danger or realize the risk presented, and (3) the utility to the possessor in maintaining the condition and the burden of eliminating the danger are slight when compared to the risk involved, then the possessor is liable for injury to the trespassing children caused by the condition if he or she fails to exercise reasonable care to *eliminate the danger or otherwise protect the children.* Note that this special duty to children is generally imposed only for "artificial" conditions (those created or maintained by the possessor), such as buildings, cranes, railroad tracks, turntables, and switchyards. The possessor's duty

may be fulfilled in some cases by a mere warning, but in others more may be required such as building fences, boarding up, locking up or tearing down offending structures, or filling in a dangerous pit.

The foregoing rule is commonly known as the **turntable doctrine,** because it originated in 1873 in *Sioux City & Pacific R. Co. v. Stout,*[25] involving a child injured while playing upon a railroad turntable. It is also frequently called the **attractive nuisance** doctrine, although this designation is somewhat misleading because there is generally no requirement that the children be allured or enticed onto the premises by the condition which causes injury. Most cases imposing liability involve children less than 12 years of age, although courts generally reject any fixed age limit. The basic test is whether the child is still too young to appreciate the particular danger presented.

Liability to Licensees. A licensee, unlike a trespasser, is upon the land with the possessor's consent. Consent to enter the premises alone, however, generally gives the licensee no right to expect that the possessor will conduct activities on the land differently or remedy dangerous conditions in order to assure the licensee's safety. Thus, as a general rule, a possessor is under a duty to carry on activities with reasonable care for the safety of licensees or make dangerous conditions safe only if (1) the possessor should expect that the licensee will not discover or realize the danger, and (2) the licensee does not know or have reason to know of the activities or conditions and the risks involved. Under this approach, once the licensee knows (through knowledge or observation, or by the possessor's warning) of the nature of the business or other activity conducted on the premises, he or she then assumes the risk involved upon entering the premises.

Liability to Invitees. The invitee, unlike a licensee, is a person who enters or remains on the land by invitation that carries with it an implied representation, assurance, or understanding that reasonable care has been used to prepare the premises and

25. 84 U.S. (17 Wall.) 657 (1873).

make them safe for the invitee's presence. A possessor, therefore, must generally exercise reasonable care to protect invitees against both dangerous activities conducted and dangerous conditions occurring on the land or at least to discover the dangerous condition or activity and give an adequate warning. What constitutes adequate preparation for the invitee's protection depends primarily on the nature of the land and the purposes for which it is used. Invitees may recover for their injuries, however, only if the possessor knows or should know that the activity or condition poses an unreasonable risk of injury, and that invitees will fail to discover or realize the danger, or protect themselves against it.

The following case illustrates the nature of the duty owed to a business invitee.

Corbin v. Safeway Stores, Inc.
648 S.W.2d 292 (Tex. 1983)

Plaintiff Gary Corbin sued defendant Safeway Stores, Inc. for damages resulting from injuries he suffered when he slipped on a grape and fell in the produce department of a supermarket owned and operated by Safeway. The evidence at trial established that Corbin slipped directly in front of a self-service grape bin. Corbin testified that he saw no mat or floor covering other than the green linoleum tiled floor. Safeway employees testified that company policy required each store to place a large non-skid, non-slip walk-off mat in front of the grape display because Safeway recognized that customers frequently dropped grapes on the floor but employees were unable to supervise the floor constantly to ensure that it remained free of grapes. Following presentation of all evidence, the trial judge granted Safeway's motion for direct verdict. The court of appeals affirmed and Corbin appealed to the Texas Supreme Court.

Spears, Justice
. . . [W]hen an occupier [of land] has actual or constructive knowledge of any condition on the premises that poses an unreasonable risk of harm to invitees, he has a duty to take whatever action is reasonably prudent under the circumstances to re-

duce or to eliminate the unreasonable risk from that condition. The occupier is considered to have constructive knowledge of any premises defects or other dangerous conditions that a reasonably careful inspection would reveal. . . .

In [previous] cases, we emphasized that an invitee's suit against a store owner is a simple negligence action. . . . As a result, the standard of conduct required of a premises occupier toward his invitees is the ordinary care that a reasonably prudent person would exercise under all the pertinent circumstances. . . . Consequently, an occupier's liability to an invitee depends on whether he acted reasonably in light of what he knew or should have known about the risks accompanying a premises condition, not on whether a specific set of facts or a specific breach of duty is established.

In this case, Corbin was Safeway's invitee. . . . To recover from Safeway, therefore, Corbin had the burden to prove (1) that Safeway had actual or constructive knowledge of some condition on the premises; (2) that the condition posed an unreasonable risk of harm to Corbin; (3) that Safeway did not exercise reasonable care to reduce or to eliminate the risk; and (4) that Safeway's failure to use such care proximately caused Corbin's personal injuries.

. . . Corbin alleged that Safeway's chosen self-service method for displaying green grapes in an open, slanted bin above a green linoleum tile floor resulted in an unreasonable risk of customers falling on grapes that have fallen or been knocked to the floor. Safeway admitted that at the time of Corbin's fall it knew of this unusually high risk associated with its grape display. It argues, however, that it is not obligated to protect customers from the acts of other customers in causing grapes to fall to the floor, regardless of whether those acts are foreseeable. Safeway believes the only duty it owes its customers with respect to the prevention of these kinds of falls is to pick up whatever objects it finds or should find on the floors of the store. We do not agree.

In all negligence actions, the foreseeability of the harmful consequences resulting from the particular conduct is the underlying basis for liability. Thus, Corbin's right to recover from Safeway depends on his showing Safeway's knowledge of the foreseeable harm of some course of conduct or method of operation. He is not required to prove one particular instance of negligence or knowledge of one specific hazard, as Safeway contends. . . .

Safeway acknowledged its full awareness of every circumstance under which it operated the self-service grape display, but contended a walk-off mat was in place at the time Corbin fell. Because the placing of such a mat in front of the grape display was a function of general store maintenance, the jury reasonably could have inferred that Safeway, through its employees, had failed to put the mat in place. This inference would satisfy the requirement of notice to Safeway. . . . A jury question existed, therefore, on whether Safeway knew or should have known of the premises condition upon which Corbin's claim is based.

The only remaining liability issues are whether the condition in which Safeway maintained its grape bin at the time Corbin was injured posed an unreasonable risk of harm; if so, whether Safeway used the ordinary care of a reasonably prudent person to reduce or to eliminate that risk; and, if Safeway was negligent, whether its negligence proximately caused Corbin's injury. . . .

The testimony of the two Safeway employees provides some probative evidence that the self-service grape bin in conjunction with the absence of any covering on the store's green linoleum tile floor posed an unusually high risk of customer falls resulting from grapes dropped on the floor. We believe that reasonable jurors could have concluded that this risk was unreasonable; accordingly, this question was a matter for the jury to determine.

On the question of the reasonableness of Safeway's conduct, there is evidence that Safeway's response to the risks accompanying the grape display was to require its stores to place walk-off mats in front of such displays. There was also evidence that no mat was in front of the grape display at the time Corbin fell. Furthermore, Safeway acknowledges that it took no other action, such as bagging the grapes, warning customers, or conducting frequent inspections, to minimize this hazard. Under these circumstances, because reasonable minds could conclude that Safeway did not use reasonable care to take some preventive measure against a foreseeable harm, the question of its negligence was for the jury to decide.

Finally, Safeway concedes that Corbin fell within a few feet of the grape display. This fact would support a jury finding that the absence of a mat or other preventive measure was a foreseeable cause-in-fact of Corbin's fall. Corbin therefore had a right to have a proximate cause issue decided by the jury. . . .

Safeway also argues that if the directed verdict is not upheld, this court will be penalizing Safeway for its diligence in instituting the limited use of walk-off mats as a company-wide safety measure. This argument reflects a misunderstanding of the basis for negligence liability. Safeway's liability to Corbin depends on its knowledge of store conditions posing risks to customers and the failure to act reasonably in response to those risks, not on the failure to comply with a company policy. If reasonable store conduct includes the use of mats or other floor coverings or even warnings in front of a particular display, then Safeway may be held liable for not using them, regardless of whether company policy requires them.

Many states now recognize that a storekeeper may be held liable for any dangerous premises condition about which he should be aware, not just for specific objects left on the floor by customers. Our holding here is consistent with the basic rule accepted by these states. . . .

[Judgment reversed and remanded for new trial.]

Modern Approach. The traditional tests outlined above impose liability upon a possessor of land based solely on the circumstances of the injured party's entry onto the property—that is, his or her status as trespasser, licensee, or invitee. This approach has been strongly criticized in recent years as awkward, complex, and mechanical in its application, and unduly protecting property interests at the expense of human safety. For these reasons, the modern trend, exhibited in decisions of approximately one-third of the states, is to abandon the traditional tripartite classification and instead apply ordinary principles of negligence in determining possessor's liability. Under this approach an owner or occupier of land: "must act as a reasonable person in maintaining his property in a reasonably safe condition in view of all the circumstances, including the likelihood of injury to others, the seriousness of the injury, and the burden on the respective parties of avoiding the risk.''[26] This approach both substantially simplifies the law, and harmonizes the land possessor's liability with that for personal negligence generally. The status of the injured party is simply one factor to be considered in assessing the possessor's reasonable care. Although the traditional approach still enjoys considerable support, the foregoing ''reasonable care under all the circumstances'' standard may ultimately become the majority rule.

Strict Liability

In certain cases, tort liability is imposed in the absence of both negligence and an intent to interfere with the plaintiff's legally protected interests. Such liability is known as **strict liability,** or liability without fault. In other words, a person is said to be ''strictly liable'' if legal responsibility is imposed even though he or she has not acted intentionally and has exercised the utmost care to prevent the harm. Two types of strict liability, imposed upon possessors of animals and those who conduct abnormally dangerous activities, are discussed below. Two other forms of strict liability, imposed upon suppliers of defective products that cause personal injury or property damage and upon common carriers for goods lost or damaged in transit, are covered in detail in Chapters 20 and 35, respectively.

Possessors of Animals

People who own or possess wild or domestic animals are often held strictly liable for damages caused when their animals trespass upon another's land, or inflict other injuries, such as bites.

Trespassing Livestock. A possessor of livestock, such as horses, cattle, pigs, sheep, and poultry, has traditionally been held strictly liable for personal injury and property damage caused if the livestock escape and trespass upon another's land. If permitted to run at large these animals often do substantial harm by eating grass or other plants, trampling crops, or injuring persons or animals. Strict liabil-

ity generally does not extend to animals, such as dogs and cats, which are not ordinarily kept under confinement and are unlikely to do significant damage by their trespass. Many states regulate animal trespass liability by statutes which often alter the common law rules.

Liability Apart from Trespass. Of course, trespass is not the only damage done by privately owned animals. Numerous cases involve dog bites and other injuries inflicted by pets. Liability of the owner generally depends upon whether the kept animal is domestic or wild.[27] Examples of the former are dogs, cats, sheep, cattle, and horses, and of the latter wolves, rattlesnakes, monkeys, and raccoons. The possessor of a wild animal is strictly liable for personal injury to another or another's animal caused by a dangerous propensity characteristic of animals of that type. On the other hand, strict liability for injuries caused by domestic animals is imposed only if the possessor knows or has reason to know of the particular animal's abnormally dangerous characteristics. Under this test, an owner is subject to strict liability for the first attack by a dog that has previously exhibited vicious tendencies.

Abnormally Dangerous Activities

A person who carries on an abnormally dangerous or ultrahazardous activity is strictly liable for personal injury and property damage resulting from that activity. An activity is abnormally dangerous if it is highly dangerous even when carefully performed and is not one, such as driving a car, that is commonly undertaken. Examples of conditions and activities meeting this test are (1) blasting or pile driving, (2) storing explosives, inflammable liquids, dangerous chemicals, or dangerous gases in quantity, (3) collecting water in a dangerous place, (4) producing, transporting, and using nuclear material, and (5) emitting noxious gases or fumes. Liability for damages caused by these activities is also often imposed on theory of nuisance

---

26. *Webb v. City and Borough of Sitka,* 561 P.2d 731, 733 (Alaska 1977).

27. A ''domestic'' animal is one ''by custom devoted to the service of mankind at the time and in the place in which it is kept.'' A ''wild'' animal is one not so devoted. *Restatement (Second) of Torts* §506.

discussed on pages 117–118. In fact, the rule of strict liability outlined above is applied by many courts under the name ''absolute nuisance.''

In the following case the court traces the development of the law governing strict liability for abnormally dangerous activities and considers whether such liability should be imposed for damages caused by toxic waste storage.

State Department of Environmental Protection v. Ventron Corporation
468 A.2d 150 (N.J. 1983)

Over a period of about 50 years, several businesses engaged in mercury processing operations on a 40 acre tract of land known as Berry's Creek, located near the Meadowlands in New Jersey. These operations created an estimated 268 tons of toxic waste, primarily mercury pollution, that contaminated Berry's Creek and adjacent land and ground waters, including the Hackensack River, with lethal mercury and threatened the environment, marine life and human health and safety. The mercury processing plant at Berry's Creek was operated from 1929 to 1960 by F. W. Berk and Company, Inc. (which went out of business in 1960) and from 1960 to 1974 by Wood Ridge Chemical Corporation (which first operated as a subsidiary of Velsicol Chemical Corporation and later was sold to Ventron Corporation). The plaintiff New Jersey Environmental Protection Agency sued numerous defendants including Wood Ridge, Velsicol and Ventron to recover damages for clean-up of the area. The lawsuit included claims for violation of state environmental statutes but also alleged several bases for common law tort liability. The trial court found the defendants strictly liable for ''unleashing a dangerous substance during non-natural use of the land.'' The appellate court affirmed and the corporate defendants appealed to the new Jersey Supreme Court. The following opinion includes only excerpts relating to common law tort liability.

Pollock, Justice
. . . We believe it is time to recognize expressly that the law of liability has evolved so that a landowner is strictly liable to others for harm caused by toxic wastes that are stored on his property and

flow onto the property of others. Therefore, we . . . adopt the principle of liability originally declared in *Rylands v. Fletcher* [L.R. 3 H.L. 330 (1868)]. The net result is that those who use, or permit others to use, land for the conduct of abnormally dangerous activities are strictly liable for resultant damages. Comprehension of the relevant legal principles, however, requires a more complete explanation of their development. . . .

[I]n 1868, the English courts decided *Rylands v. Fletcher*. In that case, defendants, mill owners in a coal-mining region, constructed a reservoir on their property. Unknown to them, the land below the reservoir was riddled with the passages and filled shafts of an abandoned coal mine. The waters of the reservoir broke through the old mine shafts and surged through the passages into the working mine of the plaintiff. . . .

The Exchequer Chamber . . . held the mill owners liable, relying on the existing rule of strict liability for damage done by trespassing cattle. The rationale was stated:

> We think that the true rule of law is that the person who for his own purposes brings on his land and collects and keeps there anything likely to do mischief if it escapes, must keep it at his peril, and if he does not do so, is *prima facie* answerable for all damage which is the natural consequence of its escape. [*Rylands v. Fletcher*, L.R. 1 Ex. 265, 279–80 (1866), aff'd, L.R. 3 H.L. 330 (1868)].

On appeal, the House of Lords limited the applicability of this strict liability rule to ''nonnatural'' uses of land. Consequently, if an accumulation of water had occurred naturally, or had been created incident to a use of the land for ''any purpose for which it might in the ordinary course of enjoyment of land be used,'' strict liability would not be imposed. *Rylands v. Fletcher*, L.R. 3 H.L. 330, 338–39. . . .

More recently, the *Restatement (Second) of Torts* reformulated the standard of landowner liability [imposing strict liability for ''abnormally dangerous'' activities] . . . and providing a list of elements to consider in applying the new standard. . . . [T]his standard incorporates the theory developed in *Rylands v. Fletcher*. Under the *Restatement* analysis, whether an activity is abnormally dangerous is to be determined on a case-by-case basis, taking all relevant circumstances into consideration. As set forth in the *Restatement:*

> In determining whether an activity is abnormally dangerous, the following factors are to be considered:
> (a) existence of a high degree of risk of some harm to the person, land or chattels of others;
> (b) likelihood that the harm that results from it will be great;
> (c) inability to eliminate the risk by the exercise of reasonable care;
> (d) extent to which the activity is not a matter of common usage;
> (e) inappropriateness of the activity to the place where it is carried on; and
> (f) extent to which its value to the community is outweighed by its dangerous attributes.
> [*Restatement (Second) of Torts* § 520 (1977)].

Pollution from toxic wastes that seeps onto the land of others and into streams necessarily harms the environment. . . . Determination of the magnitude of the damage includes recognition that the disposal of toxic waste may cause a variety of harms, including ground water contamination via leachate, surface water contamination via runoff or overflow, and poison via the food chain. . . . The lower courts found that each of those hazards was present as a result of the contamination of the entire tract. . . . Further, as was the case here, the waste

dumped may react synergistically with elements in the environment, or other waste elements, to form an even more toxic compound. . . . With respect to the ability to eliminate the risks involved in disposing of hazardous wastes by the exercise of reasonable care, no safe way exists to dispose of mercury by simply dumping it onto land or into water.

The disposal of mercury is particularly inappropriate in the Hackensack Meadowlands, an environmentally sensitive area where the arterial waterways will disperse the pollution through the entire ecosystem. Finally, the dumping of untreated hazardous waste is a critical societal problem in New Jersey, which the Environmental Protection Agency estimates is the source of more hazardous waste than any other state. . . . From the foregoing, we conclude that mercury and other toxic wastes are "abnormally dangerous", and the disposal of them, past or present, is an abnormally dangerous activity. . . .

Our examination leads to the conclusion, consistent with that of the lower courts, that defendants have violated long-standing common-law principles of landowner liability. . . . That activity has poisoned the land and Berry's Creek. Even if they did not intend to pollute or adhered to the standards of the time, all of these parties remain liable. Those who poison the land must pay for its cure. . . .

[Judgment affirmed.]

SUMMARY

1. A "tort" is generally defined as a private or civil wrong or injury, other than breach of contract, for which the law provides a remedy in the form of an action for damages. Tort law is designed to compensate the injured party and is based generally upon state common law.

2. Tort liability is imposed on three basic grounds: (1) because the defendant *intentionally* interfered with a legally protected interest of the plaintiff, or (2) because the defendant was *negligent,* or (3) because the defendant was *strictly liable,* that is, liable in the absence of either negligence or an intent to interfere with the plaintiff's interests.

3. Intentional torts are those in which the tort-feasor knows that invasion of a legally protected interest is certain, or substantially certain, to result from his or her act. Intentional torts are generally classified according to the interest protected. For example, the torts of assault, battery, false imprisonment, intentional infliction of emotional distress, defamation, invasion of privacy, and misuse of legal proceedings protect against intentional interference with a person's physical or emotional well-being. The torts of trespass, nuisance, conversion, and trespass to chattels protect against interference with the use, possession, or enjoyment of property. Business or

economic interests are protected, for example, by allowing recovery for intentional interference with performance of a contract or prospective contractual relation.

4. Most tort liability is not based upon conduct intended to cause injury; rather it is imposed for negligence—conduct which creates an unreasonable risk of injury. To avoid liability for negligence, a person must conform his or her conduct to that of a reasonable person under like circumstances.

5. To recover in an action for negligence, the plaintiff must prove some reasonable connection between the defendant's negligent conduct and the plaintiff's injury, or as is usually stated, the defendant's negligence must be the "proximate" or "legal" cause of the injury. The proximate cause requirement is actually a number of interrelated legal issues that collectively limit the defendant's liability for the consequences of his or her negligent acts.

6. When sued on the basis of negligence, various defenses based upon the plaintiff's conduct may be available to the defendant to reduce or extinguish liability to the plaintiff. Traditionally, these included contributory negligence and assumption of the risk. The contributory negligence doctrine has been supplanted in most states today by a system of comparative negligence under which the negligent plaintiff is awarded damages in proportion to his fault (negligence) in causing the injury.

7. An important area of law based upon negligence concerns the liability of owners and occupiers of land for injuries occurring on their property. Under the traditional common law rule, the liability of possessors of land to persons on the land is based upon the duty owed to the person injured. Generally, the duty owed depends upon the *status* of the injured person as a (1) trespasser, (2) licensee, or (3) invitee. The modern trend is to abandon this traditional tripartite classification system, and instead impose liability for injuries caused by the possessor's failure to exercise reasonable care under all the circumstances.

8. Tort liability may be imposed in the absence of both intent and negligence. Such "strict liability," or liability without fault, is imposed for damage caused by trespassing animals, for injuries caused by kept wild animals (and in some cases domestic animals), and for damages caused by abnormally dangerous or ultrahazardous activities.

KEY TERMS

tort	battery
tort-feasor	assault
intent	false imprisonment (false
punitive (exemplary)	arrest)
damages	defamation
libel	proximate cause
slander	contributory negligence
right to privacy	last clear chance doctrine
malicious prosecution	assumption of the risk
abuse of process	comparative negligence
trespass	trespasser
nuisance	licensee
public nuisance	invitee
private nuisance	public invitee
conversion	business invitee
trespass to chattels	turntable (attractive
negligence	nuisance) doctrine
reasonable person	strict liability

QUESTIONS AND PROBLEMS

5-1 Tort liability, like criminal liability, may be imposed either because of the defendant's fault (intentional or negligent torts) or in the absence of fault (strict liability torts). What considerations justify imposing tort responsibility in absence of fault? Do any considerations justify a more liberal use of strict liability as a basis for liability in tort rather than criminal cases?

5-2 What considerations justify a greater burden of proof in slander than libel cases? Defamation actions maintained by public officials and public figures require a showing of actual malice—that the statement was made with knowledge of its falsity or reckless disregard of the truth. Does the rule unduly protect irresponsible journalists or is it necessary to promote free discussion of and criticism of public issues and persons? Suggest other rules of liability that the courts could adopt for defamation cases to encourage discussion of public issues while protecting an individual's reputation.

5-3 Consumer advocate Ralph Nader had been a vocal critic of General Motors' products for many years. Nader filed a complaint against GM alleging that it had committed invasion of his privacy by the following acts:

1. Interviewing Nader's acquaintances and "casting aspersions upon [his] political, social, . . . racial and religious views; . . . his integrity; his sexual proclivities and inclinations; and his personal habits;"
2. Keeping him under surveillance;
3. Making threatening, harassing, and obnoxious telephone calls to him;
4. Tapping his telephone; and
5. Conducting a harassing investigation of him. Assuming that Nader can prove his allegations,

would GM's conduct constitute invasion of privacy? Why or why not?

5-4   Bertha inherited farmland that included an unoccupied house. Although she kept the house boarded up to discourage intruders and posted "no trespass" signs, trespassers broke into the house several times. Bertha and her husband Ed decided to set a "shotgun trap" to protect the property from the trespassers. They tied a loaded 20-gauge shotgun to a bed in the house and rigged a wire from the doorknob to the trigger so that the gun would fire when the door was opened. Marvin, who lived in a town near the farmhouse, thought the house had been abandoned and frequently collected antique bottles from the premises. Marvin returned to the farmhouse and entered the building removing a board from a window. When he opened the bedroom door, the gun went off causing serious injury to his leg. Marvin sued Bertha and Ed for damages. In defense they alleged that they were entitled to use a spring gun to protect their property from trespassers and burglars. How should the court rule? Explain.

5-5   Distinguish trespass and private nuisance. Why aren't all private nuisances actionable in tort? What are the advantages of using both legal (money damages) and equitable (injunction) remedies in nuisance cases?

5-6   Following lengthy negotiations, Pennzoil Co. and Getty Oil Company publicly announced that they had reached an "agreement in principle" that Pennzoil would purchase all of the stock in Getty. With knowledge of this announcement, Texaco, Inc., a competitor of Pennzoil, offered a higher price for the stock and several days later Getty entered into a contract to sell its stock to Texaco. Pennzoil sues Texaco for intentional interference with performance of a contract alleging that Pennzoil and Getty had a contract which Texaco induced Getty to breach. Just to be safe, Pennzoil also sues Texaco for intentional interference with prospective contractual relation alleging that Texaco had induced Getty not to enter into a contract with Pennzoil.

(a) Discuss the policy reasons for recognizing the torts of intentional interference with performance of contract and intentional interference with prospective contractual relation. Discuss the policy reasons for not recognizing these torts.

(b) Assume that under state law, the "agreement in principle" constituted a contract.

Should Texaco be held liable for intentional interference with performance of contract? Why or why not?

(c) If Texaco is held liable for intentional interference with performance of contract, would punitive damages be appropriate? Why or why not?

(d) Assume that the "agreement in principle" was not a contract so Pennzoil must prove intentional interference with prospective contractual relation. Should Texaco be held liable? Explain.

5-7   What social or public policies justify allowing recovery for negligently caused injury? Negligence liability is imposed for injuries caused by failure to conform conduct to that of a "reasonable person." Why are juries particularly adept at applying this standard? Could the judge acting alone perform it better?

5-8   Everett Company chartered a ship for two years and agreed to make monthly payments of $25,000 to Michaels, the owner of the ship. Every month Everett wired a telex message to his bank to transfer the monthly payment to Michaels. One month, the bank failed to act on Everett's instructions and did not transfer payment. Under the charter contract, Michaels could cancel the contract if Everett failed to make a monthly payment. Michaels cancelled the contract. As a result Everett lost profits of about $2 million because it was unable to charter another ship. Everett sued the bank and the evidence proved that the bank had acted negligently in failing to make the payment as instructed by Everett.

(a) What injury was suffered by Everett?

(b) Was the bank's negligence the proximate cause of the injury?

(c) If so, should the bank be held liable for damages of $2 million? Explain.

5-9   In each of the following cases, determine the proximate cause of the plaintiff's injuries. From whom should the plaintiff be entitled to recover?

(a) Plaintiff was dining at the Concord Cafeteria when a man ran into the restaurant, poured gasoline on the floor, and lit a match to the gasoline. During the ensuing fire, plaintiff suffered smoke inhalation and broken bones when other patrons trampled over her while trying to escape the fire. An inspection of Concord Cafeteria revealed that there were an insufficient number of fire exits and the existing exits were not adequately marked.

(b) Joe's Liquor Store sold a fifth of tequila to Randy who was seventeen years old. Randy shared the liquor with Dave and the plaintiff. Several hours later while Dave was driving his car, he made an illegal left turn and collided with another car. Dave's blood alcohol level at the time of the accident was 0.134. Plaintiff was seriously injured in the accident.

5-10 Andy was taking care of his children and cooking dinner. After placing a quiche in the oven, Andy picked up his son and walked into an adjacent room. Suddenly, the oven exploded. Andy was so startled he dropped the baby who suffered a broken arm. His other child was hit by flying debris and began bleeding. Andy grabbed both children and rushed them to the hospital. While he was gone, the house caught fire from the explosion. The flames spread to a neighbor's house and the neighbor telephoned the fire department. En route to the fire, the truck was involved in a collision causing property damage and personal injury to two firemen and to the driver of another automobile. Because of the delay, both houses burned to the ground before another firetruck arrived. Meanwhile, back at the hospital, while Andy's children were being treated, he began to suffer chest pains. Andy was hospitalized for a heart attack, which the doctor's attributed to stress and to a pre-existing heart condition.

Assume the oven was negligently designed and manufactured. Specifically, an improperly designed gas valve had caused the explosion. For which of the foregoing personal injury and property damage should the manufacturer be held liable? Explain.

5-11 Alice was seriously injured while riding a bumper car ride at Worldwide Amusement Park. The accident occurred when a bumper car being driven by Walt violently collided with a car driven by Alice. Alice sued Worldwide and Walt in a Florida court, seeking damages of $100,000. Florida imposes joint and several liability on all defendants who are liable for plaintiff's injuries. The jury found that Alice's negligence was 14% responsible for the accident, Worldwide's negligence was 1% responsible, and Walt's negligence was 85% responsible. The jury also found that Alice's total damages were $100,000.

(a) Assume that Florida follows the doctrine of contributory negligence. What is the total amount of damages for which the defendants may be held liable?

(b) Assume that Florida uses the doctrine of comparative negligence. What is the total amount of damages for which the defendants may be held liable? Further assume that Walt is a penniless pauper and that Alice will be unable to recover any damages from him. What is the total amount of damages that she could collect from Worldwide?

(c) Since the development of the doctrine of comparative negligence, most states have reconsidered whether to retain joint and several liability. Why would the doctrine of comparative negligence influence joint and several liability?

5-12 Yummy Burger is a fast food restaurant located on a busy street in Los Angeles, California. Ed Munch has sued Yummy for damages resulting from gunshot wounds that he suffered at Yummy. He has alleged that Yummy was negligent for failing to provide security guards at the restaurant. Discuss whether Yummy should be held liable under each of the following situations.

(a) Ed purchased a hamburger from Yummy and returned to his car on Yummy's parking lot. An assailant pulled a gun on Ed and demanded his money. When Ed cried for help, the assailant shot him in the leg. Although several burglaries had occurred in the neighborhood during the preceding three years, only one other person had been assaulted.

(b) Ed entered the restaurant while a robbery was in progress and was shot by one of the robbers. During the preceding three years, ten armed robberies had occurred at Yummy.

5-13 Joan was walking on a public street outside a public housing project when she was accosted by a man wielding a knife. He ordered her into a nearby unlocked apartment building, where she was robbed and sexually assaulted. The New York City Housing Authority, the owner of the apartment building, had negligently failed to keep the building's security system in good repair. May the Housing Authority be held liable to Joan because its negligence facilitated commission of a crime begun on a public street? Explain.

5-14 While shopping in a local self-service grocery store, Jasper slipped and fell, seriously injuring his back. At the time he fell, Jasper was examining merchandise on shelves displayed at eye level. According to customers standing nearby, the accident was caused by liquid, that resembled hand lotion, on the floor.

(a) If a customer had notified the store manager that she had spilled the hand lotion on the floor, would the store be liable for Jasper's injury? Explain.

(b) If none of the store employees was aware that the hand lotion was on the floor, could the store be held liable for Jasper's injury? What would Jasper have to prove to recover? Explain.

5-15 The twentieth century has witnessed a dramatic rise in commercial aviation. Under what circumstances and on what tort theories, if any, should a property owner be able to recover for over flight by aircraft in the airspace above the land? In this regard, contrast the rights of a property owner located near an airport runway with those of a farmer whose land has commercial aircraft flying over it at high altitude. Under what tort theory or theories should a property owner be able to recover for ground damage and personal injury caused by airplane crashes?

Chapter 6

Introduction to Property and the Uniform Commercial Code

This chapter introduces two fundamental topics in business law: property and the Uniform Commercial Code (UCC). A substantial portion of business law concerns the creation, protection, transfer, and enforcement of interests in property. The UCC, the most ambitious and successful uniform state law, governs many important aspects of commercial transactions. Although the two topics are discussed in great detail throughout the text, they are introduced together at this point because both subjects are necessary prerequisites to a complete understanding of the law of contracts and sales (Chapters 7–20).

The importance of these two topics to contract study lies in the fact that property principles help resolve a basic contracts issue: what law to apply to the transaction. Contract law is derived primarily from two sources: the common law and the UCC. Uniform Commercial Code contracts are limited to "transactions in goods," whereas the common law governs, among other things, contracts for the sale of land, personal service contracts, and construction contracts. Therefore, the initial determination in *every* contract case is whether the contract is governed by the common law or the UCC. Because the basic issue of what law to apply depends upon the type of property involved, it is useful, *before* studying contract law, to obtain a firm grasp of property in general and the specific property classified as goods. In addition, rights created by contract are themselves property, further underscoring the need for a basic property background.

Introduction to Property

"Property" Defined

Property is generally defined as either (1) a thing in which legal relations between persons exist, or (2) the legal relations themselves. When people think of property, they generally think of a house, an automobile, a television set, or any other *thing* having tangible, physical existence. This definition, however, fails to account for a share of stock, a patent, a copyright, the goodwill of a business, or a person's right to another's performance of a contract. Legally speaking, these things are property, even though they have no physical existence except, perhaps, as a piece of paper evidencing them.

It therefore becomes necessary to adopt the broader, and legally correct, view of property represented by the second definition. Briefly stated, **property** denotes the sum of the various legal relationships existing between identifiable persons with respect to a thing, tangible or intangible. Specifically, property concerns the relationships between the person possessing a legally protected interest in the thing, the property *owner*, and other members of society. For example, the "property" of a homeowner is not the bricks, mortar, and wood composing the physical structure, it is the extent to which the law protects the owner in his possession, transfer, use, and enjoyment of the house against appropriation, interference, or destruction by others. Thus, if the owner's neighbor carelessly damages the house, or interferes with the owner's possession, the law provides a remedy to compensate the owner for the loss. As noted in Chapter 5, this remedy is often provided by the law of torts.

In the preceding example, property exists in a tangible object (a house). Physical existence of the thing is not, however, a prerequisite to property. Assume that on June 1, a seller and a buyer enter into a contract under which the seller promises to deliver and transfer title to an automobile to the buyer on July 1, and the buyer promises to pay $2,000 to the seller on that date. The contract is the property of both the seller and the buyer. Each has the legally protected right to the other's performance of his promise. In short, all property, but not necessarily the things in which it exists, is intangible.

Property and Law

Property represents the legal relations between persons with respect to a thing. Without a system of laws designed to protect the legal relationships composing property, property as we know it would not exist. If X destroys Y's automobile, infringes upon her patent, or trespasses upon her land, the law recognizes that X has interfered with Y's property, and therefore affords Y a legal remedy. As one commentator noted,

> Property and law are born together, and die together. Before laws were made there was no property; take away laws, and property ceases.[1]

The concept of property is so firmly rooted in law that interests in property are explicitly protected by the United States Constitution. Specifically, the Fifth and Fourteenth Amendments provide that no person may be deprived of life, liberty, or *property* without due process of law. The Fifth Amendment further provides that the government may not take private property for a public use, such as a park or a highway, without providing just compensation to the owner.

The concept of property therefore requires legal sanctions protecting property rights. Without such sanctions, physical possession of tangible objects, protected only by brute force, would be all that remained. Intangibles such as contracts, stocks, bonds, checks, notes, patents, and copyrights would not exist. Society, as we know it, in which such intangibles represent an increasing percentage of total wealth, would give way to a law of the jungle.

Although property law normally confers exclusive rights in property (for example, of possession, use, and enjoyment) upon the owner, these rights are certainly not absolute. That is, the owner's rights are limited by a corresponding policy designed to protect other members of the community. For example, although a landowner may ordinarily use his property as he sees fit, local zoning ordinances or environmental protection regulations may restrict uses of the property. Similarly, the law prohibits (through principles of "nuisance") the use of property that interferes unreasonably with the right of adjoining landowners and occupiers to use their property.

In sum, property represents a set of relations, defined by law, involving both rights and limitations. As explained by one commentator, property represents a

> complex system of recognized rights and duties with reference to the control of valuable objects . . . linked with basic economic processes . . . validated by traditional beliefs, attitudes and values and sanctioned in custom and law.[2]

---

1. Bentham, *Theory of Legislation, Principles of the Civil Code,* Part I, 113, Dumont ed., Hildreth trans. (1871).

2. Hallowell, The Nature and Function of Property as a Social Institution, 1 J. Legal & Pol. Soc. 115 (1943).

Nature and Characteristics of Property Interests

It is helpful to view property as a bundle of sticks possessed by the owner. Collectively, this bundle of sticks is known as **ownership.** In common and legal speech the word **title** is frequently used to signify ownership. Property law may therefore generally be viewed as the study of ownership, with property including everything recognized by law as capable of ownership.

An owner, or a number of owners, may possess one, or several, or all of the sticks representing full ownership and each owner is said to have an "interest" in the property. In addition, he or she may create new property interests in others by relinquishing (for example, by sale, will, or gift) one or more of the sticks to others. Commonly included in the bundle of sticks representing full ownership of a thing is the right:

1. to possess it;
2. to exclude others from possession;
3. to use and enjoy it;
4. to be free from unreasonable interference by others with its use and enjoyment;
5. to dispose of it (for example, by sale, will, or gift);
6. to change its nature (for example, to make a cabinet out of an oak board);
7. to take its fruits (for example, crops from land or offspring from animals), and
8. to destroy it.

Possession is probably the most important stick in the bundle that represents property ownership. The term has major significance in many branches of law including gifts, bailments, adverse possession, secured transactions, landlord and tenant, and original acquisition. Further, both criminal and tort law protect against interference with an owner's possession, and criminal liability is imposed for possessing certain things such as illegal drugs or stolen property. However, despite the pervasive nature of possession, it resists precise, comprehensive definition. The term "possession" has a variety of meanings depending upon the context and purpose of its use. In any event, once the fact of possession is established, certain legal consequences follow (for example, acquisition of title, or commission of a crime).

The most common approach to possession regards it as the combination of two factors: 1) the physical relation of the possessor to the thing, coupled with 2) intent to exert control. Or, stated another way, the *Restatement (Second) of Torts* finds a person in possession of tangible, movable property if he has "physical control . . . with the intent to exercise such control on his own behalf, or on behalf of another."[3]

The first aspect is the actual power over the thing in question, the ability to hold and make use of it. Of course, this aspect varies depending upon the nature of the thing involved (for example, whether the thing is a watch or a farm). Coupled with this physical relation is the will or intent to control the thing. Possession additionally includes the legally protected power to exclude others from control of the thing possessed. Thus, exclusivity is also an important aspect of possession.

As previously noted, the entire bundle of sticks constituting ownership may be held by one person or may be divided in various ways that allow many people to have an interest in a given piece of property. The permissible interests existing in property may differ in duration, the extent of the interest held by the owner, the time of possession, and the number of persons concurrently holding an ownership interest. Taken collectively, the various types of interests existing in property and the rights and obligations of the parties thereto form the fundamental basis for the study of property law (see Chapters 34 through 39).

The Distinction Between Real and Personal Property

Though property is intangible in nature, property issues are commonly discussed according to the physical character (or lack thereof) of the thing in which the property exists. A fundamental distinction in property law is that between real and personal property. **Real property** generally includes

1. land (such as unimproved real estate);
2. things more or less permanently attached to land (such as a house, a barn, or a factory);

---

3. *Restatement (Second) of Torts* §216.

3. certain things affixed or annexed to land ("fixtures");
4. things growing on land in certain situations, and;
5. things belonging to or incidental to land (such as an easement for a driveway across neighboring property).

In short, real property includes land, structures, objects, and other interests attached to or closely associated with it.

Personal property, on the other hand, is everything else capable of ownership. Personal property is commonly designated either tangible (when the thing in which property rights exist has a physical existence) or intangible (when the thing has no physical existence but instead represents a valuable claim against a third person or persons). Tangible personal property includes a car, a television set, a book, a dog, or any other movable object. Intangible personal property includes patents, copyrights, trademarks, royalty rights, documents of title, commercial paper, stocks and bonds, goodwill, accounts receivable, bank accounts, security interests, or other contract rights. The foregoing are designated intangible even though their existence may be evidenced by a document (for example, such as a share of stock or promissory note).

Since early times, the terms **choses** (things) **in possession** and **choses in action** have been used to distinguish these two types of personal property. Choses in possession refers to rights in tangible physical objects. Choses in action, on the other hand, refers to property rights which, although they may be evidenced by a piece of paper, are essentially intangible because they can ultimately be claimed or enforced only by action (a legal proceeding), not by taking physical possession.

The term "personal property" does not mean that the property must be personally or individually owned, but that the property is not real property. For example, an automobile is personal property whether it is in the hands of an individual, partnership, corporation, or governmental body. The term **chattel** is frequently used to designate an article of personal property. ("Chattel" is derived from "cattle," the most common form of nonlanded,

personal wealth in early England.) Though the term "chattel" may designate both types of personal property, its use is ordinarily limited to tangible, movable objects.

The United States legal system is substantially derived from that of England,[4] and the real-personal property dichotomy evolved from early English common law. Historically, the distinction stems from the types of assets administered upon death in the courts of law and the courts of equity. The *courts of law,* concerned with preserving the feudal structure, dealt with land, the primary form of property ownership. The relative unimportance of money, goods, and things other than land in early times permitted *courts of equity* to administer these assets on the owner's death. The subsequent development of trade and commerce caused personal property to assume much greater importance, resulting in the two important categories of property, each evolving in separate courts with their own sets of rules. It has also been suggested that the distinction results from common law procedure, in which a real action was used (resulting in a return of the thing itself) when land was wrongfully detained by another. On the other hand, a personal action (resulting only in an award of money damages against the wrongdoer) was used if things other than land were involved. Thus, the thing took the name of the action, resulting in real and personal property.

Although the importance of the distinction between real and personal property has diminished somewhat in modern times, the distinction continues to be an important and viable one. In fact, the dichotomy, which is recognized to some extent in all systems of law, is essentially between movables (personal property), and immovables (real property). Thus, in the study of business law, it is helpful, *at the outset,* to determine whether real or personal property is involved in the transaction in question because applicable legal principles may vary significantly.

---

4. The law of the state of Louisiana is an exception because it is based upon the French Civil Law.

Introduction to the Uniform Commercial Code

The Background of the UCC

Business law is derived primarily from the common law and statutes, including a number of important "uniform state laws." As discussed in Chapter 1, the National Conference of Commissioners on Uniform State Laws periodically promulgates and promotes the passage of these uniform laws. The most ambitious and successful of the uniform state laws is the **Uniform Commercial Code** (UCC or Code). The UCC, which was jointly sponsored by the National Conference and the American Law Institute, represents a substantial and comprehensive modernization and expansion of prior uniform laws relating to commercial transactions.[5]

Professor Karl Llewellyn, the chief draftsman of the Code, had a profound impact on the overall text and design of the finished statute. Between 1944 and 1950, the team headed by Professor Llewellyn formulated the Code's first complete draft. After extensive consideration and debate, the first official text was promulgated in 1952. The first state to enact it was Pennsylvania in 1954. The official text was further revised in 1957, 1958, and 1962. The 1962 version remains the basis of most of the Code, although additional amendments were made to portions of the text in 1972 and 1977, and a new article was added in 1987.

The Code's reception in the various state legislatures was overwhelming. By 1968, forty-nine states, the District of Columbia, and the Virgin Islands had enacted it. The lone holdout, Louisiana, enacted a portion of the Code in 1974.

General Organization of the UCC

The UCC is divided into twelve articles. The first ten articles contain the substantive provisions, summarized below and discussed in detail at various points throughout the text.[6] Articles 10 and 11 address the mechanics of enacting the Code, such as effective date, repeal of conflicting statutes, and transition between repealed statutes and the Code. The ten substantive articles are:

Article 1	General Provisions
Article 2	Sales
Article 2A	Leases
Article 3	Commercial Paper
Article 4	Bank Deposits and Collections
Article 5	Letters of Credit
Article 6	Bulk Transfers
Article 7	Warehouse Receipts, Bills of Lading and Other Documents of Title
Article 8	Investment Securities
Article 9	Secured Transactions; Sales of Accounts and Chattel Paper

All Articles, except 5 and 6, are divided into two or more "parts" that govern differing issues within the major subject matter area. Each part is then divided into "sections" (abbreviated §). Sections are then numbered in a manner that indicates both the Article and part from which the section is taken. For example, §2-302, entitled "Unconscionable Contract or Clause," is contained in part 3 (General Obligation and Construction of Contract) of Article 2 (Sales). Thus, the first number indicates the Article and the second number the part.

After each section, the official text of the Code includes "Official Comments" on that section. These Comments, generally prepared by the drafters, state

1. the prior uniform statute or statutes, if any, from which the section is derived;
2. the purpose of the section—here the underlying legal or factual problem is commonly

---

5. These statutes and the dates of their promulgation are as follows: Uniform Negotiable Instruments Law (1896), Uniform Warehouse Receipts Act (1906), Uniform Sales Act (1906), Uniform Bills of Lading Act (1909), Uniform Stock Transfer Act (1909), Uniform Conditional Sales Act (1918), and Uniform Trust Receipts Act (1933). The Uniform Negotiable Instruments Law and the Uniform Warehouse Receipts Act had been adopted in all states. The others had varying degrees of success, yet, despite their adoption, these statutes had become outdated by the late 1930s and in need of drastic revision.

---

6. The official text of the Uniform Commercial Code is reproduced in Appendix B.

stated, important prior cases or statutes are sometimes discussed, and the intent, theory, and rationale of the section is outlined and explained;

3. cross references to related Code sections and definitions.

The various state legislatures enacted into law only the text of the statute, not the Official Comments. Courts have, however, consistently attached great weight to the Official Comments in resolving Code disputes. They have proven to be valuable aids to construction, and promote uniformity of interpretation—a basic stated purpose of the Code. The Official Comments therefore represent the most valuable tools outside the text itself for interpretation and construction of UCC provisions.

Introduction to Specific Articles

The following material provides an overview of the scope and coverage of the UCC's nine substantive Articles.

Article 1—General Provisions. Article 1, entitled "General Provisions," contains various general principles, rules of construction, and definitions applicable to the remainder of the Code. Understanding some of these fundamental concepts is necessary before undertaking a more detailed study of the UCC.

At the outset, §1–102(1) broadly states that the UCC is to be "liberally construed and applied to promote its underlying purposes and policies." Those purposes and policies, stated in §1-102(2), are:

(a) to simplify, clarify and modernize the law governing commercial transactions;

(b) to permit the continued expansion of commercial practices through custom, usage and agreement of the parties; and

(c) to make uniform the law among the various jurisdictions.

Thus, the Code initially exhorts the judiciary, which must interpret and apply it, to give the UCC a liberal construction and not to shackle it with interpretations that hamper its effectiveness or that are inconsistent with its underlying purposes and policies. The law should be allowed to develop to cover possibly unforeseen circumstances, to resolve situations not explicitly covered, or to develop new remedies.

Variation by Agreement. Although the UCC resolves a substantial number of legal issues, its provisions are not mandatory. That is, freedom of contract is a basic principle of the Code embodied in §1-102(3) that provides:

> The effect of provisions of this Act may be varied by agreement, except as otherwise provided in this Act. . . .

The parties' ability to vary the effect of Code provisions by agreement is also often explicitly stated in individual Code sections, through the language "unless otherwise agreed" or words of similar import. For example, §2-308(a) provides that "*unless otherwise agreed* the place for delivery of goods is the seller's place of business or if he has none his residence." Note, however, that the absence of "unless otherwise agreed" language in a specific Code section does not imply that its provisions cannot be varied by agreement. In other words, §1-102(3) states the general rule that all provisions of the UCC may be varied by agreement unless explicitly stated to the contrary.

Applicability of Supplementary Principles of Law. The UCC is not a comprehensive and exhaustive treatment of the entire commercial law area. It does not govern transfers of, or security interests in, real property. It does not govern bankruptcy or suretyship. It is inapplicable to many types of commercial contracts (such as insurance, employment, or construction contracts), and does not address all issues presented by the contracts it does govern. A substantial body of law existing both before and outside the Code must therefore be used to supplement its provisions. In other words, the Code supercedes prior legal principles only to the extent it explicitly covers a specific area or issue. Situations not covered by the UCC are resolved by reference to relevant pre-Code or non-Code law.

Commercial law is therefore governed primarily

by the UCC, supplemented by a variety of common law principles (drawn primarily from the law of contracts, agency, and property) and statutes (such as the Bankruptcy Code). In addition, Code provisions may be supplemented by the "law merchant," a system of rules, customs, or usages generally recognized and adopted by merchants, which either alone or as modified by common law or statute, regulate commercial transactions and the resolution of controversies.[7] Thus custom and trade usage may also supplement Code provisions. Application of supplementary legal principles to the Code is embodied in Section 1-103, which, it has been suggested, is perhaps the single most important Code provision. Of course, because the parties are generally free to alter the effect of Code provisions, much commercial law is based on private agreement, not mandated by either the Code or supplementary legal principles.

Obligation of Good Faith. Another important principle underlying the entire Code is the obligation of good faith. Like the concept of equity, good faith is a fundamental principle running through law generally and would therefore undoubtedly be applied by courts in Code litigation even in the absence of an express statutory directive. The UCC, however, makes the obligation explicit in §1-203, which states:

> Every contract or duty within this Act imposes an obligation of good faith in its performance or enforcement.

The term **good faith** is defined in §1-201(19) as

> Honesty in fact in the conduct or transaction concerned.

If the party in question is a merchant, §2-103(1)(b) provides that good faith means *both* honesty in fact and the "observance of reasonable commercial standards of fair dealing in the trade." Thus, the determination of a merchant's good faith requires an inquiry into his observance of such standards.

The presence or absence of good faith is therefore generally governed by a "subjective" test. That is, was the person whose good faith is questioned in fact (in his or her own mind) dealing honestly with the other party to the transaction? In the case of a merchant, an "objective" test is also used, meaning that good faith is measured by comparing the actor's conduct to an objective standard—reasonable commercial standards of fair dealing in the trade. Under either test, good faith "emphasizes faithfulness to an agreed common purpose and consistency with the justified expectations of the other party; it excludes a variety of types of conduct characterized as involving 'bad faith' because they violate community standards of decency, fairness, and reasonableness."[8]

General Definitions. Section 1-201, which defines forty-six terms, is the general definitional section for the entire UCC. In addition, each of the remaining Articles includes one or more sections defining terms specifically applicable to that Article. Precise use of terminology is important in the study of law generally and particularly in the study of a technical statute such as the Uniform Commercial Code. Thus, the reader must pay particular attention to the basic definitions. The terms defined in §1-201 and other definitional sections are explained throughout the remainder of this text as needed for an understanding of the underlying discussion. Access to a particular term can be obtained by using the index of statutory citations (if the particular Code section is known) or the glossary if merely the word or phrase is known.

Code provisions frequently require that actions, such as delivery or notice, be taken within a "reasonable time." Under §1-204, what constitutes a reasonable time is a question of fact dependent upon the nature, purpose, and circumstance of the action, including custom or trade usage and prior conduct of the parties. Thus, because the determination depends upon the facts of the individual case, no precise period can generally be fixed as reasonable. The UCC also commonly requires an action to be taken "seasonably." This term means that the required act must be taken at or within the

---

7. Black, *Law Dictionary* (4th ed. 1968).

8. *Restatement (Second) of Contracts* §205 comment a.

time called for by the contract, or if no time is agreed on, then at or within a reasonable time.

Article 2—Sales. Article 2 of the UCC, entitled "Sales," governs contracts for the sale of "goods." It represents a complete revision, modernization, and expansion of the Uniform Sales Act, originally promulgated by the National Conference in 1906. Article 2, the longest of the nine substantive Code Articles, is much more extensive than the old Sales Act, extending to issues not previously covered. Article 2 occupies a central position in the overall study of business law. Its provisions form much of the basis of Part II of this text (Contracts) and virtually all of Part III (Sales).

Article 2A—Leases. In 1987, the National Conference and American Law Institute added Article 2A, entitled "Leases," to the Uniform Commercial Code. Article 2A governs personal property leasing (for example, a lease by a business of its trucks or manufacturing equipment) and is designed to fill the gap between Article 2, which focuses primarily on sales, rather than lease, transactions involving personal property, and Article 9, which governs only those leases intended for security. Article 2A has been adopted in at least one state.[9] This is discussed in more detail in Chapter 16.

Article 3—Commercial Paper. Article 3, entitled "Commercial Paper," is a complete revision and modernization of the Uniform Negotiable Instruments Law originally promulgated in 1896 and subsequently adopted in every American jurisdiction. Article 3 governs specialized commercial instruments payable in money, including drafts, checks, certificates of deposit, and promissory notes. The issues addressed include the creation and transfer of such instruments and the rights and liability of various parties thereto. At the heart of Article 3 is the concept of "negotiability," which is designed to enhance the marketability and promote free transferability of the paper. Commercial paper is treated in detail in Part IV of this text.

---

9. As of this writing Article 2A has been adopted in Oklahoma.

Article 4—Bank Deposits and Collections. Article 4, entitled "Bank Deposits and Collections," contains a uniform statement of the principal rules of the bank collection process. Ordinarily, a holder of a check deposits it in an account in his own bank. This bank (the "depositary" bank) must then undertake to collect the item from the bank on which it is drawn (known as the "drawee" or "payor" bank) through one or a series of "intermediary" banks. The number of "items," mostly checks, handled by banks as part of this collection process, has grown tremendously in this century. Prior to adoption of the Code, the law applicable to the bank collection process was derived from a myriad of nonuniform sources.

Issues now covered by Article 4 include the bank collection process in general, and the rights, duties, and liabilities of a checking account depositor and his bank arising from payment or nonpayment of checks. Included in this latter category are matters such as wrongful dishonor, overdrafts, stale checks, death or incompetence of the depositor, stop payment orders, attachment and other legal process, and forgery and alteration. Article 4 is discussed in Chapter 27.

Article 5—Letters of Credit. A letter of credit is a financing, payment, and security device used in many forms in a variety of transactions. Letters of credit were originally developed and are still primarily used to finance international sales transactions between buyers and sellers not commercially acquainted with each other. In this context, the letter of credit assures payment for a sale of goods or other obligation, while providing some assurance that the obligation for which payment is requested has been performed. The letter of credit achieves this result by substituting the credit of financial institutions, such as banks, for the credit of the parties to the contract (such as a buyer and seller in a contract for the sale of goods).

Article 5 provides a system of rules governing the complicated letter of credit field. Because letters of credit were developed in international trade, some states had no law on the subject prior to enactment of Article 5. Since that time, however, the use of letters of credit has burgeoned throughout the country to include a significant number of both domestic and international applications. Letters of credit are explained in more detail in Chapter 35.

Article 6—Bulk Transfers. Article 6, entitled "Bulk Transfers," replaces no prior uniform statute, but instead supplants nonuniform bulk sales laws enacted in every United States jurisdiction. Article 6 is designed to protect creditors of a merchant who sells his entire stock in trade out of the ordinary course of business (the "bulk transfer") to an innocent purchaser, pockets the proceeds, and then disappears, leaving his creditors unpaid. Article 6 provides that such a transfer in bulk is ineffective against creditors of the seller unless they are notified of the sale in advance. Once notified, the creditors can then take steps to protect themselves prior to consummation of the sale. The operation of Article 6 is covered in more detail in Chapter 29.

Article 7—Documents of Title. Article 7 is concerned with an important part of many sales transactions: the shipment or storage of goods.[10] Although these functions may be performed by the parties, more commonly professionals such as common carriers or commercial warehousemen perform them. The instruments issued by these specialists upon receipt of goods for shipment or storage ("documents of title") governed by Article 7 simultaneously serve three functions:

1. they act as the receipt for the goods delivered to the carrier or warehouseman;
2. they contain the terms of the contract of carriage or storage between the owner and the professional; and
3. in the case of "negotiable" documents, they are a symbol standing in place of the goods, allowing a transfer of the goods simply by transferring the document.

The most common documents of title are the bill of lading (issued by carrier in exchange for goods

shipped) and the warehouse receipt (issued by a warehouseman in exchange for goods stored). The rules of Article 7 are similar in many respects to those stated in Article 3, Commercial Paper. The fundamental difference is that whereas Article 3 instruments, primarily notes and checks, are payable in money, Article 7 paper is payable in goods. Article 7 is discussed in more detail in Chapter 35.

Article 8—Investment Securities. Article 8 governs the rights and duties of persons dealing with "investment securities."[11] Although the stocks and bonds commonly traded on securities exchanges or in the "over the counter" market are the most common type of investment security, Article 8 also covers anything else that securities markets regard as suitable for trading. Article 8 determines the relative rights in investment paper of issuers, owners, purchasers, and creditors regarding transfer of the paper, notice of claims to it, registration of interests, and other issues. It therefore serves the same purpose for investment securities that Article 3 serves for promissory notes, drafts, checks, and certificates of deposit, and that Article 7 serves for documents of title. Note that Article 8 is concerned with rights in the security itself, and is not designed to prevent fraud or require disclosure in securities trading; that is the function of federal and state "securities regulation" statutes, discussed in detail in Chapter 49.

In response to the "paperwork crunch" the securities markets suffered in the late 1960s, an American Bar Association committee was formed in 1971 to determine what legislation, if any, would be advisable to eliminate or substantially reduce the use of stock certificates. It subsequently recommended that the Model Business Corporation Act[12] be amended to permit issuance of corporate stock in "uncertificated" form, and that Article 8 of the UCC be amended to govern the use of uncertificated investment securities. In response to

---

10. Article 7 represents a consolidation and revision of the Uniform Warehouse Receipts Act and the Uniform Bills of Lading Act. It also replaces certain provisions of the Uniform Sales Act relating to negotiation of documents of title.

11. It is a revision of the Uniform Stock Transfer Act, originally promulgated in 1909, but with a notable expansion in coverage to include bonds and other types of long-term indebtedness as well as stock.

12. The Model Business Corporation Act is introduced in Chapter 45.

Table 6–1	Summary of the Scope and Coverage of the Uniform Commercial Code
Article	*Provisions*
Article 1 General Provisions	States general principles, rules of construction, and definitions applicable to the rest of the Code.
Article 2 Sales	Governs contracts for the sale of goods.
Article 2A Leases	Governs leases of goods.
Article 3 Commercial Paper	Contains the law governing negotiable instruments payable in money, primarily promissory notes and checks.
Article 4 Bank Deposits and Collections	Contains rules governing the bank collection process and defines the legal relationship between a bank and its checking account customer.
Article 5 Letters of Credit	Outlines rules governing rights and obligations of parties to a letter of credit, a financing device used primarily in international trade.
Article 6 Bulk Transfers	Provides protection for creditors of a merchant who sells his entire stock in trade not in the ordinary course of business.
Article 7 Documents of Title	Governs rights and duties of parties to documents of title issued in exchange for the carriage or storage of goods.
Article 8 Investment Securities	States rules regarding transfer of stocks, bonds, and other securities traded on exchanges or in other organized markets.
Article 9 Secured Transactions	Governs all security interests in personal property created by agreement of the parties and all sales of accounts and chattel paper.

these recommendations, Article 8 was substantially amended in 1977 to provide rules for both certificated (evidenced by a written instrument) and uncertificated securities. As of this writing, the 1977 amendments have been adopted in thirty-three states.[13] Article 8 is discussed in Chapter 46.

Article 9—Secured Transactions; Sales of Accounts and Chattel Paper. Article 9 is probably

the Code's most ambitious undertaking because it consolidates under one heading all *consensual security interests in personal property* and fixtures. In addition, sales of accounts and chattel paper (basically a secured account receivable) are brought within Article 9's scope to avoid the difficult problem of distinguishing between transactions in such property intended for security and those not so intended. A secured creditor enjoys a favored position upon default by a debtor, enjoying a preferred claim against specific assets of the debtor. Upon default, a secured creditor may proceed without judgment against those assets and apply them to the unpaid debt to the exclusion of other creditors.

Prior to the adoption of Article 9, security interests in personal property were governed by a fragmented, nonuniform assortment of devices includ-

_____

13. Arkansas, California, Colorado, Connecticut, Delaware, Florida, Hawaii, Idaho, Indiana, Kansas, Kentucky, Maryland, Massachusetts, Michigan, Minnesota, Montana, Nevada, New Hampshire, New Mexico, New York, North Dakota, Ohio, Oklahoma, Oregon, Rhode Island, South Dakota, Tennessee, Texas, Virginia, Washington, West Virginia, Wisconsin, and Wyoming.

ing chattel mortgages, pledges, conditional sales contracts, factor's liens, trust receipts, and assignments of accounts receivable. Article 9 replaces these devices with a comprehensive scheme governing the creation, perfection, and foreclosure of security interests in personal property that applies without regard to the type or form of security device used by the parties. Article 9 represents a radical simplification of both the formalities for creation of security interests and of the public filing system whereby notice is given to creditors and others of the existence of a security interest in the debtor's property.

The original 1962 version of Article 9 was substantially amended in 1972 to clarify its drafting and to resolve problems not addressed by the original version. These amendments have been adopted in forty-six states.[14] Article 9 as amended in 1972 is discussed in Chapters 31–32 as part of the coverage of debtor-creditor relations. The scope and coverage of the Code's ten articles are summarized in Table 6–1.

SUMMARY

1. Property is defined as the sum of legal relations between persons with respect to a thing. The owner of a property interest is protected by law against interference with or destruction of that interest by others. Property is commonly classified as real or personal. Real property includes land, and structures, objects, and other interests closely associated with it. Personal property, on the other hand, includes everything else capable of ownership. Personal property is often classified as tangible (a chose in possession, good, or chattel) or intangible (a chose in action).

2. The Uniform Commercial Code is a widely enacted state statute governing many aspects of commercial transactions in ten substantive articles. Article 2 of the Code explicitly governs contracts for the sale of goods and is therefore integral to the study of contract law generally. Recently adopted Article 2A governs the burgeoning personal property leasing field. The Code is also the source of law governing many types of documents commonly used in business transactions including notes, checks, bills of lading, warehouse receipts, stocks, bonds, and letters of credit. The Code also addresses two issues regarding debtor-creditor relations. First, its bulk transfer provisions are designed to protect a merchant's creditors when the merchant sells his entire inventory in bulk to a third party. Second, Article 9 of the UCC provides a comprehensive framework governing all consensually created security interests in personal property.

3. The UCC is neither mandatory nor comprehensive in its coverage. Generally, the parties are free to alter the effect of Code provisions by agreement. Further, the Code, to the extent it does not address a specific issue, is liberally supplemented by legal principles existing outside the UCC.

KEY TERMS

property	choses in possession
ownership	choses in action
title	chattel
possession	Uniform Commercial
real property	Code
personal property	good faith

QUESTIONS AND PROBLEMS

6-1 Harry recently purchased a new house and three acres of adjacent land. In discussing the purchase with a friend Harry states, "It feels so good to own this property. I am king of the roost and nobody can tell me what I can or cannot do with my property." The friend replies, "You are wrong, Harry; property rights are not absolute." Who is right? Explain.

6-2 Review the definition of property and the bundle of rights constituting property. Are stolen goods property in the hands of the thief? Of anyone? Are illegal drugs, such as heroin or cocaine, property? Are human beings property?

6-3 Al, who is dining at the Corner Cafe, checks his coat at the restaurant's hat check room. Jesse, after robbing the First National Bank, runs into the Corner Cafe and stashes the money in Al's coat. After conducting a search of the restaurant, the police discover the money in Al's coat and find Jesse hiding near the check room. Posses-

---

14. The 1972 amendments to Article 9 have been enacted in every state but Vermont.

sion of stolen goods is a crime. Jesse, however, asserts that the stolen goods are not located on his person. The restaurant owner states that he does not have the goods—they are in Al's coat. Al protests that he was not even aware of the stolen goods. Which, if any, of the above parties is liable for possession of stolen goods? Explain.

6-4 UCC §1-102(3) provides that most UCC provisions may be varied by agreement of the parties to a contract. Why was §1-102(3) included in the Code? Does it not defeat the Code purpose of making commercial law uniform nationwide?

6-5 Professors James J. White and Robert S. Summers have noted, ''Section 1-103 is probably the most important single provision in the Code.'' (White & Summers, *Handbook of the Law Under the Uniform Commercial Code* 7 (2d ed. 1980)) What basis might they offer to support this assertion?

Business Crimes: The Underside of Enterprise

Thomas Donaldson

When the cops on *Miami Vice* apprehend a drug dealer, we easily label the dealer a ''crook.'' But when federal investigators discover that a successful Yale graduate working for a New York investment banking firm has bought stock in a company he knows is about to be acquired, the label seems less appropriate. Yet the latter action, known as insider trading, marks its perpetrator every bit as much a criminal as the act of dealing in drugs. By using inside information to purchase stock that will rise in price once word leaks out, he has rigged the game against other investors who lack his inside information. And he has robbed the persons from whom he purchased the stock of the increased value that their stock was bound to accrue.

The specter of business crime haunts the American economy. Some estimate that the overall cost to society from such crime—including tax evasion, illegal pollution, and inflated prices—exceeds $230 billion. Losses from bank embezzlements today exceed by five times losses from bank robberies. Computer fraud absorbs a billion dollars, and the Securities and Exchange Commission has filed more charges against insider trading in the last decade than in its previous forty-year history. Not only individuals but corporations are prey to temptation. Between 1972 and 1982, 115 of America's largest corporations were convicted of at least one major crime or paid civil penalties for serious misbehavior. One example: In 1982, the Milton Bradley Company, a major toy marketer, was fined $150,000 after pleading no contest to charges of conspiring to fix the price of crayons.

During the last three decades, public and legal attention has shifted dramatically away from conventional criminality to white-collar crime. In the 1960s the political spotlight was on the ''war on crime'' in the streets. By the 1970s, it had moved to the Watergate proceedings, and Jimmy Carter, then a candidate for the presidency, scored key points against his rival, President Ford, by criticizing Ford's pardon of Nixon. In the 1980s the headlines about white collar crime found new targets: scores of Reagan appointees, including Colonel North and Admiral Poindexter of the National Security Council, were indicted and charged with crimes, while Wall Street exploded with revelations about insider trading. At the same time, in Chicago, the F.B.I.'s ''Greylord'' investigation revealed that many of the area's respected court judges had regularly accepted bribes from people whose cases they were deciding. Many theorists have viewed this steady shift of public attention towards white-collar crime as an extension of a more fundamental erosion of confidence in government and institutional authority.

A whirlwind of new technologies aggravates the problem. High-tech systems are efficient not only for making compact disks and microcomputers, but for committing sophisticated crimes. The same computer accounting system that transfers money with great efficiency can be corrupted to misstate corporate records. In the renowned Equity Funding scandal years ago, computer experts were able to invent names for fictitious insurance policy holders, thus making Equity Funding, a company on the brink of bankruptcy, appear to be healthy. And in the E. F. Hutton debacle of the mid-1980s, high-speed money-transfer systems used by Hutton to maximize financial efficiency were manipulated to create the infamous check

Thomas Donaldson is the Wirtenberger Professor of Ethics, Loyola University of Chicago; Editor, *Soundings* Book Series on Ethics, Economics, and Business, Notre Dame University Press.

"kiting" system in which E. F. Hutton illegally earned interest on money it didn't own.

What drives well-paid executives and corporate officers to commit immoral acts? One answer may be that they carry to an extreme the motive that fuels the free-enterprise system: the drive for profit. When pursued without limit, the desire for higher salaries, bigger year-end dividends, and more attractive balance sheets corrodes corporate ethics. For firms close to bankruptcy, or executives flirting with possible demotion, the temptations can be irresistible. It was Lockheed Aircraft, nearly bankrupt and locked out of the competitive European passenger jet market, which in the 1970s decided to ensure its sale of the Tristar to Japan by bribing Japanese government officials with millions in cash. And in the 1980s it was executives of the H. J. Heinz Corporation (the makers of catsup), worried about meeting management targets, who systematically misstated corporate profits. (Executives listed as sold goods that were still lying in warehouse, and counted as expenses services that had not been rendered.)

In the corporate world the line between immorality and illegality is sometimes thin, a fact that may help explain white-collar temptation. If a member of the board of directors of a corporation arranges for a "platinum parachute," he can make a killing legally. He simply agrees with a potential buyer to drop his opposition to the purchase of the company he directs in exchange for a lump-sum payment to himself of millions of dollars (the payment is called his "platinum parachute"), even though he may be convinced that selling the company will harm shareholders and employees.

The fortune he collects is perfectly legal, although most people consider it highly immoral. Yet if the same director fails to disclose that he owns stock in a corporation that is a minor supplier of the corporation for which he is a director, he can be subject to criminal prosecution.

Some companies have spotless records, and others are always in trouble. The reason for such striking disparity may lie with the concept of "corporate culture." Many companies have traditions emphasizing honesty and fairness, and executives who set good examples for subordinates. Studies show, in fact, that the example set by one's superior is the most important factor in discouraging business crime. In the good companies word filters down that lawbreaking will not be tolerated. But in other companies, the corporate culture is lax or oriented exclusively to profit. Sometimes management-incentive programs determine salary increases by looking only at executives' achievement of profit goals, and when the goals are unrealistic, pressures can be overwhelming. And in the very worst companies (fortunately only a small percentage of United States corporations), corporate culture can actually encourage immoral behavior. Whitney North Seymour, Jr., former U.S. Attorney in New York, remarked that in such companies a "sense of clubbiness appears to attach to management so that the real sin is being caught, rather than doing something that undermines the standards of business ethics."[1]

1. *U.S. News and World Report*, September 6, 1982, p. 27.

Major Topics

- **the purpose and theoretical foundations of contracts**
- **the definitions of "promise" and "contract"**
- **the differences among various types of contracts**
- **the organizational plan for contract study in Chapters 8–15**
- **the difference between "Code" and "common law" contracts**

No aspect of modern life is free from contractual relationships. The ordinary consumer who buys a house, purchases a television or other good, borrows money, leases an apartment, rents a car, insures his or her property or life, acquires rights and obligations based on contract. Businesspeople purchasing raw materials or equipment, building a plant or retail store, selling goods or services to customers, borrowing money, selling stocks or bonds, or insuring their property are involved in contracts. Contract law provides the certainty, stability, and predictability required for the smooth and efficient performance of these and many other essential transactions.

The Law of Contracts

In its most general sense, the law of contracts concerns the legal effect of promise-making, determin-

ing when performance of a promise is legally required, and governing the relationship between parties to a contractual promise. Promises and their legal consequences are therefore the basis of contract study.

That certain promises are legally binding is fundamental to modern society. As eloquently stated by the noted legal scholar Roscoe Pound:

> In a developed economic order the claim to promised advantages is one of the most important of the individual interests that press for recognition. . . . Credit is a principal form of wealth. It is a presupposition of the whole economic order that promises will be kept. Indeed, the matter goes deeper. The social order rests upon the stability and predictability of conduct, of which keeping promises is a large item.[1]

In other words, the basic premise of contract law, expressed in the Latin phrase *pacta sunt servanda* (agreements shall be kept), reflects a more fundamental premise of human conduct generally.

The policy favoring performance of promises is supported on many theoretical grounds. Historically, giving a promise or concluding an agreement constituted a solemn commitment, based upon religious, moral, or ethical grounds, to perform. This "sanctity of contract" approach is bolstered by the

---

1. 3 Pound, *Jurisprudence* 162 (1959).

law's general recognition of private autonomy in contract matters. Under the principle of "freedom of contract," the law allows individuals to regulate their own affairs by private agreement by recognizing the promises embodied in the agreement as legally binding. Yet another approach supports enforcement of contracts on grounds that a promise, once made, induces others to rely upon it, creating an expectation of performance. Finally, and perhaps most important, promises are enforced because the needs of modern business and society generally require recognition of binding promises. Because all of the foregoing considerations—personal responsibility or morality, individual autonomy, fairness, and economic efficiency—support enforcement of promises, it is no surprise that contract principles are among the most firmly rooted in law.

Although the law generally allows individuals to order their conduct by private agreement, "freedom of contract" is certainly not absolute. Increasingly in recent years the law has imposed limitations upon private contract to prevent abuse in the bargaining process and enforcement of agreements that are illegal or otherwise contrary to public policy. These various limitations are discussed extensively throughout the contracts material.

Contract law is the basic framework of all commercial law. Therefore, although contracts are discussed here as a separate and distinct topic, many later topics are merely refined applications of contract principles. For example, rights and duties in property, commercial paper, agency, partnership, corporations, suretyship, secured transactions, and insurance are frequently determined on the basis of contractual relationships. Even when a transaction is governed by statute—such as the Uniform Commercial Code or the Uniform Partnership Act—the statutory rules may, in many cases, be changed by a contract between the parties.

Promise and Contract

Promise Defined. In legal terms, a **promise** is simply a commitment or undertaking that something will or will not happen in the future. The person making the promise is the **promisor,** and the person to whom the promise is made is the **promisee.** For example, if Sam promises to sell goods

to Betty and to deliver them in thirty days, Sam is the promisor and Betty the promisee. Sam indicates that something *will* happen in the future; goods will be delivered. Alternatively, the promisor can indicate that something will *not* happen in the future. Suppose, for example, that Sam, in exchange for an agreed sum of money, indicates that he *will not* file a lawsuit against Betty. The definition of a promise includes both types of commitments.

Contract Defined. People make promises all the time: to show up on a date, to pay back a loan, to obey certain rules. Contract law is concerned with a special class of promises, for a **contract** is "a promise or a set of promises for the breach of which the law gives a remedy, or the performance of which the law in some way recognizes as a duty."[2] Thus, not all promises are contracts. What distinguishes contractual from noncontractual promises are the consequences of failure to perform. A promisor who fails to perform a noncontractual promise incurs no legal liability. If, however, a promise is contractual, the promisee is generally entitled to a contract remedy in the event of the promisor's nonperformance or *breach*. The most common remedy available for breach of contract is an award of dollar damages. If in the opinion of the court money is an inadequate remedy, the court may force the promisor to actually *perform* the breached promise—a remedy known as *specific performance.*

For example, assume a seller and buyer, on March 1, enter into a contract for the sale of 500 fountain pens for $2,000. Delivery of the pens and payment of the price are to occur on June 1. If the seller fails to deliver on June 1, the buyer is entitled to a contract remedy—dollar damages, or, in an appropriate case, specific performance, which would require actual delivery of the 500 pens for $2,000.

Joint and Several Promises. An indefinite number of people may contract with one another. Promises may be made by or to individuals or groups acting together. If there is more than one promisor in a

---

2. *Restatement (Second) of Contracts* §1.

contract, some or all of them may promise the same performance. Rights and duties created by multiple promises of the same performance are commonly stated to be "joint," "several," or "joint and several." If two or more persons are **jointly liable** on a contract, each promisor undertakes the duty to render the same performance. In joint liability, all copromisors are liable for the entire performance, even though one or more others are also liable to perform the same duty. A joint promisor is therefore effectively liable for the performance of each one of his copromisors.

Liability of copromisors is several if (1) each promises a separate performance to be rendered respectively by each of them or (2) each makes a separate promise that the same performance will be rendered. Therefore, the term **severally liable** means that each party is liable alone or individually. Because several liability is separate and distinct, a lawsuit to enforce the contract may be brought against each several promisor independently, without joining other copromisors. For example, if Albert and Bob each promise to pay Charles $500, making a total of $1,000, their promises are several. If Albert and Bob together promise to pay Charles a total of $1,000, each to be fully responsible for the entire debt, their promises are joint.

Promises made by two or more parties can be both **joint and several** if the promisors bind themselves jointly as one party and also severally as separate parties. For example, if Albert and Bob both together and individually promise to pay Charles $1,000, their liability is joint and several. Thus, in a joint and several contract, there is one more contract (the joint contract) than there are promisors. Whether liability is joint, several, or joint and several is dependent upon the intention of the parties, determined from the language used.[3]

---

3. The joint liability concept appears at various other points throughout the text including multiple tort-feasors (see Chapter 5), cosuretyship (see Chapter 33), the liability of partners for tort, breach of trust, and contract (see Chapter 43), and the liability of two or more persons signing a negotiable instrument (see discussion of UCC §3-118(e) in Chapter 25).

Enforceable and Unenforceable Contracts

Contract law makes promises legally enforceable. A contract is legally **enforceable** if the promisee is entitled to a contract remedy if the promisor fails to perform. Generally speaking, a promise is enforceable as a contract if it meets two fundamental requirements:

1. *Agreement*—An enforceable contract requires an agreement or bargain between the parties. An agreement is created when an offer made by one party is accepted by the other.
2. *Consideration*—A promise must generally be supported by consideration to be enforceable as a contract. Consideration refers to a promise or a performance that is bargained for and given in exchange for the promise.

Taken collectively, offer, acceptance, and consideration form a conceptual unit commonly known as "contract formation." Contract formation is discussed in Chapters 8 and 9.

The existence of an agreement supported by consideration does not necessarily guarantee the enforceability of the promises contained therein. One or more formation "defects" may be present. These "defects" are generally divided into four categories: (1) lack of contractual capacity of one or both parties, (2) lack of genuine assent to the bargain due to factors such as fraud, misrepresentation, mistake, duress, or undue influence, (3) a contractual purpose that is illegal or otherwise contrary to public policy, or (4) lack of proper formality when legal formalities are required. These defects render contractual promises either *unenforceable* or *voidable*.

If a contract is **unenforceable** no contract remedy (either damages or specific performance) is available for its breach. A contract may be unenforceable, for example, because its performance would be illegal or otherwise contrary to public policy, or because it does not comply with the Statute of Frauds that requires that certain types of contracts (for example, a land-sale contract) be evidenced by a writing. Therefore, an *oral* agreement to sell land is unenforceable: A court will not award a contract remedy to either the seller or buyer if the other fails to perform.

Void and Voidable Contracts

Literally, a **void promise** or contract is one that is totally without legal force or effect. The term is, however, often used imprecisely, often simply referring to an unenforceable promise. To avoid confusion, therefore, "void" should be used to designate only those promises having no legal force or binding effect. That is, a promise is void when it lacks one of the basic elements of contract formation—agreement and consideration. For example, a promise to make a gift in the future is void because it is not supported by consideration.

A void contract must also be carefully distinguished from a **voidable** contract. A voidable contract is one in which one or more parties have the power, by electing to do so, to avoid the legal relations created by the contract. Avoidance of a voidable contract is commonly designated "disaffirmance." A voidable contract is perfectly binding and enforceable unless and until the party with the power to disaffirm elects to do so. That is, a person with a power to avoid a contract may choose instead to be bound. Such a **ratification** extinguishes that person's power of avoidance and makes the contract enforceable against her. Conversely, disaffirmance discharges the contractual duty and terminates the power of ratification. This power of ratification distinguishes a voidable from an unenforceable contract.

In most voidable contracts, only one party possesses the power to avoid, meaning that one party is bound and the other may elect whether or not to be bound. Voidable contracts of this type include those in which one party is a minor and contracts procured through fraud, misrepresentation, mistake, or duress. Assume that Michael, a minor, contracts to sell land to Anne, an adult, for $25,000. The contract is perfectly binding upon Anne if Michael wishes to enforce it. However, Michael's promise is voidable because he is a minor; that is, Michael has the power to extinguish his own right to the money and Anne's duty to pay it, and may avoid his obligation to convey the property. Although the ability to avoid is usually confined to one party, occasionally the contract may be voidable by either. Examples include contracts formed under a mutual mistake or in which both parties are minors.

Types of Contracts

Formal and Informal Contracts

Most contracts discussed in this part of the text are **informal** or **simple** contracts. If the basic elements of an enforceable contract are present, the promises involved are binding. With few exceptions,[4] no particular formalities need be observed.

On the other hand, certain contracts are governed by special rules that result from the contract's formal characteristics. The rules governing these **formal** contracts often differ from those applicable to contracts in general. Three types of formal contracts are the contract under seal, the recognizance, and the negotiable contract.

Contracts Under Seal. Since medieval times, the law has enforced promises under seal. Such promises generally lack consideration, basic to an enforceable informal contract, but are enforced because of the formality of their creation. Generally those formalities are a writing, a seal (historically, a wax seal with an impression upon it affixed to the paper), and delivery of the writing to the promisee. In many states the legal effect of the seal has been modified or abolished by statute.

Recognizance. Recognizance involves a promise in court by the promisor (recognizor) to make a certain payment unless a specified event occurs. Recognizances are used primarily to secure the recognizor's appearance in court or payment of bail.

Negotiable Contracts. Although the promise under seal and recognizance have little commercial

---

4. An exception to this rule exists for contracts subject to the "Statute of Frauds," which requires that some contracts be evidenced by a writing. The Statute of Frauds is discussed in Chapter 12.

utility, negotiable contracts are pervasive and fundamental in business. Negotiable contracts are of three types: (1) commercial paper (for example, notes and checks), (2) documents of title (for example, bills of lading and warehouse receipts), and (3) investment securities (for example, stocks and bonds). These contracts are governed by Articles 3, 7, and 8 respectively of the Uniform Commercial Code.[5]

Unilateral and Bilateral Contracts

A contractual obligation, as noted above, results from a "promise or a set of promises." Thus, a contract may involve: (1) a single promise made from a promisor to a promisee, (2) a mutual exchange of promises by two persons, or (3) any other combination of persons and promises. At least two parties are essential to a contract, but there may be an indefinitely greater number of promisors and promisees.

A contract containing only one promise is said to be **unilateral** ("one-sided"). That is, a unilateral contract involves a promise in exchange for performance of an act. For example, assume Art loses his antique gold watch and places a newspaper advertisement promising to pay a $100 reward for its return. Betty finds and returns the watch to Art. Art's promise to pay a $100 reward is binding as a contract. In this case, only Art makes a promise; Betty never promises to return the watch. Unilateral contracts therefore result when only one of the parties makes a promise.

In contrast, most contracts are **bilateral** ("two-sided"), involving at least two promises in which each party is both simultaneously a promisor and a promisee. Bilateral contracts therefore involve a promise in exchange for a return promise. For example, assume Seller and Buyer have a contract for the sale of an automobile. Seller promises to deliver and transfer title to a 1955 Chevrolet on June 1. In exchange, Buyer promises to pay $5,000 on that date. Seller is both a promisor (of the promise to deliver and transfer title to the car) and a prom-

isee (of Buyer's promise to pay $5,000). Conversely, Buyer is a promisor (of the promise to pay $5,000) and a promisee (of Seller's promise to deliver and transfer title to the car). Bilateral contracts result from a mutual exchange of promises. Figure 7–1 summarizes the difference between unilateral and bilateral contracts.

The unilateral-bilateral distinction is important in understanding the manner in which an offer to contract may be accepted, a topic discussed in Chapter 8.

Express and Implied Contracts

Express Contracts or Terms. Contracts are often characterized as either express or implied. A contract is **express** if it arises from the language, either oral or written, of the parties. Assume S states to B, "I offer to sell you my car for $1,500," and B responds, "I accept." In this case the promises involved are express.

Contracts or Terms Implied in Fact. A promise also may be inferred from conduct other than lan-

| Figure 7–1 | **Unilateral and Bilateral Contracts** |

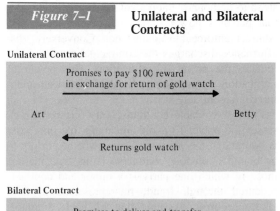

Unilateral Contract

Promises to pay $100 reward
in exchange for return of gold watch

Art → Betty

Returns gold watch

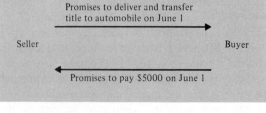

Bilateral Contract

Promises to deliver and transfer
title to automobile on June 1

Seller → Buyer

Promises to pay $5000 on June 1

---

5. Commercial paper is the subject of Part IV. Documents of title are discussed in Chapter 35 and investment securities are discussed in Chapter 46. The general scope of the various UCC articles is discussed in Chapter 6.

guage. In this case, the contract is said to be **implied in fact.**[6] Suppose A brings his turntable to B's shop for repair. A informs B of the problem and requests that he fix it. B agrees. Even though the parties are silent on the point, a promise by A to pay the cost of the repair would be inferred. Thus, a contract implied in fact is an actual contract. The intent of the parties is ascertained and enforced by the court based upon the actions of the parties, not upon their oral or written statements.

Contract Terms Supplied by Law. In addition to those arising expressly or by inference from conduct, contract terms also may be supplied by the common law. For example, contract law generally imposes a duty of good faith and fair dealing upon the parties. Thus, a duty to act in good faith might be viewed as an implied term in all contracts. Statutes are also a fertile source of implied contract terms. Certain statutes and administrative regulations, for example, prescribe standard forms for contracts such as insurance policies and bills of lading. In addition, in contracts involving goods, the Uniform Commercial Code often supplies a contract term if the parties fail to address a particular matter in their express agreement. Assume Seller agrees to sell and Buyer to buy 100 dishwashers. No other express terms are included. Article 2 of the UCC (Sales) supplies a myriad of additional terms including price, time, place, and manner of delivery, warranties, passage of title and risk of loss, and remedies.

Contracts Implied in Law. In contrast to the contract implied in fact, a contract also may be ''implied in law.'' Such a **quasi-contract** is not really a contract at all, but a form of the remedy of restitution discussed in detail in Chapter 15. Quasi-contract is designed to provide a remedy when a benefit is conferred by one party upon another, who retains the benefit. If necessary to prevent unjust enrichment of the benefited party, the law implies or imposes a promise (the quasi-contract) to pay the reasonable value of the benefit conferred. To illustrate, assume Wilson owes Carr $100. Wilson pays Carr by check but inadvertently makes it payable

for $1,000. To prevent a windfall to Carr, the court may imply a promise by Carr (the quasi-contract) to pay $900 to Wilson.

The following case illustrates the distinction between express and implied contracts.

Eaton v. Engelcke Manufacturing, Inc.
681 P.2d 1312 (Wash. App. 1984)

The defendant Engelcke Manufacturing, Inc. asked its employee, plaintiff John Eaton, whether he could design an electronic schematic for ''Whizball,'' an electronic game that Engelcke planned to design and manufacture. After Eaton stated that he estimated he could design the game in three months at a cost of $1,200–1,500, Engelcke asked him to proceed and told him the compensation would be determined when the project was complete. As Eaton worked on the design, Engelcke made several changes necessitating redesign of the electronics and circuitry. During the course of the project, Eaton and Engelcke had numerous conversations concerning additional compensation because of the increased length and complexity and Engelcke repeatedly assured Eaton that he would be paid for the work. After Eaton had worked on the project for 11 months during his off-duty hours and the schematic was 90% complete, Engelcke terminated Eaton's employment and refused to pay him for the design project.

Eaton sued Engelcke for breach of contract and the trial court awarded him damages of $5,415. On appeal, Engelcke argued that it had entered into an express contract with Eaton for production of a completed schematic design and, because Eaton had not produced the design, Engelcke owed him nothing.

Ringold, Judge
. . . The various contentions concerning liability and damages may be resolved by a careful definition of the terms involved. An express contract is one where the intentions of the parties and the terms of the agreement are expressed by the parties in writing or orally at the time it is entered into. . . . The law recognizes two classes of im-

---

6. More accurately, ''inferred from fact.''

plied contracts: those implied in fact and those implied in law. . . . A contract implied in fact

> is an agreement depending for its existence on some act or conduct of the party sought to be charged and arising by implication from circumstances which, according to common understanding, show a mutual intention on the part of the parties to contract with each other. The services must be rendered under such circumstances as to indicate that the person rendering them expected to be paid therefor, and that the recipient expected, or should have expected, to pay for them.

Johnson v. Nasi [309 P.2d 380 (Wash. 1957)]. A true implied contract, or contract implied in fact, does not describe a legal relationship which differs from an express contract: only the mode of proof is different. . . . A contract implied in law, or "quasi contract," on the other hand, arises from an implied duty of the parties not based on a contract, or on any consent or agreement. Recovery is quasi contract is based on the prevention of unjust enrichment. . . .

With these definitions in mind, we turn to the specific contentions raised by Engelcke. Its arguments against liability are premised upon the claim that the parties had an express oral contract.

The burden of proving an express contract is on the party asserting it, who must prove that the parties expressly agreed to each essential fact, including the price, time and manner of performance. . . . The trial court's findings indicate that the parties did not expressly agree to these elements. These unchallenged findings are verities on appeal, . . . and support the conclusion that the parties did not have an express contract for the design of the schematic.

In other unchallenged findings, the court found that Eaton's services in designing the prototype were rendered at Engelcke's request. The findings demonstrate that the services were "rendered under such circumstances as to indicate that the person rendering them expected to be paid therefor, and that the recipient expected, or should have expected, to pay for them." *Johnson v. Nasi, supra.* . . . These findings, in turn, support the court's legal conclusion that the parties had an en-

forceable implied in fact contract to pay Eaton the reasonable value of the services rendered. . . .

Engelcke also challenges Eaton's recovery on the ground that Engelcke received nothing of value from Eaton. This argument mistakenly assumes that the court held Engelcke liable in quasi contract and awarded damages so as to prevent Engelcke's unjust enrichment. . . . As previously indicated, Engelcke's liability was based on an implied in fact contract. The proper measure of recovery is not the benefit obtained but the reasonable value of the services rendered. . . . Eaton presented expert testimony that the reasonable value of his services was $7800. The court's award of $5415 is within the range of evidence presented at trial and will not be disturbed on appeal. . . .

[Judgment affirmed.]

Executed and Executory Contracts

As defined above, a contract consists of a legally enforceable promise or set of promises. Yet, contracting parties ordinarily do not bargain merely for promises; they seek *performance* of those promises. Thus, the ordinary contract involves an exchange of promises followed on a later date by an exchange of performances. To indicate a contract's stage of performance, the law uses the terms executory and executed.

A promise or contract is **executed** if it has been completed or performed and **executory** if it is yet to be performed. At any given time a contract may be partially executed and partially executory. Assume that on December 1, Seller contracts to sell goods to Buyer for $500. Delivery is to be made on January 1 with payment to follow on January 30. On December 1, the contract is wholly executory, yet to be performed on both sides. As of the date of delivery, the contract is partially executed (the goods have been delivered) and partially executory (the purchase price is yet to be paid). Once the money is paid, the contract is wholly executed.

If a contract is fully performed as agreed, the contractual duties are said to be discharged. To **discharge** a contractual obligation is to extinguish or terminate it. As a noun, the term discharge is sometimes used to designate the act, event, or instrument terminating the binding force of the contract. Most commonly, contractual duties are discharged by full performance by both parties. Contractual obligations may, however, be discharged prior to full performance (that is, while the contract is wholly or partially executory). A party's duty may be discharged, for example, through impracticability of performance, a mutual agreement to rescind the contract, a substitute or compromise contract, or the other party's breach. The various circumstances under which enforceable contract duties are discharged are discussed throughout the contracts chapters, most notably in the material on performance of contracts.

Scope and Organization of Contract Study

The Chronology of a Contract

Contract issues may be viewed as occurring along a time continuum from preliminary negotiations through contract formation to performance. In the preliminary negotiation stage, the parties communicate, sometimes extensively, about the subject matter of the proposed contract. Possible contract terms are suggested and accepted, rejected, or modified. Ultimately the parties reach agreement concerning both the desire to enter into a contract and the terms of that contract. That is, the parties decide what each will do or promise to do in exchange for the return promise or performance of the other. This process of contract formation is covered in Chapters 8 and 9.

Although the law usually enforces the promises made by the parties at the conclusion of their bargaining, certain factors, discussed in Chapters 10 through 12, may render otherwise binding promises either voidable or unenforceable. Chapter 10 covers contracts void or voidable because one or both parties lacks (or has limited) contractual capacity as well as contracts unenforceable in whole or in part as illegal or otherwise contrary to public policy. Chapter 11 discusses contracts voidable due to fraud, misrepresentation, mistake, duress, or undue influence in the bargaining process. Chapter 12 covers the Statute of Frauds, which requires that

certain contracts be evidenced by a writing to be enforceable.[7] In short, an agreement reached by competent parties, free from illegality, fraud, misrepresentation, mistake, or duress, and meeting any necessary writing requirements is binding as a contract.

Assuming binding contractual promises are created, the law must then determine who is entitled to enforce and who is required to perform them. Ordinarily, the promisors and promisees of the various contractual promises, known as the **parties,** are required to perform and entitled to enforce them. Occasionally, however, third parties may have rights or obligations under a contract. Simply defined, a **third party** is a person other than one of the contracting parties who is affected by the contract in question. Rights and obligations of third parties in contract are discussed in Chapter 13.

Once the foregoing issues have been resolved, a duty to perform the enforceable promises ultimately arises. This duty is breached if either party fails to perform when agreed or in some cases when a party repudiates or renounces his duty prior to the time of agreed performance. Issues arising during the performance of a contract are treated in Chapter 14.

A party who breaches a binding contractual promise is liable to the other for a contract remedy. Remedies are therefore inextricably tied to issues of performance and nonperformance. For this reason, remedies are covered in Chapter 15, immediately following the basic performance material. Figure 7–2 illustrates the life cycle of a contract.

Common Law and Code Contracts

Sources of Contract Law. As noted in Chapter 6, Article 2 of the Uniform Commercial Code (Sales) occupies an important position in the overall study of contract law. The scope of Article 2 and its relationship to contract law generally must therefore be carefully noted. Section 2-102 provides that:

> Unless the context otherwise requires, this Article applies to *transactions in goods;* it does not apply

---

7. Also discussed in Chapter 12 are other issues involving written contracts, including contract construction and interpretation, and the legal effect of the adoption of a writing.

Figure 7–2	**Life Cycle of a Contract**

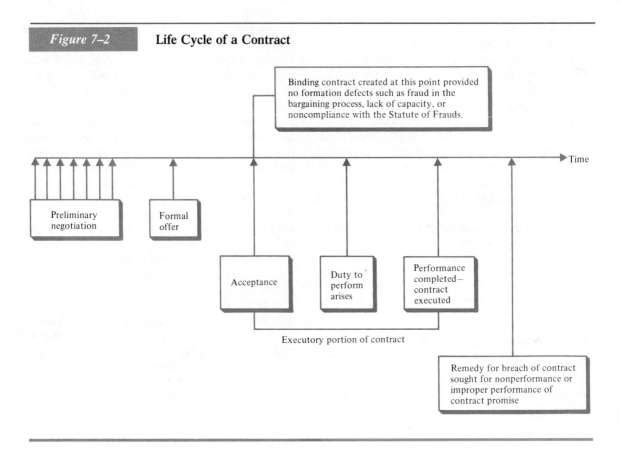

---

to any transaction which although in the form of an unconditional contract to sell or present sale is intended to operate only as a security transaction. . . .

By removing security interests in goods from the "transactions" covered,[8] the basic scope of Article 2 becomes *contracts for the sale of goods.*

Of course many contracts, such as those for the sale of land, employment and other personal services, insurance, and building construction, do not involve a sale of goods. Being outside the scope of Article 2, these contracts are governed by the vast common law of contracts. Hence, a fundamental distinction exists in contract law between "Code" and "common law" contracts.

Although code and common law contracts are governed by two different bodies of law, there is a significant overlap between them for two reasons. First, the Code is not exhaustive in the coverage of its subjects. As discussed in Chapter 6, various legal principles and doctrines existing outside the Code often supplement its provisions. For example, Article 2 includes several sections concerning formation of sales contracts, but leaves the remaining formation issues to the common law of contracts. Thus, with respect to issues not specifically addressed by the Code, common law rules govern both types of contracts. Second, courts have exhibited an increasing tendency in recent years to apply Article 2 rules by analogy to common law contracts. This trend is evidenced by the fact that the *Restatement (Second) of Contracts,* published in 1979, has adopted many Code rules as now applicable to common law contracts. In other words,

---

8. These are governed by Article 9 of the Code.

Article 2 has significantly affected the development of the common law of contracts. Although a combination of these factors provides more consistency between Code and common law rules, significant differences remain. The distinction between the two, therefore, continues to be of fundamental importance in the study of contract law.

Goods Defined. **Goods** is one of the most important terms in the study of contract law. As indicated above, if the contract in question involves a sale of *goods,* it is governed primarily by Article 2. If not, the common law of contracts provides the rules of law applicable to the transaction. Thus, resolving the initial issue in any contracts question (is this a Code or a common law contract?) requires a knowledge of what types of property are classified as goods.

Section 2-105(1) states the general rule that "goods"

> means all things (including specially manufactured goods) which are movable at the time of identification[9] to the contract for sale. . . .

Because the definition of goods is based on movability, real property (which, of course, is immovable) is not a good and therefore not within the scope of Article 2. Also excluded from the definition of goods are the money in which the price of the goods is to be paid, investment securities (such as stocks and bonds), and other intangibles. Thus, simply stated, goods are *tangible personal property:* television sets, automobiles, manufacturing equipment, appliances, clothing, books, furniture, stereo equipment, or virtually anything else sold at your local grocery store or shopping center. Living animals also are goods, as are their unborn young (in gestation), and the products of animals (for example, eggs, milk, wool). Further, money qualifies as a good if it is the commodity being sold, such as a coin collection. Growing crops, timber, fixtures, and minerals are also goods in most cases if they are to be removed and sold apart from the land to which they are attached. Article 2, therefore, governs a vast number of transactions between people in business (for example, a contract for raw materials or equipment used in manufacture), between retail merchants and consumers (for example, the sale of a refrigerator or television set), and between individuals not engaged in business (for example, the sale of a bicycle through a classified newspaper advertisement).

Merchant Defined. The term **merchant** is another important basic term used in Article 2. Under §2-104(1) a merchant is a person

1. who deals in goods of the kind, or
2. who otherwise (by her occupation or employment of an agent, broker, or other intermediary) holds herself out as having knowledge or skill peculiar to the business practices or goods involved in the transaction.

A transaction is deemed to be "between merchants" when *both* parties are chargeable with the knowledge or skill of a merchant.

Because Article 2 governs transactions in goods, its coverage is *not* limited only to transactions involving merchant buyers or sellers. As long as a sale of *goods* is involved, Article 2 applies, whether or not the parties are merchants. Many separate Code sections, however, discussed in the following contracts and sales chapters, apply different or specialized rules when one or both parties are merchants. The reason for this approach is that transactions between professionals or experts in a particular field require special rules not necessarily applicable to a casual or inexperienced buyer or seller.[10]

Note that the definition of merchant includes not only persons who deal in goods of the same kind—for example, the appliance dealer, hardware store, department store, or other seller out of inventory—but also includes persons who hold themselves out as having knowledge peculiar to the goods or practices involved in the transaction. Under the *goods*

---

9. The term "identification" is the process by which the particular goods to which the contract refers are designated or specified. Many important legal consequences depend upon whether or not goods have been identified to the contract. The effect of identification is discussed in Chapter 17.

10. UCC §2-104, Official Comment 1.

Table 7-1	Article 2—Merchants' Provisions	
Provision	Subject	Chapter and Page
§2-312(3)	Merchant sellers' warranty against infringement	Chapter 19 (The Sales Contract—Warranties) on page 426.
§2-314(1)	Implied warranty of merchantability	Chapter 19 (The Sales Contract—Warranties) on page 420.
§2-402(2)	Rule applying to merchant sellers who retain goods sold	Chapter 17 (The Sales Contract—Title and Risk of Loss) on page 385.
§2-403(2)	Effect of entrusting goods to a merchant	Chapter 17 (The Sales Contract—Title and Risk of Loss) on page 384.
§2-201(2)	Statute of Frauds exception between merchants	Chapter 12 (Written Agreements) on page 278.
§2-205	Firm offers by merchants	Chapter 8 (Contract Formation—Agreement) on page 173.
§2-207(2)	Effect of additional terms in an acceptance between merchants	Chapter 8 (Contract Formation—Agreement) on page 176.
§2-209(2)	Rule as between merchants giving effect to a provision on a form contract precluding modification unless in writing	Chapter 12 (Written Agreements) on page 283.
§2-103(1)(b)	Definition of "good faith" as applied to a merchant	Chapter 6 (Introduction to Property and the Uniform Commercial Code) on page 145.
§2-327(1)(c)	Obligations of a merchant buyer in a sale on approval	Chapter 17 (The Sales Contract—Title and Risk of Loss) on page 391.
§2-509(3)	Special residual risk of loss provision applicable to merchant sellers	Chapter 17 (The Sales Contract—Title and Risk of Loss) on page 390.
§2-603	Merchant buyer's duties with respect to 188 rightfully rejected goods	Chapter 18 (The Sales Contract—Remedies) on page 398.
§2-605(1)(b)	Rule between merchants creating waiver of buyer's objections after rejecting goods	Chapter 18 (The Sales Contract—Remedies) on page 397.
§2-609(2)	Standard for reasonableness of insecurity and assurance of performance between merchants	Chapter 14 (Performance of the Contract) on page 321.

aspect of the definition, for example, an auto mechanic selling a car would be a merchant. Under the *practices* aspect, almost any person in business is a merchant if goods are the subject matter of the transaction, because the practices referred to are ordinary business practices, such as answering mail. Under this portion of the definition, banks or universities may be merchants.[11]

The various merchants' provisions do not necessarily apply to all types of merchants listed above. The nature and purpose of the particular provision determines which merchants are included within its coverage. Table 7–1 lists the fourteen merchants' provisions contained in Article 2 and indicates where each is discussed in the text. The first four provisions apply only to persons who deal in goods of the kind. The remaining provisions apply to persons who qualify as merchants under any aspect of the definition.

---

11. UCC §2-104, Official Comment 2.

SUMMARY

1. Contract law is concerned with the legal implications of promise-making. That certain promises are made to be kept is a basic premise of contract law, consistent with human conduct generally, and necessary to the efficient operation of modern society.

2. A promise is simply a person's undertaking that something will or will not happen in the future. The person making the promise is the promisor, and the person to whom it is directed is the promisee. A contract is a promise or set of promises for breach of which the law gives a remedy or the performance of which the law recognizes as a duty. If a contractual promise is not performed, a contract remedy is available to the injured promisee.

3. Contracts are commonly classified according to their various characteristics. Contracts may be categorized as formal or informal, express or implied, unilateral or bilateral, enforceable or unenforceable, void or voidable, and executory or executed.

4. The life cycle of a contract may be viewed as occurring along a time continuum starting with preliminary negotiations and ending with full performance. This chronology provides a useful organizational basis for studying contracts.

5. Contract law is derived primarily from two sources: the common law and Article 2 of the Uniform Commercial Code. Code contracts are those involving sales of goods, generally meaning tangible personal property. Although all sales of goods are governed by Article 2, special rules are often applied to merchant buyers and sellers. Common law contracts include among others those involving land, employment and other services, and building construction. The distinction between the two types is important because Code rules of law differ from common law principles in many important respects.

KEY TERMS

promise	void promise
promisor	voidable contract
promisee	ratification
contract	informal (simple) contract
joint liability	formal contract
several liability	unilateral contract
joint and several liability	bilateral contract
enforceable contract	express contract
unenforceable contract	implied in fact contract

quasi-contract (implied in law contract)	party
	third party
executed contract	goods
executory contract	merchant
discharge	

QUESTIONS AND PROBLEMS

7-1 Contracts is the body of law making certain promises legally enforceable. It occupies a pivotal place in the study of commercial law generally. Why is it necessary to have a law of contract? What purposes do contracts serve?

7-2 Seller promises to sell Buyer a machine to be used in Buyer's factory, for which Buyer promises to pay $10,000. If later a dispute arises regarding the terms of this contract, the court may utilize several sources to determine the contract terms. What are these sources?

7-3 Eric, an adult, signs a written contract by which he promises to sell his guitar to Jimmy, a minor, for $500. Before the transaction takes place, however, another adult, Mick, offers Eric $700 for the guitar. When Eric tells Mick of the contract with Jimmy, Mick says "Don't worry. Contracts with minors are void." In fact, the law of the state in which Eric resides provides that contracts with minors are voidable by the minor.

(a) Has Mick correctly summarized the law by stating, "Contracts with minors are void"?

(b) Jimmy later tenders $500 to Eric. Eric says, "I'm sorry, Jimmy; our contract is unenforceable." Jimmy sues. Will the court enforce the contract?

7-4 Alice and Gertrude operate a restaurant and want to hire Snow Linen Co. to launder all of the restaurant's linens. At Snow Linen's request, Alice and Gertrude sign the following to evidence their agreement:

1. Snow Linen hereby agrees to pick up and launder all linens used by the Alice and Gertrude Restaurant from June 1 to October 1, at such times as agreed by the parties.

2. Alice and Gertrude jointly and each of them hereby agree to pay Snow Linen the sum of $200 per month for the services described in paragraph 1, payment to be made on the first day of July and the first day of each month thereafter.

Snow Linen provides laundering services during the months of June and July, but Alice and Gertrude fail to pay.

(a) Is the agreement a bilateral or unilateral contract? What is (are) the promise(s) made in this agreement? Identify the promisor and promisee of each promise.

(b) On August 1, is the contract executory or executed? Explain.

(c) If Snow Linen decides to sue for the $400 due under the contract, who can it sue?

(d) Assume that Alice has moved out of the country and Snow Linen sues only Gertrude. What is the maximum amount for which she can be held liable?

7-5 Tex, owner of the Silver Spur Bar and Lounge, hired Donald to manage operations beginning on January 1. They orally agreed that Donald would pay all operating and fixed costs and would retain the net revenues as his compensation. On April 1, Donald notified Tex to find a new manager because the arrangement was generating monthly net revenues of only $300. Tex offered Donald a 49% ownership interest in the bar if he would remain for two more years. When Donald rejected this offer, Tex asked Donald to continue to serve as manager while Tex investigated other alternatives. Donald continued to act as manager, receiving net revenues of about $300 per month as his only compensation. Whenever he asked Tex whether he had a new plan for com-

pensation, Tex replied "Don't you worry, we're going to make things right." On November 1, Tex hired a new manager and terminated Donald's employment. Donald sued Tex for breach of contract. An expert witness testified that reasonable compensation for management of the Silver Spur was $1,000 per month. When asked why he had not left the job earlier, Donald told the court that Tex's reassurances had convinced him that a satisfactory arrangement would be worked out.

(a) Did Donald and Tex have an express contract? Explain.

(b) Did Donald and Tex have an implied in fact contract? Explain.

(c) Assume that the court has found that a contract existed. How much should Donald be awarded as compensation?

7-6 Determine whether the following are sales of "goods" as defined in the Uniform Commercial Code:

(a) water sold by a city to its residents;

(b) electricity sold by a utility company to consumers.

7-7 A problem under §2-104, which has proven difficult for courts to resolve, is whether or not a farmer is a merchant to which the various Article 2 merchants' provisions should apply. Should a farmer be treated as a merchant under any aspect of definition stated in UCC §2-104(1)? Explain.

- the definition of an offer
- the various principles governing offers, including the master of the offer rule, the objective theory of contract, and the definiteness requirement
- the rules governing termination of offers prior to acceptance including termination by the act of the parties (revocation and rejection) and by operation of law
- the principles governing acceptance of offers, including the manner in which offers may be accepted

Chapters 8 and 9 examine contract formation, the basic process by which binding promises are created. Contract formation generally requires two elements: (1) mutual assent, or agreement, to an exchange and (2) consideration, what each party gives up in exchange for the return promise or performance of the other. The first element, agreement, is covered in this chapter. Consideration is the subject of Chapter 9.

Because most contracts are enforced without regard to form, the contract formation process usually is an informal process starting with preliminary inquiries or expressions of interest by one of the parties. These preliminary communications are often followed by more detailed inquiry, negotiation, or dickering over specific terms of the proposed contract, including price, qualities, and characteristics of any property or services involved, time or times for performance, and other rights and obligations of the parties. Specific contract terms are determined only after this often laborious process of give and take, inclusion and exclusion, proposal and counterproposal. Although not all contracts require extensive precontract negotiation, many do.

Agreement is ultimately reached when an offer is made by one party (the offeror) and accepted by the other (the offeree). Agreement analysis is therefore generally divided into two parts, offer and acceptance. This chapter follows a similar organizational approach, although offer and acceptance issues should be viewed as closely intertwined. Further, as noted above, the offer, the traditional starting point in contract formation analysis, often occurs well into the life cycle of the contract.

The Offer

Offer Defined

An **offer** is a conditional promise made by the offeror to the offeree, giving the offeree the power of acceptance, or the power to create a contract. Or, as defined in the *Restatement (Second) of Contracts:*

> An offer is the manifestation of willingness to enter into a bargain, so made as to justify another

person in understanding that his assent to that bargain is invited and will conclude it.[1]

Suppose a neighbor says to you, "I offer to sell you my car for $2,000." The neighbor has made an offer. The offer gives you, the offeree, the power to convert your neighbor's promise into a contractual obligation. If you accept and the other elements of contract formation are present, appropriate contract remedies may be recovered in the event either party fails to perform. Thus, by making an offer, the offeror agrees to be bound contractually in the event of acceptance.

Master of the Offer Rule

The offeror is the **master of the offer,** which means that the offeree must accept according to the terms of the offer. The requirements of the offer might include not only the requested promise or performance, but also the time, place, and manner of acceptance. For example, if the offer states that acceptance must take place by noon on January 10, any acceptance attempted after that time is ineffective. If the offer states how an acceptance must be communicated—perhaps by telephone, telegraph, computer mail, or letter—the offeree must use the prescribed means. In short, the offeror as the master of the offer dictates the terms under which the offer is to be accepted. Any deviation by the offeree from those terms generally results in no contract. Because the offeror incurs contract liability upon acceptance, the master of the offer rule allows the offeror to control the terms upon which he is willing to assume that liability. This concept forms the basis of several rules discussed in this chapter.

The Objective Theory of Contract

Even though the offeror is the master of the offer, the terms of the offer are judged by an *objective,* not a subjective, test. Under this test the offeror's subjective intention is generally irrelevant; rather, whatever meaning the offeror conveys either intentionally or negligently to the offeree is used. Therefore, the existence and terms of an offer are judged

from the point of view of a reasonable person in the position of the offeree.

For example, assume a fellow student sends you a letter offering to sell you her car. Although the student actually *intends* the offering price to be $2,500, she inadvertently types $2,000 in the letter. Upon receipt of the letter, a reasonable person in your position as the offeree would assume that an offer for sale has been made at $2,000. If you accept the offer without reason to know that a mistake has been made, a contract exists at $2,000. Thus, to have a binding agreement, there need be no actual "meeting of the minds" or subjective agreement between the parties. As long as there is an outward manifestation of mutual assent, a contract exists. A party is not generally allowed to assert that his subjective intention differs from his outward manifestation. This rule is known as the **objective theory of contract,** which protects the stability of contractual relationships by allowing a party to act upon reasonable appearance rather than be subject to a hidden, uncommunicated intention of the other.

The objective theory is often used to test the legal effect of various communications between the parties during the negotiating stage. Each statement is analyzed from the viewpoint of the person to whom it is made to determine whether it amounts to an offer or is merely an expression of interest, solicitation of an offer, request for clarification, or request for a better or alternative contract term. The prior relationship or conduct of the parties is often important to this inquiry. Circumstances may indicate, for instance, that a person made the alleged "offer" in jest or while intoxicated, making it difficult to construe the communication as a true "manifestation of willingness to enter into a bargain." Making this determination is often a difficult issue, as the following classic case illustrates.

Lucy v. Zehmer
84 S.E. 2d 516 (Va. 1954)

Plaintiff W. O. Lucy sued defendants A. H. Zehmer and Ida S. Zehmer, requesting that the court enforce the following written agreement: "We hereby agree to sell to W. O. Lucy the Ferguson Farm complete

---

1. *Restatement (Second) of Contracts* §24.

for $50,000.00, title satisfactory to buyer.'' The agreement, which was dated and signed by A. H. Zehmer and his wife, Ida S. Zehmer, had been written by Zehmer in a restaurant during a conversation with Lucy. The Zehmers asserted that the writing had been drawn up while Zehmer was under the influence of alcohol and had been intended as a joke. Lucy maintained that he believed the agreement was a valid contract.

The trial court held that the agreement was not legally binding and denied specific performance. Lucy appealed.

Buchanan, Justice

. . . The defendants insist that the evidence was ample to support their contention that the writing sought to be enforced was prepared as a bluff or dare to force Lucy to admit that he did not have $50,000; that the whole matter was a joke; that the writing was not delivered to Lucy and no binding contract was ever made between the parties.

It is an unusual, if not bizarre, defense. When made to the writing admittedly prepared by one of the defendants and signed by both, clear evidence is required to sustain it.

In his testimony, Zehmer claimed that he "was high as a Georgia pine," and that the transaction "was just a bunch of two doggoned drunks bluffing to see who could talk the biggest and say the most." That claim is inconsistent with his attempt to testify in great detail as to what was said and what was done. It is contradicted by other evidence as to the condition of both parties, and rendered of no weight by the testimony of his wife that when Lucy left the restaurant she suggested that Zehmer drive him home. The record is convincing that Zehmer was not intoxicated to the extent of being unable to comprehend the nature and consequences of the instrument he executed, and hence that instrument is not to be invalidated on that ground. . . .

The evidence is convincing also that Zehmer wrote two agreements, the first one beginning "I hereby agree to sell. . . ."

The appearance of the contract, the fact that it was under discussion for forty minutes or more before it was signed; Lucy's objection to the first draft because it was written in the singular, and he wanted Mrs. Zehmer to sign it also; the rewriting to meet that objection and the signing by Mrs. Zehmer; the discussion of what was to be included in the sale, the provision for the examination of the title, the completeness of the instrument that was executed, the taking possession of it by Lucy with no request or suggestion by either of the defendants that he give it back, are facts which furnish persuasive evidence that the execution of the contract was a serious business transaction rather than a casual, jesting matter as defendants now contend. . . .

Not only did Lucy actually believe, but the evidence shows he was warranted in believing, that the contract represented a serious business transaction and a good faith sale and purchase of the farm.

In the field of contracts, as generally elsewhere, "We must look to the outward expression of a person as manifesting his intention rather than to his secret and unexpressed intention. 'The law imputes to a person an intention corresponding to the reasonable meaning of his words and acts.'" [*First Nat. Exchange Bank of Roanoke v. Roanoke Oil Co.*, 192 S.E. 764, 770 (Va. 1937).]

At no time prior to the execution of the contract had Zehmer indicated to Lucy by word or act that he was not in earnest about selling the farm. . . .

The mental assent of the parties is not requisite for the formation of a contract. If the words or other acts of one of the parties have but one reasonable meaning, his undisclosed intention is immaterial except when an unreasonable meaning which he attaches to his manifestations is known to the other party. . . .

An agreement or mutual assent is of course essential to a valid contract but the law imputes to a person an intention corresponding to the reasonable meaning of his words and acts. If his words and acts, judged by a reasonable standard, manifest an intention to agree, it is immaterial what may be the real but unexpressed state of his mind. . . .

So a person cannot set up that he was merely jesting when his conduct and words would warrant a reasonable person in believing that he intended a real agreement. . . .

Whether the writing signed by the defendants and now sought to be enforced by the complainants was the result of a serious offer by Lucy and a serious acceptance by the defendants, or was a serious offer by Lucy and an acceptance in secret jest by the defendants, in either event it constituted a binding contract of sale between the parties. . . .

[Judgment reversed and remanded.]

Intent and Definiteness

Elements of an Offer. To be an offer, a communication must meet two criteria: (1) it must indicate an intention by the offeror to be contractually bound upon acceptance and (2) the terms of the offer must be reasonably certain or definite. Both issues are determined by a close analysis of the language of the communication involved and the surrounding circumstances.

The communication must first be examined to determine whether it evidences a serious intention to be legally obligated or is merely an expression of opinion, statement of intention, invitation to commence negotiation, or solicitation of an offer. Suppose Smith says to Jones: "I'm thinking of selling my house, and I'd like to get $50,000 for it." In this case, no offer for sale at $50,000 has been made to Jones. Smith is merely making a statement of intention, or at most, soliciting offers. A reasonable person in Jones's position would not assume that Smith has made a commitment to him to sell at $50,000.

Intent to be bound, by itself, is not enough. An offer must also be sufficiently definite and explicit so that, if accepted, a court in a subsequent dispute has a reasonably certain basis upon which to determine the existence of a breach and to award an appropriate remedy. In other words, this **definiteness** (or certainty) requirement means that the agreement must contain certain minimum terms. The minimum terms necessary for enforcement vary with the type of contract involved.[2]

Advertisements and Catalog Quotations. Both intent and definiteness issues are present in disputes involving the legal effect of advertisements and catalog quotations. For example, does a newspaper advertisement hawking dishwashers for $239.00 each constitute an offer to sell? Most courts hold that the ordinary newspaper or other advertisement is a mere invitation to make an offer, not a binding offer to sell at the price stated in the advertisement. This result is supported on two grounds. First, the advertiser ordinarily does not intend that legal consequences result from merely placing the advertisement. Neither the advertiser nor the reader contemplates closing a deal without further action by the seller. Rather, the reasonable inference ordinarily drawn from the advertisement is that readers are invited to come in and examine and negotiate. After such further communication and negotiation, an offer may be made and accepted, resulting in a sale of specific goods or services at an agreed price. The second reason for refusing to treat advertisements as offers is that an advertisement is generally too indefinite to constitute an offer, because it commonly omits many essential terms, most notably the *quantity*.

Offers, however, may be made by advertisement. If an advertisement is sufficiently definite and explicit to indicate an intention on the part of the advertiser to enter into a contract on those terms, courts have construed the advertisement as an offer. For example, in *Lefkowitz v. Great Minneapolis Surplus Store*,[3] the defendant store published the following advertisement in the newspaper:

Saturday 9 A.M.
2 Brand New Pastel
Mink 3-Skin Scarfs
Selling for $89.50
Out they go

Saturday. Each . . . $1.00
1 Black Lapin Stole
Beautiful, worth $139.50 . . . $1.00
First Come
First Served.

---

2. The UCC generally follows the principles outlined above for contracts involving goods. Section 2-204(3) provides that a contract will not fail for indefiniteness even if one or more terms are left open if (1) the parties have *intended* to make a contract, and (2) there is a *reasonably certain* basis for giving an appropriate remedy. As explained in Chapter 16, many of the omitted terms are supplied by the Code.

3. 86 N.W.2d 689 (Minn. 1957).

Lefkowitz, the plaintiff, was the first person in the store on Saturday, and tendered $1.00 for the black lapin (rabbit) stole. Defendant refused to sell on the basis of its "house rule" that only women were qualified to receive the bargains advertised. The court held that the advertisement was clear, definite, explicit, and left nothing open for negotiation, and thus constituted an offer. The limitation of the offer to women only, because not stated in the offer itself, was not binding on the plaintiff. Having complied with the terms of the offer, the plaintiff was therefore entitled to performance. Note that this advertisement contains two factors not present in the ordinary newspaper advertisement: the quantity is stated and promissory language indicating an intent to be legally bound is present ("First come, First served").

Communication, Effectiveness, and Duration of the Offer

Communication of the Offer. Once an offer is made, it must be communicated to the offeree, and to create a contract, the act or promise constituting acceptance must be done or made in response to the offer. In other words, the offer must *induce* the acceptance. To illustrate, suppose Sonia loses her watch, and places an advertisement in the newspaper offering a reward for its return. Bryan finds the watch and returns it to Sonia without knowledge of the reward offer. Bryan is not entitled to the reward. Because the offer has not been communicated to the offeree, his act of returning the watch does not constitute acceptance.

Not only must the offer be communicated to the offeree, it must also be communicated by the offeror or his or her authorized agent and in the manner chosen by the offeror. This requirement is merely an application of the master of the offer rule. Assume Smith directs her secretary to type a letter to Bates, offering to sell her car to Bates for $500. Prior to mailing the letter, the secretary sees Bates in the hallway and informs her of the offer. No offer has been made because the offer was not communicated either by the offeror or a person authorized by the offeror to communicate it. Assume further that after being informed of the offer, Bates walks into Smith's office and sees the letter on Smith's desk. Bates may not accept because the of-

fer has not been communicated to Bates in the medium chosen by the offeror, the mails. In these cases, however, an attempted acceptance by Bates is itself an offer, which Smith may accept if she chooses.

Effectiveness and Duration of the Offer. An offer is not effective until properly communicated to the offeree. For example, if an offer is mailed on January 1 and received on January 4, it is effective on January 4. Once an offer is effective, the offeree obtains power of acceptance—the power to create a contract. The duration of that power depends upon how long the offer is held open. The offer may state that it will be held open for a stipulated period—for example, thirty days. In this case—the offer remains open for the stipulated period, which runs from the date of the offer's effectiveness (the date of the receipt). The offeror as master of the offer, however, can provide that the time period runs from the date the offer was sent or from any other date. If no period is stipulated, the offer remains open for a reasonable time. What constitutes a "reasonable time" is a question of fact dependent upon the nature of the subject matter and all the circumstances under which the offer was made.

Effect of Mistake in Transmission. Occasionally, a mistake is made in transmitting the offer, not by the offeror, but by the chosen means of communicating it—for example, a telegraph company. A majority of courts hold that the offeror bears the risk of mistake in transmission and is thus bound to the offer *as transmitted*. An offeree who has reason to know of the mistake, however, may not take advantage of it by accepting the offer. For example, assume Smith offers to sell her car to Bates by telegraph for $950. The offer is incorrectly transmitted by the telegraph company as $905. If Bates accepts, Smith is bound to the contract at $905. Had the offer been transmitted as $95, Bates would probably have reason to know of the mistake and could therefore not accept the offer.

The majority rule appears consistent with the objective theory of contract because the offeror is held to the impression that the offer makes on the offeree. Nevertheless, the rule penalizes an offeror who has acted neither intentionally nor negligently in creating the mistaken impression. This rationale has convinced a minority of courts to hold that because the offeror is not responsible for the mistake, no contract results upon acceptance by the offeree.

Termination of the Offer Before Acceptance

Once an offer has been made, it can either be terminated prior to acceptance, or accepted, thereby creating a contract. The offer may terminate prior to acceptance because it has lapsed according to its terms or after a reasonable time has passed. In the following material, three additional situations terminating the offer before acceptance are discussed: termination by the offeror (revocation), termination by the offeree (rejection), and termination by operation of law. In studying the following contract formation issues, pay special attention to the effective dates of the various communications between the offeror and the offeree. Whether an offer results in a contract or is terminated before acceptance is determined by comparing the effective dates of each communication.

Termination by the Offeror— Revocation

Generally, an offeror may revoke an offer at any time before the offeree's acceptance becomes effective. A **revocation** is simply the offeror's statement or other conduct after the offer is made, indicating that he or she no longer intends to enter into the proposed contract. The revocation is effective when it is communicated to the offeree. In other words, the objective theory of contract applies to revocations as well as offers. It is not enough that the offeror no longer *intends* to enter into a contract. That intention must be made known to the other party.

Unlike the offer, however, the revocation may be communicated either directly or indirectly to the offeree. That is, the revocation need not be communicated by the *offeror* to become effective. Assume Smith offers to sell a car to Bates for $500, but before Bates accepts the offer, Smith sells the car to Jones. Revocation would be effective if Jones notifies Bates that the car has been sold. Effective revocation occurs when the offeree receives reliable information from a third party that would

inform a reasonable person of the offeror's intent to withdraw the offer. Note that the information received must be inconsistent with the offeror's keeping the offer open. For example, no revocation occurs if Bates merely learns that Smith has offered the car to others.

A revocation made by mail or other written communication is effective when it comes into the offeree's possession, or into the possession of some person authorized by the offeree to receive it, or when it is deposited in some authorized place, such as a post office box. Therefore, the offeree cannot avoid the revocation by failing to open or read the mail.

An offer made to the general public (such as a reward offer) may be revoked by giving equal publicity to the revocation. A reward offer made by newspaper could therefore be revoked by publishing the revocation in the same newspaper, provided no better means of notification is reasonably available.

Situations in Which the Offeror Cannot Revoke. An ordinary offer is freely revocable by the offeror at any time prior to the effectiveness of the offeree's acceptance. The law, however, recognizes several situations in which an offer cannot be revoked. Two such situations, option contracts and "firm offers" under the UCC, are discussed in the following material. A third situation, based upon the doctrine of promissory estoppel, is discussed in Chapter 9.

Option Contracts. An **option** is a contract to keep an offer open for a specified period of time. In an option contract, one party promises to hold an offer open in exchange for some consideration, usually payment by the other of a specified sum of money. An option is therefore a contract limiting the offeror's (promisor's) power to revoke an offer. Unless an option contract exists, a promise by the offeror to keep an offer open is not generally binding; it is not supported by consideration from the offeree-promisee, thus lacking a basic element of an enforceable contract. In other words, a person is usually bound to perform a promise (including one to hold an offer open) only if that promise is enforceable as a contract. Assume Stevens offers to sell Bryant a tract of land for $5,000, and promises to keep the offer open for 30 days. Stevens may revoke the offer at any time prior to the expiration of the 30-day period because his promise to keep the offer open is not supported by consideration, and is therefore not a contract. If, however, Bryant had given Stevens $5—consideration—in exchange for Stevens's promise to hold the offer open, an option contract would have been created, precluding Stevens from revoking the offer prior to expiration of the stipulated period.

When an option exists, two contracts are actually contemplated: one contract (the option contract) to keep the offer open for the specified period of time and the underlying contract that comes into existence if the option is exercised. To "exercise" an option means to accept the offer embodied in the option. In the preceding example, therefore, Bryant *exercises* the option by accepting Stevens's offer to sell the land at $5,000.

Firm Offers—UCC §2-205. Section §2-205 of the UCC contains an exception to the general rule that a promise to hold an offer open needs consideration, or something exchanged, to be binding. Under the **firm offer rule,** a written, signed offer to buy or sell goods made by a merchant stating that it will be held open is binding without consideration for the period stated. If no period is stated, the offer remains open for a reasonable time, not to exceed three months. In other words, such a written firm offer is treated as an option contract for a limited period even though no consideration supports the promise.

For the rule to apply, the offer must relate to the purchase or sale of *goods* (contracts governed by Article 2 of the UCC), the offer must be made by a *merchant,* and the offer must be made in a *signed writing.* If the term providing for irrevocability is contained in a form provided by the *offeree,* the term must be separately signed by the offeror (commonly by initialing the clause involved). This rule protects the offeror against inadvertently signing a firm offer contained in a form prepared by the offeree.

The firm offer rule supports the promise on the basis of a formality (a signed writing) as a substitute for consideration usually required to support an option. The rule applies only to current short-term, firm offers and not to long-term options. An out-side time limit of three months is set. A promise made for a longer period binds the offeror only during the first three months. The promise may be renewed, and if it ever becomes supported by consideration it may continue as long as the parties provide.

Termination by the Offeree—Rejection

Rejection is the *offeree's* statement or other conduct indicating an intention not to accept the offer. Like a revocation, a rejection is effective to terminate the offer when it is received by the offeror directly or indirectly; the rejection need not be communicated by the offeree to be effective. Because a rejection terminates an offer, the offeree may not later reconsider and accept unless the offeror revives the offer. If the offeree tries to accept after initially rejecting the offer, his purported "acceptance" simply operates as a new offer, in effect, a counteroffer.

An explicit rejection (for example, the offeree says, "I reject your offer") clearly terminates the offer. In other cases, the offeree's language and other conduct must be carefully scrutinized to determine whether a reasonable person in the offeror's position would believe that a rejection has been made. For example, no rejection occurs if an offeree merely demonstrates an intention to consider the offer further. Assume Smith offers to sell a coin collection to Bates for $2,000. Bates replies, "The price seems a little high, but let me think about it." Bates has not rejected Smith's offer.

Under an option contract, the power of acceptance is generally not terminated by the offeree's rejection. The offeror is contractually obligated not to withdraw the offer during the option period. Thus, an offeree who indicates an intent not to exercise an option may nevertheless reconsider and accept within the option period unless the offeror changes position in reliance upon the previous rejection. For example, if, after the rejection, the offeror sells the subject matter of the option to a third party, the offeree is precluded from accepting.

The "Mirror Image" Rule—Rejection by Counteroffer.
Frequently the offer is not expressly rejected. Instead, the terms of the acceptance differ from or add to the terms of the offer. The tradi-

tional common law rule differs substantially from the UCC treatment of this situation.

Under the common law, the so-called **mirror image rule** governs—the acceptance must exactly conform to (or mirror) the terms of the offer. Any deviation between an attempted acceptance and the terms of the offer is deemed a rejection of the original offer and a counteroffer[4] on the new terms.

A counteroffer, like an express rejection, terminates the offeree's power to accept the original offer. Assume Smythe offers to sell his house to Burns for $30,000. Burns responds, "I accept, but at $28,000" or "I'll pay $28,000." In effect, Burns is rejecting Smythe's $30,000 offer and counteroffering at $28,000. Burns cannot change her mind later and accept Smythe's $30,000 offer, because the original offer no longer exists. If Burns simply makes an inquiry regarding different terms, requests better terms, or comments on the terms of the offer, she does not make a counteroffer. For example, if Burns had stated, "Won't you consider less?" "Is the house air-conditioned?" or "The price seems a bit high," the original offer remains effective.

The following case illustrates the application of basic common law principles of revocation and rejection by counteroffer.

Normile v. Miller

326 S.E.2d 11 (N.C. 1985)

On August 4, 1980, Richard Byer, a real estate broker with Gallery of Homes, showed a piece of real estate owned by Hazel Miller to Michael Normile and Wawie Kurniawan. After viewing the property, Normile and Kurniawan prepared a written offer to purchase that included a provision stating "Time is of the essence, therefore this offer must be accepted on or before Aug. 5th 1980." Byer delivered the offer to Miller who signed it after making several changes in the terms. The major changes were an

increase in the earnest money deposit from $100 to $500; an increase in the down payment from $875 to $1,000; and a reduction from 25 to 20 years for the term of a loan to be made by the seller. On the evening of August 4, Byer delivered the revised document to Normile and Kurniawan, who advised the broker that they intended to wait a while before making a decision. In the early afternoon of August 5, Miller entered into a contract to sell the real estate to Lawrence Segal. At about 2:00 p.m. on that day, Byer informed Normile of the contract stating "You snooze, you lose; the property has been sold." Prior to 5:00 p.m. on August 5, Normile and Kurniawan initialed the changes on the purchase form signed by Miller and delivered it and a $500 deposit to the Gallery of Homes office.

Normile and Kurniawan (plaintiff-appellants) and Segal (plaintiff-appellee) sued defendant Miller demanding performance of the contract. The trial court ruled in favor of Segal and ordered Miller to perform the contract and convey the real estate to Segal. The Court of Appeals affirmed and Normile and Kurniawan appealed to the North Carolina Supreme Court.

Frye, Justice

. . . [W]e begin with a brief description of how a typical sale of real estate is consummated. The broker whose primary duty is to secure a ready, willing, and able buyer for the seller's property, generally initiates a potential sale by procuring the prospective purchaser's signature on an offer to purchase instrument. . . . This instrument contains the prospective purchaser's "offer" of the terms he wishes to propose to the seller. . . .

In the instant case, the offerors, plaintiff-appellants, submitted their offer to purchase defendant's property. This offer contained a Paragraph 9, requiring that "this offer must be accepted on or before 5:00 p.m. Aug. 5th 1980." Thus the offeree's, defendant-seller's, power of acceptance was controlled by the duration of time for acceptance of the offer. . . . "The offeror is the creator of the power, and before it leaves his hands, he may fashion it to his will . . . if he names a specific period for its existence, the offeree can accept only during this period." Corbin, *Offer and Acceptance, and Some of the Resulting Legal Relations,* 26 Yale L.J. 169, at 183 (1917). . . .

---

4. A counteroffer is an offer made by the offeree relating to the same subject matter proposing a substituted bargain that differs from that proposed by the original offer. *Restatement (Second) of Contracts* §39.

This offer to purchase remains only an offer until the seller accepts it on the terms contained in the original offer by the prospective purchaser. . . . If the seller does accept the terms in the purchaser's offer, he denotes this by signing the offer to purchase at the bottom, thus forming a valid, binding, and irrevocable purchase contract between the seller and purchaser. However, if the seller purports to accept but changes or modifies the terms of the offer, he makes what is generally referred to as a qualified or conditional acceptance. . . . Such a reply from the seller is actually a counter-offer and a rejection of the buyer's offer. . . .

The question then becomes, did defendant-seller accept plaintiff-appellants' offer prior to the expiration of the time limit contained within the offer? We conclude that she did not. The offeree, defendant-seller, changed the original offer in several material respects, most notably in the terms regarding payment of the purchase price. . . . This qualified acceptance was in reality a rejection of the plaintiff-appellants original offer because it was coupled with certain modifications or changes that were not contained in the original offer. . . . Additionally, defendant-seller's conditional acceptance amounted to a counteroffer to plaintiff-appellants. . . .

In substance, defendant's conditional acceptance modifying the original offer did not manifest any intent to accept the terms of the original offer, including the time-for-acceptance provision, unless and until the original offeror accepted the terms included in defendant's counteroffer. The offeree, by failing to unconditionally assent to the terms of the original offer and instead qualifying his acceptance with terms of his own, in effect says to the original offeror, "I will accept your offer; provided you [agree to my proposed terms]." *Rucker v. Sanders* [109 S.E. 857, 858 (N.C. 1921)]. Thus, the time-for-acceptance provision contained in plaintiff-appellants' original offer did not become part of the terms of the counteroffer. And, of course, if they had accepted the counteroffer from defendant, a binding purchase contract, which would have included the terms of the original offer and counteroffer, would have then resulted. . . .

Plaintiff-appellants argue that the counteroffer made by Defendant Miller to plaintiff-appellants became a binding and irrevocable option to purchase within the time for acceptance contained in their original offer to purchase. . . .

It is generally recognized that "[a]n 'option' is a contract by which the owner agrees to give another the exclusive right to buy property at a fixed price within a specified time." 8A G. Thompson, *Commentaries on the Modern Law of Real Property,* § 4443 (1963). . . . In effect, an owner of property agrees to hold his offer open for a specified period of time. . . .

[W]e conclude that defendant-seller made no promise or agreement to hold her offer open. Thus, a necessary ingredient to the creation of an option contract, *i.e.,* a promise to hold an offer open for a specified time, is not present. Accordingly, we hold that defendant's counteroffer was not transformed into an irrevocable offer for the time limit contained in the original offer because the defendant's conditional acceptance did not include the time-for-acceptance provision as part of its terms and because defendant did not make any promise to hold her counteroffer open for any stated time. . . .

[T]he next question is did plaintiff-appellants, the original offerors, accept or reject defendant-seller's counteroffer? . . . [P]laintiff-appellants did not manifest any intent to agree to or accept the terms contained in defendant's counteroffer. . . .

It is evident from the record that after plaintiff-appellants failed to accept defendant's counteroffer, there was a second purchaser, Plaintiff-appellee Segal, who submitted an offer to defendant that was accepted. This offer and acceptance between the latter parties, together with consideration in the form of an earnest money deposit from plaintiff-appellee, ripened into a valid and binding purchase contract.

By entering into the contract with Plaintiff-appellee Segal, defendant manifested her intention to revoke her previous counteroffer to plaintiff-appellants. . . . The revocation of an offer terminates it, and the offeree has no power to revive the offer by any subsequent attempts to accept. . . .

Generally, notice of the offeror's revocation must be communicated to the offeree to effectively terminate the offeree's power to accept the offer. It is enough that the offeree receives reliable information, even indirectly, "that the offeror had taken definite action inconsistent with an intention to make the contract.'' E. Farnsworth, [*Contracts,* § 3.17 (1982).] . . .

In this case, plaintiff-appellants received notice of the offeror's revocation of the counteroffer in the afternoon of August 5, when Byer saw Normile and told him, ''[Y]ou snooze, you lose; the property has been sold.'' Later that afternoon, plaintiff-appellants initialed the counteroffer and delivered it to the Gallery of Homes, along with their earnest money deposit of $500. These subsequent attempts by plaintiff-appellants to accept defendant's revoked counteroffer were fruitless, however, since their power of acceptance had been effectively terminated by the offeror's revocation. . . . Since defendant's counteroffer could not be revived, the practical effect of plaintiff-appellants' initialing defendant's counteroffer and leaving it at the broker's office before 5:00 p.m. on August 5 was to resubmit a new offer. This offer was not accepted by defendant since she had already contracted to sell her property by entering into a valid, binding, and irrevocable purchase contract with Plaintiff-appellee Segal. . . .

[Judgment modified and affirmed.]

UCC Change—§2-207. Section 2-207 of the UCC substantially alters the strict effect of the mirror image rule in contracts for the sale of goods. Under §2-207(1), a definite and seasonable[5] expression of acceptance, or a written confirmation sent within a reasonable time, operates as an acceptance resulting in a contract even though the acceptance or confirmation states terms different from, or in addition to, the offer. No contract results, however, if the acceptance is expressly made conditional on assent to the additional or different terms.

The primary reason for the Code's departure from strict compliance with the mirror image rule is the Code's attempt to resolve the ''battle of the forms'' problem. The UCC drafters found that in commercial sales contracts, the buyer and seller usually explicitly agree upon major terms such as the quantity and price of the goods sold, their quality, and the time and manner of delivery. The parties then close the deal by exchanging preprinted forms such as the buyer's ''purchase order'' and the seller's ''confirmation'' or ''acknowledgment.'' Other terms, not explicitly considered or agreed upon, are usually contained under a heading such as ''terms and conditions'' in the fine print on the standard forms. These terms commonly govern remedies, warranties and limitations upon warranties, time limits for notice of defects in goods shipped, credit terms, and the like. Because these forms are drafted by the respective parties, the preprinted terms usually favor the drafting party. As a result, when placed side by side, certain minor terms contained in the purchase order and acknowledgment form do not correspond. Therefore, a strict adherence to the common law mirror image rule would result in no contract even though the obvious intent of the parties is to enter into a contract, and they nevertheless proceed with the transaction.

Section 2-207 is primarily designed to enforce the basic intent of the parties. Neither party is allowed to escape contractual obligation because of minor discrepancies between preprinted forms. If compliance with an unnegotiated term is important, the offeree can protect himself or herself by making acceptance expressly conditional upon the offeror's assent to the term.

In addition to the battle of the forms, §2-207 also governs the written confirmation. In this case, an agreement is reached either orally—for example, by telephone—or by informal correspondence. Subsequently, a formal writing—the confirmation—is sent by one or both parties embodying the agreement but adding terms not discussed.

In both the battle of the forms and written confirmation cases, the Code relaxes somewhat the effect of the mirror image rule by making contract formation turn upon the existence of a ''definite and seasonable expression of acceptance'' by the offeree, or the timely dispatch of a written confirmation, rather than the offeree's literal compliance with the terms of the offer. The effect of the mirror image rule on Code contracts is further reduced by §2-207(3). Under this provision, even if the writ-

---

5. Under the UCC, an action is taken ''seasonably'' if it is taken at or within the time called for by the contract, or if no time is stated, then at or within a reasonable time. UCC §1-204(3).

ings exchanged by the parties do not establish an agreement, *conduct* by the parties which recognizes the existence of a contract is sufficient.

To illustrate the general operation of Section 2-207, assume S, a manufacturer of nuts, bolts, and other fasteners, and B, an appliance manufacturer, negotiate for the sale of large quantities of fasteners for use in B's manufacturing operation. The parties ultimately agree upon the quantity, assortment, price, quality, and delivery terms. These terms are typed on B's purchase order form, which is sent to S, who responds with S's preprinted confirmation form. The forms exchanged, though agreeing on the basic dickered terms, conflict somewhat in the fine print. S's form states its standard credit terms: 1/10, net 30; B's form provides 2/10, net 30. S's form states that notice of defects in deliveries must be given within 10 days; B's form allows 21 days. S's form provides for interest on overdue invoices; B's form is silent on the point. Despite these discrepancies, which would defeat contract formation under a strict application of the mirror image rule, a contract is formed under §2-207.

Terms of the Contract. Section 2-207 not only determines when a contract exists if an apparent acceptance varies the terms of the offer, but also determines the terms of that contract. Under §2-207(2), the additional terms are construed as proposals for addition to the contract. In other words, a contract is created on the *offeror's* terms, and additional terms are treated as proposals by the offeree for inclusion. In contracts between merchants, however, the additional terms become part of the contract unless:

1. The offer expressly limits acceptance to the terms of the offer,
2. The additional terms materially alter the offer, or
3. The offeror notifies the offeree of his or her objection to them within a reasonable time.

Thus, between merchants, a contract exists on the *offeree's* terms, but the offeror may be protected through the application of one of the exceptions listed above. The following case illustrates the difficulty courts have encountered in ascertaining the terms of a contract formed under §2-207.

Southern Idaho Pipe & Steel Co. v. Cal-Cut Pipe & Supply, Inc.

567 P.2d 1246 (Idaho 1977)

On August 7, 1973, Cal-Cut made a written offer to sell 40,000 feet of used steel pipe to Southern Idaho. The offer stated that the final delivery date was to be October 15, 1973. By return mail, Southern Idaho accepted the offer but changed the final delivery date to December 15, 1973. With the acceptance, Southern Idaho enclosed a check for $20,000 that Cal-Cut deposited in its bank account. On August 20, 1973, Cal-Cut sent a written confirmation to Southern Idaho. The confirmation included the original delivery date of October 15 and a note on the bottom of the confirmation stating "We will work it out." Between September 8, 1973, and October 5, 1973, Southern Idaho accepted delivery of 12,937 feet of the steel pipe. Sometime in October, Cal-Cut refused to deliver any more pipe. Southern Idaho claimed that the refusal was made around October 1 while Cal-Cut asserted that its refusal occurred on October 17. During the latter part of 1973 and during 1974, steel pipe was in short supply and the market price rose sharply.

Southern Idaho sued Cal-Cut alleging breach of contract. Cal-Cut asserted that no contract existed because the new delivery date in Southern Idaho's alleged acceptance did not constitute a valid acceptance. The trial court found that the parties had entered into a contract and ruled in favor of Southern Idaho. Cal-Cut appealed. After holding that Southern Idaho's response to Cal-Cut's offer created a binding contract under §2-207 of the UCC, the Idaho Supreme Court then discussed the terms of that contract.

Donaldson, Justice

. . . Insofar as Section . . . 2-207 was drafted primarily to create a contract where one did not exist under the common law, it does not furnish unambiguous answers to the varied problems that emerge when the legal dispute arises as to the terms of a contract after performance has begun.

In the present case, we have an acceptance that contains not additional terms, but contradictory terms. Southern Idaho in its acceptance changed the delivery date from October 15, [1973] to December 15, [1973]. We also have partial performance of the contract. . . .

The Uniform Commercial Code establishes the existence of a contract, but what terms it embodies is problematic. Section 207(2) provides guidelines for the incorporation of additional terms, but it is silent as to the reconciliation of different terms. . . .

Cal-Cut makes the argument that since its document was the offer, Southern Idaho's expression of acceptance was an acceptance of all the terms on this form, including the October 15th delivery date. Under this argument, the first party to a sales transaction will always get his own terms. In most commercial transactions, which party processes its form first is purely fortuitous. To allow the contents of a contract to be determined on this basis runs contrary to the underlying purposes of the Uniform Commercial Code of modernizing the law governing commercial transactions. . . .We cannot accept such an arbitrary solution.

Nor can we accept the solution offered in *Roto-Lith, Ltd. v. F. P. Bartlett & Co.*, 297 F.2d 497 (1st Cir. 1962). . . . The First Circuit Court held that a responding document "which states a condition materially altering the obligation solely to the disadvantage of the offeror" was "expressly conditional" within the meaning of §2-207(1). The seller's supposed acceptance was therefore a counteroffer which was accepted when the buyer received and used the goods.

Under this approach, the party who fortuitously sends the responding form, will get all of his terms. *Roto-Lith* also undermines the purposes of § . . . 2-207(1) in that it effectively reinstates the common law mirror image rule whenever, as would usually be the case, a responding document states a condition solely advantageous to the party proposing it.

The solution we choose to adopt is one suggested by Comment 6 to [§2-207] . . . Comment 6 is the only explanation the draftsmen provide for the problem of conflicting terms. We hold on its authority that where a contract is formed by conflicting documents, the conflicting terms cancel out. The contract then consists of the terms that both

parties expressly agree to with the contested terms being supplied by other sections of the Uniform Commercial Code. . . .

In the present case, the parties final delivery date of October 15, 1973 and December 15, 1973 cancel out and we must look to . . . [UCC §2-309(1)] to supply the contested term. That section provides that the "time for shipment or delivery or any other action under a contract if not provided in the chapter or agreed upon shall be a reasonable time."
. . .

The trial court found that December 15th was a reasonable termination date. The record includes evidence that supports this conclusion. Southern Idaho had to haul steel pipe from California to Idaho, the pipe was being unearthed over a forty-five mile distance, transfer commenced in early September, and 30,000 feet of pipe had to be transported. Cal-Cut knew that Southern Idaho was depending upon a December 15, [1973] termination date as is evidenced by its confirmation letter stating that "we will work it out."

. . . Given a December 15, 1973 termination date, Cal-Cut breached the contract when it declined to make further deliveries before that date.

[Judgment affirmed.]

Termination by Operation of Law

As noted above, offers are often terminated by the language or other conduct of either the offeror (revocation) or the offeree (rejection). In certain circumstances, the offer may be terminated automatically by operation of law upon the occurrence of an event without further action by the offeror or offeree. The term **operation of law** is a general legal concept used to describe the manner in which a party's rights or duties are determined automatically by the application of a rule of law to a given set of facts, without the act or cooperation of the party.[6]

---

6. Black, *Law Dictionary* (5th ed. 1979).

An offer is terminated by operation of law if before acceptance:

1. either party dies;
2. either party is deprived of contractual capacity due, for example, to a physical disability or mental illness; or
3. the subject matter of the proposed contract becomes illegal or is destroyed.

Note that these terminations become effective automatically without notice to the other party. Assume Seller offers to sell land to Buyer on January 1, dies on January 2, and Buyer learns of the death on January 3. The offer is terminated by operation of law on January 2, even though Buyer does not learn of the death until January 3. Similarly, assume that on June 1, Seller offers to sell his antique Rolls-Royce to Buyer. On June 2, while Buyer is still considering the offer, the car is destroyed by fire. The offer is terminated by operation of law on June 2.

It is important to note that although *offers* are terminated on death, *contracts* generally are not. That is, a contract is ordinarily unaffected by the death of one or both parties. To illustrate, assume Small makes an offer on June 1 to sell land to Brinkley, and agrees to hold the offer open until June 30. If Small dies on June 15, the offer is automatically revoked by Small's death; Brinkley may not accept it between the 15th and the 30th. If, however, an option contract had been created, Small's death on the 15th would not terminate Brinkley's ability to exercise the option. Brinkley still has 15 days in which to accept the offer (exercise the option), and if he elects to do so, Small's estate is bound by Brinkley's acceptance and would be required to perform the contract.

Acceptance

The offer creates the power of acceptance, the power to create a contract, in the offeree. To this point the discussion has focused upon events terminating the offer, resulting in no contractual relationship between the parties. The following material discusses **acceptance** of the offer, by which the offeree manifests assent to the terms of the offer in the manner prescribed by the offeror. Upon acceptance, the promise or promises contemplated by the offer become binding as a contract.

An offer may invite acceptance by either the offeree's *promise to perform* (that is, a promise to do or refrain from doing an act) resulting in a *bilateral* contract, or *performance* of the act requested by the offer creating a *unilateral* contract. In either case, the offer can be accepted only by a person to whom the offer has been directed, either individually, or as a member of a class (for example, an offer for a reward).

For example, assume Sam offers to sell his boat to Betty for $1,000. John overhears Sam making the offer and says, "I accept." No contract is created. Similarly, Betty could not assign or transfer Sam's offer to John or anyone else. This result is yet another application of the general principle that the offeror is the master of the offer.

Before examining acceptance principles further, it should be noted that a number of previously considered issues are closely related to acceptance. For instance, the material relating to counteroffer, mirror image, and "battle of the forms" often concerns the legal effect of an attempted, though defective, acceptance.

Manner of Acceptance in Unilateral and Bilateral Contracts

Contracts often are classified according to the manner of acceptance prescribed or authorized by the offer. If the offer invites acceptance by the offeree's return promise, the resulting contract is bilateral. A bilateral contract contains two promises— the offeror's promise in exchange for the offeree's return promise. In a bilateral contract, each party is both a promisor, a person making a promise, and a promisee, a person to whom a promise is made. Assume Zach says to Rod, "If you promise to paint my house, I promise to pay you $500." Rod says, "I accept. I promise to paint your house." A bilateral contract is created, under which Rod promises to paint the house, and Zach promises to pay $500. Each party is both a promisor and a promisee. Most contracts are bilateral in nature.

In a unilateral contract, on the other hand, the offer requests an act rather than a return promise.

An offer that says, "I promise to pay you $5 after you have completed mowing my lawn," is an offer for a unilateral contract. The offeror is not requesting a return promise (the *promise* to mow the lawn); he is requesting an *act* (mowing the lawn). The offeree must perform the act to accept the offer. Only one promise, the offeror's, is present. This promise is binding upon the offeror only after the offeree has completed the requested act (accepted the offer). Because the offeree makes no promise, he generally incurs no liability to the offeror for failure to perform the act requested in the offer.

Specific Problems of Unilateral Contracts

Unilateral contracts present unique problems for the law of offer and acceptance including: (1) the effect of the offeree's commencing performance without knowledge of the offer, (2) the revocability of unilateral offers after performance has commenced, and (3) the effect of ambiguous offers, offers that fail to clearly indicate whether a promise or performance is requested.

Commencing Performance Without Knowledge of Offer. The offer must be communicated to the offeree before acceptance can occur. If a unilateral offer is made, however, the offeree may accept even though she *started* performance without knowledge of the offer. She must only *complete* performance with knowledge of the offer. In other words, the offer need only induce completion of performance, not necessarily the entire act. Assume Audrey loses her watch and places an advertisement in the newspaper offering a reward for its return. Barbara finds the watch without knowledge of the offer. She later learns of the offer and returns the watch to Audrey. Barbara is entitled to the reward.

Revocation After Performance Commenced. The principle that unilateral offers can be accepted only by performance poses a problem commonly illustrated by the following hypothetical situation involving the Brooklyn Bridge. Suppose the offeror says to the offeree, "After you have completed walking across the Brooklyn Bridge, I promise to pay you ten dollars." The offeree then starts walking across the bridge, and as he nears the other side, the offeror yells, "I revoke." Because an offeror may generally revoke an offer prior to the effectiveness of the acceptance, and a unilateral offer is not accepted until completion of the act, one may argue that the offeror is free to revoke a unilateral offer at any time before the offeree completes performance. This is true even if, as in the above example, the offeree substantially completes performance before revocation. The rationale for this argument is that because the offeree makes no enforceable promise, the offeror should be free to withdraw before full performance.

Obviously, this result works an injustice upon an offeree who has substantially completed performance. Most courts resolve the problem by finding that once the offeree has substantially commenced performance of a unilateral contract, he must be given a reasonable opportunity to complete performance. That is, after the offeree commences performance, an option is created, making the offer irrevocable by the offeror. If the offeree completes performance within the time allowed, the offeror is bound to the promise.

Ambiguous Offers. Under the master of the offer rule, the offeror may require any mode of acceptance—promise or performance. Ordinarily, however, the offeror invites acceptance in a reasonable manner, and in case of doubt, an offer is construed as inviting the offeree to choose between promise and performance. Under both the common law and the UCC, "unless otherwise unambiguously indicated by the language or circumstances . . . an offer to make a contract shall be construed as inviting acceptance in any manner . . . reasonable in the circumstances."[7] Thus, if an offer is ambiguous or indifferent regarding the manner of acceptance, the offeree may choose either promise or performance. If the offeree chooses a promise, a bilateral contract is created. If the offeree chooses performance, Section 62 of the *Restatement (Second) of Contracts* provides that the offeree's commencement of performance constitutes an acceptance, and such an acceptance operates as a promise to render com-

---

7. UCC §2-206(1)(a); See also *Restatement (Second) of Contracts* §§30,32.

plete performance. Under this approach, a bilateral contract is created, rendering the offeree liable for breach of contract for failure to complete performance.

Expressly Unilateral Offers—UCC Approach. Under the UCC, an offer that is expressly *unilateral* may be accepted by a promise or performance. Assume B sends S an order stating, "Ship 100 dishwashers, Model 100, at once." The order is an offer for a unilateral contract, requesting shipment, not a promise to ship. However, §2-206(1)(b) provides that "an order or other offer to buy goods for prompt or current shipment" may be accepted either by a prompt promise to ship, or the prompt shipment of the goods. That is, the expressly unilateral offer ("ship at once") may be accepted either by the act, shipment, or by a promise to ship.

The "Unilateral Contract Trick." If the offeree-seller elects to ship, the UCC provides that acceptance occurs by the "prompt or current shipment of conforming or non-conforming goods." By making shipment of nonconforming goods an acceptance, the Code prevents what has been called the "unilateral contract trick." To illustrate, assume Bendix wires Star, Inc., "ship at once, 100 'deluxe' model electric typewriters." Star is out of the deluxe model, but ships instead the cheaper "student" model. Bendix rejects the shipment and sues for breach of contract. Star defends by asserting that acceptance of a unilateral offer requires performance of the requested act, here, shipment of "deluxe" typewriters. Because "student" typewriters were shipped instead, Star has not performed the act contemplated by the offer, and has therefore not accepted the offer. Because there has been no acceptance, there is no contract, and consequently no breach—the unilateral contract trick. The Code eliminates this argument by making Star's shipment of "student" typewriters (nonconforming goods) acceptance of the offer. Thus, Star's shipment simultaneously constitutes both an acceptance and a breach.

Accommodating Substitution. Occasionally, a seller will not have goods ordered by a buyer, but will ship substitute goods instead as an accommodation to the buyer. If the buyer can use them, a contract is made and the accommodation is successful; if not, the buyer simply returns them without legal consequence. To prevent the accommodating substitution from operating as an acceptance and breach under the rule outlined above, §2-206(1)(b) provides that: "a shipment of non-conforming goods does not constitute an acceptance if the seller seasonably notifies the buyer that the shipment is offered only as an accommodation to the buyer." Thus, by notifying the buyer of his intention, the seller can avoid the usual consequences of a nonconforming shipment.

The net effect of the above rules is that most offers may be accepted by a promise to perform (bilateral) or are ultimately treated as bilateral contracts. The rationale for this result is that the unilateral-bilateral distinction is essentially an artificial one, leading both the common law and the UCC to limit the importance of the dichotomy, and to treat most contracts as bilateral. Unilateral offers now include primarily reward offers, offers requesting a forebearance (for example, when the offer asks the offeree to refrain from doing an act, such as drinking, smoking, swearing), or other situations in which the offer unambiguously indicates full performance, as opposed to a promise or commencement of performance, is requested.

Notification of Acceptance in Bilateral and Unilateral Contracts

Notification is a concept appearing throughout contracts, and law generally. A person notifies or gives notice to another person by taking whatever steps are reasonably necessary to inform the other in the usual course of events. Provided these reasonable steps are taken, the notice is effective whether or not the other person actually learns of it. A person receives a notice or notification when it comes to his or her attention or is properly delivered at a place used for receipt of such communications, such as a place of business, post office box, or residence.

Generally speaking, and subject to the rules on effectiveness of an acceptance outlined below, an effective acceptance by promise—the "bilateral" contract—requires that the offeree notify the offeror of acceptance. If an offer invites acceptance by rendering a performance—the "unilateral" contract—no notification is generally necessary to make the acceptance effective. In most cases, the offeror promptly learns of the offeree's performance, thus negating any need for notification. Notice may, however, be required if the offer itself requires it or if the offeror has no adequate means of learning of the performance. Note that in any unilateral contract case, notification does not create the contract; performance or beginning performance does. Lack of notification *may,* however, discharge the offeror's duty. Notice therefore protects the offeree, who is relying upon the offer, by preventing the offeror's discharge while the offeree is performing. As previously noted, the offeree's commencement of performance often constitutes an acceptance, thereby binding him to complete performance.

The Uniform Commercial Code addresses this issue in §2-206(2) by providing that: ''Where the beginning of a requested performance is a reasonable mode of acceptance an offeror who is not notified of acceptance within a reasonable time may treat the offer as having lapsed before acceptance.'' To illustrate, assume Buyer sends Seller a written order for goods to be specially manufactured for Buyer, requesting that Seller begin at once, because manufacture will take several months. As previously discussed, acceptance may be complete when Seller begins manufacture, but Buyer's duty to pay is discharged and he may treat the offer as having lapsed before acceptance unless within a reasonable time Seller sends Buyer a notification of acceptance or unless the offer or prior dealing indicates that notice is not required. The following classic English case illustrates notification of acceptance of a unilateral offer.

Carlill v. Carbolic Smoke Ball Company
[1893] 1 Q.B. 256 (C.A.)

Defendant Carbolic Smoke Ball Company (Carbolic) published the following advertisement in several British newspapers during November 1891:

100£ reward will be paid by the Carbolic Smoke Ball Company to any person who contracts the increasing epidemic influenza, colds, or any disease caused by taking cold, after having used the ball three times daily for two weeks according to the printed directions supplied with each ball. 1,000£ is deposited with the Alliance Bank, Regent Street, showing our sincerity in the matter.

During the last epidemic of influenza, many thousand carbolic smoke balls were sold as preventives against this disease, and in no ascertained case was the disease contracted by those using the carbolic smoke ball.

One carbolic smoke ball will last a family several months, making it the cheapest remedy in the world at the price, 10s. post free. The ball can be refilled at a cost of 5s. Address, Carbolic Smoke Ball Company, 27 Princes Street, Hanover Square, London.

Plaintiff Carlill, relying on the advertisement, purchased one of the smoke balls. After using it according to the printed directions for two weeks, she contracted influenza. When she attempted to claim the 100£ reward, Carbolic refused to pay. Carlill sued Carbolic and the trial court ruled in favor of Carlill. Carbolic appealed.

Lindley, Lord Justice

. . . The first observation I would make is that we are not dealing with any inferences of fact. We are dealing with an express promise to pay 100£ in certain events. There can be no mistake about that at all. Read this advertisement how you will, and twist it about as you will, here is a distinct promise expressed in language which is perfectly unmistakable: ''100£ reward will be paid by the Carbolic Smoke Ball Company to any person who contracts the influenza after having used the ball three times daily,'' and so on.

Now one must look at it a little further, and see if this is intended to be a promise at all, or whether it is a mere puff—a sort of thing which means nothing. Is that the meaning of it? My answer to that question is No, and I base my answer upon this passage: ''1,000£ is deposited with the Alliance Bank, shewing our sincerity in the matter.'' Now, what is that deposited for? What is that put in for, except to negative the suggestion that this is a mere puff, and means nothing at all? The deposit is called in aid by the advertiser as proof of his sincerity in the matter—that is, of his intention to pay this 100£ in the events which he has specified. I make that remark, as I say, for the purpose of giving point to the observation that we are not inferring the promise from ambiguous language. Here it is, as plain as words can make it.

Then it is said that it is not binding. In the first place, it is said that it is not made with anybody in particular. Now that point is common to the words of this advertisement, as to the words of all other advertisements offering rewards. They make offers to anybody who performs the conditions named in the advertisement, and anybody who does perform the conditions accepts the offer. I take it, if you look at this advertisement, in point of law, it is an offer to pay 100£ to anybody who will perform these conditions, and the performance of the conditions is the acceptance of the offer. . . .

But then it is said, "Well, supposing that the performance of the condition is an acceptance of the offer, that acceptance ought to be notified." Unquestionably, as a general proposition, when an offer is made, you must have it not only accepted, but the acceptance notified. But is that so in cases of this kind? I apprehend that this is rather an exception to that rule, or, if not an exception, it is open to the observation that the notification of the acceptance need not precede the performance. This offer is a continuing offer; it was never revoked; and if notice of acceptance is required . . . the person who makes the offer gets the notice of acceptance contemporaneously with his notice of the performance of the condition. Anyhow, if notice is wanted, he gets it before his offer is revoked, which is all you want in principle; but I doubt very much whether the true view is not in a case of this kind that the person who makes the offer shews by his language and from the nature of the transaction that he does not expect, and does not require, notice of the acceptance apart from notice of the performance.

We have, therefore, all the elements which are necessary to form a binding contract enforceable in point of law. . . .

[Judgment affirmed.]

Silence as Acceptance. Generally, the offeree's failure to respond to the offer does not constitute acceptance. For example, suppose Seth offers to sell land to Roger stating, "If I don't hear from you by noon tomorrow, I will assume you have accepted my offer." By failing to respond, Roger has not accepted the offer. Receipt of the offer does not limit the offeree's freedom to act or refuse to act and may not require him to speak.

The offeree's explicit statements, trade custom, express agreement, or prior course of dealing between the parties may, however, lead the offeror to assume justifiably that silence is acceptance. Using the above example, suppose Roger stated to Seth, "If you don't hear from me by noon tomorrow, you can assume I have accepted." Roger's failure to respond would constitute acceptance. Or, assume Roger joins a record club. The agreement provides that the club will send a card every month indicating the current month's selection. If Roger fails to return the card, he receives the record. In this case, Roger's silence (failure to return) is an acceptance because of the prior agreement by the parties that silence operates as acceptance. Such an agreement may arise either expressly or as a result of prior dealing between the parties. Acceptance may also be inferred from silence when a person knowingly receives and accepts benefits from another while in a position to reject them. In this case, a contract implied in fact is created. That is, silence is merely one form of conduct through which a promise may be made.[8]

Effectiveness of Acceptance: "Mailbox Acceptance Rule"

The effective date of an acceptance is often governed by the doctrine known as the **mailbox acceptance rule,** or "deposited acceptance rule." This rule applies when the parties are communicating at a distance, generally by mail or telegram. Under these circumstances, an acceptance is normally effective when *sent;* that is, when the offeree relinquishes control over his acceptance. For instance, a mailed acceptance is usually effective when it is

---

8. Contracts implied in fact are discussed in Chapter 7.

placed in the mailbox, whether or not it ever reaches the offeror.[9]

For the rule to apply, the offeree must use the means of acceptance authorized by the offeror. Assume S sends B a letter offering to sell S's farm for $100,000. Assume the offer states, "You must accept by mail," or the offer says nothing about the manner or medium of acceptance. In the first situation, if the acceptance is sent by telegram, no contract is created. If sent by mail, a contract is created when the letter is placed in the mailbox. In the second situation, an acceptance either by mail or telegram would be effective when sent because the offeror, in the absence of evidence to the contrary, authorizes the means used in communicating the offer. She also impliedly authorizes any other means customarily used in similar transactions. Courts have held that both a telegraphed acceptance to a mailed offer and a mailed acceptance to a telegraphed offer meet this test. The UCC retains the mailbox rule, but divorces the rule from authorization. Under the Code, an acceptance made "by any medium reasonable in the circumstances" is effective when sent.[10]

If an unauthorized or unreasonable means of acceptance is used, the acceptance is effective when received (provided the offeror has not dictated the means which must be used). Additionally, an acceptance sent by mail or otherwise is not effective upon dispatch unless it is properly addressed, with postage or cost of transmission provided for, and with any other precautions necessary to insure a proper transmission of similar messages.[11]

The rationale for the mailbox rule is that because the offer is freely revocable by the offeror, an offeree who decides to accept needs to know precisely when an enforceable contract exists. The rule allows the offeree to rely upon the existence of the contract when he sends his acceptance. Any revocation received after this point is ineffective. Assume Sally makes an offer to sell her farm to Bob by mail on June 1. Bob accepts by mail on June 3, received by Sally on June 6. On June 4, Sally gets a better offer for the farm from Mary and telephones Bob revoking the offer. Sally's revocation is ineffective because a contract was made on June 3. Note that the rule also precludes the offeree from speculating at the offeror's expense while the acceptance is in transit. That is, the offeree's attempt to retract an acceptance after mailing is ineffective.

The rule is further justified by the fact that the offeror, being the master of the offer, can stipulate that any attempted acceptance will not be effective until actually received. In this case, the offeree cannot rely upon the contract until learning that the offeror has received the acceptance. Further, the risk of losing the acceptance in transit and the risk of a revocation becoming effective before the acceptance is received are borne by the offeree. The mailbox rule places these burdens on the offeror who was originally in a position to protect herself and failed to do so.

The mailbox rule does not apply to option contracts. An acceptance under an option contract is not effective until actually received by the offeror. Because the offer in an option contract is irrevocable by the offeror, the protection against revocation afforded the offeree by the mailbox rule is not necessary. Assume Sally grants Bob a thirty-day option to buy Sally's farm. Bob must actually notify Sally of his intent to exercise the option within the thirty-day period. Notification sent but not received within that period is ineffective.

The mailbox rule may also be inapplicable if the offeree sends both an acceptance and a rejection. For example, assume that in response to Sally's offer, Bob sends the following communications:

Bob		Sally
June 1	Rejection	June 10
(Sent)	⟶	(Received)
Bob		Sally
June 2	Acceptance	June 11
(Sent)	⟶	(Received)

---

9. Of course, if the parties are dealing face to face, or by telephone or other medium of substantially instantaneous two-way communication, the time of sending and receiving are the same.

10. UCC §2-206(1)(a).

11. Under both the common law and the Code, however, even if an unreasonable means is used, or if the instrument is improperly dispatched, the acceptance is effective when sent if actually received within the time at which it would have arrived if properly sent.

Because rejections are effective when received and acceptances are effective when sent, it appears that a contract exists on June 2. Because the offeror may rely on the rejection of June 10, however, the law recognizes an exception to the mailbox rule. On these facts, Bob's acceptance is effective when received. If received after receipt of the rejection (the case here), it is treated as a counteroffer. If received before the rejection arrives, a contract is created, because the offeror cannot rely on a rejection until received.

In the above example, the rejection is sent before the acceptance. If the acceptance is sent first, the mailbox rule still applies. To illustrate, assume that Bob responds as follows to Sally's offer:

Bob		Sally
June 1	Acceptance →	June 10
(Sent)		(Received)

Bob		Sally
June 2	Rejection →	June 9
(Sent)		(Received)

On these facts, the acceptance is effective when sent. Bob's June 2 communication is merely an attempt to retract an already binding acceptance. However, if Sally changes her position in reliance on the rejection (for example, by selling the goods she offered to Bob elsewhere upon learning of the rejection), Bob may not enforce the contract. The following case illustrates the mailbox rule.

Pribil v. Ruther
262 N.W.2d 460 (Neb. 1978)

Defendant Bertha Ruther owned a piece of real estate that she listed for sale with John Thor, a real estate broker. On April 12, 1976, plaintiff Lawrence Pribil made a written offer to purchase the property on an agreement form (known as a Uniform Purchase Agreement) that provided a space for the offeree to indicate written acceptance. Ruther signed the acceptance on April 12 and gave the form to Thor to deliver to Pribil. Thor gave the form to an employee to send to Pribil. The employee wrote a letter to Pribil dated April 14 and enclosed the signed form. The letter and form were sent by certified mail; the envelope was postmarked "April 15, 1976 P.M." Pribil received the signed acceptance form on April 16.

After signing the acceptance and giving it to Thor, Ruther decided that she did not want to accept Pribil's offer. According to Thor, Ruther telephoned Thor on April 15 at 11:42 A.M. and told him that she was going to "terminate the contract." Thor testified that immediately after that call, he telephoned Pribil and told him that Ruther had decided not to sell the property. Pribil sued Ruther alleging that a contract existed and requesting specific performance of the contract. The trial court ruled in favor of Pribil and Ruther appealed.

Boslaugh, Justice

. . . The principal issue in this case is whether the defendant had effectively rejected the plaintiff's offer and revoked her acceptance of the offer before the acceptance had been communicated to the plaintiff. . . .

Since the plaintiff sought to enforce the contract the burden was on the plaintiff to establish that there was a contract. A party who seeks to compel specific performance of a written contract has the burden of proving the contract. . . .

An express contract is proved by evidence of a definite offer and unconditional acceptance. Where the offer requires a promise on the part of the offeree, a communicated acceptance is essential. . . .

The signing of the acceptance on the Uniform Purchase Agreement by the defendant did not make the contract effective. It was necessary that there be some communication of the acceptance to the plaintiff. There must be some irrevocable element such as depositing the acceptance in the mail so that it is placed beyond the power or control of the sender before the acceptance becomes effective and the contract is made. . . . Delivery to the agent of the defendant was not delivery to the plaintiff and did not put the acceptance beyond the control of the defendant. . . .

The plaintiff contends that the deposit of the acceptance in the mail satisfied the requirement that the acceptance be communicated. Where transmission by mail is authorized, the deposit of the signed agreement in the mail with the proper address and postage will complete the contract. . . . The difficulty in this case is that there is no evidence that the acceptance was deposited in the mail before Thor called the plaintiff and informed him that the defendant would not sell the property.

The evidence is that Thor handed the purchase agreement to [his employee] with instructions to send a copy to the plaintiff. . . . Thor testified, "I can't testify when she mailed it, except by reading the postmarks on the envelope and the return receipts." The postmark indicates only that the postage was canceled sometime during the afternoon of April 15, 1976. The telephone call from the defendant was received at 11:42 A.M. The call from Thor to the plaintiff was made immediately afterward.

If we assume that transmission by mail was authorized in this case, there is no evidence to show that the acceptance was deposited in the mail before the defendant's call to Thor, and Thor's call to the plaintiff notifying him that the defendant had rejected his offer. The evidence does not show that the acceptance was communicated to the plaintiff and thus became effective before the defendant changed her mind and rejected the offer.

[Judgment reversed.]

SUMMARY

1. The first element of contract formation is an agreement embodying mutual assent to an exchange. Ordinarily, agreement is reached, after preliminary dickering or negotiation, when an offer made by one party is accepted by the other.

2. Offer and acceptance issues may be divided into three basic categories: (1) the existence, terms, and effectiveness of the offer, (2) events terminating an offer prior to acceptance, and (3) acceptance of the offer.

3. An offer is a conditional promise raising the power of acceptance, the power to create a contract, in the offeree. Because the offeror is contractually bound upon acceptance, the offeror is allowed to control the terms, duration, and manner of acceptance. This "master of the offer" rule protects the offeror by allowing him to dictate the terms on which he is willing to deal.

4. The contents of the offer and most other communications between the parties is governed by the "objective theory of contract." Under this theory the terms of a communication are determined not by the subjective intention of the communicating party, but instead by the reasonable impression the communication makes upon the other party. Judged by this test, a communication is treated as an offer if it is sufficiently definite to indicate an intention on the part of the offeror to be contractually bound and contains sufficient minimum terms. This "definiteness" requirement affords a court in a later dispute a basis to determine whether a contract exists and has been breached, and to award an appropriate remedy.

5. Once made, an offer may be terminated before acceptance, resulting in no contract. Termination may occur by act of the offeror or offeree, or by operation of law.

6. The offeror may generally terminate an offer by revoking it. An offer is generally freely revocable prior to acceptance unless the offer is itself a contract, an option, or is a "firm offer" made by a merchant to buy or sell goods in a signed writing.

7. The offeree may terminate an offer by rejecting it, including either an express rejection or counteroffer. Under the traditional common law rule, any attempted acceptance must be the "mirror image" of the offer and any variation between the two constitutes a rejection of the offer and a counteroffer on the new terms. The UCC alters this result somewhat for contracts involving goods by providing that a definite expression of acceptance or timely written confirmation operates as an acceptance even though it contains terms different from or in addition to the offer.

8. The offer may also be terminated by operation of law, most commonly upon the death of either party.

9. The offer, if not terminated, may be accepted, resulting in a contract. The offer may invite acceptance either by the offeree's return promise, creating a bilateral contract, or by the offeree's performance of an act, resulting in a unilateral contract. In general, the offeror must be notified of acceptance in a bilateral contract, although in limited circumstances the offeree's silence operates as an acceptance. In a unilateral contract, notice is usually provided by the offeree's performance of the act requested by the offer.

10. In determining the effectiveness of the various communications between offeror and offeree, the following rules apply: (1) offers, rejections (including counteroffers), and revocations are effective when received by the person to whom directed; (2) termination of an offer by operation of law is effective immediately (for exam-

ple, on death) with no notice to the other party required; and (3) subject to various exceptions, acceptances are effective when sent under the "mailbox acceptance rule." By comparing the effective dates of the various communications (for example, acceptance vs. revocation), the existence or nonexistence of a contract is determined.

KEY TERMS

offer	firm offer rule
master of the offer	rejection
objective theory of	mirror image rule
contract	operation of law
definiteness	acceptance
revocation	notification
option contract	mailbox acceptance rule

QUESTIONS AND PROBLEMS

8-1 Explain the rationale for the master of the offer rule. Is this rule consistent with the objective theory of contract?

8-2 From time to time a business may want to sell a piece of used equipment or a tract of land. The sale usually is unrelated to the firm's ordinary business activities. Although the seller may want to inform a segment of the public of the availability of the property, it also may not want such information construed as an offer. Why would a seller, who clearly wants to sell property, not want communication intended as informational to be considered an offer?

If the seller already knows the terms it is willing to accept (for example, price, financing, delivery) and wants to convey this information, it runs a greater risk that the information it communicates will be considered an offer. How can the seller protect itself from this risk?

8-3 After purchasing a new computer system, City University published a notice in the newspaper on November 1 offering to sell its used computer system to the highest bidder. The notice described the system and requested all interested parties to submit firm bids in writing to the university. Falco, a used computer dealer, submitted a letter on November 18 stating that it would purchase the system for $300,000 and that its bid would remain open through December 18.

(a) Who is the offeror? the offeree?

(b) On December 9, after learning that its bank would not lend it the money to purchase the system, Falco telephoned City University and revoked its bid. Nevertheless, on De-

cember 10, City University unequivocally accepted Falco's bid. Has a contract been formed? Explain.

8-4 (a) The Electric Cooperative, Inc. provided electric power to the town of Lindsay pursuant to a contract that expired on June 1, 1980. On March 1, 1980, the Cooperative proposed a new contract to the town. Following a vote of the city council the mayor wrote a letter dated April 1, 1980, to the Cooperative stating that the town was offering the Cooperative the right to provide electricity to Lindsay if the Cooperative would pay an annual fee of $200. The letter concluded "This agreement shall take effect upon the Cooperative's filing a written acceptance within thirty days." The Cooperative paid the $200 fee but did not file a written acceptance. On August 1, 1980, the town entered into a contract with The Peoples' Power Co. by which Peoples agreed to provide electric power to Lindsay. Electric Cooperative sued the town of Lindsay alleging that it had a contract to provide power. What result?

(b) Sea Coast Steel sells and delivers steel to automobile manufacturers. On January 4, 1984, USA Motors ordered 565 tons of steel from Sea Coast by submitting a purchase order. The final paragraph of the purchase order stated: "All deliveries to be made on or before January 15, 1984. Delivery of any item covered by this order or written approval of the order shall constitute acceptance." Sea Coast began making purchases to fill the contract. Because steel was in short supply, USA Motors wrote Sea Coast authorizing delivery on or before February 1. On January 25, Sea Coast phoned USA Motors to notify it that delivery could be made only on January 28, a Saturday. USA Motors told Sea Coast that its loading dock was closed on Saturdays so that Sea Coast should cancel the order. Sea Coast sued for breach of contract. What result?

8-5 On January 1, Franny granted Johnny a thirty-day option to purchase a farm. Johnny paid $100 for the option, which gave him the right to purchase the farm for $50,000. Determine how the court should rule in each of the following cases.

(a) On January 15, Johnny tells Franny that he is moving out of state and would not buy the farm. On January 25, Johnny tenders $50,000 to Franny, telling her he has changed his mind. Franny refuses to sell him the farm. Johnny sues.

(b) On January 10, Howard offers to purchase Franny's farm for $60,000. Franny promptly notifies Johnny that she is revoking the option unless Johnny agrees to pay $60,000. Johnny does not respond immediately but on January 22, Franny dies. On January 23, Johnny exercises his option to purchase at $50,000, but Franny's estate refuses to sell. Johnny sues.

(c) Would your answers to (a) and (b) change if Johnny had not paid $100 for the option? Explain.

(d) If the option had been for the purchase of a tractor, rather than a farm, would your answers to (a), (b), and (c) change? Explain.

8-6   On February 1, Joshua received a letter from Treasure magazine in a window envelope that permitted Joshua to read the following through the window: "JOSHUA, I'LL GIVE YOU A VERSATILE NEW CALCULATOR WATCH FREE JUST FOR OPENING THIS ENVELOPE BEFORE FEBRUARY 15." Joshua immediately opened the envelope and discovered that the letter continued "AND MAILING THIS CERTIFICATE TODAY!" By mailing the certificate, Joshua would be required to purchase a subscription to Treasure magazine. Has an offer been made? Has an acceptance been made? Has a contract been formed? Explain.

8-7   On May 20, J. W. Worth was visiting his neighbors Joe and Olive Twist when the conversation turned to taxes. Joe stated that he and his wife were considering selling some of their real estate because the taxes were too high. At Worth's request, J. W. brought out maps showing where his properties were located. Worth was especially interested in Bear Ranch and asked Joe how much he expected to sell that ranch for and Joe replied "for the assessed value." As Worth was leaving, Olive promised to send him more information about their land sales.

On June 17, Worth received a letter from the Twists that stated in part: "Enclosed is the information about the ranch sales that we discussed previously." The enclosure read as follows:

Joe and Olive Twist
R. R. 1
Hometown, Oregon

Selling Bear Ranch—approximately 2933 acres in Grant County near Seneca, Oregon at the assessed market value:

Land	$306,409
Buildings	18,010
Total	$324,419

Terms available: Buyer pays 25% down, balance over 5 years at 8% interest. Can negotiate sale date. Available after crops harvested and seller removes all equipment.

ALSO selling 250 head of cattle now located on ranch.

(a) Assume that on May 20, during his conversation with Joe Twist, Worth had stated "I accept your offer to sell Bear Ranch for the assessed value." Would a contract have been formed at that point? Explain.

(b) Assume instead that on June 21, Worth sent a letter to the Twists stating: "Re Bear Ranch. I accept your offer of June 17." Would a contract have been formed at that point? Explain. Would your answer be different if, during their meeting on May 20, the Twists had told Worth that they would sell the land only if the purchaser also agreed to buy the cattle? Explain.

(c) Assume that upon receipt of Worth's letter of June 21 (see (b) above), the Twists wrote a letter in response that stated in part "You have misconstrued our prior negotiations concerning Bear Ranch. Our letter of June 17 was not intended as an offer. In fact, we sent similar letters to three other neighbors who are also interested in the property. We are open to further negotiations." Would a contract have been formed on June 21? Explain.

(d) Assume that Worth sent his letter of June 21 but that another neighbor of the Twists also sent them a letter on June 21 accepting the offer of sale. Both Worth and the neighbor sue the Twists demanding performance of the contract. How would a court resolve the dispute?

(e) Assume that upon receipt of Worth's letter of June 21, the Twists agreed that a contract had been formed. What are the terms of the contract?

8-8   Because year end car sales were slow, Mighty Motors needed to sell some of its inventory to make room for the new 1985 model cars. Mighty Motors placed the following advertisement in the newspaper:

> BUY NOW! Buy a 1984 United Motors car now and when the 1985 models come out, we'll trade even for your '84. Your '85 car will be the same model, accessory group, etc. as the '84 that you buy now. A sure thing for you—a gamble for us, but we'll risk it!
>
> HURRY! This offer good only during September. Buyer responsible for taxes and license fees.

Mr. and Mrs. Johnson saw the ad and visited Mighty Motors. On September 20, they bought a 1984 United Motors Stingbird. When the 1985 cars came out, the Johnsons went back to Mighty Motors and requested that Mighty Motors trade in the '84 Stingbird for a new 1985 model. Mighty Motors refused stating that the Johnsons had not notified Mighty Motors in September that their purchase was being made on the terms of the advertisement. The salesman pointed out that the Johnsons had not even mentioned or discussed the ad. Mr. and Mrs. Johnson sue requesting that the court order Mighty Motors to accept their '84 car in trade for a '85 car.

(a) Mighty Motors alleged that the advertisement was not intended as an offer but was an invitation to make an offer and to come in to the dealership to bargain. Do you agree?

(b) Mr. and Mrs. Johnson alleged that the newspaper ad was an offer. If the ad was an offer, was it accepted? Was the acceptance communicated to Mighty Motors? Explain.

8-9   While Arnold and Sam were playing golf, Sam mentioned that he would like to sell his liquor store and retire. The following day, Arnold's friend Barbara said that she was interested in going into business for herself. When Arnold told her that he might be able to help her if she wanted to buy a liquor store, Barbara said she would think about it. A few days later Barbara called Arnold and requested further information about the liquor store; she also mentioned that she probably would need financing. Arnold promised to provide the information and to check into financing possibilities but added, "Under the circumstances, I would expect to be compensated if you work out a deal." Barbara responded that she would appreciate any information he had available. Thereafter, Arnold served as a go-between and arranged a sale of Sam's liquor store to Barbara for $150,000. Arnold also introduced Barbara to Peter, a local investor who provided financing for the transaction. At the closing, Arnold reminded Barbara that she had not paid him the compensation she had promised. Barbara replied that she had not promised to compensate him and that she could not afford to pay him anything. Arnold sues Barbara, alleging breach of an oral contract and requesting that the court award him a finder's fee of $7,500.

(a) At the trial, what evidence will Arnold present to establish that an offer was made? What evidence would establish acceptance?

(b) How should the court rule? Explain.

8-10   Leonard was the desk clerk at the Hospitality Hotel. One day at Leonard's request, he and the manager had a meeting in the manager's office. After discussing several matters relating to desk clerking, Leonard said that he had had a brilliant idea. When the manager did not reply, Leonard suggested that if the hotel were to open a trailer park and camping grounds adjacent to the hotel, profits would increase. Leonard also stated that he thought that 10% of the first year's profits would be reasonable compensation for his idea. The manager said he would think about it. The manager never discussed the matter with Leonard again. A few months later, Leonard quit his job. About a year later, the hotel opened a trailer park and campgrounds adjacent to the hotel. Leonard sued asking for 10% of the profits. How should the court rule?

8-11   Don owned a farm that he wanted to sell. On June 1, he mailed a letter to Barbara, who lived in a neighboring state, offering to sell the property for $100,000. The offer stipulated it would remain open for 30 days, but did not state a prescribed means of acceptance. Barbara received the offer on June 3 and immediately wrote back stating, "I accept your offer, but at $90,000; that's the most I can borrow from the bank." Don received Barbara's letter on June 10. Meanwhile, on June 3, Ed offered to buy the land from Don for $150,000. Don then promptly revoked the offer in a letter written to Barbara on June 3. On that day, Don gave the letter to his son, Jack, to mail, but Jack placed the letter in his glove compartment and forgot about it. On June 8 Don sold the land to Ed for $150,000.

On June 5, Barbara, fearing the property would be sold elsewhere if she failed to meet Don's asking price, wrote Don a letter stating "I accept your offer of the 1st." Don received Barbara's letter on June 9. On June 7, Barbara saw Jack at a cattle auction. Jack then remembered the letter in his glove compartment and handed it to her. Infuriated by the revocation Barbara immediately called Don on the phone and stated "You said the offer would remain open for thirty days. As far as I'm concerned the offer is still open. I hereby accept the offer."

Barbara sues Don for breach of contract. What result? Analyze the legal effect of the various communications between the parties to determine whether or not Don's offer was terminated prior to acceptance or was accepted while still effective resulting in a contract.

8-12 Mr. and Mrs. Brewer agreed to buy a house owned by Jane. At the same time, Jane offered to sell them some of the furnishings that the Brewers had admired. Because the Brewers were leaving on vacation, Jane agreed to provide a written statement of the furnishings she was willing to sell. Jane sent the Brewers the following:

I am willing to sell the following articles:

Antique grandfather's clock	$1,500
Spinet piano	2,000
Queen Anne chairs	1,500
Oriental rug	1,000

All of the furnishings will be left in the house. Payment of $3,000 due upon acceptance; balance of $3,000 due within sixty days. If the above is satisfactory, please sign below and return one copy with the first payment. ―――――――――――――

Six weeks later the Brewers sent the following letter to Jane.

Our trip was great! Enclosing a $3,000 check. We've misplaced the contract. Can you send another? We're moving into the house in two weeks. Please include the red secretary in the entrance foyer on the contract.

Mr. and Mrs. Brewer

After receiving the letter and $3,000 check, Jane sent the Brewers a copy of her previous letter adding the red secretary to the list of furnishings.

After the Brewers moved into the house, they asked Jane to remove the grandfather's clock and Queen Anne chairs. She refused and demanded that the Brewers pay the balance of $3,000 plus $500 for the red secretary.

(a) Jane insists that she and the Brewers had entered into a contract. Review §2-207 of the UCC and determine whether she is correct.

(b) Assuming a contract has been made, is the red secretary included in the sale? If so, at what price?

(c) The Brewers assert that no contract resulted because they did not sign and return one copy of the contract as requested by Jane. Is this argument correct? See UCC §2-206.

The second element required for contract formation is consideration. **Consideration** is what each contracting party bargains for and gives in exchange for the return promise or performance of the other party. The consideration in the form of property, services, or other conduct promised or performed provides the inducement to each party to enter into the contract.

The Doctrine of Consideration

Although the law enforces certain promises without consideration,[1] it is the basic legal doctrine deter-

mining when a promise is binding as a contract. As eloquently stated by one court:

> It is clear that not every promise is legally enforceable. Much of the vast body of law in the field of contracts is concerned with determining which promises should be legally enforced. On the one hand, in a civilized community men must be able to assume that those with whom they deal will carry out their undertakings according to reasonable expectations. On the other hand, it is neither practical nor reasonable to expect full performance of every assurance given, whether it be thoughtless, casual and gratuitous, or deliberately and seriously made.
>
> The test that has been developed by the common law for determining the enforceability of promises is the doctrine of consideration. This is a crude and not altogether successful attempt to generalize the conditions under which promises will be legally enforced.[2]

Thus consideration generally distinguishes contractual promises, which are binding on the promisor, from gratuitous or casual promises, which are not. For example, assume Sam promises to give Bill an antique gold watch in thirty days. If Sam fails to transfer the watch to Bill as promised, Sam incurs

---

1. See "promissory estoppel" beginning on page 207.

2. *Baehr v. Penn-O-Tex Oil Corporation,* 104 N.W.2d 661, 665 (Minn. 1960).

no liability because Bill has furnished no consideration to "support" the promise—that is, to make it enforceable. Sam's promise is not a contract.

Form of Consideration

Consideration capable of supporting a promise may be either (1) a promise to do something or refrain from doing something, or (2) a performance. For example, if Seth contracts to sell Bill a snowmobile for $500, Bill's promise to pay $500 provides consideration for Seth's promise to transfer title to the snowmobile. Conversely, Seth's promise to transfer title furnishes consideration for Bill's promise to pay $500. Or, suppose that Cal, as part of the sale of his restaurant to Ben for $50,000, promises *not* to open a restaurant in competition with Ben for five years. Ben's promise to pay $50,000 supports Cal's promise to transfer the restaurant's assets or stock as well as Cal's promise not to compete with Ben. Note that, as this example indicates, a single promise (or performance) may support any number of return promises.

Consideration in the form of performance may be (1) an act other than a promise, (2) a forbearance, or (3) the creation, modification, or destruction of a legal relation.[3] To illustrate, suppose Al promises to pay Bob $500. In exchange for this promise, Bob alternatively paints Al's house, refrains from smoking cigarettes for one year, or transfers title to Bob's 1955 Chevrolet to Al. In all three cases, Bob's performance is consideration for Al's promise. Keep in mind that if the consideration supporting a promise is a return promise, a bilateral contract is created; if the consideration is a performance, a unilateral contract is created.

Requirement of a Bargain

To constitute consideration, the promise or performance involved must be **bargained for.** As defined in the *Restatement (Second) of Contracts:*

> A performance or return promise is bargained for if it is sought by the promisor in exchange for his

promise, and is given by the promisee in exchange for that promise.[4]

In other words, consideration requires not only that a promise be made or a performance rendered, but also that the respective promises or performances be given in *exchange* for each other. One court explained the rationale for the bargain requirement as follows:

> Consideration requires that a contractual promise be the product of a bargain. However, in this usage, "bargain" does not mean an exchange of things of equivalent, or any, value. It means a negotiation resulting in the voluntary assumption of an obligation by one party upon condition of an act or forbearance by the other. Consideration thus insures that the promise enforced as a contract is not accidental, casual, or gratuitous, but has been uttered intentionally as the result of some deliberation, manifested by reciprocal bargaining or negotiation. . . . In substance, a contractual promise must be of the logical form: "If . . . (consideration is given) . . . then I promise that. . . ."[5]

Regarding the social utility of enforcing bargains, the *Restatement (Second) of Contracts* notes:

> Bargains are widely believed to be beneficial to the community in the provision of opportunities for freedom of individual action and exercise of judgment and as a means by which productive energy and product are apportioned in the economy. The enforcement of bargains rests in part on the common belief that enforcement enhances that utility.[6]

Ordinarily, the consideration is furnished by the promisee to the promisor. For example, if Smith promises to sell his guitar to Barker for $500, Barker, the promisee, furnishes the consideration (a

---

3. *Restatement (Second) of Contracts* §71(3).

4. *Restatement (Second) of Contracts* §71(2).
5. *Baehr v. Penn-O-Tex Oil Corporation,* 104 N.W.2d 661, 665-666 (Minn. 1960).
6. *Restatement (Second) of Contracts* §72 comment b.

promise to pay $500) supporting Smith's promise to transfer title to the guitar. The performance or return promise constituting consideration may, however, be given *to* a person other than the promisor, and may be given *by* a person other than the promisee. In other words, consideration may run from or to a third person. Assume that Doaks is negotiating for a loan from Carter. To induce Carter to make the loan, Smith promises to pay the obligation if Doaks fails to do so. Carter subsequently makes the loan to Doaks. Carter's loan to Doaks is consideration for *Smith's* promise, even though the consideration runs not to the promisor, Smith, but to a third party, Doaks.

Consideration issues can be divided into two broad areas: the nature of the promise or performance providing the consideration, and the existence of a "bargained-for exchange." This discussion begins with the nature of consideration, embodied in the concept of legal detriment. Note that throughout the chapter, various substitutes for or alternatives to consideration also are discussed. In these cases, the law enforces certain promises, (commonly because of formality, public policy, or reliance) that are not supported by consideration under traditional analysis.

Legal Detriment

Both parties to a contract must provide consideration. Generally, in a bilateral contract each party's promise supports the return promise of the other. In a unilateral contract, the offeree's performance of the requested act supplies the consideration to support the offeror's promise, the only promise made. Thus, the offeree of a unilateral contract and each party to a bilateral contract must ask, "Is the other party bound to his or her promise as a result of what I have done or promised to do?" The answer is "yes" if the party's promise or performance constitutes a **legal detriment**. A legal detriment is incurred if the promisee either:

1. refrains (or promises to refrain) from doing something that he or she has a legal right to do, or
2. does (or promises to do) something that he or she is not legally obligated to do.

The legal detriment concept is helpful in understanding a number of consideration issues and is well illustrated by a New York Court of Appeals case, *Hamer v. Sidway,*[7] decided in 1891. In this case, an uncle promised to pay his fifteen-year-old nephew the sum of $5,000 if the nephew would refrain from drinking, using tobacco, swearing, and playing cards or billiards for money until he became twenty-one. The nephew agreed to the terms of his uncle's promise and fully performed the conditions; in other words he accepted the unilateral offer by performance. The uncle died, however, without paying the $5,000 to the nephew. When the nephew attempted to enforce the contract against his uncle's estate, the executor refused to pay on the basis that the uncle's promise was not supported by consideration. The executor asserted that the promisee (the nephew) was benefited rather than harmed by refraining from the use of liquor and tobacco. Because he had done what was best for him independently of his uncle's promise, the executor asserted, the promise should not be binding unless the promisor (uncle) also was benefited.

The court rejected this argument, and held that the test of consideration is not whether the promisor or any other person benefits, but whether the promisee has incurred a detriment. The court reasoned that the nephew had a legal right to drink liquor and use tobacco. He abandoned that right for a period of years upon the strength of his uncle's promise. His forbearance, therefore, was consideration to support his uncle's promise to pay $5,000.[8]

Thus, when analyzing an alleged contract for the presence of consideration, one must examine each promise individually (the offeror's promise in a unilateral contract and both parties' promises in a bilateral contract). Look then to the promisee of that promise, and ask: "Has the promisee incurred a *detriment* in exchange for this promise?" If so, the promise is ordinarily supported by consideration and is therefore binding on the promisor.[9] As-

---

7. 27 N.E. 256 (N.Y. 1891).

8. 27 N.E. at 257.

9. As previously noted, a third party may supply the consideration to support a promise. In that case, ask whether the third party has incurred a detriment in exchange for the promise.

sume Fred promises to make a gift of a ring to Louise in thirty days. Fred is not contractually bound to perform his promise because the promisee, Louise, has incurred no detriment—done or promised to do something she is not legally obligated to do, or refrained or promised to refrain from doing something she has a legal right to do—in exchange for it. On the other hand, assume that Fred promises to sell a specified tract of land to Louise in exchange for Louise's promise to pay $10,000. To determine whether Fred's promise is binding, look to the promisee, Louise. Here, Louise has incurred a detriment in exchange for Fred's promise. She has done something she is not legally obligated to do: promised to pay Fred $10,000. Conversely, Louise's promise is supported by a detriment to the promisee, Fred, who promised to convey land to Louise, something, prior to the contract, he was under no legal obligation to do. Thus, both promises are supported by consideration and are binding upon the parties.

The following material discusses adequacy of consideration, pre-existing duty, and contract modification. These important contracts issues are all resolved, at least in part, by applying the basic legal detriment concepts outlined above.

Adequacy of Consideration

Contract law is based upon the principle of freedom of contract: the parties are generally free to determine the terms of their contract through private negotiation, subject primarily to public policy limitations. One of the terms left to private determination is the value placed upon the consideration exchanged.

For this reason, as a general rule, courts do not inquire into the adequacy of the consideration. As long as a detriment is incurred, it is irrelevant whether or not the economic value of the consideration exchanged is equivalent. In fact, the disparity may be very great. The rationale for this rule is that, in the absence of fraud, duress, or other extraordinary circumstances, the court should not intrude on the parties' freedom of contract to rescue a person from the consequences of a bad bargain. Assume Don purchases an old rocking chair from Steve at a garage sale for $25. After stripping off the old paint, Don discovers that the chair is a val-

uable antique, worth $1,000. Steve may not avoid the contract on the basis that the consideration is inadequate. Freedom of contract means freedom to make a bad as well as a good bargain.

Further, if courts became involved in comparing relative values, the adequacy of consideration would be an issue in every contract case, regardless of the underlying basis of the dispute. A party seeking to avoid performance of a contract would always assert the inadequacy of the consideration. Value determination, therefore, is left to the parties, who are in a better position than others to evaluate the circumstances of their particular agreement.

Note that the relative equivalence of the values exchanged is not totally irrelevant. Gross differences in economic value may offer strong circumstantial evidence of fraud, duress, mistake, unconscionability, lack of contractual capacity, or lack of a bargained-for exchange. These topics are considered later in the contracts material.

Pre-existing Legal Duties

The Pre-existing Duty Rule. Once made, most contracts are performed according to their original terms. The parties may, however, before or during performance desire to modify or even extinguish the obligations imposed by the contract. Perhaps the most fundamental principle based upon the legal detriment concept is the **pre-existing duty rule** governing contract modification.

Under the rule, the promise to perform (or performance of) a pre-existing legal or public duty does not furnish consideration to support a return promise. The rule is designed to prevent enforcement of promises that are supported by nothing more than the other party's promise to perform an existing legal duty. Such promises are often obtained by express or implied threat to withhold performance of the pre-existing legal duty. To prevent a contracting party from threatening breach to secure a change in the contract he or she could not secure during contract formation, the law simply provides that promising to do (or doing) what one is already legally obligated to do does not support an additional return promise.

Suppose a young actor contracts with a Broadway producer to perform in a play for $10,000. At the last moment, the actor refuses to perform unless the producer promises to pay an additional $5,000. The producer reluctantly agrees. The producer is not bound to pay the extra $5,000 because the actor has furnished no consideration (incurred no further detriment) to support the producer's promise. Thus, assuming the actor performs as agreed, the producer is bound to pay the agreed $10,000, but is not obligated on his additional $5,000 promise coerced by the actor's threat of breach.

In addition to contractual duties, the pre-existing duty rule applies to legal duties owed by public officials to members of the general public. Suppose a banker offers a reward for return of certain stolen property. A police officer who recovers the property, while acting within the scope of his duties, may not enforce the banker's promise as a contract. The officer's performance of his pre-existing public duty is not consideration for the banker's promise.

The following case illustrates the basic operation of the pre-existing duty rule.

In Re Estate of Dahn
464 P.2d 238 (Kan. 1970)

In 1965, Mamie and Louis Dahn entered into an installment contract for the purchase of a mobile home from W. W. Trailer Sales, Inc. The contract provided, in part, that if the buyers defaulted in making payment of the monthly installments, the mobile home could be repossessed and sold with the proceeds of sale to be applied to the amount owed on the contract. Mr. Dahn died two months later and Mrs. Dahn was unable to continue making the monthly payments to the bank that had financed the purchase. After the bank notified her that the payments were in arrears, Mrs. Dahn advised the bank that she could not pay the delinquent installments and arranged for the bank to pick up the trailer. The bank repossessed the mobile home and returned it to W. W. Trailer Sales, Inc. who paid the outstanding balance on the Dahns' contract. After the mobile home was sold at public sale, W. W. Trailer Sales, Inc. sued Mrs. Dahn for the difference between the amount due on the contract and the proceeds realized from the public sale. Mrs. Dahn counter-

claimed and sued the bank alleging that by oral agreement, the bank had promised to hold the mobile home until Mr. Dahn's estate had been settled. Mrs. Dahn alleged that this promise constituted an oral contract that the bank had breached by allowing the sale of the trailer. The trial court ruled in favor of W. W. Trailer Sales, Inc., and dismissed Mrs. Dahn's claims against W. W. Trailer Sales, Inc. and the bank. Mrs. Dahn appealed.

Fontron, Justice

. . . In announcing its decision the [trial] court observed that it failed to see how there was any consideration for the alleged agreement [that the bank would hold the trailer until settlement of Mr. Dahn's estate], even though it be assumed that such an agreement was reached via a telephone conversation between Mamie and a now deceased bank official.

The trial court's opinion appears to us as quite correct. Under the provisions of the conditional sale contract which Mamie and her husband both signed, the bank, as holder of the paper, was entitled to the possession of the trailer house upon default in payment. In delivering the trailer to the bank, or in permitting the bank to take possession thereof, Mamie did no more than she had agreed to do under the very terms of her own contract. When the bank obtained possession of the trailer house from Mamie it was already entitled to possession thereof by virtue of the conditional sale contract.

It is an elementary principle of law that to be enforceable a contract must be based on valuable consideration. It is also the prevailing view in this country that the performance or promise of performance of an act which the promisor is already bound to do does not constitute consideration so long as the original promise is still in effect.

The only consideration which has been suggested by Mrs. Dahn is that she peacefully, and voluntarily, gave up the trailer house. But this she was obligated by contract to do in any event, should she default in making her payments. Hence, we are constrained to hold, that in the eyes of the law, the bank received no consideration for its alleged agreement to hold the trailer. . . .

[Judgment affirmed.]

Enforceable Contract Modification—Common Law. The pre-existing duty rule prevents enforcement of promises supported solely by a promise to perform (or performance of) a pre-existing duty. It therefore follows that in both the contract and public duty cases a promise may be enforceable if the promisee incurs an additional detriment. To illustrate, using the examples in the preceding section, the police officer would be entitled to the reward if he was permitted to, and was using his free time to work on a crime outside the scope of his official responsibilities. Similarly, the producer's promise is binding if the actor changes his duty in some respect. Assume that the original contract requires the actor to perform in the play for two weeks. If the actor agrees to do one more performance in return for the $5,000, the detriment requirement is satisfied. As previously discussed, the value of the new consideration exchanged need not be equal; there must simply be some additional detriment, which reflects more than a pretense of a bargain, to support the promise.[10]

Under the pre-existing duty rule, therefore, an agreement to modify an existing common law contract—for example, contracts involving land, personal services, construction, or employment— requires consideration for the modification on both sides. In other words, a promise by one party altering his rights or duties is not binding unless the other party also incurs a further detriment. If both parties change their rights or duties, the consideration requirement is met because each has incurred a detriment. Under this analysis, mutual agreements to rescind are binding, becasue each party has given up the right to demand performance from the other.

Contract Modification Under the UCC. The Uniform Commercial Code alters the pre-existing duty rule for contracts for the sale of goods in §2-209(1) by providing that "an agreement modifying a contract within this Article needs no consideration to be binding." Assume S contracts to sell his car to B for $2,000. Prior to delivery or payment, the parties modify the contract. S agrees to include a tape player with the car with no change in price. S is obligated to include the tape player even though B has incurred no additional detriment, for instance, by agreeing to pay more money or include added property. That is, the modification needs no consideration to be binding. If both S and B had changed their duties, consideration would exist on both sides, and it would not be necessary to rely upon §2-209(1) to enforce the new agreement. It applies, as above, to make modifications binding in which one party alters his duty and the other does not. Note that nothing in §2-209 forces either party to grant a modification. It merely states that *if* a contract modification is granted by one party it needs no consideration to be binding.

As discussed in Chapter 6, an obligation of good faith is imposed upon every contract or duty governed by the UCC, including modifications under § 2-209. Therefore, coercion of a modification without legitimate commercial reason is ineffective as a violation of the duty to act in good faith.[11] In this manner, the Code, while doing away with the pre-existing duty rule for *commercially justified* contract modifications, preserves a basic advantage of the rule—the prevention of coerced contract modifications.

Contract Modifications—Unforeseen Difficulties. Section 2-209 enforces commercially justified contract modifications without consideration. A growing number of courts have applied a similar analysis to enforce modifications of common law contracts necessitated by unforeseen difficulties arising during performance of the contract. For example, the *Restatement (Second) of Contracts* provides that an agreement to modify a contract executory on both sides is binding without consideration if the modification is fair and equitable in light of circumstances that were not anticipated by the parties when the contract was made.[12] The following case illustrates the application of this evolving common law rule to a modification necessitated by unforeseen difficulties in a construction contract.

---

10. *Restatement (Second) of Contracts* §73.

11. UCC §2-209, Official Comment 2.
12. *Restatement (Second) of Contracts* §89.

Brian Construction and Development Company, Inc. v. Brighenti

405 A.2d 72 (Conn. 1978)

Plaintiff, Brian Construction and Development Company, Inc. (Brian), the contractor for construction of a post office, entered into a written contract with defendant, John Brighenti, by which Brian agreed to pay $104,326 and Brighenti agreed to perform "all Excavation, Grading, Site Work, Asphalt Pavement, Landscaping, and Concrete Work" and "everything requisite and necessary to finish the entire work properly." After Brighenti began excavation, he discovered that a factory previously had been located on the site and that "concrete foundation walls, slab floors, underground tanks, twisted metals and various combustible materials" were located beneath the surface. Because neither party to the contract had been aware of the subterranean debris (despite earlier test borings at the site), the contract did not specifically call for removal of the debris, and the cost of removal had not been included in the contract price. All parties agreed that the rubble needed to be removed before the project could be continued. Brian ordered Brighenti to perform the needed excavation pursuant to the clause by which he had agreed to do "everything requisite and necessary to finish the work properly." When Brighenti refused, they orally agreed that Brighenti would be paid his costs plus 10 percent for removing the unanticipated factory debris. Brighenti returned to work for about one week but then refused to do further excavation.

Brian completed the work and then sued Brighenti, alleging he had breached the oral agreement by abandoning the job. Brighenti alleged that the oral agreement was not a valid contract because it lacked consideration. The trial court ruled in favor of Brighenti. Brian appealed.

Loiselle, Associate Justice

. . . In *Blakeslee v. Board of Water Commissioners,* [139 A. 106, 111 (Conn. 1927)], this court . . . articulated the evolving rule that "where a contract must be performed under burdensome conditions not anticipated, and not within the contemplation of the parties at the time [when] the contract

was made, and the promisee measures up to the right standard of honesty and fair dealing, and agrees, in view of the changed conditions, to pay what is then reasonable, just, and fair, such new contract is not without consideration within the meaning of that term, either in law or in equity."

. . .

This principle has received recognition by courts of other jurisdictions confronted with situations comparable to that now before this court. In *Evergreen Amusement Corporation v. Milstead,* [112 A.2d 901 (Md. 1955)], the Maryland Court of Appeals found a subsequent oral agreement of the parties to a written construction contract valid, relying, in part, upon the theory of unforeseen circumstances. In that case, the plaintiff, operator of a drive-in movie theater, had entered into a written contract with the defendant, a contractor, pursuant to which the latter agreed to supply all the necessary materials and to perform the work needed to clear the theater site of timber, stumps, and waste material, and to grade the site as indicated on the accompanying plans. Once the work was underway, it became apparent that substantial, additional fill would be needed to complete the project, although neither party had anticipated this, both relying upon a topographical map which proved to be of doubtful accuracy. The court found that the parties, upon this discovery, entered into an oral agreement whereby the defendant would bring in the fill for additional compensation. On appeal, the plaintiff claimed that this agreement lacked consideration since the defendant promised only to do that which he had already agreed to do, i.e., to furnish all materials needed to grade the theater site. Relying upon the theory of unforeseen circumstances, the court held the agreement to be binding. . . .

The promise of additional compensation in return for the promise that the additional work required would be undertaken was held to constitute a separate, valid agreement. Such reasoning is applicable to the facts of this case. The unchallenged findings of the court reveal that the substantial rubble found beneath the surface of the site was not anticipated by either party, that its presence necessitated excavation beyond the depths required in the plans and specifications, that the cost of removing this rubble was not included in the contract price and that the parties entered into a separate oral agreement for the removal of the rubble. Under these circumstances, the subsequent oral agreement, that the defendant would remove this rubble in return for additional compensation, was binding as a new, distinct contract, supported by valid consideration. . . . The defendant's failure to comply with this agreement constitutes a breach of contract. . . .

[Judgment reversed.]

Bargained for Exchange

The second major element of consideration is that the promises or performances involved be given in exchange for each other. In other words, the existence of a detriment alone is insufficient. The promisor must make the promise because he or she wishes to exchange it for the detriment (promise or performance) incurred by the promisee and the promisee must make the promise or render a performance in order to exchange it for the promise made by the promisor. The following material examines this element of exchange required for enforcement of a promise.

Past Consideration

Typically, the promise and the consideration that supports it stand in a reciprocal relationship; the consideration induces the making of the promise and the promise induces the furnishing of the consideration. Therefore, if a promise is made or performance rendered before the return promise is made, the return promise is unenforceable because it has not been bargained for. The earlier act or promise is referred to as **past consideration.**

To illustrate, if

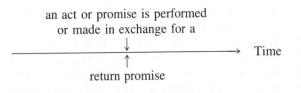

the return promise is bargained for and binding upon the promisor. If, however,

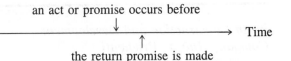

then there is no bargain for the return promise. Because no act or promise is given in exchange, the promise is not binding upon the promisor. In the eyes of the law, therefore, past consideration is no consideration. The following case illustrates an application of the past consideration principle.

Dewein v. Dewein's Estate
174 N.E.2d 875 (Ill. App. 1961)

After studying nursing, plaintiff Irene Dewein returned to her parents' home where she provided services for her parents for more than 27 years. During this period she provided nursing care for both of her parents, managed their rental properties, performed household chores, and paid all bills. Her father died in 1948, her mother, in 1957. After plaintiff's brother, Edward Dewein, died in 1959, plaintiff filed a claim against his estate alleging that her brother owed her $10,000 as a contractual obligation for the services plaintiff had rendered to their parents. In support of her claim, plaintiff offered the testimony of a neighbor who stated that she had been present with plaintiff and her brother in 1956 when the brother had stated "Sis, I am so greatful [*sic*] you are taking care of mother, and I am certainly going to see you are taken care of for life, you deserve it." The neighbor further testified that in a subsequent conversation plaintiff's brother had stated "Sis, don't you worry about the future, I am going to see you are taken care of."

The probate court denied plaintiff's claim and she appealed.

Scheineman, Justice

. . . The quoted remarks show due appreciation for what had been done, but lack the essential elements of a contract. They are more in the nature of an unenforceable promise to make a future gift as an expression of appreciation.

Certainly, the quoted remarks regarding some provision for the care of plaintiff in her declining years, so that she need not worry about the future, are very far from an agreement to pay the reasonable value of nursing services over a period of 27 years. Doubtless the persons present were assuming that plaintiff would continue to care for the woman in what must have been obviously the last days of her life. Yet the [brother's] statement contained no such condition nor any request in that regard, nor was there any indication by plaintiff that she would do so because of the [brother's] promise. Plaintiff did not give up any proposition of her own, nor change her position in any way, but simply continued for a few more months that which she had been doing of her own accord for many years. . . .

The testimony in this case fails to support the claim that plaintiff "acted in reliance upon the [brother's] promise to her." There is no indication that she had ever intended to act otherwise than the way she did. Surely, there can be no presumption or inference that after living with her mother for so many years, she was now about to desert her in the time of her greatest need, but was persuaded to stay "in reliance on promises made to her." The record contains not even a hint in that respect. The finding of the Probate Court that the evidence fails to support the claim was correct and it is affirmed.

[Judgment affirmed.]

Obligations barred by operation of law provide exceptions to the past consideration rule. A subsequent promise, for instance, to pay a contractual debt barred by the statute of limitations is binding without additional consideration. Suppose Don owes Chris $500. Chris may no longer sue Don to recover because the statute of limitations has run on the claim. However, if Don later promises Chris in writing to pay the $500, then Don's promise is binding.

Promises to perform previously voidable duties are also binding. Induced by Seller's fraud, Buyer promises to pay Seller $100 for defective merchandise. Buyer's promise is voidable. After discovering the fraud, Buyer promises to pay as agreed. Buyer's promise is binding.

Moral Consideration

One of the most common applications of the past consideration doctrine is the moral obligation case. Suppose Alice saves Stan's life, but is seriously injured while doing so. Stan, in gratitude to Alice, later promises to pay Alice $100 a month for life or pay her medical bills. Stan is not bound by his promise, because nothing has been given in exchange for it. The act giving rise to his promise (Alice saving his life) occurred before the promise was made. The past consideration provided by Alice does not support Stan's return promise. Because Stan's promise rests upon a moral but not legal obligation, past consideration in this context is often referred to as **moral consideration.**

Promises based upon moral obligations are, however, sometimes enforced. A number of courts, either by statute or through a refined application of the doctrine of quasi-contract,[13] enforce promises arising out of benefits previously conferred by the promisee upon the promisor to the extent necessary to prevent injustice or unjust enrichment of the promisor. The promises are clearly not "bargained for," but are enforced for public policy reasons. In these situations, however, the promises are not binding if their value is disproportionate to the benefit conferred.[14]

Nominal Consideration

Occasionally, a contract will state that property or services are to be exchanged "for $1.00 and other valuable consideration" or similar language. Such a statement is referred to as a recited or **nominal consideration.** Nominal consideration is often used in an effort to make gratuitous promises enforceable. The issue thus presented is whether a nominal consideration accomplishes that purpose.

Courts look generally for the existence of a bar-

---

13. Quasi-contract is introduced in Chapter 7 and covered in more detail in Chapter 15.

14. *Restatement (Second) of Contracts* §86. The rule concerning making promises arising out of benefits previously conferred enforceable in certain instances does not apply to benefits conferred as a gift or under other circumstances not involving unjust enrichment of the promisor.

gain, not the relative equivalence of the values exchanged. Nevertheless, great disparity in value may sometimes indicate that a purported exchange is not in fact bargained for, but is a mere formality. If so, a recited or nominal consideration does not support the return promise.

Assume Mark promises to paint Bob's house, a job worth $2,000. Mark's promise is stated to be "in consideration of $1.00 paid to me by Bob, the receipt of which is hereby acknowledged." If the recited amount is not paid and no other bargained for consideration is given (that is, the recital of consideration is a "sham"), the promise is unenforceable. Even if the nominal amount is paid, however, many courts still find no consideration if the return promise is not otherwise bargained for, that is, if the promise was made with the intent to make a gift.

The rules stated above concern the enforceability of *promises* supported by nominal consideration. Performance of the promise, however, may create a valid gift. That is, though a promise to make a gift is unenforceable, a gift once validly made is irrevocable by the donor.[15]

Options and Suretyship Promises. Not all promises supported solely by a nominal or recited consideration are unenforceable. Under the view taken by many courts and adopted by the *Restatement (Second) of Contracts,* an option (a promise to keep an offer open), or a suretyship promise (a promise guaranteeing payment of another's debt) is binding if it: (1) is in writing, (2) is signed by the promisor, and (3) recites a purported consideration.[16] Additionally, in the case of an option, the promise must propose an exchange on fair terms within a reasonable time. That is, nominal consideration paid or promised will support a bargained for short-term option. For example, assume S, in a signed writing, "in consideration of $1.00 paid" grants B a thirty-day option to purchase a tract of land for $15,000, a fair price. The offer is irrevocable even if the $1.00 is not in fact paid.[17] The rationale for enforcing written short-term options and suretyship promises in the absence of consideration is that such promises are often a necessary preliminary step to the conclusion of a socially useful bargain (for example, a sale of land or loan of money). Further, the formality of a signed writing executed in a commercial setting provides adequate evidence of the signer's intent to be contractually bound while minimizing the possibility of fraud.

Settlement of Claims

Accord and Satisfaction

As noted in Chapter 2, compromise is certainly the most common method of resolving disputes. An important contracts issue, grounded upon basic consideration analysis, concerns the legal effect of a compromise agreement reached to settle a pre-existing obligation. The creation and performance of the compromise agreement is known as an **accord and satisfaction.**

An accord is a contract in which a party entitled to a performance (the "creditor" below) promises to accept an alternative stated performance in full satisfaction of the original duty owed him. The effect of an accord is: (1) until performance of the accord agreement, the creditor's right to sue on the original obligation is suspended; (2) the performance of the accord agreement (satisfaction) discharges both the original duty and the duty under the accord; and (3) if the accord agreement is breached, the original duty survives and the creditor may sue on either the accord or the original duty.

In determining whether an accord and satisfaction has been created, a distinction must be made between obligations that are undisputed and liquidated, on one hand, and those that are unliquidated in amount. A claim is **disputed** if one party is contesting the *existence* of the obligation. Assume that

---

15. Gifts are discussed in Chapter 34.

16. *Restatement (Second) of Contracts* §§87(1)(a), 88(a). Options are discussed in Chapter 8. Suretyship is covered in Chapter 33.

17. This result is consistent with UCC §2-205 discussed in Chapter 8. Under that provision, short-term options to buy or sell *goods* granted by a merchant in a signed writing are binding without consideration.

S asserts that B promised to pay $500 for certain goods to be delivered by S. B admits talking to S, but denies any agreement concerning the goods was made. S's claim against B is disputed.

A claim though undisputed may be liquidated or unliquidated. A **liquidated claim** is simply one that is fixed in amount. Thus, in the preceding example, assume that B admits that an agreement to purchase the goods was made, but asserts that the price was to be left open pending further negotiation. In this case the claim is undisputed, but unliquidated. If both parties agree that a contract exists at $500, S's claim against B is both undisputed and liquidated.

If an obligation is *liquidated* and *undisputed,* courts traditionally apply the pre-existing duty rule to find that a part payment does not discharge the entire debt, even if the reduced amount is bargained for in satisfaction of the obligation. Here, the debtor is merely doing what (or in this case less than) he is already legally obligated to do. Assume Seller contracts to sell Buyer a tract of land for $4,000, payable in monthly installments over a five-year period. Two years later, Seller agrees to reduce the price to $2,500, which is ultimately paid by Buyer. In this case, Seller is not bound to his promise to accept the reduced amount in satisfaction of the $4,000 debt.

On the other hand, if a *good faith* dispute arises concerning either the existence of a claim or the amount owing, a compromise agreement to pay any definite sum of money (or render any other performance) is binding (supported by consideration) and creates an accord contract. In addition, even a liquidated and undisputed obligation may be discharged by compromise agreement involving performance significantly different from that originally agreed upon. In other words, the creditor's promise to accept substituted performance in satisfaction of the original duty is supported by consideration either because: (1) the debtor's performance differs significantly from that required by the original duty (thus it is not merely performance of a pre-existing legal duty), or (2) the existence or amount of the original duty is in doubt. The following examples illustrate the operation of an accord and satisfaction.

Using the land sale example above, assume that the Buyer, in addition to paying $2,500, agreed to paint Seller's house or transfer a fishing boat to Seller.[18] Here Buyer has substantially altered his duty, and therefore the agreement to pay money and also to provide services or property is an accord. Until Buyer performs the accord, Seller's right to sue on the original $4,000 obligation is suspended. If Buyer breaches the accord, Seller may sue either on the underlying $4,000 debt or on the accord. If Buyer properly performs the accord, both the $4,000 original debt and the accord are discharged. Or, assume that A owes B $10,000. A and B agree that A will deliver a machine to B in thirty days, which B will accept in full satisfaction of the debt. The contract is an accord. A's debt is suspended and both the debt and the accord are discharged if A delivers the machine in thirty days.

Both of the preceding examples involve undisputed, liquidated claims. To illustrate the operation of accord and satisfaction upon a disputed or unliquidated obligation, assume that Ralph performs remodeling work on Freda's house. No agreement on price is reached before work is commenced. Ralph subsequently sends Freda a bill for $1,000. Freda, thinking the bill is too high, sends a letter explaining that she thinks the amount is excessive and offering $800 in full satisfaction. Ralph accepts and Freda subsequently pays $800. An accord and satisfaction is created, discharging Ralph's claim for $1,000.

Settling Claims by Conditional Check

An accord and satisfaction is commonly created by **conditional check,** a device well illustrated by *Nardine v. Kraft Cheese Co.,*[19] decided in 1944. In this case, Kraft had shipped longhorn cheese to Nardine, a grocery store owner, on open account. A dispute developed concerning the cheese. Nardine contended that it was spoiled when received and that Kraft should take it back. Kraft asserted that the cheese was spoiled by Nardine's attempt to

18. Note that a promise to provide services or property would create a binding accord even if those services or the property were not worth $1,500. Once again, courts generally do not inquire into adequacy of consideration.

19. 52 N.E.2d 634 (Ind. App. 1944).

force cure it. In attempting to reconcile the dispute, Nardine discovered other discrepancies in the account. Finally, Nardine sent Kraft a check for approximately $146 with the notation on the check, ''This pays my account in full to date.'' Kraft certified the check and proceeded to sue Nardine for the additional sum of approximately $88 that it alleged to be still owing. In refusing to allow Kraft to recover the claimed deficiency, the court applied the now well-settled common law rule that when a bona fide dispute exists as to either the existence or the amount of a money debt, a check tendered in full satisfaction of the claim (marked ''paid in full'' or the like), which is cashed (or certified) by the other party, discharges the claim. The tender of the check is regarded as an offer for an accord. Cashing the check is simultaneous acceptance of the offer for an accord and satisfaction, which discharges both the accord and the disputed debt. Therefore, the accord and satisfaction is a defense to any subsequent suit by the creditor to collect the balance of its claim.

The creditor cannot alter this result by (1) crossing out the words ''paid in full'' on the check and then cashing it, (2) notifying the debtor that the payment is being applied on account and not in full satisfaction, or (3) by depositing the check indorsed ''under protest'' or ''with reservation of rights'' or similar language. Because the offeror is the master of the offer, the offeree may not alter its terms and create a contract on the altered terms by acceptance, as the following case illustrates.

County Fire Door Corporation v. C. F. Wooding Company

520 A.2d 1028 (Conn. 1987)

Defendant C. F. Wooding Company (Wooding) ordered several metal doors from the plaintiff County Fire Door Corporation for use at a construction site known as the Upjohn Project. After receiving the doors, Wooding informed County Fire Door that it would not pay the full sales price because of additional installation expenses that Wooding had incurred due to late delivery of the doors. After Wooding indicated its intention to pay $416.88 as the balance due on the account, County Fire Door notified Wooding that full payment of $2,618.88 was due. Wooding wrote County Fire Door reiterating its intention to pay only $416.88 and subsequently sent County Fire Door a check in the amount of $416.88 with the following statement on the reverse side: ''By its endorsement, the payee accepts this check in full satisfaction of all claims against the C. F. Wooding Co. arising out of or relating to the Upjohn Project under Purchase Order #3302, dated 11/17/81.'' County Fire Door crossed out the statement and added the following: ''This check is accepted under protest and with full reservation of rights to collect the unpaid balance for which this check is offered in settlement.''

County Fire Door indorsed the check, deposited it in its account and later and sued Wooding for the balance of approximately $2,200. The trial court ruled in favor of County Fire Door and Wooding appealed.

Peters, Chief Justice

. . . When there is a good faith dispute about the existence of a debt or about the amount that is owed, the common law authorized the debtor and the creditor to negotiate a contract of accord to settle the outstanding claim. Such a contract is often initiated by the debtor, who offers an accord by tendering a check as ''payment in full'' or ''in full satisfaction.'' If the creditor knowingly cashes such a check, or otherwise exercises full dominion over it, the creditor is deemed to have assented to the offer of accord. Upon acceptance of the offer of accord, the creditor's receipt of the promised payment discharges the underlying debt and bars any further claim relating thereto, if the contract of accord is supported by consideration. . . .

A contract of accord and satisfaction is sufficiently supported by consideration if it settles a monetary claim that is unliquidated in amount. This court has had numerous occasions to decide whether, in the context of accord and satisfaction, a claim is unliquidated when the debtor tenders payment in an amount that does not exceed that to which the creditor is concededly entitled. ''Where it is admitted that one of two specific sums is due, but there is a dispute as to which is the proper amount, the demand is regarded as unliquidated, within the meaning of that term as applied to the subject of accord and satisfaction. . . . Where the claim is unliquidated any sum, given and received in settlement of the dispute, is a sufficient consideration." *Hanley Co. v. American Cement Co.* [143 A. 566 (Conn. 1928).]. . . .

Application of these settled principles to the facts of this case establishes, as the defendant maintains, that the parties entered into a valid contract of accord and satisfaction. The defendant offered in good faith to settle an unliquidated debt by tendering, in full satisfaction, the payment of an amount less than that demanded by the plaintiff. Under the common law, the plaintiff could not simultaneously cash such a check and disown the condition on which it had been tendered. . . .

Under prevailing common law principles, . . . the parties in this case negotiated a contract of accord whose satisfaction discharged the defendant from any further monetary obligation to the plaintiff. The plaintiff might have avoided this result by returning the defendant's check uncashed, but could not simultaneously disregard the condition on which the check was tendered and deposit its proceeds in the plaintiff's bank account. . . .

[Judgment reversed and remanded.]

In determining whether a binding accord and satisfaction exists, it is irrelevant who is right or wrong in the underlying dispute; the law simply requires that a bona fide dispute exist at the time the check is tendered in full payment. In *Nardine,* for example, the court found a binding accord and satisfaction despite its additional finding that Nardine was in fact responsible for spoiling the cheese.[20] Therefore whenever accord and satisfaction is alleged on a disputed or unliquidated claim, the good faith of the party asserting the dispute is crucial. One cannot avoid a legitimate obligation merely by insisting dishonestly that a dispute exists and then tendering a part payment marked "paid in full."

In sum, if a creditor is involved in a good faith contract dispute over the existence or amount of a money debt, and a check is tendered by the debtor marked "paid in full," he should not cash or certify the check unless he agrees to the terms under which the check is tendered.

Conditional Check and the UCC

A substantial debate exists among the states regarding whether UCC §1-207 alters the common law of accord and satisfaction by conditional check outlined above. Section 1-207 provides:

> A party who with explicit reservation of rights performs or promises performance or assents to performance in a manner demanded or offered by the other party does not thereby prejudice the rights reserved. Such words as "without prejudice," "under protest" or the like are sufficient.

Section 1-207 is intended to permit contracting parties to continue performance according to their original agreement despite a pending dispute without risking a waiver of their rights.[21] Section 1-207 thus permits one party to reserve rights concerning some allegedly nonconforming aspect of the other's performance without terminating the entire underlying contract. For example, a buyer of goods may make an installment payment for or accept delivery of goods "under protest" if it believes the goods do not conform to the contract. Or, a seller may continue with performance "with reservation of rights" after the buyer has renounced or repudiated its duty under the contract.

Although most courts and commentators that have considered the issue agree that §1-207 does not alter the common law of accord and satisfaction, a minority of jurisdictions have held that this provision applies to the conditional check situation. For example, assume that a debtor tenders a check in full satisfaction of a disputed claim. The creditor may in some jurisdictions cash the check without impairing its right to proceed for any additional amount claimed if it notifies the debtor that the check is cashed with reservation of rights. Indorsing the check "under protest" or "without prejudice" is apparently sufficient. Note that in some jurisdictions adopting this approach, §1-207 applies to any "Code-covered" transaction; that is,

---

20. 52 N.E.2d at 635.

21. UCC §1-207, Official Comment 1.

as long as a check or other commercial paper (governed by UCC Article 3) is tendered in attempted satisfaction of the disputed claim, §1-207 may be used by the creditor regardless of the nature of the contract (for example, a sale of goods, services, land, or intangible personal property) underlying the parties' commercial relationship.[22]

The minority approach to §1-207 resolves a dilemma frequently faced by a creditor in a conditional check contract dispute. Assume that XYZ Corporation sells Joe Doaks goods for $20,000. Doaks asserts that the goods are defective and tenders a check for $19,000 marked "paid in full." If XYZ cashes the check, its right to recover the additional $1,000 is extinguished even though it believes that the goods are conforming. If, however, XYZ does not cash the check, it runs the risk of Doaks's later insolvency or of substantial expense and delay in recovery. In other words, the $19,000 in hand, even though less than XYZ believes to be owing, may be more acceptable than the expense and risk involved in attempting to recover the full $20,000. By indorsing the check "under protest" or "without prejudice," the creditor may cash the check without jeopardizing its right to recover the deficiency.

Mutuality of Consideration

The term **mutuality of consideration** simply means that both parties to a contract must provide consideration. Each party to a bilateral contract incurs a bargained for detriment, and it is this detriment that supports the return promise of the other. The doctrine of mutuality applies to unilateral contracts as well, even though only one promise is involved. Mutuality requires that both parties provide *consideration,* not that both parties be mutually *obligated.* In a unilateral contract, the offeror's promise becomes binding upon the offeree's performance of the requested act. Thus, both parties provide consideration. The offeree's performance is a detriment that is bargained for in exchange for the offeror's promise, making it enforceable. A

contract exists despite the fact that the offeree is never obligated to perform.[23]

Illusory Promises

Because both promises in a bilateral contract must be supported by consideration, the entire contract fails if one party's promise makes his or her performance entirely optional. In this case, the promissory language is known as an **illusory promise.** An illusory promise is not a promise at all, and therfore does not furnish consideration for a return promise. It, in effect, says, "I'll perform if I want to perform." Suppose Seller and Buyer enter into a contract in which Buyer promises to purchase "as many bicycles as I shall choose to order within the next thirty days." The buyer's "promise" is illusory, stating in effect, "I will buy as many bicycles as I want from you, but if I don't want them, I am not obligated to take them." Performance is entirely optional with the "promisor," Buyer. In other words, Buyer has incurred no detriment. Thus, Seller's promise to deliver bicycles at fixed prices is not binding.

The following material examines a number of important contracts issues in which one contracting party seeks to avoid performance for lack of mutuality (asserting that the other party's promise is illusory). Note particularly in each case the approach taken by the courts in resolving the mutuality argument.

Conditions Requiring Satisfaction

A condition is an event that must occur before a contracting party is required to perform her promise. If a promise is subject to a condition and the condition fails to occur, no duty to perform the promise arises, and the promisor incurs no liability for failure to perform. Although conditions are discussed in detail in Chapter 14,[24] conditional promises present a number of mutuality issues.

---

22. See, for example, *Horn Waterproofing Corp. v. Bushwick Iron & Steel Co., Inc.,* 488 N.E.2d 56, 61 (N.Y. 1985).

23. Under the rules discussed in Chapter 8, the offeree may become bound after she commences performance or if she treats an ambiguous offer as a bilateral offer.

24. Conditions are discussed beginning on page 308.

A contract may provide that one party's duty to perform arises only if she is "satisfied" with the performance of the other. A condition of "satisfaction" or "complete satisfaction" appears to render the promise illusory because the party whose satisfaction is required may avoid her obligation by merely stating "I'm not satisfied." Such promises, however, are not illusory. The party whose satisfaction is required must act in *good faith* and in accordance with standards of fair dealing. That is, she must be *honestly* dissatisfied and therefore may not reject the other party's performance as a means to avoid performing her own promise.

Satisfaction may be measured either by a subjective or an objective test. In a subjective test, performance is judged merely by the party's honest satisfaction or lack of satisfaction, which may be unreasonable or arbitrary. In an objective test, satisfaction is judged by determining whether a reasonable person in the position of the judging party would be satisfied. The agreement may explicitly provide the test to be used. If it does not, an objective test, if practicable, is the preferred interpretation. Absent an explicit agreement, the law does not presume that a party has assumed the risk of the other's unreasonable, even though honest, dissatisfaction. Using an objective test reduces the risk that the party subject to the condition will lose any right to recover on the contract, after partially or completely performing. Therefore, an objective test is used if

1. A subjective test (for example, "satisfaction is to be determined in buyer's sole, exclusive, and final judgment made in good faith") is not explicitly provided in the agreement, and
2. It is feasible to determine whether or not a "reasonable" person would be satisfied.

Assume Pablo contracts to paint Lee's portrait. Lee agrees to pay $2,000 only if "completely satisfied." Upon completion, Lee expresses her honest dissatisfaction, giving no further reason. According to experts in the field, the portrait has great artistic merit. Pablo may not recover $2,000 from Lee, because even though a subjective test is not explicitly required, it is not practical to apply an

objective test to the painting. That is, no objective criteria exists by which satisfaction can be measured.

In contrast, assume that Seller contracts to manufacture goods for Buyer according to explicit specifications provided by Buyer. Buyer agrees to pay $10,000 "upon satisfactory completion" of the goods. Seller tenders the completed goods to Buyer, who refuses to accept them, stating only that he is not satisfied with the finished product. According to experts in the field, the goods comply exactly with the specifications. Seller may recover the $10,000 from Buyer because subjective satisfaction is not explicitly required, and it is practicable to apply an objective test to the manufacture. That is, objective criteria exist (the specifications) to determine whether or not performance would be satisfactory to a reasonable person. Satisfaction is measured by reference to the explicit criteria imposed.

A party's satisfaction or lack thereof is a question of fact. Therefore, the promisor's assertion of dissatisfaction alone, even on the witness stand, and even if a subjective test is used, is not conclusive on the issue. The promisor must be acting honestly in withholding approval of the performance. Whether he is honestly dissatisfied or is merely attempting to avoid his obligation is determined by the trier of fact (the jury, or, if the case is tried without a jury, the court (judge)), based upon his testimony, demeanor, and other evidence adduced at the trial.

Other Conditional Promises

As the preceding discussion indicates, a party's duty to perform may be conditional upon the occurrence of a given event (for example, in the above case, satisfaction of the promisor). If the occurrence or nonoccurrence of the condition is outside the control of the promisor, his or her conditional promise clearly supports a return promise. For example, assume S contracts to sell land to B for $50,000. The buyer's promise is subject to a condition that an independent appraisal must reveal that the market value of the property is at least equal to the purchase price. B's promise supports S's return promise to convey the property, because the occurrence of the condition is not within B's control.

A promise also may be made conditional upon the occurrence or nonoccurrence of an uncertain or fortuitous event. In this situation, the promise is referred to as **aleatory**. A common aleatory promise is made in an insurance contract. Assume an insurance company promises to pay you up to $40,000 per occurrence for fire losses to your house sustained within one year. This promise supports your promise to pay the premium, even if no loss occurs within the stated period. That is, even though the company incurred no actual detriment, the *possibility* of a detriment is sufficient. Similarly, a promise is not rendered illusory because the promisor makes his duty to perform conditional upon the nonoccurrence of strikes, fires, accidents, riots, wars, floods or other Acts of God, damage or destruction of production facilities, unforeseen shutdown of sources of supply, or any other circumstances over which the promisor has no control. Such provisions (known as *force majeure* clauses) are common in contracts requiring manufacture and delivery of goods or construction of a building or other project by a stated date. A conditional promise is, however, not consideration if, at the time the promise is made, the promisor knows that the condition cannot occur.

A promise may be capable of supporting a return promise even if conditional upon occurrence of an event within the control of the promisor. For example, contracts for the sale of real estate frequently provide that the buyer's duty to perform is conditional upon her acquiring mortgage financing for the purchase in a specified amount with a given term and interest rate. At first glance, the buyer's promise to pay the purchase price seems illusory; that is, she may avoid it by failing to apply for the loan. Courts, however, find consideration in these cases by *implying a promise* on the part of the buyer to use his or her "best efforts" to obtain the financing (that is, to bring about occurrence of the condition).

A similar problem exists in exclusive dealing contracts. For example, a seller may grant a buyer an exclusive right to market the seller's products within a certain geographic area. The buyer may not be required, under the terms of the contract, to sell any products, making his promise appear "illusory." The UCC, which adopts the common law rule, finds consideration to support the seller's promise by imposing a "best efforts" requirement in the sale or promotion of the goods upon the buyer. A similar requirement to supply the goods is imposed upon the seller.[25]

Rights of Termination

A contract may contain a provision that the contract shall continue in force for a given period of time or continue indefinitely, subject to termination at the option of one or both parties. Because a party may avoid any further obligation under the contract at any time, such a promise appears illusory. Frequently, however, the right to terminate is conditional upon giving advance notice to the other party—for example, thirty, sixty, or ninety days. If a prior notice requirement exists, consideration exists, because each party has agreed to provide goods or services (or to purchase them) for at least the notice period. For example, if Seller agrees to provide Buyer with goods for a three-year period subject to cancellation on thirty-days notice by either party, both parties are bound to either buy or sell goods for at least thirty days. By doing something they are not legally required to do (buying or selling for thirty days), the requirement of legal detriment is met.

If either party has the right to terminate at will, or upon mere notification without any advance waiting period, early courts found the promises illusory. More recent cases, however, have found consideration in the act of giving reasonable advance notice in cases in which mere notice is required, or by implying a promise to give a reasonable notice of termination if a notice requirement is not explicitly stated in the contract. The UCC adopts this approach by providing in §2-309(3):

> Termination of a contract by one party except on the happening of an agreed event requires that reasonable notification be received by the other party and an agreement dispensing with notifica-

---

25. UCC §2-306(2).

tion is invalid if its operation would be unconscionable.[26]

This provision recognizes that principles of good faith and sound commercial practice normally require that sufficient notice be given to allow the other party a reasonable time within which to make a substitute arrangement.[27] It also appears to make contracts that are terminable at will by either party enforceable, because the obligation to give "reasonable notification" before termination would satisfy the consideration requirement.

In conclusion, as the entire mutuality discussion indicates, courts tend to enforce contracts despite the fact that one or both promises appear "illusory." They achieve this result by imposing an obligation to act in good faith (for example, conditions of satisfaction) or by implying a promise (for example, to use "best efforts," or to give "reasonable" notification). This tendency, exhibited in both common law decisions and by statutes such as the UCC, represents the belief by courts and legislatures that enforcement best effectuates the *intent* of the parties to enter into a *contractual* relationship. In other words, when parties make an agreement, they intend legal consequences to follow. They do not view their bargain as void, having no legal force or effect.

Promissory Estoppel

The preceding material discusses a number of situations in which the law enforces promises not otherwise supported by consideration under traditional analysis. Examples include firm offers under the UCC, promises to perform obligations barred by operation of law, and certain promises to pay for benefits previously conferred. One final exception to the consideration requirement is provided by the promissory estoppel doctrine. Under this theory a promise not otherwise binding as a contract is enforced because of the promisee's *justifiable reliance* upon it.

Estoppel is the legal principle by which a person is prevented (estopped) from asserting a position that is inconsistent with his prior conduct, if injustice would thereby result to a person who has changed position in justifiable reliance upon that conduct. Promises that are not otherwise supported by consideration may be enforceable through application of the **promissory estoppel** doctrine. Its requirements are stated in §90(1) of the *Restatement (Second) of Contracts,* which forms the basis of virtually all judicial adoptions of the doctrine:

> A promise which the promisor should reasonably expect to induce action or forbearance on the part of the promisee or a third person and which does induce such action or forbearance is binding if injustice can be avoided only by enforcement of the promise. The remedy granted for breach may be limited as justice requires.

Thus, if a promisor makes a promise knowing that the promisee or a third person will rely upon it, and the promisee or third person changes position in reliance upon the promise by acting or forbearing to act, then the promisor is bound to perform to the extent necessary to avoid injustice to the reliant party.

The promise is binding upon the promisor, not because it is supported by consideration (which it is not), but because the promisor by her conduct is precluded (estopped or prevented) from asserting a contrary position. In other words, the promise is binding without consideration because of the promisee's change of position in reliance upon it. Note that the promisor is only affected by reliance that she does or should foresee. Further, enforcement of the promise must be necessary to avoid injustice. In determining this issue, factors such as the reasonableness and character of the promisee's reliance, the formality with which the promise is made, and the possibility of unjust enrichment are considered.[28]

---

26. Unconscionability is discussed in Chapter 10. Under the UCC, "termination occurs when either party pursuant to a power created by agreement or law puts an end to the contract *otherwise than for its breach.*" §2-106(3). (Emphasis added.)

27. UCC §2-309, Official Comment 8. No notice is required if the contract provides for termination upon the occurrence of an agreed event.

---

28. *Restatement (Second) of Contracts* §90 comment b.

"Promissory" estoppel should be distinguished from **equitable estoppel** (or estoppel *in pais*). Equitable estoppel results when a person relies upon another's statement of fact (which may be made expressly, or inferred from silence or other conduct) resulting in injury. In promissory estoppel, the injured party relies upon a promise, not upon a statement of fact. Equitable estoppel prevents a party from asserting facts (including the truth) which differ from his prior representations. Promissory estoppel makes a promise binding upon the promisor, though unsupported by consideration.

In the following case the court was required to determine whether a promise should be enforced on the basis of promissory estoppel.

Hayes v. Plantations Steel Company

438 A.2d 1091 (R.I. 1982)

In January, 1972, plaintiff Edward Hayes, who had been employed by Plantations Steel Company since 1947, announced his intention to retire in July, 1972. Although Plantations maintained no formal pension plan, Hayes anticipated receiving a pension from his employer. Approximately one week before Hayes's retirement, Hugo Mainelli, Jr., an officer and shareholder of Plantations, talked briefly with Hayes and told him that the company "would take care" of him. After Hayes retired, Plantations paid him an annual pension of $5,000 until 1977 when, following several poor business years, Plantations changed ownership and management and discontinued the payments to Hayes.

Hayes sued Plantations alleging that the company was contractually obligated to continue paying the pension for his life. The trial court ruled that Plantations was required to pay Hayes a yearly pension of $5,000 on the basis of an implied in fact contract and that Hayes had demonstrated detrimental reliance sufficient to support promissory estoppel in lieu of consideration for the contract. Plantations appealed.

Shea, Justice

. . . Assuming for the purpose of this discussion that Plantations in legal effect made a promise to Hayes, we must ask whether Hayes did supply the required consideration that would make the promise binding? And, if Hayes did not supply consideration, was his alleged reliance sufficiently induced by the promise to estop defendant from denying its obligation to him? We answer both questions in the negative. . . .

Contracts implied in fact require the element of consideration to support them as is required in express contracts. The only difference between the two is the manner in which the parties manifest their assent. . . . In this jurisdiction, consideration consists either in some right, interest, or benefit accruing to one party or some forbearance, detriment, or responsibility given, suffered, or undertaken by the other. . . . Valid consideration furthermore must be bargained for. It must induce the return act or promise. To be valid, therefore, the purported consideration must not have been delivered before a promise is executed, that is, given without reference to the promise. . . . Consideration is therefore a test of the enforceability of executory promises . . . and has no legal effect when rendered in the past and apart from an alleged exchange in the present. . . .

In the case before us, Plantation's promise to pay Hayes a pension is quite clearly not supported by any consideration supplied by Hayes. Hayes had announced his intent to retire well in advance of any promise, and therefore the intention to retire was arrived at without regard to any promise by Plantations. Although Hayes may have had in mind the receipt of a pension when he first informed Plantations, his expectation was not based on any statement made to him or on any conduct of the company officer relative to him in January 1972. In deciding to retire, Hayes acted on his own initiative. Hayes's long years of dedicated service also is legally insufficient because his service too was rendered without being induced by Plantations's promise. . . .

Clearly then this is not a case in which Plantations's promise was meant to induce Hayes to refrain from retiring when he could have chosen to do so in return for further service. . . . Nor was the promise made to encourage long service from the start of his employment. . . . Instead, the testimony establishes that Plantations's promise was intended "as a token of appreciation for [Hayes's] many years of service." As such it was in the nature of a gratuity paid to Hayes for as long as the company chose. . . .

Hayes urges that in the absence of a bargained-for promise the facts require application of the doctrine of promissory estoppel. He stresses that he retired voluntarily while expecting to receive a pension. He would not have otherwise retired. Nor did he seek other employment.

We disagree with this contention largely for the reasons already stated. One of the essential elements of the doctrine of promissory estoppel is that the promise must *induce* the promisee's action of forbearance. The particular act in this regard is plaintiff's decision whether or not to retire. As we stated earlier, the record indicates that he made the decision on his own initiative. In other words, the conversation between Hayes and Mainelli which occurred a week before Hayes left his employment cannot be said to have induced his decision to leave. He had reached that decision long before.

An example taken from the restatement provides a meaningful contrast:

> "2. A promises B to pay him an annuity during B's life. B *thereupon* resigns profitable employment as *A expected* that he might. B receives the annuity for some years, in the meantime becoming disqualified from again obtaining good employment. A's promise is binding." (Emphasis added.) 1 Restatement Contracts § 90 at 111 (1932).

In *Feinberg v. Pfeiffer Co.*, 322 S.W.2d 163 (Mo.App.1959), the plaintiff-employee had worked for her employer for nearly forty years. The defendant corporation's board of directors resolved, in view of her long years of service, to obligate itself to pay "retirement privileges" to her. The resolution did not require the plaintiff to retire. Instead, the decision whether and when to retire remained entirely her own. The board then informed her of its resolution. The plaintiff worked for eighteen months more before retiring. She sued the corporation when it reduced her monthly checks seven years later. The court held that a pension contract existed between the parties. Although continued employment was not a consideration to her receipt

of retirement benefits, the court found sufficient reliance on the part of the plaintiff to support her claim. The court based its decision upon the above restatement example, that is, the defendant informed the plaintiff of its plan, and the plaintiff in reliance thereon, retired. *Feinberg* presents factors that also appear in the case at bar. There, the plaintiff had worked many years and desired to retire; she would not have left had she not been able to rely on a pension; and once retired, she sought no other employment.

However, the important distinction between *Feinberg* and the case before us is that in *Feinberg* the employer's decision definitely shaped the thinking of the plaintiff. In this case the promise did not. It is not reasonable to infer from the facts that Hugo R. Mainelli, Jr., expected retirement to result from his conversation with Hayes. Hayes had given notice of his intention seven months previously. Here there was thus no inducement to retire which would satisfy the demands of § 90 of the restatement. Nor can it be said that Hayes's refraining from other employment was "action or forbearance of a definite and substantial character." The underlying assumption of Hayes's initial decision to retire was that upon leaving the defendant's employ, he would no longer work. It is impossible to say that he changed his position any more so because of what Mainelli had told him in light of his own initial decision. These circumstances do not lead to a conclusion that injustice can be avoided only be enforcement of Plantations's promise. . . .

[Judgment reversed and remanded.]

Irrevocable Offers

As discussed in Chapter 8,[29] an offer is generally revocable by the offeror at any time prior to the effectiveness of the acceptance, unless the promise to hold the offer open is supported by consideration (creating an option contract) or subject to the "firm offer" rule of the UCC. Promissory estoppel provides a third exception to the general rule of revoc-

---

29. See revocation discussion beginning on page 172.

ability. The doctrine is particularly applicable to bids (offers) submitted by subcontractors to general contractors, which are then used in computing the general contractor's bid for the entire project.[30]

Problems relating to such bids arise from a recurring fact pattern in the construction industry that is well illustrated by the following landmark decision.

Drennan v. Star Paving Company
333 P.2d 757 (Cal. 1958)

Plaintiff William Drennan, a general contractor, submitted a bid to a school district for the construction of the Monte Viste School. As was customary in the area, various subcontractors telephoned Drennan on the day the bid was due to submit bids on subcontracting work for the project. Using the bids of the subcontractors, Drennan then submitted his bid for the entire project. Defendant Star Paving Co. (Star) telephoned Drennan and submitted a bid of $7,131.60 to perform the paving work for the Monte Viste School. Drennan incorporated this amount into his bid and listed Star as the paving contractor. Drennan was awarded the general contract. The following day, however, while Drennan was at Star's office, an employee of Star told Drennan that its bid for the paving subcontract had been incorrect and that Star could not do the work for less than $15,000. When Star refused to perform the paving work, Drennan was forced to obtain the services of another paving company that charged $10,948.60 for the paving work.

Drennan sued Star for $3,817.00 (the difference between Star's bid and the cost of paving paid by Drennan). Star alleged that no contract existed between the parties but that its bid for the paving subcontract constituted an offer which it had revoked prior to Drennan's acceptance. Drennan alleged that because of his reliance on Star's offer, the offer had

become irrevocable. The trial court entered judgment in favor of Drennan and Star appealed.

Traynor, Justice

. . . There is no evidence that defendant offered to make its bid irrevocable in exchange for plaintiff's use of its figures in computing his bid. Nor is there evidence that would warrant interpreting plaintiff's use of defendant's bid as the acceptance thereof, binding plaintiff, on condition he received the main contract, to award the subcontract to defendant. In sum, there was neither an option supported by consideration nor a bilateral contract binding on both parties.

Plaintiff contends, however, that he relied to his detriment on defendant's offer and that defendant must therefore answer in damages for its refusal to perform. Thus the question is squarely presented: Did plaintiff's reliance make defendant's offer irrevocable?

[The court then quoted Section 90 of the *Restatement of Contracts*.] . . .

The absence of consideration is not fatal to the enforcement of such a promise. . . . The very purpose of section 90 is to make a promise binding even though there was no consideration "in the sense of something that is bargained for and given in exchange." . . . Reasonable reliance serves to hold the offeror in lieu of the consideration ordinarily required to make the offer binding. . . .

When plaintiff used defendant's offer in computing his own bid, he bound himself to perform in reliance on defendant's terms. Though defendant did not bargain for this use of its bid neither did defendant make it idly, indifferent to whether it would be used or not. On the contrary it is reasonable to suppose that defendant submitted its bid to obtain the subcontract. It was bound to realize the substantial possibility that its bid would be the lowest, and that it would be included by plaintiff in his bid. It was to its own interest that the contractor be awarded the general contract; the lower the subcontract bid, the lower the general contractor's bid was likely to be and the greater its chance of acceptance and hence the greater defendant's chance of getting the paving subcontract. Defendant had reason not only to expect plaintiff to rely on its bid but to want him to. Clearly defendant had a stake in plaintiff's reliance on its bid. Given this interest and the fact

---

30. Ordinarily an offeree is not entitled to rely upon an offer prior to acceptance. If he desires protection, he should secure an option or promptly accept the offer to prevent the possibility of a timely revocation. The construction bidding case is, however, a common example of reliance upon an offer before acceptance.

that plaintiff is bound by his own bid, it is only fair that plaintiff should have at least an opportunity to accept defendant's bid after the general contract has been awarded to him. . . .

[Judgment affirmed.]

Charitable Subscriptions

Another common application of the promissory estoppel doctrine occurs in charitable subscriptions. Although a basic purpose of the consideration doctrine is to prevent enforcement of a promise to make a gift, an exception is generally recognized for promises made to charitable institutions. Some courts have sustained a charitable promise by treating it as an offer for a unilateral contract, accepted by the charity's acts in reliance. Other courts have used basic promissory estoppel principles. Under the approach followed by many courts and adopted by the *Restatement (Second) of Contracts,* a promise made to a charitable institution, which is expected to induce reliance upon it, is enforceable, even without a showing of actual reliance by the institution.[31] A mere probability of reliance is sufficient. Assume Doaks, a millionaire, promises to give $1,000,000 to the University of Illinois for expansion of the chemistry building. The university, in reliance upon Doaks's pledge and similar pledges, proceeds with the expansion plan by spending and obligating itself to spend large sums of money on the project. Doaks's promise is binding.[32] Under the *Restatement* approach, the promise would be binding even without a showing of actual reliance upon it.

SUMMARY

1. Consideration, the second basic element of contract formation, is what is given or promised by each party in exchange for and to induce the return promise or performance of the other. Consideration is the basic test developed by the law to determine which promises are legally enforceable as contracts.

2. A promise is supported by consideration and therefore binding upon the promisor if two requirements are met. First, the promisee of the promise must incur "legal detriment" by rendering a performance or making a promise. Second, the detriment incurred must be "bargained for."

3. A promisee incurs a legal detriment in exchange for a promise if she either refrains or promises to refrain from doing something that she has a legal right to do, or does or promises to do something she is under no legal obligation to do. Assuming a detriment exists, courts do not examine the relative equivalence of the values exchanged. That is, the value of the consideration is determined by the parties.

4. A promise to perform or performance of a preexisting public or statutory duty does not furnish consideration to support a return promise. This pre-existing duty rule is a direct application of the legal detriment concept, and effectively requires that modifications of existing common law contracts be supported by consideration. The UCC, however, abolishes the pre-existing duty rule for contracts involving goods by providing that a modification of a Code contract needs no consideration to be binding. Though no consideration is required, coerced contract modifications are prohibited as a violation of the duty of good faith.

5. Legal detriment analysis also forms the basis of the law governing compromise agreements reached to settle pre-existing obligations. Under principles of accord and satisfaction, a compromise agreement reached to settle a disputed or unliquidated obligation is binding. The doubt regarding either the existence or amount of the original duty—the existence of a good faith dispute—provides the consideration to support the compromise (accord) agreement. Further, even a liquidated and undisputed obligation may be discharged by a compromise agreement involving performance significantly different from that originally agreed upon.

6. To constitute consideration, the detriment must be bargained for in exchange for the promise. That is, it must be sought by the promisor in exchange for his promise and given by the promisee in exchange for that promise. For this reason if a promise is made or performance rendered before a return promise is made, the return promise is unenforceable because it has not been

---

31. *Restatement (Second) of Contracts* §90(2).

32. See *In re Field's Estate,* 172 N.Y.S.2d 740 (N.Y. Surrogate Ct. 1958).

bargained for. In other words, such "past consideration" is no consideration. Similarly, a promise purportedly given in exchange for nominal consideration is often unenforceable for lack of a bargain. In these cases, the promise usually evidences a promise to make a gift, not a contract.

7. Under the doctrine of mutuality, both parties to a contract must provide consideration. If one party's promise is illusory, making his or her performance entirely optional, no detriment is incurred, rendering any return promise unenforceable. Various types of promises including satisfaction required and other conditional promises have survived attack on grounds that they were illusory. Courts sustain these promises on various grounds, such as by imposing an obligation of good faith or implying a promise.

8. The law enforces certain promises not supported by consideration under traditional analysis. Perhaps the most important of these consideration exceptions is the promissory estoppel doctrine under which the promise is enforced because of the promisee's justifiable reliance upon it. Under the doctrine, if a promise is made with the reasonable expectation that it will be relied upon and the promisee acts or refrains from acting in reliance on the promise, then the promise is enforceable to the extent necessary to avoid injustice.

KEY TERMS

consideration	liquidated claim
bargained for exchange	conditional check
legal detriment	mutuality of consideration
pre-existing duty rule	illusory promise
past consideration	aleatory promise
moral consideration	estoppel
nominal consideration	promissory estoppel
accord and satisfaction	equitable estoppel
disputed claim	

QUESTIONS AND PROBLEMS

9-1 Most people would agree that ethical individuals and businesses keep their promises. In the United States, and in most other countries, however, not all promises are legally enforceable.
   (a) Should the law make all promises legally enforceable? Why or why not?
   (b) Suggest policy reasons supporting the general rule of law that only those promises supported by consideration are enforceable.
   (c) Name three exceptions to the general rule that only promises supported by consideration are enforceable. What are the policy reasons for these exceptions?

   (d) Often, businesspeople or businesses will perform a promise even if it is not legally enforceable. Why? If you were a business manager, under what circumstances would you recommend performance of an unenforceable promise?
   (e) Throughout this text, you will see examples of legally enforceable promises that are breached. If a person or business fails to perform a promise, is that conduct unethical? Explain.

9-2 Bob owned a vacant lot that had been appraised at $10,000. Susan owned a truck with an appraised value of $4,000. After reviewing both of the appraisals, they entered into a written agreement by which Bob agreed to sell the lot to Susan in exchange for the truck and $1,000 cash. Susan delivered the truck and money; however, Bob refused to convey the lot to her. Susan sued. Bob alleged that the contract was unenforceable because of insufficient consideration. He offered copies of the appraisals as evidence. Should the court enforce the agreement? Explain.

9-3 Al worked as a foreman for Constructo, a construction company. Al was paid on an hourly basis, and had no specific term of employment. On a particular construction project, Constructo offered to pay Al a bonus equal to one-half of the difference between the estimated and actual cost of the project. In order to earn the bonus, Al was required to remain in Constructo's employ until completion of the project and to use his extra efforts to induce workers under him to exceed union standards in construction. Al performed his duties efficiently and as a result over $30,000 in estimated labor costs were saved. Is Al entitled to a $15,000 bonus? Explain.

9-4 In the following cases, determine whether the conduct of the parties would be considered an accord and satisfaction.
   (a) Ann hired Tom's Tree Service (TTS) to cut down and remove a dead tree located in her front yard. TTS satisfactorily removed the tree and sent Ann a bill for $500. When Ann received the bill she was shocked at the high price. She sent the bill back to TTS after writing across it in red ink "This bill is outrageous!" Ann enclosed a check in the amount of $150 and wrote the following on the back of the check "In complete payment for services rendered in tree removal." TTS cashed the check then sued Ann for the unpaid $350.

(b) Wilbur bought a water heater from the J. C. Nickels store (located in Joplin, Missouri) and requested that the store deliver and install the water heater. Nickels is a national chain of department stores with billing departments centralized on a regional basis. When Wilbur received the bill from Nickels, he discovered that in addition to charging him $200 for the water heater, Nickels also charged him $10 for delivery, $75 for installation, and $15 for additional installation parts. During the next month, Wilbur telephoned, visited, and wrote to the local store manager disputing the amount of the bill. The gist of the dispute was that Wilbur believed the $200 purchase price covered delivery and installation. The store manager refused to reduce the bill. Finally, Wilbur wrote a check to Nickels in the amount of $200 and wrote on the back of the check "In full satisfaction of all outstanding claims. Negotiation of this check discharges payor of all liability for amounts owed to J. C. Nickels." Wilbur then placed the check in the preaddressed envelope provided by Nickels for its customers' convenience and mailed it to the regional billing center in Chicago. The check was cashed. J. C. Nickels then sued Wilbur for the $100 that remainded unpaid.

9-5 American Steel Co. entered into a contract to sell steel pipe to Homebuilders, Inc. for $10,000 with delivery to be made on June 1. Because the pipe was not delivered until June 15, Homebuilders notified American that it would pay only $9,000. Despite several calls from Homebuilders, American submitted an invoice on June 30 for the full $10,000. Consider the following facts in light of UCC §1-207. In either case will American be able to recover the difference between the amount paid and the invoice amount?

(a) Homebuilders submitted payment to American in the amount of $9,000 by a check containing the following notation: "Payment in full of invoice dated June 30." American cashed the check by indorsing it and adding "under protest" under the indorsement.

(b) Homebuilders submitted payment to American in the amount of $9,000 by a check containing the following notation:

Payment in full of invoice dated June 30. Upon cashing this check American agrees to discharge Homebuilders from liability for the debt arising out of invoice dated June 30 and further agrees not to reserve any rights with respect to that obligation and to waive its right to use §1-207 of the Uniform Commercial Code. The return or destruction of this check shall mean that American has rejected these conditions but the act of cashing it shall be deemed to be conclusive that American has accepted the conditions.

American cashed the check by indorsing it and adding "under protest" under the indorsement.

9-6 Seller contracts to sell a tract of land to Buyer. The land is fairly appraised at $50,000. Buyer promises to pay "$10.00 and other good and adequate consideration" for the land. Buyer pays the $10.00 but provides no other consideration. Seller subsequently refused to perform the contract. Should the court enforce it? Why or why not? Would your answer change if the $10.00 was never paid? Explain. Does resolution of this question turn primarily upon the existence of a "detriment" or the presence of a "bargained for" exchange?

9-7 Aunt Sarah owns a valuable antique silver service. Aunt Sarah telephones her niece, Lucille, and tells her "Come over to my house and I will give you my silver service." If Lucille goes to Aunt Sarah's house, would Aunt Sarah's statement become a legally enforceable contract? Explain.

9-8 Silas, a wealthy man, gave his friend Abraham a valuable stamp collection. As a result of some poor investments, Silas later lost all of his assets. Abraham, in an effort to help his friend, offered to pay $5,000 for the stamp collection and Silas reluctantly accepted the offer. If Abraham fails to pay, will Silas be able to enforce the agreement? Explain.

9-9 Consider the following fact situations:

(a) Seller sells his restaurant to Buyer. To protect Buyer's goodwill, Seller promises to pay $5,000 "if I open a competing restaurant within 3 years." Is Seller's promise illusory or is it sufficient consideration to support Buyer's return promise to pay money? Explain.

(b) A is negotiating to purchase a ship from X. A promises B, "if I decide to buy the ship, I will charter it to you." B accepts the charter. Is A's promise illusory? What has A promised to do? Has a valid enforceable contract been created?

9-10 Billie Jean is a world famous tennis player

whose endorsements of tennis balls, rackets, and shoes are valuable for marketing purposes. Billie Jean and Otis enter into an agreement by which Billie Jean grants Otis the exclusive right to use her name and to license her name in conjunction with the sale of tennis products. Otis agrees to pay Billie Jean seventy-five percent of all profits received from the licensing agreements.

Several weeks later another agent offers Billie Jean a similar deal. The agent suggests that he be given the exclusive right to license her name and in return he will pay her ninety percent of the profits. Billie Jean explains that she already has entered such a contract. After reviewing the contract, the agent concludes that it is not an enforceable contract. He points out that Otis has not promised to do anything and that, therefore, it is an illusory contract. Is the agent correct? Explain.

9-11   The U.S. government solicited bids to provide materials for a construction project at an airport. Sylvan Company submitted a bid to provide gravel of a specified quality at $5.00 per ton. The bid was submitted on a government form that stated in part: "If this bid is accepted, the bidder promises to supply the materials as required and shall deliver the materials to the site upon request of the procurement office. The U.S. Government reserves the right to cancel this contract at any time."

Sylvan's bid was accepted. Although Sylvan was willing and able to deliver the rock, the procurement office never requested delivery. Two years later, the U.S. government cancelled the contract. Sylvan sued the government alleging that the government's failure to request delivery within a reasonable time constituted a breach of contract. The government alleged that no contract existed arguing that its power to cancel at any time rendered the contract illusory. How should the court rule? Explain.

9-12   Hoffman, who owned and operated a bakery, wanted to establish a Red Owl franchise grocery store. Hoffman contacted Red Owl and after several discussions a Red Owl representative told Hoffman that if he invested $18,000, Red Owl would build and stock a store in Chilton, Wisconsin. Hoffman told the representative that he could raise the $18,000, part of which would be a loan from his father-in-law. With the advice of the representative, Hoffman bought a lot for the store in Chilton, paying $1,000 down. Hoffman and his family sold their bakery business and moved to Chilton. The Red Owl representa-

tative was aware of and encouraged all of the actions taken by Hoffman. Several weeks later, the representative increased the investment needed by Hoffman to $24,100 based on new project financial statements. Two weeks later Red Owl said it was prepared to proceed if Hoffman could raise another $2,000 for promotional purposes. After Red Owl again revised the figures and said it would require Hoffman's father-in-law to sign an agreement that his loan was a gift to Hoffman, negotiations broke off. Hoffman sues Red Owl for damages alleging that he had acted in reliance on Red Owl's promise to build a store for him. Is Hoffman entitled to recover? Explain.

9-13   Since 1900, All American Steel Corporation has operated two large steel mills in Ohio that employ over 3,500 people. In 1977, amid speculation that the mills were going to be closed, All American issued a press release stating in part:

> In response to many rumors, we wish to tell you that All American has no immediate plans to permanently shut down our Ohio mills. However, steps must be taken to improve these plants' profitability. Serious profit problems have been created by heavy imports of foreign steel, higher energy costs, higher taxes, and environmental expenditures. Continued operation of these plants is absolutely dependent upon their being profit-makers. In the months ahead, we will be calling for the full support of each and every one of you. Your cooperation and assistance are absolutely necessary if our facilities are to continue to operate.

During the following six months, employees of the plants worked diligently to improve productivity. They agreed to new working hours, assumed new duties when jobs were eliminated, and some, who had been seeking other employment, gave up new job opportunities. Within a few months productivity improved significantly and gross profit margins showed a small profit. In 1978, however, All American announced that it would close the two plants. While recognizing improved productivity, company management noted that according to net profits the plants were operating at a loss.

The employees of the two mills sued All American alleging that the company was obligated to the employees, under principles of promissory estoppel, to keep the plants open if they operated at a profit. How should the court rule?

Major Topics

- the definition of contractual capacity and the legal effects of incapacity
- the principles governing contracts made by minors and persons who are mentally ill or intoxicated
- the various types of contracts that are unenforceable on public policy grounds
- the problems created by standardized form contracts and the devices, most notably the unconscionability doctrine, that the law has developed to resolve them
- the standards governing enforceability of contracts in restraint of trade

Ordinarily, the courts will enforce a bargain evidencing mutual assent supported by consideration. Nevertheless, certain bargains, although they may meet the basic requisites of contract formation, are rendered either voidable or unenforceable for a variety of reasons including (1) a lack of contractual capacity on the part of one or both parties, (2) circumstances under which enforcement of the contract would be contrary to public policy, (3) fraud, misrepresentation, mistake, duress, or undue influence, or (4) noncompliance with certain formalities (for example, a writing) required by law for the enforcement of certain types of contracts. By treating promises made under these circumstances as either voidable or unenforceable, the law imposes special limitations on promissory liability. These limitations are treated in detail in this and the following two chapters.

Contractual Capacity

Generally, the term *capacity* refers to the ability of a person to create or enter into a legal relationship. In order to be bound to a contract both parties must have **contractual capacity.** Usually any natural[1] person has full legal capacity to incur contractual duties. Certain classes of individuals, however, possess some special characteristic that limits, or in some cases extinguishes, their contractual capacity. Examples include minors (persons under legal age), persons suffering from a mental illness or defect, and intoxicated persons. The law of contractual capacity is designed to protect these people from the effects of their own immaturity, inexperience, and lack of judgment, and to prevent another party from taking unfair advantage of them.

Lack of capacity usually renders a person's contractual obligations voidable. As previously discussed,[2] a voidable contract is one in which one or more parties have the power, by electing to do so, to avoid the legal relations created by the contract. After making the contract, the persons with limited

---

1. Contractual capacity of a corporation, an artificial person, is discussed in Chapter 45.
2. Voidable contracts are defined in Chapter 7.

capacity may elect either to be bound by the contract (to ratify it), or to avoid it. The election to avoid a contractual duty is commonly referred to as a *disaffirmance*. The other party to the contract, unless also lacking capacity or having some other grounds for avoidance, is ordinarily bound pending the election to disaffirm.

Minors' (Infants') Contracts

Most contracts voidable on capacity grounds are minors' (or infants') contracts. A **minor** or **infant** is a person who has not yet reached the age of contractual capacity. The age at which a person achieves full contractual capacity (referred to as **majority**) is determined by state statute or constitutional provision. Although the age of majority was traditionally twenty-one years, it has now been reduced in nearly all states to eighteen,[3] the voting age. A lower age of majority (for example, fifteen years) often is provided for certain types of contracts, such as life, health, or accident insurance, and student loans.

Contracts made by a minor are voidable. The minor's right to disaffirm exists whether or not the agreement is reasonable or fair to the minor and whether or not the adult knew that he was dealing with a minor. In many jurisdictions, the right to disaffirm also extends to emancipated minors. **Emancipation** occurs when the parent surrenders the right to control the minor, including the right to the care, custody, services, and earnings of the child, and renounces parental duties. In many states, emancipation also occurs by operation of law when the minor marries. As discussed later in this chapter, emancipation is important in determining a minor's liability for "necessaries" furnished to her.

Time of Disaffirmance; Ratification. Contracts made during minority are voidable by the minor prior to reaching legal age and for a reasonable time thereafter. In other words, a minor's power of avoidance is not extinguished immediately upon reaching majority. What constitutes a "reasonable time" is a question of fact dependent on all facts and circumstances. Some states, by statute, limit the minor's power of avoidance to a fixed period (for example, one year) after attaining legal age.

A minor may, after reaching majority, elect to be bound upon the previously voidable obligation. As discussed in Chapter 7, such an election, known as **ratification,** extinguishes the power of disaffirmance. Ratification may be express or implied. For example, after reaching majority a minor may communicate directly with the adult to indicate her intent to be bound on a contract made during minority. Usually, however, ratification occurs through conduct other than express statements. Such conduct frequently includes retaining and continuing to use the subject matter of the contract for more than a reasonable time after reaching majority, and failing to disaffirm within a reasonable time after reaching majority. If both factors are present, a strong case for ratification can be made.

Courts have tended, however, not to treat mere failure to disaffirm as ratification if the delay neither benefits the minor nor harms the adult. In other words, courts look to whether, based upon the facts of the case, the delay in avoidance would achieve an unfair or unreasonable result. Whether a ratification has occurred is a question of fact to be decided by the trier of fact, normally the jury, if the issue is disputed.

Restitution in Executed or Partially Executed Transactions. If a contract is wholly executory, no particular problems arise if the minor elects to avoid. If the minor disaffirms a partially or totally executed bargain, however, the law must determine to what extent the parties (particularly the adult) are entitled to be returned to their precontract positions. Courts have had substantial difficulty resolving this issue. Frequently, the policy protecting minors from improvident bargains must be weighed against the risk of forfeiture[4] by the adult and unjust enrichment of the minor.

---

3. All states fix the age of majority for contract purposes at eighteen, except Alabama (nineteen), Mississippi (twenty-one), Nebraska (nineteen), and Wyoming (nineteen). Many states fix a higher age of majority for contracts to purchase alcohol.

4. "Forfeiture" in contract law refers to the denial of compensation that results when a person entitled to performance (here the adult) loses that right (upon the minor's disaffirmance) after relying substantially (through preparation or performance) on the contract. *Restatement (Second) of Contracts* §229 comment b.

If a minor purchases goods or services from an adult on credit, the minor may plead infancy as a defense to enforcement of the contract. Generally, however, he must return any consideration passing from the adult that he still retains. He must also return any identifiable proceeds of the sale or other exchange of the consideration. Assume Andy, an adult, sells a television set to Mike, a minor, on credit. Mike may assert his infancy as a defense against Andy's action for the price, but must return the set if he still has it. It would be obviously unfair to allow Mike to keep the television, while avoiding his obligation to pay for it. Note, however, that the minor in this situation must merely return any consideration retained. The minor is not liable to the adult for (1) damage caused to the property, (2) depreciation in value of the property while in the minor's possession through normal wear and tear, (3) the rental value of the property, or (4) any profit derived by the minor from its use (for example, when goods are bought for use in the minor's business operation).

A minor who is unable to return the consideration because it has been squandered, lost, stolen, or negligently destroyed may still generally avoid the obligation to pay. Assume Seller sells a car to Buyer, a minor, on credit. The car is destroyed in a traffic accident while being driven by Buyer. Buyer may avoid her obligation to pay for the car, even though she cannot return the car or its proceeds to Seller. This result is supported by the reasoning that the same immaturity or lack of foresight that induces the minor to make the contract initially also leads to the loss or destruction of the consideration. Therefore, to force minors to return the consideration before disaffirming would deprive them of the defense, grounded in public policy, designed to protect them against the results of their indiscretion.

The rules discussed above often result in a windfall to the minor and a substantial loss to the adult. They also, in the opinion of some critics, tend to promote dishonesty by minors. For these reasons, many courts have taken steps to provide more protection for the adult when the minor disaffirms. For example, a growing number of courts have adopted a rule requiring the minor, upon disaffirmance, to compensate the adult for the value of the use and depreciation of the article while in the minor's pos-

session.[5] Some courts go further and hold the minor liable in restitution to the adult for the reasonable value of the benefits conferred on the minor. This approach protects minors against nonbeneficial transactions, while recognizing legitimate business interests of those dealing with minors.[6]

Misrepresentation of Age. A related issue concerns the rights of the parties when the minor misrepresents his or her age to the adult. Assume Sara negotiates with Beverly, a minor, for the sale of a new car. Beverly knows Sara will not deal with a minor. Therefore, to induce Sara to sell, Beverly misrepresents her age, indicating she has reached majority. This situation raises several issues.

Under the majority rule, the fact that a minor misrepresents her age does not affect the power to avoid the contract. As in other cases, the minor must return any consideration still retained in order to disaffirm. Many courts additionally protect the adult in this situation by applying the estoppel doctrine or by allowing the adult to sue the minor for fraudulent misrepresentation. Courts applying the estoppel principle hold that when the minor's fraudulent misstatement of age induces the adult to enter into the contract, an equitable estoppel (estoppel "in pais") results to prevent the minor from denying the truth of his statement. Thus, the adult is able to enforce the contract, because the minor is precluded from exercising the power of avoidance. Courts allowing recovery on the basis of fraud rely upon the basic proposition that minors, although not liable in contract, are liable for their torts. A misstatement of age, if relied upon, and causing injury, constitutes fraud, a tort. Thus, the court does not enforce the contract, but holds the minor liable in tort for damages.

Critics of both the estoppel and tort approaches argue that allowing recovery by the adult is simply an indirect means of enforcing the contract, thus

---

5. This rule is most often applied if the minor is the *plaintiff* in the suit; that is, the minor pays the purchase price, then disaffirms and sues to recover it. In the preceding discussion, the minor was the *defendant*, asserting infancy as a defense to payment. For a discussion of this plaintiff-defendant distinction, see Calamari & Perillo, *The Law of Contracts* 239-242 (2d ed. 1977).

6. Calamari & Perillo, *The Law of Contracts* 248 (2d ed. 1977).

destroying the "shield" of voidability designed to protect the minor. On the other hand, the minor should not be allowed to escape liability for her fraud by hiding behind a rule designed to protect her from the adult. The legislation in most states lowering the age of majority from twenty-one to eighteen should partly relieve this problem. Persons under age eighteen are more easily recognized as minors, and substantially fewer people (those between eighteen and twenty-one) may now avoid their contractual obligations.

Liability for "Necessaries." Though able to avoid contractual obligations, a minor may be held liable for the reasonable value of **necessaries** furnished to him. This liability, although protecting the adult supplier, is imposed to insure that the minor will be able to acquire goods and services necessary for his, and his dependents', support. The minor's liability in these cases is based, not upon the contract, but on restitutionary quasi-contract grounds.[7] Because the minor's obligation is grounded in restitution, not contract, the minor's liability is limited to the reasonable value of the benefit conferred, not necessarily the contract price. In addition, a minor is liable only for necessaries actually furnished, not an executory agreement to furnish necessaries.

Traditionally, courts have held basic items such as food, clothing, shelter, medical care, and a certain amount of education to be necessaries. Modern courts have expanded this concept of necessaries to include

> . . . such articles of property and such services as are reasonably necessary to enable the infant to earn the money required to provide the necessities of life for himself and those who are legally dependent upon him. . . .[8]

Under this test, for example, attorneys' fees, employment agency fees, and automobiles might be necessaries. Courts, however, have not applied a fixed meaning to the term. Rather, the determination is based upon the particular facts and circumstances of each case including the minor's health, marital status, and standard of living. Thus, a necessary for one minor may not be so for another.

Because a parent is liable for the support of a child, a minor is not liable upon contracts for necessaries if he has a parent or guardian who is supplying (or is willing to supply) them. A minor is liable only if the parent or guardian refuses, neglects, or is unable to supply necessaries. However, a parent who neglects the duty to support may be liable on quasi-contract grounds to a person who furnishes necessaries to his child. In other words, the person who supplies necessaries has conferred a benefit upon the delinquent parent for which the law implies a promise by the parent to pay. In the following case, the court was required to determine whether an apartment was a necessary.

Webster Street Partnership, Ltd. v. Sheridan
368 N.W.2d 439 (Neb. 1985)

Webster Street Partnership, Ltd. (Webster Street) owned an apartment building in Omaha, Nebraska. In 1982, Webster Street entered into a written apartment lease with Matthew Sheridan, who was then eighteen years of age, and Pat Wilwerding, who was seventeen years old. The age of majority in Nebraska is nineteen and the rental agent was aware that both tenants were minors. Sheridan and Wilwerding failed to pay the second month's rental payment when due and subsequently vacated the apartment.

Webster Street sued Sheridan and Wilwerding for breach of contract. They defended the suit on the ground that they were minors, thereby rendering the lease agreement voidable. The municipal court ruled in favor of Webster Street and on appeal, the district court modified the amount of damages. Webster Street appealed.

---

7. The law of restitution implies a promise to pay (a quasi-contract or contract implied in law) the reasonable value of benefits conferred by one party upon another when required to prevent "unjust enrichment". In the necessaries case, the implied promise runs from the minor to the party furnishing the goods or services. Restitution is discussed in Chapter 15.

8. *Gastonia Personnel Corporation v. Rogers,* 172 S.E. 2d 19, 24 (N.C. 1970).

Krivosha, Chief Justice

. . . As a general rule, an infant does not have the capacity to bind himself absolutely by contract. . . . The right of the infant to avoid his contract is one conferred by law for his protection against his own improvidence and the designs of others. . . . The policy of the law is to discourage adults from contracting with an infant; they cannot complain if, as a consequence of violating that rule, they are unable to enforce their contracts. . . .

However, the privilege of infancy will not enable an infant to escape liability in all cases and under all circumstances. For example, it is well established that an infant is liable for the value of necessaries furnished him. . . . [Nevertheless]

> To enable an infant to contract for articles as necessaries, he must have been in actual need of them, and obliged to procure them for himself. They are not necessaries as to him, however necessary they may be in their nature, if he was already supplied with sufficient articles of the kind, or if he had a parent or guardian who was able and willing to supply them. [*Ballinger v. Craig*, 121 N.E.2d 66, 67 (Ohio App. 1953)]

The undisputed testimony [in this case] is that both tenants were living away from home, apparently with the understanding that they could return home at any time. . . . It would therefore appear that in the present case neither Sheridan nor Wilwerding was in need of shelter but, rather, had chosen to voluntarily leave home, with the understanding that they could return whenever they desired. . . . We therefore find that both the municipal court and the district court erred in finding that the apartment, under the facts in this case, was a necessary.

Having therefore concluded that the apartment was not a necessary, the question of whether Sheridan and Wilwerding were emancipated is of no significance. The effect of emancipation is only relevant with regard to necessaries. If the minors were not emancipated, then their parents would be liable for necessaries provided to the minors. . . . If, on the other hand, it was determined that the minors were emancipated and the apartment was a necessary, then the minors would be liable. But where,

as here, we determine that the apartment was not a necessary, then neither the parents nor the infants are liable and the question of emancipation is of no moment.

Because the rental of the apartment was not a necessary, the minors had the right to avoid the contract, either during their minority or within a reasonable time after reaching their majority. . . . Disaffirmance by an infant completely puts an end to the contract's existence, both as to him and as to the adult with whom he contracted. . . . Because the parties then stand as if no contract had ever existed, the infant can recover payments made to the adult, and the adult is entitled to the return of whatever was received by the infant. . . .

[Judgment reversed and remanded.]

Mental Illness and Intoxication

In addition to infancy, contractual capacity may be restricted or extinguished due to a mental illness or defect. Contractual capacity may be affected, for example, by mental retardation, senility, brain damage resulting from accident or disease, or mental illness. Because the cause and severity of mental incompetency varies widely, the law must balance the incompetent's need for protection against the reasonable expectations of persons dealing with him.

Mental Illness. Certain persons suffering from a mental illness or defect have no contractual capacity and their contracts are void, rather than voidable. For example, severe mental or physical disability may prevent formation of the necessary intent to contract.

A person for whom a guardian has been appointed also has no contractual capacity. A **guardian** is a person appointed by the court to manage, subject to court supervision, the affairs and property of a person (referred to as a **ward**) who is considered incapable of administering her own affairs. The guardian may be appointed, for example, as a result of a person's insanity, senility, or addiction to alcohol or other drugs. The purpose of the guardianship is to protect the ward's rights and to prevent her from squandering or improvidently using her property. The guardianship proceedings provide public notice of the ward's incapacity. Thus, persons dealing with the ward are bound by the ward's incapacity, even without actual knowledge of the guardianship.[9]

Although, as indicated above, a mental infirmity may render a contract void, it more commonly renders the obligation merely voidable. Courts have developed two tests to determine when a contract is voidable due to mental incompetency. The first is the traditional ''cognitive'' test used by most courts under which the contract is voidable if the person is substantially incapable of understanding and appreciating the nature and consequences of the transaction. The second ''motivational'' or ''affective'' test is a more recent judicial development adopted in some states to supplement the cognitive test. It permits avoidance of contracts by persons who know and understand what they are doing but, due to mental illness, cannot rationally control their behavior. Under the motivational test, avoidance is allowed only if the other party to the transaction has reason to know of the mental condition.[10]

If a mentally incompetent person's contract has been partly or fully performed, it may generally be avoided by restoring the parties to their original positions, including restitution for any benefits retained by the incompetent. The court may, however, refuse to allow avoidance if the previous positions cannot be restored or if avoidance would be otherwise inequitable.

Intoxication. Contracts made by persons intoxicated through alcohol or other drug use also may be voidable. The same competency standards applied to mental illness also apply in intoxication cases. Extreme intoxication may prevent contract formation altogether. Less extreme intoxication provides a defense only if the other party has reason to know of it. Courts have, however, been less sympathetic to avoidance claims based upon intoxication than those based upon other mental infirmity.[11]

In applying both the mental illness and intoxication standard, the fairness of the transaction to the alleged incompetent and the conduct of the other party are often important. That is, if the contract is fair and reasonable, the court is more likely to find the party competent and deny the attempt to avoid. On the other hand, cases allowing avoidance often also present issues of fraud, duress, or undue influence. Thus, in many cases involving mental illness or intoxication, incapacity is not the sole basis of the court's decision.

Unenforceability on Public Policy Grounds

Contract Enforcement and Public Policy

Not all agreements made by competent parties and supported by consideration are enforceable. The courts will not enforce a promise or contract term that, either in its formation or performance, (1) violates an applicable civil or criminal statute, (2) constitutes the commission of or inducement to commit a tort, or (3) is otherwise contrary to public policy. Contracts unenforceable on this basis have traditionally been analyzed as **illegal bargains**. The concept is, however, broader than illegality—for example, a contract that violates a criminal statute. Also included are other transactions in which the interest in freedom of contract is outweighed by an overriding public interest against judicial recognition of the contract or contract term. In other words, the issue is whether the promise will be *enforced*, not necessarily whether the law has made the act of making or performing it illegal. In this manner, the law discourages certain types of promises by refusing to allow the judicial system to be used as a means to enforce them. The following material examines contracts unenforceable because they violate a statute, and those unenforceable on public policy grounds in the absence of statute.

Contracts Violating a Statute. Some contracts or contract terms are unenforceable because they violate either the letter or the policy of a state or federal statute. Only infrequently—as in the gambling or usurious contracts discussed below—will legislation explicitly provide that a contract or contract provision is unenforceable. More commonly, the statute merely prohibits certain conduct and provides a penalty, such as a fine, for a violation.

---

9. *Restatement (Second) of Contracts* §13 and comment a.

10. The approach allowing avoidance under either test has been adopted by the *Restatement (Second) of Contracts* §15.

11. See *Restatement (Second) of Contracts* §16; for a case presenting an intoxication issue, see *Lucy v. Zehmer* on page 168.

Thus, in ruling upon the enforceability of a contract that violates the statute, the court is required to balance the policy of the statute in protecting some aspect of the public welfare against the parties' interest in enforcing their promises. Frequently, to further the statutory policy, the court will find the contract wholly or partially unenforceable.

Gambling Contracts. In many states, statutes make wagering a crime and provide that promises made pursuant to such agreements are unenforceable. Assume that Tom and Margaret reside in such a state, but they agree to wager $1,000 on the outcome of the Illinois-Michigan basketball game. Tom promises to pay Margaret $1,000 if Illinois wins and Margaret promises to pay Tom $1,000 if Michigan wins. In accordance with the state statute, both of their promises are unenforceable.

Usurious Contracts. **Usurious contracts** are those in which interest rates greater than the maximum legal rate are charged. Usury statutes vary widely among the states, regarding both maximum interest rates and penalties. In some states neither principal nor interest may be recovered by the creditor if the interest rate is usurious. On the other hand, some states merely hold that interest in excess of the maximum rate is uncollectible.

To illustrate the operation of a usury statute, assume Dennis borrows $10,000 from Carol and promises to repay the loan with interest at twenty-five percent. A state statute provides that eighteen percent is the maximum rate which may be charged on such loans and provides that a promise to pay a greater sum is "void" as to *all* interest promised but not as to principal. Dennis's promise to pay interest at twenty-five percent is unenforceable. Carol may not enforce the promise to pay interest up to the maximum legal rate, because the statute provides otherwise.

A Contract to Commit a Crime. A contract to commit a murder or theft, or to give or receive a bribe, is unenforceable. The parties are also subject to criminal liability for their conduct.

Contracts Violating Licensing Statutes. City, state, and federal statutes often require that persons providing certain goods or services be licensed. A contract made by an unlicensed individual to furnish the regulated goods or services is generally unenforceable if the statute has a regulatory (as opposed to merely a revenue raising) purpose, and the public policy of the licensing or registration requirement clearly outweighs the interest in enforcement.[12]

One case of this type involves statutes requiring licensing of professionals such as physicians, dentists, and attorneys. Applying the foregoing principles, courts in these cases generally refuse to allow unlicensed practitioners to recover for their services. Assume Jones, who is not admitted to the bar, and Smith, an unlicensed physician, render services to Cox, who promises to pay for them. Cox's promises to Jones and Smith are unenforceable. This result fosters the basic regulatory purpose of professional licensing statutes: to protect the public against professional practice by incompetent or unqualified individuals. Not all licensing violation cases so clearly favor denial of enforcement, as the following case illustrates.

Asdourian v. Araj
696 P.2d 95 (Cal. 1985)

> Plaintiff Krikor Asdourian and defendant Ibrahim Araj entered into a written contract by which Asdourian agreed to remodel a garage that Araj wanted to convert into a restaurant. After Asdourian had completed substantial work, Araj refused to pay him.
>
> Asdourian sued Araj alleging breach of contract. Araj alleged that §7031 of the California Business and Professions Code barred Asdourian from bringing suit on the contract. That statute prohibits a contractor from filing suit for compensation unless the contractor was duly licensed during the performance of the contract. At the time he performed the remodeling work, Asdourian did not hold a contractors license in his own name. He previously had obtained a contractors license for his business, Artko, which he had intended to operate as a corporation. Because Asdourian had signed the contract in his own name, Araj argued that Asdourian was barred from recovery.

---

12. *Restatement (Second) of Contracts* §181.

The trial court ruled in favor of Asdourian and Araj appealed.

Bird, Chief Justice

. . . Section 7031 is a part of the Contractors License Law . . . The Contractors License Law provides a comprehensive scheme which governs contractors doing business in California. The general purpose of the law is "to guard the public against the consequences of incompetent workmanship, imposition and deception. In order to procure a license an applicant is required to make a showing of good character and of a degree of experience and general knowledge of the building, health, safety and lien laws of this state, and of the rudimentary administrative principles of the contracting business, as the board deems necessary for the safety and protection of the public." [*Howard v. State of California* 193 P. 2d 11, 13 (Cal.App. 1948).]

Section 7031 has as its purpose the enforcement of the Contractors License Law. That purpose is accomplished by denying a contractor "access to the courts to recover for the fruits of his labor . . . . when he violates the statute." [*Jackson v. Pancake,* 72 Cal.Rptr. 111, 113 (Cal.App. 1968).]

However, in exceptional circumstances the purposes of the Contractors License Law are not furthered by strict enforcement of section 7031. . . . [T]his court has employed the doctrine of "substantial compliance" to avoid the harsh consequences of strict application of section 7031.

The substantial compliance doctrine has been applied in several factual contexts. Most often, it has been applied when the contractor's license expired before completion of a project. . . ., or where the license was not obtained until after the contract was executed. . . .

The doctrine has also been applied where, following a change in the form of the contractor's business, the entity performing the contract was slightly different from the entity named on the contract. . . .

In this case, plaintiff obtained a license for his sole proprietorship under the name Artko. Plaintiff's name was on the license as the responsible managing party. At the time the license was issued, he intended to incorporate Artko. Had he done so, Artko would have become an entity separate from plaintiff. However, the incorporation never took place, and the business remained a sole proprietor-

ship. Plaintiff was personally responsible for all debts and responsibilities incurred by the business, and the assets of the business were plaintiff's assets. In essence, plaintiff *was* Artko. . . .

Since plaintiff did not have a license in his own name, . . . he was not duly licensed. If literal compliance with section 7031 is required, he cannot legally maintain these actions. However, under the circumstances of this case, the policy of the Contractors License Law has been satisfied. Defendant should not be able to avoid his obligation to compensate plaintiff for the work he performed. . . .

Here, plaintiff's firm held a valid license at the time of the contracts. The license had been issued to Artko, but bore plaintiff's name as the responsible managing party. That license provided sufficient evidence of plaintiff's qualifications. The fact that plaintiff used his own name when he entered into the contracts is technically a violation of section 7028.5. However, it did not prevent defendant from receiving the full and effective protection of the statute. . . .

Issuance of a license to Asdourian in his own name would not have provided defendant with any greater assurances that he was dealing with an experienced and competent contractor. Nor would it have provided any different information concerning the status or solvency of plaintiff's business. The business entity was precisely the same as that to which the license had been issued. The work would have been performed by the same employees, and supervised by the same person. Defendant would have obtained no better protection, and no different performance, had he contracted with Artko. . . .

Defendant attempts to rely on a technicality to defeat plaintiff's claims. This technicality is unrelated to defendant's real dispute with plaintiff—the *terms* of the remodeling agreements. . . .

Plaintiff substantially complied with the Contractors License law and should not be denied relief. . . .

[Judgment affirmed.]

Unenforceability in the Absence of Statute. Even in the absence of statute, the court frequently is required to balance public against private interests to determine enforceability. Examples of contracts or terms which have been held unenforceable on this basis include the following.

Contracts Constituting or Inducing a Tort. Courts generally do not enforce a contract or contract term that requires either party to commit a tort. Assume that A promises to pay B, who owns a newspaper, $1,000 if B will print a defamatory statement about C which both A and B know to be false. B promises to do so. Both promises are unenforceable. A's promise induced the commission of a tort and performance of B's promise would constitute commission of a tort, libel.

Promises Involving Violation of Fiduciary Duty. A fiduciary relationship is one in which one person is bound to act solely in the interest of another concerning matters within the scope of the relation. The concept is important in many areas of the law, including trusts, agency, partnership, and corporations. A fiduciary must refrain from acting for her private benefit or otherwise against the interests of the person or persons to whom she owes the fiduciary duty. Therefore, a promise to violate a fiduciary duty, or a promise made as inducement to violate that duty, is unenforceable. For example, a corporate director stands in a fiduciary relationship to a corporation. Assume X, in her capacity as director of ABC Corporation, learns trade secrets relating to ABC's manufacturing process. X promises to disclose the secrets to Y in exchange for Y's promise to pay $10,000. Because X's disclosure of the trade secrets will violate her fiduciary duty to ABC, both promises are unenforceable on grounds of public policy.

Promises Interfering With Another's Contractual Relationship. As discussed in Chapter 5, a person who intentionally and unjustifiably interferes with the performance of a contract by inducing or otherwise causing one of the parties not to perform is liable in tort to the nonbreaching party for damages resulting from the breach of the contract.[13] In other words, a contractual relationship is recognized by the law as a property right. The culpable and unjustifiable impairment or destruc-

tion of that right is a tort for which judicial relief is available.

Because intentional interference with a contractual relationship is a tort, a promise that tortiously induces a breach, as well as the return promise to commit the breach, are both unenforceable on grounds of public policy. Assume A contracts to employ B full time for three years. C, with knowledge of the existing contract and with the intent to induce B to breach it, offers B a substantially larger salary if B will begin work immediately. B accepts. Both promises are unenforceable.[14]

Exculpatory Clauses. A contract term that exempts a person from liability for his or her own torts is known as an **exculpatory clause.** An exculpatory term that seeks to excuse a person for liability for *intentional* or *reckless* conduct is always unenforceable. In contrast, parties generally may exempt themselves from liability for *negligence,* that is, failure to exercise reasonable care. This general rule is subject to several exceptions. First, a contract may not relieve an employer from liability to an employee for negligently caused injuries. Second, parties who perform a public service such as a common carrier or public utility may not avoid liability for negligence to persons they serve. Third, state statutes frequently make exculpatory clauses unenforceable in specific types of contracts. For example, in many states, a provision in a lease that exempts a landlord from liability for damages caused by the negligence of the landlord or his employees is unenforceable as contrary to public policy.[15]

Restitution In Executed and Partially Executed Transactions. If an agreement unenforceable on grounds of public policy has been partially or wholly performed, one party may seek restitution for any benefits conferred upon the other pursuant

---

13. *Restatement (Second) of Torts* §766. See discussion in Chapter 5 on page 118.

14. *Restatement (Second) of Contracts* §194 and ill. 1.

15. *Restatement (Second) of Contracts* §195. Note that a court may also refuse to enforce an exculpatory clause if its effect is unconscionable. In addition to the contracts or terms previously discussed, contract terms designed either to punish a breach or as a threat to prevent breach, known as penalties, are also unenforceable as contrary to public policy. Penalties are discussed in Chapter 15.

to the unenforceable bargain. The general rule is that the court leaves the parties as it finds them, regardless of the extent to which the contract has been performed. The court will not aid the promisee either by enforcing the promise or by granting him restitution of the benefit conferred upon the other, even if the other is also a wrongdoer. Because the rule denying restitution may result in an unjust enrichment of one party coupled with a forfeiture by the other, courts have made several exceptions to the general rule if necessary to do justice. For example, restitution has been granted: (1) if denial of restitution would effect a disproportionate forfeiture, (2) if the party claiming restitution was excusably unaware of the facts or of minor legislation, but for which the promise would be enforceable, (3) if the party claiming restitution is not equally in the wrong (*in pari delicto*) with the party from whom he seeks restitution, or (4) if the party seeking restitution withdraws from the transaction in time to prevent the accomplishment of the illegal or improper purpose for which the bargain was created. This is known as the doctrine of *locus poenitentiae,* which means literally "a place for repentance." These exceptions provide the flexibility necessary to do justice in a variety of fact situations presenting widely varying degrees of culpable behavior.[16]

Contracts of Adhesion and Unconscionability: Problems of Standardized Form Contracts

Contracts of Adhesion. Standardized form contracts, commonly known as **contracts of adhesion,** play an essential role in modern business, which requires mass production and distribution of goods and services. Form contracts can be tailored to specific transaction types, eliminating needless and repetitive detail in each individual contract, saving time and money, and allowing the parties to focus upon important particulars such as quantity and price. The forms themselves are often adapted to office routines and business machines and may be used for recordkeeping or supervisory purposes.[17]

Most contracts entered into by consumers are adhesion contracts. Examples include insurance policies, agreements for the sale or lease of personal or real property, mortgages, installment sales contracts and other agreements creating security interests, and checking and savings account agreements.

Despite their obvious utility, adhesion contracts present a major problem area in contract law. In these agreements, one party dictates many of the contract terms to the other (the "adhering" party) who generally stands in a substantially inferior bargaining position. Because the contract is drafted solely by one party and is given to the other on a "take it or leave it" basis, its terms are often unreasonably favorable to the drafting party. Contract law generally is premised upon the existence of an agreement negotiated by the parties at "arm's length." An *arm's length transaction* is one negotiated by unrelated parties, each acting in his or her own self-interest. This premise is not ordinarily present in adhesion contracts. The "adhering" party frequently must either accept the terms as written or forego the goods or services involved, because similar provisions are used by all drafting parties. The following material discusses the doctrine of unconscionability and other means developed by courts and legislatures to resolve the problems created by this disparity in bargaining power.

Unconscionability. The doctrine of **unconscionability** is an important tool used to address the problems created by adhesion contracts. The doctrine is a general principle of contract law, adopted by both the UCC and the common law. As stated in the UCC, §2-302(1), if a court as a matter of law[18] finds a contract or clause of a contract to have been

---

16. *Restatement (Second) of Contracts* §§197-199.

17. *Restatement (Second) of Contracts* §211 comment a.

18. Because the issue is a matter of *law* relief on the basis of unconscionability is granted in the discretion of the court, not as a question of fact for the jury to decide. Thus, relief granted under §2-302 is essentially equitable as opposed to legal in nature. If, however, a contract or provision is attacked as unconscionable, the parties must be afforded a reasonable opportunity to present evidence regarding its commercial setting, purpose, and effect to aid the court in making its decision. UCC §2-302(2).

unconscionable at the time it was made, the court may (1) refuse to enforce the contract, (2) enforce the remainder of the contract without the unconscionable provision, or (3) limit the effect of the unconscionable provision to avoid any unconscionable result.

"Unconscionability" is not specifically defined, but Official Comment 1 to §2-302 indicates that

> The basic test is whether, in the light of the general commercial background and the commercial needs of the particular trade or case, the clauses involved are so one-sided as to be unconscionable under the circumstances existing at the time of the making of the contract. . . . The principle is one of the prevention of *oppression and unfair surprise.* . . . (Emphasis added.)

"Oppression" or **substantive unconscionability** is present when a contract or provision is unreasonably harsh or unfair, generally extracted by a party with vastly superior bargaining power. Such contracts or terms are unenforceable as contrary to public policy. "Unfair surprise" or **procedural unconscionability** frequently occurs when a person signs a standardized form contract containing a provision, commonly in fine print, that substantially alters his or her reasonable expectations under the agreement. If procedural unconscionability is involved, enforcement is denied on the basis that the informed, voluntary mutual assent essential to a binding contract is not present. In virtually all cases in which the courts have found a contract or term unconscionable, elements of both substantive and procedural unconscionability were present.

In adhesion contracts, unconscionability may arise out of gross disparity in the values exchanged or if the form contract binds only the person who signs. Other provisions that may be unconscionable include warranty and liability disclaimers, penalties, or terms granting substantial advantages in enforcement and remedy to the drafting party. The effect of such provisions is aggravated when the person signing has limited intelligence, financial resources, education, or knowledge of the English language.

In the following opinion the court was required to determine whether a limitation of liability clause was unconscionable.

Fotomat Corporation of Florida v. Chanda

464 So.2d 626 (Fla. App. 1985)

Plaintiff Joseph Chanda, a physician, brought 28 rolls of Super-8 movie film to an outlet operated by defendant Fotomat Corporation of Florida to have the films transferred to a videotape to prevent deterioration of the pictures. The films, which were of great sentimental value, included movies from his honeymoon, graduation from medical school, his son's birth and childhood and other important family events. Upon delivery of the film, the store clerk asked Chanda to read and sign the order form which included a limitation of liability clause stating in part:

> By depositing film or other material with Fotomat, customer acknowledges and agrees that Fotomat's liability for any loss, damage, or delay to film during the processing service will be limited to the replacement cost of a non-exposed roll of film and/or a blank cassette of similar size. . . . Except for such replacement, Fotomat shall not be liable for any other loss or damage, direct, consequential, or incidental, arising out of customer's use of Fotomat's services.

The clause was printed in bold type in a conspicuous place on the order form. After reading the clause and asking the clerk about it, Chanda signed the form. While in Fotomat's possession, the films were lost prior to transfer to the videotape.

Chanda sued Fotomat for breach of contract seeking damages of $9,500, but Fotomat argued that damages should be limited to replacement of 28 rolls of unexposed Super-8 film. The trial court ruled that Fotomat's limitation of liability clause was unconscionable and ordered the jury to disregard it in determining damages. The jury found for Chanda and awarded damages of $9,500. Fotomat appealed.

Orfinger, Judge

. . . Florida has adopted the Uniform Commercial Code in dealing with commercial transactions. [The court then quoted §2-302 of the Uniform Commercial Code, "Unconscionable Contract or Clause".]

The code does not attempt to define "unconscionability." Consequently, those courts which have dealt with the problem have often looked to the common law of their respective jurisdictions because, in most, this code provision is, in reality, a codification of the common law rules. In the seminal case of *Williams v. Walker-Thomas Furniture Company*, 350 F.2d 445 (C.A.D.C. 1965), . . . the court discussed unconscionability in terms of its elements:

> Unconscionability has generally been recognized to include an absence of meaningful choice on the part of one of the parties together with contract terms which are unreasonably favorable to the other party. Whether a meaningful choice is present in a particular case can only be determined by consideration of all the circumstances surrounding the transaction. In many cases the meaningfulness of the choice is negated by a gross inequality of bargaining power. The manner in which the contract was entered is also relevant to this consideration. Did each party to the contract, considering his obvious education or lack of it, have a reasonable opportunity to understand the terms of the contract, or were the important terms hidden in a maze of fine print and minimized by deceptive sales practices? Ordinarily, one who signs an agreement without full knowledge of its terms might be held to assume the risk that he has entered a one-sided bargain. But when a party of little bargaining power, and hence little real choice, signs a commercially unreasonable contract with little or no knowledge of its terms, it is hardly likely that his consent, or even an objective manifestation of his consent, was ever given to all the terms. In such a case the usual rule that the terms of the agreement are not to be questioned should be abandoned and the court should consider whether the terms of the contract are so unfair that enforcement should be withheld.

Id. at 449-450.

Florida has long recognized the principle that the courts are not concerned with the wisdom or folly of contracts . . . but where it is perfectly plain to the court that one party has overreached the other and has gained an unjust and undeserved advantage which it would be inequitable to permit him to enforce, a court will grant relief even though the victimized parties owe their predicament largely to their own stupidity. . . .

In *Kohl v. Bay Colony Club Condominium, Inc.,* [398 So.2d 865 (Fla. App. 1981)], the court reviewed the authorities on the subject and concluded that:

> The authorities appear to be virtually unanimous in declaring (or assuming) that two elements must coalesce before a case for unconscionability is made out. The first is referred to as substantive unconscionability and the other procedural unconscionability. . . . A case is made out for substantive unconscionability by alleging and proving that the terms of the contract are unreasonable and unfair. . . . Procedural unconscionability, on the other hand, speaks to the individualized circumstances surrounding each contracting party at the time the contract was entered into. . . .

Applying the substantive prong of the test here, it cannot be said, as a matter of law, that the limitation clause here was unreasonable, when viewed in its commercial setting and when considering its purpose and effect. The charge for the processing service here was $31.00. The videocassette was priced at $18.95, and there was an additional $2.00 charge for an item not identified. There was unrebutted defense testimony that the limitation of liability provision was standard in the industry because, although loss and damage of film was relatively low in view of the tremendous volume of work done, no film processor would expose itself to liability for the unknown content of film without having to so greatly increase the cost to the public as to price the service out of the market. This is clearly a commercially reasonable consideration. . . .

The reasonableness of the clause is demonstrated by the huge loss claimed by Dr. Chanda, compared to the cost of the service. Without a doubt the film had peculiar value to the plaintiff. Some of it was irreplaceable and all of it was of great sentimental value, but that unknown "tiger" is the very reason for the inclusion of the limitation of liability provision in the transaction. There is no way the processor can conceive of the risk it takes in accepting film for processing absent an explicit agreement to accept such risk. When the customer is made aware of the provision for limitation of liability and nevertheless proceeds with the transaction he has assented to an agreement for which there is a commercial need, if the cost of the service is to be made reasonable.

Neither can we perceive that plaintiff satisfied the procedural prong of the test. The evidence reflects that Dr. Chanda saw and read the clause in question, asked a question about it and was apparently satisfied with the answer because he signed it. He had previously suffered the loss of film at a different place of business, and it had been replaced by new film. He was a doctor, well educated, experienced in business transactions, and well aware of what he was signing. While he was given no opportunity to negotiate the terms of this agremeent, he did not attempt to determine if anyone else could provide this service. Thus the evidence falls short of showing procedural unconscionability. If, as indicated by the official comment to Section 2-302 of the Uniform Commercial Code, the principle involved in the section "is one of the prevention of oppression and unfair surprise . . . and not of disturbance of allocation of risks because of superior bargaining power," no such oppression or unfair surprise is shown here. . . .

It is clear from the record here that the trial court refused to consider and apply the procedural/substantive test to determine the issue of unconscionability. Neither was any other objective analysis applied, but instead, the court appeared to view the unfairness of the agreement in retrospect, because of the result. The contract should have been reviewed in the light of the circumstances that existed when it was made. The judgment for plaintiff is reversed, and the cause is remanded to the trial court with directions to enter judgment for plaintiff for the cost of 28 rolls of unexposed Super-8 movie film.

[Judgment reversed and remanded.]

Unconscionability Between Merchants. The unconscionability doctrine has been most often applied to relieve a *consumer* from the effects of an unreasonably unfair contract. Courts have, however, been much more hesitant to apply the doctrine when the parties involved are *merchants* as the following case illustrates.

W. L. May Co., Inc. v. Philco-Ford Corporation
543 P.2d 283 (Or. 1975)

In 1962, plaintiff W. L. May Co., Inc. (May) and defendant Philco-Ford Corporation (Philco) entered into a distributorship contract by which May became the wholesale distributor of parts for repair of Philco appliances. The contract provided that either party could terminate the agreement upon 90 days written notice. The contract also required May to carry an "adequate" inventory of Philco parts and upon termination of the distributorship agreement, May was to resell to Philco from his inventory "such Philco Products and materials bearing Philco's name as Philco shall elect to repurchase, at a mutually agreed price but not in excess of Philco's current distributor price for said products and materials."

In 1971, Philco gave notice and terminated May's and all independent Philco distributorship contracts. Philco notified May that it elected not to repurchase any of May's Philco parts. Because of his inability to sell the parts, May requested that Philco repurchase them, but Philco refused. May sued Philco alleging that the termination provisions of the distributorship contract were unconscionable as defined in §2-302 of the UCC. May sought damages for the value of the Philco inventory that he had been unable to sell. The trial court held that the repurchase election provision of the contract was unconscionable and awarded May damages of $6,500. Philco appealed.

Howell, Justice

. . . We do not feel that plaintiff has shown that the repurchase provision was unconscionable within the meaning of §2-302 at the time of the formation of the contract. Plaintiff has not shown that Philco's reasons for reserving a repurchase election in its distributorship agreements were not reasonably related to the business risks involved and to Philco's reasonable commercial interests at the time of eventual termination. Although Philco presented no evidence to explain its inclusion of the repurchase election, we are not persuaded that it is unreasonable per se for a manufacturer to reserve the right to refuse to repurchase at least portions of a distributor's inventory upon termination. It may be that Philco was able to insist upon this particular allocation of risks only because of its superior bargaining power. However, under the Code, a bona fide allocation of risks will not be disturbed merely because one party had a superior bargaining position. *See* UCC §2-302, Comment 1. It may also be noted that both parties to this particular contract were sophisticated business people. This is clearly not the case of an innocent consumer who has unsuspectingly signed an adhesion contract. . . .

Similarly, we do not feel that the repurchase provision was unduly one-sided or oppressive. Although on its face that provision appears to be unqualified, in effect any exercise of the repurchase election by Philco would have been restricted by its obligation of good faith. Under the Uniform Commercial Code, a covenant of "good faith" is implied in every agreement. . . . Philco was required to exercise its repurchase election in an honest and commercially reasonable manner. So limited, the repurchase provision was not unduly one-sided and did not purport to authorize oppressive behavior. . . .

Thus, it is apparent that, *at the time of the formation of the contract,* the repurchase election provision was not unconscionable within the meaning of §2-302 of the Uniform Commercial Code. . . .

[Judgment reversed.]

Assent to Terms Not Bargained For. When determining whether a given contract or term is unconscionable, inequality of bargaining power is an important consideration. The *Restatement (Second) of Contracts* explains the relationship between bargaining power and unconscionability as follows:

> A bargain is not unconscionable merely because the parties to it are unequal in bargaining position, nor even because the inequality results in an allocation of risks to the weaker party. But gross inequality of bargaining power, together with terms unreasonably favorable to the stronger party, may confirm indications that the transaction involved elements of deception or compulsion, or may show that the weaker party had no meaningful choice, no real alternative, or did not

in fact assent or appear to assent to the unfair terms.[19]

The issue of lack of assent to the unfair terms referred to in the preceding quotation is of particular importance in the study of unconscionability and adhesion contracts. Traditionally, a person, by signing her name to a contract, manifests her assent to its terms and may not later assert that she had not read or did not understand its contents. This rule is generally stated as imposing a **duty to read** upon a person who signs a contract. In an adhesion contract, however, the party signing affirmatively assents to a few terms, commonly those that are inserted in the blanks on the standardized contract. She neither reads nor understands the printed terms contained in the remainder of the form. This fact is generally known to the drafting party. The party signing relies on the other's good faith and upon the implied representation that like terms are being accepted by others. The issue thus presented is: To what extent should the "adhering" party be bound to the unknown terms? Commenting on this issue, the court in *Williams v. Walker-Thomas Furniture Company* noted:

> Ordinarily, one who signs an agreement without full knowledge of its terms might be held to assume the risk that he has entered a one-sided bargain. But when a party of little bargaining power, and hence little real choice, signs a commercially unreasonable contract with little or no knowledge of its terms, it is hardly likely that his consent, or even an objective manifestation of his consent, was ever given to all the terms.[20]

In response to this problem, the *Restatement (Second) of Contracts* takes the position that although the person signing a standardized agreement is bound to its terms, even without reading or understanding them, he or she is not bound to "unknown terms which are beyond the range of reasonable expectation."[21] In other words, a party who signs an adhesion contract does not assent to

---

19. *Restatement (Second) of Contracts* §208 comment d.
20. 350 F.2d 445, 449 (D.C. Cir. 1965).
21. *Restatement (Second) of Contracts* §211 comment f.

a term if the drafting party has reason to believe that the signer would not have agreed to it had he known about it. The drafting party has "reason to believe" if the term is bizarre or oppressive, or substantially and adversely alters the nonstandard terms explicitly negotiated, or eliminates the dominant purpose of the transaction. Note that this approach addresses the problem of unconscionability by "unfair surprise" by refusing to enforce provisions that are contrary to reasonable expectations, indicating a lack of assent to those terms.

The unconscionability doctrine and the *Restatement* approach to nonnegotiated terms will continue to provide relief from the more onerous effects of adhesion contracts. Nevertheless, these approaches only provide protection after a person has signed an unreasonably unfair contract and is seeking to avoid its consequences in a subsequent lawsuit. They do not prevent the inclusion of such provisions initially. Additional statutory relief has been directed to this end. Many states, for example, have adopted residential landlord and tenant statutes defining rights and duties of both parties to protect tenants from the effects of one of the most troublesome adhesion contracts, the residential lease (particularly in multiunit dwellings). States have passed statutes regulating insurance policies, bills of lading, retail installment sales, and small loans. Additionally, statutes frequently provide that certain contract provisions are unenforceable for public policy reasons. At the federal level, statutes such as the Truth-in-Lending Act protect consumers in credit transactions. The Magnuson-Moss Warranty Act regulates the form and content of written warranties covering consumer goods. Statutes such as these, when coupled with diligent court policing through the unconscionability doctrine, should provide increasingly greater protection to persons signing standardized form contracts.

Covenants Not to Compete

Promises in Restraint of Trade. Both the common law and the antitrust laws have long limited enforcement of promises in **restraint of trade.** A promise is in restraint of trade if its performance would limit competition in any business or restrict the promisor in the exercise of any gainful occupation. A promise unreasonably in restraint of trade

is unenforceable on grounds of public policy. For example, assume A is considering opening a store that would compete with B's business in the same locality. B promises to pay A $10,000 in exchange for A's promise not to open a competing business. Both promises are unenforceable. Similarly, an agreement between A and B to fix the prices at which they will sell, or to divide up the existing market, are unenforceable. Such promises, which are also violations of federal and state antitrust law, are commonly designated **naked restraints** of trade, because they have no purpose other than to suppress or eliminate competition.

Despite this basic prohibition, some promises in which the promisor agrees to refrain from competition with the promisee are enforceable. To be enforceable, a promise to refrain from competition must be **ancillary** to an otherwise valid transaction or relationship. To be ancillary, as opposed to naked, a restraint must be imposed *as part of* the otherwise valid transaction. Even if a promise not to compete is ancillary to a valid transaction, it will be enforced only if:

1. the restraint is *reasonably necessary* to protect a *legitimate interest* of the promisee, and
2. the promisee's interest is not outweighed either by (a) hardship to the promisor, or (b) likely injury to the public.[22]

The most common types of promises that are judged under this test include promises (1) by the seller of a business not to compete with his buyer, (2) by an employee not to compete with his employer after termination of employment, and (3) by a partner not to compete with his former partnership.

Covenants Ancillary to Sale of a Business. A promise by a seller not to compete with his buyer is quite common when an ongoing business is sold. Such promises are enforceable under the test stated above if they are reasonable in light of the buyer's need to protect the value of the goodwill that he has purchased. Assume Seller has contracted to sell

---

22. *Restatement (Second) of Contracts* §188(1).

her bakery to Buyer. The bakery has been in business for many years and has a reputation for excellence in the community. Therefore, a significant portion of the purchase price represents goodwill.[23] On these facts, if Seller, after the sale, immediately opens a competing bakery in the same locality, the value of Buyer's goodwill is likely to be destroyed. Rather than receiving an established business of excellent reputation with the expectation of continuing profitability, the value of the purchase may now be limited to the leasehold or the building and equipment.[24]

To prevent this result, contracts for sale of a business often include a promise by the seller that she will not compete with the buyer in a certain business activity for a stated time period in a given geographic area. Such promises are generally enforceable as ancillary to an otherwise legal transaction (the sale of a business) and necessary to protect a legitimate interest of the promisee-buyer (the value of the goodwill acquired). Effectively, the seller is promising not to act in a manner that will diminish the value of what she has sold. Note, however, that the restraint must be *reasonable* in light of the interest it protects, so as not to impose an undue hardship upon the promisor.

As noted above, the extent of the restraint is measured by the activity it prohibits, its geographic scope, and its time duration. All these elements must be reasonable before the promise will be enforced. What is reasonable depends upon all circumstances including the nature and size of the business sold. To illustrate, using the preceding example, if Seller's bakery operated only in Champaign, Illinois, a restriction which included the entire state probably would be unreasonable and therefore unenforceable. Had the bakery operated interstate, however, a limitation involving the entire United States might be reasonable.

Even if the covenant is overly broad, circumstances may justify enforcement of a more narrowly drawn term. In such cases, the court, applying equitable principles, may reduce the term's scope to that which is reasonable under the circumstances, and then enforce it. Assume Seller, ancillary to the sale of the bakery, agrees not to compete with Buyer within a radius of fifty miles. The promise is fairly bargained for. Seller's promise is unreasonable because the business extends only over a two-mile radius. Although part of Seller's promise is unreasonable (from two to fifty miles), it is enforceable to the extent of two miles. Or, on the same facts, assume that the contract provides that Seller will not compete in the "bakery or other business" in the same town for three years. The term is too broad because Seller's business consisted only of a bakery. It is enforceable, however, to the extent it precludes competition in the bakery business.[25] The following case illustrates a typical dispute involving a covenant not to compete in the sale of business context. Note particularly the court's discussion of the conflicting judicial approaches to partial enforcement of overly broad covenants.

Bess v. Bothman
257 N.W.2d 791 (Minn. 1977)

Defendant Harold Bothman owned and operated an automobile repair business and towing service in Forest Lake, Minnesota. Because he wanted to seek other employment, Bothman agreed to sell two of his tow trucks to plaintiffs Robert Bess and Delmar Branum, who formed a business called "Forest Lake Towing." Bothman rented his automobile repair business on a month-to-month basis to another person. The contract for the sale of the tow trucks

---

23. That is, the purchase price exceeds the value of the assets such as land, equipment, fixtures, inventory, and leasehold.

24. A similar problem arises when the value of a corporation's business depends largely upon the goodwill of an officer or shareholder. If a major shareholder sells his shares or if the corporate business is sold, the purchaser may be injured substantially if the key figures in the enterprise are allowed to compete with the purchaser or the corporation after sale.

25. A court will only exercise its discretion to limit the effect of the restraint if the party seeking to enforce the term obtained it in good faith and in accordance with reasonable standards of fair dealing. For example, a court may refuse to rewrite an overly broad term imposed in an adhesion contract by a party with superior bargaining position.

was prepared by Bess and Branum and included the following provision:

> III.   Covenant Not to Compete
>
> Seller agrees not to hold his remaining tow vehicle out for public service, or to commit any other act detrimental to the successful operation of the business by Buyers. It is agreed that Seller will use his remaining vehicle only to tow vehicles to his place of business for repair purposes and not for towing only, unless prior agreement is obtained from Buyers.

Bothman scanned the contract, signed it, and received payment of $10,000. About a year later, he advertised a general towing service and resumed operating his business.

Bess and Branum sued seeking damages and an injunction prohibiting Bothman's conducting a general towing service. The trial court ruled in favor of plaintiffs and, after modifying the contract provision, enjoined Bothman from operating a general towing service in the Forest Lake area for a period of five years. Bothman appealed.

Kelly, Justice

. . . The district court concluded that without judicial modification the convenant not to compete was an unreasonable restraint of trade. A party may purchase the goodwill of a business and, to protect his investment, require the seller not to compete with the business sold. But such a restraint of trade is valid only if it is reasonable, and a restraint that provides more protection to the purchaser than is necessary to secure the goodwill he purchased is unreasonable and therefore illegal. . . . The district court correctly construed the contract as involving the sale of part of the goodwill of defendant's towing business, as evidenced by the covenant not to compete. But the covenant was unbounded by territorial or temporal limitations and, without limitations restricting its prohibition to protection of the goodwill of the towing business sold, the covenant embodies, as the district court found, an illegal restraint of trade. Defendant argues that the court was without authority to supply the limitations necessary to render the restraint reasonable. . . .

Although the "blue pencil" doctrine, requiring that the reasonable and unreasonable restraints be

severable, still commands a slight majority of jurisdictions, a substantial minority of courts modify unreasonable restraints of trade, whether formally divisible or not, and enforce them to the extent reasonable in the circumstances. . . .

Use of a judicial blue pencil would not aid plaintiffs here. But even if it did, we think its logic extends to the minority position. The rationale of the blue pencil doctrine is that a court is merely enforcing the legal parts of a divisible contract rather than making a new contract for the parties. . . . But this distinction and the doctrine itself emphasize form over substance. . . . No cogent reason appears to limit the partial enforcement of illegal covenants to those that are formally divisible. Moreover, under the minority position, enforcement of restrictive covenants remains a matter of equitable discretion and should be granted only when neither injury to the public interest nor injustice to the parties will result. We join the minority and hold that the district court had authority to modify and enforce the covenant not to compete. It remains to determine whether the limits established by the court were reasonable in these circumstances.

Three elements of reasonableness gauge the validity of territorial and temporal restrictions in this situation: First, whether the restriction exceeds the protection necessary to secure the goodwill purchased; second, whether the restriction places an undue hardship on the covenantor; and third, whether the restriction has a deleterious effect on the interests of the general public. . . .

Defendant essentially concedes the reasonableness of restricting the covenant's effect to the Forest Lake area. Although no evidence of the market for towing services in the area was introduced, restriction of defendant's activity within the city would seem necessary in order to protect the goodwill plaintiffs purchased. Nor would this restriction cause defendant undue hardship. The covenant permitted him to tow work in connection with his repair business; it prohibited only general towing services. The covenant also would not seem to subject the public to monopoly or other injury since other towing operations were present in the city.

The 5-year limitation is amenable to the same analysis. . . . Plaintiffs are entitled to a restriction of sufficient duration so that defendant's reentry into the field would not for that reason alone draw customers whose patronage plaintiffs had acquired. . . . The 5-year period represents a reasonable balance between protection of plaintiffs' goodwill and avoidance of undue hardship to defendant. . . .

[Judgment affirmed.]

Covenants Ancillary to Employment Relationships. Employment contracts and partnership agreements also sometimes utilize covenants not to compete. Under these covenants, the employee (or partner) agrees that upon termination of employment (or withdrawal from the partnership), he or she will not work for a competing employer or open a competing firm for a stated period of time, if ever. In many cases, the employer's reason for exacting such a promise is to prevent disclosure to a competing employer of trade secrets or confidential information acquired by the employee. Additionally, the employee may have acquired the means to lure customers away from the former employer. For example, the employee may have access to confidential customer lists, or gained the trust and confidence of existing customers, who are likely to follow the employee to a new business.

Covenants not to compete in employment contracts are enforceable subject to the same basic standards previously discussed. Courts are, however, more reluctant to enforce such covenants in employment relationships than in sales of businesses for several reasons. First, they are frequently imposed by the employer who stands in a superior bargaining position, often on the employer's standardized form contract, and may bear no substantial relationship to any information or skill peculiar to the employer's business that the employee may acquire. Second, the employer's (promisee's) interest in enforcement may be outweighed by the potential hardship upon the employee (promisor) or likely injury to the public. For example, the restraint may effectively deny the employee the means of earning a living, restrict his upward economic mobility, or deprive the public of a person whose skills are in short supply. For these reasons, some states, by statute, provide that covenants not to compete contained in employment contracts are unenforceable.

SUMMARY

1. A variety of factors may render an otherwise binding promise either unenforceable or voidable. One such factor is lack of contractual capacity. Certain persons possess special characteristics that limit, or in some cases extinguish, their contractual capacity. Examples include minors, persons suffering from a mental illness or defect, and intoxicated persons. Although lack of capacity may render a contract totally void, it more commonly renders the obligation merely voidable.

2. Minors, or infants, are persons who have not yet reached the age of contractual capacity, known as majority. A minor's contract is voidable by the minor prior to reaching legal age, usually eighteen years, and for a reasonable time thereafter. After reaching majority, however, the minor may ratify, and thereby make binding, a contract made during minority. Though not liable in contract, a minor may be held liable in restitution for the reasonable value of "necessaries," such as food, clothing, and shelter furnished to him.

3. Upon disaffirmance, the minor must generally return any consideration he still retains. If the consideration has been squandered or destroyed, the minor may nevertheless avoid the contract and recover the money or other consideration paid. In this case, however, a substantial minority of courts require the minor to account to the adult for the lost consideration. A similar duty to account is often imposed if the minor has misrepresented his age to the adult.

4. Contractual capacity also may be extinguished or limited by mental illness or defect. Persons for whom a court has appointed a guardian have no contractual capacity. If no guardian has been appointed, a contract is nevertheless voidable if made by a person who, due to a mental infirmity, is unable to reasonably understand the nature and consequences of the transaction. Some states also permit avoidance by persons who understand what they are doing but are unable to rationally control their behavior. Similar competency standards are applied to persons incapacitated due to alcohol or other drug intoxication.

5. Even if made by competent parties, a contract is rendered unenforceable if it violates an applicable

criminal or civil statute, constitutes the commission of or inducement to commit a tort, or is otherwise contrary to public policy. Examples of contracts that have been held unenforceable because they violate a statute include gambling contracts, usurious contracts, contracts made in violation of a licensing requirement, contracts to commit crimes, and unconscionable contracts or terms.

6. The unconscionability doctrine, embodied in §2-302 of the UCC, is used primarily to address problems created by standardized form contracts. Such "adhesion" contracts are drafted by one party usually with superior bargaining power and are given to the other on a "take it or leave it" basis. Because of the disparity in bargaining power, the contract may contain terms unreasonably favorable to the drafting party. To police against such terms, the unconscionability doctrine allows a court, as matter of law, to refuse to enforce or to limit the effect of any contract or term it finds to be unconscionable. Unconscionability is not explicitly defined but is characterized by an absence of meaningful choice by one party coupled with a contract or contract term that is unreasonably favorable to the other.

7. Even in the absence of a governing statute, courts are often required to balance private against public interests to determine enforceability. Examples of promises which have been held unenforceable on this basis include contracts involving the commission of a tort, contracts made by a fiduciary in violation of duty, promises interfering with another's contractual relation, exculpatory clauses, and promises in restraint of trade.

8. A promise is in restraint of trade if it limits competition in any business or restrains the promisor in the exercise of any gainful occupation. So-called naked restraints, those having no purpose other than to restrain competition, are always unenforceable and are also violations of federal and state antitrust law. A restraint imposed as part of, or "ancillary" to, an otherwise valid transaction, however, is enforceable if reasonably necessary to protect a legitimate business interest of the promisee. Common promises judged under this test include promises by the seller of a business not to compete with his buyer, by an employee not to compete with an employer after termination of employment, and by a partner not to compete with his former partnership.

KEY TERMS

contractual capacity
minor (infant)
majority
emancipation
ratification
necessaries

guardian
ward
illegal bargain
usurious contract
exculpatory clause
adhesion contract

unconscionability
substantive
  unconscionability
procedural
  unconscionability

duty to read
restraint of trade
naked restraint
ancillary restraint

QUESTIONS AND PROBLEMS

10-1 As noted in the text, the parties' freedom to contract is limited by public policy and contracts contrary to public policy are unenforceable.

(a) What is the "public policy" or the "public interest"? Is it capable of precise definition? Does the term "good faith" as discussed in Chapter 6 assist in defining the parameters of public policy?

(b) Why does contract law prevent enforcement of promises contrary to public policy? If such promises truly violate public policy, wouldn't other substantive legal areas, such as criminal or tort law, provide adequate protection?

10-2 As noted in the text, contracts by minors and others with limited contractual capacity are voidable. In modern society, do minors need protection against their own improvidence, inexperience, or lack of good judgment, allowing them to back out of a contract with an adult who is acting in good faith? Is such protection desirable, or as noted by one court, does it "lead to the corruption . . . of principles and encourage . . . habits of trickery and dishonesty"? Suggest ways that the avoidance power given minors and other incompetents actually harms, rather than benefits, them.

10-3 (a) Billy, a seventeen-year-old minor, was married and the father of a child. Billy entered into a contract to purchase a station wagon for $1,000 from Okay Used Autos. Two weeks later, the automobile began to evidence mechanical problems. After Okay refused to repair the car, Billy wrote to Okay to notify it that he was disaffirming the contract and demanding return of his $1,000. Okay did not respond so Billy sued seeking recovery of $1,000. How should the court rule? Explain.

(b) Billy also needed a job to support himself and his dependents. Billy entered into an agreement with Gaston Employment Agency by which he agreed to pay a fee if Gaston found him a job. Gaston secured employment for Billy and he accepted the job. Billy then refused to pay the agency's fee. Should a court enforce Billy's agreement with Gatson?

(c) Susie, a seventeen-year-old minor, entered into a contract with Byte Computer School for a correspondence course in computer programming. The contract provided that Susie would pay twenty-five dollars per month for three years. After Susie received her first lesson in the mail, she decided she did not want to take the lessons and returned all materials to Byte notifying it of her decision. Nevertheless, she paid the first four monthly installments. She paid three of the installments after reaching her eighteenth birthday. After Susie discontinued her payments, Byte sued Susie. Susie claimed that she was entitled to disaffirm the contract because she had been a minor. Byte argued that her payments after reaching eighteen, the age of majority, constituted a ratification of the contract. How should the court rule? Explain.

10-4 In recent years, federal and state governments have discouraged institutionalization of people with mental disabilities. As a result, many people who suffer from mental illness, senility, or mental retardation now live outside institutions and need to purchase many of the items needed for everyday life.

(a) If a person technically lacks mental capacity but lives outside an institution, should that person be able to avoid contractual obligations?

(b) Assume that you are a salesperson who suspects that a potential customer lacks mental capacity. Are there any measures you can take to protect yourself from entering into a contract with someone who is incompetent? Are protective measures available if you suspect the customer is a minor?

10-5 The unconscionability doctrine gives the court broad discretion in refusing to enforce or limiting the application of unconscionable contracts or terms. According to Official Comment 1 to §2-302, this discretion is "intended to make it possible for the courts to *police explicitly* against the contracts or clauses which they find to be unconscionable." (Emphasis added.) What does the quoted language mean? How would such "policing" be done in the absence of an unconscionability doctrine?

10-6 As the *W. L. May Co., Inc. v. Philco-Ford Corp.* case (page 227.) illustrates, courts have been very hesitant to allow unconscionability

claims in a commercial, rather than consumer, context. What factors generally preclude the application of unconscionability principles in commercial transactions?

10-7 It is generally stated that contracting parties have a "duty to read" contracts they sign. Is this a contractual "duty"? What is the effect of a failure to read? Explain the relationship between the unconscionability doctrine and the duty to read.

10-8 The Yellow Pages telephone directory is an effective advertising outlet used by many local businesses. In most cities, only one company publishes the Yellow Pages. Dr. Kathleen Schwarz, a psychologist, annually purchased a display advertisement in the Yellow Pages. One year, the Yellow Pages Co., publisher of the directory, inadvertently printed the wrong telephone number in the advertisement. Dr. Schwarz sued the Yellow Pages Co. for breach of contract alleging damages of $25,000. She is able to prove that in prior years over half of her new patients initially learned of her business through the Yellow Pages. Dr. Schwarz also can establish that her contract with Yellow Pages Co. is a form contract prepared by Yellow Pages. Yellow Pages denies liability based on the following provision in that contract: "The customer agrees that Yellow Pages Co. shall not be liable for errors and omissions of the directory beyond the amount paid for the directory advertising." Yellow Pages Co. offers to reimburse Dr. Schwarz for the cost of the advertisement.

(a) Is the contract with Yellow Pages Co. an adhesion contract?

(b) How should the court rule on Dr. Schwarz's case? Explain.

10-9 Gantos, Inc., owner and operator of a chain of clothing retail stores, purchases a portion of its inventory from Gianni Sport Ltd., a New York manufacturer and distributor of women's clothing. Gantos places its orders in writing using a form that includes the following cancellation clause: "Buyer [Gantos] reserves the right to terminate by notice to Seller [Gianni] all or any part of this order with respect to goods that have not actually been shipped by Seller."

On June 10, Gantos submitted an order for women's holiday clothing to be specially made by Gianni and delivered on October 10. On September 20, Gantos provided written notice of cancellation to Gianni. Gianni sued Gantos for breach of contract, alleging that the cancellation clause was unconscionable and, therefore, unenforceable. How should the court rule? In formulating your answer consider the following facts. Gantos and Gianni have been doing business together for over two years and all orders submitted by Gantos included the cancellation clause. Gianni's manager testifies that he had never noticed the clause in the contracts. Other buyers of women's clothing use the same clause. The women's fashion industry changes quickly so that sellers, upon receipt of cancellations, must absorb the loss or sell the goods to buyers at significantly reduced prices. The order cancelled by Gantos comprised 20% of Gianni's business for the year. Gantos' gross sales for the same year were 20 times those of Gianni.

10-10 Duane was an experienced farmer who annually purchased seeds from Joseph Seed Co. Each year a Joseph Seed salesperson visited Duane and prepared his order on a form supplied by Joseph Seed. The form included a limitation of liability provision that stated in part:

> Joseph Seed Co. warrants that seeds it sells conform to the label description. If for any reason, the seeds fail to perform as expected, Joseph Seed Co. will refund the purchase price. IN ANY EVENT JOSEPH SEED CO.'S LIABILITY FOR BREACH OF ANY WARRANTY OR CONTRACT WITH RESPECT TO SEEDS IT SELLS IS LIMITED TO THE PURCHASE PRICE OF THE SEEDS.

In 1988, Duane purchased cabbage seeds from Joseph Seed and planted them as usual. His cabbage crop failed when a fungus infected the entire crop. The fungus was caused by Joseph Seed's failure to treat the cabbage seed with a hot water process that would have killed the fungus. Duane sues Joseph Seed for damages equal to his lost profits, arguing that the limitation of liability clause is unconscionable. Duane alleges that he had not read the clause. How should the court rule in light of the following facts?

(a) In past years, Joseph Seed always had used the hot water process that would have killed the fungus. Duane did not know how cabbage seed was processed and was unaware that Joseph Seed had changed its procedures.

(b) During the visit with Duane, the Joseph Seed salesperson told Duane that Joseph Seed had decided not to use the hot water process for treating the cabbage seed in 1988.

(c) During the visit with Duane, the Joseph Seed salesperson pointed out the limitation

of liability clause and asked Duane whether he had any questions about Joseph Seed's policies. The salesperson did not discuss the hot water process.

10-11 Why are courts more hesitant to enforce covenants not to compete in an employment contract than in a sale of a business? Is not the same legal test applied to determine enforceability in either case?

10-12 While serving in the military, Donovan was trained to install glass on automobiles. Following his military discharge, Donovan accepted a job as a glass installer at Glass Specialty Co. in Kansas City, Missouri, and signed an employment contract that stated in part:

> I acknowledge that I will have access to confidential customer lists of Glass Specialty Co. and that Glass Specialty Co.'s auto glass installation business covers the entire state of Missouri and that I promise during the period of three years from and after termination of my employment, for any reason, with Glass Specialty Co. I will not associate myself with or engage in any business in competition with Glass Specialty Co. or in any other manner work for or assist any competitive automotive glass installation business in the state of Missouri.

One year later Donovan resigned from Glass Specialty Co. and, because he had no other marketable skills, he took a job as a glass installer at Custom Glass. Glass Specialty Co. sued Donovan alleging that he violated the covenant not to compete of his employment contract.

(a) Assume that Custom Glass is located in Kansas City. Should the court enforce the covenant not to compete?

(b) At trial, Donovan proved that he had no access to confidential customer lists at Glass Specialty Co. While at Glass Specialty Co. he had worked merely as an artisan, installing glass as requested by his supervisor. Would your answer to the preceding question change?

(c) Although Glass Specialty Co. agreed that Donovan had no access to customer lists, Specialty proved that Donovan had frequent contact with customers, including discussions of the optimal way to perform glass repairs. Would your answers to questions (a) or (b) change?

(d) Assume instead that Custom Glass is located in St. Louis, Missouri, which is approximately 300 miles from Kansas City. How should the court rule?

The preceding chapter discussed contracts that are voidable or unenforceable due to either lack of contractual capacity or conflict with public policy. This chapter examines additional formation defects that can render contracts voidable: fraud and misrepresentation, mistake, and duress and undue influence. Contracts involving fraud and misrepresentation are voidable because one party misleads the other concerning a fact material to the transaction. In addition, fraud is a tort for which damages are recoverable. The law of mistake concerns contracts voidable by one or both parties because of mistakes of fact not caused by the other party to the transaction. Finally, cases of duress and undue influence address problems of coercion and unfair persuasion in the bargaining process.

Fraud (Deceit) and Misrepresentation

A **misrepresentation** is an assertion that is not in accord with existing facts. That is, words or conduct asserting the existence of a fact constitute a misrepresentation if the fact does not exist. Assume Sam and Bob are negotiating for the sale of Sam's car. Sam tells Bob that the car's brakes have just been overhauled. In fact, the brakes have 75,000 miles on them. Sam has made a misrepresentation.

A misrepresentation is **fraudulent** if it is made with knowledge of its untrue character. The term **scienter** is frequently used by the courts when referring to the defendant's knowledge of falsity.

Scienter may be established in several ways. First, the statement may be made with actual knowledge of, or belief in, its falsity. Suppose S is negotiating with B for sale of S's house. In order to induce B to buy, S states, "The furnace is in perfect working order." In fact, as S is well aware, the furnace is in need of major repairs. The scienter requirement is met, because the statement is knowingly false.

Second, scienter may be inferred if the statement is made without belief in its truth or with reckless disregard of its truth or falsity. That is, a person may not actually know her assertion is false. She simply has no basis upon which to represent it as true. For example, if an auditor gives an unqualified opinion to financial statements that she has not audited, she may be liable for fraud to reliant third parties who are injured because the statements are materially misleading. The auditor may not *know* that the statements are incorrect. However, because she has not examined them, *she knows that she has no basis* upon which to assert that they fairly reflect the client's financial position. Thus, a misrepresentation may be fraudulent if the maker knows that she has neither knowledge nor belief in the existence of the matter she asserts as fact.

Not all misrepresentations are fraudulent. A person may, either negligently or innocently, make a false or inaccurate statement, believing it to be true. The legal consequences following such a nonfraudulent misrepresentation are not, as outlined below, as harsh as those imposed upon makers of fraudulent misrepresentations.

If a material misrepresentation made by one party to a contract induces the other to enter into a contract in justifiable reliance upon it, two legal consequences result. First, the contract is voidable by the reliant party on grounds of misrepresentation. Second, if the misrepresentation is fraudulent the party making the misrepresentation may be liable for damages for the tort of **fraud** (also known as "deceit" or "fraud in the inducement"). Thus, a misrepresentation has legal ramifications derived both from the law of contracts and from the law of torts.

Elements of Fraud

The party making the misrepresentation is liable for *fraud* if the plaintiff is able to prove the following elements:

1. the defendant made a fraudulent misrepresentation, with the intent to induce the plaintiff to act in reliance upon it;
2. the misrepresentation related to a material existing fact;
3. the plaintiff justifiably relied upon and acted upon the misrepresentation; and

4. the plaintiff suffered injury as a result of the reliance.[1]

No defenses are available to the defendant in fraud cases. To avoid liability, the defendant must refute one or more elements of the plaintiff's claim. Each of these elements is discussed in more detail later in this chapter. The following case illustrates the basic elements of a fraud claim in the context of the sale of a used car.

Miller v. Triangle Volkswagen, Inc.
286 S.E.2d 608 (N.C. App. 1982)

After telephoning defendant Triangle Volkswagen, Inc. (Triangle) and discussing the purchase of a used car, plaintiff James Miller visited Triangle's used-car lot to examine a 1971 Monte Carlo. Don Harmon, a salesman, told Miller that the Monte Carlo had low mileage and that Triangle had purchased it from another dealer, Phil's Auto Sales, who had purchased the car at an auction for $1,635. Nevertheless, Triangle agreed to sell the car to Miller for $1,600. Plaintiff agreed to buy the car for $1,600 and to pay an additional $45 for Triangle's performing a safety check, checking the oil and greasing the car. Triangle delivered the car to Miller with an odometer statement indicating the car had been driven approximately 24,000 miles.

In fact, Phil's Auto Sales had paid only $850 for the car at a private sale. Phil's had sold the Monte Carlo to Triangle for $1,065, and the correct mileage was 124,000 miles. Additionally, Triangle had not performed the safety check or lubrication.

Miller sued, alleging common law fraud. The trial court granted summary judgment in favor of Triangle and Miller appealed.

Martin, Judge

. . . In order to prove that defendant was guilty of fraud the plaintiff at trial must prove: (l) that a de-

---

1. *Restatement (Second) of Torts* §525.

fendant made a representation relating to some material fact; (2) that the representation was false; (3) that the defendant knew it was false or made it recklessly without any knowledge of its truth and as a positive assertion; (4) that the defendant made the representation with the intention that it should be acted upon by the plaintiff; (5) that the plaintiff reasonably relied upon the misrepresentation and acted upon it; and (6) that the plaintiff suffered injury. . . .

In this case plaintiff presented evidence on each element of fraud sufficient to withstand a motion for summary judgment. Plaintiff's evidence tended to show that the defendant through its agent, Harmon, made the material misrepresentations to the plaintiff that the car was a low mileage vehicle, with a wholesale value of $1635.00 and that Triangle had performed a safety inspection and minor repairs on the car worth $45.00. Harmon gave to plaintiff an odometer statement which verified the mileage as approximately 24,000 miles.

The plaintiff further presented evidence that these representations were false and that defendant knew they were false or made them recklessly. Phil McLamb [of Phil's Auto Sales], in his deposition, stated that he told Harmon that the car had travelled approximately 124,000 miles, not 24,000 miles. Plaintiff also presented evidence that the automobile was worth less than $1635.00, and that the safety inspection and minor repairs were not performed by defendant.

Plaintiff's evidence tended to show that defendant made these misrepresentations with the intention that they should be acted on by the plaintiff. The statements were made in a business context for the purpose of selling the car to plaintiff and the salesman Harmon took plaintiff's money on the basis of those representations.

The plaintiff purchased the automobile and drove it to Pennsylvania. This tends to show that plaintiff relied and acted upon defendant Harmon's representations.

Finally, the plaintiff's evidence indicates that he suffered injury. Defendant knew that plaintiff wanted a low mileage car. Plaintiff paid for a car that he believed had 24,000 miles, not 124,000 miles, and he paid for minor repairs and inspection of the car in the amount of $45. Plaintiff got less than he bargained for because of the misrepresentations about the car. . . .

[Judgment reversed.]

Fraud and Misrepresentation Distinguished

A plaintiff who is unable to prove fraud may nevertheless be able to avoid the contract on misrepresentation grounds. A contract is voidable on misrepresentation grounds if three elements are established.

1. the misrepresentation must be either fraudulent or material;
2. it must induce the recipient to enter into the contract; and
3. the recipient's reliance upon the misrepresented fact must be justified.[2]

If a contract procured through a fraudulent or material misrepresentation is avoided, the reliant party simply rescinds the contract, returns the subject matter, and obtains restitution of any benefit conferred upon the other party.

Note that the requirements for avoidance of the contract are less stringent than those applicable to fraud. Under tort law, fraud liability is not imposed unless the representation is *both* fraudulent *and* material, whereas contract law makes the contract voidable if the representation is *either* fraudulent *or* material. Thus, a contracting party who is unable to prove fraud may nevertheless avoid the contract if he can prove that he justifiably relied upon (1) a *nonfraudulent* misrepresentation of a material fact, or (2) a *fraudulent* misstatement not relating to a material fact. Assume S and B are negotiating for the sale of a machine to be used in B's manufacturing process. To induce B to buy, S states his good faith belief that the machine is capable of producing 100 units per hour. In fact, the machine produces only 50 units per hour. B buys the machine in reliance upon S's misrepresentation. Although B may not recover from S for fraud (because the mis-

---

2. *Restatement (Second) of Contracts* §164.

representation is not fraudulent), he may nevertheless avoid the contract.

The following material examines the various elements of fraud and misrepresentation in more detail, including the manner in which misrepresentations may be made, the various types of misrepresentations having legal consequences, when reliance upon a misrepresentation is justified, and the remedies available to a party injured by fraud or misrepresentation.[3]

Manner in Which Misrepresentation May Be Made

A misrepresentation may be made expressly, by conduct, or in some cases, by silence (nondisclosure).

Express Misrepresentation. Because a misrepresentation is a false assertion of fact, it is commonly made expressly; that is, through use of spoken or written words. For example, to induce B to buy his automobile, S states, ''This car has never been involved in an accident.'' In fact, S knows that the car has been involved in a major accident and handles poorly as a result. S has made an express misrepresentation.

Misrepresentation by Conduct (Concealment). Frequently, *conduct* other than express statements constitutes a misrepresentation. That is, action by one person that is intended or likely to prevent the other from learning of a fact is equivalent to an assertion that the fact does not exist. In this situation, misrepresentation is made by **concealment**. Assume S, an auto dealer, in order to induce B to buy a used car, turns back the odometer from 75,000 to 35,000 miles. S's conduct is a misrepresentation. Or, assume S, to induce B to purchase her house, hides the fact that her basement floods after rainstorms by painting over a section of the

basement wall to conceal water marks caused by the flooding. This concealment is equivalent to an assertion that the basement does not flood, a misrepresentation. Note that if B, while inspecting the basement asks S, ''Does the basement flood after a rainstorm?'' and S answers, ''No,'' S makes an *express* misrepresentation.

In addition to active concealment situations discussed above, a party may make a misrepresentation by successfully preventing or frustrating the other's investigation that would lead to disclosure of the fact. For example, one party may send the other searching for information on a ''wild goose chase'' to a person or place where he knows it cannot be found. Similarly, a misrepresentation is made if one party falsely denies that he has the knowledge or information requested, and the other is thereby led to believe that the facts do not exist or cannot be discovered.

Misrepresentation by Silence (Nondisclosure). Generally, a party to an arm's length business transaction is not liable for fraud simply for failing to disclose facts to the other—even facts that she knows the other would regard as material. Mere nondisclosure should be distinguished from concealment. Concealment obviously involves an element of nondisclosure, but it also involves *action* by one party that *prevents* the other from learning the fact and it is this action that constitutes the misrepresentation. On the other hand, a mere failure to speak (silence or nondisclosure) amounts to a fraudulent misrepresentation only in certain limited situations, discussed below, in which the law has imposed a duty to disclose the matter in question.

1. A person may make a statement that, when made, was true or believed to be true. Later, however, the maker may learn that the assertion was originally false or that subsequent events have rendered it false. In this situation, a person who remains silent, with knowledge that the person to whom the statement was made is relying upon it, is in the same position as if the statement had been knowingly false when made. For example, Smith and Brown are negotiating for the sale of a machine to be used in Brown's manufacturing operation. To induce Brown to buy, Smith states her good faith belief that the machine is capable of producing 100

---

3. Chapter 55 (Accountants' Liability) is based in part upon the law of fraud and negligent misrepresentation. The following material, therefore, provides the framework for understanding accountants' legal liability to third parties at common law.

units per hour. Smith subsequently discovers that the machine will produce only 50 units per hour. In this case, Smith is under a duty to correct her prior misrepresentation. Her failure to do so, with knowledge that Brown is relying upon her original assertion, constitutes a fraudulent misrepresentation that the machine is capable of producing 100 units per hour.

2. If the parties stand in a fiduciary or other relation of trust and confidence, the law imposes a duty to disclose all relevant facts. Thus, when a fiduciary duty is imposed, silence may constitute a fraudulent misrepresentation. Some of the relationships in which a person has the right to expect disclosure on this basis include those existing between: (1) a trustee and the beneficiaries of a trust, (2) an agent and principal, (3) partners, (4) a director and the corporation and its shareholders, (5) a creditor and a surety, (6) an attorney and client, (7) a physician and patient, (8) a priest and parishioner, (9) a guardian and ward, (10) tenants in common, and (11) family members.

3. A growing number of courts impose a duty to disclose under certain circumstances if one party to an agreement knows that the other is mistaken with respect to facts that are basic to the transaction. A "basic" fact goes to the substance or essence of what is bargained for. Assume that S, in order to induce B to purchase her house, fails to disclose that the house is infested with termites, a fact unknown to B. The fact withheld is basic to the transaction.

Generally, superior knowledge, skill, and experience are legitimate business advantages. A party to contract negotiations generally is not required to compensate for the other's deficiencies in investigation, experience, or judgment. For example, a buyer of property is ordinarily not expected to disclose facts to the seller that indicate that the property is more valuable than the seller believes. The law, however, somewhat limits a party's privilege to take advantage of the other's ignorance. This is particularly true when the party knows not only that the other is mistaken concerning a basic assumption but also that the other is relying upon him to disclose any facts that would substantially and adversely affect the value of the exchange. This expectation of disclosure may arise out of the relationship between the parties, customs or stan-

dards of fair dealing in the trade, or other objective circumstances. Assume Sara is negotiating with Betty for sale of Sara's house. The house is constructed over a landfill and, as a result, the foundation and other walls periodically crack. All existing cracks have been repaired, but the condition is certain to recur. In order to induce Betty to buy, Sara fails to disclose the problem. Sara knows that Betty is unaware of this fact, that it could not be discovered by ordinary inspection, and that Betty would not buy if she knew it. Sara also knows that Betty regards her as an honest and fair person who would disclose such a fundamental problem. Sara's nondisclosure here constitutes a fraudulent misrepresentation.

Material Existing Fact

To be actionable on the basis of fraud or misrepresentation, the misrepresentation must relate to a *material existing fact*. A misrepresentation is **material** if either a reasonable person would attach importance to the existence or nonexistence of the fact represented, or the person making the misrepresentation knows or should know that the other party is likely to regard the fact as important, even though it would not be important to a reasonable person.[4] In other words, both an objective and subjective test of materiality are used. Even if the matter misrepresented would not influence a reasonable person (an objective test), it is material if the maker knows that it would influence the person to whom it is made (a subjective test).

Facts include not only the existence or characteristics of a tangible thing or the occurrence of a given event or the relationship between particular persons or things, but also a state of mind, such as a statement of intention or opinion. The following material examines the various types of factual misrepresentations recognized by the courts.

Misrepresentation of Intention. Existing facts include past events as well as present circumstances, but generally do not include future events. Assume Sam contracts to sell a thoroughbred to Bill. During the negotiations, Sam asserts, "This horse will

---

4. *Restatement (Second) of Torts* §538.

win the Kentucky Derby.'' Sam generally has no liability to Bill if the horse subsequently finishes last in the race. A statement relating to the future, however, may imply a representation concerning an existing fact. The most common application of this principle concerns a person's statement of intention.

A person's assertion that he does or does not intend to do a particular thing indicates his state of mind at the time the statement is made. In the words of one court, the state of a person's mind is as much a fact as the state of his or her digestion. Thus, even though a statement of intention relates to a future event, a false representation of intent may form the basis of a fraud action, if, at the time the statement is made, the maker does not have that intention.

This rule is commonly applicable to misrepresentations of intention to perform an agreement. Normally, a person who fails to perform a contractual promise is liable for breach of contract, not fraud. For example, assume Steve agrees to sell and deliver a vacuum cleaner to Bill in thirty days in exchange for Bill's $100 cash payment. If Steve later fails to deliver because of a shortage of supply or because the agreement has become unprofitable, Steve is liable for breach of contract to Bill.

A promisor, however, by making a promise, impliedly represents to the promisee an intent to perform it. Therefore, a promise made without such intent is fraudulent. This result follows even if the promise is not legally binding as a contract—for example, if the promise is not supported by consideration. If the promise is contractually binding, however, the promisee has an action both in tort (fraud) and contract. To illustrate, using the preceding example, assume that Steve, with the intent to induce Bill to pay him $100, promises to deliver the vacuum cleaner to Bill in thirty days. Steve, when making the promise, has no intent to perform it. In fact, immediately after making the promise, Steve leaves town with the money. Steve is liable for fraud as well as breach of contract to Bill.

In some situations, however, a person may have no reason to expect that an intention will be carried out. For example, a misrepresentation of intention may be consistent with standards of fair dealing. To illustrate, assume that B is negotiating for the purchase of adjoining tracts of land owned by X, Y, and Z. B states to each seller that she intends to hold the tract as an investment. In fact, B desires the property to build a large shopping center. If, however, the sellers were aware of B's intent, they would demand a substantially higher price. A court may very well conclude that such a misrepresentation is not contrary to reasonable standards of fair dealing. Therefore, B would not be liable for misrepresentation and the sellers could not avoid their contracts.

Misrepresentation of Opinion. Like a statement of intention, a person's opinion is a fact. It represents a particular state of mind concerning the matter to which the opinion relates. Statements of opinion may take two forms. First, a person may express a *belief,* without professing actual knowledge, concerning the existence or nonexistence of a fact. Second, the person may express a *judgment* about quality, value, authenticity, or other similar matters. Thus, in an opinion, a person, rather than making a positive assertion (''this is true''), states only a belief or judgment regarding its truth (''I think this is true but I am not sure'').[5]

It is sometimes stated, erroneously, that relief on the basis of fraud is granted for misrepresentations of fact, not false statements of opinion. This blanket statement apparently is derived from the general rule that when both parties possess approximately equal competence and information with respect to the subject matter, each must trust his own judgment and, generally, neither is justified in relying upon the opinion of the other. Thus, if an ordinary commodity is sold, the purchaser is generally not entitled to rely upon the seller's opinion of its quality or worth.

The rationale for this result is the common knowledge that a seller will express a glowing opinion of whatever he has to sell. When the seller praises wares in general terms without specific representations or reference to facts, a reasonable person realizes that he or she is not entitled to rely literally on the seller's statement. This seller's hype or buildup is commonly known as ''puffing'' or ''seller's talk.'' Thus, no action for fraud lies against the used car dealer who knowingly de-

---

5. *Restatement (Second) of Torts* §538A and comment b.

scribes a defective car as a "honey," a "dandy," "the pride of the line," "a best buy," "a good little car," or the like. A court may also find that such statements are not "material" and deny recovery on that basis. Note, however, that the more specific the seller's talk becomes, the more likely a court may be to interpret the statement as a fact (that is, knowledge as opposed to opinion) supporting a fraud action. Therefore, a statement that the car is "mechanically perfect" or "in A-1 condition" may result in liability if the car is not as represented.[6]

Outside the puffing case, misrepresentations of opinion can support fraud actions. A person's opinion is a fact—her state of mind. In puffing situations recovery is denied not because the opinion is true, but because the law does not protect those who *rely* upon it. Reliance is often justified upon opinions rendered under the circumstances outlined below.

In the preceding discussion, the parties are assumed to be on an equal footing concerning the information and knowledge forming the basis of the opinion. A party may, however, assert an opinion concerning facts that are not disclosed or otherwise known to the other. Such an opinion, in certain circumstances, includes an implied representation that the maker knows facts that are sufficient to justify the opinion, or at least that he knows no facts inconsistent with it. In other words, when the parties do not possess equal information, the statement of opinion may include an implied representation of facts sufficient to support the opinion or belief.

This implied representation is particularly strong when the person rendering the opinion possesses special skill, knowledge, or judgment concerning the subject matter not possessed by the other. Thus, a misstatement of opinion by an expert may be grounds for a fraud action if the facts known to the expert do not justify the opinion. For example, An-

drew, who knows nothing about jewelry, employs Joanne, a jeweler, to appraise an antique diamond ring that Andrew is considering purchasing. Joanne states that, in her opinion, the ring is worth $1,000. In this case, Joanne is expressing more than her personal belief. In giving her opinion regarding the value of the ring, she is also giving a summary of information she has concerning the qualities and characteristics of diamonds affecting their value, as compared to the qualities of this particular ring. Thus, the statement of the jeweler is both an expression of her opinion and a conclusion of fact. The conclusion is that she has the kind of information that would justify a reasonable expert in believing that the ring is worth $1,000. If she does not possess this information, either because she has not examined the ring or has intentionally understated or overstated its value, her false opinion may subject her to liability for fraud. Therefore, when an opinion is rendered by an expert necessarily requiring a conclusion of fact supporting the opinion, the party without the special skill or expertise is entitled to rely upon the honesty of the expert's opinion and attach to it the importance warranted by the other's superior competence. Note that liability is imposed here on the basis of the *difference* in the information possessed by the respective parties.

In the following classic case, the court was required to determine whether fraud liability should be imposed for a misrepresentation of opinion.

Vokes v. Arthur Murray, Inc.
212 So.2d 906 (Fla. App. 1968)

> Plaintiff Audrey E. Vokes, a fifty-one-year-old widow without family who wanted to become an "accomplished dancer," attended a dance party at a school of dancing operated by defendants J. P. Davenport and Arthur Murray, Inc. Following the dance party, plaintiff Vokes purchased eight one-half-hour dance lessons for $14.50. Over a period of less than sixteen months, plaintiff agreed to purchase 2,302 hours of dancing lessons through fourteen dance courses for a total sales price of $31,090.45. Defendant Davenport and his teaching associates induced plaintiff to purchase the dancing lessons by a "con-

---

6. Under the UCC §2-313(1)(a), any *affirmation of fact* or promise that relates to the goods and becomes part of the basis of the bargain creates an *express warranty* that the goods will conform to the affirmation or promise. Thus, even if the seller's false statements of fact do not result in fraud liability (for example, they were not made with knowledge of falsity), the seller may be liable to the buyer for breach of express warranty. Warranties are covered in Chapter 19.

stant and continuous barrage of flattery, false praise, excessive compliments and panegyric encomiums.''

As a part of various sales promotions, Davenport encouraged Vokes to purchase additional hours of lessons to achieve first the dance studio's ''Bronze Medal,'' then the ''Silver Medal,'' and finally the ''Gold Medal.''

Vokes sued for fraud requesting the court to declare the contracts to be null and void. The trial court dismissed the complaint. Vokes appealed.

Pierce, Judge

. . . All the . . . sales promotions, illustrative of the entire fourteen separate contracts, were procured by defendant Davenport and Arthur Murray, Inc., by false representations to [Vokes] that she was improving in her dancing ability, that she had excellent potential, that she was responding to instructions in dancing grace, and that they were developing her into a beautiful dancer, whereas in truth and in fact she did not develop in her dancing ability, she had no ''dance aptitude,'' and in fact had difficulty in ''hearing the musical beat.'' . . .

Defendants contend that contracts can only be rescinded for fraud or misrepresentation when the alleged misrepresentation is as to a material fact, rather than an opinion, prediction or expectation, and that the statements and representations set forth at length in the complaint were in the category of ''trade puffing,'' within its legal orbit.

It is true that ''generally a misrepresentation, to be actionable, must be one of fact rather than of opinion''. [*Tonkovich v. South Florida Citrus Industries, Inc.,* 185 So.2d 710 (Fla. App. 1966).] . . . But this rule has significant qualifications, applicable here. It does not apply where there is a fiduciary relationship between the parties, or where there has been some artifice or trick employed by the representor, or where the parties do not in general deal at ''arm's length'' as we understand the phrase, or where the representee does not have equal opportunity to become apprised of the truth or falsity of the fact represented. . . . As stated . . . in *Ramel v. Chasebrook Construction Company* [135 So.2d 876, 879 (Fla. App. 1961).]:

> . . . A statement of a party having . . . superior knowledge may be regarded as a statement of fact

although it would be considered as opinion if the parties were dealing on equal terms.

It could be reasonably supposed here that defendants had ''superior knowledge'' as to whether plaintiff had ''dance potential'' and as to whether she was noticeably improving in the art of terpsichore. And it would be a reasonable inference from the undenied averments of the complaint that the flowery eulogiums heaped upon her by defendants as a prelude to her contracting for 1944 additional hours of instruction in order to attain the rank of the Bronze Standard, thence to the bracket of the Silver Standard, thence to the class of the Gold Bar Standard, and finally to the crowning plateau of a Life Member of the Studio, proceeded as much or more from the urge to ''ring the cash register'' as from any honest or realistic appraisal of her dancing prowess or a factual representation of her progress.

Even in contractual situations where a party to a transaction owes no duty to disclose facts within his knowledge or to answer inquiries respecting such facts, the law is if he undertakes to do so he must disclose the *whole truth*. . . . From the face of the complaint, it should have been reasonably apparent to defendants that her vast outlay of cash for the many hundreds of additional hours of instruction was not justified by her slow and awkward progress, which she would have been made well aware of if they had spoken the ''whole truth.'' . . .

In our view, from the showing made in her complaint, plaintiff is entitled to her day in Court.

[Judgment reversed.]

Misrepresentations of Law. Early courts stated, as a general rule of law, that in cases involving fraud, everyone is presumed to know the law, and, therefore, cannot be deceived by a misrepresentation of it. Under this approach, no fraud liability can result from a misrepresentation of law. The rule is apparently an extension of the principle that ignorance of the law is not a defense in a *criminal* prosecution. As the following discussion indicates, the modern approach is to treat misrepresentations of law in the same manner as any other misrepresentation.

A misrepresentation of law may be either a statement of fact or a statement of opinion. Therefore, a statement that a statute has been enacted or repealed or that a court has rendered a particular decision in a given fact situation is an assertion of fact. On the other hand, a statement of a person's judgment concerning the legal effect of a particular set of facts is a statement of opinion and is governed by the same principles applicable to other misrepresentations of opinion. Thus, as between two bargaining adversaries with equal knowledge of the facts, there can be ordinarily no justifiable reliance by one party on the other's opinion as to the legal effect of those facts. If, however, all facts are not known to both parties, a statement of opinion may carry with it the implication that the maker knows facts that justify his opinion or is unaware of facts incompatible with it. Assume a seller of real property states to a prospective buyer, "I have good title to the property." The seller's statement here is a conclusion of law. However, the buyer may be justified in interpreting the statement as the seller's assertion that she knows facts supporting her opinion (for example, she is in possession of a deed to the property and has title insurance or an attorney's opinion indicating she has good title) and that she has no information that would cause a reasonable person not to entertain the opinion expressed (for example, if the seller knows she is only a tenant under a long-term lease).

The same reasoning applies to statements of legal opinion rendered by lawyers or others who have a superior legal training, information, or expertise. Thus, a layman who requests a lawyer's opinion on a point of law is entitled to an honest opinion. He may reasonably assume the lawyer's professional honesty. The party rendering the opinion need not, however, be a lawyer. A layman dealing with an insurance agent or real estate broker is entitled to rely upon opinions of law relating to common problems related to those fields. Once again, it is the difference in the information, expertise, or skill possessed by the respective parties that makes reliance upon certain statements of opinion justified. In these cases, the opinion represents a shorthand description of the information possessed by one party over and above that possessed by the other. The following case illustrates the modern judicial approach to misrepresentations of law in fraud cases.

National Conversion Corp. v. Cedar Building Corp.

246 N.E.2d 351 (N.Y. 1969)

National Conversion Corporation (tenant) leased a commercial building from the Cedar Building Corporation (landlords). National intended to use the premises to convert garbage into fertilizer, an operation requiring that the premises be zoned for unrestricted use. During the negotiations, Cedar orally represented that the premises were in an unrestricted zone. On the basis of this representation, National was induced to enter into the lease. In fact, the premises were zoned only for light manufacturing use. As such, they could not be used by National for the intended purpose without making substantial additional expenditures necessary to control odors and to comply with other requirements of a light manufacturing zone.

National subsequently sued Cedar for fraud. The trial court found in National's favor and granted rescission of the lease and awarded over $70,000 in damages to National. Cedar appealed.

Breitel, Judge

. . . Tenant contended and proved that it had not actually known of the zoning requirement and had relied on what it was told. This proof . . . made out a classic instance of fraud in the inducement, for landlords intentionally or recklessly made false representations either as to their knowledge of the facts or the facts themselves. . . .

Landlords [however] contend that only a misrepresentation of law rather than of fact is involved and, therefore, that fraud will not lie. There is no longer any doubt that the law has recognized, even in this State, a sharp distinction between a pure opinion of law which may not, except in unusual circumstances, base an action in tort [for fraud], and a mixed statement of fact as to what the law is or whether it is applicable. . . .

[T]he law has outgrown the over-simple dichotomy between law and fact in the resolution of issues in deceit. It has been said that "a statement as to the law, like a statement as to anything else, may be intended and understood either as one of fact or one of opinion only, according to the circumstances of the case" [Prosser, *Law of Torts* 741 (3d ed. 1964)]. The statements in this case, both before the execution of the lease, and in the body of the lease, exemplify ideally an instance in which the statements are not intended or understood merely as an expression of opinion. Landlords said they knew the premises were in an unrestricted district. This meant that they knew, as a fact, that the zoning resolution did not restrict the use of the particular premises, and tenant so understood it. When coupled with the further fact that tenant's lawyer was persuaded not to verify the status of the premises on the landlords' representation, it is equally clear that tenant understood the statement to be one of fact, namely, what the zoning resolution provided by description, map, and requirements as to the area in question. The misrepresented fact, if it is at all necessary to find misrepresented facts, was what the zoning resolution contained by way of description, map, and requirements, hardly opinions as to the law albeit matters to be found in a law.

Moreover, the modern rule extends even further to cover a false opinion of law if misrepresented as a sincere opinion, as in the case of any other opinion, where there is reasonable reliance. . . . Hence, in the proper circumstances there may indeed be reliance on a fraudulently expressed statement of the law. Arguably, the facts of this case do not require so great a reach, for here the statements were keyed to the underlying data (facts) upon which the applicability of the particular zoning provisions governing the rights of owners and users were to be determined (the law). But, for the reasons indicated, it is not necessary to make the distinction rest on so narrow an analysis. . . .

[Judgment affirmed.]

Justifiable Reliance

In order to recover for loss resulting from a fraudulent misrepresentation, the party to whom it is made must rely upon the misrepresentation in act-

ing or forbearing to act, and that reliance must be justified. Reliance upon a fraudulent misrepresentation is not justified unless the misrepresentation relates to a material matter.[7]

The recipient of the fraudulent misrepresentation must *in fact* rely upon it in order to recover. It is not necessary, however, that reliance upon the truth of the assertion be the sole or decisive factor in influencing the decision. The misrepresentation need only play a substantial part. Assume S, in order to induce B to buy his house, makes three representations concerning the property. Two are true, but the third is false and fraudulent. B buys the property relying in substantial part upon the truth of all three statements. S is subject to liability for fraud to B.

Because reliance upon the misrepresentation is required, no fraud liability results if the recipient relies upon her own independent investigation concerning the matter to which the false assertion relates. Generally, a person who makes an investigation is deemed to rely upon it as to facts that it disclosed, and as to obvious facts uncovered during its course. The fraudulent party escapes liability, however, only if the other party relies solely upon the investigation and not upon the misrepresentation. That is, if reliance is partly upon the investigation and partly upon the false assertion, liability results.

The defrauded party need not only rely upon the misrepresentation, the reliance also must be justified. A person is, therefore, not justified in relying upon a statement she knows to be false or whose falsity is obvious to anyone upon a cursory examination or inspection. Additionally, early courts imposed a duty to independently investigate the truth of statements made by the other party. This view has, however, given way to the modern approach that the recipient of a fraudulent misrepresentation is justified in relying upon its truth, without undertaking an investigation, even though an investigation might have uncovered its falsity. This is true even if an investigation would be reasonable in the

---

7. Note, however, that a fraudulent assertion concerning even an immaterial matter is grounds for avoidance of the contract (see page 238).

circumstances, could be made without unreasonable expense, trouble, or delay, and even if the fact misrepresented is a matter of public record. For example, assume Susan fraudulently asserts to Dave that her land is free of all encumbrances. In fact, the land is subject to an unsatisfied mortgage, which is recorded. Dave could easily ascertain this fact by walking across the street and checking with the county recorder of deeds office. Dave, however, fails to do so and buys the land in reliance upon Susan's misrepresentation. Dave's reliance is justified. Thus, the law generally imposes no duty to investigate the truth of statements made by the other party.

The rationale for this rule is that, if a duty to investigate is imposed, the wrongdoer escapes liability for fraud as a result of the other's gullibility, credulity, or negligence. Thus, the persons with the greatest need for protection from fraud are denied recovery. The Vermont Supreme Court, in ruling upon this issue, stated:

> The defendant insists that the false representations must have been such as to deceive a man of ordinary care and prudence; i.e., if a man is not endowed with those faculties he is at the mercy of every swindler who makes him his prey, excluding from the benefits of the law the very class around whom its arm should be thrown, thus protecting the strong and robbing the weak. As well adopt Rob Roy's rule: "That they should take who have the power, and they should keep who can." No rogue should enjoy his ill-gotten plunder for the simple reason that his victim is by chance a fool.[8]

As the preceding quotation forcefully indicates, whether or not a person's reliance is justified, is not judged by comparing his conduct to that of a "reasonable person" in the circumstances—an objective test. It is determined in a subjective manner, taking into account any peculiar characteristics of the plaintiff as well as the particular facts of the case. At issue in the following case, an action for

rescission based upon innocent misrepresentation, was whether the plaintiff's reliance was justified.

Cousineau v. Walker
613 P.2d 608 (Alaska 1980)

The defendants Devon and Joan Walker owned approximately 9 acres of land that they listed for sale with a realtor. The initial listing stated that the property had 580 feet of highway frontage and that "Engineer report says over 1 million in gravel on prop." A subsequent listing agreement, which repeated that the property had 580 feet of highway frontage, stated that the land had a "minimum of 80,000 cubic yds. of gravel." An appraisal secured by the Walkers described the property as "all good gravel base . . . covered with birch and spruce trees," but did not list the highway frontage. The plaintiff Wayne Cousineau, a contractor who was also in the gravel extraction business, entered into negotiations to purchase the property. While inspecting the land, he was unable to find the boundary markers. Cousineau did not obtain a copy of the engineering report. The Walkers agreed to sell the property, including gravel rights, to Cousineau for $385,000.

After the purchase, Cousineau bought a gravel scale and contracted to have another company remove the gravel. Soon thereafter, a neighbor threatened to sue Cousineau because the company was removing gravel from the neighbor's land. A survey revealed that the property included only 415 feet of highway frontage. Further, the gravel was totally depleted after only 6,000 cubic yards had been removed. Cousineau stopped making payments to the Walkers and sued them for misrepresentation seeking rescission of the contract. The trial court ruled in favor of the Walkers and Cousineau appealed.

Boochever, Justice

. . . Numerous cases hold and the Restatement provides that an innocent misrepresentation may be the basis for rescinding a contract. There is no question, . . . that the statements made by Walker and his real estate agent in the multiple listing were false. Three questions must be resolved, however,

---

8. *Chamberlin v. Fuller,* 9 A. 832, 836 (Vt. 1887).

to determine whether Cousineau is entitled to rescission and restitution of the amount paid for the property on the basis of the misrepresentations. First, it must be determined whether Cousineau in fact relied on the statements. Second, it must be determined whether the statements were material to the transaction—that is, objectively, whether a reasonable person would have considered the statements important in deciding whether to purchase the property. Finally, assuming that Cousineau relied on the statements and that they were material, it must be determined whether his reliance was justified. . . .

In our opinion, the trial judge's finding that Cousineau and his partners did not rely on the statements made by Walker is clearly erroneous.

Regardless of the credibility of some witnesses, the uncontroverted facts are that Wayne Cousineau was in the gravel extraction business. He first became aware of the property through a multiple listing that said "1 MILLION IN GRAVEL." The subsequent listing stated that there were 80,000 cubic yards of gravel. Even if Walker might have taken the position that the sale was based on the appraisal, rather than the listings, the appraisal does not disclaim the earlier statements regarding the amount of highway frontage and the existence of gravel. In fact, the appraisal might well reaffirm a buyer's belief that gravel existed, since it stated there was a good gravel base. All the documents prepared regarding the sale from the first offer through the final deed of trust make provisions for the transfer of gravel rights. Cousineau's first act upon acquiring the property was to contract with South Construction for gravel removal, and to purchase gravel scales for $12,000.00. We conclude that the court erred in finding that Cousineau did not rely on Walker's statement that there was gravel on the property.

We are also convinced that the trial court's finding that Cousineau did not rely on Walker's statement regarding the amount of highway frontage was clearly erroneous. The Cousineaus were experienced and knowledgeable in real estate matters. In determining whether to purchase the property, they would certainly have considered the amount of highway frontage to be of importance. Despite Walker's insistence that Cousineau knew the location of the boundary markers, neither Cousineau nor the appraiser ever found them. It is improbable that Cousineau would have started removing gravel from a neighbor's property had he known the correct location of his boundary line. . . .

A material fact is one . . . which could reasonably be expected to influence someone's judgment or conduct concerning a transaction. . . . Under [§164 of the *Restatement (Second) of Contracts*], a misrepresentation may be grounds for voiding a contract if it is either fraudulent or material. . . . The reason behind the rule requiring proof of materiality is to encourage stability in contractual relations. The rule prevents parties who later become disappointed at the outcome of their bargain from capitalizing on any insignificant discrepancy to void the contract.

We conclude as a matter of law that the statements regarding highway frontage and gravel content were material. A reasonable person would be likely to consider the existence of gravel deposits an important consideration in developing a piece of property. Even if not valuable for commercial extraction, a gravel base would save the cost of obtaining suitable fill from other sources. Walker's real estate agent testified that the statements regarding gravel were placed in the listings because gravel would be among the property's "best points" and a "selling point." It seems obvious that the sellers themselves thought a buyer would consider gravel content important.

The buyers received less than three-fourths of the highway frontage described in the listings. Certainly the amount of highway frontage on a commercial tract would be considered important. . . .

The trial judge concluded as a matter of law that the plaintiffs "were not entitled to rely on the alleged misrepresentation."

The bulk of the appellee's brief is devoted to the argument that Cousineau's unquestioning reliance on Walker and his real estate agent was imprudent and unreasonable. Cousineau failed to obtain and review the engineer's report. He failed to obtain a survey or examine the plat available at the recorder's office. He failed to make calculations that would have revealed the true frontage of the lot. Although the property was covered with snow, the plaintiffs, according to Walker, had ample time to inspect it. The plaintiffs were experienced businessmen who frequently bought and sold real estate. Discrepancies existed in the various property descriptions which should have alerted Cousineau and his partners to potential problems. In short, the appellees urge that the doctrine of caveat emptor [let the buyer beware] precludes recovery.

In fashioning an appropriate rule for land sale contracts, we note initially that, in the area of commercial and consumer goods, the doctrine of caveat emptor has been nearly abolished by the Uniform Commercial Code and imposition of strict products liability. In real property transactions, the doctrine is also rapidly receding. . . .

There is a split of authority regarding a buyer's duty to investigate a vendor's fraudulent statements, but the prevailing trend is toward placing a minimal duty on a buyer. . . .

There is also authority for not applying the doctrine of caveat emptor even though the misrepresentation is innocent. The Restatements, case law, and a ready analogy to express warranties in the sale of goods support this view.

The recent draft of the Restatement of Contracts allows rescission for an innocent material misrepresentation unless a buyer's fault was so negligent as to amount to "a failure to act in good faith and in accordance with reasonable standards of fair dealing." [*Restatement (Second) of Contracts* §172 and comment b]. . . .

We do not contend that real property transactions are the same as those involving sales of goods. Nevertheless, an analogy to the applicability of the doctrine of caveat emptor under the Uniform Commercial Code is helpful. Under the Code, factual statements regarding the sale of goods constitute an express warranty. . . . Numerous cases have concluded that a buyer is entitled to rely on an express warranty, regardless of an inadequate examination of the goods.

Furthermore, the protections of the Code extend to highly sophisticated buyers in arms length transactions as well as to household consumers. Other than tradition, no reason exists for treating land sales differently from the sale of commercial goods insofar as application of the doctrine of caveat emptor is involved. We conclude that a purchaser of land may rely on material representations made by the seller and is not obligated to ascertain whether such representations are truthful.

A buyer of land, relying on an innocent misrepresentation, is barred from recovery only if the buyer's acts in failing to discover defects were wholly irrational, preposterous, or in bad faith.

Although Cousineau's actions may well have exhibited poor judgment for an experienced businessman, they were not so unreasonable or preposterous in view of Walker's description of the property that recovery should be denied. . . .

[Judgment reversed and remanded.]

Remedies for Fraud and Misrepresentation

To recover in deceit, the defrauded party must both rely upon the misrepresentation and suffer loss as a result of the reliance. That is, a fraud plaintiff may only recover for monetary injury that could reasonably be expected to result from reliance upon the misrepresentation. Assume S misrepresents the financial position of ABC Co. in order to induce B to buy his shares of stock. B buys in reliance upon the misrepresentation. Subsequently, the value of the stock deteriorates when ABC's production facilities are destroyed by fire. S is not liable for fraud to B. Although the misrepresentation caused the loss (that is, without it B would not have purchased the stock), the loss did not result from the misrepresented financial condition, but from a subsequent event unrelated to the misrepresentation. Of course, had the stock value declined as a result of ABC's impending bankruptcy, S would be liable.

In computing the amount of damages available to the injured party for fraud, most courts utilize a "benefit of the bargain test" similar to that applied in determining damages for breach of contract generally. Under this approach, the court awards the injured plaintiff the difference between the value of what the plaintiff actually received and the value of what the plaintiff would have received had the property, services, or other performance been as represented. In other words, the plaintiff recovers as if the false statements had, in fact, been true. The benefit of the bargain rule has been adopted by the great majority of courts as the basic measure of damages in fraud actions. It is also used to determine damages in fraud and misrepresentation cases arising out of contracts for the sale of goods under Article 2 of the UCC.[9]

Although commonly arising in the contract context, fraud is an intentional tort. As such, courts frequently award *punitive* damages to the plaintiff in fraud actions in addition to basic compensatory damages.

A person who merely elects to *avoid* the contract, as opposed to seeking recovery in tort for fraud, need not prove actual harm from reliance upon the misrepresentation. Rescission of the contract does not, however, bar recovery of any other damages sustained, including losses suffered as a consequence of using or preparing the subject matter of the contract prior to discovering the misrepresentation.[10]

Mistake

A **mistake** is simply a belief that does not accord with existing facts. Liability for fraud and misrepresentation results when one party acts or refrains from acting while under a mistake of fact *caused* by the other's misrepresentation. Occasionally one or both parties to a contract will be mistaken about relevant facts but for reasons not dependent upon the assertions of either party. This type of mistake is the subject of the following discussion.

As in misrepresentation, the basic remedy available in mistake cases is avoidance of the contract.[11] The availability of this remedy is closely limited by certain basic premises of contract law. Ordinarily a contracting party bears the risk that existing facts are not as he believes them to be and also that events subsequent to contract formation will make performance more expensive or burdensome. That is, freedom of contract includes the freedom to make bad bargains as well as good ones. For example, relief is ordinarily unavailable for mistaken belief concerning the value of the subject matter. To illustrate, assume Smith contracts to sell land to Bernard at a price based upon Smith's mistaken assumption that the property is suitable only for farming. Subsequently, valuable mineral deposits are discovered on the land. Smith may not avoid the contract.

Similarly, relief is not generally given for mistakes relating to the difficulty or expense of performance. Assume Alice contracts to dig a foundation for Walter's house at an agreed price, based upon Alice's mistaken assumption that the ground contains only ordinary clay and small rocks. However, during excavation, Alice discovers solid rock which substantially increases her costs, causing her to lose money on the bargain. Alice may not avoid the contract. The same result follows had Alice underestimated the labor costs on the job or if heavy rains had made performance more expensive. To allow a party to avoid his obligation on grounds of mistake in these situations would substantially impair a basic purpose of contract law: to make promises legally enforceable. In other words, a person should not be able to avoid a contract simply because it was entered into on the mistaken belief that it was a good bargain. The certainty, stability, and predictability that contractual promises provide would no longer be present. It is therefore reasonable to allocate the risk of such mistakes to the adversely affected party (Smith or Alice in the pre-

---

9. The UCC §2-721 provides that remedies for fraud and material misrepresentation include all remedies for nonfraudulent breach. Under §2-313(1)(a), a seller's misrepresentation of fact concerning his wares constitutes breach of an express warranty. Under §2-714(2), the basic measure of damages for breach of warranty is the difference between ". . . the value of the goods accepted and *the value they would have had if they had been as warranted.* . . ." (Emphasis added.) Warranties and remedies for breach of warranty are discussed in more detail in Chapter 19.

10. Remedies including punitive damages are discussed in detail in Chapter 15.

---

11. If the mistake occurs in reducing the parties' oral agreement to a writing, appropriate relief is afforded by reformation. Reformation is an equitable remedy in which the court essentially rewrites the contract to conform to the parties' actual agreement. If the mistake can be corrected by reformation, avoidance of the contract is unavailable. Reformation is discussed in Chapter 15.

ceding examples). Additionally, the contract may expressly allocate the risk to one party, or may do so by implication, as when one party undertakes to perform, knowing he has only limited knowledge concerning facts to which the mistake relates.

Unilateral Mistake

In some situations, like those discussed above, one but not both parties are mistaken regarding a basic assumption upon which the contract is made. Generally, in such a **unilateral mistake,** no relief is available to the mistaken party unless the nonmistaken party knows or has reason to know of (or was at fault in causing) the mistake. Suppose Seller and Buyer enter into a contract for sale of a machine to be used in Buyer's manufacturing process. Buyer assumes that the machine will produce 100 units per hour. In fact, the machine is capable of producing only 50 units per hour. Seller is unaware of Buyer's mistaken assumption and has made no warranties concerning the machine. Buyer may not avoid the contract. If, however, Seller knows of Buyer's mistaken belief and says nothing, Buyer may avoid the contract, not on the basis of mistake, but on the basis of fraud. The rationale for the courts' hesitancy to allow rescission on grounds of unilateral mistake is that because mistake is the exception rather than the rule, evidence of the mistake must be fairly convincing, particularly because avoidance on this ground substantially alters the reasonable expectations of the nonmistaken party. Courts have, however, shown a growing willingness to allow rescission when the consequences of the mistake are so onerous that enforcement of the contract would be unconscionable.

The most common type of unilateral mistake involves clerical errors or omissions in the computation of bids for construction contracts.[12] Assume Forbes solicits bids for construction of a building pursuant to stated specifications. Turner submits a bid of $150,000. However, Turner has (a) added incorrectly, or (b) omitted an item from the total, or (c) misunderstood Forbes's specifications. The

bid should be $200,000. If Forbes has reason to know of the mistake (for example, all other bids range between $215,000 and $275,000), he cannot accept Turner's offer. If, however, Forbes has no reason to know of the mistake and accepts, Turner may not avoid the contract *unless* the court finds that enforcement of the contract would be unconscionable. This issue will be decided in the discretion of the court based upon the extent of the loss to be incurred by Turner. If, because of the mistake, Turner will incur a $20,000 loss instead of making a $30,000 profit, the court may grant rescission. But if Forbes will make $10,000 instead of $60,000 on the contract as a result of the mistake, the court may refuse to allow rescission.

If a mistake occurs, it may be discovered immediately following formation of the contract, or after the contract has been partially or fully performed. The following case illustrates the judicial approach to a mistake discovered after the nonmistaken party had fully performed its part of the contract.

Monarch Marking System Company v. Reed's Photo Mart, Inc.
485 S.W.2d 905 (Tex. 1972)

The vice-president of defendant, Reed's Photo Mart (Reed's), mailed to plaintiff, Monarch Marking System Company (Monarch) a purchase order for five different types of labels. In the column marked quantity, the vice-president wrote "2M" for four of the labels. For the fifth label, he attached a copy of the desired label and marked the quantity as "4MM." The purchase order further requested delivery at once by parcel post. When Monarch received the purchase order it mailed the first four types of labels to Reed's. The fifth label required special printing and was forwarded to Monarch's plant. Monarch, however, changed the method of delivery from parcel post to "best way" because the shipment, which weighed 622 pounds, would have required thirty-one separate shipments to comply with parcel post requirements. Approximately two months later, Monarch sent four million labels to Reed's by motor freight. Reed's refused to accept delivery. Its vice-president immediately called Mon-

---

12. The *Drennan v. Star Paving Company* case, excerpted in Chapter 9 (page 210), is a typical example of this type of mistake.

arch claiming "a terrible mistake had been made" and explained that, Reed's had intended to order only four thousand labels, not four million.

Monarch sued Reed's for breach of contract. Reed's defended on the grounds that the quantity on the purchase order had been a mistake. The trial court ruled in favor of Monarch granting damages in the amount of $2,680 plus attorneys' fees of $750. The appellate court reversed on the grounds that the trial court had failed to consider whether Monarch should have known that the order was a mistake. Monarch appealed to the Texas Supreme Court.

Pope, Justice

. . . Most of the problems in this case are resolved by the jury findings that the term "MM" by custom and usage in the trade means one million; Monarch's method of shipping was in substantial compliance with the purchase order; the reasonable value of the labels shipped to Reed's was $2,680, and reasonable attorney fees for representing Monarch were $750. The jury refused to find that Monarch knew that the order for "4MM" labels was a mistake. . . .

The mistake was a unilateral one; it was made by Reed's, and Monarch fully performed its part of the contract. The Texas rule has long been that relief from a unilateral mistake depends upon the ability of the party mistaken to put the other party into the same situation as he was prior to the transaction in question. . . . We reaffirmed that principle in *James T. Taylor and Sons, Inc. v. Arlington I.S.D.,* [335 S.W.2d 371 (Tex. 1960)], wherein we said that one of the usual prerequisites to the granting of relief for a unilateral mistake was "(4) the parties can be placed in status quo in the equity sense, i.e., rescission must not result in prejudice to the other party except for the loss of his bargain." . . .

The treatise writers appear to be in accord with this reasoning. . . . Professor Williston says that "whatever equity there may be in favor of one who has made a unilateral mistake in the formation of a bilateral contract, the effect of it is confined to cases where the transaction is still wholly executory" [13 S. Williston, *A Treatise on the Law of Contracts* §1580, at 528 (3d. ed. 1970)] . . . .

We have in this case a fully executed contract on the part of Monarch and the record is devoid of proof of any effort on the part of Reed's to restore Monarch to the status quo even to the extent that circumstances would permit. . . .

[Judgment of the trial court affirmed.]

Mutual Mistake

When both parties, at the time of the contract, are mistaken concerning a basic assumption upon which the contract is made, the contract is voidable by the adversely affected party if (1) the mistake has a material effect on the agreed exchange of performance, and (2) the risk of the mistake has not been allocated to her. Such **mutual mistakes** occur in many different contexts. The parties may be mistaken regarding the existence, identity, quantity, or other qualities or characteristics of the subject matter. They may also be mistaken concerning the law applicable to the transaction. In all cases, the contract is voidable, if the foregoing test is met.

To illustrate, assume Sharp and Bailey enter into a contract for sale of Sharp's 1955 Chevrolet. Both parties believe that the car is still in existence, but in fact it has been destroyed by fire. The contract is voidable by Bailey. The parties here are mistaken concerning the *existence* of the subject matter.

The parties may also be mistaken as to the *identity* or *quantity* of the subject matter. Suppose S and B enter into a contract for sale of S's farm for $1,500,000. Both parties believe that the tract contains 500 acres, based upon a survey by X. X's survey is inaccurate; the farm contains only 400 acres. B may avoid the contract. If the farm actually contains 600 acres, S may avoid the contract.

Mistakes also may arise concerning the qualities or characteristics of the subject matter. In the well-known case of *Sherwood v. Walker,*[13] the seller contracted to sell a cow that both parties believed to be sterile. Because the cow was good breeding stock, the price was substantially lower than could otherwise be commanded. Before delivery, the cow was discovered to be fertile and the seller sought to

---

13. 33 N.W. 919 (Mich. 1887).

avoid the contract. The court allowed rescission on the basis that a barren cow is substantially different from a fertile one and thus the mistake went to the very nature of the thing sold. Because the facts were substantially different from those upon which the parties based their bargain, rescission was allowed.

A mistake of law providing a basis for rescission may be illustrated by the following example. Assume Tate leases commercial property from Levy for use as a fertilizer plant. As both parties know, such a use requires an unrestricted zoning classification. Both parties acting in good faith mistakenly believe that the land is located in an unrestricted zone. In fact, the land is zoned for light industrial use only, and is totally unsuitable for Tate's purposes, even with substantial additional investment. The contract is voidable by Tate.[14] In the following case the court was required to determine both the existence of a mutual mistake, and whether the parties had allocated the risk of the mistake.

Lenawee County Board of Health v. Messerly

331 N.W.2d 203 (Mich. 1982)

Carl and Nancy Pickles entered into a contract to purchase from William and Martha Messerly a 600-square-foot tract of land on which was located a three-unit apartment building. Mr. and Mrs. Pickles inspected the property prior to signing the contract. A prior owner of the apartment building had installed a septic system on the property purchased by the Pickleses. After the contract had been signed, Mr. and Mrs. Pickles visited their tenants and discovered that the septic system had malfunctioned and raw sewage was seeping out of the ground. The County Board of Health obtained an injunction prohibiting human habitation of the apartment building until a proper septic system was installed. Such a system required 2,500 square feet of property and

so could not be installed on the tract of land purchased by Mr. and Mrs. Pickles.

Mr. and Mrs. Pickles refused to pay for the property as required by the contract. The Messerlys sued for breach of contract. The Pickleses counterclaimed requesting rescission of the contract. The trial court ruled in favor of the Messerlys. The court of appeals reversed holding that the Pickleses were entitled to rescission of the contract because of mutual mistake. The Messerlys appealed.

Ryan, Justice

. . . [R]escission [for mutual mistake of fact] is indicated when the mistaken belief relates to a basic assumption of the parties upon which the contract is made, and which materially affects the agreed performances of the parties. . . . Rescission is not available, however, to relieve a party who has assumed the risk of loss in connection with the mistake. . . .

All of the parties to this contract erroneously assumed that the property transferred by the vendors to the vendees was suitable for human habitation and could be utilized to generate rental income. The fundamental nature of these assumptions is indicated by the fact that their invalidity changed the character of the property transferred, thereby frustrating, indeed precluding, Mr. and Mrs. Pickles' intended use of the real estate. Although the Pickleses are disadvantaged by enforcement of the contract, performance is advantageous to the Messerlys, as the property at issue is less valuable absent its income-earning potential. Nothing short of rescission can remedy the mistake. Thus, the parties' mistake as to a basic assumption materially affects the agreed performances of the parties.

Despite the significance of the mistake made by the parties, we reverse the Court of Appeals because we conclude that equity does not justify the remedy sought by Mr. and Mrs. Pickles. . . .

In cases of mistake by two equally innocent parties, we are required, in the exercise of our equitable powers, to determine which blameless party should assume the loss resulting from the misapprehension they shared. Normally that can only be done by drawing upon our "own notions of what is reasonable and just under all the surrounding circumstances".

Equity suggests that, in this case, the risk should

---

14. These facts are similar to those in *National Conversion Corp. v. Cedar Building Corp.*, previously excerpted in the fraud material. In that case, however, the tenant's mistaken belief was induced by the landlord's intentional misrepresentation concerning the zoning classification.

be allocated to the purchasers. . . . Section 154(a) [of the *Restatement (Second) of Contracts*] suggests that the court should look first to whether the parties have agreed to the allocation of the risk between themselves. While there is no express assumption in the contract by either party of the risk of the property becoming uninhabitable, there was indeed some agreed allocation of the risk to the vendees by the incorporation of an ''as is'' clause into the contract which, we repeat, provided:

> Purchaser has examined this property and agrees to accept same in its present condition. There are no other or additional written or oral understandings.

That is a persuasive indication that the parties considered that, as between them, such risk as related to the ''present condition'' of the property should lie with the purchaser. If the ''as is'' clause is to have any meaning at all, it must be interpreted to refer to those defects which were unknown at the time that the contract was executed. Thus, the parties themselves assigned the risk of loss to Mr. and Mrs. Pickles. . . .

[Judgment of Court of Appeals reversed.]

Effect of Misunderstanding

A problem closely related to mutual mistake concerns the effect of misunderstanding between the parties occurring in the bargaining process. Although under the objective theory of contract the parties are ordinarily bound by their outward manifestations, the parties may attach materially different meanings to those manifestations. Material differences in meaning are a major cause of contract disputes. To resolve these disputes, courts must interpret the parties' language and other conduct in light of the surrounding circumstances. The problem is illustrated by the famous case of *Raffles v. Wichelhaus*, [15] commonly known as the ''Peerless'' case. In this case the plaintiff (seller) agreed to sell cotton to the defendant (buyer). According to the contract the cotton was to arrive by the steamer *Peerless* from Bombay. By coincidence there happened to be two ships named *Peerless* sailing from Bombay, one in October and the other in December. The seller intended Peerless #2 (December) and the buyer intended Peerless #1 (October). When the seller tendered delivery from Peerless #2, buyer refused to accept or pay for the goods, resulting in the seller's suit. Because both parties attached materially different meanings to the term ''Peerless,'' and neither party knew or had reason to know that different ships were intended, the court held that no contract had been created. The same result would occur if both seller and buyer knew or had reason to know that each party meant a different ship. In other words, no contract is created if the parties attach conflicting and irreconcilable meanings to an important term that could have either but not both meanings. [16] Note that unlike the ordinary mistake cases, which may render a contract voidable, the misunderstanding outlined above prevents formation of the contract initially. The following case provides a modern example of the effect of misunderstanding.

Oswald v. Allen
417 F.2d 43 (2d Cir. 1969)

> Appellant Dr. Werner Oswald agreed to purchase some coins from appellee Mrs. Jane Allen. Mrs. Allen later refused to deliver any coins to Dr. Oswald. Dr. Oswald sued for breach of contract. The trial court held that no contract existed. Dr. Oswald appealed.

Moore, Circuit Judge

Dr. Oswald, a coin collector from Switzerland, was interested in Mrs. Allen's collection of Swiss coins. In April of 1964 Dr. Oswald was in the United States and arranged to see Mrs. Allen's coins. The parties drove to the Newburgh Savings Bank of Newburgh, New York, where two of her collections referred to as the Swiss Coin Collection and the Rarity Coin Collection were located in separate vault boxes. After examining and taking notes

---

15. 2 Hurl. & C. 906, 159 Eng. Rep. 375 (Ex. 1864).

16. *Restatement (Second) of Contracts* §20(1).

on the coins in the Swiss Coin Collection, Dr. Oswald was shown several valuable Swiss coins from the Rarity Coin Collection. He also took notes on these coins and later testified that he did not know that they were in a separate "collection." The evidence showed that each collection had a different key number and was housed in labeled cigar boxes.

On the return to New York City, Dr. Oswald sat in the front seat of the car while Mrs. Allen sat in the back with Dr. Oswald's brother, Mr. Victor Oswald, and Mr. Cantarella of the Chase Manhattan Bank's Money Museum, who had helped arrange the meeting and served as Dr. Oswald's agent. Dr. Oswald could speak practically no English and so depended on his brother to conduct the transaction. After some negotiation a price of $50,000 was agreed upon. Apparently the parties never realized that the references to "Swiss coins" and the "Swiss Coin Collection" were ambiguous. The trial judge found that Dr. Oswald thought the offer he had authorized his brother to make was for all of the Swiss coins, while Mrs. Allen thought she was selling only the Swiss Coin Collection and not the Swiss coins in the Rarity Coin Collection. . . .

Appellant attacks the conclusion of the Court below that a contract did not exist since the minds of the parties had not met. The opinion below states:

> . . . plaintiff believed that he had offered to buy all Swiss coins owned by the defendant while defendant reasonably understood the offer which she accepted to relate to those of her Swiss coins as had been segregated in the particular collection denominated by her as the "Swiss Coin Collection". . . . [285 F. Supp. 488, 492 (S.D.N.Y. 1968)]

The trial judge based his decision upon his evaluation of the credibility of the witnesses, the records of the defendant, the values of the coins involved, the circumstances of the transaction and the reasonable probabilities. . . .

In such a factual situation the law is settled that no contract exists. The *Restatement of Contracts* in section 71(a) adopts the rule of *Raffles v. Wichelhaus*. . . . Professor Young states that rule as follows:

When any of the terms used to express an agreement is ambivalent, and the parties understand it in different ways, there cannot be a contract unless one of them should have been aware of the other's understanding [Young, Equivocation in Agreements, 64 Colum.L.Rev. 619, 621 (1964).]

Even though the mental assent of the parties is not requisite for the formation of a contract . . . the facts found by the trial judge clearly place this case within the small group of exceptional cases in which there is "no sensible basis for choosing between conflicting understandings." Young, at 647. The rule of *Raffles v. Wichelhaus* is applicable here.

[Judgment affirmed.]

Duress and Undue Influence

The preceding discussion concerns contracts voidable on grounds of mistake, whether induced by the other party (fraud and misrepresentation) or otherwise. The following material examines contracts void or voidable due to an element of compulsion or coercion (duress) or unfair persuasion (undue influence) in the bargaining process. Contracts procured through duress or undue influence are generally voidable by the injured party. Unlike fraud, however, duress and undue influence are not themselves traditionally viewed as torts for which dollar damages are recoverable.

Duress

Duress may result from two forms of conduct: physical coercion and improper threat. Physical coercion ordinarily renders an obligation void (as opposed to voidable) because it lacks the manifestation of assent required for a contract. For example, assume Barry, placing a loaded gun to Short's head, forces Short to sign an instrument purportedly conveying Short's farm to Barry. Short has no knowledge of the instrument's contents. No contract is created and Short's obligation under the instrument is void.

More often duress results from a threat, not

physical compulsion. In such cases, the coerced consent (rather than as above, absence of consent) renders the contract voidable. Threats may be made expressly or by other conduct including past acts or events. Threats constituting duress are usually made by one contracting party to the other. Nevertheless, neither the person making the threat nor the person threatened need be a party to the contract, as long as the threat induces the making of the contract.

Improper threats take many forms. A threat is improper if the act threatened is itself a crime or a tort. Common examples include threats of physical violence or of wrongful seizure or retention of land or goods.

Threats of criminal prosecution also are generally improper. Either the person induced to contract or some third person (for example, a relative of the recipient) may be the object of the threatened prosecution. Threats of prosecution are usually deemed an abuse of the criminal process solely for private benefit. Assume Adams embezzles money in his capacity as Philip's agent. Philip discovers the embezzlement and threatens to file a criminal complaint against Adams unless Adams signs a promissory note for the amount stolen. Adams signs, induced by the threat. The contract is voidable by Adams. In this case, Philip has a legal right to report Adams's crime to the police. His threat to do so for private benefit is a misuse of that right. In addition, as is commonly the case, Philip may agree not to file a criminal complaint in exchange for Adams's promise. Such a promise to suppress a criminal prosecution is itself unenforceable as contrary to public policy, and may subject Philip to criminal liability.

Because the law favors free access to the courts, a threat to file a civil (rather than criminal) suit is ordinarily not improper. For example, assume Don owes Carol money for accounting services rendered by Carol. Don refuses to pay Carol's bill, thinking the amount is too high. Carol threatens to file a civil suit against Don unless Don contracts to discharge the claim at a fixed sum. To avoid going to court, Don makes the contract. Carol's threat is not improper and the contract may not be avoided by Don.

Although contracts made under threat of a civil action ordinarily are not voidable, the threat must be made in good faith. That is, a threat to pursue an action known to be without legal basis is made in bad faith and is an abuse of the judicial process. The threat is therefore improper.

To constitute duress, the threat must both be improper and induce the making of the contract. Two points regarding inducement should be noted. First, to render a contract voidable, the victim of the threat must be left with no reasonable alternative to making the contract. Second, as in cases of fraud, a subjective test of inducement is applied. That is, the threat need only induce action by the person to whom directed. The law does not require that a reasonable or prudent person (representing an objective standard) would be so induced.

As the following case illustrates, duress in modern commercial contracts often takes the form of "economic duress" or "business compulsion."

Totem Marine Tug & Barge, Inc. v. Alyeska Pipeline Service Company

584 P.2d 15 (Alaska 1978)

Plaintiff Totem Marine Tug & Barge, Inc. (Totem) and defendant Alyeska Pipeline Service Company (Alyeska) entered into an agreement by which Totem agreed to transport construction materials from Houston, Texas, to Alaska via the Panama Canal. Because of unforeseen delays, Alyeska terminated the contract and took possession of the materials at Long Beach, California. Totem then submitted a bill of approximately $300,000 to Alyeska. The bill remained unpaid for almost two months during which Totem faced bankruptcy because it lacked cash to pay its creditors. Alyeska offered to settle the bill for $97,500 if Totem would sign an agreement releasing Alyeska from all claims by Totem. Totem accepted the offer, but later sued for damages equal to the unpaid balance on the bill. Totem also requested rescission of the release agreement alleging that it had been forced to sign the agreement under duress. The trial court granted summary judgment in favor of Alyeska. Totem appealed.

Burke, Justice

. . . This court has not yet decided a case involving a claim of economic duress or what is also called business compulsion. At early common law, a contract could be avoided on the ground of duress only if a party could show that the agreement was entered into for fear of loss of life or limb, mayhem or imprisonment. . . . The threat had to be such as to overcome the will of a person of ordinary firmness and courage. . . . Subsequently, however, the concept has been broadened to include myriad forms of economic coercion which force a person to involuntarily enter into a particular transaction. The test has come to be whether the will of the person induced by the threat was overcome rather than that of a reasonably firm person. . . .

At the outset it is helpful to acknowledge the various policy considerations which are involved in cases involving economic duress. Typically, those claiming such coercion are attempting to avoid the consequences of a modification of an original contract or of a settlement and release agreement. On the one hand, courts are reluctant to set aside agreements because of the notion of freedom of contract and because of the desirability of having private dispute resolutions be final. On the other hand, there is an increasing recognition of the law's role in correcting inequitable or unequal exchanges between parties of disproportionate bargaining power and a greater willingness to not enforce agreements which were entered into under coercive circumstances.

There are various statements of what constitutes economic duress. . . . Under [the standard used by many courts], duress exists where: (1) one party involuntarily accepted the terms of another, (2) circumstances permitted no other alternative, and (3) such circumstances were the result of coercive acts of the other party. . . .

As the above indicates, one essential element of economic duress is that the plaintiff show that the other party by wrongful acts or threats, intentionally caused him to involuntarily enter into a particular transaction. Courts have not attempted to define exactly what constitutes a wrongful or coercive act, as wrongfulness depends on the particular facts in each case. This requirement may be satisfied where the alleged wrongdoer's conduct is criminal or tortious but an act or threat may also be considered wrongful if it is wrongful in the moral sense. . . .

In many cases, a threat to breach a contract or to withhold payment of an admitted debt has constituted a wrongful act. . . . Implicit in such cases is the additional requirement that the threat to breach the contract or withhold payment be done in bad faith. . . .

Economic duress does not exist, however, merely because a person has been the victim of a wrongful act; in addition, the victim must have no choice but to agree to the other party's terms or face serious financial hardship. Thus, in order to avoid a contract, a party must also show that he had no reasonable alternative to agreeing to the other party's terms, or, as it is often stated, that he had no adequate remedy if the threat were to be carried out. . . . What constitutes a reasonable alternative is a question of fact, depending on the circumstances of each case. . . .

Turning to the instant case, we believe that Totem's allegations, if proved, would support a finding that it executed a release of its contract claims against Alyeska under economic duress. Totem has alleged that Alyeska deliberately withheld payment of an acknowledged debt, knowing that Totem had no choice but to accept an inadequate sum in settlement of that debt; that Totem was faced with impending bankruptcy; that Totem was unable to meet its pressing debts other than by accepting the immediate cash payment offered by Alyeska; and that through necessity, Totem thus involuntarily accepted an inadequate settlement offer from Alyeska and executed a release of all claims under the contract. If the release was in fact executed under these circumstances, we think that under the legal principles discussed above, that this would constitute the type of wrongful conduct and lack of alternatives that would render the release voidable by Totem on the ground of economic duress. . . .

[Judgment reversed and remanded.]

Undue Influence

Contracts formed under duress are tainted by the presence of coercion in various forms and degrees. Contracts voidable for **undue influence** are characterized by a subtler type of overreaching: unfair persuasion. The cases divide themselves into two broad categories. In the first, one person so psychologically dominates another that the dominant party is able to induce the other's assent to an unreasonably unfair or disadvantageous bargain. In the second, a relation of trust and confidence exists between the parties, but it is abused by one who uses that position to unfairly persuade the other to make the contract. Examples of such confidential relationships include parent-child, husband-wife, trustee-beneficiary, guardian-ward, attorney-client, and physician-patient.

Most undue influence cases result in an unusual or uncharacteristic transaction, conferring a disproportionate benefit upon the persuading party. Commonly, the victim of the persuasion is deceased at the time of trial. Cases, therefore, usually arise between the benefited party and the relatives or the estate of the deceased, who seek to recover property transferred during life, or in some cases, to set aside a will. Because the victim of undue influence is usually unavailable to testify, circumstantial evidence of unfair persuasion is usually required including, for example, evidence of the relationship between the parties, the unfairness of the resulting contract, and the susceptibility of the person influenced.

In the following case, the court was required to decide whether a contract was procured through undue influence.

Kase v. French

325 N.W.2d 678 (S.D. 1982)

In 1973, Olivia McWilliams entered into a contract to sell her home, an adjacent smaller dwelling, two lots, and all of the personal property located in the buildings to defendants Kenneth and Betty French. The agreement provided that the Frenches would pay $40,000 plus interest of one percent, with no down payment, in installments of $184 per month, the first payment to be made two years after the signing of the contract. The contract further provided that the Frenches would allow Mrs. McWilliams to occupy, rent free, an apartment in her home for two years. After the sale, the Frenches

moved in and provided Mrs. McWilliams an apartment there for a year and a half. Mrs. McWilliams then moved into a nursing home where she later died.

The administrator of the estate of Mrs. McWilliams sued the Frenches alleging that the sales contract had been procured through undue influence. The evidence at trial established at the time of the contract Mrs. McWilliams was a widow in her eighties who lived alone in a two-story house. She had a fourth-grade education and no business experience. For several years her nephew had assisted her in her business matters. In 1971, Mr. and Mrs. French, who were in their mid-forties, purchased a grocery store. While delivering groceries to Mrs. McWilliams, Mr. French told her of her resemblance to his grandmother and introduced her to Mrs. French. They developed a friendship and Mrs. French visited Mrs. McWilliams daily and helped her with household chores. About a month after the women met, Mrs. French told Mrs. McWilliams that she need never be lonely again because the Frenches would take care of her for the rest of her life.

The terms of the contract for the sale of the house had been arranged by Mrs. McWilliams and the Frenches but the contract had been drafted by Mrs. McWilliams's attorneys. Mr. and Mrs. French had obtained an appraisal of $35,000 for the real estate. They testified that Mrs. McWilliams wanted to charge no interest but because she thought it was illegal not to charge interest, they agreed to one percent interest. At the time of the sale, interest rates were six to eight percent, although the Frenches did not advise Mrs. McWilliams of the current rates. When Mrs. McWilliams had asked her attorney to draft the contract, he had tried to dissuade her from entering into the agreement. He also had asked her nephew to try to persuade her to change the terms of the contract. When neither was able to convince her to change her mind, the attorney drafted the contract. Thereafter, Mrs. McWilliams had advised her nephew that she no longer needed his assistance in business matters because the Frenches had agreed to assist her. Mrs. McWilliams then changed her accounts to joint accounts with the Frenches.

The trial court held that Mr. and Mrs. French had not exerted undue influence over Mrs. McWilliams and upheld the validity of the contract. Mrs. Mc-

Williams's administrator appealed. After finding that a confidential relationship existed between the parties at the time of the contract, the court addressed the undue influence issue.

Wollman, Justice

. . . The indicia of undue influence are: person susceptible to undue influence, opportunity to exert undue influence and effect wrongful purpose, disposition to do so for improper purpose, and result clearly showing effect of undue influence. . . . The trial court concluded that "at all times [Mrs. McWilliams] enjoyed good health, was able to care for herself, was mentally alert and competent to the time of her death, was a strong-willed person and independent in her thinking, and was not weak willed or easily influenced." The record supports this finding. Even appellant in his brief describes Mrs. McWilliams as a "strong willed and stubborn old lady, [who] was not about to take advice."

We cannot say that the contract for deed clearly shows the effect of undue influence. The Frenches called as a witness the realtor who had appraised the property at $35,000. While the interest and down-payment terms were certainly favorable to the Frenches, Mrs. McWilliams received the favorable term of being able to live rent free in an apartment for two years. Although the promise to take care of Mrs. McWilliams for the rest of her life was not incorporated into the contract for deed, Mrs. McWilliams did, in fact, live with Mr. and Mrs. French rent free for one and a half years. Also, when Mrs. McWilliams was later placed in a nursing home, Mrs. French signed an agreement which made her the responsible party in the event of problems with payment.

This court has recognized the presence of independent legal advice as an important factor to be considered in determining whether undue influence exists. . . . Appellant attempts to undermine the importance of the advice of Mrs. McWilliams' attorney, Mr. Christol, because his advice was neither accepted nor acted upon. Appellant characterizes Mr. Christol's role as one of a draftsman who simply reduced to writing what was already agreed upon. We cannot agree with this characterization. Mr. Christol had been the attorney for Mrs. McWilliams since 1965. He had also given legal advice to her deceased husband and sister. His advice to Mrs. McWilliams was anything other than perfunctory. . . .Merely because Mrs. McWilliams chose not to follow Mr. Christol's advice does not destroy the importance of her having received that advice.

The trial court found that the Frenches had neither taken unfair advantage of Mrs. McWilliams nor exerted undue influence upon her in any of their dealings. Given the trial court's opportunity to judge the credibility of the Frenches on the basis of their courtroom demeanor and testimony, we cannot say that this finding is clearly erroneous. . . .

[Judgment affirmed.]

SUMMARY

1. Various defects in the formation process such as fraud and misrepresentation, mistake, duress, and undue influence may render otherwise binding contracts voidable.

2. A misrepresentation is an assertion that is not in accord with existing fact. A misrepresentation, made with *scienter,* is fraudulent if made with knowledge of its falsity or reckless disregard of the truth. If one party is induced to enter into a contract because of a misrepresentation by the other, the contract is voidable by the recipient. Additionally, if the misrepresentation is fraudulent, dollar damages may be recovered by the reliant party in tort for fraud.

3. Liability for fraud is imposed if one party makes a fraudulent material misrepresentation of existing fact upon which the other justifiably relies to his injury. The misrepresentation may be made by language (an express misrepresentation), by other conduct intended or likely to prevent the other from learning of the fact (concealment), or by silence (nondisclosure) in a limited class of cases in which the law imposes a duty to speak. Facts which may be misrepresented include not only the existence or characteristics of a tangible thing, the occur-

rence of an event, or the relationship between particular persons or things, but also a state of mind, such as a person's intention or opinion.

4. Regardless of the manner or content of the misrepresentation, the recipient must justifiably rely upon it. Thus, a person who knows a statement to be false or conducts an independent investigation which uncovers its falsity has not relied upon it. An independent investigation into the truth of statements made by the other party is not, however, required and whether reliance is justified is determined by considering any peculiar characteristics of the reliant party and the particular facts of the case. This approach protects persons who are gullible or negligent, those with the greatest need for protection from fraud.

5. A party seeking merely to avoid a contract on misrepresentation grounds may do so by proving that the misrepresentation was either fraudulent or material. The plaintiff need not prove actual harm resulting from reliance upon it. To recover for fraud, however, the plaintiff must prove that the misrepresentation relied upon was both fraudulent and material, and that he suffered monetary injury as a result. Most courts apply a "benefit of the bargain" test in computing damages in fraud actions. Under this test the plaintiff recovers the difference between what he actually received under the contract and what he would have received had the false statements, in fact, been true.

6. Liability for fraud and misrepresentation results from a mistake of fact caused by one of the parties. Occasionally, one or both parties are mistaken concerning a relevant fact for reasons not dependent upon the assertion of either party. Relief for such mistakes, in the form of avoidance of the contract, is given under very limited circumstances. For example, avoidance by the adversely affected party is allowed if both parties are mistaken (a mutual mistake) concerning the existence, identity, quantity, or other qualities or characteristics of the subject matter. Avoidance is not available simply because one party is mistaken concerning the value of the subject matter or the difficulty or expense of performance. Similarly, other unilateral mistakes, such as errors in computing an offer, do not provide grounds for avoidance, unless the nonmistaken party knows or should know of the mistake.

7. Contracts may also be voidable due to an element of compulsion or coercion (duress) or unfair persuasion (undue influence) in the bargaining process. Duress takes two forms, physical compulsion and improper threat. Undue influence usually results either from psychological domination of one party by the other or from abuse of a relationship of trust and confidence between the parties.

KEY TERMS

misrepresentation	mistake
fraudulent	unilateral mistake
scienter	mutual mistake
fraud (deceit)	duress
concealment	undue influence
material	

QUESTIONS AND PROBLEMS

11-1 Denise owned an appliance store that she wanted to sell. Because the business had been a perennial money loser she falsified the financial statements to indicate that the business was profitable. Claude purchased the business for $20,000, a fair price on the basis of the information supplied. Shortly thereafter he discovered the true financial picture indicating the business was worth $5,000.

(a) Assuming Claude can prove that Denise altered the financial statements, upon what legal theory should he sue her?

(b) What possible remedies could Claude obtain?

(c) If Claude attempts to prove that Denise has made a misrepresentation, could Denise defend on the ground that no misrepresentation was made because she merely supplied the financial statements, but never talked to him?

(d) The facts indicate that Claude relied upon the false financial statements. What standard is utilized to determine whether or not a person's reliance upon a representation is justified? Was Claude's reliance justifiable?

11-2 Consider whether, and under what circumstances, a fraud action could be maintained by Bob in the following situations.

(a) Sam, in order to induce Bob to buy his 100 shares of XYZ Corporation stock states to Bob that "This stock will pay dividends within five years that will equal or exceed the purchase price I am asking." Partly in reliance upon Sam's statement, Bob purchases the stock. XYZ Corporation subsequently goes bankrupt without paying any dividends.

(b) Helen, in need of money, is negotiating for a loan from Bob. Helen tells Bob that she intends to use the money to expand her business and purchase new equipment. Helen's actual intention is to use the money to invest heavily in the commodities market and speculative mining stocks. Partly in reliance on Helen's statement, Bob loans her $50,000. Helen loses everything in the commodities market.

(c) Joan and Bob are negotiating for the sale of Joan's XYZ Corporation stock. Both parties have equal access to information on the earnings of XYZ and corporate earnings generally. Joan tells Bob that in her opinion XYZ stock is a "first class security" and "worth $100 per share." In reliance on Joan's statement, Bob buys the stock which proves to be worthless.

(d) Sam is negotiating the sale of his commercial building to Bob. Tom is a tenant in the building under a long-term lease. Sam, in order to induce Bob to buy, states that, in his opinion, Tom is a "good" tenant. In fact, as Sam knew, Tom had been consistently delinquent in rent payments and had damaged the premises in the past. Partially in reliance upon Sam's statement, Bob purchased the building. Tom moved out shortly thereafter, leaving the premises in a shambles and a substantial amount of rent unpaid.

11-3 (a) Consider the *Raffles v. Wichelhaus* case (page 253). Would a contract have resulted if both parties had intended the same *Peerless*? If the same *Peerless* was intended does it make any difference whether or not the parties knew or had reason to know that there were two ships? Assume alternatively that the seller knew that two ships named *Peerless* were sailing from Bombay on different dates. Would a contract have resulted if the seller knew that the buyer intended *Peerless* #1 (October) and that the buyer was unaware that two ships existed? If a contract exists, from what ship?

(b) Consider the *Oswald v. Allen* case (page 253). Dr. Oswald was an expert in coins. Evidence adduced at the trial indicated that the coins in the "Swiss Collection" were fairly valued at at least $50,000. Additionally, the few Swiss coins in the "Rarity Collection" were themselves valued at $62,000. On these facts, the trial court found it "inconceivable" that Mrs. Allen intended to sell all of her Swiss coins for $50,000. Given these facts, is *Oswald v. Allen* an inappropriate case for application of the misunderstanding rule of *Raffles v. Wichelhaus?* Explain.

11-4 Mildred owned twenty-three acres of land at the edge of a large city. Because she was having difficulty paying the expenses of the property, Mildred entered into a contract with Robert, a real estate developer. Mildred agreed to transfer half of the property to Robert who agreed to pay some of the expenses of the property. They further agreed to develop the property into a condominium project from which Mildred and Robert would share profits. Immediately after they signed the agreement, interest rates rose causing the costs of construction to skyrocket. Additionally, the city widened a street making the property less desirable for residential units. As a result, no condominium project was built. Mildred sued Robert and requested the court to rescind the contract on the grounds that the parties had entered into the agreement under the mutual mistake that the property could be profitably developed. Should the court grant rescission? Explain.

11-5 Jewell, an elderly widow, owned several parcels of real estate. Jewell's closest relative was her nephew, Hoyt. Upon Hoyt's recommendation, Jewell executed two contracts by which she promised to sell her real property to her nephew. The contracts were prepared by Jewell's attorney. Jewell later sued to have the contracts rescinded. Although each document was clearly marked "Contract to Sell Property" she alleged that her nephew had led her to believe the documents were merely power of attorney forms. Jewell further alleged that she and her nephew stood in a confidential relationship that her nephew had exploited by exercising undue influence to induce her to sign the contracts. Is Jewell correct in asserting that undue influence is the appropriate grounds for rescission? Do the facts suggest that other grounds for rescission might exist? Explain.

11-6 In January 1977, Quinn, a stock broker employed by Humphrey Co., convinced Emma to buy 250 shares of a mutual fund by threatening her with bodily violence if she refused to buy. Emma bought the shares. Several months later Quinn was arrested on another matter and subsequently was fired by his employer. Emma continued to hold the shares of the mutual fund and received dividends until 1979 when she sold them for a loss of $35,000. Emma sued Humphrey Co. for damages based on the fact that she had been forced by duress into purchasing the shares. How should the court rule? Explain.

11-7 Beatty, a Montana rancher, sold a portion of his

land to the United States government. The government needed the land for a reservoir to be constructed in conjunction with a dam on the Missouri River. After the sale, Beatty sued the government seeking to avoid the contract alleging that he had been induced to sell the land through fear and duress. Beatty claimed that the government agents had threatened to have the property condemned through legal proceedings if he refused to sell at the price offered by the agents. Although Beatty would have received the fair market value of the land if the property were condemned, the agents stated that Beatty's attorneys' fees would consume the amount paid for the property and that Beatty might not receive payment until twenty-five years later.

The agents knew that these statements were false. Is the government guilty of duress? What factors should the court consider in resolving the dispute?

Chapter 12

Written Agreements

Major Topics

- the advantages of a written over an oral contract
- the basic principles courts use to interpret both oral and written agreements
- the parol evidence rule which determines the legal consequences of a writing adopted by contracting parties as the final expression of their agreement
- the statute of frauds, which requires that certain types of contracts be evidenced by a writing to be enforceable

Contrary to popular belief, contracts generally are not required to be written to be enforceable. Both the common law and the Uniform Commercial Code recognize and enforce a wide variety of oral contracts. A formal written contract, however, has distinct advantages over an oral contract because the writing can substantiate the existence and terms of the agreement in a dispute. A writing is particularly valuable in ongoing business relationships such as agency and employment, partnership and corporations, or when a business is sold. The use of written contracts, incorporating all agreed terms and addressing all anticipated contingencies, is a sound business practice. The more comprehensive the writing, the more protection is afforded the parties, because once a dispute arises, agreement on any issue may be impossible. In addition, costly

litigation frequently can be avoided, because rights and duties of the parties are determined in advance, and potential misunderstandings may be uncovered during the process of reducing the agreement to writing.

A written contract, however, is no insurance against controversy. In both oral and written agreements, misunderstandings, missing terms, and ambiguous language often make it difficult to determine the scope and extent of the parties' contractual undertaking. Various legal principles are designed to aid the courts in determining the meaning of a contract or term.

A common interpretation question concerns the legal effect of the adoption of a writing. Contracting parties frequently conduct lengthy preliminary negotiations ultimately incorporated into a written contract. Disputes often arise when preliminary understandings conflict with the contents of the writing. The court must then determine the terms of the contract in light of conflicting evidence presented by the parties. This issue is governed by the parol evidence rule, which generally prevents admission of evidence of preliminary negotiations or prior agreements to contradict a writing adopted as the final expression of an agreement.

Although many agreements are reduced to writing, as a general rule no writing is prerequisite to legal recognition of a contract. Contracts subject to the Statute of Frauds provide a major exception to this rule. The Statute of Frauds requires that certain types of contracts be evidenced by a writing to be enforceable. Knowing which contracts are subject to the Statute of Frauds is fundamental to basic contract study. This chapter discusses general principles of contract interpretation, the parol evidence rule, and the various types of contracts rendered unenforceable by the Statute of Frauds in the absence of a writing.

Contract Interpretation

Interpretation is the process by which a court ascertains the meaning of a contract or contract term. Courts must interpret contracts when the parties become deadlocked concerning the scope of their contractual undertakings. In these cases, the court must examine a variety of evidence in order to ascertain the *intention* of the parties, the basic inquiry in contract interpretation.

If the contract is oral, the court's interpretation process is extremely perilous. The terms of the contract must be proven by oral testimony of the parties or others and circumstantial evidence including the parties' conduct before or after making the alleged contract. Testimony on the term or issue in dispute is certain to be self-serving or ambiguous, a situation often leading the court to find that the parties had not reached agreement on the matter in question. The court, if it wishes to enforce the contract, is then required to supply the missing or disputed terms.[1]

Although a carefully drafted, comprehensive written contract unquestionably prevents countless contract disputes, potential pitfalls remain. The disputed issue may not be covered in the writing (again requiring the court to supply a term) and even if it is, the words used may be ambiguous or their meaning may be affected by the context (technical or other), by trade usage, or by typographical errors. Terms may be inadvertently included or excluded. And, even if the language is clear, the parties' subsequent conduct may indicate a modification of the term outlined in the writing.

Courts every day are required to resolve these and many other interpretation problems in a wide

variety of oral and written contracts. The law has developed various guidelines to aid courts in interpreting contracts. Initially, public policy and considerations of fairness provide a general guide to courts in determining the scope of a contractual undertaking. For example, the duty of good faith pervades contracts generally and forms the background against which all contracts are interpreted. Similarly, unconscionability and other public policy restrictions limit the range of permissible contract obligations. Interpretation standards also are derived from general contract theory, most notably the objective theory of contracts. That is, in ascertaining the extent of a contractual obligation, the courts examine the impression each party created in the other—each party's objective manifestation of assent—rather than any subjective or hidden intention.

Against this basic framework, the law supplies more specific interpretation aids.

1. Generally, a contract is interpreted as a whole and in a manner designed to give a lawful and reasonable meaning to all terms. Words or other conduct are interpreted by taking all circumstances into account, particularly the purpose and intention of the parties when making the bargain. Language is usually given its general meaning. If, however, the transaction arises in an industry or discipline using technical terms, such terms are interpreted according to their technical meaning.

2. Language within the contract is interpreted according to common sense priorities. Specific language takes precedence over conflicting general language. Separately negotiated terms or terms added to the basic bargain are preferred over conflicting language in a standardized contract.

3. Because the party choosing the language used commonly protects his own interest, any ambiguity in that language commonly is interpreted according to the other party's meaning. This principle is particularly applicable to standardized form ("adhesion") contracts in which one party drafts the entire contract and offers it to the other on a "take it or leave it" basis. In adhesion contracts, construction against the draftsman is often intertwined with the courts' refusal to enforce, as unconscionable, the term or clause involved.

4. A contract is to be interpreted in light of all circumstances including not only the express terms

---

1. Contract terms supplied by the court in absence of agreement are discussed throughout the contracts and sales material. The most notable source of such "gap fillers" is Article 2 of the UCC.

of the contract, but also the conduct of the parties, including performance under the disputed contract or other contracts. Additionally, any customs or conventions of the particular trade or business involved are considered.[2] In the following case the court was required to resolve a dispute over the meaning of the language of a written contract.

RCI Northeast Services Division v. Boston Edison Company

822 F.2d 199 (1st Cir. 1987)

In response to a request for bids from defendant Boston Edison Company (Edison), plaintiff RCI Northeast Services Division (RCI) submitted a bid to perform construction at Edison's nuclear power plant. RCI described its bid as a "cost plus percentage fee" proposal and enclosed various schedules setting forth its labor costs and equipment charges. The page describing labor costs included the following provision: "Labor cost rates include all costs, burdens, insurances and taxes applicable, based on current labor rates and are subject to escalation." Edison selected RCI to perform the contract and issued a series of purchase orders stating that the work was to be performed on a "cost plus fee basis" and that billings were to be "in accordance with the [RCI] proposal on file with Edison." RCI performed the work in 1981 and 1982 during which it submitted periodic billings. In December, 1983, eighteen months after completion of the project, RCI submitted a final bill in the amount of $185,535 claiming that the amount was an additional billing for workers' compensation insurance on the project.

After Edison refused to pay the final bill, RCI sued. The evidence established the RCI's insurer required RCI to pay estimated premiums during the project but that actual premium costs were determined following completion of the project based on job-related injuries that occurred during the construction. RCI established that this type of insurance

policy was not uncommon in the industry and had been used in contracts with other utility companies. The trial court ruled in favor of RCI and awarded damages of $185,535. Edison appealed.

Selya, Circuit Judge

. . . The issue in this case is a straightforward one. From RCI's standpoint, the contract documents specifically protected it against mounting insurance costs, thus shifting the burden of the retrospective workers' compensation premium hike to Edison. The defendant reads the same language quite differently: the base labor rate alone was subject to change, and the associated "burdens," including compensation insurance, would fluctuate only in direct proportion to, and in the same percentage as, the base labor rate itself. In short, Edison maintains that the contract price was not meant to change in accordance with increases in raw insurance costs. . . .

We start our discussion of the merits with the disputed sentence itself. We repeat it here for ease in reference:

> Labor cost rates include all costs, burdens, insurances and taxes applicable, based on current labor rates and are subject to escalation.

The least forced reading of the language is to the effect that "labor cost rates" include a variety of components—"costs, burdens, insurances and taxes"—and that these components, as well as the labor rates themselves, "are subject to escalation." Whatever may be said, pro and con, as to whether this is the *only* reasonable construction of the clause, it is surely a plausible interpretation. And Massachusetts law—which governs in this diversity action—favors the construction of terms "according to their ordinary meaning." *Thomas v. Hartford Accident & Indemnity Co.,* [500 N.E.2d 810 (Mass. 1986).]

Once the switch of inquiry is thrown, the case is made the clearer. It is hornbook law that,

> If the language of the contract is susceptible of more than one interpretation, the court should construe the contract in the light of the situation and relation of the parties at the time it was made, and, if possible, accord it a reasonable and sensible meaning, consonant with its dominant purpose.

---

2. The effect of course of performance, course of dealing, and usage of trade upon contract interpretation and the standards of preference among them are discussed later in this chapter.

Continental Bus System, Inc. v. NLRB, 325 F.2d 267, 273 (10th Cir. 1963). . . . And, as the Court has instructed,

> The intention of the parties is to be gathered, not from [a] single sentence . . . , but from the whole instrument read in the light of the circumstances existing at the time of negotiations leading up to its execution.

Miller v. Robertson, . . . 45 S.Ct. 73, 76 . . . (1924).

Here, it was Edison that determined to let the contract on the basis of the vendor's costs, supplemented by a reasonable profit. It was Edison which, in its purchase orders, stated that RCI was to perform the work "on a cost plus fee basis." The notion that RCI should absorb increases in its insurance costs for the job, rather than pass such increases along to the owner, is at odds with the "dominant purpose" of the cost-plus arrangement. [Edison] points out, correctly, that cost-plus contracts can come in varying shapes and sizes, and can be tailored to suit the specific needs of any set of contracting parties. That is certainly true—but it is of marginal relevance on the record before us. Although it would have been possible for the parties to have limited the pass-through of insurance expense in some artificial way, there is nothing in the language of the contract, the relationship of the parties, or the situation as a whole which suggests such was the case. Defining the contours of the escalator in terms of real cost increases rather than in the palpably obscure manner suggested by [Edison] fits much more comfortably into the everyday context of the deal. . . .

There would be scant utility in any further analysis. In the arena of commerce, it avails us little to stand language on its ear in an effort to rescue a firm from a sinkhole of its own design. It is no appropriate part of judicial business to rewrite contracts freely entered into between sophisticated business entities. Rather, the courts must give effect to the language of such agreements and to their discernible meaning. That is exactly what has occurred: the district judge adopted the most natural reading of the disputed sentence, ascertained that the parties intended the clause to operate in precisely that way, and decided the case accordingly.

His finding that, under the purchase orders, RCI was entitled to recoup from Edison the augmented costs attributable to the retrospective insurance premium increases enjoys adequate record support. . . .

[Judgment affirmed.]

Effect of Adoption of a Writing: The "Parol Evidence Rule"

Despite the protection offered by written contracts, they also create special interpretation problems. For example, courts frequently must determine the legal effect of a writing adopted by the parties as a final expression of their agreement. To illustrate the problem, assume Bill, a banker, is considering construction of a new, expanded bank building. Bill contacts Sam, a contractor, and the two begin preliminary negotiations for a contract to construct the building. Over a period of months, the parties meet several times to discuss various issues such as building materials, price, financing, and completion schedule. Various understandings are reached, some oral, others incorporated in informal memoranda and business correspondence. Ultimately, the parties reach final agreement and reduce their construction contract to a writing signed by both parties. Some of the previous understandings are incorporated into the writing, others are not. Some of the preliminary understandings are modified by the writing, which also includes terms not previously discussed.

If a dispute later arises concerning the terms of the construction contract, the court is often required to determine the relationship between the writing and the prior understandings and negotiations it incorporates. The basic question is to what extent, if at all, parol evidence may be admitted in court to supplement or contradict the terms contained in the writing. **Parol evidence** includes oral or written evidence of prior or contemporaneous (occurring at the same time as the final writing) agreements or negotiations and more generally anything not contained in the writing itself. The principles governing the legal effect of the writing and the admissibility of parol evidence to supplement or contradict it are embodied in the parol evidence rule.

The Parol Evidence Rule

The **parol evidence rule** provides that if the parties adopt a writing that is intended to be a final expression of some or all terms of their agreement, then all prior or contemporaneous, oral or written, agreements are discharged to the extent that they are within the scope of, or are inconsistent with, the writing. It is commonly stated that such prior agreements and negotiations are "merged" into the finalized writing. Because, under the rule, the writing effectively *becomes* the agreement, parol evidence is not admissible in court to vary or contradict the terms of the writing. The rule, however, has no application whatsoever to a subsequent modification of the final writing, whether that modification be oral or written. Figure 12–1 illustrates the application of the rule.

The parol evidence rule is designed to protect the integrity of the final writing, which is adopted to provide reliable evidence of the existence and terms of the contract, against contradiction by evidence of prior understandings, negotiations, or agreements of the parties. The rule limits what can be admitted as evidence to establish the terms of the contract in a lawsuit between the parties. It does not determine the interpretation placed upon that evidence by the trier of fact, generally the jury. In other words, when the terms of a written contract are in dispute, the jury will consider the writing together with any other evidence the court admits and reach its own conclusion concerning the scope of the parties' contractual undertaking.

"Integration" Defined. The parol evidence rule applies only to writings that constitute a final written expression of one or more terms of the agreement. This finalized writing is referred to as an **integrated agreement.** Integration may be **complete** (a complete and exclusive statement of the terms of the agreement) or **partial** (conclusive on some but not all issues). Because integration is frequently difficult to ascertain, parol evidence is admissible to establish, as a question of fact, whether or not the writing constitutes an integrated agreement and, if so, whether the integration is partial or complete.

Partial Integration. If the court finds the writing to be only a partial integration, evidence of agreements not covered by the writing is admissible. That is, because the entire agreement has not been reduced to a writing, parol evidence may be admitted, not to vary or contradict the writing, but to establish other terms or agreements necessary to ascertain the entire contract of the parties.

In the following case, the court was required to decide whether a written contract constituted a complete or merely partial integration.

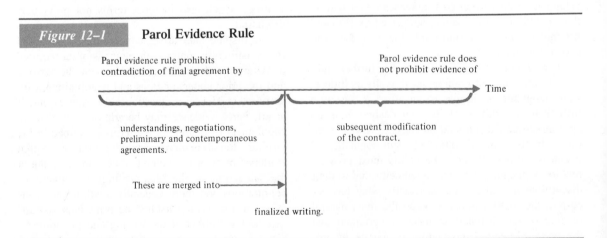

| *Figure 12–1* | **Parol Evidence Rule** |

Parol evidence rule prohibits contradiction of final agreement by

Parol evidence rule does not prohibit evidence of

→ Time

understandings, negotiations, preliminary and contemporaneous agreements.

subsequent modification of the contract.

These are merged into⟶

finalized writing.

Welborn v. Rogue Community College District

554 P.2d 535 (Or. App. 1976)

Plaintiff, Gay Welborn, accepted a teaching position at Rogue Community College commencing at the start of the 1974-1975 school year. The parties signed a one-year employment contract that the college president had sent to Welborn with a cover letter stating in part:

> It is a pleasure to send you a contract for teaching at Rogue Community College. Please sign the original copy and return it to me. It is intended that the contract for 1975-76 will be written for twelve months (240 days) beginning July 1, 1975.

During the 1974-1975 school year, the college notified Welborn that he would not be rehired for the subsequent school year.

Welborn sued defendant, Rogue Community College District, for breach of contract alleging that the college had agreed to hire him for at least a two-year period. He offered the letter from the president of the college as evidence of a two-year agreement. Welborn further alleged that prior to the signing of the contract, the dean of the college orally had agreed to a two-year period of employment. Welborn alleged that this oral agreement had not been included in the written contract because that contract was considered by the parties to be a "year-to-year formality." The College objected to the admission of any evidence of an agreement except the written one-year contract signed by the parties on the ground that such evidence was barred by the parol evidence rule.

The trial court refused to admit evidence of the oral agreement and granted judgment in the College's favor. Welborn appealed.

Tanzer, Judge

. . . The parol evidence rule is one of substantive law. It defines the contract. It is based upon the premise that the reduction to writing of any agreed upon term supersedes all negotiations and oral understandings as to that term. Therefore, parol evidence regarding terms which have been memorialized in writing is inadmissible to vary the writing, but there is no bar to parol evidence of agreements or terms of agreements which are not integrated into the writing. . . .

In this case the alleged oral agreement for a two-year contract of employment is not inconsistent with the written contract which sets out the terms of employment for the first year. Furthermore, the specific terms of employment such as salary might naturally be made as a separate agreement between the employer and employee where, as here, such terms can be expected to change annually, but the general agreement is for a longer period. Thus, parol evidence is admissible to show the co-existence of a longer term oral contract of employment with an annual collective bargaining agreement. . . .

Whether all of the terms of agreement between the parties have been integrated into the writing or whether terms exist in addition to those which were integrated into the writing is a question of fact in each case. . . . to be determined from the surrounding circumstances of the agreement. . . .

Here, the plaintiff's testimony of his agreement with representatives of the college that the contract of employment would last for at least two years and that the written contract was an annual formality, together with the reference in the college president's cover letter to the anticipated terms of the second year contract, are enough evidence to take to the jury the question of fact of whether plaintiff's allegation of the existence of a two-year contract was true. . . .

[Judgment reversed and remanded.]

Complete Integration; Collateral Contracts. As outlined above, if the parties adopt a partial integration, parol evidence is admissible to establish the remaining terms of the contract. Similarly, evidence of an agreement not within the scope of a completely integrated writing is admissible. In other words, the rule does not bar proof of a collateral contract—one related to but not part of the integrated contract, and which is not inconsistent with it. This rule, commonly referred to as the **collateral contract doctrine** is illustrated by the following case.

High Knob, Incorporated v. Allen

138 S.E.2d 49 (Va. 1964)

George Allen and J. R. Roberson, Jr. entered into separate written contracts to purchase lots in a residential subdivision developed by High Knob, Incorporated. The contracts were silent concerning the source of water for residences to be built on the lots, but a provision in the deeds provided that no well could be drilled on the property. Both Roberson and Allen testified, however, that during the course of the negotiations, Mr. McElroy, High Knob's secretary, orally stated that High Knob had a water system and would furnish water to the houses to be constructed in the subdivision for a $200 hook-up fee, which would be the only consideration paid for water service. Partially on the basis of this representation, Allen and Roberson were induced to purchase lots. After building their houses, Allen and Roberson connected to the water main and tendered the $200 fee, which was refused. Six months later, High Knob tendered a water service contract to Allen and Roberson that both refused to sign because it was not in accordance with the original oral agreement. High Knob then severed their water connections by installing cutoff valves.

Allen and Roberson sued to have water service restored. After considering all the evidence, including testimony concerning the alleged oral agreement, the trial court permanently restrained High Knob from cutting off Allen's and Roberson's supply of water. High Knob appealed, asserting that testimony concerning the oral contract should be inadmissible under the parol evidence rule because it varied the terms of the written sales contracts.

I'anson, Justice

. . . It is universally accepted that parol or extrinsic evidence will be excluded when offered to add to, subtract from, vary or contradict the terms of a written contract. But there are well-recognized exceptions to the rule. Where the entire agreement has not been reduced to writing, parol evidence is admissible, not to contradict or vary its terms but to show additional independent facts contemporaneously agreed upon, in order to establish the entire contract between the parties. This is generally referred to as the partial integration doctrine. . . .

Another exception to the rule, which is similar in many respects to the partial integration doctrine, is the collateral contract doctrine. Under this doctrine the parol evidence rule does not exclude parol proof of a prior or contemporaneous oral agreement that is independent of, collateral to and not inconsistent with the written contract, and which would not ordinarily be expected to be embodied in the writing. . . .

In the present case, the written contracts for the sale of the lots were silent as to how Allen and Roberson were to obtain water for their homes. The covenants in the deeds forbidding them from drilling a well or in any other manner taking water from the ground for use in their dwellings, indicate that since [Allen and Roberson] were unable to take water from the ground there must of necessity have been some independent, collateral agreement for obtaining water. It is inconceivable that Allen and Roberson would covenant not to take water from the ground on their own property unless there had been an agreement to obtain it from another source. The written contracts dealt with the sale of property, and since there was to be an additional consideration paid for connecting to the water system, and this subject would not ordinarily be included in a contract for the sale of land, there is a strong indication that the parties were dealing with this question in collateral agreements. The oral agreements were not inconsistent with the written sales contracts and did not vary or contradict their terms. Even High Knob recognized that the question of furnishing water was to be covered in an independent collateral agreement when it submitted water service contracts to Allen and Roberson. Thus the evidence was admissible to prove the oral agreements, and did not violate the parol evidence rule. . . .

[Judgment affirmed.]

Complete Integration; Effect of Merger Clause.

In many cases, the parties adopt a complete integration. If the writing is specific, detailed, comprehensive, and carefully drafted, the court may find that it evidences the final and complete expression of the agreement. Under the common law rule, a writing apparently complete on its face is presumed to be a complete integration in the absence of contrary evidence.

The parties sometimes explicitly indicate their intention that the writing operate as a complete integration by using a **merger** or **integration clause**. These clauses expressly state that the writing is the entire agreement of the parties, and that there are no understandings, promises, or representations except those contained therein. Merger clauses are generally valid and will be enforced by the court. The use of a merger clause generally precludes the court from finding that the writing is not a complete integration. The clause is especially useful when the parties are involved in extended negotiations, in which many proposals are made, altered, or withdrawn. When an agreement is finally reached and reduced to writing, the merger clause prevents either party from offering evidence of prior proposals or negotiations to contradict the writing.

Although a merger clause provides strong evidence that the writing is a complete integration, its use does not necessarily resolve the issue. All relevant evidence should be considered, particularly when the clause is not the result of arm's length bargaining but is imposed by one party in a standardized form (adhesion) contract. For example, merger clauses in form contracts frequently disclaim liability for statements made by the seller's agents or employees not contained in the writing. The clause in this case is inserted to protect the seller against liability for unauthorized oral representations made by an over-zealous salesperson. When used in consumer transactions, however, giving literal effect to the clause may defeat the reasonable expectations of the adhering party. For example, assume a salesperson makes representations or promises to a buyer to induce her to buy a product. When the buyer signs the seller's form contract to purchase, the representations are not included in the writing, which contains a merger clause. In these cases, the clause should be ineffective unless actually agreed upon.

The parties may create a contract orally even though they have agreed to reduce it to a later writing. Whether or not the oral agreement is binding is based upon the intent of the parties, which is frequently difficult to determine. If the parties intend not to be bound until an integrated writing is executed, no contract exists until then. In this case, the preliminary negotiations and agreements do not constitute the contract. The parties may, however, view the writing merely as a memorandum of their previous oral agreement. In this case, the oral agreement is binding even if the writing is not adopted by the parties.

Exceptions to the Parol Evidence Rule

The trend in recent years is toward a more liberal attitude concerning the admissibility of parol evidence. Courts apparently believe that the risk in hearing such evidence—the possibility, for instance, that a contract or provision based upon perjured testimony will be enforced—is outweighed by a desire to enforce the entire agreement, including terms not stated in the writing. Further, as previously noted, the inapplicability of the rule does not dictate inclusion of any term, but merely affords a party the chance to prove its existence. Courts have therefore recognized several exceptions to the parol evidence rule, which, when combined with evidence admitted under principles of integration outlined above, substantially limit the actual effect of the rule. These exceptions are discussed below.

1. Parol evidence may be admitted to establish fraud, duress, undue influence, illegality, or any other factor undermining the validity of the integrated writing. For example, if Seller and Buyer have a comprehensive written contract for the sale of land, Buyer may introduce evidence of a prior oral or written statement made by the seller that defrauded Buyer. In this case, Buyer is not trying to alter the terms of the written contract, but is attempting to show its voidable nature by virtue of fraud.

2. Parol evidence is admissible to show that the writing is subject to an oral condition. Assume a written contract requires Sam to convey land and Beth to pay the purchase price. Beth may introduce evidence that her duty was conditional upon her ability to obtain adequate mortgage financing, or subject to approval of an independent third party.

In other words, evidence of the existence of the condition is not subject to the rule.

3. Parol evidence may always be admitted to clarify ambiguous terms in the integrated writing. Ambiguity may arise either from the language used in the writing or in its application to a particular fact situation. Assume Seller and Buyer have a contract for sale of goods to be manufactured by Seller. The parties have adopted a writing in which Buyer agrees to pay Seller's "total cost." Evidence of previous negotiations of the parties is admissible to determine the meaning of "total cost."

UCC Parol Evidence Rule—§2-202

The Uniform Commercial Code retains the parol evidence rule for Code contracts. Section 2-202 provides that terms of a contract for the sale of goods

1. upon which the confirmatory memoranda of the parties agree, or
2. which are otherwise set forth in a writing intended by the parties as a final expression of their agreement with respect to the terms included in the writing,

may not be contradicted by evidence of any prior agreement or of a contemporaneous oral agreement. Under the Code, however, the contract terms may be *explained or supplemented* by (1) course of dealing, or (2) usage of trade, or (3) course of performance.[3]

A **course of dealing** is a sequence of conduct between the parties prior to the agreement establishing a common basis of understanding for interpreting their expressions and other conduct.[4] For example, previous contracts between the parties may establish a pattern of conduct useful in interpreting the disputed contract. A **usage of trade** is any regularly observed practice or method of dealing in a trade, place, or location.[5] For example, in

the lumber industry the description "2 by 4" means a board with dimensions approximately 1½" by 3½", not 2" by 4". The expression "2 by 4" is a usage of trade. Code requirements for proof of usage of trade are much less rigorous than those existing at common law. Common law courts generally required that the custom be lawful, universal, well-known, reasonable, continuous, ancient, certain, and precise. Under the UCC, the usage need only have "regularity of observance" in the place, trade, or vocation involved. This observance may exist either generally or only with respect to a special branch of the trade. The Code therefore opens the door to recognition of new customs, not just those already in existence.[6]

Course of performance is action taken by the parties pursuant to a contract involving repeated occasions for performance, such as an installment contract. In this situation, if either party has knowledge of the nature of the other's performance and an opportunity to object to it, any course of performance accepted or acquiesced in without objection is relevant to determine the meaning of the agreement. Course of performance is a valuable interpretation tool. Because the parties know best what their words of agreement mean, their subsequent conduct is the best indication of the meaning of the contract terms. In addition to aiding in interpretation, a course of performance that is inconsistent with an express term is relevant to show a waiver or modification of that term.[7]

Whenever possible in interpreting the contract, the court construes express terms as consistent with any course of performance, course of dealing, and usage of trade. If a conflict arises, however, and such a construction is unreasonable, the contract meaning is ascertained according to the following rules. The express terms control any course of performance. Course of performance controls both course of dealing and usage of trade. Course of dealing controls usage of trade.[8]

Under §2-202, evidence of *consistent additional terms* is also admissible to explain or to supplement

---

3. UCC §2-202(a).
4. UCC §1-205(1); see also *Restatement (Second) of Contracts* §223.
5. UCC §1-205(2); see also *Restatement (Second) of Contracts* §222.

6. UCC §1-205, Official Comments 5, 6, & 7.
7. UCC §2-208 and Official Comment 1.
8. UCC §§2-208(2), 1-205(4); see also *Restatement (Second) of Contracts* §§202(5), 203(b).

the writing unless the court finds that the writing was intended by both parties to be a complete and exclusive statement of the terms of the agreement—a complete integration.[9] In other words, if the writing is a complete integration, evidence of consistent additional terms is inadmissible.[10] As explained in Official Comment 3 to §2-202:

> If the additional terms are such that, if agreed upon, *they would certainly have been included* in the document in the view of the court, then evidence of their alleged making must be kept from the trier of fact. (Emphasis added.)

This approach has the effect of allowing evidence of consistent additional terms to be admitted in most cases. That is, it makes a finding of complete integration difficult, because to exclude the evidence the court must find that the offered term "would *certainly* have been included" in the writing. Therefore, unless the court makes that determination, evidence of the alleged additional term will be considered by the jury, who will then decide whether or not it was actually agreed upon.

The Statute of Frauds

One of the most important and frequently litigated contracts issues is the applicability of the **Statute of Frauds,** which simply requires that certain types of contracts be evidenced by a writing to be enforceable. The term "Statute of Frauds" was originally derived from the English or "common law" statute, but is now generally used to describe any statute imposing a writing requirement. Unless subject to some Statute of Frauds provision, a contract is enforceable in the absence of any writing.

The basic purpose of the Statute of Frauds is *evidentiary;* that is, "to require reliable evidence of the existence and terms of the contract, and to prevent enforcement through fraud or perjury of contracts never in fact made."[11] Certain Statute of Frauds provisions also perform a *cautionary* function; that is, the requirement of a writing provides additional protection to the promisor against enforcement of ill-considered, imprudent bargains. The statute also performs a *channeling* function, creating a climate in which the parties do not regard agreements as binding until put into writing and signed.

The original Statute of Frauds (formally entitled "An Act for the Prevention of Frauds and Perjuries"), usually referred to as the "common law" statute, originally was enacted in England in 1677.[12] The statute was passed when contract law was in its early developmental stages. In the fourteenth century, English courts began to enforce oral promises, commonly on the strength of oral testimony of witnesses. No distinct system of rules for excluding evidence, however, had yet been devised, and the power of courts to set aside jury verdicts contrary to the evidence was just beginning to be recognized. Further, neither the parties to the action nor persons having an interest in the outcome were competent to testify. These procedural deficiencies led to perpetration of fraud through the use of perjured testimony to bind persons to oral promises never in fact made. To illustrate, assume Brown falsely asserts that Smith has agreed to sell his farm to Brown. Brown induces Doaks to perjure himself (known as "subornation" of perjury) by saying that he had witnessed Smith's oral promise to convey. On these facts, at early common law, Smith could not testify that he made no such promise. Nor could Brown be called to testify in an effort to expose the fraud upon cross-examination.

To prevent this result, the Statute of Frauds was enacted to provide that certain *types* of contracts were unenforceable "unless the agreement . . . or some memorandum or note thereof, shall be in writing, and signed by the party to be charged. . . ."[13] A contract subject to the Statute of Frauds

---

9. UCC §2-202(b). This rule is followed for common law contracts by the *Restatement (Second) of Contracts* §216.

10. The court (judge), not the trier of fact (normally the jury), decides whether or not the writing constitutes a complete integration. The court will hear all testimony on the issue of finality and then determine whether evidence of additional terms is admissible to supplement or explain the terms of the writing which is already in evidence.

11. *Restatement (Second) of Contracts* §131 comment c.

12. 29 Car. 2, ch.3 (1677).

13. Language of §4 of the original English statute.

writing requirement is said to be "within the statute." The types of contracts within the statute, discussed below, include:

1. Suretyship contracts—promises to answer for the debt or duty of another;
2. Contracts for the sale of land or interests in land;
3. Contracts which cannot be performed within one year; and
4. Contracts made upon consideration of marriage.

Both parties need not sign the writing evidencing the contract, but the contract is only enforceable against a party who signs it. Thus, prior to a dispute, no one can determine which party's signature may be necessary. Each party therefore should be aware that it is the other party's signature that is important to enforceability. Assume S and B have a contract for the sale of land evidenced in a writing signed by S. B can enforce the contract against S, but S cannot enforce it against B.

The Statute of Frauds has been widely criticized as perpetrating far more fraud than it prevents. Even though the common law disability of a party to testify has long been removed, the statute has traditionally been interpreted as an absolute defense to enforceability. Under this approach, no matter how convincing the oral evidence may be, the contract is unenforceable if the statute's requirements are not met. Thus, parties have been able to avoid genuine bargains by hiding behind the statute, even while admitting the existence of the oral contract in court. The statute, therefore, has often been criticized as providing a "haven for welshers." The Statute of Frauds has also been criticized because the voluminous case law and numerous judge-made exceptions it has generated create uncertainty and unpredictability in the law. Further, a substantial amount of litigation has focused upon the sufficiency of the writing to the exclusion of the basic issue in dispute.

Though the original Statute of Frauds was repealed in England in 1954, statutes based upon it remain in effect in virtually all American jurisdictions. Further, additional writing requirements have been adopted, as indicated by the inclusion of several Statute of Frauds provisions in the UCC.[14] The belief apparently persists that writing requirements accomplish their desired purpose—to prevent the use of perjured testimony in contract cases. Additionally, because they create a climate in which written contracts are preferred, parties are induced, and therefore more likely, to put their deals in writing. The benefit derived from a writing in the vast bulk of cases in preventing misunderstanding and litigation may offset the occasional case in which the Statute of Frauds produces an unjust result. A writing requirement also seems to comport with the layman's conception about the enforceability of important contracts; that is, agreement is tentative until put into writing and signed.

The Common Law Statute

Suretyship Contracts—Promises to Answer for the Debt or Duty of Another. In a suretyship contract, one party (the surety) promises another (the creditor) to pay a debt owing from a debtor (or principal) to the creditor, if the debtor does not. Under the Statute of Frauds the promise by a surety to a creditor guaranteeing performance of a duty owed by a debtor to the creditor must be evidenced by a writing to be enforceable. Some states require that the writing state the consideration for the promise. Although the primary purpose of the Statute of Frauds is evidentiary, in suretyship contracts it also serves a cautionary function protecting the surety, who is commonly acting gratuitously and merely as a favor to the debtor, against ill-considered action.

To be subject to the Statute of Frauds, there must be a promise to answer for the duty of *another*. That is, the debtor (principal) must be under some duty to the promisee (the creditor) of the surety's promise. In other words, the surety's promise must be secondary (or "collateral") not primary (or "original"). Assume Dennis wishes to borrow

---

14. The Code contains four separate provisions imposing a writing requirement: (1) §2-201 relating to *goods*, (2) §8-319 relating to *securities*, (3) §9-203 covering agreements creating a *security interest* in personal property, and (4) §1-206 that concerns personal property not covered by the preceding three sections.

money or buy goods on credit from Charles. In order to induce Charles to deal with Dennis, Stan makes the following promise to Charles, "Lend money or sell property to Dennis. If he doesn't pay you, I will." Charles sells or extends credit to Dennis on this basis. In this case, the underlying duty is owed by the debtor to the creditor; Stan's promise is secondary, and is within the statute, thus requiring a writing, without regard to the dollar amount guaranteed.

On the other hand, if the debtor is under no duty to the creditor, the "surety's" promise is primary and need not be in writing unless subject to some other Statute of Frauds provision. Thus, in the preceding example, assume Stan obtains goods from Charles and orally states, "Send the bill to Dennis, if he doesn't pay, I will." Dennis has not authorized Stan to make credit purchases on his account, and makes no promise to pay for them. Stan's oral promise is enforceable because Dennis is under no duty to Charles.

A separate provision of the Statute of Frauds governs suretyship contracts made by executors or administrators. A promise by an executor or administrator of an estate to pay a debt of the deceased out of his own property is within the statute. This is merely a specialized application of the rule applicable to suretyship promises generally. As such it is subject to the same limitations and exceptions discussed above and in the following section.

The Main Purpose Rule. The **main purpose** or **leading object rule** provides an exception to the general rule requiring a writing for suretyship promises. Under the main purpose rule, a surety's oral promise is enforceable if it is made to benefit the surety's personal economic interest, rather than to aid the debtor. When the surety guarantees a debt to advance his own economic or business interests, the gratuitous element often present in suretyship is eliminated, and the commercial setting ordinarily provides evidentiary safeguards. Thus, the cautionary and evidentiary protection of the statute is not required, rendering an oral promise enforceable.[15]

---

15. *Restatement (Second) of Contracts* §116 comment a.

To illustrate, assume Shaw has a long-term contract with Bird to specially manufacture and deliver goods to Bird. Shaw encounters financial difficulty, resulting in a refusal by Shaw's suppliers to deliver additional raw materials. Bird, to ensure continued delivery from Shaw, orally promises the suppliers that if they will continue shipping to Shaw, Bird will pay if Shaw fails to do so. Bird's promise is not required to be evidenced by a writing because its primary purpose is to benefit Bird, not to accommodate Shaw. In this case, most courts would hold Bird's oral promise enforceable whether it related to past or future deliveries or both.

Assume, however, on these same facts that Shaw believes that with a little time she can extricate herself from her financial difficulties. Several of her creditors, however, are threatening legal proceeding which would force a closure of her business. Frost, a friend of Shaw, learns of her precarious financial position. In an effort to prevent Shaw's financial ruin, Frost promises the creditors that if they will postpone legal action for three months, he will pay Shaw's debts to them, if Shaw fails to do so. Frost's promise must be evidenced in writing because the consideration received for his promise (the forbearance to sue) primarily benefited Shaw. That is, the promise was made as an accommodation to Shaw; its purpose was not to further Frost's economic or business interests. In short, for the rule to apply, the circumstances must justify a conclusion that the surety's primary motive in making the promise is to advance his own interests.

The following case illustrates the application of the main purpose rule.

Graybar Electric Co. v. Sawyer

485 A.2d 1384 (Me. 1985)

Pine Tree Electrical Company, Inc. (Pine Tree), an electrical contracting firm, purchased supplies from Graybar Electric Co. (Graybar). In 1980, Hollis Sawyer invested $100,000 in Pine Tree and subsequently became vice president of the company. Later that year, Graybar cut off credit to Pine Tree because it was delinquent in paying its account. In September, Sawyer met with Graybar's finance manager and told him that if Pine Tree failed to pay its account, Sawyer would arrange to have it paid. Sawyer also provided a list of telephone numbers where he could be reached if problems arose. Graybar then wrote Sawyer a letter—which he denied having received—that stated: "Based on your willingness to have us contact you directly and your personal guarantee of payment; we will be happy to continue shipments to Pine Tree Electric." In June 1981, Pine Tree went bankrupt.

Graybar sued Sawyer for payment of Pine Tree's account. The jury found that Sawyer had agreed to guarantee the Pine Tree account and held him liable. Sawyer appealed, alleging that Graybar's suit was barred by Maine's Statute of Frauds, which requires a signed writing in a case against a person who has promised to answer for the debt of another.

McKusick, Chief Justice

. . . [T]he Statute of Frauds has . . . long been subject to an exception in a case where the promisor's main purpose in making his promise is to secure some benefit for himself. . . .

The benefit that a promisor must expect to receive under the main purpose rule in order to be held to his promise must be substantial, immediate, and pecuniary, though it may flow to the promisor through benefit to the principal obligor. . . . That is, although the promisor need not receive cash in hand from the promisee, the path of benefits flowing to the promisor must not be so circuitous or uncertain that obtaining those benefits cannot be said to have been his main purpose in making the promise. As a matter of practicality, the promisor's advantage must be served in a straightforward way in order for the main purpose rule to apply. . . .

The evidence before the jury amply supports its finding, under the instructions, that Sawyer intended by his promise to procure an immediate and substantial benefit flowing directly to himself. Sawyer had outstanding loans to Pine Tree of almost $300,000. He admitted in testimony that he needed to keep the business going in order to be paid back. The activities he undertook to get the business back on its feet financially were extensive. He followed upon his initial loan of $100,000 by lending Pine Tree further larger sums of money with the obvious purpose of keeping jobs going. . . . He guaranteed letters of credit necessary for Pine Tree to obtain two other jobs. He elected himself vice president,

and had an active hand in rejecting jobs and meeting with suppliers, and he maintained his involvement even while he was in Florida for substantial periods of time. He received interest on his loans to Pine Tree through the fall and winter of 1980 and the spring of 1981. He also received $18,000 in April of 1981 in partial repayment of the principal amount of the loans. He testified at length about his desire to increase Pine Tree's profitability so that he could be paid back. . . . Sawyer also stood to benefit in his capacity as sole preferred stockholder from any increase in the net worth of the company and from the quarterly dividends that Pine Tree was required to pay to him.

In view of the necessity of maintaining the flow of supplies to Pine Tree in order to keep the business going, and the necessity of its staying in business if Sawyer was to be repaid, the jury could reasonably find that Sawyer's oral promise, given to avoid serious difficulties for Pine Tree, was intended to confer on him a direct and substantial benefit. . . .

[T]he present case . . . falls within the accepted ambit of the main purpose doctrine.

[Judgment affirmed.]

Contracts for the Sale of Land or Interests in Land. A contract to buy or sell any interest in real property must be evidenced by a writing to be enforceable. Therefore, agreements to transfer fee simple title as well as more limited interests such as mortgages, easements, and leases are within the Statute of Frauds. Contracts creating other present or future interests such as life estates or remainders also are covered. Most Statutes of Frauds, however, exempt oral leases with a term of less than one year from the writing requirement (39 states). Some states enforce oral leases for longer terms (6 states), while others do not recognize an exception for short-term leases (5 states). The Statute of Frauds applies to any executory promise to buy or sell interests in real property regardless of the nature of the consideration exchanged—for example, money, personal property, services, or other real estate.

The "Part Performance" Doctrine. The **part performance doctrine,** which is based upon estoppel principles, provides an exception to the writing requirement for land sale contracts. For the doctrine to apply, the party seeking enforcement must show that he or she has changed position in reasonable reliance upon the oral contract. If necessary to avoid injustice, the court, exercising its equitable powers, will order performance of the contract.

The doctrine is usually applied when a seller of property refuses to convey it after the buyer has substantially relied upon an oral contract to sell existing between the parties. The buyer's reliance may take several forms including, for example, (1) payment of part or all of the purchase price, (2) taking possession of the property, and (3) making valuable improvements to the property. Generally, payment of the purchase price alone is insufficient, because returning the payment to the buyer in these cases is often an adequate remedy. Return of the price may, however, be inadequate because of an additional change in position by the buyer. Ordinarily, some combination of payment, possession, and improvements brings the doctrine into play. Assume S and B enter into an oral contract for sale of a tract of land owned by S. S allows B to take possession of the property, who pays part of the purchase price and constructs a house on the land. Two years later a dispute arises over the amount still owing and S repudiates the contract. Upon suit by B, the court may enforce the oral contract by ordering S to convey the land to B.

Contracts That Cannot Be Performed Within One Year.

The Statute of Frauds also applies to "any agreement that is not to be performed within the space of one year from the making thereof."[16] To determine whether or not a contract falls within this "one-year provision," three questions must be answered: (1) When does the one-year period commence? (2) Is the contract one that *cannot* be performed within that period? and (3) Has one party to the contract completed his performance? The answers to these questions are discussed below.

Commencement of the One-Year Period. Regarding the first question, the one-year period begins to run from the date the contract is made—when the offer is accepted—not the date on which performance is to begin. Assume A and B enter into a contract on January 1. Performance is to begin on February 1 and continue for one year from that date. The contract must be evidenced by a writing to be enforceable because the one-year period runs from January 1, not February 1. Similarly, a contract entered into on June 1, 1987, calling for performance from June 9 to June 10, 1988, must be evidenced by a writing.[17] The completion date, not the duration of performance, is relevant.

Oral leases provide an exception to the rule that the one-year period runs from the date of the contract. As previously noted, in most states an oral lease is enforceable if the term is shorter than one year. In these cases, the one-year period generally runs from the date the term begins, not the date of the agreement. For example, on June 1, L orally agrees to lease certain premises to T for one year commencing July 1. The agreement need not be in writing to be enforceable because the one-year period runs from July 1.

Possibility of Performance Within One Year. To be within the statute, the contract *by its terms* must be incapable of performance within one year. Therefore, if there is any possibility that the contract can be performed within a year of its making, it is not subject to the Statute of Frauds even though the actual performance takes more than one year. Assume Uncle says to Nephew, "If you will come and take care of me for the rest of my life, I promise to pay you $10,000." Nephew agrees and takes care of Uncle, who thereafter lives for ten years. The contract need not be evidenced by a writing to be enforceable because there was a *possibility* of performance within one year; that is, the uncle *could have* died within one year of the making of the contract. It is irrelevant that actual performance took substantially longer. The same result has been reached in contracts calling for performance "on or before," "within," or "not later than" a certain date. For example, if S agrees to deliver goods to B within thirteen months, no writing is necessary. Thus, in determining the applica-

---

16. Language of §4 of the original English statute.

17. The one-year period ends at midnight on the anniversary of the day on which the contract was made. For example, a contract entered into on December 1, 1987, requires a writing if it cannot be performed by midnight of December 1, 1988.

bility of the statute, subsequent performance is not considered. The statute does not apply, if, from the terms of the contract, there is any possibility of performance within one year.

The following case illustrates a typical application of this principle.

Chesapeake Financial Corporation v. Laird
425 A.2d 1348 (Md. 1981)

Appellees Donald Laird and Joseph Martin were real estate developers who entered into an oral contract with appellant Chesapeake Financial Corporation (Chesapeake). The contract provided that the parties would engage in a joint venture to develop a tract of real estate for which Chesapeake would provide financing. Chesapeake later refused to provide funding for the project. Laird and Martin sued Chesapeake (and one of its officers) for damages resulting from Chesapeake's alleged misrepresentation that it would provide financing for the joint venture. Chesapeake asserted that the oral promise to provide financing was unenforceable under the Maryland Statute of Frauds which provides: "No action may be brought . . . (3) [u]pon any agreement that is not to be performed within the space of one year from the making thereof; [u]nless the contract or agreement upon which the action is brought . . . is in writing and signed by the party to be charged. . . ." Chesapeake argued that because the construction project would not be performed in one year, the oral joint venture agreement was unenforceable. The trial court found in favor of Laird and Martin and awarded damages. Chesapeake appealed.

Rodowsky, Judge

. . . It appears that the joint venture project under discussion between the parties contemplated the acquisition of the 33-acre parcel, construction on it of approximately 66 dwelling units, their sale, and a division of the profits. Appellants focus on two items of testimony. Lussi, a witness called by the plaintiffs, stated on cross-examination that the "project was designed to be built in probably . . . twenty-four to thirty-six months, like any project that size." On cross-examination of Martin, the following testimony was elicited:

Q: Now, you said on direct that this would take I believe thirty-three months?
A: Thirty months.
Q: Thirty months?
A: Thirty months.
Q: If you speeded it up, could it have been done in twenty-four?
A: Yes.
Q: Yes? Much less than that?
A: Sixty-six units, no.
Q: It would take two years?
A: Minimum would be two years.
Q: Two years?
A: That is correct.
Q: There is no way you could have done it less than two years?
A: I can't say that it's impossible. It's always possible it could be built in a year, but to sell sixty-six units in this high priced market in the Baltimore area in a year—
Q: What is your answer?
A: No.

Warner v. Texas and Pacific Ry., [17 S.Ct. 147 (1896).] is . . . the leading case on the *infra annum* section of the Statute of Frauds. The Court there said:

The parties may well have expected that the contract would continue in force for more than one year; it may have been very improbable that it would not do so; and it did in fact continue in force for a much longer time. But they made no stipulation which in terms, or by reasonable inference, required that result. The question is not what the probable, or expected, or actual performance of the contract was; but whether the contract, according to the reasonable interpretation of its terms, required that it should not be performed within the year. [17 S.Ct. at 153.]

This Court has historically interpreted "literally and very narrowly" (2 A. Corbin, *On Contracts* §444, at 535 (1950)) the words of the statute which apply only to "any agreement that is not to be performed within the space of one year from the making thereof. . . ." The appellants have not clearly demonstrated that, under the terms of the alleged oral contract, as contrasted with the expectations of the parties, it could not be performed within one year.

[Judgment affirmed.]

Effect of Performance. If one party has fully performed, the one-year provision does not prevent enforcement of the remaining promises. The rule is applicable to contracts fully performed on one side when the contract is made, such as a loan of money. It also applies to any other contract fully performed on one side subsequent to its making, even if that performance takes longer than one year. If, however, either party's performance cannot be completed within a year, the statute applies to all promises in the contract including those that can or are required to be performed within a year.[18] Suppose a creditor loans money to a debtor to be repaid in installments extending beyond one year. The debtor's promise is enforceable even if not evidenced by a writing because the creditor has fully performed. Or, assume Seller and Buyer enter into an oral agreement on July 1, 1987. In exchange for Seller's promise to deliver goods on September 1, 1987, Buyer promises to pay the purchase price in three equal installments payable on January 1, 1988, July 1, 1988, and January 1, 1989. Until Seller performs, the contract is not enforceable against either Seller or Buyer because Buyer's promise cannot be performed within one year. This is true even if, as here, Seller's promise can be (in fact is required to be) performed within one year. Once Seller performs, however, Buyer's promises become enforceable even though oral.

Finally, it is important to note that the one-year provision applies independently of other Statute of Frauds requirements. For example, assume Seller and Buyer orally contract for the sale of land to be performed in two years. The requirements of both the land sale and one-year provisions of the statute must be fulfilled.

Contracts Made Upon Consideration of Marriage.
The Statute of Frauds generally covers any agreement made upon consideration of marriage. It generally applies to promises to marry bargained for and given in exchange for money or property. By judicial interpretation or amendment to the statute, mutual promises of two persons to marry each other have been excluded. A mutual promise to marry may, however, be subject to the one-year provision. Assume A and B orally agree to marry in two years. Though not subject to the marriage provision, the contract is within the one-year provision. Many states, however, prohibit actions based upon breach of promise to marry.

Uniform Commercial Code Statute—Goods (§2-201)

Rather than classifying contracts according to types, as in the common law statute, the UCC adopts a minimum dollar limitation with respect to contracts for the sale of goods. Section 2-201(1) provides that a contract for the sale of goods for the price of $500 or more[19] is not enforceable unless there is some writing sufficient to indicate that a contract for sale has been made between the parties, stating a quantity term, which is signed by the party to be charged or his authorized agent.[20]

Exceptions to the Writing Requirement under the Code.
The Code recognizes four major exceptions to the writing requirements outlined above.

Part Performance—§2-201(3)(c). Under UCC Section 2-201(3)(c), an oral contract for the sale of goods subject to the Statute of Frauds is nevertheless enforceable with respect to goods:

1. for which payment has been made (by the buyer) and accepted (by the seller), or
2. which have been received and accepted (by the buyer).

---

18. *Restatement (Second) of Contracts* §130 comment d.

19. The price may be payable in money or in services or property with a value of $500 or more. If part or all of the price is payable in an interest in real estate, Code rules (including §2-201) govern the transfer of the goods and the seller's obligations concerning them. Common law rules (including the common law Statute of Frauds) govern the transfer of the interest in land and the seller's obligations in connection with that transfer. UCC §2-304.

20. In an auction sale of goods of $500 or more, a memorandum signed by the auctioneer is generally binding on both buyer and seller.

Part performance by the buyer requires delivery of something to the seller, accepted by him as a partial performance. Thus, the buyer's part performance may consist of money, a check, services, or property that has been delivered to and accepted by the seller. In the case of the buyer, "receipt" means taking physical possession of the goods.[21] "Acceptance" is the buyer's indication of her intention to keep them, which may be made expressly, by silence, or other conduct.[22] The "part performance" exception is based upon the premise that the evidentiary function of the Statute of Frauds is satisfied by the conduct of the parties.

To illustrate the operation of this provision, assume Stein and Barth have an oral contract for the sale of auto parts for $2,000. Stein delivers parts worth $500 to Barth, and Barth accepts the goods; or alternatively, Barth makes a part payment of $500, which is accepted by Stein. In either case, to the extent of the partial performance, the contract is enforceable, even though otherwise required to be evidenced by a writing under §2-201(1). In this example, with respect to the $500 already paid or delivered, neither party can assert Statute of Frauds as a defense.

Note that part performance serves as a substitute for a writing only to the extent that payment has been made and accepted or the goods have been received and accepted. That is, part performance does not take the entire contract out of the statute. Thus, in the above example, either party may rely upon the statute as a defense to enforcement of the remaining $1,500 of the contract. This is true even if the remaining portion is less than $500. Whether or not a writing is required is determined by reference to the original amount, in this case $2,000.

This rule prevents one party from using a small *executed* oral contract to take his *fraudulent* assertion that a larger contract exists out of the Statute of Frauds. To illustrate, using the preceding example, assume Stein and Barth actually have an oral contract for $500 that has been performed. However, because the price is particularly advantageous to Barth, she fraudulently asserts that the actual agreement was $2,000, not merely $500. On these facts, the Code protects Stein by allowing him to assert the Statute of Frauds as a defense to enforcement of the fraudulently alleged contract.

Merchants' Exception—§2-201(2). Section 2-201(2) provides a special rule applicable when both parties to the contract are merchants, and one sends a writing in confirmation of the contract to the other satisfying the Statute of Frauds against the sending merchant. In this case, the confirmation satisfies the statute against the receiving merchant, unless he gives written notice of objection to its contents within ten days after receipt of the confirmation. Note that §2-201(2) is not really an exception to the writing requirement, but is instead an exception to the general rule that the writing is only enforceable against the person who signs it. If §2-201(2) applies, the Statute of Frauds is nevertheless also satisfied against the nonsigning merchant. Note that both parties must be merchants and the writing in confirmation of the contract must be sufficient to bind the sender; that is, it must be signed and state the quantity term. Further, the confirmation must be received within a reasonable time after the contract is made and written notice of objection must be given within ten days after receipt.[23] Notice of objection is effective as long as it is sent, even though not received, within ten days after receipt of the confirmation.

Section 2-201(2) is designed to prevent a type of fraud that can occur when two merchants make an oral contract over the phone. Suppose Seller and Buyer in a telephone conversation enter into a contract for sale of goods for $1,000, calling for delivery in thirty days. Seller then sends Buyer a signed written confirmation restating the terms of the agreement. Under traditional Statute of Frauds rules, the memorandum is sufficient against Seller, but not Buyer, because only Seller has signed. Because Seller is bound and Buyer is not, Buyer can back out of the contract if the market price falls below the contract price on the date of delivery, but may hold Seller liable if the market price rises. To

---

21. UCC §2-103(1)(c).
22. UCC §2-606.

23. A person "gives" a notice to another by taking whatever steps are reasonably required to inform him in the ordinary course, whether or not the other actually comes to know of it. UCC §1-201(26).

prevent this type of speculation, the Code provides that the statute is satisfied against the nonsigning merchant as well unless he gives timely notice of objection after receiving the confirmation. The rule also encourages sending written confirmations by eliminating the obvious disadvantage to the sender. Additionally, it protects the rights of both parties without requiring a second signed writing—that is, signed by Buyer.

Specially Manufactured Goods—§2-201(3)(a). Under §2-201(3)(a), an oral contract for sale of goods to be **specially manufactured** for the buyer and not suitable for sale to others in the ordinary course of the seller's business is enforceable regardless of dollar amount. This rule applies, however, only if the seller, before repudiation by the buyer, has changed her position in reliance on the contract. Reliance is shown if the seller substantially begins manufacture or makes commitments to obtain the goods under circumstances reasonably indicating that the goods are for the buyer. Therefore, the seller need not be the manufacturer to be protected by this provision. Note that this provision essentially carves another "part performance" exception out of the Code statute.

Admission in Pleading, Testimony, or Otherwise in Court—§2-201(3)(b). As discussed previously, a major criticism of the common law statute was the injustice caused when a person asserted the statute as a defense to enforcement, even while admitting the existence of the oral contract in court. The Code prevents this result in §2-201(3)(b) by denying the Statute of Frauds as a defense to a party who admits in his *pleading, testimony, or otherwise in court* that a contract for sale was made. If an admission is made, however, the contract is not enforceable beyond the *quantity* of goods admitted.

The Code drafters apparently believed that a Statute of Frauds should be retained because of its benefits in preventing enforcement of fraudulent claims, but should not be used as a device to avoid valid oral obligations. Therefore, under the Code, the Statute of Frauds may be used as a defense only if the defendant denies the existence of the contract. If he admits its existence, either voluntarily or inadvertently—for example, in his pleadings or testimony—or involuntarily—while being cross-examined by the other party—the evidentiary function of the statute is met.

Other Uniform Commercial Code Statutes

A brief discussion of three additional provisions is necessary to complete the UCC Statute of Frauds coverage.

Securities—§8-319. Under §8-319(a), any contract for the sale of securities, such as stocks and bonds, is required to be evidenced by a signed writing to be enforceable. The statute applies without regard to the dollar amount of the sale. The writing must describe the securities and state the quantity and the price. Exceptions that closely follow those contained in §2-201 are included.[24] The admission exception in §8-319(d) parallels §2-201(3)(b) except that it does not apply unless the defendant admits both the quantity and *the price*.

Security Agreements—§9-203(1)(a). A security interest is an interest in personal property (the collateral) created to secure payment or performance of an obligation, usually the repayment of a money debt. Security interests in personal property are governed by Article 9 of the UCC. Under §9-203(1)(a), an agreement which creates or provides for a security interest (a security agreement) must be in writing to be enforceable against the debtor or third parties. The agreement must be signed by the debtor and contain a description of the collateral. However, no writing is required if the collateral is in the possession of the secured party pursuant to the agreement.

Other Personal Property—§1-206. In §1-206, the Code provides a residual Statute of Frauds for the sale of personal property other than goods, securities, or security interests. Examples include intangibles such as patents, copyrights, trademarks, royalty rights, literary rights, and bilateral contract rights. A contract for sale of property subject to §1-206 must be evidenced by a writing signed by the

---

24. Compare UCC §§8-319(b), (c), and (d) with §§2-201(3)(c), 2-201(2), and 2-201(3)(b) respectively.

party to be charged if the amount sought to be enforced is over $5,000. The writing must reasonably identify the subject matter and state the price.

Other Statutes of Frauds

In addition to those previously discussed, most states impose several additional Statute of Frauds requirements. Some common examples include promises to pay debts barred by the statute of limitations, to pay a commission to a real estate broker, to make a testamentary disposition (that is, in a will), or to pay a debt contracted in infancy.

Sufficiency of the Writing

The basic purpose of the Statute of Frauds is evidentiary—to provide reliable evidence of the existence of a contract and prevent enforcement of fraudulently asserted contracts. The memorandum (writing) required by the Statute of Frauds need not satisfy rigorous formal standards. All that is required is that there be some writing indicating that a contract has been made between the parties (or offered by the signer to the other party) that states certain minimum terms, and that is signed by the party to be bound—the defendant in the contract action. Generally, for contracts subject to the "common law" statute, the memorandum must (1) identify the parties, (2) reasonably identify the subject matter, and (3) state the essential terms of the unperformed promises of the contract with reasonable certainty.

The writing need not be made as a memorandum of a contract. Generally, any writing, formal or informal, is sufficient provided it meets the requirements stated above. A **writing** for purposes of the Statute of Frauds includes handwriting, printing, typewriting, or any other intentional reduction to tangible form.[25] The writing may be made or signed at any time before or after contract formation. Therefore the Statute of Frauds may be satisfied in a will, a notation on a check, a newspaper advertisement, a receipt, an informal letter, an entry in a diary, or the minutes of a meeting. Additionally, a signed, written offer, communicated by the offeror to the offeree, and subsequently accepted orally, is sufficient to bind the offeror. A writing that has been lost or destroyed may still satisfy the statute provided its existence and terms can be proven—for example, by an unsigned copy or oral evidence.

The statute also may be satisfied in a series of documents, even though no individual writing, by itself, would be sufficient. In this case, at least one writing must be signed, and all writings taken collectively must clearly indicate that they are part of the same transaction.

In the following case, the court was required to decide whether a series of related writings constituted a sufficient memorandum under the Statute of Frauds.

Crabtree v. Elizabeth Arden Sales Corp.
110 N.E.2d 551 (N.Y. 1953)

Plaintiff Nate Crabtree sued defendant Elizabeth Arden Sales Corp., a cosmetics company, for breach of contract. The evidence adduced at trial established that in 1947 the company began negotiations to hire Crabtree as sales manager. He requested a three-year contract at $25,000 per year because he would be giving up a secure position and believed the new position might require several years to master. After further negotiations, Elizabeth Arden, the president of Elizabeth Arden Sales Corp., offered Crabtree a two-year contract on terms that were summarized in the following writing prepared by Arden's personal secretary:

EMPLOYMENT AGREEMENT WITH NATE
CRABTREE
Date Sept. 26, 1947
At 681—5th Ave   6: PM

Begin   20000.
6 months   25000.
6   "   30000.

5000. per year expense money
[2 years to make good]

---

25. UCC §1-201(46). The same definition applies when used elsewhere in this text, particularly in the commercial paper material (Chapters 21-27).

Arrangement with Mr. Crabtree by Miss Arden
Present Miss Arden
    Mr. John [sic]
    Mr. Crabtree
    Miss O'Leary

The memorandum was not signed by any of the parties.

Several days later Crabtree telephoned Robert P. Johns, the vice-president and general manager of the company, and telegraphed Arden to accept the position. When Crabtree began employment, a payroll card was made up, initialed by Johns and sent to the payroll department. The card recited that it had been prepared on September 30, 1947, was to be effective as of October 22, listed Crabtree's job classification and contained the following notation:

This employee is to be paid as follows:

First six months of
    employment $20,000. per annum
Next six months of
    employment   25,000. per annum
After one year of
    employment   30,000. per annum
        Approved by RPJ [initialed]

After six months of employment, Crabtree's salary was increased from $20,000 to $25,000. When Crabtree did not receive an increase at the end of a year, he discussed the issue with Johns and the comptroller. The comptroller prepared and signed a payroll change card that stated there was to be a "salary increase from $25,000 to $30,000 per contractual agreement with Miss Arden." Arden, however, refused to authorize the increase and after further fruitless discussion Crabtree left Arden's employ and commenced an action for breach of contract.

At the trial, Elizabeth Arden Sales Corp. denied the existence of an agreement to employ Crabtree for two years. The company further alleged that if there had been an agreement, the Statute of Frauds barred its enforcement because it had not been reduced to a written contract. The trial court ruled in favor of Crabtree and awarded $14,000 in damages. Elizabeth Arden Sales Corp. appealed.

Fuld, Judge

. . . Since the contract relied upon was not to be performed within a year, the primary question for decision is whether there was a memorandum of its terms, subscribed by defendant, to satisfy the statute of frauds. . . .

The statute of frauds does not require the "memorandum . . . to be in one document. It may be pieced together out of separate writings, connected with one another either expressly or by the internal evidence of subject-matter and occasion." [*Marks v. Cowdin*, 123 N.E. 139, 141 (N.Y. 1919)] . . . Where each of the separate writings has been subscribed by the party to be charged, little if any difficulty is encountered. . . . Where, however, some writings have been signed, and others have not—as in the case before us . . . this court has on a number of occasions approved the rule, and we now definitively adopt it, permitting the signed and unsigned writings to be read together, provided that they clearly refer to the same subject matter or transaction. . . .

Turning to the writings in the case before us— the unsigned office memo, the payroll change form initialed by the general manager Johns, and the paper signed by the comptroller Carstens—it is apparent, and most patently, that all three refer on their face to the same transaction. The parties, the position to be filled by plaintiff, the salary to be paid him, are all identically set forth; it is hardly possible that such detailed information could refer to another or a different agreement. . . . Under such circumstances, the courts below were fully justified in finding that the three papers constituted the "memorandum" of their agreement within the meaning of the statute.

Nor can there be any doubt that the memorandum contains all of the essential terms of the contract. . . . Only one term, the length of the employment, is in dispute. The September 26th office memorandum contains the notation, "2 years to make good". What purpose, other than to denote the length of the contract term, such a notation could have, is hard to imagine. . . . Quite obviously, as the courts below decided, the phrase signifies that the parties agreed to a term, a certain and definite term, of two years, after which, if plaintiff did not "make good", he would be subject to discharge. And examination of other parts

of the memorandum supports that construction. . . . Having in mind the relations of the parties, the course of the negotiations and plaintiff's
insistence upon security of employment, the purpose of the phrase—or so the trier of the facts was
warranted in finding—was to grant plaintiff the tenure he desired.

[Judgment affirmed.]

Sufficiency under the UCC. As previously noted,
the Statute of Frauds is often criticized for perpetrating far more fraud than it prevents. One reason
for this criticism is the requirement imposed by the
common law statute that the writing contain all material terms of the contract. As a result, a substantial amount of litigation under the statute has focused upon the sufficiency of the writing, even
when the existence of the underlying contract was
not in dispute. The UCC attempts to correct this
problem by providing less rigorous requirements
for the sufficiency of the writing for contracts for
the sale of goods.

Under the Code, the writing is sufficient even
though it omits or incorrectly states any agreed
term. The contract is not enforceable, however, beyond the *quantity* of goods shown in the writing.
Therefore, only three definite and invariable requirements regarding the sufficiency of the memorandum are imposed by §2-201: (1) the writing
must evidence a contract for the sale of goods; (2)
it must be signed by the party to be charged; and
(3) it must specify a quantity term. If the price is
payable in goods rather than money, the quantity
of goods must be stated.

Beyond these minimal requirements, the writing
need not state any other terms, and terms stated
(other than quantity) are not conclusive. As noted
in Official Comment 1 to §2-201: "All that is required is that the writing afford a basis for believing that the offered oral evidence rests on a real
transaction." Therefore, once the Statute of Frauds
is satisfied, the party seeking enforcement will offer evidence regarding other agreed terms. Terms
omitted from an uncontradicted writing or not otherwise proven are supplied by the Code.

The Signature Requirement. Under both the common law and the UCC, the writing satisfying the
Statute of Frauds must be signed. A **signature** includes any symbol executed or adopted by a party
with the *present intention to authenticate a writing*.[26] A person authenticates a writing when she
assents to and adopts it as her own. The signature
requirement is not rigorous. That is, a formal signature handwritten in ink is not required. A signature may be printed, stamped, or written and may
be made by initials or even a fingerprint. It may
appear on any part of the document and in some
cases may be found in a billhead or letterhead.[27]

Effect of Performance, Rescission, and Modification

Full Performance. Noncompliance with the Statute of Frauds generally renders a contract "unenforceable" not "void." Oral contracts subject to
the statute are frequently made and performed. If
the contract has been fully performed on both
sides, courts have unanimously held that the Statute
of Frauds has no effect upon the legal relations of
the parties. That is, after full performance, neither
party can maintain an action for rescission on the
basis that the contract was unenforceable under the
statute. The evidentiary function of the statute is
clearly satisfied and the parties are in the same position as if the contract had been originally enforceable.

Rescission and Modification. A commonly encountered problem concerns the extent to which the
Statute of Frauds applies to a subsequent rescission
or modification by the parties of a contract originally within the statute. Two basic issues are presented: (1) Must an agreement to rescind a contract
be in writing if the underlying contract is within the
statute? and (2) To what extent does the Statute of
Frauds apply to a contract modifying but not rescinding a prior contract?

---

26. UCC §1-201(39) which follows the common law rule.
27. UCC §1-201, Official Comment 39.

Effect of Rescission. An executory written contract subject to the Statute of Frauds may be rescinded orally. For example, assume A and B have a written contract in which A agrees to employ B for two years. Subsequently, the parties orally agree to rescind the contract. The oral agreement is effective to rescind the written contract. Under the UCC, the parties are effectively permitted to make their own statute of frauds regarding subsequent rescission or modification of a written contract for the sale of goods. Section 2-209(2) states that a signed written agreement (whether or not subject to §2-201) may provide that any future modification or rescission must be evidenced by a signed writing. If such a term is included, an oral modification or rescission is ineffective. If, however, the term is contained in a form contract (contract of adhesion) supplied by a *merchant* to a consumer, it is not binding on the consumer unless he signs the provision separately.[28] The purpose of §2-209(2) (and §2-209(3) discussed below) is to protect the parties against false allegations of oral modification.[29] Although most claims of modification are legitimate, they have frequently created policing problems for the court.

Effect of Modification. The parties may, subsequent to formation of the contract, agree to modify its terms. In determining whether or not the Statute of Frauds applies to the contract modifying but not rescinding the original agreement, the second contract is treated as containing the originally agreed terms *as modified.* The UCC reaches the same result in §2-209(3) that provides: ''The requirements of the statute of frauds section of this Article (§2-201) must be satisfied if the contract as modified is within its provisions.'' In other words, the Statute of Frauds is applied to the new contract which contains terms found in both the original and the modifying contract.

The following examples illustrate the operation of this rule, using both common law and UCC con-

tracts. Assume A, in a written contract, agrees to employ B for two years at $500 per month. When B begins work, the parties orally agree to modify the contract to provide a salary of $600 per month for six months. The second contract is enforceable even though oral (because not subject to the one-year provision) and discharges the written contract. Had the converse been true—for example, an oral contract with a six-month term modified to two years—the contract as modified would now be within the statute, requiring a writing for enforceability. Of course, had the contract been outside the statute both before and after the modification—a six-month contract modified to nine months—no writing is required in any event.

To illustrate the modification rules using UCC Section 2-201, assume that S and B have an oral contract for the sale of 500 transistors at $.95 each ($475). The oral contract is enforceable because the price is less than $500. The parties orally agree to increase the price to $1.05 without changing the quantity. The contract as modified is within the statute requiring a writing for enforceability because the price is now $525. On the other hand, if the modification had reduced the price from $1.05 to $.95, the modified contract would no longer be subject to §2-201, and would be enforceable even if oral. Once again, if the contract price is below $500 both before and after the modification, §2-201 is inapplicable both to the original contract and the modification.

The preceding discussion concerns the application of the Statute of Frauds to modifications of contracts: (1) outside the statute both before and after the modification, (2) outside the statute originally but brought within it by the modification, and (3) within the statute before but not after the modification. A particularly thorny question concerns the fourth and perhaps most common modification possibility: a contract within the statute both before and after the modification. Under the rules previously discussed, some writing satisfying the statute for the modified contract is required. The common law statute requires that all material terms be stated in the writing. As such, courts have generally held that an oral agreement modifying a material term of a contract within the statute is unenforceable unless a writing complying with requisite formalities

---

28. Note that as *between* merchants, a term in a form contract supplied by one of them preventing modification without a writing is binding without a separate signing by the other.

29. UCC §2-209, Official Comment 3.

accompanies the modification. That is, the writing satisfying the statute for the original contract does not satisfy it for the modification. A separate writing incorporating the modified term is required. The modification agreement, therefore, must satisfy the statute to the same extent as the original agreement.

Many courts considering the issue have applied this common law rule to modifications of Code contracts as well. Nevertheless, a different rule apparently should apply to contracts for the sale of goods because §2-201, as previously noted, is designed to make the writing requirement less rigorous than that imposed by the common law statute. Under the Code (§2-209(3)), if the parties modify a contract within the statute (involving goods of a price of $500 or more) both before and after the modification, parol evidence should be admissible to prove any modification except an *increase in quantity,* because the original memorandum continues to satisfy §2-201 for the contract "as modified." Because §2-201 prohibits a party from enforcing a contract beyond the quantity specified in the original memorandum, the party seeking to enforce a modification increasing quantity needs a new memorandum complying with the requirements of §2-201, specifying the new quantity in order to prevail. All other types of modifications, including a reduction in quantity, may be proven by parol evidence. In these cases, the original memorandum continues to satisfy §2-201, which is all that §2-209(3) demands. That is, both before and after the modification the contract is evidenced by a writing which: 1) indicates a contract for sale

has been made, 2) is signed by the party to be charged, and 3) states a quantity term.

Effect of Alteration

As a general rule of contract law, if a person who is owed a contractual duty fraudulently and materially alters a writing that: (1) is a complete or partial integration of the agreement, or (2) satisfies the Statute of Frauds with respect to the contract, then the duty of the other party is discharged.[30] Fraudulent material alteration of an instrument is regarded as serious enough to deprive the party responsible of the right to enforce the obligation even in its original form. That is, a duty discharged by alteration may not be revived unless the alteration is forgiven by the innocent party.[31] These rules are designed to prevent tampering with writings that determine the content or enforceability of contract duties.

An alteration may be effected by addition, deletion, unauthorized completion of a blank space in the writing, or other change. An alteration that is not both fraudulent and material does not discharge the duty, and the contract remains enforceable according to its original terms. As used in this context, an alteration is "material" if it varies the legal relations of any party with the maker of the alteration or with third parties. The meaning of the term "fraudulent" is discussed in detail in Chapter 11. Note that even if fraudulent and material, an alteration by one not a party to the contract does not result in a discharge.

SUMMARY

1. As a general rule, contracts need not be written to be enforceable. Nevertheless, written contracts have distinct advantages, both in preventing misunderstandings and omissions that cause contract disputes and in proving contract terms when a dispute does arise.

2. In both oral and written agreements, courts are often required to determine the meaning or content of a contract rendered uncertain by ambiguous language, misunderstanding, or simply because the parties failed to anticipate the contingency causing the dispute. The law has

developed various principles to aid courts in interpreting contracts.

3. When contracting parties reduce their agreement to writing, disputes often arise concerning whether evidence of preliminary negotiations and agreements (parol evidence) may be admitted in evidence in a subsequent contract dispute. The parol evidence rule generally

---

30. *Restatement (Second) of Contracts* §286.
31. *Restatement (Second) of Contracts* §287(2).

prevents admission of evidence regarding preliminary negotiations or prior agreements to contradict a writing, known as an integration, adopted by the parties as the final expression of their agreement. An integration may be complete (a complete and exclusive statement of all terms of the agreement) or partial (conclusive on some but not all issues). If an integration is merely partial, evidence of terms not governed by the writing is admissible. Further, evidence of a collateral contract—one related to but not part of the integrated contract, and not inconsistent with it—is admissible even when the parties adopt a completely integrated writing.

4. The parol evidence rule is subject to a number of exceptions. For example, parol evidence is always admissible (1) to resolve ambiguities in the writing, (2) to prove fraud, duress, undue influence, illegality, or otherwise attack the validity of the integrated writing, and (3) to prove oral conditions to the promises contained in the writing.

5. The UCC retains the parol evidence rule for contracts involving goods but provides that the terms of the writing may be explained or supplemented by course of dealing, usage of trade, course of performance, and by evidence of consistent additional terms.

6. For certain contracts—those subject to the Statute of Frauds—written evidence of the contract is required for enforceability. The original Statute of Frauds, enacted in England in 1677, requires some writing indicating that a contract has been made, stating certain minimum terms, and signed by the party to be bound for (1) contracts to answer for the debt or duty of another (suretyship contracts), (2) contracts for the sale of interests in land, (3) contracts that cannot be performed within one year, and (4) contracts made upon consideration of marriage.

7. In addition to contracts subject to the English, or common law, statute, the UCC requires that a contract for the sale of goods with a price of $500 or more be evidenced by a writing to be enforceable. No writing is required, however, if the goods are to be specially manufactured for the buyer, or if the defendant admits the existence of the contract in court. Further, no writing is required to validate a contract within the statute to the extent the agreement has been partially performed. The UCC requirements for the sufficiency of the writing are much less rigorous than those imposed by the English statute.

8. The UCC also requires a writing for contracts for the sale of securities, contracts creating security interests in personal property, and for contracts involving other personal property if the amount is over $5,000. Further, various state statutes impose writing requirements for certain types of contracts in addition to those governed by the English statute or the UCC.

9. If an oral contract subject to the Statute of Frauds is fully performed, the statute has no further legal effect; the contract is treated as if it had been originally enforceable. If the contract is still executory the parties may agree to rescind or modify it. An executory written contract subject to the statute may be rescinded orally. If the contract is modified but not rescinded, the statute's requirements must be satisfied if the contract as modified is within its provisions.

10. Generally, if a contracting party fraudulently and materially alters a writing that determines the content or enforceability of the contract, then the duty of the other party to the contract is discharged.

KEY TERMS

interpretation	course of performance
parol evidence	Statute of Frauds
parol evidence rule	main purpose (leading
integrated agreement	object) rule
complete integration	part performance doctrine
partial integration	specially manufactured
collateral contract doctrine	goods
merger (integration) clause	writing
course of dealing	signature
usage of trade	

QUESTIONS AND PROBLEMS

12-1   Hutchinson, who owned several pieces of land, entered into a contract with Contractor to build houses on the land. After the houses had been built, the parties sought court construction of the following clause in the contract:

> The ultimate cost of the houses shall include the actual cost of construction plus Contractor's fixed fee of Four Hundred Thirty-Five Dollars ($435.00), plus Owner's price of Nine Hundred Fifty Dollars ($950.00) for the land upon which each house is to be constructed. Fifty percent (50%) of any amount obtained from the sale of any house exceeding the aforementioned ultimate cost, shall be paid Contractor as additional compensation for construction of said houses.

> Contractor argued that he should be paid half of all money received from the sales of the houses in excess of the costs of construction, Contractor's fixed fee, and Hutchinson's cost of the land. Hutchinson argued that Contractor was entitled to half of the money received from the sales of the houses in excess of the costs of con-

struction, the Contractor's fixed fee, Hutchinson's cost of the land, and costs incurred by him in selling the property. That is, Hutchinson argued that he was entitled to deduct selling expenses—for example, realtors' commissions, advertising expenses, and FHA closing fees—prior to dividing the profits with Contractor. Before entering into the contract, the parties had discussed the necessity of advertising the houses and using real estate agents to market the houses. Although the sale of the houses generated a net profit, Contractor's interpretation would give him a $38,000 profit on the transaction while imposing an $18,000 loss on Hutchinson. What arguments might Hutchinson raise in support of his interpretation of the contract? What arguments might Contractor raise? Who should prevail?

12-2　Would the oral evidence offered in the following situations violate the parol evidence rule?

(a) Jude contracted to remodel Belinda's kitchen. A written contract was executed and signed by both parties, although Belinda later asserted that she thought the writing was merely an estimate. The writing also contained an integration (merger) clause. The contract required Belinda to pay 50% of the remodeling costs in advance. Belinda later refused to make this payment and Jude sued. Belinda sought to admit evidence that the contract was subject to an oral condition precedent, providing that the contract, unconditional on its face, would not become binding unless she was able to obtain financing. Because Belinda was unable to obtain financing, she asserted that her duty to perform never arose. Should the court admit the evidence?

(b) Steve, a farmer, contracted to sell grain to Oscar, a grain buyer. Steve intended to grow the crops to satisfy the contract on his own land. A written contract was executed stating nothing about the source of the grain. Steve's crop failed due to adverse weather conditions and through no fault of Steve. When Steve failed to deliver, Oscar sued for breach. Should Steve be allowed to admit oral evidence that the parties understood that the crops were to be grown only from a specified source, and that performance would be excused if that source failed?

12-3　In 1972, Stone and Pacific Co. entered into a written contract for the sale of concrete for use in the construction of the building foundation of a power plant. The contract stipulated that Stone was to supply "approximately 70,000 cubic yards" of concrete from September 1972 to June 1973. The contract further stipulated that "No conditions which are not incorporated in this contract will be recognized." By June 1973, Pacific had ordered only 12,542 cubic yards of concrete, which was the total amount needed for the construction work. Stone brought suit for breach of contract.

At trial Pacific claimed that the contract should be interpreted in light of the custom of the trade and additional terms allegedly intended by the parties. Pacific sought to admit evidence that contractors in the trade generally did not insist upon literal compliance with quantity terms in such contracts, and that in any event the parties had orally agreed prior to signing the contract that the quantity term was not mandatory and was subject to renegotiation. In effect Pacific sought to prove that the term "70,000 cubic yards" should be interpreted to mean "up to 70,000 cubic yards." Should the court admit such evidence under §2-202 of the UCC? Explain.

12-4　S entered into a contract with B for the sale of cotton. A writing exists sufficient to indicate a contract for sale signed by S, and specifying the quantity as "all the cotton to be produced on my 825 acres." Does the writing satisfy the UCC Statute of Frauds (§2-201) against S?

12-5　Yarbro, a printer, needed a photocopying machine for his shop. Because he was a poor credit risk, Xerxes Co. refused to sell Yarbro a copier. Yarbro then asked his friend Rosalie, who operated an advertising agency in an adjacent office, to purchase the copier. Xerxes agreed to sell the copier to Rosalie on credit for monthly payments of $300. After installation, Rosalie and Yarbro shared the use of the machine. Rosalie failed to make the first payment, so a Xerxes representative came to her office to repossess the copier. When Yarbro paid Xerxes the $300, Xerxes did not repossess the machine. In subsequent months, Yarbro made several other monthly payments to Xerxes. Yarbro also told the Xerxes representative "If Rosalie ever fails to make a payment, see me immediately and I will pay you." After eight months both Yarbro and Rosalie went out of business. Rosalie left town.

Xerxes sued Yarbro for the full amount of the installment contract. Yarbro alleged that he could not be held liable because his promise to pay Rosalie's debt was not in writing. How should the court rule?

12-6 Consider whether the following oral agreements are unenforceable under the one-year provision of Statute of Frauds.

(a) Andrew designed an advertisement for Beth, who paid him $42,500. Andrew alleges an oral "understanding" obligating Beth to pay Andrew $5,000 per year for every year Beth uses the ad. Beth is not obligated to use the advertisement in the future and can incur no liability for not using it. Further, Beth's failure to use the ad for any period of time, however long, does not terminate the contract.

(b) Anwar alleged that Branch, a construction company, orally agreed to pay him a fee for arranging construction of a chemical plant in Saudi Arabia. Anwar negotiated with Saudi officials, resulting in Branch's removal from an Arab blacklist and the subsequent award of a contract to Branch to construct the plant. Anwar asserted that pursuant to the oral agreement he was entitled to a substantial fee for his services. Although neither party contended that the alleged contract contained any provision regulating the time of performance, Anwar admitted that his negotiation efforts took three years, and completion of the plant took another six years.

12-7 To what extent, if at all, are the following contracts enforceable under the part performance exception to UCC §2-201?

(a) Smigel owned a 1967 Rolls-Royce "Silver Shadow." He orally offered to sell the car to Lockwood for $11,400, of which $100 was to be paid upon acceptance and the balance on delivery. Lockwood accepted the offer and paid $100 to Smigel. Smigel thereafter refused to deliver, asserting noncompliance with the Statute of Frauds.

(b) Sage is a cattle dealer. Barry is a broker who buys cattle in quantity for resale to third parties. Barry telephoned Sage in December, 1982, and allegedly agreed to purchase 2,000 head of cattle from Sage to be delivered by January 15, 1983. Barry made no payment at the time of the telephone conversation and no writings were exchanged by the parties. Subsequently, Sage delivered 222 head of cattle to Barry, but refused to deliver any more. Barry sued Sage for

breach of its duty under the alleged contract to deliver 1,778 additional head. Sage asserted the Statute of Frauds as a defense. Determine on these facts whether the contract is enforceable for (1) no cattle, (2) the 222 head delivered, or (3) 2,000 head.

12-8 LTV Corporation, a manufacturer of all-terrain vehicles, needed shipping crates to export the vehicles. LTV therefore circulated a detailed invitation to bid to obtain a local supplier who could manufacture 8,000 crates according to specifications at a total cost exceeding $50,000. Bateman submitted a written bid, which LTV accepted. LTV never signed Bateman's bid and repudiated the contract after only 1,000 crates had been ordered. Bateman sued and LTV asserted the Statute of Frauds as a defense. What result?

12-9 Under the UCC (§2-201(3)(b)), a party may not admit the existence of an oral contract in court and still rely on the Statute of Frauds as a defense. This rule has been criticized because it encourages the defendant to perjure himself by denying the existence of the contract. Is this a valid criticism given the basic purposes of the Statute of Frauds?

12-10 Consider the application of the Statute of Frauds to the following contracts:

(a) S conveyed land to B under a written contract. Subsequently, the parties agreed to rescind the transaction; S promised to return the money in exchange for B's promise to reconvey the land. Is the agreement to rescind required to be written under the Statute of Frauds?

(b) A and B make an enforceable oral contract that A will work for 30 days at $20 a day. The next day, they orally contract to substitute employment for two years at $6,000 per year. The second contract is unenforceable because a writing is required by the one-year provision of the Statute. What effect does the unenforceable modification have on the original enforceable oral contract?

12-11 On July 26, 1973, Sue Ellen, a wheat farmer, orally agreed to sell 10,000 bushels of wheat to Boggs, Inc., a grain elevator, for $2.86 per bushel, delivery to be made by September 30, 1973. Boggs sent a signed written confirmation of the contract to Sue Ellen the same day. She received the confirmation in due course but never responded to it. Boggs has a well-established reputation of never speculating on the price of grain. As soon as it purchases grain from a farmer or farmers amounting to one train carload (2,000 bushels) it places a phone call to a large regional elevator and orally sells the grain to that elevator at the prevailing price. Thereafter, a written confirmation of the contract is sent from the regional elevator to Boggs. In reliance on Sue Ellen's contract, Boggs sold the wheat to a regional elevator on July 27, 1973, for $3.46 per bushel, and received a confirmation a few days later. On August 13, 1973, Sue Ellen notified Boggs that she would not deliver the wheat. The reason for her repudiation was that the price of wheat had risen substantially during late July and early August to $4.50 per bushel. Boggs sued Sue Ellen for breach of contract.

(a) Does the confirmation sent by the regional elevator to Boggs satisfy the Statute of Frauds against Boggs for the 10,000 bushel sale at $3.46 per bushel?

(b) Does the confirmation sent by Boggs to Sue Ellen satisfy the Statute of Frauds against Sue Ellen for the sale of 10,000 bushels at $2.86 per bushel?

(c) Assuming the statute is not satisfied against Sue Ellen, should Boggs be able to assert estoppel principles (equitable or promissory) against Sue Ellen as an alternate means of enforcing the contract against her? That is, should the fact that Boggs relied upon the oral contract in selling at $3.46 to the regional elevator operate to remove the Statute of Frauds as a defense to Sue Ellen?

12-12 Trilco, a steel fabricator, telephoned Prebilt Cor-

poration, a steel wholesaler, to discuss purchasing $5,000 worth of sheet steel. Trilco then sent a written purchase order signed by Trilco describing the various sizes and quantities of steel desired. The purchase order contained the typewritten word "Confirmation" as well as the printed language "This order not valid without return acknowledgement."

Prebilt never responded to Trilco's order and never delivered any steel. When sued by Trilco for breach of contract, Prebilt asserted that the alleged agreements were unenforceable due to noncompliance with the relevant Statute of Frauds, UCC §2-201. Trilco, however, asserted that because both parties were merchants, §2-201(2) should apply. Trilco argued that its purchase orders were written confirmations of the oral agreements, sufficient to satisfy §2-201 against Trilco, and became binding upon Prebilt through its failure to object within 10 days. Is Trilco correct? What particular language contained in §2-201(2) is particularly relevant in resolving this dispute?

12-13 V orally contracts with P on March 1 to sell 200 portable window fans for $10 each, delivery to be made on April 1. Both parties sign a written memorandum specifying the quantity, but stating no other terms. Due to an exceptionally cold spring, the parties on March 25 orally agree to modify the delivery date in their agreement, making May 1 their new delivery date. Is the March 25 agreement modifying the delivery date enforceable under the Statute of Frauds? Explain.

Chapter 13   Third Parties

Major Topics

- the role played by third parties in contracts
- the law of assignment and delegation, which determines when contract rights and duties may be transferred, the rights acquired upon transfer, and the liability of the parties after transfer
- third-party beneficiary law, which determines when a person who is not a party to a contract is entitled to enforce it.

To this point in the study of contracts, we have examined the various elements of an enforceable promise and the circumstances—such as lack of capacity, illegality, misrepresentation, or absence of a writing—rendering an otherwise binding promise either voidable or unenforceable. This chapter discusses the role played by third parties in contract law. The **parties** to a contract are simply the people who have made the agreement. If Selene and Bill have a contract for the sale of Selene's boat for $500, Selene and Bill are the contracting parties. Anyone else in the world who may be affected by or have rights in the contract is referred to as a **third party**. Third parties become important in contract study in primarily two contexts: (1) in the assignment and delegation of contract rights and duties and (2) in third-party beneficiary promises.

Contracts are merely a type of property. Like other property interests, contracts are often trans-

ferred from one person to another. The law of assignment and delegation is concerned with the transfer of contract rights and duties by a contracting party to a third party. The principles of assignment and delegation are important because they form the basis for understanding many important concepts in legal subjects outside basic contracts including property, commercial paper, partnership, and secured transactions.[1]

In addition to assignment and delegation cases, third parties often become involved in contracts as third-party beneficiaries. Ordinarily only the parties to contractual promises are entitled to enforce them. Occasionally, however, a beneficiary—a person who is not a party to a contract but benefits from its performance—may enforce a contract against the original parties. This chapter first discusses basic assignment and delegation concepts, followed by coverage of third-party beneficiary promises.

---

1. Examples of subjects which are based, at least in part, upon the basic assignment and delegation material include: (1) in the law of leases, the distinction between an assignment and a sublease; (2) in the law of mortgages, the distinction between assuming and taking subject to a mortgage; (3) the law of commercial paper (UCC Article 3), particularly the holder in due course doctrine; (4) the law of partnerships relating to transfer of partners' property rights; and (5) the law of secured transactions (UCC Article 9) because it governs all sales (assignments) of accounts receivable.

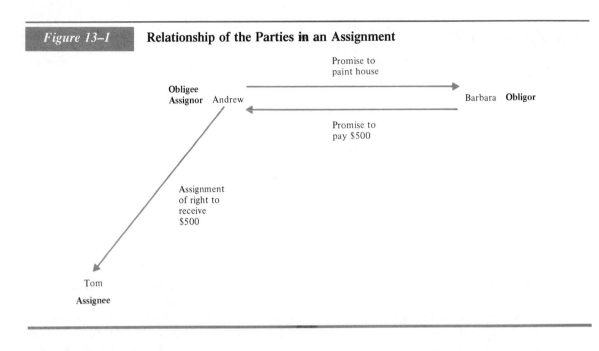

Figure 13–1   **Relationship of the Parties in an Assignment**

Assignment and Delegation

Assignment

In a bilateral contract, the parties have both rights and duties. Each party has the right to receive the other's performance as well as the duty to perform his promise. Suppose Andrew and Barbara enter into a contract in which Andrew promises to paint Barbara's house in exchange for Barbara's promise to pay $500. Both rights and duties have been created by the contract. Andrew has the right to receive $500, and the duty to paint the house. Barbara has the right to have her house painted, and the duty to pay $500.

An **assignment** is simply the transfer of the rights under a contract to a third party. The parties to an assignment are as follows: (1) the **assignor,** the person who is transferring the rights, (2) the **assignee,** the person to whom the rights are transferred, and (3) the **obligor,** or nonassigning party, the person required to render performance. To illustrate using the previous example, assume Andrew assigns his right to receive $500 to Tom. The relationship of the parties is shown in Figure 13–1.

Prior to the assignment, the assignor, Andrew, is the **obligee** of Barbara's duty, that is, the person

entitled to receive her performance. Conversely, Barbara is the obligee of Andrew's duty to paint the house, with Andrew the obligor.

The assignment of a right involves the manifestation of the assignor's intention to transfer it to the assignee. Generally, no particular formalities are necessary to make an assignment. The assignment may be made either orally or in writing.[2] By virtue of the assignment, the assignor's right to the obligor's performance is extinguished and the assignee acquires the right to that performance. Thus, in the previous example by assigning the right to Tom, Andrew's right to Barbara's performance is extinguished and Tom acquires the right to receive $500 from Barbara. Note that all or part of a right may be assigned. Therefore, although Andrew is contractually entitled to receive $500 from Barbara, he may assign any portion of it to Tom.

---

2. Various Statute of Frauds provisions require a writing for certain types of assignments. For example, a sale of securities requires a writing regardless of dollar amount (UCC §8-319) and assignments of personal property other than goods or securities need a writing if the amount is over $5,000 (UCC §1-206). Further, contracts for sale of accounts require a writing for enforceability (UCC §9-203(1)(a)). These provisions are discussed in Chapter 12.

When Contract Rights May Be Assigned. All contract rights may be assigned without the obligor's consent unless the assignment would:

1. materially change the duty of the obligor (the most common case), or
2. materially increase the burden or risk imposed on the obligor by the contract, or
3. materially impair the obligor's chance of obtaining return performance or materially reduce the performance's value.[3]

All claims to receive money may be assigned, because a change in the person to whom payment is to be made (from the assignor to the assignee) does not materially affect the duty of the nonassigning party (obligor).

To illustrate situations in which rights may not be assigned without consent, assume Alice agrees to paint Craig's picture. Craig assigns his right to have his picture painted to Mona. Alice need not perform for Mona, because her duty has been materially changed. That is, painting Mona's portrait is a materially different duty than painting Craig's portrait. The same result would follow had Alice originally agreed to give Craig violin lessons or if she had agreed to take care of Craig for life. Or, assume that Continental Casualty, a fire insurance company, agrees to insure a building owned by Sheila against fire. Sheila sells the building to Barbara and assigns the policy to her. The assignment is ineffective without Continental's consent because its risk (not its duty) has been materially changed. This result is based upon the premise that a fire insurance policy protects the insured, not the property, against loss. Therefore, the company should not be required to accept a substitute without its consent, because the decision of the company to insure is, in part, based upon the character of the insured. Once a loss occurs, however, the right to receive the proceeds is freely assignable, because it is merely a claim for money.

Revocable and Irrevocable Assignments. An assignment may be revocable or irrevocable by the assignor. An assignment is generally irrevocable if it is supported by consideration unless the contract grants the assignor a right to revoke. Similarly, an assignment made as security for, or in satisfaction of, a pre-existing debt or other obligation owed by the assignor to the assignee is irrevocable. On the other hand, a gratuitous assignment—one which is neither supported by consideration nor given as security for or in satisfaction of a debt—is generally revocable. Revocation may occur expressly, by the assignor's death, or by a subsequent assignment of the same right to another assignee. A gratuitous assignment, however, may be irrevocable if it meets the formal requirements of a valid gift. For example, a gratuitous assignment is irrevocable if the assignor delivers to the assignee a signed writing containing the assignment or any other writing that is customarily accepted as a symbol or evidence of the assigned right, such as a savings account passbook, a stock certificate, or a life insurance policy.

Delegation and Novation

A **delegation** is a transfer of the *duties* under a contract to a third party.

When Contract Duties May Be Delegated. Contract duties may be delegated without the nondelegating party's (obligee's) consent unless the obligee has a substantial interest in having his original promisor perform or control the acts required by the contract.[4] Therefore, generally, all contract duties may be delegated except those in contracts for personal services or others in which the promisor's personal skill, judgment, discretion, or supervision is required. Delegation is therefore permitted unless substantial reason can be shown why substitute performance will not be as satisfactory as personal performance.

Assume Mogul Studios hires Dustin Hoffman to act in a movie. Clearly, Dustin Hoffman could not delegate his duty to perform to his plumber, Joe Doaks, because the particular skill and reputation of Dustin Hoffman form the basis of the contract. The delegation would cause a substantial change in Mogul's expectations. However, had Mogul hired Dustin Hoffman to mow Mogul's lawn, perfor-

---

3. UCC §2-210(2); *Restatement (Second) of Contracts* §317(2).

4. UCC §2-210(1); *Restatement (Second) of Contracts* §318(2).

mance could be delegated, because substitute performance on these facts would be satisfactory. In either case, nothing prevents Dustin Hoffman's assignment of his right to receive payment under the contract. It is only delegation of performance in the first situation that is prohibited. Even in that situation, delegation would be permitted if Mogul consented. Other examples of duties that are nondelegable without consent include those owed by an attorney to a client or a doctor to a patient or, in general, any duty whose performance may be judged only by reference to subjective criteria. If there is an objective basis for judging performance—as when goods are manufactured to explicit specifications—the duties are ordinarily delegable.

In the following case, the court was required to determine whether the disputed contract involved personal services that could not be delegated.

Macke Company v. Pizza of Gaithersburg, Inc.

270 A.2d 645 (Md. 1970)

Appellee, Pizza of Gaithersburg, Inc. (PGI), operated six pizza parlors in Maryland. PGI entered into several contracts with Virginia Coffee Service, Inc. (Virginia) by which Virginia agreed to install and maintain cold drink vending machines in PGI's restaurants and to pay all necessary licenses and taxes on the machines. PGI agreed to provide electric power and water and was to receive a percentage of the profits on the machines.

Appellant, Macke Company, later purchased all of Virginia's assets and Virginia assigned the contracts with PGI to Macke. PGI refused to recognize the assignment and terminated the contract. Macke sued for breach of contract. The trial court ruled in favor of PGI, holding that the contract was a personal service contract that could not be assigned. Macke appealed.

Singley, Judge

. . . In the absence of a contrary provision—and there was none here—rights and duties under an executory bilateral contract may be assigned and delegated, subject to the exception that duties under

a contract to provide personal services may never be delegated, nor rights be assigned under a contract where *delectus personage* [choice of the person] was an ingredient of the bargain. . . .

We cannot regard the agreements as contracts for personal services. They were either a license or concession granted Virginia by the appellees, or a lease of a portion of the appellees' premises, with Virginia agreeing to pay a percentage of gross sales as a license or concession fee or as rent . . . and were assignable by Virginia unless they imposed on Virginia duties of a personal or unique character which could not be delegated. . . .

The appellees earnestly argue that they had dealt with Macke before and had chosen Virginia because they preferred the way it conducted its business. Specifically, they say that service was more personalized, since the president of Virginia kept the machines in working order, that commissions were paid in cash, and that Virginia permitted them to keep keys to the machines so that minor adjustments could be made when needed. Even if we assume all this to be true, the agreements with Virginia were silent as to the details of the working arrangements and contained only a provision requiring Virginia to ''install . . . the above listed equipment and . . . maintain the equipment in good operating order and stocked with merchandise.'' We think the Supreme Court of California put the problem of personal service in proper focus a century ago when it upheld the assignment of a contract to grade a San Francisco street:

> All painters do not paint portraits like Sir Joshua Reynolds, nor landscapes like Claude Lorraine, nor do all writers write dramas like Shakespeare or fiction like Dickens. Rare genius and extraordinary skill are not transferable, and contracts for their employment are therefore personal, and cannot be assigned. But rare genius and extraordinary skill are not indispensable to the workmanlike digging down of a sand hill or the filling up of a depression to a given level, or the construction of brick sewers with manholes and covers, and contracts for such work are not personal, and may be assigned. [*Taylor v. Palmer*, 31 Cal. 240, 247-248 (1866)]

. . . Moreover, the difference between the service the Pizza Shops happened to be getting from Virginia and what they expected to get from Macke did not mount up to such a material change in the performance of obligations under the agreements as would justify the appellees' refusal to recognize the assignment. . . .

As we see it, the delegation of duty by Virginia to Macke was entirely permissible under the terms of the agreements. . . .

[Judgment reversed.]

Effect of General Assignment. In strict legal terms, contract rights are assigned, and contract duties are delegated. Despite this distinction, the parties, as well as lawyers and courts, frequently (and confusingly) use the word "assignment" to encompass both an assignment of rights and a delegation of duties. For example, the assignor may merely state that she is assigning "the contract" or "all of my rights under the contract" to the assignee without explicitly stating whether an assignment of rights only, a delegation of duties only, or a transfer of both rights and duties is intended. Both the UCC and the common law resolve this ambiguity by treating a general assignment as both an assignment of the rights and a delegation of the duties under the contract. Acceptance of the assignment by the assignee constitutes a promise by him to perform those duties, which is enforceable by either the assignor or the other party to the original contract.[5]

Liability after Delegation; Novation. When duties are delegated, it is important to remember that one cannot avoid liability under a contract simply by transferring the duty to perform to a third party. In other words, the obligee's rights against the delegating party cannot be jeopardized without his consent. Any other rule would allow a person to avoid a contractual obligation by simply delegating it. Therefore, the delegating party remains totally liable for performance of the contract despite the delegation. The UCC succinctly states the rule in §2-210(1): "No delegation of performance relieves the

party delegating of any duty to perform or any liability for breach." After delegation the party delegating becomes a surety for the assignee's performance, liable if the assignee fails to perform as agreed.

The obligee—the person entitled to receive performance of the delegated duty—may, however, agree to release the original obligor and look only to the party to whom the duty has been delegated. In other words, one contracting party may be substituted for another. This arrangement is known as a **novation**. A novation is a special form of substituted contract,[6] which adds a new party to the contract, who was not a party to the original duty. An effective novation requires that the obligee agree to release the original obligor and that the new obligor agree to assume the delegated duty. The original obligor need not incur any additional detriment—that is, furnish additional consideration—to be discharged. By assuming the delegated duty, the new obligor satisfies the consideration requirement on his behalf. In other words, in exchange for the new obligor's promise to assume the duty, the obligee promises to discharge the original obligor's duty.[7]

For example, assume Steinberg and Brooks have a contract for the sale of goods. Steinberg assigns the entire contract to Adler including the right to receive payment as well as the duty to deliver the goods. If Adler fails to perform, Steinberg remains totally liable on the contract; she is a surety for Adler's performance. If, however, Brooks agrees to discharge Steinberg in exchange for Adler's promise to perform the delegated duty, a novation is created relieving Steinberg of liability on the contract. Note here that Adler's assumption of the delegated duty alone is insufficient to create a novation. Brooks's consent also is required. That is, Brooks's rights against Steinberg on the contract cannot be jeopardized without Brooks's consent.

---

5. UCC §2-210(4); *Restatement (Second) of Contracts* §328.

6. A substituted contract is one accepted by a contracting party in full satisfaction of an existing duty owed her. Unlike an accord, discussed in the consideration material, a substituted contract immediately discharges the original duty. Thus, breach of the substituted contract does not revive any right to sue on the original duty.

7. As discussed in Chapter 9, consideration may be given to a person other than the promisor by a person other than the promisee.

The original contract may provide for a novation. Assume Price is acting as promoter for a corporation yet to be formed, Concert, Inc. Price enters into a contract with Sounds for purchase of equipment. The contract provides that if Concert, Inc. adopts the contract after organization, Price will be released. If Concert, Inc., once formed, agrees to be bound, Price is discharged.

The following case illustrates the application of basic principles of assignment, delegation, and novation in contract law.

First American Commerce Company v. Washington Mutual Savings Bank

743 P.2d 1193 (Utah 1987)

By written contract, First Security Realty Services (Lender) agreed to make a loan to First American Commerce Company (Borrower). As security, Borrower granted Lender a mortgage in a commercial building owned by Borrower and assigned Lender the rents from the building. The contract further required Borrower to make specified improvements in the building and to obtain Lender's written consent prior to entering into any new leases on the building. Under the loan contract, Lender agreed to immediately distribute part of the loan to Borrower and to distribute the balance (described as "held-back funds") after Borrower completed the improvements to the building. Lender made the initial distribution to Borrower and then assigned the loan contract to Washington Mutual Savings Bank (Assignee). Borrower had knowledge of and consented to the assignment. After completing the building improvements, Borrower made a written request to Lender to distribute the held-back funds. Lender refused claiming that it had delegated this duty to Assignee. Borrower also contacted both Lender and Assignee to obtain consent to lease part of the building but neither would give its written consent.

Borrower sued both Lender and Assignee demanding performance of Lender's duties under the loan contract. The trial court ruled that Lender ceased to have responsibility for those duties after the assignment. Borrower appealed.

Durham, Justice

. . . Borrower argues that although Lender assigned its right to receive payments, it remained obligated to perform its duties under the loan agreement. In the absence of a novation agreement between Lender and Borrower whereby Assignee's performance would be substituted for that of Lender, Lender remained responsible for its duties under the loan. We believe that Borrower is correct.

A review of basic contract law vocabulary is helpful to a resolution of the issue. An assignment is the transfer of rights; a delegation is the transfer of duties. . . . The term "assignment" is often used imprecisely by courts. We agree with the Second Circuit Court of Appeals that "lawyers seem prone to use the word 'assignment' inartfully, frequently intending to encompass within the term the distinct [concept] of delegation. . . ." *Contemporary Mission, Inc. v. Famous Music Corp.*, 557 F.2d 918, 924 (2d Cir. 1977). . . . Regardless of the terminology they use, courts agree that a party who delegates his duties under a contract to a third person is not relieved of his responsibilities, but rather remains ultimately responsible to the party with whom he contracted for guaranteeing the successful execution of the contractual duties. . . .

Lender contends that ordinary contract law principles do not apply to bank loans and that the language of the loan documents contemplated a novation rather than an assignment. Lender's argument is that while the usual rules of contract law should apply when a party delegates a duty to provide goods or services, a bank that delegates duties under a loan agreement should have no further liability. . . . An examination of the policy underlying the general rule demonstrates the weakness of Lender's position. The usual rule requiring that a delegating party remain liable is designed to protect the expectations of the party receiving the performance. The delegating party should not be able to foist upon the other party to the contract a performer whose skills, goods, reliability, or solvency might differ from those of the delegator. . . . That reasoning applies equally to duties under loan documents. Borrower is entitled to look to Lender's reasonableness and policies respecting the approval of leases and to Lender's solvency to guarantee the release of the remainder of the loan funds.

Lender insists that whether a novation occurred is a matter of law, not of fact. Lender asserts that the language of the loan documents clearly describes a novation. We disagree with Lender on both assertions. Whether an agreement is a novation is a matter of intent. The essential element of a novation is the discharge of one of the parties to a contract and the acceptance of a new performer by the other party as a substitute for the first original party. . . . A novation must be intended by the parties to the original contract. . . .

Borrower filed an affidavit from one of its general partners stating that Borrower at all times intended to look to Lender for the held-back funds and intended to acknowledge only the assignment of money due in repayment of the loan when it acknowledged the assignment. While it is possible that a document could by its unambiguous terms provide for a novation, the documents in this case do not. . . . Further, if the parties had intended to draft a novation agreement, we think that Lender's counsel would have called the arrangement a novation or at least provided clear language consistent with the intent to substitute Assignee for Lender. . . .

[Judgment reversed and remanded.]

Contract Provisions Precluding Assignment and Delegation

Both the UCC and the common law recognize assignment and delgation as normal and permissible incidents of contracts.[8] That is, all contract rights may be assigned and all contract duties may be delegated unless the assignment or delegation would cause a substantial change in the obligation or expectation of the other contracting party. This rule applies whether or not the other party consents to the assignment or delegation. Any contract right or duty, even if it causes a substantial change, can be assigned or delegated with consent.

If the parties desire protection against an assignment or delegation, they may insert a clause in the contract prohibiting assignment without consent.

Such clauses are enforceable, even if the contract would be otherwise assignable. Their effect, however, is limited. Under both the UCC and the common law, a prohibition of assignment of "the contract" prevents only the delegation to the assignee of the assignor's performance. Thus, rights may be assigned despite the nonassignment clause.[9]

To illustrate, assume Seller and Buyer have a contract for the sale of auto parts. Because personal skill, judgment, or discretion is not involved, the duties can normally be delegated under the rules discussed above. However, the contract contains a provision prohibiting assignment of "the contract" by Seller. The clause prevents Seller from delegating its duty to perform, but does not prevent the assignment of its right to receive payment from Buyer.

Rights of the Assignee

To protect its interests, the assignee should notify the nonassigning party, or obligor, of the assignment. No particular formality is required; **notification** is effected when the assignee takes whatever steps are reasonably required to inform the obligor of the assignment. The obligor receives the notification when it comes to his attention, or is delivered at his place of business or at any other place utilized for receipt of such communications, such as an office, residence, or post office box.[10] Therefore, the obligor may have received the notification without having actual knowledge of it. The various legal issues governed by notification to the obligor are discussed below.

Duty of Obligor to Perform for Assignee. The obligor is free to perform for the assignor until she has notice of the assignment from the assignee. Obviously, the obligor cannot perform for the assignee until aware of the assignment. The assignment extinguishes the assignor's right to perfor-

---

8. UCC §2-210, Official Comment 1.

9. See UCC §2-210(3) and *Restatement (Second) of Contracts* §322(1). Note that a clause prohibiting assignment may also prohibit a transfer of rights if explicit language to that effect is used. Nevertheless, claims for money may always be assigned despite agreement otherwise.

10. UCC §1-201(26); *Restatement (Second) of Contracts* §338 comment e.

mance and transfers it to the assignee. Therefore, as soon as the obligor receives notice of the assignment, she must perform for the assignee, and performance for the assignor will not relieve her of her obligation to the assignee. To illustrate, assume that Sue and Beth have a contract for the sale of goods. Beth assigns her right to receive the goods to Alex. Once Alex notifies Sue of the assignment, she must perform for Alex. If Sue delivers the goods to Beth and Beth leaves town with them, Sue remains liable to Alex.[11]

The following case illustrates the unfortunate legal consequences of an assignee's failure to notify the obligor of an assignment.

Equilease Corporation v.
State Federal Savings and Loan Association
647 F.2d 1069 (10th Cir. 1981)

Equilease Corporation leased seven trucks to Henry Oil Company. As security for the lease Henry Oil assigned and delivered to Equilease six savings certificates that had been issued to Henry Oil by State Federal Savings and Loan Association. Equilease, however, did not notify State Federal that Henry Oil assigned the certificates to Equilease. Over a year later, after encountering financial difficulties, Henry Oil notified State Federal that the savings certificates had been lost and requested early withdrawal of the funds. State Federal allowed Henry Oil to withdraw the funds. Seven months later, after Henry Oil defaulted on one of its leases, Equilease discovered that Henry Oil had withdrawn the assigned funds. Equilease sued State Federal. The district court granted summary judgment in favor of State Federal and Equilease appealed.

Barrett, Circuit Judge

. . . It is generally agreed that prior to notification of an assignment, a debtor may pay the creditor the funds owing and such payment constitutes a

complete defense against an action brought by the undisclosed assignee against the debtor. . . .

Oklahoma has followed the general rule that an assignee must notify the debtor prior to debtor's payment to the assignor in order to bind the debtor to the obligation asserted by the assignee. . . .

Equilease's fourth cause of action alleged a breach of contract theory. The predicate was that because Equilease became the owner of the savings certificates following their pledge from Henry Oil, Equilease was entitled to rely upon the express terms of the savings certificates that no withdrawals could be expected without presentation of the passbooks issued by State Federal. In light of its failure to give notice, we hold that Equilease is not entitled to invoke a contractual obligation against State Federal. . . .

[Judgment affirmed.]

Defenses and Claims Available Against the Assignee. In an ordinary contract assignment, the assignee "steps into the shoes" of the assignor, which means that he receives rights no better or worse than the assignor had. Therefore, any claim or defense that the obligor has against the assignor also may be asserted against the assignee. As explained in comment b to Section 336 of *Restatement (Second) of Contracts*:

> [T]he assignment of a non-negotiable contractual right ordinarily transfers what the assignor has but only what he has. The assignee's right depends on the validity and enforceability of the contract creating the right, and is subject to limitations imposed by the terms of that contract and to defenses which would have been available against the obligee [assignor] had there been no assignment.

The assignee's right against the obligor is also, of course, subject to any claim or defense arising out of his own conduct.

To illustrate, assume that Aronson defrauds Barton. Aronson assigns his right to receive Barton's performance to Carlson. Carlson attempts to enforce the contract against Barton. Barton can assert Aronson's fraud as a defense against Carlson, just

---

11. Note that if Sue does deliver to Beth, Beth is deemed to hold the goods for the benefit of Alex on equitable grounds. If, however, Sue performs for Beth after notification, she bears the risk of loss in the event Beth misappropriates the goods.

as he could have asserted it against Aronson. Or, assume Spencer and Becker have a contract for the sale of goods. Spencer assigns her right to receive payment to Casey. The goods shipped by Spencer to Becker are defective. If Casey seeks enforcement of the contract against Becker, Becker can assert the defective nature of the goods as a defense to Casey's action. In both cases, the assignee takes no better rights than the assignor has.

Despite the general rule outlined above, a buyer or lessee may contractually agree not to assert against a subsequent assignee any claim or defense he may have against the seller or lender. These terms commonly are known as **waiver of defense clauses.** They are enforceable only in limited circumstances because of their potential for unconscionable application, particularly in consumer transactions.

In determining which claims or defenses may be asserted against the assignee, the time of notification of the obligor is relevant. Generally, as previously stated, the assignee is bound by the terms of the contract creating the assigned right and any claim or defense arising from it. In this situation, it makes no difference whether the breach giving rise to the defense occurs before or after the obligor is notified.[12] For example, assume Seller, on June 1, agrees to deliver goods to Buyer on June 30, and Buyer agrees to pay the purchase price within thirty days after delivery. Seller assigns her right to receive Buyer's payment to Doaks, who notifies Buyer. Seller fails to perform as promised. Buyer may assert Seller's breach as a defense to paying Doaks whether Seller's failure to deliver occurs before or after Buyer is notified. Buyer's action in this case is known as recoupment.

On the other hand, the obligor may have claims against the assignor that arise independently of the assigned contract. These claims may be asserted against the assignee only if they accrue *before* the obligor receives notice of the assignment.[13] To illustrate, using the preceding example, assume Seller properly delivers on June 30 and Buyer re-

ceives notification of the assignment on July 15. Buyer, however, has a claim against Seller resulting from Seller's breach of another contract in May. Buyer may subtract (set-off) his claim from the amount he owes Doaks by virtue of the assignment; if Buyer's claim against Seller had not accrued until after July 15, Buyer could not do so.

In cases of both recoupment and set-off, the obligor's recovery is computed as a subtraction from the assignee's claim and is therefore limited to the amount of that claim. In other words, the assignee is not liable to the obligor for amounts in excess of the assignee's claim unless he contracts to assume that liability or is himself subject to a claim by the obligor.

Variation of Assignee's Rights by Agreement of the Original Parties. Though the assignee "steps into the shoes" of the assignor and takes subject to defenses available against the assignor, she is not subject to defenses arising as a result of agreement between the assignor and obligor *after* the assignee has given notice of the assignment. In other words, once notice is received, the assignee's rights become vested and cannot be altered by later agreement between the original parties—assignor and obligor.[14] Assume S contracts to sell auto parts to B for $15,000. B assigns the contract to X, who notifies S. X's rights are vested and may not be altered by subsequent modification of the original contract by S and B.

The rule previously discussed binding the obligor to perform for the assignee after notification is merely an application of this principle. That is, once notice is received, as against the assignee, it is no defense to the obligor that he performed for the assignor. Similarly, a binding release (one supported by consideration) of the obligor by the assignor after notice is ineffective against the assignee.

Successive Assignments of the Same Right. Notification may also become an issue if there have been successive assignments of the same right. Assume Stewart is contractually obligated to deliver

---

12. See, for example, UCC §9-318(1)(a) and Official Comment 1.

13. See, for example, UCC §9-318(1)(b); *Restatement (Second) of Contracts* §336 comment d.

14. A similar rule applies to the rights of a third-party beneficiary discussed later in this chapter.

goods to Beth. For consideration, Beth assigns the right to Stewart's performance to Austin. Beth assigns the same right to Ernest, who pays cash and has no knowledge of the prior assignment. Beth has acted wrongfully in making the second assignment, and leaves town with the money received from both Austin and Ernest. As between the two innocent assignees, who has the benefit of Stewart's performance?

Two conflicting common law rules govern this situation in the absence of statute. The majority rule is that the first assignee in time prevails (in this case, Austin). This rule does not apply, however, if the first assignment was revocable (for example, because gratuitous) or voidable (for example, because of fraud or infancy) by the assignor, or if the later assignee gives value and obtains payment or satisfaction of the obligation in good faith without knowledge or reason to know of the prior assignment. The conflicting rule, arising from the early English case *Dearle v. Hall*,[15] and adopted in a number of states, is that the first assignee to notify the obligor prevails, regardless of the order in which the assignments were made. Therefore, in the preceding example under the English rule, the first assignee to notify Stewart prevails.

Statutes, particularly Article 9 of the UCC, now govern most priority problems relating to successive assignees and claims of the assignor's creditors against the assignee. The application of Article 9 to successive assignments of accounts is discussed in Chapter 32.

Assignments of Accounts

An account is a contract representing the merchant's right to payment for goods sold or services rendered to its customers, known as account debtors. A merchant's accounts receivable often occupy an important position in commercial financing. For example, financial institutions often lend money secured by a merchant's accounts or purchase them outright.

Although transactions in accounts are effectively contract assignments (with the merchant as assignor

and financial institution as assignee), all transactions in accounts are governed by Article 9 of the UCC, discussed in detail in Chapters 31 and 32. Accordingly, the rights and obligations of the parties to an account assignment are governed by Article 9, specifically §9–318, not the common law of contracts. Although §9–318 generally follows ordinary contract law principles, certain important differences, briefly discussed below, do exist.

Assignability. An account, being a claim for money, is freely assignable. Section 9-318(4) reinforces that right by providing that contract terms prohibiting assignment of accounts, or requiring the account debtor's permission for an assignment, are unenforceable. This approach facilitates the use of accounts in commercial financing.

Notification. As previously noted, various legal issues depend on notification to the obligor that an assignment has been made. If the assigned right is an account, notification of the obligor (account debtor) is governed by UCC §9-318(3). Consistent with general contract principles, the account debtor may pay the assignor until notified that the account has been assigned and that payment is to be made *to the assignee.* When accounts are assigned, collection on them can be either direct or indirect. If collection is direct, the assignee notifies the account debtor to make payments to the assignee. In indirect collection, the assignee allows the assignor to collect the accounts and remit the payments to the assignee. Both methods commonly are used in commercial financing. Thus, the account debtor in an indirect collection situation may continue to pay the assignor even after notification. An assignee who wants to take over collections must notify the account debtor to make future payments to the assignee.

Variation of Assignee's Rights by Agreement of the Original Parties. Under general contract principles, once notice of an assignment is received, the assignee's rights become vested and cannot be altered by later agreement between the original parties (assignor and obligor). Article 9 alters this rule somewhat for assignments of accounts. Section 9-318(2) provides that a good faith modification of

---

15. 3 Russ. 1, 38 Eng. Rep. 475 (Ch. 1823).

(or substitution for) an *executory* contract by the assignor and obligor (account debtor) is effective against the assignee without his consent even *after* notification. The assignee automatically acquires corresponding rights under the modified or substituted contract. The assignment may provide, however, that any such modification or substitution is a breach by the assignor. Once the services are performed or goods delivered (that is, the contract is executed), the basic vesting rule applies.

The rationale for the rule treating executed and executory contracts differently is stated in Official Comment 2 to §9-318:

> This rule may do some violence to accepted doctrines of contract law. Nevertheless it is a sound and indeed a necessary rule in view of the realities of large scale procurement. When for example it becomes necessary for a government agency to cut back or modify existing contracts, comparable arrangements must be made promptly in hundreds and even thousands of subcontracts lying in many tiers below the prime contract. Typically the right to payments under these subcontracts will have been assigned. . . . This subsection [§9-318(2)] gives the prime contractor (the account debtor) the right to make the required arrangements directly with his subcontractors without undertaking the task of procuring assents from the many banks to whom rights under the contracts may have been assigned. Assignees are protected by the provision which gives them automatically corresponding rights under the modified or substituted contract.

Third-Party Beneficiaries

In general, contracts may be enforced only by the contracting parties—the promisees of the respective broken promises. Under certain circumstances, however, a beneficiary, also known as a "third-party beneficiary," may be entitled to enforce a contract. A **beneficiary** is a person other than the promisee who will be benefited by performance of the promise. Generally, a beneficiary may enforce a contractual promise only if the promise was made with the *intent to benefit* him. The third party is then known as an **intended beneficiary**. A benefi-

ciary who is not an intended beneficiary is an incidental beneficiary.

Intended beneficiaries are commonly of two types: (1) creditor beneficiaries, and (2) donee beneficiaries. A promisor is under a duty to an intended beneficiary to perform and the beneficiary may enforce that duty. An incidental beneficiary, however, by virtue of a promise, acquires no rights upon the contract. Intended and incidental beneficiaries are discussed below.

Intended Beneficiaries

Creditor Beneficiaries. A person is a **creditor beneficiary** if performance of the promise will satisfy a debt owed by the promisee to the beneficiary. For example, assume that B purchases a car from S on credit. With $1,000 still owing on the purchase price, B sells the car to C who promises B that he will pay the remaining installments to S. Figure 13–2 illustrates this example.

Note that C's promise to pay is made to B, not to S. Thus, C is the promisor, B is the promisee, and S is the beneficiary of the promise. In this case, S is an intended beneficiary because a promise was made with the intent to benefit S, that is, to satisfy a debt owing to S. S is a creditor beneficiary because performance by C will satisfy B's (the promisee's) obligation to S.

S can enforce the promise to pay the $1,000 against either B or C. First, as against C, the promisor, S is an intended beneficiary. Second, S may recover from B if C fails to pay, because, as previously discussed, a person cannot avoid a contractual duty simply by transferring it to a third party. B becomes a surety on C's promise. Unless B is expressly released by S under circumstances creating a novation, B remains liable in the event C fails to pay. Thus, a creditor beneficiary can enforce the promise to pay against both the promisor (on the third-party beneficiary promise) and against the promisee (as surety on the original debt).

As previously discussed, the promisor is under a duty to an intended beneficiary to perform the promise and the intended beneficiary may enforce that duty. The promisee, however, as in other contractual situations, is also entitled to enforce the promise. The contract to pay the creditor is an asset

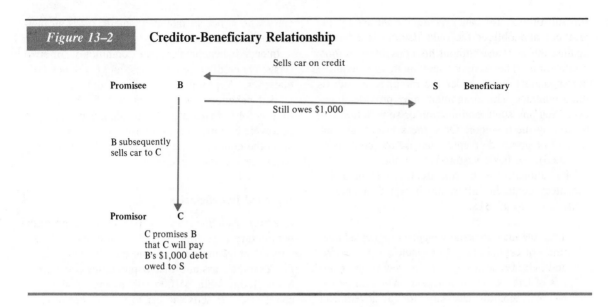

Figure 13–2 **Creditor-Beneficiary Relationship**

Sells car on credit

Promisee B   S Beneficiary

Still owes $1,000

B subsequently
sells car to C

Promisor C

C promises B
that C will pay
B's $1,000 debt
owed to S

of the promisee. If the promisor breaches, and the promisee pays the beneficiary, the promisee is entitled to reimbursement of that amount from the promisor. The promisor is therefore under a duty to both the promisee and the beneficiary.

Donee Beneficiaries. The second type of intended beneficiary is referred to as a **donee beneficiary.** A person is a donee beneficiary if the promisee in-tends to make a gift of the promisor's performance to the beneficiary. Assume that A, in exchange for B's $200 payment, promises to manufacture an oak cabinet and deliver it to C as a birthday present from B. Figure 13–3 illustrates this example.

In this case, C is a donee beneficiary of A's promise to B to manufacture and deliver the cabinet. C can enforce the promise against the promisor, A, because the promise was made with the in-

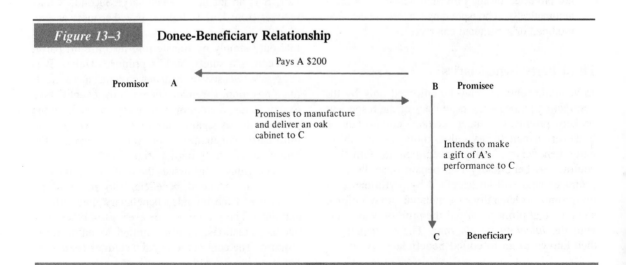

Figure 13–3 **Donee-Beneficiary Relationship**

Pays A $200

Promisor A   B Promisee

Promises to manufacture
and deliver an oak
cabinet to C

Intends to make
a gift of A's
performance to C

C Beneficiary

tent to benefit C—that is, make a gift to her. If A fails to perform, however, C may not recover against the promisee B, because B's conduct is equivalent to a promise to make a gift, which is not supported by consideration. Therefore, although the creditor beneficiary can enforce the promise against both the promisor and the promisee, the donee beneficiary may recover only against the promisor.

The most typical donee beneficiary promise is made in a life insurance contract. The promisor is the insurance company, the insured is the promisee, and the designated beneficiary under the contract is the intended beneficiary. The beneficiary, on the death of the promisee (insured) may enforce the insurance company's promise to pay the face of the policy.[16]

Other Intended Beneficiaries. Traditional creditor and donee beneficiaries are not the only beneficiaries entitled to enforce a promise. The basic test is intent to benefit the third party. Normally, only the promisee need express that intent. "If the beneficiary would be reasonable in relying on the promise as manifesting an intention to confer a right on him, he is an intended beneficiary," entitled to enforce the promise.[17] For example, lenders have been held to be third-party beneficiaries of contracts between auditors and borrowers. If the auditor knows the lender will rely upon the accuracy of the financial statements he prepares as a basis for making the loan, the lender may recover contractually as a third party beneficiary if the auditor improperly performs the audit and fails to prepare accurate statements.[18]

An intended beneficiary need not be explicitly identified when the promise is made. For example, assume B promises A that he will pay anyone to whom A becomes indebted for the purchase of an automobile. A buys a car from C. C is an intended beneficiary of B's promise. Additionally, the promise may extend to a class of persons, as the following case illustrates.

---

16. Life insurance is discussed in Chapter 56.
17. *Restatement (Second) of Contracts* §302 comment d.
18. This issue is discussed in more detail in Chapter 55.

Western Union Telegraph Company v. Massman Construction Company
402 A.2d 1275 (D.C. App. 1979)

The Washington Metropolitan Area Transit Authority (WMATA) entered into a contract with the appellees Massman Construction Company (Massman) and Fred J. Early Company (Early) by which they agreed to construct a part of the subway system. Under the contract Massman and Early agreed to "maintain, protect and restore those utilities affected by the construction, to perform the construction in such a manner as to keep existing utilities in operation and to repair at its expense all damage to utilities caused by its work." Among the utilities listed in the contract were "Telegraph Company Facilities." The contract also required Massman and Early to submit their plans to appellant Western Union Telegraph Company and other utilities for approval. During the construction, Western Union's underground equipment was damaged and Western Union submitted several bills to Massman and Early for the costs of repairing the equipment. After they refused to pay, Western sued them alleging that it was a third-party beneficiary of the contract between WMATA and Massman and Early. The trial court held that Western Union was merely an incidental beneficiary of the contract and denied recovery. Western Union appealed.

Kern, Associate Judge

. . . One who is not a party to a contract nonetheless may sue to enforce its provisions if the contracting parties intend the third party to benefit directly thereunder. . . . We will read the contract as a whole to determine whether the third party's benefit under the contract is intended or incidental. . . . Consequently, the absence of the third party's name from the contract is not fatal to his claim, especially when the surrounding circumstances tend to identify the third-party beneficiary. . . . The contract before us does not mention appellant by name, although in enumerating the various types of utilities contemplated in the contract it includes appellant under the rubric "Telegraph Company." We note that the contract, even though it is written open-endedly, does not contemplate all telegraph companies or even all the enumerated types of utilities. Rather, it must be read to refer to those utilities whose cables, wires, and other equipment ran through the underground area that was the job-site under the contract. Further, the contract contemplates appellant's role as an active participant in the work to be performed under the contract rather than as a total stranger to the contract who, by chance, enjoys an occasional benefit. Finally, the contract provides specifically that appellee should maintain and support the underground equipment of the various utilities in addition to undertaking all repairs for any damage caused. Quite clearly, this contract does more than merely indemnify WMATA for any liabilities arising out of appellees' performance. We hold, therefore, on the basis of all of these factors, that appellant was an intended beneficiary under the WMATA-Early-Massman contract and was entitled to sue to enforce its provisions. . . .

[Judgment reversed and remanded.]

Incidental Beneficiaries

Performance of a contract often benefits a third person. Unless the person is an ''intended'' beneficiary as discussed above, no duty to him is created. He is an **incidental beneficiary.** An incidental beneficiary of a promise acquires no right against either the promisor or the promisee. The following examples illustrate the incidental beneficiary concept.

1. Assume that Hughes and the State have a contract for construction of an interstate highway. Soames owns a piece of property adjoining an exit ramp on the proposed highway. The contract between the State and Hughes calls for completion by September 1. Soames therefore builds a restaurant, completed on September 1, so that she will be ready for business when the interstate opens. Hughes breaches the contract, and as a result the opening of the interstate is delayed six months. During that time, Soames's restaurant, with no ready market of interstate travelers, goes bankrupt. Clearly, Soames is a beneficiary of the promise made by Hughes to the State to complete construction by September 1. Nevertheless, on these facts, Soames cannot recover against Hughes for breach

of that promise because no intent to benefit Soames was indicated by the promise.

2. Alan contracts with Bud to dig a drainage ditch across Bud's property. The ditch would also improve drainage on Chuck's property, which is adjacent to Bud's. Alan breaches the contract. Chuck is an incidental beneficiary of Alan's promise.

3. Hammer contracts to construct a building for Cox. Berne then contracts with Hammer to supply the lumber required for the project. Cox is an incidental beneficiary of Berne's promise to supply lumber, and Berne is an incidental beneficiary of Cox's promise to pay Hammer for the building.

In the following case the court was required to determine whether the plaintiff was an intended creditor beneficiary or was merely an incidental beneficiary of a contractual promise.

Buchman Plumbing Company, Inc. v. Regents of the University of Minnesota

215 N.W.2d 479 (Minn. 1974)

The University of Minnesota entered into several contracts involving the construction of an addition to a University building. Under one contract between the University and James Steele Construction Co. (Steele), Steele agreed to serve as general contractor for the project. Plaintiff Buchman Plumbing Company (Buchman) also entered into a contract with the University by which Buchman agreed to provide all mechanical installations on the project. All contracts stated that construction would begin on April 23, 1968, and would be completed within 200 consecutive days. The project was delayed and was not completed until March 25, 1969.

Buchman sued Steele for breach of contract alleging that Steele had caused the delays and requesting damages resulting from the delay. Buchman argued that it was a third-party creditor beneficiary of the contract between the University and Steele by reason of the following provision from Article VIII of the Buchman-University contract.

The Owner [University] agrees to provide all labor and material essential to the conduct of this work not included in this contract in such a manner as not to delay its progress. . . .

The trial court held that Buchman was not a creditor beneficiary of the Steele-University contract and, therefore, dismissed the complaint. Buchman appealed.

Mullaly, Justice

. . . . It is the prevailing rule in Minnesota and other jurisdictions in the United States that a third party may sue on a contract made for his direct benefit. . . .

This court has used two tests to determine the enforceability of contracts by third-party beneficiaries. The primary test used in Minnesota in determining whether a party may sue as a third-party beneficiary is the ''intent to benefit'' test. . . . This intent must be found in the contract as read in light of all the surrounding circumstances. . . . If the intent to benefit is shown, the beneficiary is an intended beneficiary. If no intent to benefit is shown, a beneficiary is no more than an incidental beneficiary and cannot enforce the contract.

In determining whether the necessary intent to benefit is present, many courts have inquired: To whom is performance to be rendered? . . . If, by the terms of the contract, performance is directly rendered to a third party, he is intended by the promisee to be benefited. Otherwise, if the performance is directly rendered to the promisee, the third party who also may be benefited is an incidental beneficiary with no right of action. . . .

Minnesota also appears to require that the promisor's performance discharge a duty owed by the promisee to the third party. . . . In *Crow & Crow, Inc. v. St. Paul-Mercury Ind. Co.,* [77 N.W.2d 429, 431 (Minn. 1956)], this court said:

> A third-party [creditor] beneficiary is one to whom the promisee owes or is believed to owe a duty *which is discharged by the promisor's performance,* and the contractual right the third-party beneficiary acquires is to enforce a promise made for his benefit which he otherwise would not be able to enforce. (Italics supplied.)

. . . Applying the above tests, we hold that there was no ''intent to benefit'' Buchman. Steele's performance was to be rendered directly to the University. The 200-day and Article VIII clauses were intended to benefit the University. Buchman was at most an incidental beneficiary. In addition, Steele's performance of its contract with the University would not discharge the duty owed by the University to Buchman under Article VIII. . . .

[Judgment affirmed.]

As the *Buchman* case illustrates, courts often resolve the intended-incidental beneficiary issue by examining to whom the promisor renders performance. If the promisor performs directly for the promisee, the third party is usually an incidental beneficiary. If the performance runs to the third party, he or she is generally an intended beneficiary. To briefly summarize, creditor beneficiaries have rights against both the promisor and promisee, donee beneficiaries against the promisor but not the promisee, and incidental beneficiaries against neither the promisor nor the promisee.

Defenses Against Beneficiary

Against an intended beneficiary, the promisor can assert any defense that she has against the promisee. Thus, the beneficiary is in a position similar to an assignee of a right; the assignee takes subject to defenses the obligor has against the assignor. The beneficiary's right is created by the contract. If no contract exists between the promisor and promisee, or if the contract is voidable or unenforceable when formed, the infirmity can be asserted against the beneficiary as well. Therefore, defenses such as fraud, lack of consideration, lack of capacity, and Statute of Frauds are available to the promisor. For example, assume B promises A that she will pay C $100. B's promise was procured through fraud on A's part. B may assert the defense of fraud against C.

The beneficiary also is subject to any limitations or conditions imposed by the terms of the contract. Assume Multiplan, a life insurance company, insures Jim's life. Jim names Betty as beneficiary. The policy reserves to Jim the power to change the beneficiary. Betty's right is terminated if Jim changes the beneficiary before the policy maturity. Additionally, failure by the promisee to perform her return promise discharges the promisor's duty

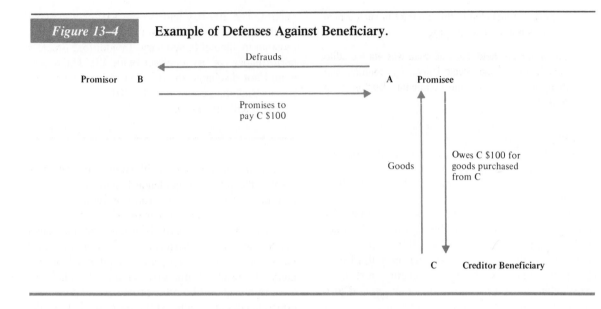

Figure 13–4   **Example of Defenses Against Beneficiary.**

to the beneficiary. For example, assume Belinda has promised Hoyt that she will pay Cathy $100. Hoyt, in return, promises to paint Belinda's house. Hoyt's failure to paint the house is a defense to Belinda when sued on her promise by Cathy.

The agreement may provide, however, that the right of the beneficiary is unaffected by defenses the promisor may have against the promisee. The "standard mortgagee clause" in fire insurance policies is an example of such a provision. These clauses provide that the insurance company (promisor) will pay the mortgagee (beneficiary) for a loss under the policy despite defenses it may have against the insured (mortgagor-promisee). This allows the mortgagee (lender holding a security interest in the property) to recover even though the insured may have violated the terms of the policy—by, for example, failure to pay the premium, storage of hazardous materials, or an intentionally set fire.[19]

Concerning other defenses that may be asserted by the promisor, the beneficiary is basically in the same position as an assignee after notification has been given to the obligor. That is, the beneficiary is bound by the terms of the contract creating his right and any defenses arising from it, but is not subject to defenses that the promisor has against the promisee arising independently of that contract. Additionally, the promisor may not assert defenses that the promisee may have against the beneficiary. Assume A owes C $100 for goods purchased from C. A then fraudulently procures B's contractual promise to pay C $100. Figure 13–4 illustrates this example.

On these facts, B may assert A's fraud as a defense to paying C. B, however, cannot assert a defense that A may have against C—for example, the goods shipped to A were defective or not as warranted.

Variation of the Duty to Beneficiary

The contract may provide that any duty to an intended beneficiary cannot be modified or discharged without the beneficiary's consent; that is, the beneficiary's rights may become vested. The most common example of such a provision is an irrevocable designation of beneficiary in a life insurance policy. In the absence of a term creating an irrevocable duty, the parties retain the power to

---

19. Insurance is discussed in Chapter 56. Mortgages are discussed in Chapter 37.

modify or discharge the duty to the beneficiary by subsequent agreement.[20]

The power to alter the duty is also terminated if the beneficiary, before receiving notice of the discharge or modification, changes position in justifiable reliance on the promise, or brings suit on the promise, or assents to the promise at either the promisor's or promisee's request.[21] Note that the beneficiary's assent to or knowledge of the contract is not necessary to give her a right of action on it. The beneficiary's assent, however, terminates the power of the parties to alter the duty to her.

SUMMARY

1. For contract purposes, the parties are simply the people who have made an agreement. Anyone else is a third party. Third parties become important in contract study primarily in two contexts: assignment and delegation and third-party beneficiary promises.

2. The law of assignment and delegation is concerned with the transfer of contract rights or duties by a contracting party to a third party. Literally, assignment is the transfer of contract rights. The assignor is the person transferring the rights and the assignee is the person to whom the rights are transferred. Delegation is transfer of contract duties. The terms assignment, assignor, and assignee are, however, often used to describe transfers of both rights and duties.

3. Generally all contract rights may be assigned and all contract duties may be delegated unless the assignment or delegation would cause a substantial change in the obligation or expectation of the other original party to the contract.

4. Although consent of the nonassigning party is not usually required, the contract may contain a provision prohibiting assignment without consent. Such a provision ordinarily prohibits only the delegation to the assignee of the assignor's performance.

5. If duties are delegated, the delegating party is not relieved of any duty to perform or any liability for breach. The delegating party may, however, be relieved of liability if a substituted contract known as a novation is effected. In a novation, the obligee—the person entitled to performance of the delegated duty—agrees to release the original contracting party and look only to the party to whom the duty has been delegated. If the new party agrees to assume the delegated duty, the original party is discharged.

6. When contract rights are assigned, the assignee should notify the obligor—the person required to render performance—that the assignment has been made. Notification resolves many legal issues occurring in assignments including (1) whether the duty of the obligor to perform for the assignee arises, (2) which defenses may be asserted against the assignee, (3) when the assignee's rights may be varied by agreement of the original parties, and (4) the effect of successive assignments of the same right.

7. When a contract is assigned, the assignee "steps into the shoes" of the assignor, meaning that the assignee acquires no better rights under the contract than the assignor has. Thus, any claim or defense that the obligor has against the assignor may also be asserted against the assignee.

8. The law of third-party beneficiaries determines when a person who is not a party to a contract but benefits from its performance—a beneficiary—is entitled to enforce it against the original contracting parties. The law provides that a third-party beneficiary may enforce a promise made with the intent to benefit the beneficiary.

9. Intended beneficiaries are most commonly creditor beneficiaries and donee beneficiaries. A creditor beneficiary is entitled to enforce a promise made to satisfy an obligation owed by the promisee to the beneficiary. A donee beneficiary is allowed to enforce a promise effecting a gift from the promisee to the beneficiary.

10. A person who benefits from performance of a contract but is not an intended beneficiary is an incidental beneficiary. An incidental beneficiary of a promise acquires no rights under the contract.

KEY TERMS

party	assignee
third party	obligor
assignment	obligee
assignor	delegation

---

20. If the third-party beneficiary promise is evidenced in an insurance policy (life or property), the power of the parties to change the beneficiary or alter the duty to him ceases when an insured loss occurs. *Restatement (Second) of Contracts* §311(2) and comment e.

---

21. *Restatement (Second) of Contracts* §311(3).

novation
notification
waiver of defense clause
beneficiary

intended beneficiary
creditor beneficiary
donee beneficiary
incidental beneficiary

QUESTIONS AND PROBLEMS

13-1 Buyer ordered 2,500 cases of light bulbs from Seller for delivery in 30 days. Seller had overestimated her inventory, and found herself unable to perform as agreed. Consequently, Seller assigned "the contract" to Crooks, who promised Seller he would perform. Crooks delivered defective merchandise to Buyer.

 (a) Is the duty in this case delegable?

 (b) Is Seller, as a result of the assignment, relieved of her duty to perform?

 (c) Who may Buyer sue for breach of contract?

 (d) Did Seller's assignment transfer the right to Buyer's payment to Crooks?

 (e) Did Seller's assignment transfer Seller's duty to perform to Crooks?

 (f) If the contract had included a provision prohibiting assignment, would the provision preclude a transfer of rights, a delegation of duties, or both, or neither?

 (g) Assume that the goods delivered under the contract conformed to the contract. Crooks had notified Buyer of the assignment. Buyer adamantly refused to pay Crooks, and instead paid Seller. Is Buyer's obligation to pay Crooks affected?

13-2 Shoemaker sold a registered stud quarterhorse to Breeder, who agreed in writing to allow Shoemaker to use the horse for two breedings per year for as long as the horse lived "regardless to whom the horse may be sold." Breeder sold the horse to Joe Doaks, who was aware of and understood the terms of the contract between Shoemaker and Breeder. Nevertheless, Doaks refused to allow Shoemaker to use the horse for breeding purposes. Shoemaker sued Doaks for damages resulting from this refusal. What result?

13-3 Consider whether the rights and duties in the following contracts are assignable.

 (a) Barbara enters into a contract with a television station in a major metropolitan area by which she agrees to render services as a news anchorwoman. The contract is for a three-year term but is renewable for two additional years at the option of the station. Six months later the owners of the station sell it to a third party and assign Barbara's contract as part of the transaction. The new owner replaces many of the personnel, including Barbara's directors, but wants Barbara to continue as anchorwoman. Barbara alleges that she is no longer obligated to perform because the contract was one for personal services which was nonassignable.

 (b) Eli, a cotton farmer, enters into a contract with the Alabama Cotton Company by which Eli agrees to sell all of the cotton grown on his 300-acre farm to Alabama Cotton for 30 cents per pound. Alabama Cotton assigns the contract to the Boll Weevil Corporation. Eli subsequently refuses to deliver the cotton to Boll Weevil alleging that the growing, harvesting, and ginning of cotton constitute personal services so that the contract may not be assigned.

 (c) Eli also alleged that he had entered into the contract with Alabama Cotton in reliance on the fact that Alabama Cotton was an established company of sound financial condition. He further alleged that Boll Weevil was not financially sound and, therefore, would have been unable to pay for Eli's cotton if the price of cotton had declined. In fact, however, the price of cotton increased substantially: at the time Eli was supposed to deliver the cotton, the market price of cotton was 80 cents per pound. Does the fact that Eli relied on Alabama Cotton's financial condition render the contract nonassignable?

13-4 Nails agreed to build a house for Brown for $30,000. Nails assigned the right to payment as well as the duty to perform to Carter. Nails then notified Brown he was leaving the construction business and would not be responsible for Carter's performance. Brown made no objection and Carter proceeded with the work. Does Brown have any rights against Nails if Carter improperly performs the house construction contract? Why or why not?

13-5 As noted in Chapter 8, an offer may be accepted only by the person or persons to whom it has been directed. That is, offers are generally nonassignable. An option, which limits the offeror's power to revoke an offer, creates contract rights in the offeree (the holder of the option). Under what circumstances, if any, should rights under an option contract be assignable? In other words, should an option holder be allowed to transfer the offer represented by the option to a third party?

13-6 In August 1972, MonArk Boat Company agreed to custom build a houseboat for Roy. As part of a corporate merger, MonArk assigned the contract to AlumaShip, Inc. in July, 1973. After AlumaShip notified Roy of the assignment, he paid the final $30,000 installment on the purchase price to AlumaShip and picked up the boat at the AlumaShip dock facilities. The boat immediately required repairs for a bent propeller. En route to a repair shop, a fire broke out on the boat, causing $37,000 damage. Roy sued MonArk alleging that it had breached the contract. In defense, MonArk argued that: (1) it could not be held liable for breach because it assigned the contract to AlumaShip, and (2) if it is held liable on the contract, Roy must make the final payment under the contract to MonArk. Is MonArk correct in either of its assertions? Explain.

13-7 Nexxus Products Company, a manufacturer and marketer of hair care products, entered into a contract with Best Company appointing Best as the exclusive distributor of Nexxus products throughout most of Texas. Subsequently, Sally Beauty Company, a distributor of beauty and hair care products in Texas, purchased all of the stock of Best and received assignment of Best's contracts, including the agreement with Nexxus. Nexxus soon learned that Sally Beauty was a wholly-owned subsidiary of Alberto-Culver, a manufacturer of hair care products and a direct competitor of Nexxus, and refused to allow Sally Beauty to act as distributor of Nexxus products. May Best's duty of performance under the exclusive distributorship be delegated to Sally Beauty without Nexxus' consent? Explain. See UCC §§2-210(1), 2-306(2).

13-8 Consider the following contracts:
(a) The State of Confusion enters into a contract with B to construct a state office building. The contract provides that B will pay damages to any person injured as a result of the construction. C is injured when she is struck by a brick falling from the partially completed building. Is C a party to the contract between B and the state? May C recover on the contract from B? On what theory?

(b) Shirley contracts to buy a new Chevette from Joe's Chevrolet, Inc. Is General Motors, the manufacturer of Chevettes, a beneficiary of either Joe's promise to deliver the car or Shirley's promise to pay for it? May General Motors recover against either Shirley or Joe if either fails to perform their respective promises? Why or why not?

(c) A promises B that A will pay B's $100 debt to C. B notifies C of the contract and C assents to it. A and B later agree to rescind the contract. Is the rescission effective against C? Explain.

13-9 Davis, who operated a ranch in New Mexico, entered into a contract with the United States Department of Agriculture by which Davis agreed to provide data to the government on cows, calves, and steers. The contract provided in part "To protect the contractor [Davis], he must carry worker's compensation insurance on all labor employed under this agreement." Davis employed Ben Cartwright, a cowboy, to perform the labor needed under the contract. Davis, however, failed to buy worker's compensation insurance. While performing his cowboy services, Ben was injured. Because he was not entitled to receive worker's compensation, Ben sued Davis alleging that Davis's failure to buy insurance constituted a breach of the contract between Davis and the government. Ben alleged that he was a third-party beneficiary under the contract thereby entitling him to damages for breach of the contract. What result?

13-10 Leroy Lear hired Phineas Phogg, an attorney, to draft a will. Because Lear's children never called or visited him, he asked Phogg to write the will leaving all of his property to Lear's friend Bill. After signing the will and paying Phogg, Lear told Bill that he would receive all of Lear's property. After Lear died, a court reviewed the will and found that it violated a state law. The will was ruled invalid and Lear's children received all of his property. Bill sued Phogg alleging that Phogg had breached the contract with Lear and that Bill was entitled to damages as an intended third-party beneficiary of the contract. How should the court rule?

- the definitions and distinguishing characteristics of various types of conditions to contractual promises
- the various doctrines distinguishing proper performance of a contract from breach, including the substantial performance doctrine, perfect tender rule, and divisibility
- the legal tools designed to protect each party's expectation of performance prior to the time of agreed performance
- the situations in which performance of a contract may be excused without liability for breach

To this point the contracts coverage has focused on how legally enforceable promises are created and transferred. Contracting parties do not, however, bargain merely for promises—they also bargain for performance of those promises. The law of contracts, therefore, also is concerned with the *performance* of contractual promises, including the standards by which performance is measured and the consequences of nonperformance or breach of a contractual duty.

Even though an enforceable contractual promise may exist, the duty to perform it may not arise because of the occurrence or nonoccurrence of an event known as a *condition*. The first step in performance analysis, therefore, is to examine the

contract to determine the existence and occurrence of any conditions to the promises contained in the contract. Once any conditions to a party's duty have occurred, failure to properly perform that duty results in liability for **breach of contract,** unless performance is excused. Breach may occur in one of two ways: either by nonperformance of a duty when performance is due or by repudiation of the duty prior to that time. If one party's conduct constitutes breach, the other is entitled to a contract remedy. This chapter defines and distinguishes the various types of contract conditions and discusses the important legal issues surrounding breach of contract.

Conditions

A **condition** is an event that must occur before the duty of performance under a contract becomes due.[1] A condition is therefore an event qualifying a contractual duty. Assume S contracts to sell his farm to B. B promises to pay $500,000 for the land but only if B is able to obtain a mortgage loan from First Bank to cover the purchase price. Obtaining the loan is a condition to B's promise to pay $500,000.

If a promise is subject to a condition, the promisor's duty to perform does not arise unless or until the condition occurs. If the condition occurs and

---

1. *Restatement (Second) of Contracts* § 224.

| Figure 14–1 | Effect of a Condition on a Contractual Promise |

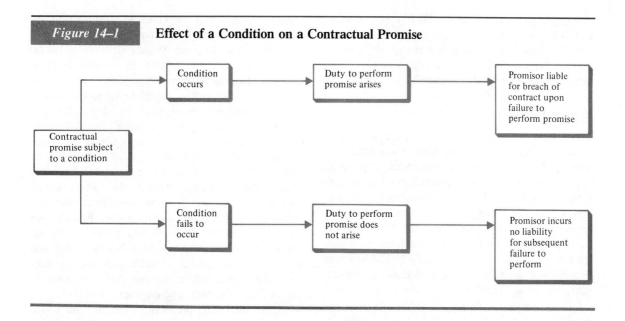

the promisor later fails to perform as agreed, liability for breach of contract usually results. On the other hand, if the condition fails to occur, the promisor's duty to perform is discharged;[2] that is, she incurs no liability for a subsequent failure to perform. Figure 14–1 illustrates the effect of a condition on a contractual promise. Because of this fundamental difference in legal effect following occurrence or nonoccurrence of a condition, determining the existence and occurrence of any conditions to a contractual promise is critical in analyzing any performance question.

Time of Occurrence—Conditions Precedent, Concurrent, and Subsequent

Conditions are frequently classified according to their time of occurrence as conditions precedent, concurrent, or subsequent. Most conditions are **precedent;** that is, they must occur *before* a duty to perform arises. The financing condition in the above example is a condition precedent.

In some contracts, performances are rendered si-

multaneously and each party's performance is a condition to the other's duty to perform; that is, the parties' performances are **concurrent conditions.** For example, in contracts for the sale of land, the seller's delivery of the deed and the buyer's payment of the purchase price are usually concurrent conditions. Concurrent conditions may therefore be viewed as mutual conditions precedent. This concept is discussed in more detail below in the material relating to conditions implied in law or "constructive" conditions.

A **condition subsequent** is an event, the occurrence or existence of which, by the terms of the contract, extinguishes a duty to perform after the duty has arisen along with any claim for breach.[3] To illustrate a condition subsequent, assume General Casualty, an insurance company, agrees to insure Marian's property against fire. The policy provides (1) that in order to recover, Marian must notify General within thirty days after the loss, and (2) no recovery under the policy is allowed unless suit is brought within two years after the loss. On these facts, notification within thirty days is a con-

---

2. The concept of "discharge" of contract is discussed in Chapter 7.

3. *Restatement (Second) of Contracts* §224 comment e, §230(1).

dition precedent to General's duty to pay. Failure to bring suit against the company within two years after the loss (the "condition subsequent") extinguishes that duty after it has arisen, along with any claim against General for breach.[4]

Express Conditions

Conditions provided for in the language (oral or written) of a promise or agreement are known as **express conditions.** The contract term creating an express condition precedent commonly begins with language such as "if," "provided that," "on condition that," or "subject to." A condition must be an event that is *not certain to occur*. Therefore, the mere passage of time is not a condition to a contractual duty. Thus, a party's duty to perform may depend both upon the passage of time and the occurrence of any conditions. Conditions commonly relate to events occurring after formation of the contract, although they may relate to a present or even a past event. The condition may also be based upon failure of an event to occur as well as occurrence of the event. Generally, exact compliance with the terms of an express condition is necessary before any duty of performance arises.

Purposes of Express Conditions. A promisor may condition his duty primarily for two reasons: (1) to shift the risk of nonoccurrence of the condition to the promisee or (2) to induce the promisee to cause the event to occur.

The first reason is perhaps most common. Unconditioned contract liability is strict liability. Ordinarily a contracting party states, in effect, "I promise to perform as agreed, under all circumstances, no matter what happens. Period." Many contracting parties are unwilling to assume this rather harsh absolute responsibility for performance, and reduce their potential liability by conditioning the promise by stating in effect "I promise to perform, if. . . ." Assume Scott wishes to contract with Branch for sale of 500 widgets, delivery to be made on June 1. Scott, however, does not have sufficient raw materials to manufacture the goods. The raw materials have been ordered from Goldberg, but the time of their delivery is uncertain. Scott knows that unless she receives them by May 1, she will have insufficient time to perform by June 1. The parties therefore agree that unless Scott receives the raw materials by May 1, her duty to deliver on June 1 will not arise. Receipt of the raw materials by May 1 is an express condition precedent. If it fails to occur, Scott's duty to perform her promise (to manufacture and deliver 500 widgets) will not arise. That is, the risk of nonoccurrence of the condition (nonreceipt of the raw materials) is borne by the promisee, Branch, not the promisor, Scott. If the raw materials are received by May 1, the condition has been met and duty to perform arises. If Scott subsequently fails to manufacture and deliver the goods by June 1, she is liable for breach of contract.

Note that in the preceding example, the occurrence or nonoccurrence of the condition—Goldberg's delivery of raw materials by May 1—was not within the control of either party. Conditions often have the effect of allocating risk from promisor to promisee even if the occurrence or nonoccurrence of the condition is wholly or partially within the promisor's control. For example, real estate contracts often condition the buyer's duty to pay the purchase price upon his or her ability to obtain adequate mortgage financing. In these cases, the buyer makes an implied promise to use best efforts to bring about occurrence of the condition.[5]

In addition to allocating risk, a condition also may be used to induce the promisee to cause the condition to occur. Assume Seller contracts to specially manufacture and deliver goods to Buyer. Buyer intends to use the goods as part of a trade show display beginning at 1 P.M. on June 1. Because later delivery would substantially impair (if not totally defeat) the value of Seller's performance to Buyer, Seller promises to deliver the goods not later than 9 A.M. on June 1 and that delivery by that time is a condition to Buyer's duty to accept and pay for the goods. A term making time of per-

---

4. A condition subsequent is not a true condition because a condition is an event that must occur *before* a duty to perform arises. A condition subsequent is an event extinguishing (discharging) a duty *after* performance has become due.

5. Conditional promises giving the promisor partial or total control over occurrence of the condition raise mutuality of consideration issues, discussed in Chapter 9.

formance a condition to the promisor's duty is commonly known as a **time of the essence** provision. On these facts, two consequences result if Seller fails to deliver by 9 A.M. First, because a condition has not occurred, Buyer's duty to perform does not arise and is discharged. Second, Seller becomes liable for breach of contract because he failed to perform his express promise.[6]

The parties should always clearly express their intent to create conditional promises, because disputes often arise when ambiguous language is used. For example, a promisor may state "I promise to pay for these goods when I get my Christmas bonus" or "I promise to pay my lawyer when he collects the debt." If a dispute over the duty to pay arises, the court must determine whether receiving the Christmas bonus or collecting the debt are express conditions to the promisor's duty.

In making this determination, courts usually state that an event is not a condition to the promisor's duty unless the promisee has control over occurrence of the event or the contract language or other circumstances clearly indicate that the promisee has assumed the risk of the event's nonoccurrence. This rule of interpretation is designed to reduce the promisee's risk of **forfeiture**—the denial of compensation that results when the promisee loses the right to the agreed exchange after relying substantially, through preparation or performance, on the expectation of that exchange.[7]

In the following case, the court was required to determine whether the contract provisions created express conditions.

A. A. Conte, Inc. v. Campbell-Lowrie-Lautermilch Corporation

477 N.E. 2d 30 (Ill. App. 1985)

Campbell-Lowrie-Lautermilch Corporation (Campbell-Lowrie), the general contractor for a construction project, entered into a contract with A. A.

Conte, Inc. (Conte), a subcontractor who was to perform excavating work on the project. The contract provided in part:

> Article 5: Material invoices submitted before the 25th of the current month will be paid by the 28th of the following month, provided the material so delivered is acceptable, and if payment for invoiced material has been received by Campbell-Lawrie-Lautermilch Corporation under its general contract. . . .

> Article 18: . . . [I]f the work has been satisfactorily performed and invoice as rendered is approved and if payment for such labor and material so invoiced has been received by Campbell-Lowrie-Lautermilch Corporation under its general contract, the subcontractor will be paid 85% of invoice as approved, less any payments previously made on account for previous periods.

After completing the excavation, Conte submitted a bill for $83,956 to Campbell-Lowrie who submitted it with other bills to the property owners in accordance with the general contract. The owners failed to pay Campbell-Lowrie and subsequently became insolvent.

Conte sued Campbell-Lowrie, demanding payment of its bill. The trial court granted summary judgment in favor of Campbell-Lowrie, holding that payment to Conte was contingent upon Campbell-Lowrie's receiving payment from the owners. Conte appealed.

Johnson, Justice

. . . The gist of Campbell-Lowrie's affirmative defense was that Article 18 of its contract with Conte set forth a condition precedent to payment. The condition was that Campbell-Lowrie must first receive payment from the owners of the project under the general contract before it was obligated to pay its subcontractors. The owners had not paid Campbell-Lowrie; therefore, Conte was not entitled to payment from Campbell-Lowrie. . . .

Campbell-Lowrie points out that the plain meaning of the language in Articles 5 and 18 of the contract creates a condition precedent to payment and that there is no ambiguity in the language. . . .

A court may not rewrite a contract to suit one of the parties but must enforce the terms as written. . . . Thus, the rights of the parties are limited by the terms expressed in the contract. . . .

---

6. Nonoccurrence of a condition is not a breach by the promisor unless he is also under a duty that the condition occur. *Restatement (Second) of Contracts* §225.

7. *Restatement (Second) of Contracts* §227 and comment b.

We do not believe that the record supports Conte's claim that its right to payment by Campbell-Lowrie was absolute and not in any way contingent upon Campbell-Lowrie's receiving payment from the owners under the general contract. Our analysis of paragraphs 5 and 18 of the contract in question convinces us that the language is clear and unambiguous and, thus, there is no need to resort to rules of construction . . . nor extrinsic evidence. . . . It is true, as pointed out by Conte, that conditions precedent are not generally favored and courts will not construe stipulations to be a condition precedent when such a construction would result in forfeiture. It is also true, as acknowledged by Conte, that plain, unambiguous language contained in the contract binds the parties to a condition precedent.

Since we have already determined that the language of the contract is plain and unambiguous, we must also conclude that the parties are bound by it. We note that the contract in question was between two entities engaged in business in the construction industry and presumably often entered into other contractual agreements of a similar nature in the course of their business. While it is clear that with the benefit of hindsight Conte may have chosen to exclude or draft differently the language of paragraphs 5 and 18, which gave rise to this dispute, this court cannot redraft the contract, and we must enforce the contract as written and agreed upon by the parties. . . .

[Judgment affirmed.]

Conditions Implied in Fact

In addition to conditions created by the express language of the parties, conditions also may be *implied* from the language or other conduct of the parties. These are **conditions implied in fact.** For example, assume Todd is a tenant in a house owned by Larry. Upon renewal of the lease, Todd agrees to do the labor necessary to remodel the bathroom and the kitchen. In exchange, Larry agrees to reduce the rent and supply the necessary materials. In this case, Todd cannot perform unless Larry performs his promise. Therefore, Larry's supplying the building materials is a condition implied in fact to Todd's duty even though not expressly stated in the contract.

Implied (Constructive) Conditions

An important class of contract conditions arise neither from the language (express conditions) nor from the other conduct (conditions implied in fact) of the parties. These conditions are imposed as a matter of law and are referred to as conditions **implied in law,** or more commonly **constructive conditions.**

Constructive Conditions of Exchange. The most important implied or constructive conditions are known as **constructive conditions of exchange.** This concept can be explained as follows: In a bilateral contract, the parties exchange promises with the expectation of a subsequent exchange of performances. That is, the parties bargain for performance, not the right to sue the other for breach. The constructive conditions doctrine is designed to protect the parties' expectation that the subsequent exchange of performances will occur. Under this approach, it is a condition to each party's duty to perform the remaining duties under a promise that there be no uncured material failure of the other party's performance due at an earlier time.[8] In other words, proper performance by each party is a constructive condition to the other's duty to render any subsequent performance.

For example, assume Bill contracts to landscape Mary's yard in exchange for Mary's promise to pay $1,000. By terms of the contract Bill is to complete the work by May 1, with Mary's payment due 10 days thereafter. Bill fails to do the work. Under the constructive conditions of exchange doctrine, Bill's proper performance is a condition to Mary's duty to pay. Because Bill did not perform, a condition to Mary's duty has not occurred; Mary is therefore not required to perform her promise (pay $1,000).

Courts and statutes frequently state that **failure of consideration** is a defense to enforcement of a contractual obligation. What this terminology actually means is "failure of performance," that is, failure of the other party to perform his promise—

---

8. *Restatement (Second) of Contracts* §237.

failure of a constructive condition of exchange. It *does not mean* lack or absence of consideration, because the consideration is provided by the exchange of promises, making them enforceable. It is the subsequent failure to perform the promises that gives rise to the defense.

As a result of constructive conditions of exchange, contractual promises are sometimes said to be **dependent** in nature, meaning that failure by one party to perform justifies the other's failure to perform. It should be noted, however, that covenants in leases and in other conveyances of land have traditionally been treated as **independent.** That is, nonperformance by one party generally does not excuse further performance by the other.[9]

Order of Performance. Frequently in contract disputes both parties fail to perform. Ascertaining the required order of performance is therefore important in determining whether a party's failure to perform constitutes a breach or is justified by the other's failure. In other words, in applying the constructive conditions of exchange doctrine, the threshold question is: who is required to perform *first?*

The order of performance may be determined by the express terms of the contract. Suppose S and B have a contract for sale of goods, calling for delivery in 30 days and payment within 10 days after delivery. On these facts, it is apparent from the terms of the contract that S is to perform first. Additionally, if the performance of one party extends over a period of time, his performance is due first unless the contract provides otherwise. This rule generally applies in contracts involving services, such as employment or construction contracts.[10]

Unless the contract or circumstances indicate otherwise, performances are due simultaneously. Simultaneous performance is possible under an agreement in the following circumstances: (1) if the same time (or period of time) is fixed for performance of each party, (2) if the time of performance is fixed for one party but not the other, or (3) if no time is fixed for the performance of either party. This approach is followed both for UCC and common law contracts.[11] As previously noted, a contract for the sale of land, for example, normally contemplates a simultaneous exchange of the deed (the conveyance of the property) and the purchase price. A contract for the sale of goods, unless otherwise agreed, requires simultaneous delivery of the goods and payment of the price.

Tender of Performance. If performance is to occur simultaneously, the concept of tender of performance becomes important. A **tender of performance** is either actual performance or an offer to perform, coupled with the manifested present ability to do so. When performances are to be exchanged simultaneously, each party's tender of performance is a condition to the other's duty. Thus, it is frequently stated that mutual tenders of performance are "concurrent conditions." A tender of performance need not be actual performance. One advantage of simultaneous performance is that one party is not required to perform without reasonable assurance that the other also will perform. Additionally, simultaneous performance avoids placing the burden on one party of financing the other's performance. In order to put the nonperforming party in breach, the injured party need not actually perform, but must only make a tender or offer to perform. Until a party has at least made an offer to perform, the other's duty does not arise. If both parties fail to make a tender, neither party is in breach.

To illustrate the operation of the preceding rules, assume Sandberg agrees to sell Bench a machine for $10,000, delivery to be made at Sandberg's warehouse on June 1. On June 1 both parties are present at the warehouse, but Sandberg neither delivers nor offers to deliver the machine and Bench neither pays nor offers to pay for the machine. Neither party can hold the other liable for breach. If Sandberg places the machine on his loading dock ready for delivery and Bench fails to pay, Sandberg

---

9. This concept is discussed in conjunction with the landlord-tenant material in Chapter 36.

10. In these cases, however, the contract generally provides for periodic or progress payments to the party rendering the longer performance. Further, most states have statutes requiring frequent periodic payment of wages in employment contracts.

11. UCC §§2-507(1), 2-511(1); *Restatement (Second) of Contracts* §234(1) and comment b.

has a claim for breach against Bench. Conversely, if Bench tenders the price to Sandberg at the agreed time and place and Sandberg fails to deliver, Sandberg is liable for breach.

Whether or not simultaneous performance is required under a contract, and unless the contract or other circumstances indicate otherwise, a party is required to render her entire performance at one time if it is possible to do so. In other words, a party is generally not entitled to perform part of her promise at a time, and the other party may not require her to do so.

Excuse of Condition

Occasionally, a duty to perform a promise will arise even though a condition to that duty has not occurred. Two common situations excusing occurrence of a condition, waiver and failure to act in good faith, are discussed below.

Waiver. **Waiver** is a term used somewhat loosely in the law. It generally is defined as the voluntary surrender or relinquishment of a known right, usually unaccompanied by consideration. In particular, a party granting a waiver effectively promises to perform a duty despite the nonoccurrence of a condition to that duty. A waiver may occur either before or after nonoccurrence of the condition.

Because a waiver effectively operates as a contract modification, the issue of consideration for the modification may arise. Generally a promise to perform a conditional duty, even though the condition has not occurred, is binding without consideration. If, however, the promise to disregard the nonoccurrence of the condition has a material effect upon what is received by the promisor or materially changes the burden or risk he has agreed to assume, consideration to support it is generally required.[12]

Therefore, the types of conditions subject to waiver without consideration under the preceding rule are those that may be viewed as merely technical or procedural in nature or conditions concerning comparatively minor matters. Examples include

conditions relating to the time or manner of performance or requirements of notice.[13]

Notwithstanding lack of consideration, waivers are frequently enforceable on the basis of estoppel. That is, if one contracting party leads the other to believe that she will not insist upon occurrence of a condition to her duty, and the other changes position in reliance on that representation—for example, by failing to cause the condition to occur—enforcement of the waiver is frequently necessary to avoid injustice to the reliant party.

Failure to Act in Good Faith—Prevention and Hindrance. Both the UCC and the common law impose a duty of good faith and fair dealing upon the parties in the performance and enforcement of the contract.[14] Though good faith is generally defined as "honesty in fact," the requirement is more expansive as it relates to the performance of the contract. For example, bad faith performance takes many forms including evasion of the spirit of the contract, lack of diligence, intentionally rendering imperfect performance, abusing a power to specify terms, and interference with, or failure to cooperate in, the other party's performance.[15] Breach of the duty to act in good faith in contract performance is commonly discussed as **prevention** or **hindrance** by one party of the other's performance. Nonperformance of this duty has two effects.

1. Because each party is under a duty to act in good faith, nonperformance of that duty is a breach of the contract. Assume Standard Packaging, Inc. agrees to manufacture and sell 100,000 plastic containers to Bottle, Inc. for $25,000. Bottle is to select an assortment of sizes and colors from a list stated in the contract. Bottle fails to make the selection within a reasonable time, and as a result, the manufacture of the containers is delayed, caus-

---

12. *Restatement (Second) of Contracts* §84(1) and comment c.

13. It should be noted, however, that, under the UCC, contract modifications need no consideration to be binding if sought in good faith. A similar rule applies to common law contracts in certain circumstances. Thus, a waiver affecting even a material part of the exchange may be binding without consideration as a contract modification.

14. UCC §§1-203, 2-103(1)(b); *Restatement (Second) of Contracts* §205; see discussion of the good faith requirement in Chapter 6.

15. *Restatement (Second) of Contracts* §205 comment d.

ing Standard loss. Because the duty of good faith requires Bottle to make the selection within a reasonable time, its failure to do so is a breach.

2. If a party's failure to act in good faith substantially contributes to the nonoccurrence of a condition to his duty, the occurrence of that condition is excused. In other words, the party who prevents or hinders the occurrence of the condition becomes liable to perform despite its nonoccurrence. Thus, if a duty to cooperate is imposed (either by the terms of the contract or as part of the duty to act in good faith), lack of cooperation results in breach. For example, assume Sullivan contracts with Bancroft to sell a tract of land for $25,000. Bancroft's duty is conditional upon her procurement of mortgage financing at a specified interest rate and term in the amount of the purchase price. Bancroft fails to make reasonable efforts to obtain financing and subsequently refuses to perform when Sullivan tenders the deed. Sullivan has a claim for breach of contract against Bancroft. Bancroft's breach of her duty to act in good faith substantially contributed to the nonoccurrence of a condition to her duty to pay the purchase price (obtaining adequate mortgage financing), thereby excusing it. To illustrate further, assume Anderson, an auditor, contracts with Nationwide, a corporation, to prepare audited financial statements as of June 30, and to issue a report by August 1, the date of the annual stockholders' meeting. Anderson is subsequently unable to complete the report by August 1 because of delays and lack of cooperation by the company's staff. In this case, because Nationwide's lack of cooperation substantially contributed to nonoccurrence of a condition to Nationwide's duty to pay (completion by August 1), the condition is excused.

Performance and Breach

Contract duties are discharged—extinguished or terminated—in various ways. For example, a contractual obligation may be discharged by a mutual agreement to rescind or modify it, a novation or other substituted contract, an accord and satisfaction, or nonoccurrence of a condition. In addition, contracts may be discharged by a promisor's bankruptcy, expiration of the statute of limitations, or through material alteration of a written agreement.

Most contracts are discharged by full performance on both sides, while others are discharged by material breach of the promises contained in the agreement. The remainder of this chapter examines the various legal doctrines that distinguish proper performance of a contract from breach, the legal tools designed to protect each party's expectation of performance prior to the time of agreed performance, and the circumstances in which contract performance is excused without liability for breach.

The "Substantial Performance" Doctrine

It is one thing to say that nonperformance of a contractual duty constitutes breach of the contract. It is quite another to apply this principle to concrete fact situations. That is, a fundamental issue in any breach of contract case is to examine the nature of the nonperformance causing the dispute. For example, the promisor may utterly fail to perform or may render virtually full performance containing only minor defects or omissions. Courts must therefore determine the legal effect of these varying degrees of contract performance.

Although simultaneous performance of contract promises is preferred, the contract may either expressly or impliedly require one party to perform before the other. Sometimes the first party to perform will render performance not literally in compliance with the contract. Contract disputes frequently arise when the party rendering such a performance asserts a right to payment on the basis of completed performance. The other party, however, refuses to perform asserting that, under the constructive conditions of exchange doctrine, she should be excused from performance because of a material defect in the first party's performance. Before one party's failure to perform causes the nonoccurrence of a constructive condition to the other's duty (thereby discharging that duty), the failure of performance must be judged **material**. The resolution of such disputes, therefore, turns upon which defects in performance are material and which are not.

The court may find that the defect in performance is immaterial or, alternatively, as is commonly stated, there has been *substantial* performance. In this situation, the constructive condition to the second party's duty has occurred, and she is required to perform her promise. This is known as the **substantial performance doctrine,** derived from the landmark case *Jacob & Youngs v. Kent* decided in 1921.[16] However, because substantial performance is not full performance, damages are recoverable for **partial breach;** damages are based only upon *part* of the right to performance under the contract. The benefit of the bargain is obtained partially through the award of damages and partially through the "substantial" performance.

The court, however, may find that the defect in performance is material. In this case, the constructive condition to the second party's duty has not occurred. Therefore, the second party's duty to perform does not arise and is discharged if the breach cannot be cured. The second party is entitled to damages for **total breach** of the contract; damages based upon *all* of his right to performance. The benefit of the bargain is obtained by completely substituting a judgment for money damages for the wrongdoer's duty to perform, and the breaching party is absolved from further duty to perform the contract. Nevertheless, the breaching party may have a claim in restitution for benefits conferred upon the other. In sum, if the failure to perform is a material breach, the injured party may sue for damages for total breach and is relieved of his corresponding duty to perform. If the breach is immaterial, the injured party must perform but is entitled to damages for partial breach.

The substantial performance doctrine must be viewed as a limited exception to the general rule that exact, literal performance of contractual promises is required for recovery. Contract law provides certainty and predictability; it is designed to protect the parties' reasonable expectations that contractual promises will be performed as agreed. To allow a party who has not literally fulfilled the terms of his promise to recover effectively binds the other to an agreement to which he has not assented. It also encourages the parties to deviate, however slightly, from the literal terms of the bargain. Both results are inconsistent with the basic purposes of contract law. Therefore, the substantial performance doctrine applies only if the departure from the agreed terms is "immaterial."

---

16. 129 N.E. 889 (N.Y. 1921).

Determining materiality is often a difficult issue, as the following case illustrates.

O. W. Grun Roofing and Construction Company v. Cope
529 S.W.2d 258 (Tex. Civ. App. 1975)

Plaintiff Mrs. Fred Cope entered into a contract with defendant O. W. Grun Roofing and Construction Company (Grun) by which Cope agreed to pay Grun $648.00 to install a new roof on her house. Grun installed the roof; however, the shingles used were not of uniform color. Grun tried to replace some of the shingles, but the colors still did not match so the roof appeared to have been patched rather than replaced. Although the roof was soundly constructed and provided protection from the elements, the color problem could be resolved only by installing a completely new roof.

Cope sued Grun for breach of contract; Grun counterclaimed for breach and requested damages of $648, the contract price. The trial court held that Grun had breached the contract and awarded damages to Cope. Grun appealed alleging that his installation of the roof constituted substantial performance of the contract thereby entitling him to the contract price.

Cadena, Justice

. . . [T]he doctrine of substantial performance . . . is especially common in cases involving building contracts, although its application is not restricted to such contracts.

It is difficult to formulate definitive rule for determining whether the contractor's performance, less than complete, amounts to "substantial performance," since the question is one of fact and of degree, and the answer depends on the particular facts of each case. . . .

[T]he following definition by the Commission of Appeals in *Atkinson v. Jackson Bros.,* 270 S.W. 848, 851 (Tex.Comm.App.1925), is a typical recital of the constituent elements of the doctrine:

To constitute substantial compliance the contractor must have in good faith intended to comply with the contract, and shall have substantially done so in the sense that the defects are not pervasive, do not constitute a deviation from the general plan contemplated for the work, and are not so essential that the object of the parties in making the contract and its purpose cannot, without difficulty, be accomplished by remedying them. Such performance permits only such omissions or deviations from the contract as are inadvertent and unintentional, are not due to bad faith, do not impair the structure as a whole, and are remediable without doing material damage to other parts of the building in tearing down and reconstructing.

. . . What was the general plan contemplated for the work in this case? What was the object and purpose of the parties? . . . Was the general plan to install a substantial roof which would serve the purpose which roofs are designed to serve? Or, rather, was the general plan to install a substantial roof of uniform color? Was the object and purpose of the contract merely to furnish such a roof, or was it to furnish such a roof which would be of a uniform color? It should not come as a shock to anyone to adopt a rule to the effect that a person has, particularly with respect to his home, to choose for himself and to contract for something which exactly satisfies that choice, and not to be compelled to accept something else. In the matter of homes and their decoration, as much as, if not more than, in many other fields, mere taste or preference, almost approaching whimsy, may be controlling with the homeowner, so that variations which might, under other circumstances, be considered trifling, may be inconsistent with that "substantial performance" on which liability to pay must be predicated. . . .

In the case before us there is evidence to support the conclusion that plaintiff can secure a roof of uniform coloring only by installing a completely new roof. We cannot say, as a matter of law, that the evidence establishes that in this case that a roof which so lacks uniformity in color as to give the appearance of a patch job serves essentially the same purpose as a roof of uniform color which has the appearance of being a new roof. We are not prepared to hold that a contractor who tenders a performance so deficient that it can be remedied only by completely redoing the work for which the contract called has established, as a matter of law,

that he has substantially performed his contractual obligation. . . .

[Judgment affirmed.]

Substantial Performance and Forfeiture

In the preceding case, O. W. Grun Roofing and Construction Company suffered a forfeiture—it was denied recovery after performing in reliance on the contract. The substantial performance doctrine is often used by the courts, in the interest of justice, when extreme forfeiture would otherwise result from the nonoccurrence of a condition. The risk of forfeiture is greatest when one party must partially or completely perform before the other party's duty to perform arises. For this reason, as the *Grun* opinion indicates, the substantial performance doctrine has been most frequently invoked in construction contracts to rescue a contractor rendering defective performance. Unfortunately for Grun Company, however, the court found that Grun's performance fell short of the substantial performance standard required for recovery under the contract.

As noted earlier in this chapter, a risk of forfeiture follows failure of an express as well as a constructive condition. Express conditions must be literally fulfilled before a duty to perform arises, in contrast to constructive conditions, which need only be substantially performed. Nevertheless, even when the parties expressly condition their duties in unmistakable language upon the occurrence of an event, the court may, in order to do justice, excuse the occurrence of the condition if necessary to avoid an extreme forfeiture unless the occurrence was a material part of the agreed exchange. This rule may apply, for example, to a "time of the essence" provision when the court finds that time of performance was not, in fact, a material part of the agreed exchange.

Substantial Performance Under the UCC—The "Perfect Tender" Rule

In contracts for the sale of goods, courts have long held that the buyer is entitled to expect strict, literal performance of the contract by the seller. Under

UCC §2-503(1), to make a valid tender of delivery the seller must "put and hold conforming goods at the buyer's disposition." Under §2-601, if the goods or the tender of delivery fail "in any respect to conform to the contract," the buyer may reject the entire shipment. Additionally, because goods may fluctuate rapidly in price, performance at the agreed time is generally essential; that is, time is of the essence. Therefore, in order to recover, the seller must tender goods conforming in every respect to the terms of the contract. This requirement is commonly known as the **perfect tender rule,** which, if interpreted literally, means that there is no "substantial performance" doctrine applicable to contracts for the sale of goods.

The Code, however, provides many exceptions to the perfect tender rule, outlined below, that create a special form of the substantial performance doctrine for sales contracts.

1. The perfect tender rule does not apply to installment contracts. An **installment contract** is one requiring or authorizing the seller to deliver the goods in separate lots to be separately accepted by the buyer. In such contracts, governed by §2-612, the buyer is entitled to reject an installment only if its nonconformity *substantially impairs* the value of that installment and cannot be corrected by the seller. Similarly, a default as to one or more installments is a breach of the whole contract only if it *substantially impairs* the value of the whole. The rationale for this approach is that "the fact of a continuing relationship normally justifies a less rigid standard for installment contracts than for contracts for a single delivery."[17]

2. Perfect tender is not required if the parties' contract allows a less strict standard of performance. The effect of UCC provisions may generally be varied by agreement of the parties under §1-102(3). As such, the parties are free to set by contract the standards by which performance is to be measured.[18]

3. Under certain circumstances, §2-508 gives a seller the opportunity to "cure" or correct a defective performance without liability for breach.

4. A buyer, entitled to reject a tender of delivery, may lose that right through failure to make an adequate rejection or failure to particularize the defects in the goods.

5. Under certain limited circumstances, a buyer may revoke a previous acceptance of goods under §2-608. The buyer may, however, revoke only if the nonconformity "substantially impairs" their value to him.

The perfect tender rule and the concepts of rejection, cure, acceptance, and revocation of acceptance are discussed in more detail in Chapter 18.

Part Performances as Agreed Equivalents—Divisibility

A contracting party may properly render part performance under a contract, but fail to properly perform her remaining obligations.[19] When a contract has been partially performed, the situation must be analyzed to determine to what extent, if at all, the party in default is entitled to recover under the contract for the performance actually rendered. The answer to this question is determined by application of the doctrine traditionally known as **divisibility.** Under the original *Restatement of Contracts* definition, a contract is divisible if by its terms: "(1) performance of each party is divided into two or more parts, and (2) the number of parts due from each party is the same, and (3) the performance of each part by one party is the agreed exchange for a corresponding part by the other party."[20] If a contract is divisible, performance of a divisible part by one party entitles her to the agreed exchange for that part, despite her nonperformance of other parts of the contract. The *Restatement (Second) of Contracts*[21] finds a contract divisible if full performance under the contract can be apportioned into corresponding pairs of part performances so that the exchange of the part performances can be regarded as **agreed equivalents.**

The rationale for the principle of divisibility and agreed equivalents is the same as that supporting the substantial performance doctrine—to reduce the risk of forefeiture to the breaching party. If the

---

17. Supplement No. 1 to the UCC, p. 1 (1955).
18. See discussion in Chapter 6.

19. The failure to render complete performance may or may not constitute a breach of the contract; for example, the party's remaining duties may be excused on grounds of impracticability (see page 325).
20. *Restatement of Contracts* §266 comment e.
21. *Restatement (Second) of Contracts* §240.

doctrine of agreed equivalents applies, the party who renders part performance is entitled to recover its agreed equivalent as if the parties had made a separate contract concerning that pair of performances. Failure to perform some other part, though possibly constituting a breach of contract, does not affect the right to recover for the part performance. Assume Seller and Buyer have a contract for the sale of 600 watches for $30,000 to extend over a one-year period. Seller is to deliver 50 watches on the first of each month. Buyer is required to pay one-twelfth of the purchase price for each shipment upon delivery. On these facts, the court may find that each delivery and the corresponding payment are agreed equivalents, making the contract divisible. Therefore, if Seller properly makes the first delivery, but subsequently breaches by refusing to render further performance, she may enforce Buyer's corresponding duty to pay for that performance (1/12 of $30,000). Buyer, however, has a claim against Seller for breaching the remainder of the contract.

Although the divisibility doctrine is primarily applicable to installment contracts, the doctrine may apply even if performance by one or both parties is to occur at the same time. For example, assume that in exchange for Barbara's promise to pay $2,000, Stan agrees to manufacture five identical oak cabinets to be delivered on June 1. Stan, however, delivers only four cabinets on June 1. Because Barbara intends to resell them through her furniture store, failure to deliver the fifth cabinet does not diminish the value of the others to her. The court may decide that manufacture and delivery of four cabinets and payment of the corresponding part of the price at the contract rate ($1,600) are agreed equivalents. Thus, Stan would be allowed to recover at the contract rate for his partial performance (4/5 of $2,000) but would be liable to Barbara for breach for failure to perform the remainder.

To apply the divisibility doctrine, the court must be able to calculate the amount due for the part performance. This calculation is possible, for example, if the prices for each performance are separately stated in the contract or can be ascertained from other sources, such as price lists. In addition to apportioning the price for the corresponding part performances, the court must also find that the corresponding pairs are agreed equivalents. That is,

the injured party should not be required to pay for a part performance unless he can make full use of that portion without the rest of the performance.[22] If the court finds that the part performance is insufficient to meet this test, the contract is generally designated **entire**. Contracts are deemed entire, for example, if performance is divided into parts representing only periodic progress payments toward the completion of a single job.

To illustrate, assume Ace Construction Company agrees to build a house for Doaks for $40,000, who agrees to finance the construction by paying one-fourth of the purchase price when the foundation is completed, one-fourth upon completion of the basic frame, one-fourth when the exterior is finished, and the final one-fourth upon receipt of the architect's certificate. Ace unjustifiably stops work upon completion of the basic frame, and sues to recover the second installment. Ace's partial performance (construction of the basic frame on the foundation) and Doaks's promise to pay $10,000 are not agreed equivalents. Ace is entitled to recover nothing from Doaks under the contract for that performance. That is, the payments are not made in exchange for a specified fraction of the building (creating in essence four separate contracts), but are part payments on the total purchase price of the house. Doaks has a claim against Ace for damages for breach of the contract.[23]

In the following case, the court was required to determine whether the contract was divisible or entire.

John v. United Advertising, Inc.
439 P.2d 53 (Colo. 1968)

> Plaintiff Dwight John, who owned and operated two motels, entered into a written contract with defendant, United Advertising, Inc. (United). The contract provided that United would construct, install, and maintain seven outdoor display signs advertis-

---

22. *Restatement (Second) of Contracts* §240 comment e.

23. Although Ace is able to recover nothing *under the contract* for its part performance, the court may, in order to avoid unjust enrichment, require Doaks to make restitution of the value of any benefit conferred upon him by Ace's performance; see the restitution discussion in Chapter 15.

ing John's motel, and John would rent the signs for $95 per month. The contract stated that the rental payment was apportioned $35 for one large sign and $10 for each of six small signs. The contract also provided that "termination or modification of any item of this agreement constitutes that part of the agreement only and does not affect any other item or part of the agreement." United failed to construct sign No. 4 and installed sign No. 5 in the wrong location. All other signs were installed in accordance with the contract.

John sued United requesting damages equal to the amount John had paid for all signs. The trial court found for John but awarded damages of only $120, representing the payments made for signs No. 4 and 5. John appealed.

McWilliams, Justice

. . . The central issue is whether the contract in question is "entire" or "severable" in nature. . . .

[I]f the contract be *severable* or *divisible,* then the plaintiff is *only* entitled to recover those monies paid defendant for signs No. 4 and 5, which sum is $120. But if the contract be deemed entire in nature, the plaintiff would be entitled to recover *all* of the monies paid by him to the defendant, which would be the sum of $680. It is in this setting that it then becomes necessary to determine the correctness of the trial court's determination that the contract is severable, and not entire.

Whether a contract is entire or severable is a matter which cannot be determined with mathematical precision. . . . The primary objective is to ascertain the intent of the contracting parties. . . . And the issue as to whether a contract is entire or severable has been characterized as a mixed question of fact and law. . . .

Plaintiff's position on this point is that it was intended that this be a "package deal," that at least four of the signs were to be so situated as to "lead" tourists to the very doorstep of his motel, and that he received *no* benefit under the contract unless all seven signs were properly erected and in place. Therefore, it is argued, the contract is entire in nature.

The defendant, on the contrary, urges that it was the intent of the parties that the contract be severable. In support thereof defendant points to the fact that the money due it from the plaintiff was not a

lump sum for the seven signs, but was apportioned as so much per individual sign. Also, the defendant argues that the termination and modification clause . . . certainly looks toward severability. Finally, defendant notes that the several billings were on a "so much per sign basis," and each sign is said to be complete within itself, with no one sign by any language printed thereon being "tied in" to any other sign.

The foregoing recital indicates that the testimony bearing on this particular matter is in at least a degree of conflict. Certainly reasonable persons could well differ as to the proper inferences to be drawn from the testimony and documentary evidence which was before the trial court. In such circumstances we are not at liberty to overturn the trial court's determination that the contract in the instant case was a severable one. . . .

[Judgment affirmed.]

Effect of Prospective Nonperformance

Each party to a contract involving an exchange of promises contemplates a subsequent exchange of performances. The preceding discussion concerned the effect of a party's failure to perform a promise when performance becomes due. Each party also expects that the other will do nothing to jeopardize the expectation of return performance *prior to* the time of agreed performance. The following two sections outline the legal tools designed to protect the *expectation* of performance. First, UCC §2-609 is discussed, which protects a party when "reasonable grounds for insecurity" arise concerning the other's ability to perform. Second, the more aggravated case, repudiation, is discussed. Here, one party, before performance is due, unequivocally indicates an intent not to perform.

Safeguarding the Expectation of Performance—UCC §2-609

The Uniform Commercial Code recognizes that the essential purpose of a contract for sale is actual performance. The parties "do not bargain merely for a promise, or for a promise plus the right to win a lawsuit. . . . [A] continuing sense of reliance and security that the promised performance will be forthcoming when due, is an important feature of the bargain.''[24] Section 2-609(1) imposes an obligation on each party that the other's expectation of receiving due performance will not be impaired. To effectuate this purpose, the Code provides that whenever reasonable grounds for insecurity arise concerning the willingness or ability of either party to perform, the insecure party may:

1. demand adequate assurance of due performance in writing, and
2. until he receives such assurance may, if commercially reasonable, suspend any performance for which he has not already received the agreed return.

Two basic legal questions are presented in applying this provision: what are **reasonable grounds for insecurity,** and what constitutes **adequate assurance of due performance?**

Concerning the first question, note that the grounds for insecurity need not be *actual,* they need only be *reasonable.* To illustrate, assume S contracts to sell 500 printed circuit boards to B for future delivery. Prior to delivery, B hears a false rumor from an apparently trustworthy source that S is making defective deliveries to other buyers (or that S is on the verge of bankruptcy). The rumor would give B reasonable grounds for insecurity about S's ability to perform. To protect her expectation of performance, B may suspend her own performance. The rumor need not actually be true; the buyer must simply have *reasonable grounds* for believing it to be true. The same reasoning applies if a seller hears a false rumor concerning the financial condition of a buyer to whom he extends credit. The obligation of good faith is, of course, imposed upon any requests for assurance. Therefore, a party may not invoke §2-609 merely as a means to delay or avoid contractual obligations.[25]

What constitutes adequate assurance of due performance is a question of fact, depending upon the circumstances of the case including the reputation of the party receiving the demand, the relationship and any prior dealings of the parties, the nature of the reason for insecurity, and whether there have been past delinquencies or defective shipments.

The test of adequate assurance is objective, not subjective; that is, the issue is whether a reasonable person would be satisfied with the assurance, not whether the demanding party is, in fact, satisfied. Under §2-609(2), between merchants, the reasonableness of grounds for insecurity and the adequacy of any assurance offered are determined according to commercial standards.

Based upon these and any other relevant factors, adequate assurance may be provided (if the problem involves defective deliveries) by a reputable seller's statement that he is giving the matter his prompt attention and that the defects will not recur. Any assurance relative to defective delivery that interferes with the buyer's use of the goods must be accompanied by replacement, repair, credit against the purchase price, or other reasonable cure. In the case of a disreputable seller, more assurance may be required, such as posting a bond or immediate replacement of the defective shipment. On the other hand, if the buyer's ability to pay is in issue, adequate assurance may simply involve a satisfactory explanation by the buyer. In more serious cases, a credit report from the buyer's banker, or a surety, or collateral to secure the debt may be required.[26]

Once a justified demand has been received, the party to whom it is directed has a reasonable time, not exceeding thirty days, to provide adequate assurances. Failure to do so constitutes a repudiation of the contract, which is then governed by the principles discussed in the following section. Assume Jake and Mike contract on January 1 for delivery of goods on June 1. In February, Mike hears a ru-

---

24. UCC §2-609, Official Comment 1.

25. A party may also invoke §2-609 in conjunction with an assignment. Under §2-210(5), the nonassigning party may treat any assignment delegating performance as creating reasonable grounds for insecurity. This rule recognizes that the nonassigning party has a substantial interest in the reliability of the person to whom the duty to perform is delegated. UCC §2-210, Official Comment 6. Assignment and delegation are discussed in Chapter 13.

26. The contract itself may contain an express provision allowing one party to (1) accelerate performance or payment, or (2) require collateral or additional collateral "at will" or "when he deems himself insecure." Consistent with the principles discussed above, this language is construed to mean that the party may invoke the provision only in the good faith belief that the prospect of receiving payment or performance is impaired. UCC §1-208.

mor concerning Jake's impending bankruptcy and demands assurances on February 15. Jake has a reasonable time from February 15 not exceeding thirty days to provide assurance. His failure to do so is a repudiation of the contract governed by principles discussed in the following section.

Note finally that §2-609 is regarded as an innovation in the law. Though applicable only to UCC contracts (sales of goods), a similar rule, based upon §2-609, has been adopted for common law contracts in the *Restatement (Second) of Contracts.*[27]

Breach by Anticipatory Repudiation

A party's conduct may go well beyond merely creating reasonable grounds for insecurity and may constitute repudiation of the contract. **Repudiation** occurs when one contracting party, by words or conduct, unequivocally indicates his inability or unwillingness to perform without breach.[28]

To constitute a repudiation, a party's statement or conduct must be sufficiently definite and positive to be reasonably interpreted by the other as indicating an unwillingness or inability to perform. Mere expressions of doubt concerning one's ability or inclination to render performance are not enough. However, an indication of possible inability to perform would certainly create reasonable grounds for insecurity, allowing the insecure party to request assurance and suspend his own performance. As noted above, failure to provide assurances within a reasonable time (not exceeding thirty days for a Code contract) would then constitute a repudiation of the contract.

A party who repudiates a duty with respect to performance not yet due commits an **anticipatory repudiation.** This term simply means that the party repudiates the duty before committing a breach by nonperformance. The effect of an anticipatory re-

pudiation is to give the other party an immediate claim against the repudiating party for damages for total breach of the contract even though the time agreed upon for performance has not yet arrived. Thus, anticipatory repudiation gives rise to what is commonly known an "anticipatory breach," or, more accurately stated, breach by anticipatory repudiation. In addition to giving rise to a claim for damages for total breach, one party's repudiation of his duty discharges the other's remaining duties to perform.[29] Assume that on April 1 Graves contracts to sell land to Brown. The contract calls for delivery of the deed and payment of the purchase price on July 30. On May 1, Graves informs Brown that she will not perform. Graves's statement is an anticipatory repudiation of the contract. Brown's duty to pay the purchase price is discharged and Brown has a claim against Graves for damages for total breach of the contract.

When faced with an anticipatory repudiation, the injured party need not elect to sue immediately for total breach, but may await the time agreed upon for performance and attempt to convince the repudiating party to retract the repudiation. During this time, the aggrieved party may elect to continue or suspend her own performance.[30]

For UCC contracts, §2-610 basically follows the principles discussed above. It provides that if either party repudiates the contract with respect to a performance not yet due, the loss of which will *substantially impair* the value of the contract to the other, the aggrieved party may (1) for a commercially reasonable time await performance by the repudiating party; or (2) resort to any Code remedy for breach even though he has notified the repudiating party that he is awaiting performance and

---

27. *Restatement (Second) of Contracts* §251.

28. *Restatement (Second) of Contracts* §250. Though repudiation is not explicitly defined in the text of the UCC, Official Comment 1 to §2-610 states: ". . . [A]nticipatory repudiation centers upon an overt communication of intention or an action which renders performance impossible or demonstrates a clear determination not to continue with performance."

29. A party may indicate that he will not perform because his performance has become impracticable or his purpose frustrated. In this case, the statement or act is *not* a repudiation because the threatened nonperformance does not constitute a breach. Therefore, no action for breach of contract arises. However, the other party's duty to render further performance is discharged. Impracticability and frustration are discussed beginning on page 325.

30. Note, however, that after repudiation, a party who continues performance or delays in attempting to find substitute performance may, under the doctrine of mitigation, be precluded from recovering damages for loss that could have been avoided. Mitigation is discussed in Chapter 15.

has urged retraction. In either case, the aggrieved party may suspend his own performance.

The following case illustrates the relationship between §2-609 (insecurity) and §2-610 (repudiation) in a modern commercial contract.

AMF, Incorporated v. McDonald's Corporation

536 F.2d 1167 (7th Cir. 1976)

Plaintiff AMF, Incorporated and defendant McDonald's Corporation entered into a contract by which McDonald's agreed to buy and AMF agreed to sell and install 16 computerized cash registers (model 72C) in McDonald's restaurants. McDonald's licensees later ordered seven more cash registers from AMF. AMF had begun marketing the cash registers in 1966 and a prototype had been installed in one of McDonald's restaurants in April, 1968. The primary contract was dated August 29, 1968. Deliveries were to begin in February, 1969 and to be completed in the first half of 1969. In February, 1969, however, AMF rescheduled the deliveries to begin in July of that year and to be completed in January, 1970. The deliveries were never made.

From the time of installation, the prototype performed poorly, requiring frequent service calls. At McDonald's request AMF removed the prototype in April, 1969. On March 18, 1969, AMF and McDonald's personnel met to discuss the problems and McDonald's requested AMF to formulate performance and reliability standards. By May 1, 1969, AMF still did not have a working machine and the parties were unable to agree on reliability standards. AMF concluded that McDonald's had cancelled the contract. At a July 29, 1969, meeting, "it was mutually understood that the 72C orders were cancelled and that none would be delivered."

AMF sued McDonald's for damages alleging that McDonald's had wrongfully cancelled and repudiated the contract. The trial court ruled in favor of McDonald's; AMF appealed.

Cummings, Circuit Judge

. . . Whether in a specific case a buyer has reasonable grounds for insecurity is a question of fact.

. . . On this record, McDonald's clearly had "reasonable grounds for insecurity" with respect to AMF's performance. At the time of the March 18, 1969, meeting, the prototype unit had performed unsatisfactorily ever since its April 1968 installation. Although AMF had projected delivery of all twenty-three units by the first half of 1969, AMF later scheduled delivery from the end of July 1969 until January 1970. When McDonald's personnel visited AMF's Vandalia, Ohio, plant on March 4, 1969, they saw that none of the 72C systems was being assembled and learned that a pilot unit would not be ready until the end of July of that year. They were informed that the engineer assigned to the project was not to commence work until March 17th. AMF's own personnel were also troubled about the design of the 72C, causing them to attempt to reduce McDonald's order to five units. Therefore, under Section 2-609 McDonald's was entitled to demand adequate assurance of performance by AMF.

However, AMF urges that Section 2-609 of the UCC . . . is inapplicable because McDonald's did not make a written demand of adequate assurance of due performance. . . . [We have] noted that the Code should be liberally construed and therefore rejected such "a formalistic approach" to Section 2-609. McDonald's failure to make a written demand was excusable because AMF's Mr. Dubosque's testimony and his April 2 and 18, 1969, memoranda about the March 18th meeting showed AMF's clear understanding that McDonald's had suspended performance until it should receive adequate assurance of due performance from AMF. . . .

After the March 18th demand, AMF never repaired the [prototype] unit satisfactorily nor replaced it. Similarly, it was unable to satisfy McDonald's that the twenty-three machines on order would work. At the May 1st meeting, AMF offered unsatisfactory assurances for only five units instead of twenty-three. The performance standards AMF tendered to McDonald's were unacceptable because they would have permitted the 72C's not to function properly for 90 hours per year, permitting as much as one failure in every fifteen days in a busy McDonald's restaurant. Also, as the district court found, AMF's Vandalia, Ohio, personnel were too inexperienced to produce a proper machine. Since

AMF did not provide adequate assurance of performance after McDonald's March 18th demand, UCC Section 2-609(1) permitted McDonald's to suspend performance. When AMF did not furnish adequate assurance of due performance at the May 1st meeting, it thereby repudiated the contract under Section 2-609(4). At that point, Section 2-610(b) . . . permitted McDonald's to cancel the orders pursuant to Section 2-711 . . . as it finally did on July 29, 1969. . . .

[Judgment affirmed.]

Retraction of Repudiation. In both UCC and common law contracts, the repudiating party may retract her repudiation unless the aggrieved party has (1) materially changed her position in reliance on the repudiation (for example, by covering; that is, procuring substitute performance), or (2) cancelled or otherwise indicated that she considers the repudiation final (for example, by bringing suit for total breach). Thus, the right to retract is entirely dependent upon action taken by the aggrieved party.[31] The retraction may be made in any manner clearly indicating the repudiating party's intention to perform. However, because the repudiation itself creates reasonable grounds for insecurity, the retraction must include any assurances justifiably demanded. An effective retraction then reinstates the repudiating party's rights under the contract.[32]

Limitation to Executory Contracts. Most courts have held that the breach by anticipatory repudiation doctrine applies only to mutually executory contracts; that is, unperformed duties must remain on both sides. Thus, an immediate action for total breach is unavailable if the aggrieved party (the plaintiff) has fully performed his obligations under the contract (the contract is executed on his side), and the repudiator's duty is still executory (requiring either the payment of money in a lump sum or installments, or other performance).[33] In other

words, a party who has fully performed cannot sue for breach of contract—even if the other party repudiates—until an actual breach by nonperformance occurs.

Assume, for example, that Smead contracts to sell a painting to Carter for $10,000 with delivery to be made on June 1 and payment to follow on July 1. Smead delivers the painting on June 1 and on June 5 Carter tells Smead that she will not make payment on July 1. Because the contract is not executory, Smead may not sue Carter for breach of contract until Carter fails to pay on July 1. This rule is especially important in installment contracts. Assume that in the preceding example, the contract provides for delivery of the painting and payment of $2,000 on June 1, with additional $2,000 payments due on July 1, August 1, September 1, and October 1. Carter makes the June and July payments and then repudiates on July 15 by indicating that she will not make any further payment. Because Smead has fully performed, she has no claim against Carter for total breach on July 15. Smead is required to sue for breach of each successive installment as it comes due.

Contracting parties often protect themselves against this result by including an **acceleration clause** in the contract. These clauses provide that upon the occurrence of a given contingency (normally a default in one or more installments), all future installments are accelerated and become immediately due and payable. In this manner the entire amount owed can be collected in a single action.

Limiting the anticipatory repudiation doctrine to wholly executory contracts has been severely criticized. It places a party who has already fully performed and faced with a repudiation at a disadvantage in remedy when compared with an injured party whose duties remain executory. In other words, the party whose duties are executory has an immediate action for total breach whereas a party who has fully performed does not. Further, the aggrieved party may be unable to collect a judgment if required to wait until the time of agreed performance to sue. For example, the repudiating party may become insolvent or leave the jurisdiction. Fortunately, this limitation is applied only infrequently because courts often protect the injured

---

31. UCC §2-611(1) and Official Comment 1; *Restatement (Second) of Contracts* §256.

32. UCC §§2-611(2)-(3).

33. *Restatement (Second) of Contracts* §253 comment c.

party by ordering restitution by the repudiator or other relief.

Excuses for Nonperformance

Contract liability is strict liability. A contracting party generally runs the risk that the contract will be more burdensome, more expensive to perform, or less desirable than anticipated, or that he paid too much or charged too little for the goods or services involved. A person can reduce these risks by incorporating special contract provisions that limit the extent of his undertaking. For example, a party may agree only to use "best efforts," or reserve a right to cancel, or limit his obligation to requirements or output, or use a "force majeure" clause, or adopt a flexible pricing arrangement, or limit liability for breach to a specified amount.

Under certain limited circumstances, however, a party who has undertaken an absolute duty is excused from performance of that duty under the doctrines of impracticability (impossibility) of performance or frustration of purpose. In these situations, generally, an extraordinary event occurs that so substantially alters the parties' reasonable expectations that the essential nature of the performance is changed. In some cases, the event rendering performance impracticable occurs before or at the time the contract is made (existing or original impracticability). Normally, however, the extraordinary event **supervenes,** meaning that it occurs after the contract is made but before performance. In such cases, the court, in the interests of justice, may discharge the obligor from his duty to perform without liability for breach. If one party's duty is discharged on impracticability or frustration grounds, the other's remaining duties are also discharged.[34] The issue is generally considered to be a question of law, not fact, and is thus for the court rather than the jury to decide. The following material examines the law governing impracticability caused by supervening events. Note that the same basic principles also govern cases of existing impracticability.

Impracticability (Impossibility)

Introduction to Impracticability. Historically, contractual duties were discharged by supervening events only if performance was objectively **impossible.** That is, relief under early common law required proof that no one could render the promised performance—the mere inability of the promisor to perform was insufficient. This statement simply means that a contracting party generally assumes the risk of his own inability to perform his duty. For example, a debtor's inability to pay a debt because of financial difficulties does not discharge the duty. Similarly, a manufacturer who contracts with the government to design and build a new computer system is not discharged if, due to its own lack of technical expertise, it is unable to produce a workable system.

Both the UCC and the *Restatement (Second) of Contracts* have abandoned the term "impossibility" in favor of the more expansive concept of **impracticability** (or **commercial impracticability**). Contract duties are discharged under the doctrine of impracticability not only if performance is objectively impossible, but also if it is rendered impracticable due to circumstances causing extreme or unreasonable difficulty or expense. The UCC impracticability doctrine is contained in §2-615, entitled "Excuse by Failure of Presupposed Conditions." Section 2-615(a) provides:

> Except so far as a seller may have assumed a greater obligation . . . delay in delivery or nondelivery in whole or in part by a seller . . . is not a breach of his duty under a contract for sale if *performance as agreed has been made impracticable by the occurrence of a contingency the non-occurrence of which was a basic assumption on which the contract was made. . . .*[35] (Emphasis added.)

---

34. As previously noted, it is a condition to each party's remaining duty to render performance that there be no material failure of the other party's performance due at an earlier time. This principle applies whether or not the failure is a breach.

35. Occasionally, the event causing impracticability will only partially prevent the seller from performing. In this situation, the seller is required to allocate production and deliveries among the customers in a fair and reasonable manner. UCC §2-615(b).

The *Restatement (Second) of Contracts* follows this basic language in formulating the doctrine applicable to common law contracts. Section 261 provides:

> Where, after a contract is made, a party's performance is made impracticable without his fault by the occurrence of an event the non-occurrence of which was a basic assumption on which the contract was made, his duty to render that performance is discharged, unless the language or the circumstances indicate the contrary.

Thus, the basic test governing discharge of a duty on grounds of impracticability is whether nonoccurrence of the event was "a basic assumption on which the contract was made."[36] As one court succinctly noted, this test "seems a somewhat complicated way of putting [the] question of how much risk the promisor assumed."[37] Impracticability analysis therefore requires resolution of three issues: (1) did an unexpected event occur after formation of the contract, (2) did that event render performance impossible or impracticable, and (3) did the promisor assume the risk that the event would occur? Relief on grounds of impracticability is unavailable if the promisor is at fault in causing the occurrence of the event. "Fault" in this context includes willful wrongs and other conduct amounting to negligence or breach of contract. In addition, under both the Code and the common law, the explicit language or other circumstances of the contract may indicate that a party has assumed an obligation to perform despite impracticability.

For the nonoccurrence of an event to be a basic assumption the parties need not consciously address themselves to that possibility. For example, death of the obligor in a personal service contract is a circumstance, the nonoccurrence of which is a basic assumption on which the contract is made, even though the parties may never consciously consider its occurrence. The fact that the event is unforeseeable strongly indicates that its nonoccurrence was a basic assumption, and therefore that the promisor did not assume the risk of its occurrence. Nevertheless, the fact that the event was foreseeable (or even foreseen) does not necessarily mean that the promisor assumed the risk because the parties may not have considered the contingency important enough to address in their agreement.

Events causing impracticability may be due either to Acts of God or acts of third parties. Both the common law and the Code deliberately refrain from any effort to list all possible contingencies. Several common fact situations to which the doctrine has been applied are discussed below.

Death or Incapacity of a Person Necessary for Performance. The most common basis for discharge on impracticability grounds is the death or incapacity of a person necessary for performance. Frequently, both parties understand that proper performance is dependent upon the continued existence or capacity of a particular person. The parties may provide that the services of a specific person are required. More frequently, however, they are silent on the point, and the court must then decide whether the duty so involves elements of personal service, expertise, judgment, or discretion that only personal performance is acceptable. If so, the duty to perform is discharged by supervening death or incapacity. Note that this approach corresponds directly to the rules relating to delegation of contract duties. That is, if the obligor could have delegated the duty, his death or incapacity does not excuse performance. In other words, upon the death of an obligor, his estate remains liable for performance of the contract unless the contract sufficiently involves elements of personal service or discretion.

Suppose Boggs hires Calhoun, a noted trial lawyer, to handle a major tort case. Calhoun dies prior to performance. Calhoun's duty is discharged by her death because performance required the exercise of Calhoun's personal skill and judgment; that is, she could not have delegated her duty to perform. Thus, Boggs has no claim against Calhoun's estate for breach of contract. On the other hand,

---

36. By its terms, UCC §2-615 only operates to discharge an aggrieved *seller*. A buyer is apparently required to proceed under the common law principles supplementing the Code through §1-103. However, the new *Restatement's* formulation of the doctrine for common law contracts makes it available to both parties. Additionally, cases decided under §2-615 have applied it to buyers.

37. *United States v. Wegematic Corporation,* 360 F.2d 674, 676 (2d Cir. 1966).

assume Seller contracts to sell and deliver 500 bales of cotton to Buyer. Seller dies prior to performance. Seller's estate remains liable to Buyer for performance of the contract. Seller could have delegated his duty to perform since his personal skill, discretion, or supervision is not necessary for performance.

Destruction of Subject Matter Necessary for Performance.

Frequently, the existence of a specific subject matter is a basic assumption on which the contract is made. Therefore, its destruction, deterioration, or failure to come into existence discharges a duty relating to it. This principle is derived from the classic early English case *Taylor v. Caldwell,* decided in 1863.[38] In this case, the defendant promised to allow the plaintiff to use the defendant's music hall for an agreed fee to give a series of four concerts. Prior to the time of agreed performance, the music hall burned down through no fault of either party. The court held that the destruction discharged the defendant's duty to perform and he was therefore not liable to the plaintiff for breach.

Failure of Anticipated Source of Supply. Perhaps the most common modern situation concerning destruction of subject matter necessary for performance occurs when the promisor's source of supply fails. For example, a seller of goods may assert impracticability if its only factory burns down. As a general rule, unless the parties make the source a basic assumption of the contract (an exclusive source agreed in the contract), its failure does not discharge the obligor's duty. Assume Swatch Textiles, Inc. contracts to sell a certain quantity of cloth to Birk. Swatch expects to manufacture the cloth in its factory. Prior to performance, however, the factory is destroyed through no fault of Swatch. Although cloth meeting the contract description is readily available on the market, Swatch refuses to purchase it in order to satisfy the contract with Birk. Swatch's duty to deliver the cloth is not discharged and it is liable to Birk for breach. Assume, however, on these same facts, that the original contract had stated that the cloth

was to be manufactured at Swatch's factory. In this situation, if the factory is subsequently destroyed, Swatch's duty to perform is discharged and it is not liable to Birk for breach because the particular source of supply was "a basic assumption on which the contract was made." Even if the contract is silent concerning the source, the court may grant relief upon its failure, if it can be shown from the circumstances, such as prior negotiations or previous contracts, that the parties had a common understanding or assumption regarding the source of supply.

Casualty to Identified Goods. The UCC resolves a related problem arising when goods which have been *identified* to the contract are destroyed prior to performance. Identification occurs when the parties designate or specify the particular goods to which the contract refers.[39] Under §2-613, if (1) the contract involves the sale of goods identified when the contract is made, and (2) the goods suffer casualty through no fault (including both willful and negligent conduct) of either party, (3) before risk of loss passes to the buyer,[40] then:

1. If the loss is total, the contract is avoided (rescinded). In this case, the burden of the casualty loss falls on the seller, but the buyer may not sue for breach of contract.

2. If the loss is partial or if the goods have deteriorated so as no longer to conform to the contract, the buyer may demand inspection and elect either to avoid the contract or accept the goods with an allowance against the price for the deterioration or deficiency in quality. As in the case of total loss, the buyer has no action for breach against the seller.

To illustrate, S, on June 1, contracts to sell three specified machines located at S's warehouse to B for $5,000. Delivery is to be made on June 30. On June 10, S's warehouse is destroyed by fire, after being struck by lightning. On these facts, S's duty to deliver the machines is discharged and S is not liable to B for breach.

---

38. 3 B. & S. 826, 122 Eng. Rep. 309 (K.B. 1863).

39. The concept and effect of identification are discussed in conjunction with the definition of "goods" in Chapter 7 and in Chapter 17.

40. Risk of loss is discussed in Chapter 17.

The principles discussed above have common application to contracts involving the sale by farmers of agricultural commodities. Here, the seller seeks to avoid his obligation on the basis of a crop failure resulting from drought, flood, or other adverse weather conditions, insects, disease, or the like. Note that growing crops are goods, identified when planted.[41] Therefore, if they are specifically identified at the time the contract is made, excuse due to their destruction may be based either upon §2-615 (Impracticability), or §2-613 (Casualty to Identified Goods). Even if the source is not explicitly stated, courts have often relieved farmers from their obligations after a crop failure. To do so, the court, based on the circumstances, finds that the parties at the time of contracting contemplated or assumed a single source of supply (the farmer's land) with no recourse to the market in case of deficiency.[42]

Supervening Illegality, Government Regulation or Order.

Parties to a contract generally assume that, subsequent to formation of a contract, the government (foreign or domestic) will not (1) make acts required for performance illegal, or (2) otherwise intervene by regulation or order to make performance impracticable. Therefore, supervening illegality, government regulation or order generally will discharge a duty on grounds of impracticability. Note that if acts required for performance were illegal at the time the contract was made, the contract is unenforceable in any event on grounds of public policy.

To illustrate, assume Signal Corp. contracts to sell oil to Hughes. Prior to performance, the government adopts an allocation plan requiring Signal to sell its entire output to Walters. Signal's duty to Hughes is discharged and Hughes has no claim against Signal for breach. Or assume Tilto, Inc.

contracts to sell pinball machines to George in a state where it is legal to own them. Prior to performance, the state passes a statute making sale, possession, and ownership of all such machines illegal. The duties of both parties are discharged.

The UCC specifically addresses the issue of government intervention in §2-615(a) by providing for the seller's discharge if performance as agreed has been made impracticable "by compliance in good faith with any applicable foreign or domestic governmental regulation or order whether or not it later proves to be invalid." Thus, the Code affords equal significance to both foreign and domestic regulation.

Increased Cost.

Circumstances making performance more expensive or difficult than anticipated usually do not form a basis for impracticability. Contracting parties generally assume the risk that performance as agreed may become more burdensome than expected. Even when dramatic increases in costs are encountered, courts in both UCC and common law contracts have generally denied relief both because the increase was insufficiently onerous to render performance impracticable and because the rise in price was foreseeable. Given the fact that one of the few certainties in modern times is that prices will rise, a contracting party can rarely prove that a price increase is an event "the nonoccurrence of which was a basic assumption on which the contract was made." For this reason, courts will likely continue to deny most impracticability claims based on increased cost, particularly because a major purpose of contract law is to protect one party against fluctuations in cost by allocating the risk of those fluctuations to the other.

In the following classic case, the court explicitly addresses the risk allocation issue.

---

41. See discussion of identification in Chapter 17. See also the discussion of goods closely associated with land in Chapter 34.

42. In addition to failure of an anticipated source of supply, occasionally the parties' intended manner of delivery or payment will fail. The Code rules dealing with this situation are contained in §2-614. Application of these rules ordinarily results in the continuation of the contract using a substitute means of delivery or payment.

Transatlantic Financing Corporation v. United States

363 F.2d 312 (D.C. Cir. 1966)

On July 26, 1956, the government of Egypt nationalized the Suez Canal Company and took over operation of the canal. On October 29, 1956, Israel invaded Egypt and two days later Great Britain and

France invaded the Suez Canal Zone. On November 2, 1956, Egypt obstructed the Suez Canal and closed it to traffic.

During this international crisis, Transatlantic Financing Corporation (Transatlantic) entered into an agreement dated October 2, 1956, with the United States to transport wheat by ship from Galveston, Texas, to Iran. The ship set sail from Galveston on October 27, 1956. Although the agreement did not specify the route the ship was to take, Transatlantic intended to use the Suez Canal. After it appeared that the United States intended to require Transatlantic to perform the agreement, the ship changed course, sailed around the Cape of Good Hope, and delivered the goods.

Transatlantic sued the United States alleging that because performance of the contract by means of the Suez Canal was impossible, the United States should pay the extra costs incurred by using the alternate route. The district court dismissed the case and Transatlantic appealed.

Wright, Circuit Judge

. . . The [impracticability] doctrine ultimately represents the ever-shifting line, drawn by courts hopefully responsive to commercial practices and mores, at which the community's interest in having contracts enforced according to their terms is outweighed by the commercial senselessness of requiring performance. When the issue is raised, the court is asked to construct a condition of performance based on the changed circumstances, a process which involves at least three reasonably definable steps. First, a contingency—something unexpected—must have occurred. Second, the risk of the unexpected occurrence must not have been allocated either by agreement or by custom. Finally, occurrence of the contingency must have rendered performance commercially impracticable. Unless the court finds these three requirements satisfied, the plea of impossibility must fail.

The first requirement was met here. It seems reasonable, where no route is mentioned in a contract, to assume the parties expected performance by the usual and customary route at the time of contract. Since the usual and customary route from Texas to Iran at the time of contract was through Suez, closure of the Canal made impossible the expected method of performance. But this unexpected development raises rather than resolves the impossibility issue, which turns additionally on whether the risk of the contingency's occurrence had been allocated and, if not, whether performance by alternative routes was rendered impracticable.

Proof that the risk of a contingency's occurrence has been allocated may be expressed in or implied from the agreement. Such proof may also be found in the surrounding circumstances, including custom and usages of the trade. . . . The contract in this case does not expressly condition performance upon availability of the Suez route. Nor does it specify "via Suez" or, on the other hand, "via Suez or Cape of Good Hope." Nor are there provisions in the contract from which we may properly imply that the continued availability of Suez was a condition of performance. Nor is there anything in custom or trade usage, or in the surrounding circumstances generally, which would support our constructing a condition of performance. The numerous cases requiring performance around the Cape when Suez was closed . . . indicate that the Cape route is generally regarded as an alternative means of performance. So the implied expectation that the route would be via Suez is hardly adequate proof of an allocation to the promisee of the risk of closure. . . .

If anything, the circumstances surrounding this contract indicate that the risk of the Canal's closure may be deemed to have been allocated to Transatlantic. We know or may safely assume that the parties were aware, as were most commercial men with interests affected by the Suez situation, . . . that the Canal might become a dangerous area. No doubt the tension affected freight rates, and it is arguable that the risk of closure became part of the dickered terms. . . . We do not deem the risk of closure so allocated, however. Foreseeability or even recognition of a risk does not necessarily prove its allocation. . . . Parties to a contract are not always able to provide for all the possibilities of which they are aware, sometimes because they cannot agree, often simply because they are too busy. Moreover, that some abnormal risk was contemplated is probative but does not necessarily establish an allocation of the risk of the contingency which actually occurs. In this case, for example, nationalization by Egypt of the Canal Corporation and formation of the Suez Users Group did not necessarily indicate that the Canal would be blocked even if a confrontation resulted. The surrounding circumstances do indicate, however, a willingness by Transatlantic to assume abnormal risks, and this fact should legitimately cause us to judge the impracticability of performance by an alternative route in stricter terms than we would were the contingency unforeseen.

We turn then to the question whether occurrence of the contingency rendered performance commercially impracticable under the circumstances of this case. The goods shipped were not subject to harm from the longer, less temperate Southern route. The vessel and crew were fit to proceed around the Cape. Transatlantic was no less able than the United States to purchase insurance to cover the contingency's occurrence. If anything, it is more reasonable to expect owner-operators of vessels to insure against the hazards of war. They are in the best position to calculate the cost of performance by alternative routes (and therefore to estimate the amount of insurance required), and are undoubtedly sensitive to international troubles which uniquely affect the demand for and cost of their services. The only factor operating here in appellant's favor is the added expense, allegedly $43,972.00 above and beyond the contract price of $305,842.92, of extending a 10,000 mile voyage by approximately 3,000 miles. While it may be an overstatement to say that increased cost and difficulty of performance never constitute impracticability, to justify relief there must be more of a variation between expected cost and the cost of performing by an available alternative than is present in this case, where the promisor can legitimately be presumed to have accepted some degree of abnormal risk, and where impracticability is urged on the basis of added expense alone.

We conclude, therefore, as have most other courts considering related issues arising out of the Suez closure, that performance of this contract was not rendered legally impossible. . . .

[Judgment affirmed.]

Frustration of Purpose

The **frustration of purpose** doctrine relieves a contracting party of her duty to perform when the un-

derlying purpose of the contract is defeated. In such cases, due to a supervening event, the value of the other party's performance becomes virtually worthless to the obligor. Note the difference between the frustration cases and the situations discussed above. In those cases, performance becomes impracticable. In the frustration cases, neither party's ability to *perform* is affected; the *purpose* of the contract is frustrated. For UCC contracts, issues of impracticability and frustration are both governed by §2-615.

The doctrine was originally adopted in the 1903 English case *Krell v. Henry*.[43] In this case, the defendant agreed to rent an apartment from the plaintiff for two days for the purpose of viewing the coronation process of King Edward VII. The King became seriously ill, and, as a result, the procession was cancelled. The defendant then refused to pay the balance on the rental agreement, resulting in the plaintiff's suit. On these facts, performance of the contract was certainly not impossible (as would be the case had the apartment burned down), but the underlying purpose for which the defendant had rented the premises (to view the coronation procession) had been defeated. On this basis, the court relieved the defendant of his duty to perform, thus creating the "frustration of purpose" doctrine.

To invoke the doctrine, the frustrated purpose must have been the principal or primary reason inducing the aggrieved party to make the contract. Both parties must understand that the transaction would make little sense in the absence of that purpose. It is not enough that the objective simply induces the making of the contract; that is, without it the party would not have made the contract. Additionally, the nonoccurrence of the frustrating event must be a basic assumption on which the contract is made. Once again, whether or not the event is foreseeable plays an important role in this determination.

Courts have been very hesitant to allow relief under this doctrine. Generally, total, not merely substantial, frustration is required. For example, in *Grace v. Croninger*,[44] a building was leased "for the purpose of therein carrying on the business of a saloon and cigar store, and for no other purpose or

---

43. [1903] 2 K.B. 740 (C.A.).
44. 55 P.2d 940 (Cal. App. 1936).

purposes whatsoever.'' Prohibition subsequently destroyed the main purpose of the lease, but because the premises could be used as a cigar store, the lessee was not excused from his duty to pay rent on the basis of frustration. Other courts have been more lenient, discharging the lessee if the principal purpose of the lease is completely frustrated. Note that this is not a case of supervening illegality because the payment of rent and occupancy of the premises were not declared illegal.

SUMMARY

1. Contracting parties do not bargain for promises alone, they bargain for performance of those promises. Generally speaking, nonperformance of a contractual promise when performance is due is breach of the contract. Before existence of breach can be determined, however, the existence and occurrence of any conditions must be determined.

2. A condition is an event qualifying a contractual promise, meaning that the duty to perform does not arise unless the condition occurs. Conditions may be classified as precedent, concurrent, or subsequent. Conditions are also designated as express or implied in fact (arising from the language or other conduct of the parties) or imposed by the law (conditions implied in law or constructive conditions).

3. Constructive conditions of exchange are the most important implied conditions. Under the constructive conditions of exchange doctrine, it is a condition to each party's duty to perform that there be no material failure of the other party's performance due at an earlier time. This doctrine prevents one party from having to perform after a material breach of duty by the other.

4. In applying the constructive conditions doctrine, the order of performance must be determined. Unless the contract or circumstances indicate otherwise, if performance can be rendered simultaneously, it is due simultaneously. Simultaneous performance assures each party that the other will perform and avoids requiring one party to finance the other's performance.

5. Nonoccurrence of a condition may be excused, due, for example, to a waiver of the condition or failure of one party to act in good faith and consistent with standards of fair dealing.

6. In contracts requiring one party to perform before the other, such as construction contracts, disputes often arise when the party rendering the first performance (for example, the contractor) asserts a right to payment on the basis that he has completed performance. The other party (for example, the owner) refuses to pay asserting that the first party's performance is defective, resulting in failure of the constructive condition of exchange. Under the ''substantial performance'' doctrine, if the failure to perform is a material breach, the other party may both sue for damages for total breach and is relieved of his obligation to perform. If the breach is not material, the other party must perform his part of the bargain but may recover damages for the partial breach.

7. In contracts for the sale of goods governed by the UCC, performance is measured by the ''perfect tender rule,'' empowering the buyer to reject goods which fail *in any respect* to conform to the contract. The UCC contains a number of provisions relieving a breaching seller from the harsh effects of the perfect tender rule, resulting in a special form of substantial performance doctrine for sales contracts.

8. A contracting party may render part performance under a contract, but fail to properly perform his remaining obligations. The contract must then be analyzed to determine to what extent, if at all, the defaulting party is entitled to recover under the contract. The result depends upon whether the contract is divisible or entire. If a contract is divisible, performance of a divisible part by one party entitles him to the agreed exchange for that part, despite nonperformance of other parts of the contract. If a contract is deemed entire, the breaching party is not entitled to recover under the contract for part performance rendered.

9. Both actual and prospective nonperformance may constitute breach of contract. Prospective nonperformance involves insecurity and repudiation. Both the UCC and the common law impose an obligation upon each party that the other's expectation of receiving due performance will not be impaired. Whenever reasonable grounds for insecurity arise concerning the willingness or ability of either party to perform, the insecure party may demand adequate assurance of due performance from the other and until he receives such assurance may suspend his own performance.

10. Anticipatory repudiation occurs when one party prior to the time of agreed performance unequivocally indicates an intent not to perform when performance is due. The effect of anticipatory repudiation is to give the injured party an immediate claim for damages for total breach of the contract even though the time of agreed performance has not yet arrived.

11. Occasionally a party will be excused from performance without liability for breach if performance as agreed has been made impracticable by the occurrence of an event, the nonoccurrence of which was a basic as-

sumption on which the contract was made. Examples of supervening events that may excuse nonperformance include death or incapacity of a party in a personal service contract, destruction of subject matter necessary for performance, failure of a specifically designated source of supply, and supervening illegality or government regulation. Even if performance is not impracticable, a promisor may be excused if the underlying purpose of the contract is frustrated.

KEY TERMS

breach of contract	substantial performance
condition	doctrine
condition precedent	partial breach
condition concurrent	total breach
condition subsequent	perfect tender rule
express condition	installment contract
time of the essence	divisibility
forfeiture	agreed equivalents
condition implied in fact	entire contract
condition implied in law	reasonable grounds for
(constructive condition)	insecurity
constructive conditions of	adequate assurance of due
exchange	performance
failure of consideration	repudiation
dependent promise	anticipatory repudiation
independent promise	acceleration clause
tender of performance	supervening event
waiver	impracticability
prevention and hindrance	(impossibility)
material breach	frustration of purpose

QUESTIONS AND PROBLEMS

14-1   Bean agreed to purchase a tract of land from Snooker for $20,000. The contract was expressly conditioned upon Bean's ability to obtain a mortgage loan to cover the purchase price. Prior to the agreed date of performance, Bean informed Snooker that he would not obtain a mortgage loan to cover the price, but would instead generate the cash by selling certain shares of stock owned by Bean. When the date of performance arrived, Snooker refused to perform, asserting that Bean's failure to obtain a loan rendered the contract null and void. Bean tendered the full purchase price in cash on the required date, and upon Snooker's refusal to convey the land, sued Snooker for breach of contract. What result?

14-2   On June 1, 1980, Eiffel contracted in writing to sell a large quantity of scrap metal to Tinker. The contract did not specify a delivery date, but provided that delivery would occur no later than September 1, 1980. On July 1, Eiffel called Tinker concerning the delivery date. Tinker replied that he was not ready to take delivery and would call Eiffel when he was. The parties had no further contact concerning the contract between July 1 and September 1, 1980. In October, Eiffel sold the scrap to others, sustaining a loss because of a decline in market price. Eiffel sued Tinker to recover the difference between the contract price and the resale price, alleging that Tinker breached the contract by failing to take delivery by September 1, and by failing to pay the agreed price. Tinker responded that he had no liability because Eiffel had not tendered delivery of the scrap metal. What result? Explain.

14-3   Pope, the general contractor on a highway construction project, hired Rail to act as subcontractor for construction of the guardrails. The rails require 30 days to install and cannot be installed until all other construction is complete. The contract between Pope and Rail stated in part:

> Rail agrees to furnish all labor, materials, equipment and services as may be necessary to complete items of work relating to installation of guardrails.
>
> Pope agrees to conduct the work for construction of the highway in such manner and with sufficient materials, equipment, and labor as are necessary to insure its completion by October 31, 1988.

The highway project ran behind schedule and was not ready for installation of the guardrails until August, 1989. When Pope requested Rail to perform, Rail refused saying its obligation of performance had been discharged for failure of conditions precedent. Do you agree? Explain.

14-4   Consider the application of the prevention or hindrance doctrine to the following facts:
(a) Kehm Corporation contracted to manufacture and deliver concrete practice bombs for the United States Navy. The completed bombs were to include tail assemblies to be furnished by the Navy. Delivery was to occur by November 1, 1980. However, Kehm failed to deliver until April, 1981. Although the government paid the contract price, Kehm sued for an additional $22,000 for damages sustained resulting from delays caused by the government which retarded completion of the contract. The evidence established that the Navy had lost interest in the concrete bomb program, had shipped

nonconforming tail assemblies for many of the bombs, thereby causing manufacturing delays, had shipped many of the tail assemblies late, and had failed to promptly accept delivery of many of the completed bombs. Has the government breached the contract?

(b) The National Rifle Association's management committee voted to move the NRA's headquarters from Washington, D.C. to Colorado. Accordingly, it engaged Shear, a real estate agent, to secure a buyer for its old headquarters building. Shear was to be paid a commission when a sale was "fully consummated." Shear obtained a buyer. A contract for sale was signed subject to approval by the management committee. Subsequently, however, a new NRA management committee was elected and voted not to move the headquarters after all. Because board approval was necessary to consummate the sale, the deal fell through and NRA then refused to pay Shear's commission. Shear sued. What result?

(c) The United States Government contracted with Arborite, a lumber company, to supply one million board feet of lumber to be used in the construction of an Army base. As Arborite knew, it was only one of several suppliers for the entire project, which required over 20 million board feet. When Arborite attempted to acquire the lumber, it was unable to do so because the demand created by the Army construction had created a market shortage. Consequently, Arborite failed to deliver and was sued by the government for breach. May Arborite avoid liability on prevention grounds?

14-5 Contractor built a country home for Owner at a cost of approximately $77,000. One of the specifications for the plumbing work provided: "All wrought-iron pipe must be well galvanized, lap welded pipe of the grade known as 'standard pipe' of Reading manufacture." Approximately nine months after completion of the house, Owner learned that only forty percent of the pipe used was manufactured by Reading, with the remainder produced by other factories. Owner then ordered Contractor to redo the work. At this point, the plumbing was encased within the walls, and compliance with the order would have required demolition of substantial parts of the completed structure. Contractor refused to comply and sued for the final installment on the purchase price ($3,500) that had not been paid.

The evidence indicated that Contractor's failure to comply was neither fraudulent nor willful, but resulted from an oversight by one of its subcontractors. Should Contractor recover? How much, and if so on what grounds? Determine whether the use of Reading pipe is an express condition to Owner's duty to pay and explain the effect of your determination on Contractor's recovery.

14-6 Sheila contracted to sell sheet metal to Bill, delivery to be made in monthly installments over a two-year period beginning June 1, 1980. Payments for the goods were to be made within ten days after each delivery. Almost from the first installment, Bill was behind in his payments, and these arrearages were often quite substantial. Sheila repeatedly called these arrearages to Bill's attention, but continued to make all shipments called for by the contract.

By March 1981, Bill became concerned about Sheila's ability to complete performance of the contract because of rumors that Sheila's plant might close and because the market price of the goods now significantly exceeded the contract price. Bill called Sheila who provided assurances of future performance even though at the time Bill still owed substantial amounts for goods already delivered. Despite Sheila's assurances Bill stopped payment on a $10,000 check given in partial payment of Bill's past due account. Bill's reason for stopping payment was that one of Sheila's truck drivers had told Bill that Sheila would make no further deliveries. Sheila's plant was forced to close in May, 1981, primarily due to Bill's refusal to accept further deliveries or pay his outstanding bill.

Sheila sued Bill for breach of contract for nonpayment of over $20,000 in accepted deliveries. Bill admitted his indebtedness but counterclaimed for damages resulting from Sheila's failure to perform the remaining installments under the contract. Should Bill prevail on his counterclaim?

14-7 In March, 1980, Semo Grain Co. contracted to buy 75,000 bushels of soybeans from Oliver Inc. at $3.10 per bushel, delivery to be made in January, 1981. Nothing in the agreement required Oliver, a farming corporation, to grow the beans, and, indeed, Oliver was not required to grow them. Oliver failed to deliver any soybeans to Semo, resulting in Semo's suit for breach of contract. Oliver asserted that adverse weather conditions excused his performance under UCC §§2-613 and 2-615. Oliver contended that although the various farms under its control planted over 3,500 acres, only 1,500 survived heavy rainfall, resulting in a harvest of less than 20,000 bushels. (a) Should Oliver be relieved of liability under §2-613? (b) Should Oliver be relieved of liability under §2-615? (c) Assuming Oliver is excused from performance under §2-615, has it complied with its obligations under that section? See §2-615(b).

14-8   Corbin went to Williston Dance Studio, Inc. to redeem a certificate entitling him to three free dancing lessons. At the time Corbin was a thirty-seven-year-old college-educated bachelor who lived alone in a one-room attic apartment. During the free lessons the instructor told Corbin that he had "exceptional potential to be a fine and accomplished dancer" and encouraged further participation. Within two years after the free lessons, Corbin had contracted for a total of 2,735 hours of lessons for which he had paid almost $25,000. Each contract signed by Corbin contained the following language in bold face type: "NONCANCELLABLE NEGOTIABLE CONTRACT. I UNDERSTAND THAT NO REFUNDS WILL BE MADE UNDER THE TERMS OF THIS CONTRACT." With 2,700 hours of lessons still remaining on his contract, Corbin was seriously injured in an automobile accident rendering him permanently disabled and unable to continue dancing lessons. Corbin then demanded his money back for the unused lessons, asserting impossibility of performance. Williston refused to return any of the money contending that the bold type phrases quoted above manifested the parties' mutual intent to waive their respective rights to invoke the doctrine of impossibility. Is Williston correct? Explain.

14-9   Florida Power & Light Co. (Florida) agreed to purchase two nuclear reactors from Westinghouse Electric Corp. (Westinghouse). Because Florida had no experience with nuclear power generation, it insisted that Westinghouse agree to remove spent nuclear fuel. To secure the contract, Westinghouse agreed in writing "to remove the irradiated fuel from the plant site and dispose of it as Westinghouse sees fit," advising Florida that it intended to have the spent fuel reprocessed. Westinghouse required the contract to include a "force majeure clause" which excused it from losses resulting from various contingencies, including "restrictions of the U.S. government." Five years later the president of the United States issued an order prohibiting

construction of nuclear fuel reprocessing plants. Thereafter, all spent nuclear fuel had to be stored in government-approved disposal sites. Westinghouse repudiated its duty to remove nuclear fuel from Florida's reactors. As a result, Florida was forced to develop a storage facility for its spent fuel at great expense. Florida sued Westinghouse for breach of contract.

(a) Westinghouse defended the suit on the grounds of impracticability under §2-615 of the UCC. How should the court rule?

(b) Westinghouse also alleged that the nonavailability of reprocessing facilities frustrated the purpose of the contract. What result?

(c) Westinghouse further alleged that it was relieved of liability under the force majeure clause. How should the court rule?

(d) Westinghouse asserted that both parties expected that the fuel would be reprocessed and that this expectation could no longer be fulfilled. Westinghouse, therefore, requested rescission on the ground of mutual mistake. What result?

14-10   In 1973, Sunflower Electric Co-op, a public utility, entered into a written contract with Tomlinson Oil Co., providing that Tomlinson would provide three million cubic feet of natural gas per day for fifteen years from the Stranger Creek gas field to Sunflower. The gas was to be piped to a storage facility from which Sunflower would pipe the gas to its customers. Tomlinson had already performed tests at Stranger Creek and its engineers concluded there was sufficient gas to meet the requirements of the contract. Sunflower immediately constructed a pipeline to the storage facility. Two years later Tomlinson provided notice that it would be unable to perform the contract. All gas wells at Stranger Creek had ceased operating because the field's gas reserves had been exhausted.

Sunflower sued Tomlinson for breach of contract. Tomlinson argued that it could not be held liable because of impracticability.

(a) Did Tomlinson assert original or supervening impracticability?

(b) The Tomlinson-Sunflower contract made no provision for the possibility that the gas at Stranger Creek would be exhausted. Who assumed the risk?

(c) How should the court rule on the case? Be sure to consider §2-615 of the UCC in resolving the case.

Major Topics

- the various judicial remedies available for breach of contract
- the interests protected by contract remedies
- the general principles used to compute money damages
- when equitable relief in the form of specific performance, injunction against breach, and reformation is available as an alternative to an award of damages
- the definition of restitution and its use as a contract remedy

The vast majority of contracts are performed as agreed, thereby discharging the duties involved. If, however, a contractual promise is not performed, or is improperly performed, the law of **contract remedies** determines the type of judicial relief available to the injured promisee.

The Role of Contract Remedies

Remedies effectuate a basic purpose of contract law to promote certainty and predictability in commercial transactions. A major reason a businessperson seeks another's contractual promise is to be assured that the promise will be performed, thus allowing planning in reliance upon the promise. The fact that contracting parties know (or should know) that legal consequences—liability for a contract rem-

edy—follow a failure to perform a contractual obligation provides a strong incentive to contracting parties to perform their promises. The traditional goal of contract remedies is to fully *compensate* the injured promisee for actual loss resulting from the breach. Thus, the underlying premise of contract remedies is compensatory, not punitive.

Types of Contract Remedies

Contract remedies are divided into three general types: (1) legal remedies (or remedies at law), (2) equitable remedies, and (3) restitution.

The **remedy at law** is, in all cases, dollar damages; that is, a party injured by breach of contract is generally entitled to money damages from the breaching party. The amount of damages is a question of fact, determined either by the jury, or by the judge in cases heard without a jury.

Contract law, therefore, usually requires a breaching promisor to pay money, not perform the broken promise. Forcing the promisor to perform as agreed forms the basis of the **equitable remedies** of specific performance and injunction against breach. Equitable remedies are available only if, in the sole discretion of the court, the remedy at law is inadequate to compensate the injured party.[1]

---

1. The derivation of the law-equity distinction and the basic relationship between the two forms of judicial relief are discussed in Chapter 1.

Finally, restitution may be available as a contract remedy. Restitution is a broad remedial concept that is used when one person confers a benefit upon another, who retains it. If necessary to prevent unjust enrichment of the benefited party, the court may order restitution, requiring payment for the reasonable value of the benefit conferred. Restitution is often used in contract cases when other remedies are unavailable. For example, a person who has breached the contract may nevertheless be entitled to restitution.

As noted in Chapter 6, the obligation of good faith applies both to the performance and *enforcement* of a contract. Parties seeking judicial remedies for breach of contract are therefore subject to a basic standard of good faith in their conduct. Bad faith enforcement may involve fabricating a dispute where none exists, falsifying facts, or asserting an interpretation contrary to one's true belief. Bad faith also has been held to include harassing demands for adequate assurance of performance, rejecting performance for unstated reasons, and abusing a power to determine compliance with or to terminate the contract. No exhaustive catalog of the possible types of bad faith is possible, of course, and each case is decided on its own peculiar facts.

Interests Protected by Contract Remedies

Contract remedies are designed to protect one or more interests of the injured promisee, including an expectation interest, a reliance interest, and a restitution interest.

Expectation Interest. The **expectation interest** is the interest most commonly protected by both legal and equitable contract remedies. Simply stated, relief on this basis seeks to give the injured party the **benefit of the bargain** by placing her in as good a position as she would have obtained had the contract been performed as agreed. In other words, when the court is presented with a contract breach, it ordinarily enforces the broken promise by protecting the injured party's expectation that the contract would be performed, not breached. Normally, a party faced with breach of contract will attempt to satisfy her expectation interest by enforcing the other party's promise against her.

Assume a seller contracts to sell and deliver machinery to a buyer for $5,000 and fails to perform. The buyer then purchases substitute goods from an alternative source for $6,000. The basic measure of damages is $1,000. The amount that the buyer actually paid ($6,000) less the damages recovered ($1,000) equals $5,000. The buyer is thus placed in the same position he would have enjoyed upon full performance. He has received the benefit of the bargain—the contracted goods for $5,000. Alternatively, had equitable relief, specific performance, been awarded, the buyer's expectation interest is satisfied by the seller's actual performance of the promise.[2]

Reliance Interest. Contract remedies also may serve to protect a promisee's **reliance interest.** A promisee may change his position in reliance on a contract, for example, by incurring expenses in preparing for, or actual, performance. In such a case, the court may allow recovery based upon a reliance, rather than expectation, interest. In this case the court requires reimbursement of the injured party sufficient to return him to the position he enjoyed before the contract was made. The reliance interest is ordinarily smaller than the expectation interest because it does not include any profit lost by the injured party on the contract. For example, a party who is unable to prove profit with reasonable certainty or who would have lost money on the contract may sue to recover damages based upon reliance rather than expectation. Under certain circumstances, courts enforce promises not otherwise binding as contracts, solely because of reliance upon them. The most notable example is the "promissory estoppel" doctrine discussed in Chapter 9.

Restitution Interest. Finally, a contract remedy may be designed to protect a promisee's **restitution interest.** In this case the court awards the promisee the value of any benefit she has conferred on the other party. The restitution interest is normally

---

2. The expectation interest is also the basis of remedy under the UCC that provides: "The remedies provided by this Act shall be liberally administered to the end that the aggrieved party may be put in as good a position as if the other party had fully performed. . . ." (§1-106(1)).

smaller than either the expectation or reliance interest because it does not include either profits or expenditures not benefiting the other party.

This chapter first examines basic principles governing the computation and award of money damages, the basic remedy in contracts cases. Second, equitable relief through specific performance and injunction against breach is covered. In either case, the basic goal is to give the injured party the benefit of his bargain or to reimburse him for loss caused by reliance on the promise. Finally, restitution is discussed both in general and as a contract remedy. The general remedies concepts discussed below are applicable to both UCC (sales of goods) and common law contracts. Additional specialized remedial rules concerning contracts for the sale of goods are discussed in Chapter 18.

Enforcement by an Award of Damages— The Remedy at Law

General Measure of Damages

As noted above, breach of contract ordinarily gives rise to a claim by the promisee for money damages to compensate for actual loss caused by the breach. In this case a dollar damages award is generally computed to include:

> General compensatory damages (the loss in the value of the other party's performance caused by failure of, or deficiency in, that performance), *plus*
> Any other loss caused by the breach, *less*
> Expenses saved as a result of the breach (expenditures or other loss the promisee avoids by not having to perform).

The manner of computing general compensatory damages for breach of contract—the loss in value caused by the breach—varies somewhat depending upon a number of factors including the type of contract, the extent and nature of the breach, and the difficulties in proving damages. In contracts involving the sale of real or personal property, damages generally are computed by comparing the contract price to the market price or to the cost incurred by the injured party in obtaining substitute performance. Thus, in contracts for the sale of

land, an injured buyer or seller who seeks money damages is ordinarily entitled to the difference between the contract price and the market price of the land on the date of the breach. In contracts involving goods, after breach by the buyer, the seller generally recovers the difference between the contract price and the market price on the date of performance, or the difference between the contract price and the resale price if the seller resells the goods. In limited circumstances—as when goods are accepted by the buyer or when the seller is unable to resell—a seller may recover the entire purchase price of goods from a breaching buyer. If the seller of goods breaches, the buyer also ordinarily recovers the difference between the contract price and the market price when the buyer learned of the breach. If, due to the breach, the buyer "covers" by acquiring substitute goods from another seller, damages equal the difference between the contract price and the cover price.

A damage award generally does not include attorneys' fees unless provided for by statute or in the agreement. **Court costs,** however, usually are assessed against the losing party. The term costs generally refers to statutory fees to which officers, jurors, witnesses, and others are entitled for their services in a lawsuit, and that are authorized by statute to be taxed and included in a judgment.[3]

Foreseeability as a Limitation on Damages—"Consequential" Damages

Loss due to breach of contract may result directly or immediately from the breach and would be suffered generally by any injured promisee. The general or basic measure of damages discussed above is designed to compensate this type of loss. In some but not all cases, however, the breach may trigger a chain of events causing additional loss as the ultimate result or consequence of the breach. In business contracts, courts have often been required to determine when a particular promisee should be entitled to recover such **consequential damages,** usually lost profits, in addition to his general damage claims.

---

3. Black, *Law Dictionary* (5th ed. 1979).

The Rule of Hadley v. Baxendale. The basic test governing the issue originally was announced in *Hadley v. Baxendale,*[4] an English case decided in 1854, and subsequently generally followed in the United States. In this case, the operators of a mill (plaintiffs) delivered a broken shaft used in the mill to a carrier (defendant) for shipment to an engineering company, which manufactured a new shaft using the broken one as a model. Through the negligence of the carrier, the return of the shaft was delayed several days and, because the mill was totally inoperative without the shaft, the plaintiffs lost several days' profits. At issue in the case was whether the lost profits (consequential damages) should be recoverable from the defendants. Note that the general measure of damages for a delay in shipment of goods would be the loss of the value of the use of the goods during the delay—that is, their rental value. In establishing the governing standard, the court stated that damages are recoverable for loss that the breaching party had *reason to foresee* when the contract was made, occurring as the probable result of its breach. Two types of loss are foreseeable and therefore recoverable under this test:

1. Losses arising in the ordinary course of events—these are commonly known as "general" damages; and
2. Losses resulting from special circumstances, beyond the ordinary course of events, of which the breaching party has reason to know. These losses are commonly labeled "special" or "consequential" damages.

Thus, losses resulting from the *special* circumstances under which a contract is made are recoverable only if the defendant is made aware of the specific consequences of a failure to perform as agreed.

In applying the rule to the facts of the case, the *Hadley* court found that the plaintiffs had communicated to the defendants only that they were mill operators and the article to be carried was a broken shaft of the mill. The fact that the mill was inoperative without the shaft was not communicated. On these facts, the court reasoned that the defendants could have assumed that the mill was shut down for independent reasons, or that the shaft was a spare. In neither case would additional profits be lost as a result of defendant's delay in delivery. Because the special circumstances were not communicated to, or known by, the defendants, the court refused to award lost profits to the plaintiff.

Hadley was a special circumstances case. Losses arising in the ordinary course of events do not have to be communicated to the defendant to be recoverable. For example, a seller of a commodity to a wholesaler would ordinarily have reason to foresee that failure to deliver as agreed would probably cause the wholesaler to lose a reasonable profit upon resale. Similarly, a seller delivering defective or nonconforming merchandise to be used in a manufacturing process has reason to know that a disruption in production will occur and profits will be lost. In addition, the seller of a machine to a manufacturer usually has reason to foresee that a delay in delivery will cause the buyer to lose the profit from its use during the period of the delay. In all such cases lost profits should be recoverable, even without explicit communication of circumstances to the defendant, because the loss involved occurs in the ordinary course of events.

The following case illustrates a modern application of the principles of *Hadley v. Baxendale.*

Spang Industries, Inc., Fort Pitt Bridge Division v. Aetna Casualty and Surety Co.
512 F.2d 365 (2d Cir. 1975)

Plaintiff Spang Industries, Inc., Fort Pitt Bridge Division (Fort Pitt) entered into a contract with Torrington Construction Co., Inc. (Torrington) to provide steel for a bridge that Torrington was constructing across the Battenkill River in northern New York state. The agreement provided "Delivery to be mutually agreed upon." On November 3, 1969, Torrington, in response to a request from Fort Pitt, notified Fort Pitt that the steel would be needed in late June, 1970. Fort Pitt replied that it would tentatively schedule delivery at that time. In January, 1970, Fort Pitt advised Torrington that it would

---

4. 9 Ex. 341, 156 Eng. Rep. 145 (Ex. 1854).

be unable to deliver in late June because of delays in an expansion program. On February 2, 1970, Torrington requested Fort Pitt to give a delivery date but the request was not answered. On May 12, 1970, Torrington again requested confirmation of the delivery date and threatened to cancel if the delivery was not reasonably close to late June. Fort Pitt responded by promising to ship the steel in August, 1970.

Most of the steel was not shipped, however, until the last week in August and the first week in September, 1970, delaying the start of construction to September 16. Because of the impending winter weather, Torrington poured the concrete for the bridge on a "crash" basis, incurring added expenses. Torrington sued Fort Pitt for damages resulting from Fort Pitt's delay. Fort Pitt appealed the trial court's damages award on the ground that the increased expenses incurred by Torrington were not within the reasonable contemplation of the parties when the contract was made.

Mulligan, Circuit Judge

. . . While the damages awarded Torrington are relatively modest ($7,653.57) in comparison with the subcontract price ($132,274.37), Fort Pitt urges that an affirmance of the award will do violence to the rule of *Hadley v. Baxendale,* . . . and create a precedent which will have a severe impact on the business of all subcontractors and suppliers.

While it is evident that the function of the award of damages for a breach of contract is to put the plaintiff in the same position he would have been in had there been no breach, *Hadley v. Baxendale* limits the recovery to those injuries which the parties could reasonably have anticipated at the time the contract was entered into. If the damages suffered do not usually flow from the breach, then it must be established that the special circumstances giving rise to them should reasonably have been anticipated at the time the contract was made.

There can be no question but that *Hadley v. Baxendale* represents the law in New York and in the United States generally. . . .

The gist of Fort Pitt's argument is that, when it entered into the subcontract to fabricate, furnish and erect the steel in September, 1969, it had received a copy of the specifications which indicated that the total work was to be completed by December 15, 1971. It could not reasonably have anticipated that Torrington would so expedite the work (which was accepted by the State on January 21, 1971) that steel delivery would be called for in 1970 rather than in 1971. Whatever knowledge Fort Pitt received after the contract was entered into, it argues, cannot expand its liability, since it is essential under *Hadley v. Baxendale* and its Yankee progeny that the notice of the facts which would give rise to special damages in case of breach be given at or before the time the contract was made. The principle urged cannot be disputed. . . . We do not, however, agree that any violence to the doctrine was done here. . . .

We conclude that, when the parties enter into a contract which, by its terms, provides that the time of performance is to be fixed at a later date, the knowledge of the consequences of a failure to perform is to be imputed to the defaulting party as of the time the parties agreed upon the date of performance. This comports, in our view, with both the logic and the spirit of *Hadley v. Baxendale.* . . . At the time Fort Pitt did become committed to a delivery date, it was aware that a June, 1970, performance was required by virtue of its own acceptance. There was no unilateral distortion of the agreement rendering Fort Pitt liable to an extent not theretofore contemplated.

Having proceeded thus far, we do not think it follows automatically that Torrington is entitled to recover the damages it seeks here; further consideration of the facts before us is warranted. Fort Pitt maintains that, under the *Hadley v. Baxendale* rubric, the damages flowing from its conceded breach are "special" or "consequential" and were not reasonably to be contemplated by the parties. Since Torrington has not proved any "general" or "direct" damages, Fort Pitt urges that the contractor is entitled to nothing. We cannot agree. . . .

It must be taken as a reasonable assumption that, when the delivery date of June, 1970, was set, Torrington planned the bridge erection within a reasonable time thereafter. It is normal construction procedure that the erection of the steel girders would be followed by the installation of a poured concrete platform and whatever railings or super-structure the platform would require. Fort Pitt was an experienced bridge fabricator supplying contractors and the sequence of the work is hardly arcane. Moreover, any delay beyond June or August would assuredly have jeopardized the pouring of the concrete and have forced the postponement of the work until the spring. The work here, as was well known to Fort Pitt, was to be performed in northern New York near the Vermont border. The court below found that continuing freezing weather would have forced the pouring to be delayed until June, 1971. Had Torrington refused delivery or had it been compelled to delay the completion of the work until the spring of 1971, the potential damage claim would have been substantial. Instead, in a good faith effort to mitigate damages, Torrington embarked upon the crash program we have described. It appears to us that this eventuality should have reasonably been anticipated by Fort Pitt as it was experienced in the trade and was supplying bridge steel in northern climes on a project requiring a concrete roadway. . . .

In this case, serious or catastrophic injury was avoided by prompt, effective and reasonable mitigation at modest cost. Had Torrington not acted, had it been forced to wait until the following spring to complete the entire job and then sued to recover the profits it would have made had there been performance by Fort Pitt according to the terms of its agreement, then we might well have an appropriate setting for a classical *Hadley v. Baxendale* controversy. As this case comes to us, it hardly presents that situation. We therefore affirm the judgment below permitting Torrington to offset its damages against the contract price. . . .

Consequential Damages under the UCC. Section 2-714(1) of the UCC adopts the rule of *Hadley* for contracts for the sale of goods by providing that a buyer may recover from a breaching seller for "loss resulting in the ordinary course of events from the seller's breach as determined in any manner which is reasonable." Section 2-715(2)(a) further authorizes buyer recovery for "any loss resulting from general or particular requirements and needs of which the seller *at the time of contracting had reason to know* and which could not reasonably be prevented by cover or otherwise." (Emphasis added.) Consistent with the preceding discussion, "particular needs of the buyer must

generally be made known to the seller while general needs must rarely be made known to charge the seller with knowledge."[5]

Under the Code a buyer's recovery is limited to those damages not preventable by cover (obtaining substitute goods from another seller) or otherwise, and are available only to the buyer. Seller's damages result from a failure by the buyer to pay the purchase price. Courts have long held such a failure to be an insufficient basis for a consequential damage award, even if consequent damage to the seller is foreseeable. Consistent with general UCC policy, consequential damages may be limited or excluded by agreement unless the provision is unconscionable.[6]

Avoidability as a Limitation on Damages—"Mitigation"

The concept of avoidability, embodied in the doctrine of **mitigation,** places an additional important limitation on damages awarded for breach of contract. Once a breach has occurred, the injured party must mitigate the damages—that is, take steps to keep damages to a minimum. The injured party may not sit idly by and allow damages to accumulate. The mitigation doctrine is designed to prevent economic waste and to assure that damages awarded do not exceed the amount necessary to compensate the injured party. Mitigation ordinarily requires suspending performance and taking affirmative steps to avoid further loss, such as making substitute arrangements. What constitutes suitable substitute performance depends upon an analysis of all circumstances including the similarity, time, and place of the alternative performance.[7]

---

5. UCC §2-715, Official Comment 3.

6. UCC §2-719(3). Unconscionability is discussed in Chapter 10. As the preceding discussion indicates, consequential damage for breach of a commercial contract is ordinarily lost profit. The UCC, however, provides that recoverable consequential damage resulting from a seller's breach also includes "*injury to person or property* proximately resulting from any breach of warranty." §2-715(2)(b). (Emphasis added.) Remedies for breach of warranty and injuries caused by defective products are discussed in Chapters 19 and 20.

7. Under the UCC, the interrelated doctrines of cover (buyer) and right to resell (seller) provide for mitigation by substitute performance in contracts for sale of goods. These concepts are discussed in Chapter 18.

Courts and commentators frequently assert that an injured party is under a "duty" to mitigate damages. This statement is incorrect, because the injured party incurs no liability for failure to mitigate. Upon failure to mitigate the injured party is simply unable to recover from the contract breacher for loss that could have been avoided by reasonable effort. The following examples illustrate this point.

1. S contracts to sell and deliver a machine to B. Prior to shipment, B repudiates the contract. Despite B's repudiation, S ships the machine to B, who refuses to receive it. S may not recover the cost of shipping the machine as part of the damages for breach.

2. Star Corp. contracts to sell production equipment to Black Mfg. Co. for $10,000, delivery to be made on June 1. Star breaches the contract by repudiating it on May 1. With reasonable effort, Black could have acquired suitable replacement equipment for $11,000 by June 1. Black fails to do so and as a result loses $15,000 in profits that would have resulted from the use of the machine. Black may not recover the $15,000 lost profit, but may recover $1,000 from Star. The $1,000 represents the general measure of a buyer's damage for nondelivery or repudiation by the seller under a contract for the sale of goods. Note that if Black, after reasonable effort, is unable to find a suitable replacement—that is, unable to cover—the $15,000 lost profits *may* be recoverable from Star as consequential damages if the test of foreseeability is met.

3. Albert hires Sally to manage Albert's business for one year for $20,000. Shortly after starting work, he fires her without cause, breaching the contract. Sally could obtain an equally good managerial job at $19,900. Sally fails to do so and remains unemployed. Her recoverable damages are $100, not the $20,000 lost earnings.[8]

Mitigation requires only that a reasonable effort to avoid loss be made. An injured party is not precluded from recovery simply because his efforts were unsuccessful in *actually* avoiding loss. Further, any incidental expenses such as commissions, storage charges, or employment agency fees incurred by the injured party in attempting to mitigate (whether successful or not) may be recovered from the breaching party. In addition, because efforts to mitigate need only be "reasonable," it is not necessary that the *maximum* possible loss under the circumstances be avoided.

The following case illustrates the mitigation doctrine applied to breach of a contract to loan money.

Utah Farm Production Credit Association v. Cox
627 P.2d 62 (Utah 1981)

Defendant Jeffrey Cox, a turkey farmer, owed about $168,000 to plaintiff, Utah Farm Production Credit Association (Utah Farm). Cox wanted to terminate his farming operations but Utah Farm proposed that he continue operations and promised to extend financing for another year. Cox then bought an additional 20,000 turkeys to raise. Utah Farm's supervisory board, however, refused to extend the financing without further collateral, which Cox could not provide.

Utah Farm sued on the outstanding debt. Cox counterclaimed for damages resulting from plaintiff's breach of its agreement to extend financing for another year. The trial court ruled in favor of Utah Farm on the debt but ruled that Utah Farm had breached the contract to provide financing to Cox. The court awarded Utah Farm damages equal to the amount due on Cox's outstanding promissory note offset by the amount of profits Cox would have realized had plaintiff not breached the financing agreement. Utah Farm appealed on the ground that Cox was not entitled to subtract the profits because he had failed to mitigate damages.

Hall, Justice

. . . Where a contractual agreement has been breached by a party thereto, the aggrieved party is entitled to those damages that will put him in as good a position as he would have been had the other party performed pursuant to the agreement. A corollary to this rule is that the aggrieved party may not, either by action or inaction, aggravate the injury occasioned by the breach, but has a duty ac-

---

8. *Restatement (Second) of Contracts* §350, ills. 2, 5, and 8.

tively to mitigate his damages. The application of these two principles to the breach of a contract to loan money yields a rule [that a] would-be borrower, upon learning that the supposed lender refuses to perform the contract, must actively seek alternative sources of financing. Only where such a search fails to yield an alternative source may the aggrieved party seek special damages, including lost profits, to compensate for the breach. The denial of special damages, and particularly lost profits, where other financing was available, or where it was not sought, is based on sound policy. Where an alternative financing source is available, other damages due to the breach are generally avoidable, and hence not compensable.

In the instant case, it is undisputed that defendant failed to seek alternative financial sources upon learning that plaintiff refused to extend the agreed-upon loan for the 1977 growing year. By defendant's own admission, the Moroni Feed Company was at least one other such source available, even if it was only for the next year's financing. Moreover, defendant did, in fact, procure short-term financing of a small sum from the Bank of Ephraim. None of these alternatives were explored upon learning of plaintiff's breach.

Defendant argues, however, that he believed such exploration to be futile in light of plaintiff's announcement of immediate foreclosure. Defendant reasoned that, as plaintiff would seek foreclosure and sale of defendant's physical facility for turkey growing, there would be little virtue in seeking an alternative loan for the 1977 growing year. As such, defendant resolved simply to sell the farm himself and seek to repay the obligation.

The argument is without merit. Had he sought alternative financing, defendant may well have been able to satisfy the debt in full, thereby rendering any threat of foreclosure meaningless. . . . At any rate, by failing to investigate such alternatives, defendant failed in his duty to mitigate damages, and the special damages contemplated by the trial court's ruling may not be allowed.

The above decision works no undue hardship on defendant. In fact, it places him in the same position in which he sought to place himself at the conclusion of the 1976 growing year. The lost profits for which he now seeks compensation are those which, but for the urgings of plaintiff, he would never have sought to earn in the first place. . . .

[Judgment reversed and remanded.]

Frequently, the injured party is able to avoid certain expenses that would have been incurred had she performed. Thus, in computing damages, her recovery is reduced by costs saved as a result of the breach. For example, Jenny Corp. contracts to build a hotel for Bart to be completed by May 1. It fails to complete performance until June 1. The cost Bart avoids by not having to operate the hotel for the month is subtracted from income lost during May in computing his damages. This same principle governs computation of damages awarded to buyers and sellers for breach of Code contracts.

Other Money Damages

Liquidated Damages. The term "liquidated" means fixed or settled in amount. By use of a **liquidated damages provision,** the parties specify in the contract the amount of damages to be awarded in the event of a breach, rather than leaving that amount to the calculation of a court or jury. These provisions reduce litigation expense and save time for courts, juries, witnesses, and parties. They are particularly useful if the amount in controversy is small.

The basic theory of contract damages is compensatory, not punitive. Thus, damages may be liquidated in the agreement, but only at an amount that is *reasonable* in light of (1) the anticipated or actual harm caused by the breach, and (2) the difficulties in proving loss.[9] The provision must therefore represent a reasonable good faith effort by the parties at the date of the contract to forecast or pre-estimate the amount of probable loss to be sustained in the event of the breach. It must not be a "penalty"; that is, a threat designed to prevent or punish breach. A term fixing unreasonably large liquidated damages is void as a penalty. Punish-

---

9. *Restatement (Second) of Contracts* §356(1); UCC §2-718(1).

ment of a promisor for his breach has no justification on economic or other grounds and a penalty is therefore unenforceable for public policy reasons. The name attached to the provision by the parties—for example, when the contract provides for the award of a fixed sum "as liquidated damages and not as a penalty"—is irrelevant in making this determination. This point is particularly important in contracts of adhesion in which the drafting party often attempts to disguise a penalty by calling it a liquidated damages clause.

The determination whether a clause fixing damages is an enforceable liquidated damages clause or an unenforceable penalty turns on an analysis of both factors listed above. This approach is taken both by the UCC and the *Restatement (Second) of Contracts*. Traditionally, however, the courts have attached more weight to the first factor. That is, if the provision is a reasonable forecast or pre-estimate of probable loss, it is often given effect even if actual damages are easily calculable.

In the following case, the court was required to determine the enforceability of a contract provision fixing damages.

Truck Rent-A-Center, Inc. v. Puritan Farms 2d, Inc.
361 N.E.2d 1015 (N.Y. 1977)

Plaintiff Truck Rent-A-Center, Inc. (TRC) and defendant Puritan Farms 2d, Inc. (Puritan) entered into a contract in 1969, by which Puritan agreed to lease a fleet of 25 new milk trucks from TRC for seven years and TRC agreed to supply and maintain the trucks. The contract included a liquidated damages clause requiring Puritan, if it breached the contract, to pay damages equal to one-half of all rentals that would have become due had the contract been fully performed. The contract also stated various factors that the parties had considered in calculating the liquidated damages: for example, the investment that TRC had made in purchasing and maintaining the trucks, the uncertainty of TRC's ability to sell or re-lease the trucks upon breach, and Puritan's savings for gas, oil, and other service items.

Almost three years later, Puritan terminated the

contract on the grounds that TRC had failed to repair and maintain the trucks. TRC sued for breach of contract alleging that it had fully maintained the trucks and that Puritan had terminated the contract because it had acquired other delivery trucks by purchasing the assets of several other dairies. The trial court held that TRC had substantially performed the contract but that Puritan had unjustifiably terminated. Using the liquidated damages clause formula, the trial court awarded TRC damages of $88,678. Puritan appealed.

Jasen, Judge
. . . The primary issue before us is whether the "liquidated damages" provision is enforceable. . . .

The rule is now well established. A contractual provision fixing damages in the event of breach will be sustained if the amount liquidated bears a reasonable proportion to the probable loss and the amount of actual loss is incapable or difficult of precise estimation. . . . If, however, the amount fixed is plainly or grossly disproportionate to the probable loss, the provision calls for a penalty and will not be enforced. . . . In interpreting a provision fixing damages, it is not material whether the parties themselves have chosen to call the provision one for "liquidated damages", as in this case, or have styled it as a penalty. . . . Such an approach would put too much faith in form and too little in substance. Similarly, the agreement should be interpreted as of the date of its making and not as of the date of its breach. . . .

In applying these principles to the case before us, we conclude that the amount stipulated by the parties as damages bears a reasonable relation to the amount of probable actual harm and is not a penalty. Hence, the provision is enforceable and the order of the Appellate Division should be affirmed.

Looking forward from the date of the lease, the parties could reasonably conclude, as they did, that there might not be an actual market for the sale or re-rental of these specialized vehicles in the event of the lessee's breach. To be sure, plaintiff's lost profit could readily be measured by the amount of the weekly rental fee. However, it was permissible for the parties, in advance, to agree that the re-

rental or sale value of the vehicles would be 50% of the weekly rental. Since there was uncertainty as to whether the trucks could be re-rented or sold, the parties could reasonably set, as they did, the value of such mitigation at 50% of the amount the lessee was obligated to pay for rental of the trucks. This would take into consideration the fact that, after being used by the lessee, the vehicles would no longer be "shiny, new trucks," but would be used, possibly battered, trucks, whose value would have declined appreciably. The parties also considered the fact that, although plaintiff, in the event of Puritan's breach, might be spared repair and maintenance costs necessitated by Puritan's use of the trucks, plaintiff would have to assume the cost of storing and maintaining trucks idled by Puritan's refusal to use them. Further, it was by no means certain, at the time of the contract, that lessee would peacefully return the trucks to the lessor after lessee had breached the contract. . . .

[Judgment affirmed.]

Punitive Damages. **Punitive,** or **exemplary damages,** are used to punish the conduct of the defendant. They usually are awarded in tort cases as a deterrent to similar future conduct by the defendant or others. Punitive damages are not awarded in contract actions unless the conduct constituting the breach is also a tort for which punitive damages may be recovered. As previously discussed, contract remedies seek to compensate the injured party, not punish the wrongdoer. A contract breach ordinarily does not involve conduct that justifies the extraordinary punitive damage remedy. If, however, the defendant has acted intentionally, maliciously, or fraudulently, or his conduct constituted gross negligence (that is, acting with reckless disregard for the consequences of his actions), punitive damages may be awarded in addition to compensatory damages.

Nominal Damages. Occasionally, the promisee of a broken contractual promise does not incur or is unable to prove loss or injury. Thus, though breach is established, damages are not. In these cases, the court may award the plaintiff **nominal damages,** such as $1.00, to acknowledge the existence of a

breach. Court costs also may be awarded in such cases.

Equitable Remedies—Specific Performance, Injunction Against Breach, and Reformation

As previously discussed, equitable remedies are granted in the discretion of the court when the remedy at law, dollar damages, is inadequate. Specific performance and injunction against breach, discussed below, represent alternatives to an award of damages as a means of enforcing a contract. Although specific performance and injunction are extraordinary remedies, modern courts have been increasingly disposed to grant them in a wide variety of situations both in UCC and common law contracts.

Specific Performance

Specific performance requires that the breaching party actually perform the contract as agreed. For example, if Seller contracts with Buyer to deliver 500 widgets and fails to do so, the remedy at law would allow compensatory damages (money) to the buyer for his loss. The remedy of specific performance, however, would actually force the seller to deliver the 500 units as promised. Specific performance is granted only if dollar damages are inadequate to compensate the injured party. Factors to be considered in determining the adequacy of legal relief include

1. The difficulty of proving damages with reasonable certainty,
2. The difficulty of procuring a suitable substitute for the performance required by the contract, and
3. The likelihood that a damage award could not be collected, due, for example, to the defendant's insolvency.[10]

Personal Property. Under the traditional test, the legal remedy is inadequate only if the subject matter is *unique.* Because most personal property is not

---

10. *Restatement (Second) of Contracts* §360.

unique, and a market for substitute property exists, dollar damages for breach are generally adequate. Specific performance may, however, properly be granted if the item is one of a kind (such as a rare painting or antique), or when the item has personal significance to one of the contracting parties. For example, a contract to purchase a family heirloom may be specifically enforced by the buyer. Additionally, contracts for the sale of patents and copyrights, shares of stock in a corporation (if substitute shares are not readily obtainable or the stock is necessary for control of a corporation whose shares are publicly traded), and businesses have been specifically enforced because the subject matter is deemed "unique." In these situations, specific performance may be granted because of the difficulty (or impossibility) of finding a suitable substitute. Further, certain types of interests cannot be valued in money, making damages difficult to prove with reasonable certainty. For example, it is difficult to value sentimental attachment to a family heirloom or loss of control over a corporation.

Land. Contracts for the sale of real property (land) are always specifically enforceable because courts long have treated each piece of, and interest in, real property as unique. Assume Steve, on March 1, contracts to sell land to Cathy for $25,000, with the conveyance of the land and payment of the purchase price to occur on August 1. Steve fails to perform. Upon suit by Cathy requesting specific performance, the court will order Steve to convey the property to Cathy, who must pay the purchase price.[11]

Note that specific performance is not available in land sale contracts if the seller, after the contract is made but before the time agreed upon to transfer the property, conveys the property to a bona fide purchaser, who takes without notice of the original buyer's interest. In these cases, the court will not order the purchaser to return the property. The original buyer's recovery is limited to the traditional measure of contract damages, that is, the difference between the fair market value and the con-

tract price on the date of performance. To illustrate using the preceding example, assume that on June 1 Steve conveyed the land to Megan, who paid fair value for the property and took it in good faith without knowledge of Cathy's interest. If Cathy later sues Steve for breach of contract, the court will not disturb the title in Megan's hands, but will instead award Cathy the remedy at law, money damages.[12]

Personal Services. Specific performance will not be granted in contracts requiring personal services or supervision, such as employment contracts, for several reasons. First, forcing an unwilling party to perform may violate the Thirteenth Amendment to the United States Constitution, which provides "neither slavery nor *involuntary servitude* . . . shall exist within the United States. . . ." (Emphasis added.) Second, such decrees are difficult for the court to supervise because, although the court may order performance, it has no way of monitoring the quality of the performance, the fundamental basis of contracts for personal services. Third, it is undesirable to compel people to continue contractual personal associations which have become unworkable.

For example, assume A agrees to act in a play being produced by B. A breaches the contract because personal animosity develops between A and B. Although A is liable for damages for her breach, the court will not order specific performance.

Specific Performance under the Uniform Commercial Code. The UCC retains but expands the common law rule of specific performance by providing in §2-716(1) that "specific performance may be decreed where the goods are *unique or in other proper circumstances.*" (Emphasis added.) The UCC initially expands the availability of specific performance by redefining "uniqueness," the traditional specific performance test, to emphasize the "commercial feasibility of replacement."[13] Un-

---

11. Although specific performance is usually awarded to buyers upon breach by a seller, sellers of land and unique personal property may also obtain specific performance.

12. In this situation the buyer under an executory contract for the sale of land may protect himself against subsequent purchasers by recording his interest, thereby giving constructive notice to would-be purchasers. The operation of the real property recording statute is discussed in Chapter 37.

13. UCC §2-716, Official Comment 2.

der the Code, goods may be "unique" even though not specific or ascertained at the time of the contract, like a family heirloom or a work of art.

Further, uniqueness is not the sole basis of the specific performance remedy under the UCC. For example, inability of the buyer to "cover"—obtain substitute goods from an alternative source—is strong evidence of "other proper circumstances" supporting specific enforcement of the contract. The buyer's inability to cover may result either from a market shortage or a monopoly on the part of the breaching party. To illustrate, assume Stern Chemical Co. has agreed to sell and deliver a certain chemical to Blake Corp. for use in Blake's manufacturing process. If Stern breaches, and Blake is unable to acquire the chemical from an alternative source, the court properly may grant specific performance.

In Code contracts, therefore, the inquiry focuses on the buyer's reasonable ability to replace the performance of the breaching seller. If replacement is not commercially feasible, specific enforcement should be decreed. If the injured buyer is able to "cover," specific performance will seldom be granted. Because a market exists for most goods, damages will ordinarily be an adequate remedy. Further, arranging for substitute performance usually avoids loss more effectively than a suit for specific performance.

Additional Reasons for Denying Specific Performance. The court may refuse to order specific performance when it would be otherwise available. For example, a court will not order one party to perform if the other party's performance cannot be secured to the court's satisfaction. If the issue is in doubt, the court may require the injured party to furnish security for performance in some form, such as simultaneous exchange, execution of a mortgage, or furnishing other collateral.

This rule is necessary because specific performance requires the breaching party to fulfill her contractual duty. Had she been sued instead for damages, the injured party's recovery would be reduced by the amount the injured party saves because she is not required to proceed with her own performance. When specific performance is sought, however, the injured party also is required to perform and some security for that performance is desirable and equitable.

A court also may deny specific performance if the character of the ordered performance would impose burdens of supervision or enforcement on the court that are disproportionate to the advantages derived from enforcement and the injury caused by its denial. As previously noted, this is one reason for denying specific performance of promises requiring personal services or supervision. In other types of contracts, however, experience has shown that potential difficulties in supervision and enforcement do not always materialize. This experience, coupled with the increasingly liberal judicial attitude toward specific performance, should result in specific enforcement orders requiring substantial court supervision, if necessary to do justice.

Injunction

An **injunction** is an order directed to a defendant by the court to do (a **mandatory injunction**) or to refrain from doing (a **prohibitory** or **negative injunction**) an act. The effect of a mandatory injunction is remedial. For example, if Bob's garage is built three feet over his property line onto Andy's property, the court may order Bob to remove the encroachment on Andy's land, a mandatory injunction. Note that in contracts, a specific performance decree is merely a mandatory injunction. That is, the court orders the defendant to perform the contract.

A negative injunction, on the other hand, is preventative in effect. For example, assume Ace Corporation's factory is polluting the air in the community. Beth, a homeowner, sues the factory in tort for the loss in value of her home and other damage to her property. If the court merely awards dollar damages to compensate for past injury, future pollution and deterioration of the property are not prevented. Payment of the money judgment would, in effect, be a license to continue polluting. Therefore, if the court determines that the remedy at law is inadequate, it may also issue an injunction preventing future damage to the property. Thus, whereas dollar damage awards are generally retroactive in effect, a negative injunction has prospective application.

Injunction is a pervasive remedy used in many areas of the law including tort (the preceding example), property, contract, antitrust, and labor law. Injunctions frequently are used in the criminal or administrative context to prevent future violations of the law. For example, the Federal Trade Commission issues "cease and desist" orders to enjoin (prevent) antitrust law violations.

Injunction Against Breach. In contract law, injunction and specific performance are closely associated remedies. Like specific performance, **injunction against breach,** a court order not to breach a contract, is available only when money damages are an inadequate remedy. Generally, a court will order a person *not* to breach a contract duty in two situations:

1. If the duty is a forbearance—a promise that something will *not* happen in the future—*or*
2. The duty is to *act* (as opposed to forbear) and specific performance would be denied by the court only for reasons inapplicable to an injunction.[14]

If the duty is merely a forbearance, the only way to specifically enforce it is through an injunction against its breach. For example, assume Mel sells his bakery to Bob. The bakery has a reputation for excellence in the community. A substantial portion of the purchase price therefore represents goodwill. In order to protect this goodwill, Mel agrees that he will *not* open a bakery in competition with Bob in the locality for five years.[15] Within one year, Mel opens a competing bakery. Bob sues for breach. Mel may properly be enjoined from opening a competing bakery.

In the second situation, the court enforces the promise indirectly by ordering forbearance from inconsistent action. For example, assume that Acme makes a contract with Fabro whereby Acme agrees to sell Fabro's appliances exclusively in Acme's stores for a period of five years. After one year, Acme breaches. Fabro sues Acme for specific performance of Acme's duty to sell Fabro's appliances and to enjoin Acme from selling appliances manufactured by others. Even if specific performance is denied on the grounds that supervision and enforcement of the order would impose an undue burden on the court, an injunction may properly be granted.

The following case discusses the distinction between specific performance and injunction against breach and illustrates a situation in which an injunction is inappropriate.

Lorch, Inc. v. Bessemer Mall Shopping Center, Inc.
310 So. 2d 872 (Ala. 1975)

Appellant Lorch, Inc. and appellee Bessemer Mall Shopping Center, Inc. (Bessemer) entered into a lease agreement by which Lorch agreed to lease a store in a shopping mall from Bessemer for a term of fifteen years. Under the lease agreement, Lorch promised "continuously and uninterruptedly to use for retail sales purposes all of the Leased Premises," "to open for business and remain open during the entire Lease Term," and not to conduct any "going out of business" sales. For over five years, Lorch operated a combination jewelry, furniture, and appliance store on the leased premises, but the store always operated at a substantial loss. During the sixth year, Lorch began advertising and conducted a going out of business sale and then notified Bessemer that it was closing the store and vacating the premises on October 1. On September 24, Bessemer sued Lorch and requested that the court issue an injunction requiring Lorch to continue operating its store at the mall. The court issued the injunction and Lorch appealed.

Merrill, Justice

. . . It is undisputed that appellant has stated its intention to go out of business. The issue on this appeal is not whether Lorch's proposed termination of its business operations at Bessemer Mall would amount to a breach of its lease. The only issue presented on this appeal is whether the trial court erred in issuing its injunction, or decree of specific performance, requiring Lorch to continue its merchandising operations at the Bessemer Mall.

The equitable remedy of specific performance and that by injunction against breach of a contract have much in common, . . . the jurisdiction exercised is

---

14. *Restatement (Second) of Contracts* §357(2).

15. The validity of convenants not to compete in the sale of a business is discussed in Chapter 10.

in substance the same, and the general rules apply in the one case as in the other. Generally, an injunction to restrain a breach of contract operates as, and affects all the purposes of, a decree for specific performance. It is one of the methods for the enforcement of contracts, and if the contract is one which would ordinarily be specifically enforced, an injunction may be awarded where this is the most appropriate form of relief. *Medical Society of Mobile County v. Walker* [16 So. 2d 321, 325 (Ala. 1944)].

In determining whether or not a temporary injunction should have issued, wide discretion is accorded the trial judge hearing the application and making the decision, and, where no abuse of that discretion is shown, his action will not be disturbed on appeal. . . .

Appellant contends that the decree of the trial court violates an established principle of equity. We agree. . . .

In *Electric Lighting Co. of Mobile v. Mobile & Spring Hill Railway Co.* [19 So. 721, 723 (Ala. 1896)], the rule was stated thusly:

> The general doctrine is that a court of equity will decree specific performance only when it can dispose of the matter in controversy by a degree capable of present performance. It will not decree a party to perform a continuous duty extending over a series of years, but will leave the aggrieved party to his remedies at law. . . .

. . . It is obvious that the relief requested in the instant case is not capable of present performance. Special knowledge, skill and judgment are necessarily involved in selecting and investing an inventory, selecting, training, and compensating adequate personnel, and innumerable other day-to-day business decisions. No case has been cited where this court has ever required continuous, affirmative acts of the type requested here. . . .

It would seem that length and complexity of performance plus difficulty of supervision may, by themselves, be sufficient grounds for denial of specific performance in cases of the type here presented.

This lease contract contained the usual covenants and provisions relating to remedies and awards of damages for noncompliance with the contract. The denial of injunctive relief does not leave the lessor without remedies at law.

[Judgment reversed and remanded.]

Injunction Against Breach of Personal Services Contracts. Although specific performance is unavailable in a personal service contract, a court may, under certain circumstances, order an injunction against the contract's breach. For example, in the well-known 1852 English case, *Lumley v. Wagner,*[16] the defendant, Johanna Wagner, a famous opera singer, contracted to sing in the plaintiff's opera house for three months and also agreed not to sing for anyone else during that time. Defendant breached the contract and prepared to sing in a competing theater. Plaintiff filed suit for breach of contract. Although refusing to order specific performance of Wagner's promise to sing, the court nevertheless granted an injunction preventing the defendant from singing for a competitor, thereby enforcing her promise not to sing elsewhere.

The rationale for an injunction in this case is similar to that supporting specific performance. That is, damages are difficult to compute and no reasonable substitute performance can be obtained. On these facts, the remedy at law (money) is inadequate because the services of the employee are unique or extraordinary. Unless the services meet this test, either because of special skill possessed by the employee or special knowledge acquired in the course of employment, dollar damages are adequate. Even if damages are inadequate, however, injunction should be denied if its effect leaves the employee without other reasonable means of making a living. In other words, the injunction should not leave the employee without alternative means of support, thereby indirectly forcing him or her to perform the contract.

Reformation

Although oral contracts are generally enforceable, the parties often commit their agreement to writing.

---

16. 1 DeG. M. & G. 604, 42 Eng. Rep. 687 (Ch. 1852).

Occasionally, mistakes are made in the process of reducing the agreement to writing. To correct such mistakes, courts of equity have developed the remedy of **reformation**. Like other equitable remedies, reformation is granted in the discretion of the court. A party requesting reformation alleges that the parties have reached an agreement which they have reduced to a writing, but because of a mistake by both parties regarding the content or effect of the writing, it fails to correctly state their agreement.[17]

The deviation between the writing and the original agreement has taken many forms. Common examples include typographical errors, computational mistakes, misdescription of the subject matter (for example, incorrect legal description of real property), omission of an agreed term, misstatement of an agreed term, or inclusion of a term not agreed upon. In these situations, the court may "reform" (rewrite) the contract to the actual agreement of the parties.

Courts are fairly hesitant to grant reformation. As illustrated by the parol evidence rule, contract law attaches great importance to integrated written contracts. Further, under the "duty to read" principle,[18] a person signing a contract is generally deemed to know its contents and agree to its terms, and may not later assert his ignorance of provisions stated in the writing. Additionally, by its very nature, reformation seeks to alter the terms of a signed written contract, which has very high probative value, by oral testimony or other evidence having significantly lower probative value. In general, then, the evidence in support of reformation must be "clear and convincing" to the court.

Restitution

Generally speaking, the term **restitution** refers to restoration, or the act of restoring something to its rightful owner, commonly to make good for some loss, damage, or injury. As a judicial remedy, all restitutionary relief is couched in terms of preventing **unjust enrichment** of one party at the expense of another. Simply stated, the law requires that "a person who has been unjustly enriched at the expense of another is required to make restitution to the other."[19]

A person is unjustly enriched if he has received a benefit from another, and it would be unjust to allow retention of the benefit without paying for it. A benefit is conferred if one party gives another possession or some other interest in real or personal property, tangible or intangible, performs services beneficial to or requested by the other, satisfies an obligation of the other, or otherwise adds to the other's security or advantage. Therefore, whereas a claim for damages seeks to *compensate* the injured plaintiff for his loss, restitution is designed to force the defendant to pay for those benefits it would be unjust for him to keep.

Restitution is a pervasive judicial remedy, available in contract or tort actions, based upon statutes or common law principles, and may be sought in law or in equity. Although the person receiving the benefit frequently acts wrongfully in acquiring it, restitution is available even from an honest or innocent defendant. That is, restitution seeks to deprive a person of benefits that in equity and good conscience he ought not be allowed to keep, though he may have acquired them honestly and with no demonstrable injury to the other party.

A person receives restitution when she is restored approximately to the position she originally occupied. In form, restitution is generally either substitutionary or *in specie*. In substitutionary restitution, the thing taken from the plaintiff is not restored. The defendant is instead required to provide some substitute, usually a payment of money. If money is awarded, measuring the appropriate amount frequently is difficult. On the other hand, if restitution is *in specie*, often called "specific restitution," certain specific property received by the defendant is restored to the plaintiff.

The distinction between substitionary and specific restitution is of critical importance in understanding the development and application of the remedy. Restitution historically developed both in courts of law and in courts of equity, governed by

---

17. If one party believes that the writing correctly expresses the prior agreement and the other knows it does not, the latter may be liable for misrepresentation (nondisclosure) and the former may be able to rescind either on that basis or on the basis of unilateral mistake.

18. "Duty to read" is discussed in Chapter 10.

19. *Restatement of Restitution* §1.

the same general principles of fairness and justice. Restitution at law developed mainly through the "quasi-contract" remedy, which is generally substitutionary, requiring a payment of *money* by the defendant. Equitable restitution developed a number of remedies, most notably the "constructive trust" doctrine, which requires return of *specific property* to the plaintiff. Note, therefore, a basic dichotomy in the law of restitution. If money is sought to prevent unjust enrichment, the legal remedy, quasi-contract, is appropriate. If, however, return of specific property is desired, the equitable constructive trust remedy may be used.

Restitution at Law—Quasi-Contract

Contract law developed through the common law action of assumpsit. By the early 1600s, assumpsit was used to enforce both express promises and those inferred from the parties' conduct (the so-called "implied in fact" contract[20]). By the mid-1600s the assumpsit action was pressed into service in cases in which no contract, express or implied in fact, existed between the parties. The purpose was restitution, achieved by the court's imposing a promise upon the defendant to pay the plaintiff for the value of the benefit conferred. So was born the **contract implied in law** or **quasi-contract.**

Early cases involved the plaintiff's payment of money by mistake to the wrong person, overpayments, and payment by a third party of money to the defendant that should have been paid to the plaintiff. For example, assume Tom owes Lew $100. He inadvertently mails a payment to Fred instead. Tom subsequently sues Fred to recover the money mistakenly paid. In this case, the court would order Fred to pay the $100 back to Tom, not on the basis of any actual contractual promise by Fred to pay $100, but on the basis of a promise "implied in law" to prevent Fred's unjust enrichment. That is, in order to prevent a windfall to Fred, the court imposes a binding promise (a quasi-contract) to pay, even though no actual agreement, express or implied in fact, exists between Tom and Fred.

Note that, unlike a contract implied in fact, the implied in law contract is not a contract at all. No

contractual relationship need exist between the parties and liability is imposed without regard to intent. The law simply requires that a benefit be conferred on the defendant which he has retained.[21] To the extent necessary to prevent a windfall, the court will imply a promise on the part of the defendant to pay the reasonable value of the benefit conferred. That is, in order to do justice, the court proceeds "as if" a contractual promise to pay exists.

The following case illustrates the operation of the quasi-contract doctrine.

Hurdis Realty, Inc. v. Town of North Providence
397 A.2d 896 (R.I. 1979)

Plaintiff Hurdis Realty, Inc. owned a commercial building in North Providence, Rhode Island. Hurdis's president was informed that sewage was not flowing properly from the building. Hurdis hired a plumber who determined that the sewer line was blocked under the city street on which the building was situated. Hurdis then requested that defendant, Town of North Providence, remedy the problem. This request was refused. Hurdis therefore hired a private contractor to do the work and sued the town for reimbursement of the contractor's $4,800 bill. The trial court found for Hurdis. North Providence appealed.

Doris, Justice

. . . Although plaintiff's complaint did not specify whether it was proceeding on a tort or contract theory, the trial justice clearly found for plaintiff on the basis of an implied-in-law contract. Unlike an express or implied-in-fact contract for which mutual assent is necessary, in an implied-in-law or quasi-contract, liability is implied by the law and arises from the facts and circumstances irrespective of any agreement or presumed intention. . . . In order to prove a quasi-contract it must be shown that: (1) the plaintiff conferred a benefit upon the defendant, (2) the defendant appreciated the bene-

---

20. Contracts implied in fact are discussed in Chapter 7.

21. Restitution is available not only when an expenditure made by one person adds to the property of another, but also when the expenditure saves the other from expense or loss.

fit, and (3) under the circumstances it would be inequitable for the defendant to retain such benefit without payment of the value thereof. . . .

A municipality, no less than a private individual, may be liable upon the principle of unjust enrichment when it has enjoyed the benefit of work performed and when no statute forbids or limits its power to contract therefor. . . . It is undisputed that municipalities have the power to enter into contracts with respect to their sewer systems. . . . The defendant concedes that it had a duty to maintain its sewer lines properly and that failure to provide proper maintenance will render it liable for resulting damages. . . .

By statute defendant is empowered to assess users of the sewer system and utilize the revenues thereby derived for the maintenance of the sewer system. . . . Even though it is subject to such an assessment, plaintiff was further required to expend its own funds to repair a damaged portion of the town's sewer lines. In so doing, plaintiff clearly conferred a benefit upon the town and fulfilled what was essentially a municipal responsibility. The town, particularly the town council president and sewer superintendent, was fully aware of the repair work. Under these circumstances it would be manifestly inequitable for defendant to benefit from the fruits of plaintiff's labor without paying for the value of that benefit. . . .

[Judgment affirmed.]

Restitution in Equity—Constructive Trust

As discussed in Chapter 1, various substantive and procedural deficiencies in the early English common law courts drove many suitors to the chancellor whose jurisdiction, grounded on equitable principles, led to the creation of chancery as an independent court. Various devices developed in courts of equity are restitutionary in nature. Among the remedies developed was the constructive trust.[22] The constructive trust concept is grounded

partially in the law of trusts, but primarily in the law of restitution. A **constructive trust** is an equitable restitutionary remedy that is used when a person who has obtained *title to property* would be unjustly enriched if permitted to retain it. In this situation, the court subjects the person holding title (the constructive trustee) to an equitable duty to convey the property to the person who should have it. The constructive trust, therefore, simply uses the trust concept (in which one person possesses title to property subject to an equitable duty to hold it for or convey it to another) as the tool to force conveyance of the property by the wrongdoer to the person who, in fairness, should have it. But for this basic similarity there is little resemblance between the constructive trust and trusts discussed in Chapter 39.

A constructive trust, therefore, bears the same relationship to an express trust that a quasi-contractual obligation bears to a contractual obligation. That is, like a quasi-contractual promise, a constructive trust is simply a fiction imposed by the court as a means of achieving justice. Constructive trusts are imposed in a variety of situations, including, for example, when property is acquired by fraud, mistake, duress, or undue influence.

Restitution as a Contract Remedy

Restitution is a common remedy in contract cases, available to a plaintiff: (1) as an alternative to enforcing the contract between the parties, (2) when, for some reason, such as his own breach, the plaintiff is precluded from enforcing the contract, or (3) upon avoidance of a contract voidable on grounds of fraud, misrepresentation, mistake, infancy, or duress. A party is entitled to restitution as a contract remedy to the extent he has conferred a benefit on the other party either through his part performance of or reliance upon the contract. Generally, a party seeking restitution of a benefit conferred is expected to return what he has received from the other party—such as land, goods, or other property. The basic objective, then, is to return the parties, as nearly as practicable, to their precontract positions.

Restitution as an Alternative to Enforcement. When faced with a breach of contract, the injured party ordinarily sues the breaching party on

---

22. Other remedies developed were (1) subrogation discussed in suretyship (Chapter 33), and in insurance (Chapter 56); (2) the accounting discussed in partnership (Chapter 42); and (3) rescission and reformation covered in this chapter.

his promise to recover money damages, or in appropriate cases, specific performance or injunction against breach. As previously noted, these remedies seek to protect the expectation (benefit of the bargain) interest, or in some instances, the reliance interest of the injured party. Alternatively, the injured party may sue in restitution to prevent unjust enrichment by recovering the value of any benefit conferred on the defendant through part performance or reliance. Although an injured party who has partially performed will usually seek damages based on his expectation interest (because this includes his lost profit on the transaction), restitution may provide a larger recovery in some cases, for example, if the injured party would have lost money on the contract.

Restitution when Plaintiff Breaches. Restitution is commonly used in contract cases to protect a party who has either breached the contract or for some other reason cannot enforce it against the other party. For example, if a contract is partially performed but is later discharged or avoided because of impracticability of performance, or noncompliance with the Statute of Frauds, restitution may be granted. In these cases, it is often unjust to allow the other party to retain the entire benefit of the part performance without paying for it. A party who has breached is entitled to restitution to the extent that the benefit received by the injured party exceeds the loss resulting from the breach. For example, assume Susan contracts to sell land to Belinda for $100,000, payment to be made in 10 equal monthly installments before transfer of title. Belinda pays $30,000, but fails to pay the remaining installments. Susan sells the land to Daniel for $95,000. Belinda can recover $25,000 from Susan; $30,000 in restitution less $5,000 damages for Belinda's breach of contract.

Restitution in Voidable Contracts. Perhaps the most common use of restitution in contract cases occurs when a party avoids a contract on grounds of infancy, mistake, duress, undue influence, misrepresentation, or fraud. In these cases, restitution is available to the party avoiding the contract for any benefit conferred on the other party resulting from part performance or reliance. Generally, the term **rescission** is used to describe the act of avoid-

ing a transaction, commonly one based upon the parties' agreement. Rescission is generally followed by restitution on both sides, thereby placing both parties in the position they occupied before the contract was made. That is, restitution is the basic remedy available when a party elects to rescind. For example, assume B, a minor, purchases a car from an adult, S, for $1,000. B subsequently avoids (rescinds) the contract on grounds of infancy. S is entitled to restitution of the car from B, and B may recover the $1,000 from S in restitution.

Election of Remedies

As the foregoing discussion indicates, a variety of remedies are available for breach of contract. Neither the UCC nor the *Restatement (Second) of Contracts* imposes any requirement that a party must elect one remedy to the exclusion of others—that is, make an **election of remedies.** The *Restatement* provides that if a party has more than one remedy, choosing one of them (for example, by bringing suit requesting a given remedy) does not bar another remedy unless (1) the remedies are inconsistent, and (2) the other party materially changes position in reliance on the initial choice of remedy.[23] The UCC adopts a similar policy by providing that Code remedies are cumulative not exclusive.[24]

For example, the remedy of specific performance and dollar damages for total breach are inconsistent. However, damages to compensate the buyer for the seller's delay in performance would not be inconsistent with the buyer's action for specific performance. To illustrate the reliance aspect of the above rule, assume Seller and Buyer have a contract for the sale of land, breached by Seller. Buyer brings an action for damages. While the suit is pending, Seller, believing that Buyer does not intend to request specific performance, makes valuable improvements to the property. Buyer then amends her complaint to ask for specific performance. Buyer's claim for specific performance is precluded, because both aspects of the above test are met.

---

23. *Restatement (Second) of Contracts* §378.
24. UCC §2-703, Official Comment 1. §2-703 and Code remedies generally are discussed in detail in Chapter 18.

Another problem of potentially inconsistent remedy exists between a claim for rescission and an action for money damages. Rescission and dollar damages achieve different results. Dollar damages place the injured party in a position approximating proper performance of the contract. Rescission and restitution return the parties to their original positions and thus treat the contract as if it never existed. Therefore, an action for dollar damages appears inconsistent with a claim for, or after, rescission. The UCC avoids this result by providing that expressions of "cancellation" or "rescission" of the contract are not construed to extinguish any claim for damages.[25] This rule is intended to safeguard the rights of an injured party, who, after a breach, ill-advisedly uses language indicating the contract is at an end. Therefore, unless the cancellation expressly states that it is "without reservation of rights," the injured party's right to recover damages is unimpaired. If the plaintiff's claim is based upon fraud or material misrepresentation, the Code reaches the same result by providing that neither rescission nor a claim for rescission is inconsistent with a claim for damages or any other Code remedy.[26]

Although remedies generally are not exclusive, a party seeking damages for breach of contract must elect whether to sue for total or merely partial breach. That is, after a breach of contract, the injured party has two basic options. Assuming the breach is material, she may choose to accept the defective performance, continue her own performance, and sue to recover damages for partial breach. Frequently, the election to continue performance is made by conduct involving an acceptance or retention for an unreasonable time of the defective performance. Alternatively, she may refuse to accept the other's performance, cancel her own performance, and sue for total breach. In other words, the election to continue performance operates as a waiver of the injured party's right to treat the contract at an end and sue for total breach. An election binds both parties; that is, if the injured party elects to continue her performance, the breaching party must also fulfill her remaining obligations.[27]

SUMMARY

1. The law of contract remedies concerns the judicial relief available when one party breaches a contractual promise. Contract remedies are of three general types: legal remedies, equitable remedies, and restitution.

2. The remedy at law is, in all cases, money damages. The traditional goal of contract remedies is to fully compensate the injured promisee for actual loss resulting from the breach. To this end, damages are generally computed to give the injured party the "benefit of the bargain." Under this test, the injured party is awarded a sum of money sufficient to place him in a position equivalent to full performance.

3. Because the underlying goal of contract remedies is to compensate the injured party, punitive damages, those designed to punish the conduct of the defendant, are not generally awarded in contract cases. In addition to basic compensatory damages, consequential damages (usually lost profits in contract cases) are recoverable for loss that the breaching party had reason to foresee when the contract was made, occurring as the probable result of its breach.

4. After breach of the contract, the injured party must take reasonable steps to mitigate damages—to keep damages to a minimum. An injured party who fails to mitigate may not recover for loss which could have been avoided by reasonable effort. The mitigation doctrine prevents economic waste by relieving the breaching party of liability for losses that the other party could have prevented.

---

25. UCC §2-720 and Official Comment. "Rescission" as used in the Code refers to a mutual agreement to discharge contractual duties. "Cancellation" occurs when either party puts an end to the contract because of a breach by the other. §2-106(4).

26. UCC §2-721.

27. The UCC adopts these principles in a number of provisions. For example, a buyer is liable for the price of goods accepted and retained, despite their nonconformity, if the goods were accepted with knowledge or reason to know the defect. §§2-607, 2-608, 2-709. However, the acceptance and retention does not prevent the buyer from recovering damages resulting from the nonconformity. §§2-607(2), 2-714(1); these provisions are discussed in detail in Chapter 18.

5. By using a liquidated damages provision the parties may specify in the contract the damages to be awarded in the event of a breach rather than leaving this determination to the court or jury. To be enforceable, damages must be liquidated at an amount which is reasonable in light of the anticipated or actual harm caused by the breach and the difficulties in proving actual loss. This limitation assures that the provision is not a "penalty"—a threat designed to prevent or punish breach.

6. If dollar damages are not adequate to remedy a breach of contract, the injured party may seek equitable relief, awarded in the discretion of the court, in the form of specific performance or injunction against breach. Both remedies effectively require the breaching party to perform the contract as agreed, rather than pay money damages for failure to perform it. Traditionally, specific performance is awarded only when the subject matter is unique, such as a rare antique or work of art. The UCC adopts a more liberal test emphasizing the commercial feasibility of replacing the promisor's performance. Contracts involving real property are always specifically enforceable because courts have long treated each piece of real property as unique. On the other hand, for various policy reasons, courts refuse to specifically enforce contracts involving personal services, such as employment contracts.

7. Another equitable remedy used in contracts cases is reformation. Reformation is used when the parties reduce their agreement to a writing, which due to a mistake fails to correctly state their agreement. If evidence of a mistake is clear and convincing, the court may reform, or rewrite, the contract to conform to the actual agreement of the parties.

8. Restitution also may be available as a contract remedy. Restitution is a broad remedial concept designed to prevent unjust enrichment of one party at the expense of another. A person who is unjustly enriched is required to make restitution either by return of a specific thing or the payment of money. Restitution developed both in courts of law and in courts of equity. If a sum of money is sought, restitution at law, or quasi-contractual relief, is appropriate. If return of specific property is desired, the equitable constructive trust doctrine is utilized. As a contract remedy, restitution may be used by a person who has breached the contract to recover the value of the benefit conferred upon the other party, and to restore the parties to their original positions after avoidance of the contract on grounds of infancy, mistake, duress, undue influence, misrepresentation, or fraud.

9. Although a variety of remedies are available for breach of contract, the law generally rejects any notion that an injured party must elect one remedy to the exclusion of others.

KEY TERMS

contract remedies	specific performance
remedy at law	injunction
equitable remedy	mandatory injunction
expectation interest	prohibitory (negative)
benefit of the bargain	injunction
reliance interest	injunction against breach
restitution interest	reformation
court costs	restitution
consequential damages	unjust enrichment
mitigation of damages	quasi-contract (contract
liquidated damages	implied in law)
provision	constructive trust
punitive (exemplary)	rescission
damages	election of remedies
nominal damages	

QUESTIONS AND PROBLEMS

15-1 Contract remedies seek to protect one or more interests of an injured promisee, including an expectation, reliance, and restitution interest. Explain and distinguish the relationship among these various interests.

15-2 Mayfield entered into a contract with Swafford by which Mayfield agreed to pay $7,000 for Swafford's construction of a swimming pool on Mayfield's property. Mayfield later sued alleging that the pool had not been constructed in a "good workmanlike manner" and requested damages equal to the cost of repair.

The evidence established that the pool was improperly constructed. Witnesses testified that substantial work was required to correct the construction—for example, removal of the concrete deck, replacement of the piping system, and realignment, replacement, and reinforcement of the walls. The trial court awarded damages of $11,381 to Mayfield, the cost to repair the defects in the pool. Is cost of repair the correct measure of damages in this case? Explain. What alternative method might the court have used?

15-3 Cricket Alley Corporation, which operates a chain of eight retail clothing stores, agreed to purchase a computerized cash register system from Data Terminal. As described by Data Terminal representatives, the system would connect the cash registers from each store to a centralized computer where records on inventory, sales, and payroll could be maintained for all stores. Data Terminal installed the new system, but it failed to operate as described. Over a period of several months, Data Terminal unsuccessfully tried to correct the problem. Finally, Cricket Alley purchased another system from Business Machinery, Inc. and sued Data Terminal for breach of contract. Cricket Alley sought damages of $50,000 representing the cost of wages it paid to employees for manually performing the tasks that the Data Terminal computer system was intended to handle. Data Terminal argued that although it knew Cricket Alley operated retail stores, it did not know of the general or particular requirements of the business at the time the contract was made. Therefore, Data Terminal claimed it could not be held liable for consequential damages—the increased cost of wages. How should the court rule?

15-4   (a) Gomer is a sales director for the Major Advertising Company located in Chicago. Major was to make an important presentation for a potential new client in New York. If the client accepted Major as its new agency, Major would earn over $1 million in the next two years. Due to unforeseen delays, the prints of the sample advertisements were not ready until the day before the presentation. Gomer rushed the prints to the Snail Express Company, an air express firm that advertised that it guaranteed overnight delivery. Gomer explained the situation to the Snail Express clerk concluding, ''So if this doesn't get to New York by tomorrow, I will lose my job and my company will lose the account which is worth over $1 million.'' The clerk nodded his head and accepted the package for shipment. The package did not arrive in New York until three days later. Gomer lost his job (which paid $125,000 per year) and Major lost the account. Gomer wants to sue Snail Express for breach of contract. Should a court award him damages? How much? If Major sues Snail Express will it be entitled to damages? How much? Explain.

        (b) Gomer's attorney writes a letter to Snail Express notifying it that Gomer intends to sue for damages. Snail Express's attorney responds that Snail Express will not pay any damages and advises the attorney to review the receipt provided to Gomer when he shipped the package. The receipt contained numerous provisions on the reverse side under the heading ''Terms and Conditions of Contract.'' Provision 23(c) states: ''Snail Express shall not be liable for any special, incidental or consequential damages, including but not limited to loss of profits or income whether or not Snail Express had knowledge that such damages might be incurred.'' Would you recommend that Gomer continue with his plans to sue? Explain.

15-5   Mr. and Mrs. Burns contracted with the Speedy Construction Company for the construction of a duplex apartment house. The Burnses intended to live in one apartment and to rent the second apartment. The contract required that the construction company would complete the building by April 1. The contract also contained the following provision:

> If the construction is not completed by April 1, Speedy Construction Company shall pay to Mr. and Mrs. Burns on an actual expense basis as established by receipts, not more than $1,000 for packing and storing of furnishings and $30 per day for temporary accommodations.

Mr. and Mrs. Burns sold their house; the purchasers were to take possession on April 1. Mr. and Mrs. Burns also found a tenant for the second apartment in the duplex and signed a one-year lease to receive $250 a month as rent. In late March, Speedy advised the Burnses that the duplex would not be completed until June 1. On April 1, the Burnses moved out of their house and into a motel that charged $50 per day. They put all of their furnishings in storage at a cost of $2,000. They advised the tenant that the apartment was not completed: the lease was terminated and the tenant moved into another apartment. By the time the Burnses finally were able to move into the new duplex, they had incurred expenses in excess of $6,000. Further, they calculated that termination of the lease cost $3,000 ($250 × twelve months).

Mr. and Mrs. Burns demanded that Speedy pay damages of $9,000 resulting from breach of the construction contract. Speedy offered to pay $1,000 plus $30 per day stating that this was the amount required under the terms of the liquidated damages clause in the contract.

        (a) Mr. and Mrs. Burns sue Speedy. They allege that the clause is not a liquidated damages clause. Are they correct? Explain.

        (b) If it is a liquidated damages clause, should it be enforced in light of the fact that the damages would be disproportionately low in relation to actual damages? Explain.

15-6 C & H operates several sugar plantations in Hawaii. In 1979, C & H decided to purchase a vessel to transport the sugar crop during the harvest. The vessel consisted of two parts, a tug boat and a barge, neither of which could be used without the other. C & H contracted to have Sun Ship construct the tug at a cost of $25 million with delivery to be made on June 30, 1981. The contract included a liquidated damages clause requiring Sun to pay $17,000 for each day that delivery was delayed past the delivery date. C & H contracted to purchase the barge from Halter at a cost of $20 million, delivery to made on June 30, 1981. A liquidated damage clause in that contract required Halter to pay $10,000 per day for late delivery. Both Sun and Halter failed to complete construction by June 30. Sun delivered the tug on March 1, 1982 (243 days late); Halter delivered the barge on July 1, 1982 (365 days late). C & H has sued both Sun and Halter for breach of contract.

(a) The court found that the liquidated damages clauses were valid and enforceable. What amount of damages should be assessed against each defendant? Explain.

(b) Assume that the contracts contained no liquidated damages provisions and that C & H suffered total damages of $370,000. How should the damages be apportioned between the defendants? Explain.

15-7 On March 1, 1984, Archie contracted to sell his farm to Beulah for $200,000, closing to occur on June 1, 1984. On April 1, Archie received a $250,000 offer from Zack. Archie accepted and the parties agreed to a May 1 closing date. Archie conveyed the land to Zack on May 1. Zack was at all times unaware of Archie's prior contract with Beulah. Beulah subsequently sued Archie for breach of contract. Is Beulah entitled to specific performance?

15-8 Campbell Soup Company entered into a contract with Wentz for sale of carrots to be grown on the Wentz farm. The contract price was $30 per ton. By the date of this contract, however, the market price had risen to $90 per ton and Wentz refused to deliver. Carrots meeting the contract description were in short supply, and could not be obtained elsewhere by Campbell. The contract, contained on a form drafted by Campbell, included the following provisions:

(1) Campbell's judgment is conclusive concerning whether or not the carrots delivered conform to the contract,

(2) Campbell may refuse carrots in excess of 12 tons per acre,

(3) The grower may not sell carrots to anyone else except carrots rejected by Campbell,

(4) A liquidated damages clause of $50 per acre upon breach by the grower (no liquidated damages clause covers a breach by Campbell),

(5) If Campbell is unable to receive the grower's carrots (for example, because of a strike or any other circumstance beyond Campbell's control), "grower may with Campbell's written consent, dispose of his carrots elsewhere. Grower may not, however, sell or otherwise dispose of any carrots which he is unable to deliver to Campbell."

Campbell sues Wentz for specific performance (or an injunction against selling the carrots to others). Should the court grant it? Should the court enforce the contract at all? Explain.

15-9 Strauss sold a racehorse to West. Upon delivery, the horse was discovered to be lame. West accordingly shipped the horse back to Strauss at Belmont Park Racetrack. Strauss refused to accept it, and the horse was shipped to Bailey's farm to be cared for. When Bailey received the horse he was aware that a dispute had arisen concerning the ownership of the horse. Two months later he sent a bill for boarding the horse to West, who replied immediately, "The horse doesn't belong to me and it was not sent to your farm at my request." Nevertheless, Bailey continued to care for the horse until he sold it to a third party four months later. In the contract dispute between Strauss and West, the court found that West was liable to Strauss for the purchase price of the horse. Bailey sued West to recover for the care, feeding, and maintenance of the horse during the six-month period. Should Bailey recover on a contract implied in fact theory? If not, should he recover on the basis of quasi-contract (a contract implied in law)?

15-10 Bill, a contractor, agreed to repair the porch on Stella's cabin, located on a remote lake in northern Wisconsin. Because the parties lived in Madison, Bill did not inspect the property at the time of the contract. Following Stella's written directions Bill located an unoccupied cabin with a dilapidated porch and spent several days repairing it. It was subsequently discovered that Bill had taken a wrong turn and had repaired Jones's cabin by mistake. Should Bill be entitled to recover the reasonable value of the improvements from Jones?

15-11 Reconsider the facts of *O. W. Grun Roofing and Construction Company v. Cope* in Chapter 14 on page 316. In this case the court held that Grun had not substantially performed and was therefore not entitled to recover under the contract. Should Grun nevertheless be entitled to restitution from the plaintiff on these facts? Why or why not? If so, in what amount?

Optimal Contract Damages under the Rule in Hadley v. Baxendale

Richard A. Epstein

Hadley v. Baxendale has long posed a difficult puzzle for theories of contract damages. As written, the opinion emphasis the importance of both general knowledge within the trade and of special circumstances of the case that the plaintiff has communicated to the defendant. The rule then holds the defendant responsible for the plaintiff's loss to the extent that they are known to or foreseeable by someone in the defendant's position. The stated goal is to put the plaintiff back in the same financial position after breach that he would have enjoyed if the defendant had performed the contract in accordance with its terms. *Hadley's* standard is a capacious one, so why then did the Court refuse to reward the plaintiff his lost profits, and require him to settle for some lower sum, such as the rental value of the shaft for the period of delay?

The traditional explanation is that the shaft need not have been the source of the plaintiff's loss. The mill could have been shut down because other equipment had been destroyed; or there may have been a spare shaft in the wings. All true, but if the test requires only reasonable foresight, then once the carrier knows that it has been entrusted with the millshaft from a mill that has stopped, it must know that there is at least a substantial probability that the want of the shaft will shut the mill down. There is no need to stretch the idea of foresight to reach every freakish event, as is done commonly in the law of torts. It takes only a little imagination to permit the recovery of lost profits under the very test *Hadley* announces. Did *Hadley* then misapply its own rule?

In order to answer this question we must take a detour from the particular issue of contract damages, and ask a question relevant in so many other contexts as well. (See, e.g. my discussion of accountant's liability, infra at 1226.) Suppose the carrier and the millowner had sat down before the

shaft was sent, and were asked to allocate by express contract the risk of loss from delay. Would they settle upon the rental value of the millshift? Lost profits? Or some other measure of damages?

Initially, there are obvious attractions to allowing full recovery for lost profits. These are real economic losses that the millowner must bear; if he were the single owner of both the carrier and the mill, he would invest substantial money to see that the millshaft was properly delivered. Damages for lost profits should give the carrier the right incentive to do the same, without forcing the millowner to monitor every detail of the carrier's operations.

Unsuspected complications are introduced because the carrier and mill have different owners. It is easy to stipulate some dollar figure for lost profits in an appellate opinion. But just how are these to be determined when the issue is sharply contested at trial, where each side has information denied the other? There is a bewildering array of fixed, variable and joint costs to take into account. It has to be asked whether the millowner could have mitigated his losses by running the mill overtime after the shaft does arrive, or perhaps, by keeping another shaft in reserve. In complex cases, it could cost an enormous amount of money to decide which of these myriad possibilities are sensible and how much money they could save. A carrier who is responsible for shipping thousands of goods of all kinds and descriptions could well refuse to enter into this "lost profits" derby every time goods are delayed in shipment. Some liquidated damage provision might be cheaper to

Richard A. Epstein is the James Parker Hall Distinguished Services Professor of Law, The University of Chicago, and Editor, Journal of Legal Studies.

administer, while providing the carrier with some tangible spur to perform on the other. The abstract damage formulas of *Hadley* might not serve the economic desires of both the millowner and the carrier to maximize the joint gains from their contract. When communication breakdown poses serious problems, lost profits need not be the best workable measure of damages.

Two sorts of evidence support this last conclusion: one from common practice, and the other from express contracts. In the law of admiralty, the traditional nineteenth measure of damages for the delayed shipment of durable fungible goods salable in a ready market was interest on the value of the goods over the period of delay. If 1000 pounds of hemp, due to arrive on June 1st when the price was $1 per pound, were delayed by the carrier's breach until July 1 when the price fell to 50¢ per pound, the measure of damage for this foreseeable loss was the one month interest on $1000, about $10, not the $500 decline in value. The outcome seems to contradict the general principle in *Hadley*, because this decline in value was surely foreseeable to the carrier, given ordinary market fluctuations. But a closer look shows the soundness of the customary rule. To be sure, the decline in prices was foreseeable, but by the same token, any increase in price attributable to the delay was equally foreseeable as well. The "compensation" the owner received from the breach was the prospect of an interim price increase. A single owner would not invest huge sums to get the cargo to market on time, why then should the damage rule require the carrier to act as the single owner would not? If the shipper did not want to take his chances, he could assign the right to the goods while in transit, with delivery at the time of arrival. There is no need for the damage rule to provide unwanted insurance.

More generally, when both ups and downs are equally foreseeable, the optimal level of contract damages is interest for the delay. When the goods could spoil in transit, however, then the proper (and customary) measure of damages was the value of the goods, for now their owner could in no way hope to profit from the carrier's breach.

Modern cases, most notably the *Heron II* decided by the House of Lords in 1967 have rejected the older admiralty practice for late delivery and have allowed the plaintiff to recover the larger $500 differential. But *Heron II* was mistaken because it ignored, as the parties would not, the owner's benefit from a price increase attributable to delay.

The second reason to believe that lost profits is not necessarily the ideal measure of damages comes the explicit provisions on consequential damages found in contracts of carriage. The Federal Express form, for example, explicitly rejects the general rule of *Hadley*. Shippers are limited to a maximum of $100 in damages for delayed shipment of goods, even where Federal Express was told about the special circumstances surrounding the shipment. Some insurance can be purchased for extra fees. Consequential damages are excluded.

The deal makes sense. Federal Express cannot make a profit if it has to pay $100 for the misdelivery of even a tiny fraction of its parcels. The customer who fears larger losses can protect himself by sending two separate packages with the same documents. The low, fixed level of damages provided by contract are not an instance of consumer exploitation, but survive in a highly competitive business environment where its customers are sophisticated firms.

Both these cases illustrate one common theme. The restrictive measure of damages awarded in *Hadley* often makes good sense in the carrier business. The nineteenth century cases that read *Hadley* narrowly, as imposing upon a defendant only those risks to which it had given tacit consent, make good commercial sense. The modern cases, and the Uniform Commercial Code, have expanded liability to cover foreseeable losses in the fashion of *Heron II*. In so doing that they have placed abstract theory above sound business practice. The first rule of damages is to let the parties decide for themselves. The second rule of damages is to fill in the gaps left by silence with those terms which maximize total gains to the parties—a test that often yields the result in *Hadley*, but not necessarily the *Hadley* rule.

Part Three

SALES

Chapter 16

The Sales Contract— Basic Obligations

Major Topics

- an introduction to the sales contract and a general comparison of Code and common law contracts
- how Article 2 of the Uniform Commercial Code supplies missing terms in the parties' agreement
- an explanation of the seller's obligations regarding delivery of the goods and the buyer's duty to pay the price
- the operation of Article 2's open price and quantity terms
- a summary of UCC rules governing auction sales
- an introduction to UCC Article 2A, which governs personal property leasing

The general law of contracts is of common law origin, developed primarily through a long series of decided cases. Indeed many fundamental contract doctrines can be traced to early decisions of English courts. The common law of contracts is continuously developing, forming an ever-expanding framework for modern commercial law.

Contracts is not, however, exclusively a common law topic. Many statutes, both state and federal, modify or replace common law contract principles in certain transactions. Perhaps the most important of these statutes is Article 2 of the Uniform Commercial Code that governs contracts for the sale of goods, or "sales contracts." Goods generally include tangible personal property, such as automobiles, appliances, and other consumer goods, business inventory and equipment, clothing, books, food, and animals. Article 2 therefore governs a wide variety of contracts made by consumers and businesspersons.

This and the following four chapters focus primarily upon issues relating to contracts for the sale of goods that have not been covered in the preceding contracts material. Although the majority of the material is drawn from specific Article 2 sections, other statutory provisions and common law doctrines also are involved.

Introduction to the Sales Contract

Article 2 and General Contract Law

Before undertaking a detailed study of sales contracts, it may be helpful to briefly review Article 2's approach to the various basic contracts issues discussed in the previous nine chapters.

Contract Formation and Modification. Article 2 generally follows the common law principles regarding contract formation, with certain notable exceptions.

Offers. Under the common law, offers are freely revocable at any time prior to the effectiveness of an acceptance unless the parties have agreed to an "option" contract to keep the offer open. Under the UCC, "firm offers" made by a merchant in a signed writing are irrevocable for up to three months, even if the offers are not supported by consideration.

Acceptance. Under the common law, unless an attempted acceptance is the mirror image of the offer, no contract results. Under the UCC, a definite and seasonable expression of acceptance operates as an acceptance even if it contains terms in addition to, or different from, the offer. This rule creates a contract even though the parties' use forms to communicate offer and acceptance containing minor differences.

Consideration. Under the pre-existing duty rule, modifications of existing common law contracts require consideration to be binding. Article 2 of the UCC provides that modifications of Code contracts, if sought in good faith, need no consideration to be binding.

Article 2 also makes minor changes in the common law approach to manner of acceptance, primarily regarding unilateral contracts. Additional issues relating to formation and terms of a sales contract are discussed throughout the following sales material.

Capacity of Parties. Article 2 effects no basic change in the law of contractual capacity. State law regarding contractual capacity generally also governs under Article 2.

Illegality; Unenforceability on Public Policy Grounds. As with capacity of parties, Article 2 leaves most illegality and public policy questions to non-Code state law. One notable exception is the unconscionability doctrine, which allows a court to refuse to enforce unreasonably unfair contracts or terms. The doctrine is most commonly applied to standardized form contracts, known as "adhesion contracts," in which the drafting party dictates terms to the other, usually a consumer, who has no power to bargain for different terms. The unconscionability doctrine is used to prevent or limit enforcement of unreasonably unfair terms contained in these contracts. Note that unconscionability principles are now generally applied to common law contracts as well.

Reality of Assent. Like capacity and legality issues, Article 2 leaves resolution of disputes involving fraud, misrepresentation, mistake, duress, and undue influence to state law existing outside the Code.

Parol Evidence Rule. Article 2 retains the parol evidence rule for sales contracts but provides that an integrated writing may be explained or supplemented by course of dealing, course of performance, usage of trade, and evidence of consistent additional terms.

Statute of Frauds. Article 2 contains an elaborate Statute of Frauds provision applicable to contracts for the sale of goods. Generally, a contract for the sale of goods with a price of $500 or more is unenforceable unless some writing exists that indicates a contract for sale has been made, is signed by party to be charged, and specifies a quantity term.

Third Parties. Article 2 generally follows common law principles regarding assignment and delegation of contracts and third-party beneficiaries. It explicitly addresses the legal effect of contract provisions prohibiting assignment and the consequences of a general assignment of a sales contract.

Performance of the Contract. The Code imposes a basic obligation of good faith in the performance and enforcement of a sales contract. Good faith requires honesty in fact and, in the case of merchants, observance of reasonable commercial standards of fair dealing in the trade. The good faith concept also applies to common law contracts.

Two basic characteristics of performance of sales contracts often distinguish them from their common law counterparts. First, unless otherwise agreed, performance by the parties occurs simultaneously. Second, the seller's performance is governed generally by the perfect tender rule, which means that if the seller's performance fails in any respect to conform to the contract, the buyer may reject the entire shipment. Thus, no "substantial performance" doctrine as it exists under the common law is applicable to sales contracts. Various Article 2 provisions, however, relieve the seller somewhat from the harsh effects of the perfect tender rule.

Both the Code and common law occasionally excuse a promisor from performance without liability for breach because of events that occur after contract formation. Article 2 excuses performance if performance as agreed has been made impracticable by the occurrence of an event the nonoccurrence of which was a basic assumption on which the contract was made. This approach expands somewhat upon the traditional common law approach requiring objective impossibility to excuse performance. The impracticability doctrine is now generally applied to both Code and common law contracts.

Although the Code's approach to anticipatory repudiation is generally similar to the common law, Article 2 adopts a unique approach to situations involving less than outright repudiation—when one party's conduct merely gives the other reasonable grounds for insecurity about the other's willingness or ability to perform. In this latter case, the Code allows the insecure party to demand adequate assurance of due performance and suspend his own performance until adequate assurance is received. Failure to provide adequate assurance within a reasonable time constitutes a repudiation of the contract. Note that the Code approach to insecurity is now recognized as an emerging principle for common law contracts as well.

Additional issues relating to performance of sales contracts are covered throughout the following sales material.

Contract Remedies. Article 2 retains the basic common law distinction between legal (money damages) and equitable (specific performance and injunction against breach) remedies available for breach of contract. Chapter 18 examines in detail how damages are computed under the Code after breach by the seller or the buyer. The Code generally follows common law principles governing mitigation of damages and adopts, with slight modification, the common law foreseeability test to determine when consequential damages should be awarded. Article 2 also generally follows common law principles governing enforcement of liquidated damages clauses.

In determining when the equitable remedies of specific performance and injunction against breach are available, Article 2 follows but expands upon the common law uniqueness test. By emphasizing the commercial feasibility of replacement rather than "one of a kind" uniqueness, the Code enhances the availability of the equitable contract remedies. Table 16–1 lists the major UCC provisions covered in the basic contracts material.

Table 16–1	Major Uniform Commercial Code Provisions Relating to Contracts Covered in Chapters 6–15	
Subject	*Code Section*	*Principle*
Coverage of UCC and Scope of Article 2	1-102	variation of Code provisions by agreement
	1-103	supplementary principles of law applicable
	1-201	general definitions
	2-102	scope of Article 2
	2-104(1),(3)	"merchant" defined
	2-105(1)	"goods" defined
Contract Formation and Modification	2-204(3)	basic contract formation requirements
	2-205	firm offers
	2-206(1)	manner and medium of acceptance
	2-206(2)	notification of acceptance
	2-207	additional or different terms in acceptance—"battle of the forms"
	2-209(1)	modification of sales contracts
General Obligations	2-306(2)	exclusive dealing contracts
	2-309(3)	notice of termination

Table 16-1	Continued	
Capacity of Parties	1-103	supplementary principles of law applicable
Illegality; Unenforceability on Public Policy Grounds	1-103 2-302	supplementary principles of law applicable unconscionability
Reality of Assent	1-103 2-721	supplementary principles of law applicable remedies for fraud and material misrepresentation
Parol Evidence Rule and Contract Interpretation	2-202 1-205(1) 1-205(2) 2-208 1-205(4) 2-208(2)	parol evidence rule "course of dealing" defined "usage of trade" defined effect of course of performance rule of construction
Statute of Frauds and Formality	2-201 8-319 9-203(1)(a) 1-206 2-209(2),(3)	Statute of Frauds—goods Statute of Frauds—securities Statute of Frauds—security interests Statute of Frauds—other personal property contract modification and the Statute of Frauds
Third Parties	2-210	assignment and delegation of sales contracts
Performance and Discharge of Contracts	1-203 1-201(19) 2-103(1)(b) 2-503(1) 2-601 2-609 2-610 2-611 2-612 2-613 2-615 1-207	obligation of good faith in performance seller's tender of delivery perfect tender rule adequate assurance of performance anticipatory repudiation retraction of repudiation breach in installment contracts casualty to identified goods impracticability settlement of claims
Contract Remedies	1-203 1-201(19) 2-103(1)(b) 1-106(1) 2-715(2)(a) 2-716(1) 2-718(1) 2-719(3) 2-720	obligation of good faith in enforcement Code remedies liberally administered buyer's consequential damages specific performance liquidated damages limitation of consequential damages effect of cancellation or rescission—election of remedy

Scope of Article 2

As discussed in Chapter 7, Article 2 governs contracts for the sale of goods. Section 2-105 defines goods generally as "all things movable at the time of identification to the contract." "Identification" refers to the process by which the particular goods to which the contract refers are designated or specified. That is, once the parties have chosen, manufactured, or otherwise designated the specific goods to be sold, they are "identified" to the contract. Sales contracts are therefore usually easily recognizable; any contract which involves the sale of a tangible, movable object is governed by Article 2.

Determining applicable law when goods are involved, however, may be difficult. For example, goods that are closely associated with land (such as crops, timber, or minerals) may be severed and sold apart from the land. In this case, UCC §2-107 determines whether the contract is for the sale of goods (governed by Article 2) or for the sale of an interest in land (governed by common law contract principles). Section 2-107 is discussed in Chapter 34 in conjunction with the coverage of the law of fixtures.

Problems in determining applicable law also have arisen if the contract involves a mixture of goods and services—for example, a contract by an artist to paint a portrait or by a plumber to deliver and install a hot water heater. The following case illustrates the principles used to determine whether such contracts are within the scope of Article 2.

Colorado Carpet Installation, Inc. v. Palermo

668 P.2d 1384 (Colo. 1983)

> Plaintiff Colorado Carpet Installation, Inc. (Colorado Carpet) sells and installs carpeting, tiles, and other flooring materials. In 1980, Fred and Zuma Palermo entered into negotiations with Colorado Carpet for the purchase and installation of flooring material at the Palermos' house. Colorado Carpet provided a written proposal to sell and install carpeting, ceramic tiles, and vinyl flooring for approximately $4,800. After Colorado Carpet had purchased the flooring materials from distributors, the Palermos refused to allow Colorado Carpet to begin installation. Colorado Carpet removed all materials and sued the Palermos for breach of contract, alleging that the Palermos had created an oral contract by orally accepting the written proposal. The Palermos asserted that they had not orally accepted the proposal. They argued further that even if an oral contract had been made, it was unenforceable because the UCC Statute of Frauds provisions require a writing for the sale of goods in excess of $500. The trial court ruled in favor of Colorado Carpet on the ground that the contract was a service contract outside the scope of the UCC. On appeal, the Colorado Court of Appeals reversed, holding that the contract was for the sale of goods and was unenforceable for lack of a writing. Colorado Carpet appealed to the Colorado Supreme Court.

Quinn, Justice

. . . In this case the subject of the contract involved "goods" because the carpeting and other materials were movable at the time that Colorado Carpet procured them for installation pursuant to the agreement. . . . The scope of the contract, however, included not only the sale of goods but also the performance of labor or service. Thus, we must determine whether such a mixed contract qualified as a contract for the sale of goods or, instead, constituted a contract for labor or service. . . .

The performance of some labor or service frequently plays a role in sales transactions. "Goods," however, are not the less "goods" merely because labor or service may be essential to their ultimate use by the purchaser. The mere furnishing of some labor or service, in our view, should not determine the ultimate character of a contract for purposes . . . of the Uniform Commercial Code. Rather, the controlling criterion should be the primary purpose of the contract—that is, whether the circumstances underlying the formation of the agreement and the performance reasonably expected of the parties demonstrate the primary purpose of the contract as the sale of goods or, in contrast, the sale of labor or service. . . .

This "primary purpose" test, we believe, is designed to promote one of the expressed statutory policies of the Uniform Commercial Code—"[t]o simplify, clarify, and modernize the law governing commercial transactions.'' [UCC §1-102(2)(a)] Useful factors to consider in determining whether ''goods'' or ''service'' predominates include the following: the contractual language used by the parties; . . . whether the agreement involves one overall price that includes both goods and labor or, instead, calls for separate and discrete billings for goods on the one hand and labor on the other; . . . the ratio that the cost of goods bears to the overall contract price; . . . and the nature and reasonableness of the purchaser's contractual expectations of acquiring a property interest in goods (goods being defined as things that are movable at the time of identification to the contract). . . .

Considering the contract under these guidelines, we are satisfied that, as a matter of law, its primary purpose was the sale of goods and not the sale of labor or service. The language in Colorado Carpet's proposal referred to the parties as ''seller'' and ''customer.'' In addition, the agreement called for an overall contract price that included both the cost of goods and labor, and . . . the charge for labor was slight in relation to the total contractual price. Finally, the carpeting and other materials were movable when Colorado Carpet procured them for the purpose of selling them to the Palermos. . . . We therefore agree with the court of appeals that the agreement between Colorado Carpet and the Palermos constituted a contract for the sale of goods, with labor or service only incidentally involved, and thus within the statute of frauds provisions of the Uniform Commercial Code. . . .

[Judgment affirmed.]

Formation and Terms of the Sales Contract

As explained in Chapter 6, the UCC is designed to simplify, clarify, and modernize commercial law and to permit continued expansion of commercial practices through custom, usage, and agreement of the parties. These policies, as applied in specific substantive Code provisions, are perhaps most evident in the various Article 2 provisions that govern the formation and terms of a sales contract.

Though its formation is governed generally by traditional contract principles, a contract for the sale of goods is easily created under the UCC. Under §2-204(1), a sales contract may be made in any manner sufficient to show agreement, including conduct by the parties recognizing the existence of the contract. Even the exact time of contract formation may be indefinite. For example, the correspondence of the parties may not disclose the exact time at which the deal was closed. Additionally, §2-204(3) provides that if (1) the parties have intended to make a contract, and (2) there is a reasonably certain basis for awarding an appropriate remedy in the event of breach, the contract will not fail for indefiniteness even though one or more of its terms are left open. The missing terms are then supplied by Code provisions often referred to as **gap fillers.** As elaborated in the Official Comment to §2-204:

> If the parties intend to enter into a binding agreement, this subsection [§2-204(3)] recognizes that agreement as valid in law, despite missing terms, if there is any reasonably certain basis for granting a remedy. . . . [C]ommercial standards on the point of ''indefiniteness'' are intended to be applied, *this Act making provision elsewhere for missing terms needed for performance, open price, remedies and the like*. (Emphasis added.)

The terms referred to above, supplied by the Code in the absence of express agreement, are discussed throughout this and the next three chapters. Examples include terms governing price, delivery, passage of title, risk of loss, remedies, and warranties.[1]

The Code additionally provides in §2-311(1) that as long as the basic formation requirements outlined above are met, a contract will not fail for indefiniteness simply because it leaves particular details of performance to be specified by one of the parties at a later date. In this situation, any such specification must be made in good faith and in a commercially reasonable manner.

Although Article 2 supplies numerous missing terms, the UCC Statute of Frauds requirement, §2-

---

1. In addition, a number of gap filling provisions (for example, §2-306(2) relating to exclusive dealing contracts) are discussed in conjunction with the basic contracts material.

201, applying to contracts for the sale of goods with a price of $500 or more, requires that the memorandum include the *quantity* term. The quantity need not be accurately stated in the memorandum, but enforcement is limited to the amount stated. Thus, at least for contracts subject to the Statute of Frauds, the agreement must contain a quantity term[2] to be enforceable.

Finally, it is important to remember that the Code generally does not limit the parties' freedom to contract, but merely supplies those terms that the parties fail to include. This freedom is expressly provided as a basic UCC principle in §1-102, which simply states that the effect of Code provisions may be varied by agreement whether or not the specific provision involved includes the language "unless otherwise agreed." Certain UCC provisions, however, explicitly provide that they may not be varied by agreement. For example, the obligations of good faith, diligence, reasonableness, and care may not be disclaimed by the parties. The standards measuring performance of these obligations, however, may be determined by agreement if the standards are not manifestly unreasonable.[3] Similarly, §2-302 (unconscionability) is not subject to variance by agreement.

In summary, Article 2 provisions taken collectively form a standardized statutory contract governing the rights, obligations, and remedies of the parties to contracts for the sale of goods. These provisions insure that bargains intended by the parties to be contracts are enforced, despite inexact expression and missing terms. Article 2's statutory contract does not, however, limit the parties' freedom of contract because its terms apply only in the absence of contrary agreement.

General Obligations of the Parties

Although sales contracts can become quite complex, the basic obligations of the parties are very straightforward. Under §2-301, the basic obligation of the seller is to transfer and deliver the goods to the buyer, who is obligated to accept and pay for the goods in accordance with the contract.

As in all contracts, the order of performance is a fundamental consideration. Under the Code, performances are to be exchanged simultaneously unless the agreement provides otherwise. §2-507(1) states:

> *Tender of delivery is a condition to the buyer's duty* to accept the goods and, unless otherwise agreed, to his duty to pay for them. (Emphasis added.)

With respect to the simultaneous obligation of the buyer, §2-511(1) provides:

> Unless otherwise agreed *tender of payment is a condition to the seller's duty* to tender and complete any delivery. (Emphasis added.)

From these basic obligations of delivery and payment a myriad of legal issues arise. The following material examines first the seller's responsibilities regarding delivery of the goods and second, the duty of the buyer to pay the price.

Seller's Duty of Delivery

The parties to a sale of goods usually expressly provide for the time, place, and manner of delivery. If they fail to do so, the UCC contains several provisions relating to delivery governing in the absence of explicit agreement. These provisions relate both to contracts requiring shipment by the seller as well as those involving parties residing in the same locality.

Time of Delivery. Under §2-309(1), if the parties fail to agree, the *time* for any shipment or delivery is a *reasonable* time. What is reasonable is a question of fact, considering all relevant factors such as the nature of the goods and market conditions, in addition to good faith and observance of reasonable commercial standards. The parties may agree to leave the time of delivery open. Unless otherwise agreed, however, arrangements relating to shipment are within the seller's discretion if seller acts

---

2. The quantity term may be either stated explicitly c measured by the requirements of the buyer or output of th seller.

3. UCC §§1-102(3)-(4).

in good faith and within the limits of commercial reasonableness.[4]

Place of Delivery. Under §2-308, unless otherwise agreed, the *place* for delivery is the *seller's* place of business, or, if he has none, then at his residence. If, however, the goods have been identified to the contract and both parties know where the goods are located, then that place is the place of delivery. For example, assume S contracts to sell B two specified spools of electrical cable. Due to lack of storage space, the spools are stored at X's warehouse, a fact known to B. Unless agreed to the contrary, X's warehouse is the place of delivery.

Manner of Delivery. The *manner* of the seller's tender of delivery is also determined by the Code in §2-503. The seller must (1) put and hold conforming goods at the buyer's disposition and (2) give the buyer reasonable notification to take delivery. Note that if the contract requires payment on delivery, the seller may retain control of the goods until payment. The tender must be at a reasonable hour and the goods must be kept available for a period long enough to allow the buyer to take possession. However, unless otherwise agreed, the *buyer* must furnish facilities (for example, a truck) for receiving the goods.

If the goods are in the possession of a bailee (generally a carrier or warehouseman) and are to be delivered without being moved, tender of delivery requires that the seller either tender a negotiable document of title covering the goods, or procure acknowledgment by the bailee that the buyer is entitled to possession of the goods. In addition, tender of a nonnegotiable document of title *or* a written direction to the bailee to deliver is sufficient tender unless the buyer objects. Thus, when documents of title are involved, proper tender basically requires action by the seller or the bailee giving the buyer the right to complete control of the goods.

Delivery in Lots. Unless the contract explicitly provides that performance is to be made in installments, §2-307 requires the seller to tender all goods called for by the contract in a single delivery and the buyer's payment is due only upon that tender. Circumstances may, however, give either party the right to make (by the seller) or demand (by the buyer) delivery in lots. A **lot** is a parcel or single article that is the subject matter of a separate sale or delivery, whether or not it is, by itself, sufficient to perform the contract.[5] For example, a seller required to deliver 10 carloads of coal could deliver in lots if only two cars were available at the time of delivery. Similarly, a buyer could receive delivery in lots if his storage facilities are inadequate to receive the entire shipment at once. In the case of a partial delivery, the price, if it can be apportioned, may be demanded for each lot. Therefore, in the above example, if the circumstances allow the seller to deliver two carloads of coal at a time, he could demand one-fifth of the price from the buyer for each delivery.

Delivery by Carrier

Frequently, the contract will require or authorize the seller to ship the goods to the buyer—for example, when the parties are at a distance. Such contracts are generally referred to as either shipment or destination contracts. In a **shipment contract,** the seller is authorized or required to ship the goods to the buyer, but is not required to deliver them at any particular destination. In a **destination contract,** the seller is required to transport the goods to a stated destination and there tender them to the buyer. Unless explicitly stated, a shipment contract is presumed. The distinction is important not only in determining the seller's obligation with respect to delivery but also in determining who bears the risk of loss if the goods are damaged or destroyed in transit.

The seller's basic obligations in a *shipment* contract are stated in §2-504. In order to make a valid tender, the seller must, unless otherwise agreed,

1. put the goods in the possession of a carrier and make a contract for their transportation to the buyer,
2. obtain and promptly deliver or tender any document necessary to enable the buyer to

---

4. UCC §2-311.

5. UCC §2-105(5).

obtain possession of the goods (or required by the agreement or trade usage), and

3. promptly notify the buyer of the shipment.

Note that the seller's failure to meet the foregoing requirements is not a grounds for rejection by the buyer unless material loss or delay ensues.

F.O.B., F.A.S., C.I.F., and C. & F. Terms Defined.

In contracts requiring shipment, the parties frequently employ specialized terminology in defining their obligations. Important examples, defined below, include F.O.B., F.A.S., C.I.F., and C. & F. terms. In shipment contract cases (such as, F.O.B. place of shipment, C.I.F., and C. & F.) the meaning of these terms is supplemented by §2-504 discussed above.

F.O.B. and F.A.S. Terms—§2-319. Unless otherwise agreed, the term **F.O.B.** (meaning "free on board") at a named place—shipping point or destination—is a *delivery* term, not a price term. Under §2-319, it imposes the following obligations on the seller. If the term is F.O.B. place of shipment, the seller is required, at that place, to ship the goods as outlined in §2-504 discussed above. In this situation, the seller bears the risk and expense of putting the goods into the carrier's possession. For example, assume S, a Chicago seller, contracts to sell and deliver steel girders to B, a New York buyer, "F.O.B. Chicago." This term creates a shipment contract. S completes its delivery obligations when it meets the three requirements for shipment imposed by Section 2-504.

In contrast, if the term is F.O.B. place of destination, the seller is required (at the seller's own expense and risk) *to transport the goods* to the named destination and there tender delivery to the buyer. This term thus creates a "destination" contract, requiring the seller to deliver at a particular destination. If the F.O.B. term (shipment or destination) is more specific, naming a vessel, car, or other vehicle, the seller is additionally obligated (at his expense and risk) to load the goods on board.

The contract may require the seller to deliver the goods to a freighter, tanker, or other vessel for further shipment. In this case, an **F.A.S.** (meaning "free alongside") term may be used. The term F.A.S. vessel at a named port (for example, F.A.S.

Jolly Roger, New York Harbor), like an F.O.B. term is a delivery term. It requires the seller to (1) deliver the goods (at the seller's expense and risk) alongside the vessel in the manner usual in that port or on a dock designated and provided by the buyer, and (2) obtain and tender to the buyer a receipt for the goods. Note that under both F.O.B. and F.A.S. terms, the buyer must promptly give the seller any instructions necessary to make delivery.

C.I.F. and C. & F. Terms— §2-320. Section 2-320 outlines the meaning and effect of C.I.F. and C. & F. terms in sales contracts. The term **C.I.F.** means that the price of the goods includes, in a lump sum, the cost of the goods, and the insurance, and freight to the named destination (for example, C.I.F. London). The term **C. & F.** (or **C.F.**) means that the price includes only the cost and freight to the named destination. A C.I.F. destination term requires the seller to (1) put the goods into the possession of the carrier and obtain a negotiable bill of lading covering the goods and a receipt from the carrier indicating payment of (or provision for) the freight charges, (2) obtain an insurance policy covering the goods providing for payment of any loss to the buyer, (3) prepare an invoice for the goods and procure any other necessary documents, and (4) promptly forward and tender all the required documents to the buyer. A C. & F. term imposes the same obligations upon the seller except that relating to insurance.

Buyer's Duty of Payment

A proper tender of delivery entitles the seller to acceptance of the goods and payment for them according to the contract. Although the contract usually provides time, place, and manner of payment, the agreement may be silent regarding one or more aspects of the buyer's payment obligation. In this case, as with delivery, the UCC fills in the gaps in the parties' agreement.

Unless otherwise agreed, payment and delivery are exchanged simultaneously in sales contracts. That is, the seller is not required to extend credit to the buyer unless the parties have explicitly agreed to a credit term. If credit is extended, the credit period generally runs from the date of shipment, or from the date of the invoice which usually indicates the time of shipment. The buyer may tender payment by check or other customary method unless the seller demands cash and gives the buyer any extension of time reasonably necessary to procure it. This rule protects the buyer against breach if the seller unexpectedly demands cash when (as is normally the case) the buyer reasonably believes that payment by a check is acceptable.[6]

Right of Inspection. Unless otherwise agreed, the buyer must tender payment at the ''time and place at which the buyer is to receive the goods.''[7] This requirement allows the buyer to exercise his preliminary right of inspection before payment stated in §2-513. As a general rule, the buyer has a right *before* payment or acceptance to inspect the goods tendered by the seller. The inspection may be at any reasonable place and time and in any reasonable manner. If the seller is required to ship the goods to the buyer, inspection may be made at the place of arrival. Note that the seller is not, however, required to relinquish physical possession of the goods to the buyer. The buyer acquires the right to possession upon tender of payment, unless the seller has agreed to extend credit. Any expense of the inspection must be borne by the buyer, but may be recovered from the seller as incidental damage if the buyer rejects the goods because of nonconformity revealed by the inspection.

In certain types of contracts, the buyer is not entitled to inspect before payment of the price. These include: (1) C.I.F. and C.F. contracts, (2) other contracts requiring payment against documents of title unless the contract provides that payment is due only after the goods become available for inspection,[8] and (3) contracts providing the delivery ''C.O.D.'' or on similar terms. Note that such contracts simply require payment before inspection. The payment neither constitutes an acceptance of the goods, nor does it impair the buyer's subsequent right to inspect. The buyer retains all rights

and remedies against the seller in the event the goods do not conform to the contract. The buyer is, however, required to proceed after making payment because the essence of such a payment term is to shift to the buyer risks which would ordinarily rest upon the seller. For example, under a C.I.F. or C.F. contract the buyer must pay for the goods upon tender of the documents, without awaiting actual arrival of the goods and with no right of inspection before payment. The reason for this requirement is that the purpose of a C.I.F. or C. & F. contract is to protect the seller against the buyer's unjustifiable rejection of the goods at a distant destination.

Open Price and Quantity Terms

Ordinarily, the parties explicitly agree upon the price to be charged and the exact quantity of goods to be delivered. Article 2, however, permits enforcement of contracts in which either the price or the quantity is left open. Sections 2-305 and 2-306 contain the principles by which price and quantity are determined in such contracts.

Open Price Term—§2-305

Under §2-305, the parties can conclude a contract for sale even though the price is not settled. Thus, the UCC recognizes that the parties may intend a binding contract even though they have not yet agreed to price or have left the price to be fixed by a market standard or a third party. If the parties intend not to be bound unless the price is later determined and, for some reason, it is not subsequently agreed or fixed, there is no contract.[9] The intention of the parties in this regard is ordinarily a question of fact.

Perhaps the most common reason the parties may leave the price open is that neither wishes to assume the risk of market fluctuations prior to delivery by agreeing to a fixed price. If the market price rises after the date of the contract, the seller may

---

6. UCC §§2-310(d), 2-511(2). The check is, however, only a conditional payment. The effect of payment by check on the obligation for which it is given is discussed in Chapter 25.

7. UCC §2-310(a).

8. In this and the C.I.F. case, the shipping documents will commonly arrive and be tendered while the goods are still in transit.

---

9. In such a case, the buyer must return any goods already received or pay their reasonable value measured on the date of delivery. The seller must return any portion of the price paid on account.

want to charge the increased price. Conversely, if the market falls, the buyer may wish to purchase the goods at the reduced rate.

Assuming a binding contract has been made without a price term, Section 2-305(1) provides that the price is a *reasonable price at the time for delivery if:*

1. nothing is said as to price,
2. the price is left to later agreement of the parties and they fail to agree, or
3. the price is to be fixed in terms of some agreed market or other standard as fixed by an agency or third person and it is not so set or recorded.

The third situation listed above occurs, for example, when the price is left to be fixed in a trade journal that subsequently ceases publication or is to be set by a third person who dies prior to fixing the price.

The obligation of good faith and commercial reasonableness imposed upon every Code contract or duty is also relevant when the price term is left open. For example, the contract may provide that the price is to be fixed by the buyer or seller. In this situation, the party empowered to set the price must act in good faith, which, in the case of a merchant, includes observance of reasonable commercial standards of fair dealing in the trade. Similarly, if the price fails to be fixed through fault of one party—for example, interference with any agreed machinery for price fixing or other failure to cooperate—the other may at his option either cancel the contract (that is, treat the conduct as a repudiation), or fix a reasonable price himself.

Open Quantity Term: Requirements and Output Contracts—§2-306

In addition to price, the parties may also contract without fixing a quantity. The most common and important of such "open quantity" contracts are requirements and output contracts. A **requirements contract** is one in which a *buyer* promises to purchase his *requirements* of a given commodity from the seller. An **output contract** is one in which a *seller* agrees to sell his entire *output* to the buyer. A requirement or output promise protects the prom-

isor against uncertainties in demand or production. That is, a business is required to purchase only its requirements or sell its output. It is not obligated to buy or sell a fixed quantity which it may not be able to use or produce.

At first glance, requirements and output promises appear illusory under principles discussed in Chapter 9. For example, a buyer could supposedly avoid obligation under a requirements contract by ceasing or changing his or her business; thus having no requirements. Similarly, a seller could cease production, generating no output. Actually, promises to purchase requirements or to sell output are not illusory. In both cases, the promisor incurs a detriment by surrendering the right to buy or sell elsewhere.

The UCC broadly validates requirements and output promises. Section 2-306(1) provides that a term that measures the quantity by the output of the seller, or the requirements of the buyer means such *actual output or requirements as may occur in good faith.* Additionally, because the quantity term is determined by actual output or requirements occurring in good faith, the contract will not fail on the basis that the quantity is too indefinite to afford an adequate remedy.

The party who determines the quantity must operate its plant or conduct its business in good faith and according to reasonable commercial standards of fair dealing in the trade. When business is conducted in this manner, the quantity purchased or produced under the contract will approximate a reasonably foreseeable figure. In other words, ceasing operations to avoid a requirements or output contract would violate the obligation of good faith imposed upon all Code contracts or duties and therefore incorporated into §2-306.

In addition to the good faith requirement, §2-306 provides that no quantity may be tendered (an output contract) or demanded (a requirements contract) that is unreasonably disproportionate (1) to any stated estimate, or (2) to any normal or otherwise comparable prior output or requirements in the absence of a stated estimate. This proviso sets reasonable limits (in addition to good faith) upon the actual quantity to be bought or sold under the contract; that is, it establishes the range within which the parties may expect the quantity to vary. Any minimum or maximum limits set in the contract clearly define intended elasticity. A stated estimate is treated as a midpoint around which the parties intend any variation to occur. The following case illustrates a typical dispute arising under a requirements contract and the resolution of that dispute under §2-306.

Orange and Rockland Utilities, Inc. v. Amerada Hess Corporation

397 N.Y.S.2d 814 (N.Y. App. 1977)

In 1969, defendant Amerada Hess Corporation (Hess) agreed to supply plaintiff Orange and Rockland Utilities, Inc., (O & R) with its requirements of fuel oil for five years to be burned to generate electricity at plaintiff's power plant. The contract fixed a price of $2.14 per barrel and included estimates of O & R's requirements for each year of the contract. Because of an anticipated lower price of natural gas, O & R intended to burn gas as its primary fuel for power generation, and expressly reserved the right to burn as much gas as it chose, notwithstanding the requirements contract.

Within five months of the execution of the contract the price of fuel oil began to rise sharply. By March 1971 the market price had reached $4.30 per barrel, more than double the contract price. As the market price of oil began to rise, O & R notified Hess on four separate occasions of substantial increases in its fuel oil requirements for the year. Hess refused to meet the revised requirements but continued to supply quantities equal to or slightly greater than those estimated in the contract. O & R purchased additional fuel oil from other suppliers and sued Hess for the difference between the market price and the contract price for the additional oil purchased. During the period in question, O & R consistently used more than double its contract estimates of oil at its generating plant, primarily because O & R had increased its sale of electricity to other utility companies and had substantially reduced its use of natural gas.

The trial court denied recovery to O & R, holding that its increased requirements were not incurred in good faith. O & R appealed. After noting that §2-306(1) of the UCC governed the dispute the appellate court rendered this opinion.

Margett, Justice

. . . Plaintiff contends on this appeal (1) that [the trial court's] finding of an absence of good faith is unsupported by the record and (2) that since its requirements for the entire term of the contract were less than twice total contract estimates, its demands were not "unreasonably disproportionate" as a matter of law. We reject both contentions upon the facts of this case and affirm [the trial court's] dismissal of the complaint. . . .

There is, as [the trial court] observed, a good deal of pre-Code case law on the requirement of "good faith." It is well settled that a buyer in a rising market cannot use a fixed price in a requirements contract for speculation. . . . Nor can a buyer arbitrarily and unilaterally change certain conditions prevailing at the time of the contract so as to take advantage of market conditions at the seller's expense. . . .

The limitation imposed by the term "unreasonably disproportionate" represents a departure from prior case law, wherein estimates were generally treated as having been made simply for the convenience of the parties and of no operative significance. . . . It is salutary in that it insures that the expectations of the parties will be more fully realized in spite of unexpected and fortuitous market conditions. . . . Thus, even where one party acts with complete good faith, the section limits the other party's risk in accordance with the reasonable expectations of the parties.

It would be unwise to attempt to define the phrase "unreasonably disproportionate" in terms of rigid quantities. In order that the limitation contemplated by the section take effect, it is not enough that a demand for requirements be disproportionate to the stated estimate; it must be *unreasonably* so in view of the expectation of the parties. A number of factors should be taken into account in the event a buyer's requirements greatly exceed the contract estimate. These include the following: (1) the amount by which the requirements exceed the contract estimate; (2) whether the seller had any reasonable basis on which to forecast or anticipate the requested increase . . .; (3) the amount, if any, by which the market price of the goods in question exceeded the contract price; (4) whether such an increase in market price was itself fortuitous; and (5) the reason for the increase in requirements.

Turning once again to the facts of the instant case, . . . it appears that in May, 1970, Hess refused an O & R demand of roughly one million barrels in excess of the contract estimate, which demand was occasioned by greatly increased sales to other utilities and a proposed release of gas which might otherwise normally have been burned for power generation. The former factor is tantamount to making the other utilities in the State silent partners to the contract . . ., while the latter factor amounts to a unilateral and arbitrary change in the conditions prevailing at the time of the contract so as to take advantage of market conditions at the seller's expense. . . . Hess was therefore justified in 1970 in refusing to meet plaintiff's demands, by reason of the fact that plaintiff's "requirements" were not incurred in good faith. . . .

We hold that under the circumstances of this case, any demand by plaintiff for more than double its contract estimates, was, as a matter of law, "unreasonably disproportionate" (UCC, §2-306, subd. [1]) to those estimates. We do not adopt the factor of more than double the contract estimates as any sort of an inflexible yardstick. Rather, we apply those standards set forth earlier in this opinion, which are calculated to limit a party's risk in accordance with the reasonable expectations of the parties. . . .

[Judgment affirmed.]

Effect of Decrease in Quantity. The *Orange and Rockland Utilities* case presents the most common requirements contract dispute, an unreasonable increase in quantity demanded by the buyer when the market price rises substantially above the contract price. A related problem concerns the legal effect of unreasonable *decreases* in quantity. Whereas the statute provides that no quantity unreasonably disproportionate to a stated estimate or prior output may be tendered or demanded, Official Comment 2 to §2-306 indicates that "good faith variations from prior requirements are permitted *even when the variation may be such as to result in discontinuance.*" (Emphasis added.) This discrepancy can be reconciled if the statutory language is interpreted to mean that a party may not *increase* demand or supply to an amount unreasonably disproportionate

to a stated estimate, or prior consumption or production. However, substantial *decreases* are permitted as long as the party who determines quantity is acting in good faith. In other words, an *increase* in quantity tendered or demanded is allowed if (1) made in good faith, *and* (2) is not unreasonably disproportionate to a stated estimate or prior experience. A *decrease* is permitted subject only to the good faith test.

This approach has received considerable support from legal commentators and in decided cases. It allows a requirements buyer to reduce purchases drastically when justified by improved equipment or operating efficiency. Assume Ben operates a steel plant requiring large amounts of natural gas to fire the furnaces. Ben contracts to buy its requirements of gas, subject to a stated estimate, from People's Gas, Inc., a public utility. Ben subsequently installs new fuel-efficient furnaces, requiring only twenty percent as much gas as the old units. Even though Ben now requires drastically reduced quantities of gas, he does not breach the contract because the reduction was undertaken in good faith. If the second "unreasonably disproportionate" test is also applied, Ben could not improve his plant without breaching the contract.

Assignability of Requirements Contracts. A recurring problem resolved by §2-306 concerns the assignability of rights under a requirements contract. Assume S agrees to sell B, a small intrastate trucking company, its requirements of gasoline for two years. B assigns the right to be supplied with gasoline to X, another trucking company (or sells the business, including the contract, to X). Under traditional common law principles of assignment discussed in Chapter 13, S need not supply X with its requirements because a substantial change in S's duty results.

Section 2-306, which now governs requirements contracts, adopts an apparently more liberal attitude than the common law, because it permits assignment if the assignee meets the section's basic guidelines. That is, after the assignment, the quantity continues to be measured by actual good faith requirements under normal operation of the business prior to the assignment. Further, the assignment does not justify a sudden or unreasonable increase or decrease in the quantity demanded. In this manner, no material change in the seller's duty is effected.[10]

Auction Sales—§2-328

Most of the sales discussed in this and the contracts material are private in nature; that is, they are the result of bargaining between parties who are known to each other. An **auction,** on the other hand, is a public sale of property (either real or personal) to the highest bidder by an auctioneer, who is authorized or licensed by law to conduct such sales.[11] The auctioneer (who is an agent of the seller) solicits bids (offers) from prospective buyers present at the sale. The UCC provides rules governing the conduct of auction sales of goods in §2-328.

The auction is complete—that is, the highest bidder's offer is accepted—when the auctioneer so announces by the fall of the hammer or in another customary manner. If a bid is made while the hammer is falling (in acceptance of a prior bid), the auctioneer may either reopen the bidding, or declare the goods sold at the bid on which the hammer was falling. If the auctioneer elects to reopen the bidding, the prior bid is discharged and further bidding continues.

As a general rule, auction sales are made **with reserve.** This means that the auctioneer (seller) may withdraw the goods at any time prior to announcing completion of the sale as indicated above. The goods, however, in explicit terms may be put up "without reserve." In this case, the auctioneer, after the calls for bids, may not withdraw an article or lot, unless no bids are received within a reasonable time. Note that the character of the sale as "with" or "without" reserve is determined as of the point when the goods are "put up" for sale. As explained in Official Comment 2 to §2-328:

> This Article accepts the view that the goods may be withdrawn before they are actually "put up," *regardless of whether the auction is advertised as one without reserve,* without liability on the part of the auction announcer to persons who are present. (Emphasis added.)

Regardless of the character of the auction, any bidder may retract his bid (withdraw his offer) prior to the auctioneer's announcement of the completion of the sale. However, one bidder's retraction does not revive any prior bid.

The seller may bid at the auction provided notice is given that liberty for such bidding is reserved. If no notice is given, and the auctioneer knowingly receives a bid on the seller's behalf or the seller makes or procures such a bid, the buyer may, at his option, either (1) avoid the sale, or (2) take the goods at the last good faith bid prior to completion of the sale. This rule does not apply if the seller's bid is made at a "forced" sale, that is, one not voluntarily made by the seller but prescribed by law to satisfy some obligation of the seller, such as a mortgage, debt, judgment, or tax lien.

A sale at auction, like other sales, may be subject to the Statute of Frauds. For example, the property sold may be land or goods with a price of $500 or more. In this situation the auctioneer is an agent of *both* parties for purposes of satisfying the statute. In other words, after accepting a bid on property subject to the Statute of Frauds, the auctioneer has an *irrevocable* power to sign the necessary memorandum for both the buyer and the seller. This power continues for a reasonable time during the day of the sale.

Personal Property Leases

Increasingly in recent years, consumers and businesses lease rather than buy goods, such as automobiles or manufacturing equipment, they use. Despite the dramatic growth of the lease as a substitute for purchase, however, a comprehensive body of law governing personal property leasing transactions has yet to be fully developed. For example, though a personal property lease is a bailment, the common law of bailments, discussed in Chapter 35, is limited in scope and does not address the myriad contract-related issues arising in the modern lease. General landlord-tenant law, discussed in detail in Chapter 36, governs real property, rather than personal property, leases. Al-

---

10. UCC §2-210, Official Comment 4; §2-306, Official Comment 4.
11. Black, *Law Dictionary* (5th ed. 1979).

though some courts have held that personal property leases are within the scope of Article 2 of the UCC as "transactions in goods,"[12] most of Article 2 focuses specifically on sales, rather than lease, transactions. Finally, Article 9 of the UCC governs only those personal property leases intended for security.

To fill this gap in the law, the American Law Institute and National Conference of Commissioners on Uniform State Laws drafted and approved in 1987 a new Article 2A of the Uniform Commercial Code, entitled "Leases." Article 2A applies to "any transaction, regardless of form, which creates a lease,"[13] and defines a lease as "a transfer of the right to possession and use of goods for a term in return for consideration."[14]

Article 2A, which is patterned generally after Article 2, divides the law governing such "true" personal property leases into five parts: (1) general provisions, (2) the formation and construction of lease contracts, (3) the effect of lease contracts, (4) the performance of lease contracts, and (5) default. Part 1 contains definitions and general provisions borrowed generally from Article 2, and an unconscionability provision. Part 2 adopts Article 2's liberal contract formation principles and contains a statute of frauds (with a $1000 minimum), a parol evidence rule, a firm offer rule, and warranty and risk of loss provisions. Part 3 includes provisions governing assignability of the lease, a subsequent lease of the goods by the lessor, a sale or sublease by the lessee, and the consequences of the leased goods becoming fixtures. Part 4 includes familiar Article 2 performance principles such as anticipatory repudiation, adequate assurance, and impracticability. Part 5 is the longest part of Article 2A, governing the rights and obligations of the parties upon default by either the lessor or lessee. Part 5 borrows heavily from Article 2 (including, for example, the concepts of acceptance, revocation of acceptance, and rejection of goods; cure; and buyers' and sellers' remedies discussed in Chapter 18) and Article 9 (for example, the right of the lessor to take possession of the goods on default without judicial process). Note that the various dollar damage remedies available to the parties (for example, upon the lessee's cover, or the lessor's disposition of the goods by a substitute lease) are computed by using present value analysis.

Article 2A has been adopted in at least one state[15] and is being considered in a number of others. Given the widespread use of personal property leases, and the inadequacy of existing law, Article 2A should ultimately be widely enacted. The text of Article 2A is reproduced in Appendix B as part of the Uniform Commercial Code.

SUMMARY

1. Contracts for the sale of goods, governed generally by Article 2 of the UCC, play an important role in modern business. The Code adopts a liberal attitude regarding formation of such contracts, enforcing them despite missing terms or inexact expression, if the parties have intended to make a contract and there is a reasonably certain basis for awarding a remedy in case of breach. Missing terms are then supplied in a variety of Article 2 "gap filling" provisions which govern generally only in the absence of contrary agreement by the parties.

2. In a sales contract the basic obligation of the seller is to transfer and deliver the goods to the buyer who is obligated to pay for the goods in accordance with the contract. The Code contains provisions governing the time, place, and manner of delivery governing in absence of agreement, and provisions defining specialized delivery terms such as F.O.B., F.A.S., C.I.F., and C. & F. The Code also contains corresponding provisions governing the time, place, and manner of the buyer's payment. In addition, the UCC outlines the legal effect of an open price and quantity term. Unless otherwise agreed, the performances of the parties are exchanged simultaneously.

3. Most sales contracts are privately negotiated. Goods may, however, be sold at auction, which is a pub-

---

12. UCC §2-102.
13. UCC §2A-102.
14. UCC §2A-103(1)(j).

15. At this writing Article 2A has been adopted in Oklahoma.

lic sale. Article 2 has specific provisions governing the conduct of auction sales.

4. Increasingly in recent years, consumers and businesses lease rather than purchase goods they use. Despite this dramatic growth in personal property leasing, the law governing such transactions remains relatively undeveloped. To fill this gap in the law, the National Conference and American Law Institute approved in 1987 new UCC Article 2A, entitled "Leases," which is patterned closely after Article 2.

KEY TERMS

gap fillers	C.I.F. term
lot	C. & F. term
shipment contract	requirements contract
destination contract	output contract
F.O.B. term	auction
F.A.S. term	sale with reserve

QUESTIONS AND PROBLEMS

16-1 Seller and Buyer have an oral agreement for the sale of 200 desk calendars. No other terms are included. Is the contract unenforceable for indefiniteness? If not, what is the price? When and where is the price to be paid? When is delivery to be made? Where is delivery to be made? What must Seller do to make an effective tender of delivery?

16-2 Seller, whose plant is located in Chicago, contracts to sell a machine tool to Buyer, a New York manufacturer. What are Seller's delivery obligations assuming the goods are shipped: (1) F.O.B. Chicago, (2) F.O.B. New York, (3) C.I.F. New York, (4) F.A.S. *Lake Queen* (a freighter)?

16-3 What are the advantages of a requirements contract to a buyer? Of an output contract to a seller?

16-4 Consider whether the following transactions are within the scope of Article 2 of the UCC.

(a) Pittsburgh-Des Moines Steel Co. (PDM) and Brookhaven enter into a written contract by which PDM agrees to construct a one-million gallon water tank on Brookhaven's property for which Brookhaven agrees to pay $175,000 within thirty days after the tank has been tested and accepted.

(b) XYZ Co. contracts to purchase a computer software package from Computech Inc. that generates spreadsheets, reports, and graphs. The package consists of various computer disks and instruction manuals.

(c) NBE, Inc. contracts to sell a computer and software to Dr. Leone. The agreement requires NBE programmers to customize the software so that it can accommodate bookkeeping and recordkeeping at the doctor's office.

16-5 Gunn, a subcontractor for a construction project at the University of Texas, needed various paving tiles for the project. Alamo, a tile manufacturer, was aware of the project and had distributed information about its tiles to various bidders, including Gunn, prior to the awarding of the subcontract. On August 31, 1983, Gunn telephoned Alamo to order two sizes of paving tiles: 4″ × 8″ and 8″ × 12″ tiles. During the conversation, neither party discussed price or time, place, or method of delivery. Alamo mailed Gunn a document called a "telephone confirmation purchase order" which described the tiles ordered by Gunn but did not specify a price or time, place, or method of delivery. Alamo delivered the 4″ × 8″ tiles and charged the prices effective on August 31, 1983. Because of production problems, Alamo was unable to furnish the 8″ × 12″ tiles. After a delay of several months, Alamo delivered 6″ × 9″ tiles which Gunn purchased "under protest." Gunn installed the tiles but incurred additional labor costs. Gunn sued Alamo for breach of contract alleging that the failure to deliver the 8″ × 12″ tiles was a breach of contract and requesting damages for the additional costs incurred by Gunn. Alamo alleged that the parties had not entered into a contract because they had not agreed to a price or date, method, or place of delivery.

(a) Have the parties made a contract?

(b) Assume the parties have made a contract. What are its terms? Has Alamo breached the contract?

16-6 Associated Hardware, Inc. sent an offer to purchase hand tools to Big Wheel Distributors for a price of "cost plus 10%." Big Wheel replied that it would sell for "dealer catolog prices less 11%," assuring Associated that its price quotation was equivalent to cost plus 10%. Although acting in good faith, Big Wheel was mistaken and the two prices were not equivalent. Associated agreed and the goods were shipped and accepted by Associated. When Big Wheel sent its bill, Associated objected because the price was not equivalent to cost plus 10%. Do the parties have a contract? If so, what is the price?

16-7 Pumpernickel, Inc., a major producer of bread and bread products, decided to sell breadcrumbs in an effort to use leftover and stale bread. Each week, Pumpernickel ground up all leftover bread products, toasted the crumbs and sold them to food processors. CTC Co., a food processor, needing a regular and large supply of breadcrumbs for its line of frozen casserole dishes, contracted to purchase breadcrumbs from Pumpernickel. A written contract provided that CTC would purchase "all breadcrumbs produced by Pumpernickel at its New York bakery at the price of 20 cents per pound." The contract was for an indefinite term but both parties had the right to cancel by giving six months' notice to the other party. After the contract had been in effect for a year, Pumpernickel's financial staff suggested that breadcrumb production terminate because the company was losing money on the operations. During several conversations with CTC personnel, Pumpernickel's sales officer indicated that breadcrumb production was likely to be terminated unless Pumpernickel could sell the crumbs for at least 25 cents per pound. Finally, without notice to CTC, Pumpernickel stopped producing breadcrumbs. The leftover bread products previously used to make the crumbs were sold to animal food manufacturers. CTC sues Pumpernickel alleging that it breached the contract. Pumpernickel argues that the contract with CTC did not require Pumpernickel to manufacture breadcrumbs but only to sell to CTC any breadcrumbs it did manufacture. How should the court rule?

Chapter 17

The Sales Contract—
Title and Risk of Loss

Major Topics

- an explanation of Code provisions governing passage of title and resolving title disputes
- the definition of "identification" and the legal consequences of identification
- Article 2 provisions regarding risk of loss in sales contracts

The Uniform Commercial Code in §2-106(1) defines a "sale" of goods as the passage of title from the seller to the buyer for a price. A number of legal issues arise in connection with this transfer of **title** (generally meaning ownership). For example, the law must determine the nature of the interest that the buyer acquires, and whether that interest is subject to claims of third parties such as the seller's creditors or prior owners of the goods. It must also ascertain when the risk of casualty to the goods is transferred to the buyer and when the buyer acquires a sufficient interest in the goods to insure against that risk. The UCC resolves these and related issues through principles of title, identification, and risk of loss.

Passage of Title

Even though title is used in the basic definition of sale, the importance of title and passage of title in Code contracts is extremely limited. As stated in

§2-401, containing the general rules relating to title:

> Each provision of this Article with regard to the rights, obligations and remedies of the seller, the buyer, purchasers or other third parties applies irrespective of title to the goods except where the provision refers to such title.[1]

One important issue resolved under the UCC without regard to title is risk of loss. **Risk of loss** rules determine the rights of the parties if the goods involved in the contract are lost, destroyed, or stolen. That is, risk of loss principles determine when the risk of such casualties passes from the seller to the buyer. If risk of loss is on the seller and the goods are destroyed, the seller bears the loss and cannot recover the price from the buyer. Additionally, the seller may also be liable for breach of contract unless he procures or manufactures substitute goods in time to perform the contract. On the other hand,

---

1. Code sections in which title *does* affect rights and duties of the parties include: (1) §2-106(1), the definition of a sale; (2) §2-312, the warranty of title discussed in Chapter 19; (3) §§2-326, 2-327, governing sale on approval and sale or return discussed on page 390; (4) §2-403(1), the voidable title rule discussed on page 382; (5) §2-501, relating to insurable interest of a seller who retains title discussed on page 386; and (6) §2-722, under which a person who has title can sue third persons for damage to goods, discussed on page 386.

if risk of loss has passed to the buyer, the buyer is liable for the price of the goods despite their destruction. Determining the precise point at which the risk passes to the buyer is therefore a fundamental issue in the sales contract.

Under the Uniform Sales Act (USA), the law that governed sales contracts prior to the UCC, the party who had title also had the risk of loss. Unfortunately, the USA rules governing passage of title were unclear and operated in many cases to transfer title (and therefore risk of loss) to the buyer while the goods were still in the seller's possession and covered by the seller's insurance. The Code drafters found that this approach caused substantial confusion, uncertainty, and litigation concerning risk of loss issues. Therefore, in order to make the rules clearer and more certain, the UCC completely divorces risk of loss (and the related issue, insurable interest) from title and instead addresses these issues in other specific Code sections. This approach has resulted in a marked reduction in litigation involving risk of loss questions. The specific rules covering insurable interest and risk of loss are discussed in detail later in this chapter.

When Title Passes

Although insurable interest and risk of loss are determined without regard to title, title is relevant in resolving a number of legal issues, both under the UCC and other state law. For example, title may be relevant in determining whether an owner's property can be attached by creditors or in assessing of property taxes. Therefore, if title becomes material, the Code contains a general provision, §2-401, governing passage of title. As a general rule, unless otherwise agreed, title passes to the buyer at the time and place at which the seller completes performance with respect to the physical delivery of the goods.

Shipment and Destination Contracts. If the contract requires or authorizes the seller to ship the goods to the buyer but does not require delivery at a particular destination—a "shipment" contract such as F.O.B. point of shipment, C.I.F., or C. & F.—title passes to the buyer at the time and place of shipment. If shipment is required or authorized

but delivery at a destination is required—a "destination" contract such as F.O.B. point of destination—title passes on tender at the destination.

Delivery Without Moving Goods. In some cases, the goods sold never move; they may, for example, be stored in a warehouse. If the parties do not explicitly agree and the goods are to be delivered without being moved, passage of title depends upon whether a document of title is involved. If the seller is to deliver a document of title, title passes at the time and place the document is delivered. If no document of title is to be delivered and the goods are identified at the time of the contract, title passes at the time and place of contracting.

Transfer of Title and Third Parties

Section 2-403 governs the extent of title acquired by a purchaser of goods. Note that the rules discussed below relate to rights acquired by *purchasers* of goods. Although "purchaser" is usually synonymous with "buyer," the term **purchaser** is defined broadly in the Code to include any person taking "by sale, discount, negotiation, mortgage, pledge, lien, issue or re-issue, gift or any other voluntary transaction creating an interest in property."[2]

The basic rule governing transfer of title to such "purchasers" is contained in §2-403(1) that states simply:

> A purchaser of goods *acquires all title which his transferor had or had power to transfer* except that a purchaser of a limited interest acquires rights only to the extent of the interest purchased. (Emphasis added.)

Thus, generally, a buyer gets whatever interest the seller had in the goods. If the seller has "good" title, the buyer gets good title. If the seller has no title—for example, she is a thief, or has acquired the goods from a thief, or an earlier transferor of the goods was a thief—the buyer gets no title. In such cases, the seller's title is referred to as "void"

---

2. UCC §§1-201(32), (33).

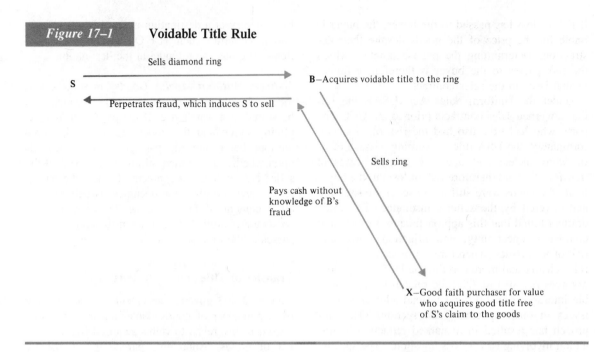

Figure 17–1 **Voidable Title Rule**

Sells diamond ring

S

B—Acquires voidable title to the ring

Perpetrates fraud, which induces S to sell

Sells ring

Pays cash without knowledge of B's fraud

X—Good faith purchaser for value who acquires good title free of S's claim to the goods

and, unless properly disclaimed, the seller breaches the warranty of title ordinarily given by a seller to a buyer.[3]

Voidable Title Rule. A special title rule, known as the **voidable title rule,** applies if a transferee of goods is a "good faith purchaser for value." Under §2-403(1):

> A person with *voidable title* has power to transfer a good title to a *good faith purchaser for value.* (Emphasis added.)

The term "voidable title" is not explicitly defined but §2-403(1) lists four situations specifically covered by the rule. To illustrate these situations, assume that S sells goods to B and that: (1) B represents herself as X in the transaction to induce S to sell; that is, B is an imposter, or (2) B pays for the goods with a check that later bounces, or (3) the parties agree that the transaction is to be a "cash

sale," which means that S and B agree that title will not pass until the price is paid, or (4) the sale was procured through fraud on B's part. B subsequently sells the goods to X, a good faith purchaser for value. In all of these situations, under the voidable title rule, B has the power subsequently to transfer good title to X. Thus, S may not recover the goods from X, but could, of course, proceed against B for damages. Figure 17–1 illustrates the operation of the rule assuming B's fraud has rendered her title voidable.

This rule does not apply to a person holding "void" title—that is, a thief or a person acquiring from or through a thief. Here, any transferee, good faith or not, takes subject to the rights of the owner. In these cases, the loss ordinarily falls on the person buying from the thief (assuming the thief cannot be held accountable).

To acquire good title under the voidable title rule, the purchaser must act in good faith and give value. **Value** is expansively defined in the UCC §1-201(44) to include, generally, any consideration sufficient to support a simple contract, including satisfying or providing security for an antecedent debt. Therefore, almost any purchaser would sat-

3. The warranty of title, contained in §2-312, is discussed in Chapter 19.

isfy the value requirement, though the amount of value given is, of course, relevant in determining whether the purchase is made in good faith or with knowledge of the original seller's claim.

In the following case the court was required to decide whether the purchaser was a good faith purchaser for value entitled to protection under the voidable title rule.

Liles Bros. & Son v. Wright
638 S.W.2d 383 (Tenn. 1982)

On November 25, 1977, Tony Mangum purchased a 580C Case backhoe and loader from plaintiff Liles Bros. & Son (Liles), a Case equipment dealer in Jackson, Tennessee, for $20,561. Mangum paid for the machine by two checks: one dated November 25 for $3,000 and the other dated December 2 for $17,561. Liles contacted Mangum's bank and ascertained there were sufficient funds to cover the $3,000 check; Mangum assured Liles that funds would be available to cover the second check by December 2.

On November 28, 1977, Mangum, posing as a heavy equipment salesman, sold the backhoe to defendant Carl Wright, an operator of a septic tank service. Wright paid $11,000 to Mangum by certified check. On December 2, Liles discovered that Mangum's check dated December 2 had been dishonored and that Mangum was in jail.

After learning that Wright had possession of the backhoe, Liles sued Wright seeking return of the machine. The trial court ruled in favor of Liles. The court of appeals reversed, holding that Wright was a bona fide purchaser for value protected under UCC §2-403. Liles appealed.

Brock, Justice

. . . Contrary to the holding of the Court of Appeals, there appears to be ample proof in the record that Wright had reason to believe that the property was stolen or obtained in a fraudulent or devious manner. The defendant's actions should not allow him to claim the status of a good faith purchaser for value.

Since 1975, Wright was engaged in the construction business operating as Carl's Septic Service. He

required the use of heavy equipment including a backhoe and loader. Wright owned two backhoes and was familiar with their operation and value.

Furthermore, Wright was in the market for a new backhoe and had recently solicited quotations from local equipment dealers. Wright contacted Mr. McKeel, an equipment dealer in Kentucky, and sought the retail price of a 580C Case backhoe. At the time of the inquiry, the machine was selling for between $18,000.00 and $19,000.00, but he was quoted a price of approximately $12,000.00 which accounted for his trade-in. By November of 1977, McKeel was selling the 580C backhoe for approximately $20,000.00. In addition, Hixson, a Ford equipment dealer from Paris, Tennessee, furnished quotations to Wright for a comparable backhoe. Hixson's quotation was approximately $20,000.00. . . . The record indicates, therefore, that Wright had ample knowledge of the true market value of the equipment which he purchased.

Other factors which would tend to indicate that Wright had notice of suspicious dealing include: the bill of sale was a blank purchase order without any reference to the name of Mangum's company, its location, its phone number, or the type of merchandise it handled; unlike previous backhoe purchases that Wright had made, he did not receive any warranty papers which is standard on a new machine; and unlike other heavy equipment dealers, such as Liles who specialized in Case equipment and Hixson who specialized in Ford equipment, Mangum specifically told Wright that he could make him a good deal on *any* kind of equipment that he wanted. Wright also admitted that he knew that quite a bit of equipment had recently been "stolen" in the western Tennessee and Kentucky area and he claimed he did not want to get involved in such dealings. Despite knowledge of the foregoing facts, Wright never inquired where Mangum's dealership or place of business was located; and, he never checked Mangum's credit reference with Watkins—the Co-op credit manager, who testified at trial that Mangum seemed to sell a lot of heavy equipment but nobody knew where it was coming from.

The Court, therefore, holds that the defendant, Wright, is not a bona fide purchaser for value. He did not conduct himself honestly in his purchase of the backhoe, and he had ample information which would have led a reasonably prudent person either to refuse to buy the backhoe or to make a considerably more detailed investigation of the facts before purchasing. Furthermore, he attempted to secrete the property so that the serial number could not be obtained when the plaintiff tried to locate the backhoe in question. . . .

If Wright was not a good faith purchaser of the backhoe, then he only has voidable title to the backhoe pursuant to . . . [UCC §2-403(1)] and Liles Bros, has the right to possession of the backhoe, under a repossession action. . . . The statute in effect recognizes that a person such as Mangum who buys goods in exchange for a check which is later dishonored only obtains voidable title, but has power to pass good title to a good faith purchaser for value. Since Wright was not a good faith purchaser of value, he too only received voidable title. Therefore, the original seller, Liles Bros., has the right to rescind its sale with Mangum, the original purchaser, who only had voidable title and reclaim the backhoe from the third party, Wright, because he, too, only had voidable title. . . .

[Judgment reversed.]

"Shelter" or "Umbrella" Protection. It is important to note the relationship between the general rule governing transfer of title and the voidable title rule. Under the general rule, the seller can generally transfer *what he has*. Therefore, a transferor with good title can transfer good title, even though the transferee might otherwise be subject to the claims of a former owner.[4] This provision creates what is commonly known as "shelter" or "umbrella" protection for the transferee. The purpose of this protection is to assure the seller a free market for what he has.

To illustrate the operation of the rule in this context, assume Bob buys a car from Sam and pays for the car with a bad check. Before Sam discovers what has happened, Bob resells the car to Tom, who pays cash and is unaware of Bob's wrongdoing. In this situation, Tom acquires good title to the car free of Sam's claim to it under the voidable title rule. Tom then sells the car to Fred, who is fully aware of (though not a party to) Bob's conduct. Fred acquires good title. (Fred would not take free of Sam's claim had he acquired the car from Bob because he is not a "good faith purchaser.") By purchasing from Tom, Fred "acquires all title which his transferor had." Fred, therefore, acquires the *rights* of a good faith purchaser without being one himself. The shelter rule protects Tom's market by allowing him to sell what he has—the rights of a good faith purchaser.

The Entrusting Rule. Under §2-403(2), any entrusting of possession of goods to a merchant who deals in goods of that kind gives the merchant the power to transfer all rights of the entruster to a buyer in the ordinary course of business. Assuming this "entrusting rule" applies, the buyer cuts off the entruster's claim to the goods. The entruster is then limited to a claim against the merchant in tort or contract. The purpose of this provision is to protect a person who buys goods in the ordinary course out of a dealer's inventory from ownership claims of third parties.[5]

Before illustrating the operation of the rule, certain terms must be defined and explained:

1. Under §2-403(3), **entrusting** includes "any delivery and any acquiescence in retention of possession" without regard to (a) any conditions attached to the delivery or retention by agreement of the parties, or (b) whether the merchant's acquisition or disposition of the goods constitutes larceny under the state criminal law.

2. The goods must be entrusted to a merchant "who deals in goods of that kind." Thus, not all persons who qualify as "merchants" for some Code provisions fall within the reach of this section.[6]

3. The merchant has the power to transfer "all rights of the entruster." Thus, if the entruster is a

---

4. A similar rule applies under UCC §3-201 to transfers of commercial paper, such as notes and checks, in which the transferee of the paper acquires the transferor's rights. Section 3-201 is discussed in Chapter 24.

5. UCC §9-307 provides similar protection to buyers against persons holding a security interest in the goods sold. Section 9-307 is discussed in Chapter 32.

6. See discussion of the definition of merchant in Chapter 7.

thief, the buyer in the ordinary course takes subject to the owner's rights.

4. The purchaser must be a "buyer in the ordinary course of business." Under §1-201(9), a **buyer in the ordinary course of business** is:

> . . . [A] person who in good faith and without knowledge that the sale to him is in violation of the ownership rights or security interest of a third party in the goods buys in ordinary course from a person in the business of selling goods of that kind but does not include a pawnbroker.

Though not explicitly stated, implicit in the definition is that the goods sold are inventory in the merchant's hands.

To illustrate the operation of the rule, assume that Joe owns a TV set in need of repair. He therefore brings it to Red's Radio & TV, Inc. for repair. Red's both repairs electronic equipment and sells new and used equipment at retail. Red repairs the set and then places it in his used equipment showroom, where it is subsequently sold to Mary, one of Red's customers. Mary cuts off Joe's ownership rights to the television. Joe has the right to recover from Red. The same result follows if the entruster leaves the goods in the merchant's possession for any other purpose. For example, Joe buys a new TV from Red and pays cash. However, because the set is a large console model, Joe leaves it in Red's possession while he gets a pick-up truck. During the hour Joe is gone, Red sells the set to Lois, another retail customer. Lois cuts off Joe's rights in the set and once again Joe's recourse is against Red.

The Ostensible Ownership Rule. It is important to note the relationship between the entrusting rule and the **ostensible ownership** rule stated in §2-402. A buyer who leaves goods in the seller's possession after sale creates the misleading impression that the seller actually owns them. This impression may deceive both buyers from and creditors of the seller. As the preceding example indicates, §2-403(2) protects most buyers in this situation against claims of the original buyer. Similarly, the seller's creditors also may be protected under the doctrine of ostensible ownership, which treats the sale as void against creditors if the seller's retention is

fraudulent under any rule of law of the state where the goods are situated. That is, unpaid creditors who seize the goods in the seller's possession (using state debt collection remedies discussed in Chapter 29) defeat the original buyer's claim to the goods.

If, however, as in the preceding example, the seller is a *merchant* dealing in goods of the kind, retention is not fraudulent as against creditors if the possession is (1) in good faith, (2) in the current course of trade, and (3) only for a commercially reasonable time. The reason for this exception is apparently that creditors of a merchant seller are less likely to be misled by his retention of the goods in a current transaction for a reasonable period of time after sale. In addition, this exception is consistent with the basic Code policy of protecting persons who buy in the ordinary course out of a merchant's inventory.

Identification

The preceding discussion explains the basic UCC principles regarding transfer of title in sales contracts. As previously noted, under the Code, title does not govern the important concepts of insurable interest and risk of loss. Rather, these issues are addressed in separate Code provisions discussed in the following material.

"Identification" Defined

Insurable interest, in addition to a number of other important legal issues under the UCC, is governed by the concept of identification. That is, many Code issues turn upon whether or not (and when) goods have become "identified" to the contract. **Identification** is the process by which the particular existing goods referred to in the contract are designated and specified. Under UCC §2-105(2), goods must be both existing and identified before any interest in them, including title, can pass. Goods not both existing and identified are known as **future goods**. For example, goods to be manufactured are not yet existing and are future goods. Ten dishwashers to be chosen out of a manufacturer's inventory of 1,000 are not yet identified and are also future goods. Of course, Article 2 governs both a present sale of goods and a sale of future goods.

Time and Manner of Identification

The UCC rules relating to identification in §2-501 provide that the parties may explicitly agree as to the time and manner of identification. In the absence of such agreement, the following rules apply.

1. If the goods are already existing and identified, identification occurs when the contract is made. For example, assume Sally offers to sell Ben her boat for $8,000. Ben comes over to Sally's house to examine the boat, which is in the driveway. After inspecting it, Ben accepts Sally's offer. The boat is identified to the contract at the time of Ben's acceptance.

2. If the goods are future goods (as defined above), identification occurs when the goods are shipped, marked, or otherwise designated by the seller as the goods to which the contract refers. For example, assume Buyer orders 100 dishwashers from Seller. Seller's warehouse contains 1,000 dishwashers (or he has no dishwashers in stock and has yet to manufacture them). Identification occurs when the seller segregates from his inventory (or manufactures and segregates) the specific 100 dishwashers to be delivered to Buyer under the contract.

3. Unborn young of animals are identified when they are conceived if the young are to be born within 12 months after contracting.

4. Growing crops are identified when they are planted if the crops are to be harvested within 12 months or the next normal harvesting season after contracting, whichever is longer.

Effect of Identification

Insurable Interest. Identification gives the buyer an *insurable interest* in the goods. Although insurable interest is discussed in more detail in the insurance material,[7] generally, in property insurance, a person has an **insurable interest** if she will be exposed to monetary injury in the event of loss, damage, destruction, or theft of the property. Insurable interest distinguishes an insurance policy from a gambling contract.

Obviously, the seller, being the owner of the goods, has an insurable interest in them. The Code designates the time of identification as the point at which the buyer obtains an insurable interest. Thus, both the buyer and the seller have an insurable interest from the point of identification. The buyer's interest, of course, continues after he acquires title. The seller retains an insurable interest as long as she has either title to, or a security interest in, the goods.

The risk of loss does not ordinarily pass to the buyer upon identification. Risk of loss rules are discussed later in this chapter. Identification merely gives the buyer the right to insure the goods to whatever extent he is exposed to the possibility of monetary loss in the event of the goods' destruction. For example, the buyer may make a down payment on the purchase price prior to the passage of title and risk of loss and would therefore have an insurable interest to that extent. Additionally, because identification and insurable interest precede transfer of risk of loss, the buyer can always be protected by insuring the goods before the risk of their loss, damage, or destruction passes to him.

Identification and Third Parties. In addition to giving the buyer an insurable interest, §2-722 provides that identification gives the buyer the right to sue third parties who tortiously damage or destroy the goods. Consistent with the rules stated above, the seller also has a right of action if he has either title to, or a security interest in, the goods. Thus, after identification, both parties may proceed against the third party. Prior to identification, only the seller has such a right.

Other Consequences of Identification. Identification has several other legal consequences, discussed in other parts of the contracts and sales material.

1. Under §2-716(3), a buyer has the right to replevy (recover possession of) *identified* goods from the seller in certain situations.

2. In certain limited circumstances, §2-502 allows a buyer may recover *identified* goods in the hands of an insolvent seller.

3. Special rules apply under §2-613 if goods

---

7. Insurance law is covered in Chapter 56.

identified when the contract is made are destroyed without fault of either party before risk of loss passes to the buyer.

4. Section 2-510(3) provides a special risk of loss rule if a buyer breaches a contract as to conforming goods *identified* to the contract.

5. Under §2-709, the seller has the right to recover the purchase price of *identified* goods in the event of a buyer's breach if the seller is unable to resell them.

6. Identification is also an integral part of the definition of "goods" in §2-105 and thus determines in part whether or not Article 2 of the UCC applies to a given transaction.[8]

Risk of Loss

Risk of loss rules determine whether the buyer or seller bears the risk of loss, damage, or destruction of the goods sold under the contract. The Code addresses risk of loss in two separate provisions, §§2-509 and 2-510.[9] The UCC divides the issue into two parts: (1) risk of loss in the absence of breach, and (2) risk of loss when either party is in breach.

Risk of Loss in Absence of Breach—§2-509

Section 2-509 governs risk of loss in the absence of breach. The basic effect of §2-509 is to place the risk on the person controlling possession of the goods, who is more likely to be insured against their loss, theft, or destruction. This approach represents a substantial improvement over the uncertainty and inequity present under prior law, the Uniform Sales Act. Section 2-509 divides risk of loss into three basic situations: (1) when the seller is required or authorized to ship the goods to the buyer, (2) when the goods are in the hands of a bailee such as a warehouseman and are to be delivered without being moved, and (3) all other cases. As with most other Code provisions, the risk of

loss rules discussed below may be changed by contrary agreement of the parties.

Risk of Loss in Shipment and Destination Contracts. If the seller is required or authorized to ship the goods to the buyer, risk of loss depends upon whether a "shipment" or "destination" contract is involved. If the seller is not required to deliver the goods at a particular destination—for example, a shipment contract such as F.O.B. shipping point or C.I.F.—risk of loss passes to the buyer when the goods are duly delivered to the carrier. Thus, risk of loss in transit in shipment contracts is borne by the buyer.[10]

If the seller is required to deliver at the destination—a destination contract, such as F.O.B. destination—the risk of loss passes to the buyer when the goods are tendered at the destination so as to enable the buyer to take delivery. Thus, risk of loss in transit in destination contracts remains on the seller.

At issue in the following case was whether the parties had contractually altered the Code rule governing risk of loss in an F.O.B. shipping point contract.

A. M. Knitwear Corp. v. All America Export-Import Corp.
359 N.E.2d 342 (N.Y. 1976)

Defendant All America Export-Import Corp. ("buyer") and plaintiff A. M. Knitwear Corp. ("seller") entered into a contract, by which the seller agreed to sell several thousand pounds of yarn to the buyer. The buyer placed the order by using its own purchase order form and filling in the information describing the goods, quantity, and the dollar amount of the order. In the column labeled "price" buyer typed: *"FOB PLANT PER LB.*

---

8. UCC §§2-716(3), 2-502, and 2-709 are discussed in Chapter 18. Section 2-613 is covered in Chapter 14, §2-105 is discussed in Chapter 7, and §2-510(3) is covered later in this chapter.

9. Risk of loss in contracts for the sale of *land* is covered in Chapter 56.

10. Note that a C.I.F. term also creates a "shipment" contract. Thus, the risk of loss, theft, or destruction in transit in such a contract is on the buyer. Although the buyer has the benefit of the insurance in this case, he bears the risk of inability to collect from the insurance company (for example, due to insolvency) or the carrier.

$1.35." In the space marked "Ship Via," buyer typed "Pick Up from your Plant to Moore-Mc-Cormak Pier for shipment to Santos, Brazil." The buyer left blank a space marked "F.O.B." where an F.O.B. term could have been added. Further shipment instructions subsequently discussed by the parties were explained by the buyer's vice-president at deposition:

> I said, "As you know, most of the goods being shipped to South America is being containerized. I have to order a container or a trailer, whatever is the simplest expression. And then in turn you will have to put it into the container."
> Mr. Lubliner [of A. M. Knitwear Corp.] said "This is no problem. Just send down the container. I will try to help you."

The buyer had an empty trailer delivered to the seller's premises and seller loaded the yarn into the trailer. Seller then notified buyer that the load was complete and buyer advised its freight forwarder to pick up the loaded trailer. Prior to the arrival of the freight forwarder, however, an unknown individual (apparently a thief) driving a tractor arrived at seller's premises, hooked up the trailer to his tractor, signed a bill of lading with an undecipherable signature, and removed the goods.

Seller sued buyer to recover payment for the goods, alleging that its contractual obligations were met when the yarn was loaded on the trailer. Buyer alleged that seller's obligations were not fulfilled until the yarn was delivered to a carrier. The trial court ruled in favor of the seller. The appellate court reversed. Seller appealed the appellate court decision.

Cooke, Judge

. . . Despite the provisions of the Code which place the risk of loss on the seller in the F.O.B. place of shipment contract until the goods are delivered to the carrier, here the seller contends that the parties "otherwise agreed" so that pursuant to its agreement, the risk of loss passed from the seller to the buyer at the time and place at which the seller completed physical delivery of the subject goods into the container supplied by the buyer for that purpose. In support of this contention, the seller alleges that the language of the purchase order "Pick Up from your Plant" is a specific delivery instruction and that the language *"FOB PLANT PER LB. $1.35,"* which appears in the price column, is a price term and not a delivery term. Further support for the seller's contention is taken from the fact that the space provided in the buyer's own purchase order form for an F.O.B. delivery instruction was left blank by the buyer. Thus, the seller contends its agreement with the buyer imposed no obligation on it to make delivery of the loaded container to the carrier. . . .

The seller's contention, that the parties intended the F.O.B. term as a price term and not a delivery term, conflicts with the code provision that states that the F.O.B. term is a delivery term "even though used *only* in connection with the stated price" (Uniform Commercial Code, §2-319, subd. [1]; emphasis added). . . .

Since the term "FOB PLANT" was a delivery term, the risk of loss was on the seller until the goods were put into the possession of the carrier—unless the parties "otherwise agreed" or there was a "contrary agreement" with respect to the risk of loss. . . .

With respect to the agreement of the parties, the seller contends that the statements in the affidavits of the parties and a portion of an examination before trial of the buyer's vice-president manifest that the parties intended that the seller's performance would be complete when the goods were loaded into the container and the buyer was notified thereof. . . .

The term "FOB PLANT" is well understood to require delivery to the carrier and does not imply any other meaning. If a contrary meaning was intended, an express statement varying the ordinary meaning is required. The statements made by an officer of the buyer and the other circumstances of this case are not enough to show that the term did not mean what it does in ordinary commercial transactions. One of the principal purposes of the code is to simplify, clarify and modernize the law governing commercial transactions. . . . To allow a commonly used term such as F.O.B. to be varied in meaning, without an express statement of the parties of an intent to do so, would not serve that purpose. . . .

[Judgment affirmed.]

Presumption of Shipment Contract. Under the UCC a shipment contract is presumed. Therefore, if no F.O.B. destination or equivalent term is used, risk of loss passes to the buyer on shipment, even if the seller has promised to pay the freight charges. That is, unless the contract specifies otherwise, the seller is not required to deliver goods at a named destination and bear the risk of loss in transit.[11]

The following case illustrates the application of this rule.

Pestana v. Karinol Corporation

367 So.2d 1096 (Fla. App. 1979)

Nahim Amar B., a resident of Mexico, entered into a contract with Karinol Corporation, an exporting company in Miami, Florida, by which Amar agreed to purchase 64 watches for $6,006. The only delivery terms in the contract provided: "Please send the merchandise in cardboard boxes duly strapped with metal bands via air parcel post to Chetumal [Mexico]. Documents to Banco de Commercio De Quintano Roo S.A." Karinol delivered the watches to its agent, American International Freight Forwarders, Inc. where they were packaged in cartons and delivered to TACA International Airlines. By prior arrangement, TACA delivered the cartons to Amar's agent. When the cartons were opened, the watches were missing. When Amar notified Karinol, both Karinol and its insurance carrier refused to cover the loss. Amar had died and a representative of his estate sued defendants Karinol, its insurer, and American International Freight Forwarding for breach of contract. The trial court ruled in favor of defendants.

Hubbart, Judge

. . . The central issue presented for review is whether a contract for the sale of goods, which stipulates the place where the goods sold are to be sent by carrier but contains (a) no explicit provisions allocating the risk of loss while the goods are in the possession of the carrier and (b) no delivery

---

11. UCC §2-503, Official Comment 5.

terms such as F.O.B. place of destination, is a shipment contract or a destination contract under the Uniform Commercial Code. We hold that such a contract, without more, constitutes a shipment contract wherein the risk of loss passes to the buyer when the seller duly delivers the goods to the carrier under a reasonable contract of carriage for shipment to the buyer. Accordingly, we affirm.

. . .

There are two types of sales contracts under Florida's Uniform Commercial Code wherein a carrier is used to transport the goods sold: a shipment contract and a destination contract. A shipment contract is considered the normal contract in which the seller is required to send the subject goods by carrier to the buyer but is not required to guarantee delivery thereof at a particular destination. . . .

A destination contract, on the other hand, is considered the variant contract in which the seller specifically agrees to deliver the goods sold to the buyer at a particular destination and to bear the risk of loss of the goods until tender of delivery. . . .

In the instant case, we deal with the normal shipment contract involving the sale of goods. The defendant Karinol pursuant to this contract agreed to send the goods sold, a shipment of watches, to . . . [Amar] in Chetumal, Mexico. There was no specific provision in the contract between the parties which allocated the risk of loss on the goods sold while in transit. In addition, there were no delivery terms such as F.O.B. Chetumal contained in the contract.

All agree that there is sufficient evidence that the defendant Karinol performed its obligations as a seller under the Uniform Commercial Code if this contract is considered a shipment contract. Karinol put the goods sold in the possession of a carrier and made a contract for the goods' safe transportation to [Amar]; Karinol also promptly notified [Amar] of the shipment and tendered to said party the necessary documents to obtain possession of the goods sold.

The plaintiff . . . contends, however, that the contract herein is a destination contract in which the risk of loss on the goods sold did not pass until delivery on such goods had been tendered to him at Chetumal, Mexico—an event which never occurred. He relies for this position on the notation at the bottom of the contract between the parties which provides that the goods were to be sent to Chetumal, Mexico. We cannot agree. A "send to" or "ship to" term is a part of every contract involving the sale of goods where carriage is contemplated and has no significance in determining whether the contract is a shipment or destination contract for risk of loss purposes. . . .

As such, the "send to" term contained in this contract cannot, without more, convert this into a destination contract.

It therefore follows that the risk of loss in this case shifted to . . . [Amar] as buyer when the defendant Karinol as seller duly delivered the goods to the defendant freight forwarder American under a reasonable contract of carriage for shipment to . . . [Amar] in Chetumal, Mexico. The defendant Karinol, its agent the defendant American, and its insurer the defendant Fidelity could not be held liable to the plaintiff in this action. . . .

[Judgment affirmed.]

Risk of Loss When Goods Not Moved. In some instances, the goods may be held by a bailee (generally a warehouseman) and are to be delivered without being moved. For example, S may sell goods stored at X's warehouse to B. In this case, risk of loss passes to the buyer:

1. on the buyer's receipt of a negotiable document of title, such as a warehouse receipt or bill of lading, covering the goods,
2. on acknowledgement by the bailee of the buyer's right to possession of the goods, or
3. after receipt of a *nonnegotiable* document of title or other written direction to the bailee to deliver.

Even though risk of loss is tied to "receipt" of a nonnegotiable document or written direction in the third case above, the risk does not actually pass when the buyer acquires physical possession of the piece of paper, as it does when a negotiable document is used. Under §2-503(4)(b), risk of loss does not pass to the buyer until the buyer has had a reasonable time to present the document or direction

to the bailee *and* the bailee has honored it. Refusal by the bailee to honor the document or to obey the direction defeats the tender.

Residual Risk of Loss Rule. In cases not governed by the rules outlined above, a residual risk of loss rule is contained in §2-509(3). Under this provision, if the seller is a *merchant,*[12] risk of loss passes when the buyer takes physical possession of the goods. If the seller is not a merchant, risk of loss passes on *tender* of delivery. Thus, in the case of a merchant seller, risk of loss may remain on the seller after a tender has been made and after title passes. Assume Bill buys a sofa from Slavin's, a furniture store. Bill pays the price and Slavin places the sofa on its loading dock. Bill, however, leaves the sofa with Slavin's while he gets a van necessary to remove it. The risk of loss remains on Slavin's until Bill returns and takes actual physical possession. This result is consistent with the basic premise of §2-509 to place the risk of loss on the person—the merchant seller in control and possession of the goods—most likely to be insured against it.

Sale on Approval, Sale or Return— §§2-326 and 2-327

Sections 2-326 and 2-327 adopt special rules regarding title and risk of loss in specialized contracts allowing a buyer to return goods already delivered even though they conform to the contract. These contracts are the "sale on approval" and the "sale or return."

If goods delivered by the seller may be returned by the buyer even though conforming, the transaction is a **sale on approval** if the goods are delivered primarily for *use*. For example, sale of a vacuum cleaner to a *consumer* on "30-day free trial" or "on satisfaction" is a sale on approval. On the other hand, the transaction is a **sale or return** if the goods are delivered primarily for resale. Assume

---

12. "Merchant" is defined in §2-104 discussed in Chapter 7. §2-509(3) applies to persons who are merchants under either the "practices" or "goods" aspect of the merchant definition. §2-104, Official Comment 2.

Electro, a manufacturer of appliances, wants Margret, an appliance dealer, to carry its line of products. Because Electro is not established in the trade, it overcomes Margret's reluctance to buy by promising to take back any goods remaining unsold in lieu of payment. The transaction is a sale or return. In short, if the goods can be returned even though they are wholly as warranted, delivery to a consumer for use is a sale on approval and delivery to a merchant for resale is a sale or return.

The *sale on approval* transaction has several legal consequences. First, unless otherwise agreed, risk of loss and title do not pass to the buyer until acceptance. "Acceptance" generally refers to conduct by the buyer indicating an intent to keep the goods. Thus, if goods on approval in the hands of the buyer are destroyed before the buyer accepts them, the seller bears the risk of loss. In this context, use of the goods for their intended purpose does not constitute acceptance, but failure to seasonably notify the seller of an election to return is an acceptance. If the goods are conforming, acceptance of any part is acceptance of the whole. If the buyer elects to return and duly notifies the seller, both the expense and risk of return are borne by the seller, but a merchant buyer must follow any reasonable instructions.

In a *sale or return*, the legal consequences are diametrically different. Even though the buyer has the right to return, risk of loss passes to the buyer upon delivery and remains with him until the goods are returned to the seller. Additionally, the return is at the buyer's expense. Also, unlike a sale on approval, acceptance of part of the goods is not acceptance of the whole. A basic purpose of a sale or return agreement is to allow the buyer to return goods remaining unsold. Therefore, the buyer, provided he acts seasonably, may return all or part of the delivery so long as the goods remain in substantially their original condition.

Rights of creditors of the buyer also differ in the two situations. Goods in the hands of a buyer on approval are not subject to the claims of his creditors until acceptance. While in the buyer's possession, however, goods delivered under a sale or return agreement are subject to the claims of the buyer's creditors. This aspect of the sale or return arrangement is discussed in more detail in the secured transactions material in Chapter 32.

Effect of Breach on Risk of Loss— §2-510

The foregoing rules apply in the absence of a breach by either party. If the seller breaches, risk of loss is governed by §§2-510(1) and (2). The effect of a buyer's breach or repudiation is stated in §2-510(3).

Seller in Breach. If the seller's tender or delivery so fails to conform to the contract as to give the buyer the right to reject the goods, risk of loss remains on the seller until cure by the seller or acceptance by the buyer. "Cure," in this context, refers to changes made in the goods already tendered such as repair or partial substitution. Risk of loss shifts when such a cure is completed. Cure by repossession and new delivery has no effect upon risk of loss for the goods originally tendered.

In the following case, the court was required to determine which party bore risk of loss after a nonconforming delivery by the seller.

Graybar Electric Company v. Shook
195 S.E.2d 514 (N.C. 1973)

> Plaintiff Graybar Electric Company and defendant Harold Shook entered into a contract by which Graybar agreed to sell three reels of underground cable to Shook. The delivery was to be made at the Six Run Grocery Store in a rural community in North Carolina. On April 6, Graybar delivered one reel of underground cable and two reels of aerial cable. Because the aerial cable was unsuitable for Shook's use, he notified Graybar that he rejected the aerial cable. He further notified Graybar that the cable would be left in a well-lit storage space he had rented behind the Six Run Grocery Store. On July 20, a reel of the aerial cable was stolen from the storage space and the second reel was stolen within a few days. Shook notified Graybar of both thefts.
>
> Graybar sued Shook for the cost of the aerial cable. The trial court dismissed the suit and the court of appeals affirmed. Graybar appealed.

Higgins, Justice

. . . The plaintiff, having made the error of delivering the nonconforming goods on a moving job in the country, was entitled to notice of the nonconformity sufficient to enable it to repossess the nonconforming goods. The plaintiff was given prompt notice but delayed action for more than three months. The cable was stolen from the defendant's regular storage space where the plaintiff had delivered it. Evidence is lacking that a safer storage space was available. The defendant's workmen moved on, leaving the cable and the responsibility for its safety to the owner.

The plaintiff, . . . contends that . . . [UCC §2-602(2)(b)] required the defendant to exercise reasonable care in holding the rejected goods pending the plaintiff's repossession and removal and that the defendant failed to exercise the required care in storage.

Actually, the plaintiff made an on the spot delivery at a store and dwelling in the country. The defendant's work force was stringing underground cable along the highway and the crew was in continual movement. Obviously the crew could not be expected to carry with it two thousand pounds of useless cable and was within its rights placing the cable in its regular storage space and notifying the plaintiff of the place of storage. Both parties realized that cable weighing almost a ton would require men and a truck to remove it. Also both parties assumed that the danger of theft from a well lighted store area was a minimal risk. The property itself was a poor candidate for larceny. The cable was permitted to remain where the plaintiff knew it was located for more than three months. The plaintiff, therefore, had ample opportunity to repossess its property.

The Uniform Commercial Code emphasizes promptness and good faith. The prospective purchaser may exercise a valid right to reject and even if he takes possession, responsibility expires after a reasonable time in which the owner has opportunity to repossess. "Where a tender or delivery of goods so fails to conform to the contract as to give a right of rejection the risk of their loss remains on the seller until cure or acceptance." . . . [UCC §2-510(1)]. The defendant did not accept the aerial cable. According to the evidence and the court's findings, the defendant acted in accordance with the request of the owner in attempting to facilitate the return of that which the defendant rejected. The plaintiff with full notice of the place of storage which was at the place of delivery did nothing but sleep on its rights for more than three months. . . .

[Judgment affirmed.]

Buyer in Breach. Under §2-510(3), if the buyer, with respect to conforming goods already identified to the contract, repudiates or otherwise breaches before risk of loss passes to him, risk of loss rests on the buyer for a commercially reasonable time to the extent the seller is not covered by insurance. Assume Seller contracts to sell identified goods for $5,000 to Buyer, delivery to be made on June 30. On June 15, Buyer repudiates the contract and on June 16 the goods are destroyed. The loss is covered by Seller's insurance to the extent of $4,000. Seller can recover $1,000 from Buyer. If the loss had been fully covered, Seller would have no claim against Buyer. If Seller is uninsured, the entire loss falls on Buyer.

A similar rule applies under §2-510(2) if the buyer accepts goods but then rightfully revokes the acceptance. (The requirements for revocation of acceptance are discussed in the next chapter.) In this case, risk of loss is deemed to rest on the seller from the beginning to the extent of any deficiency in the buyer's effective insurance coverage.

The purpose of both §§2-510(2) and 2-510(3) is to give an injured party who controls the goods the benefit of the breaching party's insurance coverage to the extent the loss or damage is not covered by the injured party's insurance. Thus, these provisions effectively place risk of loss on the injured party to the extent of his insurance.

SUMMARY

1. Article 2 defines a sale as the passing of title from the buyer to the seller for a price. Despite its use in such a basic definition, title occupies a limited role under Article 2 because issues previously resolved by title, insurable interest and risk of loss, are governed by separate Code provisions. Nevertheless, the Code contains a residual rule governing the passage of title and resolves ownership disputes arising when a person with

voidable title—for example, one acquiring property through fraud—transfers the property to a good faith purchaser. Article 2 also resolves disputes between persons who entrust goods to a merchant dealing in goods of the kind and buyers of the goods in the ordinary course of the merchant's business.

2. Risk of loss rules determine the rights of the parties if the goods involved in the contract are lost, destroyed, or stolen. Risk of loss is a fundamental issue in a sales contract because if the risk falls on the seller when the goods are destroyed, the seller is liable in damages for nondelivery unless the seller can acquire or manufacture replacement goods. On the other hand, once the risk of loss passes to the buyer, the buyer is liable to the seller for the purchase price of the goods despite the destruction. The buyer should therefore be insured prior to passage of the risk of loss. The buyer acquires an insurable interest upon identification of the goods to the contract. Identification, which is the process by which the particular goods to which the contract refers are designated or specified, always occurs before the risk passes to the buyer.

3. Article 2 contains separate provisions governing risk of loss in the absence of breach and risk of loss when either party is in breach. In the most common case, the absence of breach, separate rules govern risk of loss when (1) the seller is required or authorized to ship the goods to the buyer, (2) the goods are in the hands of a bailee, such as a warehouseman, and are to be delivered without being moved, and (3) all other cases. The basic effect of these rules is to place the risk on the person in possession, who is most likely to be insured against their casualty. If either party breaches the contract, risk of loss is placed upon the breaching party, limited in some cases, however, to the extent of any deficiency in the other party's insurance coverage.

KEY TERMS

title	ostensible ownership
risk of loss	identification of goods
purchaser	future goods
voidable title rule	insurable interest
value	sale on approval
entrusting	sale or return
buyer in the ordinary	
course of business	

QUESTIONS AND PROBLEMS

17-1 On January 1, Seller contracted to sell two photocopiers to Buyer, F.O.B shipping point. Half of the purchase price was paid on January 1, the remainder was due on delivery. On January 2,

Seller selected the two machines to be shipped to the Buyer. On January 3, Seller delivered the machines to the carrier and arranged for shipment to the Buyer. On January 4 the goods were delivered and tendered to Buyer by the carrier. Seller retains a security interest in the goods. Buyer paid final installment on January 5. On what day did title pass to the Buyer? On what day did risk of loss pass to the Buyer? On what day did the Buyer obtain an insurable interest? On what day did the Seller's insurable interest cease, if at all?

17-2 Reread Question 16-2. When should the buyer's insurance coverage be effective in each of the cases listed?

17-3 Section 2-510(1) of the UCC provides that risk of loss remains upon a seller who makes a nonconforming shipment of goods. Is this a wise rule given the basic policy underlying §2-509 (risk of loss in absence of breach)? Policy considerations aside, what problems might be encountered by courts in applying §2-510(1)?

17-4 Hollow, who owned and operated a truck dealership in Decatur, Georgia, sold a truck to Moon on June 22, 1983, promising that the truck would be delivered from Chattanooga, Tennessee where special equipment was being installed on it. Moon paid $8,800 for the truck and received an invoice and papers necessary to obtain a Georgia certificate of title. Although Moon made several inquiries to Hollow regarding date of delivery, the truck was not delivered.

On November 13, 1983, Hollow sold the same truck to Simson, who paid $8,700 for it. Hollow also told Simson the truck was in Chattanooga for installation of equipment. On November 16, Simson went to Chattanooga and took delivery of the truck.

On January 25, 1984, Moon discovered that Simson had possession of the truck. Moon then applied for a certificate of title. After learning that Hollow had absconded with all the money, Moon sued Simson to obtain possession of the truck.

How should the court rule? Cite the UCC provisions that support your answer.

17-5 We Try Harder, Inc. (WTHI) is an automobile leasing company. Although the management of WTHI is knowledgeable about car leasing, it is unfamiliar with many of the legal principles affecting its business. Consider the following events that recently occurred:

(a) WTHI leased an automobile to Al Newman.
    Al owned and operated Al's Auto Center, an

automobile dealership. Al fraudulently obtained title in the name of Al's Auto Center to the automobile from the state and placed it on the dealership lot. Marvin purchased the car for cash and title was transferred to him. Al suddenly left town and WTHI wants its automobile returned. If WTHI sues Marvin, to whom should the court award title? Explain, citing appropriate UCC provisions.

(b) To make room for a new shipment of 1985 automobiles, WTHI decided to sell its 1983 cars. WTHI consigned the automobiles to American Auto Auction (AAA), an auto wholesaler. WTHI and AAA signed a five page contract by which AAA agreed not to accept any bids on the cars without prior approval of WTHI. The contract further provided that upon WTHI's approving the acceptance of a bid, WTHI would provide the documents of title to the purchaser. AAA sold ten of the cars for cash to Sam, who owned and operated a used car lot, without providing certificates of title. AAA also sold one of the cars to Marylou for cash, again without providing a certificate of title. AAA failed to obtain WTHI's approval for the sale. AAA is in bankruptcy. If WTHI sues Sam and Marylou, to whom should the court award title? Explain, citing appropriate UCC provisions.

(c) A Cadillac was stolen from WTHI's lot. The car eventually came into the hands of a used automobile wholesaler who sold it to Silver Hill Motors. Silver Hill then sold the car to Betty Bonafide, a good faith purchaser for value. Silver Hill promised to obtain and deliver a certificate of title to Betty. Several days later, however, the police seized the Cadillac as stolen property. To whom should the court award title to the car? Explain, citing appropriate UCC provisions.

17-6 Johnson & Johnson sold goods to DAL International Trading Co., an agency of the Polish People's Republic, based upon DAL's fraudulent oral misrepresentation that the goods would be sold only in Poland. Subsequently, however, the goods were resold in the U.S. through various middlemen to Quality King Manufacturing, Inc. at prices lower than Johnson & Johnson's United States wholesale price. Johnson sued to enjoin the sale or distribution of the goods on the ground that Quality King was not a good faith purchaser under UCC §2-403(1). Johnson & Johnson argued that although Quality King had no actual knowledge of the alleged fraud, the "gray market" transaction was conducted under suspicious circumstances, and that Quality King did not act in good faith because it failed to make inquiries that would have uncovered the voidable title. Should the court grant the injunction? Explain.

17-7 Seven Seas Shipbuilders, Inc. sold a mast for a yacht to Peter Posh. Seven Seas agreed to deliver the mast after installing some hardware on it. Peter made a $4,500 down payment. Prior to completion of the installation, however, a fire destroyed Seven Seas' premises including the mast. Seven Seas' insurance covered only the buildings of its business.

(a) Who bore the risk of loss at the time of the fire? Explain, citing the appropriate UCC provisions.

(b) Prior to the fire, Seven Seas had asked Peter whether his insurance would cover it. Peter had replied that the mast would be fully covered under his insurance. Do these additional facts change your answer in (a)? Explain, citing appropriate UCC provisions.

Chapter 15 discussed the basic principles of legal and equitable remedies applicable to both Code and common law contracts. This chapter examines additional specific obligations and remedies of both the buyer and seller in contracts for the sale of goods. It will be helpful to briefly review Chapter 15 because much of the following material requires a basic understanding of contract remedies.

Remedial Philosophy of the Code

Article 2 provides both an aggrieved[1] buyer and seller with a wide variety of remedies. The UCC, however, explicitly rejects any doctrine of "election of remedy." The remedies available under the Code are not exclusive; under §1-106(1), the in-

jured party may resort to any combination of available relief in order that "the aggrieved party may be put in as good a position as if the other party had fully performed." With this goal in mind, whether pursuit of one remedy rules out another depends entirely on the facts of the case.

Contractual Modification or Limitation of Remedy

Freedom of contract is a basic policy of the Code. Consistent with this policy, §2-719 permits the parties to provide for remedies in their contract in addition to or in substitution for those outlined in the UCC and to limit or alter the measure of damages otherwise available. For example, the buyer's remedies may be limited to a return of the goods and repayment of the price, or to repair or replacement of a nonconforming delivery.

Despite the parties' ability to limit or modify remedies, there must be minimum adequate remedies available to an aggrieved buyer or seller. Inadequate contractual remedies are often present in adhesion contracts in which the drafting party dictates the relief available upon breach. If these remedies are unreasonably favorable to that party or unfairly limit available remedies, they may be deleted or modified as unconscionable under §2-302 discussed in Chapter 10. This same approach applies to consequential damages, which may be limited or excluded under §2-719(3) by contract unless the effect is unconscionable. Thus, although the

---

1. "Aggrieved party" as used in the UCC means a party entitled to resort to a remedy. §1-201(2).

contract may modify or limit remedies, such terms invite close judicial scrutiny to determine if they are unconscionable.

Unless expressly agreed to the contrary, the contractually provided remedy is optional, not exclusive. Under §2-719(2), however, if the circumstances cause an exclusive or limited remedy to "fail of its essential purpose" or to deprive either party of the substantial value of the bargain, Code remedies are reinstated. In the following case, the court was required to determine whether a limited remedy failed of its essential purpose.

Phillips Petroleum Company v. Bucyrus-Erie Company
388 N.W.2d 584 (Wis. 1986)

In the early 1970s, plaintiff Phillips Petroleum Company solicited proposals from manufacturers to construct and sell cranes to be used on Phillips' offshore oil drilling platforms located near Norway in the North Sea. Information provided by Phillips described weather conditions and wind and wave stresses under which the cranes would have to perform. Phillips accepted a written proposal submitted by defendant Bucyrus-Erie Company and the parties agreed that adapters, used to place the cranes on the drilling rigs, would be made of a grade of steel specified in design drawings approved by Phillips. The cranes and adapters were installed in 1973. On February 28, 1974, a crane broke loose from a platform and fell into the sea. Subsequent analysis revealed that the adapter rings were not constructed of the steel specified in the drawings and that Bucyrus-Erie had substituted steel that was too brittle for the intended use.

Phillips sued for damages for breach of contract but Bucyrus-Erie claimed that the written proposal limited its liability to replacement of any defective part F.O.B. Erie, Pennsylvania. This provision appeared in the proposal under the heading "Warranty." The trial court ruled that the limitation of liability clause was ineffective because it failed of its essential purpose in violation of §2-719(2) of the UCC. The court found Bucyrus-Erie liable for breach of contract and awarded damages of $1.6 million. The appellate court reversed and Phillips appealed to the Wisconsin Supreme Court.

Heffernan, Chief Justice

. . . Although we do not disagree with the trial court's conclusion that a disclaimer of liability or a limitation on damages that is inappropriately masked under a heading captioned, "Warranty," is in itself a reason to disregard it, we look to the merits of the Phillips' argument that damages ought not be limited to replacement of the defective part F.O.B. Erie because, under [§2-719(2) of the UCC]:

> "(2) Where circumstances cause an exclusive or limited remedy to fail of its essential purpose, remedy may be had as provided in [this Act]."

Here, the Phillips' argument is that to replace the adapters at Erie—a site thousands of miles from where the replacement was needed—is simply an unrealistic remedy. The adapter ring only failed on one crane, but the domino effect of that failure was that none of the Bucyrus-Erie cranes purchased by Phillips could be used until they were repaired and certified. Thus, the damage was not limited to the replacement value of a single part even on the 13 cranes. The defect resulted in the total failure of Phillips' ability to use expensive and complex equipment for a protracted period of time. This was damage caused for the "want of a horseshoe nail."

The circumstances here, the possibility of a physical failure because of wind and wave stresses of the North Sea, were those that should have been reasonably anticipated. Here the Bucyrus-Erie Company not only culpably, though perhaps inadvertently, used a type of steel that, in view of the express warranty agreed to by the seller and the buyer, was destined to fail with all the consequent, and to be anticipated, injury to the purchaser. The essential purpose of any damage award is to make the injured party whole. . . . The replacement or the supply of new conforming adapters at Erie, Pennsylvania, only minusculely compensated the purchaser. The circumstances here require that the compensation fulfill the essential purpose of all damage awards—to make the innocent party whole. It is understandable that the boilerplate limit on damages may be appropriate in most cases. In most cases, the timely supplying of the deficient part will make a party whole. Not so in this case. While both parties to this action are giants in their areas of enterprise, we do not feel that the Uniform

Commercial Code makes giant corporations fair game for either intentional sharp practices or a skewed rule of law. Under our justice system, the persona of the corporation is entitled to be treated fairly in commercial transactions. While we see no wilfulness or any evidence of subjective sharp practices in the performance of the contract, it is apparent that the remedy offered by Bucyrus-Erie's contract (concealed or masked in the warranty section) provides damages that are, in the circumstances, unconscionably low. The damage clause is unreasonable. . . . [I]t is our conclusion that the philosophy of damage awards expressed by this court . . . leads to . . . a conclusion consistent with the underlying philosophy of the Uniform Commercial Code that there be at least a fair quantum of remedy for breach of obligations. [UCC §2-719, Official Comment 1.]

Accordingly, in accordance with the code, the damage remedy is not that purportedly provided in the documents, but "remedy may be had as provided in [the UCC]" as applied by the trial court. . . .

[Judgment reversed.]

Buyers' Obligations

As noted in Chapter 14, proper performance by the seller of a Code contract is governed generally by the "perfect tender" rule of §2-601; that is, if the goods or the tender of delivery fail *in any respect* to conform[2] to the contract, the buyer is entitled to (1) *reject* the entire shipment, or (2) *accept* the entire shipment, or (3) accept any commercial unit[3] or units and reject the rest. The rights and obligations of the buyer after the seller's tender or delivery are discussed in the following material. First, the rights and obligations of the parties after a buyer's "rejection" are discussed. These include the

manner of rejection, the buyer's duties with respect to rightfully rejected goods in his possession, and the limited right of the seller to cure or correct a nonconforming delivery. Second, the concept and effect of "acceptance," and the circumstances justifying the buyer's revocation of acceptance are discussed.

Rejection—Buyers' Obligations

After delivery, the buyer generally has the right to inspect the goods. If, after inspection, the goods are found to be nonconforming, the buyer is entitled to reject them. To be effective, §2-602(1) provides that the **rejection**

1. must be made within a reasonable time after tender or delivery of the goods, and
2. the buyer must seasonably[4] notify the seller of rejection.

To fully protect a buyer's rights, the buyer should also state the particular defect or defects justifying rejection, because a buyer, under §2-605(1), may not rely upon unstated defects to justify rejection or establish breach if:

1. the seller could have corrected the defect had it been seasonably stated, and
2. as *between merchants,* the buyer, after written request by the seller, fails to provide a full and final written statement of all defects.

A buyer who rightfully rejects a delivery after taking possession of the goods must hold the goods with reasonable care for a time sufficient to allow the seller to remove them, but has no further obligation concerning them. If the seller fails to give instructions within a reasonable time after notification of rejection, the buyer (merchant or nonmerchant) may: (1) store the rejected goods, *or* (2) reship them to the seller, *or* (3) resell them for the seller's account. In all cases, the buyer is entitled to reimbursement for expenses.[5]

---

2. As used in the UCC, goods or conduct are "conforming" or "conform to the contract" when they are in accordance with the obligations under the contract. §2-106(2).

3. A "commercial unit" is a unit of goods treated as a single whole for purposes of sale and whose value is significantly impaired by division. A commercial unit may be a single article (for example, a machine), a set of articles (for example, an assortment of sizes), or a quantity (for example, a bale or carload). UCC §2-105(6).

4. The buyer acts "seasonably" by notifying the seller (1) at or within the time agreed in the contract, or (2) if no time is agreed at or within a reasonable time. UCC §1-204(3).

5. UCC §§2-602(2), 2-604.

Section 2-603 imposes certain additional responsibilities upon a *merchant* buyer who rightfully rejects goods. If the seller has no agent or place of business at the place of rejection, the buyer must follow any reasonable instructions from the seller concerning the disposition of the goods. The seller may instruct the buyer to reship, store, or resell the goods, or deliver them to a third party. The seller must, however, reimburse the buyer for any expenses incurred, including a commission if the buyer resells. If the seller gives no instructions and the goods are perishable or threaten to decline quickly in value, the buyer must make a reasonable effort to resell them on the seller's behalf. The foregoing rules are designed to give both merchant and non-merchant buyers, who reject in good faith, reasonable leeway in disposing of the goods and to prevent the buyer's conduct from being interpreted as an "acceptance" of them.

Cure—§2-508

The remedy of **cure,** stated in §2-508, protects the seller in two specific situations against the effects of a rejection by the buyer resulting from the seller's nonconforming tender or delivery. Cure is perhaps the most important of the various Code provisions relieving a seller from the harsh effect of the "perfect tender rule" generally governing sales contracts. Cure severely limits the buyer's right to reject for minor, insubstantial defects.

The seller is given the right to cure (correct a defective performance) if the buyer rejects a nonconforming tender or delivery and the *time for performance agreed in the contract has not passed.* In this situation, the seller may cure by seasonably notifying the buyer of an intention to cure, and making a conforming delivery within the time called for by the contract. Assume Charles contracts to sell and deliver 500 navy blue t-shirts to Amy for $2,000, delivery to be made "on or before June 1." On May 15, Charles inadvertently ships 500 royal blue shirts that Amy immediately rejects because they are the wrong color. Charles may cure by notifying Amy and delivering navy blue shirts by June 1.

A seller is also given an opportunity to cure when the buyer rejects a nonconforming tender that the seller *had reasonable grounds to believe would be acceptable*. In this situation, the seller may cure by seasonably notifying the buyer of an intention to cure, and substituting a conforming tender within "a further reasonable time." Note that the seller is always allowed to cure if a conforming delivery can be made within the time agreed upon for performance, but is allowed to cure after that time only if the original tender was made on the reasonable belief that it would be acceptable. In this second case, the seller is then granted a further reasonable time to cure.

The rationale for the second type of cure is to avoid injustice to the seller resulting from a surprise rejection by the buyer. The seller must, however, have "reasonable grounds to believe" that the tender would be acceptable. Thus, if a reasonable businessperson would know that the goods are unacceptable, either because of the nature of the goods themselves or the surrounding circumstances, the cure remedy is unavailable.

For example, the seller may reasonably believe that goods that are substantial equivalents of those called for, or that are a newer model, are acceptable. Or, the seller may believe that slight quantity or assortment variations will be tolerated. Or a retailer selling manufactured goods of a reputable manufacturer in the original cartons has reasonable grounds to believe that the goods will be acceptable. Commonly the seller's belief is grounded on trade usage, the contract itself, or prior dealing of the parties.

If the seller successfully cures (corrects the defective performance), the buyer may no longer *reject.* The buyer may, however, be entitled to recover damages under §2-714 (discussed in Chapter 19) governing buyer's damages for breach with respect to accepted goods. Additionally, the buyer may recover for any incidental damages.

The following case illustrates the cure remedy in a consumer sale and its relationship to the perfect tender rule.

Ramirez v. Autosport
440 A.2d 1345 (N.J. 1982)

On July 20, 1978, plaintiffs Mr. and Mrs. Ramirez entered into a contract to purchase a camper van from defendant Autosport. They were granted an allowance of $4,700 for a van that they traded in, and agreed to pay an additional $9,900 for the new van. The Ramirezes left their old van with Autosport and delivery of the new vehicle was scheduled for August 3.

On August 3, the Ramirezes returned to Autosport with a check to pick up the new camper. The vehicle, however, exhibited several defects: the paint was scratched, the electric and sewer hookups were missing, and the hubcaps had not been installed. Upon the advice of a salesman, the Ramirezes did not accept delivery because the camper was not ready. During the following days Mr. and Mrs. Ramirez called Autosport several times but were told the van was not ready. After an Autosport salesman notified them the van was ready for delivery, they went to Autosport on August 14. Workers were still touching up the paint and the dining area cushions were soaking wet because the windows had been left open, so the Ramirezes again refused to accept delivery. Autosport notified them the van would be ready on September 1; however, on that date they again were asked to wait. After waiting 1½ hours, the Ramirezes left. On October 5, they returned to Autosport with an attorney and requested return of the van they had traded in. Autosport refused and subsequently sold it to an innocent third party for $4,995.

On November 20, Mr. and Mrs. Ramirez sued Autosport seeking rescission of the contract; Autosport counterclaimed for damages for breach of contract. The trial court ruled in favor of Mr. and Mrs. Ramirez and ordered Autosport to pay $4,700 in lieu of returning the van that had been traded in. The appellate court affirmed. Autosport appealed.

Pollock, Justice

. . . This case raises several issues under the Uniform Commercial Code ("the Code" and "UCC") concerning whether a buyer may reject a tender of goods with minor defects and whether a seller may cure the defects. We consider also the remedies available to the buyer, including cancellation of the contract. The main issue is whether plaintiffs, Mr. and Mrs. Ramirez, could reject the tender by defendant, Autosport, of a camper van with minor defects and cancel the contract for the purchase of the van. . . .

Our initial inquiry is whether a consumer may reject defective goods that do not conform to the contract of sale. . . .

In the nineteenth century, sellers were required to deliver goods that complied exactly with the sales agreement. . . . That rule, known as the "perfect tender" rule, remained part of the law of sales well into the twentieth century. . . .

The chief objection to the continuation of the perfect tender rule was that buyers in a declining market would reject goods for minor nonconformities and force the loss on surprised sellers. . . .

To the extent that a buyer can reject goods for any nonconformity, the UCC retains the perfect tender rule. Section 2-106 states that goods conform to a contract "when they are in accordance with the obligations under the contract". . . . Section 2-601 authorizes a buyer to reject goods if they "or the tender of delivery fail in any respect to conform to the contract". . . . The Code, however, mitigates the harshness of the perfect tender rule and balances the interests of buyer and seller. . . . The Code achieves that result through its provisions for revocation of acceptance and cure [UCC §§2-608, 2-508]. . . .

Underlying the Code provisions is the recognition of the revolutionary change in business practices in this century. The purchase of goods is no longer a simple transaction in which a buyer purchases individually-made goods from a seller in a face-to-face transaction. Our economy depends on a complex system for the manufacture, distribution, and sale of goods, a system in which manufacturers and consumers rarely meet. Faceless manufacturers mass-produce goods for unknown consumers who purchase those goods from merchants exercising little or no control over the quality of their production. In an age of assembly lines, we are accustomed to cars with scratches, television sets without knobs and other products with all kinds of defects. Buyers no longer expect a "perfect tender". If a merchant sells defective goods, the reasonable expectation of the parties is that the buyer will return those goods and that the seller will repair or replace them.

Recognizing this commercial reality, the Code permits a seller to cure imperfect tenders. Should the seller fail to cure the defects, whether substantial or not, the balance shifts again in favor of the buyer, who has the right to cancel or seek damages [UCC §2-711]. . . . In general, economic considerations would induce sellers to cure minor defects. . . . Assuming the seller does not cure, however, the buyer should be permitted to exercise his remedies under [UCC §2-711]. . . . The Code remedies for consumers are to be liberally construed, and the buyer should have the option of cancelling if the seller does not provide conforming goods. . . .

To summarize, the UCC preserves the perfect tender rule to the extent of permitting a buyer to reject goods for any nonconformity. Nonetheless, that rejection does not automatically terminate the contract. A seller may still effect a cure and preclude unfair rejection and cancellation by the buyer. . . .

The trial court found that Mr. and Mrs. Ramirez had rejected the van within a reasonable time under [UCC §2-602]. . . . The court found that on August 3, 1978 Autosport's salesman advised the Ramirezes not to accept the van and that on August 14, they rejected delivery and Autosport agreed to replace the cushions. Those findings are supported by substantial credible evidence, and we sustain them. . . . Although the trial court did not find whether Autosport cured the defects within a reasonable time, we find that Autosport did not effect a cure. Clearly the van was not ready for delivery during August, 1978 when Mr. and Mrs. Ramirez rejected it, and Autosport had the burden of proving that it had corrected the defects. Although the Ramirezes gave Autosport ample time to correct the defects, Autosport did not demonstrate that the van conformed to the contract on September 1. In fact, on that date, when Mr. and Mrs. Ramirez returned at Autosport's invitation, all they received was discourtesy.

. . . The court properly concluded that plaintiffs were entitled to "rescind"—i.e., to "cancel"—the contract. . . .

[Judgment affirmed.]

Acceptance of Goods—§§2-606 and 2-607

The buyer's alternative to rejecting delivered goods is to "accept" them. Several important legal con-

sequences occur upon acceptance. Under §2-606, a buyer **accepts** goods in three situations. First, acceptance occurs if, after a reasonable opportunity to inspect, the buyer indicates to the seller that the goods are conforming or that he will take them despite their nonconformity. Acceptance also occurs if, after a reasonable opportunity to inspect, the buyer fails to make an effective rejection as discussed in the preceding subsection. Assume Tapeco contracts to sell 200 cases of cassette tapes to Billings, which Tapeco delivers on June 1. Billings performs an inspection and places the tapes in her warehouse. Six months later Billings attempts to reject the shipment. Billings has accepted the goods. Finally, a buyer accepts if he does any act inconsistent with an initial claim that he has rejected the goods. For example, a buyer who first attempts to reject and then acts inconsistently—such as by making part payment on the price, or using the goods in the buyer's business or manufacturing process, or modifying or repairing the goods—has accepted the goods. Note that any use of the goods by the buyer *prior to* discovering their defective nature does not constitute an acceptance.

Once a buyer has accepted goods, several important legal consequences, stated in Section 2-607, follow:

1. The buyer must pay at the contract rate for any goods accepted.

2. After acceptance, the buyer may no longer *reject* the goods. Acceptance does not, however, impair any other remedy available to the buyer for nonconformity. For example, the buyer may recover dollar damages for any defects in the goods accepted. However, it is important to note that buyers' remedies under the UCC differ depending upon whether or not the goods in question have been accepted or rejected.

3. If a tender has been accepted, the buyer must notify the seller within a reasonable time after discovery of any breach or is barred from *any* remedy.

4. After acceptance, the buyer has the burden of establishing any breach.

Revocation of Acceptance—§2-608

In certain limited circumstances, the buyer may revoke a previous acceptance of goods. The requirements for **revocation of acceptance,** stated in §2-608, are more stringent than those imposed upon the buyer rejecting the goods initially. The rationale for this approach is that, in the revocation case, the buyer has been in possession of the goods long enough to constitute an acceptance. In this situation, it is more likely that the problem was caused or at least magnified by the buyer's use of the goods, rather than any initial defect in the goods themselves. Further, due to the passage of time or other factors, the market value of the goods may have substantially deteriorated resulting in greater loss to the seller. Additionally, the buyer may have benefited by using the goods prior to revocation.

Accordingly, §2-608(1) allows a buyer to revoke a previous acceptance in two situations only if the nonconformity of the goods "substantially impairs"[6] their value to him. First, the buyer may accept goods known to be nonconforming on the reasonable assumption that the nonconformity would be corrected, or cured, by the seller. If the seller fails to cure the defect within a reasonable time, the buyer may revoke acceptance. This situation is common in sales of automobiles or other complex machinery exhibiting defects that the seller promises, but is subsequently unable, to remedy.

In this case the buyer accepts with knowledge of the defect. A buyer who is unaware of the nonconformity at the time of acceptance may revoke acceptance if acceptance was induced either by the difficulty of discovering the nonconformity before acceptance or by the seller's assurances causing the buyer to delay discovery. Absent fraud or mistake, the buyer's right to return accepted goods under the Code is limited to the two situations outlined above. That is, the concept of "revocation of acceptance" generally replaces "rescission" for Code contracts.

Revocation of acceptance must be made within a reasonable time after the buyer discovers (or should have discovered) the defect and before any substantial change in the condition of the goods. Additionally, the revocation is not effective until the buyer notifies the seller of it. The revocation and notice to the seller must occur within a reasonable time. Whether the buyer has acted within a reasonable time is a frequently litigated issue in both rejection and revocation cases. An effective revocation gives the buyer the same rights and duties regarding the goods as if he had rejected them initially.[7]

At issue in the following case was whether a buyer who accepted without knowledge of the defect had properly revoked his acceptance.

Birkner v. Purdon
183 N.W.2d 598 (Mich. App. 1970)

Defendant Robert Purdon ordered over 3,000 "Number One" Christmas trees from plaintiff Martin Birkner, a grower and wholesaler of scotch pines. "Number One" is a standard grade of tree that is over 5½ feet tall, with three good sides and without holes or gaps. When the trees were delivered, Purdon questioned whether they were of the specified quality but accepted delivery after Birkner assured him that they were good, saleable trees. After Purdon was unable to sell most of the trees, he requested that the United States Department of Agriculture (USDA) inspect the trees. The USDA inspection revealed that a large percentage of the trees were not of "Number One" quality. Purdon then sent a telegram to Birkner revoking acceptance of the Christmas trees.

Birkner sued Purdon for breach of contract to recover the purchase price of the trees; Purdon counterclaimed alleging that the trees did not meet the contract requirements. The trial court ruled in favor of Purdon and Birkner appealed.

---

6. This is the same test governing breach of Code contracts performed in installments. See discussion of §2-612 in Chapter 14.

---

7. UCC §§2-608(2), (3). As stated in §2-510(2), discussed in Chapter 17, when the buyer rightfully revokes acceptance, the risk of loss is treated as originally resting on the seller to the extent of any deficiency in the buyer's insurance coverage. However, as indicated above, to revoke an acceptance, the buyer must act before any substantial change in the condition of the goods not caused by their own defects. Therefore, if the goods are destroyed after acceptance but before revocation, the buyer is precluded from revoking acceptance and thus may not invoke §2-510(2).

Gillis, Presiding Judge

. . . We conclude there was sufficient competent evidence from which the trial judge could find plaintiff was obliged to supply good saleable trees and in fact delivered trees of inferior quality. . . .

Plaintiff . . . contends that defendant failed to reject the trees in a timely manner, thus waiving any claim of nonconformity. Defendant received the first of 5 shipments of trees on November 24, 1967. On December 21, 1967, immediately after obtaining the results of the USDA inspection and consulting with his attorney, defendant sent plaintiff a telegram revoking his acceptance of the trees.

U.C.C. §2-608 . . . provides in part:

> "(1) The buyer may revoke his acceptance of a lot or commercial unit whose nonconformity substantially impairs its value to him if he has accepted it. . . .
>
> "(b) [W]ithout discovery of such nonconformity if his acceptance was reasonably induced either by the difficulty of discovery before acceptance or by the seller's assurances. . . ."

There was testimony tending to show that immediate discovery of the defects was difficult because of the time required for the trees to open up after being flattened in transit; that on several occasions defendant had been expressly assured by plaintiff that the trees delivered were of good quality; that, because of the slow build-up of the selling season, it was difficult to judge the merchantability of the trees until the weekend of the 17th; and, finally, that defendant's relative inexperience limited his appreciation of the defects. In light of these circumstances, the question of defendant's alleged delay was one of fact for resolution by the trier. . . . The trial judge found that defendant had revoked his acceptance within a reasonable time under all the circumstances. We find no error. . . .

[Judgment affirmed.]

Buyers' Remedies

Basic Remedies

Section 2-711 lists the basic remedies available to an injured buyer in four situations: (1) when the buyer rightfully rejects the goods, (2) when the buyer justifiably revokes his acceptance, (3) when the seller fails to deliver, and (4) when the seller repudiates the contract. Note that in all of these situations, the buyer either never received the goods or justifiably returned them to the seller. If nonconforming goods are delivered and the buyer elects to accept them anyway, damages are nevertheless recoverable for breach of warranty under §2-714, the type of breach covered in the next chapter. The manner of determining damages therefore differs depending upon whether the goods have been accepted (§2-714) or not (§2-711).

Assuming the case falls into one of the four situations listed above, the buyer has various rights, outlined below.

Cancellation and Recovery of Amount Paid. The buyer may cancel the contract. **Cancellation** occurs when either party puts an end to the contract because of breach by the other. Cancellation discharges all obligations still executory on both sides. However, the cancelling party retains all remedies available for breach relating to both prior and future performance.[8] In addition to being relieved of any further obligation to pay the price, the buyer may recover whatever amounts he has already paid on the price.

Recovery of Damages. Whether or not the contract is cancelled, the buyer is entitled to recover damages in addition to prior payments on the price. Section 2-712 is used to determine damages when the buyer covers—that is, acquires substitute goods from another seller. Section 2-713 governs cases when the buyer does not cover. Both of these provisions are discussed below.

Recovery of Identified Goods or Specific Performance. If the goods have been identified to the contract, and the seller fails to deliver or repudiates, the buyer may recover them from the seller in certain limited circumstances. Additionally, as discussed in Chapter 15, specific performance may be awarded if the goods are unique or in other proper circumstances.

---

8. UCC §§2-106(3), (4).

Recovery of Damages

When the seller breaches, the buyer may elect to pursue the basic remedy at law: an award of money damages.

Cover. Under §2-712(1), after breach the buyer may **cover** by purchasing or contracting to purchase goods to substitute for those due from the seller, if the buyer acts in good faith and without unreasonable delay. Cover is a primary means used by buyers in sales contracts to mitigate damages after breach. Therefore, although the buyer is not required to cover,[9] failure to do so may prevent the buyer from recovering damages that could have been avoided by cover. Further, as stated in §2-715(2)(a), a buyer may only recover for consequential damage "which could not reasonably be prevented by cover or otherwise." Additionally, inability to cover is a strong factor to be considered in determining whether or not specific performance should be granted to the buyer. In short, it is usually in the buyer's best interest to make a good faith attempt to cover.[10]

Under §2-712(2), a buyer who covers is entitled to recover from the seller:

> the difference between the cover price and the contract price, *plus* incidental damages, *plus* consequential damages *minus* expenses saved as a consequence of the seller's breach.

Buyer's **incidental damages** stated in §2-715(1) include: (1) expense incurred in inspection, receipt, transportation, and care of rightfully rejected goods, (2) expenses and commissions incurred in effecting cover, and (3) any other reasonable expenses incident to the breach. Consequential damages are available under the *Hadley v. Baxendale* foreseeability test discussed in Chapter 15.[11] Assume Bates, Inc. contracts to purchase steel from Steelco for $10,000 to be used in Bates's manufac-

turing process. Steelco breaches the contract by failing to deliver and Bates immediately acquires substitute steel from MacGregor for $12,000. Because Bates was able to cover, it suffered no disruption in its manufacturing process and therefore lost no profits. Bates did, however, pay Smith a $200 commission for arranging the contract with MacGregor. Bates is entitled to recover $2,200 from Steelco in damages: the cover price ($12,000) less the contract price ($10,000) plus incidental damages ($200). Had Bates's production process been interrupted as a result of Steelco's breach, lost profits may be recoverable as consequential damages if they were foreseeable.

Damages in Absence of Cover. If the buyer does not cover, damages for nondelivery or repudiation are computed under §2-713(1), which awards the buyer:

> the difference between the market price at the time the buyer learned of the breach and the contract price *plus* incidental damages *plus* consequential damages *minus* expenses saved as a consequence of the seller's breach.

Under §2-713(2), "market price" is determined at the *place for tender*. In cases of rejection after arrival or revocation of acceptance, however, market price is determined at the *place of arrival*. Thus, damages are measured according to the price prevailing at the time and in the place at which the buyer would have covered had he chosen to do so.

The UCC, in §§2-723 and 2-724, adopts a liberal approach to determine market price. For example, if evidence of the price at a given time is unavailable, the court may use the prevailing price existing within any reasonable time before or after that time. If the price at a certain place is unavailable, a commercially reasonable substitute place may be used allowing, however, for the cost of transportation between the two places. Additionally, the court may use market price quotations contained in official publications, trade journals, newspapers, or periodicals to show market price of goods traded in any established market.

The §2-713(1) formula protects the buyer who does not become aware of the seller's breach immediately upon tender. That is, the market price is measured on the date the buyer learned of the

---

9. UCC §2-712(3). The buyer may choose to sue for damages for nondelivery under §2-713 discussed below.

10. The buyer's right to replevy identified goods from the seller (discussed on page 405) is also dependent upon the buyer's inability to cover. Mitigation, consequential damages, and specific performance are covered in Chapter 15.

11. UCC §2-715(2)(a). See discussion on page 340.

breach, which may be long after the seller's tender of nonconforming goods or outright failure to deliver. For example, the goods may be tendered to the distant buyer under an "F.O.B. shipping point" contract in which tender occurs on delivery to the carrier. In this case, the buyer is not jeopardized if the market price rises between the date of the breach and the date he learns of it, because damages are measured at the later date.

The following case illustrates computation of damages under §2-713. Note the important consequences of the buyer's failure to effect cover.

Panhandle Agri-Service, Inc. v. Becker
644 P.2d 413 (Kan. 1982)

Plaintiff Panhandle Agri-Service Inc. (Panhandle) and defendant Norman Becker entered into a contract by which Becker agreed to sell 10,000 tons of alfalfa (hay) to Panhandle for $45 a ton. The delivery was to be made at Becker's farm in Kansas during the 1978 hay season. Becker delivered most of the hay but was unable to deliver 912 tons, 256 pounds during 1978, so Panhandle agreed to accept the balance during the 1979 season. During the 1979 season, however, Becker refused to deliver any more hay to Panhandle.

Panhandle sued Becker for breach of contract. Testimony at trial established that Panhandle had contracted to resell the hay to a buyer in Texas for $67 per ton for a profit of $22 ($67 − $45 = $22). The trial court incorrectly used 912.256 tons (rather than 912 tons, 256 pounds) in awarding damages. The court calculated damages by multiplying 912.256 by $22 for a gross profit of $20,069.63 and then subtracted $7,371 (the cost of hauling the hay to Texas) to arrive at damages of $12,698.63. Both parties appealed. After concluding that Becker had indeed breached the contract, the Kansas Supreme Court reviewed the trial court's determination of damages.

Fromme, Justice

. . . We now turn to the question of what was the proper method of arriving at the amount of damages. As previously stated Panhandle argues on appeal it should be entitled to loss of profits of $20,069.63. Becker argues the entire judgment

should be set aside but, if not, the judgment should be reduced to . . . show a deduction from the loss of profits claimed by plaintiff of the costs of trucking from Kansas to Texas.

Under the facts of this case we believe both contentions are in error. [The court then quoted §2-713 of the UCC.]

The trial court determined that the market price of alfalfa hay at Garden City, Kansas, in 1979, was $62.00 per ton. The contract price agreed on by the parties was $45.00. So the measure of damages for nondelivery or repudiation by the seller would be $62.00 less $45.00 or $17.00 per ton, provided no incidental or consequential damages are recoverable in this case, and provided there was no evidence that "cover" was not possible. . . .

Trucking or transportation expense was not deductible from the above figure. Under the Code it is assumed the buyer will attempt to "cover" the merchandise lost by seller's nondelivery at the seller's shipping point. If the buyer seeks a replacement of the merchandise at the shipping point, he would incur replacement shipping costs roughly equivalent to those on the original contract. Thus, by comparison with such a replacement contract there would be no expenses saved in consequence of the seller's breach because we assume the buyer must pay the expenses for shipment under the new contract as well. . . .

As to incidental damages resulting from the seller's breach there was no evidence to support any of the items listed in . . . §2-715(1). Incidental damages concern expenses when goods are tendered and rejected or have to be transported and cared for, or which concern charges in connection with effecting cover.

As to consequential damages . . . §2-715(2)(a) provides:

> (2) Consequential damages resulting from the seller's breach include
>
> (a) any loss resulting from general or particular requirements and needs of which the seller at the time of contracting had reason to know and which could not reasonably be prevented by cover or otherwise.

Failure of the buyer to utilize the remedy of cover when such is reasonably available will preclude recovery of consequential damages, such as loss of profits. . . . However, . . . §2-712, which provides for cover, *i.e.,* the buyer's procurement of substitute goods, states:

> (3) Failure of the buyer to effect cover within this section does not bar him from any other remedy.

Therefore, cover is not a mandatory remedy for the buyer. The buyer is free to choose between cover and damages for nondelivery. In the present record we find no evidence which would support a finding that cover was attempted but found unavailable. We find nothing which would justify the trial court in arriving at damages using loss of business profits which are consequential damages. Consequential damages are limited under . . . §2-715(2)(a) to those instances where it is established that the loss could not reasonably be prevented by cover or otherwise. A buyer does not have to cover under . . . §2-712(3); however, on failure to attempt cover, consequential damages, including loss of profits, cannot be recovered. . . . §2-715(2)(a). . . .

The proper measure of damages under . . . §2-713 based on the evidence before the trial court in this case is the difference between the contract price of $45.00 per ton and the market price of $62.00 at the place of delivery and at the time the buyer learned of nondelivery and repudiation. There was no evidence to indicate the buyer attempted and was unable to obtain cover. The proper award in this case is to be arrived at by subtracting $45.00 from $62.00 to make $17.00 per ton, the basis for arriving at damages. Multiplying 912 tons 256 pounds by $17.00 equals $15,506.18, which is the correct amount of the judgment to be entered in favor of plaintiff, plus interest and costs.

[Judgment affirmed as modified.]

Recovery of Identified Goods

Occasionally, the seller will breach by failing to deliver goods that have been *identified* to the contract. The Code allows the buyer to recover such goods from the seller in two situations.

Replevin. Under §2-716(3) if the goods are identified, the buyer may replevy (recover possession of) them from the seller if the buyer is unable to cover or circumstances indicate that an effort to cover will be unavailing. **Replevin** is a legal remedy whereby a person entitled to possession of goods recovers them from a person who has wrongfully either taken or detained them. Assume Birch is a maker of high quality custom furniture. Birch contracts with Sawyer, a sawmill operator, to purchase 25 oak logs that Birch personally selected from Sawyer's inventory. Before the delivery date, however, the market price of oak skyrocketed due to a severe shortage of the wood. As a result, Sawyer refused to deliver the logs at the contract price. In this case, because the goods are identified to the contract and efforts to cover would be futile, Birch may replevy the logs from Sawyer under §2-716(3). Note that replevin is the buyer's equivalent to the seller's action for the purchase price discussed later in this chapter.

When used as a contract remedy to recover *identified* goods, replevin under §2-716(3) effectively orders specific performance in favor of the injured buyer. If unable to cover when the goods have *not* been identified, the buyer has a very strong case for specific performance under §2-716(1), discussed in Chapter 15. Nevertheless, because specific performance is an equitable remedy, granted only in the discretion of the court, the buyer has no *right* to the goods under these circumstances. The replevin remedy (a legal remedy) gives the buyer a *right* to the goods. The buyer who is unable to cover therefore receives somewhat greater protection if the goods are identified.

Recovery from an Insolvent Seller. A buyer is also entitled to recover identified goods from an *insolvent* seller in certain limited circumstances. Under §2-502(1) if: (1) identified goods are in the possession of the seller, and (2) the buyer has paid all or part of the purchase price, and (3) the seller becomes insolvent within ten days after receipt of the first installment on the price, *then* the buyer may recover the goods from the seller by tendering any unpaid portion of the price. Although §2-402(1) provides that unsecured creditors of the seller take subject to the buyer's rights to recover the goods under both §§2-716(3) and 2-502(1), neither section provides much protection to the buyer if the seller is bankrupt. In this case, the buyer's claim is often subordinated to the rights of the seller's other creditors.

Sellers' Remedies

A buyer may breach the contract (1) by repudiating it before the seller's performance is due, (2) by failing to pay the purchase price of goods delivered, (3) by wrongfully rejecting conforming goods, or (4) by wrongfully revoking a previous acceptance of conforming goods. In these cases, the UCC gives the seller a wide range of remedies (listed in §2-703) including the right to withhold further delivery of goods and cancel the contract. Note that these remedies often differ depending upon the existence and location of the goods. For example, a buyer may breach (1) before delivery while the seller still possesses the goods, or (2) after they have been delivered and are in the buyer's possession, or (3) before either party possesses the goods because they have not yet been procured or manufactured by the seller, or (4) while the goods are in transit (for example, in possession of a carrier such as a railroad or trucking company) from the seller to the buyer. Specific seller's remedies in these various situations are discussed below.

Sellers' Damages with Resale—§2-706

Upon repudiation, breach, or insolvency of the buyer, the seller in possession of the goods has the right to resell them to another buyer. Resale is the seller's equivalent to the buyer's remedy of "cover." If the seller resells in the manner discussed below, the seller may recover, under §2-706(1),

> the difference between the resale price and the contract price *plus* incidental damages (§2-710) *minus* expenses saved as a consequence of the buyer's breach.

Seller's incidental damages include any commercially reasonable charges incurred in connection with (1) stopping delivery, (2) transportation, care, and custody of the goods after the buyer's breach, (3) return or resale of the goods or otherwise resulting from the breach. As discussed in Chapter 15, a seller is not entitled to recover consequential damages, because the buyer's breach almost always involves a failure to pay the price. A failure to pay money has long been recognized as insufficient grounds to support a consequential damage award

even when injury to the creditor is foreseeable. For example, assume Simpson contracts to sell her living room furniture to Frost for $2,500. Frost repudiates the contract and Simpson resells the furniture to Green for $2,200 but only after spending $15 to place a classified advertisement offering the furniture for sale. Simpson's damages are $315—the difference between the resale price and the contract price ($300) plus incidental damages ($15).

Unidentified or Unfinished Goods—§2-704. When the buyer breaches, the seller may be in possession of conforming goods not yet identified to the contract. In this case, §2-704 authorizes the seller to identify them as the goods intended for the breached contract for the purposes of resale. If the goods are unfinished at the time of the breach, the seller may "in the exercise of reasonable commercial judgment for the purposes of avoiding loss" either (1) complete manufacture and wholly identify the goods to the contract, or (2) cease manufacture and resell for scrap or salvage value. Note that ordinarily mitigation principles require that an injured party suspend performance after breach to avoid further expenditure and thus further loss. Under the UCC, however, the seller is protected if he acts reasonably in completing unfinished goods even if it later appears that he could have better avoided loss by stopping manufacture. The burden is upon the buyer to prove that the seller was acting in a commercially unreasonable manner in completing manufacture. By completing manufacture (or by identifying previously unidentified goods), the seller makes the goods available for resale, and if resold, damages are computed under the formula of §2-706 discussed above.

Manner of Resale. In reselling the goods, §2-706 requires the seller to act in good faith and in a commercially reasonable manner to realize as high a price as possible under the circumstances. The resale may be made in a public (auction) or private (by solicitation and negotiation either directly or through a broker) manner. The seller is not accountable to the buyer for any profit made on resale. If resale is made privately, the seller must simply give reasonable notification to the buyer of the intent to resell. If resale is by public auction, however, the seller must reasonably notify the buyer of the time and place of the public sale unless the goods are perishable or threaten to decline speedily in value. This notice enables the buyer to bid at the sale or secure the attendance of other bidders. The seller may also bid at the auction. This right benefits the buyer because it tends to increase the resale price, thus reducing the seller's damages.

The time and place of the resale is governed by standards of "commercial reasonableness." Generally, the time for resale is a reasonable time after the buyer's breach. What is reasonable depends upon all the circumstances of the case including the nature of the goods and the condition of the market. Similarly, the place of resale is flexible so that the seller can dispose of the goods to maximum advantage. A public sale must be made at a usual place or market for such sales if one is reasonably available. The place or market must be one that prospective bidders may reasonably be expected to attend. A market may be "reasonably available" even if the goods must be shipped a considerable distance. The cost of transporting the goods may be recovered from the buyer as part of the seller's incidental damage. The buyer may benefit, however, because the goods are sold where a market for them exists, possibly resulting in a higher resale price.

Sellers' Damages Without Resale—§2-708(1)

When the buyer breaches a sales contract, resale is not always an appropriate remedy. For example, if the breach is by repudiation (as opposed to wrongful rejection or revocation of acceptance), the seller may not yet have acquired or manufactured the goods. In this situation, damages are generally determined under §2-708(1). Under this provision, the seller is entitled to recover

> the difference between the market price at the time and place for tender and the unpaid contract price *plus* incidental damages *minus* expenses saved in consequence of the buyer's breach.

Market price may be proven according to the liberal evidentiary standards discussed in the buyers' remedies material.

Lost Profits—An Alternative Measure of Damages—§2-708(2)

Frequently, the measures of damages discussed above are inadequate to place the injured seller in the same position as full performance. In this case, the Code allows the seller, as an alternative measure, to recover under §2-708(2)

> the *profit* (including reasonable overhead) which the seller would have made from full performance by the buyer *plus* incidental damages *plus* costs reasonably incurred by the seller in manufacture or procurement *minus* payments made by the buyer and proceeds of resale of the goods.

This formula is designed to compensate the seller in primarily two situations: (1) the so-called lost volume case, and (2) when the seller is to manufacture, assemble, or acquire goods for the buyer, but prior to their manufacture or acquisition the buyer breaches.

The Lost Volume Seller. Many businesses sell standardized products or products in essentially unlimited supply. The inadequacy of the basic measure of damages when the buyer breaches a contract for sale of these goods is illustrated by the following example. Silco, a seller of widgets, has an inventory of 1,000 widgets and the ability to produce more if justified by the demand. Silco contracts with Beta for the sale of 10 widgets at a total price of $1,000. Silco's profit on the sale (including reasonable overhead) is 20% of the purchase price, or $200. Beta subsequently breaches the contract, and Silco immediately resells the widgets to Miller for $1,000. In this case, the seller's basic remedy after resale (§2-706) would leave the seller uncompensated because the difference between the contract price and the resale price is zero.[12] Similarly, the difference between the contract price and the market price (§2-708(1)) is also zero. In this situation, therefore, damages under §2-708(2) are appropriate.

Note that in this case Miller didn't buy the 10

---

12. Had it been unable to resell, Silco may be entitled to the entire purchase price under §2-709 as discussed in the following subsection.

widgets because of Beta's breach. Miller would have purchased them whether or not Beta had breached. Thus, assume that Silco *actually* sold 500 widgets for the year, including the sale to Miller. But for Beta's breach, Silco *would have* sold 510 units, not 500. Silco is known as a **lost volume seller**—one who but for the buyer's breach would have had the benefit of *both* the original contract and the resale contract. As such, the proper measure of seller's damage in this case is the lost profit on the sale of 10 units, $200.

Breach Before or During Manufacture. As indicated above, §2-708(2) allows lost profits to be recovered

> together with any incidental damages provided in this article (§2-710), *due allowance for costs reasonably incurred and due credit for payments or proceeds of resale.* (Emphasis added.)

If interpreted literally, this language would deny recovery to the lost volume seller in exactly the situation §2-708(2) is designed to cover. That is, using the above example, Silco would recover lost profits, $200, plus "costs reasonably incurred," $800 (the cost of manufacture), minus "proceeds of resale," $1,000, or nothing. This result is avoided, however, because the cases, commentators, and legislative history of the UCC all indicate that the italicized language quoted above is not meant to apply to the volume seller situation; that is, damages as indicated in the preceding paragraph are appropriate. It is intended instead to apply to the situation discussed below in which the seller discovers the buyer's breach while in the process of manufacturing the goods. This language allows the injured seller to recoup expenditures made on the buyer's behalf (which now prove to be worthless to the seller and cannot be allocated to other contracts) and to realize by resale the junk or salvage value of the unfinished goods or their components, giving credit to the buyer for the proceeds of the salvage.

The application of §2-708(2) to this second situation is illustrated by the following example. Carol contracts to design and build a machine for Ezra for $20,000 to be used in Ezra's manufacturing process. Because it is specially designed, the machine when completed will have no resale value (other than for scrap) on the open market. Carol's price is calculated to include a $2,500 profit. After Carol expends $3,000 on engineering and $2,000 to acquire various component parts, Ezra repudiates the contract. Because resale of the finished machine would be impractical, Carol ceases manufacture. Neither the engineering expenses nor the acquired parts can be applied to any of Carol's other contracts. However, Carol realizes $1,000 upon resale of the component parts for scrap, but must pay Janet, a broker, a $50 commission to effect the salvage.

On these facts, damages under §§2-706 and 2-708(1) are inappropriate because Carol has no finished goods on hand to resell, or upon which to base a market price calculation. Additionally, unless she expends substantial additional sums to complete—certainly a risky alternative which a later court may interpret as a failure to mitigate damages—an action for the purchase price under §2-709, discussed in the following subsection, would be unavailable. Further, Carol has lost the profit she otherwise would have earned on the sale to Ezra. In this situation, therefore, damages computed under §2-708(2) are appropriate. Carol should therefore be entitled to lost profit ($2,500) plus incidental damage (the $50 sales commission) plus costs reasonably incurred on the buyer's behalf ($5,000) minus the proceeds of the sale of the components for scrap ($1,000), or $6,550.

Note that recovery under §2-708(2) is not limited to manufacturers or assemblers but is also available to a so-called jobber, a middleman who acquires the goods from a third party and sells them to the buyer. Assume, for example, that the buyer breaches before the jobber acquires the goods, and, because of the breach, the jobber does not obtain them. Because neither the jobber nor the buyer has the goods, both resale and an action for the purchase price are inappropriate. In such cases, the jobber's lost profit on the sale is the most accurate measure of damages.

The following case illustrates the operation of §2-708(2) and its relationship to §§2-706 and 2-708(1).

National Controls, Inc. v. Commodore Business Machines, Inc.

209 Cal. Rptr. 636 (Cal. App. 1985)

Plaintiff National Controls, Inc. (NCI), a manufacturer of electronic weighing and measuring devices, manufactures and sells the model 3221 electronic microprocessor scale, which is designed to interface with cash registers for use at check-out stands. NCI does not maintain an inventory of the 3221 scales but builds them to order to meet specifications required by different cash registers. In 1981, defendant Commodore Business Machines ordered 900 of the 3221 scales with delivery to be made in four shipments over a four month period. After accepting delivery of 50 scales, Commodore refused to accept or pay for the remaining 850. NCI then sold the 850 scales to another customer, National Semiconductor.

NCI sued Commodore for breach of contract and the trial court ruled in favor of NCI. The trial court found that NCI was a "lost volume seller" and awarded damages of $280,000, the net profit NCI would have realized had Commodore fully performed the contract. Commodore appealed.

Scott, Associate Justice

. . . Damages caused by a buyer's breach or repudiation of a sales contract are usually measured by the difference between the resale price of the goods and the contract price, as provided by Uniform Commercial Code section 2-706. When it is not appropriate to use this difference to measure the seller's loss (as when the goods have not been resold in a commercially reasonable manner), the seller's measure of damages is the difference between the market and the contract prices as provided in [UCC §2-708(1)]. Ordinarily, this measure will result in recovery equal to the value of the seller's bargain. However, under certain circumstances this formula is also not an adequate means to ascertain that value, and the seller may recover his loss of expected profits on the contract under [UCC §2-708(2)]. . . .

When buyers have repudiated a fixed price contract to purchase goods, several courts elsewhere

have construed [UCC §2-708(2)] or its state counterpart to permit the award of lost profits under the contract to the seller who establishes that he is a "lost volume seller," i.e., one who proves that even though he resold the contract goods, that sale to the third party would have been made regardless of the buyer's breach. . . .

Commodore . . . contends that if NCI was entitled to lost profits under the contract, Commodore should have received credit for the proceeds of the resale.

The literal language of [UCC §2-708(2)] does provide some support for that contention: "If the measure of damages provided in subdivision (1) is inadequate to put the seller in as good a position as performance would have done then the measure of damages is the profit (including reasonable overhead) which the seller would have made from full performance by the buyer, *together with . . . due credit for payments or proceeds of resale.*" (Emphasis added.) However, courts elsewhere have uniformly held that the underscored language does not apply to a lost volume seller. . . .

As the court in *Snyder v. Herbert Greenbaum & Assoc., Inc.,* [380 A.2d 618 (Md. 1977)], explained,

> Logically, lost volume status, which entitles the seller to the §2-708(2) formula rather than the formula found in §2-708(1), is inconsistent with a credit for the proceeds of resale. The whole concept of lost volume status is that the sale of the goods to the resale purchaser could have been made with other goods had there been no breach. In essence, the original sale and the second sale are independent events, becoming related only after breach, as the original sale goods are applied to the second sale. To require a credit for the proceeds of resale is to deny the essential element that entitles the lost volume seller to §2-708(2) in the first place—the mutual independence of the contract and the resale.
>
> Practically, if the 'due credit' clause is applied to the lost volume seller, his measure of damages is no different from his recovery under §2-708(1). Under §2-708(1) he recovers the contract/market differential and the profit he makes on resale. If the 'due credit' provision is applied, the seller recovers only the profit he makes on resale plus the difference be-

tween the resale price and the contract price, an almost identical measure to §2-708(1). If the 'due credit' clause is applied to the lost volume seller, the damage measure of 'lost profits' is rendered nugatory, and he is not put in as good a position as if there had been performance.'' [*Id.* at 625.]

In this case, the evidence was undisputed that in 1980 and 1981, NCI's manufacturing plant was operating at approximately 40 percent capacity. The production of the 900 units did not tax that capacity, and the plant could have more than doubled its output of 3221s and still have stayed within its capacity. That evidence was sufficient to support the court's findings that NCI had the capacity to supply both Commodore and National Semiconductor, and that had there been no breach by Commodore, NCI would have had the benefit of both the original contract and the resale contract. Accordingly, the trial court correctly determined that NCI was a lost volume seller, that the usual "contract price minus market price" rule set forth in [UCC §2-708(1)] was inadequate to put NCI in as good a position as performance would have done, and that NCI was therefore entitled to its lost profits on the contract with Commodore, without any set-off for profits on the resale to National Semiconductor. . . .

[Judgment affirmed.]

Sellers' Recovery of the Purchase Price—§2-709

The preceding sellers' remedies award damages based upon the difference between the contract price and the resale or market price, or upon the seller's lost profit. In three limited situations, stated in §2-709, the seller may recover the entire *purchase price* of the goods from the buyer. If the buyer fails to pay the price as it comes due, the seller is entitled to recover (together with incidental damages under §2-710) the price when

1. the goods have been accepted by the buyer, or
2. the goods have been identified to the contract and the seller cannot resell them, or

3. the goods have been damaged or destroyed after risk of loss has passed to the buyer.

These are the only situations in which an action for the price lies.

The basic thrust of the preceding rules is that the seller is generally entitled to recover the price of accepted goods (or when risk of loss has passed to the buyer) but may not recover the price of unaccepted goods unless resale is impracticable due, for example, to market conditions, obsolescence, or because the goods are specially manufactured for the buyer. Thus, unless accepted or destroyed, the burden of disposing of the goods rests on the seller, who is normally in a better position than the buyer to resell because he is in the business of selling goods of that kind. On resale the seller is then entitled to recover damages under §§2-706 or 2-708 as previously discussed.

Sellers' Remedies on Discovery of Buyer's Insolvency

A seller who discovers his buyer to be insolvent has several remedies under §§2-702 and 2-705 of the UCC.

Stopping Delivery. Assuming the buyer has not yet taken possession, §2-702(1) allows a seller who learns of his buyer's insolvency to

1. refuse delivery except for cash, including payment for prior deliveries, and
2. stop delivery of goods in the hands of a carrier or other bailee.[13]

Under §2-705, a seller is entitled to stop delivery of goods in the hands of a carrier or other bailee, such as a warehouseman, not only when the buyer is insolvent, but also when the buyer has repudiated or has failed to make a payment due before delivery. However, because stopping delivery is a burden on the carrier, the right to stop delivery for

---

13.   Section 252 of the *Restatement (Second) of Contracts* adopts a rule analogous to §2-702(1) for application to common law contracts.

reasons *other than insolvency* is limited to large shipments (for example, carload, truckload, planeload, or larger). To stop delivery, the seller must notify the bailee in such a manner to enable it, in the exercise of reasonable diligence, to prevent delivery of the goods. After notification, the bailee must hold and dispose of the goods according to the seller's directions. If a negotiable document of title covers the goods, the bailee need not obey a notification to stop until surrender of the document. If the seller's action in stopping delivery is unjustified, the seller must indemnify the bailee for any ensuing charges or damages. The seller's right to stop delivery ends when the buyer takes physical possession of the goods, or a negotiable document of title covering the goods is negotiated to the buyer, or the bailee acknowledges to the buyer that she holds the goods for the buyer.

Reclamation from an Insolvent Buyer—§2-702(2).

Once the buyer has taken possession of the goods, the seller may reclaim them only in the limited circumstances outlined in §2-702(2). Under this provision, a seller who discovers that the buyer has received goods on credit while insolvent may reclaim the goods by making a demand for their return within ten days after the goods are received by the buyer. The ten-day limit does not apply, however, if the buyer has made a written misrepresentation of solvency to the particular seller seeking to reclaim the goods within three months prior to the delivery. A successful reclamation under this rule bars the seller from recovering any other remedy with respect to them. The rationale for allowing recovery from the insolvent credit buyer is that "any receipt on credit by an insolvent buyer amounts to a tacit business misrepresentation of solvency and therefore is fraudulent as against the particular seller."[14]

Because the buyer receives the goods while insolvent, the seller's right to reclaim is often challenged by the buyer's trustee in bankruptcy, who represents all general unsecured creditors of the buyer and who may seek the goods to satisfy the claims of all creditors. The rights of the reclaiming seller under §2-702(2) as against the trustee in bankruptcy are governed by §546(c) of the Bankruptcy Code, under which the trustee must honor the seller's right to reclaim if the seller has made a written demand to reclaim the goods within ten days after their receipt by the buyer.

Although the Bankruptcy Code generally protects the seller's right to reclaim under §2-702, the requirements are more stringent; first, the demand must be in writing (no writing is explicitly required under §2-702), and second, no exception to the ten-day time limit is made when the buyer has made a written misrepresentation of solvency. Thus, a seller who seeks to use §2-702 should take care to make a written demand on the buyer within ten days. Failure to meet this requirement leaves the reclaiming seller in no better position than other unsecured creditors of a bankrupt debtor (here the buyer), receiving perhaps nothing or only a small fraction on the dollar for the claim.

Statute of Limitations—§2-725

Section 2-725 is the statute of limitations applicable to contracts for the sale of goods. Generally, an action for breach of a sales contract must be commenced within four years after the cause of action arises. The parties may by agreement reduce the limitation period to not less than one year, but may not contractually extend it. By adopting a uniform statute of limitations, the UCC avoids possible conflicting limitation periods applicable to interstate transactions in goods. Further, because most businesses retain business records at least four years, the Code statute increases the likelihood that relevant documentary and other evidence will be available to resolve the claim.

Under §2-725(2) the statute of limitations begins to run when the breach occurs, whether or not the aggrieved party knows of its occurrence. In general, a breach of warranty (discussed in the next chapter) occurs upon the seller's tender of delivery, unless the warranty explicitly extends to future performance of the goods and discovery of any breach must await the time of that performance. For example, the seller may warrant his product "for life," or for "5 years or 50,000 miles, whichever comes first." In this situation, the statute begins to run when the breach is or should be discovered.

---

14. UCC §2-702, Official Comment 2.

SUMMARY

1. The UCC contains a variety of remedies available to both buyers and sellers for breach of sales contracts. These remedies are liberally administered to place the injured party in as good a position as if the other party had fully performed. Consistent with basic Code policy, the parties may contractually provide for remedies in addition to or in lieu of those contained in Article 2.

2. Under the perfect tender rule, if the goods tendered by the seller fail in any respect to conform to the contract, the buyer may accept all of them, reject all of them, or accept some and reject the rest. An effective rejection requires that the buyer reject within a reasonable time and promptly notify the seller. After rejection by the buyer, the seller may be afforded an opportunity to cure or correct the defective performance, thus restricting the buyer's right to reject for minor defects, and often relieving the seller from the harsh effect of the perfect tender rule.

3. A buyer who fails to make an adequate rejection, or indicates that he will take them, or does an act inconsistent with the seller's ownership, accepts the goods. Generally the buyer must pay at the contract rate for goods accepted, but is entitled to damages for defects in the goods. A buyer who has accepted may, however, revoke a previous acceptance under very limited circumstances if their nonconformity substantially impairs their value.

4. Upon rejection or revocation of acceptance by the buyer, or upon the seller's repudiation or failure to deliver, the buyer is entitled to cancel the contract and recover amounts already paid on the price. The buyer is also entitled to recover damages based either upon the difference between the contract price and the market price, or the contract price and the "cover" price—the price at which the buyer acquires goods in substitution for those due from the seller. The buyer may also obtain specific performance in appropriate cases and may recover identified goods from a breaching seller under limited circumstances.

5. Seller's remedies correspond to those available to the buyer. After nonacceptance or repudiation by the buyer, the seller may recover the difference between the market price and the contract price, or if the seller resells, the difference between the resale price and the contract price. If the market price or resale remedy is inadequate to place the seller in as good a position as full performance, then the seller is entitled to recover the profit that he would have made from full performance.

The lost profit remedy is primarily appropriate when the seller is a "lost volume" seller, and when a seller ceases manufacture of, or attempts to acquire, goods after repudiation by the buyer. In lieu of the foregoing remedies, the seller may recover the entire purchase price of goods accepted by the buyer, of goods destroyed after risk of loss has passed to the buyer, and of identified goods that the seller is unable to resell. Finally, the Code provides various remedies to a seller upon discovery of his buyer's insolvency.

6. Article 2 adopts a uniform statute of limitations applicable to contracts for the sale of goods that generally requires that an action for breach of a sales contract be commenced within four years after the breach occurs.

KEY TERMS

rejection	cover
cure	incidental damages
acceptance	replevin
revocation of acceptance	lost volume seller
cancellation	

QUESTIONS AND PROBLEMS

18-1 Under what circumstances does a buyer "accept" a tender of goods under Article 2 of the Uniform Commercial Code? What are the legal consequences of "acceptance"?

18-2 Reliable Electronics has contracted to purchase 10,000 computer chips from Samson Electronics for use in Reliable's electronic calculators. The contract calls for delivery to Reliable's warehouse by June 1, 1984, with payment of the $20,000 purchase price to follow 30 days thereafter. The contract provides that defective chips may not exceed more than 0.001 of the total shipped. Because of the explicit provisions of the contract and past dealing of the parties, Samson knows that a higher defect percentage will not be tolerated, and that significant defects will cause a disruption of Reliable's assembly operation, which is currently running at full capacity.

(a) Assume the chips are delivered as agreed on June 1, 1984, what should Reliable do? If the goods are found to be nonconforming and Reliable decides to reject them, what should Reliable do? If the goods are nonconforming should Samson be given an opportunity to cure its defective performance?

What obligations does Reliable have regarding the rightfully rejected goods in its possession?

(b) Assume that the chips are delivered as agreed and pass preliminary testing. Reliable places them in its raw materials inventory and pays the purchase price. Samson, however, had improperly engineered the chips, rendering them incapable of performing an important calculating function called for by the contract. This defect could not be detected until the chip was incorporated into the calculator. As a result, the defect was not discovered until assembly of calculators utilizing the chips began August 1, 1984. What recourse, if any, does Reliable have against Samson?

(c) Assume the chips delivered do not conform to the contract or that Samson simply fails to deliver as agreed. List the basic remedial options available to Reliable under the UCC.

(d) Assume that Samson utterly fails to deliver the chips, citing increased cost. Reliable is notified of this fact shortly before June 1, 1984, the contract delivery date. As Samson knew, the 10,000 chips were to be incorporated into a shipment of calculators being specially manufactured for Sears, Roebuck & Co. The delivery date of the Sears contract is August 1, 1984. Time is of the essence under the Sears contract because the calculators are being offered as part of Sears "back to school" sale. Reliable expects to make a $20,000 profit on the Sears contract.

(1) Assume that substitute chips are available on the market for $4 each, which could be delivered in time to perform the Sears contract. Reliable must, however, incur a $500 brokerage fee and $1,000 in added shipping expenses. How much should Reliable recover from Samson for breach of contract if it buys the substitute chips? What should it recover if it elects not to cover and as a result breaches the contract with Sears?

(2) Assume that substitute chips are not otherwise available. Samson has the chips in its possession destined for the Reliable contract. What should Reliable do? Assume alternatively that Samson has not manufactured the chips but has the ability to do so in time to

enable Reliable to perform the Sears contract? What should Reliable do? Assume alternatively that Samson neither has the goods nor can it manufacture them. As a result Reliable breaches its contract with Sears. How much should Reliable recover in its subsequent breach of contract action against Samson?

18-3 Sam owns a store that sells antique furniture, as well as custom-made and stock cabinets. Doaks enters the store and indicates his interest in an antique brass bed Sam has in stock. The piece is extremely rare and after some dickering the parties agree to a price of $2,000. The bed originally cost Sam $800. Prior to the date agreed upon for delivery, Doaks phoned Sam and indicated that he would not take the bed since he had found another one at a lower price. Sam sues Doaks for breach of contract.

How would Sam's damages be computed assuming alternatively:

(1) He resells the bed to Jones for $1,500, its fair market value.

(2) He resells to Jones for $2,500, its fair market value.

(3) He does not resell but instead uses the bed in his home. At the date agreed upon for delivery the bed was worth $1,500 on the market.

18-4 Beaumont contacted Sam concerning purchase of cabinets for an apartment complex Beaumont was building. Beaumont required 500 cabinets. Two hundred and fifty were standard bathroom cabinets which Sam stocked and could be acquired in unlimited quantity from Standard Fixtures, Inc. Beaumont contracted to purchase these for $100 each. Sam paid Standard $75 for each cabinet. The remaining 250 cabinets were to be custom-made by Sam to fit the kitchens in the various apartments. Approximately 25 different sizes and styles of cabinets were involved. Sam quoted Beaumont a total price of $75,000 which included a $20,000 profit on the job. Sam acquired the raw materials for $20,000 and expended several months labor working on the cabinets. Two months before the delivery date, however, Beaumont called and indicated that financial problems had forced him to abandon the apartment project. Sam had not yet ordered the bathroom cabinets, but had completed one-third of the kitchen cabinets. They could not be resold because they had been custom built. Sam had not yet started to manufacture the remaining cabinets, and was able to resell the remaining raw lumber for $8,000. Sam sues Beaumont for breach of contract. How much should he recover? Cite relevant UCC provisions in formulating your answer.

18-5 S has sold iron rails to B for many years on open 30 day account. On June 15, S shipped $10,000 worth of rails to B (now located in B's warehouse); another $10,000 shipment was in transit via Red Ball Trucking Company on that date. B also owed an additional $5,000 for rails previously shipped, and already incorporated into B's products. B has had financial difficulty but provided a favorable financial statement to S on June 1, inducing S to make the last two $10,000 shipments. On June 21, while the second shipment was in transit, however, S discovered that the financial statement was false, and that B planned to declare bankruptcy on June 22. What should S do? Cite relevant UCC and Bankruptcy Code provisions.

18-6 Frank, a manufacturer of metal frames for motorcycles, ordered steel tubing from Karen. The tubing was delivered, accepted, and paid for by Frank. When Frank began to use the tubing, however, he discovered it was cracked and corroded. Frank wrote a letter to Karen revoking acceptance of the tubing and stating that he would hold it for 30 days after which he would sell it applying the proceeds to offset the amount to be refunded by Karen. Karen refused to pick up the tubing or to refund Frank's money. Sixty days later, Frank removed the tubing from his warehouse because he needed the storage space, and because he feared the defective tubing might inadvertently enter his production process. Frank then scrapped the tubing because its resale value as steel scrap was minimal. Frank sued Karen seeking the purchase price of the tubing as damages. Karen argued that Frank's scrapping the tubing constituted acceptance of the goods. Should the court award the damages requested by Frank? Explain, citing any relevant Code provisions.

18-7 Barb purchased a new automobile from Ed the Car Dealer. The car failed to operate properly and Barb revoked her acceptance of it. She then notified Ed that she would retain the automobile as security under UCC §2-711 and would store it until Ed returned the purchase price. Ed refused to return the purchase price so Barb sued him. The trial court ruled that the car was a "lemon" and that Barb was entitled to revoke acceptance. Barb testified that she incurred the following costs pursuant to the transaction:

Purchase price	$5,900
Storage costs (@ $30 per month)	780
Insurance on the stored automobile	250
Interest on loan (to finance the purchased car)	1,180
Cost to rent a replacement automobile (@ $150 per month)	3,900

Which of these costs is Barb entitled to recover as damages from Ed? Explain, citing appropriate Code provisions.

18-8 Acme Co. manufactures and sells "gadgets." Acme entered into a contract to sell 20,000 gadgets to Smith at $12 apiece. Because Acme's manufacturing plant was operating at full capacity Acme ordered the gadgets from Bento, a competitor, who agreed to sell the 20,000 gadgets to Acme at $8 each. After the cost of materials for gadgets suddenly increased, Bento notified Acme that it would be unable to supply the gadgets at the contract price. Acme solicited bids from other gadget manufacturers but concluded that it could manufacture the gadgets more cheaply than the current market price of $13. Therefore, Acme manufactured the gadgets at a cost of $11 each and thereby was able to fulfill its contractual obligations to Smith. Acme then sued Bento for breach of contract asserting that it had covered by buying the gadgets from itself rather than paying the market price. The court ruled in favor of Acme and awarded the following damages.

Actual damages (difference between the cover price of $11 and the contract price of $8 x 20,000 units)	$ 60,000
Potential profits (profits that Acme would have earned had it used its facilities to manufacture gadgets for other customers)	40,000

Lost profits on the Smith contract (difference between the profits of $4 apiece that Acme would have earned had Bento fulfilled the contract and the actual profits of $1 each x 20,000 units)   60,000
                                                             $160,000

Bento has appealed.

(a) Under the UCC, was Acme entitled to cover by manufacturing the gadgets itself? Explain.

(b) Assuming that the trial court's ruling was correct, did the court properly compute the damages? Explain.

18-9   By its terms, §2-713(1) is to be used to compute damages "for nondelivery *or repudiation* by the seller" in the absence of cover. Assume, therefore, that the language "learned of the breach" in §2-713(1) is interpreted to mean "learned of the repudiation" in cases based upon the seller's anticipatory repudiation. This interpretation has been adopted by a majority of courts considering the issue, but has been heavily criticized.

Consider the following example. On February 1, Jackson contracts to sell certain electronic components to Browne for $2,000 for delivery on June 1. Jackson repudiates by notifying Browne on April 1 when the market price is $3,000. Browne attempts to cover but is unable to do so because of a market shortage. By June 1 the market price has risen to $5,000. Browne sues Jackson for breach of contract proceeding under §2-713(1). To what is Browne entitled using the majority approach outlined above? Is this a fair result? Would you suggest an alternative meaning for "learned of the breach" in the repudiation case?

18-10 Under §2-713, a buyer's damages are determined according to the price prevailing at the time and place the buyer would have covered had he elected to do so. However, under §2-708(1), the corresponding seller's remedy, market price is determined "at the time and place for tender." Is this always the time or place the seller is likely to *resell* (the remedy corresponding to the buyer's cover) in the event of breach by the buyer? Explain.

Chapter 19

The Sales Contract—
Warranties

The various buyers' remedies discussed in Chapter 18 impose liability upon a seller who fails to deliver the goods required by the contract, or who delivers defective goods which the buyer ultimately rejects. A buyer may, however, *accept* goods that do not conform to the contract. In this situation, the buyer may recover damages from the seller for breach of *warranty,* the subject of this chapter.

Introduction to Warranties

In its broadest sense, a **warranty** is a statement or other representation made by a seller of goods concerning the quality, character, or capabilities of the goods sold. If the goods fail to conform to the standards created by a warranty, the seller is liable in damages for breach of warranty. The warranty concept is therefore very expansive; it essentially de-

fines the seller's obligation in a contract for the sale of goods.

Warranties may be created expressly by the language or other conduct of the seller, or may be implied—that is, imposed by law. Under the UCC, the implied warranties are merchantability and fitness for a particular purpose. In addition, the Code imposes a warranty of title and against infringement upon a seller.

Disclaimer of Warranty

Because freedom of contract is a basic principle of the UCC, the seller may, within certain limitations, undertake to contractually limit, modify, or exclude warranty liability. Although commonly used, such **warranty disclaimers** have great potential for unconscionable[1] application, particularly when the term is imposed upon a consumer buyer in a standardized form contract. The Code provisions allowing the seller to alter or eliminate warranty liability or to limit the buyer's remedy in the event of breach therefore also provide a significant amount of protection for the buyer. Additionally, at the federal level, the Magnuson-Moss Warranty Act imposes limitations on written warranty disclaimers in transactions involving consumer goods. Warranty disclaimers should therefore be studied with

---

1. Unconscionability is discussed in detail in Chapter 10.

the understanding that they are likely to invite close judicial scrutiny, regarding both compliance with relevant statutory provisions, and whether or not, in the circumstances of the case, enforcement of the disclaimer would be unconscionable.

The following material examines how the various warranties contained in the UCC are created and disclaimed, remedies for breach of warranty, and the Magnuson-Moss Warranty Act.

Express Warranties

Creation of Express Warranties—§2-313

Under §2-313 of the UCC, any *affirmation of fact or promise* made by the seller to the buyer that (1) relates to the goods, and (2) becomes part of the basis of the bargain, creates an **express warranty** that the goods will conform to the affirmation or promise. To create an express warranty, it is not necessary that the seller use the words "warrant," "warranty," or "guarantee." Nor is it necessary that the seller intend to create a warranty. Express warranties rest upon the dickered, or bargained-for, aspects of the bargain. The seller's affirmations of fact concerning the goods made during the bargaining process are basically part of the description of the goods. As stated in Official Comment 4 to §2-313: "[T]he whole purpose of the law of warranty is to determine what it is that the seller has in essence agreed to sell."

Express Warranty—Fact or Opinion. Ordinarily, express warranties are created by explicit oral or written statements made by the seller regarding the quality, character, or capabilities of the goods being sold. A major problem in this situation is to distinguish statements constituting mere "seller's talk" or "puffing" from those creating express warranties. The distinction is stated in §2-313(2):

> . . . [A]n affirmation merely of the value of the goods or a statement purporting to be merely the seller's opinion or commendation of the goods does not create a warranty.

Although the Code thus exempts a seller from warranty liability for "puffing," distinguishing such statements from those creating express warranties is extremely difficult. The line between "puffing" (for example, a used car dealer stating, "This car is a real honey.") and an "affirmation of fact" (for example, the same salesman stating, "This car has just had an engine overhaul.") is very fine. Generally, the more specific the seller's statements concerning the qualities of the goods, the more likely a court is to construe the statement as an express warranty. In addition to careful analysis of the seller's language, the court also considers the reasonableness of the buyer's reliance upon it, whether the statement was in writing, the nature of the defect, and the parties' relative knowledge concerning the characteristics of the goods. The following pre-Code classic case illustrates the fine distinction between puffing and express warranty.

Wat Henry Pontiac Co. v. Bradley
210 P.2d 348 (Okla. 1949)

In 1944, Mrs. Bradley purchased a used Buick from Wat Henry Pontiac Co. in order to travel with her seven-month-old child from Oklahoma to Mississippi to visit her husband, who was serving in the Army. During negotiations preceding the sale, the salesman assured her that the car was in good condition, "in A-1 shape," "mechanically perfect," and would get her any place she wanted to go. The car was not mechanically perfect, however, and broke down en route to Mississippi, requiring substantial repairs. Bradley therefore sued Wat Henry Pontiac for breach of warranty alleging that the salesman's statements were express oral warranties. The trial court found in Bradley's favor and awarded damages. Wat Henry Pontiac appealed.

Johnson, Justice

. . . The rule is that to constitute an express warranty no particular form of words is necessary, and any affirmation of the quality or condition of the vehicle, not uttered as a matter of opinion or belief, made by a seller at the time of sale for the purpose of assuring the buyer of the truth of the fact and inducing the buyer to make the purchase, if so received and relied on by the buyer, is an express warranty. . . .

This court in *International Harvester Co. v. Lawyer* [155 P. 617, 618 (Okla. 1916)], said:

> "Warranty" is a matter of intention. A decisive test is whether the vendor assumes to assert a fact of which the buyer is ignorant, or merely states an opinion, or his judgment, upon a matter of which the vendor has no special knowledge, and on which the buyer may also be expected to have an opinion and to exercise his judgment. In the former case there is a warranty; in the latter case there is not. . . .

The facts in this case bring it squarely within the above well-settled principles of law, and the jury was justified in finding that there was an oral warranty. . . .

The buyer here was ignorant of the facts, and the defects were hidden and not open to discovery by the buyer. The seller was an expert in handling automobiles, having served for a long period of time as an automobile mechanic before becoming a salesman; and his statements as to the condition of the car and where it could be driven constituted a warranty and not mere opinion. . . .

[Judgment affirmed.]

Express Warranty—Description. In addition to explicit verbal statements of fact or promises relating to the goods, express warranties may also be created by description. Under §2-313(1)(b), any description of the goods that is made part of the basis of the bargain creates an express warranty that the goods will conform to the description. The description may be contained in technical specifications, blueprints, or the like, or may simply arise from the seller's language. A problem arises concerning the scope of the warranty when the seller uses very general descriptive language that may consist of one word—for example, when the seller agrees to sell a "lawn mower," or an "automobile," or a "tractor" to the buyer. In this context, the court must decide what qualities or characteristics these descriptions embody. For example,

does an "automobile" have to be in running condition, or, for that matter, is it required to have an engine at all? Evidence of the negotiations of the parties and the buyer's awareness of the subject matter's condition are relevant to determine the content of the warranty.

Express Warranty—Sample or Model. Goods are often described through the use of a sample or model. Any sample or model which is made part of the basis of the bargain creates an express warranty that the goods will conform to a sample or model. A **sample** is actually drawn from the bulk of goods involved in the sale. In contrast, a **model** is not drawn from the bulk of the goods, but is offered for inspection when the goods themselves are not at hand.[2] Any item exhibited by the seller is ordinarily presumed to become part of the basis of the bargain; that is, the seller bears the burden of showing that it is not a sample or model.

Time of Express Warranty. The time when the seller's representations are made (by affirmation of fact, promise, description, sample, or model) is not material in determining whether or not they constitute express warranties. The sole test is whether they have become part of the contract. If the seller's affirmation or promise occurs after the deal is otherwise closed—for example, after the buyer has taken delivery—the warranty may be effective without additional consideration as a contract modification under §2-209(1).

Express Warranty and Fraud. Express warranty liability is based upon the seller's affirmations of fact concerning the goods, which is also the basis upon which liability for fraud and misrepresentation is imposed. Note, therefore, the relationship between fraud and express warranty.[3] A seller acting in the good faith belief in the accuracy of his statements concerning the goods may nevertheless be held liable for breach of express warranty if the

---

2. UCC §2-313(1)(c) and Official Comment 6.

3. The common law of fraud and misrepresentation discussed in Chapter 11 supplements the UCC provisions through §1-103.

goods subsequently fail to conform to the seller's statements. If the seller's representations were made with actual knowledge of their falsity, liability for fraud also may ensue.[4]

Disclaimer of Express Warranties—§2-316(1)

Warranty liability is strict liability. It is imposed whether or not the seller knows of the defect or is at fault in causing it. To avoid this essentially absolute obligation, sellers often attempt to contractually limit or extinguish their warranty liability. Disclaimers of express warranties are governed by §2-316(1). It provides that an express warranty and words or conduct tending to negate or limit that warranty are to be construed, if possible, as consistent with each other. If such a construction is unreasonable, the negation or limitation is inoperative. This language affords a court wide latitude in striking down disclaimer language it finds inconsistent with an express warranty created under §2-313. Inconsistency between warranty and disclaimer occurs primarily in two situations: (1) when both the warranty and the disclaimer are contained in the parties' written contract, and (2) when the warranty is made orally before the parties reduce the contract to a writing which contains the disclaimer.

Written Warranty and Disclaimer. Perhaps the most basic purpose of §2-316(1) is to prevent express warranties, resting upon the negotiated aspects of the bargain and incorporated into the written agreement, from being disclaimed by boilerplate language in a form contract such as "the seller hereby disclaims all warranties, express or implied." For example, assume S sells a car to B, inducing her to buy by stating "the brakes on this car were overhauled last week." This provision is included in the parties' written contract. The sales contract also contains general language dis-

claiming all warranties. Section 2-316(1) prevents the general disclaimer from excluding the warranty that the brakes are new, and thus would not prevent the buyer from recovering when she discovers that the brakes actually have 50,000 miles on them. That is, §2-316(1) protects "a buyer from *unexpected and unbargained language of disclaimer* by denying effect to such language when inconsistent with language of express warranty."[5]

Oral Warranty and Written Disclaimer. A much more troublesome problem under §2-316(1) is the effect of a written disclaimer upon oral warranties made prior to the written agreement and not incorporated into that agreement. In this case, the disclaimer issue is often complicated by a merger clause contained in the contract. For example, the contract may contain a provision generally disclaiming all warranties and a merger clause stating that the written contract, absent the warranty, represents the entire agreement of the parties. In this situation the seller may assert the Code parol evidence rule, §2-202 (discussed in Chapter 12) to prevent the buyer from introducing evidence concerning existence of the oral warranty. Assume Bob goes to Joe's Motor Sales to buy a used truck for use in his construction business. Bob examines a 1985 Chevrolet which Joe's salesman describes in glowing terms, some of which ("this is a one-owner truck," "it is in A-1 shape," "it has just had an engine overhaul") are express warranties under §2-313. Partly in reliance upon the salesman's statements, Bob buys the truck, which proves to be a lemon. Joe's written form contract, signed by Bob, does not incorporate any of the salesman's statements, but instead contains terms disclaiming all warranties and a merger clause. Bob later sues Joe's for breach of warranty. In defense, Joe's asserts that the written contract, which contains no warranties, is the final expression of the parties' agreement. Accordingly, the parol evidence rule should prevent Bob from attempting to prove existence of oral warranties contradicting the terms of the written contract.

---

4. Under UCC §2-721, remedies for fraud and material misrepresentation include all Code remedies available for nonfraudulent breach including those available for breach of warranty. The Code takes this approach to correct the situation in which common law remedies for fraud were more restricted than those available for breach of warranty.

---

5. UCC §2-316, Official Comment 1 (emphasis added).

On similar facts, a number of courts have accepted this argument and excluded the buyer's evidence of previously made oral warranties. The buyer may be protected, however, if the court finds either that the writing is not a final expression of the agreement or that enforcement of the disclaimer would be unconscionable. Nevertheless, to avoid loss of warranty protection, a buyer should always make sure that the seller's oral representations are incorporated into any subsequent written contract. Particular care must be taken when the seller uses a standardized form contract, because such contracts often contain preprinted disclaimer and merger clauses.

Implied Warranties

Unlike express warranties, which are contractual in nature, resting upon the "dickered" aspects of the bargain, **implied warranties** arise by operation of law. Two implied warranties recognized under the Code are discussed below: the warranty of merchantability and the warranty of fitness for a particular purpose. The warranty of merchantability, imposed upon a merchant seller, requires that the goods sold meet certain minimum quality standards. The warranty of fitness is given by a seller who has reason to know of a particular purpose for which the buyer requires the goods and that the buyer is relying upon the seller's skill and judgment to choose suitable goods.

Merchantability—§2-314

Elements of Merchantability. Under §2-314(1), a warranty that the goods will be **merchantable** is implied if the seller is a *merchant* with respect to goods of that kind. Section 2-3l4(2) lists six criteria to determine whether or not goods are merchantable. Note that this list contains the minimum requirements of merchantability. Other attributes of merchantability may arise in specific instances through case law or usage of trade.

1. To be merchantable, the goods must pass without objection in the trade under the contract description. That is, the goods need not be perfect, but "must be of a quality comparable to that generally acceptable in that line of trade under the description or other designation of the goods used in

the agreement."[6] Therefore, trade usage is an important factor to be considered in determining the content and scope of the warranty. In addition, price should be considered in ascertaining the extent of the seller's warranty. The warranty applies both to new and second-hand goods, but the seller's obligation with respect to used goods is somewhat more limited because that fact is part of their contract description.

2. If fungible goods are involved, §2-314(2)(b) provides that the goods must be "fair average quality within the description." This requirement is basically an extension of the first criterion above. Goods are fungible if one unit is identical to any other unit, such as grain or oil. The term "fair average," directly applicable to agricultural bulk products, means "goods centering around the middle belt of quality, not the least or the worst that can be understood in the particular trade by the designation, but such as can pass 'without objection.'"[7]

3. The goods must be fit for the ordinary purposes for which such goods are used. This is the most commonly quoted definition of merchantability, meaning that the goods must be capable of performing the tasks ordinarily required of like goods. For example, to be merchantable, a broom must be capable of sweeping; a car should be capable of providing basic transportation; food should be fit for eating. Defining the limits of "fit for the ordinary purposes" raises troublesome problems, however. For example, is whiskey not merchantable (not fit for the ordinary purposes for which it is sold) because it causes alcoholism and numerous health problems in its users or is it merchantable because it is similar to other whiskey and fit to drink? Though this question presents a somewhat extreme example, it illustrates the basic problem facing a buyer who seeks to recover for breach of the implied warranty of merchantability. He must define "the ordinary purposes for which such goods are used" before it can be determined whether or not the seller's goods are fit for those purposes.

4. The goods must run, within variations per-

---

6. UCC §2-314, Official Comment 2.
7. UCC §2-314, Official Comment 7.

mitted by the agreement or trade usage, of even kind, quality, and quantity, within each unit and among all units involved.

5. The goods must be adequately contained, packaged, and labeled as the agreement may require.

6. If any promises or affirmations of fact are made on the container or label, the goods must conform to the affirmation or promise.

Normally, the warranty of merchantability is breached because, due to the defective nature of the goods, they either do not work as anticipated—for example, a car fails to operate properly because of a defective transmission—or are unexpectedly dangerous in normal use—for example, a piece of glass found in a soda bottle.

Merchants Covered. Not all persons who qualify as "merchants" for purposes of applying some of the Code's "merchants' exceptions"[8] are merchants under §2-314. The warranty of merchantability is imposed only upon a seller who, in a professional status, sells or deals in the particular kind of goods that are the subject matter of the sale. The warranty is not given by a person, even one otherwise in business, making an isolated sale of goods. Note that to be a merchant under §2-314 the seller must both deal in goods and those goods must be involved in the sale. For example, an appliance dealer selling a dishwasher, a jeweler selling a watch, a grocer selling a loaf of bread, a restaurant owner selling a hamburger or soft drink, and generally other businesses selling goods out of inventory are "merchants" under §2-314. On the other hand, a jeweler selling a used car is not a merchant in cars, and therefore gives no warranty of merchantability to his buyer.

Fitness for a Particular Purpose—§2-315

Under §2-315, if the seller, merchant or nonmerchant, at the time of contracting, has reason to know

1. of any particular purpose for which the buyer requires the goods, *and*

2. that the buyer is relying upon the seller's skill or judgment to select or furnish suitable goods

then, unless properly disclaimed, there is an implied warranty that the goods will be fit for the buyer's particular purpose. For the warranty of **fitness for a particular purpose** to arise, the seller need only have "reason to know" (not necessarily actual knowledge) of the buyer's purpose. The buyer, however, must *actually* rely upon the seller's skill or judgment in selecting the goods.

Although both the warranties of fitness and merchantability warranties may be included in the same contract, the warranty of fitness is much narrower and more precise. That is, a particular purpose is a use peculiar to the buyer's business or specific requirements, whereas the ordinary purposes for which goods are used are uses made of the goods by buyers generally. For this reason, the goods sold under the contract may very well be merchantable under §2-314, but not fit for a particular purpose under §2-315. Assume Bonfour, who is in the process of opening a cafeteria, contacts Skillet, a restaurant equipment supplier, to purchase kitchen equipment. Bonfour has some idea of her anticipated volume, but is otherwise unfamiliar with the restaurant business, a fact that is obvious to Skillet after conversing with her. Bonfour therefore asks Skillet to recommend a commercial dishwasher capable of handling her anticipated business. After inspecting Bonfour's facilities, Skillet recommends a model thereafter purchased by Bonfour in reliance upon the recommendation. Even though her subsequent volume is less than anticipated, the dishwasher proves to be inadequate to handle the load. On these facts, even though the dishwasher is merchantable under §2-314—fit for the ordinary purposes for which dishwashers are used—it is not fit for the buyer's particular purpose. Skillet, therefore, breaches the implied warranty of fitness, but not the warranty of merchantability.

As the preceding example indicates, the implied warranty of fitness most commonly arises between merchants, although it may also be created between a merchant and a consumer. Nevertheless, §2-315 imposes no explicit requirement that the seller be a *merchant,* as in the warranty of merchantability. Ordinarily, however, only a merchant will possess

---

8. "Merchant" is defined in UCC §2–104(1). See the discussion of this definition in Chapter 7.

the necessary "skill or judgment" with respect to the goods to justify imposing the warranty.

At issue in the following case was whether an implied warranty of fitness had been created.

Ingram River Equipment, Inc. v. Pott Industries, Inc.

816 F.2d 1231 (8th Cir. 1987)

Plaintiff Ingram River Equipment, Inc., a barge operator, contracted to purchase four barges from Defendant Pott Industries, Inc., a builder of boats and barges. Ingram specified that the barges be equipped with a steam-coil system for heating heavy petroleum products and other heavy liquid cargo, which are easier to unload when heated. Plans for the steam-coil systems, which were drawn up by Pott and approved by Ingram, stipulated that furnace-weld pipe would be used. Pott constructed and delivered the barges and steam-coil systems as described in the plans. When Ingram used the barges, numerous leaks developed in the steam coils because water remained in the coils and froze. After repeated repairs, Ingram had the steam-coil systems replaced by another company whose design allowed removal of the water to prevent freezing, and used seamless pipe, which is stronger than furnace-weld pipe.

When Pott refused to pay for the replacements, Ingram sued for breach of contract. The trial court held that Pott breached its implied warranty of fitness for a particular purpose and awarded damages of $361,757. Pott appealed.

Arnold, Circuit Judge

. . . Pott's position is that several prerequisites to the creation of an implied warranty of fitness for a particular purpose were not met here. First, Pott argues that Ingram's purpose for the goods here was an ordinary rather than a particular purpose. The definition of what constitutes a particular purpose is discussed in Comment 2 to [§2-315 of the UCC], which states in pertinent part:

A "particular purpose" differs from the ordinary purpose for which the goods are used in that it en-

visages a specific use by the buyer which is peculiar to the nature of his business whereas the ordinary purposes for which goods are used are those envisaged in the concept of merchantability and go to uses which are customarily made of the goods in question. For example, shoes are generally used for the purpose of walking upon ordinary ground, but a seller may know that a particular pair was selected to be used for climbing mountains.

However, taking the Comment's illustration a step further, where shoes are sold as mountain-climbing shoes by, e.g., a store specializing in mountain-climbing gear, use of the shoes to climb mountains is not use for a particular purpose. . . .

Ingram's purpose for the goods it purchased from Pott was to use them to carry heavy petroleum products on the Mississippi and its tributaries and to heat those products to facilitate their discharge in cold climates. Pott characterizes the goods at issue as heating-coil-equipped tank barges, and argues that carrying and heating heavy petroleum products is the customary use of such products. Pott maintains that Ingram's use of the barges and the heating coils is not unique or peculiar to Ingram's business, since others use heating-coil-equipped tank barges in precisely the same manner; Pott itself had constructed over thirty such barges for use in the same manner before it built these four for Ingram.

Ingram, however, rejoins that Pott errs in suggesting that its use of the goods must be unique to fall within the fitness-for-a-particular-purpose warranty, arguing instead that the question is one of degree. According to Ingram, the proper characterization of the goods here is tank barges, rather than heating-coil-equipped tank barges. Tank barges, Ingram continues, are used to carry a multitude of cargoes, including a variety of chemicals, molasses, and oils and fuel oils of many kinds. The barges here were equipped with steam coils to enable Ingram to carry a particular kind of cargo—cargo that sometimes requires heating to aid discharge. Further, neither Pott nor Ingram deals solely or predominantly in barges that have steam coils; Pott builds and Ingram operates all sorts of barges. In these circumstances, Ingram concludes, the particular-purpose requirement is met.

We agree with Ingram that its use of the goods need not be one-of-a-kind to meet the requirements of [§2-315]. It is doubtful that even the Comment's example of using a shoe to climb mountains would qualify as a unique use of the shoe. Instead, as we read Comment 2, the key inquiry is not whether anyone else can be found who puts the goods to the same use, but whether the buyer's use is sufficiently different from the customary use of the goods to make it not an ordinary use of the goods; that a buyer's use is not entirely idiosyncratic does not mean that it is ordinary. . . . Therefore, that others put tank barges to the same use as Ingram does not preclude finding that a warranty of fitness exists.

Whether Ingram's purpose diverges sufficiently from the customary purposes of other buyers to be considered particular turns to a great extent on whether one accepts Pott's characterization of the goods as heating-coil-equipped tank barges, or instead accepts Ingram's portrayal of them as tank barges, which have been equipped with heating coils to serve a particular purpose. And this in turn hinges upon how the factual context in which Ingram and Pott struck their bargain is interpreted. To return to the Comment's shoe illustration, is this case more like one in which a buyer goes to a general shoe store and buys a pair of shoes for mountain climbing, or one in which a buyer goes to a mountain-climbing gear store to buy shoes for this purpose? This is, ultimately, a question of fact. . . . Here, since Ingram operates and Pott builds barges for a variety of uses, we are unable to conclude that the District Court was clearly erroneous in finding that an implied warranty of fitness for a particular purpose arose. . . .

Pott next argues that the warranty of fitness is inapplicable because Ingram did not communicate any particular purpose to Pott. However, Pott does not deny that it knew the barges were to be used to carry heavy petroleum products, employing the coils to heat the petroleum to make unloading easier. Instead, Pott simply reiterates its view that this was an ordinary purpose, and adds that Ingram did not communicate any other purpose. Since we have already rejected Pott's contention that Ingram's stated purpose was not particular, we reject this argument as well.

Finally, Pott assails the District Court's finding that Ingram relied upon Pott's expertise to furnish suitable barges, emphasizing that Ingram operates other such barges, that it approved the plans and specifications, and that it got Pott to alter the plans in one minor respect. We conclude, however, that there was ample evidence to support the District Court's finding. As the District Court noted, . . . the contract between Pott and Ingram stated that Ingram was interested only in the results obtained and that the manner and method of performing the work were under Pott's control. There was also testimony that Ingram's expertise in the area related primarily to operation and maintenance of barges, not to their design, . . . whereas Pott was a ship-builder, and supplied the design and specifications for the barges. That a buyer has some expertise does not bar the conclusion that he relied on a seller's superior expertise. . . . Further, Ingram's request for minor modifications in the coil design to facilitate maintenance did not negate its reliance on Pott. . . .

Accordingly, we affirm the District Court's conclusion that an implied warranty of fitness for a particular purpose was created in the sale of the barges. . . .

[Judgment affirmed.]

Disclaimer of Implied Warranties— §§2-316(2) and 2-316(3)

The UCC, in §§2-316(2) and 2-316(3), protects the buyer from surprise by permitting exclusion or modification of implied warranties only by conspicuous language or other appropriate circumstances.

Disclaiming the Warranty of Merchantability. To exclude or modify the implied warranty of merchantability, two requirements must be met: (1) the language of disclaimer must mention the word "merchantability" and (2) if the disclaimer is in writing, it must be conspicuous. Under §1-201(10), a term is **conspicuous** if "it is so written that a reasonable person against whom it is to operate ought to have noticed it." For example, a printed heading in capital letters would be conspicuous and language in the body of the contract is conspicuous if it is in larger or contrasting type or color. The basic test is "whether attention can reasonably be expected to be called to"[9] the term or clause involved. Note that an objective test is applied (a "reasonable" person should have noticed it) and the issue is one for the court, not the jury to decide.

Disclaiming the Warranty of Fitness. Unlike the warranty of merchantability, the warranty of fitness for a particular purpose may be disclaimed by general language, that is, language not specifically using the term "fitness for a particular purpose." Any disclaimer of the warranty of fitness, however, must both (1) be in writing, *and* (2) conspicuous. The following language from §2-316(2) is sufficient to exclude the warranty of fitness: "There are no warranties which extend beyond the description on the face hereof."

Disclaimer through Surrounding Circumstances. Section 2-316(3) outlines three additional situations in which implied warranties may be disclaimed without regard to the requirements outlined above. These are "common factual situations in which the circumstances surrounding the transaction are in themselves sufficient to call the buyer's attention to the fact that no implied warranties are made or that a certain implied warranty is being excluded."[10] Under §2-316(3)(a), *all* implied warranties (both merchantability and fitness) are excluded by language such as "as is," "with all faults," "as they stand," or other language which in common understanding calls the buyer's attention to the exclusion of warranties and makes it plain that no implied warranty exists. Such language in ordinary commercial usage is understood to mean that the buyer bears the entire risk as to the quality of the goods sold.

Section 2-316(3)(b) makes it clear that if the buyer, prior to entering into the contract, has ex-

amined the goods (or a sample or model) as fully as he desires or has refused to examine them, there is no implied warranty regarding defects that an examination should, in the circumstances, have revealed to him. Note that "examination" as used here is not synonymous with "inspection before acceptance," because any examination that may exclude warranty liability under this provision occurs *before* the contract is made. This rule applies whether the buyer voluntarily examines the goods before contracting or does so after a demand by the seller. Which particular defects an examination ought to reveal depends upon the nature of the defect (was it obvious or only ascertainable after chemical or metallurgical testing?), the permitted scope of the examination (was chemical analysis allowed in a case involving defective chemical composition?), and the expertise of the buyer (was he a professional or a layman?).

Finally, under §2-316(3)(c), an implied warranty may also be excluded or modified by the parties' prior course of dealing or course of performance, and by usage of trade.[11] To illustrate, assume Ohm has been selling transistors, resistors, and other electronic components in bulk to Bart for many years. The preprinted forms used by the parties to evidence their contract do not expressly disclaim implied warranties. Nevertheless the price of the components has always been "bargain basement," and over the years, Bart has routinely accepted Ohm's entire shipment, even those containing a substantial number of defective components. On these facts a court may find that the parties' prior course of dealing indicates that no implied warranty exists with respect to components retained by Bart. Note additionally that the "as is" disclaimer discussed above is merely an application of this rule allowing exclusion of implied warranty by usage of trade.

In the following case, the court considered the existence, content, breach, and disclaimer of the implied warranty of merchantability.

---

9. UCC §1-201, Official Comment 10.
10. UCC §2-316, Official Comment 6.

11. These terms, defined in §§1-205 and 2-208, are discussed in Chapter 12 in conjunction with the UCC parol evidence rule, §2-202.

Bazzini v. Garrant

455 N.Y.S.2d 77 (Dist. Ct., Suffolk County 1982)

Colaneri, Judge

This is a sad tale (or is it tail) of the noble, but late, toco toucan bird, (hereinafter Bird), which the plaintiff, Debra Bazzini, purchased from the defendants doing business as Sexy Sadie's Exotic Bird House. For Bird, a youthful creature of but 4 months, the plaintiff paid the not insubstantial sum of $1200.

Upon the sale of Bird the defendants provided the plaintiff a receipt upon which was stamped in bold red print: "HEALTH GUARANTEE FOR 48 HOURS FROM 6/3 to 6/5 EXCHANGE WILL BE MADE UPON PRESENTATION OF VETERINARIAN'S REPORT ONLY WITHIN SAID PERIOD. NOT RESPONSIBLE FOR INJURY, ACCIDENT, LOSS OR TEMPERAMENT OF LIVESTOCK AFTER PURCHASE." An oral modification of this disclaimer was granted to the extent that the plaintiff was permitted to have Bird examined within three days of the sale. That examination apparently found Bird free of any fatal malady.

Tragically, Bird's future with Mrs. Bazzini proved to be quite limited. Within two weeks after his physical, Bird suffered a seizure. (There was no evidence of fowl play.) The plaintiff contacted the veterinarian who advised her to coax Bird back to health by having him sip Gatorade. Like a champion, Bird seemed to recover. But this recovery enjoyed only the reign of a lame duck politician. Seven days later Bird was dead.

Upon the instructions of the veterinarian, the corpse of the once proud animal was stored in the plaintiff's freezer. Bird's cold, dead body was then taken to the veterinarian for autopsy.

A letter from the veterinarian indicates that the cause of Bird's demise could not be definitively established. However, the final paragraph of the letter states:

> Using the facts available it would appear the Toucan had a metabolic problem due to congenital defect, access to toxins or both. This type of problem is of

the bird itself, of a chronic nature, probably the entire, brief, life of the individual.

In life Bird was a bird—an animal of feelings, of flesh and blood and feathers. It is one of the sad aspects of the law that the heat and passion of life so often translate to cold, unfeeling words upon a page. This is such an instance for in death, notwithstanding his memory, Bird is a chattel. . . . [B]irds constitute "goods" within the contemplation of the Code and . . . the defendant was a merchant as defined in UCC §2-104(1). . . . [T]he relevant provisions of the UCC are sections 2-314 (providing for the implied warranty of merchantability) and 2-316(2) and (3) (providing for the exclusion or modification of the warranty.)

UCC §2-316(2) is not applicable since to exclude the warranty of merchantability pursuant to that section there must be mention of the word merchantability. This may seem a harsh rule to the defendants but as all entrepreneurs in the tropical bird business realize, it is a jungle out there.

UCC §2-316(3)(b) . . . provides:

> when the buyer before entering into the contract has examined the goods or the sample or model as fully as he desired or has refused to examine the goods there is no implied warranty with regard to defects which an examination ought in the circumstances to have revealed to him. . . .

Taken literally, this section does not apply to the current case. The examination of the goods, i.e., Bird's checkup, was after the sale. Further, any examination would exclude coverage of the warranty only with respect to defects which an examination ought in the circumstances to have revealed. (UCC §2-316, Official Comment 8.) Thus, by bringing Bird to a veterinarian for a physical examination, the plaintiff did everything that was practical to discover any of Bird's imperfections. No defects leading to Bird's ultimate doom were found at that time.

The proof in this small claims case is not overwhelming. Only the plaintiff and her husband testified. She also produced a notarized letter from the veterinarian and the receipt. No one testified on behalf of the defendants.

Bird was purchased on June 3, 1982. On June 27, 1982 he was dead. The issue is whether these facts establish the defendants' breach of the warranty of merchantability.

In small claims the court is not bound by the rules of evidence. . . . Thus, the veterinarian's letter may be considered. That letter suggests the probability that Bird suffered from a congenital defect. That is, to be blunt and not cagey, Bird was not fit for the ordinary purposes for which toco toucans are used. (*See* UCC §2-314(2)(c).) (At least one purpose is to stay around as a live bird.)

Further, under the circumstances the inference is permissible that Bird was not of merchantable quality at the time of sale since he ceased to function as a merchantable bird so soon thereafter. Perhaps it could be argued that this inference is unjustified. Two weeks may be a long time for fatal conditions to develop in toco toucans. But no one has offered evidence on this point. . . . Thus, it is found as a matter of fact that Bird was unmerchantable when sold.

The plaintiff is entitled to judgment in the amount of $1200. The cost of autopsy is not recoverable as incidental or consequential damages. (UCC §2-715.)

To the defendants this result will seem harsh and undoubtedly ruffle their feathers. But in a case such as this, there is a winner and a loser. It takes a tender judge to make a tough decision. Judgment for the plaintiff against the defendants in the sum of $1200, no costs, no interest.

Warranty of Title and Against Infringement

The warranties discussed to this point assure the buyer that the goods sold possess certain basic qualities and characteristics. A buyer in a sales contract, however, has an additional and more basic concern—that the seller has good title to the goods and the right to transfer them. This assurance is provided by the warranty of title.

Creation of Warranty of Title—§2-312(1)

Under §2-312(1), unless properly disclaimed, the seller in a contract for sale warrants that

1. the title conveyed will be good and its transfer rightful, and
2. the goods will be delivered free of security interests or other liens, except those known to the buyer.[12]

The basic purpose of this **warranty of title** is simply to provide what any good faith buyer of goods expects to receive, "a good, clean title transferred to him also in a rightful manner so that he will not be exposed to a lawsuit in order to protect it."[13]

A seller gives the warranty of title whether or not the seller: (1) is a merchant, (2) knew or was ignorant of the defect in title, or (3) was in possession of the goods at the time the sale or contract to sell was made. Assume Tom stole stereo equipment from Mark and later sold the equipment to Sharon, who was unaware of Tom's wrongdoing. Sharon subsequently sold the equipment to Bill through a newspaper advertisement. Ultimately, Mark, the true owner, located and repossessed the equipment from Bill. Sharon breaches the title warranty given to Bill even though she is innocent of any wrongdoing and is not a merchant. Of course, Tom, the thief, also breaches the warranty of title given in his sale to Sharon.

If the seller is a merchant, the buyer is often protected even if the seller breaches the title warranty. For example, under the "voidable title" and "entrusting" rules discussed in Chapter 17, a good faith buyer usually defeats third-party ownership claims. Further, under §9-307(1), discussed in Chapter 32, a buyer in the ordinary course of business of inventory from a merchant takes free of perfected security interests in the goods even if he knows about them.

Creation of Warranty Against Infringement—§2-312(3)

A second warranty contained in §2-312 is the **warranty against infringement.** Under §2-312(3), a

---

12. Note that with respect to liens or security interests in the goods, the buyer's *actual knowledge* is required to defeat the warranty. Therefore, the seller is not relieved if the buyer has constructive knowledge simply because a secured creditor in the goods has filed a financing statement.

13. UCC §2-312, Official Comment 1.

merchant seller dealing in goods of the kind warrants that the goods will be delivered free of any third-party claim of patent or trademark infringement. No such warranty arises by implication if the seller is not a merchant. It applies only when goods are sold as part of the seller's normal stock in the ordinary course of business.

Commercial buyers often have goods manufactured to their own particular specifications. For example, a hardware retailer may purchase its line of hand tools from a manufacturer who provides the tools according to specifications provided by the retailer. In this case, the buyer who furnishes specifications must indemnify the seller against any patent or trademark infringement claims arising out of the seller's compliance with them. That is, by providing specifications, the buyer makes a tacit representation that the seller will be safe in manufacturing according to them. The buyer is therefore required to reimburse the seller for any loss suffered if the goods infringe upon a third party's patent or trademark. Note that this provision, in essence, imposes warranty liability upon the buyer.

Disclaimer of Warranty of Title—§2-312(2)

Disclaimer of the warranty of title is governed by §2-312(2). It provides that the warranty of title may not be disclaimed by general language disclaiming all warranties, even if the buyer is aware of the general disclaimer. To effectively eliminate the warranty of title, either the seller's *specific language* (for example, "I don't have the title") or the *circumstances* must give the buyer reason to know (an objective test) that the seller does not claim title. The type of "circumstances" envisioned in §2-312(2) are sales by sheriffs, executors, and foreclosing lien holders. These sales occur outside the ordinary course of business, thereby putting the buyer on notice that the seller possesses only an unknown or limited right.

The warranty of title, like merchantability and fitness, is in effect an implied warranty because it arises automatically by operation of law. That is, the warranty is given whether or not it is explicitly or expressly stated by the seller. The title warranty is not, however, treated as an "implied" warranty for purposes of §2-316(3). Accordingly, title may

not be disclaimed by language such as "as is" or "with all faults." It may only be excluded by specific language or under the circumstances described above.

The following case illustrates the "specific language" requirement necessary to disclaim the warranty of title.

Sunseri v. RKO-Stanley Warner Theatres, Inc.
374 A.2d 1342 (Pa. Super. 1977)

Appellant RKO-Stanley Warner Theatres, Inc. (RKO) owned a theater building, part of which it leased to appellee Michael Sunseri and his partner for a recreational center. At the time the parties entered into the lease, RKO also sold some recreational equipment (bowling alleys, pool tables) to Sunseri. The equipment had been owned by Francis Zatalava, a previous lessee of the recreational center who had been forced to close his business for failure to pay taxes. After RKO's sale of the equipment to Sunseri, Zatalava sued RKO to regain possession of and title to the equipment. The court ruled that Zatalava retained title to the equipment. As a result, Sunseri lost possession of the equipment.

Sunseri then sued RKO, alleging that RKO had breached its warranty of title. RKO defended by alleging that it had disclaimed the warranty of title. The trial court ruled in favor of Sunseri and awarded him damages. RKO appealed.

Price, Judge

. . . The document which evidences the transaction between Pagano and Sunseri, as partners, and RKO is entitled "Bill of Sale" and provides, in pertinent part, as follows:

> [Seller] . . . does hereby sell, assign, convey, transfer and deliver to Buyer any right, title and interest Seller may have in the following goods and chattels. . . .

> It is expressly understood and agreed that the Seller shall in nowise be deemed or held to be obligated, liable, or accountable upon or under guaranties [sic] or warranties, in any manner or form including, but not limited to, the implied warranties

of title, merchantability, fitness for use or of quality.

The lower court found that, as a matter of law, the above-quoted language was insufficient to disclaim the warranty of title. We agree. The statutory authority in this area is section 2-312 of the Uniform Commercial Code which states, in pertinent part, the following: [The court then quoted UCC §§2-312(1) and (2)]. . . .

In the instant case, the bill of sale did not disclaim warranty of title in the "specific" language required by U.C.C. §2-312. The provision for sale of "any right, title, and interest" is clearly not a positive warning or exclusion in regard to the status of title, and would be unlikely to offend or even catch the eye of an unsophisticated buyer. . . . The second relevant provision in the sale document, stating that "Seller shall in nowise be deemed or held to be obligated, liable or accountable upon or under any guaranties [sic] or warranties" is similarly ineffective. It is couched in negative terminology, expressing what the seller will not be liable for rather than what the buyer is or is not receiving. The inadequacy of such a caveat is best illustrated by juxtaposing it with title disclaimer provisions suggested by authorities in the subject area. For example, 18 *Am. Jur. Legal Forms 2d* §253:825 (1974), provides: "Seller makes no warranty as to the title to the goods, and buyer assumes all risks of nonownership of the goods by seller." Another illustration is contained in *Purdon's Pa. Forms,* 12A P.S. §2-312, Form 2 (1970), which recommends the following language: "The seller does not warrant that he has any right to convey the title to the goods." Appellant's attempt to disclaim the warranty of title in its transaction with appellee was ineffective in that it failed to comply with the requirement, under the Uniform Commercial Code, that such a disclaimer be made in "specific language. . . ."

[Judgment affirmed.]

Conflict of Warranties—§2-317

The preceding discussion concerns the effect of a conflict between the creation of a warranty and the seller's attempt to extinguish it. A similar conflict may arise, not between warranty and disclaimer, but between two or more warranties express or implied. This problem is resolved, in a manner similar to §2-316(1) governing disclaimer of express warranties, by §2-317. This section recognizes that a seller may make several warranties concerning the same goods. To the extent they can co-exist, the buyer has the benefit of all of them. That is, the warranties are cumulative. For example, a seller may expressly warrant that fabric he sells is 100% wool. Such a warranty is not inconsistent with an implied warranty that the fabric is merchantable. Accordingly, the buyer has the benefit of both warranties.

A seller acting in good faith may, however, make inconsistent warranties. In this situation the *intent* of the parties determines which of the conflicting warranties applies. To aid the court in ascertaining intent, §2-317 states rules governing priority among conflicting warranties:

1. Exact or technical specifications displace an inconsistent (a) sample or model, or (b) general language of description.
2. A sample from an existing bulk, such as a storage bin of grain, displaces inconsistent general language of description.
3. Express warranties displace inconsistent implied warranties other than an implied warranty of fitness for a particular purpose.

The net effect of these rules is to enforce the more specific conflicting warranty. Note that for this section to apply, however, the seller must make warranties in good faith which later are shown to be irreconcilable. Under the principles of estoppel, a seller who leads the buyer to believe that all of the warranties can be performed is thereafter precluded from asserting any inconsistency as a defense.

Inconsistency between the warranties may be difficult to determine, particularly when the conflict is between an express warranty and the implied warranty of merchantability. For example, is an express warranty that a hair dryer will be free of defects in materials and workmanship for six months inconsistent with an implied warranty of merchantability? Assuming the dryer fails after seven months, the buyer may assert that a dryer lasting only seven months is not merchantable. If the court finds the two warranties inconsistent, the buyer's claim will be denied. On similar facts, however, a number of courts have permitted the buyer to recover, finding that the two warranties were consistent.

Remedies for Breach of Warranty

The discussion of buyers' remedies in Chapter 18 illustrates how UCC Article 2 measures a buyer's damages when the buyer justifiably rejects or revokes his acceptance of delivered goods, or when the seller repudiates or fails to deliver. These situations are governed generally by §§2-712 and 2-713. In warranty actions, the buyer has *accepted* the goods, but seeks to recover damages from the seller because the goods are not as warranted. Buyer's damages due to the nonconformity of accepted goods are computed under §2-714.

It is important to note that whenever the buyer asserts breach after acceptance, §2-607(3)(a) requires that the buyer notify the seller within a reasonable time after he discovers (or should have discovered) the breach. Failure to do so bars the buyer from any remedy. The notice requirement serves three purposes: (1) it affords the seller an opportunity to correct any defect; (2) it gives the seller an opportunity to prepare for negotiation and litigation; and (3) it protects the seller against stale claims asserted by the buyer after it is too late to investigate them.

Basic Measure of Damages

Under §2-714(1), a buyer who has accepted nonconforming goods and properly notified the seller of breach may recover damages for nonconformity determined in any reasonable manner. The usual and most commonly applied formula for ascertaining damages for breach of warranty is stated in §2-714(2) which allows the buyer to recover

> the difference at the time and place of acceptance between the value of the goods accepted and the value they would have had if they had been as warranted.

The most common measure of the difference in value between the goods as accepted and as war-

ranted is the cost of replacement or repair. However, to avoid a windfall to a buyer who has used the goods for a significant period of time before the breach of warranty becomes apparent, the court may reduce recovery by a reasonable allowance for depreciation. Note that the value of the goods as warranted is measured at the time and place of acceptance. This provides the most accurate measure of fair market value as warranted because the contract price may have been determined long before acceptance.

Consequential Damages

For breach of warranty actions §2-714(3), like §§2-712 and 2-713, authorizes recovery of incidental and consequential damages in appropriate cases to supplement the basic measure of damages. As discussed in Chapter 15, consequential damages, usually lost profits, may be recoverable under the foreseeability test of *Hadley v. Baxendale,* codified for Code contracts in §2-715(2)(a). In addition, §2-715(2)(b) permits recovery as consequential damages, whether or not foreseeable, for "injury to person or property proximately resulting from any breach of warranty." Thus, in a warranty action a seller may be liable not only for commercial injury (including in some cases lost profits), but also for personal injury and property damage caused by the defective product. Assume Buster purchases a clothes dryer for use in his commercial laundry from a manufacturer, Sox. The dryer fails to work properly because of a defective motor, forcing Buster's business to close for several days. Buster may recover damages under §2-714(2) for breach of warranty (here the warranty of merchantability). Additionally, if the foreseeability test is met, Buster's lost profits may be recovered as consequential damages under §2-715(2)(a). Assume further, that the defective motor overheats and causes a fire which burns down Buster's business and seriously injures him. He may recover for his personal injury and property damage as consequential damages under §2-715(2)(b), whether or not such loss was foreseeable. The application of the law of warranty to cases involving personal injury and property damage is discussed in more detail in the next chapter.

Deducting Damages from Price—§2-717

An additional remedy available to the buyer for breach of warranty is contained in §2-717. Upon notification of his intention to do so, the buyer may deduct all or any part of damages for the seller's breach from any part of the price still owing under the same contract. This provision only applies if the breach involved is of the same contract for which the price is claimed. No particular formalities for the notice are required and no further action is necessary if the seller acquiesces in the deduction.

Magnuson-Moss Warranty Act

The **Magnuson-Moss Warranty Act,** a federal statute[14] that became effective generally in June, 1975, regulates written warranties that accompany the sale of consumer goods. The Act is designed to accomplish several purposes.

1. It requires that the terms of written warranties be fully and conspicuously disclosed in simple and readily understood language.

2. It requires that such warranties be conspicuously designated as "full" or "limited." To be designated as "full," the warranty must incorporate certain minimum federal standards.

3. It prohibits the use of written warranties as a means to disclaim or modify the implied warranties of merchantability and fitness.

4. It encourages warrantors to set up informal mechanisms to settle disputes, which the consumer must use before commencing court action.

5. It allows actions for breach of warranty to be brought in federal court under limited circumstances.

Note that the Act applies only *if* the seller provides a written warranty. The law does not *require* that a consumer product or any of its components be warranted, or prescribe the duration of written warranties.

Content of Warranties

Section 2302 of the Act provides that:

In order to improve the adequacy of information available to consumers, prevent deception, and improve competition in the marketing of consumer products, any warrantor[15] warranting a consumer product to a consumer[16] by means of a written warranty[17] shall, to the extent of rules required by the [Federal Trade Commission], fully and conspicuously disclose in simple and readily understood language the terms and conditions of such warranty.

The Federal Trade Commission (FTC) has promulgated regulations requiring that written warranties covering consumer products contain the following information if the goods actually cost the consumer more than $15 exclusive of taxes:

1. the identity of the party or parties to whom the written warranty is extended;
2. a clear description and identification of products or parts covered by and excluded from the warranty;
3. a statement of what the warrantor will do in the event of a defect, malfunction, or failure to conform with the written warranty;
4. the point in time when the warranty term commences, if different from the purchase date, and the duration of the warranty;
5. a step-by-step explanation of the procedure that the consumer should follow in order to

---

14. 15 U.S.C. §§2301-2312.

15. A "supplier" is a person engaged in the business of making a consumer product available to consumers. A "warrantor" is a supplier or other person who gives a written warranty or who is obligated under an implied warranty. 15 U.S.C. §§2301(4), (5).

16. A "consumer product" is any tangible personal property normally used for personal, family, or household purposes. A "consumer" is (a) a buyer (other than for purposes of resale) of a consumer product, (b) any person to whom the product is transferred during the duration of the implied or written warranty, and (c) any other person entitled by the terms of the warranty or state law to enforce the warranty obligations. 15 U.S.C. §§2301(1), (3).

17. A "written warranty" is (a) any *written* affirmation of fact or any *written* promise made in connection with the sale of a consumer product by a supplier asserting that the material and workmanship are free of defects or will meet a specified level of performance over a specified period of time, *or* (b) any written undertaking by a supplier of a consumer product to refund, repair, replace, or take other remedial action if the product fails to meet the specifications stated in the undertaking, if the written affirmation, promise, or undertaking becomes part of the basis of the bargain. 15 U.S.C. §2301(6).

obtain performance of any warranty obligation;

6. Information about any informal dispute settlement mechanism, if any, available to the consumer;

7. any limitations on the duration of implied warranties[18] accompanied by the following statement:

Some States do not allow limitations on how long an implied warranty lasts, so the above limitation may not apply to you.

8. any limitations on relief such as incidental or consequential damages, accompanied by the following statement,

Some States do not allow the exclusion or limitation of incidental or consequential damages, so the above limitation or exclusion may not apply to you.

9. a statement in the following language:

This warranty gives you specific legal rights, and you may also have other rights which vary from State to State.[19]

The information required to be disclosed above must be made available to the consumer *prior to* the sale of the product. Additionally, to prevent deception, the FTC is empowered to determine the manner and form of presentation when the information is contained in advertising, labeling, point-of-sale material, or other written representation.

Designation of Warranties as "Full" or "Limited"

Under the Act, any written warranty covering a consumer product actually costing more than $10 must clearly and conspicuously designate the warranty as either "full" (stating the duration), or "limited." A **full warranty** is one that meets the federal minimum standards for warranty. A warranty not meeting these standards must be designated as **limited**.[20]

In order to meet federal minimum standards for full warranty, four basic elements, stated in §2304, must be contained in the warranty. These include:

1. In the event of a defect, malfunction or failure to conform with the written warranty, the seller must, at a minimum, remedy the product within a reasonable time without charge. "Remedy" means that the seller may, at his option, repair or replace the item, or may refund the purchase price. However, the seller may not elect to refund the price unless it is impracticable to repair or replace, or the buyer is willing to accept a refund.

2. No limitation may be imposed on the duration of any implied warranty.

3. Consequential damages for breach of any written or implied warranty may not be limited or excluded unless the exclusion or limitation appears conspicuously on the face of the warranty.

4. If the product (or a component part), continues to be defective after a reasonable number of attempts by the seller to resolve the problem, the seller must afford the buyer the option to elect either a refund of the purchase price or replacement. If replacement involves a component part, the seller must install the part in the product without charge.

In fulfilling the obligations outlined above, the seller may not impose any duty upon the buyer, other than notification, as a condition to securing a remedy. The seller may, however, avoid warranty obligations if he or she can establish that the defect, malfunction, or other failure to perform as warranted was caused by damage while in the consumer's possession or by the consumer's unreasonable use, including the failure to provide for reasonable and necessary maintenance. Note that nothing prevents the sale of a product with both "full" and "limited" warranties applicable to it, provided they are clearly and conspicuously designated. For example, a television set may contain a full two-year warranty on the picture tube and a limited warranty on other components—for example, restricted to parts only.

---

18. An "implied warranty" is an implied warranty arising under state law in connection with the sale, such as the warranty of merchantability and fitness arising under the UCC 15 U.S.C. §2301(7).

19. 16 C.F.R. §701.3.

20. 15 U.S.C. §2303. The rules discussed in this and the preceding section do not apply to representations of general policy regarding customer satisfaction not subject to specific limitation (for example, "satisfaction guaranteed or your money back"). 15 U.S.C. §2303(b).

Limitation of Disclaimer of Implied Warranties

One of the most important provisions of the Act is §2308(a), which prohibits disclaimer or modification of implied warranties (merchantability and fitness) by a supplier who makes any written warranty to a consumer in connection with the sale of a consumer product. Additionally, the implied warranties may not be disclaimed if, at the time of the sale or within 90 days thereafter, the supplier enters into a service contract[21] with the consumer covering the consumer product.

Although the seller may not *disclaim* implied warranties, he may *limit their duration* unless he is giving a "full" warranty. The duration of implied warranties may be limited to the duration of the written warranty if (1) the duration of the written warranty is *reasonable,* (2) the limitation is not unconscionable, and (3) it is contained in clear and unmistakable language, prominently displayed on the face of the warranty.

The prohibition against disclaimer of implied warranties is designed to prevent the unconscionable practice, widespread before passage of the Act, of using written warranties simply as a tool to disclaim implied warranties, primarily merchantability. That is, written warranties simply became a vehicle to comply with the requirements of UCC §2-316(2) concerning disclaimer of implied warranties. The written express warranty given would then be much less extensive than the disclaimed implied warranties—for example, 90 days' parts and labor on a toaster—leaving the consumer in a substantially worse position than if no written warranty had been provided. Further, the potential for unconscionability in this context was great, because by giving the warranty (generally on official-looking paper), the seller created the extremely deceptive impression that it was giving the buyer additional rights, when in fact it was taking away the buyer's existing rights.

Remedies

The stated policy of the Act is to encourage warrantors to establish informal dispute settlement mechanisms. The FTC has prescribed rules outlining the requirements for any such mechanism incorporated into a written warranty. These rules provide for participation by independent or governmental entities. If the warrantor establishes an informal dispute settlement procedure and incorporates it into the written warranty, then the consumer must first resort to the warrantor's procedure before commencing court action.

Assuming no such procedure is created, a consumer injured by a breach of warranty may bring a civil suit for damages or other relief in state court. The judgment may include court costs, attorneys' fees, and other expenses incurred in commencing and maintaining the lawsuit. The consumer may, of course, sue not only for the seller's failure to comply with Magnuson-Moss provisions, but also for breach of express or implied warranty under the UCC.

To provide a remedy in cases involving large numbers of relatively small claims, the Act allows some Magnuson-Moss Act suits to be brought in federal court. For example, in federal court suits: (1) the overall amount in controversy must exceed $50,000; (2) individual claims must exceed $25; and (3) if the action is brought as a class action there must be at least 100 named plaintiffs. These requirements are designed to facilitate relief which would otherwise be unavailable as a practical matter to individual consumers while avoiding trivial or insignificant suits being brought as class actions.

Finally, the Act explicitly provides for governmental sanctions against violators. For example, the Act allows either the Attorney General or the FTC to bring an action in federal court to enjoin (1) any warrantor from making a deceptive warranty concerning a consumer product, or (2) any person from failing to comply with any requirement or from violating any prohibition contained in the Act.[22]

---

21. A "service contract" is a written contract to maintain or repair (or both) a consumer product for a specified duration or a fixed period of time. 15 U.S.C. §2301(8). The FTC is empowered, by regulation, to prescribe the manner and form for disclosure of the terms and conditions of service contracts. 15 U.S.C §2306(a).

---

22. The Act also provides that Magnuson-Moss violations also violate Section 5 of the FTC Act. 15 U.S.C. §2310(b). Section 5 and FTC enforcement power under it are discussed in Chapter 52.

SUMMARY

1. A warranty is a seller's statement or other representation concerning the quality, character, or capabilities of the goods he sells. If the goods fail to conform to the standards created by a warranty, the seller is liable in damages for breach of warranty. The law of warranty, therefore, effectively defines the seller's obligation with respect to goods accepted by the buyer. Various types of warranties may be created under the UCC, including express warranties, implied warranties, and the warranties of title and against infringement.

2. Under the Code, any affirmation of fact or promise which relates to the goods and becomes part of the basis of the bargain creates an express warranty that the goods will conform to the affirmation or promise. Express warranties may also be created by any description, sample, or model which becomes part of the basis of the bargain. In short, express warranties rest upon the dickered, or bargained-for, aspects of the sales contract.

3. The implied warranties under the Code, which arise by operation of law, are merchantability and fitness for a particular purpose. Merchantability imposes an obligation upon a merchant seller that his wares meet minimum standards of quality. Generally, to be merchantable, the goods must be fit for the *ordinary* purposes for which such goods are used. The warranty of fitness, requiring that the goods be suitable for the buyer's *particular* purpose, is imposed upon a seller who has reason to know of the particular purpose for which the buyer requires the goods and that the buyer is relying upon the seller's skill and judgment to choose suitable goods.

4. The warranty of title simply requires the seller to provide the buyer with a good clean title free of security interests or other liens. The warranty against infringement obligates a merchant seller to deliver goods free of third-party claims of patent or trademark infringement.

5. Consistent with basic Code policy, warranties may be excluded or modified by contract. Warranty disclaimers, however, offer great potential for unconscionable application. Therefore, the Code provisions allowing the seller to alter or eliminate warranty liability or to limit the buyer's remedy in the event of breach provide a significant amount of protection to the buyer against whom the disclaimer or limitation operates. Similarly, if a seller gives more than one warranty concerning the same goods, the buyer has the benefit of all of them to the extent they can co-exist.

6. If goods accepted by the buyer are not as warranted, the buyer may generally recover as damages the difference between the value of the goods accepted and the value they would have had if they had been as warranted. The buyer may also recover incidental and consequential damages in appropriate cases. Consequential damages for breach of warranty include damages for personal injury and property damage caused by the breach.

7. Although warranties are largely governed by state law (the UCC), a federal statute—the Magnuson-Moss Warranty Act—provides additional buyer protection when written warranties are given in connection with sales of consumer goods. The Act requires that the terms of a written warranty be fully and conspicuously disclosed in simple and readily understood language, and that the warranty be designated as "full" or "limited" to indicate whether it meets certain minimum federal standards. The Act also prohibits the use of written warranties as a means to disclaim or modify the implied warranties of merchantability and fitness.

KEY TERMS

warranty	conspicuous
warranty disclaimer	warranty of title
express warranty	warranty against
sample	infringement
model	Magnuson-Moss Warranty
implied warranty	Act
merchantability	full warranty
fitness for a particular	limited warranty
purpose	

QUESTIONS AND PROBLEMS

19-1 Section 2-313 of the UCC provides that an express warranty may be created whether or not the seller uses the words "warrant," "warranty," or "guarantee." Nor is it necessary that the seller intend to create a warranty. Why does the UCC adopt such a liberal standard governing creation of express warranties?

19-2 What is the basic distinction between express and implied warranties under the UCC? Compare and contrast the implied warranty of merchantability with the warranty of fitness for a particular purpose. What is the basic distinction between remedies available for breach of warranty and the buyer's remedies discussed in Chapter 18?

19-3 Explain why courts are hesitant to allow disclaimer of express warranties created under §2-313 by general language such as "seller hereby disclaims all warranties, express or implied.''

19-4   Esther contracted Joe's Marina concerning purchase of a motorboat. Esther indicated that she needed the boat for use in a proposed water ski show, and that the boat therefore had to be capable of pulling ten skiers simultaneously at thirty-five miles per hour. Joe directed Esther to a used "Starcraft" boat with a 175 horsepower outboard motor, indicating that "this baby has more power than you'll ever need. It can pull twenty skiers at thirty-five miles per hour." After further negotiation Esther purchased the boat. Trouble, however, soon developed. With the ten skiers in a "pyramid" formation the boat could never muster more than twenty miles per hour. In addition, after only two weeks' normal use, the boat began losing power. Inspection of the engine revealed a cracked block. Esther contacted Joe who stated, "once that boat was off my property, it was yours. I never guarantee used equipment." Is Joe correct? More specifically, has Joe made any express warranties to Esther? Do any implied or other warranties run to Esther from Joe? Assuming a warranty or warranties exist, and have been breached, what remedy or remedies should Esther seek?

19-5   Jacques owned a salt water aquarium housing many expensive tropical fish. Jacques visited the Verona Rock Shop where he selected several sea shells, pieces of coral, and driftwood for his aquarium. Prior to buying the pieces, Jacques asked the sales clerk if the items were suitable for use in a salt water aquarium. The clerk said they would be suitable if they were rinsed.

Jacques rinsed the items and placed them in his aquarium. Within a week, seventeen of his fish had died. Examination of the shells revealed the presence of toxic material from the decay of creatures inhabiting the shells. The toxic material had caused the death of the fish.

Jacques sued Verona Rock Shop alleging breach of express warranty, warranty of merchantability, and warranty of fitness. Should the shop be held liable for the cost of the fish?

19-6   Jones sold a motorcycle to Jefferson and provided a title certificate which Jones registered with the state. Two years later, a police officer stopped Jefferson and asked to see some proof of title to the motorcycle. Jefferson produced the title certificate, but the identification number on the certificate did not match the identification number on the motorcycle. The police therefore seized the motorcycle. After legal proceedings, Jefferson regained possession of the vehicle. Jefferson then sued Jones alleging that Jones had breached the warranty of title and requesting reimbursement of the expenses incurred in proving to the police that Jefferson owned the motorcycle. How should the court rule?

19-7   Challenger, a manufacturer of telecommunication equipment, wanted to buy a computer system for use in its accounting department. After consulting with several computer companies, Challenger bought a system from National for $120,000. The National salesman told Challenger that the system would provide various functions including accounts receivable, payroll, inventory, and state income tax. The contract signed by the parties provided in part:

(1)   National warrants that for 12 months the computer system will perform the enumerated functions in a skillful and workmanlike manner but in case of a failure to so perform National's sole obligation is limited to correcting any error in any program or routine within 60 days after notice of said failure.

(2)   In no event shall National be liable for special or consequential damages from any cause whatsoever.

The system delivered by National failed to perform the functions enumerated in the contract. Although National continuously attempted to repair the computer, only one program was operating two years after the signing of the contract.

(a)   Challenger sued National for breach of the warranty of merchantability and fitness for a particular purpose and requested damages pursuant to UCC §2-714(2). National alleged that Challenger was not entitled to damages but that its sole remedy was to have National repair the computer. How should the court rule? Explain, citing appropriate UCC provisions.

(b)   Challenger also sought damages of $8,500 representing salaries of employees who were unable to work because of the computer failure and lost profits. National denied that Challenger was entitled to such damages. How should the court rule? Explain.

19-8   Arnie, a young golfer, purchased a device called the Golfing Gizmo to help improve his game. The Gizmo is a simple device consisting of two metal pegs, two cords—one elastic, one cotton—and a regulation golf ball. After the pegs are driven into the ground approximately 25 inches apart, the elastic cord is looped over them. The cotton cord, measuring 21 feet in length, ties to the middle of the elastic cord. The ball is attached to the end of the cotton cord. When the cords are extended, the Gizmo resembles the shape of a large letter "T," with the ball resting at the base.

The instructions state that when hit correctly, the ball will fly out and spring back near the point of impact; if the ball returns to the left, it indicates a right-hander's "slice"; a shot returning to the right indicates a right-hander's "hook." If the ball is "topped," it does not return and must be retrieved by the player. The label on the shipping carton and the cover of the instruction booklet urge players to "drive the ball with full power" and further state: "COMPLETELY SAFE BALL WILL NOT HIT PLAYER."

After using the Gizmo a few times, Arnie hit the golf ball but his club became entangled in the cord. The ball struck Arnie in the head causing serious brain damage.

(a) Arnie sued the manufacturer for breach of express warranty alleging that the statement "COMPLETELY SAFE BALL WILL NOT HIT PLAYER" constituted an express warranty. The manufacturer denied that this was an express warranty. How should the court rule? Explain.

(b) Assume that no express warranty was made concerning the Golfing Gizmo. Has the manufacturer breached the warranty of merchantability? What characteristics would a merchantable "Golfing Gizmo" exhibit?

19-9 NSP, an electrical utility, was constructing new towers to carry electric transmission lines. The towers were to be supported by wires extending to the ground where they would be attached to buried screw anchors. NSP solicited proposals from manufacturers who wanted to supply the anchors, and provided detailed technical specifications for them. Meyer, after reading the specifications, submitted a proposal, which stated in part: "The material we propose to supply meets the design requirements as specified by NSP." NSP accepted Meyer's proposal and used the Meyer anchors. Between September 27 and September 30, 1988, four towers collapsed due to a defect in the anchors. NSP immediately notified Meyer and technical personnel from both com-

panies inspected the anchors and discussed the problem. On October 15, NSP notified Meyer that it planned to remove all of the anchors. Although Meyer's technical staff believed that removal was unnecessary, Meyer did not object to NSP's plans. On February 28, 1989, NSP wrote Meyer asserting that Meyer had breached an express warranty by supplying defective anchors. A lawsuit followed.

(a) Did Meyer make an express warranty? Explain.

(b) Meyer argues that NSP failed to provide timely notice of the breach of warranty as required by UCC §2-607(3)(a). Is Meyer correct? Explain.

19-10 Section 2-314(1) provides that a "warranty that the goods shall be merchantable is implied in a contract for their sale if the seller is a *merchant with respect to goods of that kind*." (Emphasis added.)

Assume the goods sold in the following transactions are not merchantable. Are the sellers involved "merchants" who give the implied warranty of merchantability? Explain.

(a) The city of Auburn, Washington, owned and operated the only aircraft fuel service at the city airport. The fuel service delivered contaminated fuel to its customers.

(b) City Hospital furnished and billed separately four units of blood to one of its patients during major surgery. The blood was contaminated, and as a result of the transfusion the patient contracted hepatitis. (Consider also in this case (a) whether any "sale" of goods is involved and (b) whether your answer would change had the supplier been a blood bank rather than a hospital.)

(c) Wilhelm, a commercial aerial and ground crop sprayer, was engaged by Doaks to spray his wheat crop to control wild oats. Wilhelm held himself out as an expert in aerial spraying, licensed by federal and state authorities, and trained in use of crop sprays. Wilhelm had sole control over choice of the herbicide, mixing it, and applying it to Doaks's crops. After spraying Doaks's wheat became discolored and limp, ultimately yielding only six bushels per acre, compared with 16 per acre on his other fields.

(d) An association of mothers of high school band members organized a fund raising luncheon. Turkey salad prepared and sold by the association proved to be contaminated with the bacteria salmonella. One of the persons purchasing the salad became seriously ill.

(e) The City National Bank loaned money to Jones to purchase a boat and took a security interest in the boat. When Jones failed to re-

pay the loan, City repossessed the boat and sold it to Donald. The boat failed to operate properly.

(f) Would your answer in (e) above differ if the bank had sold five repossessed boats in the last year?

Major Topics

- ▧ the definition of products liability and the concept of privity
- ▧ the elements of the plaintiff's claim and defenses available under the three basic products liability theories: negligence, breach of warranty, and strict liability in tort

This chapter discusses **products liability,** the area of law imposing liability upon manufacturers and other suppliers of goods for personal injury and property damage caused by the products they sell. For example, assume XYZ Corporation manufactures hair dryers, one of which is purchased by Buyer. Because it is poorly designed, the hair dryer overheats causing a fire that injures Buyer and substantially damages Buyer's house. Buyer's right to recover against XYZ Corporation for the injury to person and property is governed by the law of products liability.

Early American courts, following seventeenth-century English precedents, imposed the harsh "caveat emptor" (let the buyer beware) doctrine upon products liability plaintiffs. Under this theory a seller had no liability in tort or contract to anyone, including a purchaser, for injuries caused by its defective product. The plaintiff's sole hope for recovery was to prove fraud or that the seller had guaranteed some specific characteristic or quality of the product.

Modern Theories of Recovery

The caveat emptor doctrine has been rejected by modern courts and replaced with three basic theories under which a manufacturer or other seller may be held liable to injured third parties. These are: (1) negligence, (2) breach of warranty, and (3) strict liability in tort. Thus, modern product liability law is grounded partially in the law of contract (warranty) and partially in the law of torts (negligence and strict liability).

The elements of the plaintiff's cause of action, particular problems, and defenses available to the seller under each theory are discussed in turn below. Although all three theories are used to impose liability on manufacturers and suppliers, the burgeoning strict liability in tort doctrine has emerged, within less than 25 years, as the primary basis for recovery by injured plaintiffs in products liability cases.

Note finally that products liability law generally compensates for *personal injury and property damage*. Recovery for direct *economic* loss and indirect *economic* consequential damage, such as lost profit, caused by defective products remains the exclusive domain of the law of warranty, discussed in Chapter 19.

Privity of Contract

A brief introduction to the "privity of contract" concept is necessary to a basic understanding of products liability. Persons who have entered into a contractual relationship with each other are said to be in **privity of contract**. For example, if Seth sells a lawnmower to Linda, he and she are in privity of contract. A basic issue in all products liability cases is to what extent injured persons not in privity with the seller may recover. Persons not in privity who are injured by the product stand in either a "horizontal" or "vertical" relationship to the manufacturer or other supplier from whom they seek to recover. A "vertical" party not in privity is a buyer of the goods who is one or more steps removed from the seller in the chain of distribution. For example, when a manufacturer sells a product to a wholesaler who sells it to a retailer who sells it to a consumer, the consumer is in privity only with the retailer. If, however, the product causes injury, the consumer may seek to recover from the wholesaler or manufacturer. The consumer's relationship to them is said to be "vertical."

"Horizontal" parties not in privity are those who are not buyers but others who by use, consumption, or other contact with the goods are injured by them. Assume Smith Corp. sells a car with defective brakes to Jones, who allows his son Art to use the car to take his girlfriend Beth to the senior prom. Art, Beth, and Carl, an innocent bystander, are injured when the car crashes because the brakes fail. Art, Beth, and Carl stand in a "horizontal" relationship to Smith but are not in privity with Smith (Jones is).

Privity issues under each theory (negligence, warranty, and strict liability) are discussed in the following subsections. It is important to note at the outset, however, that in modern product liability law, lack of privity is *not* a bar to a plaintiff seeking recovery for personal injuries caused by a seller's product.

Negligence

The basic principles of the law of negligence are covered in Chapter 5. That material examined the law primarily as applied to cases not involving products liability, to compensate, for example, for injuries caused by negligently-driven automobiles or dangerous conditions existing on land. The following material briefly reviews basic negligence law and then discusses how it has been applied to compensate persons injured by defective products.

Negligence in General

Negligence is "conduct which falls below the standard established by law for the protection of others against unreasonable risk of harm."[1] Generally, liability is imposed for injuries proximately caused by a person's failure to use **reasonable** or **ordinary care**—the amount of care a reasonably careful and prudent person would use under similar circumstances. In other words, to avoid liability for negligence, a person must conform his conduct to that of a reasonable person under like circumstances. Negligence may result from doing an act a reasonable person would not do, or neglecting to do something a reasonable person would do. The hypothetical reasonable person is not an extraordinarily cautious or skillful individual, but one possessing merely ordinary prudence and judgment. Whether the defendant's conduct falls below the standard set by the reasonable person is ordinarily a question for the jury to decide. To recover on the basis of negligence, the plaintiff must show: (1) defendant owed plaintiff a duty not to be negligent; (2) defendant breached that duty by failing to exercise reasonable or ordinary care; and (3) defendant's breach of duty proximately caused injury to the plaintiff.

Manufacturer's or Supplier's Duty

Applied to products liability, the law of negligence imposes a duty upon the manufacturer or other supplier to exercise reasonable care in the design, production, and distribution of its products. Early cases, following *Winterbottom v. Wright* (1842),[2] held that the seller's duty extended to only those persons in privity of contract with the seller. The rule in *Winterbottom* was designed to protect the newly developing industries. It was based on the assumption that "industry could not grow and prosper if it had to pay for any and all injuries its defective products caused. The assumption rested on the oft-disproved notion that wheels operate at peak efficiency when unattended by brakes."[3] The harshness of the rule was readily apparent; it left

---

1. *Restatement (Second) of Torts* §282.
2. 10 Mees. & W. 109, 152 Eng. Rep. 402 (Ex. 1842).
3. Traynor, The Ways and Meanings of Defective Products and Strict Liability, 32 Tenn. L. Rev. 363, 364 (1965).

the injured party without a remedy unless in privity with the seller. Courts quickly began to circumvent the rule by dispensing with privity when injuries were caused by "imminently or inherently dangerous" products.

The privity requirement in negligence actions for other products was first rejected in 1916 in *MacPherson v. Buick Motor Co.*[4] In this case, the defendant manufacturer sold a car to a dealer who then sold it to the plaintiff. Plaintiff was subsequently thrown out of the car and injured when a defective wheel collapsed. When sued, defendant asserted lack of privity as a defense. (Note that the plaintiff stood in a "vertical" relationship to defendant here, a buyer later in the distributive chain.) Judge Benjamin Cardozo (who later would sit on the United States Supreme Court) stated that abolition of privity should not be "limited to poisons, explosives, and things of like nature, to things which in their normal operation are implements of destruction." He went on to hold:

> If the nature of a thing is such that it is reasonably certain to place life and limb in peril when negligently made, it is then a thing of danger. Its nature gives warning of the consequences to be expected. If to the element of danger there is added knowledge that the thing *will be used by persons other than the purchaser, and used without new tests, then, irrespective of contract, the manufacturer of this thing of danger is under a duty to make it carefully.*[5]

Today, all states follow the rule adopted in *MacPherson* so that lack of privity is no longer a defense in products liability actions based on negligence. That is, a seller owes a duty to exercise reasonable care in the manufacture and distribution of its product not only to the seller's immediate purchaser, but also to all reasonably foreseeable persons who may be injured by the product.

Breach of Duty

After establishing that defendant owed the duty to exercise reasonable care, the plaintiff further must prove that defendant breached that duty—that is, that defendant failed to exercise reasonable care in the design, production, or distribution of the product that injured the plaintiff. Typically, the defendant's breach of the duty may result from the use of an unsafe design, or improper materials, failure to adequately test the product, or insufficient quality control during manufacture (for example, inspection). In some cases, even if the product is safe when properly used, reasonable care may require adequate instructions or warning if the product would be unsafe under other circumstances. In the following case, involving the adequacy of a warning, the existence of negligence and proximate causation were in issue.

Griggs v. Firestone Tire and Rubber Company
513 F.2d 851 (8th Cir. 1975)

Plaintiff Clifford Griggs suffered permanent injuries to his face and head when a tire and wheel rim assembly exploded as he was mounting a tire on a truck. The rim assembly consisted of three parts: the rim itself, a side ring, and a lock ring. The rim had been manufactured by defendant, Firestone Tire and Rubber Company (Firestone), in 1957. The side ring and lock ring were riveted together. The side ring had been manufactured in 1945. Thus, the components were mismatched and had not been intended to form a unit.

The mismatch of the rim components occurred in 1971 when the then owner of the truck had removed the original tires and rims from the truck, replacing them with extra tires and the mismatched rim components that he had accumulated. He then traded the truck in as partial payment for a new truck from Presson Ford Sales. Presson sold the truck to Murray Maynard, Griggs's employer. Griggs, a truck and tractor driver, was changing a flat tire on the truck. After reinflating the deflated tire, Griggs was tightening the lug nuts when in his words, the "tire blowed off" striking him in the face and head. In addition to suffering a fractured skull, nose, and cheekbones, Griggs lost partial vision in one eye and became subject to epileptic seizures.

Griggs sued for negligence. At trial, Firestone alleged that it had distributed catalogues warning of

---

4. 111 N.E. 1050 (N.Y. 1916).
5. 111 N.E. at 1053 (emphasis added).

the dangers posed by the wheel assemblies. Pertinent parts of those catalogues stated:

*Important Rim and Wheel
Safety Precautions*
NOTICE!

An inflated tire and rim can be very dangerous. Many accidents, some fatal, have resulted from improper handling and operation of truck rims and wheels. . . .

How to Prevent Rim Accidents During Tire Mounting . . .

Use properly matched parts only. Rim base and rings must be matched according to manufacturer, size and type. This information is stamped on each Firestone part. . . .

How to Insure Greater Safety and Service by Properly Matching Side and Lock Rings

It is important to recognize that the various types of highway rims produced by their manufacturers all differ to some degree in design. This is particularly true of removable rings and, as a result, side and lock rings of different rim types are not interchangeable. Some may appear to be, but they actually do not fit properly on the rim base. Serious accidents to personnel have resulted from the use of mismatched rings.

The catalogues had been distributed to parts distributors and manufacturers of vehicles with Firestone rims as original equipment.

The trial court ruled in favor of Griggs and awarded damages of $250,000. Firestone appealed.

Matthes, Senior Circuit Judge

. . . Some articles supplied for commerce are dangerous by their very nature, without regard to any product defect. A manufacturer or supplier of such inherently dangerous chattels is subject to a legal duty to exercise reasonable care in warning those expected to use the product of the danger presented. Liability is imposed where injury resulting from the use of the product is attributable to a breach of this "duty to warn." . . .

Defendant, by its very warning literature, implicitly acknowledges that its product is "dangerous for the use for which it is supplied" and that those "for whose use the chattel is supplied"

would not realize that dangerous condition. . . . However, defendant vigorously contests the proposition that it has failed to exercise reasonable care in warning of that danger. Additionally, defendant contends that, even should it have breached its duty to warn, its negligence could not in any event be a legal cause of plaintiff's injuries. . . .

A. Duty to Warn

. . . In the instant case we have no difficulty with the proposition that the jury reasonably could have found that defendant had not met its duty to exercise reasonable care. By any standard the danger inhering in defendant's product must be deemed great: there is an obvious potential for severe injury from wholly unanticipated explosion of a wheel assembly under great pressure in close proximity to the repairman. As Firestone acknowledges in its warning literature, the resulting harm may easily be grievous bodily injury or even death. Given this potential for severe injury, we cannot say as a matter of law that defendant discharged its duty through the informational literature which it supplied to the various parts distributors and automobile manufacturers using its rims. . . . As noted in the *Restatement* reasonable care may dictate that a warning be impressed directly on the article when (as here) the danger is great and such a warning would not be impracticable or unduly burdensome. . . . We believe the jury could reasonably have found that ordinary care required that a warning be impressed directly on this dangerous instrumentality.

In closing our discussion of this issue, we observe that the necessity for rim disassembly is not an infrequent occurrence. The record indicates that a rim may last for twenty-six years or more, and that it probably will have to be disassembled at least once a year. In the life of any given rim, therefore, there are numerous occasions when components may be mismatched and a potential "bomb" created. In calculating the warning appropriate to this danger, Firestone *assumed* that most people servicing its rims would realize the dangers presented and possess the requisite aptitude and experience to assemble the rim safely. . . .

[In] view of the inevitability of rim disassembly and the practical fact that, at least in some cases, repair is bound to be undertaken, as here, by those not familiar with the particular dangers of these multi-piece rims, the jury could find that Firestone's assumption was unreasonable and that it had failed its duty of care. . . .

B. Causation

. . . With respect to the proximate cause argument, defendant primarily contends that, even had it impressed a warning on the instant rims, the warning would have been obliterated by years of dirt and rust, and thus would not have been conveyed to the plaintiff.

While this argument was, of course, entitled to consideration by the jury, there was evidence from which the jury reasonably could conclude that a warning on these particular rims would have been visible to Griggs. . . .

Defendant also argues that legal causation has not been demonstrated in that the mismatch of rim components constitutes an independent intervening cause of plaintiff's injuries. As the trial court properly instructed, whether an intervening act will constitute an independent intervening cause is a question of foreseeability. . . . Even where the intervening act is the negligence of a third party, the act does not become a superseding cause where "a reasonable man knowing the situation existing when the act of the third person was done would not regard it as highly extraordinary that the third person had so acted." *Restatement (Second) of Torts* §447(b). Moreover, the "law does not require precision in foreseeing the exact hazard or consequence" which in fact transpires; it is sufficient "if what occurred was one of the kind of consequences which might reasonably be foreseen." *Comstock v. General Motors Corp.,* [99 N.W.2d 627, 636 (Mich. 1959)].

In this case the alleged intervening cause—the mismatch of the rim components—was precisely the event against which Firestone warned in its safety literature. It does not matter that the exact manner in which the mismatch occurred was not foreseen. Firestone cannot argue that, as a matter of law, the precise danger which it contemplated was unforeseen. Accordingly, this contention must fail. . . .

[Judgment affirmed.]

Plaintiff's Proof—"Res Ipsa Loquitur"

The plaintiff has the burden of proving by a preponderance of the evidence (meaning that it is more likely than not) defendant's negligence. In proving this issue, the plaintiff often is aided by the doctrine of **res ipsa loquitur,** literally meaning "the thing speaks for itself." Under this doctrine, it may be inferred that the harm suffered by the plaintiff has been caused by the defendant's negligence if:

1. the event is of a kind that ordinarily does not occur in the absence of negligence;
2. other responsible causes, including the conduct of the plaintiff and third persons, are sufficiently eliminated by the evidence; and
3. the indicated negligence is within the scope of the defendant's duty to the plaintiff.[6]

Provided the plaintiff is able to establish the foregoing requirements, the jury is permitted to infer (and generally will) that the defect in the product was caused by the defendant's negligence. Thus, the plaintiff will be allowed to recover even though unable to offer any direct evidence regarding the particular conduct of the defendant constituting negligence and even if the defendant introduces evidence that the event was not caused by his negligence. For example, the defendant may introduce evidence of his quality control procedures in manufacture. In other words, the jury is entitled to weigh the fact that the event did occur against the defendant's evidence of due care tending to indicate that it could not have occurred. The doctrine is most commonly applied in the products liability context when products reaching the plaintiff in sealed containers cause injury. Examples include exploding beer or soda bottles, foreign objects found in bottled, canned, or baked goods, and tainted products, such as botulism in canned beans.

Defenses

After a plaintiff proves the elements of negligence, the defendant may avoid or reduce its liability by

---

6. *Restatement (Second) of Torts* §328D.

proving one or more of the defenses to a negligence action. These defenses, which are based on the plaintiff's conduct, include assumption of the risk and contributory (or in most states today, comparative) negligence. For example, the defendant may escape liability by establishing that the plaintiff voluntarily assumed the risk of harm caused by the defendant's negligence. The defendant's liability also may be extinguished (in states recognizing contributory negligence) or reduced (in states adopting comparative negligence) upon proof that the plaintiff's own negligence contributed to her injury. These defenses are discussed in more detail in Chapter 5.

Breach of Warranty

An alternative basis for products liability recovery is the law of warranty, a branch of contract law. As explained in Chapter 19, a contract for the sale of goods may include an express warranty, an implied warranty of merchantability, or an implied warranty of fitness for a particular purpose. As with contract liability generally, warranty liability is *strict*—liability is imposed without fault. Accordingly, liability for breach of warranty does not turn upon the seller's knowledge or reason to know of the product's defectiveness or upon negligence. If the seller makes an express or implied warranty and the goods fail to perform as warranted, liability follows. Although a breach of warranty often causes merely commercial or economic injury, the UCC expressly authorizes recovery—as consequential damages—for "injury to person or property proximately resulting from any breach of warranty."[7] To recover for personal injuries or property damage under this theory, a plaintiff must prove that the seller made an express or implied warranty, that the seller breached this warranty, and that the seller's breach was the proximate cause of the plaintiff's injuries. In the following case, the court was required to determine whether express and implied Code warranties had been created.

---

7. UCC §2-715(2)(b).

Palmer v. A. H. Robins Co., Inc.
684 P.2d 187 (Colo. 1984)

In January 1973, plaintiff Carie Palmer, a twenty-four-year-old married woman and mother, visited her physician, Dr. Kenneth Petri, to obtain a prescription for birth control. After Palmer rejected birth control pills because of their potential adverse effects, Dr. Petri recommended the Dalkon Shield, an intrauterine device (IUD) manufactured by defendant A. H. Robins Co., Inc. (Robins). Based on information provided by Robins's literature and sales representatives, Dr. Petri described the Dalkon Shield as a superior IUD, safer than birth control pills and 98.9% effective in preventing pregnancy. Although Palmer was fitted with a Dalkon Shield, she became pregnant in August 1973. In November 1973, she developed a uterine infection that caused an involuntary miscarriage. She went into septic shock, a condition resulting from massive infection combined with dangerously low blood pressure. To save Palmer's life, her physicians performed a total hysterectomy.

Palmer sued Robins based on negligence, strict liability in tort, and breach of express and implied warranties. The evidence at trial established that the design of the Dalkon Shield allowed bacteria to enter the uterus causing the infection suffered by Palmer. A jury found for Palmer and awarded compensatory damages of $600,000 and punitive damages of $6,200,000. Robins appealed. In the portion of the opinion that follows, the Colorado Supreme Court considers the claims for breach of the warranties set forth in the UCC.

Quinn, Justice

. . . The Warranty Claims

. . . *Express Warranty.* Robins challenges the submission of Palmer's express warranty claim to the jury because, in its view, there was insufficient evidence to establish that Robins' claimed representations constituted part of the transaction resulting in Palmer's selection, purchase, and use of the shield. . . .

It is not necessary for an express warranty that "the seller use formal words such as 'warrant' or 'guarantee' or that he have a specific intention to make a warranty, but . . . a statement purporting to be merely the seller's opinion or commendation of the goods does not create a warranty." [UCC §] 2-313(2). Whether a particular statement constitutes an express warranty is generally an issue of fact. . . . When a warranty has been created, it "extends to any person who may reasonably be expected to use, consume, or be affected by the goods and who [was] injured by breach of the warranty." [UCC §] 2-318.

Palmer's express warranty claim was properly submitted to the jury. Palmer testified that Dr. Petri, before prescribing the shield, indicated to her that the shield was a superior IUD, safer than the birth control pill, and 98.9% effective in preventing pregnancy. Dr. Petri had drawn this information from a review of Robins' literature, [and] conversations with Robins' representatives. . . . Palmer also subsequently read literature printed by the shield's manufacturer which reiterated the safety and effectiveness claims. These statements qualify under [UCC §] 2-313(1) as affirmations of fact and product descriptions upon which Palmer relied in using the shield, as opposed to the birth control pill, as a method of contraception. There was sufficient evidence, in our view, to support a reasonable conclusion by the jury that Robins' representations concerning the superiority, effectiveness, and safety of the shield formed an essential part of Palmer's decision to have that device inserted in her body and to continue using it as a safe and effective method of contraception.

. . . Implied Warranties. Robins contends that the trial court erred in submitting to the jury Palmer's claims for breach of implied warranty of fitness for a particular purpose and implied warranty of merchantability because, according to Robins, there was no evidence establishing that the particular purpose for which Palmer selected the shield was different from its ordinary purpose.

A contract for the sale of goods by "a merchant with respect to goods of that kind" gives rise to an implied warranty of merchantability, unless properly excluded or modified. [UCC §] 2-314(1). Merchantability, as pertinent here, means that the

goods "[a]re fit for the ordinary purposes for which such goods are used," [UCC §] 2-314(2)(c), "[a]re adequately contained, packaged, and labeled," [UCC §] 2-314(2)(e), and "[c]onform to the promises or affirmations of fact made on the container or label if any," [UCC §] 2-314(2)(f). An implied warranty of fitness for a particular purpose arises "[w]here the seller at the time of contracting has reason to know any particular purpose for which the goods are required and that the buyer is relying on the seller's skill or judgment to select or furnish suitable goods." [UCC §] 2-315. . . . This is not to say, however, that implied warranties of merchantability and fitness for a particular purpose are mutually exclusive. On the contrary, Colorado case law recognizes that these warranties may coexist when there is sufficient evidence to support the creation of each warranty. . . .

There was sufficient evidence in this case to justify the submission of both warranty claims to the jury. . . . Palmer, relying on Dr. Petri's recommendation, chose the shield because she believed it would be safer than other forms of contraception and would be almost as effective as the pill in preventing pregnancy. This evidence . . . is sufficient to support Palmer's claim that she selected the shield not only to prevent pregnancy, the ordinary purpose for which an IUD is selected, but also for the particular purpose of providing her with a "safe" contraceptive device that averted such hazards as stroke, vascular clotting, and other harmful effects in the body. There can be no question that Robins knew or had reason to know of the special or particular safety features attributed to its product, since both Dr. Petri and Palmer premised their decisions on affirmative representations made by Robins. Nor can there be any question about Palmer's reliance upon Robins to furnish a product which would fulfill these particular purposes. . . .

[Judgment affirmed.]

Defenses

Because warranty is grounded in contract, the personal injury plaintiff suing for breach of warranty traditionally has encountered the seller's contract-based defenses blocking recovery. These defenses include, for example, (1) failure by the plaintiff to give timely notice of the breach to the defendant, (2) contractual limitation or exclusion of warranty protection, and (3) lack of privity of contract between the warrantor-seller and the injured plaintiff. Although these defenses often were successful in early warranty cases, the Uniform Commercial Code, which was widely adopted in the mid-1960s, and judicial decisions interpreting it eliminate or reduce the effect of these defenses in modern products liability actions based on breach of warranty.

Notice of Breach. As a condition to recovery for a breach of warranty, UCC §2-607(3)(a) requires that the buyer notify the seller of breach within a reasonable time after its discovery. Though this is a sound rule in the commercial context (it protects the seller against unreasonably delayed damage claims by a buyer), in a personal injury case, the injured plaintiff is unlikely to give notice to a remote seller with whom he has not dealt. For this reason, the Code authorizes a more relaxed notice standard for consumers than for commercial purchasers. As noted in Official Comment 4 to §2-607:

> The time of notification is to be determined by applying commercial standards to a merchant buyer. "A reasonable time" for notification from a retail consumer is to be judged by different standards so that in his case it will be extended, for the rule of requiring notification is designed to defeat commercial bad faith, not to deprive a good faith consumer of his remedy.

In addition, courts often liberally construe the notice requirement when personal, as opposed to commercial, injury is involved. For example, in some cases, the plaintiff's filing a lawsuit has been held sufficient to provide notice to the defendant. In the *Palmer* case, excerpted above, the court rejected the defendant's argument that Palmer had failed to give reasonable notice of the breach, stating:

> While [UCC §] 2-607(3)(a) provides for notification to the seller "[w]here a tender has been

accepted," we construe the word "seller," as used in that section, to refer only to the immediate seller who tendered the goods to the buyer. . . . Under this construction, as long as the buyer has given notice of the defect to his or her immediate seller, no further notification to those distributors beyond the immediate seller is required. . . .

Since the cost of the shield to Dr. Petri was included in his fee for the insertion of that device in Palmer, Dr. Petri in this case was Palmer's immediate seller. . . . Since no prescribed form of notice is required . . . there is sufficient evidence establishing that Palmer gave notice to Dr. Petri of the defective character of the shield and that this notice "came to his attention," within the meaning of [UCC §] 1-201(26), when Palmer presented herself to him in a life-threatening condition on November 18, 1973, and the days immediately following. . . .[8]

Disclaimer. Section 2-719, introduced in Chapter 18, generally allows the parties to contractually modify or limit remedies available for breach. Section 2-719(3), however, severely restricts a seller's ability to contractually disclaim warranty liability for personal, as opposed to commercial, injury. Specifically, §2-719(3) provides that consequential damages may be limited or excluded unless the limitation or exclusion is unconscionable. Limitation of consequential damage for injury to a person in cases involving consumer goods is prima facie unconscionable, but limitation when the loss is commercial is not. That is, if a clause limiting consequential damages is used, the buyer has the burden of proving its unconscionable effect unless the clause purports to limit damages for personal injury caused by a consumer good.

The following case illustrates an application of §2-719(3) and the relationship between limitations of remedy under §2-719 and warranty disclaimers under §2-316, discussed in Chapter 19.

---

8. 684 P.2d at 206-207.

McCarty v. E. J. Korvette, Inc.
347 A.2d 253 (Md. App. 1975)

Appellants Frances and Warren McCarty purchased four automobile tires from appellee E. J. Korvette, Inc. On the back of the invoice provided to the McCartys, the following statements were written under the heading "Korvette Tire Centers All-Road-Hazards Tire Guarantee":

> *The tires identified hereon are guaranteed for* the number of months (or miles) designated [*36,000 miles*] *against all road hazards* including stone bruises, impact bruises, *blow out*, tread separation, glass cuts and fabric breaks, only when used in normal, non-commercial passenger car service. *If a tire fails to give satisfactory service under the terms of this guarantee*, return it to the nearest Korvette Tire Center. *We will replace the tire* charging only the proportionate part of the sale price for each month elapsed (or mileage used) from date of purchase, plus the full federal tax.
>
> The above guarantee does not cover tires run flat, or simply worn out; tires injured by a fire, collision, vandalism, misalignment or mechanical defects of the vehicle. Radial or surface fissures, discoloration or ordinary repairable punctures, do not render tires unfit for service. Punctures will be repaired free.
>
> *Neither the manufacturer nor Korvette Tire Centers shall be liable for any consequential damage and our liability is limited solely to replacement of the product.* (Emphasis supplied.)

Five months later, the McCartys were involved in an automobile accident that caused personal injury to both of them and property damage to their car. The McCartys sued E. J. Korvette, Inc. and the tire manufacturer for damages alleging that the accident was caused by a blowout of one of the tires and further alleging that E. J. Korvette, Inc. had breached both express and implied warranties. At the conclusion of McCartys' presentation of evidence, the trial judge directed a verdict in favor of E. J. Korvette, Inc. The McCartys appealed.

Davidson, Judge

. . . The appellees initially contend that the language contained in the Korvette Tire Centers All-Road Hazard Tire Guarantee, when read as a whole, does not constitute an express warranty against blowouts, but rather constitutes a guarantee that if a blowout occurs, the tire will be replaced. . . .

Here the language on the invoice given to the buyer to the effect that "the tires identified hereon are guaranteed for 36,000 miles . . . against all road hazards, including . . . blow out . . ." constitutes an affirmation that the tires are of such existing quality, capacity and condition as to make them capable of rendering service without blowing out before they have been used for 36,000 miles. This assurance of the serviceability of the tires for a given number of miles, because it is a representation as to the existing quality, capacity and condition of the tires, constitutes an express warranty that the tires will not blow out during the first 36,000 miles of use. . . .

Here the language which says that the guarantee applies only when the tires are used in normal non-commercial passenger car service, and does not apply to tires that are run flat, or simply worn out, injured by a fire, collision, vandalism, misalignment or mechanical defects of the vehicle, constitutes a disclaimer under [UCC §2-316(1)]. The language which not only promises to replace the tire if a blowout occurs, but also attempts to avoid consequential damages and restrict the remedies of the buyer solely to replacement, constitutes a limitation of remedies under [UCC §2-316(4)], governed by the provisions of [UCC §2-719]. . . .

[UCC §2-719] gives the parties considerable latitude in which to fashion their remedies to their particular requirements. It expressly recognizes that parties may limit their remedies to repair and replacement. The parties, however, must accept the legal consequence that there be some fair remedy for breach of the obligations or duties outlined in the contract. Reasonable agreements which limit or modify remedies will be given effect, but the parties are not free to shape their remedies in an unreasonable or unconscionable way. [UCC §2719(3)] . . . establishes that limitation of consequential damages for injury to the person in the case of consumer goods is *prima facie* unconscionable.

[UCC §2-302(1)] sets forth the alternatives available to a court when it finds a limitation of remedy to be unconscionable. That section permits the court in its discretion, after a finding of unconscionability, to refuse to enforce the contract as a whole, if it is permeated by the unconscionability, or *to strike any single clause or group of clauses which are so tainted* or which are contrary to the essential purpose of the agreement, or to simply limit unconscionable clauses so as to avoid unconscionable results. Thus, any clause purporting to modify or limit remedies in an unconscionable manner is subject to deletion and will not be given effect.

Here the executory promise to replace the tire in the event of a blowout, found in the first paragraph of the warranty, . . . coupled with the clause purporting to exclude liability for consequential damages and to limit liability solely to replacement, clearly expresses an intent that replacement be the sole remedy under the contract. . . . [T]o the extent that the clause purports to limit consequential damages for personal injury, it is unconscionable as a matter of law. . . .

While there is no statutory presumption of unconscionability with respect to a limitation of consequential damages for injury to property in the case of consumer goods, . . . the clause here, which attempts to exclude liability for both personal injury and property damage is so tainted by unconscionability as to warrant deletion in its entirety. If the appellees do not want to be liable for consequential damages, they should not expressly warrant the tires against blowouts.

Under the present circumstances, the clause purporting to restrict remedies solely to replacement is ineffective. It cannot serve to convert the express warranty against blowouts into a guarantee that if a tire blew out, "the tire would be replaced." . . .

[Judgment of the trial court reversed and case remanded for a new trial.]

Privity. The UCC statutorily eliminates privity of contract as a defense to products liability cases based on breach of warranty in § 2-318, which determines which third parties, not in privity with the seller, are entitled to recover for a breach of warranty. Recognizing that states may differ on this issue, §2-318 provides three separate alternatives defining the extent of the seller's liability for breach of express or implied warranty. Alternative A, adopted in twenty-six states, is the most restrictive, allowing recovery to any natural person who is in the family or household of the buyer or who is a guest in the buyer's home if it is reasonable to expect that such person may use, consume, or be affected by the goods and who suffers personal injury because of the breach of warranty. Thus, under alternative A, liability extends horizontally beyond strict privity to the limited class of persons outlined above. In states adopting this alternative, the issue of liability to vertical parties not in privity is left to court determination through case law.[9]

The more expansive alternative B, adopted in five states, extends the seller's warranty horizontally and vertically to any natural person who may reasonably be expected to use, consume, or be affected by the goods and who suffers personal injury as a result of the breach of warranty. Alternative C, adopted in eleven states, is identical to alternative B except that liability is extended for injury to both person and *property*. Five additional states have enacted provisions similar to but more expansive than alternatives B and C, while two states have left the matter entirely to judicial determination.[10] The seller may not contractually reduce the class of persons to whom he or she would otherwise be liable for personal injury under §2-318.

Strict Liability in Tort

Development of the Doctrine

The law of warranty is designed and is well suited to compensate the immediate parties to a contract for economic or commercial injury caused by breach of warranty. Warranty law, however, even since the adoption of the UCC, often proves cumbersome when applied to personal injuries sustained by parties remote to the contract. In the early 1960s, courts therefore began to develop a new doctrine, known as **strict liability in tort,** which

---

9. As explained in Official Comment 3 to §2-318: "[T]he section in this form is neutral and is not intended to enlarge or restrict the developing case law on whether the seller's warranties, given to his buyer who resells, extend to other persons in the distributive chain."

10. Louisiana has not enacted Article 2 of the UCC.

uses a warranty concept (imposing liability without fault) but which imposes liability on the basis of tort law rather than contract law principles.

A major case in the development of the doctrine was *Henningsen v. Bloomfield Motors, Inc.* (1960),[11] in which plaintiffs sued for breach of the implied warranty of merchantability to recover for personal injuries caused by the crash of a new automobile. In finding for the plaintiffs, the court, in effect, interpreted the implied warranty of merchantability in products liability cases to mean that the product must be reasonably safe for its intended use—an implied warranty of safety. The court further found that this ''warranty'' was unencumbered by defenses traditionally available to the seller in contract warranty actions: lack of privity, lack of notice, and disclaimer. In the words of the court:

> . . . [U]nder modern marketing conditions, when a manufacturer puts a new automobile in the stream of trade and promotes its purchase by the public, an *implied warranty that it is reasonably suitable for use as such accompanies it into the hands of the ultimate purchaser.*[12]

This approach quickly evolved into the strict liability in tort doctrine, the dominant products liability theory today. The origin of the strict liability doctrine is usually traced to the following landmark case.

Greenman v. Yuba Power Products, Inc.
377 P.2d 897 (Cal. 1962)

Plaintiff William Greenman was injured while using a combination power tool manufactured by defendant Yuba Power Products, Inc. (Yuba). When using the tool as a lathe, Greenman was severely injured when the piece of wood he was working flew out of the machine and struck him. Because of defective design or construction, the set screws used to hold parts of the machine together were inade-

quate and, as a result, normal vibration during operation caused the tail stock of the lathe to move away from the wood being turned resulting in the injury.

Greenman sued on the basis of negligence and breach of express warranty contained in Yuba's brochure. Before purchase, he had studied the brochure that indicated that the product's ruggedness and positive locking aspects made it an accurate lathe. The trial court found in favor of Greenman, and awarded damages of $65,000. Yuba appealed.

Traynor, Justice

. . . The manufacturer contends, . . . that plaintiff did not give it notice of breach of warranty within a reasonable time and that therefore his cause of action for breach of warranty is barred. . . .

The notice requirement . . . however, is not an appropriate one for the court to adopt in actions by injured consumers against manufacturers with whom they have not dealt. . . . ''As between the immediate parties to the sale [the notice requirement] is a sound commercial rule, designed to protect the seller against unduly delayed claims for damages. As applied to personal injuries, and notice to a remote seller, it becomes a booby-trap for the unwary. The injured consumer is seldom 'steeped in the business practice which justifies the rule,' [James, Product Liability, 34 Tex. L. Rev. 44, 192, 197 (1955)] and at least until he has had legal advice it will not occur to him to give notice to one with whom he has had no dealings.'' [Prosser, The Assault Upon the Citadel (Strict Liability to the Consumer), 69 Yale L.J. 1099, 1130 (1960)] . . . . We conclude therefore that even if plaintiff did not give timely notice of breach of warranty to the manufacturer, his cause of action based on the representations contained in the brochure was not barred.

Moreover, to impose strict liability on the manufacturer under the circumstances of this case, it was not necessary for plaintiff to establish an express warranty. . . . A manufacturer is strictly liable in tort when an article he places on the market, knowing that it is to be used without inspection for defects, proves to have a defect that causes injury to a human being. Recognized first in the case of unwholesome food products, such liability has now

---

11. 161 A.2d 69 (N.J. 1960).
12. *Id.* at 84 (emphasis added).

been extended to a variety of other products that create as great or greater hazards if defective. . . .

Although in these cases strict liability has usually been based on the theory of an express or implied warranty running from the manufacturer to the plaintiff, the abandonment of the requirement of a contract between them, the recognition that the liability is not assumed by agreement but imposed by law . . . and the refusal to permit the manufacturer to define the scope of its own responsibility for defective products . . . make clear that the liability is not one governed by the law of contract warranties but by the law of strict liability in tort. Accordingly, rules defining and governing warranties that were developed to meet the needs of commercial transactions cannot properly be invoked to govern the manufacturer's liability to those injured by their defective products unless those rules also serve the purposes for which such liability is imposed. . . .

The purpose of such liability is to insure that the costs of injuries resulting from defective products are borne by the manufacturers that put such products on the market rather than by the injured persons who are powerless to protect themselves. Sales warranties serve this purpose fitfully at best. . . . In the present case, for example, plaintiff was able to plead and prove an express warranty only because he read and relied on the representations of the Shopsmith's ruggedness contained in the manufacturer's brochure. Implicit in the machine's presence on the market, however, was a representation that it would safely do the jobs for which it was built. Under these circumstances, it should not be controlling whether plaintiff selected the machine because of the statements in the brochure, or because of the machine's own appearance of excellence that belied the defect lurking beneath the surface, or because he merely assumed that it would safely do the jobs it was built to do. It should not be controlling whether the details of the sales from manufacturer to retailer and from retailer to [plaintiff] were such that one or more of the implied warranties of the sales act arose. . . . "The remedies of injured consumers ought not to be made to depend upon the intricacies of the law of sales." [*Ketterer v. Armour & Co.*, 200 F. 322, 323, (S.D.N.Y. 1912); *Klein v. Duchess Sandwich Co.*, 93 P.2d 799, 804 (Cal. 1939)] To establish the

manufacturer's liability it was sufficient that plaintiff proved that he was injured while using the Shopsmith in a way it was intended to be used as a result of a defect in design and manufacture of which plaintiff was not aware that made the Shopsmith unsafe for its intended use. . . .

[Judgment affirmed.]

Restatement (Second) of Torts §402A

Since the *Greenman* decision, the strict liability in tort doctrine has been adopted in virtually all states, and is today the primary basis of products liability recovery. The *Restatement (Second) of Torts* §402A, drafted shortly after the *Greenman* decision, serves as the basis for the cause of action in most states. Section 402A (entitled "Special Liability of Seller of Product for Physical Harm to User or Consumer") provides in full:

1. One who sells any product in a defective condition unreasonably dangerous to the user or consumer or to his property is subject to liability for physical harm thereby caused to the ultimate user or consumer, or to his property, if
   a. the seller is engaged in the business of selling such a product, and
   b. it is expected to and does reach the user or consumer without substantial change in the condition in which it is sold.
2. The rule stated in Subsection (1) applies although
   a. the seller has exercised all possible care in the preparation and sale of his product, and
   b. the user or consumer has not bought the product from or entered into any contractual relation with the seller.

Therefore, in order to recover against a seller in strict liability, the plaintiff generally must show that:

1. the product was in an unreasonably dangerous condition—that is, the product was "defective";

2. the unreasonably dangerous condition existed at the time the product left the seller's control; and

3. the unreasonably dangerous condition caused the plaintiff's injury or damage.

Liability exists despite the seller's lack of negligence (the "strict" aspect of the liability) and without regard to whether any contractual relationship (privity of contract) exists between the seller and the injured party.

Strict liability may be viewed therefore as an implied warranty, imposed by law and grounded on considerations of public policy, that a seller's product will not be unreasonably dangerous when used for its intended purpose. In fact, the doctrine often has been explained as nothing more than the implied warranty of merchantability stripped of the contract defenses of notice of defect, privity, and disclaimer. Because this "warranty" is very different from those traditionally found in sales of goods, however, it is much easier to regard the liability as simply "strict liability in tort."

Public Policy Grounds for Strict Liability

Courts have cited a number of important public policy considerations to support the imposition of strict tort liability upon sellers of defective products. First, the public interest in human life and health requires all the protection the law can give against the sale of unreasonably dangerous products. Second, by soliciting and inviting the use of its product through advertising, promotion, or otherwise, the seller impliedly represents the safety and suitability of the product. Having induced the use of the product, the seller should bear the liability for injury it causes. In addition, if sellers know that they are strictly liable for injuries caused by their products, they will more likely take steps to assure that those products are safe. Third, losses caused by defective products should be borne by those creating the risks and collecting the profits rather than by the injured parties who are unable to protect themselves. Further, the seller can insure itself against this liability and treat the expense as a cost of doing business, thus distributing the cost of injuries caused by defective products to the pub-

lic generally. Finally, as a general rule, the seller is in a better position than the buyer to determine whether or not the product is unreasonably dangerous, and should therefore bear the risk of injury.

"Defective" Defined

Before strict liability may be imposed upon the seller, it must be shown that the product is **unreasonably dangerous,** or **defective.** A manufacturer is not an insurer against all injuries caused by its products. Courts have used differing language to define what constitutes a defect, but all definitions are based on the common premise that a product is defective if it fails to perform in the manner reasonably to be expected in light of its nature and intended function. Therefore, a defective condition is one not contemplated by the user or consumer and that is unreasonably dangerous, that is, more dangerous than would be contemplated by the ordinary user or consumer. For example, an axe or power saw is not unreasonably dangerous because of the possibility of serious cuts, because ordinary users know the obvious dangers in using such products. If, however, the axe or saw is made of defective metal, which could break apart and cause injury during normal use, but is undetectable by prudent users, the product is defective. On the same theory, a soft drink bottler would be liable for injuries caused by chips of glass found in its bottles but would not be liable for damage caused to the consumer's teeth from the sugar in the beverage. Therefore, the condition of the product is "unreasonably dangerous" if the danger cannot reasonably be perceived and appreciated by the user or consumer.

The defect making the product unreasonably dangerous may take many forms. Defects are commonly classified as one of four types: (1) manufacturing defects, (2) design defects, (3) warning or labeling defects, and (4) packaging defects. Note that although proof of negligence is unnecessary in strict liability actions, the evidence establishing the defect also often will indicate failure to exercise reasonable care on the seller's part. Thus, imposing strict tort liability upon a negligent manufacturer may not substantially alter its legal responsibility. Strict liability has a significant effect, however, on the liability of later parties in the distributive chain, such as wholesalers and retailers, who are not themselves negligent.

Class of Permissible Plaintiffs and Defendants

Plaintiffs Protected. By its terms, §402A of the *Restatement (Second) of Torts* extends liability for personal injury and property damage only to the "ultimate user or consumer."[13] Cases subsequent to the promulgation of §402A (1965), however, have extended liability substantially to protect bystanders and others who are injured as well. The basic purpose of strict liability is to place the cost of product-related injuries upon those who place the defective products on the market. Given this purpose, no reason exists to distinguish between injuries caused to the user or consumer of the product and those caused to persons unfortunate enough to be in the vicinity when the product malfunctions. Thus, the extent of strict tort liability is now essentially the same as liability for negligence, extending to all reasonably foreseeable plaintiffs.[14]

Defendants Liable. With respect to the possible class of defendants, strict liability is imposed upon any person engaged in the business of selling products for use or consumption. It does not apply to an occasional or casual sale by one not engaged in business. Further, the imposition of liability does not depend upon whether or not a strict "sale" is involved, if the product is placed into the stream of commerce by other means. Thus, if a free sample provided by (or a product leased by) a commercial seller (or lessor) causes injury, relief on the basis of strict liability in tort is available.

Under the foregoing test, liability is imposed not only upon the manufacturer, but also upon any wholesaler, retail dealer, distributor, or the operator of a restaurant. The rationale for this result is that the position of wholesalers and retailers in the marketing process enables them to exert pressure on manufacturers to build safe products and to

---

13. This is essentially the extent of liability for breach of warranty embodied in alternative C to UCC §2-318 discussed on page 446. §2-318, Official Comment 3.

14. The class of plaintiffs protected in negligence actions and the foreseeability issue are discussed in Chapter 5.

spread the risk through insurance. Many courts, however, recognize that a seller who does not contribute to the defect has an implied indemnity remedy against the manufacturer, when sued by the injured party. That is, although strict liability is imposed upon anyone engaged in the business of selling the product, the loss should be ultimately borne by the party who created the risk—for example, the manufacturer of the defective product. The indemnity remedy becomes illusory, however, if the party creating the risk is insolvent.

Not all merchant sellers sell new products in the original chain of distribution. Many sell used goods, such as used cars. In the following case the court was asked to impose strict tort liability upon a dealer in used goods.

Tillman v. Vance Equipment Company
596 P.2d 1299 (Or. 1979)

Plaintiff Buddy Tillman was injured while performing maintenance on a 24-year-old crane owned by his employer who had purchased the crane as used goods "as is" from defendant Vance Equipment Company. Tillman sued Vance for strict liability in tort alleging that the crane was defectively designed. The trial court ruled in favor of Vance and held that a seller of used goods may not be held strictly liable in tort for a defect created by the manufacturer.

Denecke, Chief Justice

. . . [W]e have identified three justifications for the doctrine [of strict liability for defective products]:

. . . [C]ompensation (ability to spread the risk), satisfaction of the reasonable expectations of the purchaser or user (implied representational aspect), and over-all risk reduction (the impetus to manufacture a better product) . . ." [*Fulbright v. Klamath Gas Co.*, 553 P.2d 316, 321 (Or. 1975)].

While dealers in used goods are, as a class, capable like other businesses of providing for the compensation of injured parties and the allocation of the cost of injuries caused by the products they sell, we are not convinced that the other two considerations identified in *Fulbright* weigh sufficiently in this class of cases to justify imposing strict liability on sellers of used goods generally. . . .

We conclude that holding every dealer in used goods responsible regardless of fault for injuries caused by defects in his goods would not only affect the prices of used goods; it would work a significant change in the very nature of used goods markets. Those markets, generally speaking, operate on the apparent understanding that the seller, even though he is in the business of selling such goods, makes no particular representation about their quality simply by offering them for sale. If a buyer wants some assurance of quality, he typically either bargains for it in the specific transaction or seeks out a dealer who routinely offers it (by, for example, providing a guarantee, limiting his stock of goods to those of a particular quality, advertising that his used goods are specially selected, or in some other fashion). The flexibility of this kind of market appears to serve legitimate interests of buyers as well as sellers.

We are of the opinion that the sale of a used product, without more, may not be found to generate the kind of expectations of safety that the courts have held are justifiably created by the introduction of a new product into the stream of commerce.

As to the risk-reduction aspect of strict products liability, the position of the used-goods dealer is normally entirely outside the original chain of distribution of the product. As a consequence, we conclude, any risk reduction which would be accomplished by imposing strict liability on the dealer in used goods would not be significant enough to justify our taking that step. The dealer in used goods generally has no direct relationship with either manufacturers or distributors. Thus, there is no ready channel of communication by which the dealer and the manufacturer can exchange information about possible dangerous defects in particular product lines or about actual and potential liability claims.

In theory, a dealer in used goods who is held liable for injuries caused by a design defect or manufacturing flaw could obtain indemnity from the manufacturer. This possibility supports the argument that permitting strict liability claims against dealers in used goods will add to the financial incentive for manufacturers to design and build safe

products. We believe, however, that the influence of this possibility as a practical factor in risk prevention is considerably diluted where used goods are involved due to such problems as statutes of limitation and the increasing difficulty as time passes of locating a still existing and solvent manufacturer.

Both of these considerations, of course, are also obstacles to injured parties attempting to recover directly from the manufacturer. However, although the provision of an adequate remedy for persons injured by defective products has been the major impetus to the development of strict product liability, it cannot provide the sole justification for imposing liability without fault on a particular class of defendants.

For the reasons we have discussed, we have concluded that the relevant policy considerations do not justify imposing strict liability for defective products on dealers in used goods, at least in the absence of some representation of quality beyond the sale itself or of a special position vis-a-vis the original manufacturer or others in the chain of original distribution. . . .

[Judgment affirmed.]

Although the *Tillman* court refused to extend strict liability to sellers of used goods, the basic public policy considerations supporting imposition of strict tort liability generally—placing the loss upon those who profit by placing the product in the stream of commerce—appear to support application of the doctrine to merchant sellers of both new and used products. Other courts have noted that application of strict liability in tort to sellers of used products assures the consumer and the public that all reasonable efforts will be taken by the seller to see that the used product is safe, both through a reasonable inspection to discover defects and repair of those defects, however caused.

Defenses

The Restatement Approach. Section 402A of the *Restatement (Second) of Torts* announced both the criteria for imposing strict liability and the defenses available to the seller. Under the *Restatement* approach, the plaintiff's contributory negligence is not generally available to the seller as a defense, because strict liability is not based upon the seller's negligence. "Contributory negligence" as defined in the *Restatement* refers to the plaintiff's unobservant, inattentive, ignorant, or awkward failure to discover or guard against the defect causing injury. Most courts, however, define contributory negligence in this context in its ordinary tort law sense—negligence on the plaintiff's part that is a contributing cause of the plaintiff's harm.

On the other hand, the plaintiff's contributory conduct amounting to (1) an assumption of the risk, or (2) outright misuse of the product constitutes an absolute defense. As previously noted, assumption of the risk involves the plaintiff's express or implied consent to encounter a known unreasonable danger created by the defendant's conduct. **Misuse** involves use of the product for purposes neither intended nor foreseeable by the defendant. Note that the *Restatement* and many jurisdictions do not regard misuse as an affirmative defense in the true sense; rather, evidence of misuse merely rebuts proof of defective condition or causation, necessary elements of the plaintiff's strict liability case. That is, a product that causes an injury because it is used in an unforeseeable manner may very well not be defective. Similarly, if a defective product is misused, the misuse, rather than the defect, may cause the injury.

In sum, under the *Restatement* approach, the plaintiff who fails to exercise reasonable care in using the product may nevertheless recover for his injuries in strict liability. However, a plaintiff who continues to use the product *after becoming aware* of its unreasonably dangerous character, or who uses it for an unintended or unforeseeable purpose, is barred from recovery for subsequent injury caused by the product.

Comparative Fault in Strict Liability. Although many courts adhere to the position that contributory negligence does not bar recovery in strict liability, a growing number have, in recent years, applied **comparative fault** principles in strict liability actions. As discussed in Chapter 5, most American jurisdictions have abandoned contributory negligence as a defense in negligence actions and replaced it with some form of comparative negligence, in which the relative degrees of fault are

weighed by the jury and the plaintiff's total damages are reduced in proportion to his fault. Comparative negligence has the effect of providing some compensation (reduced in proportion to his fault) to a plaintiff who would be denied any recovery under the contributory negligence approach. A leading case applying comparative principles to strict liability actions is *Daly v. General Motors Corp.*[15] decided in 1978. In this case, the plaintiff was killed when a defectively designed automobile door latch failed, causing him to be forcibly thrown from the car when it collided with the median strip guard rail. The undisputed evidence indicated that the plaintiff's injuries would probably have been relatively minor had he remained in the car. Over plaintiff's objections, defendants were permitted to introduce evidence that the plaintiff had failed to use the car's safety devices (seat belts and door locks), and was intoxicated at the time of the accident. After a verdict was returned for the defendants, plaintiffs appealed. The Supreme Court of California rendered an extended opinion addressed to the central issue presented by the case: should comparative principles be applied to determine recovery in strict liability actions? The court concluded that the same reason supporting comparative negligence (a more equitable apportionment of loss) in negligence actions also supports application of comparative principles (known in this context as "comparative fault") to cases grounded in strict liability. In reaching its decision, the court stated that the fundamental purpose of comparative negligence is to "assign responsibility and liability for damage in direct proportion to the amount of negligence of each of the parties," and that this same underlying policy consideration supports an extension of comparative principles to strict liability cases "because it is fair to do so."[16]

Criticisms of Comparative Fault in Strict Liability. Critics assert that significant problems are inherent in applying comparative principles to strict liability in tort actions. First, in comparative negligence cases, the relative degrees of fault of both the plaintiff and defendant are compared to determine

---

15. 575 P.2d 1162 (Cal. 1978).
16. *Id.* at 1172.

recovery. In strict liability actions, however, liability is, by definition, not based on fault; the defendant is strictly liable. Therefore, the jury is asked to compare the defendant's liability for the defective product (not based on fault) with the plaintiff's negligence (based on fault) to determine proportionate recovery. Thus, the jury has no reasonable standard or formula (that is, no common denominator) to guide it in assigning responsibility to the parties. For example, to what can the jury compare the plaintiff's fault if the defendant's fault is not at issue? Critics argue that this problem will lead to a reduction in injured plaintiffs' recovery based solely on the jurors' instincts, speculations, conjectures or guesses as to how to allocate loss.

A second weakness cited by critics in extending comparative principles to strict liability is that it undermines a basic principle of strict liability: to insure that costs of injuries caused by defective products are borne by those who place those products on the market. By allowing sellers to escape liability because of the plaintiff's conduct, comparison in strict liability cases encourages the manufacture of defective products. As noted by Justice Mosk in his dissenting opinion in *Daly:*

> It seems self evident that procedures which evaluate the injured consumer's conduct in each instance, and thus eliminate or reduce the award against the producer or distributor of a defective product, are not designed as an effective incentive to maximum responsibility to consumers. The converse is more accurate: the motivation to avoid polluting the stream of commerce with defective products increases in direct relation to the size of potential damage awards.[17]

Conduct Compared. Although a substantial majority of jurisdictions now apply some form of comparison in strict liability cases, the precise method of comparison differs widely and is often affected by state statutes governing comparative negligence or strict liability. For example, under the form of strict liability adopted in *Restatement (Second) of Torts* §402A, ordinary contributory negligence is not a defense, but the plaintiff's mis-

use or assumption of the risk are *absolute bars* to recovery. Under some formulations of comparative fault, the plaintiff's contributory conduct, however categorized (as contributory negligence, misuse, or assumption of the risk) is compared, proportionately reducing the injured party's recovery. Some states apply comparative principles only to plaintiff conduct that would have barred recovery altogether under the original *Restatement* formulation (misuse and assumption of risk). Under this approach, the plaintiff's contributory negligence, however characterized, is not a defense and does not reduce recovery. Misuse and assumption of risk are, however, compared to proportionately reduce recovery. In contrast, still other courts apply comparative principles to any level of plaintiff culpability, including negligence, except when the plaintiff's negligence consists solely in the failure to discover or guard against the defect that caused the injury. Depending upon the form of comparison adopted, an injured plaintiff may receive more or less protection than is afforded by the original *Restatement* approach.

Applying comparative principles to strict liability actions appears to be a growing trend with the rapid growth of comparative negligence in recent years. As the preceding discussion indicates, however, the advisability of this development and the method of comparison are matters of considerable controversy. Ultimately, the proper relationship between comparative principles and strict liability will be determined only after further judicial and perhaps legislative development.

Products Liability Today

Following the development of strict liability in tort, the field of products liability grew rapidly during the 1960s and 1970s. To a large extent, the expanded scope of products liability achieved the policy objectives of strict liability. Although businesses, especially manufacturers, were exposed to increasing liability for defective products, they generally were able to cover their risk by securing insurance to cover potential legal fees and judgments. Insurance premiums became a cost of doing business incorporated into businesses' pricing policies and thereby distributed among consumers. The policies underlying products liability, however, be-

---

17. *Id.* at 1186.

came increasingly controversial during the mid-1970s and again in the early 1980s when insurance prices skyrocketed.

Both state and federal legislatures, with the encouragement of businesses, considered tort reform and, more specifically products liability reform, to reduce the potential liability of defendants for injuries resulting from their products. Proponents of reform argued that a "litigation explosion" seriously jeopardized American commerce, depriving consumers of many products and weakening the position of American business in international markets. Insurers pressed for reform asserting that premiums would continue to rise and, in some cases, insurance would be unavailable not only because of the increase in products liability cases but also because of unduly large judgments in particular cases. Opponents of reform characterized the crisis as one caused by the insurance industry, noting that the cyclical nature of the insurance industry usually was aggravated by fluctuations in interest rates. They further asserted that the claims of an explosive rate of growth in the number of cases and size of judgments were based on anecdotal evidence unsupported by statistical data. As a result of reform efforts, many states statutorily revised their tort and products liability law during the 1980s. The most common types of reform include eliminating or limiting the use of joint and several liability, placing "caps" on the amount of non-economic (pain and suffering) or punitive damages, and shortening the statute of limitations. During the last ten years, numerous bills to establish a federal products liability statute have been introduced in Congress with the purpose of providing uniformity to assist businesses that operate in interstate commerce. No bill, however, has been passed by Congress.

Changing economic and social conditions are likely to continue to influence the field of products liability. Just as industrialization and new marketing techniques were responsible for the demise of the doctrine of *caveat emptor* and the development of strict liability in tort, future business practices, new products, and changing social needs will shape the law of products liability. One of the most challenging issues facing business and the legal system today concerns "mass torts," legal claims by thousands of plaintiffs who have suffered injuries from products that were marketed for many years before their detrimental effects appeared. Today, mass torts

lawsuits seeking recovery for alleged injuries from asbestos, intrauterine devices like the Dalkon Shield and medication such as Bendectin and DES are flooding the courts. Numerous manufacturers, named as defendants for producing products as long as 50 years ago, face potential insolvency and many have filed bankruptcy. As the following case illustrates, courts often must balance competing social interests to resolve these difficult cases.

Brown v. Superior Court (Abbott Laboratories)
751 P.2d 470 (Cal. 1988)

The plaintiffs in 69 different lawsuits sued the manufacturers of diethylsilbestrol (DES), a synthetic estrogen product formerly prescribed to pregnant women to prevent miscarriages. The complaints in all of the suits included similar allegations claiming that the plaintiffs, all of whom were daughters of women who used DES, had been injured by the drug and sought to hold the drug manufacturers strictly liable for the injuries. Under special rules adopted for complex litigation, the California Supreme Court agreed to review the trial court's pretrial ruling that the defendants could not be held strictly liable for the alleged defects in DES.

Mosk, Justice

. . . The doctrine of strict liability had its genesis in a concurring opinion by Justice Roger Traynor in [which he] suggested that a manufacturer should be absolutely liable if, in placing a product on the market, it knew the product was to be used without inspection, and it proved to have a defect that caused injury. The policy considerations underlying this suggestion were that the manufacturer, unlike the public, can anticipate or guard against the recurrence of hazards, that the cost of injury may be an overwhelming misfortune to the person injured whereas the manufacturer can insure against the risk and distribute the cost among the consuming public, and that it is in the public interest to discourage the marketing of defective products. . . .

Strict liability differs from negligence in that it eliminates the necessity for the injured party to prove that the manufacturer of the product which caused injury was negligent. It focuses not on the conduct of the manufacturer but on the product itself, and holds the manufacturer liable if the product was defective. . . .

[T]he members of American Law Institute, in considering whether to adopt a rule of strict liability, pondered whether the manufacturer of a prescription drug should be subject to the doctrine. . . . [I]n 1962, section 402A [of the *Restatement (Second) of Torts*] was approved together with comment k thereto. . . .

The comment provides that the producer of a properly manufactured prescription drug may be held liable for injuries caused by the product only if it was not accompanied by a warning of dangers that the manufacturer knew or should have known about. . . .

Comment k has been analyzed and criticized by numerous commentators. While there is some disagreement as to its scope and meaning, there is a general consensus that, although it purports to explain the strict liability doctrine, in fact the principle it states is based on negligence. . . . That is, comment k would impose liability on a drug manufacturer only if it failed to warn of a defect of which it either knew or should have known . This concept focuses not on a deficiency in the product—the hallmark of strict liability—but on the fault of the producer in failing to warn of dangers inherent in the use of its product that were either known or knowable—an idea which "rings of negligence." . . .

Comment k has been adopted in the overwhelming majority of jurisdictions that have considered the matter. . . .

We shall conclude that (1) a drug manufacturer's liability for a defectively designed drug should not be measured by the standards of strict liability; [and] (2) because of the public interest in the development, availability, and reasonable price of drugs, the appropriate test for determining responsibility is the test stated in comment k. . . .

[T]here is an important distinction between prescription drugs and other products such as construction machinery, . . . a lawnmower, . . . or perfume, . . . the producers of which [have been] held strictly liable. In the latter cases, the product is used to make work easier or to provide pleasure, while in the former it may be necessary to alleviate pain and suffering or to sustain life. Moreover, un-

like other important medical products (wheelchairs, for example), harm to some users from prescription drugs is unavoidable. Because of these distinctions, the broader public interest in the availability of drugs at an affordable price must be considered in deciding the appropriate standard of liability for injuries resulting from their use.

Perhaps a drug might be made safer if it was withheld from the market until scientific skill and knowledge advanced to the point at which additional dangerous side effects would be revealed. But in most cases such a delay in marketing new drugs—added to the delay required to obtain approval for release of the product from the Food and Drug administration—would not serve the public welfare. Public policy favors the development and marketing of beneficial new drugs, even though some risks, perhaps serious ones, might accompany their introduction, because drugs can save lives and reduce pain in suffering.

If drug manufacturers were subject to strict liability, they might be reluctant to undertake research programs to develop some pharmaceuticals that would prove beneficial or to distribute others that are available to be marketed, because of the fear of large adverse monetary judgments. Further, the additional expense of insuring against such liability—assuming insurance would be available—and of research programs to reveal possible dangers not detectable by available scientific methods could place the cost of medication beyond the reach of those who need it most. . . .

The possibility that the cost of insurance and of defending against lawsuits will diminish the availability and increase the price of pharmaceuticals is far from theoretical. Defendants cite a host of examples of products which have greatly increased in price or have been withdrawn or withheld from the market because of the fear that their producers would be held liable for large judgments.

For example, according to defendant E. R. Squibb & Sons, Inc., [Bendectin], the only anti-nauseant drug available for pregnant women, was withdrawn from sale in 1983 because the cost of insurance almost equalled the entire income from sale of the drug. Before it was withdrawn, the price of [Bendectin] increased by over 300 percent. . . .

Drug manufacturers refused to supply a newly discovered vaccine for influenza on the ground that mass inoculation would subject them to enormous liability. The government therefore assumed the risk of lawsuits resulting from injuries caused by the vaccine. . . . One producer of diphtheria-tet-nus-pertussis vaccine withdrew from the market, giving as its reason "extreme liability exposure, cost of litigation and the difficulty of continuing to obtain adequate insurance." (Hearing Before Subcom. on Health and the Environment of House Com. on Energy and Commerce on Vaccine Injury Compensation, 98th Cong. 2d Sess. (Sept. 10, 1984), p. 295.) There are only two manufacturers of the vaccine remaining in the market, and the cost of each dose rose a hundredfold from 11 cents in 1982 to $11.40 in 1986, $8 of which was for an insurance reserve. The price increase roughly paralleled an increase in the number of lawsuits from one in 1978 to 219 in 1985. . . . Finally, a manufacturer was unable to market a new drug for the treatment of vision problems because it could not obtain adequate liability insurance at a reasonable cost . . . .

There is no doubt that, from the public's standpoint, these are unfortunate consequences. And they occurred even though almost all jurisdictions follow the negligence standard of comment k. It is not unreasonable to conclude in these circumstances that the imposition of a harsher test for liability would not further the public interest in the development and availability of these important products. . . .

For these same reasons of policy, we reject plaintiff's assertion that a drug manufacturer should be held strictly liable for failure to warn of risks inherent in a drug even though it neither knew nor could have known by the application of scientific knowledge available at the time of distribution that the drug could produce the undesirable side effects suffered by the plaintiff. . . .

It has been said that to "hold the manufacturer liable for failure to warn of a danger of which it would be impossible to know based on the present state of human knowledge would make the manufacturer the virtual insurer of the product. . . ." [*Woodill v. Parke Davis & Co.*, 402 N.E.2d (1.94, 199) Ill. 1980.] . . . Thus, we disagree with plaintiff's assertion that defendants should be held liable for failing to warn the physician who prescribed DES to plaintiff's mother of alleged defects in the drug that were neither known by defendants nor scientifically knowable at the time the drug was distributed. . . .

In conclusion, and in accord with almost all our sister states that have considered the issue, we hold that a manufacturer is not strictly liable for injuries caused by a prescription drug so long as the drug was properly prepared and accompanied by warnings of its dangerous propensities that were either known or reasonably scientifically knowable at the time of distribution. . . .

[Judgment affirmed.]

SUMMARY

1. The law of products liability governs the liability of manufacturers and other suppliers of goods for personal injury and property damage caused by the products they sell. Three basic legal theories are utilized to impose liability upon a seller: (1) negligence, (2) breach of warranty, and (3) strict liability in tort. Generally, under all theories, protection is extended to injured third parties, whether or not in privity of contract with the seller.

2. Under the negligence approach, the manufacturer or supplier is under a duty to exercise reasonable care in the design, production, and distribution of its products. Failure to do so constitutes negligence. If the manufacturer's or supplier's negligence causes injury, the injured party may recover damages. The injured party attempting to prove negligence may be aided by the *res ipsa loquitur*

doctrine, under which recovery is allowed even though no direct evidence regarding particular negligent conduct can be shown.

3. Breach of warranty actions have been a popular ground for recovery because warranty liability, based on contract, is strict, meaning liability is imposed without a showing of fault. If the breach of warranty causes personal injury, liability follows. Because a warranty action is based on contract, contract defenses such as lack of privity, disclaimer of warranty, and failure to give timely notice of the breach traditionally have been available to the defendant. The UCC, however, eliminates or reduces the effect of these defenses in warranty actions involving personal injury.

4. The dominant products liability theory today is the strict liability in tort doctrine, which imposes liability

without fault for injuries caused by defective products. Under this theory, the plaintiff recovers if he can prove (1) the product was defective (unreasonably dangerous), (2) the defect existed when the product left the seller's control, and (3) the defect caused the injury. Traditionally, contributory negligence was no defense to a strict products liability action, although assumption of the risk and misuse of the product were absolute bars to recovery. The modern, though controversial, approach is to apply comparative principles in strict liability actions, similar to that now applied generally in negligence cases.

KEY TERMS

products liability	strict liability in tort
privity of contract	defective (unreasonably
negligence	dangerous) product
reasonable (ordinary) care	misuse
res ipsa loquitur	comparative fault
strict liability	

QUESTIONS AND PROBLEMS

20-1 Compare and contrast the three primary bases of recovery in products liability cases. Specifically: (1) Who is entitled to sue under each theory? (2) What must the plaintiff prove under each theory? (3) Which particular sellers or suppliers may be held liable under each theory? (4) What defenses are available to a defendant seeking to avoid liability?

20-2 Shipbuilder, Inc. contracted with Transamerica, Inc. to design, manufacture, and install turbines that would be the main propulsion units for four oil tankers constructed by Shipbuilder. When the ships were chartered and put into service, the turbines on all four ships malfunctioned due to design and manufacturing defects. Only the turbines themselves were damaged. The charterers then sued Shipbuilder on products liability theories of negligence and strict liability. The court found for Shipbuilder, noting that claims regarding dissatisfaction with product quality are protected by warranty laws, rather than tort doctrines of negligence or strict liability. Is the court correct? Discuss.

20-3 In both of the following cases, the manufacturer produced a defective product. Should either manufacturer be held liable for the injuries? Explain.

(a) Juan, a security guard, was supplied with a two-way portable radio receiver to call the police if a burglary occurred. One night,

Juan discovered a burglar and called the police on the portable radio. Unknown to Juan however, the radio failed to function and when he attempted to apprehend the burglar Juan was shot and seriously injured. The radio failed to function because of a manufacturing defect.

(b) Elliott, a night clerk at a motel, purchased a mace weapon to protect himself in case of a robbery. One night an armed robber confronted Elliott, who attempted to shoot mace at the robber. The mace gun failed to function because of a defect and the robber shot and seriously wounded Elliott.

20-4 Eleanor, while grocery shopping at Dom's Market, was using a shopping cart provided by the store. The cart tipped over and Eleanor was injured as she attempted to prevent the cart from overturning. A hidden design defect had caused the cart to overturn when loaded with groceries.

(a) Eleanor sues Dom's Market, Inc. for strict liability in tort. What result?

(b) Eleanor sues the cart manufacturer for strict liability in tort. What result?

20-5 Wren, Inc. manufactures and distributes a pain reliever sold in tablet form. The product is packaged in a glass bottle with a screw top that is then placed in a small cardboard box. On the box and the bottle is printed the following statement in boldface type: THESE TABLETS ARE STRONG DRUGS. DO NOT EXCEED DOSAGE OF 2 TABLETS IN A FOUR HOUR PERIOD. The product is sold as an over-the-counter drug. Mary purchased a bottle of the pain reliever from Oswald's Drug Store. The drug store is self-service and Mary selected her purchase from an open shelf. When she returned home, Mary placed the unopened bottle in her medicine cabinet. While Mary's friend Lulu was visiting, she developed a terrible headache so she took four of the pain relievers. Within hours Lulu was dead. Examination of the bottle of pain relief tablets revealed that 10 of the tablets contained curare, a lethal poison even in small doses. A police investigation established that without a doubt, the poisoned tablets were added to the bottle after the package left the Wren plant. Lulu's family files suit against Wren and Oswald's.

(a) If the lawsuit is based on negligence, what elements will the plaintiff have to prove? Explain how the plaintiff may try to prove the case based on the preceding facts.

(b) If the lawsuit is based on strict liability in tort, what elements will the plaintiff have to prove? Explain how the plaintiff may try to prove the case based on the preceding facts.

(c) Would the defendants have any defenses available to them? Explain, specifying which defenses are likely to be asserted.

(d) If the lawsuit is based on breach of warranty, what must the plaintiff prove? What defenses might the defendant assert in a warranty action? Will the plaintiff recover? Explain.

20-6   Southland Chemicals, Inc. manufactures and markets ''Drain Clean,'' a household chemical for cleaning drain stoppages in sinks and bathtubs. The main ingredient in Drain Clean is sodium hydroxide, which when combined with water produces intense heat and steam, resulting in an explosion if the mixture is contained. The mixture is strong enough to eat away aluminum, burns and kills human tissue on contact, and causes incurable blindness if it comes in contact with the eyes even for a short period. Of course, ingestion of even small quantities of the substance causes internal bleeding and usually death. You are corporate counsel for Southland. What steps would you recommend be taken in the manufacture, marketing, labeling, and packaging of Drain Clean to minimize the risk of liability in lawsuits filed by persons injured while using the product?

20-7   Reese worked as a foreman, supervising a track repair crew for Chicago, Burlington, and Quincy Railroad. One morning the crew was loading equipment onto a flat car using a crane manufactured by Kelly Crane Co. The boom on the crane contained two cables, one being used to load equipment, and the other holding a 1,200 pound ''clam shell'' bucket suspended at the top of the boom. The bucket was not in use during the loading operation and to secure the cable holding it, the crane operator had engaged both a hand and foot brake. Either brake was intended to be independently sufficient to hold the cable fast. Reese was standing beneath the clam shell bucket supervising loading operations when the foot brake pedal ''jumped off the floor'' and the bucket fell, killing Reese instantly. Reese's estate sued Kelly in strict liability and proved that the defective design of the braking mechanism had caused it to fail. Kelly defended on the ground that Reese's conduct (standing beneath the suspended bucket) constituted alternatively:

(1) contributory negligence, (2) assumption of the risk, or (3) misuse of the product. Under §402A of the *Restatement (Second) of Torts* would Kelly escape liability on any of the foregoing theories? Would your answer change if the jurisdiction in question applies comparative fault principles in strict liability actions? Explain.

20-8   Consider whether plaintiff's alleged misuse of the product should bar recovery in the following cases:

(a) Dagwood was driving a motor home on the highway when he ran into a guardrail. The mobile home veered off the road and overturned. Because of a defective and negligent design, the gas tank was not properly protected and it exploded, seriously injuring the passengers. The defendant manufacturer argued that mobile homes are not intended to be used in accidents so that the product was being misused.

(b) Billy, a seven-year-old child, found an empty disposable beer bottle. Billy threw the bottle at a telephone pole. The bottle shattered and several pieces of glass injured Billy's eye. Defendant bottle manufacturer argued that Billy had misused the bottle.

20-9   The text discusses the pros and cons of applying the strict liability in tort doctrine to sellers of used goods. Consider the application of the doctrine to *lessors* of goods. For example, should a person in the business of renting automobiles, trailers, power tools, or other goods be held strictly liable for injuries caused by those goods? Should such *lessors* of used goods be treated differently from *sellers* of such goods? Do the policy considerations supporting strict liability require a different approach to the two cases?

20-10 Most courts have extended protection in strict liability to bystanders and others injured by defective products who are not in privity with the seller. How would you argue that a bystander should be entitled to even *greater* protection than the original user or consumer of the product?

20-11 The strict liability doctrine does not apply to an occasional or casual sale by one not engaged in business—for example, the sale of a bicycle through a classified advertisement. Why not?

20-12 Marine Manufacturing Co. manufactures diesel engines for tugboats and other water craft. The engines are distributed exclusively through franchised Marine dealers. Marine began manufacturing a new type of engine, but later learned that the fuel filter recommended for the engine would occasionally crack and rupture under pressure. Marine developed a new filter and sent letters to its franchisees instructing them to use the new filters. The letter warned that in some cases the old filter had ruptured causing fuel to spray over the engine. Boat Sales, Inc. was a franchised retailer of Marine engines and received a copy of the Marine letter. Boat Sales subsequently sold a Marine engine to Marco but installed an old filter. Boat Sales did not advise Marco of the need to use the new filters. Marco installed the engine on his tugboat. During the first voyage, the filter exploded and fuel sprayed in the engine room where it ignited. The boat burned and sank.

(a) Marco sues both Marine Manufacturing Co. and Boat Sales, Inc. for negligence. What result? Explain.

(b) Marco also sues Marine and Boat Sales Inc. under the strict liability in tort theory. What result? Explain.

(c) Assume that the court finds Marine strictly liable in tort for the personal injury and property damage caused by its defective engine. Further evidence shows, however, that Marco had been negligent for the following reasons: (1) Marco's engineer negligently left the engine room and negligently failed to observe the engine, (2) the crew was negligent for failure to take several actions to put out the fire, (3) Marco failed to provide a switch outside the engine room to turn off the engine, failed to train the crew in fire-fighting techniques, and failed to have enough fire extinguishers on board. Should Marco's conduct be considered as a basis to reduce or extinguish Marine's liability to Marco? Explain.

20-13 In *Palmer v. A. H. Robins Co. Inc.*, Robins objected to the award of over $6 million in punitive damages. Consider the following facts that were established at trial. In 1970, Robins purchased all rights to the Dalkon Shield from Dalkon Corporation, which had performed a clinical study of the IUD with 640 patients. Robins modified the Dalkon Shield and, without further clinical testing, began to market it in January 1971. In August 1971, a quality control supervisor determined that the design of the shield could introduce bacteria into the uterus. In June 1972, a Robins consultant sent a letter to Robins's man-

agement advising that the IUD be removed if a patient became pregnant. Between June 1972 and November 1973, Robins received reports of 22 miscarriages due to infections among Dalkon Shield users, including notice of one death of a user. In spite of these reports, through April 1973, Robins continued to advise physicians not to remove the Dalkon Shield from patients who became pregnant. In the fall of 1973, Robins learned that a physician was writing an article on the dangers of IUDs, particularly the Dalkon Shield, to pregnant users. In May 1974, Robins responded by warning physicians of the hazards of the Dalkon Shield to pregnant patients. In June 1974, at the request of the Food and Drug Administration, Robins ceased marketing the Dalkon Shield.

(a) In light of these facts, do you believe that punitive damages were appropriate in this case?

(b) Although Robins ceased marketing the Dalkon Shield in 1974, the company did not recall those that already had been sold. Ten years later, however, Robins began a campaign to have the Dalkon Shield removed from all users and paid the physicians' fees for removal. After Robins declared bankruptcy in 1985, it recalled all Dalkon Shields. Was Robins' conduct an example of corporate irresponsibility? Was it an example of poor business judgment? Suggest reasons why Robins did not recall the Dalkon Shield.

(c) During the time that Robins marketed the Dalkon Shield, gross sales revenues from the shield were $11 million. During that same time, Robins's net worth almost doubled to $157,695,000 in 1974 and, at the time of trial, its net worth was $240,275,000. In light of this financial information, does the punitive damage award of $6.2 million seem appropriate? Why or why not?

(d) Prior to declaring bankruptcy in 1985, Robins and its insurers had paid $378 million in 9,230 cases involving injuries from the Dalkon Shield, with 5,100 suits still pending. Its legal fees were an additional $107.3 million. In light of these awards, should any plaintiffs be awarded punitive damages? Why or why not?

The "Market Share" Doctrine in Products Liability

Gary T. Schwartz

What lawyers call "actual causation" is regarded as an essential element in every tort claim. Assume, for example, that Jim, a pedestrian, is struck by Tom, a speeding motorist, on State Street, assume that, at the same moment, Stan is speeding on Main Street a block away. Jim's lawsuit is against Tom and Tom alone. Even if Tom turns out to be uninsured and insolvent, Jim cannot bring suit against Stan, for Stan's speeding was not an actual cause of Jim's injury. Modern products liability cases generally incorporate this traditional requirement of causation. The plaintiff must prove not only that the defendant's product was in a defective condition, but also that the product defect was an actual cause of the injury he suffered.

However, in one interesting 1980 case, *Sindell v. Abbot Laboratories*, the California Supreme Court departed from a traditional application of the causation requirement. *Sindell* involved diethylstilbesterol (DES)—a drug that was marketed, mainly in the 1950s, on the idea that it would prevent miscarriages in pregnant women. Eventually, however, it was learned that DES is ineffective at discouraging miscarriages; worse yet, DES is capable of producing vaginal cancer in the daughters of the women who took DES during their pregnancy. (The latency period between the ingestion of the drug and the onset of cancer is ten years or more.) Similarly, DES can be responsible for a variety of medical conditions less serious than cancer. There is adequate reason to believe that many of the two hundred drug companies that produced DES during the 1950s failed to caution doctors (and the FDA) about the possible hazards of DES; also, these companies may have made claims about the efficacy of DES that lacked foundation.

During the relevant period of time, more than two hundred drug companies were selling DES. When a "DES daughter" seeks to bring a products liability claim, the problem she frequently encounters is that she has no way of finding out which company made the DES that her own mother took. Accordingly, if the actual causation requirement were applied in an ordinary way, it would frustrate the daughter's lawsuit. In *Sindell,* the California Supreme Court concluded that this result was unsatisfactory. The Court therefore ruled that a plaintiff, having sued certain DES manufacturers, can recover from each of them for that share of her overall damages which corresponds to the "market share" for DES held by each company during the mother's pregnancy. The Court added that a manufacturer can exculpate itself from this market-share liability by satisfactorily showing that it could *not* have been the maker of the particular DES taken by the mother.

The ingenuity of the *Sindell* market-share ruling can be appreciated from several related perspectives. Assume that there are 5,000 DES daughters and that Drug Company. A held a 20 percent share of the overall market for DES. That Company's DES products bear causal responsibility for 1,000 of the DES victims. Under a traditional application of the actual causation requirement, Company A would nevertheless be free of liability. Under *Sindell,* Company A is potentially liable for 20 percent of the harm suffered by each of 5,000 victims—a liability that is equivalent to full liability in 1,000 cases. In this way *Sindell,* even though it ignores the actual causation requirement at the case-by-case level, fully honors that requirement at an aggregate level.

Accordingly, *Sindell* is doctrinally quite defensible. Furthermore, *Sindell* is attractive from the perspectives of both fairness and safety. Because the manufacturer of a product such as DES has been the inappropriate cause of 1,000

Gary T. Schwartz is Professor of Law at the University of California—Los Angeles.

harms, to render that manufacturer liable for the equivalent of 1,000 harms is a clearly fair result. Moreover, without a *Sindell*-like liability rule, manufacturers of fungible products, anticipating that traditional causation doctrine may enable them to escape liability, may be inclined to ignore the safety incentives that the law of products liability is seeking to impose.

In sum, according to several criteria, *Sindell* is not only acceptable but praiseworthy. An additional criterion that has been neglected until now, however, is that of holding down the cost of litigation. "Market share" is the sort of issue that ordinarily is litigated in antitrust cases—each of which is likely to take years to decide. To be sure, the very high stakes in each of a very small number of antitrust cases may render the costs of litigating the market-share issue worthwhile; it hardly follows that similar litigation costs are appropriate in the "mass tort" setting of DES claims. Moreover, the very notion of "market share" proves to be deep in legal ambiguity. DES is a drug with an indefinite shelf life; what, then, is the time frame for the assessment of market share? Does *Sindell* require data about national sales? statewide sales? metropolitan sales? sales at the drugstore where the mother remembers buying her pills? What if the mother recalls buying medications at each of two drugstores, one of which (it can now be learned) sold only the DES made by Companies A and B, the second of which is now out of business? If metropolitan or drugstore information is not regarded as relevant to the issue of "market share" is it at least relevant to the question of whether a particular manufacturer can satisfy *Sindell's* exculpation doctrine? For that matter, the DES sold by some companies was tabletlike, and the DES sold by others was spherical; on the issues of both market share and exculpation, what significance should be attached to the mother's somewhat uncertain recollection of the shape of the pill she took?

The possibilities and permutations of all these questions are just about endless. The consequence is that the administrative costs of litigating DES claims are very high. In thinking about the correctness of *Sindell*, one is thus seemingly required to confront an extremely interesting yet extremely difficult question. At what point do high administrative costs render inadvisable a tort rule that otherwise can be commended by the criteria of doctrine, fairness, and deterrence? In this brief essay, I am content to pose this question for the student's consideration and to refrain from suggesting any answers. In one way, however, the question tends to answer itself. A large proportion of the costs of litigation under *Sindell* are borne by the plaintiffs who bring suit; more precisely, they are borne by those plaintiffs' lawyers, who take tort cases under a contingent-fee arrangement. In the years since 1980, plaintiffs' lawyers have come to appreciate the costliness of *Sindell* litigation. Lawyers have tended to conclude that these costs are acceptable when a DES client is suffering from cancer—for in cancer cases the prospective recovery is quite large. Yet given the expensiveness and uncertainties of *Sindell* litigation, many lawyers are now unwilling to bring suit on behalf of DES daughters whose medical conditions are less serious than cancer. In this manner, the litigation cost problem surrounding *Sindell* has generated its own solution—though this solution is, of course, both incomplete and hardly satisfying.

Moreover, in other ways, the *Sindell* opinion, despite all the hullabaloo originally surrounding it, has turned out to be interestingly limited. In post-*Sindell* ratings, courts have plausibly concluded that *Sindell* rests on the assumption of the "fungibility" of the products made by different companies. Drug products are the most likely to comply with this requirement of fungibility; therefore, the *Sindell* ruling tends to be limited to drugs. *New* drugs, moreover, are the drugs most likely to have unknown or underappreciated adverse side effects; and new drugs are generally sold by one company alone, which holds the drug's patent. A special fact about DES was that it was discovered by researchers funded by the English government, which then chose, as a matter of policy, not to secure a patent. Only this atypical circumstance led to the situation in which a new drug could be produced by many companies at the same time. It may well be, therefore, that once the DES litigation has run its course, the *Sindell* rule will have just about exhausted its range of potential major applications. Even so, however, it will remain as a wonderful heuristic in the study of tort liability rules.

Chapter 21

Introduction to Commercial Paper

This chapter and Chapters 22–26 examine the law of commercial paper—promissory notes, certificates of deposit, drafts, and checks. For centuries these commercial documents have served as primary vehicles for extending credit and as substitutes for money in the payment of debts. Commercial paper is able to perform these functions because it is easy to create and transfer. The paper itself is valuable property that can be sold or used as collateral on a loan. The rights and obligations of all parties to the paper are easily ascertained, extremely predictable, and readily enforceable in court. Commercial paper possesses these attributes because it is negotiable, a legal characteristic that promotes the free transferability and enhances the marketability of the paper.

Many legal issues arise in connection with the use of commercial paper. To a large extent these issues are resolved by Articles 3 and 4 of the Uniform Commercial Code (UCC), which form the basis of the following material.

Introduction to Article 3

Derivation of Article 3

The term **law merchant** refers to the system of routine rules, customs, or practices used in the business community to regulate transactions and solve controversies.[1] The law of commercial paper is derived from the law merchant, specifically the practices of Western European merchants who recognized centuries ago the commercial need for freely transferable substitutes for currency. The rules and principles governing these documents were absorbed into the English common law during the seventeenth and eighteenth centuries and were ultimately codified in England in 1882 by the Bills of Exchange Act.

In the United States, the law of commercial paper was first codified in the Uniform Negotiable Instruments Law (UNIL) originally promulgated in 1896. Although the UNIL was subsequently adopted in every American jurisdiction, it had significant weaknesses, including substantial nonuniformity among the states in both the statutory language adopted and in its interpretation. Further, vast changes in commercial practices concerning negotiable instruments had rendered portions of the statute obsolete. In addition, courts and commentators had long criticized the organization and lack of clarity of the statute.

---

1. Black, *Law Dictionary* (4th ed. 1968).

Because of the foregoing problems and the need to integrate the material covered by the UNIL into a comprehensive commercial statute, Article 3 of the UCC was drafted to replace the UNIL. The project took seven years to complete and condensed the UNIL's 196 sections into 79, of which 11 concern matters not treated in the earlier statute.

Although Article 3 is a complete revision and modernization of the law, it borrows heavily from the UNIL in formulating the substantive rules governing commercial paper transactions. Of all Code Articles, Article 3 departs least from the major rules and concepts of prior law. Most states have enacted the 1962 Official Text of Article 3, which forms the basis of the following discussion.

Types of Article 3 Paper Defined and Distinguished

Commercial paper governed by Article 3 is one form of "negotiable instrument." Used in law generally, the term **instrument** refers to any written document, particularly legal documents such as contracts, wills, and deeds. In our study of commercial paper, the term will be used to designate a negotiable instrument as defined in Article 3.[2]

Negotiable instruments governed by Article 3 contain a promise or order to pay *money*. This characteristic distinguishes commercial paper from other negotiable instruments such as documents of title (for example, bills of lading and warehouse receipts) and investment securities (for example, stocks and bonds) that are governed by UCC Articles 7 and 8 respectively. Although Article 3 governs negotiable instruments payable in money and makes instruments within its scope substantially equivalent to money, Article 3 does not apply to money itself. The negotiability of money is determined by common law principles and under separate statutes.

Four types of commercial paper are within the scope of Article 3: (1) notes, (2) certificates of deposit, (3) drafts, and (4) checks. Functionally, however, it is necessary to distinguish only notes and drafts, because a certificate of deposit is a spe-

cialized form of note and a check is a specialized type of draft.

Notes and Certificates of Deposit. A **note** is two-party paper involving a promise by the **maker** of the note to pay a sum certain in money to the order of the payee or to bearer on demand or at a future date.[3] An instrument may be payable to the order of a specified person, the **payee.** If no payee is specified, the instrument is payable to **bearer,** meaning anyone who lawfully possesses the instrument when it is presented to the maker for payment. If an instrument is an acknowledgment by a bank of the receipt of money with a promise to repay it, then it is known as a **certificate of deposit** (see Figure 21–1). That is, a certificate of deposit is essentially a note that the bank as the maker issues to a depositor in the bank as payee.[4]

The note's primary purpose is as a credit device; it is the usual means by which money is borrowed to be repaid at a future date or by which property or services are sold on credit. Banks, savings and loan associations, and other lenders use notes in a variety of consumer and commercial transactions. Assume Buyer desires to buy a house from Seller for $150,000, but has insufficient cash. Buyer therefore goes to First Federal Savings and Loan and arranges to borrow the purchase price. First Federal, after checking Buyer's credit, agrees to loan the money. To evidence her obligation, Buyer issues a note to the bank promising to repay the loan in monthly installments over a 25-year period. In this case, Buyer, the debtor, is the maker of the note, and First Federal is the payee. Although a note is commonly issued in exchange for a loan of money, the obligation evidenced by the note need not be a cash advance. For example, Seller may sell goods on credit to Buyer, and Buyer may issue a note to Seller for the purchase price.

"Promise" Defined. The major characteristic of a note is a promise by the maker to pay. A **promise** is defined as an undertaking to pay and must more than merely acknowledge the existence

2. UCC §3-102(1)(e).

3. UCC §3-104(2)(d).
4. UCC §3-104(2)(c).

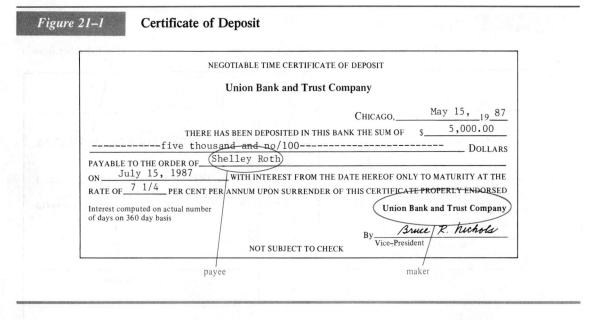

Figure 21–1 **Certificate of Deposit**

NEGOTIABLE TIME CERTIFICATE OF DEPOSIT

Union Bank and Trust Company

CHICAGO,_____May 15,___19_87_

THERE HAS BEEN DEPOSITED IN THIS BANK THE SUM OF $_____5,000.00_____

------------five thousand and no/100----------------------- _____ DOLLARS

PAYABLE TO THE ORDER OF___(Shelley Roth)_____

ON___July 15, 1987___/WITH INTEREST FROM THE DATE HEREOF ONLY TO MATURITY AT THE

RATE OF_7 1/4_ PER CENT PER ANNUM UPON SURRENDER OF THIS CERTIFICATE PROPERLY ENDORSED

Interest computed on actual number
of days on 360 day basis

Union Bank and Trust Company

By_____*Bruce R. Nichols*_____
Vice–President

NOT SUBJECT TO CHECK

payee   maker

---

of an obligation.[5] This definition makes it clear that a mere IOU is not a negotiable instrument. For example, the writing "Due X, $500 for value received, (signed) Z" contains no promise and is therefore not a note governed by Article 3. The writing may, of course, provide evidence of the existence of the debt or satisfy the Statute of Frauds against Z, but it is simply not a note to which Article 3 applies.

Drafts and Checks. Unlike notes and certificates of deposit, a **draft** (also known as a **bill of exchange**) may be designated three-party paper. The three parties are the **drawer,** the **drawee,** and the **payee.** Drafts are used both as substitutes for money and as credit devices. In drafts, the drawee and drawer generally stand in a debtor-creditor relation: the drawee owes the drawer money. A draft involves an *order* by the drawer directed to the drawee to pay to the order of the payee or to bearer a sum certain in money on demand or at a fixed or computable future date. In essence, the drawer of a draft says to the drawee, "rather than paying me

the money you owe, I order you instead to pay to the order of the payee."

Drafts are "drawn" on the drawee and may be used whenever a debtor-creditor relationship exists. One common type of draft is a **trade acceptance,** which is a draft drawn by a seller of goods on credit against his buyer. A trade acceptance is a substitute for selling goods on open account. Once the buyer assumes liability upon the trade acceptance by "accepting" it, the account becomes liquid, permitting the seller to raise money on the instrument (by selling it to a third party) before the account is due under the sales contract (see Figure 21–2).

If a draft is drawn on a bank and is payable on demand, then it is known as a **check,** certainly the most common negotiable instrument governed by Article 3.[6] In the case of a check, the drawer-depositor is a creditor of the drawee-bank because the amount on deposit in the drawer's checking account represents a debt of the bank owed to the depositor. (See Figure 21–3.)

Although a draft is three-party paper, three per-

---

5. UCC §3-102(1)(c).

6. UCC §§3-104(2)(a)–(b).

Figure 21–2 Trade Acceptance

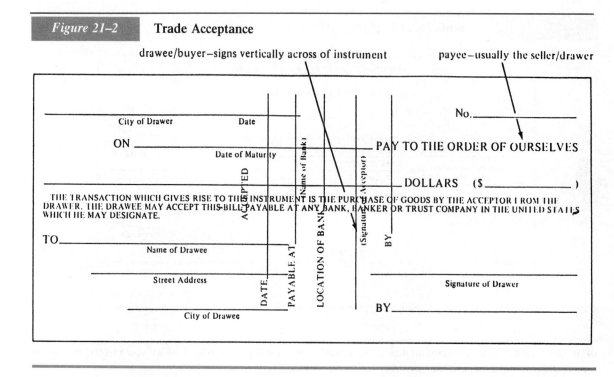

drawee/buyer–signs vertically across of instrument

payee–usually the seller/drawer

City of Drawer   Date

No.

ON _____

Date of Maturity

PAY TO THE ORDER OF OURSELVES

_____ DOLLARS   ($_____)

THE TRANSACTION WHICH GIVES RISE TO THIS INSTRUMENT IS THE PURCHASE OF GOODS BY THE ACCEPTOR FROM THE DRAWER. THE DRAWEE MAY ACCEPT THIS BILL PAYABLE AT ANY BANK, BANKER OR TRUST COMPANY IN THE UNITED STATES WHICH HE MAY DESIGNATE.

TO _____

Name of Drawee

Street Address

City of Drawee

(Signature Acceptor)
ACCEPTED
Name of Bank
LOCATION OF BANK
PAYABLE AT
DATE

BY _____

Signature of Drawer

BY _____

Figure 21–3 Check

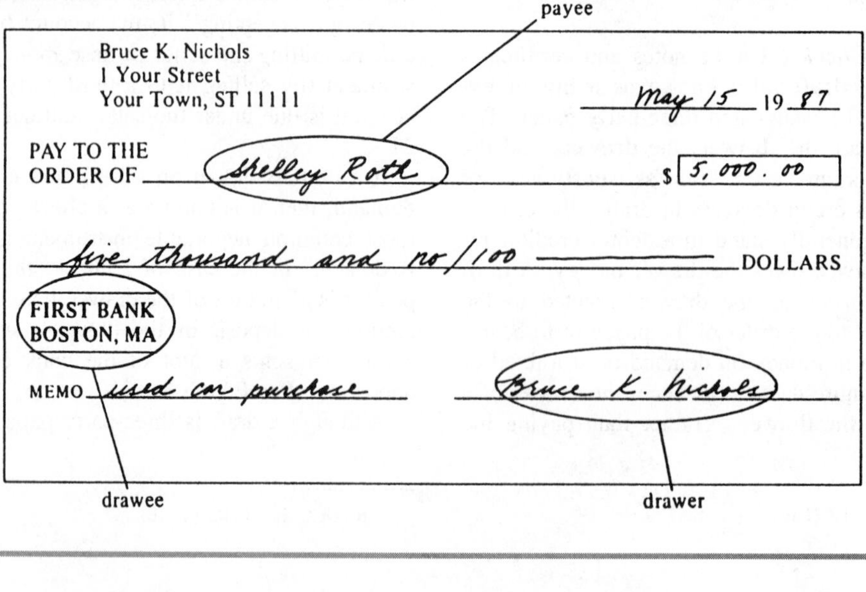

payee

Bruce K. Nichols
1 Your Street
Your Town, ST 11111

May 15 19 *87*

PAY TO THE
ORDER OF ___ *Shelley Roth* ___ $ *5,000.00*

five thousand and no/100 _____ DOLLARS

FIRST BANK
BOSTON, MA

MEMO *used car purchase*

Bruce K. Nichols

drawee

drawer

sons need not necessarily be involved because one person may fulfill two roles. In a trade acceptance, for example, the seller may make the instrument payable to himself, becoming both the drawer and the payee. Or, a person may draw a draft upon herself, becoming both the drawer and drawee.

For example, the drawer is also the drawee in a **cashier's check**—a check drawn by the issuing bank upon itself. Such a check may be procured by the payee of the instrument or a remitter. A **remitter** is a person, not a party to the instrument (that is, not the drawer, drawee, or payee), who purchases it in order to pay his own debt to the payee named in the check. Assume Bill owes Fred $5,000. Fred refuses to take Bill's personal check in payment, so Bill purchases a cashier's check from National Bank naming Fred as payee. In this case, National Bank is both drawer and drawee, Fred is the payee, and Bill is a remitter.

"Order" Defined. Unlike a note, which is characterized by a promise, a draft is an order to pay directed to the drawee. To bring the instrument within Article 3, an **order** must be a direction to pay and must be more than a mere authorization or request.[7] The word "pay" generally satisfies the order requirement in drafts. Adding words of courtesy such as "please pay" or "kindly pay" does not reduce the order to a mere request. However, language such as "I wish you would pay" would not qualify as an order. The order must identify the drawee with reasonable certainty and may be addressed to one or more drawees. The rule permitting alternative drawees allows, for example, a corporation, for commercial convenience, to draw its dividend checks upon a number of drawees (banks) usually located in different parts of the country.

Introduction to Negotiability

Advantages of Negotiability

Negotiability is a major characteristic of instruments governed by Article 3. **Negotiability** is a legal concept designed to promote the free transferability of the instrument from one owner to the next

---

7. UCC §3-102(1)(b).

and to enhance its marketability. Marketability refers to salability or liquidity—the degree to which an asset can be converted to cash without causing serious decline in its value. Negotiable instruments are *contracts*. Much of their value and usefulness in commerce lies in the ability of the owner of the instrument (for example, the payee of a note) to transfer (negotiate) it freely, unencumbered by problems attending an ordinary contract assignment.

Assignment of an Ordinary Contract. As discussed in Chapter 13, rights under a contract may ordinarily be freely assigned or transferred by a contracting party. The party transferring the rights is the assignor and the person receiving them is the assignee. The major problem facing an ordinary contract assignee is that the assignee generally "steps into the shoes" of the assignor and acquires no better rights than the assignor had. Therefore, any defense, such as fraud, breach of warranty, or failure of consideration, that the other original contracting party (obligor) can assert against the assignor can also be asserted against the assignee. The assignee also runs the risk that some third party, such as a creditor of the assignor, may claim ownership of the rights assigned. In addition, the obligor remains free to perform for the assignor until notified of the assignment. Thus, a prospective assignee of a contract is well advised to investigate the original transaction to determine its validity and whether it is subject to any claims or defenses. If no problems are found after making the investigation, the obligor must be notified of the assignment. Even then, however, the assignee is not completely protected because claims or defenses not uncovered by the investigation may still exist.

Assignment of a Negotiable Contract. If a negotiable contract is involved, many of the foregoing risks are eliminated because of the following characteristics of negotiable instruments.

Parol Evidence. In most cases, everything about a negotiable instrument, including liability of all parties, is determined by examining the instrument itself. Thus, a prospective assignee of a negotiable instrument need not "look behind" the instrument to any other document, or conduct an elaborate investigation of the original transaction giving rise to the instrument.

Transfer. Upon delivery of a negotiable instrument to the payee, the payee becomes the first "holder" of the instrument. Subsequent transferees become holders of the instrument by negotiation. Negotiation is effected simply and quickly either by mere delivery of the instrument to the transferee (assignee), or by delivery plus the signature (indorsement) of the original holder. After negotiation, the new holder of the instrument has no duty to give notice to the obligor that an assignment (negotiation) has been made. The obligor is under a duty to perform for the *holder* of a negotiable instrument, who may be someone other than the other original payee.

Freedom from Claims and Defenses. After the assignment (negotiation), an assignee (holder) who has purchased the instrument in good faith and for value takes the instrument free of all prior ownership claims and also free of most defenses asserted by other parties to the instrument. Note that the term **claim** refers to a claim of ownership of the instrument asserted either by a prior holder or by a third party not a holder. For example, a prior holder may assert that the instrument was stolen from him prior to its negotiation. Or a judgment creditor of a prior holder may claim ownership of the instrument by virtue of a judgment attaching all assets of the prior holder, including the instrument. A **defense,** on the other hand, is asserted by a party to the instrument to avoid his or her obligation to pay the instrument. Most commonly, the party asserting a defense is the maker of a note, or the drawer of a check or other draft.

Commercial Benefits of Negotiable Contracts.

The net effect of the characteristics outlined above is that the major risk undertaken by an assignee (holder) of a negotiable instrument is the solvency and capacity of prior parties, and the genuineness of the instrument itself. Eliminating other risks enhances the value of a negotiable contract on the market thus benefiting all involved. Because of reduced risk and administrative cost (from not having to make an investigation of the original transaction), an assignee is willing to pay substantially

more for a negotiable contract than a nonnegotiable one. That is, negotiable paper has a lower discount rate than nonnegotiable paper. The term **discount rate** refers to the percentage difference between the face value of an instrument at maturity and the amount an assignee, commonly a bank, is willing to pay for it prior to maturity. Although this discount, to a large extent, represents interest, it also reflects the risk of collection and costs of administering the transaction.

A lower discount rate facilitates, for example, the use by a merchant seller of his customer's promissory notes as a financing device. Assume Carter, Inc. sells manufacturing equipment to Brown on credit for $50,000. Brown issues a negotiable promissory note to Carter for the purchase price payable in one year. Carter, however, needs immediate cash to satisfy current obligations. He therefore sells the note to Regional Bank for $42,500 cash (reflecting a 15% discount rate). Because a negotiable instrument is involved, the discount rate reflects the fact that the bank will be paid even if Brown has a defense against Carter—for example, if the machinery delivered by Carter was defective. That is, because the instrument is negotiable, Brown will be required to pay the bank $50,000 at maturity even if Brown has a defense to paying Carter. Had the contract been nonnegotiable—for example, the assignment of an ordinary account receivable—the bank (the assignee) would be in no better position than Carter (the assignor) and would take subject to Brown's defense. In addition, it would incur costs in investigating the underlying transaction and notifying Brown of the assignment. As a result, the bank may be hesitant to take the paper at all, or would at least increase the discount rate to reflect the added risk and expense. Thus, if it cannot offer the bank a negotiable contract, Carter may be unable to obtain needed working capital. Brown also may be adversely affected because Carter now must charge more to realize the same amount of cash on his credit sales, or may not be able to sell on credit at all.

In addition to the benefits discussed above, various procedural rules make it easier to recover on a negotiable instrument after default than on a nonnegotiable instrument or a simple contract. When suing on a negotiable instrument, for example, the plaintiff (holder) need not plead or prove consideration, as is required in a suit on an ordinary contract. In addition, if the validity of the signatures is admitted or established, the holder is entitled to recover on the instrument merely by producing it, unless the defendant, such as the maker of a note, establishes a defense. Because signatures are generally presumed to be valid, the sole burden on the plaintiff in most cases is to produce the instrument and prove that he is a holder. The burden of proving any defense to payment rests upon the defendant.[8]

The "Holder in Due Course" Doctrine

In Article 3, negotiability is embodied in the **holder in due course doctrine,** which states that if a negotiable instrument is negotiated to a holder in due course, the holder in due course takes free of all claims and most defenses to the instrument. The holder in due course is essentially the "good faith purchaser" of the instrument entitled to the benefits of negotiability previously outlined. Under §3–302(1), a holder in due course is a holder who takes the instrument

1. for value,
2. in good faith, and
3. without notice that it is overdue, has been dishonored, or of any defense against or claim to it on the part of any person.

To illustrate the general operation of the holder in due course doctrine, assume that Sara sells a used truck to Laura for use in Laura's construction business. Because Laura is unable to pay cash for the truck, she contractually agrees to pay the $10,000 purchase price in twenty-four monthly installments. Sara, however, breaches the contract because: (1) she fails to deliver the truck, *or* (2) the truck is not as warranted (for example, it had not recently had an engine overhaul as represented by Sara), *or* (3) she defrauds Laura by turning back the truck's odometer. Before Laura discovers the problem, Sara assigns her rights under the contract to Harry, who pays cash without knowledge of Laura's defense. In this case, because an ordinary contract

assignment is involved, Harry steps into Sara's shoes and takes no better rights than she has. Therefore, Laura may assert any of the foregoing defenses against Harry when he brings an action to enforce the contract against her.

On the other hand, assume the same facts as above, except that instead of a mere contractual promise to pay, Laura issues a negotiable promissory note payable to the order of Sara. Sara immediately negotiates (assigns) the note to Harry, who pays cash without knowledge of Laura's defense; that is, Harry is a "holder in due course." In this case, Harry may compel Laura to pay the note despite Laura's defense against her original payee, Sara. Thus, the negotiability concept places the assignee of a negotiable instrument (the holder in due course, Harry) in a better position than his assignor (here, Sara). Although Sara cannot enforce the instrument against Laura, Harry (Sara's transferee) can. Simply stated, then, the net effect of the holder in due course doctrine is to negate the general principle of contract law that an assignee acquires no better rights than his assignor.

In order for an assignee to be placed in this preferred position, several requirements must be met:

1. The right assigned must be evidenced by a *negotiable instrument.* (The formal requisites of negotiability are covered in the next chapter.)
2. The instrument must be properly *negotiated* (assigned). (Negotiation is discussed in Chapter 23.)
3. The transferee of the instrument must be a *holder in due course.* (The holder in due course requirements listed above are discussed in Chapter 24.)

A person who qualifies as a holder in due course acquires various rights against other parties to the instrument and third parties. Namely, the holder in due course takes free of all claims to the instrument on the part of any person and certain defenses, commonly known as "personal" defenses, of other parties on the instrument. A holder in due course takes subject, however, to so-called real defenses. The rights of a holder in due course against persons asserting claims and defenses are covered in Chapter 24.

---

8. UCC §§3-307(1)-(2).

Parties to commercial paper, like parties to other contracts, have certain rights and duties. Generally, parties to commercial paper incur two types of liability: (1) liability for ultimate payment of the instrument (known as contract liability), and (2) liability for forgery and alteration of the instrument (known as warranty liability). Contract and warranty liability are discussed in Chapters 25 and 26 respectively. Chapter 27 concludes the commercial paper material with a discussion of special issues involving checks, including the bank collection process and the relationship between a bank and its checking account customer. Chapter 27 also discusses modern payment devices such as credit cards and electronic fund transfers.

SUMMARY

1. Article 3 of the UCC governs notes, certificates of deposit, drafts, and checks, important tools by which credit is extended and debts are paid.

2. Although Article 3 governs four types of instruments, the basic distinction is between notes, designated as "two-party" paper, and drafts, which are "three-party" paper.

3. A note involves a promise by the maker to pay a sum certain in money to the order of the payee on demand or at a definite time. A certificate of deposit, a specialized form of note, is an acknowledgment by a bank of the receipt of money with a promise to repay it.

4. A draft, unlike a note, contains an order rather than a promise. In a draft, the drawer orders the drawee, who usually is a debtor of the drawer, to pay money to the order of the payee. A draft drawn on a bank and payable on demand is known as a "check," certainly the most common type of negotiable instrument.

5. The foregoing instruments are negotiable, a characteristic that aids them in performing their valuable commercial functions. Negotiability promotes free transferability and enhances the marketability of the paper by providing (1) that all relevant information about the instrument, including liability of parties thereto, be determined from the instrument itself, (2) a simple and expeditious method of transferring the instrument, and (3) that good faith purchasers of the instrument take it free of ownership claims and free of most defenses that might be asserted by parties obligated on the paper.

KEY TERMS

law merchant
instrument
note
maker
payee
bearer
certificate of deposit
promise
draft (bill of exchange)
drawer
drawee

trade acceptance
check
cashier's check
remitter
order
negotiability
claim
defense
discount rate
holder in due course
    doctrine

QUESTIONS AND PROBLEMS

21-1 What are the basic characteristics of a negotiable, as opposed to a nonnegotiable, contract? Review the distinction between formal and informal (simple) contracts discussed in Chapter 7. Commercial paper governed by Article 3 is an important type of formal contract. Why is commercial paper a formal contract? What purposes do the formalities serve?

21-2 The law of commercial paper is primarily concerned with altering a basic principle of ordinary contract law. What is that principle? Why is it necessary to change it in commercial paper transactions?

Major Topics

- ■ the reasons why commercial paper must meet strict formal requirements
- ■ the various formal requisites of negotiability under Article 3
- ■ the rules of construction applicable to commercial paper
- ■ the legal effect of an incomplete instrument

Because of the extraordinary legal consequences of negotiability, a negotiable instrument must be readily distinguishable from a nonnegotiable one. In addition, to reduce administrative expenses and encourage widespread use, negotiable instruments must be easily created. To achieve these ends, the Uniform Commercial Code requires that a negotiable instrument within Article 3 meet strict formal requirements. Negotiability under Article 3 is strictly a matter of *form*. If the instrument in question contains the necessary formal elements, it is negotiable. All other instruments are nonnegotiable.

Formal Requisites of Negotiability

The formal requisites of negotiability under Article 3 are stated in §3-104(1). To be negotiable,

1. the instrument must be in *writing signed* by the maker or drawer,

2. the instrument must contain an *unconditional promise or order,*
3. the unconditional promise or order must be to pay a *sum certain in money,*
4. the instrument must be payable on *demand* or at a *definite time,* and
5. the instrument must be payable to *order* or to *bearer.*

Any instrument that does not meet these requirements may nevertheless be a legally binding contract on the signer. It is simply not *negotiable*. No person may therefore become a holder in due course of such an instrument with the ability to cut off prior claims and defenses. Rather, the transfer of a nonnegotiable instrument is governed by the same principles applicable to contract assignments generally—an assignee of such an instrument acquires no better rights than the assignor.

In addition to conclusively identifying negotiable contracts, formal requisites serve an additional function critical to negotiability: they assure that all relevant information about the instrument can be determined from the instrument itself. As succinctly stated in Official Comment 8 to §3-105: "[A]n instrument is not negotiable unless the holder can ascertain all of its essential terms from its face." Such terms include the amount payable, time of payment, and the liability of all parties.

The negotiability concept also requires that the information on the instrument not be subject to contradiction by evidence outside the instrument, such as oral testimony or other documents. For this reason, the UCC adopts a strict parol evidence rule applicable to commercial paper. *Everything* about Article 3 paper is determined by examining the face and back of the instrument itself. For example, all ambiguities are resolved by rules of construction provided in Article 3, and a party's liability is determined by the appearance and position of his or her signature on the paper. Further, with rare exceptions, no evidence other than what appears on the instrument itself (supplemented by UCC rules) is admissible in court to determine anything about the instrument.

A Writing Signed by the Maker or Drawer

"Writing" Defined. If a negotiable instrument is to adequately serve as a credit device or substitute for money, it must be in writing. This rule, recognized since the time of the law merchant, is necessary to promote certainty and prevent fraud. Although a writing is essential, UCC §1-201(46) defines the term **writing** broadly to include printing, typewriting, and any other intentional reduction to tangible form. A negotiable instrument therefore may be handwritten in pen or pencil on ordinary paper, carved on the top of a desk, embossed on the back of a book or a briefcase, or, for that matter, inscribed on any surface. As a practical matter, of course, virtually all commercial paper is created on forms (such as an ordinary check) printed for the purpose. Additionally, by administrative regulation or contract, banks may refuse to process checks not written on the printed form.

"Signature" Defined. To be negotiable, a note must be signed by the maker and a draft must be signed by the drawer. Like the writing, no strict formalities are imposed in defining "signature." Instead, §1-201(39) defines **signature** as "any symbol executed or adopted by a party with present intention to authenticate a writing." Section 3-401(2) adds that: "A signature is made by use of any name, including any trade or assumed name, upon an instrument, or by any word or mark used in lieu of a written signature." Thus, the signature may be handwritten, typewritten, printed, or indicated by thumbprint or other mark. Although the drawer or maker's signature ordinarily appears at the end of the writing, it may appear in the body of the instrument (for example, "I, Janice Dean, promise to pay . . . ") without any further signature.

The signature requirement is not only important in determining negotiability but also in ascertaining the contract liability of all parties to the instrument. Under §3-401(1), no person is liable on a negotiable instrument unless that person's *signature* appears on it. Signatures may be made in various capacities, which determine the nature and extent of the liability undertaken by the signer.

An Unconditional Promise or Order to Pay

A note involves a *promise* by the maker to pay money. In a draft, the drawer *orders* the drawee to pay. To be negotiable under Article 3, the note or draft must therefore contain language indicating that a promise or order has been made. Ordinarily the simple words "promise" in a note or "pay" in a draft satisfy this requirement.

The mere *existence* of a promise or order is not enough to make the instrument negotiable. The promise or order must be absolute and not conditioned upon the occurrence or nonoccurrence of any event. If paper is conditional, the holder must "look behind" the paper to see if the condition to payment has been met. The expense and delay inherent in investigating the condition defeats the basic purpose of negotiability. For this reason §3-104(1)(b) requires that, to be negotiable, an instrument must contain an *unconditional* promise or order to pay a sum certain in money and *no other* promise or order except as explicitly authorized in Article 3.

What constitutes an unconditional promise or order is sometimes a difficult question. Negotiable instruments are commonly given in exchange for a loan of money, or a sale of property or services. These instruments often contain added language referring to the underlying contract, or indicating the source of payment. The mere *existence* of a separate agreement does not affect negotiability,[1] but certain references to it may. UCC §3-105, discussed in the following three subsections, aids the

---

1. UCC §3-119(2).

court in determining whether added language renders the promise or order conditional.

Express v. Implied Conditions. The types of conditions affecting negotiability are *express*, not *implied or constructive*. Assume that, on January 1, Barker issues a $1,000 promissory note to the order of Sullivan in exchange for goods sold by Sullivan to Barker to be delivered on June 1. The note is payable on December 1 "on condition that Sullivan properly delivers the goods for which this note is issued by June 1, and that they conform to the contract of sale." In this case, Barker's promise to pay is subject to an express condition: seasonable and conforming delivery by Sullivan. The instrument is therefore nonnegotiable, because any later holder must investigate the occurrence of the condition to determine whether he or she will be paid. Negotiability is defeated because the holder cannot ascertain all essential terms from the instrument itself.

In contrast, a promise is not made conditional simply because it is subject to "implied" or "constructive" conditions under general contract law discussed in Chapter 14. For example, assume that rather than expressly conditioning his duty, Barker merely stated in the instrument that "this note is given in exchange for my purchase of goods from Sullivan which are to be delivered on June 1." As a matter of general contract law under the theory of "constructive conditions of exchange," Sullivan's failure to deliver on June 1 would justify Barker's failure to pay on December 1. One may therefore argue that the implied condition to Barker's duty destroys negotiability. The Code explicitly rejects this argument in §3-105(1)(a); implied or constructive conditions are not considered in determining negotiability.

Reference to a Separate Agreement. Negotiability is unaffected by a mere *reference to* a separate agreement to explain or provide information about the underlying transaction. In contrast, incorporation by reference[2] of the terms of a separate agreement into the instrument destroys negotiability because the holder must look to another document for terms of payment. The holder may not be required to look to other documents, even documents explicitly referred to in the instrument. The difficulty lies in determining which statements about the separate agreement *incorporate* that agreement, destroying negotiability, and which are mere references.

To resolve this problem, the UCC adopts an approach focusing upon the precise language used in the instrument. For example, under §3-105(2)(a) a promise or order is rendered conditional if the instrument states that it is "governed by" (or "conditioned by") or "subject to" any other agreement. On the other hand, negotiability is not destroyed by a simple statement that the promise or order is made, or the instrument matures, "in accordance with" or "as per" the transaction giving rise to the instrument. Without destroying negotiability, an instrument also may state its consideration or the transaction or agreement giving rise to the instrument, state that it is drawn under a letter of credit, or state that it is secured (for example, by a mortgage).[3] Such language is clearly intended to indicate the origin of the instrument and to inform, not to condition payment according to the terms of another agreement.

Courts are inclined to view the "as per–governed by" distinction as determinative. That is, an instrument made payable "as per" a separate agreement is negotiable, whereas one made "subject to" or "governed by" that agreement is not. This approach, although somewhat arbitrary, promotes certainty, which is of prime importance in the law of commercial paper.

Although requiring the holder to look to the separate agreement for essential terms ordinarily destroys negotiability, the Code does authorize certain limited incorporation by reference. For example, under §3-105(1)(c), terms giving the maker the right to prepay a note or giving the holder the right to accelerate the due date may be contained in a separate agreement without destroying negotiability.

In the following case the court was required to determine whether reference to another agreement rendered a note nonnegotiable.

---

2. Incorporation by reference is a legal doctrine under which the terms of one identifiable writing are made part of another writing by referring to, identifying, and adopting the former as part of the latter.

---

3. UCC §3-105(1).

Holly Hill Acres, Ltd. v. Charter Bank of Gainesville

314 So. 2d 209 (Fla. App. 1975)

Appellant Holly Hill Acres, Ltd. purchased land from Rogers and Blythe and executed a promissory note secured by a mortgage on the property. The note contained the following provision:

> This note with interest is secured by a mortgage on real estate, of even date herewith, made by the maker hereof in favor of the said payee, and shall be construed and enforced according to the laws of the State of Florida. *The terms of said mortgage are by this reference made a part hereof.* (Emphasis supplied.)

Rogers and Blythe assigned the promissory note and mortgage to appellee, Charter Bank of Gainesville, to secure their own note to the bank. When Holly Hill Acres defaulted on the note, Charter Bank sued to foreclose the mortgage. Holly Hill Acres defended on the ground that it had been defrauded by Rogers and Blythe in the original sale. The trial court entered summary judgment in favor of Charter Bank, holding that the note was negotiable and that the bank was a holder in due course of the note. Holly Hill Acres appealed.

Scheb, Judge

. . . Appellee Bank relies upon *Scott v. Taylor,* [58 So. 30 (Fla. 1912)], as authority for the proposition that its note is negotiable. *Scott,* however, involved a note which stated: "this note secured by mortgage." Mere reference to a note being secured by mortgage is a common commercial practice and such reference in itself does not impede the negotiability of the note. There is, however, a significant difference in a note stating that it is "secured by a mortgage" from one which provides, "the terms of said mortgage are by this reference made a part hereof." In the former instance the note merely refers to a separate agreement which does not impede its negotiability, while in the latter instance the note is rendered nonnegotiable. *See* [UCC §§ 3-105(2)(a); 3-119].

As a general rule the assignee of a mortgage se-

curing a nonnegotiable note, even though a bona fide purchaser for value, takes subject to all defenses available as against the mortgagee. . . . Appellant raised the issue of fraud as between himself and other parties to the note. . . .

The note having incorporated the terms of the purchase money mortgage was not negotiable. The appellee Bank was not a holder in due course, therefore, the appellant was entitled to raise against the appellee any defenses which could be raised between the appellant and Rogers and Blythe. . . .

The note, incorporating by reference the terms of the mortgage, did not contain the unconditional promise to pay required by [UCC] §3-104(1)(b). Rather, the note falls within the scope of [UCC] §3-105(2)(a). . . .

[Judgment reversed and remanded.]

The "Particular Fund" Doctrine. As a general proposition, persons obligated on a negotiable instrument must put all of their assets behind the instrument. For example, the maker of a note may not qualify the obligation by limiting payment to a specified part of his estate. Under §3-105(2)(b), an instrument stating that it is to be paid only out of a particular fund or source is conditional and, therefore, nonnegotiable. Thus, Mike's promissory note "payable only out of the proceeds of the sale of my 1986 soybean crop" is not negotiable whether or not sufficient proceeds actually exist to pay the note. Negotiability must be determined from the instrument itself, not extrinsic evidence. Negotiability is, however, unaffected by references in the instrument for bookkeeping or internal management purposes to the account to be debited—for example, "charge account #401"—or the source from which reimbursement is expected.

UCC §3–105(1) recognizes two exceptions to the general rule that instruments payable only out of a particular fund are nonnegotiable. First, an instrument issued by a governmental agency or unit is negotiable even if the instrument is limited to payment out of a particular fund or the proceeds of a particular source. This exception allows municipalities and other governments or governmental agencies to write checks or issue short-term warrants (notes) payable only out of the proceeds of a particular tax or other revenue source, such as a special assessment. The Code thus facilitates the use of such instruments as a method of financing public improvements and realizes the normal expectations of investors, who commonly regard such paper as negotiable.

Second, an instrument is negotiable even if it is limited to payment out of the entire assets of a partnership, unincorporated association, trust, or estate by which the instrument is issued. Paper issued by these entities frequently excludes the personal liability of the individual members of an unincorporated association, the partners of a partnership, the executor of an estate, or the trustee of a trust. Because such personal liability is viewed as an asset of the issuing entity, it may be argued that the entire credit of the obligor does not back the instrument, thus rendering it payable only out of a particular fund and, therefore, nonnegotiable. The Code nevertheless treats such instruments as negotiable, placing them on a par with instruments issued by corporations which, although backed by corporate assets, exclude the personal liability of shareholders.

Additional Terms Not Affecting Negotiability. A negotiable promise or order must be unconditional, and generally must be the *only* promise, order, power, or obligation given by the maker or drawer. For example, a note in which the maker promises to pay money and to perform services or deliver goods is nonnegotiable. Section 3-112 recognizes certain limited exceptions to this rule by allowing an instrument to contain limited obligations or powers in addition to the bare promise or order to pay money. If a note is secured, its negotiability is not affected by a promise or power stated in the instrument to maintain, protect or insure collateral, or to give additional collateral. Other than as authorized by §3-112, however, added promises, orders, powers, and obligations destroy negotiability.

A Sum Certain in Money

Article 3 paper is payable in money. Section 3-104(1)(b) states that the unconditional promise or order on the paper must be "to pay a sum certain in money." If all or part of an instrument is payable in goods or services, it cannot be negotiable

under Article 3. Requiring payment in money promotes the marketability of the paper because it is easier to ascertain the present value of a promise to pay money than a promise to deliver goods or perform services. Further, the amount of money payable must be certain, generally computable from the instrument itself.

"Money" Defined. Section 1-201(24) defines the term **money** as "a medium of exchange authorized or adopted by a domestic or foreign government as a part of its currency." An instrument payable in "currency" or "current funds" is payable in money.

Because money includes a medium of exchange authorized or adopted by a *foreign* as well as domestic government, an instrument may be negotiable under Article 3 even though payable in foreign currency. Provided it meets the other requirements, an instrument issued and to be paid in the United States, but payable in English pounds or French francs, is negotiable. If the instrument is payable in foreign currency, §3-107(2) provides that the instrument may be satisfied when due in the equivalent amount of United States dollars, unless payment in the foreign currency is specifically required by the instrument.

Sum Certain. Article 3 requires that the sum of money payable be *certain*. This **sum certain** requirement, outlined in §3-106, assures that owners or prospective owners of the instrument can readily determine its value. The holder must be able to compute the amount payable from the instrument itself. For example, assume Mary issues a note promising to pay to Peter's order "the entire proceeds of the sale of my house." In this case, Peter or a later holder must look outside the instrument to determine the amount payable (to find out what the sale proceeds, if any, were); therefore, the instrument is not negotiable.

The exact amount payable need not be explicitly stated in the instrument. As explained in Official Comment 1 to §3-106:

> It is sufficient that at *any time of payment* the holder is able to determine the amount then payable from the instrument itself with any necessary computation. (Emphasis added.)

Thus, a note issued by Mary on June 1, 1986, stating, ''I promise to pay $10,000 plus interest at an annual rate of 10% to the order of Peter on December 1, 1986,'' is negotiable.

The Code takes a similar approach to instruments payable in foreign currency. Because of fluctuations in the exchange rate, the amount for which the instrument is payable cannot be known until the payment date. Nevertheless, §3-107(2) explicitly provides that: ''A promise or order to pay a sum stated in a foreign currency is for a sum certain in money.''

A related problem concerns the effect of certain auxiliary promises on the sum certain requirement. That is, in order to increase marketability, the maker of a note may promise to pay not only principal and interest, but also exchange rates, and costs of collection and attorneys' fees upon default. Section 3-106 authorizes the inclusion of such promises, rejecting the argument that the sum payable is not certain because no one knows at the date of issue what the auxiliary costs will be. Such promises merely shift the risk of these expenses from the holder to the maker, providing more assurance that the holder will ''net'' the face amount of the instrument.

At issue in the following case was the negotiability of a note providing for a variable rate of interest.

Taylor v. Roeder

360 S.E.2d 191 (Va. 1987)

VMC Mortgage Company (VMC), was in the business of lending money to purchasers of real estate in exchange for promissory notes. To obtain loan funds, VMC borrowed money from investors, pledging as collateral the promissory notes received from the real estate purchasers. In separate transactions, VMC lent money to Olde Towne Investment Corporation of Virginia (Olde Towne) and Richard L. Saslaw and the borrowers signed promissory notes agreeing to pay back the loan amount plus interest of ''3% over Chase Manhattan Prime to be adjusted monthly.'' VMC later assigned the notes to a pension fund as security for a loan without notice to Olde Towne and Saslaw, who later repaid the full amount of the loans plus interest directly to VMC. When VMC defaulted on its loan from the pension fund and later went bankrupt, the pension fund, by its trustee William Roeder, demanded that Olde Towne and Saslaw pay the notes again, arguing that the promissory notes were negotiable instruments and that the pension fund was a holder in due course. Under the UCC, the maker of a negotiable promissory note cannot assert payment to the original obligor as a defense to paying a holder in due course who acquires the instrument without notice of the payment. The trial court ruled in favor of Roeder and ordered Olde Towne and Saslaw to pay the promissory notes to the pension fund. Olde Towne and Saslaw appealed.

Russell, Justice

The dispositive question in this case is whether a note providing for a variable rate of interest, not ascertainable from the face of the note, is a negotiable instrument. We conclude that it is not. . . .

Under the general law of contracts, if an obligor has received no notice that his debt has been assigned and is in fact unaware of the assignment, he may, with impunity, pay his original creditor and thus extinguish the obligation. His payment will be a complete defense against the claim of an assignee who failed to give him notice of the assignment. . . .

Under the law of negotiable instruments, continued in effect under the Uniform Commerical Code, the rule is different: the makers are bound by their contract to make payments to the *holder*. . . . Further, a holder in due course takes the instrument free from the maker's defense that he has made payment to the original payee, if he lacks notice of the payment and has not dealt with the maker. . . . Thus, the question whether the notes in this case were negotiable is crucial. . . .

Official Comment 1 [to §3-106 of the UCC] . . . states in part:

It is sufficient [to establish negotiability] that at any time of payment the holder is able to determine the amount then payable *from the instrument itself* with any necessary computation. . . . The computation must be one which can be made *from the instrument itself without reference to any outside source*, and this section does not make negotiable a note payable with interest "at the current rate." (Emphasis added.) . . .

We conclude that the drafters of the Uniform Commercial Code adopted criteria of negotiability intended to exclude an instrument which requires reference to any source outside the instrument itself in order to ascertain the amount due, subject only to the exceptions specifically provided for by the U.C.C. . . .

The appellee points to the Official Comment [1 to §3-104, which] states that by providing criteria for negotiability "within this Article," . . . [§3-104(1)] "leaves open the possibility that some writings may be made negotiable by other statutes or by judicial decision." The Comment continues: "The same is true as to any new type of paper which commercial practice may develop in the future." The appellee urges us to create, by judicial decision, just such as exception in favor of variable-interest notes.

Appellants concede that variable-interest loans have become a familiar device in the mortgage lending industry. Their popularity arose when lending institutions, committed to long-term loans at fixed rates of interest to their borrowers, were in turn required to borrow short-term funds at high rates during periods of rapid inflation. Variable rates protected lenders when rates rose and benefitted borrowers when rates declined. They suffer, however, from the disadvantage that the amount required to satisfy the debt cannot be ascertained without reference to an extrinsic source—in this case the varying prime rate charged by the Chase Manhattan Bank. Although that rate may readily be ascertained from published sources, it cannot be found within the "four corners" of the note.

Other courts confronted with similar questions have reached differing results. . . .

The U.C.C. introduced a degree of clarity into the law of commercial transactions which permits it to be applied by laymen daily to countless transactions without resort to judicial interpretation. The relative predictability of results made possible by that clarity constitutes the overriding benefit arising from its adoption. In our view, that factor makes it imperative that when change is thought desirable, the change should be made by statutory amendment, not through litigation and judicial interpreta-

tion. Accordingly, we decline the appellee's invitation to create an exception, by judicial interpretation, in favor of instruments providing for a variable rate of interest not ascertainable from the instrument itself. . . .

[Judgment reversed and remanded.]

Payable on Demand or at a Definite Time

To be negotiable within Article 3 an instrument must be payable either on *demand* or at a *definite time*. This requirement assures that the holder can ascertain *when* he will be paid, whereas the sum certain rule determines the *amount* payable. Both are required to compute the present value of the instrument—a basic purpose of the formal requisites.

Instruments Payable on Demand. A demand instrument is payable whenever the holder chooses to present it for payment to the maker (of a note) or the drawee (of a draft). Under §3-108, instruments payable on demand or **demand instruments** include:

1. those explicitly stated to be payable on "demand," or
2. those payable "on presentation," or
3. those payable "on sight," or
4. those in which no time for payment is stated.

The note in Figure 22–1 is a demand instrument of the first type.

The fourth type of demand instrument requires additional elaboration. Under §3-114(1), the negotiability of an instrument is unaffected by the fact that it is undated. Because the absence of a date has no effect on negotiability, an undated instrument—for example, when a blank for the date on a note or check form is not filled in—is one in which "no time for payment is stated" and is therefore payable on demand.

Negotiability of an instrument is similarly unaffected by the fact that it is antedated—for example, a check written on June 1 dated May 15—or post-dated—for example, a check written on May 15

Demand Note

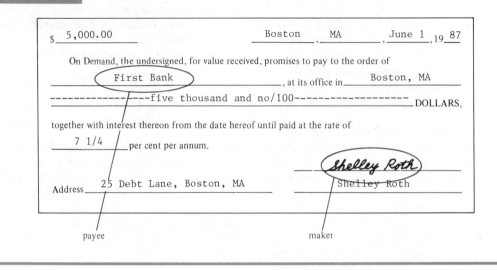

payee   maker

---

dated June 1. In either case, the time when the instrument is payable is determined by the stated date if the instrument is payable on demand. Thus, an antedated instrument may be due before it is issued. Therefore, any dated instrument not explicitly stating another time for payment is a demand instrument payable on the stated date. Checks ordinarily fall into this category.

Under §3-114(3), whenever an instrument or any signature thereon is dated, the date is presumed to be correct. In applying this rule, the court uses the stated date to determine liability of parties on the instrument without any further inquiry into the date's accuracy, unless and until evidence is introduced to the contrary.

Instruments Payable at a Definite Time. Commercial paper is frequently used as a credit device, evidencing an obligation to pay money in the future in return for goods sold, services rendered, or money loaned. The party obligated (normally the maker of a note) is not able to pay the instrument on demand but desires to postpone payment to some future date. Instruments calling for future (other than demand) payment, or **time instruments,** must be payable at a *definite time.* This re-

quirement assures that the instrument will ultimately be paid and aids in computing its value. As with other terms, the holder of such a time instrument must generally be able to compute the payment date from the instrument itself.

In §3-109(1), the UCC outlines four basic situations in which an instrument is payable at a definite time for purposes of negotiability:

1. An instrument is payable at a definite time if by its terms it is payable on or before a stated date or at a fixed period after a stated date. This is the most common time instrument. For example, Mary may issue her $10,000 promissory note dated January 1, 1983, payable "on July 1, 1983," or alternatively "6 months after date." The note in Figure 22–2 illustrates this type of time instrument. Note that if the instrument is payable at a fixed period after a stated date, the inclusion of the date is important to negotiability. Without it, the maturity of the instrument cannot be determined.

2. An instrument is payable at a definite time if by its terms it is payable at a fixed period after sight. This is a time draft. "Sight" in this case refers to "acceptance," a concept discussed in detail in Chapter 25. For example, assume Sally

| Figure 22–2 | **Time Note** |

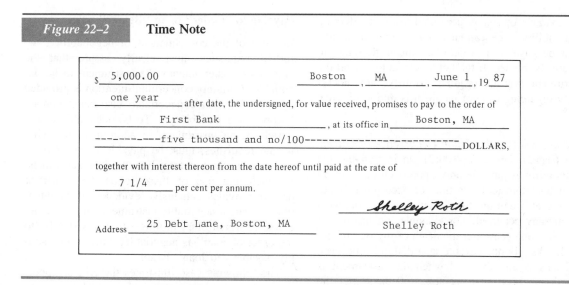

draws a draft on Bob payable to Paul's order "60 days after sight." In this case Paul must first present the draft to Bob for acceptance. The date of acceptance fixes the ultimate maturity date. That is, sixty days after the date of acceptance, Paul or a later holder will again present the instrument to Bob, this time for payment.

3. An instrument is payable at a definite time if by its terms it is payable at a definite time subject to any acceleration. Promissory notes often contain **acceleration clauses.** Such clauses generally make the note, originally payable at some fixed future date or in fixed future installments, either immediately due and payable or payable on a date sooner than originally agreed. To illustrate, assume Martin issues his $12,000 promissory note to Alice's order payable over two years in twenty-four equal monthly installments. The note contains a provision making the entire remaining balance immediately due and payable if Martin defaults on two consecutive monthly payments.

Because no one knows at the date of issue whether or not acceleration will be made, one may argue an instrument containing an acceleration clause is not payable at a definite time and should therefore be nonnegotiable. The Code decisively rejects this argument by broadly validating all ac-

celeration clauses[4] provided the instrument is ultimately payable at a definite time if no acceleration is made.

4. An instrument is payable at a definite time if by its terms it is payable at a definite time subject to: (a) *any* extension at the option of the holder, or (b) extension to a *further definite time* at the option of the maker or acceptor, or automatically upon or after occurrence of a specified act or event. An **extension clause** simply extends the maturity of an instrument (generally a note) from its original due date to a future time specified in the instrument.[5] The Code broadly validates extension clauses but places a limitation upon them if the extension occurs by the terms of the instrument or at the maker's option. That is, such an extension must be to a *further definite time.* Any other rule would allow the maker to extend the instrument indefinitely, rendering the promise to pay illusory. On the other hand, any extension (even without a time limit) at

---

4. The clause may operate at the option of the maker or holder, or automatically on occurrence of an event, and may be conditional or unrestricted. Acceleration clauses are discussed in more detail in Chapter 14.

5. Consent to extension authorizes a single extension for not longer than the original period. UCC §3-118(f).

the *holder's* option is permitted without affecting negotiability. The formal requisite that an instrument be payable at a definite time is designed to benefit the holder. If the holder elects to extend the instrument past its original maturity, any uncertainty regarding time of payment is due to his own act.[6]

Instruments Payable Upon Occurrence of Uncertain Events.

Under §3-109(2), an instrument that by its terms is payable only upon occurrence of an event uncertain as to its time of occurrence is not payable at a definite time even if the act or event has already occurred. For example, an instrument payable "one year after the death of my rich uncle, Joe Doaks" is not payable at a definite time even if Doaks is already dead when the instrument is issued. An instrument payable "60 days after the consumer price index reaches 200" or "120 years after the death of Abraham Lincoln" is similarly nonnegotiable even though the events fixing maturity have already occurred.

Such instruments are nonnegotiable for several reasons. First, if the event has not occurred, the time of payment is indeed uncertain, thwarting any effort to determine the instrument's present value, and thus defeating a basic purpose of negotiability. Second, even if the event has occurred, the holder may not know it or may not know its precise time of occurrence. The holder is therefore required to look to information beyond the face of the instrument to determine the time of payment. Third, instruments payable upon occurrence of uncertain events are used almost exclusively to borrow money in anticipation of an inheritance or receipt of a future interest. Such **post-obituary notes** are not acceptable in general commerce and are often made under unusual circumstances in which the maker's defenses should be preserved.

Payable to "Order" or to "Bearer"

Because of the consequences of negotiability, the formal requisites must clearly assure that the drawer or maker intends the instrument to be negotiable. Certainty concerning intention is provided by requiring that a negotiable instrument contain "words of negotiability." To be negotiable within Article 3, an instrument, in addition to the other formal requisites, must be payable to *order* or to *bearer* or to their statutorily authorized substitutes. By including one of these terms the maker or drawer provides conclusive evidence of an intention to issue a negotiable instrument. For example, a note in which Mary promises to pay $10,000 "to the order of Joan" is negotiable, whereas one simply payable "to Joan" is not.[7]

The following case illustrates the critical importance of the "magic words" of negotiability.

First Investment Company v. Andersen
621 P.2d 683 (Utah 1980)

Defendants Robert and Donna Andersen executed two promissory notes, each of which stated:

> For value received, Robert Andersen of Nephi, Utah, promises to pay to Great Lakes Nursery Corp. at Waukesha, Wisconsin, six thousand four hundred twelve dollars [in installments over a period of five years at 7% interest].
>
> s/ Robert Andersen
> s/ Donna Andersen

The promissory notes were executed when the Andersens entered into a franchise agreement with Greak Lakes Nursery Corp. (Nursery), which by the terms of the agreement was to provide 65,000 trees, chemicals, fertilizers, and technical training

---

6. Note that a clause authorizing extension at the holder's option gives him no greater rights against the maker or acceptor than he would have without the clause. That is, assuming no clause and no tender of full payment by the maker of a note on the due date, the holder's mere inaction would operate to extend the instrument. Under UCC §3–118(f), however, a holder may not exercise an option to extend over the objection of a maker who tenders full payment when the instrument is due.

7. Ordinarily, an instrument that does not meet the formal requisites is outside the scope of Article 3, and is treated as a simple contract. Under §3-805, however, an instrument that is nonnegotiable *solely* because it fails to include the words "order" or "bearer" (known as "almost negotiable," technically nonnegotiable," or a "mercantile specialty") is governed by Article 3 except that there can be no holder in due course of such an instrument.

to the Andersens. The Nursery assigned the Andersens' notes to plaintiff, First Investment Company. After paying several installments on the notes, the Andersens refused to make further payments on the grounds that the Nursery had failed to furnish the items and training required by the franchise agreement. First Investment sued the Andersens on the notes claiming to be a holder in due course. The trial court held that because the notes were not negotiable instruments, First Investment was not a holder in due course and, therefore, took the notes subject to the defense of failure of consideration. First Investment appealed.

Maughan, Justice

. . . Under both the N.I.L. and the U.C.C. [§3-104(1)(d)], one of the requirements to qualify a writing as a negotiable instrument is that it contain the time-honored "words of negotiability," such as "pay to the order" or "pay to the bearer." The mere promise to pay, absent the magic words "payable to order or to bearer," renders the note non-negotiable, and the liability is determined as a matter of simple contract law.

In the instant case, the notes were payable simply to the payee, and were not payable to the order of the payee or to the payee or its order and were thus not negotiable instruments. Since the notes were not negotiable, the transfer by the Nursery to plaintiff must be deemed an assignment, and the assignee (plaintiff) stood in the shoes of the assignor and took subject to existing equities and defense. . . .

[Judgment affirmed.]

The major characteristic of an instrument payable to order (so-called **order paper**) is that the payee is specifically named or otherwise designated with reasonable certainty. Conversely, **bearer paper** is payable to whoever possesses the instrument, and is therefore much like cash. The distinction between order and bearer instruments is extremely important in the law of commercial paper. As noted above, inclusion of the word "order" or "bearer" or its equivalent is essential to negotiability. In addition, the status of paper as order or bearer determines the means by which the paper is transferred (negotiated), and the liability of the parties on the instrument. The following material distinguishes instruments payable to order from those payable to bearer, and in the case of order paper, indicates to whose order the instrument is payable.

Instruments Payable to Order. Under §3-110(1), an instrument is payable to order if by its terms it is payable to the "order" or "assigns" of *any person therein specified with reasonable certainty.* Thus, a note in which the maker promises to pay $10,000 "to the order of Joe Doaks," or "to the assigns of Joe Doaks," or "to Joe Doaks or order," or "to Joe Doaks or assigns," is payable to order. Although the term "assigns" indicates an order instrument, the term "order" is, by far, the most common usage.

If the instrument is payable to a single natural person—for example, "pay to the order of John Jones"—the person to whose order the instrument is payable is clearly identified. A negotiable instrument may, however, be made payable to the order of a payee that is not a legal entity. Examples include decedent's estates, trusts, funds, partnerships, and unincorporated associations such as labor unions or business trusts. If the instrument is payable to the order of a trust, fund, or estate, it is payable to the order of the *representative* (the trustee, executor, or administrator) of such entity. Similarly, an instrument payable to the order of a partnership or unincorporated association is payable to the partnership or association. Any person authorized by the partnership or association may indorse and transfer or otherwise deal with the instrument. A similar rule applies to corporations.

An instrument also may be payable to the order of an office ("the office of the county recorder" or the "United States consulate") or to an officer by his title as such ("Treasurer of the City of Champaign" or "Clerk of the Circuit Court"). In either case, the instrument is payable to the principal, but the incumbent of the office—the current county recorder, United States consulate, city treasurer, or circuit clerk—or his successor may act as the holder for purposes of negotiating or otherwise dealing with the instrument.

A closely related situation, governed by §3-117,

arises when an instrument is payable to a *named person* with words of description. (Note that in the preceding paragraph, the incumbent in the office is not specifically named.) If an instrument is made payable to a named person, as agent or officer of a specified person (for example, "John Jones, Treasurer of XYZ Corporation," or "John Jones as agent for Joe Doaks"), the instrument is payable to the principal (XYZ Corporation or Joe Doaks) but the agent or officer (John Jones) may act as the holder.

If the words of description name the payee as a *fiduciary* of a specified person or persons, the instrument is nevertheless payable to the payee, who may negotiate, enforce, or discharge the instrument in her own name. For example, an instrument payable to "Jane Jones, trustee of City College Trust," or "Jane Jones, executor of the will of Joe Doaks," or "Jane Jones, administrator of the estate of Richard Wagner" is payable to Jane Jones. Although Jones is the proper party to negotiate or otherwise deal with the instrument, she is liable for breach of fiduciary duty if she uses the instrument for her own benefit rather than the benefit of the trust or estate.

If the instrument contains words of description other than those outlined above, the instrument is payable to the payee unconditionally and the additional words have no effect on subsequent parties. Thus, an instrument payable to "John Doe, plumber," "John Doe, trustee," "John Doe, agent," "John Doe, 421 Elm Street," "John Doe, treasurer," "John Doe, executor" is payable to John Doe unconditionally. The added language is treated merely as identification, and the payee may negotiate, discharge, or enforce the instrument even if the description is inaccurate.

Instruments Payable to Bearer. Unlike an order instrument, which is payable to a specific person, bearer paper is payable to the person possessing the instrument. Section 3-111 provides that an instrument is payable to bearer if by its terms it is payable (1) to "bearer" or the "order of bearer," or (2) to a specified person or bearer, or (3) to "cash" or the "order of cash" or *any other indication which does not purport to designate a specific payee.* The italicized language is the basic test of bearer paper. Examples of each of the three types follow.

Instruments Payable to "Bearer" or the "Order of Bearer." The "order of bearer" case ordinarily arises when the word "bearer" is written in the blank on a preprinted form such as a check.

Instruments Payable to a Specified Person or Bearer. Assume Molly issues a note promising to pay $10,000 to "John Doe or bearer." The instrument is payable to bearer. Note that in this example the word "order" does not appear. If it does, making the instrument payable "to the order of John Doe or bearer," §3-110(3) provides that the instrument "is payable to order unless the bearer words are handwritten or typewritten." Thus, §3-110(3) requires examination of the bearer language, ordinarily the word "bearer." If that language is part of a printed form (the most common case), the maker's or drawer's insertion of order language and the name of a specific payee indicates an intent that the instrument be payable to order. If, however, the word "bearer" is not part of the printed form but is instead handwritten or typewritten by the maker or drawer on the instrument, an intention to make the instrument payable to bearer is indicated. Thus, an entirely handwritten or typewritten instrument payable "to the order of John Doe or bearer" is bearer paper.

Instruments Payable to "Cash," the "Order of Cash," or Any Other Indication Which Does Not Purport to Designate a Specific Payee. Any indication not purporting to designate a specific payee results in a bearer instrument. For example, all of the following instruments are payable to bearer: "pay cash," "pay to the order of cash," "pay to the order of a keg of nails," "pay to the order of one 1955 Chevrolet," "pay a copy of the 1978 Official Text of the Uniform Commercial Code."

Rules of Construction

The formal elements of negotiability permit the essential terms of the instrument to be determined accurately and quickly from the instrument. To provide even greater certainty concerning essential terms, the UCC adopts a very strict parol evidence rule applicable to commercial paper. That is, generally the only admissible evidence concerning the essential terms of a negotiable instrument, including the liability of all parties, is the instrument itself. Ambiguities are resolved or clarified not by outside evidence, but by rules of construction stated in Article 3. In most cases, no evidence, including oral testimony or other documents, is admissible to contradict what is stated on the instrument as supplemented by Code construction rules.

Most Article 3 construction principles for ambiguous instruments are contained in §3-118. Generally, these rules cannot be altered or varied by proof that any party intended a different interpretation. Four of §3-118's construction rules are discussed below.

1. If "there is doubt whether the instrument is a draft or a note, the holder may treat it as either. A draft drawn on the drawer is effective as a note." For example, a cashier's check (one drawn by a bank upon itself) may be treated by the holder as a check on the issuing bank or a demand promissory note.

2. Language on a negotiable instrument may be printed—for example, the language of a pre-printed note or check form—typewritten, or handwritten. Anything typed or handwritten on a printed form controls an inconsistent printed term. If a conflict arises between what is typed and what is written, the handwritten term controls.

3. Notes and drafts commonly express the amount payable both in words ("one hundred dollars") and figures ($100.00). If a conflict arises between the figures and words, *words* control unless the words are ambiguous. For example, assume Ann draws a check payable to Pat's order. Ann fills in the amount as "$10.00" in figures and "one thousand dollars" in words. The instrument is payable for $1,000. In the following case the court applied this rule of construction in resolving a dispute.

Yates v. Commercial Bank & Trust Company

432 So. 2d 725 (Fla. App. 1983)

Emmett McDonald, while acting as personal representative of the estate of Marion Cahill, wrote a check drawn on the estate checking account at defendant Commercial Bank & Trust Company. The check read in pertinent part:

Pay to the order of *Emmett E. McDonald*
$10075.00 Ten hundred seventy five . . . . .Dollars.

The italicized material was handwritten; the remainder was printed.

The bank paid $10,075 to McDonald, who absconded with the funds. Plaintiff William Yates, who was appointed as successor representative for the estate, sued the bank for $9,000 representing the difference between $10,075 and $1,075. The trial court dismissed the complaint. Yates appealed.

Schwartz, Chief Judge

. . . It is clear that the complaint stated a cognizable claim against the bank. Section 673.118, Florida Statutes (1981), provides:

The following rules apply to every instrument:
. . .
(3) Words control figures except that if the words are ambiguous figures control.

Under this provision of the UCC, it was clearly improper for the bank to have paid the larger sum stated in numbers, rather than the smaller one unambiguously stated by McDonald's words. It is, therefore, prima facie liable to the estate for the excess. . . .

[Judgment reversed.]

4. An instrument may be made payable "with interest" but with no interest rate stated. Section 3-118(d) provides that such an instrument is payable with interest "at the judgment rate at the place of payment from the date of the instrument, or if it is undated from the date of issue." The **judgment rate** refers to the rate of interest required by state law to be paid on money judgments. This rate varies from state to state. For example, Illinois law provides "judgments recovered in any court shall draw interest at the rate of 9% per annum from the date of the judgment until satisfied". . . .[8]

---

8. Ill.Rev.Stat. ch. 110, ¶2-1303. Note finally that §3-118 contains additional construction rules concerning: (1) the liability of two or more persons signing the same instrument in the same capacity, and (2) the effect of a consent to extension of an instrument. These rules are discussed in the liability of parties material in Chapter 25.

Incomplete Instruments

An instrument is not negotiable unless it contains all of the formal requisites of negotiability. An instrument ultimately intended to be negotiable, which is *signed* by the maker or drawer but which omits some term or terms necessary to complete the instrument, is referred to as **incomplete**. An incomplete instrument contains blanks or spaces or otherwise indicates that additional terms are to be supplied. Usually, the omitted term or terms are some combination of the date, the payee, and the amount payable.

Under §3-115(1), an incomplete instrument "cannot be enforced until completed, but when it is completed in accordance with authority given it is effective as completed." In other words, if an incomplete instrument is completed as authorized, expressly or impliedly, by the maker or drawer, the instrument is enforceable as a negotiable instrument as completed. The instrument is treated as if completed personally by the maker or drawer. For example, assume that on June 1, Anne issues a promissory note payable to John's order "90 days after date." The instrument is complete in all respects except Anne forgets to fill in the blank for the date. Anne hands the note to John, who fails to notice the omission. At this time the instrument is incomplete and nonnegotiable because it is not payable at a definite time. The next day, John discovers the omission and fills in the date of issue on the note. The instrument is now complete and negotiable as completed.

Of course, not all completions are authorized. Assume Diane gives her roommate Joan a check signed by Diane with the date, payee, and amount blank. Diane instructs Joan to take the check to the grocery store and buy groceries for the next week, not exceeding $75 in amount. Instead of buying groceries, Joan takes Diane's check to the stereo store, uses it to purchase $2,000 worth of stereo equipment, and promptly leaves town. This is an unauthorized completion. The rules governing unauthorized completion are covered in Chapter 24.

SUMMARY

1. Article 3 requires that commercial paper meet strict formal requisites. These formalities conclusively identify negotiable instruments and assure that all relevant information regarding the instrument can be determined from the instrument itself without recourse to any other document or individual. Further, all ambiguities are resolved by rules of construction provided in Article 3.

2. To be negotiable under Article 3: (1) the instrument must be in *writing signed* by the maker or drawer; (2) the instrument must contain an *unconditional promise or order*; (3) the unconditional promise or order must be to pay a *sum certain in money*; (4) the instrument must be payable on *demand* or at a *definite time*; and (5) the instrument must be payable to *order* or to *bearer*.

3. The writing and signature requirement under the UCC are not rigorous. Though most negotiable instruments are preprinted forms such as checks, a "writing" is broadly defined to include any intentional reduction to tangible form. Similarly, a signature includes not only a formal signature, but also any other symbol adopted by a party with present intent to authenticate a writing.

4. The signed writing must contain an unconditional promise (in a note) or order (in a draft). This requirement assures that the holder need not "look behind" the instrument to determine whether any condition to payment has been met. A promise or order is not rendered conditional simply because it is subject to implied or constructive conditions under general contract law or because it refers to a separate agreement for purposes of explanation or information about the underlying transaction. Negotiability is destroyed, however, if the promise or order is subject to an express condition or incorporates the terms of a separate agreement into the instrument. Additionally, an instrument which states that it is payable only out of a particular fund or source is conditional and, therefore, nonnegotiable.

5. To allow the holder to compute the amount payable, the unconditional promise or order must be to pay a sum certain in money. Generally, no other promise or order may be included. The sum payable is certain if, at any time of payment, the holder can determine the amount then payable from the instrument itself with any necessary computation. Instruments payable in foreign currency are negotiable because "money" includes any medium of exchange adopted by a foreign or domestic government as part of its currency.

6. To be negotiable, the instrument must be payable on demand or at a definite time. Instruments payable on demand include those expressly payable "on demand,"

"on presentation," or "on sight," and those, such as checks, in which no time for payment is stated.

7. An instrument is payable at a definite time if by its terms it is payable (1) on or before a stated date or at a fixed period after a stated date, or (2) at a fixed period after sight, or (3) at a definite time subject to any acceleration, or (4) at a definite time subject to any extension at the option of the holder or to extension to a further definite time at the option of the maker or by terms of the instrument. An instrument is not payable at a definite time if it is payable only upon occurrence of an event uncertain as to its time of occurrence.

8. The final formal requirement is that the instrument be payable to "order" or to "bearer." An instrument is payable to order ("order paper") if it is payable to the order or assigns of any person specified with reasonable certainty.

9. Unlike order paper which is payable to a specific person, an instrument payable to bearer ("bearer paper") is payable to whoever possesses the instrument, and is therefore much like cash. Instruments payable to bearer include those payable (1) to "bearer," or to "the order of bearer," or (2) to a specified person or bearer, or (3) to "cash" or the "order of cash" or any other indication that does not purport to designate a specific payee.

10. Occasionally, an instrument ultimately intended to be negotiable, will be signed, but will omit some term or terms (such as the date, payee, or amount payable) necessary to complete the instrument and make it negotiable. If the instrument is completed as authorized by the drawer or maker, the instrument becomes negotiable and is enforceable as completed.

KEY TERMS

writing	extension clause
signature	post-obituary note
money	order paper
sum certain	bearer paper
demand instrument	judgment rate
time instrument	incomplete instrument
acceleration clause	

QUESTIONS AND PROBLEMS

22-1 Consider the following instrument:

XYZ Co. hereby promises to pay Joe Doaks or bearer one hundred thousand (1,000) French Francs 30 days from date, for the purchase of goods delivered on July 15, 1984, governed by agreement dated July 1, 1984, with interest. We hereby acknowledge receipt of the goods and that Joe Doaks has a security interest in the goods. XYZ Co. agrees to pay all costs of col-

lection and attorneys' fees in the event of wrongful default.

> (Signed) Sam Jones
> President, XYZ Co.

(a) Is the instrument a note or a draft?

(b) Is the instrument nonnegotiable *because* it is payable in foreign currency?

(c) Is the instrument nonnegotiable *because* the amount payable in words is different from the amount payable in figures?

(d) For what sum is the instrument payable?

(e) Is the instrument nonnegotiable *because* it is undated?

(f) Is the instrument nonnegotiable *because* it is not payable at a definite time? Could Joe Doaks complete the instrument by inserting the date? Would the instrument then be payable at a definite time?

(g) Is the instrument nonnegotiable *because* the interest rate is not stated? What is the interest rate of the instrument?

(h) Is the instrument nonnegotiable *because* it is stated to be governed by a separate agreement? Would your answer change if the instrument was stated to be payable "as per" the July 1, 1984, agreement?

(i) Is the instrument nonnegotiable *because* it states the consideration for which it was created?

(j) Is the instrument nonnegotiable *because* it states that costs of collection and attorney's fees are to be paid in event of default, rendering the sum payable not certain?

(k) Is the instrument nonnegotiable *because* it states that it is secured?

(l) Assuming the instrument is negotiable, in what currency will the holder be paid?

(m) Is the instrument nonnegotiable *because* it is not payable to the "order" of Joe Doaks?

22-2 The Werner Co. agreed to perform construction work on a shopping mall owned by Stanley. After Werner finished the work, Stanley did not have sufficient cash to pay for the work; therefore, Stanley executed the following:

Promissory Note

Stanley acknowledges that a debt of $8,000 is owed to Werner Co. as a result of construction at Plaza Shopping Mall.

This note is payable at maturity on or before May 19, 1986, plus 10% interest.

> s/ Stanley
> April 4, 1985

Is the promissory note negotiable? Explain.

22-3 The *Liberty Advertiser,* a newspaper in need of capital, borrowed $15,000 and executed the following promissory note:

> The undersigned promises to pay to the order of the Bank of Viola the sum of $15,000 payable in installments or payable $80 per week from the Jack & Jill contract.
>
> > s/ Liberty Advertiser
> > by Don Jackson,
> > President

Jack and Jill is a grocery store that contracted to advertise in the *Liberty Advertiser* for one year at $80 per week. Is the note negotiable? Explain.

22-4 M. S. Horne executed a promissory note by which he promised to pay $100,000 to the order of R. C. Clark in one year. On the note was a statement that the note could not be transferred, pledged or assigned without the written consent of Horne. In a separate letter, Horne authorized Clark to pledge the note as collateral for a loan from First State Bank. Was the original note negotiable? If not, does Horne's separate letter make it negotiable?

22-5 Peter Jones executes the following instrument:

June 15, 1984

Promissory Note

I promise to pay to the order of Max Allen the sum of $6,000.

> s/ Peter Jones

(a) Is this instrument negotiable? When is it payable?

(b) What if the note stated:

> At the earliest time possible after this date I promise to pay to the order of Max Allen the sum of $6,000.
>
> > s/ Peter Jones

Now is it negotiable? Explain.

(c) Suppose the note stated:

> As soon as I am able I promise to pay to the order of Max Allen the sum of $6,000.
>
> > s/ Peter Jones

Now is the instrument negotiable? Explain.

(d) Suppose the note stated:

> I promise to pay to the order of Max Allen the sum of $6,000 within 10 years after June 15, 1984.
>
> > s/ Peter Jones

Is the instrument negotiable? If so, what is the earliest date Max could demand payment?

22-6 On October 1, 1986, Donna agreed to purchase Sam's condominium and wrote a personal check payable to Sam for $5,000 as an earnest money deposit. Donna postdated the check to October 15 and told Sam that there would not be sufficient funds in her account to cover the check until October 15. Is the check negotiable?

22-7 Under §3-109(2), an instrument payable only upon occurrence of an event uncertain as to its time of occurrence is not payable at a definite time and is therefore not negotiable. Despite §3-109(2), is it possible under the Code to make an instrument payable upon occurrence of an uncertain event negotiable? See UCC §3-109(1)(c).

22-8 Steven Mudd served as president of Medical Interact Systems Corp. (MISC). After meeting with Mudd, Weatherford agreed to buy a computer system from MISC and mailed a $60,000 check as down payment to MISC's home office. The check was made payable to: "Stephen Mudd, President of MISC." When Mudd received the check, he indorsed it and deposited it in his personal checking account at Southeast Bank. Soon thereafter, Mudd withdrew the funds and disappeared. Weatherford sued Southeast Bank claiming that the bank wrongfully paid the check. How should the court rule?

22-9 A signed promissory note states in part

June 1, 1986

"Ninety days after date, I promise to pay to the order of *Three Thousand Four Hundred Ninety Eight and 45/100—Dollars."*

The italicized words and symbols are typed in; the remainder is printed. There are no blanks on the face of the instrument. All unused space has been filled in with hyphens. Is the instrument order or bearer paper? Is it negotiable? See UCC §§3-111, 3-115.

- ▪ **the concepts of holder and negotiation**
- ▪ **how commercial paper is negotiated**
- ▪ **the definition of indorsement and the legal effect of various types of indorsements**

The negotiability or nonnegotiability of a particular note or draft is most important upon transfer of the instrument. Only negotiable paper may be transferred free of prior claims and defenses. In Article 3, the transferee enjoying this favored position is known as a holder in due course. The term "holder in due course" embodies two substantive requirements: that the transferee be a *holder* and that he or she hold *in due course*. Therefore, before studying the qualifications of a holder in due course and the preferred status such a transferee enjoys, the subject of Chapter 24, one must first understand how a person becomes a holder of an instrument and the rights of holders generally.

Introduction to Negotiation

"Holder" Defined

Section 1-201(20) contains the basic UCC definition of holder that applies to commercial paper governed by Article 3, documents of title governed by Article 7, and investment securities governed by Article 8. As applied to Article 3, a **holder** is

A person who is in possession of [a negotiable instrument] drawn, issued, or indorsed to him or his order or to bearer or in blank.

To qualify as a holder, a person must have *possession* of the instrument. Without possession, a person cannot assert his or her status as a holder (or holder in due course) against those liable on the instrument. Every holder has the right to transfer the instrument, obtain payment of it, or sue upon it. A holder in due course, however, has rights superior to other holders if claims or defenses are asserted against the instrument.

The first holder of any instrument (note or draft) is the *payee*. The payee becomes a holder of an instrument through **issue**—by virtue of its delivery to him from the maker or drawer, or in some cases a remitter.[1] As used in Article 3, **delivery** means a "voluntary transfer of possession."[2] The instrument may be payable either to the payee's order or to bearer.

---

1. UCC §3-102(1)(a). A remitter is not a holder because the instrument, such as a cashier's check, is payable to a third party (for example, a creditor of the remitter), not the remitter. Upon delivery of the instrument from the remitter to the payee, the payee becomes a holder.

2. UCC §1-201(14). The same definition of delivery applies to documents of title (governed by Article 7) and investment securities (governed by Article 8).

"Negotiation" Defined

Free transferability is the hallmark of a negotiable instrument. Some method must therefore be available to make transferees from or after the payee holders of the instrument. This method of transfer is known as **negotiation,** which is defined in §3-202(1) as ''the transfer of an instrument in such form that the transferee becomes a holder.''

Manner of Negotiation— Order v. Bearer Paper

At this point the distinction between instruments payable to *order* and those payable to *bearer* is once again important. Under §3-202(1), if the instrument is payable to order, it is negotiated by delivery and indorsement; if the instrument is payable to bearer, it is negotiated by delivery alone. Delivery is *always* required for negotiation; it assures that the transferee has possession of the paper, the basic prerequisite to holder status. Although delivery is sufficient to negotiate a bearer instrument, an order instrument also requires an *indorsement.* The manner of indorsement and the legal effect of various types of indorsements are discussed below.

Indorsements

Indorsements in General

An **indorsement** consists of at least the payee's or other holder's *signature* but may include additional language. An indorsement usually appears on the back of the instrument. Section 3-202(2) requires that an indorsement be written by or on behalf of the *holder* either on the instrument or on a paper so firmly attached to it as to become an extension or part of the underlying instrument. This separate paper, called an **allonge,** is used when prior indorsements have exhausted the space on the back of the instrument itself. An allonge must be firmly affixed, becoming an integral part of the instrument.

Negotiation of bearer paper takes effect immediately upon delivery of the instrument. Negotiation of order paper, however, takes effect only when an indorsement is made, even if the instrument has been delivered previously. For example, if A transfers order paper to B without indorse-

ment, B does not become a holder until the date she obtains A's indorsement. Further, under §3-201(3), prior to indorsement there is no presumption that the transferee has the rights of a holder because the terms of the instrument do not run to him. Thus, although a holder is aided by the presumption that he is entitled to recover on the instrument by producing it, a possessor of unindorsed order paper ''must account for his possession of the unindorsed paper by proving the transaction through which he acquired it.''[3]

At issue in the following case was whether an order instrument had been properly indorsed.

Estrada v. River Oaks Bank & Trust Company
550 S.W.2d 719 (Tex. Civ. App. 1977)

Defendant William J. Estrada executed four promissory notes payable to the order of George Lewis. Lewis assigned the notes to River Oaks Bank & Trust Co. as security for a loan. Lewis signed only one assignment document that referred to Estrada's four promissory notes and stapled the notes to the document. He did not indorse the individual notes.

After Lewis defaulted on the loan, River Oaks sued Estrada on the notes. Estrada raised a personal defense but River Oaks claimed to be a holder in due course. The trial court ruled in favor of River Oaks. Estrada appealed.

Coulson, Justice

. . . The Estrada notes were payable to the order of Lewis and, as order instruments, could be negotiated to River Oaks only by delivery with Lewis' indorsement. River Oaks is not in possession of instruments indorsed to it or its order unless the indorsement on the collateral assignment stapled to the notes is so firmly affixed thereto as to become a part thereof. If the signature on the collateral assignment is not an indorsement of the notes, River Oaks is neither a holder nor a holder in due course. [UCC §§3-302, 1-201(20) and 3-202(1)]. . . .

---

3. UCC §3-201, Official Comment 8.

An allonge has been defined as "[a] piece of paper annexed to a bill of exchange or promissory note, on which to write endorsements for which there is no room on the instrument itself." *Black's Law Dictionary* (rev. 4th ed. 1968). . . . There is some authority for the proposition that the Code permits indorsement by allonge only if the instrument is so covered with previous indorsements that convenience or necessity requires additional space for further indorsements. . . .

We will not pass on that question. . . . [U]nder the facts of this case, the collateral assignment would not be an indorsement of the notes even if the notes were so covered with previous indorsements that use of an allonge would be an absolute necessity. All four of the Estrada notes were transferred by a single collateral assignment bearing a single signature by Lewis. River Oaks argues that this single signature is an indorsement of all four notes. We disagree. The collateral assignment cannot possibly be so firmly affixed to four notes as to become an extension or part of each one. Although the assignment could conceivably be an indorsement of one of the notes, a court could not determine which note the parties intended to indorse. . . .

We hold that the signature of Lewis on the single collateral assignment is not an indorsement of the four Estrada notes attached thereto, and, therefore, River Oaks is not a holder in due course of those four notes. . . .

Indorsement by allonge has never been considered as prudent or desirable as an indorsement on the instrument itself. . . . [Section 3-202(2)] of the Code requires that the paper be "so firmly affixed" to the instrument "as to become a part thereof." This . . . wording evidences a clear intent by the Code draftsmen to restrict, rather than expand, the use of allonges.

River Oaks had the specifically enforceable right to have the unqualified indorsement of Lewis on the Estrada notes. [UCC §3-201(3)] For reasons unknown to this court, River Oaks had Lewis sign only the collateral assignment. While this procedure may be common in the banking community, we fail to see how the simple process of having a transferor indorse his notes as well as the assignment would impede the negotiation of commercial paper. Neglecting to acquire the transferor's in-

dorsement on an instrument introduces a needless element of uncertainty into commercial transactions which should be consummated with utmost care. . . .

[Judgment reversed.]

The *Estrada* case, like many negotiation cases, involved the ill-advised use of a separate instrument (later asserted to be an allonge) to transfer the commercial paper. One is therefore well advised to heed the court's admonition against the use of allonges in commercial paper transfer.

Partial Assignment. Under §3-202(3), to be effective as a negotiation, an indorsement must convey the entire instrument or any unpaid residue. An attempt to negotiate less operates only as a partial assignment of the transferor's interest in the instrument. Assume Mark issues a $1,000 promissory note payable to Paul's order. Paul sells the note to Christie, accomplishing the sale by signing his name on the back of the note and handing it to Christie. Christie is now the holder of the instrument. If, however, Paul had turned the note over and written "pay Christie $500, (signed) Paul," or "pay Christie one-half, (signed) Paul," or "pay Christie one-third and Jane two-thirds, (signed) Paul," neither Christie nor Jane becomes a holder of the instrument.

Although an indorsement purporting to convey less than the entire instrument is ineffective as a negotiation, it does operate as a partial assignment. Whether the partial assignee acquires any rights thereby is not addressed by Article 3 and is therefore left to the general contract law of the jurisdiction. Article 3 simply states that such an assignee does not become a holder.

Incorrect Spelling. The maker or drawer often incorrectly designates the payee or misspells the name. Suppose David, intending to make his check payable to Joe Doaks, writes "Joe Dokes" in the payee blank. In this case Joe Doaks may properly indorse and negotiate the instrument either in his own name ("Joe Doaks") or in the name as improperly designated ("Joe Dokes"), or by signing both names. A person who pays or gives value for the instrument, however, such as a bank cashing the check for Doaks, may require two signatures, the correct and incorrect spelling. Signing in both names is the most proper and desirable form. It leaves no doubt concerning either the state of the title or the signer's true identity.[4]

Multiple Payees. An instrument may be made payable to the order of two or more payees.[5] For example, a check may be made payable to the order of ''A and B'' or ''A or B'' or ''A and/or B.'' Section 3-116 governs the legal effect of such instruments. An instrument payable to ''A and B'' is held by the parties as tenants in common.[6] Because they have a common interest, the instrument is payable to all of them and may be negotiated, discharged, or enforced only by all. For example, negotiation of an instrument payable to the order of ''A and B'' requires the indorsement of both parties. If one signs and the other does not, or if one signature is a forgery, the negotiation is ineffective, meaning that the subsequent transferee does not become a holder of the instrument.

On the other hand, an instrument payable to ''A or B'' is payable to *either* A or B individually. That is, the instrument is payable to either of them and may be negotiated, discharged, or enforced by whoever has possession of it. For example, an instrument payable to the order of ''A or B'' could be further negotiated by A's (or B's) indorsement alone. The same rule applies if the instrument is payable to ''A and/or B.''

Types of Indorsements

As discussed above, both indorsement and delivery are required to negotiate an instrument payable to order. Indorsement is, however, much more than a mere formal requisite of negotiation. An indorsement also determines

1. the manner of future negotiation—this issue depends upon whether the indorsement is ''blank'' or ''special.''

2. the contract liability of the indorser on the instrument—this liability differs depending upon whether the indorsement is ''qualified'' or ''unqualified.''

3. the nature and extent of the interest transferred by the indorsement—the interest transferred depends upon whether the indorsement is ''restrictive'' or ''nonrestrictive.''

Every indorsement is either blank or special, either qualified or unqualified, and either restrictive or nonrestrictive. Thus, each indorsement has three terms modifying it. Assume D issues a check payable to P's order. P indorses the check on the back with her signature alone. P's indorsement is blank, unqualified, and nonrestrictive. The three classes of indorsement are discussed in the following subsections.

Blank v. Special Indorsement. The distinction between blank and special indorsements, stated in §3-204, is important because it determines the manner of further negotiation. A **blank indorsement** is one that specifies no particular indorsee and frequently consists of the indorser's signature alone. Suppose Dave draws his check payable to the order of Pat Jones. Pat indorses the instrument simply by signing her name ''Pat Jones'' on the back. The indorsement is in blank.

A **special indorsement** specifies the person to whom or to whose order the instrument is further payable. For example, using the same instrument as above, assume Pat Jones sold the instrument to Sam Sloan and indorsed the back as follows: ''pay to Sam Sloan, (signed) Pat Jones,'' or ''pay to the order of Sam Sloan, (signed) Pat Jones.'' These are special indorsements.

An instrument originally payable to order and indorsed in blank becomes payable to *bearer* and may be further negotiated by delivery alone unless it is later specially indorsed. An instrument that is specially indorsed becomes payable to the order of the **special indorsee** (Sam Sloan in the above example), and may be further negotiated only by his indorsement. Thus, whether an indorsement is required for negotiation depends not on whether the instrument was *originally* order or bearer paper, but on the character of the *last indorsement* on the in-

---

4. UCC §3-203 and Official Comments 1-3.
5. UCC §3-110(1)(d).
6. Tenancy in common is discussed in Chapter 36.

strument as either blank or special. For example, the above instrument is, on its face, payable to order ("pay to the order of Pat Jones"). It therefore requires Pat Jones's indorsement for further negotiation. If Pat Jones indorses in blank, the instrument becomes bearer paper and all further negotiation (to one or a hundred later holders) can be accomplished by delivery alone. If Pat Jones specially indorses the paper ("pay to Sam Sloan, (signed) Pat Jones") the instrument remains order paper, requiring Sam Sloan's signature for further negotiation. If Sam Sloan indorses in blank, the instrument becomes bearer paper and remains so unless and until some later holder specially indorses it. Note that an instrument payable to bearer (either originally or by virtue of a blank indorsement) may be converted into order paper by using a special indorsement. This is true even though no indorsement is required to negotiate the instrument prior to the addition of the special indorsement.

One final point concerning the blank versus special distinction should be noted. Assume Louise issues a note payable to Don's order. As previously noted, Don may specially indorse the instrument to Worth by writing on the back "pay Worth, (signed) Don" or "pay to the order of Worth, (signed) Don." The use of the word "order" in an indorsement is not necessary, and it will not cure a defect in negotiability on the face of the instrument. For example, if Louise's note omits the word "order" or "bearer," it is nonnegotiable. This defect is not cured by use of the word "order" in an indorsement. Because the instrument is nonnegotiable, neither Worth nor Don is a holder. In short, negotiability is determined from the face of the instrument. Nothing in an indorsement can affect negotiability, either by making a nonnegotiable instrument negotiable or a negotiable instrument nonnegotiable.

Qualified v. Unqualified Indorsement.
Negotiable instruments are contracts. The extent of a person's contract liability on a negotiable instrument depends on the appearance and position of his or her *signature* thereon. By signing as an indorser, a person ordinarily undertakes "secondary contract liability" on the instrument. Under this contract, provided certain conditions are met, the indorser promises to pay the instrument if the party primarily liable, such as maker of a note or acceptor of a draft, fails to pay it.

Unless the indorsement specifically provides otherwise, the indorser undertakes secondary contract liability. Such an indorsement is **unqualified.** If, however, the indorsement contains the words "without recourse" added to the signature it is qualified. A **qualified indorsement** negates secondary contract liability; a person indorsing "without recourse" does not undertake to pay the instrument if not paid by the primary party.

An indorser would, of course, prefer to sign "without recourse" because liability on the instrument is thereby substantially reduced. Section 3-201(3), however, prevents the widespread use of qualified indorsements by providing that unless otherwise agreed, a person who gives value for an instrument (as by cashing a check) that requires an indorsement for negotiation (one payable to order or specially indorsed) is entitled to an *unqualified* indorsement from the transferor. This right is enforceable against the transferor in an action for specific performance.

Restrictive v. Nonrestrictive Indorsement.
An indorsement may transfer the holder's entire interest in the instrument. Such an indorsement is **nonrestrictive.** Or language may be added to an indorsement making it **restrictive,** limiting or restricting in some way the rights acquired by the indorsee. That is, a restrictive indorsee acquires the instrument subject to an interest of the indorser or a third person.

Section 3-205 recognizes four types of restrictive indorsement:

1. conditional indorsements,
2. indorsements purporting to prohibit further transfer of the instrument,
3. indorsements for deposit or collection, and
4. indorsements for the benefit or use of the indorser or of another person.

A brief note regarding the bank collection process is required before analyzing the legal effect of restrictive indorsements. Assume Jones draws a check on his bank in Chicago payable to Pearl, who resides in New York, in payment for goods purchased by Jones from Pearl. Pearl will commonly deposit the check in her New York bank (the depositary bank) to be collected from Jones's bank (the drawee or payor bank) in Chicago. On the way the check may be transferred to one or more intermediary banks. In some cases the payor bank may also be the depositary bank. For example, the drawer and payee may have accounts in the same bank. Section 3-206(2) provides that an intermediary bank, or a payor bank that is not also the depositary bank, is not affected by a restrictive indorsement of any person except the bank's immediate transferor or the person presenting the instrument for payment. Under this rule, liability for violating a restrictive indorsement generally is imposed only on parties outside the bank collection process and on the first bank in the collection process. Banks later in the collection process are usually exempted because they handle instruments in bulk and usually have no opportunity to consider the effect of restrictive indorsements. With this limitation in mind, the four types of restrictive indorsements are distinguished below.

Conditional Indorsements. Assume Mark issues a $1,000 promissory note payable to Paul's order on December 1. On May 1, Paul purchases a machine from Triad Co. for $1,000, delivery to be made on June 1. Paul negotiates Mark's note to Triad on May 1 in payment for the machine, using the following indorsement, "pay Triad Co. if the machine is delivered by June 1 and conforms to the contract, (signed) Paul." This is a conditional indorsement. Note that although an indorsement may impose a condition to payment, such an indorsement does not make the instrument's promise or order conditional, thereby destroying negotiability. Negotiability is determined from the face of the instrument and is unaffected by the character of any later indorsement.

The effect of a conditional indorsement is stated in §3-206(3), which provides that "[e]xcept for an intermediary bank, any transferee under an indorsement which is conditional . . . must pay or apply any value given by him for or on the security of the instrument consistently with the indorsement. . . ." Thus, nonbank transferees of an instrument bearing a conditional indorsement, as well as a depositary bank, must ascertain whether the condition has occurred. If the transferee fails to do so and the condition does not occur, the transferee

is required to pay the instrument a second time to the person imposing the condition. Conditional indorsements are rarely used.

Indorsements Purporting to Restrict Further Transfer. Occasionally, an indorsement will attempt to prohibit further transfer of the instrument by the indorsee. Suppose Timmons draws a $100 check payable to Newman's order. Newman negotiates the instrument to Joe Doaks by an indorsement stating "pay Joe Doaks only, (signed) Newman." Regarding such indorsements, §3-206(1) states simply that: "No restrictive indorsement prevents further transfer or negotiation of the instrument." An instrument negotiable on its face cannot be rendered nonnegotiable by subsequent indorsement.

Indorsements for Deposit or Collection. Certainly the most common restrictive indorsement is one containing the language "for deposit only," "for deposit and collection only," or similar terms that indicate the instrument has been negotiated solely for purposes of deposit or collection. These indorsements have the same legal effect as conditional indorsements. Under §3-206(3), "[e]xcept for an intermediary bank, any transferee under an indorsement which . . . includes the words 'for collection,' 'for deposit,' 'pay any bank,' or like terms . . . must pay or apply any value given by him for or on the security of the instrument consistently with the indorsement. . . ." Such indorsements are often used to protect a person depositing a check for collection against payment of the instrument to an unauthorized person. That is, any later transferee of the instrument is placed on notice that the person negotiating the instrument, such as a bank or bank employee, is doing so only for purposes of collecting the instrument for the payee. Thus, the transferee must assure that the instrument is applied consistently with the indorsement—deposited in the payee's account. Note that under Federal Reserve regulation, after a check in the collection process has been indorsed by a bank, only a bank may acquire the rights of a holder until the check has been either returned to the depositor, or specially indorsed by a bank to a nonbank.[7]

---

7. 12 C.F.R. §229.35(c).

Thus, a bank indorsement alone, without additional language, is a restrictive indorsement, which protects the depositor by effectively locking the instrument into bank collection channels.

Indorsements for the Benefit or Use of the Indorser or Another Person. An indorsement may expressly transfer the instrument to an indorsee for the use or benefit of the indorser or a third person. For example, an instrument payable to Paul's order may be indorsed "pay Brown in trust for Green, (signed) Paul," or "pay Brown for Green, (signed) Paul," or "pay Brown as agent for Green, (signed) Paul," or "pay Brown for account of Green, (signed) Paul." Under §3-206(4), only the first taker under such an indorsement (the person to whom Brown negotiates the instrument) must pay or apply any value given by him consistently with the indorsement (for Green's benefit). Later holders of the instrument are neither given notice nor otherwise affected by such an indorsement unless they have *actual knowledge* that the fiduciary or other person has negotiated the instrument in any transaction for his own benefit or otherwise in breach of duty.

Negotiation Subject to Rescission

Under §3-207, a negotiation, whether of order or bearer paper, is effective (the transferee becomes a holder) even though the negotiation is

1. made by an infant, a corporation exceeding its powers, or any other person lacking capacity,
2. obtained by fraud, duress, or mistake,
3. part of an illegal transaction, or
4. made in breach of duty.

As between the immediate parties to such a negotiation (or as against a later transferee not having the rights of a holder in due course), a court may allow rescission, impose a constructive trust, or afford other relief permitted by state law. For example, assume Megan issues a note payable to order of Stewart, a minor. Stewart indorses and delivers the note to Tim. Stewart's negotiation makes Tim a holder, but Stewart may rescind his negotiation and recover the instrument from Tim, because of the voidable nature of minors' contracts.

Although, as between Stewart and Tim, Stewart's negotiation can be rescinded, the fact that Tim nevertheless becomes a holder has important legal consequences. Because Tim is a holder, prior to recovery Tim may further negotiate the instrument—that is, make a transferee from Tim a holder. If this subsequent holder qualifies as a holder in due course, Stewart's right to recover the instrument is cut off. That is, the right to rescind may not be asserted against a holder in due course because a holder in due course takes an instrument free of all *claims* to it on the part of any person. Thus, a prior holder's claim to the instrument based upon lack of capacity to negotiate it or fraud inducing the negotiation may not be asserted against a holder in due course. Therefore, using the preceding example, assume that prior to any action by Stewart, Tim negotiates the note to Pat. Pat qualifies as a holder in due course because she takes in good faith, for value, and without notice of the voidable nature of Stewart's negotiation. In this situation Pat takes the note free of Stewart's claim to it. Stewart retains any rights he has against Tim under state law (for example, for the proceeds of Tim's sale of the note), but may not recover the paper from Pat.

Section 3-207 is fundamentally important in formulating the holder in due course doctrine. By making a negotiation subject to rescission effective, it enables a subsequent transferee to become a holder and, if the requirements are met, a holder in due course.

SUMMARY

1. Negotiability, by permitting transfer of commercial paper free of claims and defenses, promotes its marketability. Transferees receiving this favored position are known as holders in due course. Thus in studying the holder in due course doctrine, it is initially important to ascertain how one becomes a holder of an instrument.

2. A holder is defined as a person in possession of an instrument drawn, issued, or indorsed to her or her order or to bearer or in blank. The first holder of any

instrument is the payee. Thereafter, subsequent transferees of the instrument become holders by negotiation.

3. Negotiation is simply the transfer of an instrument in such form that the transferee becomes a holder. If the instrument is order paper, negotiation is accomplished by the holder's indorsement, which may be his or her signature alone, and delivery to the new holder. Bearer paper is negotiated by delivery alone. A negotiation is effective to make the transferee a holder even though the negotiation is subject to rescission as a result, for example, of fraud upon or infancy of the transferor.

4. An indorsement is more than a mere formal requisite of negotiation. Indorsements are of various types and govern a number of legal issues arising in connection with the paper. An indorsement may be blank or special, which determines the manner of future negotiation. It may be qualified or unqualified, which ascertains the indorser's contract liability on the instrument. It may be either restrictive or nonrestrictive, which determines the nature and extent of the interest transferred by the indorsement.

KEY TERMS

holder	special indorsement
issue	special indorsee
delivery	unqualified indorsement
negotiation	qualified indorsement
indorsement	nonrestrictive indorsement
allonge	restrictive indorsement
blank indorsement	

QUESTIONS AND PROBLEMS

23-1 To what basic principle in basic contract law does negotiation correspond? What purposes are the negotiation concepts discussed in this chapter designed to achieve?

23-2 X issued a promissory note payable to the order of P. The instrument is now in possession of Z with the following indorsements on the back.

1.	Pay to the order of A P
2.	A
3.	B, without recourse
4.	Pay C D
5.	Pay Joe Doaks if the deadbeat ever finishes painting my house C
6.	Pay E only Joe Doaks
7.	Pay F as trustee for my beloved nephew N E
8.	F
9.	Z, for deposit only

(a) If Z presents the instrument to X for payment, and the instrument is dishonored, is Z's only recourse to sue F?

(b) Was the instrument bearer paper in Z's hands?

(c) Was the instrument bearer paper in P's hands?

(d) Was C's signature necessary to negotiate the instrument?

(e) Does B have contract liability on the instrument?

(f) Does Z's indorsement prevent further negotiation?

(g) Does Joe Doaks's indorsement ''Pay E only'' prevent further negotiation?

(h) Could Z not qualify as a holder in due course because of B's indorsement?

(i) A's indorsement, consisting of his signature alone, caused the instrument to become bearer paper. Does it remain so despite the subsequent indorsements?

(j) Would Z be liable to E if F violated his trust—that is, applied the money for his own use, instead of N's?

(k) Would Z be liable to C if Joe Doaks never finished painting C's house?

23-3 On March 15, Sam Spender bought a new tennis racquet at A & J Sporting Goods. Sam paid for the racquet with a check dated March 15 payable to A & J Sporting Goods. On the back of the check, however, he wrote ''Do not deposit until April 1.'' Is the statement on the back of the check a restrictive indorsement? Explain.

23-4 Olga Blair obtained a cashier's check to pay the balance due on a charter trip to China. The check was made payable to the order of Olga Blair. Olga indorsed the check to Simone Travel Bureau, Inc. and gave the check to S. Reiss, her travel consultant. Two weeks later, a Simone Travel Bureau representative called Olga requesting final payment on her trip. At that time, Olga learned that S. Reiss had failed to give the check to the travel agency. Olga obtained the negotiated check from her bank and found the following on the back of the check:

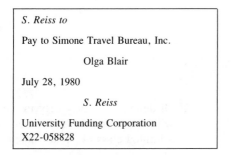

> *S. Reiss to*
>
> Pay to Simone Travel Bureau, Inc.
>
>   Olga Blair
>
> July 28, 1980
>
>   *S. Reiss*
>
> University Funding Corporation
> X22-058828

The italicized portions had been added to the check after Olga gave the check to S. Reiss. University Funding Corporation had cashed the check for Reiss, who left town with the money.
(a) Were any of the following holders of the instrument: Olga Blair, S. Reiss, Simone Travel Bureau, Inc., University Funding Corporation?
(b) List the names of all persons or corporations whose indorsement was necessary for negotiation.

23-5   Fred Klomann was payee of a promissory note issued by Sol Graff & Son. Fred Klomann then specially indorsed the note and handed it to his daughter, Candace. She examined the note and returned it to her father for collection. Subsequently Fred Klomann scratched out Candace's name in the special indorsement, inserted the name of his wife, Georgia Klomann, and delivered the note to Georgia. What interest did Fred

have in the instrument when he transferred it to Georgia? What interest did Georgia acquire? See UCC §3-201(1). Who is the holder of the instrument?

23-6   Dinah Wilson was bookkeeper for Palmer & Ray Dental Supply Inc. of Abilene. She was expressly authorized to indorse checks received from customers with a rubber stamp and deposit the checks in the firm's account in First National Bank. The rubber stamp used by Palmer & Ray to indorse the checks stated:

> Palmer & Ray Dental Supply
> Inc. of Abilene
> Box 2894
> 3110 B N. 1st
> Abilene, Texas 79603

Auditors later discovered that Wilson had cashed at the bank 35 of the checks she was supposed to deposit. Palmer & Ray sued the bank to recover the losses on these checks. What type of indorsement does the stamp create? Should Palmer & Ray prevail? Explain.

23-7   One day a male customer, James Quick, handed a check and deposit slip to Bernard, a teller at State Bank. The check was made payable to Katherine Warner and the indorsement written on the back read ''Katherine Warner For Deposit Only.'' Warner had no account at State Bank. The deposit slip instructed the bank to deposit the check in Quick's State Bank account.
(a) Should Bernard accept the check for deposit in Quick's account? Explain.
(b) Assume that Bernard refused to accept the check, but a subsequent investigation revealed that Quick had purchased the check from Warner, who negotiated it to Quick with a blank indorsement. Quick later added the ''For Deposit Only'' language before attempting to deposit the check in his State Bank account. Should Bernard now accept the check for deposit in Quick's account? Explain.

To this point, the discussion has focused on the formal requirements of a negotiable instrument and on negotiation—the manner in which a transferee of a negotiable instrument becomes a holder. This chapter examines the third element of commercial paper analysis, the qualifications and rights of a holder in due course, a holder of commercial paper who stands in a better legal position than an ordinary contract assignee.

Under ordinary contract principles, an assignee "steps into the shoes" of the assignor and takes no better rights than the assignor had. In contrast, a holder in due course often acquires rights on the instrument superior to those of the transferor. Under the Uniform Commercial Code §3-305, a holder in due course generally acquires the instrument free of

1. all claims of ownership or other claims to it on the part of any person and

2. all defenses of any party to the instrument with whom the holder has not dealt, except a limited class of "real" defenses.

The defenses defeated by a holder in due course are usually referred to as "personal" defenses. Under §3-306, a holder without holder in due course status acquires rights similar to an ordinary contract assignee, taking the instrument subject to all valid claims to it on the part of any person, and all defenses, real or personal. Thus, determining whether or not a transferee has the rights of a holder in due course becomes a critical issue in any commercial paper dispute.

Section 3-302(1) defines a **holder in due course** as a holder who takes the instrument

1. for value,
2. in good faith, and
3. without notice (a) that the instrument is overdue, or (b) that the instrument has been dishonored, or (c) of any defense against or claim to it on the part of any person.

These three elements are discussed in turn in the following three sections. Note that a holder in due course is, in essence, Article 3's "good faith purchaser for value." That is, the holder in due course receives preferred status because she gives something of value for the instrument while unaware of any legal problems affecting it.

General Requirements

Taking for Value

To qualify as a holder in due course, the holder must take the instrument "for value." Thus, one who acquires an instrument by gift is denied holder in due course status. Although the UCC generally defines **value** as the equivalent of "any consideration sufficient to support a simple contract,"[1] a specialized value definition, stated in §3-303 applies to commercial paper under Article 3. The concept of value in determining holder in due course status differs in important respects from ordinary principles of contract consideration discussed in Chapter 9.

Executory Promises Not Value. Under §3-303(a) a holder takes an instrument for value only to the extent that the agreed consideration has been performed. Under this rule, a holder who is contractually bound to pay money or perform some other act in exchange for the instrument does not give value *until* the money is paid or the act is performed. In other words, an executory promise is not value for holder in due course purposes, even though it is sufficient consideration to support a simple contract. To illustrate, assume Mark issues a $1,000 note payable in one year to Paula's order. One month later, on June 1, Paula negotiates the note to Hank in exchange for goods sold by Hank to Paula to be delivered July 1. Even though Hank becomes a holder of the instrument on June 1, he does not give value for it until July 1, when the goods are delivered. Thus, if Hank learns of a defense to payment prior to July 1—for example, that Paula had defrauded Mark—he would be denied holder in due course status. To illustrate further, assume that on June 1, Hank agrees to purchase the note from Paula for $1,000, payable $500 on June 1, and $500 on July 1. In this case, on June 1, Hank gives value and, if he meets the other requirements, qualifies as a holder in due course to the extent of $500. If Hank pays the second $500 on July 1 acting in good faith without notice of a claim or defense, he then qualifies as a holder in

due course for the face amount of the instrument, $1,000. If Hank learns of a claim or defense, such as Paula's fraud, between June 1 and July 1, Hank qualifies as a holder in due course only to the extent of $500. That is, Hank could force Mark to pay $500 despite Paula's fraud, but takes subject to Mark's defense for the remainder. Thus, the other elements of holder in due course status—good faith and lack of notice—are measured each time value is given. A holder may therefore qualify as a holder in due course to the extent of value given on one date, but not a later date, after notice of a claim or defense is acquired.

The purchaser of a negotiable instrument rarely pays face value for it. The buyer pays a discounted figure that represents interest and the risk of ultimate collection. For example, Wilcox might agree to purchase Molson's $1,000 note from Petty for $950. In this situation, Wilcox, after paying $950 may qualify as a holder in due course for the face amount of the instrument, $1,000. An excessive discount, however, may indicate lack of good faith defeating holder in due course status. Thus, if Wilcox pays $250 for the $1,000 note, the huge discount provides convincing circumstantial evidence that he knows of the legal problems affecting the instrument.

The rationale for the rule that executory promises are not value is that a holder who has not yet performed does not need the protection afforded holders in due course. That is, if the holder learns of a claim or defense to the instrument, she may simply rescind the contract to purchase the instrument and refuse to perform the promise.[2] In contrast, a holder who has performed is "out of pocket" on the instrument and would be injured by a successfully asserted claim or defense. Accordingly, the UCC protects the holder by giving her holder in due course status to the extent of performance.

At issue in the following case was whether a holder had given value sufficient to achieve holder in due course status.

---

1. UCC §1-201(44)(d).

2. The basis of this right of rescission is breach of the §3-417(2)(d) warranty made by transferors of commercial paper that no defense of any party is good against the transferor. UCC §3-303, Official Comment 3. The transfer warranties are discussed in Chapter 26.

Korzenik v. Supreme Radio, Inc.

197 N.E.2d 702 (Mass. 1964)

On October 16, 1961, Southern New England Distributing Corporation, as payee, fraudulently acquired two notes in the form of trade acceptances from defendant Supreme Radio, Inc. On October 31, 1961, Southern negotiated the instruments to its attorney, Armand Korzenik, as a retainer for legal services to be performed. Korzenik, who had no knowledge of Southern's fraud, had performed some legal services for Southern between October 25 and October 31. After Supreme failed to pay the acceptances, plaintiffs Korzenik and his law partners sued Supreme, which raised fraud as a defense. No testimony was offered as to the value of the legal services rendered between October 25 and October 31. The lower courts held that Korzenik was not a holder in due course and therefore took subject to Supreme's fraud defense. Korzenik appealed.

Whittemore, Justice

. . . Decisive of the case, as the Appellate Division held, is the correct ruling that the plaintiffs are not holders in due course under [UCC] §3-302; they have not shown to what extent they took for value under §3-303. That section provides: "A holder takes the instrument for value (a) to the extent that the agreed consideration has been performed. . . .

Under clause (a) of §3-303 the "agreed consideration" was the performance of legal services. It is often said that a lawyer is "retained" when he is engaged to perform services, and we hold that the judge spoke of "retainer" in this sense. The phrase that the judge used, "retainer *for services*" (emphasis supplied), shows his meaning as does the finding as to services already performed by Korzenik at the time of the assignments. Even if the retainer had been only a fee to insure the attorney's availability to perform future services . . ., there is no basis in the record for determining the value of this commitment for one week. . . .

[UCC] §3-307(3), provides: "After it is shown that a defense exists a person claiming the rights of a holder in due course has the burden of establishing that he or some person under whom he claims

is in all respects a holder in due course." The defence of fraud having been established this section puts the burden on the plaintiffs. The plaintiffs have failed to show "the extent . . . [to which] the agreed consideration . . . [had] been performed." . . .

[Judgment affirmed.]

Exceptions to the Rule. The UCC recognizes two related exceptions to the executory promise rule. Under §3-303(c), a holder takes an instrument for value by giving another negotiable instrument for the instrument or by making an irrevocable commitment to a third party in exchange for the instrument. To illustrate the first exception, suppose Rick is the payee of Marcia's $1,000 note. Linda purchases the note from Rick with her personal check payable to Rick's order. Linda has given value for Marcia's note, even though her check is, in essence, an executory promise. The reason for this exception is that the check, a negotiable instrument, could itself be negotiated to a holder in due course, who could force Linda to pay despite any defense she may have against Rick.

For similar reasons, the Code provides that value is given when the holder makes an irrevocable commitment to a third party (for example, to loan money) in exchange for the instrument. In this case, after the instrument is taken the holder cannot refuse to perform for the third party. Rescission and loss avoidance is therefore unavailable to the holder, justifying holder in due course protection on the instrument.

Security Interest as Value. Under §3-303(a), a holder also takes for value to the extent he or she acquires a security interest in or lien upon the instrument. In this situation, the holder takes possession of the instrument to secure payment of a debt owing to him. Such a security arrangement is known as a "pledge." The secured creditor in this case gives value only to the extent of the secured debt, not necessarily the face amount of the instrument. Assume Miller issues a $1,000 promissory note payable in one year to Parker's order in exchange for goods sold by Parker to Miller. Parker then borrows $750 from Cox and indorses and delivers Miller's note to Cox to secure the loan. In this case, Cox has given value of $750, the extent of her security interest in the note. Assuming Cox meets the other holder in due course requirements, she could force Miller to pay $750 upon Parker's default even if Miller has a personal defense to payment such as Parker's fraud or shipment of defective goods. Cox then has no further interest in the instrument because her security interest is satisfied.

Antecedent Debt as Value. Under §3-303(b), a holder takes for value when he takes the instrument in payment of or as security for an antecedent debt. The term **antecedent debt** refers simply to an old debt, one existing before the negotiation of the instrument. In this context, "value" for holder in due course purposes once again differs from general contract law consideration: payment of an antecedent debt, though value under Article 3, may, as "past consideration," be incapable of supporting an ordinary contract promise.

Assume that Stan sells goods to Betty on credit. Over a period of several years, Betty accumulates an open account balance of $10,000. Subsequently, Mary issues a $10,000 note to Betty in exchange for services performed. Betty then negotiates Mary's note to Stan in satisfaction of the $10,000 debt. Stan has given value for Mary's note for purposes of establishing Stan as a holder in due course.

Taking in Good Faith

To qualify as a holder in due course, the holder must, in addition to giving a value, take the instrument in good faith. UCC §1-201(19) defines good faith as "honesty in fact in the conduct or transaction concerned." A subjective, rather than objective, test of good faith is applied. That is, the test is not what a reasonably prudent person would have done or known on the facts presented, but what the holder in question knew. A holder who takes the instrument while acting honestly meets the good faith test even though a hypothetical "reasonable person" might not have taken the instrument under similar circumstances or would have more fully investigated the instrument's history before taking.

Taking Without Notice

In addition to value and good faith, holder in due course status requires that the holder take the instrument without notice (1) that it is overdue, (2) that it has been dishonored, or (3) of any defense against or claim to it on the part of any person. Before discussing these three elements, the term "notice" must be defined.

"Notice" Defined. Under §1-201(25), a person has **notice** of a fact in three situations. First, and most obviously, a person has notice upon acquiring actual knowledge of the fact. Second, notice is obtained upon receipt of a notice or notification of the fact. A person receives a notice or notification when it comes to her attention or is properly delivered at the "place of business through which the contract was made or at any other place held out by him as the place for receipt of such communications."[3] A person may therefore have notice of the contents of a communication delivered to her place of business, even without actual knowledge. Notice, knowledge, or notification received by an organization, such as a bank or corporation, is effective from the time it is brought to the attention of the individual conducting the transaction or, in any event, from the time it would have been brought to that person's attention had the organization exercised due diligence. Due diligence, in this context, requires that the organization maintain and comply with reasonable routines for communicating significant information within the organization. Further, to be effective a notice must be received in a time and manner sufficient to give a reasonable opportunity to act upon it.[4]

Finally, a person also has notice of a fact when the surrounding facts and circumstances known at the time in question give the person *reason to know* that it exists. An objective test is applied here: what a reasonable person would know on the facts presented. A holder in due course is therefore governed by a very strict requirement regarding knowledge of matters pertaining to the instrument—a subjective test in the good faith requirement (what

---

3. UCC §1-201(26).
4. UCC §§1-201(27), 1-201(28), 3-304(6).

did the holder *in fact* know about the instrument?) and an objective test in the notice requirement (what would a *reasonable person* have known on those facts?).

The following case examines the elements of good faith and notice in holder in due course analysis.

Money Mart Check Cashing Center, Inc. v. Epicycle Corporation

667 P.2d 1372 (Colo. 1983)

Plaintiff, Money Mart Check Cashing Center, Inc. (Money Mart), cashes payroll and government checks for a fee. On February 22, 1980, John Cronin cashed a payroll check issued to him by defendant, Epicycle Corporation, at Money Mart. Money Mart deposited the check but it was returned marked "Payment Stopped." Epicycle had stopped payment on the check because one of its employees had written the check in excess of the amount actually owed to Cronin.

Money Mart sued Epicycle for the face amount of the check. Money Mart claimed to be a holder in due course. The trial court ruled in favor of Money Mart but the appellate court reversed, holding that Money Mart was not a holder in due course because it had failed to verify that the check was good prior to cashing it. Money Mart appealed.

Rovira, Justice

. . . The question before us is whether Money Mart is a holder in due course. If it is, it takes the check free of any of Epicycle's claims to the check or defenses against Cronin. . . . That Money Mart took the check for value is undisputed, leaving the questions of "good faith" and "notice." . . .

The drafters of the Uniform Commercial Code intended that [the good faith] standard be a subjective one. . . . Thus, the question is: "[W]as this alleged holder in due course acting in good faith, however stupid and negligent his behavior might have been?" . . .

The only testimony on the question of good faith is that Money Mart cashed the check without knowing that a stop payment order had been issued on it. The Superior Court concluded that Money Mart was not a holder in due course because it

"did not inquire as to the check itself and had no knowledge as to whether the check was stolen, incomplete, or secured by fraud." Under a subjective standard, an absence of knowledge is not equivalent to a lack of good faith. . . . Consequently, if the superior Court's reversal was based upon a lack of good faith on the part of Money Mart, it was in error.

We now consider whether Money Mart had "notice" of the fact that payment had been stopped on the check or that Cronin had obtained the check improperly. [The court then quoted the Code definition of notice in §1-201(25).] As can be seen, tests other than "actual knowledge" may be used in determining whether a person is a holder in due course. . . . There is no allegation that Money Mart had received notification of the defenses, so we must now determine whether Money Mart had "reason to know" of them.

The County Court referee found that Money Mart had no reason to know of the defenses because there was nothing inherently suspicious in the transaction and Money Mart had no duty to inquire about any possible defenses or ensure that the check was good. The Superior Court held that Money Mart's failure to inquire about the validity of the check constituted negligence. However, there is nothing in the Uniform Commercial Code and nothing in the record to support such a conclusion.

A determination of whether a holder has "reason to know" is based upon "all the facts and circumstances known to him." A person "knows" of a fact when he has "actual knowledge" of it. . . . The question therefore is whether Money Mart had actual knowledge of facts giving it reason to know that a defense existed. There is nothing to distinguish the facts of this case from any other of the thousands of checks that Money Mart and others cash each year: A man came to Money Mart to cash his paycheck; Money Mart is in the business of cashing paychecks; the face of the check disclosed nothing to raise even a suspicion that there was something wrong with it.

It has often been held that where an instrument is regular on its face there is no duty to inquire as to possible defenses unless the circumstances of which the holder has knowledge are of such a nature that failure to inquire reveals a deliberate desire to evade knowledge because of a fear that investigation would disclose the existence of a defense. . . . There is nothing in using a check-cashing service instead of a bank that would lead to a rule imposing different standards on the two kinds of institutions. . . .

Accordingly, we hold that Money Mart is a holder in due course and, as such, is not subject to the defenses Epicycle may have against Cronin. . . .

[Judgment reversed.]

Note finally that under §3-304(5) the doctrine of "constructive notice" does not apply in determining notice for holder in due course purposes. That is, the public filing or recording any document, such as a financing statement creating a security interest in the instrument under UCC Article 9, does not constitute notice to a person who otherwise qualifies as a holder in due course.

Notice That Instrument is Overdue. Section 3-304(3) lists three situations giving a purchaser notice that an instrument is overdue.

Principal Overdue. A holder taking with reason to know that any part of the principal of the instrument is overdue does not qualify as a holder in due course. Frequently, the overdue nature of the instrument is apparent from the instrument itself. For example, a holder who takes a promissory note on June 10, payable by its terms on June 1, takes with notice that it is overdue.

A maker may satisfy an obligation by issuing a single note payable in a lump sum on a future date. Alternatively, the maker may issue a series of smaller individual notes with varying maturity dates or may make a single note payable in installments—for example, a $12,000 note payable in twelve equal monthly installments. In these alternate situations, known as instruments of the "same series," a holder who has reason to know that an earlier note or installment has not been paid when due, takes with notice that the instrument is overdue. Here, because all instruments or installments are intended to satisfy portions of the same obligation, default in one instrument or installment often indicates that later notes or installments also will not be paid.

Under §3-304(4)(f), knowledge that there has been a default in another instrument of the maker (not of the same series) does not of itself give the purchaser notice fatal to holder in due course status. Unless two or more notes arise out of the same transaction, nonpayment of one note does not necessarily raise an inference that the other or others will not be paid. In contrast to the rule applied to principal defaults, knowledge by the holder of nonpayment of *interest* due on the instrument does not constitute notice sufficient to defeat holder in due course status. The Code recognizes that interest payments are often delayed, without an accompanying nonpayment of principal. Accordingly, knowledge of interest payment defaults *alone* does not preclude holder in due course status.

Acceleration of the Instrument. A purchaser has notice that an instrument is overdue if he or she has reason to know that the due date of the instrument has been accelerated. For example, installment notes commonly provide that, upon default in payment of one or more installments, the holder may accelerate the instrument, making all future installments immediately due and payable. A holder taking an instrument, on its face payable on a future date, but with reason to know that the due date had been accelerated by a prior holder, could not qualify as a holder in due course.

Demand Instruments. The preceding discussion concerns time instruments, generally notes. A purchaser takes with notice that a *demand* instrument is overdue if he takes the instrument with reason to know either that a demand has already been made or that more than a reasonable length of time has passed since the instrument was issued. The most common demand instrument governed by Article 3 is a check. Section 3-304(3)(c) provides that a "reasonable length of time" for a check drawn and payable within the United States is presumed[5] to be 30 days. Therefore, the purchaser of a check over 30 days old is generally unable to qualify as a holder in due course.

---

5. The term "presumed" means that the trier of fact must assume that a fact exists unless and until evidence is introduced supporting a finding of its nonexistence. UCC §1-201(31).

Notice That Instrument Dishonored. To be a holder in due course, the purchaser must take the instrument without notice that it has been dishonored. Generally speaking, under §3-507 dishonor occurs when a draft is presented to the drawee for acceptance or payment and the drawee refuses to accept or pay it, or when a note is presented to the maker, who refuses to pay it. This fact is often noted on the instrument. Dishonor is important in determining the contract liability of parties to the instrument and is discussed more fully in Chapter 25.

Notice of Claim or Defense. A holder who takes the paper while aware of a claim or defense to it cannot qualify for holder in due course protection. Section 3-304 lists various situations deemed to place a holder on notice of a claim or defense and various facts that, of themselves, do not provide such notice.[6]

Initially, the holder may be put on notice from the appearance of the instrument itself. For example, a prospective purchaser takes with notice of a claim or defense if the instrument is substantially incomplete, bears visible evidence of forgery or alteration, or is otherwise so irregular that its validity, ownership, terms, or the party to pay are in doubt.

A purchaser also has notice of a claim or defense if she takes with notice that the obligation of any party is voidable in whole or in part (such as for fraud or material misrepresentation), or subject to other defenses (such as breach of warranty or failure of consideration), or that all parties to the instrument have been discharged. Suppose that Pat induces Mike to buy a car by fraudulently misrepresenting its mileage. Mike issues a note to Pat in exchange for the car. Pat sells and negotiates the note to Harold. Harold is not a holder in due course if he takes the instrument with notice of Pat's fraud—that is, with notice that Mike's obligation is voidable.

Finally, a purchaser has notice of a claim against the instrument if he has knowledge that a fiduciary, such as trustee of a trust, has previously negotiated the instrument in payment of or as security for his own debt or benefit, or otherwise in breach of duty. Mere knowledge that a prior holder is or was a fiduciary does not, by itself, give such notice.

The holder may receive notice of a claim or defense in various ways. The holder may receive information directly from the transferor or from the person obligated on the instrument disclosing the existence of a defense. The defense may appear in an accompanying document delivered to the holder with the instrument. Additionally, notice of a claim or defense or lack of good faith may be inferred if a close business relationship exists between the holder and the transferor.

Payee as Holder in Due Course

Ordinarily, a holder in due course is a holder who receives the instrument from the payee or a later holder. Although also a holder, the payee is usually unable to qualify as a holder in due course. As a party to the original transaction, the payee generally has notice of a claim or defense to the instrument. Assume Paula fraudulently induces Milt to issue a promissory note payable to Paula's order. Although Paula is a holder, she is not a holder in due course because she is aware of (and in fact responsible for) Milt's defense to paying the instrument.

Section 3-302(2) makes it clear, however, that a payee may qualify as a holder in due course to the same extent and in the same manner as any other holder. The payee must simply meet the requirements for holder in due course status listed in §3-302. The payee who does not deal directly with the maker or drawer asserting the defense often is able to meet these requirements. Assume Smith and Jones are co-makers of a note. Smith has induced Jones to sign through fraud. Smith, without authority from Jones, delivers the note to Black, the payee, who gives value, and takes in good faith without notice of Smith's fraud. Black is a holder in due course.

Shelter Provision—§3-201

The importance of the preferred status conferred upon a holder in due course is magnified when con-

---

6. For example, knowledge that the instrument is antedated or postdated, was issued or negotiated in exchange for an executory promise, was accompanied by a separate agreement, or that any party signed as surety for another party to the instrument, does not give notice of a defense or claim.

sidered in conjunction with §3-201(1), which provides simply that "[t]ransfer of an instrument vests in the transferee such rights as the transferor has therein. . . ." This so-called **shelter** or **umbrella provision** greatly expands the scope of the holder in due course doctrine by providing that transfer of an instrument by a holder in due course vests in the transferee the rights of a holder in due course even if the transferee does not qualify under §3-302. That is, with rare exceptions, *any transferee* (whether or not a holder) of an instrument from or after a holder in due course acquires the rights of a holder in due course and may enforce the instrument free of claims and personal defenses.

For example, Pam fraudulently induces Max to issue a note payable to her order. Pam specially indorses and delivers the instrument to Harold, a holder in due course. Harold transfers the note to Cheryl, who takes it, alternatively (1) without Harold's indorsement (that is, she is not a holder), (2) as a gift, (3) after it is overdue, or (4) with notice of (but not as a party to) Pam's fraud. In all four cases, Cheryl fails to qualify as a holder in due course under §3-302. Nevertheless, she acquires the *rights* of a holder in due course (her transferor, Harold) under §3-201, and could therefore force Max to pay the instrument despite his personal defense, fraud. Any subsequent transferee from Cheryl would acquire similar rights.

Section 3-201(2) applies the shelter rule to transfer of a limited interest in an instrument to the extent of the interest transferred. For example, transfer of a security interest in an instrument vests in the secured party (transferee) the rights of the transferor to the extent of the security interest. To illustrate, assume Sal is a holder in due course of Morey's $500 note. Sal transfers the note to Ken as security for a $250 loan from Ken to Sal. Ken acquires the rights of a holder in due course to the extent of $250.

The law generally favors free alienability (transferability) of interests in property. The shelter rule promotes free transferability of commercial paper by enabling a holder in due course to transfer what he or she has—the rights of a holder in due course. If a holder in due course could transfer those rights only to transferees capable of satisfying §3-302 on their own, the market for commercial paper would be severely restricted, thus defeating a major purpose of negotiability. To prevent this result, §3-201(1) confers de facto holder in due course status on most transferees from or after a holder in due course. Such transferees, whether or not they qualify as holders in due course under §3-302, acquire the rights of a holder in due course under §3-201. The shelter provision might therefore be viewed as an application of ordinary rules of contract assignment. The transferee steps into the shoes of the transferor (the holder in due course or transferee from such a holder) and takes the same rights (the rights of a holder in due course) that the transferor had.

Exceptions. Not all transferees from holders in due course receive the rights of a holder in due course. Any transferee who has been a party to any fraud or illegality affecting the instrument or who, as a prior holder, had notice of a claim or defense against it, cannot improve his or her position by taking from a later holder in due course. That is, these parties cannot "launder" their position by transferring the instrument to a holder in due course and later reacquiring it. To allow such "laundering" would be an open invitation to fraud. Assume Phil fraudulently induces Mary to issue a note payable to Phil's order. Phil negotiates the note to Bob, who takes with notice of Phil's fraud. Bob subsequently negotiates the instrument to Harriet, a holder in due course. Neither Phil (as a party to fraud affecting the instrument) nor Bob (as a prior holder with notice of a claim or defense) could later reacquire the instrument and assert Harriet's rights (the rights of a holder in due course) against Mary.

Rights of a Holder in Due Course

To this point we have examined how holders and transferees of a negotiable instrument achieve holder in due course status. A person enjoying this status takes the instrument free of all claims to the instrument and personal but not real defenses asserted by parties to the original transaction. These rights, embodied in UCC §3-305, are possessed by any person who qualifies as a holder in due course under §3-302, as well as any transferee acquiring the rights of a holder in due course under §3-201 discussed above.

Taking Free of Claims

Under §3-305(1), a holder in due course takes an instrument free of "all claims to it on the part of any person." Claims defeated by a holder in due course include not only claims of legal title, but also all liens, equities, or claims of any other type, including a claim for rescission of a prior negotiation. Suppose Mark issues an instrument payable to Paul's order, and indorsed by Paul in blank. Paul negotiates the instrument to Andrew. Andrew's creditor, Jerry, obtains a lien upon all of Andrew's property, including the note, to satisfy an unpaid judgment. Andrew subsequently negotiates the instrument to Bart, a minor. Bart negotiates the instrument to Carl, who negotiates it to Dave, a holder in due course. Dave takes the instrument free of (1) Jerry's claim that he has a lien upon it to satisfy the unpaid judgment against Andrew, and (2) Bart's claim that, as a minor, he is entitled to rescind the transaction with Carl, and recover the instrument.

Under §3-306(a), a person without the rights of a holder in due course takes the instrument subject to "all valid claims to it on the part of any person." Thus, a person without holder in due course rights is defeated by all adverse claimants to the instrument, including those appearing in the preceding example.

Personal Defenses

Any person possessing the rights of a holder in due course takes the instrument free from "personal" but subject to "real" defenses asserted by a party to the instrument. Most commonly, the person asserting a defense is the drawer of a check or other draft or the maker of a note. A person without the rights of a holder in due course takes subject to all defenses, real or personal. Although the UCC does not explicitly use the terms "real" and "personal" to describe the various defenses, it does retain the basic distinction between the two classes in Sections 3-305 (real defenses) and 3-306 (personal defenses). Because the rights of a holder in due course are traditionally discussed in these terms, they will be used here.

The various **personal defenses** are divided into three categories: (1) any defense to a simple contract, including fraud and misrepresentation, (2) unauthorized completion, and (3) the so-called *jus tertii* defenses of theft and violation of a restrictive indorsement. These defenses, defeated by a holder in due course, are explained below.

Any Defense to a Simple Contract. Section 3-306(b) provides that a person without the rights of a holder in due course takes the instrument subject to "all defenses of any party which would be available in an action on a simple contract." That is, ordinary contract defenses, which would be available in a contract action between the immediate parties to the instrument, may not be asserted against a holder in due course. The ability to avoid contract defenses lies at the heart of the negotiability concept and the holder in due course doctrine.

To illustrate, suppose that on March 1, Byrd issues a $15,000 promissory note payable in six months to Davenport's order to pay for 200 cameras to be delivered by Davenport to Byrd on April 1. Davenport immediately negotiates the note to a holder in due course, Harrison. In this case, Harrison could force Byrd to pay the note even though: (1) Davenport never delivers the cameras (a so-called failure of consideration), or (2) the goods are delivered by Davenport but fail to conform to the contract (a breach of warranty), or (3) a condition to either party's duty to perform had failed to occur. All of the foregoing defenses are available to Byrd against one not having the rights of a holder in due course.[7]

As with other contract defenses, common law fraud and misrepresentation, which generally render a contract voidable, are personal defenses. Assume Len sells a car to Robert, inducing Robert to buy by fraudulently turning back the odometer and making other materially false representations regarding the vehicle. To pay for the automobile, Robert issues a $1,000 promissory note payable to

---

7. In addition to "failure of consideration" (actually meaning failure of *performance*), utter lack of consideration—for example, a note issued as a gift or in exchange for an illusory promise—is merely a personal defense, and may be asserted only against persons not possessing holder in due course rights.

Len's order, which Len promptly negotiates to Steve, a holder in due course. Steve may require Robert to pay the instrument despite his fraud defense. Robert's recourse after payment is against Len.

Unauthorized Completion. As discussed in Chapter 22, an incomplete instrument is one that is *signed* while incomplete in some necessary respect, such as by omission of the payee, the amount, or in some cases, the date. Before examining the substantive rules governing incomplete instruments and holders in due course, it is important to distinguish unauthorized completion from forgery. In forgery, the *signature* of the maker or drawer is unauthorized. In **unauthorized completion,** the signature is genuine or authorized but other essential terms, such as the payee and amount, are completed in an unauthorized manner. The distinction is of fundamental importance because unauthorized completion is merely a personal defense, whereas, with rare exceptions, forgery is a real defense.

Section 3-407(3) provides that when an incomplete instrument has been completed, either as authorized or in an unauthorized manner, a subsequent holder in due course may in all cases enforce the instrument *as completed*. In addition, §4-401(2)(b) provides that a drawee bank may charge its customer's account according to the tenor of a completed item unless the bank has notice that the completion was improper. To illustrate, assume Diane gives her roommate Pam an otherwise blank check drawn on First Bank signed by Diane, with instructions to take the check to the grocery store and use it to purchase groceries for the following week, the amount not to exceed $75. Rather than obeying the instructions, Pam takes the check and Diane's identification to Red's Stereo, Inc. and uses the check to purchase $2,000 worth of stereo equipment from Red's by filling in the amount and payee blanks. Red's then presents the check to First Bank, which pays it. Pam leaves town with the equipment and is never seen again. In this situation, Red's, the payee, ordinarily qualifies as a holder in due course unless it takes with notice of Pam's wrongdoing. As a holder in due course, Red's may enforce the instrument as completed, despite the unauthorized completion, and First

Bank may charge Diane's account for $2,000. Diane thus bears the loss unless she is able to find and collect from Pam.

This rule applies even if the instrument "was not delivered by the maker or drawer."[8] Thus, an incomplete instrument stolen by a thief and later completed is enforceable as completed by a later holder in due course. Assume that Diane, in the preceding illustration, signs a blank check and places it in her desk drawer for future use. Susan burglarizes Diane's house and steals the check and Diane's identification. Susan then takes the check to Red's, represents herself as Diane, and purchases $2,000 worth of stereo equipment. Red's is once again a holder in due course and may enforce the $2,000 check against Diane, who is relegated to chasing the thief, Susan. In short, the moral of the unauthorized completion story is: never *sign* a negotiable instrument with material terms, such as the amount or payee, left blank unless you are prepared to pay the instrument according to whatever is inserted in those blanks by any person. The law properly places the loss in such cases on the person "whose conduct in signing blank paper has made the fraud possible, rather than upon the innocent purchaser."[9]

"Jus Tertii" Defenses—Theft and Violation of a Restrictive Indorsement. Ordinarily, the party to pay may assert against the holder (holder in due course or not) only his own defenses, not those based on claims of third parties to the instrument: **jus tertii defenses.** That is, the claim of a third party to the instrument is not generally available as a defense to any party liable upon the instrument unless the third party herself asserts the claim. The Code recognizes two exceptions to this rule. As against a person not having the rights of a holder in due course, the party liable may assert against the holder the defense (1) that the holder, or a person through whom he holds the instrument, acquired it by theft, or (2) that payment to such holder would violate the terms of a restrictive indorsement.[10] These defects are not available

---

8. UCC §3-115(2).
9. UCC §3-115, Official Comment 5.
10. UCC §3-306(d).

against a holder in due course, regardless of who asserts them, because a holder in due course takes free of all claims to the instrument.

To illustrate, assume Dan issues a $1,000 promissory note payable to Jack's order and subsequently indorsed in blank by Jack. While so indorsed, the instrument is stolen by Carl, who delivers it to Marge after the due date on the instrument. Marge presents the instrument to Dan for payment. Because Marge is not a holder in due course (because the paper was overdue), Dan may refuse to pay her on the grounds that she acquired it from a thief. Note that Dan here is not asserting his own defense (one arising out of his contract with Jack), but is asserting a "jus tertii" defense, one based upon a third party's (Jack's) claim to the instrument. Had Marge qualified as a holder in due course, Dan would be required to pay and she would take free of Jack's theft claim. Thus, the law refuses to permit a proved thief to recover. It also refuses to aid the thief indirectly by allowing his transferee to recover *unless* the transferee qualifies as a holder in due course.

Real Defenses

Although they acquire an instrument free of personal defenses, holders in due course are subject to a limited and extraordinary class of "real" defenses. Personal defenses are generally contractual in nature, asserted to avoid performance of an otherwise valid obligation. In contrast, most real defenses are based upon failure of the existence of an obligation initially. **Real defenses** include (1) forgery, (2) material alteration, (3) infancy, (4) other incapacity, duress, and illegality, (5) fraud in the execution, (6) discharge in bankruptcy, and (7) any other discharge known to the holder when he takes the instrument.

Forgery. Perhaps the most common real defense is **forgery.** A maker or drawer whose signature is forged has no liability on the instrument. Under §1-201(43), a forgery is one type of **unauthorized signature,** which includes both outright forgeries and a signature affixed by an agent without actual, implied, or apparent authority. Under §3-404(1), an

unauthorized signature is legally effective as the signature of the unauthorized signer in favor of any person who in good faith pays the instrument or takes it for value. It is wholly ineffective as the signature of the person whose name is signed. For example, if Tom steals Don's checkbook and forges Don's name to a check made payable to Peter, the signature by Tom in Don's name is wholly inoperative as Don's signature, but is totally effective as Tom's signature. The instrument in question is a valid check with Tom rather than Don assuming the liability of the drawer. Thus Peter or a later holder may enforce the instrument against Tom (assuming that he can be found and is solvent), but not against Don, who may assert Tom's forgery as a defense even against a holder in due course.

Effect of Negligence. The availability of forgery as a defense is limited by §3-406, which provides that a person who by his negligence substantially contributes to making an unauthorized signature is precluded from asserting the signer's lack of authority against a later holder in due course. Negligence of a drawer or maker substantially contributing to a forgery therefore changes forgery from a real to a personal defense. The rationale for this result is that the loss should fall upon the drawer or maker whose conduct (negligence contributing to a forgery) makes the fraud possible rather than upon an innocent purchaser of the paper.

The Code makes no attempt to specify any particular negligent conduct that would change an unauthorized signing into a personal defense. Instead, the matter is left for the court or jury to decide, based on the facts of the particular case. Examples of negligence include failure to secure a signature stamp or other automatic signing device, and negligent hiring or supervision of employees, such as bookkeepers, who write checks. Also included are cases in which a person learns that forgeries of her signature have been made, but subsequently fails to take steps to prevent further forgeries by the same person.

At issue in the following case was whether the drawer's conduct was negligent, converting a forgery into a mere personal defense.

Fred Meyer, Inc. v. Temco Metal Products Company

516 P.2d 80 (Or. 1973)

Plaintiff Fred Meyer, Inc., (Meyer) a department store chain, cashes payroll checks as a service for its customers if adequate identification is shown. In early October 1969, several of Meyer's branch stores cashed thirty payroll checks, each in the amount of $186.34, made payable either to Randall Lees or Anthony Haws, and drawn upon the account of defendant Temco Metal Products Company. The checks bore the signature of Temco's bookkeeper and had the amount imprinted with a check "protectograph."

Unknown to Meyer, a burglar had broken into Temco's offices and had stolen payroll checks from an unlocked filing cabinet. The burglar then used the check protectograph, which was also unlocked and unsecured, to imprint the checks. The burglar also discovered the name of Temco's bookkeeper from records in the office and had forged her name as drawer of the checks.

Meyer sued Temco to recover for losses it incurred as a result of cashing the forged checks. The trial court ruled in Temco's favor and Meyer appealed to the Oregon Supreme Court.

Tongue, Justice

. . . Plaintiff's complaint alleged that defendant was negligent (1) in failing to place the blank checks in safekeeping; (2) in failing to place its check "protectograph" in safekeeping; and (3) in failing to lock the "protectograph" so as to render it unusable. . . .

Plaintiff contends that this evidence was sufficient to present a jury question whether defendant was negligent and whether its negligence substantially contributed to the making of the forged checks, within the meaning of [§3-406] of the Uniform Commercial Code, so as to preclude defendant's assertion of forgery as against plaintiff, a holder in due course. . . .

Plaintiff calls our attention to paragraph 7 of the official comment to [§3-406] which states that:

[§3-406] applies the same rule to negligence which contributes to a forgery or other unauthorized signature. . . . The most obvious case is that of the drawer who makes use of a signature stamp or other automatic signing device and is negligent in looking after it. [§3-406] extends, however, to cases where the party had notice that forgeries of his signature have occurred and is negligent in failing to prevent further forgeries by the same person. . . .

This, however, was not a case involving a "signature stamp or other automatic signing device" where "the party had notice that forgeries of his signature have occurred," as referred to in the official comment to [§3-406]. Defendant's check "protectograph" merely stamped the amount of the checks in such a manner as to make difficult the alteration of the amount. And while such checks might appear to be more authentic than the usual checks, they still had to be signed personally by defendant's corporate secretary and bookkeeper, whose signature was forged upon these checks. Neither did plaintiff offer any evidence that defendant had been put on notice of any previous forgeries.

It is true that the blank checks were in an unlocked cabinet and that the check "protectograph" was in an unlocked desk drawer in defendant's office. The door to the office was locked, however, as well as its windows and the exterior doors to the building. In addition, there was evidence that defendant employed a security service to check its premises periodically during the night. The burglars apparently obtained entrance to the adjoining shop through a skylight and then kicked open the door to the office. . . .

[W]e conclude that defendant's conduct "clearly falls" outside what we believe to be "the community's conception of fault. . . ." [*Stewart v. Jefferson Plywood Co.,* 469 P.2d 783, 786 (Or. 1970)]

This is not a case in which conduct may be negligent for failure to foresee that such conduct may involve an unreasonable risk of harm to another person through the *negligent* conduct of a third person. Instead, this is a case in which it is contended that defendant was negligent for failure to foresee that his conduct may involve harm to another through the *criminal* conduct of a third person. . . . Under normal circumstances a person may reasonably assume that no one will violate the criminal law. . . .

[Judgment affirmed.]

Material Alteration. Commercial paper is "altered" when the holder changes its terms. Under §3-407(1), a **material alteration** is one that changes the contract of any party to the instrument in any respect. As against a person other than a subsequent holder in due course, if a holder of an instrument fraudulently and materially alters it, any party whose obligation is changed by the alteration is discharged. A subsequent holder in due course, however, may in all cases enforce the altered instrument according to its original terms.[11] Suppose Downs draws a $100 check payable to Parker's order. Parker expertly alters the amount payable to read $1,000 (a so-called "raised" check), and negotiates the check to Harris, a holder in due course. In this case, Downs may assert Parker's alteration as a defense to paying Harris, but only to the extent of the alteration, $900. Harris, as a holder in due course, may require Downs to honor the instrument according to its original amount, $100.

Effect of Negligence. As with unauthorized signatures, negligence of a drawer or maker that substantially contributes to a material alteration prevents its assertion against a later holder in due course. Negligence has been found, for example, when the drawer or maker leaves spaces in the body of the instrument allowing additional figures or words to be inserted. Drafting an instrument in pencil also might be deemed negligence, reducing a subsequent alteration to a personal defense. If negligence is found, a later holder in due course may enforce the instrument as altered. Thus, in the above example, if Downs's negligence in drafting her check allowed Parker to alter it, Harris could enforce the instrument against Downs for the full $1,000.

---

11. UCC §§3-407(2),(3).

Infancy. Under §3-305(2)(a), infancy is a real defense to the extent that it is a defense to a simple contract under state law. Thus, infancy may be asserted against a holder in due course even though the infancy renders the instrument only voidable, not void. The rule is consistent with basic contract policy protecting minors against their own immaturity, lack of judgment, and overreaching by adults. State law governing minor's contracts must be consulted to determine when infancy is available as a defense and the situations in which it may be asserted.

Although *defenses* based on infancy may be asserted against a holder in due course, *claims* may not, because holders in due course take free of all claims to the instrument. For example, assume Miller, a minor, issues a $1,000 promissory note payable to Palmer's order. Palmer negotiates the note to Foster, another minor, who negotiates it to Gregg, who negotiates it to Hatch, a holder in due course. Although Hatch takes the instrument free of any claim to the instrument asserted by Foster (attempting to rescind her negotiation to Gregg and recover the instrument), Hatch takes subject to Miller's minority defense.

Other Incapacity, Duress, and Illegality. In determining whether duress, illegality, or incapacity other than infancy constitutes a real defense, state law outside the UCC must once again be consulted. Section 3-305(2)(b) provides that such defects are real defenses *only* if their effect is to render the obligation totally *void* under state law. That is, if the incapacity, duress, or illegality renders the obligation merely *voidable*, it may not be asserted against a holder in due course. Examples of other incapacity, governed largely by statute, include mental incompetence, guardianship, or lack of capacity by a corporation. Illegality typically involves gambling contracts or those violating usury laws. Whether duress constitutes a real defense is a matter of degree. For example, the fact that the maker was induced to sign through threats of legal action or suspension of future deliveries probably could not be asserted by the maker against a later holder in due course. On the other hand, the defense that the note was signed at gunpoint should be available to the maker.

Fraud in the Execution. Although fraud generally is a personal defense, a special type of fraud, known as **fraud in the execution** (or **fraud in the essence, fraud in the factum, essential fraud,** or **real fraud**) is available even against a holder in due course. Under §3-305(2)(c), fraud in the execution occurs when a misrepresentation induces a party to sign an instrument "with neither knowledge nor reasonable opportunity to obtain knowledge of its character or its essential terms." Examples of fraud in the execution include a baseball player signing an autograph that is transmitted through carbon paper to a promissory note underneath, or when a person is tricked into believing that what he or she is signing is merely an acknowledgment or receipt rather than a negotiable instrument.

Because, as a matter of general contract law, a person is deemed to know and assent to the contents of anything she signs, fraud in the execution is very difficult to establish. The signer must prove both lack of knowledge and a lack of reasonable opportunity to obtain knowledge. Because knowledge can usually be obtained by reading the instrument, the signer is unable in most cases to meet the basic test of the defense: excusable ignorance of the contents of the writing. Extraordinary circumstances are usually present, including deficiencies of the signer in intelligence, education, business experience, or knowledge of the English language, as the following case illustrates.

Schaeffer v. United Bank and Trust Company of Maryland

360 A.2d 461 (Md. App. 1976)

James and Marie Estepp applied for a loan from appellee United Bank and Trust Company of Maryland but the bank refused to grant the loan without a real property owner acting as co-maker. The Estepps then asked appellant Marvin Schaeffer to sign the back of a promissory note prepared by the bank. After making a few payments, the Estepps moved to New Mexico. Upon the bank's request, Schaeffer provided Mr. Estepp's new telephone number and

place of employment. After the Estepps failed to make further payments, the bank sued Schaeffer.

The evidence of trial established that Schaeffer had a third grade education and limited ability to read and write. At the time the note was executed, Schaeffer had been working for James Estepp. When Schaeffer's wife had died, Estepp had assisted him in making the funeral arrangements. Schaeffer described Estepp as "a wonderful guy." Schaeffer testified that when Estepp had asked him to sign the note, Estepp had explained that Schaeffer was signing as a character witness. A bank employee who had been present when Schaeffer signed the note testified that Schaeffer appeared not to understand that he would be liable on the note. The employee had left the room to allow Estepp to explain. At the close of the evidence the trial court directed a verdict in favor of the bank. Schaeffer appealed.

Moore, Judge

. . . [T]he evidence in the light most favorable to the appellant would establish (1) that he was almost illiterate, (2) that the nature of the transaction was not explained to him by the bank, (3) that he did not understand that he was assuming any financial responsibility when he signed the note, and (4) that Mr. Estepp falsely and fraudulently misrepresented the document. This evidence mounts up to fraud in the *factum.*

Fraud in the *factum,* unaccompanied by negligence, is one of the most potent defenses in the realm of commercial law. When it is successfully interposed it bars recovery not only by the promisee on a simple contract . . . but also by a holder in due course. . . .

In discussing the elements of fraud in the *factum,* official comment 7 to §3-305 of the Commercial Law is instructive:

> The test of the defense here stated is that of excusable ignorance of the contents of the writing signed. The party must not only have been in ignorance, but must also have had no reasonable opportunity to obtain knowledge. In determining what is a reasonable opportunity all relevant factors are to be taken into account, including the age and sex of the party, his intelligence, education and business

experience; his ability to read or to understand English, the representations made to him and his reason to rely on them or to have confidence in the person making them; the presence or absence of any third person who might read or explain the instrument to him, or any other possibility of obtaining independent information; and the apparent necessity, or lack of it, for acting without delay.

Here appellant was a man of limited intelligence, little education, and virtually no ability to read English. His supervisor at work, who had assisted him in the funeral of his wife, and in whom he "had complete confidence in what he said" at the time the note was signed, misrepresented the very essence of the transaction. . . .

In the instant case the bank correctly argues that "there was no testimony or evidence of fraud perpetrated by the appellee on the appellant." This argument is, however, irrelevant. When the individual charged on a note successfully interposes the defense of fraud in the *factum* it is immaterial *who* perpetrated the fraud. . . .

Because there was evidence in this case from which a jury could have found appellant not liable on the note, it was error for the court to grant a directed verdict for the bank. . . . The motion by the bank for a directed verdict was made on the ground that Mr. Schaeffer had failed to prove any fraud or misrepresentation on the part of the bank. As we have seen, however, the absence of fraudulent conduct on the part of the payee was not dispositive of the case. . . .

[Judgment reversed and remanded for new trial.]

Discharge in Bankruptcy.

Under §3-305(2)(d), the maker's or drawer's discharge in bankruptcy may be asserted even against a holder in due course. Suppose that on June 1, Stevens issues a $1,000 promissory note payable in one year to Moore's order. Moore immediately negotiates the instrument to Hoskins, a holder in due course. Six months later, Stevens goes through bankruptcy and receives a discharge. Stevens may assert his discharge in bankruptcy as a defense to paying Hoskins.

Other Discharge.

In addition to a discharge in bankruptcy, a holder in due course takes subject to the discharge of any party to the instrument of which the holder *has notice* when he takes the instrument.[12] No discharge of any party to the instrument is effective against a later holder in due course unless the holder has notice of it when she takes the instrument.[13] For example, the Code provides that a holder may discharge any party to an instrument in any manner apparent from the face of the instrument or an indorsement such as by striking out or canceling a party's signature.[14] If a signature is so canceled, a later holder in due course takes subject to the discharge of that party, because the cancellation provides notice of the discharge. Suppose Scott is a holder in due course of Martin's $1,000 promissory note payable to Paul's order and indorsed by Paul, Alan, Bob, Carl, and Don. Scott acquired the instrument from Don, who as a favor to Bob, had crossed out Bob's indorsement. Scott takes with notice of and subject to Bob's discharge. All other parties (Martin, Paul, Alan, Carl, and Don) remain liable on their basic contracts. This contract liability is discussed in detail in Chapter 25.

Effect of Payment.

Although payment of an instrument normally discharges a party,[15] such a discharge, as noted above, is ineffective against a subsequent holder in due course without a notice of the discharge. Assume Burton issues a $1,000 demand promissory note payable to Fisher's order. One month later Fisher demands and receives payment from Burton, who does not require Fisher to surrender the instrument. Fisher subsequently negotiates the instrument to Holly, a holder in due course. Holly may require Burton to pay the note again because Holly took without notice of and therefore free from Burton's discharge based on his payment of the instrument. Any person paying an instrument should therefore require the holder to surrender it.

---

12. UCC §3-305(2)(e).
13. UCC §3-602.
14. UCC §3-605.
15. UCC §3-603.

Federal Trade Commission Rule

The holder in due course doctrine has been severely restricted in consumer credit transactions because of the potential for abuse illustrated by the following example. Assume Perkins, a dealer in shoddy merchandise (or services), sells Masters a television set. Because Masters is unable to pay cash she buys under a "conditional sales contract" consisting of a promissory note for the purchase price payable in installments and a security agreement giving Perkins the right to repossess the television if Masters fails to pay the note. Immediately after the sale to Masters, Perkins sells the contract for cash to a bank or finance company, which usually qualifies as a holder in due course under Article 3. Therefore, even if the television later proves defective, Masters, the consumer, is required to pay the purchase price to the bank or finance company. The consumer's most valuable remedy against a breaching seller, withholding the purchase price, is therefore extinguished under a strict application of the holder in due course doctrine.

Because of this perceived abuse, most states either by statute or judicial decision have imposed some restriction on the holder in due course doctrine in consumer transactions. Further, the Federal Trade Commission (FTC) promulgated rules and regulations effective since 1976 effectively abolishing the holder in due course doctrine in credit sales of goods or services to a consumer. Under these regulations,[16] the seller[17] must include the following notice (in at least ten-point boldface type) in any contract evidencing a sale or lease of goods or services to a consumer[18] on credit:

NOTICE

ANY HOLDER OF THIS CONSUMER CREDIT CONTRACT IS SUBJECT TO ALL CLAIMS AND DEFENSES WHICH THE DEBTOR COULD ASSERT AGAINST THE SELLER OF GOODS OR SERVICES OBTAINED PURSUANT HERETO OR WITH THE PROCEEDS HEREOF. RECOVERY HEREUNDER BY THE DEBTOR SHALL NOT EXCEED AMOUNTS PAID BY THE DEBTOR HEREUNDER.[19]

Failure to include this notice is deemed an unfair or deceptive trade practice, violating Section 5 of the Federal Trade Commission Act.[20]

The effect of including the above notice is that no transferee of the contract, such as a bank or finance company, acquires the rights of a holder in due course. That is, including the quoted notice renders the debtor's promise conditional defeating negotiability. Thus, the assignee of such consumer paper takes no better rights than its assignor, the seller, had.

Two points concerning the scope and operation of the FTC rule should be noted. First, it applies only to consumer, not business or commercial transactions. Second, it effects no change in Article 3 of the UCC or any other state law. It simply requires inclusion of the quoted notice to avoid violating the Federal Trade Commission Act. Note that a business transferee of consumer paper without the required notice may be unable to qualify as a holder in due course in any event, because it should know that the notice is required and therefore does not take the paper in good faith.

---

16. 16 C.F.R. §§433.1-433.3.

17. The regulations define "seller" as "a person who, in the ordinary course of business, sells or leases goods or services to consumers." 16 C.F.R. §433.1(j).

18. The regulations define "consumer" as "a natural person who seeks or acquires goods or services for personal, family, or household use." 16 C.F.R. §433.1(b).

---

19. 16 C.F.R §433.2.

20. The FTC Act and the Federal Trade Commission's authority under §5 thereunder are discussed in Chapter 52.

SUMMARY

1. A holder in due course is a specialized transferee of commercial paper who stands in a better legal position than an ordinary contract assignee. A holder in due course takes the instrument free of all claims to it and personal, but not real, defenses asserted by a party to the instrument. A person without the rights of a holder in due course takes the instrument subject to all claims to it and all defenses, real or personal.

2. To qualify as a holder in due course, the holder must take the instrument (1) for value, (2) in good faith, and (3) without notice that the instrument is overdue, or has been dishonored, or of any defense against or claim to it on the part of any person.

3. Generally speaking, any transferee who takes the instrument from or after a holder in due course acquires the rights of a holder in due course, whether or not the transferee meets the requirements listed above. This so-called shelter or umbrella rule assures marketability of the paper, and expands substantially the number of transferees afforded holder in due course status.

4. Holders in due course take free of personal but not real defenses asserted by a party to the instrument, usually the maker of a note or drawer of a check or other draft. Personal defenses include (1) any defense to a simple contract, including fraud and misrepresentation, (2) unauthorized completion, and (3) the "jus tertii" defenses of theft and violation of a restrictive indorsement.

5. Real defenses include (1) forgery, (2) material alteration, (3) infancy, (4) other incapacity, duress, and illegality, (5) fraud in the execution, (6) discharge in bankruptcy, and (7) any other discharge known to the holder when he takes the instrument.

6. The holder in due course doctrine has been severely restricted in consumer credit transactions by Federal Trade Commission rule. Under this rule, any contract evidencing a sale or lease of goods to a consumer on credit must include a notice making the transferee subject to claims and defenses which the consumer could assert against the seller of the goods or services.

KEY TERMS

holder in due course	unauthorized completion
value	jus tertii defenses
antecedent debt	real defenses
notice	forgery
shelter (umbrella)	unauthorized signature
provision	material alteration
personal defenses	fraud in the execution

QUESTIONS AND PROBLEMS

24-1 To be a holder in due course, a person must take an instrument in good faith (imposing a subjective standard) and without notice (imposing an objective standard) of various problems with the instrument. Why does the law impose both types of standards upon those it protects as holders in due course?

24-2 Consider the following facts.
(a) Samson sold goods to Baily for $500 on June 1. Baily gave Samson a check, which Samson promptly sold the same day to Lawson for $500, payable $150 on June 3, $150 on June 5, and $200 on June 7. Assume that the goods Samson sold to Baily were not as warranted. Lawson became aware of this fact on June 6. Assuming he meets the other requirements, for what amount could Lawson qualify as a holder in due course?
(b) Miller issued a note payable to the order of Pierce in the amount of $1,000. Pierce sold the note to East for $980. East paid Pierce $300 cash, a $300 check made payable to East to Pierce, and canceled a prior loan of $380 that Pierce owed East. Assuming he meets all other requirements, for what amount could East qualify as a holder in due course?

24-3 Consider the following situations.
(a) Alexander sues Benedict. After some negotiation, Alexander agrees to dismiss the lawsuit if Benedict will execute a promissory note for $1,000 payable in 60 days. Benedict executes the promissory note payable to Alexander who negotiates it to First Bank as collateral for an $800 loan. On the due date, First Bank demands payment from Benedict. He refuses claiming that the promissory note is not supported by consideration because Alexander failed to dismiss the lawsuit.
   (1) Is First Bank a holder in due course? To what extent? Explain.
   (2) Is Benedict's defense legal grounds for refusing to pay the note? Explain.
(b) On July 1, Annette gave Frankie a $500 promissory note due on December 1 in exchange for a motorcycle sold by Frankie to Annette. On July 15 Frankie negotiated the note to Connie in payment for a used car that Connie promised to deliver on August

1. Annette has a defense to paying the note because Frankie fraudulently misrepresented the motorcycle's mechanical condition. Could Connie be a holder in due course on these facts? If so, when and under what circumstances would she achieve that status? If Connie qualifies as a holder in due course, would she take the instrument free of Annette's defense?

24-4 On August 1, Ralph sold real property located in Macon County to Mary Maker who in partial payment executed a promissory note for $15,000 payable to the order of Ralph. The note was secured by a mortgage on the real property. On August 15, Carl Creditor sued Ralph and took a judgment for $10,000 which Carl recorded on August 15 in the Macon County recorder's office, a place of public record. Recording the judgment gave Carl a lien on Ralph's property, including the note. On September 1, Ralph negotiated Mary Maker's promissory note to First State Bank as collateral for a loan.

(a) Has First State Bank taken the note for value? Explain.

(b) Ralph later defaulted on the loan. Both Carl and First State Bank assert a right to Mary's payment on the promissory note. First State Bank claims that it is a holder in due course. Carl alleges that the bank cannot be a holder in due course because it had constructive notice of Carl's lien because the lien was recorded. Who is correct? Explain.

24-5 Brown sold some property to Jones in exchange for a negotiable promissory note for $100,000. Brown, without indorsing the note, delivered it to his daughter Belle stating "I want you to have this note as a gift." After Belle notified Jones of the gift, he began making payments to her. Brown died and his estate claimed that Brown owned the promissory note at his death.

(a) Assume that the promissory note was payable to bearer. Is Belle a holder? A holder in due course? Explain.

(b) Assume that the promissory note was payable to the order of Brown. Is Belle a holder? A holder in due course? Does Belle have any rights in the note? Explain.

(c) Assume that Belle refused to accept the note as a gift but instead paid her father the present value of the note. Is she a holder? A holder in due course? Does it matter whether the note is made payable to bearer or to the order of Brown? Explain.

24-6 On October 1, 1988, Hunt sold some cattle to Pierre who paid for them by check payable to Hunt in the amount of $30,000. When Pierre returned to his ranch, he discovered that the cattle had been miscounted and he had received more than he had paid for. Pierre called Hunt and told her he would send a new check in the proper amount of $35,000 and asked her to destroy the check. Approximately one year later in October, 1989, Hunt was in financial difficulties and Creditor demanded that she make payments on a loan owed to Creditor. Hunt began searching through her files and discovered the two checks from Pierre. Hunt indorsed the checks and delivered them to Creditor. After noticing that the checks were almost a year old, Creditor called Pierre and told him that he would be depositing some "old checks" drawn on Pierre's account. Creditor then deposited the properly indorsed checks and Pierre's bank paid both. When reconciling his bank account the following month, Pierre realized that Creditor had cashed the check that Hunt should have destroyed. After the bank refused to recredit his account for $30,000, Pierre sued Creditor.

How should the court rule? In formulating your answer, consider whether Creditor is a holder in due course and discuss the effect of Creditor's telephone call notifying Pierre of the proposed deposit of the checks.

24-7 John bought a printing press from Leonard and paid for it with a check. Leonard indorsed the check to Virginia in payment of a pre-existing debt. Virginia gave the check to Vanessa, her sister, and suggested she use it to buy herself a birthday present. Vanessa deposited the check in her account but it was returned marked "payment stopped." Vanessa telephoned John who said he had stopped payment on the check because the printing press was defective. When Vanessa threatened to sue, John told her she would lose the case because she had not given value for the check and, therefore, was not a holder in due course.

(a) Is Vanessa a holder in due course? Explain.

(b) If Vanessa sues, who will win? Explain.

24-8 On January 1, Smith executed a $1,000 negotiable promissory note payable on January 30 to the order of Jones for goods to be delivered by Jones to Smith. Jones breached the contract and the goods were never delivered. On January 2, Jones negotiated the note to Zimmer who had no knowledge of the breach. Zimmer agreed to pay

$975, payment to be made on January 10. Zimmer, on January 3, negotiated the note to his nephew, Claypool, as a graduation present. Claypool then sold the note to Faust who paid $975 cash and had no knowledge of any defenses against the instrument. Faust then sold the note to Wilson for $959, who took on January 29, with knowledge that Jones had breached the contract.

(a) Is Zimmer is a holder in due course?

(b) Is Claypool is a holder in due course?

(c) Is Faust is a holder in due course?

(d) Is Wilson a holder in due course?

(e) Would Wilson take the note subject to Smith's defense against Jones?

24-9 Kroyden Industries, Inc. was enjoined by the court from committing specified unfair trade practices in connection with its sale of carpeting to consumers. In violation of the injunction, Kroyden obtained a $1,500 promissory note from Doaks for purchase of carpeting. Kroyden negotiated the note to Harris, a holder in due course. When Doaks refused to pay the note, Harris sued. Doaks asserted illegality as a real defense. He argued that because the transaction which resulted in the execution of his note was a violation of the injunctive order, the transaction was ''illegal'' and thus a nullity under UCC §3-305(2)(b). Is Doaks correct? Explain.

24-10 Louis Guerra entered into a retail installment contract agreeing to pay $10,000 to Modern Builders to install new siding on Guerra's home. After Modern Builders installed the siding, Guerra executed a negotiable promissory note in the amount of $10,000 payable to Modern Builders and requiring Guerra to pay $1,000 per year plus interest at 8%. Modern Builders assigned the note and contract to Home Savings and notified Guerra of the assignment. After Guerra had made the first annual payment of $1,800, the siding began to peel and fall from the house. Another siding dealer told Guerra that Modern Builders had improperly installed the siding and had used inappropriate materials. The dealer estimated that the cost of removing the old siding and installing new siding would be $12,000.

(a) Home Savings has sued Guerra for failing to make further payments on his promissory note. May Guerra assert Modern Builder's breach of contract as a defense to payment to Home Savings? Explain.

(b) Guerra has counterclaimed against Home Savings and Modern Builders. Assume that Guerra can prove damages of $12,000 for breach of the siding contract. Would Guerra be entitled to recover any damages from Home Savings? Explain.

Chapter 25

Liability of Parties—
Contract Liability

Major Topics

- the distinction between primary and secondary contract liability on commercial paper
- the nature of primary liability and which parties assume that liability
- the nature of secondary liability and which parties assume that liability
- the conditions precedent to secondary liability
- the contract liability of accommodation parties and guarantors on commercial paper

Commercial paper, governed by Article 3, is a formal contract that requires a payment of money. As in other contracts, the parties to commercial paper acquire certain rights and undertake certain duties. An important inquiry in commercial paper analysis is, therefore, to define and distinguish the various obligations of the maker of a note, the drawer and drawee of a draft, and an indorser or other transferee of either type of instrument.

Broadly speaking, parties to commercial paper incur two types of liability: contract and warranty. Whereas warranty liability generally imposes responsibility for forgery and alteration, contract liability concerns the obligation of the various parties for ultimate *payment* of the instrument.

This chapter explains and distinguishes the contractual undertakings of the parties and examines how those obligations are discharged or extin-

guished. Chapter 26 explains the circumstances under which the law imposes warranty liability for forgery and alteration.

Liability Based Upon Signature

Signature in General

Although the nature and extent of commercial paper contract liability differs, all contract liability is imposed in the same manner. Under §3-401(1) no person is liable on an instrument unless and until he or she signs it. As noted in Chapter 22, a signature includes any symbol used by the party to authenticate a writing, including, for example, a handwritten signature, an "X," and a signature stamp or other automatic device. The signature may be made using a trade or assumed name and, in appropriate cases, may be affixed by an authorized agent or other representative of the signer. Parties to commercial paper generally sign in one of four capacities: (1) the maker of a note, (2) the drawer of a check or other draft, (3) the acceptor of a check or other draft, or (4) an indorser of any instrument. Therefore, in order to determine the contract liability of a party, one must simply examine the instrument to ascertain the capacity in which the party signed.

Identifying Capacity of Signer. To aid in conclusively determining the capacity of a signature, §3-402 provides simply that "[u]nless the instrument *clearly indicates* that a signature is made in some other capacity it is an indorsement.'' (Emphasis added.) Therefore, no person is liable on an instrument unless her signature appears thereon, and any signature in an ambiguous capacity is an indorsement. All ambiguities are resolved from the instrument alone, providing yet another example of the strict parol evidence rule applicable to commercial paper.

Because all ambiguous signatures are indorsements, it is necessary to identify those signatures that clearly indicate another capacity. Another capacity is most commonly indicated by the position of the signature on the instrument. For example, the drawer of a check or other draft and the maker of a note generally sign in the lower right-hand corner on the face of the instrument. A signature appearing in the lower right-hand corner is therefore presumed to be the signature of a drawer or maker. Similarly, a signature appearing on the back of an instrument is generally deemed an indorsement.

The capacity of the signer is also clearly indicated if words of description are used. For example, a signature appearing anywhere on an instrument stating, ''Joe Doaks, maker'' imposes liability upon Joe Doaks as a maker, whereas a signature ''Joe Doaks, witness'' imposes no liability upon him. Similarly, a signature appearing in the body of an instrument often clearly indicates the signer's capacity. For example, if an instrument states ''I, Jane Adams, promise to pay . . . ,'' Jane Adams is obviously signing as the maker of a note.

Joint and Several Liability. Under §3-118(e), if two or more persons sign as maker, drawer, acceptor, or indorser and as part of the same transaction, they are jointly and severally liable. The signers may be sued together (jointly) or individually (severally) on the obligation and the entire amount owing may be collected from any one of them. Assume A and B co-sign as makers of a $1,000 promissory note payable to P's order. P or a later holder may collect the entire $1,000 from either A or B, or from A and B together.[1]

---

1. Joint and several liability is discussed in more detail in Chapter 7.

Signature by Authorized Representative

Individuals in business often act through agents. Corporations, which are artificial persons, act only through agents. Accordingly, §3-403(1) provides that a negotiable instrument may be signed by an authorized representative or agent, such as the treasurer, controller, or officer of a corporation. The representative's authority to sign is determined by principles of agency law, discussed in detail in Chapter 40. Under ordinary agency principles, if the agent is authorized to sign, the principal, such as the corporation, becomes liable on the instrument as signer, and the agent or representative has no liability upon it. Because the representative generally signs his or her own name to the instrument, however, care must be taken to disclose the representative capacity. Otherwise, later holders of the instrument may be misled concerning the extent of the signer's obligation. The Code resolves the problem by imposing *personal liability* on the instrument (as maker, drawer, acceptor, or indorser) upon an agent who fails to properly indicate his or her representative capacity. Because this issue has resulted in a substantial amount of litigation, persons in business must be familiar with the Code's approach to representative signatures.

Section 3-403(2) provides that an authorized representative who signs his or her own name to an instrument is personally obligated on the instrument if the instrument:

1. neither names the person represented nor shows that the agent signed in a representative capacity, or
2. names the person represented but does not show that the agent signed in a representative capacity, or
3. does not name the person represented but does show that the agent signed in a representative capacity.

If a dispute arises concerning the agent's liability, the agent may attempt to introduce parol evidence—evidence other than the instrument itself, such as oral testimony—to prove her representative capacity. Section 2-403 makes it clear that parol evidence is never admissible in court to change the result dictated above if the party seeking to recover is a later holder of the instrument who did not deal with the agent. If, however, the lawsuit involves the agent-signer and the person with whom she dealt (such as the payee of a check signed by the agent), parol evidence is admissible in cases 2 and 3 above to prove representative capacity. If the evidence shows that these "immediate parties" did not intend the agent to be personally liable, the agent is excused from liability. In the first case—in which the signer neither names the person represented nor his representative capacity—parol evidence is never admissible. That is, an agent who signs her name *only* may not introduce evidence of her agency capacity even against a person taking the instrument from the agent who knows the agent intended to sign on another's behalf.

The following example, contained in Official Comment 3 to §3-403, illustrates the operation of the foregoing principles. Assume that Peter Pringle has appointed Arthur Adams as his agent with authority to sign negotiable instruments on Pringle's behalf. Alternatively, an instrument might bear one of the following signatures affixed by Adams:

1. "Peter Pringle," or
2. "Arthur Adams," or
3. "Peter Pringle by Arthur Adams, Agent," or
4. "Arthur Adams, Agent," or
5. "Peter Pringle, Arthur Adams"

In case 1, assuming Adams is authorized, Pringle is liable on the instrument and Adams is not. In case 2, Adams is personally liable and parol evidence is inadmissible against anyone to extinguish his obligation. Case 3 is the preferred method of signing; Pringle is liable on the instrument and Adams is not. In cases 4 and 5, Adams is personally liable on the instrument. If, however, the litigation involves the immediate parties, Adams may attempt to prove by parol evidence, such as oral testimony, that he signed only as an agent for Pringle.

The principal may be a corporation or other organization rather than an individual. In this case, the name of an organization preceded or followed by the name and office of an authorized individual is a signature made in a representative capacity. For example, the signature "XYZ Corporation, by

Arthur Adams, Treasurer" imposes no personal liability upon Adams.[2]

In the following case the court was required to determine whether a signature was made in a representative or in an individual capacity.

Valley National Bank, Sunnymead v. Cook
665 P.2d 576 (Ariz. App. 1983)

> Arizona Auto Auction, Inc. issued three checks payable to Central Motors Company. The checks were drawn on the account of Arizona Auto Auction at First National Bank of Arizona and were signed by defendant, J. M. Cook, the company's treasurer. Although "Arizona Auto Auction, Inc." was imprinted on the checks, there was no indication on the checks that J. M. Cook was an officer. One of the instruments in question is shown in Figure 25-1.
>
> Central Motors deposited the checks in its account at Valley National Bank, Sunnymead. When Valley National Bank presented the checks for payment, First National Bank dishonored the checks because a stop payment order had been issued. Valley National Bank was unable to recover payment from Central Motors.
>
> Plaintiff Valley National Bank, as a holder in due course, sued defendants Arizona Auto Auction, Inc. and J. M. Cook. The trial court held that Arizona Auto Auction, Inc. was liable on the checks but held that J. M. Cook was not personally liable. Valley National Bank appealed from the ruling in favor of J. M. Cook.

Corcoran, Judge
The issue raised in this appeal is whether an individual who signs a check without indicating her representative capacity is personally liable on the obligation evidenced by the check when the check has the name of the corporate principal printed on it. . . .

---

2. UCC §3-403(3). The preceding discussion assumes that the agent's signature, however affixed, is authorized. The legal effect of an unauthorized signature is discussed in the next chapter.

| Figure 25–1 | **Valley National Bank, Sunnymead v. Cook Instrument** |

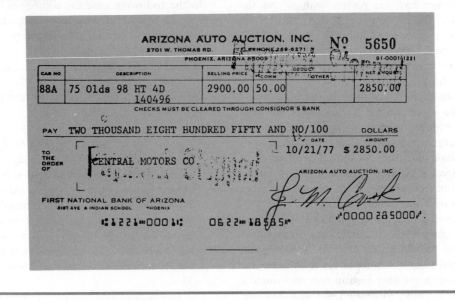

The question of whether Cook signed in her individual or representative capacity is governed by section 3-403 of the Uniform Commercial Code (UCC). . . .

The Bank argues that this section conclusively establishes Cook's personal liability on the checks. We do not agree. Admittedly, the checks fail to specifically show the office held by Cook. However, we do not find that this fact conclusively establishes liability since [UCC §3-403] imposes personal liability on an agent who signs his or her own name to an instrument only "if the instrument . . . does not show that the representative signed in a representative capacity." Thus, we must look to the entire instrument for evidence of the capacity of the signer. . . .

The checks are in evidence and are boldly imprinted at the top "Arizona Auto Auction, Inc." and also "Arizona Auto Auction, Inc." is imprinted above a signature line appearing at the lower righthand corner. Under the imprinted name of the corporate defendant appears the signature of appellee Cook without any designation of office or capacity on each of the checks before us on appeal. Appellee Cook did not endorse the checks on the

back. The record does not reflect appellee Cook made any personal guaranty of these checks or any other corporate obligation. . . .

The Superior Court of Pennsylvania was confronted with a similar situation in *Pollin v. Mindy Mfg. Co., Inc.,* [236 A.2d 542 (Pa. Super. 1967)]. There the court denied recovery by a third party endorsee against one who affixed his signature to a payroll check directly beneath the printed corporate name without indicating his representative capacity. . . .

The difference in outcome in the *Pollin* case and the cases cited by the Bank in which corporate agents were held liable for failing to show a corporate title reflects the *Pollin* court's emphasis on *business expectations,* an emphasis which is proper and entirely consistent with the spirit of UCC §3-403. . . . In determining what these expectations might be, it is important to draw a distinction between a check and a note. . . . [W]hile it may be common for creditors of small corporations to demand that corporate officers personally obligate themselves on corporate notes, it would be most unusual to demand the individual obligation of an officer on corporate checks.

The fact that common business expectations may not be consistent with a strict reading of UCC §3-403(2), as that section relates to corporate checks, as opposed to notes, is exemplified by the record before us. . . .

[T]he testimony is consistent with the common business and banking expectation that where a corporate name is printed on a check any accompanying signatures relating to the corporate drawer will be the signatures of officers authorized by the by-laws or corporate resolutions to sign the instrument in a representative capacity, without regard to whether there is a specific reference to the representative capacity. This is especially clear where, as here, the check is drawn against a corporate checking account.

In this case the checks clearly show the name of the corporation in two places and the money was payable from the account of Arizona Auto Auction, Inc., over which Cook as an individual had no control. Considering the instruments as a whole, we conclude under these circumstances that they sufficiently disclose that Cook signed them in a representative and not an individual capacity. . . .

[Judgment affirmed.]

In contrast to the approach taken by the court in *Valley National Bank,* a number of cases have imposed personal liability upon a corporate officer who signs a check on a corporate account without explicitly disclosing his or her representative capacity. For this reason a corporate agent, like an agent of an individual principal, is well advised to comply literally with §3-403 by disclosing both the identity of the principal and the agent's representative capacity—as in ''Arizona Auto Auction, Inc. by J. M. Cook, Treasurer.''

Primary Liability

Contract liability is either primary (incurred by primary parties) or secondary (incurred by secondary parties). A person having **primary liability** undertakes an absolute obligation to pay the instrument. The primary parties are the maker of a note and the acceptor of a draft. An acceptor is simply a drawee who undertakes to pay a draft. Unlike primary liability, **secondary liability** is conditional; a secondary party agrees to pay only if the primary party does not and certain formal conditions are met. The secondary parties on commercial paper are the drawer of a draft or check and the indorser of any instrument. Whether liability is primary or secondary, subsequent events ultimately occur that discharge it. As in contracts generally, to ''discharge'' a duty means to extinguish or cancel it. The following material examines the contract liability of the various parties whose signatures appear upon a negotiable instrument. Primary liability is covered first followed by a discussion of secondary liability.

Maker of a Note

Section 3-413(1) provides that the maker of a note promises to pay the instrument according to its terms when he or she signed. The maker's liability is primary because the maker undertakes an absolute obligation to pay the note, and no conditions to that liability (such as a demand for payment) exist. Assume Matson issues a $1,000 promissory note on June 1, 1983, payable with interest to Peter's order on June 1, 1984. Matson is obligated to pay Peter (or a later holder) $1,000 plus interest as of June 1, 1984. The holder's failure to present the instrument to Matson on that date, however, has no effect on Matson's liability. Further, until a tender of payment by Matson or expiration of the statute of limitations, interest on the note continues to run after June 1, 1984.

Acceptor of a Draft

''Acceptance'' Defined. Primary liability on a draft, including a check, requires a basic understanding of *acceptance,* a concept unique to drafts. Clearly, the drawee is the person who should pay a draft, because the essence of a draft is an order by the drawer to the drawee to pay. It is equally clear that drawer should not be able to impose primary liability upon the drawee without the drawee's consent. The drawee's consent to assume primary liability on a draft is known as **acceptance**—defined in §3-410(1) as the drawee's signed engagement to honor (pay) a draft as presented. Therefore, prior to acceptance, *no one* has primary liability on a draft. After acceptance the drawee has an absolute

obligation to pay the draft when it is due to the payee or later holder.

An acceptance must be written on the draft and may consist of the drawee's signature alone. A drawee who accepts a draft is known as an **acceptor.** Although an acceptance is usually written vertically across the face of the instrument, the drawee's signature appearing anywhere on a draft is an acceptance. Because a drawee has no reason to sign a draft other than to accept it, the signature itself, regardless of its position, "clearly indicates" the capacity of the signer.

Demand and Time Drafts. Like notes, drafts may, by their terms, be payable on demand (a **demand draft**), or at some fixed or determinable future time (a **time draft**). The concept of acceptance is important only in a time draft. That is, a demand draft is given by the drawer to the payee and then presented to the drawee only once: for payment. Such drafts are commonly known as **sight drafts** because they are to be paid by the drawee on "sight." A demand draft is not presented to the drawee for acceptance (the drawee's *promise* to pay it); it is presented for *payment.* The drawee therefore never assumes primary liability on a demand draft: the drawee either pays the instrument or doesn't. If the drawee pays it, the transaction is at an end. If the drawee fails to pay (dishonors) it, the liability of the secondary party or parties (here, the drawer) ensues.

In time drafts, on the other hand, two presentments are required, the first for acceptance and the second for payment. Acceptance not only initiates the drawee's liability on the instrument, it also commonly fixes the date for payment. For example, time drafts are often stated to be payable a fixed period after "acceptance" or "sight."[3]

To illustrate, assume Bill Brown owes Susan Simon $1,000 for goods bought from Simon. In order to pay an obligation owed by Simon to Paul Potts, Simon draws a draft upon Bill Brown (see Figure 25–2). On June 2, Potts takes the instrument to Brown for acceptance. Brown accepts by signing "Bill Brown, accepted" across the face of the draft and dating his signature. By accepting, Brown has

Figure 25–2   **Time Draft**

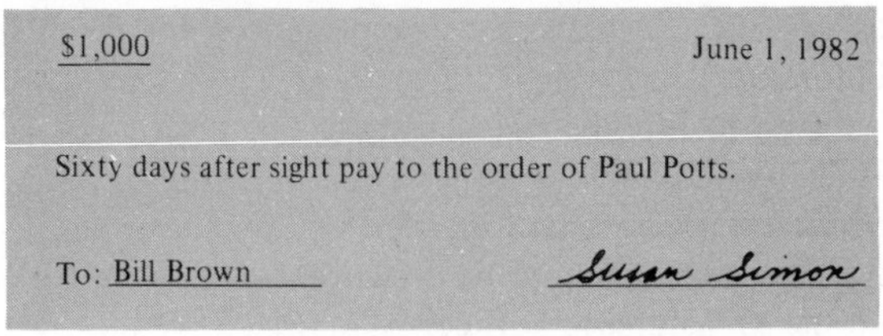

$1,000   June 1, 1982

Sixty days after sight pay to the order of Paul Potts.

To: Bill Brown   *Susan Simon*

undertaken the absolute obligation to pay the instrument to Paul Potts (or to a later holder if Potts transfers the instrument) sixty days after June 2. Note that the instrument is ultimately presented twice to Brown, once for acceptance (in this case on June 2) and again for payment (sixty days thereafter).

A drawee incurs no liability to the holder of an instrument for failure to accept because prior to acceptance the drawee's signature does not appear on the instrument. This rule applies even if the drawer and drawee stand in a contractual relationship that requires the drawee to accept drafts drawn by the drawer. After acceptance, however, the drawee is primarily liable to the holder of the instrument.

Certified Checks. Because a check is a demand draft, the drawee bank ordinarily has no obligation to the payee or to a later holder to pay the check. Because a check is presented for payment, not acceptance, the bank never undertakes primary liability upon it. If the bank refuses to pay, the holder simply proceeds against the drawer and any indorsers on their *secondary* contract liability.

Although under no obligation to do so, a bank may agree to accept or "certify" a check. **Certification** occurs when an authorized representative of a bank signs or stamps language on the face of the check indicating the bank's undertaking to pay. A certified check is therefore one that is *accepted* rather than *paid* by the bank. It is more valuable than an ordinary check because of the bank's undertaking to stand behind it. A certified check is similar in effect to a time draft because two presentments are made, one for acceptance (certifica-

---

3. "Sight" in this context refers to acceptance.

tion) and subsequently for payment. Unlike a time draft, however, a certified check is paid on demand by the bank at any time after certification.

At issue in the following case was whether a check had been properly certified.

Menke v. Board of Education, Independent School District of West Burlington
211 N.W.2d 601 (Iowa 1973)

Plaintiff Menke Plumbing-Heating & Sheet Metal Work (Menke) submitted a bid to perform construction work at the West Burlington High School. The bidding rules required all bidders to submit a certified check with their bids to demonstrate good faith. Although Menke's bid was the lowest, the Board of Education refused to award it the contract for failure to submit a certified check. Menke had submitted a check that he had asked the drawee State Central Savings Bank to certify. The bank had stamped the following on the check:

CERTIFIED

June 30, 1970

The State Central Savings Bank

West Point Office, West Point, Iowa

Manager

$6,300.00

The blank line was for a bank officer's signature; however, no officer had signed.

Menke sued both State Central Savings Bank and the Board of Education. The trial court held that the check had not been certified. Menke and the bank appealed.

Rees, Justice

. . . The principal issue presented by the Bank's appeal is whether a check stamped as was the check in the case here is properly certified as a matter of law. The Bank claims the stamp placed upon the check by it is adequate to constitute a certification. The lower court held, and plaintiff Menke and defendant Board assert in this appeal

that the stamped words indicating certification without the signature of a bank official do not as a matter of law suffice to effect proper certification of the check. We are persuaded the trial court was correct in its ruling, and agree with plaintiff and defendant Board.

We are unable to find precedent holding that there is any specified form essential to the certification of a check. . . . [§3-411(1) of] the Uniform Commercial Code provisions defines certification of a check to be acceptance. "Acceptance" consists of "the drawee's *signed* engagement to honor the draft as presented. It must be written on the draft, and may consist of his signature alone." (Emphasis added). . . .

From the foregoing provisions of the Uniform Commercial Code, the following inferences are presented: (1) Certification must be in writing, at least as opposed to parol evidence. . . . (2) If an acceptance can consist of a signature alone, the logical conclusion would seem to be that a certification consists of no less than a signature and possibly other words indicating acceptance. . . .

We note the definition of the word "signed" in [§1-201(39) of the UCC] includes "any symbol executed or adopted by a party *with present intention to authenticate a writing*." (Emphasis supplied). Authentication must be discernable when viewed in the light of commercial reasonableness. The defendant Bank here affixed a stamp bearing words of certification with a blank line for a bank official's signature to assure the holder or third parties that the check was certified by the bank and that the certification was authentic. Rubber-stamps may be easily copied and secured with facility, and fraudulent certification accomplished by the use thereof would be detrimental to the interests of a bank. We therefore feel it is consistent with customary certification practice, as hereinabove referred to, to conclude that defendant Bank had adopted the stamp, but that a "present intention to authenticate" a check required the script signature of a bank official to indicate certification. . . .

We hold, therefore, that a check stamped with words of certification and a signature line, but without any written, printed, stamped or facsimile signature thereon, does not provide sufficient evidence of intent to authenticate certification by a bank to a holder in a commercial transaction, and as a matter of law does not comply with the statutory requirements for certification. . . .

[Judgment affirmed.]

Effect of Alteration Before Acceptance. Under §3-413(1), the acceptor of a draft, like the maker of a note, binds himself to "pay the instrument according to its tenor at the time of his engagement." A maker is therefore primarily liable on the note as executed when it is issued, and an acceptor is liable on a draft as worded when he accepts it. Thus, a drawee who accepts an instrument that has been altered prior to acceptance is liable on the instrument as altered, not as originally drawn. Assume Donna draws a draft against Art ordering Art to pay $100 to Peter's order "30 days after acceptance." Peter takes the instrument from Donna and raises it to $1,000. Peter then negotiates it to Harry, who presents it to Art for acceptance. If Art accepts he is liable for the full $1,000.[4] If the instrument is altered after acceptance, §3-407(3) provides that the acceptor remains liable on the instrument according to its original tenor (as accepted) to a subsequent holder in due course.

Effect of Acceptance Varying Draft. Occasionally, a drawee will accept an instrument but attempt to vary the terms of the draft as presented. Suppose Denise draws a draft against Larry ordering him to pay $100 to Polly's order "30 days after acceptance." Polly indorses the instrument to Tony, who presents it to Larry for acceptance. Assume alternatively that Larry writes on the face of the instrument "accepted, Larry, but only if I receive the proceeds of the sale of my house within 30 days," or "accepted, Larry, payable in 60 days," or "accepted, Larry, for $75 because that is all I owe to Denise." In these situations, §3-412 gives the holder, Tony, two options. One option is to treat the drawee's variant acceptance as a dishonor and proceed immediately against Polly and Denise on their secondary contract liability. If the holder

chooses this option, the drawee's acceptance is canceled. Alternatively, the holder may assent to the variance. In this case, each drawer and indorser who does not agree to the variance is discharged. Thus, if Tony acquiesces in Larry's altered acceptance, Tony has no recourse against Polly or Denise if Larry fails to pay the instrument when due.

Secondary Liability

Nature of Secondary Contract Liability

Upon signing, the maker of a note or acceptor of a draft undertakes primary liability, an absolute obligation to pay the instrument. In contrast, the drawer of a check or other draft and the indorser of any instrument assume only secondary contract liability, promising to pay only if the primary party does not. By virtue of their signatures, drawers and indorsers effectively make the following promise to every later holder of the instrument: "Present this instrument to the party primarily liable. If he or she doesn't pay (or accept) it, and you notify me of that fact, then I will pay the instrument." Note that the person who draws or indorses "without recourse" (a "qualified" indorsement) effectively negates this secondary contract obligation. A qualified indorser therefore assumes no liability to pay the instrument if the primary party does not.

Order of Liability. Frequently, more than one person assumes secondary contract liability on an instrument. For example, a check is signed by the drawer and is usually indorsed by the payee. Both notes and drafts often change hands before payment, requiring a number of indorsements. In such cases, the order of liability among those secondarily liable must be determined. Section 3-414(2) states that indorsers are liable to each other in the order in which they indorse, which is presumed to be the order in which their names appear on the instrument. Assume Mark issues a $1,000 promissory note payable to Paul's order in one year. The note is subsequently negotiated several times resulting in the following indorsements on the back (see Figure 25–3). Ed, the last holder of the instrument, presents it on the due date to Mark, who refuses to pay it. In this situation, assuming Ed properly notifies them, Dave, Charles, Barbara,

---

4. As developed in the next chapter, however, Art has recourse against Harry and Peter based upon their "warranty" liability on the instrument.

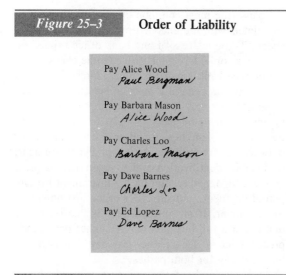

Figure 25–3   **Order of Liability**

Pay Alice Wood
Paul Bergman

Pay Barbara Mason
Alice Wood

Pay Charles Loo
Barbara Mason

Pay Dave Barnes
Charles Loo

Pay Ed Lopez
Dave Barnes

Alice, and Paul as indorsers all have secondary contract liability and are liable to Ed in the amount of the note. Ed is not, however, entitled to collect $5,000 ($1,000 each from Dave, Charles, Barbara, Alice, and Paul). The parties are liable successively in the order in which they sign. That is, if Ed collects $1,000 from Dave, Dave could collect $1,000 from Charles, who could collect $1,000 from Barbara, who could collect $1,000 from Alice, who would finally recover $1,000 from Paul. Thus the ultimate loss from Mark's dishonor falls upon Paul assuming he is solvent. If not, the loss falls upon Alice, and so on. Note that in the case of a check or other draft an additional secondary party, the drawer, is present. Thus, the payee of a draft has recourse against the drawer. In sum, assuming the solvency of all parties, the ultimate loss upon dishonor by the primary party falls upon the payee of a note and the drawer of a check or other draft.

Conditions Precedent

As noted above, secondary liability is conditional, not absolute. The **conditions precedent** to secondary contract liability are:

1. *presentment* to the primary party,
2. *dishonor* by the primary party, and
3. *notice of dishonor* to the secondary parties.

The Code prescribes clear time limits within which presentment to the primary party must be made and notice of dishonor must be given. An unexcused[5] delay in presentment or notice absolutely discharges all *indorsers* from any liability on the instrument.

Presentment. Before secondary liability can be imposed, the primary party must first be given the opportunity to accept or pay the instrument. This is accomplished by **presentment,** defined in §3-504(1) as a demand for payment or acceptance made by the holder upon the maker, acceptor, or drawee. An instrument may be presented for payment (to the maker of a note or drawee of a draft) or for acceptance (to the drawee of a time draft).

Time of Presentment—Time Instruments. The time of presentment, governed by §3-503, depends upon the nature of the instrument. A time instrument must generally be presented on the date on which it is payable. For example, a promissory note, due by its terms on June 1, 1984, must be presented to the maker on that date. If a draft is payable after acceptance—for example, payable "30 days after acceptance"—it must be presented to the drawee for acceptance within a reasonable time after it is drawn. Similarly, if an instrument such as a promissory note is accelerated, it must be presented for payment within a reasonable time after acceleration.

Time of Presentment—Checks and Other Demand Instruments. If a demand instrument is involved, presentment must be made within a reasonable time after the drawer or indorser signs the instrument. Ordinarily, what constitutes a reasonable time for presentment varies depending upon the nature of the instrument, any banking or trade usage, and the particular facts of the case. For the

---

5. The UCC, in §3-511, lists various situations in which a secondary party remains liable despite noncompliance or delay in compliance with the conditions precedent. For example, the drawer or indorser may waive the requirements. A waiver of presentment or notice may be embodied in the instrument itself or may be written above the signature of an indorser. In the former case the waiver is binding upon all secondary parties; in the latter, it is binding only upon the particular indorser.

most common demand instrument, an ordinary check, the following are presumed to be reasonable periods within which to present the instrument for payment or initiate the bank collection process. In order to hold the drawer liable, presentment must be made within thirty days after issue or the date of the instrument, whichever is later. To hold an indorser liable, presentment must be made within seven days after his indorsement. To illustrate, assume that on January 1, Don draws a check payable to Pat's order in payment for a television set purchased from Pat. On January 5, Pat indorses and negotiates the check to Catherine. On January 10, she indorses and negotiates the check to Albert. On January 15, he presents the check to the drawee bank. The bank refuses payment because Don has no money in his account. On these facts, the holder, Albert, will proceed against the indorsers, Pat and Catherine, and the drawer, Don, on their secondary contract liability. Catherine is liable because presentment was made within seven days after her signature. Pat, however, is discharged because presentment was not made within seven days after his signature. Don is liable because presentment was made within thirty days after the date of the check.

Note that in most cases Don, the drawer, would remain liable even if presentment is delayed beyond the 30-day period. Section 3-502(1)(b) provides that the *drawer* is discharged by a delay in presentment only if the failure or other insolvency of the drawee bank causes the drawer to lose funds on deposit that would have been available to pay the instrument had it been properly presented. In most cases, therefore, the drawer of a check is not relieved of secondary contract liability because of the holder's delay in presentment.

Manner of Presentment. Presentment may be made in person or by the mails, or in the case of ordinary checks, through normal banking channels. The instrument generally must be presented at the place specified in it, such as a bank or place of business. If no place is stated, presentment should be made at the place of business or residence of the party to accept or pay. Federal Reserve regulations specify that for ordinary checks the drawee bank must accept presentment of checks at: 1) a location, including a check processing center, requested by

the bank (the most common case); 2) a bank office associated with the encoded routing number on the check; 3) the address of any bank office printed on the check; or 4) any bank office, if the check states the drawee bank's name without address.[6]

Instruments generally must be presented at a reasonable hour and, if at a bank, presentment must be made when the bank is open to the public to conduct its banking functions. The maker or drawee may require exhibition of the instrument, reasonable identification of the person making presentment, a signed receipt on the instrument for any partial payment, and surrender of the instrument on full payment. If any presentment is due on a day that is not a full business day for either party, then presentment is due on the next day that is a full business day for both parties.[7]

At issue in the following case was whether a proper presentment had been made.

Estate of Kohlhepp v. Mason
478 P.2d 339 (Utah 1970)

Hannah Kohlhepp died leaving a will that granted appellant Hal Mason the right to purchase her farm for $10,000. Although Mason notified the executor of the estate that he intended to exercise the option, payment was delayed several times because of problems encountered by Mason's lender, Financial Service Company. Finally, the court ordered that unless Mason delivered the $10,000 by 5:00 P.M. on Friday, November 7, 1969, his option to purchase would terminate. On the afternoon of November 7, Financial Service Company deposited a check for $10,000 with the clerk of the court.

The following Monday the executor's secretary picked up the check from the court and, with the attorney representing one of the heirs of the estate, visited the bank on which the check was drawn. They asked the vice-president of the bank whether the check could be paid if it were presented for pay-

---

6. 12 C.F.R. §229.36(b).
7. See UCC §§3-503(3)-(4), 3-504(2), 3-505(1), 4-104(1)(c).

ment. The vice-president said it would not and put the notation "Drawn against uncollected funds" on the check. The secretary then delivered a photocopy of the check to the executor who notified Mason and the court that the option had expired because the bank had refused to pay the check. Upon petition of the executor, the court held that the option had terminated because the check deposited with the court was unacceptable to the bank. Mason appealed.

Callister, Justice

. . . In the instant action, has the check ever been presented for payment? The check was drawn to the order of "Mervin E. Holt Executor for the estate of Hannah Kohlhepp."

Presentment is a demand for acceptance or *payment made upon* the maker, acceptor, *drawee* or other payor *by or on behalf of the holder.* [UCC §3-504(1)]

"Holder" means a person who is in possession of a document of title or an instrument or an investment security drawn, issued or endorsed to him or his order or to bearer or in blank. [UCC §1-201(20)]

Executor Holt testified that he has neither had possession of the check nor presented it for payment or deposit. He further stated that his instructions to his secretary were to go pick up the check so that he might endorse it and present it for payment. There is no evidence in the record whereby he authorized his secretary or Mr. Mann to demand payment of the check on his behalf, and neither of the parties who went to the bank occupied the status of a holder under [UCC §1-201(20)].

A check does not itself operate as an assignment of any funds in the bank, [UCC §3-409(1)], but suspends the underlying obligation until the instrument is presented, [UCC §3-802(1)(b)]. . . . The drawer's contract is that he will pay the amount of an uncertified check upon dishonor and notice thereof, [UCC §3-413(2)]. Under the foregoing provisions a check is not payment until presented and paid, unless the parties agree otherwise. Since the court and the executor did not agree otherwise, we must conclude that the check was not a payment at the time of deposit [with the clerk of the court], but a promise of future payment at the time of presentation. The trial court erred when it concluded that the check was not payment in accordance with

its order because the payee had never presented the check and demanded payment.

This cause is reversed and remanded to the district court with an order to give devisee, Mason, a reasonable time in which to pay the $10,000.

[Judgment reversed and remanded.]

Dishonor. A **dishonor** occurs when, after proper presentment, the drawee or maker refuses to pay an instrument presented for payment or the drawee refuses to accept an instrument presented for acceptance. In the case of a check, the following notations stamped or printed on the instrument indicate dishonor: "not sufficient funds" (NSF), "account garnished," "no account," "account closed," or "payment stopped." A bank does not dishonor a check by returning it because: (1) the drawer's signature or an indorsement is missing, illegible, or forged, (2) the instrument has been altered, (3) the check is postdated and presented before that date, or (4) the instrument is presented to the wrong bank.

Section 3-506 provides that the drawee or maker need not accept or pay the instrument immediately upon presentment. If the instrument is presented for acceptance, the drawee may defer acceptance without dishonor until the close of the next business day following presentment. In addition, the holder in a good faith effort to obtain acceptance may allow the drawee an additional business day to accept. Such an extension is not a dishonor of the instrument and therefore does not discharge the secondary parties to it, such as the drawer or prior indorsers. Suppose Winston is the payee of a draft drawn upon Cook by Daley, the drawer. The instrument is dated June 1, and is payable "30 days after acceptance." Winston presents to Cook for acceptance on June 3, a Monday. Cook has until the close of business Tuesday to accept or refuse to accept (dishonor). Winston *may* allow Cook until the close of business Wednesday to accept without discharging the secondary party, Daley.

If the instrument is presented for payment, the drawee or maker must act within a much shorter time to avoid dishonor. Although payment may be deferred pending examination of the instrument, payment must ultimately be made before the close of business on the day of presentment. A longer time is allowed for acceptance than for payment because acceptance is sought merely to secure the drawee's undertaking to pay and fix the final date of payment. A holder presenting for payment expects immediate satisfaction of the instrument.

Notice of Dishonor. Upon dishonor, the holder has an immediate right to sue any person primarily liable on the instrument (the maker of a note or the acceptor of a draft) and also has immediate recourse against all secondary parties (drawers and indorsers). The holder, therefore, need not pursue the primary party first, but may elect to proceed directly against the secondary parties. Indeed, in an ordinary check, no one has primary liability, meaning that the holder's only recourse is against secondary parties.

Time of Notice. To hold the secondary parties liable, however, they must be given timely notice that the instrument has been dishonored. **Notice of dishonor,** governed by §3-508, may be given to any person liable on the instrument by or on behalf of: (1) the holder, (2) any party who has received notice, or (3) any other party who can be compelled to pay the instrument. A proper notice benefits all parties with rights on the instrument against the party notified. That is, anyone who may be required to pay the instrument may notify anyone who may be liable upon it.

Under the UCC, if given by a bank, notice must be given by the bank's **midnight deadline,** meaning midnight of the next banking day following dishonor or receipt of notice of dishonor. For ordinary checks, however, Federal Reserve regulations discussed in Chapter 27 require the drawee and other banks in the collection process to notify the depositary bank of dishonor within generally a much shorter period. If given by a person other than a bank, notice must be given before midnight of the third business day after dishonor or receipt of notice of dishonor.

For example, assume a note originally payable to Paul containing the following indorsements has been presented by Don and dishonored by the maker (see Figure 25–4). Because indorsers are secondarily liable in the order in which they sign, Don may recover from Carl, who may recover

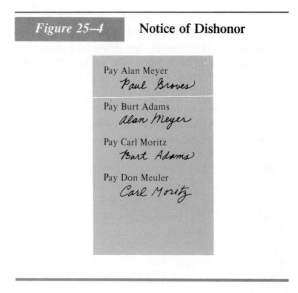

| Figure 25–4 | **Notice of Dishonor** |

Pay Alan Meyer
Paul Broves

Pay Burt Adams
Alan Meyer

Pay Carl Moritz
Burt Adams

Pay Don Meuler
Carl Moritz

from Burt, who may recover from Alan, who may recover from Paul. Assuming all parties are nonbanks, Don has three business days after dishonor to notify Carl, who has three more days to notify Burt, and so on.

Although Don may be protected merely by notifying his immediate transferor, Carl, Don should notify all persons having secondary liability on the instrument (drawers and indorsers). In this manner, Don, the only person who has not yet been paid, assures that the conditions precedent are satisfied against all parties potentially liable to him. In this manner the bankruptcy or inability to locate one indorser will not affect his rights against the others. To illustrate, using the preceding example, assume Don merely notifies Carl. Carl flees the jurisdiction to avoid paying Don (or is bankrupt) without notifying Burt, Alan, or Paul. Because Burt, Alan, and Paul have not received notice, their secondary contract liability is discharged, leaving Don to proceed only against the maker, who also may be bankrupt or have a valid defense to payment. By giving proper notice himself to all secondary parties, Don has the potential liability of Alan, Burt, Carl, and Paul. In short, upon dishonor, the holder is well advised to notify all secondary parties.

Manner of Notice; Protest. Generally, notice of dishonor may be given in any reasonable manner. It may be oral or written (including a stamp or other notation on the instrument) simply identifying the instrument and stating that it has been dishonored. A written notice is effective when properly sent, even if never received.

Although informal notice is usually sufficient, occasionally a formal "protest" is required. Under §3-509(1), a **protest** is a certificate of dishonor signed and sealed by a United States consul or vice consul, a notary public, or any other person authorized by local law to certify dishonor.

Under §3-501(3), a protest is required only upon dishonor of a draft drawn or payable outside the United States. It is therefore never necessary for notes and only infrequently required for an ordinary check. For example, a protest would be required upon dishonor of a draft drawn in Chicago upon a drawee in Montreal.

A protest facilitates proof of dishonor in a subsequent lawsuit on the instrument. Thus, a protest may be advantageous to the holder of either a foreign or domestic instrument. For this reason, optional protest of any instrument is authorized by the Code, whether or not legally required. If protest is required, however, failure to protest within the prescribed time discharges both the drawer and the indorsers without a showing of injury.[8]

Effect of Certification on Secondary Liability

As previously noted, a bank has no obligation to a holder either to pay or to certify a check. If the bank does certify, however, the liability of secondary parties to the instrument may be affected. Under §3-411(1), if the *drawer* procures the certification, his or her secondary liability on the instrument is unaffected. If, however, a holder procures the certification, the drawer and all prior indorsers are discharged. Assume Diane draws a check on First Bank made payable to Pat and has it certified by the bank before giving it to Pat in payment for a house. The bank is primarily liable and Diane is secondarily liable on the check. Assume, alternatively, that Diane draws a check on

First Bank payable to Pat's order. Pat negotiates the check to Hal. Hal takes the check to First Bank and requests certification. First Bank, although under no obligation to do so, certifies the check. In this case, the bank is primarily liable on the instrument, and Pat and Diane are discharged. That is, Pat and Diane have no liability to Hal or a later holder if First Bank subsequently fails to pay.

Accommodation Parties and Guarantors

Contract of Accommodation Party

The concept of "security" underlies much of the law governing debtor-creditor relations. In a typical security arrangement, a creditor loans money or sells goods on credit to a debtor. At the creditor's request, the debtor's promise to pay is backed by some form of security, providing the creditor an independent source of payment if the debtor defaults. One important type of security device is a suretyship arrangement, discussed in Chapter 33, under which a person known as a "surety" undertakes to satisfy the obligation if the debtor does not. The essence of suretyship is that although both the surety and principal debtor are liable to the creditor, the debtor, not the surety, should pay. Thus, under general suretyship principles, a surety who is required to pay the creditor is entitled to full reimbursement from the debtor.

Parties to commercial paper undertake a contractual obligation to pay money. That obligation, like any other, may be backed by a surety's promise. A surety on commercial paper is referred to as an **accommodation party**, which is simply defined in §3-415(1) as a person who signs an instrument in any capacity (maker, indorser, acceptor) for the purpose of lending his name or credit to another party to the instrument. Thus, an accommodation party is simply a surety whose obligation is on the instrument itself, guaranteeing the performance of another party to the paper, the accommodated party. The liability of the accommodation party is, therefore, determined by the capacity in which he signs the instrument. For example, an accommodation maker or acceptor assumes primary contract liability on the instrument. An accommodation indorser is liable only after the conditions precedent—presentment, dishonor, and notice of dis-

---

8. UCC §3-502(2); this rule differs from the general rule that a drawer is discharged through failure of the conditions precedent only if actual loss results.

honor—are met. Section 3-415(5), however, follows general suretyship principles by providing that the accommodation party has no liability to the party accommodated, and if required to pay, has a right of recourse on the instrument against that party.

To illustrate, assume Mary purchases a car from Rod and proposes to pay for it by issuing a promissory note. Because Mary's credit rating is not good, Rod refuses to take her note unless she obtains a surety. Mary convinces her father, Fred, to act as an accommodation party. Fred could sign as an accommodation maker, as shown in Figure 25–5. In this case Fred is liable as a maker. When the instrument is due, Rod may present it to either Mary or Fred for payment. If Fred pays, he may recover $1,000 from Mary (if she is solvent). If Mary pays, she is entitled to nothing from Fred. That is, Fred as an accommodation party is not liable to the party accommodated, Mary.[9]

Alternatively, Fred may sign as an accommodation indorser, as in Figure 25–6. In this case, Fred is liable as an indorser. That is, to hold Fred, Rod must present the instrument to Mary on the due date, and if it is dishonored must give Fred timely notice of dishonor. Note that in this case Fred's indorsement is not in the chain of title. That is, his signature is not necessary to negotiate the instrument; Rod's is. Section 3-415(4) provides that such an **irregular** or **anomalous indorsement** is notice to later holders of its accommodation status, even though it contains no additional words of description. Once again, if Fred is required to pay he may recover the amount paid from Mary.

Contract of Guarantor

Occasionally, a party will sign an instrument, usually as maker or indorser of a note, adding specific words of guaranty, such as "payment guaranteed" or "collection guaranteed." The legal effect of this

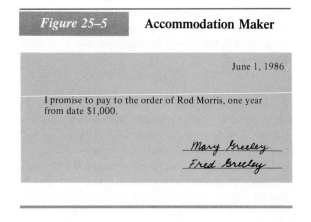

Figure 25–5   **Accommodation Maker**

June 1, 1986

I promise to pay to the order of Rod Morris, one year from date $1,000.

Mary Greeley
Fred Greeley

language is stated in §3-416. A person who adds the words **payment guaranteed** to her signature promises that if the instrument is not paid when due that she will pay it without resort by the holder to any other party. **Collection guaranteed** added to a signature is a more limited undertaking, meaning that if the instrument is not paid when due, the signer will pay it but only if (1) the holder has reduced her claim against the maker or acceptor to judgment, and that execution on the judgment has

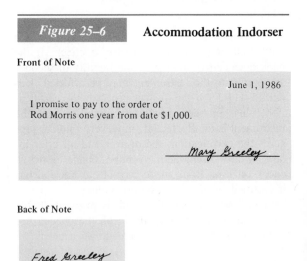

Figure 25–6   **Accommodation Indorser**

Front of Note

June 1, 1986

I promise to pay to the order of Rod Morris one year from date $1,000.

Mary Greeley

Back of Note

Fred Greeley

---

9. Note that ordinary co-makers are jointly and severally liable. A joint and several promisor is entitled to contribution from the others upon paying more than his proportionate share. Thus if Mary and Fred were ordinary co-makers, not principal and surety, one who pays the entire amount is entitled to $500 in contribution from the other. Joint and several liability and its relationship to suretyship is discussed in Chapter 33.

been returned unsatisfied, or (2) the maker or acceptor is insolvent or it is otherwise apparent that it is useless to proceed against her. Words of guarantee that do not otherwise specify, such as "I guarantee the instrument," guarantee payment. In sum, whereas a person guaranteeing payment is liable immediately upon default, the guarantor of collection is liable only after the holder exhausts all legal remedies against the primary party.

Words of guaranty added to the signature of a sole maker or acceptor have no effect upon his liability. For example, assume Jones issues a note payable to Paul's order. Jones's liability is the same whether he signs the instrument "Jones" or "Jones, payment guaranteed." If words of guaranty (payment or collection) are used in an indorsement, the conditions precedent to secondary contract liability, presentment, and notice of dishonor or protest are waived. Thus, a person who indorses a note "payment guaranteed" is essentially liable as a co-maker. A "collection guaranteed" indorser waives the benefit of conditions precedent, but is not liable until all attempts to collect from the maker have proven futile.

The following case illustrates the critical distinction between a guarantor and an accommodation party.

First National Bank of Ceredo v. Linn
282 S.E.2d 52 (W. Va. 1981)

Karl and Linda Estep purchased a trailer from P & S Trailer Sales, Inc. (P & S Trailer) and executed a promissory note payable to P & S Trailer. P & S Trailer sold the note to appellant First National Bank of Ceredo, which agreed to purchase the note only if it was indorsed by P & S Trailer and two of its officers, appellees George Linn and Harry F. Thompson, Jr. Therefore, the following was added to the note prior to the assignment to the bank:

WITH RECOURSE

Seller guarantees payment of the amount due on said contract as and when the same shall become due, waiving any extension of time made by LENDER and agrees to repurchase said contract at any time upon demand after any default by Buyer. Seller waives notice of acceptance of this guaranty and notices of nonpayment and nonperformance.

> P & S Trailer Sales, Inc.
> Seller
>
> By /s/ George Linn
> Its *President*
>
> /s/ George Linn
> /s/ Harry F. Thompson, Jr.

Subsequently, the Esteps defaulted on the note and P & S Trailer went out of business. The bank sued Linn and Thompson. The trial court ruled in favor of Linn and Thompson; First National Bank of Ceredo appealed.

Miller, Justice

This appeal involves the application of certain principles set out in our Uniform Commercial Code to determine whether the appellees, Messrs. Linn and Thompson, were indorsers under . . . §3-414 or guarantors under . . . §3-416. The resolution of appellees' standing determines their liability on a note since the appellant, First National Bank of Ceredo (Bank), failed to give them notice of dishonor after the primary obligor did not pay on the note. The requirement of notice of dishonor is necessary to affix liability on an indorser but is not required for guarantors of an instrument. . . .

Despite the acknowledgement that the language in the "With Recourse" paragraph is that of guaranty, we do not believe that Linn and Thompson became guarantors for two reasons. First, the language in the guaranty paragraph speaks solely of the "Seller." The Seller is clearly identified in other portions of the document as P & S Trailer, and, of course, from a factual standpoint, it was the seller of the trailer. . . .

A second factor involved in this case is what is known as the presumption of indorsement arising from [UCC §3-402]: "Unless the instrument clearly indicates that a signature is made in some other capacity it is an indorsement."

. . . In the present case, it is clear that the Esteps, as buyers of the trailer with an unpaid balance due on the purchase price, were the makers of the note. The payee of the note was P & S Trailer. Linn and Thompson's signatures do not appear on the face of the note but follow the "With Recourse" signature of P & S. Trailer, which corporate signature followed the corporate guaranty made at the time P & S Trailer transferred the note to the Bank. We have previously pointed out that the guaranty language was narrowly drawn to encompass only the Seller, P & S Trailer. Consequently, in view of the limited language in the guaranty provision, we cannot say . . . that there is a clear indication that Linn and Thompson signed as guarantors. As a result, under this statute, they are deemed indorsers. . . .

Once Linn and Thompson's status is established as indorsers, it is clear from [UCC §3-414(1)], that upon dishonor they were required to be given the necessary notice of dishonor. . . .

From a purely technical standpoint, Linn and Thompson were accommodation indorsers by virtue of [UCC §3-415(4)] relating to the contract of an accommodation party which states: "An indorsement which shows that it is not in the chain of title is notice of its accommodation character." . . . Here, Linn and Thompson were neither makers nor payees of the note; therefore, their signatures were not necessary to transfer title of the note to the Bank. Thus, they were not in the chain of title to the note and are accommodation indorsers. . . .

Their status as accommodation indorsers does not change their obligation as indorsers and, as we have previously discussed, an indorser is not liable unless there is presentment, notice of dishonor and protest. Had the Bank upon the default in the monthly payments by the makers, the Esteps, given notice to Linn and Thompson of the default and made demand for their payment, the result in this case would have been different. With such notice of default and demand for payment, Linn and Thompson could have then proceeded to make the monthly payments instead of being confronted, as here, at a later time with the entire deficiency balance due. One of the reasons for requiring such notification to a party secondarily liable, such as an indorser, is to enable him to assume the payments rather than be held accountable for the entire unpaid obligation. The contract of an indorser is that he "engages that upon dishonor and any necessary notice of dishonor . . . he will pay the instrument *according to its tenor*." [UCC §3-414] (Emphasis added)

The trial court was correct in holding Linn and

Thompson not liable since no notice of dishonor was given them and its judgment is, therefore, affirmed.

[Judgment affirmed.]

Effect of Instrument on Underlying Obligation

Whether commercial paper liability is primary or secondary, subsequent events, usually proper payment of the instrument, discharge it. Other circumstances, discussed throughout this and the next chapter, that extinguish a party's liability include, for example, fraudulent and material alteration, certification of a check, acceptance varying a draft, and unexcused delay in presentment or notice of dishonor or protest. An additional discharge issue, relevant in lawsuits regarding negotiable instruments, concerns the effect of an instrument on the obligation for which it is given. Notes and checks are given, for example, in exchange for loans of money or sales of goods or services. The effect of the negotiable contract (the note or check) on the "underlying contract" (for example, the sale of goods or services) must therefore be carefully noted.

Generally speaking, a check or other negotiable instrument is treated as **conditional payment**. This means that the payee, by taking the instrument, surrenders the right to sue on the underlying obligation until the instrument is due. If the instrument is not paid when due, the right to sue on the underlying obligation is "revived," and the holder is given the option to sue either on the instrument (with the relaxed procedural requirements applicable to commercial paper) or on the underlying obligation. Under §3-802, however, if a party to the instrument (such as the drawer of a check) is discharged on the *instrument* for one of the reasons previously noted, he or she is also discharged on the *underlying obligation*.

If a certified check is involved, the conditional payment rule may be altered. As noted earlier in this chapter, if a holder procures certification of a check, the drawer is discharged on the instrument. Thus, upon certification of the check the original obligation is treated as paid and the holder's only recourse is against the bank, not the drawer. Suppose Dick draws a $1,000 check on First Bank payable to Art to pay for a car sold by Art to Dick. Art takes the check to First Bank, which certifies it. Dick is discharged on the instrument and upon the underlying obligation to pay for the car. Thus, if Art is subsequently unable to collect from the bank—for example, due to bank failure—Art has no recourse against Dick.

SUMMARY

1. Negotiable instruments under Article 3 are formal contracts requiring a payment of money. Contract liability is imposed when a person signs the instrument as (1) the maker of a note, (2) the drawer of a check or other draft, (3) the acceptor of a check or other draft, or (4) an indorser of any instrument. Any signature in an ambiguous capacity is an indorsement.

2. Contract liability on commercial paper is of two general types: primary and secondary. Primary liability is undertaken by the maker of a note and the acceptor of a draft. These parties undertake an absolute obligation to pay the instrument. The maker of a note promises to pay the instrument according to its terms when signed. The drawee of a draft assumes primary liability upon it by acceptance, making the drawee an acceptor. Prior to acceptance no one has primary liability on a draft. Because a check is a demand instrument, it is generally presented to the drawee bank only once—for payment. The bank may, however, accept the check, thereby undertaking an absolute obligation to pay. Such an acceptance is known as "certification."

3. Secondary contract liability is undertaken by the drawer of a check or other draft and the indorser of any instrument. These secondary parties agree to pay the instrument if the primary party does not, provided certain "conditions precedent" to that liability are met. The conditions precedent are presentment of the instrument to the primary party, dishonor of the instrument by that party, and notice of dishonor to the secondary parties. Article 3 prescribes explicit time limits within which presentment and notice must be made. Although no particular formalities for notice of dishonor are generally imposed, a formal certificate of dishonor known as a "protest" is required for drafts drawn or payable outside the United States. If more than one person assumes secondary liability, the parties are liable in the order in which they sign, which is presumed to be the order in which their names appear on the instrument.

4. Occasionally, a person signs an instrument in order to lend his name or credit to another party to the instrument. Such an "accommodation party" is liable in the capacity in which he signs (for example, as a maker, acceptor, drawer, or indorser), but under general suretyship principles is not liable to the party accommodated. Thus, an accommodation party who is required to pay is entitled to reimbursement from the party accommodated. In addition to outlining the general liability of an accommodation party, Article 3 also governs the legal effect of words of guaranty added to a signature such as "payment guaranteed" and "collection guaranteed."

5. A check or other negotiable instrument ordinarily operates as a conditional payment. This means that the payee, by taking the instrument, surrenders the right to sue on the underlying obligation until the instrument is due. If not paid when due, the holder may sue either on the instrument or on the underlying debt.

KEY TERMS

primary liability	dishonor
secondary liability	notice of dishonor
acceptance	midnight deadline
acceptor	protest
demand draft	accommodation party
time draft	irregular (anomalous)
sight draft	indorsement
certification	payment guaranteed
conditions precedent	collection guaranteed
presentment	conditional payment

QUESTIONS AND PROBLEMS

25-1 A signature on an instrument in an ambiguous capacity is always treated as an indorsement. What is the purpose of this rule?

25-2 Simpson Co. recently hired efficiency experts to help increase company profits. The experts discovered that Simpson was holding several overdue promissory notes. Management reported that it had never tried to collect the notes and had not even asked the makers for payment. One of the notes read:

> January 1, 1964
>
> I hereby promise to pay $50,000 to the order of Simpson Co. on December 1, 1964, with interest at 4% per annum.
>
> /s/ Peter Potts
> /s/ Willie Wilson

The efficiency experts are able to locate Willie Wilson and recommend that Simpson sue him.

(a) Who is the maker of the note? In what capacity has Willie Wilson signed?

(b) Willie argues that he is an indorser of the note but Simpson argues that he is a maker. What difference would it make whether Willie signed as maker or indorser?

25-3 Mr. Carl's Fashion, Inc. was a Texas corporation that operated beauty salons. Carl Nichols was the president of Mr. Carl's Fashion, Inc. Seale Enterprises loaned $10,000 for improvements to one of the beauty salons in return for a promissory note that was signed as follows:

Carl V. Nichols (typewritten)

/s/ Carl V. Nichols (handwritten)

No payments were made on the note so Seale sued Carl Nichols.

(a) Carl alleges that he signed the note in his representative capacity as president of Mr. Carl's Fashion, Inc. so that he should not be held personally liable. How should the court rule? Explain, citing appropriate Code sections.

(b) The court evidence establishes that Carl and the president of Seale Enterprises discussed the transaction and both believed that Carl was signing in his representative capacity as president of Mr. Carl's Fashion, Inc. How should the court rule? Explain citing appropriate Code sections.

(c) Assume instead that Seale transferred the note to First State Bank, a holder in due course, who sues Carl on the note. The evidence in (b) above was established but First State Bank proves that it was not aware that Carl had signed in his representative capacity. What result? Explain.

25-4 Norton and Keller sold $800 worth of farm equipment to Miles Knapp. Miles orally promised to pay the $800. Because Norton and Keller owed $800 to Exchange Bank, it prepared the following sight draft:

$800   April 18, 1982

At sight pay to the order of Exchange Bank $800, value received and charge to the account of Norton and Keller.

/s/ Norton and Keller

To: Miles Knapp

Exchange Bank presented the draft to Miles Knapp who wrote on the back

Kiss my foot.

/s/ Miles Knapp

When Miles Knapp refused to pay the draft, Norton and Keller sued him. Knapp argued that he could not be held liable on the instrument because he had not contracted to pay anything. Norton and Keller argued that by signing the back of the draft, Knapp had accepted it and could be held contractually liable under §3-413(1). What result? Explain.

25-5 Paula is the chief operating officer of Theta Corp. Theta executed a promissory note payable to First Bank on which Paula personally signed as an accommodation indorser. On the due date First Bank presented the note to Theta which dishonored it. First Bank sued Paula six months later. Paula claimed that she was discharged from liability because the bank had failed to provide notice of dishonor to her. The bank claimed that as president of Theta, Paula knew of the dishonor so that notice was unnecessary. What result? Explain. See §3-511.

25-6 E. J. V. Drywall Co., Inc. (Drywall) issued a promissory note payable to the order of plaintiff Community National Bank in the amount of $9,082.50. A bank officer required Edward J. Varrichione, Drywall's president, to sign the back of the note under the words "Assenting to Terms and Waivers on the Face of this Note." After Drywall defaulted on the note, Community National Bank sued Varrichione alleging that he was an indorser on the note. Varrichione alleged that he had not signed as an indorser but as an accommodation to the bank merely indicating his assent to the terms of the note. Varrichione received none of the proceeds of the note, which were used solely by Drywall.

(a) In what capacity, if any, is Varrichione liable on the instrument? Explain.

(b) Assuming Varrichione is liable, what defenses might he assert?

25-7 Aloysius borrowed $20,000 from and executed a promissory note payable to Second National Bank. Bartholomew and Chauncey agreed to serve as accommodation indorsers. Bartholomew first signed his name to the back of the note, and Chauncey signed immediately thereafter. Aloysius defaulted on the note and Second National Bank sued Bartholomew and Chauncey. Bartholomew argued that the indorsers were jointly and severally liable pursuant to UCC §3-118(e) while Chauncey argued that pursuant to §3-414(2) of the Code, the indorsers were liable in the order in which they signed. Who is correct? Explain.

Chapter 26

Liability of Parties—
Forgery and Alteration

Major Topics

- the legal effect of unauthorized signatures and material alteration
- the presentment and transfer warranties under Article 3
- the legal effect of payment of an instrument bearing forgeries or material alterations

To this point, the discussion of liability of parties has focused on contract liability. This liability, based on a party's signature, determines the responsibility for ultimate payment of the instrument and the relationship among the various parties liable. The material in this chapter addresses a significant problem in commercial paper analysis: the effects of forged or otherwise unauthorized signatures and of material alteration of an instrument. In most cases, the party responsible for the forgery or alteration has disappeared, or is insolvent, or is in jail, or otherwise cannot be held accountable for such actions. The law is therefore primarily concerned with resolving disputes among the various innocent parties affected by the wrongdoer's conduct.

Basic Concepts of Forgery and Alteration

To understand Article 3's approach to the forgery and alteration problem, one must be familiar with three basic concepts: (1) the definition and effect of an unauthorized signature, (2) the definition and ef-

fect of a material alteration, and (3) the content and effect of the presentment and transfer "warranties."

Unauthorized Signatures

Effect of Unauthorized Signature. Signatures determine the contract liability of all parties to the instrument and also are often essential to transfer (negotiate) the instrument. Unfortunately, forged or otherwise unauthorized signatures are commonplace in commercial paper transactions, requiring the law to address specifically the effect of the "unauthorized" signature.

As discussed in Chapter 24, an "unauthorized signature" includes both an outright forgery and a signature affixed by an agent exceeding his or her authority. Any unauthorized signature is legally effective as the signature of the unauthorized signer in favor of any person who in good faith pays the instrument or takes it for value. It is wholly ineffective as the signature of the person whose name is signed. Suppose Faye forges Mary's signature as maker of a note payable to Paul. Mary has no liability on the instrument; Faye is liable on it as a maker.

Forged Drawer's or Maker's Signature and Forged Indorsement. It is important to distinguish between the legal effect of a forged drawer's or maker's signature (illustrated above) and a forged indorsement. When a drawer's or maker's signature is forged, a valid negotiable instrument is created. The unauthorized signer, however, not the person whose name is signed, is the maker or drawer of the instrument. It therefore follows that the payee and subsequent transferees may be holders of the instrument, and if they qualify, holders in due course.

A forged indorsement, however, presents an entirely different situation. To illustrate, assume Dan draws a check payable to the order of Jean. The check is stolen by Sue who forges Jean's indorsement on the back and delivers the instrument to Cal who cashes it without knowledge of the forgery. Sue's signature in Jean's name is wholly inoperative as Jean's signature, but is wholly effective as Sue's signature. The instrument is, however, payable to Jean's order, requiring Jean's, not Sue's, signature (indorsement) for further negotiation. Thus, Sue's signature in Jean's name is ineffective to negotiate the instrument, and neither Cal nor any subsequent transferee from or after Cal becomes a holder of the instrument. Because there can be no holders after forgery of Jean's signature, there also can be no holders in due course.

In sum, although there may be holders and holders in due course of an instrument on which the *drawer's or maker's* signature is forged, there can be no holder or holder in due course after forgery of any *indorsement* necessary to negotiate the instrument. The liability of parties in both forgery situations is discussed later in this chapter.

Effect of Material Alteration

As noted in Chapter 24, under §3-407(1) an instrument is altered when the holder changes its terms, and a material alteration is one that changes the contract of any party to the instrument in any respect. Material alterations may change the number or relation of the parties, or add to or remove any part of the original signed writing. Examples include changing the name of the payee or the date or place the instrument is payable and, most often, raising the amount payable. Under §3-407(2)(a), a fraudulent material alteration by the holder of an instrument generally discharges any party whose contract is thereby changed. If, however, an altered instrument is negotiated to a holder in due course, the holder in due course may always enforce the instrument according to its original terms. Assume

that June issues a $100 note payable to Sam's order. Sam alters the instrument by raising the amount to $1,000 and negotiates it to Harold. If Harold is not a holder in due course, June is completely discharged on the instrument; that is, June has no liability either to Sam or Harold. If Harold is a holder in due course, June is liable to him for the original amount of the instrument, $100.[1]

Warranties on Presentment and Transfer

In addition to secondary *contract* liability, various holders of commercial paper have *warranty* liability on the instrument. Whereas contract liability is based upon a party's signature, warranty liability is imposed (1) upon *presentment* of the instrument to the primary party for payment or acceptance, and (2) upon any *transfer* of the instrument for consideration. These warranties stated in UCC sections 3-417 and 4-207 are made (1) without regard to the holder's intent, (2) by banks transferring or presenting instruments in the bank collection process and holders who transfer or present an instrument outside that process, and (3) whether the holder transfers the instrument by indorsement and delivery or by delivery alone. Thus, transferors of bearer paper without indorsement incur warranty liability, even though they have no contract liability.

Presentment Warranties. **Presentment warranties** are given *to* the party who is to pay or accept the instrument (including the maker of a note or the drawee or acceptor of a draft) *by* (1) any person presenting the instrument for payment or acceptance, and (2) any prior transferor of the instrument. Assume Molly issues a note payable to Joanne's order. Joanne indorses in blank and delivers the instrument to Walt, who delivers to Sonia, who delivers to Ken, who delivers to Bill. Bill presents the instrument to Molly for payment. Bill, Ken, Sonia, Walt, and Joanne all make three presentment warranties to Molly.

First, a person making a presentment warranty warrants that he or she has good title to the instru-

---

1. Note that an alteration made by a person not a holder (a spoliation) or an immaterial or nonfraudulent alteration does not discharge any party to the instrument. In such cases a later holder, whether or not a holder in due course, may enforce the instrument according to its original tenor. UCC §3-407(2)(b).

ment, meaning that no indorsements on the instrument are forged. Second, the person warrants that he or she has *no knowledge* that the signature of the maker or drawer is forged or otherwise unauthorized. This warranty is not, however, given by a holder in due course acting in good faith to (1) a maker with respect to the maker's own signature, or (2) to a drawer with respect to the drawer's own signature, or (3) to the acceptor of a draft if the holder took the draft after acceptance or obtained acceptance without knowledge that the drawer's signature was unauthorized. In these three cases, the warranty is not given because the party to whom the instrument has been presented is deemed to be in a better position than the holder to verify the signature in question.

The final presentment warranty is that the instrument has not been materially altered. This warranty is not given by a holder in due course acting in good faith to (1) the maker of a note, (2) the drawer of a draft, (3) the acceptor of a draft regarding an alteration made prior to acceptance if the holder took after acceptance, or (4) the acceptor of a draft regarding an alteration made after acceptance. The rationale for these exceptions is, once again, that the holder in due course should not be required to make warranties regarding information that should be readily available to the party to whom presentment is made.

Transfer Warranties. Unlike the presentment warranties, which run to the primary party on the instrument, **transfer warranties** run *to* the various holders or other transferees of the instrument and are given *by* any person who transfers an instrument for consideration. Such a transferor warrants that

1. he or she has good title to the instrument, and
2. all signatures are genuine or authorized, and
3. the instrument has not been materially altered, and
4. no defense of any party is good against the transferor, and
5. he or she has no knowledge of any insolvency proceeding (for example, bankruptcy) pending against the maker or acceptor or the drawer of an unaccepted draft.

If the transfer is by indorsement, these warranties run from the transferor to all later holders of the instrument. If the transfer is made by delivery alone—for example, when the instrument is in bearer form—the warranties run only to the immediate transferee. Therefore, even though a transferor of bearer paper has no contract liability, because his signature does not appear on the instrument, he does have warranty liability. This liability extends, however, only to an immediate transferee, not to all later holders of the instrument. For example, assume Marge issues a note payable to Pam's order. Pam indorses the note specially to Quincy, who indorses specially to Robert. Robert indorses the instrument in blank and delivers it to Sally, who delivers it to Ted, who delivers it to Una, who presents the note to Marge. These transactions are summarized in Figure 26–1.

In this situation, because Pam, Quincy, and Robert transferred by indorsement, their transfer warranties run to every subsequent holder of the instrument; Pam's run to Quincy, Robert, Sally, Ted, and Una; Quincy's run to Robert, Sally, Ted, and Una; and Robert's run to Sally, Ted, and Una. The warranties of the later holders, because transfer occurred by delivery alone, run only to immediate transferees. Thus, Sally's warranties run only to Ted; and Ted's run only to Una. Thus, the final holder, Una, has the benefit of warranties running from Ted, Robert, Quincy, and Pam. Of course, Una is entitled to only one recovery, and assuming the warranties are breached (for example, Marge's signature is a forgery), the warrantors are liable in

---

Figure 26–1   **Transfer Warranty**

Back of Instrument

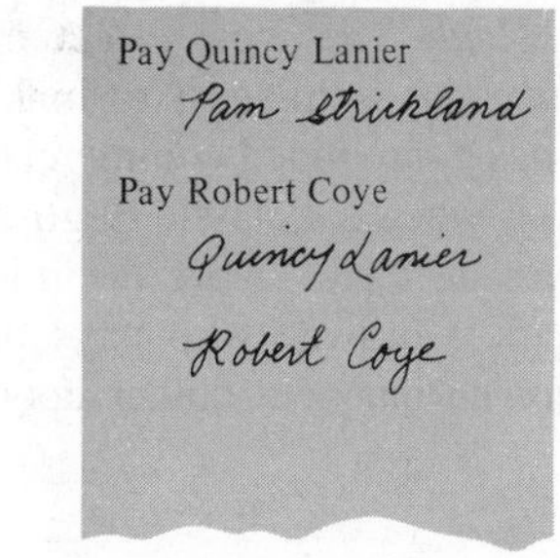

Pay Quincy Lanier
Pam Strickland

Pay Robert Coye
Quincy Lanier

Robert Coye

Robert then delivers to Sally who delivers to Ted who delivers to Una who presents the note to Marge

the order in which they transferred. For example, if Una recovered from Ted, Ted might proceed against Sally, who could proceed against Robert, who could recover from Quincy, who could recover from Pam.

If an indorser signs "without recourse," a qualified indorsement, all transfer warranties remain the same, except that the fourth warranty is changed from an absolute promise that no defense is good against her to a more limited warranty that she has *no knowledge* of such a defense. Therefore, even though a "without recourse" indorsement negates secondary contract liability, it has only a very limited effect upon the indorser's transfer warranties.

The transferor does not warrant that the primary party is solvent. The buyer is required to determine the financial condition of the party to pay before taking the instrument. Nevertheless, a transferor who knows, but fails to disclose, that insolvency proceedings have been instituted against the party to pay, commits a fraud upon the buyer. The fifth transfer warranty accordingly protects the purchaser against such a knowing concealment.

Forgery and Alteration—Specific Problems

The principles governing unauthorized signature, material alteration, and warranty liability help to resolve three important commercial paper issues: (1) the effect of payment of an instrument upon which the drawer's or maker's signature is forged, (2) the effect of payment of an instrument containing a forged indorsement, and (3) the effect of paying a materially altered instrument. These issues are discussed below.

Effect of Payment on Forged Drawer's or Maker's Signature

The Rule of Price v. Neal. The legal effect of paying an instrument on which a drawer's or maker's signature is forged has confounded commercial paper students since 1762, when the classic English case, *Price v. Neal,*[2] was decided. Under the rule adopted in *Price v. Neal,* a drawee who pays or accepts an instrument for an innocent holder upon

which the drawer's signature is forged is bound by the acceptance and cannot recover back the payment. The same rule applies if a maker pays a note upon which his or her signature is forged. The UCC codifies *Price v. Neal* in §3-418, which provides that: "Payment or acceptance of any instrument is final in favor of a holder in due course, or a person who has in good faith changed his position in reliance on the payment." The traditional justification for this rule is that the drawee (such as a bank) is in a better position than the holder to know the drawer's signature and recognize a forgery. Although this rationale is questionable when applied to our modern banking system that processes thousands of checks daily, it is more convincing when applied to the maker of a note who pays an instrument on which his or her own signature is forged. An alternative justification, suggested in Official Comment 1 to §3-418, is that "it is highly desirable to end the transaction on an instrument when it is paid rather than reopen and upset a series of commercial transactions at a later date when the forgery is discovered." Although this reasoning has also been heavily criticized, the rule of *Price v. Neal* remains firmly entrenched in the law of commercial paper.

To illustrate the operation of the rule, assume that Thomas steals Dwyer's checkbook and forges Dwyer's name to a check made payable to Peters. Peters negotiates the instrument to Holt, a holder in due course.[3] Holt presents the instrument to First State Bank, the drawee. First State pays the instrument. On these facts, First State may not charge Dwyer's account for the amount of the check. It has not paid according to Dwyer's order, which is the basic contract between Dwyer and the bank. That is, §4-401(1) permits a bank to charge its checking account customer's account only for checks that are "properly payable." A check bearing a forged drawer's signature is not properly payable. Further, under *Price v. Neal* as codified in UCC §3-418, the bank may not recover the amount it paid from Holt. Note that Holt does not breach her presentment warranty to the bank, because a

---

2. 3 Burr. 1354, 97 Eng. Rep. 871 (K.B. 1762).

3. Note here that Holt may be a holder and therefore a holder in due course because the check is a valid negotiable instrument with Thomas, rather than Dwyer, as drawer.

presenting holder does not absolutely warrant the validity of the drawer's signature to the drawee. The holder merely warrants that he or she has *no knowledge* that the drawer's signature is forged. Therefore, the bank bears the loss unless it can find and recover from the forger, Thomas, (an unlikely prospect) or from a prior holder who obtained payment with knowledge of the forgery. For example, assume Peters knew of Thomas's forgery when he sold the instrument to Holt. In this case, Peters breaches his presentment warranty to First State that he had no knowledge that the signature of the drawer was unauthorized.

If the bank discovers the forgery, it is, of course, not required to pay the check. The bank may return the instrument to the holder who is then required to proceed against prior transferors for breach of the transfer warranties. Thus, in the preceding example, assume Holt presents the instrument to First State Bank, which discovers the forgery and refuses to pay. The bank returns the check to Holt, who is required to proceed against Peters for breach of Peters's transfer warranty that all signatures are genuine or authorized. Peters is then faced with the unenviable task of finding and recovering from Thomas.

Effect of Negligence. As noted in Chapter 24, a person whose negligence substantially contributes to a forgery may not assert the forgery as a defense against a holder in due course. Section 3-406 also prevents the negligent party from asserting the unauthorized signature against "a drawee or other payor who pays the instrument in good faith and in accordance with the reasonable commercial standards of the drawee's or payor's business." Thus, although a drawee bank that pays an instrument bearing a forged drawer's signature may not generally charge the drawer's account, it may do so if the drawer's negligence substantially contributed to the forgery. Such negligence may occur, for example, if the drawer uses a stamp or other automatic signature device and fails to adequately safeguard it.

Effect of "Double Forgery." Check forgery schemes often involve the so-called double forgery. In this case the wrongdoer forges both the drawer's and the payee's signature. The payee is usually fic-

titious, but even if not, the forger intends the payee to have no interest in the instrument. In these cases, the bank paying the instrument attempts to characterize the case as one involving a forged indorsement (in which it can shift the loss to prior parties for breach of warranty of title under principles discussed below) rather than one involving a forged drawer's signature (in which it is bound by its payment under *Price v. Neal*). Courts considering this argument have generally held that the double forgery situation is treated as a forged drawer's signature case leaving the loss on the drawee bank paying the check. The basic rationale for this result is that because the payee is not entitled to payment in any event, the drawee bank could never be required to pay the instrument twice. The bank's loss is not caused by paying the wrong person because of a forged indorsement. It results from paying the instrument at all because of the forged drawer's signature.[4]

Effect of Payment on a Forged Indorsement

The legal principles applied to forgery of an indorsement differ substantially from those governing forgery of the drawer's or maker's signature. This difference stems from the basic fact that there can be no holder or holder in due course of any instrument bearing a forgery of any indorsement *necessary to negotiate the instrument*. Further, any person who pays a note or draft bearing a forged necessary indorsement *converts* it,[5] meaning that any person paying is liable to the person whose name is forged for the face amount of the instrument.[6]

To illustrate the legal effect of payment on a forged indorsement, assume Diane draws a check

---

4. O'Malley, The Code and Double Forgeries, 19 Syracuse L. Rev. 36, 43-44 (1967). See, for example, *Perini Corporation v. First National Bank of Habersham County*, 553 F.2d 398, 414-16 (5th Cir. 1977).

5. UCC §3-419(1)(c). "Conversion" is a tort defined as "an intentional exercise of dominion or control over a chattel which so seriously interferes with the right of another to control it that the actor may justly be required to pay the other the full value of the chattel." *Restatement (Second) of Torts* §222A. See discussion of conversion in Chapter 5.

6. UCC §3-419(2).

on First Bank payable to Pam's order. The check is subsequently stolen by Tod who forges Pam's indorsement and cashes the check at Joe's Currency Exchange. Joe's presents the check to First Bank, which pays it. On these facts, note that although Tod's signature in Pam's name is effective as Tod's signature, it is wholly ineffective as Pam's signature. Because the check is an order instrument (payable to the order of Pam), Pam's signature is necessary to further negotiate it. Her signature, however, does not appear on the instrument. It therefore follows that no one possessing the check after Pam (Tod and Joe's) becomes a holder.

Because a forged indorsement is wholly inoperative and ineffective to negotiate the instrument, a check bearing a forged indorsement is not properly payable. That is, the drawee bank may apply funds from the drawer's account to paying an order instrument only upon receiving the payee's or special indorsee's authorized indorsement. Accordingly, as when the drawer's signature is forged, a drawee bank that pays an instrument bearing a forged indorsement may not charge its customer's account. Thus, in this case, First Bank may not charge Diane's account for the amount of the check.

In addition, Joe's and First Bank, who paid the instrument on a forged indorsement, are both liable in conversion to Pam. Joe's, however, is liable to First Bank for breach of the presentment warranty that it had good title to the instrument. That is, Joe's is not a holder and therefore has no title. In short, unlike the forged drawer's signature case in which the bank is bound by its payment, a bank that pays on a forged indorsement, though it may not charge its customer's account, may recover from prior transferors for breach of the presentment warranties. Therefore, the ultimate loss (assuming the forger cannot be found) falls upon the person who received the instrument from the forger, in this case, Joe's.[7] Note here that assuming Pam recovers from Joe's, First Bank may then charge the drawer's, Diane's, account for the amount of the check.

---

7. If, after the forgery, the instrument is transferred several times before presentment, the same result follows. The person dealing with the forger is liable to the drawee for breach of the *presentment* warranty of title (§3-417(1)(a)) and to later transferees for breach of the *transfer* warranty of title (§3-417(2)(a)).

The check has now been paid according to Diane's order; the intended payee, Pam, has been paid by Joe's.

The following case represents a somewhat unique application of the principles governing forged indorsements. Note the bank's defense in this case.

Eatinger v. First National Bank of Lewistown
649 P.2d 1253 (Mont. 1982)

Plaintiff Ruth Eatinger employed Ervan Glover as a contractor to perform construction work for her. After Glover requested Eatinger to pay for materials he needed for the construction, she wrote a check in the amount of $7,128.32 payable to Intermountain Company, a material supplier, and gave it to Glover to pay for the materials. Several weeks later, she wrote another check for supplies in the amount of $5,500 payable to Custom Corrugating and Supply and again delivered it to Glover.

Glover took each of the checks to the defendant, First National Bank of Lewistown, the drawee. He indorsed the first check "for exchange only to Intermountain Company by Ervan Glover" and then asked the bank to issue a cashier's check in the same amount payable to Intermountain Company. He indorsed the second check in a similar manner and obtained a cashier's check payable to Custom Corrugating and Supply. Glover then gave the cashier's checks to the respective companies for payment on his own accounts rather than for purchase of materials for Eatinger.

When Eatinger received her bank statement and canceled checks, she noticed that Glover had indorsed the checks and she notified the bank. A bank employee told her not to worry because the cashier's checks had been made payable to the same payees. Two months later Glover notified plaintiff that he was unable to complete the construction work because he was out of money. Glover later disappeared.

Eatinger sued the bank for conversion of the checks. A jury found in favor of the bank and Eatinger appealed.

Haswell, Chief Justice

. . . Here the defendant accepted and negotiated two checks which were not endorsed by the payees or by anyone who was clothed with apparent or actual authority to so act for them. Glover was not connected with the payees in any way.

[Section 4-401(1) of the UCC] provides that a bank may charge a customer's account for an item that is "properly payable." There are a number of cases which have interpreted this language to require proper endorsements. . . .

Here, the bank accepted and charged against plaintiff's account two checks which were not properly endorsed and therefore not properly payable. The bank may not charge plaintiff's account therefor.

The bank's defense on the grounds that the proceeds of the checks reached the intended payees must similarly fail. . . . [Cases from other jurisdictions have held] that in a forged endorsement or absent endorsement case, even though the intended payee may receive the proceeds of a check, if the funds are not applied for the purpose for which they were intended the bank may be held liable. . . . Here it is uncontroverted that plaintiff suffered substantial losses because she did not receive the building materials for which the checks were drawn. . . .

[Judgment reversed.]

The forged indorsement rules outlined above provide substantial protection to a payee or later holder whose indorsement is forged and highlight a recurring problem in commercial paper analysis: the danger of possessing an instrument indorsed in blank or otherwise payable to bearer. Because an instrument indorsed in blank is payable to bearer, the holder of such paper runs essentially the same risk of theft or loss as the possessor of cash. Suppose that Dawson draws a check payable to Patterson's order. Patterson indorses in blank and delivers to Hart in satisfaction of a debt owed to Hart by Patterson. Timms steals the check and takes it to Carver who cashes it without knowledge of the theft. In this case, Timms is not a holder because there has been no delivery (*voluntary* transfer of possession) to him. However, Timms's transfer of

the instrument to Carver is a delivery. Because the instrument is bearer paper, this delivery alone is sufficient to negotiate the instrument and make Carver a holder. If Carver additionally qualifies as a holder in due course (which the facts given indicate she does), she takes the instrument free of Hart's claim that it was stolen from him. That is, she will be paid out of Dawson's account, and Hart faces the unenviable task of trying to find and collect from Timms.

On the other hand, had the instrument been specially indorsed—for example, "pay Hart, (signed) Patterson"—it would be order paper when stolen by Timms. He must therefore forge Hart's indorsement to transfer the instrument. Assuming he does so, his transferee, Carver, does not become a holder and converts the instrument against Hart. A holder of commercial paper is therefore well advised *never* to carry around an instrument indorsed in blank. If the instrument must remain in the holder's possession prior to further negotiation it should be in order form. If payable to order when stolen, a necessary indorsement must be forged, meaning there can be no further holder of the instrument.

Recognizing the risk inherent in possessing paper indorsed in blank, §3-204(3) allows the holder to protect herself by converting a blank indorsement into a special indorsement. The holder may do this by writing above the blank indorser's signature "any contract consistent with the character of the indorsement." Assume, as above, that Hart is the holder of Dawson's check originally payable to Patterson and indorsed in blank. Hart may convert the paper into an order instrument simply by writing "Pay Hart" above Patterson's signature. The paper is now specially indorsed, payable to Hart's order and cannot be further negotiated without his signature.

Impostors and Fictitious Payees

The law recognizes an exception to the rules that generally govern forged indorsements in the "impostor" and "fictitious payee" cases described in the following three situations.

1. Smith, who bears a remarkable likeness to Joe Doaks, impersonates Doaks and induces Michelle to issue a check made payable to Doaks's order. Smith indorses Doaks's name on the check.

First Bank cashes the check, knowing nothing of Smith's fraud.

2. Smith, treasurer of XYZ Corporation, makes a payroll check payable to Joe Doaks, a name picked at random out of the Chicago telephone directory. Smith has prepared phony documentation showing Joe Doaks as an employee of XYZ Corporation. Every week when payroll checks are distributed, Smith removes the check payable to Joe Doaks and indorses "Joe Doaks" on the back. First Bank cashes the check unaware of Smith's fraud.

3. Smith, a dishonest payroll clerk of XYZ Corporation, prepares a payroll check payable to Joe Doaks, a fictitious person. Smith gives the check, together with legitimate employee checks, to the treasurer of the corporation for signature. The treasurer signs and returns the checks to Smith for distribution, unaware of Smith's fraud. Smith removes the check and indorses it "Joe Doaks." First Bank cashes the check without notice of Smith's wrongdoing.

Situations 2 and 3 are commonly referred to as "payroll padding" schemes.

Section 3-405 adopts a single rule to resolve the three situations outlined above. It provides simply that in these cases an indorsement *by any person* in the name of the named payee is effective to negotiate the instrument. Thus, in the preceding examples, the indorsements affixed by Smith in Joe Doaks's name are not treated as forgeries. Therefore, First Bank in all three cases becomes a holder (and most likely a holder in due course) of the instrument and has not paid an instrument bearing a forged indorsement. This rule applies both when the payee actually exists, as in cases 1 and 2, and when the payee is fictitious or non-existent, as in case 3. The test applied in all cases is whether the person indorsing *intends that the payee shall have no interest in the instrument*. The instrument does not become bearer paper. An apparently regular chain of indorsements must appear on the instrument, but *any person* may effectively indorse the instrument in the name of the payee.

Assuming the dishonest party cannot be found or held accountable, this rule places the loss upon the drawer or maker of the instrument rather than upon an innocent later holder or drawee who purchases or cashes it. The rationale for this result is that the loss should fall upon the party originally in the best position to protect himself. That party is clearly the maker or drawer of the instrument who is responsible for the defective instrument's appearance in the stream of commerce. That is, the drawer's or maker's failure to obtain adequate identification from the payee or to maintain adequate accounting controls over payroll enabled the fraud to occur. In addition, losses caused by dishonest employees can be insured against, and the cost of such insurance should be viewed as an expense of the drawer's rather than the holder's or drawee's business. Thus in the preceding examples, First Bank would be paid on the instrument, and, if the drawee, could charge the drawer's account. The drawers, Michelle and XYZ Corporation, would bear the loss unless they could recover from the wrongdoer, Smith. If Smith's indorsements in the payee's names had been treated as forgeries, the loss would fall upon First Bank under the rules governing forged indorsements previously discussed.

Although any person may effectively indorse an instrument procured under the circumstances outlined above, this rule has no effect on the civil or criminal liability of the indorser. For example, the fact that Smith's signatures are effective indorsements of the phony payroll checks has no effect upon Smith's probable criminal liability for embezzlement, or Smith's civil liability in tort to XYZ Corporation. Additionally, Smith's signatures in the payees' names are effective to impose secondary contract liability upon him as an indorser on the instrument.

The following case illustrates the basic operation of §3-405.

Clinton Weilbacher Builder, Inc. v. Kirby State Bank

643 S.W.2d 473 (Tex. App. 1982)

Plaintiff Clinton Weilbacher Builder, Inc. sued defendant Kirby State Bank to recover $22,738 that Weilbacher alleged was wrongfully paid from its checking account at Kirby State Bank on forged indorsements. The evidence showed that over a fourteen month period, Weilbacher's bookkeeper Norma Wilson prepared thirty-two checks made payable to various creditors, which were then signed by Clinton Weilbacher. Wilson then forged the payee's names to the checks, deposited them in her personal checking account, and subsequently withdrew the proceeds. Kirby, in the course of regular banking transactions, accepted the forged checks, honored them, and charged the amounts against Weilbacher's checking account. The trial court granted summary judgment in favor of Kirby State Bank and Weilbacher appealed.

Cadena, Chief Justice

. . . Defendant's answer alleged . . . that plaintiff's claim is barred by [UCC §3-405(a)(3)], which provides:

> (a) An indorsement by any person in the name of a named payee is effective if . . . (3) an agent or employee of the maker or drawer has supplied him with the name of the payee intending the latter to have no [interest in the instrument]. . . .

The evidence that the payees named in the forged checks had all been paid for services previously rendered, and that they were not entitled to and never received proceeds from the forged checks, without more, is susceptible of only one conclusion. It is unlikely that reasonable minds could differ on whether Wilson intended the payees to receive proceeds from the forged instrument on these facts, when there is no evidence they were even aware the checks existed or of Wilson's scheme. Clearly the payees were not intended to receive the money in question. . . .

The parties are not in dispute as to the basic law applicable to this case. All concede that [UCC §3-405(a)(3)] governs its disposition.

Section 3-405 . . . places the loss attributable to forgery and caused by the conduct of a "faithless employee" upon the employer rather than the bank. The Code comments state that in a fictitious payee situation the loss should fall upon the employer as a risk of his bûsiness enterprise rather than upon the subsequent holder or drawee. The reasons given are that the employer is normally in a better position to prevent such forgeries by reasonable care in the selection or supervision of his employees. If he is not, he is at least in a better position to cover the loss by fidelity insurance, a cost more properly an expense of his business rather than of the business of the holder or drawee. . . .

The loss is shifted by making the indorsement effective rather than by explicitly imposing it upon the drawer. By declaring a forged indorsement effective, a collecting bank's liability on a Section 4-207 warranty and a drawee bank's liability to its customer under Section 4-401 are precluded with the result that the loss is borne by the drawer. . . . The instant case is directly on point with the typical situations cited as examples in the Code commentary. . . .

We hold that Section 3-405 bars plaintiff's recovery in this case as a matter of law.

[Judgment affirmed.]

An often litigated issue under §3-405 concerns whether the negligence or lack of good faith on the part of the drawee or other person dealing with the wrongdoer should deny that person the protection of §3-405. The following case illustrates one court's approach to the problem.

Kraftsman Container Corporation v. United Counties Trust Company

404 A.2d 1288 (N.J. Super. 1979)

> Plaintiff Kraftsman Container Corporation maintained a checking account at defendant, United Counties Trust Company. Kraftsman's treasurer was authorized to draw and sign checks on behalf of Kraftsman. Over a four year period the treasurer converted the proceeds of over 100 checks to his own use by making the checks payable to fictitious payees or actual creditors but cashing them himself. The treasurer had indorsed most of the checks illegibly, but others had no indorsement. United Counties Trust cashed all the checks.
>
> Kraftsman sued United Counties Trust for paying over a forged indorsement. United Counties Trust alleged that under UCC §3-405 the loss should be borne by Kraftsman, the employer. Kraftsman argued that because of United Counties Trust's negligence, §3-405 should not apply. In the following

opinion, the superior court of New Jersey ruled on a motion for summary judgment.

Dreier, Judge, Superior Court

. . . The basic rule is that a bank which pays a check on a forged indorsement is liable, since a forged indorsement is wholly inoperative as the signature of the actual payee (§3-404), and is thus not properly payable under §4-401. A check validly issued but wrongfully paid by the bank on a forged indorsement entitles the customer to a credit. . . .

The risk of loss may shift. Section 3-405 deems effective an indorsement by anyone in the name of a fictitious payee. The treasurer in the instant case, drawing and signing checks on behalf of the customer, plainly had the requisite intent under the statute. . . .

There is no qualifying language in §3-405 setting forth a standard of care to be applied to either the bank or its customer. This is in contrast to §3-406, which would specifically penalize the customer for negligence substantially contributing to a material alteration or an unauthorized signature. In that situation a bank is required to pay the item "in good faith and in accordance with the reasonable commercial standards of the drawee's or payor's business." . . . The conspicuous absence in §3-405 of either an "ordinary care" or "good faith" standard signals that a test for a bank's liability for payment on improper indorsements must be found elsewhere. . . . Plaintiff urges that a standard of simple negligence applies. Defendant asserts that it is shielded from liability by §3-405. There are no New Jersey cases construing the standard to be applied.

Read independently of other U.C.C. provisions, §3-405 apparently shifts the fictitious-payee indorsement loss to the customer without regard to any lack of care on the part of the bank. . . . Yet the bank may not pay over such an indorsement with impunity. Section 1-203 of the U.C.C. imposes on every contract subject to its provisions an obligation of good faith which, under §1-102(3), may not be disclaimed by agreement. Although §4-103(1) specifies that a bank may not disclaim responsibility for its own lack of good faith or failure to exercise ordinary care, §4-401(2) allows the bank to charge its customer's account only when

payment has been in good faith. "Good faith" itself is defined in §1-201(19) as "honesty in fact in the conduct or transaction concerned."

While the good faith requirement is invariable throughout the U.C.C. by way of §1-102(3), the more rigorous and objective negligence standard of ordinary care does not have such general applicability. Simple negligence on the part of a bank should not, and has been found not to affect the operation of §3-405; only bad faith should bar the bank from invoking §3-405 to defeat the customer's claim. . . .

The bank must fulfill at least a threshold requirement to invoke the protection of §3-405. The provision requires "[a]n indorsement by any person in the name of a named payee." . . .

Defendant bank seeks here to invoke §3-405(1)(b) to defeat plaintiff customer's claim. The bank must have at the very least required indorsements in the name of the named payee. . . . This court construes §3-405 as requiring an indorsement substantially identical to the name of the named payee.

Those checks cashed by defendant bank without any indorsement must be excluded from §3-405 protection. Summary judgment is therefore denied the bank regarding the unindorsed checks. Summary judgment is also denied as to those checks exhibiting illegible indorsements; the illegibility of the indorsements raises a question of fact as to whether payment by the bank constituted a lack of "good faith" on the part of the bank. . . .

Finally, plaintiff has raised a material question of fact as to the propriety of the bank's conduct over the entire four-year period. The transactions are to be viewed as a whole, since bad faith may be evidenced by a consistent failure by the bank to monitor and investigate a series of irregular transactions. . . . Effective indorsements do not relieve the bank from liability if there is proof of a course of dealing so irregular in nature that the bank is shown to have violated its own policies and to have failed to act according to the standard of honesty-in-fact. . . . Although there is no evidence that any bank employees were acting as confederates, not once was the treasurer asked to indorse the checks himself; nor was he ever questioned regarding the illegible or missing payee indorsements.

Viewing all of the evidence in the light most favorable to the customer, this court cannot say that as a matter of law defendant bank acted in good faith. . . .

[Motion for summary judgment denied.]

Effect of Payment of an Altered Instrument

This section examines the effect of material alteration. As in forgery cases, the party altering the instrument is usually unavailable to answer for the wrongdoing. The law is, therefore, again primarily concerned with sorting out the rights of the various innocent parties injured by the alteration.

As a general rule, §4-401(2) allows a bank that pays an altered check to charge the drawer's account according to the original tenor of the instrument. For example, a drawee bank that pays a check raised from $100 to $1,000 may generally charge the drawer's account for $100. In some alteration cases, however, the bank may not charge the account. For example, if the name of the payee is changed, the instrument bears a forged indorsement, and the rules discussed above apply. In any event, the drawee bank or other person paying an altered instrument may recover from prior parties for breach of the presentment warranty that the instrument has not been materially altered. Prior parties in turn may recover in the order of transfer for breach of the *transfer* warranty of no material alteration. Thus, as in the forged indorsement case, the ultimate loss usually falls upon the person who takes the instrument from the wrongdoer.

To illustrate, assume that Delbert draws a $100 check on Second Bank payable to Pauline's order. Pauline raises the check to $1,000 and cashes it at Joe's Currency Exchange, which deposits the check in its account in First Bank. First Bank ultimately presents the check to the drawee, Second Bank, which pays it. Pauline, of course, cannot be found when the alteration is discovered. In this case, Second Bank, the drawee, may charge Delbert's account for $100, the original amount of the instrument. Pauline, Joe's, and First Bank are all liable to Second Bank for $900 for breach of the *presentment* warranty against material alteration. Further, Pauline is liable to Joe's, who is liable to First Bank for breach of the *transfer* warranty against material alteration. Therefore, if Second Bank collects from First Bank, First Bank could collect from Joe's, who bears the task of collecting from Pauline.

As in the unauthorized signature case, §3-406 provides that a drawer whose negligence substantially contributes to a material alteration of his instrument may not assert the alteration as a defense against a later holder in due course or a drawee or other person paying the instrument in good faith according to reasonable commercial standards of the payor's business. Therefore, in the preceding example, if Delbert's carelessness in drafting the check—for example, by writing it in pencil or by leaving spaces where words or numbers could be inserted—provided the opportunity for Pauline to alter it, Delbert could not assert the alteration against later parties to the instrument. That is, Second Bank could charge Delbert's account for the full $1,000 and Delbert would be required to attempt to find and collect from Pauline.

SUMMARY

1. The law of commercial paper must often resolve disputes involving forged or otherwise unauthorized signatures and material alteration of an instrument. These problems are generally resolved through application of three basic concepts including (1) the legal effect of an unauthorized signature, (2) the legal effect of material alteration, and (3) the content and effect of the presentment and transfer warranties.

2. An unauthorized signature, which includes a forgery, is wholly ineffective as that of the person whose name is signed, but operates as the signature of the unauthorized signer. For this reason the forgery of a drawer's or maker's signature creates a valid negotiable instrument (with the unauthorized signer liable as drawer or maker). On the other hand, forgery of a necessary indorsement is ineffective to negotiate the instrument, meaning that no later transferee becomes a holder.

3. An instrument is materially altered when the contract of any party to the instrument is changed in any respect by the holder. Although a fraudulent material alteration ordinarily discharges any party whose contract is thereby changed, a subsequent holder in due course may always enforce the instrument according to its original tenor.

4. The UCC imposes liability for forgery and alteration generally through use of the presentment and transfer warranties stated in §§3-417 and 4-207. Presentment warranties are given by the party presenting an instrument for payment or acceptance and any prior transferor to the maker of a note or the drawee-acceptor of a draft. Each person making a presentment warranty warrants that (1) he has good title to the instrument, (2) he has no knowledge that the signature of the maker or drawer is unauthorized, and (3) the instrument has not been materially altered.

5. Transfer warranties are given by any person who transfers an instrument for consideration to later holders. Such a transferor warrants that (1) he has good title to the instrument, (2) all signatures are genuine or authorized, (3) the instrument has not been materially altered, (4) no defense of any party is good against him, and (5) he has no knowledge of any insolvency proceeding pending against the party to pay the instrument.

6. Application of the foregoing principles resolves common problems including the effect of payment of an instrument (1) upon which the drawer's or maker's signature is forged, (2) upon which a necessary indorsement is forged, and (3) which has been materially altered. If the drawee or maker pays an instrument to a holder in due course upon which the drawer's or maker's signature is forged, the payment cannot be recovered from the holder paid, and the drawee or maker ordinarily bears the loss (assuming the wrongdoer cannot be found). If the drawee or maker discovers the forgery and refuses to pay, the loss usually falls upon the person who dealt with the forger.

7. If an instrument is paid upon which a necessary indorsement is forged, any person paying does not become a holder of the instrument and converts it against the person whose name is forged. In these cases the loss ultimately falls upon the person dealing with the forger. An exception to this result is the ''impostor'' and ''fictitious payee'' case in which the loss falls not on the holder dealing with the wrongdoer but upon the drawer or maker of the instrument.

8. General principles similar to those governing forged indorsements apply to material alteration. That is, the loss generally falls upon the person who takes the instrument from the person altering it.

KEY TERMS

presentment warranties
transfer warranties

QUESTIONS AND PROBLEMS

26-1 Greer stole an automobile that was the property of Brown. Brown's title to the automobile and other identification papers were in the automobile. Greer represented himself as Brown and sold the automobile to Alm Auto Co., which paid Greer with a check payable to the order of Brown. Greer indorsed the check with Brown's name and sold it to Clancy.
   (a) Is Greer's indorsement in Brown's name effective?
   (b) Does Clancy become a holder of the instrument?
   (c) Assuming Greer cannot be found, who will bear the ultimate loss on the instrument?
   (d) Does Greer's signature in Brown's name effectively bind Greer personally on the instrument as an indorser to Clancy? Explain.

26-2 Zack stole Sid's checkbook and forged Sid's signature to a check made payable to Terry. Terry indorsed the check to Hugh, a holder in due course. Hugh took the check to the drawee bank and the bank paid the check.
   (a) May the bank deduct the amount of the check from Sid's account? Explain.
   (b) May the bank recover the amount it paid from Hugh? Explain.

26-3 Dick drew a check on First Bank payable to the order of Paul. The check was stolen from Paul by John who forged Paul's signature and sold the check to Herb, who knew nothing of the theft. Herb then indorsed the instrument over to Mark in satisfaction of a debt owed by Herb to Mark. Mark presented the check to First Bank, and the bank paid it.
   (a) Could Mark be a holder in due course of the instrument?
   (b) Could Herb be a holder in due course of the instrument?
   (c) May the bank recover the amount of the check from Mark?
   (d) May Mark recover the amount of the check from Herb, if Mark is required to pay First Bank?
   (e) Do Herb, Mark, and the bank have any liability to Paul?

(f) If the bank pays Paul, can it charge Dick's account?

26-4 Dykstra entered a written agreement to purchase a Cadillac purportedly owned by James and Peggy Bateman. Dykstra presented James Bateman with a personal check for $9,000 drawn upon National Bank of South Dakota payable to "James Bateman and Peggy Bateman." The bank knew that Dykstra, a customer of twenty years, had made a deal on a Cadillac because the bank had loaned Dykstra money to purchase the automobile. James Bateman appeared at bank's main office and, in the presence of bank officer James Murphy, endorsed "James Bateman and Peggy Bateman" on Dykstra's check. It was subsequently discovered that Peggy Bateman did not exist and James Bateman was not the owner of the Cadillac. Dykstra promptly informed the bank of the fraud. The true owner of the Cadillac subsequently repossessed the car. Dykstra sues the bank for wrongfully cashing the check. Should Dykstra prevail? Consider particularly the application of UCC §§3-405 (impostor-fictitious payee rule) and 3-406 (negligence contributing to forgery or alteration).

26-5 Fred, while visiting Chicago, asked Lloyd, a local business associate, for assistance in cashing a check. Fred accompanied Lloyd to Lloyd's office, ABT, Inc. where the treasurer agreed to cash the check so long as Lloyd indorsed it. Fred handed Lloyd a check drawn on American Bank payable to Henry Sherman, Inc. The back of the check was indorsed Henry Sherman and Lloyd added his signature. The treasurer cashed the check and handed the money to Lloyd who immediately gave it to Fred. ABT deposited the check at Belmont Bank. Belmont presented the check to American, which dishonored it, because it had been notified that Sherman's indorsement was a forgery. Due to inadvertence, however, Lloyd was not notified of the dishonor until a month later. Fred has fled the country. ABT sued Lloyd to recover the amount of the check.

(a) In what capacity is Lloyd liable on the instrument?

(b) Does Lloyd have contract liability on the instrument to ABT? Explain.

(c) Does Lloyd have any warranty liability on the instrument to ABT? Explain.

26-6 Should a person paying an instrument bearing a missing necessary indorsement incur the same liability as one paying on a forged indorsement? Explain.

26-7 To assist in keeping the books of their auto repair business, Gordon and Mildred Neely hired Louise Bradshaw as a part-time bookkeeper. Although the business bank account was maintained at First Alabama Bank, the Neelys accepted Bradshaw's recommendation to open a second account for personal expenditures and corporate payroll at American National Bank. She explained that checks could be drawn on the First Alabama account to fund the second account at American National. Bradshaw also kept her personal account at American National. The Neelys signed the bank signature card authorizing them to draw checks on the account. They entrusted Bradshaw with the documents to return them to the bank. Without the knowledge or authorization of the Neelys, Bradshaw signed the signature card and added her name in a noticeably different type.

Subsequently, Bradshaw filled out checks drawn on the First Alabama account made payable to American National and with a large space to the left of the amount written on the designated lines. Mrs. Neely signed these checks being fully aware of these large gaps. Bradshaw altered the checks either by adding a digit or two to the left of the original amount, or by raising the first digit after using liquid erasure. She then deposited the original amount into Neely's American National payroll account, and depositing to her account or taking in cash the difference between the original and altered amounts.

When the bank statements were received, Bradshaw realtered the checks using liquid erasure. Bradshaw and Mrs. Neely then reconciled the statements with Mrs. Neely calling out the information from her journal entry and with Bradshaw responding from the bank statements and items. Consequently, Mrs. Neely never saw the altered checks or the statements. A new accountant later discovered the defalcations, which totaled over $17,000. Bradshaw has disappeared. The Neelys sued American National Bank to recover the amounts paid on the altered instruments. Who should prevail? Explain.

26-8 Nora Ray, an eighty-year-old woman, gave a check to a man claiming to be Robert Freeman, an employee of the utility company. Mrs. Ray had admitted Freeman to her home when he stated he needed to check the electricity because of a power outage. After checking the outlets, Freeman told Mrs. Ray he would return but that she was required to pay a $1.50 service fee for which the utility company only accepted payment by check. Freeman wrote out the check in ink and Mrs. Ray signed it.

When Freeman failed to return, Mrs. Ray telephoned the bank to stop payment on the check because she believed that he had not earned the service fee. She then learned that Freeman had altered the check and had cashed it for $1,851.50 instead of $1.50. When Freeman had written out the check at Mrs. Ray's home, he had left enough room to allow his later alteration. The bank had cashed the check after Freeman produced two identification cards.

Nora Ray sued the bank to recover the $1,850 that it had paid on the altered check. The bank asserted that because Mrs. Ray's negligence had contributed to the alteration she should be denied recovery. What factors should the court consider in resolving the case? Who should prevail?

26-9   American Savings and Loan Association was a holder in due course of two Manville Corporation bearer notes due September 2, 1982, and payable at Morgan Guaranty Trust Company. On August 26, 1982, Manville filed a Chapter 11 bankruptcy petition. American, who was aware of the bankruptcy, did not anticipate payment on September 2. Nevertheless, Chase Manhattan, who held the notes for American, presented them on September 2 through the New York Clearing House. Although Morgan had instituted special procedures to process Manville notes and checks, it failed to dishonor the notes by the clearing house deadline. Morgan sought return of the money but American refused, arguing that Morgan's restitution claim was barred by §3-418, the UCC's codification of *Price v. Neal*, which provides generally that payment of an instrument is final in favor of a holder in due course. Is American correct? Explain.

Chapter 27

Bank Deposits and Collections; Credit Cards and Electronic Fund Transfers

- the operation and legal aspects of the check collection process
- the legal relationship between a bank and its checking account customer
- the law governing credit cards and electronic fund transfers

Checks are by far the most common type of commercial paper, used in millions of transactions every day and processed in large quantities by various banks and other financial institutions across the country. Although checks are governed by the same basic principles that apply to all commercial paper, the law provides special additional rules that govern the manner in which checks are processed through the banking system and the relationship between a bank and its checking account customers. These special principles are contained in federal statutes and administrative regulations, and in Article 4 of the UCC, "Bank Deposits and Collections."

This chapter covers the basic principles governing the check collection process and the bank-customer relationship, and then discusses modern alternatives to payment by check, such as credit cards and electronic fund transfers.

The Check Collection Process

Assume that Doaks, a Chicago retailer, owes Crenshaw, a Boston manufacturer, $1,000 for goods sold to Doaks. Doaks draws a check payable to Crenshaw upon his checking account in First State Bank of Chicago, and mails it to Crenshaw in Boston. Crenshaw then deposits the check in its account in the City Bank of Boston. Because it is not the drawee, City Bank does not pay the check. Rather, City Bank collects it from the drawee, First State. The process by which the check is transmitted and presented to the drawee, paid, and the proceeds transferred and credited to the depositor's account is known as the bank collection or **check collection process.**

UCC §§4-104 and 4-105 define a number of terms important to understanding the check collection process.[1] In the preceding example, both Doaks and Crenshaw are customers of their respective banks. A **customer** is any person having an account with a bank or for whom the bank has agreed to collect a check. City Bank is referred to as the **depositary bank** meaning the first bank to which the check is transferred for collection. First Bank, the drawee, is the **payor bank**—the bank by which the check is payable.

Although the check may be presented directly by the depositary bank to the payor bank, it more commonly passes through one or more intermediary banks or a clearing house before reaching the

---

1. Federal statutes and regulations governing the check collection process, discussed later in this chapter, use terminology generally corresponding to that appearing in Article 4.

payor bank. An **intermediary bank** is any bank to which a check is transferred in the course of collection other than the depositary or payor bank. Checks often pass through intermediary banks when the payor and depositary banks are in different cities or states. The Federal Reserve Banks located in major cities across the country serve as the major intermediary banks in a nationwide check collection and clearing system. If both the depositary and payor banks are located in the same city or region, a local or regional clearing house may be used to present the check. A **clearing house** is an association of banks or other payors regularly clearing checks. All banks handling checks for collection are designated **collecting banks** and the one ultimately presenting the check to the payor bank is the **presenting bank**. The process by which the various banks outlined above send checks to the payor-drawee bank for payment is known as "forward collection." Figure 27–1 illustrates the various stages of the forward check collection process.

The preceding discussion illustrates the most common check collection case, the "transit check"—a check deposited in one bank but payable by another. In some cases, the depositary bank will also be the payor bank. This occurs, for example, if both the drawer and payee maintain an account in the same bank or when the payee cashes the check at the payor bank. Such checks are referred to as "on us" checks.

The law governing bank deposits and collections focuses on two separate legal relationships. The first concerns checks *deposited* in the customer's account, and the second involves checks *drawn upon* the account. The following material therefore examines first the legal relationship among the customer, collecting banks, and the payor bank in the check collection process and then the relationship of the payor bank to its customer, the drawer of the check.

Legal Aspects of the Check Collection Process

A checking account deposit triggers a chain of legally significant events involving the customer (the payee or other holder of the check), the various collecting banks, and the bank upon which the check is drawn, the payor bank.

Collection and Payment of a Check

When depositing a check, the customer negotiates it to his or her bank for purposes of collection. If

---

Figure 27–1   **The Check Collection Process**

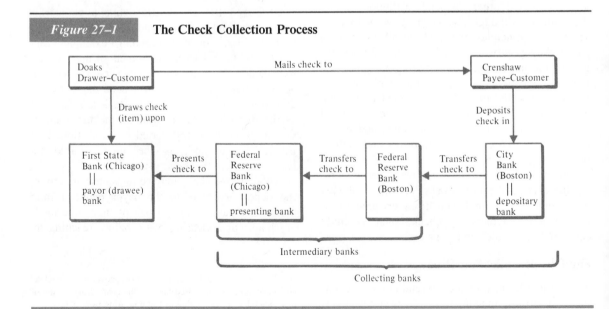

the instrument is order paper—for example, a check made payable "to the order of Joe Doaks"—the customer must indorse the check upon deposit. This indorsement may be blank or special (payable to the bank's order), but should also contain restrictive language such as "for deposit only." As noted in Chapter 23, such a restrictive indorsement requires the depositary bank to make sure that the amount of the check gets into the depositor's account and effectively prevents a finder, thief, or anyone else outside the bank collection process from negotiating the check.

Upon deposit, the depositary bank becomes a *holder,* but not the *owner* of the check. The depositor is the owner. Under §4-201(1), the bank is merely an agent of the owner to collect the check from the drawee and to credit the proceeds of the check to the depositor-owner's account. The same agency relationship exists between the depositor and other collecting banks. Thus, in the example above, City Bank of Boston (the depositary bank) and the Federal Reserve Banks (intermediary banks) are all agents for the owner of the check (Crenshaw) to collect the check from the drawee, First State Bank of Chicago.

The check collection process is designed to secure final payment of the check from the drawee-payor bank. Upon final payment (1) the drawer's (the payor bank's customer) account is reduced by debiting or charging it in the amount of the instrument, (2) the contract liability of the drawer and prior indorsers on the instrument is discharged, and (3) the payor bank and other collecting banks become accountable for the amount of the check to its owner, the depositor. This result may be explained as follows. Before payment the drawee-payor bank has no liability on the check.[2] Under §3-603, however, when the bank pays the holder, the various other parties to the instrument are discharged. Thus, the payor bank by paying the check discharges the contract liability of prior parties to it including the drawer and any indorser. The bank is now accountable for the amount of the check to the holder who presented it, the presenting bank.[3] The presenting bank is, in turn, accountable to the person or bank forwarding or depositing the check, and so on. Thus, accountability moves down the so-called "remittance chain," ultimately ending with the depositary bank's liability to pay its customer, the depositor of the check.

Final payment is generally accomplished through a series of "settlements" made among the various banks in the collection process. Settlement is accomplished by paying the check in cash, by adjusting and offsetting the banks' clearing house balances, by debiting or crediting accounts between banks, or by forwarding various types of remittance instruments.

Return of Dishonored Checks

Although most checks are paid,[4] the payor-drawee bank may refuse to honor a check upon presentment—due, for example, to insufficient funds in the drawer's account. If the check is dishonored when presented, the payor bank will return it (often through the same chain of intermediary banks, now known as "returning" banks, used for forward collection) to the depositary bank, which ultimately returns the check to its customer, the depositor; that is, the check "bounces". The payor and other returning banks then settle for the dishonored check with each other and the depositary bank, which in turn settles with the depositor. Because a check presented through the forward collection process may not be paid, many depositary banks place "holds" on checks deposited in their customers' accounts, refusing to allow funds to be withdrawn pending payment of the check by the payor bank. These holds are designed to protect the depositary bank against the risk inherent in allowing its depositor to withdraw funds that the bank has not yet collected.

Critics have long asserted that holds placed by many banks are unduly long and that bank customers have a right to prompter access to their deposits. Banks, however, have argued that the holds merely reflect the time needed for the attempted

---

2. UCC §§3-401(1), 3-409(1).
3. UCC §§3-301, 4-213(1).

4. A 1985 study estimated that approximately 350 million checks are returned annually, a figure representing less than 1% of all checks processed. *Return Items Study, Final Report,* prepared for the Bank Administration Institute by J. D. Carreker and Associates, Inc. (May 1985).

collection and return of unpaid checks, noting that the current check return system is a slow, relatively labor-intensive, and costly process, due to the number of returning banks that must process a check on its trip from the payor to depositary bank. For example, a study prepared for the Bank Administration Institute[5] concluded that although the forward collection process takes an average of 1.6 days to complete, the return process averages 5.2 days. The study found that approximately forty percent of checks take seven days or longer to complete the collection and return cycle and that fifteen percent take ten days or longer. The study further estimated that the average returned check is handled by 3.4 banks (the payor and depositary banks, and an average of 1.4 returning banks).

Expedited Funds Availability Act

In response to this problem, Congress in 1987 passed the **Expedited Funds Availability Act**.[6] The Act requires banks to make funds available to depositors within specified time frames, and to disclose their funds availability policies in writing to depositors. The Act also mandates that improvements be made in the check collection and return process to reduce the risk of loss to banks resulting from the expedited funds availability requirement. In addition, for interest bearing accounts, the Act requires banks to begin accruing interest not later than the day the bank receives credit for the deposit (one or two days after deposit for most checks). The Act delegates broad authority to the Federal Reserve Board (Board) to implement its provisions, including the authority to regulate "any aspect of the payment system, including the receipt, payment, collection, or clearing of checks; and . . . any related function of the payment system with respect to checks."[7] Pursuant to this authority, the Board adopted **Regulation CC**,[8] which became effective on September 1, 1988. Because the Act and Regulation CC are federal law, they preempt any

inconsistent Uniform Commercial Code provisions but only to the extent of the inconsistency.[9]

Funds Availability Schedules. Under the Act as implemented by Regulation CC, funds availability depends on the type of deposit. For the following types of deposits, the funds can generally be withdrawn by cash or check on the first business day[10] following the banking day[11] of deposit: cash; electronic payments; checks drawn on the United States Treasury, a Federal Reserve Bank, or a Federal Home Loan Bank; checks drawn by a state or a unit of general local government; U.S. Postal Service money orders; cashier's or certified checks; "on us" checks (checks deposited in a branch of the depositary bank and drawn on the same or another branch of the same bank, if both branches are located in the same state or check processing region); and the first $100 of any amount deposited by checks not subject to next day availability.[12]

The availability of other checks deposited in an account depends upon whether they are "local" or "nonlocal." A "local" check is one deposited in a bank located in the same Federal Reserve processing region as the drawee-payor bank. (There are 48 Federal Reserve processing regions in the United States.) A "nonlocal" check is a check deposited in a bank located in a different check processing region than the payor-drawee bank.[13] Approximately one-third of the checks handled by the Federal Reserve Banks are nonlocal.

Under temporary availability schedules in effect from September 1, 1988, through August 31, 1990, local checks must be available for withdrawal by the third business day after the banking day of deposit, and nonlocal checks must be available no later than the seventh business day after the banking day of deposit. These time limits are reduced

---

5. *Return Items Study, Final Report,* prepared for the Bank Administration Institute by J. D. Carreker and Associates, Inc. (May 1985).

6. 12 U.S.C. §§4001-4010.

7. 12 U.S.C. §4008(c).

8. 12 C.F.R. part 229.

9. 12 C.F.R. §229.41.

10. A "business day" is generally a calendar day other than Saturdays, Sundays, and holidays. 12 C.F.R. §229.2(g).

11. A "banking day" is that part of any business day on which an office of a bank is open to the public for carrying on substantially all of its banking functions. 12 C.F.R. §229.2(f); UCC §4-104(1)(c).

12. 12 U.S.C. §4002(a); 12 C.F.R. §229.10.

13. 12 U.S.C. §§4001(13), (15); 12 C.F.R. §§229.2(r), (s),(v),(w).

under permanent availability schedules effective September 1, 1990 to two business days after deposit for local checks, and five business days after deposit for nonlocal checks.[14]

The law recognizes limited exceptions to the availability schedules for new accounts, deposits exceeding $5,000 on any one banking day, redeposited checks, accounts with repeated overdrafts, deposits that the depositary bank has reasonable cause to believe are uncollectible from the drawee-payor bank, and deposits made under emergency conditions, such as computer or communications equipment failure. The exceptions generally permit the bank to delay funds availability for a "reasonable period" after the day dictated by the applicable availability schedule. Under Regulation CC, an extension of up to four business days is a reasonable period. The bank has the burden of proving that any longer extension is reasonable.[15]

Check Collection System Improvements. Under Article 4 of the UCC, a drawee-payor bank that decides not to pay a check must return the check or give notice of dishonor by its "midnight deadline" (midnight of the next banking day following the banking day on which the bank receives the check for payment). Failure to make a timely return renders the payor bank accountable for the amount of the check. The bank's return obligation may be satisfied by dispatching the returned check by mail or private courier, or in accordance with clearing house rules or other agreement among banks. Intermediary returning banks similarly must act to dispatch returned checks by their midnight deadlines. Under Article 4, the payor and returning banks have little incentive beyond meeting their midnight deadlines to speed the return process.

To implement the Act's mandate to improve the check processing system, Regulation CC alters this result by requiring that payor and other banks return dishonored checks to the depositary bank in an "expeditious manner," thus providing an incentive to banks to speed the flow of returned checks. Generally, the payor and returning banks act "expedi-

tiously" by: (1) processing and dispatching returned checks in the same general manner as forward collection checks,[16] or (2) returning dishonored checks to the depositary bank within two (for local checks), or four (for nonlocal checks) business days following presentment to the payor bank.[17]

If the dishonored check is for $2,500 or more, any notice of nonpayment must be received by the depositary bank by 4:00 p.m. (local time) on the second business day following presentment of the check.[18] A payor bank may be held accountable for the amount of the check for failure to meet either the Article 4 midnight deadline or the Regulation CC deadlines, but not both.[19]

A bank returning a dishonored check obtains credit for it by, in effect, presenting the check to the depositary bank for payment in a manner similar to presentment of the instrument to the payor bank during forward collection. The depositary bank must pay the payor bank or other bank returning the check prior to close of business on the day the depositary bank receives the check.[20]

The Federal Reserve has implemented a number of new returned check services to assist banks in complying with their obligations under Regulation CC. One of the most significant improvements is the increased use of "direct returns," under which the Federal Reserve banks deliver returned checks directly to the depositary banks, bypassing the various intermediary banks that processed the check during forward collection, thereby minimizing the number of banks that must handle a returned check. Another device with significant potential to expe-

---

14. 12 U.S.C. §§4002(b),(c); 12 C.F.R. §§229.11, 229.12.

15. 12 U.S.C. §4003; 12 C.F.R. §229.13.

16. The specifics of this requirement are explained in the Federal Reserve's overview of Regulation CC as follows: "[T]he paying bank must dispatch returned checks with the same speed and diligence that it would dispatch forward collection checks received for deposit by noon on the banking day after the day of presentment of the returned check. This means that a check presented to the paying bank on Monday that is not paid must be dispatched as quickly as a check deposited in that bank on Tuesday morning that is drawn on the depositary bank."

17. 12 C.F.R. §§229.30-229.31.

18. 12 C.F.R. §229.33.

19. 12 C.F.R. §229.38(b).

20. 12 C.F.R. §229.32.

dite the check collection and return system is check "truncation," now used in several Federal Reserve Banks. In truncation, checks are not physically transported to the drawee-payor bank. Rather, the Federal Reserve Bank transmits the coded information on the check electronically to the payor bank, and indexes, microfilms, and stores the paper checks. If the payor bank decides to dishonor the check, it notifies the Federal Reserve Bank by a published deadline. The Federal Reserve Bank then retrieves the physical check and initiates the return process to the depositary bank. The payor bank may also request retrieval services, such as a copy of the check. The Federal Reserve stores the checks and microfilm for a negotiated period, usually 90 days and seven years respectively, after which they are destroyed.

Duties of Collecting Banks

The UCC explicitly imposes a duty of ordinary care upon collecting banks. For example, under §4-202(1) a collecting bank must use ordinary care in (1) presenting an item or sending it for presentment, (2) sending a notice of dishonor or returning a dishonored item, (3) settling for an item when it receives settlement, (4) making or providing for any necessary protest, and (5) notifying its transferor of any loss or delay of an instrument in transit within a reasonable time after the loss or delay is discovered. Regulation CC imposes a similar duty of good faith and ordinary care upon all banks in the collection process.[21]

In addition to the duty of care, §4-207 imposes transfer and presentment warranties upon collecting banks and upon the customer depositing the check for collection that are virtually identical to those discussed in the preceding chapter. Thus, the payor and the various collecting banks receive the protection against forgery and alteration these warranties provide. Despite warranty liability, a collecting bank is an agent of the owner of the check, not the other collecting banks. It is therefore not liable for the insolvency, negligence, or other misconduct of other banks or for the loss or destruction of a check in the possession of others.[22]

Collecting Banks as Holders in Due Course

Although banks in the collection process are holders, they qualify as holders in due course only under limited circumstances. To illustrate, assume Daniel draws a $500 check on State Bank payable to Nancy's order in exchange for goods purchased from Nancy. Nancy deposits the check in her account in National Bank, and the bank credits her account for $500. In this case, the bank has not yet given value for the instrument, a prerequisite to holder in due course status, because its deposit credit is a mere executory promise under §3-303(a).

Under §4-208(1), however, the bank acquires a *security interest* in the deposited item (and therefore gives value) to the extent it (1) allows the depositor to withdraw the deposit credit prior to collecting the check, (2) gives a deposit credit available for withdrawal as of right, whether or not the depositor actually withdraws it, or (3) makes an advance on or against the check—for example, loans money secured by the deposited check. In short, the bank gives value to the extent it extends credit on items in the course of collection.

To illustrate using the preceding example, assume National Bank allows Nancy to withdraw $400 from her account prior to collecting Daniel's check from State Bank. National Bank has a $400 security interest in (and has therefore given value for) the instrument. Under §4-209, if National Bank meets the other requirements, it therefore qualifies as a holder in due course of the check for $400. National Bank could therefore collect $400 on the instrument from Daniel even if he stops payment on the check and has a valid personal defense to paying Nancy—for example, if the goods delivered by Nancy to Daniel were defective.

---

21. 12 C.F.R. §229.38(a).

22. UCC §4-202(3); 12 C.F.R. §229.38(a). A collecting bank is, however, required to follow instructions regarding the instrument given by its immediate transferor, but may disregard instructions given by anyone else. UCC §4-203.

Frequently, a number of checks are deposited either simultaneously or successively in the same account. If the bank permits the depositor to withdraw a part of the total of all checks prior to collection, the law must determine how the bank's security interest is allocated among the various checks deposited. Section 4-208(2) resolves the problem by providing that the bank's security interest is spread proportionally over all checks in a single deposit. If checks are deposited successively, credits first given are first withdrawn. That is, the Code adopts a "first-in, first-out rule" for successive deposits. Assume that on Monday Pam deposits five checks in her account in Security Bank, drawn by Albert, Bob, Carol, Don, and Ed respectively, each for $200. Security Bank permits Pam to withdraw $800 on Tuesday prior to collecting any of the checks. The bank gives value for each check to the extent of $160 (0.8 × $200). Assume alternatively that Albert's and Bob's checks are deposited on Monday, Carol's and Don's Tuesday, and Ed's on Wednesday. On Wednesday, the bank permits Pam to withdraw $800 prior to collecting any of the checks. Security Bank has given value for the first $800 worth of checks, those drawn by Albert, Bob, Carol, and Don.

Relationship Between Payor Bank and Its Customer

To this point the discussion has focused upon the legal principles governing the collection of a check *deposited* in a customer's account. This section examines the nature of the relationship existing between the customer and the bank regarding checks *drawn upon* the account.

Contract Between Payor Bank and Customer

When a person opens a checking account by depositing a sum of money with a local bank, a contract is created between the customer and the bank. The money becomes the property of the bank (cash) and the duty to repay it a general current liability (a demand deposit). The bank and its customer therefore stand in a simple creditor-debtor relation.

The contract between the customer and the bank is usually informal in nature. The depositor fills out an account application, submits identification, signs a signature card, and makes an initial deposit. By signing the signature card, the customer usually agrees to abide by the bank's rules governing checking accounts. These rules are usually stated on the signature card, the deposit receipt, or some separate writing provided to the customer. The remaining terms of the contract are supplied by Articles 3 and 4 of the UCC, other statutes or common law doctrines, and banking custom.

Checks Properly Payable. Upon creation of the checking account the bank acknowledges its indebtedness for the balance in the account and agrees to pay demand drafts (checks) within that balance to the customer's order upon presentment. In other words, the bank obligates itself to pay according to the customer's (drawer's) order. If the bank does so, it is entitled to charge (debit) the customer's account for the amount of the check. If the bank pays contrary to its customer's order, it has violated its basic contract and may not charge its customer's account. This basic contract is stated in §4-401, which provides that a bank may charge its customer's account only for checks that are "properly payable."

For example, suppose Carr has a checking account in First Bank. A check bearing Carr's signature is presented to First Bank ordering it to pay $1,000 to Paul's order. In this case, First Bank can charge Carr's account for $1,000 if it pays $1,000 to Paul. If the check is not properly payable—for example, because it bears a forged drawer's signature or forged indorsement or has been materially altered—the bank has not paid according to its customer's order and may therefore charge the drawer's account only under circumstances outlined in Chapter 26.

The bank is not obligated to pay a check that results in an overdraft. If the bank does pay, however, it may charge the drawer's account for the full amount of the check. That is, a check creating an overdraft authorizes payment from the drawer's account and creates an implied promise to reimburse the drawee bank on demand.[23]

---

23. UCC §4-401(1) and Official Comment 1.

In addition to checks properly payable under the preceding analysis, a bank may charge its customer's account in two other situations. Section 4-401(2) permits a bank paying a holder in good faith to charge the account according to (1) the original tenor of an altered check, or (2) the tenor of a completed check, even though the bank knows the check has been completed unless the bank has notice that completion was improper.

Order of Payment. Under §4-303(2), the bank may pay checks presented to it in any order convenient to the bank. If the account balance is insufficient to pay all checks presented at any one time, the bank must honor checks in any order it chooses until the account balance is too small to pay any remaining check. The remaining checks may then be dishonored. Although the bank may pay checks in any order, it must continue to pay until the balance will not cover any remaining check. The bank may not dishonor all checks simply because the account balance is insufficient to cover all of them.

Liability for Wrongful Dishonor. If the bank refuses or neglects to honor a properly payable check, it is liable to its customer for damages proximately caused by its wrongful dishonor. If, as is usually the case, the check is dishonored by mistake, liability is limited to actual damages proved. Recovery may include damages for an arrest or prosecution of the customer—for example, for writing a bad check—or other consequential damages such as loss of credit rating. If the dishonor is intentional, punitive damages may also be available if permitted by state law outside the Code. The burden of proving the existence and amount of damages rests upon the customer.[24]

Stop Payment Orders

The bank is contractually obligated to pay checks according to the drawer's order. This order is communicated to the bank when the check is presented to it for payment. Occasionally, however, the

drawer may issue a check but subsequently discover that the check should not be paid. For example, the drawer may issue a check in payment for goods, but later learn that the payee has defrauded him or that the goods involved are defective. In such cases, the Code, in §4-403, recognizes the right of the customer to countermand, or "stop," the order represented by a check. If payment is effectively stopped, the check will not be paid when presented to the payor-drawee bank. Rather the check will be returned, and the bank will not charge the drawer's account.

Most **stop payment orders** are given to the bank by telephone and later confirmed in writing. The Code authorizes oral stop orders but provides that they are binding on the bank only for fourteen calendar days unless renewed in writing during that time. A written order is binding for six months but may be renewed in writing. Because it is inconvenient and expensive to stop payment, most banks charge for the service.

Only the drawer may stop payment on a check; the payee or other holder of the check has no such right. The customer, however, has no right to stop payment on a certified check, regardless of who procures certification. The certified check is the bank's own obligation, and the drawer has no right to require the bank to impair its own credit by dishonoring a certified check.

At issue in the following case is whether the purchaser of a cashier's check has a right to stop its payment.

State of Missouri ex rel. Chan Siew Lai v. Powell

536 S.W.2d 14 (Mo. 1976)

In December of 1974, Chao Kin Tak (Kin Tak), a broker from Hong Kong, entered into a contract to purchase 60,000 metric tons of fertilizer from Nathanial Gunn (Gunn) to be delivered the following year to certain customers of Kin Tak in Indonesia. As part of the agreement Gunn was to pay a commission to Kin Tak as broker. Gunn delivered and received payment for 10,000 tons in early 1975. In April of 1975, Kin Tak requested partial advance

---

24. UCC §§4-402, 1-106(1).

payment of his commission for the balance of the sale. Gunn agreed and purchased and delivered to Kin Tak a cashier's check for $150,000 payable to Kin Tak. Unknown to Gunn, however, Kin Tak's customers had canceled their order for the remaining 50,000 tons of fertilizer and had so notified Kin Tak in March, 1975. When Gunn learned that the order had been canceled, he notified the bank to stop payment on the check. When the bank refused, Gunn petitioned the court for an injunction ordering the bank to stop payment.

The evidence established that the cashier's check had been negotiated to Chan Siew Lai, a holder in due course. Nevertheless, the trial court agreed to enjoin the bank from paying the check. Chan Siew Lai appealed.

Henley, Judge

. . . A cashier's check, unlike an ordinary check, is a check drawn by a bank on itself and is accepted by the mere act of its issuance. . . . It is sometimes, as here, purchased by a party from a bank for issuance payable to the order of another as payee. Thus, when issued, it becomes the primary obligation of the bank (rather than the purchaser) to pay it from its own assets upon demand, and the purchaser has no authority to countermand a cashier's check because of fraud allegedly practiced on the purchaser by the payee. . . .

The nature and usage of cashier's checks in the commercial world is such that public policy does not favor a rule that would permit stopping payment of them. It is aptly stated in *National Newark & Essex Bank v. Giordano,* [268 A.2d 327, 329 (N.J. Super. 1970)]: "A cashier's check circulates in the commercial world as the equivalent of cash. . . . People accept a cashier's check as a substitute for cash because the bank stands behind it, rather than an individual. In effect, the bank becomes a guarantor of the value of the check and pledges its resources to the payment of the amount represented upon presentation. To allow the bank to stop payment on such an instrument would be inconsistent with the representation it makes in issuing the check. Such a rule would undermine the public confidence in the bank and its checks and thereby deprive the cashier's check of the essential incident which makes it useful. People would no longer be willing to accept it as a substitute for cash if they could not be sure that there would be no difficulty in converting it into cash."

The stop order given by Gunn and the legal process issued in connection with the injunction suit were received by and served upon the Bank after it had issued the cashier's check and came too late to terminate or suspend the Bank's obligation to honor and pay it. Furthermore, the fraud allegedly practiced on Gunn by Kin Tak, if true, afforded him no standing or authority to countermand the Bank's obligation to pay its check on demand; his remedy is by action against Kin Tak.

Gunn's petition alleges facts which show . . . that he has no claim for injunctive relief against the Bank. . . .

[Judgment reversed.]

Effectiveness of Stop Order. Section 4-403(1) provides that to be effective, a stop order must be received by the bank at a *time,* and in a *manner* sufficient to give the bank a reasonable opportunity to act upon it. Thus, a telephoned stop order is not effective immediately when the bank's switchboard operator answers the phone; it must be brought to the attention of the person responsible for processing such orders. Under §4-303(1) a stop order comes too late to bind the bank if, prior to receipt of the order, the bank has (1) accepted or certified the check, (2) paid it in cash, (3) completed the process of posting the check to the drawer's account,[25] or (4) otherwise become accountable for the amount of the check. In these cases, the amount of the check may be charged to (deducted from) the drawer's account despite the stop order.

At issue in the following case was whether a stop order had been given in a proper manner.

---

25. The "process of posting" means the usual internal procedure used by the payor bank to determine whether to pay a check and to record the payment. This procedure may include, for example, verifying signatures, ascertaining whether sufficient funds are available, affixing a "paid" or other stamp, and making an entry charging the customer's account, UCC §4-109 and Official Comment. Although the procedure varies among banks, the process of posting is complete when two basic events have occurred: a decision to pay and some recording of payment.

FJS Electronics, Inc. v. Fidelity Bank
431 A.2d 326 (Pa. Super. 1981)

On February 27, 1976, plaintiff FJS Electronics, Inc. (FJS) drew a check in the amount of $1,844.98 on its account at defendant Fidelity Bank. On March 9, 1976, FJS telephoned a stop payment order on the check to Fidelity and later provided written confirmation of the stop order. Both the oral and written order indicated the amount of the check to be $1,844.48. All other information, including the number of the check and the payee, was correct. On March 15, 1976, Fidelity paid the check.

FJS sued Fidelity. The evidence at trial established that Fidelity used a computer to detect checks subject to stop payment orders. The computer was programmed to pull checks according to the dollar amount of the check. Thus, if the dollar amount was incorrect, the check would not be detected. The trial court ruled in favor of FJS; Fidelity appealed.

Brosky, Judge
. . . The central issue for our determination is whether a bank had a reasonable opportunity to stop payment on a check in the sum of $1,844.98 when the amount given by the customer was $1,844.48, hence, inaccurate. . . .

It is clear that the order here was timely received. The court below determined that even though it contained an error, the order was given in such manner as to give the bank a reasonable opportunity to act. Fidelity, in essence, asserts that [§4-403(1)] should be read to require compliance with the procedures of a particular bank, regardless of what they are and regardless of whether the customer has been made aware of them. Fidelity argues that since its technique for ascertaining whether payment had been stopped required absolute accuracy as to the amount of a stopped check, this section would require absolute precision in order for the notice to be reasonable. Such a narrow view is not consistent with the intent [of] §4-403, expressed in Comment 2 following the section:

. . . [S]topping payment is a service which depositors expect and are entitled to receive from banks notwithstanding its difficulty, inconvenience and expense. The inevitable occasional losses

through failure to stop should be borne by the banks as a cost of the business of banking.

Fidelity does not contend that it could not have used a technique which required less precision in the stop payment order. It does not contend that it could not have found the check had it used a more thorough system. It merely asserts that since it chose a system which searched only by amount, notice is not reasonable unless it conforms to the requirements of this system.

Fidelity made a choice when it elected to employ a technique which searched for stopped checks by amount alone. It evidently found benefits to this technique which outweighed the risk that an item might be inaccurately described in a stop order. This is precisely the type of inevitable loss which was contemplated by the code drafters and addressed by the comment quoted above. The focus of §4-403 is the service which may be expected by the *customer,* and a customer may expect a check to be stopped after the bank is given reasonable notice. A bank's decision to reduce operating costs by using a system which increases the risk that checks as to which there is an outstanding stop payment order will be paid invites liability when such items are paid.

An error of fifty cents in the amount of a stop payment order does not deprive the bank of a reasonable opportunity to act on the order. . . .

[Judgment affirmed.]

Payment Over a Stop Order. A bank may receive a stop order, but due to inadvertence or neglect, pay the check anyway. In this case, the bank is liable to its customer because the bank has not paid according to the customer's order. Nevertheless, §4-403(3) imposes the burden of proving loss due to payment over the stop order upon the customer. If the customer is unable to prove loss, the bank may charge her account even though it failed to honor the stop order. Further, under §4-407, a bank that pays a check over a stop order is subrogated to (succeeds to) the rights of

1. the payee or other holder against the drawer,

2. the drawer against the payee or other holder of the check, and

3. any holder in due course against the drawer.

To illustrate the third subrogation case above, assume that Dan draws a check upon First Bank payable to Pam for the purchase of a car. Pam defrauds Dan, who later discovers the fraud and stops payment on the check. Pam negotiates the check to Hal, a holder in due course, who presents the check to First Bank. First Bank inadvertently pays over Dan's stop order. In this case, First Bank may charge Dan's account because Dan can prove no loss due to the bank's improper payment. Hal, as a holder in due course, could have forced Dan to pay in any event because Dan's defense (fraud) is merely personal. First Bank, upon payment, succeeds to Hal's rights against Dan and could also therefore force Dan to pay.

In sum, the stop payment order provides somewhat limited protection to the drawer. The order, if honored, simply prevents the check from being paid initially out of the drawer's account. It does not prevent the payee or other holder from later suing the drawer on the underlying obligation for which the check was given. Further, even if the bank fails to honor the order, it is subrogated to the rights of the payee or later holder. If, as is commonly the case, the person presenting the check is a holder in due course—for example, a currency exchange that cashes the check in good faith for the fraudulent payee—the bank may pay over the order and charge the account unless the drawer has a real defense.

Effect of Customer's Death or Incompetence

A checking account customer may deposit checks in or draw checks upon an account shortly before death or, less frequently, before being adjudicated mentally incompetent. Section 4-405(1) provides that a payor or collecting bank's authority to pay, certify, or collect an item is not revoked by the death or incompetence of a customer until the bank knows of the death or adjudication of incompetence and has a reasonable opportunity to act upon it. Under this rule, banks need not verify the continuing vitality and competence of their customers be-

fore paying or collecting checks. Any other rule would be unworkable given the staggering volume of checks processed by modern banks.

Section 4-405(2) provides an additional rule governing checks drawn shortly before death. Even with knowledge of the death, the bank may continue to pay checks drawn against the account for a period of ten days after the date of death unless ordered to stop payment by some person claiming an interest in the account such as a creditor of the drawer, or the executor of the drawer's estate. This rule allows holders of checks issued shortly before death to cash them without having to file a claim against the deceased drawer's estate. Because these checks usually are given in immediate satisfaction of an obligation (for example, the grocery bill) and no defense to payment exists, filing a claim usually is a needless formality burdensome on the bank, the probate court, the executor of the estate, and the holder of the check.

Stale Checks

In banking and commercial practice a check more than six months old is considered a **stale check.** Under §4-404, a bank is under no obligation to pay a stale check and, therefore, its failure to pay is not a wrongful dishonor. The bank *may,* however, pay a stale check and charge its customer's account provided it acts in good faith. Thus, the bank has the option to pay the check and charge its customer's account or refuse to pay it with no liability for dishonor. Although not required to do so, many banks will consult the customer for instructions when presented with a stale check.

The preceding rule does not apply to a certified check. The drawer's account is charged when the check is certified and it thereafter becomes the bank's obligation. This obligation extends to the holder of the check until the local statute of limitations governing such instruments expires.

Customer's Duty to Discover Forgery and Alteration

As noted in Chapter 26, a drawee bank that pays an altered check may charge its customer's account only for the original tenor of the item, and if it pays a check bearing a forged drawer's signature, it may not charge the account at all. Section 3-406 provides, however, that a drawer whose negligence "substantially contributes" to the forgery or alteration may not assert the alteration or lack of authority against the drawee bank who pays the instrument in good faith. A bank that pays a forged or altered instrument therefore may escape liability if its customer has failed to exercise reasonable care in preparing or safeguarding checks.

A checking account customer who is negligent in examining bank statements also may be prevented from asserting certain forgery and alteration against the bank under §4-406. In other words, a customer may be liable for negligent conduct both before and after the forgery or alteration has occurred. Under §4-406(1), when a bank sends its customer a statement of account accompanied by the checks paid in good faith, the customer must exercise reasonable care and promptness to examine the statement and the checks to discover forgeries of his signature and alterations, and to notify the bank promptly if a forgery or alteration is discovered.

Under §4-406(2)(a), if the bank is able to prove loss caused by the customer's failure to perform these duties, the customer may not assert a forgery of his or her signature or an alteration against the bank. For example, the bank may be able to prove that with prompt notice it could have located and recovered from the wrongdoer but that it cannot now do so. In this case, the customer could not force the bank to recredit the account.

Effect of Successive Forgery or Alteration. Occasionally, a series of checks are forged or altered by the same wrongdoer, usually a relative or employee of the drawer. In this case, the relationship between the drawer and the bank is governed by §4-406(2)(b). Under this provision, the drawer-customer is liable upon any forged or altered instrument paid by the bank after the first such instrument and bank statement is made available to the customer for a reasonable time (not exceeding 14 calendar days) and before the customer notifies the bank of the problem. Losses resulting from successive forgeries or alterations by the same person can usually be traced to the customer's negligence in failing to examine bank statements and notify the bank of objections. Because this failure prevents the bank from avoiding payment of the later checks

and allows the wrongdoer to continue his misdeeds, the law places the loss on the customer.

To illustrate, assume Don maintains a checking account at First Bank. On November 15, Nick, Don's dishonest nephew, steals three checks from Don's checkbook. Nick forges Don's signature to the first check, makes it payable to cash, and cashes it at a currency exchange. First Bank pays the check on November 17. On December 2, Don receives his monthly bank statement from First Bank containing the forged check. On December 12, First Bank pays a second check forged by Nick, and on December 20 pays the third. On December 22, Don notifies the bank of the forgeries. On these facts the bank may not charge Don's account for the first check it paid. Concerning the second check, paid within the fourteen-day period, the jury is required to decide as a matter of fact whether Don had the statement in his possession long enough (a "reasonable period") to allow him to examine it, discover the forgery, and notify the bank. On these facts Don had the statement for 10 days (December 2 to December 12) before the second check was paid. If the jury finds that this was sufficient time to take action, the bank may charge his account despite the forgery. Finally, the third check was paid on December 20, well beyond the fourteen-day period prescribed by the Code. Thus, First Bank may charge Don's account for the amount of the check. Even if the customer is negligent under the principles outlined above, the bank nevertheless remains liable under §4-406(3) if the customer is able to prove that the bank was itself negligent in paying the forged or altered check.

The following case illustrates the general operation of §4-406.

Ossip-Harris Insurance, Inc. v.
Barnett Bank of South Florida
428 So.2d 363 (Fla. App. 1983)

Plaintiff Ossip-Harris Insurance, Inc. (Ossip) maintained a checking account at defendant Barnett Bank. Between May, 1980, and June, 1981, Ossip's bookkeeper forged the signature of Edward Harris, Ossip's president, on ninety-nine checks and wrongfully diverted almost $20,000. During the year-long period, Harris periodically reviewed the bank statements but did not detect the forgeries until June, 1981.

Ossip sued Barnett Bank for wrongful payment of forged checks. Barnett alleged that Ossip should be denied recovery because it had been negligent in failing to detect and report the forgeries. The trial court ruled in favor of Barnett Bank. Ossip appealed.

Hendry, Judge

. . . Resolution of this dispute turns on the provisions of subsections (1) through (3) of [§4-406 of the UCC]. . . .

We find that Barnett met its burden . . . of conclusively showing that Ossip failed to meet its initial burden under [§4-406(1)] in that it did not "exercise reasonable care and promptness to examine the statement and items to discover" the unauthorized signatures. The undisputed evidence demonstrates that Ossip received bank statements from Barnett each month from May 1980 to June 1981 and that the statements contained the cancelled checks alleged to be forgeries. In response to a question posed by Ossip's own attorney, Edward Harris admitted that he did not actually review the signature on all of the company's cancelled checks and even admitted that he didn't pay attention to the signatures on the checks but was more concerned with the amounts and whether it was "the kind of check [Ossip-Harris] would normally pay." The checks were thus not scrutinized for unauthorized signatures as required by statute, nor was reasonable notice given to Barnett of any wrongdoing after the first statement and checks were made available to Ossip within the meaning of [UCC §4-406(2)(b)]. Consequently, the evidence supports the conclusion, as a matter of law, that Ossip failed to exercise the degree of care required by statute . . . [and] is therefore precluded from recovering against Barnett unless it can establish lack of ordinary care by Barnett in paying the forgeries.

Under [UCC §4-406(3)], the burden of proving Barnett's lack of ordinary care falls squarely on Ossip-Harris. . . . Deposition testimony by Estella Brown, an employee of Barnett that handled the Ossip-Harris account, established that she had received six months of on-the-job training and that she examined each check against the signature card

on file with the bank to determine the validity of the signature. When any problems arose with regard to signatures, she would bring the checks to the attention of her supervisor. Ossip presented no evidence of either the accepted standard of ordinary care in the banking world, or that Barnett's method of detecting forgeries did not meet this standard. Ossip's only argument in this regard, that the bank was negligent in not detecting the forgery, is particularly unavailing in light of the fact that Edward Harris failed to detect the forgery of *his own signature*. To require Barnett's employees to be handwriting experts as Ossip seems to imply, would establish a higher standard than that required by the statute, which is simply *ordinary* care. . . .

[Judgment affirmed.]

Statute of Limitations. Regardless of the care or lack of care exercised by either the customer or the bank, §4-406(4) places an absolute time limit within which the customer must act. If the instrument is altered or the drawer's signature is forged, the customer must discover and report that fact to the bank within one year after the statement containing the offending instrument is made available to her. With respect to a forged indorsement, the customer must act within three years. The longer time limit for forged indorsements is allowed because, although the customer should easily detect an alteration of her own check or forgery of her own signature, she is unfamiliar with the indorser's signatures and may not learn of the forgery immediately. Failure to discover and report the problem to the bank within the prescribed time limits prevents the customer from asserting the forgery or alteration against the bank.

Credit Cards

A **credit card** is simply a device, such as a card or plate, for obtaining money, property, or services on credit. As a money substitute and a credit device, credit cards perform commercial functions similar to those performed by notes and checks. For example, a person often uses a credit card to satisfy obligations that would otherwise be paid in cash or by check. Credit cards are also often used to borrow money or purchase goods or services on credit to be paid in future installments. This section examines the various types of credit cards and the legal principles governing them.

Types of Credit Cards

Credit cards are generally classified as single-party, dual-party, or multiparty. Through use of a **single-party credit card,** the oldest type, the issuer of the card sells goods or services on credit to its customer, the cardholder. This sale may be made by the card issuer directly or through an agent or franchised dealer. The cardholder is subsequently billed, commonly on a monthly basis, for the charges incurred on the card. Thus, a single-party transaction is a simple credit sale with the card used to identify persons to whom credit should be extended. Common examples of single-party cards are those issued by oil companies and department stores.

In a **dual-party credit card,** the card issuer does not sell goods or services but instead provides credit and collection services for those who do. The card issuer has two classes of customers, its cardholders and the merchants who honor its cards. Under a dual-party plan the cardholder uses the card to buy goods or services from a merchant belonging to the plan. The merchant is then reimbursed, less a discount, for charges incurred by cardholders. The issuer then undertakes to collect the outstanding balances from various cardholders. Examples of dual-party cards are American Express and Diner's Club cards.

Closely related to dual-party cards are **multiparty** bank cards, such as Visa and Master Card. Under bank card plans, a participating bank enlists both cardholders and merchants. Like the dual-party cards, merchants are paid by the bank that enlisted them in the plan, and the bank bills its cardholders periodically for charges incurred against the card. In the multiparty card, however, merchants honor cards issued by any participating bank. Thus, when a bank pays its customer, the merchant, the bank may be required to collect the charge from another bank that issued the card. The collection process is similar to that used for ordinary checks.

Regardless of the type of card involved, two principal legal problems have arisen: (1) the effect of unauthorized use of the card, and (2) when a cardholder may assert defenses against the card issuer. Although initially matters of state law, these and other credit card issues are now primarily governed by federal legislation. The federal approach is embodied in portions of the Federal Truth in Lending Act,[26] discussed below.

Liability of Cardholder for Unauthorized Use

Perhaps the most common legal problem presented by credit cards is the effect of unauthorized use—the extent of a cardholder's liability when the card is used by a thief or a person acting without authority. The common law reached differing results on this issue depending upon the type of card involved.

The Truth in Lending Act provides for extremely limited liability for unauthorized use of a consumer's credit card, regardless of type. Under this statute,[27] the cardholder is liable for unauthorized charges on the card occurring before notifying the card issuer up to the *lesser* of $50 or the amount of money, property, or services obtained by the unauthorized use of the card. This liability attaches only if the following three conditions are met:

1. The card involved must be an "accepted" credit card—one that the cardholder has requested or applied for and received, or has signed or used to obtain credit. Thus, a cardholder has no liability for unauthorized use of cards mailed on an unsolicited basis.

2. The issuer must provide adequate notice to the cardholder of the maximum potential liability outlined above and of means such as a telephone number or address by which the issuer may be notified orally or in writing of loss or theft of the card.

3. The issuer must provide a method whereby the user of the card can be identified as the person authorized to use it. Most commonly, the method

---

26. The "Truth in Lending Act" is the popular name for Subchapter I of the Consumer Credit Protection Act, 15 U.S.C. §1601 *et seq.*

27. 15 U.S.C. §1643, 12 C.F.R. §226.12.

of identification is the cardholder's signature appearing on the card.

Even if the foregoing conditions are met, the cardholder may nevertheless escape even the limited liability imposed by the statute if no liability would have been imposed upon him under state common law. For example, at common law, the holder of a single-party card is not responsible in most states for unauthorized use. Thus, the federal law does not expand the liability of the single-party cardholder up to the $50 maximum. Rather, it limits liability to $50 or less in cases in which state law would have imposed greater responsibility. For example, in dual-party or multiparty cards some states have held a cardholder liable for all unauthorized charges made before the cardholder notifies the issuer.

The limitations outlined above apply only to consumer credit transactions, not to transactions involving extensions of credit for business, commercial, or agricultural purposes, or to organizations, such as corporations or government agencies. Credit card transactions in these cases continue, therefore, to be governed by state law.[28]

Assertion of Defenses Against Issuer

Even when their use is authorized, credit cards are sometimes used to purchase defective goods or services. The law must, therefore, determine when a cardholder may assert against the card issuer defenses he or she may have against the merchant providing the defective goods or services. As with unauthorized use, the issue is governed primarily by federal law, and single-party cards are treated differently from other types.

In a single-party card transaction, the card issuer is also effectively the seller of the goods or services involved. The single-party cardholder may therefore assert any defective performance by the seller's company-owned outlet, agent, or franchised dealer against the parent company issuing the card. Suppose Sue Cohen uses her Standard Oil card to purchase a battery from Bill's Amoco of Chicago, Illinois. If the battery proves defective, Sue may assert the defect as a defense to paying the bill sub-

mitted by Standard Oil Company, provided she first makes an effort to settle the dispute with Bill's. That is, Sue's defense against Bill's may be asserted against Standard.

Dual-party and multiparty cards present more difficult problems because the card issuer—for example, American Express or a bank issuing a Visa card—is not the seller of the defective goods or services, but instead merely provides a credit and collection service for the merchants. Because card issuers enlist participating merchants, however, they do have some ability to screen and police against troublesome merchants honoring their cards. For this reason, federal law[29] allows a cardholder to assert defenses against credit card issuers if

1. the cardholder first makes a good faith effort to resolve the dispute with the merchant honoring the card,
2. the amount of the initial transaction exceeds $50,
3. the merchant's place of business is located either in the same state as the cardholder's billing address or within 100 miles of that address.

Note that only the first limitation (good faith effort to resolve the dispute) applies (1) to single-party cards, and (2) when the issuer of a dual- or multiparty card induces its cardholder through a mail solicitation to use the card to purchase the goods which prove defective. For example, Master Card and Visa bills commonly include promotional literature for products that can be purchased by mail and billed to the card. The card issuer is subject to defenses arising out of sales of these goods without regard to the dollar or geographic limitations outlined above. If the cardholder is able to assert a defense, the *amount* asserted may not exceed the amount of credit outstanding with respect to the transaction at the time the cardholder first notifies the card issuer or the offending merchant of the problem.[30]

---

28. 15 U.S.C. §1603(1).

29. 15 U.S.C. §1666i(a).
30. 15 U.S.C. §1666i(b).

Limitations on Credit Card Issuers

To protect cardholders and merchants against certain unfair or anticompetitive practices, the Truth in Lending Act imposes several limitations upon credit card issuers. For example, consumer holders of bank cards, such as Visa or Master Card, often maintain checking accounts in the bank issuing the card. In such cases, the bank may not, either before or after credit card privileges are revoked, offset amounts owing on credit card transactions against funds held on deposit with the bank. The bank must instead resort to ordinary creditors' remedies, available under either federal or state law, to collect the amount due.[31]

The law also provides that no card issuer may prohibit a merchant from offering a discount to any consumer to pay by cash, check, or similar means other than the credit card.[32] Further, the merchant may not be required, as a condition to participating in a credit card plan, to open an account with (or procure any other service from) the card issuer not essential to the operation of the plan.[33]

Electronic Fund Transfers

In recent years, many banks have installed automated teller machines as part of their drive-up or walk-up facilities or in remote locations such as shopping centers. These machines enable bank customers, using a special card and identification number, to deposit or withdraw money from their accounts electronically.

In 1978, Congress enacted the Electronic Fund Transfer Act[34] to establish a basic framework for the rights, liabilities, and responsibilities of participants in electronic funds transfer systems such as automated tellers. The Act is limited in scope. It concerns only consumer transfers, not the substantial volume of transfers occurring among banks and other large business organizations. Further, the Act does not displace all state law on the subject; it supplants state law only if state law provides less protection to consumers than the federal statute.

As defined in the Act, an **electronic fund transfer** includes any transfer of funds other than one initiated by check, draft, or similar paper instrument that is initiated through an electronic terminal, telephone, computer, or magnetic tape, and that orders, authorizes, or instructs a financial institution to debit or credit an account. The term includes transfers through point of sale terminals and automated teller machines, preauthorized direct deposits and withdrawal of funds, and transfers initiated by telephone pursuant to a prearranged plan. The Act prescribes guidelines for the contract between a bank and its customer regarding electronic transfers, requires that the bank provide written documentation of such transfers including a periodic statement, and imposes limited consumer liability for unauthorized transfers involving the account.

As with credit cards, the consumer has no liability for unauthorized transfers unless the card or other means of access used for the transfer is accepted and the bank provides a means whereby the card user can be identified as the person authorized to use the card. This is commonly accomplished by a personal identification number, which the customer is supposed to keep secret and separate from the access card. If these two conditions are met and the card is lost, the customer is liable up to a maximum of $50 for unauthorized transfers occurring before he notifies the bank. The customer has no liability for unauthorized transfers occurring after the bank is notified.

Liability is expanded up to a $500 maximum if the bank is able to prove that the unauthorized transfer was caused by the customer's failure to report an unauthorized transfer within sixty days after transmittal of the bank statement disclosing the transfer. Liability also is increased if the unauthorized transfer is caused by the customer's failure to report any loss or theft of a card within two business days after learning of it.

---

31. 15 U.S.C. §1666h.

32. 15 U.S.C §1666f, 12 C.F.R. §226.12(f)(1).

33. An account solely for clearing purposes may be used, but no finance charges or minimum balance requirements may be imposed. 15 U.S.C. §1666g, 12 C.F.R. §226.12(f)(2).

34. 15 U.S.C. §§1693-1693r. Subchapter VI of the Consumer Credit Protection Act; 12 C.F.R. part 205.

SUMMARY

1. Federal statutes and administrative regulations, and Article 4 of the UCC, entitled "Bank Deposits and Collections," contain the rules governing the check collection process—the process by which a check is presented to the drawee bank, paid, and the proceeds transferred and credited to the depositor's account.

2. To assure that checking account customers have prompt access to their funds, Congress, in 1987, enacted the Expedited Funds Availability Act. The Act requires banks to make funds available to depositors within specified time frames, and mandates that improvements be made in the check collection process, primarily to speed the return of unpaid checks. The Federal Reserve Board has adopted comprehensive Regulation CC to implement the Act's provisions.

3. Article 4 of the UCC governs the legal relationship between a bank and its checking account customer. A checking account involves a contract requiring the bank to pay checks within the balance of the account according to the customer's (drawer's) order.

4. The order to pay is communicated to the bank when the check is presented to it for payment. Prior to that time the drawer may countermand or stop the order to pay embodied in a check. If the bank, due to negligence or inadvertence, pays the check after receiving a stop order, it is liable to its customer for breach of its basic contract. Nevertheless, the burden of proving loss due to payment over a stop order rests upon the customer. Further, after payment the bank is subrogated to the rights of the payee or other holder against the drawer, the drawer against the payee or other holder, and any holder in due course against the drawer.

5. In addition to governing the basic contract between the customer and the bank and the legal implication of stop payment orders, Article 4 also resolves additional issues arising in the bank-depositor relationship. These include, for example, the effect of the customer's death or incompetence, payment of stale checks, and the customer's duty to examine bank statements to discover forgery and alteration.

6. In addition to checks and notes, credit cards are often used as a method to purchase goods or services. A credit card is simply a device, such as card or plate, utilized to obtain money, goods, or services on credit. Cards are often designated as single-party (for example, an oil company card), dual-party (for example, an American Express Card), or multiparty (for example, a Visa or Master Card). Regardless of the type of card used, two principal legal problems have arisen: first, the effect of unauthorized use of the card, and second, when a cardholder may assert defenses against the card issuer arising out of the underlying transaction. Although initially matters of state law these and other credit card issues are now governed primarily by explicit provisions of the federal Truth in Lending Act.

7. Like credit cards, electronic fund transfers are also substantially governed by federal law. Electronic fund transfers include generally any transfer of funds initiated through an electronic terminal, such as an automated teller machine, which authorizes a financial institution to debit or credit an account.

KEY TERMS

check collection process
customer
depository bank
payor bank
intermediary bank
clearing house
collecting bank
presenting bank
Expedited Funds
 Availability Act
Regulation CC
stop payment order
stale check
credit card
single-party credit card
dual-party credit card
multiparty credit card
electronic fund transfer

QUESTIONS AND PROBLEMS

27-1 Explain the general operation of the bank collection process, including the sequence of events occurring when the check is honored and when it is dishonored. Why are banks required to return dishonored checks promptly?

27-2 Michael drew a check upon his checking account in Gulfstream Bank payable to Paul's order. The check was signed but blank in amount. Paul was to fill in the amount at a future date for carpentry work to be performed by Paul. Before the check was presented Michael closed his account at Gulfstream Bank. After Paul performed the work, he filled in the check in the amount of $100 and presented it to the bank, which paid it creating an overdraft on Michael's closed account. On these facts may Gulfstream recover the amount of the check from Michael? On what theory?

27-3 James, who maintained a checking account at Highland National Bank, died on June 1, 1985.

Two days later, before the bank had notice of James's death, James's sister, Stella, appeared at the bank with checks signed in blank by James and informed bank officials that James had sent her to close out his account. She inquired as to the balance of the account and filled in the check payable to herself for the amount of that balance. The bank verified the authenticity of James's signature and Stella's identity. Stella subsequently cashed the check at a currency exchange and fled the country. In fact, Stella had no authority to make the withdrawal, and the executor of James's estate sued the bank to recover the amount paid. What result?

27-4   Tusso delivered a $600 check drawn on Security National Bank to Adamson Construction Co. in payment for work performed by Adamson. The payment was made by mistake, however, because Adamson had already been paid for the services as part of a previous bill. Realizing the mistake, Tusso went to the bank the next day at 9 A.M., stopped payment on the check, and paid the required fee. At 10:30 the same morning, Adamson presented the check to the bank, which paid it. On these facts, may Security charge Tusso's account for the amount of the check? If not, does Security have any rights against Adamson?

27-5   On September 14, 1983, Siegel drew a check on First Bank payable to Peter's order, postdated to November 14, 1983. Peter immediately deposited the check in his account and First Bank paid it on September 17, 1983. Does Siegel have any recourse against the bank? Assuming it is required to recredit Siegel's account, what recourse might the bank have? Explain.

27-6   Nu-Way Services, Inc. (Nu-Way), a truck repair company, maintained a checking account at Mercantile Trust Company. Over a period of approximately six months James Ussery, Nu-Way's night manager, altered seven checks prepared by Nu-Way to pay for auto parts by substituting his name as payee. Additionally, Ussery stole forty-three of Nu-Way's blank checks and forged the signature of Nu-Way's president, Mariano Costello. Although Nu-Way received the canceled and altered checks with its monthly bank statements, the clerk who reconciled the statements failed to detect the alterations or forgeries. When one of Nu-Way's vendors notified Costello of a check made payable to Ussery, Costello discovered Ussery's wrongdoing.

Costello notified Mercantile of the alterations and forgeries, but Mercantile refused to recredit Costello's account. Costello sued Mercantile to recover on the checks. The evidence established that the forgeries were expertly done and several bank employees were unable to distinguish between the forgeries and the genuine signatures. The alterations, however, were crudely done, accomplished by making obvious erasures on the instrument. How should the court rule in this case?

27-7   The use of credit cards and electronic fund transfers certainly eliminates the need for many checks. For example, a hotel bill formerly paid by check is now often paid by credit card. Automatic teller devices eliminate the need for many checks formerly written simply to obtain cash. Do you think these devices will ever eliminate the need for ordinary checks? What future role do you see for checks? What are the relative advantages and disadvantages of payment by check as opposed to credit card and electronic fund transactions?

27-8   A common practice among hotels, car rental companies, and other merchants is to utilize a so-called "open" credit card slip as a means of securing payment. Under this arrangement, the customer allows the merchant to take an impression of the credit card and the voucher is then signed by the customer. The amount is not filled in but the merchant retains the voucher as security for ultimate payment of the bill. Eventually, the merchant fills in the amount and gives the customer a copy of the voucher. The arrangement is therefore similar to giving the merchant a check, otherwise blank, signed by the drawer. The risks to the drawer of unauthorized completion of a check are outlined in Chapter 24. Does a credit card customer using the open credit card voucher run similar risks? Explain.

27-9   Antone D. Silvia maintained a checking account in Industrial National Bank. For more than 25 years, John J. Mahoney had calculated and prepared Silvia's taxes. After the return was prepared, Mahoney would write out a check to the Internal Revenue Service, obtain Silvia's signature, and mail the check and tax return. After preparing the 1967 tax return and obtaining a check from Silvia, Mahoney altered the check so that it was payable to "Internal Revenue Services by John J. Mahoney." Mahoney then indorsed the check "Internal Revenue Services by John J. Mahoney," presented the check to the drawee, Industrial, and obtained several cashier's checks.

Silvia received the canceled check with a bank statement in February, 1968, but failed to notice the alteration or indorsement. In April, 1969, the Internal Revenue Service notified Silvia that he had failed to file a 1967 tax return. Silvia then discovered the altered check and requested Industrial to credit his account but the bank refused. Silvia sued Industrial.

Industrial argued that because Silvia had failed to report the alteration within one year as required by UCC §4-406(4), he was precluded from asserting the claim against the bank. Silvia argued that although he is precluded from recovery on the material alteration by the one-year discovery and notice limitation of UCC §4-406(4), he may still recover on the unauthorized indorsement under the three-year provision of that section. Who is correct?

Emerging and Percolating Issues in the Payment System

© *Edward L. Rubin, 1988*

"Commercial Paper," the subject of Chapters 21–27, is a legal term, whose boundaries were established by the conceptual exigencies of pre-modern law. At present, it covers two quite separate functions, credit and payment. Credit involves the extension of value in return for the promise of its future return (with interest, generally). Payment is the process by which value is transferred in exchange for goods and services. Recently, the non-cash mechanisms by which payment is effected (mainly checks, credit cards and electronic fund transfers) have become a matter of rapid technological change and substantial legal controversy. Since the changes are quite technical, and the controversies are complex and varied, the subject is best approached in terms of a general, analytic framework.

The two main social purposes that are implicated by the payment system, and by the laws which govern it, are social equity and economic efficiency. Social equity issues arise if one identifiable group in society is significantly disadvantaged. In the payment system, the predominant claim of social disadvantage is that certain groups do not have access to standard payment instruments such as credit cards or checking accounts. It is undoubtedly true that lower income people do not have equal access to credit cards, but this is generally considered unavoidable, since the card also involves an extension of credit. There have been claims, however, that even creditworthy persons were being denied credit cards on the basis of race or sex. Such discrimination was made illegal in the Equal Credit Opportunity Act (1974).

The controversial issue at present is whether minorities, the elderly or lower income people are being systematically denied access to payment instruments which do not have a credit feature, specifically checking accounts. Consumer advocates have argued that this has in fact occurred, and have urged legislatures to enact "lifeline" banking laws that would require banks to offer low-cost accounts. Banks respond that they cannot operate such accounts at a profit, and that, for people with limited funds, cash, money orders and check cashing services are more economical.

An optimal resolution of the lifeline services controversy requires both empirical data and normative judgments. To begin with, it would be necessary to determine precisely how much low-income people are paying for their payment services. If banks can offer lower-cost services and still make a profit, a lifeline law could then be enacted without imposing additional costs on them. If banks cannot offer such services profitably, there remains the question whether the existing services are inequitably expensive. Those who conclude that these services are not inequitable would have no reason to favor a lifeline law. Those who reach the contrary conclusion might favor such a law, even though it imposed losses on the banks. If such a law were passed, banks would presumably raise the price of their other services; in other words, the result would be that existing bank customers would be subsidizing those who held lifeline accounts. Cross subsidies of this kind are regarded by economists as less efficient than a direct subsidy. But they are often more politically palatable because they do not increase public expenditures; whether this political advantage is more important than the inefficiency depends on the strength of one's commitment to the social equity advantage of lifeline accounts.

Edward L. Rubin is Professor of Law at the University of California, Berkeley.

The second policy involved in the payment system is economic efficiency. In this context, efficiency simply means that a given payment is effectuated at the lowest cost. Payments are governed by private agreement, and economic theory holds that these agreements will be efficient, in the absence of a market failure. But many observers have argued that there exist extensive market failures in the payment system—not with respect to price perhaps, but with respect to secondary matters that consumers do not shop for. One such matter may be the time in which a bank makes deposited funds available to the customer for withdrawal. In the early 1980s, Congress became concerned about these "holds" that banks were placing on deposited funds. Its concern culminated in the Expedited Funds Availability Act of 1987, which requires banks to make funds available according to a fixed time schedule and to disclose this schedule to the customer. The Act represents good social policy if there truly is a market failure in funds availability policies, and if the Congressional solution does not impose costs which exceed the net benefit to customers from accelerated availability.

Having decided to legislate, Congress did not stop with the availability schedule. Instead, it granted the Federal Reserve Board plenary control over the check collection system, and urged it to adopt a number of innovations in the collection process. The Federal Reserve has already exercised its authority by promulgating a massive regulation, designated "Regulation CC" (1988). This not only implements the availability schedule, but also transforms the process by which dishonored checks are returned. It thus displaces a large part of the Uniform Commercial Code (under the Constitution a federal regulation pre-empts any state enactment). Given its mandate from Congress, it is quite likely that the Fed will promulgate further regulations, governing forward collection as well, and pre-empt even more of the UCC. These operational rules are desirable policy if there is a market failure in banks' ability to reach optimal agreements among themselves for check collection. Such a failure may very well exist, given the vast number of banks in the U.S., and the complexity of the collection process.

Another area where there is a potential market failure is the allocation of losses due to fraud and forgery. Most individuals and many small businesses are unaware of bank loss allocation practices, and unable to estimate their economic significance. There is thus a strong argument for legal regulation in this area. The Uniform Commercial Code governs this subject with respect to checks, and this is one part of the UCC which will probably not be pre-empted by the Fed. Losses on credit cards and electronic fund transfers are governed by two federal statutes that are essentially consumer protection laws—the Truth in Lending Act (1970 Amendments) and the Expedited Funds Availability Act (1978). In the late 1970s, the New Payments Code, attempted to establish uniform rules governing losses for all these payment instruments. It ran into determined opposition from banking interests, however, who felt that the revision would make the pro-bank UCC rules more consumer oriented, but not affect the pro-consumer federal laws. In response, the UCC's sponsors abandoned the New Payments Code, and proceeded with a more limited project to revise the existing UCC provisions, and to add one new section governing wholesale (but not consumer) electronic fund transfers.

In terms of the policy of economic efficiency, loss allocation rules should minimize the aggregate social cost of losses. One way to do so is to spread the losses across the entire customer base. This can be achieved by holding banks liable for losses. Another way to lower social cost is to enact rules that induce customers and banks to take precautions against loss; this requires that some liability be imposed on each party. Thus the two methods seem to suggest opposing solutions. The federal statutes resolve this conflict by holding consumers liable for a small, fixed amount of each loss and imposing the remainder on the bank. This gives both parties an incentive to take precaution, without visiting consumers with excessive losses. The UCC does not take this approach at present, and the pending revision would not do so either. Rather, they impose liability on the party who seems most at fault, an approach that is consistent with traditional legal rules, but not with principles of economic efficiency. This may also be inconsistent with social equity, depending how broadly one defines this latter policy.

Part Five

DEBTOR-CREDITOR RELATIONS

Chapter 28

Introduction to Debtor-Creditor Relations

Major Topics

- an overview of credit transactions, including types of credit, the creditor's decision to extend credit, and the risks of extending credit
- an introduction to the law of debtors and creditors, including the source of the law, the concept of priority among creditors, and the definition of the concept of security
- discussion of federal and state laws affecting credit transactions

Millions of debtor-creditor relationships occur each day in a wide variety of situations. A consumer may buy a dishwasher on credit from a local appliance store, borrow money from a bank to buy a new car or house, contract with a local builder to remodel the kitchen, or simply become indebted to pay the phone or utility bills. In the commercial setting, businesses often borrow money to finance inventory, acquire equipment, construct buildings, or to provide working capital. Businesses also often purchase goods and services on credit.

In each of these transactions, one party—the **debtor**—has incurred an obligation or debt that is owed to a second party—the **creditor**. Although most debtor-creditor relationships are created voluntarily by contract or agreement of the parties, the relationship often arises by operation of law without the consent of the debtor. If, for example, one person sues another and wins a judgment for damages, the judgment becomes a legally enforceable obligation owed by the losing party, the **judgment debtor,** to the person who has won the judgment, the **judgment creditor.** In addition, a person may involuntarily become a debtor of a local, state, or federal government after incurring liability to pay property or income taxes, penalties, or fines.

The Law of Debtors and Creditors

Most substantive law governing debtor-creditor relations is derived from state statutes including Articles 6 and 9 of the Uniform Commercial Code. Superimposed upon this state law system is the federal law of bankruptcy. In addition, federal law regulates, particularly for consumer transactions, much of the process of extending credit and collecting debts from recalcitrant debtors. The foregoing statutes and regulations form the basis of this and the following chapters on debtor-creditor relations.

Types of Credit

Financial institutions, retailers, and other businesses provide many types of credit. Credit that is extended to businesses frequently is called **commercial** (or business) **credit,** while credit to persons for personal, family, or household purposes usually is called **consumer credit.** In **closed-end credit,** the amount of the debt is fixed and a repayment date is specified. In closed-end credit transactions, the parties agree at the time the credit is extended to the number of payments, due date, and amount of each payment. The typical car loan is a closed-end credit transaction. The debtor borrows a fixed amount of money and agrees to repay the debt through fixed monthly payments over a specified period.

In contrast, **open-end credit** is credit extended on an account in which the debtor will incur obligations in a series of transactions. Although the terms of open-end credit, such as the billing period and interest rate, are usually established in advance, neither the amount of the debt nor the specific due date is set. The amount of the debt fluctuates as the debtor makes purchases and remits payment on the account, with an agreed interest rate charged on the outstanding balance. Credit card accounts offered by retailers and banks are examples of open-end credit.

Credit may also be secured or unsecured. For reasons developed later in this chapter, secured creditors enjoy substantial advantages over unsecured creditors when the debtor encounters financial difficulty.

The Credit Decision

To determine whether an applicant is worthy of credit, most creditors require a potential debtor to complete a credit application. Of course, the creditor's primary concern is whether the debtor will repay the debt. Creditors consider many factors in making this determination. For commercial credit, the creditor usually reviews the business's accounting records, especially items such as current assets, current liabilities, profitability, and asset and inventory turnover. For consumer credit, the creditor usually reviews the applicant's assets (such as real estate and checking and savings accounts), employment and other sources of income, outstanding debts, and credit history. Most creditors verify the information a credit applicant provides and often obtain further information from a credit bureau. Credit bureaus compile information on individuals from public records, such as the courts, the recorder of deeds, and other recording agencies, and regularly obtain reports from retailers and financial institutions on delinquent accounts.

To simplify the credit decision, many creditors use credit scoring systems developed by credit specialists. Most systems list several factors as indicators of a debtor's creditworthiness. The creditor assigns each factor a number of points and establishes a minimum score for creditworthiness. Many creditors that use credit scoring systems supplement the information with subjective criteria.

The credit decision also includes the terms upon which credit will be extended. Financial institutions frequently set the amount of the credit, the interest rate, the payment schedule, and other terms according to the perceived risk of the obligation. Retailers and credit card issuers using open-end credit generally extend credit on the same terms to all debtors but establish individualized credit limits.

Risks of Extending Credit—Default and Bankruptcy

Creditors run two basic risks in extending credit: that the debtor will default and that the debtor will become insolvent. Default is simply the debtor's failure to pay or perform the obligation. **Insolvency** occurs when a debtor has insufficient assets to meet his total obligations or is unable to pay debts as they come due. A debtor generally reveals insolvency by defaulting on one or more outstanding obligations.

A debtor who has become insolvent may commence a bankruptcy proceeding under federal law. Bankruptcy law is designed to relieve an honest debtor from overburdensome financial obligations by granting a discharge if certain legal requirements are met. This discharge gives the debtor a fresh start, free of claims of former creditors. That is, a creditor who is not paid in full in the bankruptcy proceeding is generally precluded thereafter from asserting a claim against the debtor. To protect creditors claiming against a debtor's limited assets, the law also provides an elaborate priority system to assure equitable treatment of competing creditors. Bankruptcy is discussed in detail in Chapter 30.

Liens, Priorities, and General Creditors

When a debtor is insolvent, bankrupt, or otherwise possesses limited financial ability, questions of priority arise. That is, because the debtor's assets are insufficient to pay all creditors in full, the order in which competing creditors are paid must be determined. A creditor who is paid before another is said to have a "priority" over that creditor. Creditors may achieve priority in many ways. Perhaps the most common method of establishing priority is by creating a lien upon all or a specified portion of the debtor's property, real or personal.

Liens. A **lien** is an interest in property designed to secure the payment or other performance of an obligation. A lien gives the creditor recourse to the specific property in which the lien exists to satisfy the obligation secured by the lien. That is, if property is subject to a lien and the obligation secured by the lien is unpaid, the creditor may sell the property and apply the proceeds to the unpaid debt to the exclusion of other creditors. A lien, therefore, gives such a creditor priority over other creditors in the specific property subject to the lien. Frequently, two or more creditors will hold a lien upon the same property owned by the debtor. In these cases, debtor-creditor law also determines the priority among competing lien creditors.

Consensual Liens. Liens may be created with the debtor's consent, usually evidenced in a contract. Consensually created liens are introduced in the introduction to security on page 576.

Statutory Liens. Some liens are created by operation of law. Most of these are **statutory liens,** imposed or authorized solely by statute, that arise when specified circumstances or conditions occur. Many statutory liens are descendants of liens originally granted to certain creditors at common law. These **common law liens** generally allowed creditors such as landlords, bailees, and innkeepers to retain possession of the debtor's property until the debt was paid.

Some of the most common statutory liens are discussed below. As in other liens, if the debt secured by a statutory lien remains unpaid, the property may be sold and the proceeds applied to the debt.

An **artisan's lien** is the right of an artisan to retain possession of the object repaired or worked upon (such as an automobile) until receipt of payment for the work performed. An artisan is a skilled worker, such as a tailor, carpenter, or auto mechanic, in a trade requiring manual dexterity.

A **bailee's lien** is granted to carriers and warehousemen allowing them to retain possession of goods entrusted to them pending payment for the shipment or storage charges.[1]

A **landlord's lien** secures payment of rent by giving the landlord a lien upon the tenant's personal property located on the leased premises and, in the case of farmland, crops grown thereon.

A **mechanic's lien** is given to persons who supply services, labor, or material in the construction or improvement of real property. For example, a mechanic's lien may be used to secure payment for labor and materials of a contractor who remodels a property owner's kitchen. A mechanic's lien is recorded in the real estate records to provide constructive notice of its existence. If the debt secured by the lien is not paid, the lien is ultimately satisfied out of the proceeds of the next sale of the underlying real property.

A **tax lien** is held by the state or federal government or a governmental subdivision to secure payment of delinquent taxes. For example, a tax lien may be imposed in favor of a state or local government upon real property to secure unpaid real property taxes. Additionally, a federal tax lien is imposed upon all property of a taxpayer who refuses or neglects to pay a tax for which he is liable.

Judicial Liens. A third type of lien is a **judicial lien,** created by judicial action. Judicial liens include those created by judgment, levy, garnishment, or other legal or equitable process or proceeding. Judicial liens are discussed in the following chapter.

Priorities. In some cases, a creditor without a lien is granted a priority in payment over certain other creditors. Unlike liens, which may be created by contract, these **priorities** are almost always created by statute, most notably federal bankruptcy law. For example, bankruptcy law provides that admin-

---

1. Such liens are expressly authorized in §§7-209, 7-210 (warehousemen), 7-307, 7-308 (carriers) of the UCC and in the Federal Bills of Lading Act (49 U.S.C. §§105-106).

istrative expenses and employee claims for wages, among others, are given a priority in distribution of the bankrupt's limited assets. This priority exists even though the creditors involved have no lien upon specific property of the debtor.

General Creditors. A creditor who has neither a lien nor a priority is known as a **general creditor.** General creditors of a consumer debtor often include the power or phone company, and sellers of goods or services on credit. General creditors, of course, stand in the worst possible position when financial difficulty arises because they are paid only after creditors with a lien or statutorily authorized priority are paid. For this reason, the bulk of debtor-creditor law concerns when and how creditors establish a priority in distribution of the debtor's assets, thereby avoiding the unenviable general creditor status.

In summary, in the distribution of a debtor's assets, creditors with a lien are ordinarily paid first out of the proceeds of the property subject to the lien. If more than one creditor holds a lien on the same property, the law provides rules to establish priority among the competing lienholders. If assets remain that are not subject to liens, their proceeds are distributed first to creditors given a priority by statute. Any remaining assets are then distributed to general creditors.

Introduction to Security

To protect themselves against other creditors in the event of bankruptcy and to provide for expeditious collection upon default, creditors often insist upon some form of **security.** Virtually all security issues are based on a common situation. One person (the creditor) loans money to, sells property to, or performs services for another (the debtor) who then becomes bound to repay the loan or pay for the property or services. Because of the debtor's credit history, financial position, or other reason, the creditor desires more than merely the debtor's personal promise to pay. The creditor wants some additional "security" to satisfy the obligation in whole or in part if the debtor defaults.

Security is most commonly provided by a contractually created lien in the debtor's property. That

is, the debtor and creditor enter into a contract creating a lien in specific property owned by the debtor, often known as the "collateral." The contract provides that if the obligation secured by the collateral is not paid, the creditor may take possession of and sell the collateral to satisfy the debt. This right is known as the secured party's **right of foreclosure.** If the collateral (security) is *real property,* the transaction is governed by the law of mortgages discussed in Chapter 37. If the security is *personal property,* the arrangement is known as a "secured transaction" and is governed by Article 9 of the UCC. Secured transactions under Article 9 are discussed in detail in Chapters 31 and 32.

A creditor who has a contractually created lien is usually known as a **secured creditor,** and has important advantages over unsecured creditors. Upon default a secured creditor has recourse to specific assets of the debtor, often without the necessity of a judicial proceeding. These assets may then be sold and the proceeds applied to reduce or extinguish the secured debt to the exclusion of unsecured claims. In contrast, an unpaid unsecured creditor must first obtain a judgment and then may have a court officer seize and sell the debtor's assets to satisfy the debt. The unsecured creditor, however, often finds that the assets have been dissipated, are statutorily exempt from his claim, or are subject to secured creditors' claims.

In addition to liens created in specific property, security also may be provided by the contractual promise of someone other than the debtor to satisfy the obligation if the debtor does not. Such a security arrangement is known as "suretyship" and the third party guaranteeing the debt is a "surety." Suretyship is a common and important security device, and suretyship principles underlie many basic legal concepts. Suretyship is the subject of Chapter 33.

Government Regulation of Credit

In most consumer credit transactions, the creditor possesses greater bargaining power than the debtor. Some creditors have abused this power by arbitrarily refusing credit to deserving consumers or by misrepresenting contractual credit terms. To help eliminate these abusive practices, the federal government has enacted the **Consumer Credit Protec-tion Act** (CCPA)[2], which includes three major statutes relating to the extension of consumer credit: the Equal Credit Opportunity Act, the Fair Credit Reporting Act, and the Truth-in-Lending Act. These statutes are supplemented by state laws that further regulate credit transactions.

Equal Credit Opportunity Act

The **Equal Credit Opportunity Act (ECOA)**[3] prohibits discrimination in credit transactions on the basis of sex, marital status, religion, race, color, national origin, or age. The ECOA also prohibits discrimination because all or part of a credit applicant's income is derived from a public assistance program or because the applicant has in good faith exercised any right under the Consumer Credit Protection Act. The purpose of ECOA is to prevent creditors from depriving a person access to credit because of factors unrelated to creditworthiness. The Federal Reserve Board has issued **Regulation B**[4] to implement the ECOA.

The Credit Application. The ECOA restricts the type of information that a creditor may request on a credit application and limits the use of that information. A credit application, which includes both oral and written requests for credit, cannot request the applicant's race, color, religion, or national origin. Although the creditor may sometimes ask the applicant's sex, marital status, or age, this information may be used only for limited purposes. A creditor may not ask for data concerning the applicant's spouse unless both spouses are applying for use of the credit (for example, a joint credit card account). Creditors may request some types of information only if they advise the applicant that providing the information is optional. For example, a credit application may ask the applicant's title (Mr., Ms., Miss, Mrs.) if the application states that responding is optional. Disclosure that a person re-

ceives alimony, maintenance, or child support is allowed only if the applicant relies on these payments as an income source for credit purposes. To ensure that applicants are aware of their rights, the creditor must provide notice of the general provisions of the ECOA.

Use of Information. The ECOA prohibits the creditor from using any information about the applicant to discriminate on the basis of sex, marital status, age, religion, race, color, or national origin. Acts of intentional discrimination and practices with discriminatory effect are illegal. A creditor, therefore, cannot deny an applicant credit because she is a married woman or because he is Moslem or Hispanic. Credit practices have discriminatory effect if they create a disparate impact on persons protected by the ECOA. A creditor, for example, cannot routinely disregard part-time employment, alimony, or child support as sources of income because statistics show that women are more likely to rely on these sources of income. By disregarding these resources, the creditor would commit sex-based discrimination, illegal under the ECOA. Compliance with the ECOA requires that creditors evaluate the reliability of income from part-time employment, alimony, or child support in the same manner as they evaluate other sources of income.

The ECOA also prohibits certain discriminatory practices in the actual extension of credit, which are based on race, color, national origin, age, sex, or marital status. For example, a credit card company cannot impose a $300 credit line for a woman applicant while setting a $500 credit limit for a man with similar qualifications.

Notification of Credit Decision. One of the most important provisions of ECOA requires a creditor to notify the applicant of the creditor's decision to extend or not to extend credit within thirty days after receiving the application. A creditor who takes adverse action must state specific reasons for the action taken. Adverse action includes a denial or revocation of credit, changing the terms of an existing credit arrangement, or refusing to extend credit in the amount or on the terms requested. A creditor who uses a credit scoring system cannot merely indicate that the applicant failed to achieve

---

2. 15 U.S.C. §§1601-1693r.

3. 15 U.S.C. §§1691-1691f (Subchapter IV of the Consumer Credit Protection Act).

4. 12 C.F.R. part 202.

the requisite number of points, but must state the factors that most significantly affected the adverse score.

Remedies. A variety of federal administrative agencies, including the Federal Trade Commission (FTC), are charged with enforcing compliance with ECOA requirements. The ECOA also creates a statutory civil cause of action for violation of the statute. A successful plaintiff may recover actual damages and reasonable attorneys' fees and may recover up to $10,000 in punitive damages.

Fair Credit Reporting Act

The federal **Fair Credit Reporting Act (FCRA)**,[5] protects consumers from inaccurate and obsolete information contained in reports of consumer reporting agencies. A **consumer reporting agency** is a person or organization that for a fee or on a cooperative nonprofit basis regularly assembles or evaluates credit or other information on consumers for use by third parties. The most common type of agency is a credit bureau that provides reports to financial institutions, retailers, and other creditors for use in making credit decisions. Consumer reporting agencies do not include creditors that provide information to third parties concerning only the creditor's own experiences with the consumer.

Scope. The FCRA regulates the use of two types of reports prepared by consumer reporting agencies: consumer reports and investigative consumer reports. Consumer reports are oral or written reports from a consumer reporting agency that concern a consumer's creditworthiness, credit standing, credit capacity, character, general reputation, personal characteristics, or mode of living. These reports are used or collected to establish a consumer's eligibility for credit, consumer insurance, or employment. Consumer reports generally contain information collected by the agency from public records and the consumer's creditors. Investigative consumer reports contain information concerning the consumer's character, general reputation, per-

sonal characteristics, or mode of living, collected by personal interviews with the consumer's neighbors, friends, or acquaintances. A creditor may not request an investigative consumer report without disclosing to the consumer that such a report will be obtained as part of the credit decision.

A consumer reporting agency is authorized to provide consumer reports only to persons that the agency has reason to believe will use the information in connection with the extension of credit or review of a credit account, or that intend to use the information for employment or insurance purposes. The agency also may release a consumer report to a court or to the consumer on whom the report is made.

Obsolete Information. To ensure that the information in a consumer report is accurate and current, the FCRA prohibits consumer reporting agencies from disclosing obsolete adverse information in a consumer report. Such information includes bankruptcies that antedate the report by more than ten years and other adverse information that antedates the report by more than seven years, such as lawsuits and judgments (although judgment records may be disclosed throughout the statute of limitations period if longer than seven years), paid tax liens, accounts placed for collection, and criminal records of arrest, indictment, or conviction. In addition, before releasing information from an investigative consumer report, the agency must reverify any adverse information that was obtained more than three months prior to the date of the report.

Inaccurate Information. The FCRA also allows consumers access to their credit reports and a method of verifying accuracy. A creditor who denies consumer credit because of a consumer report must notify the credit applicant of the name and address of the consumer reporting agency that provided the report. The consumer then may request the agency to disclose the nature and substance of the information in the agency's file as well as the sources of information and recipients of reports during the preceding six months. If the consumer disputes the accuracy of any information, the consumer reporting agency must reinvestigate and delete any inaccurate information. If the agency finds

---

5. 15 U.S.C. §§1681-1681t (Subchapter III of the Consumer Credit Protection Act).

that the information is accurate, the consumer is entitled to file a statement explaining the dispute. Upon request of the consumer, the consumer reporting agency must provide notice of a deletion or the consumer's statement explaining a dispute to creditors who received the report during the previous six months. In all subsequent reports, the agency must include the consumer's statement explaining the dispute or a summary of that statement.

The following case illustrates application of some of the provisions of the FCRA to records maintained by a credit bureau.

Thompson v. San Antonio Retail Merchants Association

682 F.2d 509 (5th Cir. 1982)

San Antonio Retail Merchants Association (SARMA) provides computerized credit reporting services on a subscription basis to local businesses. Subscribers gain access to the information by calling SARMA's central computer from their own computer terminals and entering the name or social security number of an individual. The computer displays records of all persons with similar names and the subscriber selects the appropriate record. If a business accepts a record of a particular consumer, SARMA's central computer data base "automatically captures" any other information in that business's data base concerning the consumer.

In 1978, the plaintiff William Douglas Thompson, III applied for a Gulf Oil Corporation credit card. Gulf requested a credit search from SARMA and mistakenly accepted the record of William Daniel Thompson, Jr. which listed a bad debt report from Gordon's Jewelers. Through the automatic capture feature, the SARMA computer added all information on William Douglas Thompson, III from Gulf's data base to William Daniel Thompson, Jr.'s credit file. The data included William Douglas Thompson, III's social security number, his wife's name, and his place of employment. Thereafter, SARMA's files contained a garbled record of credit information on both men.

Although Gulf asked SARMA to verify the bad account from Gordon's, the errors were not discovered and Gulf denied Thompson's credit application. William Douglas Thompson, III subsequently applied two times for credit with Montgomery Ward but was denied credit because of the adverse report from Gordon's. Thompson never requested the reason for the credit denials. In June of 1979, Mrs. William Douglas Thompson, III applied for a loan from her credit union and first learned of the adverse report from Gordon's. During the next four months, she and her husband visited and wrote to Gordon's and SARMA requesting correction of the records. Despite Gordon's and SARMA's acknowledgment of the errors, the records were not corrected.

Mr. and Mrs. William Douglas Thompson, III sued SARMA. The trial court held that SARMA had failed to follow reasonable procedures to assure maximum possible accuracy of its files. The Thompsons were awarded damages of $10,000 plus attorneys' fees of $4,485. SARMA appealed.

Per Curiam

. . . [The Fair Credit Reporting Act] does not impose strict liability for any inaccurate credit report, but only a duty of reasonable care in preparation of the report. That duty extends to updating procedures, because "preparation" of a consumer report should be viewed as a continuing process and the obligation to insure accuracy arises with every addition of information. . . .

Applying the reasonable-person standard, the district court found two acts of negligence in SARMA's updating procedures. First, SARMA failed to exercise reasonable care in programming its computer to automatically capture information into a file without requiring any minimum number of "points of correspondence" between the consumer and the file or having an adequate auditing procedure to foster accuracy. Second, SARMA failed to employ reasonable procedures designed to learn the disparity in social security numbers for the two Thompsons. . . .

With respect to the first act of negligence, George Zepeda, SARMA's manager, testified that SARMA's computer had no minimum number of points of correspondence to be satisfied before an inquiring subscriber could accept credit information. Moreover, SARMA had no way of knowing if the information supplied by the subscriber was correct. Although SARMA did conduct spot audits to verify social security numbers, it did not audit all subscribers. With respect to the second act of negligence, SARMA's verification process failed to uncover the erroneous social security number even though Gulf made a specific request for a "revision" to check the adverse credit history ascribed to the plaintiff. SARMA's manager, Mr. Zepeda, testified that what should have been done upon the request for a revision, was to pick up the phone and check with Gordon's and learn, among other things, the social security number for William Daniel Thompson, Jr. It was the manager's further testimony that the social security number is the single most important information in a consumer's credit file. In light of this evidence, this Court cannot conclude that the district court was clearly erroneous in finding negligent violation of [the Fair Credit Reporting Act]. . . .

The district court's award of $10,000 in actual damages was based on humiliation and mental distress to the plaintiff. Even when there are no out-of-pocket expenses, humiliation and mental distress do constitute recoverable elements of damage under the Act. . . .

[T]he inaccurate information remained in SARMA's files for almost one and one-half years after the inaccurate information was inserted. Even after the error was discovered, Thompson spent months pressing SARMA to correct its mistakes and fully succeeded only after bringing a lawsuit against SARMA. . . .

[Judgment affirmed.]

Remedies. The FCRA provides for administrative enforcement by the FTC and other federal agencies. It also provides both civil remedies and criminal penalties for violation of its provisions. A consumer may sue a credit reporting agency for actual damages and punitive damages (if the violation was willful) and may be awarded reasonable attorneys' fees. Obtaining information on a consumer from a credit reporting agency under false pretenses is punishable by a fine of up to $5,000 or imprisonment for up to one year, or both. An employee or officer of the agency who knowingly or willfully provides information to an unauthorized person is subject to the same penalties.

Truth-in-Lending Act

The most comprehensive federal statute concerning consumer credit is the **Truth-in-Lending Act (TILA),**[6] which requires creditors to disclose to consumers specified contractual terms of credit transactions. **Regulation Z,**[7] issued by the Federal Reserve Board, implements the TILA.

Scope. The TILA applies only to consumer credit transactions, those in which the debtor is a natural person seeking credit for personal, family, or household purposes. The TILA applies only to creditors who regularly extend credit and to whom the debt is initially payable. Accordingly, banks, savings and loan institutions, credit card companies, retailers, and professionals who make loans or sell goods or services on credit generally are subject to the provisions of the TILA. Under the TILA, a transaction involves the extension of credit if the creditor imposes a finance charge or if the debt is payable in more than four installments (even if no finance charge is imposed). Most credit transactions in excess of $25,000 are exempted. If, however, the transaction involves consumer real property (for example, a loan to purchase a house), or if the creditor takes a security interest in personal property that is the consumer's primary dwelling (for example, a mobile home), the creditor must comply with the TILA regardless of the amount of credit.

Disclosure Requirements. Regulation Z specifies the credit terms that a creditor must disclose and requires the disclosures to be made "clearly and conspicuously" in a written form that the consumer may keep.[8] Two of the most important credit terms are the "finance charge" and the "annual percentage rate," which must be disclosed more conspicuously than other information provided except the creditor's identity.

The **finance charge** is the cost of consumer credit expressed in a dollar amount. It includes all

---

6. 15 U.S.C. §§1601-1667e (Subchapter I of the Consumer Credit Protection Act).
7. 12 C.F.R. part 226.
8. 15 U.S.C. §1632(a); 12 C.F.R. §§226.5(a), 226.17(a).

charges imposed by the creditor upon the consumer incident to or as a condition of extending credit. Under the TILA, therefore, a finance charge includes not only interest or a time-price differential but also other fees that the creditor requires the debtor to pay to obtain credit. Such fees include service or carrying charges, loan fees, finder's fees, fees for appraisals and credit reports, charges for insurance paid by the debtor to protect the creditor if the debtor defaults, and certain other insurance premiums.[9]

The **annual percentage rate (APR)** generally is the finance charge on an annual basis expressed as a percentage of the amount of credit. Thus, whereas the finance charge is the cost of credit expressed in a dollar amount, the APR is its cost expressed as a yearly percentage rate. The TILA and Regulation Z provide a detailed explanation of the method of calculating the APR. Regulation Z also includes tables to assist the creditor.[10]

The TILA establishes different disclosure requirements for open-end and closed-end credit plans.[11] A creditor entering into an open-end agreement must make certain disclosures in writing in a statement issued at the time the account is opened and in statements issued on a periodic basis according to the creditor's billing cycle for periods in which the account has a debit or credit balance or in which a finance charge is made. The opening statement must include the conditions under which a finance charge is made, the method of determining the finance charge, the method of determining the balance upon which the finance charge is based, the periodic rate (for example, $1\frac{1}{2}\%$ per month), and the APR. The periodic statement provides similar information applied to specific transactions that occurred during the billing period: the previous balance, identification of each transaction, credits and payments, the balance subject to the finance charge, the finance charge and the periodic rate, and the APR. The TILA also requires the creditor to make other disclosures when changes in credit terms or other changes occur.

Prior to entering into a closed-end credit transaction, the creditor must provide a written disclosure statement that includes the identity of the creditor, the finance charge, the APR, the amount financed, the total of payments (amount financed plus finance charge), and the number, amount, and due dates of payments, and late fees (expressed in a dollar amount or on a percentage basis). If the creditor is taking a security interest in the debtor's property, the security interest must be disclosed. If the creditor is also the seller of the property for which the credit transaction was arranged, the disclosure statement also must show the "total sales price," indicating the cash price plus additional charges plus the finance charge. Figure 28-1, taken from Regulation Z, is a model disclosure form for a closed-end credit sale.

Other Provisions. In addition to disclosures concerning the costs of credit, the TILA includes other statutory requirements concerning credit transactions. The statute grants consumers a limited right to rescind certain credit transactions in which the creditor will acquire a security interest in the debtor's principal residence.[12] Another part of the TILA is **Fair Credit Billing Act,**[13] which regulates billing practices and disputes for open-end credit accounts. The Fair Credit Billing Act includes procedures that the debtor and creditor must follow when billing errors occur. Each year the creditor must furnish the debtor with a statement outlining the debtor's rights and creditor's responsibilities under the Act.

Remedies. The TILA creates a civil cause of action for failure to comply with its disclosure requirements. A consumer who successfully sues a creditor for violation of the TILA may be awarded actual damages, plus a penalty generally equal to twice the finance charge. The TILA, however, creates a minimum penalty of $100 and a maximum penalty of $1,000 in an individual suit. The successful consumer may also recover court costs and a reasonable attorneys' fee. Damages are generally recoverable only if the creditor's violation relates

---

9. 15 U.S.C. §1605; 12 C.F.R. §226.4.

10. 15 U.S.C. §1606(a); 12 C.F.R. part 226, Appendices F, J.

11. 15 U.S.C. §§1637-1638.

---

12. 15 U.S.C. §1635.

13. 15 U.S.C. §1666-1666j.

Figure 28–1	Credit Sale Sample

Big Wheel Auto   Carmen Green

ANNUAL PERCENTAGE RATE The cost of your credit as a yearly rate.	FINANCE CHARGE The dollar amount the credit will cost you.	Amount Financed The amount of credit provided to you or on your behalf.	Total of Payments The amount you will have paid after you have made all payments as scheduled.	Total Sale Price The total cost of your purchase on credit, including your downpayment of $ 1500–
14.84%	$ 1496.80	$ 6107.50	$ 7604.30	$ 9129.30

You have the right to receive at this time an itemization of the Amount Financed.
☐ I want an itemization.   ☒ I do not want an itemization.

Your payment schedule will be:

Number of Payments	Amount of Payments	When Payments Are Due
36	$211.23	Monthly beginning 6-1-87

Insurance
Credit life insurance and credit disability insurance are not required to obtain credit, and will not be provided unless you sign and agree to pay the additional cost.

Type	Premium	Signature	
Credit Life	$120–	I want credit life insurance.	Carmen Green Signature
Credit Disability		I want credit disability insurance.	Signature
Credit Life and Disability		I want credit life and disability insurance.	Signature

Security: You are giving a security interest in:
☒   the goods being purchased.
☐ _____

Filing fees $ 12.50 _____   Non-filing insurance $_____

Late charge: If a payment is late, you will be charged $10.

Prepayment: If you pay off early, you
☐ may   ☐ will not   have to pay a penalty.
☒ may   ☐ will not   be entitled to a refund of part of the finance charge.

See your contract documents for any additional information about nonpayment, default, any required repayment in full before the scheduled date, and prepayment refunds and penalties.

I have received a copy of this statement.

Carmen Green   5-1-87
Signature   Date

e means an estimate

to disclosures of material importance. A creditor may avoid liability by proving that its failure to comply resulted from a bona fide error (for example, a printing error or computer malfunction). To encourage creditors to correct disclosure violations, the TILA exempts from civil liability a creditor who discovers an error, notifies the debtor, and makes any necessary adjustments within sixty days after discovering the error, provided that the debtor is notified of correction before the debtor institutes a lawsuit or gives written notice of the error to the creditor.

A creditor also may be subject to criminal penalties of a maximum fine of $5,000 and up to one year imprisonment, or both, for willfully and knowingly providing false or inaccurate information required by the Act or Regulation Z.[14]

State Regulation of Credit Transactions

Many states have adopted statutes similar to the ECOA, the FCRA, and the TILA that govern credit transactions within the individual state. In general, state statutes supplement the provisions of federal law, and creditors must comply with both federal and state law. State statutes vary considerably but many provide more stringent requirements or more severe penalties than the federal laws. Almost every state has adopted some form of disclosure law concerning certain types of consumer transactions. These statutes have a variety of names, including the "Retail Installment Act," "State Truth in Lending Act," and "Motor Vehicle Sales Act."

The **Uniform Consumer Credit Code (UCCC)**, originally promulgated in 1968 and revised in 1974, has been enacted in some form in eleven states.[15] It is designed to replace piecemeal state consumer credit laws with a single comprehensive code. The UCCC regulates, for example, interest rates, garnishment, home solicitation and referral sales, credit insurance, contract terms and disclosure, and creditors' remedies.

Usury Laws. Every state has adopted some form of usury statute that establishes a maximum rate of interest that may be charged for credit transactions. **Usury** is the act of charging an interest rate in excess of that allowed by state law.

State law often establishes two maximum interest rates. The "legal rate" applies to transactions in which the parties did not agree on an interest rate. For example, if a person or business buys goods or services on an open account and fails to pay, the creditor generally may charge the legal rate of interest on the outstanding balance. In most states, this rate is between six percent and nine percent.

The second maximum interest rate is the "contract rate," which applies to transactions in which the parties have agreed to a specified rate of interest. The maximum contract rate usually is higher than the legal rate. Frequently, commercial credit transactions are exempted from the laws concerning the contract rate. That is, in transactions between two businesses, the parties may be free to establish as high a level of interest as they desire. Many states establish different contract rates for open-end and closed-end credit transactions, allowing a higher interest rate for open-end transactions.

A creditor is well advised to review state usury laws prior to entering into a credit transaction. Some states provide that the penalty for violating the usury law is forfeiture of the interest in excess of the allowed rate while other states penalize usury by requiring forfeiture of all interest or even by voiding the contract.

SUMMARY

1. The debtor-creditor relation is governed primarily by state statutes, including Articles 6 and 9 of the UCC, and the federal law of bankruptcy. In addition, federal law regulates, particularly for consumer transactions, much of the process of extending credit and collecting debts from recalcitrant debtors.

2. In many debtor-creditor disputes, two or more creditors hold claims that, taken collectively, exceed the debtor's total assets. In this case, the order on priority in which competing creditors are paid must be determined.

3. One method used by creditors to establish priority in distribution of a debtor's assets is to create a lien upon all or some of the debtor's property. A lien—an interest in property securing payment or other performance of an obligation—gives a creditor recourse to specific property in which the lien exists to the exclusion of other creditors. Liens may be created with the debtor's consent, by statute or common law doctrine, or by judicial action.

4. In some cases, a creditor without a lien is granted a priority by statute in payment over certain other credi-

---

14. 15 U.S.C. §§1611, 1640.

15. States enacting the UCCC include Colorado, Idaho, Indiana, Iowa, Kansas, Maine, Oklahoma, South Carolina, Utah, Wisconsin, and Wyoming. State adoptions are not, however, uniform.

tors. For example, federal bankruptcy law grants a priority in the distribution of the debtor's limited assets to certain creditors, such as employees, who do not possess a lien upon the debtor's property. General creditors, who possess neither a lien nor a priority, are paid only after creditors with a lien or statutorily authorized priority.

5. To protect themselves against other creditors and to expedite collection upon default, creditors often insist upon some form of security. A contractually created lien in the debtor's property is the most common form of security. If the debtor's real property forms the security, the transaction is governed by the law of mortgages; if the debtor's personal property provides the security, the transaction is governed by Article 9 of the UCC. Another form of security is suretyship, in which a third party, the surety, is obligated to satisfy the obligation if the debtor does not.

6. To help eliminate abusive practices by creditors, the federal government has adopted the Consumer Credit Protection Act which includes three statutes governing the extension of consumer credit, the Equal Credit Opportunity Act, the Fair Credit Reporting Act, and the Truth-in-Lending Act.

7. The Equal Credit Opportunity Act (ECOA) prohibits discrimination in credit transactions on the basis of sex, marital status, religion, race, color, national origin, age, or the applicant's receiving public assistance.

8. The Fair Credit Reporting Act (FCRA), which regulates consumer reporting agencies, limits the use of obsolete and inaccurate information in consumer credit reports, and provides a mechanism to facilitate consumers' correcting and supplementing information in those reports.

9. The Truth-in-Lending Act (TILA) requires disclosure of specified credit terms in consumer credit transactions.

10. Many states have adopted statutes regulating consumer credit transactions which supplement federal law. In addition, state usury laws establish a maximum interest rate that may be charged in credit transactions.

KEY TERMS

debtor
creditor
judgment debtor
judgment creditor
commercial credit
consumer credit
closed-end credit
open-end credit
insolvency

lien
statutory lien
common law lien
artisan's lien
bailee's lien
landlord's lien
mechanic's lien
tax lien
judicial lien

priorities
general creditor
security
right of foreclosure
secured creditor
Consumer Credit
  Protection Act (CCPA)
Equal Credit Opportunity
  Act (ECOA)
Regulation B
Fair Credit Reporting Act
  (FCRA)

consumer reporting
  agency
Truth-in-Lending Act
  (TILA)
Regulation Z
finance charge
annual percentage rate
  (APR)
Fair Credit Billing Act
Uniform Consumer Credit
  Code (UCCC)
usury

QUESTIONS AND PROBLEMS

28-1 As discussed in the text, general creditors are in the worst position when a debtor encounters financial difficulty. Why would a creditor extend credit without taking security—that is, does a creditor ever act reasonably by becoming a general creditor?

28-2 Major Department Store uses a credit scoring system to determine an applicant's creditworthiness. One of the factors used in the system is the zip code. If an applicant's residence is in zip code 12345, the applicant receives five points. If the applicant's residence is in zip code 67890, the applicant receives negative five points. Zip code 12345 is an upper middle-class suburb with predominantly white residents. Zip code 67890 is an inner city neighborhood with predominantly black residents. Does this system violate the ECOA?

28-3 Patsy Anderson, a married woman, has applied for a loan from United Finance Co. United verified Anderson's credit background and agreed to lend her the money provided she grants a security interest in her household goods. United has prepared a promissory note that requires both Anderson's and her husband's signature. United also has prepared a security agreement for both of their signatures. Anderson has explained to United that the loan is for her own use and she—not her husband—will repay it. Nevertheless, United has insisted that both parties sign because the household goods that will serve as collateral are jointly owned by Anderson and her husband. Has United violated the ECOA?

28-4 Mr. and Mrs. Freeman borrowed money from Southern Bank. Although the Freemans fully repaid the loan, Southern Bank has on several occasions sent reports to the local credit bureau

Figure 28–2	Statement of Disclosure and Loan Register

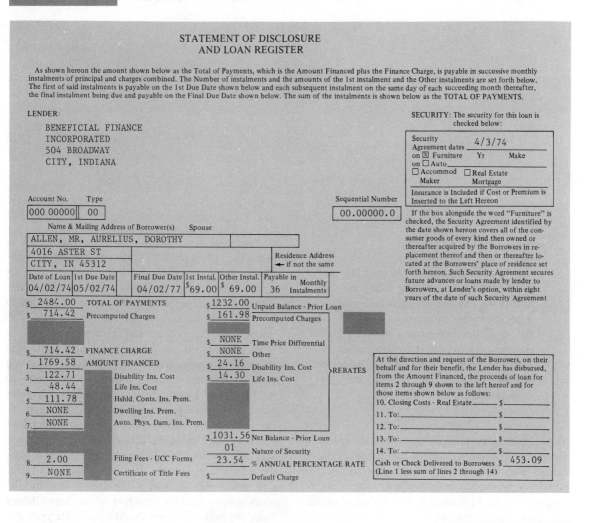

STATEMENT OF DISCLOSURE
AND LOAN REGISTER

As shown hereon the amount shown below as the Total of Payments, which is the Amount Financed plus the Finance Charge, is payable in successive monthly instalments of principal and charges combined. The Number of instalments and the amounts of the 1st instalment and the Other instalments are set forth below. The first of said instalments is payable on the 1st Due Date shown below and each subsequent instalment on the same day of each succeeding month thereafter, the final instalment being due and payable on the Final Due Date shown below. The sum of the instalments is shown below as the TOTAL OF PAYMENTS.

LENDER:

BENEFICIAL FINANCE
INCORPORATED
504 BROADWAY
CITY, INDIANA

SECURITY: The security for this loan is checked below:

Security Agreement dates 4/3/74 on ☒ Furniture Yr Make on ☐ Auto_____ ☐ Accommod Maker ☐ Real Estate Mortgage

Insurance is Included if Cost or Premium is Inserted to the Left Hereon

If the box alongside the word "Furniture" is checked, the Security Agreement identified by the date shown hereon covers all of the consumer goods of every kind then owned or thereafter acquired by the Borrowers in replacement thereof and then or thereafter located at the Borrowers' place of residence set forth hereon. Such Security Agreement secures future advances or loans made by lender to Borrowers, at Lender's option, within eight years of the date of such Security Agreement

Account No. Type
| 000 00000 | 00 |

Sequential Number
| 00.00000.0 |

Name & Mailing Address of Borrower(s)   Spouse

ALLEN, MR, AURELIUS, DOROTHY

4016 ASTER ST
CITY, IN 45312

Residence Address ◄— if not the same

Date of Loan	1st Due Date	Final Due Date	1st Instal.	Other Instal.	Payable in
04/02/74	05/02/74	04/02/77	$69.00	$ 69.00	36 Monthly Instalments

$ 2484.00 TOTAL OF PAYMENTS
$ 714.42 Precomputed Charges

$ 714.42 FINANCE CHARGE
1. 1769.58 AMOUNT FINANCED
3. 122.71 Disability Ins. Cost
4. 48.44 Life Ins. Cost
5. 111.78 Hshld. Conts. Ins. Prem.
6. NONE Dwelling Ins. Prem.
7. NONE Auto. Phys. Dam. Ins. Prem.

8. 2.00 Filing Fees · UCC Forms
9. NONE Certificate of Title Fees

$ 1232.00 Unpaid Balance · Prior Loan
$ 161.98 Precomputed Charges

$ NONE Time Price Differential
$ NONE Other
$ 24.16 Disability Ins. Cost
$ 14.30 Life Ins. Cost

}REBATES

2. 1031.56 Net Balance · Prior Loan
01 Nature of Security
23.54 % ANNUAL PERCENTAGE RATE
$_____ Default Charge

At the direction and request of the Borrowers, on their behalf and for their benefit, the Lender has disbursed, from the Amount Financed, the proceeds of loan for items 2 through 9 shown to the left hereof and for those items shown below as follows:
10. Closing Costs · Real Estate_____ $_____
11. To:_____ $_____
12. To:_____ $_____
13. To:_____ $_____
14. To:_____ $_____
Cash or Check Delivered to Borrowers $ 453.09
(Line 1 less sum of lines 2 through 14)

and to other creditors stating that the Freemans have failed to repay the loan.

(a) The Freemans have filed a lawsuit alleging that Southern Bank has violated the Fair Credit Reporting Act. How should the court rule on their complaint?

(b) What other remedies are available to the Freemans?

28-5   Figure 28–2 is part of a disclosure form provided by a finance company to a borrower in connection with a consumer loan. Does this form meet the requirement of the Truth-in-Lending Act that disclosures be made "clearly and conspicuously"?

Chapter 29

Creditors' Remedies

Most debtors promptly pay their obligations as they come due. The law of debtors and creditors is concerned with those who do not. A debtor may be unwilling or unable to pay a legitimate debt for various reasons. The debtor may be overextended due to poor management of his or her business or finances, or because of illness or disability. Or the debtor may have fraudulently incurred the obligation, with no intent to repay it or at least with no qualms about leaving creditors unpaid at the first sign of financial difficulty. Whatever the reason for nonpayment, in debtor-creditor law the validity of the plaintiff-creditor's claim usually is not in question. Rather, the law generally addresses two basic issues: debt collection remedies and priority disputes.

This chapter examines the first of these issues, the various remedies available under state law to aid creditors in collecting debts from unwilling or dishonest debtors. These remedies, which may be available either before or after a judgment is obtained, are designed to locate and apply to the debt assets held (1) by the debtor, (2) by third parties indebted to the debtor, or (3) by third parties to whom the debtor has transferred the property with intent to frustrate or defraud creditors.

In addition to providing basic debt collection remedies, debtor-creditor law resolves so-called priority disputes among competing creditors all holding valid claims against the debtor. Disputes often arise among secured creditors, between secured creditors and creditors holding judicial or statutory liens upon the debtor's property, between secured creditors and buyers of the collateral from the debtor, and between secured creditors and general unsecured creditors of the debtor. Priority disputes among various creditors of the same debtor form the bulk of debtor-creditor law. They are the basic focus of the law of secured transactions (discussed in Chapters 31 and 32), mortgages (covered in Chapter 37), and bankruptcy (discussed in Chapter 30).

State Debt Collection Remedies

If an individual fails to pay a debt when due, the creditor usually first tries nonjudicial means of collection including phone calls, letters threatening legal action (''dunning letters''), or personal visits. If these efforts fail, the creditor may turn to the legal system.

Although judicial debt collection remedies are designed to reach the debtor's assets and apply them to the unpaid debt, every state, by statute or constitutional provision, exempts certain property from creditors' claims. These state **exemption statutes** protect the debtor or her family from total destitution. Although individual state statutes vary widely, all exempt certain personal property identified by type or value. Real property used as a residence may be exempt under a "homestead" exemption. State statutes usually protect certain forms of income, such as income from trusts and wages. In most states, both the proceeds and cash surrender value of a life insurance policy also are exempt. Although many exemption statutes are archaic and provide for unequal treatment of debtors, states have been slow to change them.[1]

The following material discusses the state debt collection remedies used by creditors to reach a debtor's nonexempt assets.

The Judgment

Under the Fifth and Fourteenth Amendments to the Constitution, no person may be deprived of life, liberty, or property without due process of law. Due process generally includes notice to the defendant and a hearing relevant to the nature of the case. In the debtor-creditor context, therefore, a debtor generally may not be forced to part with property (money) without a judicial determination of the validity of the creditor's claim. This judicial determination is embodied in a judgment rendered by a court.

To obtain a judgment, the creditor files a lawsuit against the debtor alleging facts supporting the existence of the debt and the debtor's default. A copy of the complaint and summons are then served upon the debtor (service of process), which satisfies the notice aspect of the due process requirement. The debtor is then given the opportunity to appear in court to contest the existence or amount of the debt. If the debtor contests the claim, a trial is held (the hearing aspect of the due process requirement) after which the court may find for the debtor or

may render judgment against the debtor for all or part of the creditor's claim. If the debtor fails to answer the complaint or appear in court, a **default judgment** will be entered for the creditor for the amount stated in the complaint. Collection lawsuits usually result in a default judgment in the creditor's favor.

A creditor desires to obtain a judgment as quickly and cheaply as possible after default to take advantage of the collection remedies available to a judgment creditor. One device traditionally used by creditors to expedite the process of obtaining judgment is the **cognovit** or **confession of judgment clause.** A cognovit clause is a term contained in the original contract creating the debt, such as a lease or promissory note, authorizing the creditor to obtain a judgment against the debtor upon default without notice to the debtor or a hearing. The clause generally authorizes the creditor to choose an attorney to appear in court and confess judgment against the debtor for the amount in default along with other charges, usually including attorneys' fees. Because their basic operation is diametrically at odds with the Due Process Clause, cognovit clauses have been harshly received by the courts. Although the Supreme Court has not declared cognovit clauses unconstitutional per se,[2] most states, by statute, have either abolished them or severely limited their use. The legal attitude toward cognovit clauses is particularly harsh if they are imposed in adhesion contracts governing consumer transactions such as residential leases or installment sales of consumer goods.

Both secured and unsecured creditors may obtain a judgment because both have a personal right against the debtor for the amount of the debt. The secured creditor, additionally, has rights in the collateral that may or may not require a judicial proceeding to enforce. If a secured creditor obtains a judgment and the value of the collateral is insufficient to discharge it, the balance due is known as a **deficiency judgment.** The creditor may then attempt to collect the deficiency from the debtor's remaining assets by using the various collection remedies outlined below.

---

1. The federal Bankruptcy Code also contains an exempt property provision discussed in Chapter 30.

2. See *D. H. Overmyer Co., Inc., of Ohio v. Frick Company*, 92 S. Ct. 775 (1972).

Prejudgment (Provisional) Remedies

In certain limited situations, a creditor may have rights to the debtor's assets before judgment. For example, a secured creditor may, as part of the security agreement, be entitled to repossess the debtor's assets upon default without judicial authorization. Further, an unsecured creditor may acquire rights in the debtor's property before the validity of the creditor's claim is determined by using prejudgment or "provisional" remedies. Prejudgment remedies are extraordinary and provisional because the creditor's ultimate right to the assets is dependent upon his or her later obtaining a judgment against the debtor. Prejudgment remedies also are subject to constitutional due process limitations outlined later in this chapter.

Attachment. **Attachment,** originally developed in early English common law, is a prejudgment remedy now generally governed by statute and is designed to reach assets in the hands of the debtor. Attachment is primarily used by a creditor who fears that the debtor may dissipate, squander, fraudulently transfer, or conceal assets during the course of the lawsuit establishing the validity of the creditor's claim. To assure that assets are available when a judgment is obtained, state statutes authorize the use of a **writ of attachment.** The writ of attachment directs the sheriff to take custody of the debtor's personal or real property and hold the property during the trial of the case to assure its availability if and when the creditor obtains a judgment. The sheriff's act in taking custody of the debtor's property is known as **levy.** If the creditor obtains a judgment, the seized assets are then used to satisfy it.

A creditor seeking attachment must usually post a bond to reimburse the debtor for losses if the debtor successfully defends the creditor's action on the underlying debt. All states allow the debtor to recover damages from the creditor for a wrongful attachment.

Attachment creates a lien upon the property levied. The lien is effective from the date the levy is made, or in some states, from the date the writ is delivered to the sheriff. If a judgment is subsequently obtained, the attaching creditor generally has priority over other liens that took effect after the effective date of the attachment lien.

Prejudgment Garnishment. **Garnishment** (in some states known as "trustee process") is a collection remedy directed to a third party (the "garnishee") who holds property of, or is indebted to, the debtor. Garnishment is both a prejudgment and postjudgment remedy.

In prejudgment garnishment, the court directs the garnishee not to pay the debtor until the creditor's suit against the debtor has concluded and any judgment rendered therein paid. Most garnishees are either banks in which the debtor maintains an account or employers owing wages to the debtor. Prejudgment garnishment is similar to attachment in that both remedies preserve assets which may be used to satisfy a later judgment. Additionally, both remedies create a lien upon the property involved. In garnishment the lien usually is effective from the date process is served on the garnishee.

Replevin and Self-Help. **Replevin** is a statutory prejudgment remedy enabling the plaintiff to recover possession of specific goods wrongfully taken or detained. Unlike attachment, which may be used to reach all nonexempt property of the debtor, replevin is available only to a creditor who has a lien upon the property involved or the right to possession. As such, replevin is primarily used by secured creditors to recover possession of (repossess) property in which they have a security interest after default by the debtor. For example, a replevin action might be used by a bank to repossess an automobile after default by a borrower on an auto loan. In most states, the plaintiff obtains a writ of replevin by filing an affidavit with the clerk of the court and posting a bond. The sheriff then "replevies" (seizes) the property and turns it over to the plaintiff pending resolution of the suit over the right to possession.

Closely related to replevin is the ancient remedy of **self-help,** widely used in secured lending. Under self-help, upon default by the debtor, the creditor simply repossesses the collateral (such as an automobile) without resort to judicial process. The self-help remedy may be provided for in the contract between debtor and creditor, and its use is explicitly authorized by Article 9 of the Uniform Commercial Code. Self-help is quicker and cheaper than obtaining a writ of replevin, but replevin is more appropriate if the creditor fears that the debtor will resist attempts at self-help repossession.

Receivership. A **receiver** is a person appointed by the court to take possession of and administer, preserve, or manage the debtor's property under court direction. Appointment of a receiver is an extraordinary equitable remedy, available only when the remedy at law, such as attachment, is inadequate. Like garnishment, receivership is both a prejudgment and postjudgment remedy.

A receiver is a neutral, disinterested party, possessing only those powers and duties conferred by the court. Usually those powers are limited to taking possession of (but not title to) specified property and preserving it pending the outcome of the litigation. Additionally, limited management duties, such as collection of rent, may be imposed.

Unlike other provisional remedies, appointment of a receiver does not create a lien upon or affect title to the property. Existing liens on the property remain valid and subsequent judgment creditors, including the petitioning creditor, may obtain liens upon it. Receivership therefore benefits all creditors by preserving the property while conflicting creditors' claims to it are resolved.

Constitutional Limitations on Prejudgment Remedies.
Attachment, garnishment, replevin, and other prejudgment remedies deprive the debtor of property before the validity of the creditor's claim is determined. For this reason, state prejudgment remedies have often been attacked as a taking of property without due process of law, thereby violating the Fourteenth Amendment. Since the classic case of *Sniadach v. Family Finance Corporation of Bay View,* decided in 1969, the Supreme Court has held in a series of cases that prejudgment remedies are subject to constitutional due process limitations generally requiring notice to the debtor and an opportunity for a hearing before state governmental agents (such as a court officer, marshall, or sheriff)

seize the debtor's property, or other procedural safeguards to provide debtor protection.[3] In the following case, the Supreme Court considered the constitutionality of a statute authorizing prejudgment replevin.

Fuentes v. Shevin
92 S.Ct. 1983 (1972)

Appellant Margarita Fuentes entered into an installment contract to purchase a stove and stereo from Firestone Tire and Rubber Company (Firestone). Under the contract, Firestone retained title to the goods until Fuentes had paid the full purchase price and finance charges, but Fuentes was entitled to possession of the goods as long as she made the installment payments. Fuentes allegedly defaulted on the payments after having paid approximately two-thirds of the amount owed. Firestone obtained a writ of replevin ordering the sheriff to seize the stove and stereo. On the same day, Firestone filed a lawsuit against Fuentes seeking return of the goods. Prior to the hearing on the lawsuit, the deputy sheriff seized the goods from Fuentes's home.

Under Florida statute, a court clerk issued a writ of replevin to any person who completed a form alleging that his or her goods had been "wrongfully detained" by another if the person also instituted a lawsuit to recover the goods. The person obtaining the writ also was required to file a bond equal to twice the value of the goods to be seized.

Fuentes filed a lawsuit alleging that the Florida replevin statute violated the Due Process Clause of the Constitution. The trial court upheld the constitutionality of the statute and Fuentes appealed to the Supreme Court. The case was consolidated with another case challenging a similar replevin statute of Pennsylvania.

---

3. See *Sniadach v. Family Finance Corporation of Bay View,* 89 S. Ct. 1820 (1969); *Mitchell v. W. T. Grant Company,* 94 S. Ct. 1895 (1974); *North Georgia Finishing, Inc. v. Di-Chem, Inc.,* 95 S. Ct. 719 (1975).

Justice Stewart

. . . The question is whether these statutory procedures violate the Fourteenth Amendment's guarantee that no State shall deprive any person of property without due process of law. . . .

As in the present cases, such statutes are most commonly used by creditors to seize goods allegedly wrongfully detained . . . by debtors. . . .

For more than a century the central meaning of procedural due process has been clear: "Parties whose rights are to be affected are entitled to be heard; and in order that they may enjoy that right they must first be notified." [*Baldwin v. Hale*, 68 U.S. (1 Wall.) 223, 233 (1863).] . . . It is equally fundamental that the right to notice and an opportunity to be heard "must be granted at a meaningful time and in a meaningful manner." [*Armstrong v. Manzo*, 85 S. Ct. 1187, 1191 (1965).] . . . .

The primary question in the present cases is whether these state statutes are constitutionally defective in failing to provide for hearings "at a meaningful time." . . . [N]either the Florida nor the Pennsylvania statute provides for notice or an opportunity to be heard *before* the seizure. The issue is whether procedural due process in the context of these cases requires an opportunity for a hearing *before* the State authorizes its agents to seize property in the possession of a person upon the application of another.

The constitutional right to be heard is a basic aspect of the duty of government to follow a fair process of decision-making when it acts to deprive a person of his possessions. The purpose of this requirement is not only to ensure abstract fair play to the individual. Its purpose, more particularly, is to protect his use and possession of property from arbitrary encroachment—to minimize substantively unfair or mistaken deprivations of property, a danger that is especially great when the State seizes goods simply upon the application of and for the benefit of a private party. . . .

The requirement of notice and an opportunity to be heard raises no impenetrable barrier to the taking of a person's possessions. But the fair process of decision-making that it guarantees works, by itself, to protect against arbitrary deprivation of property. For when a person has an opportunity to speak up in his own defense, and when the State must listen to what he has to say, substantively unfair and simply mistaken deprivations of property interests can be prevented. . . .

If the right to notice and a hearing is to serve its full purpose, then, it is clear that it must be granted at a time when the deprivation can still be prevented. At a later hearing, an individual's possessions can be returned to him if they were unfairly or mistakenly taken in the first place. Damages may even be awarded to him for the wrongful deprivation. But no later hearing and no damage award can undo the fact that the arbitrary taking that was subject to the right of procedural due process has already occurred. . . .

The right to a prior hearing, of course, attaches only to the deprivation of an interest encompassed within the Fourteenth Amendment's protection. . . .

The appellants who signed conditional sales contracts lacked full legal title to the replevied goods. The Fourteenth Amendment's protection of "property," however, has never been interpreted to safeguard only the rights of undisputed ownership. Rather, it has been read broadly to extend protection to "any significant property interest," [*Boddie v. Connecticut*, 91 S. Ct. 780, 786 (1971).] including statutory entitlements.

The appellants were deprived of such an interest in the replevied goods—the interest in continued possession and use of the goods. . . . They had acquired this interest under the conditional sales contracts that entitled them to possession and use of the chattels before transfer of title. In exchange for immediate possession, the appellants had agreed to pay a major financing charge beyond the basic price of the merchandise. Moreover, by the time the goods were summarily repossessed, they had made substantial installment payments. Clearly, their possessory interest in the goods, dearly bought and protected by contract, was sufficient to invoke the protection of the Due Process Clause. . . .

The statutes, moreover, abdicate effective state control over state power. Private parties, serving their own private advantage, may unilaterally invoke state power to replevy goods from another. No state official participates in the decision to seek a writ; no state official reviews the basis for the claim to repossession; and no state official evaluates the need for immediate seizure. There is not even a requirement that the plaintiff provide any information to the court on these matters. The State acts largely in the dark. . . .

We hold that the Florida and Pennsylvania prejudgment replevin provisions work a deprivation of property without due process of law insofar as they deny the right to a prior opportunity to be heard before chattels are taken from their possessor. . . .

[Judgments vacated and remanded.]

Postjudgment Collection Remedies

Because most collection lawsuits result in a default judgment for the creditor, obtaining a judgment against the debtor is frequently a simple task. Collecting the judgment usually is much more difficult. The law provides various remedies designed to assist the creditor in locating, seizing, and converting to cash, assets necessary to pay the judgment creditor.

Judgment Liens. In most states, a judgment creates a lien upon the judgment debtor's real property. In some states, the **judgment lien** is created the moment the judgment is rendered. In others, the lien does not arise until the judgment is docketed or recorded with an appropriate public officer, such as the county recorder of deeds. The priority between the judgment lienor and other competing interests in the property is generally determined by the order of recording or docketing.

Execution. A judgment and judgment lien do not put money into the creditor's pocket. Payment is ultimately made through the judicial process of **execution,** which is similar in many ways to attachment. The creditor possessing an unpaid judgment petitions the clerk of the court to issue a **writ of execution** directed to the sheriff or other appropriate public official. The writ directs the sheriff to levy upon (seize) the debtor's real and personal property, sell the property at public sale (an **execution sale**), and apply the proceeds to the unpaid judgment.

The writ specifies a ''return date'' by which the sheriff must return it to the issuing clerk indicating

which assets were seized and sold or that no assets could be found. If no leviable assets are found, the writ is returned unsatisfied and is usually marked ''nulla bona.'' Note that unlike attachment (after which the sheriff holds the assets pending the outcome of the litigation), a levy in execution anticipates sale of the assets to satisfy the judgment.

The judgment creditor possesses a lien upon the debtor's *real property* due to his judgment lien. The judgment creditor obtains a lien upon *personal property* through the writ of execution. In most states, the lien does not attach until the sheriff actually levies upon the property involved. In a few states, however, the lien attaches when the writ is delivered to the sheriff. Priority among execution liens is therefore determined by the order of delivery of the writ or order of levy, depending on the state.

Postjudgment Garnishment. In postjudgment garnishment, the creditor files a complaint alleging that he or she holds an unpaid judgment against the debtor and that the garnishee holds property belonging to the debtor that may be used to satisfy the judgment. A copy of the complaint and summons is then served on the garnishee and in many states notice is also served upon the judgment debtor. The garnishee then has a stated period within which to file an answer to the complaint stating the property, wages, or other liability, if any, owing to the debtor. If the garnishee admits liability to the debtor, the garnishee is required to turn the property over to the court for disposition to the judgment creditor. If the garnishee contests the existence or amount of any obligation to the debtor, a proceeding is held in which the liability of the garnishee to the judgment debtor is determined.

Certainly the most common garnishee is an employer owing wages to an employee-debtor. Wage garnishments, made either before or after judgment, are subject to important limitations imposed by federal law. Under Subchapter II of the Consumer Credit Protection Act,[4] creditors may garnish no more than twenty-five percent of the debt-

---

4. 15 U.S.C. §§1671-1677.

or's weekly disposable earnings,[5] *or* the amount by which his weekly disposable earnings exceed thirty times the federal minimum wage, whichever is less. The law authorizes a larger garnishment percentage (fifty to sixty-five percent of disposable earnings) to satisfy orders for support of a spouse or child. Orders issued by a court pursuant to a rehabilitation plan under federal bankruptcy law, and debts due for any state or federal tax, are not subject to these basic restrictions. In addition to limiting the amount of wages that may be garnished, the law also precludes the employer from discharging any employee because his or her earnings have been garnished for any one indebtedness.

Creditor's Bill and Supplementary Proceedings. Lack of knowledge concerning the existence or whereabouts of the debtor's assets often hampers a creditor's efforts to enforce a judgment by execution or garnishment. To aid the creditor in discovering assets and to prevent the debtor from conveying or encumbering them, the law provides two related remedies, the creditor's bill and supplementary proceedings.

At early common law, a writ of execution could not be used to reach equitable assets, such as a beneficiary's interest in a trust, or intangibles. To correct this deficiency in the legal remedy, courts of equity developed the **creditor's bill,** under which the creditor files a "bill" with the court requesting that the debtor be ordered to turn over his equitable and intangible assets for sale in satisfaction of the judgment. Commonly, part of the creditor's bill is a bill of discovery under which the debtor and third parties can be examined in court in an effort to locate assets.

The importance of the creditor's bill has diminished somewhat in recent times. Most modern execution statutes now reach equitable and intangible assets in the debtor's hands and garnishment may be used to reach claims owed to the debtor by third parties. Further, the discovery function of the creditor's bill is now commonly accomplished by simpler, more expeditious supplementary proceedings.

Unlike the creditor's bill, which is a separate equitable action commenced by the creditor, **supplementary proceedings** are summary in nature and used as part of the original lawsuit. Supplementary proceedings may generally be used as soon as the judgment is rendered, and provide for discovery of assets, injunctions against transfer, and discretionary power to appoint receivers. Although supplementary proceedings are cheaper and quicker than a creditor's bill, they may provide less protection to the judgment creditor. Whereas the service of process upon the debtor under the creditor's bill generally creates a lien upon the debtor's assets, supplementary proceedings do not create a lien in some states.

Although largely supplanted by supplementary proceedings, the creditor's bill is, however, still the primary device used to recover property transferred by the debtor to third parties with intent to hinder, delay, or defraud creditors. The law of such "fraudulent conveyances" is discussed later in this chapter.

Debtor Protection

The Debt Collection Problem. If informal creditor efforts at debt collection fail, merchants often turn the collection effort over to a collection agency. Because a collection agency is called in only after polite request and persuasion have failed, some collection agencies, which often operate on a fifty percent commission, have resorted to questionable, extrajudicial tactics to collect. These tactics have included use of obscene or profane language, threats of violence, harassing or anonymous telephone calls at unreasonable hours, misrepresenting the consumer's legal rights, obtaining information by false pretenses, impersonating public officials and attorneys, sending documents that appear to be judicial process, publishing "deadbeat" lists, contacting and disclosing the debtor's personal affairs to friends, neighbors, and employers, collecting more than is legally owing, and misusing postdated checks.

Individual states have taken steps to curb collection abuse. For example, harassed debtors have been allowed to recover damages under common law tort theories such as defamation, invasion of the right of privacy, interference with contractual

---

5. "Disposable earnings" means the employee's wages, salary, or commissions less deductions required by law, such as federal and state income tax withholding and Social Security.

relations, and malicious prosecution. In addition, many states have enacted legislation requiring licensing and regulation of collection agencies. These state efforts were largely ineffective. General tort theories required the expense and delay of a lawsuit and were available only in aggravated cases. State legislation was piecemeal, often providing no civil damage remedy to injured debtors, and was unable to control debt collectors operating in interstate commerce.

The Fair Debt Collection Practices Act. In response to these inadequate state law remedies, Congress in 1977 enacted the **Fair Debt Collection Practices Act (FDCPA)**.[6] The FDCPA applies to collection of debts contracted by consumers for personal, family, or household purposes. It imposes various restrictions and obligations upon independent "debt collectors," which generally include all third persons such as collection agencies regularly engaged in the business of collecting debts for others. Debt collectors also include attorneys who collect debts on behalf of their clients. The FDCPA preempts state law governing debt collection practices only to the extent that the state law is "inconsistent" with the Act's provisions. A state providing greater debtor protection than the FDCPA is not deemed to be inconsistent. The major substantive provisions of the FDCPA are discussed below.

Obtaining Location Information. Debt collectors may communicate with third parties only to determine the debtor's whereabouts, including the debtor's residence, telephone number, and place of employment. In these communications the debt collector may not state that the debtor owes any debt and may not use language, symbols, or mail indicating that the correspondence relates to debt collection. The debt collector generally may contact a third party only once unless further contact is necessary to obtain complete information. Additionally, once the debt collector learns that the debtor is represented by an attorney, all further communication with third parties must stop unless

the attorney fails to answer the debt collector's communications.

Communication with the Debtor. The debt collector may not communicate with the debtor at an inconvenient time (between 9 P.M. and 8 A.M.) or place, if the debt collector knows the debtor is represented by an attorney, or at the debtor's place of employment if the debt collector knows that the debtor's employer prohibits such communications. Generally, all debtor contact must cease after the debtor notifies the debt collector in writing that the debtor refuses to pay the debt or desires further communication to cease.

Prohibited Practices. Debt collection practices designed to harass, oppress, or abuse the debtor, such as the various tactics previously listed, are expressly prohibited.

Validation of Debts. A debt collector must provide the debtor with written notice of the amount of the debt and the creditor to whom it is owed. The debtor then has thirty days to contest the validity of the debt. If the debtor does so, collection efforts must cease until the debt collector sends the debtor verification, such as a copy of a judgment rendered against the debtor. This requirement prevents collection efforts against the wrong person or concerning previously paid debts.

Forum Abuse. To prevent "forum abuse," debt collectors may not institute legal proceedings in courts distant from or inconvenient to the debtor. Collection proceedings must be brought in the judicial district where the debtor resides or the underlying contract was signed. If real property is involved, the action must be brought where the land is located.

Remedies. The FDCPA is primarily self-enforcing through private civil damage actions maintained by injured debtors. Debt collectors who violate the Act are liable for actual damages sustained, additional damages, not exceeding $1,000, as the court may allow, court costs, and attorneys' fees. Actions may be maintained in either state or federal court, subject to a one-year statute of limitations.

---

6. 15 U.S.C. §§1692-1692o (Subchapter V of the Consumer Credit Protection Act).

Fraudulent Conveyances and Bulk Transfers

Creditors attempting to locate and seize assets may find that the debtor has conveyed away his or her property to third parties, such as friends and relatives, in an effort to prevent creditors from reaching them. For over four centuries, the law has protected creditors against such **fraudulent conveyances** or transfers by allowing them to recover the property from the transferee. The remainder of this chapter discusses fraudulent conveyance law and its counterpart, the law of bulk transfers.

Fraudulent Conveyances

Development of the Law. The origin of fraudulent conveyance law is generally traced to the **Statute of Elizabeth,** enacted in England in 1570.[7] This statute provides generally that any transfer of property made with the "end purpose and intent, to delay, hinder or defraud creditors" is "utterly void." Although the statute rendered such transfers void, subsequent judicial interpretation held the transfers merely *voidable* by the transferor's creditors. That is, a fraudulent conveyance is valid as between the transferor and transferee.

Because the statute required proof of an actual intent to defraud—a difficult issue to prove—courts soon developed various circumstantial criteria, known as **badges of fraud,** to distinguish fraudulent from nonfraudulent transfers. Typically, a transfer evidencing one or more of the following characteristics is treated by the court as a fraudulent conveyance, voidable by the transferor's creditors: (1) if the transfer is general—involving all or substantially all of the debtor's assets; (2) if the transferor retains possession or the beneficial use of the property after transfer; (3) if the transfer is made in secret; (4) if the transfer is made to a family member, such as a spouse or child; (5) if the transfer is made without consideration or for less than full and adequate consideration; or (6) if the transfer is made in anticipation of or during litigation, or in anticipation of financial difficulty.[8]

In most American states, the Statute of Elizabeth was either recognized as part of the common law inherited from England or the statute or its equivalent was legislatively enacted. Despite its common origin, state fraudulent conveyance law varied widely among states. To provide uniformity of the law and to reach injurious transfers made without *actual* intent to defraud, the National Conference of Commissioners on Uniform State Laws drafted the **Uniform Fraudulent Conveyance Act (UFCA)** in 1918. In 1984, the National Conference adopted a revision of the UFCA, known as the **Uniform Fraudulent Transfer Act (UFTA),** which is designed to integrate fraudulent conveyance law with the Uniform Commercial Code and the federal Bankruptcy Code. The UFCA has been enacted in sixteen states and the UFTA has been adopted in seventeen states.[9]

Types of Fraudulent Transfers. As under the Statute of Elizabeth, both the UFCA and UFTA provide that a transfer[10] made or obligation incurred with *actual* intent to hinder, delay, or defraud any creditor is fraudulent against both present creditors (those whose claims arose before the transfer was made) and future creditors.[11] Both Acts also state that a transfer made or obligation incurred by a person who receives less than reasonably equivalent value in exchange is constructively fraudulent (that is, fraudulent without regard to the debtor's actual intent) in three cases:

  1) if the debtor after the transfer or obligation is left with assets that are unreasonably

---

7. 13 Eliz., ch. 5 (1570).

8. The badges of fraud concept was originally announced in *Twyne's Case,* 3 Co. Rep. 80b, 76 Eng. Rep. 809 (K.B.1601).

9. States enacting the UFCA include Arizona, Delaware, Maryland, Massachusetts, Michigan, Montana, Nebraska, New Jersey, New Mexico, New York, Ohio, Pennsylvania, Tennessee, Utah, Wisconsin, and Wyoming. The UFTA has been enacted in Arkansas, California, Florida, Hawaii, Idaho, Maine, Minnesota, Nevada, New Hampshire, North Dakota, Oklahoma, Oregon, Rhode Island, South Dakota, Texas, Washington, and West Virginia.

10. The UFTA defines "transfer" as "every mode, direct or indirect, absolute or conditional, voluntary or involuntary, of disposing of or parting with an asset or an interest in an asset, and includes payment of money, release, lease, and creation of a lien or other encumbrance." UFTA §1(12). This definition corresponds generally to the definition of "conveyance" under §1 of the UFCA.

11. UFCA §7, UFTA §4(a)(1).

small to conduct the business or transaction in which she is engaged (fraudulent as to present and future creditors);[12]

2) if the debtor intended to incur, or believed that she would incur, debts beyond her ability to pay as they mature (fraudulent as to present and future creditors);[13]

3) if the debtor was insolvent at the time of or as a result of the transfer (fraudulent as to present creditors only).[14]

The UFTA also recognizes a new form of fraudulent transfer—a preferential transfer to an insider such as a relative of or corporation controlled by an individual debtor, a director or officer of a corporate debtor, or a partner of a partnership debtor. Specifically, a transfer is fraudulent as to present creditors if: (1) the transfer was made to an insider for an antecedent debt, (2) the debtor was insolvent at the time of the transfer, and (3) the insider had reasonable cause to believe that the debtor was insolvent.[15]

Remedies. If a fraudulent conveyance is made, an injured creditor has a choice of remedies. The creditor may maintain an action, generally a creditor's bill, to have the conveyance set aside. Alternatively, the creditor may disregard the conveyance and attach or levy execution directly upon the property conveyed in the hands of the transferee. Other remedies may also be available to the creditor. For example, the court may enjoin the debtor from making further disposition of property, and in aggravated cases, may appoint a receiver to take charge of the debtor's property.

In the following case, decided under the UFCA, the court was required to determine whether two transfers of real property were fraudulent conveyances.

---

12. UFCA §5, UFTA §4(a)(2)(i).

13. UFCA §6, UFTA §4(a)(2)(ii).

14. UFCA §4, UFTA §5(a). Note that §8 of the UFCA provides that any transfer made or obligation incurred by an insolvent partnership to a partner is fraudulent without regard to intent or adequacy of consideration. The UFTA does not contain a provision aimed specifically at transfers or obligations of insolvent partnership debtors.

15. UFTA §5(b). The bankruptcy implications of preferential transfers to insiders are discussed in Chapter 30.

Montana National Bank v. Michels
631 P.2d 1260 (Mont. 1981)

On December 11, 1973, defendant Roy E. Michels, Jr. executed a promissory note due in one year payable to Montana National Bank (Bank) in the sum of approximately $75,000. At that time Michels owned an interest in 280 acres of land in Montana that he was purchasing on an installment contract. On December 16, 1974, Michels conveyed the real estate to his wife Shirley Michels for consideration of $1.00. Following the conveyance to his wife, Michels was insolvent, with a net worth of negative $11,662. On February 19, 1975, Shirley and Roy Michels, Jr. conveyed the real estate to Roy Michels's uncle James Cybulski, who agreed to pay the real estate installment contract and forgave a debt of $1,200 owed to him by Roy Michels. Cybulski also paid $11,879 that Michels owed to various creditors.

After discovering that Michels had transferred his real estate interest, the Bank sued the Michelses and Cybulski alleging that the transfers constituted fraudulent conveyances. The trial court ruled in favor of the Bank and set aside both conveyances. The Michelses and Cybulski appealed.

Daly, Justice

. . . Actual fraudulent intent within the meaning of the Uniform Fraudulent Conveyance Act may be established by circumstantial evidence. . . . Where the effect of a particular transaction with a debtor is to hinder, delay or defraud creditors, the law infers or supplies the intent, even though there may be no direct evidence of a dishonorable motive but, on the contrary, an actual, honest, but mistaken, motive exists. . . .

We have previously used "badges of fraud" to determine if a conveyance is fraudulent and should be set aside. . . .

This Court has said on many occasions that a court cannot scrutinize too closely the relation between husband and wife with respect to business dealings between them where creditors are concerned. . . . The marital relation is often a convenient means for the perpetration of a fraud, and when claims of indebtedness are made between husband and wife, they must be subjected to the most searching examination, if not indeed suspicion. . . .

Based on appraisals given at trial the fair market value of the land at the time of conveyance to Shirley Michels was $41,508. However, she paid only one dollar in consideration. We have long recognized inadequacy of consideration as a badge of fraud. . . .

At the time of the conveyance to his wife, Roy Michels was indebted to plaintiff in the amount of approximately $80,000. This debt was in addition to various other liabilities.

In financial statements submitted to the Bank by Roy Michels, the subject land represents a substantial asset. Michels, however, failed to notify the Bank of a planned or consummated conveyance to his wife. In fact, it was not until February 17, 1975, that plaintiff Bank learned of the conveyance through its own investigations.

After the conveyance, Roy Michels retained possession of the land. His explanation of the transfer was that it was for estate planning purposes and to provide security for his wife in the event of his death. However, in light of the above facts surrounding the transaction and the conveyance of the land to Cybulski two months later, this explanation bears no logical relationship to the events which actually occurred.

We hold the foregoing evidence substantiates a finding that the conveyance of December 16, 1974, was made with actual intent on the part of Roy Michels, Jr., to hinder, defraud and delay plaintiff Bank as a creditor. We also agree with the District Court that Shirley Michels was not a bona fide purchaser for value and that the Bank is entitled to have the conveyance declared fraudulent and set aside.

On February 17, 1975, defendant Roy Michels and his attorney met with Bank officials to discuss Michels' financial problems and possible solutions. At this meeting, liquidation of assets and bankruptcy were discussed. The vice president of the Bank testified that the meeting was the first time the Bank learned of the conveyance from Roy to Shirley Michels. At that time defendant promised officials that he would not transfer the land for a period of ninety days.

Two days after this meeting, on February 19, 1975, without notifying the Bank, defendants Roy

and Shirley Michels conveyed and assigned all interests in the real property to defendant Cybulski, the uncle of Roy Michels. This transaction occurred after only four or five days of negotiations. . . . [S]ecret or hurried transactions or transactions made under threat of litigation are considered badges of fraud. . . .

Once again, after the conveyance to Cybulski, both Roy and Shirley Michels retained possession and lived on the property without paying any rent.

At the time of conveyance to Cybulski, the fair market value of the land was $41,508. As purported consideration, Cybulski (1) assumed the outstanding principal and interest on the contract for deed amounting to $25,483.30, of which $19,577.73 was actually paid at the time of trial; (2) paid numerous creditors of Roy Michels in the amount of $11,879.26; and (3) forgave an antecedent debt owed to him by defendant in the amount of $1,200. We agree with the trial court that the last two items given did not consist of valid consideration for the reason that Shirley Michels, as grantor, was not obligated under the indebtedness paid or forgiven by Cybulski. . . .

We hold that the secret conveyance of February 19, 1975, for inadequate consideration, while defendant was indebted to the Bank and under the threat of bankruptcy, was made with the actual intent on the part of Roy E. Michels, Jr., to defraud, hinder and delay the Bank as creditor, and, therefore, must be set aside as a fraudulent conveyance.

[Judgment affirmed.]

The law does not protect creditors against all fraudulent conveyances. For example, both Acts[16] provide that a creditor may not recover a transfer from a good faith purchaser for value—one who pays reasonably equivalent value for the property and has no knowledge of the fraud at the time of the purchase. Thus, creditors generally are allowed to subject fraudulently transferred property to their claims only if the transferee has participated in the scheme to hinder or defraud creditors, has taken

---

16. UFCA §9, UFTA §8(a).

with notice of the fraud, or is a donee or has taken for less than full and adequate consideration.

Bulk Transfers—UCC Article 6

Development of the Law. An important and common form of fraudulent conveyance, which is not voidable under ordinary fraudulent conveyance law, is the bulk transfer. In the typical case, a merchant, owing debts, sells all or a major part of his inventory at once out of the ordinary course of business (the "bulk sale" or "bulk transfer") to an innocent purchaser, pockets the proceeds, and then disappears, leaving unsecured creditors unpaid. Note that in the bulk sales case the transferee buys the merchant's stock in trade for adequate consideration with no knowledge of, or participation in, the seller's scheme to defraud his creditors. Thus, creditors may generally not avoid the transfer as a fraudulent conveyance, and may not levy upon or otherwise reach the assets in the purchaser's hands. Absent additional legal protection, therefore, the unpaid unsecured creditors have no recourse unless they can establish that the purchaser has assumed the merchant's existing debts.

Beginning in the late nineteenth century, the bulk transfer became a common method used by dishonest merchants to defeat their creditors' claims. To protect creditors in this case and to close the bulk transfer loophole in state fraudulent conveyance law, every state enacted "bulk sales" legislation. By the mid-twentieth century these statutes had become outdated, causing substantial uncertainty and litigation. Additionally, the lack of uniformity of the various enactments made it difficult for creditors involved in interstate transactions to protect themselves.

For these reasons, the drafters of the UCC prepared Article 6, "Bulk Transfers," to provide a uniform bulk transfer law, embodying the better rules of the prior statutes. Article 6 provides creditor protection primarily by requiring advance notice of the transfer so that creditors may take steps to protect themselves before the assets are transferred and before the purchase price is paid. If the required notice is not given, the transfer is "ineffective" as against the seller's creditors. This means that the creditors can disregard the sale and reach the goods in the transferee's hands to satisfy their claims, even though the transferee is a good faith purchaser for adequate consideration.

Article 6 is also designed to prevent a second type of commercial fraud occurring when a "merchant, owing debts, . . . sells out his stock in trade to a friend for less than it is worth, pays his creditors less than he owes them, and hopes to come back into the business through the back door some time in the future."[17] Though this situation is within the scope of state fraudulent conveyance laws, the bulk transfer rules provide for advance notice of the sale. After receiving the notice, the creditors can investigate the price and other circumstances of the sale to determine whether they should try to stop it.

Article 6 has long been criticized as being loosely drafted and insufficiently specific. In response to this criticism, the Corporation, Banking, and Business Law Section of the American Bar Association established a committee in 1975 to study the problem and to draft and recommend adoption of desirable amendments. Eventually, many of the committee's recommendations should be incorporated into a revised Article 6, which will then be submitted to the states for adoption.

"Bulk Transfer" Defined. A **bulk transfer** is defined in §6-102(1) as

> any transfer in bulk and not in the ordinary course of the transferor's business of a major part of the materials, supplies, merchandise or other inventory . . . of an enterprise subject to this Article.

Although the term "major part" of the transferor's inventory is not defined, most courts have construed the term to mean "greater than 50%," measured as a percentage of the total value of the inventory rather than total volume.

Under §6-102(3), enterprises subject to Article 6 are "those whose principal business is the sale of merchandise from stock, including those who manufacture what they sell." Businesses principally engaged in the sale of services, such as farming,

---

17. UCC §6-101, Official Comment 2.

professional services, cleaning shops, barber shops, hotels, and restaurants, are exempted.

To be subject to Article 6, the property transferred must be *goods,* more specifically inventory. "Inventory" generally includes property held by a person for immediate or ultimate *sale* in the ordinary course of business. A transfer of a substantial part of the merchant's equipment[18] is not a bulk transfer unless made in connection with a bulk transfer of inventory. Transfers of intangibles, such as stocks, bonds, notes, checks, and accounts, are governed by other UCC Articles and do not generally present any substantial bulk sales risk.

Compliance Requirements. If the transfer qualifies as a "bulk transfer," the sale is ineffective against any creditor[19] of the seller unless four basic requirements, stated in Sections 6-104 and 6-105, are met:

1. The buyer must require the seller to furnish a signed and sworn list of his existing creditors. The list must contain the names and addresses of all creditors, even those whose claims are disputed. The seller bears the responsibility for the completeness and accuracy of the list, and the transfer is not rendered ineffective due to errors or omissions unless the buyer knows of them.

2. The parties must prepare a schedule of the property transferred sufficient to identify it.

3. The buyer must preserve the list and schedule for six months after the transfer and either permit inspection or copying of both documents by any creditor of the seller, or file the list and schedule in a designated public office.

4. The buyer must give written notice of the transfer to all persons included on the list of creditors furnished by the seller, and all other persons known by the buyer to hold or assert claims against the seller.[20] The notice must be given at least 10 days before the buyer takes possession of the goods or pays for them, whichever occurs earlier. For example, if the buyer takes possession on June 1, and makes payment on June 15, the notice must be given at least 10 days prior to June 1.[21]

A buyer who fails to comply with the obligations outlined above incurs no liability if the seller's debts are paid as they mature. Similarly, any defect in compliance can always be cured by paying off the creditors.

Content of the Notice. The content of the notice is provided in §6-107. A so-called short form notice is used when the seller's debts are to be paid in full as they come due from the proceeds of the sale. The short form includes the fact that a bulk transfer is about to be made, the names and business addresses of the parties, and where creditors should file their claims. If the proceeds of the transaction will not be used to satisfy creditors' claims or if the buyer is in doubt on the issue, the "long form" notice must be used. The long form should always be used because the buyer may not be certain that the seller will use the proceeds to pay her debts (even though she has promised to do so), or of the actual extent of those debts. The long form notice requires the following additional information: the location and general description of the property transferred; the estimated total of the seller's debts; the address where the list of creditors and schedule of property may be inspected; whether the transfer is being made to satisfy an existing debt (or debts) and if so, the amount of the debt (debts) and to whom owing; and whether new consideration is to be paid for the transfer and if so the time and place of payment.

Optional Requirement. Article 6 contains an optional provision, §6-106, which has been

---

18. "Equipment" is property used or bought primarily for use in business. UCC §9-109(2).

19. The term "creditor" is broadly defined in the Code to include "a general creditor, a secured creditor, a lien creditor and any representative of creditors, including an assignee for the benefit of creditors, a trustee in bankruptcy, a receiver in equity and an executor or administrator of an insolvent debtor's or assignor's estate." UCC §1-201(12).

20. Creditors protected under Article 6 are those holding claims based on transactions or events occurring before the bulk transfer. Persons becoming creditors after notice is given are not entitled to notice. UCC §6-109(1).

21. The 10-day period is measured from the date the notice is properly sent, not the date the creditor receives it. See UCC §§1-201(26), (38).

adopted in twenty states[22] and imposes a duty upon a buyer who gives new consideration for the transfer to assure that the proceeds of the sale are applied to satisfy creditors' claims. This section gives the transferor's creditors direct protection against the seller's improper dissipation of the proceeds by ensuring that the money paid to the seller is in fact used to pay his debts.[23]

Statute of Limitations. Because Article 6 imposes unusual obligations upon the transferee, it provides a short statute of limitations within which the unpaid creditors must proceed against the noncomplying buyer. Section 6-111 provides that no action may be brought nor any levy made more than six months after the transferee takes possession of the goods. If the transfer has been concealed, however, actions may be brought or levies may be made within six months after discovery of the transfer.

At issue in the following case was whether a bulk transfer had been concealed for purposes of applying the statute of limitations.

Columbian Rope Company v. Rinek Cordage Company

461 A.2d 312 (Pa. Super. 1983)

In 1972 Rinek Cordage Company (Cordage) executed a promissory note payable to appellant Columbian Rope Company (Columbian) in partial payment for yarn Columbian had supplied to Cordage. In April, 1974, Cordage made a bulk sale of all of its inventory to Rinek Rope Co. (Rope) in exchange

---

22. States adopting optional §6-106 include: Alaska, California, Florida, Idaho, Kansas, Kentucky, Maryland, Minnesota, Mississippi, Montana, New Jersey, North Dakota, Oklahoma, Pennsylvania, South Dakota, Tennessee, Texas, Utah, Washington, and West Virginia.

23. The buyer may meet this obligation by (1) agreement with the seller that the buyer will retain the sales proceeds until all creditors are ascertained and paid, or (2) depositing the proceeds in a bank account requiring the buyer's counter-signature, or (3) depositing the money with an independent escrow agent, or (4) if creditors' claims are disputed, the buyer may pay the price into the court and interplead the seller's creditors.

---

for Rope's president's forgiving a $17,589 debt Cordage owed him. Rope did not notify Cordage's creditors of the bulk transfer, and continued to operate the business from the same address used by Cordage.

In November, 1976, Columbian sued Cordage, Rope, and Rope's president seeking payment of the unpaid balance of the promissory note. Rope alleged that the claim against it was barred by the statute of limitations because the lawsuit was begun more than six months after the bulk transfer. Columbian alleged that the statute of limitations began to run from the time that it discovered the transfer because Rope had concealed the bulk transfer. The trial court ruled in favor of Rope and Columbian appealed.

Hoffman, Judge

. . . The Uniform Commercial Code, Article 6, concerning bulk transfers, as enacted in Pennsylvania . . . is designed to remedy the "major bulk sales risk" of the merchant, owing debts, who sells away virtually all his stock in trade and disappears leaving his creditors unpaid. Uniform Commercial Code, §6-101, Comments 2, 4. . . . The statute's basic mechanism is to require the prospective transferee to give advance notice to the transferor's creditors of the impending bulk sale. . . . The prior notice affords the creditors an opportunity to participate in structuring the transfer or commence legal action against their debtor, the transferor, before the assets are sold away. . . . [I]f the transferee does not give the required notice, the transfer will be "ineffective" against the transferor's creditors, [UCC] §6-105, who may then commence actions for the transferor's debts against the transferee within the six months following the transfer. [UCC] §6-111. . . . [I]f the transferee's failure to give notice is not simply noncompliance with the statute but amounts to "concealment" of the bulk transfer, the transferee is subject to actions by the transferor's creditors commenced within six months of when the creditor discovers the concealed bulk transfer. [UCC] §6-111. The question we face here is whether a completely undisclosed bulk transfer should be treated as "concealed" for purposes of the U.C.C.'s statute of limitations. . . .

We find that the complete failure to give notice

of the impending bulk transfer is not merely non-compliance, but "concealment."

Treating complete failure to give notice merely as noncompliance and not concealment would undermine the legislature's scheme to promote advance notice of bulk transfers. . . . Sending the statutory notice stirs up the transferor's creditors, possibly delaying the transfer and increasing the risk of creditor action adverse to the transferee's interests. Less formal notice would likely have similar consequences, and also gives creditors essential information to promptly begin action. However, when no notice at all is given, creditors have little means to discover the completely undisclosed transfer, identify the transferee, and commence action all within six months of the transfer. Prudent transferees would thus, despite the legislative intent, regularly choose the alternative of complete nondisclosure unless such complete nondisclosure were considered concealment. . . .

Interpreting "concealment" to include complete nondisclosure is, on the other hand, consistent with the legislature's scheme and eminently fair to both transferees and creditors. The transferee's protection from creditors is more reliably based on the notice given. The time limits on creditors' actions become more reasonably related to their opportunity to act. . . . Creditors must still act within six months of discovering the transfer so that transferees are spared prolonged liability for the transferor's stale debts. . . .

Finally, the legislative scheme does not suggest that the concealment must be intentional or affirmative. . . . Inadvertent as well as conscious failures to make any disclosure of a bulk transfer both occasion the major bulk sales risk of a transferor merchant disposing of his stock in trade and disappearing, leaving his creditors unpaid. . . . Consequently, a complete failure to notify the transferor's creditors should be considered "concealment" of the bulk transfer for purposes of calculating the statute of limitations under [UCC] §6-111.

Applying these principles, the record reveals that the bulk transfer here was wholly undisclosed, and thus concealed. No notice, formal or informal, was sent to Cordage's two outstanding creditors, apparently because Rope's and Cordage's officers did not think it necessary. . . . The circumstances in no way revealed to creditors that the transfer had

occurred. Both transferor and transferee operated out of the same business address, with Cordage owning the premises and Rope leasing space. Both used the "Rinek" name. . . . Accordingly, even though the record contains no proof of deceptive intent, the bulk transfer was effectively "concealed" from creditors by the complete nondisclosure. . . . We thus reverse the lower court's dismissal of the action against Rope, and remand for findings of fact to determine whether appellant commenced action within six months of its discovering the bulk transfer. . . .

[Judgment reversed and remanded.]

Exempted Transfers. Certain bulk transfers are exempted from compliance with Article 6 by §6-103. These exemptions include

1. A transfer of inventory to a new business enterprise organized to take over and continue the business (for example, when a proprietorship is incorporated and the assets of the original business are transferred to the corporation);
2. A transfer to a person maintaining a known place of business in the state who agrees to pay the debts of the transferor in full and gives public notice of that fact and who is solvent after assuming the transferor's debts;
3. A transfer made as security for performance of an obligation or in settlement or realization of a lien or other security interest;[24]
4. A general assignment for the benefit of creditors;[25]
5. Sales by executors, administrators, receivers, trustees in bankruptcy, or any public officer under judicial process;
6. Sales made in the course of judicial or ad-

---

24. Under the UCC, security interests in all types of personal property are governed by Article 9 (Secured Transactions) discussed in Chapters 31 and 32. Such transfers are therefore excluded from Article 6 coverage. See UCC §9-111.

25. Assignments for the benefit of creditors are discussed in Chapter 30.

ministrative proceedings for dissolution or reorganization of a corporation of which creditors are notified; and

7. Transfers of property exempt from execution.

Auction Sales. In addition to privately negotiated transactions, Article 6 applies to bulk transfers made by sale at auction. In this case, §6-108 requires the seller to furnish a list of creditors and to assist the auctioneer in preparing a schedule of property to be sold. The auctioneer is responsible for retaining the list and schedule and for notifying the listed creditors. Failure by the auctioneer to perform these duties does not affect the title acquired by purchasers at the auction. Nevertheless, a noncomplying auctioneer who knows that the auction constitutes a bulk transfer may be held liable to the seller's creditors up to the net proceeds of the auction.

SUMMARY

1. State debtor-creditor law provides the various remedies designed to aid a creditor in collecting an obligation from an unwilling or dishonest debtor, and resolves disputes among competing creditors all holding valid claims against the debtor.

2. Some state law remedies are available before a judgment is obtained against the debtor on the underlying debt. These prejudgment, or provisional, remedies include, for example, attachment, prejudgment garnishment, replevin and self-help, and receivership. Prejudgment remedies generally are subject to constitutional due process limitations.

3. After a judgment has been obtained, state laws provide various remedies designed to discover the debtor's assets, liquidate them, and apply them to the debt. These include, for example, foreclosing judgment liens, execution, postjudgment garnishment, creditor's bills, and supplementary proceedings.

4. To protect debtors against abusive and deceptive debt collection practices, both state and federal law regulate conduct of independent collection agencies. Because state remedies were perceived as inadequate, Congress in 1977 enacted the Fair Debt Collection Practices Act.

5. Creditors' remedies are generally designed to reach assets in the possession either of the debtor or of third parties indebted to the debtor. A debtor may, however, transfer his or her property to third parties with actual or implied intent to hinder, delay, or defraud creditors. Such "fraudulent conveyances" are generally voidable by creditors, under ancient legal principles embodied in many states today in the Uniform Fraudulent Conveyance Act, or the Uniform Fraudulent Transfer Act.

6. Traditional fraudulent conveyance law does not protect creditors against a "bulk transfer" type of fraud, under which a fraudulent merchant sells his entire inventory to a good faith purchaser, pockets the proceeds, and disappears, leaving creditors unpaid. Bulk transfer law, now codified in Article 6 of the UCC, protects creditors in this case by requiring that they be given advance notice of the sale.

KEY TERMS

exemption statute	execution sale
default judgment	creditor's bill
cognovit (confession of judgment) clause	supplementary proceedings
deficiency judgment	Fair Debt Collection Practices Act (FDCPA)
attachment	
writ of attachment	fraudulent conveyance
levy	Statute of Elizabeth
garnishment	badges of fraud
replevin	Uniform Fraudulent Conveyance Act (UFCA)
self-help	
receiver	
judgment lien	Uniform Fraudulent Transfer Act (UFTA)
execution	
writ of execution	bulk transfer

QUESTIONS AND PROBLEMS

29-1   In 1983, Terry Hanson borrowed $10,000 from Interfirst Bank to purchase an automobile. Hanson promised to repay the loan in 36 monthly payments, and the bank retained a security interest in the car. The contract authorized self-help repossession by the bank upon default. In 1984, Hanson stopped making monthly car payments. Interfirst sent Hanson a notice demanding payment and later hired a company to repossess the car. On August 12, 1984, Interfirst filed a replevin action and the court set a hearing for a prejudgment writ of replevin on August 27. In the meantime, the repossession company located the car and repossessed it on August 21. Hanson challenged the repossession as a violation of the due process clause. Hanson argued that once the bank sought intervention of the court in the replevin action, the right to self-help repossession without a hearing was extinguished. Is Hanson correct?

29-2 Collection Accounts Terminal, Inc. is a debt collection agency that has been considering new procedures to make its debt collection operations more efficient. It has decided to send each debtor a series of three form letters described below. Do any of these procedures violate the FDCPA? Explain.

(a) The first letter will notify the debtor that his or her account has been placed with Collection Accounts Terminal, Inc. and will request the debtor to contact the agency. The letter will be written on stationery and mailed in envelopes with Collection Accounts Terminal's name and address written prominently so the debtor will know whom to contact.

(b) If the debtor fails to contact the agency, it will send a second letter stating the following: "Our field investigator has been instructed to make an investigation in your neighborhood and to personally call on your employer. The immediate payment of your account or a personal visit to our office will spare you this embarrassment." Nevertheless, the agency does not intend to visit neighbors or employers.

(c) If the debtor still fails to respond, the agency will send a third letter stating: "Unless you pay your account in full, it may be referred to an attorney with instructions to commence legal proceedings." Collection Accounts Terminal has retained an attorney and intends to refer most of its large accounts to her for filing lawsuits.

29-3 In 1984, Abraham borrowed $30,000 from Albuquerque Bank and signed a promissory note for that amount plus interest. At the time he signed the note, Abraham owned one large piece of real estate plus several smaller tracts, all located in New Mexico. Late in 1985, Abraham conveyed the large piece of real estate to his sister in exchange for a loan of $37,000. The real estate then held a fair market value of $177,000. At the time of the conveyance to his sister, Abraham owed various creditors a total of $71,000. Albuquerque Bank recently discovered that Abraham conveyed the property to his sister and is now considering filing a lawsuit to have the transfer set aside as a fraudulent conveyance. Would you recommend that the bank take this action? Explain.

29-4 United Coal Corporation was in financial difficulty with multi-million dollar liabilities for federal income taxes, trade accounts, pension fund contributions, strip mining and back-filling obligations, and municipal real estate taxes. United's president organized a small group of investors to buy the company, who borrowed substantially all of the purchase price at high interest rates secured by mortgages on United's assets. Although a majority of the purchase price went to selling shareholders, after the buyout, the corporation lacked funds to pay its routine operating expenses or real estate taxes. The United States government later filed suit to reduce certain corporate federal tax assessments to judgment and argued that the mortgages executed in connection with the buyout should be set aside as fraudulent conveyances under the UFCA. Should the UFCA apply in the context of such a "leveraged buyout"? Explain.

29-5 M & L, Inc. operated a retail jewelry store. M & L purchased on credit diamonds valued at $3,000 from Gem Importers. Without repaying Gem Importers, M & L sold all of its office furnishings, equipment, and customer lists to New Jewelers, Inc., another retailer. Neither party notified M & L's creditors of the transfer. Gem Importers has sued New Jewelers for the $3,000 debt alleging the transfer violated the bulk transfer provisions of the UCC. How should the court rule? Explain.

29-6 On August 29, 1984, Canyon Culvert Company sold almost all of its manufacturing equipment to Armco, Inc. Between September 4 and October 15, 1984, Canyon Culvert transferred the rest of its equipment, its office furniture and its inventory to Canyon Steel, a newly formed corporation. After learning of these transactions, Republic Steel, a creditor of Canyon Culvert, sued Armco alleging that the sale of equipment to Armco, made shortly before the sale of inventory to Canyon Steel, was a transfer of equipment "made in connection with a bulk transfer of inventory" under §6-102(2). Republic therefore asserted that the transfer to Armco was ineffective against Republic's claim as creditor because Armco had failed to provide the statutory bulk sales notice required by Article 6 of the UCC. Is Republic correct? Explain.

State law collection remedies generally reward the creditor or creditors who act first in proceeding against the debtor's assets, and are not generally designed to promote equal or equitable treatment of creditors when the debtor's assets are insufficient to pay all creditor claims. In addition, state remedies do not protect an honest, though hopelessly indebted, person from repeated and often harassing creditor attempts at collection.

Resolving these problems is the function of the law of bankruptcy. Bankruptcy is simultaneously a collective creditors' remedy and debtor relief provision embodied in a federal statute. It is designed to serve two fundamental purposes: (1) to relieve an honest debtor from overburdensome financial obligations and give him or her a fresh start, free of claims of former creditors, and (2) to provide for equitable treatment of creditors who are competing for the debtor's limited assets.

Introduction to Bankruptcy

Bankruptcy is federal law. One of the powers granted to Congress in the Constitution is the power to establish "uniform Laws on the subject of Bankruptcies throughout the United States."[1] Congress first exercised this power in 1800 and subsequently enacted bankruptcy statutes in 1841, 1867, 1898, and 1978. This chapter is based upon the Bankruptcy Reform Act of 1978, as substantially amended in 1984 and 1986.

General Organization and Operation of the Statute

The law of bankruptcy is contained in Title 11 of the United States Code, commonly referred to as the "Bankruptcy Code." Title 11 is divided into eight substantive "chapters," which are organized as follows:

Chapter 1   General Provisions
Chapter 3   Case Administration

---

1. U.S. Const. art. I, §8, cl. 4.

The relief afforded by the statute is of two general types: liquidation (governed by Chapter 7) and rehabilitation (the subject of Chapters 9, 11, 12 and 13). Chapters 1, 3, and 5, governing the general operation of the bankruptcy proceeding, apply generally to both liquidation cases (under Chapter 7) and rehabilitation cases (under Chapters 11, 12, and 13).[2]

Most bankruptcies (70–80%) are liquidation cases involving nonbusiness debtors (80–90%). In a **liquidation case,** usually known as **straight bankruptcy,** the debtor surrenders all nonexempt assets, the bankruptcy "estate," to a "trustee in bankruptcy." The trustee in bankruptcy collects the estate's assets, converts them to cash, and distributes the proceeds to creditors who have filed claims against the estate according to a priority scheme provided in the Bankruptcy Code. Unless the debtor is guilty of certain specified conduct, he or she is "discharged" from liability upon any debts remaining unpaid, except those that may not be discharged under bankruptcy law.

In a **rehabilitation case** under Chapters 11, 12, and 13, the debtor's assets are not liquidated. Rather, the debtor retains them and pays creditors out of future earnings pursuant to a plan filed with and approved by the court. Chapter 11 addresses primarily business or corporate rehabilitation. Chapter 13 governs rehabilitation of individual or consumer debtors, plus some eligible businesses. Chapter 12 provides relief for certain persons engaged in farming operations whose debts do not ex-ceed prescribed limits. Most rehabilitation plans are unsuccessful, ultimately being converted into liquidation cases.

Bankruptcy Courts and Jurisdiction

Because bankruptcy is federal law, bankruptcy cases are tried in federal courts. The various federal district courts have original and exclusive jurisdiction of all cases under Title 11 and acquire exclusive jurisdiction over all property, wherever located, of the debtor as of the commencement of the case. The district courts may also hear civil cases arising in or related to a case commenced under Title 11. For example, the district court could (but is not required to) adjudicate a breach of contract case between a bankrupt debtor and one of its suppliers or customers.

Although the federal courts have jurisdiction, federal district judges do not ordinarily hear bankruptcy cases. Rather, the law provides for the creation in each judicial district of a **bankruptcy court,** a unit of the district court staffed by **bankruptcy judges.** Whereas federal district judges appointed under Article III of the Constitution enjoy life tenure (subject to impeachment), bankruptcy judges are appointed to fourteen-year terms by the Court of Appeals for the circuit in which the judge sits. Further, federal judges' compensation may not be reduced during their continuance in office.[3] Because bankruptcy judges are not appointed under Article III, their jurisdictional powers are limited and their decisions subject to review by the federal district court.[4]

To relieve bankruptcy judges of burdensome administrative and supervisory duties, Congress in 1978 created a pilot United States Trustee system, which became permanent and nationwide in 1986.[5] The system is under the control of the Attorney General of the United States, who appoints for a five year term a United States Trustee and one or more Assistant United States Trustees to each of 21

---

2. 11 U.S.C. §103(a). Chapter 9 is generally self-contained and is supplemented only by provisions of Chapter 1. 11 U.S.C. §103(e).

3. U.S. Const. art. III, §1.

4. The provisions governing creation of bankruptcy courts, appointment of bankruptcy judges, and the relationship between the bankruptcy courts and the district courts are contained in 28 U.S.C. §§151-158.

5. 28 U.S.C. §§581-589a.

geographic regions. The United States Trustee establishes and supervises a panel of private trustees to serve in Chapter 7 cases, appoints or serves as standing trustee in Chapter 12 and 13 cases, and when necessary, appoints a Chapter 11 trustee. The United States Trustee also generally supervises the administration of bankruptcy cases, including, for example, monitoring the progress of cases to prevent undue delay, monitoring rehabilitation plans, and ensuring that the debtor timely files all reports, schedules, and fees required by law.

Consumer and Business Bankruptcy

Though much of bankruptcy law applies both to business bankruptcies and those involving individual consumers, certain areas of the law are much more important in one type than the other. For example, in consumer bankruptcies, the debtor is likely to have few assets that are not exempt or already subject to secured creditors' claims. Accordingly, consumer bankruptcy usually generates little creditor interest. Legal disputes are likely to focus upon whether the debtor or a given debt should be discharged or whether certain property should be exempt from creditors' claims. In contrast, a business bankrupt is likely to have substantial assets, generating heated disputes among creditors over priority in distribution of those assets. Thus in business bankruptcy, the orderly collection and distribution of the estate is the basic issue, whereas in consumer bankruptcy, discharge is the focus. Indeed, in most consumer bankruptcies there are no assets to liquidate and distribute, and in most corporate bankruptcies, discharge is irrelevant. A bankrupt corporate shell with no assets has little need for a "fresh start."

Straight Bankruptcy—Chapter 7

Commencing a Chapter 7 Case

Under the Bankruptcy Code a liquidation (Chapter 7) proceeding may be either voluntary (debtor initiated) or involuntary (creditor initiated).[6] In a **voluntary case,** the debtor files a petition with the

bankruptcy court requesting the relief afforded by Chapter 7. Filing the petition constitutes an automatic "order for relief." Generally, any individual, partnership, or corporation may file a voluntary bankruptcy petition under Chapter 7. Railroads, banking institutions, and insurance companies, however, are ineligible.[7] Approximately 99 percent of liquidation cases are commenced voluntarily by the debtor.

Creditors may also force a debtor involuntarily into a Chapter 7 bankruptcy proceeding by filing a petition with the bankruptcy court, provided (1) the aggregate claims of petitioning creditors are at least $5,000, and (2) if the debtor has twelve or more creditors, at least three join in the petition. If the debtor has fewer than twelve unsecured creditors, only one need file.

Unlike a voluntary case, the mere filing of an **involuntary case** petition does not constitute an "order for relief." The debtor may challenge the creditors' attempt to force him into bankruptcy. After the petition and summons are served, the debtor has twenty days to file defenses and objections.[8] If the debtor fails to object, the court enters an order for relief. If the debtor timely objects, a trial is held, which may be heard by the court sitting without a jury. After the trial, the court is required to order relief against the debtor if it finds either that the debtor is not paying undisputed debts as they become due *or* a custodian has been appointed for or has taken possession of substantially all of the debtor's property within 120 days preceding the filing of the petition.

The first test—failure to pay debts as they come due—is known as the "equity" or "accounting" definition of insolvency.[9] The second test—appointment of a custodian within 120 days before the petition—creates an irrefutable presumption

---

6. 11 U.S.C. §§301, 303.

7. Railroad bankruptcies are governed by Subchapter IV of Chapter 11 of the Bankruptcy Code. 11 U.S.C. §§1161-1174. Bank and insurance company liquidations are governed by other state and federal regulatory statutes. 11 U.S.C. §109(b).

8. Bankruptcy Rule 1011, 11 U.S.C.

9. This test differs from the insolvency definition used elsewhere in the Bankruptcy Code, requiring balance sheet insolvency, meaning that total liabilities exceed total assets at fair valuation. 11 U.S.C. §101(31).

that the debtor is unable to pay his debts as they mature. If the creditors fail to seek bankruptcy liquidation within 120 days after the appointment, they are not precluded from filing an involuntary petition. They are, however, required to prove equity insolvency rather than the more easily provable custodian test. The custodian test is covered in more detail later in this chapter in conjunction with collective creditor remedies outside bankruptcy.

Certain debtors, such as railroads, banking institutions, and insurance companies, may not be forced into involuntary bankruptcy. In addition, creditors may not commence involuntary cases against farmers or non-profit corporations, such as churches, schools, and charitable organizations.

Because an involuntary petition adversely affects the debtor's business operation and reputation, the Bankruptcy Code includes provisions to discourage frivolous claims. For example, if the court finds that the petition was filed in bad faith, it may dismiss the case and may award the debtor court costs, attorneys' fees, and punitive and other damages.

Automatic Stay. The **automatic stay**[10] is an important legal consequence of filing either a voluntary or involuntary bankruptcy petition. Simply stated, filing the petition "stays" or prevents further efforts by creditors to collect their debts. Efforts stayed by the bankruptcy include the judicial debt collection remedies discussed in Chapter 29 as well as informal collection efforts such as phone calls and letters. Also stayed is the creation, perfection, or enforcement of any lien upon the debtor's property.

The stay generally continues until the case is closed or dismissed, or the debtor is granted or denied a discharge. If the debtor receives a discharge, the debtor's liability to pay most of the debts stayed is permanently extinguished. Note that certain debts survive a bankruptcy proceeding and certain debtors are denied discharges. After the stay is lifted, therefore, collection efforts may continue against such debts or debtors.

Upon a creditor's request, the bankruptcy court

may terminate or otherwise modify the automatic stay. Relief from the stay primarily aids secured creditors, whose interest in specific property of the debtor may be jeopardized if the stay is continued. At issue in the following case was whether a creditor had violated the automatic stay.

In the Matter of Holland
21 B.R. 681 (Bkrtcy. N.D. Ind. 1982)

Wilbert Glenn Holland (debtor) borrowed money from the Dana Corporation Federal Credit Union (Credit Union) and authorized his employer to transfer $80.00 from his weekly paycheck to the Credit Union for repayment of the loan. Every week the Credit Union deposited the payroll deduction into Holland's share draft account, and once a month the Credit Union transferred the deductions to its loan department where they were applied toward payment of the loan.

On November 21, 1980, Holland filed a petition for bankruptcy and the bankruptcy court sent a notice of the bankruptcy and automatic stay to the Credit Union. Shortly after November 21, 1980, Holland went to the Credit Union with copies of the bankruptcy petition to request termination of the payroll deduction. Credit Union procedures required that Holland complete a form to be delivered to his employer to terminate the payroll deductions. Despite Holland's visit and subsequent telephone calls to the Credit Union, none of the Credit Union's employees advised him of the procedure or provided the necessary forms. As a result, the payroll deductions continued and the Credit Union applied the deductions to repay the loan.

Holland filed a motion with the bankruptcy court seeking an order finding the Credit Union in violation of the automatic stay.

Rodibaugh, Bankruptcy Judge
. . . For the reasons stated below, the Court . . . finds that the Credit Union has violated the Automatic Stay of §362(a)(6) of the Bankruptcy Code. . . .

There is no doubt that the Credit Union had ac-

---

tual notice of the debtor's petition in bankruptcy and of the automatic stay before it continued to make transfers from the debtor's share draft account to the loan account with the Credit Union. There is no question that at the time the Credit Union made these transfers it had notice and actual knowledge that the debtor no longer wanted his post-petition earnings to be applied against his loan with the Credit Union. . . .

The Credit Union contends it did not violate the stay because it took *no act* to collect the debt. Rather it just received the debtor's voluntary payments of the debt through payroll deduction arrangement. . . .

[W]e do not hold that the Credit Union violated the stay by receiving money pursuant to the arrangement in this case and depositing it into the debtor's account. This alone would not be an act to collect a debt. However, when the credit union transfers the money to pay a pre-petition debt owed to itself it has then committed an act to collect a claim and thereby violates the stay unless . . . there is clear evidence that, post-petition, the debtor demonstrated willingness to voluntarily have these earnings applied to the debt. . . .

This result is consistent with the plain language of §362(a)(6), with the intent of Congress as demonstrated in the Legislative History, and with case law. . . .

Congressional intent seems clear. "The automatic stay is one of the fundamental debtor protections provided by the bankruptcy laws. It gives the debtor a breathing spell from his creditors. It stops *all collection efforts* (emphasis added), all harassment and all foreclosure actions." H. R. Rep. No. 595, 95 Cong. 1st Sess. 340 (1977). . . . "Paragraph (6) prevents creditors from attempting in *any way* (emphasis added) to collect a pre-petition debt." Id. at 342. . . . Section 362 was added to the bankruptcy laws to protect the inexperienced, frightened, or ill-counseled debtors who might succumb to attempts to evade the purpose of the bankruptcy laws by sophisticated creditors. Id. at 342.

Furthermore, courts have held that inactivity on the part of a creditor with notice of the bankruptcy which permits the forces of collection to go forward is as offensive to the automatic stay provision as is activity. . . .

Acts taken in violation of the automatic stay are void ab initio. . . . Consequently all transfers to the loan account made after the date of the petition (November 21, 1980) must be returned to the debtor plus the interest that would have been earned had that money remained in the debtor's share draft account. . . .

[So ordered.]

Trustee Election and Duties; Creditors' Meeting. Once the bankruptcy proceeding begins, the debtor's property is effectively held in trust for the benefit of her creditors. The trustee of the property, known as the **trustee in bankruptcy,** occupies a pivotal role in the bankruptcy proceeding. The trustee in bankruptcy is responsible for investigating the debtor's financial affairs; locating and collecting the debtor's property; invalidating certain transfers of property made by the debtor; reducing the assets to cash; determining the validity of creditor claims against the estate; distributing the money to creditors according to the priorities provided by the Bankruptcy Code; and, in some cases, operating the debtor's business and opposing the debtor's discharge. The trustee in bankruptcy is a private citizen, not a government employee or judicial officer.

Promptly after the order for relief is entered, the court appoints an "interim trustee" from a panel of private trustees established and maintained by the United States Trustee. The interim trustee serves at least until the creditors' meeting, which is held within a reasonable time after the order for relief. The debtor must appear at this meeting and submit to examination under oath. Creditors and the trustee may question the debtor concerning his or her conduct, property, or any other matter affecting administration of the estate or the debtor's right to a discharge. This examination is designed to determine whether assets have been improperly disposed of or concealed or if grounds exist for objection to the debtor's discharge. In addition to examining the debtor, the meeting affords the debtor's general unsecured creditors an opportunity to elect the trustee in bankruptcy. If the creditors fail to elect a trustee, the interim trustee appointed by the court serves as permanent trustee in the case. The bankruptcy judge may not attend the meeting.

Property of the Estate

Filing a bankruptcy petition, either voluntarily or involuntarily, creates an **estate**.[11] In a liquidation case, the property of the estate passes to the trustee in bankruptcy and is distributed to the debtor's creditors. The estate contains all legal or equitable, tangible or intangible, property interests owned by the debtor wherever located and by whomever held.

Generally, property acquired after the filing of the petition does not become "property of the estate." If the debtor receives a discharge, such post-petition property may not therefore be subjected to most prepetition claims with the following exceptions: (1) property acquired by the debtor within 180 days after the filing of the petition acquired (a) as a bequest, devise, or inheritance (that is, by will or intestate succession), (b) as a result of a property settlement agreement with the debtor's spouse, and (c) as a beneficiary of a life insurance policy; (2) proceeds, products, offspring, rents, or profits received from property of the estate (such as interest on bonds, rent from an apartment building, or insurance proceeds); (3) property recovered by the trustee under the avoidance powers discussed later in this chapter; and (4) property acquired by the *estate* after commencement of the case.

Exempt Property. The Bankruptcy Code allows the debtor to exempt various types of property of the estate from creditors' claims.[12] Additionally, as noted in Chapter 29, each state has enacted an exemption statute insulating certain property. The Bankruptcy Code provides the debtor with a choice between exemptions allowed under state law and under federal statutes other than the Bankruptcy Code,[13] or those provided by the Bankruptcy Code. Individual states may, by statute, require the debtor

to use state exemptions. A majority of states have enacted such legislation.

Bankruptcy Code exemptions, if available, include the following:

1. Certain sources of income and compensation for losses—such as unemployment compensation; public assistance; social security, veterans, disability, and crime victim reparation benefits; alimony, child support, and separate maintenance payments; certain pension, annuity, and profit-sharing benefits; payments resulting from the death of a person supporting the debtor; and payments to compensate for personal injury or lost income of the debtor or a person supporting the debtor.

2. Certain specific property without dollar limitation—such as professionally prescribed health aids and unmatured life insurance contracts.

3. Certain specific property with dollar limitation—such as the debtor's equity interest in real or personal property used as a residence, not exceeding $7,500 (homestead exemption); a motor vehicle not exceeding $1,200; household furnishings, clothes, appliances, and other goods held for consumer purposes not exceeding $200 per item or $4,000 in aggregate value; jewelry not exceeding $500; implements, books, or tools of the debtor's trade not exceeding $750; and the loan value of the debtor's life insurance policy not exceeding $4,000.

4. Unspecified property with dollar limitation—such as $400 in any property plus up to $3,750 in the unused amount of the homestead exemption.

Note that any waiver of exemptions, state or federal, executed by the debtor in favor of a creditor, made either before or after bankruptcy, is unenforceable.

Collecting Estate Property—General Trustee Powers

The trustee in bankruptcy is the representative of the estate, with the capacity to sue and be sued. As previously noted, the trustee's principal duty is to collect the property of the estate, convert it to cash, and pay competing creditors according to the priorities provided by law. A variety of Bankruptcy Code provisions aid the trustee in maximizing the value of the estate for distribution to creditors.

---

11. 11 U.S.C. §541.

12. 11 U.S.C. §522.

13. For example, federal law outside Title 11 exempts social security benefits, railroad retirement annuities, civil service retirement benefits, and veteran's benefits, among others.

Initially, the law imposes various duties upon the debtor regarding the property of the estate. For example, the debtor must (1) appear and submit to examination under oath at the meeting of creditors concerning the nature, location, and extent of his property, (2) submit a list of creditors, a schedule of assets and liabilities, and a statement of the debtor's financial affairs, (3) cooperate with the trustee to enable the trustee to perform his or her duties, and (4) surrender to the trustee all property of the estate including books, documents, records, and papers relating to that property.

The law also requires that persons in possession of the debtor's property or those owing money to the debtor turn it over to the trustee. Additionally, the court may order third parties, such as attorneys and accountants possessing books, documents, or records regarding the debtor's property or financial affairs, to turn over or disclose that information. Because the basic duty of the trustee is to maximize the value of the estate for the benefit of creditors, the court may authorize or order the trustee to abandon property that is burdensome to the estate or is of inconsequential value.

If the estate includes a business owned by the debtor, the court may authorize the trustee to operate the business for a limited period if the continued operation is in the best interest of the estate and is consistent with an orderly liquidation. Such an authorization might be made, for example, to convert work in process into finished goods that can be sold at a much higher price than the unfinished goods.

Executory Contracts and Unexpired Leases. In addition to buildings, equipment, inventory, and other tangible property, the estate may also contain intangible property, including any rights the debtor may have under executory contracts (contracts on which performance remains due to some extent on both sides) and unexpired leases. For example, assume D, a boat manufacturer, has filed for bankruptcy. Property of the estate would include the rights D possesses under an existing supply contract with S, a manufacturer of fiberglass, and the rights D has under a ten-year lease with L on the building housing D's manufacturing operation. Filing a bankruptcy petition does not terminate executory contracts and unexpired leases, even if the contract or lease contains a "bankruptcy clause" or "*ipso facto* clause" that purports to terminate the contract or lease upon bankruptcy. Such clauses are unenforceable in bankruptcy.

After commencement of the case, the lease or contract continues in force, and the trustee in bankruptcy is given the option, subject to court approval, to (1) assume and perform the lease or contract, (2) assume and assign the lease or contract to a third party, or (3) reject the lease or contract. In a liquidation case, the trustee must act to assume within sixty days after the order for relief is entered. If not assumed within this time, the contract or lease is deemed rejected.

The options outlined above allow the trustee to retain leases or contracts beneficial to the estate, and to rid the estate of those that burden it.[14] For example, a building leased by the debtor may be in a good business location at a reasonable rent. A new tenant might be willing to pay the trustee for an assignment of the lease. In this case, assumption and assignment of the lease by the trustee would be in the best interest of the estate. In a liquidation case, leases and contracts are ordinarily rejected. In this case, the nonbankrupt party may file a claim against the estate as a general unsecured creditor for breach of the lease or contract.

Collecting Estate Property— Trustee's Avoidance Powers

Bankruptcy law gives the trustee certain extraordinary "avoidance" powers to defeat claims of certain creditors and to recover property of the estate held by third parties. Lawsuits by the trustee under these "avoidance powers" may generally be commenced up until the case is closed or dimissed, or within two years after the trustee's appointment, whichever occurs first.[15]

Defenses of the Estate. Initially, the trustee "steps into the shoes" of the debtor and may assert any defense the debtor has against a creditor's claim. For example, suppose Carl fraudulently induces Donna to purchase a car on credit for $1,000

---

14. 11 U.S.C. §365.
15. 11 U.S.C. §546(a).

by misrepresenting its mechanical condition. Donna files for bankruptcy and Carl files a $1,000 claim against the estate. Donna's trustee in bankruptcy acquires her rights and therefore may assert Carl's fraud as a defense to paying Carl's claim. Had Donna already paid Carl, Donna's trustee could use the fraud as a basis to recover the money from Carl.[16]

Rights of Actual Creditors. In addition to assuming the debtor's position, the trustee assumes the position of actual unsecured creditors who have valid claims against the debtor.[17] Therefore, the trustee may avoid any transfer of property by the debtor or any obligation incurred by the debtor that could be attacked under state or federal law by the debtor's unsecured creditors. For example, assume Day owes Carter $10,000. Subsequently, Day, a merchant, sells his entire inventory to Smith for $200,000. Smith does not notify Carter of the transfer. Smith, therefore, fails to comply with Article 6 of the Uniform Commercial Code governing bulk transfers, discussed in Chapter 29. Under Article 6, the transfer to Smith is thus ineffective against Carter. Day files for bankruptcy. Because Carter, an actual unsecured creditor of Day, can avoid the transfer, Day's trustee in bankruptcy may also avoid it.[18] The trustee in this case would not be aided merely by stepping into Day's shoes; that is, Day could not avoid the transfer to Smith.

Rights of Hypothetical Creditors—"Strong-Arm" Clause. The trustee is not limited to the rights possessed by the debtor's *actual* creditors. Under the so-called strong-arm clause of the Bankruptcy Code,[19] the trustee may also assert the rights of "hypothetical" lien creditors or bona fide purchasers. Specifically, under this clause the trustee may avoid any transfer of property or any obligation incurred by the debtor that could be avoided by: (1) a creditor who extends credit to the debtor and obtains a judicial lien on the debtor's property (a lien creditor), (2) a creditor with an unsatisfied writ of execution against the debtor's property (a judgment creditor), and (3) a bona fide purchaser of the debtor's real property, *whether or not such a creditor or purchaser actually exists.* This power is particularly helpful to the trustee when no actual creditor of the estate possesses the power transferred to the trustee under the strong-arm clause.

For example, assume Crenshaw loans Doaks $25,000. Doaks gives Crenshaw a mortgage on real property owned by Doaks to secure repayment of the loan. Crenshaw, however, fails to record the mortgage. A bona fide purchaser of the property from Doaks would therefore take it free of Crenshaw's mortgage. Doaks subsequently files for bankruptcy, while still owning the real property. Doaks's trustee in bankruptcy takes the land free of Crenshaw's mortgage under the strong-arm clause. Note that the trustee acquires the rights of a bona fide purchaser of the land, even though no such purchaser actually exists; Doaks did not sell the land prior to bankruptcy.

Preferences. Shortly before bankruptcy, a debtor has insufficient assets to pay all creditors. With the limited assets remaining, however, the debtor may pay one or more creditors to the exclusion of others. Because a basic purpose of bankruptcy is to insure the equitable treatment of similarly situated creditors, bankruptcy law[20] allows the trustee to recover certain prebankruptcy transfers known as **preferences** that favor one creditor over another. Preferences are recoverable from a favored creditor if the trustee is able to prove the following five conditions.

1. The transfer was made to or for the benefit of a creditor.
2. The transfer was made for or on account of an "antecedent debt," one owed by the debtor before the transfer was made.
3. The debtor was insolvent when the transfer was made. The debtor is presumed to be insolvent during the 90 days immediately preceding the filing of the petition.

---

16. 11 U.S.C. §558.

17. 11 U.S.C. §544(b).

18. The trustee may avoid the entire transfer and recover the property for the benefit of the estate. The trustee's recovery is not limited to the amount of Carter's claim. See *Moore v. Bay,* 52 S. Ct. 3 (1931).

19. 11 U.S.C. §544(a).

20. 11 U.S.C. §547.

4. The transfer was made (a) on or within 90 days immediately preceding the filing of the petition, or (b) between 90 days and one year before the petition was filed if the creditor was an **insider.** An insider is a person in a sufficiently close relationship to the debtor that his or her conduct is subject to closer scrutiny than creditors dealing with the debtor at arm's length. Examples include a relative of (or corporation controlled by) an individual debtor, a general partner of a partnership debtor, and a director, officer, or controlling shareholder of a corporate debtor.

5. The creditor, by virtue of the transfer, receives more than would have been received in a Chapter 7 bankruptcy proceeding if the transfer had not been made.

In short, a preference occurs when a debtor pays off an old debt shortly before bankruptcy to the detriment of other creditors. A preference, unlike a fraudulent conveyance discussed in the next section, does not reduce the net worth of the estate. Assets and liabilities are reduced equally. Preferences involve payment of legitimate debts and do not constitute fraud on the debtor's part. The evil of a preference is its inequitable treatment of competing creditors.

Preference Analysis. In analyzing preference cases, three dates are relevant: (1) the date of the debt, (2) the date of the transfer, and (3) the date of bankruptcy. The date of the debt must precede the date of the transfer. This requirement establishes the "antecedent" nature of the debt; it is not a preference to pay current debts as they come due. The 90-day (or in insider cases, up to one year) period within which the trustee may recover is measured between dates (2) and (3) above, that is, between the date of transfer and the date of bankruptcy.

To illustrate, assume that on January 1, Adams, Baxter, and Charles each ship $10,000 worth of goods to Dodd on open account for use in Dodd's business. Dodd makes no payment on these accounts during the next six months. On July 1, Dodd's financial position has deteriorated to the point where his only remaining assets are a build-

ing worth $10,000 and $10,000 cash. Dodd pays Adams $10,000. On August 1, Dodd files a bankruptcy petition. The $10,000 payment to Adams is a preference recoverable by the trustee for the benefit of the estate. The relevant dates are as follows:

1. Date of Debt . . . . Jan. 1 ⎫ Establishes
2. Date of Transfer . . . . July 1 ⎭ antecedent debt

3. Date of Bankruptcy . . . . Aug. 1   Occurs within 90 days of transfer

The adverse effect of the transfer to Adams upon Dodd's other creditors is clear. Assuming no other expenses or creditors, but for the transfer Adams, Baxter, and Charles would each receive $6,667. That is,

$$\frac{\text{assets}}{\text{claims}} \quad \frac{\$20,000}{\$30,000} = 66\text{¢ on the dollar}$$

Because of the July 1 transfer, Adams receives $10,000, which is more than she would receive in the bankruptcy proceeding if the transfer had not been made. Adams will be required to return the $10,000 payment to the trustee, but will then be entitled to file a $10,000 claim in Dodd's bankruptcy proceeding.

Payments of current obligations are not subject to preference attack. Using the above example, assume that on July 1, Adams delivers an additional $10,000 worth of goods and Dodd pays for them in cash. No preference occurs because there is no antecedent debt. Various provisions of the Bankruptcy Code clarify which transactions are treated as current and therefore not subject to avoidance as a preference.

Fraudulent Conveyances. The Bankruptcy Code[21] permits the trustee in bankruptcy to avoid fraudulent conveyances made or obligations incurred on or within one year prior to the date the bankruptcy petition is filed. Specifically, the trustee may avoid any transfer of property or obligation made with actual intent to hinder, delay, or defraud past or

---

21. 11 U.S.C. §548.

future creditors. Additionally, the trustee may avoid any transfer or obligation for which the debtor received less than a reasonably equivalent value if the debtor (1) was insolvent at the time of the transfer or was rendered insolvent by the transfer, or (2) was engaged (or about to engage) in business for which the debtor's remaining property was an unreasonably small capital, or (3) intended to incur or believed that he would incur debts beyond his ability to pay. These provisions are substantially similar to those contained in the Uniform Fraudulent Conveyance Act, and Uniform Fraudulent Transfer Act, discussed in Chapter 29. As under state law, the Bankruptcy Code protects a transferee who receives the property from the debtor in good faith and for value.

Statutory, Judicial, and Consensual Liens.

To assure equitable treatment of creditors, the trustee in bankruptcy has significant power to avoid various liens that attach to the debtor's property prior to bankruptcy. The trustee may avoid statutory liens, such as mechanics liens and various tax liens, if (1) the lien first becomes effective because of the debtor's financial difficulty or when a bankruptcy petition is filed, or (2) the lien is not perfected and enforceable at the time the case is commenced against a bona fide purchaser of the property subject to the lien. The trustee also may avoid any statutory lien possessed by a landlord for unpaid rent.[22]

Judicial liens (judgment liens and other liens obtained by legal or equitable proceedings) may be avoided if they arise within 90 days prior to filing of the bankruptcy petition. That is, judicial liens obtained within ninety days of bankruptcy are simply preferences that are defeated by the trustee under principles previously discussed.

The trustee also may avoid consensual liens (those created by contract between the debtor and a creditor) in certain cases. Generally, to defeat the trustee in bankruptcy, creditors holding a security interest in the debtor's *real* property (a mortgage) must properly record their interest prior to bankruptcy in an appropriate public office, usually the county recorder of deeds. Similarly, creditors with security interests in personal property, such as inventory and equipment, defeat the trustee in bankruptcy if their interests are "perfected" prior to bankruptcy. Perfection usually requires that a "financing statement" be publicly filed, commonly with the secretary of state. As with judicial liens, consensual liens recorded or filed within 90 days prior to bankruptcy may often be avoided by the trustee as preferences. Consensual liens in personal property are covered in detail in the next two chapters. Recording and mortgages are discussed in Chapter 37.

Postpetition Transfers.

The trustee in bankruptcy does not take possession of the debtor's property immediately after the petition is filed. A period of time elapses before the property is turned over. During this "gap," the debtor may transfer property belonging to the estate to a third party. Subject to certain exceptions, the trustee may avoid transfers made by the debtor after the case is commenced.[23] The proceeds of any postpetition transfer that is not avoided become property of the estate.

Distributing Property of the Estate

Claims.

After the bankruptcy petition is filed and the debtor files a list of creditors, the court sends a notice of the bankruptcy proceeding to the listed creditors. To participate in the assets of the estate, creditors usually must file a proof of claim with the court within 90 days after the date set for the meeting of creditors.[24] **Claims** include any right to payment or to receive any equitable remedy, such as specific performance of a contract. Shareholders of a bankrupt corporation may file a proof of interest.

Once filed, a proof of claim is prima facie evidence of the creditor's claim. As such it is **allowed**—participates in the distribution of the estate's assets—unless another creditor or the bankruptcy trustee objects. In that event the court, after notice and a hearing, determines the validity

22. 11 U.S.C. §545.

23. 11 U.S.C. §549.
24. Bankruptcy Rule 3002(c), 11 U.S.C.

and amount of the claim and then allows it, subject to the following exceptions and limitations.[25]

1. The claim is disallowed to the extent it is unenforceable against the debtor or his property.
2. A claim is disallowed to the extent it represents interest accruing on the debtor's obligations after the petition is filed.
3. Claims for property taxes are disallowed to the extent the tax claim exceeds the value of the debtor's interest in the land.
4. Claims for services rendered by the debtor's attorney or an "insider" are allowed only to the extent of the reasonable value of the services.
5. Claims for postpetition alimony, maintenance, or child support are disallowed.[26]
6. Claims of the debtor's landlord for future rent due on a lease terminated in bankruptcy (for example, if the trustee rejects the lease) are limited.[27]
7. Claims of the debtor's employees for future compensation due under employment contracts are limited.
8. Federal tax claims resulting from the debtor's late payment of state unemployment taxes are disallowed.

Generally, only claims arising before the petition is filed are allowed. Certain claims arising thereafter, however, may be allowed. Such claims include (1) in an involuntary case, any claim arising in the ordinary course of the debtor's business after the filing, but before the order for relief or appointment of the trustee, whichever occurs first, (2) claims arising from the trustee's rejection of executory contracts or unexpired leases, (3) claims of a person from whom property was recovered by the trustee as a preference or fraudulent conveyance, and (4) certain tax claims entitled to priority in distribution of the estate.

Priorities. Once the trustee has collected the assets of the estate, the trustee sells them and distributes the proceeds to the various creditors with allowable claims. Distribution is made first to secured creditors and then to unsecured creditors according to Bankruptcy Code priority rules.

Secured Creditors. Assuming a creditor has obtained a lien upon the debtor's property that is valid against the trustee in bankruptcy, that creditor is paid out of the collateral to the exclusion of other creditors.[28] Various methods may be used to apply the collateral to the secured debt. The court may order the automatic stay imposed at the commencement of the case lifted, allowing the creditor to seize the property and sell it in satisfaction of the debt. Alternatively, the trustee may simply abandon the encumbered property to the creditor with the same result. If these alternatives are not used, the property will ultimately be sold by the trustee and the proceeds distributed to the secured creditor, less the costs incurred by the trustee in preserving and selling the collateral.

If the collateral is insufficient to satisfy the underlying debt in full, the excess is treated as a general creditor's unsecured claim, and receives a percentage distribution equal to that received by other unsecured claims.[29]

Unsecured Creditors. After secured creditors are paid, the remaining nonexempt property of the estate is applied to pay the administrative expenses of the bankruptcy and unsecured creditors in the order outlined below.[30] All claims of one class are paid in full before the next class receives anything.

---

25. Rules relating to allowance of claims or interests are contained in 11 U.S.C. §502.

26. These debts are not discharged in bankruptcy and may therefore be satisfied out of the debtor's postpetition assets. 11 U.S.C. §502(b)(5).

27. Claims for rent accruing before either bankruptcy or the debtor ceased possessing the property, whichever is earlier, are not limited. Claims accruing after that time are limited to rent payable under the lease for the longer of the following two periods: (1) one year, or (2) 15% of the remaining term of the lease not to exceed three years. 11 U.S.C. §502(b)(6).

---

28. 11 U.S.C. §725.

29. 11 U.S.C. §506(a).

30. These priorities are contained in 11 U.S.C. §507.

If the assets are insufficient to pay all claims of a given class, the claimants share pro rata:

1. Administrative expenses of the bankruptcy such as the costs of maintaining and selling property of the estate, the trustee's compensation, and the debtor's and the trustee's attorneys' fees;

2. In an involuntary case, certain claims arising in the ordinary course of the debtor's business arising after the petition is filed but before the order for relief is entered or the trustee is appointed, whichever occurs first;

3. Claims of employees against a bankrupt employer for wages, salaries, and commissions (including vacation, severance, and sick leave pay) up to $2,000 per employee earned within ninety days prior to the date the petition was filed or the date the debtor ceased business operations, whichever occurred first;

4. Claims for contributions to employee benefit plans that arise from services rendered by the employee within 180 days prior to the filing of the petition (or cessation of the debtor's business, whichever is earlier) and that are limited in amount to $2,000 multiplied by the number of employees covered by the plan, *less* any amount paid to employees under the third priority listed above;

5. Claims of farmers who stored grain in a bankrupt grain elevator and fishermen who sold or transferred fish to a bankrupt fish produce storage or processing facility up to $2,000 per individual;

6. Claims of consumers who paid money to a bankrupt business for goods or services to be provided at a later date, which were not provided, up to $900 per individual;

7. Tax claims including income or gross receipts taxes, property taxes, any tax required to be withheld or collected, employment taxes, excise taxes, and customs duties arising from the importation of merchandise;

8. Claims of general unsecured creditors whose claims are timely filed.

In computing total general creditor claims, deficiencies in secured creditor's claims and priority claims exceeding the time or amount limitations outlined above are included. Because assets are usually insufficient to pay general creditor claims in full, claimants share pro rata. For example, if $10,000 remains after payment of priority claims and allowed unsecured claims total $100,000, each creditor receives ten percent of his claim

$$\frac{\$10,000 \text{ assets}}{\$100,000 \text{ claims}}$$

or ten cents on the dollar. The distribution to general creditors is often known as the **dividend** and the percentage of their claims general creditors are paid is the **dividend percentage.**

Discharge

Effect of Discharge. A basic purpose of bankruptcy, in addition to equitable treatment of creditors, is debtor relief. In bankruptcy law, debtor relief is embodied in the form of the discharge, designed to give the debtor a ''fresh start'' free of claims of former creditors. A **discharge in bankruptcy** releases the debtor from any further liability for most debts that arose prior to the date the order for relief is entered. Discharge is generally granted whether or not a proof of claim was filed for the debt in question and whether or not the claim based on the debt was allowed.

A discharge voids any judgment against the debtor imposing personal liability for a prepetition debt and prevents creditors from commencing or continuing any legal proceeding or other act to collect a discharged debt. Thus, the discharge constitutes a total prohibition of debt collection efforts, including informal action such as telephone calls, letters, and personal contacts.

Not all debtors and not all debts are discharged in bankruptcy. A debtor who is denied a discharge occupies an unenviable position. All nonexempt assets are seized, liquidated, and distributed to satisfy creditors' claims. The remaining balances of all prepetition creditor claims survive and may be asserted against the debtor after bankruptcy. Even if the debtor is granted a discharge, some specific debts survive the proceeding and may be collected after bankruptcy. Note that if the debtor is denied a discharge, *all* creditor claims survive. If the debtor is discharged, only specifically enumerated debts survive; the remainder are discharged.

Debtors Not Discharged. The Bankruptcy Code provides that the court is to grant the debtor a discharge unless a creditor or the trustee in bankruptcy objects and establishes a ground for denying a discharge.[31] These grounds are generally based upon the debtor's dishonesty or lack of cooperation in the bankruptcy proceeding. When the court has determined whether to grant the debtor a discharge, the court holds a hearing to inform the debtor that a discharge has been granted or the reason why a discharge has been denied. A debtor is denied a discharge if one of the following grounds is proven.

1. The debtor is not an individual. (Corporations and partnerships are ineligible for discharge under Chapter 7.)

2. The debtor made a fraudulent conveyance of property, either before or after the case was commenced.

3. The debtor concealed, destroyed, falsified, or failed to keep or preserve financial books and records from which the debtor's financial condition or business transactions could be ascertained.

4. The debtor knowingly and fraudulently: (a) made a false oath or account, (b) presented or used a false claim, (c) received consideration for acting or failing to act in connection with the bankruptcy, or (d) withheld financial books and records from the bankruptcy trustee.

5. The debtor failed to explain satisfactorily any loss or deficiency of assets necessary to meet liabilities.

6. The debtor (a) refused to obey any lawful order of the court, (b) failed to respond on the ground of privilege against self-incrimination to a material question approved by the court after being granted immunity, or (c) when self-incrimination is not involved, failed to testify or to respond to a material question approved by the court.

7. The debtor committed any of the acts specified in paragraphs 2 through 6 above in connection with a separate bankruptcy case involving an "insider" within one year prior to the debtor's bankruptcy petition.

8. The debtor signs a written waiver of discharge approved by the court after the order for relief is entered.

A discharge previously granted may be revoked on the request of the trustee or a creditor, upon

proof that the discharge was obtained through fraud, or that the debtor knowingly and fraudulently retained property belonging to the estate or failed to obey a court order. In addition, the Bankruptcy Code limits the frequency of a bankruptcy discharge. In a liquidation case, the debtor may receive a discharge only once every six years, measured between the dates on which bankruptcy petitions are filed.

At issue in the following case was whether the debtor should be denied a discharge.

In the Matter of Hugh D. Reed
700 F.2d 986 (5th Cir. 1983)

Hugh D. Reed filed for bankruptcy in December, 1979, but the bankruptcy court denied Reed a discharge in bankruptcy. At the time he filed bankruptcy, Reed owed a bank approximately $200,000 for a loan extended to Reed's Men's Wear, a retail store he operated that became insolvent in 1979. Reed also owed money to other creditors of the business.

The primary reason for the court's denial of discharge was that shortly before declaring bankruptcy, Reed had converted his property into assets exempt from the claims of creditors. Under Texas law, a person's homestead is exempt from the claims of general creditors in bankruptcy. During November and December of 1979, Reed had sold much of his property—including his stock and collections of antiques, coins, and guns—and had used the proceeds to pay off loans secured by mortgages on his home.

The federal district court upheld the denial of discharge. On appeal to the court of appeals, Reed argued that under bankruptcy law he was entitled to use exemptions allowed by state law rather than those provided by federal bankruptcy law. He further argued that by denying him a discharge in bankruptcy, the court effectively had denied him the right to use the exemptions allowed under state law.

Rubin, Circuit Judge
. . . The Bankruptcy Code provides that a debtor may be denied discharge if he has transferred property "with intent to hinder, delay, or defraud a creditor" [11 U.S.C. §727(a)(2)]. . . .

31. 11 U.S.C. §727.

In considering the effect of Reed's transfer of assets, we distinguish, as did the careful opinion of the bankruptcy court, the debtor's entitlement to the exemption of property from the claims of his creditors and his right to a discharge from his debts. The Bankruptcy Code allows a debtor to retain property exempt either (1) under the provisions of the Bankruptcy Code, if not forbidden by state law, . . . or (2) under the provisions of state law and federal law other than the minimum allowances in the Bankruptcy Code. . . .

Reed elected to claim his exemptions under state law. The bankruptcy judge, therefore, referred to Texas law to determine both what property was exempt and whether the exemption was defeated by the eleventh-hour conversion. Texas constitutional and statutory protection of the homestead is absolute, and the bankruptcy judge interpreted Texas law to allow the exemption in full regardless of Reed's intent. . . .

While the Code requires that, when the debtor claims a state-created exemption, the scope of the claim is determined by state law, it sets separate standards for determining whether the debtor shall be denied a discharge. The debtor's entitlement to a discharge must, therefore, be determined by federal, not state, law. In this respect, 11 U.S.C. §727(a)(2) is absolute: the discharge shall be denied a debtor who has transferred property with intent to defraud his creditors. . . . [M]ere conversion [of property to exempt assets] is not to be considered fraudulent unless other evidence proves actual intent to defraud creditors. . . . For example, evidence that the debtor, on the eve of bankruptcy, borrowed money that was then converted into exempt assets would suffice to support a finding of actual intent to defraud. Only if such a finding is made may a discharge be denied.

The evidence amply supports the bankruptcy court's finding that Reed had an actual intent to defraud. Reed's whole pattern of conduct evinces that intent. . . . His rapid conversion of nonexempt assets to extinguish one home mortgage and to reduce another four months before bankruptcy, after arranging with his creditors to be free of payment obligations until the following year, speaks for itself as a transfer of property in fraud of creditors. His diversion of the daily receipts of Reed's Men's Wear into an account unknown to his creditors and management consultant and his subsequent use of the receipts to repay a loan that had been a vehicle for this conversion confirm his fraudulent motivation. . . .

The denial of a discharge on this ground . . . was appropriate. It would constitute a perversion of the purposes of the Bankruptcy Code to permit a debtor earning $180,000 a year to convert every one of his major nonexempt assets into sheltered property on the eve of bankruptcy with actual intent to defraud his creditors and then emerge washed clean of future obligation by carefully concocted immersion in bankruptcy waters.

Reed asserts that denial of a discharge makes the exemption meaningless. This is but fulmination. Reed may retain his home, mortgages substantially reduced, free of claims by his creditors. In light of the ample evidence, aside from the conversion itself, that Reed had an actual intent to defraud his creditors, he simply is not entitled to a discharge despite the fact that a generous state law may protect his exemption.

[Judgment affirmed.]

Debts Not Discharged. Even if the debtor receives a discharge, the Bankruptcy Code provides[32] that certain prepetition debts survive the proceeding and may be collected against the debtor's postbankruptcy assets. Debts not discharged include

1. most taxes;
2. money, property, or services obtained through misrepresentation or fraud;
3. money, property, or services obtained through use of a materially false and fraudulent written financial statement;
4. liability for "luxury goods" obtained by the debtor on or within forty days prior to the order for relief from a single creditor with a total value exceeding $500;
5. cash advances obtained within twenty days prior to the order for relief totaling more than $1,000 that are extensions of

---

32. 11 U.S.C. §523.

consumer credit under an open end credit plan (such as a credit card);

6. debts that the debtor fails to include on his or her list of creditors if as a result the unlisted creditor is unable to file a timely claim in the proceeding;

7. debts resulting from the debtor's fraud or embezzlement while acting in a fiduciary capacity, such as a trustee;

8. debts resulting from embezzlement or larceny;

9. debts to a spouse or former spouse for alimony, separate maintenance, or child support;

10. debts resulting from the debtor's willful and malicious injury of another person or his property;

11. liability for fines, penalties, or forfeitures payable to governmental units;

12. student loans, unless the loan first became due at least five years before the bankruptcy petition was filed;

13. debts, such as a tort judgment, incurred by the debtor as a result of driving a motor vehicle while legally intoxicated; and

14. debts from a prior bankruptcy in which the debtor was denied a discharge.

Reaffirmation Agreements. A debtor may promise in a **reaffirmation agreement** to pay a debt discharged in bankruptcy. To prevent erosion of the fresh start aspect of bankruptcy, the Bankruptcy Code severely limits enforcement of such agreements. To be enforceable, a reaffirmation agreement must be made before the discharge is granted, be filed with the court, and contain a clear and conspicuous statement that it may be rescinded by the debtor at any time prior to discharge or within 60 days after being filed with the court, whichever occurs later. If the debtor is represented by an attorney, the attorney must file an affadavit that the agreement represents the debtor's fully informed and voluntary agreement and does not impose undue hardship on the debtor. If the debtor is not represented by an attorney during negotiation of the reaffirmation agreement, the agreement must be approved by the court. Additionally, at the discharge hearing the court must inform the debtor that reaffirmation agreements are not required by law and

explain the consequences of reaffirmation. Note that the foregoing requirements do not prevent a debtor from voluntarily repaying any debt.[33]

Rehabilitation—Chapters 11, 12, and 13

An alternative to liquidation, often more advantageous to all concerned, is to keep the financially troubled debtor in business, postponing, compromising, or altering creditor claims, and allowing the debtor to attempt to work out his problems. Such debtor "rehabilitation" arrangements are often preferable to general creditors who usually receive little or nothing upon liquidation. Four chapters of the Bankruptcy Code are concerned with debtor rehabilitation: Chapter 9 (Adjustment of Debts of a Municipality), Chapter 11 (Reorganization), Chapter 12 (Adjustment of Debts of a Family Farmer With Regular Annual Income), and Chapter 13 (Adjustment of Debts of an Individual With Regular Income). In all cases, rehabilitation "plans" are adopted under which creditor claims are reduced, converted into other forms of debt or equity, or the time of payment extended. In corporate reorganization, claims of equity security holders (shareholders) may also be affected.

A debtor, at any time during pendency of a Chapter 7 case (either voluntary or involuntary), has an absolute one-time right to convert the case to a proceeding under Chapter 11, 12, or 13.[34] This conversion privilege assures the debtor is always given an opportunity to repay debts. If a rehabilitation plan under Chapter 11, 12, or 13 is unsuccessful, the case may be converted by the debtor, or in some cases his creditors, to a Chapter 7 liquidation proceeding.

Chapter 11—Reorganization

Commencement of the Case. Chapter 11 is the primary device used to rehabilitate corporate, as opposed to individual, debtors in financial difficulty. A Chapter 11 case may be commenced in various ways. The case may be commenced either voluntarily (by the debtor) or involuntarily (by

---

33. 11 U.S.C. §§524(c)-(f).
34. 11 U.S.C. §706(a).

creditors) using the same requirements discussed earlier in this chapter. Second, upon request of the trustee or creditor, the court may, after notice and a hearing, convert a Chapter 7 case into a Chapter 11 case. Finally, the debtor may commence the case through conversion from a Chapter 7 case.

In reorganization cases, unlike those under Chapter 7, the debtor usually retains possession of property of the estate and continues to manage and operate the business as a "debtor in possession." No trustee in bankruptcy is appointed; rather, the debtor in possession has the rights and powers, and performs the functions and duties, of the trustee. After commencement of the case, but before confirmation of the plan, however, the court may appoint a trustee for cause, including fraud, dishonesty, incompetence, or gross mismanagement by the debtor's current management, or if the court finds the appointment to be in the best interest of creditors, shareholders, or others interested in the estate. Even if the court finds it unnecessary to appoint a trustee, it may appoint an examiner to investigate any allegations of fraud, dishonesty, misconduct, or other irregularity.

Under Chapter 11, like Chapter 7, the debtor is required to file a list of creditors, a schedule of assets and liabilities, and a statement of the debtor's financial affairs. A creditor's proof of claim (or proof of interest in the case of a shareholder) is deemed to be filed if it appears in the above schedules, unless the claim or interest is disputed, contingent, or unliquidated. Chapter 11 therefore does not require that every creditor or shareholder file a proof of claim or interest in a reorganization case.

Because a Chapter 11 debtor often has hundreds or thousands of creditors, after the order for relief, the court is required to appoint a committee of creditors holding unsecured claims. The court may also appoint committees representing other classes of creditors or shareholders. A **creditors' committee** ordinarily consists of persons holding the seven largest claims against the debtor of the type represented by the committee. Creditors' committees perform various functions such as consulting with the trustee or debtor in possession regarding administration of the case, investigating the debtor's conduct, participating in the formulation of the reorganization plan, and requesting the appointment of a trustee or examiner.

Formulation of the Plan. The proposal and acceptance of a **reorganization plan** and its confirmation by the court make up the major part of a Chapter 11 proceeding. The debtor may file a reorganization plan at any time, with the exclusive right to do so during the first 120 days after the order for relief is entered. Any party may file a plan if the debtor has not filed within 120 days, if a trustee has been appointed, or if the debtor's plan is not accepted by creditors or shareholders.[35] Most plans are the result of intensive negotiations among the debtor, its creditors, and shareholders.

Because creditors and equity security holders in reorganization cases are so numerous, the plan generally divides the claimants into "classes," consisting of claims or interests that are substantially similar. The plan then designates how creditors within each class are treated. Generally, the plan must provide the same treatment for each claim or interest of a particular class.

Adequate Protection. As previously discussed, secured creditors holding consensual liens in the debtor's real or personal property will defeat the trustee in bankruptcy's claim to the property if their interests are properly recorded or filed prior to bankruptcy. Despite this basic protection, secured creditors are often adversely affected by the debtor's bankruptcy, particularly a Chapter 11 reorganization. Initially, the automatic stay prevents the creditor from collecting the secured debt or from repossessing and selling its collateral. In addition, the Bankruptcy Code[36] permits the trustee (or debtor in possession in a Chapter 11 case) to use, sell, or lease estate property that is subject to a security interest. Thus, in a Chapter 11 reorganization, the debtor in possession often retains and uses property that, but for the bankruptcy, could be repossessed and sold by a secured creditor. Bankruptcy law, however, requires that the debtor in such a case provide the secured party with "adequate protection" of its interest in the collateral while enforcement efforts are prevented by the automatic stay. If the debtor fails to provide adequate protection, the secured creditor may file a motion

---

35. 11 U.S.C. §1121.
36. 11 U.S.C. §363.

with the court to lift the automatic stay to permit foreclosure. Such motions are common and lack of adequate protection is the primary basis for lifting the automatic stay in reorganization cases.

Although the term is not explicitly defined, the Bankruptcy Code[37] lists various methods of providing adequate protection. One method is to require cash payments or additional or replacement liens on estate property to compensate the secured party for any decrease in the value of the collateral resulting either from the delay of the automatic stay or the debtor's use of the property. Adequate protection also may be provided by granting such other relief as will provide the secured party with the "indubitable equivalent" of its interest in the collateral.[38]

Confirmation of the Plan. Once formulated, plans are submitted to the various classes of creditors and shareholders for approval. In addition to the plan or a summary thereof, the holders of claims or interests receive a written disclosure statement approved by the court, containing information adequate to enable them to make an informed judgment about the plan.[39] To be accepted by a class of creditors, the plan must be approved by those holding at least two-thirds in dollar amount and more than one-half in number of allowed claims. To be accepted by a class of equity security holders, persons holding at least two-thirds in dollar amount of a given class of security must approve. No vote is required of any class whose claims or interests are unimpaired by the plan (who are deemed to accept it) or of any class that receives nothing under the plan (who are deemed to reject it).[40]

After the vote, the court is required to hold a hearing on confirmation of the plan. Generally, the court must confirm the plan if it has been proposed in good faith, each class of creditors or shareholders has either accepted the plan or the class's interests are not impaired by the plan, and various additional conditions prescribed by the Bankruptcy Code are met.[41] Even if a class rejects the plan,

however, the court may confirm the plan if it finds that the plan does not discriminate unfairly and is fair and equitable to the impaired class's interest.[42] Confirmation of the plan over the objection of one or more classes of creditors or interests is appropriately known as a **cramdown.**

Specifically, cramdown is allowed if the impaired class and all below it are treated according to a rule of "absolute priority," meaning that the dissenting class must be paid in full before any junior class receives anything. Under this rule, objecting secured creditors may be bound by the plan if they are allowed to retain their security interest in the collateral and are to receive payments with a present value equal to the value of the collateral. Objecting unsecured creditors may be bound if under the plan either (1) their claims are to be paid in full, or (2) no class junior to them is entitled to share under the plan. An analogous rule applies to various classes of shareholders. Under these rules, for example, a trade creditor owed $500 must be paid in full if the shareholders are to receive anything.

In the following case, the court was required to determine whether a plan should be confirmed over a creditor's objection.

In Re White
41 B.R. 227 (Bkrtcy. M.D. Tenn. 1984)

> Thomas C. White, owner and operator of Thomas C. White & Associates, a land surveying business, filed a petition for reorganization under Chapter 11 of the Bankruptcy Code. White filed a plan of reorganization that was accepted by all creditors except Midland Bank and Trust Company, which held two claims against White. Under the plan, one claim in the amount of $12,000 was to be paid at the rate of $270 per month plus interest. The second claim in the amount of $88,200 was to be paid over ten years with interest. The larger debt, which was secured by a real estate mortgage, was to be prepaid if White succeeded in subdividing and selling a portion of the real estate. The plan was based on a pro-

37. 11 U.S.C. §361.
38. 11 U.S.C. §361(3).
39. 11 U.S.C. §1125.
40. 11 U.S.C. §1126.
41. 11 U.S.C. §1129(a).

42. 11 U.S.C. §1129(b).

jection that White's gross income for the next year would be about $103,000, although gross income for each of the two previous years had averaged $52,000. The plan also projected that the real estate could be prepared for sale at a nominal cost, but Midland maintained that improvements costing at least $30,000 were necessary.

Midland objected to the plan on the grounds that it was not feasible, that it had not been proposed in good faith, and that it was not fair and equitable.

Paine, Bankruptcy Judge

. . . In order for a plan of reorganization to be approved by this court, the plan must comply with all the requirements of Chapter 11 as stated in 11 U.S.C. §1129(a)(1). The court has a duty to examine the plan and determine whether or not the plan conforms to the requirements of 11 U.S.C. §1129, regardless of whether objections are filed. . . . In fulfilling this duty, the court concludes that the specific objections raised by Midland are without merit.

First, Midland asserts that the plan was not proposed in good faith as required by 11 U.S.C. §1129(a)(3). Essentially, a reorganization plan is proposed in good faith when there is "a reasonable likelihood that the plan will achieve a result consistent with the objectives and purposes of the Bankruptcy Code." *In re Nite Lite Inns,* 17 B.R. 367, 371 (Bankr. S.D. Cal. 1982). . . . Herein, the debtors have proposed a plan which provides for payments to both secured and unsecured creditors. The secured creditors will receive the value of their collateral plus interest while the unsecured creditors will receive payment contingent upon both the surveying business and the subdivision of the debtors' property. The court finds that the financial assumptions underlying the debtors' plan are reasonable and there is a likelihood of success. Thus, the requisite good faith has been established by the debtors.

Midland also claims that the proposed plan does not comply with §1129(a)(11) in that it is not feasible and will most likely be followed by liquidation. Courts have held that in order to determine whether a plan is feasible, the court must examine ". . . the adequacy of the capital structures; the business's earning power; economic conditions; management's ability; the probability of the present management's continuation; and any other factors

related to the successful performance of the plan." *In re Polytherm Industries, Inc.,* 33 B.R. 823, 831 (W.D. Wis. 1983). . . . The court need not find that the plan is guaranteed of success, but only that a reasonable expectation of success exists. . . . At trial, the court heard testimony concerning the present earning power of the surveying business and the projected earning power of the business based on work in progress. The court also heard testimony concerning prospective purchasers of the subdivided farm land. Based on this evidence, as well as the debtors' demonstrated expertise in the surveying business, the court has determined that the plan is feasible within the meaning of §1129(a)(11).

Finally, Midland alleges that the debtors' plan does not meet the fair and equitable requirements of §1129(b)(2) [the "cramdown" provision] and thus, may not be confirmed over its objection. The court finds that the debtors' plan allows Midland to retain its lien on the property securing its claims, provides Midland with deferred cash payments totaling the allowed amount of its claims plus appropriate interest, and provides that Midland receive any proceeds obtained from the sale of its collateral. With respect to Midland, the court finds that the debtors' plan meets both the fair and equitable requirement of §1129(b)(2) and the requirement that the plan not discriminate unfairly pursuant to §1129(b)(1). . . .

The plan proposed by the debtor not only conforms to all of the applicable requirements of §1129(a) but it also conforms to the requirements of §1129(b) with respect to each class of dissenting creditors. . . .

[Reorganization plan confirmed.]

Implementation of the Plan. Once confirmed, the provisions of the plan are binding on the debtor and anyone issuing securities or acquiring property under the plan. The debtor's creditors or shareholders are also bound including those whose claims or interests were impaired and those who voted against the plan.[43] Thus, after confirmation, creditor and shareholder rights and interests are determined by

---

43. 11 U.S.C. §1141(a).

the terms of the plan and preconfirmation rights and interests are extinguished.

Chapter 13—Adjustment of Debts of an Individual with Regular Income

Chapter 13 governs rehabilitation of individual debtors. Under prior law, individual rehabilitation was limited to "wage earners," but relief under Chapter 13 of the current Bankruptcy Code is available to any individual with a "regular income" who owes, on the date the petition is filed, fixed unsecured debts of less than $100,000 and fixed secured debts of less than $350,000. Thus, Chapter 13 is available to wage earners, sole proprietors, and other persons in business with a regular income, for whom a full-blown reorganization under Chapter 11 is too cumbersome.[44]

Commencement of the Case. Like other bankruptcy proceedings, a Chapter 13 case commences with the filing of a petition. A Chapter 13 case may be commenced *only* by the debtor, who may convert a Chapter 13 case to a Chapter 7 case or may dismiss it at any time.[45]

Under Chapter 13, like Chapter 11, the debtor generally retains possession of all property of the estate, and a debtor engaged in business continues to operate the business unless the court orders otherwise. In a Chapter 13 case, however, after the case is commenced, a trustee is appointed to oversee performance of the debtor's rehabilitation plan. A Chapter 13 trustee has many of the same duties as the trustee in a liquidation case. Under Chapter 13, property of the estate includes all property acquired and earnings received by the debtor both before and after the case is commenced.

Formulation of the Plan. Chapter 13 is designed as a flexible tool for planned repayment of all or part of the debtor's obligations. Under Chapter 13 only the debtor may file a plan of repayment, which at a minimum must: (1) provide for submission to the trustee of whatever portion of the debtor's future income is necessary to implement the plan, (2) provide for full payment of claims entitled

to priority, and (3) provide identical treatment of all claims within a particular class. Although payments under the plan must generally be made within three years, the court may approve a longer period not exceeding five years.[46]

Confirmation of the Plan. Once the plan is formulated, the court holds a hearing on confirmation. Unlike Chapter 11, creditors do not vote to accept or reject a Chapter 13 plan. The plan requires court approval only. To confirm the plan, the court must find that it meets the following criteria:

1. the plan contains terms required or authorized by Chapter 13 or other applicable provisions of the Bankruptcy Code;
2. the filing fee has been paid;
3. the plan was proposed in good faith;
4. unsecured creditors receive an amount under the plan at least equal to the amount that would be paid to them in a Chapter 7 liquidation (sometimes called the "best interests" test);
5. interests of secured creditors are protected under the plan; and
6. the debtor will be able to make all required payments and otherwise comply with the plan.[47]

In addition to the above requirements, if the trustee or an unsecured creditor objects to confirmation, the court may not approve the plan unless either

1. the amount to be distributed under the plan pays the objecting creditor's claim in full, or
2. the plan provides that all of the debtor's projected "disposable income" to be received for three years after payments commence is to be used to make payments under the plan.[48]

The provisions of a confirmed plan are binding upon both the debtor and creditors, and vest title to all property of the estate in the debtor.

---

44. 11 U.S.C. §109(e).
45. 11 U.S.C. §1307.

46. 11 U.S.C. §§1321, 1322.
47. 11 U.S.C. §1325(a).
48. 11 U.S.C. §1325(b).

After confirmation, the debtor makes payments to the trustee, who in turn pays the creditors according to the terms of the plan. To expedite the plan's implementation, the debtor must start making payments proposed by the plan within thirty days after the plan is filed. Once payments under the plan are completed, the debtor receives a discharge of all debts provided for by the plan. Even if all payments have not been made, the court may grant a ''hardship'' discharge to the debtor if the debtor's failure was due to circumstances beyond the debtor's control, creditors have already been paid at least what they would have received in a Chapter 7 proceeding, and modification of the plan is not practicable.

Debtor Advantages of Chapter 13. Since its enactment in 1978, Chapter 13 has become an increasingly popular vehicle for consumer bankruptcy. Chapter 13 provides several advantages over a Chapter 7 liquidation proceeding. First, upon successful completion of a Chapter 13 plan, the debtor is entitled to a discharge of all debts provided for in the plan including a variety of debts that are not discharged in a Chapter 7 proceeding. Second, a Chapter 13 debtor can generally retain collateral and require secured creditors to continue financing the debt (for example, an auto loan secured by the car). Under Chapter 7, to retain the collateral, the debtor must pay in cash the lesser of the balance of the loan or the fair market value of the collateral. Third, Chapter 13 contains a cramdown provision, allowing approval of the plan over creditor objection.

The following case explains the reasons for the differences between Chapters 7 and 13, and highlights the problem of balancing debtor and creditor interests in bankruptcy.

In Re Rimgale

669 F.2d 426 (7th Cir. 1982)

Donald Rimgale filed a Chapter 13 bankruptcy petition and in July, 1980, proposed a plan to pay $120 per month for 42 months to seven creditors. Rimgale owed approximately $6,200, representing unsecured consumer debts, to six of the creditors.

Rimgale also owed approximately $50,000 to Mary Ravenot resulting from a tort judgment awarded to Ravenot in 1979. Rimgale's wife, a psychiatric nurse, had cared for Ravenot, a twenty-six-year-old widow then undergoing psychiatric treatment and later adjudged incompetent. The Rimgales first won Mrs. Ravenot's confidence, then induced her to turn over to them all the proceeds of her husband's life insurance.

Under the proposed plan, Ravenot would have received a total of $2,700. Over Ravenot's objection, the bankruptcy judge confirmed the plan. Ravenot appealed the confirmation order to the federal district court alleging that the plan failed to meet the ''best interests'' test of §1325(a)(4) of the Bankruptcy Code and that the plan had not been proposed in good faith as required by §1325(a)(3) of the Code. District Court Judge Decker held that the proposed plan did not satisfy the best interests test because under the Chapter 13 plan Ravenot would receive only $2,700, an amount less than she would have received if Rimgale had filed for bankruptcy under Chapter 7. In a Chapter 7 liquidation, Ravenot's intentional tort claim would not have been discharged. Rimgale appealed to the federal court of appeals.

Cummings, Chief Judge

. . . One of Congress' purposes in enacting the Bankruptcy Reform Act of 1978 was to make the old Chapter XIII provisions more accessible and attractive to individual debtors. Liberalized provisions, Congress reasoned, would benefit both debtors and creditors. Debtors would be given more latitude to work out debt composition plans, thus avoiding the stigma of straight bankruptcy. Creditors would receive total or substantial repayment under a Chapter 13 plan, but little or nothing in a Chapter 7 liquidation.

To make Chapter 13 work, Congress . . . expanded the class of debtors who could take advantage of Chapter 13[,] . . . eliminated the requirement that a plan be approved by a majority of unsecured creditors [and] . . . added an incentive for debtors to complete performance under the confirmed plan. 11 U.S.C. §1328 provides that a debtor who has carried out his plan is entitled to a discharge of virtually all debts provided for in the plan or disallowed. Thus a Chapter 13 debtor may be discharged from a variety of debts that a Chapter 7 bankrupt remains obligated to pay at the conclusion of a liquidation.

The statutory modification of Chapter 13 has had both intended and unintended effects. The number of Chapter 13 cases has increased sharply. Many of them correspond closely to the idealized case Congress had in mind when it wrote the legislation: the debtor, given time and relief from harassment, is able to pay all or most of his debts. Increasingly, however, bankruptcy courts are seeing cases like the one before us, in which debtors propose less substantial, or even nominal, payments under a Chapter 13 plan, in order eventually to take advantage of Chapter 13's generous discharge provisions. Our task is to determine whether such a plan is permissible under the legislation Congress has drafted. In so doing, we are not free to rewrite the legislation as we think best, but neither are we able to ignore the broad equitable principles that have characteristically animated American bankruptcy law. . . .

Judge Decker based his decision for Mrs. Ravenot on the . . . ground . . . that the claim under Chapter 7 was worth more than the $2,700 she would receive over a forty-two month period under the Chapter 13 plan. . . .

Donald Rimgale has challenged Judge Decker's interpretation of the statute in this Court. We agree that Judge Decker's analysis cannot stand. . . . What is to be compared is the total of the payments to the creditor, discounted to present value, and the amount the creditor would receive in a straight liquidation. . . . If Judge Decker's interpretation were right, any creditor with a nondischargeable debt could block a Chapter 13 plan by insisting that his claim might some day be satisfiable in full. Such a creditor would have a virtual veto over a Chapter 13 plan, while ordinary unsecured creditors have not even a vote. The generous discharge provisions of Chapter 13 would be illusory. . . . In short, this reading of the "best interests" test undercuts the limiting of creditors' power and the inducement of broad discharges, both integral parts of Congress' revision of Chapter 13. . . .

In eliminating the requirement that a majority of creditors approve a plan, Congress did not also eliminate all scrutiny of plans. Instead it transferred the decision to the bankruptcy judge, aided by the Chapter 13 trustee. It is the bankruptcy court's duty to evaluate the good faith of the plan under §1325(a)(3). As the Eighth Circuit has noted,

> [a] comprehensive definition of good faith is not practical. Broadly speaking, the basic inquiry should be whether or not under the circumstances of the case there has been abuse of the provisions, purpose, or spirit of [the Chapter] in the proposal. . . . [*In re Terry*, 630 F.2d 634, 635 (8th Cir. 1980), quoting 9 *Collier on Bankruptcy*, ¶9.20 at 319 (14th ed. 1978)].

This inquiry imposes a considerable responsibility on bankruptcy judges. And the conduct comprehended under the rubric "good faith" will have to be defined on a case-by-case basis as the courts encounter various problems in the administration of Chapter 13's provisions. . . .

Congress eschewed setting any minimum levels of repayment that a debtor must propose to qualify for Chapter 13 relief. Thus good faith cannot be treated as a license to read into the statute requirements Congress did not enact, *e.g.*, a requirement that a plan pay 70% of unsecured claims to qualify for the discharge benefits. . . .

We therefore agree with the analysis of District Judge Ingram in *In re Burrell*. . . .

> The correct approach . . . is to treat the issues of substantiality and best effort as elements of good faith. Unless the courts have discretion to consider such factors, the danger exists that Chapter 13 plans could become shams that would emasculate the safeguards that Congress has included in Chapter 7 to prevent debtor abuse of the bankruptcy laws. The courts retain discretion to prevent such abuse, and that discretion can be exercised effectively through a meaningful interpretation of the good faith requirement of §1325(a)(3). In each case, the bankruptcy court must consider the debtor's entire circumstances to determine whether his plan proposes to make meaningful payments to unsecured creditors. In making that determination, the courts should be mindful of the fact that the unsecured creditors must rely on the court to give meaning to the congressional intent that they receive substantial payments. Within these guidelines, the courts should proceed on a case-by-case basis. [6 B.R. 360, 366 (N.D. Cal. 1980)]. . . .

[Vacated and remanded to the bankruptcy court to determine the good faith of Rimgale's petition.]

Chapter 13 has been severely criticized as unfair to creditors. A basic objection, as *Rimgale* illustrates, is use of Chapter 13 as a quasi-liquidation, rather than rehabilitation, device. That is, ideally, Chapter 13 is designed to provide for debtor relief from harassment and payment of all or a substantial portion of debt over an extended period of time. Increasingly, however, debtors seek to take advantage of Chapter 13's liberal discharge provisions by proposing small or even nominal payments under a Chapter 13 plan, over frequent creditor objection that the plan is not proposed in good faith. Courts have then been required to determine the debtor's good faith under principles outlined in *Rimgale* and a number of other cases. Although Chapter 13 was amended in 1984 to provide more creditor protection, Congress has thus far refused to prohibit use of Chapter 13 as a quasi-liquidation device.

Chapter 12—Adjustment of Debts of a Family Farmer with Regular Annual Income

In 1986, Congress added Chapter 12, entitled "Adjustment of Debts of a Family Farmer with Regular Annual Income," to the Bankruptcy Code. Relief under this rehabilitation chapter is available to a "family farmer," defined generally as an individual (or individual and spouse) engaged in farming operations who meets the following criteria: (1) total debts do not exceed $1.5 million; (2) at least 80 percent of the total fixed debt arises out of a farming operation owned or operated by the debtor; and (3) at least 50 percent of the debtor's gross income is derived from the farming operation. A partnership or corporation also may qualify as a debtor under Chapter 12 if: (1) it meets the first two criteria outlined above; (2) more than 80 percent of its assets are related to the farming operation; and (3) more than half of its stock or equity is owned by members of the same family, who conduct the farming operation.[49]

Chapter 12 was enacted to provide an effective rehabilitation alternative to small farmers affected by low crop prices and dramatically dropping farmland values. As noted in the Conference Report accompanying the bill enacting Chapter 12:

> Under current law, family farmers in need of financial rehabilitation may proceed under either Chapter 11 or Chapter 13 of the Bankruptcy Code. Most family farmers have too much debt to qualify as debtors under Chapter 13 and are thus limited to relief under Chapter 11. Unfortunately, many family farmers have found Chapter 11 needlessly complicated, unduly time-consuming, inordinately expensive and, in too many cases, unworkable.[50]

Chapter 12 is modeled closely upon Chapter 13. The debtor files a plan of reorganization within 90 days after the petition is filed. At the confirmation hearing, which must be concluded within 45 days after the plan is filed, the court confirms the plan if it meets standards similar to those applied under Chapter 13, including the "disposable income" requirement. Although similar to Chapter 13, Chapter 12 alters certain provisions that Congress deemed inappropriate for family farm reorganization. For example, Chapter 12 raises the debt limits for qualification, and extends the time limits for filing the plan and for commencing payments under a confirmed plan. Because it aids a particular class of debtors, Chapter 12 automatically will be repealed on October 1, 1993 unless Congress affirmatively extends its effectiveness.

Collective Creditor Remedies Outside Bankruptcy

Unlike state law collection remedies, bankruptcy law is designed to achieve equitable treatment of competing creditors by requiring that creditors act together rather than individually. Bankruptcy, however, is expensive and time-consuming. As a result, the law has developed various collective remedies outside bankruptcy through which creditors,

---

49. 11 U.S.C. §101(17).

50. H.R. Rep. No. 99-958, 99th Cong., 2d Sess. 48 (1986).

though not paid in full, often receive a larger percentage on their claims than would be available in bankruptcy. The primary remedies of this type are assignments for the benefit of creditors, and composition and extension agreements. These remedies are usually initiated by the debtor.

Assignments for the Benefit of Creditors

In an **assignment for the benefit of creditors**, a financially troubled debtor transfers all nonexempt assets to an assignee or trustee who liquidates the assets and distributes the proceeds to the debtor's creditors. An assignment for the benefit of creditors is therefore the common law or state statutory counterpart to a liquidation under Chapter 7, although significant differences exist between the two devices.

Creditor consent is not required for an assignment for benefit of creditors. Nevertheless, because the assignment transfers title to the debtor's property to the assignee, it may be challenged as a fraudulent conveyance. To avoid this result, the assignment must be "general," conveying all of the debtor's property without restriction to the assignee.

After the assignment, the assignee sells the assets and distributes the cash to creditors. Secured creditors satisfy their claims out of the collateral and the remaining creditors are treated equally, each receiving the same pro rata share of the proceeds. After an assignment, the debtor is not discharged from any debts remaining unpaid because bankruptcy law preempts the states' right to grant discharges. For this reason, assignments for the benefit of creditors are used primarily by corporate rather than individual debtors.

Although an assignment for the benefit of creditors is of common law origin, the device is regulated by statute in over forty states. Many of these statutes are permissive, allowing the debtor to choose between a common law or a statutory assignment. Statutes generally require recording of the assignment and provide procedures for notifying creditors and filing schedules of assets and liabilities.

It is important to note that an assignment for the benefit of creditors provides a basis for creditors to file an involuntary bankruptcy petition against the debtor. Because a custodian (the assignee) takes possession of substantially all of the debtor's property, one of the two alternative bases for involuntary bankruptcy has been met. Creditors dissatisfied with the assignment therefore have an absolute right to have the liquidation proceed in a bankruptcy court under bankruptcy law with the creditor protection that law provides.

Compositions and Extensions

A **composition** is a contract between the debtor and two or more creditors under which the creditors agree to accept a partial payment in full satisfaction of their claim. An **extension** is a similar agreement that extends the time of payment. Generally, debtor-creditor agreements of this type involve elements of both composition and extension; creditors accept a reduced amount, payable over a longer period.

Compositions and extensions are governed by ordinary contract law principles. Consideration supporting the agreement is the promise of other creditors to accept less or extend time of payment. Accordingly, a binding composition or extension agreement requires promises by the debtor and at least two creditors.

In contrast to an assignment for the benefit of creditors, a binding composition or extension agreement discharges the debts covered by the arrangement. This discharge is effected, however, not by the law of bankruptcy, but simply by the binding contractual promises of the debtor and his creditors. Therefore, the rights of creditors who are not parties to the agreement are unaffected.

Composition and extension agreements are primarily rehabilitation, not liquidation, devices. The debtor retains property except as provided in the agreement, and continues to operate her business. The agreement is not a basis for an involuntary bankruptcy proceeding. Although consent of all creditors is not required, effective rehabilitation will not be achieved unless most creditors participate. Accordingly, the agreement should be comprehensive and designed to secure wide creditor participation. To protect the agreement against later avoidance on fraud grounds, the debtor should fully and honestly disclose all relevant information to creditors and no creditor should receive secret consideration preferring him over others.

SUMMARY

1. Bankruptcy is a collective creditors' remedy and debtor relief provision, governed by the federal Bankruptcy Code. It serves two fundamental purposes: (1) to relieve an honest debtor from overburdensome financial obligations, giving him or her a fresh start free of former creditors' claims, and (2) to provide for equitable treatment of creditors competing for the limited assets of the debtor.

2. Bankruptcy cases are heard in the bankruptcy court, a unit of the federal district court, that is staffed by bankruptcy judges.

3. Bankruptcy relief is of two general types: liquidation, or "straight" bankruptcy, and rehabilitation. Liquidation is governed by Chapter 7 of the Bankruptcy Code and debtor rehabilitation is the subject of Chapters 9, 11, 12, and 13.

4. All bankruptcy cases are commenced by filing a petition with the court. A liquidation case may be commenced upon the debtor's own petition (a voluntary case) or upon the petition of his creditors (an involuntary case). After the petition is filed, further creditor action against the debtor is "stayed" and the court enters an order for relief provided certain requirements are met.

5. Upon entry of the order for relief, the debtor surrenders all nonexempt property to a trustee in bankruptcy who is appointed by the court or elected by creditors. The property transferred creates the bankruptcy estate.

6. The trustee in bankruptcy represents the debtor's general unsecured creditors. The trustee's duties include collecting the debtor's assets, converting them to cash, and distributing the proceeds to creditors who file allowable claims against the estate according to priorities provided in the Bankruptcy Code.

7. The trustee possesses significant "avoidance powers," which enable the trustee to defeat certain creditor claims. For example, the trustee may assert any defenses the debtor has against any creditor. The trustee may also avoid any transfer of property by the debtor or any obligation incurred by the debtor that could be attacked either by the debtor's actual unsecured creditors, or by a lien creditor, judgment creditor, or bona fide purchaser of real property, whether or not such a creditor or purchaser actually exists.

8. The trustee may also recover, for the benefit of the estate, certain property transferred by the debtor to third parties, such as: (1) preferences—transfers of property made shortly before bankruptcy by an insolvent debtor in payment of an antecedent debt that prefers one creditor over others; (2) fraudulent conveyances—generally transfers made with actual or implied intent to hinder, delay, or defraud creditors; and (3) postpetition transfers.

9. Once the property is collected, it is distributed to creditors, who file allowable claims against the estate. Secured creditors are paid first to the extent of the value of their collateral. Unsecured creditors are paid next according to the priorities outlined in the Bankruptcy Code. After secured and priority claims are paid, any remaining assets are distributed to general creditors.

10. After the bankruptcy proceedings, most debtors receive a discharge in bankruptcy, releasing the debtor from liability for most debts that arose prior to bankruptcy. Certain debtors, however, such as those who were dishonest or failed to cooperate in the bankruptcy, are denied a discharge. Further, even if the debtor receives a discharge, certain specific debts survive the proceeding and may be collected against the debtor's postbankruptcy assets.

11. Chapter 7 liquidation is the harshest bankruptcy remedy. Bankruptcy law also provides for debtor rehabilitation, which pays creditors from future income while postponing, compromising, or altering creditor claims. Rehabilitation involves formulation and confirmation of a rehabilitation plan. Bankruptcy Code rehabilitation provisions are contained in Chapter 11 (Reorganization), Chapter 12 (Adjustment of Debts of a Family Farmer With Regular Annual Income), and Chapter 13 (Adjustment of Debts of an Individual With Regular Income).

12. State law provides collective remedies that often are more advantageous to creditors than bankruptcy because they are quicker and less costly. Among these are the assignment for the benefit of creditors and composition and extension agreements.

KEY TERMS

liquidation (straight bankruptcy) case	allowed claim
rehabilitation case	dividend
bankruptcy court	dividend percentage
bankruptcy judge	discharge in bankruptcy
voluntary case	reaffirmation agreement
involuntary case	creditors' committee
automatic stay	reorganization plan
trustee in bankruptcy	cramdown
estate	assignment for the benefit of creditors
preference	composition
insider	extension
claim	

QUESTIONS AND PROBLEMS

30-1 The basic purposes of bankruptcy are to provide the debtor with a fresh start free of claims of former creditors and to provide equitable treatment of the debtor's creditors. Summarize the specific Bankruptcy Code provisions that effectuate these purposes under Chapters 7, 11, 12, and 13.

30-2 As bankruptcy law has developed, it has provided increasingly greater debtor protection. For example, prior to the Bankruptcy Act of 1898, consent of a majority of creditors was required for discharge. Why has the law changed to provide for automatic discharge, subject to limited exceptions? Should debtors be discharged in bankruptcy? What are the arguments for and against a discharge in bankruptcy?

30-3 The automatic stay has sometimes been described as the most important provision in the Bankruptcy Code. Why is the automatic stay so valuable to debtors? Consider both individual and business debtors.

30-4 In 1981, the Senate held hearings on a bill that would have added the following provision to the Bankruptcy Code: "An individual may be a debtor under Chapter 7 only if such individual cannot pay a reasonable part of his debts out of his anticipated future income." Under this bill, such a debtor would be required to seek relief under Chapter 13. Should this bill be enacted? What arguments support its passage? What are the arguments against it?

30-5 What policies justify bankruptcy law's failure to provide a discharge of certain debtors? Of certain debts? Consider each ground individually.

30-6 Loman has filed a petition for straight bankruptcy. The total value of his nonexempt assets is $6,000 and his total debts are $15,000. During the meeting of creditors, Loman testified that he owned an interest in a pension plan that he had not included in his list of assets. The creditors have discovered that XYZ Bank manages the pension plan and holds all the pension assets in trust. Loman has contributed $100 per month to the pension plan. When he reaches age 65 he will be entitled to receive $1,000 per month from the pension plan. Loman is now 47 years of age and the value of his contributions to the pension plan is $35,000. The creditors request that the bankruptcy judge order XYZ Bank to transfer the $35,000 to the trustee in bankruptcy for inclusion in the bankrupt's estate. Should the judge order the transfer? Explain the reasons for your answer.

30-7 In July 1986, CP & A Accounting Services prepared financial statements for Sharpe Construction Company. Sharpe used the statements in an effort to obtain a bank loan but failed to qualify for the loan. Sharpe paid CP & A $500 in July prior to preparation of the statements and the balance of $2,000 in October. In December Sharpe declared bankruptcy.
(a) Were the payments to CP & A avoidable preferences? Explain.
(b) CP & A has argued to the court that even if the payments were preferences, the court should grant the firm's expenses a priority as an administrative expense. CP & A has pointed out that the trustee used the financial statements thereby reducing the costs of administration of the estate. Should CP & A's expenses be granted priority as administrative expenses?

30-8 Prestige Manufacturing Co. began having financial problems in January 1980. Norman Noles, the sole shareholder of Prestige, attributed the problems to a general economic recession and was confident that the company would weather the bad period. To alleviate cash flow problems, Norman frequently advanced money to the company from his own savings account to meet the company payroll. Within a few months, Prestige generally repaid the advances to Norman. The recession lasted longer than Norman had anticipated, and in January 1983 Prestige filed a petition in bankruptcy under Chapter 7. A review of the company checking account revealed that Prestige had paid Norman $2,000 in October 1982, $3,500 in November 1982, and $4,000 in December 1982. Norman testified that these checks represented repayments of advances that Norman had made to pay the company payroll in the summer of 1982.
(a) The trustee in bankruptcy has requested that Norman repay $9,500 because the transfers were fraudulent. Norman has testified that he had no intent to hinder or delay creditors but rather that he was attempting to keep the company afloat to protect creditors. Were the transfers to Norman fraudulent conveyances? Explain.
(b) Discuss any other provisions of the Bankruptcy Code that might help the trustee to obtain turnover of the payments to Norman.

30-9 Parr Meadows Racing Association, Inc. borrowed approximately $14 million from Flushing Bank for construction of a racetrack. Because of financial difficulties, Parr Meadows defaulted in repaying the loan. On June 11, Parr Meadows transferred ownership of the racetrack to its president Ronald Parr. On June 12, Parr declared bankruptcy. Flushing Bank sued Parr Meadows and Parr seeking to have the transfer set aside as a fraudulent conveyance. At trial, Parr testified that the transfer was not made with the intent to hinder, delay, or defraud creditors. Parr explained that because of the automatic stay provisions of bankruptcy law, he believed that the transfer served to preserve the racetrack as an asset. He believed that if the racetrack was able to continue its operations, sufficient moneys would be earned to allow payment to Flushing Bank and other creditors. Thus, he argued that the transfer actually preserved assets for the creditors. Was the conveyance a fraudulent conveyance? Explain.

30-10   Under a reaffirmation agreement, a debtor may promise to pay a debt discharged in bankruptcy. Under what circumstances would a debtor want to enter into a reaffirmation agreement?

30-11   The first form of adequate protection outlined in the text (cash payments or additional or replacement liens) assures that the value of the collateral remains relatively constant during the course of the bankruptcy proceeding. It does not compensate for the interest the secured party could have earned had it been allowed to immediately foreclose and sell the collateral and reinvest the proceeds. Should a secured party in a Chapter 11 proceeding be able to recover such interest or ''lost opportunity cost'' under the second form of adequate protection, which provides the secured party with the ''indubitable equivalent'' of its interest in the property?

30-12   Is the use of Chapter 13 as a liquidation device an abuse which should be corrected? If so, what changes would you make in the statute?

30-13   In *In re Burrell*, Judge Ingram states that bankruptcy judges have the power to insure that debtors do not abuse the liberal discharge provisions of Chapter 13 of the Bankruptcy Code by considering whether proposed repayment plans are made in good faith. Judge Ingram suggests that the bankruptcy judge examine ''the debtor's entire circumstances'' in considering the proposed plan. In general, what factors would be relevant to determining whether the debtor has shown good faith?

30-14   Consider the following plans and determine whether they were made in good faith and whether they provide substantial repayment to creditors.

(a) Debtor is a school teacher with monthly net earnings of about $1,300. Two years prior to filing bankruptcy under Chapter 13, the debtor purchased an $18,000 automobile, which is subject to a purchase money security interest. He owes a balance of about $8,000 to GMAC for the car. The debtor's unsecured debts total approximately $7,500, including a school loan with a balance including interest of $3,900. The debtor's assets primarily consist of household goods. The debtor has proposed a plan to pay $300 a month for three years to his creditors. Most of the payment will be made to GMAC and the debtor will retain title to the automobile. According to the debtor's calculations, his other monthly expenses total $950, so that after his monthly $300 payment, his discretionary income will be $50. GMAC will receive about $10,000 under the plan. At the termination of the plan, the debtor will have paid about one percent of the claims of the unsecured creditors. Should the bankruptcy court approve the plan? Explain.

(b) The debtor is a dentist who established his own office after graduating from dental school. While self-employed, he earned a gross income of approximately $14,000 per year. Two years prior to filing the Chapter 13 petition, the debtor discontinued his own practice and went to work for an established dentist who pays the debtor net wages of $24,000 per year. The debtor's only assets are household goods. He owes the following debts: $8,900 in back taxes due to the IRS and $48,000 due to ten unsecured creditors, including approximately $31,500 in student loans. The debtor's estimated monthly living expenses are $1,748. He is unmarried and has no dependents. The debtor proposes to pay $252 per month to his creditors for five years. At the termination of the plan, the debtor will have paid the tax claim in full without interest and will have paid approximately ten percent of the unsecured claims. Should the bankruptcy judge approve the plan? Explain.

(c) The debtor graduated from medical school several months prior to filing a Chapter 13 bankruptcy petition. She is employed as a resident physician specializing in internal medicine and her net income is about $1,320 per month. The debtor's only assets are household goods. She owes approximately $95,000 in unsecured debts to four creditors. The debtor, who is unmarried and has no dependents, has estimated monthly living expenses of $1,146. She proposes a plan to pay $162 per month to her creditors for a period of five years. At the termination of the plan, she will have paid approximately ten percent of the debts. Should the bankruptcy judge approve the plan? Explain.

Chapter 31

Introduction to Secured Transactions

Because of the risks involved in making loans or extending credit, many debtor-creditor relationships involve some form of security. Secured creditors enjoy a substantial advantage in remedy over unsecured creditors in the event of a debtor's financial difficulty or bankruptcy. The secured creditor possesses a property interest—a security interest—in specific assets of the debtor. Upon the debtor's default the secured creditor may proceed against those assets and apply them to the unpaid debt to the exclusion of other creditors. If the security interest

exists in real property, the arrangement is governed by the law of mortgages, discussed in Chapter 37. If the encumbered property is personal property, a "secured transaction" is involved, governed by Article 9 of the Uniform Commercial Code. For example, assume Ann borrows $25,000 from First Bank. Ann gives First Bank a security interest in her house to satisfy the debt in event of Ann's default. This situation is governed by the law of mortgages. Had Ann instead given the bank a security interest in her inventory or equipment, which are personal property, a secured transaction is created, governed by UCC Article 9.

Introduction to Article 9 of the Uniform Commercial Code

Although Article 9 represents a vast improvement over pre-Code law governing personal property security, it had become apparent by 1966 that the original 1962 version of Article 9 needed revision. Many sections had been amended by individual adopting states, defeating uniformity of the law among the various jurisdictions. Additionally, attorneys and law teachers had indicated areas requiring improvement. In response, an Article 9 Review Committee was formed and submitted recommendations for change, which were ultimately approved by both the National Conference of Commissioners on Uniform State Laws and the American Law Institute. These amendments, promulgated in 1972, clarify the drafting of some Article

9 sections and answer certain questions not resolved under the original version. As of this writing, the 1972 amendments have been adopted in forty-nine states.[1] For this reason, the secured transactions material that follows is based upon Article 9 as amended in 1972. The text also incorporates certain changes made in Article 9 as part of the 1977 amendments to Article 8. These amendments, discussed in Chapter 46, enable investment securities such as stocks and bonds to be issued and transferred in both uncertificated (not evidenced by a stock certificate or other instrument) and certificated form.

Basic Definitions

In a **secured transaction,** a borrower or buyer gives a lender or seller an interest in personal property or fixtures to secure performance of an obligation. Under §1-201(37), the interest created in the property is known as a **security interest.** The secured obligation is virtually always a duty to pay money, either in repayment of a loan or for the purchase price of property sold on credit. The **debtor** is the party who owes the obligation and is giving security. The **secured party** is the lender, seller, or other party in whose favor a security interest exists. Property in which the secured party's security interest exists is known as the **collateral.** These four terms are used in every transaction governed by Article 9.

Article 9 covers generally any consensual or contractual security interest created in personal property. The contract creating the security interest is known as the **security agreement.**[2]

Types of Security Interests

Various functionally different types of security interest are recognized under Article 9. For example, a security interest may be possessory or non-possessory. In a **possessory security interest,** the debtor delivers possession of the collateral to the secured party, who retains the property until the debt is paid. Such an arrangement is known as a **pledge,** the simplest form of secured transaction. A pledge is in essence a bailment[3] for security with the debtor-bailor the "pledgor" and the secured party-bailee the "pledgee."

In a **non-possessory security interest,** the debtor retains possession of the collateral that is subject to the security interest. Non-possessory interests are the most important modern security arrangements, as illustrated by the inventory financing devices discussed in the next chapter.

A security interest may also be purchase-money or non-purchase-money. Under Section 9-107, a security interest is a **purchase money security interest** to the extent that it is (1) taken or retained by a seller of the collateral to secure all or part of its price, or (2) taken by a person who makes an advance or incurs an obligation that enables the debtor to acquire rights in collateral. All other security interests are non-purchase-money.

In many instances, Article 9 provides special priority rules applicable to purchase money security interests. To recognize a purchase money security interest, ask two questions: (1) What is the collateral? and (2) What is the debt? If the debt is all or part of the purchase price of the collateral, the interest is a purchase money security interest.

Assume Alice's TV sells a television set to Bill on credit, taking a security interest in the television set to secure payment. Alice's interest is a purchase money security interest. Or assume that First Bank loans Bill the money to buy the television set from Alice's for cash. First Bank takes a security interest in the set to secure payment of the debt. First Bank has a purchase money security interest. In both cases the secured debt is the purchase price of the collateral, the television set.

Types of Collateral

The study of personal property security is complicated by the fact that personal property takes many forms, and Article 9 priority rules differ in most cases depending upon the type of collateral in-

---

1. The 1972 amendments to Article 9 have been enacted in every state except Vermont.

2. Article 9's basic definitions and an index of definitions are contained in §9-105.

---

3. Bailments are discussed in Chapter 35.

volved. Three major types of personal property collateral are recognized: goods, semi-intangibles, and intangibles.

Goods. Under Article 9, as under Article 2, goods generally include *tangible personal property*.[4] Section 9-109 divides goods into four categories: consumer goods, farm products, inventory, and equipment.

Consumer Goods. **Consumer goods** are those used or bought for use primarily for personal, family, or household purposes.

Farm Products. **Farm products** include crops or livestock, products of crops or livestock in the unmanufactured state, and supplies used or produced in farming operations. Milk, eggs, and wool are examples of farm products. To be classified as farm products, goods must be in possession of a debtor engaged in farming, and must not have been subjected to a manufacturing process. If the farm products have been subjected to a manufacturing process, they then become inventory in the farmer's hands.

Inventory. Goods are **inventory** if they are held primarily for immediate or ultimate resale in the ordinary course of the seller's business. Inventory also includes raw materials, work in process, and materials used or consumed in a business, such as fuel consumed in operations and containers used to package goods.

Equipment. **Equipment** includes goods used or bought for use primarily in business, including a profession or farming. Trucks, rolling stock, tools, and machinery are examples of equipment.

The four classes of goods outlined above are exhaustive and mutually exclusive. Any goods not covered by one of the other definitions are treated as equipment.

In order to determine the proper classification of the collateral, one must first identify the debtor, because the same piece of collateral may change classifications depending on the debtor's identity. Suppose Joe's Appliances purchases several television sets from Zenith Radio Corporation on credit, giving Zenith a security interest in the sets. Joe's sells one set to Connie on credit for Connie's home use, taking a security interest in the set. Joe's sells five other sets to Northern University for use in its audio-visual program. Northern University borrowed money to finance the purchase, using the sets as collateral on the loan. In these examples, the TV sets are (1) inventory—in Zenith's and Joe's hands, (2) consumer goods—in Connie's hands, and (3) equipment—in Northern University's hands.

Semi-intangible Collateral. Three types of semi-intangible collateral are recognized under Article 9: documents of title, chattel paper, and instruments. This collateral, though intangible in the sense that it represents a valuable claim against a third party, is evidenced by an indispensible document showing the existence of the property.

Documents of Title. **Documents of title,** discussed in detail in Chapter 35, are documents issued by specialized bailees such as carriers or warehousemen evidencing the right to receive, hold, and dispose of goods in storage or transit. Examples include bills of lading and warehouse receipts. These documents, which may be negotiable or nonnegotiable, are governed in part by Article 7 of the UCC.

Chattel Paper. Chattel paper is often involved in inventory financing, a major concern of Article 9. Under §9-105(1)(b), **chattel paper** is a writing or writings that evidence both an obligation to pay money and a security interest in or a lease of specific goods. To illustrate how chattel paper is created, assume that Dealer sells a photocopier to Customer on credit. Customer signs a promissory note for the price and gives Dealer a security interest in the machine to secure the debt. This arrangement is usually known as a **conditional sales contract.** In this case, (1) Dealer is the secured party; (2) Customer is the debtor; (3) the conditional sales contract is the security agreement; and (4) the photocopier is collateral—equipment in Customer's hands.

Assume that Dealer needs additional cash to finance its business. Dealer therefore borrows money

---

4. UCC §9-105(1)(h).

from First Bank using the conditional sales contract from Customer as collateral to secure its loan. In this case, (1) Dealer is the debtor; (2) First Bank is the secured party; (3) the conditional sales contract is the collateral—chattel paper, an obligation to pay money (from Customer to Dealer), and a security interest in specific goods (the photocopier); and (4) Customer is now an **account debtor** defined in §9-105(1)(a) as a person obligated on an account, chattel paper, or general intangible.

Chattel paper may also be created through a lease of specific goods. Assume Dealer leased instead of sold the photocopier to Customer and then used the lease as collateral on the loan from First Bank. In this case, the lease is chattel paper in the transaction between Dealer and First Bank.

Instruments. Section 9-105(1)(i) defines **instruments** to include (1) commercial paper, such as notes, checks, and other drafts, (2) certificated securities, such as stocks and bonds represented by an instrument, and (3) any other writing that evidences a right to the payment of money and is not itself a security agreement or lease and which is transferred in the ordinary course of business by delivery with any necessary indorsement or assignment.

Intangible Collateral. Two types of intangible collateral are defined in §9-106: accounts and general intangibles.

Accounts. An **account** is any right to payment for goods sold (or to be sold) or for services rendered (or to be rendered) that is not evidenced by either an instrument or chattel paper. An account is, therefore, the ordinary open account receivable. Such a right to payment is an account even though not "earned by performance," that is, even though the seller has not yet delivered the goods or rendered the services in question.

General Intangibles. **General intangibles** are any personal property other than goods, accounts, chattel paper, documents, instruments, and money. This catch-all category includes any item of personal property not previously discussed, such as goodwill, trademarks, patents, literary rights, royalty rights, or copyrights.

Scope of Article 9

Transactions Intended for Security. Prior to enactment of Article 9, personal property security was governed by a fragmented, nonuniform assortment of devices including chattel mortgages, pledges, conditional sales contracts, factors liens, trust receipts, and assignments of accounts receivable. Article 9 replaces these devices with a comprehensive scheme governing the creation, priority, and foreclosure of security interests in personal property. Section 9-102 creates a single security device applicable to any transaction, *regardless of its form,* that is intended to create a security interest in personal property or fixtures including goods, documents, instruments, general intangibles, chattel paper, and accounts. All consensual security interests in personal property or fixtures are therefore governed by Article 9. Article 9 does not expressly abolish pre-Code security devices, and indeed they continue to be used. Whatever form the transaction takes, however, the rights and obligations of the parties and third parties are determined by Article 9 if the transaction is intended to have effect as security.

To illustrate, suppose that Seller sells goods to Buyer on credit. Seller reserves title in herself until Buyer pays purchase price. The reservation does not prevent title from passing to Buyer. It does, however, create a security interest in the goods sold in favor of Seller. That is, Seller intended to create a security interest in the goods sold by reserving title. The transaction is governed by Article 9.

A lease may also be used to create a security interest in personal property governed by Article 9. Assume Lessor leases a cash register to Lessee, who agrees to pay monthly rental for twenty-four months. At the end of the term, Lessee has the option to purchase the cash register for little or no additional consideration. In this case, the "lease" is governed by Article 9 because it is *intended* to create a security interest in the cash register. The arrangement is not a true lease, but is in reality a disguised credit sale of the cash register, using the cash register as collateral to secure payment of Lessee's obligation. The arrangement is designed to allow Lessor to repossess the cash register (by asserting that he is only leasing it) upon Lessee's default in payment of the monthly installments.

Generally, whether a personal property lease is intended for security is determined by examining the particular facts of each case. Note that under §1-201(37)(a), inclusion of an option to purchase in a personal property lease does not necessarily make the lease one intended for security. Under §1-201(37)(b), however, a lease is intended for security when, as above, the lessee has the option to become the owner of the property for no additional or nominal consideration. In the following case, the court was required to determine whether a personal property lease was intended for security. Note the important legal consequences of this determination.

In the Matter of Marhoefer Packing Company, Inc.

674 F.2d 1139 (7th Cir. 1982)

Robert Reiser & Company, Inc. (Reiser) leased a Vemag sausage stuffing machine to Marhoefer Packing Company, Inc. (Marhoefer). The lease agreement provided that Marhoefer would pay $665 per month for a period of 48 months. At the end of the fourth year Marhoefer could purchase the machine for $9,968 or could renew the lease for another term of 4 years at a rental rate of $2,990 per year. If the lease were renewed, Marhoefer could purchase the sausage stuffer for one dollar at the end of the second term. Approximately 1 year after Reiser delivered the machine, Marhoefer filed a voluntary petition in bankruptcy.

The trustee in bankruptcy alleged that the sausage stuffer constituted an asset of the bankrupt corporation on the ground that the lease agreement between Reiser and Marhoefer was a lease intended as security as described in UCC §1-201(37)(b) rather than a true lease. Because Reiser had not perfected its security interest, the trustee requested the bankruptcy court to rule that the sausage stuffer was property of the bankrupt free and clear of any liens.

The bankruptcy court held that the lease agreement was a true lease and ordered the trustee to return the machine to Reiser. On appeal, the district court reversed, holding that the lease was intended as security. Reiser appealed to the Seventh Circuit Court of Appeals.

Pell, Circuit Judge

. . . The primary issue to be decided in determining whether a lease is "intended as security" is whether it is in effect a conditional sale in which the "lessor" retains an interest in the "leased" goods as security for the purchase price. . . . By defining the term "security interest" to include a lease intended as security, the drafters of the Code intended such disguised security interests to be governed by the same rules that apply to other security interests. . . . In this respect, §1-201(37) represents the drafter's refusal to recognize form over substance.

Clearly, where a lease is structured so that the lessee is contractually bound to pay rent over a set period of time at the conclusion of which he automatically or for only nominal consideration becomes the owner of the leased goods, the transaction is in substance a conditional sale and should be treated as such. It is to this type of lease that clause (b) properly applies. Here, however, Marhoefer was under no contractual obligation to pay rent until such time as the option to purchase the Vemag stuffer for one dollar was to arise. In fact, in order to acquire that option, Marhoefer would have had to exercise its earlier option to renew the lease for a second 4-year term and pay Reiser an additional $11,960 in "rent." In effect, Marhoefer was given a right to terminate the agreement after the first four years and cease making payments without that option ever becoming operative.

Despite this fact, the district court concluded as a matter of law that the lease was intended as security. It held that, under clause (b) of §1-201(37), a lease containing an option for the lessee to purchase the leased goods for nominal consideration is conclusively presumed to be one intended as security. This presumption applies, the court concluded, regardless of any other options the lease may contain.

We think the district court's reading of clause (b) is in error. In our view, the conclusive presumption provided under clause (b) applies only where the option to purchase for nominal consideration necessarily arises upon compliance with the lease. . . . It does not apply where the lessee has the right to terminate the lease before that option arises with no further obligation to continue paying rent. . . . For where the lessee has the right to terminate the transaction, it is not a conditional sale. . . .

We therefore hold that while §1-201(37)(b) does provide a conclusive test of when a lease is intended as security, that test does not apply in every case in which the disputed lease contains an option to purchase for nominal or no consideration. . . .

[S]ection 1-201(37) states that "[w]hether a lease is intended as security is to be determined by the facts of each case." . . . Consideration of the facts of this case . . . leads us to conclude that the lease in question was not intended as security.

First, Marhoefer was under no obligation to pay the full purchase price for the stuffer. . . . The fact that the total amount of rent Marhoefer was to pay under the lease was substantially less than the [purchase price] shows that a sale was not intended. . . .

It is also significant that the useful life of the Vemag stuffer exceeded the term of the lease. An essential characteristic of a true lease is that there be something of value to return to the lessor after the term. . . .

Finally, the bankruptcy court specifically found that "there was no express or implied provision in the lease agreement dated February 28, 1977, which gave Marhoefer any equity interest in the leased Vemag stuffer." . . .

From all of the facts surrounding the transactions, we conclude that the agreement between Marhoefer and Reiser is a true lease. . . .

[Judgment reversed.]

Cases such as *Marhoefer*, involving a dispute between an alleged "lessor" of goods and the "lessee's" trustee in bankruptcy, are extremely common. One reason for the large volume of litigation distinguishing true leases from those creating security interests, is that §1-201(37)'s intent standard is vague and difficult to apply. For this reason, new Article 2A of the Uniform Commercial Code, which governs personal property leasing and is discussed in Chapter 16, includes a revised version of §1-201(37). This new section is designed to clarify the distinction between leases and security interests

by focusing on the economic consequences of the transaction rather than the parties' subjective intent.[5]

Sales of Accounts and Chattel Paper. In addition to consensual security interests in personal property, Article 9 governs *any sale* of accounts or chattel paper, *whether or not intended for security*. In this case, Article 9's scope is expanded to avoid the often difficult problem of distinguishing between transactions in accounts and chattel paper intended for security and those that are not. If the transaction involves the sale of accounts or chattel paper, the seller is the "debtor," the buyer is the "secured party," the buyer's interest is a "security interest," and the accounts or chattel paper are the "collateral."

Transactions Excluded from Article 9. Article 9 is primarily concerned with commercial financing, particularly involving inventory, arising by contract between a lender and borrower or buyer and seller. Article 9 therefore excludes from its scope, in §9-104, certain transactions such as the following that do not fit this mold.

1. Liens arising under statute or common law by virtue of status, not by the consent or agreement of the parties, such as federal liens and liens given by statute to suppliers of services or materials.

2. Any interest in or lien upon real estate, including a lease or a landlord's lien.

3. Transactions not related to commercial financing, such as (a) a sale of accounts or chattel paper as part of a sale of the business out of which they arose, (b) assignments of accounts or chattel paper for purposes of collection, (c) transfer of a right to payment under a contract to an assignee who is to perform the duties under the contract, and (d) a transfer of a single account to an assignee in whole or partial satisfaction of a pre-existing debt.

4. Security transactions using property that does not customarily serve as commercial collat-

---

5. The text of Article 2A, including revised §1-201(37), is reproduced in Appendix B.

eral, such as rights under life insurance policies and deposit accounts, tort claims, and judgments.

Creation and Perfection of a Security Interest

Article 9 provides creditor protection by creating a security interest in the debtor's property as security for an obligation owed to the creditor. To provide this protection, Article 9 addresses two fundamental issues: how a legally enforceable security interest is created between the debtor and the secured party and how a creditor holding a security interest is protected against claims of third parties to the collateral.

Under Article 9, a security interest is effective between the immediate parties upon **attachment**. That is, after attachment, if the debtor defaults, the secured party has the right to foreclose or otherwise use the collateral to satisfy the claim. Prior to attachment the secured party has no such right. Enforceability against the debtor alone provides little protection to a secured creditor, however. Upon default, other secured creditors may assert claims to the same collateral and unsecured creditors may attempt to levy upon it if they obtain judgments. Further, if the security interest is non-possessory, the debtor may have previously sold the collateral. To be protected against such third-party claims, the secured party must "perfect" its interest in the collateral. In short, attachment governs the rights of the secured party against the debtor and **perfection** determines the secured party's rights against third-party claimants to the collateral.

Note that under §9-303(1), a security interest is perfected only after it has attached and all the applicable steps required for perfection have been met. The steps for attachment and perfection may occur in any order. If, however, the steps necessary to perfect are taken before the security interest attaches, the interest is not perfected until it attaches. That is, a security interest cannot be perfected until it has attached. The date of perfection is, of course, very important in determining priorities among various claimants to the collateral.

Attachment of a Security Interest

Under §9-203(1), a security interest is not enforceable against the debtor or third parties until it has attached to the collateral. Attachment requires the co-existence of three elements, which may occur in any order. That is, the interest attaches when the last of the following three events occurs:

1. there must be an enforceable security agreement;
2. the secured party must give value; and
3. the debtor must have rights in the collateral.

The Agreement

Attachment requires the existence of a valid security agreement, the agreement creating or providing for a security interest. To be enforceable, §9-203(1)(a) requires that the security agreement be in writing, be signed by the debtor, and contain a description of the collateral. These formalities are designed to provide reliable evidence concerning the existence and terms of the security agreement, including the property serving as collateral.

The Writing Requirement. The UCC provides that a security agreement must be in writing unless the secured party is in possession of the collateral pursuant to the agreement. When the secured party takes possession of the collateral, the evidentiary need for a writing is not as great as when the debtor retains possession. The writing requirement is both a condition to the enforceability of the security interest against third parties and is also effectively a statute of frauds. That is, unless the secured party is in possession of the collateral, the security interest, if not in writing, is unenforceable even against the debtor. Because the term "security interest" under §1-201(37) includes a buyer's interest in accounts and chattel paper, an agreement for the sale (assignment) of such property is also a "security agreement," required to be in writing.

The Signature Requirement. The written security agreement must be signed by the debtor.

Description of the Collateral. The security agreement must contain a description of the collateral sufficient to identify it. The test for sufficiency of the description is contained in §9-110, which provides that any description of personal property or

| Figure 31-1 | **Simple Security Agreement** |

Date _____

_____ ("Debtor") hereby grants to
Name   No. and Street   City   County   State   Zip

_____ ("Secured Party") a security
Name   No. and Street   City   County   State   Zip

interest in the following property ("Collateral"): _____

_____

_____

to secure payment and performance of obligations identified or set out
as follows ("Obligations"):   _____

_____

_____

   Default in payment or performance of any of the Obligations or default under any agreement evidencing any of the Obligations is a default
under this agreement. Upon such default Secured Party may declare all
Obligations immediately due and payable and shall have the remedies of
a secured party under the _____Uniform Commercial Code.

   Signed in (duplicate) triplicate.

Debtor _____   Secured Party _____

By _____   By _____

---

real estate is sufficient whether or not it is specific
if it "reasonably identifies what is described."
Thus, the description requirement under the Code
is not rigorous. For example, assume XYZ Corporation borrows money from First Bank, giving the
bank a security interest in its inventory. A statement in the agreement that the loan is secured by
"the inventory of XYZ Corporation" would be a
sufficient description for Article 9 purposes. Serial
numbers and detailed listing of the inventory are
not required. Figure 31-1 illustrates a simple security agreement form.
   In the following case, the court was required to

determine whether an enforceable security agreement had been created.

Pontchartrain State Bank v. Poulson
684 F.2d 704 (10th Cir. 1982)

   In March 1976, D & D Mining Corporation (D &
D) borrowed $100,000 from Pontchartrain State
Bank (Bank). On March 2, the Bank filed a financ-
ing statement, naming D & D as debtor and the
Bank as secured party, that listed various pieces of

equipment identified by serial number as the collateral. On March 2, Richard Sonberg, D & D's attorney, sent a letter to the Bank stating that the Bank held a security interest in the equipment listed on the financing statement. On March 16, D & D, by two of its officers, Siegel and Johnston, executed a promissory note for the $100,000 loan. The note stated that the loan was secured by ''various equipment totaling $158,600 located at Haskel County, Oklahoma.'' D & D defaulted in its payment on the note late in 1976. After the default, the Bank learned that Ed Poulson had purchased two pieces of the equipment listed on the financing statement.

The Bank sued Poulson alleging that he had converted equipment that was subject to its security agreement. Poulson alleged that the Bank and D & D had not signed a security agreement as required by UCC §9-203 and, therefore, the Bank did not hold a security interest in the equipment. The trial court ruled in favor of Poulson holding that the Bank did not have a valid security interest. The Bank appealed.

Barrett, Circuit Judge

. . . A security agreement, as defined by [UCC] §9-105, is ''an agreement which creates or provides for a security interest.'' Traditionally, the security agreement was contained in a separate security instrument. Recently, however, some courts have construed other documents, such as promissory notes or financing statements, as security agreements if they otherwise satisfy the requirements of Article 9 and contain language creating or providing for a security interest. . . .

There appears to be a split among the courts regarding the language which is needed to give rise to a security agreement, however. Some courts [including Oklahoma] have held that a document, to be a security agreement, must contain language specifically granting a security interest in collateral. . . .

Other courts have been more flexible . . . [and have] rejected the argument that a security agreement must contain language explicitly conveying a security interest. . . .

The promissory note in this case provided that it was '' . . . secured by pledge and delivery of the securities or property mentioned on the reverse . . .'' thereto. The note does not specifically grant a security interest to Bank; thus, under the law of

this Circuit interpreting the Oklahoma Commercial Code, it does not satisfy the requirements for the creation of a security agreement.

Even if the language is construed to give rise to a security agreement, however, the note is still not enforceable because it fails to satisfy the other requirements of §9-203. Section 9-203 also requires that the security agreement contain a description of the collateral. Section 9-110 provides that any description of property is sufficient, whether or not it is specific, ''if it reasonably identifies what is described.'' A generic description of property is usually sufficient if the description is adequate to make identification possible through reasonable effort and inspection. . . .

The promissory note described the collateral as: ''various equipment totaling $158,600.00 located in Haskel County, Oklahoma.'' Bank argues that Siegel, during the negotiation of the loan, gave Bank a list of Johnston's equipment totaling $158,600 to be used as collateral. Therefore, according to Bank, inasmuch as the dollar figure refers to the equipment on the list, which was identified by serial number, the description was adequate.

In support of its contention, Bank cites several cases which have found a generic description adequate to satisfy the Article 9 requirements. The description in those cases referred to ''all equipment'' or ''all goods.'' The general description was upheld because all of the debtor's goods or equipment were included and thus a creditor would know at all times what items were encumbered. In this case, on the other hand, while the figure $158,600 refers to some equipment, there is no hint as to which specific equipment is covered. Moreover, although some courts have held that a security agreement may incorporate other documents by reference and thereby satisfy the dictates of Article 9, the doctrine of incorporation by reference is not applicable in this case because the promissory note makes no reference to the list. . . .

Bank also argues that the March 2, 1976, letter from Sonberg to Bank suffices as a security agreement. The letter stated that D & D was vesting Bank with ''a security interest in certain business equipment and machinery described and identified on the financing statement.''

The letter arguably grants a security interest to Bank and adequately describes the collateral by means of the doctrine of incorporation by reference but it fails to fulfill the third §9-203 requirement. Section 9-203 specifically requires that the *debtor* sign the agreement, that is, an agent of D & D. The letter, although written at the request of Dale Johnston, was signed only by Richard T. Sonberg. Sonberg was not an agent of D & D; he acted solely as its attorney and thus does not come under §9-203. That the letter incorporates the financing statement which was signed by Siegel, the treasurer of D & D, is of no moment as the financing statement serves only to identify the collateral and does not serve as the security agreement. Section 9-203 requires that the *agreement* be signed by the debtor.

None of the documents proffered by Bank individually provides evidence of the existence of an enforceable security agreement. Nor do the documents, taken as a whole, satisfy the requirements of §9-203. . . .

Inasmuch as the other requirements for a security agreement were not satisfied, the fact that D & D filed a financing statement is not significant. . . .

[Judgment affirmed.]

Value Given by Secured Party

Section 9-203(1)(b) requires that the secured party must give value before a security interest can attach. For Article 9 purposes, **value** generally includes any consideration sufficient to support a simple contract. In most cases, the secured party gives value by loaning money to or selling goods on credit to the debtor. A creditor's binding contractual promise to extend credit or loan money in the future also constitutes value as of the time the promise is made. Further, a secured party who takes a security interest in the debtor's property to secure a pre-existing debt owed by the debtor gives value.[6]

Debtor's Rights in the Collateral

A debtor must have an interest in a specified piece of property to use it as collateral. Accordingly, §9-

203(1)(c) provides that attachment cannot occur until "the debtor has rights in the collateral." The debtor's rights may constitute full ownership or a lesser interest. For example, the debtor may own property as a tenant in common with another. A debtor with a limited interest, however, has only limited rights to use as collateral.

The debtor often has rights in the collateral at the time the secured party gives value. Article 9, however, also broadly validates so-called after-acquired property clauses allowing obligations covered by the security agreement to be secured both by the debtor's currently owned property and property acquired by the debtor in the future.[7]

Perfection of a Security Interest

The Secured Party and Third Parties

Attachment of the security interest makes the security arrangement enforceable against the debtor, thereby allowing the secured party to resort to the collateral upon default. Perfection determines the rights of the secured party against third parties asserting an interest in the collateral. The secured party must be protected against three classes of third parties:

1. creditors of the debtor, including lien creditors;
2. buyers of the collateral from the debtor; and
3. other secured parties claiming an interest in the same collateral.

Examples illustrating how competing claims arise follow. As with other statutes involving debtors and creditors, Article 9 perfection rules generate a system of priorities determining the order in which creditors are paid out of the debtor's limited assets.

Creditors of the Debtor. Fundamentally, a secured party needs protection against claims of the debtor's other creditors. Although unpaid general creditors (those with neither a lien nor a priority) often assert an interest in the debtor's property, a secured party is primarily concerned with lien cred-

---

6. UCC §1-201(44).

7. See discussion of UCC §9-204 in Chapter 32.

itors. Under Article 9, a **lien creditor** is a creditor who has acquired a lien upon the property involved by attachment, levy, or other judicial process and includes an assignee for the benefit of creditors (from the time of the assignment), the trustee in bankruptcy (from the date the petition is filed), and a receiver in equity (as of the date the court appoints the receiver).

The most common lien creditors are judgment creditors and the trustee in bankruptcy. For example, assume Charles loans Dana $500. Dana gives Charles a security interest in a painting she owns to satisfy the debt in event of default. Dana negligently runs a stop sign and destroys a car owned by Jim. Jim sues her for damages and the court awards him a $5,000 judgment. Dana fails to pay the judgment, and also defaults on Charles's loan. Jim brings an action to enforce the judgment, which results in issuance of a writ of execution against Dana's property including the painting. Jim is a lien creditor, and the rules of perfection determine whether Charles or Jim will get the painting.

To illustrate further, assume the same facts as above, except that after the loan, Dana files a bankruptcy petition. The trustee in bankruptcy is a lien creditor and wishes to seize and sell the painting for benefit of all creditors. The rules of perfection determine whether the trustee or Charles will have benefit of the painting. It is important to note that defeating the trustee in bankruptcy's claim is the fundamental purpose of any secured transaction. That is, the debtor's default, raising the need for recourse to the collateral, is often followed by bankruptcy. The secured party must therefore, at a minimum, take the steps necessary to assure a preferred claim to the collateral as against the debtor's bankruptcy trustee.

Buyer of the Collateral. Most modern secured transactions are non-possessory; that is, the debtor retains possession of the collateral that secures the obligation. In this case, the debtor may sell the collateral to a third party, who may or may not be aware of the secured party's claim. The rules of perfection determine whether the buyer or the secured party is entitled to such collateral upon the debtor's default.

Conflicting Security Interests in the Same Collateral. A common priority problem arises when two or more *secured* creditors assert an interest in the same collateral. For example, assume that Dana borrows $500 from Charles and gives him a security interest in her painting. She retains possession of the painting. Dana then borrows $500 from Bob, giving him a security interest in the same painting. Dana leaves town, leaving both debts unpaid. The rules of perfection determine which creditor will have the benefit of the painting to satisfy the debt.

A secured party with a perfected security interest is not protected under *all* circumstances against *all* third-party claims. That is, "perfection" is not a synonym for "absolute protection." More accurately, a secured party with a perfected interest is protected against some, but not necessarily all, third-party claims, and in some cases only for a limited period. The extent of protection provided depends upon a combination of three interrelated factors: (1) the identity of the third-party claimant, (2) the type of collateral involved, and (3) the method of perfection. In analyzing any secured transaction dispute, therefore, each of these three factors must be carefully considered.

Purposes and Methods of Perfection

A creditor with a perfected security interest enjoys a preferred claim to the debtor's assets to the exclusion of other creditors and others claiming an interest in those assets. The rules of perfection are designed to insure that a creditor granted this preferred status has taken steps necessary to put third parties on notice of the secured party's claim. These steps generally involve either taking possession of the collateral or filing a document giving public notice of the interest. Once notified, other creditors and buyers will not be misled concerning the nature and extent of the debtor's interest in the property. Thus, perfection by possession or filing protects both the secured party—by preserving a preferred claim to the property—and others who, once notified, will not be induced to lend money secured by, or to purchase, previously encumbered property. In certain limited situations, however, the UCC authorizes "automatic" perfection, protecting a secured party who has neither filed nor taken possession. In these cases, the administrative costs of providing notice are deemed to outweigh the benefits of public notice.

The following material discusses the three methods of perfecting a security interest recognized by Article 9:

1. perfection by taking possession of the collateral;
2. perfection by filing a "financing statement" in an appropriate public office; and
3. automatic perfection occurring upon attachment with no further action by the secured party.

The discussion that follows assumes that the security interest has attached. As previously noted, if the steps necessary for perfection occur first, the interest is perfected at the time it attaches.

Perfection by Possession

The simplest and oldest method of perfection, authorized by §9-305, is the pledge—perfection by the creditor's possession of the collateral. A security interest in most types of collateral—including goods, instruments (other than certificated securities), money, negotiable documents of title, and chattel paper—may be perfected by possession. Possession is the only way to perfect a security interest in instruments and money.

The secured party's possession puts third parties on notice of the secured interest and no further notice or filing is required. A security interest is perfected by possession from the time the secured party takes possession and continues as long as possession is retained. Possession may be taken by the secured party or an agent on the secured party's behalf. The debtor or a person controlled by the debtor may not act as the secured party's agent for this purpose.[8] As the following case illustrates, the debtor's possession, even on the secured party's behalf, will not put third parties on notice of the secured party's interest.

---

8. UCC §9-305, Official Comment 2.

In re Stewart

74 B.R. 359 (Bkrtcy. M.D. Ga. 1987)

Plaintiff First American Bank & Trust Company lent the debtor Thomas Stewart money in exchange for a promissory note secured by a diamond ring owned by Stewart. At the time of the loan, the bank took possession of the ring but later released it to Stewart who intended to sell it. Upon receipt of the ring, Stewart signed the following document prepared by the bank:

> Athens, GA., September 14, 1984
> RECEIVED from FIRST AMERICAN BANK & TRUST COMPANY, ATHENS, GEORGIA the following property, held by the Bank as collateral security: 1 ladies' Diamond Ring and in consideration thereof I HEREBY AGREE TO HOLD SAID PROPERTY IN TRUST for the following purposes, viz: give to Armonds Diamond Center for Sale and I will return the said property, or Cash Equivalent with due diligence to the Bank, the intention of this arrangement being to protect and preserve unimpaired the lien of FIRST AMERICAN BANK & TRUST COMPANY on said property.
>
> /s/ Thomas Stewart

Stewart took the ring to Armond Parks Diamond Center, which sold the ring to a third party in exchange for another diamond ring and $4,917. Stewart did not return the cash or ring to the bank and several months later he filed for bankruptcy. American Bank & Trust Company sued the trustee in bankruptcy seeking delivery of the diamond ring and $4,917, which had been recovered by the trustee in bankruptcy from Armond Parks. The trustee argued that the bank did not have a perfected security interest in the diamond ring or its proceeds and, therefore, the bank was not entitled to the cash or ring.

Hershner, Bankruptcy Judge

. . . To perfect a security interest, a secured party must file a financing statement unless the secured party elects to take possession of the collateral as provided for under [§9-305 of the UCC]. . . .

Under Georgia law, the court concludes that Plaintiff had a perfected security interest in the diamond ring prior to the release of the diamond ring to Debtor under the document executed on September 14, 1984. The security interest had attached because Plaintiff had possession of the diamond ring pursuant to the security agreement between Plaintiff and Debtor; value had been given; and Debtor had rights in the diamond ring. Plaintiff perfected its security interest in the diamond ring by taking possession of it. . . .

The real issue for the court to determine is what effect the September 14, 1984, document plaintiff and Debtor executed had upon plaintiff's security interest which it had perfected by possession. The court notes that the primary purpose behind requiring a secured party to comply with the perfecting provisions under Article 9 is to "put a diligent searcher on notice of the secured party's claim." J. White & R. Summers, Handbook of the Law Under the Uniform Commercial Code §23-5 (2d ed. 1980). Actual possession of the collateral in which the secured party claims a security interest "gives notice to the world that the debtor does not have full use of the collateral." 9 R. Anderson, Anderson on the Uniform Commercial Code §9-305:7 (3d ed. 1985). Subsequent lenders and creditors thus are adequately informed of the possible existence of a perfected security interest in the collateral, and they can inquire of the secured party the extent of the secured party's interest in the collateral. . . .

Plaintiff asserts that pursuant to the September 14, 1984, document, it did not release its perfected security interest in the diamond ring because under the terms of that document, Debtor held the diamond ring in trust for plaintiff. Official Comment 2 to §9-305 of the Uniform Commercial Code provides that "[p]ossession may be by the secured party himself or by an agent on his behalf; it is of course clear, however, that the debtor or a person controlled by him cannot qualify as such an agent for the secured party." Official Comment 2, U.C.C. §9-305. The argument that a debtor possesses collateral on behalf of a secured party for the purpose of perfection by possession has been uniformly rejected because possession by the debtor does not give adequate notice to other creditors of the secured party's interest in the collateral. . . .

By relinquishing possession of the diamond ring, Plaintiff lost its perfected security interest in the diamond ring because it failed to perfect its security interest by one of the other methods of perfection provided for by the Georgia commercial code. The September 14, 1984, document simply does not qualify as one of these methods. The court notes that potential lenders and creditors were not put on notice of plaintiff's security interest in the diamond ring even though Debtor possessed the diamond ring pursuant to a trust arrangement. This is evidenced by Mr. Parks' testimony. Mr. Parks testified that he thought Debtor owned the diamond ring and that he was completely unaware of any claim plaintiff had to the diamond ring. The court therefore concludes that as of the date Debtor filed his bankruptcy petition, plaintiff's security interest in the diamond ring was unperfected. . . .

[Judgment for defendant.]

Perfection of any security interest in securities, certificated or uncertificated, is governed by §8-321, which provides that the security interest both attaches and is perfected when the security is transferred pursuant to agreement by a debtor who has rights in the security to a secured party who has given value. "Transfer" of a security, governed by §8-313(1), requires either possession or its functional equivalent.

Perfection by Filing

For many types of collateral, a secured party may perfect a security interest by filing a **financing statement** in an appropriate public office. Filing a financing statement is by far the most common method of perfection because in most cases the debtor requires possession and use of the collateral, such as inventory or equipment, in order to repay the loan. Security interests in goods, negotiable documents of title, and chattel paper may be perfected by filing as an alternative to taking possession. Collateral incapable of possession, such as accounts and general intangibles, may be perfected only by filing. If the collateral is goods covered by a nonnegotiable document of title (or otherwise possessed by a bailee who has not issued a negotiable document), §9-304(3) provides a special perfection rule. It states that the security interest is perfected when (1) the bailee issues a document of title in the name of the secured party, (2) the bailee is notified of the secured party's interest, or (3) the secured party files a financing statement covering the goods.

Contents of Financing Statement. Like taking possession, filing is designed to put third parties on notice of an interest in the debtor's property. A third party who desires further information may then contact the debtor or secured party for details. Consistent with the basic notice function, under §9-402 a financing statement is sufficient if it (1) contains the names of the debtor and the secured party; (2) gives an address of the secured party from which information concerning the security interest may be obtained; (3) gives an address of the debtor; (4) contains a statement indicating the types, or describing the items of collateral; and (5) is signed by the debtor.

Although not required, a copy of the security agreement may be used as a financing statement if it meets the above requirements and is signed by the debtor. A filed financing statement is not, however, a substitute for a written security agreement necessary for attachment. Although the financing statement need only be signed by the debtor, any amendments to the financing statement must be signed by both parties.

In the following case the sufficiency of the description of the collateral in the financing statement was at issue.

Thorp Commercial Corporation v. Northgate Industries, Inc.

654 F.2d 1245 (8th Cir. 1981)

On May 13, 1971, Franklin National Bank (Bank) loaned Northgate Industries, Inc. (Northgate) $6,500. On May 21, 1971, the Bank filed a financing statement with the Minnesota secretary of state that described the collateral as "assignment accounts receivable" and "proceeds." The Bank subsequently advanced further loans to Northgate. On April 4, 1972, Thorp Commercial Corporation (Thorp), pursuant to its own loan agreement with Northgate, filed a financing statement listing as collateral Northgate's existing and subsequently acquired accounts receivable. Thorp also made subsequent loans to Northgate.

Northgate went out of business owing approximately $60,000 to the Bank and $100,000 to Thorp. The Bank sued Thorp alleging that Thorp had converted some of Northgate's accounts receivable, which rightfully belonged to the Bank because its security interest had been perfected by the filing of the financing statement in 1971. Thorp alleged that the Bank held a security interest only in accounts receivable in existence at the time the Bank had filed its financing statement. The trial court ruled in favor of Thorp holding that the Bank's financing statement failed to cover subsequently acquired accounts receivable. The Bank appealed.

McMillian, Circuit Judge

. . . The security agreement and financing statement have different functions under the UCC. The security agreement defines what the collateral is so that, if necessary, the creditor can identify and claim it, and the debtor or other interested parties can limit the creditor's rights in the collateral given as security. The security agreement must therefore describe the collateral. [UCC] §9-203(1). The financing statement, on the other hand, serves the purpose of putting subsequent creditors on notice that the debtor's property is encumbered. The description of collateral in the financing statement does not function to identify the collateral and define property which the creditor may claim, but rather to warn other subsequent creditors of the prior interest. The financing statement, which limits the prior creditor's rights vis-a-vis subsequent creditors, must therefore contain a description only of the type of collateral. . . .

A split in authority exists [concerning the description of collateral in the financing statement]. . . .

Under one view a financing statement adequately covers collateral if it reasonably puts a subsequent creditor on notice of a need for further inquiry about the possibility that the collateral is subject to a prior security interest. . . .

Under the second view of Article 9, a financing statement suffices to perfect a security interest in collateral if the financing statement itself contains a reasonable description of the collateral. . . .

The approach of . . . courts which require that the financing statement by its own terms describe the collateral cannot be supported under Article 9. Article 9 simply does not require that the financing statement describe anything more than the type of collateral and leaves to interested parties the burden of seeking more information. . . . One central purpose of allowing a broad financing statement is to allow a creditor that envisions an ongoing financing arrangement to protect the priority of its interest by filing at an early date a notice to third parties which will cover the existing arrangement and broad range of potential future modifications. By requiring a description of the collateral in the financing statement itself, courts would destroy this flexibility.

Minnesota . . . appears to be one of the jurisdictions which has adopted the first view discussed above, that a financing statement covers the collateral in question if it merely makes it reasonable for a subsequent creditor interested in the collateral to make further inquiries. . . .

If the financing statement covers not only existing security interests in the type of collateral described but also security interests which may arise in the future, then a financing statement covering "assignment accounts receivable" would cover any assignment of the debtor's accounts receivable that might exist or be made in the future. The word "assignment" might mean a specific assignment of named accounts receivable but is broad enough to refer to a general assignment of all the debtor's accounts receivable, including those acquired in the future. A subsequent creditor, faced with notice that a security interest may exist or be created in any or all of the debtor's accounts, would certainly have reasonable grounds for inquiring further before relying on any of the debtor's accounts for collateral. We conclude that under Minnesota law applying the UCC the financing statement covering "assignment accounts receivable" was adequate to perfect the Bank's security interest in accounts acquired subsequent to the filing of the financing statement, whether or not there was a specific assignment of particular accounts. . . .

[Judgment reversed and remanded.]

Effectiveness, Duration, and Termination of Financing Statement. Under §9-403, the financing statement is deemed filed when it is presented to and accepted by the recording officer together with payment of any necessary filing fee. Upon filing, the filing officer marks each statement with a file number, the date, and the hour of filing, indexes it under the debtor's name, and holds it for public inspection. A financing statement is effective for a period of five years from the date it is filed. It thereafter lapses unless the secured party files a **continuation statement** within six months prior to expiration of the five-year period. The continuation statement must be signed by the secured party, identify the original financing statement by file number, and state that the original statement remains effective. Succeeding continuation statements may be filed to continue the effectiveness of the original statement. In this way, Article 9 provides a self-clearing public filing system because filings older than five years, for which no continuation statement is filed, automatically become ineffective.

A debtor who has satisfied the obligation for which the security interest was created may require the secured party to file a **termination statement** to publicly note that the financing arrangement has been terminated. Because most financing statements expire automatically in five years, under §9-404, the secured party generally is not required to file a termination statement unless one is explicitly demanded by the debtor. If, however, the collateral is consumer goods, the secured party must file a termination statement within one month or within ten days following written demand by the debtor after the secured obligation is satisfied. Such termination statements are only infrequently required because many security interests in consumer goods are perfected without filing under the automatic perfection rules discussed later in this chapter.

Place of Filing. Article 9 replaces a wide variety of state notice systems involving various types of collateral. To accommodate differences among individual states, Article 9's drafters, in §9-401(1), allowed states to choose one of three alternatives concerning the proper place of filing.

The first alternative provides for local filing

when the collateral is (1) timber to be cut, (2) minerals, including oil and gas, (3) accounts arising from the sale of minerals including oil and gas at the minehead or wellhead, and (4) when the financing statement is filed as a "fixture filing." In these cases, the filing is made in the local public office, usually the county recorder's office, where a mortgage on the underlying real estate would be recorded. All other filings are made centrally, usually in the state secretary of state's office.

The second alternative provides initially for local filing for the types of collateral listed above. Local filing is also required for (1) farm collateral such as equipment used in farming operations, farm products, or accounts or general intangibles arising from the sale of farm products, (2) crops, and (3) consumer goods. In all other cases, central filing is required.

Alternative three is identical to the second regarding local filing. In cases requiring central filing, however, the secured party must file both in the secretary of state's office and in the county in which the debtor has a place of business if that place of business is located only in one county. If the debtor has no place of business in the state but resides in the state, the second filing must be made in the county where the debtor resides. Although alternative two, enacted in about one-half of the states, enjoys the widest following, state adoptions of it and the other alternatives often vary from the official text. Figure 31–2 is a facsimile of a financing statement form used for local filings in Illinois, a jurisdiction that has adopted alternative two.

The net effect of the various filing alternatives is that security arrangements of essentially local character or involving local real estate usually are filed locally, and commercial financing arrangements (involving, for example, inventory or equipment) are filed centrally.

Article 9 is not the only recording system governing security interests in personal property. Indeed, Article 9 explicitly exempts from its filing provisions transactions for which an adequate public notice filing system already exists under state or federal law. For example, alternative federal filing systems exist for security interests in ships, railroad equipment, copyrights, patents, and civil aircraft. At the state level, "certificate of title" statutes commonly require that security interests in motor vehicles be noted on the title document. If a filing system which supplants Article 9 exists, the secured party must comply with that system. Perfection under such an alternative system, however, has the same legal consequences as an Article 9 perfection.

Automatic Perfection

Article 9 provides a number of "automatic" perfection rules under which a security interest is perfected upon attachment without requiring that the secured party either file or take possession. Automatic perfection is provided for situations in which possession of the collateral is not feasible, but in which requiring filing would impose an undue burden on Article 9's recording system. That is, automatic perfection rules are applied when the public notice benefits of filing are deemed outweighed by potential clogging of the recording system. Article 9's automatic perfection rules, most of which are discussed below, are generally characterized by one or more limiting factors: (1) they apply only to certain types of collateral, (2) they do not protect the secured party against all third-party claimants, and (3) they are often limited in duration.

Purchase Money Security Interests in Consumer Goods. Perhaps Article 9's most important automatic perfection rule is contained in §9-302(1)(d), which provides that a purchase money security interest in consumer goods is perfected automatically upon attachment without filing.[9] For this rule to apply the security interest must be a purchase money security interest *and* the collateral must be consumer goods. Thus, a financing statement must be filed to perfect purchase money security interests in other types of collateral such as equipment or inventory. The rationale for the automatic perfection rule in consumer goods cases is that such goods are frequently financed on a purchase money basis and that filing a financing statement with respect to every purchase creates a costly burden on sellers.

---

9. Filing is required for a motor vehicle required to be registered.

Figure 31–2	**Financing Statement—Local Filing**

STATE OF ILLINOIS

UNIFORM COMMERCIAL CODE—FINANCING STATEMENT—FORM UCC–2

INSTRUCTIONS:
1. PLEASE TYPE this form. Fold only along perforation for mailing.
2. Remove Secured Party and Debtor copies and send other 3 copies with interleaved carbon paper to the filing officer. Enclose filing fee.
3. If the space provided for any item(s) on the form is inadequate the item(s) should be continued on additional sheets, preferably 5" x 8"
   or 8" x 10". Only one copy of such additional sheets need be presented to the filing officer with a set of three copies of the
   financing statement. Long schedules of collateral, indentures, etc., may be on any size paper that is convenient for the secured party.

This STATEMENT is presented to a filing officer for filing pursuant ot the Uniform Commercial Code.

Debtor(s) (Last Name First) and address(es)

Secured Party(ies) and address(es)

For Filing Officer
(Date, Time, Number, and Filing Office)

1. This financing statement covers the following types (or items) of property:

ASSIGNEE OF SECURED PARTY

2. (If collateral is crops) The above described crops are growing or are to be grown on:
   (Describe Real Estate)

3. (If applicable) The above goods are to become fixtures on (The above timber is standing on...) (The above minerals or
   the like (including oil and gas) or accounts will be financed at the wellhead or minehead of the well or mine located on...)
   (Strike what is inapplicable) (Describe Real Estate)

and this financing statement is to be filed in the real estate records. (If the debtor does not have an interest of record)
The name of a record owner is

4. ☐ Products of Collateral are also covered.

_____ Additional sheets presented.
_____ Filed with Recorder's Office of _____ County, Illinois

By _____
Signature of (Debtor)

(Secured Party)*

*Signature of Debtor required in most cases
Signature of Secured Party in Cases Covered By UCC §9-402 (2)

This form of financing statement is approved by the Secretary of State.

In addition, automatic perfection prevents burdening the filing system with thousands of financing statements covering very small amounts. Further, other creditors are unlikely to be injured by automatic perfection. Creditors other than the seller rarely lend against consumer goods due to their limited value and rapid depreciation.

Automatic perfection in consumer goods protects the seller against claims of the debtor's other creditors but does not protect the seller, under certain circumstances, against a sale of the collateral by the debtor. Under §9-307(2), a buyer of consumer goods takes free of a perfected security interest if he or she (1) buys without knowledge of the security interest, (2) gives value, (3) buys for his or her own personal, family, or household purposes, and (4) before a financing statement is filed. Thus, a secured party who desires protection against a sale of the collateral by the debtor to a bona fide purchaser for consumer purposes must file a financing statement. Because the risk presented by such sales is small in relation to the cost of filing financing statements, most sellers assume the risk and do not file.

To illustrate the operation of these provisions, assume that Art's Appliances, a retailer, sells a television set on credit to Roe. Roe signs a security agreement promising to pay the purchase price and giving Art's a security interest in the set to secure payment—a conditional sales contract. Art's security interest is perfected automatically upon attachment. Thus, even without filing, Art's will have the benefit of the television to the exclusion of Roe's other creditors in the event of Roe's nonpayment or bankruptcy. Assume, however, that Roe subsequently sells the television for cash to Doaks, who buys it for use in his home with no knowledge of Art's security interest. In this case, unless Art's has filed a financing statement covering the set before its sale to Doaks, Doaks acquires the set free of Art's interest.

Sales of Certain Accounts. Assignments of a merchant's accounts, either as an outright sale or as security for a loan, often form an integral part of commercial financing. In these cases, the assignee must file a financing statement to perfect his interest in the accounts. Section 9-302(1)(e) provides that a financing statement is not necessary to perfect an assignment of accounts that does not (either alone or in conjunction with other assignments to the same assignee) transfer a *significant part* of the assignor's outstanding accounts. This section is designed to exempt from filing casual or isolated assignments of a single account or small group of accounts under circumstances not related to business financing. Because all transactions in accounts are governed by Article 9, and accounts are so

commonly involved in financing, §9-302(1)(e) must be viewed as a limited exception to the filing requirement. As Official Comment 5 to §9-302 cautions: "Any person who regularly takes assignments of any debtor's accounts should file."

Twenty-one-day Perfection in Instruments or Documents. Provided certain conditions are met, Article 9 recognizes two situations in which a security interest in *instruments* (other than certificated securities, which are governed by §8-321) or *documents of title* becomes or remains perfected for a twenty-one-day period even though the secured party does not have possession of the collateral and has not filed a financing statement.[10] Section 9-304(4) provides that a security interest in instruments (other than certificated securities such as stocks and bonds) or negotiable documents of title is perfected without filing or taking possession for a period of twenty-one days after attachment to the extent it arises (1) for new value given, (2) under a written security agreement. This section provides limited protection to a lender who loans money secured by instruments or negotiable documents before taking possession or, with respect to negotiable documents, before filing. Under §9-304(5), a creditor who has perfected a security interest in instruments or documents of title by taking possession retains a perfected interest for twenty-one days after relinquishing possession if the delivery of the collateral to the debtor is to allow the debtor (a) to sell or exchange the goods covered by the document or to store, load, unload, ship, process, or otherwise deal with the goods in a manner preliminary to their sale or exchange, or (b) to sell, exchange, present, or collect the instrument.[11] The rationale for both of the twenty-one-day rules discussed above is explained in Official Comment 4

---

10. Filing a financing statement is ineffective to perfect an interest in instruments in any event.

11. Under UCC §§9-304(4) and 9-304(5), transfer of the instrument by the debtor to a holder in due course (or due negotiation of a document of title) during the twenty-one-day period would cut off the rights of the secured party. UCC §9-309. Further, after the twenty-one-day period has expired the secured party has a totally unperfected interest, and must take additional steps to be protected against any third party. UCC §9-304(6).

to §9-304, which states, "There are a variety of legitimate reasons . . . why such collateral has to be temporarily released to a debtor and no useful purpose would be served by cluttering the files with records of such exceedingly short term transactions."

Default

The secured party's rights in specific property owned by the debtor—the collateral—distinguish a secured from an unsecured obligation. These rights are commonly triggered by the debtor's **default,** which generally involves the debtor's nonpayment of the secured obligation as it comes due. Part 5 of Article 9 contains the various provisions relating to default. Article 9 does not define "default," instead allowing the parties to define it in their security agreement. Accordingly, security agreements often incorporate elaborate default provisions.

Assuming the secured party has created a security interest that is enforceable against the debtor (attachment) and defeats third-party claims (perfection), after default, the secured party generally has the right to take possession of the collateral and dispose of it in satisfaction of the debt.

Taking Possession of the Collateral

Unless otherwise agreed, a secured party has the right to take possession of the collateral upon the debtor's default. In taking possession the secured party may proceed without judicial process, if possession can be obtained without breach of the peace, or may proceed by a legal action, such as replevin. The UCC therefore authorizes "self-help" repossession provided the creditor's action does not result in breach of the peace. "Breach of the peace" is not defined in Article 9, but its meaning has been at issue in many pre-Code and post-Code cases. Generally, a creditor may not enter the debtor's house to repossess collateral without consent and may not repossess collateral located elsewhere over the debtor's unequivocal protest. However, clandestine repossessions of cars from driveways, parking lots, or public streets are generally upheld, as the following case illustrates.

Census Federal Credit Union v. Wann
403 N.E.2d 348 (Ind. App. 1980)

Defendant Census Federal Credit Union (Credit Union) loaned money to plaintiff Richard Wann, who granted the Credit Union a security interest in his automobile. After Wann defaulted in repaying the loan, the Credit Union demanded that Wann deliver possession of the automobile to the Credit Union. Wann refused and the Credit Union, through its agents, repossessed the car from the parking lot of the apartment building where Wann lived at approximately 12:30 A.M.

Wann sued the Credit Union, alleging that it had breached the peace in violation of §9-503 of the UCC and had committed trespass in repossessing the automobile. The trial court ruled in favor of Wann and the Credit Union appealed.

Neal, Judge

. . . The sole issue in this case is whether defendant was subject to any civil liability under the facts herein stated for exercising self-help repossession of the automobile under the authority of [UCC §] 9-503. Defendant contends that under this statute it had every right to take possession of the automobile without judicial process so long as it committed no breach of the peace in doing so. Plaintiff concedes that this general statement of the law is correct, but argues that defendant committed a breach of the peace by its actions. . . .

A breach of the peace includes all violations of public peace, order, or decorum. A breach of the peace is a violation or disturbance of the public tranquility or order, and the offense includes breaking or disturbing the public peace by any riotous, forceful, or unlawful proceedings. . . .

Cases in other jurisdictions have held that absence of consent of the defaulting party to repossession is immaterial to the right of a secured party to repossess without judicial process. . . .This, of course, is a necessary result, for contrary to the argument of plaintiff, [UCC §] 9-503, by its very existence, presupposes that the defaulting party did not consent. Should the defaulting party consent, no statutory authority would be required for a secured party to repossess, with or without judicial process. To hold otherwise would emasculate that statute.

Analysis of the above authorities reveals no substantial conflict. They reveal to us, in regard to the right of a secured party to repossess a chattel upon default without resort to judicial process pursuant to [UCC §] 9-503, a proscription of a secured party's use of force, intimidation, or harassment in the repossession of a chattel. The secured party may not in the process of repossession break into or enter into homes or other buildings or enclosed spaces, or commit any crime against the defaulting party, or disturb the peace, or otherwise commit any breach of the peace. Repossession upon default is not, in and of itself, a criminal trespass. . . . The secured party may, in repossession without judicial process [UCC §] 9-503, take a chattel off a street, parking lot or unenclosed space. However, even in the attempted repossession of a chattel off a street, parking lot or unenclosed space, if the repossession is verbally or otherwise contested at the actual time of and in the immediate vicinity of the attempted repossession by the defaulting party or other person in control of the chattel, the secured party must desist and pursue his remedy in court. We approve the reasoning contained in these authorities.

Plaintiff has not cited any authority, nor have we found any, in Indiana or elsewhere, that holds that the secured party cannot, under the self-help provisions of the U.C.C., repossess an automobile off a street, parking lot, or unenclosed space in absence of the defaulting party or any person in control of the chattel, as was done here. The plain policy of the law . . . is to forbid acts that tend to provoke violence or any breach of the peace. We are of the opinion that under the facts of this case the act of the defendant in repossessing the automobile by taking it off the parking lot late at night, in absence of plaintiff or other person in immediate control of the vehicle, did not constitute a breach of the peace for the purposes of [UCC §] 9-503.

[Judgment reversed.]

Disposition of the Collateral

Once in possession of the collateral, the secured party has two alternatives: (1) retain the collateral in full satisfaction of the debt—a "strict foreclosure," or (2) sell the collateral and apply the proceeds to the unpaid obligation.

Strict Foreclosure. Under **strict foreclosure,** authorized in §9-505(2), after default and repossession, the secured party merely retains the collateral in full satisfaction of the debt. If this remedy is used, the secured party foregoes the right to sue the debtor for any deficiency—the difference between the unpaid debt and the value of the collateral. A secured party who intends to use strict foreclosure must send written notice to the debtor unless the debtor has, after default, waived or modified his right to notice. The secured party also must notify other secured parties known to have an interest in the collateral. If the secured party receives written objection from a person notified within twenty-one days after the notice was sent, the secured party must dispose of the collateral by resale. If no one objects, the secured party may retain the collateral in full satisfaction of the debt.

Under §9-505(1), if the collateral is consumer goods and the debtor has already paid sixty percent or more of the price, the secured party must dispose of the collateral by resale unless the debtor, after default, signs an agreement renouncing or modifying his rights. The reason that strict foreclosure is unavailable in this case is that a debtor who has paid sixty percent of the price has probably built up equity in the goods, so that a resale would result in a surplus to be returned to the debtor.

Resale of the Collateral. Because repossessed collateral is often worth less than the unpaid debt, secured creditors usually have little desire to retain the collateral and forego their rights to sue for the deficiency. Accordingly, sale of the collateral is the most common remedy used by secured creditors after default.

Under §9-504, after default and repossession, a secured party may sell, lease, or otherwise dispose of the collateral, either "as is" or following any commercially reasonable preparation or processing. The proceeds of this disposition are applied in the following order:

1. reasonable expenses incurred by the secured party in disposing of the collateral—for example, expenses of re-taking, preparation for sale, and if the security agreement provides, attorneys' fees;
2. the satisfaction of the indebtedness owed to the secured party; and, finally,
3. the satisfaction of any indebtedness owed to any subordinate secured party in the same collateral.

Any surplus is to be returned to the debtor and, unless otherwise agreed, the debtor is liable for any deficiency.

The collateral may be sold either by public or private sale. Two basic requirements govern the conduct of the sale. First, the secured party must give reasonable notification to the debtor of the time and place of any public sale, or of the time after which a private sale will be made. Unless the goods in question are consumer goods, the secured party must also notify any subordinate secured party from whom he or she has received written notice. Second, every aspect of the disposition including the method, manner, time, place, and terms of the sale must be commercially reasonable. The secured party may buy the collateral at any public sale. If the collateral is of a type customarily sold in a recognized market, or is of a type that is the subject of widely distributed standard price quotations, the secured party may also buy at a private sale.

Secured Party's Collection Rights. Problems of disposition inherent in a sale of goods, such as inventory or equipment, are not present if the collateral is accounts receivable, chattel paper, or instruments. Accounts receivable, for example, represent the most liquid asset in the debtor's business, and may be collected without any interruption of the business. As a result, §9-502(1) provides that upon default, the secured party is entitled to notify the persons obligated on the accounts, chattel paper, or instruments to make payments directly to the secured party. This right exists whether the method of collection contemplated by the security agreement before default was *direct* (account debtors making payments directly to the secured party, referred to as "notification" financing) or *indirect* (payment by the account debtors to the debtor, referred to as "non-notification" financing). The security agreement may grant the secured party the right to give notice and make collections before default. Section 9-502, however, automatically gives the secured party this right after default.

SUMMARY

1. In a secured transaction, governed by Article 9 of the Uniform Commercial Code, a borrower or buyer gives a lender or seller a security interest in personal property or fixtures to secure performance of an obligation. The debtor is the party who owes the obligation and is giving security. The secured party is the lender, seller, or other party in whose favor a security interest exists. The property providing the security is the collateral. Security interests may be possessory or non-possessory, purchase money or non-purchase-money.

2. The major types of personal property collateral are goods, semi-intangibles, and intangibles. Goods include consumer goods, farm products, equipment, and inventory. Semi-intangibles include documents of title, chattel paper, and instruments. Intangibles include accounts and general intangibles.

3. Article 9 governs any transaction that, regardless of its form, is intended to create a security interest in personal property or fixtures. Article 9 excludes from its coverage security transactions that do not arise by agreement of the parties and transactions not related to commercial financing. Article 9 also governs any sale of accounts or chattel paper, whether or not intended for security.

4. Before a security interest is effective between the debtor and secured party, it must attach to the collateral. Attachment requires the co-existence of three elements: (1) an enforceable security agreement must exist; (2) the

secured party must give value; and (3) the debtor must have rights in the collateral.

5. Perfection determines the secured party's rights against third-party claimants to the collateral. These third parties include: (1) creditors of the debtor, including lien creditors such as the debtor's trustee in bankruptcy, (2) buyers of the collateral from the debtor, and (3) other secured parties claiming an interest in the collateral.

6. Article 9 recognizes three methods of perfecting a security interest:

1. perfection by taking possession of the collateral;
2. perfection by filing a "financing statement" in an appropriate public office; and
3. automatic perfection occurring upon attachment with no further action by the secured party.

7. Security interests in money and instruments may be perfected only by taking possession. Security interests in accounts and general intangibles may be perfected only by filing. Security interests in other types of collateral including goods, negotiable documents of title, and chattel paper may be perfected either by filing or taking possession.

8. Automatic perfection rules apply only to certain types of collateral, do not protect the secured party against all third parties, and are often limited in duration. Article 9's most important automatic perfection rule provides that a purchase money security interest in consumer goods is perfected automatically upon attachment without filing.

9. The secured party's rights in specific property owned by the debtor—the collateral—distinguish a secured from an unsecured obligation. These rights are triggered by the debtor's default, which usually involves the debtor's nonpayment of the secured obligation as it comes due. After default the secured party generally has the right to take possession of the collateral and dispose of it in satisfaction of the debt.

10. In taking possession of the collateral the secured party may proceed without judicial process (self-help) if possession can be obtained without breach of the peace, or may proceed by judicial proceeding such as a replevin action.

11. Once in possession of the collateral, the secured party may either retain the collateral in full satisfaction of the debt—a strict foreclosure—or may sell the collateral at public or private sale and apply the proceeds to the debt. If the collateral involved is accounts receivable, chattel paper, or instruments, Article 9 permits the secured party upon default to notify account debtors to make payments directly to the secured party.

KEY TERMS

secured transaction	document of title
security interest	chattel paper
debtor	conditional sales contract
secured party	account debtor
collateral	instruments
security agreement	account
possessory security interest (pledge)	general intangibles
	attachment
non-possessory security interest	perfection
	value
purchase money security interest	lien creditor
	financing statement
consumer goods	continuation statement
farm products	termination statement
inventory	default
equipment	strict foreclosure

QUESTIONS AND PROBLEMS

31-1 Compare and contrast the concepts of attachment and perfection under Article 9 of the UCC. What are the basic requirements for attachment? What functions do these requirements serve? Indicate the possible method or methods of perfecting a security interest in the various types of collateral discussed in the text.

31-2 Consider whether each of the following descriptions of collateral is sufficient to identify a security interest (a) in the security agreement and (b) in the financing statement. See §§9-110 and 9-402 of the Code:

(a) Consumer goods of the debtor.

(b) All of the contents of Joe's Diner.

(c) All farm equipment.

(d) Inventory.

31-3 First State Bank has agreed to lend Mrs. Carraway $30,000 and to take a security interest in three certificates of deposit that she owns. The certificates are nonnegotiable and nontransferable. How should the bank perfect its security interest?

31-4 Richard Valway owned a restaurant named Ricardo's. Gregg Equipment Co. sold restaurant equipment to Valway pursuant to a written security agreement retaining a purchase money security interest in the equipment. Gregg filed a financing statement listing the debtor as "Ricardo's." Does Gregg hold a perfected security interest? Why or why not?

31-5 Woofer and Tweeter, Inc. sold a stereo system on credit to Mr. and Mrs. Brown and retained a security interest in the stereo. After the Browns defaulted in making monthly payments, an employee of Woofer and Tweeter went to the Brown home to repossess the stereo. The employee was accompanied by a deputy sheriff in full uniform. The employee explained that he wanted the stereo and the Browns allowed him to take it with no argument. The deputy merely stood at the door while the repossession took place. The Browns then sued Woofer and Tweeter for unlawful repossession.

(a) Did a breach of the peace occur?

(b) Should the court uphold the repossession? Explain.

31-6   The Money Bank loaned Darla money to purchase a mobile home. The parties signed a written agreement granting the bank a security interest in the mobile home. Darla defaulted in repaying the loan but refused to give the bank possession of the mobile home. Rinaldo, an employee of the bank, went to Darla's home while she was at work, used a crowbar to remove a lock from the door, released Darla's dog, and tied it to a nearby tree. Rinaldo then removed the mobile home from its concrete foundation and hauled the mobile home to the bank. Darla sued the bank alleging that the repossession constituted a breach of the peace. How should the court rule? Explain.

31-7   Rinaldo also repossessed a car subject to the Money Bank's security interest. He visited the debtor and asked for return of the automobile. The debtor asserted that he had made all the necessary loan payments, so Rinaldo suggested that the debtor go to the bank with Rinaldo to verify his payment record. While the debtor was reviewing his account with the loan officer, Rinaldo towed the car from the bank's parking lot to a nearby garage. Even though the bank records confirmed that the debtor was one payment in arrears, the debtor sued the bank alleging that the repossession violated §9-503 of the UCC. How should the court rule? Explain.

Chapter 32

Secured Transactions— Priorities

Major Topics

- the general rules governing priority between a secured party and third-party claimants to the collateral, including general creditors, lien creditors, buyers of the collateral, and other secured parties
- an explanation of the "floating lien" and how the priority disputes it creates are resolved
- Article 9's treatment of priorities in fixtures and accessions
- a discussion of specialized secured transaction issues including field warehousing and security interests as preferences in bankruptcy

Like much of debtor-creditor law, Article 9 of the Uniform Commercial Code is primarily concerned with resolving disputes among creditors competing for the limited assets of a defaulting debtor. The basic intent of any Article 9 secured creditor is to have a priority claim to the collateral. How effective a given security interest is in achieving that result is the subject of the following material.

General Rules of Priority

The value of perfected security interest is most easily illustrated by first examining the priority between an unperfected security interest and the various types of claimants discussed in the preceding chapter, and then comparing those results with the

position enjoyed by a perfected secured party against the same claimants.

Unperfected Security Interests

Versus General Creditors. Under §9-201, a security agreement is effective according to its terms against the debtor's unsecured creditors. That is, an unsecured general creditor has no lien upon any specific property belonging to the debtor. In contrast, a secured party whose interest has attached (but has not been perfected) has a lien upon the collateral. Accordingly, the unperfected secured party may repossess the collateral upon default and defeat an unsecured creditor's claim to the property.

Versus Lien Creditors. A secured party is primarily interested in defeating lien creditors, particularly the debtor's trustee in bankruptcy. Indeed, the acid test of any secured transaction is determining whether it will enjoy a priority in the debtor's bankruptcy. The trustee in bankruptcy, who represents the debtor's general creditors, often seeks to avoid the security interest and use the collateral to satisfy the general creditors' claims. Herein lies the weakness of an unperfected security interest. Under §9-301(1)(b), the rights of a holder of an unperfected security interest are subordinate to the rights of a person who becomes a lien creditor before the security interest is perfected. For example, assume Roberts loans $1,000 to Simpson on June 1, taking a security interest in a stamp collection in the possession of Simpson pursuant to a written agreement. Roberts does not file a financing statement. On August 1, a petition in bankruptcy is filed against Simpson. Simpson's trustee in bankruptcy becomes a lien creditor on August 1. The trustee in bankruptcy prevails over Roberts with respect to the stamp collection, because the trustee became a lien creditor before Roberts's interest was perfected.

Under §9-301(2), if the security interest in question is a purchase money security interest that must be perfected by filing—that is, it is not a purchase money security interest in consumer goods—a secured party who files a financing statement within 10 days after the debtor receives possession of the collateral will take priority over the rights of a lien creditor arising between the time the security interest attaches and the time of filing.

The following case illustrates a priority dispute between a secured party and the trustee in bankruptcy in the context of a typical "certificate of title" statute.

In the Matter of Keidel
613 F.2d 172 (7th Cir. 1980)

On May 17, 1977, Esther Keidel borrowed $3,500 from the First National Bank of Wood River to purchase a mobile home. After Keidel signed a promissory note and security agreement giving the bank a security interest in the mobile home, the bank issued a check payable jointly to Keidel, the sellers, and Olin Employees' Credit Union, which held a lien on the mobile home. When Keidel delivered the check to the Credit Union, she was given a certificate of title indicating that the Credit Union had released its lien and had named First National Bank of Wood River as lienholder. A Credit Union employee advised Keidel to send the certificate of title to the secretary of state. Keidel failed to file the certificate.

On November 7, 1977, Keidel filed for bankruptcy. Soon thereafter, First National Bank of Wood River filed the certificate of title to the mobile home with the secretary of state, and on December 15, 1977, a new certificate showing the bank as

lienholder was issued. The bank also repossessed the mobile home.

The trustee in bankruptcy filed a complaint with the bankruptcy court alleging that the mobile home was a part of the bankrupt's estate. The bankruptcy judge ordered First National Bank of Wood River to pay $3,500, representing the value of the mobile home, to the trustee. The district court affirmed and the bank appealed.

Cudahy, Circuit Judge

. . . Under Illinois law, security interests in personal property are, in general, governed by the Uniform Commercial Code as adopted in Illinois. . . . With respect to the means of perfection of security interests in motor vehicles (including mobile homes), however, the Illinois Vehicle Code exclusively controls. . . . Thus, the Illinois Vehicle Code provides that:

> A security interest is perfected by delivery to the Secretary of State of the existing certificate of title, if any, an application for a certificate of title containing the name and address of the lienholder and the date of his security agreement, and the required fee. It is perfected as of the time of its creation if the delivery is completed within 21 days thereafter, otherwise as of the time of the delivery. Ill. Rev. Stat. ch. 95½, §3-202(b).

In the instant case the old certificate of title and an application for a new certificate were not delivered to the Secretary of State until shortly before December 15, 1977. But the security interest of the First National Bank of Wood River was created on May 17, 1977, when the security agreement and the promissory note were signed. [UCC] §9-203(1) and (2). . . . Therefore, since the security interest was not perfected within 21 days of its creation, it was not perfected until the application was delivered to the Secretary of State—well after the date of bankruptcy (Nov. 7, 1977). . . . On November 7, 1977, therefore, the security interest of the Bank was unperfected. . . .

Hence, as of the date of the bankruptcy, the rights of the Bank, as the holder of an unperfected security interest, were subordinate to those of the trustee in bankruptcy, who stood in the position of a lien creditor or lienholder. . . . This result illustrates the general rule that a lien creditor or lien-holder (in whose shoes the trustee stands) prevails over the holder of an unperfected security interest but is defeated by the holder of a perfected security interest. . . .

The Bank contends that the result here produces a windfall for the bankrupt's estate at the expense of the secured creditor, which furnished the purchase price of the mobile home. This may indeed be the result in this case, but the Bank has only itself to blame for failure to perform its statutory duty prescribing application for a new title. The Illinois law applicable to secured transactions in personal property, including motor vehicles, places strong emphasis on the need for diligence in perfection of the security interest in accordance with the statutory method. . . . The strong policy favoring diligence in perfection (and the consequent gain in certainty and regularity) outweighs the possibility here of "unjust enrichment" or a "windfall."

[Judgment affirmed.]

Versus Buyer of the Collateral. Under §§9-301(1)(c)-(d), a buyer of the collateral from the debtor prevails against an unperfected security interest in the collateral if the buyer (1) gives value and (2) receives delivery of the collateral without knowledge of the security interest and before the interest is perfected. For example, assume that on June 1, Carol loans Don $10,000, taking a security interest in Don's equipment. On June 2, Don contracts to sell a lathe (a piece of his equipment) to Janet, who pays $5,000. On June 3, Carol files a financing statement covering the equipment. On June 4, Janet picks up the lathe from Don without knowledge of Carol's interest. Carol will prevail, because, though Janet gave value before perfection, she did not take possession before perfection.

Priority Among Unperfected Security Interests. Under §9-312(5)(b), if two or more unperfected secured parties claim an interest in the same collateral, the first to attach will prevail. To illustrate, on June 1, Roberts loans Simpson $1,000, taking an enforceable security interest in Simpson's stamp collection. Roberts does not file. On July 1,

Carter loans Simpson $1,000 and takes an enforceable security interest in the same collection. Carter does not file. As between Roberts and Carter, Roberts prevails, because her interest attached first, that is, on June 1.

Perfected Security Interests

A secured party with a perfected security interest fares much better than unperfected secured parties in the various priority contests with third parties claiming an interest in the collateral.

Versus General Creditors. As noted above, even an unperfected security interest defeats a general creditor's claim to the collateral. Perfected interests therefore also defeat a general creditor's claims.

Versus Lien Creditors. The ability to defeat a lien creditor is the hallmark of a perfected security interest. Under §9-301(4), a perfected security interest takes priority over the claims of a lien creditor to the extent that the security interest secures advances made before the person became a lien creditor or within forty-five days thereafter. The primary value of §9-301(4) to the secured party is that it protects the secured party against the most potent lien creditor—the debtor's trustee in bankruptcy. That is, a creditor who obtains a perfected security interest before the date the bankruptcy petition is filed (the date on which the trustee becomes a lien creditor) will have the benefit of the collateral free of the trustee's claim to it.[1]

Versus Buyer of Collateral. As a general rule, under §9-306(2) the holder of a perfected security interest defeats subsequent buyers of the collateral from the debtor unless the secured party has authorized the disposition. This rule is subject to a number of important exceptions that substantially limit its effect. For example, as previously noted, a purchase money security interest in consumer goods is perfected automatically upon attachment. If, however, the secured party does not file, a consumer

---

1. The debtor's trustee in bankruptcy may avoid certain security interests perfected shortly before bankruptcy as preferences under principles discussed later in this chapter.

buyer of the collateral from the debtor defeats the secured party's claim to the goods. Three additional important exceptions are discussed below.

Buyers in the Ordinary Course of Business. Under §1-201(9), a **buyer in the ordinary course of business** is a person who in good faith and without knowledge that the sale to him is in violation of the ownership rights or security interest of a third party in the goods, buys goods in the ordinary course from a person in the business of selling goods of that kind. Although not explicitly stated in the definition, a buyer in the ordinary course of business is primarily a purchaser of *inventory* from a person in the business of selling that inventory. For example, a person buying a diamond ring from a jeweler or a dishwasher from an appliance dealer is a buyer in the ordinary course of business. §9-307(1) provides that such a buyer takes the goods free of a security interest created by his seller even though the security interest is perfected, and even though the buyer knows of its existence. To illustrate, assume that First Bank loans money to Red's Television and to secure repayment takes a security interest in Red's inventory. First Bank files a financing statement covering the transaction in an appropriate public office. James, a customer, walks into Red's store and buys a television set. In this case, James is a buyer in the ordinary course of business. James takes the set free of First Bank's security interest, even though the interest is perfected (by filing) and even if he knows of the bank's security interest, unless he knows that the sale is in violation of the security agreement. Note that §9-307(1) protects the buyer when the debtor's sale of the collateral is unauthorized. If the secured party has authorized the sale in the security agreement or otherwise, the buyer, under §9-306(2), takes the property free of the security interest.

Two important reasons justify the rule protecting buyers in the ordinary course of business against pre-existing security interests in the inventory. First, a buyer of inventory should not be required in every transaction with a merchant to determine whether a security interest exists in the goods or whether they might be repossessed by a secured party. Second, and perhaps more important, any other rule would permit merchants who purchase inventory without creating a security interest to offer their goods for sale free and clear of creditors'

interests, while those who finance their inventory on a secured basis could not. This result would place the merchants who finance inventory at a definite competitive disadvantage, making it difficult for them to generate cash through the sale of inventory to repay their loans.

A buyer in the ordinary course of business does not take free of all pre-existing security interests in the goods. As the following case illustrates, §9-307(1) protects the buyer only against a security interest "created by his seller."

National Shawmut Bank of Boston v. Jones
236 A.2d 484 (N.H. 1967)

> Robert Wever purchased a Dodge Dart automobile from Wentworth Motor Company under a conditional sale contract by which Wentworth retained a security interest in the car. Wentworth assigned the contract to plaintiff National Shawmut Bank of Boston, which perfected the security interest by filing a financing statement in the office of the town clerk. Wever, without the permission of the bank, sold the car to Hanson-Rock, Inc. of Hampton, N.H., another automobile dealer, which later sold the car to defendant Victor Jones. Hanson-Rock and Jones had no knowledge of the bank's security interest and neither examined the town clerk's records to search for prior security interests.
>
> National Shawmut Bank sued Jones for return of the car or for damages of $1,490 representing the unpaid balance due on Wever's contract. The trial court transferred the case to the New Hampshire Supreme Court for rulings on several issues of law.

Grimes, Justice

. . . Since Wever purchased for personal, family or household purposes, the Dart is classified as consumer goods. [UCC §] 9-109. The plaintiff's security interest was perfected by filing the financing statement with the Town Clerk of Hampton where Wever resided, ([UCC §] 9-401(1)(a)), and continues when the collateral is sold without its consent as was the case here unless Article 9 provides otherwise. [UCC §] 9-306(2). In the case of buyers of goods, [UCC §] 9-307(1) does provide otherwise in certain instances. . . .

Since defendant purchased in good faith without

knowledge that the sale to him was in violation of the security interest of another and bought in the ordinary course from a person in the business of selling automobiles, he was a "buyer in the ordinary course of business." [UCC §] 1-201(9). However, §9-307(1) permits him to take free only of "a security interest created by his seller." The security interest of the plaintiff was not created by Hanson-Rock, Inc., the defendant's seller, but by [Wever in favor of] Wentworth Motor Co., Inc. Defendant, therefore, does not take free of the plaintiff's security interest under this section. . . .

[Remanded.]

Repeal of Farm Products Exception. By its terms, the rule of §9-307(1) does not apply to a person who is buying farm products from a person engaged in farming operations. Under this so-called "farm products" exception, the purchaser of farm products is not protected against liens created by his seller and thus effectively becomes a guarantor of the loan made to the agricultural borrower secured by the farm products. Though harshly criticized as paternalistic and failing to recognize that agricultural finance is now simply another form of modern commercial finance, the farm products exception survived the 1972 Article 9 amendments after heated debate between organized farm lenders and processors of agricultural products. A number of states nevertheless enacted nonuniform amendments to provide greater purchaser protection.

Congress ultimately ended the debate by enacting §1324 of the Food Security Act of 1985, which repeals the farm products exception on a nationwide basis. Under the statute, "notwithstanding any other provision of Federal, State, or local law," a buyer in the ordinary course of business who buys a farm product from a seller engaged in farming operations takes free of a security interest created by the seller, even though the security interest is perfected and the buyer knows of its existence.[2] A similar rule protects commission merchants or selling agents who sell farm products for others in the ordinary course of business. Under the law the secured party may, however, protect itself by giving advance notice to the purchaser, commission merchant, or selling agent of the security interest. Notice may be given directly by the secured party. Alternatively, the statute authorizes the states to establish an optional central filing system, which generates state-wide lists of security interests that are furnished to prospective purchasers, commission merchants, or selling agents.

Purchasers of Instruments, Documents, and Securities. Section 9-309 provides that Article 9 does not limit the rights of (1) a holder in due course of a negotiable instrument (such as a note or check), (2) a holder to whom a negotiable document of title (such as a warehouse receipt or bill of lading) has been duly negotiated, or (3) a bona fide purchaser of a security (such as a stock or bond). Thus, a holder in due course of a negotiable instrument or bona fide purchaser of a security would take priority over an earlier nonpossessory, and therefore unperfected, security interest in an instrument or security. (Remember that a secured party may perfect a security interest in a negotiable instrument or security only by taking possession.) In addition, a holder to whom a negotiable document of title has been duly negotiated takes priority over an earlier security interest in the document which is perfected by filing. Note that filing a financing statement, which provides constructive notice to most third parties, is not notice to the holders or purchasers listed in §9-309.[3] For example, assume Canfield, Inc. loans Delbert $10,000 secured by negotiable warehouse receipts belonging to Delbert. Delbert retains possession of the receipts and Canfield perfects its interest in the receipts by filing a financing statement. Subsequently, Delbert duly negotiates[4] the receipts to Holbrook. Holbrook cuts off Canfield's rights to the receipts, even though Canfield's interest is perfected. To be protected against holders such as Holbrook, therefore, a secured party must take possession.

Purchasers of Chattel Paper and Instruments. When chattel paper is used as collateral, the

---

2. 7 U.S.C. §1631(d).

3. See, for example, UCC §3-304(5).

4. The due negotiation doctrine applicable to negotiable documents of title under Article 7 is discussed in Chapter 35.

secured party may take possession of the paper, notify the account debtors, and make collections. This approach is a "notification" or "direct collection" arrangement. Alternatively, the secured party may perfect by filing and leave the debtor in possession of the paper to make collections and remit the proceeds to the secured party. This method is known as a "non-notification" or "indirect collection" arrangement. Because both methods are widely used, and because chattel paper is not negotiable, Article 9 permits perfection of security interests in chattel paper either by filing or taking possession.

Perfection by filing may, however, provide more limited protection to the secured party. Under §9-308(a), a purchaser of chattel paper or an instrument who (1) gives new value and (2) takes possession of it in the ordinary course of the purchaser's business has priority over a security interest in the chattel paper or instrument even though perfected, if the purchaser buys the paper without knowledge that the chattel paper or instrument is subject to a security interest. Note that this rule applies only if the paper is purchased in the ordinary course of the *purchaser's* business. As such, only purchasers in the business of buying such paper, such as banks or finance companies, qualify for protection under this provision.

For example, Dealer, an appliance retailer, sells goods on credit to customers under conditional sales contracts giving Dealer a security interest in the goods sold. Dealer then borrows money from First Bank, giving the bank a security interest in the contracts to secure repayment. The bank files but leaves Dealer in possession of the paper in order to make collections. Dealer subsequently sells the paper to Finance Company, who pays cash and takes possession of the paper in the ordinary course of its business without knowledge of the bank's security interest. Dealer subsequently defaults on the loan and First Bank seeks to use the paper purchased by Finance to satisfy the unpaid debt. In this case, Finance will take the paper free of the bank's claim even though that claim is perfected.

First Bank can easily protect itself from the effect of §9-308(a) by stamping (with a rubber stamp) or noting on the paper itself that it is subject to a security interest in favor of the bank. In this manner, the bank can allow the debtor to retain possession of the paper to collect on it from the account debtors but is protected from purchasers such as Finance who can no longer meet the requirement that they take without knowledge of the bank's security interest.

Priority Among Perfected Security Interests. The most important priority rule in Article 9 is §9-312(5)(a), which governs priority between two or more secured parties, all of whom have perfected their interests. Section 9-312(5) is a catch-all rule, governing situations not otherwise specifically addressed. It adopts a "first in time, first in right" rule with the "time" computed as the *earlier* of (1) the date on which the financing statement is filed, or (2) the date of perfection. That is, each secured party gets its "better date" (the earlier date) in determining priority in relation to other perfected secured creditors. If one security interest is perfected and another is not, the perfected secured party, of course, has priority.

Security Interests Versus Liens Arising by Operation of Law

Under state common law or statute, persons who regularly repair or improve goods obtain a possessory lien upon the goods (an "artisan's lien") to secure payment for labor or material charges. The priority between such a possessory lien and a prior security interest in the goods is governed by §9-310. The operation of §9-310 is explained and illustrated in the following case.

National Bank of Joliet v. Bergeron Cadillac, Inc.
361 N.E.2d 1116 (Ill. 1977).

In February of 1973, plaintiff National Bank of Joliet loaned Gladys Schmidt $4,120 to purchase an automobile. The bank took and perfected a security interest in the automobile. In August of 1973, defendant Bergeron Cadillac, Inc. (Bergeron) performed repairs costing approximately $2,000 on the automobile. When Schmidt failed to pay for the repairs, Bergeron retained possession of the car. Under Illinois law, a common law lien is created when a repairman retains possession of a vehicle to secure payment for repairs performed on the vehicle.

When Schmidt defaulted in paying the loan, the bank sued Bergeron demanding delivery of the car. Bergeron alleged that its common law lien had priority over the bank's security interest. Both the trial and appellate courts ruled in favor of Bergeron. The bank appealed.

Ward, Chief Justice

. . . The plain language of §9-310 gives the lien of persons furnishing services or materials upon goods in their possession priority over a perfected security interest unless the lien is created by statute and the statute expressly provides otherwise.

The comment of Anderson (Anderson, Uniform Commercial Code) is:

> Such a lien is, basically, the artisan's lien of the common law. Whether such a lien is based upon decision or statute law, Code [§9-310] gives it priority, with one exception, over a pre-existing security interest in the goods. . . .
>
> The single exception relates to a lien created by statute; such a lien does not have such priority if the statute expressly provides otherwise. Accordingly, the lien has priority when it is based upon the common law or decision, or when it is based upon a statute which is silent as to priorities or which gives the lien priority. The lien is subordinated to the security interest only when the lien statute expressly so declares. 4 Anderson, Uniform Commercial Code sec. 9-310, at 341-42 (2d ed. 1971). . . .

The artisan's possessory lien of the common law is recognized in Illinois. . . .

As the defendant had a common law possessory lien for services and materials in connection with the repairs it made, its lien takes priority over the plaintiff's earlier perfected security interest under the provisions of [§9-310]. . . .

[Judgment affirmed.]

The "Floating Lien" Priority Rules

Article 9 is primarily concerned with commercial financing arrangements whereby a merchant uses its business assets—such as inventory, equipment,

accounts receivable, or chattel paper—as collateral on a loan or other obligation. If the business debtor encounters financial difficulty or bankruptcy, these commercial financing arrangements present a myriad of priority problems. These problems are complicated by the "floating lien" often used in inventory and accounts financing and the need for determining priority not only in the original collateral, but also in the "proceeds" of its sale or exchange. The following material explains how Article 9 resolves the problems presented by common commercial financing arrangements.

After-Acquired Property Clauses

Although inventory commonly serves as collateral in business financing arrangements, its use presents an obvious problem: inventory is sold to third parties in the ordinary course of the debtor's business to generate funds to repay the loan secured by the inventory, and to purchase additional inventory. Because a merchant's inventory is constantly changing, an inventory financier usually desires a security interest not only in the original inventory, but also in additional inventory later acquired by the debtor. This result is accomplished by including an **after-acquired property clause** in the security agreement. Such clauses are expressly validated in §9-204(1), which states that a security agreement may provide that any or all obligations covered by the agreement are to be secured by after-acquired collateral. The after-acquired property clause creates a **floating lien,** or a **floating charge.** That is, the lien "floats" over the debtor's ever-changing stock, covering whatever inventory is found there. Inventory financing secured by after-acquired inventory is often referred to as **floor planning.**[5]

The converse of the rule discussed above is also true. Under §9-204(3), a security agreement may provide that existing collateral will secure additional advances of money from the secured party. In addition, although the UCC broadly validates the floating lien in commercial financing arrangements, the lien's use in consumer lending is severely re-

---

5. Although some courts have held that a floating lien attaches only when the debtor acquires rights in the new collateral, most courts now hold that attachment relates back to the date of the original agreement.

stricted. Under §9-204(2), after-acquired consumer goods may be used to provide additional security only if the debtor acquires them within 10 days after the secured party gives value. Of course, in the commercial lending context, collateral subject to the floating lien is commonly acquired months or even years after the original agreement.

Most Article 9 priority provisions are designed to systematically resolve the various conflicts created by the inventory floating lien. The following material examines the major Code provisions that resolve the conflicts created when a bank or other lender loans money to a debtor to finance the debtor's inventory and takes a security interest in that inventory, both presently existing and after-acquired.

Introduction to Proceeds

Under §9-306(1), **proceeds** include whatever is received upon the sale, exchange, collection, or other disposition of the collateral. Money, checks, deposit accounts, and the like are "cash proceeds." All others are "noncash proceeds." Under §9-306(2), a security interest continues in: (1) collateral notwithstanding a sale, exchange, or other disposition (unless otherwise provided in Article 9 or unless the disposition of the collateral was authorized by the secured party), and (2) any identifiable proceeds received by the debtor.

In the inventory financing case, under §§9-307(1) or 9-306(2), the secured party's right in the collateral—the inventory—is defeated by the buyer in the ordinary course of business. Therefore, after the sale, the secured party's interest extends only to the *proceeds* of the sale of the inventory. Under §9-203(3), this right to proceeds exists automatically whether or not a specific provision including proceeds is contained in the security agreement.

The secured party has a *continuously perfected* security interest in the proceeds if the interest in the original collateral was perfected—no additional action by the secured party is necessary to perfect this interest. The secured party's perfected interest in proceeds is often limited in duration, however. Under §9-306(3), a security interest in proceeds becomes unperfected ten days after receipt of the proceeds by the debtor unless: (1) a filed financing statement covers the original collateral (here inventory) and the proceeds are collateral in which a security interest may be perfected by filing in the office or offices where the financing statement covering the inventory has been filed, or (2) a filed financing statement covers the original collateral and the proceeds are identifiable cash proceeds, or (3) the security interest in the proceeds is separately perfected within the ten-day period.

Although a security interest in inventory is cut off when the debtor sells it to a buyer in the ordinary course of business and the interest in proceeds often is perfected only for a short period of time, a floating lien is nevertheless valuable to a secured party. The proceeds of the sale of the inventory are ultimately converted to cash, which is then used to purchase more *inventory* subject to the secured party's floating lien. This process of converting the proceeds of the sale of inventory to cash which is used to purchase more inventory is known as the **recoupment cycle**. At some point in the recoupment cycle, the debtor uses some of the money to pay his salary, overhead, and other fixed expenses. This process is referred to as **extraction**. What remains of the money is used to purchase additional inventory, which then becomes subject to the secured party's security interest. The secured party protects its security interest by making periodic surprise counts of the inventory. If the inventory level remains at a reasonably constant level, the secured party is assured that there has not been excessive extraction, either by fraudulent conduct or by the debtor's poor business practices. If the inventory level dips significantly, the secured party is alerted to potentially excessive extraction of cash from the proceeds, and can then take steps to determine the reason for the excessive extraction, enforce its security interest against the collateral, or accelerate the debt. Such remedies available to the secured party are normally contained in the security agreement itself.

The following material examines the common priority problems arising when a debtor whose property is subject to a floating lien encounters financial difficulty. The rules are most easily understood by assuming that the debtor is in bankruptcy, possessing on the date of bankruptcy specific assets including inventory and proceeds of the sale of inventory in various forms. Various creditors, including the trustee in bankruptcy, seek to use these lim-

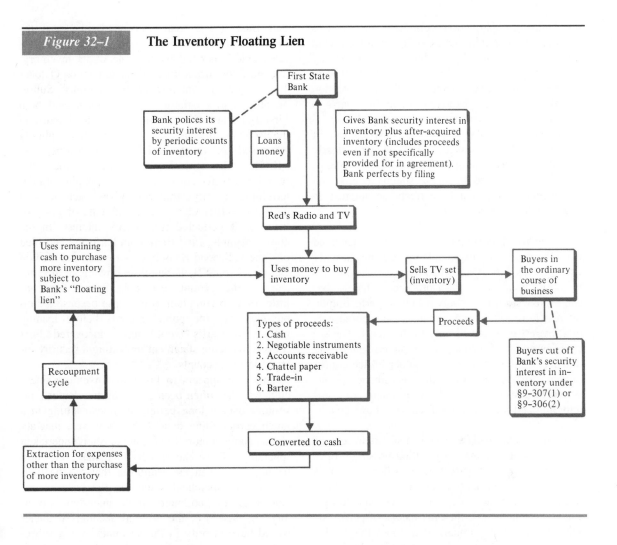

| Figure 32-1 | **The Inventory Floating Lien** |

ited assets to satisfy their unpaid claims. The secured party holding a floating lien is protected against such claims in two ways. First, the normal operation of the recoupment cycle provides a continuing stock of inventory subject to the security interest. Second, some protection is provided in the proceeds themselves. Proceeds generated by the sale of inventory fall into six general categories: (1) cash, (2) instruments, (3) accounts receivable, (4) chattel paper, (5) trade-ins, and (6) barter.

Figure 32–1 illustrates the floating lien situation, the recoupment cycle, and the types of proceeds that may be generated by the sale of inventory. The extent of the secured party's protection in these proceeds is covered below.

Specific Proceeds Priority Rules

Cash. If a buyer in the ordinary course of business pays cash for the inventory, the security interest in cash proceeds is automatically perfected, but only for ten days. The interest becomes unperfected thereafter because filing, which is the means of perfection for the inventory, is an inappropriate means of perfection for cash, for which the only means of perfection is possession. While the proceeds remain in a cash state, the secured party enjoys very limited protection in them. Taking possession of cash is not normally a viable alternative because cash is necessary for the continued operation of the business. Further, even during the ten-day automatic perfection period, if the cash is transferred to a third party or commingled with other cash generated by the business, the security interest in the cash proceeds is cut off. A prudent secured lender may obtain significant protection through the simple expedient of including a term in the security agreement requiring the debtor to promptly deposit all cash proceeds from the sale of the collateral in a separate bank account clearly identified as containing only proceeds. As previously noted, a filed financing statement covering the inventory indefinitely perfects an interest in "identifiable cash proceeds."[6]

Instruments. Frequently the proceeds received from the buyers are negotiable instruments, usually checks. This case is governed by principles similar to those applicable to cash proceeds. That is, because possession is the only means of perfecting an interest in negotiable instruments, the secured party's interest is perfected only for ten days. The secured party is, of course, *not* protected against the transfer of the instrument to a holder in due course (under §9-309), and once the instrument is converted to cash or deposited, the problems of commingling and identification discussed above arise.

Accounts Receivable. Merchants often extend credit to their customers by selling goods on open account. A secured party holding a floating lien in the inventory sold enjoys substantial protection in such accounts receivable proceeds, because filing a financing statement is the only means of perfection with respect to accounts. Therefore, the bank's original financing statement relating to the inventory gives the bank a continuously perfected security interest in the accounts receivable that are proceeds. To illustrate a possible priority problem relating to such accounts, suppose that First Bank loans money to Carl's Appliances. To secure repayment, First Bank takes a security interest in Carl's present and after-acquired inventory including proceeds, and files a financing statement covering the transaction on June 1. Subsequently, Carl's finds itself short of cash and approaches Sec-

ond Bank for a loan. Second Bank loans the money, taking a security interest in Carl's accounts receivable generated by the sale of its inventory. Second Bank files a financing statement on October 1 to perfect its interest in the accounts. Subsequently, Carl's defaults on both loans and both First Bank and Second Bank claim an interest in the accounts. Because this situation is not explicitly addressed in other Article 9 provisions, §9-312(5)(a), the general rule governing priority between two perfected secured parties, applies. In determining priority, this rule gives each secured party the earlier of two dates: its date of filing or the date it perfected its security interest. In the above example, First Bank both perfected and filed on June 1; Second Bank both perfected and filed on October 1. First Bank therefore prevails in the contest over the accounts receivable. Second Bank has little room to complain in this case because a simple check of the public records before loaning money to Carl's would have uncovered First Bank's financing statement indicating a security interest in the accounts.

This rule appears to favor the inventory financier, who has often been financing the debtor's inventory over a long period of time resulting in a much earlier filing date. Note, however, that accounts and inventory financing are often undertaken separately. Thus, the earlier filing may very well belong to a financial institution that has been financing the merchant solely on the basis of accounts claiming no interest in the underlying inventory. In this case, the original accounts financier would have priority in the accounts over a subsequent inventory financier claiming the accounts as proceeds.

Chattel Paper. Section 9-308(b) resolves a commonly encountered priority problem relating to chattel paper as proceeds of the sale of inventory subject to a security interest. The rule provides that a purchaser of chattel paper or an instrument, who gives new value and takes possession of it in the ordinary course of the purchaser's business, has priority over a security interest in the chattel paper or instrument that is claimed merely as *proceeds of the sale of inventory* subject to a security interest, even though the purchaser knows that the specific paper or instrument is subject to the security inter-

---

6. UCC §9-306(3)(b). See §9-306(4) for the specifics of a secured party's rights in identifiable proceeds.

est. To illustrate the operation of this rule, assume as before that First Bank loans money to Carl's Appliances and acquires a floating lien including proceeds in Carl's inventory, perfected by filing. Carl's sells microwave ovens on credit to customers using a conditional sales contract giving Carl's a security interest in the goods sold. Carl's, in need of cash, then sells the conditional sales contracts to Discounters, a finance company. Discounters pays cash (gives value) and takes possession of the paper with knowledge that the paper is subject to First Bank's security interest.

If Carl's subsequently defaults upon its loan, First Bank may attempt to claim an interest in the chattel paper in Discounter's hands as proceeds of the sale of inventory subject to its security interest. In this case, Discounters' claim to the paper as a purchaser will prevail over the bank's claim to the paper as proceeds. Therefore, persons in the business of buying chattel paper are protected without examining the public record, a result consistent with ordinary business expectations. This rule gives the debtor a ready market for its paper, and therefore indirectly benefits a secured party holding a floating lien. That is, §9-308(b) makes it easier for the debtor (Carl's) to convert the proceeds to cash that can be used to pay off the loan or buy more inventory subject to the bank's interest.

It is important to note the distinction between §9-308(b) and §9-308(a). The secured party is afforded greater protection in §9-308(a)—the purchaser prevails only if it takes without knowledge of the secured party's interest—because in that situation, the chattel paper in question *is* the underlying collateral securing the debt. The paper is left in the debtor's possession primarily to facilitate collection. In §9-308(b), however, the chattel paper is claimed merely as proceeds of the sale of inventory subject to a security interest. The inventory, not the paper, provides the primary security in this case.

Trade-In. Frequently, part of the consideration for the sale of inventory will be a trade-in. For example, a buyer in the ordinary course of business may purchase a new television set and pay for it partly in cash and partly with a trade-in of the old set. The old set is proceeds of the sale of inventory subject to a security interest. The trade-in item then becomes inventory in the debtor's hands subject to the bank's security interest.

Barter. Occasionally, part of the consideration for the sale of inventory is a bartered item. For example, assume Fred's Video sells a video cassette recorder to a buyer, and the buyer pays for the item by transferring a used car to Fred's Video, which Fred's plans to use in its business. In this case, the secured party must assure itself that its filing with respect to the inventory is a proper means of perfection with respect to the bartered item. In the above example, the car is now equipment in the hands of Fred's. Filing is an appropriate means of perfecting an interest in equipment. In this example, however, because the bartered item has a title document, the proper means of perfection is to note the security interest on the title document, which the secured party should do. Further, the secured party should assure itself that it has filed its financing statement in the proper office for the type of property that the bartered item represents.

Conflicting Security Interests in the Same Collateral

The following material discusses two important rules governing priority between the holder of the floating lien in inventory or equipment and other creditors holding a conflicting security interest in the same collateral.

Purchase Money Security Interests in Inventory—§9-312(3). The secured party polices the floating lien arrangement by periodically counting the debtor's inventory. This policing effort can be defeated by a dishonest debtor who purchases additional inventory, not for cash, but on credit from a supplier, giving the supplier a purchase money security interest in the inventory sold. In this manner, when the original secured party counts the inventory, the level is high. Unknown to the secured party, however, some or all of the inventory is subject to a security interest of the purchase money supplier. If the debtor subsequently goes bankrupt or absconds, a priority contest arises between the bank's floating lien on after-acquired inventory and the supplier's purchase money security interest in that inventory.

Section 9-312(3) resolves this conflict as follows. The purchase money supplier of the inventory will prevail over the bank's after-acquired clause if the supplier (1) perfects its interest by filing a financing statement covering the inventory, *and* (2) gives written notice to the prior secured party that it has or expects to acquire a purchase money security interest in the debtor's inventory. Both the perfection and the notice must occur *before* the debtor receives possession of the inventory from the supplier. Note that the notice to the prior party is, like a financing statement, valid for five years. Thus, once notice is given, the supplier can continue to sell on a purchase money basis for five years and defeat any claim to the inventory under the prior secured party's after-acquired property clause.

To illustrate, assume that First Bank loans money to Red's Radio and acquires a floating lien in Red's inventory, which is perfected by filing. Rather than pumping the proceeds of the sale of inventory back into the business, Red instead pockets the money. To keep the inventory level high and avoid alerting First Bank of any problem, Red approaches Ace Electronics, a manufacturer of radios, and purchases radios on credit giving Ace a purchase money security interest in the radios to secure the payment of the purchase price. As a result, when First Bank counts the inventory, the level remains high, in spite of Red's excessive extraction.

When the underlying loans to Ace and First Bank are not repaid, both parties claim an interest in Red's inventory (Ace on the basis of its purchase money security interest and First Bank on the basis of its after-acquired clause). In this context First Bank will win unless Ace both perfects its interest by filing (note that the bank's interest is already perfected) and notifies the bank in writing before it delivers the inventory to Red's.

The foregoing rule benefits all parties to the transaction. The bank holding the floating lien enjoys a priority in the inventory shipped on a purchase money basis unless the supplier meets the requirements outlined above. Once notified of its debtor's attempt to buy inventory on credit, it can proceed to ascertain the reason for excessive extraction. The purchase money inventory supplier who meets the §9-312(3) requirements obtains a priority over a *prior perfected* security interest in inventory. Section 9-312(3) also allows the debtor

to give a purchase money supplier a security interest in the inventory, which enjoys a priority over a prior secured lender. Without such a rule an honest debtor's ability to obtain additional credit would be severely limited if a prior secured lender insists upon retaining a floating lien on the debtor's inventory but refuses to advance additional money.

Consignments. A device often used in inventory financing having important secured transactions implications is the consignment. A **consignment** may be succinctly defined as a bailment[7] for sale. In a consignment, the owner of the goods (the "consignor"), who retains title, delivers possession of them to the "consignee." The consignee, who is commonly a merchant dealing in goods of the kind, then attempts to sell the consigned goods. Consignments may be either: (1) "intended as security" or (2) "true." In a **consignment intended as security,** the bailee-consignee assumes initial responsibility for the purchase price of the goods, whether or not he or she sells or otherwise disposes of them. This type of consignment is functionally equivalent to the conditional sale discussed above. That is, a debtor-creditor relationship exists between the parties with a reservation of title in the seller to secure payment of the purchase price of goods in the consignee's possession. Because the transaction is intended to create a security interest in personal property, it is, of course, governed by Article 9.

In contrast, a **true consignment** is a principal-agent relationship. The consignee is merely the consignor's agent for the purpose of selling the consigned goods to third parties. In a true consignment, the title remains in the consignor, but the consignee does not undertake an absolute obligation to pay for them upon receipt of the goods. That is, the true consignee is not a buyer, but merely an agent, who may return unsold goods. Upon a sale of consigned goods, title moves from the consignor to the purchaser. The consignee becomes liable to pay for them only upon a sale, appropriation to his own use, or violation of the agency contract.

Either type of consignment creates a "secret lien" against other creditors of the consignee. In

---

7. Bailments are discussed in detail in Chapter 35.

other words, consigned goods in the possession of and apparently owned by the consignee are likely to mislead other creditors concerning the consignee's financial position. For this reason, many disputes have arisen between consignors and the consignee's creditors upon insolvency of the consignee.

Priority rules resolving such disputes are contained in UCC Section 2-326(3) and in various provisions of Article 9.[8] Although the precise relationship among these provisions is far from clear, it is apparent that most consignments, whether intended for security or not, are governed by Article 9. That is, the Code effectively abolishes the "secret lien" aspect of a consignment by requiring that all consignors provide some public notice of the consignment—usually by filing a financing statement—to obtain priority in the consigned goods over other creditors of the consignee.

For example, §2-326 provides that goods delivered on a true consignment to a merchant dealing in goods of the kind are subject to the claims of the consignee's (merchant's) creditors unless the consignor (1) complies with an applicable law providing for a consignor's interest to be evidenced by a sign (a "sign statute"), or (2) establishes that the merchant is generally known by its creditors to be substantially engaged in selling goods of others, or (3) complies with the filing requirements of Article 9. The first two requirements have virtually never been applied in decided cases. Thus, filing an Article 9 financing statement is the sole practical method of protecting the consignor's interest in the goods against other creditors' claims.

Further, if the consignee is already financing inventory under a floating lien, the consignor must do more than merely file to be protected. Assume Monty ships television sets to Roberta, a dealer, under a true consignment arrangement. Roberta finances her inventory through First Bank, which holds a floating lien in Roberta's inventory. Monty obtains a priority in the consigned inventory over First Bank only by complying with §9-114, which imposes notice and filing requirements virtually identical to those imposed under §9-312(3) discussed above. That is, the consignor prevails only

by filing a financing statement and notifying the prior secured party before delivering the consigned goods to the merchant.

Non-inventory Purchase Money Security Interests—§9-312(4). Section 9-312(4) provides a rule governing purchase money security interests in collateral other than inventory. In this situation, a purchase money supplier—usually of equipment—has priority over a prior secured party's after-acquired clause if the purchase money security interest is perfected at the time the debtor receives possession of the collateral, or within ten days thereafter. This provision differs in two important respects from the inventory rule previously discussed. First, a ten-day grace period for perfection is provided. This approach is consistent with the ten-day period generally applicable to purchase money security interests. Second, no notice to the prior secured party is required.

To illustrate the operation of §9-312(4) assume Rachel's Discount store borrows money from First Bank, giving the bank a security interest in its equipment (for example, counters, repair equipment, delivery, and service trucks) plus after-acquired equipment. First Bank perfects its interest by filing. Rachel's buys a typewriter on credit for use in its business from Alpha Business Supply, which takes a purchase money security interest to secure the price. If Rachel's defaults on all loans, Alpha will have priority in the typewriter over the bank proceeding under its after-acquired equipment clause if Alpha's interest is perfected (by filing) at the time Rachel's receives possession of the equipment *or* within ten days thereafter. Alpha is not required to notify First Bank. In the following case, the court was required to determine when the debtor received possession of the collateral for purposes of applying §9-312(4).

In re Acme Motors, Inc.

68 B.R. 701 (Bkrtcy. D.R.I. 1986)

Acme Motors, Inc. contracted to lease a telephone system from CIT Financial Services Corporation, which retained a purchase money security interest. Tele-Dynamics, Inc. delivered the system, began installation on November 12, and completed instal-

---

8. UCC §2-326 is discussed in general in Chapter 17. Article 9 provisions include §§9-102, 9-114, and 9-408.

lation on November 13, 1985. On Monday, November 25, 1985, CIT filed a UCC financing statement describing its purchase money security interest in the telephone system and in any proceeds from the sale of the system. After Acme later filed for bankruptcy, the telephone system was sold for $12,000, which was held in escrow by order of the bankruptcy court. CIT claimed that it was entitled to the proceeds in accordance with the purchase money security interest and financing statement. William and Irving Gabrilowitz, who were secured creditors of Acme, asserted that CIT's security interest was invalid because it was not properly perfected.

Votolato, Bankruptcy Judge

. . . To perfect a security interest in equipment, a financing statement must be filed, . . . and the priority of competing security interests is governed by [UCC §9-312]. . . . Subsection four states:

> (4) A purchase money security interest in collateral other than inventory has priority over a conflicting security interest in the same collateral or its proceeds if the purchase money security interest is perfected at the time the debtor receives possession of the collateral or within ten (10) days thereafter.

If CIT's purchase money security interest is properly perfected, it takes priority over the Gabrilowitz's secured claim in the amount of $329,763 . . . and, of course, over unperfected security interests. . . .

The Gabrilowitzs argue that the correct date for determining the time period within which CIT could perfect its security interest is November 12, when installation of the system was commenced. They reason that "[i]f there was installation on November 12, 1985, there must have been delivery on or before November 12, 1985. Further, if Acme received *possession* of the collateral on November 12, 1985, the 10-day filing period would have begun on November 12, 1985 and would have expired on Friday, November 22, 1985." . . . They rely upon *In re Automated Bookbinding Services, Inc.*, 471 F.2d 546 (4th Cir. 1972). In that case the debtor entered into a contract to purchase a bookbinding machine whose component parts were delivered during the period May 26 to June 2,

1970. . . . The contract provided for a purchase price of $84,265 for the machine, and a separate installation charge of $2160. Installation began on May 27, and the purchaser acknowledged satisfactory completion of installation on June 18. The financing statement was filed on June 15. . . . The court held that the ten day period allowed by §9-312(4) within which to file the [financing statement] began to run on June 2, when the purchaser received possesion of the last shipment of component parts for the machine. Since the financing statement was filed more than ten days after June 2, the court held that the supplier of the machinery lost "its favored position under §9-312(4)" and that the holder of the security interest through an after acquired property clause was entitled to the equipment. . . .

We agree with [*Automated Bookbinding*] . . . that possession of the collateral is the controlling factor for determining the beginning of the ten day filing period of [UCC §9-312(4)]. However, [*Automated Bookbinding*] is clearly distinguishable from the case at bar. . . . [I]n *Automated Bookbinding*, there were two transactions—(1) an agreement to purchase the machine and (2) a separate contract to install it. In the instant matter we have a single contract covering both the delivery and installation of the telephone system. . . . [W]e conclude that the agreement contemplated that Acme Motors obtain possession of an operating telephone system to be installed by the supplier, Tele-Dynamics, Inc. Since the supplier is not the secured party, it has no interest in being able to manipulate the period within which to file the financing statement. It was the ability of the secured party to affect the filing date which concerned the *Automated Bookbinding* court. . . . [The court] was concerned with the policy of disclosure underlying Article 9, which allows prospective lenders to learn of any preexisting security interests before they extend credit. The court stated that if possession were defined "as requiring completion of tender of delivery terms . . . a secured creditor [could] delay performance of a tender of delivery term, and thereby avoid the filing requirement indefinitely." [471 F.2d at 553.] In that case such a holding would have given the secured party a twenty-six day period after the purchaser acquired possession, within which to perfect the security interest, from

June 2 to June 28. That concern is not present in the instant matter. . . . Here, CIT, the secured creditor, and Tele-Dynamics, Inc., the supplier-installer, are separate entities. The ability to affect the "tender of delivery" and, in turn delay the time for filing the security interest, are not in the same hands, as they were [in *Automated Bookbinding*]. . . . [T]he purposes of Article 9 will not be frustrated by a holding that CIT's security interest was recorded in time. Accordingly, we conclude that Acme Motors, Inc. received possession of the collateral on November 13, 1985, when the installation of the telephone system was complete, and not until then. . . .

A determination that Acme Motors received possession on November 13 does not fully resolve this dispute, however, since CIT filed its financing statement with the Secretary of State on *Monday*, November 25, 1985, twelve days after delivery. As to this, CIT argues that because the tenth day after Acme Motors received possession, November 23, was a Saturday, when the Secretary of State's office was closed, a Monday filing is permitted. . . . R.I.GEN.LAWS §25-1-5 (1985 Reenactment) provides:

> 25-1-5. Saturday closing of public offices. If any state . . . administrative offices, or any branch, division or independent agency thereof, shall close on any Saturday pursuant to the provisions of this section, any act which would otherwise be required to be performed on any such Saturday at or by such administrative office . . . if such administrative office . . . were not so closed, shall be so performed on the next succeeding business day. . . . No liability or loss of rights of any kind shall result from the failure to perform any of such acts on any such Saturday.

Since the last day for CIT to perfect its security interests fell on Saturday, §25-1-5 protects CIT from a "loss of rights of any kind . . . from the failure to perform any of such acts on any such Saturday." At least one other court has followed an approach similar to this in interpreting the interplay between U.C.C. §9-312(4) and a state statute dealing with official offices closed on the last day for perfecting a purchase money security interest. . . . To hold otherwise would, impermissibly,

in our view, establish a nine-day period within which to perfect a purchase money security interest under . . . [UCC §§9-302 and 9-312(4)] whenever the tenth day fell on a Saturday.

Accordingly, we find that Acme Motors received possession of the completed telephone system on November 13, 1985, and conclude that CIT's filing of its financing statement in the office of the Secretary of State on November 25, 1985, gave it a perfected security interest in the collateral, which continues in the proceeds of the collateral currently held in escrow by order of this Court. . . .

Priorities in Fixtures and Accessions

Fixture Priorities—§9-313

Security interests in real property (mortgages) are governed by state law outside the UCC. A public "recording" system similar to, but separate from, Article 9's filing system exists for real property interests including mortgages. That is, persons holding security interests in real property (mortgagees) provide public notice of their interest by recording it in a public office, usually the County Recorder of Deeds.[9]

Although real estate priorities are generally determined by non-Code law, Article 9 does address one important security issue affecting real property—the priority between personal property security interests in fixtures and persons holding an interest in the land to which the fixture is attached. A fixture is an item of personal property that has become so closely related to particular real estate that it is treated in law as part of the land. The following discussion assumes that the disputed property has become a fixture under the state property law principles discussed in Chapter 34.

Fixture priorities are governed by §9-313, which initially introduces the "fixture filing" concept. A fixture filing may be required to provide protection against certain real estate interests. Under §9-313(1)(b), a **fixture filing** involves filing a financ-

---

9. Mortgages and the operation of the real property recording system are discussed in detail in Chapter 37.

ing statement in the office where a mortgage on the underlying real estate would be recorded covering goods that are or are to become fixtures. Under §9-402(5), the financing statement in this case must state that it covers fixtures, recite that it is to be filed for record in the real estate records, and contain a description of the real estate. If the debtor is not the owner of the land (for example, a lessee), the record owner's name also must be included.

Note that a fixture filing, when required, protects the secured party against claims of persons who hold an interest in the *real property* and claim the fixture as part of that property. An ordinary filing that complies with §9-401(1) protects the secured party against everyone else. Because a fixture filing is filed for record and indexed, it assures that any person examining the real estate records will discover the secured party's interest.

Given this basic background, three common priority disputes governed by §9-313 are illustrated below using the following example. Assume Tom owns a house. The house is in need of a new furnace, but Tom is short of cash. Accordingly, he approaches Joe's Plumbing and Heating, which agrees to install a new furnace on credit, taking a security interest in the furnace to secure payment of the purchase price. In the following discussion Joe's will be referred to as the "fixture financier."

Fixture Financier v. Lien Creditor. Assume Tom fails to pay off the loan and subsequently goes bankrupt. Tom's trustee in bankruptcy (a lien creditor) claims the furnace for the benefit of all creditors. Under §9-313(4)(d), a fixture financier prevails over any person becoming a lien creditor after the security interest is perfected by any method permitted by Article 9—for example, an ordinary filing or automatic perfection of a purchase money security interest in consumer goods. Fixture filing is not required to defeat a lien creditor, because lien creditors, such as judgment creditors and the trustee in bankruptcy, do not extend credit in reliance upon the real estate records. Thus, Joe's would prevail over Tom's bankruptcy trustee if his interest is perfected by any method before the bankruptcy petition is filed.

Fixture Financier v. Mortgagee. Assume that prior to Joe's installation of the furnace Tom had

borrowed money to buy the house from First Bank. Tom gave First Bank a mortgage on the house to secure repayment which First Bank properly recorded. After installation of the furnace, Tom borrowed additional funds from Second Bank, giving Second Bank a mortgage on the house, which the bank recorded. If Tom later defaults on all three loans, Section 9-313 determines who has the benefit of the furnace. It adopts two different rules, one applicable to prior real estate interests (here First Bank) and the other applicable to subsequent real estate interests (here Second Bank). To defeat a pre-existing real estate interest, four requirements, stated in §9-313(4)(a), must be met: (1) the security interest in fixtures must be a purchase money security interest; (2) the interest must be perfected by fixture filing; (3) the filing must be made before the goods become fixtures or within ten days thereafter; and (4) the debtor must have a record interest in or be in possession of the real estate. In the above example, therefore, Joe's will prevail over First Bank if it made a fixture filing covering the furnace within ten days after it was installed in Tom's house. This rule, which gives the fixture financier priority over a prior real estate interest, promotes the availability of short-term credit for modernization and improvement of the real estate. These improvements, once paid for, ultimately benefit the long-term real estate lenders.

Concerning subsequent real estate interests, §9-313(4)(b) provides that the first secured party to file or record prevails. The fixture financier must perfect by fixture filing. In the above example, therefore, Joe's will prevail against Second Bank if it perfects by fixture filing before Second Bank records its mortgage.[10]

Fixture Financier v. Buyer of Real Estate. The priority between the fixture financier and a subsequent buyer of the real estate from the debtor is governed by the general "first to file or record" rule explained above. Thus, Joe's would prevail against a buyer of the house in which the furnace is installed if its security interest is perfected by fixture filing before the buyer recorded his deed.

---

10. No ten-day grace period for filing is provided in this case. Whoever records or files first wins. The ten-day period provides protection only against *prior* real estate interests.

Accession Priorities—§9-314

Section 9-314 provides the priority rule determining when a secured party claiming an interest in accessions—goods installed in or affixed to other goods—is entitled to priority over a person holding a security interest in the whole. As a general rule a security interest that attaches to the collateral before it is affixed to the whole has priority over a security interest in the whole existing at the time of affixation. Perfection is not required; protection against a conflicting interest in the whole is provided merely by attachment.[11] Under §9-314(3), however, the security interest must be perfected to protect the secured party against the following third parties who have no knowledge of the security interest in accessions: (1) a subsequent purchaser for value of any interest in the whole, (2) a creditor (such as a judgment creditor or trustee in bankruptcy) who subsequently obtains a lien upon the whole by judicial proceedings, and (3) a creditor with a prior perfected security in the whole to the extent that he makes subsequent advances.

Assume Jane owns a marina and uses a large boat as part of her business equipment. First Bank has a perfected security interest in the boat to secure a loan owed by Jane to the bank. The diesel engine in the boat malfunctions and Jane replaces it with one manufactured and installed by Caterpillar Tractor, Inc. Jane purchases the engine on credit, giving Caterpillar a security interest in the engine which fully attaches before Caterpillar installs the engine. Assuming Jane defaults on both the Caterpillar and First Bank loans, Caterpillar has a superior claim to the engine over First Bank and may remove it from the boat. Caterpillar should, however, perfect its interest—for example, by filing a financing statement covering the engine—to protect itself against a purchaser of the boat who is unaware of Caterpillar's interest, or a creditor who obtains a lien upon the boat by judicial proceedings without knowledge of Caterpillar's interest. In addition, if Caterpillar's interest is not perfected and

First Bank has no actual knowledge of it, First Bank, as a prior perfected secured party in the whole, enjoys a priority in the engine to the extent it loans additional money secured by the boat after the engine is installed. In short, the prudent creditor with a security interest in accessions should perfect its interest.

Note finally that if the whole is subject to a security interest, the owner may place his own accessions upon it. For example, an owner may buy tires for cash and place them on a car that is subject to a security interest in favor of a bank. In this case the accessions simply become part of the car and provide added collateral to the holder of the security interest in the whole.

Special Topics

Field Warehousing

A security device commonly used in inventory financing is a field warehouse. Field warehousing uses warehouse receipts covering inventory to provide a secured lender with effective control over disposition of the debtor's inventory.

To illustrate warehouse receipts financing, assume that Doaks Novelties, Inc., a manufacturer of Christmas decorations, needs working capital to finance its operations during the off-season summer months. Doaks therefore approaches First Bank for a loan, proposing to use its large inventory of Christmas lights as collateral. First Bank agrees, but desires complete control over the inventory but does not, of course, want to take possession. Doaks therefore transports the inventory to Gray's Terminal Storage, Inc., a commercial warehouse. Gray's issues a negotiable warehouse receipt to Doaks covering the inventory, which Doaks then pledges to the bank as collateral on the loan. First Bank is protected because it now possesses the warehouse receipt and Gray's will not surrender the inventory without it.

Although this arrangement provides significant protection to the secured party, it has distinct disadvantages for the debtor. For example, the debtor incurs substantial time and expense in transporting inventory to and from the warehouse and must pay storage charges. Additionally, the inventory is not immediately available to the debtor when needed

---

11. A security interest that attaches to the goods *after* they become part of the chattel is subordinate to a pre-existing security interest in the chattel unless the prior secured party in writing consents to the security interest or disclaims any interest in the accessions. UCC §9-314(2).

for sale or to finish work on it. These problems are resolved by using a field warehouse arrangement. Simply stated, **field warehousing** involves the creation of a warehouse on the debtor's premises—the "field" warehouse—into which inventory is placed. Warehouse receipts are issued from this warehouse, which are then used by the debtor as collateral on the loan.

To create a field warehouse the debtor must first obtain a warehouseman, who must be independent of the debtor. Several commercial warehouse companies specialize in field warehouse arrangements. Space on the debtor's property is then selected as the site for the warehouse, and leased to the warehouse company, usually at a nominal rent. The warehouse company then segregates the leased area by setting up fences, locks, and gates to establish control over the property within the field warehouse, and hires a warehouse manager. The manager, who is covered by a fidelity bond and is usually an employee of the debtor, is authorized to issue warehouse receipts and is instructed when to allow inventory out of the warehouse.

Once established, the debtor stores inventory in the field warehouse and receives warehouse receipts, which are used as collateral to secure a loan. The bank may police the stored inventory loosely or strictly depending upon its arrangement with the debtor. Although the warehouse receipts may be negotiable, nonnegotiable receipts are more commonly used because they do not have to be obtained from the bank and surrendered to the warehouseman each time inventory is removed from the warehouse. Rather, the lender gives the warehouse company written instructions outlining the circumstances under which inventory is to be released.

Courts often have invalidated field warehousing arrangements either because the warehouseman was not independent of the debtor or had not established actual and exclusive control over the stored inventory. In many of these cases, the field warehouse lender had perfected its security interest only in the now invalid documents (for example, by taking possession of negotiable warehouse receipts). As a result, the lender was left with an unperfected security interest in the underlying inventory. For this reason, a field warehouse should be used as a policing device, not an independent method of creating and perfecting a security interest in the stored inventory. To be protected against other creditors claiming an interest in the stored inventory if the field warehouse is ruled invalid, the secured party always should obtain a written security agreement covering the inventory and perfect its interest in that inventory by filing a financing statement.

Security Interests as Preferences in Bankruptcy

Because a perfected secured party enjoys a preferred position in the debtor's bankruptcy, a security interest perfected shortly before bankruptcy to secure an old debt may effectively prefer the secured creditor over other creditors of the debtor. That is, if the interest is recognized in bankruptcy, the secured creditor is preferred in the same manner as if the debtor had sold the underlying property and then paid the creditor directly.

To prevent this result, the federal Bankruptcy Code provides that the creation of a security interest in the debtor's property, like an outright transfer of that property, may constitute a voidable preference. Specifically, the trustee in bankruptcy may avoid security interests that secure antecedent debts and that are perfected or recorded within 90 days prior to bankruptcy. That is, for security interests, the date of the transfer (date 2 in basic preference analysis) is generally the date on which a mortgagee records its mortgage (if the security interest is a real property mortgage) or the date on which the secured party files a financing statement (if the security interest is created in personal property governed by Article 9 of the UCC).[12]

Assume that on January 1, Alan, Bob, and Chris each ships $10,000 worth of goods to Donna on open account for use in her business. Donna makes no payment on these accounts during the next 6 months. On July 1, when Donna's only remaining assets are equipment worth $10,000 and $10,000 cash, she gives Alan a security interest in the equipment to secure his $10,000 debt. Alan promptly files a financing statement. On August 1, Donna declares bankruptcy. On these facts, Alan's security interest constitutes a preference. The date of the transfer (date 2) is July 1, the date of filing. The date of transfer (July 1) follows the date of the debt it secures (January 1) creating the essence of

---

12. 11 U.S.C. §547(e)(1).

a preference—transfer to a creditor on account of an antecedent debt. The date of bankruptcy (August 1) follows the transfer (occurring on July 1) by less than 90 days resulting in a voidable preference.

To protect bona fide secured parties who delay, through inadvertence or otherwise, in perfecting their security interests, the Bankruptcy Code provides a ten-day "grace period" after the debt in which to file or record the security interest. If the interest is perfected by filing or recording within the ten-day period, the date of transfer "relates back" to the date of the debt; thus, there is no transfer on account of an antecedent debt, and therefore no preference.[13] Assume that on June 1, Cathy loans $10,000 to Donald, secured by Donald's equipment. If Cathy files a financing statement within ten days after June 1, her security interest may not be avoided as a preference. If, however, Cathy delays filing her financing statement until June 15, and Donald goes bankrupt within ninety days after June 15, the trustee in bankruptcy will be able to avoid Cathy's security interest as a preference. A prudent secured lender, therefore, whether in real or personal property, should always take steps to perfect his interest within ten days after the debt is created to avoid potential preference attack.

When the trustee avoids an outright transfer as a preference, the property is recovered from the transferee and becomes property of the estate. When the trustee avoids a preferential security interest, the property simply enters the estate free of any lien. The preferred creditor, as in absolute transfers, then files a claim against the estate for the amount of the debt and receives the same distribution from the estate as other creditors of his class.

The "Floating Lien" as a Preference.

Though it is an extremely useful financing tool, the "floating lien" in inventory discussed earlier in this chapter may operate unfairly to prefer its holder over other creditors if the debtor is allowed to build up its inventory shortly before bankruptcy. Although under UCC §9-108, the mere existence of a secured party's floating lien does not create a preference, the Bankruptcy Code provides[14] that a creditor holding a floating lien is subject to preference attack to the extent that it improves its position during the ninety-day period preceding bankruptcy. This "improvement in position" test requires a determination of the creditor's position ninety days before the petition and on the date the petition is filed. The creditor's "position" is computed by subtracting the value of the collateral from the amount of the debt, yielding the amount of unsecured debt. A creditor improves its position to the extent the amount of unsecured debt is reduced. Assume Dan, an appliance dealer, files for bankruptcy on June 1. On that date, Dan owes First Bank $85,000 secured by a floating lien in his inventory, which is worth $70,000. Ninety days prior to bankruptcy, the outstanding loan was $100,000 secured by $50,000 in inventory. First Bank has improved its position during the ninety days preceding bankruptcy and has therefore received a voidable preference of $35,000 computed as follows:

	90 days prior to bankruptcy	Date of bankruptcy	
Amount of debt	$100,000	$85,000	
Amount of collateral	⟨50,000⟩	⟨70,000⟩	
Amount of unsecured debt	$ 50,000	− $15,000	= $35,000—amount of voidable preference

In this case, therefore, the trustee in bankruptcy is able to avoid $35,000 of First Bank's $70,000 security interest in Don's inventory. Thus, the bank will file an $85,000 claim against the estate, $35,000 of which is secured by Don's inventory. Regarding the remaining $50,000, First Bank is a general creditor and will receive the same percentage on the dollar as other general creditors. Note that the bank is relegated to the same position it occupied 90 days before bankruptcy—$50,000 of its loan is not secured.

---

13. 11 U.S.C. §547(e)(2).

14. 11 U.S.C. §547(c)(5).

SUMMARY

1. Like much of debtor-creditor law, Article 9 is primarily concerned with resolving priority disputes among creditors competing for the limited assets of debtors who default. Analysis of the general rules of priority reveals that unperfected security interests have priority over general creditors, but are subordinate to most other third-party claimants to the collateral, including the debtor's trustee in bankruptcy. Perfected interests, on the other hand, defeat most third-party claims.

2. Inventory financing is often conducted by using a "floating lien," under which the secured party loans money and to secure repayment takes a security interest in all the debtor's inventory, both presently existing and after-acquired. The UCC broadly validates such after-acquired property clauses and then systematically resolves the various priority disputes they create.

3. When a merchant finances its inventory using a floating lien, the merchant's customers who buy the inventory, "buyers in the ordinary course of business," take the inventory free of the secured party's claim to it even though the security interest is perfected and the buyer knows of its existence. Although the secured party's claim to the inventory is thus extinguished upon sale, the security interest continues in the proceeds of sale, including cash, instruments, accounts receivable, chattel paper, trade-ins, or bartered items. Article 9 contains several provisions resolving disputes between the secured party and various third-party purchasers and creditors claiming an interest in these proceeds.

4. Suppliers of inventory and equipment often sell on credit taking a purchase money security interest in the goods sold. Article 9 allows the purchase money supplier of inventory to prevail in this case over a prior perfected floating lien in inventory provided it perfects its interest and notifies the prior secured party before delivering the inventory to the debtor. A similar rule applies to suppliers of inventory on consignment. The purchase money supplier of equipment prevails over a prior secured party merely by perfecting its interest within ten days after the debtor receives possession of the collateral.

5. Article 9 contains specialized provisions governing priority in fixtures and accessions. These provisions generally allow a creditor holding a security interest in fixtures attached to real property or in accessions incorporated into personal property to protect its interest against third-party purchasers or creditors asserting a claim to the collateral.

6. Field warehousing is a device using warehouse receipts as a method of providing a secured lender with effective control over disposition of the debtor's inventory. In field warehousing, a warehouse is created on the debtor's premises—the "field" warehouse—into which inventory is placed. Warehouse receipts are issued from this warehouse which are then used by the debtor as collateral on the loan.

7. Bankruptcy law prevents secured transactions from being used as an indirect method to give one creditor a preference. The law allows the trustee in bankruptcy to avoid security interests perfected within ninety days prior to bankruptcy that secure antecedent debts. The law also prevents the holder of a "floating lien" from improving its position (reducing the amount of unsecured debt) within the ninety days immediately preceding bankruptcy.

KEY TERMS

buyer in the ordinary course of business	recoupment cycle
after-acquired property clause	extraction
floating lien (floating charge)	consignment
floor planning	consignment intended as security
proceeds	true consignment
	fixture filing
	field warehousing

QUESTIONS AND PROBLEMS

32-1   Shepler borrowed money for plant expansion from Myertown Bank and executed a security agreement. The bank filed a financing statement that covered all "present and future inventory." Shepler was a dealer in farm machinery. Moline entered into a contract with Shepler whereby Moline appointed Shepler its franchise dealer for Moline farm machinery. The franchise provided that title to the farm machinery would remain in Moline until the purchase price was paid in full. The agreement was not filed or recorded. Shepler is now bankrupt. At the time of the adjudication of bankruptcy, Shepler had $15,000 worth of inventory delivered to him by Moline in his possession.

(a) Did the bank's security interest attach to the inventory?

(b) Was the description of the collateral insufficient?

(c) Was the bank's security interest valid only insofar as it was limited to Shepler's presently existing inventory?

(d) Was the bank's security interest unperfected because only the financing statement was filed, rather than the security agreement?

(e) Did Moline's security interest attach to the inventory shipped by Moline?

(f) Does Moline have a purchase money security interest?

(g) Does the bank have a purchase money security interest?

(h) Does Moline have a perfected security interest?

(i) As between Moline and the bank, who will have the benefit of the $15,000 of inventory?

32-2 Franklin Novelties borrowed $25,000 from Commercial Bank secured by certain chattel paper in the possession of Franklin. The paper in question was purchased by Franklin from various retailers and was treated by Franklin as a short-term investment. The bank filed a financing statement covering the transaction. Franklin finances its inventory through First State Bank. Because its products are expensive, Franklin routinely accepts conditional installment sales contracts for the sale of inventory evidencing both an obligation to pay the purchase price and creating a security interest in the item sold. First State Bank has filed a financing statement covering the inventory. Franklin is now in financial difficulty. In an effort to generate cash, Franklin sold all of the paper in its possession (that is, both held for investment and arising from the sale of inventory) to Money, Inc., a finance company. Money paid cash and took possession of the paper with full knowledge of Commercial Bank's and First State Bank's security interest.

(a) Does First State's security interest extend to the contracts which were generated by sale of the inventory?

(b) May Commercial Bank recover the paper from Money, Inc. to satisfy its debt?

(c) May First State Bank recover the paper from Money, Inc. to satisfy its debt?

32-3 Shady Characters, Inc. is a dealer in masks and magic supplies. Shady borrowed $90,000 from Regional Bank on June 1 to finance a purchase of inventory. Regional Bank took a security interest in inventory plus after-acquired inventory as well as Shady's equipment, both current and after-acquired. Regional Bank immediately filed a financing statement covering the transaction. Shady maintains open accounts with many of its large customers. In an effort to generate more working capital, Shady borrowed $10,000 from

Downstate Bank, using the accounts receivable as collateral to secure the loan. Downstate Bank immediately filed a financing statement on July 1. Shortly thereafter, Sam, owner of Shady, approached Monsters, Inc. and purchased $10,000 worth of masks on credit, giving Monsters a security interest in the masks to secure payment of the purchase price. Monsters made delivery on August 15 and filed a financing statement on August 16. On August 17, Sam then approached City Office Supply and purchased $10,000 worth of office equipment on credit giving City a security interest in the equipment to secure payment of the purchase price. City delivered on August 18 and filed a financing statement on August 30 covering the transaction. Shady, on October 1, was adjudicated a bankrupt. The trustee in bankruptcy now claims all inventory, accounts, and equipment to satisfy claims of general unsecured creditors, a sum in excess of $100,000. Assume Regional Bank's claim remains totally unpaid. Regional Bank asserts a security interest in all inventory and equipment on hand as well as the accounts receivable being used to secure the loan from Downstate Bank.

(a) As between Regional Bank and Downstate Bank, who has priority in the accounts? Explain, citing relevant Code sections.

(b) As between Regional Bank and Monsters, Inc., who has priority in the masks? Explain, citing relevant Code sections.

(c) As between Regional Bank and City Office Supply, who has priority in the equipment? Explain, citing relevant Code sections.

(d) Is Regional Bank's security interest valid against the trustee in bankruptcy? If so, in what collateral?

32-4 Donald purchased a 2.5 carat diamond ring from Mayor Jewelry Co. as an anniversary present for his wife Lorraine. Donald signed a written contract, agreeing to pay for the ring in forty-eight monthly installments and granted Mayor a security interest in the ring. Donald took possession of the ring. The owner of Mayor Jewelry Co. advised the store manager to be certain that she perfected the security interest immediately. The store manager did not file a financing statement.

(a) The owner of Mayor Jewelry Co. hears a rumor that Donald is about to go bankrupt. Mayor's owner asks the store manager if she has perfected the security interest and she replies ''Of course—there's nothing to worry about.'' Is she correct? Explain.

(b) Instead of giving the ring to his wife, Donald sells the ring for $10,000 to his friend Ronald who retains it for his own use. Prior to purchasing the ring, Ronald asks Donald if the ring is free and clear of all liens and Donald replies "Yes." One year later Donald declares bankruptcy still owing $7,500 to Mayor Jewelry Co. After Ronald refuses to give the ring to Mayor, Mayor sues Ronald. To whom should the court award possession of the ring? Explain. Would your answer be different if Mayor had filed a financing statement? Explain. (See UCC §9-307.)

(c) Instead of selling the ring to Ronald, Donald sells the ring to Acme Jewelers, a jewelry retailer. Donald declares bankruptcy still owing Mayor Jewelry Co. $7,500. Mayor sues Acme. To whom should the court award the ring? Explain. (See UCC §§9-306 and 9-307.)

(d) Instead of selling the ring, Donald gives it to his wife Lorraine as he had intended. Donald declares bankruptcy still owing Mayor $7,500. Mayor sues Lorraine. To whom should the court award possession of the ring?

(e) Instead of selling the ring or giving it to his wife, Donald uses the ring as collateral to borrow $10,000 from First National Bank. He signs a security agreement giving the bank a security interest in the ring. For safekeeping, the bank stores the ring in its vault. Donald declares bankruptcy. To whom should the court award the ring, Mayor Jewelry Co. or First National Bank? Would your answer be different if Mayor Jewelry Co. or First National Bank had filed a financing statement? (See UCC §9-312.)

32-5 A-1 Auto Sales, a retailer of new and used automobiles, has requested American State Bank to act as inventory financier. You are the bank's loan officer who has been assigned to handle the transaction. You have agreed to lend up to $100,000 to A-1 each month to purchase inventory and you also have agreed to allow A-1 to sell the inventory to its customers. To secure the loan, you require A-1 to grant American a security interest in all inventory it purchases with money obtained from American.

(a) How would you perfect the security interest? Explain and include in your explanation the exact description of the collateral that should be used in the financing statement.

(b) Describe the procedures you would use after

making the loan to ensure that A-1 complies with the terms of your agreement.

(c) Assume that A-1 sells to Carla one of the cars in the inventory purchased with the loan from American. Carla pays for the car with funds borrowed from Federal Bank pursuant to a written loan and security agreement. To secure the loan, Federal takes and perfects a security interest in the car. Federal then transfers $10,000, the cost of the car, to A-1 but A-1 fails to pay any of that amount to American. Carla defaults in paying Federal and Federal takes possession of the car. Meanwhile American learns of the sale to Carla and demands payment from A-1 who no longer has the money. You call an officer of Federal claiming a prior security interest in the car. Federal asserts that its security interest takes priority. Who is correct? Explain. (See UCC §§9-307 and 9-308.)

(d) A-1 has encountered financial difficulties and needs cash quickly. Jones, an officer of A-1, develops a scheme to obtain the money. He completes a purchase and security agreement showing a sale of a car to John Smith by which Smith promises to pay $10,000 to A-1 and grants a security interest in a car as security. Jones takes the agreement to Fidelity Loan Co., a company to which A-1 frequently sells chattel paper, which pays A-1 $7,500 for the contract. Fidelity perfects a security interest in the car. By the time Fidelity discovers that the transaction was a sham, Jones has left town and A-1 is bankrupt. During the bankruptcy proceeding, Fidelity discovers that the car described in the contract purchased from A-1 is listed among A-1's inventory. Fidelity requests that it be awarded possession of the car but American claims a prior security interest. To whom should the car be awarded? Explain, citing pertinent Code provisions and discussing any relevant policy issues.

(e) Although Fidelity wants to continue purchasing chattel paper from auto retailers, it also wants to avoid sham transactions such as the one by Jones. What procedures might Fidelity adopt to protect itself in the future?

32-6 On February 1, 1984, Herman purchased a computer from Computers Galore, a retailer. Herman paid the purchase price in full and requested delivery to his office on February 15. Computers Galore's inventory was financed by Second Bank and Trust which retained a security interest perfected in 1983 in all inventory and proceeds. The security agreement between the bank and Computers Galore allowed the retailer to sell the inventory. On February 12, 1984, Computers Galore defaulted in its payments to the bank and the bank took possession of all of the inventory of Computers Galore. Included in the inventory was the computer that Herman had purchased. Herman sued Second Bank and Trust demanding delivery of his computer. How should the court rule? Explain.

32-7 Nelson Company, a sporting goods manufacturer, is considering selling inventory to Haggett's Sport Shop on credit, retaining a security interest in the inventory. Nelson has searched the UCC filing system records and discovered a financing statement dated two years earlier showing that Haggett owed money to First State Bank. The financing statement states that the bank holds a security interest in "all accounts receivable and/or inventory in connection with a retail sporting goods shop."

(a) Nelson must determine whether to make the sale to Haggett. If Nelson takes a security interest in the items of inventory it sells to Haggett, will First State Bank's interest conflict with Haggett's?

(b) Suggest steps that Nelson might take to protect itself if it makes the sale.

32-8 Marina Boat Co. is a retailer of boats and sailing equipment. On June 1, 1982, Warner Bank agreed to act as Marina's primary inventory financier and took a security interest in all of Marina's inventory, including after-acquired inventory. Warner properly filed a financing statement the same day. On April 1, 1985, Crestliner Boat Builders sold Marina seven boats for its inventory pursuant to a written credit agreement by which Crestliner retained a purchase money security interest in the seven boats. Crestliner properly perfected its security interest on April 1 and delivered the boats to Marina on April 5. Prior to selling the boats to Marina, Crestliner had requested a search of the UCC records.

(a) The search of the UCC records had revealed Warner's security interest in inventory. On April 2, Crestliner provided a written notice to Warner notifying it that Crestliner was selling seven boats to Marina and was retaining a purchase money security in the boats. The notification included a description and serial number for each boat. On September 1, 1985, Marina declared bankruptcy. Both Warner and Crestliner claimed

a perfected security interest in the seven boats. Whose interest takes priority? Explain. See UCC §9-312.

(b) Disregard the facts stated in the preceding paragraph. Assume instead that Crestliner's search of the UCC records revealed no prior security interests. On May 1, Warner extended further credit to Marina, relying on its previously filed financing statement. On September 1, Marina declared bankruptcy. Both Warner and Crestliner claim a security interest in the seven boats. The evidence at trial reveals that the secretary of state had filed Warner's financing statement under "Warner Bank" instead of "Marina Boat Co." thus explaining why Crestliner's search had not revealed Warner's prior interest. To whom should the court award possession of the boats? Explain, including a discussion of the policy issues.

32-9 COF, Inc. sells several items of inventory to Sullivan, a retailer, retaining a security interest in the specified items of inventory and their proceeds. COF perfects its security interest and opens a special bank account into which Sullivan agrees to deposit the proceeds. Sullivan sells the inventory over a period of six months but deposits the proceeds in his own bank account rather than in the special account. Thus the proceeds become intermingled with money from other sales. Sullivan also pays other creditors from his bank account. COF sues Sullivan demanding payment of $20,000, the value of the inventory that it had sold to Sullivan. Sullivan's only assets are his inventory, which is subject to perfected security interests of other creditors, and $20,000 that is deposited in his bank account. In addition to his debt to COF, Sullivan owes approximately $30,000 to general creditors, who also have sued Sullivan. The court is attempting to determine to whom it should award the money in Sullivan's bank account.

(a) Consider §§9-306(1) and (2) of the UCC. Explain how COF could identify and trace the proceeds of the sale of the inventory it sold to Sullivan.

(b) Assume that in the period following Sullivan's sale of the inventory purchased from COF, Sullivan's bank account has always had a balance of at least $20,000. To whom should the court award the bank account?

(c) Assume instead that during the period following Sullivan's sale of the inventory purchased from COF, Sullivan's bank balance has fluctuated. At one time the balance was as low as $2,500. To whom should the court award the bank account?

32-10 On October 17, 1979, First Security Bank lent Elliot $10,000 to be used for renovating and redecorating a business he operated called "Elliot's Paint and Supply." Elliot executed a promissory note and security agreement granting First Security a security interest in all inventory, including after-acquired inventory. First Security perfected the security interest. Most of Elliot's inventory consisted of paint that he sold at retail. He purchased his paint inventory on open account from Absco, Inc. On the date of the bank loan Elliot's inventory was valued at $17,000. During the following year, the value of the inventory fluctuated between $15,000 and $20,000. In late November of 1980, a bank officer paid a routine visit to Elliot's Paint and Supply and discovered the store was closed and vacant. The bank later discovered that in early November, Elliot had returned paints valued at $12,000 to Absco for credit on his open account. First Security Bank sued Absco alleging that Absco had converted the bank's property. Absco alleged that the bank's security agreement with Elliot permitted him to "sell and dispose of the collateral in the ordinary course of business." Absco provided evidence showing that Elliot regularly returned slow-moving inventory to Absco for credit.

(a) Was Elliot's return of his paint inventory to Absco "in the ordinary course of business"?

(b) How should the court decide the case?

32-11 On June 30, 1968, Cudmore-Neiber Shoe Company sold a business known as "The Bootery" to Merlyn Pugh. Cudmore-Neiber financed the sale through an installment contract and retained a security interest in the business including inventory, accounts receivable, fixtures, and all after-acquired property. Cudmore-Neiber filed a financing statement in the county recorder's office on May 29, 1973, and in the secretary of state's office on June 17, 1975.

While Pugh was operating The Bootery, he purchased inventory from United States Shoe Company. Pugh defaulted in paying the purchase contract and Cudmore-Neiber repossessed the business on May 29, 1973. At that time, Pugh owed United States Shoe Company over $10,000.

United States Shoe Company sued Cudmore-Neiber alleging that its repossession of The Bootery was unlawful because Cudmore-Neiber had not perfected its security interest prior to the repossession. Is United States Shoe Company correct? Explain.

32-12 In 1981, Union State Bank loaned Cockrum a large sum of money to finance his farm and hog confinement operation. To secure repayment Union obtained and perfected a security interest in Cockrum's presently existing and after acquired equipment and farm products, including livestock. In 1983, Farmers Cooperative Elevator Company sold Cockrum livestock feed on credit, taking a purchase money security interest in the feed. Farmers perfected its interest by filing a financing statement when the feed was delivered to Cockrum. After Cockrum defaulted on both loans, Farmers claimed priority over Union Bank in Cockrum's remaining feed. Farmers also asserted that it was entitled to priority in Cockrum's hogs, which had eaten much of the feed, alleging that the hogs were "proceeds" of Farmers' collateral, the feed, and were automatically subject to Farmers' security interest under §9-203(3). Farmers argued that §9-306(1) defines proceeds to include whatever is received upon the sale, exchange, collection, or "other disposition" of the collateral, a definition broad enough to include hogs as proceeds of feed.

(a) Does Farmers have a priority over Union Bank in the feed remaining in Cockrum's possession? Explain.

(b) Does Farmers have a priority over Union Bank in the hogs which ate the feed supplied by Farmers? Explain.

32-13 Mr. and Mrs. Gerayne Poole operated Greenway Elevator Co., a grain elevator, in Clay County, Arkansas. On March 17, 1976, Corning Bank loaned money to the Pooles for the purchase of grain bins. Corning Bank took a security interest in the grain bins and filed a financing statement in the Clay County circuit clerk's office on March 19, 1976. The financing statement described the grain bins as "goods" to be retained at the place of business of Greenway Elevator Co., Post Office Box 94, Greenway, Arkansas. The financing statement contained no description of any real estate and no indication that the property described was attached to, or to become attached to land. Accordingly, the clerk filed the financing statement under the Pooles' name in the UCC records for security interests in goods; the instrument was not recorded or noted in the real estate records.

On May 17, 1976, Bank of Rector loaned money to the Pooles and recorded a mortgage showing that it held a security interest in the real estate on which Greenway Elevator Co. was located. The mortgage was filed in the county real estate records.

The Pooles subsequently defaulted in their loan payments to both banks and a dispute arose between Bank of Rector and Corning Bank as to who had a priority security interest in the grain bins. Bank of Rector argued that the bins constituted fixtures for which no proper financing statement had been filed and, therefore, the Bank of Rector was entitled to foreclose on the grain bins as a part of the real estate. Corning Bank argued that the grain bins were goods subject to its perfected security interest so that Corning Bank was entitled to the bins. Who is correct? Explain.

32-14 Assume you are a loan officer of First State Bank, which is considering lending money to Chips, Inc., a manufacturer of integrated circuits and other electronic components. Chips has proposed and the bank has accepted a field warehousing arrangement to provide security for a $500,000 loan. What steps would you take in the creation and operation of the field warehouse to provide maximum security to the bank in the event of Chips, Inc.'s default or bankruptcy?

32-15 On June 1, Barry borrowed $10,000 from Lois giving her a security interest in a valuable painting owned by Barry. Lois did not file a financing statement covering the transaction at that time. On August 1, she discovered that Barry was insolvent and immediately filed a financing statement. Barry filed a voluntary bankruptcy petition on September 1. Who will have the benefit of the painting, Lois or the trustee in bankruptcy? Explain. Would the trustee have the benefit of the painting if Barry's bankruptcy petition had been filed on December 15? Would the trustee have the benefit of the painting if Lois had filed her financing statement on June 9? Explain.

Chapter 33

Suretyship

In the secured transactions discussed in the preceding two chapters, the secured party has recourse to specific property belonging to the debtor if the debtor defaults upon the secured obligation. Instead of (or in addition to) a security interest in the debtor's property, security may also be provided by the promise of a third party (a surety) to perform the obligation if the debtor does not. Many legal issues arise in this situation that are resolved by the common law of *suretyship,* the subject of this chapter.[1]

Introduction to Suretyship

Suretyship is the legal relationship existing when

1. one party, the *principal,* is legally bound to a *creditor* who is entitled to but one satisfaction;
2. another party, the *surety,* has bound himself, by contract, to the creditor to perform the same acts for which the principal is liable; and
3. as between the two who are bound (principal and surety), the principal rather than the surety should perform.[2]

Thus, suretyship always involves at least three parties: the **principal,** the person for whose debt or default the surety is liable; the **creditor,** the person to whom both the surety and principal owe their duties; and the **surety,** the person liable on the debt or obligation of another, the principal. Although both the principal and surety are liable on the same obligation to the creditor, as between the two, the principal rather than the surety should perform. In other words, in suretyship the creditor has rights against both the principal and surety, but the surety

---

1. If a surety becomes bound upon a negotiable instrument, the rights and duties of the surety (known as an "accom-

modation party") are governed by Article 3 of the UCC and by the common law of suretyship that supplements Article 3 through UCC §1-103. Accommodation parties are discussed in Chapter 25.

2. *Restatement of Security* §82.

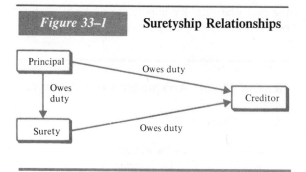

Figure 33–1   **Suretyship Relationships**

may shift the ultimate loss to the principal. This latter characteristic marks the arrangement as a suretyship. The relationship may therefore be characterized as shown in Figure 33–1. The principal's duty to the creditor is commonly called the "principal obligation," suggesting that its performance is secured by another promise, the surety's, known as a "collateral" or "accessorial" obligation.

To illustrate the typical case, assume Paula needs $10,000 to open a business. She, therefore, approaches Chris for a loan. Because of Paula's somewhat precarious financial condition, Chris agrees to loan the money only if Paula provides collateral or obtains a surety who will guarantee repayment of the loan. Because Paula has no (or insufficient) collateral, Paula convinces her rich aunt, Stella, to act as a surety. Stella promises Chris that if he will loan money to Paula, Stella will repay the loan if Paula fails to do so. Chris then loans the money to Paula. In Chris's eyes, both Paula and Stella are liable on the $10,000 debt, though Chris is entitled to only one recovery—that is, $10,000, not $20,000. As between Paula and Stella, however, Paula should pay.

Creation of Suretyship

Suretyship is usually created by express contract with the creditor in which the surety intends at the time of contracting to become a surety. The surety's promise may be made either in the same instrument evidencing the principal's contract or in a separate instrument. The surety may agree to guarantee all or merely a specified portion of the principal's obligation.

Ordinarily, the surety is obtained with the con-

sent of, or at the request of, the principal. Suretyship is not, however, dependent upon any agreement between the surety and principal that the principal should perform. The surety may have undertaken his or her obligation by dealing directly with the creditor without the consent or even knowledge of the principal.

In addition to express contract, suretyship may also arise by operation of law, as a consequence of new contractual relations with third parties. For example, a suretyship by operation of law is usually created after assignment of a contract. That is, in the absence of a novation, after an assignment that delegates a duty to perform, the assignee becomes the principal and the assignor becomes a surety guaranteeing the assignee's performance of the contract. A suretyship is created because two people, assignor and assignee, are liable on the same debt to a creditor, the other original party to the contract, who is entitled to but one performance. As between the two who are liable, however, one, the assignee, rather than the other, the assignor, should perform.[3]

Compensated and Uncompensated Sureties

The law of suretyship distinguishes between **compensated** or **corporate** sureties, and other sureties, commonly referred to as **accommodation, uncompensated,** or **gratuitous** sureties. A compensated surety, normally a corporation, is one engaged in the business of executing surety contracts for compensation known as a "premium." Premiums are determined by computing risk on an actuarial basis. Contracts executed by compensated sureties are commonly known as **bonds.** Common types of bonds are the **fidelity bond,** securing an employer against embezzlement or defalcation by an employee, and a **performance bond** securing an owner (commonly a governmental body) for the proper performance of a building construction contract by a contractor.

---

3. Assignment, delegation, and novation are discussed in detail in Chapter 13. Another common example of suretyship created by operation of law occurs when real property burdened by a mortgage is transferred, and the transferee assumes the mortgage. This situation is explained in Chapter 37.

Most other sureties are not principally engaged in entering into suretyship contracts for a fee. Their contracts are occasional and incidental to other business. Such sureties may act gratuitously—for example, a father guaranteeing his son's credit purchase of an automobile—or may receive some pecuniary advantage—for example, a shareholder guaranteeing a loan to her corporation.

The distinction between compensated and other sureties is important because, in certain cases, compensated sureties are governed by legal principles that differ from those applied to other sureties. In general, these specialized rules impose greater liability upon the compensated surety because one engaged in the business of executing suretyship contracts can be expected to have contemplated and provided for (in computing the premium) certain risks not assumed by other sureties. Unless specifically noted, however, the rules outlined in this chapter apply to both types of surety.

Sureties and Guarantors

Suretyship law distinguishes between persons answering for the debt of another, based upon whether the promise is "primary" or "secondary." An undertaking involving the promisor's direct and absolute promise to perform, one not conditioned upon another's failure to perform, is a "primary" obligation. On the other hand, the term "secondary obligation" means that the promisor has undertaken to perform only if another person fails to perform. A "surety," pursuant to a contract of *suretyship,* makes a primary promise, whereas a "guarantor," pursuant to a contract of **guaranty,** makes a secondary promise.

A special type of guaranty contract is the **guaranty of collection** (sometimes known as a **conditional guaranty** or **guaranty of collectibility**). In the ordinary or "absolute" guaranty, the creditor may proceed against the guarantor *immediately* upon the principal's default. In the guaranty of collection, however, the creditor must put the principal in default and *additionally* exhaust all legal remedies against the principal before suing the guarantor. These remedies might include, for example, obtaining a judgment against the defaulting debtor and applying any collateral possessed by the creditor to reduce the guaranteed debt. The follow-

ing case illustrates the importance of the distinction between a surety and a guarantor.

General Motors Acceptance Corporation v. Daniels

492 A.2d 1306 (Md. 1985)

In June 1981, John Daniels agreed to buy a used car from Lindsay Cadillac Company (Lindsay). Because John had a poor credit rating, his brother, defendant Seymoure Daniels, agreed to co-sign the installment sales contract. Both John and Seymoure signed the contract at the same time on lines designated "buyer" and "co-buyer." Lindsay assigned the contract to plaintiff General Motors Acceptance Corporation (GMAC). In May 1982, GMAC declared the contract in default and sued Seymoure for the unpaid balance because John could not be located. The trial and appellate courts found that Seymoure was a guarantor of the contract between John and GMAC, and as a result GMAC was required to bring suit first against John before it could sue Seymoure. GMAC appealed to the Court of Appeals of Maryland.

Cole, Judge

We shall decide in this case whether a person who signs an installment sales contract for the sole purpose of lending his credit to the purchaser makes the contract of a surety or the contract of a guarantor. . . .

A contract of suretyship is a tripartite agreement among a principal obligor, his obligee, and a surety. This contract is a direct and original undertaking under which the surety is primarily or jointly liable with the principal obligor, . . . and therefore is responsible at once if the principal obligor fails to perform. A surety is usually bound with his principal by the same instrument, executed at the same time, and on the same consideration. . . .

Ultimate liability rests upon the principal obligor rather than the surety, but the obligee has remedy against both. . . . With respect to notice of default, the surety is ordinarily held to know every default of his principal because he is under a duty to make inquiry and ascertain whether the principal obligor is discharging the obligation resting on him. . . . Consequently, the surety is ordinarily liable without notice.

A contract of guaranty, similar to a contract of suretyship, is an accessory contract. . . . Despite this similarity, a contract of guaranty has several distinguishing characteristics. First, this particular contract is collateral to and independent of the principal contract that is guaranteed and, as a result, the guarantor is not a party to the principal obligation. A guarantor is therefore secondarily liable to the creditor on his contract and his promise to answer for the debt, default, or miscarriage of another becomes absolute upon default of the principal debtor and the satisfaction of the conditions precedent to liability. . . . Second, the original contract of the principal is not the guarantor's contract, and the guarantor is not bound to take notice of its nonperformance. Rather, the guarantor agrees that the principal is able to and will perform a contract that he has made or is about to make, and that if he defaults the guarantor will pay the resulting damages provided the guarantor is notified of the principal's default. As such, the guarantor insures the ability or solvency of the principal. Third, the contract of guaranty is often founded upon a separate consideration from that supporting the contract of the principal and, consequently, the consideration for the guarantor's promise moves wholly or in part to him. Fourth, and in sum, the guarantor promises to perform if the principal does not. By contrast, a surety promises to do the same thing that the principal undertakes. . . .

Our review of the evidence in this case convinces us that the District Court erred in finding that Seymoure was a guarantor rather than a surety with respect to the installment sales contract. . . .

Seymoure agreed to purchase the subject automobile by affixing his signature to the installment sales contract on the line designated "Buyer." The contract clearly stated that all buyers agreed to be jointly and severally liable for the purchase of that vehicle. . . .

Seymoure executed the same contract as his brother, thereby making himself a party to the original contract. There is no evidence that Seymoure executed an agreement collateral to and independent of this contract. This fact, standing alone, ordinarily negates the existence of a guaranty. . . .

Both Seymoure and John signed the contract at the same time. . . . Furthermore, there are no competent facts indicating that Seymoure expressly agreed to pay for the automobile only upon the default of John. Seymoure also did not qualify his signature in any manner. Thus, by the terms of the contract Seymoure agreed to be primarily and jointly liable with John for the purchase of the automobile. GMAC was therefore not required to proceed against John in the first instance, and the failure of GMAC promptly to notify Seymoure of the default in payments and of the lapse in physical damage insurance coverage does not constitute a discharge.

Finally, on the facts of this case it is immaterial that the contract did not expressly designate Seymoure as a "surety." Whether a party has entered into a contract of suretyship or guaranty is to be determined by the substance of the agreement and not by its nomenclature. . . .

[Judgment reversed.]

Despite the basic distinction between sureties and guarantors outlined above, the term "surety" is generally used in a broad sense to include not only strict sureties (primary promisors) but also guarantors. This approach is consistent with the emphasis in suretyship upon the principal-surety relationship and has the support of most courts, commentators, and the *Restatement of Security*.[4] Because most of the legal consequences of suretyship and guaranty are the same, and to avoid needless duplication of terms, in the material that follows the term "surety" is used to include both a surety and guarantor, unless otherwise noted.

The Suretyship Contract

Rights and duties of the parties in suretyship are governed almost exclusively by agreement. Therefore, basic contract principles, discussed in Part II of this book, govern many problems raised in suretyship cases. The following material focuses upon

---

4. This approach also accords with the definition of the term "surety" in the Uniform Commercial Code. See UCC §1-201(40).

a few important contracts issues as they apply to suretyship.

Interpreting Suretyship Contracts

Courts and commentators often state that the uncompensated surety is a "favorite of the law," subjecting his or her contracts to a special standard requiring an interpretation strictly in favor of the surety (a rule of *strictissimi juris*). The rationale for this statement is that the uncompensated surety commonly binds himself or herself as a favor to another, without receiving any personal benefit or direct compensation. In contrast, the compensated surety is said not to be a favorite of the law, requiring ambiguous language to be strictly construed against the surety (its own language because the compensated surety virtually always drafts the contract). In fact, no special standard of interpretation applies to suretyship contracts. The judicial attitude apparently favoring the accommodation surety is often no more than an application of the general interpretation rule that ambiguous language is construed most strongly against its user. As with all contracts, careful drafting that anticipates and resolves potential contingencies prevents many disputes.

Formation of the Contract

A suretyship contract must meet the same basic requirements for enforceability as other contracts. There must be an agreement supported by consideration, which may not be rendered unenforceable or voidable by defects such as fraud, misrepresentation, illegal purpose, lack of contractual capacity, or noncompliance with the Statute of Frauds.

Offer and Acceptance. In suretyship, the initial element, the agreement (or mutual manifestation of assent) is usually evidenced by an offer made by the surety and an acceptance made by the creditor. Like other offers, the surety's offer may be accepted only by or for the benefit of the person to whom it is made. If the offer is made to a particular individual (an offer for a **special guaranty**), only he or she can accept it. On the other hand, an offer for a **general guaranty** is limited by its terms to no particular individual and may be accepted by any person to whom the principal communicates

the offer and who accepts it by extending the credit contemplated by the offer. An offer of suretyship is frequently of a continuing nature, that is, a **continuing guaranty**, rather than for a single extension of credit.

A surety usually offers to guarantee the principal's performance of a *contractual* obligation, such as repayment of a debt or proper performance of a construction contract (a performance bond). In a fidelity bond, however, the surety may guarantee performance of a public duty owed by the principal, such as faithful performance of his function as a public fiscal officer.

Consideration. The consideration supporting the uncompensated, or accommodation, surety's promise is the creditor's extension of (or promise to extend) credit to the principal. If the surety is obtained after credit is extended, the prior extension of credit is "past consideration" and will not support the surety's promise. Unlike most contracts, in which the benefit of each promise runs to the promisee, in suretyship the benefit of the creditor's promise or performance runs to the principal, not the surety (promisee).

The compensated surety, of course, receives direct consideration in the form of the premium paid by the creditor, such as the principal's employer, to the surety. The compensated surety is therefore bound whether it is obtained before or after the principal obligation arises.

Capacity and Formality

A natural person having general contractual capacity also has capacity to become a surety. A business corporation also generally has the power to act as a surety.[5] Indeed, most modern sureties, such as bonding companies, are corporations.

The promise of the surety to answer for the duty of another is within the common law Statute of Frauds. Therefore, a signed writing is usually necessary to make the surety's promise enforceable against him.

---

5. The Model Business Corporation Act provides that corporations have the power "to make contracts and guarantees" and incur liabilities. MBCA §4(h), RMBCA §3.02(7). Further, suretyship contracts fall within broadly drafted corporate purposes clauses in the corporate charter, now in widespread use.

Relationship Between Surety and Principal

The primary characteristic of a suretyship relation is that although both the surety and the principal are liable to the creditor, as between the two, the principal should perform. The surety's rights against the principal are equitable in nature and origin and are embodied in three basic doctrines: reimbursement, exoneration, and subrogation.

Reimbursement

Reimbursement is the surety's right to be reimbursed by the principal *after* paying or otherwise performing the principal obligation. The principal is under a duty to reimburse the surety if either (1) the surety's undertaking was obtained at the request of the principal or with the principal's consent,[6] or (2) the principal has assumed a duty, once the primary obligation of the surety—for example, a contract assignment.

The right of reimbursement does not permit the surety to profit at the principal's expense. If the surety satisfies his or her own obligation and discharges the principal's duty by paying less than the amount nominally due, reimbursement is limited to the amount paid. Similarly, if the surety transfers property or performs services in fulfillment of the obligation, reimbursement is limited to the reasonable value of the property or services.

Exoneration

Exoneration is the surety's right, *before* paying the creditor, to compel the principal to perform. Thus, whereas reimbursement forces the principal to pay the *surety*, exoneration forces him or her to pay the *creditor*.

Exoneration, which is equitable in nature, is based on the premise that the principal owes the surety a duty to perform the principal obligation, thereby "exonerating" the surety from suit by the creditor. It is inequitable to subject the surety to the inconvenience and temporary loss involved in performing the obligation if the principal is able to do so.

Subrogation

A surety who satisfies the principal obligation succeeds to the position ("steps into the shoes") of the creditor for purposes of proceeding against the principal. This is known as the surety's right of **subrogation.** Subrogation is grounded in restitution and is designed to prevent unjust enrichment of the principal (whose obligation has been paid in full) at the surety's expense. Subrogation operates as an equitable assignment (or assignment by operation of law) of the creditor's rights to the surety after the obligation to the creditor has been satisfied. Note that reimbursement and exoneration give the surety direct rights against the principal, whereas in subrogation, the surety proceeds indirectly by asserting the creditor's rights against the principal.

Subrogation therefore entitles the surety, after payment, to use any remedy against the principal that the creditor could have used and to succeed to any other advantage enjoyed by the creditor including (1) a mortgage or other lien on the principal's property, (2) the right to proceed against any third party who has promised or is otherwise liable to either the creditor or principal to pay the debt, and (3) any priority (for example, in the principal's bankruptcy proceeding) that the creditor possesses. To illustrate the first situation above, assume Sam is a surety on Paul's $100,000 obligation to Cathy. The debt is secured by a mortgage on Paul's real property and by Paul's coin collection in Cathy's possession. Upon Paul's default, Sam satisfies the obligation. He is now entitled by subrogation to the benefit of the mortgage and the coin collection limited by the amount that he has paid.

Relationship Between Surety and Creditor—In General

The following material is divided into two parts and examines the various aspects of the relationship between the creditor and surety. The first part surveys the mutual rights and duties of the surety and creditor. The second part discusses the defenses

---

6. The duty to reimburse is commonly based on an express or implied contract (a contract "implied in fact") between the principal and surety. If the surety becomes bound without the principal's knowledge or consent, many courts recognize the surety's right to recover in restitution (quasi-contract—a contract "implied in law") in order to prevent the principal's unjust enrichment. Some courts, however, treat the nonconsensual surety as a mere volunteer.

available to the surety to avoid paying the creditor after the principal's default.

Enforcement of Creditor's Claim Against Principal

Surety's Right to Compel Creditor to Proceed Against Principal. A suretyship promise provides both assurance of payment to the creditor and protects the creditor against the burden and delay required to collect the debt from the principal through judicial proceeding. Thus, as a general rule, the surety has no right to compel the creditor to enforce its claim against the principal, and is not discharged by the creditor's failure to attempt collection of the debt from the principal. A surety who intends to be bound only after exhaustion of remedies against the principal should contract as a guarantor of collection.

A number of states that follow the doctrine of *Pain v. Packard* (1816)[7] alter this rule by statutes that enable the surety to compel the creditor to sue the principal. Under these statutes, if the creditor after receiving written notice fails or refuses to sue the principal, the surety is discharged to the extent of the loss caused by the creditor's failure or refusal to proceed.

Application of Collateral Held by Creditor. The principal obligation may be secured both by the surety's promise and by a security interest in specific property owned by the debtor. As a general rule, a creditor having a security interest in the principal's property may, on default, compel the surety to pay without first resorting to the collateral. This rule effectuates a primary purpose of suretyship: to assure the creditor's immediate payment, without the expense and delay inherent in proceeding against the principal (or in this case, his or her collateral). That expense and delay is borne by the surety as part of the suretyship undertaking.[8] A surety who pays the creditor is, of course, sub-

rogated to the creditor's position, and may use the collateral to obtain reimbursement.

A court of equity may protect the surety from the operation of this rule, forcing the creditor to proceed first against the collateral if "his failure to do so will result in unusual hardship to the surety and doing so will not prejudice the creditor."[9] That is, a balancing test is applied, balancing the relative hardship on the surety against the burden enforcing the security would impose on the creditor.

Application of Payments to Creditors

Frequently, the principal owes several separate obligations to the same creditor. Some of these obligations may be totally unsecured, while others may be secured by collateral or a surety's promise, or both. In this situation, a dispute may arise over proper allocation of part payments by the principal debtor to the various obligations. For example, assume Sally is surety on Pam's $1,000 obligation to Carla. Pam also owes Carla $2,000 on a separate unsecured debt. Pam pays Carla $1,000. How is the $1,000 part payment to be applied to the outstanding obligations?

As a general rule, the creditor is bound to follow the principal's directions regarding the application of a payment. If the principal fails to direct application of a part payment between two or more matured debts, the payment is applied at the *creditor's* discretion. Therefore, in the preceding example, if Pam pays Carla $1,000 without instructions, Carla may apply the payment as she sees fit. In this case, Carla would most likely apply the payment to the unsecured obligation, leaving the $1,000 debt on which Sally is a surety outstanding.

Similar rules apply to application of the proceeds of collateral held by the creditor. If the creditor holds security for performance of the obligation guaranteed by the surety, proceeds of the sale of that security must be applied to reduce the surety's ultimate liability. If, however, the creditor holds security from the principal to secure all debts, including those not secured by the surety, the creditor is under no obligation to apply any of the proceeds of the security for the surety's benefit. Therefore,

---

7. 13 Johns. 174 (N.Y. 1816).

8. This rule does not apply if the surety is merely a guarantor of collection, because such a guarantor is obligated to pay only after the creditor has exhausted all legal remedies against the principal, including the enforcement of any collateral.

---

9. *Restatement of Security* §131(2).

the original agreement between creditor and principal fixes the subsequent rights of the parties concerning application of the collateral.

Relationship Between Surety and Creditor—Surety's Defenses

Certain events, occurring either during the formation of the principal's or surety's contract or subsequently, may extinguish or reduce the surety's duty to the creditor. The events collectively composing the surety's defenses are usually (though not necessarily) caused by the conduct of either the creditor or the principal, or both. Most of the defenses are applications of one or more of the following general concepts.

1. As a general rule, the surety is not liable to the creditor unless the principal is liable. Accordingly, defenses available to the principal against the creditor (allowing the principal to avoid performance of the obligation to the creditor) are also available to the surety. Notable exceptions to this rule are the incapacity or bankruptcy of the principal.

2. Generally, defenses arising between the surety and principal, such as fraud perpetrated by the principal on the surety, are not available to the surety as a defense to paying the creditor.

3. Conduct by the creditor (or by the creditor and principal) that has the effect of discharging the principal, altering the principal obligation, or increasing the surety's risk, discharges the surety.

4. The creditor must act reasonably, and therefore a surety is liable only for losses that could not have been prevented through the creditor's exercise of reasonable diligence.

5. Frequently, compensated sureties are held liable to the suretyship contract in situations that would discharge an uncompensated surety.

Defenses Arising During Contract Formation

Infancy or Other Incapacity of the Principal. The principal's lack of capacity to contract, due to mental incompetence or more commonly, infancy, is not a defense available to the surety against the creditor. One of the major reasons a creditor obtains a surety is to be protected against the principal's incapacity to contract that insulates the principal from suit by the creditor.

Fraud or Duress upon the Principal or Surety. If the principal has been induced to contract as a result of the fraud or duress of the creditor, the surety is not liable to the creditor. In this case, the creditor has concealed facts (the duress or fraudulent misrepresentations) that make performance by the principal less likely and thus increase the surety's risk beyond that originally contemplated. Thus, two separate defenses are involved, one available to the principal, the other to the surety.

A related problem arises when the *surety* is induced to become bound due to fraud or duress upon him or her by the principal. As a general rule, the principal's fraud or duress gives the surety no defense against the creditor unless the creditor has knowingly accepted the advantages of the fraud or has taken no action in reliance on the surety's promise.

Fraud by Creditor upon Surety. Fraud by the creditor upon the surety is a defense to the surety. Fraud may result from the creditor's express misrepresentations, concealment, or nondisclosure of material facts. For example, if the surety requests information from the creditor, the creditor must fully disclose all material facts. Disclosure is required when the creditor knows facts unknown to the surety that materially increase the surety's risk. Material facts include the principal's financial condition, his past conduct (for example, performance of prior contracts or dishonesty as an employee), or secret agreements between creditor and principal (for example, that the actual contract between principal and creditor differs from the one upon which the surety is relying).

Effect of Discharge of Principal Obligation

Nonperformance by Creditor. The suretyship contract is collateral or ancillary to the principal obligation. Therefore, as a general rule, the surety is not liable unless the principal is liable. The surety may plead most defenses available to the principal when sued by the creditor. Possibly the most basic defense available to any contracting party is that the other party failed to perform as agreed. For example, the creditor may fail to lend money, sell goods, or perform services as provided in the contract with the principal. In this case, the principal has a defense to performance that is also available to the surety.

Performance by Principal. Because the creditor is entitled to only one performance, performance by the principal, or by another on his or her behalf, discharges the surety to the extent of the performance.

The following case illustrates both the extent of a surety's liability to the creditor and the effect of the principal's performance on that liability.

State ex rel. Mayle v. Aetna Casualty and Surety Company

166 S.E.2d 133 (W. Va. 1969)

Aetna Casualty and Surety Company was a surety on a performance bond for which Gary Wade and Frank Surina, two state conservation officers, were the principals. Wade and Surina, while in the performance of their jobs, were involved in a shooting incident in which Adair Kennedy was killed. The administratrix of Kennedy's estate sued Wade and Surina for wrongful death and sued Aetna as surety. Following a trial, the jury returned a verdict against Wade for $300 and against Surina for $300. The jury also returned a verdict against Aetna for $3,500 as Wade's surety and for $3,500 as Surina's surety. Wade and Surina paid the judgments but Aetna appealed.

Caplan, Judge

. . . An official bond is collateral security for the faithful performance of an officer in the discharge of his official duties. It is an obligation binding the surety on the bond to make good that officer's default, if any should occur. Should there be no default, no liability is incurred by the surety. However, should the principal become liable for some breach of his official duties, the surety is called upon, in accordance with the terms and to the ex-

tent of the bond, to pay the amount of the principal's liability.

It is a well settled principle of law that the extent of liability of the surety is limited by the penalty of the bond and is otherwise the same as that of the principal. . . . As long ago as 1866, the Supreme Court of the United States declared in *United States v. Burbank and Allsbury,* [71 U.S. (4 Wall.) 186 (1866)]. "It is unnecessary to refer to authorities to show that the liability of the surety cannot exceed that of his principal." . . .

Applying the principles expressed above to the instant case it becomes quite evident that Aetna Casualty and Surety Company, the surety on the bonds of Gary L. Wade and Frank Surina, Jr., can be charged with no greater liability than that found against the principals. Therefore, since each of said principals became liable for $300.00, the surety could be liable on each bond for no more than that amount.

It is the further position of the appellant, Aetna, that inasmuch as the principals under the bonds have satisfied the judgments against them, it can no longer be liable on such bonds and should be discharged. Here the principals, Wade and Surina, elected to pay the judgments against them and the plaintiff expressed satisfaction with the jury verdicts by accepting such sums from Wade and Surina. Only Aetna appealed.

As a general rule, the liability of the surety is coextensive with that of the principal. . . . When a principal purchases a bond he does not purchase insurance from liability. A bond is issued for the protection of those with whom the principal deals. Therefore, when the injured party is made whole by the principal, the obligation of the surety is extinguished. . . .

[Judgment reversed and remanded.]

Tender of Performance by Principal. As indicated in Chapter 14, a tender is an offer of performance coupled with the present ability to perform. If accepted, the tender becomes performance, discharging both principal and surety. If the creditor refuses to accept the principal's tender of performance the surety, as a general rule, is discharged. The principal is not fully discharged by the refusal but is discharged to the extent of all subsequent liability for interest, costs, and attorneys' fees.[10] Courts also universally hold that tender of performance by the surety that is refused discharges the surety. The principal nevertheless remains liable after the surety's tender. In both cases, the surety is discharged because the suretyship undertaking is not intended to protect against loss resulting from the creditor's refusal to accept payment.

Impracticability of Performance. As discussed in Chapter 14, events occurring subsequent to formation of the contract may render performance by one or both parties impracticable, excusing performance of the duties involved. If performance of the principal obligation becomes impracticable, giving the principal a defense to its enforcement, the defense is also available to the surety unless the surety has contracted otherwise with the creditor.

Release of the Principal Debtor. The surety is obtained to protect the creditor against the principal's unwillingness or inability to perform. If the creditor assures that nonperformance by releasing the principal, the creditor should have no recourse against the surety. Accordingly, as a general rule, the creditor's release of the principal discharges the surety.

The law recognizes two important exceptions to this rule. First, the surety is not discharged if the creditor in the instrument containing the release *reserves his or her rights* against the surety. This rule may be explained as follows. After the creditor unconditionally releases the principal, the underlying obligation is extinguished. The surety is also discharged because the surety's rights of reimbursement and subrogation have been destroyed by the creditor's conduct.

A release with a reservation of rights, however, is regarded as preserving the surety's rights of both reimbursement and subrogation. That is, the debt is not discharged by a release with reservation; it is treated merely as an executory covenant by the creditor not to sue the principal. The surety may therefore satisfy the obligation and proceed immediately against the principal on subrogation or reimbursement grounds. Because the surety's rights are unaffected by the release, the surety is not discharged. Thus, the reservation subjects the principal to the risk (and puts him or her on notice) that the protection afforded by the release may be illusory.

The law recognizes a second exception to the rule if the surety consents to remain bound despite the release. By assenting to become the principal debtor, the surety waives the normal incidents of the principal's release, and is not discharged, as the following case illustrates.

Hickory Springs Manufacturing Company, Inc. v. Evans
541 S.W.2d 97 (Tenn. 1976)

In 1970, Hickory Springs Manufacturing Company, Inc., agreed to extend credit to Star-Line Manufacturing Company. Glenn Evans and Howard Gose, the only shareholders of Star-Line, personally guaranteed Star-Line's indebtedness to a maximum of $10,000. In 1972, Gose sold his stock in Star-Line to Evans but did not revoke the guaranty. By late 1973, Star-Line had encountered financial difficulties and owed Hickory Springs almost $35,000. Evans began to negotiate the sale of his stock to Mr. Jarnagin. Jarnagin contacted Hickory Springs and negotiated a deal by which Hickory Springs would accept payment of $17,433.45 from Star-Line in full settlement of the debt it owed to Hickory Springs. Hickory Springs agreed to this compromise because it realized that if Jarnagin did not purchase Star-Line, the company would file for bankruptcy. Jarnagin purchased all of the stock in Star-Line and paid $17,433.45 to Hickory Springs and Hickory Springs released Star-Line from further liability on the debt. Hickory Springs then sued Evans and Gose for $10,000 pursuant to the guaranty they had signed in 1970. The trial court dismissed the case holding that Hickory Springs' release of the principal Star-Line discharged the sureties. After the appellate court affirmed the judgment, Hickory Springs appealed to the Tennessee Supreme Court.

---

10. See, for example, UCC §3-604(1).

Fones, Chief Justice

. . . The applicable provisions of the guaranty agreement are as follows:

> The liability of the undersigned shall not exceed the sum of Ten Thousand Dollars ($10,000.00) but such liability shall extend to all present and future indebtedness from time to time of said debtor [Star-Line Manufacturing Co.] to creditor and shall not be affected by said debtor's insolvency, at any time . . . or by creditor's acceptance of any composition, plan of reorganization, settlement, compromise, dividend, composition, payment of distribution. . . .

Under the general principles of suretyship law, a release of the principal also releases the surety to the extent that the principal is released. . . . The surety is not released, however, if the creditor in the release reserves his rights against the surety, or if the surety consents to remain liable notwithstanding release of the principal. . . .

In the guaranty agreement quoted above, respondents clearly consented to remain liable notwithstanding any "settlement" or "compromise." By the terms of the agreement, the guaranty is not expressly limited to involuntary situations, nor do we think the parties intended the agreement to be so limited. As the terms of a commercial guaranty agreement are to be construed as strongly against the guarantor as the sense will admit, . . . we hold that the agreement contemplated voluntary as well as involuntary settlements and compromises, and that respondents remain liable on their guaranty. . . .

In their cross-complaint, respondents maintain that if they are found liable on their guaranty agreement, they should be subrogated to the rights of the creditor and entitled to reimbursement from the successors in interest of the principal, Star-Line. Respondents misconstrue the law of subrogation.

The doctrine of subrogation is an equitable one, and it is recognized that the payment of an obligation by a surety entitles him to stand in the place of the creditor and be substituted to all of the rights of the creditor against the principal. . . .

Here the creditor's rights against the principal have been extinguished by the complete release given Star-Line. The debt having been extin-

guished, there remains nothing to which respondents could be substituted. They expressly agreed to this legal consequence by contracting to remain liable in spite of any compromise settlement of the debt. . . .

[Judgment reversed and remanded.]

Principal's Discharge in Bankruptcy. Various provisions of the federal Bankruptcy Code are concerned with the rights of sureties in the principal's bankruptcy proceeding. The Bankruptcy Code expressly provides[11] that a surety's liability is not affected by the principal's discharge in bankruptcy. That is, although the discharge destroys the rights of both the surety and creditor against the principal, it does not alter the surety's obligation to the creditor. This result is consistent with the intention of the parties, because protecting the creditor against the principal's discharge in bankruptcy is a fundamental purpose of suretyship.

Modification of Principal's Duty

If, without the surety's consent, the principal and creditor modify the principal's contract, the surety (other than a compensated surety) is discharged unless the modification, by its very nature, can only be beneficial to the surety. For example, a modification that raises the interest rate on an obligation, changes the specifications on a building contract, or substitutes delivery of a different commodity or performance of a different service from that originally agreed, would discharge the surety. In contrast, a modification lowering the interest rate or the total amount due on the principal obligation, reducing rental payments, or requiring the principal to provide additional security to the creditor, would not discharge the surety. The rationale for the rule is that the surety contracts to be bound for the principal's performance of a particular duty or set of duties. If the principal and creditor, by agreement to which the surety is not a party, change that duty, the new obligation is not the one guaranteed by the

---

11. 11 U.S.C. §524(e).

surety. It therefore follows that the surety should be discharged.

A more restrictive rule, from the surety's standpoint, is applied to modifications of contracts secured by a compensated surety. Under the approach taken by the *Restatement of Security,* discharge of a compensated surety is tied to increased risk. The surety is discharged only if the modification materially increases the risk. If, however, the risk is not materially increased, the surety remains liable but the obligation is reduced to the extent of any loss due to the modification.

Extension of Time for Payment. Generally, if the principal and creditor, without the surety's consent, make a binding agreement to extend the time for payment by the principal, the surety is discharged unless the creditor reserves his or her rights against the surety in the extension agreement. To discharge the surety, the extension agreement must be binding as a contract between principal and creditor. Therefore, if the agreement is not supported by consideration or is voidable by the creditor (for example, due to fraud), the surety remains liable.

Assuming the agreement for extension between principal and creditor is binding as a contract, the creditor may nevertheless retain the surety's liability by reserving his rights against the surety in the extension agreement. This characteristic distinguishes the extension of time from other modifications of the principal's duty. Like the release with reservation previously discussed, the extension with reservation does not discharge the original contract but is instead treated as a covenant by the creditor not to sue the principal during the extension period. The surety's rights are unaffected because he or she may pay the debt immediately and proceed against the principal for reimbursement. By accepting the extension with reservation of rights against the surety, the principal cannot complain if the surety ignores the extension, pays the debt, and sues the principal immediately.

A different rule is applied to extensions of time on obligations guaranteed by a compensated surety. A binding extension without reservation does not discharge the compensated surety. Such a surety is only discharged to the extent that it is harmed by the extension.

Impairment of Security

After paying the creditor, the surety succeeds by subrogation to the creditor's rights in any collateral held by the creditor. Because of the surety's inherent interest in the security, the creditor is under a duty not to destroy or reduce its value. Therefore, *if* a creditor who has security from the principal and knows of the surety's obligation

1. surrenders or releases the security to the principal, or
2. willfully or negligently harms it, or
3. fails to take reasonable steps to preserve its value,

then the surety's obligation is reduced to the extent of the value of the lost security.

A closely related problem is the creditor's premature payment to the principal. For example, construction contracts frequently provide that a certain percentage of the contract price is to be withheld from amounts paid by the owner to the contractor, as security for the latter's proper performance of the contract. If the owner nevertheless pays the amount to be withheld, courts generally hold that the surety is completely discharged, due to a material alteration of the surety's contract varying his risk. A number of jurisdictions, however, hold that a compensated surety is only discharged to the extent of actual loss due to the payment. Under this approach, the surety remains liable if the principal uses the payment in performance of the contract guaranteed by the surety.

Co-sureties

Frequently, two or more persons are bound to the same obligation in a suretyship capacity. This section is concerned with the rights and duties of these co-sureties.

"Co-suretyship" Defined

Co-suretyship is defined as

> The relation between two or more sureties who are bound to answer for the *same duty* of the principal, and who as between themselves should

share the loss caused by the default of the principal.[12]

Apportioning the loss caused by the principal's default may be required by an express contract between the parties, but more commonly results from the application of equitable principles. Co-sureties may be bound upon the same or different instruments. Their obligations may be in differing amounts and may arise at different times. Co-sureties need not know of each other's existence when undertaking their obligations.

Contribution

The chief characteristic of co-suretyship is the proportionate sharing of the loss caused by the principal's default, a process known as **contribution.** Contribution is equitable in nature, required because of the benefit conferred upon one co-surety by another's performance. The right may be modified by contract between the sureties, but is not affected by the fact that one or more co-sureties is compensated.

Computation of Contribution. Because the right to contribution depends upon the proportionate shares of the various co-sureties, the law has developed rules to determine how those shares are computed.

Equal Shares. In many cases, the liability of each surety for the principal's default is equal. This result occurs, for example, if all sureties guarantee performance of the principal's duty generally or stipulate equal amounts, or fail to contract beween themselves for other than equal shares. In this situation, the proportionate share is determined by dividing the loss by the number of *solvent* sureties within the jurisdiction. In computing the loss, a surety's contributive share is reduced by any part performance by the principal.

For example, assume Jack, Kelly, Laura, and Mark are co-sureties for Pam's $150,000 debt to Calvin. All sureties have agreed to guarantee the entire debt. Pam pays $30,000 and then defaults.

The proportionate share of each surety for purposes of contribution is $30,000 [($150,000 − $30,000) ÷ 4]. If one or more of the sureties is insolvent or outside the jurisdiction of the court, the remaining sureties must contribute a proportionate amount of the loss so caused. Thus, if Mark is insolvent, the contributive share of Jack, Kelly, and Laura is $40,000. These rules apply only in determining the amount of contribution one co-surety may obtain from another. They have no effect on each surety's liability to the *creditor.* Thus, if Laura, Kelly, and Mark are all insolvent upon Pam's default, Jack can be held liable for the full $120,000 loss, because he did not limit his liability to Calvin. That is, the extent of a surety's liability is dependent upon his agreement with the creditor. That liability is unaffected by the surety's inability to obtain contribution from co-sureties.

A surety is entitled to contribution from a co-surety only after discharging *more* than his or her proportionate share of the principal's obligation. For example, assume Alice and Betty are co-sureties on Patty's $10,000 debt to Cindy. Patty defaults and Alice pays Cindy $5,000 (her proportionate share—one half of the loss). Alice is not entitled to contribution from Betty. Had Alice paid $6,000, she would be entitled to $1,000 contribution from Betty.

Unequal Shares—All Obligations Specified. Because co-sureties enter into separate contracts with the creditor, the individual suretyship obligations may be restricted to specific amounts that vary among the sureties. In this situation, if the amounts guaranteed are unequal, the surety's shares are determined in proportion to the risk assumed by each. For example, assume Jack, Kelly, and Laura are co-sureties on Pam's $50,000 debt to Calvin. Jack has agreed to guarantee $35,000, Kelly, $15,000, and Laura, $10,000. Pam pays $20,000 and then defaults. The sureties' contributive shares toward the $30,000 loss are as follows:

Surety	Liability Assumed	Fraction	Loss	Contributive Share
Jack	$35,000	35/60	× $30,000	$17,500
Kelly	15,000	15/60	× 30,000	7,500
Laura	10,000	10/60	× 30,000	5,000
				$30,000

---

12. *Restatement of Security* §144. (Emphasis added.)

If Laura becomes insolvent, the shares would be computed as follows:

Surety	Liability Assumed	Fraction		Loss	Contributive Share
Jack	$35,000	35/50	×	$30,000	$21,000
Kelly	15,000	15/50	×	30,000	9,000
					$30,000

If Jack becomes insolvent, the shares would be computed as follows:

Surety	Liability Assumed	Fraction		Loss	Contributive Share
Kelly	$15,000	15/25	×	$30,000	$18,000
Laura	10,000	10/25	×	30,000	12,000
					$30,000*

*Total liability only $25,000.

Note in this last case that because Kelly and Laura have limited their total liability to $25,000 ($15,000 and $10,000 respectively), they cannot be compelled to pay the entire $30,000 loss. In this case, Calvin will not be able to collect the $5,000 deficiency from any surety because Jack is insolvent and Kelly and Laura have fully performed their suretyship obligations.

Unequal Shares—All Obligations Not Specified. Occasionally, one surety assumes liability without limit and the remaining sureties limit their obligations to stated amounts. In this case, contributive shares are determined by comparing the loss with the amount guaranteed by the surety who assumes the largest *stipulated* obligation. If the loss is *less than or equal to* the amount guaranteed by the largest stipulated surety, then contributive shares are computed as if the surety without limit guaranteed the same amount as the largest stipulated surety. If the loss is *more than* the amount guaranteed by the largest stipulated surety, then the surety without limit is required to contribute as if he had guaranteed the amount of the *default*. Assume Jack, Kelly, and Laura are sureties on Pam's debt to Calvin, an open line of credit. Jack has agreed to guarantee payment up to the full amount of the obligation as it finally accrues. Kelly has limited her liability to $15,000 and Laura to

$10,000. Assuming Pam's ultimate default is $8,000, Jack's contributive share is computed as if he had guaranteed $15,000. In this case, the amount of the loss ($8,000) is less than the amount guaranteed by the largest stipulated surety (Kelly— $15,000) and therefore the first rule above applies. The contributive shares are as follows:

Sureties	Liability Assumed	Fraction		Loss	Contributive Share
Jack	$15,000	15/40	×	$8,000	$3,000
Kelly	15,000	15/40	×	8,000	3,000
Laura	10,000	10/40	×	8,000	2,000
					$8,000

If, however, the loss is $25,000, Jack's contributive share is computed as if he had guaranteed the amount of the default because the default ($25,000) is greater than the amount guaranteed by the largest stipulated surety (Kelly—$15,000). In this case, the respective shares are therefore computed as follows:

Sureties	Liability Assumed	Fraction		Loss	Contributive Share
Jack	$25,000	25/50	×	$25,000	$12,500
Kelly	15,000	15/50	×	25,000	7,500
Laura	10,000	10/50	×	25,000	5,000
					$25,000

Effect of Settlement and Existence of Security. If the principal defaults, and one co-surety settles with the creditor at less than the amount nominally due from the principal, co-sureties are entitled to the benefit of the settlement. For example, assume Frank, Gayle, and Harry are co-sureties on Peter's $30,000 obligation to Cameron. Peter defaults and Cameron agrees with Frank to accept a stamp collection fairly valued at $24,000 in full satisfaction of the debt. Frank can recover $8,000 each from Gayle and Harry.

A surety may receive security from the principal to secure the surety's right of reimbursement. Although the existence of the security does not affect the duty of other sureties to contribute, the surety receiving the security must share it with co-sureties. That is, in settling the sureties' ultimate liability, each co-surety is entitled to an interest in the security in proportion to his liability for the principal's default. Because of this duty to account, a surety's right of contribution is reduced by a pro rata share of the security if he or she loses, destroys, or releases it to the principal. Assume Frank and Gayle are co-sureties on Peter's $10,000 obligation to Cameron. Frank has received rare coins worth $5,000 from Peter as security for Frank's reimbursement. Peter defaults, and Frank pays Cameron $10,000. Frank has a right of contribution from Gayle for $5,000 but must share the security with her. Thus, ultimately both Frank and Gayle will contribute $2,500. The same result follows had Frank sold the coins for $5,000, negligently lost them, failed to realize their fair value on sale, or released them to Peter.

Effect of Release of Co-surety.
Occasionally, the creditor will release one co-surety from his or her obligation. Although such a release does not discharge the remaining co-sureties, it does extinguish their ability to obtain contribution from the released co-surety. Therefore, when the creditor releases one of several co-sureties, the obligation of the remaining co-sureties is reduced by the amount the released co-surety could have been compelled to make contribution.[13] That is, the ultimate liability of each co-surety is computed as if the released surety had contributed. For example, assume Smith and Thompson are co-sureties on Palmer's $10,000 obligation to Clark. Clark releases Thompson, and Palmer defaults. Clark can collect no more than $5,000 from Smith, because Thompson could have been compelled to contribute one-half of the loss.

If, as part of the release of one surety, the creditor *reserves his or her rights* against co-sureties, the obligations of the remaining sureties are not discharged or reduced. In this case, the reservation of rights puts the released surety on notice that the release is effective only between that surety and the creditor and does not affect the rights of other sureties. Thus, if the remaining sureties pay more than their proportionate share, they are entitled to contribution from the released surety.

---

13. If the creditor can show that the released co-surety is insolvent, the release has no effect on the remaining co-sureties' shares, because they could not have obtained contribution from the released co-surety.

Contribution Among Co-promisors.
As discussed in Chapter 7, several people may promise to render the same performance making their contractual liability joint or joint and several. When multiple promises of the same performance are made, a suretyship relation necessarily exists between the promisors. That is, whenever two people promise the same performance, either (1) one is the principal obligor and the other a surety, or (2) each is *both* a principal obligor *and* a surety. Assume that Art agrees to act as a surety on Ben's $10,000 debt to Corrine. In this case, only Ben (the principal) has assumed ultimate liability. If Art is required to pay, he as a surety may obtain reimbursement from Ben for the full amount. Thus, assuming Ben is solvent, Art, in the final analysis, should pay nothing to Corrine.

Assume, alternatively, that Art and Ben are jointly liable on the $10,000 obligation to Corrine. In this case, both Art and Ben have ultimate liability to pay Corrine $10,000. In addition, Art is a surety for Ben's performance and Ben is a surety for Art's performance. That is, Art and Ben are co-sureties. Therefore, if Ben defaults and Art pays Corrine $10,000, Art is entitled to $5,000 in contribution from Ben, under the general principles discussed above.

Exoneration

In the principal-surety context, exoneration is the surety's equitable right to compel the principal to pay the *creditor*. A similar right exists among co-sureties. Because each co-surety is liable only for part of the loss, exoneration is limited to the amount that the suing surety would be entitled to receive as contribution had he or she paid the entire debt. Assume Redman and Story are co-sureties on Pendleton's $10,000 obligation to Coffin. Pendleton defaults. If Redman sues Story in exoneration, Story will be required to pay Coffin $5,000.

Subrogation

A surety who satisfies the creditor's claim is subrogated to the creditor's rights against the principal. Such a surety also succeeds to the creditor's position as against *co-sureties*, but may receive only his *contributive share* from any co-surety, because as among the co-sureties, the subrogated surety should bear a portion of the loss. This principle is most commonly applied upon bankruptcy of a co-surety. Suppose Ruth and Sarah are co-sureties on Phil's $10,000 debt to Cindy. Phil defaults and Sarah is petitioned into bankruptcy. Ruth pays Cindy $10,000. Ruth may file a $10,000 claim (as subrogee of Cindy's rights) in Sarah's bankruptcy proceeding. Ruth is then entitled to dividends from Sarah's bankrupt estate, but not exceeding $5,000,

the extent of Ruth's right of contribution against Sarah. Thus, even if Sarah's estate pays a 60% dividend to creditors, Ruth receives only $5,000 on her $10,000 claim.

A surety, after paying the creditor, is similarly subrogated to the creditor's rights in any collateral received from co-sureties. Once again, the surety may use such collateral only to the extent necessary to satisfy his or her right of contribution from the other co-sureties.

SUMMARY

1. Suretyship provides security to a creditor by the promise of a third party (the surety) to perform the obligation if the debtor does not. Suretyship is a contractual arrangement created when two parties, principal and surety, become legally bound to a creditor for the same performance. Though both principal and surety are liable, as between the two, the principal rather than the surety should perform.

2. Suretyship law recognizes a distinction between compensated (or corporate) sureties and uncompensated (accommodation or gratuitous) sureties. The law, in certain cases, imposes greater liability upon compensated sureties, who assume risks not undertaken by other sureties.

3. A surety's liability may be primary (a contract of suretyship) or secondary (a contract of guaranty). In the former the surety's liability is coextensive with the principal's; in the latter, the surety is liable only after the principal's default. In a specialized guaranty contract, a "guaranty of collection," the creditor must both put the principal in default and exhaust all legal remedies against the principal before proceeding against the surety.

4. An offer for a suretyship contract usually is made by the surety to the creditor, and may be made to one creditor (a special guaranty) or to a group of creditors (a general guaranty), and may guarantee a single obligation or successive extensions of credit (a continuing guaranty). The consideration supporting the compensated surety's promise is the premium. An uncompensated surety's promise is supported by the creditor's extending credit to the principal.

5. The surety has three basic rights against the principal: (1) reimbursement—the surety's right to be reimbursed by the debtor *after* paying or otherwise performing the principal obligation, (2) exoneration—the surety's right, *before* paying the creditor, to compel the principal to perform, and (3) subrogation—the right of

the surety to succeed to the rights of ("step into the shoes of") the creditor against the principal, after satisfying the principal's duty to the creditor.

6. Suretyship protects the creditor against the burden and delay required to collect the debt from the principal. Accordingly, the surety generally has no right to compel the creditor to attempt collection of the debt from the principal before proceeding against the surety. Similarly, the surety may not generally require the creditor to apply any collateral received from the principal to the debt before proceeding against the surety.

7. Various defenses are available to a surety to reduce or extinguish his obligation to the creditor. These defenses arise from (1) events, such as fraud, occurring during formation of the principal or suretyship contract, (2) events discharging the principal obligation, (3) modification of the principal's duty without the surety's consent, and (4) impairment of security by the creditor.

8. If two or more sureties are bound to answer for the same duty of the principal, they are co-sureties who share the loss caused by the principal's default. The process of sharing the ultimate burden among co-sureties is known as "contribution." The law has developed detailed rules governing computation of co-sureties' shares. In addition to the right of contribution, a surety also possesses rights against co-sureties based on exoneration and subrogation.

KEY TERMS

suretyship	bond
principal	fidelity bond
creditor	performance bond
surety	guaranty
compensated (corporate)	guaranty of collection
surety	(conditional guaranty,
uncompensated (gratuitous	guaranty of
or accommodation)	collectibility)
surety	special guaranty

general guaranty   subrogation
continuing guaranty   co-suretyship
reimbursement   contribution
exoneration

QUESTIONS AND PROBLEMS

33-1   Creditors often obtain security by contractually creating an interest, a lien, in specific real or personal property belonging to the debtor. Obtaining a surety is an alternative or additional method of providing security. What are the advantages to a creditor of suretyship over other types of security? What advantages do contractually created liens have over suretyship?

33-2   Courts and commentators frequently state that an accommodation surety is a ''favorite of the law.'' Why? Should accommodation sureties be treated any differently from corporate sureties? Explain.

33-3   Farmers Produce Co. purchased goods on account from Acme Feed and Supplies, Inc. By March 1986, Farmers owed over $8,000 on account. Acme refused to make further sales on credit unless Farmers obtained a surety. National Insurance Co. agreed to act as surety for debts incurred after March 1986 and Acme extended an additional $5,000 worth of supplies on credit. In July, Farmers advised National that it was in default on the payments to Acme but that Farmers would be able to pay the bills after the fall harvest. National provided $1,000 to Farmers to make a payment on its bill to Acme. Farmers made the payment without giving instructions regarding the application of the payment.

(a) Acme applied the payment to Farmers' oldest bill dating back to March of 1985. Does Acme have the right to apply the payment in this manner? Explain.

(b) Assume you work for National Insurance Co. You are the officer who decided to advance $1,000 for the payment to Acme. Would you have handled the transaction differently? Explain.

33-4   Watkins Co. is a wholesale supplier of beauty salon products. Pierre, a beauty salon operator, has purchased supplies on credit from Watkins for over ten years. During the last year, however, Pierre had written four checks to Watkins that were returned for insufficient funds. Pierre later covered the checks with cash payments. Watkins called several of Pierre's other creditors and learned that they too had received bad checks from Pierre.

Pierre placed an order for $5,000 worth of supplies from Watkins. Watkins advised Pierre that it would sell the goods on credit only if Pierre obtained a surety. Pierre asked his friend Ruth to act as surety.

(a) Ruth asked Pierre if he had ever had financial problems or trouble paying his bills. Pierre denied having had such problems even though during the last six months his business had suffered severe cash flow problems. Ruth then agreed to become Pierre's surety. Pierre filed for bankruptcy and Watkins sued Ruth for the $5,000 debt. Ruth alleged that Pierre had defrauded her by misrepresenting his financial problems. Assuming that the misrepresentation constituted fraud, would Pierre's fraudulent misrepresentation be grounds for relieving Ruth from liability as a surety to Watkins? Explain.

(b) Assume that the discussion between Pierre and Ruth had occurred while a representative of Watkins was present. The representative knew that Pierre had had financial problems but was unsure whether to mention the problems. Would you recommend that the representative advise Ruth of Pierre's recent financial difficulties? Explain.

(c) Disregard the facts in (a) and (b), above. Assume that after Pierre asked Ruth to serve as surety, Ruth immediately visited Watkins Co.'s office to sign the necessary papers. Does Watkins Co. have any obligation to advise Ruth that Pierre had recently written several bad checks? Explain.

33-5   Wally agreed to purchase a house from Stanley and on March 30, 1984, signed a promissory note by which he agreed to pay $50,000 on March 30, 1985. Wally's wife Rebecca signed the promissory note as an accommodation maker. On March 1, 1985, Wally and Stanley entered into a second agreement by which Stanley agreed to accept five monthly installments of $10,000 (with the first payment due in March) in lieu of $50,000 on March 30. Rebecca was not advised of the second agreement. One provision of the agreement stated ''Wally and Stanley agree that Stanley's forbearance on the full payment due on March 30, 1985, does not waive any of the terms of the original note and that all rights and obligations set forth therein are binding in all respects.''

Wally defaulted in making the monthly payments. Stanley demanded that Rebecca, as surety, make the $50,000 payment. Rebecca refused saying that Stanley's extension of the time to make payments without her consent discharged her from liability. Is she correct? Explain.

33-6 Third State Bank loaned $10,000 to Dewey to purchase a car. The bank took a security interest in the car and also required Dewey to obtain a surety. Dewey's uncle Jack agreed to serve as surety. Dewey later filed for bankruptcy. At the bankruptcy hearing, Jack discovered that the bank had failed to perfect its security interest in the car. When the bank sued Jack as surety, Jack alleged that he could not be held liable because the bank's failure to perfect its security interest constituted an impairment of collateral. How should the court rule? Explain.

Toxic Waste, Corporate Regulation, and Bankruptcy

*Thomas H. Jackson**

Cases involving insolvent firms responsible for toxic waste sites illustrate the problems of resolving untested legal issues in bankruptcy proceedings. The conflicts arise both in liquidating corporations and reorganizing corporations. The basic facts are the following: a firm that handles toxic wastes maintains a site where leakage or improper storage has created a health hazard. The state obtains a judicial order directing the firm to clean up the wastes but, before the firm does so, it files for bankruptcy.

The principle case involving a liquidating corporation is the 1986 Supreme Court case *Midlantic National Bank* (106 S.Ct. 755) in which the debtor was liquidating under Chapter 7 of the Bankruptcy Code. The cost of cleaning up a toxic waste site far exceeded its cleaned-up value, and the trustee sought to abandon the site pursuant to Section 554 of the Code which provides that "[a]fter notice and a hearing, the trustee may abandon any property of the estate that is burdensome to the estate. . . ." Responding to objections raised by state and municipal authorities, the Supreme Court, by a bare majority, held that Section 554 did not permit abandonment in this case. The Court reasoned that because prior bankruptcy law had recognized a "narrow" exception for important health and safety issues, Congress must have intended to continue this exception when it codified the abandonment notion. The dissent argued that the language of Section 554 had no qualification, and none should be added by the Court.

In *Penn Terra* (733 F. 2d 267), a 1984 Third Circuit case, the issue was similar: whether bankruptcy's law, automatic stay—which basically prohibits prebankruptcy creditors from taking actions that dismember an estate—applied to an action by the state requiring Penn Terra to reclaim land it had strip mined. Penn Terra's trustee

argued that this violated the automatic stay and sought to enjoin the state from enforcing its injunction.

The focus was on two Bankruptcy Code provisions. The first excepted from the automatic stay "the commencement or continuation of an action or proceeding by a governmental unit to enforce such governmental unit's police or regulatory power." The second narrowed this exception by providing that, while the exception applies to the enforcement of judgments obtained in such actions, it does not apply to the enforcement of *money* judgments. The Third Circuit concluded that the state's action constituted an exercise of police power and the injunction was not "an attempt to enforce a money judgment," even though the expenditure of money was required. The state's action was taken to prevent future harms and the automatic stay did not preclude the state from enforcing its injunction.

Both *Midlantic* and *Penn Terra* involved liquidating corporations, and therefore, the main issue ultimately was that of the *priority* of cleanup claims, not Bankruptcy Code provisions such as the abandonment and automatic stay sections. Bankruptcy marshals assets and distributes them in a prescribed order to those who have rights against the assets. Who has these rights, as well as their relevant priority, however, are determined, with a few exceptions not relevant here, by applying nonbankruptcy law.

Assume that a firm owns land in Virginia on which it has dumped toxic wastes in violation of state law. Including the land, which is valued at $50,000 without the toxic wastes, the firm has $500,000 in assets. At the request of the state, the

*Arnold Leon Professor of Law and Dean, University of Virginia, School of Law

court has ordered the firm to clean up the wastes at a cost of $200,000. The firm also owes $800,000 to a number of general creditors. Who gets what portion of the $500,000 in assets?

Imagine that no bankruptcy petition is filed and the assets are distributed pursuant to state law dissolution. Virginia will get the $50,000 value of the land, given that under the federal Comprehensive Environmental Response, Compensation, and Liability Act of 1980, any owner of the land will bear the clean-up costs. This would leave it a $150,000 claim which it would share with the other creditors pro rata in the remaining $450,000 of assets. (In a few states, statutes have been enacted giving environmental clean-up orders priority as to *all* assets of the polluter. In those states, pro rata sharing would not be the rule.)

Imagine now that the firm files for bankruptcy before dissolving. Those with priority in a distribution pursuant to state law should have priority in bankruptcy's distribution as well. This result may be altered, however, if the court focuses on the Bankruptcy Code without giving adequate attention to pertinent state law. Consider *Midlantic,* where the Court focused on the abandonment issue. Neither the majority nor the dissent adopted the most logical reading of the abandonment section. Although Section 554 does not explicity restrict the abandonment power, the logical reading is that the trustee's powers are limited by ''applicable nonbankruptcy law.'' This point is hammered home by 28 U.S.C. §959(b) which commands the trustee (or debtor in possession) ''to manage and operate the property in his possession . . . according to the requirements of the various laws of the State in which such property is situated, in the same manner that the owner or possessor thereof would be bound to do if in possession thereof.'' Recognizing this fact, however, does not resolve the case because the court still must determine the way to distribute the assets of the dissolving corporation even if state law does not permit that corporation to ''abandon'' the asset and its associate liability prior to dissolution itself.

Consider, then, the automatic stay issue raised by *Penn Terra*. If the automatic stay does not apply and (to continue with the example) the firm has to do the cleanup, it will spend $200,000. Unless Virginia's status is that of a creditor with a priority right to all of the firm's assets (which is a question of state law), Virginia has no right to get $200,000 ahead of the other creditors. If lifting the stay would have that effect, then lifting it incorrectly resolves the priority question in the case of a liquidating corporation. If Virginia wants to clean up the toxic waste site, it should be able to do so, but it will have to spend $200,000 of its ''own'' money to do that. It would then have a claim for that amount against the firm and get paid according to its entitlements. If Virginia has a priority right to all the assets, it will get paid in full. If Virginia *is* in fact entitled to be paid ahead of others because of the effect of nonbankruptcy law, then there may be a good reason to lift the stay. It has to pay $200,000 to Virginia anyway, and it might better do so sooner than later.

Because liquidating corporations like Midlantic and Penn Terra have no future business, the priority question is clear; but the priority question is not necessarily the same in cases when corporations continue in business.

There are certain costs to running a business, in or out of bankruptcy. A firm might be required to have environmental smokestacks or to file reports on environmental compliance. There is no reason why a debtor in bankruptcy should be relieved of such costs. The argument that a firm can make more money by producing its product while polluting the environment is irrelevant in a world which forbids it. If the state can shut down a business that has not cleaned up its toxic waste, then—even though it lacks such status in a liquidation case—it may have something *tantamount* to a priority right to all the assets if that firm continues.

The lesson of the interplay between the Bankruptcy Code and toxic waste issues, then contains a broader message. The basic problem is the one that occurs when there are too many liabilities chasing too few assets. Nothing bankruptcy law can do can change that fact. The courts must be cautious about making something a bankruptcy issue that it is not; in the process they may miss what is likely to be the real issue.

Part Six   PROPERTY

- an introduction to property ownership and transfer
- an introduction to the law of intellectual property: patents, copyrights, and trademarks
- discussion of various methods of acquiring title to or an interest in personal property
- coverage of the law of fixtures, which resolves ownership disputes concerning personal property that has become closely annexed or adapted to real property

Property acquisition, ownership, use, possession, and disposition pervade both personal and commercial life. Individuals and businesses own vast quantities of land devoted to agriculture, manufacturing, product distribution, and retailing. They buy and sell equipment, inventory and other businesses, enter into contracts, issue stocks and bonds, and secure patents and copyrights. Individuals acquire and dispose of goods (such as appliances, household furnishings, and clothing) for personal use, invest or borrow money, buy and sell homes, and provide for disposition of property on death.

As noted in Chapter 6, property denotes the totality of legal relations among persons with respect to a thing, tangible or intangible. Specifically, the law of property addresses the legal relationships existing between a person or persons possessing a legally protected interest in the thing, the owner,

and other members of society. Legally protected interests in land are called "real property." Personal property includes everything else capable of ownership. Personal property may be tangible (such as an automobile, stereo equipment, a cat, or any other object that can be moved) or intangible (such as patents, copyrights, negotiable instruments, stocks and bonds, accounts receivable, or other contract rights).

The law of property is largely concerned with the creation of, transfer of, and limitations on the various ownership interests in the property. This and the following five chapters expand on the basic property introduction in Chapter 6 by examining these issues for both personal and real property.

Introduction to Property Ownership and Transfer

Character of Property Ownership

The totality of rights constituting full ownership of property may be held by one person or may be divided in a variety of ways, resulting in multiple interests in the same property. The permissible ownership interests existing in property known as "estates" differ in several major respects:

1. *Duration*. A property interest may be created to last infinitely or indefinitely or to terminate at a given time or upon the occurrence of an event.

2. *Extent of interest held by the owner*. A

property owner may have full ownership or may have a more limited interest such as merely a right to possess the property or to receive the income from it.

3. *Time of possession.* Property interests may be split successively with the present right to possession held by one person and the future right to possession (a "future interest") resting in another.

4. *Number of persons concurrently holding a possessory interest.* Two or more persons may simultaneously have the right to possess the same property.

As each property issue is discussed in the following chapters, note how the bundle of rights representing full ownership has been divided. In this manner, the various property subjects can more easily be contrasted and distinguished.

Property Transfer

The holder of an interest in either real or personal property usually acquires it by transfer from a prior owner. The law ordinarily favors the free transferability (alienability) of interests in both real and personal property. In general, interests in property may be transferred either voluntarily or involuntarily during the life of the owner (designated *inter vivos* transfers) or on the death of the owner.

Voluntary Transfers. Voluntary transfers—those intentionally made without coercion during the life of the transferor—are made either by sale or by gift. An inter vivos transfer of an interest in real property is known as a **conveyance** or a **grant** and is accomplished by using a formal document known as a deed. The party making the transfer is known as the grantor and the party to whom the transfer is made is the grantee.

Unlike real property, interests in personal property may generally be transferred inter vivos without formality. For example, title to most tangible personal property may be acquired by sale or gift simply by transferring possession from one owner to the next. This general rule is subject to a number of exceptions. For example, statutes commonly provide that certain types of property, such as automobiles, may be transferred only through a formal title certificate. In addition, intangibles, such

as accounts, notes, checks, stocks, and bonds require formalities for transfer dictated by statute.

A person may voluntarily transfer his or her entire interest in property or may create a more limited interest in the transferee. For example, the owner may transfer the right to possession of the property for a period of time without surrendering ownership. If real property is involved, such a transfer creates a landlord-tenant relationship. If the right to use but not possess the land is transferred, the interest created is an easement. If possession but not ownership of personal property is transferred, a bailment is established.[1]

Involuntary Transfers. Under certain circumstances, property interests may also be transferred involuntarily—without the owner's consent. For example, in real property, the doctrine of adverse possession effects an involuntary transfer when the statute of limitations expires. Further, the eminent domain power allows governmental bodies to take private property for public use if just compensation is provided.[2] In addition, both real and personal property transfers may occur upon the bankruptcy of the owner, enforcement of a security interest in the property, or a judicial sale to satisfy an unpaid judgment.

Transfers on Death and in Trust. A person may also effect a transfer of property at death. The ability to do so is recognized by the law as one of the bundle of rights included in the concept of private ownership of property. Transfers on death are accomplished either through a will or by the operation of state "intestate succession" statutes if a person fails to leave a valid will. A transfer of property by will is commonly known as a devise and the transferees known as devisees. Takers of property through intestate succession statutes are known as heirs. Property transfers by will or intestate succession are in essence gifts, but differ from ordinary gifts in that they take effect after the death of the transferor.

---

1. Landlord-tenant, easements, and bailments are discussed in Chapters 36, 38, and 35.

2. Adverse possession and eminent domain are discussed in Chapters 37 and 38.

An additional method of property disposition is a trust. A property owner may transfer property in trust either during his lifetime or upon death. The essence of a trust is a "splitting" of ownership between the trustee who takes and holds legal title to the property and the beneficiaries who hold the equitable or beneficial title.

The property issues outlined above are covered in the following five chapters. This chapter examines intellectual property (such as patents and copyrights), the various methods of acquiring title to or an interest in personal property during life other than by sale or trust, and the law of fixtures. Chapter 35 concludes the personal property material with coverage of the law of bailments and documents of title. Chapters 36 through 38 comprise the real property coverage, addressing the fundamental principles of land ownership and transfer and land use regulation. Finally, Chapter 39 discusses transfers of both real and personal property on death and in trust.

Intellectual Property

The legal principles governing personal property discussed later in this chapter and in Chapter 35 affect primarily goods (tangible personal property) or intangibles (such as stocks, bonds, and documents of title) commonly evidenced by a writing. The following material discusses an important and unique form of intangible personal property known as "intellectual property." **Intellectual property** is the bundle of rights associated with ideas and creative thoughts. Generally, these rights are created only after novel ideas are reduced to a tangible medium. Historically, intellectual property has included literary and artistic works and inventions. With the increasing sophistication of modern marketing and communication, intellectual property has expanded to include audio and video recordings and computer programs.

In the United States, intellectual property rights are regulated primarily by federal law. Article I, Section 8, Clause 8 of the Constitution states "The Congress shall have Power . . . To promote the Progress of Science and useful Arts, by securing for limited Times to Authors and Inventors the exclusive Right to their respective Writings and Discoveries." Pursuant to this grant of power, Congress has enacted the Patent Act[3] and the Copyright Act.[4] Additionally, under its power to regulate interstate commerce, Congress has adopted the Lanham Act, which governs the interstate use of trademarks. These three areas of law—patents, copyrights, and trademarks—form the traditional basis for the study of intellectual property.

Patents

A **patent** is a grant of the exclusive right to make, use, and sell an invention for a term of years. Under the federal Patent Act, the United States Patent and Trademark Office, a branch of the federal Department of Commerce, grants a patent to an inventor, usually for a period of seventeen years. After the patent expires, the invention becomes part of the public domain. By granting the inventor a limited monopoly of the invention, federal patent law encourages innovation and full disclosure of inventions that eventually will become available for public use.

Patentability. Not all inventions are patentable. The Patent Act empowers the federal government to grant three general types of patents: utility patents, design patents, and plant patents.

A **utility patent,** the most common type, is granted to a person who invents or discovers "any new and useful process, machine, manufacture, or composition of matter, or any new and useful improvement thereof."[5] A "process" is a method of achieving a certain result, such as a method of making a metal alloy, chemical, or drug. Even if the end product of the process is not patentable, the process itself may be patented. A "machine" is an apparatus, such as a drill press, used to achieve a certain result or to perform a function. A "manufacture" is "the production of articles for use from raw or prepared materials by giving to these materials new forms, qualities, properties, or combinations, whether by hand-labor or by machinery."[6] A

---

3. 35 U.S.C. §1 *et seq.*
4. 17 U.S.C. §101 *et seq.*
5. 35 U.S.C. §101.
6. *American Fruit Growers, Inc. v. Brogdex Co.,* 51 S. Ct. 328, 330 (1931).

"composition of matter" includes "all compositions of two or more substances . . . whether they be results of chemical union, or of mechanical mixture, or whether they be gases, fluids, powders or solids."[7] An improvement of a process, machine, manufacture, or composition of matter also may be patentable.

The second type of patent is the **design patent,** which may be issued for "any new, original and ornamental design for an article of manufacture."[8] The design patent concerns the appearance of a manufactured article rather than its use or operation. **Plant patents,** which are the third type of patent, may be issued to anyone who "invents or discovers and asexually reproduces any distinct and new variety of plant."[9] A plant patent may be granted only for plants that are cultivated and developed by human beings, such as hybrid vegetables or flowers that do not occur naturally.

At issue in the following utility patent case was whether a living microorganism was a patentable "manufacture" or "composition of matter."

Diamond v. Chakrabarty
100 S.Ct. 2204 (1980)

In 1972, respondent Ananda M. Chakrabarty, a microbiologist, applied for a patent for a human-made, genetically engineered bacterium capable of breaking down multiple components of crude oil. Because of this property, which is possessed by no naturally occurring bacteria, Chakrabarty's invention is believed to have significant potential value for treating oil spills. The Patent and Trademark Office denied the patent on the ground that living things are not patentable under the Patent Act.

The Court of Customs and Patent Appeals reversed the decision and the Supreme Court granted the Commissioner of Patents and Trademarks' petition for certiorari.

Chief Justice Burger

. . . [W]e must determine whether respondent's micro-organism constitutes a "manufacture" or "composition of matter" within the meaning of [§101 of the Patent Act]. . . .

In choosing such expansive terms as "manufacture" and "composition of matter," modified by the comprehensive "any," Congress plainly contemplated that the patent laws would be given wide scope.

The relevant legislative history also supports a broad construction. . . . The Committee Reports accompanying the 1952 Act inform us that Congress intended statutory subject matter to "include anything under the sun that is made by man." . . .

This is not to suggest that §101 has no limits or that it embraces every discovery. The laws of nature, physical phenomena, and abstract ideas have been held not patentable. . . . Thus, a new mineral discovered in the earth or a new plant found in the wild is not patentable subject matter. Likewise, Einstein could not patent his celebrated law that $E = mc^2$; nor could Newton have patented the law of gravity. Such discoveries are "manifestations of . . . nature, free to all men and reserved exclusively to none." [*Funk Brothers Seed Co. v. Kalo Inoculant Co.,* 68 S.Ct. 440, 441 (1948)]

Judged in this light, respondent's micro-organism plainly qualifies as patentable subject matter. His claim is not to a hitherto unknown natural phenomenon, but to a nonnaturally occurring manufacture or composition of matter—a product of human ingenuity. . . .

. . . [T]he patentee has produced a new bacterium with markedly different characteristics from any found in nature and one having the potential for significant utility. His discovery is not nature's handiwork, but his own; accordingly it is patentable subject matter under §101. . . .

[Judgment affirmed.]

Securing a Patent. To secure a patent, the inventor must submit an application to the United States Patent and Trademark Office. Only the inventor may apply for a patent. Because the procedures of

---

7. *Shell Development Company v. Watson,* 149 F. Supp. 279, 280 (D.C. 1957).
8. 35 U.S.C. §171.
9. 35 U.S.C. §161.

the Patent Office are very technical, most inventors employ a patent attorney to handle the application process.

An important part of the patent application is the specification, a detailed and complete description of the invention sufficient to enable someone skilled in the technical area of the invention to duplicate it. The utility patent applicant must establish that the invention is novel. Novelty is lacking if the invention was known or used by others in the United States or if it was patented or described in a printed publication in the United States or a foreign country prior to its invention by the applicant. To determine the invention's novelty, the applicant generally will search prior patents and other technical literature and will distinguish the invention from other similar inventions. The utility patent applicant also must prove that the invention has utility or usefulness and is nonobvious, that is, that the invention is not obvious to a person skilled in the art to which it pertains. Although both design and plant patents require novelty, and must be nonobvious, they do not require utility. A patentable plant need not be useful, only distinctive. Design patents require ornamentality rather than utility.

After the patent application is filed in the Patent Office, a patent examiner reviews the application to determine whether the invention meets the statutory requirements. The examiner will conduct an independent search of the technical literature to determine whether the invention is novel and will verify the inventor's claims. If the examiner finds that the application meets the statutory requirements, the Patent and Trademark Office will issue a patent to the applicant. If the patent application is rejected, an appeal procedure, ultimately allowing judicial review, is available.

Property Rights of the Patent Holder.
The inventor who secures a United States utility or design patent has the exclusive right to make, use, or sell the invention in this country for a period of seventeen years (fourteen years for design patents). The plant patent holder has the exclusive right to reproduce the plant for seventeen years.[10] The property

10. 35 U.S.C. §§154, 163, 173.

rights of the inventor in other countries depend on compliance with patent laws in the individual countries. A patent holder who produces, assigns, or otherwise uses the patented product is said to "work the invention." In general, under United States law, the patent holder is not obligated to work the invention. Nevertheless, because the patent becomes a part of the public domain after seventeen years, an inventor seeking financial benefit will work the invention.

The inventor may assign all or part of the right, title, and interest in the patent to another. An assignment is a conveyance of title to the patent entitling the assignee full right to work the invention. Assignments of patents should be recorded in the Patent and Trademark Office to protect the assignee from conflicting claims of subsequent assignees.

Instead of assigning the patent, the inventor may retain legal title and grant a "license" of all or some of the rights to another. A license entitles the licensee to use the patent for the purposes and for the period of time specified in the licensing agreement. In exchange for the license, the licensee usually pays a royalty to the inventor. The royalty may be a lump sum payment or may be based on a percentage of sales or production. A license may be exclusive, thereby preventing the patent holder from granting other licenses. Some agreements create "cross-licenses" by which one patent holder grants a license in one invention in exchange for a license in a different patent from another patent holder. Although assignment and licensing of patent rights are legal, misuse of these rights, for example to restrain trade in violation of antitrust laws, may be illegal.

Trade Secrets.
Federal patent law promotes development of new products and manufacturing processes by giving the inventor a monopoly or right of exclusion for a limited period of time in exchange for full disclosure of the invention. State law, most notably state tort law that protects wrongful disclosure or use of trade secrets, may also protect certain forms of invention. A **trade secret** is

any formula, pattern, device or compilation of information which is used in one's business, and which gives him an opportunity to obtain an advantage over competitors who do not know or use it. It may be a formula for a chemical compound, a process of manufacturing, treating or preserving materials, a pattern for a machine or other device, or a list of customers.[11]

As the term indicates, the subject of a trade secret must be secret—not generally known to the public or to other competitors in the trade or business. It may or may not be patentable. Novelty, as used in patent law, is not required.

Unlike patents, which confer a right to exclude all others from using the invention, trade secrets are protected against unauthorized use only if the secret is obtained through a breach of a confidential relationship or other improper means. Thus, an employer who confides the secret to key employees under an express or implied restriction against disclosure or use would be protected if the employees subsequently used the secret for personal use or disclosed it to a competitor. In addition, the holder of a trade secret is protected against knowledge gained by improper means such as physical force, burglary, theft, wiretapping, or other forms of industrial espionage. The trade secret holder, accordingly, is not protected against discovery of the secret by honest means, independent invention, or reverse engineering (analyzing the product embodying the secret to determine how it was developed or manufactured). Thus, tort liability is imposed not for using a trade secret, but rather for employing improper means to procure it.[12] A person injured by tortious use or disclosure of a trade secret may recover damages for past injury and may, in some cases, obtain an injunction against future use of the secret.

A patent provides in some ways more, and in other ways less, protection than a trade secret. For example, trade secrets may last indefinitely and are not limited to patentable inventions. In contrast, patent law protects inventions that are not secret even against persons who independently and honestly discover the patented product or process.

Copyrights

A **copyright** is the exclusive right to reproduce a creative work. Prior to 1976, copyrights were governed by both state common law and federal statute. Copyrights are now regulated solely by a comprehensive federal statute, the Copyright Act of 1976.

Copyrightability. The Copyright Act lists seven categories of creative works to illustrate the types of material that qualify for copyrights: literary works; musical works; dramatic works; pantomime and choreographic works; pictorial, graphic, and sculptural works; motion pictures and other audiovisual works; and sound recordings.[13] A 1980 amendment to the Act makes it clear that computer programs are literary works that may be copyrighted. The creator of any type of copyrightable work is called the "author."

The critical criterion for determining whether a work may be copyrighted is originality; that is, the work must originate with the author. The work need not be novel, unique, or artistic. It need only be original.

Securing a Copyright. Unlike patents, copyrights are not granted by the federal government. Instead, the author of an original work automatically secures a copyright when the work becomes "fixed in any tangible medium of expression . . . from which [it] can be perceived, reproduced, or otherwise communicated, either directly or with the aid of a machine or device."[14] A notice of copyright must be placed on all copies of the work after publication. Generally, publication is considered to have occurred when the work is publicly distributed or displayed. The notice should include three elements: (1) the word "copyright," abbreviation "Copr.," or the symbol ©, or in the case of sound recordings, the symbol ℗, (2) the date of first publication, and (3) the name of the copyright owner.

Under the Copyright Act of 1976, the author is required to register the work and deposit two copies of it with the Copyright Office within three months of publication. An author who fails to register a

---

11. *Restatement of Torts* §757 comment b.

12. At issue in *E. I. du Pont de Nemours & Company, Inc. v. Christopher* excerpted in the Guide to Reading Legal Case Excerpts was whether the defendant had used "improper means" to obtain another's trade secret.

13. 17 U.S.C. §102.

14. *Id.*

work is not denied copyright protection, but may not sue for unauthorized reproduction of the work until registration. If an author has failed to include the copyright notice on the work, copyright protection will not be forfeited if the work is registered within five years of publication and a good faith effort is made to affix the notice on remaining copies.

Property Rights of the Copyright Holder.

In most cases, the author is the initial copyright holder. If, however, a person is hired for the purpose of creating the work, the person's employer is entitled to the initial copyright and is considered the author in law. Generally, the copyright exists for the life of the author plus fifty years. If the work was created for hire, however, the copyright expires seventy-five years after publication or 100 years after creation, whichever occurs first.

The author of a copyrighted work has five exclusive rights that are enumerated in the Copyright Act: (1) the right to reproduce the work, (2) the right to prepare derivative works based on the copyrighted work, (3) the right to public distribution of copies of the work, (4) the right to public performance of the work, and (5) the right to public display of the work. The author of a copyrighted work may assign all or some of these rights. The assignment must be in writing and signed by the holder of the copyright and should be recorded with the Copyright Office. A copyright holder also may license all or part of the rights. Most licensing agreements provide for the payment of royalties.

Despite the rights granted to the copyright holder under the Act, "fair use" of a copyrighted work is permitted. The Act does not define the elements of fair use. In general, however, limited use of a portion of the work for purposes of review or critique, for teaching or instructional activities, or for news reporting qualifies for fair use. The purpose of the fair use doctrine is to prevent restraint of discussion and exchange of information concerning a work.

Trademarks

Trademarks are words or symbols used in marketing that identify the source of a product. The modern law of trademarks developed through the common law. The federal Lanham Act,[15] which codifies much of this common law, regulates the interstate use of trademarks and other similar marks. The statute is supplemented by state statutory and common law. International use of trademarks is subject to the laws of the individual countries where the marks are to be used.

Types of Marks.

Trademarks and service marks comprise most of the marks protected under state and federal law. A **trademark** is identified by the Lanham Act as ''any word, name, symbol, or device or any combination thereof adopted and used by a manufacturer or merchant to identify and distinguish his goods, including a unique product, from those manufactured or sold by others and to indicate the source of the goods, even if that source is unknown.''[16] Examples of trademarks include the words ''Pepsi'' and ''Pepsi-Cola,'' the red flag displaying the word ''French's'' on mustard and condiments, the Coca-Cola bottle, and the picture of the black-hatted man on Quaker products. **Service marks** are similar to trademarks but are used in the sale and advertising of services rather than products. The words ''American Express'' and the picture of the greyhound dog on Greyhound buses are examples of service marks. Service marks are particularly useful in franchising. ''McDonald's,'' ''Pizza Hut,'' and other names and symbols associated with fast-food restaurants are franchised service marks.

The Lanham Act also recognizes collective marks and certification marks. A **collective mark** is a trademark or service mark used by members of a collective group, such as a union or trade association, to identify that its goods or services are produced by members of the group. Many realtors, for example, display a symbol reading ''MLS'' indicating that they are members of Multiple Listing Service, a real estate cooperative. A **certification mark** is a mark that attests to a specified quality, material, or origin from a certain region. The symbol ''UL,'' for example, certifies that a product is in compliance with the standards of Underwriters' Laboratories, Inc. Textile and clothing manufactur-

---

15. 15 U.S.C. §1051 *et seq.*
16. 15 U.S.C. §1127.

ers often use a symbol that certifies their goods are made, for example, of 100% cotton or wool.

Registration. The Lanham Act establishes a system of federal registration of marks with the Patent and Trademark Office. In addition to complying with procedural requirements, the owner of the mark must prove that it has adopted and used the mark in interstate commerce. The registrant also must establish that the mark distinguishes the owner's products from those of others. This requirement means that the mark cannot be merely generic or descriptive. For example, the term "sugar substitute" cannot be registered because it is descriptive. Similarly, the words "saccharine" or "aspartame," generic terms for types of sugar substitutes, cannot be registered. The terms "Sweet 'N Low" and "Nutrasweet," however, are registered trademarks for sugar substitutes. Marks that are primarily surnames also cannot be registered unless the surname has acquired a secondary meaning through its association with a product or service. The Lanham Act prohibits registration of scandalous, immoral, or deceptive marks, and of those consisting of the flag, coat of arms, or other insignia of the United States, a state, a municipality, or a foreign country.

A mark meeting the requirements of the Lanham Act may be registered on the Principal Register of the Patent and Trademark Office and provides notice that the owner has adopted and used the mark. Most states also maintain systems for registering marks used intrastate.

Rights of the Owner of the Mark. The most important property right created by ownership of a mark is the right to license its use. Soft drink companies, for example, generally license the use of their trademarks to bottlers for use in selling beverages made according to the company's formulas. Many fast-food businesses have successfully licensed their service marks as a part of franchise arrangements.

Trademarks and service marks also may be completely assigned to other persons and businesses. An assignment of a mark, however, must be made in conjunction with the assignment of the goodwill of the business in which the mark is used. In other words, an assignment of a mark "in gross" is in-

effective. This rule naturally arises from the fact that marks are protected only when used in the marketing of a good or service. Assignments of marks should be recorded at the Patent and Trademark Office.

Infringement

The unauthorized use of intellectual property is called **infringement.** Specifically, patent infringement is the unauthorized manufacture, sale, or use of a patented invention. Copyright infringement includes, for example, verbatim copying of the copyrighted work and copying the work in a substantially similar work. Infringement of a mark is the use of a mark that is so similar to another's mark that purchasers are likely to be confused as to the source of the products or services.

An intellectual property owner injured by infringement may bring suit in federal court. In addition, most states recognize a cause of action for infringement of trademarks and other marks. In these suits, a variety of remedies are available, including injunctions, dollar damages, equitable accounting, and in some cases attorneys' fees.

In the following copyright infringement case, the court examined the nature of and limits upon copyright protection in computer programs.

Apple Computer, Inc. v. Franklin Computer Corporation
714 F.2d 1240 (3d Cir. 1983)

Apple Computer, Inc. manufactures and markets microcomputers, peripheral equipment, and computer programs, including application programs and operating system programs. An application program allows the user to perform a specific task, such as word processing, while an operating system program manages the internal functions of a computer or facilitates the use of an application program. An operating system program, for example, might translate commands written in BASIC or FORTRAN to a machine language that can be interpreted by the central processing unit of a computer. Computer programs can be stored on semi-conductor chips that are incorporated into the circuitry of a computer or on floppy disks used with computer disk drives.

Franklin Computer Corporation manufactures and sells microcomputers designed to be compatible with Apple peripherals and software programs. Apple sued Franklin for copyright infringement, alleging that Franklin had copied and sold fourteen operating system programs that Apple had developed and copyrighted. Some of the programs were stored on ROM (Read Only Memory) semi-conductor chips within the Apple microcomputer and other programs were stored on floppy disks. Franklin admitted that it had copied the programs but alleged that because the programs were operating system programs, they were not copyrightable. Apple made a motion for a preliminary injunction to restrain Franklin from using, copying, selling, or infringing Apple's copyrighted programs. After the district court denied the motion, Apple appealed to the Third Circuit Court of Appeals.

Sloviter, Circuit Judge

. . . Franklin contends that operating system programs are *per se* excluded from copyright protection under the express terms of section 102(b) of the Copyright Act. . . .

Section 102(b) of the Copyright Act . . . provides:

> In no case does copyright protection for an original work of authorship extend to any idea, procedure, process, system, method of operation, concept, principle, or discovery, regardless of the form in which it is described, explained, illustrated, or embodied in such work. . . .

Franklin argues that an operating system program is either a "process," "system," or "method of operation" and hence uncopyrightable. Franklin correctly notes that underlying section 102(b) . . . is the distinction which must be made between property subject to the patent law, which protects discoveries, and that subject to copyright law, which protects the writings describing such discoveries. However, Franklin's argument misapplies that distinction in this case. Apple does not seek to copyright the method which instructs the computer to perform its operating functions but only the instructions themselves. The method would be protected, if at all, by the patent law, an issue as yet unresolved. . . .

Both [operating system programs and application programs] instruct the computer to do something. Therefore, it should make no difference for purposes of section 102(b) whether these instructions tell the computer to help prepare an income tax return (the task of an application program) or to translate a high level language program from source code into its binary language object code form (the task of an operating system program such as "Applesoft". . .). Since it is only the instructions which are protected, a "process" is no more involved because the instructions in an operating system program may be used to activate the operation of the computer than it would be if instructions were written in ordinary English in a manual which described the necessary steps to activate an intricate complicated machine. There is, therefore, no reason to afford any less copyright protection to the instructions in an operating system program than to the instructions in an application program.

Franklin's argument . . . that an operating system program is part of a machine mistakenly focuses on the physical characteristics of the instructions. But the medium is not the message. . . . The mere fact that the operating system program may be etched on a ROM does not make the program either a machine, part of a machine or its equivalent. . . . In fact, some of the operating systems at issue were on diskette. . . .

Perhaps the most convincing item leading us to reject Franklin's argument is that the statutory definition of a computer program as a set of instructions to be used in a computer in order to bring about a certain result, 17 U.S.C. §101, makes no distinction between application programs and operating programs. . . .

Franklin's other challenge to copyright of operating system programs relies on the line which is drawn between ideas and their expression. . . .

The expression/idea dichotomy is now expressly recognized in section 102(b) which precludes copyright for "any idea." . . . The legislative history indicates that section 102(b) was intended "to make clear that the expression adopted by the programmer is the copyrightable element in a computer program, and that the actual processes or methods embodied in the program are not within the scope of the copyright law.'' [H.R. Rep. No. 1476, 94th Cong., 2d Sess. 54, 57.]

Many of the courts which have sought to draw the line between an idea and expression have found difficulty in articulating where it falls. . . . [We previously have] quoted approvingly the following passage from *Dymow v. Bolton,* 11 F.2d 690, 691 (2d Cir. 1926):

> Just as a patent affords protection only to the means of reducing an inventive idea to practice, so the copyright law protects the means of expressing an idea; and it is as near the whole truth as generalization can usually reach that, *if the same idea can be expressed in a plurality of totally different manners, a plurality of copyrights may result,* and no infringement will exist. (Emphasis added.)

We adopt the suggestion in the above language and thus focus on whether the idea is capable of various modes of expression. If other programs can be written or created which perform the same function as an Apple's operating system program, then that program is an expression of the idea and hence copyrightable. In essence, this inquiry is no different than that made to determine whether the expression and idea have merged, which has been stated to occur where there are no or few other ways of expressing a particular idea. . . .

The district court made no findings as to whether some or all of Apple's operating programs represent the only means of expression of the idea underlying them. . . . Therefore, if the issue is pressed on remand, the necessary finding can be made at that time. . . .

In summary, Franklin's contentions that operating system programs are *per se* not copyrightable is unpersuasive. . . . We believe that the 1980 amendments reflect Congress' receptivity to new technology and its desire to encourage, through the copyright laws, continued imagination and creativity in computer programming. . . .

[Judgment reversed and remanded.]

Acquiring Title to or an Interest in Personal Property

Gifts

A **gift** is a voluntary transfer of an interest in property by the owner (the **donor**) to another (the **donee**) without any consideration or compensation. This lack of consideration distinguishes a gift from a transfer by contract or sale. To be legally effective to transfer title to the donee a gift must meet three requirements, designed generally to prevent fraud:

1. delivery of the subject matter to the donee,
2. present intent by a competent donor to make the gift, and
3. acceptance of the gift by the donee.

The burden of proving these requirements rests with the donee. If they are proven, the gift is said to be ''valid'' and is generally irrevocable by the donor or those who would otherwise take the property by will or intestate succession upon the donor's death. Note that a gift is an inter vivos transfer of property. Any purported gift that is to take effect only upon the donor's death is invalid. Transfers on death are legally effective only if made in compliance with state statutes governing the validity of wills.

Although both real and personal property may be the subject of gift, the law of gifts is primarily concerned with personal property. Real property transfers, whether by sale or gift, are accompanied by substantial formality—for example, the execution and delivery of a deed to the transferee. Compliance with these formalities generally leaves little doubt regarding the existence of the gift. Most personal property, however, is easily transferable without particular formality, and the owner often has no formal evidence of title. In this context, the alleged donee's possession of the subject matter may be the only hard evidence that a gift has been made. For this reason, most gift disputes arise after the donor's death. The parties to the dispute are usually the alleged donee and the donor's heirs or devisees who assert that they are entitled to the property because no valid gift had been made during the donor's life. The person best qualified to resolve the dispute, the donor, is obviously unavailable to testify concerning how the alleged donee acquired possession.

Delivery. **Delivery** is the transfer of possession of the subject matter from the donor to the donee. Delivery requires that the donor absolutely relinquish the power to use, manage, or otherwise control the property. If the alleged donor fails to do so, no valid gift is made. For example, if the donor states her intent to make a gift of an antique gold watch, but retains it in a safe deposit box to which only she has access, the gift fails for lack of delivery.[17]

The delivery requirement accomplishes several purposes. First, the formality inherent in making delivery serves a cautionary function, protecting the donor against ill-advised or impulsive gifts. Second, delivery is important in determining whether the owner actually *intended* to make a gift, a basic issue in gift cases. The donor's surrender of control over the property to the donee is strong evidence of intent to make a gift and thus helps resolve cases in which other evidence of intent is ambiguous or sketchy. Third, the delivery requirement protects the donor against fraudulent assertions by others that a gift has been made.

Symbolic or Constructive Delivery. The manner of delivery varies depending on the nature of the subject matter, its location, and the location and physical condition of the parties. As a general rule, if the object of gift is capable of manual transfer—for example, a watch, jewelry, or a television set—physical delivery of the object itself is required. The donee need not actually take physical possession as long as the object is placed within her control and out of the control of the donor. For example, the property may be placed in a bank account, trunk, or other receptacle owned by the donor.

Frequently, manual delivery is impossible or impractical because of the size or location of the subject matter. To address this situation, the doctrines of symbolic and constructive delivery have been developed. A **symbolic delivery** occurs when another object is delivered in place of the actual subject matter. A **constructive delivery** involves a transfer to the donee of the means to obtain possession and control of the property involved.[18]

The most common type of constructive delivery involves the transfer of a key to a safe deposit box, trunk, or other locked receptacle in order to make a gift of the contents. Courts generally sustain constructive deliveries when physical transfer of the contents is inconvenient or impractical (for example, when the donor is bedridden), or the subject matter is large or bulky or located at a site remote to the parties.

Constructive deliveries have been sustained, however, even if the property can be manually transferred. For example, delivery of keys to a locked box located in the bedridden donor's room may be an effective delivery of the contents. Most cases appear to turn on whether, after considering all facts and circumstances of the individual case, the court is convinced that the alleged donor did in fact intend to make a gift of the property in dispute.

In addition to tangible personal property capable of manual delivery (a "chose in possession"), intangible property consisting of a claim by one person against another for the performance or transfer of something valuable (a "chose in action") may be the subject of gift. Examples include ordinary debts and contract rights, bank accounts, checks and notes, bonds, shares of stock, and life insurance policies. As a general rule, a gift of such assets may be accomplished by delivering either the writing customarily accepted as evidence of the obligation (such as shares of stock, an insurance policy, or a savings account passbook) or a writing signed by the donor.

In the following case, the court considered whether the donor had made delivery of a gift of stock.

---

17. A valid delivery may be made before, at the same time as, or after the words of gift or other expression of intent. Thus, no re-delivery is required if the owner decides to make a gift of property already in the donee's possession.

18. As used in law, the term "constructive" means that a given legal result is implied, inferred, or deduced, by law when certain facts are present. The term is used as a modifier to mean, in essence, "as if."

Estate of Ross v. Ross

626 P.2d 489 (Utah 1981)

David Ross was a corporate officer and director in five family-owned corporations. In 1972, David's son Rod began working for one of the corporations, Equitable Life and Casualty Insurance. Between 1974 and 1978 David told several persons that he wanted to reward Rod for his work with Equitable Life by giving him company stock. David exchanged some of his stock in Equitable for new shares issued in Rod's name. Both the corporate records and the stock certificates listed Rod as owner. David, however, kept the certificates in an envelope in a bank safety deposit box with certificates of other family members. The stock later was moved to a safe in the company office to which only David and his brother had access. When stock dividends were issued, David placed the new certificates in Rod's envelope in the safe. All cash dividends were paid to Rod, who attended and voted at shareholders' meetings.

David died in 1978 after having transferred twenty-five percent of his stock in the family businesses to Rod. David's will divided his estate equally among his three children. Thus, in combination with the lifetime transfers, Rod would have owned fifty percent of his father's stock while his brother and sister each would have received twenty-five percent.

The brother and sister filed a claim in probate court alleging that the lifetime transfers were not valid gifts because David had failed to deliver the stock certificates to Rod. The trial court ruled that David had made a valid lifetime gift of twenty-five percent of his stock to Rod. Appellants, Rod's brother and sister, appealed.

Howe, Justice

. . . Appellants assert that three elements must be proven for a person to claim valid title to property by inter vivos gift: a clear and unmistakable intention on the part of the donor to pass immediate ownership, an irrevocable delivery, and acceptance. . . . They contend . . . that the court's decision was erroneous in that the element of irrev-

ocable delivery was not established by clear and convincing evidence.

An important purpose of the delivery requirement is to avoid the hedging of a would-be donor who wishes to retain certain benefits of ownership, including the control of the gift property, while designating another as the recipient of the property during the donor's lifetime. If a gift is not completed before one's death, of course, it is subject to the formalities of testamentary disposition. In the instant case, therefore, the finding of a gift must be based on the decedent's voluntary parting with the control of the stock during his lifetime.

It is appellants' position that decedent should have parted with his dominion over the certificates by physically delivering them to Rod and that the transfer of ownership on the corporate records was insufficient to meet the requirements of delivery. . . .

Viewing the facts of this case in light of the requirements of inter vivos gifts, we find the gifts of stock to Rod were complete and valid. Evidence of decedent's intention that Rod be made the owner of the stock in question during his lifetime was uncontroverted. Appellants do not challenge the sufficiency of the evidence as to donative intent nor the finding of the trial court that the change in ownership was recorded on the corporate books. New certificates were issued in Rod's name. The decedent did not thereafter exercise control over the stocks. On the contrary, Rod voted the stock as its legal owner and received cash and stock dividends.

The fact that the stock certificates were kept in a safe to which decedent, but not Rod, had access is not fatal to the finding of a completed gift. The decedent had physical possession of stock certificates belonging to a number of other Ross family members. There was no assertion or evidence that he exerted control or possessory rights over any of that stock. His custody of Rod's stock was simply consistent with the practice within the family businesses of keeping the stock certificates in a central location clearly identified as to the owners of the shares. Individual envelopes carried owners' names, stock certificate numbers, and the number of shares represented by the certificates.

We find no error in the trial court's . . . conclusion that the inter vivos gifts to Rod were valid. . . .

[Judgment affirmed.]

Intent. A valid gift requires proof of the donor's intent to transfer title gratuitously. The person to whom the property is delivered must become the new owner rather than a custodian of the property, or an agent for the original owner. Evidence of the donor's express statements, the relationship of the parties, the size of the gift, and the donor's financial situation may be used to show an intent to gratuitously pass title. The donor also must possess sufficient mental capacity to appreciate the nature of his action. A gift induced by fraud, undue influence, or duress may be avoided by the donor or his estate.

Even if intention can be shown, the gift fails in the absence of proper delivery. That is, a gift that is to take effect in the future is simply a promise to make a gift and is unenforceable for lack of consideration. Suppose that at a family reunion rich uncle Arthur states to his favorite nephew John, ''I promise to give you my antique gold watch at your college graduation ceremony next Saturday.'' Arthur incurs no liability for a subsequent failure to make the gift.

Acceptance. Acceptance is the final element of a valid gift. Because a person cannot, in an inter vivos transaction, have property forced upon her against her will, acceptance is required. If, however, the gift is beneficial, acceptance by the donee is presumed. This presumption is used to sustain gifts made to a third party on the donee's behalf unknown to the donee until after the donor's death, and gifts to minors and mental incompetents.

Gifts Causa Mortis. Two basic types of gifts are recognized: inter vivos gifts (the subject of the preceding discussion) and gifts *causa mortis*. Both require the basic elements of intent, delivery, and acceptance. The **gift causa mortis** differs from an inter vivos gift in two basic respects. First, it is made in anticipation or contemplation of the donor's imminent death. Second, it is revocable by the donor at any time prior to his death and is au-

tomatically revoked upon the donor's recovery or delivery from the illness, injury, or peril inducing the gift, or if the donee fails to outlive the donor.

A gift causa mortis is similar to a testamentary (by will) transfer because it is not finally and irrevocably effective until the donor's death. Nevertheless, in order to fulfill the donor's intention, courts do not treat a gift causa mortis as an invalid attempt to circumvent the formalities of a will. Instead, the deathbed gift is deemed a present transfer, subject to revocation as indicated above. To prevent fraud such deathbed gifts are usually validated only if evidence of their existence is clear and convincing.

Original Acquisition

At any given time, certain tangible objects may not be owned by anyone. Two primary examples of unowned property are: (1) wild animals, birds, and fish in their natural state, and (2) abandoned property. Title to unowned goods may be acquired by **original acquisition** by taking possession.

Title acquired by capturing or killing wild animals is subject to applicable game laws and the rights of the owner of the land on which the animal is captured. Although a landowner does not own the wildlife on his or her property until reducing it to possession, the landowner is given superior rights to game killed or caught on the land by a trespasser. In addition, mere pursuit of a wild animal does not constitute possession, allowing an intervening party to acquire title. Nevertheless, animals or fish caught in a trap or net are in the ''constructive possession,'' and therefore owned, by the person owning the trap or net. If the animal escapes, possession and ownership cease, meaning that any person subsequently capturing the animal becomes the owner.[19]

Title to abandoned property may also be acquired by taking possession. To establish **abandonment** the owner must have *intended* to permanently and absolutely relinquish all interest in the property. Most disputes arise when no positive evidence

---

19. These rules apply only to wild animals. Domestic animals are governed generally by the same rules of law applicable to inanimate, tangible personal property, such as a car or television set.

of abandonment exists—for example, the owner's express statements or conduct—and intent must be inferred from the owner's failure after a lapse of time to make an effort to reclaim the property. A common form of abandoned property is marine wreckage, which is governed by special principles of admiralty law.

Accession

Accession (literally meaning "something added") occurs when value in the form of labor or property, or both, is added to tangible personal property. The doctrine, in one form, supports the right of an owner to all that his property produces. For example, the offspring of an animal belongs to its owner. These are "natural" accessions in contrast to "artificial" accessions in which value is added to one person's property by the labor or materials or both of another. Most disputes involve artificial accessions after either the property improved or property added has been "converted,"[20] that is, after the owner has been *wrongfully* deprived of her property either by the person making the improvements or another. The law must then determine the state of the title to the new article created and the rights of the respective parties.

Resolution of accession disputes requires a determination of whether labor, materials, or both are added by the converter. If labor alone is added—for example, the owner's lumber is converted into a cabinet—the result appears to turn on a combination of two factors:

1. *The increase in the value of the property caused by the addition of labor.* As the disparity in value, before and after, increases, the court is more likely to hold that the converter has acquired title to the finished product. In this case, the original owner is entitled to money damages for the value of the property before conversion.

2. *Whether the conversion was innocent or willful.* As a general rule, a willful converter may not acquire title to a chattel because of added value caused by his labor. That is, the finished product remains the property of the original owner, regardless of the increase in value.

If *goods* of one owner are added to those of another, the resulting product generally belongs to the owner of the principal goods. This result follows even if the owner of the principal goods acts wrongfully in acquiring and incorporating the accessions into the property. Assume Joan fraudulently acquires fabric from Bob and uses it to reupholster the interior of her car. Both the fabric and the car belong to Joan. Bob, of course, is entitled to recover money damages. This principle has been applied in some cases even if the accessions can be removed without substantial damage to the principal good.

Confusion

Like accession, confusion arises when combining property of two or more persons causes conflicting claims to the resulting whole. In **confusion,** however, the combination involves mere *commingling* of similar goods rather than a change in the nature of the goods (by adding labor or combining them with other goods) characteristic of accession. The goods involved in confusion disputes are commonly **fungible,** meaning that one unit of the combined mass is indistinguishable from another. Fungible goods, which are usually sold by weight or measure, include oil, sand, gravel, other minerals, timber, and grain. No confusion arises if the specific property of the individual owners remains segregated or can be identified. Disputes arise when goods, though physically unchanged, have become so commingled that it is impossible to ascertain and return specific property.

If the confused goods are similar in grade and quality, and the proportion contributed by each owner can be established, each owner is generally entitled to take his or her proportionate share. This approach achieves an equitable result even when the commingling is fraudulent or intentional, because the innocent party receives goods similar in grade, quality, and amount to those confused.

If the proportions contributed by each owner cannot be ascertained, either because the respective quantities are unknown or because the goods are not of like grade and quality, some courts award the entire mass to the innocent party if the confusion is fraudulent or willful. This harsh forfeiture remedy has been applied by some courts even to a

---

20. Conversion is discussed in Chapter 5.

careless or negligent commingling. A more equitable approach to both the willful and the negligent case resolves the problem by allocating the burden of proof. Once the innocent party has established the commingling, the burden shifts to the wrongdoer to prove what portion of the combined property he or she owns. If the wrongdoer is unable to do so, the entire mass belongs to the innocent party. Thus, the innocent party is protected to the full value of his contribution in either case, but a forfeiture of any excess is prevented if the wrongdoer can prove his share.

If the commingling is not negligent or willful but instead occurs (1) with the consent of the parties, (2) by an act of a third party, or (3) by an Act of God, the parties are treated as tenants in common[21] of the resulting mass in proportion to their contributed share. If the amounts contributed cannot be ascertained, rough justice can often be achieved by treating the owners as holding equal shares.

Finding Lost Property

Personal property is **lost** when its owner casually and involuntarily parts with it without recalling either the circumstances or place of the loss. A **finder** is a person who discovers the lost property and reduces it to possession. The finder does not obtain title to lost goods against the owner, but has superior title against all persons but the true owner. Assume Andrew finds a watch belonging to Oscar. Before Oscar is located, Andrew loses the watch, which is subsequently found by Bart. Andrew may recover the watch from Bart. The same result follows had Bart stolen the watch from Andrew.

After taking possession, the finder must make a reasonable effort to locate the owner and restore the property to her. In many states, procedures to be followed are governed by **estray statutes,** which commonly provide for advertisement of the goods found followed by a stated period after which the property belongs absolutely to the finder, to the state, or partly to each. A finder who knows or learns the identity of the owner, but fails to take reasonable measures to restore the property to the owner is guilty of theft.

The finder's title and right to possession are not affected by the ownership of the property in or on which it is found. This rule is subject to a number of exceptions, the most important of which is based upon the distinction between "lost" and "mislaid" property.

Property is "lost" casually and involuntarily. In contrast, the owner may intentionally and voluntarily lay down an article and then depart, forgetting to take the property. Such property is deemed **misplaced** or **mislaid,** not lost. Under the traditional rule, mislaid property belongs to the owner of the property where it is found, not to the finder. This rule is designed to facilitate return of the item to its true owner. That is, once the owner discovers the property missing, the owner may remember where she left it and return there.

Distinguishing lost from mislaid property is an often difficult issue resolved after considering a number of factors including the nature of the property, the place where it is found, and the circumstances of the original parting. The following case illustrates the importance of the lost-mislaid distinction in resolving a dispute regarding ownership of property.

Paset v. Old Orchard Bank and Trust Company
378 N.E.2d 1264 (Ill. App. 1978)

Plaintiff Bernice Paset found $6,325 on the seat of a chair in a booth in the safety deposit vault of defendant Old Orchard Bank and Trust Company in Illinois. Paset, who rented one of the safety deposit boxes, turned the money over to the bank. Although the bank notified its customers that property had been found in the vault, no one claimed the money.

The Illinois estray statute provides that if a person finds lost property, the person shall file an affidavit with the circuit judge who will file public notice of the finding of the property. If no one claims the property within one year, title vests in the finder. After complying with the statute, Paset claimed that she owned the money, but the bank refused to return the money to her.

Paset sued to recover the money. The trial court, noting that the money was "mislaid property," not

---

"lost property," held that the bank should hold the money on behalf of its owner. Paset appealed.

Simon, Justice

. . . The Illinois estray statute's principal purposes are to encourage and facilitate the return of property to the true owner, and then to reward a finder for his honesty if the property remains unclaimed. The statute provides an incentive for finders to report their discoveries by making it possible for them, after the passage of the requisite time, to acquire legal title to the property they have found. . . .

Traditionally, the common law has treated lost and mislaid property differently for the purposes of determining ownership of property someone has found. Mislaid property is that which is intentionally put in a certain place and later forgotten; at common law a finder acquires no rights to mislaid property. The element of intentional deposit present in the case of mislaid property is absent in the case of lost property, for property is deemed lost when it is unintentionally separated from the dominion of its owner. The general rule is that the finder is entitled to possession of lost property against everyone except the true owner. . . .

As is usual in cases involving a determination of whether property is lost or mislaid, this court is not here assisted by direct evidence, for, obviously, the true owner is not available to state what his intent was. . . . Our conclusion is that the estray statute should be applied, and ownership of the money vested in the plaintiff finder.

Thus, we do not accept the bank's initial argument that the money was mislaid rather than lost. It is complete speculation to infer, as the bank urges, that the money was deliberately placed by its owner on the chair located partially under a table in the examining booth, and then forgotten. If the money was intentionally placed on the chair by someone who forgot where he left it, the bank's notice to safety deposit box subscribers should have alerted the owner. The failure of an owner to appear to claim the money in the interval since its discovery is affirmative evidence that the property was not mislaid. . . .

We also reject the bank's alternative argument that the money, having been found in a place from which the general public was excluded, was always

in the bank's constructive custody or possession, and therefore could not have been "lost," as that word is used in the estray statute. . . .

[W]e conclude that the estray statute vested ownership in the finder of the property in this case when the owner did not appear after the legislatively designated time of 1 year—at which point the bank's temporary custody and possession was terminated. . . .

[Judgment reversed.]

Fixtures

A **fixture** is an item of personal property that, by virtue of its attachment to, or close association with, land, is regarded as part of the land. The essence of a fixture is that what was once tangible movable personal property (hereafter called a "chattel") subsequently becomes part of the real estate with which it is associated. Although treated as part of the real estate, a fixture such as a furnace, hot water heater, or chandelier does not lose its basic identity. Personal property integrated into the basic structure of a building such as boards, nails, bricks, and plaster is governed generally by the law of accession.

Fixture disputes generally arise between a person (or persons) claiming an interest in the chattel as *personal property* and another (or others) holding an interest in the *land* on which the article is located, asserting that it has become a fixture and therefore part of the real estate. The basic question for judicial determination is whether the chattel, by definition originally personal property, has become so closely related to real estate that it should now be legally treated as real property. Typical fixture disputes, usually classified as involving either "common stem" or "divided" ownership, are discussed below.

Common Stem Ownership

The **common stem ownership** situation is the simplest and most frequently encountered case. In these cases the **annexor** (person placing the chattel on the real estate) owns *both* the chattel and the land to which it is annexed. To illustrate, assume

Vicky, a property owner, makes an improvement to her property by installing a furnace, central air conditioning, a chandelier, kitchen cabinets, or a hot water heater. Subsequently she sells the house to Walter. Nothing is said about the improvement in the contract for sale. After moving in, Walter discovers that Vicky has taken the article with her. Was Vicky entitled to do so, or did the chattel pass to Walter with the ownership of the real estate? The answer to this question depends upon whether the property in question is a fixture. A fixture, as part of the land, passes with ownership of the real estate. Thus, if the article is deemed a fixture Walter prevails; if not, Vicky prevails. Fixtures also pass as real property under a will, are part of any security covered by a mortgage, and are subject to a real property tax.

Whether or not a chattel has become a fixture is a legal conclusion, usually a question of fact for the jury to decide. To guide the jury, various tests for distinguishing a fixture have been developed by statute and judicial decision. Certainly the most commonly recited test is the three-part standard originally adopted by the Ohio Supreme Court in 1853 in *Teaff v. Hewitt*.[22] In that case, the court stated that a fixture is characterized by (1) actual *annexation* of the chattel to the realty, (2) *appropriation* or adaptation to the use or purpose of the realty to which the chattel is connected, and (3) *intention* by the annexor to make the chattel a permanent part of the land.[23] The *Teaff* court stated that each aspect of the test must be satisfied to designate the chattel a fixture.

Modern cases, though they frequently recite the *Teaff* tripartite standard, place primary emphasis on the third aspect, the *intent* of the annexor at the time of annexation to permanently improve the property. All other factors are merely circumstantial evidence of that intent. Resort to circumstantial evidence is necessary because the annexor has not expressly indicated intent. Further, relevant intent is not subjective (what the annexor intended in his or her own mind) but objective (what impression the annexor's conduct created in others, such as creditors or purchasers).

Determining Intent. In resolving the basic issue of intent, important factors that should be considered suggested by the foregoing discussion include the following.

Mode and Degree of Annexation. This factor often, although not necessarily, provides the strongest guidance toward resolving the issue. The inquiry generally focuses on whether the chattel may be removed without substantial damage either to it or to the premises to which it is attached. For example, a central air conditioning system is more likely to be held a fixture than a window air conditioner.

Extent to Which the Article is Specially Adapted to the Premises. This factor may be used, for example, to find keys, storm windows, screens, gas stoves, refrigerators, and rollaway beds to be fixtures even though the degree of annexation is slight or nonexistent.

Time and Place the Case Arises. Storm windows may be more likely to be held fixtures in northern climates, whereas an air conditioner may be more often designated a fixture in the south.

No one factor is determinative. All the surrounding circumstances are considered together to resolve the ultimate issue: *intent* as objectively manifested by the annexor.

Divided Ownership

A second type of fixture dispute, the **divided ownership** case, arises when the owner of a chattel annexes it to the land of another, requiring a determination of whether the attached article now belongs to the landowner. Although this divided ownership may arise with respect to chattels annexed by a life tenant, or even a trespasser, it most commonly occurs when a tenant makes improvements on the landlord's property and then seeks to remove them at the expiration of the lease. Although the basic issue is again intent, tenants are not as likely as owners to intend to permanently improve the real estate. Accordingly, courts have generally allowed removal of chattels affixed by tenants.

If the chattels are attached for use in the tenant's

---

22. 1 Ohio St. 511 (1853).
23. *Id.* 529–530.

trade or business (for example, counters, machinery, shelves, or light fixtures), the tenant's right to remove them is well settled. Such articles are somewhat confusingly known as **trade fixtures,** which are not fixtures at all because they do not pass to the owner of the underlying real property interest, the landlord. This right of removal has generally been liberally construed in the tenant's favor to include chattels affixed either for particular business or agricultural needs, and the right commonly extends even to substantial structures on the land, such as a barn or shed. In fact, tenants have been allowed to remove structures, even if the structure is thereby reduced to its raw materials.

Despite this broad policy favoring the tenant in these cases, limitations on the right of removal exist that arise either expressly or from the surrounding circumstances:

1. Because the lease is a contract, the parties may explicitly provide for disposition of the chattels, making items otherwise removable nonremovable, and vice versa.

2. Courts commonly draw a distinction between those articles affixed to further the tenant's particular needs (allowing removal) and those that amount to a permanent improvement of the lessor's premises (more hesitant to allow removal).

3. The tenant must generally remove the chattels during the term of the lease. This approach prevents the disturbance of the succeeding possessory interest (landlord or subsequent tenant) caused by the former tenant's entry to remove the chattel.

The following divided ownership case illustrates the application of the three-part standard to resolve whether certain chattels should be classified as personal property or as fixtures.

T-V Transmission, Inc. v. County Board of Equalization

338 N.W.2d 752 (Neb. 1983)

Plaintiff, T-V Transmission, Inc., (T-V) furnishes cable television service to subscribers in Pawnee County, Nebraska. The company operates an antenna that feeds signals to a cable that T-V has constructed and attached to utility poles throughout the area. When a person subscribes to the cable televi-

sion service, T-V runs an additional cable and support wire (known as "station connects" or "aerial housedrops") from the utility pole to the subscriber's house. If a subscriber discontinues cable television service, service is cut off at the utility pole by installation of a terminator, but the aerial housedrop remains in place.

The defendant, County Board of Equalization, assesses taxes on personal property in the county. The board assessed taxes against T-V for all aerial housedrops it had installed in the county. T-V appealed, alleging that upon installation, the aerial housedrops became fixtures. The trial court held that the housedrops were personal property. T-V appealed.

Hastings, Justice

. . . [T]he defendant County Board of Equalization of Pawnee County . . . assessed "station connects," or aerial housedrops, as personal property belonging to the plaintiff rather than as fixtures attached to the real estate of each individual homeowner subscriber. . . .

The plaintiff has no agreement with its subscribers which would prevent the subscribers' use of these materials, and the plaintiff makes no claim on these cables nor seeks to recover or retrieve them when there has been a disconnection of the service. The plaintiff has no easement across the yards of subscribers to install or remove the cables, and, as a matter of fact, according to the plaintiff's witness, the "station connects," or housedrops, have very little salvage value and are really abandoned by the company. The hope of the plaintiff is, of course, that when a different person occupies that house he will request a reconnection of the service. . . .

The basic question involved in this appeal may be quite simply stated to be, Are the "station connects," or aerial drops, together with the enclosed cables, personal property which remain in the ownership of the plaintiff, or are they fixtures affixed to and which become a part of the real estate? The answer would appear to be deceptively simple:

> In determining this question, the following tests, while not all inclusive, have received general approval, viz: 1st. Actual annexation to the realty, or something appurtenant thereto. 2d. Appropriation to the use or purpose of that part of the realty

with which it is connected. 3d. The intention of the party making the annexation to make the article a permanent accession to the freehold. This intention being inferred from the nature of the articles affixed, the relation and situation of the party making the annexation, the structure and mode of annexation, and the purpose or use for which the annexation has been made. . . . The third test, namely that of ''intention,'' appears by the clear weight of modern authority to be the controlling consideration. [*Swift Lumber & Fuel Co. v. Elwanger* 256 N.W. 875, 877 (Neb. 1934).]

We believe that there is little doubt that the entire system from the utility pole inward, was annexed to the realty and was appropriated solely for the use of the occupants of that realty.

As to the remaining question, concerning the intention of the party making the annexation, we have both the testimony and the practice of the plaintiff that it had no right or intention of removing the property, and in fact had not done so but had abandoned, in favor of the homeowner, all claim to the property that it might otherwise have had. . . .

[Judgment reversed.]

Sale of Goods Apart From Land— Applicable Law

A property owner may desire to sever an item that is a fixture or otherwise part of the land and sell, use, or otherwise dispose of it *apart* from the land. When goods closely associated with real estate are sold, the law must determine whether a sale of real or personal property is involved. If the item is real property, the transaction is governed by common law contract and property principles. If the item is personal property, the transaction is a sale of goods governed by Article 2 of the UCC.

The rules determining the law applicable to sales of goods apart from the land are stated in §2-107, summarized below.

1. A contract for the sale of (1) minerals (including oil and gas) to be extracted, or (2) a structure or its materials to be removed from the land (for example, an old barn to be torn down and its lumber salvaged) is a contract for the sale of *goods* subject to Article 2 if the seller is required to sever. If the buyer is to sever, the transaction is considered one affecting *land* and is subject to the law governing real estate transfers. Assume Seller contracts to sell to Buyer an old barn that is to be torn down and removed from the land. The contract is governed by Article 2 if Seller is to sever, but is a sale of an interest in land (and thus outside the scope of Article 2) if Buyer is to sever.

2. A contract for the sale apart from the underlying real estate of growing crops, timber to be cut, or fixtures is a sale of goods governed by Article 2 regardless of who severs even though they form part of the land at the time of the contract. Assume Seller owns a house containing an ornate chandelier. Seller sells the chandelier to Buyer under a contract requiring Buyer (or Seller) to remove it from the house. The chandelier is a good and its sale is therefore governed by Article 2. Note that Article 2 governs only the basic contract for sale. It does not resolve the various disputes arising concerning ownership of such property. These are left primarily to the common law of fixtures.

SUMMARY

1. The law of both real and personal property is primarily concerned with the creation and transfer of various ownership interests in the property. Property ownership may be held by one person or by a number of persons who may hold widely varying interests in the same property. Whatever their nature or extent, ownership interests usually are acquired by transfer from a prior owner. Property may be transferred either voluntarily or involuntarily during the owner's life or on the owner's death.

2. Intellectual property is a form of intangible personal property relating to ideas and creative thoughts. The major forms of intellectual property are patents, copyrights, and trademarks. Unlike most property, intellectual property rights are governed primarily by federal law.

3. In addition to transfers by contract or in trust, an

interest in personal property may be acquired during the owner's life by gift, original acquisition, accession, confusion, and by finding lost property.

4. A gift is a voluntary transfer of an interest in property by the donor to the donee without consideration or compensation. To be valid, and thus irrevocable by the donor, the gift must meet three requirements: (1) delivery of the subject matter to the donee, (2) present intention by a competent donor to make the gift, and (3) acceptance by the donee. Even if these three elements are met, a gift made in anticipation of death (a gift "causa mortis") is revocable by the donor at any time prior to death and is automatically revoked if the donor recovers.

5. Title to personal property may also be acquired by original acquisition by reducing previously unowned property to possession. Two primary examples of property that may be acquired by original acquisition are wild animals, birds, and fish in their natural state and abandoned property.

6. The law of accession has been developed to resolve disputes arising when the labor and materials of one person are added to the property of another. The law determines the state of the title to the new article created and the rights of the respective parties.

7. Confusion occurs when similar property of two or more persons becomes so commingled that the specific property of each can no longer be ascertained. The law of confusion determines the proportionate share of the commingled goods owned by each party.

8. Property is lost when the owner involuntarily parts with it without recalling the circumstances or the place of the loss. In this case, a finder who subsequently reduces the property to possession has superior rights in it against all but the true owner. The finder's title and right to possession are not generally affected by the ownership of the land in or on which property is found. This rule is subject to a number of exceptions, the most important of which is based on the distinction between "lost" and "mislaid" property.

9. Disputes may arise when items of personal property become closely affixed or adapted to a particular tract of real property. In this case, two competing parties, one holding an interest in the chattel as personal property and another holding an interest in the land to which the property is attached, may claim an interest in the chattel. These disputes are resolved by the law of fixtures. The UCC resolves a related question determining whether goods severed and sold apart from land, such as crops, timber, or minerals, are treated as real or personal property.

KEY TERMS

conveyance (grant)	constructive delivery
intellectual property	gift causa mortis
patent	original acquisition
utility patent	abandonment
design patent	accession
plant patent	confusion
trade secret	fungible goods
copyright	lost property
trademark	finder
service mark	estray statute
collective mark	misplaced (mislaid)
certification mark	property
infringement	fixture
gift	common stem ownership
donor	annexor
donee	divided ownership
delivery	trade fixtures
symbolic delivery	

QUESTIONS AND PROBLEMS

34-1   Carla has manufactured and patented a unique composition known by the chemical name "fluoricose." The product may be substituted for sugar in any recipe but fluoricose has no calories and prevents tooth decay by covering teeth with a protective coating.

    (a) Carla intends to market her invention and is trying to develop a trademark for it. Why would she want to obtain a trademark if she already has a patent?

    (b) Could Carla obtain a trademark if she adopted and used the name "fluoricose?" Explain.

    (c) Could Carla obtain a trademark if she adopted and used the name "Sugar Substitute?" Explain.

    (d) Could Carla obtain a trademark if she adopted and used the name "Sweet and Toothy"? Explain.

34-2   Video cassette recorders (VCRs) allow the user to record television programs and replay the recording. Bill Green owned a Sunny brand VCR and used it to record the film *Snow White,* which had been copyrighted by Walt Disney Productions.

    (a) Has Bill violated the Copyright Act of 1976? Explain.

    (b) Has Sunny violated the Copyright Act of 1976 by manufacturing a machine that facilitates the copying of copyrighted material? Explain.

34-3 In Japan, the government issues patents under a system similar to the United States system. The Japanese government, however, may order the patent holder to grant a nonexclusive license if the invention has not been worked sufficiently for three or more years.

(a) What is the purpose of such compulsory licensing?

(b) Should the United States adopt a provision for compulsory licensing? Explain.

34-4 Assume Dave transfers a diamond ring to Carl with instructions to deliver the ring to Dave's daughter Sue as a gift. Under what circumstances would Dave's transfer of the ring to Carl constitute a valid delivery of the ring to Sue? When would such a transfer not be a valid delivery? Would a valid gift be made if Dave had directed Carl to deliver the ring only after Dave's death?

34-5 William and Beth were engaged to be married in June. In January, William purchased a diamond engagement ring and gave it to Beth. In May Beth broke the engagement. William sued Beth demanding return of the engagement ring. Beth alleged that the ring was a gift. What result? Explain.

34-6 Father opened a joint savings account with his adult Son. Both Father and Son provided specimen signatures and Father told Son, "This account is to be for your benefit." For the next 10 years, Father kept the account passbook, made deposits and withdrawals, and declared the interest as his income for tax purposes. Assume that Son obtains the passbook and withdraws all of the funds in the account. Father demands return of the funds and Son refuses saying Father had made a gift of the account to Son. Father explains that it was his intention that Son have the account only after Father's death. Did Father make a valid gift? Explain.

34-7 Henry suffered a severe heart attack and was admitted to the hospital in critical condition. When his good friend Theresa came to visit him, Henry told her to go to his house and to take the envelope on the top of his desk saying, "The envelope is for you." With another friend, Ther-esa picked up the envelope and found that it contained several certificates of deposit. Henry died the following day. The heirs claim that the certificates of deposit were estate assets. Theresa claimed the certificates of deposit were a gift causa mortis to her.

(a) What arguments should the heirs raise to prove that the gift was invalid?

(b) What arguments should Theresa raise to prove the gift was valid?

34-8 A state has enacted a statute imposing a tax on "real property and improvements thereon and fixtures attached thereto." The state tax assessor has decided the following property may be taxed under the statute. Is the assessor correct?

(a) A storage shed located on Fred's farm. Fred purchased the prefabricated shed at a hardware store and placed it on his property, using a concrete foundation.

(b) A specially constructed bank vault door (fair market value of $100,000). First National Bank installed the door when it created a vault room on its premises to provide safety deposit storage for its customers.

(c) A crystal chandelier recently installed in Nelson's palatial mansion. Nelson purchased the chandelier in Europe where it had been hanging in the castle of a German baron. The chandelier was installed in Nelson's mansion by bolting it to an electrical socket in the ceiling.

34-9 Clarence purchased a radio transmission tower on an installment contract from Motorola Communications. Clarence then leased a parcel of land from the Industrial Corporation. Clarence installed the tower on the land. The tower was 400 feet tall and was anchored to the ground by a concrete slab measuring ten feet square and extending eight feet into the ground. Additionally, guy wires secured the tower and were attached to rods sunk six feet in the ground. Two years after installing the tower Clarence defaulted in making payments to both Motorola and Industrial. Motorola attempted to repossess the tower but Industrial asserted that the tower had become a fixture. Who owns the tower? Explain.

Chapter 35

*Bailments, Documents of
Title, and Letters of Credit*

Bailments are a common fact of modern life. Whenever you loan a book to a friend, borrow your neighbor's lawnmower, drop your car off for repairs, ship goods by air express, or store goods in a warehouse, a bailment exists. In its broadest sense a **bailment** is simply the rightful possession of goods by someone not the owner. A bailment is typically created by delivery of tangible personal property from a person in possession (the **bailor**) to another (the **bailee**) for a specified purpose without transfer of title. The bailor retains ownership and expects that the property will be returned upon completion of the bailment.

Bailments are fundamentally different from sales or gifts. In a sale or gift, title to the property and the unlimited right to possess and use it pass to the buyer or donee. In a bailment, title remains in the bailor and the bailee's use of the property is limited by the terms of the bailment. In addition, a sale or gift does not envision a return of the property to the owner present in a bailment.

Introduction to Bailments

Types of Bailments

Most bailments arise out of contract between the bailor and bailee, such as leases of personal property and bailments for repair, shipment, or storage. Thus, the rental of a car or the shipment of goods by rail or truck creates a bailment. Bailments may also be created gratuitously. For example, a person may lend her binoculars to a friend to use at a football game.

Although most bailments result from an agreement between the parties, occasionally a person obtains possession of another's goods without either his knowledge or consent. Most courts classify this arrangement as an **involuntary, constructive,** or **quasi-bailment.** Examples include the finder of lost articles, a person in possession of goods delivered by mistake or deposited on his land by accident or force of nature, and a landlord in possession of goods left by a tenant upon termination of a lease.

The law of bailments primarily concerns the bailee's liability for (1) the loss, theft, damage, or destruction of goods in the bailee's possession and (2) misdelivery—delivery of the goods to a person other than the bailor or otherwise contrary to the terms of the bailment. Bailment law is derived from several sources: the common law, state statutes (most notably Article 7 of the Uniform Commercial Code), and federal law. This chapter divides the substantive law of bailments into two general parts: bailee's liability in general and the specialized liability of professional bailees (warehousemen and carriers).

Possession in Bailments

The bailee's possession of the property is the essence of a bailment. Without possession, no bailment exists, and the legal consequences discussed later in this chapter do not arise. Possession generally requires physical control over the property involved coupled with the intent to exercise such control.

Physical Control. "Parking lot" cases illustrate the concept of possession in bailments. Ann, a car owner, parks her auto for a fee in a parking lot or garage owned by Ben. While still on the lot, the car is damaged or stolen. In determining Ben's liability (if any) for the theft or damage, the nature of the relationship between Ann and Ben must be ascertained. If Ann merely rents a reserved space from Ben, but parks the car herself and keeps the key, the relationship may be characterized as a lease of land or in some cases a license (a revocable privilege to use another person's land). No bailment has been created because Ann did not transfer possession of the car to Ben. Parking garage receipts commonly state explicitly that no bailment results from parking the car (for reasons that will become apparent below). On the other hand, if Ben directs Ann to leave the keys in the car, issues a claim check, and then has the car parked by an attendant, a bailment is created because possession has been transferred from Ann to Ben.

Intent to Exert Control. Because the bailee must not only have physical control, but must also intend to exercise control, a bailment may not be forced upon the bailee without consent. The intent requirement helps determine the identity of the prop-

erty subject to bailment. Suppose Art delivers a coat to Beth for safekeeping. Unknown to Beth, a valuable diamond has been sewn into the coat's lining. Beth is a bailee of the coat, but not necessarily the diamond. A bailee is therefore not responsible for items the existence or value of which she is unaware. Bailees have, however, been held liable for the contents of bailed articles, if the presence and value of the contents could reasonably be anticipated by the bailee—for example, gloves in the pocket of a coat or a tire in the trunk of a car.

General Liability of the Bailee

Liability for Theft, Damage, or Destruction of the Bailed Goods

Article 2 of the UCC determines risk of loss in contracts for the *sale* of goods without regard to the passage of title from seller to buyer.[1] In bailments, however, risk of loss is tied to title. Because a bailment involves only a transfer of *possession,* and not title, the risk of loss, theft, damage, or destruction of the goods in the bailee's possession is ordinarily borne by the bailor.

In some cases, a bailee may be liable for casualty to the bailed goods. Since the classic case of *Coggs v. Bernard,*[2] the law is well settled that a bailee, although not an *insurer* of goods under his control, is liable for loss or damage for which he is at *fault.* In determining the degree of fault necessary to impose liability upon the bailee, courts have traditionally employed a three-part test based on whether the bailment is (1) for the benefit of the bailor, (2) for the benefit of the bailee, or (3) for the mutual benefit of the parties.

Bailor's Benefit. A bailment may be created for the sole benefit of the bailor. In this case, the bailee performs a service without compensation concerning the bailed property. Under the traditional rule, such a "gratuitous bailee" is responsible only if casualty to the goods is caused by his "gross neg-

---

1. Risk of loss in contracts for sale of goods is governed by UCC §§2-509 and 2-510, which are discussed in Chapter 17.

2. 2 Ld. Raym. 909, 92 Eng. Rep. 107 (K. B. 1703).

ligence." In other words, the gratuitous bailee is required to exercise only "slight care."

Suppose Alan, an auto mechanic, as a favor agrees to tune up his friend Nancy's car for free. Nancy delivers the car to Alan's house. In this case, a bailment is created for the benefit of Nancy, the bailor. The car is subsequently destroyed by fire while parked in Alan's garage. The fire started after Alan inadvertently kicked over a gasoline can. Nancy sues him for the loss. On these facts Alan escapes liability for the destruction of Nancy's car unless the trier of fact, usually the jury, finds that his conduct was grossly negligent.

Bailee's Benefit. A bailment also may be created solely for the bailee's benefit—for example, when a friend or neighbor borrows your car, lawn mower, or power tool. In this case, the bailee is traditionally required to use "extraordinary care" in preserving the goods against loss or injury. In other words, the bailee is liable for damage or destruction caused by her "slight negligence."

Mutual Benefit. Bailments are also commonly created for the benefit of both parties. Mutual benefit bailments include rentals of motor vehicles and other property and bailments in which the bailee performs services to the bailed article for a price. For example, delivering a car to a mechanic for repair creates a mutual benefit bailment. In these cases, the bailee is required to exercise "ordinary care" in handling the goods. Ordinary care, in this context, means the amount of care a reasonably prudent person would exercise in the preservation of his or her own goods under similar circumstances. Therefore, in the mutual benefit bailment, the bailee is liable for simple negligence.

In the following case, the proper classification of the bailment under the three-part test was in issue.

American Enka Company v.
Wicaco Machine Corp.
686 F.2d 1050 (3rd Cir. 1982)

Plaintiff American Enka Company (Enka) planned to construct a rayon manufacturing plant in Tennessee. Defendant Wicaco Machine Corp. (Wicaco)

was employed as a subcontractor to manufacture machinery for the plant. In preparing to make the machinery (spinnerettes), Wicaco purchased 6,000 pounds of hastelloy (a special alloy of nickel, chromium, molybdenum, and carbon) in October, 1974. Enka paid for the hastelloy but it was stored at Wicaco's plant. In April, 1977, Enka cancelled construction of the new plant due to declining demand for rayon. Wicaco agreed to hold the hastelloy until Enka was able to find a use for it. In January, 1979, Enka requested return of the hastelloy, at which time Wicaco discovered that the metal had disappeared.

Enka sued Wicaco for damages. The trial court ruled that Wicaco was a bailee for the mutual benefit of Enka and Wicaco. The trial court held that Wicaco had breached its duty to exercise reasonable care and awarded damages to Enka. Wicaco appealed alleging that it had acted as a gratuitous bailee.

Aldisert, Circuit Judge

. . . The dispute in this case is whether the facts establish a bailment for mutual benefit or one for the sole benefit of Enka. Wicaco argues that although the bailment began as one for mutual benefit because of its expectation of profit in making the spinnerettes, once Enka notified it that the Tennessee project was cancelled, Wicaco's agreement to continue holding the ingots without charge converted the bailment to one for the sole benefit of the bailor. Accordingly, it contends that it can be held liable only for gross neglect.

Classification of a bailment as one for mutual benefit does not require the bailor to demonstrate a specific, tangible benefit or compensation running to the bailee. Pennsylvania's appellate courts have said that "a possibility or chance of expected profit to accrue" from the bailment is sufficient to make the relationship one for mutual benefit. . . . The specific question presented for review is whether, as the district court found, Wicaco retained a realistic expectation of profit from the bailment relationship after the Tennessee project was cancelled. Because the nature of the relationship in this case turns on the objective expectations of the bailee, it is a question of fact, and our review of the district court's decision is limited. . . .

We conclude that the district court's findings

were supported by the evidence and we reject Wicaco's argument because it ignores the business realities of Wicaco's relationship with Enka. As evidenced by the testimony of Wicaco president Donald F. Palmer, Wicaco expected either that the Tennessee project would be revived or that it would receive future orders from Enka and Chemtex, or Chemtex alone, allowing use of the bailed hastelloy. Indeed, in June 1977 Enka solicited a Wicaco bid for the manufacture of spinnerettes for use in existing Enka plants. Because Wicaco is in the business of manufacturing mill equipment, not the storage of metal alloys, an expectation of future orders would be sufficient to make the bailment one for mutual benefit. We therefore conclude that the district court's finding that the bailment was for mutual benefit was not clearly erroneous. . . .

[Affirmed as to the issue of liability.]

Modern Approach. The traditional tripartite test, in which a bailee's liability turns upon the benefit accruing to each party, has been widely criticized for various reasons. The standards of care (slight, ordinary, extraordinary) are difficult to apply to specific fact situations, and as the preceding case indicates, it is often difficult to determine which type of bailment is involved. For these reasons, modern decisions in many states impose liability, *in all cases,* for failure to exercise ordinary care under the circumstances. The relative benefits conferred on the parties—for example, a compensated versus a gratuitous bailment—are still relevant, but are only one factor considered by the court in determining whether the bailee exercised ordinary care. Other factors include the nature and value of the property, the business or specialized skill, if any, of the bailee, and the place where the goods are delivered.

Burden of Proof

The bailor seeking to recover for loss or damage to the bailed goods must prove (under the modern approach) that the bailee failed to exercise ordinary care in handling the goods. Proving the bailee's negligence is often a difficult task, because the bailee's acts of negligence occur while the goods are

in the bailee's possession and are known only to the bailee. In other words, on the issue of negligence, the bailor can prove that the bailee failed to return the property or returned it in a damaged condition but little else. For this reason, courts generally hold that the bailor establishes a "prima facie" case for recovery once the bailor proves both

1. the existence of the bailment (delivery of the property to the bailee) and
2. either the bailee's failure to return the goods or the damaged condition of the returned goods.

If these two requirements are proven, the burden of proof shifts to the bailee; that is, negligence of the bailee is presumed. In order to rebut the presumption and prevent an adverse judgment, the bailee must then introduce some evidence showing lack of fault in causing the damage or loss.

Contractual Limitation or Exclusion of Liability

Bailments are often created by contract between the bailor and bailee—for example, for repair, storage, or use of the bailed article. As part of that contract, the parties are generally free to limit the bailee's potential liability for casualty to the bailed goods. Courts will enforce a contractual limitation of liability reached after arms length bargaining between the parties. For example, a commercial bailee such as a warehouseman may agree to accept a reduced fee in exchange for reduced liability.

Disputes often arise, however, when a warehouseman, coat check room operator, or parking lot operator seeks to limit liability for damage or loss of goods by posting a sign noting the limitation and also by placing the limitation on the claim check or ticket evidencing the bailment. Because any attempted liability limitation is legally effective only if the parties mutually agree to it, a bailee cannot limit the liability otherwise imposed by law without proof that the bailor knew and accepted the terms of the bailment. Thus, a bailor who does not read the sign is not bound to a limitation stated on it. In addition, customers (bailors) ordinarily view a claim check or parking lot ticket as merely an identification token, *not* a writing evidencing the terms of the contract between the parties. There-fore, a bailor without reason to know that the token purports to be a contract should not be bound by terms printed on it.

At issue in the following case was enforceability of a liability limitation provision.

Carter v. Reichlin Furriers

386 A.2d 647 (Conn. Super. 1977)

In April, 1973, plaintiff Florence Carter brought her coat to defendant Reichlin Furriers for cleaning and storage until the following winter. Reichlin's employee gave her a receipt form. When Carter returned for the coat in the fall, Reichlin informed her that the coat was lost.

Carter sued Reichlin for $450, the fair market value of the coat. Reichlin alleged that its liability was limited to $100. The evidence at trial established that Reichlin's employee had listed the value of the coat as $100 on the receipt. The back of the receipt limited Reichlin's liability to "depositor's valuation appearing in this receipt." Although the receipt provided a place for both parties' signatures, it was unsigned. Carter testified that she had not discussed valuation of the coat with the employee and that she had not read the receipt until the coat was lost.

The trial court awarded plaintiff Carter $450 as damages; defendant Reichlin appealed.

Shea, Judge

. . . It has been the law of this state that a provision in a receipt wholly relieving a bailee from liability for the loss of property is contrary to public policy and invalid. . . . On the other hand, a limitation placed by the parties on the extent of the bailee's liability for loss of the goods has been expressly sanctioned. . . .

Whether or not a particular provision forms part of a contract is ordinarily a factual question for the trier. The finding that the plaintiff was unaware of the valuation of her coat marked upon her receipt would not be conclusive. An actual "meeting of the minds" would not be required if, under all the circumstances, the plaintiff's conduct would warrant a reasonable belief that she had assented to the

terms of the receipt which she received and held for approximately six months. . . . Some authorities hold that the acceptance of a warehouse receipt containing a stipulation limiting the liability of the bailee makes the limitation binding as a part of the storage contract if the receipt was received at the time the goods were delivered, regardless of actual notice of the stipulation. . . . The modern tendency, however, is to draw a distinction between the bailor who is a business man and one who is a member of the public. . . . In Connecticut provisions exculpating a bailee or limiting his liability are not necessarily a part of the bailment contract in the absence of actual knowledge of them. . . . The mere handing of a receipt containing such a limitation to a bailor has been held insufficient to require a finding of constructive notice. . . . In the present case the trial court found that the plaintiff never read the receipt and that the valuation inserted was never discussed with her. It was not the "depositor's valuation" referred to in the limitation provision, but, rather, that of the defendant's employee. The receipt was not signed by either party although spaces were provided for that purpose by the draftsman of the document. Nothing in the evidence would compel a conclusion that the plaintiff's conduct justified a reasonable person in assuming that she had consented to the limitation of damages contained in the receipt. . . .

[Judgment affirmed.]

Unconscionable Limitations. In the preceding case, the bailor was not informed of and did not consent to the limitation. In contrast, a limitation in a sign or claim check made known to the bailor, who subsequently enters into the bailment, is generally enforceable. In this case, however, the bailor is bound to an "adhesion" contract, a standardized contract drafted by the bailee and presented on a "take it or leave it" basis. The bailor's freedom of choice is often limited by the fact that the bailee possesses a virtual monopoly—for example, the only parking garage at an airport—or that similar terms are used by all bailees. On similar facts, courts have refused to enforce an *unreasonable* limitation on grounds of unconscionability—absence of meaningful choice coupled with contract terms that are unreasonably favorable to one party. In other words, the mere fact that a liability limitation is made known to the bailor does not insure its enforcement.

Exculpatory Clauses. The preceding discussion examines the enforceability of liability *limitations.* The bailee may attempt, through an **exculpatory clause,** to *exempt* himself completely from liability for negligence. Clearly, a contract term relieving a party from tort liability for reckless or intentional conduct is unenforceable on grounds of public policy. Modern courts (and legislatures) also tend to deny enforcement of disclaimers of liability for negligence both in bailments and other areas of law.

Effect of Misdelivery

Once the purposes of the bailment have been accomplished, the bailee is under a duty to redeliver the bailed goods to the bailor on demand. Unlike the standard applied to the bailee's conduct while in possession of the goods (reasonable care), the bailee's duty to redeliver is absolute. For example, a bailee who refuses to redeliver the property upon completion of the bailment is liable to the bailor for the tort of conversion. A bailee who delivers the property to an unauthorized person or one who has no rightful claim to the goods against the bailor is liable for conversion of the goods or for damages for breach of contract, even if the bailee is acting in good faith and without negligence. For example, delivery to an imposter who has cleverly forged an order to deliver renders the bailee liable. Bailees protect themselves in some cases by requiring presentation of a ticket or claim check as a condition to redelivery. The bailee then has the obligation to redeliver the goods in good faith to the person in possession of the ticket.

Although ordinary bailees are generally subject to absolute liability for misdelivery, involuntary bailees such as finders of lost articles are liable for misdelivery only if negligent. The basis of this rule is that an involuntary bailee, who does not willingly assume a bailee's obligations, should be held liable only to a general duty to exercise reasonable care.

Third-Party Claims. The bailee faces a dilemma if a third party, such as a creditor or person alleging ownership, asserts a claim to the goods adverse to the bailor. A bailee delivering to such a third party incurs absolute liability to the bailor for misdelivery if the claim is later found invalid. The bailee is excused from liability if delivery is made under valid legal process, such as a writ of attachment or execution,[3] or if the third-party claim is later determined to be valid. For example, the bailee has no liability if the bailor is a thief.

Absent compulsory legal process, however, the bailee must initially determine the validity of the adverse claim. This determination is often made in an *interpleader* action, in which the bailee surrenders the property to the court (and is relieved of further liability) and the bailor and third party are required to litigate their conflict concerning the property. In other words, the bailee faced with conflicting claims may compel the claimants to litigate their claims with each other rather than with the bailee.

Effect of Use Contrary to Terms of the Bailment

In addition to misdelivery, the bailee may also be subject to expanded liability for using the bailed property in an unauthorized manner. In general, the bailee's right to possess and use the bailed property is determined by the terms of the bailment. These terms may be expressly stated in the bailment contract or may be implied based on the circumstances of the case. For example, the use may be necessary for the care of the bailed chattel or may be a method of compensating the bailee for her services concerning the property. In determining the implied limits of permitted use, the basic test is whether a reasonable person, after considering all circumstances, would regard the use as one that would have been included in the agreement had the parties anticipated the occasion for such a use.

The bailee may, however, go beyond the scope of the bailment by (1) selling the bailed property, (2) using it as collateral on a loan, or (3) using it

---

3. State debt collection remedies, including writs of attachment and execution, are covered in Chapter 29.

for purposes not contemplated or authorized by the bailment. For example, an auto mechanic may accept a car for storage or repair but subsequently use the property for personal or business purposes. These acts generally constitute a conversion of the property, rendering the bailee liable to pay the bailor the full value of the property. Whether the bailee's use is serious enough to constitute a conversion is frequently a difficult question. Most unpermitted uses are serious enough to impose liability. Nevertheless, a minor, temporary deviation that does not damage the property or inconvenience the bailor and that is not intended as a defiance or repudiation of the bailor's rights does not constitute a conversion.

Bailment disputes over unauthorized use normally arise because the bailed property is damaged or destroyed while in the bailee's possession. Although generally liable only for injury to the property caused by negligence, a bailee who departs from the terms of the bailment effectively becomes an insurer of the goods. That is, the bailee becomes responsible for all injury to the goods whether or not caused by negligence and whether or not the bailee's conduct constitutes a conversion. Assume Joan takes her car to Sam, an auto dealer, with instructions to sell it. In violation of this agreement, Sam drives the car 5,000 miles on personal business. While so using the car, it is destroyed by lightning. Because Sam has converted the car, he is liable to Joan for its full value even though he was not at fault in causing the loss. Assume alternatively that Sam does not regularly use the car on personal business, but on one occasion drives the car five miles on a personal errand. During this trip the auto is destroyed by lightning. Even though the use is not a conversion and the destruction is not due to Sam's negligence, Sam is liable to Joan for the value of the property. Of course, had the car been destroyed by lightning on Sam's lot, while being displayed for sale, Joan bears the loss because Sam was neither negligent nor had he departed from the scope of the bailment.

Innkeepers' Liability

A special form of bailee liability is imposed upon hotels and innkeepers for theft or destruction of goods of their guests. The liability includes not only goods within the actual physical control of the innkeeper—for example, valuables stored in the hotel safe—but also the guest's property located in his or her room. Although the latter situation arguably involves no transfer of possession, courts have treated it as a bailment for purposes of imposing liability.

Under the majority common law rule, an innkeeper is a qualified insurer of the goods of guests, relieved of liability only by proving that the loss resulted from an Act of God or an act of a public enemy, the inherent nature of the goods, or the contributory fault of the guest. The common law subjects the innkeeper to a strict liability standard similar to that governing common carriers discussed below. This extraordinary liability originally developed centuries ago when travelers were easy prey for bandits and thieves, and innkeepers were expected to provide protection as well as lodging and food for guests.

The common law rule has been modified by statute in most states. These statutes are far from uniform. Most state statutes repudiate the common law doctrine, strictly limiting the dollar amount of an innkeeper's liability for loss of, or damage to, a guest's property. A copy of the innkeeper's statute usually is posted in each guest room. A guest carrying valuable articles is therefore well advised to read and comply with its terms. If the statutory liability limitation does not cover the value of the articles, the guest should make special arrangements with the hotel or others for their safekeeping.

Bailments for Shipment or Storage

Documents of Title Under UCC Article 7

An important branch of the law of bailments involves the rights, duties, and liabilities of carriers and warehousemen in performing two fundamental commercial functions: the shipment and the storage of goods. Carriers and warehousemen use specialized instruments known as "documents of title" in performing these functions. For example, a person wishing to store goods may deliver them to a commercial warehouse (a bailee), which issues a document of title known as a "warehouse receipt" to the storer (bailor). Or, a person desiring to ship goods may deliver them to a carrier (a bailee), which issues a document of title known as a "bill of lading" to the shipper (bailor).

"Document of Title" Defined. Article 7 of the UCC governs documents of title and the rights and obligations of persons issuing them. A **document of title** is defined in §1-201(15) as any document accepted in business or financing transactions as adequately evidencing that the person who possesses it is entitled to receive, hold, and dispose of the document and the goods it covers. Documents of title, which cover goods in the bailee's possession, include a bill of lading, dock warrant, dock receipt, warehouse receipt, or order for the delivery of goods. Although documents of title are ordinarily issued by the bailee, an order for delivery of goods (a **delivery order**) is issued by a shipper or storer addressed to a carrier or warehouseman ordering it to deliver goods in its possession to a specified person.[4]

"Bill of Lading" Defined. Section 1-201(6) defines a **bill of lading** as a document evidencing receipt of goods for *shipment* issued by a person engaged in the business of transporting or forwarding goods. The term includes an "airbill"—a document that serves for air transportation as a bill of lading does for marine, truck, or rail transportation. The definition also includes bills issued by **freight forwarders**—those in the business of consolidating less than carload shipments to obtain the benefit of lower rail and truck rates—in addition to carriers such as railroads and trucking companies.

The person named in a bill of lading as the person *from* whom the goods have been received for shipment is known as the **consignor**. The person named in the bill *to* whom or to whose order the bill promises delivery is the **consignee**.[5] A **through bill of lading** is one issued by the first of two or more carriers when the carriage is to be performed in part by connecting carriers other than the issuer.

A bill of lading is commonly issued by the carrier to the consignor at the place of shipment. The carrier may, however, at the request of the consignor, issue a **destination bill**. Such bills are issued at the destination or at any other place designated in the request. A destination bill assures that the bill of lading will be available to the person taking delivery at the destination in advance of actual arrival of the goods.

"Warehouse Receipt" Defined. Section 1-201(45) defines a **warehouse receipt** as "a receipt issued by a person engaged in the business of storing goods for hire."[6] A person engaged in the business of storing goods for hire is a **warehouseman**.[7] Under §7-207, a warehouseman is generally required to keep the goods covered by each receipt separate to permit identification and delivery of the particular goods stored. Different lots of fungible goods, such as oil or grain, may, however, be commingled. In this case the owners become tenants in common of the resulting mass.

Negotiable and Nonnegotiable Documents of Title. A warehouse receipt, bill of lading, or other document of title may be either negotiable or nonnegotiable. Under §7-104(1), a document of title is **negotiable** if

1. by its terms the goods are to be delivered to *bearer* or to the *order* of a named person, or
2. where recognized in overseas trade, it runs to a named person or assigns.

Any other document is *nonnegotiable*. Negotiable bills of lading are required, by Interstate Commerce Commission (ICC) regulation, to be printed on yellow paper, whereas nonnegotiable, or "straight" bills, are printed on white paper. Nonnegotiable documents are more common. For example, most interstate railroad shipments are carried under straight bills of lading. Further, airbills issued by air express companies commonly are nonnegotiable.

The distinction between negotiability and nonnegotiability is important for several reasons. For

---

4. UCC §7-102(1)(d).
5. UCC §§7-102(1)(b)-(c).

6. Because the definition applies to storing goods "for hire," not "for profit," state operated and cooperative warehouses are included. UCC §7-102, Official Comment 2.
7. UCC §7-102(1)(h).

example, the person entitled to delivery differs depending on the type of document involved, and a negotiable document constitutes much more effective control of the goods because it must be surrendered to obtain delivery. In addition, a transferee of a negotiable document may acquire more rights than the transferor had. These issues are discussed in more detail later in this chapter. Finally, as outlined in Chapter 16, the negotiable-nonnegotiable distinction is important in determining risk of loss, passage of title, and manner of seller's delivery when goods covered by a document of title are sold.

Scope of Article 7. Article 7 represents a consolidation and revision of two prior uniform state laws, the Uniform Bills of Lading Act and the Uniform Warehouse Receipts Act. In 1916, Congress enacted the Federal Bills of Lading Act (FBLA)[8] that is, in most respects, identical to the Uniform Bills of Lading Act. Thus, warehouse receipts are governed by Article 7, but bills of lading are governed by both state (UCC Article 7) and federal law.

Generally, the FBLA governs any bill of lading issued by a common carrier (defined below) for the transportation of goods in interstate or foreign commerce.[9] Article 7 governs bills issued for intrastate shipments and for shipment from a foreign country into a state. Although the FBLA closely follows the provisions of Article 7, it does not reflect certain additions and clarifications contained in Article 7.

In addition to the FBLA, carriers are also substantially governed by the Interstate Commerce Act, as revised and codified in 1978,[10] regulations of the Interstate Commerce Commission, and numerous other federal statutes of limited scope.

The bailee issuing a document of title acknowledges possession of the goods and contracts to deliver them. From this basic obligation, three fundamental issues arise: (1) liability for loss, damage, or destruction of the goods while in the bailee's possession, (2) contractual limitation or exclusion of that liability, and (3) the bailee's duty to deliver

---

8. 49 U.S.C. §§81-124.
9. 49 U.S.C. §81.
10. 49 U.S.C. §10101 *et seq.*

the goods upon termination of the carriage or storage.

Liability for Loss, Damage, or Destruction of Bailed Goods— Warehousemen

Under Article 7, a warehouseman's liability for damage to, or destruction of, stored goods is governed by the same standard as that applied to ordinary bailees at common law. Section 7-204(1) provides that a warehouseman is liable for casualty to stored goods "caused by his failure to exercise such care in regard to them as a reasonably careful man would exercise under like circumstances." Thus, the warehouseman, like most other bailees, is liable only for damage or destruction caused by negligence—failure to exercise reasonable care.

Liability for Loss, Damage, or Destruction of the Bailed Goods— Common Carriers

The extent of a carrier's liability for loss or destruction of goods in its possession depends upon whether it is a "common" as opposed to a "private" or "special" carrier. Whereas a private carrier is subject to the same standard imposed on other bailees—liability for loss or destruction caused by negligence—a common carrier is a qualified insurer of goods entrusted to it by the shipper. Thus, a carrier's status as common or private is an initial and fundamental determination in ascertaining liability.

The common law definition of common carrier, articulated in many decisions, involves three basic elements. To be a **common carrier,** a person must undertake or hold out to perform (1) carriage, (2) for hire, (3) for all those who apply. The essence of this definition is the public holding out.

Rule of Liability. A person classified as a common carrier is, subject to five limited exceptions, absolutely liable for loss, damage, or destruction of goods in transit. Although the early common law justified the rule as necessary to prevent collusion with robbers and thieves, modern authorities recognize broader grounds for imposing a qualified insurer's liability upon a common carrier, including (1) stimulating care and fidelity on the carrier's part, (2) the carrier's exclusive possession of evidence concerning circumstances of the loss, (3) the difficulties in discovering and proving the carrier's fault, and (4) the carrier's ability to adjust its rates to cover hazards. Whatever the justification, the principle of absolute liability prevailing under the common law is adopted and applied to common carriers issuing bills of lading under both federal law[11] and Article 7.[12]

Exceptions to Liability. The law has long recognized five exceptions to the general rule of absolute liability. The carrier may escape liability by proving that the loss was caused by

1. an Act of God,
2. an act of a public enemy,
3. an act of public authority,
4. an act of the shipper, or
5. the inherent nature of the goods.

Even if the loss is caused by one of the recognized exceptions, the carrier nevertheless remains liable unless it also establishes that it used *reasonable care* to prevent losses from the excepted causes. A discussion of the five exceptions to absolute liability follows.

Act of God. Though the term is probably incapable of precise definition applicable to all cases, damage or destruction generally occurs by Act of God if it results from the operation solely of natural forces without human intervention. Sudden and violent disturbances such as lightning, earthquakes, wind, tornadoes, hurricanes, or other violent storms are considered Acts of God.

Act of a Public Enemy. A carrier is not liable for destruction caused by an act of an organized military or naval force with which the carrier's country is at war. This exception does not apply to acts of robbers or thieves such as hijackers, nor generally to civil disturbances. Perhaps because of improved communications and intelligence, allowing carriers to avoid potential trouble spots, this exception has not been recently applied.

Act of Public Authority. The carrier is excused from its absolute duty to deliver if the goods involved have been taken by valid legal process—for example, replevin, execution, or attachment to satisfy an unpaid judgment against the owner—or under the state's police power—for example, a seizure of stolen goods, drugs, liquor, or other contraband. If the goods are taken by public authority, the carrier is under a duty to promptly notify the shipper of the seizure so that it may appear in the proceedings and defend its interest.

Act of the Shipper. The carrier is not liable for loss caused solely by the shipper's act or default. Most commonly in this context, the loss results from the shipper's improper loading or packaging of the shipped goods. Although the carrier ordinarily is not liable for such losses, if the defect in packaging or loading is apparent or "patent"—for example, the carrier knew or should have known that the shipper's packing or loading was defective—the carrier that accepts the goods remains an insurer of their safety in transit.

Inherent Nature of the Goods. A common carrier is not liable for losses resulting from the inherent nature of the goods shipped. Examples include perishable items such as fruits, vegetables, and livestock. Once again, the carrier bears the burden of showing that the loss was due solely to the inherent nature of the goods and that the carrier's negligence did not contribute to the loss. For example, a negligent delay in transporting perishable

---

11. The so-called "Carmack Amendment" to the Interstate Commerce Act (49 U.S.C. §11707) provides that a common carrier issuing a receipt or bill of lading and any other common carrier delivering the goods are liable to the full extent of common law liability to the person entitled to recover under the receipt or bill. Either of these carriers is liable for damage caused by any carrier used in the trip—for example, under a "through" bill of lading. The initiating or delivering carrier may then recover from any connecting carrier responsible for the loss. Although the Carmack Amendment does not explicitly restate the common law rule, the Supreme Court in *Missouri Pacific Railroad Company v. Elmore & Stahl,* 84 S. Ct. 1142, 1144 (1964), has held that this statute codifies the common law approach.

12. UCC §7-309(1).

goods resulting in spoilage subjects the carrier to liability.

In summary, to recover from the carrier for damage or destruction of a shipment, the shipper must prove delivery of the goods to the carrier in good condition, the carrier's subsequent nondelivery or delivery in a damaged condition, and the amount of damages. The burden of proof then shifts to the carrier, who escapes liability only by proving *both* that the damage or destruction was caused by an excepted peril and that the carrier's negligence did not contribute to the loss. The following case illustrates the basic principles governing carrier liability.

Martin Imports v. Courier-Newsom Express, Inc.

580 F.2d 240 (7th Cir. 1978)

Martin Imports hired the Courier-Newsom Express, Inc., a motor common carrier, to ship 250 cases of wine from Chicago to Rockford, Illinois. The usual transit time for the trip was one day. A driver picked up the shipment from Martin Imports at 4:30 P.M. on December 23. The driver delivered the wine in an unheated tractor-trailer to Courier-Newsom's terminal in Rockford at 5:00 A.M. on December 24. The terminal, however, was closed because Courier-Newsom's employees' collective bargaining agreement required that December 24 and 25 were nonwork days. No attempt was made to notify the consignee of the arrival of the shipment. The trailer remained at Courier-Newsom's terminal until the morning of December 26. During that period, the temperature in Rockford was below freezing. When Courier-Newsom tendered delivery to the consignee on December 26, the consignee refused to accept the shipment because the wine had frozen and many of the bottles had exploded.

Martin Imports sued Courier-Newsom to recover the value of the wine. The trial court held in favor of Courier-Newsom, the appellee; Martin Imports, the appellant, appealed.

Jameson, Senior District Judge

. . . [The trial] court concluded that appellee had not been negligent in its handling of the wine ship-

ment [and] that the damage was due to one of the excepted causes relieving a carrier of liability, namely the inherent vice or nature of the commodity shipped. . . .

Appellee's manager testified . . . that appellee knew when it accepted the shipment that it contained wine and knew that due to the collective bargaining agreement it would not be delivered the next day, as shipments tendered on Mondays normally would be. He said appellee also knew that the shipment would remain in the trailer and the trailer would be left outside until its employees returned to work on the 26th. And, after the shipment arrived in Rockford, there was no attempt to communicate with or notify the consignee of its arrival until the 26th. Under these circumstances we can only conclude that appellee was negligent in failing to advise the appellant that its shipment would not be delivered according to appellee's normal schedule, due to the fact that under the collective bargaining agreement not only was Christmas day a holiday, but the preceding day as well. While the delay in delivery of the wine arguably may have been reasonable, the failure to advise the shipper in advance of the abnormally long delivery time was not.

We find nothing in the record that would impute knowledge of the collective bargaining agreement to appellant. In appellant's business the day preceding Christmas is apparently among its busiest of the year. It was not unreasonable for it to assume that the carrier would also be open for business that day. It is reasonable to infer that if appellant had any reason to believe that the wine would not be delivered on the 24th according to the normal transit schedule, it would not have tendered the shipment in the first place. . . .

Appellee accepted the shipment knowing that it was wine, that sub-freezing temperatures would be encountered, and that there would be a delay in delivery of 48 hours in excess of the normal transit schedule. Appellee was negligent in failing to advise appellant that the wine would not be delivered until December 26—two full days after the normal time of delivery. . . .

[Judgment reversed.]

Commencement and Termination of Liability. Because a carrier bears an extraordinary liability, an often pivotal issue is to determine precisely when that liability begins and ends. Ordinarily, absolute liability commences when the goods are delivered into the carrier's possession and accepted for immediate shipment. Thus, a carrier who is in possession of the goods awaiting shipping instructions incurs the liability of a warehouseman—for negligence only. Once the goods have been transported to the destination, the carrier's strict liability ceases when the carrier tenders delivery to the consignee at a suitable time and place giving the consignee a reasonable opportunity to receive the goods. If the goods remain in the carrier's possession after that time, liability is reduced to that of an ordinary bailee or warehouseman.

At issue in the following case was whether a carrier held goods as a warehouseman or a carrier at the time of the loss.

Armour & Co., Inc. v. Rush Delivery Service, Inc.

409 N.E.2d 792 (Mass. App. 1980)

Plaintiff, Armour & Co., Inc. (Armour) hired defendant, Rush Delivery Service, Inc. (Rush), a licensed common carrier, to transport and deliver a shipment of meat from the Penn Central yards to four different buyers. Rush picked up the shipment but when it attempted to deliver to the first consignee, the buyer informed the driver it was too late in the day to accept delivery. The driver telephoned for instructions and Armour told Rush to deliver the goods the following morning. Armour advised Rush that it could leave the truck in a nearby yard owned by Armour. After securing the vehicle, the driver left the truck in Armour's yard and took the keys with him. When the driver returned the following morning, the truck was missing.

Armour sued Rush for the value of the lost shipment. At trial, the jury found in favor of Armour and Rush appealed.

Dreben, Justice

. . . Rush acknowledged at trial that if it had common carrier status at the time of the theft, it would be strictly liable for the loss without any showing of negligence. . . . On the other hand, if Rush had warehouseman status, it would only be liable for negligence. . . . [I]t was agreed that Rush would only be liable if it were found to have common carrier status. . . .

Rush argues that it lost its common carrier status when it parked the trailer in Armour's yard because the owner, Armour, had taken possession of the meat. We disagree, as the jury could have found from the evidence set forth above that Armour did not take control or possession of the trailer but had merely allowed Rush to use its yard as a parking place for the trailer.

Rush also argues that although it originally was a common carrier, its status as a common carrier terminated and was never revived. It points out that although it was a common carrier when it picked up the trailer at the Penn Central yards, once it had tendered delivery to the consignee and the consignee refused to accept the shipment, its status as common carrier terminated, and it became a warehouseman. . . . The question, however, is whether it continued as a warehouseman or whether its status again shifted to that of common carrier. . . .

We think there was sufficient evidence for the jury to find that Rush's common carrier status was revived, and we agree with the following conclusions of the trial judge which he set forth in his memorandum . . . : "[T]he jury could have found that, after rejection by the primary consignee, Rush had been instructed by Armour to make delivery of the shipment the next morning to that consignee; that Rush had expressly or impliedly agreed to do so; that Rush drove the trailer to the Southampton premises with the understanding and intention that it would make or continue the delivery the next morning and with the further understanding that in the interim the responsibility for the shipment remained with Rush until picked up the next morning."

Although Rush argues that the evidence does not support a finding that it agreed to assume responsibility for the shipment as a common carrier rather than as a warehouseman, the determination of the capacity in which the responsibility was accepted by Rush as well as "the precise period of time" when Rush's liability as a common carrier commenced were questions of fact for the jury. . . .

The judge carefully and properly instructed the jury that if they found that Rush had agreed to the resumption of common carrier status, they would also have to decide when that resumption took place. On the basis of the evidence before them, it was open to the jury to find that Rush had agreed to accept responsibility as a common carrier at the time the arrangements to park the trailer in Armour's yard were made. . . .

[Judgment affirmed.]

Contractual Limitation of Liability

Like ordinary bailees, carriers and warehousemen often contractually limit their liability for loss, damage, or destruction of goods received for shipment or storage. If the bailee is a warehouseman, §7-204(2) provides that liability for loss or destruction of stored goods may be limited by a term in the warehouse receipt or storage agreement. The bailor is not, however, required to accept the warehouseman's liability limitation. Instead, the bailor may, at the time he signs the storage agreement or within a reasonable time after receipt of the warehouse receipt, request that the warehouseman's liability be increased on all or part of the stored goods. In this situation, the warehouseman may charge an increased rate, but must assume the added liability. Section 7-204(2) authorizes liability limitations only. It does not allow the warehouseman to wholly exclude or disclaim all liability for negligence.

A common carrier, like the warehouseman and ordinary bailee, is permitted to limit the amount of liability (except for conversion) in a written contract with the shipper. Both the Interstate Commerce Act and Article 7 adopt a rule consistent with that applied to warehouse receipts, allowing rates to be varied depending on the value of the goods shipped.[13] In addition, carriers commonly disclaim responsibility for undeclared articles of extraordinary value, hidden from view. Thus, although the common carrier's liability at common law is nearly absolute, the extent of that liability is frequently limited by contract between the carrier and shipper exchanging a reduced rate for reduced liability.

Note that under Article 7, no contractual limitation is effective to limit liability for conversion of the goods to the carrier's or warehouseman's own use.

The Duty of Delivery

Consistent with the common law approach, Article 7 imposes absolute liability upon carriers and warehousemen for misdelivery. Under §7-403(1), absent a valid excuse, carriers and warehousemen must deliver to "a person entitled under the document."[14] The person entitled to delivery may or may not be the original storer (in a warehouse receipt) or consignee (in a bill of lading). That is, documents of title often are used to transfer title to (or a security interest in) the goods from the person originally entitled to delivery under the document to another. The bailee's delivery obligation differs depending on whether the document of title covering the goods is negotiable or nonnegotiable.

Negotiable Documents. If a negotiable document is involved, §7-403(4) provides that delivery must be made to the **holder** of the document. The first holder is usually the storer or consignee to whom the document is originally issued. Holders also include any person to whom the document has been *negotiated* by the storer or consignee or a later holder. **Negotiation** is effected by delivery of the document to the transferee if the document is in bearer form, or by indorsement and delivery if the document requires delivery to the order of a named person.[15] These rules are virtually identical to those governing transfer of notes and checks.

A negotiable document of title represents the

---

13. 49 U.S.C. §§11707(c), 10730; UCC §7-309(2). Rates are fixed in published "tariffs" filed with the Interstate Commerce Commission. The tariff, a public document, also sets forth the services offered by a common carrier and the rules, regulations, and procedures relating to those services.

14. A similar standard is imposed for federal bills of lading under the FBLA. 49 U.S.C. §88-89.

15. UCC §7-501. The FBLA contains substantially identical provisions governing interstate bills of lading. 49 U.S.C. §§107-110.

goods and provides effective control over them. Under §7-403(3), a bailee (carrier or warehouseman) who delivers goods covered by a negotiable document without requiring surrender of the document for cancellation (or notation for partial deliveries) is liable for misdelivery to any person to whom the document is later negotiated. Because of this liability, a bailee will not deliver goods governed by a negotiable document without the document. The person controlling the document therefore controls the goods.

Nonnegotiable Documents. If a nonnegotiable document is involved, §7-403(4) requires the bailee to deliver according to its specific promise made in the document. In a bill of lading the bailee usually promises to deliver to the consignee and in a warehouse receipt to the storer. The bailee may also deliver according to written instructions from a person authorized in the document to give them.

Under negotiable and nonnegotiable documents, as a prerequisite to delivery, the person obtaining the goods must pay the charges for storage or shipment[16] and must be ready and willing to sign, if requested, an acknowledgement that the goods have been delivered.

At issue in the following case involving a nonnegotiable bill of lading was whether the carrier should be held liable for misdelivery.

Refrigerated Transport Co., Inc. v. Hernando Packing Co., Inc.
544 S.W.2d 613 (Tenn. 1976)

Plaintiff, Hernando Packing Co., Inc. (Hernando) of Memphis, Tennessee, received a telephone order from Al Hark of J&A Trading Company (J&A) requesting delivery of a truckload of meat to Fort Lauderdale, Florida. Hernando shipped the meat via defendant Refrigerated Transport Co., Inc. (Refrigerated) for delivery to Broward Cold Storage, a

public warehouse in Fort Lauderdale. Hernando completed the bill of lading as follows:

> To BROWARD COLD STORAGE
> (acct. of J&A Trading Co.)
> 3220 S.W. 2nd Avenue
> Fort Lauderdale, Florida.

When Refrigerated's truck arrived at Fort Lauderdale, a person identifying himself as Al Hark of J&A Trading Co. met the truck across the street from Broward. Hark requested delivery of part of the meat to another location to which the truck driver agreed. The following morning, Hark met the truck at the Broward loading dock and transferred some of the meat to another truck. The remainder of the load was stored at Broward. When Hernando telephoned J&A to notify it of the pending delivery, Hernando learned that J&A had gone out of business. Hernando then telephoned Broward and learned of the delivery to Al Hark, who had disappeared.

Hernando sued Refrigerated alleging that the trucker had failed to deliver the meat to Broward as required by the bill of lading. The trial court ruled in favor of Hernando and Refrigerated appealed.

Henry, Justice

. . . This controversy pivots upon the precise provisions of the bill of lading, viz: the consignment to "Broward Cold Storage (account of J&A Trading Co.)." Refrigerated earnestly insists that this, in effect, was a consignment to "J&A Trading Co., care of Broward Cold Storage." While this position is plausible, when consideration is given to the nature and purpose of bills of lading, the duties and obligations arising thereunder, and to the plain terms of the consignment, we cannot embrace this theory of the case.

At the very outset we point out that we are dealing with a "straight" bill of lading . . . which is not negotiable. . . .

Delivery under a straight bill of lading may only be made to "[a] person lawfully entitled to the possession of the goods, or (b) the consignee named" therein. 49 U.S.C. Sec. 89.

While there are various areas of potential disagreement in this controversy they all boil down to a single question: Who was the consignee under the bill of lading?

---

16. Article 7 gives warehousemen (under §§7-209, 7-210) and carriers (under §§7-307, 7-308), a lien upon goods received for shipment or storage to secure payment of charges incident to the bailment. A similar lien is imposed for federal bills of lading under the FBLA. 49 U.S.C. §105.

In our view, there is no ambiguity. The consignment was to Broward. The parenthetical matter inserted simply advised the warehouse as to the identity of the ultimate receiver of the goods upon Broward's reconsignment. The only address inserted was that of Broward. Al Hark's name does not appear on the bill. It is fairly inferable that the consignment was to Broward as a precautionary measure against an unknown purchaser. Such would have been reasonable and prudent. But we need not speculate since the language was clear. There is no way that this delivery could have been properly made except to Broward and at Broward's address. Most assuredly a street corner delivery to a stranger not named in the bill and not shown by the record to have presented any credentials or authority cannot constitute valid delivery. All the driver ever had to do was to present his bill of lading to an authorized representative of Broward. The failure to do so was a breach of the contract of carriage.

To constitute a valid delivery, absent special circumstances, it is imperative that delivery be made to the right person, at the proper time and place and in a proper manner. This is implicit in the Contract of Carriage. . . .

We hold that Refrigerated breached its duty to deliver the cargo to Broward, the party designated in the bill of lading; that delivery to Al Hark was at Refrigerated's peril; that the burden of validating this delivery by establishing Al Hark's ownership and right to possession was upon Refrigerated and that it failed to carry that burden.

While we make this holding within the context of our view that Broward was the consignee, had we adopted Refrigerated's view that J&A Trading Company was the consignee, with the goods being shipped "in care of" Broward, the result would be the same. This necessarily follows from the facts that J&A was not in existence; that Al Hark had no connection with J&A; and that delivery was made to him without proper inquiry and without notice to Broward, or J&A. Had such inquiry been made and such notice given the driver would have discovered that he was dealing with an imposter. . . .

[Judgment affirmed.]

Excuse and Delay. A bailee may escape liability for misdelivery if it establishes the existence of a lawful excuse, including delivery to a person with paramount title, destruction or damage to the goods for which it is not liable, that the property has previously been sold in lawful enforcement of the carrier's lien, stoppage of delivery in transit by the seller under UCC §2-705, delivery of goods under court order, destruction of hazardous goods, refusal to deliver pending interpleader, and compliance with authorized changes in delivery instructions.[17] Although a carrier is responsible for unexcused nondelivery or misdelivery, a carrier who merely delays delivery is liable only if the carrier's negligence caused the delay.

The "Due Negotiation" Doctrine

Vast quantities of goods in storage or transit are bought and sold every day simply by transferring the documents of title that cover them. After a document is issued and transferred, disputes often arise when two or more persons claim ownership of either the document or the goods it covers.

As previously noted, a carrier or warehouseman is obligated to deliver to the holder of a *negotiable* document. As against the bailee, therefore, any holder is entitled to the goods. As against third parties claiming superior rights in the goods or the documents, the holder's rights depend on whether the document was acquired by due negotiation. To constitute **due negotiation,** §7-501(4) states that a negotiable document of title must be negotiated to a holder (1) who purchases it in good faith without notice of any defense against or claim to it on the part of any person, (2) for value, (3) in the regular course of business or financing, (4) in a transaction not involving mere settlement or payment of a money obligation. Under §7-502(1), a holder to whom a negotiable document of title has been duly negotiated acquires title to both the document and the goods it covers, because transfer of the document is the exclusive method of transferring title to both the document and the goods.

A holder by due negotiation of a negotiable document acquires the same rights against the carrier

---

17. UCC §7-403(1).

or warehouseman as any other holder (the duties of delivery and care) and in addition defeats virtually all outstanding prior equities and claims both to the document and the goods. Assume Olsen stores goods with White, who issues a negotiable warehouse receipt requiring delivery to Olsen's order. Olsen duly negotiates the receipt to Henry. Subsequently, White sells the stored goods to Zimmer, an innocent purchaser. Henry cuts off Zimmer's claim to the goods. Or, assume Pam directs Art to take goods to White for storage and obtain a negotiable warehouse receipt to Pam's order. Art delivers the goods to White, obtains a negotiable bearer receipt, duly negotiates it to Henry, and disappears with the money. Henry defeats Pam's claim to the goods and the document.

Not all third-party claims are cut off by good faith purchasers of negotiable documents. For example, if a necessary indorsement on the document is forged, the transferee does not become a holder and therefore does not defeat the claim of the person whose name is forged. A good faith purchaser is also not protected if the original bailor was a thief. A thief cannot acquire the power to transfer a good title simply by storing or shipping the stolen goods.

The due negotiation doctrine, the Article 7 counterpart of the holder in due course doctrine applied to commercial paper, applies only to negotiable documents. Under §7-504(1), transferees of nonnegotiable documents (and holders of negotiable documents who do not take by due negotiation) acquire "the title and rights which his transferor had or had actual authority to convey." Thus, the transferee "steps into the shoes" of the transferor and is subject to any defects in the transferor's title. For example, assume Doaks acquires goods from Olsen by fraud or with a bad check, and delivers the goods to White who issues a nonnegotiable warehouse receipt. Doaks subsequently transfers the receipt to Barnett. Olsen may recover the goods from Barnett.

Letters of Credit

A letter of credit is an important financing, payment, and security device widely used both in international and domestic trade. Letters of credit are governed by Article 5 of the UCC. Article 5, how-

ever, covers some but not all of the rules and concepts concerning letters of credit, and its provisions are almost completely subject to variation by agreement. This approach permits continued development of the law and provides flexibility.

As defined in UCC §5-103(1)(a), a **letter of credit** is an "engagement by a bank or other person made at the request of a customer . . . that the issuer will honor drafts or other demands for payment upon compliance with the conditions specified in the credit." Letters of credit are of two basic types, the traditional or "commercial" letter of credit, and the standby letter of credit.

Commercial Letters of Credit

Documents of title and letters of credit often are used to facilitate financing sales of goods between buyers and sellers not commercially acquainted with each other. These devices substantially reduce the risk of nondelivery of the goods by the seller and nonpayment of the price by the buyer. To illustrate, assume Barker, a New York buyer, wishes to purchase $500,000 worth of perfume from Sylvan, a Paris manufacturer. Neither party has previously dealt with the other. Several methods of financing the transaction may be used. First, the buyer could send cash or a check with the order. This approach, of course, presents substantial risks to the buyer because the seller might abscond with the money without shipping the goods or may ship inferior goods. If nonconforming goods are shipped, Barker would probably have to sue Sylvan for breach of contract in France. Further, even if Sylvan properly performs, Barker is out-of-pocket the purchase price until the goods arrive and are sold. Conversely, if Sylvan ships the goods and awaits Barker's remittance, it runs similar risks: Barker's dishonesty, rejection of the goods at the destination, and delay in receiving payment.

A better, though not ideal alternative, is the **shipment under reservation,** or documentary sale. Under this approach, Sylvan draws a draft for the purchase price against Barker and forwards it, together with a bill of lading covering the goods, to a New York bank with instructions not to surrender the bill of lading (which allows Barker to obtain the goods on arrival) until Barker accepts or pays the draft. Shipment under reservation assures that

Barker cannot obtain the goods until paying for them but does not guard against its possible insolvency or refusal to pay for the goods when they arrive. If Barker defaults, Sylvan must dispose of the goods at a distant port or pay freight charges back to France. In addition, any breach of contract action against Barker probably must be maintained in New York.

A commercial letter of credit solves most of the problems inherent in the foregoing financing methods, by effectively substituting a bank's credit for that of the buyer. Under this approach, Barker (the customer) requests its bank (the issuer) to write a letter of credit directed to Sylvan (or Sylvan's bank) that provides that Barker's bank will honor a draft drawn against it for the purchase price, provided the draft is accompanied by certain documents relating to the goods. These documents commonly include a bill of lading, an invoice, and an insurance policy covering the goods. If Sylvan (the beneficiary) complies with the terms of the letter, it is assured of payment by Barker's bank. Barker promises to reimburse its bank and pays a small commission.

Both parties benefit from this form of financing. The buyer is assured that the goods have been shipped that (at least on the face of the documents) conform to the contract. Further, after payment, the bank may turn the bill of lading over to the buyer, allowing the buyer to obtain the goods and then repay the bank out of the proceeds of their resale. On the other hand, the seller is virtually assured of payment upon compliance with the letter, because a bank's credit is substituted for the buyer's. Further, the letter of credit creates an absolute, independent obligation to pay upon presentation of conforming documents without regard to any dispute existing between the buyer and seller on the underlying sales contract. In addition, the draft backed by the letter of credit may be readily discounted, often allowing the seller to obtain payment as soon as the goods are shipped.

Standby Letters of Credit

Although letters of credit were developed and are still primarily used to finance international sales transactions, they also are widely used, both do-

mestically and internationally, outside the sale of goods field. One of the most common modern applications is the **standby letter of credit** in which the customer's *default* in performance of a financial or other obligation (such as repayment of a loan or proper completion of a construction contract) triggers the issuer's duty to pay the beneficiary. Thus, whereas the traditional or commerical letter of credit contemplates payment upon proper *performance* of an obligation (the beneficiary-seller's delivery of documents indicating shipment of goods), a standby letter of credit is paid upon *nonperformance*. For example, assume Lender contracts to loan Borrower $1 million to be repaid in periodic installments. To secure repayment, Lender requires Borrower to obtain a standby letter of credit from First Bank. Borrower (the customer) then fills out an application requesting First Bank (the issuer) to issue a letter of credit obligating the bank to honor Lender's (the beneficiary) draft for payment upon Lender's presentation of a statement specifying default by Borrower on the loan repayment obligation. If the bank agrees to issue the letter of credit, Borrower contractually will be required to reimburse the bank for sums expended under the letter, an obligation which often is secured by collateral.

Although it often serves the same basic function as the suretyship or guaranty contract discussed in Chapter 33, the standby letter of credit differs from a guaranty in two important respects. First, because the guarantor's obligation is secondary, the guarantor generally may assert contract defenses the principal debtor has against the creditor. In contrast, the issuer's obligation to pay the beneficiary under a letter of credit is primary and independent of other contracts or relationships involved in the transaction. Thus, the issuer may not assert either: (1) a defense the customer (Borrower) has against the beneficiary (Lender), or (2) a defense the issuer has against the customer, to avoid paying the beneficiary upon default. Second, a guarantor is liable upon the debtor's actual default. In contrast, letters of credit require payment upon presentation of conforming documents. Thus, the issuer under a standby letter of credit is obligated to pay when the beneficiary presents it with a draft and statement certifying default which conforms to the terms of the letter, whether or not the customer has *in fact* defaulted.[18]

Standby letters of credit assure prompt and certain payment and have proven popular both with users and banks.[19] In addition to the standard loan guaranty outlined above, standby letters have been adapted to a wide variety of transactions in which the parties desire firm assurance of payment.

SUMMARY

1. A bailment involves a transfer of possession of tangible personal property from its owner or other person in possession (the bailor) to another (the bailee) for a specified purpose. In its broadest sense, a bailment is simply the rightful possession of goods by someone not the owner. The law of bailments primarily concerns the bailee's liability for loss, theft, damage, or destruction of the bailed goods in its possession, and for misdelivery.

2. A bailee is generally liable for loss of or damage to the bailed goods for which he is at fault. Traditionally, the degree of fault necessary to impose liability depends on whether the bailment is for the bailor's benefit, the bailee's benefit, or for the mutual benefit of the parties. The modern approach, however, requires the bailee simply to exercise reasonable care under the circumstances. Under appropriate circumstances, this liability may be altered by contract.

3. Unlike the reasonable care standard applied to the bailee's possession, the bailee's duty to deliver is absolute. Thus, a bailee who delivers the property to an unauthorized person is liable to the bailor even though acting in good faith and free from negligence. Similarly, if the bailee uses the property in an unauthorized manner, the bailee is absolutely liable for loss or destruction of the property whether or not caused by negligence.

4. At common law, an innkeeper was a qualified insurer of its guests' goods. This standard, similar to that imposed upon common carriers, has been modified in most states by statutes that strictly limit the dollar amount of an innkeeper's liability.

5. The most important modern bailments are those for carriage and storage of goods undertaken by professional bailees—known as "carriers" and "warehousemen." In exchange for goods received for shipment or storage, these bailees issue documents of title to the bailors. Warehousemen issue warehouse receipts and carriers issue bills of lading.

6. Although warehousemen are ordinarily subject only to the same negligence standard applied to other bailees, common carriers (those who perform carriage for hire for all who apply) are qualified insurers of goods they carry. That is, a common carrier is absolutely liable for loss, damage, or destruction of goods in transit unless it proves both its freedom from negligence and that the loss was caused by an Act of God, an act of a public enemy, public authority, or the shipper, or the inherent nature of the goods. As in ordinary bailments, this liability may be altered by contract.

7. Carriers and warehousemen are obligated to deliver the goods to the person entitled under the document of title. The person entitled to delivery is the holder of a negotiable document and the person to whom the bailee promises delivery in a nonnegotiable document.

8. The rights of the parties upon transfer of a document of title also depend upon negotiability. If a negotiable document is "duly negotiated" the holder obtains title both to the document and to the goods it covers. A holder by due negotiation therefore defeats virtually all outstanding claims and equities both to the document and the goods. A holder of a negotiable document who does not take by due negotiation or the transferee of a nonnegotiable document acquires only the rights that his or her transferor had.

9. The letter of credit, governed by Article 5 of the UCC, is a useful financing, payment, and security device widely used in a variety of domestic and international transactions. Letters of credit are of two basic types, the traditional or commercial letter of credit, and the standby letter of credit.

KEY TERMS

bailment	involuntary (constructive)
bailor	(quasi) bailment
bailee	exculpatory clause

---

18. White & Summers, *Handbook of the Law Under the Uniform Commercial Code* 711-713 (2d ed. 1980).

19. In June 1985, for example, outstanding standby letters of credit issued by banks in the United States amounted to $153.2 billion. Federal Reserve Bank of San Francisco, *Winter 1986 Economic Review* 20.

document of title
delivery order
bill of lading
freight forwarder
consignor
consignee
through bill of lading
destination bill of lading
warehouse receipt
warehouseman

negotiable document of
 title
common carrier
holder
negotiation
due negotiation
letter of credit
shipment under
 reservation
standby letter of credit

QUESTIONS AND PROBLEMS

35-1 In each of the following cases, determine whether a bailment has been created and if so, identify the bailee and the bailor. Determine the standard of care to which the bailee should be held in determining liability for the loss or destruction of the bailed property.

(a) Great Dane Trailers, a manufacturer of trailers for tractor-trailer trucks, manufactures a trailer in Detroit that must be delivered to Houston. Central Transport, Inc., a trucking company, agrees to haul the trailer to Houston at no charge if it may use the trailer to haul freight on the trip. The trailer is stolen by an unknown party during the trip.

(b) While at a party, Fred finds an unusual and valuable bracelet that he recognizes as one owned by Marsha. Fred telephones Marsha to tell her he has found her bracelet. Several days later Marsha comes to Fred's house to pick up the bracelet. Fred cannot find the bracelet.

(c) Leo borrows Louise's minicomputer to help prepare his tax returns. While using the computer, he notices a small mechanical problem. When Leo tries to fix the computer, it explodes and is totally destroyed.

35-2 Evelyn delivered two rings to Gem Jewelers, Inc. to have the stones reset. Gem stored the rings in its walk-in fireproof vault that was reinforced with steel and concrete. One night a burglar broke into the store, gained access to the vault by ripping the door off, and stole the contents including Evelyn's rings. The store had not previously been burglarized. Evelyn sues Gem for the value of her rings. Should Gem be held liable? Explain.

35-3 Consider whether bailments have been created in the following situations.

(a) Seth drives his car to a municipal airport parking lot. Although he parks the car himself, the lot management requires presentation of a claim check to retrieve it. Further, the municipal lot is the only available parking at the airport. Is the city a bailee of Seth's car?

(b) Seth rents a safe-deposit box at First State Bank. Two keys are needed to open the box, one of which is retained by Seth. Is the bank a bailee of the contents of the box?

35-4 Marlene, a jewelry designer, sent a package of jewelry to one of her salesmen who was staying at the Baltimore Hotel. Marlene insured the package and put her return address on the outside of the package. It was sent by United Parcel Service, a private delivery company. Although the salesman checked at the hotel desk several times a day, the package did not arrive before he had to check out of the hotel. Before leaving, the salesman gave the hotel desk clerk written instructions not to accept the package and to have it returned to the sender. Despite the instructions the hotel accepted the package when it was delivered. The hotel held the package for thirty days and when no one claimed it, the hotel turned the package over to the local post office marked return to sender. The hotel did not check its records to see if the addressee had ever been registered there. The post office lost the package. Marlene sues United Parcel Service, the Baltimore Hotel, and the post office. Who should be held liable? Why?

35-5 Assume goods being shipped by Red Ball Express, a common carrier, are destroyed. Red Ball is liable for their destruction under the principles discussed in the text. The goods were being shipped by Seller (located in New York) to Buyer (located in Chicago) pursuant to a contract for sale of the goods. To whom is Red Ball liable? Explain.

35-6 Assume Malloy acquires goods from Olson by fraud. Malloy delivers the goods to William, who issues a negotiable warehouse receipt. Malloy duly negotiates the document to Briggs. May Olson recover the goods from Briggs? Assume the document was nonnegotiable. May Olson recover the goods from Briggs? Assume no document of title was issued. After acquiring the goods from Olson, Malloy sold them to Briggs, who paid fair value and was unaware of Malloy's wrongdoing. May Olson recover the goods from Briggs?

35-7 In anticipation of moving out of state, Mr. and Mrs. Turner stored all of their household goods with Pilgrim Co., a moving and storage company. Pilgrim issued a nonnegotiable bill of lading to Mr. and Mrs. Turner. Mrs. Turner writes to the Pilgrim office explaining that the Turners' plans have changed and they have decided to get a divorce. She requests that Pilgrim hold the goods until further notice.

(a) Mr. Turner appears at the Pilgrim office requesting delivery of the goods. What should Pilgrim do? Explain.

(b) Assume instead that Mr. Turner forges a letter over Mrs. Turner's signature requesting delivery of the goods to 123 Oak Street. Pilgrim delivers the goods. The house is owned by a woman friend of Mr. Turner who accepts the goods. Pilgrim asks for the bill of lading but the woman says it has been lost. Mrs. Turner sues Pilgrim for its misdelivery of the goods. What result? Explain.

35-8 El Paso Coin Co. delivered four boxes of valuable coins to Panhandle Airways, an air common carrier, to ship to New York's LaGuardia Airport. Panhandle issued a bill of lading and flew the coins to Dallas where it transferred the four boxes of coins to World Airlines because Panhandle did not fly to New York. A consignee picked up the coins in New York; however, only three boxes arrived. The fourth disappeared and was never found. El Paso sued Panhandle. Should Panhandle be held responsible for the loss? Explain.

35-9 Norfolk & Western Railway, a common carrier, agreed to transport sixteen shipments of lumber for Masonite Corp. During one of the early shipments, some of the lumber shifted and almost fell from the railroad car. Norfolk & Western notified Masonite of the problem and requested that Masonite pack the subsequent shipments in a safer manner and directed Masonite to have the packing checked thoroughly by the Norfolk & Western safety inspector prior to shipping. Masonite failed to follow Norfolk and Western's request. The final shipments were placed on the railroad car and were subjected only to the railway's external inspection. En route, the lumber shifted because of the poor packing and fell from the train causing a derailment that destroyed all of the lumber.

Masonite sued Norfolk & Western claiming the railway company should be held strictly liable as a common carrier. Norfolk & Western defended by alleging that it could not be held responsible for latent defects in packing. How should the court rule? Explain.

American property law, like much of our legal system, is derived from English common law. Originally grounded in feudal society, the concept of estates has developed as the basic scheme of land ownership in the United States. Simply stated, an **estate** is an ownership interest in property. This ownership interest may be absolute (subject only to governmental control for the needs of society generally) or may be limited as to its nature, quality, quantity, duration, or time or extent of possession.

Traditionally, estates are classified as either **freehold** or **nonfreehold**. This distinction, also derived from the English feudal system, provides a convenient basis for organizing our discussion of the various property interests. Freehold estates are characterized by their uncertain or potentially unlimited duration. In contrast, nonfreehold estates have a fixed or determinate duration and are considered lesser interests in property than freeholds. The various freehold estates are covered below followed by a discussion of co-ownership, in which two or more persons simultaneously have the right to possess the same property. The chapter concludes with coverage of nonfreehold estates, the basis of the law of landlord and tenant.

Freehold Estates in Property

Introduction to Future Interests

Before discussing the various freehold estates, one must distinguish present possessory estates from future interests in property. A **present possessory estate** is one in which the owner has the present right to *possession* of the property. As discussed below, full property ownership may be split into lesser estates, which take effect in possession and enjoyment *successively*. In other words, the owner or group of owners of an estate may not have the present right to possess the property, because they must await the termination of the preceding estate, or estates, in the property. In this situation the owner possesses a **future interest,** one that takes effect in possession and enjoyment, if at all, at some future time. Note that the owner of a future interest may never acquire the right to possess the property or, on the other hand, may be assured of that right. Resolution of this issue depends upon the nature of the future interest in relation to the preceding estates, or upon the occurrence or non-occurrence of uncertain events. Thus, future interests are in fact present interests in property. "Future" simply refers to the *time* of possession (whether or not the right to possession is assured), not the *existence* of the interest. Because a future interest takes effect in the future, its owner may be dead when the interest becomes possessory. In this situation, the property passes to the owner's estate and is distributed according to the owner's will or by the state intestate succession statute if the owner fails to leave a will. In other words, unless explicitly stated in the instrument creating the interest, the holder of a future interest need not outlive the preceding estates in order to take.

The Fee Simple

The Fee Simple Absolute. The law recognizes two types of fee simple estates: the fee simple absolute and the defeasible, or qualified, fee simple. The fee simple absolute is the most common of all estates and comports closely with the layman's understanding of ownership. The **fee simple absolute** (commonly shortened to "fee simple" or "fee") is the entire bundle of rights a person may possess in property—the largest quantity of ownership interest recognized by the law.

The fee simple is potentially unlimited in duration and is freely transferable by sale or gift during the owner's lifetime; it passes by will or intestate succession after death. In such cases, the transferee then receives a fee simple that continues indefinitely until transferred as outlined above. The owner need not convey his or her entire fee simple interest but may transfer only a part. Further,

whether or not the entire interest is transferred, the owner may create lesser estates in any number of transferees.

At common law, a fee simple could only be transferred inter vivos by use of the language "to (the grantee) and his heirs" in the deed. Today, by statute in most states, this formal language is no longer required, and unless it appears from the instrument (deed or will) that a lesser estate is intended, a fee simple absolute is presumed. Therefore, a simple grant of property "to B" would now vest fee simple title in B.

Defeasible Fees and Related Future Interests. The **defeasible,** or **qualified, fee**[1] contains all of the incidents of the fee simple absolute except that it is subject to a condition: it can be terminated by the occurrence or nonoccurrence of an event stated in the instrument, such as a will or deed, creating the estate. The three basic types of defeasible fee simple estates are

1. the fee simple determinable,
2. the fee simple subject to a condition subsequent, and
3. the fee simple subject to an executory limitation.

Fee Simple Determinable. The **fee simple determinable** (known also as a "fee on common law limitation" or "modified fee") is commonly characterized by use of the words "so long as," "until," "during," or "while" preceding the language qualifying the interest. Assume Smith sells a building to Jones using the following language in the deed: "To Jones and his heirs so long as the premises are not used for the sale of alcoholic liquor." This language creates a fee simple determinable in Jones. In this situation, Jones has all of the incidents of absolute ownership subject, however, to *automatic* termination if the property is used for the sale of liquor. This same limitation is also imposed upon a buyer of the property from Jones, a taker through Jones's will or by intestate succession, and other persons later in the chain of ownership. Upon

---

1. Defeasible fees also are referred to as "determinable" or "base" fees.

termination, the property passes in fee simple absolute back to Smith, or her heirs or devisees if Smith is deceased. After creating the fee simple determinable, Smith, or her successors in interest, possess a future interest in the property known as a **possibility of reverter.**

Fee Simple Subject to a Condition Subsequent. The **fee simple subject to a condition subsequent** is similar to the fee simple determinable but differs in one important respect. Whereas a fee simple determinable ends automatically and the property reverts to the grantor on occurrence or nonoccurrence of the stated event, the fee simple subject to a condition subsequent continues until the grantor or his successors in interest take some affirmative steps (such as entering the premises or commencing a lawsuit to enter) to terminate the estate. The fee simple subject to a condition subsequent usually is created by the language ''upon condition that'' or ''provided that'' preceding the condition, coupled with language allowing termination upon failure of the condition. A fee simple subject to a condition subsequent would, for example, be created by Smith's conveyance to ''Jones and his heirs on condition that the premises are never used for the sale of alcoholic liquor, and if they are so used then Smith or her heirs may enter and terminate the estate hereby conveyed.'' The future interest possessed by Smith or her successors in interest in this case is known as a **right of entry for condition broken** or more commonly, a **power of termination.**

Because the possibility of reverter and power of termination can exist for a potentially indefinite period, they often cloud land titles. For example, as time passes and conditions change, a remote buyer may wish to use the property for purposes prohibited by terms of the defeasible estate. In this case, the buyer must acquire the defeasible fee from its current owner, and must extinguish the future interest. Because the original grantor and immediate heirs are long dead, tracking down remote heirs and purchasing their interests is required. To reduce this problem, many states have enacted statutes (1) requiring that action be taken within a limited time (for example, seven years) after occurrence of the prohibited event, or (2) limiting the overall duration of the interest (for example, to

forty years), or (3) restricting the transferability of the interest.

Fee Simple Subject to an Executory Limitation. The third type of defeasible interest is the **fee simple subject to an executory limitation.** It differs from the interests discussed above in that, upon termination of the fee simple estate, the property passes to a *third party,* someone other than the grantor or her heirs. Transfer of the interest to the third party is, as in a fee simple determinable, effected *automatically* upon occurrence or nonoccurrence of the stated event. For example, assume White conveys property ''to Brown and his heirs, but if Brown dies without leaving children surviving him, then to Cox and her heirs.'' Brown, in this case, has a fee simple subject to an executory limitation and Cox has a future interest in the property known as an **executory interest** or **executory limitation,** which cuts off and divests Brown's fee simple estate if Brown dies without children surviving him. Note that Cox's interest in the property is known as a ''shifting'' use or interest because it destroys an estate vested in a grantee and ''shifts'' it to the holder of the executory interest—in this case, Cox.

Executory interests also may be designated as ''springing'' uses or interests, which destroy an existing estate held by the *grantor.* For example, Nelson by deed may convey property to ''Black and her heirs, Black's interest to begin one year from the date of this deed.'' In this situation, Nelson has a fee simple subject to an executory limitation. Black has a ''springing'' executory interest because it ''springs'' into existence in one year, destroying the estate of the grantor, Nelson. In most states, executory interests are freely transferable *inter vivos* by deed, and pass on death by will or intestate succession.

Life Estates

A **life estate** is an interest in property limited in duration to the life or lives of one or more persons. After the fee simple absolute, life estates represent the most common type of freehold interest. Life estates are created primarily in connection with family settlements or estate planning. For example, a person with a family may wish to leave property to a surviving spouse to provide for him or her until death and then ultimately transfer the property to the children.

Life estates are generally created by explicit language contained in a deed or will. If a deed is used, the estate may be created in the grantor by reservation—for example, when the grantor conveys a fee simple in the property but reserves to herself a present life estate—or in a person other than the grantor. The holder of a life estate is known as the **life tenant** and it is most frequently his or her life that determines the duration of the estate. For example, a conveyance of property ''to Ann for life'' creates a life estate in Ann terminating on Ann's death. The life tenant need not, however, be the measuring life. The duration of the estate may be determined by the life of another. This is known as a life estate *pur autre vie*. The person whose life is used as the measuring stick, the *cestui que vie,* takes nothing as a result of the grant. For example, property conveyed ''to Ann for the life of Bob'' creates a life estate ''pur autre vie.'' Ann is the ''life tenant'' and Bob is the ''cestui que vie''.[2]

Life estates, like most other property interests, are freely transferable. Of course, the estate normally ends at the owner's death. Therefore, if James owns a life estate and sells it to Ron, Ron's interest ordinarily terminates on James's death.[3] Further, because the life estate terminates on death, no interest ordinarily passes to the life tenant's heirs or persons taking under a will. In the estate pur autre vie, however, the life tenant may predecease the measuring life. For example, if property is conveyed ''to James for the life of Ron,'' James may die before Ron. In this situation, the life estate passes by will or intestate succession, like other property interests, and ultimately terminates on the death of the cestui que vie, in this case, Ron.

Life estates, like fee simple estates, may be defeasible. Assume Alan, in his will, leaves a house ''to my wife, Beth, for life, so long as she continues to occupy it as her residence.'' In this case, the life estate is defeasible (or determinable) subject to

termination before Beth's death if she ceases to occupy the premises.

The life tenant is in essence treated as the owner of the property for the duration of the estate. As such, he or she is entitled to the use and possession of the property, including any rents or profits the property generates. Because other interests in the property follow the life estate, however, the law protects these interests against unreasonable reduction in value. This protection is provided by imposing a duty on the life tenant not to commit waste. **Waste** is conduct by the life tenant in the use of the land resulting in a substantial and unreasonable reduction in the value of the property passing to the following estates. If the life tenant is committing waste, the holder of the subsequent injured estate may bring an action for damages or an injunction.

Other Future Interests

Reversions. A **reversion** is a future interest remaining in a *grantor* of property who transfers away less than his entire interest in the property. No reversion may, therefore, be created when the grantor conveys a fee simple absolute to the grantee.[4] Reversions arise automatically by operation of law; they need not be expressly created. Assume Sarah, by deed or will, transfers land ''to Bob for life.'' Because Sarah has not transferred her entire interest in the property—she has not stated what happens to the property on Bob's death—a reversion is created in Sarah. Therefore, on Bob's death, fee simple title ''reverts'' to Sarah. More accurately stated, the right to possession reverts to Sarah. The reversion itself essentially *remains in* the grantor since she has transferred less than her entire interest. Sarah is free, during her lifetime, to convey her reversionary interest by deed. On Sarah's death, it passes to whoever is entitled to her property under her will or by intestate succession.

The grantor need not possess fee simple title to create a reversion. For example, the owner of a life estate may convey an estate for years (that is, a leasehold interest) to a grantee. On termination of

---

2. There may be more than one measuring life. In this case, the estate continues until the death of the last surviving cestui que vie.

3. That is, Ron's life estate is an estate pur autre vie.

---

4. Other future interests, such as a possibility of reverter or power of termination may arise in a grantor in conjunction with transfer of a fee simple interest.

the leasehold, the right to possession of the property reverts to the life tenant for the duration of his life estate.

Remainders. In contrast to a reversion, which arises in a *grantor,* a **remainder** is a future interest that arises in a third party (someone other than the grantor) that takes effect in possession and enjoyment on the natural termination of the preceding estate. Assume Carol conveys property "to Alice for life, then to Ted in fee simple absolute." In this case, Alice has a life estate, and Ted has a remainder, taking effect on the natural termination of Alice's estate, Alice's death. Ted, the owner of the remainder, is known as the "remainderman." In this case, no reversion is created in Carol because she has transferred her entire interest in the property. Like most other future interests, remainders are freely transferable during life, and pass by will or intestate succession on death.

A remainder need not confer a fee simple interest. Suppose Carol conveys property "to Alice for life, remainder to Ted for life." In this case, Ted owns a remainder—a future interest created in someone other than the grantor becoming possessory upon the natural termination of the preceding estate, Alice's death. Carol, in this case, retains a reversion that takes effect on Ted's death.

Vested and Contingent Remainders. Remainders are classified as either vested or contingent. A remainder is vested when the remainderman is unconditionally entitled to possession immediately upon termination of the prior possessory estate (normally a life estate). Assume Mark conveys property "to Greg for life, remainder to Dan." Dan's remainder is absolutely vested.

If the identity of the remainderman is uncertain or if his or her interest depends on occurrence or nonoccurrence of an event, the remainder is contingent. In other words, a contingent remainder is a remainder subject to a condition precedent. Suppose Larry conveys property "to Darrell for life, remainder to Darrell's first-born child in fee simple absolute." At the time of the grant, Darrell has no children. In this case, Darrell has a life estate, Darrell's first-born child has a "contingent" remainder, contingent upon being born alive. If a child is born alive, the remainder becomes vested. The

child need not then outlive Darrell in order to take. The remainder would then simply pass to the child's estate. The original grant could, however, have required that the child survive Darrell or attain a certain age. In that case, a second contingency would be imposed upon the remainder; the child must both be born and survive Darrell or attain a minimum age.

If the contingencies governing the remainder fail to occur and the grantor has not provided for disposition of the property in that event, a reversion is created in the grantor. Thus, using the preceding example, if Darrell dies childless, the grant becomes simply "to Darrell for life" and the property reverts to Larry or those taking through his will or by descent. Therefore, unless the grantor provides for alternative disposition of the property, a reversion always accompanies a contingent remainder.[5]

Because a contingent remainder creates only an expectancy or possibility of an interest, the early common law refused to recognize it as an estate in land. As such, the interest could not be transferred either inter vivos or on death. In most states, however, contingent remainders are now freely alienable like other future interests.

Co-ownership of Property

Two or more persons often simultaneously hold an interest in the same property. The nature of these interests varies greatly. For example, a life tenant and remainderman hold interests representing a successive right to possession of or income from property. The material that follows addresses a particular type of simultaneous interest, **co-ownership** or **concurrent ownership,** in which two or more persons, known as "co-owners" or, more commonly, "co-tenants," have a concurrent right to *possession* of the same property. In concurrent ownership, each co-tenant holds an "undivided" interest in the property. This means that each co-tenant has a simultaneous, proportionate share of the entire property, but no separate interest in any

---

5. Even though the reversion itself is contingent (that is, on failure of the condition attached to the remainder), the grantor's interest is still known as a reversion, not a "contingent" reversion.

particular or identifiable portion of it. For example, assume Ann, Barbara, Carol, and Dawn are co-owners of a farm, each holding an undivided one-fourth interest. In this situation, Ann owns one-fourth of the entire property and has equal right to possession and enjoyment of the farm subject to the rights of the other co-tenants. This is the unity of possession common to all forms of co-ownership. The interest is undivided because there is no designation regarding which particular one-fourth of the farm each co-tenant owns—for example, that Ann owns the northeast quarter, Barbara the northwest quarter, and so on. Although co-ownership originally developed in the real property context, personal property such as bank accounts, government bonds, or other securities also may be jointly owned.

Joint Tenancy and Tenancy in Common Distinguished

Three basic forms of co-ownership are recognized: **joint tenancy,** tenancy by the entirety (a specialized form of joint tenancy recognized in some states between husband and wife), and tenancy in common.[6] The fundamental difference among these forms of ownership is the **right of survivorship** existing in joint tenancies and tenancies by the entirety but not tenancies in common. Under the right of survivorship, if one of two joint tenants or tenants by the entirety dies, the deceased's share is owned by the other, who becomes sole owner. If the property is owned by more than two joint tenants, the deceased's share belongs to the survivors jointly.

Assume Hart, Sloan, and Davis own real estate in fee simple as joint tenants each owning an undivided one-third interest. Assume Hart leaves a will leaving all of his property to Rogers. On Hart's death, his one-third interest remains in the surviving joint tenants, Sloan and Davis, equally; that is, after Hart's death, Sloan and Davis each own an undivided one-half interest in the property in joint tenancy. On Sloan's death, the survivor, Davis, owns the entire property in fee simple.

---

6. A fourth type, community property, is discussed in Chapter 39.

Thus, if property is held in joint tenancy and the joint tenancy is not severed prior to the death of any joint tenant, the joint tenant who lives the longest ultimately becomes sole owner of the property.

When a person dies an "estate" is created. This estate is distributed, after paying creditors' claims, by the terms of the decedent's will or by state "intestate succession" statutes if the decedent does not leave a valid will. Because a joint tenant's interest does not pass to his or her estate on death, Rogers, the taker under Hart's will, has no claim to Hart's one-third joint tenancy interest. That interest automatically resides in the survivors, Sloan and Davis.

A **tenancy in common,** on the other hand, has no right of survivorship. On death of a tenant in common, the tenant's interest passes, like any other property (such as a car, television set, or house) to the tenant's estate. Thus, whoever is designated to take the property by will or intestate succession is entitled to the decedent's interest. To illustrate using the preceding example, assume Hart, Sloan, and Davis own the farm as tenants in common. In this case, on Hart's death, his interest passes by the will to Rogers.

Creditors' Claims. Because joint tenancy property never gets into the decedent's estate, it is also not generally subject to claims of the deceased joint tenant's creditors. Assume for example, on the above facts, that Savin is Hart's creditor, holding a valid $10,000 claim. On Hart's death, Savin may not reach Hart's one-third interest in the farm in the hands of Sloan and Davis to satisfy the debt. If, however, Hart, Sloan, and Davis hold the farm as tenants in common, Hart's one-third interest passes to his estate and, like most other property in his estate, is subject to claims of his creditors. A creditor of a person owning joint tenancy property may be protected by forcing a severance of the joint tenancy prior to death, under principles outlined later in this chapter.

Effect of Simultaneous Death. Because rights in a joint tenancy or tenancy by the entirety depend on survivorship, disputes have arisen if the co-tenants die in a common disaster. The **Uniform Simultaneous Death Act,** adopted in 47 states, partially resolves this problem by providing that joint tenants or tenants by the entirety who die simultaneously are treated as having died as tenants in common holding equal shares.[7]

Creation and Termination of Co-ownership

Presumption of Tenancy in Common. At early common law, a conveyance of property to two or more persons, if ambiguous, was presumed to create a joint tenancy. Because this presumption often results in transfer of the property on death contrary to the decedent's intent, the modern presumption is that a grant of property to two or more persons creates a tenancy in common unless the intent to form a joint tenancy is clearly indicated in the instrument creating the interest. Thus, today a conveyance of property "to Andrew and Robert," or "to Andrew and Robert equally," or "to Andrew and Robert jointly" should create a tenancy in common. To create a joint tenancy, the grantor should make his intent clear by using language such as "to A and B, as joint tenants, and not as tenants in common, with right of survivorship." Some states, by statute, have either abolished the joint tenancy entirely or have removed its primary incident, the right of survivorship.

In the following case, the court was required to determine whether the language of a deed was sufficient to create a joint tenancy.

In re Estate of Michael
218 A.2d 338 (Pa. 1966)

In 1947, Harry and Bertha Michael and Ford and Helen Michael acquired joint ownership of the King Farm. The deed conveyed the farm to

> Harry L. Michael and Bertha M. Michael, his wife, tenants by the entireties and Ford W. Michael and Helen M. Michael, his wife, as tenants by the entireties, with right of survivorship.

---

7. Uniform Simultaneous Death Act §3. The Act has been adopted in all states except Louisiana, Montana, and Ohio. Problems of simultaneous death in wills and intestate succession are discussed in Chapter 39.

Following the death of her husband, Bertha Michael died, leaving by will her interest in the King Farm to her son, Robert.

In a declaratory judgment action, Ford and Helen Michael, both of whom had survived Bertha Michael, alleged that the two married couples had held the farm as joint tenants. Because Harry and Bertha Michael had predeceased Ford and Helen Michael, they argued that they owned the entire farm by right of survivorship. Robert Michael argued that the two couples had held the farm as tenants in common, with each couple owning an undivided one-half interest, thereby entitling him to ownership of a one-half interest in the farm.

The trial court ruled in favor of Ford and Helen Michael holding that the 1947 deed had created a joint tenancy with right of survivorship between the two couples. Robert Michael appealed.

Jones, Justice

. . . At common law, joint tenancies were favored, and the doctrine of survivorship was a recognized incident to a joint estate. The courts of the United States have generally been opposed to the creation of such estates, the presumption being that all tenants hold jointly as tenants in common, unless a clear intention to the contrary is shown. . . .

In Pennsylvania, by the Act of 1812 [68 P.S. §110.], the incident of survivorship in joint tenancies was eliminated unless the instrument creating the estate expressly provided that such incident should exist. The Act . . . does not *forbid* creation of a joint tenancy if the language creating it *clearly* expresses that intent. . . .

[I]n order to engraft the right of survivorship on a co-tenancy which might otherwise be a tenancy in common, the intent to do so must be expressed with sufficient clarity to overcome the statutory presumption that survivorship is not intended. . . . Whether or not survivorship was intended is to be gathered from the instrument and its language . . ., but no particular form of words is required to manifest such intention. . . .

The phrase, "with right of survivorship," is capable, as appellant properly urges, of at least three possible interpretations: (1) explanatory of the one of the incidents of the estate, known as tenancy by the entirety; (2) explanatory of the one tenancy by the entirety, the creation of which it follows; or (3), as the appellee and the lower court contend, indicative of the creation of a right of survivorship as between the two sets of spouses. Any one of these interpretations is a *possibility* but deciding which was intended by the parties would involve nothing but a mere guess. Such ambiguous terminology falls far short of the *clear* expression of intent required to overcome the statutory presumption.

Nowhere in the deed is the term "joint tenants" employed. To create a right of survivorship the *normal* procedure is to employ the phrase "joint tenants, with a right of survivorship, and not as tenants in common" in describing the manner in which the grantees are to take or hold the property being conveyed or transferred. . . .

We cannot find within the four corners of this deed a *clearly* expressed intention to create a joint tenancy with the right of survivorship. Having failed to find a *clear* intention to overcome the statutory presumption against such estates, the Act of 1812 compels us to find that the deed of 1947 created a tenancy in common as between the two sets of married couples, each couple holding its undivided one-half interest as tenants by the entireties.

[Judgment reversed.]

Creation of Co-ownership.

To create a joint tenancy, four elements, commonly known as the **four unities**, must be present. These unities are

1. *Time*—all joint tenancy interests must vest at the same time.
2. *Title*—all joint tenants must acquire their interests in the same instrument, such as a deed or will.
3. *Interest*—the interest of each co-owner must be identical. This means that fractional shares must be equal—for example, three joint tenants each must have a one-third interest—and the type and duration of the estate must be the same—for example, all must be life estates or fee simples.
4. *Possession*—all joint tenants have an undivided interest in the property and an equal right to possess the entire property subject to the rights of the other co-tenants.

In a tenancy in common, only the unity of possession need be present. Therefore, a tenancy in common may be created with unequal fractional shares. For example, A, B, and C may be tenants in common holding one-half, one-third, and one-sixth interests. Tenants in common may also have differing interests acquired at different times. For example, Rose may, during her lifetime, convey a one-half interest in her farm to Sally in fee simple, and leave a life estate in the remaining one-half to Tom in her will. Sally and Tom are tenants in common.

Termination of Joint Tenancy.

Once created, a joint tenancy may be terminated or severed whenever one of the four unities ceases to be present. This is easily accomplished when one joint tenant, during his lifetime, transfers his interest to a third party. In this case, the unities of time and title are destroyed and a tenancy in common is created.

For example, assume Art and Bob are joint tenants. Bob sells his interest to Joan. Because the four unities are not present between Art and Joan, they hold the property as tenants in common. Assume further that Ann, Betty, and Carol are joint tenants. Carol sells her interest to Mark. As between Ann and Betty, the unities are still present and therefore Ann and Betty hold an undivided two-thirds of the property as joint tenants. Mark, however, holds his one-third as a tenant in common with Ann and Betty. Therefore, on Mark's death, his one-third passes to his estate, but on Betty's death her one-third interest goes to Ann by right of survivorship. Similarly, if Carol sells her interest to Ann, Ann (now owning two-thirds) holds one-third of the property as a joint tenant with Betty, and one-third as a tenant in common. Thus, if Ann predeceases Betty, one-third of the property goes to Betty by right of survivorship and one-third passes to Ann's estate. If Betty predeceases Ann, Ann then owns the entire property.

Severance of a joint tenancy may occur either voluntarily or involuntarily. For example, a person's creditors may force a sale of property held in joint tenancy to satisfy an unpaid judgment. The consent of the remaining joint tenants is not necessary to sever the joint tenancy in this manner.

Termination of Co-ownership.

Severance of the joint tenancy generally results in a tenancy in common. The co-tenants of either a joint tenancy or tenancy in common may, however, desire to terminate concurrent ownership altogether. This result is accomplished by **partition**—physically dividing the property into distinct portions resulting in individual ownership by the former co-tenants of each portion. Partition destroys the undivided nature of co-ownership and may be accomplished either by agreement of the parties or by order of the court. Judicial partition is generally available to any co-tenant as an absolute right under statutory procedures that vary among the states. The property may be physically divided, or "partitioned in kind," if such a division is possible. More commonly, however, the property is sold at judicial sale and the proceeds apportioned among the co-tenants.

Tenancy by the Entirety

A **tenancy by the entirety** is a specialized form of joint tenancy with right of survivorship existing between co-tenants who are husband and wife. The estate is based on the common law concept of "spousal unity"—that husband and wife are one person. At common law, therefore, a transfer of property to husband and wife resulted in only one estate, an entirety. In this estate, the spouses own the whole interest collectively but no undivided individual share. In contrast, in a joint tenancy the tenants own both the whole and an undivided share.

The legal effect of this distinction is as follows. First, the tenancy by the entirety may not be partitioned except with the consent of both parties or by divorce. A joint tenancy may be partitioned at the request of one joint tenant. Second, a tenancy by the entirety may not be severed by the act of a single spouse. A joint tenancy, on the other hand, is severed when one joint tenant voluntarily or involuntarily conveys his or her interest.

With the modern erosion of the fiction that husband and wife are one, most states have abolished the tenancy by the entirety, with the result that a conveyance of property to husband and wife creates either a joint tenancy or tenancy in common, depending upon the language used. In states that still retain the interest (limited in many states to real property), the spouses are usually given equal rights in the control and enjoyment of the property. At common law, these rights were possessed solely by the husband.

Cooperatives and Condominiums

Two other forms of joint property ownership, the cooperative and the condominium, provide a method for ownership of multiple-unit dwellings. Although both the cooperative and condominium have long been used in high-density areas such as large cities, their use has become more widespread in recent years as the general costs of owning real estate have increased.

The **cooperative** is a form of real estate ownership by which residents in a multiple-unit building own shares in a corporation that owns the building. Ownership of shares in the corporation entitles each resident to lease a unit in the building and to use common areas of the building. As part of a shareholder agreement, each resident makes a monthly payment that represents a prorated share of the cost of repaying the loan that the corporation has secured to purchase the building and a share of the building maintenance costs. Generally, each tenant is jointly and severally liable on the loan. Therefore, if any resident fails to make a monthly payment, the other tenants must arrange to pay the tenant's share of the loan to avoid default.

Because of the problems created by the joint and several liability aspect of the cooperative, the condominium has evolved as a more popular form of ownership for multiple-dwelling buildings. In a **condominium** system, each resident purchases a living unit in the building and all residents own common areas, such as hallways, basement storage areas, roads, and recreation facilities, as tenants in common. Although a resident may secure a loan to finance the purchase of an individual unit, the other residents assume no liability for that loan. Condominiums maintain a condominium association of which each resident is a member and that is responsible for operation of the building. Residents pay a monthly fee to the condominium association to cover the costs of maintaining common areas. Most states regulate condominium ownership by statutes that require condominium developers to adopt a master deed and condominium association bylaws. These documents describe the interests held by each condominium owner and the methods of maintaining and paying the expenses for the common areas. Under most statutes, a purchaser of a condominium unit is entitled to receive copies of these documents prior to transfer of ownership.

Introduction to Landlord and Tenant

Leases of real property are among the most common legal relationships entered into by both consumers and persons in business. Individuals often rent rather than buy their homes or apartments. Businesses routinely rent the land and buildings used to conduct their retail, wholesale, manufacturing, and service operations. A **lease** creates a **landlord-tenant relationship**, which arises upon a *transfer of the right to possession of real property* from the owner—the **lessor** or **landlord**—to another—the **lessee** or **tenant**—for consideration known as "rent." Thus, in a lease a real property owner, the lessor, relinquishes possession of the property but retains ownership. A lease creates a possessory "nonfreehold" estate in the property in the tenant. This estate is often known as a "leasehold." The landlord, who conveys away less than her entire interest in the land, retains a reversion that takes effect upon termination of the agreed lease term. The landlord also has the right to receive rents for the duration of the lease. The landlord's reversion plus her right to receive rent is collectively known as the "leased fee."

Elements of a Valid Lease

A lease is a conveyance of the property for a given period of time during which rights and obligations of the parties are governed by their express agreement. The promises made by the landlord and tenant to each other in the lease to do or not to do certain acts are known as "covenants." A lease, therefore, contains elements of two major substantive legal areas: property and contracts. The trend in recent years is away from the older property-oriented approach, placing more emphasis on the contract aspects of a lease in determining rights and duties of the parties.

Statute of Frauds. A lease, like an agreement to transfer a fee simple interest in land, is generally enforceable only if it is evidenced by a writing signed by the party to be charged. This requirement was first imposed by the English (or "common law") Statute of Frauds,[8] which has been adopted, with modifications, in virtually all states. Most state enactments, however, exempt leases with a term of one year or less from the operation of the Statute of Frauds, rendering such leases enforceable even if oral.

Essential Terms. The legal requirements for an enforceable lease are not rigorous. No formal words of leasing are required. Proof of intent to transfer possession and create the relationship is sufficient. The minimum terms necessary to create an enforceable lease are (1) the names of the parties, (2) a description of the property, (3) the term of the lease, (4) the amount of the rent, and (5) the time of payment. Many of the minimum terms are supplied by law if not explicitly stated. For example, if not stated, the amount of rent is assumed to be the reasonable value of the premises, with payment due at the end of the term.

Even though a writing is not always required for enforceability, a written lease that outlines the rights and obligations of the parties and resolves as many contingencies as possible is always desirable. An integrated written lease provides maximum protection to the parties in the event of a dispute, and the act of reducing the agreement to writing frequently uncovers misunderstandings that can then be resolved. In addition to the basic provisions outlined above, other terms commonly appearing in a lease include restrictions on use of the property; rights of inspection; disposition of fixtures; liability for repairs, maintenance, taxes, utilities, and insurance; effect of destruction of premises, or taking by eminent domain; default and remedies for default; rights of tenant to assign or sublease premises; security for payment of rent or damage to property and application of security; and termination or renewal of lease including effect of tenant's holding over.

Effect of Recording. Most states also have statutes providing that leases of longer than a statutorily specified duration are recordable interests in land. The statutory period varies substantially from state to state.[9] Thus, long-term leases are often recorded

---

8. 29 Car. 2, ch. 3, §1 (1677). The common law statute is discussed in detail in Chapter 12.

9. For a listing of the various statutory periods see Statutory Note to §2.1 of the *Restatement (Second) of Property (Landlord and Tenant)*.

with the local recorder of deeds to give constructive notice to third parties of the lessee's interest in the property. The importance and effect of recording is discussed in detail in Chapter 37.

Duration of the Lease— "Nonfreehold" Estates

A lease creates an interest in the land in the tenant known as a "nonfreehold" estate. Unlike the freehold estates, which are ordinarily created by deed or will and have unlimited or indeterminate duration, nonfreehold estates are created by contract and are terminated upon expiration of the lease term, by acts of the parties, or upon occurrence of an agreed condition. Even though the nonfreehold is an estate in land and immovable, it is personal property, a so-called "chattel-real." This anomaly is a historical remnant of early judicial hostility toward nonfreehold estates.

The duration of a lease depends on the type of nonfreehold estate created. These estates (or "tenancies") are generally classified as one of four types: the estate for years, the estate from period to period, the estate at will, and the estate at sufferance.

The Estate for Years. The **estate for years** is the most prevalent form of nonfreehold estate, characterized by a fixed beginning and ending date. Assume that on June 1, 1981, L agrees to lease real property to T, beginning July 1, 1981, and running for five years, ending June 30, 1986. The parties have created an estate for years. Note that the duration of the estate is unimportant. Any lease for a fixed period, however long or short, is designated an estate for years. For example, an estate for years is created if L leases the premises for one day or ninety-nine years.

The estate expires automatically at the conclusion of the stated period. Absent a contrary provision in the lease, no notice of termination is required by either party. The estate may, however, be subject to termination before expiration of the period upon occurrence of an agreed event, such as tenant's nonpayment of rent.

Estate from Period to Period. An **estate from period to period** or **periodic tenancy** continues indefinitely for successive periods (week to week, month to month, year to year) until notice of termination is given by either party. Periodic tenancies may be created expressly. For example, L may lease property to T from year to year. More commonly, however, periodic tenancies arise by implication when the parties fail to specify the duration of the lease. In this case, if the tenant pays rent periodically—by the week or month—a period to period lease is created for successive one-week or one-month periods that continues indefinitely until terminated by proper notice of either party.

The required notice period is now governed by statute in most states, and therefore individual state law must be consulted. For year to year tenancies, the statutory periods range between thirty days and six months, whereas tenancies for shorter periods generally require thirty days advance notice.

A periodic tenancy also may arise when a tenant continues in possession, or "holds over," after expiration of an estate for years. In this case, the landlord may elect to treat the tenant as a trespasser and evict her, or may choose to continue to recognize her as a tenant, generally by accepting further rental payments. If the landlord elects the latter alternative, a periodic tenancy is created by implication and the tenant's lack of intent to renew is irrelevant. If the duration of the original lease is greater than one year, and the landlord elects to treat the holdover as a tenant, a periodic tenancy from year to year is created. If the term of the original lease is less than one year, the term of the new tenancy is equal to the term of the previous lease. Some courts, in this situation, find that the new tenancy is based on the period for which rent is payable, not the term of the original lease.

The new lease created by the tenant's holding over and the landlord's acceptance of rent is governed generally by terms of the old lease with the exception of the term. The landlord may, however, prior to expiration of the lease, notify the tenant that new terms will be applicable in the event the tenant holds over. In this case, the tenant is bound to the new terms if he or she elects to remain in possession.

The Estate at Will. If the landlord leases property "to T at the will of L" or "to T as long as L wishes," an **estate (tenancy) at will** is created.

This estate may be terminated at the will of either T or L.[10] The tenancy at will is the lowest form of leasehold interest but is recognized as an estate because it confers the right of exclusive possession upon the tenant. This characteristic distinguishes a tenant at will from a mere "licensee"[11] or lodger. At common law, no notice by either party was necessary to terminate the tenancy. Many states today, however, have statutes requiring minimum advance notice, such as thirty days.

Ordinarily, tenancies at will arise by implication. For example, if a tenant takes possession with no explicit agreement regarding payment of rent, a tenancy at will arises. In most states, however, this tenancy at will is quickly converted into a period to period tenancy upon payment of rent based upon the period for which rent is paid. Similarly, a tenant in possession under an invalid lease—for example, due to noncompliance with the Statute of Frauds—is, in most states, a tenant at will until periodic rental payments are made, thereby creating a period to period lease. Other examples of tenants at will include a purchaser of property who takes possession prior to receiving legal title or pursuant to an unenforceable contract for sale and a tenant for years who holds over with the landlord's consent.

The Estate at Sufferance. The **estate at sufferance** is not an estate at all. It arises when a holdover tenant wrongfully remains in possession upon expiration of the lease term. The landlord may elect to treat the holdover tenant either as a trespasser or as a tenant under a new periodic tenancy. If the landlord elects the first alternative, the former tenant possesses merely at the "sufferance" of the landlord, pending the landlord's efforts to evict. A tenant at sufferance differs from an ordinary trespasser only in that his or her original possession was rightful.

Effect of Death of Either Party. Unless provided otherwise in the lease, an estate for years or a periodic tenancy is not terminated by the death of either party. The interest passes as part of the decedent's estate by will or intestate succession and the rights and duties under the lease are enforceable by or against the estate. The lease continues until expiration of the term (in an estate for years), or until termination by proper notice (in a periodic tenancy).

A tenancy at will depends upon the continuing will of both landlord and tenant that the tenancy continue. The death of either extinguishes the will of the deceased and therefore terminates the tenancy on the date the survivor becomes aware of the death.

Rights and Obligations of Landlord and Tenant

The rights and obligations of landlord and tenant to each other arise both from the express terms of the lease and from the law governing the landlord-tenant relation generally. The basic obligations on the lease are implicit in its definition—the landlord transfers exclusive possession of the property for the agreed term to the tenant who becomes obligated to pay rent.

Possession and Use of the Property

Because a lease involves a transfer of the exclusive right to possession, the landlord has no right to enter the premises to inspect or effect repairs and maintenance, unless she has reserved the right to do so. In other words, the landlord who enters the premises during the lease term without authorization in the lease or consent of the tenant is liable as a trespasser.[12]

Absent a provision in the lease to the contrary, the tenant may use the premises for any reasonable, legal purpose. For this reason, landlords often insert a provision in the lease restricting the use of the property—for example, to residential purposes only—or by prohibiting certain uses. Because the law does not favor restrictions on land use, such

---

10. If the lease is to T "as long as T wishes," some states find a tenancy at will terminable by either party but others find a life estate in T.

11. Licenses are discussed in Chapter 38.

---

12. The landlord may, however, show the premises to prospective tenants after receiving notice of termination.

terms often are construed strictly against the landlord.

Regardless of the use of the property, the tenant is under a duty not to commit waste. This duty requires that the tenant's use of the property results in no permanent or lasting injury to the property—the landlord's reversion. In other words, the tenant ordinarily must return the property in its original condition, excepting ordinary wear and tear.

Duty to Pay Rent and Events Terminating the Duty

Corresponding to the landlord's duty to deliver possession is the tenant's duty to pay rent. Rent is most commonly payable in money but the lease may provide payment in services or property. The time of payment is almost always specified, but rent is due at the end of the term (or each period) if not stated. Most leases explicitly provide that rent is payable in advance periodically over the term of the lease.

The amount of rent may be fixed or variable depending on whether a gross, net, or percentage lease is used. In a gross lease, the tenant pays a flat sum out of which the landlord is required to pay expenses such as taxes, utilities, and insurance. A net lease requires the tenant to pay, in addition to rent, expenses such as those listed above. A percentage lease is commonly used when the business location of the property is an important part of its value. The amount of rent is computed as a percentage of gross sales, gross profits or net profits of a business conducted by the lessee on the premises, usually in addition to a minimum stipulated rent.

Effect of Destruction of the Property. The duty to pay rent ordinarily continues until the normal termination of the lease term. As a general rule, this duty continues even if the leased premises are accidentally destroyed by fire or other casualty during the term. That is, under the traditional majority view, unless the lease provides otherwise, the tenant assumes the risk of loss and must continue to pay rent even though improvements on the land are damaged or destroyed. The reasoning for this result is that the tenant still possesses the *land* and could

have protected any interest in the improvements by insurance.[13]

If fire or casualty destroys the entire subject matter of the lease, leaving nothing for the tenant to occupy, the lease is terminated. This result occurs, for example, in a lease of an apartment or single room in a building. Because of the hardship inherent in forcing continued payment of rent on a building damaged or destroyed through no fault of the tenant, most leases expressly provide for the contingency to alter or extinguish the tenant's duty to pay rent.

Effect of Surrender and Abandonment. The tenant's duty to pay rent may also be extinguished by surrender. A **surrender** is a contract involving either the transfer of the landlord's reversion to the tenant or of the tenant's nonfreehold estate to the landlord. In either case, one party acquires fee simple title through the merger of the reversion and the nonfreehold estate. A surrender requires mutual agreement of the parties. This agreement may be either express (arising out of the language used by the parties) or implied from the conduct of the landlord and tenant. Implied surrender occurs when the parties' conduct is inconsistent with the continuation of the landlord-tenant relationship—for example, when the landlord resumes possession of the premises after a relinquishment of possession by the tenant. A tenant's surrender extinguishes both his interest in the property and any further duty to pay rent.

Claims of implied surrender commonly are made after abandonment by the tenant. **Abandonment** is the wrongful *unilateral* act of the tenant in vacating the premises without further intent to abide by terms of the lease. In contrast, surrender is a *mutual agreement* between landlord and tenant to terminate the lease. After abandonment, the tenant's duty to pay rent continues unaffected. Abandonment, however, is viewed as an offer for surrender, and subsequent conduct by the landlord, such as

---

13. Although both parties have an insurable interest, neither the landlord nor the tenant is under any obligation to insure, unless the duty is imposed by the lease.

leasing the premises to another, may be viewed as acceptance of the offer, thereby creating an implied surrender extinguishing the tenant's further duty to pay rent.

Breach of Covenant of Quiet Enjoyment—Eviction and Constructive Eviction.

After the tenant has taken possession, the landlord may not interfere with the tenant's possession and enjoyment of the property. This duty is imposed through an implied **covenant of quiet enjoyment,** generally arising independent of the lease by operation of law. The covenant is breached by an **eviction.** Acts constituting an eviction may be taken by the landlord, someone acting under the landlord's authority, or a person having title to the property superior (paramount) to the landlord's.

Evictions are of two types, actual and constructive. In either case, an eviction terminates the tenant's further liability for rent and gives the tenant an action for damages against the landlord for breach of the covenant of quiet enjoyment. An actual eviction occurs when the tenant is physically removed from all or part of the premises. More commonly, however, eviction is **constructive.** In constructive eviction the landlord does not actually deprive the tenant of possession. Instead, the landlord, by conduct or neglect, so substantially disturbs or interferes with the tenant's right of possession and enjoyment that the premises are rendered uninhabitable. For example, constructive eviction may be shown by the landlord's failure to provide heat, running water, or other essential services, or to perform a covenant to repair necessary to make the property fit for occupancy.

In order to assert constructive eviction as a defense to paying rent, the tenant must *vacate* the premises within a reasonable time after occurrence of the event constituting eviction. The vacating tenant bears the burden of showing not only that the conduct of the landlord constitutes an eviction but also that she moved out within a reasonable time thereafter. If eviction is shown, the tenant's duty to pay rent is suspended from the time possession is abandoned.

In the following case, the court determined whether the landlord's conduct effected a constructive eviction.

Reste Realty Corporation v. Cooper
251 A.2d 268 (N.J. 1969)

In April, 1959, Joy Cooper leased a basement office in a commercial office building to use for training sales personnel in her jewelry business. The lessor was a corporation that owned the building and employed a resident manager. Whenever it rained, Cooper's office flooded. During the first two years of the lease, she called the resident manager when the flooding occurred and he helped to remove the water. The manager died in March, 1961, and the office building was sold to Reste Realty Corporation. Thereafter, despite Cooper's complaints, she received no assistance when the basement flooded and she was forced to postpone or to hold sales meetings at other locations during the flooding. In December, 1961, a heavy rainstorm occurred during a major sales meeting causing five inches of water to accumulate in the office. Cooper sent the landlord a notice of vacation and abandoned the premises.

Plaintiff Reste Realty Corporation sued defendant Cooper to recover the rent for the remaining term of the lease. In her defense, Cooper alleged that the flooding constituted a constructive eviction thus relieving her from the obligation to pay rent.

The trial court ruled in favor of Cooper but the appellate court reversed. Cooper appealed to the Supreme Court of New Jersey.

Francis, Justice

. . . [T]he lease in question contains an express covenant of quiet enjoyment for the term fixed. Where there is such a covenant, whether express or implied, and it is breached substantially by the landlord, the courts have applied the doctrine of constructive eviction as a remedy for the tenant. Under this rule any act or omission of the landlord or of anyone who acts under authority or legal right from the landlord, or of someone having superior title to that of the landlord, which renders the premises substantially unsuitable for the purpose for which they are leased, or which seriously interferes with the beneficial enjoyment of the premises, is a breach of the covenant of quiet enjoyment and constitutes a constructive eviction of the tenant. . . .

[T]he trial court found sufficient interference with the use and enjoyment of the leased premises to justify the tenant's departure and to relieve her from the obligation to pay further rent. In our view the evidence was sufficient to warrant that conclusion, and the Appellate Division erred in reversing it. Plaintiff argued and the Appellate Division agreed that a constructive eviction cannot arise unless the condition interferes with the use in a permanent sense. It is true that the word "permanent" appears in many of the early cases. . . . But it is equally obvious that permanent does not signify that water in a basement in a case like this one must be an everlasting and unending condition. If its recurrence follows regularly upon rainstorms and is sufficiently serious in extent to amount to a substantial interference with use and enjoyment of the premises for the purpose of the lease, the test for constructive eviction has been met. . . .

Plaintiff's final claim is that assuming the tenant was exposed to a constructive eviction, she waived it by remaining on the premises for an unreasonable period of time thereafter. The general rule is, of course, that a tenant's right to claim a constructive eviction will be lost if he does not vacate the premises within a reasonable time after the right comes into existence. . . . What constitutes a reasonable time depends upon the circumstances of each case. In considering the problem courts must be sympathetic toward the tenant's plight. Vacation of the premises is a drastic course and must be taken at his peril. If he vacates, and it is held at a later time in a suit for rent for the unexpired term that the landlord's course of action did not reach the dimensions of constructive eviction, a substantial liability may be imposed upon him. That risk and the practical inconvenience and difficulties attendant upon finding and moving to suitable quarters counsel caution.

Here, plaintiff's cooperative building manager died about nine months before the removal. During that period the tenant complained, patiently waited, hoped for relief from the landlord, and tried to take care of the water problem that accompanied the recurring rainstorms. But when relief did not come and the "crowning blow" put five inches of water in the leased offices and meeting rooms on December 20, 1961, the tolerance ended and the vacation came ten days later after notice to the landlord. The

trial court found as a fact that under the circumstances such vacation was within a reasonable time, and the delay was not sufficient to establish a waiver of the constructive eviction. We find adequate evidence to support the conclusion and are of the view that the Appellate Division should not have reversed it. . . .

[Judgment of Appellate Division reversed and judgment of trial court reinstated.]

Condition of the Leased Property

Common Law Approach. Under the traditional common law rule, the landlord makes no implied covenant that the premises are suitable for any particular purpose including habitation and is not liable for dangerous conditions existing on the property. The tenant, therefore, is responsible for determining the safety, fitness, and suitability of the property. In addition, under traditional common law principles, the landlord has no duty to repair the leased premises, absent an express provision in the lease requiring repair. The landlord is, however, bound to repair portions of the property not transferred to the lessee, such as the common areas of an apartment building such as elevators, stairs, hallways, sidewalks, fire escapes, and porches.

These principles were developed in an agrarian society and are based on the assumption that (1) the land (commonly unimproved farm land) was the most important feature of the leasehold, (2) the tenant could be expected to personally ascertain the quality and characteristics of the property and make most necessary repairs, and (3) the lease was a result of arms length bargaining between parties with relatively equal bargaining power. These assumptions are no longer true when applied to the modern urban residential lease.

Modern urban tenants, most of whom live in multi-unit apartment buildings, are interested not in land, but in a dwelling suitable for habitation. These tenants are usually unskilled in maintenance and repair work, may not have the financial resources to contract for repairs, and have little incentive to undertake repairs because they have no long-term interest in the property. Further, the modern residential lease is commonly an adhesion contract (a standardized form contract) given to the tenant on a "take it or leave it" basis.[14] It usually deals almost exclusively with landlord's rights and tenant's duties and imposes no express obligations on the landlord to repair or deliver and maintain the property in a habitable condition.

Even if the lease contains covenants of suitability or fitness or imposes a duty to repair, the common law tenant is faced with the "independent covenants" doctrine. Under this doctrine, grounded upon the common law emphasis on the lease as a conveyance of an interest in land, covenants between landlord and tenant are deemed "independent." Promises are independent if the failure by one party to perform a promise does not excuse the other's duty to perform a corresponding promise. Assume the landlord has promised to repair the premises. Under traditional doctrine, the landlord's failure to do so does not excuse the tenant's duty to pay rent. The tenant is relegated to an action for damages for breach of covenant against the landlord but is still obligated to pay rent. Because of the time and expense of a lawsuit and the economic and social position of many tenants, recovery on this basis is not a practical reality. In addition, the tenant is precluded from using the most valuable weapon against the breaching landlord: withholding rent. This result is a substantial departure from the constructive conditions of exchange doctrine discussed in Chapter 14 normally applicable to *contracts,* which makes promises between contracting parties dependent. Briefly stated, in contract law, failure by one party to perform justifies the other's subsequent failure to perform.

The constructive eviction doctrine also provides little help to the residential tenant. The doctrine can be applied only in fairly aggravated cases, and even then the tenant must vacate promptly before the liability for rent is extinguished. Further, a tenant who moves out does so at his peril because a court may later find the landlord's conduct insufficient to constitute a constructive eviction. Of course, constructive eviction is an inherently inadequate tenant's remedy because it does nothing to assure the tenant a habitable place to live after moving out and does not provide compensation for any moving expenses.

Implied Warranty of Habitability. Because of the harsh results imposed on tenants when traditional common law principles are applied to modern residential leases, courts developed the **implied warranty of habitability.** This warranty effects two major changes in the traditional common law doctrine.

First, it imposes an implied covenant in the lease that the premises will meet certain minimum standards of habitability. The warranty is breached if the premises are unsuitable for residential use. Although other modes of proof may be acceptable, the minimum standards of fitness for human habitation imposed by law are commonly measured by the objective legislative standard stated in local housing, safety, sanitary, or health codes, or similar public regulation. Many jurisdictions use substantial code violations as the basic test, while others require additional evidence of unsuitability.

Second, the implied warranty of habitability makes the residential landlord and tenant relation governed by contract rather than property principles. As such, the tenant's duty to pay rent and the landlord's duty to deliver and maintain the premises in a habitable condition are mutually dependent. Failure of the landlord to maintain the property in a habitable condition extinguishes the tenant's duty to pay rent. After breach, the tenant may elect to terminate the lease and vacate the premises or affirm the lease and remain in possession, and may assert the landlord's breach either as a "sword" (tenant as plaintiff to recover damages) or a "shield" (tenant as defendant in landlord's suit for nonpayment of rent).

Today, the vast majority of states impose a warranty of habitability in residential leases. Though initially created by judicial decision, the issue is now governed by statute in many states. For example, the **Uniform Residential Landlord and Tenant Act (URLTA),** governing residential leases in fifteen states,[15] imposes explicit duties upon landlords regarding habitability of residential property.

---

14. Adhesion contracts are discussed in Chapter 10.

15. The URLTA has been enacted, with modification, in Alaska, Arizona, Florida, Hawaii, Iowa, Kansas, Kentucky, Montana, Nebraska, New Mexico, Oregon, Rhode Island, South Carolina, Tennessee, and Virginia.

Commercial Leases. The implied warranty of habitability was developed to protect urban residential tenants. Courts traditionally have been reluctant to extend implied warranty principles to leases of commercial or industrial property for several reasons. First, the parties are likely to possess relatively equal bargaining power. Second, the commercial tenant frequently occupies an entire building under a long-term lease. The business tenant is therefore much closer to being the owner of the property than the apartment dweller, and as a businessperson can be expected to effect, or contract for, needed repairs. Third, commercial leases often contemplate substantial renovation or adaptation of the property to the tenant's use—for example, conversion of a warehouse into a restaurant. Despite these differences a number of courts recently have extended implied warranty principles to commercial leases. The reasons for this approach are explained in the following case.

Davidow v. Inwood North Professional Group—Phase I

747 S.W.2d 373 (Tex. 1988)

> Defendant Joseph Davidow, a physician, entered into a written five-year lease with plaintiff Inwood North Professional Group—Phase I (Inwood) for medical office space. The lease required Inwood to provide air conditioning, electricity, hot water, janitorial and maintenance services, light fixtures, and security services. Davidow encountered numerous problems with the leased premises. Because the air conditioning did not work properly, office temperatures often exceeded eighty-five degrees. The roof leaked whenever it rained preventing use of part of the waiting room and causing stained tiles and rotting, mildewed carpet. Inwood did not provide cleaning and maintenance so that pests and rodents often infested the office, and the parking lot was constantly littered with trash. Hot water was not provided and the electricity was turned off for several days after Inwood failed to pay the electric bill. Several burglaries and incidents of vandalism also occurred. Fourteen months prior to the lease expiration, Davidow moved to a new office and refused to continue paying the rent.

> Inwood sued Davidow for the unpaid rent and Davidow counterclaimed, alleging breach of an implied warranty that the premises were suitable for use as a medical office. The trial court ruled in favor of Davidow, but the court of appeals reversed and rendered judgment for Inwood for the unpaid rent. Davidow appealed to the Texas Supreme Court.

Spears, Justice

This case presents the question of whether there is an implied warranty by a commercial landlord that the leased premises are suitable for their intended commercial purpose. . . .

At common law, the lease was traditionally regarded as a conveyance of an interest in land, subject to the doctrine of *caveat emptor*. The landlord was required only to deliver the right of possession to the tenant; the tenant, in return, was required to pay rent to the landlord. Once the landlord delivered the right of possession, his part of the agreement was completed. The tenant's duty to pay rent continued as long as he retained possession, even if the buildings on the leasehold were destroyed or became uninhabitable. The landlord's breach of a lease covenant did not relieve the tenant of his duty to pay rent for the remainder of the term because the tenant still retained everything he was entitled to under the lease—the right of possession. All lease covenants were therefore considered independent. . . .

In the past, this court has attempted to provide a more equitable and contemporary solution to landlord-tenant problems by easing the burden placed on tenants as a result of the independence of lease covenants and the doctrine of *caveat emptor*. . . . The land is of minimal importance to the modern tenant; rather, the primary subject of most leases is the structure located on the land and the services which are to be provided to the tenant. The modern residential tenant seeks to lease a dwelling suitable for living purposes. The landlord usually has knowledge of any defects in the premises that may render it uninhabitable. In addition, the landlord, as permanent owner of the premises, should rightfully bear the cost of any necessary repairs. In most instances the landlord is in a much better bargaining position than the tenant. Accordingly, we [previously have held] that the landlord impliedly warrants that the premises are habitable and fit for living. We further implicitly recognized that the residential tenant's obligation to pay rent is dependent upon the landlord's performance under his warranty of habitability. . . .

When a commercial tenant such as Dr. Davidow leases office space, many of the same considerations are involved. A significant number of commentators have recognized the similarities between residential and commercial tenants and concluded that residential warranties should be expanded to cover commercial property. . . .

It cannot be assumed that a commercial tenant is more knowledgeable about the quality of the structure than a residential tenant. A businessman cannot be expected to possess the expertise necessary to adequately inspect and repair the premises, and many commercial tenants lack the financial resources to hire inspectors and repairmen to assure the suitability of the premises. . . . Additionally, because commercial tenants often enter into short-term leases, the tenants have limited economic incentive to make any extensive repairs to their premises. . . . Consequently, commercial tenants generally rely on their landlords' greater abilities to inspect and repair the premises. . . .

In light of the many similarities between residential and commercial tenants and the modern trend towards increased consumer protection, a number of courts have indicated a willingness to apply residential property warranties to commercial tenancy situations. . . .

There is no valid reason to imply a warranty of habitability in residential leases and not in commercial leases. Although minor distinctions can be drawn between residential and commercial tenants, those differences do not justify limiting the warranty to residential leaseholds. Therefore, we hold there is an implied warranty of suitability by the landlord in a commercial lease that the premises are suitable for their intended commercial purpose. This warranty means that at the inception of the lease there are no latent defects in the facilities that are vital to the use of the premises for their intended commercial purpose and that these essential facilities will remain in a suitable condition. If, however, the parties to a lease expressly agree that the tenant will repair certain defects, then the provisions of the lease will control. . . .

A commercial tenant desires to lease premises suitable for their intended commercial use. A commercial landlord impliedly represents that the premises are in fact suitable for that use and will remain in a suitable condition. The tenant's obligation to pay rent and the landlord's implied warranty of suitability are therefore mutually dependent.

The existence of a breach of the implied warranty of suitability in commercial leases is usually a fact question to be determined from the particular circumstances of each case. Among the factors to be considered when determining whether there has been a breach of this warranty are: the nature of the defect; its effect on the tenant's use of the premises; the length of time the defect persisted; the age of the structure; the amount of the rent; the area in which the premises are located; whether the tenant waived the defects; and whether the defect resulted from any unusual or abnormal use by the tenant. . . .

The jury found that Inwood leased the space to Dr. Davidow for use as a medical office and that Inwood knew of the intended use. The evidence and jury findings further indicate that Dr. Davidow was unable to use the space for the intended purpose because acts and omissions by Inwood rendered the space unsuitable for use as a medical office. The jury findings establish that Inwood breached the implied warranty of suitability. Dr. Davidow was therefore justified in abandoning the premises and discontinuing his rent payments. . . .

[Judgment reversed.]

Transferring Interests in Leased Property

The interests of both the landlord and tenant in the leased property are freely assignable or transferable without consent unless: (1) a tenancy at will is involved, (2) the lease requires significant personal services from either party and transfer of one party's interest would substantially impair the other's chance of obtaining those services, or (3) the parties to the lease validly agree otherwise. An interest in leased property may be transferred in any manner complying with the formalities dictated by governing law. For example, the interest of both landlord and tenant may generally be transferred by will or intestate succession on death. During life, the landlord's interest is transferred by deed. Approximately one-half of the states require a writing to transfer the tenant's interest in leased property, generally if the term of the original lease is greater than one year.

Assuming none of the exceptions outlined above are applicable (or if applicable, consent is obtained), the interest of either party may be transferred. The following material details the effect of a transfer of the landlord's or tenant's interest.

Transfer of the Tenant's Interest

Assignment and Sublease Defined. The liability of parties when the tenant transfers her interest depends upon whether the transfer is an "assignment" or a "sublease." An **assignment** occurs when the tenant transfers away her entire interest under the lease. In a **sublease,** the tenant transfers all or part of her interest in the property for a period less than the entire term. Further, a transfer, originally for the entire term, is a sublease if the tenant may reacquire the right to possession upon occurrence of an event. In other words, the tenant wishing to create an assignment may not retain any reversionary interest in the leased property. If the transfer is an assignment, the original tenant is the "assignor" and the transferee is the "assignee." In a sublease, the original tenant is the "sublessor" and the transferee is the "sublessee."

For example, assume Lang leases property to Turner for 10 years. With eight years remaining on the lease, Turner transfers the entire property to McGrath for the balance of the term. The transfer is an assignment. McGrath holds the property under Lang. If Turner transfers the entire property to McGrath for five years, the transfer is a sublease. McGrath holds the property under Turner for the five years that he is entitled to possession. During the five-year period, Turner continues to hold under Lang. Similarly, assume Turner transfers the entire property to McGrath for the balance of the term but reserves the right to take possession of the leased property if McGrath uses the property for other than residential purposes. The transfer is a sublease. The foregoing traditional test for distinguishing an assignment from a sublease, based upon the

transferor's retention of a reversion, continues to be generally applied. Some courts, however, resolve the issue by examining the intent of the parties, determined from all surrounding circumstances including the name the parties attach to the transfer.

Liability of Parties after Transfer. Classifying the transfer as an assignment or a sublease has important legal consequences for both the transferor and the transferee. The basic issue presented is the liability of the parties after the transfer for performance of "covenants running with the land." Common examples of covenants running with the land include promises to repair, to pay rent, to build on the land, to renew or extend the lease, to pay taxes, to supply heat and hot water, or restricting use of the property—for example, to residential purposes.

Consistent with the general principles of assignment discussed in Chapter 13, the tenant is not relieved of liability on the lease simply by transferring an interest in the property, whether by assignment or sublease. In other words, the original tenant's liability to the landlord is based on contract. To be relieved of this liability, the tenant must obtain a release from the person entitled to the benefit of the tenant's promise, the landlord. This release is accomplished through a novation, which occurs if the transferee promises to perform the tenant's promises and the landlord in return agrees to release the original tenant from any further liability on the lease.

Effect of Assignment. Assuming the transfer is an assignment, the liability of the assignee to the landlord for performance of covenants running with the land depends upon whether the assignee assumes or does not assume the lease. The assignee assumes the lease if he promises either the landlord or the tenant[16] that he will assume and agree to perform the lease during the balance of the term. An assignee who assumes the lease may be held liable for performance of covenants running with

---

16. If the promise is made to the tenant, the landlord is a third-party beneficiary of the assignee's promise to perform the lease. Third-party beneficiary promises are discussed in detail in Chapter 13.

the land both during the period of his occupancy *and after reassignment.* By assuming the lease, the assignee incurs contract liability to the landlord which, like the liability of the original tenant, is not extinguished by a later transfer of the property, absent a novation. The assignee's liability extends to the landlord, the original tenant, and any intermediate assignee, who, being obligated to do so, has performed the lease.

On the other hand, an assignment may be made in which the assignee does *not* agree to perform the lease during the balance of the term. In this case, the assignee may be held liable by the assignor or by the landlord for performance of covenants running with the land but only during the *period of the assignee's occupancy.* An assignee who does not assume, therefore, has no liability if a subsequent assignee defaults on the lease.

Note that after an assignment, in the absence of a novation, both the assignor and the assignee are liable to the landlord. As between the assignor and the assignee, ordinary principles of suretyship (discussed in Chapter 33) apply to determine who ultimately pays. After an assignment, the assignee becomes primarily liable on the lease and the assignor becomes secondarily liable—that is, the assignor is a surety for the assignee's performance. If the assignee defaults and the assignor-surety is required to pay the landlord, the assignor-surety is entitled to reimbursement from the assignee.

Effect of Sublease. The foregoing rules determine the rights and liabilities of the parties after an *assignment.* If the tenant *subleases* the premises by retaining a reversionary interest, however small, in the leased property, no legal relationship is created between the sublessee and the landlord. As a result, the landlord has no right of action against a sublessee for breach of covenants contained in the lease. The sublessee is merely a tenant of the original tenant, who continues to be primarily liable on the obligations under the lease. The rights and duties of the parties on the sublease are determined by the agreement between the sublessor (original tenant) and sublessee. A sublessee, though not liable on the lease, may be evicted by the landlord if covenants contained in the lease are not performed. For example, assume Larson leases property to Towe for 10 years. After two years, Towe subleases the

property for six years to Stans. Stans, as a sublessee, has no obligation on the original lease between Larson and Towe. Stans holds under Towe and Stans's rights and duties are determined by the sublease agreement with Towe. If, however, the terms of the original lease are not performed, Stans, or anyone else possessing the property, could be evicted by Larson.

Effect of Provision Precluding Assignment. The parties to a lease may validly contract that the interest of either party may not be transferred without consent. Provisions precluding transfer by the tenant without the landlord's consent are by far the most common type, because the landlord usually has a substantial interest in the personal qualities of a tenant, particularly the tenant's reputation for meeting financial obligations. On the other hand, only infrequently does the tenant's use and enjoyment of the property depend significantly on the landlord's continued ownership.

Despite their basic validity, restraints on alienation are strictly construed because of the fundamental policy favoring free transferability of property interests. For example, it is well settled that a provision in a lease prohibiting assignment is not breached by a sublease. Conversely, a prohibition against subleasing is not violated by an assignment. If the lease contains a prohibition against assignment by the tenant without the landlord's consent, and consent to an assignment is subsequently granted, most courts hold that consent to one assignment does not extinguish the landlord's right to approve future assignments, unless the lease indicates to the contrary.

Under the traditional majority rule, the party whose consent is required (generally the landlord) is entitled to withhold consent for any reason or arbitrarily. The minority view, however, provides that consent cannot be unreasonably withheld, unless a freely negotiated provision in the lease confers an absolute right to withhold consent. This latter approach, which has been adopted by the *Restatement (Second) of Property,*[17] is more con-

---

17. *Restatement (Second) of Property (Landlord and Tenant)* §15.2.

sistent with the basic policy favoring free alienability of interests in property.

In the following case, the Supreme Court of California, after analyzing the policy reasons for both approaches, adopted the minority rule.

Kendall v. Ernest Pestana, Inc.

709 P.2d 837 (Cal. 1985)

The City of San Jose owned approximately 14,000 feet of hangar space at San Jose Municipal Airport which it leased to Irving and Janice Perlitch. In 1970, the Perlitches subleased the space for a term of 25 years to Robert Bixler who operated an airplane maintenance business. Under the terms of the written sublease agreement, the lessee (Bixler) could not assign or sublease the property without the written consent of the lessors (Perlitches). Subsequently, the Perlitches assigned their interest in the lease to Ernest Pestana, Inc. In 1981, Bixler agreed to sell his airplane maintenance business, including equipment, inventory, and the existing lease, to Jack Kendall and Grady and Vicki O'Hara. Although the purchasers had a stronger financial statement and greater net worth than Bixler, Ernest Pestana, Inc. refused to consent to the assignment of the lease unless the assignees agreed to an increased rent. Kendall and the O'Haras sued alleging that Ernest Pestana, Inc.'s refusal to consent to the assignment was an unlawful and unreasonable restraint on the freedom of alienation. The trial court dismissed the complaint and Kendall and the O'Haras appealed to the California Supreme Court.

Broussard, Justice

This case concerns the effect of a provision in a commercial lease that the lessee may not assign the lease or sublet the premises without the lessor's prior written consent. The question we address is whether, in the absence of a provision that such consent will not be unreasonably withheld, a lessor may unreasonably and arbitrarily withhold his or her consent to an assignment. . . .

The law generally favors free alienability of property, and California follows the common law rule that a leasehold interest is freely aliena-

ble. . . . Contractual restrictions on the alienability of leasehold interests are, however, permitted. . . .

The common law's hostility toward restraints on alienation has caused such restraints on leasehold interests to be strictly construed against the lessor. . . .

Nevertheless, a majority of jurisdictions have long adhered to the rule that where a lease contains an approval clause (a clause stating that the lease cannot be assigned without the prior consent of the lessor), the lessor may arbitrarily refuse to approve a proposed assignee no matter how suitable the assignee appears to be and no matter how unreasonable the lessor's objection. . . .

The traditional majority rule has come under steady attack in recent years. A growing minority of jurisdictions now hold that where a lease provides for assignment only with the prior consent of the lessor, such consent may be withheld *only where the lessor has a commercially reasonable objection to the assignment,* even in the absence of a provision in the lease stating that consent to assignment will not be unreasonably withheld. . . .

For the reasons discussed below, we conclude that the minority rule is the preferable position. . . .

The impetus for change in the majority rule has come from two directions, reflecting the dual nature of a lease as a conveyance of a leasehold interest and a contract. . . . The policy against restraints on alienation pertains to leases in their nature as *conveyances.* Numerous courts and commentators have recognized that "[i]n recent times the necessity of permitting reasonable alienation of commercial space has become paramount in our increasingly urban society." [*Schweiso v. Williams,* 198 Cal. Rptr. 238 (Cal. App. 1984).] . . .

The second impetus for change in the majority rule comes from the nature of a lease as a *contract.* As the Court of Appeal observed in *Cohen v. Ratinoff,* [195 Cal. Rptr. 84 (Cal. App. 1983)], . . . "there has been an increased recognition of and emphasis on the duty of good faith and fair dealing inherent in every contract." . . . "[W]here a contract confers on one party a discretionary power affecting the rights of the other, a duty is imposed to exercise that discretion in good faith and in accordance with fair dealing." [*Cal. Lettuce Growers v. Union Sugar Co.*, 289 P.2d 785 (Cal. 1955).] . . . Here the lessor retains the discretionary power to approve or disapprove an assignee proposed by the other party to the contract; this discretionary power should therefore be exercised in accordance with commercially reasonable standards. . . .

Under the minority rule, the determination whether a lessor's refusal to consent was reasonable is a question of fact. Some of the factors that the trier of fact may properly consider in applying the standards of good faith and commercial reasonableness are: financial responsibility of the proposed assignee; suitability of the use for the particular property; legality of the proposed use; need for alteration of the premises; and nature of the occupancy, i.e., office, factory, clinic, etc. . . .

Denying consent solely on the basis of personal taste, convenience or sensibility is not commercially reasonable. . . . Nor is it reasonable to deny consent "in order that the landlord may charge a higher rent than originally contracted for." [*Schweiso v. Williams*, 198 Cal. Rptr. 238 (Cal. App. 1984).] . . . This is because the lessor's desire for a better bargain than contracted for has nothing to do with the permissible purposes of the restraint on alienation—to protect the lessor's interest in the preservation of the property and the performance of the lease covenants. . . .

[T]he majority rule has traditionally been justified on three grounds. . . . None of these do we find compelling.

First, it is said that a lease is a conveyance of an interest in real property, and that the lessor, having exercised a personal choice in the selection of a tenant and provided that no substitute shall be acceptable without prior consent, is under no obligation to look to anyone but the lessee for the rent. . . .

A lessor's freedom at common law to look to no one but the lessee for the rent has, however, been undermined by the adoption in California of a rule that lessors—like all other contracting parties—have a duty to mitigate damages upon the lessee's abandonment of the property by seeking a substitute lessee. . . . Furthermore, the values that go into the personal selection of a lessee are preserved under the minority rule in the lessor's right to re-

fuse consent to assignment on any commercially reasonable grounds. Such grounds include not only the obvious objections to an assignee's financial stability or proposed use of the premises, but a variety of other commercially reasonable objections as well. . . .

The second justification advanced in support of the majority rule is that an approval clause is an unambiguous reservation of absolute discretion in the lessor over assignments of the lease. The lessee could have bargained for the addition of a reasonableness clause to the lease (i.e., "consent to assignment will not be unreasonably withheld"). The lessee having failed to do so, the law should not rewrite the parties' contract for them. . . .

Numerous authorities have taken a different view of the meaning and effect of an approval clause in a lease, indicating that the clause is not "clear and unambiguous," as respondent suggests. . . .

It is not a rewriting of a contract, as respondent suggests, to recognize the obligations imposed by the duty of good faith and fair dealing, which duty is implied by law in every contract.

The third justification advanced in support of the majority rule is essentially based on the doctrine of stare decisis. It is argued that the courts should not depart from the common law majority rule because "many leases now in effect covering a substantial amount of real property and creating valuable property rights were carefully prepared by competent counsel in reliance upon the majority viewpoint." [*Gruman v. Investors Diversified Services*, 78 N.W.2d 377, 381 (Minn. 1956).]. . . As pointed out above, however, the majority viewpoint has been far from universally held and has never been adopted by this court. Moreover, the trend in favor of the minority rule should come as no surprise to observers of the changing state of real property law in the 20th century. The minority rule is part of an increasing recognition of the contractual nature of leases and the implications in terms of contractual duties that flow therefrom. . . .

In conclusion, both the policy against restraints on alienation and the implied contractual duty of good faith and fair dealing militate in favor of adoption of the rule that where a commercial lease provides for assignment only with the prior consent of the lessor, such consent may be withheld only where the lessor has a commercially reasonable objection to the assignee or the proposed use. . . .

[Judgment reversed.]

Effect of Sale or Mortgage of Leased Property by the Landlord

The landlord's reversion and right to receive periodic rental payments (the "leased fee") are generally freely transferable. After the transfer, the tenant's rights and liabilities on the lease remain the same; that is, the buyer takes subject to valid existing leases on the property. The buyer has constructive notice of the leasehold interest because of the tenant's possession of the property, or the recording of the lease.

The buyer is generally entitled to receive rental payments accruing after the transfer as an incident of the transfer of the underlying property (the reversion). The seller may, however, expressly reserve the right to receive future rents. If the seller does so, only the bare reversion is transferred to the buyer.

After the transfer, the landlord remains liable to the tenant on covenants contained in the lease. The buyer, in addition to receiving the benefits, becomes liable for all obligations under the lease arising after the transfer. The buyer is not liable for obligations arising under the lease prior to the transfer unless he expressly assumes them.

Leased property is often subject to a mortgage in favor of a lending institution. If the landlord defaults on the underlying loan secured by the mortgage, the law must determine whether the tenant can be evicted by a subsequent foreclosure by the mortgagee. The issue is resolved by determining which came first, the mortgage or the lease. If the mortgage precedes the lease, the tenant takes the property with notice of the mortgage, assuming it is recorded. The tenant's rights may therefore be extinguished by foreclosure of the mortgage. If, however, the lease is made before the mortgage, the mortgagee takes subject to the tenant's rights. In this situation, the later mortgagee (like the buyer discussed above) is put on notice of the lessee's interest by virtue of his or her possession of the mortgaged property or recordation of the lease. Thus, despite foreclosure, the tenant cannot be evicted before expiration of the lease. For example, assume that in 1975 Lawrence borrows $50,000 from First Bank secured by a mortgage on Lawrence's warehouse, which is promptly recorded by the bank. In 1980, Lawrence leases the warehouse to Trent for five years. In 1982, Lawrence defaults on the loan and First Bank forecloses the mortgage. Trent may be evicted by the foreclosure. However, had Lawrence mortgaged the property in 1981, the bank, after Lawrence's default, is required to honor the remaining term of Trent's lease.

SUMMARY

1. Ownership interests in land, known as "estates," differ in several major respects including the duration of the interest, the extent of the interest held by the owner, the time of possession, and the number of persons simultaneously holding an interest. Traditionally, estates are classified as either "freehold" or "nonfreehold." Freehold estates are characterized by indefinite or indeterminate duration. Nonfreeholds form the basis of the law of landlord and tenant. Estates are also classified as either present or future interests according to the time when the owner becomes entitled to possession.

2. The freehold estates include the fee simple absolute, the defeasible or qualified fees simple, and the life estate. The fee simple absolute is the largest ownership interest recognized by law.

3. The defeasible fees simple include the fee simple determinable, the fee simple subject to a condition subsequent, and the fee simple subject to an executory limitation. If a defeasible estate is terminated, the property is transferred to the holder of a future interest in the property known respectively as a "possibility of reverter," a "power of termination," and an "executory interest."

4. A life estate is an interest in property limited in duration to the life or lives of one or more persons. After a life estate, the property is generally acquired by the

holder of either a reversion or remainder interest in the property.

5. Co-ownership occurs when two or more persons simultaneously have the right to possess the same property. The major forms of co-ownership are the joint tenancy and the tenancy in common. A third type, the tenancy by the entirety, is a specialized form of joint tenancy recognized in some states existing between husband and wife. In addition, the cooperative and condominium provide a method for co-ownership of multiple-unit dwellings.

6. A lease creates a landlord-tenant relationship arising upon a transfer of the right to possession of real property from the owner, the lessor or landlord, to another, the tenant or lessee, in consideration of rent. A lease creates an interest in the property in the tenant known as a "nonfreehold estate" or "leasehold." The landlord's interest in the property is known as the "leased fee."

7. The duration of the lease depends upon the type of estate created in the tenant. Nonfreehold estates include an estate for years, an estate from period to period, and an estate at will. The estate at sufferance is not an estate at all, but is used to describe the possession of a tenant who wrongfully holds over upon termination of a lease.

8. The basic obligations of the parties to a lease are implicit in its definition: the landlord transfers exclusive possession of the property to the tenant who becomes obligated to pay rent. The parties also frequently agree to assume other obligations such as duties to insure, repair, or pay taxes.

9. The tenant's duty to pay rent ordinarily continues until expiration of a fixed lease term or proper notice in a periodic tenancy. The duty may be terminated prior to that time by events such as (1) the destruction of the leased property, (2) a surrender involving a mutual agreement by the parties to terminate the lease, and (3) breach by the landlord of the implied covenant of quiet enjoyment involving an actual or constructive eviction of the tenant.

10. Under traditional common law rules, the landlord makes no implied covenant that the leased premises are safe or fit for any particular purpose, including habitation. The landlord also has no duty to repair absent an express provision in the lease, and covenants between landlord and tenant are independent. Because these rules cause substantial hardship to urban residential tenants, the law developed a "warranty of habitability" in residential leases. This warranty imposes an implied covenant in the lease that the premises will meet certain minimum standards of habitability. It also makes covenants between landlord and tenant mutually dependent, thereby allowing the tenant to withhold rent as a remedy for the landlord's failure to deliver and maintain the premises in a habitable condition. Some jurisdictions have extended implied warranty principles to commercial leases.

11. Like other property interests, the interest of both landlord and tenant in the leased property usually are freely transferable. The liability of parties upon a tenant's transfer depends upon whether the tenant assigns or subleases his interest.

12. The landlord's reversion and right to receive periodic rental payments may also be transferred or mortgaged. The buyer or mortgagee, however, takes subject to valid existing leases on the property.

KEY TERMS

estate	four unities
freehold estate	partition
nonfreehold estate	tenancy by the entirety
present possessory estate	cooperative
future interest	condominium
fee simple absolute	lease
defeasible (qualified) fee	landlord-tenant
fee simple determinable	relationship
possibility of reverter	landlord (lessor)
fee simple subject to a	tenant (lessee)
condition subsequent	estate for years
power of termination	estate from period to
(right of entry for	period (periodic
condition broken)	tenancy)
fee simple subject to an	estate (tenancy) at will
executory limitation	estate at sufferance
executory interest	surrender
(executory limitation)	abandonment
life estate	covenant of quiet
life tenant	enjoyment
waste	eviction
reversion	constructive eviction
remainder	implied warranty of
concurrent ownership (co-	habitability
ownership)	Uniform Residential
joint tenancy	Landlord and Tenant
right of survivorship	Act (URLTA)
tenancy in common	assignment of lease
Uniform Simultaneous	sublease
Death Act	

QUESTIONS AND PROBLEMS

36-1   Courts frequently are required to construe deeds and wills in which the parties have not clearly stated what type of estate is being conveyed. American courts frequently state that they will presume a fee simple absolute was granted unless the grantor's intention clearly is otherwise. Similarly, the courts will presume that a conveyance to more than one person creates a tenancy in common rather than a joint tenancy. Why have the courts adopted these presumptions? Explain.

36-2 Donovan devised his farm to the Boy Scouts by his will that provided:

> I give, devise and bequeath to the Boy Scouts of America my farm located in Madison County to be retained and used by the Boy Scouts for the purposes of that organization.

The Boy Scouts accepted the devise but later entered into a contract to sell the farm with the intention of using the proceeds of sale to support scouting programs.

Donovan's heirs sued the Boy Scouts alleging that the Boy Scouts did not have the power to sell the farm. The heirs sought to have the farm transferred to them.

(a) On what grounds could the heirs allege that they were entitled to the property? Explain.

(b) How should the court rule? Explain.

36-3 Marie died and left a will that stated:

> I give all of my property to my husband Melvin for and during his lifetime with the power to use, consume or sell the property as he sees fit. All of my property remaining at the death of my husband I give to my daughter Dixie.

(a) What interest does Melvin own in the property?

(b) During his lifetime, Melvin gave all of Marie's valuable antique furniture to his second wife. Dixie sued to prevent the gift to the second wife. What result?

(c) Melvin died. His will provided that the house which had been owned by Marie was to be given to his son Howard. Dixie sues alleging that the house is her property. What result?

36-4 Pearl owned a life estate in a tract of land covered by woods. From time to time, Pearl cut and sold timber from the woods. Bobby, who owned the remainder interest in the property, sued Pearl alleging that cutting timber from the property constituted waste. Should the court enjoin Pearl from cutting timber? Explain.

36-5 Edith, a widow, wanted to buy a house. Because she did not have enough money to pay for the house, her son Mike and his wife Gloria helped finance the purchase. The seller deeded the property as follows:

> To Mike and Gloria, husband and wife, and Edith, a single woman, as joint tenants and not as tenants in common. It is seller's intention to convey to Mike and Gloria, husband and wife, an undivided one-half interest and to Edith, a single woman, an undivided one-half interest.

(a) A state statute provides that any conveyance to a husband and wife creates a tenancy by the entirety. What interest in the property is held by each of the parties? Assume that Mike dies, what interest would Gloria and Edith hold?

(b) Assume instead that Mike and Gloria obtained a divorce. The following year Edith died. What interest would Mike and Gloria own in the property?

36-6 Consider the following cases to determine whether the lease has been renewed.

(a) Tenant and Landlord signed a ten-year lease that provided that "Tenant has the option to re-lease the premises for an additional term provided that if Tenant exercises the option, Landlord may increase the rental payments by ten percent." At the end of the ten-year term, Tenant provided no notice to Landlord but the Tenant held over and pays the rent.

(b) Lessor and Lessee entered into a four-year commercial lease for which Lessee agreed to pay forty cents per square foot. The lease provided that "Lessee has a two-year option under the same conditions except rental will increase to forty-three cents per square foot." The lease also provides "In the event Lessee holds over after the expiration of the term, such holding over shall not be deemed to extend or renew the term of this lease but such tenancy thereafter shall continue on a month to month basis upon all terms and conditions of this lease." At the end of four years, Lessee sent his rental payment calculated at forty cents per square foot. Lessor provided a notice that the lease was to terminate in thirty days. Lessee then sent a notice of his exercise of the option and enclosed a check for the additional rent under the option.

(c) Tenant and Landlord enter into a lease for a

term of five years that includes the following provision: "Tenant shall have the option to take a renewal lease for a further term of three years at a monthly rate to be negotiated by the parties." Tenant provides notice of exercise of the option but Tenant and Landlord are unable to agree on the rental amount. The parties ask the court to set the rent.

36-7 On August 1, 1986, Tenant and Landlord enter into a written lease for office space. The lease provides that Tenant is entitled to possession of the premises on September 1.

(a) On September 1, Landlord informs Tenant that the construction of the office building is not complete so the office will not be ready for occupancy until October 1. Tenant refuses to pay the rent and moves his office to another building. Landlord sues Tenant for breach of the lease. What result?

(b) Instead, on September 1, Tenant discovers that the current occupant of the office space whose lease expired on August 31 has not vacated the office. Tenant refuses to pay the rent and moves his office to another building. Landlord sues Tenant for breach of the lease. What result?

36-8 Fast Foods Co. leases a vacant lot on Main Street from Leasehold, Inc. for a term of twenty years. The lease requires Fast Foods to construct a drive-in restaurant building, parking lot, and driveways on the property and to obtain all necessary permits to operate the restaurant. After preparing architectural plans for the restaurant, Fast Foods applies to the city for a permit to construct a driveway to provide access to Main Street. The city refuses to grant the driveway permit because increased traffic would create unsafe traffic conditions. As a result, the restaurant would be inaccessible to automobiles. Fast Foods notifies Leasehold that it is terminating the lease. Should Leasehold try to enforce the lease? Explain.

36-9 Nathan leased an apartment in his eight-unit apartment building to Florence. Although the back entrance to the building was locked, the front entrance had no lock. One afternoon while Florence was returning to her apartment, an assailant attacked her in the hallway and stole her purse. She suffered serious injurious requiring hospitalization.

Florence sued Nathan alleging that his failure to provide security for the building, specifically a lock on the front door, constituted a breach of the implied warranty of habitability. State law provides that a warranty of habitability extends to all "facilities vital to the use of the premises for residential purposes." Evidence introduced at trial established that in the three years preceding the attack on Florence, numerous burglaries and street muggings had occurred in the neighborhood. Has Nathan breached the implied warranty of habitability by failing to provide adequate security in the building? Explain.

36-10 On January 1, Anchor Inn entered into a ten-year lease of a building from Lessor to be used as a restaurant. The lease provided that "Lessor will be responsible for maintaining the heating and air conditioning system, including the replacement thereof if necessary." Anchor Inn spent substantial amounts remodeling the building and operated the restaurant successfully for several months. When the weather became warm, however, the air conditioning system began to malfunction. Lessor sent in numerous repairmen, all of whom told Lessor that the air conditioning system was not large enough to cool the premises. Lessor refused to install a new system. Anchor Inn was uncertain what action to take. It could not afford to move to a new building. Nevertheless, it also was losing customers because of the heat in the restaurant. What should Anchor Inn do? Explain.

36-11 In anticipation of his upcoming marriage, Sonny entered into a one-year lease for an apartment in Newtown, a city to which he and his new wife planned to move on July 1. A few weeks before the wedding, his fiancee broke the engagement. On May 15, Sonny wrote to the landlord and asked to break the lease and explained the circumstances. The landlord did not reply. A year later, however, the landlord sued Sonny requesting as damages the rental payments for the year term of the lease. The evidence at trial established that the landlord had made no attempt to re-lease the apartment after receiving Sonny's letter. How should the court rule? Why? Would your answer be different if the evidence also showed that the landlord had received inquiries about renting the apartment but that she had told all persons that the apartment already was rented? Explain.

36-12 United Industries Co. leased a building from Landowner for a term of ten years. After two years, United subleased the building to Maplewood Furniture Co. Maplewood occupied the building for the remaining eight years and paid the rent to Landlord in a timely fashion. After Maplewood vacated the premises, Landlord discovered that the building had suffered excessive damage. Landlord sued United for waste. United established that all damage had occurred during Maplewood's occupation of the premises. Should the court hold United liable for the waste?

36-13   E & S Realty leased a building for $3,000 per month to Healthco, which operated a dental laboratory known as Denthetics in the building. The lease restricted use of the building to medical or dental facilities. The lease also stated that the tenant could not assign the lease "without the written consent of the Landlord, which consent the Landlord shall not unreasonably withhold." Five years later, Healthco sold Denthetics to H & M Laboratory Services, which continued to operate a dental laboratory with no change in personnel or services. H & M Laboratory Services was a well-known dental laboratory in excellent financial condition. As part of the sale, Healthco assigned its interest in the lease and later notified E & S of the assignment. Upon receipt of the notice, E & S advised H & M that it was a tenant at will responsible to pay $5,500 per month, and notified Healthco that it had breached the lease. Is E & S correct?

Transfers of both real and personal property by sale occupy an especially important position in the study of business law. The purpose of many contracts is to transfer land, or tangible or intangible personal property, for consideration. The law of sales and commercial paper is concerned with bargained-for transfers of special types of personal property: goods, promissory notes, and drafts. This chapter expands the coverage of property transfers by discussing **conveyancing,** the performance of the various functions, including financing, necessary to effect transfer of real property interests.

Voluntary Transfer of Real Property by Sale—Conveyancing

The basic land sale contract contains the seller's legally enforceable promise to convey fee simple title to the property to the buyer in exchange for the buyer's promise to pay the purchase price. In the absence of an express contrary provision, it is *implied* that the seller is to convey a fee simple absolute to the buyer and that the title to be conveyed is marketable or merchantable. A **marketable title** is one that a reasonably prudent and legally well-informed buyer is willing to take and pay for. Title is marketable if no reasonable doubt exists concerning its validity and if it is unlikely that the buyer will be exposed to a lawsuit in order to defend it. Existence of marketable title is determined by the court of equity, which will not force the grantee to buy a lawsuit.

The Real Estate Contract

Although real property may be conveyed without a formal written contract, one is almost always used for several reasons. First, the Statute of Frauds requires that contracts for the sale of interests in land be evidenced by a written memorandum to be enforceable. The minimum terms necessary for enforcement are the identity of the parties, a sufficient identification of the property, and the purchase price. Second, a real estate transfer is a complicated transaction. For example, the buyer must be sure before conveyance that title to the property is marketable and must make arrangements for financing. In addition, the parties should agree upon risk of loss, payment of taxes, rights on default, the condition of the premises (including the plumbing, heating, air conditioning, and electrical systems), and the effect of the discovery of termites or other structural defects. These issues are best handled in a comprehensive written contract outlining the rights and duties of both parties.

In addition to the basic contract to convey the real property interest, other contracts are usually present in the typical real estate transaction. For example, the seller may employ a real estate agent using a listing agreement to aid in procuring a buyer. Further, because financing is usually required, the buyer often contracts with a lending institution for a loan to be secured by the property purchased. This security interest, known as a "mortgage," is discussed later in this chapter.

The contract usually fixes a date for performance, known as the "law day," commonly three to five weeks after the contract is made. Unless otherwise agreed, real estate contracts require simultaneous performance by the parties. Thus, on the law day the seller usually conveys the property by delivering a formal document known as a "deed" to the buyer and the buyer pays the purchase price. This performance is known as **title closing, closing,** or **settlement.** In addition to the basic duties of conveyance and payment of the price, other expenses incident to the transfer, including, for example, the costs of financing and establishing a merchantable title, are paid at the closing. For residential property, the **Real Estate Settlement Procedures Act (RESPA),** a federal statute, requires advance itemized disclosure of closing costs to the buyer. If either party fails to perform (breaches the contract), the other is entitled to an appropriate contract remedy, either money damages or, as is always available in land sale contracts, specific performance.[1]

The Deed

A **deed** is a written instrument used to transfer (convey) an interest in real property. The parties to a deed are the **grantor** (the person transferring the interest), and the **grantee** (the person to whom the interest is transferred). A deed is used to convey any interest in real property (a fee simple or a lesser estate), by sale or by gift.

Formalities of a Valid Deed. To be valid and effective to transfer the interest, a deed must comply with certain formalities, generally prescribed by statute. Although the requirements vary somewhat among states, generally a deed must (1) be in writing, (2) identify both the grantor and grantee, (3) contain words of conveyance (such as "convey," "grant," or "bargain and sell") to indicate the grantor's intent to transfer an interest to the grantee, (4) indicate the nature of the estate taken by the grantee (for example, fee simple absolute or life estate), and (5) contain a sufficient legal description of the property.

Legal Description. A deed fails because of an insufficient description if it is possible that more than one tract of land could be identified by the language used. No particular method of description is required by law. Courts often sustain informal or imprecise descriptions because the parties, merely by drafting the deed, indicate an obvious intent to transfer some interest. Nevertheless, to avoid confusion and litigation, and to protect marketability of the title, a more precise formal description is always advisable. Well-drafted deeds commonly describe the property by metes and bounds, the rectangular survey system, or reference to a subdivision plat or map.

Under a "metes and bounds" description, the oldest method, distances (metes) and directions (bounds) are used to trace the perimeter of the described property by starting from a fixed point then

---

1. Specific performance is discussed in Chapter 15.

moving either clockwise or counterclockwise and ultimately returning to the starting point. This method is used throughout most of the eastern United States. The rectangular survey system adopted by the Continental Congress in 1785 is the dominant form of legal description used in thirty states.[2] Under this system, property is described based on a government survey conducted to facilitate development and settlement of areas west of the original thirteen colonies. The survey divides the country into a grid formed by thirty-five north-south lines, known as "principal meridians," and east-west lines known as "principal base lines." The grid is further subdivided into a series of "townships," the basic unit of measurement, each 6 miles square. The township is further divided into thirty-six "sections," each one mile square containing 640 acres. The rectangular survey system is primarily used to describe large agricultural areas. Finally, subdivided land in urban areas is usually described by reference to a plat or map prepared by a surveyor or engineer and recorded in the local county recorder of deeds office. Lots within the plat are numbered or lettered and the property is subsequently described by that number or letter, the subdivision name, and reference by page to the book in the county recorder's office containing the map. The plat frequently contains additional information about easements, setback and sidelot restrictions, and lot measurements. These become part of the description and are incorporated into the deed by reference.

In the following case, the sufficiency of the legal description was in issue.

Overton v. Boyce

221 S.E.2d 347 (N.C. 1976)

Plaintiffs Penelope Badham Overton and Alexander Badham and defendant A. C. Boyce claimed title to a tract of land located in North Carolina. The deed

---

2. These include all states north of the Ohio River, those west of the Mississippi (except Texas), and Alabama, Florida, and Mississippi.

under which the plaintiffs based their claim described the land in dispute as follows:

> [T]he following real estate in Chowan County, to wit: A certain tract of Pocosin Land adjoining the lands of the late Henderson Luton & others, containing, by estimation, Three Hundred and Nineteen Acres.

Plaintiffs filed suit against Boyce in an effort to quiet title to the land. The trial court granted summary judgment to Boyce holding that the description of the land in the plaintiffs' deed did not describe the property sufficiently to identify it. Plaintiffs appealed and the appellate court reversed, holding that the plaintiffs should have been allowed to offer extrinsic evidence that allegedly identified the land. Boyce appealed.

Lake, Justice

. . . When it is apparent upon the face of the deed, itself, that there is uncertainty as to the land intended to be conveyed and the deed, itself, refers to nothing extrinsic by which such uncertainty can be resolved, the description is said to be patently ambiguous. . . . Parol evidence may not be introduced to remove a patent ambiguity since to do so would not be a use of such evidence to fit the description to the land but a use of such evidence to create a description by adding to the words of the instrument. . . .

The description in the deed under which the plaintiffs claim title is patently ambiguous. It refers to nothing extrinsic to which one may turn in order to identify with certainty the land intended to be conveyed. All that the deed tells us about the land is that it is "pocosin land," i.e., swamp land, in Chowan County, it adjoins the lands of the late Henderson Luton and contains, *by estimation,* 319 acres. It is a matter of common knowledge that there are numerous, extensive tracts of pocosin land in Chowan County. The deed leaves the reader of it in doubt as to each of the following things: (1) The exact area of the tract intended to be conveyed, (2) whether the tract intended to be conveyed is all or only part of a single pocosin area, (3) assuming the "Henderson Luton" tract can be located with certainty, on which side of it lies the land here intended to be conveyed, and (4) the length of the common boundary between the "Henderson Luton" tract and the land here intended to be conveyed. Furthermore, the record shows, and the Superior Court found, there were recorded in the office of the Register of Deeds of Chowan County three separate deeds conveying large tracts of land in Chowan County to Henderson Luton and another deed conveying a smaller tract to Henderson Luton and another. The descriptions of the three larger tracts conveyed to Henderson Luton alone show that each of these tracts had one or more boundary lines running along or through a swamp or along the Chowan River.

Since the description in the deed under which the plaintiffs claim is patently ambiguous, the deed is void and cannot be the basis for a valid claim of title in the plaintiffs to the land now claimed by them. . . .

[Judgment reversed.]

Execution of a Deed. In addition to the basic formal requirements, the deed must be properly executed before it is effective to convey the interest to the grantee. The requirements for a valid execution are sometimes summarized by the expression "signed, sealed, and delivered." In addition, attestation or acknowledgment of the instrument may be required.

Signature. The deed must be signed by the grantor. Although the grantee must be identified in the deed, the grantee need not (and rarely will) sign. A deed signed only by the grantor is known as a deed "poll." Almost all deeds are of this type. A deed signed by both parties is known as an indenture.

Seal. The seal, used to authenticate an instrument in an era when few could write, has little modern significance. Most states no longer require a seal on deeds or other written instruments. Nevertheless, seals are still used as a matter of custom in many cases. At common law, the seal was a wax impression, but in modern deeds it is simply evidenced by the word "Seal" or "L.S." printed on the standard form.

Delivery and Acceptance. To be effective the deed must be delivered to and accepted by the grantee. By accepting the deed, the grantee is bound by its terms, thus eliminating the need for his or her signature. The deed is effective to transfer title on the date it is delivered to the grantee.

Attestation and Acknowledgment. Approximately one-fifth of the states require that deeds be attested to be effective to transfer title. Attestation refers to the act of witnessing the execution of a written instrument, at the request of the person making it, and subscribing it as a witness.[3] Other states, as proof of authenticity, require attestation as a prerequisite to recording the deed in the recorder of deeds office. Many states require acknowledgment as a condition to recording. Acknowledgment is a more formal witnessing by a public officer, such as a notary public or justice of the peace, of the grantor's declaration that the execution is his or her free and voluntary act.

Consideration. A deed simply transfers an interest in land and is not itself a contract. No consideration therefore need be paid or stated for the conveyance to be valid. Because a consideration clause was required in certain early common law deeds, modern deeds customarily contain a clause reciting a purported or nominal consideration such as one dollar. The nominal recital of consideration in the deed is purely a matter of form and bears no relationship to the amount paid by the grantee for the property.

Warranty Deeds. Two types of deeds are commonly used to convey real property interests, the warranty deed and the quitclaim deed. The **warranty deed** contains a number of promises, known as **covenants for title,** concerning the status of the grantor's title. The common or usual covenants contained in a general or full warranty deed are the covenants of seisin and right to convey, the covenant against encumbrances, and the covenant of quiet enjoyment.

---

3. Black, *Law Dictionary* (5th ed. 1979).

Covenants of Seisin and Right to Convey. These two covenants in effect mean that the grantor owns the estate she purports to convey, usually a fee simple absolute, and has the right and power to transfer it.

Covenant Against Encumbrances. This covenant means that the property is transferred free of encumbrances not specifically stated in the deed. An **encumbrance** is a right or interest in land, which diminishes its value, but does not prevent transfer of a fee simple. Encumbrances are of three basic types: (1) liens against the property to satisfy monetary obligations such as mortgages, taxes, special assessments, or judgments, (2) interests less than a fee simple such as leaseholds and life estates, and (3) restrictions on the use of the property evidenced, for example, by easements or restrictive covenants. To avoid breaching this warranty, deeds generally state that the property is subject to real estate taxes, covenants, conditions, restrictions, and easements apparent or disclosed by the public record and all applicable zoning laws and ordinances.

Covenant of Quiet Enjoyment. This covenant promises that the grantee will enjoy the quiet and peaceable possession of the property and will not be evicted by a person holding a better title.

Although the foregoing warranties are commonly set forth in full in the deed, many states authorize a statutory "short-form" deed. If the form dictated by statute is used—for example, if the grantor "conveys and warrants" the property to the grantee—the warranties are included even though not expressly stated in the deed.

Limited Warranty Deeds. Discussed above are the covenants contained in the "full" or "general" warranty deed. Fewer warranties are given if a "special" or "limited" warranty deed is used. In a special warranty deed, the grantor warrants only against defects arising since he acquired title, but not against defects or third-party claims arising prior to that time. Language used to create a special warranty deed generally is governed by statute. For example, in Illinois, a deed using the language of conveyance, "grant," "bargain," or "sell," or a

combination thereof, is deemed to include the following covenants: (1) that the grantor owns an indefeasible fee simple estate, (2) that the property is free from encumbrances created by the grantor, and (3) that the grantee will have quiet enjoyment of the property against the grantor and those taking through the grantor.[4]

Breach of Covenant. If a covenant for title is breached, the injured party generally is entitled to money damages. The buyer may be entitled to a return of the entire purchase price plus interest for a total failure of title, or to a proportionate reduction for a partial failure. If the grantor conveys a lesser estate than warranted (for example, a life estate when a fee simple is warranted), damages equal the price paid less the value of the estate received. If the breach involves an encumbrance, the amount paid to remove it and clear the title, not exceeding the purchase price, may be recovered. If the easement or other encroachment cannot be removed, damages measured by the reduction in value of the burdened property are appropriate.

Merger. Delivery of a deed of a type required by the contract discharges the seller's obligations. Under the doctrine of merger, the purchaser's acceptance of the deed extinguishes many of his or her rights under the contract. Therefore, if title later proves defective, the buyer's recourse is for breach of the covenants in the deed, not the contract provisions. Generally, however, merger applies only to matters of title, and not to collateral promises, such as the seller's promise to build or to make improvements or repairs. These promises survive the deed and may form the basis of a subsequent suit by the buyer.

Quitclaim Deeds. The **quitclaim deed,** unlike a warranty deed, makes no warranties or promises regarding title to the grantee. The grantor of a quitclaim deed states in effect, "Whatever interest I may have in the property (and I may have none), I convey to you." Thus, the grantee may obtain a fee simple title or no title upon acceptance of a quitclaim deed and has no recourse against the

---

4. Ill. Rev. Stat. ch. 30, ¶ 7.

grantor for any failure of title. Examples of operative language used in quitclaim deeds include "Grantor hereby releases, surrenders, and relinquishes any right, title or interest that he may have. . ." or "The grantor does remise, release and quitclaim . . ." or in an Illinois short form deed simply "Grantor conveys and quitclaims . . . ". Quitclaim deeds are used when the grantor is uncertain of his interest, to clear up defects in the chain of title, to transfer an interest from one co-tenant to another, and to transfer an interest from one spouse to the other pursuant to a divorce settlement.

Recording Statutes

Even though the seller may be obligated by the contract or deed to transfer fee simple title, any deed, regardless of type, transfers only the seller's interest in the property. Thus, the seller's representations regarding title are only valuable to the buyer if the seller either possesses the promised interest or is solvent and available to be sued when a problem arises. Because title assurance based upon the seller's representations provides such limited protection to the buyer, the buyer must, before delivery of the deed, independently determine whether the seller in fact possesses the interest she purports to convey. This task is accomplished by professional examination of the public record of land titles generated by state **recording statutes**.

Each state has enacted a recording statute designed to provide reliable public information regarding the status of real estate titles. By examining this public record, a prospective purchaser or lender can determine whether the seller or debtor possesses the interest he contracts to convey or use as security for payment of an obligation, and whether any liens or encumbrances exist against the property.

As a general rule, any document concerning the creation or transfer of an interest in real property, including deeds, wills, contracts, mortgages, leases, assessments, tax liens, and mechanic's liens, are recordable. The documents evidencing the interest are recorded in a local office variously known as the **recorder of deeds, county recorder,** or **registry** (or **registrar**) **of deeds.** Because these are usually county offices, the proper place of re-

cording usually is the recorder's office in the county where the land is located. Ordinarily, documents accepted for recording must meet certain statutory formalities to insure authenticity, such as attestation or acknowledgment.

Effect of Recording. Recording is not required to make the instrument effective between the *immediate parties* to the transaction. For example, a deed is effective to transfer an interest from the grantor to the grantee upon delivery even though never recorded. A deed of mortgage given by a debtor (mortgagor) to a lender (mortgagee) is effective to create a security interest in the debtor's property even if not recorded by the mortgagee.[5] The recording statute is designed to protect the purchaser or mortgagee against conflicting claims to, or interests in, the same property by *third parties—*persons other than the original grantor or mortgagor. Simply stated, the recording statute protects purchasers and mortgagees acting in good faith against prior unrecorded recordable interests in the property. Recording is constructive notice to third parties of the recording party's interest.[6]

Constructive notice means that later third parties are deemed to know of a prior recorded interest, and therefore take subject to it, even if they have no *actual* knowledge of its existence. Therefore a transferee who fails to record her interest is protected only against her transferor and those who have *actual* knowledge of the transfer. Recording provides protection against everyone else. A purchaser or mortgagee is thus protected by the recording statute in two ways: (1) she takes free of prior unrecorded interests in the property, and (2) recording is constructive notice to all third parties of her interest.

Generally, recording statutes protect only those purchasers or lenders who act in good faith and give value or consideration for their interest in the

---

5. As discussed later in this chapter, a mortgage is an interest in real property created by a "mortgagor" in favor of a "mortgagee" as security for performance of an obligation.

6. Just as failure to record does not affect the validity of an instrument between parties, recording does not validate an otherwise invalid instrument. Recording simply provides constructive notice of the *existence,* not necessarily the legal effectiveness, of the instrument.

property. To meet the good faith standard, the purchaser or lender must take without either actual subjective knowledge or constructive notice via the recording statute. Further, a purchaser or lender who has knowledge of facts that would induce a reasonable person to investigate further is charged with notice of facts that would be disclosed by a reasonable inquiry. This inquiry notice commonly arises when someone other than the grantor occupies the property at the time of the conveyance. Donees of property and persons taking under a will or by intestate succession receive property gratuitously. Because these transferees do not give value, they are not protected by the recording statute and therefore take the property subject to prior unrecorded interests.

The recording statute serves two basic closely related functions in protecting land titles. First, it provides a public record that prospective purchasers and lenders can examine to verify the truth and completeness of the owner's representations concerning the property. Second, it determines priority among *successive* purchasers and mortgagees of the same property. These functions are discussed in more detail below.

The Title Search. Because each document affecting ownership of property is recorded, a chronological public record of transactions concerning the property is created. Systematic examination of this record is known as a **title search.** By means of a title search, a prospective purchaser or lender ascertains whether the seller actually owns the interest she purports to convey and what interest others, including creditors, may hold in the property.

To facilitate locating documents affecting the particular property under examination, all recording statutes mandate that instruments accepted for recording be indexed. In most states, instruments are indexed alphabetically under the name of both the grantor and the grantee (a grantor-grantee index). In other states, instruments are indexed according to the legal description of the land involved (a tract index).

A prospective purchaser or lender has constructive notice of all instruments recorded within the chain of title of the particular tract in question. The **chain of title** refers to the succession of deeds, wills, and other instruments by which the ownership of the property and other interests in it can be traced from the present owner back to the original patent or deed from a governmental authority to the first private owner. All land titles originate in a grant from a sovereign including the United States, Spain, France, Mexico, England, or the original thirteen states depending upon the area of the country involved.

In some states, the title is searched back to the original grant from a sovereign. In others, search of a more limited period—for example, 30 to 100 years—is undertaken. Several states have adopted **Marketable Title Acts** that reduce the period of title search by extinguishing all claims and title defects automatically after a fixed period, such as thirty to forty years, unless preserved by filing a statutory notice.

Even if a title search establishes an unbroken chain of ownership or good "record title," the prospective purchaser may not receive a clear, unencumbered title due to events not disclosed by the recording statute. Examples include defects in a conveyance in the chain, such as forgery of a grantor's signature; fraud or duress inducing a grantor to execute the instrument, minority or other incapacity of a grantor, failure of delivery of a deed in the chain; misrepresentation of marital status by a grantor (leaving the possibility of a claim by the spouse or spouse's heirs); or failure of all persons holding an interest in property to join in a conveyance (leaving the possibility of a claim by an omitted person or his heirs). In addition, errors such as an incorrectly filed document may exist in the record itself.

The county recorder's office is not the only source of public information concerning land titles. For example, court records may indicate an outstanding judgment against the record owner affecting his title. In addition, probate, tax, and assessment records contain important information. A thorough title search therefore requires examination of all relevant public records.

In addition to searching the public record, the title searcher should always physically inspect the premises to determine the rights of parties in possession and other information that may not be disclosed by the public record. This physical inspection should, in all cases, include a precise determination of lot boundary lines. Unless the property lines are known (by locating surveyor's stakes or from a prior survey), a survey may be required. The physical inspection and survey are of particular importance because neither an attorney's opinion nor title insurance (discussed below) protects the buyer against defects an inspection or survey would uncover.

In virtually all states private abstract or title companies maintain a private duplicate set of real estate records. These records are kept up to date on a daily basis by information obtained from the recorder's office. The information obtained by the abstract company over time is used to prepare an **abstract of title,** which is a chronological summary of the contents of all recorded instruments pertaining to a particular tract of land. The abstract is then rented to persons desiring to examine the title. Thus, although the buyer, lender, seller, or their attorneys could conduct the title search, this task is ordinarily contracted to a professional abstracter. A seller or borrower is ordinarily under no duty to furnish an abstract to the buyer or lender in the absence of specific agreement to do so. The parties customarily provide by contract, however, that the seller or borrower furnish the abstract.

The Attorney's Opinion and Title Insurance.

Once an abstract of title has been prepared, it is examined by an attorney who renders a professional opinion concerning the status of the title through either an attorney's opinion or title insurance. In an **attorney's opinion,** an attorney examines the title as disclosed by the abstract and renders a formal written opinion regarding its marketability. The opinion will note any areas for concern and list any liens or encumbrances burdening the property. The attorney does not insure the title, but is only liable for injury caused by negligent errors or omissions.

An alternative form of title protection is afforded by title insurance. **Title insurance** is a contract between the insurer—a title insurance company—and an insured—a property owner or person lending money secured by real property. The insurer agrees to indemnify or reimburse the insured against losses resulting from certain specified defects in the title to the covered property. Note that the *title* is not really insured, the owner or lender is merely indemnified against loss resulting from failure of the title.

Title insurance is, like the attorney's opinion, based upon a search of the public record. Usually, attorneys employed by the title insurance company render the opinion after examining the private land records maintained by the insurance or abstract company. Title insurance provides somewhat more protection than an attorney's opinion because the owner need not show negligence in order to recover, defects not of record may be covered, and the insurance company bears the expense of defending any suit necessary to protect the title.

The "Torrens" System.

Under the recording statute, the instruments constituting evidence of various interests in or claims to property such as deeds, mortgages, and easements are recorded. From this ever-expanding body of information, the prospective buyer or lender must draw a conclusion concerning the status of the seller or borrower's title. This is an expensive, cumbersome process, requiring multiple searches and examinations of the same title as the property is transferred from one owner to the next.

The **Torrens system** is an alternative method involving registration of title to property, instead of recording evidence of that title. Under the Torrens system, the title is registered in a judicial proceeding in which all parties claiming an interest in the property are notified and given the opportunity to assert their claims. After a hearing, a certificate of title, similar to an automobile title, is issued to the person found to be the owner. The certificate indicates the nature of the owner's title (usually a fee simple) and any liens or encumbrances against the property. Once the title is registered, the owner, as well as subsequent buyers or lien holders, takes free of all claims or interests, except those noted on the certificate. To transfer the property, the owner simply executes a deed to the grantee. The deed and the owner's certificate are filed with the registrar of titles (the Torrens equivalent of the recorder of deeds), who simply cancels the grantor's certificate and issues a new one to the grantee. Any liens or encumbrances surviving against the grantee are noted on the new certificate. Thus, after registration, title can be transferred quickly and without a costly title search.

Despite its apparent advantages, the Torrens system has not achieved widespread acceptance in the United States. Today, fewer than one-fourth of the states have enabling statutes providing for land title registration under the Torrens system. Even in those states, registration is optional with the owner, and may exist only in certain geographic areas.

Priority Among Successive Purchasers.

A basic purpose of the recording statute is to protect purchasers or mortgagees by providing a public record disclosing the condition of title to land they are about to purchase or lend against. To accomplish this purpose, the recording statute effectively gives a property owner the *power* to make successive conveyances of the same property, even though he or she may have no *right* to do so. The problem is simply illustrated by the following example. Ann, the fee simple owner of a tract of land, sells it by warranty deed to Bob, who pays fair market value. One week later, Ann conveys the same property by warranty deed to Carl, who also pays fair value. Ann pockets the proceeds of both sales and disappears. As between Bob and Carl, the innocent purchasers left behind, who is entitled to the land? In the absence of any recording statute, the common law rule, known as "first in time, first in right," provides that the first purchaser *in time* (in this case, Bob) prevails. That is, after the conveyance to Bob, Ann has no interest remaining to transfer to Carl.

With a recording statute in effect, however, priority is determined by the terms of the recording statute, not by chronological order of conveyance. This approach is designed to protect the integrity of the recording system and enable a prospective purchaser to rely upon the public record as indicating the state of the title. Statutes are generally classified as one of three types according to the manner of resolving the priority issue. The characteristics of each type are discussed below.

Pure Race Statute.

Pure race statutes are in effect only in five states and even in those states do not apply to all recorded instruments. Under this type, the first purchaser to record prevails; that is, the purchaser who wins the "race" to the county recorder's office prevails. This result follows even if the first person to record takes with actual knowledge of a prior unrecorded conveyance.

Pure Notice Statute.

Under a **pure notice statute,** in effect in twenty-five states, a subsequent purchaser who takes without actual knowledge of a prior unrecorded conveyance prevails, regardless of who later records first. To illustrate using the preceding example, assume Bob fails to record before Ann's conveyance to Carl. Carl wins if at the time of the conveyance to him, he has no *actual* knowledge of Bob's interest regardless of whether Bob or Carl later records first. If Bob had recorded prior to Ann's conveyance to Carl, Bob prevails because Carl takes the property with constructive notice of Bob's interest.

Race-Notice Statute.

Race-notice statutes, a combination of the first two, govern in approximately one-half of the states. Under a race-notice statute, the subsequent purchaser prevails if he or she *both* (1) takes without actual knowledge of the prior conveyance, and (2) records first. Thus, under a race-notice statute, even if Carl takes without actual knowledge of Bob's interest, Bob prevails if he records first.

In the following case, the court used Wisconsin's race-notice statute to resolve a dispute between two competing grantees of the same property.

Kordecki v. Rizzo
317 N.W.2d 479 (Wis. 1982)

In 1974 the Garcias entered into a contract to purchase a piece of real property from the Katts. In 1977, the Garcias defaulted on the contract and the Katts brought a foreclosure suit. At the same time, the Katts filed with the registrar of deeds a notice—called a *lis pendens* (Latin: a pending suit)—stating that title to the property was in litigation. As part of the settlement of the foreclosure suit, the Garcias deeded their interest in the real property to Bruno Rizzo as trustee in November, 1977. Rizzo recorded the deed on March 28, 1978.

On December 12, 1977, however, the Garcias sold the same property to plaintiff, Larry Kordecki. The Garcias quitclaimed the property to Kordecki who recorded the deed on December 14, 1977. Kordecki did not perform a title search.

Plaintiff Kordecki sued defendant Rizzo alleging that Kordecki owned title to the property because his deed had been recorded prior to that of Rizzo.

Wisconsin has adopted the following race-notice recording statute:

> Every conveyance . . . which is not recorded as provided by law shall be void as against any subsequent purchaser in good faith and for a valuable consideration of the same real estate or any portion thereof whose conveyance shall first be duly recorded.

The trial court ruled in favor of Kordecki. On appeal, the court of appeals reversed. Kordecki appealed to the Wisconsin Supreme Court.

Abrahamson, Justice

. . . The Garcias are the common grantors of the two competing grantees. The Garcias conveyed their interest in the property to Rizzo as trustee in November, 1977. Thereafter, the Garcias conveyed their interest in the property to Kordecki. Under the law of conveyancing (without considering the recording statute), because Garcia had already passed title to Rizzo as trustee, Garcia could convey no interest to Kordecki and Kordecki could acquire no interest in the land under the quit claim deed. Hence under the law of conveyancing, Rizzo takes priority over Kordecki. . . . [The Wisconsin recording statute] is a notice-race recording statute and changes the common law of conveyancing. When we consider the recording statute, we must recognize that since Rizzo did not record the Garcias' deed to him, Rizzo's title is subject to defenses existing by reason of his failure to record. Kordecki recorded his deed before Rizzo recorded his.

The recording statute is designed (1) to force the recording of all instruments so that the record will show a complete history of the title and (2) to protect purchasers who rely on the record and purchase in good faith and for value over those who have not recorded their interest in the real estate thereby possibly misleading others. In other words, the purpose of the recording statute is to render record title authoritative to protect a purchaser who relies on the record and is a purchaser in good faith and for a valuable consideration.

In determining rights under the recording statute, in contrast with determining rights under the common law of conveyancing, the initial question is not what the Garcias actually owned when they conveyed the property to Kordecki but what the record shows they owned. To claim the benefits of . . . a purchaser in good faith, Kordecki is deemed to have examined the record and to have notice of the contents of all instruments in the chain of title and of the contents of instruments referred to in an instrument in the chain of title. A purchaser in good faith is one without notice, constructive or actual, of a prior conveyance. . . .

Had Kordecki examined the record, which he did not, he would have found the lis pendens which would have led him to the Kenosha county circuit court file on the proceedings to foreclose the land contract. . . . Thus Kordecki is viewed as having constructive notice from the recorded instruments that Garcia had no power to sell the property on December 12, 1977, that there may be unrecorded conveyances and that the proffered deed might be a nullity. Despite Rizzo's failure to record, the record gave Kordecki notice of defects of his grantor's title and the possibility of unrecorded conveyances. . . .

Because Kordecki cannot claim sanctuary under the notice-race recording statute, we affirm the decision of the court of appeals.

In addition to purchasers of and lenders against the real estate, real property recording statutes also may affect the rights of purchasers of goods closely associated with the land but sold apart from it, such as minerals, structures, crops, timber, or fixtures. Under §2-107(3) of the Uniform Commercial Code, the buyer of such goods takes subject to rights of a *prior* purchaser or mortgagee of the underlying real estate who records his or her interest. The buyer of the goods may also be jeopardized by *subsequently* created interests in the land. For example, a purchaser of real estate commonly receives crops growing on it, raising the possibility of conflicting claims between the buyer of the growing crops and a person who later purchases the underlying land before the crops are harvested. To protect the crop buyer in this situation, §2-107(3) provides that the crop sale contract may be recorded in the real estate records where it provides constructive notice to third parties of the buyer's rights under the contract. Some courts protect the crop buyer in this situation even if he or she fails to record by holding that the crops are personalty to which the recording act does not apply or that a "constructive severance" is effected at the time the crops are sold.

Financing Real Property

A real estate buyer seldom has the financial resources to pay cash for the property. Normally, the buyer makes a down payment and must borrow the remainder of the purchase price. Creditors financing real property usually require security. This security is generally provided by a mortgage, or in some cases an installment contract.

Introduction to Mortgages

A **mortgage** is an interest in real property that is created to secure performance of an obligation, normally repayment of a debt. The person creating the mortgage and giving the security is known as the **mortgagor**. The person receiving the benefit of the security afforded by the mortgage is known as the **mortgagee**. The mortgage gives the mortgagee a security interest in specific real estate owned by the mortgagor. If the obligation secured by the mortgage is not performed, the mortgagee has recourse against the property to satisfy the obligation. In other words, in a mortgage, real property serves as collateral for a loan or other obligation.

The mortgage is not the debt; the debt is usually evidenced by a promissory note signed by the mortgagor. This note, usually payable in installments over an extended period, evidences what is known as the "underlying debt." Most mortgage notes are of the "direct reduction" or "amortizing" type, in which each equal installment payment is part principal and part interest. Thus, the principal amount is gradually reduced (amortized) over the term of the loan and interest is charged on the unpaid balance. An increasing proportion of each payment is allocated to principal as the debtor builds equity in the property.[7]

To illustrate, assume Burns contracts to buy a house from Smith for $50,000. To finance the purchase, Burns borrows $50,000 from First Federal Savings and Loan and executes a promissory note payable to the order of First Federal for $50,000. Burns then pays the $50,000 to Smith, who conveys the property to Burns. In addition, Burns gives First Federal a mortgage on the property purchased to secure repayment of the promissory note. If Burns defaults, First Federal is entitled to the mortgaged property to satisfy any unpaid portion of the debt.

Under the traditional definition, if the *seller,* rather than a third party, finances the buyer, a "purchase money" mortgage is created. The buyer pays the seller an agreed down payment and the seller conveys the property to the buyer. The remainder of the purchase price is then paid in installments to the seller, who takes a mortgage on the property to secure the unpaid balance. Today, in a majority of states, any mortgage given on property to secure its purchase price is known as a "purchase money" mortgage no matter who (the seller or a third party) provides the financing.[8]

Creation of a Mortgage. A mortgage, like other interests in real property, is created by use of a deed, a mortgage deed, in which the mortgagor conveys the property to be used as security to the mortgagee. The mortgage deed, like the general warranty deed, contains the names of the parties, a legal description of the property, covenants for title, language of conveyance, and is signed by the grantor (mortgagor). In addition, the deed describes the underlying loan secured by the mortgage. It also contains additional covenants designed to protect the mortgagee's interest in the property, such as the mortgagor's promise to pay the underlying indebtedness, to keep the premises insured and in good repair, and to pay taxes, other liens, and assessments against the property.

In approximately one-third of the states, a security device known as a **deed of trust** or **trust deed**

---

7. Equity refers to the difference between the market value of the property (evidenced by the purchase price) and the outstanding indebtedness.

8. This approach is consistent with the "purchase money security interest" definition applicable to personal property under Article 9 of the UCC. See discussion of UCC §9-107 in Chapter 31.

may be used as the functional equivalent of a mortgage. A deed of trust, like other trusts, uses three parties instead of the two (mortgagor-mortgagee) present in the ordinary mortgage. The borrower (settlor or trustor) transfers the property to the trustee who holds it in trust for the benefit of the lender (beneficiary) as security for payment of the debt. The rights of the parties are determined by the trust instrument, including the borrower's right to reconveyance upon satisfaction of the obligation and the lender's rights on default.

"Title" versus "Lien" Theory of Mortgages. The law has developed two basic theories to describe the nature of the property interest created by a mortgage. Traditionally, under the "title theory" of mortgages, a mortgage is an outright conveyance of the property to the mortgagee (who at early common law took possession of the property) subject to reconveyance upon satisfaction of the secured obligation.[9] Under this theory, if the mortgagor defaults, the mortgagee retains the property even if the value of the property exceeds the amount owing on the secured debt at the time of default.

Because strict application of the title theory may result in a windfall to the mortgagee (the difference between the outstanding debt and the value of the property), the "lien theory" is now generally applied to characterize a mortgage. Under this approach, because the mortgage is created only as *security* for a debt, the mortgagee's interest in the property is limited to the amount of the outstanding obligation. If upon default the value of the property exceeds the unpaid balance, any surplus is returned to the mortgagor. Many states reach this "lien theory" result even though they treat a mortgage technically as an outright conveyance of the property. In other words, a hybrid "title-lien" approach is used.

Liability on the Underlying Debt. The mortgagor ordinarily is personally liable for payment of the debt secured by the mortgage because he or she also has signed the underlying promissory note. This liability is important in the event of a deficiency. A deficiency occurs when, after default, the mortgaged property is worth less than the outstanding debt. Because the mortgage is given as security for payment of the debt, not as a substitute for it, a mortgagor who also signs the note is generally liable for any deficiency upon default. Conversely, a property owner may be liable on the mortgage but not on the secured debt. In this case, the mortgagor loses his or her interest in the property, but has no liability for any deficiency.

Priority Among Successive Mortgagees

A property owner may borrow money from two or more lenders and give each a mortgage on the same property. In this case, legal disputes commonly arise when the mortgagor defaults and the value of the mortgaged property is less than the total of the outstanding obligations it secures—for example, two $50,000 loans secured by a mortgage on property worth $75,000. Priority of the various mortgagees in distribution of this limited fund must then be determined.

Priority among successive mortgagees, like priority among successive purchasers, is determined by the recording statute regardless of which mortgage occurred first in time. A mortgage is an interest in land, and the mortgage deed, like other deeds, is a recordable instrument. Recording protects the mortgagee against a subsequent sale or mortgage of the same property to another. If the mortgagee fails to record, subsequent buyers or mortgagees without actual notice take free of the unrecorded mortgagee's claim.

Therefore, if a dispute arises, generally the first mortgage to record is paid first (a "first mortgage"), the second to record is paid second (a "second mortgage"), and so on until the sum generated on sale of the property is exhausted. For this reason, a first mortgage is often termed a "senior" mortgage and second and subsequent mortgages are referred to as "junior" mortgages. Although rights of successive mortgagees are usually determined by

---

9. Under the title theory, a mortgage is similar to the fee simple subject to a condition subsequent (discussed in Chapter 36). That is, title to the property remains in the mortgagee until repayment of the underlying debt—occurrence of the condition subsequent.

the recording statute, a mortgagee may, by "subordination" agreement, contractually relinquish a right to priority it would otherwise possess.

Although no rule theoretically limits the number of mortgages that may burden a given parcel of land, there are seldom more than two. Many lenders, by statute or as a matter of policy, will loan only upon first mortgage security. Additionally, second and subsequent mortgages are commonly available only for shorter terms at higher interest rates.

A mortgagor who satisfies the secured obligation is entitled to have the encumbrance evidenced by the mortgage removed from the public record. This result is accomplished by a written release executed by the mortgagee in a form necessary for recording. The release is then recorded, clearing the mortgagor's title.

Sale of Mortgaged Property

As a general rule, and in the absence of contrary agreement, the mortgagor is free to sell the mortgaged property without consent of the mortgagee. The sale, however, has no effect upon either the mortgage itself or the mortgagor's liability on the underlying debt. In other words, the mortgagee's rights against both the mortgagor and the property are unaffected by the sale. The sale may be effected with or without retiring the existing mortgage.

Refinancing. Most commonly the buyer will "refinance." That is, the buyer pays the purchase price in cash, part of which is paid to the mortgagee to extinguish the mortgage debt (and the mortgage) with the remainder paid to the seller. Both the seller and the original mortgagee are thus paid in full. Because the buyer is rarely in a position to finance the purchase himself, he generally borrows the necessary funds from a lending institution securing the loan with a new mortgage on the property purchased.

Taking "Subject to" or "Assuming" Mortgage. The property may also be sold without retiring the existing mortgage. The buyer simply pays the seller for the seller's equity in the property, continues to make payments on the mortgage, and takes either "subject to" the existing mortgage, or agrees to "assume" the mortgage debt. A buyer who takes "subject to" the mortgage incurs no personal liability for payment of the debt that the mortgage secures. Thus, if the buyer fails to repay the debt, he or she will lose the property if the mortgagee subsequently forecloses, but is not liable if the amount realized when the property is sold is insufficient to satisfy the outstanding debt. If the foreclosure sale realizes more than the remaining debt, the excess is paid to the buyer because the seller has already been paid for her equity in the property.[10]

Alternatively, the buyer may agree to "assume" the underlying mortgage indebtedness. Although it is frequently stated that the buyer "assumes the mortgage," the buyer actually assumes, and thereby becomes personally obligated to pay, the underlying loan that the mortgage secures.[11] Under traditional contract principles, the seller remains totally liable for repayment of the debt despite the buyer's assumption. That is, a suretyship relation is created between the seller and buyer upon assumption of the mortgage. If the buyer defaults, the seller may be compelled to satisfy the unpaid obligation. The seller may, however, be relieved of liability if the mortgagee agrees to release her and look only to the buyer for payment. In this case a novation is created in which one contracting party, the buyer, is substituted for another, the seller, whose liability is extinguished.[12]

---

10. Even if the deed or contract fails to mention that the conveyance is "subject to the mortgage," the result is effectively the same as outlined above provided the mortgage is recorded. In other words, a seller cannot transfer property free of an existing recorded mortgage.

11. The buyer's promise to assume the mortgage debt may be made either to the seller or the bank. In either case, it is enforceable by the bank. That is, the bank, as a third-party creditor beneficiary, may enforce the promise against the buyer, even if the promise is not made to the bank directly. Third-party beneficiary promises are discussed in Chapter 13.

12. The elements of a novation are discussed in conjunction with the law of assignment and delegation in Chapter 13 and in Chapter 36 in conjunction with coverage of landlord-tenant law.

The following case illustrates the effect of default after a mortgage assumption on the original mortgagor's liability.

Berg v. Liberty Federal Savings and Loan Association

428 A.2d 347 (Del. 1981)

In 1970 Howard and Sandra Berg signed a note for a loan secured by a mortgage on real estate in favor of Liberty Federal Savings and Loan Association (lender). In 1973 the Bergs sold the real estate to a third party (grantee) who assumed liability for the note. During the following four years the grantee made loan payments and corresponded directly with the lender. In 1978, the grantee defaulted on the loan.

After notifying the Bergs of the default, the lender sued the Bergs for the amount due on the note. In defense of the suit the Bergs argued that the lender was required to foreclose on the mortgage prior to suing on the note. They further argued that the lender could sue only the grantee, alleging that the lender had released the Bergs by accepting payments from and corresponding with the grantee.

The trial court ruled in favor of Liberty Federal Savings and the Bergs appealed.

Horsey, Justice

. . . As between a mortgage lender and a borrower-mortgagor who, by bond or note is personally bound, the law is clear and undisputed as to the creditor's rights: that on debtor's default, lender may, at its option, either sue on the bond or foreclose on the mortgage. . . . No implication arises from the mere taking of collateral security that a creditor will look only or primarily to the security for repayment of the loan. . . . A creditor-mortgagee may pursue all available remedies concurrently or successively, to the extent that separate and distinct remedies are recognized at law or in the controlling instrument. . . .

Absent a release or contract of novation, a mortgagor is not exonerated from personal liability on his bond or note by conveying the mortgaged premises to a third party who assumes the mortgage—regardless of lender's acceptance of grant-ee's payments on the mortgage, assuming the terms of repayment are not varied. . . .

A novation will not be presumed but must be proved, with the burden of proof thereof resting on the proponent. . . . It has been held that a creditor's knowledge of a debt assumption and acceptance of payments on the debt from assumptor is not sufficient to effect a novation or release of the original debtor. Creditor's expressed assent to give up the original debt is required. . . .

Here there is no allegation or evidence that lender varied the terms of the debt instruments after grantee assumed the mortgage and became the primary obligor. . . .

Lender's acceptance of timely mortgage payments from grantee over a period of four years and related correspondence was insufficient as a matter of law to alter lender's right—under the terms of mortgagor's bond and firmly established precedent—to proceed, on default, as its option either on the bond or to foreclose on the mortgage. . . .

[Judgment affirmed.]

Effect of Due-on-Sale Clause. A **due-on-sale clause** is a contractual provision contained in the promissory note or mortgage, permitting the mortgagee, at its option, to declare the entire balance of the mortgage immediately due and payable if the property secured is sold or otherwise transferred without the prior consent of the mortgagee. Due-on-sale clauses originally were designed to protect the mortgagee against impairment of its security or increased risk of default caused by a sale. That is, the mortgagee could investigate the creditworthiness of a prospective buyer and invoke the clause if the buyer proved financially irresponsible. In recent years, however, due-on-sale clauses have been used primarily to retire old, unprofitable mortgages when the encumbered property is sold, thereby enabling the mortgagee to maintain its long-term portfolio at current interest rates. For example, if a due-on-sale clause is exercised, the seller-mortgagor is unable to offer a prospective buyer an assumption of his long-term, low-interest fixed rate mortgage as a financing device. Although prior to 1982 many state courts refused to enforce due-on-sale clauses as unreasonable restraints on alienation, federal law[13] now makes them generally enforceable.

Regulations issued by the Federal Home Loan Bank Board provide that if a mortgage contains a due-on-sale clause, the lender is not required to exercise it upon sale, but may instead waive it and allow the buyer to assume the existing mortgage. The assumption agreement must be in writing and executed before the transfer is made. In this case, the buyer becomes contractually obligated on the original loan and the lender is allowed to adjust the interest rate upward. After the assumption, however, the lender must release the original borrower (seller) from all obligations under the loan.[14] This result differs from the traditional contract approach discussed above under which the original mortgagor remains liable after assumption.

Transfer of Mortgagee's Interest. The mortgagor's promissory note secured by the mortgage is freely transferable by the mortgagee. Because the mortgage merely secures the note, they must be transferred together. Sale of the mortgage without the debt is ineffective, and sale of the note automatically carries with it the security provided by the mortgage; that is, the mortgage "follows" the debt.

Rights on Default; Foreclosure

After default, the mortgagee may always proceed upon the underlying note, obtain a judgment, and seek to enforce it against the debtor's general assets. Because these assets are usually insufficient or subject to other creditors' claims, however, the mortgagee usually desires to enforce its interest in the security. **Foreclosure** is the method by which the mortgaged property, or proceeds of its sale, is applied in satisfaction of the debt.

Literally, the term "foreclosure" refers to barring or terminating the mortgagor's "equity of redemption." The **equity of redemption** concept

was developed to allow the mortgagor to "redeem" his property by satisfying the debt plus interest within a reasonable time after default. Because the mortgagee could not sell or otherwise dispose of the property while a possibility of redemption remained, a method of fixing the duration of the mortgagor's equity of redemption was required. The method developed was the mortgagee's suit to foreclose or extinguish the mortgagor's equity of redemption.

In early foreclosure actions, the mortgagee filed a petition with the court alleging default by the mortgagor and obtained a court decree ordering payment within a fixed time. Failure to pay within that time, such as six months to a year, forever extinguished the equity of redemption and vested title absolutely in the mortgagee without any sale of the property. This is known as "strict" foreclosure and survives to a limited extent in only a few states today.

In modern times foreclosure by sale has supplanted strict foreclosure as the primary means of enforcing the mortgagee's security. Two types of foreclosure involve sale of the mortgaged property: (1) foreclosure by judicial sale, and (2) foreclosure by power of sale. Foreclosure by judicial sale is the most common means used in the United States. The procedure varies somewhat among the states. Generally, the mortgagee files a complaint alleging default by the mortgagor. If the court finds in the mortgagee's favor after a hearing, it renders a decree or judgment of foreclosure giving the mortgagor a specified period of time (the equity of redemption) to pay the obligation, after which the property is sold at public auction. A majority of states also give the mortgagor an additional "statutory" right of redemption, allowing him to reclaim the property even after sale. The period of redemption is most commonly either six months or one year after sale. Ultimately the proceeds of the sale are used first to pay the mortgagee's debt and then any junior lenders in the order of their priority. Any surplus remaining after all secured parties are paid is returned to the mortgagor.

Although judicial foreclosure is available in all states and is by far the most common method used, it is expensive and time-consuming. A cheaper, more expeditious method, authorized in over one-third of the states, is foreclosure by power of sale.

13. See *Fidelity Federal Savings and Loan Association v. de la Cuesta*, 102 S. Ct. 3014 (1982); §341 of Garn-St. Germain Depository Institutions Act of 1982, 12 U.S.C. §1701j-3; 12 C.F.R. §§591.1–591.6.

14. 12 C.F.R. §591.5(b)(4).

Under this method, a foreclosure sale may be conducted without recourse to the courts if the mortgage instrument itself gives the mortgagee the power to sell the property in the event of default. Conduct of the sale, by public auction, is strictly regulated by statute to protect the mortgagor.

If the proceeds of the sale are insufficient to satisfy the costs of the proceeding and secured debts, the mortgagee may, in the vast majority of states, obtain a deficiency judgment, which may be satisfied out of the debtor's other assets. A few states have enacted ''antideficiency'' statutes preventing the mortgagee from obtaining a deficiency judgment after foreclosure of a purchase money mortgage. A few other states limit any deficiency judgment to the difference between the fair market value of the mortgaged property and the debt. This approach reduces the amount of the deficiency because the amount realized on public sale commonly is less than would be realized through arms length bargaining.

Installment Sales Contracts

In mortgage financing, as discussed above, the buyer makes a down payment, borrows the remainder of the purchase price from the seller or a third party, and receives a deed from the seller. The contract remains executory (yet to be performed) only for a relatively short period—that is, the time between the date of the contract and the seller's delivery of the deed at closing. If mortgage financing is unavailable due to a tight money market or inability of the buyer to make a sufficient down payment, an **installment sales contract** (also known as a ''contract for deed,'' ''agreement for deed,'' or ''land contract'') may be used.

In an installment contract, the seller finances the buyer who generally takes possession of the property, makes periodic installment payments against the price, and is usually responsible for payment of taxes, assessments, insurance, and repairs on the property. The seller retains title as security for performance of the contract and delivers the deed only after the purchase price is paid. Thus, unlike the ordinary real estate contract, the installment contract remains executory for an extended period, commonly several years. Because the purchaser has no deed during the executory period, a memoran-

dum of the contract should be recorded when the contract is made to provide constructive notice to third parties of the purchaser's interest in the property. Recording, for example, protects the buyer against a subsequent sale or mortgage of the property by the seller.

Escrow Agreements

An escrow is a convenient and flexible device for closing many types of real estate transactions including installment contracts. In an **escrow,** one party to the contract deposits a deed, other instrument, or money with a third party (known as an ''escrowee,'' ''escrow agent,'' or ''escrow holder''), who holds the deposited instrument or funds until the performance of a condition or happening of an event outlined in the ''escrow agreement.'' Upon occurrence of the agreed condition or conditions, the escrow agent is authorized to deliver the deposited instrument or funds to another party to the arrangement.

To illustrate the operation of an escrow arrangement, assume that Smith contracts to sell her apartment building to Black for $100,000. Although both Black and the building are located in Illinois, Smith currently resides in California. Because the parties are dealing at a distance, neither wants to risk performing without assurance that the other also will perform. This assurance is provided by an escrow arrangement, involving an Illinois bank or trust company where Black resides acting as escrow agent. Smith simply sends a deed to the property, executed naming Black as grantee, to the bank with instructions to deliver the deed to Black when he deposits the purchase price to Smith's account. In this manner, Black is assured that he will receive the deed upon payment of the price, and Smith is assured that the property will not be conveyed to Black unless and until Smith receives the purchase price.

Escrows also are commonly used in installment sales contracts. Because the seller retains title in such contracts until the purchaser performs, the purchaser runs the risk that the seller will be unwilling or unable to convey the property at the time contractually agreed. For example, the seller may be dead, incompetent, or absent from the jurisdiction when the duty to convey arises. To prevent this result, installment contracts commonly require the seller to deposit a deed to the property with an escrow agent to be delivered to the buyer upon payment of the purchase price.

An escrow is an agency relationship resulting from the agreement between the parties and the escrow agent. As an agent of both buyer and seller, the escrowee stands in a fiduciary relationship to both parties concerning both the deposited property and performance of escrow agreement.[15] Once created, the escrow agent's authority is not terminated or otherwise affected by the death or incapacity of either party prior to performance of the conditions.[16]

Transfer of Real Property by Adverse Possession

The preceding discussion concerns voluntary transfer of real property by sale. The following material examines adverse possession, which transfers real property involuntarily, without the owner's consent.

Introduction to Adverse Possession

Adverse possession is a method of acquiring title to real property through operation of the statute of limitations.[17] Statutes of limitation generally are designed to avoid prejudice to the defendant and to encourage prompt resolution of a dispute by requiring that a prospective plaintiff file a lawsuit within a specified period of time after his or her cause of action arises or be barred from recovery. Statutes of limitation vary depending upon the nature of the claim.

The adverse possession doctrine is based upon the statute of limitations applicable to an action by an owner of real property against a person wrong-

fully possessing it. Although the limitation period varies between five and thirty years among the states, approximately one-fourth of states use a twenty-year limitation and the vast majority (approximately eighty percent) provide for periods between ten and twenty years. If the owner fails to file his or her suit for recovery of possession from the **adverse possessor** within the statutory period, two legal results follow: (1) the owner's claim against the possessor is extinguished, and (2) the adverse possessor acquires title to the property.

For example, assume Sam and Bob own adjoining lots in a residential subdivision. Sam constructs a fence in his backyard six feet over the property line resulting in Sam's wrongful possession of a strip of Bob's land. The possession continues for the statutory period and the other elements of adverse possession outlined below are met. In this case, Bob may no longer sue Sam to recover possession of the disputed strip of land, and Sam, the adverse possessor, acquires title to it.

The principal purpose of the adverse possession doctrine is neither to punish the negligent owner for sleeping on his rights nor to reward the adverse possessor for his wrong. It is instead to strengthen the title of the possessor of land, thereby quieting titles through the passage of time and correcting technical errors in conveyancing.

The adverse possessor's title is a new or original[18] title, destroying the record owner's title and vesting automatically by operation of law when the legal requirements are met. A person may therefore have acquired title by adverse possession, even though the public record discloses record title in another. The adverse possessor need not publicly announce the interest by recording it to be protected against purchasers from the original owner. For this reason, a prospective buyer of real property should always conduct a physical inspection or survey of the property to precisely determine boundary lines. In this manner, adverse possession claims, not disclosed by an ordinary title examination, may be discovered.

Title to property owned by the federal or state

---

15. The nature of the fiduciary duty owed by an agent to a principal is discussed in Chapter 40.

16. The escrow arrangement discussed above should be distinguished from an "escrow account." An escrow account is a bank account commonly maintained in the name of a mortgagor and mortgagee into which the mortgagor makes periodic payments to satisfy recurring charges such as property taxes and insurance premiums.

17. Statutes of limitation are introduced in Chapter 1.

---

18. The title is said to be "original" as opposed to "derivative." Title is derivative if acquired through the original owner by sale, gift, will, or intestate succession.

government or governmental entity may generally not be acquired by adverse possession. This result is dictated by statute in many states. Even in the absence of statute, the general common law rule is simply that the statute of limitations does not run against the government. Similarly, no title may be acquired by adverse possession against land registered under the Torrens system.

Elements of Adverse Possession

Adverse possession cases usually arise when the original owner discovers the possession and files suit to recover the property. The possessor then defends by asserting that he has acquired title to the property by adverse possession. To prevail the adverse possessor must generally prove that his possession was (1) in an open and notorious manner, (2) hostile, exclusive, and adverse to the original owner's interest and under a claim of right, and (3) continuous over the period of the statute of limitations.

Open, Visible, and Notorious Possession. To establish title by adverse possession, the occupation of the property must be sufficiently obvious to put the owner on notice of the possession. The owner need not actually know of the possession, but is deemed to know facts that would have been discovered had he or she conducted a reasonable inspection of the property. For example, an adverse interest may run against an absentee landowner who is not physically present and therefore unaware of the possession. The "open and notorious" requirement provides the landowner an opportunity to protect his or her interest.

Hostile, Exclusive, and Adverse Possession Under a Claim of Right. The term "hostile," as used in the law of adverse possession, does not refer to antagonistic, belligerent, or threatening conduct on the possessor's part. It simply means that the possession is without the permission, express or implied, of the owner; that is, the possession must be wrongful on the possessor's part. The possession must also generally be under a "claim of right," meaning that the adverse possessor must indicate an intent to possess the land as against the whole world, including the true owner. In other words, mere trespass or simple possession is not enough.

The possessor must intend to claim the title as owner.

Some question exists concerning whether hostile possession requires an intentional usurpation of another's land, or whether mistaken or innocent possession is also sufficient. For example, assume A and B are adjoining property owners. A plants a hedge or builds a fence on what he mistakenly believes to be the property line. In fact, the fence or hedge is several feet over the property line, resulting in A's wrongful possession of a strip of B's land.

On these facts, most courts hold that subjective intention of the possessor is irrelevant. Mere physical possession over the property line whether intentional or mistaken is sufficient to make the possession hostile and adverse under a claim of right. That is, the only intent required is the intent to possess.

The person claiming title by adverse possession also must prove that his or her possession was exclusive over the statutory period. Thus, mere shared or common possession with the record owner generally defeats any adverse possession claim. Further, exclusive possession of land by one co-tenant (a joint tenant or tenant in common) is generally not deemed hostile to the interests of the other co-tenants. Nevertheless, if actual "ouster" can be shown (conduct by the co-tenant in possession excluding the others and indicating that he holds adversely to their interests), the statute of limitations begins to run against the ousted co-tenants.

Continuous and Uninterrupted Possession Over the Statutory Period. Generally, the statute of limitations begins to run when the possessor commences hostile and adverse, open and notorious possession. Once commenced, possession must be continuous and uninterrupted for the statutory period. Continuous does not mean constant, but instead depends upon the nature of the land involved. For example, possession of farming or grazing land is continuous if used in an open and notorious manner for its intended purpose during appropriate times of the year. Possession may therefore be continuous even though the adverse possessor is not physically present every day of the year. A break in this continuity of possession places constructive possession back in the legal owner. The statute of limitations then stops running and a new statutory period commences upon retaking possession.

Because of the length of the limitation period in adverse possession cases, the law has been required to determine the legal effect of successive adverse possessors of the same property, none of whom individually holds the property for the required period. In this case, the successive adverse possessors may add, or "tack," their respective holding periods to establish possession for the period required by the statute of limitations if they are in "privity," or as is frequently stated "in privity of blood or contract." This simply means that tacking of holding periods is permitted if there is some connection between the successive possessors—for example, by deed, will, intestate succession, contract, or even oral permission or consent. Note that transfer of the adversely possessed property by the record owner does not interrupt the running of the statute.

Adverse Possession Under Color of Title

The adverse possessor usually occupies the property wrongfully without any semblance of actual ti-tle prior to expiration of the statutory period. The original possession may, however, occur under **color of title.** In this situation, the possessor claims the land under an instrument purporting to pass title but which is ineffective to operate as a conveyance. Examples include a deed to which the grantor's signature is forged, or a deed executed by a grantor with defective or nonexistent title. Some but not all states require that the instrument constituting color of title be recorded.

The effect of possession under a color of title differs from possession under a claim of right. In many states the statutory period of possession is shortened if possession is under a color of title provided the possessor pays the annual property taxes assessed against the property.[19] The extent of the property acquired also differs when property is held under color of title. Ordinarily, the adverse possessor may claim only that portion of the land actually possessed and occupied during the statutory period. A person holding under color of title may acquire title to the entire tract, if adequately described in the instrument, even though actual possession is limited to a portion of the property.

SUMMARY

1. A transfer of an interest in real property is known as a "conveyance" and, collectively, the performance of the various functions necessary to effect the transfer is known as "conveyancing." A real estate transfer usually is accomplished pursuant to a contract requiring the seller to convey marketable title to the property to the buyer in exchange for some consideration, usually the payment of money. Performance of the contract occurs at the title closing, when the seller delivers a deed to the property to the buyer, who pays the purchase price.

2. The deed is simply an instrument used to transfer an interest in real property. To be effective the deed must meet formal requirements prescribed by state law. Generally the deed must be in writing, identifying the grantor and the grantee, containing words of conveyance, and a legal description of the property. The deed generally is effective to transfer the property once it is signed by the grantor and delivered to the grantee.

3. Deeds are of two general types: the warranty deed and the quitclaim deed. A warranty deed contains a number of promises ("covenants for title") concerning the status of the grantor's title. If a covenant for title is breached, the injured grantee may recover damages from the grantor. In contrast, the quitclaim deed simply transfers whatever interest, if any, the grantor possesses.

4. Before delivery of the deed, the real estate buyer must be assured that the seller possesses the interest he has contracted to convey. Such title assurance is provided primarily by professional examination of public land records generated by state recording statutes.

5. Each state has a recording statute, designed to provide reliable public information concerning the ownership of and other interests in real property. Recording statutes permit recordation of various instruments affect-

---

19. In most states, when occupancy is not based upon color of title, the adverse possessor need not pay taxes to mature his title. Thus, the legal owner may pay the taxes and still lose the property.

ing land ownership, and a purchaser of property generally takes it free of a prior unrecorded instrument. The ownership of a particular tract and other interests in it can be ascertained by searching the public record created by the recording statute. In addition, recording statutes also resolve priority disputes among persons successively acquiring an interest in a given piece of property.

6. Once the various interests in the land have been determined from the public record, the record is then examined by an attorney, who renders an opinion concerning the marketability of the title. This opinion may be embodied in a formal attorney's opinion or may be backed by a title insurance policy.

7. Under the Torrens system, an alternative to title assurance based upon examining the instruments evidencing title, a legal proceeding is held in which the title itself is registered and a certificate of title is issued to the owner. Once registered, the land is subsequently transferred merely by issuing a new certificate of title to the buyer, avoiding the necessity of a title search before each transfer.

8. Creditors financing real estate purchases usually require security. This security usually is provided by a mortgage, an interest in real property that is created to secure performance of an obligation, usually repayment of a debt. Like other real property interests, a mortgage is created by deed, a mortgage deed, in which the mortgagor conveys an interest in the property to be used as security to the mortgagee.

9. A property owner may borrow money from two or more lenders and give each a mortgage on the same property. If the value of the mortgaged property is less than the total of the outstanding obligations it secures, priority of the various mortgagees is determined by the real property recording statute.

10. The mortgagor is generally free to sell or otherwise transfer the mortgaged property without the mortgagee's consent. If the property is sold without paying off the underlying debt and retiring the mortgage, the buyer takes the property either "subject to" the existing mortgage, or "assumes" the mortgage debt. A buyer who takes "subject to" the mortgage incurs no personal liability for payment of the debt which the mortgage secures, whereas one who "assumes" does undertake such liability.

11. "Foreclosure" is the method by which the mortgaged property, or its proceeds, is applied in satisfaction of the debt. Judicial sale is the most common foreclosure method used in the United States.

12. An alternative to conventional mortgage financing is the "installment sales contract" or "contract for deed." In this case, the seller finances the buyer who takes possession of the property and makes periodic installment payments against the price. The seller retains title as security for the buyer's performance and delivers the deed only after the purchase price is paid in full.

13. An "escrow" agreement is often used as a convenient and flexible tool for closing real estate transactions including installment sales contracts.

14. Although real property transfers are usually voluntary, a transfer may be effected without the owner's consent by adverse possession. Under this doctrine a person wrongfully possessing another's property, the adverse possessor, acquires title to it provided the possession is (1) in an open and notorious manner, (2) hostile, exclusive, and adverse to the original owner's interest under a claim of right, and (3) continuous over the period of the statute of limitations. The adverse possession doctrine stabilizes land titles by recognizing long-standing possession of property.

KEY TERMS

conveyancing	abstract of title
marketable title	attorney's opinion
title closing (settlement)	title insurance
Real Estate Settlement Procedures Act (RESPA)	Torrens system
	pure race statute
deed	pure notice statute
grantor	race-notice statute
grantee	mortgage
warranty deed	mortgagor
covenants for title	mortgagee
encumbrance	deed of trust (trust deed)
quitclaim deed	due-on-sale clause
recording statute	foreclosure
recorder of deeds	equity of redemption
constructive notice	installment sales contract
title search	escrow
chain of title	adverse possession
Marketable Title Acts	adverse possessor
	color of title

QUESTIONS AND PROBLEMS

37-1 You are considering purchasing a home in Shady Acres, a residential subdivision. You have begun preliminary negotiations with the seller of the property. What issues should be addressed in the contract for sale? Assuming you decide to purchase the property, what steps should be taken prior to conveyance to assure that you receive a good title?

37-2 Most real estate contracts require that the seller convey the property by warranty deed. What protection does a warranty deed provide the purchaser? Under what circumstances might the buyer be willing to accept a quitclaim deed?

37-3 Fred and Ethel, residents of New Jersey, applied to First National Bank for a loan. As collateral for the loan, they offered to pledge a house in Missouri. Fred and Ethel explained that they owned the house; however, Ethel's retired parents had rented the property and were living there.

A junior loan officer had a title seach performed and all records indicated that Fred and Ethel owned the property. A bank representative also drove by the house and noticed an elderly couple working in the garden.

You are the senior loan officer at the bank. The junior loan officer states that the value of the house is more than the requested loan and recommends that the loan be approved without further investigation. Missouri has adopted a race-notice recording statute. Would you approve the loan? Explain.

37-4 In 1972, Russell fraudulently obtained title to seventy-five acres of land in Florida owned by Mrs. Elliott, an elderly, uneducated woman. Mrs. Elliott had agreed to sell Russell fifteen acres but Russell prepared a deed conveying seventy-five acres. Because Mrs. Elliott could not read well, she relied on Russell's statement that the deed conveyed only fifteen acres and signed the deed. Russell recorded the deed.

(a) Russell enlisted the aid of a shady friend, Boris. Russell explained how he had fooled Mrs. Elliott and offered to sell the property to Boris for $25,000, the fair market value of the property. Boris paid $25,000 and Russell deeded the property to Boris who recorded the deed. Mrs. Elliott sues Boris claiming that she owns the property. Who owns the property? Explain.

(b) Assume instead that Boris immediately offers to sell the property to an acquaintance, Rocky. Rocky performed a title search and traced the chain of title to Boris. Rocky paid $25,000 and Boris deeded the property to Rocky. Mrs. Elliott sues Rocky. Who owns the property? Explain.

37-5 By warranty deed, Adam conveys Blackacre to Eve. Eve records the deed at the recorder's office. The recorder inadvertently misfiles the deed. Adam later conveys the same property to Joseph by quitclaim deed. Joseph searches the title at the recorder's office and, because of Eve's misfiled deed, finds that Adam is shown as the title holder. Joseph records his deed. Who owns Blackacre? Explain.

37-6 Installment land contracts sometimes are used

to effect a "silent sale." In the silent sale the contract is used to transfer the property without notifying the seller's mortgagee of the sale, thereby preventing it from exercising its due-on-sale clause. The buyer is therefore effectively able to assume the seller's low interest rate mortgage. To prevent the mortgagee from learning of the sale the parties do not record a memorandum of the contract in the recorder's office. In addition, the seller continues making payments on the mortgage, and taxes, utilities, and insurance continue to be carried in the seller's name. What risks do silent sales pose to the parties involved: the buyer, the seller, their attorneys, title companies, and real estate brokers?

37-7 Because adverse possession constitutes an involuntary transfer of property, the interest of an owner by adverse possession usually will not show up in a title search. How is a person who purchases property protected from the claims of an adverse possessor? Explain.

37-8 In 1928, Katy and Adolph conveyed by warranty deed a portion of their real property to Adam, an adjoining landowner. For almost fifty years, Adam did not develop the property. Katy and Adolph, however, continued to use the property. They stored farm equipment on it and planted and maintained a garden there. In 1975, Adam died and devised the property to his son who began construction of a house on the property. Katy and Adolph sue to enjoin the construction, alleging that they had acquired title to the property by adverse possession.

(a) Should the court grant or allow Katy and Adolph's claim of adverse possession? Explain.

(b) Would your answer be different if the 1928 deed to Adam had been a quitclaim deed? Explain.

37-9 As noted in the text, most courts hold that in adverse possession cases, mistaken or innocent possession is sufficient to constitute hostile possession. A minority of courts hold that if a person possesses property up to the boundary without knowledge of the actual property line, but intending only to possess up to the true property line, his possession does not meet the hostility requirement. Thus, under the minority rule, the subjective intention of the adverse possessor is determinative. Do you agree with this approach? What problems might a court encounter in applying it?

37-10 In 1933, Ben purchased a piece of land suitable

for cattle grazing and took title by warranty deed. Adam owned a ranch which adjoined the piece of land. In 1934 Adam erected a fence around his ranch and fenced in approximately 100 acres of Ben's land. During the next forty years, Adam allowed his cattle to graze on the land three or four weeks each year. Although Ben did not use the land, he paid the real estate taxes on it every year. Adam claims title to the land by adverse possession. Who owns the land? Explain.

37-11   In 1977, Vincent conveyed a parcel of land by warranty deed to Wanda. Wanda later learned that Lee claimed title to the land by adverse possession. Wanda sued Lee to clear title to the land.

(a) Assume that Lee fails to prove title by adverse possession because he has had possession of the land for only three years. Has Vincent breached any of the warranties of the warranty deed?

(b) Assume instead that Lee's claim to title by adverse possession is valid because he possessed the land for over twenty years. Has Vincent breached any of the warranties of the warranty deed? Explain.

37-12   Ernest signed an agreement to sell a piece of land to Ricardo and agreed to provide an abstract of title. At Ernest's request, First Title Service prepared an abstract but negligently failed to find a prior deed by which Ernest had conveyed the property to Sam. Ernest paid First Title's abstract fee and provided a copy of the abstract to Ricardo. Ricardo took the abstract to Sun City Bank and relying on the abstract the bank loaned Ricardo $100,000 secured by a mortgage on the land. Ricardo defaulted on the loan and the bank began foreclosure proceedings. Sun City then discovered that Sam owned the property.

Sun City sued First Title Service Company alleging that its negligence in failing to find Sam's deed had caused Sun City to lose $100,000. How should the court rule? Explain.

- an introduction to the various methods by which land use is regulated by private agreement or governmental action
- discussion of the law of easements, which creates a limited property interest in the use of another's land
- coverage of promises governing land use, most notably restrictive covenants that limit land use by private agreement
- discussion of the law of zoning, which imposes governmental land use regulations through exercise of the state's police power
- coverage of the law of eminent domain, which authorizes the actual taking of private property for public uses

Many of the rights constituting property ownership protect the owner's possession and use after acquisition. Balanced against the owner's right of use and enjoyment is a countervailing policy protecting other landowners and occupiers in the use of their property. In other words, ownership rights are not absolute; they are subject to rights of neighboring property owners and other members of the community. This chapter focuses upon various limitations and privileges of use of land imposed either by private agreement or by act of public authority including federal, state, or local government. Private individuals may regulate land use by creating easements and profits, which are limited interests in the use of the property itself, or by covenants imposed by contract.

Public regulation is of two general types: zoning, in which the use and physical configuration of property is regulated or restricted, and eminent domain, under which private property is taken from its owner and applied to a public use.

Private Regulation of Land Use

Easements and Profits

An **easement** is an interest in land that gives its owner the right either to use another person's land for a limited and specified purpose, or to prevent another person from using his land in a specified way. The most common easements are "rights of way" that give a person the right to pass over or under another's land, such as driveways, roads, sidewalks, and footpaths. Easements granted to public utilities to run power or telephone lines, underground cables, pipelines, and sewer lines are also common. The list of possible uses for which an easement may be created is endless, limited only by the specific needs of the parties.

An easement is a *nonpossessory interest*. The owner of the property burdened by the easement has the full right to possess and use the property subject only to the easement. Assume Ann and Beth are adjoining property owners. Ann grants Beth an easement across a sixteen foot strip of her property for driveway and sidewalk purposes. In this case, Beth has an interest in Ann's land, the easement, allowing her to *use* Ann's property for a specified purpose—as a driveway and sidewalk. Beth has no right to use the strip of land for any other purpose—for example, to run a drainage tile or to use portions of Ann's property not covered by the easement for the stated purpose. The right to possess and use the property remains in Ann, subject only to Beth's right of way. Had Beth desired the unrestricted possession and use of the property to plant a garden or build a garage, she could purchase fee simple title or possibly lease the premises from Ann. The nonpossessory aspect of an easement is, therefore, an important factor distinguishing it from other property interests.

If the right of use in another's property involves the right to *remove* part of the land or products of the land, it is known as a **profit,** or more fully, a **profit à prendre.** Through a profit, a landowner may transfer the right to remove sand, dirt, gravel, other minerals, or grass or timber from the land. A profit carries with it the right to enter the property, make use of the property necessary to sever the minerals or products, and the right to remove them from the property. The right to take from the property (the profit) distinguishes the profit from an ordinary easement. Generally, the same legal principles govern both interests.

Because an easement is a nonpossessory estate, the owner of the land subject to the easement usually is permitted to share in the use permitted by the easement. This rule is particularly important if the easement includes a profit, because it allows the landowner to join the easement holder in the extraction of minerals or other natural resources.

Affirmative and Negative Easements. The easements illustrated above are known as ''affirmative easements.'' An affirmative easement allows its holder to use or do some act on another's land that would be unlawful without the easement. In contrast, a ''negative'' easement does not permit the holder to use another's land. Instead, it prevents the owner of the burdened property from doing something otherwise lawful upon his or her own land. Assume Ann and Beth are adjoining property owners. In order to preserve the free flow of light or air across her property, or to preserve an unobstructed view, Beth purchases an easement from Ann preventing Ann from building on her property or limiting the height of any structures erected on Ann's land. Beth has no right to use Ann's property for any purpose. The easement in this case limits Ann's use of her own land.

Easements Appurtenant and Easements in Gross. Easements also are classified as appurtenant or in gross. An **easement appurtenant** involves two tracts of land, one benefited by the easement, known as the ''dominant tenement'' or ''dominant estate,'' and one burdened by the easement, referred to as the ''servient tenement'' or ''servient estate.'' An easement appurtenant benefits land owned by the holder of the easement—the dominant tenement. The preceding examples are easements appurtenant. In both cases, Beth's land, the dominant tenement, is benefited by the easement, either because of the right to use a driveway across Ann's land, or the right to have an unrestricted view or flow of light or air across Ann's land. Ann's land, the servient estate, is burdened because her use of the property is restricted by the easement. Easements appurtenant commonly, although not necessarily, involve adjoining tracts of land.

An **easement in gross,** on the other hand, is not obtained for the benefit of land owned by the holder of the easement. In other words, in an easement in gross, there is no dominant tenement. The most common example of an easement in gross is a public utility right of way for purposes of running lines, poles, or underground cables. Profits are also commonly in gross, because the right to enter the land to remove minerals, timber, or other resources frequently exists independently of the holder's ownership of land.

Creation of Easements

Easements are usually created by an express act of the parties, by implication, by prescription, or by eminent domain.

By Express Act of the Parties. Like other interests in land, most easements are created upon delivery of a deed describing the nature and extent of the interest conveyed. A deed may create the easement in either the grantor or the grantee. Assume Sally and Bob own adjoining tracts of land. In exchange for an agreed sum, Sally, the grantor, conveys an easement to Bob, granting him the right to run a drainage tile across Sally's land. Bob, the grantee, has obtained an easement by "express grant."

An easement may be created in the grantor by "exception" or "reservation." Assume Sally owns a tract of land that has a highway running along its southern border, but no other access to a public street. Sally conveys the south one-half of the tract to Bob. In order to assure continued access to the highway, Sally, as part of the conveyance to Bob, creates or retains an easement in herself across the property transferred for driveway and sidewalk purposes. Sally, the grantor, has created an easement by reservation or exception.

By Implication. Easements may also be created in favor of either the grantor or grantee by implication. These easements, which are based upon the inferred or presumed intention of the parties, arise when an owner of a tract of land divides it into two or more parts and conveys one or more of the parts to others. Implied easements are of two types: easements implied from quasi-easements and easements implied from necessity.

Frequently, a property owner will use one part of her land to benefit another part. Assume Susan owns a tract of land that abuts a highway running along its southern boundary. She resides in a farm house located on the northern one-half of the land, and constructs a driveway across the southern one-half providing access to the road. Because a person cannot possess an easement in his or her own land, the tract's southern one-half is said to be burdened by a "quasi-easement" (the driveway running across it). Susan subsequently sells the northern one-half of the tract to Betty. The deed of conveyance makes no mention of any easement for driveway purposes across the tract's southern one-half. On these facts, an easement may be implied in favor of the grantee, Betty, resulting from the quasi-easement originally existing on the land. If Susan had sold the southern one-half of the tract, an easement across it may be implied (an implied reservation) in favor of Susan, the grantor.

An easement also may be implied because of *necessity,* regardless of any prior use made of the property. An "easement by necessity" (or "way

by necessity") arises when an owner of a single tract conveys part of it, and thereby "landlocks" the portion retained or conveyed, leaving no way to enter or exit the land without trespassing upon neighboring property. In this case, an easement by necessity is created in favor of the grantor if the landlocked land is retained, or the grantee if the landlocked land is conveyed. Unlike an easement implied from a quasi-easement, which continues indefinitely, an easement created by necessity continues only so long as the need for the use continues.

By Prescription. Fee simple title, a possessory interest in property, may be acquired through a person's adverse *possession* of another's property for the period of the statute of limitations. Similarly, an easement, a nonpossessory interest, may be obtained through adverse *use* for the statutory period. In this case, an easement (known as a "prescriptive easement") is created by **prescription**. The requirements necessary to create an easement by prescription are similar to those needed to acquire title by adverse possession. Thus, an easement by prescription may be created by *use* of another's land (such as for a footpath or driveway) if the use is hostile, open and notorious, and is continuous and uninterrupted for the period of the statute of limitations.

By Eminent Domain. Unlike easements created by express grant or reservation, prescriptive easements are created involuntarily. An easement also may arise involuntarily through the sovereign's exercise of its eminent domain power: the power of the government to take private property for public use. In the majority of cases involving a taking of land by eminent domain, the interest acquired is merely an easement, not a fee simple. Easements are commonly taken by eminent domain for highways, streets, railroads, utility lines, subterranean pipes or cables, flowage (the right to overflow, flood, and submerge the servient land), and for overflight and clearance near airports.

Scope of Easement

An easement involves a limited right to use land of another. The scope of an easement varies according to the purpose and type of use permitted (such as for a driveway, drainage ditch, or for light and air), the specific portion of the servient tenement burdened by the easement (the location of the use), the manner of exercise, and the duration of the use (for a limited period or indefinitely).

The method of creating an easement necessarily fixes its extent. Thus, the scope of an expressly created easement is limited by the specific terms of the instrument (deed or will) creating it. Because they are not evidenced by a written instrument, the extent of easements by necessity, implication, and prescription must be determined solely from the circumstances of their creation.

Transfer of Easements

Like most other property interests, both easements appurtenant and easements in gross are freely transferable. As a general rule, the easement follows the ownership or possession of the dominant estate in an easement appurtenant. Similarly, a transferee of the servient estate takes subject to the easement. This rule applies to all easements appurtenant whether created by grant, reservation, implication, or prescription. Assume Bob and Carol own adjoining tracts of land. Bob also holds an easement across Carol's land for driveway and sidewalk purposes to reach a public street. Bob sells his land to Ted. Ted has the benefit of the easement across Carol's land even if the instrument of conveyance makes no mention of the easement. If Carol sells or leases her land to Alice, Alice takes subject to the burdens imposed by the easement. In other words, an easement appurtenant is unaffected by a transfer of possession of either the dominant or servient estate.[1]

In contrast, under the "English Rule," an easement in gross created only individual or personal rights, which could not be transferred. This approach generally is not followed in the United States, where easements in gross, except those clearly intended to benefit only the original ease-

ment holder, are transferable during life or at death.

Termination of Easements

Easements may terminate by expiration according to the intent manifested by the parties when they created the interest, or by extinguishment resulting from events occurring after its creation. Upon termination, the burden imposed upon the servient estate by the easement is removed.

By Expiration. Although the duration of easements usually is indefinite, easements may be created to last for a specified period of time or to accomplish a given purpose. Assume that Alan grants Bob a right of way across his land for the term of a lease of adjoining property by Alan to Bob. Here, the easement terminates upon expiration of the lease. Or assume XYZ Corporation is constructing a factory on its property. To provide access for construction equipment during the period of construction, XYZ purchases a right of way across Joe Doaks's land to continue until construction is finished. Upon completion of the factory, XYZ's easement terminates.

By Extinguishment. An easement may be terminated by events not contemplated by the parties when they created the easement. In this case, termination is by extinguishment. Extinguishment may be complete or partial, depending upon the nature of the easement and the manner of termination. An easement usually is extinguished by conduct of the dominant owner, conduct of the servient owner, or conduct of both parties.

Conduct of the Dominant Owner. The dominant owner may extinguish the easement by release or abandonment. Release simply transfers the easement back to the owner of the servient estate. A release by sale or gift is made by deed (normally a quitclaim), and a release on death must be contained in a valid will. Extinguishment by abandonment occurs if the dominant owner's conduct indicates an intent to relinquish the right to use the easement further. Intent to abandon is determined from all surrounding circumstances including the dominant owner's nonuse of the easement, verbal

---

1. An easement appurtenant cannot be transferred apart from the dominant estate to which it is attached, unless the transfer is made to the owner of the servient estate as a means of extinguishing the easement.

statements of an intention to abandon, or other conduct inconsistent with further use of the easement. For example, a railroad may abandon a right of way by tearing up and removing rails and ties.

Conduct of the Servient Owner. Extinguishment may also result from acts of the servient owner. Just as an easement may be created by prescription, it may also be terminated by the servient owner's adverse use of the easement (for example, by building a fence across a right of way) over the period of the statute of limitations.

Conduct of Both Parties. The conduct of both parties may terminate the easement by merger. A merger occurs when the holder of an easement in gross becomes the owner of the servient estate, or in an easement appurtenant, the same person acquires both the dominant and servient estates. In these cases, the easement is permanently terminated because the lesser estate (the easement) is merged into the greater (the fee simple).

"Licenses" Distinguished

Not every privilege to use the land of another is an easement. A privilege to enter upon or perform acts on another's land that lacks one or more of the elements essential to create an easement is known as a **license**. The person in possession of the land who grants the right of use is the "licensor" and the person empowered to use the land is the "licensee." A license, which results from the consent of the licensor to allow the use, simply gives the licensee the right to use another's land without incurring liability as a trespasser.

Unlike an easement, which continues until it expires by its terms or is extinguished, a license is always revocable at the will of the property owner, the licensor. Intent to revoke may be exhibited expressly or by using the property inconsistently with the license. A license also ends upon the death of either party, a conveyance of the servient estate by the licensor, or upon the licensee's attempt to transfer the license.

Although a license is an interest in land, the formalities necessary to create other interests in land, such as a deed, are not applicable to licenses. A license is therefore created whether the initial consent is express or implied, oral or written. Further, a defective attempt to create an easement creates a license. Assume Sam attempts to grant to his neighbor, Bill, an easement across Sam's yard for use as a footpath. However, Sam's attempt is made orally or in a deed that Sam does not sign. On these facts, Bill acquires a license rather than an easement to use Sam's land. Sam may revoke the license at any time by indicating his intent to end it.

Covenants

An easement alters the normal incidents of land ownership and possession by creating a limited property interest in the servient estate. In addition, subject to public policy limitations, all conceivable land uses may be regulated privately by contract.

Covenants are contractual promises concerning land use. An **affirmative covenant** requires the promisor (covenantor) to do something on his land, such as building or maintaining a party wall,[2] irrigation or drainage ditch, or structure such as a dam or bridge. A **negative**, or **restrictive, covenant** restricts or limits the permissible uses of the land or the acts that may be performed upon it. Like a negative easement, a restrictive covenant limits the property owner in the use of his or her own land. A landowner who breaches a restrictive covenant may be liable to neighboring property owners for money damages and may be enjoined by the court against further breach of the covenant. Restrictive covenants compose the vast majority of covenants affecting land use.

Restrictive covenants most commonly are used in residential subdivisions to achieve a coordinated, consistent pattern of land use within the area covered by the covenants. When so used, the covenants are commonly known as "building restrictions" and are generally intended to maintain property values and to preserve the residential character of the area. Common examples of restrictive covenants in this context include those (1) restricting the use of all lots or certain lots to residential purposes only (or prohibiting certain uses); (2) im-

---

2. A party wall is a wall built next to, or astride, a boundary line designed to serve simultaneously as a common wall of two adjoining structures.

posing minimum cost or square footage requirements on any building constructed in the subdivision; and (3) requiring that any building
constructed on a lot must be located a minimum
distance from streets (a setback restriction), or from
an adjoining lot (a sidelot restriction), or from the
rear lot line. As with easements, the list of possible
restrictions is potentially infinite, limited only by
the needs of the property owners.

Although most restrictions are upheld as beneficial and essential tools of private land use control,
courts refuse to enforce covenants that are illegal,
unconstitutional, or otherwise contrary to public
policy. For example, in the famous case *Shelley v.
Kraemer*,[3] the Supreme Court refused to enforce on
constitutional grounds a restrictive covenant prohibiting "any person not of the Caucasian race"
from residing on a specified street. If a prohibited
covenant is involved, neither the deed containing it
nor other permissible restrictions are affected; the
offending covenant is simply void.

Creation of Covenants

Covenants governing land use may be imposed
with or without the conveyance of any land. Assume Adams and Branch are adjoining owners of
large tracts of scenic rural land. To assure a continued unobstructed view, Adams and Branch, by
contract, agree that no structures may be built
within 500 feet of either side of their mutual
boundary line. Adams and Branch have created a
restrictive covenant by contract without conveyance.

Usually, however, restrictive covenants are created by the grantor upon a conveyance of land, and
limit the grantee's use of the land. The restrictive
covenant may be contained in the deed itself. If the
property is located in a residential subdivision, an
alternative method generally is used. When property is subdivided, a plat or map of the subdivision
is filed in the county recorder's office and is the
basis for the legal description of property located
within the area covered by the map. A list or declaration of restrictions imposed by the person sub-
dividing the property also is filed for record in con-

junction with the map. These restrictions are
incorporated by reference into the individual deeds
to lots within the subdivision, even though they are
not set out in full in each deed. The person performing a title search on property in a subdivision
must therefore read the plat restrictions to determine whether the property under examination complies with limitations imposed on its use.

To be enforceable, promises concerning land use
generally are required under the Statute of Frauds
to be in writing. Ordinarily, the Statute of Frauds
requires that the writing be signed by the person
against whom enforcement is sought. Although
covenants are often contained in or incorporated
into the deed, and modern deeds usually are signed
only by the grantor, most courts hold that the grantee, by accepting the deed, is bound by covenants
contained in the deed, even without signing it.

Effect Upon Subsequent Transferees

Property subject to restrictive covenants is often
transferred from one owner to another. A basic
question arising when the property is transferred is
the extent to which the covenant runs with the land.
A covenant **runs with the land** if either the liability to perform it or the right to take advantage of it
passes to a transferee of the property.

Either the benefit or the burden, or both, of the
covenant may run. Assume Art and Bob own adjoining tracts of land. In order to preserve his view
of the ocean, Art secures Bob's covenant not to
build any structure more than one story tall on
Bob's land. Art subsequently sells his land to Carol
and Bob sells his tract to Diane. If the covenant
runs with the land, Carol may enforce the restriction against Diane. That is, the benefit of the covenant runs to Carol with the sale of Art's tract, and
the burden runs to Diane upon transfer of Bob's
land.

Originally, covenants running with the land were
enforced in courts of law. Beginning with the English case *Tulk v. Moxhay*,[4] decided in 1848,
courts of equity began to enforce promises respecting land use by imposing an **equitable servitude**
upon the burdened land. Courts of equity became

---

3. 68 S. Ct. 836 (1948).

4. 2 Ph. 774, 41 Eng. Rep. 1143 (Ch. 1848).

involved because the stringent requirements for covenants running with the land at law prevented judicial enforcement of many beneficial covenants. The equitable servitude has emerged as the primary tool for developing restricted areas, residential or otherwise, in modern times.

Even in equity, however, not all covenants are enforceable by or against subsequent transferees. An equitable servitude, which is treated as an interest in land, runs with the land if four basic elements are present.

1. The restriction must be contained in a *writing* that satisfies the Statute of Frauds.

2. The original parties must *intend* that a restriction be imposed on the use of the land involved. Intention that the covenant run is easily established if the covenant, by terms of the creating instrument, expressly binds "assigns" or "successors." Express language is not, however, required. Intent is ascertained after considering all surrounding circumstances.

3. The restriction must *touch and concern* the land. The burden of a covenant touches and concerns land if it decreases the utility or value of the land in the hands of its owner, the covenantor (promisor). Conversely, the benefit of a covenant touches and concerns the land if it increases the utility or value of the affected land in the hands of its owner, the covenantee (promisee). The subdivision restrictions previously listed illustrate covenants that touch and concern the land.

4. The subsequent purchaser must take with actual or constructive *notice* of the restriction. Notice usually is provided by recording a document containing the restrictions in the county recorder's office. If the covenant is not properly recorded, a bona fide purchaser of the property without actual notice takes free of the restriction.

At issue in the following case was whether the purchaser had been adequately notified of the restriction.

Davis v. Huey

620 S.W.2d 561 (Tex. 1981)

In 1965, after planning and developing a residential subdivision near Austin, Texas, plaintiff Austin Corporation filed a document listing restrictive covenants applicable to the subdivision with the recorder of deeds. Paragraph 7 of the document established setback, front-line, side-line, and rear-line limits for each of the lots. Paragraph 8 provided in part:

> No building, wall or other structure shall be placed upon such lot until the plan therefor and the plot plan have been approved in writing by the Developers. Refusal of approval of plans and specifications by the Developers . . . may be based on any ground, including purely aesthetic grounds, which in the sole and uncontrolled discretion of the Developers . . . shall seem sufficient.

In May 1976, defendants Tom and Hattie Davis purchased a lot in the subdivision adjacent to a lot owned by plaintiffs Robert and Mary Huey. The Davises submitted plans for a house to Austin Corporation which refused to approve them because the proposed placement of the house was inconsistent with the general plan of the subdivision. The plans, which complied with Paragraph 7 of the restrictive covenants, provided that the house would be placed near the rear-line of the property while all other houses in the subdivision were located much closer to the front-line of the lots. After negotiations failed, the Davises began construction of their house. The Hueys and Austin Corporation sued the Davises requesting an injunction to halt construction and alleging that the house would reduce the value of surrounding property and would block the views from the houses of the Hueys and other neighbors. The trial court granted the injunction. After the appellate court affirmed, the Davises appealed to the Texas Supreme Court.

Wallace, Justice

. . . It has been stated that housing today is ordinarily developed by subdividers, who, through the use of restrictive covenants, guarantee to the homeowner that his house will be protected against adjacent construction which will impair its value, and that a general plan of construction will be followed. . . . Restrictions enhance the value of the subdivision property and form an inducement for purchasers to buy lots within the subdivision. . . . A covenant requiring submission of plans and prior approval before construction is one method by which guarantees of value and of adherence to a general scheme of development can be accomplished and maintained. . . .

Although covenants restricting the free use of property are not favored, when restrictions are confined to a lawful purpose and are within reasonable bounds and the language employed is clear, such covenants will be enforced. . . . However, a purchaser is bound by only those restrictive covenants attaching to the property of which he has actual or constructive notice. One who purchases for value and without notice takes the land free from the restriction. . . .

The majority view with respect to covenants requiring submission of plans and consent prior to construction is that such clauses, even if vesting the approving authority with broad discretionary powers, are valid and enforceable so long as the authority to consent is exercised reasonably and in good faith. Other cases have apparently taken the position that a discretionary approval covenant will not permit the approving authority to impose limitations more restrictive than those specific restrictions affecting the lot owner's use of the property. Under this view, a restriction requiring approval of plans will not justify the imposition of building design or site requirements which are more onerous than those specifically stipulated by other restrictions of record.

We find that the better reasoned view is that covenants requiring submission of plans and prior consent before construction are valid insofar as they furnish adequate notice to the property owner of the specific restriction sought to be enforced. Therefore, the question before this Court is whether the approval clause set out in Paragraph 8 of the restrictions placed the Davises on notice that their lot was subject to more stringent building site restrictions than those set out in the specific restriction governing set-back and side-lines, Paragraph 7. We hold that as a matter of law Paragraph 8 failed to provide the Davises with notice of the placement restrictions sought to be enforced and therefore the developer's refusal to approve the plans exceeded the authority granted by the restrictive covenants and was void. . . .

It is undisputed that Austin Corporation, by impressing upon all lots in Section 7 a uniform set of restrictive covenants, intended to establish a scheme or plan to insure the development of a "residential area of high standards." There is also little dispute that the developer has implemented in the subdivision a general scheme or plan which has resulted in a residential area of high standards. David B. Barrow, Jr., who, acting on behalf of Austin Corporation, refused to approve the Davises' plans testified . . . that in the area of the Davises' lot all the houses are located roughly equidistant from the street, have a rear area or back yard, have only minor variations in size, and are located on their lots so as to avoid interference with neighbors' views. Barrow stated that the Davises' house was incompatible with the surrounding houses because of its larger dimensions, its placement near the rear of the lot, and its obstruction of the views from neighboring houses. However, it is to be emphasized that Barrow also acknowledged that "in the abstract," the Davises' house would not detract from and was not inconsistent with a residential area of high standards. Thus, it is apparent that in the view of Barrow, the Davises' plans were consistent with a residential area of high standards but were incompatible with a general plan or scheme involving the placement of houses on lots in Section 7.

However, there is nothing in the record which will support a holding that a general plan or scheme had been adopted by the developer with respect to placement so as to place the Davises on notice of such restrictions. Barrow testified that at the time the restrictions were filed, the developers had no definite intentions concerning the regulation of placement under Paragraph 8. In addition, other than the specific restrictions on building site and size, there is no language in any of the covenants, particularly in Paragraph 8, which would place a purchaser on notice that his lot was subject to the placement limitation sought to be enforced. . . .

Based on the language of the restrictive covenants and Barrow's testimony, it is clear that a general scheme regarding the placement of houses on lots in Section 7 did not exist at the time the restrictions were filed but that the placement restrictions sought to be imposed were in response to developing conditions in the subdivision. Thus, the limitations on the Davises' free use of their property were not based on the restrictive covenants but rather on the voluntary decisions of neighboring lot owners who had the good fortune to construct their houses prior to the Davises. The personal decisions of adjoining lot owners do not appear in the Davises' chain of title or in any other instrument of record. Therefore, the Davises did not purchase with notice of the limitation sought to be imposed and their lot is not burdened by the placement restriction. . . .

A contrary holding would be inconsistent with the basic concept underlying the use of restrictive covenants that each purchaser in a restricted subdivision is subjected to the burden and entitled to the benefit of the covenant. In the instant case, under the theory advanced by the developer, lot owners who built their houses early in the development of the subdivision had a relatively free hand in deciding on placement of their houses on their lots, limited only by the specific restrictions. However, once these houses were constructed the surrounding undeveloped lots were burdened to the extent that placement of houses on these lots could not be inconsistent with the developed lots as determined by the approving authority in the subdivision. Thus, lot owners who built their houses early in the development of the subdivision received the benefits of the covenants but not the burdens. In contrast, the Davises were burdened by the restrictions but essentially will receive no benefits because their house was constructed after other lot owners had decided on placement of their houses. . . . Thus, the placement restriction sought to be enforced in this cause clearly lacks the mutuality of obligation central to the purpose of restrictive covenants. . . .

Accordingly, we hold that the refusal of the developer to approve the Davises' plans exceeded his authority under the restrictive covenants and was void. . . .

[Judgment reversed and remanded.]

Termination of Covenants

The duration of convenants varies depending upon a number of factors, such as the intent of the original parties, statutory restrictions, and subsequent events. Because covenants impose a limitation on the free use of land, their unlimited duration is not favored. The parties may explicitly provide for termination by fixing a definite period—for example, 20-50 years—after which the limitation expires. Covenants also frequently contain explicit provisions allowing termination by the original grantor or by a vote of all (or a portion of) the affected landowners.[5] Many states, either by statute or judicial decision, limit the permissible duration of covenants regulating land use.

Subsequent events may extinguish an existing covenant prior to the time it would otherwise terminate. Covenants may be terminated if neighborhood conditions have so changed since the creation of the covenants that it is impossible to secure, to a substantial degree, the intended purposes or benefits of the restrictions. The change of condition may result from acts of one or both parties or their successors or from a change in the character of the area—for example, from residential to commercial use.

Public Regulation of Land Use

Easements and restrictive covenants govern land use by private agreement. Land use also may be regulated by governmental action. For example, the sovereign may impose limitations on land use through zoning. In addition, private property may be involuntarily taken for a public use under the sovereign's power of eminent domain.

Introduction to Zoning

Zoning is the process by which a municipality regulates the use that may be made of property and the physical configuration of the development of land within its jurisdiction. The power to zone is derived from the state's police power that authorizes legislation for the protection of the public health, safety, welfare, and morals.[6] Although zoning ordinarily is done by local government, the power to zone is derived from the various state legislatures that have passed enabling statutes delegating the power to lo-

---

5. Even without an explicit provision, covenants may be extinguished or amended by agreement of all affected owners.

6. The state police power is discussed in more detail in Chapter 4.

cal government, or by constitutional provision giving localities the specific authority to zone. In most states, this authorization is patterned, in whole or in part, upon the provisions of the **Standard State Zoning Enabling Act,** which was originally drafted in 1924.

Under traditional zoning, the land affected by the ordinance is divided into zones or districts, with only certain uses permitted within each zone. Zoning restrictions are of three general types: limitations on the use of property within each zone; height, bulk, and area restrictions; and architectural limitations on the exterior design of buildings. Use districts are frequently of four major types: residential, commercial, industrial, and special.

Constitutional Limitations on Zoning Power

Although police power, the basis of zoning, is certainly the most extensive and pervasive power of state government, it is not without limitations. A valid exercise of police power (including zoning) requires a showing that the regulation bears a substantial relation to public health, safety, morals, or general welfare. In essence, this means that a zoning restriction must be reasonable both by its terms and in its application. Thus, zoning restrictions that impose an arbitrary, unreasonable, oppressive, or unduly discriminatory interference with the rights of property owners are constitutionally impermissible. The specific constitutional provisions imposing such a limitation are the Due Process and Equal Protection Clauses of the Fourteenth Amendment.[7]

Early state cases did not uniformly uphold the validity of comprehensive zoning ordinances. However, two landmark United States Supreme Court cases firmly established the constitutional validity of and limitations upon the zoning power. In *Village of Euclid, Ohio v. Ambler Realty Co.,* decided in 1926,[8] the Court upheld comprehensive

zoning regulation as a valid exercise of the state's police power that did not involve an unconstitutional deprivation of property.

In the case that follows, the Court determined whether a zoning ordinance may be unconstitutional as applied to a particular piece of property.

Nectow v. City of Cambridge
48 S. Ct. 447 (1928)

Saul Nectow owned a tract of land in the city of Cambridge, Massachusetts. The city enacted a zoning ordinance fixing a boundary that placed approximately 20% of Nectow's land within a residential zone, with the remainder unrestricted. Because adjacent property was used for railroad and industrial purposes, the tract in question had no practical value for residential use. Nectow sued the city alleging that, as applied to his land, the zoning ordinance deprived him of property without due process of law in violation of the Fourteenth Amendment. The Massachusetts state courts sustained the ordinance as applied to Nectow and he appealed to the United States Supreme Court.

Sutherland, Justice

. . . A zoning ordinance of the city of Cambridge divides the city into three kinds of districts, residential, business, and unrestricted. . . . The ordinance is an elaborate one, and of the same general character as that considered by this court in *Euclid v. Ambler Co.* . . . In its general scope it is conceded to be constitutional within that decision. [Nectow's land] was put in district R-3, in which are permitted only dwellings, hotels, clubs, churches, schools, philanthropic institutions, greenhouses and gardening, with customary incidental accessories. . . .

[B]ecause of the industrial and railroad purposes to which the immediately adjoining lands to the south and east have been devoted and for which they are zoned, the locus is of comparatively little value for the limited uses permitted by the ordinance. . . .

An inspection of a plat of the city upon which the zoning districts are outlined, taken in connec-

---

7. In relevant part, the Fourteenth Amendment provides that ''No state shall . . . deprive any person of life, liberty, or property, without due process of law; nor deny to any person within its jurisdiction the equal protection of the laws.''

8. 47 S. Ct. 114 (1926).

tion with the [trial court's] findings, shows with reasonable certainty that the inclusion of the locus in question is not indispensable to the general plan. The boundary line of the residential district before reaching the locus runs for some distance along the streets, and to exclude the locus from the residential district requires only that such line shall be continued 100 feet further. . . . There does not appear to be any reason why this should not be done. Nevertheless, if that were all, we should not be warranted in substituting our judgment for that of the zoning authorities primarily charged with the duty and responsibility of determining the question. . . . But that is not all. The governmental power to interfere by zoning regulations with the general rights of the land owner by restricting the character of his use, is not unlimited, and, other questions aside, such restriction cannot be imposed if it does not bear a substantial relation to the public health, safety, morals, or general welfare. . . . Here, the express finding of the . . . court below, is that the health, safety, convenience, and general welfare of the inhabitants of the part of the city affected will not be promoted by the disposition made by the ordinance of the locus in question. This finding . . . after a hearing and an inspection of the entire area affected, supported, as we think it is, by other findings of fact, is determinative of the case. That the invasion of the property of plaintiff in error was serious and highly injurious is clearly established; and, since a necessary basis for the support of that invasion is wanting, the action of the zoning authorities comes within the ban of the Fourteenth Amendment and cannot be sustained.

[Judgment reversed.]

State courts, following *Nectow,* continue to test the validity of zoning regulations as applied to particular parcels of land on a case-by-case basis. This approach allows the court to relieve landowners from excessively burdensome restrictions without striking down an entire ordinance. Nevertheless, a zoning ordinance, like all exercises of the police power, usually is given a strong presumption of validity. That is, courts ordinarily defer to the legis-lative judgment that the particular regulation bears a substantial relationship to the public health, morals, safety, or welfare.

Objectives of Zoning

To avoid constitutional objections, all zoning regulation must be based upon a comprehensive plan. The comprehensive plan is an overall program for the future physical development of an area, including furnishing city services, such as streets, mass transit, sewers, and police and fire protection. Responsibility for the comprehensive plan ordinarily rests with the city zoning or planning commission. In addition to formulating the plan, zoning commissions study and determine the community's zoning needs and necessary changes, give notice and hold hearings, and make recommendations to the municipal legislative body.

The comprehensive plan must be consistent with the objectives for which zoning ordinances may be enacted—protecting public health, safety, welfare, and morals. For example, regulations that insure adequate light and air, and limit the density of land use (such as building height and lot size restrictions) are designed to protect public health. Regulations aimed at reducing the risk of fire (by restricting the location or existence of gasoline stations or refineries), or street congestion (by regulating the existence of multifamily dwellings in single family residential districts and the location of shopping centers, hospitals, and public facilities) are justified on grounds of public safety. Aesthetic zoning, or zoning to enhance community appearance, is justified as promoting the general welfare. Included under this heading are regulation of junkyards and mobile homes, and zoning to preserve open spaces, and historical districts and buildings. Ordinances regulating the location of adult bookstores and theaters by dispersing them throughout allowable districts or concentrating them into one district are attempts to protect public morals and property values of nearby residences and businesses.

Altering the Zoning Plan

Zoning enabling statutes require that zoning regulations be uniform for each class or kind of building throughout each district. The uniform operation of zoning classifications may be reduced by various devices, including nonconforming uses, amendments, variances, and special permits. Substantial use of these devices can defeat the essential purpose of comprehensive land use planning.

Nonconforming Uses. When a zoning ordinance is enacted, it affects previously developed land as well as undeveloped land. Invariably, certain developed property is used for purposes now prohibited by the new ordinance, such as a drugstore in a newly established residential zone. In this case, the affected property is known as a **nonconforming use,** meaning that it does not conform to the current restrictions on the zoned area, but lawfully existed when the ordinance went into effect and has continued in existence since that time.

Zoning ordinances usually permit nonconforming uses to continue, thereby reducing both political opposition to the passage of the ordinance and the likelihood that the ordinance will be declared unconstitutional as a deprivation of property without due process of law. The ordinance may permit the nonconforming use to continue indefinitely or may require it to be amortized and gradually eliminated within a specified period of time. Eliminating nonconforming uses has, however, proven a difficult task.

Amendments. The local legislative body, which enacted the zoning ordinance, may alter the plan by amendment. Amendments commonly take one of two forms: reclassification of property to a different zone known as **rezoning,** or changes made in the uses allowed in a particular zone. Amendments must be enacted in accordance with the comprehensive plan. If not, they are subject to judicial attack as invalid spot zoning. **Spot zoning** occurs when a zoning amendment classifies a single property or group of properties within a district to a use that is inconsistent with the general zoning pattern of the surrounding area, and is designed primarily for the economic benefit of the owner.

Variances. Zoning amendments involve a legislative change in the ordinance itself. In addition, zoning ordinances usually provide for administra-

tive relief—for example, from a zoning board of appeals, zoning board of review, or board of adjustment—by allowing an adversely affected landowner to apply for a variance or special permit under certain circumstances. **Variances,** which are designed to prevent rigidity, are commonly of two types: *use variances,* which permit a different use than that authorized by ordinance, and *area variances,* which permit modification of area, yard, height, setback, or similar restrictions. An area variance is less disruptive of the zoning plan because it does not threaten neighboring property with an incompatible use, and is therefore more commonly granted.

Special Permits. Another type of administrative remedy that adds flexibility to the zoning ordinance is the **special permit,** also known as a ''special use permit,'' ''special exception,'' or ''conditional use.'' Unlike the variance, which involves a use prohibited by the ordinance, special permits allow a landowner to use his or her land in a manner expressly *permitted* by the ordinance, provided that certain conditions and standards set forth in the zoning regulations are met. A basic function of the administrative zoning board is to hear and act on applications for special permits. Special permits commonly are used to control: uses posing safety, traffic, or noise problems to neighboring property; uses that are necessary but incompatible within a specific zone; and facilities customarily located in residential zones that attract large numbers of people. Uses commonly allowed by special permit include gas stations, parking lots, churches, schools, parks, utility substations, funeral homes, and certain recreational uses such as bowling alleys or golf courses.

Introduction to Eminent Domain

Increasingly in recent years, private property has been required by local, state, and federal government for public purposes such as community facilities, housing, highways, airports, schools, public utilities, and a host of other public needs. The power, inherent in a sovereign, to take, or authorize the taking of, private property for public use without the owner's consent upon making just compensation is known as **eminent domain.**[9] Use of eminent domain power is authorized by act of the legislature. The power may be exercised by the federal or state legislature itself or may be delegated to a municipal corporation or other governmental subdivision or public corporation, or in some cases, to a private corporation or individual, such as a railroad or utility.

The eminent domain power is inherent in the power of the sovereign to enact laws affecting persons or property within its jurisdiction. Like all governmental action, however, the eminent domain power is subject to restrictions imposed by the United States Constitution. State governments also are subject to the strictures of individual state constitutions. The federal Constitution contains two provisions limiting the eminent domain power. The last clause of the Fifth Amendment states:

> . . . Nor shall private property be taken for public use, without just compensation.

The various state constitutions contain similar language. For example, the constitution of Illinois (1970) provides:

> Private property shall not be taken or damaged for public use without just compensation as provided by law.

Both the Fifth Amendment (applicable by its terms to action of the federal government) and the Fourteenth Amendment (applicable by its terms to the states) also contain a "due process" clause providing that no person shall be deprived of:

> . . . life, liberty, or *property,* without due process of law . . . (Emphasis added.)

The term "due process" means that before a person may be deprived of life, liberty, or property,

he or she must be afforded notice of the potential deprivation and a hearing relevant to the nature of the case.

By placing the Eminent Domain and Due Process clauses together, the basic procedure and issues in eminent domain are highlighted. If the government or governmental agency desires property for a public use, such as an interstate highway, it will offer to buy the property for a stated price from the owner. If the owner refuses to sell at the price offered and subsequent negotiations do not result in agreement, the government initiates a legal action, known as a **condemnation proceeding,** to exercise its eminent domain power. The government or government agency seeking condemnation is the "condemnor," and the person whose property is to be taken, or condemned, is the "condemnee." The condemnation proceeding is necessary to satisfy the requirements of due process that the owner be afforded notice and a hearing before his or her property is taken. The issues decided in that hearing are dictated by the Eminent Domain Clause of the Constitution: (1) is there a *taking,* (2) is the taking for a *public use,* and (3) if the taking is for a public use, how much money is necessary to provide *just compensation* to the owner whose property is taken? The answers to these questions form the major issues in eminent domain cases.

A condemnation proceeding is unlike an ordinary lawsuit because the government, the party initiating the suit (the plaintiff), is required to pay damages (just compensation). Ordinarily the plaintiff seeks to recover damages from the defendant. Occasionally, in a proceeding known as **inverse condemnation,** the property owner initiates the suit. The basic premise in inverse condemnation is that, although the sovereign has in fact taken private property for public use, it has done so without resort to a formal condemnation procedure and without compensation. Inverse condemnation therefore represents an alternative method to recover compensation in the absence of the usual formal procedure initiated by the government.

A Taking

At the heart of the eminent domain power is a taking of private property by the sovereign for public use. Compensation is required whether the taking

---

9. The term "eminent domain" apparently originated in 1625 with the Dutch statesman, Hugo Grotius, who commented that the property of individual citizens is under the "eminent domain" of the state so that the state or its representative may transfer or destroy it. Although the power to take private property for public use is now generally considered to be based upon the sovereignty of the state, the term "eminent domain" has been commonly accepted in this country to describe the power.

is total or partial, and whether a fee simple or lesser interest, such as an easement, is appropriated. If the property owner actually is deprived of possession of his property, the existence of a taking is apparent. For example, the state may condemn a portion of privately owned farmland in order to construct a highway or public building. A taking also may occur without formally divesting the owner of title to or possession of the property. For example, the construction of a ditch, drain, fence, or elevated railway over property is a taking because the usefulness, though not necessarily possession, of the property is impaired. Furthermore, a law that limits the height of buildings near a public park in order to preserve its beauty appropriates for public use an interest in the adjoining property (an easement) requiring compensation.

Examples of takings are endless and ever-expanding. Therefore, whether compensation is constitutionally required under the Eminent Domain Clause cannot be determined by mechanical rules that are readily applicable to all cases. Each case must be decided on its own merits until the courts, by the gradual process of inclusion and exclusion, determine which injuries to private property rights must be compensated. A substantial body of case law at both the federal and state level already exists to aid the property owner or her attorney in making this determination.

Exercise of "Police Power" Compared. Not every governmental interference with the possession, use, or enjoyment of private property is compensable under the Eminent Domain Clause. In fact, most governmental restriction concerning private property, such as zoning, is constitutionally valid *without compensation* as an exercise of the sovereign's police power. The fundamental distinction between the eminent domain and the police power is that in eminent domain, an interest in the property is *taken* from the owner and applied to a use beneficial to the public. In contrast, the police power does not appropriate private property for public use, but simply *regulates* its use and enjoyment by the owner to prevent use in a manner detrimental to the public interest. This distinction between taking and regulating is vital because an exercise of the eminent domain power requires that the affected property owner receive just compensation for the tak-

ing. No compensation, however, is paid upon a valid exercise of the police power, even though the owner's rights in the property have been diminished because of the limitations imposed on its use.

Public Use

Only public uses justify the exercise of the eminent domain power against private property. The Constitution forbids a governmental appropriation of private property for purely or predominantly private purposes. As with the term "taking," a comprehensive definition of "public use" necessarily evolves on a case-by-case basis through judicial inclusion and exclusion. In addition, the character, commercial development of land in the region, and local conditions frequently determine which uses are public. In other words, the various states, by judicial decision and constitutional provision, define "public" differently based upon the history and the particular needs and problems of the region.

Although no comprehensive definition of "public use" is available to cover all cases, three general classes of uses emerge as public thereby allowing a taking by eminent domain. The first class includes government buildings, libraries, schools, museums, highways, airports, parks, bridges, subways, public parking lots, sewage treatment plants, public housing, and urban redevelopment. In the second category, private property is taken for the benefit of a railroad for its roadbed or for a utility, such as a telephone or power company, to run lines or cables. In the third category are uses that, though essentially private, are recognized as public on historical grounds or because of abnormal local conditions. For example, in some states mining, logging, or irrigation is vital to the economic welfare of the state, and is treated as public in character for the purposes of eminent domain; in other states, use of eminent domain power for these purposes is denied because of the private use involved.

Just Compensation

Fundamental to the meaning and exercise of eminent domain power is the constitutional requirement that the owner whose property is taken receive just compensation.[10] The prohibition against uncompensated taking is designed to prevent the injustice that results if benefits are conferred upon the public to the detriment of the individual property owner. The condemnor satisfies the compensation requirement by paying to the condemnee a sum of money equivalent to the loss sustained.

Although the existence of the right to compensation is unquestioned, the amount that is constitutionally required is a difficult issue. Just compensation generally equals the fair market value[11] of the property taken on the date of the taking. In the case of a partial taking, just compensation equals the depreciation in value of the land remaining.

The amount of compensation has long been held to be a judicial, not a legislative, question. The trier of fact, which in most states is the court (judge) sitting without a jury, determines just compensation based upon the testimony presented.[12] Evidence of value is commonly provided by testimony of professional appraisers. These experts are hired by the respective parties and often give widely varying opinions concerning the value of the property. Generally, neither the property owner's attorneys' fees nor payments to appraisers acting as expert witnesses are taken into account in computing the award.

The owner is compensated for the land and not for the loss of its particular use. Under the general common law rule, therefore, the owner is generally not entitled to recover for the value of any business conducted on the property or loss of goodwill. This approach, though failing to compensate an important element of the owner's damage, is commonly justified on the grounds that the owner's property, not his right to conduct a business, is taken by the sovereign.

---

10. This right is constitutionally guaranteed at both the federal and state levels as a limitation on the exercise of eminent domain power. Even in the absence of an eminent domain clause, however, just compensation for public taking would undoubtedly be required as an essential element of due process.

11. Though "fair market value" has been defined in various ways, the term generally means the amount of money that a willing purchaser would pay to a willing owner considering all uses for which the land is suited or might be applied.

12. Many states, however, require by constitutional provision that the value of property taken by eminent domain be ascertained by a jury in all or certain types of cases.

Some states have statutes specifically authorizing recovery for the going concern value of a business in eminent domain cases. Other states, which follow the common law rule, recognize exceptions to its application, as the following case illustrates.

City of Detroit v. Michael's Prescriptions
373 N.W.2d 219 (Mich. App. 1985)

As part of a large project involving condemnation of 465 acres in an area of Detroit known as Poletown, the city of Detroit condemned a pharmacy that had operated as Michael's Prescriptions for over 40 years. A jury awarded the owner of Michael's Prescriptions $275,000 as compensation for the city's taking of the property. The judgment included compensation for the goodwill or going concern value of the business. The City of Detroit appealed.

Kelly, Presiding Judge

. . . The law of eminent domain is governed in Michigan by the Constitution and by statute. . . . While intangible property interests are compensable,. . . no formula or artificial measure of damages will apply in all cases and the amount to be recovered by the owner of the condemned property will generally be left to the discretion of the trier of fact based on the evidence presented. Just compensation should, however, place the owner of the property in as good a position as was occupied before the taking. . . .

The general rule of law is that, unless a business is taken for use as a going concern, the owner of the business located on a condemned parcel of realty will not be compensated for the good will or going concern value of the business. . . . The justification for this general rule is that the owner of a successful business may generally transfer that business to another location. Where the government does not appropriate the business for its value as a going concern, the owner of that interest need not be compensated since nothing is taken. . . .

As with most general principles of law, however, the rule prohibiting recovery is not without exception. . . .

[I]t is clear that recovery of the going concern value of a business lost to condemnation will depend on the transferability of that business to another location. If the business can be transferred, nothing is taken and compensation is therefore not required. Whether a business is transferable will be decided on a case by case basis inasmuch as a specific factual analysis is required. Generally, however, recovery will be allowed where the business derives its success from a location not easily duplicated or where relocation is foreclosed for reasons relating to the entire condemnation project. In large scale condemnation projects such as Poletown, involving the elimination of an entire segment of the residential and business community, transferability of neighborhood businesses is often foreclosed.

Michael's Prescriptions was located directly across the street from the entrance to St. Joseph Mercy Hospital. The Samaritan Medical Clinic was located one block away and at some point during the condemnation project occupied the same building that housed Michael's Prescriptions. Also in the same building were two physicians' offices. Michael's Prescriptions sold only pharmaceuticals, measured 20 feet by 28 feet, and was operated by Mr. Kablak, whose severe hearing impairment necessitated both amplified telephones and his son's assistance in filling prescriptions.

Respondent's accountant testified that due to the unique location of the pharmacy and monopolization of the prescription business of St. Joseph Mercy Hospital's emergency room, Michael's Prescriptions generated phenomenal gross sales of pharmaceuticals. Testimony established that when Michael's Prescriptions and St. Joseph Mercy Hospital were the only businesses operating in the condemned area, Michael's Prescriptions still generated its highest sales and most profitable year. The accountant classified the condemned property as a neighborhood pharmacy but considered it unique because of its location, operation and high income in comparison to eight other prescription pharmacies that he represented.

Evidence presented at trial regarding relocation efforts suggest that Michael's Prescriptions was nontransferable. Mr. Kablak and a professional realtor were unsuccessful in their attempts to find a location with a similar traffic pattern. While the business did relocate 12 blocks away from its original vantage point, sales and profits have already declined and evidence introduced at trial established that the trend would continue.

In our view, a significant factor in the inability of Michael's Prescriptions to relocate as a going concern is the nature of the condemnation project itself. . . . The success of Michael's Prescriptions was attributable in part to the locational advantage of being so near a hospital, an emergency room, a clinic, and two physicians' offices. Its success also derived in no small part from the character of the neighborhood as described above and the good will of its established customers. Because of the condemnation of the entire surrounding neighborhood, the relocation of Michael's Prescriptions and other similar neighborhood businesses was realistically foreclosed by the scattering of established customers throughout the metropolitan area and by the elimination of other "business-generating businesses". . . .

In the instant case, Michael's Prescriptions lost its leasehold interest in the underlying realty, its established customers and the prescription market generated by the neighborhood hospital, clinic and physicians' offices. . . .

We conclude that the trial court did not err in allowing the introduction of evidence as to the going concern value of Michael's Prescriptions. . . .

[Judgment affirmed.]

Federal Relocation Assistance and Land Acquisition Policy

In recent years, the federal government, acting on its own behalf or by providing funds to various state governments, has become increasingly involved in major public works projects requiring exercise of eminent domain power. Projects such as the interstate highway program, public housing, and urban renewal have required an unprecedented taking of private property, displacing vast numbers of people, often in densely populated urban areas. In order to provide for uniform and equitable treatment of persons displaced from their homes, businesses, and farms by federal and federally assisted programs, and to establish uniform and equitable land acquisition policies for these programs, Congress passed the **Uniform Relocation Assistance and Real Property Acquisition Policies Act** in 1970.[13]

The Act provides relocation assistance to persons who are forced to move from real property because the property is acquired for a program or project undertaken by a federal agency or with federal financial assistance. The assistance takes one of three general forms: (1) moving expenses for persons occupying the property as a dwelling, (2) compensation for moving or other expenses relating to a business or farming operation conducted on the property taken, and (3) payments for replacement housing for owners and tenants. The Act also establishes a uniform land acquisition policy containing policy provisions designed to guide federal agencies (and state agencies acting with federal assistance) in acquiring land for public projects. These policies are designed to encourage real property acquisition by agreement rather than litigation, to assure consistent treatment of property owners affected by the many federal programs, and to promote public confidence in federal land acquisition practices.[14]

SUMMARY

1. An owner's right to possess, use, and enjoy land may be limited by private agreement or by act of public authority. Land use may be regulated privately either by creating a limited interest of use (an easement) in the property itself or by contract. The government may also impose land use restrictions through exercise of its police power and its eminent domain power.

2. An easement is an interest in land giving its owner the right either to use the land of another for a limited and specified purpose, or to prevent the other from doing something otherwise lawful upon his or her land. Easements may be obtained for the benefit of land owned by the easement holder (an easement appurtenant) or the right of use may exist independently of the holder's ownership of any land (an easement in gross). Easements may be created by express act of the parties, implication, prescription, and eminent domain. Like most other property interests, easements are freely transferable. Although the duration of an easement is often indefinite, easements may terminate by their terms (expiration) or may be extinguished by events, such as an abandonment, occurring after creation.

3. Not every privilege to use another's land is an easement. Privileges of use that lack the formalities necessary to create an interest in land result in a license. A license, unlike an easement, is freely revocable by the property owner granting it.

4. Land use may be regulated privately by contract as well as conveyance. Promises concerning land use, usually known as "covenants," may require a landowner to do something on his or her land, such as maintain a fence. More commonly, covenants are negative or restrictive, limiting the permissible uses of the land or the acts that may be performed upon it. Restrictive covenants often are used in residential subdivisions to maintain property values and preserve residential character.

5. Covenants governing land use usually are created upon coveyance of the land and are generally imposed by the grantor to limit the grantee's use of the land. If the property is transferred later, the liability to perform the covenant or the right to take advantage of it passes to the transferee of the property (the covenant "runs with the land") if certain criteria are met. Once created, a covenant may terminate according to its own terms, by vote of all or a portion of the affected landowners, or by subsequent events such as changed neighborhood conditions.

6. The law of zoning is perhaps the most common exercise of the state police power affecting rights in real property. Zoning is the process by which a municipality regulates the permissible uses of property and the physical configuration of land within its jurisdiction. Zoning ordinances usually divide land into zones or districts, permitting only certain uses within each zone. The ordinance must be adopted pursuant to a comprehensive plan of development. The plan may be altered thereafter by permitting nonconforming uses, rezoning particular parcels, and allowing variances. In addition, uses may be authorized by special permit.

---

13. 42 U.S.C. §§4601-4655.

14. 42 U.S.C. §4651.

7. Through its eminent domain power, the sovereign may *take* private property for a public use, such as a road, park, or public building. If the parties are unable to agree to a voluntary sale, the government may initiate a condemnation proceeding to force a conveyance of the property. To satisfy constitutional requirements, however, the owner must be paid just compensation for the property that is involuntarily transferred. In addition, federal law provides for relocation expenses for persons displaced by federal or federally funded projects.

KEY TERMS

easement
profit (profit à prendre)
easement appurtenant
easement in gross
prescription
license
affirmative covenant
negative (restrictive)
  covenant
covenants running with
  the land
equitable servitude
zoning
Standard State Zoning
  Enabling Act

nonconforming use
rezoning
spot zoning
variance
special permit
eminent domain
condemnation proceeding
inverse condemnation
Uniform Relocation
  Assistance and Real
  Property Acquisition
  Policies Act

QUESTIONS AND PROBLEMS

38-1 This chapter discusses various methods of regulating or restricting land use. Should the law generally favor restrictions on land use? For what purposes are private restrictions, such as easements and restrictive covenants, imposed? For what purposes are public restrictions, such as zoning ordinances and takings by eminent domain, imposed? What criteria do courts employ in determining the validity of private restrictions? Do these differ from those used to judge public restrictions?

38-2 During the oil crisis of the 1970s, Efficient Company, Inc. constructed a new office building heated only by solar energy. The new heating system worked well until 1985 when the adjoining landowner began construction of a new high-rise office building. Efficient realized that the new building would block the sun and make the solar heating system inoperable. Efficient sues to enjoin construction of the building.
  (a) Efficient argues that it has obtained a pre-

scriptive easement in the area over the neighbor's land. Should the court grant the injunction?
  (b) What steps might Efficient have taken to better protect itself?

38-3 The ABC Shipping Co. owns a large tract of land near the riverfront in St. Louis. The city has proposed to create several new, wide streets in the area to relieve traffic congestion. A city official meets with the president of ABC concerning acquiring part of ABC's land for a new street. Because the street will benefit ABC's property, the president has no objection to relinquishing some of the land to the city for street purposes. The land to be sold, however, would be useful in any future expansion of ABC's businesses at the site. The president, therefore, desires assurance that if the proposed streets are not built, ABC may reacquire the property for use in its business. Offer some suggestions concerning how the assurance could be accomplished.

38-4 Rock Promotions, Inc. owns a large theater that it uses for rock concerts. Fred Stone buys a ticket from Rock Promotions and attends a concert. Soon after the performance begins, several members of the audience sitting near Fred become rowdy and unruly. Two employees of Rock Promotions eject not only the unruly people but also Fred. When Fred complains, a Rock Promotions employee states that the company has the right to revoke Fred's ticket at will. Is the employee correct? What type of legal relationship is created between the owner of a theater or arena and the holder of a ticket to an event held on the property?

38-5 In each of the following cases, the court must decide whether the restrictive covenant should be enforced. How should the court rule? Explain.
  (a) Plaintiffs own a lot in the Myers Park subdivision, an area developed pursuant to a common plan in 1950. The deeds to all of the lots provide that each lot shall be used only for residential purposes. In 1954, all of the property owners signed an agreement allowing construction of a library on one lot. In 1970, an apartment building was built on one lot. In 1975, a bank branch office was opened in a house located on one lot. The remaining thirty lots are improved with single family dwellings. Much of the surrounding neighborhood is commercial property.

Plaintiffs want to build an office building and allege that the restrictive covenant should not be enforced.

(b) Defendants own property in the Sun and Fun Subdivision, a residential community in Florida developed pursuant to a common plan. The deeds to all of the lots in the subdivision contain a covenant that provides that all homeowners agree that no child under the age of twenty-one shall be a permanent resident. Bob and Marylou bought a house in the subdivision in 1970. In 1975, Marylou became pregnant unexpectedly. The day that she arrived home from the hospital with the baby, the other homeowners delivered a letter requesting that Bob, Marylou, and the baby vacate the premises to comply with the covenant. Bob and Marylou sue to have the covenant lifted.

(c) Homer and Hannah live in a subdivision that maintains a swimming pool and park for the residents. The deed to each lot in the subdivision provides that the owner will pay a $100 annual fee to a homeowners association for upkeep of the pool and park. The deed further provides that the covenant is to run with the land. Because Homer and Hannah have never used the recreational facilities, they refuse to pay the fee. The homeowners association sues them to enforce the covenant.

38-6 In May of 1975, Ida purchased a lot on Green Hill Beach in the city of Kingston for the purpose of building a residence. Three months later the Kingston Zoning Board declared Green Hill Beach to be a High Flood Danger Zone and passed an ordinance prohibiting the construction of any buildings on the beach. The purpose of the ordinance was to protect the beach from erosion that would lead to flooding of the town and would create a hazard to public health and safety. Ida sued the city alleging that the ordinance was in effect a taking of her property and sought compensation for inverse condemnation.

The city argued that the ordinance merely was an exercise of its police powers for which no compensation was necessary. How should the court decide the case? Explain.

38-7 Peaceville is a city that prides itself on being a quiet and safe place to live. In 1975, Donald purchased two acres of land in Peaceville where he planned to construct a low-income housing project. Because the land was zoned for single-family residences only, Donald applied to the Peaceville zoning commission to have the property rezoned for multifamily dwellings. The city refused to rezone and Donald sued.

(a) At the trial Donald offers in evidence the minutes of the zoning commission meeting containing several statements from commission members that they were opposed to the rezoning because it would lead to an influx of "minorities and other undesirables." How should the court rule?

(b) Assume instead that there are no minutes of the zoning commission meeting. Nevertheless, Donald offers evidence to show that many potential residents of the housing project are minority members. Donald argues that the refusal has the effect of discriminating on the basis of race. How should the court rule? Explain.

38-8 The city of Detroit sought to obtain 465 acres of land within a residential area of the city known as "Poletown." After obtaining the property, the city intended to sell it to General Motors Corporation as the site for a new automobile assembly plant. Although the city was willing to pay the fair market value for the property, many Poletown residents opposed the project because they would lose their homes. The city, however, believed the project would help to alleviate the 18% unemployment rate in Detroit. A group of Poletown residents sued the city alleging that it had misused its powers of eminent domain by taking property for a private rather than public use. How should the court decide the case? Explain.

Chapter 39

Decedents' Estates and Trusts

Property law is primarily the study of the ownership and transfer of legally recognized property interests. Earlier chapters have focused upon transfers by an owner through sale or gift. This chapter examines two additional methods of transferring either real or personal property interests: wills and intestate succession statutes, which effect transfers upon an owner's death; and trusts, which may be used to transfer property either during or after the owner's life.

Introduction to Transfers on Death

Methods of Transfer

For purposes of transfers made on death, a person (the "decedent") may die in one of two ways, testate or intestate. A person who leaves a valid will directing the disposition of his or her property dies **testate**. A **will** is simply a formal instrument by which a person makes a disposition of his or her property to take effect after death. A person making the will is known as a **testator**. A transfer of property through a will is known as a **testamentary disposition**. A person who (1) fails to leave a will, (2) fails to leave a "valid" will (the requirements of which are discussed later in this chapter), or (3) leaves a valid will that does not dispose of all of the testator's property dies **intestate**. If a valid will fails to dispose of all the testator's property, the decedent dies partially testate and partially intestate. If a person dies intestate, his or her property is distributed to persons known as "heirs" according to rules provided in state **intestate succession statutes**.

Estates and Estate Administration

On a person's death, an **estate** is created, which includes all property, real and personal, tangible and intangible, owned by the decedent. The administration of a decedent's estate is within the jurisdiction of the **probate court**. A probate court has primarily two functions. First, assuming the decedent leaves a will, the court must determine whether it complies with the statutory requirements. Second, the court supervises the administration of the estate. Estate administration includes locating and collecting the decedent's assets, ascertaining and paying taxes, funeral expenses, and other creditors' claims against the estate, and distributing the remaining assets according to the terms of the will or intestate succession statute. Though literally referring only to the first function (to probate or prove the will), the term **probate** is generally used to refer to any matter or proceeding pertaining to the administration of a decedent's estate. A decedent's estate is probated in the state in which the decedent was domiciled at the time of death. **Domicile** generally refers to a person's permanent residence to which he or she intends to return.

Although the court supervises the administration of the estate, actual responsibility for discovery, collection, and distribution of the decedent's assets and payment of lawful claims and taxes against the estate generally falls upon the **executor** (female, **executrix**). The executor is often named by the testator in the will. Nevertheless, the named executor must be appointed or authorized by the probate court to serve in that capacity. If the testator leaves a will, but no executor is named in the will, or if the named executor is deceased, incompetent, or refuses to serve, the court appoints an administrator "c.t.a." (short for *cum testamento annexo* meaning "with the will annexed"). In an intestate estate, the court appoints an **administrator** (female, **administratrix**) to perform the functions outlined above. The formal instruments issued by the court appointing and authorizing the executor or administrator to act are known as "letters testamentary" or "letters of administration" respectively. Executors and administrators are known as "personal representatives" of the estate.

The executor is entitled to be compensated for his duties and may be a beneficiary (even a principal beneficiary) under the will. The executor is, however, a *fiduciary* with respect to the estate and, in dealing with its assets, must observe the same standards that would be followed by a prudent person dealing with the property of another.[1]

Each state has enacted a "probate act" or "probate code." These statutes contain, for example, the requirements of a valid will and a plan of intestate succession. They also prescribe rules relating to estate administration, relating to the duties, qualifications, and appointment of executors and administrators, notification of creditors, time limits within which creditors' claims must be filed, the priority for payment of claims against the estate, and the manner of ultimate distribution of the remaining assets and closing the estate.

Probate statutes vary widely from state to state. In an effort to modernize probate law and provide greater uniformity among the states, the National Conference of Commissioners on Uniform State Laws has drafted a **Uniform Probate Code (UPC)**. Completed in 1969, the UPC has now been enacted in fifteen states.[2]

In the following case, the U.S. Supreme Court discusses administration of a probate estate and notification of creditors with claims against the estate.

Tulsa Professional Collection Services, Inc. v. Pope
108 S. Ct. 1340 (1988)

Following five months of hospitalization at St. John Medical Center, H. Everett Pope, Jr. died testate on April 2, 1979. At the time of his death, Pope owed St. John Medical Center for the costs of his medical care. Pope's wife, appellee JoAnne Pope, initiated probate proceedings and was appointed executrix of the estate. As required by Oklahoma statute, the executrix published a notice beginning on July 17, 1979 and continuing for two consecutive weeks in the Tulsa Daily Legal News that advised creditors

---

1. The fiduciary concept is discussed in more detail later in this chapter in the material on trusts, and appears in various other contexts throughout this text.

2. States enacting the UPC include Alaska, Arizona, Colorado, Florida, Hawaii, Idaho, Maine, Michigan, Minnesota, Montana, Nebraska, New Mexico, North Dakota, South Carolina, and Utah. Kentucky has enacted a small portion of the UPC.

that they must file any claims against the estate within two months. St. John Medical Center did not file a claim against the estate within the two-month period, but in 1983 appellant Tulsa Professional Collection Services, Inc., a subsidiary of the hospital responsible for collecting overdue bills, filed a claim with the probate court. The court rejected the claim on the ground that it had not been filed within the statutory claim period. Both the appellate court and state supreme court affirmed. On appeal to the U.S. Supreme Court, Tulsa Professional Collection Services, Inc. argued that the Oklahoma statute violated due process because it failed to require actual notice of probate proceedings to known creditors of a deceased debtor.

O'Connor, Justice

. . . Oklahoma's probate code requires creditors to file claims against an estate within a specified time period, and generally bars untimely claims. . . . Such "nonclaim statutes" are almost universally included in state probate codes. . . . Giving creditors a limited time in which to file claims against the estate serves the State's interest in facilitating the administration and expeditious closing of estates. . . . Most States also provide that creditors are to be notified of the requirement to file claims imposed by the nonclaim statutes solely by publication [in a newspaper]. Indeed, in most jurisdictions it is the publication of notice that triggers the nonclaim statute. The Uniform Probate Code, for example, provides that creditors have 4 months from publication in which to file claims. . . .

Under Oklahoma's probate code, any party interested in the estate may initiate probate proceedings by petitioning the court to have the will proved. . . . The court is then required to set a hearing date on the petition, . . . and to mail notice of the hearing "to all heirs, legatees and devisees, at their places of residence," [Okla. Stat. Title 58, §§25, 26.] If no person appears at the hearing to contest the will, the court may admit the will to probate on the testimony of one of the subscribing witnesses to the will. . . . After the will is admitted to probate, the court must order appointment of an executor or executrix, issuing letters testamentary to the named executor or execu-

trix if that person appears, is competent and qualified, and no objections are made. . . .

Immediately after appointment, the executor or executrix is required to "give notice to the creditors of the deceased." [Okla. Stat. Title 58, §331.] Proof of compliance with this requirement must be filed with the court. . . This notice is to advise creditors that they must present their claims to the executor or executrix within 2 months of the date of the first publication. As for the method of notice, the statute requires only publication: "[S]uch notice must be published in some newspaper in [the] county once each week for two (2) consecutive weeks." [Okla. Stat. Title 58, §331.] A creditor's failure to file a claim within the 2-month period generally bars it forever. . . .

Appellant's interest is an unsecured claim, a cause of action against the estate for an unpaid bill. Little doubt remains that such an intangible interest is property protected by the Fourteenth Amendment. . . . Appellant's claim, therefore, is properly considered a protected property interest.

The Fourteenth Amendment protects this interest, however, only from a deprivation by state action. Private use of state sanctioned private remedies or procedures does not rise to the level of state action. . . . But when private parties make use of state procedures with the overt, significant assistance of state officials, state action may be found. . . . The question here is whether the State's involvement with the nonclaim statute is substantial enough to implicate the Due Process Clause. . . .

Here . . . there is significant state action. The probate court is intimately involved throughout, and without that involvement the time bar is never activated. The nonclaim statute becomes operative only after probate proceedings have been commenced in state court. The court must appoint the executor or executrix before notice, which triggers the time bar, can be given. Only after this court appointment is made does the statute provide for any notice; §331 directs the executor or executrix to publish notice "immediately" after appointment. . . . Finally, copies of the notice and an affidavit of publication must be filed with the court. . . . It is only after all of these actions take place that the time period begins to run, and in every one of these actions, the court is intimately involved. This involvement is so pervasive and substantial that it must be considered state action subject to the restrictions of the Fourteenth Amendment.

Where the legal proceedings themselves trigger the time bar, . . . due process is directly implicated and actual notice generally is required. . . .

Creditors, who have a strong interest in maintaining the integrity of their relationship with their debtors, are particularly unlikely to benefit from publication notice. As a class, creditors may not be aware of a debtor's death or of the institution of probate proceedings. Moreover, the executor or executrix will often be, as is the case here, a party with a beneficial interest in the estate. This could diminish an executor's or executrix's inclination to call attention to the potential expiration of a creditor's claim. There is thus a substantial practical need for actual notice in this setting.

At the same time, the State undeniably has a legitimate interest in the expeditious resolution of probate proceedings. Death transforms the decedent's legal relationships and a State could reasonably conclude that swift settlement of estates is so important that it calls for very short time deadlines for filing claims. . . . Providing actual notice to known or reasonably ascertainable creditors, however, is not inconsistent with the goals reflected in nonclaim statutes. Actual notice need not be inefficient or burdensome. We have repeatedly recognized that mail service is an inexpensive and efficient mechanism that is reasonably calculated to provide actual notice. . . .

On balance then, a requirement of actual notice to known or reasonably ascertainable creditors is not so cumbersome as to unduly hinder the dispatch with which probate proceedings are conducted. . . .

Whether appellant's identity as a creditor was known or reasonably ascertainable by appellee cannot be answered on this record. . . . If appellant's identity was known or "reasonably ascertainable," then termination of appellant's claim without actual notice violated due process. . . .

[Judgment reversed and remanded.]

Wills and Intestate Succession

Since ancient times, the law has allowed persons to dispose of personal property by will. The ability to transfer real property, however, is a more recent development, derived primarily from the English Statute of Wills,[3] enacted in 1540.

A transfer of real property by will is known as a **devise**. A person receiving a devise is a "devisee." A gift of money by will is known as a **legacy,** received by a "legatee." The term **bequest** describes any form of personal property passing by will and is hence a broader term than "legacy." The UPC abolishes the distinction and treats any disposition by will of either real or personal property as a "devise" and any person designated in the will to receive a devise as a "devisee." For the sake of simplicity, the UPC approach is used in the following material.

Devises of property are commonly classified as specific, general, or demonstrative. A **specific devise** is one of particularly designated property—for example, the testator may leave "my 1955 Chevrolet" or "my house at 203 Elm Street" to X. A **general devise** is a gift payable out of the general assets of the testator's estate—for example, "I leave $2,000 to Z." A **demonstrative devise** is one payable out of specific property or a specific fund—for example, the testator may leave $1,000 payable "from my savings account at First Federal Savings."

The "Valid" Will

Formalities of Execution. In order to control the disposition of his or her property after death, a person must leave a valid will. The term "valid" means that the will satisfies all formalities prescribed by state statute. These formalities are designed to prevent fraud, and, as previously indicated, compliance with them is determined by the

---

3. 32 Hen. 8, ch. 1 (1540). Traditionally, a "will" referred only to an instrument transferring real property, whereas a "testament" transferred personal property—hence the term "last will and testament." The term "will," however, is now used to designate a document disposing of both real and personal property interests.

probate court. The modern trend, evidenced by the UPC provisions, is to simplify the requirements for execution of a valid will, and to validate the will whenever possible, so that more people may use wills to transfer property on death. A few states even have statutory will forms that the testator completes simply by filling in appropriate blanks. Despite these developments, a majority of persons owning property die intestate.

Modern state will statutes are based upon early English statutes, but vary somewhat among the states. Generally, a valid will must be in writing, signed by the testator, and witnessed. Under the UPC, the witnesses must witness either the signing of the will by the testator, an acknowledgment by the testator that the signature is his, or an acknowledgment by the testator that the document is his will. Though only the signature of the witnesses is *required,* wills often contain an **attestation clause** signed by the witnesses, simply reciting that the statutory formalities necessary for proper execution have been observed. The use of an attestation clause aids in subsequently establishing the validity of the will in probate or if contested.

Although the UPC and most other statutes require the signature of only two witnesses, a few states require three. To assure the validity of the will wherever the testator is domiciled on death, the testator is therefore well advised to have three witnesses in all cases. Nevertheless, the UPC and many other statutes provide that a will is deemed validly executed if it complies with the law in the state of its execution.

As illustrated in the following case, courts strictly enforce the statutory formalities even if the result may defeat the testator's clear intentions.

Matter of Will of Daly

402 N.Y.S.2d 747 (N.Y. Surrogate Ct. 1978)

Robert M. Daly, a resident of New York, died leaving an estate of approximately $175,000. Although Daly was married and had three children, he devised most of his property to friends in a will that Daly had prepared without the advice of an attorney.

The evidence established that two of Daly's employees had signed the will as witnesses. Daly's

children requested summary judgment denying probate of the will because it had not been executed in accordance with the New York statute that provided:

> The signature of the testator shall be affixed to the will in the presence of each of the attesting witnesses, or shall be acknowledged by the testator to each of them to have been affixed by him or by his direction. The testator may either sign in the presence of, or acknowledge his signature to each attesting witness separately.

In the following opinion, the surrogate court ruled on the admissibility of the will.

Kahn, Surrogate

. . . The pertinent subdivision mandates that the testator's signature be made in the presence of each of the subscribing witnesses, or be acknowledged by him to have been so made. The testator may either sign in their presence or acknowledge his signature to each attesting witness separately. Two facts are essential—that the testator sign his name, and that the witnesses see him sign or that he acknowledges his signature to them. It is not required that the signing or acknowledgment be in the presence of both witnesses at the same time. . . .

It is clear from reading the statute that the procedural formalities called for have not been complied with in the factual setting hereinabove described. What is not clear, however, is how far the courts have gone in allowing deviations from those prescribed procedural formalities, particularly where the instrument in question has not been executed under the auspices of an attorney. Not surprisingly there are numerous precedents which have addressed themselves to just that issue now before the Court. . . .

In summarizing the . . . precedents, it can be stated that where the witnesses cannot recollect the circumstances surrounding the execution of the instrument, the document may be admitted to probate. . . . Given considerable weight in such cases is the length of time elapsing between the execution of the document and its being offered for probate.

Where however there is no question that the testator did not sign his name in the presence of the witness and further failed to acknowledge his signature, then in such a case a motion for Summary Judgment would indeed be appropriate. . . .

The instrument before the Court is dated December 29, 1976. The witnesses' testimony was taken only four (4) months thereafter on May 2, 1977. The first witness has testified that he was not told what he was signing; that the testator did not sign his name in the witness' presence; that the document was so folded that he could not tell whether the testator's signature was on the document and that the testator never acknowledged any signature to him. The testimony of the second witness is equivocal and covers the widest range of possibilities. Alternatively, he testified that the testator's signature was on the document, was not on the document, or that he did not recall whether it was or was not upon the document. In any event, said "signature," was in no way or manner acknowledged by decedent to this witness.

Based on the testimony adduced, as well as the precedents examined, the Court finds that the testator's signature was not acknowledged to either witness as required by statute. . . .

Finally, this Court must note how this proceeding once again points up the disastrous results which can occur when a lay person takes it upon himself to do his own will. In this case, decedent was a young and intelligent person who was knowledgeable in death and estate matters due to his professional status as a funeral director. Nevertheless, his do-it-yourself will did not meet the requirements of law, with the unfortunate result that his intentions as expressed in the purported will were thwarted. The Court cannot ignore this opportunity to warn others to seek professional legal advice and guidance before they execute such a vitally important document as their Last Will and Testament.

A common problem regarding execution arises if a witness is "interested"—that is, a beneficiary under the will. Most modern statutes provide that the use of an interested witness does not affect the validity of the will, but that the interested witness's share under the will is limited to whatever he or she would have received had there been no will. Some statutes provide that the right of an interested

witness to take under the will is unaffected if a sufficient number of disinterested witnesses have signed to satisfy statutory requirements. The UPC provides that neither the will nor any provision is invalidated because it is signed by an interested witness. Thus, under the UPC, the interested witness takes the share outlined in the will.

Age and Capacity Requirements. In addition to formalities of execution, certain minimum age and capacity requirements are imposed. For example, the UPC provides that any person eighteen years of age or older who is of sound mind may make a will. The eighteen-year age requirement, now effective in most states, represents a reduction from the traditional requirement, twenty-one years. That the testator be of "sound mind" generally requires that, at the time of execution of the will, he can understand in a general way (1) the nature and extent of his property, (2) the persons who are the natural objects of his bounty, and (3) the disposition that he is making of his property. In addition, the testator must be capable of appreciating these elements in relation to each other and forming an orderly plan regarding the disposition of the property.[4]

Lack of testamentary capacity is not established merely because the testator's disposition is unfair or excludes persons who are the natural objects of his bounty. The will, however, may be invalidated by proof of fraud or undue influence on the testator. Influence is "undue" if it destroys free choice and allows substitution of another's volition for that of the testator.

Nuncupative and Holographic Wills. In some states, the nuncupative will and the holographic will are valid, even though they fail to meet the basic formalities outlined above. A **nuncupative will** is an *oral* will dictated by the testator during his or her last illness before a sufficient number of witnesses and later reduced to a writing. Not all states recognize such wills and those that do impose restrictions upon their use. For example, stat-

---

4. These criteria govern only a person's mental capacity to make a will. A person may have testamentary capacity even though he is under guardianship or has no contractual capacity.

utes generally limit the amount or type of property that may be transferred and require a reduction to writing within a specified number of days. The nuncupative will therefore represents a limited exception to the general rule that wills be in writing.

Holographic wills constitute an exception to the requirement that wills be witnessed. **Holographic wills** are those, according to most statutes, written entirely in the handwriting of the testator. Holographic wills are validated without witnesses because the fact that the will is entirely in the testator's handwriting reduces the risk of fraud that the formalities are designed to prevent. Although many states do not recognize the validity of holographic wills, the UPC expressly authorizes their use.

Revocation of Wills

A will is "ambulatory," which means that it takes effect only upon the testator's death and until that time he or she is free to alter or revoke it. A will may be revoked by physical act, a subsequent writing, or by operation of law.

Revocation by Physical Act. State statutes prescribe specific physical acts that constitute revocation. Under the UPC, revocation by physical act occurs if the will is "burned, torn, canceled, obliterated, or destroyed, with the intent and for the purpose of revoking it. . . ." The UPC also permits *partial* revocation by physical act—the obliteration of a devise by crossing it out. Many states prohibit such partial revocations and instead require a subsequent document complying with the state wills statute to accomplish this result.

Revocation by Subsequent Writing. A will also may be revoked in whole or in part through the use of a written instrument that is itself given testamentary effect because of statutory compliance. This subsequent instrument may be (1) a will, (2) an instrument that revokes the prior will but does not itself dispose of any property, or (3) a codicil. A **codicil** is an addition or supplement to the will that may add to, subtract from, modify, or revoke provisions of an existing will. Ordinarily, it leaves the will intact except for the changes indicated; that is, a codicil generally does not purport to dispose of all of the testator's property or completely revoke

the existing will. All of the foregoing instruments are given effect because they comply with the formalities necessary for creation of a valid will generally.

Revocation by Operation of Law. A will, or part thereof, also may be revoked by operation of law due to changes in the testator's circumstances. For example, some states provide that marriage or marriage plus the birth of a child after the execution of a will revokes it automatically. Many state statutes also provide that a divorce, subsequent to execution of a will, revokes any disposition of property to the former spouse. Under the UPC, however, only a divorce revokes a will by operation of law.

Dependent Relative Revocation. Occasionally, the testator will revoke a will while under a mistaken assumption of law or fact. In order to best carry out the testator's intent—the basic issue in all will construction—courts often apply the **dependent relative revocation doctrine.** Under this doctrine, if the court finds that the testator's revocation is dependent, or conditional, upon the truth of his or her assumption, then the revocation is ineffective if the assumption is, *in fact,* false. For example, the doctrine is commonly applied when the testator destroys the will on the mistaken assumption that a subsequently executed will is valid. If the later will proves invalid—for example, due to noncompliance with the will formalities—the court may apply the doctrine to reinstate the prior will by treating the revocation as conditional on the validity of the second will.

Effect of Subsequent Events

Even if the will has not been revoked, persons named in the will nevertheless may be prevented from receiving property because of events occurring after the execution of the will.

Lapse. Generally, to take property under a will, devisees or legatees must survive (outlive) the testator. If a beneficiary predeceases the testator, the beneficiary's gift is said to **lapse.** The effect of a lapse is dependent on a number of factors. Ordinarily, a will contains a "residuary" clause disposing of all property not otherwise provided for in the will. For example, Todd may leave a valid will devising his farm to Carol and leaving the "rest, residue, and remainder" of his estate to Michael. If Carol predeceases Todd her gift then passes under the residuary clause to Michael. If Michael predeceases Todd, the property in the residuary is distributed as if Todd died intestate. Similarly, if Todd had not included a residuary clause, the property would pass by intestacy.

Most states have enacted anti-lapse statutes, which vary significantly from state to state, to prevent this result in certain situations. Under the UPC, for example, if the deceased devisee is a relative[5] of the testator and leaves "issue" surviving the testator, then the surviving issue of the deceased devisee take the gift in his place. **Issue** generally means lineal descendants, for example, a father's sons and daughters, grandsons and granddaughters, and so on. Lineal descendants are distinguished from "collateral" descendants, such as nieces and nephews.

Ademption. A second doctrine that may prevent a beneficiary from receiving property provided for him in the will is ademption. **Ademption by extinction** occurs when the subject matter of the gift is not in the testator's estate at the time of death. For example, the testator may execute a will devising her farm to X, but subsequently sell the property prior to her death. In this situation, the gift fails and X gets nothing; X usually is not entitled to the proceeds of the sale. The doctrine of ademption by extinction applies only to *specific* bequests and devises—for example, when the testator leaves "my house at 203 Elm Street" to X.

The testator may, after execution of the will but during his lifetime, make a gift of property to a beneficiary under the will. If the testator intends the gift to be in lieu of the bequest or devise, the lifetime gift operates as a partial or total **ademption by satisfaction** of the testamentary disposition. Ademption by satisfaction occurs only when the decedent leaves a valid will. If he or she dies intestate, the analogous doctrine of **advancement** may operate to reduce the amount of property that otherwise would pass to an heir. Under the UPC, lifetime gifts do not operate to reduce the share of a person who would otherwise take, absent some clear indication that the gift is in satisfaction or is an advancement.

Abatement. A beneficiary's share under a will also may be reduced or extinguished by **abatement.** Abatement—or reduction—must occur when there is insufficient property in the estate to satisfy all gifts provided in the will after creditors' claims, taxes, and administration expenses have been paid. An abatement statute determines the order in which the testator's property is applied to satisfy his obligations. The UPC, which is similar to the law applied in most states, provides first that any intention of the testator, either as expressed in the will or implied by the testamentary plan, controls. In the absence of a showing of intention, shares abate without any preference between real or personal property in the following order: (1) property not disposed of by the will (intestate property); (2) residuary devises; (3) general devises; (4) specific devises. If the assets of the estate are insufficient to pay all devises within a given classification, the beneficiaries share those assets pro rata. For example, assume Tom leaves $6,000 to Pam and $4,000 to Sarah. After payment of claims only $5,000 remains to be distributed for general devises. Pam receives $3,000 and Sarah receives $2,000.

Protection of the Testator's Family

Although a person is generally free to dispose of her property on death as she sees fit, the law imposes certain limitations on the ability to disinherit a surviving spouse. At common law, a surviving widow was entitled to **dower,** a life estate[6] in one-third of all real estate owned by the husband at any time during the marriage. A widower, under the comparable right of **curtesy,** was entitled to a life estate in all of his wife's real estate if a child was born alive during the marriage. Dower and curtesy

---

5. For purposes of the UPC statute, "relatives" of the testator include a grandparent or a lineal descendant of a grandparent and do not include persons related to the testator by marriage.

6. Life estates are discussed in Chapter 36.

encumber land titles and provide inadequate protection for surviving spouses because most wealth today is held in the form of personal property. As a result, common law dower and curtesy have been abolished in most jurisdictions.

Most states now protect the spouse through ''forced share'' or ''elective share'' statutes. These statutes give the surviving spouse the option either to take under the testator's will or reject the provisions of the will and receive a share prescribed by statute. This share is commonly either one-third to one-half of the estate, or the share that would have passed to the spouse had the decedent died intestate. If the surviving spouse elects to take the forced share, the estate is not thereby rendered intestate. However, the shares of other beneficiaries must be reduced because by electing, the surviving spouse generally receives more than is provided in the will.

A minority of states[7] provide for spousal protection through the **community property doctrine,** derived from the French and Spanish civil law. In the majority of states (designated ''common law'' states) each spouse owns whatever he or she has earned. In community property states, husband and wife, however, are treated as equal co-owners of property (community property) acquired with the earnings of either during marriage without regard to which spouse actually supports the family. Also included as community property is the income from, or proceeds of, the sale of community property. Property owned by either spouse before marriage or acquired by gift, inheritance, or devise thereafter and the income therefrom are deemed separate property. Therefore, on death, either spouse can dispose of only one-half of the community property. The other one-half belongs to the surviving spouse. Thus, the decedent may transfer by will or intestate succession only his or her separate property and one-half of the community property.

Some degree of protection also is provided to the family by statutes, varying considerably from state to state, that give the surviving spouse and children a preference in certain property over unsecured creditors of the estate and persons to whom the property has been devised by will. These exemptions or allowances are commonly of three types: the homestead exemption, personal property exemptions, and the family allowance. The purpose of a homestead exemption, available in most states, is to protect the family unit by exempting a certain portion of the family residence from creditors' claims. The homestead exemption generally is expressed in terms of a dollar amount, commonly between $1,000 and $10,000, continuing after the death of the head of the family for the benefit of the surviving spouse and minor or dependent children.

In addition to the homestead exemption, the decedent's family generally is entitled to certain items of personal property (such as household furniture, automobiles, appliances, and personal effects) free of general creditors' claims. Finally, most states provide a family allowance during administration of the estate. The allowance entitles the surviving spouse and children to a specified sum of money or property for the support and maintenance of the family while the estate is being administered. Generally the homestead exemption, personal property exemption, and family allowance are in addition to any property otherwise passing to the spouse or children.

Intestate Succession

A person who fails to leave a valid will dies intestate. A person who dies leaving a will that does not dispose of his or her entire estate, whether by the terms of the will or by partial revocation or lapse, dies partially intestate. Intestate property is transferred as provided in state intestate succession statutes, frequently designated ''statutes of descent and distribution.'' ''Descent'' refers to the transfer of real property and ''distribution'' to personal property. Some states provide for differing distribution of real and personal property. Under the UPC, and many other state statutes, all of the decedent's intestate property passes in the same manner.

Persons entitled to the decedent's property if he dies intestate are known as **heirs.** A person has heirs, determined at his death, whether or not he

---

7. Arizona, California, Idaho, Louisiana, Nevada, New Mexico, Texas, and Washington.

leaves a valid will. If the decedent leaves a valid will, the heirs take nothing, unless (as is commonly the case) provision is made for one or more of them in the will. If, however, the decedent is wholly or partially intestate, intestate property passes to the heirs. Thus, if the validity of a will is contested, the parties are commonly the beneficiaries under the will on one side and the heirs on the other.

Operation of a Typical Statute. Statutes of descent and distribution vary substantially from state to state. Typically, property is first distributed to any surviving spouse or children of the decedent. If both survive, they share the estate—for example, one-half goes to the spouse and one-half to the children. If the decedent leaves no surviving spouse or children, the property is distributed to the decedent's parents and their descendants (the brothers, sisters, nieces, and nephews of the decedent). If no persons survive in this class, distribution is made to the decedent's grandparents and their descendants (the uncles, aunts, and cousins of the decedent), great grandparents and their descendants, and so on.

If there are no takers alive in any of the classes listed above, the intestate estate then passes or "escheats" to the state. Note that the UPC, unlike many other state intestate succession statutes, prohibits inheritance by persons more remote than grandparents and their descendants. This approach, in line with modern policy, simplifies proof of heirship and eliminates will contests by remote relatives (so-called laughing heirs), who are ordinarily well beyond the limits of the decedent's probable donative intent.

Degree of Kinship and Representation. As noted above, the portion of the intestate estate not passing to the surviving spouse (or the entire estate if there is no surviving spouse) is distributed first to any surviving descendants (children, grandchildren, etc.) of the decedent. If all descendants are of the same degree of kinship to the decedent, they take equally. If they are of unequal degree, those of more remote degree take by representation.

In the United States the degree of kinship (blood relationship) is determined according to the civil law method. Under this method, degree of relation-

ship between the decedent and collateral relatives is determined by counting the number of generations from the decedent to the common ancestor and from that ancestor down to the relative. In the lineal line (grandparent, parent, child, grandchild), it is simply necessary to count the number of generations, up or down. By applying these rules, the degrees of kinship for common relatives are as follows:

1st degree—the decedent's children and his parents;

2nd degree—the decedent's brothers, sisters, grandparents, and grandchildren;

3rd degree—the decedent's aunts, uncles, nieces, nephews, great grandparents, and great grandchildren;

4th degree—the decedent's great uncles and great aunts (sons and daughters of great grandparents), first cousins (sons and daughters of uncles and aunts), grandnephews and grandnieces (sons and daughters of nephews and nieces), great-great grandparents, and great-great grandchildren.

Assume that Donald dies intestate, survived only by his three children: Alan, Bonnie, and Charles (no surviving spouse). Because they are all of equal degree (first), they share equally; each takes one-third of the estate. Assume, however, that Alan has predeceased Donald, leaving two children surviving, Robert and Sally. Because Robert and Sally are of more remote degree than Bonnie and Charles—Robert and Sally are of second degree (grandchildren), whereas Bonnie and Charles are of first degree (children)—they take by "representation."

Taking by **representation,** commonly known as taking **per stirpes** or **by stocks,** means that the lineal descendants or "issue" of a deceased heir inherit the share of an estate (the intestate's) that their immediate ancestor would have inherited had he survived (outlived) the intestate. To illustrate, because Alan has predeceased Donald, his share passes by representation to his children Robert and Sally equally; each takes one-sixth of Donald's estate. Note that Robert and Sally are not entitled to inherit from Donald if Alan is still alive. If both Alan and Sally predecease Donald, but Sally leaves three children surviving (Donald's great grandchildren), Ed, Frank, and Gail, they share Sally's one-

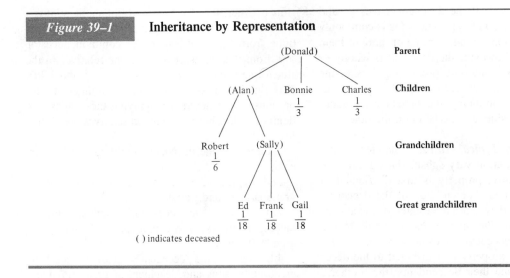

Figure 39–1 **Inheritance by Representation**

( ) indicates deceased

sixth equally (that is, one-eighteenth each). Donald's estate is thus divided as shown in Figure 39–1.

In contrast to per stirpes distribution, a will or intestate succession statute may provide that property is to be distributed **per capita.** Under this method, the estate is simply divided by the number of surviving descendants, regardless of degree. Thus in the preceding example, under a per capita distribution, Bonnie, Charles, Robert, Ed, Frank, and Gail each take one-sixth of Donald's estate.

Simultaneous Death. Rights of heirs in inheritance cases depend upon surviving (outliving) the intestate. A common problem in estate administration arises when several family members are involved in a common disaster and die simultaneously or within a few days of each other. The frequency of this problem is, of course, aggravated by modern life with its increased mobility and multiple forms of transportation. To resolve one aspect of this issue, forty-seven states and the District of Columbia have adopted the **Uniform Simultaneous Death Act.** Section 1 of the Act provides that if the disposition of property by will or intestate succession depends upon priority of death *and* there is no sufficient evidence that persons have died otherwise than simultaneously, each person's property is distributed as if she had survived. This

rule represents only a partial solution to the problem, however, because if evidence can be adduced regarding who survived, even if only for a second, the survivor is entitled to inherit. As a result, considerable litigation has been generated on the grisly issue of who lived longest after a common tragedy, necessitating multiple administrations of the same property. The UPC, borrowing a tool long used in wills and trusts, resolves the problem for most cases by requiring an heir to survive the intestate by five days (120 hours) in order to inherit from him. In other words, a person who fails to outlive the decedent by 120 hours is deemed to have predeceased him for purposes of intestate succession. The UPC applies the same rule to those taking under a will. An exception to this requirement is made if its application would cause the estate to escheat to the state. In other words, no minimum survivorship requirement is imposed upon the last eligible relative of the intestate.

Introduction to Trusts

A trust is an extremely useful tool for family settlement, as well as for tax and estate planning. It is simply one of the various methods by which property may be transferred. Other methods include sale or gift during life and will or intestate succession on death.

A **trust,** in essence, *splits* title to property between the **trustee,** who holds legal title, and the **beneficiary** or beneficiaries who hold beneficial or equitable title. The trustee is subject to various duties, imposed by law or the terms of the trust, to deal with the property for the benefit of the beneficiaries. The person creating the trust is known as the **settlor** or **trustor.** The property subject to the trust is variously known as the **trust property, trust res, corpus,** or simply "subject matter of the trust." The benefit may be conferred by a trust created during the settlor's lifetime—an **inter vivos trust**—or in his will on death—a **testamentary trust.** The settlor's *intention* is paramount in construing the terms of the trust to determine the duties and powers of the trustee and rights of the beneficiaries.

Types of Trusts

Express Trusts. Trusts are generally classified as either "express" or "implied." An **express trust** arises as a result of the settlor's *language* indicating her intent to create it. Express trusts are either private or charitable. In a **private trust,** the most common type, the trust property is devoted to the use of specified persons designated as beneficiaries. In a **charitable trust,** the property is devoted to charitable purposes beneficial to the community in favor of a class of beneficiaries who are not specifically designated.

Purposes of Express Trusts. The basic motivation for creation of a trust is donative: the settlor wishes to confer the benefit of the property upon the beneficiary. The settlor usually transfers the property in trust, rather than by outright gift or devise, to provide for the management and possession of the property by someone other than the person or persons who are to enjoy the benefits of the property. The settlor may desire this separation of management and enjoyment for many reasons. For example, the beneficiaries may be children or others who through mental infirmity, senility, illness, drug or alcohol addiction, or mere immaturity or improvidence are unable, in the settlor's estimation, to adequately manage the property. The settlor also may wish to limit the permissible uses of the property—

for example, to the support, maintenance, or education of the beneficiary or for charitable purposes. The trust may also be used to provide for successive beneficiaries. For example, the settlor may, in a will, leave an apartment building in trust to pay the income to her ailing mother for life for her support and care, with the remainder in fee simple passing to her children.

Implied Trusts. **Implied trusts** arise by operation of law, not by the express language of the settlor. They are of two types: resulting trusts and constructive trusts. A resulting trust, like an express trust, is based on the intent of the person creating it. In a resulting trust, however, intent is presumed when the surrounding circumstances indicate that the settlor does not intend that the person taking or holding the property should have the beneficial interest in it. Resulting trusts are discussed later in this chapter.

A constructive trust, unlike any of the foregoing trusts, is not based upon intent but is imposed to redress wrong or prevent unjust enrichment and is therefore remedial in nature. Because a constructive trust is merely one form of restitution, constructive trusts are covered in the basic restitution discussion in Chapter 15.

Creation, Modification, and Termination of Trusts

The private express trust results from the settlor's indication of an intention to create it. In addition to intent, a trust requires trust property, a trustee, and a beneficiary.

Methods of Creating a Trust

The settlor must own or control the property that is to become the trust corpus. Either real—for example, an apartment building—or personal—for example, stocks and bonds—property may be used. A trust is most commonly created by a *transfer* of the property from the settlor to another person as trustee for the beneficiary or beneficiaries. This transfer may be accomplished during the settlor's life creating an inter vivos trust or upon her death by will forming a testamentary trust. Creation of a trust, therefore, ordinarily involves at least three people (the settlor, trustee, and beneficiary) requiring a transfer of the property from the settlor to the trustee.

A trust may also be created by the settlor's *declaration* that he holds the property as trustee for another person. In this case, the trust arises without any transfer of title to the property. Assume Andrew, the owner of a bond, declares himself as its trustee for specified beneficiaries. Andrew, the settlor, is also trustee of the bond for the beneficiaries. The settlor has the capacity to create a trust by declaration or inter vivos transfer to the extent he has capacity to transfer the same property outright. He must have a testamentary capacity to create a trust by will.

Intention to Create a Trust

A trust is created only if the settlor properly manifests an intention to create it. This manifestation may be made by conduct or more commonly by written or spoken words. Generally, no particular form of words or conduct is required to manifest this intention. Courts are, however, often required to determine whether the settlor's language evidences an intent to make a trust or is merely "precatory." Precatory words are those amounting merely to the transferor's suggestion or hope that the transferee will use or dispose of the property in a given way, but allowing the transferee full discretion in deciding whether or not to follow the suggestion or comply with the wish. For example, rather than transferring property "to Carol in trust for Bob," the language used may instead be "to Carol hoping (wishing, desiring, recommending, relying, requesting, on confidence) that she will use the income from the property to care for Bob." In these situations, the court must interpret the language used, often contained in a decedent's will, to determine whether a trust is created under which Carol is trustee of the property for Bob's benefit, or whether she is entitled to the property beneficially, subject at most to a moral or ethical obligation.

In the case that follows, the court considers whether a valid trust has been created.

Cabaniss v. Cabaniss
464 A.2d 87 (D.C. App. 1983)

Charles Cabaniss committed suicide on September 16, 1979, leaving a will naming his wife (appellant) as executrix. Two days before his suicide Cabaniss telephoned his daughter Stephanie (appellee) and asked her to keep some checks that he had set aside for another daughter, Carla, who was incompetent. The following day Cabaniss took the checks to Stephanie's home and told her to set up a joint checking account for Carla's benefit. Cabaniss also wrote a letter to his attorney giving him power of attorney to provide Stephanie the authority to open a bank account for the benefit of Carla with some checks endorsed by Cabaniss. A postscript to the letter stated that Stephanie was "to act as trustee and withdrawals are to be used only for the benefit of Carla." Cabaniss then told Stephanie he would "check out" the letter with his attorney and implied that he would accompany her to the bank at a later time. Cabaniss endorsed the checks which he left with the letter in a file cabinet at Stephanie's house. Stephanie then left town for the day. When she returned, she found that Cabaniss had left his key to her house inside the house. The following day Cabaniss committed suicide in his office.

The issue before the trial court was whether the checks in Stephanie's possession constituted part of Cabaniss' estate or whether the checks were trust property that passed outside the probate estate. The trial court ruled that Cabaniss had created a trust funded with the checks of which Stephanie was trustee and Carla was beneficiary. Appellant appealed.

Belson, Associate Judge

. . . The elements of a trust, including an *inter vivos* trust created for the benefit of a third person, are the following: (1) a trustee, who holds the trust property and is subject to equitable duties to deal with it for the benefit of another; (2) a beneficiary, to whom the trustee owes equitable duties to deal with the trust property for his benefit; (3) trust property, which is held by the trustee for the beneficiary. . . .

Unless otherwise provided by statute, such as the

Statute of Frauds or Statute of Wills, an enforceable trust can be created without a writing. . . . Essential to the creation of a trust is the settlor's manifestation or external expression of his intention to create a trust. . . . Such manifestation may be by written or spoken language or by conduct, in light of all surrounding circumstances. . . .

Appellant contends that decedent failed to demonstrate sufficiently his intention to create a trust by his incomplete testamentary transfer of the endorsed checks to Stephanie. . . . She also contends that decedent simply designated Stephanie as his agent to hold the checks for safekeeping pending his further instructions regarding their disposition, and that such agency authority terminated with his death. Alternatively appellant asserts that decedent failed to manifest an unambiguous firm intention to create a present trust. . . . In support of this contention appellant maintains that decedent specifically conditioned any trust arrangement upon his accompanying Stephanie to the bank to open up the trust account following a disposition of the trust funds with attorney Dolphin. Appellant also asserts that decedent, at most, delivered possession of the endorsed checks to Stephanie, and not title, because he retained access to and subsequent control over them. . . .

We agree with the trial court that decedent adequately manifested his intention to create a trust and subsequently complied with the formalities necessary to bring about that result. In his oral declarations to Stephanie and in his letters executed in Stephanie's presence, decedent imperatively and unambiguously designated his daughter Carla as beneficiary, appointed Stephanie trustee, and identified the endorsed checks as the trust property. Simultaneously, decedent unconditionally negotiated the checks to Stephanie by endorsing them in blank and by delivering them to, and leaving them in, Stephanie's exclusive possession. . . . Moreover, decedent's later surrender of his key to Stephanie's house confirms that he relinquished all control of the trust property to Stephanie. . . . Such definitive acts negate any inference that Stephanie held the checks as decedent's agent, subject to his further instructions regarding disposition of the checks. . . .

We also conclude that the record does not support appellant's contention that decedent manifested his intention to create a trust *only* when, but not until, he initiated a trip to the bank with Stephanie or discussed the trust arrangements with Dolphin. It was Stephanie who raised the possibility that decedent's cooperation might be needed to open a savings account. Decedent had already made clear that he was creating the trust, and his agreement to comply with any requirements of a savings institution did not alter that fact. Nor did the agreement to review the matter with attorney Dolphin have that effect. We are satisfied that Dr. Cabaniss went to his unfortunate death in the belief that he had taken additional steps to assure the well-being of his incompetent daughter.

We conclude that the trial court correctly ruled that decedent had unconditionally manifested his intention to create a trust, that the trust was created for the benefit of Carla. . . .

[Judgment affirmed.]

Formalities of Creation

Requirement of a Writing. Unless otherwise required by statute, an enforceable inter vivos trust can be created without a writing. Thus, oral trusts in personal property are recognized as valid and enforceable. Almost all jurisdictions, however, require that express trusts of real property be evidenced by a writing.

Testamentary Trusts. A valid will is necessary to create a trust by testamentary disposition. In order to create a valid trust by will, the will must indicate an intention to create a trust, the identity of the beneficiaries, the identity of the trust property, and the purposes of the trust.

Frequently, the testator desires, not to create a trust in a will, but, by testamentary disposition, to add property to a trust created inter vivos. Such a trust is commonly known as a **pour over trust** because on death property is "poured over," or into, the living trust.

Pour over trusts are advantageous because they eliminate the necessity of repeating the terms of the trust, which may be long and involved, in the will, and remove property so transferred from involvement in probate proceedings. As a result, these trusts have been upheld as valid on several theories against attack on the grounds that they constitute an invalid testamentary disposition. Today, the problem is resolved in forty-three states by the **Uniform Testamentary Additions to Trusts Act**, which also is included as part of the Uniform Probate Code. Under §1 of the Act, if the trust is identified in the testator's will,[8] and its terms are set forth in a written instrument (other than a will), and it is executed before or concurrently with execution of the testator's will, then a devise or bequest to the trust is valid even if the trust is amendable or revocable, or both, and even if the trust is in fact amended after execution of the will.

The Trustee

Title to trust property is held by the trustee subject to equitable duties to deal with it for the benefit of another, the beneficiary. Unless the settlor manifests an intention to the contrary, a trust is created even though no trustee is named in the instrument creating the trust, or the named trustee is dead or otherwise incapable of taking title to the property, or the named trustee refuses to serve. This rule applies to inter vivos and testamentary trusts and in both cases the court appoints a trustee to administer the trust.

The settlor may appoint a single trustee or may name two or more co-trustees, whose functions, powers, and duties may differ. Co-trustees hold legal title to the property as joint tenants.

As a general rule, any natural person may take and hold property in trust to the extent that he may do so for his own benefit. Private corporations (artificial persons), such as trust companies or banks, are capable of holding and administering property in trust subject to statutes governing corporate existence, and if the purposes of the trust are consistent with those for which the corporation is created. Similarly, a sovereign, such as the United States, a state, or municipality, may hold and administer property in trust.

Because a trust may be created by declaration,

the settlor is capable of acting as trustee. A beneficiary also may be a trustee unless he is both the sole beneficiary and sole trustee. In that situation, the legal and equitable interests in the property "merge" and the beneficiary owns the property free of any trust.

The trustee is entitled to compensation out of the trust property for his or her services, but may waive this right. The amount of compensation (usually a percentage of income or principal) may be fixed by statute, the terms of the trust, or by the court.

The Beneficiary

Because a trust is a means of making a disposition of property, the person receiving the beneficial interest, the beneficiary, must be definitely ascertained. The description is sufficiently definite if (1) the beneficiary is specifically named in the trust instrument, or (2) his or her identity may either be ascertained from facts existing when the trust is created or, in most circumstances, facts occurring thereafter.

The trust may designate one or several beneficiaries. If there is more than one beneficiary, the beneficial interest may be held simultaneously (as joint tenants or tenants in common) or successively (one beneficiary may be a life tenant and another a remainderman). Any natural person or corporation having capacity to take and hold legal title to property has capacity to be a beneficiary of a trust of that property.

The trust may designate a definite class of persons as beneficiaries. A class is definite as long as the identity of its members is ascertainable, even though it consists of a changing or shifting group, which may increase or decrease in size—for example, the class may be affected by births, deaths, or other events. The settlor may specifically name the members of the class or may use more general language, transferring property in trust, for example, for the benefit of "children," "grandchildren," "nephews," or "issue."

A settlor may transfer the property in trust for the erection or maintenance of tombstones or monuments, the care of graves, or the care of specific animals. Because there is no beneficiary to enforce the trust, such a distribution is not a trust at all

---

8. The testator need not be the settlor of the trust, which could therefore be created in another person's will.

under the basic definition, but is commonly known as an **honorary trust**. Legal recognition of honorary trusts varies from state to state, though many jurisdictions, by statute, validate provisions for the maintenance of graves and monuments. In any event, the purported trustee is not allowed to keep the property. He must either apply it for the stated purpose or return it to the settlor.

Nature, Extent, and Transfer of the Beneficiary's Interest. Modern trust law treats the beneficiary as owning an equitable interest in the underlying trust property. The extent of the beneficiary's interest in that property depends upon the settlor's intent. For example, the beneficiary may have an absolute right to the property, or may merely have a contingent interest. His or her share of trust property may be explicitly stated or may, by the terms of the trust, be subject to the trustee's uncontrolled discretion (a "discretionary" trust). The trustee may have the power to exclude the beneficiary altogether. The beneficiary's interest may begin or cease only upon occurrence of a designated event such as marriage, starting college, or reaching a stated age. The duration of the interest may be fixed or indefinite. The trust may provide that the trustee will pay or apply only so much of the trust property and income therefrom as is necessary for the education or support of the beneficiary (a "support" trust). In short, the trust instrument determines the extent of the beneficiary's interest.

Unless the beneficiary's interest is one that terminates on death, such as a life estate, it passes, like other property, by will or intestate succession at the death of the beneficiary. The interest also may be transferred inter vivos (by sale, gift, or through attachment by creditors), unless the interest is subject to a spendthrift clause. In a **spendthrift trust** the beneficiary may not voluntarily transfer the interest, and creditors of the beneficiary may not reach it to satisfy their claims. In other words, the beneficiary may not transfer the interest either voluntarily or involuntarily. The spendthrift aspect of the trust may be imposed either by the terms of the trust, or, in some states, by statute.

Spendthrift trusts are designed to protect the beneficiary against his or her own wastefulness, incompetence, inexperience, or improvidence. A settlor may not create a spendthrift trust for himself, because this would be a simple way to frustrate his creditors. Spendthrift clauses are upheld in most United States jurisdictions on the ground that the settlor, as owner of property, should be able to qualify the interest transferred to the beneficiary as long as no violation of public policy is involved.

Modification and Termination of Trusts

As a general rule, the settlor has no power to revoke or modify a properly created trust *unless* he or she has reserved such a power by the terms of the trust. Even if the settlor fails to reserve a power of revocation or fails to exercise a reserved power, the trust may terminate upon expiration of the time period for which the trust was created or upon the happening of a certain event, such as the completion of the beneficiary's college education. The trust also may be terminated by consent of the parties in certain situations. For example, if all beneficiaries consent, the trust will be terminated if all beneficiaries have capacity and the material purposes of the trust have been accomplished.

Even if trust purposes have not been accomplished *and* the settlor has not reserved a power of revocation or modification, the trust may be modified or revoked with the consent of all of the beneficiaries and the settlor. This rule only applies if the trust is created inter vivos and the settlor is still living. This method would, for example, be a means of terminating a spendthrift trust, which could not be terminated by consent of the beneficiaries alone.

In the course of administering a private trust, it may become impossible or illegal to follow the settlor's directions, or due to circumstances unknown to or not anticipated by the settlor, following them will defeat or substantially impair accomplishment of the trust purposes. In such cases, the court may permit or direct the trustee not to comply with the direction in the trust, to perform an act not authorized, or even to do an act forbidden by terms of the trust.[9]

---

9. A similar, though distinguishable, problem arising in charitable trusts is governed by the *cy pres* doctrine, discussed later in this chapter.

Trust Administration

The trustee is under a duty to administer the trust. In an inter vivos trust, the trustee derives his or her authority from the trust instrument and administers the trust without court supervision. A testamentary trustee, like an executor or administrator, is appointed by the court and usually is accountable to it.

Powers of the Trustee

The trustee may exercise those powers conferred upon him by the terms of the trust (express powers), or those necessary and appropriate to carry out the purposes of the trust (implied powers), which are not forbidden by terms of the trust. Modern trusts generally grant the trustee very broad powers in accomplishing trust purposes. These powers allow the trustee to act quickly in an emergency and to adapt the trust to changing circumstances without obtaining court authorization. In many states, statutes such as the Uniform Trustee's Powers Act confer a large number of customary powers upon the trustee. Express powers may be "mandatory," requiring the trustee to do an act such as invest in a certain type of property or "discretionary," giving the trustee the privilege but not the duty to perform. The trustee incurs no liability for exercising or failing to exercise a discretionary power, unless he has abused his discretion. Generally, the court will not interfere and substitute its judgment for that of the trustee even if the court would act differently in the situation.

Duties of the Trustee

The "Fiduciary" Relationship. The most important duty imposed upon the trustee is "loyalty," requiring the trustee to administer the trust solely in the interest of the beneficiary. This duty embodies the fiduciary relationship existing between the trustee and beneficiary. A **fiduciary relationship** is simply one in which one person is under a duty to act solely for the benefit of another concerning matters within the scope of the relation. In addition to trustee and beneficiary, other fiduciary relationships exist, for example, between guardian and ward, attorney and client, agent and principal, and partners. The extent of the obligations imposed differs somewhat among the various fiduciary relations. The duties of the trustee are the most intensive of any fiduciary.

The fiduciary duty of loyalty imposes a duty upon the trustee

1. not to profit at the expense of the beneficiary, or use trust property for the trustee's personal benefit;
2. not to enter into competition with the beneficiary without the beneficiary's consent, unless authorized to do so by the terms of the trust or the court;
3. not to sell property to or buy property from the trust, without court approval, regardless of the trustee's good faith, the fairness of the transaction, or whether the trustee makes a profit;[10]
4. not to disclose to third persons information acquired as trustee, if the effect of the disclosure would be detrimental to the beneficiary's interest; and
5. not to delegate the administration of the trust to a third party.

Other duties owed by the trustee to the beneficiary include the duty to

1. keep and render clear and accurate accounts concerning trust administration;
2. give, on request, complete and accurate information regarding the nature and amount of trust property, and to permit inspection of trust property and records;
3. take, keep control of, and preserve the trust property;
4. take reasonable steps to enforce claims that the trustee holds against third parties concerning the trust, and to defend actions that may result in a loss of the trust estate;
5. prevent commingling of trust property with the trustee's own property or that held by the trustee upon other trusts, and to ear-

---

10. Additionally, a trustee may not purchase for personal benefit property that he or she is under a duty to purchase for the trust. The court may allow the trustee to buy trust property only if it finds the purchase to be in the best interests of the beneficiary.

mark the property as belonging to the trust; and

6. deal impartially with the beneficiaries, if there are two or more, and if the trust is created to pay income to the beneficiary, to pay the net income at reasonable intervals, or according to terms of the trust.

The "Prudent Person" Rule. The trust estate is ordinarily composed of income producing property, such as cash, stocks, bonds, rental real property, a farm, or a business. The trustee usually is required to make periodic payments of the income from the property to the beneficiaries. In managing the property, the trustee must use reasonable care and skill to preserve it and also is under a duty to make it productive. These duties require the trustee to invest the property or to periodically sell a trust asset and reinvest the proceeds. The settlor often specifies permissible types of trust investments which, of course, are binding upon the trustee.

In the absence of the settlor's express direction, many states have statutes governing investments by trustees. A few of these statutes are of the so-called "legal list" type, limiting the trustee to certain specified types of investments. Most states, however, either by statute or judicial decision, judge trustees' investments by the **prudent person rule.** Under this approach, the trustee is under a duty to the beneficiary to make only those investments that a prudent person would make of his or her own property taking into consideration both the preservation of the estate and the amount and regularity of the income to be generated. The prudent person rule requires the trustee to make a reasonable investigation into the safety of the investment and probable income to be generated. This investigation ordinarily involves securing customary financial information and may include consideration of advice from bankers, lawyers, accountants, or brokers.

Regardless of the rule generally applied, the terms of the trust determine proper trust investments. That is, an investment permitted either by a legal list or the prudent person approach may be prohibited in the trust instrument. Conversely, a speculative investment, not otherwise permissible, may be authorized. Therefore, as in almost all trust issues, the terms of the trust must be carefully consulted.

Liability of the Trustee

A trustee who violates the duty of loyalty, or any other duty owed to the beneficiary, commits a "breach of trust." A breach of trust renders the trustee liable to the beneficiary for any loss or depreciation in value of the trust property resulting from the breach, any profit resulting from the breach of trust, and any profit that would have been made by the trust had there been no breach. For example, the trustee is liable if he or she is directed by terms of the trust to purchase IBM stock and fails to do so, resulting in loss when the price of the stock rises. The trustee would also be liable for profits made by using trust property for personal business.

The trustee is not liable for loss or depreciation of the property or for failure to make a profit in the absence of a breach of trust. Thus, if through no fault of the trustee trust property is lost or stolen, or if the trustee fails to buy profitable securities that he is authorized but under no duty to purchase, no liability follows.

As a general rule, only the beneficiary can maintain a suit against the trustee to enforce the trust or for breach of trust. In an action by the beneficiary, the court may compel the trustee to perform duties under the trust, issue an order preventing the trustee from committing a breach of trust, compel the trustee to redress a prior breach of trust, or remove the trustee. The settlor may not sue to enforce the trust or for breach of trust unless he or she has retained some interest, such as a power of revocation, in the trust property.

The trustee is entitled to indemnity from the trust estate for expenses properly incurred in trust administration. The trustee also is entitled to indemnity for liability incurred in contract or tort arising in the proper course of trust administration.

In the following case, the court was required to determine whether the trustee committed a breach of trust.

Allard v. Pacific National Bank
663 P.2d 104 (Wash. 1983)

J. T. and Georgiana Stone created testamentary trusts known as the "Stone Trusts" naming defendant Pacific National Bank as trustee and plaintiffs Freeman Allard and Evelyn Orkney as beneficiaries. In 1978, the sole asset of the Stone Trusts was a piece of real property located in downtown Seattle that was subject to a 99-year lease that J. T. and Georgiana Stone had entered into with Seafirst Bank in 1952. The lease also provided that Seafirst had the right of first refusal to purchase the property. In 1977, Seafirst assigned its interest in the lease to Seattle Credit Union (Credit Union). In 1978, Credit Union offered to purchase the property from the trustee for $139,900. The trustee rejected the offer but offered to sell the property to Credit Union for $200,000. Credit Union accepted the offer and paid $200,000 to the trustee who then deeded the property to Credit Union.

The beneficiaries sued the trustee alleging that it had breached its fiduciary duties. The trial court ruled in favor of the trustee, holding that it had acted in good faith when it sold the property. The beneficiaries appealed.

Dolliver, Justice

. . . Plaintiffs' argument regarding Pacific Bank's alleged breach of its fiduciary duties is twofold. First, Pacific Bank had a duty to inform them of the sale of the Third and Columbia property. Second, Pacific Bank breached its fiduciary duties by failing either to obtain an independent appraisal of the Third and Columbia property or to place the property on the open market prior to selling it to Seattle Credit Union. We agree with plaintiffs' position in both instances and hold defendant breached its fiduciary duty in its management of the trusts. . . .

The Stone Trusts gave Pacific Bank "full power to . . . manage, improve, sell, lease, mortgage, pledge, encumber, and exchange the whole or any part of the assets of [the] trust estate". Under such an agreement, the trustee is not required to secure the consent of trust beneficiaries before selling trust assets. . . . The trustee owes to the beneficiaries, however, the highest degree of good faith, care, loyalty, and integrity. . . .

Pacific Bank claims it was obligated to sell the property to Credit Union since Credit Union, as assignee of the lease agreement with Seafirst Bank, had a right of first refusal to purchase the property.

Since it did not need to obtain the consent of the beneficiaries before selling trust assets, Pacific Bank argues it also was not required to inform the beneficiaries of the sale. We disagree. The beneficiaries could have offered to purchase the property at a higher price than the offer by Credit Union, thereby forcing Credit Union to pay a higher price to exercise its right of first refusal as assignee of the lease agreement. Furthermore, letters from the beneficiaries to Pacific Bank indicated their desire to retain the Third and Columbia property. While the beneficiaries could not have prevented Pacific Bank from selling the property, they presumably could have outbid Credit Union for the property. This opportunity should have been afforded to them. . . .

That the settlor had created a trust and thus required the beneficiaries to enjoy their property interests indirectly does not imply the beneficiaries are to be kept in ignorance of the trust, the nature of the trust property, and the details of its administration. . . . If the beneficiaries are able to hold the trustee to proper standards of care and honesty and procure the benefits to which they are entitled, they must know of what the trust property consists and how it is being managed. . . .

The trustee must inform beneficiaries . . . of all material facts in connection with a nonroutine transaction which significantly affects the trust estate and the interests of the beneficiaries prior to the transaction taking place. The duty to inform is particularly required in this case where the only asset of the trusts was the property on the corner of Third and Columbia. Under the circumstances found in this case failure to inform was an egregious breach of fiduciary duty and defies the course of conduct any reasonable person would take, much less a prudent investor.

We also conclude Pacific Bank breached its fiduciary duties regarding management of the Stone trusts by failing to obtain the best possible price for the Third and Columbia property. Pacific Bank made no attempt to obtain a more favorable price for the property from Credit Union by, for example, negotiating to cancel the restrictive provisions in the lease originally negotiated with Seafirst Bank. . . . The bank neither offered the property for sale on the open market, . . . nor did it obtain an independent outside appraisal of the Third and Columbia property to determine its fair market value. . . .

Washington courts have not yet considered the nature of a trustee's duty of care regarding the sale of trust assets. Other courts, however, generally require that a trustee when selling trust assets try to obtain the maximum price for the asset. . . . Some courts specifically require trustees to obtain an independent appraisal of the property. . . . Other courts merely require that a trustee determine fair market value by placing the property on the open market. . . .

We agree . . . that a trustee may determine the best possible price for trust property either by obtaining an independent appraisal of the property or by "testing the market" to determine what a willing buyer would pay. The record discloses none of these actions were taken by the defendant. By its failure to obtain the best possible price for the Third and Columbia property, defendant breached its fiduciary duty as the prudent manager of the trusts. . . .

We hold defendant breached its fiduciary duty and reverse the trial court on this issue. . . .

[Judgment reversed and remanded.]

Principal and Income Allocation

In many trusts, the interests of the beneficiaries are successive. In this situation, one beneficiary, the income beneficiary, is entitled to income from the trust property, commonly for life. A later beneficiary is then to receive the trust property, or principal, outright on the termination of the income beneficiary's interest. For example, assume Oliver, in his will, leaves an apartment building and stocks and bonds to First National Bank in trust, to pay the income annually to Oliver's wife Wanda for her life. On Wanda's death, the property is to be conveyed to Oliver's son Fred, in fee simple; Wanda has a life estate and Fred a remainder. Because Wanda and Fred have separate and distinct interests in the property, during Wanda's life the trustee must allocate receipts and expenditures relating to the property between the two beneficiaries. A common trust administration problem is to determine how much to pay the income beneficiary each year or, stated conversely, how much to retain for the remainderman. The net income payable currently to the income beneficiary is ascertained by subtracting expenditures allocable to income from receipts allocable to income. This process of apportionment is commonly known as **principal and income allocation.**

As always, the trust instrument may dictate how various receipts and expenditures are to be allocated. In the absence of such express provision, the issue is resolved in most states by the **Uniform Principal and Income Act,** originally promulgated in 1931, and revised in 1962. Nine states have adopted the 1931 version,[11] and thirty have enacted the revised 1962 Act.[12] The following general allocation rules are derived from the 1962 Act.

General Allocation Rules

Income is the return in money or property derived from the use of, or as profit produced by, the principal. Thus, ordinary current receipts are credited to income. Against these gross receipts, ordinary current expenses, including repairs and a reasonable allowance for depreciation, incurred in managing the trust property are deducted.[13] Thus, the income beneficiary generally is entitled to the net income of any business or farming operation conducted by the trust, computed in accordance with generally accepted accounting principles. Any tax paid by the trustee upon income is charged against income.

---

11. Alabama, Colorado, Kentucky, Oklahoma, Pennsylvania, Tennessee, Vermont, Virginia, and West Virginia.

12. Alaska, Arizona, Arkansas, California, Connecticut, Florida, Hawaii, Idaho, Illinois, Indiana, Kansas, Maryland, Michigan, Minnesota, Mississippi, Montana, Nebraska, Nevada, New Mexico, New York, North Carolina, North Dakota, Oregon, South Carolina, South Dakota, Texas, Utah, Washington, Wisconsin, and Wyoming.

13. Interest received and paid on trust property, being income statement items, are allocated to income. If trust property is subject to a mortgage, only the portion of any mortgage payment constituting interest is charged to income. The portion that reduces the principal of the indebtedness is deducted from principal.

In contrast, principal is the property set aside by the settlor to be held in trust and eventually delivered to the remainderman, while its return or use is in the meantime taken or received by the income beneficiary. Principal also includes property received in substitution for, or as a change in form of, the original principal. Therefore, proceeds from the sale or exchange of the trust property are principal. Any gain or loss resulting from such a disposition is allocated to principal. Conversely, losses incurred in the sale, exchange, destruction, or casualty of the trust property are charged against principal, but any insurance proceeds received upon loss, damage, theft, or destruction of trust property are added to principal. Additionally, proceeds of property taken on condemnation (eminent domain) proceedings are principal.

Deducted from amounts allocated to principal are costs incurred in investing and reinvesting principal, expenses in preparation of principal for rental or sale, and expenses incurred in maintaining or defending any action to construe the trust, to protect it or the property, or assure the title of any trust property. In addition, the cost of extraordinary repairs, or expenditures incurred in making a capital improvement to the property, are payable out of principal. Similarly, the cost of special assessments levied against the trust property for improvements are also charged to principal.

Finally, the cost of periodic judicial accounting, the trustee's regular compensation, and the trust's current management expenses are divided equally between principal and income. In order to equalize income distributions from year to year, the trustee may estimate expenditures out of income in advance, and withhold sufficient income from distribution to build up a reserve to meet them. Similarly, a trustee who incurs unanticipated, large expenses out of income may spread the payment over several years.

Unproductive and Wasting Property

When a trust is created for successive beneficiaries, the trustee is under a duty to the income beneficiary both to preserve the property and to make it productive in order to produce a reasonable income. The trustee owes the beneficiary entitled to the principal the duty to preserve the trust estate. The trustee must therefore balance the two interests. The law addresses this balancing problem under the related concepts of unproductive and wasting property.

Trust property is or may become unproductive or underproductive. That is, property may be valuable but yield no income, or income substantially lower than the current rate of return on trust investments. Because the trustee is required to make the trust property productive, he is under a duty to the income beneficiary to sell such property within a reasonable time and invest the proceeds in income producing property, even if not directed to do so by the settlor. The terms of the trust may, however, direct or permit the trustee to retain unproductive or underproductive property.

Wasting property consists of interests that terminate or necessarily depreciate over time either because of the nature of the interest or because of the character of the property involved. Examples of such property include leaseholds and other property generating income only for a limited period, royalties, patent rights, assets consumed or depleted by use (such as mines, oil and gas wells, quarries, and timber land), or property worn out by use (such as buildings, machinery, or farm implements).

If part of the trust estate is wasting property, the trustee is under a duty to the beneficiary entitled to principal to either make a provision for amortization—that is, periodically set aside from the receipts generated by the property a sum necessary to replace the depreciation of the property—or sell the property. Note that apportioning receipts between successive beneficiaries when trust property is unproductive protects the *income beneficiary,* whereas apportionment when the property is wasting protects the remainderman entitled to *principal.*

Securities as Trust Property

Frequently the trust property will include securities such as stocks and bonds. Securities present several principal and income allocation problems.

Share Dividends and Share Splits. Corporate distributions in the form of a share split or share dividend are principal. For example, assume B holds shares of XYZ Co. as trustee to pay the income to

C for life, remainder to D. Assume the company declares a dividend payable in its own shares, or a "2 for 1" share split. In either case, the additional shares are added to principal. Note that dividends payable in share or other securities of a company other than the one declaring the dividend are income. Therefore, if XYZ Co. declares a dividend payable in shares of ABC Co., the distribution is income.

Cash Dividends and Other Distributions. Dividends payable in cash or property other than shares of the declaring corporation, whether ordinary or extraordinary, are income. If the trustee has the option of receiving a dividend either in cash or in shares of the distributing corporation, the dividend is income regardless of the option chosen by the trustee. Distributions made pursuant to a total or partial liquidation of the corporation, including a merger, consolidation, or reorganization, are principal. The trustee is entitled to rely upon any statement by the corporation concerning the source or character of any dividend or other distribution.

Rights to Subscribe. A right given to shareholders to subscribe to shares or other securities issued by the *distributing* corporation and the proceeds of any sale of that right is *principal*. In contrast, rights to subscribe to shares or securities of *other* corporations and the proceeds of their sale are income. For example, if by virtue of owning XYZ Co. shares the trustee obtains the right to subscribe to additional XYZ Co. shares and ABC Co. shares, the former rights are principal and the latter are income.

Bond Premium and Discount. In addition to stock, bonds are also frequently held as trust investments. Clearly the income beneficiary is entitled to the interest from these securities, but an allocation problem arises if they are purchased by the trust at a premium or a discount. For example, a bond with a purchase price greater than its face value is purchased at a premium: the trustee may pay $1,050 for a bond with a face value of $1,000 payable in 3 years. In this situation, the bond is in essence a wasting asset, and one may argue that periodic amortization deductions should be made from amounts paid to the income beneficiary. Con-

versely, when bonds are purchased at a discount— for example, a bond purchased at $950 paying $1,000 in 3 years—the income beneficiary may argue that the difference between the cost of the bond and the amount paid at maturity is income to which he is entitled in addition to periodic interest payments. These arguments are rejected by the Uniform Principal and Income Act for the sake of convenience and ease of trust administration. Under the Act, all interest on bonds purchased by the trustee at a *premium* is income. If the bond is purchased at a *discount,* the entire amount collected at maturity is principal. Thus, in both cases, the income beneficiary is entitled to the periodic interest payments, no more and no less, whereas the principal receives the face of the bond at maturity, no more and no less. The Act recognizes an exception to this rule for bonds "payable at a future time in accordance with a fixed schedule of appreciation in excess of the price at which it was issued," such as U.S. savings bonds. These bonds bear no interest but appreciate in value as they reach maturity. In this case, the incremental appreciation in value is distributed as income.

Charitable Trusts

In a private trust the property is applied to the use of certain specified persons designated as beneficiaries. In a charitable trust, the property is devoted to purposes beneficial to the public. Charitable purposes include, for example, the relief of poverty, the advancement of education, the promotion of health, governmental or municipal purposes, and other purposes beneficial to the community. Although private and charitable trusts have much in common, significant differences exist regarding the validity, enforcement, and modification of the trust.

Because a charitable trust is designed to accomplish public purposes and not to give a beneficial interest to individual beneficiaries, persons who are to receive benefits from a charitable trust need not be designated. In other words, the individuals to whom the benefits accrue are not the beneficiaries. Rather, by aiding them, the interests of the real beneficiary, the public, are served.

Because the public generally is the beneficiary, a charitable trust is enforced differently from a private trust. In a private trust, the named beneficiary is entitled to enforce it. In a charitable trust, the attorney general of the state in which the trust is to be administered, as a representative of the public, is empowered to enforce the trust. A person with a special interest in performance of the trust—such as a specific charity or agency, which, by terms of the trust, is to be benefited—also may enforce it. Neither the settlor nor members of the public generally may maintain an enforcement action.

Alteration of Charitable Trusts— The "Cy Pres" Doctrine

As previously discussed, the court, in both private and charitable trusts, may permit the trustee to deviate from a trust term if compliance becomes impossible, illegal, or would, due to circumstances unforeseen by the settlor, defeat or substantially impair trust purposes. The **cy pres doctrine**, which is applicable only to charitable trusts, is an analogous but more extensive principle, under which the court permits or directs the application of the trust property to a charitable purpose different from that designated by the settlor.

The doctrine applies if the designated charitable purpose becomes impossible, impracticable, or illegal, *and* the settlor has manifested a more general intention to devote the property to charitable purposes. In this situation, the trust will not fail. Instead, upon application by the trustee, attorney general, or other interested party, the court will direct that the property be applied to some other charitable purpose falling within the settlor's general charitable intention. In other words, the property is applied to charitable purposes "as near as possible" (from the French phrase "cy pres comme possible") to those intended by the settlor.

The settlor's intended purpose may fail for a variety of reasons. For example, if the settlor leaves property in trust to establish a hospital and the amount proves insufficient for that purpose, the court may direct application of the property to benefit an existing hospital or otherwise for the promotion of health, provided the settlor has indicated a general charitable intent to aid the sick. Although "cy pres" literally requires application of the property to a purpose "as near as possible" to that en-

visioned by the settlor, courts have recognized that, in choosing among possible alternatives, it is not necessary to choose the one closest to the settlor's plan. The basic test is to choose the approach that seems best suited to accomplish the settlor's general charitable purpose.

Resulting Trusts

A **resulting trust** arises when a person makes a disposition of property under circumstances indicating that he or she does not intend that the person taking or holding the property should have the beneficial interest in it. A resulting trust, like an express trust, is dependent upon the settlor's intent, but intent is *presumed* or *implied,* rather than explicitly stated. Because the person holding the property (the trustee of the resulting trust) is not entitled to it, the beneficial interest springs back or "results" to the transferor or his estate. A resulting trust is "passive"; that is, the only duty of the trustee is to convey the property to the beneficiary (the original transferor) or according to his direction.

A resulting trust arises if an express private or charitable trust fails, or is fully performed without exhausting the trust property. In these cases, the trustee, who generally has no beneficial interest, should not be entitled to keep the trust property but rather should be compelled to return it to the settlor or his estate. For example, assume that Gene transfers $10,000 to First State Bank in trust to pay the income to Chris for life. On Chris's death, First State Bank holds the $10,000 upon a resulting trust for Gene or his estate. Or, assume Gene transfers $50,000 to First State Bank in trust to build a hospital. If the amount proves insufficient to accomplish the charitable purpose, and Gene has not indicated a general charitable intent, the trust fails. The bank then holds the money upon a resulting trust for Gene or his estate.

In the foregoing examples, the settlor could have created an express (as opposed to resulting) trust by stating as a trust term what disposition should be made of the property upon termination or failure of the trust. In the absence of such a term, however, the resulting trust is used to achieve the settlor's probable or presumed intent.

SUMMARY

1. Upon death, an estate is created containing all of the property formerly owned by the decedent. This property is distributed under the supervision of a state probate court according to the terms of a will or through operation of an "intestate succession" statute.

2. A will is simply a formal instrument by which a person, known as a "testator," makes a disposition of property to take effect after death. If the will meets the formal requirements prescribed by state law, the decedent's property will be distributed, after payment of lawful claims against the estate, according to the terms of the will. If the decedent fails to leave a valid will, the estate is distributed according to state intestate succession statutes.

3. A will has no legal effect before death and until that time may be altered or revoked by the testator. A will may be revoked by physical act, a subsequent writing complying with the formalities of a will revoking the former will, or by certain changes in the testator's circumstances, such as divorce. Even if the will meets the statutory formalities and is not revoked, persons named in the will may be prevented from receiving their designated share of the estate through the doctrines of lapse, ademption, and abatement.

4. Although the testator generally is allowed to dispose of property on death as he or she desires, the law imposes certain limitations, such as forced share statutes, on the ability to disinherit a surviving spouse. The testator's family also is protected by statutes creating a homestead exemption, exempt property, and a family allowance. These statutes give the surviving spouse and children a preference in certain property over unsecured creditors and other persons named in the will.

5. A trust splits the ownership of property between the trustee, who holds legal title, and the beneficiary, who holds equitable or beneficial title. Most trusts are created expressly, arising as a result of a property owner's language, indicating an intention to create it. The owner, or settlor, usually creates the trust by transferring the property to the trustee either during life (an inter vivos trust) or in the settlor's will on death (a testamentary trust). Trusts also are created during life by the settlor's declaration that he holds the property as trustee for another.

6. The powers and duties of the trustee and the nature and extent of the beneficiary's interest are determined by the instrument creating the trust. The settlor has no power to modify or terminate the trust unless such a power has been reserved in the terms of the trust. Even in the absence of a power to revoke, the trust may terminate for various reasons, such as completion of the purpose for which the trust was created.

7. The trustee is under a duty to administer the trust. The law imposes various duties upon the trustee in this capacity, such as the fiduciary duty of loyalty, and the duty to make only those investments of trust property that a prudent person would make. Failure to properly perform any duty imposed by law or the terms of the trust renders the trustee liable to the beneficiary for damages for breach of trust.

8. If the interests of the trust beneficiaries are successive, the trustee must allocate receipts and expenditures arising from managing the trust property between the income beneficiary and remainderman. This process of apportionment, known as "principal and income allocation," may be governed by the trust instrument. In the absence of an express provision, trustees are guided by statutes such as the Uniform Principal and Income Act.

9. Express trusts may be either private or charitable. Although the two have much in common, significant differences exist between the two regarding the validity, modification, and enforcement of the trust.

10. A resulting trust, like an express trust, is dependent upon the settlor's intent, but intent is presumed or implied, rather than explicitly stated. Resulting trusts arise when a person transfers property under circumstances indicating that he or she does not intend that the person possessing the property should have the beneficial interest in it.

KEY TERMS

testate	legacy
will	bequest
testator	specific devise
testamentary disposition	general devise
intestate	demonstrative devise
intestate succession statute	attestation clause
estate	nuncupative will
probate court	holographic will
probate	codicil
domicile	dependent relative revocation
executor (executrix)	doctrine
administrator (administratrix)	lapse
Uniform Probate Code (UPC)	issue
devise	ademption by extinction

ademption by satisfaction
advancement
abatement
dower
curtesy
community property
   doctrine
heirs
per stirpes distribution
   (taking by
   representation)
per capita distribution
Uniform Simultaneous
   Death Act
trust
trustee
beneficiary
settlor (trustor)
trust property (res, corpus)

inter vivos trust
testamentary trust
express trust
private trust
charitable trust
implied trust
pour over trust
Uniform Testamentary
   Additions to Trusts Act
honorary trust
spendthrift trust
fiduciary relationship
prudent person rule
principal and income
   allocation
Uniform Principal and
   Income Act
cy pres doctrine
resulting trust

QUESTIONS AND PROBLEMS

39-1　The requirements for a valid will often have been criticized as a trap for the unwary. This criticism seems especially valid in cases such as *Matter of Will of Daly*. Why do states continue to adhere strictly to the will formalities?

·39-2　Why do most people in the United States die intestate? Given this fact, what factors should the legislature consider in enacting an intestate succession statute?

39-3　In September, 1975, Theresa gave her friend Jean a check in the amount of $5,000 with a note stating "Jean, I'm leaving you this check rather than putting you in my will. I hope I will have enough money to cover the check in my account after I die." Theresa died in October, 1975. When Jean tried to cash the check, the bank refused to honor it because of Theresa's death, Jean petitioned the probate court requesting a distribution of $5,000 from Theresa's estate. How should the court rule? Explain.

39-4　Leonard died in an automobile accident in which his automobile was destroyed totally. Leonard's insurance company paid $3,500, the value of the car, to his estate. Leonard's will provided:

> To my brother, David, I will any automobile which I may own at my death. The rest, residue and remainder of my property, I devise to my daughter Carol.

Is David entitled to any distribution from Leonard's estate? Explain.

39-5　In 1975, Harry executed a will leaving his farm, a savings account at ABC Bank, and some personal property to his daughter Emily. The will further provided that if Harry sold the farm during his lifetime, he bequeathed an additional $20,000 to Emily. In June, 1978, Harry sold the farm for $25,000. In August of 1978, Harry deposited $20,000 in the savings account at ABC Bank. Harry died in September, 1978. The executor of his estate petitioned to allow distribution of the savings account, the personal property, and $20,000 to Emily. The residuary legatees objected to this distribution arguing that Harry's transfer of the $20,000 to the savings account during his lifetime was an ademption by satisfaction. How should the court rule?

39-6　June Cleaver died leaving the following will:

LAST WILL AND TESTAMENT

I, June Cleaver, being of sound mind make this my last will and testament and revoke all prior wills.

1. I give all of my real property to my husband, Ward, if he survives me.

2. I give my diamond ring to my sister, May.

3. I give $50,000 to my son, Wallace, and $100,000 to my son, Theodore.

4. I give my car to my son's friend, Eddy Haskell.

5. All of the rest, residue and remainder of my property I give, devise and bequeath to my brother, Herbert.

6. I appoint Eddy Haskell to be executor of this my last will and testament.

IN WITNESS WHEREOF, I hereunto have signed my name this 2d day of July, 1963.

        s/June Cleaver
        _____

WITNESSED　s/May Reed
        _____

At the time of her death, June resided in the state of Michigan which has enacted the Uniform Probate Code. Answer each of the following questions concerning her will.

(a) At the time she executed the will, June lived in a state that required only one witness to a will. Michigan law, however, requires two witnesses. Is the will valid? Explain.

(b) May Reed is an interested witness. Is she entitled to receive the diamond ring? Explain.

(c) June had executed a will in 1961 and in a codicil in 1962 she bequeathed her diamond ring to another sister, April. Who is entitled to receive the ring? Explain.

(d) At the time she executed the will, June owned a 1960 Chevrolet. She later sold this car and purchased a 1985 Mercedes Benz. Has the bequest to Eddy been adeemed?

(e) June's son Wallace, predeceased her. Wallace's wife and daughter were living at the time of June's death; however, the daughter died the day after June died. Who is entitled to the $50,000 left to Wallace? Explain.

39-7   A, during his lifetime, executes and delivers to B an instrument purporting to transfer to B in trust for C "such shares of IBM common stock as I shall own at the time of my death." Is a trust created at the time A executed and delivered the instrument? Is a trust created upon A's death? Assuming A dies owning IBM stock, who is entitled to it? Does that person take the property subject to any trust?

39-8   Christie deposits $10,000 in a savings account in First Federal Savings and Loan. The deposit was made in Christie's name "as trustee for my beloved daughter, Kay." Is a trust created? If a trust is created, is it revocable or irrevocable? Assume Christie dies without withdrawing any part of the deposit. Christie left a will leaving her entire estate to Sam. Should Kay be entitled to the $10,000 in the account? Why or why not?

39-9   Oliver died leaving the following will:

> I hereby devise that all of my property be placed in trust and that the income be paid in equal shares to my wife so long as she shall not remarry and to my sister for her life.

Oliver was survived by both his wife and sister as well as by his son.

(a) Oliver's son files suit alleging that the will did not create a valid trust. Do you agree? Explain.

(b) Assume that the court determines that the trust is valid. For five years, Oliver's wife and sister share the income. Then Oliver's wife remarries. How should the income be paid?

(c) Three years after Oliver's wife remarries, his sister dies. Now how should the income be paid?

39-10   Pearl died leaving a will with a residuary clause that provided:

> All the rest and residue of my estate, I give, devise and bequeath to my nephew Kenneth to distribute among my relatives as he sees fit.

The executor of Pearl's estate determines that Pearl intended to establish a trust and notifies the probate court that he intends to transfer the residuary assets to Kenneth in trust. Pearl's husband files a complaint with the court objecting to the trust. He asserts that Pearl failed to create a trust so that the property should be distributed to him in accordance with the intestacy laws. Kenneth argues that if the court should find that no trust was created then the residuary assets should be distributed to Kenneth outright.

How should the court rule? Explain.

39-11   Calvin established an inter vivos trust naming First National Bank as trustee. The trust instrument provided that all income should be paid to Calvin during his life. It also provided:

> At the death of the Settlor, the net income of the trust property in the discretion of the trustee may be used for the following:
>
> a) an annual donation to St. Phillip's Church to assist in the maintenance and upkeep of the church or for the operation of the recreational center owned by the church
>
> b) scholarships for boys or girls attending St. Phillip's Church who desire to go to college
>
> c) annual donations to local or national civil rights organizations for work in voter registration and political education of minorities

At Calvin's death, Calvin's sole heir, his sister, sued the trustee for the trust assets. She alleged that the trust should fail because Calvin used only precatory language and because the trust beneficiaries were indefinite. What result? Explain.

39-12   When Mary was twenty-one, her father died leaving her a large amount of money. Upon the recommendation of her attorney, Mary established an irrevocable spendthrift trust and transferred all of the money to First State Bank as trustee. The trust provided that the trustee should pay all income to Mary during her life, remainder to be distributed as Mary provided in her will. Three years later, Mary requested that the trustee terminate the trust and transfer the trust corpus to Mary. The bank refused to terminate the trust and Mary sued.

At trial, a representative of the bank testified

that Mary had had no experience with financial matters. He also testified that Mary had become a member of a religious cult to which she had donated almost all of the income paid to her. How should the court rule? Explain.

39-13   Consider the following facts and determine whether the trustee has committed a breach of trust.

(a) The trust holds a farm appraised at $100,000. Because the trust is not generating sufficient income, the trustee decides to sell the farm. After receiving several offers of less than $100,000, the trustee purchases the farm for his own use for $105,000.

(b) Trustee is an insurance agent. The trust assets include several buildings that must be insured. The trustee takes out insurance and pays himself the usual commission for such a sale.

(c) Trustee is a bank. As part of the securities portfolio of the trust, trustee invests in its own bank stock.

(d) Trustee is a bank. The trust maintains a checking and savings account at the bank.

39-14   Charles Xavier died leaving a will that named Central National Bank as trustee of a trust for the benefit of two beneficiaries. The trust estate included 4300 shares of Sears Roebuck & Co. common stock that had a value of $117 per share on the date of Xavier's death. The Sears stock comprised 70% of the trust estate and 97% of the stock of the trust estate. The trustee retained the Sears stock and in less than 18 months its value had dropped to $88 per share. The beneficiaries sued Central National alleging that it had breached its fiduciary duties by mismanaging the trust assets. Specifically, the beneficiaries claimed that the trustee should have diversified the stock holdings within three months after the trust was established. How should the court rule?

39-15   Josie established a testamentary trust from which all income was to be paid to the Cancer Research Fund. The trustee determines that there is not and has never been any organization known as the ''Cancer Research Fund.'' In another provision of the will, Josie stated her intention to disinherit her heirs. The trustee petitions the court for instructions as to whether the trust should be dissolved. How should the court rule?

Viewpoint

Emerging Issues in Property Law: Time Sharing, Implied Warranties, and Eminent Domain

James E. Krier

Property is ownership, or so goes the ordinary notion. But the reader of Chapters 34–39 will appreciate that, for better or worse, this ordinary conception is regarded by lawyers as simplistic. For lawyers, property consists of a bundle of rights, and each of the rights, or any cluster of them, might be held in ways so numerous and varied as to confound any one-dimensional notion, such as "property is ownership." And to confound students of property as well: property rights might be possessory or not; present or future; certain or contingent; exclusive or shared; of limited or unlimited duration; and so on.

Notwithstanding this complexity, property law is relatively stable as legal doctrine goes (a blessing at least in that it makes learning more manageable): by and large, its rich history of accretion from something rather simple to something awesomely complex is exactly that— history. But "relatively stable" does not mean perfectly static, and significant developments are always under way. The purpose here is to mention a few of them.

Cooperatives and condominiums were discussed in Chapter 36; although these forms of ownership have ancient roots, their flowering is remarkably recent. Even more recent is a related form, time sharing, which creates an entirely new sort of property interest. Time sharing, it appears, actually started as a product of condominiums, for time-sharing agreements generally relate to the sharing by several persons of condominiums in resort areas. The Uniform Condominium Act recognizes a time-share estate, perhaps the newest entry in the property lexicon, and there is now a Model Real Estate Time-Share Act. As you might expect, time-sharing agreements themselves can be complicated and of various forms. The general idea, however, is ownership by a group, each

member of which has the right to exclusive possession for a designated period.

Time sharing is of obvious interest to real estate developers, but its novelty will naturally give rise to problems and risks until the law of the time-share estate becomes more settled. Some states have statutes governing time-sharing agreements; in others the only resort is to the old common law system of estates, which must be twisted and bent to suit the developers' (and the owners') purposes. Co-ownership in any form always gives rise to nice disputes about the sharing of benefits and burdens, and time sharing will not be an exception—especially because the number of owners per unit of capital will be large, and most of them will wish to be in the same place at the same (most desirable) time. The astute developer will, of course, anticipate problems and specify their resolution in the time-sharing agreement. But given the novelty of time sharing, anticipation will be imperfect at the very best.

Real estate developers will also want to keep a close eye on the developing law of implied warranties—in leased premises (the implied warranty of habitability, discussed in Chapter 36) and in premises built and sold in fee simple (the implied warranty of fitness, of quality). In both instances, it appeared for a time that these warranties might apply only to residential premises, but the situation is ripe for change. The implied warranty of fitness has already found some application to sales of commercial real estate, and the Uniform Land Transactions Act would carry the application further. The Act has not yet been adopted by any state, but it is likely

James E. Krier is the Earl Warren DeLano Professor of Law at the University of Michigan.

to influence the decisions of state courts nevertheless. As to leases of property, the implied warranty of habitability similarly remains almost entirely limited to residential premises, but legal commentators have urged extension to commercial tenancies and a few court decisions have taken tentative steps in that direction (for example, the warranty has been implied in the case of a lease of a small building to a handful of professionals engaged in providing personal services). Moreover, the general obligations of residential landlords continue to expand (a fact itself troublesome to real estate investors) and could spill over into the commercial context. A recent California case enlarged a residential landlord's tort liability on grounds that would appear to apply to commercial landlords as well.

A final warning to developers. The law of takings (see Chapter 38) implies that private property may be condemned by the government (that is, taken by the government against the owner's will) only for public use, and only upon payment of just compensation. Recent decisions of two sorts are important here.

First, it is now clear that "public use" is essentially devoid of meaning, with the result that the government is practically unconstrained in its power of eminent domain. When the City of Oakland, California, recently sought to condemn the Raiders football team in order to keep the franchise in the area, the owners objected that the taking would not be for a public use. The California Supreme Court was inclined to disagree. And when the state of Hawaii sought through its power of eminent domain to force the compensated transfer of vast amounts of land from the hands of its few owners to the holders (by lease) of residential tracts of the land, the oligopolist owners objected that there would be no public use because the land would be transferred directly to private parties. The United States Supreme Court thought otherwise.

The alert reader will wonder why the owners in these cases are so concerned, given that they receive just compensation. The answer is straightforward: the constitutional measure of compensation is commonly short of what owners could get in the market.

The second sort of important recent decision relates to this last remark, and illustrates the fact that sometimes takings are not compensated at all. The topic here is the implicit taking that arises, not when the government exercises its power of eminent domain, but when it regulates pursuant to the police power and allegedly goes too far, substantially reducing the value of the regulated property. The law of implicit takings is a mire thick and deep, but still one can see something in it. Government regulatory activities can go far indeed in their negative influence on property values without triggering the obligation to compensate, even when the loss of property value is very large and very focused. For example, the owners of Grand Central Station were effectively denied the extraordinarily valuable right to develop the airspace above the terminal, yet the United States Supreme Court held that the New York City regulations working this result did not amount to a taking. But that was a decade ago, and a more recent decision (1987) by the Court intimates that it will look more closely than before at the basis for intrusive land-use regulations; those without substantial (as opposed to arguable) governmental justification may now be found to have taken property, when in the past the finding would have been otherwise. If a taking is found in such cases, the government is then free, of course, to invalidate the offending regulation rather than keep it in place and pay the just compensation required by the Constitution. Invalidation, however, will not always undo losses that property owners might have suffered while the regulation was in effect. May property owners recover those temporary losses from the government? The answer in the past was generally no, except for a very limited range of cases. But again change is in the air. In yet another 1987 decision the Court held that governments might be liable in damages for temporary takings. The reach of the decision is far from clear, but it and the other 1987 case discussed above are likely to dampen the zeal of land-use regulators. Is that a good thing?

Several years ago a well-known observer said that "we are in the midst of a major transformation in which property rights are being fundamentally redefined to the disadvantage of property owners." The statement was probably an oversimplification at the time. The new decisions of the Supreme Court only make it more so.

BUSINESS ORGANIZATIONS

The law of agency concerns the legal rights and duties that arise when persons act on behalf of others. Agency relationships are a basic institution in a capitalistic economy, enabling employers to conduct many business activities in many places simultaneously. Even the smallest business owned by a single individual proprietor usually must hire employees, and even completely self-employed and self-sufficient individuals conduct business with others through their agents. As a business grows in size and adopts a formal structure, agency becomes increasingly important. For example, the partnership is largely a mutual agency relationship existing among the co-owners of the business, the partners. The corporation, the dominant organizational form for modern business, is an artificial person which acts only through agents.

Agency is a consensual fiduciary relationship in which one party, an **agent,** agrees to act on behalf of and under the control of another, known as the **principal.**[1] The principal is the person for whom an action is to be taken and the agent is the person who is to act. Either of the parties to the relation may be a natural person, a partnership, or a corporation.

Agency is based upon the premise that a person who acts through another, acts himself.[2] That is, the acts of the agent are treated in law as the acts of the principal. Accordingly, the benefits, as well as the liabilities, derived from the agent's conduct accrue to the principal.

The law of agency encompasses the legal relationship existing between principal and agent[3] and the legal relationship of principal and agent to third parties. The first category involves such issues as the creation of the relationship, the capacity of parties, and the duties of principal and agent to each other. The second category comprises the bulk of agency law, and divides into two broad areas: liability to third parties in *contract* and liability to third parties in *tort.* Separate and distinct rules apply to contract and tort liability. Therefore, in analyzing a third-party agency question, one must

---

1. *Restatement (Second) of Agency* §1.
2. This paraphrases the old maxim *qui facit per alium facit per se.*
3. This relationship is sometimes referred to as the relationship *inter se.*

first determine whether the agent has committed a tort against a third party, or has entered into a contract with a third party. Having made this determination one can apply the relevant legal principles to the issues raised by the question.

In addition to determining the liability for contracts made and for injuries caused *by* agents, the law of agency addresses the liability for accidental injuries or death inflicted *upon* agents acting within the scope of their employment. Traditionally governed by the common law of agency, this issue is now largely governed by state "workers' compensation" statutes.

This chapter examines the basic relationship between principal and agent, and the law of agency and contract, including the legal effect of notice or knowledge acquired by an agent and the principles governing termination of agency powers. Chapter 41 addresses agency and torts, including a discussion of workers' compensation statutes.

General Principles of Agency

Creation and Formality

According to the *Restatement (Second) of Agency,* an agency relationship results from "the manifestation of consent by one person to another that the other shall act on his behalf and subject to his control, and consent by the other so to act."[4] Although agency relationships often are created by contract, no contractual relationship is required. Assume Jane Doaks asks her friend Moe to purchase an antique lamp at an auction Moe plans to attend. If Moe consents to act, an agency relationship exists between the parties even though no contract is present. Agencies are also created by **power of attorney,** a written instrument by which one person authorizes another to act as her agent.[5]

Agents often are empowered to enter into contracts on behalf of their principals. The Statute of Frauds may apply to these contracts, requiring a writing for enforceability. Assume Paul appoints Alice as agent to purchase a machine for Paul for

$1,000. Alice subsequently contracts to purchase the machine from Ted. Because the contract involves a sale of goods with a price exceeding $500, a writing is required for enforceability under §2-201 of the Uniform Commercial Code. As Paul's authorized agent, however, Alice may sign the writing on Paul's behalf, thereby satisfying the Statute of Frauds against Paul.

As a general rule, an agent need not be authorized in writing to act as an agent unless a statute specifically provides otherwise. This rule applies even if the agent is authorized to enter into written contracts and even if those contracts must be evidenced by a writing under the Statute of Frauds. State statutes, however, often provide that if the contract to be negotiated by the agent is within the Statute of Frauds, the authorization must also be written.[6] These statutes are the modern embodiments of the **equal dignity rule** existing at common law requiring written agents' authorization. For example, if Paul appoints Alice as agent to purchase land on his behalf in a state that has adopted a statutory equal dignity rule, Alice's authorization also must be in writing.

Types of Agents

Agents may perform a wide variety of tasks for their principals. They may buy or sell property, pay or collect money, drive motor vehicles or operate machinery, manage people and assets, and more generally, perform any task a person could do without an agent. Various terms, defined below, have developed to describe the functions and characteristics of certain agents.

General and Special Agents. A **general agent** is one "authorized to conduct a series of transactions involving a continuity of service."[7] General agents are characterized by continuous service, not the degree of skill or discretion exercised. Thus, managers, clerks, and sales and purchasing agents are all general agents. They are an integral part of a business enterprise, not requiring additional authoriza-

---

4. *Restatement (Second) of Agency* §1.
5. Note that a person designated an agent under a power of attorney need not be an attorney.

6. Some states impose this requirement for all contracts within the statute; others impose it for land sale contracts only.
7. *Restatement (Second) of Agency* §3(1).

tion for each transaction conducted on the principal's behalf.

A **special agent,** in contrast, is one who conducts "a single transaction or a series of transactions not involving continuity of service."[8] Thus, a real estate broker or auctioneer employed to sell the principal's house or other property, a stockbroker empowered to buy certain securities, or an attorney hired to negotiate a contract are special agents. The distinction between general and special agents is important in determining the extent and termination of the agent's authority to bind the principal to contracts made by the agent with third parties.

Masters and Servants. A **servant** is an agent whose *physical conduct* in the performance of his duties is subject to the control or right of control of the principal. A principal who has the control or right to control an agent's physical conduct is known as a **master.** Most typical employees, such as managers, clerks, truck drivers, salesmen, or factory workers, are servants, and their employers are masters. A servant should be distinguished from an **independent contractor,** a person who contracts to do something for another but whose physical conduct in the performance of the undertaking is not subject to the other's control or right of control. An independent contractor may be, but is not necessarily, an agent.[9] The master-servant relationship, discussed in detail in Chapter 41, is a basic prerequisite to imposing liability upon a principal for torts committed by agents against third parties.

Brokers, Factors, and Del Credere Agents. A **broker** is simply an agent empowered to make or procure contracts on her principal's behalf for compensation, usually called a "commission." Perhaps the most common brokers are real estate brokers (those empowered to procure the purchase or sale of land) and stockbrokers (those employed to buy or sell stocks, bonds, or other securities).

A **factor,** or **commission merchant,** on the other hand, is an agent entrusted with possession and control of the principal's goods for purposes of sale, compensated by a commission or "factorage." A factor, unlike a broker, is commonly in possession and control of the property involved and sells in her own, rather than her principal's name.

A **del credere agent** is simply a factor who sells goods on credit and then guarantees to the principal the purchaser's solvency and the purchaser's performance of the contract. In other words, the del credere agent acts as a surety, liable to the principal if the purchaser defaults. The agent is normally compensated for his suretyship promise by an additional commission (a del credere commission) on the sale. Because the main purpose of the agent's promise is to benefit the agent, not to accommodate the principal, the promise of a del credere agent need not be in writing under the Statute of Frauds like other suretyship promises.

Capacity of Parties

Because agency is not necessarily a contractual relationship, a person need not have contractual capacity to be a principal. Agency is based upon consent, and therefore only the capacity to give legally operative consent is required. Most natural persons and corporations meet this test. In fact, without capacity to appoint agents, a corporation could not act. In addition, persons with limited capacity, such as minors, may be principals. Nevertheless, the creation of the agency and the transactions made under it are affected by the principal's limited capacity. For example, assume Mel, a minor, appoints Alan as his agent to purchase a car from Tom. Alan later purchases the car from Tom. Both the appointment of Alan as agent and the subsequent contract with Tom are voidable by Mel.[10]

On the other hand, a person has capacity to be an agent even though she has no capacity to be a principal. Capacity to have rights or be subject to duties is not required. To illustrate, suppose Joe tells his daughter Mary, a minor, to go to the hardware store, purchase an electric drill, and charge the purchase to Joe's account. In this case, Mary

---

8. *Restatement (Second) of Agency* §3(2).
9. *Restatement (Second) of Agency* §2.

10. Alan may incur liability to Tom in this situation for breach of the agent's warranty of authority discussed later in this chapter.

has capacity to be an agent, and is thereby able to bind Joe to the contract, even though Mary could not have been bound to the same contract herself because she has limited contractual capacity.

Duties of Agent to Principal

The basic rights and obligations of principal and agent are often determined by an express contract. Failure of either party to perform results in liability for breach. Thus, in determining the scope of an agency relation, the explicit terms of any contract existing between the parties must first be examined.

Unless the parties otherwise agree, the law imposes various duties upon both principal and agent, which are inferred from the conduct of the parties based upon common experience and understanding and basic notions of fairness. Among these duties are the duties of loyalty and obedience owed by an agent to a principal, and the correlative duties of compensation, indemnity, and protection owed by a principal to an agent. A party injured by breach of these duties may sue for damages or other appropriate judicial relief.

Duties of Service and Obedience. A basic characteristic of agency is that the agent acts under the direction and control of the principal. Various specific duties imposed upon the agent effectuate this purpose.

Duty of Obedience. The agent is under a duty to obey all reasonable instructions from the principal regarding the manner of performing the agency. The extent of obedience required and the manner of the agent's performance are determined by the agency contract or by the character of the agency. In master-servant relationships, for example, the master usually closely controls and supervises the servant's activities. In other agencies, however, certain customary aspects of the agent's performance are left to the agent's discretion. Clients, for example, may not usually interfere in the specific details of their attorney's performance, including the conduct of court proceedings.[11]

Duty to Act as Authorized. Principles of "authorization," discussed in detail later in this chapter, determine when principal and agent are liable on contracts made by the agent with third parties. An agent has a duty to act only as authorized by the principal, and not to act on the principal's behalf after her authority is terminated. An agent breaches this duty, for example, by making an unauthorized contract for which the principal is liable or by improperly delegating her authority.

Duty to Keep and Render Accounts. The agent must keep and render accurate accounts of money or property received or disbursed on the principal's behalf. The duty extends to the amounts of receipts or payments and other relevant information such as the persons involved and the dates of transactions. The extent of the duty to account varies with the nature of the agency and business custom. For example, a traveling salesperson has more extensive accounting duties than a store clerk.

Duty to Give Information. The agent is required to keep the principal informed of important facts acquired during the course of the agency that may affect the principal's interests. The duty to disclose such information is particularly important because notice or knowledge acquired by an agent during the course of his employment may be imputed to the principal, whether or not actually communicated.

Duty of Care and Skill. The agent also has a duty to exercise reasonable care and skill in the performance of her work, and in addition, to exercise any special skill she may have. Under this duty, for example, the principal may recover for an agent's negligent destruction of the principal's goods. A client may recover from an attorney whose negligent failure to file a lawsuit in a timely fashion, or to be aware of changes in the law, causes loss to the client. The principal also may sue the agent for conduct that subjects the principal to tort liability to third parties under principles outlined in Chapter 41.

Duties of Loyalty. Agency is a fiduciary relationship imposing duties of utmost trust and confidence upon an agent. That is, an agent acts on behalf of

---

11. *Restatement (Second) of Agency* §385 and comment a.

and subject to the control of the principal, and is a fiduciary in the performance of those acts. The fiduciary nature of an agent's obligation is embodied in the **duty of loyalty,** under which the agent is required to act solely for the benefit of the principal regarding all matters within the scope of the agency. An agent's fiduciary obligation closely parallels that owed by a trustee to the beneficiaries of a trust.

The duty of loyalty requires the agent to account for all profits arising out of the agency, including incidental or unusual profits, whether or not received in a breach of the agent's duty. Assume Art is a salesperson in Penny's store. Thelma purchases goods from Art, but inadvertently overpays her bill by ten dollars. Thelma disappears before the mistake can be corrected. Art must account to Penny for the overpayment. In addition to the basic duty to account, the agent also is required to have title to property obtained on the principal's behalf held in the principal's name and not to commingle the principal's property with his own.

The duty of loyalty also prevents the agent from competing with the principal concerning matters within the scope of the agency. Assume Ann is an agent to buy and sell antiques for Paul. Unknown to Paul, Ann maintains a personal stock of antiques which she sells to Paul's customers and periodically replenishes with purchases from Paul's customers. Ann has committed a breach of her duty of loyalty to Paul. Note that competition by the agent is permitted with the principal's consent, and in areas outside the scope of the agency. For example, an agent employed to buy and sell land may compete with the principal in the sale of goods.

The duty of loyalty also prevents an agent from disclosing or otherwise using confidential information acquired during the course of the agency to the principal's detriment. The agent may not use the information for his own benefit or disclose it to a competitor of the principal. Protected information includes specialized business practices or trade secrets, customer lists, and other matters peculiar to the principal's business, such as the principal's intention to buy or sell property, issue securities, declare dividends, or merge with another business. The agent is accountable for any profits made by the use or disclosure of confidential information whether or not the principal has been harmed

thereby. This rule is designed to foster the free flow of sensitive business information between principal and agent.

At issue in the following case was whether an agent had breached his fiduciary duty of loyalty.

H-B Ltd. Partnership v. Wimmer
257 S.E.2d 770 (Va. 1979)

Cheryl Switzer and George Vincent, doing business as H-B Ltd. Partnership, employed Edgar Wimmer, a realtor, to act as their agent to obtain commercial property in Stafford County, Virginia. In December 1976, Switzer and Vincent discovered a parcel of land that they were interested in purchasing and Wimmer agreed to locate and contact the owner to ascertain whether the property was for sale. In January 1977, Wimmer advised Switzer and Vincent that he had met with the owner who lived in Washington, D.C., and that she had agreed to sell the land for $60,000. Wimmer further advised them that his realtor's fee would be $5,000. Switzer and Vincent agreed to purchase the property and requested Wimmer to draw up a contract.

In February 1977, Wimmer notified Switzer that he feared the owner might change her mind about the sale if signing the contract were delayed, so Wimmer agreed to sign the contract as purchaser and then assign the property to H-B Ltd. Partnership upon payment of the $65,000. On March 2, Switzer and Vincent signed an agreement with Wimmer. In May, Switzer and Vincent learned that the owner of the property had conveyed it to Wimmer for a price of $36,000. When Wimmer refused to convey the property to them for $36,000, they sued Wimmer, alleging that he had breached his fiduciary duty as agent, and requested that the court find that Wimmer held the property in constructive trust for Switzer and Vincent. The trial court ruled in favor of Wimmer, and Switzer and Vincent appealed.

I'anson, Chief Justice

. . . An agent is a fiduciary with respect to the matters within the scope of his agency. A fiduciary relationship exists in all cases when special confidence has been reposed in one who in equity and good conscience is bound to act in good faith and with due regard for the interests of the one reposing the confidence. . . .

When an agent is employed on an oral agreement to purchase real property for his principal, and buys the property with his own funds and takes a conveyance to himself, thereby violating his fiduciary relationship with his principal, he will be deemed in equity to hold the title thereto as a constructive trustee for the principal. . . .

In the present case, the uncontradicted evidence shows that Wimmer was employed by Switzer and Vincent as their agent to ascertain the owner of the property in question and to negotiate on their behalf for its purchase. Wimmer fraudulently and in breach of faith and confidence reposed in him by his principals had the property conveyed to himself. By misleading Switzer and Vincent into believing that the sales price was $60,000, Wimmer would have made a secret profit of $24,000 for himself in addition to a real estate agency commission of $5,000. The unconscionable conduct of Wimmer was a breach of the confidence and faith reposed in him by his principals. Hence, under the uncontradicted evidence, a constructive trust was created by operation of law and Wimmer held the property as trustee for Switzer and Vincent. . . .

[Judgment reversed and remanded.]

Duties of Principal to Agent

Although an agency is a fiduciary relationship, imposing a duty of loyalty upon the agent in his dealings with the principal, no such fiduciary duty is imposed upon the principal. That is, the principal is generally under no duty to act solely for the agent's interest in matters within the scope of the agency. The principal does, however, owe various duties to the agent, most notably the duties of compensation, indemnity, and protection.

In the absence of agreement to serve gratuitously, an agent is entitled to compensation for work performed on the principal's behalf. If no specific amount is stated in the agency agreement, the agent is entitled to the fair value of the services performed. In the ordinary employment (master-servant) relationship, the employer must generally maintain and render accurate accounts of amounts due the employees. Other agents, such as factors, brokers, and auctioneers, maintain an independent business and commonly keep their own accounts of amounts due from the principal.

In addition to the duty to compensate, the principal is required to indemnify, or reimburse, the agent for expenses reasonably and properly incurred on the principal's behalf in the conduct of the agency. The principal must also reimburse the agent for losses incurred through no fault of the agent in transactions the principal authorizes. This duty often arises either expressly or by implication from the agency contract between the parties. It may also be restitutionary, imposed to prevent unjust enrichment of the principal after the agent personally satisfies an obligation of the principal, or suffers a loss that, in fairness, the principal should bear.

The principal also owes a general duty to use reasonable care to prevent agents from being injured during their performance of the agency. In master-servant relationships, for example, breach of this duty of care provides a basis for employees to recover from their employers for job-related injuries. The common law governing employer liability for injuries to employees and the impact of state workers' compensation statutes on that liability are discussed in Chapter 41.

Agency and Contracts

Perhaps the most pervasive agency issue concerns the liability of the principal and agent for *contracts* made by the agent with third parties on the principal's behalf. The law addresses two basic questions: When is an agent personally liable upon a contract made on the principal's behalf? and When is the principal liable upon a contract made by an agent? Both questions are answered by applying fairly straightforward rules that require an initial understanding of the concept of ''authority.''

General Principles of Contract Liability

The Concept of Authority. Every day agents enter into contracts that may be enforced by or against their principals. An agent's power to bind the principal to a contract is derived from the principal's directions or instructions to the agent concerning the extent of the agent's power. This power is referred to as the agent's **authority**.[12] The extent of the agent's authority is determined by examining the principal's words (oral or written) or other conduct indicating the principal's consent that the agent act on the principal's behalf. Thus, authority is based upon a manifestation of consent running from the principal to the agent. The existence and extent of authority is important because a principal is generally liable upon contracts he has authorized the agent to make, but not for an agent's unauthorized contracts. To illustrate, assume Parker authorizes Andrews in writing to sell Parker's car at a price not less than $500. Andrews contracts to sell the car to Thomas for $600. Andrews also contracts with Sax to sell Parker's house for $50,000. Parker is bound to the contract with Thomas, but not with Sax. Andrews has authority to sell the car but not the house.

Express and Implied Authority. An agent's authority may be either express or implied. **Express authority** is based upon explicit oral or written statements defining the agent's power. Thus, in the preceding example, Andrews is expressly authorized to transfer title to Parker's car in exchange for money. Most authority is not express but arises by implication. Authority is often **implied** because the express language is very general in nature. For example, Carol may appoint Jean to "manage" Carol's grocery store or apartment building. In this case, much of Jean's authority is implied from the general express grant; that is, it flows as a natural or logical consequence of the express authority granted. For example, a person hired to manage a business possesses implied authority to (1) make contracts reasonably necessary to conduct the business, (2) procure equipment and supplies and make necessary repairs, (3) hire, supervise, and fire employees, (4) sell goods or services in the ordinary course of business, (5) receive money and pay debts arising from the operation of the business,

and (6) otherwise direct the ordinary operation of the business.[13]

Implied authority extends only to those acts incident and necessary to exercise the express authority granted. That is, implied authority may not contradict the express grant in any way. To determine the extent of implied authority, therefore, one must carefully examine the express authority granted. To illustrate, assume P hires A to manage P's business, but reserves the sole power to hire and fire employees. A has no implied authority to hire and fire employees.

Agent's Warranty of Authority. A person who purports to make a contract for a principal impliedly represents that he has the power to bind the principal. An agent who has no such authority breaches this **implied warranty of authority** and is liable in damages to the third party. The warranty is breached even if the agent is reasonably mistaken concerning the existence or extent of his authority. For example, assume Johnson hires Acheson as a sales representative with authority only to solicit orders for Johnson's products, fabrics and carpeting. Acheson, representing herself as Johnson's purchasing agent, contracts to purchase carpeting from Dalton Mill, Inc., a carpet manufacturer. Johnson has no liability on the contract, and Acheson is liable to Dalton for breach of the implied warranty of authority. Note that even if Acheson reasonably believed that she had authority to make the purchase, she is still liable.

An agent may also be liable if the principal lacks contractual capacity. For example, an agent acting on behalf of a totally incompetent principal breaches the warranty of authority. The mere fact that the principal's contracts are voidable, however, does not render the agent liable. For example, an agent acting on behalf of a minor principal is not necessarily liable to the third party if the minor later disaffirms the contract. The agent is liable in this case, however, if she either represents to the third party that the principal has full capacity, or knows of the principal's incapacity and the third party's ignorance of that fact. An agent represent-

---

12. *Restatement (Second) of Agency* §7.

13. *Restatement (Second) of Agency* §73.

ing a principal with limited capacity should, therefore, disclose that fact to the third party to avoid potential liability.

Contract Liability—Undisclosed Principals

A principal is **disclosed** if the third party knows both that the agent is acting for a principal and the principal's identity. In this the most common agency arrangement, if the agent is authorized the principal is liable on the contract—that is, becomes a party to the contract—and the agent is not. An agent acting on behalf of a disclosed principal does not intend to become personally liable on the contract. Rather, the intent of all concerned is that the principal and the third party are to be the contracting parties.

Agents may, however, act on behalf of partially disclosed or undisclosed principals. A principal is **partially disclosed** if the principal's existence, but not identity, is known to the third party. For example, assume Allison is acting as agent for Peter to purchase land. She communicates with Thomas, a prospective seller, and states "I am acting as an agent in this transaction but I am not at liberty to disclose my principal's name." Peter is a partially disclosed principal. A principal is **undisclosed** if neither the existence nor identity of the principal is known to the third party at the time of the contract. Suppose Peter wants to acquire a large block of land from several sellers for a shopping center. To avoid provoking a drastic increase in price, Peter appoints Allison as an agent to purchase the various parcels of land. Allison is instructed not to tell prospective sellers that she is acting for Peter. Various owners later enter into contracts with Allison to sell, unaware that she is acting as Peter's agent. As far as the individual sellers are concerned, they are dealing only with Allison. In this case, Peter is an undisclosed principal.[14]

A principal is always liable if the agent is authorized. Thus, a principal's liability is the same whether the principal is disclosed, partially disclosed, or undisclosed. An agent's liability, however, differs. Unlike the agent acting for a disclosed principal, the agent acting for a partially disclosed or undisclosed principal becomes a party to, and therefore personally liable upon, the contract. Thus, when an authorized agent acts on behalf of a partially disclosed or undisclosed principal, *both* principal and agent are liable to the third party on the contract. That is, the law recognizes the existence of *two* contracts.

Under the traditional common law rule both principal and agent are liable, but their liability is not joint and several. Rather, the liability is essentially in the *alternative,* governed by the doctrine of **election.** Under this doctrine, after discovering the existence and identity of the principal, the third party may elect to hold either the principal or the agent liable on the contract. For example, assume Callahan is appointed by Potter, an undisclosed principal, to purchase land for a shopping center. Stiller contracts with Callahan to sell a tract of land. In this case Stiller will initially look to Callahan for performance of the contract because Stiller is unaware of the agency. Once Stiller discovers Potter's existence and identity, however, Stiller may elect to hold Callahan liable on the contract, thereby releasing Potter, or may elect to hold Potter liable, thereby releasing Callahan. No election can be made unless and until the third party discovers the principal's existence and identity.

The election rule has been harshly criticized in recent years as outdated and unjust, and a minority of courts are rejecting it as the following case illustrates.

Crown Controls, Inc. v. Smiley
756 P.2d 717 (Wash. 1988)

Jim Smiley owned 75% of the stock of North American Drill Supply, Inc. (Drill Supply), an Oregon corporation. Drill Supply registered ownership of the trade name "Industrial Associates" with the state of Oregon as required by law, listing Smiley as its authorized representative. In a number of conversations with Crown Controls, Inc., a sales representative for suppliers of chemical control equip-

---

14. *Restatement (Second) of Agency* §4.

ment, Smiley identified himself as an agent of Industrial Associates but did not mention the existence of Drill Supply. Smiley ordered equipment from Crown Controls, which delivered the equipment and submitted a bill to Industrial Associates for $9,136. The bill was not paid and, after discovering that Industrial Associates was a trade name owned by Drill Supply, Crown Controls sued both Smiley and Drill Supply for breach of contract. The court granted summary judgment against Drill Supply doing business as Industrial Associates, but ordered a trial to determine whether Smiley was personally liable for the debt. Crown Controls unsuccessfully tried to recover the judgment from Drill Supply. After a trial, the court ruled that although Smiley was personally liable to Crown Controls for breach of contract as an agent of an undisclosed principal, Drill Supply, Crown Controls was required to elect whether to pursue Smiley or Drill Supply in collecting its judgment. The court of appeals reversed the ruling concerning election of remedies and held that Smiley and Drill Supply were jointly and severally liable for the judgment. The Washington Supreme Court granted Smiley's petition for review.

Durham, Justice

. . . Smiley argues that by obtaining a judgment against Drill Supply, and by attempting to collect on that judgment, Crown Controls elected to give up their rights against him. In support, Smiley points to this state's "election of remedies" doctrine. Under that doctrine, the liability of an agent and his undisclosed principal on a contract is only in the alternative. In other words, after learning all the relevant facts, a creditor must elect whether he will hold the agent or the principal liable for the debt. . . . A creditor who elects to hold the previously undisclosed principal liable thereby discharges the agent, even if the creditor subsequently discovers that the principal is insolvent. . . . Furthermore, the entry of a judgment against the principal amounts to an election to forego collecting from the agent. . . .

Evaluation of the relative merits of the "election of remedies" doctrine in this context can be reduced to the following dilemma: legal commentators generally consider joint and several liability to be

the better reasoned approach, but alternative liability has been the rule in this state for decades and it has long been the majority rule in other jurisdictions as well. For example, the Reporter for the American Law Institute stated that the Restatement [of Agency] adopted the theory of alternative liability because it felt bound by judicial precedent in the majority of jurisdictions, but felt the minority rule to be better reasoned. . . .

This latter rule can be described more generally as joint and several liability, because it allows a creditor to collect from the agent, the principal, or both, until the judgment has been fully satisfied. . . .

[T]he "election of remedies" rule in the context of undisclosed principals was traditionally justified by three arguments. . . . These arguments can be summarized as follows. First, alternative liability was intended to protect the principal from the vexation of having to defend two suits, one brought by the creditor and the other brought by the agent seeking indemnity for his own liability. This argument, however, does not adequately support the current theory of alternative liability, because modern pleading practice allows for impleading and consolidation of actions. Second, the theory was traditionally predicated on merger analysis, which stated that two rights of action brought against different parties, but based on the same set of facts, could not coexist when one action has been reduced to judgment. Merger analysis fails, however, in explaining why recovery of judgment against the agent before learning about the existence of an undisclosed principal does not bar a subsequent action against the principal. . . . The remaining argument justifying the tradition of alternative liability is the "one contract-no windfall" rationale. According to this rationale, the plaintiff has only contracted for one cause of action and would receive an unjustified windfall if the creditor were allowed to sue the agent and the principal simultaneously. . . .

However, opponents of alternative liability stress that a creditor has two distinct causes of action, both arising from the failure to perform the obligations of the contract. The undisclosed principal becomes liable because he initiates the contract and profits by it; the agent becomes liable because of his promise. These opponents maintain that the assertion of liability of either the agent or the principal is entirely in harmony with a claim against the other. . . .

Furthermore, there is no "windfall" to the creditor. Although he can seek to recover damages from more than one party, his aggregate recovery is limited by the amount of the judgment. Indeed, as the Court of Appeals pointed out, retention of the current law constitutes an unjustified windfall for the debtors who are able to use the doctrine to avoid debts that they are otherwise obligated to pay. . . .

We conclude that the . . . rule of joint and several liability is the better reasoned approach, and that coexistent remedies against the agent and principal would be neither inconsistent nor repugnant. . . .

In conclusion, we hold that the liability of an agent and his previously undisclosed principal is no longer alternative, but is joint and several. Accordingly, a creditor may recover judgments against both the principal and the agent, may attempt to collect its judgment against either party, and, to the extent that the judgment remains unsatisfied, may subsequently pursue collection from the other party. . . .

[Judgment affirmed.]

The preceding discussion generates two simple rules governing most agency contract situations:

1. An agent is liable on a contract made in an agency capacity unless both (a) the agent is authorized, and (b) the principal is disclosed.
2. The principal (disclosed, partially disclosed, or undisclosed) is liable upon contracts made on his behalf if the agent is authorized to act.

The doctrines of ratification and apparent authority, discussed below, may be viewed as exceptions to the general rule that the principal is liable only if the agent is authorized.

Ratification

Ratification involves words or other conduct on the part of the principal indicating an intent to be bound upon (to treat as authorized) a previously unauthorized contract made on her behalf. Ratification may be inferred from various types of conduct including express statements to the third party of a willingness to be bound, silence indicating consent, accepting the benefits of the contract, or bringing suit to enforce the contract. If disputed, the ratification issue is a question of fact for the jury to decide.

A ratification automatically "relates back" to the date of the unauthorized contract, which is then treated as originally authorized. After ratification, therefore, the agent's liability to the third party for breach of the warranty of authority is terminated, and no notice of the ratification need be given to the third party to bind him. Nevertheless, the third party is permitted to withdraw from the unauthorized contract at any time *prior to* ratification. Similarly, the death or incapacity of the third party extinguishes the principal's power to ratify. The principal also may not ratify if circumstances have so materially changed since the contract was made that it would be inequitable to subject the third party to liability.

To illustrate, assume that Page is the owner of a stable and several thoroughbreds. Page hires Archer to manage the stable, but gives Archer no authority to buy or sell any horse. On June 1, Archer sells one of Page's horses to Tudor. At this point, Page is not liable on the contract because Archer is unauthorized. Archer is liable to Tudor for breach of the warranty of authority. Although unauthorized, Archer has exacted a good price for the horse, and Page decides to go through with the sale. On June 10, the day Tudor is to pick up the horse, Page assists in readying the horse for transport and prepares the papers necessary to effect the sale. When Tudor arrives, the transfer is made with no mention of Archer's lack of authority. Page's conduct constitutes ratification of Archer's contract. Although Tudor could have withdrawn from the contract prior to ratification (between June 1 and June 10), once ratified, Tudor is bound as if the contract had been originally authorized. Tudor may not now avoid the contract on the grounds that it was unauthorized when made, and Archer has no liability to Tudor for breach of the warranty of authority. If the horse had died on June 5, however, Page could not ratify the contract.

Prerequisites to Ratification. There are three basic prerequisites to an effective ratification. First, the principal must have capacity both at the time of the unauthorized act and at the time of ratification. A person who has no capacity to authorize an act may not later ratify it. For example, persons organizing a corporation (corporate promoters) often purport to contract on its behalf before the corporation is formed. Because the corporation is not a legal entity when the contracts are made, the corporation may not ratify them when it comes into existence.[15]

A second requirement for effective ratification is that the person making the contract must purport to be acting for, and on behalf of, the person subsequently ratifying the contract. No pre-existing agency relationship need exist between the parties. The person acting must simply purport to act as an agent for another, who need not be identified. Thus, a wholly undisclosed principal may not ratify an unauthorized contract. The rationale for this requirement is that "one reason for allowing ratification to be effective as prior authorization is to give to the other party what the other expected to get in dealing with the agent. This reason does not exist if the other party does not intend to deal with the principal."[16]

Finally, an effective ratification requires that the principal ratify either with full knowledge of all material facts regarding the actions taken on her behalf, or at least while aware that she does not know all the facts. That is, a principal who affirms an unauthorized contract without investigation, while aware of her ignorance of all facts, assumes the risk of the unknown facts. For example, assume Ashby, purporting to act for Peterson but lacking authority, contracts to sell to Taylor land owned by

Peterson. To induce Taylor to buy, Ashby fraudulently misrepresents the condition of the house located on the land. When informed of the contract, and without knowing the details, Peterson ratifies the contract indicating an intent to "back Ashby up on the contract, whatever happened." Peterson may not later avoid the ratification upon learning of Ashby's conduct, and is subject to liability to Taylor for fraud. As this example illustrates, a principal must ratify the entire transaction and may ratify an agent's tort as well as an unauthorized contract. Thus, Peterson could not ratify Ashby's contract without also assuming the liability resulting from Ashby's fraud. In the following case the court was required to determine whether a principal had ratified its agent's contracts.

Perkins v. Rich
415 N.E.2d 895 (Mass. App. 1981)

Paul John Rich was pastor of First Parish Unitarian Church of East Bridgewater, Massachusetts. The church by-laws provided that a committee of parish members were in "general charge of all business affairs and property" of the church. In the mid-1960s Rich began to assume responsibility for the church's financial affairs. Without approval of the committee, Rich, on behalf of the church, borrowed large sums of money to renovate the church property and to acquire new property. The loans were secured by mortgages on the church's property. Rich intended to create a village similar to Williamsburg, Virginia, featuring museums, galleries, and exhibits. By 1973, construction had progressed to include interior renovation of the church, installation of two swimming pools, extensive landscaping, establishment of an art gallery, and construction of parking lots. During 1977, the church defaulted in payment of the loans.

The church members elected a new committee that sued Rich and Bay State Federal Savings & Loan Association and Shawmut First County Bank, both of which had lent money to the church. The committee alleged that the loans and mortgages were invalid because Rich had lacked the authority to enter into the transactions. A special master ap-

---

15. Concerning promoter's liability, see discussion in Chapter 45.

16. *Restatement (Second) of Agency* §85 comment a.

pointed by the trial court found that Rich was without authority to enter into the loan and mortgage agreements but further found that the committee's failure to disavow the transactions constituted ratification. The committee appealed.

Brown, Judge

. . . The Committee claims that it did not know of the existence of the mortgages and thus that its failure to repudiate the mortgages resulted not from a ratification of the transactions, but from ignorance of essential facts. Generally, in order to establish ratification of unauthorized acts of an agent, a principal must have "full knowledge of all material facts." [*Combs v. Scott*, 94 Mass. 493, 496 (1866).] . . . Ignorance of such facts will not lead to liability. . . . However, a qualification to this rule is that one cannot "purposefully shut his eyes to means of information within his own possession and control" (id. at 497), having only that knowledge "which he cares to have." [*Kelley v. Newburyport & Amesbury Horse R.R.*, 6 N.E. 745, 748 (Mass. 1886).] . . . This is especially true of the Committee, which functioned as the "business center" of the Church and had a duty to keep itself informed of Church business. . . .

Further, as found by the master, the Committee was not totally ignorant of Rich's actions. . . . From the many indicia of the radical physical and structural changes to the church and its surroundings, it should have been obvious to the Church that "something [was] afoot." The very nature of the construction and renovation indicated that large expenditures were being made. Although Rich was far from candid in his disclosures, he did inform Church members of various projects at Church events and through annual reports and publications. The Committee, whose responsibility was to approve payment of all bills, and Church members in general, deliberately ignored these facts. . . . By not asking the simple question—"What is going on?"—as suggested by the master, the Committee assumed the risk of what its investigation might have disclosed. . . .

We thus conclude that the Committee's knowledge of substantial and costly physical changes at the Church should have provoked an investigation by the Committee which would have led to the discovery of the mortgages. . . . By failing to disavow the mortgages, the Church ratified the transactions, a ratification which may be inferred without a vote by the Committee. . . .

Accordingly, the mortgages are valid and binding upon the Church, and the judgments of the Superior Court must be affirmed.

Apparent Authority

As outlined above, a principal is personally liable for the authorized acts of an agent and for those unauthorized acts that he ratifies. The principal also may be bound because of the agent's apparent authority.[17] Unlike *actual authority*, which is based upon the principal's conduct toward the *agent*, **apparent authority** is based upon the principal's conduct toward *third parties* who deal with the agent or purported agent. To illustrate:

$$\text{Principal} \longrightarrow \text{Agent}$$
$$\text{Actual Authority}$$

$$\text{Principal} \longrightarrow \text{Third Party}$$
$$\text{Apparent Authority}$$

Apparent authority is based on estoppel principles, which were discussed in the contracts material. Apparent authority is created when a principal, by words or conduct, leads a third party to believe that another person is an agent, vested with certain authority. In fact, the person possesses no actual authority or less authority than the third parties are led to believe. In reliance upon the principal's representations, and while unaware of the agent's lack of actual authority, the third party contracts with the agent on the principal's behalf. In this case, the principal is liable on the contract, not because the agent is authorized, but because the principal has created "apparent authority" in the agent. After creating apparent authority by inducing reliance upon the apparent agency, the principal is es-

---

17. In some states, apparent authority is referred to as "ostensible" authority.

topped, or prevented, from asserting the agent's lack of actual authority as a defense to enforcement of the contract. Note that a contract made by an apparent agent may be enforced both against and by the principal. That is, an apparent agent may confer both contractual rights and liabilities upon the principal. Suppose Ashe, without actual authority, represents herself to Trotter as Park's agent to purchase supplies for Park's business. Park is present while Ashe makes the representation and says nothing. Trotter enters into a contract with Ashe. Park is bound because his conduct—in this case silence in the face of Ashe's false statements—indicates to Trotter that Ashe is authorized to contract for Park. Ashe has apparent authority with no actual authority.

Although no pre-existing agency relationship is required, apparent authority is most commonly used to expand the authority of an existing agent. For example, Austen, acting as agent for Parish, is expressly authorized to enter into contracts on Parish's behalf for the purchase of goods not exceeding $500. Austen and Trevor negotiate a contract in the amount of $600. Trevor is aware of Austen's limitation and informs Parish of the proposed purchase. Parish says to Trevor, "Don't worry about it." Austen then enters into a contract with Trevor for $600. In this case, Parish's conduct toward Trevor has created apparent authority in Austen to enter into a contract for $600, thereby expanding Austen's authority. Note that Austen has no actual or implied authority to enter into a contract for $600 because actual authority runs from the principal to the agent. In this case, Parish's representation of authority to Trevor creates apparent authority in Austen.

Apparent authority is similarly created in an agent when a principal repeatedly ratifies the agent's unauthorized conduct. Using the preceding example, assume that Austen enters into several $600 contracts with Trevor over a period of time. Parish consistently ratifies Austen's conduct by remaining silent and performing the contracts. Parish's repeated ratification has created apparent authority in Austen to enter into contracts for that amount. Once again, the apparent authority is created by Parish's conduct toward Trevor, leading Trevor to believe that Austen possesses the requisite authority.

Apparent authority also may expand the authority of an existing agent when the agent's actual authorization is narrow or is limited in some respect by the principal, but the agent is appointed to a position, such as manager or treasurer, that involves certain generally recognized duties. The very title "manager," for example, is a representation that the agent has certain powers normally incident to that position. Therefore, any limitation placed upon these normal and ordinary incidents by the principal, known as a **secret limitation,** is not binding upon third parties who have no notice of the limitation. The agent, by virtue of his position, possesses apparent authority. For example, assume A is hired to manage P's apartment building, but is given no authority to collect rent checks. This limitation is not binding upon tenants without notice of the limitation, because a normal incident of an apartment building manager's duties is to collect the rent.

It is important to note that an agent acting on behalf of an undisclosed principal generally possesses no apparent authority to bind the principal. That is, because the third party is unaware of the principal's existence, the principal makes no representations or manifestations to the third party concerning the agent's authority. Thus, the undisclosed principal usually is bound only for acts within the scope of the agent's actual authority. As noted above, however, courts have held that placing a person in a position, such as manager, involving generally recognized powers and duties, is a sufficient representation to create apparent authority in the agent even without direct communication between the principal and third party. Under this theory, an undisclosed principal may be held liable for an agent's unauthorized acts if the agent is placed in a position in which the agent appears to be the owner or manager of a business or property. As noted by one court:

> The typical application of this rule is to a going concern with an established place of business and obvious assets operated by one who ostensibly is the proprietor but secretly is agent for an undisclosed principal. . . . In such cases liability is imposed upon the undisclosed principal because he has placed the agent in such apparent relationship to an observable enterprise as is likely to in-

duce reliance upon him as a responsible proprietor.[18]

Finally, creation of apparent authority must be carefully distinguished from an agent's attempt to "bootstrap" authority. To illustrate, assume Anson, with intent to perpetrate a fraud, represents himself to Teller as Palmer's purchasing agent. In fact, Palmer has never even seen Anson. Anson then purchases goods from Teller for Palmer's account, and leaves town with the merchandise. In this case Palmer has no liability on the contract to Teller. Anson has neither actual nor apparent authority, but has attempted to bootstrap authority. That is, authority capable of binding the principal runs from the principal to agent or principal to third party, *not* from the agent to the third party. In the following case, both the agent's actual and apparent authority were in issue.

Ripani v. Liberty Loan Corporation of Carmichael

157 Cal. Rptr. 272 (Cal. App. 1979)

Plaintiff Joseph Ripani owned a commercial building which he leased to defendant Liberty Loan Corporation of Carmichael. Liberty Loan had an option to renew the lease for an additional two years by giving thirty days written notice to Ripani. Two months prior to expiration of the lease, Ripani went to Liberty Loan's office to collect the rent. He reminded Michael Anderson, Liberty Loan's branch manager, that the lease would soon expire. Anderson prepared, signed, and delivered to Ripani a notice that Liberty Loan was exercising its option to renew the lease for two years. Two months later, Liberty Loan advised Ripani that it would not renew the lease and vacated the premises.

Ripani sued Liberty Loan for rent due under the two-year renewal. Liberty Loan alleged that Anderson did not have the authority to exercise the option to renew on its behalf. The trial court entered judgment in favor of Ripani and Liberty Loan appealed.

---

18. *Senor v. Bangor Mills, Inc.*, 211 F.2d 685, 688 (3d Cir. 1954).

Kleaver, Associate Justice

. . . An agent has such authority as a principal actually or ostensibly confers upon him. . . .

In order to establish actual or ostensible authority of an agent, the principal's consent need not be express, but may be implied from the facts of a particular case. . . . An agent's authority may be established by circumstantial evidence, and the testimony of the agent is admissible to prove both the fact of the agency and the extent of the authority conferred. . . . We proceed to examine the evidence to determine whether it supports a finding of either actual or ostensible authority.

Anderson was the branch manager of the office. As branch manager, his duties included approving loans, supervising personnel, handling collections and repossessions, hiring and terminating employees, and signing checks on behalf of the company. Anderson would pay miscellaneous bills, office expenses, supplies, rent and attorneys' fees by check. The rent under the terms of the lease was paid to plaintiff by check signed by Anderson. Prior to the time Anderson executed the option, he had discussed with his superior the possibility of moving the business to a larger office. At his superior's direction he discussed the amount of space available with at least one lessor, and the amount the rent would be. After reporting the results of his search to his superior Anderson was told not to search for other space, that the company had decided to retain plaintiff's space. Anderson signed the exercise of the lease option because he believed defendant intended to retain the office and he had the authority to exercise the option as branch manager of the office. The evidence supports a finding that Anderson had the actual authority to exercise the option in the lease.

The evidence further supports a finding that Anderson had ostensible authority to exercise the option. All dealings plaintiff ever had with the company were with the branch manager. Rent was paid by the branch manager by check signed by the branch manager. Any maintenance problem or duty plaintiff had under the lease was reported to him by the branch manager. The original lease, although signed by company officers and not the branch manager, was presented to plaintiff for his signature by the branch manager and plaintiff never met with anyone else from the company. Throughout the eight years plaintiff leased the premises to defendant, defendant always dealt with plaintiff through branch managers. Defendant placed a branch manager in the office with the extensive authority to operate the business and the apparent authority to deal with matters under the lease. These facts could properly indicate to plaintiff that the branch manager had the authority to exercise the option in the lease. . . .

[Judgment affirmed.]

Liability of Principal for Notice or Knowledge of Agent

In the course of performing their duties, agents often acquire knowledge or receive notification of facts having actual or potential legal significance to the principal. The law of agency determines when notice to or knowledge of an agent is legally effective as if given to or acquired by the principal directly. Before discussing this issue the distinction between notice and knowledge should be noted.

Notice and Knowledge Defined

Notification is a formal act intended to affect the legal relations between the notifier and the person notified. A person has notice of a fact if he has actual knowledge of it, has received a notice or notification of it, or from all facts and circumstances known to him at the time has reason to know that it exists.[19] **Knowledge,** on the other hand, is a more limited concept, referring to a person's subjective conscious belief in the truth of a fact or condition.[20] A person therefore may have notice of a fact without actual knowledge. For example, recording a deed or mortgage provides constructive notice to the entire world of the recording party's interest, even though most persons have no actual knowledge of the recording.

Agent's Notice

As a general rule, a notification given to an agent is notice to the principal if the agent is actually or apparently authorized to receive it. Conversely, notifications given by an authorized agent are notifications by the principal. The agent's notice is often said to be "imputed" to the principal, based upon the legal fiction that principal and authorized agent are one person.

For example, assume Price appoints Abram to manage a number of commercial buildings leased by Price to various businesses. Abram is authorized to lease the buildings, contract for their repair, settle disputes with tenants, hire and fire employees, and give and receive notifications in connection with the property. Tate is a tenant in one of the buildings. A provision in the lease provides that it may be terminated by either party upon ninety days advance notice. Tate notifies Abram of her intent to terminate the lease and move out in ninety days. Tate's notification to Abram is notice to Price, whether or not Abram communicates it to Price. Note that the same result follows even if Price had previously fired Abram, if Tate has no notice of the firing. That is, Abram still possesses apparent though not actual authority. Had Tate instead notified a repairman employed by Price, the notice would not be imputed to Price. The repairman, unlike Abram, is not actually or apparently authorized to receive such notification.

Agent's Knowledge

An agent's knowledge may also be imputed to the principal. Generally, the principal is deemed to have the knowledge of facts known to an agent if that knowledge is important in the transaction the agent is authorized to conduct. Suppose Amy is Paula's agent to buy and sell antiques. Amy defrauds Terry into buying a worthless vase by knowingly representing it as a valuable antique. Paula is liable to Terry for fraud, because Amy's knowledge of falsity is imputed to Paula. Similarly, Paula could not retain property acquired for her through Amy's fraud or other wrongdoing. The following case illustrates an important exception to the general rule that an agent's knowledge is imputed to the principal.

---

19. UCC §1-201(25); *Restatement (Second) of Agency* §9(1).

20. *Restatement (Second) of Agency* §9 comment c.

McKey & Poague, Inc. v. Stackler

379 N.E.2d 1198 (Ill. App. 1978)

George Hiles and Eugene F. Migely were licensed real estate brokers who were employed by McKey & Poague, Inc. In 1973, a federal court ruled that Hiles and Migely had been involved in illegal racial discrimination in conjunction with the rental of an apartment owned by Presbitero. Subsequently, Ronald E. Stackler, Director of the Department of Registration and Education of the State of Illinois, suspended both Hiles's and Migely's real estate licenses because of their practicing racial discrimination. The director also suspended the license of McKey & Poague, Inc. as employer of Hiles and Migely. Hiles, Migely, and McKey & Poague, Inc. appealed the decision to the Illinois circuit court, which reversed the decision to suspend the licenses. The director of the Department of Registration and Education appealed.

Lorenz, Justice

. . . Although we uphold the decision of the Department as to the individuals who actually participated in the unlawful racial discrimination, we have found no evidence in the record indicating that McKey & Poague authorized, was aware of, or in any manner condoned the discrimination. The record is devoid of any evidence to support the decision that McKey & Poague was itself guilty of racial discrimination, and the decision of the Department as to McKey & Poague is therefore against the manifest weight of the evidence. Indeed, the testimony indicates that McKey & Poague expressly forbids its employees, including Hiles and Migely, from engaging in racial discrimination, requiring each employee to sign an agreement to adhere to fair housing laws and displaying posters containing anti-discrimination laws in each office. The record reflects no corporate departure from this enunciated policy.

While the actions of the two employees were proper grounds for a suspension of their individual licenses, those actions do not constitute a basis under the facts here for the suspension of the corporate certificate of the employer, McKey & Poague. . . .

The evidence presented to the Department does not demonstrate that McKey & Poague as employer of Hiles and Migely was aware of their illegal conduct. Furthermore, although the Department properly found that Hiles and Migely were aware of the discriminatory policies of Presbitero, we do not believe that such knowledge under these facts can be imputed to McKey & Poague. Although knowledge acquired by an agent within the scope of his agency will generally be imputed to his principal, knowledge will not be imputed where the agent has a motive or interest in concealing the facts from the principal. . . . Where Hiles and Migely were acting in violation of both the law and their employment agreements, they certainly possessed a motive or interest in concealing Presbitero's policies from their employer, and the knowledge should not, therefore, be imputed to McKey & Poague. . . .

For the foregoing reasons that portion of the judgment of the circuit court reversing and vacating the Department's suspension of McKey & Poague's certificate is affirmed. The remainder of the judgment . . . is reversed. . . .

[Judgment affirmed in part and reversed in part.]

Termination of Agency Powers

At some point, the agent's authority to affect the legal relations of the principal terminates. After termination the agent no longer has the power to bind the principal to contracts with third parties. The following material examines the various methods by which an agent's actual and apparent authority are extinguished.

Termination of Actual Authority

Effect of Subsequent Events. An agent's actual authority is created by the principal's manifestation of consent to the agent. Similarly, actual authority is terminated when the agent, based upon the principal's words or conduct, is led to believe that the principal no longer desires the agency to continue. This intent may be inferred from the original authorization in light of subsequent events. Agencies often terminate according to the terms of the agency contract, or the occurrence of a given event, or on completion of the purpose for which the agency was initially created. To illustrate, assume A agrees to work for P for a period of three years. At the end of three years the agency is terminated according to the terms of the contract. Or, assume P appoints A as agent to sell his car. After A sells the car, the agency is terminated because the act authorized by the agency has been accomplished. In these cases, the agency is terminated by events clearly indicated in the original authorization.

An agent's authority also terminates upon occurrence of an unspecified event or a substantial change in circumstances from which the agent should reasonably infer that the principal no longer consents to a continuation of the agency. Under this rule, for example, an agent's authority terminates upon the loss, destruction, or substantial change in value of the subject matter; a substantial change in business conditions; a loss of (or failure to acquire) qualification of either principal or agent or a change in law that makes it illegal to carry out an authorized act; or a serious breach of the duty of loyalty by the agent. For example, assume A is appointed P's agent to sell P's antique Rolls-Royce. Prior to the sale, the car is destroyed by fire as A knows. A's authority is terminated. Or assume P hires A, an attorney, to represent him in a divorce suit. A is subsequently disbarred. A's authority is terminated.

A similar analysis is applied to the bankruptcy of either principal or agent. If the agency is one dependent upon the continued solvency or credit rating of either party, bankruptcy terminates the agency. If not so dependent, the agent's authority to act is unaffected. For example, assume P appoints A as agent to purchase raw materials on credit for use in P's business ventures. P subsequently becomes bankrupt and A learns of that fact. A's authority to make further contracts for P is terminated. Note that on these same facts, A's bankruptcy would not necessarily terminate the agency.

Effect of Death or Incapacity.
An agency is terminated automatically by operation of law upon the death or incapacity of either the principal or agent. Because no notice to the other party is required, an agent may be held liable for breach of the warranty

of authority on contracts made after the principal's death, but without knowledge of it. Some courts protect the agent in this case by providing that the warranty of authority is not breached unless the agent contracts with actual knowledge of the principal's death. Under this approach, if the agent enters into a contract with a third party after the principal's death but before learning of the death, neither the agent nor the principal's estate is liable on the contract.

Termination by Acts of the Parties—Agency for Agreed Term.
In many cases the parties contractually agree that the agency will continue for a fixed term. For example, P may hire A to act as her purchasing agent for a three year period. Nevertheless, because an agency is a consensual relationship, the parties may always *mutually* agree to terminate the agency, regardless of any prior agreement or authorization. Further, either party may *unilaterally* terminate the agency at any time, even if contractually obligated to continue the agency. Generally, agency authority is extinguished when the intent to terminate is communicated to the other party. A party wrongfully terminating the agency is, however, liable to the other for breach of the agency contract. In short, both the principal and the agent have the power, but not necessarily the right, to terminate the agency at any time.

Termination by Acts of the Parties—Agency for Indefinite Term; Employment at Will Doctrine.
In the absence of an agreement regarding the period of employment, the agency is generally terminable upon notice by either party.[21] Traditionally, this rule also has applied to the employer-employee relationship, permitting employers to fire employees "at will," if the employee is hired for an indefinite period of time without an employment contract. During the last twenty-five years, however, a majority of states have recognized exceptions to this **employment at will doctrine** prohibiting employers from discharging employees if the dismissal would violate principles of public policy,

---

21. *Restatement (Second) of Agency* §442.

implied contractual conditions, or an implied in fact contract.[22]

Public Policy. Over half of the states have adopted the rule that termination of an employee is unlawful if it violates clearly mandated public policy. Some states recognize a tort action, called unlawful or retaliatory discharge, for employee dismissals in violation of public policy. Others consider a termination in violation of public policy to be a breach of contract. In applying this exception to the employment at will doctrine, courts first must determine what constitutes public policy. One court succinctly summarized the issue as follows:

> In determining whether a clear mandate of public policy is violated, courts should inquire whether the employer's conduct contravenes the letter or purpose of a constitutional, statutory, or regulatory provision or scheme. Prior judicial decisions may also establish the relevant public policy. However, courts should proceed cautiously if called upon to declare public policy absent some prior legislative or judicial expression on the subject.[23]

Under the public policy exception, courts have found dismissal to be unlawful if the employee was discharged for reporting the employer's illegal acts to authorities (whistleblowing) or for refusing to engage in illegal acts such as committing perjury, falsifying company records, or participating in price fixing schemes. Courts also have found a violation of public policy when an employee was discharged for exercising legal rights or complying with a statutory duty, for example, by filing a workers' compensation claim, for serving jury duty, or for obeying a subpoena and appearing at a

hearing. The following case discusses the public policy exception to the employment at will doctrine.

McClanahan v. Remington Freight Lines, Inc.
517 N.E.2d 390 (Ind. 1988)

Plaintiff John McClanahan began working as an interstate truck driver for defendant Remington Freight Lines, Inc. in November 1981. In March 1982, Remington's safety director, Richard Barbour, instructed McClanahan to travel to New York to pick up a load of freight and to deliver it to Minnesota by a route designated by Barbour. After picking up the load, McClanahan informed Barbour that it weighed 78,000 pounds and, therefore, would exceed the maximum weight limit of 75,000 pounds allowed on the Illinois roads on the designated route. Barbour replied that McClanahan probably would not be caught by authorities because of the absence of permanent scales on the Illinois route and further assured McClanahan that Remington would pay any fine he incurred. After refusing to drive the overweight load through Illinois, McClanahan was fired by Barbour for refusing to carry a load. McClanahan sued Remington in tort for wrongful discharge. Remington argued that McClanahan was an employee at will who could be fired for any reason. McClanahan acknowledged that he was an employee at will but claimed that he could not be discharged for refusing to commit an illegal act. The trial court granted Remington's motion for summary judgment. After the appellate court reversed in part, McClanahan appealed to the Indiana Supreme Court.

Shepard, Chief Justice
. . . The American employment-at-will doctrine gained strength and reached its peak by the beginning of the twentieth century. At that time, the employer's right to discharge at his whim was virtually absolute. With the advent of federal and state legislation, collective bargaining, and employment contracts, the vitality of that rule has dwindled. The essence of the modern rule is that an employ-

---

22. The exceptions to the employment at will doctrine discussed in this chapter have developed primarily through state common law. An employer's power to discharge an employee may be limited further by state or federal statutes. Chapter 53 discusses various federal statutes, including Title VII of the Civil Rights Act of 1964 and labor laws, that restrict an employer's power to fire employees.

23. *Parnar v. Americana Hotels, Inc.*, 652 P.2d 625, 631 (Hawaii 1982).

ment contract of indefinite duration is presumptively terminable at the will of either party. . . .

In recent years the employment at will doctrine has come under particular attack in the courts, which have been asked to create modifications or exceptions to the doctrine to avoid potentially harsh results. A common plea by discharged plaintiffs is that an employer should be subjected to tort liability if his firing of the employee contravenes a well-defined public policy. The judicial response to pleas for a public policy exception to the employment at will doctrine has been mixed.

This Court has recognized such an exception to the employment at will doctrine when an employee was discharged for filing a workmen's compensation claim. . . .

We agree with the Court of Appeals that firing an employee for refusing to commit an illegal act for which he would be personally liable is as much a violation of public policy declared by the legislature as firing an employee for filing a workmen's compensation claim. A separate but tightly defined exception to the employment at will doctrine is appropriate under these facts. . . .

No Indiana statute explicitly states that public policy is violated by committing an illegal act or requiring an employee to do so at the risk of his job. Nonetheless, the idea that individuals contravene public policy when they violate the law is so basic to our social and political order that a legislative pronouncement of that concept is hardly necessary. Some states interpret the penal code as a statement of public policy; when the law is violated, so is the public policy. . . .

If McClanahan had chosen to drive his overweight truck through Illinois, he would have been personally liable for violation of Illinois law and subject to a fine. . . . Furthermore, he would have been jointly and severally liable for the cost of repairing any damage to the highway or highway structures caused by his overweight vehicle. . . .

Depriving McClanahan of any legal recourse under these circumstances would encourage criminal conduct by both the employee and the employer. Employees faced with the choice of losing their jobs or committing an illegal act for which they might not be caught would feel pressure to break the law simply out of financial necessity. Employ-

ers, knowing the employees' susceptibility to such threats and the absence of civil retribution, would be prompted to present such an ultimatum.

The law will not countenance such a situation. . . .

McClanahan stated a cause of action when he alleged he was wrongfully discharged for refusing to commit an illegal act for which he would have been personally liable. Accepting as true the facts alleged by McClanahan, we conclude that McClanahan clearly has presented sufficient evidence to overcome the defendants' motion for summary judgment. . . .

[Judgment affirmed.]

Implied Contract Conditions. A second exception to the employment at will doctrine is based on the principle of general contract law implying a covenant of good faith and fair dealing in all contracts. As applied to an employment contract, this rule imposes liability for breach of contract on an employer who discharges an employee in bad faith. Few cases have used the covenant of good faith and fair dealing as the sole basis for finding an unlawful discharge. Employers have been held liable for breach of the covenant, however, for discharging an employee who refused to date her foreman and for firing a salesman to avoid paying him sales bonuses.

Implied in Fact Contract. In some cases, termination of an at will employee may be unlawful because it would violate an implied in fact contract or contract term. As discussed in Chapter 7, an implied in fact contract is inferred from the conduct of the parties. In the employment context, implied in fact contracts limiting the employer's power of termination often arise from statements made by company officials or officers or from written policies distributed by the employer. Assume, for example, that Enid operates a business and when hiring Frank, she tells him that he will not be terminated without just cause. Because Enid's statement creates an implied in fact contract term, Frank is not considered an at will employee and, therefore, may not be terminated arbitrarily or without cause.

With a large company or corporation, an implied in fact contract is more likely to arise from provisions in a personnel manual adopted by the employer to inform employees of policies such as working hours, vacation and sick leave, appropriate dress and conduct, and other related matters. A majority of states now recognize that the statements included in those manuals may create implied in fact contract provisions. If, for example, the handbook states that an employee can be terminated only for just cause, arbitrary dismissal constitutes a breach of contract. Courts also have held that a company's failure to follow a dismissal procedure outlined in an employee manual may constitute breach of contract. Assume that the XYZ Co. personnel manual states that continued employment will be based on satisfactory annual performance reviews and that XYZ will provide two warnings prior to discharging an employee. Dismissal of an employee who has received only excellent performance evaluations or who has not received two written warnings would constitute breach of contract. In such cases, many courts have concluded that strict adherence to the employment at will doctrine despite the provisions of an employment manual unfairly favors the employer. One court explained:

> It is patently unjust to allow an employer to couch a handbook, bulletin, or other similar material in mandatory terms and then allow him to ignore these very policies as 'a gratuitous, non-binding statement of general policy' whenever it works to his disadvantage. Assuredly, the employer would view these policies differently if it were the employee who failed to follow them.[24]

As a result of judicial decisions finding implied in fact contracts, many employers now use written agreements stating that employment is at will or include disclaimers or provisions in personnel manuals clearly indicating that they do not constitute terms of employment.

Termination of Apparent Authority

Agents often possess both actual and apparent authority. Termination of actual authority does not terminate apparent authority, because apparent authority is based upon the principal's representations to third persons, not to the agent. If an agent possesses apparent authority, therefore, the principal desiring to terminate the agency must extinguish both types of authority.

Actual authority is terminated in the same manner as it is created—by the principal's manifestation to the agent. Apparent authority is also extinguished as it is created—by the principal's manifestations to third parties. That is, apparent authority is extinguished by giving notice to third parties that the agent no longer has authority to bind the principal. This notice is accomplished in one of two ways depending upon the relationship of the particular third party to the agent. Persons who have previously extended credit to, or received credit from, the principal through the agent are entitled to actual oral or written notice of the agent's lack of continuing authority. Other third parties entitled to actual notice include persons who have been specially invited by the principal to deal with the agent (the specially accredited agent), persons with whom the principal knows the agent has begun to deal, and persons who rely upon a writing, such as a power of attorney, indicating the agent's authority entrusted to the agent by the principal. All other persons, including those who have not previously dealt with the agent or who have dealt with him on a cash basis, are entitled to notice by publication. **Notice by publication** is accomplished by advertising the termination in a newspaper of general circulation in the area where the agent operates or publicizing the termination by another effective means.[25]

The rules outlined above apply only to general agents. Generally, if the principal represents to a third party that an agent is employed as a special

---

24. *Small v. Springs Industries, Inc.*, 357 S.E.2d 452, 455 (S.C. 1987).

25. *Restatement (Second) of Agency* §136.

agent, the agent's apparent authority is extinguished upon termination of his actual authority. That is, no notice is required to terminate the apparent authority of a special agent, unless the principal leads the third party to believe that he will receive notice of termination. Further, any agent's apparent authority terminates automatically without notice upon the death or incapacity of the principal.[26]

Termination of a Power Given as Security

In an ordinary agency relationship, the agent acts on behalf of and subject to the control of the principal. The agency device may, however, be used to create powers in the agent to be used for the agent's rather than the principal's benefit, usually used to secure performance of an obligation owing from the principal to the agent. In this case, the parties create in the "agent" a **power given as security** (sometimes known as an **agency coupled with an interest**). For example, assume A agrees to loan money to P, but only if P provides some collateral to secure the loan. P therefore delivers a valuable stamp collection to A, and gives A the power to sell the stamp collection in the event P defaults. A has a power given as security.

A power given as security is not a true agency, because the agent (creditor) does not act subject to the principal's (debtor's) control, or for his benefit. As such it may not be terminated in the same manner as authority or apparent authority. As a general rule, a power given as security is irrevocable by the person granting it and is not extinguished by the death or incapacity of either party. In other words, a power given as security is generally terminated only with the consent of the holder of the power or upon satisfaction of the obligation secured by the power. Thus, in the preceding example, if P repays the loan, A's power to sell is terminated. Assuming, however, that the loan remains unpaid, the power may not be revoked unilaterally by P, and is unaffected by the death or incapacity of either A or P.

---

26. *Restatement (Second) of Agency* §§132-133.

SUMMARY

1. Agency is a fiduciary relationship in which one party, an agent, agrees to act on behalf of and under the control of another, the principal. An agency is created by the manifestation of consent by both parties. Although agency relationships are often created by contract, no contractual relationship is required, and the parties need not have contractual capacity. The law of agency primarily addresses the relationship between principal and agent and the relationship of principal and agent to third parties in both contract and tort.

2. An agency is a fiduciary relationship imposing various duties upon the parties. Most important is the duty of loyalty owed by the agent to the principal. This duty requires the agent to act solely for the benefit of the principal regarding matters within the scope of the agency. The agent also owes the principal various duties of service and obedience. Although no duty of loyalty is owed by the principal to the agent, the principal is under a duty to compensate the agent, to reimburse him for expenses and losses incurred during the course of the agency, and to use reasonable care to prevent injury to the agent during performance of the agency.

3. The legal effect of contracts made by the agent on the principal's behalf depends upon whether the agent is authorized and whether the principal's existence and identity are disclosed to the third party contracting with the agent. The extent of an agent's authority, which may be express or implied, is determined by examining the principal's words or other conduct toward the agent indicating the principal's consent that the agent act on the principal's behalf.

4. Two basic rules govern most agency and contracts cases: (1) an agent is liable on a contract made in an agency capacity unless both the agent is authorized, and the principal is disclosed; and (2) the principal (disclosed, partially disclosed, or undisclosed) is liable upon contracts made on his behalf if the agent is authorized to act. In the partially disclosed and undisclosed principal cases, in which both principal and agent are liable, the traditional common law rule requires the third party, after discovering the existence and identity of the principal,

to elect to hold either the principal or the agent liable. A minority of jurisdictions reject this approach and hold the principal and agent jointly and severally liable.

5. Two important doctrines may be viewed as exceptions to the general rule that the principal is liable if the agent is authorized—ratification and apparent authority. Ratification is conduct by the principal indicating an intent to be bound upon a previously unauthorized contract made on his behalf. After ratification, the principal is bound as if the contract had been originally authorized. An effective ratification requires that (1) the principal have capacity both at the time of the unauthorized act and at the time of ratification, (2) the person making the contract purport to be acting on behalf of the person subsequently ratifying, and (3) the principal ratify either with full knowledge of the facts surrounding the contract or while aware that he does not know all facts.

6. Unlike actual authority, which is based upon the principal's conduct toward the agent, apparent authority is based upon the principal's conduct toward *third parties* who deal with the agent or purported agent. Apparent authority, based upon estoppel principles, is created when a principal, by words or conduct, leads a third party to believe that another person is an agent, vested with certain authority. After creating apparent authority by inducing reliance upon the apparent agency, the principal is estopped, or prevented, from asserting the agent's lack of actual authority as a defense to enforcement of a contract made by the apparent agent.

7. In addition to liability upon contracts made by agents, a principal's legal relations may also be affected by notice or knowledge acquired by an agent. As a general rule, a notification given to an agent is notice to the principal if the agent is actually or apparently authorized to receive it. An agent's knowledge is imputed to the principal if that knowledge is important to the transaction the agent is authorized to conduct.

8. Agency relationships generally are terminated in the same manner in which they were created. For example, an agent's actual authority ceases when the agent, based upon the principal's words or conduct, is led to believe that the principal no longer desires the agency to continue. An agency also is terminated automatically by operation of law upon death or incapacity of either party. Apparent authority is terminated by giving notice to third parties that the agent no longer has authority to bind the principal. A power given as security, or "agency coupled with an interest," is not a true agency and therefore may not be terminated in the same manner as actual or apparent authority. Such a power is generally irrevocable by the person granting it and is not extinguished by the death or incapacity of either party.

KEY TERMS

agency	implied warranty of
agent	authority
principal	disclosed principal
power of attorney	partially disclosed
equal dignity rule	principal
general agent	undisclosed principal
special agent	election
servant	ratification
master	apparent authority
independent contractor	secret limitation
broker	notification
factor (commission	knowledge
merchant)	employment at will
del credere agent	doctrine
duty of loyalty	notice by publication
authority	power given as security
express authority	(agency coupled with
implied authority	an interest)

QUESTIONS AND PROBLEMS

40-1   What business functions are served by allowing agents to bind their principals to contracts? Consider both corporate and individual principals. Summarize the basic methods by which a principal can be held liable upon contracts made by an agent.

40-2   Laverne was manager of a store operated by Hartford Co. Over a period of several months Laverne embezzled funds belonging to Hartford.
   (a) Has Laverne violated any of her fiduciary obligations to Hartford? Explain.
   (b) Hartford sued Laverne for repayment of the misappropriated funds. Hartford also demanded repayment of all wages that it had paid to Laverne during the period that the embezzlement occurred. Should Laverne be required to repay the wages? Explain.

40-3   Peter Novera was a gardener who worked for Phillip Lederle. Novera advised Lederle that a tree on Lederle's property had died and Lederle asked Novera to find someone to remove the tree. Novera called Jacob Wing, a tree surgeon, and they met on the grounds near the dead tree. After discussing removal of the tree, Wing pointed out some other trees that needed special care. Novera authorized Wing to remove the tree and to spray and trim the other trees. Wing sent a bill to Novera who then advised Wing that the property belonged to Lederle. Wing then sent the bill to Lederle. Lederle paid for the removal of the dead tree but refused to pay for the other services. Wing has sued Lederle. Is Lederle liable for payment of the bill? Explain.

40-4 Crystal Computers planned to have a sales show of its new products at the Brandywine Hilton Hotel. Crystal and Brandywine entered into a contract by which Crystal agreed to rent six of the hotel's meeting rooms for a three-day period. Several days before the show, Brandywine notified Crystal that construction of the meeting rooms was not complete and the sales show would have to be cancelled. Crystal filed a lawsuit for breach of contract naming both Brandywine and the Hilton Corporation as defendants. Hilton Corporation denied that Brandywine was its agent. Crystal, however, entered evidence to support its allegation that Brandywine had the apparent authority to act as Hilton's agent. The evidence showed that Brandywine was owned by a group of businessmen pursuant to a franchise agreement with Hilton. Hilton required Brandywine to display the Hilton logo and sign. The architectural style of the hotel, its furnishings and color schemes all were subject to approval of Hilton. Linens, matches, and ashtrays of the hotel bore the Hilton logo. The president of Crystal testified that at all times he believed he was dealing with the Hilton Corporation even though the rental contract listed Brandywine Hilton Hotel as the renting party. Did Brandywine have the apparent authority to act as Hilton's agent? Explain.

40-5 Lewis University and Canel Management Co. entered into an agreement by which Canel agreed to provide all maintenance services for the university campus. The agreement provided that Canel had the power to "contract on behalf of Lewis for the purchase of any items necessary and incidental to Canel's performing its duties." The agreement was signed by the president of Lewis University and the president of Canel. Canel appointed its employee Don Boyd to supervise the maintenance at the university. Boyd signed a contract with Roscoe Co. which agreed to provide 1,000 cases of soap and cleansers at a cost of $50 per case. Boyd signed the agreement "Lewis University by Don Boyd, its agent." Lewis University refused to pay for the soap and cleanser claiming that Boyd lacked the authority to enter into the contract. Roscoe has sued both Lewis University and Don Boyd. Who is liable on the contract? Explain.

40-6 Gloria operates a store and gas station that allows customers to charge purchases on an open account. Ronald Abare opened an account in the name of "Abare Wells" and periodically purchased on credit gasoline that was pumped into trucks bearing the name Abare & Sons Artesian Well Drilling Co. Monthly bills were paid by checks with the name Abare & Sons Artesian Well Drilling Co. on them. After several bills were left unpaid, Gloria sued Ronald Abare for the amounts due on the account. Abare claimed that the account was for a corporation, Abare & Sons Artesian Well Drilling Co., and that he should not be held personally liable. How should the court rule?

40-7 (a) Emard, quality control director at Frosted Foods, Inc., wrote a memo to his supervisor advising him that substandard ingredients were being used in the company's products. Emard noted that the use of these ingredients was inconsistent with the products' labels thereby violating the state Food, Drug, and Cosmetic Act. Shortly thereafter, Frosted Foods, Inc. fired Emard. Emard sued Frosted Foods alleging that he was discharged in retaliation for attempting to correct the labeling of the company's products. Assuming that Emard can prove his allegations, how should the court rule?

(b) Murphy was assistant treasurer of AHP Corp. While reviewing financial statements he discovered that the accounts had been illegally manipulated to show $50 million growth in income that enabled several officers to receive bonuses. Murphy notified top management of the improprieties and was fired several weeks later. Was Murphy's dismissal unlawful? Explain.

40-8 Valley View Hospital hired Clara as operating room supervisor in 1972 but no employment agreement was signed. After starting work she received a copy of the Valley View Policy Manual, a twenty-page pamphlet summarizing various general matters such as holidays, sick leave, insurance, dress code, wages and hours, termination procedure, and grievance proceedings. In 1978, following several promotions, Clara was fired. The Policy Manual included the following provision: "The discharged employee who feels himself aggrieved by the terms of the discharge may appeal to Administration and will be granted hearing." Clara requested a hearing but it was denied.

(a) Clara has sued Valley View for breach of contract. Valley View alleges that Clara's employment was terminable at will. How should the court rule?

(b) Would your answer to (a) be different if Valley View could prove that Clara did not read the Policy Manual until after she had been fired? Why or why not?

(c) Assume that you have been hired by Valley View as personnel administrator. Suggest provisions that might be included in the Policy Manual to minimize the likelihood that the manual would be considered part of an employment contract.

- introduction to the general liability of principal and agent for torts committed against third parties
- discussion of the *respondeat superior* doctrine, which imposes liability without fault upon a principal for torts committed by an agent
- coverage of the law governing compensation of employees for job-related injuries including the operation of a typical workers' compensation statute

Whereas Chapter 40 examines the liability of principal and agent for *contracts* made on the principal's behalf, this chapter covers the tort aspects of the agency relationship. It focuses first upon the tort liability of the parties when the agent injures a third party while acting for the principal, and concludes with a discussion of liability for injuries inflicted upon an agent that occur during the course of employment.

Tort Liability of Principal and Agent

As a basic principle of tort law a person is always liable for her own torts. The fact that a person is acting in an agency capacity therefore does not reduce the *agent's* liability for her wrong. Rather, the law of agency and torts determines when the *principal* is liable to third parties for torts committed

by the agent. Generally the principal may be held liable on one of two theories. First, the principal may be liable for his own intentional or negligent conduct in causing the injury. Second, the principal may be liable "vicariously" for the agent's tortious conduct under the *respondeat superior* doctrine.

Liability of Principal for Principal's Torts

A person is always liable for an intentional wrong he directs another to do. A principal is therefore liable for harm caused to a third person by an agent resulting from the principal's express direction. Assume Peterson, with intent to disrupt Todd's business, directs Archer to cut the electrical and telephone lines to Todd's store. Archer cuts the lines. Peterson is liable in tort to Todd.

In addition to express direction, a principal may be liable for his own negligence in conducting the agency that results in harm to a third person. In this context, negligence may take many forms including giving improper or ambiguous orders, failing to establish proper working rules and regulations, or failing to exercise reasonable care in the selection, training, or supervision of employees. Assume Pennington, a courier service, hires Amber to drive one of its trucks. Amber, as Pennington knows, has a history of erratic driving behavior including several accidents and traffic citations. Amber is subsequently involved in a traffic accident that destroys Terry's car. Pennington may be liable to

Terry for negligence in choosing Amber as a driver. The same result follows had Pennington failed to adequately train Amber or supervise Amber's conduct.[1]

Liability of Principal for Agent's Torts—Respondeat Superior

Although the principal may be held liable for her own negligent or intentional conduct resulting in injury to a third party, liability is often imposed upon completely innocent principals for torts committed by their agents under the **respondeat superior** (Latin: "let the master respond") doctrine. This doctrine imposes liability without fault upon the principal in a "master-servant" relationship. Under this doctrine "a master is subject to liability for the torts of his servants committed while acting in the scope of their employment."[2] Liability under the respondeat superior doctrine is **vicarious**.[3] The master is liable for the *servant's* tortious conduct. Liability is imposed without regard to the negligence or other fault of the master.

Most employment arrangements create a master-servant relationship between employer and employee. One rationale for holding an employer liable for an employee's torts is that the master both selects and controls the servant and should therefore be responsible for his conduct. Another rationale for the doctrine is that the employer reaps the benefit of the employee's labor and places the employee in a position where the employee may injure third parties. The employer should therefore also bear the responsibility for the employee's actions, treating them as an ordinary cost of doing business, rather than imposing the loss upon the innocent third parties who have been injured. The employer can insure against this liability and pass the cost of insurance along to all of its customers, thereby spreading the loss among those who benefit from the employer's business. An added rationale is that

imposing liability upon the master for the servant's conduct induces employers to be more careful in choosing, training, instructing, and supervising their employees. Finally, the doctrine increases the likelihood that injured third parties will be compensated. That is, the employer, backed by insurance coverage, provides a "deep pocket" more likely to be able to pay a judgment than the servant causing the injury. Whatever the justification, the respondeat superior doctrine is firmly entrenched in the law, with precedents dating back nearly three centuries.[4]

Liability is imposed under the respondeat superior doctrine if two elements are present:

1. a *master-servant relationship* exists between principal and agent; and
2. the agent (servant) was acting in the *scope of employment* when the tort was committed.

These elements are discussed in more detail below.

The Master-Servant Relationship. As noted in Chapter 40, master and servant are specialized forms of principal and agent. A master is a principal who employs an agent and who has the right to control the physical conduct of the agent's activities. A servant is the agent who performs continuous service for another and whose physical conduct is subject to control by the other. Thus all masters are principals, but not all principals are masters, because not all principals possess the right to control the physical conduct of their agents. Similarly, all servants are agents, but not all agents are servants because certain agents are not subject to the principal's physical control in the performance of their duties. Note that a servant is characterized by continuous service, not by the character or quality of the service rendered. Thus, servants include not only manual laborers but also ship captains and corporate managers. In addition, although control or right of control by the master is essential, this requirement is easily established. For example, corporate managers and cooks are servants even

---

1. On these facts Pennington is probably also liable to Terry on the respondeat superior theory discussed below. Nevertheless, the fact that the employer is also negligent may provide the injured party with certain advantages in remedy.

2. *Restatement (Second) of Agency* §219(1).

3. Sometimes also referred to as "derivative" or "secondary."

---

4. See, for example, *Jones v. Hart,* Holt, K.B. 642, 90 Eng. Rep. 1255 (K.B. 1698).

though it is often understood, if not explicitly stated, that they have wide latitude and discretion in performing their duties.

A servant must be carefully distinguished from an independent contractor. An independent contractor is a person who contracts with another to do something but who is not subject to the other's control or right of control in the performance of the undertaking. That is, an independent contractor contracts with another to render a service, but retains control over the manner in which the acts constituting performance are performed. An independent contractor may or may not be an agent.[5] Assume P appoints A, a real estate broker, as agent to sell P's land. A is an agent, but is an independent contractor, not a servant. Or, assume P contracts with A, a building contractor, to build an office building for P at an agreed price. A is an independent contractor, but is neither an agent nor a servant.

The distinction between a servant and an independent contractor is an important one. A master is responsible for the physical conduct of servants and is therefore liable for torts committed by servants against third persons. On the other hand, with certain exceptions, an employer is not responsible for the physical conduct, and therefore the torts, of an independent contractor. Because imposition of liability turns upon the distinction, courts often have been required to determine whether a person committing a tort is a servant or independent contractor. The major factors to be examined by the court in making this determination are listed in §220 of the *Restatement (Second) of Agency.* No one factor alone is determinative; all relevant facts are considered. The following case explains and applies the *Restatement* test.

Eden v. Spaulding
359 N.W.2d 758 (Neb. 1984)

Plaintiff Ronald Eden was injured in a traffic accident involving a truck driven by defendant Dennis Spaulding, a truck driver employed by defendant

---

5. *Restatement (Second) of Agency* §2(3).

Ernest Fundum. At the time of the accident, Spaulding was en route to pick up newspapers from the defendant Omaha World-Herald Company (World-Herald) for delivery to Norfolk, Nebraska. Eden sued the three defendants for damages and a jury returned a verdict in favor of Eden, awarding total damages of $3 million.

All of the defendants appealed and World-Herald specifically appealed the finding that Fundum was an agent of World-Herald. The company argued that Fundum was an independent contractor and, therefore, World-Herald could not be held liable for his negligence or that of his employees.

Per Curiam

. . . We . . . hold that, as a matter of law, no agency existed between [World-Herald and Fundum] and that Fundum, in his relationship with the World-Herald, was an independent contractor. . . .

We [previously have] set forth 10 factors from the *Restatement (Second) of Agency* §220 (1958) which must be considered in determining the nature of the relationship. An application of these factors to the instant case shows as a matter of law that Fundum was an independent contractor rather than an agent.

As set out in *Maricle v. Spiegel,* [329 N.W.2d 80, 87 (Neb. 1983)]: "Generally, control, or the right of control, is the chief criterion in determining whether someone acts as an independent contractor." . . . The control exercisable by the World-Herald was minimal. It could only suggest a pickup time to Fundum. Fundum's arrival at a later time would be "inconvenient" to both parties, but the decision as to when to pick up the papers was nonetheless within his discretion. The World-Herald could not object to drivers hired by Fundum to drive his trucks. The World-Herald did not dictate the route a truck was to follow from Norfolk to Omaha and return. Fundum paid for all the gas and oil used by his trucks in the trips. There were no other intimations in the record which would suggest a right of control on the part of the World-Herald. It is clear that the World-Herald possessed no such right. . . .

The second factor . . . is whether or not the one employed is engaged in a distinct occupation or business. Clearly, Fundum was engaged in a distinct occupation. The hauling for the World-Herald was not his only business. . . . [H]e also had two [post office] "star routes." He had three vans and a truck to use in his business. Thus, it cannot be said that his trucking business, though small, was non-existent.

The third factor includes the kind of occupation involved—whether, in the locality, the job is usually supervised by the employer. Clearly, this is not the case. Other "star route" drivers were hauling for the World-Herald under similar contracts. There was very little World-Herald supervision. There were no fixed routes, no regulations concerning carrying passengers, and no restrictions on the carriage of other baggage.

The fourth suggested consideration—the skill required in the particular occupation—is not very enlightening in this fact pattern. Regardless of whether driving a truck of this type is an unskilled or highly skilled trade, there are great numbers of people who engage in it as independent contractors and as employees.

"That the worker supplies his own materials and tools may be indicative of contractor status." *Voycheske v. Osborn* [244 N.W.2d 74, 76 (Neb. 1976)]. It is undisputed that Fundum supplied his own truck. He was also responsible for furnishing the necessary oil, grease, gasoline, and repairs to the truck. When one truck wore out, Fundum replaced it on his own, without consulting the World-Herald. On the night of the accident it was Fundum who paid for a substitute truck to haul the newspapers.

The length of time which a person is employed is another element of the test. Again, this factor is not particularly illuminating. While we agree that where the right to terminate without penalty exists, the employee is usually a servant . . . , we note that any motor carrier's hauling contract could be terminated in such a manner, if the contract permitted such termination.

The seventh criterion deals with the method of payment. "Normally an employee is compensated while he works. An independent contractor's compensation, on the other hand, usually depends upon whether he makes a profit from the contract." *Stephens v. Celeryvale Transport, Inc.,* [286 N.W.2d 420, 426 (Neb. 1979)]. Fundum was clearly operating to realize a profit. He was paid a monthly

sum. If, after paying his employees' salaries and other operating expenses, there was a surplus, Fundum would make money. If there was a deficit, he would lose money.

Whether or not the work is part of the regular business of the employer also must be examined. While the World-Herald had its own distribution system within the city, it had no trucks which delivered the papers outside of the city. Carriage of newspapers to distribution centers outside the city was contracted out by the World-Herald.

[W]hether the parties believed they were creating a master-servant relationship is an important guideline. The contrary is clearly true in this case. The World-Herald withheld no income taxes, Social Security, or any other deduction. It carried no workmen's compensation coverage on Fundum. It made no attempt to regulate him. Fundum, on the other hand, made all the necessary deductions from his drivers' paychecks, provided workmen's compensation coverage to his drivers, and issued directions to his drivers. The parties were unquestionably acting in the belief that their relationship was that of independent contractor.

The final factor . . . is whether or not the principal is in business. This question is not germane to the issue at hand. If the principal is not in business, an independent contractor's status will be found. This factor is inapplicable here. . . .

For the reasons hereinbefore set out we find that the trial court erred in submitting the agency question to the jury and failing to find as a matter of law that Fundum was an independent contractor. . . .

[Judgment reversed and remanded with directions to dismiss Omaha World-Herald Company.]

Table 41–1 summarizes some of the important differences between a servant and an independent contractor.

Scope of Employment. Under the respondeat superior doctrine, a master is liable only for those torts committed within the scope of the servant's employment. The *Restatement (Second) of Agency* finds a servant's conduct within the **scope of employment** if it is of the kind he is employed to

Table 41–1	Differences Between Servants and Independent Contractors	

Characteristics of a Servant	*Characteristics of an Independent Contractor*
Salaried or working for hourly wage.	Paid for a completed job.
Works for employer who supervises or has right to supervise the work.	Engaged in a distinct business or occupation of his own with no outside supervision or control of the work.
Works continuously for same employer over long period with regular hours, specific area of employment, or fixed route.	Works for another only long enough to complete the job.
Uses employer's tools, equipment, or works on property owned by employer.	Uses own equipment, tools, and may work at his own place of business.

perform; occurs substantially within authorized time and space limitations; and is motivated, at least in part, by a purpose to serve the master.[6] Note that, with a number of exceptions, an employee who commits a tort on her way to or from work is not within the scope of employment for purposes of imposing liability upon the employer.

Scope of employment is a broad concept that includes not only those acts authorized by the master, but also many acts expressly forbidden by the master. In other words, scope of employment is not tied to authority or authorization discussed in the agency and contracts material. If it were, the master could simply state that employees are not authorized to commit torts in the course of their work and could avoid respondeat superior liability accordingly. The basic question for judicial determination is whether the employee's deviation from his employment either in time, place, act, or motive is so great that the employer should no longer be held accountable for the employee's actions.

The classic statement of the test governing scope of employment is the "frolic-detour" dichotomy originally announced in 1834 in *Joel v. Morison*.[7] In this case, the plaintiff broke his leg when a cart and horse negligently driven by the defendant's servants ran him over. The accident occurred on a highway outside the normal route used by the servants. The plaintiff sued the master for damages and the issue for the jury was whether the servants

had departed from the scope of employment relieving the master of liability. On this issue, the court instructed the jury (which found for the plaintiff):

> If the servants, being on their master's business, took a detour to call upon a friend, the master will be responsible. . . . The master is only liable where the servant is acting in the course of his employment. If he was going out of his way, against his master's implied commands, when driving on his master's business, he will make his master liable; but if he was going on a frolic of his own, without being at all on his master's business, the master will not be liable.[8]

Thus, a servant who embarks upon a **frolic** departs from the scope of employment, relieving the master of liability for the servant's torts. A mere **detour,** however, is a less severe deviation, insufficient to remove the servant from the scope of employment. Although the test of scope of employment announced in *Joel v. Morison* and rephrased in the *Restatement (Second) of Agency* is not precise, no more rigid test is possible. If an act is clearly outside the scope of employment, the court resolves the issue. In most cases, however, the scope of employment issue is a close factual question and is decided by the jury.

A related question concerns when a servant, who has clearly departed from the scope of employment (embarked on a "frolic") sufficiently returns to the

---

6. *Restatement (Second) of Agency* §228(1).
7. 6 Car. & P. 501, 172 Eng. Rep. 1338 (N. P. 1834).

8. 6 Car. & P. at 503, 172 Eng. Rep. at 1338–1339.

scope of employment to reimpose tort liability upon the master. To re-enter the scope of employment the servant must again be reasonably near the authorized geographic and time limitations of employment and must be acting with an intent to perform assigned duties. This issue, like scope of employment, often presents a close factual question, and is usually left to the jury in difficult cases. In the following case the court was required to decide whether an employee's negligent conduct occurred within the scope of employment.

Edgewater Motels, Inc. v. Gatzke

277 N.W.2d 11 (Minn. 1979)

Defendant A. J. Gatzke was employed as a district manager for defendant Walgreen Co. During August, 1973, Gatzke spent several weeks in Duluth, Minnesota, supervising the opening of a new Walgreen's restaurant. While in Duluth he stayed at plaintiff Edgewater Motel. Walgreen's paid Gatzke's hotel bill, all living expenses, and entertainment expenses. Gatzke was on call twenty-four hours a day to handle problems arising in all Walgreen's restaurants located in his district.

On August 23, 1977, Gatzke worked for seventeen hours at the new Walgreen's restaurant. With another district manager, Gatzke then went to the Bellows restaurant to have a drink. The two managers spent part of the time at the Bellows discussing operations of Walgreen's restaurants. Gatzke also discussed the mixing and pricing of drinks with the Bellows bartender. Gatzke was interested in this information because the Walgreen's restaurant served liquor. After having four drinks Gatzke returned to his hotel room where he began working on his expense account.

A fire broke out in Gatzke's room later that evening. Edgewater Motel sued Gatzke and Walgreen Company for damages of $330,360 resulting from Gatzke's negligent smoking of a cigarette in his hotel room. The jury found that Gatzke had been negligent and also found Walgreen Co. to be liable under the doctrine of respondeat superior. The trial court set aside the verdict as to Walgreen Co. on the ground that Gatzke's negligence had not occurred in

the scope of his employment. Edgewater Motel appealed.

Scott, Justice

. . . The question raised here is whether the facts of this case reasonably support the imposition of vicarious liability on Walgreen's for the conceded negligent act of its employee.

It is well settled that for an employer to be held vicariously liable for an employee's negligent conduct the employee's wrongful act must be committed within the scope of his employment. . . .

To support a finding that an employee's negligent act occurred within his scope of employment, it must be shown that his conduct was, to some degree, in furtherance of the interests of his employer. . . . Other factors to be considered in the scope of employment determination are whether the conduct is of the kind that the employee is authorized to perform and whether the act occurs substantially within authorized time and space restrictions. . . . No hard and fast rule can be applied to resolve the "scope of employment" inquiry. Rather, each case must be decided on its own individual facts. . . .

The initial question raised by the instant factual situation is whether an employee's smoking of a cigarette can constitute conduct within his scope of employment. . . .

[A]fter careful consideration of the issue we are persuaded by the reasoning of the courts which hold that smoking can be an act within an employee's scope of employment. It seems only logical to conclude that an employee does not abandon his employment as a matter of law while temporarily acting for his personal comfort when such activities involve only slight deviations from work that are reasonable under the circumstances, such as eating, drinking, or smoking. . . .

We . . . hereby hold that an employer can be held vicariously liable for his employee's negligent smoking of a cigarette [if] he was otherwise acting in the scope of his employment at the time of the negligent act.

Thus, we must next determine whether Gatzke was otherwise in the scope of his employment at the time of his negligent act. . . . It appears that the district court felt that Gatzke was outside the scope of his employment while he was at the Bellows, and thus was similarly outside his scope of employment when he returned to his room to fill out his expense account. The record, however, contains a reasonable basis from which a jury could find that Gatzke was involved in serving his employer's interests at the time he was at the bar. Gatzke testified that, while at the Bellows, he discussed the operation of the newly-opened Walgreen's restaurant with Hubbard. Also, the bartender stated that on that night ''[a] few times we [Gatzke and the bartender] would talk about his business and my business, how to make drinks, prices.''

But more importantly, even assuming that Gatzke was outside the scope of his employment while he was at the bar, there is evidence from which a jury could reasonably find that Gatzke resumed his employment activities after he returned to his motel room and filled out his expense account. The expense account was, of course, completed so that Gatzke could be reimbursed by Walgreen's for his work-related expenses. In this sense, Gatzke is performing an act for his own personal benefit. However, the completion of the expense account furthers the employer's business in that it provides detailed documentation of business expenses so that they are properly deductible for tax purposes. . . . In this light, the filling out of the expense form can be viewed as serving a dual purpose; that of furthering Gatzke's personal interests and promoting his employer's business purposes. Accordingly, it is reasonable for the jury to find that the completion of the expense account is an act done in furtherance of the employer's business purposes.

Additionally, the record indicates that Gatzke was an executive type of employee who had no set working hours. He considered himself a 24-hour-a-day man; his room at the Edgewater Motel was his ''office away from home.'' It was therefore also reasonable for the jury to determine that the filling out of his expense account was done within authorized time and space limits of his employment.

In light of the above, we hold that it was reasonable for the jury to find that Gatzke was acting within the scope of his employment when he completed his expense account. Accordingly, we set aside the trial court's grant of judgment for Walgreen's and reinstate the jury's determination that Gatzke was working within the scope of his employment at the time of his negligent act. . . .

[Judgment reversed.]

Borrowed Servants. Occasionally, one master may permit or direct his servant to perform services for another. ABC Construction may rent a dump truck and driver to XYZ Construction for temporary use in a construction project undertaken by XYZ. If the servant loaned or rented then negligently injures a third party, the law must determine which of the two masters should bear the loss. To make this choice, courts traditionally analyze the factors previously discussed to determine whether a master-servant relationship exists, emphasizing particularly the factor of control. The court then imposes liability upon the master with the right to control or direct the elements of the specific act that caused the injury. Such a master is deemed to be in the best position to prevent the injury. Under this approach, although the servant is employed by two masters, only one of them is held responsible for the servant's torts.

This approach to the ''borrowed servant'' problem has been harshly criticized for reaching inconsistent results within and among the various jurisdictions and because no convincing policy reasons exist for placing the loss on one employer rather than the other. That is, the servant is subject to a significant degree of control by both masters and is furthering the business interests of both masters. For this reason, an increasing number of jurisdictions reject the borrowed servant rule, and apportion the loss between the two masters.

Liability for Use of Force. In most cases imposing vicarious liability upon the master, the servant's negligence (failure to exercise reasonable care) is the cause of the injury to the third party. Occasionally, however, injury results from the servant's intentional rather than merely negligent conduct, often involving a use of force against the third party. A servant's intentional torts frequently are viewed as outside the scope of employment. Courts, nevertheless, often impose liability upon the master if a particular use of force was foreseeable by the master due to the nature of the employment. Situations in which courts have imposed liability on the master for a servant's tortious use of force include the following.

1. If the use of force is expressly ordered or authorized by the master, liability clearly follows. A principal is always liable for his directed acts.

2. In certain employment relationships, use of force is an integral part of the job. A master is therefore liable for intentional harm inflicted by such servants as bouncers, bodyguards, or persons employed to repossess goods from defaulting debtors.

3. Employers are often held liable for intentional torts committed by the servant in the protection or recovery of the master's property or otherwise in furtherance of the master's business. In these cases, the conduct involved is neither expressly or impliedly authorized by the master nor may it actually benefit or protect the master's business or property. For example, suppose Adelman was hired by Perez to manage a jewelry store. One Sunday, while the store was closed, Adelman drove by and observed Toomey walk out of the rear entrance, get into a car, and drive away. Believing Toomey to be a burglar, Adelman gave chase and ultimately drove Toomey off the road, severely injuring him. Toomey was in fact an employee of the gas company who had been called out on an emergency basis to investigate a reported gas leak in the building. Perez may be liable to Toomey because Adelman's tort, though intentional, was committed in Adelman's good faith, though mistaken, belief that he was protecting Perez's property.

4. A master may be held liable for intentional torts that are caused by friction inherent in the employment situation. That is, a master who places a servant in a position requiring contacts with third persons under circumstances likely to lead to conflict may be held liable for injuries inflicted by the servant. For example, assume Ahern is hired by Peake to drive a delivery truck. Ahern works long hours in heavy traffic and is frequently required to carry heavy parcels in extreme weather conditions. Near the end of a long day, Ahern backs into a car owned by Tully, causing minor damage. Tully proceeds to yell at Ahern and in the ensuing argument

Ahern punches Tully, breaking his jaw. Peake may be held liable for the intentional tort committed by Ahern, because such a situation is likely to arise in the performance of Ahern's job.

In the following case, the court was required to determine whether liability should be imposed upon an employer for its employee's intentional tort.

Johnson v. Dixon
457 So. 2d 79 (La. App. 1984)

Kenneth Johnson, an employee of Amax Nickel Refining Company, Inc. (Amax), became involved in an argument with Gregory Dixon, an employee of Louisiana Industrial Coatings (LIC), an independent contractor performing painting work at the Amax plant. The argument began when Dixon who was applying spray paint above Johnson's work area sprayed coal tar on Johnson. Johnson demanded that Dixon discontinue painting but Dixon, who had been advised that his work had "top priority," refused. An argument, including name calling, ensued and Dixon shoved Johnson against a steel beam.

Johnson sued Dixon and LIC alleging injuries caused by Dixon's having committed a battery. The trial court held Dixon and LIC liable for Johnson's injuries. LIC appealed arguing that it could not be held liable under the doctrine of respondeat superior because Dixon had acted outside the scope of his employment.

Gulotta, Judge

. . . We . . . reject LIC's argument that its employee Dixon was not acting within the course and scope of his employment during the incident. According to LIC, Dixon's personal motives to punish Johnson for racial taunts and to "appease his own machismo" were not in furtherance of LIC's interests as an independent contractor at the Amax plant. We disagree.

An employer's liability under the doctrine of respondeat superior for the tortious act of its employee depends on the facts and circumstances of each case, including whether the employee's conduct is closely related in time, place and causation to his employment. . . . When a dispute involving an employee erupts into violence, the question is whether it was "primarily employment-rooted" and regarded as "a risk of harm fairly attributable to the employer's business, as compared with conduct motivated by purely personal considerations entirely extraneous to the employer's business interests." *LeBrane v. Lewis*, 292 So. 2d 216 (La. 1974). . . .

In the instant case, the dispute between Johnson and Dixon concerned which worker had priority to perform his job in the area. Dixon understood that LIC painters were not to stop spraying unless so instructed by an LIC supervisor, whereas Johnson believed that Amax employees had priority and could stop LIC painters if they interfered with Amax work.

Dixon testified that he had approached Johnson to explain that he could not stop spraying at his request and to inform him of the proper procedure, as well as to see if Johnson would carry out his threat to kick him. According to Johnson, the dispute began when Dixon sprayed him and said he would not stop for him or anyone but his supervisor. In an accident investigation report of the incident, Ronald Burmaster, an Amax supervisor, indicated that Dixon and Johnson's working in the same area and the painters' instructions "not to shut down their operation, unless notified by their foreman" were the conditions contributing most directly to the accident.

Although racial slurs and some personal bravado were undoubtedly involved, it is clear that this argument between these workers was primarily employment-rooted and reasonably incidental to the performance of each worker's duties in furtherance of his employer's business. Accordingly, we find no error in the trial judge's conclusion that Dixon acted in the course and scope of his employment, thereby making LIC . . . liable under the doctrine of *respondeat superior* for his tortious conduct. . . .

[Judgment affirmed.]

Liability of Servant to Master. When an employer is held liable to a third party for its employee's tort, the law must determine whether the employer may in turn recover from the employee responsible for the injury. As a general rule, unless authorized to

act in the manner causing the injury, an employee who subjects the employer to liability under respondeat superior for a negligent or other wrongful act in the course of employment is liable to the employer for the loss incurred. This result has been criticized as inconsistent with the basic policy of the respondeat superior doctrine. As noted by one court:

> [R]*espondeat superior* rests upon a public policy that the employer bear the burden as an expense of the operation he expands through the employment of others. . . . The theoretical liability of an employee to reimburse the employer is quite anachronistic. The rule would surprise the modern employer no less than his employee. Both expect the employer to save harmless the employee rather than the other way round, the employer routinely purchasing insurance which protects the employee as well.[9]

Despite this criticism, most courts continue to permit the employer's suit against the negligent employee for indemnity. Such suits, though uncommon, may be valuable if the employee, such as a corporate officer or manager, has substantial personal assets or separate insurance coverage.

Liability for Agent's Fraud. In addition to liability for use of force, a principal may be legally responsible for intentional torts of agents not involving physical conduct, most commonly fraud. A rule similar to that applied to agency and contracts governs the principal's liability for the agent's fraud. That is, a principal is liable for an agent's fraudulent misrepresentation if the agent is actually or apparently authorized to make the representation. For example, assume Paula appoints Ann as agent with full authority to negotiate the sale of Paula's house. Ann defrauds Tina by fraudulently representing that the house is free of termites. In reliance upon Ann's statement, Tina purchases the house. Paula is liable for fraud to Tina. Whereas liability for most torts is based upon respondeat superior and requires a master-servant relation, the rule govern-

---

9. Chief Justice Weintraub in *Eule v. Eule Motor Sales*, 170 A.2d 241, 242 (N.J. 1961).

ing nonphysical conduct torts is based upon contract principles. Thus, liability may be imposed upon any principal, whether or not a master.

Workers' Compensation

History

The respondeat superior doctrine imposes liability without fault upon an employer for torts committed by employees acting within the scope of employment. A related issue, now governed largely by state "workers' compensation" statutes, concerns employer liability for work-related injuries sustained by their employees.

The common law approach to this problem, developed in the early days of the industrial revolution, was to impose liability on the employer only for those injuries caused by the negligence or other fault of the employer. Thus, although the employer was liable without fault for injuries caused to third parties *by* employees under respondeat superior, injuries *to* employees were compensated only if the employer was at fault, making employee recovery difficult. This difficulty was magnified by the development of three defenses available to the employer in a suit by an injured employee: (1) the "fellow servant" doctrine, (2) assumption of the risk, and (3) contributory negligence.

Beginning in 1837[10] courts created a **fellow-servant exception** to the principle of employer liability. Under this doctrine, an employer was not liable for negligent injury to an employee caused by the conduct of a fellow employee. Many jurisdictions later began to carve a "vice-principal" exception to the fellow-servant rule, under which the employer was held liable for injuries caused by employees in supervisory capacities, such as foremen.

Under the *assumption of the risk* defense, an employee who was aware of the dangerous conditions existing in the employment, but nevertheless voluntarily continued to work, was denied recovery. That is, even if the master had been negligent in creating the defect or dangerous condition causing the injury—for example, by failing to properly

maintain a machine—the servant who was aware of the condition had "assumed the risk."

Under the *contributory negligence* defense, even if the employer's negligence could be clearly established, recovery was denied if the employee's negligence, however slight, also contributed to the injury.

In order to recover at common law, therefore, an injured employee had to prove not only the employer's negligence proximately causing the injury, but also (1) that the employee's own negligence did not contribute to the injury, (2) that he had not voluntarily accepted the risk of a known danger, and (3) that the injury was not caused by the conduct of a fellow employee. The net effect of the common law fault approach, bolstered by these three defenses, was to deny any recovery to employees for job-related injuries in the vast majority of cases, or to allow recovery only after a lengthy court battle. Alarmingly, this contraction in employee protection coincided with a sharp increase in industrial accidents occasioned by the industrial revolution. By the late nineteenth century, it had become apparent that a radical change in employee compensation law was necessary.

In response to this problem the various states began to enact workers' compensation statutes, modeled upon systems first adopted in Germany and England. By 1920 all but eight states had workers' compensation statutes and by 1949 every state had enacted one. Because workers' compensation laws are state statutes, the employers and employees covered, and benefits paid, vary greatly among the states. For example, agricultural workers, domestic servants, and casual laborers are excluded under the laws of many states, as are nonprofit organizations and employers having a small number of employees. Although individual statutes are thus far from uniform, the following material outlines the basic operation of a typical workers' compensation act.

Operation of a Typical Statute

In contrast to the common law approach based upon fault, **workers' compensation statutes** typically provide that an injured employee is automatically entitled to benefits prescribed by statute if the injury (1) was accidental, and (2) arose out of and

---

10. *Priestley v. Fowler*, 3 M. & W. 1, 150 Eng. Rep. 1030 (Ex. 1837).

in the course of employment. Negligence or fault of either the employer or employee are generally irrelevant. That is, an employee whose own negligence caused or contributed to the injury is nevertheless entitled to recover, and an employer who is completely free from fault is not excused from liability.

Employers unilaterally fund workers' compensation systems. Statutes generally require the employer to secure this liability through a private insurance policy, a state insurance fund, or in some cases by self-insurance. Premiums are commonly based upon an employer's or industry's injury-experience rating, increased or decreased on the basis of prior accident and liability record. In this manner, employment-related injuries are treated as a business expense with the cost distributed among the consumers of the employer's product. Workers' compensation and respondeat superior therefore both rest upon the policy that employment-related injuries are a cost of doing business and should therefore be borne by business enterprise, not the individuals injured as a result.

In most jurisdictions, workers' compensation coverage is compulsory. In the minority of states providing for "elective" or "optional" workers' compensation coverage, the employer may elect either to be covered under workers' compensation, or be subject to a common law negligence action by injured employees, without the benefit of the common law defenses previously discussed. Today, most employers in states permitting election choose compensation coverage. Note that an employer in a compulsory jurisdiction who fails to obtain coverage is similarly subjected to common law actions without benefit of the defenses.[11]

The benefits paid under workers' compensation are prescribed by statute. Generally, only injuries that produce disability or death (thus affecting the employee's earning power) are compensable. Compensation is usually measured as a percentage (commonly one-half to two-thirds) of the employee's average wage. Maximum dollar limitations are, however, usually imposed, often reducing recovery below this amount. Overall duration of payments also is often limited.

In exchange for these somewhat modest benefits guaranteed under workers' compensation, the employee surrenders the common law right to sue the employer for negligence in causing the injury. A workers' compensation recovery does not, however, prevent an employee from suing any other third party responsible for the accident. For example, if an employee is injured while using a defectively manufactured machine, a workers' compensation award would not preclude a suit against the manufacturer of the machine. If the employee recovers from the third party, however, the proceeds are first applied to reimburse the employer for the compensation award, with any balance paid to the employee.

Workers' compensation statutes cover work-related injuries to employees, not independent contractors. Both courts and legislatures have, however, expanded "employee" status in borderline workers' compensation cases to cover individuals who would not be servants under traditional tort analysis. Generally, if the work is done as an integral part of the employer's business and the worker has no independent business or profession of his own, employee status is established. This theory better assures that the cost of an industrial accident is borne by the consumer as part of the cost of the employer's product.

To expedite the processing of claims, most workers' compensation laws are administered by special workers' compensation boards or commissions, rather than by courts. Typically, an injured employee must give prompt notice of injury to his employer and then file a claim with the administrative agency within a stated period, usually one to two years. Commonly, a single hearing officer or examiner makes initial findings that are later affirmed, modified, or rejected by the full board or commission. Rules of procedure and evidence are generally relaxed before these administrative tribunals.

Final decisions of the workers' compensation board are then reviewable, like other administrative agency decisions, by the courts. Judicial review is, however, limited to questions of law. The reviewing court generally accepts the commission's find-

---

11. Some states protect injured employees of uninsured employers by providing for state payment of the claim. The state then proceeds against the employer to recover the payments and impose fines or other penalties.

ings of fact if supported by any evidence, even if the court would have ruled differently on the same facts.

Requirements for Compensation

Most litigation in the compensation field is generated by the application of the basic coverage formula. In most states, to be eligible for compensation an employee must suffer "personal injury by accident arising out of and in the course of employment."

Personal Injury by Accident. An accidental injury is an unexpected mishap or event, which is usually traceable to a specific time, place, and cause. The most common industrial accidents result from motor vehicle collisions, explosions, slips and falls, and contact with factory machinery. In these cases both the cause and the result of the accident are unexpected. Compensation is also generally granted for an accidental result alone—that is, when the injury is an unexpected consequence of the routine performance of the employee's job. Under this test most states provide compensation for heart attacks, hernias, strokes, or back injuries resulting from the normal exertion or exposure of the employee's duties.

Injuries caused by employment-related diseases also are often compensable. For example, in many states, pre-existing diseases, such as heart disease, aggravated by the employment are compensable. Diseases of exposure (such as pneumonia) and infectious or contagious diseases acquired during employment are covered. Further, all states provide compensation for occupational diseases, which are caused by prolonged exposure to the normal, but harmful, conditions of a particular employment.

Arising out of and in the Course of Employment. To be compensable, the accidental injury must both "arise out of" and occur "in the course of" the employment. The requirement that the injury "arise out of" the employment establishes the causal connection between the employment and the injury. Under the traditional approach, causality is established by proof that the injury resulted from risks distinctly associated with the employment. Under the more modern positional risk test, em-

braced in a growing number of jurisdictions, an injury arises out of the employment if the conditions of employment placed the employee in the position (time and place) where he or she was injured. This approach provides compensation for injuries caused by so-called neutral risks such as stray bullets, random acts of violence, or Acts of God. These risks are termed "neutral" because they are neither clearly employment-related nor personal to the employee.

An injury arises in the course of employment if it occurs (1) during the time of the employment, (2) at a place where the employee should or may be expected to be, and (3) while the employee is performing her duties or acts incidental to those duties. This test, which judges the connection between the employment and the time, place, and circumstances of the accident, is generally similar to the "scope of employment" test used in respondeat superior cases. In many cases, however, courts have allowed workers' compensation to an injured worker who would probably be deemed outside the scope of employment for tort purposes. In the following case, the court was required to determine whether an employee was entitled to workers' compensation benefits.

Union Packing Company of Omaha v. Klauschie

314 N.W.2d 25 (Neb. 1982)

Henry Klauschie, an employee of Union Packing Company of Omaha, worked as a meat trimmer in a meat packing plant. His duties required him to stand most of the working day. For health and safety reasons, Union Packing required that he wear rubber boots while working. In March 1979, Klauschie noticed a small blister on his foot. Although the blister did not heal, it caused no pain or swelling until late June 1979. The foot then began to swell and the blister darkened. In July 1979, Klauschie consulted Dr. Charles Brannen, who diagnosed a severe infection. Klauschie was hospitalized and, after treatment of the infection failed, Dr. Richard Gross amputated a part of Klauschie's foot in August 1979.

Klauschie filed a workers' compensation claim and the Nebraska Workmen's Compensation Court found that he had suffered a compensable injury. Union Packing appealed.

Hastings, Justice

. . . The critical issue for us to decide is whether or not the bacterial invasion of Mr. Klauschie's system was an accident arising out of and in the course of his employment by Union Packing, as determined by the Workmen's Compensation Court. . . .

Dr. Brannen testified that the sole cause of Mr. Klauschie's injury and disability was the result of his employment, i.e., the wearing of the boots. The physician performing the surgery, Dr. Gross, stated that in his opinion all of Mr. Klauschie's troubles related back to the pressure injury caused by wearing the boots. Finally, Dr. Davis, although expressing no opinion as to the cause of the sore on Mr. Klauschie's foot, did say that it was almost unheard of for either bacteria to invade the skin in the absence of a preexisting wound or infection in that area. Although the medical testimony differs as to whether the skin break, the vascular injury, or the bacterial invasion was the causative factor in the resultant amputation and disability, . . . we have said that where a record presents nothing more than conflicting medical testimony, we will not substitute our judgment for that of the Workmen's Compensation Court. . . .

The next question to consider is whether or not there was an accident arising out of the employment. . . . An accident is defined as "an unexpected or unforeseen injury happening suddenly and violently . . . and producing at the time objective symptoms of an injury." Neb. Rev. Stat. §48-151(2) (Reissue 1978). "The terms injury and personal injuries shall mean only violence to the physical structure of the body and such disease or infection as naturally results therefrom." §48-151(4). In dealing with these definitions, we have said that "the accident requirement of the act was satisfied if the cause of the injury was of accidental character or the effect was unexpected or unforeseen, and happened suddenly and violently. We also said that it was no longer necessary that the injury be caused by a single traumatic event, but the exertion in the employment must contribute in some material and substantial degree to cause the injury." *Crosby v. American Stores,* . . . 298 N.W.2d 157, 159 (1980).

In our opinion, the blister or vascular injury which manifested itself in the early stages prior to April 15, 1979, as disclosed by the testimony cited above, constituted an accidental injury arising out of Mr. Klauschie's employment. . . .

We conclude that the infection and subsequent amputation and disability were phases in a whole group of events having their origin with the manifestation of the "pressure sore" discovered prior to April 15, 1979. Therefore, the Workmen's Compensation Court was correct in determining that Mr. Klauschie suffered a compensable injury and is entitled to benefits as determined by its award. . . .

[Judgment affirmed in part and reversed and remanded in part.]

SUMMARY

1. The law of agency addresses the tort liability of the parties when the agent injures a third party while acting for the principal. Because a person is always liable for his own torts, the fact that a person is acting as an agent does not reduce the agent's tort liability. Similarly, the principal is liable for tortious acts he directs an agent to do and for negligence in the selection, training, or supervision of agents. The law of agency also imposes "vicarious" liability upon completely innocent principals for torts of agents under the doctrine of respondeat superior.

2. Liability is imposed under the respondeat superior doctrine if (1) a master-servant relationship exists between principal and agent (a principal has no liability for torts of independent contractors), and (2) the agent (servant) was acting within the scope of employment when the tort was committed. A servant's conduct is within the scope of employment if it is of the kind he is employed to perform, occurs substantially within authorized time and space limitations, and is motivated, at least in part, by a purpose to serve the master.

3. Although vicarious liability is generally imposed for a servant's negligent rather than intentional torts, a

master may be held liable for a servant's use of force if the use of force is expressly ordered or authorized by the master, if force is an integral part of the job, if force was used to protect or recover the master's property or otherwise in furtherance of the master's business, or if the use of force was caused by friction inherent in the employment situation. A principal is liable for intentional torts not involving physical conduct, such as fraud, if the agent is actually or apparently authorized to act.

4. In addition to liability for torts committed by agents, the law of agency is also concerned with on the job injuries incurred by employees. Traditionally, the law imposed liability upon an employer whose negligence caused the employee's injury. Three defenses available to the employer—the fellow-servant doctrine, contributory negligence, and assumption of risk—made employee recovery difficult.

5. To provide greater employee protection in the face of increasing industrial accidents, states have replaced the common law negligence approach with workers' compensation statutes that typically provide that an injured employee is entitled to specified benefits if the injury was (1) accidental, and (2) arose out of and in the course of employment. Under these statutes, which are funded unilaterally by the employer, the negligence or fault of either the employer or employee are generally irrelevant. Like the respondeat superior doctrine, workers' compensation is designed to treat employment related injuries as a cost of doing business, borne by business enterprise, not the injured individuals.

KEY TERMS

respondeat superior doctrine	detour
vicarious liability	fellow-servant exception
scope of employment	workers' compensation statute
frolic	

QUESTIONS AND PROBLEMS

41-1   Which of the various policy reasons supporting the respondeat superior doctrine is most important? Should employers be held vicariously liable for the torts of their employees?

41-2   Workers' compensation statutes are designed to remedy the serious deficiencies in the traditional common law approach to employee compensation for work-related injuries. Given the relatively modest benefits paid under workers' compensation, what are its advantages to the employee over even a liberal common law recovery? What are the advantages to the em-ployer of workers' compensation over common law tort recovery?

41-3   Western Company owned an office building in which Adams Box Co. rented an office. Western hired STOP Corp. to remove and replace some pipes and valves located in the basement of the office building. STOP agreed to complete the work within a two-week period and to provide all specialized equipment necessary for the job. An employee of STOP was using a blowtorch to cut through a pipe when a small explosion occurred followed by a fire. The offices of Adams Box Co. were destroyed. An inspection revealed that the blowtorch had been used improperly and negligently.

(a) If Adams Box Co. sues STOP Corp. for negligence, should the court hold STOP liable? Explain.

(b) If Adams Box Co. sues Western Company for negligence, should the court hold Western liable? Explain.

41-4   Clearwater Drilling Company was drilling a well and setting a water line for a restaurant under construction. Kastner had been hired by Clearwater to lay pipe for the water line. As was its custom, Clearwater leased a backhoe and driver on an hourly basis from Toombs Construction Co. to dig the water line ditch. The backhoe driver, Malcolm, was instructed by Clearwater to dig the ditch to a depth of six feet. Malcolm warned Clearwater that the soil was soft and might cave in, but was instructed to dig the six-foot trench anyway. Although Malcolm knew that a six-foot trench was unsafe without reinforcement, Malcolm followed Clearwater's instructions and dug the ditch. Subsequently, Kastner was seriously injured when the ditch caved in. Kastner sued Malcolm, Toombs, and Clearwater to recover for his injuries. Which, if any, of the defendants should be held liable to Kastner and on what theory?

41-5   T & G Realtors, Inc. agreed to serve as real estate brokers for Mr. and Mrs. Feldman who were trying to sell their home. While answering questions in preparing the listing agreement, the Feldmans said they had never had problems with leakage or water in the basement. Mr. and Mrs. Thurston were interested in purchasing a house and Lois, a T & G real estate agent, took them on a tour of the Feldmans' home. The Thurstons asked if the owners had had problems with water in the basement. After consulting the information sheet prepared by the Feldmans, Lois replied in the negative. The Thurstons purchased the house and subsequently learned that while the Feldmans owned the home, the basement had flooded every spring. The Thurstons sued the Feldmans, T & G Realtors, Inc., and Lois for fraud and misrepresentation. Who among the defendants should be held liable? Explain.

41-6 In each of the following cases, the employee was involved in an automobile accident. Consider whether at the time of the accident the employee was acting in the scope of employment, so that the employer should be held liable for the damages caused by the employee.

(a) Elliott worked as a clerk at Stop and Save, a twenty-four-hour convenience store, located on Green Street. Elliott also lived on Green Street approximately two miles from the Stop and Save. Every day Elliott drove his car down Green Street to the Stop and Save. One day Elliott negligently failed to stop at the stop sign on First Street and collided with a car driven by Mrs. Sanchez. Mrs. Sanchez sued both Elliott and Stop and Save. Should Stop and Save be held vicariously liable for Elliott's negligence?

(b) Elliott's supervisor asked him to drive to the office of Stop and Save's accountant to pick up some papers. The accountant's office also was located on Green Street. Elliott drove to the office, picked up the papers, and decided to drop off his laundry at the cleaners on First Street. Elliott then drove down First Street and was making the turn on Green Street to return to the Stop and Save. While making the turn, Elliott negligently drove his car onto the sidewalk injuring Mr. Smith. Mr. Smith sued Elliott and Stop and Save. Should Stop and Save be held liable?

(c) Elliott's supervisor requested Elliott to drop off some papers at the accountant's office on Green Street. While driving down Green Street, Elliott engaged in a "drag race" with another driver and collided with a car driven by Ms. Jay. She sued Elliott and Stop and Save. Is Stop and Save liable?

(d) Assume that in each of the previous situations, Elliott also was injured and filed a workers' compensation claim against Stop and Save. Did Elliott's injuries "arise out of and in the course of employment?" Should the court consider the same factors it does when determining whether a tort occurred "in the scope of employment?" Explain.

41-7 Ronnell was a salesman employed by National Biscuit Co. While visiting Jerome's Grocery Store, Ronnell and Jerome became involved in an argument stemming from Jerome's complaint that Ronnell was using too much shelf space for display of National Biscuit products. Ronnell assaulted Jerome who was seriously injured by the attack.

(a) Jerome sued National Biscuit Co. seeking damages under the doctrine of respondeat superior. How should the court rule?

(b) Assume that National Biscuit Co. had received complaints about Ronnell's aggressive conduct from other grocers prior to the incident at Jerome's Grocery Store. Would your answer to part (a) differ based on this information? Suggest another basis for suing National Biscuit Co., assuming that it was aware of Ronnell's violent tendencies.

41-8 Fred Jones worked as a brakeman for Penn Central. After completing 24 hours on duty, Jones left the train and flagged a taxicab. The taxi driver requested that Jones wait a few minutes while the driver used the restroom facilities in the train station. Jones became angry and kicked the taxi driver breaking his leg. The taxi driver sued Penn Central seeking damages resulting from the injuries caused by its employee, Jones.

(a) Assume that Jones had intended to take the cab to another train station to continue his work for Penn Central. How should the court rule?

(b) If Jones had intended to take the cab home, how should the court rule?

41-9 Edmund was a sales agent for Family Insurance, a job requiring him to visit customers and potential customers at their homes or offices to discuss insurance coverage. On May 22, Edmund visited the Greens at their home to complete an insurance transaction requiring the legal description of their home. While Edmund was present, the Greens produced their lockbox containing the deed to their home as well as jewelry and other valuables. Five weeks later, the Greens' house was burglarized and the lockbox and contents were stolen. Later police investigations revealed that Edmund had hired two convicts to commit the burglary. The Greens have sued Edmund and Family Insurance seeking damages for the tort of conversion, alleging that Family Insurance should be held liable under the doctrine of respondeat superior. How should the court rule?

41-10 In each of the following cases, determine

whether the employee suffered an accident or injury that should be compensated under workers' compensation.

(a) Osgood, an electrician, spent the morning installing wiring in a factory. The work included carrying and lifting fixtures weighing about twenty pounds. In the early afternoon while Osgood was taking a coffee break in the cafeteria, he suddenly slumped over and fell from his chair. A doctor found that Osgood suffered a heart attack.

(b) Would your answer in part (a) be different if the evidence showed that Osgood had suffered from heart disease for several years?

(c) Carlos worked as a bookbinder, a job that required him to lift paper bundles weighing 100 pounds each from the floor to his work bench. In January he began to experience back pain and by February 1, Carlos could no longer lift the bundles and entered a hospital for back surgery. Carlos could not remember a specific day or incident when his back pains had begun.

(d) Due to severe job stress, Deather suffered a mental breakdown and attempted to commit suicide. Deather later filed a claim for workers' compensation for the mental breakdown.

This chapter begins the text's coverage of business organizations, the various forms in which capital, labor, and management are combined in an undertaking for profit. The three principal forms of business organization used in the United States are the sole proprietorship, the partnership, and the business corporation.

The Law of Partnership

Types of Business Organizations

The simplest and most common form of business organization, in absolute numbers, is the sole pro-

prietorship, a business owned and controlled exclusively by one person. The proprietor reaps all profits, bears all losses, and exercises sole management responsibility. He or she is personally liable for all obligations incurred in operating the business, whether created by tort or contract. Although commanding a substantial edge in absolute numbers, the sole proprietorship accounts for a relatively small percentage of total business receipts in the United States.

In contrast to the proprietorship with its total lack of organizational formality and internal management structure, the corporation is the most sophisticated and formalized type of business organization. A corporation may be created only by complying with state statutes allowing the corporate form. The corporation becomes a separate legal entity apart from its owners, who transfer assets to it in exchange for evidence of ownership, shares of stock. The owners, the shareholders, do not directly manage the business, but instead periodically elect directors who are required by statute to manage the enterprise. The directors, in turn, select officers to manage the daily operation of the firm. Because the corporation is a separate legal entity, shareholders, directors, and officers generally have no personal liability for corporate obligations, and the corporation is unaffected by death or withdrawal of its shareholders, directors, or officers or by transfer of its shares. Losses are borne by the corporation to the extent of its assets. Profits are either distributed to the shareholders as dividends or are retained in the business at the directors' discretion.

A partnership is the simplest form of business organization involving two or more owners. It is a common and useful form for small business of almost any type and often is used to combine services of some partners with property or money of others. A partnership is like a proprietorship except that there are two or more owners who generally have equal right to participate in management and deal with third parties, and who are personally liable for all debts incurred by the business. Any profits of the firm are shared according to the agreement of the partners. The business may be altered or even destroyed by the death or withdrawal of a partner, or the transfer of a partner's interest. Most partnerships, unlike corporations, are created without formality, and are often as simple as an oral understanding to pool assets and talents and split the profits. A partnership might therefore be viewed as a residual organizational form, used when two or more people combine in a business venture, but fail to adopt the more formal corporate structure.

General and Limited Partners

Partners are characterized as general or limited. A **general partner** is one who is personally liable to partnership creditors for the full amount of all debts and obligations incurred by the partnership. Most partnerships are composed wholly of general partners, and are known as "general partnerships." A **limited partner,** on the other hand, is a person whose liability to creditors of the partnership is limited to the amount of capital he or she has contributed to the partnership. A partnership composed of one or more general partners and one or more limited partners is known as a "limited partnership."

Sources of Partnership Law

In early English law, legal disputes among merchants were resolved primarily by distinct and varied mercantile courts, which existed apart from the English common law courts. These courts recognized two forms of partnership already used in continental Europe, the *societas* (the general partnership) and the *commendam* or *société en commandité* (the limited partnership). In the eighteenth century, merchants' cases, including partnership cases, began to appear more frequently in the regular English courts as the common law developed its principles of commercial law. The nineteenth century saw the rise of the partnership as a popular organizational form and the development of the common law of partnership. The law generated so much confusion and uncertainty, however, that statutory relief became necessary resulting in England in enactment of the Partnership Act of 1890.[1]

During the late nineteenth century the United States was experiencing similar difficulties with its common law of partnership, which lacked uniformity among the states, lacked a consistent legal theory, and failed to address many recurring problems. To resolve this situation, in 1902 the National Conference of Commissioners on Uniform State Laws[2] commissioned the drafting of a uniform law on partnership. The result, completed in 1914, was the **Uniform Partnership Act (UPA),** which has been enacted in forty-nine states and the District of Columbia.[3] The UPA is therefore the basis of the following basic partnership discussion.

To govern limited partnership, the National Conference drafted the Uniform Limited Partnership Act (ULPA) completed in 1916 and revised in 1976 in the Revised Uniform Limited Partnership Act (RULPA). The RULPA was itself amended in 1985. These statutes, which are supplemented in many respects by provisions of the UPA, form the basis of the limited partnership discussion in Chapter 43.

The UPA, ULPA, and RULPA are not the sole sources of law governing partnership. Partnership law also borrows heavily from basic principles of contracts, estoppel, property, and agency.[4] Indeed, a partnership is often described as a mutual agency relation, with each partner acting as both principal and agent. In addition to common law doctrines, state and federal statutes supplement partnership

---

1. 53-54 Vict., ch. 39 (1890).
2. See discussion of the National Conference in Chapter 1.
3. All states except Louisiana have enacted the UPA.
4. UPA §4.

law. Examples include state statutes governing lawsuits by and against the partners in the firm name, the Statute of Frauds, statutes relating to capacity of persons to become partners, and federal bankruptcy law.

This chapter discusses the legal principles governing the creation of a general partnership and the relation of partners among themselves.

Nature and Formation of Partnership

Partnership Defined

A substantial portion of partnership case law concerns whether two or more persons are, in fact, partners. In these cases, courts usually must determine whether the disadvantages of partnership status (usually personal liability for a partnership debt) should be imposed upon a person who denies he is a partner. In most disputes, a creditor who has loaned money or sold goods or services on credit to one person (who is now insolvent or otherwise unwilling or unable to pay) seeks to hold another liable for payment, asserting that the two are partners. If the creditor succeeds in proving that the parties are partners, the creditor can collect from either. If the parties are not partners but are, for example, buyer and seller, landlord and tenant, lender and borrower, employer and employee, or co-tenants, one party cannot be held vicariously responsible for the other's obligations. The law must therefore distinguish those joint business arrangements that are partnerships from those that are not.

To make this distinction, the UPA defines a **partnership** as "an association of two or more persons to carry on as co-owners a business for profit."[5]

"An Association." A partnership requires an association, a voluntary collection, uniting, or a coming together of two or more persons for a certain purpose. The term connotes both voluntariness and intent to be a member of the association. Thus, a person cannot become a partner without his or her consent and "no person can become a member of a partnership without the consent of all the part-

ners."[6] A partner's right to exercise choice and preference regarding admission of new members to the firm is known as *delectus personae* (Latin: "choice of the person"). Consent to become a partner is ordinarily expressed in a formal or informal agreement or contract between the parties, the partnership agreement. The partnership agreement is discussed in more detail later in this chapter.

Although a partnership is a voluntary, intentional relationship, the parties need not intend to create a partnership or call themselves "partners." They must simply intend to create a relationship that includes the essential elements of a partnership outlined below. Indeed, the basic issue in many partnership disputes is whether partnership status should be imposed upon a person who denies she intended to be a partner.

"Of Two or More Persons." A partnership requires an association of two or more "persons." The UPA defines persons to include individuals, partnerships, corporations, and other associations.[7] Most partners are natural persons. Any natural person with general contractual capacity has capacity to become a partner. A minor may also become a partner. Because a minor's contracts are voidable, however, he may disaffirm both the partnership agreement and personal liability to creditors on partnership debts. Nevertheless, the minor's capital contribution is subject to the claims of firm creditors.

Under the UPA definition, a corporation may become a partner. A corporation's capacity to become a partner, however, has generally been governed by state corporation law and the articles of incorporation, rather than partnership law. Early cases held that becoming a member of a partnership was beyond the scope of corporate power because membership required an excessive delegation of management power by the board of directors. Modern corporation statutes, however, reject this view and permit a corporation to become a partner. For example, the Revised Model Business Corporation Act provides that each corporation has the power "to be a promoter, partner, member, associate, or

---

5. UPA §6(1).

6. UPA §18(g).
7. UPA §2.

manager of any partnership, joint venture, trust, or other entity.''[8]

"To Carry on . . . A Business." To be a partnership, the association of two or more persons must be formed "to carry on . . . a business." The UPA defines a business to include "every trade, occupation, or profession."[9] The term "business" implies continuity, a series of acts directed toward a profit-making end rather than a single or isolated undertaking. An association of two or more persons to carry out a single enterprise, specific transaction, or single series of transactions for profit is known as a **joint venture.** Generally, the same legal principles govern both partnerships and joint ventures.[10]

Even though a partnership is formed to carry on a business, partnership status does not require that any business actually be transacted. For example, assume Art and Bob agree to pool their resources to buy souvenirs to sell at football games. After each has contributed money to a common fund, Art refuses to carry on the business as agreed. A partnership has nevertheless been created.

"As Co-owners." Co-ownership of the business is a hallmark of partnership. Nevertheless, the UPA makes it clear that mere co-ownership of income producing property, such as in joint tenancy or tenancy in common, does not of itself establish a partnership, whether or not the co-owners share profits made by the use of the property.[11] These co-ownership arrangements often are not commercial in nature and may not even involve a voluntary association. For example, two sisters, Pam and Sally, may inherit income producing farm land as joint tenants from their deceased grandmother. Pam and Sally are not partners. In addition, the concept of "business" generally contemplates more than mere passive co-ownership or investment. The greater the degree of activity, the more likely a business, and therefore a partnership, exists. Thus, if Pam

and Sally in the above example agree to subdivide the property inherited into lots, build homes, and split the profits, they are partners. Two basic components characterize co-ownership arrangements recognized as partnerships: profit sharing and joint control.

Profit Sharing. Profit (and loss) sharing is the most critical attribute of partnership. Indeed, except for the specific situations outlined below, the UPA provides that "the receipt by a person of a share of the profits of a business is *prima facie* evidence that he is a partner in the business."[12] Note that partners share profits (receipts minus expenses); sharing gross receipts, a much more limited participation in a business, does not of itself establish a partnership.[13] For example, an author receiving royalties is not thereby a partner with her publisher. An insurance company charging a premium based upon the insured's gross receipts is not thereby a partner of the insured.

Although sharing profits is usually prima facie evidence of partnership, §7(4) of the UPA provides that profit sharing *alone* is insufficient to establish partnership status if the profits were received in payment:

1. Of a debt by installments or otherwise, or as interest on a loan, even if the amount of payment varies with the profits of the business. For example, assume Carl loans Diane $10,000 for use in Diane's clothing store and Diane agrees to make monthly payments to Carl equal to one-half of Diane's monthly profits. Sharing profits in this manner, alone, does not make Carl a partner in Diane's business.

2. As wages of an employee. For example, assume Ed, a manager of Joe's store, is paid a fixed salary plus a percentage of monthly profits. Ed, because of this fact alone, does not become a partner.

3. As rent to a landlord. For example, assume Laura leases her commercial building for five years to Tim, who intends to open a restaurant on the premises. Rent is computed as a percentage of Tim's net profits from the restaurant. Laura, by this fact alone, does not become a partner in Tim's restaurant.

---

8. RMBCA §3.02(9), MBCA §4(p).

9. UPA §2.

10. One difference that has been noted between a joint venture and a partnership is that each partner is a general agent of the partnership, but each joint adventurer is not an agent for other joint venturers.

11. UPA §7(2).

---

12. UPA §7(4).

13. UPA §7(3).

4. As an annuity to a widow or other representative of a deceased partner. When a partner dies, the partner's widow or widower or estate often desires to keep the business going and participate in the profits of the business, rather than accept a lump sum settlement for the deceased partner's interest. Sharing profits in this manner, alone, does not make the widow or widower or other representative a partner.

5. As consideration for the sale of business goodwill or other property. When a business or other income producing property is sold, the purchase price may be computed as a percentage of income generated by the asset after sale. For example, Sam may sell his business to Beth in exchange for Beth's promise to pay Sam twenty-five percent of the profits derived by Beth from the business. This fact alone does not make Sam a partner in Beth's business.

Note that the situations described above, standing alone, do not create partnerships. Additional facts, such as participation in management and control of the business, may make the creditor, employee, landlord, widow, or seller a partner.

Control Sharing. A common interest in management and control of the business is also essential to partnership. That is, "to state that partners are co-owners of a business is to state that they each have the power of ultimate control."[14] Control sharing is what distinguishes a partnership from an agency relation. An agent, unlike a partner, is not a co-principal with equal right to participate in management and control of the business.

The power of control is affirmative, involving, for example, the power to set prices, control costs, hire and fire employees, and make other business decisions. Negative control, such as veto power over a certain transaction or prior consultation rights, is often used by lenders to protect their investment. This indirect or incidental control generally indicates a debtor-creditor, not a partnership relation.

"For Profit." A partnership is a business association organized "for profit." Accordingly, noncommercial, nonprofit associations, organized, for example, for civic, religious, fraternal, or charitable purposes, are not partnerships. In addition, labor unions and trade associations are not partnerships. To be a partnership, an association need only be organized with the *expectation* of profit. Failure to make a profit does not defeat partnership status. In the following case the court was required to determine whether partnership liability should be imposed upon a person insisting that he was merely a creditor, not a partner.

Lupien v. Malsbenden

477 A.2d 746 (Me. 1984)

Plaintiff Robert Lupien entered into a written agreement with Stephen Cragin, doing business as "York Motor Mart," by which Cragin agreed to construct a Bradley automobile. Lupien agreed to pay $4,450 and to trade in his pickup truck in payment for the Bradley. After Lupien had paid the full purchase price, Cragin failed to deliver the Bradley and disappeared.

Lupien sued defendant Frederick Malsbenden alleging that Malsbenden and Cragin had operated York Motor Mart as partners. At trial Malsbenden testified that he was not Cragin's partner but that he had loaned Cragin $85,000, without interest, to finance the construction of Bradley cars. The loan was to be repaid from the proceeds of the sales of the cars. Malsbenden stated that he had purchased for York Motor Mart the kits from which the cars were constructed and other equipment. Malsbenden testified that after Cragin's disappearance in May 1980, Malsbenden had taken control of York Motor Mart only to dispose of the assets. Malsbenden considered himself to be Cragin's "banker," not a partner.

The trial court held that Malsbenden and Cragin were operating their business as partners and held Malsbenden liable on the contract with Lupien. Malsbenden appealed.

McKusick, Chief Justice

. . . The Uniform Partnership Act, adopted in Maine . . . defines a partnership as "an association of 2 or more persons . . . to carry on as co-owners a business for profit." . . . Whether a partnership exists is an inference of law based on

---

14. UPA §6, Official Comment.

established facts. . . . A finding that the relationship between two persons constitutes a partnership may be based upon evidence of an agreement, either express or implied,

> to place their money, effects, labor, and skill, or some or all of them, in lawful commerce or business with the understanding that a community of profits will be shared. . . . No one factor is alone determinative of the existence of a partnership. . . .

Dalton v. Austin, [432 A.2d 774, 777 (Me. 1981)]. If the arrangement between the parties otherwise qualifies as a partnership, it is of no matter that the parties did not expressly agree to form a partnership or did not even intend to form one. . . .

Here the trial justice concluded that, notwithstanding Malsbenden's assertion that he was only a "banker," his "total involvement" in the Bradley operation was that of a partner. The testimony at trial, both respecting Malsbenden's financial interest in the enterprise and his involvement in day-to-day business operations, amply supported the Superior Court's conclusion. Malsbenden had a financial interest of $85,000 in the Bradley portion of York Motor Mart's operations. Although Malsbenden termed the investment a loan, significantly he conceded that the "loan" carried no interest. His "loan" was not made in the form of a fixed payment or payments, but was made to the business, at least in substantial part, in the form of day-to-day purchases of Bradley kits, other parts and equipment, and in the payment of wages. Furthermore, the "loan" was not to be repaid in fixed amounts or at fixed times, but rather only upon the sale of Bradley automobiles.

The evidence also showed that, unlike a banker, Malsbenden had the right to participate in control of the business and in fact did so on a day-to-day basis. According to Urbin Savaria, who worked at York Motor Mart from late April through June 1980, Malsbenden during that time opened the business establishment each morning, remained present through part of every day, had final say on the ordering of parts, paid for parts and equipment, and paid Savaria's salary. On plaintiff's frequent visits to York Motor Mart, he generally dealt with Malsbenden because Cragin was not present. It was

Malsbenden who insisted that plaintiff trade in his truck prior to the completion of the Bradley because the proceeds from the sale of the truck were needed to complete the Bradley. . . . As of three years after the making of the contract now in litigation, Malsbenden was still doing business at York Motor Mart, "just disposing of property."

Malsbenden and Cragin may well have viewed their relationship to be that of creditor-borrower, rather than a partnership. At trial Malsbenden so asserts, and Cragin's departure from the scene in the spring of 1980 deprives us of the benefit of his view of his business arrangement with Malsbenden. In any event, whatever the intent of these two men as to their respective involvements in the business of making and selling Bradley cars, there is no clear error in the Superior Court's finding that the Bradley car operation represented a pooling of Malsbenden's capital and Cragin's automotive skills, with joint control over the business and intent to share the fruits of the enterprise. As a matter of law, that arrangement amounted to a partnership. . . .

[Judgment affirmed.]

The *Lupien* case is typical of those involving the definition of partnership: a creditor of the alleged partnership seeks to impose personal liability upon a person who denies he or she is a partner. The following case illustrates the definition in a somewhat different context.

Chaiken v. Employment Security Commission

274 A.2d 707 (Del. Super. 1971)

The Delaware Employment Security Commission (the Commission) levied an assessment against Richard K. Chaiken for failure to file unemployment compensation contributions for two barbers who worked in a barber shop operated by Chaiken. Chaiken alleged that the barbers were not employees but were partners for whom he was not required to pay unemployment compensation contributions. The evidence established that Chaiken had registered the business as a partnership and that he and the two barbers had filed federal partnership tax returns. Chaiken also offered into evidence two partnership agreements. The first paragraph of the agreements declared the creation of the partnership. Under the second paragraph, Chaiken agreed to provide the barber chairs, supplies, and licenses and the barbers agreed to furnish their own tools. That section also provided that upon dissolution ownership of these items would revert to the person who had provided them. Paragraph three provided a formula for division of the income among Chaiken and the two barbers. The fourth paragraph declared that Chaiken would decide all partnership policy. The final paragraph stated the barbers' hours of work and holidays.

The Commission held that the business was not a partnership. Chaiken appealed.

Storey, Judge

. . . The mere existence of an agreement labelled "partnership" agreement and the characterization of signatories as "partners" does not conclusively prove the existence of a partnership. Rather, the intention of the parties, as explained by the wording of the agreement, is paramount. . . .

A partnership is defined as an association of two or more persons to carry on as co-owners a business for profit. . . . As co-owners of a business, partners have an equal right in the decision making process. . . . But this right may be abrogated by agreement of the parties without destroying the partnership concept, provided other partnership elements are present. . . .

Thus, while paragraph four reserves for Chaiken all rights to determine partnership policy, it is not standing alone, fatal to the partnership concept. Co-owners should also contribute valuable consideration for the creation of the business. Under paragraph two, however, Chaiken provides the barber chair (and implicitly the barber shop itself), mirror, licenses and linen, while the other partners merely provide their tools and labor—nothing more than any barber-employee would furnish. Standing alone, however, mere contribution of work and skill can be valuable consideration for a partnership agreement. . . .

[D]istribution of partnership assets to the partners upon dissolution is only allowed after all partnership liabilities are satisfied. . . . But paragraph two of the agreement, in stating the ground rules for dissolution, makes no declaration that the partnership assets will be utilized to pay partnership expenses before reversion to their original owners. This deficiency militates against a finding in favor of partnership intent since it is assumed Chaiken would have inserted such provision had he thought his lesser partners would accept such liability. Partners do accept such liability, employees do not.

Most importantly, co-owners carry on "a business for profit." The phrase has been interpreted to mean that partners share in the profits and the losses of the business. The intent to divide the profits is an indispensable requisite of partnership. . . . Paragraph three of the agreement declares that each partner shall share in the income of the business. There is no sharing of the profits, and as the agreement is drafted, there are no profits. Merely sharing the gross returns does not establish a partnership. . . . Nor is the sharing of profits prima facie evidence of a partnership where the profits received are in payment of wages. . . .

The failure to share profits therefore, is fatal to the partnership concept here.

Evaluating Chaiken's agreement in the light of the elements implicit in a partnership, no partnership intent can be found. The absence of the important right of decision making or the important duty to share liabilities upon dissolution individually may not be fatal to a partnership. But when both are absent, coupled with the absence of profit sharing, they become strong factors in discrediting the partnership argument. . . .

In addition, the total circumstances of the case taken together indicate the employer-employee relationship between Chaiken and his barbers. The agreement set forth the hours of work and days off—unusual subjects for partnership agreements. The barbers brought into the relationship only the equipment required of all barber shop operators. And each barber had his own individual "partnership" with Chaiken. Furthermore, Chaiken conducted all transactions with suppliers, and purchased licenses, insurance, and the lease for the business property in his own name. Finally, the name "Richard's Barber Shop" continued to be used after the execution of the so-called partnership agreements.

It is the conclusion of this Court that Chaiken did not carry the burden of proving the existence of partnerships. . . .

[Judgment affirmed.]

Partnership Name and Registration Requirements

Although not required, most partnerships use a firm name. The partnership may do business in the name of one or more partners—for example, Joe Doaks and Millie Hobbs may transact business under the name "Doaks and Hobbs"—or may use a fictitious, assumed, or trade name, such as "Star Bar & Grill," or "The Record Service," or "A-1 Tire & Battery," or "ABC Home Remodelers." The firm name of a successful business often acquires substantial value.

Most states have fictitious or **assumed business name statutes** that require that a certificate listing the names and addresses of persons conducting business under an assumed or trade name be filed in the public records (for example, the county clerk's office). Some states also require that a notice of the filing be published in a newspaper of general circulation for a stated period (for example, once a week for three consecutive weeks). These statutes provide public information of business ownership to interested persons such as creditors. In some states, no filing is required if the partnership name consists solely of the owners' surnames.

Sanctions for noncompliance vary among the states, and range from a fine to, occasionally, imprisonment. Early statutes rendered the noncomplying firm's contracts unenforceable. Many modern statutes, however, simply deny the firm access to the state court system to sue on its contracts or other transactions until it complies.

Entity and Aggregate Characteristics of Partnership

An issue that has long troubled partnership law is whether a partnership is merely an aggregate of the individual partners, or is a legal entity or legal person, like a corporation, existing apart from its owners. Many legal issues are resolved differently, depending upon the theory chosen. Under an aggregate theory, for example, a partnership cannot be sued in the firm name; rather, each individual partner must be named as a defendant in the lawsuit. An entity approach, in contrast, would permit suits in the firm name.

Under the traditional aggregate, or common law, theory, the rights and obligations created by partnership activities are those of the partners; the partnership is not recognized as a legal person. The UPA adopts instead a hybrid approach, treating the partnership as an entity for some purposes and an aggregate for others, with the entity theory predominant. For example, although the partners are personally liable for firm debts, the partnership is an entity for purposes of acquiring, holding, and transferring property; and each partner is considered an agent of the partnership. Further, partnership assets, liabilities, and transactions are separate and distinct from those of the partners. As the operative UPA provisions are discussed in the following material, the text will indicate whether the Act is following an aggregate or entity theory of partnership.

Like the UPA, other modern statutes often treat a partnership as an entity for specific purposes. For example, both federal bankruptcy law and the Uniform Commercial Code define "person" to include a partnership.[15] Modern procedural statutes generally permit a partnership to sue and be sued in the firm name. On the other hand, federal tax law treats the partnership as an aggregate, attributing income or losses incurred by the partnership to the individual partners. The partnership is not viewed as a taxpaying entity.

Relationship Among Partners

Assuming a partnership exists, a number of important legal issues arise during the course of carrying on the partnership business. The law must initially determine the nature of the partners' interest in the partnership and partnership property, and the legal relationship among partners. These issues are discussed below.

---

15. 11 U.S.C. §101(35); UCC §§1-201(28),(30).

The Partnership Agreement

Existence and Formality. The primary and most important source of "law" governing the legal relationship among partners is a private contract, known as the **partnership agreement** (or sometimes **articles of partnership**). This contract governs the rights and obligations of the various partners and the internal structure of the partnership. As one court long ago noted, the agreement is "the law of [the] partnership, made by the parties, . . . which a court of equity ought to regard as the rule in all questions arising between them."[16] This principle is carefully followed by the UPA, which precisely regulates the rights of partners as against *third parties* but allows the partners great flexibility to govern relations among themselves by contract. The UPA does, however, include a number of provisions governing the relation of partners to one another which apply in the absence of agreement among them.

Although governed essentially by contract, the law usually does not require a written agreement to create or maintain a partnership. The common law Statute of Frauds, however, does require a writing if the partnership is, by terms of the agreement, to continue for more than one year.[17] Nevertheless, unwritten partnership agreements without fixed terms are generally deemed to continue "at will" and are terminated upon death or at the will of any partner. Accordingly, such oral agreements are capable of performance within one year and are enforceable without a writing.

Even though a formal written contract is not generally required, a comprehensive, attorney drafted, carefully negotiated, written partnership agreement is always advisable. Casually created business relations, including partnerships, are a fruitful source of litigation. A comprehensive written contract prevents many disputes, because potential problems are anticipated and ambiguities resolved while reducing the agreement to writing. Additionally, the writing can be used by the court to resolve any later dispute between the parties, eliminating the need to prove the existence and terms of a disputed oral contract.

Terms of the Agreement. The partnership agreement should include all terms necessary to the orderly operation and liquidation of the partnership. Although specific provisions vary based upon such factors as the type of business and number of partners, the following issues should be addressed explicitly in the agreement. The operation of many of these terms is covered in more detail throughout the partnership material.

General Provisions. Included in this category, for example, are terms stating the names of the partners, and the name, purpose, term, and place of business of the partnership.

Capitalization. The agreement should contain provisions indicating the initial and subsequent capital contributions of each partner, whether separate capital, income, and drawing accounts are to be maintained, and limitations or restrictions on withdrawals.

Other Financial and Accounting Matters. The agreement should include provisions determining the accounting method, fiscal year, profit-and-loss-sharing ratio, compensation of partners, and the right of partners to be reimbursed for business expenses. Provision for firm bank accounts and maintenance and inspection of partnership books should also be made.

Property. The agreement should clearly state what property is partnership property, what property, if any, belonging to individual partners is to be made available for partnership use, and how title to partnership property is to be held.

Management. The agreement should outline the rights of each partner in the management of the business, the voting requirements for taking partnership action, the powers, limitations, and authority of each partner, and the amount of time each partner is expected to spend on firm business.

Dissolution. The agreement should state which events dissolve the partnership, whether the

---

16. *Jacob C. Slemmer's Appeal,* 58 Pa. 168, 176 (1868).

17. The common law Statute of Frauds and the "one year" provision are discussed in detail in Chapter 12.

business is to be continued after dissolution, how the value of a withdrawing or deceased partner's interest is computed, and the procedure for liquidating and distributing partnership assets.

Partners' Compensation

Profit sharing, the hallmark of partnership, is the primary method of compensating partners. The partnership agreement often provides for unequal shares among the partners (for example, A, B, and C may agree to share profit fifty, thirty, and twenty percent respectively) and may provide loss sharing ratios that differ from those governing profit sharing. Unless otherwise agreed, however, the UPA provides that profits and losses are shared equally, even if the partners have unequal capital contributions. If a profit-sharing ratio is agreed upon (for example, 5:3:2) but nothing is provided regarding losses, losses are shared in the same percentage as profits.[18]

Each partner is generally required to render services to the partnership in the conduct of its business. Absent contrary agreement, however, a partner is not entitled to compensation for services rendered to the firm, to rent upon property she permits the partnership to use, or to interest on her capital contribution.[19] Partners are compensated by a share of profits; other forms of compensation, such as salaries, rents, and interest, must be explicitly agreed upon. In many partnerships one or more partners manage the day-to-day affairs of the partnership and receive salaries, while others are inactive. The rule denying compensation in addition to profits is subject to one notable exception. Upon dissolution of a partnership, a surviving partner is entitled to reasonable compensation for her services in winding up the partnership affairs.[20] In addition to any basic compensation, the partnership is required to reimburse a partner who makes payments from her own funds or reasonably incurs personal

liabilities in the ordinary and proper conduct of the firm's business or for the preservation of its business or property.[21]

Participation in Management

Unless otherwise agreed, all partners have equal rights in the management and control of the partnership business.[22] In many partnerships, however, the partnership agreement vests management authority in a small group of partners or, in some cases, one partner. Among partners entitled to vote, any disagreement arising out of ordinary partnership affairs may be decided by a majority vote of the partners.[23] For example, a majority vote could authorize ordinary business transactions such as borrowing money, approving accounts, and hiring and firing employees. In many cases, a partner's authority to act for the partnership is explicitly stated in the partnership agreement. For example, the agreement may give one partner exclusive authority to buy raw materials for use in the business. No further vote of the partners is required to authorize that partner to purchase raw materials.

Certain extraordinary business matters require a unanimous vote of the partners. For example, a unanimous vote is required

1. to admit a new partner;[24]
2. to change, or do any act that violates, the partnership agreement;[25]
3. to change the capital of the firm;
4. to change the scope of the partnership business; or
5. to change the place of the firm business.

In addition, the UPA states that a partner or group of partners acting without the unanimous consent of the others have no authority to

1. assign partnership property for the benefit of creditors;

---

18. UPA §18(a).
19. Although a partner is not generally entitled to interest on his or her capital contribution, interest is payable from the date when repayment of the contribution should be made. UPA §18(d).
20. UPA §18(f).

21. UPA §18(b).
22. UPA §18(e).
23. UPA §18(h).
24. UPA §18(g).
25. UPA §18(h).

2. dispose of partnership goodwill;
3. do any other act that would make it impossible to carry on ordinary partnership business;
4. confess a judgment binding upon a co-partner, the partnership, or partnership property; or
5. submit a partnership claim or liability to arbitration.[26]

The voting requirements outlined above often are changed by agreement of the partners. For example, less than or greater than a majority of votes may be required for certain actions. Some partners may receive more than one vote based upon capital contribution, profit-and-loss-sharing ratio, or seniority.

Whatever voting requirements a partnership adopts determines a partner's actual authority to deal with third parties on behalf of the firm. Accordingly, the preceding discussion is an important prerequisite to understanding the relationship between partners and third parties discussed in Chapter 43.

Duty to Keep Books and Render Information

Adequate accounting records are particularly important in a partnership, which requires accurate computation of the ever-changing interests of multiple owners. Accordingly, the UPA requires that accounting books and records be kept, and unless the partners otherwise agree, the books are to be kept at the partnership's principal place of business. Wherever the books are kept, each partner "shall at all times have access to and may inspect and copy any of them."[27]

The partnership books provide important information to each partner concerning partnership affairs. To supplement this information, the UPA also requires each partner to render on demand to any other partner true and full information regard-

ing all matters affecting the partnership. Each partner also must render information to the legal representative of any partner who is deceased or under a legal disability. The duty extends to both general and limited partners for transactions occurring from formation through the operation and liquidation of the firm.

Collectively, the firm books and each partner's duty to render accurate and complete information provide each partner with the tools to discover and investigate breaches of perhaps the most important duty existing among partners—the fiduciary duty of loyalty.

The Partner as Fiduciary

A partnership is a fiduciary relationship similar to that existing between trustee and beneficiary, principal and agent, and director and corporation. The fiduciary duty of loyalty imposes an obligation upon each partner to act solely for the benefit of the other partners or the partnership in matters within the scope of the partnership relation. The relationship is one of strict trust and confidence, requiring the partner to subordinate personal interests to those of fellow partners. The UPA holds a partner liable as a fiduciary by requiring every partner to

> account to the partnership for any benefit, and hold as trustee for it any profits derived by him without the consent of the other partners from any transaction connected with the formation, conduct, or liquidation of the partnership or from any use by him of its property.[28]

A vast number of litigated cases involve breach of a partner's fiduciary duties. Prohibited conduct includes, for example, the following.

1. A partner may not divert a partnership opportunity for personal benefit. A partnership opportunity includes any business transaction (1) neces-

---

26. UPA §9(3). Assignments for the benefit of creditors are discussed in Chapter 30. Confession of judgment is discussed in Chapter 29. Arbitration is discussed in Chapter 2.

27. UPA §19.

28. UPA §21(1). This fiduciary standard also applies to the representative of a deceased partner engaged in liquidating partnership affairs as the personal representative of the last surviving partner. UPA §21(2).

sary or related to partnership business, (2) offered to or learned about through the partnership, and (3) developed with partnership funds or facilities.

2. A partner may not secretly use or deal in the partnership assets for personal benefit, personally acquire a partnership asset, or otherwise use the partnership or its property in ways not contemplated by the partnership agreement.

3. A partner may not compete with the partnership in transactions within the scope of partnership business, and must account to co-partners for all "secret" profits realized in transactions injurious to partnership interests.

4. A partner must disclose all material facts to co-partners concerning his ownership of property, business dealings, future plans, potential conflicts of interest, and any other matter indicating an actual or potential interest adverse to the partnership. Disclosure is required under these circumstances, whether or not information is specifically requested by other partners. A partner who is purchasing another partner's interest in the firm owes a similar duty of full and honest disclosure.

The following classic case explains the nature of the fiduciary relationship among partners.

Clement v. Clement
260 A.2d 728 (Pa. 1970)

In 1923 L. W. Clement and his brother Charles formed a partnership engaged in the plumbing business and operated under the name "Clement Brothers." L. W. assumed complete control over the business finances for over forty years. In 1964, the two partners entered into negotiations for L. W. to purchase Charles's interest in the partnership.

Charles filed a suit in equity requesting dissolution of the partnership and an accounting. The chancellor found that L. W. had diverted partnership funds to purchase real estate and insurance policies. The chancellor awarded Charles a one-half interest in the real estate and insurance. L. W. appealed and the appellate court en banc reversed, holding that Charles had failed to prove that L. W. had committed fraud and that under the doctrine of laches Charles's delay in bringing suit precluded his recov-

ery. Charles Clement appealed to the Supreme Court of Pennsylvania.

Roberts, Justice

. . . [P]artners owe a fiduciary duty one to another. . . . One should not have to deal with his partner as though he were the opposite party in an arm's length transaction. One should be allowed to trust his partner, to expect that he is pursuing a common goal and not working at cross-purposes. This concept of the partnership entity was expressed most ably by Mr. Justice, then Judge, Cardozo in *Meinhard v. Salmon,* [164 N.E. 545, 546 (N.Y. 1928)]:

> Joint adventurers, like copartners, owe to one another, while the enterprise continues, the duty of the finest loyalty. Many forms of conduct permissible in a workaday world for those acting at arm's length, are forbidden to those bound by fiduciary ties. A trustee is held to something stricter than the morals of the marketplace. Not honesty alone, but the punctilio of an honor the most sensitive, is then the standard of behavior. As to this there has developed a tradition that is unbending and inveterate. Uncompromising rigidity has been the attitude of courts of equity when petitioned to undermine the rule of undivided loyalty by the "disintegrating erosion" of particular exceptions. . . . Only thus has the level of conduct for fiduciaries been kept at a level higher than that trodden by the crowd. It will not consciously be lowered by any judgment of this court. . . .

It would be unduly harsh to require that one must prove actual fraud before he can recover for a partner's derelictions. Where one partner has so dealt with the partnership as to raise the probability of wrongdoing it ought to be his responsibility to negate that inference. It has been held that "where a partner fails to keep a record of partnership transactions, and is unable to account for them, every presumption will be made against him." *Bracht v. Connell,* [170 A. 297, 301 (Pa. 1933)]. Likewise, where a partner commingles partnership funds with his own and generally deals loosely with partnership assets he ought to have to shoulder the task of demonstrating the probity of his conduct.

In the instant case L. W. dealt loosely with partnership funds. At various times he made substantial investments in his own name. He was totally unable to explain where he got the funds to make these investments. The court en banc held that Charles had no claim on the fruits of these investments because he could not trace the money that was invested therein dollar for dollar from the partnership. Charles should not have had this burden. He did show that his brother diverted substantial sums from the partnership funds under his control. The inference that these funds provided L. W. with the wherewithall to make his investments was a perfectly reasonable one for the chancellor to make and his decision should have been allowed to stand.

The doctrine of laches has no role to play in the decision of this case. It is true that the transactions complained of cover a period of many years. However, we do not think that it can be said that Charles negligently slept on his rights to the detriment of his brother. L. W. actively concealed much of his wrongdoing. He cannot now rely upon the doctrine of laches—that defense was not intended to reward the successful wrongdoer. . . .

[Judgment vacated and remanded.]

Right to an Accounting

Under ordinary circumstances the partners, all of whom have access to the firm books and property, are able to ascertain for themselves the status of partnership affairs. Under certain extraordinary circumstances, however, a more formal comprehensive review is undertaken in an **accounting,** an equitable proceeding in which the court directs[29] a comprehensive investigation of the partners' and partnership transactions in order to adjudicate the rights of the various partners. The accounting determines, for example, the amount of cash or other assets invested by each partner, actual profit (or loss) from operations, the extent of partnership property, and ultimately the status of the various partners' capital accounts. Once it is completed, the court then renders a money judgment for or

against each partner in the amounts determined by the accounting.

Traditionally, an accounting was available only upon dissolution of the firm. The UPA, however, expands the availability of the remedy by providing that a partner is entitled to a formal accounting

1. whenever co-partners wrongfully exclude him or her from the partnership business or possession of partnership property;
2. when the partnership agreement provides for the right to an accounting;
3. whenever another partner has violated his or her fiduciary duty; or
4. whenever other circumstances render an accounting just and reasonable.[30]

An accounting is a potent remedy, enabling an aggrieved partner to obtain fair treatment, and providing a basis to examine and reconcile a number of often complex partnership transactions. It is generally a partner's sole remedy for breach of the various contractual and fiduciary obligations existing between a partner and the partnership. The accounting ascertains rights and obligations among all partners, determining what each owes and is owed. Separate suits for damages by and against individual partners cannot achieve this comprehensive result.

Partners' Property Rights

Section 24 of the UPA provides that the property rights of a partner include (1) rights in specific partnership property, (2) an interest in the partnership, and (3) a right to participate in the management. Participation in management has been previously discussed. Partnership property, the character of the partners' interest in it, and the nature of a partner's interest in the partnership are discussed below.

Partnership Property

Partnership business usually commences after the partners have made their capital contributions to the

---

29. Ordinarily, the accounting is conducted by an auditor, referee, or master, subject to court review.

30. UPA §22.

firm. The partners may contribute property or services. Property contributed may be of any type, real or personal, tangible or intangible, and often includes money. This property is then used to generate or purchase other property in the course of the firm's business.

Distinguishing Partnership from Individual Property.

Distinguishing partnership property from property that, though used in the business, belongs to an individual partner is a basic problem in partnership law. The distinction is important in resolving a number of legal issues including, for example, the disposition of the property upon the death of a partner or dissolution of the firm, the right of firm creditors to reach the property, whether income or loss from use or disposition of the property is to be shared by the partners, and who is entitled to transfer the property.

Generally speaking, the partners' intention, as outlined in the partnership agreement, determines whether specific property belongs to an individual partner or the partnership. If the agreement fails to address the issue, the status of the property may be ambiguous, and ultimately lead to a dispute that the court must resolve by inferring the parties' intent from their conduct.

Section 8(1) of the UPA provides generally that partnership property includes all property originally brought into the partnership or subsequently acquired by purchase or otherwise, on account of the partnership. This general statement provides little guidance in concrete fact situations and courts must look to more specific indicia of partnership ownership. For example, generally, property acquired with partnership funds is partnership property.[31] Property with a record title, such as automobiles, real estate, or stock certificates, is presumed to be partnership property if title is held in the firm name. Firm ownership is also indicated if the partnership pays for taxes, repairs, and insurance on the property, or if the property is entered and carried on the partnership books. On the other hand, mere partnership use, possession, or occupancy of property owned by one partner raises no presumption of firm ownership. Partners often mix personal and partnership affairs, especially in family partnerships.

Title to Partnership Property.

Partnerships have long been allowed to hold and convey title to tangible and intangible personal property, such as automobiles, stocks, and bonds, in the firm name. At common law, however, a partnership could not take or hold title to real property in the firm name because it was not a legal entity. Rather, title was held in the names of one or more partners who, in essence, held the property in trust for the partnership. Section 8(3) of the UPA resolves this problem by providing that any estate in real property may be acquired in the firm name. Title so acquired can be conveyed only in the partnership name. In other words, under the UPA a partnership is treated as a legal entity for purposes of acquiring, holding, and transferring interests in real property.

Rights in Specific Partnership Property—Tenancy in Partnership

Partnership property takes many forms including, for example, cash, equipment, inventory, accounts receivable, land, and buildings. Under §25 of the UPA, partners hold title to specific partnership property under a special form of co-ownership known as **tenancy in partnership**. The characteristics of this tenancy are as follows.

1. Each partner has an equal right with his or her partners to possess specific partnership property for *partnership purposes* but no right to possess such property for any *other* purpose without the consent of the other partners.

2. A partner may not assign his or her right in specific partnership property except as part of an assignment by all partners of their rights in the same property.

3. A creditor of an *individual partner* may not, by attachment or execution, reach that partner's right in specific partnership property. That is, a partner may neither voluntarily nor involuntarily (through action of his personal creditors) assign his interest in specific partnership property. The firm's property may, however, be seized to satisfy the claims of unpaid *partnership* creditors.

---

31. UPA §8(2).

4. As in a joint tenancy,[32] on the death of a partner, her right in specific partnership property vests in the surviving partner or partners. The surviving partner or partners (or the legal representative of the last surviving partner) may possess the property only for partnership purposes.

To illustrate the incidents of tenancy in partnership, assume A and B are partners in a printing shop. Partnership property includes the building (contributed by A) in which the shop is located and various printing presses and other equipment (contributed by B). A and B hold the property in tenancy in partnership. Both parties may possess the property for partnership purposes, but neither has the right to possess it for personal use without the consent of the other. Neither A nor B can independently sell or otherwise assign any interest in specific partnership property (for example, a printing press) to a third party. A and B acting together, however, could transfer title to specific property. Personal creditors of A or B may not, by judicial process, seize specific partnership property to satisfy an unpaid personal debt. Creditors of the partnership could, however, force a seizure and sale of the specific property to satisfy a partnership debt. On A's death, title to the partnership property vests in B. A's estate receives no interest in the specific property now vested in B, who may possess the property only for partnership purposes.

Although under the UPA a tenancy in partnership is a special form of co-ownership, it has few of the legal attributes characteristic of other forms of co-ownership such as the joint tenancy and tenancy in common. As one commentator succinctly noted: "The incidents of this tenancy are so negligible that ownership of the property is, for all practical purposes, in the partnership, not in the partners."[33] In other words, the partnership is the functional owner of the partnership property and is recognized as a legal entity for that purpose.

Partner's Interest in the Partnership

Even though the partnership is the de facto owner of the partnership property, the partners collectively own the partnership. An individual partner's ownership interest is embodied in his or her **partnership interest,** which is defined in UPA §26 as the partner's share of the profits and surplus of the business. That is, the partnership interest is essentially each partner's share of the difference between the firm's assets and liabilities. For example, if A and B are equal partners with equal capital contributions in a partnership with assets of $150,000 and liabilities of $100,000, each partner has a $25,000 interest in the firm. Like a share of corporate stock, a partnership interest is intangible personal property.

A partner, through the partnership interest, possesses most of the incidents of individual ownership not existing in specific partnership property. For example, a partner's interest may be individually assigned, personal creditors may reach it, and it may be transferred to the partner's estate on death.

Assignment of Partnership Interest. An individual partner may sell or otherwise assign his interest in the partnership. The assignment does not dissolve the partnership and, unless otherwise agreed, the assignee is not entitled (1) to participate in the management or administration of the business, (2) to require any information or account of partnership transactions, or (3) to inspect partnership books. In short, the assignee does not become a partner—that requires unanimous consent of the other partners. Rather, the assignee is entitled to receive, according to his contract, the profits to which the assigning partner would otherwise be entitled.[34] If the partnership is liquidated, the assignee also is entitled to any surplus—share of undistributed profits and return of capital contribution—to which the assigning partner would have been entitled.

Creditors' Rights. Although a partner's personal creditors may not reach specific partnership property to satisfy their claims, they may reach the partner's interest in the partnership either voluntarily, through an assignment by the partner, or involuntarily through a **charging order.** To use this device, the creditor first reduces its claim against the

---

32. Joint tenancies are discussed in Chapter 36.
33. Crane & Bromberg, *Law of Partnership* 228 (1968).
34. UPA §27(1).

debtor partner to judgment, and then petitions the court to "charge" that partner's partnership interest with payment of the unsatisfied debt.[35] The court may then order that payments, including distributions of profits and withdrawals of capital, to which the partner becomes entitled are to be made to the creditor. A charging order is generally viewed as a creditor's sole remedy to reach a debtor partner's interest in the partnership. The creditor, like the assignee, does not become a partner, has no right in specific partnership property, and has no right to participate in management. The debtor partner continues as a partner, except that distributions otherwise payable to the partner are paid to the creditor.

Ordinarily, the charging order operates as a type of lien on the partner's interest and continues until the judgment debt is repaid. The creditor's claim may, however, be so large that the partner's periodic income from the firm will not satisfy the debt within a reasonable time. In this case, the court may order a sale of the debtor's partnership interest, with the proceeds to be paid to the creditor.

Inheritability. Upon death of a partner, the partnership interest generally passes as personal property according to the terms of his or her will, or by intestate succession. The partner's devisee or heir (for example, a surviving spouse) is then paid for the value of the deceased partner's interest in the firm through, for example, an accounting action involving liquidation of the firm and distribution of the proceeds. Alternatively, the partnership agreement may provide for continuation of the firm after death of a partner by stating that a deceased partner's interest passes to the surviving partner or partners who are required to purchase it from the partner's estate. To prevent liquidation of the firm to pay for a deceased partner's interest, these buy-out arrangements often are funded by life insurance policies maintained on the life of each partner. The effect of death of a partner and the method of computing his interest should be clearly outlined in the partnership agreement.

SUMMARY

1. The three primary forms of business organization used in the United States are the sole proprietorship, the partnership, and the corporation. A partnership is the simplest organizational form involving two or more owners. Partners may be general (possessing unlimited liability for firm debts) or limited (liable only to the extent of investment in the business). Partnership law is based upon the Uniform Partnership Act (UPA), the Uniform Limited Partnership Act (ULPA), and the Revised Uniform Limited Partnership Act (RULPA), which are liberally supplemented by common law principles of contracts, estoppel, property, and agency.

2. A partnership is defined in the UPA as "an association of two or more persons to carry on as co-owners a business for profit." Although each element of the definition must be met, sharing profits and losses is the most important attribute of partnership. For some purposes, such as taxation and legal liability, a partnership is merely an aggregate of the individual partners. For others, such as property ownership and litigation, the

partnership is a legal entity or legal person, like a corporation, existing apart from its owners.

3. Rights and obligations of the partners and internal structure are generally determined by contract among them, the partnership agreement. This agreement commonly contains detailed provisions governing capitalization, other financial and accounting matters, partnership property, management, and dissolution. In the absence of contrary agreement, partners are compensated by a share of profits generated by the business, and each partner has an equal voice in the management and control of the business.

4. The UPA requires that partnership books and records be kept and that each partner render accurate and complete information to co-partners regarding partnership affairs. Each partner also owes a fiduciary duty of loyalty to the other partners and the partnership, which prevents a partner from diverting a partnership opportunity for personal benefit or from competing with the partnership. Partnership disputes, including those involving breaches of duty, generally are resolved in an equitable proceeding known as an accounting.

5. The UPA provides that the property rights of a partner include (1) rights in specific partnership property, (2) an interest in the partnership, and (3) a right to par-

---

35. UPA §28(1).

ticipate in the management. Partnership property includes all property originally brought into the partnership or subsequently acquired on account of the partnership. Under the UPA specific partnership property is held by the partners in tenancy in partnership. The incidents of this tenancy are so minimal, however, that partnership property is effectively owned by the partnership, not the partners. Rather, a partner's ownership of the partnership is embodied in his or her interest in the partnership—a share of the profits and surplus of the business. Unlike specific partnership property, a partnership interest may be assigned by an individual partner, reached by creditors of an individual partner, and transferred on death by a partner.

KEY TERMS

general partner
limited partner
Uniform Partnership Act
  (UPA)
partnership
joint venture
assumed business name
  statutes

partnership agreement
  (articles of partnership)
accounting
tenancy in partnership
partnership interest
charging order

QUESTIONS AND PROBLEMS

42-1 After reading the text and cases regarding the definition of partnership, what steps would you take to avoid being treated as a partner
 (a) of a debtor (if you are a creditor)?
 (b) of a tenant (if you are a landlord)?
 (c) of an employer (if you are an employee)?
 (d) of a buyer of a business (if you are the seller)?

42-2 In each of the following questions, determine whether the parties are partners.
 (a) In 1975, Dale entered into a long-term lease of a building. For three years, he subleased the building to a business that operated a bar on the premises. In 1978, the subtenant moved and Dale made an oral agreement with Frances for operation of the bar. Frances agreed to manage the bar by purchasing supplies, paying bills, keeping the records, and hiring and firing employees. Frances and Dale agreed that each would receive $200 per week plus one-half of the profits. Frances agreed to provide a monthly accounting to Dale. Dale claims that he owns the business and Frances is an employee. Frances believes she and Dale are

partners. Are Frances and Dale partners? Explain.
 (b) Elwood, a bachelor, inherited a farm from his father in 1940. Soon thereafter, he and his sister Nora moved into the farmhouse and began farming operations. Elwood raised the crops and livestock while Nora handled the cooking and housework and kept the books. A sign on the land read "The Elwood and Nora Farms." Elwood and Nora discussed all major purchases such as equipment and livestock. Nora wrote all checks but the checks were drawn on account solely in Elwood's name. All property was registered in Elwood's name. Elwood annually filed an individual tax return and Nora filed no tax returns. All profits were reinvested in the farming operation. On several occasions in discussion with friends, Elwood referred to Nora as his partner. Are Elwood and Nora partners? Explain.

42-3 Joe and Tony were partners who operated a grocery store for over twenty years. They both worked full time in the store until 1980 when they decided they could no longer work together because of irreconcilable differences. Joe advised Tony that he wanted to terminate the partnership and requested that Tony make available all of the accounting records. Although Tony had kept complete records during the term of the partnership, most of the records had been inadvertently destroyed when Tony's son had cleaned the basement of their house. After Joe's request to terminate the business, Tony changed the sign on the store to read "Tony's Supermarket" but continued to operate the store. Despite Joe's frequent requests for his assets in the business, Tony refused to pay any money to Joe. In 1984, Joe sued Tony requesting $750,000 as his half of the profits. Tony countersued claiming that he was entitled to wages for the three years he had solely operated the business. Tony also claimed that $750,000 was greater than half of the profit but could not provide a more accurate figure because of destruction of the records. How should the court rule? Explain.

42-4 In *Clement v. Clement* (see page 894), one of the justices filed a dissent stating in part:

> In 1923, L. W. Clement and his younger brother, Charles, formed a partnership for the purpose of engaging in the plumbing business under the name of Clement Brothers. They agreed to share the profits

of the business equally after payment of the debts. L. W. was the more alert and aggressive of the two. He attended special training schools to upgrade his plumbing skills, and became a master plumber. He alone conducted the business here involved, and had complete control of its finances. He frequently worked nights, Sundays and holidays. Charles, on the other hand, refused to be "bothered" with the administration of the business or its finances. He insisted also on limiting his work to a regular eight-hour shift and confining his contribution to the business to the performance of various plumbing jobs assigned to him.

(a) Should these facts affect the outcome of the case? Explain.

(b) The dissenting justice further stated:

> Over the years, L. W. accumulated assets which eventually became quite valuable. For instance, in 1945 he purchased two lots of land for $5,500, and subsequently constructed a commercial building thereon. This construction was financed in most part by money secured through placing a mortgage on the property.

Assume that the original $5,500 used to purchase the land had been diverted from the partnership. Do you think Charles was entitled to one-half of the value of the property? Explain.

(c) In explaining the importance of partners' fiduciary duties, one text states: "Without the protection of fiduciary duties, each [partner] is at the other's mercy." Crane & Bromberg, *Law of Partnership* 389 (1968). What does this statement mean?

(d) If you had been advising L. W. Clement, what suggestions would you have made to ensure that L. W.'s investments did not become partnership property?

42-5 Heloise applied to First State Bank for a personal loan of $10,000. When Bart, the lending officer, inquired about her assets, Heloise explained that she was the owner of Heloise's Antique Shop and provided an appraisal showing the value of the inventory to be $100,000. Bart verified that the inventory was not subject to a security interest. Bart then recommended to his supervisor that the bank grant the loan. The supervisor suggested that Bart check the county clerk's records where he discovered that Heloise's Antique Shop was operated as a partnership by Heloise and Abelard.

(a) Bart still recommended that the loan be granted explaining that one-half of the inventory would be valued at $50,000, more than enough to cover the value of the loan. Is Bart's explanation correct? Explain.

(b) What further information would you request prior to determining whether to grant the loan?

42-6 In many partnership agreements, the partners agree to purchase life insurance on the life of each partner naming the partnership (or the partners) as the beneficiaries. The face amount of each policy usually is an amount approximately equal to the value of the partner's interest in the partnership. Why would such a policy be advisable for the partnership and for the insured partner?

42-7 In 1970, David purchased a piece of real estate for $10,000 on which he constructed an automobile repair shop. In 1972, David and Jonathan formed a partnership to operate the repair shop. David contributed the land and shop and Jonathan contributed $15,000 in cash. In 1980, Jonathan died leaving his entire estate to his daughter Esther. Later that year, David agreed to sell the land and repair shop to Peter. After Peter checked the real estate records and found that the property was registered in David's name, Peter paid $50,000 to David. After Esther learned of the sale, she filed a lawsuit against Peter, claiming that one-half of the real estate belonged to her, and demanding that Peter convey one-half of the property to her.

(a) Does Esther own a one-half interest in the real estate? Explain.

(b) Should the court award anything to Esther? Explain.

Major Topics

- the nature of a general partner's liability to third parties in contract or tort
- how a partner acquires actual or apparent authority to bind the partnership to contracts
- the criteria determining when liability is imposed upon the partnership for torts or crimes of a partner
- a discussion of the law governing creation and operation of limited partnership, including the relationship among general partners, limited partners, and third parties

In the course of its business, a partnership frequently enters into contracts with third parties, such as lenders, customers, and suppliers of goods or services. These contractual obligations are often incurred by one or more, but fewer than all, partners acting or purporting to act on behalf of the partnership. In addition to making contracts, an individual partner, in the course of partnership business, may tortiously injure a third party through negligent or intentional conduct. The first part of this chapter examines the law determining when co-partners should be held liable for contracts made or torts committed by other partners.

The second part discusses the limited partnership, a device through which some participants, the limited partners, escape personal liability to third parties for acts of the general partners. Rather, limited partners, like corporate shareholders, are liable upon firm obligations only to the extent of their investment in the business.

General Partners and Third Parties

Nature of Partners' Liability

Under the Uniform Partnership Act, partners are jointly and severally liable for partnership torts and breaches of trust and jointly liable on partnership contracts.[1] Thus, for tort obligations the partners are bound both individually (severally) and as a unit (jointly). Procedurally, this means that an injured third party may sue one or more partners separately or all of them together at her option. For contracts, the partners' joint liability may require the third-party plaintiff to join all partners as defendants in the suit. Procedural reforms in most states, however, effectively or explicitly convert joint liability into joint and several liability. In addition, at least ten states[2] have amended the UPA itself to impose joint and several liability in both tort and contract.

Whether liable jointly or jointly and severally,

---

1. UPA §15. Joint and several promises are discussed in Chapters 7 and 33.

2. These states include Alabama, Arizona, Colorado, Georgia, Kansas, Mississippi, Missouri, North Carolina, Tennessee, and Texas.

each partner has unlimited liability to pay all debts and obligations of the firm. That is, the partners usually agree *among themselves* to share losses. Creditors are not bound by this arrangement and may collect the entire amount of a partnership debt from any one partner. The paying partner must then attempt to recover a proportionate share of the loss from co-partners. To illustrate, assume Smith, Jones, and White are equal partners. White enters into a contract with (or tortiously injures) Brown. Brown sues Smith, Jones, and White as partners for damages. Jones, White, and the partnership are all insolvent. Smith is independently wealthy. Despite Smith's inability to obtain any reimbursement from Jones or White, partnership law may hold Smith personally liable for the entire debt owing to Brown and other partnership creditors. The principles determining when that liability is to be imposed are discussed below.

Contract Liability—In General

The law of agency supplements the UPA and the Act explicitly provides that "every partner is an agent of the partnership for the purpose of its business."[3] Accordingly, the power of a partner to bind the partnership to contracts with third parties is governed by the same principles that enable an ordinary agent to bind her principal. In short, the partnership is bound on contracts made by a partner acting within the scope of her (1) express actual authority, (2) implied actual authority, and (3) apparent authority. In addition the partnership is bound on contracts outside the scope of the partner's actual or apparent authority if it ratifies them.[4]

Partners' Authority—Actual. The basic methods of conferring actual authority upon a partner have already been discussed. For example, the partnership agreement often expressly authorizes one or more partners to contract for purchases of inventory and supplies, to hire employees, to purchase equipment, and to make other contracts normally incident to the partnership business. A contract made pursuant to such an authorization binds the partnership without further action by the partners. Actions not expressly authorized by the partnership agreement may be authorized by vote of the partners. If the voting percentages required for a given action are not outlined in the partnership agreement, the voting rules outlined in the UPA apply.

Partners' Authority—Apparent. A partner possesses perhaps the greatest apparent authority of any agent. That is, "partner," like "manager," or "treasurer," is itself an implied representation to third parties that the person bearing the title possesses certain generally recognized powers. Thus, §9(1) of the UPA provides that the act of every partner "for apparently carrying on in the usual way the business of the partnership" binds the partnership, unless the acting partner has no actual authority to act for the partnership in the transaction, and the person with whom he is dealing has knowledge of that fact. Courts ordinarily interpret the UPA language to mean that a partner has apparent authority to perform acts "usual" for the particular partnership and those usual for similar partnerships in the locality.

In determining a partner's apparent authority, courts often have drawn a distinction between "trading" and "nontrading" partnerships. A **trading partnership** is a commercial or merchandising business, one involved in maintaining an inventory and buying and selling it for profit. Other partnerships not so involved (such as law firms, insurance, and loan businesses) are referred to as "nontrading partnerships." Courts traditionally hold that partners in trading partnerships have much broader apparent authority to buy and sell goods, borrow money, and execute negotiable instruments. As more modern nontrading businesses use the partnership form, however, the distinction between trading and nontrading partnerships has become less important. Partners generally have apparent authority to make representations to customers, hire and fire employees, make contracts for compensation, and receive delivery of property or payments from third parties.

Acts not within the apparent scope of partnership business do not bind the partnership unless actually authorized by the other partners. Traditional ex-

3. UPA §§9(1), 4(3).

4. See discussion of these issues in the agency material in Chapter 40.

amples of such acts include contracts for guaranty or suretyship, using firm assets to pay individual debts, and giving away partnership property. In addition, fewer than all partners have no authority to do any of the acts discussed in Chapter 42 for which the UPA requires consent of all partners.[5]

Contract Liability—Partnership by Estoppel

Liability of Nonpartners. As a general rule, persons who are not partners among themselves are not partners as to third parties.[6] A notable exception to this rule is **partnership by estoppel,** under which basic equitable estoppel principles are used to impose partnership liability upon a person who is not, in fact, a partner. Such a person is known as a ''partner by estoppel,'' ''ostensible partner,'' or ''apparent partner.''

As noted in Chapter 9, estoppel[7] is the legal principle under which a person is estopped, or prevented, from asserting a position inconsistent with her prior conduct if injustice would thereby result to a person who changes position in justifiable reliance on that conduct. The UPA uses estoppel principles to establish partnership liability in §16(1), which provides in part that

> When a person, by words spoken or written or by conduct, represents himself, or consents to another representing him to any one, as a partner in an existing partnership or with one or more persons not actual partners, he is liable to any such person to whom such representation has been made, who has, on the faith of such representation, given credit to the actual or apparent partnership. . . .

A nonpartner may be represented as a partner in various ways. For example, the representation may be made in a private manner, such as a face-to-face conversation in which the person directly represents

himself, or permits others to represent him, as a partner. In this case, only the person to whom the representation is made may hold the apparent partner liable. A person also may be held out as a partner in a public manner. For example, the person's name may appear in a public document such as an assumed name certificate or license application, or may be used in the firm name, letterhead, or advertising. A person who makes or consents to a public representation is liable to any person extending credit to whom the representation is communicated in any manner. That is, liability is imposed even if the form of representation upon which the creditor relies in extending credit (for example, a printed circular or word of mouth) is not the form of representation to which the apparent partner has consented (for example, a newspaper advertisement). Note that in both the public and private cases, the creditor must in fact rely upon the representation of partnership in extending credit.

The following case illustrates the operation of partnership by estoppel principles.

Anderson Hay and Grain Co. v. Dunn
467 P.2d 5 (N.M. 1970)

In 1968, Virgil Welch entered into a lease that entitled him to operate the feed concession at the Ruidoso Downs racetrack. To secure the lease, Welch signed a note for $65,000, which was guaranteed by Sam Dunn. Welch and Dunn then entered into a written agreement granting Dunn the exclusive right to maintain the accounting records, inventory controls, and accounts receivable of the feed concession. They opened a bank account under the name ''Ruidoso Downs Feed Concession'' and both Dunn and Welch were authorized to sign checks and make withdrawals. In 1968 Welch filed a partnership tax return for the business.

Appellant Anderson Hay and Grain Co. sold feed to Ruidoso Downs Feed Concession and, based on Dunn's financial responsibility, extended credit to the business. When payments were late on the account, Anderson Hay and Grain Co. contacted Dunn, who would pay the account.

After the account became delinquent, Anderson Hay and Grain Co. sued Welch and Dunn for

---

5. UPA §§9(2), 9(3). See discussion of acts requiring unanimous consent in Chapter 42.

6. UPA §7(1).

7. The UPA explicitly provides that the law of estoppel applies under the Act. UPA §4(2).

$13,568, alleging that they were partners of Ruidoso Downs Feed Concession. Welch admitted that they were partners but Dunn denied the existence of a partnership. At trial, other persons doing business at the racetrack testified that they believed Dunn and Welch were partners and that Dunn had characterized Welch as his partner. The trial court held Welch liable on the contract, but dismissed the claim against Dunn. Anderson Hay and Grain Co. appealed.

Tackett, Justice
. . . The only issue before this court is whether Dunn was a partner in the operation of the Ruidoso Downs Feed Concession. The evidence reveals that Dunn was a partner by estoppel as a matter of law. . . . [The court then quoted UPA §16.]

Dunn, by his conduct, actions and words, furnishes substantial evidence that he and Welch were partners. . . . It is immaterial that the parties do not designate the relationship as a partnership, or realize that they are partners, for the intent may be implied from their acts. . . .

If Dunn did not want to be considered or held out as a partner in the feed business, he should not have allowed himself to be so associated. He consented to being held out as a partner by his actions. . . . When appellant demanded money from Dunn on account, Dunn never said he was not a partner. When payments were past due, appellant called Dunn on the telephone and Dunn would send a check. A reasonable conclusion to draw from such occurrences is that Dunn was the responsible partner. It is sufficient if the course of conduct is such as to induce a reasonable and prudent man to believe that which the conduct would imply. . . .

Dunn conducted himself so as to induce appellant to deal with him in the belief that he was a partner and, by so doing, created a partnership by estoppel. . . .

The case is reversed and remanded to the trial court with instructions to reinstate it on the docket and enter a new judgment against Dunn and Welch, jointly and severally. . . .

Liability of Partners and Partnership. The doctrine of partnership by estoppel is used to impose contractual liability upon the ostensible partner.

Under ordinary principles of apparent authority, acts of the ostensible partner may also contractually bind his supposed partners. A person who has been represented as a partner in an existing partnership (or with one or more persons not actual partners) is an agent of the persons consenting to the representations. Thus, the ostensible partner may contractually bind those consenting to the same extent and in the same manner as an actual partner to third persons who rely upon the representation. If all members of an existing partnership consent to the representation, a partnership obligation results; otherwise, the liability is the joint obligation of the person acting and those consenting to the representation.[8] For example, Addison, Burke, and Crabbe (ABC) are partners in the business of buying and selling used cars. Dunne, a car dealer, but not a partner, represents himself to Thacker as a partner in ABC partnership. Addison and Burke are present when the representation is made, but say nothing. Thacker, believing that he is dealing with the partnership, contracts to sell cars to Dunne. On these facts, Dunne, Addison, and Burke are jointly liable on the contract to Thacker; that is, by their silence, Addison and Burke created apparent authority in Dunne to bind them. Neither Crabbe nor the partnership is liable on the contract.

Conveyance of Partnership Real Property

Although the UPA allows title to real property to be acquired and conveyed in the firm name, real property owned by the firm often is held or transferred in the names of one or more of the partners. Section 10 of the UPA states the rules governing how title to real property is conveyed in various situations and the legal effect of such conveyances on the rights of the partners and third parties.

If title to real property is held in the partnership name, any partner may convey the property by a deed executed in the partnership name. The partnership may recover the property from the grantee if the partner executing the deed had no actual or apparent authority to make the conveyance. If, however, the grantee subsequently conveys the property to a good faith purchaser, the partnership's

---

8. UPA §16(2).

right to recover the property is extinguished and its sole recourse is against the wrongdoing partner.

If title is held in the firm name, a partner may convey the property in his or her own name. For example, assume Allen and Barker are partners doing business as "Realty Associates." Barker conveys a tract of land held by the partnership in the firm name to Crenshaw, but signs the deed in his own name, "Barker." In this case, if Barker is authorized to act, Crenshaw receives an equitable interest in the property. This means that Crenshaw may maintain an equitable action against the partners to compel either of them to sign the deed in the firm name, thereby conveying legal title to the property.

If partnership property is held in the name of one or more, but not all, partners and the firm's interest is not disclosed, those partners may transfer good title to the property by conveyance in their names. In this case, if the partners' act is unauthorized, the partnership may recover the property unless the transferee is a good faith purchaser.

Occasionally, one partner signing a deed in her own name or the partnership name will attempt to convey firm property held either (1) in the name of one or more or all partners, or (2) by a third party in trust for the partnership. For example, A, by signing a deed in her own name, may convey partnership property held in the names of A, B, and C, all partners in ABCD partnership. In this case the transferee receives equitable title to the property if the conveying partner's act was authorized. The transferee then has the right to compel the remaining partners (or trustee) to sign the deed to transfer legal title.

Finally, complete title to firm real property held in the names of all partners may be transferred by a deed signed by all partners.

At issue in the following case, decided under §§9 and 10 of the UPA, was whether a partner possessed actual or apparent authority to convey partnership real estate.

Hodge v. Garrett

614 P.2d 420 (Idaho 1980)

Plaintiff Bill Hodge entered into a written contract to purchase a small parcel of land adjacent to Pay-

Ont Drive-In Theatre. The contract listed "Pay-Ont Drive-In Theatre, a partnership" as seller and Rex E. Voeller, managing partner of Pay-Ont, signed on behalf of the partnership. After the partnership refused to perform the contract, Hodge sued the partners and partnership for breach of contract. The trial court found that Voeller had actual and apparent authority to execute the contract on behalf of the partnership and ordered specific performance. The partners and partnership appealed.

Bistline, Justice

. . . At common law one partner could not, "without the concurrence of his copartners, convey away the real estate of the partnership, bind his partners by a deed, or transfer the title and interest of his copartners in the firm real estate." 60 *Am.Jur.2d Partnership* §149 (1972). . . . This rule was changed by the adoption of the Uniform Partnership Act. The relevant provisions are currently embodied in [§§9 and 10]. . . .

The meaning of these provisions was stated in one text as follows:

> "If record title is in the partnership and a partner conveys in the partnership name, legal title passes. But the partnership may recover the property (except from a bona fide purchaser from the grantee) if it can show (A) that the conveying partner was not apparently carrying on business in the usual way or (B) that he had in fact no authority and the grantee had knowledge of that fact. The burden of proof with respect to authority is thus on the partnership." Crane and Bromberg on Partnership §50A (1968). . . .

Thus this contract is enforceable if Voeller had the actual authority to sell the property or, even if Voeller did not have such authority, the contract is still enforceable if the sale was in the usual way of carrying on the business and Hodge did not know that Voeller did not have this authority. . . .

Although [actual] authority may be implied from the nature of the business, . . . or from similar past transactions, . . . nothing in the record in this case indicates that Voeller had express or implied authority to sell real property belonging to the partnership. There is no evidence that Voeller had sold property belonging to the partnership in the past, and obviously the partnership was not engaged in the business of buying and selling real estate.

The next question, since actual authority has not been shown, is whether Voeller was conducting the partnership business in the usual way in selling this parcel of land such that the contract is binding under [§§9 and 10 of the Uniform Partnership Act], i.e., whether Voeller had apparent authority. Here the evidence showed, and the trial court found:

> "That at the inception of the partnership, and at all times thereafter, Rex E. Voeller was the exclusive, managing partner of the partnership and had the full authority to make all decisions pertaining to the partnership affairs, including paying the bills, preparing profit and loss statements, income tax returns and the ordering of any goods or services necessary to the operation of the business."

The court made no finding that it was customary for Voeller to sell real property, or even personal property, belonging to the partnership. Nor was there any evidence to this effect. Nor did the court discuss whether it was in the usual course of business for the managing partner of a theater to sell real property. Yet the trial court found that Voeller had apparent authority to sell the property. From this it must be inferred that the trial court believed it to be in the usual course of business for a partner who has exclusive control of the partnership business to sell real property belonging to the partnership, where that property is not being used in the partnership business. We cannot agree with this conclusion. For a theater, "carrying on in the usual way the business of the partnership," . . . means running the operations of the theater; it does not mean selling a parcel of property adjacent to the theater. Here the contract of sale stated that the land belonged to the partnership, and, even if Hodge believed that Voeller as the exclusive manager had authority to transact all business for the firm, Voeller still could not bind the partnership through a unilateral act which was not in the usual business of the partnership. . . .

[Judgment reversed.]

Partnership Tort Liability

Partnership tort liability, like contract liability, is based upon general agency principles. Accordingly, the partnership is liable to third parties injured by tortious acts or omissions of partners acting in the ordinary course of the partnership business. Partners are also liable for tortious acts of other partners which they have expressly authorized or ratified.[9]

As in ordinary agency, tort liability is most commonly imposed for a partner's negligent conduct causing injury. For example, assume A, a partner in ABC Partnership, is driving a firm vehicle (or her own vehicle) to make a call on a prospective customer. En route, A negligently runs a stop sign and collides with T, another motorist. The partnership is liable to T for A's tort. Whether a partner has deviated sufficiently from the ordinary course of partnership business to relieve the partnership from liability is determined by the principles governing scope of employment that were previously discussed in the agency material.

Liability for negligence may also be imposed in professional partnerships. For example, a law firm is liable for damages caused by incorrect advice negligently furnished by a partner to a client. Similarly, a partnership of physicians is liable for one partner's negligent treatment of a patient.

Not all partnership tort liability is based upon negligence. A partnership may be liable for intentional torts committed by a partner in the scope of partnership business, such as fraud, misrepresentation, defamation, trespass, or conversion. Suppose A is a partner in ABC Partnership, which buys and sells used cars. A fraudulently induces T to buy a car by turning back the odometer and falsely represents that the car has never been involved in an accident. The partnership is liable to T for A's fraud because the representations were made in the ordinary course of the partnership business.

In addition to basic tort liability, a partnership also is bound by an individual partner's breach of trust. For example, a partner in an investment firm may be actually or apparently authorized to receive, hold, and invest money or property of oth-

---

9. UPA §13.

ers. In this case, the partnership is liable if the partner misapplies the money or property received (for example, uses it to pay personal debts). Liability similarly is imposed if money or property received by the partnership is misapplied by any partner while in the custody of the partnership.[10]

At issue in the following case was whether a partnership should be held liable for compensatory and punitive damages resulting from a partner's fraud and breach of trust.

Husted v. McCloud
450 N.E.2d 491 (Ind. 1983)

Appellee Herman McCloud retained Husted and Husted, a law firm operating as a partnership, to represent him as executor of his mother's estate. Edgar Husted, a partner of the firm, advised McCloud that estate tax was due to the Internal Revenue Service. At Husted's request, McCloud issued a check in the amount of $18,800 payable to the Husted and Husted Trust Account and Husted agreed to pay the estate tax and retain a portion of the payment as attorneys' fees. Instead, Husted deposited the check in his personal account and converted the money to his own use. The Internal Revenue Service later notified McCloud of the outstanding tax liability and McCloud paid the tax plus interest.

McCloud sued Edgar Husted, and Husted and Husted for conversion of the $18,800. The trial court held both Edgar Husted and the law firm liable for compensatory and punitive damages and the appellate court affirmed. The Indiana Supreme Court accepted the case for review.

Pivarnik, Justice

. . . The trial court and the Court of Appeals determined that . . . the partnership [was] liable to the same extent as Edgar Husted for any civil penalty imposed in this case. The partnership claims that Edgar's criminal acts were not within the ordinary course of partnership business. Furthermore, the partnership claims that it never had possession

of the certain funds converted and therefore the partnership cannot be held liable for Edgar's acts with respect to said funds. There were two partners in the partnership law firm, Edgar Husted and Selwyn Husted, Edgar's father. McCloud clearly was a client of the partnership since McCloud dealt with both Selwyn and Edgar on his estate case. In fact, Selwyn was the partner who first brought McCloud's case into the partnership's office. Edgar was acting within the ordinary course of the partnership's business and with apparent authority since Edgar's request for and acceptance of money from McCloud to pay McCloud's estate tax liability was well within the work parameters of an attorney properly handling a decedent's estate. We therefore find that even though fraud and conversion of a client's funds are not part of the ordinary course of a law partnership's business, the trial court correctly found . . . that the partnership was responsible for partner Edgar in taking money entrusted to him and misapplying it. We also find that the trial court was justified in finding that McCloud's money was in the partnership's possession when it was in Edgar's possession since Edgar deviated from McCloud's plan and converted the money to his own use only after he received it in the ordinary course of the partnership's business. Accordingly, the trial court did not err by holding the partnership responsible to McCloud for compensatory damages.

Whether Appellant partnership is liable for punitive damages, however, is another story. Husted & Husted argues that the cases . . . have generally held that where a partnership is sued for a partner's intentional tort, the partnership's liability turns on whether the purpose or effect of the tortious act was to benefit the partnership's business or whether the tort was so removed from the ordinary course of that business that it could not be considered within the implicit authorization of the co-partners. . . .

We . . . agree with Appellant partnership that the rationale behind punitive damages in Indiana prohibits awarding such damages against an individual who is personally innocent of any wrongdoing. Punitive damages are not intended to compensate a plaintiff but rather are intended to punish the wrongdoer and thereby deter others from engaging in similar conduct in the future. . . . Ac-

---

10. UPA §14.

cordingly, we now hold that the trial court erred by adjudging the innocent partner in this case responsible for punitive damages. . . .

[Judgment of the Court of Appeals vacated and remanded.]

Partnership Criminal Liability

The preceding discussion concerns partnership civil liability for an individual partner's tort or breach of trust. Responsibility for a partner's criminal acts is generally not imposed upon co-partners unless they participate in the crime, authorize it, or assent to it. All partners may, however, be held liable for crimes committed by one of them in the course of business for which no criminal intent is required. These so-called strict liability crimes include, for example, violations of pure food and drug laws and illegal sales of liquor. In addition, the partnership (rather than the individual partners) may be held criminally responsible and punished, for example, by a fine levied against partnership assets.

Notice or Knowledge of Partner

In the course of their duties, partners often acquire knowledge or receive notification of facts having actual or potential legal significance to the partnership. Consistent with general agency principles, notice to, or knowledge of, any partner concerning any matter relating to partnership affairs operates as notice to, or knowledge of, the partnership.[11] For example, notice of a license revocation hearing given to one partner is notice to the partnership, whether or not communicated to the other partners.

Knowledge of the partnership may be acquired either by the partner acting in the transaction or other partners. If acquired by other partners, the knowledge is imputed to the partnership if they could and should have communicated it to the acting partner.[12] Assume Park fraudulently induces

Morley to issue a promissory note payable to the order of Park. Park negotiates the note to Adams, a partner in ABC Partnership, in the usual course of partnership business. Although Adams has no knowledge of Park's fraud, Baxter, another partner, is aware of Park's wrongdoing. Baxter also knows that the partnership was considering purchasing Morley's note and could have communicated his knowledge to Adams. Baxter's knowledge is imputed to the partnership, and as a result it could not qualify as a holder in due course of Morley's note.

The UPA recognizes an important exception to the rule that knowledge of a partner is knowledge of the partnership: the partnership is not charged with knowledge of a fraud on the partnership committed by or with the consent of a partner.

Limited Partnership

Introduction to Limited Partnership

Unlimited personal liability for firm debts and obligations is a distinct disadvantage of partnership, particularly for partners who merely invest capital but take no active role in management of the business. The law has therefore long recognized the need for a form of business organization that allows persons to invest in the firm and share in profits with no management responsibility and with no liability for firm obligations beyond the amount invested in the business. Although the corporation primarily fulfills this need today, the limited partnership was the first, and remains an alternative, device for profit sharing coupled with limited liability for losses.

Applicable Law. During the Middle Ages, an arrangement known as the *commendam* allowed a financier to share in the profits of another's trade without personal liability for losses. This device was ultimately incorporated into the French Commercial Code of 1807, which formed the basis of early American limited partnership acts first enacted in New York (1822), Connecticut (1822), and Pennsylvania (1836). In 1916, the National Conference of Commissioners on Uniform State Laws adopted the **Uniform Limited Partnership Act (ULPA),** which was later revised by the Conference in 1976 in the **Revised Uniform Limited**

---

11. UPA §§3, 12. The liability of a principal for notice to or knowledge of an agent is discussed in the agency material in Chapter 40.

12. UPA §12. Knowledge acquired by a partner while a partner is imputed to the partnership. If acquired prior to becoming a partner knowledge is imputed if present in the partner's mind at the time of the transaction in question.

Partnership Act (RULPA). The RULPA was itself amended in 1985. At this writing, the ULPA governs limited partnerships in twelve states[13] and the District of Columbia. The RULPA governs in thirty-seven states.[14] The RULPA differs from the ULPA primarily by assimilating concepts of corporation law into the law of limited partnership. The drafters adopted this approach because a limited partnership and a corporation, both with limited liability, have always been alternative forms of business organization. Because both statutes currently enjoy considerable support, important provisions of the RULPA and the ULPA will be compared and contrasted in the following material. In addition, selected important changes made in the RULPA in the 1985 amendments will be noted.

Limited Partnership Defined. A **limited partnership** is a partnership formed by two or more persons under a limited partnership statute having as members one or more general partners and one or more limited partners.[15] In a limited partnership, therefore, at least one partner (a general partner) has unlimited liability for firm debts and obligations characteristic of partners generally. In contrast, the limited partner or partners are not personally liable for partnership obligations and therefore have no liability for partnership losses beyond the amount invested in the firm. Both Acts allow a person to be simultaneously both a general and limited partner in the same partnership possessing the rights and obligations of both.[16] In addition, a majority of states now allow a corporation to be a general partner, which renders the requirement that at least one partner have unlimited liability illusory in many cases.

---

13. These include Alaska, Georgia, Hawaii, Indiana, Kentucky, Maine, New Mexico, New York, Pennsylvania, Tennessee, Utah, and Vermont.

14. States enacting the RULPA include Alabama, Arizona, Arkansas, California, Colorado, Connecticut, Delaware, Florida, Idaho, Illinois, Iowa, Kansas, Maryland, Massachusetts, Michigan, Minnesota, Mississippi, Missouri, Montana, Nebraska, Nevada, New Hampshire, New Jersey, North Carolina, North Dakota, Ohio, Oklahoma, Oregon, Rhode Island, South Carolina, South Dakota, Texas, Virginia, Washington, West Virginia, Wisconsin, and Wyoming. Louisiana has not enacted either the ULPA or RULPA.

15. ULPA §1, RULPA §101(7).

16. ULPA §12, RULPA §404.

Restrictions on Limited Partnership Status. In exchange for limited liability, the law imposes two important restrictions on the formation and operation of a limited partnership. First, unlike a general partnership, which may be created simply by private agreement, a limited partnership may be formed only by complying with specific statutory formalities provided in the ULPA or the RULPA. These formalities provide public notice to creditors that some firm members have only limited liability for firm debts. Second, limited partners, unlike general partners, may not participate in the management and control of the business. That is, limited partnership law refuses to insulate persons who actually participate in the management of the business from liability for partnership obligations. These two important concepts are developed in more detail below.

Formation of Limited Partnership

Formal Requirements. To create a limited partnership under the ULPA and 1976 RULPA, its members must sign a certificate that states basic information about the business, including the name of the partnership and character of its business, its term and location, the identity of the limited and general partners and their addresses, the amount of cash or other property contributed by the limited partners, the limited partners' share in profits, the methods for admitting new limited partners or assigning a partnership interest, and any provisions relating to continuance of the business upon death, retirement, or incapacity of a general partner.[17] Under the 1985 amendments to the RULPA, the certificate need only contain the name of the limited partnership, the address of its office, the name and address of each general partner and of an agent for service of process on the limited partnership, and the latest date upon which the limited partnership is to dissolve.

Once executed, the certificate is filed in an appropriate public office where it is available for continuous public inspection. Under the ULPA filing is generally local, for example, in the office of the recorder of deeds or the county clerk of the county

---

17. For a detailed listing of the information required in the certificate, see ULPA §2(1)(a).

where the partnership's principal office is located. Under the RULPA, central filing in the secretary of state's office is required. Under both Acts, technical defects in the certificate do not prevent formation of a limited partnership. A limited partnership is formed if there has been substantial compliance in good faith with the filing requirements.[18]

During the term of the partnership, a certificate of amendment must be filed to reflect important changes in partnership structure or capitalization. For example, new or additional capital contributions may be made or required, new partners may be added, others may withdraw, or the business may be continued after withdrawal of a general partner. The certificate, with amendments, provides accurate information about the partnership on a continuing basis. It is not designed to speak only as of the date of its original execution. A similar procedure is followed upon dissolution and winding up of the partnership, or at any other time when no limited partners remain. In this case, a certificate of cancellation must be filed.[19]

The certificate of limited partnership is a formal document filed to provide basic information about the partnership to interested third parties. It is not an exhaustive statement of the partners' rights and obligations. As in a general partnership, the partners usually execute a separate private partnership agreement governing the affairs of the partnership and the conduct of its business.

The following case, decided under the ULPA, illustrates the purpose of the statutory formalities and the effect of noncompliance.

Dwinell's Central Neon v. Cosmopolitan Chinook Hotel

587 P.2d 191 (Wash. App. 1978)

On October 25, 1972, Cosmopolitan Chinook Hotel entered into a contract to purchase neon signs from Dwinell's Central Neon. The contract was signed, on behalf of Cosmopolitan, "Evan Bargman, V.P., R. Powers, President." In October, 1976, following

Cosmopolitan's default in payments, Dwinell's sued Cosmopolitan for the balance due on the contract. The complaint alleged that Cosmopolitan was a general partnership, but Cosmopolitan alleged that it was a limited partnership.

The evidence established that at the time Cosmopolitan and Dwinell's entered into the contract, Cosmopolitan had taken no steps to comply with a Washington state statute (the ULPA) requiring a limited partnership to file a certificate of limited partnership with the county clerk. In February, 1973, Cosmopolitan filed the certificate. Cosmopolitan also alleged that at the time of the contract Dwinell's was aware that Cosmopolitan was a limited partnership because the parties had signed as officers of the corporate general partner rather than as general partners, and because Cosmopolitan's limited partnership status was a matter of common knowledge in the community.

The trial court ruled that Cosmopolitan was liable on the contract as a general partnership. Cosmopolitan and its partners appealed.

McInturff, Judge

. . . [A] third party's knowledge regarding the status of a limited partnership is irrelevant when at the time of contracting, the partners have made no attempt to comply with the statutory information and filing requirements of the Limited Partnership Act. . . .

Limited partnerships were unknown at common law and are purely creatures of statute. Parties seeking the protection of limited liability within the context of a partnership must follow the statutory requirements. . . . To form a limited partnership, a certificate of limited partnership must be drafted and filed with the county clerk. . . . While our courts no longer require literal compliance with the statute at one's peril . . ., the statute does contemplate at least "substantial compliance with the requirements." . . . Here, there was no compliance with the statute at the time of contracting and the certificate of limited partnership was not filed until several months later. The object of statutory regulation of limited partnerships is to insure that limited partners do not find themselves exposed to the unlimited liability of a general partner.

The statute specifies the acts which must be performed by persons desiring to become limited part-

---

18. ULPA §2(2), RULPA §201(b).
19. ULPA §24, RULPA §§202, 203.

ners. Cosmopolitan had not complied with any requirements of the statute at the time it entered into the contract with Dwinell's. Obviously, the purpose of the filing requirement was thwarted, that is, to acquaint third persons dealing with the partnership of the details of the partnership arrangement. A creditor has a right to rely upon there being substantial compliance with [the statute] before the protection of its provisions are afforded to any member of a partnership. . . . Here there was no compliance.

Cosmopolitan . . . contends that because [the statute] is silent as to when the certificate must be filed, a reasonable time is implied. Cosmopolitan submits that it substantially complied with the requirements of the statute by filing a certificate of limited partnership some 90 days *after* the contract went into effect. . . . Cosmopolitan wants the effect of filing the certificate of limited partnership to relate back to a contract previously entered into. To adopt this reasoning would render the statutory requirement . . . meaningless and business relationships would be rendered unstable and unpredictable.

Thus, since there was no compliance with the Limited Partnership Act, the court was correct in holding as a matter of law that Cosmopolitan was liable as a general partnership on the contract with Dwinell's. . . .

[Judgment affirmed.]

Since this case was decided, Washington has enacted the RULPA, which explicitly addresses the time of formation issue considered by the court. Consistent with the court's reasoning interpreting the ULPA, §201(b) of the RULPA provides that a limited partnership is formed either at the time that the certificate of limited partnership is filed with the secretary of state, or at any *later* time specified in the certificate.

Type of Business Conducted.
A limited partnership may conduct any business that a general partnership may, except those expressly excluded by statute. Many states, for example, prevent limited partnerships from engaging in insurance or banking activities. These are regulated industries that may generally be conducted only by entities organized under special statutes. Many limited partnerships are organized to finance and manage commercial real estate such as apartment complexes, office buildings, and shopping centers.

Partnership Name.
For the protection of creditors, the law imposes limitations on the name that a limited partnership may use. Under both the ULPA and RULPA, the surname of a limited partner may not appear in the partnership name unless it is also the name of a general partner, or unless the limited partnership had used that name before admitting the limited partner.[20] A limited partner whose name appears in the partnership name in violation of the above prohibition may be held liable as a general partner to creditors who extend credit to the partnership without actual knowledge that the limited partner is not a general partner.[21]

The RULPA imposes additional explicit firm name limitations. For example, the words "limited partnership" must appear in the firm name. In addition, the name may not be the same, or deceptively similar to, the name of any corporation or other limited partnership.[22]

Partnership Office, Agent, and Records.
The ULPA contains no provision for maintenance of an office or registered agent or for partnership recordkeeping. In contrast, the RULPA requires a limited partnership to continuously maintain an office, which need not be its place of business, in the state. At this office, the partnership is required to keep (1) a current list of the names and addresses of all partners, (2) a copy of the certificate of limited partnership and any amendments, (3) a copy of all financial statements and tax returns for the three most recent years, and (4) a copy of any written partnership agreement binding on the partners. The

---

20. ULPA §5(1), RULPA §102(2).

21. ULPA §5(2), RULPA §303(d). Note that the RULPA imposes general partner liability only upon a limited partner who *knowingly* permits his name to be used in the name of the limited partnership.

22. RULPA §§102(1),(3).

1985 amendments to the RULPA require that certain additional information (such as the partners' contributions and events causing dissolution) be kept at the office unless already contained in a written partnership agreement. These records must be kept available for inspection and copying by any partner during ordinary business hours.[23]

In addition to an office, the RULPA requires the partnership to maintain an agent in the state for service of process on the limited partnership. The office, recordkeeping, and agent requirements of the RULPA assure that the limited partnership has certain minimum contacts with its state of organization. They also assure that the limited partners, whose participation is passive in nature, will have access to the basic documents affecting the partnership.[24]

Foreign Limited Partnership. The ULPA does not refer to the "foreign" limited partnership, one doing business in a state other than that of its formation. The RULPA requires foreign limited partnerships to apply for and obtain a certificate of registration from states in which it seeks to do business. The application, filed with the secretary of state, requires disclosure of certain basic information regarding the partnership. Foreign limited partnerships must also maintain an agent for service of process in the state. Until it registers, a foreign limited partnership may not sue in the foreign state. Further, the state may bring an action to restrain an unregistered partnership from doing business in the state. Failure to register does not, however, impair the validity of any contract or act of the foreign limited partnership, or prevent it from defending a lawsuit in the state.[25] The requirements for registration of foreign limited partnerships are similar to those discussed in Chapter 45 imposed upon foreign corporations.

Relationship Among Partners

Capital Contribution. Under both the ULPA and RULPA, a limited partner's capital contribution may consist of cash or property, including a promissory note or other obligation to contribute cash or property in the future.[26] The Acts differ, however, regarding services. Whereas under the ULPA a limited partner may not contribute services, the RULPA permits both services rendered and an obligation to perform services in the future to constitute a partner's capital contribution.[27]

Regardless of the character of the contribution, a limited partner is obligated to the partnership to make any contribution stated in the certificate, even if he is unable to perform because of death, disability, or any other reason. If a partner does not make a required contribution of property or services, the partner or his estate is obligated to contribute cash equal to the value of the contribution that has not been made.[28] A limited partner also holds as trustee for the partnership (1) any specific property stated in the certificate as contributed by him but which was not contributed or has been wrongfully returned, and (2) any money or property wrongfully paid to him on account of his contribution.[29] In short, a limited partner is liable to the extent of his investment in the partnership, which includes the amount actually contributed, any amount the partner is obligated to contribute in the future, and any cash or property wrongfully withheld from or wrongfully distributed by the partnership.

Profits and Losses. The profits and losses (and other distributions of cash or property) of a limited partnership are allocated among the partners in the manner provided in the partnership agreement. The ULPA does not explicitly provide a basis for sharing profits, losses, and distributions in the absence of agreement. In contrast, the RULPA states that if the partnership agreement is silent, profits, losses, and distributions are allocated "on the basis of the values as stated in the partnership records . . . , of the contributions made by each partner to the extent they have been received by the partnership and have not been returned."[30]

---

23. RULPA §§104(1), 105.
24. RULPA §§104(2), 105.
25. RULPA §§902, 907, 908.

26. ULPA §4, 17(1)(b); RULPA §501.
27. RULPA §501.
28. ULPA §17(1), RULPA §502.
29. ULPA §17(2).
30. RULPA §§503, 504; note that this rule differs from that applied to general partnerships in which profits and losses are shared equally in the absence of agreement. UPA §18(a).

Management and Control. In a limited partnership, the general partner or partners manage the business and incur personal liability to creditors. Limited partners are passive investors who do not participate in management and are therefore exempted from personal liability for firm debts. Nevertheless, limited partners may, in some circumstances, have a voice in the conduct of partnership affairs.

In a limited partnership, the general partners enjoy all the rights and powers, and are subject to the same liabilities, as exist in a general partnership.[31] Accordingly, management powers and authority of general partners are generally stated in the agreement and actions not explicitly authorized are taken by appropriate vote of the general partners. Without unanimous consent of all limited partners, however, under the ULPA a general partner or all general partners have no authority to

1. do any act in violation of the certificate;
2. do any act that would make it impossible to carry on the ordinary business of the partnership;
3. confess a judgment against the partnership;
4. possess or assign partnership property for other than partnership purposes;
5. admit a person as a general partner;
6. admit a person as a limited partner unless the right to do so is given in the certificate; or
7. continue the business with partnership property on the death, retirement, or incapacity of a general partner unless the right to do so is given in the certificate.[32]

In contrast, the RULPA only requires unanimous consent to admit a general partner. (Under the 1985 amendments to the RULPA, additional general partners also may be admitted as provided in writing in the partnership agreement.) Other than this requirement, the RULPA does not grant the limited partners any right to vote as a class on specific partnership matters.[33] Under both Acts, however, the partnership agreement may grant limited partners the right to vote on any matter.

Business Transactions with the Partnership. Under both Acts, a limited partner may loan money to, or transact other business with, the partnership.[34] The ULPA, however, prohibits a limited partner from making loans to the partnership secured by firm assets, and forbids repayment of loans made by limited partners if the payment would render the firm unable to pay debts to nonpartner creditors. Such acts are deemed a fraud upon partnership creditors.[35] The RULPA omits these provisions, leaving the issue to each state's fraudulent conveyance statute.[36]

Information. A limited partner is entitled to information on important matters affecting the partnership business. To this end, both Acts provide that limited partners have a right at all times to inspect and copy any of the partnership books and records. In addition, limited partners have the right to obtain upon reasonable demand from general partners (1) true and full information regarding the business and financial condition of the partnership, (2) a copy of the partnership's tax returns as they become available, and (3) other information concerning partnership affairs as is "just and reasonable."[37]

Limited Partners and Third Parties

A basic purpose of a limited partnership is to insulate the limited partners from personal liability for firm debts and obligations. A limited partner may, however, take certain actions that will render her liable as a general partner to firm creditors. For example, as previously discussed, a limited partner whose name appears in the firm name may be held personally liable to partnership creditors. Other circumstances imposing unlimited liability upon a limited partner are discussed below.

Participation in Control. In exchange for limited liability, limited partners must refrain from active

---

31. ULPA §9(1), RULPA §403.
32. ULPA §9.
33. RULPA §§401, 405 and Comment.

34. ULPA §13(1), RULPA §107.
35. ULPA §13.
36. RULPA §107, Comment. Fraudulent conveyances are discussed in Chapter 29.
37. ULPA §10(1), RULPA §305.

participation in the management of the business. Under both Acts, therefore, a limited partner who "takes part in the control of the business"[38] becomes personally liable for partnership obligations as a general partner. Determining when review, advisory, management selection, veto, or other power exercised by a limited partner constitutes an improper exercise of control is one of the most troublesome issues in limited partnership law.

The RULPA attempts to clarify the issue by including a "safe harbor" provision listing activities that, by themselves, do not constitute participation in the control of the business. Some of these activities include

1. being a contractor for, or an agent or employee of, the limited partnership or of a general partner;
2. consulting with and advising a general partner concerning the limited partnership business;
3. acting as a surety for the limited partnership;
4. requesting or attending a meeting of partners; or
5. voting on important partnership matters such as dissolution and winding up, a change in the nature of the business, or the admission or removal of a general partner.

The enumeration is not exhaustive or exclusive; that is, a limited partner may possess other powers that also would not constitute participation in control of the business.[39]

Unlike the ULPA, the RULPA provides that a limited partner who participates in control of the business is liable only to persons who transact business with the partnership with *actual knowledge* of the limited partner's participation. Liability may be imposed without actual knowledge of participation, however, if the limited partner exercises powers substantially the same as those of a general partner.[40] The 1985 amendments to the RULPA alter this requirement and impose liability in all cases

only to persons who transact business with the partnership reasonably believing (based upon the limited partner's conduct) that the limited partner is a general partner.

In the case that follows, decided under the ULPA, the court was required to determine whether a limited partner should be held liable as a general partner for taking part in the control of the business.

Western Camps, Inc. v. Riverway Ranch Enterprises

138 Cal. Rptr. 918 (Cal. App. 1977)

Constructors Research Corporation (CRC) was a general partner of a limited partnership known as Riverway Ranch Enterprises (Riverway). Wallace McCoy was a limited partner of Riverway and an officer of CRC. Riverway was the lessee of forty acres of land in California, and in 1970 subleased the land to plaintiff Western Camps, Inc. The sublease agreement was negotiated by Stanford Oken, president of Western Camps, and McCoy. The agreement provided that Riverway would pay Western Camps $60,000 if Riverway terminated the lease within ten years. In 1971, Riverway terminated the lease but refused to pay $60,000 to Western Camps.

Plaintiff Western Camps sued defendants Riverway and McCoy for breach of contract. The trial court ruled in favor of Western Camps and held that both Riverway and McCoy were liable for the damages. McCoy appealed.

Dunn, Associate Justice

. . . A limited partner is not bound by the obligations of the limited partnership, and is not liable as a general partner, unless he takes part in the control of the partnership business. . . . The trial court found that at the time the sublease was negotiated McCoy, in addition to being a limited partner, also was one of the three officers, directors and shareholders of CRC, the corporate general partner. The court further found that McCoy exercised complete management and control in the negotiations for the sublease and in its termination, and acted without the advice or guidance of the other officers and directors of CRC. Pointing out that a corporation may be a general partner in a limited partnership

---

38. ULPA §7, RULPA §303(a). "Participates" is substituted for "takes part" in the 1985 amendments to the RULPA.
39. RULPA §303(b),(c).
40. RULPA §303(a).

. . . and that a corporation may act only through its agents, . . . McCoy argues that he is not liable as a general partner because, in the transactions regarding the sublease, he was acting in his capacity as agent of the corporate general partner, not in his capacity as a limited partner. The question thus presented is whether a limited partner in a limited partnership becomes liable as a general partner if he takes part in the control of the partnership business while acting as an agent of the corporation which is the sole general partner of the limited partnership.

This question apparently has not been considered in California. In two other jurisdictions, conflicting conclusions have been reached on the point. In *Delaney v. Fidelity Lease Limited,* 526 S.W.2d 543, 545 (Tex. 1975), it was held that ''the personal liability, which attaches to a limited partner when 'he takes part in the control and management of the business,' cannot be evaded merely by acting through a corporation.'' The court rejected the argument that, for the purpose of fixing personal liability upon a limited partner, the ''control'' test should be coupled with a determination of whether the limited partner held himself out as being a general partner having personal liability to the extent that the third party (or plaintiff) relied upon the limited partner's general liability. In this regard, the opinion pointed out that Section 7 of the Uniform Limited Partnership Act simply provides that a limited partner who takes part in the control of the business subjects himself to personal liability as a general partner, and does not mention any requirement of reliance on the part of the party attempting to hold the limited partner personally liable. The court further expressed concern that the statutory requirement of at least one general partner with general liability in a limited partnership could be circumvented by limited partners operating the partnership through a corporation with minimum capitalization and, therefore, with limited liability.

In *Frigidaire Sales Corp. v. Union Properties, Inc.,* . . . [544 P.2d 781 (Wash.App. 1976)], the court rejected the reasoning of the *Delaney* case and concluded that the dominant consideration in determining the personal liability of the limited partner is reliance by the third party, not control by the limited partner. It was there stated (pp. 784–785): ''If a corporate general partner in a limited partnership is organized without sufficient capitali-

zation so that it was foreseeable that it would not have sufficient assets to meet its obligations, the corporate entity could be disregarded to avoid injustice. We find no substantive difference between the creditor who does business with a corporation that is the general partner in a limited partnership and a creditor who simply does business with a corporation. In the absence of fraud or other inequitable conduct, the corporate entity should be respected. . . . A limited partner is made liable as a general partner when he participates in the 'control' of the business in order to protect third parties from dealing with the partnership under the mistaken assumption that the limited partner is a general partner with general liability. . . . A third party dealing with a corporation must reasonably rely on the solvency of the corporate entity. It makes little difference if the corporation is or is not the general partner in a limited partnership. In either instance, the third party cannot justifiably rely on the solvency of the individuals who own the corporation.'' . . .

We agree with the views expressed in the *Frigidaire* case, and accordingly apply the principles there stated to the facts in the instant case. Such facts are: before the sublease was negotiated, Oken was aware of the corporate capacity of CRC, the general partner, and he knew that McCoy was one of its ''principles.'' In June or July 1970 Oken asked Dick Browne, then the president of CRC, who would be representing CRC in its negotiations with plaintiff regarding the sublease. Browne replied that McCoy would be ''making the decisions.'' McCoy signed the sublease on behalf of Riverway, adding after his signature the words ''for CRC.'' Moreover, the trial court found, as a fact, that ''CRC was organized in good faith and had an adequate capitalization necessary to liquidate its indebtedness.'' Under these circumstances, no fraud or injustice to plaintiff results from respecting the corporate entity of the general partner. . . . We hold, therefore, that CRC, the corporate general partner, is solely liable for the obligations of the limited partnership under the sublease, and that McCoy, a limited partner, has no personal liability for such obligations.

[Judgment against defendant McCoy reversed.]

Liability for False Statements in the Certificate. Both limited and general partners may be held liable to third parties for false statements contained in the limited partnership certificate. Under both Acts, any person who signs the certificate knowing that it contains a false statement is liable to any person who subsequently suffers loss by relying on the statement.[41] Moreover, after formation of the partnership, circumstances may change and render a statement in the initial certificate inaccurate. In this case, the partners are liable to persons who rely upon the original, now misleading, certificate after sufficient time has passed to enable the partners to amend or cancel the certificate. Although the ULPA imposes liability for failure to amend the certificate in light of future events upon both general and limited partners, the RULPA confines the obligation to general partners.[42]

Mistaken Belief of Limited Partner Status. A person may contribute capital to a business, erroneously, but in good faith, believing that she has become a limited partner. Under the ULPA, such a person is not treated as a general partner if, upon discovering the mistake, she renounces her interest in the profits of the business or any other compensation.[43] Under the RULPA, the person escapes liability as a general partner if she (1) causes an appropriate certificate or amendment of limited partnership to be executed and filed, or (2) withdraws from future equity participation in the enterprise.[44] No renunciation, withdrawal, or filing is effective, however, to avoid liability to a third person who had previously transacted business with the enterprise believing the mistaken contributor to be a general partner.[45]

Assignment of Partnership Interest. Like a general partner's interest, a limited partner's interest is personal property and is freely assignable in whole or in part.[46] A limited partner's interest includes the right to receive a share of profits or other compensation as stipulated in the certificate and a return of capital contribution.[47] The assignment does not dissolve the limited partnership nor does it entitle the assignee to exercise any of the rights of a limited partner (for example, to inspect books and records and to be kept informed of firm business matters). The assignment merely entitles the assignee to receive, to the extent assigned, any distribution to which the assigning partner would otherwise be entitled.[48]

An assignee of a partnership interest may become a limited partner if either the assignor gives the assignee that right according to authority granted in the partnership agreement, or all other partners consent. An assignee who becomes a limited partner succeeds to the rights and liabilities of the old limited partner, but is not obligated for unknown liabilities. After the assignment, the assignor remains liable for any required unpaid capital contribution and for false statements in the certificate.[49]

If a partner dies or is adjudged incompetent, his executor, administrator, guardian, or other legal representative may exercise all of that partner's rights for the purpose of settling his estate or administering his property. In this capacity, the legal representative may exercise any power the partner had to give an assignee the right to become a limited partner. The estate of a deceased limited partner remains liable for obligations incurred by the partner.[50]

A limited partner's interest, like that of a general partner, may be assigned involuntarily through a charging order to satisfy a debt owed to a creditor of the partner. To the extent charged, the creditor has only the rights of an assignee of the partner's interest; that is, the creditor does not become a limited partner by virtue of the charging order.[51]

---

41. ULPA §6(a), RULPA §207(1).

42. ULPA §6(b), RULPA §207(2).

43. ULPA §11.

44. RULPA §304(a). Under the RULPA, the person who withdraws from the enterprise in order to be protected from liability need only renounce his future, not current, interest in the profits of the business.

45. RULPA §304(b).

46. ULPA §§18, 19(1); RULPA §§701, 702.

47. ULPA §10(2).

48. ULPA §19(3), RULPA §702.

49. ULPA §§19(4),(6),(7); RULPA §704.

50. ULPA §21, RULPA §705.

51. ULPA §22, RULPA §703.

SUMMARY

1. Partnership law determines when partners are held liable for contracts made or torts committed by other partners. Partners are generally jointly and severally liable for partnership torts, breaches of trust, and contracts. Each partner, therefore, has unlimited liability for all debts and obligations of the firm.

2. Every partner is an agent of the partnership for the purpose of its business. Accordingly, the power of a partner to bind the partnership to contracts with third parties is determined by general agency principles. The partnership is therefore bound on contracts made by a partner acting within the scope of his (1) express actual authority, (2) implied actual authority, and (3) apparent authority. In addition, the partnership is bound upon contracts outside the scope of the partner's actual or apparent authority if it ratifies them.

3. Persons who are not partners among themselves generally are not partners as to third parties. An exception to this rule is partnership by estoppel, under which basic equitable estoppel principles are used to impose partnership liability upon a person who is not, in fact, a partner.

4. Although the UPA allows title to real property to be acquired and conveyed in the firm name, real property owned by the firm is often held or transferred in the names of one or more of the partners. The UPA governs how title to real property is conveyed in various situations and the legal effect of such conveyances on the rights of the partners and third parties.

5. Partnership tort liability, like contract liability, is based on general agency principles. Thus, the partnership is liable to third parties injured by a negligent act or omission of any partner acting in the ordinary course of the partnership business. A partnership also may be liable for intentional torts committed by a partner in the scope of partnership business, such as fraud, misrepresentation, defamation, trespass, or conversion. A partnership is also bound by an individual partner's breach of trust and, in certain limited cases, for a partner's criminal act.

6. Notice to, or knowledge of, any partner concerning any matter relating to partnership affairs operates as notice to, or knowledge of, the partnership.

7. The limited partnership and the corporation are two organizational forms that couple profit sharing with limited liability for losses. Limited partnerships are governed in some states by the Uniform Limited Partnership Act (ULPA) and in others by the Revised Uniform Limited Partnership Act (RULPA). The RULPA differs from the ULPA primarily in its attempt to assimilate corporation law concepts into the law of limited partnership.

8. A limited partnership is a partnership formed by two or more persons under a limited partnership statute (the ULPA or RULPA) having as members one or more general partners and one or more limited partners. The general partners manage the business and have unlimited liability for firm debts; the limited partners are passive investors whose liability is generally limited to the extent of their investment. The relationship among limited and general partners is governed by the partnership agreement, supplemented both by the UPA and the applicable Limited Partnership Act.

9. The law imposes two important restrictions on formation and operation of a limited partnership. First, unlike a general partnership which may be created informally, a limited partnership may be formed only by complying with formalities provided in the ULPA or RULPA. These formalities provide public notice to creditors that some firm members have only limited liability for firm debts. Second, limited partners may not participate in management and control of the business. Those who do may be held liable to third parties as general partners. A limited partner also may be liable to third parties for false statements in the limited partnership certificate and for failure to take action after discovering that the limited partnership was defectively formed.

KEY TERMS

trading partnership
partnership by estoppel
Uniform Limited
 Partnership Act (ULPA)
Revised Uniform Limited
 Partnership Act
 (RULPA)
limited partnership

QUESTIONS AND PROBLEMS

43-1 Courts and commentators often state that a partnership is a mutual agency relationship. What are the similarities and differences between the rights and obligations of a partner and an ordinary agent?

43-2 Consider the effect of the various changes discussed in the text made in limited partnership law by the Revised Uniform Limited Partnership Act. Are all of the changes advisable? Explain.

43-3 For many years J. T. Katz and A. Z. Downs operated the Food Town grocery store as partners. Although their partnership agreement placed no restrictions on either partner's powers,

Katz handled the bookkeeping and Downs operated the grocery store. Katz and Downs purchased their inventory from Ace Food Suppliers on open account and always paid their bills from a partnership bank account.

(a) One day, Katz telephoned Ace and notified the company that he no longer would be responsible for purchases made from Ace. Ace's president asked if Katz and Downs were dissolving their partnership, and Katz replied in the negative, explaining that he believed inventory could be purchased elsewhere at cheaper prices. The following day, Downs placed a $5,000 order with Ace. Ace delivered the goods but never received payment. Ace sued Katz and Downs. Can Katz be held liable on the bill? Explain.

(b) Disregard the facts in part (a). Assume instead that Downs placed an order with Ace and asked for delivery at Food Town. When Ace's salesclerk began to write the order to the account of Katz and Downs, Downs asked that it be charged only in his name. After Ace failed to receive payment, it sued Katz and Downs. Can Katz be held liable? Explain.

43-4 Jeanette Kinkaid and Barry Haught are general partners in Barrikaid Leasing Company, a general partnership. The partnership borrowed $1 million from Belmont Bank to finance its operations and executed a promissory note that was signed as follows:

BARRIKAID LEASING CO.
a West Virginia general partnership

By /s/ Barry D. Haught
_____
    Barry D. Haught, a General Partner

By /s/ Jeannette E. Kinkaid
_____
    Jeannette E. Kinkaid, a General Partner

/s/ Barry D. Haught
_____
Barry D. Haught, Individually

/s/ Peggy L. Haught
_____
Peggy L. Haught, Individually

/s/ Jeannette E. Kinkaid
_____
Jeannette E. Kinkaid, Individually

Peggy Haught, Barry Haught's wife, had no interest in the business and received nothing from

the loan. She signed the note solely as an accommodation maker. (See UCC §3-415 discussed in Chapter 25). In contrast, Jeannette Kinkaid and Barry Haught signed the note both as general partners of Barrikaid Leasing Company and individually as accommodation makers.

After the partnership defaulted on the loan, Jeannette Kinkaid paid it, and sought contribution from Barry and Peggy Haught, as cosureties on the loan. Is Jeannette entitled to contribution from Barry? Is Jeannette entitled to contribution from Peggy? Explain.

43-5 Charlie McLain and his brother, Lance, formed a partnership to operate C & L Farms. They signed a short agreement which provided that Charlie would manage the farm on a full-time basis and receive seventy-five percent of the profits while Lance would be a nonworking partner and receive twenty-five percent of the profits. The only other provision of the agreement stated that all losses would be split fifty-fifty. In 1983, Charlie and Lance borrowed $20,000 from First National Bank to finance the purchase of hogs. Both brothers signed a promissory note. When the note came due, the bank agreed to renew it, and Charlie and Lance signed a renewal promissory note. When the renewal note matured, it was again renewed; but because Lance was out of town, only Charlie signed the renewal note as follows: "C & L Farms by Charlie McLain and Lance McLain." When the note came due, First National wrote a letter to both Charlie and Lance requesting payment. Lance responded that he was not responsible for payment of the note because he had not authorized Charlie to sign his name. Is Lance liable on the note? What other information is necessary to determine Lance's liability? Explain.

43-6 In the fall of 1983, Frank Burger, a traveling salesman of restaurant supplies, visited Roberts Town and Country Restaurant in an effort to sell supplies to Mr. Roberts, the owner of the restaurant. Roberts declined to purchase any supplies. In the spring of 1984, Burger again visited Roberts Town and Country Restaurant and talked to Hank Hanna. Hanna agreed to buy supplies costing $5,000. They signed a sales agreement listing Burger as seller and Town and Country Restaurant as buyer. Burger delivered the supplies but Hanna failed to pay for them. Burger sued Mr. Roberts and Hank Hanna, a partnership, doing business as Roberts Town and Country Restaurant. The evidence at trial established that during January of 1984, Mr. Roberts had leased the restaurant to Hanna. Roberts had not participated in the operation of the restaurant since that time. Roberts, however, had left a neon sign reading "Roberts Town and Country Restaurant" on the building. Should the court hold Mr. Roberts liable on the contract as a partner by estoppel? Explain.

43-7 Warren Lyons, an attorney, was a partner in Lyons, Taylor, and Benson, a partnership organized solely for the practice of law. Lyons represented Dorothy in a divorce action. During meetings with Lyons, Dorothy mentioned that she had recently inherited $50,000 from an aunt in Kansas and asked Lyons whether he could recommend someone to help her invest the money. Lyons explained that he recently had invested in a Yummers fast food franchise at considerable profit. At his suggestion, Dorothy invested $50,000 in Yummers, Inc., a corporation of which he was an officer. Dorothy wrote a check payable to "Warren Lyons as Attorney for Dorothy" and Lyons purchased stock in Yummers, Inc. in Dorothy's name. Yummers, Inc. went bankrupt, and Dorothy sued Lyons and Lyons, Taylor, and Benson for fraud. Lyons admitted his liability. Should the court hold Lyons, Taylor, and Benson liable? Explain.

43-8 A federal statute provides that any person who knowingly transports explosive and dangerous articles in interstate commerce is guilty of a misdemeanor. A & P Trucking Co., a partnership operating in Missouri and Illinois, was charged with violation of the statute. A & P Trucking Co. has moved for dismissal of the indictment.

(a) How should the court rule? Explain.

(b) Assume that an employee who was not a partner was the only person who knew that the truck was carrying explosives. Can the individual partners be convicted and sentenced to prison? Explain.

43-9 Ralph purchased Mac's Restaurant for $50,000. Because he needed additional capital, he entered into a limited partnership agreement, with Arnold serving as limited partner and Ralph serving as general partner. Ralph contributed the restaurant, and Arnold contributed $50,000 cash to the limited partnership. Arnold also took a security interest in the restaurant and equipment to secure his $50,000 investment. The restaurant failed to show a profit and eventually closed owing general creditors $75,000. The general creditors have won a judgment and have requested that the court order a judicial sale of the restaurant to pay the judgment. Arnold, however, claims that he now is entitled to foreclose on the restaurant, and that the general creditors may receive the proceeds in excess of $50,000. How should the court rule? Explain.

43-10 Hacienda Farms, Ltd. was a limited partnership with Ricardo de Escamilla as general partner and James Russell and H. W. Andrews as limited partners. The operation went bankrupt and creditors attempted to have Russell and Andrews held liable as general partners. The partnership agreement required all checks to be signed by a limited partner and a general partner or by both limited partners; the general partner had no power to withdraw money from the account. De Escamilla testified that he always consulted with Russell and Andrews prior to deciding what crops to plant. One year prior to bankruptcy, Andrews and Russell had asked de Escamilla to resign as manager of the farm and they hired a new farm manager.

(a) Under the ULPA, would Andrews and Russell be held liable? Explain.

(b) Under the RULPA, would Andrews and Russell be held liable? Explain.

Chapter 44

Partnership Dissolution and Winding Up

- the distinctions among dissolution, winding up, and termination of partnership
- the legal causes of dissolution of general and limited partnership
- the consequences of dissolution on continued operation of the business, partners' authority to bind the partnership, and partners' liability for firm debts
- how partnership assets are distributed upon liquidation of both general and limited partnerships

A partnership does not continue indefinitely. The cessation of partnership existence occurs in three stages: dissolution, winding up, and termination. **Dissolution** is "the change in the relation of the partners caused by any partner ceasing to be associated in the carrying on . . . of the business."[1] Upon dissolution, the partnership is not terminated, but continues until "winding up" of partnership affairs is completed.[2] **Winding up,** often referred to as **liquidation,** is the series of transactions necessary to settle partnership affairs after dissolution. During winding up, the partnership's uncompleted transactions are finished, assets are converted to

cash, debts are paid, and the excess, if any, is distributed to partners. When winding up is completed the partnership is **terminated.** These basic principles apply both to general and limited partnerships.

The result outlined above may generally be altered by agreement of the partners. Such an agreement is often advisable, because the dissolution-winding up-termination process may result in the destructive liquidation of a valuable ongoing business. The partners should therefore anticipate and control both the causes and consequences of dissolution in their partnership agreement. The material that follows examines the principles under the Uniform Partnership Act, the Uniform Limited Partnership Act, and the Revised Uniform Limited Partnership Act governing dissolution and winding up that apply when the partners' agreement is silent on the issue.

Causes of Dissolution

A partnership may be dissolved by operation of law, by court decree, and by an act of a partner in violation of the partnership agreement.

Operation of Law

Under §31 of the UPA, a partnership is dissolved automatically by operation of law under the following circumstances.

1. A partnership is dissolved upon expiration of a definite term (for example, five years) or com-

---

1. UPA §29.
2. UPA §30.

pletion of a particular undertaking (for example, to build an apartment building) specified in the agreement.

2. The partnership may be dissolved by unanimous consent of all partners even before expiration of an agreed term or accomplishment of a specified purpose.[3]

3. If no definite term or particular undertaking is specified, a partnership "at will" is created, which may be dissolved by the express will of any partner at any time.

4. The partnership agreement may confer a power upon partners to expel another partner under certain circumstances. Although such provisions are rare because of the possibility of oppression of one partner by the others, expulsion of a partner in accordance with the agreement dissolves the partnership.

5. A partnership is dissolved by any event that makes the partnership unlawful, or for the members to carry it on as a partnership.

6. The death of any partner dissolves the partnership.

7. The bankruptcy of any partner or the partnership dissolves the partnership.

Although not explicitly stated in the UPA, retirement of a partner dissolves the partnership. In this case, the retiring partner ceases to be associated with the business causing a dissolution under the general definition. Note that admission of a new partner generally does not cause dissolution.

Court Decree

Under §32 of the UPA, dissolution may be ordered by court decree upon application of any partner in the following circumstances.

1. A partner may become physically or mentally incapacitated or otherwise be unable to discharge his partnership responsibilities. In this case, to protect both the incapacitated partner and other partners, the court may order the partnership dissolved.

2. Conduct by a partner that prejudicially interferes with (or makes it impracticable to conduct) partnership business and willful or persistent breaches of the partnership agreement are grounds for judicial dissolution at the request of the injured partners. On this basis, for example, the court may order dissolution for irreconcilable differences or deadlock between partners, misappropriation of partnership assets, neglect of business responsibilities, or exclusion of one or more partners from management.

3. The court may order dissolution if the business can only be carried on at a loss.

4. As noted in Chapter 43, assignment of a partner's interest does not of itself dissolve the partnership. If, however, the agreed term of the partnership has expired, its particular undertaking completed, or if the partnership is "at will," the purchaser of a partner's interest may petition the court for dissolution. A similar right is granted the purchaser of a partner's interest resulting from a charging order.

5. To provide flexibility to resolve unusual situations, the court may also decree dissolution whenever "other circumstances render a dissolution equitable."[4]

At issue in the following case was whether the trial court properly ordered dissolution of a limited partnership.

Mandell v. Centrum Frontier Corporation
407 N.E.2d 821 (Ill. App. 1980)

In 1976, Frontier Investment Associates was organized as a limited partnership composed of four limited partners and Centrum Frontier Corporation and William P. Thompson as general partners. The sole asset of the limited partnership was Park Place, a 900-unit apartment building in Chicago, which was purchased in 1978 with a bank loan obtained by the limited partners, who also had loaned money to the partnership. The limited partnership agreement pro-

---

3. The consent of any partner who has assigned her interest or whose interest has been subjected to a charging order is not required to effect dissolution in this manner. UPA §31(1)(c). This provision allows the remaining partners to dissolve after one partner's interest has been assigned to a stranger or encumbered by a charging order.

4. UPA §32(1)(f).

vided that the general partners could not sell the apartment building or convert it to condominiums without approval of the limited partners.

Thompson managed Frontier for over a year during which it suffered substantial cash losses. The limited partners began efforts to sell Park Place but Thompson refused to cooperate with these efforts even after a purchaser had been found. Instead Thompson proposed converting Park Place to condominiums, a plan that the limited partners rejected.

On September 27, 1979, plaintiffs, the limited partners, filed suit against defendants Thompson and Centrum seeking dissolution of the limited partnership. The trial court granted dissolution on the grounds that the limited partnership could only be operated at a loss and that the general and limited partners had reached a deadlock. The court ordered that Park Place be sold at a judicial sale. Thompson and Centrum appealed.

O'Connor, Justice

. . . A court will dissolve a partnership when it is reasonably certain that the business of the partnership cannot be carried on at a profit. . . . A history of past losses is an indication that future profits are not to be expected. . . .

Because the partnership had a negative cash flow during 15 months of the 17 months prior to filing this suit and the losses continued even after the trial court had ordered Park Place sold, we find that the trial court properly decreed dissolution of the partnership on the ground that Frontier could only be carried on at a loss.

Defendants argue further that the trial court erred when it refused to consider the tax benefits received by virtue of their participation in the partnership. The substance of defendants' argument is that because the partnership never operated at a real economic loss as to the individual plaintiffs, the partnership should not have been dissolved. We disagree. The focus is to be placed on the losses of the partnership as an entity and not the losses of the individual partners. . . .

Defendants also argue that because the ultimate purpose of the partnership included the future development and sale of Park Place, the trial court erred when it failed to consider that the partnership would be enormously profitable if Park Place was

sold as condominiums. We disagree. Even assuming that the business of the partnership was to sell Park Place and that such a sale would be enormously profitable, under the existing circumstances conversion was not possible. Section 11.9 of the partnership agreement prohibited the general partners from converting without the approval of the limited partners and the limited partners refused to agree to Thompson's conversion proposal. . . . [P]laintiffs had no duty or obligation to agree to the conversion. . . .

Defendants next contend that the trial court erred in also basing dissolution of the partnership on the ground that there existed a deadlock between the general partners and the limited partners. The trial court found that where neither the general partners nor the limited partners could sell or convert without the consent of all the partners, a deadlock existed which rendered operation of the partnership totally ineffective. . . .

When the purposes of a business relationship are being defeated by deadlock, a court can declare the business relationship at an end. . . . Dissolution of a partnership is proper where relations existing between partners render it impractical for them to conduct business beneficially. . . .

In the instant case, Frontier's purpose as stated in the partnership agreement was "the acquisition, ownership, development, leasing, management and sale" of Park Place. Holding the building as rental property was resulting in daily losses to the partnership. A sale of Park Place appeared attractive to both the limited partners and Thompson. However, the parties could not agree as to whether to sell the property to a third party developer or to sell the units as condominiums. By virtue of the amendment to Section 11.9 of the partnership agreement, the general partners could not convert Park Place to condominiums without the consent of a majority of the limited partners and the limited partners refused to agree to a conversion proposal. The partnership agreement provided that partnership assets could not be sold without the approval of all the partners and the general partners refused to agree to a sale of Park Place to a third party unless Thompson could participate in any future conversion of the property. Because only a sale of Park Place would result in profit to the partnership, the trial court did not err when it also based dissolution of the partnership on the ground that deadlock existed between the two groups of partners. . . .

[Judgment affirmed.]

Violation of Partnership Agreement

A partnership is a mutual agency relation with each partner acting both as a principal and as agent for the other partners. Like other agencies, a partnership is a personal relationship, resting on mutual consent. This consent may be withdrawn by any partner at any time, even if the acting partner is contractually obligated to continue the partnership. That is, all partners have the *power,* but not necessarily the *right,* to dissolve the partnership at any time.[5] For example, assume A, B, and C are partners in an auto repair business. Their partnership agreement provides that the partnership will continue for three years. Though the business is profitable, B becomes dissatisfied with the arrangement after one year. B may dissolve the partnership even though his act violates the partnership agreement, rendering him liable for damages to the other partners.

Consequences of Dissolution

Liquidation or Continuation

Upon dissolution, the partnership has two basic alternatives: liquidation or continuation of the business. Liquidation involves a sale of all assets, payment of creditors, and distribution of any excess to the partners. Alternatively, the business may be continued with a different ownership agreement and a financial settlement with the outgoing partner or partners.

General Rule—Liquidation. Under §38(1) of the UPA, upon dissolution "each partner . . . may have the partnership property applied to discharge its liabilities, and the surplus applied to pay in cash

the net amount owing to the respective partners." Thus, as a general rule, any partner has the right to compel liquidation of the partnership after any type of dissolution. This "liquidation right" imposes a corresponding duty upon the partners to wind up and terminate the business. It may be asserted by any partner or by the heir or personal representative of a deceased partner.

The liquidation is generally conducted by the partners or the legal representative of the last surviving partner. A partner who is bankrupt or has wrongfully caused the dissolution has no right to participate in the liquidation. As an alternative to liquidation by the partners, any partner may, for good cause shown (for example, fraud by co-partners) obtain winding up by the court. Court supervised liquidation is usually accomplished by appointment of a receiver.[6]

Exceptions to Liquidation Rule. The UPA recognizes three important exceptions to the rule permitting forced liquidation upon dissolution. These include (1) when the dissolution is caused in violation of the partnership agreement, (2) when dissolution is caused by expulsion of a partner pursuant to the partnership agreement, and (3) when continuation is allowed by agreement of the partners.

Dissolution in Violation of the Agreement. A partner who, in violation of the agreement, causes a dissolution has no liquidation right. Rather, under UPA §38(2), the remaining partners can either (1) liquidate the business and sue the dissolving partner for damages for breach of the partnership agreement, or (2) continue the business, using the firm name and property, either by themselves or with new partners. If the remaining partners continue the business, they must pay (or secure payment to) the dissolving partner for the value of her interest, less damages for breach of the partnership agreement, and less any value attributable to the goodwill of the business. The continuing partners also must indemnify the dissolving partner against all present and future partnership liabilities.

---

5. UPA §31(2).

6. UPA §37.

Dissolution by Expulsion of Partner. A partner who is expelled from the partnership through operation of an express provision in the partnership agreement is not entitled to liquidation. Rather, the remaining partners may continue the business, and the expelled partner is entitled to be paid in cash for the net amount owed him by the firm. The expelled partner also is entitled to be discharged from all partnership liabilities.[7]

Continuation Agreement. In many cases, liquidation causes substantial injury to the partners. That is, the partnership often possesses substantially more value as a viable, going concern than it does upon a forced sale of its assets. In addition, the partnership often represents an employment opportunity for the partners not available elsewhere. The foregoing exceptions provide very limited protection to partners against forced liquidation upon dissolution. Fortunately, however, the UPA provides that the liquidation right is granted only "unless otherwise agreed."[8] Thus, the partners may, by **continuation agreement,** restrict or deny the liquidation right generally arising upon dissolution.

A continuation agreement may be made at the time of dissolution or may be part of the original partnership agreement. Because dissolution is so fundamental, however, and the effects of liquidation so potentially ruinous, a comprehensive continuation provision usually should be incorporated into the basic partnership agreement. Issues that should be addressed by the continuation provision include, for example, the causes of dissolution, the method of computing the value of the departing partner's interest, the method and medium of payment for that interest, the method of funding the buy out (such as insurance owned by the firm or partners, or firm assets, or the partners' individual assets), and the method of protecting outgoing interests against firm debts. A carefully drafted continuation agreement will give the partnership continuity of existence similar to a corporation, efficiently compensating partners who leave the business, and allowing liquidation only in situations that can be anticipated and controlled by the partners.

Partners' Authority

The following material examines the effect of a dissolution upon the actual and apparent authority of the partners.

Termination of Actual Authority. Unless the business is to be continued (as authorized by a continuation agreement or the UPA), dissolution "terminates all authority of any partner to act for the partnership."[9] The partners, nevertheless, retain authority for transactions appropriate to winding up partnership affairs, and to complete transactions unfinished at dissolution.[10] The UPA recognizes an exception to the rule that a partner's authority terminates immediately upon a dissolution if dissolution is caused by the act, death, or bankruptcy of a partner. In these cases, a partner may hold co-partners liable for their proportionate share of any liability created after dissolution if the acting partner had no knowledge of a dissolution caused by the act of another partner, or no knowledge or notice of a dissolution caused by the death or bankruptcy of another partner.[11]

Termination of Apparent Authority. Although dissolution terminates the actual authority of the partners, persons who have previously dealt with the firm and others who know of its existence may be unaware of the firm's dissolution. The partners still possess apparent authority to bind the partnership to such persons. Therefore, to prevent one partner from creating new partnership obligations (those not necessary to wind up the business) after dissolution, the partners must take affirmative steps to terminate each partner's apparent authority.

As with other agents, a partner's apparent authority is terminated by giving appropriate notice to third parties of the partner's lack of authority.[12]

---

7. UPA §§38(1), 36(2).
8. UPA §38(1).

9. UPA §33.
10. UPA §35(1)(a).
11. UPA §§33(1), 34.
12. UPA §35(1)(b).

Persons who have extended credit to the partnership prior to dissolution are entitled to actual notice of the dissolution. Persons who have not extended credit to the partnership but know of its existence are entitled to notice of dissolution by publication in a newspaper of general circulation in the locality where the partnership conducted business. Until proper notice is given, any partner has continuing authority to bind the others after dissolution to contracts with third parties.

Continuing apparent authority is most often used to hold a retiring partner liable for obligations incurred by former partners after dissolution. Assume Allen, Branch, and Cox are partners in a clothing store. Cox retires, dissolving the partnership. Although the partners' actual authority is terminated upon dissolution for all purposes except winding up, their apparent authority continues until extinguished by notification. Thus, assume Branch, after dissolution, contracts on behalf of the partnership to purchase on credit a shipment of suits from Simpson. Simpson, who had been supplying clothes to the firm for many years, had no knowledge or notice of the dissolution. Both Allen and Cox may be held liable on the contract to Simpson.

Partners' Liability

Over the life of the partnership, partners may die, retire, or be expelled from the firm and new partners may be admitted. Dissolution of the partnership caused by changes in membership does not of itself affect the existing liability of any partner to firm creditors.[13] Any other rule would allow partners to avoid firm debts simply by dissolving. For example, if the partnership is dissolved by retirement of a partner, all partners remain liable for firm debts incurred during the operation of the partnership. If the remaining partners continue the business after dissolution, with or without new partners, creditors of the dissolved partnership are also creditors of the new firm continuing the business.[14]

Upon retirement of a partner, remaining partners who continue the business often assume the burden of paying firm creditors as part of the settlement of the departing partner's interest. Although such an agreement is binding among the partners, it has no effect upon the creditors; the retiring partner remains liable for all debts incurred while a partner,[15] becoming a surety for the assuming partners' performance. The retiring partner is, however, discharged from partnership debts if the creditors consent to a novation, under which the continuing partners assume the duty to perform existing obligations and the retiring partner is released.

A person who is admitted as a partner in an existing partnership is liable for partnership debts incurred before she became a partner, as if she had been a partner when the obligations were incurred. This liability may, however, be satisfied only out of partnership property; that is, the incoming partner is generally liable for pre-existing firm debts only to the extent of her capital contribution.[16] The new partner is, of course, personally liable for all debts incurred after becoming a partner.

At issue in the following case was whether a partnership debt had been incurred before or after a person became a partner.

Moseley v. Commercial State Bank
457 So. 2d 967 (Ala. 1984)

> Southern Distilleries was a general partnership organized in 1980 to produce gasahol. The partnership agreement provided that any three partners having at least an aggregate sixty percent interest in the partnership were authorized to borrow money and execute promissory notes on behalf of the partnership. On December 19, 1980, Southern Distilleries, by three of its partners, borrowed $140,184 from Commercial State Bank and signed two promissory notes that were due March 19, 1981. Southern Distilleries failed to pay the notes when due.
>
> On April 2, 1981, the partnership agreement was

---

13. UPA §36(1).
14. UPA §41.

15. As noted in the preceding section, such a partner may be liable for obligations incurred thereafter unless third party creditors are properly notified.
16. UPA §17.

amended to add three new partners including Julius Moseley who contributed $100,000 to the capital account of the partnership. On July 21, 1981, Southern Distilleries paid the interest on the notes and three partners executed a new note in the amount of $140,000. Commercial State Bank marked the December 19 notes "Paid."

After Southern Distilleries failed to pay the July 21 note, Commercial State Bank sued Southern Distilleries and each of the partners. The trial court held the partnership and the partners jointly and severally liable. Moseley appealed.

Faulkner, Justice

. . . Execution of an instrument in the partnership's name for the purpose of carrying on the usual business of the partnership binds the partners, unless the partner executing the instrument has no authority to act and the person with whom he is dealing has knowledge that he has no authority to act. . . . A person admitted as a partner into an existing partnership is liable for partnership obligations arising before his admission into the partnership. His liability for pre-existing obligations can be satisfied only out of partnership property, however. . . .

The bank's judgment is against Moseley personally. The dispositive issue of this case, therefore, is whether the obligation sued on arose before Moseley's admission into the partnership. In support of Mosely's contention that the debt pre-existed his admission into the partnership, Moseley argues that the new note was merely a renewal of a pre-existing obligation. . . .

There is no dispute in this case as to the material facts. Moseley entered into a general partnership agreement with other individuals doing business under the name Southern Distilleries. The partners who executed the note sued on were expressly authorized to bind the other partners. Although the defendant chooses to categorize the debt created by the note sued on as the renewal of a pre-existing debt, it is clear that the obligation created by the old note terminated when the bank accepted the new note. Prior to the execution of the new note the bank could have brought an action to collect the debt. After it accepted the new note and satisfied the old one, there was no obligation which was due and payable to the bank until the new note ma-

tured. In agreeing to the forebearance of its rights to collect the money owed it by Southern Distilleries, the bank relied on the representations of the partnership agreement that the partners, including Moseley, would be bound by the new note. Since the contract sued on was entered into by a partnership which included Moseley, and since there was valid consideration for the contract sued on, the plaintiff is entitled to enforce the contract against the defendant. . . .

We understand that Moseley had no knowledge of the day-to-day operations of the partnership and that he did not find out about the note until the bank brought this action. While Moseley apparently considered his interest in the firm to be that of merely an investor (he categorizes his $100,000.00 contribution to the firm's capital account as a "loan"), he signed an agreement granting him all the rights of a general partner in the firm and authorizing the other partners to obligate him as a general partner, which they did. This is not a case where fraud or overreaching was alleged. The partnership agreement was not an adhesion contract entered into by parties with unequal bargaining strength. The parties are competent business men dealing at arm's length, who presumably have ample access to counsel. If Moseley had wished to limit his exposure to liability he should have taken steps to do so when he chose to become involved in the enterprise. . . .

[Judgment affirmed.]

Distribution Priorities—General Partnership

Solvent Partnerships

If, upon dissolution, the business is liquidated, partnership assets are reduced to cash and distributed to partnership creditors and partners. Property subject to distribution upon liquidation includes both the partnership property and any additional contributions collected from the partners necessary to pay partnership obligations.[17] This principle sim-

---

17. UPA §40(a).

ply recognizes that the partners are personally liable for firm obligations and may therefore be required to contribute additional funds to cover any deficiency between firm assets and liabilities. The duty to contribute to firm losses may be enforced against living partners and the estate of a deceased partner. The duty may be enforced by any partner or his legal representative, or by representatives of creditors.[18]

The UPA specifies the order in which assets are distributed.[19] First, claims of partnership creditors (other than partners) are paid. Second, claims of partners other than for capital contributions or profits are paid. These include advances or loans made by a partner to the partnership. A partner is entitled to be paid interest on such advances.[20] Third, partners' capital contributions are returned. Finally, any amount remaining is distributed to the partners as profits.

For example, suppose A, B, and C are equal partners who have each contributed $25,000 to the business. In addition B has loaned the partnership $25,000. Upon liquidation, firm assets are sold for $200,000 and creditors' claims total $50,000. The $200,000 would be distributed $50,000 to creditors, then $25,000 to B to repay his loan, then $75,000 to the partners in repayment of their capital contributions. The remaining $50,000 would be divided equally among the partners as profits.

If firm assets are insufficient to repay in full partnership creditors, advances or loans made by partners, or capital contributions, the loss is shared (subject to contrary agreement) in the same proportion as the partners share profits. If, in the example above, firm assets are sold for $135,000, A, B, and C would each receive $20,000 as a return on their capital contributions. That is, after paying creditors (including B) $60,000 remains to cover the partners' $75,000 in capital contributions. This results in a $15,000 loss shared equally by the partners.

To illustrate the distribution rules further, assume that A, B, and C are partners. A contributed $20,000, B, $15,000, and C, $10,000. On liquidation, after all creditors are paid, $12,000 remains

to be distributed to the partners. They have agreed to share profits and losses equally. The $33,000 loss ($45,000 − $12,000) is allocated equally to the partners as follows:

	A	B	C
Capital	$ 20,000	$ 15,000	$ 10,000
Loss	(11,000)	(11,000)	(11,000)
	$ 9,000	$ 4,000	$ (1,000)

When finally settled, C must contribute an additional $1,000 from his personal assets. This $1,000 plus the $12,000 will be used to pay A $9,000 and B $4,000. If C is insolvent and unable to contribute additionally, A and B share this loss equally ($500 each) and of the $12,000, A is entitled to $8,500 and B, $3,500.

In the following case the court was required to determine the proper allocation of assets among partners on liquidation. Note the special rule applicable to a partner who contributes services but not money or property to the partnership.

Langness v. The "O" Street Carpet Shop, Inc.
353 N.W.2d 709 (Neb. 1984)

Herbert J. Friedman, Strelsa Langness, and The "O" Street Carpet Shop, Inc. formed a general partnership in 1973. Langness contributed $14,000 in cash, and Friedman contributed his legal services, upon which no value was placed in the articles of partnership. "O" Street Carpet contributed a real estate contract entitling it to purchase for $56,000 a piece of rental property valued at $65,000. The partnership used $6,000 of the cash as a down payment on the real estate and $8,000 was given to "O" Street Carpet for its operations. The articles provided that the partnership would pay $116.66 per month to Langness, and Gerald Neva, president of "O" Street Carpet, personally guaranteed the payments.

In 1978, the partnership sold the rental property and the partners agreed to dissolve the partnership. Following payments of its debts, the partnership's

---

18. UPA §§40(e),(f),(g).
19. UPA §40(b).
20. UPA §18(c).

net assets were $48,824.41 which were distributed as follows:

Langness	$16,792.01
''O'' Street Carpet	26,808.58
Friedman	5,223.82

Langness sued ''O'' Street Carpet and Friedman alleging that she was entitled to a greater share of the assets. The trial court held that Friedman and ''O'' Street Carpet were jointly and severally liable to Langness for $7,290.42. Friedman appealed.

Per Curiam

. . . Friedman's first three assignments of error are best analyzed by reviewing the capital contributions made by the parties, the nature of the payments made to Langness, and the distributions made to each of the three partners upon the winding up of the partnership.

. . . [A]t the time the partnership was formed, ''O'' Street Carpet contributed a $56,000 purchase agreement on property with a fair market value of $65,000, for a contribution of property worth $9,000. However, $8,000 of the $14,000 contributed by Langness went to ''O'' Street Carpet, thereby reducing its capital contribution at that time to $1,000. During the life of the partnership, ''O'' Street Carpet contributed an additional $4,005 in capital. Thus, ''O'' Street Carpet's total capital contribution is $5,005.

Friedman contributed no money or property. It is the general rule that a partner who contributes only services to the partnership is not deemed to have made a capital contribution to the partnership such as to require capital repayment upon dissolution unless the parties have agreed to the contrary. . . .

Friedman argues that since, by the agreement, he was given 10 percent of the partnership, he was entitled to be credited with a like amount of the partnership capital upon dissolution. While the agreement specifically states that Friedman is entitled to 10 percent of the partnership profits, it mentions nothing concerning his rights to partnership capital upon dissolution. We see nothing in the agreement which indicates the general rule is not to apply. Therefore, Friedman made no capital contribution to the venture.

We next address the nature of the payments made to Langness. The articles of partnership called for the partnership to pay to Langness $116.66 per month for the life of the partnership. While this provision of the articles is found under a section labeled *''Distribution of Profits and Losses,''* the agreement does not state whether it is to be treated as an advance on profits or a capital withdrawal. The personal guarantee executed by Neva labeled it a ''return on the $14,000.00 investment.'' Both accountants who testified at the trial stated that the payments were treated as capital withdrawals. Langness treated the payments as such when preparing her tax returns. The tax returns of the partnership did not treat them as expenses. Although Friedman argues that they should be treated as advances against Langness' future profits, we do not see any reason to do so when the partnership itself treated them otherwise.

From our review of . . . a ledger of the payments made by checks issued by NFL Associates, we find that Langness was issued 47 checks for $116.66, 3 checks for $233.32, and 1 check for $117.32. We calculate her total capital withdrawals as $6,300.30, a figure different than that urged upon us by the parties or found by the district court. This $6,300.30 reduced her capital in the partnership to $7,699.70.

We now reach the question of the appropriate amounts of the distribution to each of the partners. The partnership agreement provides: ''Upon the dissolution of the partnership after settlement of all of it's [sic] debts, liabilities, and other obligations, the partners are entitled to all remaining assets of the partnership in equal proportions in liquidation of all of their respective interests in the partnership.'' Amounts owing to partners to reimburse them for capital contributions are liabilities of the partnership and take priority over amounts owing to partners in respect to profits. . . .

Of the $48,824.41 in assets remaining after payment of the partnership's debts, $7,699.70 is to be paid to Langness for her capital contribution and $5,005 to ''O'' Street Carpet for its capital contribution. The remaining $36,119.71 is to be divided according to the partners' share in the profits, which is on a 45-45-10 basis. This calculation requires $16,253.87 to be paid to Langness for profit, the same amount to ''O'' Street Carpet, and

$3,611.97 to Friedman. At the time of the winding up of the partnership, the distributions should have been as follows:

	Return of Capital	+	*Share of Profits*	=	*Total*
Langness	$ 7,699.70		$16,253.87		$23,953.57
"O" Street Carpet	5,005.00		16,253.87		21,258.87
Friedman	0.00		3,611.97		3,611.97
	$12,704.70		$36,119.71		$48,824.41

Since Langness was paid only $16,792.01, she is entitled to an additional $7,161.56. . . .

Therefore, the judgment of the district court is modified as follows: Langness shall have judgment against and recover from Friedman the sum of $1,611.85, the difference between the amount he received, $5,223.82, and the amount he should have received, $3,611.97. Further, Langness shall have judgment against and recover from "O" Street Carpet the amount of $5,549.71, the difference between the amount it received, $26,808.58, and the amount it should have received, $21,258.87. . . .

[Judgment affirmed as modified.]

Insolvent Partnerships

In the preceding examples, the partnership assets were sufficient to pay outside creditors' claims in full; that is, the partnerships were solvent. Because individual partners may be compelled to contribute toward firm losses, any partnership is solvent as long as any partner is solvent.[21] Both the partnership and the partners may, however, be insolvent with the assets of each being administered in a bankruptcy proceeding. In this situation, a dispute may arise between creditors of the partnership and creditors of the individual partners concerning distribution of partnership and individual assets.

Traditionally, this problem was resolved both under federal bankruptcy law[22] and the UPA[23] by the rule of "dual priorities," often known as the "jingle rule." This rule gave partnership creditors priority in the distribution of partnership assets, and creditors of individual partners priority in distribution of a partner's individual assets. The rule permitted partnership creditors to proceed against a partner's individual assets only after individual creditors had been paid. Conversely, individual creditors could attach an individual partner's interest in the partnership only after firm creditors had been paid.

The jingle rule was harshly criticized for many years for destroying or diminishing partnership creditors' rights against the partners' separate property. That is, the rule that paid partner's individual creditors first from individual assets undermined the principle that partners are personally liable for firm debts. For this reason, the Bankruptcy Reform Act of 1978 repealed the jingle rule insofar as it insulates a partner's separate property from claims of partnership creditors until the partner's individual creditors are paid in full. Under the new Bankruptcy Code, partnership creditors retain their priority in partnership assets, but share equally with individual creditors in individual assets.[24]

Dissolution and Winding Up—Limited Partnership

Causes of Dissolution

The principles governing dissolution and winding up of limited partnerships are similar to those applicable to general partnerships. After an event causing dissolution occurs, the partnership is wound up (liquidated) and terminated, unless some provision is made to continue the business. The following events cause dissolution of a limited partnership.

1. The partnership is dissolved at the time or upon occurrence of events specified in the certifi-

---

21. Under federal bankruptcy law, a partnership is insolvent if firm debts exceed the sum of partnership assets and each individual partner's net worth (nonpartnership assets less nonpartnership debts). 11 U.S.C. §101(31)(B).

22. Bankruptcy Act §5g, 11 U.S.C. §23(g) (repealed 1978).

23. UPA §§40(b),(h),(i); 36(4).

24. 11 U.S.C. §723.

cate of limited partnership or partnership agreement.[25]

2. The partnership also may be dissolved by court decree, upon application of any partner, if the court finds that it is not reasonably practicable to carry on the business in conformity with the partnership agreement.[26]

3. The partnership may be dissolved by the unanimous written consent of all partners.[27]

4. The partnership is dissolved upon withdrawal of a general partner unless the right to continue the business with the remaining general partner or partners is stated in the partnership agreement or all partners consent to continuance.[28] Under both the ULPA and RULPA, "withdrawal" occurs upon the voluntary withdrawal (for example, retirement) of the general partner from the business, even if the withdrawal violates the partnership agreement,[29] and upon the death or adjudicated incapacity of a general partner.[30] Under the RULPA, withdrawal also occurs upon the dissolution of a corporate general partner,[31] the assignment of the general partner's interest, the removal of the general partner in accordance with the partnership agreement, and the bankruptcy of a general partner.[32]

Distribution Priorities

If, upon dissolution, the partnership business is not continued, firm assets are liquidated and distributed according to priorities outlined by statute. The ULPA and RULPA have substantially different provisions governing distribution of assets upon liquidation.

Under the ULPA,[33] assets are distributed according to the following priorities:

First, outside creditors are paid. Claims of limited partners for money loaned to the partnership share assets pro rata with general creditors.[34]

Second, limited partners' claims for profits are paid.

Third, limited partners' capital contributions are returned.

Fourth, loans to general partners are paid.

Fifth, general partners' claims for profits are paid.

Finally, general partners' capital contributions are returned.

The RULPA[35] uses the following priorities:

First, creditors are paid. Claims of outside creditors, claims for money loaned by limited partners, and claims for money loaned by general partners all share available assets pro rata.

Second, partners and ex-partners who have become entitled to a distribution of income or capital upon their withdrawal from the partnership are paid.

Third, unless otherwise provided in the partnership agreement, the capital contributions of both limited and general partners are returned.

Finally, unless otherwise agreed, any remaining assets are paid to both general and limited partners for their interest in the partnership (profits).

Note that the RULPA treats limited and general partners equally regarding repayment of loans, return of capital contribution, and distribution of profits, unless otherwise provided in the partnership agreement. In contrast, under the ULPA limited partners' claims for loans, profits, and capital are paid before general partners receive anything. The effect of the RULPA approach, therefore, is to downgrade the rights of limited partners upon liquidation of the partnership.

---

25. RULPA §801(1), (2).
26. RULPA §§801(5), 802.
27. RULPA §801(3).
28. ULPA §§9(1)(g), 20; RULPA §801(4).
29. ULPA §20, RULPA §§402(1), 602.
30. ULPA §20, RULPA §402(6). The death or withdrawal of a limited partner does not affect the continued existence of the partnership.
31. RULPA §402(9). Termination of a trust that is a general partner, distribution of an estate that is a general partner, and winding up of a separate partnership that is a general partner also constitutes withdrawal. RULPA §§402(7), (8), (10).
32. RULPA §§402(2)-(5).

---

33. ULPA §23.
34. ULPA §13. Note that limited partners may not be secured creditors under ULPA §13(1)(a).
35. RULPA §804.

SUMMARY

1. Dissolution is the change in the relationship of the partners caused when any partner ceases to be associated with carrying on the business. Dissolution may occur by operation of law, by court decree, or by a partner withdrawing in violation of the partnership agreement.

2. Generally, any partner has the right to compel liquidation of the partnership after any type of dissolution. This "liquidation right" imposes a corresponding duty upon the partners to wind up and terminate the business. The UPA recognizes three important exceptions to the rule permitting forced liquidation upon dissolution: (1) when the dissolution is caused in violation of the partnership agreement, (2) when dissolution is caused by expulsion of a partner pursuant to the partnership agreement; and (3) when continuation is allowed by agreement of the partners.

3. Dissolution generally terminates actual authority of any partner to act for the partnership, except for transactions necessary to wind up partnership affairs and to complete transactions unfinished at dissolution. Partners' apparent authority continues after dissolution until proper notification of dissolution is given to third parties.

4. A partnership may be dissolved by changes in membership. For example, partners may retire and others may be admitted. Generally, dissolution does not affect the existing liability of any partner. A newly admitted partner is liable for pre-existing firm debts but only to the extent of her capital contribution.

5. If, upon dissolution, the partnership is liquidated rather than continued, partnership assets are reduced to cash and distributed to partnership creditors and partners. The UPA specifies that assets are distributed first to creditors, then to partners for claims other than capital or profit, then to partners to return their capital contribution. Any amount remaining is distributed to the partners as profits.

6. If the partnership is insolvent, a dispute may arise between creditors of the partnership and creditors of the individual partners over distribution of partnership and individual assets. This situation is governed by the federal Bankruptcy Code.

7. Distribution priorities upon liquidation of a limited partnership differ depending upon which limited partnership statute is in effect. Under the ULPA, limited partners' claims for loans, capital, and profits are paid before general partners receive anything. Under the RULPA, limited and general partners are treated equally regarding repayment of loans, return of capital contribution, and distribution of profits, unless otherwise provided in the partnership agreement.

KEY TERMS

dissolution	termination
winding up (liquidation)	continuation agreement

QUESTIONS AND PROBLEMS

44-1 On May 1, 1978, Larry, Carl, and Mike formed Nuway Developers, a partnership for the purchase, development, and sale of real estate. On February 15, 1985, Larry signed a contract agreeing to buy a piece of real estate from Landowner. Landowner had not previously dealt with Nuway Developers and was not aware that Larry was a partner in the firm. On March 15, 1985, after Larry had failed to pay Landowner, Landowner demanded that the partnership perform the contract. In each of the following cases, determine the date the partnership was dissolved and whether the partnership is liable on the contract. Explain your reasoning.

(a) On February 10, 1985, Carl wrote a letter to his partners stating, "I hereby notify you that I am terminating the partnership and request that steps be taken to liquidate the partnership assets." Although the partners held several meetings to discuss liquidation, they were unable to agree on the proper procedure for liquidation. On March 1, 1985, Carl died.

(b) On December 1, 1984, Mike told his partners, "I want to terminate this partnership as soon as possible." Nevertheless, he continued to perform work for the partnership on an intermittent basis until March 1, 1985, when he left town and began to work full time as a realtor for a corporation. On March 15, 1985, Mike filed a lawsuit demanding an accounting and dissolution of the partnership.

44-2 Lewis and Collins formed a partnership to construct and operate a restaurant. Lewis was to construct and equip the restaurant while Collins was to operate the restaurant. Due to unexpected expenses, the cost of constructing the restaurant greatly exceeded estimates. As a result, Lewis was forced to obtain a loan that was due in two years. Because of the need to repay the loan, Lewis was quite anxious to see the restaurant show a profit. In the first few months of operation, the business broke even, but Lewis demanded that Collins manage the business in a different manner. Lewis regularly interfered with operations. Finally, Lewis demanded that the partnership be dissolved. When Collins refused, Lewis filed suit requesting the court to dissolve the business. Following presentation of evidence, the jury found that the restaurant could reasonably be expected to operate at a profit and that Lewis's interference had caused the restaurant to operate at a loss. How should the court resolve the dispute? Explain.

44-3   Harry and Jeff formed a partnership for the operation of a retail furniture store. The partnership agreement provided:

> If either partner dies, the surviving partner agrees to pay to the estate of the surviving partner an amount equal to the value of the deceased partner's interest in the partnership property as of the date of death.

Harry died on June 1, 1985. As of that date, the partnership property consisted entirely of inventory—i.e., furniture located in the store's showroom. The furniture had been purchased from a wholesaler for $100,000. Retail markup on the furniture was approximately 150%. The firm's liabilities were $10,000.

(a) If you were the surviving partner, what amount would you think was the proper amount to pay to the deceased partner's estate? Explain your calculations.

(b) If you were the administrator of the deceased partner's estate, what amount would you expect the estate to receive? Explain your calculations.

(c) What is the correct amount to be paid to the estate?

44-4   Lee and his sister Bea want to form a partnership to operate a manufacturing firm. The business will be capital intensive requiring them to borrow a substantial amount of money. Nevertheless, Lee and Bea have projected that the income from the business will be sufficient to repay the loans and generate substantial profits. Recognizing the difficulty that would be caused by liquidation of the operation, they wish to include in the partnership agreement provisions for continuation of the business in case either of the partners dies, especially during the early years of the partnership. If either of them dies, each wants to be sure that his or her spouse and children will receive adequate income. Unfortunately, because of a hereditary disease, neither Bea nor Lee is insurable except at a prohibitive cost. Recommend provisions for them to include in a continuation agreement that would take effect upon the death of either partner.

Major Topics

- the nature and types of corporations and the development of American corporation law
- the various factors to consider in choosing the form of a business organization
- the law governing transactions by persons who organize and plan the creation of a corporation
- how a corporation is formed and is qualified to do business outside its state of incorporation
- the situations in which a defectively organized corporation will be legally recognized, and the situations in which the existence of a duly formed corporation will be disregarded

Although the partnership provides a flexible and easily created organizational form for many businesses, it has a number of disadvantages. Partners have unlimited personal liability for firm debts and obligations. Partnerships often are of limited duration and ownership interests are difficult to transfer. As the number of investors increases, lack of centralized management may make operating the partnership unwieldy. In addition, new partners participate in management, making it difficult to raise large amounts of equity capital without diluting control. To remedy these and other problems, the law has developed the corporation, the dominant form of organization for modern business.

The Law of Corporations

Nature of a Corporation

The basic advantage of a corporation over a partnership is that a **corporation** is recognized as a legal entity, existing apart from, and independent of, its owners or investors. That is, provided certain statutory formalities are met, the law recognizes a corporation as a fictitious being or artificial person. The corporate person is owned by shareholders, or stockholders, who transfer assets to it in exchange for shares of stock. The shareholders do not manage the corporation directly, but rather elect directors who have a statutory responsibility to manage or direct its business and affairs. The directors, in turn, appoint officers who handle the day-to-day operation of the business.

The corporation has unlimited liability for corporate obligations. Its owners, the shareholders, are generally liable only to the extent of their investment. They enjoy limited liability because corporate debts are obligations of the artificial person, the corporation, not the shareholders. The corporation is not affected by changes in ownership. Existing shareholders may die, go bankrupt, or transfer their shares, and new investors may be added by the sale of additional stock without affecting the corporation. Like a natural person, the corporation can own property, enter into contracts, and sue and be sued. Similarly, corporations may be subject to criminal liability and are entitled to many of the protections accorded natural persons in the federal and state constitutions.

Types of Corporations

Corporations are commonly classified as either "public" or "private." A **public corporation** (sometimes called a "municipal" or "political" corporation) is one created by the government for political purposes to administer civil government, often vested with local legislative powers. Examples include cities, counties, towns, and school districts. The federal government also has created public corporations, such as the Federal Savings and Loan Insurance Corporation, to administer specific federal programs. **Private corporations** are those formed by private individuals for private purposes and include generally nonprofit and business corporations. **Nonprofit corporations** include, for example, those organized for religious, educational, or philanthropic purposes. Income from such corporations is applied to the specific purpose or purposes for which the organization is created (such as to provide scholarships), rather than the personal enrichment of the persons who own or operate it. In contrast, **business corporations,** the subject of this and the following three chapters, generally include those organized to carry on a definite business for profit.

Although only about one-fifth of all business enterprises in the United States are business corporations, economically they clearly dominate unincorporated business organizations. For example, the 500 largest American business corporations account for nearly two-thirds of all nonagricultural economic activity and employ one out of every six nongovernment workers. Business corporations also employ three-fourths of the nation's work force.[1]

Closely-Held and Publicly-Held Corporations.
Business corporations are often described as either "closely-held" or "publicly-held." A **closely-held corporation**[2] is one whose shares are owned by one shareholder or a closely knit group of shareholders. The vast majority of business corporations are closely held and they usually, though not necessarily, are relatively small business enterprises. In the typical closely-held corporation, all or most of the shareholders are also directors or officers, no public market exists for the corporation's shares, and the parties may impose restrictions on transfer of shares. In short, most closely-held corporations operate internally like proprietorships or partnerships, but use the corporate form for limited liability or tax advantages.

A **publicly-held corporation** is one whose shares are owned by many people. Examples of publicly-held corporations are those that have shares traded on established securities exchanges, or for which public share price quotations exist. Unlike shareholders in closely-held corporations, those in publicly-held corporations have little voice in management. Their participation is limited to electing corporate directors and voting upon major corporate changes. In addition, shares are freely transferable, with a public market for the shares. Publicly-held corporations must comply with many federal and state regulatory statutes that govern the conduct and operation of larger corporations. The major regulatory statutes primarily affecting large corporations are discussed in detail in Part VIII of this text (Government Regulation of Business).

Despite significant differences between closely- and publicly-held corporations, both are generally organized and operate under the same state corporation statutes governing all corporations. Some states, however, provide special provisions addressing specific problems of closely-held corporations.

Professional Corporations.
The **professional corporation** or association is a closely-held corporation formed by professionals such as doctors, lawyers, accountants, and engineers. All states and the District of Columbia have passed enabling statutes allowing professionals to incorporate. These statutes normally require that all shareholders of the corporation be licensed in the particular profession involved. In addition, the shareholders remain personally liable for their professional acts to third parties. Traditionally, professionals incorporated to take advantage of retirement and other tax advantages available to corporate "employees" but not

---

1. Henn & Alexander, *Laws of Corporations* 5 (3d ed. 1983).

2. Closely-held corporations also are called "close corporations," "closed corporations," and "incorporated partnerships."

self-employed individuals such as proprietors and partners. Federal tax law was amended effective in 1984, however, to provide substantially similar benefits under both self-employed and corporate retirement plans.[3]

Development of American Corporation Law

Unlike a partnership, which may be created by informal agreement of the parties, a corporation is created only by complying with a statute authorizing or enabling business organization in the corporate form. The federal government has no express power to authorize incorporation and has not generally sought to regulate incorporation through its enumerated powers, such as the Commerce Clause. As a result, virtually all modern business corporations are organized under state corporate enabling statutes, often known as "business corporation acts."

In the late 1700s, incorporation was an infrequently used and closely guarded legislative function granted only with specific legislative approval, that is, by "special incorporation." Spurred by the industrial revolution, however, in the early 1800s the states began enacting general incorporation statutes, which allowed persons to form corporations by complying with certain formalities without specific legislative consent.

Early general incorporation statutes often imposed limitations and restrictions regarding corporate size and duration, invested capital, and corporate powers and purposes. These restrictions were effective as long as businesses remained local. With the rise of the railroads and other interstate operations, however, businesses could shop among the various states to find the least restrictive incorporation statute. In the early twentieth century, many states began to "liberalize" their incorporation statutes to attract incorporation business. Liberalization involved, for example, provisions weakening shareholder control, abolishing maximum capitalization and indebtedness requirements, and expanding permissible corporate purposes and powers. To avoid losing incorporation business,

states with restrictive statutes also were forced to relax their statutes.

The state of Delaware is the clear winner of this competition for corporate charters. Since 1899, it has had the most flexible incorporation statute, particularly attractive to large corporations and corporate management. The Delaware bar and legislature also have made a concerted and continuous effort to maintain a well-settled and predictable body of corporate law. Their efforts have been very successful in attracting large corporations. Thirty of the fifty largest American corporations, one-third of the 500 largest corporations, and forty percent of corporations listed on the New York Stock Exchange are incorporated in Delaware. Many states have modeled their business corporation acts upon the Delaware statute.

Although Delaware law has distinct advantages for incorporation of large, publicly-held, interstate businesses, most small businesses are incorporated under the law of the jurisdiction in which their property and principal place of business are located. In many jurisdictions, corporation law is heavily influenced by the **Model Business Corporation Act (MBCA)**, which was drafted by a committee of the American Bar Association. The MBCA was first published as a complete statute in 1950, and is today the basis of, or influenced the drafting of, incorporation statutes in thirty-nine states[4] and the District of Columbia. The Act has been amended many times since its first publication and was completely overhauled and renumbered in 1984 in the **Revised Model Business Corporation Act (RMBCA)**.[5] These model acts are designed to balance the interests of management, the shareholders, corporations, and the public. Recent revi-

---

3. Tax Equity and Fiscal Responsibility Act of 1982, P.L. 97-248, 97th Cong., 2d Sess. (1982).

---

4. Jurisdictions that have statutes based, at least in part, upon the MBCA include Alabama, Alaska, Arizona, Arkansas, Colorado, Connecticut, Florida, Georgia, Hawaii, Idaho, Illinois, Iowa, Kentucky, Louisiana, Maine, Maryland, Massachusetts, Michigan, Mississippi, Montana, Nebraska, New Jersey, New Mexico, New York, North Carolina, North Dakota, Oregon, Rhode Island, South Carolina, South Dakota, Tennessee, Texas, Utah, Vermont, Virginia, Washington, West Virginia, Wisconsin, and Wyoming.

5. The RMBCA, and a conversion table between the MBCA and RMBCA are included in Appendix F. Citations in the footnotes generally include the original section numbers and the corresponding sections in the Revised Act.

sions, however, have become more management-oriented.

Although state competition to attract local incorporation business and the MBCA have tended to promote uniformity in corporate law, substantial differences remain among the various jurisdictions. Even among MBCA jurisdictions, significant differences are found because the Act has been frequently amended and is intended merely as a drafting guide, not a uniform statute. For this reason, this text discusses generally applied corporate law principles, with specific statutory provisions from the MBCA and RMBCA used for illustrative purposes.

The Organizational Form

Before discussing the substantive law of corporations, it is important to examine the differences between a corporation and the unincorporated business organizations to determine when a corporation is the appropriate organizational form.

Comparison of Forms of Business Organization

A person or persons embarking upon a business venture must adopt some organizational form. In most cases, the choices are among (1) a proprietorship, (2) a partnership, (3) a limited partnership, and (4) a corporation. Table 45–1 compares the four organizational forms according to the ease and cost of creation; the ease and cost of operation; the extent of liability of the owners; the method of management and control; the continuity of existence after changes in ownership; the transferability of ownership interest; the ability of the organization to raise additional debt or equity capital; and federal income tax considerations.

Selecting the Organizational Form

Table 45–1 merely highlights the major differences among the various organizational forms. A particular business must, of course, operate in one of the four forms, and selection of that form may or may not involve a conscious choice. For example, a self-employed individual operating a grocery store is a proprietorship. If two brothers jointly operate a landscaping business, a partnership is created. Prudent business planning, however, requires that the owners consciously select the most appropriate form for their particular business.

Generally, no one form is inherently more desirable than another. Nevertheless, because a corporation has substantial organizational and operational formalities and is expensive and cumbersome to create and operate, it should be chosen only after carefully considering the nature and size of the business and the financial, personal, and tax characteristics of the owner or owners. That is, before incorporating, the following factors should be noted.

1. Limited liability is a distinct advantage of the corporate form but it is an advantage that may be overestimated, particularly in a relatively small business. For example, both partners and corporations may obtain insurance against many business risks such as tort liability or casualty to firm assets. In addition, in small corporations lenders often insist that shareholders personally guarantee corporate obligations.

2. As a partnership increases in size, management and control of the business becomes increasingly cumbersome. The limited partnership provides more effective centralization of management by vesting control in the hands of one or a few general partners and effectively excluding (under threat of unlimited liability) limited partners from participation in management. In a limited partnership, however, the managers (the general partners) are participants in the business. If outside management expertise is needed, the corporate form is appropriate. In a corporation, neither the officers nor directors need have any ownership interest in the corporation. In short, if it is desired to centralize management in fewer than all owners or in persons not owners, the corporation is the preferred form.[6]

3. In large corporations, continuity of existence is advantageous because ownership, and often management, are constantly changing. In small businesses, however, the advantage of corporate continuity may be more apparent than real in many

---

6. If the general partner of a limited partnership is itself a corporation, outside managers can be used in the limited partnership setting.

cases. For example, partnership agreements often provide for continuation of the business after events which would otherwise cause dissolution. In addition, in many small businesses death, retirement, bankruptcy, or incapacity of key personnel often effectively terminates the business, regardless of the organizational form used.

4. Although free transferability of ownership interest is an advantage of the corporate form, its value in a small business should not be overestimated. By agreement, partners can also make partnership interests freely transferable. In addition, in a closely-held corporation free transferability may mean little because no ready market may exist for the shares.

5. As a corporation grows in size, its ability to raise large amounts of capital while maintaining centralized management becomes a distinct advantage of corporate form. Various combinations and types of securities may be issued to fit a particular need. In addition, earnings may often be retained in the business to fuel corporate growth with shareholders enjoying appreciated share values rather than current dividend distributions.

6. Federal income tax considerations often are determinative in choice of organizational form. Whether a partnership or corporation is more advantageous from an income tax perspective requires consideration of a number of factors. These include the financial condition, age, and estate plans of the owners; the likely income or loss to be generated by the business; whether some or all owners intend to work in the business; whether income is to be retained in the business or distributed; and whether some investors' contributions are to be treated as loans rather than capital contributions.

To Incorporate or Not to Incorporate? Various distinctive attributes, such as centralization of management, free transferability of interest, perpetual existence, and limited liability are characteristic of the corporate form. These and other factors make the corporation an ideal device for large business. For small businesses, however, the apparent advantages of corporate form often are illusory. Centralized management, transferability of interest, and business continuity, can, if desired, be provided by agreement in a partnership. Corporate limited liability may be of little value if creditors require the

shareholders to personally guarantee corporate obligations. Creating and operating a corporation involves cost, complexity, and formality not present in a partnership. In short, the corporation often is not the most desirable form for small business. Incorporation is perhaps most commonly indicated if limited liability is an important consideration and is reasonably attainable in corporate form and federal income tax consequences are favorable.

Preincorporation Transactions

If the parties decide that a corporation is appropriate, they must take affirmative steps to bring the corporation into existence. Because a corporation is a creature of statute, corporate existence requires compliance with statutory procedures in the jurisdiction chosen for incorporation. Before these steps are taken and, therefore, before corporate existence begins, the person or persons organizing and planning the corporation, known as **promoters**, often enter into contracts or other transactions on behalf of the corporation yet to be formed. Promoters' activities include, for example, discovering and developing the business opportunity, arranging the necessary capital, obtaining the property and personnel required to conduct the business, and complying with the statutory formalities for forming the corporation.

The corporation may be formed before activities on its behalf are taken. In this case, authorized contracts made in the corporate name are binding upon the corporation but not the promoter under ordinary principles of agency. Frequently, however, the corporation is not yet in existence during the promotional stage. In this case, the law must determine (1) to what extent the promoters are personally liable upon contracts made with third parties on behalf of the corporation, and (2) to what extent the corporation, upon coming into existence, is liable upon contracts made by the promoters. Basic principles, borrowed generally from the law of agency and contracts, govern these issues.

Promoters' Liability

A promoter who contracts on behalf of a corporation not yet formed, without disclosing that fact, is personally liable on the contract. In addition, a pro-

	Table 45-1	Comparison of Forms of Business Organization		
	Proprietorship	*Partnership*	*Limited Partnership*	*Corporation*
Ease and cost of creation	Proprietorship is automatically created when there is one owner and no other form is selected.	Partnership is automatically created when there are two or more owners and no other form is selected.	Limited partnership is created by complying with state statute authorizing limited partnership form. Detailed documents must be filed with appropriate public officials.	Corporation is created by complying with state statute authorizing corporate form. Detailed documents must be filed with appropriate public officials.
Ease and cost of operation	Proprietorship operates under few legal restraints.	Partnership operates under few legal restraints.	Limited partnership operates under more restrictions than partnership. For example, certificate of limited partnership must periodically be amended to reflect changes in capitalization or composition.	Operations are subject to substantial legal formality. For example, corporate minutes must be kept; meetings and elections must be held; franchise, share transfer, and other taxes must be paid; a registered office and agent must be maintained; and if the corporation does business in another state, it must qualify there as a foreign corporation.
Extent of liability	Proprietor has unlimited personal liability for all business debts and obligations.	Partners have unlimited personal liability for all business debts and obligations.	General partners have unlimited personal liabilities for all business debts and obligations; limited partners' liability is limited to the extent of their investment in the business unless they participate in management and control or allow their names to be used in the firm name.	Corporate shareholders are liable only to the extent of their investment in the business, and may also participate in management if they are officers or directors of the corporation.
Management and control	Proprietor has exclusive right to manage the business.	Absent contrary agreement, all partners have equal voice in management.	Control is vested in one or more general partners; limited partners are excluded from participation in management under threat of unlimited liability.	Centralized management is created when shareholders elect directors who appoint officers to manage business.

Table 45–1   (continued)

	Proprietorship	Partnership	Limited Partnership	Corporation
Continuity of existence	Proprietorship ceases when the proprietor dies or abandons the business.	Partnership is dissolved by death or withdrawal of a partner and a variety of other events, but continuity may be provided by agreement.	Partnership is dissolved by death or withdrawal of a partner and a variety of other events, but continuity may be provided by agreement.	A corporation, as a legal entity, possesses perpetual existence unless terminated in a manner prescribed by law.
Transferability of interest	Proprietor's interest is freely transferable.	Absent contrary agreement, partner may not transfer entire interest without consent of other partners.	Transferability is similar to a partnership, but the partnership agreement may allow a limited partner to confer limited partnership status upon a transferee.	Ownership interests in a corporation, evidenced by shares of stock, may generally be freely sold, assigned, or otherwise transferred.
Access to capital	Credit is available to the extent of the value of assets committed to business and the personal assets of the proprietor.	Credit is available to extent of value of assets committed to business and the personal assets of the partners. New equity investment requires admitting new partners which dilutes control.	Limited partnership may attract additional equity by selling additional limited partnership interests without diluting control of general partners.	In a small corporation, credit availability is generally similar to a partnership. As a corporation grows in size, substantial corporate assets, a public market for its shares, free transferability of its securities, and predictable limited liability of investors facilitate corporate expansion through issuance of debt or equity securities without diluting control.
Income tax considerations	Proprietor's business income or loss combined with other income or loss and taxed on the proprietor's individual return.	Partnership pays no tax, but files an information return indicating each partner's proportionate share of profit or loss. Respective shares of income or loss are then included on each partner's individual return.	Tax treatment is similar to general partnership.	Corporation is an entity for tax purposes, leading to "double taxation." Its income is taxed to the corporation on a corporation tax return and again to the shareholders on their individual returns when later distributed as dividends.

moter who represents that the corporation is in existence, when in fact it is not, incurs personal liability to the third party for breach of the warranty of competent principal made by agents generally, or upon misrepresentation grounds. More commonly, however, a promoter contracts for the corporation and discloses to the third party that the corporation is not yet formed. In this case, the result depends upon how the parties characterize the transaction. For example, the promoter might escape personal liability if the arrangement is framed as a revocable or irrevocable offer running to the corporation, to be accepted or rejected after formation. Or the arrangement may provide that the promoter is initially bound but will be released if the corporation is later formed and assumes liability on the contract.[7] Alternatively, the parties may provide that the promoter remains liable, even if the corporation is formed and assumes liability on the contract. To avoid litigation, the extent of the promoter's undertaking should be carefully drafted into the agreement between the promoter and third party.

Corporate Liability Upon Promoters' Contracts

The corporation, upon coming into existence, is not immediately liable upon promoters' contracts. That is, the promoter cannot bind the corporation as its agent because the corporation (the principal) was not in existence when the contract was made. For the same reason, the corporation does not generally incur liability by "ratifying" promoters' contracts, as that term is used in agency law. Rather, the corporation becomes liable by "accepting" the third party's offer, or "adopting" or "assuming" the contract, or by taking an "assignment" of the contract from the promoter. However characterized, corporate liability requires some affirmative act by the corporation indicating its assent to the preincorporation transaction.

Promoters' Fiduciary Duties

Frequently, two or more persons are actively involved in promoting a corporation. During the promotional stage, co-promoters are treated as joint venturers or partners, and therefore owe each other the strict fiduciary duties of fair dealing and disclosure generally existing among partners. Promoters also owe similar fiduciary duties to the corporation and its shareholders after incorporation. For example, a promoter who sells property to the corporation in exchange for stock or cash owes duties of good faith, fair dealing, and full disclosure to the corporation's board of directors and shareholders. Secret profits obtained by the promoter in violation of these duties may be recovered by the corporation.

A promoter may provide full disclosure to parties involved with the corporation at the time of the transaction (or when the promoter is the sole shareholder), but not to persons *subsequently* investing in or lending money to the corporation as part of the original promotion plan. These parties may later assert that the promoters' services or property were overvalued. In this situation, the authorities are split, but the trend appears to allow recovery by later parties in the absence of full disclosure.

The following case illustrates the nature of a promoter's duty to the corporation and its shareholders.

Golden v. Oahe Enterprises, Inc.
295 N.W.2d 160 (S.D. 1980)

In October 1966, Donald Emmick and J. B. Morris incorporated Oahe Enterprises, Inc. to operate a ranch owned by Morris. Morris contributed the ranch to the corporation in exchange for Oahe stock. Emmick contributed 6,315 shares of Colonial Manors, Inc. stock (CM stock) in exchange for Oahe stock. Emmick represented that the CM stock was worth $19 per share and the number of shares of Oahe stock issued to Emmick was based on this value. Later in 1966, Warren Golden became a shareholder of Oahe. By 1970, Emmick had purchased all of the shares of Oahe stock except those owned by Golden.

---

7. That is, the promoter and third party may contract in advance for a novation, releasing the promoter and substituting the corporation.

In 1974, the South Dakota Supreme Court ordered that Oahe be dissolved and that the corporate assets be distributed between Golden and Emmick in proportions based on the number of shares owned by each. Golden argued that Emmick had obtained his original shares in Oahe through fraud and misrepresentation because the true value of the CM stock had been far less than $19 per share. The trial court held that Emmick had not committed fraud. Golden appealed.

Wollman, Chief Justice

. . . As we interpret it, Golden's real complaint is that Emmick was allowed to use as the value of his CM stock a value arbitrarily affixed by the CM board of directors for a strictly internal purpose—that of raising badly needed funds for CM by offering stock options at a desperate juncture in its corporate life. This value admittedly bore no relationship to the book value of CM stock, which the trial court found to be forty-seven cents per share. Emmick admitted that he used for his valuation of CM stock the internal stock option price set by the CM board of directors. Yet when that same board reduced the CM stock option price to $9.50 per share on September 16, 1966, a fact Emmick knew, this reduction was not reflected in the value Emmick set on the CM shares transferred into Oahe a month and a half later. . . .

[W]here a promoter through . . . overvaluation of property exchanged for stock and failure to disclose all material facts regarding such exchange, takes more from the corporation than he transfers in, he is held liable for what courts term secret profit. . . .

As a promoter of Oahe, Emmick stood in a fiduciary relationship to both the corporation and its stockholders and was bound to deal with them in the utmost good faith. "The obtaining of a secret profit by a promoter through the sale of property to a corporation is uniformly held to be a fraud on the corporation and stockholders, and the promoter may be required to account for such profit." Annot., 84 A.L.R.3d 163, 164, §2[a] (1978).

The valuation of the CM stock was based on Emmick's self-serving estimate of matters well known to him as a CM insider and was warped by Emmick's self-interest. Emmick was not trading stock that had an easily ascertainable value; he was not dealing with people experienced in transactions of this type. He failed to make known facts of which he, as an insider of CM, was aware. . . . In addition to being an insider of CM, he was both a director of and the dominant and controlling force in Oahe. We hold, therefore, that he failed in his duty to the corporation to disclose information regarding stock he intended to transfer into Oahe for Oahe shares and is therefore liable for the shortfall to the corporation therefrom.

We conclude that the CM stock that Emmick transferred into Oahe was greatly overvalued at its $19.00 per share figure. . . .

The $19.00 per share valuation had no basis in fact and was meaningless except as an internal stock option price for sale to CM shareholders. Accordingly, we hold that the trial court erred in concluding that the value set by Emmick on the CM stock in the Emmick/Oahe transaction of $19.00 per share did not constitute fraud, deceit or misrepresentation. . . .

Because the total value of the CM stock Emmick transferred to Oahe was less than the value Emmick received in Oahe stock, the difference can be equalized by canceling the number of Oahe shares held by Emmick that is proportional to the overvaluation. . . .

[Judgment reversed and remanded.]

Incorporation and Admission

During the promotional stage of any corporation, often after preliminary arrangements for corporate capital, assets, and personnel have been made, the promoter or promoters must arrange for formation of the corporation. Once the corporation is created, the parties must also take steps to qualify it to do business in states outside the jurisdiction chosen for incorporation.

Procedures for Incorporation

Although the details vary among the states, the basic procedure for incorporation is similar. One or more persons (who may be corporations themselves), known as *incorporators,* prepare a document usually known as the *articles of incorporation.*[8] The articles of incorporation are then filed, together with any necessary fee, with an appropriate state official, usually the secretary of state, who reviews the application. If the articles conform to legal requirements, the secretary will issue a *certificate of incorporation.* Typically, corporate existence begins either when the secretary of state issues the certificate or on the date the articles are filed. In some states, additional requirements must be met, such as filing or recording in a local office or publishing the articles in a newspaper.

Contents of Articles. The articles of incorporation must contain certain information prescribed by statute. In many states, official forms for the articles are used. Although the contents of the articles vary among the states and modern corporate statutes tend to minimize the mandatory requirements of the articles,[9] the following information is typically required: (1) the name of the corporation, (2) its duration, (3) the purpose or purposes for which the corporation is organized, (4) information concerning shares of stock including the number authorized, the designation of classes of stock, and rights and preferences of shares or shareholders, (5) the address of the registered office and the name of the corporation's registered agent, (6) the number, names, and addresses of the initial board of directors, and (7) the name and address of each incorporator.[10] In addition to mandatory information, the articles may contain provisions concerning regulation of the internal affairs of the corporation. The following material elaborates upon certain typical provisions of the articles.

Corporate Name. Generally the corporate name must include language indicating corporate form such as ''corporation,'' ''company,'' ''incorporated,'' or ''limited,'' and may not be the same as or deceptively similar to any other corporate name. Secretaries of state generally maintain lists of existing corporate names against which new corporate applications are checked. The prohibition against deceptively similar names is designed to prevent unfair competition.

Corporate names are generally allocated on a first-come, first-served basis. Many corporation statutes, however, permit reservation of available corporate names for a limited period.[11]

Corporate Duration. Some older corporation statutes limited corporate duration. Virtually all modern statutes permit perpetual corporate existence, which often is presumed unless a limited period of duration is stated in the articles.

Corporate Purposes. Although many statutes require that corporate purposes be fully stated, the modern trend is to authorize extremely broad corporate purposes clauses. For example, the MBCA states that corporate purposes ''may be stated to be, or to include, the transaction of any or all lawful business for which corporations may be incorporated under this Act.''[12] The RMBCA does not even require that the articles contain a purposes clause, but simply presumes that every corporation is organized to conduct any lawful business unless a narrower purpose is outlined in the articles of incorporation.[13]

Registered Office and Agent. A corporation is required to maintain a registered office with a registered agent in the state of incorporation. The registered office need not be the corporation's place of business. The registered agent is the corporation's agent to receive service of process on the corpora-

---

8. Traditionally, at least three natural persons were required to act as incorporators. Modern statutes, however, typically require only one incorporator, who may be either a natural person or a corporation. See, for example, MBCA §53, RMBCA §2.01.

9. See, for example, RMBCA §2.02(a).

10. This list is drawn from MBCA §54.

---

11. For example, the Model Business Corporation Act allows names to be reserved, upon application to the secretary of state, for a nonrenewable 120-day period. See MBCA §9, RMBCA §4.02.

12. MBCA §54.

13. RMBCA §§2.02(b), 3.01(a). Certain purposes, however, are beyond the scope of even a broadly drafted purposes clause. For example, banks and insurance companies are regulated under separate statutes and may therefore not be incorporated under the state's general business corporation act. MBCA §3, RMBCA §3.01(b).

tion, other notices or demands, and official communications from the state. If a corporation fails to maintain a registered agent, under the MBCA the secretary of state becomes its agent for these purposes. Under the RMBCA, such a corporation may be served by registered or certified mail, addressed to the secretary of the corporation at its principal office. Changes in the registered office or agent may be made by filing a statement outlining the change with the secretary of state.[14]

Organization of the Corporation. After issuance of the certificate of incorporation, the directors named in the articles hold a meeting to complete the organization of the corporation. If directors are not named in the articles, the incorporators hold the meeting.[15] This meeting is often orchestrated by the parties' attorney, with minutes prepared in advance to assure that all necessary legal formalities have been met. At the meeting, typically, directors are formally elected, officers are appointed to manage the corporation, preincorporation contracts are adopted or rejected, shares of stock are issued and consideration for shares is established, a resolution is made opening a corporate bank account that designates the persons authorized to sign checks, and a corporate seal is adopted. In addition, corporate bylaws, if desired, are adopted.

Bylaws are a set of rules governing the corporation's internal affairs. Bylaws may contain any provision for the management of corporate affairs not inconsistent with law or the articles of incorporation. Unlike the articles of incorporation, the bylaws are not filed with the secretary of state.[16] Generally, the power to make, alter, amend, or repeal any bylaw is vested in the board of directors unless reserved to the shareholders in the articles of incor-

poration.[17] Bylaws generally may be amended much more easily than the articles of incorporation.

Corporate Powers

Statutory Powers. To implement the corporate purposes stated in the articles of incorporation, every state corporation statute includes an extensive list of powers possessed by businesses incorporated in the jurisdiction. For example, the MBCA provides that each corporation has the power

1. to have perpetual existence, unless limited in the articles of incorporation;
2. to sue, be sued, and defend in the corporate name;
3. to acquire, own, hold, improve, and use any interest in either real or personal property including stocks or bonds;
4. to sell, convey, mortgage, pledge, lease, or otherwise transfer any or all of its property;
5. to lend money and take a security interest in either real or personal property to secure its repayment;
6. to make contracts and guarantees (that is, act as a surety), to borrow money and issue notes, bonds, or other obligations that may be secured by corporate assets;
7. to make charitable contributions;
8. to be the member of any partnership or joint venture;
9. to exercise other powers necessary and convenient to effect its purposes including the power to conduct its business, maintain offices, elect officers and directors, adopt bylaws regulating its internal affairs, and establish pensions, profit-sharing, and other incentive plans for its officers, directors, and employees.

This enumeration gives a corporation virtually the same powers as a natural person.[18] Although not always legally required,[19] articles of incorporation often include powers clauses which restate or ex-

---

14. See, for example, MBCA §§12-14, RMBCA §§5.01-5.04. Note that under the MBCA, a secretary of state who receives service of process for a corporation that fails to maintain a registered agent is required to forward a copy by registered mail to the corporation's registered office.

15. MBCA §57, RMBCA §2.05.

16. Nevertheless, the articles often address, as optional provisions, matters which are or could be covered in the bylaws. Conversely, provisions of the articles of incorporation are often repeated in the bylaws. In the event of conflict, provisions of the articles of incorporation control.

17. MBCA §27, RMBCA §§2.06, 10.20.

18. MBCA §4, RMBCA §3.02.

19. See, for example, MBCA §54, RMBCA §2.02(c).

pand upon the statutory list, or provide more limited corporate powers.

"Ultra Vires" Acts. A corporation which acts beyond the scope of its powers or stated purposes acts **ultra vires.** *Ultra vires* acts include both those expressly prohibited and those in excess of granted powers or purposes. Traditionally, ultra vires corporate contracts, if fully performed, would not be rescinded. If the contract was wholly executory, however, ultra vires provided a good defense to enforcement by either party. If the contract was partially executed, an ultra vires defense remained, but relief in restitution (quasi-contract) was available to recover the value of the benefit conferred by the part performance. The courts applied these rules erratically and often defeated the legitimate expectations of the parties. As a result, modern corporation law severely limits the use of the ultra vires defense.

Because modern corporation statutes authorize extremely general purposes clauses (for example, "the transaction of any or all lawful business"), few corporate activities are ultra vires. In addition, even if corporate purposes or powers are restricted, the MBCA and many state statutes provide that no corporate act or conveyance is invalid because the corporation lacked the power to act, except in three limited circumstances. These circumstances include (1) a suit by a shareholder against the corporation to enjoin it from doing an act, (2) a proceeding by the corporation against incumbent or former officers or directors for their unauthorized acts, and (3) a suit by the state attorney general to dissolve the corporation or to enjoin it from transacting unauthorized business.[20]

Admission of Foreign Corporations

A corporation organized under the laws of a given state is referred to as a **domestic corporation** in that state. For example, in Illinois, a corporation incorporated under the laws of Illinois is a domestic corporation. If such a corporation does business in another state, it is referred to as a **foreign corporation** in that state. Thus, an Illinois corporation

doing business in Indiana is a foreign corporation in Indiana. Because corporate status is a privilege granted by state law, foreign corporations must qualify to do business in states outside the state of incorporation. In order to qualify, the corporation must obtain a "certificate of authority" from the secretary of state of each state in which it is a foreign corporation.[21]

To obtain a certificate of authority, the foreign corporation must generally file an application with the secretary of state. The foreign corporation also must file a verified copy of its articles of incorporation and pay all required fees or taxes. If the application is in order, the secretary of state will issue the certificate that authorizes the corporation to transact business in the state for the purposes set forth in the application.[22]

Once authorized to do business, the foreign corporation must continuously maintain both a registered office and a registered agent in the state.[23] Under the MBCA, if the foreign corporation fails to maintain a registered agent in the state or if its certificate of authority has been suspended or revoked, the corporation automatically appoints the secretary of state as its agent to receive service of process.[24] Under the RMBCA, such a foreign corporation may be served by registered or certified mail, addressed to the secretary of the corporation at its principal office.

Until it obtains a certificate of authority, a foreign corporation is denied the use of the courts of the state: it is not permitted to maintain any action or suit in the state with respect to its business. Failure to obtain the certificate does not, however, prevent it from defending a suit in the state, and does not impair the validity of any contract the corporation makes. A foreign corporation that transacts business without a certificate of authority is liable for all fees or franchise taxes that would have been

---

20. MBCA §7, RMBCA §3.04.

21. See, for example, MBCA §106, RMBCA §15.01.

22. See generally MBCA §§110-112, RMBCA §§15.03, 15.05.

23. See generally MBCA §§113, 115, RMBCA §§15.07, 15.10.

24. Under the MBCA, a secretary of state who receives service of process in this manner is generally required to forward a copy by registered mail to the corporation's principal office in the state where it was incorporated. See MBCA §115.

imposed if the corporation had obtained the certificate, and all penalties imposed for failure to pay the fees or taxes. Proceedings to recover these amounts are brought by the state attorney general.[25]

At issue in the following case was whether a corporation's activities within a state constituted "doing business," requiring it to qualify as a foreign corporation.

Goodwin Brothers Leasing, Inc. v. Nousis
366 N.E.2d 38 (Mass. 1977)

Plaintiff Goodwin Brothers Leasing, Inc. (Goodwin), a Kentucky corporation, leased a pressure fryer to defendant Katherine Nousis who operated a pizza parlor in Massachusetts. After Nousis defaulted in making the lease payments, Goodwin sued her in a Massachusetts trial court. The court ruled in favor of Goodwin and awarded it damages.

Chapter 181, §4 of the Massachusetts General Laws requires foreign corporations doing business in Massachusetts to file a certificate of registration. Corporations that fail to comply with the registration requirement are barred from filing lawsuits in the Massachusetts courts.

Nousis appealed on the ground that Goodwin's failure to file a certificate of registration barred it from filing suit against her. The court of appeals affirmed the trial court's ruling in favor of Goodwin. Nousis appealed to the Massachusetts Supreme Judicial Court.

Abrams, Justice

. . . [A] State cannot constitutionally require a foreign corporation to obtain a certificate of authority to do business in the State if its participation in the trade is limited to wholly interstate business. . . . Moreover a State cannot properly bar a foreign corporation's access to its courts where that corporation is engaged solely in interstate commerce. . . .

Given these limitations on the legislative power . . . , we conclude that the activities engaged in by Goodwin do not constitute doing business in a manner which would invoke the filing requirements of c.181, §4.

Intrastate commerce cannot be distinguished from its interstate counterpart by reference to any precise rule. Resolution of the question is dependent on the facts and circumstances of each particular case. . . . We must, however, look beyond the individual transaction which gave rise to the present controversy, as all the corporation's activity within the Commonwealth should be scrutinized prior to making that determination. . . . We note additionally, that the constitutionally required minimal in-State contacts for purposes of subjecting a foreign corporation to the State's qualification requirements are greater than the contacts required for purposes of long-arm jurisdiction. . . .

We review the salient features of Goodwin's business involvement within the Commonwealth. Goodwin is a duly incorporated Kentucky corporation engaged in the business of leasing equipment throughout the country. It has no usual place of business in Massachusetts; it does not have any employees located here; and it maintains no inventory of goods within the Commonwealth. Goodwin does not solicit potential lessees of its equipment in Massachusetts. Instead, it solicits business from manufacturers who themselves find customers interested in obtaining the equipment; as a means of financing, the manufacturer sells the item to Goodwin which in turn leases the equipment to the customers which the manufacturer has already found. Goodwin's bills are mailed from offices in Kentucky, and rental payments are sent by its customers to the same address. At present, Goodwin maintains similar arrangements in Massachusetts for the rental of two other pressure frying machines.

On the basis of the above recited facts, we do not believe that the provisions of c.181 apply to operations similar to the one under present scrutiny. Goodwin is engaged only in interstate commerce, and the several machines which it owns and leases out within the Commonwealth are mere incidents of its interstate business. . . .

[Judgment affirmed.]

25. See MBCA §124, RMBCA §15.02.

Recognition or Disregard of Corporate Form

One purpose of incorporating is to insulate the shareholders from unlimited personal liability for corporate obligations. Corporation law, however, through the doctrines of "de facto incorporation" and "corporation by estoppel," occasionally provides limited liability to persons who do business as a corporation without complying with corporate formalities. On the other hand, in some instances, courts "pierce the corporate veil" to impose personal liability on shareholders of a duly formed corporation. These problems of recognition or disregard of corporate form are discussed below.

Defective Incorporation

A **de jure corporation** is one formed in compliance with all mandatory state requirements. A *de jure* corporation is recognized as a corporation for all purposes and its existence is not subject to attack either by the state or by creditors.

The incorporators may, however, attempt to comply with the provisions authorizing corporate status but fail in some respect, resulting either in delay in or failure of corporate formation. For example, the secretary of state may return the initial application to correct a technical defect, or the parties may prepare but inadvertently fail to file the articles. Despite the problem, the parties conduct business as a corporation. Subsequently, firm creditors seek to hold the shareholders personally liable as partners for business debts, citing the defective incorporation. In this situation the common law has recognized two doctrines to protect shareholders of the defectively organized corporation: the "de facto incorporation doctrine" and "corporation by estoppel."

Under the traditional test, a **de facto corporation** is created if (1) an enabling statute exists permitting corporate form, (2) the parties have made a good faith effort to comply with the statute, and (3) the parties subsequently conduct business as a corporation. If these requirements are met, only the state can challenge corporate existence. Third parties, such as creditors, may not assert lack of cor-

porate status as a basis to impose personal liability on the owners.

Another common law doctrine used to insulate owners of defectively organized corporations is **corporation by estoppel.** This doctrine has been applied, for example, when a third party transacts business with a corporation, unaware of its defective organization and relying solely upon the corporation's credit. Subsequently, after discovering that a corporation has not been formed, the third party seeks to hold the promoters or shareholders personally liable on the obligation as partners. On these facts, the third party is often estopped, or prevented, from holding the owners personally liable. Courts have reasoned that it is unjust to allow a person who has relied only upon corporate credit to impose personal liability upon shareholders and promoters, especially when the failure of incorporation was not caused by negligence or willful failure to comply with statutory requirements.

The problem of defective incorporation often is addressed explicitly by statute. For example, under the MBCA and many state statutes, issuance of the certificate by the secretary of state begins corporate existence and is conclusive evidence that all conditions precedent to proper incorporation have been met. Subsequently, corporate existence may be attacked only by the state in a proceeding to cancel or revoke the certificate of incorporation or for involuntary dissolution of the corporation.[26] Under this approach, if the secretary of state accepts the filing and issues the certificate, a de jure corporation is created, despite technical defects in the filing. Because any steps short of obtaining a certificate of incorporation do not constitute substantial or apparent compliance, a number of courts have concluded that the MBCA and similar statutes have abolished both the de facto incorporation doctrine and corporation by estoppel principles.

The following case illustrates the traditional approach to a defective incorporation problem.

---

26. MBCA §56, RMBCA §2.03. Note that under the RMBCA, corporate existence begins when the articles of incorporation are filed. The secretary of state's filing of the articles is conclusive proof that all conditions precedent to proper incorporation have been met.

Cantor v. Sunshine Greenery, Inc.

398 A.2d 571 (N.J. Super. 1979)

On December 16, 1974, plaintiffs Edward Cantor and Leo Masin agreed to lease a building to Sunshine Greenery, Inc. Plaintiffs prepared a lease naming Sunshine Greenery, Inc. as tenant, which defendant William J. Brunetti, as president of Sunshine Greenery, Inc., signed. The corporation defaulted in paying the lease. Plaintiffs sued Sunshine Greenery, Inc. and Brunetti for damages.

Plaintiffs alleged that Brunetti should be held liable on the lease because at the time the lease was signed, the certificate of incorporation for Sunshine Greenery, Inc. had not been officially filed with the secretary of state. The evidence showed Brunetti had mailed the certificate to the secretary of state on December 3, 1974, but that the secretary of state's office had not filed the certificate until December 18, 1974.

The trial court held Brunetti individually liable on the lease. Brunetti appealed.

Larner, Judge Appellate Division

. . . In view of the late filing, Sunshine Greenery, Inc. was not a *de jure* corporation on December 16, 1974 when the lease was signed. . . . Nevertheless, there is ample evidence of the fact that it was a *de facto* corporation in that there was a *bona fide* attempt to organize the corporation some time before the consummation of the contract and there was an actual exercise of the corporate powers by the negotiations with plaintiffs and the execution of the contract involved in this litigation. When this is considered in the light of the concession that plaintiffs knew that they were dealing with that corporate entity and not with Brunetti individually, it becomes evident that the *de facto* status of the corporation suffices to absolve Brunetti from individual liability. Plaintiffs in effect are estopped from attacking the legal existence of the corporation collaterally because of the nonfiling in order to impose liability on the individual when they have admittedly contracted with a corporate entity which had de facto status. . . .

Although Cantor had considerable experience in ownership and leasing of commercial property to individuals and corporations, he did not request a personal guarantee from Brunetti, nor did he make inquiry as to his financial status or background. Without question, he knew and expected that the lease agreement was undertaken by the corporation and not by Brunetti individually, and that the corporation would be responsible thereunder. . . .

To deny [the existence of a *de facto* corporation] because of a mere technicality caused by administrative delay in filing runs counter to the purpose of the *de facto* concept, and would accomplish an unjust and inequitable result in favor of plaintiffs contrary to their own contractual expectations. . . .

[Judgment reversed and remanded.]

Disregarding Corporate Existence— "Piercing the Corporate Veil"

Because the basic purpose of corporate form is limited liability, courts generally recognize the separate legal existence of a corporation formed in full compliance with state law. Accordingly, if a corporation incurs obligations in excess of its assets, creditors' claims usually are satisfied only out of corporate property, however limited. If, however, unfairness or injustice will result if shareholders are permitted to hide behind the corporate form, courts disregard the corporate entity, or "pierce the corporate veil," to impose personal liability upon shareholders for corporate obligations.

Cases that impose shareholder responsibility for corporate debt often include some or all of the following characteristics: (1) insufficient capital contributed to the business in relation to the nature of the business and its risks, (2) excessive fragmentation of a single business into separate corporations, (3) failure to observe corporate formalities, such as meetings and issuance of stock, (4) failure to separate corporate from shareholder affairs, such as failure to keep separate corporate records, commingling shareholder and corporate assets, or paying personal debts with corporate assets (or vice versa), or (5) evidence of affirmative wrongdoing or fraud such as creating the corporation to avoid an existing obligation or siphoning off corporate funds by a dominant shareholder. Cases on piercing the corporate veil most commonly arise in one-person, family, or other closely-held corporations (for example, when the corporation is used merely as a facade for the shareholders' personal dealings) and in subsidiary or other affiliated corporations (for example, when a corporation uses an undercapitalized subsidiary to undertake a particularly risky venture).

The corporate claim asserted against the shareholders may result either from a contract between the creditor and the corporation, or from a tort committed by the corporation. For example, a person injured in an auto accident by the negligent driving of a corporate agent may seek to recover from the corporation. Courts are more reluctant to pierce the corporate veil in contract cases than in tort cases. A contract claimant deals with the corporation voluntarily and may be able to secure the personal guarantee of shareholders on corporate debts. If corporate credit is unacceptable and shareholders refuse to incur personal liability, the third party may refuse to deal with the corporation. Tort claimants, on the other hand, are involuntary creditors. Their claims may easily be frustrated by undercapitalized, underinsured corporations. In these cases, courts are more likely to impose personal responsibility upon the shareholders.

In the following contract case, the court was required to decide whether a shareholder should be held personally liable on a corporate obligation.

Victoria Elevator Company of Minneapolis v. Meriden Grain Co.

283 N.W.2d 509 (Minn. 1979)

Defendant Harold Schroeder operated Schroeder's Cashway, a sole proprietorship that sold feed, seed, and other agricultural products. In 1969, Schroeder entered into an agreement with Gerald Robinson and Paul Soli by which they agreed to form a corporation to be called Meriden Grain Co. Although the corporation was formed, Robinson and Soli failed to contribute any capital and Schroeder and his wife became the sole shareholders of Meriden. Schroeder contributed cash and the inventory of Schroeder's Cashway to the corporation. In 1972, Meriden built two grain storage bins. The Schroeders owned all

other property used by the corporation including land, buildings, machinery, and equipment. In some tax returns and financial statements prepared by Meriden, these assets were listed as corporate property.

Plaintiff Victoria Elevator Co. entered into fourteen contracts to purchase corn from Meriden. After Meriden failed to perform the contracts, Victoria Elevator sued Meriden and was awarded damages in August 1974. In September and November 1974, Meriden transferred ownership of the grain storage bins to the Schroeders and to Meriden Farm Center. The trial court "pierced the corporate veil" and held that Schroeder was personally liable for the judgment owed to Victoria Elevator. Schroeder appealed.

Yetka, Justice

. . . [F]raud may often be cited as a ground for disregarding the corporate entity, but it is not the only ground for such a finding. Courts have also relied upon the "alter ego" or "instrumentality" theory to impose liability on an individual shareholder. . . . Factors considered significant in the determination include: insufficient capitalization for purposes of corporate undertaking, failure to observe corporate formalities, nonpayment of dividends, insolvency of debtor corporation at time of transaction in question, siphoning of funds by dominant shareholder, nonfunctioning of other officers and directors, absence of corporate records, and existence of corporation as merely facade for individual dealings. . . .

Disregard of the corporate entity requires not only that a number of these factors be present, but also that there be an element of injustice or fundamental unfairness. . . . Where the above factors are present, to allow an individual to escape liability because he does his business under a corporate form is to allow him an advantage he does not deserve. Doing business in a corporate form in order to limit individual liability is not wrong; it is, in fact, one purpose for incorporating. But where the formalities of corporate existence are disregarded by one seeking to use it, corporate existence cannot be allowed to shield the individual from liability for damages incurred by those dealing with the corporation.

In the instant case, we have an individual who

did not clearly distinguish between property owned by himself as an individual and property owned by the corporation. He combined the tax returns of the corporation and his sole proprietorship, using the wrong forms for both. He allowed the corporation to take deductions for depreciation on property not owned by the corporation. The corporation paid no rent for its use of property owned by defendant as an individual. He misrepresented corporate assets to state and federal agencies. Defendant withdrew funds (allegedly as wages) from the corporation at a time when the corporation was in financial trouble.

Other facts of defendant's conduct also support finding him individually liable. Although the defendant observed corporate formality by holding shareholders' and directors' meetings and issuing stock certificates, he failed to make formal distinctions between corporate and individual property. There are no documents clearly indicating transfer of individual property to the corporation. Even the cash contributions to the corporation were not clearly marked. The corporation paid no dividends. Only defendant managed the corporation; voting at meetings by defendant and his wife was apparently a mere formality.

It is clear from the evidence in this case that defendant did not treat the corporation as a separate entity. He lent it the use of his money and property—sometimes calling it a loan, sometimes calling it a transfer of assets, rarely making a formal record of the transaction. In a letter . . . in Nober 1969, he stated that the business had incorporated and was going under a new name: "Meriden is run the same as before and everything is the same as before except name only. P. S. We have just transferred our assets over to Meriden Grain so there should be no problem." This letter seems to suggest that defendant thought only the name had changed. His method of filing his tax returns and of moving money in and out of the two businesses indicates that he did not differentiate between the sole proprietorship and the corporation. Since defendant did not treat the corporation as a separate legal entity, he should not be entitled to its protection against personal liability. . . .

[Judgment affirmed.]

In the following case, the court was required to determine whether a parent corporation should be held liable for torts committed by its subsidiary.

United States v. Jon-T Chemicals, Inc.
768 F.2d 686 (5th Cir. 1985)

Defendant Jon-T Chemicals, Inc. (Chemicals) was incorporated in 1969 as a fertilizer and chemicals business. In 1971, Chemicals formed Jon-T Farms, Inc. (Farms) as a wholly-owned subsidiary corporation to engage in farming and land-leasing. Chemicals invested $10,000 as its capital contribution. From 1970 through 1973, John H. Thomas served as president and chairman of the boards of both corporations and the directors and officers of Chemicals also served in the same positions with Farms. Farms used Chemicals's offices, computer and accountant without paying any fee and Chemicals paid the salary of Farms's only employee. Chemicals also made numerous informal advances to Farms to pay its expenses.

In 1972 and 1973, Thomas and other business associates formed two cotton farming ventures that leased land from Farms. On behalf of the ventures, Thomas and Farms submitted fraudulent applications for federal agricultural subsidies and the ventures received approximately $2.5 million in subsidies from the federal government. Subsequently, the plaintiff United States sued Thomas and Farms for false representations and conversion and obtained a judgment of $4.7 million. After Thomas and Farms became insolvent, the federal government sought to hold Chemicals liable, alleging that Farms was the alter ego of Chemicals. The trial court ruled in favor of the United States and pierced the corporate veil to hold Chemicals, as owner of Farms, liable for $4.7 million. Chemicals appealed.

Goldberg, Circuit Judge
. . . Under the doctrine of limited liability, the owner of a corporation is not liable for the corporation's debts. Creditors of the corporation have recourse only against the corporation itself, not against its parent company or shareholders. . . .

While limited liability remains the norm in American corporation law, certain equitable exceptions to the doctrine have developed. The most common exception is for fraud. . . . Another exception arises where, as here, a parent company totally dominates and controls its subsidiary, operating the subsidiary as its business conduit or agent. . . . In such cases, the subsidiary is considered the "alter ego," "agent," or "instrumentality" of the parent company, and the district court, acting in its equitable capacity, is entitled to pierce the corporate veil.

The complementary theories of limited liability and piercing the corporate veil have provoked consternation among courts and legal scholars alike. They have been variously described as a "legal quagmire." . . . Nowhere is this more true than in the case of the alter ego doctrine. In some sense, every subsidiary is the alter ego of its parent company. Where the subsidiary is wholly-owned by the parent and has the same directors and officers, operating the subsidiary independently of the parent company not only has little practical meaning, it would also constitute a breach both of the subsidiary's duty to further the interests of its owner, and of the directors' and officers' duty towards the parent company. Nevertheless, our cases are clear that one-hundred percent ownership and identity of directors and officers are, even together, an insufficient basis for applying the alter ego theory to pierce the corporate veil. . . . Instead, we maintain the fiction that an officer or director of both corporations can change hats and represent the two corporations separately, despite their common ownership.

In lieu of articulating a coherent doctrinal basis for the alter ego theory, we have instead developed a laundry list of factors to be used in determining whether a subsidiary is the alter ego of its parent. These include whether:

(1) the parent and the subsidiary have common stock ownership;

(2) the parent and the subsidiary have common directors or officers;

(3) the parent and the subsidiary have common business departments;

(4) the parent and the subsidiary file consolidated financial statements and tax returns;

(5) the parent finances the subsidiary;

(6) the parent caused the incorporation of the subsidiary;

(7) the subsidiary operates with grossly inadequate capital;

(8) the parent pays the salaries and other expenses of the subsidiary;

(9) the subsidiary receives no business except that given to it by the parent;

(10) the parent uses the subsidiary's property as its own;

(11) the daily operations of the two corporations are not kept separate; and

(12) the subsidiary does not observe the basic corporate formalities, such as keeping separate books and records and holding shareholder and board meetings. . . .

Chemicals . . . contends that the district court gave insufficient weight to the fact that Farms observed all of the formalities required by corporation law, including keeping separate books and records and holding regular meetings of shareholders and of the board of directors. According to Chemicals, as long as corporate forms were observed by the subsidiary, then the corporate form must also be observed by the courts.

Our only reply is that Chemicals puts form ahead of substance. . . . In determining whether a subsidiary is the alter ego of its parent, we apply a multifactor test. One of these factors is whether the corporate formalities were observed—but this is only one of several factors; it is not determinative. Thus, Chemicals' argument that Farms observed the corporate formalities goes merely to the weight of the evidence, not to the correctness of the legal standard applied by the district court. . . .

Here, the district court based its ultimate alter ego finding on a number of subsidiary findings. . . . We consider them first and then turn to the court's ultimate finding regarding Farms's alter ego status.

First, Chemicals challenges the district court's findings that Farms "operated with a grossly inadequate capital." . . . Chemicals claims that although Farms initially had only $10,000 in capital, it subsequently received millions of dollars in advances for working capital from Chemicals. . . . In our view, Chemicals' argument misses the point. The underlying question is whether Farms was an economically viable, independent entity or whether it operated merely as the adjunct or alter ego of Chemicals. The fact that Farms continually had net operating losses and survived due to massive and ongoing transfusions from Chemicals does not indicate that Farms ever stood on its own two feet. Quite the contrary; it reinforces the district court's conclusion that Farms did not have any separate financial existence. . . .

The district court's finding that there was a commingling of the corporate funds of Chemicals and Farms is similarly supported by the record. . . .

Having found the district court's subsidiary findings to be supported by the record, we have little trouble in affirming the court's ultimate finding that Farms is the alter ego of Chemicals. . . . To mention just some of the evidence supporting the district court's alter ego holding, all of the directors and officers of Farms served as directors and officers of Chemicals; Farms was wholly owned by Chemicals; Chemicals paid many of the bills, invoices, and expenses of Farms; it covered Farms's overdrafts; it made substantial loans to Farms (at one time amounting to $7 million) without corporate resolutions authorizing the loans and without demanding any collateral or interest; Chemicals and Farms filed consolidated financial statements and tax returns; Farms used the offices and computer of Chemicals without paying any rent; the salary of

Farms's one regular employee was paid by Chemicals; and employees of Chemicals performed services for Farms without charging for their time. Chemicals also advanced money and provided services on an informal basis to the joint ventures. . . .

Finally, Chemicals argues that the Government never proved that Chemicals participated in the joint ventures, and, in particular, in the wrongdoing resulting in the improper subsidy payments. According to Chemicals, it cannot be held responsible because it did not engage in any wrongdoing. This argument, however, begs the alter ego question. The purpose of the alter ego analysis is to determine whether Chemicals is vicariously liable for Farms's actions—that is, whether actions by Farms are considered to be actions by Chemicals. Thus, even if Chemicals were correct that Thomas filed the false forms and improperly converted the five sight drafts in his capacity as president of Farms rather than of Chemicals, this is irrelevant given the district court's ultimate finding, based on a consideration of the evidence as a whole, that Farms was the alter ego of Chemicals. . . .

[Judgment affirmed.]

SUMMARY

1. The most dominant form of organization for modern business is the business corporation. A corporation is recognized as a legal entity, an artificial person existing apart from, and independent of, its owners, the shareholders, who enjoy limited liability for corporate obligations.

2. Business corporations often are classified as either publicly-held or closely-held. Whereas a publicly-held company has many shareholders whose shares are traded in a public market, a closely-held company has shares owned by one or a closely knit group of shareholders. The professional corporation, composed of professionals such as doctors, lawyers, and accountants, is one type of closely-held corporation.

3. A corporation is created only by complying with state business corporation acts, which authorize or enable business organization in the corporate form. Corporation law has been heavily influenced by the flexible Delaware statute and the Model Business Corporation Act.

4. A person or persons embarking upon a business venture must adopt some organizational form. In most cases, the choices are among (1) a proprietorship, (2) a partnership, (3) a limited partnership, and (4) a corporation. The choice must be based upon the particular business under examination, taking into account the nature and size of the business and the financial, personal, and tax characteristics of the owner or owners. Although the corporate form usually is preferred for large enterprises, it often is not the most desirable form for small business.

5. The persons organizing and planning the corporation, known as "promoters," often enter into contracts on behalf of the corporation yet to be formed. In this case, the law must determine (1) to what extent the promoters are personally liable upon contracts made with third parties on behalf of the corporation and (2) to what extent the corporation, upon coming into existence, is liable upon contracts made by the promoters. Principles borrowed from the law of agency and contracts govern these issues. In addition to contract liability, promoters may also owe fiduciary duties to the corporation and its shareholders.

6. A corporation is formed by complying with formalities outlined in the business corporation act of the state chosen for incorporation. Typically, one or more persons, known as "incorporators," prepare the "articles of incorporation" which then are filed with the secretary of state. The articles contain information on the corporation's business and capital structure, its registered office, and agent. If the articles conform to law, the secretary of state issues a "certificate of incorporation," and the directors named in the articles hold a meeting to complete the organization of the corporation. Once legally created, the corporation has most of the same legal powers as a natural person.

7. If the corporation does business in states outside its state of incorporation, it must qualify to do business in those states as a foreign corporation. In order to qualify, the corporation must obtain a "certificate of authority" from the secretary of state of each state in which it is a foreign corporation. Various legal sanctions are imposed against foreign corporations that fail to obtain certificates of authority.

8. One purpose of incorporating is to insulate the shareholders from unlimited personal liability for corporate obligations. Corporation law, however, through the doctrines of "de facto incorporation" and "corporation by estoppel" occasionally provides limited liability to persons who do business as a corporation without complying with corporate formalities. Conversely, in some instances, courts "pierce the corporate veil" to impose personal liability on shareholders of a duly formed corporation.

KEY TERMS

corporation	Revised Model Business
public corporation	Corporation Act
private corporation	(RMBCA)
nonprofit corporation	promoter
business corporation	bylaws
closely-held corporation	ultra vires
publicly-held corporation	domestic corporation
professional corporation	foreign corporation
Model Business	de jure corporation
Corporation Act	de facto corporation
(MBCA)	corporation by estoppel

QUESTIONS AND PROBLEMS

45-1 Bob and Cara wanted to open a retail clothing store but needed $100,000 capital to do so. Their life savings amounted to $3,000. Nevertheless, they formed a corporation named "Craig Place Ltd." and found four investors who were willing to invest $12,000 each. Craig Place Ltd. issued 12,000 shares of stock to each of the investors. Bob and Cara promised to provide the remaining $52,000. They requested a loan from First State Bank, which refused to lend the money to Bob and Cara but agreed to lend $50,000 to Craig Place Ltd. Bob and Cara personally guaranteed the loan. They took the money, added $2,000 from their savings, and deposited it in Craig Place Ltd.'s bank account. In exchange they received 52,000 shares of stock. The retail clothing store failed. Following payment of all creditors except the bank the corporation's total assets were $40,000. First State Bank has filed a lawsuit claiming that it is entitled to the money because it is a creditor of the corporation. The four investors claim that they should receive the money.

(a) Do Bob and Cara have any liability to the corporation or minority shareholders for using a bank loan to the corporation to pay for stock issued to them? On what theory?

(b) Assuming Bob and Cara are insolvent, how should the court distribute the $40,000 remaining upon liquidation of the corporation?

(c) Would your answer in (b) be different if the investors were able to prove that the bank knew Bob and Cara were using the money to purchase their shares in Craig Place Ltd.? Explain.

45-2 On April 1, 1985, How and Associates, an architectural firm, and Ed Boss signed a written contract by which How agreed to develop an architectural plan for a hotel and restaurant complex for payment of $50,000. Ed Boss signed the contract as follows: "Ed Boss, as agent for a corporation to be formed which will be the obligor." On May 15, 1985, the Hunter Hotel Co. was incorporated. On July 1, 1985, How received a check for $10,000 from the Hunter Hotel Co. as partial payment for "architectural plans for hotel complex per contract dated April 1, 1985." The check was signed by "Ed Boss, President Hunter Hotel Corp."

(a) Assume that How completed the architectural plans but received no further payments. Is Hunter Hotel Co. liable for the $40,000 owed to How? Explain.

(b) Assume that How completed the architectural plans and then learned that Hunter Hotel Co. was insolvent. Is Ed Boss liable for the $40,000 owed to How? Explain.

(c) Assume that Ed Boss formed a new corporation called Boss Corp. on August 1, 1985, and submitted $50,000 to How "in full payment per contract dated April 1, 1985.'' Hunter Hotel Co. notifies How that although Ed Boss has resigned from Hunter, Hunter intends to honor its April 1, 1985, contract with How. Both Boss Corp. and Hunter request delivery of the architectural plans. With which party does How have a contract? Explain.

45-3 On October 15, 1982, Arnold personally borrowed $10,000 from First City Bank. First City required that Arnold obtain a guarantor for his promissory note. Westover, Inc., a real estate corporation of which Arnold was a director, agreed to guarantee payment of the note. On November 15, 1982, Morton and Edith purchased all of the shares of Westover. On October 15, 1983, Arnold failed to repay the note and First City sued Westover. Morton, who is now president of Westover, requests that the court refuse to enforce the guaranty on the ground that Westover acted ultra vires by guaranteeing the note. Westover's bylaws provide that it was formed for the purpose of ''transacting business relating to real estate.'' Has the corporation acted ultra vires?

45-4 In January, 1985, Bennett and Davenport agreed to form a corporation to be called ''Aero-Fabb Co.'' They submitted articles of incorporation to the state on January 22 in which both were named as corporate directors. Both parties actively participated in the policy and operational decisions of the organization. On February 15 Davenport, on behalf of Aero-Fabb Co., signed two contracts by which the company agreed to rent equipment from Timberline Equipment, Inc. Davenport signed one contract ''Kenneth L. Davenport d/b/a Aero-Fabb Co.'' and the other contract ''Kenneth L. Davenport d/b/a/ Aero Fabb Corp.'' On March 1, 1985, the secretary of state notified Bennett and Davenport that the articles of incorporation that they had submitted were incomplete. They provided the additional requested information and on April 1, 1985, the state issued a certificate of incorporation to Aero-Fabb Co. The corporation was not successful and defaulted in payments on the contracts with Timberline. Timberline filed suit naming Aero-Fabb Co., Bennett, and Davenport as defendants.

(a) Bennett and Davenport alleged that the contracts were with Aero-Fabb Co., a de facto corporation. Explain what is meant by de facto corporation and why Bennett and Davenport would raise it as a defense. Assuming

the doctrine is recognized in the state, can Bennett and Davenport establish it?

(b) Bennett and Davenport allege that the doctrine of corporation by estoppel precludes their being held personally liable on the contract. Explain the applicability of corporation by estoppel to these facts.

(c) The state Business Corporation Act contains the following provision

> All persons who assume to act as a corporation without the authority of a certificate of incorporation issued by the Corporation Commissioner, shall be jointly and severally liable for all debts and liabilities incurred or arising as a result thereof.

Bennett asserts that he cannot be held personally liable on the Timberline contracts because he did not sign them. Should Bennett be held liable under the above provision? Would your answer change if Bennett was merely an investor who did not participate in management?

45-5 Trucking Brothers, Inc. is a corporation formed by Ray and Ed who each contributed $2,500 to the corporation. Trucking Brothers is engaged in the business of selling produce on a commission basis. The growers of the produce deliver it to Trucking Brothers, which then arranges a sale to a wholesaler or retailer and delivers the produce to the purchaser. Trucking Brothers requires payment on delivery, and after deducting twenty-five percent as its commission, pays the grower the proceeds of sale. Trucking Brothers uses Ray's truck to deliver the produce. Frank delivered a shipment of artichokes to Trucking Brothers, which sold them to a grocery store. Trucking Brothers failed to pay Frank for the artichokes.

(a) Frank sues Ray and Ed seeking to hold them personally liable on the contract. He alleges that the corporate veil should be disregarded because Trucking Brothers was inadequately capitalized. What factors should the court consider in determining inadequate capitalization?

(b) Other than capitalization, what other factors might affect the court's determination? Suggest further general information that would be helpful to the court.

45-6 Archie was a cab driver in New York City. State law required that every cab carry liability insurance of at least $10,000. Archie formed five corporations; he was the sole shareholder of each corporation. Each corporation owned only one asset—a taxicab which carried $10,000 liability insurance. Archie maintained separate records for each corporation and did not intermingle corporate funds with his own funds. While riding in a taxicab owned by one of Archie's corporations, Gloria suffered serious injuries. She sued not only the corporation that owned the taxi in which she had been riding, but also the four other corporations and Archie. Gloria alleged that the court should "pierce the corporate veil" and hold Archie personally liable for her injuries. How should the court rule? Explain.

45-7   Plaintiff was injured while using fireworks distributed by Oriental Fireworks Co. Because Oriental Fireworks carried no liability insurance and had assets less than $12,000, plaintiff requested the court to pierce the corporate veil and hold

J. C. Chou liable for the injuries. Evidence at trial revealed that Oriental Fireworks had never carried insurance and that its assets never exceeded $13,000. J. C. Chou owned one-half of the shares of Oriental Fireworks and his wife owned the other half. They were the only officers of the corporation. The Chous were unable to provide evidence that they had paid consideration for their shares or that the corporation had ever held meetings. No corporate records could be found. How should the court rule?

45-8   Courts must often decide whether to disregard the corporate entity to hold the shareholders liable for a corporate obligation. Should the courts apply different criteria to claims based upon contracts between the plaintiff and the corporation from those based upon a tort committed by the corporation?

Chapter 46

Corporate Financial Structure

Major Topics

- an introduction to corporate financial structure, including the various types of debt and equity securities, and the factors considered in selection of capital structure
- the legal requirements governing issuance of, and payment for, shares of stock
- the law relating to ownership and transfer of corporate securities, governed by Article 8 of the Uniform Commercial Code
- a discussion of corporate dividends and other distributions of corporate assets to shareholders

Like an individual or unincorporated association, a corporation must have a source of funds to acquire assets and finance its business operations. In ongoing corporations, most funds are generated by reinvesting, or "plowing back," all or part of corporate earnings into the business. An additional, and usually the initial, method of raising corporate funds is the issuance of corporate "securities" in exchange for transfer of cash, property, or services to the corporation.

Introduction to Corporate Financial Structure

Sources of Corporate Funds

A **security** is a share, participation, or other interest in the property of the issuing corporation (an equity security), or an obligation of the issuer (a debt security).[1] **Equity securities,** such as shares of stock, are those that create an ownership interest in the business. The owners of the equity securities, and therefore the corporation, are the shareholders or stockholders. In contrast to equity securities, which represent an investment in the business, **debt securities** represent obligations that must ultimately be repaid and create a debtor-creditor relationship between their holders and the corporation. Common debt securities include notes, debentures, and bonds. Many corporations use both debt and equity securities to finance the business, and the combination of the two for a particular corporation is known as its "capital structure."

Types of Equity Securities

A corporation's equity securities, its shares of stock, are the "units into which the proprietary interests in a corporation are divided."[2] They represent the underlying ownership interest of the corporation and confer three basic rights upon shareholders: (1) the right to share in distributions of corporate income (dividends) when declared by the board of directors, (2) the right to vote on important corporate matters and thereby participate in

---

1. UCC §8-102(1) (1977).
2. MBCA §2(d), RMBCA §1.40(21).

control, and (3) the right to a proportionate share of net assets upon liquidation of the firm.

Preferred and Common Shares. Not all shares are created equal with respect to these rights. The articles of incorporation may divide shares into classes. If classes are authorized, the articles must describe the designations, preferences, limitations, and relative rights of each class. Voting rights of any class of shares may be limited or denied, or special voting rights may be provided. In addition, a corporation may issue stock in preferred or special classes that have preference over other classes in the payment of dividends or in the assets of the corporation upon liquidation, or both.[3] Classes of shares that have such preferential rights are known as **preferred shares**. Preferred shares generally are nonvoting.

In contrast, **common shares** are the residual ownership interest in the corporation. Common shares are entitled to dividends only after shares with a dividend preference are paid. They are entitled to distributions on liquidation only after creditors (including holders of debt securities) and equity securities with a liquidation preference are paid. If a corporation has only one class of shares, they are, in effect, common shares. A corporation need not, however, have only one class of common shares. State corporation statutes generally authorize creation of various classes of common shares with each possessing different rights and privileges.

Redeemable and Convertible Shares. The articles of incorporation may make certain classes of stock subject to reacquisition, or redemption, by the corporation at a fixed price.[4] Although such redemption or "call" provisions generally apply only to preferred shares, some states permit redeemable common shares if there is at least one class of voting common shares not subject to redemption. Redemption of a class of shares may be mandatory or optional, as well as total or partial.

The articles of incorporation also may provide that shares of a given class may be convertible into shares of another class on some predetermined ratio. This ratio usually takes stock dividends and splits into account to protect the conversion privilege against dilution. The MBCA and some state statutes prohibit conversion of one class of stock into a class having prior or superior rights to dividends or to corporate assets upon liquidation.[5] Under these provisions, for example, preferred stock may be convertible into common, but not vice versa.

A given class of security often possesses both redemption and conversion privileges. In this situation, after the call for redemption, the shareholder usually has a limited period within which to exercise the conversion right. Note that redemption and conversion provisions also are common in debt securities.

Options, Warrants, and Rights. A corporation may create and issue rights or options that entitle their holders to purchase a specified number of shares of a given class of stock from the corporation at a specified price usually within a limited period of time. Rights or options may be issued in conjunction with, or independently of, the corporation's issue of other securities, and may be issued as incentives to corporate directors, officers, or employees.[6]

Share options usually are evidenced by certificates known as "warrants," which are generally long-term in nature. In contrast, short-term share options are known as "rights," which are often issued in lieu of dividends or in conjunction with the issuance of debt securities or preferred stock. Both warrants and rights of publicly-held companies are freely transferable and publicly traded. Their value depends upon the difference between the stock's market price and the option price.

Issuance of Shares

A corporation has the power to create and issue the number of shares stated or authorized in its articles of incorporation.[7] The law generally places no limit

---

3. See, for example, MBCA §15, RMBCA §6.01.
4. See, for example, MBCA §15(a), RMBCA §6.01(c)(2).

5. MBCA §15(e).
6. See, for example, MBCA §20, RMBCA §6.24.
7. See, for example, MBCA §15, RMBCA §6.03(a).

on the number of shares of various classes that may be authorized and does not require that all authorized shares be issued. Some states, however, impose an organization tax based on authorized shares, which creates a practical limit on the number of such shares. Nevertheless, sufficient shares should be authorized to meet both present and future financing needs to avoid the need to later amend the articles of incorporation.

Some or all of the authorized shares will be issued to shareholders in exchange for consideration and are then said to be "outstanding." Shares are outstanding until they are later reacquired by the corporation through redemption, exercise of conversion privilege, or purchase. Such shares often are known as "treasury shares" or "treasury stock."

Shares may generally be issued with a "par" or "stated" value or may be "no par" shares. **Par value** of a share is simply the amount designated as par value for the share in the articles of incorporation. In contrast, "no par" shares are simply those that are stated in the articles to have no par value.

Consideration for Shares. Both par and no par shares are issued for consideration, expressed in dollars, determined by the board of directors, unless that right is reserved to the shareholders in the articles of incorporation. Historically, if par value stock was used, the par value was the selling price of the stock. Today, par value usually bears no relation to the issue price. Stock may not, however, be sold for less than par value. For this reason, among others, modern corporate par value stock usually bears a nominal par value, such as one dollar. In the absence of fraud in the transaction the judgment of the board of directors regarding the value of the consideration received for stock, or for stock rights or options, is generally conclusive.[8] Note that treasury stock may be sold for any price fixed by the board of directors without regard to any par value stated on the stock.

Minimum Capital Requirements. Statutes in several jurisdictions prohibit a corporation from commencing business until a certain minimum capital has been received in exchange for issuance of shares. Although $1,000 is the most common minimum, some states require $500, and others require that a specified minimum percentage of authorized capital be contributed. Because minimum capital provisions take no account of the actual capital needs of the business and generally involve nominal amounts, they provide no real creditor protection. For this reason, the MBCA, the RMBCA, and many state statutes have eliminated any minimum capitalization requirement.

Stated Capital and Capital Surplus. The par-no par distinction not only affects the consideration requirements for the issue of shares but also determines the composition of the corporation's stated capital and capital surplus accounts. If the corporation issues par value stock, the par value of the shares is credited to the "stated capital" account and the difference between the selling price and par value is credited to a "capital surplus" account. As defined in many state statutes, "surplus" of a corporation is the amount by which the net assets (assets minus liabilities) exceed its stated capital. Surplus of the corporation is of two basic types, capital surplus and earned surplus (retained earnings). In a newly formed corporation with no accumulated earnings, the entire surplus, if any, of the corporation will be capital surplus.

Assume ABC Corporation issues 10,000 shares of stock sold for $10 per share with a par value of $1 per share. Stated capital is $10,000 (10,000 × $1) and capital surplus is $90,000 (10,000 × ($10 − $1)). The balance sheet of the corporation after issuing the stock is therefore

Assets		*Liabilities*	
Cash	$100,000		-0-
		Capital Accounts	
		Stated Capital	$ 10,000
		Capital Surplus	90,000
		Earned Surplus	-0-
	$100,000		$100,000

Under most state statutes, if the corporation issues no par stock, the entire consideration received for

---

8. MBCA §§18-20, RMBCA §§6.21, 6.24.

the shares is allocated to stated capital. The board of directors may, however, allocate some or all of the consideration to capital surplus within a specified time after the stock is issued. Most state statutes impose no limitation upon the amount that may be allocated from stated capital to capital surplus. For example, assume DEF Corporation issues 10,000 shares of no par stock, selling for $20 per share. Stated capital is $200,000 (10,000 × $20). If the board of directors later votes to transfer $19 per share to capital surplus, stated capital would be $10,000 ($200,000 − (10,000 × $19)) and capital surplus $190,000.

How a corporation divides its capital contribution between capital surplus and stated capital may have important legal consequences. Many jurisdictions provide that corporate funds may be expended to pay dividends or to repurchase or redeem outstanding shares to the extent of amounts in the corporation's earned surplus (retained earnings) account and in some cases, its capital surplus account. Stated capital, in contrast, is effectively locked into the corporation and may usually be distributed only upon liquidation of the firm. Accordingly, allocating a substantial portion of the consideration for stock to capital surplus gives the corporation more future flexibility to pay dividends or reacquire its stock. This result accounts in part for the common use of nominal par value stock.

Allocating a corporation's capital contribution between stated capital and capital surplus is artificial and provides no real protection to creditors against excessive distribution of corporate assets to shareholders. For this reason the RMBCA and many modern state statutes eliminate the concept of par value and any legal consequences attached to the distinction between stated capital and capital surplus. Under this approach, the validity of corporate distributions is determined solely by the insolvency test discussed later in this chapter.

Payment for Shares

Stock Subscriptions. A corporation has no need to issue and set the consideration for stock unless it has investors willing and able to buy it. A stock subscription is one method used to acquire investment capital or the assurance of such capital. A **stock subscription** is an offer or agreement by a ''subscriber'' to purchase and pay for a specified number of previously unissued shares of the corporation. Stock subscriptions may be postincorporation or preincorporation. Postincorporation stock subscriptions are ordinary bilateral contracts between the subscriber and the corporation.[9] Preincorporation subscriptions are, however, complicated by the fact that the corporation is not a legal entity at the time of the subscription. Accordingly, under the traditional approach, a preincorporation subscription was a mere offer, revocable by the subscriber until accepted by the corporation after its formation. This result created uncertainty regarding corporate capitalization until after incorporation.

To prevent this result, state corporation statutes make preincorporation subscriptions enforceable for a limited period. For example, the MBCA and RMBCA provide that a subscription for shares of a corporation to be organized is irrevocable for six months unless the subscription agreement provides otherwise or all other subscribers agree to revocation.[10] Modern statutes also frequently provide for automatic acceptance of the subscription upon incorporation and require that the subscription be in writing signed by the subscriber.

The payment terms of a stock subscription, unless specified in the subscription itself, are determined by the board of directors. Any call by the board of directors for payment of subscriptions must be uniform as to all shares of the same class. Generally, the stock certificate is issued when the subscription price is fully paid. If a subscriber defaults in payment under the agreement the corporation may proceed to collect it in the same manner as any other debt owed to the corporation.

Note that modern distribution techniques and securities registration requirements generally prevent the use of stock subscriptions in connection with securities issued by publicly-held corporations.

Shareholder Liability for Watered Shares. In exchange for the issuance of shares, shareholders and subscribers are legally obligated to pay to the corporation the consideration fixed by the board of directors. Although the consideration for shares is

---

9. A share subscription contained in the articles of incorporation is also generally irrevocable and is binding upon the corporation.

10. MBCA §17, RMBCA §6.20.

expressed in dollars, cash is not the only permissible consideration. Many state statutes and constitutions provide that consideration for the issuance of shares may be paid in money, property, or services actually performed for the corporation. Under this approach, neither promissory notes nor the promise of future services constitute payment or part payment for issuance of shares. The RMBCA, however, permits stock to be issued for promissory notes or contracts for future services.[11]

Shares issued for the full eligible consideration are deemed validly issued, fully paid, and nonassessable.[12] Shares issued to persons who pay less than the law requires are called "bonus," "discount," or "watered" shares. Bonus shares are those for which no lawful consideration is received by the corporation. Discount shares are shares issued for cash less than the fixed consideration. Watered shares are those issued for property or services worth less than the required consideration. The term **watered shares** usually is used to describe all three types.

Watered shares in a corporation's capital structure may injure both the corporation's creditors and its shareholders. Creditors may be injured because watered shares artificially inflate the corporation's capitalization. If creditors are involved, the shareholder may be compelled to contribute additional consideration to make up the difference between the consideration fixed by the board of directors and the amount of valid consideration paid. If a holder of watered shares later sells them, a good faith purchaser incurs no liability to the corporation or its creditors for any unpaid consideration. Similarly, a creditor to whom the holder transfers the shares as collateral is not personally liable as a shareholder. In both cases, however, the transferor remains liable despite the transfer.[13]

Creditor claims involving watered shares are rare today primarily because of federal and state securities regulation statutes. In modern cases, the complaining parties usually are other shareholders of the corporation whose equity in the corporate assets is unfairly diluted by issuance of new shares without lawful consideration. In these cases, the appropriate remedy is to cancel the offending shares.

Although share consideration requirements protect shareholders, certain shareholders may be denied the benefit of that protection, as the following case illustrates.

Frasier v. Trans-Western Land Corporation
316 N.W.2d 612 (Neb. 1982)

Ted Deyle, his nephew G. Frederic Wood, and William Frasier agreed to form a corporation for the purpose of buying and developing real estate. In a preincorporation agreement, the three men stated their intent to be equal shareholders with Deyle to provide all funds necessary for the real estate development and Frasier and Wood to handle all duties relative to development.

Trans-Western Land Corporation was incorporated in January, 1978, and Deyle, Frasier, and Wood each received 5,000 shares of common stock with a par value of $0.50 per share. Deyle transferred cash to the corporation for the purchase of land. Neither Frasier nor Wood paid any cash to the corporation but they did begin the land development. In May, 1978, at Wood's suggestion, both Wood and Frasier wrote checks for $2,500 to Trans-Western for payment of their stock, but the corporation immediately reissued a check in the same amount to each of them. In February, 1979, Wood paid $2,500 to the corporation for his stock but Frasier maintained that he was to receive the stock for his work for the corporation. Frasier later resigned as an officer and director of Trans-Western. The board of directors then decided to cancel Frasier's stock. In August, 1979, the board of directors decided to sell all of the corporation's assets.

Frasier sued Trans-Western, Deyle, and Wood alleging that he should have received notice of the sale. The trial court held that Frasier was not entitled to notice because his shares were void for lack of consideration. Frasier appealed.

Krivosha, Chief Justice

. . . [Section 21-2018 of the Nebraska Revised Statutes] provides in part: "No corporation shall be permitted to issue stock except for an equivalent in money paid or labor done, or property actually re-

---

11. RMBCA §6.21(b).
12. MBCA §19, RMBCA §§6.21(d).
13. MBCA §25, RMBCA §6.22.

ceived and applied to the purpose for which such corporation was created. Neither promissory notes nor future services shall constitute payment or part payment for issuance of shares of a corporation. . . .''

The real question we must answer by this appeal is whether the stock allegedly issued in violation of §21-2018, but in accordance with an agreement between all of the stockholders, is void in its inception or merely voidable as to certain persons under certain conditions. A reading of the Nebraska Business Corporation Act leads us to the conclusion that a violation of §21-2018 may cause the stock to be voidable but not void. . . .

We must not lose sight of the fact that this is a suit between informed and consenting stockholders, as opposed to creditors or uninformed stockholders. The distinction is legally significant.

. . . [I]t is clear that the rule which permits a corporation in the first instance and a court thereafter to declare the issuance of stock void or to otherwise obligate a stockholder to make further payment is applied in one manner as it relates to creditors of the corporation and in a totally different manner to stockholders who, with knowledge, participated in the plan which is thereafter attacked by the participating stockholders. . . .

Appellees argue that the provisions of §21-2018 require our finding that the issuance of stock for less than full value is void regardless of who is involved. The language they rely upon is that portion of §21-2018 which provides: ''. . . and all *fictitious increase* of stock shall be void.'' (Emphasis supplied.) We believe that appellees misread the statute. What it provides is that the *fictitious increase* is void, not the *stock* itself. This language makes it clear that, notwithstanding that the stock may recite that it is fully paid and nonassessable, creditors may impose liability upon the holders of such stock. . . .

The provision of §21-2018 making all fictitious increases of stock void relates to a creditor's right against a holder of ''watered stock'' and not to the validity of the stock itself. The creditor has a cause of action against the individual holder because, indeed, the individual holder is a stockholder. Were the courts to hold the stock itself void, the holder could not be liable to the creditor. This is true even though the corporation itself cannot maintain an action. . . .

An entire examination of this record makes it quite clear that, creditors aside, the payment for the stock was not critical to the operation of this corporation or its success. What appears to be more critical were the efforts made by the parties, including Frasier. It strikes us as being wholly inequitable and improper to permit the corporation and its remaining stockholders to allow Frasier to operate under the belief embodied in the written agreement that he was a stockholder and then remove him just at a point when it appears that a profit would be realized because of his refusal to make a cash capital contribution of funds not needed and previously waived. We believe that the issuance of the stock was only voidable and not void, and neither Wood nor Deyle was in a position to object. They participated and acquiesced in the manner in which the stock was issued to [Frasier]. The fact that a creditor may have another right against the corporation is not significant to this case. . . .

[Judgment reversed and remanded.]

Debt Securities

Debt securities are issued in exchange for loans made to the corporation. Like other loans, debt securities require periodic interest payments and ultimately must be repaid. Thus, whereas the holder of an equity security is an owner of the corporation, the holder of a debt security is a creditor. Holders of debt securities, as creditors, enjoy a claim on corporate assets prior to shareholders.

Publicly-held corporations commonly issue debt securities known as ''bonds'' and ''debentures.'' Technically, a **debenture** is an unsecured obligation rendering debenture holders general creditors of the corporation. In contrast, a **bond** is an obligation secured by a lien or mortgage upon specific corporate property. Despite this difference, the term ''bond'' is often used to describe both bonds and debentures. Bonds and debentures are commonly long-term obligations issued in $1,000 denominations (or multiples thereof) with a fixed interest rate, often known as the ''coupon'' rate.

Both bonds and debentures typically are issued and administered under an **indenture** (sometimes called a ''trust agreement'' or ''deed of trust'') between the corporation issuing the securities and a trustee, usually a financial institution. The indenture contains the basic terms of the issuance, including any redemption or conversion provisions, the nature and extent of any security, and protective provisions such as minimum ratios of assets to liabilities, restrictions on dividends or share redemption, and limitations on additional issues of securities. The trustee generally represents the interests of the various security holders.[14]

Bonds and debentures are not the only source of corporate debt financing. Long- and short-term notes from commercial banks and insurance companies also are commonly used. In addition, suppliers of goods or services often extend credit to corporations on a secured or unsecured basis.

Selection of Capital Structure

Although every corporation issues some stock, corporate management enjoys considerable flexibility in determining the corporation's particular mix of debt and equity securities, its capital structure. Management considers various factors including market conditions, stability of corporate earnings, interest rates, the nature and extent of corporate assets, and the amount of capital required. In addition, tax considerations also weigh heavily in the decision.

Shareholder Debt. Shareholders often lend a portion of their investment to the corporation, rather than contributing it outright for shares of stock. Because interest payments on the debt are deductible by the corporation and dividend payments are not, such debt reduces the problem of corporate "double taxation." In addition, the ultimate repayment of the debt may receive more favorable tax treatment than a repurchase or redemption of equity securities.

Because of the tax advantages of corporate debt payable to shareholders, a substantial body of tax law has evolved from Internal Revenue Service attempts to reclassify corporate debt as stock in cor-

porations with excessive debt capitalization. A corporation with a high debt to equity ratio (for example, four to one or higher) is commonly known as a "thin" corporation. The Internal Revenue Code and IRS regulations provide guidelines distinguishing debt from share interests.

In addition to tax advantages, shareholders who loan money to the corporation may, as creditors, enjoy greater rights upon bankruptcy or insolvency of the corporation than ordinary shareholders. Shareholder debt is often, however, subordinated to the claims of outside general creditors in a bankruptcy proceeding. The principles governing such subordination are discussed in the following case.

Tanzi v. Fiberglass Swimming Pools, Inc.
414 A.2d 484 (R.I. 1980)

In 1968, plaintiff Richard Tanzi incorporated Fiberglass Swimming Pools, Inc. as a business selling and installing swimming pools. Tanzi and his parents made an initial capital contribution of $3,000. During the first few years of operation, Tanzi used his personal funds to finance pool installations during the spring and then retained profits received later in the season. In 1972, Tanzi transferred approximately $18,675 of his personal funds and $25,000 obtained from his mother to Fiberglass which used the money to purchase equipment. These amounts were listed as outstanding loans on the corporation's 1973 financial statements. In 1973, gross sales reached $238,000 and Fiberglass repaid $5,000 to Tanzi. On November 23, 1973, Fiberglass executed a promissory note payable to Tanzi and his mother in the amount of $40,818.76 and the Tanzis filed a financing statement listing various pieces of equipment as security for the note. In the following years, the business began to decline and in 1976 Fiberglass went into receivership.

During the receivership proceedings, Tanzi filed a petition to reclaim certain corporate equipment alleging that it was security for the loans made to Fiberglass by his mother and him. The receiver asserted that the money transferred by the Tanzis constituted capital contributions rather than loans. The trial court ruled in favor of the receiver and the Tanzis appealed.

---

14. The issuance of debt securities to the public may be subject to the federal Trust Indenture Act of 1939, discussed in Chapter 49.

Kelleher, Justice

. . . [A]s a matter of law there is nothing to prevent *"bona fide* transactions between a corporation and its principal shareholder, including those which result in the shareholder's becoming a creditor of the corporation." Henn, *Corporations* §152 at 269 (2d ed. 1970). . . .

The question of what treatment is to be accorded such claims most often arises in receivership or bankruptcy proceedings. . . . Even though a shareholder loan is not per se invalid, . . . obviously the transaction is subject to strict judicial scrutiny. . . . The general rule would also permit corporate directors and officers as well as shareholders to attain creditor status for loans advanced to the corporation. . . . It goes without saying that courts are particularly watchful in all these situations because of the fiduciary status that officers and dominant shareholders must observe vis-a-vis the corporation when the individual acts both for himself and for the corporation. . . .

With this background in mind, we now proceed to consider the Tanzis' contention that their claim should have received priority because they were secured creditors of Fiberglass. The issue narrows to whether these transactions by the Tanzis first met the requirements of valid loans in that a debtor-creditor relationship ever existed between them and Fiberglass. The trial justice remained unconvinced, as do we. Clearly, persons making capital contributions are not corporate creditors. . . .

In *In re Mader's Store for Men,* [254 N.W.2d 171 (Wis. 1977)], the court collected and analyzed cases in which advances to a corporation were subordinated on the capital contribution theory and extracted the following relevant factors: (1) was the claimant in a position to control corporate affairs "at least to the extent of determining the form of the transaction . . . "; (2) were the advances intended to be repaid in the ordinary course of the corporation's business; and (3) was the paid-in stated capital "unreasonably small in view of the nature and size of the business in which the corporation was engaged." . . . 254 N.W.2d at 186. . . .

In the bankruptcy context, the following criteria have been considered in determining the treatment of the disputed advancements: the adequacy of capital contribution, the ratio of shareholder loans to capital, the amount of shareholder control, the

availability of similar loans from outside lenders, and certain relevant questions, such as, whether the ultimate financial failure was caused by under-capitalization, whether the note included repayment provisions and a fixed maturity date, whether a note or debt document was executed, whether proceeds were used to acquire capital assets, and how the debt was treated in the corporate records. . . .

Applying the criteria enunciated earlier to the facts in this case, we conclude that the trial justice was justified in finding that the cash advancements to Fiberglass were contributions to risk capital rather than bona fide loans to the corporation. We feel that the initial risk capital of $3,000 was inadequate to sustain corporate sales in excess of $200,000. Furthermore, Richard Tanzi completely controlled the corporation, a factor to which the trial justice specifically alluded as follows: "As long as it [Fiberglass] was making profits, he was taking the profits out. When he needed money to buy additional assets or run the business, he put money in." On balance, the transaction itself bore very few earmarks of an arm's length bargain. The note lacked either interest, repayment, or default provisions and had no fixed maturity date. Although an actual repayment of $5,000 was made to Richard Tanzi, this factor is offset by the fact that the proceeds, in reality, were used to acquire capital assets necessary for corporate expansion. Finally, the belated execution of the promissory note strongly suggests that it was an attempt in form rather than in substance to protect the family investment. Surely, under these circumstances, in which repayment safeguards were virtually nonexistent, an outside lender would have been foolhardy to risk its funds. The Tanzis' "loan," therefore, qualified as a contribution to capital that was correctly subordinated to the claims of the general creditors. . . .

[Judgment affirmed.]

Leverage. If money can be borrowed from outside creditors, another possible advantage of debt financing is "leverage" or "trading on equity." Leverage occurs if the total investment in the business (debt and equity) yields a higher rate of return than the interest cost of borrowing money. For example, a business with a $500,000 total investment may generate $75,000 per year in earnings (a fifteen percent rate of return) when the interest rate on borrowed funds is twelve percent. Under these circumstances, the business should borrow as much of the $500,000 investment as possible. The entire difference between the rate of return on total investment and the interest payments on the borrowed portion of that investment is profit which magnifies the rate of return on the equity securities. If earnings are poor and insufficient to cover the fixed interest payments, however, losses on equity capital also are magnified.

Ownership and Transfer of Securities

Certificated and Uncertificated Securities

Corporate debt and equity securities generally are evidenced by a document—for example, a stock certificate—and are known as **certificated securities.** Certificated securities are, like commercial paper and some documents of title, negotiable instruments.[15] Alternatively, some state corporation statutes, to relieve the "paperwork crunch" in securities markets, authorize corporations to issue securities in **uncertificated** form, not represented by an instrument. Article 8 of the Uniform Commercial Code, entitled "Investment Securities," states rules governing the transfer of the rights constituting securities and how those rights are established against the issuer and third parties. Article 8 was amended in 1977 to resolve these issues for uncertificated, as well as certificated, securities. Note that revised Article 8 does not require or authorize the use of uncertificated securities. It simply provides the governing rules if uncertificated securities are authorized by state law and a particular corporation elects to issue securities in that form. At this writing, thirty-three states have enacted the 1977 revision of Article 8.[16]

---

15. UCC §§8-102(1)(a), 8-105(1) (1977).

16. These include Arkansas, California, Colorado, Connecticut, Delaware, Florida, Hawaii, Idaho, Indiana, Kansas, Kentucky, Maryland, Massachusetts, Michigan, Minnesota, Montana, Nevada, New Hampshire, New Mexico, New York, North Dakota, Ohio, Oklahoma, Oregon, Rhode Island, South Dakota, Tennessee, Texas, Virginia, Washington, West Virginia, Wisconsin, and Wyoming.

Ownership and Transfer of Certificated Securities

Registered and Bearer Securities. Certificated securities may be issued in registered or bearer form. A certificated security is in "registered" form if (1) it specifies the person entitled to the security, and (2) its transfer may be registered upon books maintained for that purpose by or on behalf of the issuer. A certificated security is in "bearer" form if it runs to bearer according to its terms.[17] A certificated security in bearer form is transferred simply by delivery of the certificate to the transferee or to a "financial intermediary," such as a stockbroker, bank, clearing corporation, or other entity that ordinarily maintains security accounts for its customers. If in registered form, the transfer requires both delivery and a proper indorsement. The transferor indorses by signing an assignment or transfer of the instrument on the instrument or on a separate document, or by affixing his or her signature to the back of the security. As in commercial paper, the indorsement may be blank (the holder's signature alone) or special (specifying to whom the security is to be transferred). If indorsed in blank the security becomes a bearer instrument and may subsequently be transferred by delivery alone. If specially indorsed, the special indorsee's indorsement is required for further transfer. After the transfer, the security may be presented to the issuer for registration, who will register the transfer to designate the transferee as the new registered owner.

Debt Securities. Debt securities, such as bonds and debentures, usually are freely transferable bearer instruments. Interest payments are made to bearers of interest "coupons" that are periodically clipped from the instrument and submitted for payment. If the instrument is registered with the issuer, the periodic interest payments, and the principal at maturity, are paid to the registered owner. Coupon securities also may be registered as to principal ("registered coupon" form). In this case, principal is payable to the registered owner upon maturity,

---

17. UCC §§8-102(1)(d),(e) (1977).

but interest is payable to the bearers of the individual interest coupons.

Equity Securities. Certificated shares of stock, like debt securities, are generally freely transferable. Restrictions on transfer may, however, be imposed by appropriate provisions in the articles of incorporation or bylaws. Share transfer restrictions commonly are used in closely-held corporations as a control device and are sometimes required for securities issued under securities regulation exemptions discussed in Chapter 49. Under UCC §8-204(a), any share transfer restriction imposed by the issuer must be conspicuously noted on the share certificate to be effective against any person without actual knowledge of the restriction.

State corporation statutes require that corporations maintain a record of their shareholders, showing the class and number of shares held by each shareholder.[18] These records are sometimes known as "share books" or "share ledgers" and in small corporations the stubs in the share certificate book serve as the record of shareholders. In larger corporations, transfers of shares are recorded by a "stock transfer" agent, but in smaller corporations this task may be handled by the corporate secretary or other officer. Statutes generally allow the corporation to rely upon record ownership to determine which shareholders are entitled to vote, to be sent notices, to receive dividends, and otherwise to exercise the rights and powers of a shareholder.[19] A substantial number of shares are not registered in the name of the investor, but are held by brokers in their own names or in the names of certain Wall Street brokers (street names) or by clearinghouses. These securities generally are left in the broker's possession to facilitate further trading.

Ownership and Transfer of Uncertificated Securities

An uncertificated security is recorded on the books of the issuer, though there is no instrument evidencing the holder's interest in or claim against the corporation. Because there are no certificates to indorse or deliver, uncertificated debt or equity securities are transferred by registering the transfer with the issuer, according to the transferor's instructions. Within two business days after the transfer of an uncertificated security has been registered, the issuer must send an **initial transaction statement** (ITS) to the new registered owner, which is signed by the issuer and contains a description of the issue of which the security is a part, the number of shares or units transferred, the new registered owner's name and address, and the date the transfer was registered. In addition, the ITS must note any liens existing against or adverse claims to the security that have been previously communicated by third parties to the issuer and any restrictions, such as share transfer restrictions imposed by the issuer.[20] A similar statement is furnished to the transferor.

A purchaser of a certificated security generally may assume that the holder of the instrument owns and may transfer it. The instrument itself is prima facie evidence of the holder's rights. In contrast, an initial transaction statement is neither a negotiable instrument nor a security, and a conspicuous legend to that effect must appear on the statement. It is merely a record of the rights of the purchaser against the issuer at the time of issuance.[21] Accordingly, subsequent purchasers cannot justifiably rely on the contents of an initial transaction statement. Assume that on December 1, 1985, Seller exhibits a "clean" ITS to Buyer, dated December 1, 1984, indicating that Seller owns 1,000 shares of ABC Co. stock. Buyer has absolutely no assurance that Seller now owns any ABC Co. stock. That is, during the year, Seller may have sold the stock, pledged it as security for a loan, or a judgment creditor may have acquired a lien upon it. Buyer acquires no rights against ABC Co. in the stock until he receives his own ITS.

Rights of Purchasers

The buyer of a security expects to receive a good title, rightfully transferred, free of liens or claims.

---

18. See, for example, RMBCA §16.01(c).
19. See, for example, UCC §8-207(1) (1977).
20. UCC §8-408 (1977).
21. UCC §8-408(9) (1977).

Section 8-306 of the UCC provides for the buyer's basic title need by imposing warranty liability upon sellers who transfer certificated securities or originate instructions to transfer uncertificated securities. A person transferring a certificated security to a purchaser for value warrants that the transfer is effective and rightful, that the security is genuine and has not been materially altered, and that she knows of no fact that might impair the security's validity. The seller who originates instructions to transfer an uncertificated security undertakes substantially the same obligation, a warranty of absence of defects.

Under §8-301, upon transfer of a security, the purchaser acquires whatever rights in the instrument the transferor had or had authority to convey. This provision creates a "shelter rule" for investment securities identical to the one applicable to sales of goods (§2-403(1)) and commercial paper (§3-201(1)). In addition to acquiring the rights of his transferor, under §8-302 a "bona fide" purchaser acquires the security free of any adverse claim. Adverse claims include, for example, an assertion by a third party that the transfer is wrongful or that he or she is the owner of or has an interest in the security. A bona fide purchaser is one to whom a certificated security has been delivered with any necessary indorsement, or to whom the transfer of an uncertificated security is registered on the issuer's books, who pays value for the security in good faith without notice of any adverse claim to it. Thus, a bona fide purchaser is Article 8's equivalent to the holder in due course of commercial paper.

A purchaser of a certificated security generally is charged with notice only of facts apparent when he takes delivery of the security. Accordingly, most purchasers, who are not familiar with the history of a particular certificate, take the instrument free of liens, defenses, restrictions, or adverse claims not noted on or otherwise disclosed by the security itself. The purchaser of an uncertificated security, on the other hand, is charged with notice of what appears in the initial transaction statement sent by the issuer upon registration of the transfer, and acquires the security free of liens, defenses, restrictions, or adverse claims other than those noted in that statement. Thus, with an uncertificated security, the purchaser enjoys bona fide purchaser status

only after receiving a "clean" initial transaction statement.[22]

A bona fide purchaser acquires a security free of most claims and defenses. Lack of genuineness of a certificated security or initial transaction statement, however, may constitute a complete defense against even a bona fide purchaser, as the following case illustrates.

New Jersey Bank, N.A. v. Bradford Securities Operations, Inc.
690 F.2d 339 (3d Cir. 1982)

Bankers Trust Company was transfer agent for Southern California Edison Company (SCE). In 1976, Bankers Trust appointed Bradford Securities Operations, Inc. (BSOI) to serve as agent in issuing and transferring SCE stock. BSOI retained several thousand of SCE's blank stock certificates. When a new certificate was to be issued, BSOI filled in the owner's name and signed the certificate as transfer agent. BSOI then sent the certificate to Manufacturers Hanover Trust Company, which countersigned the certificate as registrar and recorded the shareholder's name. The certificate then was mailed to the owner.

In July 1977, BSOI discovered that 500 SCE certificates were missing from its vault. Although an investigation disclosed that the certificates had been removed in March 1977, the investigators failed to discover who had stolen them. Fifty of the missing certificates were found at New Jersey Bank (NJB). The bank had accepted the stock certificates as collateral for a loan made to Herman Rhodes in March 1977.

After Rhodes failed to pay the loan, NJB demanded that BSOI pay the face value of the certificates. When BSOI refused, NJB sued BSOI and Manufacturers Hanover. The trial court held that

---

22. A purchaser should not, therefore, release the purchase price to the seller unless and until a clean initial transaction statement is received. A purchaser who pays the seller first, and subsequently receives a statement indicating defects in the seller's title, is relegated to a claim against the seller for breach of warranty.

under Article 8 of the UCC, BSOI was not liable on the certificates. NJB appealed.

Becker, Circuit Judge

. . .[A]ssuming the certificates to be "securities," we agree with the district court that they are invalid under [UCC §]8-202(3). That section states: "Except as otherwise provided in the case of certain unauthorized signatures on issue (§8-205), lack of genuineness of a security is a *complete defense* even against a purchaser for value and without notice." (Emphasis added.) Section 8-205 sets out the exception specified in §8-202(3): an issuer will be liable to a bona fide purchaser if, but only if, the unauthorized signature is that of an employee or agent of the issuer entrusted with the signing of the certificates or with the responsible handling of such documents. . . .

BSOI argued that NJB failed to produce at trial any evidence that the signatures were those of BSOI employees authorized to sign the certificates. The district court agreed, finding no merit in the contention that the mere fact of theft from BSOI's custody was sufficient evidence that a BSOI employee was responsible for the unauthorized signatures. Nor did the court see any evidence of a link between an employee of BSOI and Rhodes. Having determined that NJB failed to prove that the certificates fell within §8-205's exception, the court concluded that §8-202(3)'s lack-of-genuineness defense was available to BSOI.

NJB nevertheless contends here, as it did below, that the certificates are valid whether the signatures are real or forged, interpreting the introductory language of §8-205 . . . to make *all* unauthorized signatures, including forgeries . . . effective against a bona fide purchaser. . . .

We disagree. NJB ignores the clear language of §8-205, which declares *all* unauthorized signatures, including forgeries, to be ineffective. The special rule for a bona fide purchaser applies only if (1) the purchaser has taken the certificates for value and without notice *and* (2) the signature is that of a person either responsible for the certificates or authorized to sign. This exception to the lack-of-genuineness defense, as we interpret it, protects an innocent third party from losses occasioned by a dishonest employee of the issuer or

transfer agent. But the issuer or its agent bears the risk of loss only when employees within its control are responsible for the unauthorized signature; when a person outside this group commits the forgery, even a bona fide purchaser must succumb to the familiar principle of *caveat emptor*. . . .

We therefore agree with the district court that NJB cannot invoke this exception unless it can prove that the certificates had been signed by someone entrusted by SCE or its agents with responsibility for signing or handling the documents. We also agree that NJB failed to adduce any evidence implicating a BSOI employee as the forger. The certificates accordingly are without effect even though NJB claims as a bona fide purchaser, and the district court was correct in ruling against NJB on its UCC claim. . . .

[Judgment affirmed.]

Lost, Destroyed, or Stolen Certificated Securities

A certificated security may be lost, destroyed, or stolen. The issuer who issues a replacement security runs the risk that the original certificate will later appear in the hands of a bona fide purchaser. Accordingly, §8-405 requires the issuer to issue a replacement security only if the owner (1) makes a request for a new security before the issuer has notice that the security has been acquired by a bona fide purchaser, (2) furnishes an adequate bond to indemnify the corporation if the original security is later presented for registration, and (3) satisfies any other reasonable requirements imposed by the issuer. An owner who fails to notify the issuer promptly that a security has been lost, destroyed, or stolen may not assert any claim against the issuer either for improperly registering a subsequent transfer or for a replacement security.

After the corporation issues a new certificate, a bona fide purchaser of the original certificate may present it for registration. In this situation, the corporation must register the transfer, but may then recover on the indemnity bond and may also recover the new certificate unless it has been transferred to a bona fide purchaser.

Dividends, Distributions, and Redemptions

Corporate **distributions** are transfers of money or other property by the corporation to its shareholders. A distribution out of a corporation's current or past earnings is a **dividend**.[23] Corporate distributions, whether of earnings or capital, may be proportionate or disproportionate to share ownership. For example, preferred shares may have preferential rights either to dividends or distributions in liquidation or both over other shares. In addition, a corporation's redemption, repurchase, or other acquisition of some of its shares may effect a disproportionate distribution. Because any corporate distribution may affect the rights of various classes of shareholders and, most important, corporate creditors, the law imposes limitations and restrictions on distributions of corporate assets to shareholders. These issues are discussed below.

Kinds of Dividends

Dividends are divided into three types: (1) cash, (2) property, and (3) share or stock. A cash dividend, the most common type, is a distribution of legally available funds to the shareholders. The amount of the dividend is commonly stated on a cents or dollars per share basis, or as a percentage of the stated or par value of the shares. Property dividends, or dividends-in-kind, are those consisting of property other than cash or the corporation's own shares. Shares of a subsidiary or other corporation or other securities commonly are used for such dividends.

Unlike cash or property dividends, share dividends do not distribute corporate assets to the shareholder. Rather, a share dividend distributes to shareholders additional shares of the declaring corporation, or fractions thereof, for each share owned. For example, in a ten percent share dividend, each shareholder receives an additional one share for each ten shares owned. A share dividend

---

23. The term dividend also is commonly used to describe distributions from capital, or distributions in partial liquidation, as well as distributions of earnings and profits. More appropriately, however, transfers from capital should simply be referred to as distributions, not dividends.

increases the total number of shares representing the corporation's equity, and proportionately reduces the percentage ownership each share represents. Usually, but not necessarily, the additional shares are of the same class as the original shares.

Shareholders owning fewer than the minimum number of shares or an amount not divisible by the minimum may receive fractional shares. Alternatively, **scrip,** a certificate representing the right to receive a portion of a share, may be used. Scrip, unlike fractional shares, confers neither voting, dividend, nor liquidation rights upon its holder. Scrip may, however, be bought and sold, and when combined with sufficient additional scrip, is surrendered to the corporation in exchange for a full share.

Closely related to a share dividend is a share split, because both increase the number of outstanding shares but do not distribute assets. They differ, however, in their effect on the corporate capital accounts. In a share dividend, the par value or in some cases the fair market value of the dividend shares is capitalized, transferred from the earned surplus to the stated capital or capital surplus account. In a share split, there is no transfer of earnings to capital.

Dividend Preferences

As a general rule, shareholders participate in dividends declared by the corporation in proportion to share ownership. The articles of incorporation may grant one or more classes of shares—preferred shares—the right to receive dividends or distributions in liquidation of the corporation, before the common shares. Dividend preferences usually are fixed in the articles in an amount expressed in dollars or as a percentage of the par value of the stock and may be cumulative, noncumulative, or cumulative-to-the-extent-earned. A **cumulative dividend preference** entitles a shareholder to receive a prescribed dividend for the current year and all prior years in which the preferred dividend was not paid, before any dividend may be paid on the common shares. If a dividend preference is **noncumulative,** preferred dividends not paid in prior years do not accumulate and need not be satisfied before dividends are subsequently paid to shares with subordinate dividend rights. Only the current year's preference need be satisfied.

A dividend preference that is **cumulative-to-the-extent-earned** entitles preferred shareholders to carry forward and accumulate unpaid dividends to the extent that the corporation had earnings available to pay the dividend in the year or years that the dividend was omitted. For example, assume a corporation had no earnings in 1985, but substantial earnings in 1986 and 1987. If the preferred is cumulative-to-the-extent-earned and dividends are to be paid in 1987, the preferred dividends for 1986 and 1987 must be satisfied before any dividend is paid to the common.

Preferred shares, whether cumulative, noncumulative, or cumulative-to-the-extent-earned, may or may not be entitled to additional dividends beyond their fixed dividend preference. Shares that are entitled to receive the amount of the stated dividend preference and no more are **nonparticipating.** In contrast, **participating** preferred are entitled to share in dividends with other classes of shares in addition to the dividend preference. The articles of incorporation outline whether preferred shares are participating or not and the nature of that participation—for example, equally with other shares, in a fixed ratio, after other classes have been paid, or upon occurrence of a condition.

The Dividend Decision

A corporation pays dividends if, when, and as declared by the board of directors. Once declared, a dividend becomes a legally enforceable obligation of the corporation and cannot be repealed or retracted by the board. Dividend policy is influenced by factors such as corporate earnings, future capital needs of the business, and shareholder expectations. In closely-held corporations, federal income tax consequences of distribution or retention to major shareholders often is determinative.

The decision to pay dividends, even upon shares with a dividend preference, is within the business judgment and therefore the discretion of the board. Courts generally will not intervene to compel payment of dividends unless a complaining shareholder proves an abuse of that discretion. Abuse of discretion may be found, for example, if the directors' conduct is fraudulent, dishonest, or clearly unrea-

sonable. Although relief has been granted in very few cases, such as the following, preferred shareholders and shareholders in closely-held corporations have been the most successful in suits to compel dividend distributions.

Dodge v. Ford Motor Co.
170 N.W. 668 (Mich. 1919)

Defendant Ford Motor Company (Ford) was organized and incorporated in 1903. In 1916, plaintiffs John and Horace Dodge, who owned ten percent of the stock of Ford, sued the corporation demanding that it pay dividends to the shareholders.

The evidence at trial established that Ford had paid regular annual dividends of $1.2 million and from 1911 through 1915 had paid additional "special dividends" totalling $41 million. After the board of directors adopted a plan to expand the company by increasing the plant and equipment, Ford began to accumulate a large surplus to finance the expansion.

The trial court ruled in favor of the Dodges and ordered Ford Motor Company to pay a dividend of $10 million. Ford appealed.

Ostrander, Chief Justice

. . . When plaintiffs made their complaint and demand for further dividends, the Ford Motor Company had concluded its most prosperous year of business. The demand for its cars at the price of the preceding year continued. It could make and could market in the year beginning August 1, 1916, more than 500,000 cars. Sales of parts and repairs would necessarily increase. The cost of materials was likely to advance, and perhaps the price of labor; but it reasonably might have expected a profit for the year of upwards of $60,000,000. It had assets of more than $132,000,000, a surplus of almost $112,000,000, and its cash on hand and municipal bonds were nearly $54,000,000. Its total liabilities including capital stock, was a little over $20,000,000. It had declared no special dividend during the business year except the October, 1915, dividend. It had been the practice, under similar circumstances, to declare larger dividends. Considering only these facts, a refusal to declare and pay further dividends appears to be not an exercise of discretion on the part of the directors, but an arbitrary refusal to do what the circumstances required to be done. These facts and others call upon the directors to justify their action, or failure or refusal to act. . . .

A business corporation is organized and carried on primarily for the profit of the stockholders. The powers of the directors are to be employed for that end. The discretion of directors is to be exercised in the choice of means to attain that end, and does not extend to a change in the end itself, to the reduction of profits, or to the nondistribution of profits among stockholders in order to devote them to other purposes. . . .

We are not, however, persuaded that we should interfere with the proposed expansion of the business of the Ford Motor Company. . . .

Assuming . . . that the plan and policy and the details agreed upon were for the best ultimate interest of the company and therefore of its shareholders, what does it amount to in justification of a refusal to declare and pay a special dividend or dividends? The Ford Motor Company was able to estimate with nicety its income and profit. It could sell more cars than it could make. . . . [T]he yearly income and profit was determinable, and, within slight variations, was certain. . . .

The company was continuing business, at a profit—a cash business. If the total cost of proposed expenditures had been immediately withdrawn in cash from the cash surplus (money and bonds) on hand August 1, 1916, there would have remained nearly $30,000,000.

Defendants say, and it is true, that a considerable cash balance must be at all times carried by such a concern. But, as has been stated, there was a large daily, weekly, monthly, receipt of cash. The output was practically continuous and was continuously, and within a few days, turned into cash. Moreover, the contemplated expenditures were not to be immediately made. The large sum appropriated for the smelter plant was payable over a considerable period of time. So that, without going further, it would appear that, accepting and approving the plan of the directors, it was their duty to distribute on or near the 1st of August, 1916, a very large sum of money to stockholders. . . .

The decree of the court below fixing and deter-

mining the specific amount to be distributed to stockholders is affirmed. . . .

Funds Legally Available for Dividends

To protect corporate creditors and, in some instances, preferred shareholders, the law limits distributions of corporate assets to shareholders. State business corporation acts determine which funds are legally available for dividends and impose widely varying requirements. Some of the tests used include the following.

1. In all states, a dividend payment is prohibited if the corporation is insolvent or would be rendered insolvent by the distribution. Insolvency is commonly defined as inability to pay debts as they come due in the ordinary course of business (equity insolvency) or an excess of total liabilities over total assets (bankruptcy insolvency).[24]

2. Assuming solvency, all jurisdictions permit dividends to be paid to the extent of the corporation's unrestricted and unreserved earned surplus (retained earnings). Earned surplus consists of accumulated profits earned by the corporation since its formation reduced primarily by prior dividend distributions.

3. Assuming solvency, some states permit corporate distributions to be made out of any surplus, capital, earned or both. These statutes are commonly said to prohibit an "impairment" of stated capital by a dividend. Distributions from capital surplus may, however, be limited if the corporation has no earned surplus.

4. Some states permit dividends to be paid from current profits even if a deficit exists in the earned surplus account from losses incurred in prior periods. These are known as "nimble" dividends.

The various dividend tests tied to surplus are confusing and provide little creditor protection. For

---

24. Even in the absence of a provision in a state's corporation statute, distribution of assets to shareholders by an insolvent corporation would probably be voidable by creditors as a fraudulent conveyance under state debtor-creditor law. Fraudulent conveyances are discussed in Chapter 29.

this reason, the MBCA, as amended in 1979, and the RMBCA eliminate the concept of par value, surplus, and stated capital, and make validity of corporate distributions turn solely upon whether the corporation is insolvent in either the equity or bankruptcy sense immediately after the distribution.[25]

State corporate statutes generally impose liability upon directors for unlawful dividends or other distributions. For example, under the MBCA and RMBCA, a director who votes for or assents to the declaration of any dividend or other distribution in violation of statutory limitations or the articles of incorporation is liable to the corporation for the amount by which the dividend or distribution exceeds that legally permissible.[26] A defense to liability is recognized if the director exercised due care in making the distribution by relying upon financial statements or opinions provided by corporate officers, employees, accountants, or attorneys.

Repurchase or Redemption

A corporation has the power to acquire its own shares.[27] It may also issue stock, generally preferred, that may be redeemed by the corporation. The shares (sometimes called "treasury shares") acquired by the corporation are functionally equivalent to authorized but unissued shares.[28] Accordingly, after the repurchase or redemption, the re-

maining outstanding shares each represent a proportionately larger interest in a reduced pool of assets.

A repurchase or redemption is similar in effect to a dividend; in both cases, the corporation distributes corporate assets to its shareholders without consideration. Unlike a dividend, however, a redemption or repurchase involves an element of exchange—shares of stock for corporate assets. It also effects a disproportionate distribution of corporate assets to the selling shareholders. Dividends are usually paid to all shareholders in proportion to their holdings.

A corporation may repurchase its own shares for a variety of reasons. In a closely-held corporation, for example, the repurchase may be used to buy out one or more shareholders. In a publicly-held corporation, repurchased shares may be used for employee compensation plans or to purchase other corporations. Additionally, substantial repurchases may drive up the price of remaining shares and may thus be used as a defensive measure to defeat a hostile takeover bid.

To protect creditors, reacquisitions and redemptions are subject to legal restrictions similar to those applicable to dividends. Indeed, the MBCA and RMBCA apply the same insolvency standard previously described to all corporate distributions including dividends and repurchase and redemption of shares.[29]

SUMMARY

1. In ongoing corporations, most funds are generated by reinvesting some portion of corporate earnings into the business. An initial, and often continuing, method of raising corporate funds is to issue corporate "securities" in exchange for cash, property, or services. Securities are of two basic types: equity and debt. Equity securities, such as shares of common and preferred

stock, create an ownership interest in the business. In contrast, debt securities, such as notes, bonds, and debentures, are issued in exchange for loans made to the corporation. Corporate management usually has flexibility in determining the corporation's mix of debt and equity securities, its capital structure.

2. A corporation has the power to create and issue as many shares of stock as are authorized in its articles of incorporation. These shares may be preferred (enjoying a preference over other shares for dividends or for amounts distributed on liquidation, or both) or common, and may be redeemable by the corporation or convertible into another class of shares.

3. In exchange for shares issued, shareholders and

---

25. MBCA §45, RMBCA §6.40(c).

26. MBCA §48, RMBCA §8.33.

27. See, for example, MBCA §6, RMBCA §6.31.

28. The articles of incorporation may prohibit reissue of reacquired shares. In this case, the acquired shares are cancelled and the number of authorized shares is reduced by the number of shares acquired. See MBCA §6, RMBCA §6.31.

29. MBCA §45, RMBCA §6.40.

subscribers are legally obligated to pay to the corporation the amount determined by the board of directors. If a purchaser fails to pay full consideration for shares, the shares may be cancelled, or alternatively, the shareholder may be compelled to contribute additional consideration.

4. Publicly-held corporations commonly issue debt securities known as bonds and debentures. These securities are often issued and administered under an indenture between the issuing corporation and a trustee, usually a financial institution.

5. Corporate debt and equity securities are generally evidenced by a document—for example, a stock certificate—and are known as "certificated securities." Certificated securities may be issued in registered or bearer form. A certificated security is transferred by delivery of a bearer security or indorsement and delivery of a registered security. After the transfer, the security may be presented to the issuer for registration of the transferee as the new registered owner. An uncertificated security is recorded on the books of the issuer though there is no instrument evidencing the holder's interest in or claim against the corporation. Uncertificated debt or equity securities are transferred by registering the transfer with the issuer according to the transferor's instructions.

6. Rights of purchasers of investment securities are governed by principles similar to those applied to transferees of commercial paper. Article 8 of the Uniform Commercial Code imposes warranty liability upon transferors for title and other defects, and transferees have the benefit of a "shelter" rule. Further, a "bona fide" purchaser, the Article 8 equivalent of a holder in due course, acquires the security free of any adverse claim.

7. A certificated security may be lost, destroyed, or stolen. The issuer is required to issue a new security only if the owner meets specific legal requirements designed to protect the issuer.

8. Corporate distributions are transfers of money or other property by the corporation to its shareholders. A distribution out of a corporation's current or past earnings is a dividend. Other distributions include repurchases and redemptions of outstanding shares.

9. Dividends are of three types: cash, property, and share. Although shareholders generally participate in dividends declared by the corporation in proportion to share ownership, the articles of incorporation may grant one or more classes of shares—preferred shares—the right to receive dividends or distributions in liquidation of the corporation, before the common shares. Dividend preferences may be cumulative, cumulative-to-the-extent-earned, or noncumulative, and may be participating or nonparticipating. A corporation pays dividends if, when, and as declared by the board of directors.

10. To protect corporate creditors and in some instances, preferred shareholders, the law limits the extent to which a corporation may distribute dividends to shareholders. Funds legally available for dividends are determined by various tests tied to insolvency, earned or other surplus, or existence of net profits.

11. A corporation has the power to acquire its own shares and may issue stock that may be redeemed by the corporation. Legal restrictions, similar to those governing dividends, are imposed to protect creditors in reacquisitions and redemptions.

KEY TERMS

security	initial transaction
equity securities	statement (ITS)
debt securities	distribution
preferred shares	dividend
common shares	scrip
par value	cumulative dividend
stock subscription	preference
watered shares	noncumulative dividend
debenture	preference
bond	cumulative-to-the-extent-
indenture	earned dividend
certificated securities	preference
uncertificated securities	nonparticipating
	participating

QUESTIONS AND PROBLEMS

46-1   State statutes traditionally have allowed issuance of corporate shares only in exchange for cash, property, or services previously performed for the corporation. The Revised Model Business Corporation Act, however, allows shares to be issued for future services, promissory notes, or any tangible or intangible property or benefit to the corporation. (See RMBCA §6.21(b).)

(a) What is the purpose of the traditional requirement that stock be issued only for money, property, or services previously performed?

(b) Suggest reasons warranting the relaxed standards contained in the Revised Model Business Corporation Act.

46-2   A partnership known as "Leonard Plumbing and Heating Supply Co." was organized in October 1980. The three partners, Fazio, Ambrose, and B. T. Leonard, had capital contributions as of September 1984 totalling $51,620.78, distributed as follows: Fazio, $43,169.61; Ambrose, $6,451.17; and Leonard, $2,000.

In the fall of that year, it was decided to incorporate the business. In contemplation of this step, Fazio and Ambrose, on September 15,

1984, withdrew all but $2,000 apiece of their capital contributions to the business. This was accomplished by the issuance to them, on that date, of partnership promissory notes in the sum of $41,169.61 and $4,451.17, respectively. These were demand notes, no interest being specified. The capital contribution to the partnership business then stood at $6,000—$2,000 for each partner.

During 1984 the corporation lost $22,000 on sales of $400,000. The firm's ratio of current assets to current liabilities was 1:1. In June 1986, after suffering additional losses, the corporation filed a voluntary bankruptcy petition. Fazio and Ambrose filed claims against the estate for the promissory notes given to them upon incorporation. Over the objection of the trustee in bankruptcy, the bankruptcy court allowed their claims finding that the paid-in capital at the time of incorporation was adequate, and that Fazio and Ambrose had not mismanaged the business, or practiced fraud or deception.

(a) Do you agree with this conclusion or should the claims of Fazio and Ambrose be subordinated to the claims of the corporation's other unsecured creditors?

(b) The issue of undercapitalization of a corporation usually arises, as in this case, only after the corporation has become insolvent or bankrupt. How can a business person know whether an ongoing business is undercapitalized?

46-3 Review the facts presented in the *New Jersey Bank* case at page 965. NJB also alleged that its losses were due to BSOI's negligence in safeguarding the certificates. The evidence showed that BSOI kept a log system for tracking the certificates and conducted monthly random audits of certificates in the vault.

(a) Does BSOI's system provide sufficient protection to withstand allegations of negligence?

(b) Recommend ways that the system could be improved keeping in mind the necessity for cost effectiveness.

(c) Does the fact that the court found against NJB on the Article 8 claim excerpted in the text preclude NJB's recovery on the basis of the common law tort of negligence, assuming negligence is proven? What sections of the UCC would be relevant in resolving the issue?

46-4 Glenn owned 100 shares of Moonlight Co. common stock. After Glenn died on September 23,

his brother Roy was appointed executor and began to collect the assets of Glenn's estate. The task was difficult because Glenn had been in the habit of hiding important papers in his house. Roy thoroughly searched Glenn's house four times between October 1 and November 1 but could not find the certificates for the Moonlight stock. On November 15, Roy wrote to the Moonlight Co. transfer agent requesting information on replacing the stock certificates. Roy's letter stated "Although we continue to search for the certificates, we now assume they have been lost."

(a) What procedure should the transfer agent recommend?

(b) Pursuant to instructions from his attorney, on December 28, Roy sent a "stop order" to the transfer agent requesting that it not transfer Glenn's shares of Moonlight Co. because the certificates had been lost. The transfer agent replied by notifying Roy that his stop order had arrived too late: the stock had been sold on October 29 and Glenn's signature had been forged. The purchaser had bought the shares through a broker and had paid market price for the shares. The transfer agent claims that it owes nothing to Glenn's estate. Is the transfer agent correct? Explain.

46-5 Park Corporation has issued 50,000 shares of cumulative, preferred stock. Park's bylaws provide: "The holders of the preferred stock shall be entitled to receive, and the Corporation shall be bound to pay thereon, but only out of the net profits of the Corporation, a fixed yearly dividend of one dollar ($1.00) per share."

(a) In 1983, Park operated at a loss and had no net profit. Are the preferred shareholders entitled to receive a dividend? Explain.

(b) In 1984, Park had net profits of $35,000. Are the preferred shareholders entitled to a dividend? Explain.

(c) In 1985, Park Corporation's net profits exceeded $200,000. Are the preferred shareholders entitled to a dividend? Explain.

46-6 Explain the similarities and differences between a dividend and a redemption or repurchase of shares. Summarize the various types of legal restrictions on corporate distributions. What purpose are these restrictions designed to serve?

46-7 The decision to pay corporate dividends is within the discretion of the board of directors. Why are courts hesitant to disturb the board's decision regarding the timing and amount of dividends?

Chapter 47

Corporate Management—Structure and Duties

Major Topics

- a discussion of the management structure of a corporation, including the functions and powers of the shareholders, directors, and officers
- coverage of the various duties owed by corporate management to the corporation and its shareholders, including the primary duties of care and loyalty

Once created, a corporation must be managed by natural persons, whose functions, rights, powers, and duties are determined by constitutions, statutes, administrative rules and regulations, and a variety of intracorporate sources such as the articles of incorporation, bylaws, resolutions, and private contracts. Corporate management powers are divided among the shareholders, the board of directors, and corporate officers. The shareholders, the owners of the corporation, periodically elect the board of directors, who have ultimate responsibility to manage the corporation. The board of directors, in turn, appoints corporate officers and delegates to them the authority to operate the corporation consistent with management policy determined by the board. The officers often appoint additional executive officers and employees to manage day-to-day business activities. Collectively, the officers and directors of a corporation are known as its "management." In closely-held corporations the same persons are of-

ten simultaneously shareholders, directors, and officers.

Corporate Management Structure

Shareholders—Meetings

Although the shareholders are the owners of the corporation, their participation in management is generally limited to voting on the election of directors and upon extraordinary corporate matters such as amendments to the articles of incorporation, dissolution, merger or consolidation, or sale of corporate assets outside the ordinary course of business. In addition, the power to amend, adopt, or repeal bylaws may be reserved to the shareholders in the articles of incorporation, and shareholders may generally repeal or change bylaws adopted by the directors.[1]

Shareholder votes are normally taken at either annual or special meetings. Corporations usually are required to hold an annual shareholders' meeting at a time stated in, or fixed by, the bylaws.[2] Although the primary purpose of the annual meeting is to elect some or all of the directors, other business also may be conducted. For example, management reports may be made, bylaws may be amended or repealed, and shareholder or manage-

---

1. See, for example, MBCA §27, RMBCA §10.20.
2. See, for example, MBCA §28, RMBCA §7.01(a).

ment resolutions may be considered and submitted for a vote. In addition to the annual meeting, special meetings addressing specific issues may be called by the board of directors, the holders of a specified number of shares, or other persons specified in the articles of incorporation or bylaws. Written advance notice of the time, place, and the date of both annual and special meetings must be given to each shareholder entitled to vote. Notice of a special meeting must include a description of its purpose, and only business within that purpose may be conducted at the meeting.[3]

At annual and special meetings, shareholders may vote in person or may authorize other persons to vote their shares by proxy. To conduct business, a quorum must be present—usually a majority of shares entitled to vote, represented either in person or by proxy.[4] Although the articles of incorporation may provide a different quorum percentage, many state statutes provide that a quorum may not be less than one-third of shares entitled to vote. Unless otherwise stated in the articles or bylaws, a majority vote of a quorum constitutes the act of the shareholders.

The MBCA and many state statutes permit shareholders to take action without a meeting if written consent to the action is signed by all shareholders entitled to vote on the issue. The consent device eliminates unnecessary formal meetings and is particularly useful in closely-held corporations in which many decisions are unanimous.[5]

To determine which shareholders are entitled to notice of a meeting, to demand a special meeting, to vote, or to take other shareholder action, the bylaws or board of directors may fix a "record date." Persons listed on the corporate books as the registered owners of shares on the record date are entitled to vote. Statutes generally require that the record date be fixed within a limited period preceding the meeting, for example, not more than seventy days before the meeting.[6] Once the record date is established, the officer or agent in charge of the stock transfer books prepares a complete "voting list" or "voting record" of shareholders entitled to vote. This list must be made available to shareholders for inspection and copying at the meeting and under some statutes, in advance of the meeting.[7]

Shareholders—Voting

Unless otherwise provided in the articles of incorporation, each outstanding share, regardless of class, is entitled to one vote on each matter presented at the meeting. The articles may provide for more than one vote for any share. Treasury shares and shares held by other corporations controlled by the issuing corporation are not entitled to vote and are not counted in determining the number of outstanding shares. Redeemable shares are not entitled to vote after notice of redemption is mailed and money sufficient to redeem the shares has been deposited with a financial institution.[8]

Voting rights of any class of shares may be limited or denied in the articles of incorporation. The MBCA provides, however, that shareholders are entitled to vote as a class, even if otherwise denied voting rights, if an amendment to the articles of incorporation is proposed that would alter the rights of that class (for example, a change in number of authorized shares, preferences, or preemptive rights).[9] A similar rule applies to votes concerning merger or voluntary dissolution of the corporation.

Election of Directors—Straight and Cumulative Voting. Voting to elect the board of directors may be either straight or cumulative. **Straight voting** is the usual method of shareholder voting. Under this approach, each share is entitled to one vote on each matter, including one vote for each vacant directorship. Because directors are elected by a plurality of votes, the shareholder with the largest block of shares elects all the directors.

To assure minority representation on the board of directors, many states require cumulative voting. In other states, cumulative voting may be provided for or excluded in the articles of incorporation.

---

3. See MBCA §§28, 29; RMBCA §§7.01, 7.02, 7.05.
4. MBCA §32, RMBCA §7.25.
5. MBCA §145, RMBCA §7.04.
6. RMBCA §7.07(b). If the corporation fails to fix a record date, eligibility to vote is often determined as of the date the notice of the meeting is mailed.

---

7. MBCA §31, RMBCA §7.20.
8. See, for example, MBCA §33, RMBCA §7.21.
9. See MBCA §60, RMBCA §10.04.

Under **cumulative voting**, which applies only to the election of directors, the number of votes each shareholder receives is equal to the number of his or her shares multiplied by the number of directorships to be filled. Therefore, if seven directors are to be elected, a shareholder owning 300 shares receives 2,100 votes, all of which may be cast for one director or may be distributed as the shareholder sees fit.[10]

As the number of directors to be elected decreases, an increasingly greater number of minority shares is required to elect one director. Thus the value of cumulative voting decreases with the size of the board of directors. In addition, as discussed later in this chapter, the MBCA and most other state statutes authorize classification of directors, which further minimizes the effect of cumulative voting as a means of assuring minority representation.

Proxies and Proxy Voting. The grant of authority by a shareholder to another to vote his or her shares is a **proxy**. In large publicly-held corporations, management must usually solicit proxies to obtain a quorum at a meeting, because few shareholders personally attend.[11] Many statutes require that the proxy be in a writing signed by the shareholder.[12] The proxy holder, the agent appointed to vote the shares, need not be a shareholder but must have capacity to act as an agent. A general proxy authorizes the proxy holder to vote on all issues presented at the meeting. The duration of the proxy varies among the states. The MBCA and RMBCA provide that a proxy is valid for eleven months, unless a longer period is provided in the proxy.[13]

Like other agencies, appointment of a proxy is generally revocable by the shareholder; revocation may also occur by operation of law upon the shareholder's death or incapacity. Some statutes, however, provide that revocation by operation of law is ineffective, unless notice of the death or incapacity is communicated to the corporation before the proxy is exercised.[14] A proxy may, however, be irrevocable if it is "coupled with an interest" or "given as security." For example, a shareholder may pledge her shares to a creditor as collateral on a loan, appointing the creditor irrevocably as proxy holder.[15] Such a proxy is, however, revoked when the interest with which it is coupled is extinguished—for example, when the debt secured by the shares is paid.[16]

Voting Trusts and Voting Agreements. A person who accumulates sufficient proxies from shareholders can obtain control of the corporation or at least assure representation on the board of directors. Voting trusts and voting agreements also may be used to control large blocks of stock. A **voting trust** is created when a group of shareholders transfer legal title to their shares to a trustee in exchange for "voting trust certificates." The trustee has the power to vote the shares subject to any limitations in the trust agreement. Corporate dividends and other distributions are usually passed through the trust to the equitable owners of the shares, the holders of the voting trust certificates. The voting trust certificates often are freely transferable, like the shares they represent.

Early cases refused to enforce voting trusts, holding that separating the right to vote from other

---

10. To determine the number of shares necessary to elect a given number of directors under cumulative voting the following formula is applied:

$$X = \frac{Y \times N^1}{N + 1} + 1$$

X is equal to the number of shares needed to elect a given number of directors. Y equals the total number of shares voted at the meeting. N^1 equals the number of directors the minority shareholder wishes to elect. N equals the total number of directors to be elected at the meeting. For example, assume a minority shareholder wishes to elect two directors to a nine-member board. One thousand shares will be voted at the meeting. The number of shares necessary equals:

$$\frac{1,000 \times 2}{9 + 1} + 1 = 201 \text{ shares.}$$

11. Important federal laws governing solicitation of proxies from shareholders of publicly-held corporations by management and nonmanagement groups are discussed in detail in Chapter 49 (Securities Regulation).

12. See, for example, MBCA §33, RMBCA §7.22(b).

13. MBCA §33, RMBCA §7.22(c).

14. See, for example, RMBCA §7.22(e). Revocation of agency is discussed in Chapter 40.

15. Other types of irrevocable proxies are listed in RMBCA §7.22(d).

16. See RMBCA §7.22(f).

incidents of share ownership was contrary to public policy. Modern corporation statutes, however, uniformly authorize voting trusts subject to certain restrictions. For example, under the RMBCA, to be enforceable, a voting trust must be in writing signed by the participating shareholders, and is not valid for more than ten years unless the parties extend it.[17]

The voting trust may concentrate control of a large block of shares in one or a few persons, who can thereby elect directors and control the corporation. Voting trusts often are used in corporate reorganizations to give control to former creditors whose debt has been reclassified as stock as part of the reorganization plan.

The shareholder **voting agreement** (or **pooling agreement**) is a less formal control device. Unlike the voting trust, which involves a transfer of title to the shares to a third party, a shareholder voting agreement is simply a contract between two or more shareholders providing how their shares will be voted on certain matters, usually the election of directors. Shareholder agreements are enforceable under basic contract principles and generally are expressly authorized by statute.[18] Shareholder agreements often are used to allocate and maintain control in closely-held corporations. Their use in that context is discussed in more detail in Chapter 48.

Shareholders—Right to Information

Corporate Records. Each corporation is required by law to keep appropriate accounting books and records, minutes of its shareholders' and board of directors' meetings, and a detailed record of its shareholders. These records must be maintained in written form or in another form that can be reduced to writing within a reasonable time.[19]

Shareholder Inspection of Records. Shareholders have a right to be kept informed of corporate affairs. To effectuate this purpose, both common law and statute confer upon shareholders a qualified right to inspect corporate books and records. Apart from statute, shareholders have the common law right to inspect books and records for "proper purposes."

State business corporation acts generally supplement the common law right with a statutory inspection right. The statutory right is typically limited to persons who own at least a minimum number of shares or who have been shareholders for a minimum period, or both. For example, under many state statutes, a shareholder who owns at least five percent of the outstanding stock or who has been a shareholder for at least six months is entitled to inspect books and records. This right is exercised by written demand on the corporation stating the purpose of the demand. The statutory right may extend only to certain books and records, preserving the shareholder's common law right for others. Penalties for failure to honor a statutory demand for inspection vary among the states.[20]

By statute, a shareholder's right to inspect certain records, such as the articles of incorporation or bylaws, may be absolute. Inspection of other records, however, such as accounting records or the list of shareholders, commonly requires that the demand be made in good faith and for a proper purpose.[21] A proper purpose is one designed to obtain information to protect the shareholder's interest in the corporation. Proper purposes include, for example, ascertaining the financial condition of the corporation, the value of shares, the propriety of dividend payments, discovering the existence of dishonesty or mismanagement by corporate officers or directors, and communicating with other shareholders to solicit proxies or publicize mismanagement. Improper purposes include harassment or extortion, acquiring trade secrets for personal benefit or a corporate competitor, and obtaining the shareholder list to sell for profit.

The line between proper and improper purposes is imprecise and has generated a substantial volume of litigation, illustrated by the following case.

---

17. RMBCA §7.30.
18. See, for example, MBCA §34, RMBCA §7.31.
19. See, for example, RMBCA §§16.01 (a)-(d).

20. Under the MBCA, for example, corporate officers who refuse to permit inspection after a proper demand are subjected to a statutory penalty equal to 10% of the value of the shareholder's shares in addition to other damages sustained. MBCA §52.
21. See, for example, RMBCA §16.02.

Weigel v. O'Connor

373 N.E.2d 421 (Ill. App. 1978)

Plaintiff John Weigel organized Weigel Broadcasting Company in 1962. In 1966, defendants J. W. O'Connor and Howard Shapiro acquired more than two-thirds of the company's common stock. O'Connor became chairman of the board and Shapiro was elected president. Weigel retained approximately nine percent of the company's stock.

In a letter dated July 22, 1975, Weigel made a formal demand to inspect specified corporate books and records, including certain contracts, invoices, and accounting records. The demand stated several purposes for the inspection, including ascertaining the value of the corporate stock, the financial condition of the corporation and its sources of revenue, the officers' compensation, and the amount of broadcasting time given as trade-outs (sales of advertising time for goods or services rather than cash). After the corporation failed to respond to the demand, Weigel filed a lawsuit seeking a court order to allow the inspection. At trial, Weigel testified that corporate employees had informed him of several incidents of misconduct and mismanagement. Weigel also testified that he had questioned Shapiro and O'Connor about the incidents but had received inadequate responses. The trial court ordered the corporate officers to provide some of the documents requested by Weigel but held that Weigel had failed to establish a proper purpose for the other books and records. Weigel appealed.

Linn, Justice

. . . Section 45 of the Illinois Business Corporation Act gives a stockholder in a corporation, who otherwise qualifies under the provisions of the statute, the right to examine "in person, or by agent or attorney, at any reasonable time or times, for any proper purpose, its books and records of accounts, minutes and record of shareholders and to make extracts therefrom." . . . The Illinois Supreme Court has interpreted the phrase "for any proper purpose" to include "honest motive" and "good faith." . . . A proper purpose is one which seeks to protect the interests of the corporation as well as the interests of the shareholder seeking the

information. . . . A shareholder is legitimately entitled to know anything and everything which the records, books and papers of the company would show so as to protect his interest and so long as he has an honest motive and is not proceeding for vexatious or speculative reasons. . . .

A stockholder must be seeking something more than satisfaction of his curiosity and must not be conducting a general fishing expedition. . . .

Although the burden of proving good faith and proper purpose rests with the stockholder . . . , proof of actual mismanagement or wrongdoing is not necessary. Good faith fears of mismanagement are sufficient. . . .

In support of the plaintiff's claim of proper purpose the following evidence was adduced at trial. Weigel was the founder and a longtime shareholder in the corporation in which he retained a substantial investment. Although not always in agreement with current management, the plaintiff actively participated in shareholders' meetings and corresponded with other minority shareholders. Weigel's testimony indicated that, based on information received from corporate insiders, he had reason to fear that the financial security of the corporation was being jeopardized by the personal use of trade-outs by corporate officers, the giving of kick-backs to advertising agents and the uncompensated use of corporate property for the benefit of another corporation. In an attempt to verify the insider information the plaintiff unsuccessfully questioned two of the defendant corporate officers. These factors, coupled with the history of the lack of dividend payments, are sufficient indications of proper purpose to support plaintiff's demand. . . .

A single proper purpose is sufficient to satisfy the statutory requirement. . . . Once that purpose has been established, the shareholder's right of inspection extends to all books and records necessary to make an intelligent and searching investigation. . . . The language "books and records" has been construed to extend to contracts and other papers. . . .

A shareholder need not establish a proper purpose in respect to each document he desires to examine; a proper purpose which would entitle him to the right of inspection generally is sufficient. . . . Here, the plaintiff made a specific demand for designated documents, not a blanket de-

mand for all books and records of the corporation, although such omnibus demands have been upheld.
. . .

Plaintiff argues convincingly that all the records included in his demand must be examined together in order to reveal a true picture of the corporate operations. We agree. It is elementary that if corporate mismanagement or the misuse of corporate property exists (and we do not assert that it does exist in this case), it will best be shown by a total examination of all reasonably required books and records of the corporation. . . .

[Judgment reversed and remanded.]

Shareholders—Preemptive Rights

Frequently, an existing corporation will issue additional shares of stock to finance corporate operations or expansion. Existing shareholders may enjoy "preemptive rights" in such new shares issued by an ongoing corporate concern. A **preemptive right** allows an existing shareholder to purchase a new issue of shares in proportion to his present interest in the corporation, before the shares are sold to others. A preemptive right, if exercised, prevents dilution of a shareholder's financial or voting interest in the corporation. Though initially recognized by judicial decision, preemptive rights now generally are governed by statutes that usually provide that preemptive rights may be limited or denied by appropriate provision in the articles of incorporation.

Even if preemptive rights are permitted, both the common law and statutes recognize a number of exceptions. For example, preemptive rights generally apply only to new issues, not to shares which were previously authorized but unissued. In addition, no preemptive right generally exists to acquire shares issued for property or services rather than cash; shares issued in connection with a merger, consolidation, or reorganization; shares issued to satisfy conversion or option rights; treasury shares; and shares issued to officers, directors, or employees under incentive or compensation plans.[22]

Preemptive rights are likely to be valuable to shareholders of a closely-held corporation to protect proportionate interests in control, dividends, and surplus. In contrast, most shareholders in publicly-held corporations own an insignificant percentage of its stock and possess a minimal voice in control of the business. In this situation, denial of preemptive rights has little effect upon shareholders, and proportionate ownership can be maintained, if desired, by purchasing shares on the market.

Directors

All corporate powers are exercised by, or under the authority of, the board of directors. In addition, the business and affairs of the corporation are managed under the direction of the board.[23]

As part of its management function the board: (1) makes basic policy decisions concerning, for example, products, services, prices, or labor relations, (2) selects, supervises, and removes corporate officers and other executive personnel and delegates authority to them, (3) determines executive compensation including pension and retirement plans, (4) determines if, when, and in what form or amount dividends will be paid, (5) determines financing and capital changes, (6) adopts, amends, and repeals bylaws, (7) participates with shareholders in effecting major corporate changes such as merger or dissolution, and (8) supervises the overall operation of the enterprise.[24] Directors may be insiders—persons who are also officers or employees of the corporation or its affiliates. The board also may include "outside" directors, persons not affiliated with management. Increasingly in recent years, boards of large publicly-held companies include a mixture of both inside and outside directors.

Election, Constitution, and Tenure of Board of Directors. Although older corporation statutes required that the board consist of at least three directors, modern statutes commonly permit one- or

---

22. See, for example, MBCA §§26, 26A; RMBCA §6.30.

23. See MBCA §35, RMBCA §8.01(b).
24. Henn & Alexander, *Laws of Corporations* 564 (3d ed. 1983).

two-person boards.[25] The number and qualifications of directors must be specified in the articles of incorporation or bylaws.

The initial board of directors, named in the articles of incorporation or elected by the incorporators, serves until the first annual meeting of shareholders, which is usually held shortly after incorporation. Permanent directors are elected at that meeting and at each annual meeting thereafter. Under the MBCA and RMBCA, if a corporation has nine or more directors, the articles of incorporation may provide for two or three classes of directors. If there are two classes, each class comes up for election every other year; that is, each serves a two-year term. Because the terms are staggered, only one class's term expires in any given year. In the absence of classification, all directors are elected each year.[26] After incorporation, the number of directors may be increased or decreased by appropriate amendment of the articles of incorporation or bylaws. A reduction in the number of directors does not shorten any incumbent director's term.

A director whose term has expired continues to serve until a successor is elected and qualified. Under this rule, corporate power to transact business is unaffected by failure to hold an annual meeting because existing directors continue in office. Vacancies on the board are filled as provided by statute or the bylaws. Under modern statutes, vacancies caused by death or resignation usually are filled by the board of directors. Vacancies caused by an increase in the number of board members also are often filled by the board, although some states require shareholder action. A director elected to fill a vacancy generally serves until the next meeting of shareholders at which directors are elected.[27]

During their terms of office, directors may be removed by the shareholders for cause, such as fraud or breach of duty, usually by majority vote. Modern statutes, such as the MBCA and RMBCA, also permit removal without cause by shareholder

vote, unless the articles of incorporation provide otherwise.[28]

Formalities of Board Action. Corporate management authority is vested in the board of directors as a body, not in individual directors. Accordingly, directors usually must act in properly constituted meetings, affording opportunity for discussion, deliberation, and collective judgment. The timing and other aspects of board of directors' meetings usually are governed by detailed bylaw provisions. Meetings are either regular or special and may be held either within or outside the state of incorporation. Although all types of business may be conducted at both regular and special meetings, directors generally are entitled to advance written notice of special, but not regular, meetings.[29]

Absent a provision to the contrary, a majority of the number of directors fixed in the bylaws or articles of incorporation constitutes a quorum for transaction of business. The articles or bylaws may provide greater quorum requirements, and some states permit less than a majority of the board—for example, one-third—to constitute a quorum. Many states also permit board members to participate in meetings by telephone.[30] If a quorum is present, the vote of a majority of directors present is the act of the board unless the articles or bylaws prescribe a greater number. Each director is entitled to one vote and may generally not vote by proxy.[31] Although the board usually acts in a meeting, the MBCA, the RMBCA, and most state statutes permit directors to act without a meeting if a written consent, stating the action taken, is signed by all directors. Such a consent has the same legal effect as a unanimous vote.[32]

A director who objects to an action authorized by a majority of the board must either request that a dissent be entered in the minutes of the meeting

---

25. MBCA §36, RMBCA §8.03(a).

26. MBCA §§36, 37, RMBCA §§8.05, 8.06.

27. See generally MBCA §36, RMBCA §8.05.

28. See MBCA §39, RMBCA §8.08.

29. See, for example, MBCA §43, RMBCA §§8.20, 8.22, 8.23.

30. See MBCA §§40, 43; RMBCA §§8.20, 8.24.

31. Although a quorum usually is required for director action, vacancies on the board of directors may generally be filled by majority vote of the directors remaining in office, even if this number is less than a quorum. See MBCA §38, RMBCA §8.10.

32. See, for example, MBCA §44, RMBCA §8.21.

or give written notice of dissent. Either action eliminates the dissenting director's potential personal liability for the action taken.[33]

Committees of Directors. Typically, the board of directors of a large corporation delegates much of its management authority to corporate officers and to executive and other committees of the board. If allowed by the articles of incorporation or bylaws, the board of directors may establish one or more committees and appoint members of the board to serve on them. Once created, a committee may exercise the board's authority to the extent specified by the board or provided in the articles or bylaws.

The executive committee, which performs board functions between meetings of the full board, is the most common committee. Other committees may include, for example, an audit, a nominating, a compensation, and a finance committee. To prevent excessive delegation of board authority to committees, their powers are limited by statute. For example, the MBCA and RMBCA provide that a committee may not (1) authorize distributions, (2) approve actions requiring shareholder vote or a merger not requiring shareholder vote, (3) fill vacancies on the board, (4) adopt, amend, or repeal bylaws, or (5) authorize or approve reacquisition or sale of shares. These important matters must be undertaken by vote of the full board.[34]

Officers

Functions of Officers. Corporate officers who conduct the day-to-day affairs of the business are appointed and removed by the board of directors. Officers are agents of the corporation to whom the board delegates authority to execute and administer board policy decisions. Although corporate management is legally under direction of the board, in many large corporations the officers effectively manage the corporation, and the board merely ratifies their decisions.

State corporation statutes require or authorize a corporation to have certain officers. Typically, a corporation will have a president, who is the principal executive officer of the corporation, one or more vice-presidents in charge of various aspects of the business (for example, marketing, sales, or finance), a treasurer, and a secretary. In addition, numerous junior officers may be appointed such as assistant treasurer, assistant secretary, assistant vice-president, comptroller, cashier, or loan officer. The duties of the various corporate officers generally are outlined in the bylaws.

Although officers usually are appointed by the board of directors, some statutes provide for shareholder election. Officers usually serve at the pleasure of the board of directors, subject to removal at any time. If a valid employment contract exists between the officer and the corporation, however, premature termination constitutes a breach of contract.

Officers' Authority. Because officers, unlike directors, are agents of the corporation, their authority to bind the corporation is governed by general principles of agency law, discussed in Chapters 40–41. Indeed, much of the modern law of agency concerns the liability of a corporation (the principal) for the acts of corporate officers (agents) on its behalf.[35] Like other agents, a corporate officer's authority to act for the corporation is derived from (1) actual authority—express or implied, (2) apparent authority, or (3) corporate ratification of a previously unauthorized act. An officer's express authority is derived primarily from four sources: the state corporation statute, the articles of incorporation, the bylaws, and resolutions of the board of directors. The most common and reliable of these sources is a resolution adopted by the board of directors authorizing the transaction in question.

Like other agents, corporate officers may possess a degree of implied authority that flows from their express authority. Most corporate officers, such as secretaries, treasurers, or vice-presidents, possess little, if any, implied authority by virtue of their

---

33. See MBCA §35, RMBCA §8.24(d).
34. MBCA §42, RMBCA §8.25.

35. In addition, the principles governing the liability of persons signing negotiable instruments and other contracts in a representative capacity, discussed in Chapter 25, most commonly are applied in the corporate context.

offices. Although many older cases held that a corporation's principal executive officer also had no implied authority to bind the corporation, many modern courts have expanded the implied authority of corporate presidents to include transactions within the corporation's ordinary or everyday course of business. Other courts give a president implied authority to bind the corporation to any contract that the board of directors could authorize or ratify. Despite this modern trend, prudent third parties always should require a board of directors' authorizing resolution to insure corporate liability upon important transactions negotiated by the officers. This approach provides maximum third-party protection by recognizing that the directors, not the officers, are the ultimate source of corporate authority.

Even if a corporate officer possesses no express or implied actual authority, the corporation may be bound by the officer's apparent authority or on grounds of ratification. As discussed in Chapter 40, apparent authority arises when a person (here the corporation) leads third parties to believe that another (here the corporate officer) has authority to act on its behalf. Third parties who reasonably rely upon the officer's apparent authority may bind the corporation despite the officer's lack of actual authority. Even if the officer's conduct is beyond the scope of her actual or apparent authority, the corporation may be bound if it ratifies the previously unauthorized act of the officer.

Duties of Management

Corporate management, including directors, officers, and, in some cases, controlling shareholders, owes various legal duties to the corporation, and in certain instances, its shareholders and creditors. These duties, which have generated a substantial amount of litigation, are derived from a variety of sources including both state and federal law. Management duties existing under state law are discussed in the material that follows. Liability imposed under federal law, specifically federal securities law, is covered in Chapter 49.

The most important duties imposed upon management under state law are derived from the common law, and include primarily (1) the duty to exercise reasonable care in managing the corporation and (2) the fiduciary duty of loyalty to the corporation. In some jurisdictions, one or both of these duties are codified by statute.[36]

In addition to the duties of care and loyalty, state business corporation acts commonly impose liability upon officers and directors for violations of specific statutory directives. For example, directors may be held liable for commencing business before the required minimum capital has been contributed. Other provisions impose liability for improper dividends or repurchase of the corporation's shares, improper distribution of assets to shareholders upon liquidation of the corporation, and unlawful loans to corporate directors, officers, or shareholders.

Duty of Care

The duty of care is perhaps the most basic duty imposed upon corporate management. As defined by the MBCA and RMBCA, directors and officers must discharge their duties in good faith, in a manner they reasonably believe to be in the best interests of the corporation, and with the care an ordinarily prudent person in a like position would exercise under similar circumstances.[37] Although other formulations abound, this duty simply renders directors and officers liable to the corporation for negligence in the performance of their responsibilities. The duty of care does not, however, render management liable for every mistake or error in judgment. Under the **business judgment rule,** officers and directors have no liability for honest, unbiased transactions undertaken with reasonable care, even if it later appears that the act was ill-advised or mistaken.

Negligent management may take many forms, including negligent selection or supervision of employees, inadequate consideration or research of major decisions, or authorizing unnecessarily risky or unusual transactions. Directors and officers also are required to keep reasonably informed of corporate affairs. To help them accomplish this duty, the MBCA and many state statutes permit officers

---

36. See, for example, MBCA §35, RMBCA §8.30.
37. MBCA §35, RMBCA §§8.30, 8.42.

and directors who act in good faith to rely upon information prepared by other corporate officers or employees, legal counsel, public accountants, or a committee of the board of directors.

Although the business judgment rule insulates most management decisions from attack, courts will impose liability in appropriate circumstances, as the following case demonstrates.

Smith v. Van Gorkom
488 A.2d 858 (Del. 1985)

Trans Union Corporation was a publicly-held Delaware corporation. Although Trans Union had an annual cash flow of hundreds of millions of dollars, the corporation was unable to use all of its available investment tax credits. In 1980, company management began considering strategic alternatives, including the possibility of selling Trans Union to a company that could take advantage of the tax credits. Trans Union's chief financial officer suggested a leveraged buy-out by management and calculated the feasibility of a buy-out if Trans Union's shares were sold at $50 and $60 per share. The officer selected these figures merely for purposes of illustration; they did not reflect the officer's valuation of Trans Union stock.

Jerome Van Gorkom, Trans Union's chairman and chief executive officer, vetoed the suggestion of a leveraged buy-out by management but, without the knowledge of other officers, approached Jay Pritzker to discuss his purchasing Trans Union. On September 18, after several meetings with Van Gorkom, Pritzker offered to purchase Trans Union at $55 per share, a figure that Van Gorkom had suggested because a leveraged buy-out would be feasible at that price. Pritzker advised Van Gorkom that the board of directors must act on the offer no later than September 21. Van Gorkom called a board meeting for September 20 at which he explained Pritzker's proposal in a twenty-minute presentation. Following the two-hour meeting, the board of directors approved Pritzker's offer on the condition that Trans Union could accept any better offer. That evening Van Gorkom signed a merger agreement while attending a social event. On Feb-

ruary 10, Trans Union's shareholders approved the merger with seventy percent of the shareholders voting in favor, seven percent opposed, and twenty-three percent not voting.

Plaintiffs, shareholders of Trans Union, brought a class action suit against the board of directors alleging that the board had violated its fiduciary duty by approving the merger at the meeting on September 20. The trial court ruled in favor of the board of directors. Plaintiffs appealed.

Horsey, Justice

. . . A director's duty to inform himself in preparation for a decision derives from the fiduciary capacity in which he serves the corporation and its stockholders. . . . Since a director is vested with the responsibility for the management of the affairs of the corporation, he must execute that duty with the recognition that he acts on behalf of others. Such obligation does not tolerate faithlessness or self dealing. But fulfillment of the fiduciary function requires more than the mere absence of bad faith or fraud. Representation of the financial interests of others imposes on a director an affirmative duty to protect those interests and to proceed with a critical eye in assessing information of the type and under the circumstances present here. . . .

Thus, a director's duty to exercise an informed business judgment is in the nature of a duty of care, as distinguished from a duty of loyalty. . . .

In the specific context of a proposed merger of domestic corporations, a director has a duty . . . , along with his fellow directors, to act in an informed and deliberate manner in determining whether to approve an agreement of merger before submitting the proposal to the stockholders. . . .

On the record before us, we must conclude that the Board of Directors did not reach an informed business judgment on September 20, 1980 in voting to "sell" the Company for $55 per share pursuant to the Pritzker cash-out merger proposal. Our reasons, in summary, are as follows:

The directors (1) did not adequately inform themselves as to Van Gorkom's role in forcing the "sale" of the Company and in establishing the per share purchase price; (2) were uninformed as to the intrinsic value of the Company; and (3) given these circumstances, at a minimum, were grossly negligent in approving the "sale" of the Company upon two hours' consideration, without prior notice, and without the exigency of a crisis or emergency.

. . . [T]he Board based its September 20 decision to approve the cash-out merger primarily on Van Gorkom's representations. None of the directors, other than Van Gorkom and Chelberg, had any prior knowledge that the purpose of the meeting was to propose a cash-out merger of Trans Union. . . .

Without any documents before them concerning the proposed transaction, the members of the Board were required to rely entirely upon Van Gorkom's 20-minute oral presentation of the proposal. No written summary of the terms of the merger was presented; the directors were given no documentation to support the adequacy of the $55 price per share for sale of the Company; and the Board had before it nothing more than Van Gorkom's statement of his understanding of the substance of an agreement which he admittedly had never read, nor which any member of the Board had ever seen. . . .

As of September 20, the Board had made no evaluation of the Company designed to value the entire enterprise, nor had the Board ever previously considered selling the Company or consenting to a buy-out merger. . . .

Despite the foregoing facts and circumstances, there was no call by the Board, either on September 20 or thereafter, for any valuation study or documentation of the $55 price per share as a measure of the fair value of the Company in a cash-out context. . . .

The record also establishes that the Board accepted without scrutiny Van Gorkom's representation as to the fairness of the $55 price per share for sale of the Company—a subject that the Board had never previously considered. The Board thereby failed to discover that Van Gorkom had suggested the $55 price to Pritzker and, most crucially, that Van Gorkom had arrived at the $55 figure based on calculations designed solely to determine the feasibility of a leveraged buy-out. . . .

None of the directors, Management or outside, were investment bankers or financial analysts. Yet the Board did not consider recessing the meeting until a later hour that day (or requesting an exten-

sion of Pritzker's Sunday evening deadline) to give it time to elicit more information as to the sufficiency of the offer, either from inside Management . . . or from Trans Union's own investment banker, Salomon Brothers, whose Chicago specialist in merger and acquisitions was known to the Board and familiar with Trans Union's affairs.

Thus, the record compels the conclusion that on September 20 the Board lacked valuation information adequate to reach an informed business judgment as to the fairness of $55 per share for sale of the Company. . . .

[W]e hold that the directors of Trans Union breached their fiduciary duty to their stockholders . . . by their failure to inform themselves of all information reasonably available to them and relevant to their decision to recommend the Pritzker merger. . . .

[Judgment reversed and remanded for determination of damages.]

The Duty of Loyalty

Officers and directors owe a fiduciary duty of loyalty to the corporation. Like other fiduciaries discussed in this text—trustees, agents, and partners—corporate directors and officers are under a strict duty to act honestly, and in good faith, and solely in the interest of another, here the corporation, regarding matters within the scope of the relation. As noted by one court, a director or officer

> owes loyalty and allegiance to the company—a loyalty that is undivided and an allegiance that is influenced in action by no consideration other than the welfare of the corporation. Any adverse interest of a director will be subjected to a scrutiny rigid and uncompromising.[38]

Cases alleging breach of the duty of loyalty are often litigated, and occur in a wide variety of fact situations. In the following case, a director's non-

---

38. *Litwin v. Allen,* 25 N.Y.S.2d 667, 677 (N.Y.Sup. Ct. 1940).

disclosure was attacked as a breach of fiduciary duty.

Midwest Management Corporation v. Stephens

353 N.W.2d 76 (Iowa 1984)

Morris Stephens served as director and chairman of the investment committee of Midwest Management Corporation (Midwest) from August 1969 through December 1971. In the summer of 1970, while Midwest was investigating investment opportunities, Stephens' son and his business colleagues were looking for financing to open a securities broker-dealer business. Stephens proposed that Midwest provide the financing. After negotiation, Midwest agreed to propose for its shareholders' approval a plan by which Midwest would invest $250,000 in the new business provided that Stephens would manage the business and would purchase 100,000 shares of stock in the new company. Although Stephens later denied that he agreed to purchase the stock, he was present at shareholders' meetings held on July 29 and September 19, 1970. At both of the meetings, Midwest's directors told the shareholders that Stephens had agreed to purchase 100,000 shares of the stock.

The shareholders approved the proposal and Midwest invested $250,000 in the business. The new company suffered losses and Midwest invested another $150,000. The business closed in the fall of 1971, and Midwest lost over $325,000. Midwest then learned that Stephens never had purchased any of the company's stock. Midwest sued Stephens for breach of his fiduciary duties. The trial court awarded compensatory and punitive damages. Stephens appealed.

Uhlenhopp, Justice

. . . A director of a corporation owes the corporation complete loyalty, honesty, and good faith. . . That duty is owed the corporation and its shareholders whenever the action of the director concerns "matters affecting the general well being of the corporation." [*Yerke v. Batman*, 376 N.E.2d 1211, 1214 (Ind. App. 1978).] . . .

As a fiduciary, Stephens' first duty was "to act in all things of trust wholly for the benefit of his corporation." [*Perlman v. Feldmann*, 219 F.2d 173, 176 (2d Cir. 1955), *cert. denied*, 75 S. Ct. 880 (1955)]. This encompassed a duty to disclose information to those who have a right to know the facts. . . . Upon hearing statements in unequivocal terms at meetings on July 29 and September 19, 1970, that he had agreed to purchase 100,000 shares of Midwest stock at $1.50 per share, Stephens was bound to disclose the facts, as he perceived them, to the shareholders. He did not do so and knowingly permitted the shareholders to be led to believe statements which he now says are untrue and to give their approval to the broker-dealer business. . . .

Midwest made its investment in the broker-dealer business knowing that the venture was risky. Stephens points to this known risk and argues that his failure to purchase stock had no causal relation to the failure of the business. For all that appears from the evidence, this is true; the business would have failed even if Stephens had acquired the stock.

The evidence also demonstrates, however, that Midwest's shareholders were willing to take the risk of the broker-dealer business only if Stephens took the risk with them. By concealing his intention, Stephens led them to believe he would join in the risk. He is the one who induced them by this ruse to go into the venture, and his concealment of his intention is the wrong which determines the damages. But for that concealment the stockholders would not have authorized the venture in the first place. Their loss flows from their joining in the venture, and their joining in the venture flows from Stephens' concealment. . . . We thus find Stephens liable for Midwest's loss of $325,741.11. He must place the shareholders in the same financial situation as if he had not concealed his intention and they had not authorized Midwest to go into the venture. . . .

The trial court also awarded Midwest $25,000 in punitive damages. Defendant contends the award is unjustified. . . .

We find the award in this case was justified. Shareholders at the meetings on July 29 and September 19, 1970, had a right to know Stephens' true position, but he, a fiduciary, knowingly and purposely failed to inform them of his actual intention. . . .

[Judgment modified on other grounds and remanded.]

Conflict of Interest. The duty of loyalty may be breached when an officer or director has an interest actually or potentially in conflict with the interest of the corporation. Conflict of interest may arise, for example, in transactions between the fiduciary and the corporation—such as a sale of corporate property to a director, a sale of property by the director to the corporation, or other contracts between the director and the corporation. Conflicts may also arise in transactions between two corporations having common directors.

Fiduciary transactions involving outright fraud or bad faith are voidable by the corporation. Further, under the modern approach, other transactions in which an officer or director has an interest are voidable by the corporation unless the contract or transaction is fair to the corporation, or is approved, ratified, or authorized by a vote of the disinterested members of the board or of the shareholders after full disclosure of all relevant facts. "Fairness" in this context is determined by deciding whether an independent corporate fiduciary dealing at arm's length would have entered into the transaction. The officer or director asserting the validity of the transaction usually has the burden of proving fairness. These principles, which are derived from the common law and statutory provisions, apply to contracts or transactions between the corporation and the fiduciary individually, or another entity in which the fiduciary is an officer, director, partner, or is otherwise financially interested.[39]

Competing with the Corporation. Officers and directors may not compete with the corporation in business transactions within the scope of their corporate responsibilities. The rule prevents fiduciaries from using the corporate position to unfairly or inequitably favor personal over corporate interests. For example, an officer or director may not use corporate assets or personnel to conduct personal business, use corporate trade secrets or customer lists for personal benefit or sell them to others, solicit corporate customers or employees for personal ventures, receive secret profits, kickbacks, or commissions on corporate transactions, or breach reasonable and enforceable covenants not to compete after leaving corporate employment.[40] A fiduciary who wrongfully competes is liable to the corporation for money damages and may hold any property acquired in breach of duty on a constructive trust for the benefit of the corporation.

Many wrongful competition cases involve the **corporate opportunity doctrine,** which prevents corporate officers and directors from usurping and diverting to themselves a business opportunity in which the corporation has an expectancy, property interest or right, or that in fairness should belong to the corporation.[41] In determining what constitutes a corporate opportunity, many modern courts adopt a line of business test that holds that corporate opportunities are those closely associated with or related to actual, planned, or potential business activities of the corporation. Other courts have applied a narrower test, finding corporate opportunities only in pre-existing business relationships. Though proximity of the opportunity to existing or prospective corporate business is important, it is not the sole test of liability. In each case, the court's perception of permissible business ethics and of the fairness of the transaction to the corporation often is determinative.

In some cases, corporate fiduciaries have been permitted to divert opportunities that the corporation is unwilling or unable to pursue because, for example, the corporation lacked the financial ability to undertake the transaction or because the persons offering the opportunity refused to deal with the corporation. Recognizing corporate inability as a defense to diversion, however, reduces manage-

---

39. See MBCA §41, RMBCA §§8.60–8.63.

40. Henn & Alexander, *Laws of Corporations* 629 (3d ed. 1983).
41. *Id.* at 632.

ment incentive to use best efforts to obtain corporate financing and resolve other problems. The following case illustrates the modern judicial approach to the defense of financial inability in corporate opportunity cases.

Klinicki v. Lundgren

695 P.2d 906 (Or. 1985)

Plaintiff F. R. Klinicki was a shareholder, director, and vice-president of Berlinair, Inc., a closely-held corporation that provided air taxi service. Defendant Kim Lundgren was a shareholder, director, and president of Berlinair. In 1977, Klinicki and Lundgren met with representatives of Berliner Flug Ring (BFR), a group of travel agents who chartered flights for German tourists, to discuss a contract by which Berlinair would provide charter flights for BFR. No agreement was reached but in June of 1978 Lundgren learned that BFR might be willing to enter into a charter contract. On July 7, 1978, Lundgren incorporated Air Berlin Charter Company (ABC) and became its sole shareholder. On August 20, 1978, ABC presented BFR a charter contract proposal. After a series of discussions BFR entered into a contract with ABC on September 1, 1978.

Klinicki filed a shareholder derivative suit on behalf of Berlinair against Lundgren alleging that he had breached his fiduciary obligations as president and director of Berlinair by diverting a corporate opportunity to ABC. Lundgren argued that Berlinair had lacked the financial resources to handle the BFR contract and, therefore, the contract could not have been a corporate opportunity for Berlinair. The trial court held Lundgren liable for diversion of corporate opportunity and the Oregon court of appeals affirmed. Lundgren appealed to the Oregon Supreme Court.

Jones, Justice

. . .While courts universally stress the high standard of fiduciary duty owed by directors and officers to their corporation, there are distinct schools of thought on the circumstances in which business opportunities may be taken for personal advantage. One group of jurisdictions severely restricts the

corporate official's freedom to take advantage of opportunities by saying that the ability to undertake the opportunity is irrelevant and usurpation is essentially prohibited; other jurisdictions use a test which gives relatively wide latitude to the corporate official on the theory that financial ability to undertake a corporate opportunity is a prerequisite to the existence of a corporate opportunity. . . .

Counsel for defendant . . . contends there is no corporate opportunity if there is no capacity to take advantage of the corporate opportunity. We reject this argument. By the same token, we reject plaintiff's contention . . . that financial ability is totally irrelevant in an unlawful taking of a corporate opportunity. . . .

Where a director or principal senior executive of a close corporation wishes to take personal advantage of a "corporate opportunity," . . . the director or principal senior executive must comply strictly with the following procedure:

(1) the director or principal senior executive must promptly offer the opportunity and disclose all material facts known regarding the opportunity to the disinterested directors or, if there is no disinterested director, to the disinterested shareholders. If the director or principal senior executive learns of other material facts after such disclosure, the director or principal senior executive must disclose these additional facts in a like manner before personally taking the opportunity.

(2) The director or principal senior executive may take advantage of the corporate opportunity only after full disclosure and only if the opportunity is rejected by a majority of the disinterested directors or, if there are no disinterested directors, by a majority of the disinterested shareholders. If, after full disclosure, the disinterested directors or shareholders unreasonably fail to reject the offer, the interested director or principal senior executive may proceed to take the opportunity if he can prove the taking was otherwise "fair" to the corporation. Full disclosure to the appropriate corporate body is, however, an absolute condition precedent to the validity of any forthcoming rejection as well as to the availability to the director or principal senior executive of the defense of fairness.

(3) An appropriation of a corporate opportunity may be ratified by rejection of the opportunity by a majority of disinterested directors or a majority of

disinterested shareholders, after full disclosure subject to the same rules as set out above for prior offer, disclosure and rejection. Where a director or principal senior executive of a close corporation appropriates a corporate opportunity without first fully disclosing the opportunity and offering it to the corporation, absent ratification, that director or principal senior executive holds the opportunity in trust for the corporation.

Applying these rules to the facts in this case, we conclude:

(1) Lundgren, as director and principal executive officer of Berlinair, owed a fiduciary duty to Berlinair.

(2) The BFR contract was a "corporate opportunity" of Berlinair.

(3) Lundgren formed ABC for the purpose of usurping the opportunity presented to Berlinair by the BFR contract.

(4) Lundgren did not offer Berlinair the BFR contract.

(5) Lundgren did not attempt to obtain the consent of Berlinair to his taking of the BFR corporate opportunity.

(6) Lundgren did not fully disclose to Berlinair his intent to appropriate the opportunity for himself and ABC.

(7) Berlinair never rejected the opportunity presented by the BFR contract.

(8) Berlinair never ratified the appropriation of the BFR contract.

(9) Lundgren, acting for ABC, misappropriated the BFR contract. Because of the above, the defendant may not now contend that Berlinair did not have the financial ability to successfully pursue the BFR contract. . . .

[Judgment affirmed.]

Duties to Minority Shareholders

Directors. A number of cases have considered the nature of the duty owed by corporate directors and controlling shareholders to shareholders owning a minority of the corporation's stock. Directors are under a statutory duty to manage in the best interests of the corporation as a whole, and are subject to fiduciary duties when undertaking corporate actions such as issuance or redemption of shares, amending the articles of incorporation, or authorizing a plan of merger or dissolution. These duties require the directors to treat each class of shareholders fairly in taking corporation action and preclude attempts to favor one intracorporate group at the expense of another. For example, directors who authorize issuance of additional shares in an attempt to unfairly dilute the voting power of minority shareholders (freeze them out) violate their fiduciary duties.

Controlling Shareholders. The ordinary shareholder has no fiduciary duty to the corporation and is entitled to vote her shares for directors or other corporate actions as desired. Courts have, however, subjected a shareholder who possesses a controlling block of stock to fiduciary duties. Thus, controlling shareholders, through their ability to elect directors or approve extraordinary corporate matters, may not cause the corporation to take action that unfairly and adversely affects the rights of minority shareholders.

Controlling shareholders also may be subject to both the duty of care and fiduciary duties when selling their stock, and therefore control of the corporation, to a third party. For example, a controlling block may be sold to unscrupulous purchasers who steal corporate assets after sale ("loot" the corporation) to the detriment of minority shareholders. On similar facts, many courts have imposed liability for negligence upon controlling shareholders who failed to make a reasonably adequate investigation of the potential purchasers and their motives.

Another issue often arising in connection with the sale of a controlling block is the disposition of the "control premium"—the difference in value between a block of shares carrying the right to control the corporation and other shares not part of the control block. A number of cases, on varying legal theories including diversion of corporate opportunity or sale of a corporate asset, have required the controlling shareholder to share any control premium with the minority shareholders or the corporation. Other courts have allowed the selling shareholder to retain the control premium.

SUMMARY

1. Corporate management powers are divided among the shareholders, the board of directors, and corporate officers. The shareholders, who are the owners of the corporation, periodically elect the board of directors, who have ultimate management responsibility. The board of directors, in turn, appoints corporate officers and delegates to them the authority to operate the corporation consistent with board policy.

2. Shareholders generally are entitled to elect directors and approve certain extraordinary corporate matters. Shareholder votes normally are taken at annual or special meetings, at which a shareholder may vote either in person or by proxy. To assure minority representation on the board of directors, many states require cumulative voting. In addition to accumulating proxies, large blocks of stock may be controlled through voting trusts and voting agreements.

3. Both common law and statute confer upon shareholders a qualified right to inspect corporate books and records.

4. To prevent dilution of a shareholder's proportionate financial or voting interest upon issuance of new shares, the articles of incorporation may provide for preemptive rights. A preemptive right allows an existing shareholder to purchase a new issue of shares in proportion to his or her present interest in the corporation, before the shares are sold to others.

5. All corporate powers are exercised by, or under the authority of, the board of directors. In addition, the business and affairs of the corporation are managed under the direction of the board. The number and qualifications of directors are specified in the articles of incorporation or bylaws. Unless the board is divided into classes with staggered terms, all directors are elected annually.

6. Corporate management authority is vested in the board of directors as a body, not in individual directors. Accordingly, directors must usually act in properly constituted meetings. The timing, quorum requirements, and other aspects of directors' meetings are usually governed by detailed bylaw provisions. Further, if allowed by the articles of incorporation or bylaws, the board of directors may establish committees of board members.

7. The officers conduct the day-to-day business of a corporation and are appointed and removed by the board of directors. Officers are agents of the corporation to whom the board delegates authority. As an agent, an officer's authority to bind the corporation is governed by general principles of agency law.

8. Corporate management, including directors, officers, and in some cases controlling shareholders, owe various legal duties to the corporation, and in certain instances its shareholders and creditors. The primary duties of management under state law are (1) a duty to exercise reasonable or due care in managing the corporation and (2) the fiduciary duty of loyalty to the corporation.

KEY TERMS

straight voting
cumulative voting
proxy
voting trust
voting (pooling)
  agreement

preemptive right
business judgment rule
corporate opportunity
  doctrine

QUESTIONS AND PROBLEMS

47-1   Melvin, a shareholder of Peoples State Bank, requested to inspect all of the bank's books and records to determine whether the bank directors had abused their fiduciary duties by diverting corporate assets to directors or by providing favorable treatment to certain bank customers who were friends and relatives of directors.

(a) Should the bank allow Melvin to inspect the books and records? Explain.

(b) The bank president is willing to allow Melvin access to some of the books and records. The president maintains, however, that allowing access to certain records would breach the bank's confidential relationship with its customers and would constitute an invasion of the customers' privacy. Melvin sues the bank to obtain all books and records. How should the court rule? Explain.

47-2   The bylaws of most corporations include a provision that allows the officers or directors to call special meetings of the board of directors. These provisions generally require that a notice of the special meeting be mailed to all directors within a given number of days prior to the meeting and that the notice specify the purpose of the meeting. In the absence of proper notice, any action of the board is invalid unless later ratified by the absent directors. Assume that Doaks, a director of Davidson Company, sent a notice of a special meeting to other directors for the purpose of "analyzing and discussing financial and legal problems facing the corporation and for the purpose of authorizing any action necessary for resolving such financial and legal matters.'' Jones, another director of the company, received the notice but decided to attend an important golf match rather than the special meeting. At the meeting, the other directors voted to dissolve the corporation. Jones, who strongly opposed dissolution, challenged the decision reached at the special meeting. Should the decision be enforced by a court? Why or why not?

47-3 Florence Barth owned the common shares of Barth, Inc. Its principal asset was an apartment complex managed by Florence. In addition to the common shares, preferred shares had been issued to the Federal Housing Administration, which had guaranteed corporate indebtedness for the purchase price of the apartment complex. To protect the FHA's interest, the articles of incorporation, which were duly filed and a matter of public record, provided that the corporation could not take the following actions without prior consent of the preferred shareholders: (1) pay for repairs from a reserve fund, (2) remodel, reconstruct, or demolish the apartment house, (3) rent apartments below a fixed rate, (4) carry out any basic change in corporate structure such as consolidation, merger, or voluntary liquidation, (5) amend the articles of incorporation, or (6) assign, transfer, dispose of, or encumber any real or personal property. Despite this limitation, Florence, without the knowledge or consent of the FHA, contracted to sell the apartment building to Newberry, who was unaware of the corporation's existence. When the FHA learned of the sale, it sought to avoid the contract on the basis of Florence's lack of authority. Newberry asserted that he believed that Florence was the owner of the property, or that in any event Florence had actual or apparent authority to sell because of her position as secretary-treasurer of the corporation, sole common shareholder, and apartment manager. Who should prevail? Explain.

47-4 Directors of corporations often are persons of diverse backgrounds: business and financial experts, civic leaders, family members of major shareholders, and officers of universities and charitable organizations. Should all corporate directors be held to the same standard of care or should the standard of care depend on the director's educational and business background? Explain.

47-5 Major Equipment Co. and four of its employees were convicted in federal court of illegal price fixing. The company paid a $1 million fine. Several shareholders brought a derivative suit against the directors of Major Equipment Co. alleging that they had breached their duty of care by failing to discover the employees' illegal acts. Although the shareholders could not prove that the directors had actual knowledge of the price fixing, the shareholders alleged that the failure to detect the price fixing was evidence of negligence by the directors.

(a) Do you agree with the shareholders' reasoning? Explain.

(b) Would your answer differ if Major Equipment Co. was a large corporation with tens of thousands of employees or if it was a small corporation with only a few employees?

47-6 Reconsider the facts of *Smith v. Van Gorkom* (see page 982). On appeal, the directors argued that even if they had breached their duty of care, they should not be held liable because the shareholders had ultimately approved the transaction. Under what circumstances, if any, should shareholder ratification of the actions of officers or directors relieve them of their liability for breach of duty?

47-7 (a) In many corporations, directors receive compensation from the corporation either for serving as directors or for serving as corporate officers. If a director participates in the approval of his own compensation, has the director engaged in self-dealing or a conflict of interest? What actions might a board of directors take to minimize their potential liability for breach of their fiduciary duties?

(b) In recent years, numerous large corporations have become involved in ''hostile'' takeovers. Corporate managers have developed innovative methods to protect officers of corporations that may become takeover targets. For example, some corporations have granted ''golden parachutes'' to their top executives. These golden parachute contracts guarantee the executives compensation for several years if the corporation is taken over by another corporation. If officers or directors approve a golden parachute contract, have they violated their fiduciary duties?

47-8 By January 1, 1986, Lunken Corp., a Delaware corporation, had issued approximately 400,000 shares of common stock and was authorized to issue an additional 75,000 shares. During early 1986, Condec, Inc. acquired approximately one-half of Lunken's outstanding stock through tender offers to the shareholders. On May 1, 1986, Lunken's board approved sale of all of its assets to U.S. Industries on the condition that the sale be approved by Lunken's shareholders. On May 2, 1986, Lunken sold its 75,000 unissued shares to a subsidiary of U.S. Industries for 75,000 shares of U.S. Industries preferred stock. Lunken agreed to repurchase the 75,000 shares if Lunken's shareholders failed to approve sale of the entire company to U.S. Industries.

Condec sued Lunken and its board of directors alleging that the issuance of the 75,000 shares of its stock served no legitimate corporate purpose and had been designed merely to prevent control of Lunken by Condec. Testimony at trial established that if Condec obtained control of Lunken, Condec intended to replace the officers and directors.

(a) Delaware law provides that shares of a corporation cannot be issued for an improper purpose. What do you think was the purpose of issuing the 75,000 to U.S. Industries' subsidiary? Is this a proper purpose?

(b) Have the officers and directors of Lunken violated their fiduciary duty? Why or why not?

47-9 SAC is a corporation that manufactures and sells computer graphic equipment. Albert and Stanley were employees of SAC who managed the research and development of the corporation. Dr. Brennan, a university professor, invented a new type of computer graphic equipment and asked Albert and Stanley if they would like to form a business with him to market the machine. Albert suggested that Dr. Brennan allow SAC to market his invention, but Brennan stated that he was unwilling to allow his concept to be disclosed to or used by SAC. Further, due to poor financial condition, SAC was at the time neither inclined nor able to develop new products.

For six months Albert and Stanley worked with Brennan to establish a new company. During this time, they continued their employment with SAC. Finally, they quit SAC and devoted their full efforts to operating the new business.

(a) Have Albert and Stanley violated their fiduciary duties as agents of SAC?

(b) If Albert and Stanley had been officers or directors of SAC, would their conduct have violated their fiduciary duties?

Chapter 48

*Corporate Management—
Special Topics*

Major Topics

- the method used to effect major corporate changes such as amendment of the articles of incorporation, merger or consolidation, or corporate dissolution
- discussion of the special problems encountered in managing closely-held corporations
- special problems regarding litigation by and against corporations, including shareholder derivative suits

Chapter 47 examined the basic corporate management structure, including the roles, powers, and duties of shareholders, directors, and officers. This chapter examines important specialized topics in corporate management, including how major corporate changes are accomplished; the problems of operating a closely-held corporation under traditional principles of corporate governance; and the principles governing litigation by or against the corporation, its officers, or directors.

Extraordinary Corporate Matters

Although voting for directors is the usual extent of shareholder management participation, shareholder approval also is required to authorize certain extraordinary corporate transactions deemed beyond the scope of ordinary powers delegated to the board. These matters generally include amendments to the articles of incorporation, merger and consolidation, sale of substantially all corporate assets, and voluntary dissolution.

The procedure for effecting extraordinary corporate transactions is governed by statute. Generally, the board of directors adopts a resolution setting forth the proposed transaction. Written notice of the proposal is given to shareholders, who then vote upon it at either an annual or special shareholders' meeting. Unless a greater percentage is required by the articles of incorporation, a majority vote of all shares entitled to vote on the proposal is usually required for approval. For some transactions, approval of specific classes of shareholders also may be required. Once approved, documents reflecting the change are filed with the secretary of state of the state of incorporation. To protect minority shareholders who dissent from major corporate changes, the law provides a statutory "appraisal" remedy, through which dissenting shareholders are paid in cash for their shares. In addition, even if statutory procedures are met, courts may intervene on equitable grounds to prevent oppression of minority shareholders.

Amendment of Articles of Incorporation

A corporation has the power to amend its articles of incorporation. The amended articles may contain any provision that could have been included in original articles filed at the time of amendment.[1] Although changes may be made in any of the articles' provisions, amendments most commonly involve the corporate capital structure. If the amendment involves a change in shares or rights of shareholders, the procedures necessary to effect the action should be included in the articles.

Although certain minor changes in the articles may be made by the directors alone, most amendments require approval by shareholder vote. Because many article amendments adversely affect the rights of one or more classes of shareholders, specific approval by vote (generally either a majority or two-thirds) of the adversely affected class may also be required.[2] Dissenting minority members of the class are generally bound by the majority vote but may assert the statutory appraisal rights discussed later in this chapter.

Combinations

Corporate combinations are extraordinary corporate transactions that often require shareholder approval. Combination occurs by merger or consolidation, or acquisition by one corporation of the assets or stock of another corporation.

Statutory Merger. Any two or more corporations may be merged into one of them (referred to as the "surviving" corporation) or may consolidate into a "new" corporation. In a merger, one survives and the other dissolves. In contrast, in a consolidation, both constituent corporations dissolve upon the creation of the new corporation. Shareholders of the disappearing corporations commonly receive shares of the surviving or new corporation in exchange for their shares. The surviving or new corporation succeeds to all rights and property of the dissolved corporation, as well as all liabilities of the constituent corporations, by operation of law. Therefore, no creditors' rights are adversely affected by the combination.

To achieve the combination, a plan of merger or consolidation is approved by resolution of the respective boards of directors and is submitted for approval by vote of shareholders of both corporations. An appraisal remedy generally is available to dissenting shareholders of either corporation. Corporate combination using the method described above is commonly known as "statutory merger."

Before combining, corporations may be wholly independent or may stand in a parent-subsidiary relationship. Many states have adopted "short-form" merger statutes to provide a summary procedure for merger of parents and wholly owned or substantially wholly owned subsidiaries.[3] Under the MBCA and RMBCA, for example, a parent owning ninety percent or more of the outstanding subsidiary shares may, by resolution of the parent board, merge the subsidiary into the parent without a vote by the shareholders of either corporation.[4] Short-form merger statutes generally create no appraisal remedy for the parent's minority shareholders. Dissenting shareholders of the subsidiary, however, are generally accorded an appraisal remedy.

Asset or Stock Purchase. Corporate combination also may occur if one corporation buys all, or substantially all, of the assets of another corporation. In this case, the corporate existence of both corporations is unaffected. Rather, the form of corporate assets is changed. For example, the selling corporation's assets now may consist solely of cash or securities rather than the inventory, equipment, land, or buildings, which were sold. After the sale, the selling corporation may liquidate and distribute its assets to shareholders or may remain in existence as a holding or investment company.

The sale or lease of all, or substantially all, corporate assets outside the ordinary course of business is an extraordinary transaction, requiring board resolution and shareholder approval. Dissenting shareholders generally are entitled to an appraisal remedy. In contrast, shareholder vote of the acquiring corporation is not required, and share-

---

1. See MBCA §58, RMBCA §10.01.
2. See MBCA §60, RMBCA §10.04.

3. The merger of a subsidiary into a parent is known as an "upstream" merger; a merger of the parent into the subsidiary is referred to as a "downstream" merger.
4. See MBCA §75, RMBCA §11.04.

holders of the acquiring corporation who object to the purchase have no appraisal remedy.

Corporate combination also may be achieved if one corporation purchases all, or a controlling block, of another corporation's stock. The purchase may be accomplished by negotiated sale with a major stockholder or stockholders, by purchases on the open market, or by tender offer to existing shareholders. No overall shareholder approval is required; rather, individual shareholders of the target company decide whether or not to sell their shares. If the buyer accumulates enough shares to control the corporation, it may be operated as a subsidiary, liquidated, or merged into the acquiring corporation. Because the sale involves no action by the acquired company's board and no formal shareholder approval, appraisal remedies are not available.

When one company is purchased by another, rights of the selling corporation's creditors may be affected, as the following case illustrates.

Bullington v. Union Tool Corp.

328 S.E.2d 726 (Ga. 1985)

Marsha Bullington brought a products liability suit against Union Tool Corp. seeking damages for injuries that she suffered while operating a table saw on April 3, 1981. The saw had been designed and manufactured sometime prior to 1956 by Indiana Foundry Machine & Supply Co., Inc. (the old corporation). In 1956, Indiana Foundry Machine & Supply, Inc. (the new corporation) was incorporated and purchased the real estate and most of the assets of the old corporation for adequate consideration. After the sale, the old corporation ceased doing business. None of the shareholders, officers, or directors of the new corporation had owned or managed the old corporation. The new corporation manufactured and sold many of the same products as the old corporation and continued to market them under the trade name "Indiana Line," which also had been used by the old corporation. The new corporation used the same manufacturing facilities and sales office that had been used by the old corporation. Most of the employees of the old corporation

continued to work for the new corporation. The new corporation, however, never manufactured table saws of any kind, including the type that injured Bullington. In 1962, the new corporation merged with Union Tool Corp., which, by written agreement, assumed all liabilities of the new corporation.

The trial court granted Union Tool's motion for summary judgment holding that Union Tool was not liable as a successor corporation for the torts of the company that designed and manufactured the table saw. The appellate court affirmed, and appellant Bullington appealed to the Georgia Supreme Court.

Clarke, Justice

. . . The issue before the court is the effect of the 1956 sale on tort liability.

Generally, a purchasing corporation does not assume the liabilities of the seller unless: (1) there is an agreement to assume liabilities; (2) the transaction is, in fact, a merger; (3) the transaction is a fraudulent attempt to avoid liabilities; or (4) the purchaser is a mere continuation of the predecessor corporation. . . .

The appellants contend that the new corporation should be held liable under the theory that it is a continuation of the old corporation. . . . In Georgia, the common law continuation theory has been applied where there was some identity of ownership. . . .

The appellant concedes that there is no identity of ownership in the present case, but contends that the continuation theory should be expanded in product liability cases because of the policies behind manufacturers' liability. The court in *Cyr v. B. Offen & Co., Inc.,* 501 F.2d 1145 (1st Cir. 1974), expanded the continuation exception to successor liability where the successor was a group of employees of the predecessor who formed the new corporation, and continued to produce the same product in the same place and manner as the predecessor. In discussing the policy of spreading the risk of injury so that one who places a defective product into commerce should bear the cost of the injuries from that product the court states that a "successor carrying over the experience and expertise of the manufacturer, is likewise in a better position than the consumer to gauge the risks and the costs of meeting them. The successor knows the product, is able to calculate the risks of defects as the predecessor, is in a position to insure therefor and reflect such costs in sale negotiations, and is the only entity capable of improving the quality of the product.'' *Cyr,* at 1154. . . .

Other states have adopted the rule set forth in *Ray v. Alad Corp.,* [560 P.2d 3 (Cal. 1974)], of expanding successor liability in product liability cases where 1) the predecessor is liquidated after the transfer, 2) the successor holds itself out to [the] public as a continuation and produces the same product line, thus having the knowledge needed to weigh the risk of injury and 3) where the successor is benefiting from the good will of the prior manufacturer and should also assume the burden for defects in previously sold products. . . .

Other courts, while recognizing these . . . policy differences in debtor-creditor cases from which the common law exceptions have evolved and products liability cases, have declined to expand or judicially modify the continuation exception. . . .

Although urged by appellant . . . to expand the continuation exception in this case we decline to do so. We acknowledge the new corporation operated with many of the same employees, at the same location, and with a similar company name. Nevertheless, the facts in this case do not fit the holdings in previous Georgia cases because there was no common ownership and fall outside the holdings in [*Cyr* and *Ray*] because the product alleged to be defective was not produced or sold by the new corporation. The rationale underlying the holding in *Cyr* is that the successor was in a position to improve the quality of the product in question or to reflect the possible defects in the cost of the product. Since the new corporation never produced the product, this rationale does not apply. *Ray* actually requires that the new corporation produce the same product line. . . .

[Judgment affirmed.]

Dissolution and Liquidation

Unless its duration is limited in the articles of incorporation, a corporation enjoys indefinite or perpetual existence. Therefore, once created, some formal action must be taken by the corporation or others to terminate it. Corporation statutes include procedures for voluntary or nonjudicial dissolution. In addition, both statutes and the common law permit involuntary, or judicial, dissolution by court decree in certain circumstances.

Voluntary Dissolution. The procedure for voluntary dissolution is similar to that for other major corporate changes. The board of directors adopts a resolution that must be approved by shareholder vote. Appraisal remedies are not available to dissenting shareholders. Alternatively, under the MBCA, dissolution may be authorized without board action by unanimous written consent of all shareholders. This device is widely used in closely-held corporations. The decision to dissolve is then reflected in documents filed with the secretary of state.[5] Upon dissolution, corporate assets are liquidated, creditors are paid, and what remains is distributed, subject to any liquidation preference, proportionately to the shareholders.

To protect creditors in the dissolution and liquidation process, notice of dissolution is given to creditors directly and by publication. In addition, the corporation continues for a stated period after dissolution to wind up corporate affairs. During this period, the corporation may sue and be sued on predissolution claims. For example, the MBCA provides that the dissolution of a corporation does not eliminate or impair any remedy available to or against the corporation, its directors, officers, or shareholders for any predissolution claim or liability if a lawsuit is commenced on the claim or liability within two years after dissolution.[6]

Involuntary Dissolution. State corporation statutes also provide for involuntary dissolution by judicial decree in some cases. Proceedings for involuntary dissolution may be maintained by the state attorney general, the secretary of state, sharehold-

---

5. See MBCA §§83-84, RMBCA §§14.02-14.03. In addition, voluntary dissolution by incorporators or initial directors is automatically allowed for any corporation that has not commenced business or issued any shares. MBCA §82, RMBCA §14.01.

6. MBCA §105. Contrast RMBCA §§14.06–14.07.

ers, or creditors. For example, under the MBCA, a corporation may be dissolved in an action filed by the attorney general if it is established that the corporation has (1) failed timely to file its annual report or to pay its franchise tax, (2) procured its articles of incorporation through fraud, (3) exceeded or abused its legal authority, or (4) failed to maintain or appoint a registered agent or notify the state of a change in registered agent.[7]

In an action maintained by shareholders, the court may order liquidation of the corporation if it is proven that (1) the directors are deadlocked in the management of corporate affairs and the shareholders are unable to break the deadlock, which threatens irreparable injury to the corporation; (2) the acts of the directors or those controlling the corporation are illegal, oppressive, or fraudulent; (3) corporate assets are being misapplied or wasted; or (4) the shareholders are deadlocked in voting power and have failed for at least two consecutive annual meetings to elect successors to directors whose terms have expired or would have expired upon election of new directors. Note that even in the absence of statutory authorization, courts often have ordered dissolution upon proof of mismanagement or deadlock.

A creditor may obtain judicial dissolution by proving (1) that it has obtained a judgment against the corporation, the judgment is unsatisfied, and the corporation is insolvent, or (2) that the corporation has admitted in writing that the creditor's claim is due and owing and that the corporation is insolvent.[8]

Appraisal Remedies

State statutes afford shareholders a right to dissent from certain extraordinary corporate transactions and obtain payment in cash for their shares. This statutory "appraisal" remedy generally awards the dissenting shareholder the "fair value" of his shares. Fair value is defined as the value of the shares immediately before the action to which the dissenter objects is taken. Any appreciation or depreciation in anticipation of the proposed corporate action is generally excluded from the fair value determination. Fair value must be determined by judicial proceeding—the "appraisal" aspect of the remedy—only if the corporation and the shareholder cannot voluntarily agree upon a fair price for the shares.

The appraisal remedy generally is available to shareholders who dissent from major corporate action requiring shareholder approval, including mergers and consolidations (subsidiary shareholders only in short-form mergers), sales of substantially all corporate assets outside the ordinary course of business, and amendments of the articles of incorporation that materially and adversely affect the rights of shares owned by the dissenting shareholder.[9]

The statutory procedures for dissenting are complex and vary among the states. Strict time limits attend virtually every action taken by either party. If statutory procedures are not literally followed, the right to dissent is lost and the shareholder must accept the objectionable transaction.

Typically, if a proposed corporate action is one that creates dissenters' rights, the notice of the shareholders' meeting at which the vote will be taken must inform the shareholders of their right to dissent. Before the vote, an objecting shareholder must file with the corporation a written notice of intention to demand that she be paid fair compensation for her shares and refrain from voting the shares in approval of the action. After the shareholder demands payment, the corporation offers or pays each dissenter the amount the corporation estimates to be the value of the shares. A shareholder who is dissatisfied with the payment or offer files another demand for payment with the corporation indicating her own estimate of the fair value of the shares. If the parties do not agree upon a fair value of the shares within a specific time, the corporation files suit to judicially determine their value. Based

---

7. MBCA §94, RMBCA §§14.20, 14.30.
8. MBCA §97, RMBCA §14.30.

---

9. Under the MBCA, for example, dissenters' rights are available for article amendments that (1) alter or abolish a preferential or preemptive right of the dissenters' shares, (2) create, alter, or abolish a right of redemption applicable to the shares, or (3) exclude or limit the right of the shares to vote on any matter or to cumulate votes. MBCA §80, RMBCA §13.02.

upon the evidence, usually including the testimony of one or more appraisers, the court determines the value of the shares and renders judgment for the shareholder in that amount with interest.[10]

A substantial number of filed dissents, because they must be paid in cash, may block a proposed action. Because of the expense and delay involved in judicially determining value, however, the appraisal remedy is not a popular shareholder remedy.

Valuation of Shares

In appraisal and other judicial proceedings, the court is required to determine the fair value of shares. The case that follows explains the factors considered by modern courts in valuing shares.

Weinberger v. UOP, Inc.
457 A.2d 701 (Del. 1983)

In 1975, The Signal Companies, Inc. (Signal) acquired 50.5% of UOP, Inc.'s outstanding shares. Signal appointed six directors to UOP's board of directors, including Charles Arledge and Andrew Chitiea who also both served as officers and directors of Signal. In 1977, Signal requested Arledge and Chitiea to prepare a feasibility study concerning Signal's potential acquisition of the remaining 49.5% of UOP stock. The study concluded that the UOP stock would be a good investment for Signal at any price up to $24 per share. Signal's executive committee decided to offer $20 to $21 per share for UOP's outstanding shares.

UOP retained Lehman Brothers Kuhn Loeb, Inc., an investment banker, to render an opinion as to the fairness of the offer. In less than a week Lehman Brothers examined UOP's records and facilities and prepared a written opinion letter stating that $20 or $21 per share would be a fair price to UOP's minority shareholders. After the president of UOP also indicated his belief that $21 per share was a fair price, the UOP board of directors met and voted to approve the merger. The UOP directors appointed

by Signal abstained. UOP then sent a letter to its shareholders recommending the merger at $21 per share. The merger was approved at a shareholders' meeting at which 56% of the minority shareholders voted.

Plaintiff William Weinberger, representing the class of minority shareholders who refused the offer of $21 per share, sued Signal, UOP, and certain officers and directors. Weinberger alleged that the merger was unfair because the defendants had not fully disclosed all information to the minority shareholders. The evidence established that the Arledge-Chitiea report had not been made available to UOP's directors or its shareholders. The Chancery Court ruled that the merger was fair to the minority shareholders.

Weinberger appealed. After concluding that the merger was not fair to the minority shareholders because UOP had not disclosed sufficient information to them, the Delaware Supreme Court turned to the issue of the fair price of UOP stock.

Moore, Justice
. . . The concept of fairness has two basic aspects: fair dealing and fair price. . . . The latter aspect of fairness relates to the economic and financial considerations of the proposed merger, including all relevant factors: assets, market value, earnings, future prospects, and any other elements that affect the intrinsic or inherent value of a company's stock. . . .

[Plaintiff's] evidence was that on the date the merger was approved the stock was worth at least $26 per share. In support, he offered the testimony of a chartered investment analyst who used two basic approaches to valuation: a comparative analysis of the premium paid over market in ten other tender offer–merger combinations, and a discounted cash flow analysis.

In this breach of fiduciary duty case, the Chancellor perceived that the approach to valuation was the same as that in an appraisal proceeding. Consistent with precedent, he rejected plaintiff's method of proof and accepted defendants' evidence of value as being in accord with practice under prior case law. This means that the so-called "Delaware block" or weighted average method was employed wherein the elements of value, i.e., assets, market price, earnings, etc., were assigned a par-

---

10. See generally MBCA §81, RMBCA §§13.01-13.31.

ticular weight and the resulting amounts added to determine the value per share. This procedure has been in use for decades. . . . However, to the extent it excludes other generally accepted techniques used in the financial community and the courts, it is now clearly outmoded. It is time we recognize this in appraisal and other stock valuation proceedings and bring our law current on the subject.

While the Chancellor rejected plaintiff's discounted cash flow method of valuing UOP's stock, as not corresponding with "either logic or the existing law" (426 A.2d at 1360), it is significant that this was essentially the focus, i.e., earnings potential of UOP, of Messrs. Arledge and Chitiea in their evaluation of the merger. Accordingly, the standard "Delaware block" or weighted average method of valuation, formerly employed in appraisal and other stock valuation cases, shall no longer exclusively control such proceedings. We believe that a more liberal approach must include proof of value by any techniques or methods which are generally considered acceptable in the financial community and otherwise admissible in court, subject only to our interpretation of [the Delaware appraisal statute]. . . . This will obviate the very structured and mechanistic procedure that has heretofore governed such matters. . . .

Fair price obviously requires consideration of all relevant factors involving the value of a company. . . . This is not only in accord with the realities of present day affairs, but it is thoroughly consonant with the purpose and intent of our statutory law. . . .

It is significant that [the Delaware appraisal statute] now mandates the determination of "fair" value based upon "all relevant factors". Only the speculative elements of value that may arise from the "accomplishment or expectation" of the merger are excluded. We take this to be a very narrow exception to the appraisal process, designed to eliminate use of *pro forma* data and projections of a speculative variety relating to the completion of a merger. But elements of future value, including the nature of the enterprise, which are known or susceptible of proof as of the date of the merger and not the product of speculation, may be considered. When the trial court deems it appropriate, fair value also includes any damages, resulting from the taking, which the stockholders sustain as a class. If

that was not the case, then the obligation to consider "all relevant factors" in the valuation process would be eroded. . . .

On remand the plaintiff will be permitted to test the fairness of the $21 price by the standards we herein establish, in conformity with the principle applicable to an appraisal—that fair value be determined by taking "into account all relevant factors." . . .

While a plaintiff's monetary remedy ordinarily should be confined to the more liberalized appraisal proceeding herein established, we do not intend any limitation on the historic powers of the Chancellor to grant such other relief as the facts of a particular case may dictate. . . . Since it is apparent that this long completed transaction is too involved to undo, and in view of the Chancellor's discretion, the award, if any, should be in the form of monetary damages based upon entire fairness standards, i.e., fair dealing and fair price. . . .

[Judgment reversed and remanded.]

The Closely-Held Corporation— Special Problems

State business corporation statutes are designed to govern creation and operation of all corporations, regardless of size or number of shareholders. Typically, however, these statutes envision a fairly large business with numerous stockholders who exercise little management control beyond their ability to elect directors. Shares are freely transferable and a public market often exists for the shares. The board of directors, which consists of at least three, and usually more, persons, exercises broad discretion in management of corporate affairs and appoints additional persons as officers to run the business. Board action is taken by majority vote with each director entitled to one vote. Formal meetings of directors and shareholders at which votes are taken are held periodically.

Most corporations, however, do not fit this statutory mold. They are closely-held corporations in which the few stockholders participate substantially in management, simultaneously serving as officers and directors. Corporate management is conducted on an informal basis, usually by unanimous shareholder consent. In addition, no public market exists for the shares. In this context, special problems are created not addressed by general corporation statutes. Although some state statutes have subchapters or groups of sections applicable, by election or otherwise, to closely-held corporations, many do not. In any event these statutes have proven to be of limited utility. The shareholders of a closely-held corporation must, therefore, by careful drafting of the articles of incorporation and other corporate documents, anticipate and resolve in advance the problems peculiar to such a corporation within the confines of the state's general business corporation act. Some of those problems are discussed below.

Distribution of Management Power

Business corporation acts adopt a tripartite management scheme involving shareholders, directors, and officers, each with specific responsibilities and rights in corporate management. In a closely-held corporation in which shareholders are involved in daily management as both officers and directors, a realistic separation of powers is not attainable and corporate formalities such as votes and meetings may be ignored. Rather, the business may operate by unanimous or majority shareholder consent, indistinguishable from a partnership.

Ignoring corporate formality and blurring management functions in a closely-held corporation causes various problems. For example, disregard of corporate formality is one factor often considered in a court's decision to "pierce the corporate veil" to impose personal liability upon shareholders for corporate obligations.[11] Another issue is the extent to which management functions may be governed by private agreements that vary the statutory scheme of corporate control. Note that agreements among shareholders to exercise their functions as shareholders—for example, to vote for certain persons as directors—are perfectly valid and enforceable. Such agreements, together with share transfer restrictions, help assure that control will remain in the hands of specified individuals, preventing a transfer of ownership or management power to potentially undesirable outsiders.

In contrast, however, shareholders may, by agreement among them, attempt to dictate the decisions they will make in their capacities *as directors*. These agreements may relate, for example, to directors' decisions to pay dividends, or to employ a shareholder as an officer of the corporation. Such agreements often have been successfully attacked as limiting or extinguishing the *discretionary* power of the board, conferred by statute, to manage the corporation in the best interests of the corporation. The agreements are said to "fetter" or in some cases "sterilize" the board of directors.

The modern legal trend, however, permits enforcement of shareholder agreements governing director functions in closely-held corporations. For example, statutes in a growing number of states expressly permit such agreements and may allow closely-held corporations to dispense with the board of directors entirely.[12] Further, modern judicial decisions also have permitted more flexibility in management of closely-held corporations. As noted in the classic Illinois Supreme Court case, *Galler v. Galler* (1964):

> [S]hareholder agreements . . . are often, as a practical consideration, quite necessary for the protection of those financially interested in the close corporation. While the shareholder of a public-issue corporation may readily sell his shares on the open market should management fail to use, in his opinion, sound business judgment, his counterpart of the close corporation often has a large total of his entire capital invested in the business and has no ready market for his shares should he desire to sell. He feels, understandably, that he is more than a mere investor and that his voice should be heard concerning all corporate activity. Without a shareholder agreement, specifically enforceable by the courts, insuring him a modicum of control, a large minority shareholder might find himself at the mercy of an oppressive or unknowledgeable majority. Moreover, . . . the shareholders of a close corporation are often also the directors and officers thereof. With substantial shareholding interests abiding in each member of the board of directors, it is often quite impossible to secure, as in the

---

11. Disregard of corporateness, or "piercing the corporate veil," is discussed in Chapter 45.

12. See, for example, RMBCA §8.01(c).

large public-issue corporation, independent board judgment free from personal motivations concerning corporate policy. For these and other reasons . . ., often the only sound basis for protection is afforded by a lengthy, detailed shareholder agreement securing the rights and obligations of all concerned. . . .

This court has recognized . . . the significant conceptual differences between the close corporation and its public-issue counterpart. . . . [Where] no complaining minority interest appears, no fraud or apparent injury to the public or creditors is present, and no clearly prohibitory statutory language is violated, we can see no valid reason for precluding the parties [in a closely-held corporation] from reaching any arrangements concerning the management of the corporation which are agreeable to all.[13]

Whether or not shareholder agreements are used, operating the closely-held business as a corporation often leads to dispute, as the following case illustrates.

Fournier v. Fournier

479 A.2d 708 (R.I. 1984)

E. P. Fournier Co., a Rhode Island corporation founded by Ernest P. Fournier in 1953, sold and serviced new and used automobiles. Two of Fournier's sons, Paul and Roland, worked for the corporation. In 1962, after Paul had expressed dissatisfaction with the business operations, the board of directors entered into written agreements by which Paul was authorized to "act as general manager of the Corporation with full authority to hire, approve sales and contribute to policy decisions" and Roland was named assistant manager in charge of used car operations.

Following the death of Ernest Fournier, all of the corporation's stock was owned by his five sons. Paul, who continued to serve as general manager, was president and treasurer; Roland served as assistant manager and was vice-president and secretary. Paul and Roland also were the only directors. In

October 1980, Paul terminated Roland's employment with the corporation.

Roland and two of his other brothers sued Paul and E. P. Fournier Co. seeking reinstatement of Roland as assistant manager. The trial court held that Paul lacked the authority to terminate Roland's appointment as assistant manager. Paul appealed.

Weisberger, Justice

. . .The court is faced with what essentially amounts to a family dispute cloaked in corporate structure. . . . The principal source of contention lies in the apparent breakdown of the combined business and fraternal relationships of two of the brothers, namely Paul J. Fournier and Roland A. Fournier. . . .

We hold that the authority to remove Roland from his position as assistant manager of the E. P. Fournier Co., as well as from the offices of vice president and secretary, lies with the board of directors and not with Paul pursuant to any of his individual, corporate capacities. The power of removal is often explicitly conferred by a corporation's own law in its charter or bylaws, or by statute. Neither the charter of E. P. Fournier Co. nor its bylaws contain provisions in respect to the removal of officers or agents. . . .

It is the prevailing view that the power to remove officers and agents of a corporation resides in the body that appointed or elected them. . . . The authority to remove is inherent in and incident to the authority to select. They are corollary powers.

The bylaws of E. P. Fournier Co. imposed on its board of directors the duty to manage the business and affairs of the corporation. On June 1, 1960, the shareholders added a provision to the bylaws which authorized the board of directors to enter into agreements for management of the business with any individuals it deemed necessary as manager or assistant manager. . . . Indeed, on the same day, the board entered into such contracts employing Paul as manager and Roland as assistant manager. By means of its employment contract with Roland, the board delegated to him some of the powers, duties, and liabilities imposed on it under its bylaws. Having charged Roland to act for it in the first instance, the board of directors possessed the inherent right and authority to remove from him such aspects of managerial authority as it had bestowed on him. This we find is consistent with gen-

---

13. 203 N.E.2d 577, 583-585 (Ill. 1964).

eral principles of agency which give a principal the right to revoke the agency. . . .

Paul asserts that his employment agreement with the board of directors making him manager of the corporation in 1960 effectively conferred on him all of the board's authority to manage the corporation, including its power to remove Roland. In short, he asserts that by the agreement, the board of directors stripped itself of all managerial and decision-making functions. This we find contravenes both the theory inherent in the corporate structure and our corporate statutes.

Section 7-1.1-33 [of the Rhode Island Business Corporation Act] provides that "[t]he business and affairs of a corporation shall be managed by a board of directors." Although this section grants to the board sole original power to manage the affairs of the corporation, the authority of corporate directors may be limited by other statutory provisions or by the corporation's own law through its charter or bylaws. Under the authority of the bylaws of E. P. Fournier Co., the board of directors entered into management contracts with Paul and Roland, thereby delegating in part its authority to manage the corporation. Although we recognize that in Paul's appointment as manager the board delegated the authority to carry on the day-to-day business of the corporation, we do not believe that the board completely abdicated its power, as Paul suggests. The duties and powers of a general manager, while extensive, do not result in the deprivation of all statutory authority and responsibilities of the directors. . . . Too broad a delegation of powers, either express or implied, may be interpreted as an unlawful abdication by the board of directors of its management functions. . . . Moreover, this aspect of Paul's argument is not supported by the facts. Subsequent to Paul's assuming the position of manager, the board-of-directors continued to function as a body. Many affairs of the corporation requiring board action and approval were conducted by the directors. There were board-of-directors meetings. The directors entered into the December 1962 agreement. Directors met to select new officers after the death of Ernest P. Fournier. We believe, therefore, that Paul's claim that he has effectively been the board of directors of E. P. Fournier Co. since 1960 has no basis in law or in fact. That being so, a formal board meeting should have been called for the purpose of terminating Roland. It is

noteworthy in this instance that a meeting of the board of directors comprised of Paul and Roland would probably lead to deadlock on this matter. Nothing short of a stockholders' meeting could accomplish Roland's removal. These procedural obstacles, however, cannot justify Paul's unilateral action. The formalities of board-of-director or stockholder action were required. . . .

We agree with the decision of the trial justice that Roland's termination was ineffective and improper and that he should be reinstated to the active position of assistant manager. . . .

[Judgment affirmed.]

Oppression of Minority Shareholders

As noted by the court in *Galler,* a major reason for shareholder agreements regarding shareholder and director functions is to maintain control of the corporation and to prevent oppression of minority shareholders. Oppression of the minority is a distinct risk in closely-held corporations. Because corporate statutes provide that corporate action is taken by majority vote of directors, a faction within the corporation with the power to elect a majority of directors may consistently outvote the minority and, therefore, exclude them from corporate management. The majority may "freeze out" the minority by refusing to pay dividends, and may drain off corporate earnings in the form of salaries, bonuses, or rents payable to majority shareholders. The majority may also deprive minority shareholders of corporate offices or employment and may purchase corporate assets at inadequate prices.

Because no outside market exists for shares of the corporation, which may also be subject to share transfer restrictions, a disgruntled minority shareholder may be locked into the corporation, excluded from management, employment, or dividends, but unable to sell out or force liquidation of the business (which would require 50% share ownership). These problems are exacerbated by the fact that all or most shareholders are involved in day-to-day management, increasing the likelihood of disputes and acrimony.

Various devices have been developed to protect minority interests in closely-held corporations, devices that should be negotiated during corporate formation and may be included in the articles of incorporation, bylaws, or shareholder agreements. One device is to provide for greater than majority (commonly unanimous) voting requirements for shareholder or director action. This approach gives the minority an effective veto power over unfair or high-handed majority action. Another method is to create separate classes of stock for the majority and minority shareholder, with the majority shares entitled to superior dividend rights but with both classes entitled to elect an equal number of directors. Another protection device is a mandatory agreement among shareholders requiring the majority shareholders of the corporation to buy out the minority at a price fixed by a predetermined formula.

The following case illustrates one form of oppression in a closely-held corporation and analyzes the nature of the relationship between majority and minority shareholders.

Wilkes v. Springside Nursing Home, Inc.
353 N.E.2d 657 (Mass. 1976)

In 1951, plaintiff Stanley Wilkes, T. Edward Quinn, Leon Riche, and Hubert Pipkin formed Springside Nursing Home, Inc., a Massachusetts corporation. Each of the men invested $1,000 and received 10 shares of stock. They agreed that each shareholder would serve as a director and they divided the duties of operating the nursing home among themselves. In 1952, the corporation began paying each of the shareholders a weekly salary. In 1959, Pipkin sold all of his stock to Lawrence O'-Connor but, otherwise, the corporation continued to operate as originally planned. Following a disagreement between Quinn and Wilkes in 1965, the relationship among all shareholders began to deteriorate. In 1967, Wilkes announced his intention to sell his shares but refused an offer from the other three shareholders because the price was too low. In February 1967, the corporation terminated Wilkes's salary. At the annual meeting in March, the three other shareholders failed to re-elect Wilkes as a director or officer and he was advised that his services were no longer needed.

Wilkes sued Springside, Quinn, Riche, and O'-Connor alleging that they had breached their fidu-

ciary duties. The trial court ruled in favor of the majority shareholders. Wilkes appealed.

Hennessey, Chief Justice

. . . [W]e do not consider it vital to our approach to this case whether the claim is governed by partnership law or the law applicable to business corporations. This is so because, as all the parties agree, Springside was at all times relevant to this action, a close corporation. . . .

"[S]tockholders in the close corporation owe one another substantially the same fiduciary duty in the operation of the enterprise that partners owe to one another." [*Donahue v. Rodd Electrotype Co. of New England, Inc.*, 328 N.E.2d 505 (Mass. 1975)]. As determined in previous decisions of this court, the standard of duty owed by partners to one another is one of "utmost good faith and loyalty." [*Cardullo v. Landau*, 105 N.E.2d 843 (Mass. 1952)]. . . .

In the *Donahue* case we recognized that one peculiar aspect of close corporations was the opportunity afforded to majority stockholders to oppress, disadvantage or "freeze out" minority shareholders. In *Donahue* itself, for example, the majority refused the minority an equal opportunity to sell a ratable number of shares to the corporation at the same price available to the majority. The net result of this refusal, we said, was that the minority could be forced to "sell out at less than fair value," . . . 328 N.E.2d at 515, since there is by definition no ready market for minority stock in a close corporation.

"Freeze outs," however, may be accomplished by the use of other devices. One such device which has proved to be particularly effective in accomplishing the purpose of the majority is to deprive minority stockholders of corporate offices and of employment with the corporation. . . . This "freeze-out" technique has been successful because courts fairly consistently have been disinclined to interfere in those facets of internal corporate operations, such as the selection and retention or dismissal of officers, directors and employees, which essentially involve management decisions subject to the principle of majority control. . . .

The denial of employment to the minority at the hands of the majority is especially pernicious in some instances. A guaranty of employment with the corporation may have been one of the ''basic reason[s] why a minority owner has invested capital in the firm.'' Symposium—The Close Corporation, 52 Nw.U.L.Rev. 345, 392 (1957). . . . The minority stockholder typically depends on his salary as the principal return on his investment. . . . Other noneconomic interests of the minority stockholder are likewise injuriously affected by barring him from corporate office. . . . Such action severely restricts his participation in the management of the enterprise, and he is relegated to enjoying those benefits incident to his status as a stockholder. . . . In sum, by terminating a minority stockholder's employment or by severing him from a position as an officer or director, the majority effectively frustrate the minority stockholder's purpose in entering on the corporate venture and also deny him an equal return on his investment.

. . . [A] strict obligation [is imposed] on the part of majority stockholders in a close corporation to deal with the minority with the utmost good faith and loyalty. On its face, this strict standard is applicable in the instant case. . . . Nevertheless, we are concerned that untempered application of the strict good faith standard . . . to cases such as the one before us will result in the imposition of limitations on legitimate action by the controlling group in a close corporation which will unduly hamper its effectiveness in managing the corporation in the best interests of all concerned. The majority, concededly, have certain rights to what has been termed ''selfish ownership'' in the corporation which should be balanced against the concept of their fiduciary obligation to the minority. . . .

Therefore, when minority stockholders in a close corporation bring suit against the majority alleging a breach of the strict good faith duty owed to them by the majority, we must carefully analyze the action taken by the controlling stockholders in the individual case. It must be asked whether the controlling group can demonstrate a legitimate business purpose for its action. . . . In asking this question, we acknowledge the fact that the controlling group in a close corporation must have some room to maneuver in establishing the business policy of the corporation. It must have a large measure of discretion, for example, in declaring or withholding dividends, deciding whether to merge or consolidate, establishing the salaries of corporate officers, dismissing directors with or without cause, and hiring and firing corporate employees. . . .

If called on to settle a dispute, our courts must weigh the legitimate business purpose, if any, against the practicability of a less harmful alternative.

Applying this approach to the instant case it is apparent that the majority stockholders in Springside have not shown a legitimate business purpose for severing Wilkes from the payroll of the corporation or for refusing to reelect him as a salaried officer and director. . . . There was no showing of misconduct on Wilkes's part as a director, officer or employee of the corporation which would lead us to approve the majority action as a legitimate response to the disruptive nature of an undesirable individual bent on injuring or destroying the corporation. On the contrary, it appears that Wilkes had always accomplished his assigned share of the duties competently, and that he had never indicated an unwillingness to continue to do so.

It is an inescapable conclusion from all the evidence that the action of the majority stockholders here was a designed ''freeze out'' for which no legitimate business purpose has been suggested. Furthermore, we may infer that a design to pressure Wilkes into selling his shares to the corporation at a price below their value well may have been at the heart of the majority's plan.

In the context of this case, several factors bear directly on the duty owed to Wilkes by his associates. At a minimum, the duty of utmost good faith and loyalty would demand that the majority consider that their action was in disregard of a longstanding policy of the stockholders that each would be a director of the corporation and that employment with the corporation would go hand in hand with stock ownership; that Wilkes was one of the four originators of the nursing home venture; and that Wilkes, like the others, had invested his capital and time for more than fifteen years with the expectation that he would continue to participate in corporate decisions. Most important is the plain fact that the cutting off of Wilkes's salary, together with the fact that the corporation never declared a dividend . . . assured that Wilkes would receive no return at all from the corporation.

[Judgment reversed and remanded for determination of damages.]

Deadlock

Control devices designed to protect the minority create serious risk of deadlock at either the shareholder or director level. That is, with unanimous voting requirements, one dissenting vote can cripple corporate action. If the majority and minority each have the power to elect, for example, two directors, a 2–2 vote is not an unlikely possibility.

Various devices can be built into the corporate structure to control deadlock, such as providing that if the board is unable to agree for a specified time, then the dispute will be submitted to an arbitrator for a binding decision. Provisions concerning how the arbitrator is to be chosen and the extent of the arbitrator's power must be carefully drafted. Another device is to require one competing faction to buy out the other. Determining which faction buys and which sells, and at what price, is often a difficult issue.

The most drastic deadlock remedy is voluntary or involuntary liquidation of the corporation. To protect minority shareholders, modern courts and legislatures increasingly provide involuntary liquidation as a remedy in both deadlock and oppression cases. Alternatively, the parties may prescribe in advance the circumstances and procedures for corporate liquidation.

Corporate Litigation

As a legal entity, a corporation has the capacity to sue and be sued in the corporate name. Lawsuits for injury to the corporation may be maintained by corporate management directly, by shareholders "derivatively," or by others on behalf of the corporation. Claims against the corporation may be asserted by a variety of third parties such as creditors, federal or state governments, or shareholders (for example, to recover dividends or to examine corporate records). As previously discussed, notice of a lawsuit against a corporation is provided by serving process on the corporation's registered agent.

Important issues peculiar to corporate litigation include shareholder derivative suits and indemnification for litigation expenses of officers and directors.

Shareholder Derivative Suits

A corporation may sustain serious injury from a breach of duty, negligence, or other wrongdoing of corporate officers or directors. For example, officers or directors may have converted a corporate opportunity for personal profit. Although the corporation is a legal entity, capable of suing in its own name to recover for such an injury, corporate management has no interest in maintaining suit because it is allegedly involved in the wrongdoing. To provide a remedy in this case and others in which corporate management refuses to act, the law allows one or more shareholders to bring a **derivative suit** in the corporate name to enforce a corporate cause of action. That is, in a derivative suit, shareholders sue not in their individual capacities, but as representatives of the corporation. The corporation is the plaintiff in the case, though it is often a nominal defendant for procedural purposes. Any judgment in a derivative action is paid to the corporation, not the shareholders. The judgment nevertheless benefits both corporate creditors and shareholders indirectly by protecting the value of their investment in the corporation. If the suit is successful, however, the plaintiff-shareholder is entitled to reimbursement by the corporation for reasonable expenses, including attorneys' fees.

Prerequisites for Derivative Suits. Although derivative actions are a valuable tool for policing management conduct, they have been used as abusive "strike suits," suits brought not to redress a corporate wrong, but to secure a favorable private settlement for the shareholders and their attorneys. To prevent abuse, the law imposes a number of restrictions upon shareholder derivative actions that are discussed below. These restrictions are derived from the Federal Rules of Civil Procedure,[14] state civil procedure statutes, state business corporation acts,[15] and case law. Note that most modern share-

---

14. Fed. R. Civ. P. Rule 23.1, 28 U.S.C.
15. See MCBA §49, RMBCA §7.40.

holder derivative suits are brought in federal court under the federal securities laws or on diversity of citizenship grounds.

The various legal and procedural requirements that must be met to maintain a derivative action include, for example, the following.

Exhaustion of Intracorporate Remedies. Before commencing a derivative action, the shareholder must first make a demand upon the board of directors (or in some cases other shareholders) to enforce the claim, or prove that such an appeal would be futile—for example, that the wrongdoers control the corporation. That is, before proceeding derivatively, the shareholder must exhaust remedies available within the corporation.

Contemporaneous Share Ownership. Under the "contemporaneous share ownership" requirement, the plaintiff must have been a shareholder at the time when the alleged wrong took place. Persons acquiring shares after that time by operation of law (for example, by will or intestate succession) also are eligible plaintiffs. In addition, the plaintiff must own shares when the action is commenced, during its pendency, and through entry of final judgment. These requirements assure that the plaintiff has a financial stake in a corporate recovery, prevents the plaintiff from "buying a lawsuit," and, in federal cases, prevents collusion in establishing diversity of citizenship.

Security for Expenses. In approximately one-fifth of the states, plaintiffs who own less than a minimum amount of the corporation's stock[16] may be required, upon application by the corporation, to provide security (usually a bond) for reasonable expenses including attorneys' fees that may be incurred by the corporation or others in defending the suit. These "security for expenses" statutes are designed to prevent strike suits and have been upheld as constitutional even though they affect only small

shareholders. Courts often permit the plaintiff to bring additional shareholders into the suit in order to meet the minimum shareholding requirement, thereby eliminating the need to provide security.[17]

The following case discusses the rationale for the requirement that a shareholder must exhaust intracorporate remedies before commencing a derivative suit.

Aronson v. Lewis

473 A.2d 805 (Del. 1984)

Leo Fink was a director, and owned 47% of the stock, of Meyers Parking System, Inc. (Meyers). In 1981, Meyers's board of directors approved an employment agreement by which Meyers would pay Fink $150,000 per year plus a bonus of 5% of its pretax profits over $2,400,000. Fink agreed to devote his best efforts to "advancing Meyers's interest." The agreement was for a five-year term with automatic renewal annually. Although Fink could terminate the contract at will, Meyers was required to provide six months notice for termination. Even if Meyers terminated the agreement, Meyers was required to pay at least $100,000 per year to Fink for his life in exchange for Fink's serving as a consultant. At the time of the agreement, Fink was seventy-five years of age. Meyers's board of directors also approved the corporation's making interest-free loans of $225,000 to Fink.

Plaintiff Harry Lewis, a shareholder of Meyers, brought a shareholder derivative suit against Meyers and ten of its directors seeking cancellation of the employment agreement with Fink. The defendants argued that Lewis was required to make a written demand to the corporation's board of directors requesting it to correct its allegedly wrongful conduct.

---

16. Minimum stockholding usually is measured as a percentage of outstanding shares (for example, 5 percent) or minimum value (for example, $25,000 or $50,000).

---

17. Note that if a bond is posted and the suit is unsuccessful, the corporation has recourse to the security for reimbursement. In contrast, if no bond is required, the corporation generally is not entitled to reimbursement for expenses of an unsuccessful suit. Thus, a plaintiff who is required to provide security may be required to pay the litigation expenses of both parties.

The court ruled that Lewis was excused from making a written demand because it would have been futile. Defendants appealed.

Moore, Justice

. . . A cardinal precept of the General Corporation Law of the State of Delaware is that directors, rather than shareholders, manage the business and affairs of the corporation. . . . The existence and exercise of this power carries with it certain fundamental fiduciary obligations to the corporation and its shareholders. . . . Moreover, a stockholder is not powerless to challenge director action which results in harm to the corporation. The machinery of corporate democracy and the derivative suit are potent tools to redress the conduct of a torpid or unfaithful management. . . .

By its very nature the derivative action impinges on the managerial freedom of directors. Hence, the demand requirement . . . exists at the threshold, first to insure that a stockholder exhausts his intracorporate remedies, and then to provide a safeguard against strike suits. Thus, by promoting this form of alternate dispute resolution, rather than immediate recourse to litigation, the demand requirement is a recognition of the fundamental precept that directors manage the business and affairs of corporations.

In our view the entire question of demand futility is inextricably bound to issues of business judgment and the standards of that doctrine's applicability. . . . It is a presumption that in making a business decision the directors of a corporation acted on an informed basis, in good faith and in the honest belief that the action taken was in the best interests of the company. . . . Absent an abuse of discretion, that judgment will be respected by the courts. . . .

Delaware courts have addressed the issue of demand futility on several earlier occasions. . . . The rule emerging from these decisions is that where officers and directors are under an influence which sterilizes their discretion, they cannot be considered proper persons to conduct litigation on behalf of the corporation. Thus, demand would be futile. . . .

Our view is that in determining demand futility the Court of Chancery in the proper exercise of its discretion must decide whether, under the particularized facts alleged, a reasonable doubt is created that: (1) the directors are disinterested and independent and (2) the challenged transaction was otherwise the product of a valid exercise of business judgment. . . .

Having outlined the legal framework within which these issues are to be determined, we consider plaintiff's claim . . . of futility here: Fink's domination and control of the directors. . . .

Plaintiff's claim that Fink dominates and controls the Meyers's board is based on: (1) Fink's 47% ownership of Meyers's outstanding stock, and (2) that he "personally selected" each Meyers director. Plaintiff also alleges that mere approval of the employment agreement illustrates Fink's domination and control of the board. In addition, plaintiff argued on appeal that 47% stock ownership, though less than a majority, constituted control given the large number of shares outstanding, 1,245,745.

Such contentions do not support any claim under Delaware law that these directors lack independence. . . . [P]roof of majority ownership of a company does not strip the directors of the presumptions of independence. . . . There must be coupled with the allegation of control such facts as would demonstrate that through personal or other relationships the directors are beholden to the controlling person. . . .

The requirement of director independence inheres in the conception and rationale of the business judgment rule. . . . Independence means that a director's decision is based on the corporate merits of the subject before the board rather than extraneous considerations or influences. While directors may confer, debate, and resolve their differences . . . , the end result . . . must be that each director has brought his or her own informed business judgment to bear with specificity upon the corporate merits of the issues without regard for or succumbing to influences which convert an otherwise valid business decision into a faithless act.

Thus, it is not enough to charge that a director was nominated by or elected at the behest of those controlling the outcome of a corporate election. That is the usual way a person becomes a corporate director. It is the care, attention and sense of individual responsibility to the performance of one's duties, not the method of election, that generally touches on independence. . . .

Here, plaintiff has not alleged any facts sufficient to support a claim of control. . . . Therefore, we cannot conclude that the complaint factually particularizes any circumstances of control and domination to overcome the presumption of board independence, and thus render the demand futile. . . .

[Judgment reversed and remanded.]

Settlement of Derivative Suits. To discourage "strike suits" and unfair settlements, the Federal Rules of Civil Procedure[18] and a number of state statutes require court approval for dismissal or compromise of derivative suits, and notice to other shareholders of the terms of the dismissal or compromise. In approving the settlement, the court considers various factors including the size of the settlement in relation to the value of the claim and the difficulty in proving it, the solvency of the defendants, and objections or proposals of other shareholders. Note that any settlement secretly paid to an individual plaintiff-shareholder generally may be recovered for the benefit of the corporation in another derivative action.

Indemnification for Litigation Expenses

Directors, officers, and other corporate personnel often must defend lawsuits brought against them based upon the conduct of their corporate responsibilities. These suits may be civil, criminal, administrative, or investigatory in nature and maintained by either private or governmental plaintiffs. A question that has long concerned the law of corporations is the extent to which corporate personnel are entitled to be indemnified or reimbursed by the corporation for expenses of litigation brought against them in their corporate capacities. These expenses include primarily attorneys' fees and amounts paid in settlement of a suit or satisfaction of a judgment.

Although originally addressed by common law, indemnification is now governed by statute in all states. Although the statutes vary widely, many are modeled upon Section 5 of the MBCA. Under this provision, indemnification is allowed generally if the defendant acted in good faith and in a manner reasonably believed to be in the best interests of the corporation. If the action was criminal in nature, the defendant must additionally have had no reasonable cause to believe that his conduct was unlawful.[19]

If the suit is maintained by or on behalf of the corporation—for example, a shareholder derivative suit—rather than an outsider, indemnification is generally allowed subject to the "good faith" and "best interests" tests outlined above. In these cases, however, no indemnification is permitted if the defendant is adjudged liable for negligence or misconduct in the performance of his duty to the corporation unless the court determines that indemnification of some or all expenses is proper in light of the circumstances of the case.

A defendant who is successful on the merits or otherwise in defense of any suit described above is entitled to indemnification for expenses actually and reasonably incurred. Any other indemnification (unless ordered by the court) is made only as authorized in the specific case upon a determination that the person seeking reimbursement has met the standards of conduct discussed above. The determination is made by vote of the board of directors, or in some cases, by independent legal counsel or the shareholders.

The various statutory indemnification provisions generally are not exclusive. Many corporations, therefore, have detailed provisions governing the issue in their articles of incorporation or bylaws.

Directors' and Officers' Liability Insurance

A corporation may purchase and maintain insurance on behalf of officers, directors, employees, or agents against any liability incurred by them in their corporate capacities whether or not the corporation has the power to indemnify the loss. Such insurance usually is called "D & O liability insurance." The policy usually covers both the corpo-

---

18. Fed. R. Civ. P. Rule 23.1, 28 U.S.C.

19. MBCA §5. Compare RMBCA §§8.50-8.58.

ration for amounts paid to indemnify corporate personnel, and officers and directors for amounts not indemnifiable by the corporation (for example—liability for negligence). The corporation and the person covered, therefore, often share the cost of the premium. Although the insurance protects against negligence, it does not cover liabilities incurred through self-dealing, dishonesty, knowing violation of securities law, or other intentional misconduct.

SUMMARY

1. Although voting for directors is the usual extent of shareholder management participation, shareholder approval is also required for certain extraordinary corporate transactions deemed beyond the ordinary powers of the board. These matters generally include amendments to the articles of incorporation, merger and consolidation, sale of substantially all corporate assets, and voluntary dissolution. State statutes afford shareholders a right to dissent from certain extraordinary corporate transactions and obtain payment in cash for their shares. This statutory "appraisal" remedy generally awards the dissenting shareholder the "fair value" of his shares.

2. State business corporation statutes are designed to govern creation and operation of all corporations, regardless of size or the number of shareholders. Closely-held corporations, however, create management problems not addressed by general corporation statutes. For this reason, shareholders in a closely-held corporation should by careful negotiation and drafting anticipate and resolve in advance problems relating to distribution of management power and control, oppression of minority shareholders, and deadlock in corporate management.

3. As a legal entity, a corporation has capacity to sue and be sued. Lawsuits for injury to the corporation may be maintained by corporate management directly. Alternatively, shareholders may sue "derivatively" as representatives of the corporation to recover for injury to the corporation caused by the negligence, breach of duty, or other wrongdoing of corporate officers or directors. To prevent abuse, derivative suits are subject to strict procedural limitations.

4. Subject to a number of limitations, state corporation statutes, and in some cases the articles of incorporation or bylaws, allow indemnification of directors, officers, and other corporate personnel for expenses of litigation brought against them in their corporate capacities. Indemnification often is funded by insurance that protects both the corporation and corporate personnel.

KEY TERM

shareholder derivative suit

QUESTIONS AND PROBLEMS

48-1 Big Bank shareholders approved a merger with First Bank Corp. Hanson, who owned 200 shares of Big Bank, voted against the merger and elected to exercise a statutory right to appraisal. After the appraisers valued the stock, Big Bank offered to pay Hanson the appraised price for his shares but he refused stating that he wished to withdraw from the appraisal process. Big Bank sued Hanson demanding that he tender his shares for the appraised price. Should the court allow Hanson to withdraw from the appraisal process? Why or why not?

48-2 Assume that you, your father, your brother, and a close family friend desire to create a corporation with equal shares to build and operate a restaurant. The family friend has the expertise in restaurant management, your brother will do the accounting, and you and your father are providing most of the capital, but will stay out of the day-to-day operations. What provisions should be included in the articles of incorporation, bylaws, or shareholder agreements to provide harmonious management, prompt resolution of disputes, prevent deadlock, prevent oppression of a dissenting shareholder, and provide orderly liquidation of the business, if necessary?

48-3 In 1978, five members of the Gray family formed a corporation to operate its farming and ranching operations. The family members also entered into a written agreement that provided in part: "So long as all of the original stockholders are alive, they shall not sell, trade, encumber or otherwise dispose of the stock which they now own or later may acquire without the written consent of the remaining stockholders." In 1985, Robert, one of the shareholders, notified the corporation of his desire to sell his stock. The other four shareholders refused to consent to the sale. Robert filed suit requesting the court to hold that the consent provision was unenforceable. He argued that the provision in effect permanently prohibited his right to sell his property. How should the court rule?

48-4   A plaintiff who wishes to initiate a shareholder derivative suit must meet a variety of requirements (for example, demand on directors, ownership of stock at the time the wrongdoing occurred) not generally imposed on plaintiffs. Why have courts adopted these requirements?

48-5   On September 1, Harris purchased fifty shares of Raygo Co. In October, Raygo purchased a small company owned by Raygo's president's sister for a price of $100 million. Harris immediately wrote to the president of Raygo demanding that the sale be rescinded because the purchase price far exceeded the value of the small company. Because Harris received no reply, she sold all of her shares of Raygo Co. on November 15. On December 1, Harris brought a shareholder derivative suit alleging that the president of Raygo had breached his fiduciary duties. The state statute concerning derivative suits provides in part:

> In a derivative action brought by one or more shareholders to enforce a right which may properly be enforced by the corporation, the plaintiff shareholder shall have been a shareholder at the time of the transaction of which he complains.

   (a) Assume that Harris did not own any stock at the time she filed the derivative suit. Under the statute is she entitled to bring the suit? Explain.

   (b) Assume instead that on November 31, Harris purchased one share of Raygo. Would she legally be entitled to bring the derivative suit under the statute? Explain.

48-6   In 1984, General Motors Corporation (GM) acquired 100% of the stock of EDS, a corporation founded by H. Ross Perot. The sales agreement provided that Perot would exchange his shares of EDS stock for shares of GM stock and would remain as chairman of EDS. Perot also was elected to GM's board of directors. Within 2 years, major disagreements arose between Perot and GM and Perot repeatedly criticized GM management in public. In 1986, Perot offered to sell his GM stock to GM and after negotiations Perot and GM officers agreed to the terms of a repurchase agreement which then was submitted to a committee of three GM outside directors who unanimously recommended board approval. The following day GM's board of directors approved the agreement which required Perot to transfer all of his GM stock to GM, to resign from GM's board, and to resign as chairman of

EDS. Under the agreement, Perot also agreed to stop criticizing GM management, not to purchase GM stock or engage in a proxy contest against GM's board of directors for five years, and not to compete with EDS for three years or recruit EDS executives for eighteen months. In exchange, GM agreed to pay Perot approximately $740 million, which was about twice the market value of Perot's stock. A group of GM shareholders filed a shareholder derivative suit against GM, Perot, and GM's board of directors, alleging that they had violated their fiduciary duties by paying a grossly excessive price to Perot and by wasting company assets by paying "hush mail" to Perot. The defendants moved to dismiss the suit on the ground that plaintiffs had failed to make a written demand to GM's board of directors seeking corrective action prior to filing the suit. The plantiffs contended that such a written demand would have been futile. How should the court rule?

48-7   The bylaws of Elmira Corporation provide in part:

> Every person who is or was a director, officer or employee of Elmira Corporation shall be indemnified by the Corporation against any and all liability and reasonable expense that may be incurred by him in connection with or resulting from any claim, action, suit or proceeding, civil or criminal, or in connection with an appeal relating thereto, in which he may be involved as a party or otherwise, by reason of his being or having been a director, officer or employee of the Corporation.

   (a) While Annabelle Jones was serving as a director of Elmira Corporation, she became involved in a struggle for control of the corporation. Jones and three other directors sued the remaining directors alleging that they had violated state law in a recent board of directors' election. The case later was dismissed by the court. Jones sought indemnification of her attorneys' fees and court costs from Elmira. Under the bylaws, is she entitled to indemnification? Explain.

   (b) Leon Lynch, treasurer of Elmira, embezzled several million dollars from the corporation. Elmira sued Leon and won a judgment against him. Is Leon entitled to indemnification of his legal expenses? Explain.

   (c) Many state statutes provide that a corporation may not indemnify an officer or director for defending a suit in which the officer or director is found liable for negligence or misconduct. Other statutes allow indemnification of an officer or director who has been found liable for negligence or misconduct only if the court approves the indemnification. Still other statutes allow indemnification regardless of the officer's or director's liability. Explain the advantages and disadvantages of each type of statute.

The Conflict Between Shareholders and Managers: New Light and New Issues

John C. Coffee, Jr.

For more than a half-century, the most debated issue in corporate law has been that raised by Adolf Berle and Gardiner Means in *The Modern Corporation and Private Property* (1933). Essentially, they claimed that ownership and control had become separated in the public corporation, with the result that management was largely autonomous. In their view, management was unchecked either by shareholders, who were widely dispersed and for whom opposition was too costly to organize, or by market forces, because corporations could finance themselves through retained earnings. Much subsequent writing about corporate law and behavior has debated the accuracy of this premise of managerial autonomy. During the 1960s a school of academics known as the "managerialists" developed a behavioral model of the firm theorizing that managers sought to maximize not profits, but sales, growth, and firm size.[1] Maximizing firm size—that is, "empire building"— was in the manager's self-interest, they claimed, because it increased their security, psychic income, and compensation (which tends to be positively correlated with firm size).[2] Empirical work during this period contrasted "management controlled" firms with "shareholder controlled" firms (that is, firms having a substantial or controlling shareholder) and found that the former category of firm typically had a much lower rate of return on its retained earnings.[3] This finding suggested the existence of an "earnings retention bias" in management controlled firms under which funds that could have been paid out as dividends were instead retained and expended on marginally profitable projects.

Today, the view of management as a self-contained, insulated bureaucracy appears to have been the product of unique historical circumstances. During the 1970s, a variety of forces—international competition, the oil crisis, the rise of the hostile takeover, and the growing power of institutional investors—appear to have significantly curbed managerial discretion. Critics of the Berle-Means thesis have also challenged its basic premise that shareholders are dispersed and powerless. One recent survey of over 500 large corporations found that the five largest ownership interests controlled on the average more than 25 percent of the shares, a statistic that implies that shareholders normally constitute a strong monitoring force.[4] In addition, the stock market could represent a powerful constraint on management, even if managers principally relied on internal cash flow to finance expansion, because the shareholders could design compensation systems using stock options and similar techniques that gave managers a strong interest in maximizing the value of the firm's stock.[5]

Still, economists recognize that managers, as agents, can have interests that conflict with those of their principals, the shareholders. Indeed, modern finance theory has formalized the Berle-Means line of analysis by developing a theory of "agency costs"—namely, the costs that are incident to any principal/agent relationship, such as that between shareholders and their managers. These costs consist basically of the monitoring costs that shareholders must incur to hold their agents faithful to their interests plus the residual loss that it is not cost efficient to prevent.[6] Agency costs are also borne by managers, however, because to the extent shareholders cannot effectively prevent misbehavior by their agents, shareholders should pay less for their shares. As a result, it is often in the interest of managers to undertake measures limiting their own ability to engage in opportunistic behavior. Today, most commentators would probably conclude that improved monitoring controls

John C. Coffee, Jr. is Adolf A. Berle Professor of Law, Columbia University Law School.

and modern developments in the internal structure of the firm have reduced much of the opportunities for managerial self-dealing that were prevalent at the time Berle and Means wrote.[7]

At the same time, neoclassical economists have correspondingly come to acknowledge that firms have a tendency to grow beyond their optimal size and to retain earnings that could be paid out to shareholders and invested elsewhere at a higher rate of return.[8] What explains this phenomenon? If it were only managers' desire to maximize their salaries, this tendency could be easily overcome by adjusting compensation formulas. But more basic factors may be at work. One factor may be a "risk aversion differential," under which managers are more risk averse than shareholders because they have more of their wealth (and expectations for future wealth) invested in the firm. Although shareholders tend to hold diversified portfolios, managers tend to be over-invested in their own firm; in short shareholders own many stocks, but managers have only one job. This lack of diversification creates a rational incentive to reduce the risks to which their firm is subject by causing it to grow and diversify—even if this growth (particularly through conglomerate acquisitions) reduces the value of the firm's shares.[9]

These theories help explain recent developments in the market for corporate control—that is, the world of takeovers and tender offers. Since the early 1980s, a new breed of financial entrepreneur—typified by Carl Icahn and Boone Pickens—has begun to make takeover bids with a view not to managing the acquired firm's assets, but to liquidating it. Such "bust-up takeovers" make economic sense for target firms that expanded inefficiently, because the stock price of such firms should decline below their asset liquidation value, and this discount invites a takeover. In this view, the market for corporate control is essentially disciplining unprofitable growth by target firms. During the mid-1980s, a surge in restructuring and spinoffs by firms thought to be potential takeover targets suggests that the deterrent threat of the hostile takeover has at least partially corrected this managerial tendency toward excessive growth.

Currently, the premia offered by bidders in tender offers averages approximately 50 percent more than the pre-bid market price of the target. As noted above, this could imply that there are enormous agency costs which are reduced when the target's assets are removed from the control of its incumbent management (possibly because target management inefficiently expanded or overinvested in staff or perquisites). Another plausible explanation for the consistently high premia paid in takeovers is overpayment by bidders. After all, if corporations tend to expand inefficiently, this bias for inefficient growth could affect takeover bidders as well as other corporations. Some recent data support this possibility that takeovers may often produce wealth transfers from bidder shareholders to target shareholders. One recent study of 236 matched pairs (that is, bidder and target corporations, taken together) between 1962 and 1987 found that, following the takeover, the combined stock value of each pair of target and bidder firms increased on average by 7.5 percent.[10] In three out of four cases, the gains exceeded the losses (thus leaving, however, 25 percent in which the net impact of the takeover, as determined by the stock market reaction, was negative). Even more revealing is the fact that during the 1960's, acquiring firms experienced statistically significant gains in their stock prices following takeovers, while during the 1970s they experienced no statistically significant gains, and, during the 1980s, bidders incurred statistically significant losses equal to about 3 percent of their market value (or $27 million per takeover on average). Still, on an aggregate basis, this study found a net increase in shareholder wealth from takeovers, because the gains received by target shareholders exceeded the losses experienced by the bidder shareholders.

What can explain this puzzling pattern? Increasingly, during the 1970s and 1980s, tender offers by one bidder elicited counteroffers by rival bidders (sometimes called "white knights"), thereby leading to sustained auction contests. In these auctions, the eventual victor often might be the party that most overestimated the target's value (some economists call this the "winner's curse" problem). Curiously, it may imply that the real victims in takeovers are the bidder's shareholders.

In this light, it seems ironic that the potential victim that has most concerned the states are the target shareholders. A majority of the states (currently 34) have recently enacted anti-takeover statutes to "protect" target shareholders from being "coerced" into tendering. Because the typical premia in takeovers are high (50 percent on average today) and most offers are for all outstanding common shares, this prospect of coercion seems minimal. Still, the real concern of state legislatures may be for the employees, managers, creditors of the target firm and the surrounding local communities—all of whom may be exposed to real losses from takeovers. By chilling takeovers, these constituencies are protected, but possibly at a loss in overall economic efficiency. Part of the problem about state regulation of takeovers is that those who experience losses—chiefly, employees and local communities—tend to be clustered in the state of incorporation and thus can effectively lobby for protection, while the beneficiaries of takeovers (shareholders) tend to be dispersed nationally and lack effective local political clout. Until 1987, the ability of states to regulate tender offers seemed constitutionally doubtful (largely on the ground that state takeover regulation was preempted by the Williams Act, the federal statute regulating takeovers, and also burdened interstate commerce in violation of the Commerce Clause of the U.S. Constitution). In 1987, however, the Supreme Court upheld an Indiana anti-takeover statute in *CTS Corp. v. Dynamics Corp. of America*,[11] and a wave of new state statutes has followed. The constitutionality of many of these statutes is still in doubt, but state regulation has clearly become the newest force in takeover regulation.

The debate over the impact of hostile takeovers on economic efficiency has recently intensified. While financial economists point to stock price studies that seem to show that shareholders gain in the aggregate, industrial organization economists have conducted follow-up studies that have not found any increase in profitability, market share, or other measures of efficiency following a takeover.[12] Critics also increasingly blame the takeover movement for, among other things, higher corporate leverage (and thus an increased risk of bankruptcy), disruption of longer-term planning, declining emphasis on research and development, and unfair exploitation of workers.[13] This debate will undoubtedly continue, and the evidence to date is certainly open to reasonable dispute. One conclusion seems, however, certain: takeovers,

more than any other development in modern American corporate history, have exposed basic tensions among shareholders, managers, and other constituencies in the publicly held corporation.

1. See W. Baumol, Business Behavior Value and Growth (1959); R. Marris, The Economic Theory of Managerial Capitalism (1962); R. Cyert and J. March, A Behavioral Theory of the Firm (1963).   2. There has been a substantial debate over whether executive compensation is determined more by firm size or firm profitability. For a review, see W. McEachern, Managerial Control and Performance (1975).   3. See Baumol, Heim, Malkiel, and Quandt, Earnings Retention, New Capital and the Growth of the Firm, 52 Rev. Econ. & Statistics 128 (1973) (finding that corporations that avoided the capital markets had low rates of return—often near zero—on their retained earnings).   4. Demsetz and Lehn, The Structure of Corporate Ownership: Causes and Consequences, 93 J. Pol. Econ. 1155 (1985).   5. Jensen and Meckling, Theory of the Firm: Managerial Behavior, Agency Costs and Ownership Structure, 3 J. Fin. Econ. 305 (1976).   6. Agency theory dates essentially from a seminal article by Jensen and Meckling, supra note 6.   7. Williamson, The Modern Corporation: Origins, Evolution, Attributes, 19 J. Econ. Lit. 1537 (1981).   8. Jensen, Agency Cost of Free Cash Flow, Corporate Finance, and Takeovers, 76 Am. Econ. Rev. 323 (1986).   9. See Amihud and Lev, Risk Reduction as a Managerial Motive for Conglomerate Mergers, 12 Bell J. Econ. 605 (1981). Another explanation is that managers are seeking to protect their "firm specific" human capital (namely, experience and knowledge that they have acquired which is valuable to their own firm, but not to the market generally) by increasing the size of the firm to protect it from bankruptcy or hostile takeovers. For a discussion of these and other explanations of the "bust-up takeover", see Coffee, *Shareholders Versus Managers: The Strain in the Corporate Web*, 85 Mich. L. Rev. 1 (1987).   10. Bradley, DeSai and Kim, *Synergistic Gains from Corporate Acquisitions and their Division Between the Stockholders of Target and Acquiring Firms*, (forthcoming in the Journal of Financial Economics).   11. 107 S. Ct. 1637 (1987).   12. See, e.g., D. Ravenscraft and F. M. Scherer, "Mergers and Managerial Performance" in Coffee, Lowenstein and Rose-Ackerman, (eds.), KNIGHTS, RAIDERS & TARGETS: The Impact of the Hostile Takeover (1988); D. Mueller, *Mergers and Market Share*, 67 Review of Economics and Statistics 259 (1985). Other studies have found that target corporations do not differ significantly in their financial characteristics from other firms in their same industry. See, e.g., Merck, Shleifer and Visny, *Characteristics of Hostile and Friendly Takeover Targets*, NBER Working Paper (June 1987).   13. For a recent study of labor's response to the growing significance of takeovers (which involves increasing demands to participate in corporate governance and to limit the mobility of capital), see Stone, *Labor and the Corporate Structure: Changing Conceptions and Emerging Possibilities*, 55 U. Chi. L. Rev. 73 (1988). Some economists have also argued that takeovers can breach prior implicit contracts between labor and management. See Schleifer and Summers, *Hostile Takeovers As Breaches of Trust* (National Bureau of Economic Research 1987).

Part Eight

GOVERNMENT REGULATION OF BUSINESS

Chapter 49   *Securities Regulation*

Major Topics

- an introduction to securities regulation, including the development of the law, overview of major statutes, and the definition of security
- a discussion of the Securities Act of 1933 governing public distribution of securities
- coverage of the Securities Exchange Act of 1934, which created the Securities and Exchange Commission, and regulates secondary trading in securities and securities markets

Corporate securities, such as stocks and bonds, represent claims against and ownership interests in a corporation, and are therefore only as valuable as the assets and the ongoing business that underlie them. Because corporate securities have no intrinsic value, but are a popular medium for investment, they often have been used in schemes intended to mislead or defraud investors. To prevent fraud and to assure the orderly functioning of the securities markets, the states and the federal government have enacted comprehensive securities regulation statutes. These statutes require full and honest disclosure of relevant business information by persons who offer or sell securities to the public. To promote public confidence, these laws also regulate the operation of the securities markets and the qualifications of the people who operate them.

Introduction to Securities Regulation

Development of the Law—State Regulation

The rapid industrial growth of the late nineteenth century was fueled to a great extent by the sale of corporate securities. Though most of these sales represented legitimate investments, many did not, and state legislatures were soon pressured to enact remedial legislation. In 1911, Kansas passed the first state statute regulating the distribution and sale of securities. Other states soon followed and all states now have such legislation. To this day, these statutes are known as **blue sky laws,** because their basic purpose is to prevent fraud perpetrated through ''speculative schemes which have no more basis than so many feet of 'blue sky.'''[1]

State blue sky legislation typically requires registration of securities brokers and dealers, registration of securities offered or traded in the state, and proscribes certain fraudulent conduct. State statutes commonly require both disclosure of relevant information and qualification of the security. Under the qualification procedure, the state securities commissioner evaluates the merits of the proposed investment before the securities can be offered for sale. Although most blue sky statutes are based in

---

1. *Hall v. Geiger-Jones Company,* 37 S. Ct. 217, 220-221 (1917).

whole or in part upon the Uniform Securities Act, promulgated in 1956, significant differences in language and interpretation exist among the states.

State securities regulation proved inadequate in policing securities frauds, however, especially those operating on a national scale. After the stock market crash of 1929, which was precipitated in large part by vast quantities of fraudulent securities, Congress acted. Federal securities law, the subject of the remainder of this chapter, is based upon six statutes enacted between 1933 and 1940 pursuant to Congress's power to regulate interstate commerce.[2]

Federal Securities Regulation Statutes

Congress initiated federal securities regulation with the **Securities Act of 1933** (the 1933 Act),[3] which governs the public distribution of securities. With certain exceptions, it prohibits the offer or sale of securities to the public unless the offering is properly registered. Rejecting the state "qualification" or "merit" approach, the 1933 Act requires broad disclosure of relevant corporate information to prospective investors, provides civil remedies for violations, and prohibits fraudulent or deceptive practices in the sale of securities.

To complement the 1933 Act, Congress enacted the **Securities Exchange Act of 1934** (the 1934 Act).[4] The 1934 Act created the **Securities and Exchange Commission** (SEC) to administer federal securities law and created a comprehensive plan regulating public "trading" in securities. Thus, whereas the 1933 Act governs distributions by an issuer to the public for the first time, the 1934 Act governs subsequent trading in those securities among private investors on the various securities exchanges or in the more informal over-the-counter markets. The 1934 Act also requires comprehensive periodic disclosure of business information by companies with publicly traded securities, and imposes significant federal regulation on the securities markets.

Collectively, the 1933 and 1934 Acts are the heart of federal securities regulation. To supplement these statutes, Congress enacted four regulatory statutes of more limited scope between 1935 and 1940. These include: (1) the **Public Utility Holding Company Act of 1935**,[5] correcting abuses in the financing and operation of electric and gas utilities owned by holding companies, (2) the **Trust Indenture Act of 1939**,[6] protecting bondholders by regulating the terms of bond indentures under which large issues of corporate debt securities are administered, (3) the **Investment Company Act of 1940**,[7] regulating publicly-owned companies, such as mutual funds, which are engaged in the business of investing and trading in securities, and (4) the **Investment Advisers Act of 1940**,[8] regulating persons who are in the business of rendering investment advice but are not securities brokers or dealers.

The Securities and Exchange Commission

The Securities and Exchange Commission is composed of five commissioners, appointed by the president, each serving five-year terms. The terms are staggered so that one commissioner's term expires each year, and no more than three commissioners may be members of the same political party. Although the SEC itself has basic responsibility for SEC action and decisions, its staff is responsible for the day-to-day operations. The SEC operates from a head office in Washington, D.C. and nine regional and six branch offices. It is divided into five major divisions governing enforcement, corporation finance, market regulation, investment management, and corporate regulation. Like other major federal agencies, the SEC possesses quasi-legislative (rule-making) power, the power to investigate violations of the statutes it administers, and the power to adjudicate those violations and impose penalties.

---

2. The power of Congress to regulate interstate commerce under the Commerce Clause of the Constitution is discussed in detail in Chapter 4.

3. 15 U.S.C. §77a *et seq.* The Securities Act is sometimes known as the "Truth in Securities" Act.

4. 15 U.S.C. §78a *et seq.*

5. 15 U.S.C. §79 *et seq.*

6. 15 U.S.C. §77aaa *et seq.*

7. 15 U.S.C. §80a-1 *et seq.*

8. 15 U.S.C. §80b-1 *et seq.*

The SEC has exercised its rule-making power extensively to promulgate rules governing procedural and technical matters, defining terms used in the various acts, and stating substantive principles of law. These rules are published in Volume 17 of the Code of Federal Regulations. The SEC also has adopted detailed forms that are used to comply with the disclosure and filing requirements of the securities laws. The SEC also periodically publishes "releases," which include guidelines for statutory or rule interpretation and outline the commission's position on current issues, and responds to individual inquiries regarding compliance with the law through its "no action" letters.

As part of its enforcement and adjudicatory powers, the SEC has supervisory and disciplinary power over persons registered with it including brokers, dealers, investment companies, investment advisers, securities exchanges, and attorneys and accountants who practice before the SEC. The commission also may proceed against persons distributing securities in violation of the 1933 Act registration provisions. Although many violations are handled through administrative sanctions, the SEC sometimes proceeds in federal court to enjoin future violations of the law and may refer serious violations to the Justice Department for criminal prosecution.

Definition of "Security"

One of the most basic securities law issues is whether a particular investment transaction constitutes a **security.** Resolving the issue determines whether securities law registration requirements or antifraud provisions, or both, apply to the transaction. Both federal and state securities laws define "security" broadly to cover a wide range of investment instruments. For example, the definitions include traditional securities such as stocks and bonds and catchall categories such as "investment contracts" and "any interest or instrument commonly known as a security."[9]

Courts often must decide whether an unconventional investment transaction is a security, usually as an "investment contract." The leading case formulating the judicial definition of investment contract is *Securities and Exchange Commission v. W. J. Howey Co.,* decided by the Supreme Court in 1946.[10] In this case, W. J. Howey Co. offered for sale to the public individual rows of trees in a citrus grove, conveying the land by deed to the purchasers. In conjunction with the sale, a service company affiliated with Howey offered the purchasers a service contract under which the company would cultivate, harvest, and market the fruit and distribute the net profit to the owner. In holding that the sale-service contract promotion was an "investment contract" and therefore a "security" requiring registration under the 1933 Act, the Court announced the now famous *Howey* test:

> [A]n investment contract for purposes of the Securities Act means a contract, transaction or scheme whereby a person invests his money in a common enterprise and is led to expect profits solely from the efforts of the promoter or a third party. . . .[11]

The Court noted that a security may be found under the test even if no formal stock or other certificate is used and even if, as in *Howey,* the investors have nominal interests in the physical assets of the enterprise. The test "embodies a flexible rather than a static principle, one that is capable of adaptation to meet the countless and variable schemes devised

---

9. Under §2(1) of the Securities Act of 1933: "The term 'security' means any note, stock, treasury stock, bond, debenture, evidence of indebtedness, certificate of interest or participation in any profit-sharing agreement, collateral-trust certificate, preorganization certificate or subscription, transferable share, investment contract, voting-trust certificate, certificate of deposit for a security, fractional undivided interest in oil, gas, or other mineral rights, any put, call, straddle, option, or privilege on any security, certificate of deposit, or group or index of securities (including any interest therein or based on the value thereof), or any put, call, straddle, option, or privilege entered into on a national securities exchange relating to foreign currency, or, in general, any interest or instrument commonly known as a 'security,' or any certificate of interest or participation in, temporary or interim certificate for, receipt for, guarantee of, or warrant or right to subscribe to or purchase, any of the foregoing." Virtually identical definitions of security are found in the other federal securities laws and in most state blue sky laws.

10. 66 S. Ct. 1100 (1946).

11. *Id.* at 1103.

by those who seek the use of the money of others on the promise of profits.''[12]

The *Howey* test has been applied to hold a wide variety of investment schemes ''securities'' including, for example, sales of limited partnership interests, interests in oil and gas leases, withdrawable capital shares in a savings and loan association, variable annuities, and interests in whiskey warehouse receipts. The guiding principle in all cases is whether the investors need the protection of the securities laws. Indeed, in several cases, courts have refused to apply the securities laws when other federal regulations adequately protect the parties.

The following case illustrates the application of the *Howey* test.

Hocking v. Dubois

839 F.2d 560 (9th Cir. 1988)

Defendant Maylee Dubois, a licensed realtor in Hawaii, arranged the sale of a condominium located in a resort complex in Hawaii to plaintiff Gerald Hocking. Dubois informed Hocking that the sale included an option to participate in a rental pool arrangement (RPA) operated by an agent of the resort complex. Under the RPA, the agent rented condominiums to vacationers, pooled the rental income and, after assessing management costs, distributed the net income pro rata to the RPA participants. During each distribution period every participating owner received a pro rata share of the net income whether or not that owner's condominium had been rented during the period. Hocking elected to participate in the RPA.

Hocking subsequently sued Dubois alleging that she had violated §10(b) of the Securities Exchange Act and Rule 10b–5 promulgated thereunder by committing fraud in inducing him to buy the condominium. The trial court, after finding that the sale of the condominium was not a sale of a security as defined in federal securities law, granted summary judgment to Dubois. Hocking appealed.

---

12. *Id.*

Reinhardt, Circuit Judge

. . . The term ''security'' is defined in section 2 of the Securities Act of 1933 . . . and in section 3 of the Securities Exchange Act of 1934. . . . The sections, which are substantially identical . . . define a security to include any ''investment contract.'' . . .

The now classic definition of an investment contract is found in *SEC v. W. J. Howey Co.*, [66 S.Ct. 1100 (1946)]. . . . Under *Howey*, . . . an investment contract consists of (1) an investment of money, (2) in a common enterprise, (3) with the expectation of profits produced by the efforts of others.

Generally, simple transactions in real estate, without more, do not satisfy the *Howey* criteria. . . . When a purchaser is motivated exclusively by a desire to occupy or develop the land personally, no security is involved. . . .

Real estate transactions may involve an offer of securities when an investor is offered both an interest in real estate *and* a collateral expectation of profits. . . . However, drawing the line between the offering of land sales contracts and investment contracts has not been easy. To resolve this difficulty, at least in the area of condominiums, the Securities and Exchange Commission issued guidelines in 1973 on the applicability of federal securities laws to the burgeoning resort condominium market. . . .

[T]he Commission states unequivocally that it will view a condominium as a security if it is offered with any one of three specified rental arrangements. The second of these arrangements, the controlling one here, is ''[t]he offering of participation in a rental pool arrangement.'' 38 Fed. Reg. 1735, 1736 (1973). . . . [T]he offering of a condominium with an RPA *automatically* makes the investment a security. . . .

Even apart from the guidelines, we find that under the three *Howey* criteria an offer of a condominium with an RPA constitutes an offer of an investment contract.

1. *Investment of Money.* Defendants do not dispute that the condominium purchase satisifed *Howey's* first requirement. Hocking invested money in the condominium.

2. *Common Enterprise.* There has been some disagreement among the circuit courts of appeals

on what satisfies the requirement of a common enterprise. . . .

Horizontal commonality describes the relationship shared by two or more investors who pool their investments together and split the net profits and losses in accordance with their pro rata investments. . . . By pooling their assets and giving up their claims to any profit or loss attributable to their particular investments, investors make their collective fortunes dependent on the success of a single common enterprise. Clearly, horizontal commonality describes the relationship that purchasers of a company's securities share with one another. This is the standard, run-of-the-mill situation for which the securities laws were designed to apply. . . .

A rental pool arrangement creates *horizontal* commonality with other parties involved in the RPA. If Dubois' offer to sell the condominium did not include the option of joining the RPA, then Hocking's investment in the condominium would be his alone and not an investment in a common venture. In the absence of other investors, there would be no horizontal commonality. . . . [T]he offer of a condominium to Hocking did include an offer of an option to enter an RPA. Accordingly, horizontal commonality exists.

It is readily apparent that an RPA for condominiums is a common enterprise. Each investor buys one share—a condominium—in a common venture that pools the rents from all of the units. The success of each participant's individual investment clearly depends on the entire RPA's success. At least with respect to the common enterprise prong of *Howey*, this is precisely the reason why the SEC felt that an offer of a condominium with an option for RPA *automatically* constitutes the offer of a security.

3. *Expectation of Profits Produced by Others' Efforts*. With respect to the third prong of *Howey*, i.e., the expectation of profits produced by the efforts of others, we conclude that this requisite is met *whenever* a condominium is sold with an RPA option. This is what the Commission has done in its guidelines for condominiums. . . .

The SEC and its advisory committee recognized the wisdom of having a rule that would make the sale of all the condominiums in a particular condominium development subject to the securities laws or would exclude the sale of all those units—

regardless of the fortuity of the individual economic expectations of the particular buyer. A rule, the applicability of which depended on the subjective intentions of each individual prospective purchaser of each separate unit, would be extremely difficult to administer and would be arbitrary inasmuch as it would make the seller's—and any broker's—liability depend on the undisclosed and often unformed thoughts of the buyer. Even a specific condominium unit could on one day be a security and the next not, depending on the investment attitudes of a particular prospective purchaser on a particular day. For these reasons the SEC's Real Estate Advisory Committee was willing to recommend "rather mechanical tests" with respect to condominium investments, which the SEC adopted in its guidelines. . . . We agree, and believe that the Release's bright line rule reflects the only proper interpretation of *Howey* as applied to condominiums. The purchase of a condominium with an RPA option thus meets the third *Howey* requisite that there be an expectation of profits based upon the entrepreneurial or managerial efforts of others.

Not only, then, does the alleged transaction at issue constitute the offer of a security under the SEC guidelines, but it also constitutes a security under the test set forth in *Howey*. . . .

[Judgment reversed and remanded.]

The Securities Act of 1933

The Securities Act of 1933 is concerned with distributions of securities—the process by which a corporation or other issuer offers and sells its securities to the public for the first time. It protects investors by requiring full and fair disclosure of relevant information regarding the securities offered and the issuer. The heart of the 1933 Act is §5, which provides that no security may be offered or sold to the public unless a "registration statement" has been filed with the SEC. Major 1933 Act provisions are discussed below.

Public Distribution of Securities

A corporation may be able to finance its operations or expansion out of its earnings or from private sources such as bank loans. Alternatively, it may raise necessary funds through a transaction exempt from securities law registration. If large sums of money are required, however, or if the company desires additional equity rather than debt financing, it may undertake a registered public offering of securities.

A public offering is not without its hazards. Registration is an extremely expensive and time-consuming process requiring extensive public disclosure of corporate affairs. Periodic reporting requirements under the 1934 Act impose additional expense. The offering may fall upon an unreceptive market. Dividend policy and control of the business will be affected.

If the corporation chooses public financing, it must devise some method to offer and sell the securities to members of the public. Although the corporation may undertake the task itself, most issuers have neither the expertise nor the personnel to make a public offering. Rather, the issuer enlists a network of underwriters and dealers registered with the SEC and appropriate state agencies. Under §2(11) of the 1933 Act, an **underwriter** is a person who purchases securities from an issuer with a view toward distribution to the public, and any person who participates in the underwriting effort. Under §2(12), a **dealer** is any person who engages in the business of offering, buying or selling, or otherwise trading in securities issued by others.

Typically, securities in an underwritten offering are sold by the issuer to the underwriters, who sell them to dealers, who in turn sell them to the public. In a "firm commitment" underwriting, the underwriters purchase an allotment of securities outright from the issuer and resell them at a markup to the dealers. In this case, the underwriters bear the expense of any unsold securities. In a "best-efforts" underwriting, commonly used by less established issuers, underwriters attempt to sell what they can on a commission basis, with no liability for unsold shares.

1933 Act Disclosure Requirements

Superimposed upon this distribution scheme is the Securities Act of 1933 that requires that issuers file a **registration statement** with the SEC before securities are offered or sold to the public. The first part of the registration statement is the **prospectus,** a copy of which must be delivered to persons to whom the security is offered or sold. The contents of the prospectus are outlined in §10 of the Act and SEC rules. The remainder of the registration statement (Part II) contains information that, though not distributed to all investors, is available for public inspection in the SEC files.

The registration statement contains exhaustive disclosure of the issuer's affairs, including detailed information about the issuer, its directors and major stockholders, the issuer's capitalization, the price and nature of the securities offered (including the amount and intended use of the proceeds), information concerning underwriters and counsel, and a current balance sheet and income statement. The second part of the registration statement contains copies of agreements with underwriters, opinions of counsel, certain major contracts, the articles of incorporation, and agreements or indentures affecting the security offered.

Various forms of registration statements are available, depending upon the nature of the issuer, the surrounding circumstances, and the type of security. To ease the burden imposed upon issuers by federal securities regulation, in 1982 the SEC adopted a system integrating the disclosure requirements of the 1933 and 1934 Acts. This system permits issuers who are already registered and periodically reporting substantial corporate information under the 1934 Act to use special forms that require less detailed disclosure than the basic long-form registration statement. These forms incorporate by reference much of the information already on file with the SEC under the 1934 Act reporting requirements.

The Registration Process

Section 5 of the 1933 Act divides the registration process into three periods: the pre-filing period (the period before the registration statement has been completed and filed with the SEC), the waiting period (the period between the filing date and the date the registration statement becomes "effective"), and the post-effective period. The registration process may be illustrated as follows:

Pre-filing period	Waiting period	Post-effective period

Time

Filing date   Effective date

Permissible selling efforts differ depending on how far the registration process has progressed, reflecting the level of public information about the offering.

The Pre-filing Period. Before a registration statement is filed, both sales of securities and oral or written offers to buy or sell securities are prohibited. Although preliminary negotiations between the issuer and underwriters and among underwriters are exempted from the definition of "offer," virtually any other selling effort during the prefiling period, including offers to or by dealers, is a violation of the Act.[13]

The Waiting Period—Duration. Section 8(a) of the Act provides that the registration statement becomes "effective" twenty days after it is filed with the SEC, but that a new twenty-day period begins to run upon the filing of any subsequent amendment to the registration statement. Although the statutory waiting period is twenty days, the period usually is in fact much longer. Section 8 empowers the SEC to issue a "refusal" or "stop" order to suspend the effectiveness of an inaccurate or incomplete registration statement or one that contains a material misrepresentation or omission. Rather than using the refusal or stop order procedures, however, the SEC usually proceeds to correct deficiencies through a more informal "deficiency letter" or "letter of comment" procedure.

Common deficiencies in the registration statement include inadequate disclosure of specific sources of corporate income or loss; inadequate ex-

planation of the use of the proceeds of the offering; inadequate disclosure of transactions between the issuer and insiders, such as officers, directors, or major shareholders; and failure to make the prospectus readable. In response to the SEC's recommendations, the issuer then files an amendment, which commences a new twenty-day waiting period. Virtually all registration statements require at least one such amendment.

The Waiting Period—Permissible Selling Efforts. As in the pre-filing period, no sales of securities are permitted during the waiting period. Offers to buy or sell are, however, allowed. Although the Act imposes no restrictions upon oral offers (made either in person or over the telephone) during the waiting period, written offers are closely regulated. As a general rule, two types of written offering materials are permitted: the preliminary or "red herring" prospectus and the "tombstone" advertisement.

Preliminary Prospectus. The 1933 Act makes it unlawful to transmit any prospectus (defined in §2(10) to include all written offers to sell a security) after the registration statement is filed that does not disclose all relevant information about the issuer outlined in §10. Because the offering price (and information dependent upon the offering price) generally is unavailable during the waiting period, the 1933 Act authorizes the use of a preliminary prospectus during the waiting period. Such a prospectus must contain a legend in red ink (hence the term "red herring") that a registration statement has been filed but has not yet become effective, that information in the prospectus is subject to completion or amendment, and that sales may be made only after the registration statement becomes effective.

Tombstone Advertisement. The 1933 Act excludes from the definition of prospectus any written communication that merely identifies the security and its price, states by whom orders will be executed and from whom a prospectus may be obtained, and contains other information which may be authorized or required by SEC rules and regu-

---

13. The term "offer" is broadly defined to include any activity reasonably calculated to solicit or create buying interest. Securities Act §2(3).

Table 49-1	**Overview of 1933 Act Security and Transaction Exemptions**
Exemptions	*Securities or Transactions Covered*
Exempt Securities	- Government, bank, and certain insurance company securities - Short term commercial paper - Securities issued by certain not-for-profit organizations - Savings and loan securities - Securities issued by federally regulated common carriers - Insurance policies and annuity contracts §§3(a)(2)-(6), (8)

Exempt Distributions by Issuers	- Small or limited offerings—§§4(2), 3(b), and 4(6)
	    Securities Act Rules 251-264 (Regulation A)
	    Securities Act Rules 501-506 (Regulation D)
	- Intrastate offerings—§3(a)(11)
	    Securities Act Rule 147
	- Securities exchanged by issuer with existing security holders or in corporate
	    reorganization, and certificates issued in bankruptcy proceedings—§§3(a)(7), (9), (10)

Secondary Trading Exemptions	- Transactions by persons other than issuers, underwriters, or dealers—§4(1) Securities Act Rule 144 - Most transactions by dealers—§§4(3) and 4(4)

lations.[14] Communications of this type are known as "tombstone advertisements" because they are customarily framed by a black border. Most financial publications contain a number of these notices in each issue.

The Post-effective Period. Once the registration statement becomes effective, the underwriters and dealers are free to make offers and sales of the registered securities. The Act provides, however, that a registered security delivered for sale must be accompanied or preceded by a copy of the final prospectus. Dealers must deliver a prospectus in conjunction with the original sale of the security distributed by the issuer or an underwriter. They also must furnish a prospectus upon certain resales of securities reacquired by the dealer and resold within a specified time after the initial public offering. A prospectus used more than nine months after the registration statement becomes effective must

be updated so that its information is no more than sixteen months old.[15] In addition, whether or not the nine-month period has expired, the prospectus must be updated to reflect any development occurring after the effective date, such as a change in earnings, that would make the original prospectus materially misleading.

Exemption from 1933 Act Registration

Sections 3 and 4 of the 1933 Act exempt certain securities and security transactions from the registration requirements outlined above. These provisions are heavily supplemented by various SEC rules and releases. Although the exemptions excuse registration or impose alternative requirements, they do not alter liability under the Act's antifraud provisions (discussed later in the chapter). In addition, exemptions generally are strictly construed and the person claiming an exemption has the burden of proving its availability. Table 49-1 provides

---

14. Pursuant to this authority, the SEC has adopted Rule 134, which specifically outlines the various categories of information that may be included.

15. Securities Act §10(a)(3).

an overview of the various security and transaction exemptions in the 1933 Act, which are discussed in detail below.

Exempt Securities and Transactions. Section 3(a) of the 1933 Act exempts various securities from registration based upon the nature of the security or its issuer. These include (1) qualified securities issued or guaranteed by state, local, and federal governments and governmental organizations, federal reserve banks, and certain insurance companies, (2) commercial paper, such as a promissory note, if the paper has a maturity date not exceeding nine months, (3) securities issued by a not-for-profit organization organized and operated solely for religious, educational, benevolent, fraternal, charitable, or reformatory purposes, (4) securities issued by savings and loan associations or similar institutions supervised or examined by state or federal authorities, and by farmers' cooperatives exempt from federal taxation, (5) certain securities issued by federally regulated common carriers, and (6) insurance policies and annuity contracts issued by companies supervised by a state insurance commissioner or similar officer.[16]

In addition to specific securities, the Act exempts from registration securities distributed in certain types of transactions. Unlike exempt securities, those sold under a transaction exemption may not, in many cases, be resold without registration or compliance with another transaction exemption. A transaction exemption is available, for example, for securities exchanged by the issuer exclusively with existing security holders; securities issued in exchange for securities, claims, or property interests in a judicially or administratively approved corporate reorganization plan; and certificates issued by a receiver, trustee, or debtor in possession with court approval in a federal bankruptcy proceeding.[17] The Act also exempts from registration (1) certain transactions involving small or limited offerings, (2) purely intrastate offerings, and (3) transactions by persons other than issuers, underwriters, or dealers. The following sections discuss these important transaction exemptions.

Small or Limited Offering Exemptions. The exhaustive disclosures required in a 1933 Act registration impose an onerous and expensive burden upon issuers. Because of this expense, public financing often is not a viable alternative for smaller businesses or small issues of securities. To resolve this problem, the 1933 Act and SEC rules provide a number of exemptions for small issues, which provide less burdensome disclosure requirements than those imposed in a full-blown 1933 Act registration.

The limited issue exemptions are derived primarily from three separate sections of the 1933 Act.

1. Section 4(2) of the Act exempts from registration "transactions by an issuer not involving any public offering." Significant amounts of securities are sold pursuant to this "private placement" exemption, which may be used to sell a large block of securities to an institutional investor, such as an insurance company, or to a small group of private individuals. In both cases, the exemption is based on the fact that the purchasers are sophisticated and possess the bargaining power necessary to require the disclosures that registration would provide. If the class of persons to whom the securities are offered is shown to need the protection of the Act, the exemption is lost. General solicitation of purchasers is not permitted and resale of the securities is restricted.

2. Section 3(b) authorizes the SEC, through its rules and regulations, to exempt offerings not exceeding $5 million if it finds that registration "is not necessary in the public interest and for the protection of investors by reason of the small amount involved or the limited character of the public offering."

3. Section 4(6), added in 1980, exempts sales not exceeding $5 million made exclusively to any number of "accredited investors." Accredited investors include virtually all types of institutional investors (such as banks, insurance companies, registered investment companies, savings and loan associations, credit unions, and securities brokers or dealers); directors, executive officers, or general partners of the issuer; certain partnerships, corporations, and trusts with total assets exceeding $5 million; and individuals meeting certain minimum net worth or income requirements. Though no specific information need be furnished, general solici-

---

16. Securities Act §§3(a)(2)-(6), (8).
17. Securities Act §§3(a)(7), (9), (10).

tation of purchasers is not permitted and resale is restricted.

Pursuant to its statutory authority under these provisions, the SEC has adopted various rules governing limited offerings. The most important of these rules are contained in Regulation A (Securities Act Rules 251–264), adopted in 1956, and Regulation D (Securities Act Rules 501–506), adopted in 1982. Regulation A provides a somewhat simplified form of registration for small issues, while Regulation D simplifies and coordinates the various limited offering exemptions.[18]

Regulation A. Adopted under §3(b) of the Act, Regulation A imposes registration and disclosure requirements similar to, but much less expensive and burdensome than, a full-blown 1933 Act registration. If the issuer qualifies for the exemption, Regulation A may be used to issue not more than $1.5 million in securities during any twelve-month period. Securities issued under Regulation A can be resold without restriction.

To use Regulation A, the issuer files an "offering statement" with the SEC's nearest regional office, containing a "notification" and "offering circular." The information required in the offering statement is less detailed than a 1933 Act registration statement, and prospectus and financial statements need not be audited. After a ten-day waiting period (usually extended by the SEC letter of comment procedure previously discussed), selling efforts may commence and offerees and purchasers must be furnished with a copy of the offering circular.

Regulation D. Regulation D provides a comprehensive framework governing many small issues and issuers. It consists of SEC Rules 501 through 506. Rules 501–503 contain the definitions, conditions, and filing and disclosure requirements applicable to the three specific exemptions contained in Rules 504, 505, and 506. Although Regulation D provides an exemption from *federal* registration,

it does not excuse compliance with any applicable state "blue sky" law.

1. *Rule 501.* Rule 501 defines certain important terms used in Regulation D.

2. *Rule 502.* Rule 502 specifies the type of information which must be furnished to purchasers in offerings exempted by Regulation D. If the sales are made under Rule 504 or to accredited investors only, no specific information need be furnished. If, however, sales are made to nonaccredited purchasers under Rules 505 or 506, specific financial and other information must be supplied to all purchasers. The amount and format of this information differs depending upon whether the issuer is registered under the 1934 Act. The rule also provides that securities exempted under Regulation D may not be offered or sold by any form of general solicitation or advertising, including newspaper, radio, or television advertisements. Finally, Rule 502 provides that securities sold under Regulation D cannot be resold by the purchasers without registration or an independent exemption. The issuer must place a legend on the certificates stating that the securities are not registered and that their transfer is restricted.

3. *Rule 503.* Rule 503 states that notice of exempt sales made under Regulation D must be filed with the SEC.

4. *Rule 504. Exemption for issues not exceeding $1 million.* Rule 504 permits an issuer to sell a total of up to $1 million of securities to an unlimited number of investors in any twelve-month period as long as no more than $500,000 of the securities are offered and sold without registration under state blue sky laws. The exemption is not available to investment companies or to companies subject to the registration and reporting requirements of the 1934 Act. The manner of offering and resale restrictions imposed by Regulation D do not apply to sales made in compliance with a state blue sky law requiring registration of the securities and delivery of a disclosure document before sale. In addition, Regulation D restrictions do not apply to sales of up to $500,000 made in states that have no such statute if: (1) the securities have been sold in at least one state in compliance with that state's registration and disclosure statute, and (2) the disclosure document is in fact delivered to all purchasers in the nonqualifying states before the se-

---

18. In addition to these regulations, the SEC has adopted Regulation E (Securities Act Rules 601-610a), under §3(c) of the Act, which provides an exemption for offerings by certain investment companies not exceeding $5 million.

curities are sold. Rule 504 imposes no requirement that any specific information be furnished to purchasers.

5. *Rule 505. Exemption for limited offerings not exceeding $5 million.* Rule 505 permits an issuer to sell up to $5 million in securities in any twelve-month period to any number of accredited investors and up to thirty-five other purchasers. If, however, at least one purchaser is not an accredited investor, the disclosures required by Rule 502 must be furnished to all purchasers. The exemption may be used by all issuers except investment companies and issuers who have been convicted of securities offenses or subject to SEC disciplinary proceedings within specified time periods.

6. *Rule 506. Private placement safe harbor.* Federal case law provides general guidelines for availability of the private placement exemption under §4(2). To provide greater certainty in corporate planning, Rule 506 provides a safe harbor for the exemption. That is, compliance with Rule 506 assures availability of the private placement exemption, but failure to satisfy its provisions does not necessarily mean that the exemption is unavailable. Rule 506, which is available to all issuers, permits issuers to sell an unlimited amount of securities to an unlimited number of accredited investors and up to thirty-five other buyers. If sales are made to nonaccredited buyers, the issuer must reasonably believe that the purchaser, either alone or with a representative, "has such knowledge and experience in financial and business matters that he is capable of evaluating the merits and risks of the prospective investment."[19] As under Rule 505, if there are any nonaccredited buyers, the disclosures required by Rule 502 must be furnished to all purchasers.

Intrastate Offering Exemption. Section 3(a)(11) of the 1933 Act exempts from federal registration "any security which is a part of an issue offered and sold only to persons resident within a single State . . ., where the issuer of such security is . . . a corporation, incorporated by and doing business within, such State. . . ." State blue sky laws continue to apply, however, if the offer is made to the public. Both the courts and the SEC have interpreted this "intrastate offering" exemption very narrowly. It exempts only those issues that "represent local financing by local industries, carried out through local investment."[20]

Rule 147. To provide greater certainty to corporate planners intending to use the intrastate exemption, the SEC in 1974 adopted Rule 147, which defines certain terms of the statute. Rule 147, like Rule 506 discussed above, provides a "safe harbor."

The statute itself provides that the exemption is available only if all purchasers *and* offerees are residents of a single state and the issuer is incorporated by and doing business in that state. Thus, a corporation operating solely in Illinois, but incorporated in Delaware to take advantage of Delaware's liberal corporation law, could not qualify for the exemption. Rule 147 provides that an issuer is presumed to be "doing business" in the state if (1) it derives at least eighty percent of its annual gross revenues from activities in the state, (2) at least eighty percent of its assets are located in the state, (3) at least eighty percent of the proceeds of the offering are to be used in the state, and (4) the issuer's principal office is located in the state.

Even if the foregoing requirements are met, the exemption is lost for the entire offering if securities sold under the exemption are subsequently resold to nonresidents. This approach applies both to intrastate transfers intended merely as a first step in an interstate distribution and to inadvertent later sales to nonresidents. Rule 147 provides, however, that the exemption is preserved if no resales are made to nonresidents within nine months after the initial sale by the issuer is completed. To protect against interstate offers and sales, Rule 147 requires the issuer to (1) place a legend on the stock certificate indicating that the securities are unregistered and cannot be resold interstate, (2) issue stop transfer instructions to the issuer's transfer agent, and (3) obtain a written statement from each purchaser regarding his or her residence. Table 49–2 summarizes the major 1933 Act transaction exemptions discussed above.

---

19. Securities Act Rule 506(b)(2)(ii).

20. Securities Act Release 4434, 26 Fed. Reg. 11896, 11897 (Dec. 6, 1961).

Table 49–2	Summary of Major 1933 Act Transaction Exemptions*					
Exemption	Total Offering Price Limitation	Number of Investors	Investor Qualification	Manner of Offering— Limitations	Resale Limitations	Disclosures
Regulation A	$1.5 million during any 12-month period	Unlimited	None	Offering circular; limited advertising permitted	None	Offering circular furnished to offerees and purchasers
Rule 504	$1 million in any 12-month period	Unlimited	None	General solicitation not permitted unless conducted (at least in part) in compliance with state blue sky law requiring delivery of disclosure document before sale	Restricted unless offering conducted (at least in part) in compliance with state blue sky law requiring delivery of disclosure document before sale	None required
Rule 505	$5.0 million in any 12-month period	Unlimited number of accredited investors and up to 35 other purchasers	Accredited investors or none required	General solicitation not permitted	Restricted	If purchased solely by accredited investors, none required. If any non-accredited purchasers, disclosures required by Rule 502 must be furnished to all purchasers.

Table 49–2 Continued

Exemption	Total Offering Price Limitation	Number of Investors	Investor Qualification	Manner of Offering—Limitations	Resale Limitations	Disclosures
Section 4(2)—Rule 506	Unlimited	Unlimited number of accredited investors and up to 35 other purchasers	Sophisticated investors only; accredited investors presumed qualified	General solicitation not permitted	Restricted	If purchased solely by accredited investors, none required. If any non-accredited purchasers, disclosures required by Rule 502 must be furnished to all purchasers.
Section 4(6)	$5.0 million	Unlimited number of accredited investors	Accredited investors only	General solicitation not permitted	Restricted	None required
Section 3(a)(11)—Intrastate Exemption—Rule 147	Unlimited	Unlimited	All offerees and purchasers must be residents of the same state in which issuer is incorporated and doing business	May be public or private offering	Unlimited resales to residents; resales to nonresidents permitted after 9 months	State blue sky laws apply if public offering

*This table is adapted from Hazen, *The Law of Securities Regulation* 107–109 (1985).

Secondary Trading Exemptions. Unless specifically exempted, the 1933 Act requires registration of all security transactions. To this point the discussion has examined the transaction exemptions used by issuers to avoid registering an initial distribution of securities. Most security transactions, however, are not part of the original distribution but involve secondary trading—for example, on a stock exchange—of securities already issued and outstanding.

Section 4(1) of the 1933 Act provides that the Act's registration provisions apply only to issuers, underwriters, and dealers, thus exempting transactions by nonprofessionals. Section 4(3) then exempts all transactions by securities dealers, except for sales that are part of the original distribution and resales made within a limited time after the registration statement becomes effective. Section 4(4) further exempts unsolicited "brokers transactions" executed upon customers' orders upon a securities exchange or in the over-the-counter market.[21] Collectively, these provisions exempt most day-to-day secondary trading occurring upon securities exchanges and over-the-counter markets from the Act's registration requirements.

Liability of Underwriters. Despite the exclusion of most brokers' and dealers' transactions, underwriters, like issuers, remain subject to the Act's registration requirements. As previously noted, underwriters generally include persons who purchase securities from the issuer for public distribution. For purposes of defining "underwriter," however, the term "issuer" includes both the corporation and any person who controls it.[22] Because "underwriters" therefore include those who sell securities for a person who controls a corporation, underwriter liability is imposed upon persons not otherwise engaged in the investment banking business in two important situations:

1. A controlling person may sell all or a portion of his or her stock in stock exchange or over-the-counter transactions effected through securities brokers or dealers. In this case, the broker or dealer is not insulated by the "brokers" transaction exemption and may be held liable as an "underwriter" for selling unregistered securities to the public. The selling controlling person is liable as an "issuer."

2. A person may purchase securities from an issuer in a transaction exempt from registration as a private placement or under Regulation D. Subsequently, the purchaser may wish to resell these "restricted" securities. If the purchaser is deemed to have purchased the securities from an issuer with a view to distribution, resale will render the purchaser liable as an underwriter for selling unregistered securities.

Rule 144. To provide practical guidance in determining when a registration statement must be filed for these secondary distributions, the SEC in 1972 adopted Rule 144. If the sale is made in compliance with the Rule, a person selling restricted or other securities on behalf of a controlling person (case 1 above) and a person reselling restricted securities (case 2 above) are deemed not to be engaged in the distribution of securities, and therefore not underwriters. The rule imposes the following "safe harbor" requirements:

1. sufficient current public information must be available about the issuer;
2. securities acquired in a nonpublic transaction must be held by the purchaser for two years before resale;
3. once the two-year period has expired, the amount of any securities resold during any three-month period may not exceed the greater of (a) one percent of the shares of that class currently outstanding, or (b) the average weekly trading volume in the securities for the previous four weeks;
4. sales must be made through brokers' transactions or in transactions directly with a "market maker"—a dealer who maintains a trading market for over-the-counter securities; and
5. notice of the sales must be filed with the SEC.

---

21. A broker is simply a person engaged in the business of effecting securities transactions as agent for others.

22. Securities Act §2(11). "Control" is a question of fact, defined in Securities Act Rule 405 to include "the power to direct or cause the direction of the management and policies of a person, whether through the ownership of voting securities, by contract, or otherwise."

Liability Under the 1933 Act

The 1933 Act contains specific remedies to prevent the sale of unregistered securities and to assure the accuracy of the registration materials. These remedies may be enforced by SEC administrative proceedings, court injunctions, and, in some cases, criminal prosecution. In addition, various civil remedies are available to private individuals injured by violations of the Act.

Liability for Failure to Register—Section 12(1). Section 12(1) of the Act provides that any person who offers or sells a security in violation of §5 is liable for damages to the person purchasing the security. For purposes of §12(1), a "seller" includes not only the owner of the security who passes title, but also any nonowner, such as a broker, who successfully solicits the purchase and who is motivated at least partially by a desire to serve his own financial interests or those of the security's owner. The purchaser may sue either in state or federal court to rescind the sale and recover the purchase price of the security plus interest in exchange for the security. A purchaser who no longer owns the security may recover money damages equal to the difference between the original purchase price and subsequent selling price. A §12(1) action must be brought within one year after the violation upon which it is based, but may not be maintained more than three years after the security was offered to the public.

Liability for False Registration Statement—§11. Section 11 of the 1933 Act imposes liability for misstatements and omissions in the registration statement. Under §11(a), if the registration statement, when it becomes effective, contains an untrue statement of material fact or omits to state a material fact, any person acquiring the security (either as part of the original distribution or in subsequent secondary trading) may maintain a civil suit against specified persons either in state or federal court. The injured purchaser may recover damages equal to the difference between the purchase price of the security and its value at the time of suit, or its selling price if the plaintiff no longer owns it. Persons liable, jointly and severally, to injured purchasers include:

1. every person who signed the registration statement;[23]
2. every director;
3. every person who consents to being named in the registration statement as being or about to become a director;
4. every accountant, engineer, appraiser, or other expert who has, with his or her consent, been named as having prepared or certified any part of the registration statement; and
5. every underwriter.

To recover under §11, the purchaser simply must prove loss and the existence of an untruth or omission in the registration statement. Proof of reliance on the registration statement is not required unless the buyer acquires the security after the issuer has published an earnings statement covering at least twelve months beginning after the effective date of the registration statement. A §11 action must be filed within one year after the purchaser discovers or should have discovered the untrue statement or omission, but may not be brought more than three years after the security is offered to the public.

Defenses. Persons charged with violating §11 may assert a number of affirmative defenses. For example, defendants may escape liability by proving either that the purchaser knew of the untruth or omission in the registration statement when acquiring the security, or that the decline in the security's value had been caused by factors other than the material falsities and omissions. An additional, and the most important, defense to §11 liability is the "due diligence" defense contained in §11(b)(3). This defense is available to all defendants except the issuer, who is strictly liable for all errors or omissions in the registration statement.

The due diligence defense imposes differing standards of conduct upon the various parties to the registration statement and absolves them from liability if they meet that standard. Regarding parts of

---

23. Section 6 of the Act requires that the registration statement be signed by the issuer, its principal executive officer or officers, its principal financial and accounting officer, and the majority of its board of directors.

the registration statement either prepared by an expert *other than the defendant* (for example, audited financial statements prepared by a certified public accountant) or made by a public official or public official document, a defendant must prove that he had no reasonable grounds to believe that there were any material misrepresentations or omissions. With respect to other parts of the registration statement, a nonexpert defendant escapes liability by proving that he made a reasonable investigation, which provided a reasonable ground for belief that the registration statement was true. An expert defendant, such as an accountant, engineer, or appraiser, is subject to the same "reasonable investigation" standard for parts of the registration statement prepared by the expert. The standard of reasonableness for "reasonable investigation" and "reasonable grounds to believe" is "that required of a prudent man in the management of his own property."[24]

Although potential §11 liability is a fundamental concern of all persons involved in preparing the registration statement, it has generated surprisingly little litigation. Indeed, the most definitive interpretation of §11 is *Escott v. BarChris Construction Corporation,* a classic federal district court decision decided thirty-five years after the Act was passed.[25] *Escott* and subsequent cases indicate that the standard of care required to avoid §11 liability differs depending upon the nature of the defendant, the issuer, and the defendant's participation in the registration process. In 1982, the SEC adopted Rule 176, which attempts to codify the relevant factors to be considered.

Antifraud Provisions—§§12(2) and 17(a). The 1933 Act contains two provisions imposing liability for fraud and misrepresentation in securities sales, §§12(2) and 17(a). Section 12(2) permits a purchaser to recover from a person who offers or sells a security (whether or not required to be registered) by oral or written communication that contains material misstatements or omissions. As under §12(1),

under §12(2) the purchaser may sue only his seller, the remedy is either rescission or money damages, and suit may be maintained either in state or federal court. An affirmative defense is available to a seller who can prove that she neither knew, nor should have known, of the untruth or omission. Suit must be filed within one year after the untruth or omission was discovered or should have been discovered, but not more than three years after the security was sold.

Section 17(a) is the 1933 Act's general antifraud provision providing a remedy for fraud, material misrepresentations, and omissions in the sale of securities. The remedy governs activities of offerors and sellers, not purchasers, but applies to all securities whether registered or exempt from registration. It supplements the express civil liability provisions (§§11 and 12) and may be enforced in state or federal court through SEC civil suit or criminal proceedings. Courts are divided concerning whether a private remedy should be implied under §17(a). Section 17(a)'s counterparts in the 1934 Act, §10(b) and Rule 10b–5, are discussed later in this chapter. Table 49–3 summarizes the civil remedies available under the 1933 Act.

1933 Act Criminal Liability. Under §24 of the Securities Act of 1933[26] any person who willfully violates any provision of the Act, its rules and regulations, or willfully makes a material misstatement in a registration statement, is guilty of a crime. Offenders may be punished by fines of up to $10,000, or imprisonment not exceeding five years, or both.

The Securities Exchange Act of 1934

The Securities Exchange Act of 1934 regulates secondary trading in securities, the securities markets, and persons conducting securities transactions. The 1934 Act imposes registration and disclosure requirements upon many issuers, the securities exchanges, self-regulatory organizations, and securities brokers and dealers. It also regulates proxy solicitation, tender offers, insider trading, and fraud and manipulative practices in securities trading.

---

24. Securities Act §11(c).

25. The facts of the case and the portion of the opinion concerning the liability of an independent public accountant under §11 are included in Chapter 55 (Accountants' Liability).

26. 15 U.S.C. §77x.

Table 49–3	Summary of 1933 Act Remedies			
Section	Conduct Proscribed	Permissible Plaintiffs	Permissible Defendants	Securities Covered
12(1)	Offer or sale of security in violation of §5.	Purchaser	Seller	Securities required to be registered.
11	Misrepresentations or omissions in registration statement.	Purchaser	Persons signing registration statement, directors, experts, and underwriters.	Securities covered by registration statement.
12(2)	Offer or sale of security by written communications containing material misstatements or omissions.	Purchaser	Seller	Any security, whether or not requiring registration.
17(a)	Fraud, material misrepresentations, and omissions in sale of securities.	SEC civil suit or government criminal suit; courts split on availability of implied private remedy for purchaser.	Offerors and sellers.	Any security, whether or not requiring registration.

1934 Act Registration and Reporting Requirements

The 1934 Act requires the following companies to register with the SEC: (1) issuers that have securities traded on a national securities exchange, (2) issuers that have both a class of equity securities held by at least 500 shareholders and total assets exceeding $5 million,[27] and (3) all issuers with outstanding securities sold under a 1933 Act registration. Note that 1934 Act registration is in addition to any registration of a specific securities offering required by the 1933 Act.

Initial registration under the 1934 Act requires detailed disclosure of information regarding the issuer's organization, capital structure, officers and directors, financial condition, and major contracts. In addition, under §13 of the Act, registered companies are required to file annual and other periodic reports with the SEC. These reports include the Form 10-K annual report, the Form 10-Q quarterly report, and a Form 8-K current report, which must be filed when certain specified changes in the issuer's condition or operations occur. These reports assure continuing public availability of current information about companies whose securities are publicly traded.

Financial and Accounting Requirements. The 1934 Act imposes a number of financial reporting and accounting requirements. The SEC generally adheres to generally accepted accounting principles (GAAP) and generally accepted auditing standards (GAAS) used by the private sector, but closely guides the form and substance of financial disclosure. The Act also imposes, as part of the **Foreign Corrupt Practices Act of 1977,**[28] substantial internal control requirements upon reporting companies. Under the Act, reporting issuers must maintain books and accounts that accurately and fairly reflect

27. Securities Exchange Act §12(g)(1). Note that the statute requires registration of issuers with assets exceeding $1 million, but Securities Exchange Act Rule 12g-1 exempts issuers with less than $5 million in assets.

28. Pub. L. No. 95-213, 91 Stat. 1494 (Dec. 19, 1977); 15 U.S.C. §§78m(b), 78dd-1, 78dd-2, 78ff.

"in reasonable detail" the issuer's transactions and disposition of its assets. In addition, the issuer must devise and maintain a system of internal accounting control sufficient to assure that (1) transactions are executed according to management's general or specific authorization, (2) all transactions are accounted for according to generally accepted accounting principles, (3) access to corporate assets is permitted only with management's general or specific authorization, and (4) the recorded accountability for assets is periodically compared with existing assets, and appropriate action is taken to reconcile any difference.

Liability for Misleading Statements in Filed Documents—§18(a).

To assure accurate disclosure, §18(a) of the 1934 Act imposes liability upon any person who is responsible for any false or misleading statement in any application, document, or report filed with the SEC under the terms of the 1934 Act or its rules and regulations. Liability extends to the issuer and its officers and directors, particularly those who sign the filed documents. Relief is available to any investor who reads the filed document, relies upon it, and is injured by purchasing or selling a security at a price affected by the statement.

A defendant may escape liability under §18(a) by proving that "he acted in good faith and had no knowledge that such statement was false or misleading." This defense is similar to, but somewhat less rigorous than, the due diligence defense of §11 of the 1933 Act for misrepresentations in a registration statement. Suit under §18(a) must be commenced within one year after discovery of the violation, and in any event within three years after the facts constituting the cause of action occurred.

In addition to periodic reporting requirements, 1934 Act registration triggers a number of other disclosure and remedial provisions relating to proxies, tender offers, insider short-swing profits, and fraud and manipulative practices in connection with the purchase or sale of a security. These provisions are discussed in more detail below.

1934 Act Criminal Liability.

Section 32 of the Securities Exchange Act of 1934[29] provides that any person who willfully violates any provision of the 1934 Act, its rules and regulations, or who willfully and knowingly makes materially false or misleading statements in any document filed with the SEC is guilty of a crime. Punishment may include a fine of up to $100,000, or imprisonment not exceeding five years, or both.

Proxy Regulation

Under the statutory scheme of corporate control discussed in Chapter 47, shareholders participate in management through their power to vote on the election of directors and upon certain extraordinary corporate transactions such as merger or dissolution. In large corporations in which shareholders are widely scattered, shareholder votes often are made by proxies, solicited either by existing corporate management or by "insurgent" groups seeking to change corporate policy. Section 14(a) of the 1934 Act makes it unlawful for a registered company to solicit proxies from its shareholders that violate rules and regulations the SEC may adopt "as necessary or appropriate in the public interest or for the protection of investors." As with much of federal securities law, the basic goal of proxy regulation is to provide full disclosure of accurate information to investors.

SEC Rule 14a–3 requires that each person whose vote is solicited must be furnished with a "proxy statement" containing a detailed list of specific information. Disclosures required include, for example, whether the proxy is revocable, whether statutory appraisal remedies are available, a description of the person making the solicitation, the interests and compensation of persons taking an active role in the solicitation, and other information relating to specific matters presented for shareholder vote. If proxies are being solicited by the issuer in advance of an annual meeting at which directors will be elected, an annual report of the issuer's operations also must be included. In addition to the proxy statement and annual report, shareholders also are furnished with a proxy form on which they record their votes (to approve, disapprove, or abstain) on the proposals to be presented at the meeting.

To assure accurate proxy solicitation materials, Rule 14a–9 makes it unlawful to solicit proxies by

---

29. 15 U.S.C. §78ff.

any oral or written communication containing any statement that is "false or misleading." The Supreme Court has long recognized an implied private remedy in favor of persons injured through violation of Rule 14a–9's general antifraud provisions. In addition, courts have upheld Rule 14a–9 claims involving mere negligence in the preparation of proxy materials without proof of actual "scienter," or intent to deceive. Permissible remedies include money damages, attorneys' fees, and injunctive relief requiring resolicitation of proxies and a new vote based on corrected materials.

The SEC proxy rules apply generally to all solicitation of proxies, consents, or authorizations from shareholders, either by management or others. To assure adequate disclosure of relevant information on both sides of any issue, shareholders are entitled to information, including in some cases a mailing list of persons entitled to vote, relevant to matters to be voted upon at the meeting. Rule 14a–8 also requires management to include shareholder proposals and a brief supporting statement in its proxy solicitation material. To prevent abuse, certain shareholder eligibility and timeliness requirements are imposed. The issuer also may refuse to include some shareholder proposals such as those relating to personal grievances against the issuer, the conduct of the issuer's ordinary business operations, matters not subject to shareholder vote under state law, and proposals that are duplicative or have previously been submitted to a vote.

Tender Offer Regulation

The tender offer is an increasingly popular method of acquiring control of a corporation. It is a public offer made directly to the shareholders of a target company to sell their shares, usually for a cash price fixed far in excess of current market price, and usually contingent upon various factors such as tender of a minimum total number of shares and prompt action by shareholders. Such tender offers or "take-over bids" require no shareholder votes like a statutory merger and no participation by the target company's management.

Not surprisingly, tender offers are often bitterly opposed by incumbent management of the target companies, leading to heated control battles. Target management may undertake a variety of defensive

tactics including, for example, seeking a friendly merger partner, selling off the company's most desirable assets, reacquiring a significant portion of its stock, issuing additional shares of stock, adopting restrictive bylaw or charter provisions, staggering directors' terms of office, adopting long-term employment contracts for top management, or making a tender offer for shares of the original bidder. These corporate control battles are routinely followed by the national media, which has coined a laundry list of distinctly nonlegal terms to describe the various actors and tactics in the war for control, such as "white ("black," "gray") knights," "crown jewels," "greenmail," "golden parachutes," "midnight specials," "bear hugs," "sharks," "shark repellants," and "poison pills" among many others.

Unregulated tender offers have significant potential for abuse. Shareholders of the target company are likely to be misled by confusing and conflicting claims of the combatants, and little time may be provided to make a decision whether to sell. Additionally, a tender offeror may hide his or her intentions, commitments, or even identity, cloaking the entire transaction in secrecy.

Prior to the 1960s, corporate takeover attempts usually involved either proxy solicitations, regulated by §14 of the 1934 Act discussed above, or exchange offers of securities subject to registration requirements of the 1933 Act. When tender offers began to increase in popularity in the 1960s, many corporate control battles were outside the reach of existing securities law. To eliminate this loophole, Congress enacted the Williams Act amendments to the 1934 Act in 1968.[30] The Williams Act protects investors by subjecting tender offerors to advance disclosure requirements, protects target shareholders who elect to tender their stock, and prohibits fraud and deception in tender offers.

The Williams Act's major provisions, 1934 Act §§13(d), 14(d), and 14(e) are discussed below.

Filing Requirements—§13(d). Under §13(d) of the 1934 Act, any person or group other than the issuer who acquires more than five percent of any

---

30. Pub. L. No. 90-439, 82 Stat. 454 (July 29, 1968); 15 U.S.C. §§78m(d), 78n(d), 78n(e).

class of equity securities registered under the Act must file disclosures with the issuer, the SEC, and securities exchanges within ten days after the acquisition. The disclosure statement must include (1) the purchaser's background and identity, (2) the source and amount of funds used for the acquisition, (3) the purpose of the purchase (for example, investment or control), (4) the number of shares owned, and (5) information concerning any contracts, arrangements, or understandings regarding the issuer's securities. Note that an issuer's purchase of its own shares is subject to similar disclosure requirements under §13(e).

Tender Offer Procedures—§14(d). Section 13(d) is designed to mandate disclosure *after* a person or group has acquired over five percent of any class of registered equity security. These acquisitions may be made in market transactions or in privately negotiated purchases of large blocks of shares. In contrast, §14(d) applies to shares acquired by tender offer. Under this provision, a person making a tender offer that would result in acquisition of more than five percent of any class of equity security registered under the 1934 Act must file with the SEC all advertising and solicitation material to be used in the offer and the information required by §13(d). Similar information must be furnished to the issuer. Filings under §14(d) must be made *before* distribution of tender offer materials to target company shareholders.[31]

Section 14(d)'s preacquisition filing requirements are triggered by existence of a "tender offer." The Williams Act does not define "tender offer," allowing the SEC and the federal courts to develop a definition, which has included both open market and privately negotiated purchases. The following case illustrates the dynamics of a takeover battle and that the definition of "tender offer" under §14(d) is far broader than traditional takeover attempts involving widespread public solicitation.

---

31. The SEC has promulgated a detailed set of regulations under Section 14(d) governing the content and dissemination of statements and obligations of target management. Regulation 14D, Securities Exchange Act Rule 14d-1 *et seq.*

Wellman v. Dickinson

475 F. Supp. 783 (S.D.N.Y. 1979), *aff'd*, 682 F.2d 355 (2d Cir. 1982)

In 1977, following a bitter power struggle, Fairleigh S. Dickinson, Jr. was removed from his position as chairman of the board of Becton, Dickinson & Company (BD), a corporation that had been founded by Dickinson's father. At the time of his ouster, Dickinson owned 4.2 percent of BD's outstanding stock and the Dickinson family owned an additional one percent. Dickinson hired two investment banking and brokerage firms, Salomon Brothers (Salomon) and F. Eberstadt & Company, Inc. (Eberstadt) to find a corporation that would be willing to purchase Dickinson's shares of BD as the first stage of a takeover of BD. Dickinson also arranged for several other sympathetic BD shareholders to make their shares available to a corporate purchaser.

Salomon and Eberstadt presented Dickinson's proposals to several corporations, explaining to each that they readily could arrange a sale of thirteen percent of BD's shares to an interested buyer. Sun Company, Inc. (Sun), a corporation in the oil and gas business, became interested in acquiring BD. After considering a conventional tender offer to all BD shareholders, Sun decided to attempt to secretly purchase the BD stock owned by Dickinson and his friends as well as several large blocks of BD stock held by institutional shareholders. The executive committee authorized Sun to solicit and purchase thirty-four percent of BD's shares from large individual and institutional shareholders using a two-tier offer: the shareholder could agree to sell at $40 per share reserving the right to receive the highest price paid to any subsequent shareholder solicited by Sun, or the shareholder could agree to sell at $45 with no recourse. The offer was to be conditioned on Sun's obtaining at least twenty-five percent (subsequently lowered to twenty percent) of BD's outstanding shares.

On January 14, 1978, Salomon and Eberstadt presented the offer to Dickinson who accepted at $45 per share. During the following three days, Dickinson's friends and several other shareholders also agreed to sell their BD shares. Salomon and

Eberstadt then contacted and presented the offer to purchase to thirty institutional shareholders. In most of the presentations, Sun's identity was not disclosed and the solicitee was asked to respond within one hour. By the evening of January 16, Sun had received verbal commitments from approximately thirty-three individual and institutional shareholders owning twenty percent of BD's stock. On January 16, BD's closing price on the New York Stock Exchange was 32 7/8. On January 17 and 18, couriers were sent to all of those who had made verbal commitments; purchase agreements were signed, and Sun paid for the stock. On January 19, Sun, Dickinson, and Dickinson's daughter each filed a §13(d) statement.

BD and the SEC sued Sun alleging that it had violated §14(d) of the Williams Act by failing to file a disclosure statement prior to making a tender offer. Sun alleged that the transactions were "privately negotiated" purchases and that it had made no tender offer.

Carter, District Judge

. . . One of the chief concerns of Congress in enacting the Williams Act provisions was to remove the secrecy which had heretofore cloaked transactions involving a shift in corporate control. Defendants concede this purpose but contend that the transaction at issue here requires a post-acquisition Section 13(d) filing rather than a pre-acquisition Section 14(d) filing. . . .

Sun's acquisition is infected with the basic evil which Congress sought to cure by enacting the law. This purchase was designed in intent, purpose and effect to effectuate a transfer of at least 20% controlling interest in BD to Sun in a swift, masked maneuver. It would surely undermine the remedial purposes of the Act to hold that this secret operation, which in all germane respects meets the accepted definition of a tender offer, is not covered by Section 14(d)'s pre-acquisition filing requirements. . . .

[T]he concept of a tender offer has never been precisely defined either in the Williams Act itself or by the [Securities and Exchange] Commission. Congress left to the Commission the task of providing through its experience concrete meaning to the term. The Commission has not yet created an exact

definition, but in this case and in others, it suggests some seven elements as being characteristic of a tender offer: (1) active and widespread solicitation of public shareholders for the shares of an issuer; (2) solicitation made for a substantial percentage of the issuer's stock; (3) offer to purchase made at a premium over the prevailing market price; (4) terms of the offer are firm rather than negotiable; (5) offer contingent on the tender of a fixed number of shares, often subject to a fixed maximum number to be purchased; (6) offer open only a limited period of time; (7) offeree subjected to pressure to sell his stock. . . . [T]he Commission also [has] listed an 8th characteristic not included here—whether the public announcements of a purchasing program concerning the target company precede or accompany rapid accumulation of large amounts of the target company's securities. The reason this last characteristic was left out undoubtedly was because publicity was not a feature of this transaction.

At any rate, it seems to me that the list of characteristics stressed by the Commission are the qualities that set a tender offer apart from open market purchases, privately negotiated transactions or other kinds of public solicitations. With the exception of publicity, all the characteristics of a tender offer, as that term is understood, are present in this transaction. The absence of one particular factor, however, is not necessarily fatal to the Commission's argument because depending upon the circumstances involved in the particular case, one or more of the above features may be more compelling and determinative than the others. . . .

Accordingly, in acquiring 34% of BD stock in the transaction at issue here, Sun made a tender offer for BD stock without a pre-acquisition filing in violation of Section 14(d) of the Williams Act.

SEC Rules[32] outline the basic procedures by which the tender offer is conducted. In general, the offer must be commenced within five business days

---

32. Regulation 14D, Securities Exchange Act Rules 14d-1 to 14d-101; Regulation 14E, Securities Exchange Act Rules 14e-1 to 14e-3; Securities Exchange Act Rule 10b-13.

after the offeror publicly announces its identity and that of the target company, the offering price, and the number and class of shares sought. Materials containing the required disclosures and describing the offer are filed and are distributed, either by the offeror or the target, to the shareholders. Target management also must file disclosure documents and must provide shareholders with a written statement of its position on the offer within ten days after the offer is made. The tender offer generally must be kept open for twenty business days. If the percentage of the class of securities being sought or the consideration offered is increased or decreased, the offer must remain open for ten business days from the date that notice of the change is provided to shareholders. While the offer is pending the offeror must purchase shares exclusively through the offer. Shareholders who tender their shares are allowed to withdraw them throughout the offering period. If a tender offer is made for less than all of the outstanding shares and more than the requested number are tendered, the offeror must purchase the securities on a pro-rata basis from all shareholders who tender during the period the offer is open. Finally, the tender offer must be open to all holders of the class of securities subject to the tender offer, and if the offering price is increased during the term of the offer, all tendering shareholders are entitled to receive the increased consideration.

Liability for Misstatements in Tender Offers—§14(e).

Section 14(e) of the 1934 Act makes it unlawful for any person to misstate or omit to state any material fact, or to engage in any fraudulent, deceptive, or manipulative acts or practices in connection with any tender offer.[33] Because §14(e) provides no express remedy for injured investors,[34] a recurring issue under §14(e) is whether a private remedy for damages should be *implied*. On this issue the Supreme Court in 1977 held in *Piper v.*

Chris-Craft Industries, Inc.,[35] that a defeated tender offeror could not maintain a private action for damages resulting from alleged misstatements made by its opponents in a takeover battle. Later cases have, however, permitted target company shareholders who rely upon a misrepresentation or omission to recover damages for violation of §14(e). In addition, courts have allowed target company management and competing tender offerors to obtain injunctions against misleading statements by their opponents. Section 14(e) prohibits "fraudulent, deceptive or manipulative acts or practices, in connection with any tender offer." The Supreme Court has held that the term "manipulative" as used in §14(e) requires misrepresentation or nondisclosure.[36] It connotes "conduct designed to deceive or defraud investors by controlling or artificially affecting the price of securities."[37] Target company shareholders seeking to recover under §14(e) from the offeror or target management must prove reliance upon the misrepresentation or omission of a material fact.

Even if target management's defensive tactics do not violate §14(e), they may constitute breach of a fiduciary or other duty owed shareholders under state law. Frequently, however, management defensive tactics are found to be within the protection of the "business judgment" rule.

State Tender Offer Regulation.

In addition to federal law, most states have enacted legislation governing tender offers. In contrast to the Williams Act, which is intended to provide a neutral setting giving the offeror and management an equal opportunity to present their cases, early state legislation strongly favored incumbent target management, impeding takeover attempts. In *Edgar v. Mite Corporation* (1982),[38] the Supreme Court held that an Illinois tender offer statute of this type, which unduly favored target management, was pre-empted under the Supremacy Clause by the Williams Act. The Court also found that the statute unduly bur-

---

33. Note that §14(e), unlike other Williams Act provisions, applies whether or not the target company is subject to 1934 Act registration.

34. Section 18(a), however, provides an express remedy to persons injured by false or misleading statements in reports or documents filed under the 1934 Act, including Williams Act filings. See discussion on pages 1032.

35. 97 S. Ct. 926 (1977).

36. *Schreiber v. Burlington Northern, Inc.*, 105 S. Ct. 2458, 2465 (1985).

37. *Ernst & Ernst v. Hochfelder*, 96 S. Ct. 1375, 1384 (1976).

38. 102 S. Ct. 2629 (1982).

dened interstate commerce thereby violating the Commerce Clause of the Constitution.[39] To cure these constitutional infirmities, states began drafting statutes to regulate tender offers through corporate governance law rather than through state securities laws or administrative regulations. One statute of this type is Indiana's Control Share Acquisition Act, which provides that whenever a purchaser acquires "control shares" in an Indiana corporation, the purchaser acquires voting rights only to the extent granted by resolution of a majority of all disinterested shareholders. The practical effect of the statute is to condition acquisition of corporate control on approval of a majority of preexisting disinterested shareholders. In 1987, the Supreme Court, in *CTS Corp. v. Dynamics Corporation of America* (1987),[40] held that the Indiana statute was not pre-empted by the Williams Act and did not violate the Commerce Clause. On the preemption issue, the Court noted that because offerors can physically comply with both statutes, the state statute can be pre-empted only if it frustrates the purposes of the federal law. The court found that the Indiana statute protected the independent shareholders against the contending parties by allowing them to vote as a group, thus furthering a basic purpose of the William Act to place investors on an equal footing with the takeover bidder. The court distinguished the Illinois statute condemned in *Edgar*, which operated to favor management against offerors.

On the Commerce Clause issue the Court held that the Act's limited effect on interstate commerce was justified by the State's interests in defining the attributes of shares in its corporations and in protecting shareholders. In reaching this conclusion, the Court noted that the Act did not discriminate against interstate commerce because it applied equally to both resident and nonresident offerors, and did not create a risk of inconsistent tender offer regulation by different states. The Court also noted that the states, as the traditional overseers of corporations, have an interest in promoting stable relationships among the parties and in ensuring that investors have an effective voice in corporate affairs.

Since the Supreme Court's decision in *CTS Corp.*, a number of states have adopted new takeover statutes, some modeled on the Indiana control share approach. The constitutionality of many of these statutes has yet to be determined. In addition, support is growing in Congress for federal legislation to explicitly pre-empt state tender offer regulation. In short, the legal status of state tender offer regulation must await significant future judicial and perhaps legislative developments.

Insider Reporting and Trading Regulation—§ 16

Section 16 of the 1934 Act prevents short-term trading and other transactions in a corporation's securities by corporate insiders. Its purpose is to prevent "the unfair use of information which may have been obtained"[41] by the insider as a result of his or her relationship to the issuer.

To monitor insider transactions, §16(a) imposes reporting requirements upon all persons who beneficially own, directly or indirectly, more than ten percent of a class of equity securities registered under §12 of the 1934 Act, and every officer and director of an issuer of such a security. These persons are required to file an ownership statement with the SEC after becoming an officer, director, or beneficial owner, and at the end of any month in which the insider buys or sells the corporation's equity securities. Although no private remedy is available for violation of §16(a)'s reporting requirements, SEC administrative and criminal sanctions may be imposed.

Section 16(b) restricts short-term trading in the issuer's stock by persons subject to §16(a)'s reporting requirements. Under this provision the issuer (or a shareholder suing on behalf of the issuer) may recover any profit realized by the insider from any purchase and sale, or any sale and purchase, of the issuer's stock within any six-month period. For purposes of §16(b), "profit" is computed by comparing the highest sales price against the lowest

---

39. The Supremacy Clause is discussed in Chapter 1; federal and state regulation under the Commerce Clause is covered in Chapter 4.

40. 107 S. Ct. 1637 (1987).

41. Securities Exchange Act §16(b).

purchase price within any six-month period. This approach can result in a recoverable "profit" even though the insider may have incurred an out-of-pocket loss from a series of transactions during the six-month period.

Section 16 authorizes recovery of so-called "short-swing" profits to prevent unfair use of inside information. No proof is, however, required that the insider actually used inside information in deciding whether to buy or sell. That is, liability is strict requiring disgorgement of profit in the absence of any wrongdoing.

A §16(b) suit must be maintained in federal court subject to a two-year statute of limitations running from the date of the transaction that creates §16(b) profits. Suit is maintained by the corporation or a shareholder suing derivatively, and recovery inures to the corporation. The SEC has no enforcement authority under §16(b).

1934 Act Antifraud Provision—§10(b) and Rule 10b-5

In federal securities law, general "antifraud" provisions often supplement the specific statutory requirements and express remedies.[42] The general antifraud provision under the 1934 Act is §10(b), which provides that it is unlawful

> [t]o use or employ, in connection with the purchase or sale of any security . . ., any manipulative or deceptive device or contrivance in contravention of such rules and regulations as the Commission may prescribe as necessary or appropriate in the public interest or for the protection of investors.

Pursuant to this authority the SEC has adopted rules[43] prohibiting a variety of specific manipulative or deceptive conduct. In addition to these specific prohibitions, the SEC in 1942 adopted Rule 10b-5, a general antifraud provision, which states in full:

It shall be unlawful for any person, directly or indirectly, by the use of any means or instrumentality of interstate commerce, or of the mails or of any facility of any national security exchange,

(a) To employ any device, scheme, or artifice to defraud,

(b) To make any untrue statement of a material fact or to omit to state a material fact necessary in order to make the statements made, in the light of the circumstances under which they were made, not misleading, or

(c) To engage in any act, practice, or course of business which operates or would operate as a fraud or deceit upon any person, in connection with the purchase or sale of any security.

Implied Private Remedy. Although Rule 10b-5 creates no express private remedy for violations, lower federal courts starting in 1946[44] began to imply a private remedy for injured investors, a remedy formally recognized by the Supreme Court in 1971.[45] During its early years the Rule 10b-5 implied remedy received an expansive judicial interpretation. Supreme Court decisions since 1975 have, however, somewhat limited its availability. Two important points in this regard should be noted.

1. Rule 10b-5, by its terms, prohibits fraud or deception in the purchase or sale of any security by any person. All securities are covered, whether registered or exempted from registration under the 1933 or 1934 Acts, and whether issued by publicly-held or closely-held corporations. Despite this expansive coverage, the Supreme Court has held that to maintain a private action under Rule 10b-5, the plaintiff must be either a purchaser or seller of the securities involved.[46]

2. The Supreme Court held in *Ernst & Ernst v. Hochfelder*[47] that a private cause of action for damages under Rule 10b-5 requires proof of scien-

---

42. For example, §17(a) is the 1933 Act's general antifraud provision. Section 14(e) of the 1934 Act imposes liability for fraud and deception in tender offers.

43. Securities Exchange Act Rules 10b-1 to 10b-21.

44. *Kardon v. National Gypsum Co.,* 69 F. Supp. 512 (E.D. Pa. 1946).

45. *Superintendent of Insurance v. Bankers Life and Casualty Company,* 92 S. Ct. 165 (1971).

46. *Blue Chip Stamps v. Manor Drug Stores,* 95 S. Ct. 1917 (1975).

47. 96 S. Ct. 1375 (1976).

ter—an intent to deceive, manipulate, or defraud. The defendant's negligent conduct alone is insufficient to invoke Rule 10b-5 liability.[48] Although not yet resolved by the Supreme Court, most lower federal court decisions have held that statements made in reckless disregard of the truth also meet the scienter requirement and are therefore actionable under Rule 10b-5.

Application of Rule 10b-5. Rule 10b-5's broad antifraud proscription has been applied to a wide variety of fact situations generally divided into three broad areas.

Corporate Mismanagement. In a number of early cases, minority shareholders used Rule 10b-5 as a remedy to redress abuses by corporate management or controlling shareholders involving transactions in stock. Examples include sales of controlling stock interests at a premium and mergers that freeze out the minority shareholders. Although these abuses also often violate fiduciary obligations imposed by state law, a Rule 10b-5 claim, if available, may present fewer substantive or procedural obstacles. In 1977, however, the Supreme Court decided *Santa Fe Industries, Inc. v. Green*,[49] which substantially limited the use of Rule 10b-5 as a remedy for corporate mismanagement. In this case, the Court reaffirmed its *Hochfelder* holding that Rule 10b-5 reaches only manipulative or deceptive conduct. Although a number of lower courts have given *Santa Fe* a narrow reading, the law is clear that claims based solely on breach of fiduciary duty or internal corporate mismanagement under state law do not involve manipulation or deception sufficient to support a Rule 10b-5 action.

Corporate Misstatements. Various securities law provisions are designed to assure the accuracy of specific documents such as registration statements and proxy solicitation materials. Rule 10b-5 provides an additional remedy for misstatements in these and other corporate documents such as press releases and reports.

In the following case, involving alleged corporate misstatements, the Supreme Court addressed two important elements of a Rule 10b-5 claim, materiality and reliance.

Basic, Incorporated v. Levinson
108 S.Ct. 978 (1988)

Beginning in September 1976, representatives of Combustion Engineering, Inc. held a series of meetings and telephone conversations with officers and directors of Basic, Incorporated concerning the possibility of a merger. During 1977 and 1978, addressing the issue of increased trading in Basic stock, Basic made three public statements denying that it was engaged in merger negotiations. On October 21, 1977, an article in the Cleveland Plain Dealer stated that Basic's president had said that "no negotiations were under way with any company for a merger." On September 25, 1978, Basic issued a release stating that "management is unaware of any present or pending company development that would result in the abnormally heavy trading activity and price fluctuations in company shares." Basic reiterated this statement in a report to shareholders on November 6, 1978. On December 18, 1978, Basic requested the New York Stock Exchange to suspend trading in its shares because Basic had been approached by another company concerning a merger. Two days later, Basic publicly announced its approval of Combustion's tender offer of $46 per share for all outstanding shares.

Plaintiff Max Levinson, a former Basic shareholder, brought a class action against the defendants, Basic and its directors, on behalf of all shareholders who had sold their stock after Basic's statement on October 21, 1977 and before suspension of trading on December 18, 1978. Plaintiffs alleged that the defendants had violated section 10(b) of the Securities Exchange Act and Rule 10b-5 by issuing three false or misleading statements in 1977 and 1978, thereby causing injury to plaintiffs who had sold their stock at artificially depressed prices. The trial court ruled that plaintiffs' reliance on the

---

48. The Supreme Court has held that the scienter standard applies both to a private action for damages and to a civil enforcement action brought by the SEC to enjoin violations of Rule 10b-5.

49. 97 S. Ct. 1292 (1977).

statements could be presumed based on the fraud-on-the-market theory. Nevertheless, the trial court held that any misstatements were immaterial and granted summary judgment in favor of the defendants. The Sixth Circuit Court of Appeals reversed. The Supreme Court granted certiorari.

Justice Blackmun

. . . The Court previously . . . has defined a standard of materiality under the securities laws, . . . concluding in the proxy-solicitation context that "[a]n omitted fact is material if there is a substantial likelihood that a reasonable shareholder would consider it important in deciding how to vote." [*TSC Industries, Inc. v. Northway, Inc.*, 96 S. Ct. 2126, 2132 (1976)]. . . . It further explained that to fulfill the materiality requirement "there must be a substantial likelihood that the disclosure of the omitted fact would have been viewed by the reasonable investor as having significantly altered the 'total mix' of information made available." [*Id.*]. We now expressly adopt the *TSC Industries* standard of materiality for the §10(b) and Rule 10b-5 context.

. . . The application of this materiality standard to preliminary merger discussions is not self-evident. Where the impact of the corporate development on the target's fortune is certain and clear, the *TSC Industries* materiality definition admits straightforward application. Where, on the other hand, the event is contingent or speculative in nature, it is difficult to ascertain whether the "reasonable investor" would have considered the omitted information significant at the time. Merger negotiations, because of the ever-present possibility that the contemplated transaction will not be effectuated, fall into the latter category. . . .

Even before this Court's decision in *TSC Industries*, the Second Circuit had explained the role of the materiality requirement of Rule 10b-5, with respect to contingent or speculative information or events, in a manner that gave that term meaning that is independent of the other provisions of the Rule. Under such circumstances, materiality "will depend at any given time upon a balancing of both the indicated probability that the event will occur and the anticipated magnitude of the event in light of the totality of the company activity." *SEC v.*

Texas Gulf Sulphur Co., [401 F.2d 833, 849 (2d Cir. 1968)]. . . .

Whether merger discussions in any particular case are material therefore depends on the facts. Generally, in order to assess the probability that the event will occur, a factfinder will need to look to indicia of interest in the transaction at the highest corporate levels. Without attempting to catalog all such possible factors, we note by way of example that board resolutions, instructions to investment bankers, and actual negotiations between principals or their intermediaries may serve as indicia of interest. To assess the magnitude of the transaction to the issuer of the securities allegedly manipulated, a factfinder will need to consider such facts as the size of the two corporate entities and of the potential premiums over market value. No particular event or factor short of closing the transaction need be either necessary or sufficient by itself to render merger discussions material.

As we clarify today, materiality depends on the significance the reasonable investor would place on the withheld or misrepresented information. . . .

We turn to the question of reliance and the fraud-on-the-market theory. Succinctly put:

> The fraud on the market theory is based on the hypothesis that, in an open and developed securities market, the price of a company's stock is determined by the available material information regarding the company and its business. . . . Misleading statements will therefore defraud purchasers of stock even if the purchasers do not directly rely on the misstatements. . . . The causal connection between the defendants' fraud and the plaintiffs' purchase of stock in such a case is no less significant than in a case of direct reliance on misrepresentations. *Peil v. Speiser*, 806 F.2d 1154, 1160–1161 (3d Cir. 1986).

Our task, of course, is not to assess the general validity of the theory, but to consider whether it was proper for the courts below to apply a rebuttable presumption of reliance, supported in part by the fraud-on-the-market theory. . . .

Petitioners . . . complain that the fraud-on-the-market theory effectively eliminates the requirement that a plaintiff asserting a claim under Rule 10b-5 prove reliance. . . .

We agree that reliance is an element of a Rule 10b-5 cause of action. . . . Reliance provides the requisite causal connection between a defendant's misrepresentation and a plaintiff's injury. . . . There is, however, more than one way to demonstrate the causal connection. . . .

The modern securities markets, literally involving millions of shares changing hands daily, differ from the face-to-face transactions contemplated by early fraud cases, and our understanding of Rule 10b-5's reliance requirement must encompass these differences.

> In face-to-face transactions, the inquiry into an investor's reliance upon information is into the subjective pricing of that information by that investor. With the presence of a market, the market is interposed between seller and buyer and, ideally, transmits information to the investor in the processed form of a market price. Thus the market is performing a substantial part of the valuation process performed by the investor in a face-to-face transaction. The market is acting as the unpaid agent of the investor, informing him that given all the information available to it, the value of the stock is worth the market price. *In re LTV Securities Litigation*, 88 F. R. D. 134, 143 (N. D. Tex. 1980). . . .

Presumptions typically serve to assist courts in managing circumstances in which direct proof, for one reason or another, is rendered difficult. . . . The courts below accepted a presumption, created by the fraud-on-the-market theory and subject to rebuttal by petitioners, that persons who had traded Basic shares had done so in reliance on the integrity of the price set by the market, but because of petitioners' material misrepresentations that price had been fraudulently depressed. Requiring a plaintiff to show a speculative state of facts, *i.e.*, how he would have acted if omitted material information had been disclosed . . . or if the misrepresentation had not been made, . . . would place an unnecessarily unrealistic evidentiary burden on the Rule 10b-5 plaintiff who has traded on an impersonal market. . . .

Arising out of considerations of fairness, public policy, and probability, as well as judicial economy, presumptions are also useful devices for allocating the burdens of proof between parties. . . .

An investor who buys or sells stock at the price set by the market does so in reliance on the integrity of that price. Because most publicly available information is reflected in market price, an investor's reliance on any public material misrepresentations, therefore, may be presumed for purposes of a Rule 10b-5 action. . . .

Any showing that severs the link between the alleged misrepresentation and either the price received (or paid) by the plaintiff, or his decision to trade at a fair market price, will be sufficient to rebut the presumption of reliance. For example, if petitioners could show that the "market makers" were privy to the truth about the merger discussions here with Combustion, and thus that the market price would not have been affected by their misrepresentations, the causal connection could be broken: the basis for finding that the fraud had been transmitted through market price would be gone. Similarly, if, despite petitioners' allegedly fraudulent attempt to manipulate market price, news of the merger discussions credibly entered the market and dissipated the effects of the misstatements, those who traded Basic shares after the corrective statements would have no direct or indirect connection with the fraud. Petitioners also could rebut the presumption of reliance as to plaintiffs who would have divested themselves of their Basic shares without relying on the integrity of the market. . . .

[Judgment vacated and remanded.]

Insider Trading. Rule 10b-5's most important function is to police against **insider trading**—buying and selling securities based upon access to confidential or proprietary information not available to the public. Insider trading destroys the integrity of the securities markets and undermines the basic "full disclosure" philosophy of federal securities law. Its abolition is one of the SEC's top enforcement priorities. In most cases, insider trading is attacked under Rule 10b-5(c), which prohibits acts or practices that operate as a fraud on any person.

Insider Trading and Rule 10b-5. The following case, decided by the SEC, established the basic standards governing insider trading under Rule 10b-5.

In the Matter of Cady, Roberts & Co.
40 S.E.C. 907 (1961)

Shortly after 11 A.M. on November 25, 1959, Robert M. Gintel, a securities broker and partner in Cady, Roberts & Co. (Registrant) received a telephone message from J. Cheever Cowdin, a director of Curtiss-Wright Corporation who also was affiliated with Cady, Roberts & Co., stating that Curtiss-Wright's quarterly dividend had been cut. Cowdin had phoned during a recess in Curtiss-Wright's board meeting, before news of the board's decision had been communicated to the New York Stock Exchange or the Dow Jones News Ticker Service. Gintel immediately entered orders to sell or sell short 7,000 shares of Curtiss-Wright stock for his various customer accounts. These orders were executed by 11:18 A.M. at over $40 per share. When the dividend announcement appeared on the Dow Jones tape at 11:48 A.M., the New York Stock Exchange suspended trading in Curtiss-Wright stock because of the large number of sell orders. Though trading resumed at 1:59 P.M., the stock price plunged and closed the day under $35.

The SEC instituted proceedings to determine whether Cady, Roberts & Co. and Gintel willfully violated the antifraud provisions of §10(b) of the 1934 Act, Rule 10b-5 issued under that Act, and §17(a) of the 1933 Act.

Cary, Chairman

. . . So many times that citation is unnecessary, we have indicated that the purchase and sale of securities is a field in special need of regulation for the protection of investors. To this end one of the major purposes of the securities acts is the prevention of fraud, manipulation or deception in connection with securities transactions. Consistent with this objective, Section 17(a) of the Securities Act, Section 10(b) of the Exchange Act and Rule 10b-5, issued under that Section, are broad remedial provisions aimed at reaching misleading or decep-

tive activities, whether or not they are precisely and technically sufficient to sustain a common law action for fraud and deceit. . . .

These anti-fraud provisions are not intended as a specification of particular acts or practices which constitute fraud, but rather are designed to encompass the infinite variety of devices by which undue advantage may be taken of investors and others.

Section 17 and Rule 10b-5 apply to securities transactions by "any person." Misrepresentations will lie within their ambit, no matter who the speaker may be. An affirmative duty to disclose material information has been traditionally imposed on corporate "insiders," particularly officers, directors, or controlling stockholders. We, and the courts have consistently held that insiders must disclose material facts which are known to them by virtue of their position but which are not known to persons with whom they deal and which, if known, would affect their investment judgment. Failure to make disclosure in these circumstances constitutes a violation of the anti-fraud provisions. If, on the other hand, disclosure prior to effecting a purchase or sale would be improper or unrealistic under the circumstances, we believe the alternative is to forego the transaction.

The ingredients are here and we accordingly find that Gintel willfully violated Sections 17(a) and 10(b) and Rule 10b-5. We also find a similar violation by the registrant, since the actions of Gintel, a member of registrant, in the course of his employment are to be regarded as actions of registrant itself. It was obvious that a reduction in the quarterly dividend by the Board of Directors was a material fact which could be expected to have an adverse impact on the market price of the company's stock. The rapidity with which Gintel acted upon receipt of the information confirms his own recognition of that conclusion.

We have already noted that the anti-fraud provisions are phrased in terms of "any person" and that a special obligation has been traditionally required of corporate insiders, e.g., officers, directors and controlling stockholders. These three groups, however, do not exhaust the classes of persons upon whom there is such an obligation. Analytically, the obligation rests on two principal elements; first, the existence of a relationship giving access, directly or indirectly, to information intended to be available only for a corporate purpose and not for the personal benefit of anyone, and second, the inherent unfairness involved where a party takes advantage of such information knowing it is unavailable to those with whom he is dealing. In considering these elements under the broad language of the anti-fraud provisions we are not to be circumscribed by fine distinctions and rigid classifications. Thus our task here is to identify those persons who are in a special relationship with a company and privy to its internal affairs, and thereby suffer correlative duties in trading in its securities. Intimacy demands restraint lest the uninformed be exploited.

The facts here impose on Gintel the responsibilities of those commonly referred to as "insiders." He received the information prior to its public release from a director of Curtiss-Wright, Cowdin, who was associated with the registrant. Cowdin's relationship to the company clearly prohibited him from selling the securities affected by the information without disclosure. By logical sequence, it should prohibit Gintel, a partner of registrant. This prohibition extends not only over his own account, but to selling for discretionary accounts and soliciting and executing other orders. . . .

The three main subdivisions of Section 17 and Rule 10b-5 have been considered to be mutually supporting rather than mutually exclusive. Thus, a breach of duty of disclosure may be viewed as a device or scheme, an implied misrepresentation, and an act or practice, violative of all three subdivisions. Respondents argue that only clause (3) may be applicable here. We hold that, in these circumstances, Gintel's conduct at least violated clause (3) as a practice which operated as a fraud or deceit upon the purchasers. Therefore, we need not decide the scope of clauses (1) and (2). . . .

Cady, Roberts and subsequent cases make it clear that insiders possessing material, nonpublic information have a duty either to disclose it or abstain from trading. This duty extends not only to classic corporate insiders such as officers, directors, and controlling shareholders, but also to employees such as engineers who acquire material information from a corporate source. Liability also extends to tippees, such as the broker in *Cady,* who acquire information from or through insiders who have breached their duties, and to tippers, who pass on the information but do not themselves trade in the stock.

In the following case the Supreme Court articulated the standard for analyzing certain cases involving trading on material nonpublic information by people other than classic insiders.

Dirks v. Securities and Exchange Commission
103 S. Ct. 3255 (1983)

Petitioner Raymond Dirks, an officer of a New York broker-dealer firm, specialized in providing investment analysis of insurance company securities. On March 6, 1973, Ronald Secrist, a former officer of the insurance company Equity Funding of America, advised Dirks that Equity Funding's assets were vastly overstated as a result of fraudulent corporate practices. Dirks visited Equity Funding's headquarters to investigate the charges. Although senior management denied any wrongdoing, several employees corroborated Secrist's allegations. Dirks contacted a *Wall Street Journal* reporter and urged him to write a story on the charges but the reporter declined because of fears of a libel suit. Dirks also discussed the information with several clients including five investment advisors for institutional investors who liquidated more than $16 million of holdings in Equity Funding securities. During Dirks' two-week investigation Equity Funding stock fell from $26 per share to less than $15 per share. On March 27, the New York Stock Exchange halted trading of Equity Funding securities. Subsequently, California insurance authorities uncovered evidence of fraud from Equity Funding's records and the company went into receivership.

The SEC charged Dirks with aiding and abetting violations of the antifraud provisions of the Securities Act of 1933 and the Securities Exchange Act of 1934 by repeating the allegations of Equity Funding's fraud to investors who traded on the information. Following an administrative hearing, the SEC found Dirks guilty of the charges but only censured him because of his role in uncovering the Equity

Funding fraud. The court of appeals affirmed and the United States Supreme Court granted certiorari.

Justice Powell

. . . Petitioner Raymond Dirks received material nonpublic information from "insiders" of a corporation with which he had no connection. He disclosed this information to investors who relied on it in trading in the shares of the corporation. The question is whether Dirks violated the antifraud provisions of the federal securities laws by this disclosure. . . .

[A]n insider will be liable under Rule 10b-5 for inside trading only where he fails to disclose material nonpublic information before trading on it and thus makes "secret profits." [*In the Matter of Cady, Roberts, & Co.*, 40 S.E.C. 907, 916, n. 31 (1961).] . . . .

The SEC's position, as stated in its opinion in this case, is that a tippee "inherits" the *Cady, Roberts* obligation to shareholders whenever he receives inside information from an insider. . . .

In effect, the SEC's theory of tippee liability . . . appears rooted in the idea that the antifraud provisions require equal information among all traders. This conflicts with the principle set forth in [*Chiarella v. United States*, 100 S. Ct. 1108 (1980)], that only some persons, under some circumstances, will be barred from trading while in possession of material nonpublic information. . . . We reaffirm today that "[a] duty [to disclose] arises from the relationship between parties . . . and not merely from one's ability to acquire information because of his position in the market." [100 S. Ct. at 1116-1117, n.14.] . . .

The conclusion that recipients of inside information do not invariably acquire a duty to disclose or abstain does not mean that such tippees always are free to trade on the information. The need for a ban on some tippee trading is clear. Not only are insiders forbidden by their fiduciary relationship from personally using undisclosed corporate information to their advantage, but they may not give such information to an outsider for the same improper purpose of exploiting the information for their personal gain. . . . Thus, the tippee's duty to disclose or abstain is derivative from that of the insider's duty. . . . As we noted in *Chiarella*, "[t]he tippee's obligation has been viewed as arising from his role as a participant after the fact in the insider's breach of a fiduciary duty." [100 S. Ct. at 1115, n. 12.]

Thus, some tippees must assume an insider's duty to the shareholders not because they receive inside information, but rather because it has been made available to them *improperly*. And for Rule 10b-5 purposes, the insider's disclosure is improper only where it would violate his *Cady, Roberts* duty. Thus, a tippee assumes a fiduciary duty to the shareholders of a corporation not to trade on material nonpublic information only when the insider has breached his fiduciary duty to the shareholders by disclosing the information to the tippee and the tippee knows or should know that there has been a breach. . . . Tipping thus properly is viewed only as a means of indirectly violating the *Cady, Roberts* disclose-or-abstain rule. . . .

Whether disclosure is a breach of [the insider's fiduciary duty] depends in large part on the purpose of the disclosure. . . . [T]he test is whether the insider personally will benefit, directly or indirectly, from his disclosure. Absent some personal gain, there has been no breach of duty to stockholders. And absent a breach by the insider, there is no derivative breach. . . .

Under the inside-trading and tipping rules set forth above, we find that there was no actionable violation by Dirks. It is undisputed that Dirks himself was a stranger to Equity Funding, with no preexisting fiduciary duty to its shareholders. He took no action, directly or indirectly, that induced the shareholders or officers of Equity Funding to repose trust or confidence in him. There was no expectation by Dirks' sources that he would keep their information in confidence. Nor did Dirks misappropriate or illegally obtain the information about Equity Funding. Unless the insiders breached their *Cady, Roberts* duty to shareholders in disclosing the nonpublic information to Dirks, he breached no duty when he passed it on to investors as well as to the *Wall Street Journal*.

It is clear that neither Secrist nor the other Equity Funding employees violated their *Cady, Roberts* duty to the corporation's shareholders by providing information to Dirks. The tippers received no monetary or personal benefit for revealing Equity Funding's secrets, nor was their purpose to make a gift of valuable information to Dirks. As the facts of this case clearly indicate, the tippers were motivated by a desire to expose the fraud. . . .

We conclude that Dirks, in the circumstances of this case, had no duty to abstain from use of the inside information that he obtained.

[Judgment reversed.]

Under *Dirks,*

> a tippee assumes a fiduciary duty to the shareholders of a corporation not to trade on material nonpublic information only when the insider has breached his fiduciary duty to the shareholders by disclosing the information to the tippee and the tippee knows or should know that there has been a breach.[50]

Although this approach is restrictive, courts have recognized additional theories of liability for outsiders who trade on inside information. For example, footnote 14 of the *Dirks* opinion itself recognizes that when corporate information is revealed legitimately to an underwriter, accountant, lawyer, or consultant working for the corporation, these outsiders (sometimes called "temporary insiders") may become fiduciaries of the shareholders. In this case, a duty to disclose or abstain is imposed, if the corporation expects the outsider to keep the disclosed nonpublic information confidential, and the relationship between the parties at least implies a duty of confidentiality. The fiduciary duty in this case is based upon the existence of a special confidential relationship giving the outsider access to information solely for corporate purposes.

An additional theory of outsider liability is the "misappropriation" theory adopted by the Second Circuit Court of Appeals in *United States v. Newman,*[51] under which:

> one who misappropriates nonpublic information in breach of a fiduciary duty and trades on that information to his own advantage violates §10(b) and Rule 10b-5.[52]

This theory has been used, for example, to support criminal prosecutions and SEC injunctive proceedings against employees who breach an employer-imposed duty of confidentiality by stealing and subsequently trading upon material nonpublic information entrusted to the employers (such as investment banks, financial printers, or law firms) by their clients. The Supreme Court has not yet explicitly accepted the misappropriation theory as a basis for insider trading liability.[53]

Insider Trading Sanctions Act. Partially in response to the *Chiarella* and *Dirks* decisions, Congress enacted the **Insider Trading Sanctions Act of 1984.**[54] The Act permits the SEC to file suit against anyone violating the 1934 Act or rules by "purchasing or selling a security while in possession of material nonpublic information." The SEC may recover a civil penalty from the violator not exceeding three times the profit gained or loss avoided as a result of the unlawful purchase or sale. Persons who aid and abet a violation by communicating material nonpublic information also may beheld liable. In addition, the Act raises the maximum criminal fine for willful 1934 Act violations from $10,000 to $100,000.

Foreign Corrupt Practices Act of 1977

SEC investigations conducted in the 1970s revealed corporate bribery of foreign officials by over 300 United States companies involving hundreds of millions of dollars. In many cases, the bribery had been facilitated and concealed by falsification of corporate records. In order to deter corporate bribery of foreign government officials, Congress, in 1977, added the Foreign Corrupt Practices Act to the Securities Exchange Act of 1934.[55] The Act adopts a two-fold approach. First, as previously noted, it requires companies to maintain strict ac-

---

50. 103 S. Ct. at 3264.

51. 664 F.2d 12 (2d Cir. 1981).

52. *Securities and Exchange Commission v. Materia*, 745 F.2d 197, 203 (2d Cir. 1984).

---

53. In *Carpenter v. United States*, 108 S. Ct. 316 (1987), the Supreme Court was evenly divided regarding whether the misappropriation theory should be recognized under Rule 10b-5. Accordingly, the Court affirmed the defendants' convictions based on that theory.

54. Pub. L. No. 98-376, 98 Stat. 1264 (Aug. 10, 1984); 15 U.S.C. §§78u(d)(2), 78ff.

55. Pub. L. No. 95-213, 91 Stat. 1494 (Dec. 19, 1977); 15 U.S.C. §§78m(b), 78dd-1, 78dd-2, 78ff.

Table 49–4	Summary of 1934 Act Remedies		
Provision	*Conduct Proscribed*	*Permissible Plaintiffs*	*Permissible Defendants*
§18(a)	False or misleading statement in any document filed under 1934 Act or Rules.	Investors who purchase or sell in reliance upon document.	Issuer, its officers, and directors.
Rule 14a-9	False or misleading proxy solicitation materials.	Government enforcement; private actions for damages.	All persons soliciting proxies.
§14(e)	Fraud or misrepresentation in tender offers.	Government enforcement; private action for damages limited.	Any person making misrepresentation or omission in tender offer.
§16(a)	Insiders' failure to report ownership of or transactions in corporation's stock.	SEC administrative and civil proceedings.	Officers, directors, and shareholders owning more than 10% of company's stock.
§16(b)	Profit realized by insiders who buy or sell corporation's stock within any six month period.	Issuer (or shareholder acting on issuer's behalf).	Officers, directors, and shareholders owning more than 10% of company's stock.
Rule 10b-5	Fraud in connection with purchase or sale of any security.	SEC enforcement; purchaser or seller of security.	Any person who commits fraud or deception in sale of any security; proof of scienter required.
Foreign Corrupt Practices Act	Bribery of foreign officials.	Government criminal and civil enforcement.	Issuers with securities registered under 1934 Act and other "domestic concerns."

counting standards and management control over their assets. Second, the Act makes it a crime for United States companies and individuals to bribe foreign officials for specific corrupt purposes.

The Act's criminal provisions apply to issuers with securities registered under the 1934 Act, other "domestic concerns,"[56] and their officers, directors, employees, or agents. The Act prohibits persons covered from corruptly offering or transferring anything of value directly or indirectly to a foreign official, foreign political party, or official thereof. To be illegal the purpose of the payment must be

1. to influence any action or decision of the official or political party in his or its official capacity, or
2. to induce the foreign official or party to use his or its influence to affect an act or decision of the government,

in order to assist persons making payment in obtaining, retaining, or directing business to any person.

Corporate violators are subject to a fine of up to $1 million. Individual offenders may be fined up to $10,000, imprisoned for up to five years, or both. Fines imposed upon individuals may not be paid, directly or indirectly, by the corporation. The Act also empowers the attorney general to maintain a civil action in federal court to enjoin violations. Table 49–4 summarizes the various 1934 Act remedies discussed above.

---

56. "Domestic concerns" include individual citizens or residents of the United States, and any corporation, partnership, or sole proprietorship which has its principal place of business in the United States or is organized under the laws of one of the United States.

SUMMARY

1. Because corporate securities often have been used in schemes intended to mislead or defraud investors, the states have regulated distribution and sale of securities through "blue sky" laws since the early 1900s. State securities regulation proved inadequate in policing securities frauds, however, especially those operating on a national scale. The stock market crash of 1929 provided the impetus for federal regulation embodied in the Securities Act of 1933, the Securities Exchange Act of 1934, the Public Utility Holding Company Act of 1935, the Trust Indenture Act of 1939, the Investment Company Act of 1940, and the Investment Advisers Act of 1940. These statutes are administered by the Securities and Exchange Commission and generally provide investor protection by requiring full disclosure of accurate information to investors.

2. One of the most basic issues in securities law is to determine whether a particular investment transaction constitutes a security. Although the definition includes prototypical securities such as stocks and bonds, the law is broadly drafted to bring a wide range of investment instruments within the securities laws.

3. The Securities Act of 1933 governs the process by which a corporation or other issuer offers and sells its securities to the public for the first time. It provides generally that no security may be offered or sold to the public unless a registration statement has been filed with the SEC and become effective. Through a prospectus, certain information in the registration statement is provided to investors. The 1933 Act protects investors by providing full and fair disclosure of relevant information regarding the securities offered and the issuer.

4. The registration process under the 1933 Act is divided into three periods: the pre-filing period (the period before the registration statement has been completed and filed with the SEC), the waiting period (the period between the filing date and the date the registration statement becomes "effective"), and the post-effective period. Permissible selling efforts differ depending on how far the registration process has progressed, reflecting the level of public information about the offering.

5. Certain securities and security transactions are exempt from the 1933 Act's registration requirement. Major exempt transactions include (1) certain transactions involving small or limited offerings, (2) purely intrastate offerings, and (3) transactions by persons other than issuers, underwriters, or dealers.

6. The 1933 Act contains a variety of specific remedies designed to prevent the sale of unregistered securities and to assure the accuracy of the registration ma-

terials. These include §§12(1) and 11, which impose liability for selling unregistered securities and for deficiencies in registration statements, and §§12(2) and 17(a), which provide remedies for fraudulent conduct in the sale of securities.

7. The Securities Exchange Act of 1934 regulates secondary trading in securities, the securities markets, and persons conducting securities transactions. The 1934 Act, for example, imposes registration and disclosure requirements upon many issuers, the securities exchanges, self-regulatory organizations, and securities brokers and dealers. It also regulates proxy solicitation, tender offers, insider trading, fraud and manipulative practices in securities trading, and corporate bribery of foreign officials.

8. One of the most important 1934 Act provisions is Rule 10b-5 adopted by the SEC, which prohibits fraud in the purchase or sale of any security. Courts have long recognized an implied private remedy under Rule 10b-5 for injured investors. The plaintiff must be a purchaser or seller of the securities involved and the defendant must have acted with scienter or intent to deceive.

9. Rule 10b-5's broad antifraud proscription has been applied to a wide variety of fact situations generally divided into three general areas: (1) corporate mismanagement, (2) corporate misstatements, and (3) insider trading. Rule 10b-5's most important function is its use in policing against insider trading—buying and selling securities based on access to information not available to the public.

KEY TERMS

blue sky laws
Securities Act of 1933
Securities Exchange Act of 1934
Securities and Exchange Commission
Public Utility Holding Company Act of 1935
Trust Indenture Act of 1939
Investment Company Act of 1940
Investment Advisers Act of 1940
security
underwriter
dealer
registration statement
prospectus
Foreign Corrupt Practices Act of 1977
insider trading
Insider Trading Sanctions Act of 1984

QUESTIONS AND PROBLEMS

49-1   Federal securities laws provide investor protection by requiring full disclosure of accurate and timely information to investors, who can then make an informed choice concerning a securities transaction. Is this approach sufficient to protect investors? Should the SEC impose substantive requirements on issuers and "insiders" beyond full disclosure? Should federal law adopt a "merit" system to monitor which securities may be publicly offered?

49-2 Koscot Interplanetary, Inc. provides the opportunity for participation in the distribution and sale of cosmetics. A person may become a "beauty advisor" by purchasing Koscot cosmetics at a discount of 45% off the retail price. The beauty advisor then may sell the cosmetics at the retail price. A person may become a "supervisor" or "retail manager" by paying $1,000 to Koscot in return for the right to purchase Koscot cosmetics for a 55% discount. The supervisor then may sell the cosmetics directly to the public or may sell them to beauty advisors. A person who wishes to become a distributor pays $5,000 to Koscot and is entitled to receive cosmetics at a 65% discount which then may be sold to beauty advisors or supervisors. A supervisor or distributor who enlists another person to become part of the organization receives $600 for enlisting a supervisor or $3,000 for enlisting a distributor. Supervisors and distributors are encouraged to enlist others to join the organization by inviting them to "Opportunity Meetings" where Koscot employees attempt to recruit them to become beauty advisors, supervisors, or distributors.

(a) Mary White has paid $1,000 to Koscot to become a supervisor. How is she likely to make a profit from this investment? Explain.

(b) Harry Smith has paid $5,000 to become a distributor. How would he anticipate making a profit? Explain.

(c) Would either White's or Smith's investments be considered the purchase of a security under the federal securities laws? Explain.

49-3 As part of a collective bargaining agreement, various trucking companies employing Teamsters Union members agreed to pay $20 per week to the Teamsters Union Pension Trust Fund for each union member who was employed at one of the companies. A union member who worked in the union for at least 20 years would be entitled to receive a monthly pension of approximately $500 from the Trust Fund upon retirement. Each employee is required to participate in the pension plan so that employees do not have the option to receive direct payment

from the employer in lieu of a contribution to the pension plan. Is the employer's contribution to the pension fund an investment on behalf of the employee? Would the contribution be considered a security under federal securities law? Explain.

49-4 Manor Nursing Centers, Inc. submitted a registration statement to the SEC in conjunction with the issuance of new securities. The effective date was December 8, 1969. Manor then issued the securities which were accompanied by a prospectus containing the information set forth in the registration statement. Although the registration statement was accurate and correct on December 8, subsequent business developments rendered the information false and misleading. Was Manor required to correct this information? Explain. What, if any, statutes were violated?

49-5 Amexco, Inc. made a proposal to the management of McGraw Co. suggesting that the two companies merge. McGraw's board of directors rejected the proposal in a letter that McGraw released to the public. The letter characterized Amexco's offer as being "reckless, illegal, and improper." Amexco then filed a written notification with the SEC stating that Amexco intended to make a cash tender offer for all of McGraw's stock at a price of $40 provided that McGraw's management did not oppose the merger. McGraw replied by notifying Amexco that it would oppose the merger and issued a press release stating that $40 per share was an unfair price and that Amexco had engaged in illegal trade practices. Amexco decided not to pursue the tender offer.

Amexco has sued McGraw alleging that its public charges that Amexco's initial proposal was "reckless, illegal, and improper" were false, as were McGraw's statements that $40 per share was unfair and that Amexco had engaged in illegal trade practices. Can McGraw be held liable for violating Section 14(e) of the Williams Act? Explain.

49-6 Alphonse made the following transactions in Aladdin Lamp Co. stock:

Date	Transaction	Number of Shares	Price Per Share
2/1/87	Bought	15,000	$24
4/3/87	Sold	15,000	40
5/5/87	Bought	5,000	35
9/1/87	Sold	5,000	30
10/15/87	Bought	5,000	25

(a) Determine whether Alphonse would be subject to the provisions of §16(b) of the Securities Exchange Act of 1934 if:
(1) Alphonse was president of Aladdin and on 1/3/87 owned 2.2% of Aladdin stock;
(2) Alphonse was a director of Aladdin;
(3) Alphonse's wife was president of Aladdin;
(4) Alphonse was not an officer or director of Aladdin. On 1/31/87, Alphonse owned 15,000 shares (all of which he had purchased in 1985) of a total of 200,000 shares of outstanding Aladdin stock.

(b) Assume that Alphonse was subject to the provisions of §16(b) and that prior to 2/1/87 he owned 10% of Aladdin stock. Aladdin has demanded that he turn over the profits he has realized in 1987. What amount does Alphonse owe to Aladdin?

49-7 In 1984, the *Wall Street Journal* reported that it had fired a reporter who wrote a column entitled "Heard on the Street." The column, a popular feature of the newspaper, discusses market developments affecting individual stocks. The sources for the column's information are security analysts and buyers and sellers of the stock, rather than the corporation or its officers. The *Wall Street Journal* reported that it had discovered that the reporter frequently leaked information to his friends concerning the topics of upcoming "Heard on the Street" columns.

(a) Had the reporter violated Rule 10b-5 by leaking advance information to his friends? Explain.

(b) Consider the following facts included in the *Wall Street Journal* report. On February 13, 1984, Beatrice had closed at approximately $31 per share. On February 17, 1984, "Heard on the Street" reported that Nestle Corporation was preparing to buy Beatrice Foods Corporation for $45 a share. On that date, Beatrice stock closed at approximately $35 1/2 per share.

Assume that on February 13, the reporter had leaked the information contained in the February 17 article to a friend who had purchased 5,000 shares of Beatrice on February 13. The friend sold the stock on February 17. Would your answer to the question in part (a) be different in light of this information? Explain.

49-8 Dr. Annabelle Stephens appeared on the nationally broadcast television show Investigative Report on April 6, 1985, to report on her findings that a new drug Espadril was unsafe and possibly carcinogenic. Espadril is manufactured by Drugco. On April 1, 1985, Dr. Stephens had purchased "put" options on Drugco stock. The put options entitled Dr. Stephens to sell the stock at a price of $50 during the following ninety-day period. On April 1, the market price of Drugco.'s stock was selling at $55 per share.

(a) Immediately following the broadcast of Investigative Report, the market price of Drugco stock dropped to $40 and Dr. Stephens exercised her put options. Has she violated any securities laws? Explain.

(b) The April 6 edition of Investigative Report was broadcast opposite a special showing of "Flames of Passion," an immensely popular soap opera. During the following week, the market price of Drugco stock climbed to $60 per share and Dr. Stephens lost a great deal of money. Has Dr. Stephens violated any securities laws? Explain.

49-9 The *New York Stock Exchange Company Manual* provides in part:

The market action of a corporation's securities should be closely watched at a time when consideration is being given to significant corporate matters. If rumors or unusual market activity indicate that information on impending developments has leaked out, a frank and explicit announcement is clearly required. If rumors are in fact false or inaccurate, they should be promptly denied or clarified. . . . If rumors are correct or there are developments, an immediate, candid statement to the public as to the state of negotiations or the state of development of corporate plans in the rumored area must be made directly and openly.

(a) Discuss the advantages and disadvantages both to the public and to a corporation of requiring a company to provide the information described above in the *New York Stock Exchange Company Manual*.

(b) Assume that ABC Corporation's primary business is the mining and sale of copper ore. The market price of ABC stock began to climb due to rumors that ABC geologists had discovered a rich copper deposit. A *Wall Street Journal* reporter called ABC for a verification of the rumors. ABC's publicity office issued the following statement:

> Reports that ABC has discovered a large lode of copper ore are premature and possibly misleading. During the last six years ABC has been conducting explorations in Canada for copper ore. A recent report concerning one site has led to a recommendation that more samples should be evaluated. The work done to date has not been sufficient to reach any definite conclusions. Prior press reports that mention statistics of size and grade of ore are without factual basis and have originated by speculation of people not associated with ABC. When reasonable conclusions can be made, ABC will issue a definite statement to its stockholders and to the public.

Assume that at the time of this press release, ABC had received reports from its geologists that there was a 75% likelihood that a major deposit had been discovered. Has ABC engaged in a "manipulative or deceptive practice" in violation of Rule 10b-5? What other factors might be relevant in making this determination? Explain.

(c) Assume that market analysts have issued a report estimating XYZ's earnings in the next year. The report is very optimistic and far exceeds XYZ's own estimate of earnings. Does XYZ have an obligation to release its own earnings estimate? If XYZ did not release its own estimate, could XYZ be held liable under Rule 10b-5 to purchasers who bought XYZ stock based on the market analysts' optimistic reports? Explain.

(d) Assume that XYZ issued a press release in January 1986 projecting its earnings in the next two years. By March 1986, corporate officers realized that the projections were inaccurate and that its earnings would be far less than projected. Does XYZ have an obligation to release information correcting its projections?

Major Topics

- **an introduction to antitrust law, including its historical background, major statutory provisions, enforcement tools, and its scope and exemptions**

Antitrust law is concerned primarily with three federal statutes: the Sherman Antitrust Act, passed in 1890, and the Clayton Act and Federal Trade Commission Act, both enacted in 1914. These statutes, supplemented by state legislation, are designed to promote and preserve competition in a free and open market, and to prevent a firm or group of firms from acquiring or maintaining monopoly power—the power to establish prices above competitive equilibrium. The strong public policy favoring preservation of competition and prevention of monopoly is at the heart of our free enterprise system.

This and the following two chapters examine the antitrust laws, detailing the conduct they proscribe, the remedies they make available, and the analysis used by the courts in determining violations.

Historical Background

The Birth of Federal Regulation

The drafters of the Constitution incorporated various devices into our political system designed to prevent concentration of political power. A similar decentralization policy prevailed in the development of the American economic system. A major cause of the colonists' hostility toward England was dissatisfaction with the mercantilist system, which was characterized by government regulation of industry and commerce, and restrictions upon individual economic effort. Early Americans, self-sufficient and free of the rigid class system prevailing in Europe, readily embraced a policy of economic individualism with minimal government interference in economic affairs. Thus, free enterprise and *laissez-faire* capitalism, like political liberty, were cornerstones of the new American system.

By the mid-nineteenth century, the development of the telegraph and improvements in transportation, most notably the railroad, made large, centralized businesses feasible. A new form of business organization, the corporation, emerged to manage the vast amounts of capital and economic power aggregated by rapid industrialization. Increasing business concentration threatened the continued vitality of the free enterprise system by vesting excessive economic and political power in the hands of a few, whose conduct in acquiring and maintaining that power was certainly less than exemplary.

The trend toward economic concentration and its consequent abuses began with the railroads. To counter the effects of previous, often bitter, rate wars, individual railroads began to act in concert by forming "pools," first implemented in the early 1870s. The pools were used to divide traffic, earnings, and geographic markets, discriminate in price among various shippers and localities, and grant secret rebates to preferred shippers and buyers.

In response to the abusive railroad practices, inadequate state regulation, and widespread public concern, Congress passed the Interstate Commerce Act in 1887. It proscribed the "pool" arrangement, assured just and reasonable rates, and prohibited rate discrimination. The Act also created the Interstate Commerce Commission (ICC) to enforce its provisions. Thus began what has become a recurring theme in government regulation of business: a pervasive federal regulatory statute coupled with enforcement by a strong federal administrative agency.

The Movement Toward "Antitrust"

The railroad "pools" were not the only combinations threatening the free enterprise system in the late nineteenth century. Depending upon voluntary adherence, the pool was a less than ideal method of expeditious, consistent, concerted action. To achieve a more effective business organization, attorneys for the Standard Oil Company devised an arrangement patterned after a shareholders' voting trust.[1] The trust agreement provided that the owners of stock in several companies would transfer their securities to a board of trustees who had full management control. In exchange, the stockholders received trust certificates that entitled them to a percentage of the earnings of the jointly controlled companies.

By 1887, the trust device had been used to monopolize entire industries, including fuel oil, cotton, linseed oil, sugar, lead, and whiskey. The trusts were inherently destructive of competition and their conduct in acquiring and maintaining power was frequently ruthless. For example, trusts often would enter a market selling at well below cost to drive competitors out of business or force them to sell (predatory pricing). Once competition was eliminated, the trust would raise the price far

above that obtained under competitive conditions. Other unscrupulous trust practices included stock fraud and other financial scandals, political bribery, and labor oppression. By the presidential election of 1888, a strong bipartisan movement, including small business, labor, and agrarian interests, was calling for strong remedial "antitrust" legislation. The result was the **Sherman Antitrust Act,**[2] introduced by Senator John Sherman of Ohio and signed into law by President Benjamin Harrison on July 2, 1890. Although the holding company soon superseded the trust as the primary device for effecting business combination, the term **antitrust** has survived and today designates both the state and federal laws designed to promote competition and prevent monopoly.

The Sherman Act

Backed by criminal, civil, and equitable sanctions, the Sherman Antitrust Act is the primary tool of antitrust enforcement in the United States. The Sherman Act contains only two substantive provisions. Section 1 provides that:

> Every contract, combination in the form of trust or otherwise, or conspiracy, in restraint of trade or commerce among the several States, or with foreign nations, is declared to be illegal.

Section 2 states that:

> Every person who shall monopolize, or attempt to monopolize, or combine or conspire with any other person or persons, to monopolize any part of the trade or commerce among the several States, or with foreign nations, shall be deemed guilty of a felony. . . .

The Act is not specific concerning the particular conduct it seeks to prevent and makes no effort even to define its basic concepts of "restraint of trade" or "monopolization." Rather, the Sherman Act serves as a broad and general "charter of freedom," allowing the federal courts (and most im-

---

1. Shareholders' voting trusts are covered in Chapter 47.

2. 15 U.S.C. §§1–7.

portant, the Supreme Court) to develop a common law of antitrust to preserve and promote competition and prevent monopoly. This statutory charter is general enough to allow the court flexibility in determining whether, on the unique facts of a specific case, the basic policy objectives of antitrust are violated.

Sections 1 and 2 of the Sherman Act exhibit both fundamental differences and fundamental similarities. Section 1 is concerned with *contracts, combinations, and conspiracies* in restraint of trade. Thus, §1 violations require *two or more persons* banding together (for example, to fix prices or divide markets) to achieve the anticompetitive result. The existence of a combination is therefore always at the heart of any §1 violation. In contrast, although §2 speaks of conspiracies to monopolize (which also would be §1 violations), it is primarily concerned with single-firm conduct (such as predatory pricing) or a structural condition likely to create or maintain a monopoly in a particular market. Despite this basic difference, both sections may be viewed as complementary methods of achieving the same goal: to prevent monopoly. Both aim at acts or practices that tend to control markets or reduce competition.

Within twenty years after its enactment in 1890, the courts had interpreted the Sherman Act to prohibit price fixing by combining railroads, a massive merger of two western railroads, and to declare the trusts controlling the meat, tobacco, and oil industries to be illegal monopolies. Despite these successes and the widespread public support for antitrust, early enforcement of the Sherman Act was characterized by judicial hostility and government indifference. Critics assailed both the judicial interpretation of the Act and the law itself, which appeared to reach only anticompetitive conduct in fruition, not trade restraints in their incipiency or simply unfair trade practices or methods of competition. Critics also believed new enforcement techniques were required, given the somewhat inconsistent performance by the Department of Justice.

By the presidential election of 1912, bipartisan support was once again mustered for antitrust reform. Upon his election in 1912, Woodrow Wilson promptly urged the passage of new legislation to both strengthen the antitrust laws and create a federal administrative agency entrusted with enforcement responsibilities. Consequently, Congress, in 1914, passed the Clayton Act and the Federal Trade Commission Act. Since 1914 there have been no further major antitrust enactments.

The Clayton Act

The **Clayton Act**[3] was designed to strengthen the Sherman Act by bringing certain specific monopolistic or restrictive practices within the reach of the antitrust laws. It contains four basic substantive provisions discussed more fully in later material:

1. Section 2, as amended in 1936 by the Robinson-Patman Act, prohibits certain types of price discrimination.
2. Section 3 prohibits certain sales made on condition that the buyer not deal with the seller's competitors.
3. Section 7 prohibits certain corporate mergers.
4. Section 8 prohibits a person from serving on the board of directors of two competing companies (an "interlocking directorate") if one or both companies are larger than a given size.

Unlike the Sherman Act, which generally requires proof of actual and substantial anticompetitive effect, the Clayton Act is designed to reach anticompetitive acts or practices in their *incipiency*. Thus, the Clayton Act §§2, 3, and 7[4] all are appended by language that finds a violation if the effect of the price discrimination, exclusive contract, or merger "*may* be to substantially lessen competition or *tend* to create a monopoly in any line of commerce."[5]

Thus, a showing of probable, rather than actual, adverse competitive effect is sufficient to establish

---

3. 15 U.S.C. §§12-27.
4. Section 8 imposes a fixed dollar limitation for violation.
5. Language of §3 Clayton Act (emphasis added).

a Clayton Act violation. In other words, the Clayton Act is, at least in theory, more sensitive to anticompetitive conduct than the Sherman Act.

The Federal Trade Commission Act

Due to public dissatisfaction with both the adequacy of antitrust law and the zeal of the Justice Department, Congress determined that a strong federal administrative agency was needed to aid in antitrust enforcement, monitor business conduct, and advise business, the courts, and Congress on antitrust matters. Consequently, in 1914, Congress enacted the **Federal Trade Commission Act**,[6] which created the **Federal Trade Commission (FTC)**. The commission is composed of five commissioners, appointed by the president to seven-year terms, and approved by the Senate. No more than three of the commissioners may be members of the same political party. The FTC is empowered to enforce both the Clayton and Federal Trade Commission Acts, but not the Sherman Act. The FTC Act's sole substantive provision is §5, which authorizes the FTC to issue "cease and desist" orders prohibiting "unfair methods of competition" and "unfair or deceptive acts or practices." Note that §5 not only is a tool of antitrust enforcement, but also is the basis of the FTC's consumer protection activities.

The legal principles governing violations of the Sherman, Clayton, and FTC Acts are covered in the next two chapters. The following material provides an overview of the legal remedies available for antitrust violations, and the persons and conduct covered.

Enforcing the Antitrust Laws

The basic remedies available for antitrust violations include (1) criminal sanctions, (2) equitable proceedings by either government or private plaintiffs, (3) private actions for money damages, and (4) forfeiture.

---

6. 15 U.S.C. §§41-58.

Criminal Sanctions

Violations of both §§1 and 2 of the Sherman Act are felonies punishable by imprisonment of up to three years and fines of up to $100,000, or both, for individuals, and fines of up to $1,000,000 for corporations. The Antitrust Division of the Department of Justice or a local United States attorney under the direction of the attorney general can initiate criminal prosecution. Like other federal felonies, prosecution commences after indictment returned by a grand jury. Criminal prosecution under the Sherman Act generally has been used only when the challenged conduct is particularly aggravated and of unquestioned illegality. With two rarely invoked exceptions, no criminal sanctions are imposed for violations of the Clayton Act or the FTC Act.[7]

Equitable Remedies

Civil equitable actions maintained either by the government or private plaintiffs are far more common than criminal proceedings as a method of antitrust enforcement. Both the Sherman Act and the Clayton Act[8] confer jurisdiction upon the federal courts to "prevent and restrain" violations and impose a duty upon the attorney general to institute proceedings in equity for that purpose. Similarly, §16 of the Clayton Act authorizes private plaintiffs (such as an injured competitor) to maintain actions to enjoin actual or threatened injury resulting from violation of either the Sherman Act or the Clayton Act.

The relief afforded in a civil equitable action is remedial rather than punitive. As in all cases of equity, the court has broad discretion in fashioning an appropriate remedy. As a result, antitrust decrees have, for example, (1) restrained certain acts

---

7. Violations of §3 of the Robinson-Patman Act (15 U.S.C. §13a) are punishable by imprisonment of up to one year and a $5,000 fine or both. Individuals who violate §10 of the Clayton Act (15 U.S.C. §20), concerning certain dealings between a common carrier and another firm with interlocking directors or officers, are similarly punishable.

8. Sherman Act §4, (15 U.S.C. §4), Clayton Act §15 (15 U.S.C. §25).

or conduct, (2) ordered divestiture of subsidiary companies, (3) created new companies; (4) ordered patents, trade secrets, or technology made available to competitors, and (5) cancelled or modified contracts. After entry of the judgment, the court often retains jurisdiction in order to modify or supervise performance of the decree.

Consent Decrees. When the government commences a civil antitrust action, both parties often have a strong incentive to settle rather than litigate the dispute. Suits often take years to resolve and legal fees commonly are measured in the millions of dollars. The disruption and adverse publicity occasioned by major antitrust litigation are detrimental to a company. An adjudication of liability in a government antitrust suit also opens the door for subsequent private suits for damages. From the Justice Department's point of view, settlement frees limited resources to pursue other cases.

For these reasons, approximately seventy-five to eighty percent of civil suits instituted by the government are settled through **consent decrees**. Under this procedure, a compromise agreement between the government and the defendant is filed with the federal court, and, if the court approves of the settlement, it is incorporated into a judicial order known as a consent decree. Once entered, the consent decree has the same effect as any other judicial order and may be subsequently modified only upon court approval. Even though the defendant is bound by its terms once entered, the consent decree generally is neither an adjudication nor admission of liability for antitrust violations. Accordingly, private plaintiffs may not use it to establish the defendant's liability in subsequent civil suits for damages.

Cease and Desist Orders. The FTC possesses significant antitrust enforcement powers because it is able to issue **cease and desist orders**. These orders provide injunctive relief by preventing or restraining unlawful conduct. A cease and desist order is thus prospective in effect, imposing neither criminal nor other civil penalties for past conduct. Like Justice Department civil proceedings, most FTC investigations are settled by a consent order procedure. If negotiations are unavailing, the commis-

sion initiates the formal adjudication process by filing a complaint outlining the alleged antitrust violation.[9] After an opportunity for preparation, a hearing is held before an administrative law judge appointed by the commission. The findings and orders of the judge may then be appealed to the full commission, allowed as a matter of right. The commission's decision (for example, to issue a cease and desist order) may then be appealed to the court of appeals. Note that reviewing courts seldom overturn FTC decisions, commonly deferring to the commission's expertise and findings of fact. Although no criminal sanctions or private damage remedies are imposed for FTC Act violations, violation of a final cease and desist order carries a $10,000 per day civil penalty. In addition, the federal district courts are empowered to grant mandatory injunctions and other appropriate equitable relief to enforce final FTC orders.[10]

Private Action for Damages

"Treble" Damages. Because of the limited resources of the Justice Department and FTC, public antitrust enforcement is necessarily selective, focusing on major industries or flagrant violations. Private enforcement, by individuals or businesses injured by antitrust violations, is therefore necessary to supplement government efforts. To this end, the Clayton Act includes private remedies, legal and equitable in nature, for violations of both the Sherman and Clayton Acts. Equitable relief, under §16 of the Clayton Act, was discussed above. Legal relief, a private action for money damages, is authorized by §4 of the Clayton Act which provides:

> [A]ny person who shall be injured in his business or property by reason of anything forbidden in the antitrust laws[11] may sue therefor [in a federal

---

9. That is, of §§2, 3, 7, or 8 of the Clayton Act, or §5 of the FTC Act.

10. Federal Trade Commission Act §5(l) (15 U.S.C. §45(l)).

11. Under §1(a) of the Clayton Act (15 U.S.C. §12(a)), the term "antitrust laws" includes the Sherman Act, the Clayton Act, and the Wilson Tariff Act (15 U.S.C. §§8-11).

district court of competent jurisdiction], and shall recover threefold the damages by him sustained, and the cost of suit, including a reasonable attorney's fee.[12]

Note that a private plaintiff proceeding under this provision recovers *three* times its actual damages. That is, damages sustained are tripled or "trebled" in computing the ultimate recovery. The prospect of a treble damage award provides a strong incentive for private antitrust enforcement, increasing the likelihood that antitrust violations will be discovered. This increased risk, coupled with the severe treble damage penalty, helps deter illegal conduct. Suits under §4 must be commenced within four years after the cause of action accrues.

Class of Permissible Plaintiffs—Standing to Sue. Though Clayton Act §4 literally allows *any* person to recover damages for injury caused by antitrust violations, it requires that a prospective plaintiff be injured "in his *business or property.*" Read restrictively, this language applies only to injury to commercial (business) interests or enterprises. Although many cases use this definition,[13] courts have not strictly adhered to it, and have allowed recovery by nonprofit or professional groups and ultimate consumers. For example, in *Reiter v. Sonotone Corporation* (1979),[14] the Supreme Court held that consumers who, because of antitrust violations, pay a higher price for goods purchased for personal use, sustain an injury to their "property" within the meaning of §4.

Consumer recovery is limited, however, by the general requirement that purchasers entitled to sue under §4 must be "direct" or immediate. For example, a consumer who purchases directly from M, a manufacturer involved in a price-fixing conspiracy, is allowed to recover. If the manufacturer first sells to an innocent middleman, from whom the consumer purchases, the middleman is a "direct"

purchaser entitled to recover treble damages, whereas the consumer is said to be an "indirect" purchaser, precluded from recovery.[15] Although treble damage recovery is thus limited to direct purchasers, indirect purchasers are not precluded from seeking equitable relief under §16.

Note that purchasers are not the only persons entitled to recover under §4. For example, suppliers or competitors of an antitrust violator also may be injured in their "business or property," therefore entitled to maintain a damage action.

Relationship to Government Suits. Under Clayton Act §5(a), a final judgment or decree rendered in any civil or criminal proceeding brought by the United States finding that the defendant has violated the antitrust laws is prima facie evidence against that defendant in an action maintained by any other party concerning matters determined in the government suit. This provision greatly benefits subsequent private plaintiffs seeking treble damages. In a private action under §4, the plaintiff must ordinarily prove both the existence of an antitrust violation, and damages resulting from that violation. If the *existence* of the violation is already established in the prior government suit (by a plea of guilty or a conviction after trial in a criminal case or a finding of liability in a civil case), the private plaintiff may recover merely by proving damages.

Because private plaintiffs may number in the thousands and damages are trebled, an adverse determination in a government suit may have disastrous financial consequences. As a result, antitrust defendants often have a strong incentive to settle the government's suit in a manner that is not conclusive in subsequent cases. If the government action is civil, a consent decree is frequently sought because it is ordinarily neither an adjudication on the merits nor an admission of liability by the defendant. In a criminal case, the court may allow the defendant to plead "nolo contendere" or "no contest" to the charge. Through such a plea the defendant accepts the punishment for the crime charged

---

12. Note that §16 (15 U.S.C. §26) differs from §4 (15 U.S.C. §15) in that §16 requires merely threatened rather than actual injury, and injunctive relief is not necessarily limited to injuries to business or property interests.

13. See, for example, *Hawaii v. Standard Oil Company of California*, 92 S. Ct. 885, 892 (1972).

14. 99 S. Ct. 2326 (1979).

15. See *Hanover Shoe, Inc. v. United Shoe Machinery Corp.*, 88 S. Ct. 2224 (1968); and *Illinois Brick Company v. Illinois*, 97 S. Ct. 2061 (1977).

but does not admit guilt. Because, under §5(a), neither a consent decree nor a "nolo" plea involves a finding of antitrust violation, subsequent private plaintiffs must prove both the existence of the violation and damages in order to recover.

Forfeiture

Section 6 of the Sherman Act contains the seldom used forfeiture remedy. It provides for the forfeiture to the United States of any property being transported interstate (or to a foreign country) if the property is owned under, and the subject of, a contract, combination, or conspiracy in restraint of trade violating §1 of the Sherman Act. The property may be seized in proceedings similar to those used for property illegally imported into the country.

The Reach of the Antitrust Laws— Scope and Exemptions

Although the basic policy underlying the antitrust laws is the preservation of competition and prevention of monopoly, the antitrust laws do not enjoy universal application. For example, wholly intrastate activity is outside the reach of federal antitrust law, and certain anticompetitive conduct enjoys limited antitrust immunity. The remainder of this chapter examines the various limitations on antitrust application.

The Interstate Commerce Requirement

The Sherman Act prohibits both restraints (§1) and monopolization (§2) of "trade or commerce among the several States." This interstate commerce requirement is imposed because the antitrust laws, like other federal regulatory statutes, were enacted pursuant to the Commerce Clause, giving Congress the power "to regulate Commerce . . . . among the several States."[16]

Congressional authority to regulate under the Commerce Clause has long been interpreted to ex-

tend beyond activities actually *in* interstate commerce to reach other activities, even wholly local in character, which nevertheless substantially *affect* interstate commerce.[17] The Supreme Court has adopted a correspondingly broad interpretation in applying the Sherman Act, as *McLain v. Real Estate Board of New Orleans, Inc.,* excerpted in Chapter 4, indicates.

In contrast to the Sherman Act, the Clayton Act generally imposes a stricter jurisdictional requirement under the Commerce Clause. Although §7 reaches mergers of firms engaged "in any activity affecting commerce," §2 (as amended by the Robinson-Patman Act) and §3 (exclusive dealings) both apply only to persons engaged in "commerce" and conduct occurring "in the course of such commerce." Section 8 (interlocking directorates) applies to corporations "engaged in whole or in part in commerce."

The Federal Trade Commission Act (§5) allows the FTC to enjoin unfair methods of competition and unfair or deceptive trade practices "in or affecting commerce." No satisfactory explanation exists for the differing jurisdictional reach of the various antitrust provisions.

State law may govern conduct arguably beyond the reach of federal antitrust law. For example, virtually all states have antitrust statutes similar to federal law, applicable to intrastate activity. State tort law also often provides a private remedy for certain unfair competitive acts or practices.

Exemptions

Certain types of conduct receive a limited exemption from the antitrust laws. For example, labor unions, agricultural cooperatives, and export associations, which are in effect combinations in restraint of trade, are exempt. Certain industries that are regulated by state or federal administrative agencies are exempt. Further, action taken by state governments or governmental entities and private conduct intended to influence government action may be beyond the reach of antitrust law. The scope of and rationale for these exemptions vary

---

16. U.S. Const. art. I, §8, cl. 3. The Commerce Clause is discussed in Chapter 4.

17. See, for example, *Wickard v. Filburn,* 63 S. Ct. 82 (1942).

widely. Some are expressly stated in the antitrust laws, some are express or implied in other statutes, and some are judicially created through statutory interpretation.[18]

Regulated Industries. Many private industries are extensively regulated by state or federal administrative agencies. The most prevalent regulation of this type is of natural monopolies, such as utilities. Also regulated are common carriers, banks, stock exchanges, and television and radio communication. The rationale for regulation varies with the industry. For example, utility regulation is designed to temper monopolistic practices and provide a substitute for competition, whereas communications regulation provides for fair and orderly use of the limited radio and television broadcast spectrum.

Regulated industries are not entirely free from antitrust scrutiny. The statutory framework itself commonly substitutes a scheme of regulated rates and services for competition, providing protection for other firms and the public generally. If rates and services are not regulated, antitrust law may apply in full force. Modern courts have increasingly subjected regulated industries to the antitrust laws unless they conflict with "clear, discernible regulatory objectives expressed or implied in the regulatory statute."[19]

Labor Unions, Agricultural Cooperatives, and Export Associations. Labor unions are essentially labor monopolies that collectively determine wages and other conditions of employment. Without antitrust exemption, therefore, labor unions could be attacked as illegal combinations in restraint of trade. In response to several early Sherman Act cases questioning the legality of unions, Congress enacted §6 of the Clayton Act in 1914, which provides that the antitrust laws shall not be construed to (1) forbid the existence and operation of labor organizations, (2) forbid or restrain individual members of such organizations from lawfully carrying out their legitimate ends, or (3) find a labor organization, or its members, to be an illegal combination or conspiracy in restraint of trade. Clayton Act §20[20] restricts the power of federal courts to grant injunctions in labor disputes, and exempts from antitrust scrutiny employee conduct, such as strikes and boycotts, arising during the course of disputes concerning terms and conditions of employment. The Norris-LaGuardia Act of 1932[21] also generally prohibits injunctions in labor disputes. Collectively, these statutes and subsequent cases exempt most union activity and collective bargaining agreements from the antitrust laws.

The scope of the labor antitrust exemption is, however, limited. Conduct that would violate the Sherman Act in the absence of union involvement is not immunized by the participation of the union. For example, a union may not band together with a nonlabor party, such as a contractor or manufacturer, to achieve a result forbidden by the antitrust laws.

Agricultural cooperatives, fishermen's organizations, and export trade associations also enjoy a limited antitrust exemption.[22] In these cases, persons who would otherwise be in competition (farmers, fishermen, exporters) are allowed to form associations to collectively prepare and market their products, including fixing prices at which the association will sell. As with labor unions, however, the exemption extends to the existence and operation of such organizations, not to combinations or conspiracies in restraint of trade with persons not so exempted.

Antitrust Immunity of State Governmental Entities: The "State Action" Exemption. The Sher-

---

18. Patent law (discussed in Chapter 34) also effectively provides a limited exemption from antitrust in order to promote innovation and invention. That is, an inventor is granted a limited monopoly–the exclusive right to make, use, or sell his invention for a period of seventeen years. 35 U.S.C. §154. In the case of patents, one public policy (promotion of invention) is deemed to outweigh another (preservation of competition). Patents do, however, create a host of antitrust problems.

19. Sullivan, *The Law of Antitrust* 746 (1977).

20. 29 U.S.C. §52.

21. 29 U.S.C. §§101-115.

22. The agricultural exemption is contained in §6 of the Clayton Act and the Capper-Volstead Act of 1922 (7 U.S.C. §§291-292). The fisherman's exemption is stated in the Fisherman's Cooperative Marketing Act (15 U.S.C. §§521-522), and the export exemption is provided in the Webb-Pomerene Act (15 U.S.C. §§61-66).

man Act does not apply to actions of the federal government. It is also generally inapplicable to actions of state legislatures and state administrative agencies. The landmark case establishing this so-called "state action" exemption is *Parker v. Brown* (1943).[23] In this case, the Court stated that neither the language nor the legislative history of the Sherman Act suggests that it was intended to restrain state action or official action directed by a state. Rather, the Act must be taken as a prohibition solely on individual or corporate action. On the authority of *Parker*, however, state legislative action, or action by state officials or agencies, is not entirely free of Sherman Act scrutiny. Federal antitrust policy mandates competition as the governing standard. In contrast, state economic regulatory statutes may substitute public regulation for private competition or may dictate or permit a result contrary to basic antitrust principles. In all cases asserting the "state action" exemption, the purpose and effect of the state action must be weighed against countervailing antitrust or other federal policy to determine whether antitrust immunity is available. The following case summarizes the legal standard for antitrust immunity under *Parker v. Brown.*

California Retail Liquor Dealers Association v. Midcal Aluminum, Inc.
100 S. Ct. 937 (1980)

A California statute required wine producers and wholesalers to file fair trade contracts or price schedules with the state. The fair trade contracts established the sales price at which wines were to be sold to retailers and consumers. If a producer did not use a fair trade contract, the wholesaler was required to file and post a schedule of the sales prices for the wines. The law prohibited state licensed wine merchants from selling wines except at the price set in a fair trade contract or price schedule.

The California Department of Alcoholic Beverage Control charged that Midcal Aluminum, Inc., a wholesale wine distributor, sold Gallo wine for

prices less than those established by E. & J. Gallo Winery's price schedule. Midcal admitted the charges but requested the California court of appeal to enjoin the state's wine pricing system alleging that it violated the federal Sherman Act. The court of appeal granted the injunction. The California Retail Liquor Dealers Association sought review by the United States Supreme Court, which granted a writ of certiorari.

Justice Powell

. . . The threshold question is whether California's plan for wine pricing violates the Sherman Act. . . .

California's system for wine pricing plainly constitutes resale price maintenance in violation of the Sherman Act. . . . The wine producer holds the power to prevent price competition by dictating the prices charged by wholesalers. . . .

Thus, we must consider whether the State's involvement in the price-setting program is sufficient to establish antitrust immunity under *Parker v. Brown* [63 S. Ct. 307 (1943)]. That immunity for state regulatory programs is grounded in our federal structure. "In a dual system of government in which, under the Constitution, the states are sovereign, save only as Congress may constitutionally subtract from their authority, an unexpressed purpose to nullify a state's control over its officers and agents is not lightly to be attributed to Congress." [*Id.*, at 313.] In *Parker v. Brown*, this Court found in the Sherman Act no purpose to nullify state powers. Because the Act is directed against "individual and not state action," the Court concluded that state regulatory programs could not violate it. [*Id.*, at 314.]

Under the program challenged in *Parker*, the State Agricultural Prorate Advisory Commission authorized the organization of local cooperatives to develop marketing policies for the raisin crop. The Court emphasized that the Advisory Commission, which was appointed by the Governor, had to approve cooperative policies following public hearings: "It is the state which has created the machinery for establishing the prorate program. . . . [I]t is the state, acting through the Commission, which adopts the program and enforces it. . . ." *Ibid.* In view of this extensive official oversight, the Court wrote, the Sherman Act did not apply.

---

23. 63 S. Ct. 307 (1943).

Without such oversight, the result could have been different. The Court expressly noted that "a state does not give immunity to those who violate the Sherman Act by authorizing them to violate it, or by declaring that their action is lawful. . . ." [*Id.*, at 314.]

Several recent decisions have applied *Parker*'s analysis. In *Goldfarb v. Virginia State Bar* [95 S. Ct. 2004 (1975)], the Court concluded that [attorneys'] fee schedules enforced by a state bar association were not mandated by ethical standards established by the State Supreme Court. The fee schedules therefore were not immune from antitrust attack. "It is not enough that . . . anticompetitive conduct is 'prompted' by state action; rather, anticompetitive activities must be compelled by direction of the State acting as a sovereign." [*Id.*, at 2015.] Similarly, in *Cantor v. Detroit Edison Co.* [96 S. Ct. 3110 (1976)], a majority of the Court found that no antitrust immunity was conferred when a state agency passively accepted a public utility's tariff. In contrast, Arizona rules against lawyer advertising were held immune from Sherman Act challenge because they "reflect[ed] a clear articulation of the State's policy with regard to professional behavior" and were "subject to pointed reexamination by the policymaker—the Arizona Supreme Court—in enforcement proceedings." *Bates v. State Bar of Arizona* [97 S. Ct. 2691, 2698 (1977)].

Only last Term, this Court found antitrust immunity for a California program requiring state approval of the location of new automobile dealerships. *New Motor Vehicle Bd. of Cal. v. Orrin W. Fox Co.* [99 S. Ct. 403 (1978)]. That program provided that the State would hold a hearing if an automobile franchisee protested the establishment or relocation of a competing dealership. [*Id.*, at 408.] In view of the State's active role, the Court held, the program was not subject to the Sherman Act. The "clearly articulated and affirmatively expressed" goal of the state policy was to "displace unfettered business freedom in the matter of the establishment and relocation of automobile dealerships." [*Id.*, at 412.]

These decisions establish two standards for antitrust immunity under *Parker v. Brown*. First, the challenged restraint must be "one clearly articulated and affirmatively expressed as state policy";

second, the policy must be "actively supervised" by the State itself. *City of Lafayette v. Louisiana Power & Light Co.* [98 S. Ct. 1123, 1135 (1978)] (opinion of Brennan, J.). The California system for wine pricing satisfies the first standard. The legislative policy is forthrightly stated and clear in its purpose to permit resale price maintenance. The program, however, does not meet the second requirement for *Parker* immunity. The State simply authorizes price setting and enforces the prices established by private parties. The State neither establishes prices nor reviews the reasonableness of the price schedules; nor does it regulate the terms of fair trade contracts. The State does not monitor market conditions or engage in any "pointed reexamination" of the program. The national policy in favor of competition cannot be thwarted by casting such a gauzy cloak of state involvement over what is essentially a private price-fixing arrangement.

[Judgment affirmed.]

Attempts to Influence Government Action: The Noerr-Pennington Doctrine. A problem related to state action immunity concerns the antitrust implications of private efforts to influence government action. Simply stated, may a competitor or group of competitors petition the government or a government agency to take an action that would injure the petitioners' competitors? The landmark case addressing this issue is *Eastern Railroads Presidents Conference v. Noerr Motor Freight, Inc.*[24] In this case, the Supreme Court reasoned that the whole concept of representative government depends upon the ability of people to make their wishes, however selfish, known to their representatives and that the Sherman Act was designed to reach business, not political, conduct. The Court also stated that the right to petition the government is a freedom protected by the Bill of Rights. The Court therefore held that no violation of the Sherman Act can be predicated upon mere attempts to influence the passage or enforcement of laws. The Court further held that the Act does not prohibit two or more persons from associating together (that is, a com-

---

24. 81 S. Ct. 523 (1961).

bination) in an effort to persuade the legislature or executive to take particular action concerning a law that would produce a trade restraint or a monopoly.

In a later case, *United Mine Workers of America v. Pennington*,[25] the Supreme Court made it clear that

> *Noerr* shields from the Sherman Act a concerted effort to influence public officials regardless of intent of purpose. . . . Joint efforts to influence public officials do not violate the antitrust laws even though intended to eliminate competition. Such conduct is not illegal, either standing alone or as part of a broader scheme itself violative of the Sherman Act.[26]

Despite the apparent broad antitrust exemption for lobbying activities embodied in this *Noerr-Pennington* doctrine, *Noerr* itself stated that there may be instances in which the alleged conspiracy

> . . .ostensibly directed toward influencing governmental action, is a mere sham to cover what is actually nothing more than an attempt to interfere directly with the business relationships of a competitor. . . .[27]

In such a case, the Court indicated that Sherman Act liability would indeed be appropriate.

Both *Noerr* and *Pennington* involved allegedly illegal attempts to influence legislative and executive action. The Supreme Court has held that the *Noerr-Pennington* doctrine and its "sham" exception quoted above also apply to attempts to influence adjudicative bodies, such as administrative agencies and courts.[28] The sham exception may be applied in this context, for example, if the defendant files a series of baseless, repetitive lawsuits designed to prevent a competitor from entering the market or obtaining necessary administrative permits or approvals.

In the following case the Supreme Court considered whether anticompetitive efforts to affect the product-standard setting process of a private association are immune from antitrust liability under the *Noerr-Pennington* doctrine.

Allied Tube & Conduit Corporation v. Indian Head, Inc.

108 S. Ct. 1931 (1988)

The National Fire Protection Association (Association)—a private organization with more than 31,500 members representing industry, labor, academia, insurers, organized medicine, firefighters, and government—publishes product standards and codes relating to fire protection. In its National Electric Code (Code), the Association establishes product and performance requirements for the design and installation of electric wiring systems. A substantial number of states and local governments routinely adopt the Code into law and many private certification laboratories, insurance underwriters, electrical inspectors, and contractors accept and adopt the standards listed in the Code. For many years, the Code had approved the use of steel electrical conduit (the tubing used to carry electrical wires through the walls and floors of buildings) and steel was the primary material used for conduit. In 1980, after respondent Indian Head, Inc., began manufacturing plastic conduit made of polyvinyl chloride, the Association placed on the agenda of its annual meeting a proposal to include plastic conduit as an approved material in the Code. Petitioner Allied Tube & Conduit Corporation, the nation's largest producer of steel conduit, met with its independent sales agents, other steel conduit manufacturers and members of the steel industry to plan strategy to prevent the Association's approval of plastic conduit. They agreed to pack the annual meeting with new members whose sole function was to vote against the polyvinyl chloride proposal. The steel interests recruited 230 persons (of which 155 were recruited by Allied Tube & Conduit) to join the Association and paid over $100,000 for their membership, registration and attendance expenses. At the Association's annual meeting, the proposal to approve polyvinyl chloride conduit was rejected by a vote of 394 to 390.

Indian Head sued Allied Tube & Conduit, alleg-

---

25. 85 S. Ct. 1585 (1965).
26. *Id.* at 1593.
27. 81 S. Ct. at 533.
28. *California Motor Transport Co. v. Trucking Unlimited*, 92 S. Ct. 609 (1972).

ing that it had violated federal antitrust laws by conspiring with other steel interests to restrain trade in the electrical conduit market. The trial court ruled in favor of Allied Tube & Conduit, reasoning that its conduct was protected under the *Noerr-Pennington* doctrine because the Association was "akin to a legislature" and Allied Tube & Conduit's activities were protected political activity intended to influence state and local government. The Court of Appeals reversed and the United States Supreme Court granted certiorari.

Justice Brennan

. . . Concerted efforts to restrain or monopolize trade by petitioning government officials are protected from antitrust liability under the [*Noerr-Pennington* doctrine]. . . . The validity of such efforts, and thus the applicability of *Noerr* immunity, varies with the context and nature of the activity. A publicity campaign directed at the general public, seeking legislation or executive action, enjoys antitrust immunity even when the campaign employs unethical and deceptive methods. . . . But in less political arenas, unethical and deceptive practices can constitute abuses of administrative or judicial processes that may result in antitrust violations. . . .

In this case, the restraint of trade on which liability was predicated was the Association's exclusion of respondent's product from the Code, and no damages were imposed for the incorporation of that Code by any government. The relevant context is thus the standard-setting process of a private association. Typically, private standard-setting associations, like the Association in this case, include members having horizontal and vertical business relations. . . . There is no doubt that the members of such associations often have economic incentives to restrain competition and that the product standards set by such associations have a serious potential for anticompetitive harm. . . . Agreement on a product standard is, after all, implicitly an agreement not to manufacture, distribute, or purchase certain types of products. Accordingly, private standard-setting associations have traditionally been objects of antitrust scrutiny. . . . When, however, private associations promulgate safety standards based on the merits of objective expert judgments and through procedures that prevent the standard-setting process from being biased by members with economic interests in stifling product competition, . . . those private standards can have significant procompetitive advantages. . . .

Given this context, petitioner does not enjoy the immunity accorded those who merely urge the government to restrain trade. We agree with the Court of Appeals that the Association cannot be treated as a "quasi-legislative" body simply because legislatures routinely adopt the Code the Association publishes. . . . [W]here, as here, the restraint is imposed by persons unaccountable to the public and without official authority, many of whom have personal financial interests in restraining competition, we have no difficulty concluding that the restraint has resulted from private action. . . .

Here the context and nature of the activity do not counsel against inquiry into its validity. Unlike the publicity campaign in *Noerr,* the activity at issue here did not take place in the open political arena, where partisanship is the hallmark of decisionmaking, but within the confines of a private standard-setting process. . . . [P]etitioner did not confine itself to efforts to persuade an independent decisionmaker; . . . rather, it organized and orchestrated the actual exercise of the Association's decisionmaking authority in setting a standard. Nor can the setting of the Association's Code be characterized as merely an exercise of the power of persuasion, for it in part involves the exercise of market power. The Association's members, after all, include consumers, distributors, and manufacturers of electrical conduit, and any agreement to exclude polyvinyl chloride conduit from the Code is in part an implicit agreement not to trade in that type of electrical conduit. . . . Although one could reason backwards from the legislative impact of the Code to the conclusion that the conduct at issue here is "political," we think that, given the context and nature of the conduct, it can more aptly be characterized as commercial activity with a political impact. . . . [T]he antitrust laws should not necessarily immunize what are in essence commercial activities simply because they have a political impact. . . .

Although we do not here set forth the rules of antitrust liability governing the private standard-setting process, we hold that at least where, as here, an economically interested party exercises decisionmaking authority in formulating a product standard for a private association that comprises market participants, that party enjoys no *Noerr* immunity from any antitrust liability flowing from the effect the standard has of its own force in the marketplace.

This conclusion does not deprive state and local governments of input and information from interested individuals or organizations or leave petitioner without ample means to petition those governments. . . . Petitioner, and others concerned about the safety or competitive threat of polyvinyl chloride conduit, can, with full antitrust immunity, engage in concerted efforts to influence those governments through direct lobbying, publicity campaigns, and other traditional avenues of political expression. To the extent state and local governments are more difficult to persuade through these other avenues, that no doubt reflects their preference for and confidence in the nonpartisan consensus process that petitioner has undermined. Petitioner remains free to take advantage of the forum provided by the standard-setting process by presenting and vigorously arguing accurate scientific evidence before a nonpartisan private standard-setting body. And petitioner can avoid the strictures of the private standard-setting process by attempting to influence legislatures through other forums. What petitioner may not do (without exposing itself to possible antitrust liability for direct injuries) is bias the process by, as in this case, stacking the private standard-setting body with decisionmakers sharing their economic interest in restraining competition. . . .

[Judgment affirmed.]

Economics and Antitrust

The basic policy underpinnings of antitrust, preserving competition and preventing monopoly, are rooted in history, experience, and economic theory. Any basic economics text will ably illustrate the evils of monopoly. These include, for example, restricted output at higher prices resulting in inefficient resource allocation, lack of incentive to improve or innovate, and concentration of economic power with attendant undue political influence.

Conversely, competition is said to result in efficient pricing and resource allocation, provide an incentive for innovation and efficiency, give purchasers a wider range of choice, improve quality, and result in diversification of economic power more consistent with a democratic society.

In recent years, economic analysis has assumed an increasingly larger role both in the development of substantive antitrust rules and in the resolution of individual cases. For example, many antitrust scholars argue that economic efficiency should be the exclusive goal of the antitrust laws. This approach, which guided government enforcement policy during the 1980s, has greatly influenced the development of many antitrust principles, such as the law governing vertical restraints of trade discussed in the next chapter. In addition, many antitrust cases, particularly those involving mergers or monopolization, require a determination of relevant market, market structure, and the effect of certain conduct on competition. In making these determinations, courts usually are guided, in part, by the testimony of witnesses expert in economics.

The importance of economics in antitrust should not, however, be overestimated. Economics is a theoretical social science. Conflicting theories and approaches abound. Antitrust is law. Like all areas of law, antitrust must be used to resolve specific, concrete disputes, requiring application of relevant legal rules to the facts of a particular case. The rules governing antitrust cases come not from economic theory, but from relevant statutes (the Sherman, Clayton, and Federal Trade Commission Acts) and federal (most notably Supreme Court) cases interpreting them. In short, whereas economic theory currently plays an increasingly important role in the *development* of antitrust rules, it is no substitute for a detailed study of relevant precedent. As one jurist succinctly stated: "Economics informs the law. . . . It is not the case that economics is the law."[29]

In addition, many antitrust theorists believe that efficient resource allocation and prevention of en-

29. Stephen B. Breyer, judge of the United States Court of Appeals for the First Circuit as quoted in T. Lewin, "Antitrust Ideas: 3 Problems," *The New York Times*, March 8, 1983, p. D2.

hanced prices are not the sole objects of antitrust policy. Antitrust law is grounded in a populist tradition. As noted by one commentator, the law recognizes various additional policy objectives of antitrust including for example, a preference for: (1) decentralization of economic power, (2) reduction of the range within which private choice may be exercised in matters materially affecting others, (3) enhancement of opportunity for independent entre-preneurship, and (4) small over large.[30] These factors are recurrent themes in antitrust legislation and judicial decisions. Antitrust policy also is affected by the prevailing political and social climate.

In sum, although economics provides a useful tool in formulating antitrust policy, it is for the courts and legislatures to balance economic and other goals of antitrust, and to develop a comprehensive body of law.

SUMMARY

1. Antitrust law is designed to promote and preserve competition in a free and open market, and to prevent the acquisition or maintenance of monopoly power. The law is based primarily upon three federal statutes: the Sherman Act, passed in 1890, and the Clayton Act and Federal Trade Commission Act, both enacted in 1914.

2. The Sherman Act contains only two substantive provisions. Section 1 declares contracts, combinations, and conspiracies in restraint of trade to be illegal. Section 2 proscribes monopolization, and attempts and conspiracies to monopolize.

3. The Clayton Act was designed to strengthen the basic Sherman Act prohibitions by bringing certain specific monopolistic or restrictive practices within the reach of the antitrust laws. It contains four basic substantive provisions: (1) §2, as amended in 1936 by the Robinson-Patman Act, prohibits certain types of price discrimination; (2) §3 prohibits certain sales made on condition that the buyer not deal with the seller's competitors; (3) §7 prohibits certain corporate mergers; (4) §8 prohibits a person from serving on the board of directors of two competing companies (an "interlocking directorate") if one or both companies are larger than a given size.

4. The Federal Trade Commission Act created the Federal Trade Commission and prohibits unfair methods of competition and unfair or deceptive trade practices.

5. Four basic remedies are available for antitrust violations: (1) criminal sanctions, (2) equitable proceedings by both government and private plaintiffs, (3) private actions for money damages, and (4) forfeiture.

6. The antitrust laws do not enjoy universal application. Wholly intrastate activity is outside the reach of federal antitrust law. In addition, certain anticompetitive conduct enjoys limited antitrust immunity. For example, certain combinations in restraint of trade, such as labor unions, agricultural cooperatives, and export associations, are exempt. Antitrust law also does not apply to certain industries regulated by state or federal administrative agencies. Finally, action taken by state governments or governmental entities and private conduct intended to influence government action may be beyond the reach of antitrust law.

KEY TERMS

Sherman Antitrust Act	Federal Trade
antitrust	Commission (FTC)
Clayton Act	consent decrees
Federal Trade	cease and desist order
Commission Act	

QUESTIONS AND PROBLEMS

50-1   Under the common law of contracts, discussed in Part II of the text, a promise is in restraint of trade if its performance would: (1) limit competition in any business, or (2) restrict the promisor in the exercise of any gainful occupation. A promise in restraint of trade is generally unenforceable as contrary to public policy unless it is both (1) reasonable, and (2) ancillary to an otherwise valid transaction or relationship. The railroad pools and trusts discussed above were certainly effective restraints of trade of the first type, limiting or eliminating competition in the industry involved. They were also patently unreasonable "naked" restraints with no purpose other than the suppression of competition. Why then was the common law of restraint of trade an ineffective method of antitrust enforcement necessitating enactment of major federal remedial legislation?

50-2   In what respect is antitrust law similar to constitutional law?

---

30. Sullivan, *The Law of Antitrust* 11 (1977).

50-3   What are the advantages and disadvantages of awarding treble damages to private plaintiffs injured through violation of the antitrust laws?

50-4   Union electrical workers in New York City exacted an agreement from local contractors to purchase electrical equipment only from local manufacturers who had closed-shop agreements with the union. The union also agreed with several local manufacturers to confine local sales to contractors employing union members. The combination between the union, contractors, and manufacturers was successful for all concerned. Electrical equipment manufactured outside New York was effectively excluded from the market. Prices of New York electrical equipment soared, to the great profit of local manufacturers and contractors. Wages went up, hours were shortened, and union employment multiplied. Is the union in this case immune from antitrust liability under the labor exemption?

50-5   Detroit Edison distributed "free" light bulbs to residential customers and recovered the cost as part of its charges for electricity. The light bulb arrangement was described in the utility's tariff that had been approved by the Michigan regulatory commission. By law, the tariff could not be changed without commission approval. The practice was challenged as an illegal tying arrangement (tying the sale of bulbs to electricity). Is the challenged tie immune from antitrust scrutiny as state action?

50-6   Hahn and Codding develop and operate shopping centers. Both Hahn and Codding submitted offers to develop a proposed shopping center in downtown Santa Rosa, California. In 1972, the Urban Renewal Agency (Agency) selected Hahn as the exclusive developer of the center. To finance purchase of the land for the project, the Agency decided to issue municipal bonds. Beginning in 1973, Codding filed a series of nine lawsuits challenging various aspects of the shopping center development and Codding financed four lawsuits filed by other parties. Although each of the lawsuits was dismissed, the development of the shopping center was delayed because the bonds could not be issued until all litigation had been resolved.

Hahn sued Codding alleging that he had violated §1 of the Sherman Act. Hahn asserted that by filing "a series of overlapping, repetitive and baseless lawsuits," Codding had conspired to eliminate potential competition from the new shopping center. The trial court held that Codding's involvement in the lawsuits was protected conduct under the *Noerr-Pennington* doctrine. Is the court correct? Explain.

Although the Sherman Act is almost a century old, it remains the primary tool of antitrust enforcement in the United States. The Sherman Act's two substantive provisions have been applied in hundreds of federal cases to proscribe a wide variety of anticompetitive conduct. This chapter examines the principles developed by the Supreme Court governing trade restraints and monopolization under §§1 and 2 of the Sherman Act.

Introduction to §1

Section 1 of the Sherman Act declares *contracts, combinations,* and *conspiracies* in restraint of trade

to be illegal. Section 1 therefore reaches concerted action by separate firms; it does not reach unilateral conduct. In §1 violations, the parties involved remain under separate ownership and control, but they combine or conspire together to obtain or exercise market power. Occasionally, proof of conspiracy is the pivotal issue in the case. The first part of this chapter explores the various types of loose-knit combinations that violate the Sherman Act. Unlike monopolization, which requires elaborate analysis of market structure, Section 1 violations are generally conduct oriented.

Development of the Legal Standard for §1 Violations

By its terms, §1 of the Sherman Act condemns "every" contract combination or conspiracy in restraint of trade. Early in Sherman Act history, however, it became apparent that such a literal interpretation was unworkable. In a sense, every contract restrains trade. For example, if Seller contracts to sell fifty bicycles to Buyer for $5,000, trade is thereby restrained because Buyer foregoes the opportunity to buy from other sellers and Seller surrenders the opportunity to sell to other buyers. In short, a literal interpretation of the Sherman Act condemns contract law generally, a result certainly not intended by the statute. Some standard therefore had to be established to separate those contracts or combinations that violate the statute from those that do not.

The Rule of Reason. In 1711, the common law of contracts adopted the standard of *reasonableness* in *Mitchel v. Reynolds,*[1] a standard it continues to apply in judging the enforceability of promises in restraint of trade. In the landmark case *Standard Oil Company v. United States,*[2] decided in 1911, Chief Justice White adopted a similar standard to judge Sherman Act violations. Under this **rule of reason** the Sherman Act does not condemn all restraints of trade, but only those restraints whose character or effect is unreasonably anticompetitive. In applying the rule of reason the court hears evidence concerning three basic issues: (1) what harm to competition results from the challenged restraint, (2) what is the purpose of the restraint, and is it legitimate and important, and (3) are there alternative means, less restrictive to competition, to achieve the same result? For most Sherman Act cases, the rule of reason continues to be the standard by which violations of the Act are judged.[3]

Note that the standard dictated by the Sherman Act is *competition.* As the following case indicates, courts will not balance the anticompetitive effect of the restraint against social goals other than the maintenance of competition.

National Society of Professional Engineers v. United States
98 S. Ct. 1355 (1978)

The National Society of Professional Engineers (Society) was organized to govern the nontechnical aspects of engineering practice, including promotion of professional, social, and economic interests of its members. Its canon of ethics prohibited engineers

---

1. 1 P. Wms. 181, 24 Eng. Rep. 347 (Ch. 1711). See Chapter 10.

2. 31 S. Ct. 502 (1911).

3. By announcing the rule of reason in the *Standard Oil* case, the Supreme Court pleased neither antitrust reformers nor business interests. The reformers thought the rule rendered the Act vague and general and delegated too much power in antitrust policy to the judicial branch. Business complained that the rule provided no specific guidelines, making it difficult to predict the legality of any proposed business conduct. This dissatisfaction was a major reason for passage of the Clayton Act and Federal Trade Commission Act in 1914.

from discussing the fee to be charged until after the client had selected the engineer for a particular project. The United States filed a civil antitrust action against the Society, alleging that the canon prohibiting submission of competitive bids for engineering services suppressed price competition and deprived customers of the benefits of free and open competition in violation of §1 of the Sherman Act. The Society defended on grounds that awarding engineering services to the lowest bidder would produce inferior engineering work, endangering the public safety. For this reason, it argued that the canons were not an unreasonable restraint of trade in violation of the Sherman Act. The District Court granted an injunction against the canon and the Court of Appeals affirmed. Both courts found the canon unlawful on its face and therefore illegal without regard to claimed or possible benefits. The Supreme Court granted certiorari.

Justice Stevens

. . . This is a civil antitrust case brought by the United States to nullify an association's canon of ethics prohibiting competitive bidding by its members. The question is whether the canon may be justified under the Sherman Act . . ., because it was adopted by members of a learned profession for the purpose of minimizing the risk that competition would produce inferior engineering work endangering the public safety. . . .

To evaluate this argument it is necessary to identify the contours of the Rule of Reason and to discuss its application to the kind of justification asserted by petitioner. . . .

The test prescribed in *Standard Oil* is whether the challenged tracts or acts "were unreasonably restrictive of competitive conditions." Unreasonableness under that test could be based either (1) on the nature or character of the contracts, or (2) on surrounding circumstances giving rise to the inference or presumption that they were intended to restrain trade and enhance prices. Under either branch of the test, the inquiry is confined to a consideration of impact on competitive conditions. . . .

[T]he purpose of the analysis is to form a judgment about the competitive significance of the restraint; it is not to decide whether a policy favoring competition is in the public interest, or in the interest of the members of an industry. Subject to exceptions defined by statute, that policy decision has been made by the Congress. . . .

Price is the "central nervous system of the economy," *United States v. Socony-Vacuum Oil Co.,* [60 S. Ct. 811, 845 (1940)], and an agreement that "interfere[s] with the setting of price by free market forces" is illegal on its face. . . . In this case we are presented with an agreement among competitors to refuse to discuss prices with potential customers until after negotiations have resulted in the initial selection of an engineer. While this is not price fixing as such, no elaborate industry analysis is required to demonstrate the anticompetitive character of such an agreement. It operates as an absolute ban on competitive bidding, applying with equal force to both complicated and simple projects and to both inexperienced and sophisticated customers. . . .

The Sherman Act does not require competitive bidding; it prohibits unreasonable restraints on competition. Petitioner's ban on competitive bidding prevents all customers from making price comparisons in the initial selection of an engineer, and imposes the Society's views of the costs and benefits of competition on the entire marketplace. It is this restraint that must be justified under the Rule of Reason, and petitioner's attempt to do so on the basis of the potential threat that competition poses to the public safety and the ethics of its profession is nothing less than a frontal assault on the basic policy of the Sherman Act.

The Sherman Act reflects a legislative judgment that ultimately competition will produce not only lower prices, but also better goods and services. . . . The assumption that competition is the best method of allocating resources in a free market recognizes that all elements of a bargain—quality, service, safety, and durability—and not just the immediate cost, are favorably affected by the free opportunity to select among alternative offers. Even assuming occasional exceptions to the presumed consequences of competition, the statutory policy precludes inquiry into the question whether competition is good or bad. . . .

[B]y their nature, professional services may differ significantly from other business services, and, accordingly, the nature of the competition in such services may vary. Ethical norms may serve to regulate and promote this competition, and thus fall within the Rule of Reason. But the Society's argument in this case is a far cry from such a position. We are faced with a contention that a total ban on competitive bidding is necessary because otherwise engineers will be tempted to submit deceptively low bids. Certainly, the problem of professional deception is a proper subject of an ethical canon. But, once again, the equation of competition with deception, like the similar equation with safety hazards, is simply too broad; we may assume that competition is not entirely conducive to ethical behavior, but that is not a reason, cognizable under the Sherman Act, for doing away with competition.

In sum, the Rule of Reason does not support a defense based on the assumption that competition itself is unreasonable. . . .

[Judgment affirmed.]

Although *reasonableness* remains the sole standard governing Sherman Act violations, courts use two approaches to determine reasonableness. In most cases, the rule of reason allows the defendant to introduce evidence of the reasonableness of the restraint to avoid a violation. The Supreme Court has, however, declared that certain specific practices or business relationships are so inherently destructive of competition that they are unreasonable **per se**; that is, "conclusively presumed to be unreasonable and therefore illegal without elaborate inquiry as to the precise harm they have caused or the business excuse for their use."[4] Per se illegality has been imposed, on a case by case basis, on a variety of conduct including price fixing, division of markets, group boycotts, and tying arrrangements.

The defendant is not permitted to justify conduct in the per se category because the Court has already determined, through considerable experience with the practice or device, that it has no purpose other than to destroy or stifle competition. Per se rules simplify enforcement of the Act, and reduce the length of litigation because the plaintiff is not re-

---

4. *Northern Pacific Railway Company v. United States,* 78 S. Ct. 514, 518 (1958).

quired to refute the defendant's justification. Per se rules also provide greater predictability and therefore greater deterrence against conduct the law finds particularly offensive. When studying the various §1 issues outlined below, note whether the business practice in question is governed by the rule of reason or has been branded a per se violation.

Types of Trade Restraints

In analyzing §1 cases, one must initially characterize the nature of the restraint. Restraints of trade are of two types: "horizontal" and "vertical." A **horizontal restraint** is an agreement among competitors; persons at the same functional level. For example, an agreement among competing manufacturers to fix prices of commodities they sell imposes a horizontal restraint. A similar agreement among wholesalers or among retailers also is horizontal. In contrast, a **vertical restraint** is an agreement between persons standing in a buyer-seller or supplier-supplied relationship. For example, assume a manufacturer sells loudspeakers to a retailer on condition that the retailer resell the speakers to its customers only at prices set by the manufacturer. Such a "resale price maintenance" arrangement imposes a vertical restraint.

Horizontal and vertical restraints tested under §1 are discussed below. Horizontal restraints covered include price fixing, division of markets, concerted refusals to deal (group boycotts), and exchange of market information. Vertical restraints discussed include resale price maintenance; location, territory, and customer restrictions; and tying and exclusive dealing contracts.

Horizontal Restraints

Introduction to Cartels

Agreements among competitors to restrain trade are a major concern under §1, reaching full blown **cartels** (agreements among competitors to restrict output and raise prices) as well as other types of concerted conduct having some cartel effects.

The anticompetitive impact of cartels can readily be illustrated. Microeconomic theory teaches that the monopolist will maximize its return at a lower output and therefore a higher price than would prevail in a competitive industry. This restricted output and higher price is antitrust law's basic concern. Monopoly effects may, however, be achieved without a monopolist if firms in an industry who would otherwise compete instead agree to cooperate on matters of price and output. This is the classic cartel, through which the parties, acting collectively rather than independently, reduce output and reap and share the extraordinary profit characteristic of a monopolist. Section 1 of the Sherman Act is the primary legal tool used to attack such combinations.

Despite their promise of shared monopoly profit, cartels do not pervade American industry for various reasons. Initially, a cartel is plagued by problems of administration. The parties must devise some mechanism to restrict and divide output or fix prices among participating firms, and to police the arrangement to assure compliance. This mechanism must be sophisticated because the decisions involved are complex. For example, an agreement on optimum price and output is difficult, because the profit-maximizing price for the industry as a whole will be too high for some firms and too low for others.[5] The cartel also must be geared to operate in secret because the entire arrangement is, of course, illegal. These administrative difficulties commonly preclude cartelization if the number of firms in the industry is large, but may be overcome if the market structure is oligopolistic, in which a few large firms dominate the industry.

Once a cartel is in operation and a price is successfully set, cartel members have a strong incentive to cheat. Because the cartel price is higher than that prevailing under competitive conditions, each cartel member could lower its price and still make a profit. Thus, as long as other firms can be relied upon to honor the cartel price, and undercutting that price can be done without alerting them, a firm can substantially increase sales and profits by cheating. This is the ideal situation for a cartel member: competing while the others do not. Once

---

5. This assumes that the conspirators actually know what output will maximize profit in the short run, an amount that is difficult if not impossible to determine accurately.

discovered, cheating causes the cartel to break down.

Despite these problems, cartels do exist and their operation, even for a limited period, exacts a great social and economic cost. The following material discusses various types of horizontal arrangements, from classic cartels involving blatant price fixing or market division to more subtle devices used to control or affect output or price.

Price Fixing

Price fixing is the cooperative setting of price levels or ranges by competing firms.[6] In its various forms, price fixing is the most onerous conduct reached by the antitrust laws, and has been treated accordingly by the courts.

The classic case outlining the judicial approach to price fixing is *United States v. Socony-Vacuum Oil Co.,*[7] decided in 1940. In this case, a group of major oil-refining companies were indicted and convicted for conspiring to raise prices of gasoline sold in the midwestern area. Through a concerted program of bidding for and buying gasoline and then storing it when necessary, the defendants were able to affect the quantity and therefore the price of gasoline sold in the market. The case reached the Supreme Court, and the opinion, rendered by Justice Douglas, remains the definitive statement regarding the application of the Sherman Act to price fixing.

The Court initially reaffirmed that the standard dictated by the Sherman Act is *competition,* and upheld the defendants' conviction concluding that:

> [u]nder the Sherman Act a combination formed for the purpose and with the effect of raising, depressing, fixing, pegging, or stabilizing the price of a commodity in interstate or foreign commerce is illegal per se.[8]

Socony-Vacuum was the first case to use the now familiar "per se" language to characterize certain §1 violations.

In addition to announcing a per se rule for horizontal price fixing, the court indicated that the definition of price fixing is expansive: any agreement between competitors that affects or is intended to affect price, however accomplished, is price fixing. As noted by the court:

> [P]rices are fixed . . . if the range within which purchases or sales will be made is agreed upon, if the prices paid or charged are to be at a certain level or on ascending or descending scales, if they are to be uniform, or if by various formulae they are related to market prices. They are fixed because they are *agreed upon.*[9]

Applying this test to the facts, the Court labeled the concerted buying program of the oil companies price fixing, because its effect was to establish a floor price in the spot market, effectively manipulating that market, and resulting in higher prices than would otherwise have prevailed.

Under the test announced by the Court, a wide variety of business conduct constitutes price fixing. Agreements to pay or charge a fixed price or a minimum or maximum price, to confine prices within a given range, or to tie price to some external standard all are per se illegal. Similarly, fixing trade-in allowances, mark-ups, discounts, or the spread between premium and nonpremium products is illegal. These arrangements might be termed direct price fixing. As *Socony-Vacuum* indicates, however, indirect arrangements affecting price are equally suspect. For example, the defendants in that case manipulated price by reducing supply (by purchasing and storing gasoline). A similar agreement among buyers to limit purchases, thereby driving price down, or by sellers to limit output, driving prices up, is per se illegal. Another form of price fixing is "bid rigging," which is common in the construction industry. Government contracts usually are awarded by competitive bidding. Contractors can manipulate the bidding process by collusively submitting bids higher than would exist under competitive conditions, frequently taking turns submitting the "low" bid. In this case, the conspirators fix prices by concertedly tampering with the *offers* they make. In short, any agreement between competitors that has or may have an effect

---

6. Black, *Law Dictionary* (5th ed. 1979).
7. 60 S. Ct. 811 (1940).
8. *Id.* at 844.

9. *Id.* (Emphasis added).

on the price the competitors charge or offer is suspect under the Sherman Act, including agreements that merely affect a part of the price (for example, agreements fixing discounts or credit terms) and those that alter the mechanisms by which price is determined (for example, agreements restricting output).

In addition to accepting an expansive definition of price fixing, *Socony-Vacuum* stated in its now celebrated footnote 59 that the power to fix prices is not necessary to establish an illegal conspiracy under §1. The plaintiff need prove only an act of conspiring, not that the conspirators had the means available to accomplish their objective.

Socony-Vacuum and other cases also address the applicability of two defenses commonly raised by persons charged with illegal price fixing: (1) that price fixing was necessary to prevent ruinous or cut-throat competition destructive of the industry, and (2) that in any event the prices fixed were reasonable. Regarding the first defense, early §1 cases clearly establish that competition is the standard mandated by the Sherman Act. Conduct that destroys competition is prohibited, even if in the opinion of the defendants or others some other arrangement (for example, a cartel) would be more beneficial to the industry or the public. The reasonable price defense has suffered a similar fate. Price, under competition, is determined by market and cost conditions. Therefore, a reasonable price is one determined in response to those conditions, which are ever changing. Thus, any price set by collusive behavior manipulates and distorts normal price-setting mechanisms and is inherently unreasonable.

Horizontal Market Division

Agreements among competitors to divide the market in which they would otherwise compete inherently destroy competition. Market division schemes come in many forms. Competing firms may agree to divide a market geographically by allocating a specific territory to each firm. For example, Anson and Barber, competing manufacturers, may agree to divide the country in half, with Anson selling in the East and Barber selling only in the West. Or, firms may divide a market by customers. For example, Anson may agree to sell only to wholesalers, and Barber to retailers. Or, the conspirators

may divide a product market. For example, if Anson and Barber manufacture products X and Y, Anson may agree to sell only X in the future and Barber only Y.

The problem of any market division is that the firms involved agree not to compete with one another in the divided market. By removing competitors or potential competitors from the market, supply is reduced and price is raised. Further, if no independent firms (that is, those not a party to the conspiracy) compete, the division may award its members a monopoly of their respective shares. For these reasons, courts have long condemned horizontal market division, regardless of form, as inherently anticompetitive.

In *United States v. Topco Associates, Inc.,*[10] decided in 1972, the Supreme Court announced explicitly what had been implicit in a host of earlier decisions: horizontal market division is a per se violation of §1. In the words of the Court:

> It is only after considerable experience with certain business relationships that courts classify them as *per se* violations of the Sherman Act. . . . One of the classic examples of *per se* violation of §1 is an agreement between competitors at the same level of the market structure to allocate territories in order to minimize competition. . . . This Court has reiterated time and time again that horizontal territorial limitations are naked restraints of trade with no purpose except stifling of competition. . . . Such limitations are *per se* violations of the Sherman Act.[11]

The Court went on to hold that horizontal market division is per se illegal whether or not accompanied by other antitrust violations.[12]

Group Boycotts—Concerted Refusals to Deal

Purpose and Effect of Boycotts. A **group boycott**, or **concerted refusal to deal**, is a horizontal combination intended to *eliminate* (or prevent the entry of) a competitor of the parties to the combi-

---

10. 92 S. Ct. 1126 (1972).
11. *Id.* at 1133–1134.
12. *Id.* at 1134 n. 9.

nation. Group boycotts usually span more than one functional level (that is, manufacturer, wholesaler, retailer). In the classic case, a group of competitors at one level desire, for whatever reason, to eliminate a competitor at their level. For example, assume Adams, Bowman, Cox, and Davis are wholesalers. Davis is troublesome to the others because she engages in rigorous price competition, which Adams, Bowman, and Cox wish to avoid. To eliminate Davis from the market, the other three approach Martin, a major supplier of all four wholesalers and indicate that they will refuse to buy from Martin unless he stops selling to Davis. If Martin fears the loss of the conspirators' business he may be persuaded to go along and cease selling to Davis. If this happens, Davis is cut off from a trade relationship she needs to compete effectively and the conspirators may achieve their intended result. Note that this case, like virtually all boycotts, involves an element of coercion to achieve cooperation.

Although boycotts usually involve two functional levels and some concerted refusal to deal, neither is absolutely required to achieve the anticompetitive result of a boycott. For example, assume Adams, Bowman, Cox, and Davis are all brokers. To be effective, a broker requires the cooperation of fellow brokers. Adams, Bowman, and Cox could effectively eliminate Davis by refusing to deal with him. In this case the concerted refusal to deal is aimed at the intended victim, Davis (rather than against a person above or below the victim in the distribution chain) and includes only one functional level. Or, assume Adams, Bowman, and Cox, retailers, persuade Martin, a manufacturer, not to deal with their competitor, Davis, by circulating false rumors concerning her financial position. The three have not refused to deal with anyone, and Martin's refusal to sell to Davis is unilateral, not concerted. Nevertheless, the effect is the same: elimination of a competitor of the conspirators.

Thus, neither "concerted refusal to deal" nor "boycott" fully describes the conduct subject to antitrust scrutiny in this context. The law merely requires that, regardless of the means used, a group of competitors concertedly act to deprive an actual or potential competitor of suppliers, customers, or other essential trade relationships needed to compete with those conspiring.

Legal Test Governing Group Boycotts. Classic group boycotts have been declared in a number of Supreme Court cases to be per se violations of §1 of the Sherman Act. These arrangements clearly injure competition and exhibit no countervailing procompetitive effects. Nevertheless, not all concerted activity that excludes a competitor is per se illegal. Many exclusionary devices have purposes not solely related to the self-interest of the challenged combination and are tested under a less harsh rule of reason standard. For example, industry self-regulation plans designed to prevent fraud or establish safety standards frequently have boycott effects, yet are not categorically declared illegal. Such plans are nevertheless subject to close antitrust scrutiny.

In the following case the court was required to determine whether a per se or rule-of-reason approach should be applied to a challenged business practice.

Northwest Wholesale Stationers, Inc. v. Pacific Stationery and Printing Co.
105 S. Ct. 2613 (1985)

Northwest Wholesale Stationers (Northwest) is a purchasing cooperative composed of approximately 100 office supply retailers in the Pacific Northwest. It acts as primary wholesaler for the member retailers. Although nonmember retailers may purchase wholesale supplies at the same price as members, Northwest distributes its profits to members at the end of each year in the form of a percentage rebate on purchases. Accordingly, members effectively purchase supplies at a price significantly lower than nonmembers.

Pacific Stationery, Inc. (Pacific), which became a member of Northwest in 1958, sells office supplies at both retail and wholesale. In 1974, Northwest amended its bylaws to prohibit wholesale activities by its members, but explicitly excluded Pacific from the prohibition. In 1977, a controlling stock interest in Pacific was sold, but the new owners did not notify Northwest as required by its bylaws. In 1978, the membership of Northwest voted to expel Pacific.

Pacific sued Northwest in federal court alleging a violation of §1 of the Sherman Act. Pacific alleged that its expulsion resulted from Pacific's decision to maintain a wholesale operation, and was a group boycott limiting its ability to compete. Northwest contended that the expulsion resulted from Pacific's failure to notify cooperative members of the change in stock ownership.

The district court rejected application of a per se rule to the challenged conduct and held instead that rule of reason analysis should govern the case. Finding no anticompetitive effect, the court granted summary judgment for Northwest. The court of appeals reversed holding that the facts supported a finding of per se liability. The Supreme Court granted certiorari.

Justice Brennan

. . . This case requires that we decide . . . when *per se* antitrust analysis is appropriately applied to joint activity that is susceptible of being characterized as a concerted refusal to deal. . . .

This Court has long held that certain concerted refusals to deal or group boycotts are so likely to restrict competition without any offsetting efficiency gains that they should be condemned as *per se* violations of §1 of the Sherman Act. . . .

This case therefore turns . . . on whether the decision to expel Pacific is properly viewed as a group boycott or concerted refusal to deal mandating *per se* invalidation. . . .

Cases to which this Court has applied the *per se* approach have generally involved joint efforts by a firm or firms to disadvantage competitors by "either directly denying or persuading or coercing suppliers or customers to deny relationships the competitors need in the competitive struggle." [Sullivan, *Law of Antitrust* 261-262 (1977).] . . . In these cases, the boycott often cut off access to a supply, facility, or market necessary to enable the boycotted firm to compete . . . and frequently the boycotting firms possessed a dominant position in the relevant market. . . . In addition, the practices were generally not justified by plausible arguments that they were intended to enhance overall efficiency and make markets more competitive. Under such circumstances the likelihood of anticompetitive effects is clear and the possibility of countervailing procompetitive effects is remote.

Although a concerted refusal to deal need not necessarily possess all of these traits to merit *per se* treatment, not every cooperative activity involving a restraint or exclusion will share with the *per se* forbidden boycotts the likelihood of predominantly anticompetitive consequences. . . .

Wholesale purchasing cooperatives such as Northwest are not a form of concerted activity characteristically likely to result in predominantly anticompetitive effects. Rather, such cooperative arrangements would seem to be "designed to increase economic efficiency and render markets more, rather than less, competitive." [*Broadcast Music, Inc. v. Columbia Broadcasting System, Inc.*, 99 S. Ct. 1551, 1562 (1979).] The arrangement permits the participating retailers to achieve economies of scale in both the purchase and warehousing of wholesale supplies, and also ensures ready access to a stock of goods that might otherwise be unavailable on short notice. The cost savings and order-filling guarantees enable smaller retailers to reduce prices and maintain their retail stock so as to compete more effectively with larger retailers.

Pacific, of course, does not object to the existence of the cooperative arrangement, but rather raises an antitrust challenge to Northwest's decision to bar Pacific from continued membership. It is therefore the action of expulsion that must be evaluated to determine whether *per se* treatment is appropriate. The act of expulsion from a wholesale cooperative does not necessarily imply anticompetitive animus and thereby raise a probability of anticompetitive effect. . . . Wholesale purchasing cooperatives must establish and enforce reasonable rules in order to function effectively. Disclosure rules, such as the one on which Northwest relies, may well provide the cooperative with a needed means for monitoring the creditworthiness of its members. Nor would the expulsion characteristically be likely to result in predominantly anticompetitive effects, at least in the type of situation this case presents. Unless the cooperative possesses market power or exclusive access to an element essential to effective competition, the conclusion that expulsion is virtually always likely to have an anticompetitive effect is not warranted. . . . Absent such a showing with respect to a cooperative buying arrangement, courts should apply a rule-of-reason analysis. At no time has Pacific made a threshold showing that these structural characteristics are present in this case. . . .

The District Court appears to have followed the correct path of analysis—recognizing that not all concerted refusals to deal should be accorded *per se* treatment and deciding this one should not. . . . [I]n our judgment the District Court's rejection of *per se* analysis in this case was correct. A plaintiff seeking application of the *per se* rule must present a threshold case that the challenged activity falls into a category likely to have predominantly anticompetitive effects. The mere allegation of a concerted refusal to deal does not suffice because not all concerted refusals to deal are predominantly anticompetitive. When the plaintiff challenges expulsion from a joint buying cooperative, some showing must be made that the cooperative possesses market power or unique access to a business element necessary for effective competition. . . .

[Judgment reversed and remanded.]

Exchange of Market Information

Trade Associations Generally. In the United States, literally thousands of trade associations operate at the local, state, and national levels. Although individual characteristics vary somewhat, they are generally nonprofit organizations in which membership is voluntary and whose members are business entities engaged in a single line of commercial endeavor. There are trade associations of petroleum refiners, lawn mower manufacturers, retail druggists, restaurateurs, insurance agents, automobile dealers, potato chip and snack food manufacturers, hairdressers, home builders, and so on. Perhaps no industry or industrial subgroup, organized by functional level (for example, manufacturers, wholesalers, retailers) or geographic area (for example, local, state, regional, or national) is without its trade association. There are even associations of associations, known as "federations."

Trade associations generally perform functions that individual businesses are incapable of performing on their own including (1) collection and dissemination of statistical information, including prices, and production and distribution costs, both from the industry and outside it, (2) publishing bulletins and magazines, and sponsoring conventions and other meetings of various types, (3) effecting product standardization programs, (4) inspecting,

grading, or certifying individual member's products to assure quality, (5) conducting industrial, labor, and market research programs, and (6) conducting public relations and sales promotion campaigns.

Although many of these activities appear consistent with antitrust's goal of maintaining competition, trade association activities always deserve close antitrust scrutiny because, by definition, a trade association is a horizontal combination of competitors. The association therefore provides the opportunity to engage in collusive or interdependent conduct in restraint of trade. Indeed, trade associations have been used in a number of cases to implement and police express, patently unlawful activities, such as price fixing, market division, and group boycotts. Although such aggravated conduct is subject to per se treatment, the legality of most trade association activity is tested under the rule of reason.

Legal Standard Governing Data Dissemination. Local, regional, and national trade associations often disseminate information about prices, production and other industry statistics. Although rapid and wide dissemination of price information is essential to a competitive market, the competitive effect of such programs varies greatly depending upon the kind of information distributed and the structure of the industry. For example, if the data submitted is very explicit and detailed, outlining specific prices charged to specific customers, the program may be used as a policing device for a price fixing or market division conspiracy. If an industry is oligopolistic, price information exchanges may facilitate a program of collusion or price leadership (in which all firms follow prices set by the industry leader). In contrast, in an industry involving a large number of small firms, widely distributed price information may stimulate competition. Because the effect of exchange of price information differs, each program is tested under the rule of reason to determine its impact on competition.

Under the approach taken by the early cases, the purpose and effect of the information exchange was analyzed by examining the details of the individual plan. Provided certain types of information were not exchanged (such as future estimates of price or production or specific information on individual transactions), the plan was legal. More recent cases, most notably the following, have recognized the importance of industry structure in analyzing market information plans.

United States v. Container Corporation of America

89 S. Ct. 510 (1969)

> A group of manufacturers that accounted for ninety percent of the total production of corrugated cardboard containers in the southeastern United States instituted a plan whereby, on an irregular basis, each participant in the plan would supply on demand the most recent price it quoted or charged. The United States instituted a civil antitrust action alleging that the arrangement was a price-fixing agreement in violation of §1 of the Sherman Act. The district court dismissed the complaint and the government appealed to the Supreme Court.

Justice Douglas

. . . The case as proved is unlike any of other price decisions we have rendered. There was here an exchange of price information but no agreement to adhere to a price schedule. . . . There was here an exchange of information concerning specific sales to identified customers, not a statistical report on the average cost to all members, without identifying the parties to specific transactions. . . .

Here all that was present was a request by each defendant of its competitor for information as to the most recent price charged or quoted, whenever it needed such information and whenever it was not available from another source. Each defendant on receiving that request usually furnished the data with the expectation that it would be furnished reciprocal information when it wanted it. That concerted action is of course sufficient to establish the combination or conspiracy, the initial ingredient of a violation of §1 of the Sherman Act. . . .

There was to be sure an infrequency and irregularity of price exchanges between the defendants; and often the data were available from the records of the defendants or from the customers themselves. Yet the essence of the agreement was to furnish price information whenever requested.

Moreover, although the most recent price charged or quoted was sometimes fragmentary, each defendant had the manuals with which it could compute the price charged by a competitor on a specific order to a specific customer. . . .

The defendants account for about 90% of the shipment of corrugated containers from plants in the Southeastern United States. While containers vary as to dimensions, weight, color, and so on, they are substantially identical, no matter who produces them, when made to particular specifications. The prices paid depend on price alternatives. Suppliers when seeking new or additional business or keeping old customers, do not exceed a competitor's price. It is common for purchasers to buy from two or more suppliers concurrently. A defendant supplying a customer with containers would usually quote the same price on additional orders, unless costs had changed. Yet where a competitor was charging a particular price, a defendant would normally quote the same price or even a lower price.

The exchange of price information seemed to have the effect of keeping prices within a fairly narrow ambit. Capacity has exceeded the demand from 1955 to 1963, the period covered by the complaint, and the trend of corrugated container prices has been downward. Yet despite this excess capacity and the downward trend of prices, the industry has expanded in the Southeast from 30 manufacturers with 49 plants to 51 manufacturers with 98 plants. An abundance of raw materials and machinery makes entry into the industry easy with an investment of $50,000 to $75,000.

The result of this reciprocal exchange of prices was to stabilize prices though at a downward level. Knowledge of a competitor's price usually meant matching that price. The continuation of some price competition is not fatal to the Government's case. The limitation or reduction of price competition brings the case within the ban, for as we held in *United States v. Socony-Vacuum Oil Co.,* [60 S. Ct. 811, 844 (1940)], interference with the setting of price by free market forces is unlawful *per se*. Price information exchanged in some markets may have no effect on a truly competitive price. But the corrugated container industry is dominated by relatively few sellers. The produce is fungible and the competition for sales is price. The demand is inelastic, as buyers place orders only for immediate, short-run needs. The exchange of price data tends toward price uniformity. For a lower price does not mean a larger share of the available business but a sharing of the existing business at a lower return. Stabilizing prices as well as raising them is within the ban of §1 of the Sherman Act. . . . The inferences are irresistible that the exchange of price information has had an anticompetitive effect in the industry, chilling the vigor of price competition. . . .

Price is too critical, too sensitive a control to allow it to be used even in an informal manner to restrain competition.

[Judgment reversed.]

Container Corporation represents a refinement in the judicial approach to exchange of market information by competitors. In this case, the court examined both the conduct involved (exchange of price information upon request) and the structure of the industry (including number and size of firms, ease of entry, elasticity of demand, nature of competition) to determine the effect of the price exchange on competition. Although the court's structural analysis in this case is subject to criticism,[13] the approach is consistent with that developed in monopoly and merger cases, and supplies a common thread for application of the rule of reason in all cases; that is, reasonableness is determined by examining the challenged conduct in the context of the particular industry structure.

Proof of Conspiracy

To establish a §1 violation, the antitrust plaintiff must prove the existence of "contract, combination, or conspiracy." That is, persons acting independently may legally act in ways that would be illegal if performed by two or more persons in con-

cert. An express agreement effected through oral or written language of the parties is not required to establish a horizontal conspiracy. Joint action must simply be contemplated and undertaken. In fact, the Supreme Court has repeatedly stated that the act of conspiring alone is sufficient to violate §1. Because most combinations, express or implied, are effectuated through covert action, evidence of joint action frequently must be inferred from the surrounding circumstances, including correspondence, meetings, or other communication.

The first case addressing the problem of proving conspiracy absent direct evidence of concerted activity is *Interstate Circuit, Inc. v. United States* (1939).[14] In this case, the court stated that:

> It is elementary that an unlawful conspiracy may be and often is formed without simultaneous action or agreement on the part of the conspirators. . . . Acceptance by competitors, without previous agreement, of an invitation to participate in a plan, the necessary consequence of which, if carried out, is restraint of interstate commerce, is sufficient to establish an unlawful conspiracy under the Sherman Act.[15]

Interstate Circuit and cases following it establish the **conscious parallelism** doctrine, under which conspiracy may be proven by evidence that two or more firms acted in the same way with knowledge of the other's actions. Uniformity of action *alone* is, however, insufficient to prove conspiracy. Uniformity *plus* some other factor or group of factors pointing toward collusive conduct is required. These "plus factors"[16] take many forms including a proposal for joint action; a complex yet uniform set of responses; failure to deny the conspiracy; direct communication, or the opportunity for direct communication, through meetings, correspondence, telephone calls; and circumstances alerting each participant that joint action will be beneficial only if all others participate.[17]

---

13. For example, although market structure was somewhat oligopolistic, entry was easy and there was little showing that individual firms possessed market power. Existing over capacity would seem to preclude exacting monopoly profits. Further, meeting a competitor's price after learning it might be deemed a competitive rather than collusive response.

---

14. 59 S. Ct. 467 (1939).

15. *Id.* at 474.

16. This term was initially used in *C-O Two Fire Equipment Co. v. United States,* 197 F.2d 489, 497 (9th Cir. 1952).

17. Sullivan, *The Law of Antitrust* 317 (1977).

Vertical Restraints

Vertical trade restraints exist between parties standing in a buyer-seller or customer-supplier relation. In other words, whereas horizontal combinations exist among parties at one function level, vertical combinations include parties at two or more levels. Unlike horizontal restraints, which usually are informal aggregations, vertical restraints usually are imposed by express contract between the parties. This agreement supplies the "contract, combination, or conspiracy" necessary to establish jurisdiction under §1 of the Sherman Act.

Although firms at different functional levels are not in competition, vertically imposed restraints do significantly affect competition in the markets occupied by the parties to the restraint. Many vertical restraints are imposed in the chain of a product's distribution, as for example, a contractual restriction imposed by a manufacturer upon a retailer dictating the price at which the retailer resells or dictating where or to whom he may sell. Such "distributional" restraints compose the first two sections of the following material. Following the treatment of distributional restraints, tying and other exclusive dealing contracts are discussed.

Resale Price Maintenance (Vertical Price Fixing)

Per Se Illegality of Vertical Price Restrictions. Few rules of antitrust law are as long standing as that governing an agreement between a seller and a buyer fixing the price at which the buyer may resell the goods purchased. Simply stated, such a **resale price maintenance** contract constitutes a per se violation of §1 of the Sherman Act. For example, assume M, a manufacturer sells a television to R, a retailer, for $250. As part of the contract, R agrees that he will not resell the set to a retail customer for less than $500. The contract constitutes a per se §1 violation. Since the landmark case, *Dr. Miles Medical Company v. John D. Park & Sons Company,*[18] decided in 1911, courts have held that resale price maintenance is both an unreasonable restraint on a buyer's right to transfer the item sold, and unreasonably forecloses price competition among traders competing in reselling the restricted article. Further, the seller has no legitimate countervailing interest to justify such a restraint.

Motives for Resale Price Maintenance. In resale price maintenance, a manufacturer commonly fixes its retailers' resale price at a level higher than would prevail under competitive conditions. Because the quantity demanded falls as price rises, resale price maintenance generally results in fewer sales by manufacturers to retailers than would be made had the retailers competed. Ordinarily, however, a manufacturer maximizes profits by selling to retailers at a price satisfactory to itself and then stimulating competition at the retail level. Competition among retailers reduces the price to consumers, and increases the number of units sold. Competition also reduces dealer profits, thereby minimizing the cost to the manufacturer of having the retail function performed. Why, then, would a manufacturer want to contractually fix its dealers' resale prices at a level that may reduce the number of units sold and increase dealer profits?

One purpose of resale price maintenance is to facilitate or disguise a cartel among retailers. Pressure to impose resale price restrictions usually comes from *retailers,* not manufacturers. Retailer cartelization through resale price maintenance is possible if the manufacturer sells a branded or differentiated product and retailers are sufficiently powerful to induce the manufacturer to "impose" resale price restrictions at prices exceeding those prevailing under competitive conditions.

Even without a push from below, a substantial number of manufacturers have, over the years, formulated and maintained complicated resale price maintenance plans because of perceived benefits to the manufacturer. For example, the Supreme Court has noted that when total consumer demand

> is affected less by price than by the number of retail outlets for the product, the availability of dealer services, or the impact of advertising and promotion, it will be in the interest of manufacturers to squelch price competition through a scheme of resale price maintenance in order to concentrate on nonprice competition.[19]

---

18. 31 S. Ct. 376 (1911).

19. *Albrecht v. The Herald Company,* 88 S. Ct. 869, 872 n.7 (1968).

Manufacturers also sometimes assert that fixing resale prices allows them to achieve more efficient distribution of their products. For example, resale price maintenance is sometimes justified on grounds that (1) it provides a larger profit margin for retailers, inducing them to carry the product, to promote it effectively, and to provide necessary ancillary services, (2) it prevents a larger dealer from using the product as a "loss leader," selling it below cost to the detriment of other dealers, (3) it cultivates a "prestige" image accompanying a high price, and (4) the manufacturer is better able than retailers to determine the optimum price at which its products should be sold.

These and other distributional justifications are open to criticism, either on theoretical grounds, or because the same result can be achieved in less anticompetitive ways. For example, competing independent retailers, each acting in response to changing costs and market conditions, should be better able to identify the optimum price that a manufacturer who is removed from the retail market. Further, little evidence exists that loss-leader tactics either are prevalent or have any significant effect. Additionally, a high resale price can be maintained by charging an appropriately high price to retailers. Promotion can be done directly by the manufacturer, or a high wholesale price may be coupled with an allowance to dealers who provide promotional services, or the manufacturer can require promotional expenditures as a condition of sale.

Attempts to Circumvent the Prohibition Against Resale Price Maintenance.

Despite long-standing judicial hostility, both buyers and sellers frequently have sought to legalize resale price maintenance schemes, either through statutory authorization or imaginative characterization. On one hand, between 1937 and 1975, federal law provided an exemption for certain price maintenance agreements authorized under state "fair trade" laws. Such legislation was enacted in response to intense lobbying by retail trade associations. On the other, parties often have attempted to avoid an antitrust violation by characterizing the arrangement as (1) an agency or consignment (resulting in no "sale" of the restricted product to the nominal agent or consignee) or (2) a unilateral refusal by a seller to deal with buyers who fail to observe its resale price restric-

tions (resulting in no "combination" triggering operation of §1).

Agency and Consignment Arrangements. A consignment is, in essence, a bailment for sale. The owner of personal property (the consignor) transfers its possession to the consignee, who acts as the owner-consignor's agent to sell the item. The consignor retains title and sets the price at which he is willing to sell. After sale, the consignee pays the consignor the purchase price less a commission. Because the seller retains title to the merchandise and can therefore dictate the selling price, consignment arrangements often have been used to implement resale price maintenance schemes.

Although early cases validated resale price maintenance effected through consignment arrangements, the Supreme Court has more recently taken a harsher approach. For example, in the 1964 landmark decision, *Simpson v. Union Oil Company*,[20] Union Oil Company "consigned" rather than sold gasoline to over 4,000 retail stations in the eight western states in order to fix the resale prices charged by the independent dealers. In holding that Union's "consignment" arrangement violated §1, the Supreme Court stated:

> One who sends a rug or a painting or other work of art to a merchant or a gallery for sale at a minimum price can, of course, hold the consignee to the bargain. . . . When, however, a "consignment" device is used to cover a vast gasoline distribution system, fixing prices through many retail outlets, the antitrust laws prevent calling the "consignment" an agency, for then the end result of *United States v. Socony-Vacuum Oil Co.* . . . . would be avoided merely by clever manipulation of words, not by differences in substance. The present, coercive "consignment" device, if successful against challenge under the antitrust laws, furnishes a wooden formula for administering prices on a vast scale.[21]

Under the rationale of *Simpson,* consignments used to comprehensively and coercively administer resale prices among independent businesspersons on

---

20. 84 S. Ct. 1051 (1964).
21. *Id.* at 1055, 1057.

a large scale are unlikely to survive judicial scrutiny under the Sherman Act.

Unilateral Refusals to Deal—The Colgate *Doctrine.* Sellers often have attempted to legalize resale price restrictions by simply refusing to deal with buyers who fail to observe a resale price maintenance policy. Legal support for such a "unilateral refusal to deal" is found in the Supreme Court's early decision, *United States v. Colgate & Co.* (1919),[22] in which the Supreme Court stated:

> In the absence of any purpose to create or maintain a monopoly, the [Sherman Act] does not restrict the long recognized right of trader or manufacturer engaged in an entirely private business, freely to exercise his own independent discretion as to parties with whom he will deal; and, of course, he may announce in advance the circumstances under which he will refuse to sell.[23]

Thus, under the "*Colgate* doctrine" as it has come to be known, a seller may avoid antitrust liability if it does nothing more than announce a resale price maintenance policy and refuse to deal with buyers (wholesalers, retailers, or both) who fail to observe it. The doctrine considers the seller to be acting unilaterally, not in combination with its wholesalers and retailers, and therefore outside the scope of the Sherman Act. Because use of the *Colgate* doctrine eliminates competition in the sellers' product among wholesalers and retailers, a result that would be per se illegal if attempted by any of the parties through express contract, the Supreme Court has in a number of cases distinguished and qualified the doctrine. Perhaps the most notable of these cases follows.

United States v. Parke, Davis & Company

80 S. Ct. 503 (1960)

Parke, Davis & Company, a pharmaceutical manufacturer, adopted a policy of selling only to wholesalers and retailers that maintained resale prices specified by Parke Davis. In enforcing its policy, Parke Davis promptly cut off wholesalers who sold to retailers at prices different from Parke Davis's "net price selling schedule." It also refused to sell to any wholesaler who supplied Parke Davis products to a retailer who did not observe the manufacturer's minimum retail price. In so doing, Parke Davis coercively enlisted wholesalers to police its price maintenance policy against recalcitrant retailers. If a retailer violated the policy, Parke Davis would supply the retailer's name to its wholesaler, who (to avoid the risk of itself being cut off) promptly stopped selling to the offending retailer. Parke Davis also induced retailers not to advertise discount prices on Parke Davis products by convincing a major retailer to refrain from advertising discounts and then using that cooperation as leverage to obtain others' acquiescence.

The federal government sought injunctive relief against Parke Davis, alleging that Parke Davis's enforcement efforts had gone beyond mere customer selection, and instead constituted an illegal combination in restraint of trade. The district court dismissed the government's complaint and the government appealed to the United States Supreme Court.

Justice Brennan

. . . [W]hatever uncertainty previously existed as to the scope of the *Colgate* doctrine, *Bausch & Lomb* and *Beech-Nut* [earlier cases examining the doctrine] plainly fashioned its dimensions as meaning no more than that a simple refusal to sell to customers who will not resell at prices suggested by the seller is permissible under the Sherman Act. In other words, an unlawful combination is not just such as arises from a price maintenance *agreement,* express or implied; such a combination is also organized if the producer secures adherence to his suggested prices by means which go beyond his mere declination to sell to a customer who will not observe his announced policy. . . .

The Sherman Act forbids combinations of traders to suppress competition. True, there results the same economic effect as is accomplished by a prohibited combination to suppress price competition if each customer, although induced to do so solely by a manufacturer's announced policy, independently decides to observe specified resale prices. So

---

22. 39 S. Ct. 465 (1919).
23. *Id.* at 468.

long as *Colgate* is not overruled, this result is tolerated but only when it is the consequence of a mere refusal to sell in the exercise of the manufacturer's right "freely to exercise his own independent discretion as to parties with whom he will deal." [39 S. Ct. 468.] When the manufacturer's actions, as here, go beyond mere announcement of his policy and the simple refusal to deal, and he employs other means which effect adherence to his resale prices, this countervailing consideration is not present and therefore he has put together a combination in violation of the Sherman Act. . . .

The program upon which Parke Davis embarked to promote general compliance with its suggested resale prices plainly exceeded the limitations of the *Colgate* doctrine and . . . effected arrangements which violated the Sherman Act. Parke Davis did not content itself with announcing its policy regarding retail prices and following this with a simple refusal to have business relations with any retailers who disregarded that policy. Instead Parke Davis used the refusal to deal with the wholesalers in order to elicit their willingness to deny Parke Davis products to retailers and thereby help gain the retailers' adherence to its suggested minimum retail prices. . . . In thus involving the wholesalers to stop the flow of Parke Davis products to the retailers, thereby inducing retailers' adherence to its suggested retail prices, Parke Davis created a combination with the retailers and the wholesalers to maintain retail prices and violated the Sherman Act. . . .

Moreover, . . . Parke Davis went beyond the limits of the *Colgate* doctrine [in another way]. With regard to the retailers' suspension of advertising, Parke Davis did not rest with the simple announcement to the trade of its policy in that regard followed by a refusal to sell to the retailers who would not observe it. . . . Parke Davis sought assurances of compliance and got them, as well as the compliance itself. It was only by actively bringing about substantial unanimity among the competitors that Parke Davis was able to gain adherence to its policy. . . . [I]f a manufacturer is unwilling to rely on individual self-interest to bring about general voluntary acquiescence which has the collateral effect of eliminating price competition, and takes affirmative action to achieve uniform adherence by inducing each customer to adhere to avoid

such price competition, the customers' acquiescence is not then a matter of individual free choice prompted alone by the desirability of the product. The product then comes packaged in a competition-free wrapping—a valuable feature in itself—by virtue of concerted action induced by the manufacturer. The manufacturer is thus the organizer of a price-maintenance combination or conspiracy in violation of the Sherman Act. . . .

[Judgment reversed and remanded.]

Parke Davis illustrates the judicial hostility toward using the *Colgate* doctrine to condone conduct that would be unlawful if effected by direct agreement. No seller today may safely rely upon a unilateral refusal to deal as a viable means of imposing and enforcing resale price maintenance. Courts are quick to find a combination in virtually any effort to police the arrangement. This combination may be found between competitors, the seller and buyer, or simply among the seller and confederates it enlists to help enforce the arrangement. As a noted judge once stated, observing the Supreme Court's approach to the issue: "there is no 'combination' when a manufacturer simply states a resale price and announces that he will not deal with those who depart from it; there is a combination when the manufacturer goes one inch further."[24]

Nonprice Vertical Restraints

Territorial, Customer, and Location Restrictions. Resale price maintenance is not the only form of vertical distribution restraint. Sellers also may impose *nonprice* vertical restraints including location, territorial, and customer restrictions. Under a "location" restriction, the seller contractually requires the buyer to resell only from a stated lo-

---

24. *Albrecht v. The Herald Company,* 88 S. Ct. 869, 878–879 (1968) (dissenting opinion of Justice Harlan). The preceding discussion concerns a manufacturer's setting price *floors;* a minimum resale price. The Supreme Court has held that maximum resale prices, like minimum prices, when imposed or enforced by combination are per se illegal.

cation, such as the buyer's existing retail store. A "territorial" restriction requires a buyer to confine its sales to a given geographic area, such as a city or county or portion thereof. A "customer" restriction requires, for example, a retailer to sell goods purchased only to consumers and not to other retailers.

Nonprice vertical restraints most commonly arise in franchising arrangements. In one sense, a **franchise** is simply a license from the owner of a trademark or trade name (the franchisor) permitting another (the franchisee) to sell a product or service under that name or mark.[25] The term today has, however, developed a broader meaning encompassing the "elaborate agreement under which the franchisee undertakes to conduct a business or sell a product or service in accordance with methods and procedures prescribed by the franchisor and the franchisor undertakes to assist the franchisee through advertising, promotion and other advisory services."[26] This "elaborate agreement" is usually the source of the vertical restrictions subject to antitrust scrutiny.

Franchise arrangements vary in many ways. For example, the relationship between franchisor and franchisee may simply be one of buyer and seller; or the franchisee may be designated an "authorized dealer" with certain additional manufacturer control over the franchisee's business operation; or the franchisor may have almost total control over all aspects of the business, as in a fast food restaurant. The franchisee may carry only the franchisor's products or it may carry competing lines; it may be large or small, well financed or short of funds, experienced in the business or a novice. Each of these factors may be relevant in ruling on the legality of vertical restraints imposed by the franchisor.

All franchise arrangements, however, have one thing in common: the franchisees are independent businesspersons. In all cases, the manufacturer has determined, for whatever reason, that it can more efficiently distribute its product or service through independent wholesale or retail outlets rather than through a company-owned (vertically integrated)

distribution system. If the manufacturer declines to make the substantial investment required for vertical integration, the antitrust question presented is: to what extent should the law permit a manufacturer to interfere with the decisions of its buyers concerning how they compete in reselling the goods? As to resale price maintenance, the Supreme Court has long prohibited such interference in the harshest terms. We turn now to its treatment of nonprice vertical restraints.

Legal Standard Governing Nonprice Vertical Restraints. The current legal standard for vertical nonprice restraints was announced in *Continental T.V., Inc. v. GTE Sylvania, Incorporated,*[27] decided in 1977. In this case, Sylvania, a manufacturer of television sets, sold directly to franchised retail dealers. The franchise agreement contained a location clause, allowing the franchisee to sell only from a designated location or locations. The agreement did not grant territorial exclusivity to franchisees (that is, Sylvania was free to license new dealers in competition with an existing franchisee), but did not preclude franchisees from selling competing brands. The case arose when Sylvania franchised Young Brothers, an established San Francisco television retailer, as an additional retail outlet one mile from Continental T.V., Inc., one of Sylvania's most successful franchised dealers. In displeasure over Sylvania's decision, Continental canceled a large order, and indicated an intent to begin selling Sylvania televisions in Sacramento, in violation of the location restriction. Upon termination of the franchise,[28] Continental sued Sylvania challenging the legality of Sylvania's location clause under §1 of the Sherman Act. The trial court held that Sylvania's location restriction constituted a per se §1 violation. The Supreme Court granted certiorari and held that the legality of nonprice vertical restraints should be governed by a rule of reason rather than the harsh per se standard applicable to vertical *price* restraints (resale price maintenance). In authorizing rule of reason analysis, the Court stated that

---

25. Black, *Law Dictionary* (5th ed. 1979).

26. *H & R Block, Inc. v. Lovelace,* 493 P.2d 205, 212 (Kan. 1972).

27. 97 S. Ct. 2549 (1977).

28. Note that many, if not most, antitrust cases testing vertical restrictions arise out of franchise terminations.

The market impact of vertical restrictions is complex because of their potential for a simultaneous reduction of intrabrand competition and stimulation of interbrand competition. . . .

Vertical restrictions promote interbrand competition by allowing the manufacturer to achieve certain efficiencies in the distribution of his products. . . . For example, new manufacturers and manufacturers entering new markets can use the restrictions in order to induce competent and aggressive retailers to make the kind of investment of capital and labor that is often required in the distribution of products unknown to the consumer. Established manufacturers can use them to induce retailers to engage in promotional activities or to provide service and repair facilities necessary to the efficient marketing of their products. Service and repair are vital for many products, such as automobiles and major household appliances. The availability and quality of such services affect a manufacturer's goodwill and the competitiveness of his product. Because of market imperfections such as the so-called "free rider" effect, these services might not be provided by retailers in a purely competitive situation, despite the fact that each retailer's benefit would be greater if all provided the services than if none did.[29]

Although these justifications for nonprice vertical restraints enjoy a wide following, their validity is questionable. Initially, any argument made in favor of nonprice vertical restrictions can also be used to justify resale price maintenance, long a per se Sherman Act violation. Further, although vertical nonprice restrictions do not fix resale prices, they eliminate or significantly reduce competition, including *price* competition, between dealers governed by the restrictions. That is, by insulating dealers who might otherwise compete in the sale of a product, vertical nonprice restrictions may indirectly achieve resale price maintenance. Further, because they obviously restrict intrabrand competition, any argument against treating territorial, customer, or location restrictions as per se violations must be based on some offsetting benefit to competition. The asserted benefit in this case is that intrabrand insulation encourages greater selling effort by dealers, stimulating interbrand competition. But, as noted by one commentator:

> We may assume, in general, that the more competition a dealer faces, the more vigorous will that dealer be obliged to be; and this holds true whether the competition is interbrand or intrabrand. A dealer worried about losing even those buyers with some pre-commitment to its brand will hustle more earnestly than a dealer free of intrabrand competition and which must worry about losing only those prospective customers who lack a clear preference for the brand. "Effort" is encouraged not by freeing a dealer from important competitive pressures, but by subjecting each dealer to whatever competitive pressure the market generates.[30]

In sum, the current and more lenient "rule of reason" standard for vertical nonprice restraints may not be justified. The approach undercuts the long-standing prohibition against resale price maintenance and the arguments supporting it are controversial.

Termination of One Dealer at the Request of Another

Among the most frequently litigated modern antitrust cases are those in which one retail or wholesale dealer is terminated by the manufacturer at the request of another dealer or group of dealers. To illustrate the typical case, assume that Manufacturer A has four franchised wholesale distributors W, X, Y, and Z serving a given geographic area. Z is a low overhead, aggressive price cutter, who is luring customers away from W, X, and Y, who complain to A about Z's price cutting. Shortly thereafter, A terminates Z's franchise. Determining the appropriate legal standard to resolve cases of this type has proven to be perhaps the single most controversial modern antitrust issue.

The Supreme Court traditionally treated such a case as a classic horizontal group boycott. For ex-

---

29. 97 S. Ct. at 2558, 2560.

30. Sullivan, *The Law of Antitrust* 419 (1977).

ample, in *United States v. General Motors Corporation* (1966),[31] certain franchised Los Angeles area Chevrolet dealers sold some of their cars through "referral outlets" or "discount houses," which resold the cars at extremely low prices. After numerous other franchised dealers complained, General Motors telephoned all area dealers, both to identify those associated with the discounters and to induce the offenders to stop dealing with the discounters. GM, through coercion, quickly elicited from each dealer its promise to refrain from dealing with the discounters. To police the agreement GM and its dealer associations jointly financed "shopping" of the discounters, which was successful in assuring that no Chevrolet dealer continued to supply them with cars.

The government sued for an injunction, alleging that GM and its dealers were participating in a conspiracy in restraint of trade in violation of §1 of the Sherman Act. At trial, GM argued that the dealers' involvement with discounters violated a location clause in the franchise agreement by establishing unauthorized additional sales outlets. GM further argued that the clause was lawful and that GM, its dealers and their associations were merely seeking to vindicate a legitimate interest in uniform compliance with the franchise agreement. The court rejected this argument noting that the facts presented a clearly horizontal rather than vertical problem:

> We need not . . . decide whether the "location clause" may be construed to prohibit a dealer, party to it, from selling through discounters, or whether General Motors could by unilateral action enforce the clause, so construed. We have here a classic conspiracy in restraint of trade: joint, collaborative action by dealers, the appellee associations, and General Motors to eliminate a class of competitors by terminating business dealings between them and a minority of Chevrolet dealers and to deprive franchised dealers of their freedom to deal through discounters if they so choose. . . .
>
> Elimination, by joint collaborative action, of discounters from access to the market is a *per se* violation of the Act. . . .

> [I]nherent in the success of the combination in this case was a substantial restraint on price competition—a goal unlawful *per se* when sought to be effected by combination or conspiracy. . . .[32]

The *General Motors* court had little difficulty finding a horizontal conspiracy on the facts presented. In the 1984 case, *Monsanto Company v. Spray-Rite Service Corporation*,[33] however, the Supreme Court focused on the vertical rather than horizontal aspects of dealer terminations, and adopted a strict evidentiary standard regarding proof of conspiracy to be applied in such cases. Monsanto terminated the distributorship of Spray-Rite after receiving numerous complaints from competing Monsanto distributors about Spray-Rite's price cutting practices. The Court initially discussed the distinction between independent and concerted activity, and the differing standards applicable to price and nonprice vertical restraints. It then rejected the Court of Appeals' holding that an antitrust plaintiff can survive a motion for a directed verdict (that is, the Court will permit the jury to decide whether an unlawful agreement or conspiracy exists) if the plaintiff proves that a manufacturer terminated a price-cutting distributor in response to or following complaints by other distributors. The Court stated:

> Permitting an agreement to be inferred merely from the existence of complaints, or even from the fact that termination came about "in response to" complaints, could deter or penalize perfectly legitimate conduct. As Monsanto points out, complaints about price cutters "are natural—and from the manufacturer's perspective, unavoidable—reactions by distributors to the activities of their rivals." . . .
>
> Thus, *something more than evidence of complaints is needed. There must be evidence that tends to exclude the possibility that the manufacturer and nonterminated distributors were acting independently.* . . . [T]he antitrust plaintiff should present direct or circumstantial evidence that reasonably tends to prove that the manufac-

---

31. 86 S. Ct. 1321 (1966).

32. *Id*. at 1327–1328, 1330–1331.
33. 104 S. Ct. 1464 (1984).

turer and others "had a conscious commitment to a common scheme designed to achieve an unlawful objective." [*Edward J. Sweeney & Sons, Inc., v. Texaco, Inc.*, 637 F.2d 105, 111 (3rd Cir. 1980).][34]

Applying this standard to the facts, the Court found sufficient evidence to support the jury finding of unlawful conspiracy.

In 1988, the Court decided another important dealer termination case, which follows. Justice Stevens's dissent illustrates the deep philosophical differences that exist among courts and commentators concerning the appropriate characterization of such cases for purposes of imposing antitrust liability.

Business Electronics Corporation v. Sharp Electronics Corporation

108 S.Ct. 1515 (1988)

In 1968, respondent Sharp Electronics Corporation appointed petitioner Business Electronics Corporation as the exclusive retailer in Houston, Texas of Sharp's electronic calculators. In 1972, Sharp appointed Gilbert Hartwell as a second retailer in Houston. Although Sharp published a list of suggested minimum retail prices, the retailers were not required to adhere to the price list. Business Electronics usually sold Sharp calculators at prices lower than Sharp's suggested minimum prices and lower than those charged by Hartwell. In June 1973, after complaining several times to Sharp about Business Electronics's prices, Hartwell notified Sharp that he would terminate his dealership unless Sharp ended its relationship with Business Electronics within 30 days. Sharp terminated the Business Electronics dealership in July, 1973.

Business Electronics sued Sharp and Hartwell alleging that they had conspired to terminate its dealership in violation of §1 of the Sherman Act. The trial court instructed the jury that an agreement to terminate a dealer because of price cutting was a per se violation of §1. The jury found for Business Electronics and awarded damages of $600,000. On appeal, the Fifth Circuit Court of Appeals reversed, holding that an agreement between a manufacturer and dealer to terminate another dealer was a per se violation of §1 of the Sherman Act only if the agreement required the surviving dealer to set prices at a particular level. The U.S. Supreme Court granted review of the case.

Justice Scalia

. . . Although vertical agreements on resale prices have been illegal *per se* since *Dr. Miles Medical Co. v. John D. Park & Sons Co.*, [31 S. Ct. 376 (1911)], we have recognized that the scope of *per se* illegality should be narrow in the context of vertical restraints. In *Continental T.V., Inc. v. GTE Sylvania Inc.*, [97 S. Ct. 2549 (1977)], we refused to extend *per se* illegality to vertical nonprice restraints, specifically to a manufacturer's termination of one dealer pursuant to an exclusive territory agreement with another. . . . Rather, we found [that vertical nonprice restraints] had real potential to stimulate interbrand competition, "the primary concern of antitrust law". . . .

Moreover, we observed that a rule of *per se* illegality for vertical nonprice restraints was not needed or effective to protect *intra*brand competition. . . . [S]o long as interbrand competition existed, that would provide a "significant check" on any attempt to exploit intrabrand market power. . . . In fact, in order to meet that interbrand competition, a manufacturer's dominant incentive is to lower resale prices. . . .

Our approach to the question presented in the present case is guided by the premises of *GTE Sylvania* and *Monsanto:* that there is a presumption in favor of a rule-of-reason standard; that departure from that standard must be justified by demonstrable economic effect, such as the facilitation of cartelizing, rather than formalistic distinctions; that interbrand competition is the primary concern of the antitrust laws; and that rules in this area should be formulated with a view towards protecting the doctrine of *GTE Sylvania*. These premises lead us to conclude that the line drawn by the Fifth Circuit is the most appropriate one.

There has been no showing here that an agreement between a manufacturer and a dealer to terminate a "price cutter," without a further agree-

---

34. *Id.* at 1470-1471 (Emphasis added).

ment on the price or price levels to be charged by the remaining dealer, almost always tends to restrict competition and reduce output. Any assistance to cartelizing that such an agreement might provide cannot be distinguished from the sort of minimal assistance that might be provided by vertical nonprice agreements like the exclusive territory agreement in *GTE Sylvania,* and is insufficient to justify a *per se* rule. Cartels are neither easy to form nor easy to maintain. Uncertainty over the terms of the cartel, particularly the prices to be charged in the future, obstructs both formation and adherence by making cheating easier. . . . Without an agreement with the remaining dealer on price, the manufacturer both retains its incentive to cheat on any manufacturer-level cartel (since lower prices can still be passed on to consumers) and cannot as easily be used to organize and hold together a retailer-level cartel.

The District Court's rule on the scope of *per se* illegality for vertical restraints would threaten to dismantle the doctrine of *GTE Sylvania.* Any agreement between a manufacturer and a dealer to terminate another dealer who happens to have charged lower prices can be alleged to have been directed against the terminated dealer's "price cutting." In the vast majority of cases, it will be extremely difficult for the manufacturer to convince a jury that its motivation was to ensure adequate services, since price cutting and some measure of service cutting usually go hand in hand. Accordingly, a manufacturer that agrees to give one dealer an exclusive territory and terminates another dealer pursuant to that agreement, or even a manufacturer that agrees with one dealer to terminate another for failure to provide contractually-obligated services, exposes itself to the highly plausible claim that its real motivation was to terminate a price cutter. Moreover, even vertical restraints that do not result in dealer termination, such as the initial granting of an exclusive territory or the requirement that certain services be provided, can be attacked as designed to allow existing dealers to charge higher prices. Manufacturers would be likely to forego legitimate and competitively useful conduct rather than risk treble damages and perhaps even criminal penalties. . . .

In sum, economic analysis supports the view, and no precedent opposes it, that a vertical restraint

is not illegal *per se* unless it includes some agreement on price or price levels. . . .

[Judgment affirmed.]

Justice Stevens, with whom Justice White joins, dissenting.

In its opinion the majority assumes, without analysis, that the question presented by this case concerns the legality of a "vertical nonprice restraint." As I shall demonstrate, the restraint that results when one or more dealers threatens to boycott a manufacturer unless it terminates its relationship with a price-cutting retailer is more properly viewed as a "horizontal restraint." Moreover, an agreement to terminate a dealer because of its price cutting is most certainly not a "nonprice restraint." The distinction between "vertical nonprice restraints" and "vertical price restraints," on which the majority focuses its attention, is therefore quite irrelevant to the outcome of this case. Of much greater importance is the distinction between "naked restraints" and "ancillary restraints" that has been a part of our law since [1899]. . . .

In this case, it does not appear that respondent imposed any vertical nonprice restraints upon either petitioner or Hartwell. . . . This therefore is not a case in which a manufacturer's right to grant exclusive territorites, or to change the identity of the dealer in an established exclusive territory, is implicated. The case is one in which one of two competing dealers entered into an agreement with the manufacturer to terminate a particular competitor without making any promise to provide better or more efficient services and without receiving any guarantee of exclusively in the future. . . .

The termination was motivated by the ultimatum that respondent received from Hartwell and that ultimatum, in turn, was the culmination of Hartwell's complaints about petitioner's competitive price cutting. The termination was plainly the product of coercion by the stronger of two dealers rather than an attempt to maintain an orderly and efficient system of distribution.

In sum, this case does not involve the reasonableness of any vertical restraint imposed on one or more dealers by a manufacturer in its basic franchise agreement. What the jury found was a simple and naked "agreement between Sharp and Hartwell to terminate Business Electronics because of Business Electronics' price cutting.''. . .

This is the sort of agreement that scholars readily characterize as ''inherently suspect.'' When a manufacturer responds to coercion from a dealer, instead of making an independent decision to enforce a predetermined distribution policy, the anticompetitive character of the response is evident. . . . If two critical facts are present—a naked purpose to eliminate price competition as such and coercion of the manufacturer—the conflict with antitrust policy is manifest.

Indeed, since the economic consequences of Hartwell's ultimatum to respondent are identical to those that would result from a comparable ultimatum by two of three dealers in a market—and since a two-party price-fixing agreement is just as unlawful as a three-party price-fixing agreement—it is appropriate to employ the term ''boycott'' to characterize this agreement. In my judgment the case is therefore controlled by our decision in *United States v. General Motors Corp.*, [86 S.Ct. 1321 (1966)]. . . . Precisely the same goal was sought and effected in this case—the elimination of price competition at the dealer level. Moreover, the method of achieving that goal was precisely the same in both cases—the manufacturer's refusal to sell to discounting dealers. . . .

In sum, this simply is not a case in which procompetitive vertical nonprice restraints have been imposed; in fact, it is not a case in which *any* procompetitive agreement is at issue. The sole purpose of the agreement between respondent and Hartwell was to eliminate price competition at Hartwell's level. . . .

I respectfully dissent.

The clear consequence of cases such as *Monsanto* and *Business Electronics* is to insulate most manufacturers from Sherman Act suits by terminated dealers, even if the motive for termination was partially, or even largely, the dealer's price cutting activities. For example, by 1987, the *Monsanto* case had spawned over seventy lower federal court opinions. In many of these cases, the plaintiff-terminated distributor was unable to survive the defendant's motion for summary judgment or directed

verdict under the heightened burden of proof standard announced in *Monsanto*. As a result, many plaintiffs were denied recovery with no opportunity even to present evidence to a jury that the defendant manufacturer's conduct was concerted not unilateral. The *Business Electronics* case erects yet another evidentiary barrier to plaintiff recovery in dealer termination cases.

Justice Stevens' dissent illustrates the dissatisfaction among many in the legal community with the current Supreme Court approach. Bills currently are pending in both Houses of Congress that would codify the rule of *Dr. Miles Medical Company* and make all forms of resale price maintenance per se illegal under §1 of the Sherman Act, including: (1) agreements between a supplier and distributor to eliminate or restrict a distributor's full latitude to determine prices that it will charge; (2) agreements between a supplier and a distributor to eliminate or restrict the freedom of a second distributor freely to determine what price it will charge; and (3) agreements like those in *Monsanto* and *Business Electronics* in which a supplier and distributor agree to terminate or cut off supply to a second distributor because of the second distributor's pricing policies. The pending bills also would overrule *Monsanto* by providing that an inference of concerted action is raised upon proof that the manufacturer terminated or refused to supply goods or services to the plaintiff-dealer in response to communications from a competing dealer or dealers regarding price competition by the plaintiff. Once the inference of concerted activity is thus raised, the jury then decides whether §1 has been violated.

Tying Arrangements

A **tying contract** is one in which a seller agrees to sell one product (the so-called tying product) only if the buyer also purchases a second product (the tied product) from the seller. For example, a manufacturer might sell its photocopier only to buyers who also agree to buy paper from the manufacturer. In this case, the photocopier is the tying product, and the paper is the tied product. In a tying agreement, the buyer, in order to get something it wants, is required to buy something it either doesn't want or can obtain on more favorable terms from another supplier. The basis of antitrust concern over tying arrangements is that the buyer should be able to obtain the tied products or services separately if it so desires.

Applicable Statutory Provisions. Tying and other exclusive dealing contracts are governed both by §1 of the Sherman Act (as contracts in restraint of trade) and by §3 of the Clayton Act. Section 3 provides in relevant part:

> It shall be unlawful for any person engaged in commerce, in the course of such commerce, to lease or make a sale or contract for sale of goods, . . . whether patented or unpatented, . . . on the condition, agreement, or understanding that the lessee or purchaser thereof shall not use or deal in the goods . . . of a competitor or competitors of the lessor or seller, where the effect . . . may be to substantially lessen competition or tend to create a monopoly in any line of commerce.

Although §3 is theoretically more sensitive to a violation than §1 of the Sherman Act (it reaches conduct that "may" substantially lessen competition or "tend" to create a monopoly), it is more limited in scope. That is, §3 applies only to sales or leases of "goods, wares, merchandise, machinery, supplies, or other commodities"—in short, tangible personal property. It does not apply to tying or other exclusive arrangements involving services, intangible property, or land. Because §1 must be used in cases not involving goods, the judicial criteria for establishing a violation have tended to merge, whether the court is applying §1 or §3.

Purposes of Tying Arrangements. Tying arrangements often constitute a seller's attempt to use power over one product (the tying product) to obtain power over another, or otherwise distort or foreclose freedom of trade in the second (tied) product. To effect a tying arrangement, therefore, the seller must have some market power in the tying product. That is, the seller cannot use a generic product as the tying device because buyers will simply buy substitute goods from other sellers. For example, a grocer who tells his patrons "I will sell you apples only if you also buy oranges" is not likely to foreclose competition in oranges, because

buyers desiring only apples will go to another grocer. If, however, the tying product is unique, the seller may attempt to parlay its preferred position in that product into a similar position in the tied product, over which it would otherwise hold no particular competitive advantage. Buyers of the tied product are thereby injured because their preference for the seller's tying product artificially forces them to make a less than optimal choice for the tied product. Judicial hostility to tying is based on the fact that a single seller should not be able to restrict competition in a product the seller does not lawfully monopolize.

Legal Standard Governing Tying Arrangements. Because a successful tie requires some market power in the tying product, many tying cases involve patented products, which by definition give the seller an effective monopoly over the patented article. Courts have maintained a strict antitying stance in patent law cases under the patent misuse doctrine. For example, in *Morton Salt Co. v. G. S. Suppiger Co.* (1942),[35] Morton Salt held a patent on a machine that added salt tablets in the canning process, and sought to force machine buyers to purchase its salt tablets as well. In announcing the patent misuse doctrine, the Supreme Court held that Morton Salt had misused its patent by attempting to tie nonpatented supplies (salt tablets) to it, and accordingly could not recover for even a direct infringement of its patent[36] until the misuse was terminated and its effects abated. The patent misuse doctrine has proven a strong deterrent to attempts to use patented products to stifle competition in unpatented ancillaries or supplies.

Consistent with its patent law underpinnings, courts applying the Sherman and Clayton Acts have taken a harsh approach to tying arrangements. The basic legal standard was developed in a line of cases beginning in the mid-1930s and culminating in the 1958 landmark, *Northern Pacific Railway Company v. United States.*[37] During the 1860s

---

35. 62 S. Ct. 402 (1942).
36. In this case, the defendant manufactured and sold a machine violating the patent.
37. 78 S. Ct. 514 (1958).

Congress had granted Northern Pacific approximately forty million acres of land in several northwestern states to facilitate railroad construction from Lake Superior to Puget Sound. By 1949, the railroad had sold over ninety percent of the land, but retained mineral rights to much of it. Most of the unsold land was leased for one purpose or another.

The suit arose out of Northern Pacific's "preferential routing" clauses contained in both its contracts leasing or selling the land. These clauses compelled the buyer or lessee to ship all commodities produced or manufactured on the land over Northern Pacific's lines provided that its rates were equal to those of competing carriers. Alternative means of transportation existed for many of the covered shipments, including two major rail carriers. The government challenged the preferential routing clause as an unlawful tying device under §1 of the Sherman Act, tying freight service (the tied product) to the sale or lease of the land (the tying product).[38]

After noting the difference between agreements or practices governed by the rule of reason and those relegated to per se illegality, the Supreme Court placed tying arrangements into the per se category stating that tying contracts

> serve hardly any purpose beyond the suppression of competition. . . . They deny competitors free access to the market for the tied product, not because the party imposing the tying requirements has a better product or a lower price but because of his power or leverage in another market. At the same time buyers are forced to forego their free choice between competing products. For these reasons . . . tying agreements fare harshly under the laws forbidding restraints of trade. . . . They are unreasonable in and of themselves whenever a party has sufficient economic power with respect to the tying product to appreciably restrain free competition in the market for the tied product and a "not insubstantial" amount of interstate commerce is affected.[39]

---

38. Note that §3 of the Clayton Act is not involved here because land and services, not goods, were the subject of the arrangement.

39. 78 S. Ct. at 518.

As the language quoted above indicates, the Court applies a two-fold test in determining the legality of tying arrangements under antitrust law. A violation is established upon proof that (1) the defendant possesses sufficient economic power in the market for the "tying" product and (2) a substantial volume of commerce in the market for the "tied" product is restrained by the tie. Applying this test, the court found that Northern Pacific possessed substantial economic power by virtue of its extensive landholdings, using these as leverage to induce large numbers of purchasers and lessees to give it preferential treatment, thereby excluding competing carriers. Thus finding both power and foreclosure of substantial competition, the Court held Northern Pacific guilty of a per se Sherman Act violation.

In the following case the Supreme Court was required to determine whether a tying contract should be declared per se illegal.

Jefferson Parish Hospital District No. 2 v. Hyde
104 S. Ct. 1551 (1984)

In July 1977 Dr. Edwin Hyde, a board certified anesthesiologist, applied for admission to the medical staff of East Jefferson Hospital. Although the credentials committee and medical staff executive committee recommended approval, the hospital board denied the application because the hospital was a party to a contract providing that all anesthesia services required by the hospital's patients would be performed by Roux & Associates, a professional corporation.

Hyde sued in federal court alleging that the exclusive contract violated §1 of the Sherman Act. The district court denied relief finding that the anticompetitive consequences of the Roux contract were minimal and outweighed by benefits of improved patient care. The court of appeals reversed, finding the contract illegal per se. The Supreme Court granted certiorari.

Justice Stevens

. . . At issue in this case is the validity of an exclusive contract between a hospital and a firm of anesthesiologists. We must decide whether the contract gives rise to a per se violation of §1 of the Sherman Act because every patient undergoing surgery at the hospital must use the services of one firm of anesthesiologists, and, if not, whether the contract is nevertheless illegal because it unreasonably restrains competition among anesthesiologists. . . .

Certain types of contractual arrangements are deemed unreasonable as a matter of law. . . . It is far too late in the history of our antitrust jurisprudence to question the proposition that certain tying arrangements pose an unacceptable risk of stifling competition and therefore are unreasonable *per se*. . . .

It is clear, however, that every refusal to sell two products separately cannot be said to restrain competition. If each of the products may be purchased separately in a competitive market, one seller's decision to sell the two in a single package imposes no unreasonable restraint on either market, particularly if competing suppliers are free to sell either the entire package or its several parts. . . .

Our cases have concluded that the essential characteristic of an invalid tying arrangement lies in the seller's exploitation of its control over the tying product to force the buyer into the purchase of a tied product that the buyer either did not want at all, or might have preferred to purchase elsewhere on different terms. When such "forcing" is present, competition on the merits in the market for the tied item is restrained and the Sherman Act is violated. . . .

[P]er se prohibition is appropriate if anticompetitive forcing is likely. . . .

In sum, any inquiry into the validity of a tying arrangement must focus on the market or markets in which the two products are sold, for that is where the anticompetitive forcing has its impact. Thus, in this case our analysis of the tying issue must focus on the hospital's sale of services to its patients, rather than its contractual arrangements with the providers of anesthesiological services. In making that analysis, we must consider whether petitioners are selling two separate products that may be tied together, and, if so, whether they have used their market power to force their patients to accept the tying arrangement.

The hospital has provided its patients with a package that includes the range of facilities and services required for a variety of surgical operations. At East Jefferson Hospital the package includes the services of the anesthesiologist. Petitioners argue that the package does not involve a tying arrangement at all—that they are merely providing a functionally integrated package of services. . . .

As a matter of actual practice, anesthesiological services are billed separately from the hospital services petitioners provide. There was ample and uncontroverted testimony that patients or surgeons often request specific anesthesiologists. . . . The record amply supports the conclusion that consumers differentiate between anesthesiological services and the other hospital services provided by petitioners.

Thus, the hospital's requirement that its patients obtain necessary anesthesiological services from Roux combined the purchase of two distinguishable services in a single transaction. . . . The fact that petitioners' patients are required to purchase two separate items is only the beginning of the appropriate inquiry.

The question remains whether this arrangement involves the use of market power to force patients to buy services they would not otherwise purchase. Respondent's only basis for invoking the *per se* rule against tying and thereby avoiding analysis of actual market conditions is by relying on the preference of persons residing in Jefferson Parish to go to East Jefferson, the closest hospital. A preference of this kind, however, is not necessarily probative of significant market power.

Seventy percent of the patients residing in Jefferson Parish enter hospitals other than East Jefferson. . . . Thus East Jefferson's "dominance" over persons residing in Jefferson Parish is far from overwhelming. The fact that a substantial majority of the parish's residents elect not to enter East Jefferson means that the geographic data does not establish the kind of dominant market position that obviates the need for further inquiry into actual competitive conditions. . . .

[T]his record contains no evidence that the hospital "forced" any such services on unwilling patients. The record therefore does not provide a basis for applying the *per se* rule against tying to this arrangement.

In order to prevail in the absence of per se liability, respondent has the burden of proving that the Roux contract violated the Sherman Act because it unreasonably restrained competition. . . .

[T]here is no evidence that any patient who was sophisticated enough to know the difference between two anesthesiologists was not also able to go to a hospital that would provide him with the anesthesiologist of his choice.

. . . [A]ll that the record establishes is that the choice of anesthesiologists at East Jefferson has been limited to one of the four doctors who are associated with Roux and therefore have staff privileges. . . .

Petitioners' closed policy may raise questions of medical ethics, and may have inconvenienced some patients who would prefer to have their anesthesia administered by someone other than a member of Roux & Associates, but it does not have the obviously unreasonable impact on purchasers that has characterized the tying arrangements that this Court has branded unlawful. There is no evidence that the price, the quality, or the supply or demand for either the "tying product" or the "tied product" involved in this case has been adversely affected by the exclusive contract between Roux and the hospital. It may well be true that the contract made it necessary for Dr. Hyde and others to practice elsewhere, rather than at East Jefferson. But there has been no showing that the market as a whole has been affected at all by the contract. . . .

[Judgment reversed and remanded.]

Exclusive Dealing

In an **exclusive dealing contract** a buyer agrees to deal only with a particular seller, or alternatively, not to deal in the goods of the seller's competitors. Tying arrangements are one form of exclusive dealing. In requirements contracts,[40] another form of exclusive dealing, a buyer agrees to purchase all of its requirements of a given commodity from the seller. For example, P, a publisher, might contract to purchase its "requirements" (rather than a fixed quantity) of paper from a particular paper company. This arrangement involves exclusive dealing,

not tied to any other product sold by the paper company.

Antitrust law is concerned with requirements contracts because they effectively prevent the seller's competitors from competing for the buyer's business. They also restrict the buyer's freedom of choice to deal with a number of suppliers. For these reasons, requirements contracts and other exclusive dealings (such as a franchise under which a retailer agrees to carry only one manufacturer's line) are, like tying contracts, subject to antitrust scrutiny under both §1 of the Sherman Act and §3 of the Clayton Act.

Unlike tying contracts, requirements contracts have legitimate commercial purposes. Accordingly, requirements contracts have fared better under judicial examination than have tying arrangements. As noted by Justice Frankfurter in *Standard Oil Co. of California and Standard Stations, Inc. v. United States* (1949):[41]

> Requirements contracts . . . may well be of economic advantage to buyers as well as to sellers, and thus indirectly of advantage to the consuming public. In the case of the buyer, they may assure supply, afford protection against rises in price, enable long-term planning on the basis of known costs, and obviate the expense and risk of storage in the quantity necessary for a commodity having a fluctuating demand. From the seller's point of view, requirements contracts may make possible the substantial reduction of selling expenses, give protection against price fluctuations, and—of particular advantage to a newcomer to the field to whom it is important to know what capital expenditures are justified—offer the possibility of a predictable market. . . . They may be useful, moreover, to a seller trying to establish a foothold against the counterattacks of entrenched competitors.[42]

Because of the significant economic advantages of requirements contracts, the judicial approach to determining their legality differs substantially from that used for tying arrangements. Tying devices

---

40. Requirements and output contracts are discussed in Chapter 16. A brief review of that material is helpful in understanding this section.

41. 69 S. Ct. 1051 (1949).
42. *Id.* at 1058–1059.

may be declared illegal merely upon a showing of some market power in the tying product and foreclosure of substantial dollar amount of commerce in the tied product. In contrast, for requirements contracts, the Court has rejected simple "quantitative substantiality." An exclusive dealing arrangement does not violate §3 unless "the court believes it probable that performance of the contract will foreclose competition in a substantial share of the line of commerce affected."[43] In applying this test a court first determines the line of commerce (the type of goods or services involved), and the geographic market (the market area in which the seller operates and to which the purchaser can practicably turn for suppliers). The court then determines whether the competition foreclosed by the contract constitutes a substantial share of the relevant market. This more considered judicial treatment is warranted because of the numerous beneficial aspects of requirements contracts not present in tying arrangements. The three-step analysis used here, defining product market, geographic market, and then analyzing competitive impact, is similar to that used in monopolization cases under §2 of the Sherman Act covered in the next part of this chapter, and merger cases under §7 of the Clayton Act discussed in the next chapter.

Monopolization

Section 2 of the Sherman Act specifies that it is a crime to (1) monopolize, (2) attempt to monopolize, or (3) conspire to monopolize any part of interstate or foreign commerce.

Whereas §1 of the Sherman Act is concerned with concerted or joint conduct in restraint of trade, §2 is violated when a single firm obtains or seeks to obtain a position of such size and power that it is able to assert an extreme degree of market power known as "monopoly power." Simply defined, a seller has market power if it has the power to affect the price prevailing in the market for its goods or services. Most sellers possess little or no market power because there are adequate substitutes for

their products. Therefore, although a seller without market power can sell all it wants at the prevailing market price, buyers will acquire substitute goods from other sellers if the seller attempts to charge more.

If, however, the market is dominated by a single seller, there are few, if any, adequate substitutes. Such a seller faces essentially a downward sloping demand curve for its products, similar to that representing total market demand for products produced by many sellers. Such a seller has market power. It can sell a relatively small quantity, exacting a high price for each item sold or it can sell a large quantity at a somewhat lower price. If the degree of market power has ripened into monopoly, basic microeconomic theory teaches that prices will be higher and output lower than under competitive conditions. In addition to exacting this so-called monopoly profit, which distorts allocation of resources, the monopolist may use its size and power to consolidate or expand its position by practices which operate to exclude or eliminate actual or potential competitors from the market.

The initial element in the offense of monopolization under §2 is the possession of monopoly power. "Monopoly power" is the power to fix or otherwise control price in, or exclude competition from, the relevant market. Possession of monopoly power *alone* is not, however, sufficient to establish a violation. That is, being a monopoly is not necessarily illegal. For example, monopolies are commonly granted by federal, state, or municipal governments because certain functions, such as public utilities, are best performed by a single supplier. Or, monopoly may be "thrust upon" a firm because of superior business skill or efficiency, or a superior product, or because the local economy is capable of supporting only one enterprise of that type, such as a newspaper. The mere existence of monopoly is not proscribed. What is forbidden is the act of monopolization, and the attempt or conspiracy to do so. The offense of monopolization therefore requires not only proof of monopoly power in the relevant market but also that the challenged firm has deliberately followed a course of market conduct through which it has acquired or maintained that power. The plaintiff (often the government) bears the burden of proving both of the foregoing elements of the §2 offense.

---

43. *Tampa Electric Company v. Nashville Coal Company*, 81 S. Ct. 623, 628 (1961).

Early Interpretations—The Conduct Approach

Although §2 was initially applied to condemn a massive railroad merger,[44] the early landmark monopolization cases involved attacks on the classic "trusts," controlling the oil and tobacco industries. Both cases, *Standard Oil Company v. United States*[45] and *United States v. American Tobacco Company,*[46] were decided by the Supreme Court in 1911.

In both cases the court focused its inquiry on the monopoly power issue and quickly concluded that power over price existed and was being exercised by the defendants. The court held that the second element, illegal purpose and intent to monopolize, could be established by proof of trade practices that would violate §1 of the Sherman Act (as unreasonable restraints of trade) if performed by two or more parties in combination. Applying this standard to the facts, the court found both the tobacco and oil trusts guilty of violating §2. Both defendants possessed unquestioned monopoly power, and both exhibited a history of malicious and predatory conduct in acquiring that power, illustrating an illegal intent. The two elements of a violation, power plus intent, were established.

These early cases imposed a "conduct" standard for violation. Conduct rules govern many, if not most, antitrust issues. For example, it is against the law for competitors to enter into agreements on price. Conduct rules, in many contexts, provide workable legal norms reasonably capable of judicial application and enforcement. In monopolization cases, however, a conduct, or "bad acts" test, has significant limitations. First, the test provides no workable formula for determining the existence of monopoly power, the first element of the monopolization offense. Secondly, it does not address monopoly power acquired through normal and reasonable business practices, rather than the vicious conduct characteristic of the early trusts.

Modern Monopolization Analysis— The "Structural" Approach

Because of the foregoing limitations, it soon became apparent that a new, more sophisticated, judicial approach was needed to resolve monopolization issues. This new approach which examines market structure was provided in 1945 by Judge Learned Hand in the celebrated case, *United States v. Aluminum Co. of America (Alcoa).*[47]

Market Definition. Market structure refers to a market's basic characteristics and organization. The following factors, among others, are relevant in the analysis of market structure: (1) the degree of concentration in the market—the number and size of competing firms, (2) barriers to entry—barriers may be created, for example, by patents, huge capital requirements, or exclusionary practices of existing firms, (3) the degree of product differentiation—whether consumers perceive one firm's product as a substitute for another and the manner in which differentiation is achieved, (4) the degree of product diversity, (5) the degree of vertical integration—that is, the extent to which a single firm controls successive stages of production and distribution (for example, supply of raw materials or retail outlets), and (6) industry cost structure—the relationship of fixed to variable costs.[48]

In *Alcoa,* Judge Hand used a structural analysis of the aluminum industry to determine the existence and extent of Alcoa's market power, the threshold inquiry in monopolization cases. The analysis proceeds in two steps. First, the court determines the relevant product and geographic market. Second, it computes the defendant's share of that market and uses that share as a basis for judging the extent of the defendant's market power. That is, monopoly power is inferred if the defendant controls an undue percentage of transactions occurring in the market. Although no precise threshold percentage has been established, either legislatively or judicially, cases have held fifty percent or less insufficient but seventy-five to eighty percent sufficient. Although the threshold percent-

---

44. *Northern Securities Company v. United States,* 24 S. Ct. 436 (1904).

45. 31 S. Ct. 502 (1911).

46. 31 S. Ct. 632 (1911).

47. 148 F.2d 416 (2d Cir. 1945).

48. See Sullivan, *The Law of Antitrust* 24–25 (1977).

age necessarily varies with the type and characteristics of a particular market, control in the sixty-five to seventy-five percent range is likely to invite antitrust scrutiny.

A significant problem with this structural approach is defining the relevant market. The defendant will attempt to expansively define the market, so that its overall percentage is low. The government will attempt to define the market narrowly so that the defendant's share is large. For example, assume Coca-Cola Bottling Company is the sole manufacturer and licensor of Coca-Cola and that the relevant geographic market is the entire world. If the product market is defined as Coca-Cola, the manufacturer controls 100% of the market. If it is defined as all cola drinks, the percentage drops. If defined as all soft drinks, it falls even further. If it is defined as all beverages, including, for example, coffee, tea, milk, and beer, the percentage becomes miniscule. This process of inclusion and exclusion frequently dominates monopolization cases.

Purpose and Intent to Monopolize. Determining the relevant market and the defendant's share does not end the inquiry; it is simply a standard against which the existence of monopoly power may be inferred. The second element of the monopolization offense also must be proved: a deliberate course of market conduct evidencing a purpose and intent to monopolize. Unlike the early cases, which inferred illegal intent to monopolize from predatory conduct violating §1 of the Sherman Act, under the structural approach, acts "honestly industrial" and legal in themselves, are sufficient if their effect is to exclude competitors or erect barriers to entry.

At issue in the following case was whether the defendant's conduct evidenced a purpose and intent to monopolize.

Bonjorno v. Kaiser Aluminum and Chemical Corporation
752 F.2d 802 (3d Cir. 1984)

> Columbia Metal Culvert Co., Inc. fabricated aluminum drainage pipe from corrugated aluminum sheet and aluminum coil. Between 1962 and 1972, Co-

lumbia purchased these raw materials from defendant Kaiser Aluminum and Chemical Corporation (Kaiser) through its distributor Kaiser Aluminum and Chemical Sales, Inc. (KACSI). Following a falling out with Kaiser, Columbia began purchasing its raw materials from Alcoa and Reynolds. In 1973, Kaiser opened a pipe fabrication plant a few miles from Columbia's plant and Robert Kennedy, Columbia's best salesman, left Columbia to become an independent distributor of Kaiser's aluminum pipe. In 1974, Kaiser and other major aluminum producers raised the price of aluminum sheet and coil to approximately the same price that Kaiser charged for finished aluminum pipe. Following a period of financial difficulty, Columbia stopped producing aluminum pipe in 1975. In 1978, Columbia sold its assets to a third party who then sold the remaining Columbia assets to Kaiser in 1981.

> In 1974, the plaintiffs, the sole shareholders of Columbia, sued Kaiser alleging that it had violated §2 of the Sherman Act by monopolizing the aluminum drainage pipe market in the Mid-Atlantic region of the United States. The case was tried by a jury that found that Kaiser had violated §2. Kaiser appealed on the ground that the evidence was insufficient to send to the jury.

Seitz, Circuit Judge

. . . There are two main elements in monopolization: "(1) the possession of monopoly power in a relevant market, and (2) the willful acquisition or maintenance of that power as distinguished from growth or development as a consequence of a superior product, business acumen, or historical accident." [*United States v. Grinnell,* 86 S. Ct. 1698, 1703–1704 (1966)]. . . .

Kaiser's contentions on liability in this appeal go to the question of whether there is insufficient evidence that its alleged conduct demonstrates the willful acquisition or maintenance of monopoly power. . . .

1. *Kaiser Attempted to Control Its Competition.* There was evidence that Kaiser attempted to control the independent fabricators by requiring them to purchase all of their raw materials from Kaiser. Mr. Bonjorno of Columbia, and Mr. Arvay of U.S. Aluminum, a South Carolina fabricator, both testified that Kaiser attempted to coerce the

fabricators into purchasing only from Kaiser. There was testimony that Holmes Collins, the Kaiser manager of the division that manufactured and marketed the aluminum pipe, threatened to open a pipe fabrication plant "across the street" from Columbia if it purchased its raw materials from other sources. There were threats that if Kaiser saw so much as one pound of metal from another producer that it would terminate its relationship with Columbia. When Columbia did purchase aluminum from another company, Kaiser carried through with its threats by locating a pipe plant only 40 miles from Columbia's and by refusing to sell any more coil to Columbia. Finally, there was evidence that Holmes Collins told Columbia's owners that Kaiser would control Columbia's growth and market. . . .

2. *Kaiser's Actions to Destroy Columbia.* In addition to locating a plant near Columbia's, the plaintiffs allege that Kaiser engaged in a series of deliberate acts to drive Columbia out of the pipe market. The most serious claim is that Kaiser deliberately raised the price of the raw materials to the same level as the price that it charged for the finished pipe, thus making it impossible for Columbia to operate at a profit if it sold pipe competitively with Kaiser. The plaintiffs term this price condition a "price squeeze."

The evidence and the record show that for a significant period of time in 1974, the distributor list price of Kaiser's aluminum pipe, per pound, was just above, or even below, the market price for aluminum coil. The mere existence, however, of a "price squeeze" is not necessarily an antitrust violation. The plaintiff must present evidence that the defendants deliberately produced the effect, sufficient to provide a reasonable basis for the jury to conclude that the "squeeze" was not the result of natural market forces such as supply and demand or legitimate competition. . . .

To show that the price squeeze was a deliberate act on the part of Kaiser, the plaintiffs produced evidence that Kaiser controlled both the price of the raw material and the price of the finished pipe, and that Kaiser exercised that power. That Kaiser could control the price of the finished pipe is evident. By setting the price at which it sold to distributors, Kaiser effectively controlled the prices at which the distributors bid to contractors. Further, because of

Kaiser's large market share, it was likely that it or one of its distributors would be bidding on nearly every job. In this fashion, Kaiser, if it desired, could keep the prices of the pipe low. . . .

Kaiser was not the largest supplier of aluminum coil or sheet to independent fabricators, although if the aluminum used by its own pipe plants were included, it produced over 80% of the aluminum used for making pipe. Kaiser contends that since it was not the dominant force in the commodity price market for aluminum coil and sheet, it did not control the prices of the raw materials. The plaintiffs' theory, however, was that Kaiser was a price leader, and that Reynolds and Alcoa, the other major aluminum producers, usually followed Kaiser's pricing strategy. Thus, Kaiser's prices would determine the market prices.

The principal evidence in support of this theory was the testimony of Professor Oliver Williamson, an economist and expert in antitrust. He testified that the aluminum industry was an oligopoly limited to a few major producers of aluminum, and that in particular lines of aluminum products, one of the producers became dominant and set the pricing strategy for the rest of the industry. He indicated that the other aluminum producers usually followed the price leader because if an aluminum producer did not comply, he would not be followed in the areas where it was dominant. He further indicated that there were economic studies that tended to show that the price leadership phenomenon was especially noticeable during the early to mid-1970's and that aluminum prices were kept high by the producers during the relevant period.

Further, Dr. Williamson testified that he believed that Kaiser was the dominant firm in setting the prices for aluminum coil and sheet used in making pipe. . . .

Given that Dr. Williamson's opinion was well supported by the evidence, we cannot say that the question of price leadership should not have gone to the jury.

The next question is whether the evidence shows that Kaiser deliberately manipulated the coil and pipe prices to create a squeeze. There was evidence that the squeeze was not caused by natural market forces.

The most significant evidence of deliberate manipulation of the coil prices was Kaiser's withdrawal of the commodity price for coil in January of 1974. This caused a steep rise in the price of coil from about 38 cents per pound to about 44 cents per pound. . . . Kaiser's manager, Holmes Collins, testified that the commodity price was withdrawn because Kaiser no longer wished to sell to independent fabricators. Thus, Collins' testimony supported an inference that the price change was not related to costs but was intended to affect the independent competition.

Perhaps some of the strongest evidence that the price squeeze was deliberate lies in the relationship of the price of coil charged by Kaiser and its distributor price for pipe. If the coil prices charged by KACSI truly reflected the cost of the coil plus a fair return, then the price of the finished pipe should be higher by at least the fabrication cost of the pipe. However, the price of the pipe was often below the price of the coil during the first six months of 1974. Alternatively, if the price of the pipe reflected Kaiser's true costs plus a fair return, then the price of the raw material should be less by at least the cost of the fabrication. Thus, either the pipe prices were too low, or the raw material prices too high. . . .

Given these facts, there was sufficient evidence for the jury to conclude that Kaiser not only possessed the power to create the price squeeze, but that it exercised that power to destroy its competition. . . .

There is additional evidence that Kaiser sought to destroy Columbia by setting up Robert Kennedy as a distributor. There is evidence that Kaiser extended credit to Kennedy even though its credit department concluded that Kennedy's operation was an "unacceptable credit risk." . . . The jury could infer that by going against the very strong recommendation of its credit department, Kaiser displayed its intent to drive Columbia out of business. . . .

When a monopolist competes by denying a source of supply to his competitors, raises his competitor's price for raw materials without affecting his own costs, lowers his price for the finished goods, and threatens his competitors with sustained competition if they do not accede to his anticompetitive designs, then his actions have crossed the shadowy barrier of the Sherman Act. . . . Given the evidence of Kaiser's anticompetitive behavior, we hold that there was sufficient evidence to permit the monopolization claim to go to the jury.

[Judgment affirmed.]

Attempt and Conspiracy to Monopolize

Section 2 of the Sherman Act prohibits not only monopolization, but also *attempts* and *conspiracies* to monopolize. The Supreme Court has recognized each as an independent offense, distinct from monopolization.[49]

In *Swift & Company v. United States* (1905), the Supreme Court stated that two elements must be proven to establish the offense of attempt to monopolize; (1) a specific intent to monopolize and (2) a dangerous probability of success.

Unlike monopolization, which requires only proof of general intent (intent to do the acts that are ultimately analyzed as creating or maintaining a monopoly), the attempt offense requires a *specific* intent. The defendant must exhibit an intent to destroy competition or obtain a monopoly.[50] Because the defendant will seldom announce such a design publicly, intent generally is inferred from proof of conduct that is clearly destructive of competition, and that has no social, commercial, or economic justification. Thus, predatory price cutting or coercive refusals to deal would certainly establish the requisite intent although less aggravated conduct by an already dominant firm may suffice if the effect is to exclude competition.

In addition to specific intent, *Swift* and later cases suggest that an attempt to monopolize requires a showing of a "dangerous probability of success." In fact, however, the plaintiff need not

---

49. Attempt to monopolize was recognized as a separate offense in *Swift & Company v. United States*, 25 S. Ct. 276 (1905), and conspiracy to monopolize was so recognized in *American Tobacco Co. v. United States*, 66 S. Ct. 1125 (1946).

50. *Times-Picayune Pub. Co. v. United States*, 73 S. Ct. 872, 890 (1953).

prove that the defendant already possesses sufficient market power *actually* to monopolize the market. That is, the defendant's predatory or coercive conduct evidencing a specific intent to monopolize may be proscribed whether or not the defendant, through its use, could have achieved the prohibited result.

Conspiracy to monopolize involves an agreement by two or more firms or individuals to commit the prohibited act. Monopolization, in contrast, is concerned primarily with single-firm conduct. Conspiracy to monopolize further differs from monopolization in that (1) specific intent is required as in attempt and (2) no showing of monopoly power is required. Because it involves concerted conduct, a conspiracy to monopolize also may violate §1 of the Sherman Act as a conspiracy in restraint of trade.

SUMMARY

1. Section 1 of the Sherman Act declares contracts, combinations, and conspiracies in restraint of trade to be illegal. It prohibits only unreasonable restraints of trade, and violations are generally analyzed under the rule of reason. Inherently anticompetitive and unreasonable conduct, however, may be condemned under §1 without any elaborate inquiry into its reasonableness or business justification. That is, the Supreme Court has held that certain specific practices or business relationships are so inherently anticompetitive that they are unreasonable "per se."

2. Trade restraints governed by §1 are of two types: horizontal and vertical. A horizontal restraint is an agreement among competitors or persons at the same functional level. A vertical restraint exists between persons in a buyer-seller or supplier-supplied relationship.

3. Horizontal restraints governed by §1 include price fixing, division of markets, concerted refusals to deal, and market information exchanges. Price fixing and division of markets have long been treated as per se violations of the Act. Although some concerted refusals to deal are per se illegal, others are governed by rule of reason analysis. Exchanges of market information, primarily through trade associations, generally are judged under the rule of reason.

4. Vertical restraints judged under §1 include resale price maintenance, nonprice vertical restraints (such as territory, location, and customer restrictions), and tying and other exclusive dealing contracts. Although resale price maintenance has long been a per se Sherman Act violation, nonprice vertical restraints now are judged by the rule of reason. Although certain tying arrangements also have been ruled per se illegal, not every refusal to sell two products separately has automatically been condemned. Unlike tying contracts, other exclusive dealing arrangements, such as requirements contracts, have legitimate commercial purposes. For this reason, requirements contracts receive a more considered judicial treatment involving market definition and analysis of competitive impact. Tying and other exclusive dealing contracts are judged both under §1 of the Sherman Act and §3 of the Clayton Act.

5. The offense of monopolization under §2 of the Sherman Act has two elements: (1) the possession of monopoly power in the relevant market and (2) the willful acquisition or maintenance of that power as distinguished from growth or development as a consequence of a superior product, business acumen, or historic accident. Although early cases used a "conduct" approach for violation, modern cases analyze market structure.

6. Section 2 of the Sherman Act prohibits not only monopolization, but also attempt and conspiracies to monopolize.

KEY TERMS

rule of reason	conscious parallelism
per se violation	resale price maintenance
horizontal restraint	franchise
vertical restraint	tying contract
cartel	exclusive dealing contract
price fixing	
group boycott (concerted refusal to deal)	

QUESTIONS AND PROBLEMS

51-1 A group of independent grocery store chains desired to sell "house brand" or "private label" products to enable them to better compete with national and regional supermarket chains. Because none of the independent operations was large enough to market a house brand alone, they formed Topco to act as purchasing agent for goods to bear the Topco brand and to license the individual members to sell those products. Topco purchased products bearing the brand from packers and distributed them to participating stores. Ultimately, over 1,000 different items bearing the Topco name were marketed through member supermarket chains. The members completely controlled Topco's operations. Topco's bylaws provided for exclusive or in fact exclusive territorial licenses. Members were authorized to sell Topco products in a specific geographic territory and were precluded from selling outside that territory. Existing licensees also had an effective veto power over admission of a new member into their area. Thus, the members effectively divided up the geographic market for Topco products and had the ability to prevent another licensee from competing in their respective territories. Does this arrangement violate the Sherman Act as a division of markets because it effectively prohibits competition in Topco-brand products among member retail grocery chains?

51-2 Fashion Originators Guild of America (FOGA) was an association of manufacturers of textiles and women's garments—chiefly dresses. The manufacturers claimed to be creators of distinctive and original designs and fabrics for fashionable women's clothes. Guild members were, however, plagued by problems of "style piracy." After Guild manufactured garments reached the market, other manufacturers would systematically make and sell copies of them, usually selling at lower prices. Although Guild designs were neither patented nor copyrighted, Guild members believed the practice to be immoral and unethical, constituting a tortious invasion of their rights and an unfair trade practice. To eliminate the "style pirates," all Guild members agreed not to sell garments to retailers who also sold garments of other manufacturers copied from Guild designs. An elaborate policing mechanism was set up to "shop" the retailers to assure compliance and to determine whether a competing garment was, in fact, a copy of a Guild design. Does this arrangement violate the Sherman Act? FOGA asserted in defense that the boycott was necessary to eliminate the "devastating evils" of style piracy, which the Guild believed to be tortious. Should the court accept this argument?

51-3 Radiant Burners, Inc. manufactured and sold the "Radiant Burner," a ceramic gas burner for use in heating houses and other buildings. American Gas Association (a trade association including public utilities, gas pipeline companies, and manufacturers of gas burners) maintained laboratories in which it tested the safety, utility, and durability of gas burners. After successful testing, the Association affixed a "seal of approval" that was important to burner manufacturers since utilities would not supply gas to unapproved burners. The Association failed to approve the plaintiff's "Radiant Burner." Does American Gas Association's refusal to approve the "Radiant Burner" violate §1 of the Sherman Act? What additional facts regarding the "seal of approval" process would be important in making this determination?

51-4 Molinas, a star basketball player, was suspended indefinitely by the National Basketball Association for betting on league games. He sued, alleging that the league and its members had engaged in an illegal boycott. Is Molinas correct?

51-5 The American Hardwood Association, representing producers of one-third of all hardwood produced in the United States, adopted a so-called open competition plan. Under the plan members were required to submit to the Association daily reports of all sales and shipments, monthly reports of inventory and production, and price lists including immediate reporting of price changes. Information also was required concerning estimated future production and market conditions. Members were subject to inspection and audit, and penalties resulted from failure to report. The Association then sent each member weekly or monthly reports based upon the information submitted. These reports were detailed, including, for example, every sale price and the name of the purchaser. The Association's "manager of statistics" also circulated a monthly market report letter in part based upon the estimates of future market conditions and production submitted by the members. What is the probable effect of the "open competition" plan on competition among hardwood producers? Does the plan violate §1 of the Sherman Act?

51-6 Interstate Circuit, a large theater chain, simultaneously sent a letter to eight film distributors stating that it would refuse to deal with any distributor who also distributed first-run films to "second-run" theaters in competition with Interstate Circuit, unless the admission price in such theaters exceeded $2.00 and no double features were shown. The names of all addressees were listed on each letter. After conferences between representatives of Interstate and the distributors, each distributor agreed to impose the demanded restrictions upon their subsequent run theaters. Do the facts indicate a conspiracy in violation of the Sherman Act?

51-7 General Electric "consigned" electric lamps to independent retail dealers, thereby fixing the price at which the dealers sold to consumers. The dealers assumed all expenses of storage, cartage, transportation, handling, sale, and distribution of the lamps. General Electric, on the other hand, paid the cost of shipment to the dealer and assumed the risk of loss (for example, due to fire, flood, obsolescence, or price decline), insured the goods, and paid all taxes assessed upon them. Does General Electric's consignment arrangement violate §1 of the Sherman Act? Explain.

51-8 Tying arrangements foreclose freedom of trade and competition in the tied product. What other anticompetitive effects might a tying arrangement have?

51-9 IBM sold its patented computer on condition that disks manufactured by IBM be used in the machine. IBM's justification for the arrangement was that use of other manufacturer's disks would impair the computer's performance, thereby impairing or "debasing" IBM's goodwill. Should this justification absolve IBM from antitrust liability for tying?

51-10 Price leadership refers to an industry or market practice in which price pronouncements of one firm, the "price leader" are followed by some, if not all, of the firm's competitors. Price leadership is common in many American industries including steel, automobiles, and banking. Conditions favorable to price leadership include standardized products, oligopolistic market structure, and formula pricing. Commentators have expressed conflicting views on the economic and antitrust significance of price leadership. Are competitors who announce identical price increases within days or even hours of the price leader's exercising their "independent business judgment" or are they engaged in unlawful conspiracy?

51-11 Telex manufactured peripheral equipment, such as tape drives and printers, that were "plug compatible" (plugging directly into) with IBM central processing units. Telex began cutting into IBM's sales of such equipment, so in response IBM lowered its price on certain units and adopted its competition's policy of granting discounts on long term leases of equipment. Is IBM guilty of monopolizing the market for peripheral equipment plug compatible with its machines? What factors should the court consider in making this determination?

51-12 *Lorain Journal,* a newspaper, had enjoyed a substantial monopoly in the dissemination of news and advertising in Lorain, Ohio, for many years. However, in 1948 WEOL, a radio station, was licensed to operate, and soon began competing with the *Journal* for advertising revenue. The *Journal* responded by announcing to its advertisers that it would refuse to accept advertising from anyone who also advertised on radio. Since the *Journal* reached 99 percent of Lorain families, it was an indispensable advertising medium for many Lorain concerns. Is *Lorain Journal* guilty of an attempt to monopolize? Explain.

Chapter 52

The Clayton Act and Federal Trade Commission Act

Major Topics

- discussion of the Robinson-Patman Act, which prohibits certain forms of price discrimination
- coverage of antitrust law governing mergers including the legal standards applied and the potential anticompetitive effects of various types of mergers
- discussion of antitrust enforcement and consumer protection under the Federal Trade Commission Act

As outlined in Chapter 50, the Clayton Act contains four substantive provisions including §2, as amended by the Robinson-Patman Act—prohibiting price discrimination by a seller among various buyers in certain circumstances; §3—testing the legality of tying and other exclusive dealing arrangements; §7—prohibiting certain corporate mergers; and §8—prohibiting a person from simultaneously serving on the board of directors of two or more competing corporations of a given size. With the exception of §3 (which was discussed in Chapter 51 in conjunction with vertical restraints of trade), each of these provisions is covered in the material that follows. The chapter concludes with a discussion of the role of §5 of the Federal Trade Commission Act in antitrust enforcement and consumer protection.

Price Discrimination—The "Robinson-Patman" Act

Section 2 of the Clayton Act, as amended in 1936 by the Robinson-Patman Act, prohibits price discrimination under certain circumstances. Price discrimination occurs when a seller charges one buyer more than another for the same commodity. Discrimination by a seller among its buyers, like the vertical restraints discussed in the previous chapter, may have anticompetitive impact at both the seller and buyer levels. For example, a seller operating in a number of markets may cut its price in one market in order to drive out local competition, while maintaining a higher price elsewhere. Such "predatory" pricing affects competitors of the discriminating seller (that is, injury occurs at the functional level horizontal to the seller) and causes **primary line competitive injury,** or injury at the same functional level as the discriminating seller.

On the other hand, discrimination may affect competition at the buyer's level. For example, assume a manufacturer ordinarily sells its widgets to retailers for $10. A large retailer that purchases in huge quantity is able to coerce the manufacturer into selling to it for $8. The manufacturer continues to sell to small retailers for $10. As a result of the discrimination the large buyer is able to undercut its competition in the market for resale of the goods. In this case, competitive injury occurs at the **secondary line,** among buyers at a functional level below (or vertical to) the discriminating seller. If the buyer receiving the discrimination itself resells (for example, a wholesaler receiving a discrimination passes the lower price onto its retail buyers), competition may be affected two functional levels below the discriminating seller. In this case, injury occurs to competitors of the buyer's customers and is known as **third line** or **tertiary line** injury.

As originally drafted in 1914, §2 was intended to reach only primary line discrimination—predatory, geographic price cutting. After the First World War, however, mass buyers, including mail-order houses and chain stores, began to appear in the American marketplace. Aided partially by discriminatory price concessions from suppliers that were beyond the reach of §2, these large buyers were able to undercut independent retailers, jeopardizing their existence. Following a Federal Trade Commission inquiry, in 1936 Congress passed the **Robinson-Patman Act,**[1] which amended original §2 of the Clayton Act to reach secondary competitive effects and to outlaw certain of the more flagrant devices used by the chains to exact price concessions. Note that unlike other antitrust laws, the Robinson-Patman Act is primarily concerned with protection of small competitors, not competitive structure or process.

The principal enforcement body for the Act is the FTC, which proceeds against violators either informally or through the formal complaint procedure that may result in issuance of a cease and desist order. Robinson-Patman enforcement also may be undertaken by the Department of Justice. In Justice Department actions, Robinson-Patman charges usually accompany complaints alleging other antitrust violations. In addition, private plaintiffs injured by price discrimination may maintain treble damage actions authorized under §4 of the Clayton Act.

As amended by the Robinson-Patman Act, Clayton Act §2 contains six subsections, §§2(a) through 2(f).[2] These provisions are discussed below beginning with the elements of the "prima facie" case.

---

1. 15 U.S.C. §§13(a)-13(f).

2. The Act contains an additional provision, §3, which makes certain price discrimination a criminal offense. 15 U.S.C. §13a.

The Prima Facie Case—§2(a)

Section 2(a) is the heart of the Robinson-Patman Act, stating the basic elements, which if proven, and in the absence of a defense, establish a violation, (the "prima facie" case). Section 2(a) states in part:

> It shall be unlawful for any person engaged in commerce, in the course of such commerce, either directly or indirectly, to discriminate in price between different purchasers of commodities of like grade and quality, where either or any of the purchases involved in such discrimination are in commerce . . . , and where the effect of such discrimination may be substantially to lessen competition or tend to create a monopoly in any line of commerce, or to injure, destroy, or prevent competition with any person who either grants or knowingly receives the benefit of such discrimination, or with customers of either of them.

To facilitate discussion of §2(a), the text that follows divides the statutory language into a series of shorter, more manageable phrases, and examines separately.

The "In Commerce" Requirement. The Robinson-Patman Act imposes a stringent in commerce requirement. The person charged with price discrimination (normally the seller) must be "engaged in commerce," the discrimination must occur "in the course of such commerce," and "either or any of the purchases involved in such discrimination" must be in commerce. Taken collectively, these three commerce related requirements mean that at least one of the sales challenged as part of a pattern of price discrimination must cross a state boundary. Thus, a defendant with strictly intrastate sales is beyond the reach of the statute.

Discrimination in Price. The Act makes it illegal "either directly or indirectly, to discriminate in price." Indirect price discrimination comes in many forms. For example, a seller, although selling the same goods to different buyers at the same price, may give one purchaser more favorable credit or delivery terms, return privileges, or product-related services. Certain indirect forms of price discrimination effectuated through preferential brokerage, advertising, or promotional allowances are addressed explicitly in §§2(c) through 2(e) of the Act, discussed below. Even without these sections, however, the conduct involved would be subject to attack under §2(a) as an indirect form of price discrimination.

The Robinson-Patman Act specifically reaches the quantity discount, a major form of price discrimination. Quantity discounts are lower prices charged to buyers of large quantities of the seller's product. A stated purpose of the Robinson-Patman Act was to limit

> the use of quantity price differentials to the sphere of actual cost differences. Otherwise, such differentials would become instruments of favor and privilege and weapons of competitive oppression.[3]

To violate the statute, the discrimination in price must be "between different purchasers." Thus, the Act applies only to sales,[4] not to leases, agency or consignment arrangements, licenses, or refusals to deal (that is, selling to one firm while refusing to deal with another).[5]

Commodities of Like Grade and Quality. The Act requires that the discriminatory sales be "of commodities of like grade and quality." Because Robinson-Patman applies only to sales of "commodities" (tangible personal property), it does not reach price discrimination in the sale of services or of intangibles such as advertising.

The "like grade and quality" requirement has generated many interpretation problems. Though

sales of goods with "actual and genuine physical differentiations" at different prices are clearly beyond the reach of the Act,[6] how should the law treat physically identical goods that are differentiated solely because one carries a popular brand name and the other does not? The Supreme Court addressed this question directly in 1966 in *Federal Trade Commission v. Borden Company.*[7]

In this case, Borden produced and sold its evaporated milk under stomers. Although all milk distributed under the Borden name was physically and chemically identical, the private label milk regularly sold at lower prices than the Borden brand milk. The FTC found the milk sold under the Borden and private labels to be of "like grade and quality," held the price differential discriminatory in violation of the Robinson-Patman Act, and issued a cease and desist order. The Court of Appeals reversed holding that, as a matter of law, the customer label milk was not of the same grade and quality as Borden's brand. The Supreme Court reversed and remanded holding that when physical differences between products are trivial or nonexistent, they are of "like grade and quality," even though sold under different brand names or labels with varying consumer acceptance. As noted by the Court:

> If two products, physically identical but differently branded, are to be deemed of different grade because the seller regularly and successfully markets some quantity of both at different prices, the seller could, as far as §2(a) is concerned, make either product available to some customers and deny it to others, however discriminatory this might be and however damaging to competition. Those who were offered only one of the two products would be barred from competing for those customers who want or might buy the other. The retailer who was permitted to buy and sell only the more expensive brand would have no chance to sell to those who always buy the cheaper product or to convince others, by

---

3. H. R. Rep. No. 2287, 74th Cong., 2d Sess. 9 (1936).

4. Sales to certain purchasers, such as governmental bodies or non-profit institutions are exempt. A seller may therefore charge such buyers a lower price than its other customers without violating the Act.

5. A proviso to §2(a) provides that "nothing herein contained shall prevent persons engaged in selling goods . . . from selecting their own customers in bona fide transactions and not in restraint of trade."

---

6. *Report of the Attorney General's National Committee to Study the Antitrust Laws* 158 (1955).

7. 86 S. Ct. 1092 (1966).

experience or otherwise, of the fact which he and all other dealers already know—that the cheaper product is actually identical with that carrying the more expensive label.[8]

Thus, under *Borden* "the economic factors inherent in brand names and national advertising should not be considered in the jurisdictional inquiry under the statutory 'like grade and quality' test."[9] In other words, physically identical goods are of like grade and quality, regardless of market acceptance. As such, sales of these goods at different prices are within the basic reach of the Robinson-Patman Act §2(a), and further inquiry is then made to determine whether the arrangement is discriminatory, having an adverse effect on competition.

Anticompetitive Effect. As the final element of the prima facie case, the Robinson-Patman Act requires examination of the competitive impact of the challenged conduct. A price discrimination meeting the foregoing requirements is illegal if its effect "may be substantially to lessen competition or tend to create a monopoly in any line of commerce." This test parallels that contained in Clayton Act §§3 and 7, and original §2, and requires analysis of adverse competitive effect in the overall relevant market. Additionally, in language unique to the Robinson-Patman Act, violation also results if the effect of the discrimination may be to injure, prevent, or destroy competition (1) with the discriminating seller (primary line injury), or (2) among customers of the discriminating seller (secondary line injury), or (3) among customers of customers of the discriminating seller (third or "tertiary" line injury). The Act thus explicitly addresses secondary line injury as well as primary line injury. Further, by focusing upon the impact of discrimination on competitors, rather than competition, the new test eliminates the need for exhaustive market analysis in every case. For this reason, many Robinson-Patman cases use this test in establishing a violation.

Although the Robinson-Patman Act protects against injury at the seller's level, the great majority of cases decided since 1936 examine the effect of price differentials on competition among customers of the discriminating seller. In sharp contrast to primary-line cases (which require a showing of substantial adverse competitive impact absent proof of predatory intent), both the FTC and the courts have generally assumed that *any* price discrimination has the requisite anticompetitive effect. That is, the mere showing that competing buyers were charged different prices is generally sufficient to establish a prima facie Robinson-Patman violation in a secondary-line case. Despite this almost per se standard, price discriminations found illegal tend to be substantial in amount, systematic and continuing, and involve items for which resale profit margins are low and competition keen. Additionally, there must be proof that the buyers involved are in competition both at the functional level (manufacturer, wholesaler, or retailer) and in the geographic area.

In the following case, the court was required to determine whether there was sufficient proof of competitive injury to establish a Robinson-Patman Act violation.

Falls City Industries, Inc. v. Vanco Beverage, Inc.
103 S. Ct. 1282 (1983)

Between 1972 and 1978, Falls City Industries, Inc. (Falls City) sold its beer to Vanco Beverage, Inc. (Vanco), the sole wholesale distributor for Falls City Beer in Evansville, Indiana, at a higher price than it charged its wholesale distributor Dawson Springs, Inc. (Dawson Springs) in Henderson, Kentucky. The two cities form a single metropolitan area across a state line. The two distributors did not compete for sales to the same retailers because Indiana law prohibited Indiana wholesalers from selling to out-of-state retailers and Indiana retailers were prohibited from buying from out-of-state wholesalers. Indiana law also required brewers to sell to all Indiana wholesalers at a single price. Because Dawson Springs passed its cost savings on to retailers, Falls City's pricing policy resulted in

8. *Id.* at 1097.
9. *Id.* at 1098, quoting *Report of the Attorney General's National Committee to Study the Antitrust Laws* 158 (1955).

lower retail beer prices in Henderson than in Evansville. Accordingly, many Indiana consumers crossed the border to purchase cheaper beer in Kentucky. As a result, Vanco sold less beer to Indiana retailers than would have been sold had Vanco been able to charge a competitive price.

Vanco sued Falls City alleging that its pricing policy violated the Robinson-Patman Act. Both the trial court and the Court of Appeals found that Vanco had established a prima facie case of illegal price discrimination. The Supreme Court granted certiorari.

Justice Blackmun

. . . To establish a prima facie violation of §2(a), one of the elements a plaintiff must show is a reasonable possibility that a price difference may harm competition. . . . This reasonable possibility of harm is often referred to as competitive injury. . . .

Falls City contends that the Court of Appeals erred in relying on *FTC v. Morton Salt Co.* [68 S. Ct. 822 (1948)], to uphold the District Court's finding of competitive injury. In *Morton Salt* this Court held that, for the purposes of §2(a), injury to competition is established prima facie by proof of a substantial price discrimination between competing purchasers over time. . . . In the absence of direct evidence of displaced sales, this inference may be overcome by evidence breaking the causal connection between a price differential and lost sales or profits. . . .

According to Falls City, the *Morton Salt* rule should be applied only in cases involving "large buyer preference or seller predation." . . . Falls City does not, however, suggest any economic reason why *Morton Salt's* . . . inference should not apply when the favored competitor is not extraordinarily large. Although concerns about the excessive market power of large purchasers were primarily responsible for passage of the Robinson-Patman Act, . . . the Act "is of general applicability and prohibits discriminations generally." *FTC v. Sun Oil Co.* [83 S. Ct. 358, 368 (1963)]. . . .

The *Morton Salt* rule was not misapplied in this case. In a strictly literal sense, this case differs from *Morton Salt* because Vanco and Dawson Springs did not compete with each other at the wholesale level; Vanco sold only to Indiana retailers and Dawson Springs sold only to Kentucky retailers. But the competitive injury component of a Robinson-Patman Act violation is not limited to the injury to competition between the favored and the disfavored purchaser; it also encompasses the injury to competition between their customers—in this case the competition between Kentucky retailers and Indiana retailers who, under a District Court finding not challenged in this Court, were selling in a single, interstate retail market.

After observing that Falls City had maintained a substantial price difference between Vanco and Dawson Springs over a significant period of time, the Court of Appeals, like the District Court, considered the evidence that Vanco's loss of Falls City beer sales was attributable to factors other than the price difference, particularly the marketwide decline of Falls City beer. Both courts found it likely that this overall decline accounted for some—or even most—of Vanco's lost sales. Nevertheless, if some of Vanco's injury was attributable to the price discrimination, Falls City is responsible to that extent. . . .

The Court of Appeals agreed with the District Court's findings that "the major reason for the higher Indiana retail beer prices was the higher prices charged Indiana distributors," and "the lower retail prices in Henderson County attracted Indiana customers away from Indiana retailers, thereby causing the retailers to curtail purchases from Vanco." 654 F.2d, at 1229. These findings were supported by direct evidence of diverted sales, and more than established the competitive injury required for a prima facie case under §2(a). . . .

[Although the Court affirmed the Court of Appeals' holding that Vanco had established a prima facie case, it vacated and remanded the judgment on other grounds.]

Brokerage and Promotional Allowances

Before the Robinson-Patman Act was passed, large buyers obtained competitive advantages over smaller purchasers in several ways other than through direct reductions in price. One method commonly used was to set up a "dummy" broker, employed by the buyer who, in many cases, rendered no services. The buyer then demanded that the seller pay "brokerage" to these ficticious brokers who then turned it over to the buyer. Another method of disguising price discrimination was to provide large buyers with more favorable promotional allowances or services (such as advertising, in-store displays, and special packaging) than those provided to other customers. To curb these specific abuses, Congress enacted §§2(c), 2(d), and 2(e), supplementing the basic price discrimination prohibitions of §2(a). The scope and operation of these provisions are discussed below.

Brokerage Under §2(c). Section 2(c) makes it unlawful for a buyer to exact price concessions through brokerage commissions paid to itself or its agents. More specifically, the statute makes it unlawful for any person either to pay or to receive anything of value as a commission, brokerage, or other compensation, except for services rendered in connection with the purchase or sale of goods.

Section 2(c) is self-contained and effectively imposes a rule of per se illegality on conduct within its scope. For example, the defenses available to a §2(a) charge to not apply to §2(c) actions, and no showing of anticompetitive effect is required under §2(c). Also, unlike §2(a), §2(c) requires only one transaction (commonly a payment by the seller to the buyer's broker) to establish violation. In short, the seller may generally legally make payments only to an independent broker retained and controlled by the seller. Most cases have held that only the seller's broker renders any real services within the meaning of the statute.[10]

Promotional Allowances and Services Under §§2(d) and 2(e). In addition to prohibiting price discrimination disguised as brokerage, the Robinson-Patman Act also prevents indirect price discrimination through discriminatory promotional allowances under §2(d), and services under §2(e). Allowances or services covered by the Act take many forms including advertising, catalogues, demonstrations, in-store displays and demonstrations, special packaging, warehouse facilities, ac-

cepting returns for credit, prizes or merchandise used in promotional contests, or any other service designed to promote resale of the product.

Sections 2(d) and 2(e) are similar in operation to §2(a) in that they prohibit discriminatory treatment of purchasers who compete in the resale of the goods for which the promotional allowances or services are provided. To avoid Robinson-Patman liability, any promotional allowances or services granted by the seller must be made "available on proportionally equal terms" to all competing purchasers.

The concept of "availability" involves two elements. First, the seller must take affirmative steps to notify all competing buyers of the various types of promotional assistance offered by the seller. Second, the type of program offered by the seller must be usable by all competing customers. It is of little use to a buyer to be notified of a program that, though nominally available to all, is in fact limited only to large buyers. For example, a seller may offer to reimburse customers for a portion of television advertising expenses. If some customers are too small to use television advertising and no comparable benefits are provided these purchasers, the seller violates §2(d). Similarly, a seller would violate the Act by providing in-store demonstrators, who because of sales volume are practically available only to large department stores.

Assuming promotional allowances and services are "available," they must be furnished on "proportionally equal terms." This requirement can generally be satisfied by "basing the payments made or the services furnished on the dollar volume or on the quantity of goods purchased during a specified period."[11] For example, assume during a given year S sells $10,000 worth of goods for resale to B, and $20,000 to B1. If S provides promotional services or allowances with a cost of $500 to B, it should provide $1000 to B1.

Defenses to a Robinson-Patman Act Violation

Proof of a prima facie case of price discrimination under §2(a) does not necessarily result in liability. The seller may avoid the consequences of the discrimination by proving one of three defenses: the

---

10. Most cases have held that a buyer's broker does not render services to the seller, even if it performs some function, like warehousing or breaking bulk.

11. FTC Guides, 16 C.F.R. §240.7.

"cost justification" defense, the "meeting competition" defense, or the "changing conditions" defense. The burden of proving a defense is on the discriminating seller. That is, they are "affirmative" defenses.

The "Cost Justification" Defense.

The Robinson-Patman Act does not prohibit price discrimination that is cost justified, or that reflects differences in the cost of selling to different purchasers. Specifically, the Act contains a proviso[12] to §2(a) that

> [n]othing herein contained shall prevent price differentials which make only due allowance for differences in the cost of manufacture, sale, or delivery, resulting from the differing methods or quantities in which such commodities are to such purchasers sold or delivered.[13]

Although the Act broadly authorizes a seller to pass on cost savings whether occurring in the manufacture or distribution of the goods, in most cases the alleged savings result from lower distribution or direct-selling costs. Some of the distribution costs that may vary among customers include transportation, warehousing and storage, sales promotion and advertising, administrative salaries and expenses, and special services to the customer.

Although, when comparing customers, the *existence* of savings in cost is evident, the *amount* of savings frequently is very difficult to prove because cost accounting in distribution is expensive and inexact. Many costs must be allocated in any attempt to prove the cost of serving a particular customer, and the FTC has not been content with accounting estimates based on ordinary business records. A detailed cost study is required, involving perhaps stopwatch studies of time spent by personnel such as salesmen or truck drivers, and other quantitative measurement of the business operation. These problems led the Supreme Court to lament: "Proof of a cost justification being what it is, too often no one can ascertain whether a price is cost-justified."[14]

The problem of proof, coupled with the fact that Robinson-Patman coverage may be avoided altogether by relatively minor changes in "grade and quality," explain why the cost justification defense has been rarely invoked as a defense.

The "Meeting Competition" Defense.

The "meeting competition" defense, contained in §2(b), provides that a seller may escape liability by showing that

> his lower price or the furnishing of services or facilities to any purchaser or purchasers was made in good faith to meet an equally low price of a competitor, or the services or facilities furnished by a competitor.

The "meeting competition" defense is available in an action for price discrimination under §2(a) or for disproportionate promotional allowances and services under §§2(d) and 2(e) respectively. Meeting competition is not a defense to discriminatory brokerage payments violative of §2(c). Like cost justification, meeting competition is an affirmative defense, difficult to prove, and made more difficult by a restrictive FTC view of its application.

The effect of the meeting competition defense is to allow the seller to lower its price to one customer to meet the competition without lowering its price to all customers. Because of the difficulty in drawing a workable line between "new" and "old" customers, courts have held that if a reduction is made in good faith to match a competitor's price, the meeting competition defense is available either to retain an existing customer or to acquire new customers. To establish the defense the seller must show that the lower price in issue is *its* competitor's price, not the lower price of its buyer's competitor. For example, assume S sells goods for

---

12. A "proviso" is a clause or part of a clause contained in a statute which either excepts something from the enacting clause, qualifies, modifies, or restrains its generality, or excludes some possible ground of misinterpretation concerning its extent. Black, *Law Dictionary* (5th ed. 1979). Provisos usually are preceded by the words "provided," "provided that," or "provided, however." In the Robinson-Patman Act, provisos are used to introduce the defenses.

13. Note that cost justification is a defense only to violations of §2(a) and §2(f) (relating to buyer liability). It does not provide a shield against discriminatory brokerage payments or disproportionate promotional allowances and services under §§2(c), 2(d), and 2(e).

14. *Automatic Canteen Co. v. Federal Trade Commission*, 73 S. Ct. 1017, 1027 (1953).

resale to B, X, Y, and Z. B2, a competitor of B but not a customer of S, substantially undercuts B's price. S may not, consistent with the meeting competition defense, lower its price to B alone (that is, to B but not to X, Y, and Z) to meet B2's competition. The defense, if applicable, would allow S to lower its price to B to meet a price offered to B by a seller in competition with S.

The "Changing Conditions" Defense. The last proviso to §2(a) provides that the Act is not designed to prohibit price differentials made in response to changing conditions affecting either the market for or the marketability of the goods concerned. The proviso gives examples of such changing conditions including actual or imminent deterioration of perishable goods, obsolescence of seasonal goods, distress sales under court process, and sales discontinuing business in the goods concerned.

The defense envisions two separate situations justifying price differentials. First, changing market conditions, and second, an alteration in the marketability of the product. Defendants have been much more successful using the defense in the second case, when the desirability of the product itself is diminished. Examples include reducing price on 1986 automobiles once the 1987 models are introduced, or on fruits and vegetables in danger of spoiling.

The marketability of most products varies over time, or depends upon the time of year in which the goods (for example, Christmas ornaments) are sold. As a result, a seller charging different prices on sales widely separated in time may not be engaged in price discrimination prohibited by the Robinson-Patman Act. That is, an implied element of the prima facie case under §2(a) is that the different prices creating the discrimination must be charged in transactions reasonably contemporaneous in time.

Buyer Liability Under the Robinson-Patman Act

To this point the discussion has concerned statutory liability of sellers engaged in discriminatory pricing practices. The following material discusses the provisions penalizing buyers for their involvement in

such discrimination: §§2(f) and 2(c) of the Robinson-Patman Act, and §5 of the FTC Act.

Buyer Liability for Inducing or Receiving Price Discrimination—§2(f). Section 2(f) of the Act provides:

> It shall be unlawful for any person engaged in commerce, in the course of such commerce, knowingly to induce or receive a discrimination in price which is prohibited by this section.

Thus, liability for illegal price discrimination under §2(a) extends both to the seller granting the discrimination and to any buyer knowingly receiving it.

Section 2(f) is, in essence, a corollary to §2(a), and liability is derivative. That is, a buyer cannot be held liable under §2(f) if a prima facie case under §2(a) could not be established against the seller or if the seller has an affirmative defense, such as cost justification or meeting competition. In either case, there is no price discrimination "prohibited by this section" triggering §2(f) liability.

Buyer Liability Under §2(c), 2(d), and 2(e). Buyer liability also is imposed for receiving brokerage on promotional allowances and services in violation of §§2(c), 2(d), or 2(e) respectively.

Section 2(c), as previously noted is self-contained, and explicitly provides that it is unlawful either "to pay or grant, or to receive or accept" an unlawful brokerage. Thus, the prohibition applies both to buyers and sellers.

Sections 2(d) and 2(e) are explicitly aimed at sellers and make no mention of buyer liability. Early decisions nevertheless held §2(f) applicable to discriminatory promotional allowances and services even though §2(f) explicitly reaches only "discrimination in price." More recently the FTC has attacked buyers receiving discriminatory promotional allowances and services under §5 of the FTC Act as an unfair method of competition.

Mergers—Clayton Act §7

The antitrust movement grew in the late 1800s out of widespread concern over the competitive abuses of the early consolidations of industrial power, the trusts. Thus, antitrust is concerned not only with anticompetitive activities of competitors or buyers and sellers, but also with the permanent consolidation of previously separate enterprises into a single economic entity.

Antitrust analysis commonly uses the term "merger" to describe such a union. For antitrust purposes, "merger" is broadly defined. It generally makes no difference whether either or both corporations survive as a matter of state corporation law. The terms "merger," "consolidation," "acquisition," and "amalgamation" may generally be used interchangeably. The characteristic of antitrust concern is the imposition of unified control upon previously independent business entities.

Introduction to Merger Law

Mergers Classified. Mergers usually are classified and analyzed according to the business or market relationship of the parties. These classifications are useful in analyzing the competitive impact of a merger and will be used throughout the following discussion. A **horizontal merger** is one between former competitors. A **vertical merger** occurs when a firm acquires a supplier or customer. If a business acquires a supplier, it is said to vertically integrate "backward" or "upstream." Conversely, when a firm acquires a customer (for example, a manufacturer acquiring a chain of retail outlets), "forward" or "downstream" vertical integration occurs. A **conglomerate merger** involves parties who were neither former competitors nor in the same supply chain. Each type of merger outlined above may be subject to antitrust attack. Although mergers may be scrutinized under §1 of the Sherman Act, §7 of the Clayton Act is the most important provision testing the legality of a merger.

Statutory Basis of Merger Law. Originally §7 of the Clayton Act was directed primarily at the development of holding companies,[15] and at the secret acquisition of *competitors* through purchase of all or part of a competitor's *stock.* Subsequent

amendments have extended the Act's coverage to include both asset and stock acquisitions. The Act now also covers both mergers between actual competitors and vertical and conglomerate mergers having the requisite anticompetitive effect. Section 7 of the Clayton Act[16] now states in relevant part:

> No person engaged in commerce or in any activity affecting commerce shall acquire, directly or indirectly, the whole or any part of the stock or other share capital and no person subject to the jurisdiction of the Federal Trade Commission shall acquire the whole or any part of the assets of another person engaged also in commerce or in any activity affecting commerce, where in any line of commerce or in any activity affecting commerce in any section of the country, the effect of such acquisition may be substantially to lessen competition, or to tend to create a monopoly.

The statutory language highlights the elements of a §7 proceeding. First, the relevant product (the "line of commerce") and geographic market (the "section of the country") must be defined. Then, the competitive impact of the merger is analyzed within that market. If the merger's "effect may be substantially to lessen competition, or to tend to create a monopoly," it is prohibited.

Remedies; Merger Guidelines; Premerger Notification. Private plaintiffs, the FTC, and the Justice Department may maintain proceedings under §7. Because of the prohibitive expense and complexity of merger litigation, however, the Antitrust Division of the Justice Department maintains most suits. If the court finds a violation, the usual remedy is divestiture, although this remedy may not be available in a private suit. Preliminary injunction also may be decreed pending determination of the merger's legality.

Because the Department of Justice is the primary enforcement body of §7, and because §7 uses general language, the Department recently issued **merger guidelines** that detail the general principles and specific standards used to determine which mergers are likely to be challenged. These new

---

15. A holding company is one that confines its activities to owning stock in, and supervising management of, other companies. Black, *Law Dictionary* (5th ed. 1979).

16. 15 U.S.C. §18.

guidelines, issued June 14, 1984,[17] replace those promulgated by the Department in 1982 and 1968. To aid in enforcement of §7, Clayton Act §7A, enacted in 1976, requires that advance notice be given the FTC and the Justice Department of certain large mergers.

Market Definition in Merger Cases. Section 7 proscribes only those mergers whose effect "may be substantially to lessen competition, or to tend to create a monopoly." To resolve this issue the relevant *market* within which competitive impact is to be analyzed must first be determined. Because §7 indicates that competitive effect may occur "in any line of commerce . . . in any section of the country," both a product and geographic market must be defined. The product market may consist of one or more products or services offered by either company. The geographic market includes the area within which either firm, or both combined, conducts business. The market definition process under §7 is similar to that undertaken in monopolization cases under §2 of the Sherman Act. Under that statute, monopoly power is in issue. Market definition establishes the boundaries within which a firm's power is measured. Merger involves a change in market structure. Market definition in this context establishes the framework to analyze probable anticompetitive consequences of that change. As suggested by the Justice Department in introducing the 1982 merger guidelines: "The goal of market definition is to identify and consider all the firms that would have to cooperate in order to raise prices above the competitive level and keep them there."[18]

Product Market. In determining which products or services to include in the relevant "line of commerce" for §7 purposes, the Supreme Court in *Brown Shoe Co. v. United States* (1962) stated: "The outer boundaries of a product market are determined by the reasonable interchangeability of use or the cross-elasticity of demand between the product itself and substitutes for it."[19] Thus, product substitutability defines the outer limits of the relevant product market.

Geographic Market. The criteria used to determine the appropriate geographic market are the same as those used for the product market. Geographic substitutability defines the market. Depending on the facts, the relevant market may range in size from a part of a single metropolitan area to the entire nation.

Geographic market definition is designed to establish a boundary separating firms that are important in analyzing the competitive effect of the merger from those that are not. The Supreme Court has stated that the relevant geographic market consists of "the area in which the goods or services at issue are marketed to a significant degree by the acquired firm."[20]

The size of this "area" varies depending upon such factors as transportation costs, extent of distribution facilities, or customer inconvenience. For example, if the relevant product is ready-mix concrete, the geographic market would be necessarily small because of prohibitive transportation costs. Similarly, certain industries generally are localized in nature such as retail sale of groceries and commercial banking. On the other hand, other industries such as steel and automobile manufacture involve a national geographic market.

Once the relevant market is defined, the competitive effect of the merger within that market is analyzed. The following material examines the potential competitive impact of horizontal, vertical, and conglomerate mergers, and the standards developed by the courts to decide when a given merger violates §7.

Horizontal Merger

The majority of mergers posing competitive problems are horizontal—between existing competitors. A horizontal merger, like a price-fixing agreement, eliminates competition among the parties, but does so permanently. For example, whereas A and B as

---

17. 1984 Merger Guidelines, 49 Fed. Reg. 26,823-26,837 (June 29, 1984).

18. 4 Trade Regulation Reporter ¶13102 at 20529.

19. 82 S. Ct. 1502, 1523–1524 (1962).

20. *United States v. Marine Bancorporation, Inc.*, 94 S. Ct. 2856, 2869 (1974).

individual competitors may not legally agree on prices to charge their customers, A and B as merger partners, now members of a single integrated economic entity, may. The parties may thus accomplish by merger what they are prohibited from doing by ordinary agreement. Further, by successive merger, a firm capable of exerting monopoly power may result.

Nevertheless, antitrust law has always been more hospitable to mergers than to cartels. The reasons for this approach are varied including that (1) merger may achieve economies of scale or permit other genuine economic efficiencies, such as integration of production, (2) merger promotes free alienability (transferability) of assets, allowing owners of the acquired corporation to sell out, (3) merger may be an expeditious method of diversification, entry into a new market, or acquisition of a needed asset (for example, a patent) or technology, (4) merger allows productive assets to be quickly diverted to more beneficial purposes, (5) merger may expedite installation of more efficient management, and penalize inefficient operation, and (6) merger may occur for competitively neutral reasons, such as tax advantage. In short, the reasons for merger are widely varied, some beneficial to competition, others neutral, and still others injurious. Although the law is more tolerant of merger than loose-knit cartelization, it must still identify and proscribe mergers detrimental to competition.

The basic danger of horizontal merger is market concentration. **Market concentration** is a function of the number of firms in a market and their respective market shares. Markets can range from atomistic (in which very large numbers of firms compete, each small relative to the overall size of the market) to monopolistic (in which one firm controls the entire market). Of great antitrust concern is a market in which a relatively small number of firms account for most market sales. A market dominated by a small number of large firms is said to be "highly concentrated." High concentration increases the likelihood that one firm, or a small number of firms, can successfully exercise market power.[21]

---

21. 1984 Merger Guidelines, 49 Fed. Reg. at 26,830.

Legal Standard Governing Horizontal Merger. A horizontal merger eliminates one competitor and concentrates the power of two firms into one. Depending upon market structure, this result may or may not be of antitrust concern. If a large number of competitors still remain in the market and the resulting firm is small, the competitive impact may be negligible. But if the merger partners are large and the market concentrated, the anticompetitive potential is magnified. The law must draw the line between those mergers which would increase concentration, and thus the risk of collusion and interdependence, and those which are harmless or beneficial to competition.

The following landmark case best articulates the legal standard by which horizontal mergers are judged.

United States v. Philadelphia National Bank
83 S.Ct. 1715 (1963)

The Justice Department filed a civil action to enjoin the proposed merger of Philadelphia National Bank (PNB) and Girard Trust Corn Exchange Bank (Girard), the second and third largest commercial banks in the four-county area including and surrounding Philadelphia. The merger would result in a firm controlling about 30 percent of that market, the same as the largest bank. The market share held by the top two firms would then have increased from 45 to 60 percent. The market exhibited an increasing trend toward concentration, frequently accomplished through merger. During the 14 years preceding the suit, for example, the number of commercial banks in the Philadelphia area had declined from 108 to 42. In addition, much of the growth of the proposed merger partners had been achieved through merger.

The District Court rendered judgment for the defendants holding that the four county Philadelphia metropolitan area was not the relevant geographic market because PNB and Girard actively competed with other banks throughout the northeastern United States. The court also held that even assuming that the four-county area was the relevant market, there was no reasonable probability that competition among commercial banks in the area would be substantially lessened as a result of the merger. The United States appealed to the Supreme Court.

Justice Brennan

. . . The statutory test is whether the effect of the merger "may be substantially to lessen competition" "in any line of commerce in any section of the country." . . .

We have no difficulty in determining the "line of commerce" (relevant product or services market) and "section of the country" (relevant geographical market) in which to appraise the probable competitive effects of appellees' proposed merger. We agree with the District Court that the cluster of products (various kinds of credit) and services (such as checking accounts and trust administration) denoted by the term "commercial banking," . . . composes a distinct line of commerce. . . .

We part company with the District Court on the determination of the appropriate "section of the country." The proper question to be asked in this case is not where the parties to the merger do business or even where they compete, but where, within the area of competitive overlap, the effect of the merger on competition will be direct and immediate. . . . In banking, as in most service industries, convenience of location is essential to effective competition. Individuals and corporations typically confer the bulk of their patronage on banks in their local community; they find it impractical to conduct their banking business at a distance. . . . The factor of inconvenience localizes banking competition as effectively as high transportation costs in other industries. . . . Therefore, since, as we recently said in a related context, the "area of effective competition in the known line of commerce must be charted by careful selection of the market area in which the seller operates, *and to which the purchaser can practicably turn for supplies.*" [*Tampa Electric Company v. Nashville Coal Company,* 81 S. Ct. 623, 628 (1961) (emphasis supplied).]; . . . the four-county area in which appellees' offices are located would seem to be the relevant geographical market. . . .

Having determined the relevant market, we come to the ultimate question under §7: whether the effect of the merger "may be substantially to lessen competition" in the relevant market. Clearly, this is not the kind of question which is susceptible of a ready and precise answer in most cases. It requires not merely an appraisal of the immediate impact of the merger upon competition, but a prediction of its impact upon competitive conditions in the future; this is what is meant when it is said that the amended §7 was intended to arrest anticompetitive tendencies in their "incipiency." . . .

[W]e think that a merger which produces a firm controlling an undue percentage share of the relevant market, and results in a significant increase in the concentration of firms in that market is so inherently likely to lessen competition substantially that it must be enjoined in the absence of evidence clearly showing that the merger is not likely to have such anticompetitive effects. . . .

The merger of appellees will result in a single bank's controlling at least 30% of the commercial banking business in the four-county Philadelphia metropolitan area. Without attempting to specify the smallest market share which would still be considered to threaten undue concentration, we are clear that 30% presents that threat. Further, whereas presently the two largest banks in the area (First Pennsylvania and PNB) control between them approximately 44% of the area's commercial banking business, the two largest after the merger (PNB-Girard and First Pennsylvania) will control 59%. Plainly, we think, this increase of more than 33% in concentration must be regarded as significant. . . .

There is nothing in the record of this case to rebut the inherently anticompetitive tendency manifested by these percentages. . . .

Of . . . little value, we think, are the assurances offered by appellees' witnesses that customers dissatisfied with the services of the resulting bank may readily turn to the 40 other banks in the Philadelphia area. In every case short of outright monopoly, the disgruntled customer has alternatives; even in tightly oligopolistic markets, there may be small firms operating. A fundamental purpose of amending §7 was to arrest the trend toward concentration, the *tendency* to monopoly, before the consumer's alternatives disappeared through merger, and that purpose would be ill-served if the law stayed its hand until 10, or 20, or 30 more Philadelphia banks were absorbed. This is not a fanciful eventuality in view of the strong trend toward mergers evident in the area. . . .

[I]t is suggested that the increased lending limit of the resulting bank will enable it to compete with the large out-of-state bank, particularly the New York banks, for very large loans. We reject this application of the concept of "countervailing power." . . . If anticompetitive effects in one market could be justified by procompetitive consequences in another, the logical upshot would be that every firm in an industry could, without violating §7, embark on a series of mergers that would make it in the end as large as the industry leader. For if all the commercial banks in the Philadelphia area merged into one, it would be smaller than the largest bank in New York City. This is not a case, plainly, where two small firms in a market propose to merge in order to be able to compete more successfully with the leading firms in that market. Nor is it a case in which lack of adequate banking facilities is causing hardships to individuals or businesses in the community. The present two largest banks in Philadelphia have lending limits of $8,000,000 each. The only businesses located in the Philadelphia area which find such limits inadequate are large enough readily to obtain bank credit in other cities. . . .

[Judgment reversed and remanded with direction to enter judgment enjoining the proposed merger.]

The Court in *Philadelphia Bank* thus announced a two-part market concentration test establishing a prima facie violation of §7. That is, absent proof by the defendants that the merger is not likely to injure competition, a horizontal merger violates 7 if it (1) produces a firm controlling an undue percentage of the relevant market, and (2) results in a significant increase in concentration in that market.

Justice Department Guidelines—Horizontal Merger. In determining which mergers meet this test, the Justice Department has announced in its recent merger guidelines that it will use the **Herfindahl-Hirschman Index (HHI)** as an aid to interpreting market concentration data. The HHI is computed by summing the squares of the individual market shares of all firms included in the market. The HHI reflects both the distribution of market shares of the top firms as well as the composition

of the remaining firms. It also gives proportionally greater weight to the shares of the larger firms.

The HHI ranges from 10,000 (a pure monopoly—$100 \times 100 = 10,000$) to a number approaching zero in an atomistic market. Most markets will, of course, fall somewhere in between. For example, a market in which 10 firms each control a 10 percent share has an HHI of 1,000 ($10^2 \times 10 = 1,000$). A more concentrated market consisting of four firms with market shares of 30, 30, 20, and 20 percent has an HHI of 2,600 ($30^2 + 30^2 + 20^2 + 20^2 = 2,600$).

In evaluating horizontal mergers, the Department, consistent with the *Philadelphia Bank* standard, considers both postmerger market concentration and the increase in concentration resulting from the merger. Increase in concentration is measured by doubling the product of the market shares of the merging firms.[22] For example, the merger of firms with 5 and 10 percent market shares would increase HHI by 100 points ($5 \times 10 \times 2 = 100$).

The Justice Department guidelines divide the range of market concentration measured by the HHI into three categories: unconcentrated (postmerger HHI below 1,000), moderately concentrated (postmerger HHI between 1,000 and 1,800), and highly concentrated (postmerger HHI over 1,800).[23] If the postmerger market is unconcentrated, the Justice Department is unlikely to challenge any merger. If the postmerger market is moderately concentrated, a challenge is unlikely for any merger increasing the HHI by less than 100 points. If the merger increases the index by more than 100 points, a challenge is more likely than not, with the decision based upon the extent of the increase, ease of entry into the market, and other relevant factors.[24] If the postmerger market is highly concentrated, challenge is unlikely if the merger increases

---

22. This formula is explained as follows: Before the merger the market shares of the merging firms are squared individually (for example, $a^2 + b^2$). After the merger, the sum of those shares is squared, that is $(a + b)^2$, which equals $a^2 + 2ab + b^2$. The increase in the HHI is therefore $2ab$.

23. An HHI of 1,800 indicates a level of concentration existing, for example, in a market of approximately six equal-sized firms.

24. Among the other factors considered are the nature of the product and terms of sale, availability of information about specific transactions, previous conduct of firms in the market, and overall market performance.

the index by fewer than 50 points, more likely than not with a 50–100 point increase, and very likely if the increase exceeds 100 points. If the leading firm in the market has a share of 35 percent or more, however, the department is likely to challenge any merger by the leader with any firm possessing at least one percent of the market.

Because the merger guidelines are promulgated by an arm of the executive branch (the Justice Department), not a court or legislature, they do not have the effect of law. Thus, a merger challenged by the Justice Department is not necessarily illegal. The elements of a §7 violation must still be proven in court. The guidelines are useful, however, as a guide to firms contemplating a merger.

Interlocking Directorates—Clayton Act §8. Although it does not directly address the horizontal merger problem, §8 of the Clayton Act[25] concerns a closely related issue: interlocking directorates. An interlocking directorate occurs when one person simultaneously serves on the board of directors of two or more competing corporations. Section 8 forbids a person from serving as a director of two or more corporations if:

1. the corporations involved are engaged in whole or in part in interstate commerce;
2. one of the corporations has combined capital, surplus, and undivided profits exceeding $1 million; and
3. the corporations are or shall have been competitors "so that the elimination of competition by agreement between them" would violate "any of the provisions of any of the antitrust laws."

The basic remedy for a Section 8 violation is to require the offending director to resign one of the posts.[26]

Unlike the other substantive Clayton Act provisions (§2, 3, and 7), Section 8 requires no showing of probable anticompetitive effect. Liability follows upon proof of the basic elements outlined above. Section 8 has been applied sparingly; the first case construing it arose almost 40 years after its passage.[27]

Vertical Merger

Anticompetitive Effects. Vertical merger combines firms formerly in a supplier-customer relationship. The most commonly noted anticompetitive consequence of vertical merger is **foreclosure**. To illustrate, assume that a given industry consists of three equal-sized manufacturers A, B, and C, which sell to three equal-sized retailers X, Y, and Z. All retailers buy from all manufacturers. C subsequently integrates vertically by merging with Z. If C now acts as Z's sole supplier, A and B are "foreclosed" from selling to one-third of the retail market. Conversely, if C now sells only to Z, X and Y are "foreclosed" from buying from one-third of the supply market. The degree of foreclosure caused by a merger is an important factor in testing its legality.

Vertical integration by merger also may create competitively objectionable barriers to entry. A firm seeking to enter the market might find that, because of substantial vertical integration, it has too few potential customers (in case of entry at the supplier level) or suppliers (in case of entry at the customer level) to enter either market alone. Though entering both markets simultaneously may be possible, the incremental cost of entering two markets rather than one may be sufficient to deter entry at all. If existing market structure is conducive to monopolization or collusion (for example, highly concentrated), such a barrier may adversely affect future market performance.

Vertical merger may also facilitate collusion among competitors in violation of the Sherman Act. Because retail prices are generally more visible than prices in upstream markets, substantial vertical integration to the retail level may facilitate a price fixing arrangement among manufacturers by making it easier to monitor price and police violations. Further, even without collusion, substantial

---

25. 15 U.S.C. §19.

26. §8 has additional provisions concerning banks and trust companies, now largely supplanted by The Depository Institution Management Interlocks Act, 12 U.S.C. §§3201-3208. Clayton Act §10 (15 U.S.C. §20) supplements §8 and proscribes certain purchases by common carriers from another corporation when directors or managers interlock.

27. *United States v. Sears, Roebuck & Co.*, 111 F. Supp. 614 (S.D.N.Y. 1953).

vertical integration into the retail market reduces the number of independent firms competing at that level.

Elements of a §7 Violation. As with horizontal mergers, the courts have devised a test to determine which vertical mergers are likely to have significant anticompetitive consequences. Initially, the relevant market is defined, usually to include the product that the acquired customer or supplier bought from or sold to the acquiring firm. Then, probable anticompetitive effect is estimated by determining what percentage of the unintegrated portion of the customer or supply market is being foreclosed by the merger. The larger the percentage, the greater likelihood of a §7 violation. For example, assume five manufacturers supply a given market, each having a roughly equal market share. If there are approximately 1,000 customers in the market, merger by a manufacturer with one of them may foreclose the remaining 999 customers from a substantial share of the supply market. On the other hand if 100 independent manufacturers previously supplied the market, a supplier-customer merger may not present significant foreclosure problems. Thus, as in horizontal mergers, the degree of concentration (in this case in either the upstream or downstream market) is a critical factor in judging legality.

The merger guidelines indicate that the Justice Department is likely to challenge vertical mergers which increase barriers to entry (for example, because of the need to enter both the customer and supplier market simultaneously), or those which facilitate collusion. The guidelines indicate that challenge to a vertical merger is unlikely unless one of the affected markets is highly concentrated. The guidelines use an 1,800 HHI as the threshold.

Conglomerate Merger

A conglomerate merger combines firms that neither compete nor stand in a buyer-seller relationship. Three types of corporate combination are generally categorized as "conglomerate." First, a "pure" conglomerate merger involves firms engaged in unrelated businesses (for example, an oil company acquiring a movie studio). Second, a **market extension merger** joins firms selling the same product, but operating in different geographic markets.

A market extension merger, though closely related to a horizontal merger, differs in that it does not eliminate existing direct competition between the parties. Third, a **product extension merger** combines firms producing related, though not identical, products. In this manner, the acquiring firm adds a product to its line. The acquired firm's product may generally be produced by similar facilities, marketed through the same channels, and advertised in the same media. An excellent example of a product extension merger is Procter and Gamble's 1957 aquisition of Clorox Chemical Co. Here, a large diversified manufacturer of low-price, high-turnover household products added liquid bleach by merger to its product line.

Although the dangers of concentration and foreclosure inherent in horizontal and vertical mergers are not present in conglomerate mergers, such mergers may injure "potential" competition and create the danger of reciprocal buying and entrenchment.

The "Potential Competition" Doctrine. In "market extension" and "product extension" mergers, the acquiring firm expands by merger to sell the same product in a different geographic market or to add a related product to its line. In this case, injury may occur to "potential" rather than actual competition, because prior to the merger the acquiring company is a "potential entrant" into the geographic or product market in which the acquired firm operates. Depending upon the characteristics of the merging firms and the structure of the target market, the loss of the potential competition occasioned by the merger may have sufficient anticompetitive effect to condemn the merger under §7.

The term "potential competitor" was first used by the Supreme Court in 1964 in *United States v. El Paso Natural Gas Company*[28] and the **potential competition doctrine** was developed in a series of cases decided over the following ten years.[29] In developing and applying the doctrine, the Supreme

---

28. 84 S. Ct. 1044 (1964).

29. The major cases in this line are *United States v. Penn-Olin Chemical Company*, 84 S. Ct. 1710 (1964); *Federal Trade Commission v. Procter & Gamble Company*, 87 S. Ct. 1224 (1967); *United States v. Falstaff Brewing Corporation*, 93 S. Ct. 1096 (1973); and *United States v. Marine Bancorporation, Inc.*, 94 S. Ct. 2856 (1974).

Court has recognized that market or product extension mergers may violate §7 on potential competition grounds if:

1. the target market (the new geographic or product market) is substantially concentrated;

2. the acquiring firm has the characteristics, capabilities, and economic incentive to render it a potential "de novo" entrant (that is, an entrant by internal expansion rather than by merger); and

3. the acquiring firm's premerger presence on the fringe of the target market in fact temper oligopolistic behavior by participants in that market.

The Supreme Court has thus recognized a "wings effect" in interpreting §7. That is, if the preceding elements are present, the acquiring firm probably prompted premerger procompetitive effects in the target market by being perceived by firms in that market as likely to enter "de novo." Eliminating these procompetitive effects by removing the potential competitor may render the merger unlawful under §7.

The size of the firm in the target market also is relevant in determining a merger's legality. If the acquired firm is already dominant, merger with a large potential competitor may both remove the competitor from the market and reinforce the dominant firm's position, thus perpetuating the oligopoly and raising barriers to entry. These effects would not necessarily follow had a small existing competitor been acquired. Accordingly, the law recognizes that "toe hold" acquisitions by potential competitors might not violate §7.

The merger guidelines indicate that the Justice Department will continue to challenge conglomerate mergers eliminating potential competitors. The guidelines state that a merger in a highly concentrated target market (HHI 1,800 or above) is likely to be challenged if the acquired firm's market share exceeds twenty percent, may be challenged if the share is between five and twenty percent, and is unlikely to be attacked if the share is five percent or less.

Reciprocity and Entrenchment. Creating a market structure conducive to "reciprocity" or "reciprocal

dealing" is another possible anticompetitive consequence of conglomerate merger. A **reciprocal dealing** arrangement arises when two parties are related as buyer to seller in one or more markets and seller to buyer in another or others. In this situation the parties may agree, in effect, "I'll buy from you, if you buy from me." The goods purchased under reciprocal buying arrangements are frequently dissimilar in kind, which could ordinarily be purchased from other sources on similar or even more advantageous terms. If the arrangement is well established, it prevents competitors of each company from selling to the other, and awards each party with the added size and strength attributable to its position as an assured supplier of the other.

Reciprocity may be challenged under §1 of the Sherman Act but a conglomerate merger may also be challenged under §7 as a dangerous step toward reciprocity. That is, opportunities for reciprocity increase greatly if several firms operate in a number of different markets.[30] For example, assume A, a steel manufacturer, merges with a chain of hardware stores. B fabricates and sells steel bolts and other fasteners. A might agree to buy fasteners (for its hardware stores) from B only if B buys its raw steel from A (the steel manufacturer). Reciprocity possibilities increase as the number of firms controlled by conglomerates and the number of conglomerates grow.

In addition to reciprocity, conglomerate merger may cause competitive problems resulting from disparity in size of the acquiring firm relative to firms in the target market. If a company already dominant in a market is acquired by a large powerful firm, the dominant firm might become **entrenched.** That is, the "deep pockets" of the acquiring firm might discourage entry into the market as well as competitive challenges from existing competitors, who might fear retaliation by the dominant firm.

Federal Trade Commission Act

Section 5 of the Federal Trade Commission Act, which is enforced exclusively by the FTC through administrative proceedings, states:

---

30. That is, a much greater possibility exists that the parties will simultaneously be buyer-seller and seller-buyer.

Unfair methods of competition in or affecting commerce, and unfair or deceptive acts or practices in or affecting commerce, are declared unlawful.[31]

Section 5 as originally drafted proscribed only "unfair methods of competition" occurring in interstate commerce. The Wheeler-Lea Act of 1938 added the prohibition of "unfair or deceptive acts or practices." In addition, §5 was amended in 1975 to extend the FTC's jurisdiction to matters merely "affecting" interstate commerce.

Under §5, as amended, the FTC has a dual role. First, through its power to prohibit "unfair methods of competition," the FTC protects the competitive system by prohibiting anticompetitive practices. In this context, §5 is a tool of antitrust enforcement, supplementing the Sherman and Clayton Acts. Second, by exercising its power to proscribe "unfair or deceptive acts or practices," the FTC protects consumers who are injured by practices such as deceptive advertising or labeling without regard to any effect on competitors. The Act does not define the specific conduct prohibited as unfair, but allows the FTC to develop a flexible standard on a case-by-case basis.

Antitrust Enforcement Under §5

As noted in Chapter 50, two federal agencies enforce the antitrust laws. The Justice Department enforces the Sherman and Clayton Acts through suits maintained in federal court. The FTC enforces the Clayton and FTC Acts through administrative proceedings resulting in issuance of a cease and desist order. Though the FTC, therefore, has no explicit Sherman Act enforcement power, a number of cases have held that "unfair methods of competition" include acts or practices that violate the Sherman or Clayton Acts, as well as conduct arguably beyond their scope. The antitrust laws therefore exhibit an increasing sensitivity to anticompetitive conduct. The Sherman Act generally requires proof of actual adverse effect on competition. The Clayton Act is violated if the challenged conduct *may* substantially lessen competition or *tend* to create a monopoly. Section 5 of the FTC Act authorizes the

FTC to stop acts or practices: (1) in their incipiency which, if allowed to continue, would violate the Sherman and Clayton Acts, (2) that merely violate the "spirit" of those Acts, and (3) that are otherwise "unfair." Thus, although not explicitly empowered to do so, the FTC frequently enforces the Sherman Act indirectly through §5, and also enjoins conduct beyond the reach of either the Sherman or Clayton Acts.

Consumer Protection Under §5

Deceptive Advertising. A major purpose of the Wheeler-Lea Amendment to §5 was to protect consumers against deceptive advertising claims. Accordingly, much of the FTC's consumer protection activity has focused on misleading claims relating to product quality, quantity and price, and deceptive endorsements and testimonials.

In a FTC proceeding to restrain promotional activity injurious to consumers, the FTC must generally show that the practice has the capacity to deceive consumers and to affect materially their purchasing decision. Promotional activities with the capacity to deceive include generally express or implied misrepresentations or material nondisclosures. In the following case the court was required to determine what facts constitute a material factor in a consumer's purchasing decision.

Federal Trade Commission v. Colgate-Palmolive Co.
85 S.Ct. 1036 (1965)

In a television commercial for Rapid Shave brand shaving cream, respondent Colgate-Palmolive Co. demonstrated a "sandpaper test." While an announcer stated, "To prove Rapid Shave's super-moisturizing power, we put it right from the can onto this tough, dry, sandpaper," the television picture showed application of Rapid Shave to a substance that appeared to be sandpaper followed by a picture of a razor shaving the substance clean. The FTC (Commission) issued a complaint against Colgate-Palmolive alleging that the commercial was false and deceptive. The evidence established that sandpaper could be shaved clean after application of Rapid Shave only after soaking for about 80 min-

31. 15 U.S.C. §45(a)(1).

utes. The evidence also showed that the substance that appeared to be sandpaper in the commercial was a piece of plexiglass to which sand had been applied. The Commission found that Colgate-Palmolive had misrepresented Rapid Shave's moisturizing power by failing to indicate the elapsed time prior to shaving. The Commission also found that failure to disclose the use of the plexiglass was a material misrepresentation. Colgate-Palmolive appealed the Commission's ruling concerning the use of the plexiglass. After the First Circuit Court of Appeals set aside the Commission's order, the Commission was granted a writ of certiorari by the U.S. Supreme Court.

Chief Justice Warren

. . . The basic question before us is whether it is a deceptive trade practice, prohibited by §5 of the Federal Trade Commission Act, to represent falsely that a televised test, experiment, or demonstration provides a viewer with visual proof of a product claim, regardless of whether the product claim is itself true. . . .

We granted certiorari to consider the Commission's conclusion that even if an advertiser has himself conducted a test, experiment or demonstration which he honestly believes will prove a certain product claim, he may not convey to television viewers the false impression that they are seeing the test, experiment or demonstration for themselves, when they are not because of the undisclosed use of mockups. . . .

The parties agree that §5 prohibits the intentional misrepresentation of any fact which would constitute a material factor in a purchaser's decision whether to buy. They differ, however, in their conception of what "facts" constitute a "material factor" in a purchaser's decision to buy. Respondents submit, in effect, that the only material facts are those which deal with the substantive qualities of a product. The Commission, on the other hand, submits that the misrepresentation of *any* fact so long as it materially induces a purchaser's decision to buy is a deception prohibited by §5.

The Commission's interpretation of what is a deceptive practice seems more in line with the decided cases than that of respondents. . . . It has long been considered a deceptive practice to state falsely that a product ordinarily sells for an inflated

price but that it is being offered at a special reduced price, even if the offered price represents the actual value of the product and the purchaser is receiving his money's worth. . . .

It has also been held a violation of §5 for a seller to misrepresent to the public that he is in a certain line of business, even though the misstatement in no way affects the qualities of the product. As was said in *Federal Trade Comm. v. Royal Milling Co.* [53 S. Ct. 335, 336 (1933)]:

> If consumers or dealers prefer to purchase a given article because it was made by a particular manufacturer or class of manufacturers, they have a right to do so, and this right cannot be satisfied by imposing upon them an exactly similar article, or one equally as good, but having a different origin.

The courts of appeals have applied this reasoning to the merchandising of reprocessed products that are as good as new, without a disclosure that they are in fact reprocessed. And it has also been held that it is a deceptive practice to misappropriate the trade name of another.

Respondents claim that all these cases are irrelevant to our decision because they involve misrepresentations related to the product itself and not merely to the manner in which an advertising message is communicated. This distinction misses the mark for two reasons. In the first place, the present case is not concerned with a mode of word. Secondly, all of the above cases, like the present case, deal with methods designed to get a consumer to purchase a product, not with whether the product, when purchased, will perform up to expectations. . . . In each the seller has used a misrepresentation to break known brands regardless of a product's actual qualities, the prejudice against reprocessed goods, and the desire for verification of a product claim. In each case the seller reasons that when the habit is broken the buyer will be satisfied with the performance of the product he receives. Yet, a misrepresentation has been used to break the habit and . . . a misrepresentation for such an end is not permitted. . . .

We agree with the Commission, therefore, that the undisclosed use of plexiglass in the present commercials was a material deceptive practice, independent and separate from the other misrepresentation found. We find unpersuasive respondents' other objections to this conclusion. Respondents claim that it will be impractical to inform the viewing public that it is not seeing an actual test, experiment or demonstration, but we think it inconceivable that the ingenious advertising world will be unable, if it so desires, to conform to the Commission's insistence that the public be not misinformed. If, however, it becomes impossible or impractical to show simulated demonstrations on television in a truthful manner, this indicates that television is not a medium that lends itself to this type of commercial, not that the commercial must survive at all costs. Similarly unpersuasive is respondents' objection that the Commission's decision discriminates against sellers whose product claims cannot be "verified" on television without the use of simulations. All methods of advertising do not equally favor every seller. If the inherent limitations of a method do not permit its use in the way a seller desires, the seller cannot by material misrepresentation compensate for those limitations. . . .

[Judgment reversed and remanded for entry of judgment enforcing the Commission's order.]

Consumer Unfairness Rule-making Authority.

The FTC is authorized to restrain both deceptive and unfair trade practices injuring consumers. Although Commission actions often have been based on alternate theories of deception and unfairness, more recently the FTC has used consumer unfairness as an independent basis for its actions. Congress facilitated the development of a consumer unfairness doctrine by adding §18 to the FTC Act in 1975,[32] in response to concern that the FTC cease and desist order procedure was ineffective in safeguarding the consumer public against unfair trade practices. Section 18 empowers the FTC to promulgate trade regulation rules that define specifically which acts or practices are unfair under §5. Violation of a trade regulation rule, which may be designed to prevent future conduct, is a §5 violation.

Before promulgating a rule, the FTC must publish notice of the proposed rule-making, allow interested parties to submit written comments, and provide opportunity for an informal hearing. After the rule (including a statement of its basis and purpose) is promulgated, persons objecting to the rule may obtain judicial review from a federal court of appeals.

Section 18 does not provide standards to be used in identifying unfair practices. Accordingly, the FTC's rule-making authority was soon criticized as overly vague and broad, particularly after the FTC proposed a rule in the late 1970's that would have completely prohibited television advertising of certain products during children's programming. In 1980, Congress responded to this criticism by limiting somewhat the FTC's rule-making authority. At Congress's request, the FTC also issued a policy statement,[33] which articulates the standard used to identify unfair consumer practices that may be proscribed by FTC rule:

> To justify a finding of unfairness the injury must satisfy three tests. It must be substantial; it must not be outweighed by any countervailing benefits to consumers or competition that the practice produces; and it must be an injury that consumers themselves could not reasonably have avoided.[34]

Although the Commission's standard, emphasizing "unjustified consumer injury," specifies guideposts for judicial review of FTC rules, it does not delineate specific kinds of practices or consumer injuries it covers. Nevertheless, neither Congress nor the FTC has provided a more specific definition, and FTC rules governing funeral industry and consumer credit practices have been upheld by federal courts reviewing them under the three-part consumer injury standard.[35]

---

32. 15 U.S.C. §57a, part of the Magnuson–Moss Warranty–Federal Trade Commission Improvement Act.

33. Letter from FTC to Senators Ford and Danforth (Dec. 17, 1980), *reprinted in* H.R. Rep. No. 156, Pt. 1, 98th Cong., 1st Sess. 33–40 (1983).

34. *Id.* at 36.

35. See *Harry & Bryant Co. v. Federal Trade Commission,* 726 F.2d 993 (4th Cir. 1984); *American Financial Services Association v. Federal Trade Commission,* 767 F.2d 957 (D.C. Cir. 1985).

Scope of Remedial Orders. After finding a violation of §5 or trade regulation rule, the FTC issues a cease and desist order. The Commission has wide latitude in determining the type of order necessary to alleviate the particular unfair or deceptive practice, and courts usually defer to Commission discretion in framing remedies. For example, in antitrust cases cease and desist orders have required patent licensing and divestiture of corporations acquired in violation of §7 of the Clayton Act. In the following consumer unfairness case, the court reviewed the legality of an FTC order.

Orkin Exterminating Co., Inc. v. Federal Trade Commission

849 F.2d 1354 (11th Cir. 1988)

Between January 1966 and February 1975, Orkin Exterminating Company, a pest control company that treats houses and buildings to destroy termites, offered its customers a "continuous protection guarantee." The guarantee provided that after initial treatment of a structure against termites, customers could obtain annual reinspections and retreatment, if necessary, for the lifetime of the structure by paying an annual fee specified in the contract. In 1980, Orkin decided to increase the annual fee required for the continuous protection guarantee by the greater of $25 or 40% of the original fee. Orkin notified approximately 207,000 customers who had obtained the guarantee between 1966 and 1975 that their annual fee would be increased because of inflation. In 1984, the Federal Trade Commission (FTC) issued an administrative complaint charging Orkin with commission of an unfair act or practice in violation of §5 of the FTC Act. The complaint alleged that Orkin had violated the guarantee contracts by unilaterally raising the fees specified in the contracts. The administrative law judge ruled in favor of the FTC and ordered Orkin to roll back its prices to the fees set forth in the guarantee contracts. The FTC affirmed the decision and Orkin appealed to the federal court of appeals.

Clark, Circuit Judge

. . . Section 5 declares that "unfair or deceptive acts or practices in or affecting commerce" are un-lawful, . . . ; it also empowers the Commission to prevent certain entities from engaging in behavior that constitute "unfair or deceptive acts or practices.". . .

Orkin contends that a "mere breach of contract," which does not involve some sort of deceptive or fraudulent behavior, is outside the ambit of section 5. . . .

Orkin's argument is clearly inconsistent with the ways in which the FTC's unfairness authority has developed, as a result of both legislation and judicial interpretation. . . . The Supreme Court, for example, has "put its stamp of approval on the Commission's evolving use of a consumer unfairness doctrine not moored in the traditional rationales of anticompetitiveness or deception." [*American Financial Services v. FTC*, 767 F.2d 957, 971 (D.C. Cir. 1985).] . . .

In 1980, the Commission promulgated a policy statement containing an abstract definition of "unfairness" which focuses upon unjustified customer injury. . . . [The court then quoted the FTC policy statement.] . . . [A]s the ultimate authority charged with the construction of federal statutes, the courts must set aside Commission orders which are inconsistent with its statutory mandate or the intent of Congress. . . .

We must therefore decide whether the Commission exceeded its authority in deciding that one company's unilateral breach of 207,000 consumer contracts could meet the Commission's definition of unfairness. . . . Of course, the Commission's three-part standard does little to isolate the specific types of practices and consumer injuries which are cognizable. But "the consumer injury test is the most precise definition of unfairness articulated by either the Commission or Congress"; consequently, we must resolve the validity of the Commission's order "by reviewing the reasonableness of the Commission's application of the consumer injury test to the facts of this case, and the consistency of that application with congressional policy and prior Commission precedent." [*Id.* at 972.]

The first prong of the unfairness standard requires a finding of substantial injury to consumers. . . . The Commission's finding of "substantial" injury is supported by the undisputed fact that Orkin's breach of its pre-1975 contracts generated, during a four-year period, more than $7,000,000 in revenues from renewal fees to which the Company was not entitled. As the Commission noted, although the actual injury to individual customers may be small on an annual basis, this does not mean that such injury is not "substantial." . . .

As for the second prong of the unfairness standard, the Commission noted that "conduct can create a mixture of both beneficial and adverse consequences." 108 F.T.C. at 364. . . . But because "[t]he increase in the fee was not accompanied by an increase in the level of service provided or an enhancement of its quality," the Commission concluded that no consumer benefit had resulted from Orkin's conduct. [*Id.*] . . . On appeal, Orkin has not challenged [either] the Commission's conclusions regarding consumer benefits and benefits to competition . . . [, or] the Commission's finding that consumers could [not] have reasonably avoided the harm caused by Orkin's conduct. . . .

The Commission's conclusion was simply that it was an "unfair" practice to breach over 200,000 contracts. We think this was a reasonable application of the Commission's unfairness standard.

There remains, however, the question whether this case represents a significant departure from prior Commission precedent. . . . We think it important to remember . . . that section 5 by its very terms makes deceptive and unfair practices distinct lines of inquiry which the Commission may pursue. As is suggested above, while a practice may be both deceptive and unfair, it may be unfair without being deceptive. . . . Furthermore, the Commission has explained in its Policy Statement that it operates under the assumption that the unfairness doctrine "differs from, and supplements, the prohibition against consumer deception." H.R. Rep. 156, Pt. 1, 98th Cong., 1st Sess. 34 (1983). . . .

An adoption of Orkin's position would mean that the Commission could never proscribe widespread breaches of retail consumer contracts unless there was evidence of deception or fraud. . . . The statutory scheme at issue here "necessarily gives the Commission an influential role in interpreting section 5 and in applying it to facts of particular cases arising out of *unprecedented situations.*" *F.T.C. v. Colgate-Palmolive, Co.,* [85 S. Ct. 1035, 1042 (1965)] (emphasis added). . . . [A]s the D.C. Circuit has observed,

> the Commission has, for all practical purposes, been left to develop its unfairness doctrine on an incremental, evolutionary basis. At this juncture, it is not for this court to step in and confine, by judicial fiat, the Commission's unfairness authority to acts or practices found to be deceptive or coercive. Our role is simply to review the Commission's exercise of its unfairness authority in this case.

[*American Financial Services v. F.T.C.,* 767 F.2d 957, 982 (D.C. Cir. 1985).] This case may be "unprecedented" to the extent it concerns non-deceptive contract breaches. But given the extraordinary level of consumer injury which Orkin has caused and the fact that deceptiveness is often not a component of the unfairness inquiry, we think the limitation of the Commission's section 5 authority urged by Orkin would be inconsistent with the broad mandate conferred upon the Commission by Congress. Thus, because the Commission's decision fully and clearly comports with the standard set forth in its Policy Statement, we conclude that the Commission acted within its section 5 authority. . . .

[FTC order affirmed.]

SUMMARY

1. Section 2 of the Clayton Act, as amended in 1936 by the Robinson-Patman Act prohibits price discrimination under certain circumstances. The Act covers primarily primary line discrimination (causing injury at the same functional level as the seller) and secondary line discrimination (causing injury to buyers from the dis-criminating seller who must compete in the resale of the commodities sold).

2. A prima facie case of price discrimination violating the Robinson-Patman Act requires that a seller engaged in interstate commerce discriminate in price between different purchasers. The discriminatory sales must be of commodities of like grade and quality and must cause competitive injury. Liability for illegal price

discrimination under §2(a) extends both to the seller who grants the discrimination and to any buyer who knowingly receives it.

3. The Robinson-Patman Act was enacted primarily to curb and prohibit all devices by which large buyers use their purchasing power to exact discriminatory preferences from sellers. To curb specific abuses, the Robinson-Patman Act supplements its general price discrimination prohibition by explicitly prohibiting discriminatory brokerage and promotional allowances and services.

4. The Robinson-Patman Act recognizes three major defenses to a violation: the cost justification defense, the meeting competition defense, and the changing conditions defense.

5. Antitrust law addresses the permanent consolidation of previously separate enterprises through merger in §7 of the Clayton Act. Section 7 applies to horizontal, vertical and conglomerate mergers, and prohibits those mergers which substantially lessen competition or tend to create a monopoly in any line of commerce in any section of the country. Section 7 cases require that the relevant product and geographic markets be established followed by analysis of the competitive impact of the merger in that market.

6. Horizontal mergers may adversely affect competition by creating excessive market concentration. Vertical mergers pose the risk of foreclosure. Conglomerate mergers may eliminate a potential competitor from the market, and create risk of reciprocal dealing and entrenchment. The courts have established tests to govern the legality of each type of merger, and the Justice Department has published "merger guidelines" indicating which mergers are likely to be challenged by the government.

7. Under §5 of the Federal Trade Commission Act, the FTC enforces the antitrust laws (through its power to restrain "unfair methods of competition") and protects consumers (by proscribing "unfair or deceptive acts or practices"). In antitrust enforcement, §5 may be used to reach incipient violations of the Sherman and Clayton Acts. In protecting consumers against unfair trade practices, the FTC may promulgate trade regulation rules outlawing specific practices that are unfair to consumers.

KEY TERMS

primary-line competitive
  injury
secondary-line competitive
  injury
third line (tertiary line)
  competitive injury

Robinson-Patman Act
horizontal merger
vertical merger
conglomerate merger
merger guidelines
market concentration

Herfindahl-Hirschman
  Index (HHI)
foreclosure
market extension merger
product extension merger

potential competition
  doctrine
reciprocal dealing
entrenchment

QUESTIONS AND PROBLEMS

52-1   The Robinson-Patman Act is often criticized for not being effectively integrated with the rest of antitrust law. Is the Robinson-Patman Act a beneficial statute or should it be repealed?

52-2   Morton Salt sold its Blue Label salt to wholesalers and large retailers under a standard quantity discount system available to all customers. Under this system a buyer's per case price was reduced as its purchases increased, as follows:

	Per Case
Less than (rail) carload purchases	$1.60
Carload purchases	1.50
5,000-case purchases within any 12 months	1.40
50,000-case purchases within any 12 months	1.35

Only five companies, operators of large chains of retail grocery stores, purchased in sufficient quantity to obtain the $1.35 per case price. As a result of this low price, the chains were able to sell salt at retail cheaper than wholesale purchasers from Morton could resell to independent retailers, many of whom competed with local outlets of the five chain stores. Morton was charged with violating the Robinson-Patman Act and defended on the ground that its quantity discount was not discriminatory because it was available to all on equal terms. Is Morton correct? Explain. Morton also contended that because salt is a small item in most wholesale and retail businesses, and in consumer's budgets, the competitive effect of its program was insufficient to violate the Act. Is Morton correct? Explain.

52-3   A seller may sell to two wholesalers at different prices. The favored wholesaler (the one receiving the lower price) may pass the savings along to his retail customers, giving them a competitive advantage over customers of the disfavored wholesaler. Injury here occurs at the third line; among customers (retailers) of customers (wholesalers) of the seller granting the discrimination. Although tertiary (third) line injury is covered under the Robinson-Patman Act, very few cases have considered injury beyond secondary line. Why?

52-4 Summarize the potential anticompetitive effects of the various types of mergers governed by §7 of the Clayton Act. Are the merger guidelines too lenient, allowing certain mergers which should be prohibited?

52-5 Sidney Weinberg held directorships in both B. F. Goodrich and Sears, competitors in the sale of tires and tubes, and six other classes of goods sold at retail. Upon Justice Department attack under §8 of the Clayton Act, he defended on the ground that the statute requires proof that a hypothetical merger between the corporations involved would violate §7. Is Weinberg correct?

52-6 Consider whether the following advertising techniques are false or deceptive in violation of §5 of the FTC Act.

(a) In a newspaper advertisement, MC Paint Company advertised a gallon of paint for $10.00 and stated that the purchaser would receive a free can of paint of equal quality with each can purchased. Prior to the advertising campaign MC had sold the advertised paint for $5.00 per can.

(b) Would your answer to question (a) change if MC could prove that paint of comparable quality sold for $10.00 per can in other stores?

(c) Guten Tag, Inc. ran a television advertisement for its vanilla ice cream showing happy children eating the ice cream. Because ice cream rapidly melts under lights used to film the ads, Guten Tag used mashed potatoes in place of the ice cream.

(d) Yummy Soups Company ran a magazine advertisement showing a picture of a bowl of Yummy's vegetable soup. Yummy placed clear marbles in the bottom of the bowl causing all of the vegetables to rise to the surface of the soup, thus giving the soup the appearance of being thicker than it really was.

52-7 In 1971, Sears, Roebuck and Co. began an advertising campaign as part of a new marketing program for its Lady Kenmore brand dishwasher. The advertisements claimed that the dishwasher cleaned all dishes without prerinsing or scraping and washed dishes on the top rack as clean as those on the bottom rack. These claims were false and tests conducted by Sears established their falsity. During the first three years of the advertising program, sales of Lady Kenmore dishwashers rose 300 percent.

Following an investigation, the Federal Trade Commission charged Sears with disseminating deceptive and unfair advertisements in violation of §5 of the FTC Act. After a hearing, an administrative law judge found that Sears' advertising claims were false and ordered Sears to cease and desist from making the false claims. The judge also ordered Sears not to make any performance claims for its major home appliances without "competent and reliable tests" or other evidence that substantiated the claims. Sears appealed the order to the court of appeals on the ground that the order was overly broad because it extended to appliances other than the Lady Kenmore dishwasher. Sears argued that because the FTC complaint alleged a §5 violation only with respect to Sears' dishwasher advertising, the FTC lacked the power to issue an order covering any product except dishwashers. In Sears correct? Why would the FTC want to issue an order covering all of Sears' major home appliances in this case?

The relationship between employers and employees is a form of the principal-agent relationship described in Chapters 40-41. Historically, employment law, like agency, was governed by state common law, which, to encourage industrialization, imposed only minimal obligations on employers. By the late 1800s, some states began to enact statutes, such as the workers' compensation laws discussed in Chapter 41, to protect employees. When the Depression created a national labor crisis in the 1930s, the federal Congress, exercising its constitutional power to regulate interstate commerce, abandoned the policy of leaving employment regulation to the states, and enacted a series of statutes designed to alleviate the crisis. For many years, the federal government restricted its regulation to establishing minimum compensation, protecting children in the labor force, and guaranteeing employees the right to organize by forming unions. Today, however, federal regulation has expanded to other areas of employment, including hiring, firing, and

promotion practices, pension and retirement plans, and safety and health in the workplace. Although some employment matters are still governed by state statutes and common law doctrines, most notably workers' compensation and the employment at will doctrine discussed in Chapter 40, federal statutes comprehensively regulate the rights and duties of employees and employers. This chapter examines the most significant of these statutes.

Employee Protection Statutes

Fair Labor Standards Act

The **Fair Labor Standards Act (FLSA)**,[1] enacted in 1938, regulates minimum wages, hours of employment, and child labor. Though numerous exceptions and exemptions apply, most employers and employees engaged in interstate commerce or in the production of goods for interstate commerce are subject to the Act. The Act, for example, does not apply to managerial, administrative, and professional employees or to "mom and pop" businesses employing only the owner's immediate family.

The FLSA requires employers to pay employees a minimum wage, currently $3.35 per hour. An employer cannot require employees to work more than forty hours per week unless they are paid time

---

1. 29 U.S.C. §201 *et seq.*

and one-half their regular rate for hours worked in excess of forty hours. Special rules allow an employer to pay less than the minimum wage to students, apprentices, and handicapped workers if the employer obtains authorization from the Secretary of Labor. In some cases, the Act allows wages to be computed on a piece-rate, rather than an hourly basis.

The FLSA also prohibits oppressive child labor. The Secretary of Labor issues regulations governing the types of jobs that children may hold and the maximum number of hours they may work. Generally, children of age sixteen or seventeen may work unlimited hours in nonhazardous jobs. Fourteen and fifteen-year old children may work limited hours only in nonhazardous jobs and may not work in manufacturing or mining. The FLSA provides special rules for children employed in farm labor, generally allowing them to work longer hours at a younger age.

The Wage and Hour Division of the Department of Labor administers the FLSA. It investigates possible violations of the Act and may issue subpoenas compelling attendance of witnesses and production of employment records. Civil and criminal penalties may be imposed for violations of the Act. Workers who have received subminimum wages may file a civil suit under the Act for twice the amount of back pay plus attorneys' fees and costs.

Social Security Act

Congress enacted the **Social Security Act**[2] in 1935 to provide income to retired workers and later amended the Act to include benefits to others including disabled workers and dependents of deceased workers. The Social Security Act also provides hospitalization and medical benefits for the elderly. Social Security programs are funded by taxes imposed on employers, employees, and self-employed persons.

Under the Federal Insurance Contributions Act (FICA),[3] both employers and employees must make annual contributions of Social Security taxes. Determination of whether an employer-employee relationship exists is made using the common law standard.[4] Generally, any person who has the right to control and direct the result and means by which an individual's services are rendered is considered an employer. In 1988 and 1989, each employee must contribute 7.51% of his or her gross annual wages (subject to the ceiling discussed below) and the employer must contribute an equal amount. The tax will rise to 7.65% in 1990. Thus, beginning in 1990, the total Social Security tax for each employee will be 15.3% (7.65% contributed by the employee; 7.65% contributed by the employer) of that employee's gross annual wages. Wages include all cash payments—including salary, commissions, bonuses and vacation pay—as well as the cash value of other forms of compensation—such as meals, lodging, clothing, and services. The Act establishes a ceiling that fixes the maximum amount of annual wages subject to the tax. The ceiling, which was $45,000 in 1988, is adjusted annually based on an escalator formula. Wages in excess of the ceiling are not subject to Social Security tax. The employer must withhold the employee's share of the tax from wages, submit payment of both the employee's and employer's contributions, and maintain records of the employee's earnings. The employer is primarily liable for payment of the employee's share of the tax even if the employer fails to withhold the tax from the employee's wages. An employer who fails to submit taxes to the federal government when due must pay a penalty and interest and may be subject to criminal liability.

Self-employed persons who receive earnings from carrying on a trade or business also must pay Social Security taxes under the Self-Employment Contributions Act.[5] Prior to 1990 self-employed persons are taxed at a special rate, but beginning in 1990, a self-employed person must contribute taxes at an annual rate equal to the combined employer-employee rate of 15.3% of net self-employment earnings. The maximum self-employment earnings subject to the tax are limited to the same ceiling applied to wages of an employed person. An individual who receives wages from an employer, as

---

2. 42 U.S.C. §301 *et seq.*
3. 26 U.S.C. §§3101-3126.

4. See discussion in Chapter 41 of the text.
5. 26 U.S.C. §§1401-1403.

well as self-employment earnings, is entitled to offset the gross wages against this ceiling in determining the amount of self-employment earnings subject to the tax. A self-employed person who fails to pay the taxes when due must pay a penalty and interest and may be subject to criminal liability.

Social Security programs are administered by the Social Security Administration which determines who is entitled to benefits and their amount. Employees who have accumulated sufficient credits while employed become eligible for retirement benefits at age 65, but may retire at age 62 and receive lower monthly benefits. In general, a person who qualifies for retirement benefits is entitled to them regardless of other retirement income such as private pensions. In some cases, however, a portion of the benefits may be subject to federal income taxation if the person's adjusted gross income exceeds $25,000. A worker who becomes totally disabled prior to age 65 may qualify for disability benefits. In some cases, even persons who made no contributions to Social Security, such as the spouse or minor children of a deceased or disabled worker, may qualify for benefits under survivors' or dependents' programs.

In addition to a portion of the Social Security tax, employers are required to fund unemployment compensation for workers who are temporarily unemployed. The federal unemployment compensation program, embodied in the Federal Unemployment Tax Act (FUTA),[6] is coordinated with state programs, and employers receive a credit against the federal unemployment tax for taxes paid to qualified state unemployment funds. The duration and amount of unemployment benefits paid and the employees eligible to receive benefits vary among the states.

Employee Retirement Income Security Act

Although federal law does not require employers to provide pension programs, many private businesses offer retirement and pension plans as employee benefits. Because of abuses and mishandling of private pension funds, Congress adopted the **Employee Retirement Income Security Act (ERISA)**[7] in 1974 to regulate most private pension programs that provide retirement income to employees or that allow employee deferral of income to termination of employment.

Two general types of pension plans are recognized under ERISA: defined benefit plans and defined contribution plans. Defined benefit plans specify the retirement benefits that an employee will receive, usually calculated by formulas based on the employee's compensation and years of service. Under a defined benefit plan, for example, employees may be entitled to receive annual retirement benefits equal to seventy-five percent of the average of their yearly earnings during the highest three years of earnings. Defined contribution plans assign each employee separate accounts to which a specified amount is deposited annually. Upon retirement, the employees are entitled to receive pensions based on the amounts (including interest or other investment income) available in their accounts. Pension plans may be contributory or noncontributory. Under a "contributory" plan both the employee and employer make contributions to the plan while only the employer contributes to a "noncontributory" plan. "Qualified" pension plans are those that comply with Internal Revenue Service requirements entitling the employer to deduct its contributions for federal tax purposes and allow earnings on contributions to accumulate without tax recognition.

ERISA requires all pension plans to be in writing and to name a plan manager. All assets (other than insurance) must be held in trust, and ERISA imposes a fiduciary duty on the manager and advisers who, therefore, must exercise the care that a prudent person would exercise in managing his or her own assets. ERISA restricts the plan's investments by prohibiting certain transactions (such as loans and leases) with the sponsoring employer or certain employees, officers, directors, and major shareholders of the employer. A pension plan may invest in securities issued by the employer although such investments are subject to some limitations under

---

6. 26 U.S.C. §§3301-3311.

7. 29 U.S.C. §1001 *et seq.*

defined benefit plans. As further protection, ERISA created the Pension Benefit Guaranty Corporation to provide insurance of pension benefits in case the plan fails or terminates. All plans must maintain such insurance.

ERISA provided important reforms of pension plan vesting requirements. **Vesting** occurs when the employees' rights to their interests in the pension plan cannot be forfeited or taken away. Prior to ERISA, many employers postponed vesting until immediately prior to the employee's retirement age. An employee who changed jobs or was discharged forfeited all rights to pension benefits and the employer recouped its contributions. Under contributory plans, ERISA requires that employees' rights to their own contributions vest immediately. Thus, the employees never forfeit their contributions. ERISA establishes minimum vesting requirements for employer contributions under both contributory and noncontributory plans. In general, employees' rights to employer contributions must fully vest within five or seven years in accordance with formulas set forth in ERISA.

ERISA also establishes reporting and disclosure requirements for pension plans. Plan managers must keep detailed records of investments and distributions and must submit periodic reports to the IRS. the Department of Labor, and the Pension Benefit Guaranty Corporation. Employees also are entitled to receive periodic statements covering their interests in the plan.

The Department of Labor and the Department of the Treasury are responsible for enforcing ERISA. Criminal penalties may be imposed for failure to comply with disclosure requirements. The statute also allows civil suits, including those for breach of fiduciary duties, for violations of the Act.

Occupational Safety and Health Act

In 1970, Congress adopted the federal **Occupational Safety and Health Act (OSHA)**[8] to ensure "safe and healthful working conditions and to pre-serve our human resources."[9] With the exception of federal, state, and local governments, almost every employer whose business affects interstate commerce is subject to the provisions of the Act although some special accommodations are made for small businesses. The **Occupational Safety and Health Administration** (also called "OSHA") of the Department of Labor has primary responsibility for administration and enforcement of the Act. If, however, a state law meets requirements set by OSHA, the state regulates safety and health standards within its borders.

OSHA imposes a general duty on the employer to provide "employment and a place of employment which are free from recognized hazards that are causing or are likely to cause death or serious physical harm to his employees."[10] A "recognized hazard" is a dangerous condition or activity of which the employer has actual knowledge or of which the employer should have known based on the standard of knowledge in the industry. An employer is obligated to eliminate recognized hazards if feasible.

The Secretary of Labor also issues regulations setting standards for specific industries and the employer must comply with the standards set for its industry. These regulations are adopted through a notice and hearing procedure that allows input from interested parties including employers and employees.

OSHA standards vary considerably from industry to industry and cover a variety of conditions in the workplace. They include, for example, maximum noise levels, air quality standards in the workplace, permissible locations for equipment and machinery, and safety procedures for employees. Because of widespread criticisms of OSHA's overly-detailed regulations, unnecessarily strict enforcement, and attention to safety rather than health hazards, OSHA has attempted in the last few years to simplify its rules and reduce the number of regulations. Nevertheless, the cost of compliance with OSHA standards is a frequent subject of litigation as illustrated in the following case.

---

8. 29 U.S.C. §§651-678.

9. 29 U.S.C. §651(b).
10. 29 U.S.C. §654(a)(1).

American Textile Manufacturers Institute, Inc. v. Donovan

101 S. Ct. 2478 (1981)

Byssinosis, a respiratory disease that may resemble chronic bronchitis or emphysema, is primarily caused by inhalation of cotton dust released during the handling and processing of cotton. Studies estimate that over 25% of all active cotton mill workers suffer from some form of the disease and that approximately one in twelve cotton mill workers suffer from the most disabling form of byssinosis.

In 1978, the Secretary of Labor and OSHA promulgated standards establishing maximum limits of cotton dust permissible in the air in workplaces maintained by the cotton industry. OSHA mandated installation of ventilation systems and special floor sweeping procedures to reduce cotton dust and required employers to monitor cotton dust exposure and to provide medical surveillance including annual employee medical examinations. Prior to adopting the regulations, OSHA held public hearings and received comments from interested parties.

Petitioners, American Textile Manufacturers Institute and others representing the cotton industry, sued the Secretary of Labor alleging that the standards were invalid because OSHA had failed to demonstrate a reasonable relationship between the costs and benefits of the cotton dust standard. The court of appeals (the court of original jurisdiction) upheld the validity of the standard. The Supreme Court granted certiorari to the petitioners.

Justice Brennan

. . . The principal question presented in these cases is whether the Occupational Safety and Health Act requires the Secretary, in promulgating a standard pursuant to §6(b)(5) of the Act . . . to determine that the costs of the standard bear a reasonable relationship to its benefits. . . . [P]etitioners urge not only that OSHA must show that a standard addresses a significant risk of material health impairment . . . but also that OSHA must demonstrate that the reduction in risk of material health impairment is significant in light of the costs of attaining that reduction. . . . Respondents on the other hand contend that the Act requires OSHA to promulgate standards that eliminate or reduce such risks "to the extent such protection is technologically and economically feasible." . . .

Section 6(b)(5) of the Act . . . (emphasis added), provides:

> The Secretary, in promulgating standards dealing with toxic materials or harmful physical agents under this subsection, shall set the standard which most adequately assures, *to the extent feasible,* on the basis of the best available evidence, that no employee will suffer material impairment of health or functional capacity even if such employee has regular exposure to the hazard dealt with by such standard for the period of his working life. . . .

The plain meaning of the word "feasible" supports respondents' interpretation of the statute. According to Webster's Third New International Dictionary of the English Language 831 (1976), "feasible" means "capable of being done, executed, or effected." . . . Thus, §6(b)(5) directs the Secretary to issue the standard that "most adequately assures . . . that no employee will suffer material impairment of health," limited only by the extent to which this is "capable of being done." In effect then, as the Court of Appeals held, Congress itself defined the basic relationship between costs and benefits, by placing the "benefit" of worker health above all other considerations save those making attainment of this "benefit" unachievable. Any standard based on a balancing of costs and benefits by the Secretary that strikes a different balance than that struck by Congress would be inconsistent with the command set forth in §6(b)(5). Thus, cost-benefit analysis by OSHA is not required by the statute because feasibility analysis is. . . .

When Congress has intended that an agency engage in cost-benefit analysis, it has clearly indicated such intent on the face of the statute. . . . Certainly in light of its ordinary meaning, the word "feasible" cannot be construed to articulate such congressional intent. We therefore reject the argument that Congress required cost-benefit analysis in §6(b)(5). . . .

[Judgment affirmed.]

OSHA also requires businesses to maintain records documenting employee accidents and illnesses and records concerning particular hazards, including exposure to toxic substances. Employees and their unions have a right to inspect some records concerning hazards.

OSHA's most effective tool for investigating and discovering safety and health hazards is inspection of business workplaces. Such inspections are subject to the constitutional requirements of administrative searches discussed in Chapter 4. Employees and unions also report hazards to OSHA. Upon discovering violations, OSHA issues a written citation to the employer providing a time limit for correction. The employer may challenge the citation through an administrative hearing process and the decision ultimately may be appealed to federal court. Employers who violate the Act or OSHA standards are subject to both civil and criminal penalties.

Employee Polygraph Protection Act

The federal **Employee Polygraph Protection Act** of 1988[11] limits private employers' use of lie detectors and other mechanisms designed to determine a person's honesty. The statute, which generally prohibits most uses of lie detectors by employers in industries operating in or affecting interstate commerce, bars employers from discharging, disciplining, discriminating, or denying employment or promotion to employees or prospective employees on the basis of the results of a lie detector test. Under the Act, however, employers may request current employees to submit to polygraph examinations while investigating incidents causing economic loss, such as theft, embezzlement, or industrial espionage or sabotage, if the employer has reasonable suspicion that the employee was involved in the incident and had access to the property subject to the investigation. The statute exempts the federal and state government and also allows limited use of lie detectors in matters dealing with national defense and security. Other exemptions allow the use of lie detectors by security services in hiring employees who will protect facilities or materials with significant impact on the health and safety of the state or national security of the United States (including electric, nuclear power, or public water facilities, public transportation, and toxic waste), or by employers who manufacture or distribute certain drugs in hiring employees who will have access to those drugs. Even those employers who are exempt may not use lie detector results (or refusal to submit to a lie detector test) as the sole basis for discharging an employee or refusing to hire an applicant. The Act further establishes testing procedures for private employers who are allowed to use polygraph examinations. The employer must provide written notice to the employee, must use licensed examiners and must not ask questions about certain subjects (such as questions about sexual behavior or those relating to religious, racial, or political beliefs or affiliations).

The Secretary of Labor, who is responsible for administering the Act and adopting regulations, may assess a $10,000 civil penalty against employers who violate the Act and may seek legal or injunctive relief against violators in federal district courts. An employer who violates the Act also may be liable for damages and attorneys' fees of an employee or prospective employee injured by the violation.

Worker Adjustment and Retraining Notification Act

In 1988, Congress also enacted the **Worker Adjustment and Retraining Notification Act**[12], a statute that requires businesses to provide advance notification of certain plant closings or mass layoffs of employees. The Act applies only to employers with 100 or more full-time employees or 100 or more employees who in the aggregate work at least 4,000 hours per week (excluding overtime). The notification is required if an employer permanently or temporarily closes a plant causing employment loss to 50 or more full-time employees during a 30-day period or reduces the labor force causing employment loss to: 1) at least 500 full-time employees at the site, or 2) at least 50 full-time employees that comprise at least one-third of the employees at

---

11. 29 U.S.C. §§2001–2009.

12. 29 U.S.C. §§2101–2109.

the site. Under the Act, "employment loss" is considered to be termination (other than discharge for cause or voluntary departure or retirement), a layoff exceeding 6 months, or a reduction in working hours of more than 50% during each month of a six-month period. Sixty days prior to a plant closing or layoff that creates such an employment loss, the employer must provide written notice to each affected employee (or if the employees are unionized, to the union representative), to the chief elected official of the community in which the plant is located, and to certain other state officials. A plant closing or layoff is allowed without the 60-day notice if, at the time the notice was due, the employer was attempting to obtain capital or business that would have prevented or postponed the closing or layoff and the employer reasonably and in good faith believed that the notice would have prevented its obtaining the capital or business. Further, the 60-day notice is not required if the closing or layoff was caused by natural disaster or by business circumstances that could not be reasonably foreseen. An employer that orders a plant closing or mass layoff without providing the 60-day notice may be held civilly liable to pay 60 days' compensation and benefits to the affected employees.

Equal Employment Opportunity Statutes

In the wake of the civil rights movement of the 1950s and 1960s, the federal government enacted several statutes to guarantee employment opportunities to women and minority groups who historically had suffered discriminatory treatment by public and private employers. These statutes generally are referred to as equal employment opportunity laws.

Equal Pay Act

One of the earliest of these laws was the **Equal Pay Act**[13] of l963, an amendment to the Fair Labor Standards Act. The statute requires employers to pay equivalent wages to employees of both sexes who perform equal work on jobs requiring equal skill, effort, and responsibility under similar working conditions. Pay differences based on seniority

or merit, however, are permissible. An employer who violates the statute must raise the pay of the employee receiving lower wages and may not lower the wages of the higher paid employee.

Title VII of the Civil Rights Act of 1964

Title VII of the Civil Rights Act of 1964[14] as amended by the Equal Employment Opportunity Act of 1972 provides a more comprehensive approach to eliminating unfair discrimination in employment. Title VII prohibits employment discrimination on the basis of race, color, national origin, religion, and sex.

The provisions of Title VII apply to all employers with fifteen or more employees in industries affecting interstate commerce. Many businesses with fewer than fifteen employees are subject to state or local statutes similar to Title VII. State governments and most agencies of the federal government also must comply with Title VII.

Title VII's prohibitions against discrimination apply to most employment practices. An employment agency cannot refer or fail to refer an individual for employment based on race, color, national origin, religion or sex. An employer cannot use these classifications as a basis for hiring, discharging, or granting promotion, compensation or other conditions or privileges of employment to employees. Employment benefits such as training opportunities, life and health insurance and pension plans also must be administered without discrimination based on the prohibited classifications. Segregation or classification of employees on the basis of race, color, national origin, religion or sex is illegal if such classification adversely affects employment opportunities. As illustrated in the following case, sexual harassment of an employee also may violate Title VII.

Meritor Savings Bank v. Vinson
106 S. Ct. 2399 (1986)

In 1974, respondent Mechelle Vinson began employment as a teller-trainee at petitioner Meritor

---

13. 29 U.S.C. §206(d).

14. 42 U.S.C. §§2000e to 2000e-17.

Savings Bank under the supervision of Sidney Taylor. During the following years, Vinson was promoted to teller, head teller, and assistant branch manager. In September 1978, Vinson took sick leave for an indefinite period and in November 1978, the bank discharged her for excessive use of sick leave.

Vinson sued Taylor and Meritor Savings Bank, alleging that she had been subject to sexual harassment in violation of Title VII. At trial, Vinson testified that Taylor had invited her to dinner and suggested that they go to a motel to have sexual relations. After first refusing, Vinson eventually agreed because of fear of losing her job. She testified that Taylor subsequently made repeated demands for sexual favors both during and after business hours. She estimated that she had intercourse with Taylor forty to fifty times. Vinson further testified that Taylor fondled her in front of other employees and forcibly raped her on several occasions. These activities ceased after 1977 when Vinson began dating a steady boyfriend. Taylor denied all of Vinson's allegations and testified that she had made the accusations in response to a business-related dispute.

The trial court ruled that Vinson "was not the victim of sexual harassment . . . [nor of] sexual discrimination" and held that if Vinson and Taylor had engaged in a sexual relationship, the relationship was a voluntary one. The court of appeals reversed and remanded the case for further proceedings. The Supreme Court accepted the case for review.

Justice Rehnquist

. . . Title VII of the Civil Rights Act of 1964 makes it "an unlawful employment practice for an employer . . . to discriminate against any individual with respect to his compensation, terms, conditions, or privileges of employment, because of such individual's race, color, religion, sex, or national origin." 42 U.S.C. § 2000e-2(a)(1). . . .

Without question, when a supervisor sexually harasses a subordinate because of the subordinate's sex, that supervisor "discriminate[s]" on the basis of sex. Petitioner apparently does not challenge this proposition. It contends instead that in prohibiting discrimination with respect to "compensation, terms, conditions, or privileges" of employment,

Congress was concerned with what petitioner describes as "tangible loss" of "an economic character," not "purely psychological aspects of the workplace environment." . . .

We reject petitioner's view. First, the language of Title VII is not limited to "economic" or "tangible" discrimination. The phrase "terms, conditions, or privileges of employment" evinces a congressional intent "to strike at the entire spectrum of disparate treatment of men and women" in employment. *Los Angeles Department of Water and Power v. Manhart,* [98 S. Ct. 1370, 1375 n. 13 (1978)], quoting *Sprogis v. United Air Lines, Inc.,* 444 F.2d 1194, 1198 (7th Cir. 1971). Petitioner has pointed to nothing in the Act to suggest that Congress contemplated the limitation urged here.

Second, in 1980 the EEOC issued guidelines specifying that "sexual harassment," as there defined, is a form of sex discrimination prohibited by Title VII. . . . The EEOC guidelines fully support the view that harassment leading to noneconomic injury can violate Title VII.

In defining "sexual harassment," the guidelines first describe the kinds of workplace conduct that may be actionable under Title VII. These include "[u]nwelcome sexual advances, requests for sexual favors, and other verbal or physical conduct of a sexual nature." 29 CFR §1604.11(a) (1985). Relevant to the charges at issue in this case, the guidelines provide that such sexual misconduct constitutes prohibited "sexual harassment," whether or not it is directly linked to the grant or denial of an economic *quid pro quo,* where "such conduct has the purpose or effect of unreasonably interfering with an individual's work performance or creating an intimidating, hostile, or offensive working environment." §1604.11(a)(3).

In concluding that so-called "hostile environment" (*i.e.,* non *quid pro quo*) harassment violates Title VII, the EEOC drew upon a substantial body of judicial decisions and EEOC precedent holding that Title VII affords employees the right to work in an environment free from discriminatory intimidation, ridicule, and insult. . . .

Since the guidelines were issued, courts have uniformly held, and we agree, that a plaintiff may establish a violation of Title VII by proving that discrimination based on sex has created a hostile or abusive work environment. As the Court of Appeals for the Eleventh Circuit wrote in *Henson v. Dundee*, 682 F.2d 897, 902 (1982):

> "Sexual harassment which creates a hostile or offensive environment for members of one sex is every bit the arbitrary barrier to sexual equality at the workplace that racial harassment is to racial equality. Surely, a requirement that a man or woman run a gauntlet of sexual abuse in return for the privilege of being allowed to work and make a living can be as demeaning and disconcerting as the harshest of racial epithets." . . .

Of course, . . . not all workplace conduct that may be described as "harassment" affects a "term, condition, or privilege" of employment within the meaning of Title VII. . . . For sexual harassment to be actionable, it must be sufficiently severe or pervasive "to alter the conditions of [the victim's] employment and create an abusive working environment." [*Henson*, at 904.] Respondent's allegations in this case—which include not only pervasive harassment but also criminal conduct of the most serious nature—are plainly sufficient to state a claim for "hostile environment" sexual harassment. . . .

[T]he fact that sex-related conduct was "voluntary," in the sense that the complainant was not forced to participate against her will, is not a defense to a sexual harassment suit brought under Title VII. The gravamen of any sexual harassment claim is that the alleged sexual advances were "unwelcome." . . . The correct inquiry is whether respondent by her conduct indicated that the alleged sexual advances were unwelcome, not whether her actual participation in sexual intercourse was voluntary. . . .

While "voluntariness" in the sense of consent is not a defense to such a claim, it does not follow that a complainant's sexually provocative speech or dress is irrelevant as a matter of law in determining whether he or she found particular sexual advances unwelcome. To the contrary, such evidence is obviously relevant. The EEOC guidelines emphasize that the trier of fact must determine the existence of sexual harassment in light of "the record as a whole" and "the totality of circumstances, such as the nature of the sexual advances and the context in which the alleged incidents occurred." 29 CFR §1604.11(b) (1985). . . .

In sum, we hold that a claim of "hostile environment" sex discrimination is actionable under Title VII, that the District Court's findings were insufficient to dispose of respondent's hostile environment claim, and that the District Court did not err in admitting testimony about respondent's sexually provocative speech and dress. . . .

[Judgment of the Court of Appeals affirmed and remanded to District Court for further proceedings.]

Bona Fide Occupational Qualifications. Title VII, however, recognizes one general exception—known as the **bona fide occupational qualification (BFOQ)**—to its prohibitions against discrimination. If religion, sex, or national origin is a "bona fide occupational qualification reasonably necessary to the normal operation of [a] particular business,"[15] the employer may use these criteria for hiring, training or promotion. Race or color never may be used as bona fide occupational qualifications.

The BFOQ exception, which has been raised primarily in cases involving sex discrimination, has been construed narrowly by the courts. Restricting jobs to members of one sex based on stereotyped characterizations is not sufficient to meet the BFOQ exception. One court, for example, has held that an employer could not limit a switchman's job to men merely because the employer assumed that women could not perform heavy lifting required for the job.[16] In a similar case involving a job that required strenuous manual labor, the court held that sex was not a BFOQ. Instead, the court suggested that each applicant's ability to perform the tasks should be considered on an individual basis regardless of the applicant's sex.[17] Customer preference also is not

---

15. 42 U.S.C. §2000e-2(e). Title VII also exempts religious corporations, associations, educational institutions, or societies "with respect to the employment of individuals of a particular religion to perform work connected with the carrying on . . . of . . . activities" of such organizations. 42 U.S.C. §2000e-1.

16. *Weeks v. Southern Bell Telephone & Telegraph Company*, 408 F.2d 228 (5th Cir. 1969).

17. *Rosenfeld v. Southern Pacific Company*, 444 F.2d 1219 (9th Cir. 1971).

sufficient to justify sex discrimination. For example, an airline that restricted flight attendant jobs to women argued that being of the female sex was a BFOQ because customers preferred women attendants. Noting that employing only female attendants was not a business necessity, the court rejected the airline's argument.[18]

In some cases involving privacy and safety considerations, however, the courts have recognized the BFOQ exception. For example, the Supreme Court upheld excluding women from jobs as guards at maximum security penitentiaries in Alabama. The prisons, which were understaffed and had a history of violence, housed only male inmates, including a substantial number of sex offenders, in a dormitory setting.[19] In subsequent cases, though, courts have held that excluding women from jobs as prison guards or deputy sheriffs under less hostile circumstances violated Title VII.[20] The privacy rights of prisoners may require that some duties (such as strip searches, supervision of showering or dressing) be conducted by employees of the same sex as the prisoners. Nevertheless, several courts have suggested that rather than excluding employees of the opposite sex from the job, the employer should accommodate privacy rights by assigning only those duties based on sex.[21]

Disparate Treatment and Disparate Impact.
Employer practices subject to challenge under Title VII include intentional discrimination as well as conduct that has the effect of discrimination. Intentional discrimination based on race, color, national origin, religion, or sex is illegal **disparate treatment**. For example, a company's refusal to hire blacks or to promote women to supervisory positions is illegal disparate treatment of blacks and women. In contrast, an employment practice that is neutral on its face but has an adverse impact on those of a certain race, color, national origin, religion or sex causes illegal **disparate impact**. Requiring all salespeople to be at least six feet tall, for example, has a disparate impact on women.

An employee or applicant who has been the subject of disparate treatment can prove a violation of Title VII by establishing that the employer based its decision on illegal criteria. Even if a plaintiff cannot prove that the employer engaged in overt discrimination, courts recognize a prima facie case of disparate treatment if by proof of the following elements: (1) the plaintiff belongs to a protected class, (2) the plaintiff applied for a job for which the employer was seeking applicants, (3) the plaintiff was qualified for the job, (4) the plaintiff was denied the job, and (5) the job remained open and the employer continued to accept applications. After the plaintiff proves a prima facie case, the burden of proof shifts to the employer who must prove a legitimate business reason for rejecting the plaintiff's application.[22]

In recent years, many Title VII cases have challenged employment practices that have a disparate impact on women or minorities. The first Supreme Court case to recognize disparate impact as a violation of Title VII was *Griggs v. Duke Power Co.,*[23] in which the employer required the employees to hold a high school diploma to secure more desirable positions in the company. This requirement affected black employees more adversely than white employees because a greater proportion of black employees had not earned the diploma. The Court held the requirement violated Title VII stating:

> The Act [Title VII] proscribes not only overt discrimination but also practices that are fair in form, but discriminatory in operation. The touchstone in business necessity. If an employment practice which operates to excludes Negroes cannot be shown to be related to job performance, the practice is prohibited.[24]

To prove a prima facie case of disparate impact, a plaintiff must prove that a facially neutral employment practice had a significant discriminatory

---

18. *Diaz v. Pan American World Airways, Inc.*, 442 F.2d 385 (5th Cir. 1971).

19. *Dothard v. Rawlinson*, 97 S. Ct. 2720 (1977).

20. See *Gunther v. Iowa State Men's Reformatory*, 612 F.2d 1079 (8th Cir. 1980); *Hardin v. Stynchcomb*, 691 F.2d 1364 (11th Cir. 1982).

21. *Id.*

---

22. *McDonnell Douglas Corporation v. Green*, 93 S. Ct. 1817, 1824 (1973).

23. 91 S. Ct. 849 (1971).

24. *Id.* at 853.

impact on women or minorities. The burden of proof then shifts to the employer who, to avoid liability, must prove that the practice results from business necessity. Many disparate impact cases challenge the use of objective criteria, such as test scores or minimum educational requirements, that may have a discriminatory effect on minorities, or minimum height and weight standards, that adversely affect women and certain minority groups. Recently, however, the Supreme Court held that the use of subjective criteria also may have a disparate impact on groups protected by Title VII. Subjective criteria may include, for example, an interviewer's evaluation of a person's common sense, business judgment, creativity, loyalty, or ambition. Recognizing that an interviewer without discriminatory intent subconsciously could be affected by stereotypes and prejudices, the Court held that subjective or discretionary employment practices that have a disparate impact could violate Title VII.[25]

In the following case, the Supreme Court reviews the purposes of Title VII in light of a novel defense raised in a disparate impact case.

Connecticut v. Teal
102 S. Ct. 2525 (1982)

Respondents, Winnie Teal and three other black employees of the Connecticut Department of Income Maintenance, sought promotion to supervisory positions. The first requirement for promotion was to take and pass a written examination. Respondents took the exam but did not achieve a passing score. Only 54.17% of all black employees who took the exam passed it while 79.54% of the white employees who took the test passed.

Following administration of the exam, the state promoted forty-six (11 black and 35 white) employees who had passed the exam to supervisory positions. Among those who had taken the exam, 22.9% of the black employees and 13.5% of the white employees received promotions.

Respondents sued petitioners, the state of Connecticut and the Department of Income Mainte-

nance, alleging that use of the written examination violated Title VII by excluding a disproportionate number of black employees from promotion to supervisory positions. Petitioners argued that the "bottom line" result of the examination was not discriminatory because a greater percentage of black employees than white employees were promoted. The District Court dismissed respondents' claim holding they had not established a prima facie case of discrimination. The Court of Appeals reversed and the Supreme Court granted certiorari to the petitioners.

Justice Brennan

. . . We must first decide whether an examination that bars a disparate number of black employees from consideration for promotion, and that has not been shown to be job-related, presents a claim cognizable under Title VII. Section 703(a)(2) of Title VII provides in pertinent part:

> It shall be an unlawful employment practice for an employer— . . .
> (2) to limit, segregate, or classify his employees or applicants for employment in any way which would deprive or tend to deprive any individual of employment opportunities or otherwise adversely affect his status as an employee, because of such individual's race, color, religion, sex, or national origin. . . .

Petitioners' examination, which barred promotion and had a discriminatory impact on black employees, clearly falls within the literal language of §703(a)(2), as interpreted by *Griggs*. The statute speaks, not in terms of jobs and promotions, but in terms of *limitations* and *classifications* that would deprive any individual of employment *opportunities*. A disparate-impact claim reflects the language of §703(a)(2) and Congress' basic objectives in enacting that statute: "to achieve equality of employment *opportunities* and remove barriers that have operated in the past to favor an identifiable group of white employees over other employees." [91 S. Ct. at 853](emphasis added). When an employer uses a nonjob-related barrier in order to deny a minority or woman applicant employment or promotion, and that barrier has a significant adverse effect on minorities or women, then the applicant has

---

25. *Watson v. Fort Worth Bank and Trust*, 108 S. Ct. 2777 (1988).

been deprived of an employment *opportunity* "because of . . . race, color, religion, sex, or national origin." . . .

In considering claims of disparate impact under §703(a)(2) this Court has consistently focused on employment and promotion requirements that create a discriminatory bar to *opportunities*. This Court has never read §703(a)(2) as requiring the focus to be placed instead on the overall number of minority or female applicants actually hired or promoted. . . .

In sum, respondents' claim of disparate impact from the examination, a pass-fail barrier to employment opportunity, states a prima facie case of employment discrimination under §703(a)(2). . . .

Having determined that respondents' claim comes within the terms of Title VII, we must address the suggestion of petitioners . . . that we recognize an exception, either in the nature of an additional burden on plaintiffs seeking to establish a prima facie case or in the nature of an affirmative defense, for cases in which an employer has compensated for a discriminatory pass-fail barrier by hiring or promoting a sufficient number of black employees to reach a nondiscriminatory "bottom line." We reject this suggestion which is in essence nothing more than a request that we redefine the protections guaranteed by Title VII.

Section 703(a)(2) prohibits practices that would deprive or tend to deprive "*any individual* of employment opportunities." The principal focus of the statute is the protection of the individual employee, rather than the protection of the minority group as a whole. Indeed, the entire statute and its legislative history are replete with references to protection for the individual employee. . . .

[P]etitioners seek simply to justify discrimination against respondents on the basis of their favorable treatment of other members of respondents' racial group. . . .

It is clear that Congress never intended to give an employer license to discriminate against some employees on the basis of race or sex merely because he favorably treats other members of the employees' group. . . .

Title VII does not permit the victim of a facially discriminatory policy to be told that he has not been wronged because other persons of his or her race or sex were hired. . . . Every *individual* employee is protected against both discriminatory

treatment and "practices that are fair in form, but discriminatory in operation." *Griggs v. Duke Power Co.,* [91 S. Ct. at 853.] . . .

In sum, petitioners' nondiscriminatory "bottom line" is no answer, under the terms of Title VII, to respondents' prima facie claim of employment discrimination. . . .

[Judgment affirmed and remanded.]

Seniority Systems. Seniority systems create special problems in Title VII litigation. Seniority systems generally grant employees special privileges—such as greater job security, vacation and pension benefits and promotion and transfer opportunities—based on their tenure with a company. In many companies, minority members and women have the least seniority because employment opportunities only recently have been available to them. As a result, they are unable to enjoy the benefits of those with greater seniority. Further, when employers layoff employees, those with the least seniority are the first to be discharged. In essence, seniority systems may have a disparate impact on women and minority members and may serve to perpetuate discrimination that existed prior to the enactment of Title VII.

The Supreme Court has held that bona fide seniority systems that were not adopted with the intent of discriminating against protected classes do not violate Title VII.[26] The Court also has held, however, that those who have been actual victims of discrimination may be awarded greater seniority than that to which they would be entitled based on years of employment.[27] Thus, while recognizing the potential discriminatory impact of seniority systems because of historical discrimination, the Supreme Court has extended special protection under Title VII only to those who have personally suffered from discriminatory practices.

Affirmative Action and Reverse Discrimination. Some companies adopt **affirmative action pro-**

---

26. *International Brotherhood of Teamsters v. United States,* 97 S. Ct. 1843 (1977).

27. *Id.*

grams to encourage hiring women or members of certain minority groups that are underrepresented in the company. These efforts have been subject to criticism because they may result in **reverse discrimination**—discrimination in favor of minorities and women. The issues raised by affirmative action and reverse discrimination have not yet been fully resolved by the legislature or the courts. In *United Steelworkers of America v. Weber*, the Supreme Court upheld the validity of voluntary affirmative action plans "designed to eliminate conspicuous racial unbalance in traditionally segregated job categories."[28] Courts have approved adoption of affirmative action programs to compensate for past intentional discrimination against women and minorities, even if those who benefit from the programs were not actual victims of discrimination.[29] Generally, programs that establish hiring preferences or goals that favor women or minorities are more likely to be approved than are programs that establish hiring quotas that restrict a fixed number of jobs for women or minorities. If Title VII achieves its purpose of providing equal employment opportunity, affirmative action eventually will become unnecessary. Until that time, however, courts will continue individual review of affirmative action cases in an attempt to balance the equities of the parties involved in the suit.

Enforcement. The **Equal Employment Opportunity Commission** (EEOC) is responsible for enforcing Title VII. Actions under Title VII must be initiated by filing a claim with the EEOC, which notifies the employer of the charge. After investigation of the complaint, the EEOC may dismiss the charge if it finds no reasonable cause for the allegations of wrongdoing. The complaining party then may file a civil action in federal district court. If the EEOC finds reasonable cause for the charge, it must attempt to obtain a conciliation agreement by the parties. The EEOC may file a civil action in the federal district court if a conciliation agreement is not obtained, or the EEOC may issue a "right to sue" letter notifying the complaining party that he or she may file a federal civil suit.

A successful plaintiff in a Title VII action may be awarded damages equal to the back pay to which the plaintiff would have been entitled had the discrimination not occurred, limited to that which accrued within two years prior to filing the charge. Injunctive relief also is available. Most courts refuse to award punitive damages. The court may award attorneys' fees to the prevailing party in the suit.

Other Equal Employment Opportunity Laws

Other federal statutes adopted to protect employees from unfair discrimination are the Pregnancy Discrimination Act and the Age Discrimination in Employment Act.

Pregnancy Discrimination Act. The **Pregnancy Discrimination Act** of 1978,[30] which amends Title VII, prohibits employment discrimination based on pregnancy. Under the statute an employer may not discharge or refuse to hire or promote a woman solely because she is pregnant. An employer also may not require pregnant women to take leave at a specified time during pregnancy but instead must base mandatory leaves on the individual woman's inability to continue working. The Act also grants some reinstatement rights to women who take leave because of pregnancy and requires employers to treat pregnancy, childbirth, and related medical conditions in the same way they treat other causes of disability under fringe benefit plans.

Age Discrimination in Employment Act. The **Age Discrimination in Employment Act** (ADEA) of 1967[31] as amended in 1986 prohibits both private and governmental employers from discriminating on the basis of age against persons over the age of 40 years. Under the Act, which has many provisions similar to those of Title VII, an employer may not discharge or fail or refuse to hire a person because of age and may not discriminate in grant-

28. 99 S. Ct. 2721, 2730 (1979).

29. *Local 28 of Sheet Metal Workers' International Association v. Equal Employment Opportunity Commission*, 106 S. Ct. 3019 (1986); *Local Number 93, International Association of Firefighters v. City of Cleveland*, 106 S. Ct. 3063 (1986).

30. 42 U.S.C. §2000e(k).

31. 29 U.S.C. §§621-634.

ing compensation, conditions, or privileges of employment. Generally, an employer may not establish a compulsory retirement age for employees except for certain executives or high policy-making employees who are entitled to nonforfeitable annual retirement benefits. An employer who willfully violates the ADEA may be subject to liquidated damages equal to twice the plaintiff's compensatory damages.

As with Title VII violations, an employee may prove age discrimination by establishing either disparate treatment or disparate impact. A plaintiff who alleges intentional discrimination under ADEA must prove that age was a determinative, but not necessarily the sole, reason for the employer's discriminatory action. If a plaintiff establishes age discrimination, the burden shifts to the employer who can avoid liability by proving a legitimate, nondiscriminatory reason for the allegedly illegal conduct.

An employer may use age as a criterion in employment decisions if age is a bona fide occupational qualification reasonably necessary to the normal operation of the particular business. In *Western Air Lines, Inc. v. Criswell,* (1985)[32] the Supreme Court held that the BFOQ defense must be narrowly construed and ruled that an airline's requiring all flight engineers to retire at age 60 was not based on a valid BFOQ. The Court stated that to justify the use of a mandatory retirement age for safety reasons the employer must prove that it had reasonable cause to believe that all or substantially all persons over the age qualification were unable to perform safely the duties of the job or that it was highly impractical to test the employee's ability to perform the job on an individualized basis.

Cases alleging age discrimination have increased substantially during the last few years. One of the most difficult issues presented by these cases involves companies that are attempting to reduce costs through job elimination or consolidation. In some cases, upper level employees, who frequently are older and earn higher salaries and benefits, have been offered special incentives for early retirement. Although such programs have been challenged as discriminatory practices, courts have upheld the validity of early termination if voluntarily made by

---

32. 105 S. Ct. 2743 (1985).

the employee. As illustrated by the following case, businesses must be especially careful not to violate the ADEA when formulating and implementing cost saving programs involving employment.

Metz v. Transit Mix, Inc.
828 F.2d 1202 (7th Cir. 1987)

Defendant Transit Mix, Inc., a business selling concrete to construction contractors, discharged plaintiff Wayne Metz, who had worked for the company for 27 years. At the time of his discharge, Metz was manager of Transit Mix's Knox, Indiana plant. Following three years of financial problems due to a decline in local construction, Transit Mix decided to close the Knox plant for the winter of 1983-84 and temporarily laid off Metz in December, 1983. In April 1984, Transit Mix discharged Metz and assigned management of the Knox plant to Donald Burzloff, assistant manager of the Plymouth, Indiana plant. At the time of Metz's termination, he was 54 years old and earned approximately $15.75 per hour. Burzloff then was 43 years old and earned about $8.05 an hour.

Metz sued Transit Mix alleging that his discharge violated the ADEA. Following a trial, the district court ruled in favor of Transit Mix and Metz appealed.

Cudahy, Circuit Judge

. . . The ADEA prohibits employers from discriminating against employees on the basis of age. . . . Its objective in part is to promote employment of older workers on the basis of their abilities rather than their age. . . . The statute does not, however, prevent an employer from terminating an older worker based on reasonable factors other than age. . . . When, as in the present case, a plaintiff is proceeding on a disparate treatment analysis, the plaintiff may recover only if the defendant in discharging the plaintiff was motivated by a discriminatory animus; that is, the plaintiff may recover only if his or her age was a determining factor in the employer's decision.

Proving intentional discrimination is often difficult, so a plaintiff may do so by presenting either direct or indirect evidence of discrimination. . . .

In order to permit recovery for an ADEA claim through indirect means, this circuit has adopted a variation of the burden-shifting analysis set forth by the Supreme Court in the Title VII context for establishing a prima facie case of employment discrimination. . . . As applied to an ADEA claim, this analysis requires that a plaintiff show that he or she: 1) belongs to the protected class (age forty or older); 2) was qualified for his or her position; 3) was terminated; and 4) was replaced by a younger person. After the plaintiff has established a prima facie case, the defendant employer then has the burden of presenting evidence that the plaintiff's discharge was a result of "some legitimate, nondiscriminatory reason." If the defendant meets this burden of production, the burden shifts to the plaintiff to prove that the reasons proffered by the employer for the discharge were merely a pretext for discrimination. . . . Throughout the trial, the burden remains with the plaintiff to prove there was discrimination, rather than with the employer to prove the absence of discrimination. . . .

The district court found that Metz had established a prima facie case of age discrimination. The court further found that a determining factor in Transit Mix's decision to replace Metz with Burzloff was a desire to save the higher cost of Metz's salary and that this factor "bore a relationship to Mr. Metz's age." . . . The court held, however, that this was not age discrimination in violation of the ADEA because it was based on an assessment of the cost of employing an individual employee, namely, Metz, rather than an impermissible assessment of the costs of employing Transit Mix's older employees as a group. The sole issue on appeal is whether the salary savings that can be realized by replacing a single employee in the ADEA age-protected range with a younger, lower-salaried employee constitutes a permissible, nondiscriminatory justification for the replacement.

Congress enacted the ADEA in response to the problems that the older worker faces in the job market, including the obstacles that the long-term employee encounters when he or she is suddenly without work. . . . These difficulties have been attributed in large part to the worker's development of firm-specific skills not easily transferable to a different job setting. . . . Therefore, while the older employee's higher salary reflects the value of improved skills and the increased productivity that results, it is also indicative of one of the very problems the ADEA was intended to address: the likelihood that the employee will be less employable in other settings.

The ADEA has consistently been interpreted by the administrative agencies charged with its enforcement and the courts to prohibit an employer from replacing higher paid employees with lower paid employees in order to save money. The Equal Employment Opportunity Commission guidelines expressly provide that "A differentiation based on the average cost of employing older employees as a group is unlawful except with respect to [certain] employee benefit plans . . . 29 C.F.R. §1625.7(f) (1986). . . .

Neither the district court nor Transit Mix on appeal takes issue with this interpretation of the ADEA in the context of policies that eliminate older employees as a group based on their higher salaries. Rather, they argue for a distinction based on whether the employer's employment action, motivated by a desire to save costs, affects a group of employees or an individual employee. . . .

The same ADEA policy concern that forms the basis for rejecting cost-based employer practices that have an adverse impact upon older workers as a group is present in the case of Metz's discharge: Given the correlation between Metz's higher salary and his years of satisfactory service, allowing Transit Mix to replace Metz based on the higher cost of employing him would defeat the intent of the statute. . . .

Metz's relatively high salary was the result of annual raises that were given to him by Transit Mix regardless of how the company was doing financially. . . . Metz's salary therefore reflected his twenty-seven years of service to Transit Mix. When Lawrence, the president of Transit Mix, decided that the company's poor performance no longer justified the salary that the company had given Metz, Lawrence replaced Metz because of that salary without first asking Metz to take a pay cut. Given these facts, Lawrence's desire to save costs was not a permissible, nondiscriminatory reason for replacing Metz with the younger, less-costly Burzloff; by thus replacing Metz, Transit Mix violated Metz's rights under the ADEA. . . .

We are, of course, aware that employers must

control costs if they are to remain competitive and that this imperative of survival will inevitably create tensions with the legal prohibitions against age discrimination. We think it would be unwise, however, to translate this imperative into a rule that an older employee can be fired and replaced by an equally proficient younger employee merely because the older employee happens to be earning more money at the moment. There are a number of less burdensome measures that can be introduced if necessary before "industrial capital punishment" is brought into play. . . .

[Judgment reversed and remanded.]

Labor Law

The preceding sections of this chapter discussed employment laws that protect an individual employee's rights and equal employment opportunities. The remainder of the chapter concerns labor law, a body of federal statutory, administrative, and case law governing employees' collective action though the formation and operation of labor organizations and unions.

Federal Statutes

During the late nineteenth and early twentieth centuries, employees began to form labor organizations in an attempt to strengthen their power to bargain for favorable employment contracts, especially with corporate employers. Using the common law to resolve labor disputes, the judiciary demonstrated a strong bias in favor of employers by enjoining most union activities including strikes, picketing, and boycotts. Federal regulation of labor-management relations began in 1932 when Congress adopted the **Norris-LaGuardia Act**[33] that restricted the federal courts' power to issue injunctions in labor disputes. Three years later, Congress enacted the **National Labor Relations Act**[34] (the NLRA, or often called the **Wagner Act**) which was amended in 1947 by the **Labor-Management Relations Act**[35] (usually called the **Taft-Hartley Act**) and again in 1959 by the **Labor-Management Reporting and Disclosure Act**[36] (usually called the **Landrum-Griffin Act**).

Wagner Act. The Wagner Act established employees' basic rights to engage in collective action: (1) the right to form, join, or assist unions, (2) the right to bargain collectively through a union chosen by the employees, and (3) the right to engage in concerted activities for the purpose of collective bargaining or other mutual aid or protection.[37] To secure and implement these rights, the Act defined a series of **unfair labor practices**, illegal conduct that was prohibited by the Wagner Act. All unfair labor practices defined in the Wagner Act were practices committed by employers and, therefore, the Act significantly limited employers' powers to oppose unionization. The Wagner Act also created the **National Labor Relations Board (NLRB),** a federal agency responsible for administering the NLRA and issuing rules and regulations. The NLRB also was granted the power to investigate and prosecute alleged unfair labor practice cases and to provide administrative hearings for violations of the NLRA.

Taft-Hartley Act. Following a period of dramatic growth of unions, Congress amended the NLRA with the Taft-Hartley Act in an effort to assume a more neutral federal policy toward labor-management relations. Although the NLRA continued to guarantee employees' rights to engage in union activities, the Taft-Hartley Act made illegal certain unfair labor practices committed by unions and employees, thereby protecting employers from abusive conduct by unions. The Act also reorganized the NLRB by better separating its prosecutorial functions from its adjudicative duties.

Landrum-Griffin Act. Congress added the second major amendment to the NLRA by adopting the Landrum-Griffin Act in 1959 in response to wide-

---

33. 29 U.S.C. §§101-115.
34. 29 U.S.C. §151 *et seq.*

---

35. 29 U.S.C. §141 *et seq.*
36. 29 U.S.C. §§153, 158-160, 164, 186, 187, 401 *et seq.*
37. 29 U.S.C. §157.

spread corruption within union administration. The Landrum-Griffin Act created a bill of rights that protects union members from improper treatment by unions. Some of these rights include voting and membership rights, the right to freedom of speech and assembly, the right to sue a union or its officers, and the right to procedural safeguards prior to discipline by a union. The Landrum-Griffin Act also requires unions to adopt constitutions and by-laws and to submit periodic financial reports to the Secretary of Labor.

Unfair Labor Practices in Labor-Management Relations

Today the NLRA as amended remains the most significant statute regulating labor-management relations. Its coverage extends to employees of most businesses affecting interstate commerce except employees of federal and state governments, non-profit hospitals, agricultural laborers, and workers subject to the Railway Labor Act.

The NLRA imposes on employers a general duty not to interfere with employees' rights to form, join, or assist unions, or to engage in concerted activities. Similarly, unions are prohibited from restraining or coercing employees exercising these rights. Violation of these statutory requirements by an employer or union is an unfair labor practice. The NLRA also establishes more specific unfair labor practices addressed to tactics frequently used by unions or management. The material that follows discusses the major unfair labor practices arising from labor-management relations.

Election of the Collective Bargaining Representative. Unionization begins with the employees' selection of a union to act as their collective bargaining representative to engage in negotiations called **collective bargaining** with the employer. The objective of the negotiation is to obtain a **collective bargaining contract,** a formal agreement covering wages, hours, and conditions of employment.

A union or employees initiate a campaign for selection of the bargaining representative. A union that obtains sufficient support, documented by authorization cards signed by the employees, may demand that the employer recognize the union as the bargaining representative. The employer may vol-

untarily recognize the union and proceed to collective bargaining, but in such a case the union is not officially certified as the collective bargaining representative by the NLRB. If the employer refuses to grant recognition, the union, an employee, or the employer may file a petition for representation election with the NLRB.

The NLRB investigates the petition to determine that an adequate number of employees support a union (generally 30% of the employees as documented by authorization cards). The NLRB also determines the appropriate bargaining unit for the election. The bargaining unit consists of the employees who will be entitled to vote in the election and who will be represented by the union if it is elected. The unit may consist of the entire business, one department, one or more plants, or one or more stores or offices of the business. With the consent of the union and the employer, the NLRB then sets the date for the election that is conducted under the supervision of an NLRB representative. With limited exceptions, all nonsupervisory and nonmanagerial employees within the unit are entitled to vote. Following the election the NLRB certifies the union as the collective bargaining representative if a majority of the voting employees have voted for a union. If the employees reject the union, the NLRB certifies the election results.

During the union campaign and election, an employer can engage only in limited activities in opposition to unionization. The employer is entitled to express its opinion of a union or unionization through speeches, literature, or other means provided the employer does not interfere with, restrain, or coerce employees who are exercising their rights to organize. If, for example, the employer threatens reprisals for organizational activities[38] or grants benefits during an election campaign to induce employees to reject the union, the employer commits an unfair labor practice. Withholding existing benefits or revoking planned increased benefits during the election campaign also may be unlawful.

The employer also is prohibited from unduly interfering with the union and employees' rights to distribute information to employees and to solicit employees' votes. In general, the employer may

---

38. 29 U.S.C. §158(c).

prevent or limit dissemination of literature or solicitation of votes by employees during working time. The employer, however, may not restrict these activities by employees in nonworking areas during nonworking time—such as lunch hours or breaks—without a showing of special circumstances. A retail business, for example, may prohibit employee solicitation activities on the sales floor during employees' nonworking time if the activities would disrupt business.

Unions also are prohibited from interfering with employees' organizational rights. Threats against employees for refusal to join the union are unlawful. The union cannot grant special benefits or privileges—such as waiver of membership fees—to employees who vote in favor of the union.

The Collective Bargaining Process. After a union has been certified or recognized as the collective bargaining representative, it is the exclusive representative for all employees in the unit. Both the union and the employer have a duty to bargain in good faith on wages, rates of pay, hours of employment, or other conditions of employment. Failure or refusal to bargain in good faith is an unfair labor practice.

At a minimum, the duty to bargain in good faith requires both parties to meet at reasonable times and places and attempt to reach an agreement by offering and considering proposals. Although the duty to bargain in good faith does not require either the union or the employer to make concessions or to reach an agreement, offering proposals, counterproposals, and concessions may demonstrate that a party has fulfilled its duty to bargain in good faith. If the union and management reach an impasse, they need not continue futile negotiations. In determining whether the parties have fulfilled their duty to bargain, the courts and the NLRB will examine their conduct during the entire course of negotiations.

The duty to bargain in good faith applies only to mandatory subjects of bargaining—those within the category of "wages, hours and other terms and conditions of employment," including discharge of employees, seniority, work schedules, retirement and pension plans, insurance plans, and grievances. The parties are prohibited from negotiating illegal subjects of bargaining, which are proposals that violate the labor statutes. For example, "featherbedding"—paying employees for services that are not performed or not intended to be performed—is illegal under the NLRA and, therefore, may not be the subject of bargaining or may not be required under the collective bargaining agreement. All topics other than mandatory or illegal subjects of bargaining are considered voluntary or permissive subjects of bargaining which, if both parties agree, may be negotiated and included in the collective bargaining agreement.

In the case that follows, the Supreme Court considers collective bargaining and mandatory subjects of bargaining.

Ford Motor Company v. National Labor Relations Board
99 S. Ct. 1842 (1979)

Petitioner Ford Motor Company operates a parts stamping plant employing 3,600 employees who are represented by the International Union, United Automobile, Aerospace, and Agricultural Implement Workers of America (the Union). Because no restaurants are located near the plant, Ford provides in-plant cafeterias and vending machines managed by ARA Services, Inc., an independent caterer. By contract with Ford, ARA furnishes food, management, machines, and personnel in exchange for reimbursement of all direct costs plus 9% of net receipts. If receipts exceed costs plus the 9% surcharge, Ford retains the excess but if the receipts are less than the costs and surcharge, Ford is obligated to pay ARA the deficit up to $52,000 per year. Ford has the right to review and approve the quality, quantity, and price of the food served by ARA.

In 1976, Ford notified the Union that cafeteria and vending machine prices were to be increased. The Union requested that Ford bargain over the prices and services but Ford refused maintaining that these matters were not mandatory subjects of bargaining. The Union filed an unfair labor practice charge with the National Labor Relations Board (the Board) alleging that Ford had refused to bargain over a mandatory bargaining subject.

The Board ruled that Ford had violated its duty to bargain in good faith. Ford appealed to the Seventh Circuit Court of Appeals, which held that the cafeteria and vending machine food prices and services were mandatory subjects of bargaining. The Supreme Court granted Ford's petition for review.

Justice, White

. . . The principal question in this case is whether prices for in-plant cafeteria and vending machine food and beverages are "terms and conditions of employment" subject to mandatory collective bargaining. . . .

The Board has consistently held that in-plant food prices are among those terms and conditions of employment defined in §8(d) [of the National Labor Relations Act] and about which the employer and union must bargain. . . .

Construing and applying the duty to bargain and the language of §8(d), "other terms and conditions of employment," are tasks lying at the heart of the Board's function. . . . [W]e conclude that the Board's consistent view that in-plant food prices and services are mandatory bargaining subjects is not an unreasonable or unprincipled construction of the statute and that it should be accepted and enforced.

It is not suggested by petitioner that an employee should work a full 8-hour shift without stopping to eat. It reasonably follows that the availability of food during working hours and the conditions under which it is to be consumed are matters of deep concern to workers, and one need not strain to consider them to be among those "conditions" of employment that should be subject to the mutual duty to bargain. By the same token, where the employer has chosen, apparently in his own interest, to make available a system of in-plant feeding facilities for his employees, the prices at which food is offered and other aspects of this service may reasonably be considered among those subjects about which management and union must bargain. The terms and conditions under which food is available on the job are plainly germane to the "working environment." *Fibreboard Paper Products Corp. v. NLRB*, [85 S. Ct. 398,409 (1964)] (Stewart, J., concurring). Furthermore, the company is not in the business of selling food to its employees, and the establishment of in-plant food prices is not among those "managerial decisions, which lie at the core of entrepreneurial control." [*Id.* at 409] (Stewart, J., concurring). The Board is in no sense

attempting to permit the Union to usurp managerial decision-making; nor is it seeking to regulate an area from which Congress intended to exclude it.

Including within §8(d) the prices of in-plant-supplied food and beverages would also serve the ends of the National Labor Relations Act. . . . As illustrated by the facts of this case, substantial disputes can arise over the pricing of in-plant-supplied food and beverages. National labor policy contemplates that areas of common dispute between employers and employees be funneled into collective bargaining. The assumption is that this is preferable to allowing recurring disputes to fester outside the negotiation process until strikes or other forms of economic warfare occur.

The trend of industrial practice supports this conclusion. In response to increasing employee concern over the issue, many contracts are now being negotiated that contain provisions concerning in-plant food services. . . . Although not conclusive, current industrial practice is highly relevant in construing the phrase "terms and conditions of employment." . . .

We affirm, therefore, the Court of Appeals' judgment upholding the Board's determination in this case that in-plant food services and prices are "terms and conditions of employment" subject to mandatory bargaining under §§8(a)(5) and 8(d) of the National Labor Relations Act.

[Judgment affirmed.]

The purpose of the collective bargaining process is to secure a collective bargaining agreement to govern the relations between the employer and employees and the union and the employer. This agreement is not an employment contract; employees are hired individually. The collective bargaining contract usually covers wages, hours, promotions, health insurance, pensions, vacations, holidays, and seniority. Almost all collective bargaining agreements provide a grievance procedure for resolving disputes in interpreting and applying the provisions of the agreement. Most collective bargaining agreements also require that disputes not settled through the grievance procedure be submitted to arbitration. With rare exceptions, the courts will enforce the arbitrator's decision so that court resolution of contract disputes occurs only infrequently.

Even after a collective bargaining agreement is made, the duty to bargain in good faith continues. As a result, modifications of the bargaining contract or resolution of issues not covered in the contract may require further negotiations by the parties.

If the union and employer are unable to reach a collective bargaining contract or to resolve mandatory bargaining subjects, the federal government provides mediation services through the Federal Mediation and Conciliation Service, a federal agency. Many states offer similar services. Although mediation is not binding, mediators often succeed in bringing the opposing parties to an agreement.

Hiring and Employment Practices. Under the NLRA, an employer commits an unfair labor practice "by discrimination in regard to hire or tenure of employment or any term or condition of employment to encourage or discourage membership in any labor organization."[39] Thus, a business may not discharge or refuse to hire a person because of involvement in union activities. The **yellow dog contract**—an employee's agreement as a condition of employment not to join or retain membership in a union—also is illegal. Similarly, the employer cannot fire or discriminate against employees because they have filed charges against an employer under the NLRA or have testified at a hearing or trial brought under the Act.

Unions also are prohibited from causing employers to discriminate against employees because of their union membership. The **closed shop**—an employer's agreement to hire only members of a union—is illegal. Nevertheless, under current labor law, some union shop and agency shop agreements are legal. A **union shop** agreement requires newly hired employees to join the union within a specified period after beginning employment. Union shop agreements are legal only if union membership is required on or after the thirtieth day following the beginning of employment. An **agency shop** agreement requires employees who do not join the union

to pay for the union's services through fees that usually are equivalent to members' dues and fees. A legal agency shop cannot require the employee to pay such fees earlier than thirty days after beginning employment.

The NLRA, however, allows states to enact **right-to-work laws** that prohibit union and agency shops. Almost half of the states, located primarily in the South and Southwest, have adopted right-to-work laws. In those states, union and agency shops are illegal.

Strikes. The ultimate negotiating weapon of a union is a **strike,** a concerted work stoppage by the employees. During a labor dispute or contract negotiation, the threat of a strike strengthens the union's bargaining power. Strikes generally represent legal conduct protected under labor law. As a general rule, the employer may not discharge or otherwise discipline employees who engage in strikes. Nevertheless, employers are not required to pay striking employees and may hire replacements to perform the strikers' work.

When employees engage in a strike for illegal purposes or participate in illegal strike activities, they lose their protection under the labor statutes and are subject to dismissal and discipline. For example, a strike to compel the employer or to allow the union to commit an unfair labor practice is illegal. Employees who strike in breach of a no-strike clause in a collective bargaining agreement also lose the protection of the labor laws as do those who engage in **wildcat strikes,** which are strikes by a minority of employees without authorization of the union. Both types of strikers are entitled to contest any discipline or dismissal for their conduct through the grievance procedure.

Federal law prohibits a strike during a statutory "cooling off period." The union or employer who seeks to modify or terminate a contract, for example, must provide notice to the other party giving rise to a sixty-day cooling off period. A union cannot strike until the earlier of sixty days following the notice or the termination of the contract. Further, if a strike would create a national emergency, a federal court, upon request of the president, may issue an injunction creating an eighty-day cooling off period.

Federal labor law protects the rights of employ-

---

39. 29 U.S.C. §158(a)(3).

ees who engage in lawful strikes but their rights depend on the type of strike in which they participate. An **unfair labor practice strike** is caused in whole or in part by the employer's commission of an unfair labor practice. Employees who engage in unfair labor practice strikes are entitled to reinstatement in their jobs upon request, even if the employer has hired replacements. Any strike that is not an unfair labor practice strike is called an **economic strike** because such strikes frequently concern employees' demands for economic benefits. If permanent replacements have not been hired, economic strikers are entitled to reinstatement in their former jobs. The employer, however, need not reinstate economic strikers whose jobs have been filled by permanent replacements. Nevertheless, the economic strikers who have not secured comparable employment elsewhere receive preferential treatment to reinstatement if their former job or a job for which they are qualified becomes vacant at a later date.

Picketing. Picketing provides an opportunity for the union and employees to publicize disputes with the employer. Frequently strikes are accompanied by picketing. **Primary picketing**—picketing the business with which the union has a genuine dispute—generally is legal and protected under the labor laws. In refusing to enjoin primary picketing, courts have noted that it is an exercise of the right of free speech. Such picketing may be illegal, however, if it is accompanied by violence or is likely to lead to violence. Courts usually may enjoin picketing on the private property of the employer.

Secondary Boycotts. Federal protection of strikes and picketing generally extends only to concerted activities directed at the primary employer; that is, the business with which the union has a genuine dispute. A **secondary boycott** is a union tactic of pressuring the primary employer by striking, picketing, or otherwise boycotting a business with which the primary employer does business. Inducing or engaging in a secondary boycott is an unfair labor practice under the NLRA.

Assume, for example, that the employees of Manufacturer Co. are striking their employer for higher wages and that Supplier, Inc. and Retailer Corp. both do business with Manufacturer Co. The striking employees may picket Manufacturer and may appeal to the employees of Supplier and Retailer not to cross the picket line. Manufacturer's employees also may request that Supplier and Retailer discontinue doing business with Manufacturer. All of such activities are considered to be primary activities directed at Manufacturer, the primary employer. If, however, Manufacturer's employees are unsuccessful in discouraging others from dealing with Manufacturer, the employees cannot apply pressure to those secondary parties. Manufacturer's employees cannot try to induce Supplier's or Retailer's employees to strike their own employer or even to engage in a concerted refusal to handle Manufacturer's products because such conduct is a secondary boycott. Similarly, Manufacturer's employees cannot picket Supplier or Retailer in an effort to discourage their employees or customers from dealing with Supplier or Retailer. Such secondary picketing also is an unfair labor practice.

A hot cargo clause also is an unfair labor practice under federal labor law. A **hot cargo clause** is a provision in a collective bargaining agreement by which an employer voluntarily agrees not to do business with a nonunion company or a company involved in a labor dispute. By prohibiting hot cargo agreements, the NLRA effectively eliminates voluntary secondary boycotts.

Certain secondary activities do not violate the NLRA. Under the ally doctrine, for example, a union may strike, picket, or boycott a second business that is an ally of the primary company. An ally, however, is narrowly defined as a business with which the primary employer has common ownership of capital plus either common management or interrelated and dependent activities.

Another exception to the secondary boycott rules allows employees to engage in informational picketing that is directed at the public to encourage boycott of a particular product at a secondary site. For example, striking employees of Manufacturer Co. may picket Retailer Co. to inform the public that Retailer sells a specific product of Manufacturer. Such picketing is legal if the public could boycott purchasing just one product without boycotting the secondary employer's entire business. Similarly, the union or employees of Manufacturer may publicize by a method other than picketing that another business distributes Manufacturer's products. The publicity must identify the primary employer and describe the labor dispute and may not contain information about the secondary employer other than the fact that it distributes the primary employer's products.

Employer Lockouts. A **lockout**—the temporary closing of all or part of a business by refusal to allow employees to work—is an employer tactic analogous to a strike. Some lockouts are defensive in nature. An employer, for example, may close a plant in anticipation of a strike to prevent work stoppage at an inopportune time, such as in the middle of the food manufacture process when spoilage would be very costly. Other lockouts are taken for offensive purposes to put economic pressure on employees to accept bargaining proposals.

The legality of a lockout depends on the employer's intent. If the employer locks out employees to avoid its bargaining duties, to destroy the union, or to penalize employees for engaging in union activities, the lockout constitutes an unfair labor practice. If, however, the lockout is motivated by legitimate business or economic reasons, the lockout usually does not violate the law.

Employer Reorganization of Business. Though a lockout temporarily closes a business, an employer may permanently close all or part of its unionized operations. The Supreme Court considered the legality of permanent closings in *Textile Workers Union of America v. Darlington Manufacturing Company* (1965)[40] and held:

> . . . [W]hen an employer closes his entire business, even if the liquidation is motivated by vindictiveness toward the union, such action is not an unfair labor practice. . . . [A] partial closing is an unfair labor practice . . . if motivated by a purpose to chill unionism in any of the remaining plants of the single employer and if the employer may reasonably have foreseen that such closing would likely have that effect.[41]

Thus, terminating a business is allowed for any reason, but a partial closing—for example, eliminating one plant or facility—is illegal if the employer does so to discourage union activities at other facilities. The **runaway shop,** which is closing one facility or moving its operations to another facility to avoid having to bargain with a union, also is an unfair labor practice. In some cases, however, a plant closing motivated by economic reasons, such as high labor costs that may be attributable to union bargaining, may be legal.

Economic problems also may cause an employer to seek reorganization under the bankruptcy laws. As part of the reorganization, the employer may want to reject or modify an existing collective bargaining agreement. The Bankruptcy Code[42] requires that, before filing an application with the court to reject the agreement, the trustee in bankruptcy or debtor in possession (the employer) make a proposal to the bargaining representative that outlines all modifications to the agreement that may be necessary for reorganization and that assures that all affected parties are treated "fairly and equitably." The union is entitled to receive all relevant information, such as financial statements, necessary to evaluate the proposal. Often the union and employees will cooperate with the trustee or employer to reach acceptable modifications in an effort to preserve their jobs for the long term. The law explicitly requires the parties to meet and confer in good faith in an attempt to reach mutually satisfactory modifications to the agreement.

If the union does not agree to the proposed modifications, the Bankruptcy Court may determine whether to reject the collective bargaining agreement. Following a hearing at which all interested parties may testify, the court may approve rejection of the agreement if it finds that the union refused the proposed modification without good cause and that the balance of equities clearly favors rejection. While the proposed rejection is under consideration by the court, the judge may authorize a temporary change in the terms of the collective bargaining agreement.

---

40. 85 S. Ct. 994 (1965).
41. *Id.* at 1001-1002.

42. 11 U.S.C. §1113.

SUMMARY

1. During the last fifty years the federal government has increased regulation of employer-employee relations. Various statutes regulate employee compensation and safety. For example, the Fair Labor Standards Act guarantees a minimum wage and regulates child labor. The Social Security Act provides benefits to retired workers funded by a tax on employers, employees, and self-employed persons. The Employee Retirement Income Security Act regulates private pension plans to ensure that anticipated pensions are available for retired employees. The Occupational Safety and Health Act requires employers to provide a workplace free from recognized hazards.

2. Other employee protection statutes include the Employee Polygraph Protection Act of 1988, which restricts private employers' use of lie detectors for hiring, firing, and disciplinary purposes; and the Worker Adjustment and Retraining Notification Act, which requires businesses to provide advance notification of certain plant closings or mass layoffs.

3. In the wake of the civil rights movement of the 1950s and 1960s, Congress enacted several statutes to guarantee equal employment opportunities to women and minority groups. Title VII of the Civil Rights Act of 1964 is the most important of these statutes. Title VII prohibits employment discrimination based on race, color, national origin, religion, and sex. It permits employment practices based on sex, religion, or national origin if the classification is necessary for a bona fide occupational qualification. Title VII prohibits practices that result in disparate treatment of or disparate impact on certain persons because of race, color, national origin, religion, or sex.

4. Other equal employment opportunity laws include the Equal Pay Act of 1963, which requires equal pay for employees of either sex who perform equal work; the Pregnancy Discrimination Act, which prohibits employment discrimination based on pregnancy; and the Age Discrimination in Employment Act, which prohibits employment discrimination based on age against persons over forty years of age.

5. Federal labor law is the body of federal statutory, administrative, and case law governing labor organizations. The National Labor Relations Act as amended by the Taft-Hartley Act and the Landrum-Griffin Act is the most significant federal labor statute.

6. Under federal labor law employees are entitled to organize and elect a collective bargaining representative. The collective bargaining agent and the employer have a duty to bargain in good faith concerning wages, hours, and other terms and conditions of employment.

7. Certain acts committed by employers or employees are made illegal under federal labor law as "unfair labor practices." By prohibiting unfair labor practices, the law seeks to prevent employers from interfering with employees' rights to form, join, or assist unions, or to engage in concerted activities, and to prevent unions from restraining or coercing employees.

KEY TERMS

Fair Labor Standards Act (FLSA)
Social Security Act
Employee Retirement Income Security Act (ERISA)
vesting
Occupational Safety and Health Act (OSHA)
Occupational Safety and Health Administration
Employee Polygraph Protection Act
Worker Adjustment and Retraining Notification Act
Equal Pay Act
Title VII of the Civil Rights Act of 1964
bona fide occupational qualification (BFOQ)
disparate treatment
disparate impact
affirmative action programs
reverse discrimination
Equal Employment Opportunity Commission (EEOC)
Pregnancy Discrimination Act
Age Discrimination in Employment Act (ADEA)

Norris-LaGuardia Act
National Labor Relations Act (Wagner Act)
Labor-Management Relations Act (Taft-Hartley Act)
Labor-Management Reporting and Disclosure Act (Landrum-Griffin Act)
unfair labor practices
National Labor Relations Board (NLRB)
collective bargaining
collective bargaining contract
yellow dog contract
closed shop
union shop
agency shop
right-to-work laws
strike
wildcat strike
unfair labor practice strike
economic strike
primary picketing
secondary boycott
hot cargo clause
lockout
runaway shop

QUESTIONS AND PROBLEMS

53-1   The unemployment rate for young workers, especially unskilled workers less than twenty years of age, tends to be higher than the unemployment rate for other workers. Some politicians have suggested that these workers be exempted from the provisions of the FLSA. Would such an exemption resolve the unemployment problem? Explain. Does the FLSA create unemployment? Explain.

53-2 In *Meritor Savings Bank v. Vinson* (see page 1128), the bank argued that it could not be held liable for the acts of its employee Taylor because the bank had not been notified that Taylor was harassing Vinson.

(a) Under what circumstances should an employer be held liable for sexual harassment committed by one of its employees? Consider whether different standards should apply depending on whether the employer is an individual or a corporation.

(b) Meritor Bank had a grievance procedure that employees could use to resolve work-related problems or complaints, but Vinson failed to use the grievance procedure. If Vinson is able to prove that she was subjected to sexual harassment, should she be denied the opportunity to recover damages from the bank because she failed to use the grievance procedure? Explain.

(c) The grievance procedure adopted by Meritor Bank required Vinson to file a complaint with her immediate supervisor, Taylor. If Taylor failed to resolve the complaint, Vinson would have had the opportunity to appeal the grievance to higher level bank officials. Do these facts affect your answer to part (b)?

53-3 Actuarial data establish that, in general, women live longer than men. As a result, the cost of pensions for the average woman are higher than those for the average man. May an employer legally require a female employee participating in a contributory pension plan to make larger contributions than male employees? May the employer legally pay a smaller monthly pension to a retired woman than to a retired man? Explain.

53-4 Discuss whether the employer's conduct in the following cases violates the Age Discrimination in Employment Act.

(a) Julian, a 61 year old manager, has worked for Whitney Co. for 20 years. Whitney has suffered substantial losses during the last few years and is reorganizing its workforce. As part of its reorganization, Whitney offers Julian and all employees over the age of 60

a lump sum payment based on their salary in exchange for their election to retire immediately. After explaining the terms of the offer, Julian's supervisor tells Julian that he must reply within one week. Julian accepts the retirement offer but later decides that he was treated unfairly and sues Whitney alleging that it violated the ADEA.

(b) Assume that during its reorganization, Whitney offered Julian a new position (in lieu of retirement) as assistant sales manager of a local office because a new 38 year-old employee would be assuming the responsibilities currently handled by Julian and two other managers. The position would be a substantial demotion for Julian. Other assistant sales managers earn approximately 50% as much as Julian currently earns and work irregular hours. Julian assumes that he would be subject to the same pay and working conditions. Julian rejects the offer of a new position, resigns, and sues Whitney for violation of the ADEA.

53-5 A hospital has adopted a rule prohibiting union solicitation in all patient-access areas of the hospital. As a result, union solicitation was restricted to several employee-only restrooms and locker areas that served approximately one-third of the employees. An employee decided to distribute a union newsletter in the hospital cafeteria. Prior to giving the newsletter to any person, she first asked if the person was an employee. The hospital reprimanded the employee for violation of the solicitation rule and the employee filed unfair labor practice charges. Is the hospital's solicitation rule an unfair labor practice? Explain.

53-6 During an organization campaign at Sinclair Co., Sinclair's president made an effort to talk to all employees about unionization. The president reminded the employees that a strike fifteen years earlier had "almost put our company out of business" and stated that the company was on "thin ice" financially. The president also pointed out that many unionized companies in the area had gone out of business at a loss of 3,500 jobs. Has the president committed an unfair labor practice? Explain.

53-7 During an organization campaign, a union requested employees to sign "recognition slips." Any employee who signed a slip prior to the representation election would be entitled to a waiver of the initiation fee required to join the union. The employer charged that use of the recognition slips was an unfair labor practice. How should the court rule? Explain.

53-8 American Space Co. manufactures jets, rockets, and other products used in the aerospace industry. The company has a collective bargaining agreement with the Space Industry Workers Union. During the last year, American has noticed a substantial decline in the quality of the construction of its products and is concerned that the poor quality may affect the safety of the products and ultimately may lead to a decline in sales. Attributing the poor quality to increased use of drugs and alcohol by its employees, American unilaterally announced that all employees would be subject to random testing for drugs and alcohol. The union files an unfair labor claim alleging that the testing program is a mandatory bargaining subject. How should the court rule? Explain.

53-9 DeBartolo Corp. owns East Lake Mall and leases shops in the mall to various retailers. Wilson's Department Store, which leases space in the mall, decided to rebuild its store and hired High Co., a nonunion company, to perform the construction work. Under the terms of its lease, Wilson's may hire any construction company it wishes without obtaining approval of DeBartolo or other mall tenants. Members of a local construction workers union began distributing handbills at the mall entrances. The leaflets stated:

PLEASE DO NOT SHOP AT EAST LAKE MALL. WILSON'S DEPARTMENT STORE, NOW UNDER CONSTRUCTION AT EAST LAKE, PAYS SUBSTANDARD WAGES AND FRINGE BENEFITS. WE ASK THAT YOU SHOW YOUR OPPOSITION TO SUBSTANDARD WAGES AND FRINGE BENEFITS BY REFUSING TO PATRONIZE THE TENANTS OF EAST LAKE MALL.

The handbill distribution was peaceful and caused no disruption at the mall. DeBartolo Corp. filed unfair labor practice charges with the NLRB alleging that the union's activities constituted an illegal secondary boycott. How should the Board rule?

Chapter 54

Environmental Law

Major Topics

- an introduction to the common law and federal remedies used to address environmental problems
- coverage of the federal statutes designed to control air and water pollution, toxic substances, and radiation
- the federal government policy to consider the environment in decision making

Environmental law has emerged as a distinct field of legal practice and study only in the last twenty years. Although environmental problems—such as air and water pollution and waste disposal—existed prior to that time, they were subject only to minimal regulation. During the mid-1960s, however, a broadly based political movement emerged demanding improved environmental quality. Congress responded by adopting legislation that amended existing statutes and created new statutes to protect the environment and regulate the use of the nation's resources. Many states also enacted laws to provide similar, and sometimes more stringent, regulation within their boundaries. This chapter discusses environmental law including common law remedies, federal regulation of air and water pollution and toxic and hazardous substances, federal environmental policy, and federal control of radiation associated with nuclear power.

Introduction to Environmental Law

Common Law Remedies

Under the common law, the tort actions of trespass, negligence, and nuisance may provide a remedy for personal injury and property damage caused by environmental pollution. Businesses that produce industrial dirt and smoke, for example, have been held liable for unlawful trespass. Odors, noise, toxic substances, and air and water pollution created by industries have been held to be public and private nuisances.

During the 1960s, it became clear that these common law remedies were inadequate to protect those injured by environmental pollution. Because of the widespread effects of industrial pollution, some injured parties were unable to prove the special injury necessary to proving private nuisance cases. Yet, many local officials were reluctant to prosecute public nuisance actions against powerful companies that provided employment and economic support to their community. In heavily industrialized areas, where pollution damage resulted from the cumulative effects of many manufacturers, courts were unwilling to hold one company responsible for environmental injuries.

Lawsuits based on the common law presented other issues that were difficult for judicial resolution. Many courts lacked the expertise to handle the complex scientific and technical evidence of environmental suits. Further, the courts were unable to fashion appropriate remedies because of underlying economic, social, and political concerns that hindered equitable resolution of individual cases. The following case illustrates some of the limitations of the common law and the judicial system to provide an effective forum for resolving environmental issues.

Boomer v. Atlantic Cement Company
257 N.E.2d 870 (N. Y. 1970)

The defendant Atlantic Cement Company had invested more than $45 million in a New York cement manufacturing plant that employed over 300 people. The plaintiffs, a group of landowners who lived near the plant, sued Atlantic seeking an injunction to restrain operation of the plant and damages for injuries to their property caused by dirt, smoke, and vibrations from Atlantic's operations. The trial and appellate courts denied the injunction but held that plaintiffs were entitled to damages incurred to the date of the trial. The courts also noted that plaintiffs could bring successive lawsuits as further damages were incurred. Plaintiffs appealed to the New York Court of Appeals.

Bergan, Judge
. . . The threshold question . . . on this appeal is whether the court should resolve the litigation between the parties now before it as equitably as seems possible; or whether, seeking promotion of the general public welfare, it should channel private litigation into broad public objectives. . . .

Effective control of air pollution is a problem presently far from solution even with the full public and financial powers of government. In large measure adequate technical procedures are yet to be developed and some that appear possible may be economically impracticable.

It seems apparent that the amelioration of air pollution will depend on technical research in great depth; on a carefully balanced consideration of the economic impact of close regulation; and of the actual effect on public health. It is likely to require massive public expenditure and to demand more than any local community can accomplish and to depend on regional and interstate controls.

A court should not try to do this on its own as a by-product of private litigation and it seems manifest that the judicial establishment is neither equipped in the limited nature of any judgment it can pronounce nor prepared to lay down and implement an effective policy for the elimination of air pollution. This is an area beyond the circumference of one private lawsuit. It is a direct responsibility for government and should not thus be undertaken as an incident to solving a dispute between property owners and a single cement plant—one of many—in the Hudson River valley. . . .

The ground for the denial of injunction, notwithstanding the finding both that there is a nuisance and that plaintiffs have been damaged substantially, is the large disparity in economic consequences of the nuisance and of the injunction. . . .

The rule in New York has been that such a nuisance will be enjoined although marked disparity be shown in economic consequence between the effect of the injunction and the effect of the nuisance. . . .

. . . [T]o follow the rule literally in these cases would be to close down the plant at once. This court is fully agreed to avoid that immediately drastic remedy; the difference in view is how best to avoid it.

One alternative is to grant the injunction but postpone its effect to a specified future date to give opportunity for technical advances to permit defendant to eliminate the nuisance; another is to grant the injunction conditioned on the payment of permanent damages to plaintiffs which would compensate them for the total economic loss to their property present and future caused by defendant's operations. . . .

[T]echniques to eliminate dust and other annoying by-products of cement making are unlikely to be developed by any research the defendant can undertake within any short period, but will depend on the total resources of the cement industry nationwide and throughout the world. The problem is universal whenever cement is made.

For obvious reasons the rate of the research is beyond control of defendant. If at the end of 18 months the whole industry has not found a technical solution a court would be hard put to close down this one cement plant if due regard be given to equitable principles.

On the other hand, to grant the injunction unless defendant pays plaintiffs such permanent damages as may be fixed by the court seems to do justice between the contending parties. All of the attributions of economic loss to the properties on which plaintiffs' complaints are based will have been redressed. . . .

Thus it seems fair to both sides to grant permanent damages to plaintiffs which will terminate this private litigation. The theory of damage is the "servitude on land" of plaintiffs imposed by defendant's nuisance. . . .

[Reversed and remanded to trial court for determination of permanent damages.]

Despite its limitations, public and private plaintiffs continue to use the common law as a basis for obtaining damages and injunctive relief for injuries from industrial pollution. As a clearer public environmental policy has emerged, courts increasingly have applied tort principles in combination with federal statutory law to resolve difficult environmental problems.

Federal Regulation

Congress began comprehensive federal regulation of environmental matters in the late 1960s. The National Environmental Policy Act, enacted in 1969, articulated a federal policy to "create and maintain conditions under which man and nature can exist in productive harmony."[1] The Act also created the **Council on Environmental Quality (CEQ)** to advise the president on environmental matters. By executive order, President Nixon created the **Environmental Protection Agency (EPA)** to centralize federal environmental regulation. The EPA, which now is one of the largest federal administrative agencies, is the primary agency responsible for protecting the nation's environment. Authority for regulating some specific environmental matters, however, has been retained by over a dozen other federal agencies and departments, including, for example, the Department of the Inte-

rior, the Department of Defense, the Department of Labor, the Food and Drug Administration, and the Nuclear Regulatory Commission.

Federal statutes form the core of environmental law today. Although over twenty federal statutes specifically address environmental concerns, only those statutes that substantially affect business and industry are discussed in this chapter.

Technology and Environmental Law

Science and technology have affected environmental law more than any other area of law. Before examining specific statutes, therefore, one should consider the effect of technological research and knowledge on the implementation of environmental statutes.

Most environmental laws direct the EPA to develop regulations and procedures to implement general policy set forth in a statute. The EPA, for example, has been required to establish standards that limit specific pollutants to levels that are safe to human health, and to control products that provide an unreasonable risk to health or the environment. The scientific community, however, has been unable to provide the EPA with definite and clear information necessary to set many of these standards. Because the EPA has had to evaluate vast numbers of reports and conflicting data, federal statutes have been implemented more slowly than initially anticipated by Congress. Due to technological lags, many statutes and regulations have been amended and substantially revised over a period of less than twenty years. The lack of precise data also has required the EPA to establish some environmental standards on the basis of risk analysis, rather than on quantitative information. Enforcement has been delayed while regulated businesses and industries have challenged in court the reliability of the data supporting EPA standards.

Even when the EPA has been able to establish clear standards and procedures, technology has limited implementation of environmental programs in other ways. In some cases the technology has not been available to attain satisfactory environmental quality. Some statutes and regulations are intended to be "technology-forcing"; that is, they require industry to invent and adopt new technology. In 1970, for example, Congress established

---

1. 42 U.S.C. §4331(a).

auto emission standards that were beyond the technological capabilities of the auto makers. Although new inventions have significantly reduced emissions, Congress has been forced to extend compliance deadlines on several occasions because of technological delays.

Other environmental laws are "technology-based" or "technology-limited"; that is, they take into consideration the limits of technology. For example, some regulations require industry to use the best available technology or to demonstrate the lowest achievable emission rate. Nevertheless, state of the art technology often is extremely expensive for businesses. Although most federal statutes incorporate some form of cost-benefit balancing test, businesses frequently have challenged federal statutes and EPA regulations that impose high costs on industry. In considering the material that follows, give special attention to ascertaining the extent to which costs should be considered in achieving the environmental benefits of the federal statutes.

Clean Air Act

Air Pollution

Air pollution consists of air-borne particles and gases that endanger human health, damage property, or destroy or interfere with plant and animal life. Although air pollution occurs naturally (for example, volcanoes emit pollutants), major pollution usually is the by-product of industrial activities. Some of these industrial by-products, such as soot and dust, are harmful when produced while others, such as nitrogen oxides and hydrocarbons, become hazardous when they combine with one another or with other substances in the air. Air pollution is created by both stationary sources, including factories, power plants, or other industrial sites, and mobile sources, such as cars, aircraft, and other movable objects.

Regulatory Framework

The federal **Clean Air Act**[2] as amended by the Clean Air Act Amendments of 1970 and 1977 es-

tablishes the current framework for regulation of air pollution. The statute requires the federal government, especially the EPA, to improve air quality in the United States. Under the Clean Air Act as amended, the states, under the EPA's direction, are responsible for regulating some sources of air pollution. Other sources of pollution are regulated directly by the federal government.

Federal Emission Standards

The federal government sets specific standards for two pollutant sources: mobile sources and new stationary sources. In the Clean Air Act Amendments of 1970, Congress required manufacturers of automobiles and light trucks to reduce emission levels of specified substances by 90 percent from the 1970 emission levels. Some of the requirements later were eliminated and deadlines for others were extended into the 1980s. The Clean Air Act Amendments of 1977 set emission standards for heavy-duty vehicles. Although mobile source emissions have been reduced substantially since 1970, the objectives set at that time have not yet been attained.

Other pollutant sources subject to federal emission standards are newly constructed or modified stationary sources. The EPA establishes the emission standards for such stationary sources based on the best available control technology, taking into consideration the costs of compliance.

The EPA also establishes national emission standards for hazardous air pollutants. The EPA has identified four substances—asbestos, beryllium, mercury, and vinyl chloride—as hazardous pollutants that cause serious illness or mortality. Because of the extreme danger caused by these substances the EPA standards are set without regard to economic or technical feasibility.

State Implementation Plans

A major objective of the Clean Air Act Amendments of 1970 was the reduction of air pollution from existing stationary sources. To achieve this objective Congress developed a statutory program by which the federal EPA establishes air quality standards while the states develop and implement plans to attain those standards. The EPA has adopted **national ambient air quality standards**

---

2. 42 U.S.C. §7401 *et seq.*

(NAAQS) for seven identified pollutants: particulate matter, sulfur oxides, carbon monoxide, nitrogen oxides, ozone, hydrocarbons,[3] and lead. The NAAQS specify two maximum air concentration levels for each pollutant. "Primary" standard levels are set to protect human health with an adequate margin of safety, and "secondary" standard levels are set to protect plant and animal life, property, and the aesthetic aspects of the environment.

As required by the Clean Air Act Amendments of 1970, the states develop **state implementation plans (SIPs)** designed to attain the air quality established by the NAAQS. Following public hearing, each state submits a SIP to the EPA for approval. If the EPA deems that the plan is inadequate, the EPA may supplement the SIP. After the EPA approves a SIP, its provisions are enforceable by both the state and federal governments.

The SIPs were supposed to attain the primary standard levels of the NAAQS within three years and the secondary levels within a reasonable time. The provisions of each SIP vary depending on the extent and sources of pollution within the state. Generally a SIP includes an inventory of the sources of the pollutants listed in the NAAQS and a compliance schedule for reducing the pollutants. Most SIPs set maximum emission levels for the pollutant sources and in some cases specify the type of control device necessary for the source. SIPs also include monitoring and reporting requirements and enforcement procedures. The following case discusses the roles of the EPA and the state in adopting a SIP.

Union Electric Company v. Environmental Protection Agency

96 S. Ct. 2518 (1976)

In 1971 the EPA promulgated NAAQS for sulfur dioxide, a by-product of coal burning. The following year the EPA approved an SIP submitted by the state of Missouri that set more stringent sulfur dioxide emission limitations for metropolitan St. Louis.

Petitioner, Union Electric Company, an electric utility company with three coal-fired generating plants in the St. Louis area, was unable to comply with the sulfur dioxide emission levels. The state granted Union Electric a variance that permitted it to exceed the limitations for one year.

Following expiration of the variance, the EPA notified Union Electric that sulfur dioxide emissions from its plants violated the Missouri SIP. Union Electric filed a petition in the federal court of appeals requesting judicial review of the EPA's approval of the Missouri SIP. Union Electric alleged that the EPA should not have approved the SIP because the sulfur dioxide emission limitations were economically and technologically infeasible. The court dismissed the petition holding that the EPA was not authorized to consider economic or technological infeasibility during the SIP approval process. The United States Supreme Court granted Union Electric's petition for review.

Justice Marshall

. . . [T]he 1970 Amendments to the Clean Air Act were a drastic remedy to what was perceived as a serious and otherwise uncheckable problem of air pollution. The Amendments place the primary responsibility for formulating pollution control strategies on the States, but nonetheless subject the States to strict minimum compliance requirements. These requirements are of a "technology-forcing character," . . . and are expressly designed to force regulated sources to develop pollution control devices that might at the time appear to be economically or technologically infeasible. . . .

[T]he entire Congress accepted the Senate's three-year mandate for the achievement of primary air quality standards, and the clear import of that decision is that the Administrator [of the EPA] must approve a plan that provides for attainment of the primary standards in three years even if attainment does not appear feasible. . . . [T]he primary standards had to be met in less than three years if possible; they had to be met "as expeditiously as practicable." §110(a)(2)(A). . . .

It is argued that when such a state plan calls for proceeding more rapidly than economics and the available technology appear to allow, the plan must be rejected as not "practicable." . . . The Administrator's position is that §110(a)(2)(A) sets only a

---

3. Hydrocarbon NAAQS were revoked in 1983.

minimum standard that the States may exceed in their discretion, so that he has no power to reject an infeasible state plan that surpasses the minimum federal requirements—a plan that reflects a state decision to engage in technology forcing on its own and to proceed more expeditiously than is practicable. . . .

We read the [Act] to demand only that the implementation plan submitted by the State meet the "minimum conditions" of the Amendments. . . . Beyond that, if a State makes the legislative determination that it desires a particular air quality by a certain date and that it is willing to force technology to attain it—or lose a certain industry if attainment is not possible—such a determination is fully consistent with the structure and purpose of the Amendments. . . .

In sum, we have concluded that claims of economic or technological infeasibility may not be considered by the Administrator in evaluating a state requirement that primary ambient air quality standards be met in the mandatory three years. And, since we further conclude that the States may submit implementation plans more stringent than federal law requires and that the Administrator must approve such plans if they meet the minimum requirements of §110(a)(2), it follows that the [Act] provides no basis for the Administrator ever to reject a state implementation plan on the ground that it is economically or technologically infeasible. . . .

Our conclusion is bolstered by recognition that the Amendments do allow claims of technological and economic infeasibility to be raised in situations where consideration of such claims will not substantially interfere with the primary congressional purpose of prompt attainment of the national air quality standards. . . .

Perhaps the most important forum for consideration of claims of economic and technological infeasibility is before the state agency formulating the implementation plan. So long as the national standards are met, the State may select whatever mix of control devices it desires . . . and industries with particular economic or technological problems may seek special treatment in the plan itself. . . . Moreover, if the industry is not exempted from, or accommodated by, the original plan, it may obtain a variance, as petitioner did in this case. . . .

In short, the Amendments offer ample opportunity for consideration of claims of technological and economic infeasibility. . . . Allowing such claims to be raised by appealing the Administrator's approval of an implementation plan, as petitioner suggests, would frustrate congressional intent. It would permit a proposed plan to be struck down as infeasible before it is given a chance to work, even though Congress clearly contemplated that some plans would be infeasible when proposed. . . .

[Judgment affirmed.]

The SIPs demonstrated only limited success in achieving the goals of the 1970 Clean Air Act Amendments. As a result, the 1977 Amendments included stricter regulation of the states. Congress directed all states to review their SIPs and imposed more stringent requirements in regions called "dirty air areas" or "nonattainment areas" that had failed to reach the NAAQS primary standard levels. In some cases, these requirements limit new construction and modification of existing pollution sources.

The 1977 Amendments to the Clean Air Act also require that the states develop standards for maintaining air quality and preventing significant deterioration in areas that were in compliance with the NAAQS. To accommodate industrial growth, the SIPs may allow limited deterioration in air quality.

Enforcement

Both civil and criminal remedies are available for violations of the Clean Air Act. Civil penalties of up to $25,000 per day for violation of emission limits have been the primary enforcement tool used by the EPA. Because paying these penalties may be more cost-effective than compliance, the Act also authorizes the EPA to obtain civil penalties equal to the violator's economic benefits from noncompliance. The EPA has not frequently employed this form of penalty, perhaps because of the difficulty in computing the appropriate amount. Private citizens also may bring civil suits against those who violate emission standards or EPA orders. Criminal fines are limited to those who knowingly violate the

Clean Air Act or who make false statements under reporting requirements (for example, by falsely reporting emission data).

Clean Water Act

Water Pollution

The primary cause of water pollution is **effluent,** the discharge of waste substances into rivers, lakes, and oceans. Industrial, agricultural, and municipal waste accounts for almost all water pollution. Manufacturing industries dispose of waste by-products in lakes and rivers. Electric power plants and heavy industrial plants, which use water for cooling, discharge heated water into lakes and rivers. Agriculture creates animal waste and chemical fertilizers that add to water pollution. Finally, municipal waste treatment plants discharge large amounts of organic waste and chemicals.

Some chemical and toxic pollutants produce almost immediate harmful effects by contaminating the water, plants, and animals rendering them unfit for human use or consumption. Other pollutants interfere with biological and chemical processes. Heavy water pollution, for example, may slow the decomposition of organic waste, and heated water interferes with fish reproduction. Chemicals, organic waste, or heated water also can accelerate plant growth causing eutrophication—the dying of lakes.

Regulatory Framework

Federal regulation of water pollution began with the Federal Water Pollution Control Act that placed the primary burden of reducing water pollution on state and local government. The 1972 Amendments to the Act adopted a new federally-oriented approach to regulation. In 1977, the Act was again amended and reorganized as the **Clean Water Act,**[4] which was further amended by the Water Quality Act of 1987. The objective of the Clean Water Act is to restore and maintain the chemical, physical and biological integrity of the waters of the United States through a variety of federally su-

pervised programs. Publicly owned waste treatment works combine local and regional planning for municipal waste treatment and disposal with a federal program of funding through grants and loans. Industries that discharge waste into publicly owned waste treatment works generally must pre-treat waste to reduce certain pollutants. Under the Clean Water Act, control of "nonpoint sources" of pollution, which are nonspecific sources such as runoff from farmland or mines, was left primarily to the states. Because an increasing amount of water pollution was caused by these nonpoint sources, the Water Quality Act of 1987 increased federal regulation by requiring the states to evaluate these pollution sources and to develop management programs that must be approved by the EPA.

National Pollutant Discharge Elimination System

The Clean Water Act also created the **National Pollutant Discharge Elimination System (NPDES)** for the control of "point source" pollution—discharges of polluting substances into a body of water through a confined and discrete conveyance such as a pipe, ditch, or conduit. Every public or private facility that discharges waste through a point source must obtain an NPDES permit from the EPA or from an EPA approved state program. Permit holders are required to maintain records and monitoring programs established by the EPA. Under the NPDES system, the EPA sets **effluent limitations** based on different types of available technology and each permit holder determines what type of control devices to use to achieve the federally established standards. The EPA sets these effluent limitations through regulations that classify all industries into approximately forty categories. For each category, the EPA then establishes specific point source effluent limitations using technological standards created by Congress in federal statutes.

Initially, under the 1972 Amendments, Congress directed the EPA to establish effluent limitations for each type of pollutant according to the "best practicable technology" (BPT) currently available and according to the more stringent "best available technology" (BAT) economically achievable. Industrial polluters were supposed to comply with the

---

4. 33 U.S.C. §1251 *et seq.*

BPT standards by 1977 and the BAT standards by 1983. Because of problems both with establishing and meeting these standards, Congress revised the process for setting effluent limitations in the Clean Water Act. For toxic substances, the EPA was to set effluent limitations according to the most stringent BAT. Most nontoxic substances, such as biochemical oxygen-demanding substances, total suspended solids, pH, oil and grease, were classified as conventional pollutants. The EPA was directed to set effluent limitations for conventional pollutants from existing point sources according to the "best conventional technology" (BCT), a new standard incorporating a cost-benefit analysis, that in practice is at least as stringent as BPT. For all new point sources, the EPA was to develop effluent limitations using BAT standards. Although the 1977 Amendments established deadlines by which NPDES permit holders were supposed to comply with appropriate standards, many of these deadlines were not met, often because the EPA failed either to set the limitations or to allow adequate time for industries to adopt necessary technology. In recognition of these difficulties, the Water Quality Act of 1987 directs the EPA to develop guidelines "as expeditiously as possible" and requires compliance by the earlier of three years after guidelines are established or March 31, 1989. Nevertheless, in conference reports, Congress approved the EPA's policy of extending deadlines for industries for which the EPA has failed to issue effluent limitations.

Enforcement

Violators of the NPDES requirements for effluent limitations and statutory provisions are subject to both administrative and judicially imposed penalties. The EPA is authorized to assess two classes of administrative penalties: Class I penalties may not exceed $10,000 per day up to a maximum of $25,000 per violation, and Class II penalties may not exceed $10,000 per day up to a maximum of $125,000 per violation. Class II penalties may be assessed only after a full hearing on the record while Class I penalties require only written notice to the violator who may request a less formal hearing. Those who commit statutory violations or fail to comply with an administrative order also may be

subject to a judicial civil penalty of up to $25,000 per day. The Water Quality Act of 1987 requires the EPA and courts in determining appropriate administrative or civil penalties to consider specific factors, such as the seriousness of the violation, the violator's compliance history, the violator's ability to pay, and the economic benefit or savings resulting from the violation.

Violators also may be criminally prosecuted. Negligent violations by first offenders are punishable by fines of between $2,500 and $25,000 per day, and imprisonment up to one year, or both. For subsequent offenders, the potential maximum penalty may be increased to $50,000 per day and imprisonment up to two years, or both. Anyone who knowingly commits violations is subject to more severe criminal penalties including fines of between $5,000 and $50,000 per day, and imprisonment of up to three years, or both. The maximum penalties also may be doubled for subsequent knowing violations. Finally, very severe penalties of up to 15 years' imprisonment and a fine up to $250,000 may be imposed against individuals who commit a violation with knowledge that it places another person in imminent danger of death or serious bodily injury. An organization that commits such a violation is subject to a criminal fine of up to $1 million.

Regulation of Toxic and Hazardous Substances

In recent years, scientific evidence has revealed the potential toxicity of many synthetic chemicals that have been produced and used for decades. These chemicals have significantly benefited society, for example, by increasing agricultural production with fertilizers and pesticides, and by enabling development of new building materials, plastics, fibers, paper products, food preservatives, and drugs. Many of the synthetic substances that are the products and by-products of commercial and industrial activities, however, are hazardous to human beings, even in minute quantities. Some chemicals accumulate in plants and animals thereby multiplying their dangerous effects, while other chemicals fail to break down for long periods and, thus, retain their toxic potential. The toxic effects of many of these substances do not appear until many years after exposure.

Since the 1970s Congress has increased regulation of toxic substances by amending existing statutes and creating new statutes. The Clean Air Act and the Clean Water Act include provisions concerning hazardous substances in the air and water. Other federal statutes regulating toxic substances are discussed in the material that follows.

Federal Insecticide, Fungicide, and Rodenticide Act

The **Federal Insecticide, Fungicide, and Rodenticide Act (FIFRA)**[5] requires manufacturers of pesticides to register their products with the EPA and to meet labeling requirements on proper use and safety precautions. To initiate registration of a pesticide, the manufacturer must submit the chemical formula, the proposed label, and comprehensive data about its probable effects on human beings based on animal studies. The EPA must register the pesticide if the chemical composition warrants the claims as to its efficacy, the manufacturer has complied with labeling and data submission requirements, and the product will not cause unreasonable adverse effects on the environment when it is used as intended and in accordance with widespread and commonly used practices. The EPA may register the pesticide for general use or, if the product is especially hazardous, for restricted use by certified applicators. In determining whether the product will produce unreasonable adverse effects in the environment, the EPA employs a cost-benefit analysis weighing the economic, social, and environmental costs and benefits. Following registration, the pesticide may be manufactured and distributed, but the EPA must review the registration at least every five years.

After a pesticide has been registered, the EPA may cancel the registration if it determines that the pesticide causes unreasonable adverse effects on the environment. Upon the manufacturer's request, however, the EPA must hold an adjudicatory hearing prior to cancellation. If the pesticide creates an imminent hazard or emergency, the EPA may suspend the registration, thus banning production and distribution of the pesticide until completion of the hearing process.

At the cancellation hearing the manufacturer effectively bears the burden of proving that the pesticide poses only a minimal risk or that its benefits outweigh the risk. If the manufacturer is unable to establish the necessary proof, the registration may be cancelled and further manufacture or sale of the pesticide is illegal. Alternatively, the registration may be cancelled only in part by restricting use of the product or requiring labels that set forth precautions for its use.

Toxic Substances Control Act

In 1976, Congress enacted the **Toxic Substances Control Act (TSCA)**,[6] a statute that was intended to provide comprehensive regulation of toxic substances. As required by TCSA, the EPA has compiled an inventory of all existing chemicals, which it intends to update periodically. At least 90 days prior to beginning commercial production of a new chemical—one that is not included in the EPA inventory—the manufacturer must provide a premanufacturing notice (PMN) to the EPA. A similar notice must be provided if the manufacturer intends to apply an existing chemical to a significant new use.

Under TSCA generally a chemical is presumed to be marketable; the EPA does not license or affirmatively approve manufacture of a chemical. Nevertheless, the EPA has the power to limit use of a chemical if the EPA finds that it presents an unreasonable risk to health or the environment. If, for example, the PMN does not include sufficient data for the EPA to determine the risks of the chemical, the EPA can delay manufacture or distribution until the data are available. If the EPA finds that any chemical (whether new or on the existing inventory) presents, or will present, an unreasonable risk to health or the environment, the EPA may restrict marketing of the chemical. The EPA can prohibit use of the product, establish production quotas,

---

5. 7 U.S.C. §136 *et seq.*

6. 15 U.S.C. §2601 *et seq.*

limit its use, or require special labeling. The EPA's decision to restrict the use is subject to review through a hearing process. The manufacturer, however, bears the burden of proving that the chemical does not present an unreasonable risk to health or to the environment.

One objective of the TSCA was to enable the government to collect comprehensive data on potentially hazardous chemical substances. TSCA, for example, requires manufacturers to notify the EPA of any information that reasonably shows that a chemical presents a substantial risk of injury to health or to the environment. Manufacturers also must maintain records of significant adverse reactions allegedly caused by a chemical. TSCA further allows the EPA to request companies to conduct tests and to submit test data on chemicals suspected of being hazardous. To encourage the cooperation of businesses, TSCA prohibits the EPA from releasing to the public certain confidential information such as trade secrets and commercial information. As illustrated by the following case, TSCA has been subject to some criticism from businesses.

Dow Chemical Company v. United States Environmental Protection Agency

605 F.2d 673 (3d Cir. 1979)

Under authority of TSCA, the EPA issued regulations requiring manufacturers, processors, and distributors of ten chemicals suspected of being hazardous to submit to the EPA lists of studies initiated or conducted by the company. The regulation required such lists even from companies that were manufacturing or using the chemicals only for research purposes. Dow Chemical Company filed a petition in the Third Circuit Court of Appeals challenging the EPA's authority to require the tests from those using the chemicals for research purposes.

After analyzing the statute and regulations and reviewing the statutory history, the court held that the EPA had acted within the scope of its authority. The court then addressed Dow's arguments that the statute and regulations would discourage product research and development.

Adams, Circuit Judge

. . . The result we reach today may understandably cause concern to those troubled about the relative decline of technological innovation in the United States. If companies are required to submit to a federal administrative agency the results of tests they perform in the process of developing new products their chances of realizing a substantial competitive advantage may be measurably reduced. With the opportunity for [competitive advantage] diminished in this fashion, corporate research may concentrate on substances that are *not* presently subject to the agency's scrutiny. The result may be a net reduction of general research on the very substances—hazardous chemicals—on which research is greatly needed. Were this to come about, it would presumably conflict with one of Congress' purposes in passing the Act. Alternatively, companies may simply reduce their research and development spending altogether, particularly since the Toxic Substances Control Act is not the only current disincentive to innovation.

Of course, in the present case good arguments may be made for the Act as drafted. It is fair to doubt whether the primary commitment of large corporations is to the health of our citizenry—and reasonable for the government to seek to learn about and more carefully control toxic substances. The drafting of legislation often entails difficult policy choices, and the statute at issue here is no exception. But the issue for this Court cannot be whether we would have drafted [the statute] so as to provide greater protection for product research and development. Nor is the question whether the regulation actually promulgated is a desirable one. We recognize the potentially unfortunate consequences of the EPA's regulation and of our reading of the Act. Our role, however, is confined to construing the statute so as to give effect to the legislation as written and to the intent of Congress in enacting such legislation. In so doing we have determined that Congress delegated to the EPA the authority to promulgate the regulation that is under challenge here. Perhaps the public may have reason to regret this result, but the possibility that the Act as drafted may inhibit technological innovation may not be relied upon as a justification for ignoring the apparent congressional decision in the drafting of the statute. Rather, any change in this regard is for the Congress to consider. . . .

[Petition for review denied.]

Resource Conservation and Recovery Act

One of the first incidents to awaken the general public to the dangers of improper disposal of toxic substances occurred at Love Canal, New York. During the late 1970s, synthetic chemical substances began to percolate to the surface of land in an area near Niagara Falls. Research revealed that Hooker Chemical Company had disposed of over 20,000 tons of chemical waste (including toxic benzene, PCBs, and pesticides) in an abandoned mile-long canal. Hooker had discontinued using the canal as a waste site in the mid 1940s and in 1953, after the site had been filled in, Hooker donated the property to the local board of education. A school and private residences were constructed on the site. During the 1970s, about the same time that the chemicals surfaced, Love Canal residents began to display an unusually high incidence of cancer, birth defects, neurological disorders, and other health problems.

Due to the increased awareness of the problems of hazardous waste disposal, Congress enacted the **Resource Conservation and Recovery Act (RCRA)**[7] in 1976. Whereas TSCA was designed to control the manufacture, distribution, and sale of chemicals, RCRA established a plan for the transportation and disposal of hazardous waste. RCRA defines hazardous waste as

> solid waste, or combination of solid wastes, which because of its quantity, concentration, or physical, chemical, or infectious characteristics may—(A) cause, or significantly contribute to an increase in mortality or an increase in serious irreversible, or incapacitating reversible, illness; or (B) pose a substantial present or potential hazard to human health or the environment when im-

properly treated, stored, transported, or disposed of, or otherwise managed.[8]

The EPA uses four criteria for identifying hazardous waste: ignitability, corrosivity, reactivity, and toxicity. The EPA has identified over 300 products that it deems hazardous.

The RCRA requires generators—producers—of hazardous waste to maintain records on the quantity and composition of their waste products and to comply with EPA standards for labeling, storage, and transportation of the waste. A generator who disposes of the hazardous waste off-site must comply with a transport procedure established under the RCRA. A manifest, a written document describing the hazardous waste and designating the facility to which it is being transported, must accompany all shipments of hazardous waste to disposal sites. The manifest must be returned to the generator after delivery. The generator must notify the EPA if the manifest is not returned within thirty-five days.

The RCRA also requires facilities that treat, store, or dispose of hazardous waste—including the generator if it uses on-site disposal—to obtain an operating permit from the EPA. Permit holders must provide monitoring, employee training, emergency procedures, and fencing and warning signs. Permit holders also must carry insurance to cover potential liability for injuries from hazardous waste. The EPA has established disposal techniques for hazardous waste including, for example, incineration, deep-well injection, discharge into waters or oceans, and land disposal. Permit holders must comply with standards set by the EPA in disposing of the hazardous waste. Because of leakage problems with land disposal techniques, Congress amended the RCRA in 1984 to require phase-out of land disposal unless more permanent containment can be attained. At present such technology is not available.

The RCRA provides criminal penalties for knowingly or willfully violating the Act. Violation of the transportation, treatment, storage, or disposal provisions may be punished by a fine of $50,000 per day, or imprisonment up to two years,

---

7. 42 U.S.C. §6901 *et seq.*

8. 42 U.S.C. §6903(5).

or both. Violations of record keeping provisions are punishable by fines of $25,000 per day and imprisonment up to one year or both for a first conviction and $50,000 per day and imprisonment up to two years or both for subsequent convictions. Civil penalties up to $25,000 per day may be imposed for failure to comply with a state or EPA compliance order.

Comprehensive Environmental Response, Compensation, and Liability Act

Congress adopted the **Comprehensive Environmental Response, Compensation, and Liability Act (CERCLA)**[9] in 1980 to provide a system for cleanup of abandoned hazardous waste sites and accidental spills and leakage of hazardous waste. In 1986, Congress amended the statute to strengthen cleanup standards and to extend coverage of the Act to both private and government hazardous waste disposal sites. The 1986 amendments also added "right-to-know" provisions that require businesses to disclose annual emissions of specified chemical substances and to notify state and local governments immediately after emergency release of certain chemicals or hazardous substances.

CERCLA directed the EPA to prepare a National Contingency Plan with procedures for governmental response to the release of hazardous substances. The statute defines hazardous substances by reference to substances identified under the Clean Air Act, the Clean Water Act, TSCA, and RCRA. One of the most important elements of the National Contingency Plan is a priority list of hazardous waste sites to be cleaned up by the federal government. By 1986, fewer than 25 identified hazardous waste sites had been cleaned up under CERCLA. Under the 1986 amendments, as many as 2,000 sites may be added to the priority list and the EPA is required to begin cleanup of at least 375 sites by 1990.

CERCLA also established the Hazardous Substance Response Trust Fund—the Superfund—to finance cleanup of hazardous waste sites. The Superfund provided $1.6 billion for cleanup programs during the first five years. In 1986, an additional

$9.0 billion was allocated to Superfund for the next five years. The Superfund is funded by excise taxes on oil, certain chemical feedstocks, and motor fuel as well as by general government revenues and by a special tax included in the corporate alternative minimum income tax. The EPA may use the Superfund to finance cleanup of abandoned hazardous waste sites. A state or private party also may clean up a hazardous waste site and then seek reimbursement from the Superfund. The EPA then may sue the potentially responsible parties (PRPs) for the costs (response costs) borne by the Superfund.

Some of the most controversial provisions of CERCLA concern the PRPs who include previous operators as well as generators and transporters of waste to the site. CERCLA imposes strict liability, or liability without fault. Because responsible parties are jointly and severally liable, a financially sound business may have to bear all of the costs that other responsible parties are unable to pay. Prior to undertaking cleanup of a hazardous waste site, the EPA may order the PRPs to perform the cleanup. A party that fails to do so and subsequently is found liable for the response costs may be liable for treble damages.

Lawsuits brought under CERCLA have proved to be complex, expensive, and time consuming. Resolution of technical legal matters has impeded the cleanup process. Because of the problems associated with those suits, settlement agreements set forth in consent decrees have become an attractive alternative to both the EPA and industry. The 1986 amendments to CERCLA encourage consent decrees subject to public review to resolve hazardous waste site cleanup litigation. The 1985 settlement of a major lawsuit involving a waste site in Ohio maintained by Chem-Dyne Corporation may serve as a model for resolution of future cases.

During the 1970s, hundreds of companies disposed of waste at the Chem-Dyne site. By 1982, the site required cleanup because of leakage of hazardous substances from storage drums and tanks which contaminated soil and groundwater. Approximately 300 companies were identified as PRPs. In August 1982, 112 of the PRPs agreed to pay $2.5 million to the government in exchange for release from liability for cleanup of the surface of the site. The federal government then sued twenty-three additional PRPs for surface cleanup costs. That suit

---

9. 42 U.S.C. §9601 *et seq.*

was expanded to add defendants and claims for the costs of cleaning up the subsurface contamination. In 1984, following two years of pleadings and discovery, over 160 PRPs had been named as defendants in the suit. The parties then engaged in almost a year and a half of negotiation that led to settlement through a consent decree. The decree establishes a procedure for cleaning up the Chem-Dyne site and provides a formula to allocate the cleanup costs among the defendants.[10]

National Environmental Policy Act

One of the first federal statutes concerning the environment was the **National Environmental Policy Act (NEPA).**[11] Unlike the other statutes discussed in this chapter, NEPA is not a pollution control statute. Instead, NEPA imposes a duty on federal agencies to consider environmental matters in administering their programs. As a result, NEPA affects private business and industry only indirectly.

NEPA requires all federal agencies to include an **environmental impact statement (EIS)** with every proposal for legislation or major federal action that will significantly affect the environment. The Council on Environmental Quality has developed regulations governing the EIS process. In general, an agency must prepare an environmental assessment for any project subject to federal control. These projects include not only direct federal actions, such as construction of a federal highway or dam, but also private projects requiring a federal license or financed by federal funds. The environmental assessment addresses the issue of whether an EIS is necessary. If the agency determines that the project will not have a significant impact on the environment, it will not prepare an EIS. If it does prepare an EIS, the agency seeks input from the public and other agencies. It then prepares a report detailing the environmental impact of the project, unavoidable adverse environmental effects, and alternatives to the proposed action.

The provisions of NEPA are enforceable by judicial review. Many cases arise when an interested party challenges an agency's decision to proceed with a project despite its adverse environmental impact. In such cases, the courts usually review the case to determine that the agency has followed the proper procedure but limit substantive review to whether the agency action was arbitrary or capricious. The following case involves judicial review of an agency's decision not to prepare an EIS.

Thomas v. Peterson
753 F.2d 754 (9th Cir. 1985)

In 1980, the United States Forest Service proposed construction of a gravel road in the Jersey Jack area of the Nezperce National Forest in Idaho. One purpose of the road construction was to provide access to timberland in Jersey Jack that was to be opened to commercial timber development. The Forest Service prepared an environmental assessment (EA) that concluded that an environmental impact statement (EIS) was not required because the road would have no significant environmental impact. The EA, however, discussed only the environmental impact of the road and did not consider the impact of the planned timber development.

The plaintiffs—landowners, ranchers, miners, hunters, fishermen, and several conservation and recreational organizations—appealed the decision not to prepare an EIS. After the chief of the Forest Service affirmed the decision, the plaintiffs appealed to the Ninth Circuit Court of Appeals.

Sneed, Circuit Judge
. . . Section 102(2)(C) of NEPA requires an EIS for "major Federal actions significantly affecting the quality of the human environment." 42 U.S.C. §4332(2)(C) (1982). While it is true that administrative agencies must be given considerable discretion in defining the scope of environmental impact statements, . . . there are situations in which an agency is required to consider several related actions in a single EIS. . . . Not to require this would permit dividing a project into multiple "actions," each of which individually has an insignificant environmental impact, but which collectively have a substantial impact. . . .

---

10. For a more complete discussion of the case, see The Second Chem-Dyne Settlement, 15 Envtl. L. Rptr. 10208 (1985).

11. 42 U.S.C. §4321 *et seq*.

[T]he Council on Environmental Quality (CEQ) has issued regulations that . . . require "connected actions" to be considered together in a single EIS. . . .

It is clear that the timber sales cannot proceed without the road, and the road would not be built but for the contemplated timber sales. . . . The Forest Service's cost-benefit analysis of the road considered the timber to be the benefit of the road, and while the Service has stated that the road will yield other benefits, it does not claim that such other benefits would justify the road in the absence of the timber sales. . . .

We conclude, therefore, that the road construction and the contemplated timber sales are inextricably intertwined, and that they are "connected actions" within the meaning of the CEQ regulations.

The CEQ regulations also require that "cumulative actions" be considered together in a single EIS. . . . "Cumulative actions" are defined as actions "which when viewed with other proposed actions have cumulatively significant impacts." [40 C.F.R. §1508.25(a)(2).] The record in this case contains considerable evidence to suggest that the road and the timber sales will have cumulatively significant impacts. The U.S. Fish & Wildlife Service, the Environmental Protection Agency, and the Idaho Department of Fish & Game have asserted that the road and the timber sales will have significant cumulative effects that should be considered in an EIS. The primary cumulative effects, according to these agencies, are the deposit of sediments in the Salmon River to the detriment of that river's population of salmon and steelhead trout . . . and the destruction of critical habitat for the endangered Rocky Mountain Gray Wolf. . . .

The Forest Service argues that the cumulative environmental effects of the road and the timber sales will be adequately analyzed and considered in the EA's and/or EIS's that it will prepare on the individual timber sales. The EA or EIS on each action, it contends, will document the cumulative impacts of that action and all previous actions.

We believe that consideration of cumulative impacts after the road has already been approved is insufficient to fulfill the mandate of NEPA. A central purpose of an EIS is to force the consideration of environmental impacts in the decisionmaking process. . . . That purpose requires that the NEPA process be integrated with agency planning "at the earliest possible time," 40 C.F.R. §1501.2, and the purpose cannot be fully served if consideration of the cumulative effects of successive, interdependent steps is delayed until the first step has already been taken.

The location, the timing, or other aspects of the timber sales, or even the decision whether to sell any timber at all, affects the location, routing, construction techniques, and other aspects of the road, or even the need for its construction. But the consideration of cumulative impacts will serve little purpose if the road has already been built. Building the road swings the balance decidedly in favor of timber sales even if such sales would have been disfavored had road and sales been considered together before the road was built. Only by selling timber can the bulk of the expense of building the road be recovered. . . . Therefore, the cumulative environmental impacts of the road and the timber sales must be assessed before the road is approved. . . .

We therefore reverse the district court on the NEPA issue and hold that, before deciding whether to approve the proposed road, the Forest Service is required to prepare and consider an environmental impact statement that analyzes the combined impacts of the road and the timber sales that the road is designed to facilitate. . . .

[Judgment reversed and remanded.]

Radiation Control

During the 1950s, the federal government and private industry began development of nuclear power as an energy source. Nuclear power generally was regarded as a cleaner and less expensive alternative to petroleum and coal. As construction and operation of nuclear plants progressed, however, problems began to emerge. Nuclear energy became increasingly expensive due to escalating costs for the construction of nuclear power plants. Despite research efforts, scientists were unable to develop methods for long-term disposal of nuclear waste created by the power plants. Moreover, an accident in 1979 at the Three Mile Island nuclear power plant in Pennsylvania and a more serious accident at Chernobyl in the Soviet Union in 1986 heightened public concern about the safety of nuclear power plants. Because nuclear power continues to be a significant energy source, the control of radiation associated with nuclear power is an important aspect of environmental law.

The federal government has exclusive authority to regulate construction and operation of nuclear power plants. The **Nuclear Regulatory Commission (NRC)** (formerly the Atomic Energy Commission) is the federal agency responsible for civilian nuclear regulation. The NRC controls nuclear materials, such as plutonium and uranium, that produce nuclear power and by-product materials that become radioactive during the production of nuclear energy. Nuclear power plants generally are constructed and operated by private industry subject to federal regulation.

The NRC has established regulations for construction of nuclear power plants and issues construction permits only after review of the proposed plant for safety factors. Prior to approving construction of a plant, the NRC must prepare an EIS that examines the environmental impact of the proposed plant including the impact if an accident causing radiation release were to occur. Following construction of a nuclear plant, operation may begin and continue only if the NRC issues a license. Following the Three Mile Island accident, the NRC began licensing nuclear plant operators. NRC regulations also govern the operation of the plants and the use and disposal of nuclear materials and by-products.

Perhaps the most controversial aspect of nuclear regulation is permanent disposal of nuclear waste. All nuclear plants create low-level radioactive waste. Plants may transfer the low-level waste to recipients, licensed by the NRC, who bury, incinerate, or dump the waste at sea. Spent nuclear fuel maintains a high level of radioactivity and currently no permanent disposal techniques are available. At present most spent nuclear fuel is stored on an interim basis at nuclear power plants under permits issued by the NRC. In accordance with **The Nuclear Waste Policy Act**[12] the Federal government is supervising the selection and development of a

---
12. 42 U.S.C. §10101 *et seq.*

site to serve as a permanent repository for high level nuclear waste and spent fuel from nuclear reactors. This repository is scheduled to open sometime after the year 2000.

In light of the unavailability of permanent waste sites and methods of disposal, some individuals have questioned the NRC's judgment in issuing new nuclear plant licenses. As described in the following case, the issue of nuclear waste disposal frequently arises in judicial review of an EIS prepared in conjunction with a proposed nuclear power plant.

Baltimore Gas and Electric Co. v. Natural Resources Defense Council, Inc.
103 S. Ct. 2246 (1983)

In 1974 the Nuclear Regulatory Commission (Commission) adopted Table S-3 to summarize the environmental costs associated with the nuclear fuel cycle of a nuclear power plant. The Commission uses the table as part of EISs required for federal licensing of individual nuclear plants. One item in Table S-3 is the "zero-release assumption"—a statement that radioactive nuclear waste will have no long-term environmental effect based on the assumption that the waste would not escape once it was properly stored. In a suit brought by the National Resources Defense Council, Inc. against the Commission, the federal court of appeals ruled that Table S-3 was invalid for NEPA purposes because the zero-release assumption was arbitrary and capricious. The United States Supreme Court accepted the case for review.

Justice O'Connor
. . . We are acutely aware that the extent to which this Nation should rely on nuclear power as a source of energy is an important and sensitive issue. Much of the debate focuses on whether development of nuclear generation facilities should proceed in the face of uncertainties about their long-term effects on the environment. Resolution of these fundamental policy questions lies, however, with Congress and the agencies to which Congress has delegated authority, as well as with state legislatures and, ultimately, the populace as a whole. Congress has assigned the courts only the limited,

albeit important, task of reviewing agency action to determine whether the agency conformed with controlling statutes. . . .

The controlling statute at issue here is the National Environmental Policy Act. . . . Congress in enacting NEPA, however, did not require agencies to elevate environmental concerns over other appropriate considerations. . . . Rather, it required only that the agency take a "hard look" at the environmental consequences before taking a major action. . . . The role of the courts is simply to ensure that the agency has adequately considered and disclosed the environmental impact of its actions and that its decision is not arbitrary or capricious. . . .

In its Table S–3 Rule here, the Commission has determined that the probabilities favor the zero-release assumption, because the Nation is likely to develop methods to store the wastes with no leakage to the environment. . . . The Commission recognized, however, that the geological, chemical, physical and other data it relied on in making this prediction were based, in part, on assumptions which involve substantial uncertainties. Again no one suggests that the uncertainties are trivial or the potential effects insignificant if time proves the zero-release assumption to have been seriously wrong. After confronting the issue, though, the Commission has determined that the uncertainties concerning the development of nuclear waste storage facilities are not sufficient to affect the outcome of any individual licensing decision.

It is clear that the Commission, in making this determination, has made the careful consideration and disclosure required by NEPA. . . .

The Commission's decision to affix a zero value to the environmental impact of long-term storage would violate NEPA . . . only if the Commission acted arbitrarily and capriciously in deciding gener-

ically that the uncertainty was insufficient to affect any individual licensing decision. In assessing whether the Commission's decision is arbitrary and capricious, it is crucial to place the zero-release assumption in context. Three factors are particularly important. First is the Commission's repeated emphasis that the . . . purpose of the rule was not to evaluate or select the most effective long-term waste disposal technology or develop site selection criteria. A separate and comprehensive series of programs has been undertaken to serve these broader purposes. . . .

Second, the Commission emphasizes that the zero-release assumption is but a single figure in an entire Table, which the Commission expressly designed as a risk-averse estimate of the environmental impact of the fuel cycle. . . .

Third, a reviewing court must remember that the Commission is making predictions, within its area of special expertise, at the frontiers of science. When examining this kind of scientific determination, as opposed to simple findings of fact, a reviewing court must generally be at its most deferential. . . .

[W]e think that the zero-release assumption—a policy judgment concerning one line in a conservative Table designed for the limited purpose of individual licensing decisions—is within the bounds of reasoned decisionmaking. It is not our task to determine what decision we, as Commissioners, would have reached. Our only task is to determine whether the Commission has considered the relevant factors and articulated a rational connection between the facts found and the choice made. . . . Under this standard, we think the Commission's zero-release assumption, within the context of Table S–3 as a whole, was not arbitrary and capricious.

[Judgment reversed.]

SUMMARY

1. The tort actions of trespass, negligence, and nuisance provide remedies to those injured by environmental pollution. Although early cases based on these actions provided inadequate relief, the common law tort remedies can be used to resolve environmental matters.

2. Comprehensive federal regulation of the environ-

ment began in the 1960s. The EPA is the primary federal agency responsible for administering environmental regulation.

3. Limited and conflicting scientific data, technological lags, and the costs of adopting expensive technology have delayed implementation of federal environmental law.

4. The Clean Air Act regulates air pollution through NAAQS established by the federal EPA that are implemented through SIPs adopted by the states. Mobile air pollution sources, new stationary sources, and hazardous air pollutants are directly regulated by the EPA.

5. The Clean Water Act requires the EPA to establish effluent standards that must be met by industrial polluters under a federal permit system.

6. Toxic and hazardous substances are subject to federal control under various statutes. FIFRA provides a registration system for pesticides and TSCA provides a similar system for registration of other chemicals. The EPA may cancel registration and restrict production and distribution of pesticides and chemicals that present a risk to the environment.

7. RCRA and CERCLA regulate hazardous waste. Under RCRA, the transportation, storage, and disposal of hazardous waste must comply with EPA regulations. CERCLA provides funding to clean up hazardous waste sites and establishes a procedure for recovering clean-up costs from responsible parties.

8. NEPA requires federal administrative agencies to consider the environmental impact of proposed major federal actions in an EIS.

9. The NRC has the authority to regulate nuclear energy by controlling nuclear materials and licensing the construction and operation of nuclear power plants. Under the Nuclear Waste Policy Act the federal government must develop a site for permanent disposal of radioactive waste.

KEY TERMS

Council on Environmental Quality (CEQ)
Environmental Protection Agency (EPA)
Clean Air Act
national ambient air quality standards (NAAQS)
state implementation plan (SIP)
effluent
Clean Water Act
National Pollutant Discharge Elimination System (NPDES)
effluent limitations
Federal Insecticide, Fungicide, and Rodenticide Act (FIFRA)

Toxic Substances Control Act (TSCA)
Resource Conservation and Recovery Act (RCRA)
Comprehensive Environmental Response, Compensation, and Liability Act (CERCLA)
National Environmental Policy Act (NEPA)
environmental impact statement (EIS)
Nuclear Regulatory Commission (NRC)
Nuclear Waste Policy Act

QUESTIONS AND PROBLEMS

54-1 Various alternatives to the current statutes regulating air and water pollution have been suggested. Discuss the advantages and disadvantages of the following alternatives.
(a) All sources of pollution in a given area should be required to reduce their emissions by a uniform percentage.
(b) All sources of pollution in a given area should be required to limit their air or water pollution to a certain number of pounds per day.

54-2 The regulatory framework of the Clean Air Act is based on federally established uniform air quality standards, while the Clean Water Act is based on federally established uniform effluent limitations.
(a) Suggest reasons for the different approaches that the two statutes use for eliminating pollution.
(b) Which type of regulatory system is easier to enforce? Explain.
(c) Consider the statutes from the viewpoint of a business or industry. Which approach would you prefer? Explain.

54-3 Are the provisions of the Clean Water Act technology-forcing or technology-based? Explain.

54-4 When the EPA cancelled registration under FIFRA of the pesticide DDT, the manufacturer challenged the EPA cancellation. The producers of DDT argued that the EPA had failed to prove that DDT use was harmful to human beings.
(a) The EPA based its conclusion that DDT posed an imminent hazard by relying on test data showing that DDT probably was carcinogenic (cancer causing) to mice and rats. Should the EPA be required to prove conclusively that a substance is hazardous to human beings before being allowed to cancel registration? Explain.
(b) Producers of DDT argued that the EPA should be required to prove that the benefits of cancelling registration and use of a pesticide outweigh the benefits derived from the pesticide. Do you agree with the DDT producers? Explain.
(c) In the DDT cases, the court effectively held that in a registration cancellation hearing the producers of the pesticide must bear the burden of proving that the product causes only minimal risk and that the benefits of its use outweigh the costs. How would a producer of a pesticide prove these elements? Do you

believe the allocation of the burden of proof in such cases is proper? Explain.

54-5 The Resource Conservation and Recovery Act has been described as a system for regulating hazardous wastes from "cradle to grave." What is meant by this description? Is it accurate? Explain.

54-6 Under CERCLA, the EPA may clean up a hazardous waste site and then sue some or all of the potentially responsible parties to recover the costs. The EPA, however, has entered into many settlement agreements (such as the one involving the Chem-Dyne site, discussed in the text) in which the PRPs perform and pay for the cleanup. Both the EPA and private industry have suggested that cleanup by the polluters is less expensive and more efficient. Many members of Congress, however, do not favor cleanup by private industry.

(a) Why would members of Congress be opposed to settlements in which industry performs the cleanup?

(b) What incentives can the EPA offer to encourage industries to cooperate in cleanup of hazardous waste sites?

54-7 EISs generally consider the impact of federal projects on the natural environment, for example, the quality of air, and loss of resources such as plant and wildlife. An EIS, however, is required for all "major Federal actions significantly affecting the quality of the human environment." (42 U.S.C. §4332(2)(C).) Consider the requirements of an EIS in light of the following facts.

(a) The federal government proposes to construct a prison in New York City. What environmental factors should be considered in the EIS?

(b) Metropolitan Edison Co. requests the NRC's permission to restart one of the undamaged nuclear reactors at Three Mile Island. A local citizens group asserts that the NRC must prepare an EIS that considers the severe psychological damage that might be caused to local residents. Is this potential psychological damage an environmental impact? Explain.

54-8 Review the cases excerpted in this chapter. Does the judiciary appear willing to assume an active role in establishing substantive rules for environmental regulation? Explain. Suggest reasons for this judicial attitude toward environmental law.

Emerging Issues in Environmental Law: Control Costs, Incentive Programs, and the Regulation of Toxic Wastes

James E. Krier

Government regulation of business is a large topic, and this essay is focused on only one of its aspects: environmental law, considered in Chapter 54. But environmental regulation is a particularly active and innovative area, and one of growing importance to business people and corporate firms. The freshness of the field may account for its vitality. It is an old saw among students of regulation that government programs, like people, have a life cycle: they start off loud and kicking, they experience a troubled and rebellious adolescence, they mellow into middle age, and they become old, sedentary, set in their ways. Environmental regulation is something short of middle-aged. This description applies especially to the federal government's programs, and it is *federal* environmental law that matters most today. At least until the turn of the century, environmental problems were largely the province of state courts applying routine common law (tort and property) doctrine. But the spread of people and technology, and with them the spread of pollution problems of various sorts, enlarged environmental problems beyond common law capacities, and first local and then state governments responded with more or less centralized programs of legislative and administrative control. There was some early federal regulation, but it was piecemeal and passive, existing primarily as a means of support for state and local efforts. This situation changed dramatically beginning around 1970. Since then, environmental law has come to mean federal programs—about air pollution, water pollution, and hazardous substances especially.

The move from courts to legislatures and agencies, and the more recent (and related) move from local to state to federal authority, are two impor-

tant themes in the history of environmental law. Right now there is modest momentum to decentralize environmental controls once again, and to give some authority back to the states. A reason—but hardly a conclusive one—to decentralize has to do with the costs of uniformity in a universe of diverse conditions. Federal intervention has meant largely uniform requirements, such as the same air and water quality standards everywhere, and uniform requirements can be troublingly inefficient when, as has come to be, the costs and benefits of achieving them vary dramatically from place to place. Does it really make sense to have the air in Los Angeles as clean as the air in Los Altos, given that the meteorological and demographic characteristics of Los Angeles are atypical? (Though not, we should realize, utterly unique: a number of other major metropolitan areas share them to considerable degree.) Should water quality be uniform when the costs and benefits of controlling water pollution differ from one body of water in an area to another body of water in the same area, and from area to area as well? Economists in particular are inclined to answer no, and to argue for variations in standards of quality. For now they win the argument by default, because the uniformity required by law is still to be achieved in fact; as to the future, one manifestation of the movement for decentralization is likely to be federal environmental quality standards set on a nonuniform basis. A more substantial manifestation, but also a highly unlikely one, would be a return to state standard setting.

The foregoing discussion is about *ambient*

James E. Krier is the Earl Warren DeLano Professor of Law at the University of Michigan.

standards—those that dictate the quality of the receiving medium, whether air, water, or land. Related issues arise in the case of *source* standards, the actual regulatory requirements applied to polluters in order to achieve the desired levels of ambient quality. Here the typical pattern has again been uniformity, at least for all sources within a given category. But because some of the sources in a category are likely to be capable of controlling more cheaply than others, it would be less costly overall to have them control more and the others less. One could, of course, set regulatory standards that take this variability into account, but the process becomes cumbersome. At the extreme, each plant could require its own peculiar standard. Hence economists suggest that standard setting should be abandoned in favor of alternative techniques—emission fees and marketable rights—that have the effect of charging each polluter for each unit of pollution output. Under the constraint of having to pay to pollute, firms with low control costs would control more, and those with high control costs less, and the resulting aggregate amount of control would be achieved at minimal cost.

Neither emission fees nor marketable rights have been enacted in pure form, but—perhaps as a product of the innovative youth of environmental regulation—variants are being used. With regard to certain requirements of the Clean Air Act, for instance, sources are permitted to avoid expensive controls on one stack by providing for controls on another more manageable stack (in some cases, one owned by another company) beyond the ordinary requirements, thus offsetting the increase at one point with the reduction at the other. This application of the marketable-rights approach is called a "bubble": attention is directed not to the output from each individual stack, but rather to the amount of pollution coming from a hole in the top of an imaginary bubble put over all the point sources.

Emission fees and marketable rights are examples of an incentives-based approach to control, and one (though not the only) end they have in mind is minimizing costs. Cost minimization becomes more and more important as growth—in population, production, consumption, and knowl-edge about the effects of environmental pollution—moves us in the direction of ever greater degrees of control. High levels of control are expensive, and economy becomes crucial. It is likely, then, that we will see a gradual shift from technology-based to incentives-based standards. Those in the world of business will find it in their interest to become familiar with the characteristics, and the advantages and disadvantages, of each of the various techniques.

Until very recently, environmental regulation has been obsessed with *conventional* pollutants—well-known (and sometimes visible) agents that cause acute effects at relatively high concentrations. But advances in control and in scientific understanding have revealed the terrible importance of *unconventional* pollutants, most notably toxic substances. Here effects are often chronic, building up over a lifetime of exposure and manifested only after a long period of latency. Once discovered, they may be irreversible—and catastrophic as well. The mechanisms underlying the exposure-effect relationship are poorly understood, dangerous concentration levels may be infinitesimal, and the probability that exposure will lead to disease is often very remote. In short, toxic substances entail high stakes and great uncertainty, and these make regulatory efforts exceedingly difficult. History shows that, for conventional pollutants, regulatory uncertainty has been resolved by trial and error—an approach to which toxic substances hardly lend themselves. Unhappily, however, present regulatory programs are (perhaps necessarily) crude. Because toxic substances move sinuously throughout the environmental media, for example, integrated management—of air, water, and land as a whole—becomes exceedingly important. Yet segmented thinking continues to dominate. For example, RCRA (discussed in Chapter 54), regulates the (usually land) disposal of hazardous substances. But now, by virtue of 1984 amendments, Congress has come close to banning land disposal of these substances altogether. Where, then, are they to go? Into the air? The water?

We could, of course, simply ban hazardous substances, period. But they are ubiquitous, an inherent part—or so it seems—of the mixed blessings of modern life.

Chapter 55

Accountants' Liability

Major Topics

- the common law theories, including breach of contract, negligence, and fraud, under which an auditor may be held liable to the client or third parties
- the major theories of accountants' civil liability under federal securities law
- major grounds of accountants' criminal liability under federal law
- a discussion of the law governing accountant-client privilege
- income tax preparers' liability under the Internal Revenue Code

In periodic audits, independent certified public accountants (CPAs) review, examine, and test a company's financial statements. The accountant's objective is to express an opinion regarding whether the financial statements fairly present financial position, results of operation, and changes in financial position.[1] The independent CPA communicates this opinion in an audit report, which usually states that the audit was conducted in conformity with **generally accepted auditing standards (GAAS),** and (if the opinion is unqualified) that the financial state-

ments are fairly presented in conformity with **generally accepted accounting principles (GAAP).**[2] The client then often distributes the audit report and financial statements to interested third parties, including shareholders, creditors, lenders, and potential investors. The audit report assists these people in evaluating the company's financial health before making a business decision.

Independent auditors render important services to their clients including evaluating and suggesting improvements in internal control procedures and, in some cases, detecting fraud or embezzlement by the client's employees. The auditor's undertaking also serves an important public function in our economic system. As noted by one commentator: "The functioning and, indeed, the perpetuation of our private enterprise system depends on the continuing confidence of investors and creditors in the reliability of financial statements. To provide this

---

1. 1 AICPA Professional Standards, Statements on Auditing Standards §110.01 (1972).

---

2. The auditor may issue four different types of audit opinions. If the auditor conducts an audit conforming to GAAS and (1) believes that the financial statements are presented in conformity with GAAP, then the auditor should issue an unqualified opinion, (2) believes that the overall financial statements are fairly presented with some specific exceptions, then the auditor should issue a qualified opinion, (3) believes that the financial statements are *not* fairly presented in conformity with GAAP, then the auditor should issue an adverse opinion, (4) cannot satisfy himself regarding whether the financial statements are presented fairly, then the auditor should issue a disclaimer of opinion.

confidence is precisely the role that the auditor assumes.''[3] Both the Securities and Exchange Commission and the American Institute of Certified Public Accountants (AICPA), the profession's oversight body, emphasize the public accountant's responsibility to safeguard the public interest, ''a responsibility that has grown as the number of investors has grown, as the relationship between corporate managers and stockholders has become more impersonal, and as government increasingly relies on accounting information.''[4]

Occasionally, auditors have failed to meet their public responsibility by certifying as accurate financial statements that are materially inaccurate or misleading. In such cases, third parties who rely on the audit report and suffer damages often look to the auditor for compensation. To illustrate a typical case, assume Blake Company hires auditing firm Arthur Ross to perform an audit. Blake needs the audit report to obtain a loan from First National Bank, which intends to use the audit information to evaluate Blake's loan application. Relying on Arthur Ross's report, the bank makes the loan. A short time later Blake Company declares bankruptcy and defaults on the loan. First National later learns that Arthur Ross failed to discover an irregularity—for example, that the treasurer had been embezzling large sums of money—that rendered the audited statements materially misleading. The bank sues Arthur Ross for damages, alleging that it would not have made the loan had the irregularity been detected.

Accountants may be held liable to their clients and to third parties such as First National Bank on a variety of legal theories. Under the common law, liability may be based upon breach of contract, negligence, or fraud. Statutory liability usually is based upon the federal securities laws that are discussed in detail in Chapter 49. This chapter examines the major legal theories underlying accountants' liability, beginning with common law liability.

Common Law Liability

Contract Liability

The employment of an accountant is a contractual undertaking. Because the rights and obligations of the parties are controlled by private agreement, the auditor must properly perform the agreed undertaking to be entitled to compensation. The accountant's primary duties usually are expressed in the engagement letter, a contract between the auditor and the client. The letter normally specifies the nature of the auditor's examination, the responsibilities assumed, and limitations on the scope of the audit. In addition, implied in every contract for work or services is the duty to perform it skillfully, carefully, diligently, and in a workmanlike manner. The auditor may be liable to the client for breach of contract, for example, if the auditor issues a standard audit report without making an examination in accordance with GAAS, fails to deliver the audit report on time, violates the client's confidential relationship, or otherwise fails to perform.

An accountant's contract liability also may extend to third-party beneficiaries of the contract. As discussed in Chapter 13, a beneficiary (a person who benefits from performance of a contract but is not a party to it) may enforce a contract made with the intent to benefit the beneficiary. In the accountants' liability context, for example, an audit may be undertaken for the express purpose of providing financial statements to a specific lender as part of a loan application. In this case, the bank or other lender may be an intended beneficiary of the contract between the auditor and client, entitled to recover damages for the auditor's breach. Few reported cases have used the third-party beneficiary theory, suggesting that this theory has not yet been fully developed by the courts.

Negligence Liability

An accountant may incur liability for negligence to two classes of people: clients and third parties.

Liability to the Client. Negligence is conduct which falls below the standard established by law to protect others against unreasonable risk of

---

3. Former AICPA Vice-President Leonard Savoie, quoted in ''Why Accountants Need to Tell a Fuller Story,'' *Business Week,* February 6, 1971, at 87.

4. 2 AICPA Professional Standards, Code of Professional Ethics §51.04 (1984).

harm.[5] In most cases, the standard to which a person must conform to avoid liability for negligence is that of a reasonable person under similar circumstances. A client seeking to recover against an accountant in an action based on negligence must satisfy four requirements. First, the plaintiff must show that the accountant had a duty not to be negligent. Second, the accountant must have breached that duty by failure to exercise reasonable care. Third, the plaintiff must establish a causal connection between the negligence and the injury. Finally, the plaintiff must prove damage or actual loss. Many suits brought against an accountant for negligence involve failure to discover defalcations involving, for example, check kiting, concealment of inventory shortages, and embezzlement. The material that follows briefly outlines the elements of a negligence action in the accountants' liability context.

Duty. In most circumstances the accountant is engaged to issue a "certified" report. The standard audit report usually states that "our examination was made in accordance with generally accepted auditing standards . . . " and that the audited financial statements present fairly the client's financial position "in conformity with generally accepted accounting principles applied on a basis consistent with that of the preceding year." Auditing standards concern how the work of the particular audit is performed. For example, auditing standards determine what books, records, and assets are examined; how accounts such as cash and accounts receivable are verified; and how internal control is evaluated. In contrast, accounting principles determine how the completed work is presented in the financial statements. Accounting principles, for example, determine when contingency reserve is required and how to account for a decline in the value of inventory. These standards and principles are derived from published pronouncements of the AICPA, state accounting boards and CPA societies, the Financial Accounting Standards Board (FASB), and SEC and IRS rules and releases. In determining negligence, the court examines the auditor's compliance with both appropriate auditing standards and accounting principles. That is, liability may be imposed for lack of reasonable care either in conducting the audit or in presenting its results in the audit report.

As a professional, an accountant is held to possess the degree of skill, knowledge, and judgment commonly possessed by other members of the profession in the locality. Accordingly, the accountant is held to a higher standard of care than the ordinary "reasonable person." Generally to avoid liability, an accountant must act as a reasonably prudent accountant would act under similar circumstances. For this reason, negligence often must be proven or disproven by expert accounting testimony.

Note that failure to follow GAAS and GAAP, the custom of the profession, generally indicates negligence in the conduct of the audit. Literal adherence to customary practice, however, does not necessarily indicate lack of negligence. Compliance with GAAS and GAAP is merely one factor to be considered in evaluating the accountant's reasonable care.

Many clients believe that an audit can be relied on to detect fraud. Although under a duty to search for errors and irregularities, an auditor is not a guarantor of the accuracy of the financial statements. That is,

> [a]n auditor is not bound to be a detective, or . . . to approach his work with suspicion or with a foregone conclusion that there is something wrong. He is a watch-dog, but not a bloodhound. He is justified in believing tried servants of the company in whom confidence is placed by the company. He is entitled to assume that they are honest, and to rely upon their representations, provided he takes reasonable care. If there is anything calculated to excite suspicion he should probe it to the bottom; but in the absence of anything of that kind he is only bound to be reasonably cautious and careful.[6]

---

5. *Restatement (Second) of Torts* §282. The basic principles of negligence are introduced in Chapter 5.

6. *In re Kingston Cotton Mill Company,* [1896] 2 Ch. 279, 288–289 (C.A.).

Though an audit cannot be relied upon to disclose defalcations or management fraud, failure to uncover certain frauds may be negligence. For example, GAAS are designed in part to uncover deliberate misrepresentations by management, but are less effective at detecting frauds involving collusion, forgery, or unrecorded transactions. Thus an auditor who fails to follow GAAS may be liable in negligence for failure to uncover a fraud that would have been found had those standards been properly applied.

Breach of Duty. Once the legal duty is established, the plaintiff in a negligence suit must prove the accountant's breach of duty. The accountant may breach the duty by using inadequate procedures and methods to ascertain the information on which the audit report is based. For example, an engagement to perform an audit implies the duties to verify cash, confirm accounts receivable, observe physical inventories, and generally adhere to professional standards. Failure properly to perform these tasks may constitute negligence. In addition, the accountant may be negligent in communicating the information to the client. For example, the accountant may be negligent for issuing an unqualified opinion when a qualified opinion is appropriate.

Causation and Damages. Once negligence is established, the plaintiff must establish the amount of his damage with reasonable certainty, and demonstrate that the accountant's acts or omissions were the cause of the loss. Causation is apparent if the client sues for losses caused by an employee's embezzlement that the accountant should have detected. More difficult cases arise if the plaintiff seeks recovery for losses resulting from bad business investments or decisions made in reliance on the audit report.

Liability to Third Parties. Although an audit is designed to inform management of inefficiencies and irregularities in the business, increasingly, audited financial statements are used by third parties who have no contractual relation with the accountant. Third parties such as banks, potential investors, and shareholders who are injured by relying upon negligently certified financial statements may sue the auditor. The following material examines the conflicting legal theories governing accountants' liability to third parties for negligence.

The **Ultramares** *Rule.* The landmark case concerning accountants' liability to third parties for negligence is *Ultramares Corporation v. Touche* decided by the New York Court of Appeals in 1931.[7] In this case, Fred Stern and Co., a firm engaged in the importation and sale of rubber, required extensive use of credit to finance its operations. The defendant, Touche, Niven & Co., was hired by Stern to prepare and certify a December 31, 1923, balance sheet. The defendants certified thirty-two copies of the financial statements knowing that the balance sheet would be used by Stern to obtain credit. The defendants certified the balance sheet even though Fred Stern & Co. was insolvent with $706,000 in fictitious receivables on the books. On the faith of the certified financial statements, Ultramares Corporation loaned money to Stern. Shortly thereafter, Stern went bankrupt and Ultramares sued the accountant alleging that the accountant's misrepresentations were both negligent and fraudulent.

Judge Benjamin Cardozo, writing for a unanimous court, found negligence on the part of the accountant. Nevertheless, he held that the accountant had no liability to third parties for ordinary negligence even though liability to third parties could be imposed for fraud or gross negligence. Judge Cardozo, concerned with expansive accountants' liability to third parties, stated:

> If liability for negligence exists [between the accountant and unknown third party], a thoughtless slip or blunder, the failure to detect a theft or forgery beneath the cover of deceptive entries, may expose accountants to a liability in an indeterminate amount for an indeterminate time to an indeterminate class. . . . Our holding does not emancipate accountants from the consequences of fraud. It does not relieve them if their audit has been so negligent as to justify a finding that they had no genuine belief in its adequacy, for this again is fraud. It does no more than say that, if

---

7. 174 N.E. 441 (N.Y. 1931).

less than this is proved, if there has been neither reckless misstatement nor insincere profession of an opinion, but only honest blunder, the ensuing liability for negligence is one that is bounded by the contract, and is to be enforced between the parties by whom the contract has been made.[8]

The *Ultramares* case therefore takes a very restrictive view of an accountant's liability to third parties for negligence, allowing recovery only by persons in privity of contract with the accountant. Applying this test, the court refused to hold the negligent accountants liable to Ultramares, a lender with whom they had no contractual privity.

The New York Court of Appeals reaffirmed its support for the *Ultramares* privity rule and refined it in *Credit Alliance Corporation v. Arthur Andersen & Co.* (1985)[9] in which the court stated:

[T]his court [has since] reiterated the requirement for a "contractual relationship or its equivalent." . . . Before accountants may be held liable in negligence to noncontractual parties who rely to their detriment on inaccurate financial reports, certain prerequisites must be satisfied: (1) the accountants must have been aware that the financial reports were to be used for a particular purpose or purposes; (2) in the furtherance of which a known party or parties was intended to rely; and (3) there must have been some conduct on the part of the accountants linking them to that party or parties, which evinces the accountants' understanding of that party or parties' reliance. While these criteria permit some flexibility in the application of the doctrine of privity to accountants' liability, they do not represent a departure from the principles articulated in *Ultramares*, . . . but, rather, they are intended to preserve the wisdom and policy set forth therein.[10]

Alternatives to Ultramares. Both courts and commentators have harshly criticized the *Ultramares* doctrine for unreasonably insulating negligent CPAs from third-party liability. Although a majority of the courts continue to follow the *Ultra-*

mares rule of privity, many courts are rejecting it and extending accountants' liability for negligence to third parties. One alternative to the *Ultramares* privity doctrine is the rule stated in §552 of the *Restatement (Second) of Torts,* which has received considerable support. Section 552, entitled "Information Negligently Supplied for the Guidance of Others," provides in relevant part:

(1) One who, in the course of his business, profession or employment, or in any other transaction in which he has a pecuniary interest, supplies false information for the guidance of others in their business transactions, is subject to liability for pecuniary loss caused to them by their justifiable reliance upon the information, if he fails to exercise reasonable care or competence in obtaining or communicating the information.
(2) . . . [T]he liability stated in Subsection (1) is limited to loss suffered
    (a) by the person or one of a limited group of persons for whose benefit and guidance he intends to supply the information or knows that the recipient intends to supply it; and
    (b) through reliance upon it in a transaction that he intends the information to influence or knows that the recipient so intends or in a substantially similar transaction.

Under §552 an auditor owes a duty (1) to his client, (2) to intended or known third-party users of financial statements, and (3) to any individually unknown third parties who are members of a known or intended *class* of third-party users of financial statements. The *Restatement* extends liability beyond *Ultramares* in that the auditor need not know the plaintiff's identity, if the plaintiff belongs to an identifiable group to whom the information was intended to be furnished. For example, an auditor who knows that a report is to be prepared for bank borrowing would be liable to the particular bank to whom the client delivers the opinion.

Under either the *Ultramares* or *Restatement* approach, almost all third-party users of financial statements are precluded from suing negligent accountants at common law. That is, shareholders, creditors, and other third parties are in most cases merely "reasonably foreseeable" third parties; they are not known or intended ones. Accordingly, they are denied recovery under both the *Restatement* and

---

8. *Id.* at 444, 448.
9. 483 N.E.2d 110 (N.Y. 1985).
10. *Id.* at 117–118.

Ultramares. For this reason, a few courts have adopted a third approach that extends an auditor's duty of reasonable care to reasonably foreseeable plaintiffs who are neither known nor a member of an intended class. In the following case, the court weighs the advantages and disadvantages of the various approaches to accountants' liability to third parties for negligence.

Raritan River Steel Company v. Cherry, Bekaert & Holland

367 S.E.2d 609 (N.C. 1988)

> Intercontinental Metals Corporation (IMC) retained defendants Cherry, Bekaert & Holland, a firm of certified public accountants, to audit the company's financial statements for the years ending September 30, 1980 and September 30, 1981. Plaintiff Sidbec-Dosco, Inc. extended credit to IMC in reliance on information contained in the audit report prepared by defendants for IMC. Subsequently, plaintiff sued defendants, alleging that they were negligent in their preparation of the report, resulting in an overstatement of IMC's net worth, and causing loss to the plaintiff. The trial court dismissed the complaint and the court of appeals reversed in part. The Supreme Court of North Carolina granted defendants' petition for review to determine the scope of an accountant's liability to third parties for negligent misrepresentations contained in an audit report.

Exum, Chief Justice

. . . Courts in our sister states have recognized . . . different approaches to determine the scope of an accountant's liability for negligent misrepresentation in the context of financial audits. The most restrictive standard was first enunciated in an opinion by then Chief Judge Cardozo of the New York Court of Appeals, in which the Court concluded that to be liable for negligent misrepresentation, an accountant must be in privity of contract with the person seeking to impose liability or there must be "[a] bond . . . so close as to approach that of privity." [*Ultramares Corp. v. Touche, Niven & Co.*, 174 N.E. 441, 446 (N.Y. 1931).] Several jurisdictions follow this restrictive view. . . . Recently the New York Court of Appeals reaffirmed its reliance on the *Ultramares* ap-

proach and announced criteria with which to determine whether the "privity or near-privity" standard has been met. [*Credit Alliance Corp. v. Arthur Andersen & Co.*, 483 N.E.2d 110 (N.Y. 1985).] . . .

A less restrictive rule is set forth in the *Restatement (Second) of Torts* §552 (1977). . . . As we understand it, under the Restatement approach an accountant who audits or prepares financial information for a client owes a duty of care not only to the client but to any other person, or one of a group of persons, whom the accountant or his client intends the information to benefit; and that person reasonably relies on the information in a transaction, or one substantially similar to it, that the accountant or his client intends the information to influence. If the requisite intent is that of the client and not the accountant, then the accountant must know of his client's intent at the time the accountant audits or prepares the information. A number of jurisdictions adhere to the Restatement standard. . . .

The courts of three states have recently adopted a position which extends an accountant's liability to all persons whom the accountant should reasonably foresee might obtain and rely on the accountant's work. . . .

We reject the *Ultramares* "privity or near-privity" approach, as elucidated in *Credit Alliance*, because it provides inadequately for the central role independent accountants play in the financial world. Accountants' audit opinions are increasingly relied upon by the investing and lending public in making financial decisions. . . . The accounting profession itself has recognized as much. . . . Because of this heavy public reliance on audited financial information we believe an approach that protects those persons, or classes of persons, whom an accountant knows will rely on his audit opinion, but who may not otherwise be in "privity or near-privity," with him is desirable.

Although the *Ultramares* approach to accountants' liability seems unduly restrictive, we also decline to adopt the "reasonably foreseeable" test because it would result in liability more expansive than an accountant should be expected to bear. Courts which extend an accountant's liability to all reasonably foreseen users of his financial information do so on the ground that there is no good reason to exempt accountants from the general rule that a negligent actor is liable for all reasonably foreseeable consequences of his negligence. . . . The reasoning [of the court in *H. Rosenblum, Inc. v. Adler*, 461 A.2d 138 (N.J. 1983),] is representative. It analogized a negligent misrepresentation claim against an accountant to a products liability claim against a manufacturer and concluded that public policy did not justify disparate negligence standards. . . .

Between the production and distribution of an accountant's audit report and the design and manufacture of a product we perceive significant differences which justify establishing a narrower class of plaintiffs to whom the accountant owes a duty of care. Designers and manufacturers have control over the processes by which the products enter the stream of commerce. . . . Manufacturers, and to a lesser extent designers, can limit their potential liability by controlling the number of products they release into the marketplace. Auditors, on the other hand, have no control over the distribution of their reports, and hence lack control over their exposure to liability. Moreover, . . . auditors do not control their client's accounting records and processes. . . . While, in the final analysis, an auditor renders an opinion concerning the accuracy of his client's records, he necessarily relies, in some measure, on the client for the records' contents. Because of the accountant's inability to control the distribution of his report, as well as his lack of control over some of the contents of the statements he assesses, a standard which limits his potential liability is appropriate.

A more fundamental difference between product designers and manufacturers and accountants lies in their differing expectations concerning their work product. Manufacturers and designers fully expect that their products will be used by a wide variety of unknown members of the public. Indeed, this is their hope, for with wider use will come increased profits. This is not the case when an accountant prepares an audit. An accountant performs an audit pursuant to a contract with an individual client. The client may or may not intend to use the report for other than internal purposes. It does not benefit the accountant if his client distributes the audit opinion to others. Instead, it merely exposes his work to many whom he may have had no idea would scrutinize his efforts. We believe that in fairness accountants should not be liable in circumstances where they are unaware of the use to which their opinions will be put. Instead, their liability should be commensurate with those persons or classes of persons whom they know will rely on their work. With such knowledge the auditor can, through purchase of liability insurance, setting fees, and adopting other protective measures appropriate to the risk, prepare accordingly. . . .

We conclude that the standard set forth in the *Restatement (Second) of Torts* §552 (1977) represents the soundest approach to accountants' liability for negligent misrepresentation. It constitutes a middle ground between the restrictive *Ultramares* approach advocated by defendants and the expansive "reasonably foreseeable" approach advanced by plaintiffs. It recognizes that liability should extend not only to those with whom the accountant is in privity or near privity, but also to those persons, or classes of persons, whom he knows and intends will rely on his opinion, or whom he knows his client intends will so rely. On the other hand, as the commentary makes clear, it prevents extension of liability in situations where the accountant "merely knows of the ever-present possibility of repetition to anyone, and the possibility of action in reliance upon [the audited financial statements], on the part of anyone to whom it may be repeated." *Restatement (Second) of Torts* §552, Comment h. As such it balances, more so than the other standards, the need to hold accountants to a standard that accounts for their contemporary role in the financial world with the need to protect them from liability that unreasonably exceeds the bounds of their real undertaking.

We acknowledge that courts have not been uniform in their application of the Restatement approach. . . . Some [have construed §552] to mean that liability turns on whether the accountant's client specifically mentions a person or class of persons who are to receive the audited financial statements. . . . The Restatement's text does not demand that the accountant be informed by the client himself of the audit report's intended use. The text requires only that the auditor *know* that his client intends to supply information to another person or limited group of persons. Whether the auditor acquires this knowledge from his client or elsewhere should make no difference. If he knows at the time he prepares his report that specific persons, or a limited group of persons, will rely on his work, and intends or knows that his client intends such reliance, his duty of care should extend to them.

Applying the Restatement test to Sidbec-Dosco's complaint, we conclude Sidbec-Dosco has stated a legally sufficient claim against defendants for negligent misrepresentation. Sidbec-Dosco alleges that when defendants prepared the audited financial statements for IMC they knew: (1) the statements would be used by IMC to represent its financial condition to creditors who would extend credit on the basis of them; and (2) plaintiff and other creditors would rely upon these statements. These allegations are sufficient to impose upon defendants a duty of care to Sidbec-Dosco under the Restatement approach as we have interpreted and adopted it herein. . . .

[Judgment affirmed.]

The *Ultramares* doctrine of privity has been eroded in the past decade with the adoption of §552 of the *Restatement (Second) of Torts* in a number of jurisdictions, and the even more expansive liability imposed by courts adopting a "reasonable foreseeability" standard. Nevertheless, the recent reaffirmation of the *Ultramares* doctrine by the influential New York Court of Appeals indicates that the common law regarding accountants' liability to third parties for negligence is likely to remain unsettled among the various jurisdictions.

In addition, some states have legislatively altered the extent of an accountant's liability. For example, an Illinois statute enacted in 1986 generally limits an accountant's liability for negligence to persons in privity of contract. Third parties may recover only if the accountant was aware that the client's "primary intent . . . was for the professional services to benefit or influence the particular person bringing the action."[11]

Fraud Liability

Under the *Ultramares* rule, privity is required in negligence cases, but not in suits brought by injured third parties on the basis of fraud. That is, an accountant may be held liable to reliant third par-

ties whom the accountant intended to deceive by his reports. Consequently, in a jurisdiction following the *Ultramares* rule of privity, third-party plaintiffs often base their cause of action on fraud to avoid the privity requirement applicable to negligence actions. To be liable for fraud: (1) the defendant must make a misrepresentation with knowledge of its falsity (scienter) and with the intent to induce the plaintiff to act in reliance upon it, (2) the misrepresentation must relate to a material fact, (3) the plaintiff must justifiably rely upon and act upon the misrepresentation, and (4) the plaintiff must suffer injury as a result of the reliance. Proving scienter is the major hurdle in an accountants' liability case based on fraud. The plaintiff must establish that the defendant lacked a genuine belief that the information disclosed was accurate and complete in all material respects. Scienter may be proven by either direct or circumstantial evidence of the defendant's state of mind.

In a number of cases courts have recognized that acts constituting gross negligence raise an inference of fraud sufficient to support third-party recovery against an accountant. In *State Street Trust Co. v. Ernst*,[12] for example, the court stated:

> Accountants . . . may be liable to third parties, even where there is lacking deliberate or active fraud. A representation certified as true to the knowledge of the accountants when knowledge there is none, a reckless misstatement, or an opinion based on grounds so flimsy as to lead to the conclusion that there was no genuine belief in its truth, are all sufficient upon which to base liability. A refusal to see the obvious, a failure to investigate the doubtful, if sufficiently gross, may furnish evidence leading to an inference of fraud so as to impose liability for losses suffered by those who rely on the balance sheet. In other words, heedlessness and reckless disregard of consequence may take the place of deliberate intention.[13]

Liability Under Federal Securities Law

The federal securities laws discussed in Chapter 49 provide investor protection by requiring full and

---

11. ¶. Rev. Stat. ch. 111, π5535.1.

12. 15 N.E.2d 416 (N.Y. 1938).
13. *Id.* at 418–419.

accurate public disclosure of relevant information. Many of the required disclosures are accomplished through examinations and reports prepared by independent accountants. Regarding the accountant's function under the securities laws the SEC has noted:

> A public accountant's examination is intended to be an independent check upon management's accounting of its stewardship. Thus he ha[s] a direct and unavoidable responsibility of his own, particularly where his engagement relates to a company which makes filings with the Commission or in which there is a substantial public interest.[14]

The securities laws impose substantial responsibilities and potential liabilities upon accountants who evaluate the fairness and accuracy of financial statements issued by publicly-held companies. Initially, the SEC, through various rules and releases, regulates accounting practices and the form of financial statements used in SEC filings. The SEC also has the power to discipline accountants who prepare documents filed with the commission who are unqualified, have engaged in unethical or improper professional conduct, or who have willfully violated (or aided and abetted others to violate) any provision of the federal securities laws.[15] In addition to administrative sanctions, accountants may be held liable to third parties for damages under the various civil liability provisions of the Securities Act of 1933 and the Securities Exchange Act of 1934, which are discussed in detail in Chapter 49. The material that follows highlights the civil liability provisions of particular concern to accountants.

Liability Under §11 of the 1933 Act

Section 11 of the Securities Act of 1933, which imposes liability for misstatements or omissions in a registration statement filed under the 1933 Act, applies to accountants, engineers, or other experts who prepare or certify parts of the registration statement. Note that §11 measures the accuracy of the registration statement at the time it becomes effective. Thus, the auditor must undertake a review covering the period between the date of the audit report and the date of public sale of the securities to assure that the financial statements are accurate on the registration statement's effective date.

A number of defenses are available to defeat liability under §11. The most important of these is the "due diligence" defense, discussed as applied to an accountant in the following landmark case.

Escott v. BarChris Construction Corporation
283 F. Supp. 643 (S.D.N.Y. 1968)

> BarChris Construction Corporation was engaged in the construction of bowling alleys. Generally, BarChris entered into a contract with a customer receiving only a small down payment on the purchase price. When the building was finished, the customer paid the balance of the contract price in notes, payable in installments over a period of years. Because BarChris was compelled to expend considerable sums in construction before receiving reimbursement, it was in constant need of cash to finance operations. Accordingly, it made a public offering of debentures in early 1961, pursuant to a registration statement filed with the SEC on March 30, 1961, and which became effective May 16, 1961. By that time BarChris was experiencing difficulty collecting amounts due from some of its customers. Because of overbuilding in the industry, bowling alley operations had begun to fail. After an abortive attempt to obtain additional financing, BarChris filed for bankruptcy reorganization in October 1962 and defaulted upon the debentures.
>
> The buyers of the debentures maintained a class action under §11 of the Securities Act of 1933 against the persons who signed the registration statement, the underwriters, and Peat, Marwick, Mitchell & Co., BarChris's auditors. Plaintiffs alleged that the registration statement contained a number of material false statements and omissions. The court found that the 1960 sales figures in the financial statements prepared by Peat, Marwick included the contract price of completed alleys which

---

14. *In re Kerlin,* SEC Accounting Series Release No. 105 (1966).

15. SEC Rule of Practice 2(e); 17 C.F.R. §201.2(e).

in fact had not been sold by BarChris. For example, BarChris originally contracted to build Heavenly Lanes (also known as "Capitol Lanes") for an outside purchaser. When the contract fell through, BarChris built the alley and leased it to its wholly owned subsidiary, Capitol Lanes, Inc., which operated the alley beginning in December 1960. By listing Heavenly Lanes in the 1960 sales figures as a completed contract, though it was never sold to any outside interest, 1960 sales were inflated by $330,000, and liabilities were understated by a similar amount. The court also found that the prospectus contained other misstatements and omissions including a failure to disclose unpaid officers' loans, failure to disclose that most of the debenture proceeds would be used to pay pre-existing debts rather than to provide additional working capital for the expansion of alley construction, failure to disclose substantial customer delinquencies, and failure to disclose that BarChris was already engaged in the operation of bowling alleys and would soon be engaged in operating alleys repossessed from defaulting customers.

To avoid liability for the false statements and omissions, each defendant asserted the "due diligence" defense contained in Section 11(b) of the 1933 Act. In the following portion of the opinion, the court considered whether Peat, Marwick had established the defense.

McLean, District Judge

. . . The part of the registration statement purporting to be made upon the authority of Peat, Marwick as an expert was . . . the 1960 figures. But because the statute requires the court to determine Peat, Marwick's belief, and the grounds thereof, "at the time such part of the registration statement became effective," for the purposes of this affirmative defense, the matter must be viewed as of May 16, 1961, and the question is whether at that time Peat, Marwick, after reasonable investigation, had reasonable ground to believe and did believe that the 1960 figures were true and that no material fact had been omitted from the registration statement which should have been included in order to make the 1960 figures not misleading. In deciding this issue, the court must consider not only what Peat, Marwick did in its 1960 audit, but also what

it did in its subsequent "S-1 review." The proper scope of that review must also be determined. . . .

The 1960 Audit

Peat, Marwick's work was in general charge of a member of the firm, Cummings, and more immediately in charge of Peat, Marwick's manager, Logan. Most of the actual work was performed by a senior accountant, Berardi, who had junior assistants, one of whom was Kennedy.

Berardi was then about thirty years old. He was not yet a C.P.A. He had had no previous experience with the bowling industry. This was his first job as a senior accountant. He could hardly have been given a more difficult assignment. . . .

It is unnecessary to recount everything that Berardi did in the course of the audit. We are concerned only with the evidence relating to what Berardi did or did not do with respect to those items which I have found to have been incorrectly reported in the 1960 figures in the prospectus. More narrowly, we are directly concerned only with such of those items as I have found to be material.

Capitol Lanes

First and foremost is Berardi's failure to discover that Capitol Lanes had not been sold. This error affected both the sales figure and the liability side of the balance sheet. Fundamentally, the error stemmed from the fact that Berardi never realized that Heavenly Lanes and Capitol were two different names for the same alley. . . .

Berardi assumed that Heavenly was to be treated like any other completed job. He included it in all his computations.

The evidence is conflicting as to whether BarChris's officers expressly informed Berardi that Heavenly and Capitol were the same thing and that BarChris was operating Capitol and had not sold it. I find that they did not so inform him.

Berardi did become aware that there were references here and there in BarChris's records to something called Capitol Lanes. He also knew that there were indications that at some time BarChris might operate an alley of that name. . . .

Berardi testified that he inquired of Russo

[BarChris's chief executive officer] about Capitol Lanes and that Russo told him that Capitol Lanes, Inc. was going to operate an alley some day but as yet it had no alley. Berardi testified that he understood that the alley had not been built. . . .

I am not satisfied with this testimony. If Berardi did hold this belief, he should not have held it. The entries [in Peat, Marwick's work papers] as to insurance and as to "operation of alley" should have alerted him to the fact that an alley existed. He should have made further inquiry on the subject. It is apparent that Berardi did not understand this transaction. . . .

The burden of proof on this issue is on Peat, Marwick. . . . Peat, Marwick has not proved that Berardi made a reasonable investigation as far as Capitol Lanes was concerned and that his ignorance of the true facts was justified. . . .

The S–1 Review

The purpose of reviewing events subsequent to the date of a certified balance sheet (referred to as an S–1 review when made with reference to a registration statement) is to ascertain whether any material change has occurred in the company's financial position which should be disclosed in order to prevent the balance sheet figures from being misleading. The scope of such a review, under generally accepted auditing standards, is limited. It does not amount to a complete audit.

Peat, Marwick prepared a written program for such a review. I find that this program conformed to generally accepted auditing standards. . . .

Berardi made the S–1 review in May 1961. He devoted a little over two days to it, a total of 20½ hours. He did not discover any of the errors or omissions pertaining to the state of affairs in 1961 which I have previously discussed at length, all of which were material. The question is whether, despite his failure to find out anything, his investigation was reasonable within the meaning of the statute.

What Berardi did was to look at a consolidating trial balance as of March 31, 1961 which had been prepared by BarChris, compare it with the audited December 31, 1960 figures, discuss with Trilling [BarChris's controller] certain unfavorable developments which the comparison disclosed, and read certain minutes. He did not examine any "important financial records" other than the trial balance. . . .

In substance . . . Berardi . . . asked questions, he got answers which he considered satisfactory, and he did nothing to verify them. . . .

There had been a material change for the worse in BarChris's financial position. That change was sufficiently serious so that the failure to disclose it made the 1960 figures misleading. Berardi did not discover it. As far as results were concerned, his S–1 review was useless.

Accountants should not be held to a standard higher than that recognized in their profession. I do not do so here. Berardi's review did not come up to that standard. He did not take some of the steps which Peat, Marwick's written program prescribed. He did not spend an adequate amount of time on a task of this magnitude. Most important of all, he was too easily satisfied with glib answers to his inquiries.

This is not to say that he should have made a complete audit. But there were enough danger signals in the materials which he did examine to require some further investigation on his part. Generally accepted accounting standards required such further investigation under these circumstances. It is not always sufficient merely to ask questions.

Here again, the burden of proof is on Peat, Marwick. I find that . . . Peat, Marwick has not established its due diligence defense. . . .

1934 Act Liability

Under §18(a) of the Securities Exchange Act of 1934, accountants may be held liable for material misstatements or omissions in documents they prepare which are filed with the SEC. Accountants also have been found civilly liable under §14 for their role in preparing false or misleading proxy solicitation material. In addition, an accountant may be held liable under §10(b) and Rule 10b–5 for fraud in the purchase or sale of any security. In the following case the court was required to determine whether an accountant could be held liable under Rule 10b–5 for failing to disclose a securities fraud perpetrated by another.

Rudolph v. Arthur Andersen & Co.

800 F.2d 1040 (11th Cir. 1986)

John DeLorean set up DeLorean Research Limited Partnership (DRLP) and, on March 23, 1978, issued a private placement memorandum stating that the funds raised by the limited partnership offering would be used for research and development related to production of a new sports car. The automobile venture failed and plaintiff Sidney Rudolph and other investors lost their investments. Rudolph sued the defendant Arthur Andersen & Co. (Andersen), an accounting firm, claiming that it had violated §10(b) of the Securities Exchange Act of 1934 and Rule 10b-5. Rudolph later requested leave to amend his complaint with allegations of fact demonstrating Andersen's participation in the fraud. The proposed amendment alleged that the limited partnership placement memorandum included audit reports and other financial statements prepared by Andersen concerning the financial condition of various DeLorean ventures for the years 1976 and 1977 and further alleged that Andersen continued to perform substantial non-auditing services for DeLorean after 1977. Rudolph alleged that sometime after July 28, 1978, DeLorean determined that the funds raised by DRLP were not needed for research and development and that he diverted the funds for other uses without notifying the investors. Rudolph claimed that the diversion was a fraud and that, because of its business relationship with DeLorean, Andersen knew or recklessly failed to learn of the fraud. Rudolph concluded that Andersen's willful or reckless failure to disclose the alleged fraud constituted a violation of §10(b) and Rule 10b-5. The trial court refused to allow Rudolph to file the amended complaint on the ground that even if proved the facts would not establish a violation of federal securities laws. After the trial court dismissed Rudolph's complaint, he appealed.

Vance, Circuit Judge

. . . Our role . . . is limited to determining whether the proposed complaint fails to state a claim under Rule 10b-5. . . .

There can be no doubt that plaintiffs' complaint contains sufficient allegations to support a Rule 10b-5 claim against DeLorean. Plaintiffs allege that in the course of selling securities—the partnership investment units—DeLorean continuously represented that the partnership funds would be used for research and development, while actually deciding at some point during the sale to use the funds for some other purpose. This is surely the type of "untrue statement of a material fact . . . in connection with" the sale of securities that Rule 10b-5 was intended to prohibit.

It is also clear that if read literally, Rule 10b-5 would reach the alleged conduct of Andersen. The rule prohibits "omit[ting] to state a material fact" necessary to make the statements made not misleading. Plaintiffs' complaint accuses Andersen of doing just that, and of thereby leading to plaintiffs' injury.

Rule 10b-5, however, is not read literally. Instead, a defendant's omission to state a material fact is proscribed only when the defendant has a duty to disclose. Such a duty may exist "where the law imposes special obligations, as for accountants, brokers, or other experts, depending on the circumstances of the case." *Woodward v. Metro Bank*, 522 F.2d 84, 97 n. 28 (5th Cir. 1975). . . . A duty to disclose may also be created by a defendant's previous decision to speak voluntarily. Where a defendant's failure to speak would render the defendant's *own* prior speech misleading or deceptive, a duty to disclose arises. . . .

We have not held these factors to be exclusive; there may be others which may properly be taken into account in a particular situation. For instance, the extent of the defendant's knowledge and the significance of the misstatement, fraud or omission might be relevant. A defendant who *intentionally* did not reveal what he *knew* to be fraud might more reasonably be expected to speak out than a defendant who merely failed to learn of a material but ambiguous omission. The extent of the defendant's participation in the fraud might also be important. . . .

Although this court has not considered the issue, . . . other courts have held that accountants "have a duty to take reasonable steps to correct misstatements they have discovered in previous financial statements on which they know the public is relying." *IIT, An International Investment Trust v. Cornfeld*, 619 F.2d 909, 927 (2d Cir. 1980). . . .

This duty arises from the fact that investors are likely to rely on an accountant's work.

> Where it gives an opinion or certifies statements, an auditing firm publicly assumes a role that carries a special relationship of trust vis-à-vis the public. The auditor in such a case holds itself out as an independent professional source of assurance that the audited company's financial presentations are accurate and reliable. . . . . The importance of the act of certifying is such that a continuing duty to disclose has been imposed where the auditor learns facts revealing that a certification believed correct when issued was actually unwarranted. . . . *Gold v. DCL, Inc.*, 399 F.Supp. 1123, 1127 (S.D.N.Y. 1973) . . . .

On the other hand, courts have refused to hold accountants liable for not disclosing ordinary business information discovered after the completion of a report, where the information did not indicate that the report was inaccurate as of the date it was issued. . . .

Although informative, these principles do not resolve this case. Here there is no allegation that Andersen's statements and reports were misleading *as of the time they were issued.* However, the information Andersen allegedly possessed without disclosing was not comprised of mere facts and figures casting some possible doubt on the continued usefulness of its earlier conclusions. Rather, Andersen is alleged to have known that DeLorean was using its statements and reports to commit a significant fraud.

The rule that an accountant is under no duty to disclose ordinary business information, unless it shows a previous report to have been misleading or incorrect when issued, is a sensible one. It would be asking too much to expect accountants to make difficult and time-consuming judgment calls about the nature of routine facts and figures turned up after a report has been completed. The situation is quite different, however, where the issue is disclosure of actual knowledge of fraud. Standing idly by while knowing one's good name is being used to perpetrate a fraud is inherently misleading. An investor might reasonably assume that an accounting firm would not permit inclusion of an audit report it prepared in a placement memo for an offering the firm knew to be fraudulent, and that such a firm would let it be known if it discovered to be fraudulent an offering with which it was associated. It is not unreasonable to expect an accountant . . . to disclose fraud in this type of circumstance, where the accountant's information is obviously superior to that of the investor, the cost to the accountant of revealing the information minimal, and the cost to investors of the information remaining secret potentially enormous. . . .

The complaint clearly alleges fraud on the part of DeLorean, and plaintiffs may be able to prove that fraud at trial. The complaint also alleges that Andersen performed non-auditing business services for DeLorean. Plaintiffs possibly could prove at trial that through these services Andersen was involved in the fraud itself. It is also likely that the evidence will show that Andersen had spoken previously with respect to the DRLP offering, through its audit reports and statements included in the placement memo, and that Andersen knew investors would rely to some extent on those reports and statements. Plaintiffs might also prove that Andersen failed to disclose DeLorean's fraud even though it had *actual knowledge* of that fraud, and that Andersen's access to information concerning the fraud was far greater than plaintiffs.' Proof of these circumstances would be sufficient to establish that Andersen had a duty to disclose. . . .

[Judgment reversed and remanded.]

Criminal Liability

In addition to civil liability to injured third parties, accountants may be subject to criminal liability under various federal statutes. For example, as discussed in Chapter 49, it is a crime willfully to violate any provision of the federal securities laws (including rules and regulations adopted under those laws), or to make material misstatements in registration statements or other documents filed with the SEC.[16] In addition, the Federal False Statements Statute[17] makes it a crime to knowingly

---

16. Securities Act of 1933 §24, 15 U.S.C. §77x; Securities Exchange Act of 1934 §32, 15 U.S.C. §78ff.
17. 18 U.S.C. §1001.

and willfully make false statements in matters within the jurisdiction of federal departments or agencies. Violations of the statute, which include false SEC filings, carry fines of up to $10,000, imprisonment of up to five years, or both. Collectively, these statutes have been used to impose liability on accountants for their role in preparing false or misleading proxy materials or financial statements, commonly that conceal misconduct by management insiders. Because the statutes require "knowing" or "willful" conduct and the accountant usually receives no financial gain other than his legitimate fee, the cases often turn on distinguishing simple errors of judgment from accounting errors made with sufficient criminal intent to support a conviction.[18] Note that because a number of people often are involved and the mails are used to distribute the misleading documents, federal conspiracy and mail fraud may also be charged.[19]

Accountant-Client Privilege

Generally, AICPA ethics standards prohibit an accountant from disclosing confidential information obtained from clients except (1) when the client consents, (2) when disclosure is necessary to comply with an enforceable subpoena or summons, (3) when necessary to avoid violation of GAAS and GAAP, or (4) when necessary to respond to an inquiry of the AICPA ethics division or trial board, or state CPA society or regulatory authority.[20] Although accountant-client communications are confidential and should not be disclosed to third parties unless the courts require it, they generally are not "privileged."

A **rule of privilege** enables a person to prevent certain information from being introduced into evidence in court. Examples include the Fifth Amendment privilege that protects a witness against self-incrimination, and privileges that protect communications between parties to confidential relationships such as physician and patient, priest and penitent, attorney and client, and husband and wife. Under privileged communication rules, for example, a physician, priest, attorney, or spouse may not be compelled to disclose information in court over the objection of the patient, penitent, client, or other spouse. Rules of privileged communication are designed to preserve the confidentiality of the relation and to protect relationships whose social importance justifies some sacrifice in availability of evidence necessary to administration of justice.[21]

Although no accountant-client privilege is recognized at common law, approximately one-third of the states have conferred such a privilege by statute. These statutes vary widely concerning the persons, accounting services, and legal proceedings covered by the privilege. No accountant-client privilege is recognized under federal law. For this reason, a state-created privilege is inapplicable in federal tax cases, federal criminal cases, and federal administrative proceedings.

Important policy reasons justify a refusal to recognize an accountant-client privilege. In *United States v. Arthur Young & Company* (1984),[22] the Supreme Court recently reaffirmed the general federal rule by holding that no confidential accountant-client privilege exists for the client for tax accrual work papers held by an accountant and sought by the IRS as part of a criminal investigation of the client's tax returns. In explaining its holding the Court noted the difference between the attorney-client relationship (in which a privilege is recognized) and the accountant-client relation:

> [T]he private attorney's role [is] as the client's confidential advisor and advocate, a loyal representative whose duty it is to present the client's case in the most favorable possible light. An independent certified public accountant performs a different role. By certifying the public reports that collectively depict a corporation's financial status, the independent auditor assumes a *public* responsibility transcending any employment relationship with the client. The independent public accountant performing this special function owes

---

18. See *United States v. Simon,* 425 F.2d 796 (2d Cir. 1969; *United States v. Natelli,* 527 F 2d 311 2d Cir 1975).

19. The federal conspiracy and mail fraud statutes are discussed in Chapter 3.

20. 2 AICPA Professional Standards, Code of Professional Ethics §301.01 (1973).

---

21. McCormick, *Law of Evidence* 171 (3d ed. 1984).

22. 104 S.Ct. 1495 (1984).

ultimate allegiance to the corporation's creditors and stockholders, as well as to investing public. This "public watchdog" function demands that the accountant maintain total independence from the client at all times and requires complete fidelity to the public trust. To insulate from disclosure a certified public accountant's interpretations of the client's financial statements would be to ignore the significance of the accountant's role as a disinterested analyst charged with public obligations.[23]

As noted by another writer:

> A . . . valid criticism of a privilege statute in the auditing area is that it is inconsistent with the auditor's *appearance* of independence. . . . For the client to be able to silence legally the CPA who is expressing a professional opinion concerning the financial statements on which the public relies creates an appearance which is incompatible with the very nature of an independent public servant. If a privilege statute were enacted in the auditing area, the client would be able to silence the independent public accountant in a court proceeding to the possible detriment of those segments of the public relying on these statements. It seems inconsistent to have an independent auditor (who is attempting to protect third party interests) prohibited from testifying as to certain information because the client will not give his consent, when at the same time a stockholder or third party believes a fraud or wrong has been perpetrated and needs such testimony to support the existence of the wrong.[24]

Tax Return Preparation Liability

The recent rapid growth in the number of persons preparing tax returns for compensation has led to a corresponding increase in the number of improperly prepared returns. To address this problem, the Tax Reform Act of 1976 included several provisions regulating the conduct of paid income tax preparers. The law defines an income tax return preparer as any person who prepares for compensation, or who employs one or more persons to prepare for compensation, all or a substantial portion of any income tax return or claim for refund.[25] The bases of liability under the law are understatement of a taxpayer's liability and failure to meet certain disclosure, ministerial, or recordkeeping requirements. The rules are enforced by a series of sanctions against tax preparers who violate the rules, including monetary penalties and injunctive relief.

An understatement of liability occurs if the net amount of taxes payable are understated *or* if the amount of a refund or credit is overstated. A tax preparer who negligently or intentionally disregards IRS rules and regulations resulting in an understatement of liability is subject to a $100 penalty. Although due diligence in applying the rules or regulations is a defense, the preparer bears the burden of proof regarding good faith and reasonable basis for his position. A tax preparer who willfully understates the taxpayer's liability is subject to a $500 penalty.[26]

The tax preparer may also be subject to various penalties for failure to meet a number of technical requirements. For example, a $25 penalty may be imposed upon a preparer for each failure to furnish the taxpayer with a completed copy of the tax return, sign the return, or furnish an identifying number on the return. A $50 penalty is imposed for each failure to keep copies or lists of returns prepared up to a maximum of $25,000 per return period. A $100 fine is assessed against a preparer for each failure to retain and make available a list of return preparers employed during the return period up to a maximum of $20,000 per return period. The tax return preparer has a defense to the foregoing penalties if the failure to comply is due to "reasonable cause," not willful neglect. Finally, a $500 penalty is imposed upon any preparer who negotiates or indorses a refund check issued to a taxpayer regarding a return or claim for refund prepared by the preparer.[27]

---

23. *Id.* at 1503.

24. Weygandt, The CPA and His Duty to Silence, *The Accounting Review,* January, 1970, at 73.

25. 26 U.S.C. §7701(a)(36).

26. 26 U.S.C. §6694.

27. 26 U.S.C. §6695.

In addition to liability under the Internal Revenue Code, tax return preparers may be held liable to their clients if they are negligent in preparing the return. Negligence takes many forms including erroneous advice, failure to file the return in a timely fashion, or computational errors. Damages are commonly measured by the tax losses including penalties incurred by the client.

SUMMARY

1. Through periodic audits, independent public accountants render an important service to their clients and third parties. The audit assists the client in discovering inefficiencies and irregularities in its business, and third parties such as shareholders, creditors, and potential investors in evaluating the financial health of the client before making a business decision. Recipients of inaccurate audit reports who suffer injury often seek compensation from the accountants. Accountants may be held liable to their client and, in some cases, third parties on various theories, based both upon the common law and statute.

2. Common law theories of recovery include breach of contract, negligence, and fraud. In contract, liability is limited to the client, and third parties may recover only if they qualify as third-party beneficiaries of the contract. In negligence actions, courts are split. Under the traditional *Ultramares* rule, liability extends only to persons in privity of contract with the accountant. Under the conflicting approach, liability extends to certain third parties who are injured by the accountant's negligence. Which third parties are protected varies somewhat among the states recognizing third-party liability. In contrast to negligence, fraud liability extends to relying third parties whom the accountant intends to deceive by his reports.

3. Statutory accountants' liability is based primarily upon the civil liability provisions of the federal securities laws. In addition, various federal statutes may impose criminal liability upon accountants for intentionally preparing false or misleading financial statements or other documents.

4. Although full disclosure between client and accountant is in the public interest, no accountant-client privilege is recognized at common law or under federal law. Some states, however, confer such a privilege by statute.

5. The Tax Reform Act of 1976 included several provisions regulating the conduct of paid income tax return preparers. Liability is based upon understatement of the taxpayer's liability and failure to meet certain disclosure requirements. In addition, an accountant who negligently prepares a tax return may be held liable to the client.

KEY TERMS

generally accepted auditing standards (GAAS)

generally accepted accounting principles (GAAP)

rule of privilege

QUESTIONS AND PROBLEMS

55-1 Compare the various approaches to accountants' liability to third parties for negligence discussed in the text. Review the policy reasons justifying each theory of liability. Which approach is preferable?

55-2 A public accountant was under contract to prepare a corporate tax return on or before March 15. The accountant failed to file on time. The corporation brought suit to recover for penalties paid due to the accountant's negligence in failing to timely file. Assume that no negligence is proven. Is the corporation without a remedy?

55-3 Jones, Inc. is negotiating for a loan from First Bank. The bank requests audited financial statements. Jones engages Doaks & Co. CPAs to perform the audit, telling Doaks that the statements will be used to negotiate a loan from First Bank. Doaks issues an unqualified opinion, negligently failing to discover material overstatements of assets. Jones delivers the statements to First Bank, which denies the loan. Without communicating with Doaks, Jones then uses the statements to obtain a loan from Second Bank. In addition, Jones shows the statements to his friend, Fred, who buys stock in Jones, Inc. in reliance on the statements. When the errors are discovered, Jones, Inc. declares bankruptcy and both Second Bank and Fred lose their entire investments. Would Doaks be liable to Second Bank under *Ultramares?* The *Restatement?* The rule of reasonable foreseeability? Assuming negligence recovery is unavailable, could Second Bank proceed on any other theory? Would any of your answers change if Jones had originally told Doaks that he needed the audited statement "to negotiate a bank loan"? Would Doaks be liable to Fred under *Ultramares?* The *Restatement?* The rule of reasonable foreseeability?

55-4   An auditor certified its client's balance sheet which listed accounts receivable at $2,000,000 without disclosing that $768,000 of the accounts were probably uncollectible. The auditor also failed to physically inspect the inventory, relying instead upon the client's balance sheet figure of $4,000,000. The auditor had been made aware that the financial statements were to be used for the purpose of obtaining credit. The client subsequently declared bankruptcy. On what theory or theories might a creditor who loaned money to the client on the basis of the financial statements recover from the auditor?

55-5   Assuming third-party negligence actions are allowed against accountants, should the client's negligence (for example, in permitting an embezzlement scheme to continue) contributing to the loss be a total or partial bar to recovery under principles of contributory or comparative negligence?

55-6   Ernst & Ernst performed periodic audits of First Securities Company, a small securities brokerage firm, and prepared annual reports for filing with the SEC under the 1934 Act. Nay, the president of the firm, fraudulently induced various customers to invest in "escrow" accounts that he represented would yield a high rate of return. In fact, no escrow accounts existed and Nay converted his customer's funds to personal use immediately upon receipt. The accounts were not reflected on First Securities' books. Ernst & Ernst did not uncover the fraud because it failed to use appropriate auditing procedures to discover certain internal practices that prevented an effective audit. One such practice was Nay's rule that only he could open mail addressed to him at First Securities, even if it arrived in his absence. If the audit had been properly performed, the "mail rule" would have been discovered and reported to the SEC as an irregular procedure, leading to an investigation that would have revealed the fraud. The fraud was finally discovered only after Nay committed suicide leaving a note describing the escrow accounts as "spurious" and First Securities as bankrupt.

(a) Customers who lost money subsequently sued Ernst & Ernst alleging that it had "aided and abetted" Nay's violation of Rule 10b–5. Has Ernst & Ernst violated Rule 10b–5? Explain.

(b) Could Ernst & Ernst be held liable under any other civil liability provision of the securities laws?

(c) Could Ernst & Ernst be held liable to the customers for negligence under any of the theories of third-party liability discussed in the text?

55-7   Summarize the policy reasons for and against recognition of an accountant-client privilege. Should such a privilege be recognized?

55-8   In *United States v. Arthur Young & Company,* the IRS sought Arthur Young's tax accrual workpapers for use in a criminal tax investigation. These workpapers pinpoint "soft spots" on the corporation's tax returns, highlighting those areas in which the taxpayer has taken a position that may at some later date require payment of additional taxes. The court of appeals recognized a privilege as necessary to promote full disclosure to public accountants and insure the integrity of the securities markets. The court of appeals feared that were the IRS to have access to tax accrual workpapers, a corporation might be tempted to withhold from its auditor certain information relevant and material to a proper evaluation of its financial statements. The Supreme Court rejected this argument. Why?

Major Topics

- an introduction to the law of insurance, including the regulation of insurance and the types and interpretation of insurance contracts
- the concept of insurable interest and the principle of indemnity
- the persons and interests protected by insurance and the nature of the risk transferred to the insurer
- the obligations of an insured following a loss and the measure of recovery for various types of insurance
- defenses available to an insurer and the rights an insurer acquires through subrogation

Insurance is a contractual arrangement used to transfer and distribute risk.[1] Through an insurance contract, an insurer—an entity engaged primarily in the business of insurance—promises to pay another, the insured, a sum of money or provide other value upon the occurrence of some harmful event. The insurer distributes the risk among a substantial number of persons who pay premiums to the insurer based upon the total estimated losses to be incurred by members of the insured class. In insur-

ance, therefore, the insured in effect exchanges a fixed, certain loss—the cost of the premium—to avoid a catastrophic loss caused by a risk insured against. Risk sharing among the insured class, under which all members contribute to pay the losses of a few, is a fundamental characteristic of insurance.[2]

Although insurance law is basically a branch of contract law, a number of characteristics distinguish it from ordinary contract law. For example, although insurance is a basic tool of business and estate planning, insurance contracts are not individually negotiated. Rather, they are complex adhesion contracts, which often are neither read nor understood by insureds. Accordingly, both courts and legislatures have actively policed insurance contracts and companies to protect the reasonable expectations of the insured. This policing includes extensive government regulation of the insurance industry, strict construction of contract terms against the insurance company, and in some cases, statutorily mandated contracts. Insurance contracts also present a "moral risk." The presence of insurance often has motivated schemes to defraud

---

1. Keeton, *Insurance Law* 2 (1971).

---

2. In some cases, the insurer will spread the loss even further through reinsurance. Under this arrangement, another insurance company contracts with the original insurer to reimburse it for liability under its own policies. Thus, in reinsurance, the original insurer becomes an insured (or reinsured) and another company becomes an insurer (or reinsurer).

and even to murder. In addition, absent "insurable interest" insurance contracts can be used as a gambling device. Thus, a basic role of the law of insurance is to police abuses by both insurers and insureds while preserving the fundamental business and personal protection afforded by insurance.

Introduction to Insurance

Regulation of Insurance

Insurance companies engage in the sale and drafting of insurance contracts (policies), collecting information necessary to compute premiums; investigating, paying, and defending claims for insured losses; and managing vast amounts of cash collected from policyholders. Regulating insurance company activities has traditionally been a state, rather than federal, activity.

In 1944, however, the Supreme Court held that the business of insurance involved interstate commerce and was therefore subject to federal regulation under the Commerce Clause of the Constitution.[3] Lobbying by the insurance industry, however, led to passage in 1945 of the McCarran-Ferguson Act.[4] It provided for continued regulation of insurance by the states, but stated that federal antitrust law would be applicable to the business of insurance if not regulated by state law. To prevent federal regulation, the National Association of Insurance Commissioners (NAIC) and an "All-Industry Committee" promptly drafted comprehensive model legislation, which has been widely adopted by the states. State statutes, administered through a state "commissioner of insurance," commonly require licensing of insurance companies (local and out-of-state), insurance agents, and brokers. Statutes also regulate insurance rates to prevent inadequate, excessive, or discriminatory rates, prevent unfair trade practices, monitor the financial condition of insurers, provide for service of process upon out-of-state insurers, and monitor the terms of insurance policies.

---

3. *United States v. South-Eastern Underwriters Ass'n,* 64 S. Ct. 1162 (1944). Federal regulation under the Commerce Clause is discussed in Chapter 4.

4. 15 U.S.C. §§1011–1015.

Types of Insurance

Insurance contracts commonly are classified according to the nature of the risk covered as (1) life insurance, (2) fire and marine insurance, and (3) casualty insurance. Although a number of insurers write all lines of insurance, many specialize in one or more types of coverage.

Life Insurance. **Life insurance** is a contract to make designated payments upon the death of the person whose life is insured. In a life insurance policy the insurer contracts with the "owner" of the policy to pay a specified amount—the proceeds—to a beneficiary upon the death of a named person—the *cestui que vie.* The owner of the policy pays the premiums, may in certain cases assign the policy or borrow against it, may elect among various options concerning distribution of proceeds, and has the power to name and in most cases change the beneficiary. The three roles (owner, cestui que vie, beneficiary) may be fulfilled by separate individuals or by one person. For example, a person may purchase a life insurance policy on her own life naming her estate as beneficiary.

Life insurance is commonly designated wholelife, endowment, or term. A whole-life policy provides coverage for the entire life of the insured. Premiums generally are paid for life or until the insured reaches a prescribed advanced age. The policy matures for payment only upon the death of the person insured. An endowment policy provides for payment of the proceeds upon the death of the insured within the endowment period (for example, twenty years) or at the end of that period if the insured survives. A term policy pays a specified amount only if death occurs within a term or period specified in the policy.

Both whole-life and endowment policies involve an element of savings or investment because it is certain that if the policy is kept in force, proceeds ultimately will be paid. Both types accumulate a cash surrender value after the policy has been in force for a given period such as two or three years. Generally, the insured may borrow from the insurance company against the cash surrender value, or may use the policy as collateral on a loan from another creditor. If the policy is terminated before the death of the person whose life is insured, the cash surrender value may be returned to the insured, or used to fund some other option offered by the insurance company (for example, to purchase a lesser face amount of fully paid-up insurance).

In contrast to whole-life and endowment, payment under a term policy occurs only if the insured dies within the stated period. A term policy accumulates no cash surrender value and involves no certainty of payment. Accordingly, a term policy does not incorporate elements of saving or investment characteristic of the other forms.[5]

Fire and Marine Insurance. **Fire insurance** covers losses to specifically listed property (such as a building or its contents) caused by fire or lightning. Fire insurance does not cover fires intentionally set by the insured, and coverage usually is limited to losses caused by a hostile fire (one not occurring or contained in a place intended for a fire, such as a stove or fireplace). Fire insurance policies also commonly cover damage from wind, rain, collision, explosion, water damage, and earthquake.

Marine insurance developed in the 1600s to protect ships and their cargos from "perils of the sea." Modern marine policies are substantially similar to the one adopted in 1779 by the Society of Underwriters operating from Lloyd's Coffee House in London. Because marine policies did not cover ships or cargo transported on inland waterways, **inland marine insurance** was developed. Inland marine insurance has been extended in modern times to cover transportation risks generally; bridges, tunnels, and other devices of transportation and communication; and goods which may be affected by movement. A common type of inland marine policy is a personal property "floater" that protects, for example, the inventory or equipment of a business.

Casualty Insurance. **Casualty insurance** is designed to cover a variety of risks including legal liability, burglary and theft, accident and illness, collision, workers' compensation, and property damage. Collectively, fire and casualty insurance provide the basic coverage for real property and personal property such as boats, airplanes, and motor vehicles.

The Insurance Contract

Formation and Terms. Most insurance contracts are contained on standardized written forms drafted by the insurer. Typically, the insured makes the offer through an application to the company, which can accept the offer by issuing, or in some cases, delivering the policy to the insured. During the interim between application and issuance, the insurer may provide temporary coverage through "binding receipts" or "conditional binding receipts" in life insurance, or "binders" in other types of insurance. Although temporary coverage in life insurance usually requires a premium payment, property insurance binders often are issued in advance of any premium payment.

In exchange for the premium, the insurer agrees to pay specified benefits upon occurrence of stated contingencies. Pecuniary liability limits are included, which in the case of liability insurance may be stated on a per person or per accident basis. The duration of the coverage is explicitly stated in the policy and may indicate that coverage begins on a specified date (for example, "April 15, 1985, 12:01 A.M. standard time at the address of the named insured"). Coverage in a life insurance policy commonly commences upon delivery of the policy to the insured in good health and payment of the first premium. Constructive delivery of the policy (for example, to the insurance agent) may be sufficient for this purpose.

Although insurance contracts commonly cover a single insured, many standard forms of insurance such as life, health, accident, and hospitalization are marketed under group insurance plans. In group insurance, a master policy is issued to the person, such as an employer, who negotiates the contract with the insurer. Certificates of participation are then furnished to group members covered by the

---

5. In contrast to ordinary life insurance, which protects against hardship caused by the insured's premature death, an annuity contract protects against economic problems of the insured's long life. Under an annuity, payments begin on a specified date and continue for the life of the insured.

plan. The premium may be paid entirely by the employer (a noncontributory plan) or in whole or in part by the employees (a contributory plan). Premium costs in a group policy commonly are lower because of the insurer's reduced administrative expense.

Interpretation of Insurance Contracts. Courts often protect an insured by construing language of insurance contracts in favor of coverage. Perhaps because insurance is a fundamental tool of personal, business, and estate planning, courts believe that the public interest is best served by compensating insureds, even if the literal language of the contract could be interpreted to deny coverage. Another factor influencing judicial treatment of insurance contracts is the nature of the contract itself. An insurance contract is the classic adhesion contract—a standardized form contract, loaded with fine print, given to the insured on a take-it-or-leave-it basis. Accordingly, a basic issue in many insurance cases is whether the court should refuse to enforce a provision in the standardized form under one of the various legal theories designed to protect the adhering party. In the following case, the court discusses whether the theories of unconscionability and "reasonable expectations" (discussed in Chapter 10), and breach of warranty (discussed in Chapter 19) should operate to prevent enforcement of a term in an insurance contract.

C & J Fertilizer, Inc. v. Allied Mutual Insurance Company
227 N.W.2d 169 (Iowa 1975)

Plaintiff, C & J Fertilizer, Inc. operated a fertilizer plant in Olds, Iowa. Plaintiff was insured under two policies issued by defendant, Allied Mutual Insurance Company, titled "BROAD FORM STOREKEEPERS POLICY" and "MERCANTILE BURGLARY AND ROBBERY POLICY." The policies were issued after defendant's agent, at plaintiff's request, inspected the building and explained the coverage. The agent pointed out that the policy covered only third-party burglary and not an "inside job" and that some hard visible evidence of burglary was

required to establish a third party's responsibility for the crime. The plaintiff's president, a thirty-seven-year-old farmer with a high school education, examined the coverages and amounts but did not read the fine print defining "burglary" on page three of the policies. Each policy defined "burglary" as meaning,

> . . . the felonious abstraction of insured property (1) from within the premises by a person making felonious entry therein by actual force and violence, of which force and violence there are visible marks made by tools, explosives, electricity or chemicals upon, or physical damage to, the exterior of the premises at the place of such entry. . . .

On Saturday, April 18, 1970, plaintiff's employees locked all exterior doors upon leaving at the end of the business day. On Monday, April 20, 1970, when the employees reported for work, the outside doors were locked, but the front office door was unlocked. Truck tire tread marks were visible in the mud in the driveway leading to and from a plexiglas door entrance to the warehouse. No marks apparently made by tools, explosives, electricity, or chemicals were visible on the exterior of the building and there was no physical damage to the exterior.

Chemicals and office and shop equipment worth approximately $10,000 had been taken from the warehouse over the weekend. The door to the interior room where the chemicals were stored was physically damaged and carried visible marks made by tools. The police officer investigating the crime demonstrated that the exterior plexiglas door could be opened without leaving visible marks by leaning on the door while turning the locked handle.

Plaintiff sued defendant for the burglary loss under the two policies. The trial court denied recovery, holding that under the definition of burglary in the policy there was no physical damage to the exterior of the building to indicate felonious entry by force and violence. Plaintiff appealed to the Iowa Supreme Court.

The Supreme Court initially noted that insurance policies are adhesion contracts tendered to the insured on a take-it-or-leave-it basis. The court also stated that courts and commentators generally recognize that an insured will not read a detailed, cross-referenced, standardized, mass-produced insurance form, and will not understand it if he does. Against this background the court considered the plaintiff's theories of recovery based upon "reasonable expectations," implied warranty, and unconscionability.

Reynoldson, Justice

. . . Reasonable Expectations

This court adopted the doctrine of reasonable expectations in *Rodman v. State Farm Mutual Ins. Co.*, 208 N.W.2d 903, 905–908 (Iowa 1973). The *Rodman* court approved the following articulation of that concept:

> "The objectively reasonable expectations of applicants and intended beneficiaries regarding the terms of insurance contracts will be honored even though painstaking study of the policy provisions would have negated those expectations."—208 N.W.2d at 906. . . .

[It cannot] be asserted the above doctrine does not apply here because plaintiff knew the policy contained the provision now complained of and cannot be heard to say it reasonably expected what it knew was not there. A search of the record discloses no such knowledge.

The evidence does show . . . a "dicker" for burglary insurance coverage on chemicals and equipment. The negotiation was for what was actually expressed in the policies' "Insuring Agreements": the insurer's promise "To pay for loss by burglary or by robbery of a watchman, while the premises are not open for business, of merchandise, furniture, fixtures and equipment within the premises. . . ."

In addition, the conversation included statements from which the plaintiff should have understood defendant's obligation to pay would not arise where the burglary was an "inside job." Thus the following exclusion should have been reasonably anticipated:

> "Exclusions
> "This policy does not apply: . . .
> "(b) to loss due to any fraudulent, dishonest or criminal act by any Insured, a partner therein, or an

officer, employee, director, trustee or authorized representative thereof. . . ."

But there was nothing relating to the negotiations with defendant's agent which would have led plaintiff to reasonably anticipate defendant would bury within the definition of "burglary" another exclusion denying coverage when, no matter how extensive the proof of a third-party burglary, no marks were left on the exterior of the premises. This escape clause, here triggered by the burglar's talent . . . was never read to or by plaintiff's personnel, nor was the substance explained by defendant's agent.

Moreover, the burglary "definition" which crept into this policy comports neither with the concept a layman might have of that crime nor with a legal interpretation. . . .

The most plaintiff might have reasonably anticipated was a policy requirement of visual evidence (abundant here) indicating the burglary was an "outside" not an "inside" job. The exclusion in issue, masking as a definition, makes insurer's obligation to pay turn on the skill of the burglar, not on the event the parties bargained for: a bona-fide third-party burglary resulting in loss of plaintiff's chemicals and equipment. . . .

Appropriately applied to this case, the [reasonable expectations] doctrine demands reversal and judgment for plaintiff.

Implied Warranty

Plaintiff should also prevail because defendant breached an implied warranty that the policy later delivered would be reasonably fit for its intended purpose: to set out in writing the obligations of the parties (1) without altering or impairing the fair meaning of the protection bargained for when read alone, and (2) in terms that are neither in the particular nor in the net manifestly unreasonable and unfair. . . .

We would be derelict in our duty to administer justice if we were not to judicially know that modern insurance companies have turned to mass advertising to sell "protection." A person who has been incessantly assured a given company's policies will afford him complete protection is unlikely to be wary enough to search his policy to find a provision nullifying his burglary protection if the burglar breaks open an inside, but not an outside, door.

There is little justification in depriving purchasers of merchandized "protection" of those remedies long available to purchasers of goods [under the UCC warranty of fitness for a particular purpose]. . . .

Effective imposition of an implied warranty would encourage insurers to make known to insurance buyers those provisions which would limit the implied warranty inherent in the situation. These exclusions would then become part of the initial bargaining. Such provisions, mandated by the Uniform Commercial Code to be "conspicuous" in the sale of goods . . . should be conspicuously presented by the insurer in the sale of protection. This would be no more difficult than the manner in which they advertise their product's desirable features. . . . From a public policy viewpoint, such a requirement (in order to enforce what is essentially an exclusion) might promote meaningful competition among insurers in eliminating technical policy provisions which drain away bargained-for protection. The ultimate benefit would be a chance for knowledgeable selection by insurance purchasers among various coverages. . . .

In *Mease v. Fox*, 200 N.W.2d 791 (Iowa 1972) we joined a scant handful of courts pioneering the concept that implied warranty relief was not the captive of chattel sales law, but was available to resolve long-standing inequities in the law of dwelling leases. It is now time to provide buyers of protection the same safeguards provided for buyers of personalty and lessees of dwellings.

The policy provided by defendant in this instance breached the implied warranty of fitness for its intended purpose. It altered and impaired the fair meaning of the bargain these parties made for plaintiff's insurance protection. . . .

Unconscionability

Plaintiff is also entitled to a reversal because the liability-avoiding provision in the definition of the burglary is, in the circumstances of this case, unconscionable. . . .

The policies in question contain a classic example of that proverbial fine print (six point type as compared with the twenty-four point type appearing on the face of the policies: "BROAD FORM STOREKEEPERS POLICY" and "MERCANTILE BURGLARY AND ROBBERY POLICY") which "becomes visible only after the event." Such print is additionally suspect when, instead of appearing logically in the "exclusions" of the policies, it poses as a part of an esoteric definition of burglary. . . .

Commentators suggest a court considering a claim of unconscionability should examine the factors of assent, unfair surprise, notice, disparity of bargaining power and substantive unfairness. . . .

[P]laintiff's evidence demonstrated the definitional provision was unconscionable. Defendant never offered any evidence . . . which might support a conclusion the provision in issue, considered in its commercial setting, was either a reasonable limitation on the protection it offered or should have been reasonably anticipated by plaintiff. . . .

[Judgment reversed.]

Insurable Interest

The Principle of Indemnity

Contracts of insurance, other than life insurance, generally are characterized as indemnity contracts. An **indemnity contract** is one in which the promisor (indemnitor) agrees to save the promisee (indemnitee) harmless from ("indemnify" or "reimburse" him for) the legal consequences of the promisee's conduct or that of some other person. Assume General Casualty, an insurance company, agrees to insure Mary against any liability she may incur as a result of harm to others caused by Mary's operation of her automobile—a contract of indemnity. Mary, while driving negligently, injures Tom, who sustains $10,000 damages. Under the contract, General Casualty is required to reimburse or indemnify Mary for the $10,000 obligation she owes to Tom. In addition, the contract requires General Casualty to indemnify Mary for any loss caused by the collision of her automobile with another object. Mary's automobile, worth $5,000, is destroyed in the accident. General Casualty's $5,000 payment to

Mary protects her from the liability for the collision loss.[6]

Insurance therefore transfers the loss from the insured to the insurer. The indemnity concept implies that the benefit conferred by the insurer may not exceed the loss suffered by the insured. That is, an insured should not be able to realize a net profit through insurance. The law recognizes two reasons for this approach. First, the possibility of profit through insurance is an inducement to use insurance as a wagering or gambling device. Second, the prospect of profit may provide inducement for intentionally destroying the insured life or property. The legal principles designed to prevent net profit from occurrence of insured events are embodied in the concept of **insurable interest**. That is, to prevent use of the policy as a wagering contract and to minimize any inducement to cause the event insured against, the person who recovers under the policy must have an insurable interest in the property or person insured. Although the law of insurable interest is primarily common law or judgement in nature, many states have statutes on the subject.

Though the purposes of the doctrine are the same for both forms of insurance, property and life insurance are governed by substantially different insurable interest rules. Differences exist primarily because the indemnity principle is much less pervasive in life insurance than in property insurance. These differing approaches to insurable interest are outlined below.

Insurable Interest in Property

Because property insurance is based on indemnity, a person possesses an insurable interest in property to the extent he or she may be subjected to economic injury if the property is lost, destroyed, or damaged. Generally, in property insurance, insurable interest need exist only at the time of the loss, not necessarily when the policy is acquired.

Persons Having Insurable Interest. Persons holding a legal interest in the property have an insurable interest to the extent of the value of the interest. Such persons include the outright owner of property, a life tenant, a remainderman or holder of other future interest in property, and a lessor, lessee, or sublessee of the same property. Persons having legal title in a representative capacity, such as trustees and executors, also have an insurable interest in property under their control. Proceeds of any insurance would then be held for the benefit of the person or persons (for example, beneficiaries of a trust) for whom the representative acts. In addition, a shareholder has an insurable interest in corporate property to the extent of the shareholder's proportionate share of corporate assets on liquidation.

Persons holding equitable interests also qualify. For example, the beneficiary of a trust has an insurable interest in the trust property. Even in the absence of a legal or equitable interest, a mere possessor of property has an insurable interest to the extent of the property's value. This category includes, for example, a bailee who may be liable to the bailor if the property is destroyed.

Although an unsecured creditor has no insurable interest in the debtor's property, a secured creditor does have an insurable interest in property subject to the security interest. The security interest may arise by contract (such as a mortgage of real property or secured transaction of personal property) or otherwise (for example, a mechanic's or artisan's lien). The creditor's insurable interest is limited to the amount of the secured obligation, not necessarily the full value of the property.

Buyers and Sellers of Property. As noted in Chapter 17, in a contract for the sale of goods, once risk of loss passes to the buyer, the buyer is obligated to pay the purchase price of the goods even if they have been lost or destroyed. To protect against this risk, the UCC gives the buyer an insurable interest in the goods at the time they are iden-

---

6. An indemnity contract often is confused with a suretyship contract, discussed in Chapter 33. Though both types of contracts protect the promisee against loss, in suretyship, the promisee is a *creditor* who has or is about to extend credit to a third party, the principal. The surety's (promisor's) promise is made to the creditor to protect him against the principal's failure to perform. In contrast, in indemnity, the promisee is a *debtor or obligor*, present or prospective. Thus, a basic indemnity contract involves two parties (indemnitor, indemnitee), whereas suretyship always involves three parties (surety, principal, creditor).

tified to the contract, which occurs before risk of loss passes.

The UCC risk of loss rules generally place the loss in contracts involving *goods* upon the party who controls possession of the goods. In contrast, in contracts for the sale of *land,* some courts, following the English "equitable conversion" doctrine,[7] hold that risk of loss passes to the buyer upon creation of an enforceable contract. Under this approach, based on the theory that the buyer under an enforceable contract is the equitable owner of the property, risk of loss passes before the buyer has either possession or title. Although the buyer as equitable owner has an insurable interest upon signing the contract, he or she is likely to be unaware that the casualty risk has passed. For this reason, a number of states have enacted the **Uniform Vendor and Purchaser Risk Act,**[8] which basically provides that risk of loss does not pass until the buyer acquires either legal title (for example, receives delivery of the deed) or possession of the property. A number of states have adopted a similar approach by judicial decision. To avoid disputes, the buyer and seller should always explicitly address the risk of loss issue in the contract, and alter or acquire insurance coverage to comply with their agreement.

Insurable Interest in Life

Insurable interest in life insurance arises in two contexts: obtaining insurance on one's own life and obtaining insurance on the life of another. A person always has an unlimited insurable interest in his or her own life. Inherent safeguards against the dangers of gambling or murder generally eliminate the need for an inquiry into insurable interest. A person who takes out a policy on his own life and pays the premiums may designate his estate or another person as beneficiary. The beneficiary need not have an insurable interest in the insured's life.

In contrast, to have an insurable interest in *another's* life, a person must have some pecuniary interest in the continued vitality of the cestui que vie. In addition, the consent of the person whose death triggers payment generally is required. In certain cases, pecuniary interest or benefit is presumed because the individuals are closely related by blood or law. For example, spouses and parents and minor children automatically have insurable interests in each other's lives. In addition, most courts considering the issue have held that a person has an insurable interest in the life of a brother or sister. Other relationships more remote, however, such as aunts, uncles, and cousins, commonly require some additional proof of economic interest (for example, if the insured supports the beneficiary). If insurable interest in life is based upon a familial relationship, no limit usually is placed upon the dollar amount of insurance that may be obtained.

Insurable interest in another's life also may be based upon a business relationship. For example, a creditor has an insurable interest in his or her debtor's life. Partners have insurable interests in each other's lives. Indeed, life insurance policies are frequently used to fund a buy-out arrangement upon a partner's death. If insurable interest in life is based upon a commercial relationship, the insurance obtained may not greatly exceed the value of that interest.

In cases involving insurable interest in life, courts often have been required to determine (1) who may challenge the beneficiary's lack of insurable interest, and (2) when insurable interest must exist. The following case explains the general principles governing these two issues.

Secor v. Pioneer Foundry Company

173 N.W.2d 780 (Mich. App. 1970)

Defendant, Pioneer Foundry Company (Pioneer), employed Jack Secor from 1954 to 1963. In 1960, Pioneer obtained a $50,000 "keyman" insurance policy on Secor's life. Pioneer was the applicant, owner, and beneficiary of the policy, and paid the premiums. After the employment relationship terminated in July, 1963, Pioneer paid the March 1964

---

7. *Paine v. Meller,* 6 Ves. Jun. 349, 31 Eng. Rep. 1088 (Ch. 1801).

8. The Uniform Vendor and Purchaser Risk Act has been adopted in California, Hawaii, Illinois, Michigan, Nevada, New York, North Carolina, Oklahoma, Oregon, South Dakota, and Wisconsin.

annual premium, raising the total premiums paid to over $28,000. Secor died in April, 1964, and the insurer paid the proceeds of the policy to Pioneer.

Plaintiff, Secor's widow and administratrix of his estate, sued Pioneer to recover the proceeds, arguing that after the termination of Secor's employment Pioneer Foundry lost whatever insurable interest it had in Secor's life. The trial court ruled that the plaintiff had no cause of action against Pioneer and she appealed to the appellate court.

Levin, Judge

. . . A preliminary issue—whether the plaintiff has standing to complain—is dispositive of plaintiff's contention that Pioneer Foundry no longer had an insurable interest after Secor left its employ. In *Hicks v. Cary* [52 N.W.2d 351 (Mich. 1952)], on facts similar to those before us, the Michigan Supreme Court declared that the insurer alone may assert that the beneficiary of a life policy does not have an insurable interest. . . . The rule that only the insurer can raise the question of lack of insurable interest appears to be well supported in other jurisdictions.

In the present case, the insurer . . . paid the proceeds of the policy to Pioneer Foundry in May, 1964, without asserting this possible defense.

The plaintiff argues that, apart from whether she has standing to raise the insurable interest defense, the underlying premise of the insurable interest requirement—the public policy against speculation on the life of another—is so pervasive that Pioneer Foundry could not lawfully retain insurance on Secor's life after the termination of his employment. . . .

The purchaser of ordinary life insurance, as distinguished from casualty or property insurance, buys not only indemnification in a specific amount against a particular peril or potential loss but also makes an investment. To terminate the rights of the owner or beneficiary of ordinary life insurance because the relationship to the life insured has changed, perhaps after many years of making premium payments, at a time when death is bound to be more imminent than it was at the time the policy was issued, would not only adversely affect this investment quality of life insurance but would also confer an unanticipated and unwarranted windfall on the insurer.

In recognition of these considerations the almost universal rule of law in this country is that if the insurable interest requirement is satisfied at the time the policy is issued, the proceeds of the policy must be paid upon the death of the life insured without regard to whether the beneficiary has an insurable interest at the time of death. It has, accordingly, been held that an employer who is the beneficiary of a policy insuring the life of one of his employees may collect proceeds which become payable under the policy even though the employee's death occurs after the termination of his employment.

The ordinary life insurance policy issued to the defendant corporation is referred to in the insurance industry as "keyman" life insurance. The plaintiff emphasizes that the typical life insurance policy is purchased to provide for loss by family members who may be expected to suffer a personal as well as a financial loss upon the death of the life insured. From this she argues that keyman life insurance should not be governed by the same rules as apply to life insurance generally. The proffered distinction is not, in our opinion, meaningful. Life insurance is not meant to assuage grief; its primary function is monetary. It serves fundamentally the same purpose whether the beneficiary is a widow or a business; it seeks to replace with a sum of money the earning capacity of the life insured.

The plaintiff's analogy to the public policy against a murderer collecting insurance on the life of the victim is inapposite. Pioneer Foundry's act of paying the yearly premium after Secor left its employ is not (contrary to plaintiff's argument) at all analogous to murdering him. Given the general rule that the beneficiary of a life policy may collect its proceeds although the insurable interest which existed when the policy was issued subsequently terminates, it would make no sense to hold that the act of paying the premium (necessary to the full preservation of the owner's rights under the policy) somehow or other brings about a termination of the owner-beneficiary's rights.

We also decline to limit Pioneer Foundry's recovery to the amount of its investment in the policy and its financial loss (probably nil) upon Secor's death. Pioneer Foundry's investment in the policy was large both quantitatively and relatively. It chose to make the premium payment due eight months after Secor's employment terminated to preserve recovery of its prior expenditures. It did this in its own interest; it has not been suggested that it was acting for, or because of any obligation it had assumed to, Secor or his family. . . .

[Judgment affirmed.]

Persons and Interests Protected; Risk Transferred

Like other contracts, an insurance contract outlines the legally enforceable rights and obligations of the parties. Important provisions in insurance policies include those identifying the person or persons who are entitled to benefits under the policy, the interests of those persons that are protected, and the extent and nature of the risk transferred to the insurer.

Property and Casualty Insurance

Persons Insured. In property and casualty insurance, the "insured" generally refers to the person or persons whose loss triggers the insurer's liability to pay benefits. The insured is designated in the policy by inserting his or her name in a blank following the words "does insure" or similar language. Additional insureds may subsequently be added by indorsements to the policy.

The interest of the insured or insureds in the property may or may not be designated. For example, two insureds might be designated "owner" and "mortgagee" or "life tenant" and "remainderman." Insurable interest principles define and limit an insured's potential recovery under the policy. Thus, if more than one insured is listed, proceeds are commonly payable "as their interests may appear," meaning that proceeds are paid "in proportion to the damage to their respective interests in the insured property."[9]

In addition to the insureds stated in the policy and added by indorsement, insureds may be added by explicit policy provisions. Important provisions of this type include the "omnibus" and "standard mortgage" clause. An **omnibus clause** defines additional insureds as a class bearing a specified relationship to the named insured. For example, an automobile policy often contains an omnibus clause that extends policy protection to the insured, members of the insured's household, and persons driving the car with permission of the named insured. These clauses, designed to protect both the named insured and potential accident victims, originally applied only to automobile legal liability coverage. They now commonly apply to collision and medical payment coverage as well.

A **standard mortgage clause,** generally appearing in fire insurance or homeowner's policies, is designed to protect the lender holding a mortgage on the insured property. Under the clause, the mortgagee becomes an insured and loss is payable to the mortgagor and mortgagee "as interests appear." The clause further provides that the mortgagee may collect for losses under the policy even if the mortgagor would be denied recovery. For example, the mortgagor might be denied recovery for breaching a condition in the policy, such as by storing hazardous materials on the property. Or, the mortgagor may have previously sold the property, thereby extinguishing insurable interest. To recover, the mortgagee must generally pay any premium left unpaid by the mortgagor. The standard mortgage clause places the mortgagee in a better position than a mere assignee of the policy proceeds from the mortgagor. Under ordinary contract principles, the lender as mere assignee would take subject to any defenses the insurer has against the mortgagor.

Effect of Assignment. When an insured loss occurs, the proceeds of the insurance ordinarily are paid to the insured—for example, a homeowner covered by a fire insurance policy whose home is destroyed by fire. An insured may, however, designate a third party (such as a creditor) to receive the proceeds of the policy. Such an assignment may be made in the policy or in a separate contract, and may occur before or after the loss. The right transferred, merely a claim for money due from the insurance company, is freely assignable without the insurer's consent.

In an assignment of proceeds, the designation of insureds in the policy is not affected and the property insured is not transferred. In contrast, the in-

---

9. Keeton, *Insurance Law* 179 (1971).

sured may sell the insured property and attempt to transfer his entire interest in the policy to the buyer, who then becomes a new substituted insured. In this case, the insurer's consent is required, because an insurer bases its decision to insure in part upon the character of the individual insured. That is, a property insurance contract does not run with the land; rather, a novation must be effected among the parties substituting the buyer for the seller with the insurer's consent.

Life Insurance

Designation of Beneficiary. In life insurance, the owner of the policy (who usually also is the cestui que vie) commonly designates a beneficiary to receive the proceeds, and retains the other rights of ownership. The beneficiary of a life insurance policy may be named irrevocably or revocably. In an irrevocable designation the owner has no power to change the beneficiary. More commonly, the policy expressly permits the owner to change the beneficiary at any time prior to the death of the cestui que vie. Policies also commonly provide for contingent or secondary beneficiaries who receive the proceeds if the primary beneficiary predeceases the cestui que vie. The policy owner's estate usually is designated as final contingent beneficiary.

Effect of Assignment. The owner of a life insurance policy may assign the entire policy, including the various incidents of ownership, such as the right to borrow money from the insurer secured by the policy and the duty to pay premiums. The person whose death triggers payment of the proceeds remains the same after the assignment. A life insurance policy generally may be freely assigned without the insurer's consent, even to a person without an insurable interest in the cestui que vie. If the beneficiary has been irrevocably designated, however, the beneficiary's right to proceeds cannot be impaired without his or her consent.

If the beneficiary designation is revocable, the assignee will simply change the beneficiary after the assignment. Occasionally, however, the assignee will neglect to comply with the formalities outlined in the policy either for assignment or change of beneficiary, leading to a dispute over the proceeds between the assignee and beneficiary. To promote assignability of life insurance contracts, courts generally have favored the assignee in these cases.

An assignment of a life insurance policy may be made to a creditor other than the insurer to provide collateral on a loan from the creditor to the owner-assignor. On the owner's death, if the policy proceeds exceed the amount of the debt, other persons may assert a claim to the excess. Although the intent of the parties is controlling, most decisions have permitted the creditor to retain no more than the amount of the debt plus interest and charges, reasoning that the assignment or designation was intended merely as security for payment of the debt and no more.

Risk Transferred

The scope of an insurer's obligation regarding both the risk covered and the duration of coverage is determined by the express language of the insurance contract. In defining the risk insured against, policies commonly are designated either all-risk or specified-risk policies. An all-risk policy covers damage to the insured subject matter from any cause except those explicitly stated in the policy through exception, exclusion, or condition. A specified-risk policy, in contrast, covers injury caused only by the risks listed.

Marine and inland marine insurance are typical all-risk policies, whereas fire and automobile insurance are specified-risk contracts. Life insurance also may be viewed as an all-risk policy because it pays upon the death of the insured from any cause, except those specifically excepted (for example, suicide during the first year of the policy). Characterizing a policy as all-risk or specified-risk has important legal consequences. For example, in a specified-risk policy the insured has the burden of proving that the loss resulted from one of the specified causes. In an all-risk policy, once existence of the loss is proven, the insurer must prove that the loss fell within some exception or exclusion to the policy coverage to escape liability. This allocation of the burden of proof substantially aids the insured if the precise cause of the loss cannot be determined.

In addition, as the following case indicates, an all-risk policy reduces gaps in coverage and therefore the likelihood that a court will find a given loss outside the protection of the policy.

Northwest Airlines, Inc. v. Globe Indemnity Company
225 N.W.2d 831 (Minn. 1975)

In 1965, plaintiff Northwest Airlines, Inc. and defendant Globe Indemnity Company entered into an insurance contract entitled "Blanket Crime Policy" providing indemnity for covered losses up to $250,000 less a $20,000 deductible. On November 24, 1971, a man ticketed under the name D. B. Cooper boarded a Northwest flight in Portland, Oregon, bound for Seattle, Washington. The man hijacked the plane by threatening to detonate what appeared to be a bomb concealed in his briefcase unless the following demands were met: (1) $200,000 cash to be delivered to the plane in Seattle, (2) four parachutes to be delivered with the money, (3) no police interference, and (4) refueling of the plane at Seattle. After communicating with company officials, the pilot decided to cooperate with the hijacker.

Northwest's Seattle ground personnel were notified of the hijacking and received home office authorization to procure the money and parachutes. Arrangements were made to obtain the money from Seattle First National Bank, whose personnel transported the money from its downtown facility to the airport. The release of cash funds resulted in a debit to Northwest's account which it repaid the next day.

Bank employees proceeded to Northwest's air freight terminal, a "premises" insured under the Blanket Crime Policy. Inside the terminal a Northwest official gave the bank employees a receipt for the money. Another Northwest official transported the money to the plane, where it and the parachutes were given to the hijacker, who released the passengers. Under directions from the hijacker, the crew then was directed to fly to Mexico. Shortly after takeoff, the hijacker lowered the rear stairs of the plane and jumped. Neither the hijacker nor the money has ever been located.

Northwest sued the Globe Indemnity to recover under the following insuring agreements in the blanket crime policy:

LOSS INSIDE THE PREMISES COVERAGE
II. Loss of Money and Securities by the actual destruction, disappearance or *wrongful abstraction* thereof *within the Premises* or within any Banking Premises or similar recognized places of safe deposit. . . .

LOSS OUTSIDE THE PREMISES COVERAGE
III. Loss of Money and Securities by the actual destruction, disappearance or *wrongful abstraction* thereof outside the Premises while being conveyed by a *Messenger* or any armored motor vehicle company, or while within the living quarters in the home of any Messenger.

Loss of other property by Robbery or attempt thereat outside the Premises while being conveyed by a *Messenger* or any armored motor vehicle company, or by theft while within the living quarters in the home of any Messenger. (Italics supplied.) . . .

The trial court ruled that there had been a wrongful abstraction of money from within Northwest's premises or from within Northwest's bank premises, and also outside the premises while the money was being conveyed by a messenger as defined in the policy. The court therefore rendered judgment for Northwest in the amount of $180,000, and Globe Indemnity appealed to the Supreme Court of Minnesota.

Yetka, Justice
. . . To recover, defendant correctly states that plaintiff must establish:

(1) That it suffered a loss of money.

(2) That the loss resulted from the actual wrongful abstraction thereof.

(3) That the wrongful abstraction is a risk covered in the policy. Defendant attacks the first element on grounds that the trial court's finding that plaintiff "suffered a loss of $200,000 in money by means of wrongful abstraction thereof within the meaning of the contract of insurance" is too general. . . .

[W]e cannot agree that the taking of the $200,000 is not a "loss of money" as defined in the policy. . . .

The second requisite element, wrongful abstraction, is not defined in the policy and the parties agree that said term is unambiguous. . . .

Defendant characterizes the hijacking as extortion, which is "wrongful" according to the definition of extortion provided by defendant. Thus, the hijacking was wrongful. The term "abstract" is defined in Webster's New International Dictionary (2d ed. 1947) p. 10, as "to take secretly or dishonestly." . . . . [I]t would appear clear that airline hijacking for ransom is indeed wrongful abstraction.

Defendant argues also that extortion is not a peril insured against by the policy. Defendant proposes that the rule of "expressio unius est exclusio alteris" [the expression of one thing is the exclusion of another] is applicable because the inclusion of coverage for wrongful abstraction thereby excludes coverage for extortion and hijacking losses. We do not agree with these contentions. . . .

[I]t is fair to state that the term "wrongful abstraction" is as broad in scope as it is possible to envision. Had defendant desired to couch coverage in more restrictive terms, it was its duty to do so since it is obvious that plaintiff would not voluntarily suggest more restrictive language which would naturally work to its detriment. . . .

When [the] policy is read as a whole, we find it to be in the nature of a blanket or all-risk policy, as opposed to one which covers only specified risks. As defendant's counsel admitted in oral argument, mere unforeseeability of the manner in which the loss was sustained will not *per se* constitute grounds for the insurer to deny coverage. In the present case, where there is blanket coverage and the risk at issue was not excluded, the insurer must fulfill its contractual obligation to indemnify the insured. . . .

[Judgment affirmed.]

Claims and Recovery

Parties' Duties After Loss

Both life and property insurance policies explicitly outline appropriate procedures for filing a claim to recover for a covered loss. In a life insurance policy, due proof of death of the insured and surrender of the policy are common prerequisites to payment of insurance proceeds. Property and liability insurance policies usually require that the insured give prompt notice of any loss to the insurer or its agent. The insured also may be required to furnish the names of persons injured and of any witnesses and to prevent further damage to the property. Within a stated period after the loss or after the insurer's request (for example, sixty days) the insured also must provide a "proof of loss." The proof of loss provides details of the accident, other insurance that may cover the loss, the interest of the insured and others in the property, receipts for repairs, detailed repair or replacement estimates, and inventories of lost or damaged personal property. The insured also is usually required to cooperate with the insurer regarding any investigation, settlement, or defense of any claim; forward copies of legal documents received; and submit to physical examinations or to questions under oath.

As illustrated by the following case, the insured's duty to comply with a policy's claim procedures can be of critical importance.

Commercial Union Insurance Company v. International Flavors & Fragrances, Inc.
822 F.2d 267 (2d Cir. 1987)

Under a comprehensive liability insurance policy issued to defendant International Flavors & Fragrances, Inc. (IFF) in 1976 and renewed through 1979, plaintiff Commercial Union Insurance Company (CU) agreed to indemnify IFF and to provide a defense in lawsuits within the policy's coverage. As a condition of coverage, IFF was required to give written notice of any "occurrence" to CU "as soon as practicable." This notice of occurrence provision became the subject of litigation after CU refused to defend or indemnify IFF in conjunction with a lawsuit brought by Plough, Inc.

The action arose from a contract by which IFF, between 1975 and 1977, had supplied 62,000 pounds of banana-coconut fragrance used in Plough's Tropical Blend suntan lotion. In 1976, Plough notified IFF and the Food and Drug Administration (FDA) that fifteen persons had reported skin reactions after using Tropical Blend. During the next year Plough and IFF employees consulted in an attempt to identify the cause of the skin reactions. By July 1977, after fifty cases had been reported, dermatologists conducting clinical tests concluded that the skin reactions were caused by a photoallergenic reaction to 6-methyl coumarin (6-MC), a chemical agent that IFF used in the banana-coconut fragrance. In September 1977, Plough notified IFF officers of these results. In December 1978, the FDA notified IFF that 6-MC was being banned from use in suncare products and IFF informed its insurance broker of the FDA's action. In March 1979, Plough sued IFF, which shortly thereafter notified CU of the suit.

CU filed suit seeking a declaratory judgment that it had no duty to defend or indemnify IFF because of its failure to give timely notice of the occurrence. Although the jury found in favor of CU, the trial judge granted in part a motion for judgment notwithstanding the verdict and ruled that CU had no duty to indemnify IFF but had a duty to defend the suit. CU and IFF appealed to the Second Circuit Court of Appeals.

Winter, Circuit Judge

. . . Notice-of-occurrence provisions have several purposes. . . . They enable insurers to make a timely investigation of relevant events and exercise early control over a claim. Early control may lead to a settlement before litigation and enable insurers to take steps to eliminate the risk of similar occurrences in the future. When insurers have timely notice of relevant occurrences, they can establish more accurate renewal premiums and maintain adequate reserves. . . .

[T]he photoallergenic nature of 6-MC was totally unknown and unexpected prior to the events giving rise to the instant action. . . . Plough did its best in 1977 and 1978 to avoid any public disclosure that its Tropical Blend products might be harmful. However, we cannot agree with the suggestion that these facts excuse IFF from complying with the notice-of-occurrence provision as a matter of law. As noted above, a principal purpose of such a provision is to enable insurers to reduce future risks to the public by preventing the continued use of known harmful substances by their insureds. Had IFF given timely notice, CU could have taken steps to protect the public from further exposure to 6-MC. Indeed, Plough's attempts to avoid publicity were feasible *only* because IFF, which also had a financial interest in concealment, did not give notice to CU. We believe that a rule of law that would inhibit insurance companies from eliminating risks known to manufacturers and sellers but concealed for purposes of commercial advantage is undesirable.

Under New York law, compliance with a notice-of-occurrence provision in an insurance policy is a condition precedent to an insurer's liability under the policy. . . . An insured's failure to give timely notice to its insurer may be excused, however, by proof that the insured either lacked knowledge of the occurrence or had a reasonable belief of nonliability. . . . Viewing the evidence, as we must, in the light most favorable to CU, . . . we conclude that it was more than sufficient to support the . . . jury's finding of an unexcused breach of the notice-of-occurrence provision.

The test for determining whether the notice provision has been triggered is whether the circumstances known to the insured at that time would have suggested to a reasonable person the possibility of a claim. . . . By September 1977, some eighteen months before Plough began its litigation, IFF executives knew, *inter alia*, that: (1) 6-MC was photoallergenic; (2) Plough had contracted to pay IFF over $700,000 for a fragrance containing 6-MC; (3) Plough had spent thousands of dollars to determine the cause of the Tropical Blend problem; (4) millions of units of Tropical Blend could not be sold and would have to be destroyed; and (5) many individuals had suffered personal injuries, some severe, because of the fragrance. Subsequent events merely confirmed 6-MC's photoallergenicity. The fact that this harmful property was unknown prior to September 1977 is of no aid to IFF in view of its failure to give the required notice until March 1979. A jury might thus easily have concluded that a reasonable person, knowing in September 1977 that IFF's product had caused and was causing great losses to Plough, would have realized that there had been an occurrence possibly giving rise to a claim covered by the policy. . . .

Judge Pollack correctly held that IFF's breach of the notice-of-occurrence clause would relieve CU of its duty to indemnify IFF for Plough's recovery. He also concluded that this breach would not justify CU's refusal to defend the Plough lawsuit, however, because an insurer's duty to defend is broader than its duty to indemnify. . . . That was error. While an insurer's obligation to furnish a defense is indeed separate from and broader than its obligation to indemnify, . . . the added breadth arises out of the duty to provide a defense against even wholly frivolous, and thus non-indemnifiable, claims so long as the allegations fall within the policy's coverage. IFF's compliance with the notice requirement, however, was a condition precedent to all of CU's duties under the policy, including the duty to defend. . . . The . . . jury's finding that IFF had not complied with the notice provision thus excused CU's refusal to defend without reservation as well as its refusal to indemnify. . . .

[Judgment reversed and remanded.]

Once a claim is properly filed, the insurer evaluates, processes, and pays or denies it. A growing number of courts recognize that, in handling a claim, the insurer is under a duty to act in good faith and consistent with standards of fair dealing. Breach of this duty may, as the following case illustrates, subject an insurer to tort liability to its insured.

Arnold v. National County Mutual Fire Insurance Company

725 S.W.2d 165 (Tex. 1987)

Plaintiff Glen Arnold was severely injured in June 1974 when the motorcycle he was operating was struck by a car driven by an uninsured motorist. Arnold was insured by defendant National County Mutual Insurance Company (NCM) under a policy that included uninsured motorist protection with a limit of $10,000. Arnold requested NCM to pay him the limit under the policy and an independent insurance adjusting firm recommended NCM to pay Arnold. NCM, however, refused to pay or to negotiate a settlement with Arnold. NCM's refusal was based on its attorney's suggestion that Arnold may have been driving too fast for conditions and may have been intoxicated, but NCM failed to investigate either of these matters. After suing the uninsured motorist and NCM, Arnold was awarded a judgment in the amount of $17,975 in December, 1977. NCM then paid Arnold $10,000. Arnold sued NCM in tort alleging that the insurer had breached its duty of good faith and fair dealing in handling the claim. The trial court granted summary judgment in favor of NCM

and the court of appeals affirmed. Arnold appealed to the Supreme Court of Texas.

Ray, Justice

. . . Arnold raises the issue of whether there is a duty on the part of insurers to deal fairly and in good faith with their insureds. We hold that such a duty of good faith and fair dealing exists. . . .

While this court has declined to impose an implied *covenant* of good faith and fair dealing in every contract, we have recognized that a duty of good faith and fair dealing may arise as a result of a special relationship between the parties governed or created by a contract. . . .

In the insurance context a special relationship arises out of the parties' unequal bargaining power and the nature of insurance contracts which would allow unscrupulous insurers to take advantage of their insureds' misfortunes in bargaining for settlement or resolution of claims. In addition, without such a cause of action insurers can arbitrarily deny coverage and delay payment of a claim with no more penalty than interest on the amount owed. An insurance company has exclusive control over the evaluation, processing and denial of claims. . . .

A cause of action for breach of the duty of good faith and fair dealing is stated when it is alleged that there is no reasonable basis for denial of a claim or delay in payment or a failure on the part of the insurer to determine whether there is any reasonable basis for the denial or delay. Arnold pleaded and produced sufficient summary judgment proof to raise an issue of material fact that NCM had no reasonable basis for its refusal to pay his uninsured motorist claim and with actual knowledge of that, forced him to a trial on the accident before it would pay the claim.

Arnold further complains that the trial court erred in granting summary judgment by ruling that he was not entitled to recover exemplary damages and mental anguish damages. . . . However, we would point out that exemplary damages and mental anguish damages are recoverable for a breach of the duty of good faith and fair dealing under the same principles allowing recovery of those damages in other tort actions. . . .

[Judgment reversed and remanded.]

Measure of Recovery

In a life insurance policy, the company pays to the beneficiary of record the amount fixed in the policy less the amount of any policy loans outstanding at the insured's death. Other policies, such as accident insurance, also may provide for fixed benefits.

In liability insurance, the insurer agrees to pay damages for personal injury and property damage that the insured becomes legally responsible to pay. Liability usually is limited to a specified maximum for each injured person and a total maximum for each accident or occurrence. The insurer also undertakes to provide a legal defense or settle at its expense any lawsuit or claim brought against the insured requesting damages.

In property insurance, recovery generally is based upon "actual cash value" at the time of the loss. For replaceable commodities with a fixed market price, that price usually is the measure of actual cash value. In many cases, however, actual cash value is determined only after the court has considered a combination of relevant factors including replacement cost, depreciation, and the effect of obsolescence of the insured property.

Doelger and Kirsten, Inc. v. National Union Fire Ins. Co.

167 N.W.2d 198 (Wis. 1969)

> Plaintiff Doelger and Kirsten, Inc. sued defendant National Union Fire Insurance Co. to recover for the loss of certain wooden patterns stored in a barn that was destroyed by fire. The insurance policy restricted liability to the "actual cash value of the property." The trial court found that replacement cost of the patterns was $12,100 but that, because of obsolescence, the plaintiff's actual loss was $4,840. The defendant appealed this judgment to the Supreme Court of Wisconsin.

Hansen, Justice

What is the proper measuring stick to use in determining the "actual cash value" of wooden patterns of uncertain age, apparently more than 30 years old, last used in 1958 or 1959 and useable only for the producing of castings for alligator shears, an item of heavy industrial equipment for which there no longer seems to be much public demand?

Plaintiff contends that the proper measuring stick is a replacement cost. Evidence from an expert pattern maker was offered that the cost of reproduction of the destroyed patterns was $12,100.00. Such cost of reproduction, the plaintiff spiritedly contends, is the sole test of value.

Defendant counters that the measuring stick to be used is that of present market value, actually contending that alligator shears, and consequently patterns used to make them, are obsolete and of no value at all. It is conceded that the patterns had not been used since 1956, and were moved to the barn for storage in 1963. The bottom dropped out of the alligator shears market in the mid-fifties with the development of the guillotine shears, a new and improved type of cutting machine. As background it should be mentioned that we deal here with a piece of expensive equipment. An alligator shears is no scissors to remove warts from crocodiles. One such shears costs $30,000. At the peak of demand, orders came in only two, three or four times a year.

By the replacement test plaintiff would get $12,100. By the present market value test, plaintiff would get nothing or very near to that. The trial court adopted the measuring stick of replacement cost, minus physical depreciation and minus obsolescence. . . .

This is in accord with the opinion of experts in valuation of property.

> For example, in the case of used patterns, molds, and designs used as equipment by a manufacturer it has been held that their replacement cost new is not a fair test and that their obsolescence as well as their physical depreciation must be taken into account. [1 Bonbright, Valuation of Property 383.]

Applied to the type of equipment here involved and the type of situation here presented, this appears to be a common sense approach to determining present "actual cash value." In the absence of any evidence as to physical depreciation, the trial court made no deduction for the attrition of the aging process, holding that to do so would be "pure speculation." Giving weight both to evidence as to absence of orders and the presence of continuing inquiries as to availability of alligator shears, the trial court found evidence of "substantial obsolescence." On this record, . . . it was for the trial court to determine the degree of obsolescence, if the equipment was found to have some value rather than no value.

Admittedly, this was no easy assignment. Under the fact situation here presented, the court could not be expected to ascertain the "actual cash value" with exact mathematical precision. It was for the trier of fact to set the damages at a reasonable amount, using an acceptable measuring stick. This is what he did.

Perhaps as a footnote only, we add the warning that sustaining the trial judge here is not laying down an invariable test to be applied in ascertaining "actual cash value" in all fire insurance cases. Actually, this court has consistently followed what has been termed the "broad evidence rule" giving considerable leeway and latitude to the trier of facts. In practice, this broad rule gives to the trial forum the right to consider in a given case all facts reasonably tending to throw light upon the subject. In a post-Volstead Act [Prohibition] case involving the destruction of buildings designed and used for the manufacture of malt used in the brewing of beer, the New York State appellate court well stated this "broad evidence rule":

> Where insured buildings have been destroyed, the trier of fact, may, and should, call to its aid, in order to effectuate complete indemnity, every fact and circumstance which would logically tend to the formation of a correct estimate of the loss. It may consider original cost and cost of reproduction; the opinions upon value given by qualified witnesses; the declarations against interest which may have been made by the assured; the gainful uses to which the buildings might have been put; as well as any other fact reasonably tending to throw light upon the subject. [*McAnarney v. Newark Fire Insurance Co.,* 159 N.E. 902, 905 (N.Y. 1928).]

Under the "broad evidence rule," we need not find the route travelled by the trier of fact in this case to be the only route that could have been travelled. We need only to find it a proper and acceptable one. This we do. That both parties are outraged by the result reached may be some reasurance that the trial court found and followed a via media between two extremes. . . .

[Judgment affirmed.]

If the insured property is residential real estate, indemnity based upon replacement cost less depreciation usually is insufficient to allow the homeowner to rebuild. For this reason, modern comprehensive homeowner's policies often provide replacement cost insurance. Typically, such a provision states that if, at the time of the loss, the amount of insurance on the damaged building is 80 percent or more of the full replacement cost of the building immediately before the loss, then coverage is extended to include the full cost of repair or replacement without deduction for depreciation. Note that, for reasons developed below, replacement cost insurance induces the owner to insure the property for close to its full replacement cost.

Coinsurance. Nonmarine property insurance rates are fixed as a percentage of the total amount of insurance under the policy. Thus, the insured pays the same amount for the first and last thousand dollars' worth of coverage. Most property losses are, however, partial, meaning that the lower levels of coverage cost more to provide. In addition, because most losses are partial, insureds are induced to underinsure their property.

Coinsurance is one device developed by insurers to induce owners to insure their property for an amount close to its full value. Under a coinsurance clause, recovery for a partial loss is limited (that is, the insured becomes a coinsurer) unless the owner insures the property for at least a specified percentage (usually 80 percent) of its full value. Recovery under a coinsurance clause is computed using the following formula:

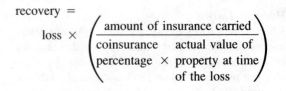

$$\text{recovery} = \text{loss} \times \left(\frac{\text{amount of insurance carried}}{\genfrac{}{}{0pt}{}{\text{coinsurance}}{\text{percentage}} \times \genfrac{}{}{0pt}{}{\text{actual value of}}{\genfrac{}{}{0pt}{}{\text{property at time}}{\text{of the loss}}} \right)$$

For example, assume property worth $200,000 sustains an $80,000 fire loss. The owner has insured the property for $100,000 under a policy containing an 80 percent coinsurance clause. The owner's recovery would be $50,000 computed as follows:

$$\$50,000 = \$80,000 \times \left(\frac{\$100,000}{0.8 \times \$200,000}\right).$$

On these facts, therefore, the owner bears $30,000 of the $80,000 loss. Had the owner insured the property for $160,000, recovery would be $80,000. That is:

$$\$80,000 = \$80,000 \times \left(\frac{\$160,000}{0.8 \times \$200,000}\right).$$

Thus, by insuring the property consistently with the coinsurance percentage, the owner recovers in full for any partial loss up to the policy limit, $160,000.

Note that coinsurance applies to partial not total losses; after a total loss, the owner may recover the face amount of the policy. In the first example, therefore, if the building had been completely destroyed, the owner could recover $100,000.

Other Insurance. An insured may take out more than one policy of insurance upon his or her life or property. The face amount of all life insurance policies will be paid on death. In contrast, to prevent the moral risk of net profit from overinsurance, property insurers use **other insurance clauses** to limit effective coverage if the insured obtains additional insurance on the same property. These clauses typically provide that each insurer pays the proportion of the loss that the face amount of each policy bears to the total amount of insurance carried. For example, if an owner insures property for its full value with two insurers and suffers a total loss, each insurer would be required to pay one-half of the loss.

Rights and Defenses of Insurer

Defenses of Insurer

An insured possesses information not known to the insurer, such as the state of his health, medical history, or the condition, type, or use of property owned. Such information is, of course, important to the insurer in evaluating the risk to determine whether to insure and at what premium. Insurers elicit the information from the insured through representations or warranties. A representation is a statement regarding the subject of insurance that forms part of the basis of the insurer's decision to insure. Generally, a material misrepresentation, whether or not intentionally (fraudulently) made, relied upon by the insurer is grounds for avoiding the policy. The insurer generally has the burden of proving that the misrepresentation was material. Intentional concealment of a material fact is likewise a basis for avoidance, though an innocent failure to disclose may not be, except in marine policies.

In contrast to representations, certain statements or promises made by the insured may be expressly incorporated into the contract. Such "warranties" or "conditions" are affirmative—a statement asserting that certain facts are true when the contract is made—or promissory—that the facts will continue to be true throughout the life of the policy. Unlike representations, warranties are presumed to be material, and generally must be strictly observed to prevent avoidance by the insurer. For example, if the insured warrants that no flammable liquids will be stored on the insured property during the life of the policy, recovery for any fire loss may be denied if gasoline is stored on the premises. Because of its harsh effect upon the rights of the insured, a warranty must be expressly and conspicuously included in the policy and must clearly indicate that the insured's rights depend upon compliance.

To protect insureds, courts construe ambiguous language as representations rather than warranties, and ambiguous warranties as affirmative rather than promissory. In addition, various statutes prevent denial of recovery under a life insurance policy based upon immaterial technicalities. For example, to avoid upsetting the estate and financial planning of an insured, many states require that life insurance policies contain a clause making the policy incontestable (except for nonpayment of premiums) after the policy has been in effect for a given period, such as one or two years. If the insured survives the stated period, an **incontestable clause** prevents the insurer from asserting a misrepresentation or breach of warranty as a basis to avoid the contract. The law usually takes a similar approach to suicide; that is, the insured's suicide is not grounds for denial of recovery unless it occurs within a stated period after inception of the policy. A limited defense is, however, provided for the insured's misrepresentation of age. In this case, the amount payable on the insured's death is the amount of insurance the premiums actually paid would have purchased if the age had been correctly stated.

Subrogation

As noted in Chapter 33 (Suretyship), **subrogation** is an equitable remedy grounded in restitution designed to prevent unjust enrichment. In insurance law, the insurance company after paying the insured succeeds to, or is subrogated to, the insured's rights in contract or tort against any third party causing the loss. An insurer has no right of subrogation against its own insured. Subrogation is de-

signed to prevent a double recovery by the insured (one from the insurer and another from the person causing the loss) and to place the ultimate loss upon the party responsible for the injury. For example, assume Tim negligently destroys John's car. Continental Casualty, John's insurer, indemnifies him for the loss. Continental is subrogated to John's tort claim against Tim to the extent of Continental's payments to John. Subrogation rights arise by operation of law and therefore need not be expressly provided for in the insurance contract.

Although the law recognizes a right of subrogation for amounts paid under property and liability insurance policies, subrogation generally has been denied in life insurance. In life insurance, the insurer is obligated to pay a fixed sum on death. Because indemnity for determinable economic loss is not the basis of recovery, there is no possibility of double recovery by the beneficiary. Thus, the beneficiary or other family member (not the insurer) also may recover in tort against any third party wrongfully causing the death of the insured.

SUMMARY

1. Insurance is a contractual arrangement for transferring and distributing risk. In an insurance contract, an insurer, an entity engaged in the business of insurance, promises to pay another, the insured, a sum of money or provide other value upon occurrence of some harmful event during a specified period. In exchange for this promise, the insured pays a premium. Insurance contracts and insurance company activities are regulated by the states.

2. Insurance contracts are of three basic types: (1) life insurance, (2) fire and marine insurance, and (3) casualty insurance. Insurance contracts are standardized form contracts tendered to the insured on a take-it-or-leave-it basis. To protect insureds, courts often construe insurance contracts to provide coverage for a given loss, and use contract doctrines, such as unconscionability, to police against unreasonably unfair terms.

3. Most insurance contracts are contracts of indemnity under which the insurance company promises to indemnify or reimburse the insured for some accrued or anticipated liability. Under the indemnity concept, the benefit conferred by the insurer may not exceed the loss suffered by the insured. This approach, prohibiting net

profit from insurance, prevents use of an insurance contract as a gambling device, and eliminates any inducement for the insured to cause the event insured against. The legal principles designed to prevent net profit from insurance are embodied in the concept of insurable interest.

4. In property and casualty insurance the insured generally is the person or persons whose loss triggers the insurer's liability to pay benefits. Persons insured may be explicitly named in the policy, subsequently added by indorsement, or included by operation of policy provisions such as an "omnibus" or "standard mortgage" clause. Although the insured usually receives the proceeds, the right may be assigned to a party not named as an insured under the policy.

5. A life insurance policy creates various rights in favor of its owner that generally may be assigned. The rights of the beneficiary of the policy depend upon whether the beneficiary is named revocably or irrevocably.

6. The scope of the insurer's obligation regarding both the risk covered and the duration of coverage are determined by express terms of the insurance contract. In defining the insured risk, policies are commonly designated either "all-risk" or "specified-risk."

7. Life and property insurance policies explicitly outline appropriate procedures for filing a claim to recover for an insured loss. In life insurance, proceeds are fixed in the policy, but in property insurance, recovery is based upon the actual cash value of the insured property at the time of the loss. The amount of recovery also may be affected by the operation of a coinsurance or other insurance clause.

8. An insurer relies upon information provided by the insured in evaluating risk and computing the premium. Certain misrepresentations by the insured or the insured's failure to comply with written warranties incorporated into the contract may provide a basis to avoid the contract. To protect insureds, courts and legislatures have devised various devices such as "incontestable clauses" to prevent denial of recovery based upon immaterial technicalities.

9. In insurance law, the insurer after paying the insured is subrogated to the insured's rights against any third party causing the loss. The right of subrogation, which prevents double recovery by the insured, is not recognized in some forms of insurance.

KEY TERMS

insurance
life insurance
fire insurance
marine insurance
inland marine insurance
casualty insurance
indemnity contract
insurable interest

Uniform Vendor and
  Purchaser Risk Act
omnibus clause
standard mortgage
  clause
coinsurance clause
other insurance clause
incontestable clause
subrogation

QUESTIONS AND PROBLEMS

56-1 Insurance is a method of transferring and distributing risk. What is risk? What benefits does a life insurance policy provide for an insured and the beneficiaries? What benefits do fire and casualty insurance provide to a business?

56-2 Life insurance is often characterized as a contract of investment rather than indemnity. How does life insurance differ from other forms of insurance? How is it similar? Is it accurate to say that life insurance is not a contract of indemnity? Explain.

56-3 A homeowner's policy provides that "we do not insure . . . any loss arising out of any act committed: (1) by or at the direction of the insured; and (2) with the intent to cause a loss." Why? Should an employer's insurance provide protec-

tion for deliberate acts of employees? Should recovery be denied for losses caused by the negligent (rather than intentional) conduct of an insured? Explain.

56-4 Omnibus clauses have bred litigation because they tie expanded coverage to the "permission" of the insured. How could the clause be redrafted to prevent this litigation?

56-5 What factors might the court take into account in determining the amount of insured's recovery for a fire loss to (1) income producing property, such as an apartment or office building, (2) a residence, (3) personal property, such as household furnishings, (4) an automobile, (5) inventory?

56-6 Bailey owned a fraternity house on the University of Oklahoma campus that he insured against fire with Gulf Insurance Company. The house fell into disrepair and was declared a public nuisance by the city. The city condemned the building and ordered it torn down. Subsequently, the building was severely damaged by an accidental fire. Should Bailey be entitled to recover anything under the policy? If so, how should recovery be computed?

56-7 In 1976, James Butler purchased a used 1967 Austin-Healey sports car, and acquired an auto insurance policy covering the car from Farmers Insurance Company. Two years later, it was discovered that, unknown to Butler, the car previously had been stolen. The police seized the car and returned it to its rightful owner. Butler sought to recover under a provision in the policy under which Farmers agreed to pay "for loss to the described automobile caused by accidental means." Farmers denied liability on the grounds that (1) Butler had no insurable interest in the automobile, and (2) that, in any event, repossession of the auto by the rightful owner was not a loss covered by the policy. Is Farmers correct? Explain.

56-8 To recover under a property insurance policy, the insured must show that an insured event caused the loss. In determining causation, some courts use a proximate cause test analogous to that used in tort cases discussed in Chapter 5. Other courts use a "contemplated damages" test and hold the insurer liable only for losses within the contemplation of the parties when the policy was issued. In the following fact situations, determine whether the insured should recover under either test.

(a) The policy covered "direct loss by windstorm." The insured livestock, exposed to a cold wind, took shelter on a frozen pond and drowned when the ice broke.

(b) The policy covered "loss by windstorm." A high wind blew down power lines, cutting off power to the insured's freezer, causing its contents to spoil.

(c) The policy covered "direct loss by vandalism and malicious mischief." Vandals threw cans onto the roof of insured's bowling alley. The cans clogged the downspouts, causing rainwater to accumulate on the roof, which collapsed.

56-9 In his will, Joe Doaks left his house to his daughter Gertrude for life, with the remainder in fee simple absolute passing to John Jones. Gertrude occupied the house and insured it against fire loss under a policy issued by Home Insurance Company, naming Gertrude as sole insured. While the policy was in force, a fire destroyed the house. Gertrude died in the fire, approximately twenty minutes after it began. Gertrude's estate filed a claim against Home for the fire loss. Home denied liability, asserting that because Gertrude had only a life estate in the house, her insurable interest terminated by operation of law on her death and accordingly neither she nor her estate suffered any pecuniary loss from the fire. Is Home Insurance correct? Explain.

Major Topics

- an introduction to international law and its sources, and the functions of international organizations
- how power over foreign affairs is distributed between the state and federal government in the United States
- the role of national courts in civil and criminal cases involving foreign parties, property, or events
- international law standards protecting foreign nationals and their property
- the role of national courts in disputes involving a foreign sovereign or its public acts

To this point, the text has examined the organization and operation of the American legal system, the basic legal principles governing rights and duties of private parties in commercial transactions, and the role of the government in regulating business activity. The United States legal system is, of course, only one among many. This chapter provides an overview of the legal concepts governing the legal relationship among sovereign states, the role of the state and federal government in international affairs, and the power of United States courts to adjudicate matters affecting foreign nations and their citizens.

International Law and Organizations

International law, often known as "public international law" or the "law of nations," is the system of law that governs relationships among states. A state exhibits three basic characteristics: it must have a territory, a population, and a sovereign government capable of controlling its territory and conducting international relations with other states.[1] States possess sovereignty, which might be viewed as the supreme political authority from which the state derives other specific political powers. Sovereignty provides the international independence of a state and the right and power to regulate its internal affairs free of foreign interference.

International law should be distinguished from an individual state's internal law, also known as its "national," "municipal," or "local" law. A country's national law may affect various aspects of international relations, though the extraterritorial effect of one country's law is necessarily limited by the sovereignty of other countries. For example, almost every country has developed a system of **private international law,** a branch of conflicts of law that determines (1) when a domestic court should exercise jurisdiction over a case involving foreign persons or territories, (2) when foreign

---

1. Akehurst, *A Modern Introduction to International Law* 1, 53 (6th ed. 1987).

rather than domestic law should apply to a case, and (3) when judgments rendered by foreign courts should be recognized and enforced in a domestic court.

In the United States and other countries a legislature enacts law. The executive, among other functions, enforces it and the judiciary tries violations of criminal law and resolves civil disputes. Violations of law are backed by legal sanctions including money damages, injunctions, fines, and imprisonment. Among the sovereign states no centralized legislature exists, no court possesses mandatory jurisdiction, and no executive body imposes legally enforceable sanctions. This lack of sanctions—lack of an obligatory judicial forum whose judgments are enforceable by executive authority—has led some observers to conclude that the norms that govern human conduct in the world arena are not "law," in the traditional sense of the term, at all. Nevertheless, states normally obey principles of international law, which are derived from consensus or formal agreement, because it is in their individual self-interest to do so. States are few in number and cannot move; economic and other needs force most states to cooperate with their neighbors and to be reasonably reliable in international dealing. Violation of a rule may lead to retaliation by other states, an unacceptable result in light of increasing interdependence among states.

Sources of International Law

Modern international law began to develop in the sixteenth and seventeenth centuries, corresponding to the development of modern Western European states. Article 38(1) of the Statute of the International Court of Justice provides the most widely accepted list of the sources of international law. It states:

> The Court, whose function is to decide in accordance with international law such disputes as are submitted to it, shall apply:
> (a) international conventions, whether general or particular, establishing rules expressly recognized by the contesting states;
> (b) international custom, as evidence of a general practice accepted as law;

> (c) the general principles of law recognized by civilized nations;
> (d) . . . judicial decisions and the teachings of the most highly qualified publicists of the various nations, as subsidiary means for the determination of rules of law.

Treaties. The first source, "international conventions" refers to treaties. A **treaty** is an agreement or contract between two or more nations or sovereigns, formally signed by an authorized representative and ratified by the sovereign or supreme power of each state. Because modern technology, communication, and trade have made states increasingly interdependent and willing to cooperate on a variety of common problems, treaties occupy an ever-expanding role in the orderly conduct of international relations. Some address critical national interests of a political character, such as alliances, peace settlements, and bans on atomic testing. Others involve less politically charged relationships between governments and government agencies, such as agreements on foreign aid or cooperation in provision of government services such as weather forecasting. Still others, such as tariff treaties, tax conventions, and treaties of friendship, commerce, and navigation, regulate business relationships between nationals or residents of the participating countries.

Custom. Custom is the original source of international law. A practice is recognized as part of international custom if it involves a consistent course of conduct by a number of states over a considerable period, a recognition that the practice is consistent with or required by international law, and general acquiescence in the practice by other states.[2] Many international customs have been codified in treaties in recent years, providing more precision and predictability in the law.

General Principles of Law. "General principles of law" provide the third source of international law. These principles, derived primarily from the national law of the developed countries, supplement

---

2. Steiner & Vagts, *Transnational Legal Problems* 298 (3d ed. 1986).

and fill in the gaps in treaties and customary law, the primary sources of international law. Examples of general legal principles used by international tribunals include estoppel, laches, and *res judicata*.

Judicial Decisions and Learned Writers. Although international courts are not required to follow previous decisions (that is, to observe the principle of *stare decisis* applicable under American law), they commonly do, particularly as the body of decided case law in international tribunals increases. Judgments of national courts also play a subsidiary role in developing rules of international law; for example, rules of law on subjects such as diplomatic immunity have been developed by national courts. Writings of legal commentators, like judicial decisions, also can provide evidence of customary law and play a role in developing new international rules.

International Organizations

Primarily since the end of World War II, treaties have been used to create international organizations using a permanent staff, buildings, and other assets to maintain continuous activity. These organizations play an important role in addressing international legal problems not easily resolved through customary international law, or noninstitutional bilateral or multilateral treaties. The organizations are formed for various purposes including peace-keeping and world order, and regulating, facilitating, and developing commercial or economic activities among member states. Some of the more important organizations are briefly introduced below.

United Nations. The United Nations was created at the end of the Second World War to promote peaceful resolution of international disputes and provide for collective action to stop aggression. The United Nations also is concerned with economic development, social welfare, and human rights.

The United Nations Charter divides the organization into constituent parts. The Security Council is vested with primary responsibility for the maintenance of international peace and security. The Council's nonprocedural decisions are subject to veto by its permanent members: China, France, the Soviet Union, the United Kingdom, and the United States. The General Assembly is composed of representatives from all member states. Resolutions of the General Assembly have, in recent years, increasingly addressed trade, investment, and economic matters, rather than peace-keeping issues. General Assembly resolutions enjoy rather limited adherence in the international arena. The Secretariat, headed by the secretary general, administers the day-to-day affairs of the United Nations, and occasionally takes initiative in political matters.

International Court of Justice. Perhaps the most important United Nations body from a legal standpoint is its judicial branch, the International Court of Justice (ICJ). The ICJ issues advisory opinions and decides actual disputes. Its jurisdiction is limited by two basic principles. First, only states may be parties to litigation before the ICJ. Second, jurisdiction is not compulsory but is based upon the state's consent. The Court consists of fifteen judges, no more than two of whom may be from the same country. Judges are elected by the General Assembly and the Security Council to nine-year terms with one-third of the Court being re-elected or replaced every three years.

The ICJ is not the only international tribunal. Other international courts have been created, for example, under regional treaties of economic or political cooperation. Most notable among these is the Court of Justice of the European Economic Community.

General Agreement on Tariffs and Trade. From a commercial standpoint, an important international organization is the General Agreement on Tariffs and Trade (GATT). GATT is the product of post World War II meetings designed to reduce trade barriers to foster free trade. GATT became effective in 1948 and is an executive agreement rather than a treaty under United States law. Its cardinal objectives stated in its preamble are the "substantial reduction of tariffs and other barriers to trade" and the "elimination of discriminatory treatment." GATT provides rules for tariff negotiations that result in tariff schedules, rules governing conduct of international trade and liberalization of restrictive policies, and provisions for meeting and consultation among members to discuss policy and settle disputes. Over 100 countries are parties to or are guided by GATT in the conduct of their international trade policy. Under its auspices, periodic, multinational trade negotiations ("rounds") have been held resulting in significant tariff (import and export duty) concessions as well as reduction of nontariff trade barriers such as import quotas and complex customs procedures.

International Monetary Fund. The same concern over protectionist trade measures that led to GATT also motivated the Bretton Woods Conference of 1944 that created the International Monetary Fund (IMF), to which the United States adhered in 1945. Most U.N. members belong to the IMF, which seeks to eliminate foreign exchange restrictions, stabilize currency exchange rates, and resolve balance of payments problems. This it achieves in part through a complex lending system which permits a country to borrow money necessary to maintain the stability of the currency relative to other currencies.

European Economic Community (Common Market). Political and economic instability in western Europe following World War II inspired various movements for western European unity to prevent another war among them and to accelerate economic revival. In 1952, a treaty among Belgium, the Federal Republic of Germany, France, Italy, Luxembourg, and the Netherlands created the European Coal and Steel Community (ECSC), which created a common market in these basic commodities. This action was followed in 1957 by the Treaty of Rome that created the European Economic Community (EEC) and the European Atomic Energy Community (Euratom). Collectively these three agreements create the European Economic Community, or Common Market, the largest single market for exports from the United States. In addition to the original six members, Denmark, Greece, Ireland, Portugal, Spain, and the United Kingdom subsequently have joined.

The EEC is a supranational organization with a developed institutional structure and the equivalent of its own executive, legislative, and judicial branches. Its basic purpose is to establish a customs union among member states through elimination of internal tariffs and creation of a common external tariff. It also promotes free competition, free movement of labor services and capital, common agricultural and transportation policies, and harmony among laws of the member states.

Distribution of National Powers Over Foreign Affairs

Public international law governs the relationship among sovereign states. The following material examines how the power to address foreign affairs issues is distributed among the various branches of the United States government, and between the federal government and the states.

Regulation of Foreign Affairs

In the United States, a federal form of government, power to regulate internal affairs is divided by the Constitution between the federal government and the states. International law and United States constitutional law, however, regard the federal state rather than member states as the sovereign for purposes of conducting international relations.

Various constitutional provisions and Supreme Court opinions establish the primacy of the federal over the state governments in foreign affairs. For example, Article I, Section 8, Clause 3 of the Constitution vests in Congress the power "to regulate Commerce with foreign Nations." Both state and federal courts often have used this "Foreign Commerce Clause" to declare unconstitutional state and local laws that unduly burden international commerce or impermissibly interfere with congressional power to regulate foreign commerce.

The Supreme Court has noted that the Constitution in literal terms does not vest exclusive power over foreign affairs in the national government. Nevertheless, the Court has indicated that the power is inherently vested in the federal government as a necessary incident of nationality. As summarized by the Court in *United States v. Belmont* (1937):[3]

> [T]he external powers of the United States are to be exercised without regard to state laws or policies. . . . [C]omplete power over international

---

3. 57 S. Ct. 758, 761 (1937).

affairs is in the national government and is not and cannot be subject to any curtailment or interference on the part of the several states.

In the external sphere occupied by the federal government, the president, the chief of the executive branch, is the constitutional representative of the United States. That is, the president is generally viewed as the sole agent of the nation regarding external relations and its sole representative with foreign nations.

The Treaty Power

In exercising power over foreign relations, the president commonly acts through treaties or executive agreements. Article 2, Section 2, Clause 2 of the United States Constitution (the Treaty Clause) provides that the president "shall have Power, by and with the Advice and Consent of the Senate to make Treaties, provided two-thirds of the Senators present concur." Some treaties, such as those requiring appropriation of money, require passage by both houses of Congress like ordinary federal legislation before they become effective. Most treaties are, however, "self-executing." That is, they require only approval by two-thirds of the Senate and presidential ratification to become part of judicially enforceable federal domestic law. Thus, in the United States most treaties become part of national law and international law simultaneously.

International accords also are made by executive agreement. Executive agreements require no approval of either house of Congress to become law. Although executive agreements are not explicitly mentioned in the Constitution, courts have upheld them as authorized either by an implied delegation of congressional authority over foreign commerce or as an inherent executive power. Because it is simpler and quicker, the executive agreement has become an increasingly popular tool of international accord. For example, between 1946 and 1972, executive agreements outnumbered treaties by 5,590 to 368.[4]

Relationship of Treaties to Other National Law

Under the Supremacy Clause, contained in Article VI of the Constitution, the federal Constitution, federal statutes, and treaties are the supreme law of the land, and therefore supercede any inconsistent state law.[5] The relationship between a treaty and other federal law is more troublesome. Although a treaty supercedes a prior inconsistent federal statute, Congress may effectively repeal or modify a treaty commitment by a statute enacted after the treaty. As noted by one court: "Under our constitutional scheme, Congress can denounce treaties if it sees fit to do so, and there is nothing the other branches of government can do about it."[6] Such a treaty termination or modification may, of course, be a violation of international law.

Federal statutes and treaties thus enjoy relatively equal status in the hierarchy of federal law. The following classic case illustrates the relationship between a treaty and the third source of federal law, the United States Constitution.

Reid v. Covert
77 S. Ct. 1222 (1957)

> Mrs. Clarice Covert was arrested and charged with murdering her husband, a sergeant in the United States Air Force, at an airbase in England. Mrs. Covert resided with her husband on the base, but was not a member of the armed services. She was tried by court martial under the Uniform Code of Military Justice (UCMJ). A number of Bill of Rights guarantees, such as the right to a jury trial and the right to grand jury indictment, available to civilian criminal defendants, are not available to persons tried under the UCMJ. The terms of Article 2(11) of the UCMJ provided that it applied to "all persons serving with, employed by, or accompanying the armed forces without the continental limits of the United States" but "subject to the provisions of any treaty or agreement to which the United

---

4. Steiner & Vagts, *Transnational Legal Problems*, 611 (3d ed. 1986).

5. The Supremacy Clause is introduced in Chapter 1.

6. *Diggs v. Schultz*, 470 F.2d 461, 466 (D.C. Cir. 1972).

States is or may be a party or to any accepted rule of international law.''

The military tribunal found Mrs. Covert guilty of murder and sentenced her to life imprisonment. She petitioned the federal district court for a writ of habeas corpus to set her free on the ground that the Constitution forbade her trial by military authorities. The district court agreed and ordered her released. The government appealed directly to the Supreme Court.

Justice Black,

. . . [This case raises] basic constitutional issues of the utmost concern. [It involves] the power of Congress to expose civilians to trial by military tribunals, under military regulations and procedures, for offenses against the United States thereby depriving them of trial in civilian courts, under civilian laws and procedures and with all the safeguards of the Bill of Rights. . . .

At the beginning we reject the idea that when the United States acts against citizens abroad it can do so free of the Bill of Rights. The United States is entirely a creature of the Constitution. Its power and authority have no other source. It can only act in accordance with all the limitations imposed by the Constitution. When the Government reaches out to punish a citizen who is abroad, the shield which the Bill of Rights and other parts of the Constitution provide to protect his life and liberty should not be stripped away just because he happens to be in another land. . . .

At the time of Mrs. Covert's alleged offense, an executive agreement was in effect between the United States and Great Britain which permitted United States' military courts to exercise exclusive jurisdiction over offenses committed in Great Britain by American servicemen or their dependents. For its part, the United States agreed that these military courts would be willing and able to try and to punish all offenses against the laws of Great Britain by such persons. . . . Even though a court-martial does not give an accused trial by jury and other Bill of Rights protections, the Government contends that article 2(11) of UCMJ, insofar as it provides for the military trial of dependents accompanying the armed forces in Great Britain . . . can be sustained as legislation which is necessary and proper to carry out the United States' obligations under the international agreements made with [that country].

The obvious and decisive answer to this, of course, is that no agreement with a foreign nation can confer power on the Congress, or on any other branch of Government, which is free from the restraints of the Constitution. . . .

There is nothing in [the language of the Supremacy Clause] which intimates that treaties and laws enacted pursuant to them do not have to comply with the provisions of the Constitution. Nor is there anything in the debates which accompanied the drafting and ratification of the Constitution which even suggests such a result. . . . It would be manifestly contrary to the objectives of those who created the Constitution, as well as those who were responsible for the Bill of Rights—let alone alien to our entire constitutional history and tradition—to construe Article VI as permitting the United States to exercise power under an international agreement without observing constitutional prohibitions. In effect, such construction would permit amendment of that document in a manner not sanctioned by Article V. The prohibitions of the Constitution were designed to apply to all branches of the National Government and they cannot be nullified by the Executive or by the Executive and the Senate combined.

There is nothing new or unique about what we say here. This Court has regularly and uniformly recognized the supremacy of the Constitution over a treaty. . . .

In summary, we conclude that the Constitution in its entirety applied to the trial [of] Mrs. Covert. Since [her] court-martial did not meet the requirements of Art. III, §2, or the Fifth and Sixth Amendments we are compelled to determine if there is anything *within* the Constitution which authorizes the military trial of dependents accompanying the armed forces overseas. . . .

[The Court found no constitutional authorization for such trials and accordingly affirmed the judgment of the district court.]

National Courts in the International Setting

To this point, this chapter has examined the nature and sources of international law, the law governing relations among states, and the distribution of government power within the United States over foreign affairs. The following material examines some of the legal issues presented when a municipal or national court tries a case involving a foreign country or its agencies, foreign citizens, or events occurring beyond national boundaries.

Jurisdiction of National Courts

As noted in Chapter 1, the term "jurisdiction" refers to the power of a court to hear and render a binding judgment in a case. In the international context, the term refers to the capacity of a state to prescribe or to enforce a rule of law.[7] If the persons, property, or events involved touch more than one country, the appropriate jurisdiction of a given nation's courts must be determined. Generally, jurisdiction of a national court is determined by national law, subject to a few restrictions imposed by international law. That is, international law seldom requires a court to hear a case, but instead is concerned with the limits upon individual state discretion.

Criminal Cases. In determining national court jurisdiction, criminal and civil cases must be distinguished. A number of international law theories have been developed to define the criminal jurisdiction of a country's courts. In criminal cases, every country enjoys jurisdiction over crimes committed within its territory (a territorial principle) and over crimes committed by its own citizens anywhere in the world (a nationality principle). Other, less widely accepted, bases of criminal jurisdiction include the "protective" principle (allowing a state to punish acts injurious to its security, even when committed by foreigners abroad), the "passive personality" principle (allowing jurisdiction based upon the nationality of the persons injured), and the "universality" principle (allowing jurisdiction over all crimes, even crimes committed by foreigners abroad if the wrongdoer is arrested within the prosecuting state). Though English-speaking countries generally regard universality jurisdiction as a violation of international law, it is less objectionable when applied to acts threatening the entire international community and which are criminal in all states such as hijacking, piracy, war crimes, violence against diplomats, and certain forms of international terrorism.

Whatever the basis of jurisdiction, the criminal defendant must be brought before the courts of the country asserting jurisdiction. A defendant who has taken refuge in another country must be extradited. Generally, a country has no duty to extradite criminal defendants to other countries in absence of treaty. Though many extradition treaties are in force, deportation has become a common substitute for extradition.

Civil Cases. Unlike criminal law, international law imposes few restrictions upon jurisdiction of national courts in civil cases. Various theories of national law, however, limit the reach of a country's courts in civil litigation. For example, the doctrines of sovereign immunity and act of state discussed later in this chapter, are national law theories that limit the civil jurisdiction of a nation's courts. In addition, courts often are hesitant to take jurisdiction and impose local law upon conduct occurring at least in part outside the territorial limits of their country. Attempts by a nation to apply its law outside its borders create resentment in other countries, who regard the attempt as an unwarranted and illegal intrusion into their sovereignty.

Perhaps the most controversy in this area has arisen regarding judicial attempts to apply United States antitrust law extraterritorially. The question involves a delicate balancing of the interests of the United States against the adverse effect upon foreign harmony. Although courts have long held that the place or location of anticompetitive *effects* (as opposed to the conduct) determines whether United States antitrust law applies to a given transaction,[8] they have articulated different formulations of the nature and amount of effects needed. To eliminate this uncertainty, Congress enacted the Foreign Trade Antitrust Improvements Act[9] in 1982, which provides that United States antitrust law applies to foreign business transactions only when the con-

---

7. *Restatement (Second) of Foreign Relations Law of the United States* §6.

8. Judge Learned Hand announced this approach in the antitrust landmark *United States v. Aluminum Co. of America,* 148 F.2d 416, 443-444 (2d Cir. 1945), discussed in Chapter 51.
9. 15 U.S.C. §§6a, 45(a)(3).

duct giving rise to the claim has a "direct, substantial, and reasonably foreseeable" anticompetitive effect on United States domestic, import, or export commerce. Anticompetitive conduct lacking the required domestic effect is exempt even if it originates in the United States or involves American-owned businesses operating abroad.

International Civil Dispute Resolution

Unlike criminal law, which is designed to punish socially harmful conduct, the civil law is remedial in nature, designed to resolve disputes between private individuals, corporations, or other entities. If all parties are located within a single country, the problems presented are matters of national law (state or federal) resolved in national courts. If, however, one or more parties is a foreign citizen, property is located in a foreign country, or events occur abroad, a myriad of additional problems arise. For example, assume B, a New York retailer, wishes to buy $500,000 worth of perfume from S, a manufacturer located in Paris, France. Even if no dispute arises, factors not present in domestic transactions must be considered. For example, the parties must consider the tariff, import-export and currency regulations of both countries to arrange for payment for the goods. If a dispute arises (for example, the goods shipped are defective), other issues arise including what country's law applies, how the dispute will be resolved, and the location of the forum. In international transactions, the parties often resolve these issues expressly in their original contract.

International Arbitration. Because of uncertainty regarding substantive and procedural laws of the various nations, arbitration provisions are a popular method of dispute resolution in international business transactions. A contractual arbitration provision may provide for the creation of a panel of members representing each party concerned or may refer the dispute to a neutral international organization such as the International Chamber of Commerce. Enforcement of contractual arbitration clauses is facilitated by provisions of individual treaties of friendship, commerce, and navigation, and by the United Nations Convention on the Rec-

ognition and Enforcement of Foreign Arbitral Awards, which has been implemented in over fifty countries, including the United States.[10]

If the contract contains no arbitration provision, disputes are likely to result in litigation. To eliminate uncertainty regarding the proper court for resolution of the dispute and the law to be applied in that court, the contract may include a "choice of forum" or "choice of law" clause. A choice of forum clause enables the parties to specify in advance which country's courts shall hear disputes. Such clauses, if reasonable, generally are enforceable in most countries. A choice of law clause specifies which country's law is to be applied to a prospective dispute. Most nations enforce a choice of law clause if the body of law specified bears a substantial relationship to the parties and the transaction.

Note that each country's body of law generally includes choice of law rules determining which country's substantive law is to apply to an international dispute. That is, the forum country may be directed by its own law to apply another country's law to a particular transaction. Thus, in the absence of choice of forum and choice of law provisions in the contract, legal proceedings in two or more countries may result, with each court applying its own choice of law rules to determine the applicable body of substantive law.

Recognition and Enforcement of Foreign Judgments. Assume Seller, a citizen of France, sues Buyer, a citizen of the United States, in a French court for breach of contract. If the court renders a judgment in favor of Seller, Seller may attempt to enforce the judgment in the United States to reach assets owned by Buyer there. In the United States, courts generally enforce foreign judgments based on comity (courtesy or deference to the foreign court), provided no strong public policy is violated. The fairness of the trial, the voluntary appearance of the defendant, and lack of prejudice or fraud are factors favoring enforcement of foreign judgments.[11] Other legal systems enforce foreign judgments in varying circumstances, but generally are

---

10. 9 U.S.C. §201 *et seq.*
11. *Hilton v. Guyot,* 16 S. Ct. 139 (1895).

not as accommodating as the United States. Various bilateral and multilateral treaties and regional conventions now address the issue and have somewhat increased the enforceability of foreign judgments.[12]

United Nations Convention for International Sales.

In October, 1986, the U.S. Senate unanimously ratified the 1980 United Nations Convention on Contracts for the International Sale of Goods (CISG), which became effective among the initial contracting states on January 1, 1988. The CISG, which applies in the absence of contrary agreement by the parties, states substantive rules governing formation of international sales contracts, and the rights and duties of the buyer and seller. It is designed to minimize conflicts of law problems in international sales transactions and to provide a basis for settling issues that the parties have not resolved by contract. As of 1988, the CISG, which more closely resembles Article 2 of the UCC than any foreign sales law, had been ratified by sixteen countries.

Treatment of Foreign Nationals and Their Property

Potential civil disputes with foreign citizens are not the only risk of international transactions. Individuals or business entities living, investing, or transacting business in a foreign country may be injured by acts of the foreign sovereign itself. Nationalistic trends in developing countries resulting from colonialism and perceived economic imperialism have long created concern among western governments over the security of the person and property of nationals operating abroad. Not surprisingly, the western view regarding treatment of aliens and their property differs somewhat from that embraced by the developing countries. Note that the host state's duties are owed not to the injured alien but to the alien's sovereign, which makes a claim through diplomatic channels for compensation or other remedy. Disputes that cannot be settled by negotiation may, if the parties consent, be referred to arbitration or to an international tribunal.

Protection of the Person

A person who resides or acquires property in a foreign country is subject to the laws or customs of that country. The United States and Western European countries have long asserted, however, that a claim against the host country may be justified if the foreign state's laws or conduct falls below a "minimum international standard." Although the elements of such a standard are disputed, it might include a prohibition against torturing or wrongfully killing or imprisoning the alien, looting or destroying his property, or maintaining excessively severe or unfair procedures or punishments.

In contrast, other states—including a number of Latin American, South American, Asian, and African countries—reject any minimum international standard, opting instead for a "national standard." Under this theory, aliens who establish themselves in a foreign country are entitled to the same rights of protection as nationals, but no more. Aliens are thus entitled to nondiscriminatory treatment, but otherwise consent to be treated as nationals.

Expropriation

In addition to protecting its citizens abroad, a country also has a significant stake in safeguarding the property and investments of its nationals in foreign countries. Although foreign investment takes many forms, foreign direct investment has had the greatest impact. Direct investment creates a sufficient ownership interest in a foreign asset or enterprise (usually twenty-five percent or more) to provide a significant degree of control.

The most important vehicle for foreign direct investment is the multinational corporation. Such enterprises engage in business activities that traverse national borders and take a variety of forms. A multinational corporation may initially export goods to markets abroad, then establish foreign sales organizations, and finally create foreign manufacturing facilities. Wholly-owned subsidiaries of the multinational parent often are used to oversee foreign operations.

Foreign direct investment poses significant risks,

---

12. Note that enforcement of sister-state judgments within the United States is guaranteed by the Full Faith and Credit Clause of the Constitution discussed in Chapter 2.

the most important of which is the risk of **nationalization,** the forced taking of the foreign assets by the host government. This power has been exercised more than 260 times in the last twenty years. Nationalism and resentment against foreign exploitation have, among other factors, prompted these actions. Although investment nationalizations primarily have occurred in underdeveloped countries whose economies are dominated by foreign corporations, western nations such as Canada and England also have nationalized commercial enterprises.

Legal Standard Governing Nationalization. International law generally recognizes a sovereign's right to nationalize foreign investments to promote the national welfare. The power generally is recognized as a basic incident of a state's sovereignty over its national resources and economic activities.[13] A taking in accordance with national law is known as an **expropriation;** an unlawful taking is a **confiscation.**

Western countries have long asserted the existence of a two-fold minimum international standard governing expropriation based upon customary international law. Under this standard, a lawful taking (1) must be for a "public purpose," and (2) must be accompanied by payment of "just compensation" or "prompt, adequate and effective compensation" for the investor's loss.[14] In contrast, the Soviet Union and other communist countries take the position that international law imposes no legal obligation to pay compensation upon taking of a foreign investor's property. The developing countries commonly take a middle position asserting that existence of a public purpose is an issue decided solely by the taking state and that any compensation payable is determined by all surrounding circumstances including the economic and political priorities of the taking state.

Disputes between states over expropriated property generally are settled by compromise, with the expropriating state paying part of the value of the property taken. The compromise payment usually covers all claims made by one state arising out of another's nationalization program. For example, since 1948, thirty-five countries have resolved expropriation claims through negotiated lump sum payments to the United States government. Customary international law generally imposes no duty upon a state to pursue expropriation claims of its nationals or to remit any recovery to the injured investors. Nevertheless, money received under such a blanket settlement, which usually represents only a fraction of the taken property's value, usually is distributed to former owners through an administrative tribunal, known in the United States as the Foreign Claims Settlement Commission.

Investment Protection. In order to attract new investment to developing countries, both developed and developing countries have taken steps to protect foreign investment. For example, many developing countries have constitutional provisions or statutes prohibiting expropriation for a stated period or guaranteeing a right to compensation. More important, a number of developing countries have entered into treaties with western nations including similar guarantees, which provide much greater certainty than customary international principles.

The United States, the United Kingdom, and other western countries also encourage foreign investment by insuring their nationals, for a premium, against certain political and other risks. In the United States, for example, insurance is available through the Overseas Private Investment Corporation (OPIC),[15] an agency of the United States under the policy guidance of the secretary of state. OPIC insures citizens of the United States and business entities substantially owned by United States' citizens against losses and business interruption caused by (1) a foreign government prohibiting conversion of foreign earnings into dollars or repatriation of investor capital, (2) expropriation or confiscation of assets including wrongful repudiation by the host government of its own contracts with the investor, and (3) war, revolution, insurrec-

---

13. United Nations General Assembly Resolution 3201 (1974).

14. Note that this standard is similar to that governing exercise of eminent domain power in the United States, discussed in Chapter 38.

15. Created by Public Law 91-175 as part of the Foreign Assistance Act of 1969, 22 U.S.C. §§2191-2200a.

tion, and civil strife.[16] An investor is charged an annual premium for OPIC insurance based upon the value of the investment and the type of risk (inconvertibility, expropriation, or war) covered. In addition to government insurance agencies such as OPIC, private insurers substantially are engaged in insuring a wide variety of international investment risks.

National Courts and Foreign Sovereignty

An investor who suffers an investment loss because of the act of a host state may attempt to recover through private civil litigation maintained in another country. Two legal theories, the doctrines of "sovereign immunity" and "act of state," may prevent or limit such litigation.

Sovereign Immunity

Sovereign immunity is a doctrine of international law under which domestic courts, in certain circumstances, will not exercise jurisdiction over a foreign state or its instrumentalities. The doctrine in the United States and elsewhere developed as a matter of grace or comity to promote good international relations. Traditionally, foreign sovereigns enjoyed complete immunity from suits in United States' courts. This rule of "absolute immunity" is still followed by many countries. In 1952, however, the State Department in the so-called "Tate Letter" adopted the "restrictive" or "qualified" theory of foreign sovereign immunity that also is accepted by a majority of Western European states. Under this theory "immunity is confined to suits involving the foreign sovereign's public acts, and does not extend to cases arising out of a foreign state's strictly commercial acts."[17]

This theory is now codified as a matter of federal law in the Foreign Sovereign Immunities Act of 1976.[18] The Act contains the legal standards governing claims of immunity in civil actions against a foreign state or its political subdivisions, agencies, or instrumentalities. The Act provides that a for-

eign state is normally immune from the jurisdiction of state and federal courts, subject to specified exceptions. These exceptions include, for example, actions in which the foreign state has waived its immunity and actions based upon the commercial activities of the foreign sovereign carried on in the United States or causing a direct effect in the United States. If an exception applies the foreign state is liable in the same manner and to the same extent as a private individual in the circumstances. Although cases may be maintained either in federal or state court, the sovereign defendant has the right to remove any civil action from a state to a federal court.

The governmental-commercial distinction embraced by the restrictive immunity approach is based upon the appropriateness of local court involvement in the dispute. Acts that can be performed only by states, such as expropriating property, involve sensitive international political issues, which should not be relegated to local courts for determination. In contrast, commercial activity, such as making contracts to purchase building materials, can and are performed both by states and individuals. In this context, the state is no different from any private litigant, and local courts are fully suited to resolve such disputes. In addition, refusal by local courts to hear such cases would impose needless hardship on the other party, who would be left without an effective remedy.

In determining which acts are commercial and which governmental, the Act states that "commercial activity" means either a regular course of commercial conduct or a particular commercial transaction or act. A commercial activity is one that an individual might carry on for profit, and is determined by the nature of the transaction or course of conduct rather than its purpose.[19]

The Act of State Doctrine

The **act of state doctrine,** like sovereign immunity, is a principle of judicial restraint designed in part to prevent the judiciary from embarrassing and interfering with the executive in the conduct of foreign affairs. The doctrine prevents the courts of one

---

16. 22 U.S.C. §2194.

17. *Verlinden B.V. v. Central Bank of Nigeria,* 103 S. Ct. 1962, 1968 (1983).

18. 28 U.S.C. §§1602-1611.

---

19. 28 U.S.C. §1603(d).

state from challenging the validity of public acts that a recognized foreign sovereign commits within its own territory. Unlike sovereign immunity (which applies when a person seeks to make the state a *party* to the litigation), the act of state doctrine often applies in suits between two private litigants in which action taken by a state is relevant. If applicable, it prevents a court from finding state action invalid, thus protecting a party who bases a claim or defense upon actions of a foreign state. For example, assume State X expropriates without compensation property belonging to Doaks, a citizen of State Y. The expropriation is the act of state. Subsequently, State X sells the expropriated property to Jones, a citizen of State Y. Doaks sues Jones and State X in State Y to recover the property or its value. If applicable, the act of state doctrine would provide a defense to Jones and State X to Doaks's claim. State X, of course, also may assert the doctrine of sovereign immunity.

Although most act of state litigation involves expropriation of alien-owned property within a foreign state, it also has been applied in foreign trade antitrust cases. The following case discusses the doctrine in that context.

Timberlane Lumber Co. v. Bank of America National Trust and Savings Association

549 F.2d 597 (9th Cir. 1976)

> Timberlane Lumber Co. is an Oregon partnership principally involved in the purchase and distribution of lumber at wholesale in the United States and the importation of lumber into the United States for sale and use. To provide an alternative source of lumber for delivery to its distribution system on the East Coast of the United States, Timberlane decided to develop forest land and milling facilities in Honduras. Timberlane's efforts to establish operations in Honduras were thwarted, according to Timberlane, by a conspiracy among officials of the Bank of America (Bank) and others, located in both the United States and Honduras, designed to maintain control of the Honduran lumber export business in the hands of a few select individuals financed and controlled by the Bank.
>
> Specifically, Timberlane alleged that it attempted

to procure a milling facility originally owned by the Lima family. The Lima business had encountered financial difficulty and its assets had passed to its creditors including one Casanova, the Bank of America, and a group of unpaid Lima employees. Timberlane purchased the employees' interest and reactivated the Lima mill. Although Timberlane made a substantial cash offer to the Bank to purchase its interest, the offer was refused. Instead the Bank and Casanova assigned their interests to Caminals, who went to court to enforce them. Caminals obtained an "embargo" on the property—a court-ordered attachment preventing its sale. The court also appointed a judicial officer known as an "interventor" to prevent any diminution in the value of the property. In enforcing the embargo, guards and troops were used to cripple and for a time completely shut down Timberlane's milling operation. In addition, the conspirators allegedly caused Timberlane's manager to be falsely arrested and were responsible for several defamatory articles about Timberlane in the Honduran press.

Timberlane sued Bank of America and various other defendants alleging violations of United States antitrust law, primarily §§1 and 2 of the Sherman Act. The district court dismissed the complaint under the act of state doctrine and for lack of subject matter jurisdiction. Timberlane appealed. In the following excerpt from the opinion the court of appeals considered whether the act of state doctrine barred Timberlane's claim.

Choy, Circuit Judge

. . . The classic enunciation of the act of state doctrine is found in *Underhill v. Hernandez*, [18 S. Ct. 83, 84 (1897)]:

> Every sovereign State is bound to respect the independence of every other sovereign State, and the courts of one country will not sit in judgment on the acts of the government of another done within its own territory.

From the beginning, this principle has been applied in foreign trade antitrust cases. In *American Banana Co. v. United Fruit Co.* [29 S. Ct. 511 (1909)], the first such case of significance, the American owner of a banana plantation caught in a border dispute between Panama and Costa Rica claimed that a competitor violated the Sherman Act by persuading the Costa Rican government to seize his lands. The act complained of would have required an adjudication of the legality of the Costa Rican seizure, an action which the Supreme Court said our courts could not challenge. . . .

The defendants argue—as the district court apparently held—that the injuries allegedly suffered by Timberlane resulted from acts of the Honduran government, principally in connection with the enforcement of the security interests in the [Lima mill], which American courts cannot review. Such an application of the act of state doctrine seems to us to be erroneous. Even if the *coup de grace* to Timberlane's enterprise in Honduras was applied by official authorities, we do not agree that the doctrine necessarily shelters these defendants or requires dismissal of the Timberlane action.

The leading modern statement of the act of state doctrine appears in *Banco Nacional de Cuba v. Sabbatino* [84 S. Ct. 923 (1964)]. . . . [T]he Court concluded that the doctrine was not compelled by the nature of sovereignty, by international law, or by the text of the Constitution. . . . Rather, it derives from the judiciary's concern for its possible interference with the conduct of foreign affairs by the political branches of the government. . . . The Court recognized that not every case is identical in its potential impact on our relations with other nations [and] . . . [w]hether forbearance by an American court in a given situation is advisable or appropriate depends upon the "balance of relevant considerations. . . . [T]he less important the implications of an issue are for our foreign relations, the weaker the justification for exclusivity in the political branches." [84 S. Ct. at 940.]

While we do not wish to impugn or question the nobility of a foreign nation's motivation, we are necessarily interested in the depth and nature of its interest. The *Restatement (Second) of Foreign Relations Law of the United States* §41 (1965) makes an important distinction on this basis in limiting the deference of American courts:

> [A] court in the United States . . . will refrain from examining the validity of an act of a foreign state by which that state has exercised its jurisdiction *to give effect to its public interests.* [Emphasis added.]

The "public interest" qualification is intentional and significant in the context of Timberlane's action, as a comment to §41 makes plain:

> *Comment d. Nature of act of state.* An "act of state" as the term is used in this Title involves the public interests of a state as a state, as distinct from its interest in providing the means of adjudicating disputes or claims that arise within its territory. . . . A judgment of a court may be an act of state. Usually it is not, because it involves the interests of private litigants or because court adjudication is not the usual way in which the state exercises its jurisdiction to give effect to public interests. . .

On the basis of the foregoing analysis, we conclude that the court below erred in dismissing the instant suit. . . . The actions of the Honduran government that are involved here—including the application by its courts and their agents of the Honduran laws concerning security interests and the protection of the underlying property against diminution . . . consisted of judicial proceedings which were initiated by Caminals, a private party and one of the alleged co-conspirators, not by the Honduran government itself. . . . Timberlane does not seek to name Honduras or any Honduran officer as a defendant or co-conspirator, nor does it challenge Honduran policy or sovereignty in any fashion that appears on its face to hold any threat to relations between Honduras and the United States. In fact, there is no indication that the actions of the Honduran court and authorities reflected a sovereign decision that Timberlane's efforts should be crippled or that trade with the United States should be restrained. . . . Moreover, . . . plaintiffs here apparently complain of additional agreements and actions which are totally unrelated to the Honduran government. These separate activities would clearly be unprotected even if procurement of a Honduran act of state were one part of defendants' overall scheme. . . .

Under these circumstances, it is clear that the "act of state" doctrine does not require dismissal of the Timberlane action. . . .

We, therefore, vacate the dismissal and remand the Timberlane action.

SUMMARY

1. International law is the system of law governing the relationship among states. Unlike a state's internal or national law, which may be enforced in an obligatory judicial forum whose judgments are enforceable by executive authority, international law is characterized by lack of binding sanctions.

2. International law is derived primarily from (1) treaties, (2) custom, (3) general principles of law, and (4) judicial decisions and writing of legal commentators.

3. International organizations created by treaty serve important functions in international affairs, including peace-keeping and regulation and development of economic and commercial activities. Some important international organizations include the United Nations (including its judicial arm, the International Court of Justice), the General Agreement on Tariffs and Trade, and the European Economic Community, or Common Market.

4. In the United States, power to regulate foreign commerce and conduct foreign affairs rests exclusively with the federal government, not the states. In this external sphere the president, the chief of the executive branch, is the representative of the United States.

5. In conducting foreign affairs, the president commonly acts through treaties or executive agreements. Although treaties must be approved by two-thirds vote of the Senate, executive agreements require no Senate approval. Although treaties enjoy a status equal to federal statutes (and thus take priority over inconsistent state legislation), treaties must comply with the provisions of the United States Constitution.

6. A national court may be presented with a case involving foreign citizens or property or events occurring in a foreign country. Various theories of international and national law operate to limit the jurisdiction of national courts in criminal and civil cases.

7. Because of uncertainty regarding the substantive and procedural laws of various countries and doubt regarding enforceability of foreign judgments, parties to international business transactions often use contractual provisions to govern any disputes arising out of their agreement. Common examples are arbitration, choice of forum, and choice of law clauses.

8. Individuals or business entities living or investing abroad may be harmed by acts of the foreign government. Although a foreign national living abroad is subject to foreign law, western states have long asserted that treatment of aliens must meet a "minimum international standard." In contrast, other countries assert that a "na-

tional" standard is appropriate under which aliens are entitled to the same rights of protection as nationals, but no more.

9. In addition to protecting its citizens abroad, a country also has a stake in safeguarding property and investments of its nationals in foreign countries. Nevertheless, international law generally recognizes a sovereign's right to nationalize or expropriate foreign investment to promote the national welfare. Western countries assert that international law requires that any taking (1) must be for a public purpose, and (2) must be accompanied by prompt and just compensation of the owner. Other countries impose a more limited legal obligation upon the expropriating country. The expropriation risk may be reduced by treaty or by private or public insurance.

10. A private litigant may attempt to sue a foreign state or question an act of a foreign state in a national court. The national court may refuse to exercise jurisdiction in such a case under the doctrines of "sovereign immunity" or "act of state." These doctrines are designed in part to prevent the judiciary from embarrassing and interfering with the executive in the conduct of foreign affairs.

KEY TERMS

international law	expropriation
private international law	confiscation
treaty	sovereign immunity
nationalization	act of state doctrine

QUESTIONS AND PROBLEMS

57-1 The California Buy American Act requires that contracts for the construction of public works or the purchase of materials for public use be awarded only to persons who will agree to use or supply materials which have been manufactured in the United States. Ducommun, Inc. submitted a bid to the city of Los Angeles for steel beams to be used in constructing a bridge. Though Ducommun's bid was lowest, the city rejected it because it was based upon steel to be manufactured in Japan. Ducommun sued the city alleging that the statute is unconstitutional. What is the basis of Ducommun's claim? Should Ducommun prevail?

57-2 Asakura, a Japanese citizen, resides in Seattle,

Washington, and has been engaged in business there as a pawnbroker since 1975. In 1985, the city passed an ordinance requiring licensing of pawnbrokers and providing that "no license shall be granted unless the applicant is a citizen of the United States." A treaty between the United States and Japan provides "The citizens or subjects of each of the high contracting parties shall have liberty to enter, travel and reside in the territories of the other to carry on trade, . . . and generally to do anything incident to or necessary for trade upon the same terms as native citizens or subjects, submitting themselves to the laws and regulations there established." Does the statute violate the treaty? If so, should it be invalidated? On what grounds?

57-3 Sumitomo Shoji America, Inc., is a New York corporation and a wholly owned subsidiary of a Japanese general trading company. Lisa Avagliano, a secretarial employee of Sumitomo and a United States citizen, sued Sumitomo in federal district court, claiming that its alleged practice of hiring only male Japanese citizens to fill executive, managerial, and sales positions violated Title VII of the Civil Rights Act of 1964. Sumitomo moved to dismiss the complaint on the ground that its practices were protected under Art. VIII(1) of the Friendship, Commerce and Navigation Treaty between the United States and Japan. Article VIII(1) provides that the "companies of either Party shall be permitted to engage, within the territories of the other Party, accountants and other technical experts, executive personnel, attorneys, agents and other specialists of their choice." The primary purpose of the provision was to give corporations of each signatory legal status in the territory of the other party and to allow them to conduct business in the other country on a comparable basis with domestic firms. Should the district court dismiss the complaint? Explain.

57-4 A French merchant ship collided with a Turkish merchant ship on the high seas. The Turkish ship sank and several Turkish citizens were drowned. The accident was caused by criminal negligence of Lieutenant Demons, an officer on the French ship. When the French ship docked in Turkey, Turkish police arrested him. Does France have jurisdiction to try Lieutenant Demons? On what basis? Does Turkey have jurisdiction to try Lieutenant Demons? On what basis? Does the United States have jurisdiction to try Lieutenant Demons? On what basis?

57-5 On March 17, 1975, Nigeria and Ipitrade International entered into a written commercial contract for the purchase and sale of cement. By entering into the contract, Nigeria expressly agreed that the construction, validity, and performance of the contract would be governed by the laws of Switzerland and that any disputes arising under the contract would be submitted to arbitration by the International Chamber of Commerce, Paris, France. During 1975 and 1976 various disputes arose with respect to the contract and on May 12, 1976, Ipitrade filed a demand for arbitration with the Secretariat of the Court of Arbitration of the International Chamber of Commerce. Thereafter, an arbitration proceeding was conducted in which the Federal Republic of Nigeria refused to participate, relying on the legal defense of sovereign immunity. Is Nigeria correct? Explain.

57-6 The Shanghai-Nanking Railway Administration, an official agency of the Republic of China, established in 1948 a $200,000 bank account in National City Bank of New York. Subsequently, China sought to withdraw the funds but National refused to pay. China sued National in United States federal district court to recover the money. National asserted a counterclaim against China seeking a judgment for $1.6 million on defaulted treasury notes issued by China owned by the bank. China asserted that it was immune from suit on the counterclaim under principles of sovereign immunity. Is China correct?

57-7 During the early 1900s, American corporations acquired interests in copper properties in Chile. By the early 1970s, two companies—the Anaconda Company and Kennecott Copper Corporation—held vast stakes in these properties. In 1971, the Chilean government expropriated the mining assets of both companies. In computing the compensation due Kennecott, Chile contended that compensation need be paid only for plant and equipment taken, not for the vast mineral deposits in place. President Salvadore Allende, however, subsequently determined that "excess profits" previously withdrawn by Kennecott offset any compensation that might otherwise have been paid to Kennecott on account of the nationalization. Kennecott then filed suit in five European countries against various buyers of Chilean copper, requesting that the court order the buyers to pay amounts owed for the copper to Kennecott rather than the Chilean government. What factors should the European courts consider in determining whether to grant Kennecott's request? Should Kennecott prevail?

57-8 In addition to the act of state issue, a basic question in the *Timberlane* case excerpted in the text was whether United States antitrust law should apply to the controversy. Apply the Foreign Trade Antitrust Improvements Act of 1982 to determine whether the court should exercise jurisdiction. In making your determination note that (1) Honduras has no antitrust law and competitors are allowed to allocate markets, and restrict price or output, and (2) during the period in question Honduran lumber constituted approximately five percent of total United States lumber imports. Consider also the following analysis suggested by the *Timberlane* court:

The elements to be weighed include the degree of conflict with foreign law or policy, the nationality or allegiance of the parties and the locations or principal places of business of corporations, the extent to which enforcement by either state can be expected to achieve compliance, the relative significance of effects on the United States as compared with those elsewhere, the extent to which there is explicit purpose to harm or affect American commerce, the foreseeability of such effect, and the relative importance to the violations charged of conduct within the United States as compared with conduct abroad. (549 F.2d at 614.)

Liability of Accountants for Negligence: How Can We Tell the Best Rule?

Richard A. Epstein

Accountant's liability to third parties for negligence is one of the most hotly contested issues in modern business law, as the sharp division of opinion between the New York Court, both in *Ultramares* and *Credit Alliance,* and the New Jersey Court in *Rosenblum* reveals. Why does this impasse arise and how might it be resolved?

Prevention and compensation are the two major functions most frequently assigned to the tort law. Prevention is served because the threat of liability induces firms to take care to avoid inflicting losses on others. Compensation is achieved by having negligent defendants pay injured plaintiffs. Satisfying both objectives simultaneously generally works to improve the overall efficiency of the system. Loss prevention ensures that there is more wealth to go around, while loss spreading, coupled with insurance, spares individual victims the sting of large losses. It is hard to conceive of any legal system ignoring these twin considerations.

At first glance, these two goals seem to make the case of accountants' liability for negligence easy. If the accountant was negligent, then by definition the loss to investors who relied on their statements could have been prevented at reasonable cost. Similarly, any crushing losses could be passed on by price increases or funded by insurance. The New Jersey Court in *Rosenblum* adopted just this view when it jettisoned the traditional privity rule, which barred the accountant's liability to anyone other than his own client. That court held that privity made no more sense for words than for things. Privity had long been abandoned in product liability cases. Now the accountants' cases have been brought into line.

This last comparison gives us reason to pause: the remorseless expansion of product liability law

has wrought serious, unintended consequences in both product and insurance markets, leading to widespread calls for legislative reform. Debates over accountants' liability have not reached the same fever pitch, but reputable accounting firms are united in their opposition to the expansion of liability *Rosenblum* demands. If these rules were efficient, why the opposition? The accountant's additional liabilities could be more than offset by the higher fees collected from clients. The clients in turn could recoup their additional costs by obtaining a lower interest rates on loans or a higher price on the sale of stock or assets. After all, the accountant's liability for faulty audits should reduce the risk to any prospective lender or purchaser, a benefit worth paying for. Yet opposition persists.

To see why, it is important to understand the total environment in which the accountant functions. The accountant must charge a fee sufficient to cover the cost of doing business, with allowance for a normal profit. The increased cost of loss prevention and insurance under an expanded negligence rule are two relevant components of cost. In setting his fee therefore the accountant must have some sense of the uses to be made of his audit statements. It makes a big difference whether the client wants $10,000 or $1,000,000 in loans. When the use of the audit statement is not fixed or known in advance, it is difficult to set the proper fee. Without the privity limitation, the accounting firm finds cannot reliably estimate its potential exposure for loss. The accountant's insurer faces the identical problem in trying to set its own premium. Privity

Richard A. Epstein is the James Parker Hall Professor of Law, The University of Chicago, and Editor, Journal of Legal Studies.

has one unsuspected virtue. It aids in the quantification of relevant business risks.

Next it is necessary to define the events for which compensation is payable. Negligence is at best an uncertain standard now that customary industry standards are no longer dispositive. The error rate in individual cases will be high, and legal fees will necessarily increase both with the uncertainty of the outcome and the size of the stakes. Think only of what could happen when the auditor of a bankrupt public power system is sued for billions by hundreds of disappointed bondholders. The potential of huge losses always calls for an exacting, but ad hoc, review. After the fact, a jury might find that no matter how much the accountant did, it still did not do enough. These litigation and error costs must be factored back into the overall situation. Yet unlike the payment of dollars from accountant to bondholders, these costs provide neither client nor bondholders with any gain. Rather these costs drive a wedge between what the accountant pays and the third-party investor collects. From the whole picture, we have no obvious way of telling whether the price of negligence liability is too high, too low, or just right: does the negligence system create superior incentives that justify its high administrative and error costs. The implicit guess of the New Jersey Court was that good incentives dominated administrative costs. The sense of the New York Court was that they did not. Who's right.

Try this thought experiment. Assume that all three parties to the drama—the client, lender or purchaser, and accountant—could be placed in a single closed room where they are asked to allocate by agreement any future risk of loss. Privity is no longer an issue, for by hypothesis the accountant has entered into an agreement with the prospective lender or purchaser. What will that agreement provide? This question is instructive because it forces the third-party to decide before the fact whether it is worth paying the additional costs necessary to fund the contingent liability for negligent misrepresentation under the New Jersey rule.

Ordinary commercial contracts typically contain language limiting the defendant's liability for consequential damages. Complex negligence principles are replaced with strict liability rules, coupled with very limited damages. (See my discussion of *Hadley v. Baxendale,* supra at 358 and 359) One point of low damages is to induce the plaintiff (who still bears part of the loss even when he or she recovers) also to take precautions against the loss. That opportunity, while not much discussed in the cases, surely exists here. Lenders and buyers are sophisticated parties, typically represented by their own accountants. They able to obtain insurance against some risks, and to diversify their purchases and loans to reduce the risks that remain. Loss prevention rests as much on them as on the accountants for sellers and borrowers. In many contexts joint care by all parties may be desired.

It is difficult in the abstract, however, to determine the *relative* capacities of the parties to avoid and spread loss. No single rule can perfectly handle the wide variation among cases. No one therefore can speak with great confidence if forced to choose across the board between the New York and the New Jersey rules. That is why the disagreement persists. In a critical sense, however, the courts have asked the wrong question. The proper issue is not how courts should impose liability on accountants, but how private parties might allocate loss by agreement.

One possible way to encourage the contract solution is to allow auditors to place conspicuous disclaimers on their audit statements. The auditor would not find that decision an easy one, because the stronger the disclaimer, the less useful the statement to the client, and the lower the accountant's fee. The auditor therefore will have to decide how to frame that disclaimer: liability for fraud only?, for negligence? liability, but only for a certain percentage of loss?, liability only for out-of-pocket expenses? If a buyer wants greater protection, he can now negotiate directly with the auditor in order to purchase that protection. It is far easier for the prospective purchaser to seek out a known auditor than it is for an auditor to seek out each of many unidentified possible purchasers. The emerging pattern of disclaimers and contracts in the marketplace would then allow us to decide whether the lion's share of the truth lay with the New York Court, the New Jersey Court, or as seems likely, somewhere in between.

abandonment 1. in landlord-tenant law, the wrongful unilateral act of the tenant in vacating the premises without further intent to abide by terms of the lease. 2. the intentional, permanent, and absolute relinquishment of all interest in an item of personal property by the owner.

abatement doctrine that operates to reduce or extinguish a beneficiary's share when there is insufficient property in a decedent's estate to satisfy all gifts provided in the will after creditor's claims, taxes, and administrative expenses have been paid.

abstract of title a chronological summary of the contents of all recorded instruments pertaining to a particular tract of land.

abuse of process the use of a legal process to accomplish a purpose for which it was neither designed nor intended.

acceleration clause contractual clause providing that upon occurrence of a given contingency (such as default in one or more installments in a promissory note), all future installments are accelerated and become immediately due and payable, or payable on a date sooner than originally agreed.

acceptance 1. in commercial paper, the drawee's signed engagement to honor (pay) a draft as presented. See UCC §3-410(1). 2. in general contract law, the act by which an offeree manifests assent to the terms of an offer in the manner prescribed by the offeror. 3. in sales law, the buyer's indication of an intent to retain (rather than reject and return) goods delivered by a seller. See UCC §2-606.

acceptor a drawee who accepts a draft.

accession process by which value in the form of labor or property, or both, is added to tangible personal property.

accommodation (uncompensated or gratuitous) surety a surety that is not principally engaged in entering into suretyship contracts for a fee. An accommodation surety's contracts are occasional and incidental to other business. See *compensated (corporate) surety.*

accommodation party a person who signs an instrument in any capacity (maker, indorser, acceptor) for the purpose of lending his or her name or credit to another party to the instrument. See UCC §3-415(1).

accord and satisfaction the creation and performance of a compromise agreement used to settle a preexisting, usually disputed or unliquidated, obligation. Specifically, an accord is a contract in which a party entitled to a performance promises to accept an alternative stated performance in full satisfaction of the original duty owed. Satisfaction is the performance of the accord agreement.

account any right to payment for goods sold (or to be sold) or for services rendered (or to be rendered) that is not evidenced by either an instrument or chattel paper. See UCC §9-106.

account debtor a person obligated on an account, chattel paper, or general intangible. See UCC §9-105(1)(a).

accounting in partnership law, an equitable proceeding in which the court directs a comprehensive investigation of the partners' and partnership transactions in order to adjudicate the rights of various partners.

acknowledgment formal witnessing of the signing of an instrument, such as a deed, by a public officer such as a notary public or justice of the peace of the signer's declaration that the execution is his or her voluntary act.

act of state doctrine doctrine of judicial restraint designed in part to prevent the judiciary from embarrassing and interfering with the executive in the conduct of foreign affairs. The doctrine prevents the courts of one state from challenging the validity of public acts that a recognized foreign sovereign state commits within its own territory.

ademption by extinction   a doctrine of the law of wills that may prevent a beneficiary from receiving property provided for him or her in the will. Ademption by extinction occurs when the subject matter of the gift is not in the testator's estate at the time of death. See *ademption by satisfaction.*

ademption by satisfaction   A doctrine of the law of wills that may prevent a beneficiary from receiving property provided for him or her in the will. Ademption by satisfaction occurs when the testator, after execution of the will but during his or her lifetime, makes a gift of property to a beneficiary under the will, that serves in lieu of the bequest or devise. See *advancement.*

adequate assurance of due performance   in contract and sales law, when "reasonable grounds for insecurity" arise with respect to the performance of either party, the other party may demand adequate assurance of due performance and, until he or she receives such assurance, may suspend any performance for which he or she has not already received the agreed return. What constitutes adequate assurance is a question of fact, depending upon the circumstances of the case. The grounds for insecurity need only be "reasonable," not actual. See UCC §2-609.

adhesion contract   a standardized form contract in which one party dictates many of the contract terms to the other (the adhering party).

administrative order   judgment that terminates an administrative hearing.

Administrative Procedure Act   comprehensive federal statute that sets forth procedures federal administrative agencies must follow when engaging in rulemaking or adjudication and that regulates dissemination of information gathered by agencies.

administrative search   usually a governmental civil inspection of a residential or commercial building to determine compliance with fire, health, and other safety codes.

administrator (administratrix)   a person appointed by a probate court to fulfill an executor's functions in an intestate estate.

advancement   doctrine that operates to reduce the amount of property that otherwise would pass to an heir if a person dies intestate. It is analogous to the doctrine of ademption by satisfaction applied when the decedent leaves a will. See *intestate, ademption by satisfaction.*

adverse possession   a method of acquiring title to real property through operation of the statute of limitations.

adverse possessor   a person wrongfully possessing real property who may acquire title through the operation of the adverse possession doctrine. See *adverse possession.*

affirm   action of an appellate court that confirms the judgment of a lower court.

affirmative action programs   programs adopted to encourage hiring women or members of minority groups that are underrepresented in the company or institution.

affirmative covenant   in property law, a covenant that requires the promisor (covenantor) to do something on his or her land, such as building or maintaining a party wall, irrigation or drainage ditch, or structure such as a dam or bridge. See *covenant.*

affirmative defense   facts that the law recognizes as a bar to the plaintiff's claim if proven by the defendant. Examples include expiration of the status of limitation, discharge of the claim in bankruptcy, or prior adjudication of the claim.

after-acquired property clause   clause that can be included in a security agreement, which provides that any or all obligations covered by the security agreement are to be secured by after-acquired collateral. See UCC §9-204(1).

Age Discrimination in Employment Act   federal statute enacted in 1967 prohibiting employment discrimination against persons over forty years of age.

agency   a consensual fiduciary relationship in which one party, or agent, agrees to act on behalf of and under the control of another, known as the principal.

agency coupled with an interest   see *power as given security.*

agency shop   agreement requiring employees who do not join the union to pay for the union's services through fees that usually are equivalent to members' dues and fees.

agent   see *agency.*

agreed equivalents   see *divisibility.*

airbill   a document of title serving for air transportation as a bill of lading does for marine or rail transportation. See *bill of lading, document of title.* See UCC §1-201(6).

aleatory promise   a contractual promise made conditional upon the occurrence or nonoccurrence of an uncertain or fortuitous event.

alteration   in commercial paper law, a change in the terms of an instrument by the holder. See *material alteration.*

allonge   in commercial paper, a separate paper, used for indorsements when prior indorsements have exhausted the space on the back of an instrument. An allonge must be firmly affixed and an integral part of the instrument. See *indorsement.* See UCC §3-202(2).

allowed claim   in a bankruptcy case, a claim that participates in the distribution of the estate's assets.

ancillary restraint   a promise in restraint of trade made as part of an otherwise valid transaction, such as a sale of a business. See *restraint of trade, naked restraint.*

annexor   in the law of fixtures, the person who places the chattel on real estate.

annual percentage rate (APR)   under the Truth-in-Lending Act, the finance charge on an annual basis expressed as a percentage of the amount of credit.

answer   the pleading in a civil case in which a defendant replies to each allegation of a complaint.

antecedent debt   an old debt, one existing before the

negotiation of an instrument, or transfer of money or other property to satisfy it.

anticipatory repudiation a repudiation of a contractual duty that occurs before the repudiating party commits a breach by nonperformance. See *repudiation.*

antitrust laws state and federal laws designed to promote competition and prevent monopoly.

apparent authority conduct of the principal toward third parties who deal with the agent or purported agent, creating authority in the agent to bind the principal.

appellant party to a lawsuit seeking an appeal.

appellate jurisdiction jurisdiction possessed by courts that are empowered to review cases that have been tried by a court of original jurisdiction.

appellee in an appeal, the party against whom an appeal is taken.

arbitration method of resolving disputes in which an objective third party proposes a resolution that the two parties are bound by law to accept.

arraignment in criminal law, a hearing before the court at which the indictment or information is read to the defendant.

artificial persons entities such as corporations that are treated in law as persons. See *natural person.*

artisan a skilled worker, such as a tailor, carpenter, or auto mechanic, in a trade requiring manual dexterity.

artisan's lien the right of an artisan to retain possession of an object repaired or worked upon until receipt of payment for the work performed.

assignee in a contract assignment, the person to whom rights are transferred.

assignment the transfer of the rights under a contract to a third party. The term is sometimes used to designate both a transfer of rights and a delegation of duties under the contract.

assignment for the benefit of creditors the transfer of all nonexempt assets by a debtor to an assignee or trustee, who liquidates the assets and distributes the proceeds to the debtor's creditors.

assignment of lease the transfer by the tenant of his or her entire remaining interest under the lease.

assignor in a contract assignment, the person transferring rights under the contract.

association a voluntary collection, uniting, or coming together of two or more persons for a certain purpose. The term connotes both voluntariness and intent to be a member of an association. See, for example, *partnership.*

assumed business name statute a state law requiring that a certificate listing the names and addresses of persons conducting business under an assumed name or trade name be filed in the public records.

assumption of the risk in tort law, a defense to liability based on the plaintiff's consent (express or implied) to encounter a known unreasonable danger created by the defendant's conduct.

attachment 1. in secured transactions law, the process

making the security interest effective between the immediate parties: the debtor and secured party. See UCC §9-203. 2. in debtor-creditor law, a prejudgment remedy, generally governed by statute, designed to reach assets in the hands of the debtor and hold them to assure their availability if and when the creditor obtains a judgment.

attempt in criminal law, act or acts committed by the defendant with the intent to commit a crime, constituting a substantial step toward the commission of that crime.

attestation the act of witnessing the execution of a written instrument, at the request of the person making it, and subscribing it as a witness.

attestation clause a clause in a will, signed by the witnesses, stating that the statutory formalities necessary for proper execution have been observed.

attorney a person who has been authorized by one or more states to practice law on behalf of clients.

attorney's opinion a formal written opinion regarding the marketability of title to real property that is rendered by an attorney after examining the title as disclosed by an abstract of title.

attractive nuisance doctrine rule of tort law stating the conditions under which a possessor of land is liable for injury to trespassing children. See also *turnable doctrine.*

auction a public sale of property (either real or personal) to the highest bidder by an auctioneer who is authorized or licensed by law to conduct such sales.

authority in agency law, the power of an agent to bind the principal to a contract, derived from the principal's directions or instructions to the agent about the extent of the agent's power.

automatic stay a legal consequence of filing a bankruptcy petition that prevents further efforts by creditors to collect their debts.

badges of fraud in the law of fraudulent conveyances, circumstantial criteria used to distinguish fraudulent from nonfraudulent transfers of assets.

bail a security or obligation given by an accused person or another to obtain the accused's release from custody.

bailee in a bailment, a person in rightful possession of goods of another.

bailee's lien a lien granted to carriers and warehousemen allowing them to retain possession of goods entrusted to them pending payment for the shipment or storage charges. See UCC §§7-209, 7-210, 7-307, 7-308.

bailment the rightful possession of goods by someone who is not the owner.

bailor in a bailment, a person originally in possession of goods who delivers them to another (the bailee) for a specified purpose without transfer of title.

banking day that part of any day on which a bank is

open to the public to perform substantially all of its banking functions. See UCC §4-104(1)(c).

bankruptcy court a unit of the federal district court created to hear bankruptcy cases.

bankruptcy judge a judge appointed to a bankruptcy court to hear bankruptcy cases. Jurisdictional powers of bankruptcy judges are limited and their decisions are subject to review by the federal district court.

bargain an agreement to exchange a promise for a promise or a promise for a performance. Most agreements recognized as contracts are bargains. See *contract*.

bargained-for exchange in contract law, a performance or return promise is "bargained for" if it is sought by the promisor in exchange for his promise, and is given by the promisee in exchange for that promise.

battery a harmful or offensive contact with a person that is intended by the actor to cause such a contact.

bearer A person in possession of an instrument, document of title, or certificated security payable to bearer or indorsed in blank. See UCC §1-201(5).

bearer paper in the law of commercial paper, an instrument payable to bearer or indorsed in blank. See UCC §3-111. See *order paper*.

beneficiary in contract law, a person other than the promisee who will be benefited by performance of a promise. See *trust*.

benefit of the bargain in contract law, after breach, the injured promisee receives the "benefit of the bargain" if the judicial relief awarded places him or her in as good a position as he or she would have obtained had the contract been performed as agreed. See *expectation interest*.

bequest a term generally describing any form of personal property passing by will.

bilateral contract contract involving a promise in exchange for a return promise. A bilateral contract therefore involves at least two promises in which each party is both simultaneously a promisor and a promisee. See *unilateral contract*.

bill of lading a document evidencing receipt of goods for shipment issued by a person engaged in the business of transporting or forwarding goods. See UCC §1-201(6).

blank indorsement an indorsement that specifies no particular indorsee and frequently consists of the indorser's signature alone. See *indorsement*.

blue-sky laws state laws regulating the distribution and sale of securities designed primarily to prevent fraud.

bona fide occupational qualification (BFOQ) exception to Title VII's prohibition against employment discrimination. If religion, sex, or national origin is a bona fide occupational qualification reasonably necessary to the normal operation of a particular business, the employer may use these criteria for hiring, training, or promotion. See *Title VII*.

bond 1. in corporation law, an obligation secured by a lien or mortgage upon specific corporate property. 2. in suretyship law, a contract executed by a compensated surety.

booking in criminal law, an administrative procedure carried out after the arrest of a suspect in which the suspect's name, time of arrest, and alleged crime are recorded in police records.

breach of contract generally, failure to perform a contract once any conditions to a party's duty have occurred. Breach may occur either by nonperformance of a duty when performance is due, or by repudiation of the duty prior to that time.

brief written document summarizing the legal errors that the appellant alleges occurred at trial and for which he or she requests review by the appellate court.

broker an agent empowered to make or procure contracts on his or her principal's behalf for compensation, usually called a commission.

bulk transfer any transfer in bulk and not in the ordinary course of the transferor's business of a major part of the materials, supplies, merchandise, or other inventory of an enterprise subject to UCC Article 6. See UCC §6-102(1).

burden of proof the duty or obligation to prove the disputed fact or facts constituting a cause of action or affirmative defense.

business corporation corporation organized to carry on a definite business for profit. See also *corporation*.

business invitee a person invited to enter or remain on another's land for purposes connected with business dealings with the possessor of the land.

business judgment rule rule of corporation law under which officers and directors have no liability for honest, unbiased transactions undertaken with reasonable care, even if it later appears that the act was ill-advised or mistaken.

buyer in the ordinary course of business a person who, in good faith and without knowledge that the sale to him or her is in violation of the ownership rights or security interest of a third party in the goods, buys in ordinary course from a person–not including a pawnbroker–in the business of selling goods of that kind. See UCC §1-201(9).

bylaws a set of rules governing a corporation's internal affairs. See *corporation*.

C. & F. term term indicating that the price of goods includes the cost of the goods and freight to the named destination. See UCC §2-320.

C.I.F. term term indicating that the price of goods includes, in a lump sum, the cost of the goods, the insurance, and the freight to the named destination. See UCC §2-320.

cancellation occurs when either party puts an end to a sales contract because of breach by the other party. See UCC §2-106(4).

capacity the ability of a person to create or enter into a legal relationship.

cartel an agreement among competitors to restrict output and raise prices.

cashier's check a check drawn by the issuing bank upon itself. See *check*.

cause of action a fact or set of facts that, if proven, entitle a plaintiff to judicial relief. Statutory law and the common law establish the elements of a cause of action.

cease and desist order order issued by an administrative law judge or administrative agency that commands a wrongdoer to stop an illegal practice. A cease and desist order provides injunctive relief by preventing or restraining unlawful conduct.

certificate of deposit an instrument that is an acknowledgment by a bank of the receipt of money with a promise to repay it. See UCC §3-104(2)(c).

certificated securities corporate debt or equity securities evidenced by a document, such as a stock certificate. See UCC §8-102(1). See also *uncertificated securities*.

certification acceptance of a check by the drawee bank. Certification occurs when an authorized representative of a bank signs or stamps language on the face of a check to indicate the bank's undertaking to pay. See UCC §3-411.

certification mark a mark attesting to a specified quality, material, or origin from a certain region.

chain of title the succession of deeds, wills, and other instruments by which the ownership of property can be traced back to the original patent or deed from a governmental authority to the first private owner.

charging order device through which a judgment creditor can reach a debtor partner's interest in the partnership involuntarily to satisfy an unpaid debt.

charitable trust trust in which the property is devoted in charitable purposes beneficial to the community in favor of a class of beneficiaries who are not specifically designated. See *trust*.

chattel an article of personal property. The term is usually used to describe tangible, movable objects, such as automobiles.

chattel paper a writing or writings that evidence both an obligation to pay money and a security interest in or a lease of specific goods. See UCC §9-105(1)(b).

check a draft drawn on a bank and payable on demand. See UCC §3-104(2)(b).

check collection process the process by which a check is transmitted and presented to the drawee, paid, and the proceeds transferred and credited to the depositor's account.

chose thing.

choses in action property rights for intangible things that can be claimed or enforced by action, not by taking physical possession; intangible personal property. See *choses in possession*.

choses in possession property rights in tangible physical objects; goods. See *choses in action*.

civil law law that establishes standards of conduct for relations between individuals and provides compensation to injured parties; areas of law other than criminal law. See *criminal law*.

claim 1. in bankruptcy law, any right to payment or to receive any equitable remedy, such as specific performance of a contract. 2. in commercial paper, a term referring to a claim of ownership of the instrument asserted against a holder either by a prior holder or a third party not a holder.

class action lawsuit involving numerous plaintiffs in which one or more persons file suit on their own behalf and on behalf of all persons (the class) having claims based on common issues of fact and law.

Clayton Act federal antitrust law enacted in 1914 prohibiting certain types of price discrimination, certain sales made on condition that the buyer not deal with seller's competitors, certain corporate mergers, and certain interlocking directorates. See *Sherman Act*.

Clean Air Act federal statute establishing the current framework for regulating air pollution.

Clean Water Act federal statute establishing the regulatory framework for water pollution control.

clearing house an association of banks or other payors regularly clearing items. See UCC §4-104(1)(d).

closed-end credit credit arrangement involving a fixed amount of debt and a specified repayment date.

closed shop illegal agreement under federal labor law by which an employer agrees to hire only members of a union.

closely-held corporation corporation whose shares are owned by one shareholder or a closely knit group of shareholders. See also *corporation*.

codicil an addition or supplement to a will that may add to, subtract from, modify, or revoke provisions of an existing will.

cognovit (confession of judgment) clause a term in an original contract creating a debt, such as a lease or promissory note, which authorizes the creditor to obtain a judgment against the debtor upon default without notice to the debtor or a hearing.

collateral in a secured transaction, property in which the secured party's security interest exists. See UCC §9-105(1)(c).

collateral contract doctrine doctrine providing that the parol evidence rule does not bar admission of evidence of an agreement not within the scope of a completely integrated writing. In other words, the parol evidence rule does not bar proof of a related agreement that is neither inconsistent with nor part of the integrated contract.

collateral estoppel doctrine providing that issues actually decided in one lawsuit are conclusively determined for later lawsuits between the same parties involving different causes of action.

collecting bank   any bank handling checks for collection except the payor bank. See UCC §4-105(d).

collection guaranteed   words added to a signature on a negotiable instrument meaning that if the instrument is not paid when due, the signer will pay, but only if the holder exhausts legal remedies against the primary party, or circumstances indicate that proceeding against the primary party would be useless. See UCC §3-416.

collective bargaining   negotiations between the employer and a union representing the employees.

collective-bargaining contract   a formal agreement between an employer and labor union covering wages, hours, and conditions of employment secured by collective bargaining.

collective mark   a trademark or service mark used by members of a collective group to identify that its goods or services are produced by members of the group.

color of title   a person who possesses land under an instrument that purports to pass title but which is ineffective to operate as a conveyance is said to possess under color of title.

Commerce Clause   clause of the Constitution granting Congress the power to regulate commerce with foreign nations, among the states, and with the Indian tribes.

commercial credit   credit that is extended for businesses.

commercial speech   expression for business purposes, such as an advertisement for a product or service.

common carrier   a person who undertakes or holds out to perform carriage, for hire, for all those who apply.

common law   rules and principles of law embodied in cases previously decided by the courts.

common law liens   liens created by judicial decision that allow creditors such as landlords, bailees, and innkeepers to retain possession of a debtor's property until the debt is paid.

common shares   shares representing the residual ownership interest in a coporation.

common stem ownership   fixture dispute in which the annexor (person placing the chattel on the real estate) owns both the chattel and the land to which it is annexed.

community property doctrine   doctrine in which husband and wife are treated as equal co-owners of property acquired with the earnings of either during the marriage without regard to which spouse actually supports the family.

comparative fault   in products liability cases based on strict liability, the assignment of responsibility and liability for damage in direct proportion to the degree of fault of each of the parties.

comparative negligence   rule of negligence law in which a negligent plaintiff is awarded damages reduced in proportion to his or her fault (negligence) in causing the injury.

compensated (corporate) surety   a surety, normally a corporation, which is engaged in the business of executing surety contracts for compensation known as a premium.

complaint   the initial pleading filed by the plaintiff that initiates a civil lawsuit.

complete integration   in contract law, a writing intended by the parties to be a complete and exclusive statement of the terms of the agreement. See *integrated agreement*.

composition   a contract between a debtor and two or more creditors under which the creditors agree to accept partial payment in full satisfaction of their claim.

Comprehensive Environmental Response, Compensation, and Liability Act (CERCLA)   federal statute that provides a system for cleaning up abandoned hazardous waste sites and accidental spills and leakage of hazardous waste.

concealment   misrepresentation by conduct other than express statements; that is, action by one person which is intended or likely to prevent another from learning of a fact.

concurrent conditions   in contract law, when performances of the parties are due simultaneously, each party's tender of performance is a condition to the other's duty. These mutual tenders of performance are often known as concurrent conditions. See *tender*.

concurrent ownership (co-ownership)   type of simultaneous ownership interest in which two or more persons have a concurrent right to possession of the same property.

condemnation proceeding   a legal action initiated by the government to exercise its eminent-domain power. See *eminent domain*.

condition   an event that must occur before the duty of performance under a contract becomes due.

condition implied in fact   a condition implied from the language or other conduct of the parties. See *express condition*.

condition implied in law (constructive condition)   a condition imposed by law, arising from neither the language nor other conduct of the parties. See *express condition, condition implied in fact*.

condition precedent   a condition that must occur before a duty to perform arises. See *condition*.

conditional check   a method of creating an accord and satisfaction in which a check is tendered in full satisfaction of a disputed claim. Cashing a check is deemed acceptance of an offer for an accord and satisfaction of the accord, thereby discharging the disputed claim.

conditional payment   effect of a check or other instrument on the obligation for which it is given. This means that the payee, by taking the instrument, surrenders the right to sue on the underlying debt until the instrument is due. If the instrument is not paid when due, the holder may sue either on the debt or the instrument. See UCC §3-802.

conditional sales contract security transaction in which a seller sells goods on credit to a buyer and takes a security interest in the goods sold to secure payment.

conditions precedent in commercial paper, the conditions to secondary contract liability: presentment to the primary party, dishonor by the primary party, and notice of dishonor to the secondary parties. See UCC §§3-413, 3-414.

condition subsequent an event, the occurrence of which, by the terms of the contract, extinguishes a duty to perform after the duty has arisen along with any claim for breach. See *condition*.

condominium form of ownership for multiple-dwelling buildings in which each resident purchases a living unit in the building and all residents own common areas as tenants in common.

confiscation an unlawful taking of foreign assets by a host government. See *nationalization, expropriation*.

conflict of laws rules of law adopted by a state to determine when and how its courts will apply another state's law.

confusion commingling of fungible goods (such as grain) of two or more owners in such a manner that the specific property of individual owners cannot be identified.

conglomerate merger a merger between firms who were neither former competitors nor in the same supply chain. See *product extension merger, market extension merger*.

conscious parallelism doctrine of antitrust law under which conspiracy in violation of §1 of the Sherman Act may be proven by evidence that two or more firms acted in the same way, each with knowledge of the other's actions.

consent decrees judicial orders that incorporate a compromise agreement between the government and the defendant in settlement of antitrust suits.

consent order order issued by an administrative law judge in which a party, without admitting guilt, agrees to stop an allegedly illegal practice.

consequential damages damages which do not flow directly and immediately from a breach of contract, but rather from the consequences or results of the breach. Consequential damages include, for example, lost profits, and personal injury and property damage.

consideration a promise or performance each contracting party bargains for and gives in exchange for the return promise or performance of the other party.

consignee in the law of documents of title, the person named in a bill of lading as the person to whom or to whose order the bill promises delivery. See UCC §7-102(1)(b).

consignment a bailment for sale. In a consignment, the owner of the goods (the consignor), who retains title, delivers possession of them to the consignee, who then attempts to sell them.

consignment intended as security type of consignment creating a debtor-creditor relationship in which the bailee-consignee assumes initial responsibility for the purchase price of goods, whether or not he or she sells or otherwise disposes of them. The consignor retains title to the goods to secure payment for the goods in the consignee's possession. See *true consignment*.

consignor in the law of documents of title, the person named in a bill of lading as the one from whom the goods have been received for shipment. See UCC §7-102(1)(c).

conspicuous contract term or clause so written that a reasonable person against whom it is to operate ought to have noticed it. See UCC §1-201(10).

conspiracy an inchoate crime committed when a person, with intent that a crime be committed, agrees with another or others to the commission of that offense.

constitution document that establishes the basic principles, governmental structure, and law of a state or nation. The Constitution of the United States is reprinted in Appendix A.

constructive a term used as a modifier (for example, constructive delivery, notice, or eviction) meaning that the given legal result (for example, delivery, notice, or eviction) is implied, inferred, or deduced, by law, when certain facts are present. The term as so used means in essence "as if."

constructive conditions of exchange a doctrine of contract law which provides that it is a condition to each party's duty to perform the remaining duties under a promise that there be no uncured material failure of the other party's performance due at an earlier time.

constructive delivery in the law of gifts, a transfer to the donee of the means to obtain possession and control of the subject matter.

constructive eviction form of eviction in which the landlord, by conduct or neglect, so substantially interferes with the tenant's right of possession and enjoyment that the premises are rendered uninhabitable.

constructive notice effect of filing or recording certain documents, such as deeds and financing statements, in an appropriate public office. As a result of filing or recording, later third parties are deemed to know (they have constructive notice) of a prior recorded interest, even if they have no actual knowledge of its existence.

constructive trust an equitable restitutionary remedy that is used to restore property to its rightful owner when a person who has obtained title to the property would be unjustly enriched if permitted to retain it.

consumer credit credit that is extended to persons for personal, family, or household purposes.

Consumer Credit Protection Act (CCPA) federal statute regulating consumer credit transactions that includes the Electronic Fund Transfer Act, the Equal Credit Opportunity Act, the Fair Credit Reporting Act, the Truth-in-Lending Act, the Fair Debt Collection Practices Act, and imposes restrictions on wage garnishments.

consumer goods goods used or bought primarily for personal, family, or household use. See UCC §9-109(1).

consumer reporting agency a person or organization that for a fee or on a cooperative nonprofit basis regularly assembles or evaluates credit or other information on consumers for use by third parties.

continuation agreement in partnership law, agreement through which partners may restrict or deny the liquidation right generally arising upon dissolution. See *dissolution*.

continuation statement in the law of secured transactions, a statement filed in an appropriate public office which extends the effectiveness of a financing statement.

continuing guaranty guaranty that is of a continuing nature, rather than for a single extension of credit.

contract a promise or a set of promises for the breach of which the law gives a remedy, or the performance of which the law in some way recognizes as a duty.

Contract Clause constitutional provision prohibiting the states from passing any law impairing the obligation of contracts.

contract remedies judicial relief available to an injured promisee, when a contractual promise is not performed or is improperly performed.

contractual capacity the ability of a person to create or enter into a contract, that is, to incur contractual duties.

contribution in cosuretyship, the process of proportionately sharing the loss among cosureties caused by the principal's default.

contributory negligence negligence on the plaintiff's part which, combining with the defendant's negligence, causes the plaintiff harm.

conversion a tort occurring when one person intentionally excercises control over a chattel belonging to another which so seriously interferes with the other's right to control it that the possessor is required to pay the full value of the chattel.

conveyance (grant) a transfer of an interest in real property made during the life of the transferor, accomplished by using a formal document known as a deed.

conveyancing the performance of the various functions, including financing, necessary to effect transfer of real property interests.

cooperative a form of real estate ownership by which residents in a multiple-unit building own shares in a corporation that owns the building.

copyright the exclusive right to reproduce a creative work.

corporate opportunity doctrine doctrine of corporation law that prevents corporate officers and directors from usurping and diverting to themselves a business opportunity in which the corporation has an expectancy, property interest or right, or which in fairness should belong to the corporation.

corporation an artificial person or a legal entity created by compliance with laws authorizing the corporate form. A corporation exists apart from and independent of its owners or investors, possesses powers similar to those of natural persons, and generally enjoys continuous existence despite changes in ownership.

corporation by estoppel common law doctrine used to insulate owners of defectively organized corporations from personal liability for corporate debts.

cosuretyship the relation between two or more sureties who are bound to answer for the same duty of the principal, and who as between themselves should share the loss caused by the default of the principal.

Council on Environmental Quality (CEQ) council created by the National Environmental Policy Act to advise the president on environmental matters.

counterclaim a complaint filed by the defendant against the plaintiff in a civil case.

course of dealing a sequence of conduct between parties prior to an agreement establishing a common basis of understanding for interpreting their expressions and other conduct. See UCC §1-205(1).

course of performance action taken by the parties pursuant to a contract involving repeated occasions for performance, such as an installment contract. See UCC §2-208(1).

court costs statutory fees to which officers, jurors, witnesses, and others are entitled for their services in a lawsuit, and that are authorized by statute to be taxed and included in a judgment.

courts of chancery (equity) courts that were developed to provide appropriate relief when no satisfactory remedy was available in the common law courts.

courts of equity see *courts of chancery*.

covenant promise; term is used primarily in the real property context (for example, conveyancing and landlord-tenant law) to describe promises made by the parties in leases, deeds, and contracts.

covenant of quiet enjoyment in landlord-tenant law, an implied covenant between landlord and tenant that after the tenant has taken possession, the landlord may not interefere with the tenant's possession and enjoyment of the property. The covenant is breached by eviction.

covenants for title in a warranty deed, promises concerning the status of the grantor's title. They include generally the covenants of seisin and right to convey, the covenant against encumbrances, and the covenant of quiet enjoyment.

covenants running with the land in real property law, a covenant under which either the liability to perform it, or the right to take advantage of it, passes to a transferee of the property.

cover a buyer's remedy in a sales contract by which

the buyer purchases or contracts to purchase goods to substitute for those due from the breaching seller. See UCC §2-712.

cramdown in a bankruptcy case, the confirmation of a reorganization plan over the objection of one or more classes of creditors or interests.

credit card a device, such as a card or plate, used to obtain money, property, or services on credit.

creditor a person to whom a debt is owed by a person known as a debtor. See UCC §1-201(12).

creditor beneficiary in contract law, a type of intended beneficiary. A person is a creditor beneficiary if performance of the promise will satisfy a debt owed by the promisee to the beneficiary. See *beneficiary*.

creditor's bill historically, a bill filed by a creditor with the court requesting that a debtor be ordered to turn over his or her equitable and intangible assets for sale in satisfaction of the judgment. It often contained a bill of discovery. It is now used primarily to recover fraudulent conveyances.

creditor's committee in bankruptcy reorganization, a committee of persons holding large unsecured claims against the debtor of a particular type. Creditors' committees perform various functions in the reorganization, including participation in formulation of the reorganization plan.

crime an act or failure to act, which is injurious to the public welfare, that violates a law prohibiting or commanding the act, and subjects the offender to punishment prescribed by law.

criminal law principles and rules of law that protect society by establishing minimum standards of socially acceptable conduct and punishing those who fail to meet these standards. See *civil law*.

criminal procedure the law that governs the various steps of a criminal proceeding from preliminary investigation to arrest to trial through termination of punishment.

crossclaims in a civil lawsuit, complaints by a named defendant against other parties listed as defendants in the lawsuit.

cross-examination examination of a witness in a trial or hearing by the party opposed to the one who produced the witness, concerning the witness's testimony elicited on direct examination.

cumulative dividend preference in corporation law, dividend preference that entitles a shareholder to receive a prescribed dividend for the current year and all prior years in which the preferred dividend was not paid before any dividend may be paid on the common shares. See *preferred shares*.

cumulative-to-the-extent-earned preference in corporation law, dividend preference that entitles preferred shareholders to carry forward and accumulate unpaid dividends to the extent that the corporation had earnings available to pay the dividends in the year or years in which the dividends were omitted. See *preferred shares*.

cumulative voting in corporation law, method of shareholder voting, which applies only to the election of directors, in which the number of votes each shareholder receives is equal to the number of his or her shares multiplied by the number of directorships to be filled.

cure a seller's remedy under Article 2 of the UCC, which permits a seller, in limited situations, to cure (correct a defective performance) without liability for breach. See UCC §2-508.

curtesy the common law right of a widower to a life estate in all of his wife's real estate if a child was born alive during the marriage. See *dower*.

customer in the law of bank deposits and collections, any person having an account with a bank or for whom the bank has agreed to collect an item. See UCC §4-104(1)(e).

cy pres doctrine doctrine, applicable only to charitable trusts, under which the court permits or directs the application of the trust property to a charitable purpose different from that designated by the settlor. The doctrine applies if the designated charitable purpose fails, and the settlor has manifested a more general intention to devote the property to charitable purposes.

damages a monetary award recovered in court by a person who has suffered injury through the wrongful conduct, such as tort or breach of contract, of another.

de facto incorporation doctrine common law doctrine used to insulate shareholders of a defectively organized corporation from personal liability for corporate debts. It applies if an enabling statute exists permitting corporate formation, the parties having made a good-faith effort to comply with the statute, and the parties subsequently conduct business as a corporation. See *corporation*.

de jure corporation corporation formed in compliance with all mandatory state requirements whose existence is not subject to attack either by the state or by creditors.

dealer person who engages in the business of offering, buying, selling, or otherwise trading in securities issued by others.

debenture a type of corporate debt security, specifically an unsecured obligation rendering debenture holders general creditors of the corporation.

debt securities corporate securities representing obligations that must ultimately be repaid and create a debtor-creditor relationship between their holders and the corporation. Examples include notes, debentures, and bonds. See *security*.

debtor 1. a party who has incurred an obligation or debt that is owed to another, the creditor. 2. in a secured transaction, the party who owes the obligation and is giving security, and includes a seller of accounts or chattel paper. See UCC §9-105(1)(d).

deed   a written instrument used to transfer (convey) an interest in real property.

deed of trust (trust deed)   a security device used in some states as the functional equivalent of a mortgage. A deed of trust, like other trusts, uses three parties (settlor, trustee, beneficiary) instead of two (mortgagor, mortgagee) present in the ordinary mortgage.

deed poll   deed signed only by the grantor.

defamation   a tort action that protects a person's interest in his or her reputation and good name. Liability is imposed if a false and defamatory statement is made and communicated to a third party, and the defendant was at fault in disseminating the statement. See *libel, slander*.

defamatory communication   one which tends to so harm the reputation of another as to lower him or her in the estimation of the community or to deter third persons from dealing with him or her.

default judgment   judgment that is entered for the plaintiff in a civil case if the defendant fails to answer the complaint or file a motion to dismiss within the time specified in the summons.

defeasible (qualified) fee   a fee simple ownership interest in property that is subject to a condition; that is, it can be terminated by the occurrence or nonoccurrence of an event stated in the instrument creating the estate.

defective (unreasonably dangerous) product   a product that fails to perform in the manner reasonably to be expected in light of its nature and intended function.

defendant   party from whom a plaintiff seeks some form of judicial relief or recovery in a legal proceeding.

defense   as used in the law of commercial paper, facts (such as fraud) asserted by a party to a negotiable instrument (usually the maker of a note or the drawer of a draft) to avoid his or her obligation to pay the instrument.

deficiency judgment   the balance due to a secured creditor who obtains a judgment and the value of the collateral is insufficient to discharge it.

definiteness   a requirement that an offer be sufficiently definite and explicit so that if accepted, a court in a subsequent dispute has a reasonably certain basis upon which to determine the existence of a breach and to award an appropriate remedy. See UCC §2-204(3).

del credere agent   a factor who sells goods on credit and then guarantees to the principal the purchaser's solvency and the purchaser's performance of the contract.

delegation   the transfer of the duties under a contract to a third party.

delivery   1. in the law of gifts, the transfer of possession of the subject matter of the gift from the donor to the donee. Proper delivery requires that the donor absolutely relinquish the right to use, manage, or control

the property. 2. with respect to instruments, documents of title, chattel paper or certificated securities, delivery means a voluntary transfer of possession. See UCC §1-201(14).

delivery order   an order for delivery of goods that is issued by a shipper or storer, and addressed to a carrier or warehouseman, ordering it to deliver goods in its possession to a specified person. See UCC §7-102(1)(d).

demand draft   a draft that is payable on demand.

demand instrument   instrument payable whenever the holder chooses to present it for payment to the maker (of a note) or the drawee (of a draft). See *instrument*.

demonstrative devise   devise payable out of specific property or a specific fund in a testator's estate.

dependent promises   in contract law, a term used to mean that failure by one party to perform justifies the other's later failure to perform. It essentially describes the constructive conditions of exchange doctrine generally applicable to contracts.

dependent relative revocation doctrine   principle of the law of wills holding that if a court finds a testator's revocation of a will is dependent, or conditional, upon the truth of an assumption of law or fact then the revocation is ineffective if the assumption is, in fact, false.

deposition   the testimony under oath of a person (the deponent) who is examined (deposed) out of court by a party to a lawsuit.

depository bank   the first bank to which a check is transferred for collection. See UCC §4-105(a).

design patent   a patent that may be issued for any new, original, and ornamental design for an article of manufacture.

destination bill of lading   bill of lading that is issued at the destination (rather than the place of shipment) or at any other place designated in the request to ensure that the bill of lading will be available at the destination in advance of actual arrival of the goods.

destination contract   a sales contract in which the seller is required to transport goods to a stated destination and there tender them to a buyer.

detour   deviation by a servant from the scope of employment, but which is insufficient to remove the servant from the scope of employment and relieve the master of liability for the servant's torts. See *scope of employment, respondeat superior doctrine*.

devise   traditionally, a transfer of real property by will. Modern statutes, such as the UPC, treat any transfer of property by will, real or personal, as a device.

direct examination   the first examination or interrogation of a witness by the party on whose behalf the witness is called.

disability   see *immunity*.

discharge   in contract law, to extinguish or terminate a contractual obligation.

discharge in bankruptcy   in a bankruptcy case, a discharge that releases the debtor from any further liability for most debts that arose prior to the date the order for relief is entered.

disclosed principal in agency law, a principal whose identity and existence are known to the third party.

discount rate term referring to the percentage difference between the face value of an instrument at maturity and the amount an assignee, commonly a bank, is willing to pay for it prior to maturity.

discovery process that allows each party in a lawsuit to discover all relevant facts prior to trial.

dishonor in commercial paper, dishonor occurs if, after proper presentment, the drawee or maker refuses to pay an instrument presented for payment, or the drawee refuses to accept an instrument presented for acceptance.

disparate impact condition arising from an employment practice that is neutral on its face but which has an adverse impact on those of a certain race, color, national origin, religion, or sex. Employment practices causing disparate impact are illegal under Title VII of the Civil Rights Act of 1964.

disparate treatment intentional employment discrimination based on race, color, national origin, religion, or sex. Employment practices involving disparate treatment are illegal under Title VII of the Civil Rights Act of 1964.

disputed claim situation in which one party contests the existence of an obligation.

dissolution the change in the relation of the partners caused by any partner ceasing to be associated in the carrying on of the business. See UPA §29.

distributions transfers of money or other property by the corporation to its shareholders.

diversity jurisdiction one type of subject matter jurisdiction which may be exercised by the federal courts. Generally, federal courts have jurisdiction over cases in which the plaintiff and defendant are citizens of different states and the amount in controversy exceeds $10,000.

divided ownership type of fixture dispute that arises when the owner of a chattel (for example, a tenant) annexes it to the land of another (for example, a landlord), requiring a determination of whether the attached article now belongs to the landowner.

dividend 1. a distribution out of a corporation's current or past earnings. 2. in a bankruptcy case, the amount of money distributed to general creditors.

dividend percentage in a bankruptcy case, the percentage of their claims that general creditors are paid.

divisibility a contract doctrine used to determine when a party who has partically performed, but has failed to render complete performance, is entitled to recover for the part performance. If a contract is divisible, performance of a divisible part entitles a party to the agreed exchange for that part, despite nonperformance of other parts of the contract. Generally, a contract is divisible if full performance can be divided into corresponding pairs of part performances, so that the exchange of part performances can be regarded as agreed equivalents.

doctrine of judicial review doctrine that gives federal courts the power to determine whether the acts of the legislative and executive branches of government comply with the Constitution and to refuse to enforce those acts that violate it.

document of title any document accepted in business or financing transactions as adequately evidencing that the person who possesses it is entitled to receive, hold, and dispose of the document and the goods it covers. Examples include bills of lading and warehouse receipts. See UCC §1-201(9).

documentary draft a draft the honor of which is conditioned upon the presentation of a document or documents. The drafts used in shipments under reservation and letters of credit are documentary drafts. See UCC §5-103(1)(b).

domicile a person's permanent residence, to which he or she intends to return.

donee the person to whom a gift is made. See *gift*.

donee beneficiary in contract law, one type of intended beneficiary. A person is a donee beneficiary if the promisee intends to make a gift of the promisor's performance to the beneficiary. See *beneficiary*.

donor one who makes a gift. See *gift*.

Double Jeopardy Clause a provision of the Fifth Amendment to the Constitution prohibiting a criminal defendant from being tried twice for the same offense in most circumstances.

dower common law right of a surviving widow to a life estate in one-third of the real estate owned by her husband at any time during the marriage. See *curtesy*.

draft (bill of exchange) a writing signed by the drawer containing an unconditional order by the drawer directed to the drawee to pay to the order of the payee or to bearer a sum certain in money on demand or at a definite time. See UCC §§3-104(1), 3-104(2)(a).

drawee the person to whom a draft is directed and who is ordered to pay the amount of the draft.

drawer the person drawing a draft and addressing it to the drawee.

dual-party credit card credit card issued by a card issuer who does not sell goods or services but instead provides credit and collection services for those who do. The card issuer has two classes of customers, its cardholders and the merchants who honor its cards.

due negotiation negotiation of a negotiable document of title to a holder (1) who purchases it in good faith without notice of any defense against or claim to it on the part of any person, (2) for value, (3) in the regular course of business or financing, and (4) in a transaction not involving mere settlement or payment of a money obligation. See UCC §7-501(4).

due-on-sale clause a contract provision contained in the promissory note or mortgage, permitting the mortgagee, at its option, to declare the entire balance of the mortgage immediately due and payable if the property secured is sold or otherwise transferred without the mortgagee's consent.

Due Process Clause a clause in the Fifth and Fourteenth Amendments to the Constitution which provides that no person shall be deprived of life, liberty, or property without due process of law. The clause generally requires that parties to civil and criminal cases receive "procedural" due process—notice and a hearing—before a deprivation of life, liberty, or property.

duress an element of compulsion or coercion in the bargaining process, resulting from either physical coercion or improper threat, which renders a contract voidable.

duty see *right*.

duty of loyalty duty imposed upon agents, partners, corporate directors, and trustees. It requires these parties to act solely for the benefit of others (for example, the principal, other partners, the corporation, or beneficiaries of a trust) regarding all matters within the scope of the relation. See *fiduciary*.

duty to read rule of contract law stating that a person who signs her name to a contract manifests her assent to its terms and may not later assert that she had not read or did not understand its contents.

easement an interest in land that gives its owner the right either to use another person's land for a limited and specified purpose, or to prevent another person from using his or her land in a specified way.

easement appurtenant an easement involving two tracts of land, one benefited by the easement and (known as the "dominant tenement" or "dominant estate"), and one burdened by the easement (known as the "servient tenement" or "servient estate"). An easement appurtenant benefits land—the dominant tenement—owned by the holder of the easement. See *easement*.

easement in gross an easement obtained other than for the benefit of land owned by the holder of the easement. In an easement in gross, there is no dominant tenement. See *easement, easement appurtenant*.

economic strike strike based on employees' demands for economic benefits.

effluent the discharge of waste substances into rivers, lakes, and oceans.

effluent limitations limitations set by the EPA for those who discharge pollutants into lakes, rivers, or oceans.

election doctrine of the law of agency and contracts, applied when the principal is partially disclosed or undisclosed. Under this doctrine, after discovering the existence and identity of the principal, the third party may elect to hold either the principal or the agent liable on the contract.

election of remedies choice by a party of one contract remedy to the exclusion of others. Contract law generally rejects any requirement that an injured promisee make an election of remedies.

electronic fund transfer any transfer of funds other than one initiated by check, draft, or similar paper instrument which is initiated through an electronic terminal, telephone, computer, or magnetic tape, and which orders, authorizes, or instructs a financial institution to debit or credit an account.

emancipation a state that occurs when a parent surrenders the right to control a minor, including the right to the care, custody, services, and earnings of the child, and renounces parental duties.

eminent domain the power, inherent in a sovereign, to take, or authorize the taking of, private property for public use without the owner's consent upon making just compensation.

Employee Retirement Income Security Act (ERISA) federal statute enacted in 1974 to regulate most private pension programs that provide retirement income to employees or which allow employee deferral of income to termination of employment.

employment at will doctrine traditional doctrine of agency law permitting an employer to fire an employee for any reason ("at will") if the employee is hired for an indefinite term without an employment contract. Most states now recognize a number of exceptions to the doctrine.

encumbrance a right or interest in land which diminishes its value but does not prevent transfer of a fee simple.

enforceable contract term describing a contract in which the promisee is entitled to a contract remedy if the promisor fails to perform.

entire contract a contract that is not divisible; that is, a contract in which corresponding part performances are not agreed equivalents. See *divisibility*.

entrenchment condition that may occur if a company already dominant in a market is acquired by a larger, powerful firm.

entrusting any delivery of goods to (and any acquiescence in retention of possession of goods by) a merchant who deals in goods of the kind. See UCC §2-403(3).

Environmental Impact Statement (EIS) a report required by the National Environmental Policy Act which federal agencies must include in every proposal for legislation or major federal action that will significantly affect the environment.

Environmental Protection Agency (EPA) agency created to centralize federal environmental regulation.

Equal Credit Opportunity Act (ECOA) federal statute prohibiting discrimination in credit transactions on the basis of sex, martial status, religion, race, color, national origin, or age.

equal dignity rule common law principle providing that if the contract to be negotiated by an agent is within the Statute of Frauds, the agent's authorization must also be written.

Equal Employment Opportunity Commission (EEOC) commission responsible for enforcing Title VII of the Civil Rights Act of 1964. See *Title VII*.

Equal Pay Act federal statute enacted in 1963 requiring employers to pay equivalent wages to employees of both sexes who perform equal work on jobs requiring equal skill, effort, and responsibility under similar working conditions.

Equal Protection Clause provision of the Fourteenth Amendment to the Constitution stating that no state shall deny to any person within its jurisdiction the equal protection of the laws.

equipment goods used or bought for use primarily in business, including a profession or farming. See UCC §9-109(2).

equitable estoppel (estoppel "in pais") estoppel that results when a person relies upon another's statement of *fact* (which may be made expressly, or inferred from silence or other conduct) resulting in injury. See *estoppel, promissory estoppel*.

equitable remedy judicial remedy available if, in the discretion of the court, the remedy at law (money damages) is inadequate to compensate the injured party.

equitable servitude device developed in courts of equity to enforce promises respecting land use.

equity in real property law, term referring to the difference between the market value of property and the outstanding indebtedness it secures.

equity of redemption concept developed in the law of mortgages which allows a mortgagor to redeem his or her property by satisfying the debt plus interest within a reasonable time after default.

equity securities securities, such as shares of stock, that create an ownership interest in the business. See *security*.

escrow a flexible device for closing many types of real estate transactions, including installment contracts. In an escrow, one party to the contract deposits a deed, other instrument, or money with an escrow agent, who holds the deposited instrument or funds until occurrence of an event outlined in the escrow agreement.

escrow account a bank account commonly maintained in the name of a mortgagor and mortgagee into which the mortgagor makes periodic payments to satisfy recurring charges such as property taxes and insurance premiums.

essential fraud See *fraud in the execution*.

estate 1. all legal or equitable, tangible or intangible property interests owned by the debtor in a bankruptcy case. 2. an ownership interest in property. 3. the combination of all property, real and personal, tangible and intangible, owned by a decedent.

estate at sufferance term used to describe the possession of a holdover tenant who wrongfully remains in possession of property upon expiration of the lease term.

estate for years in landlord-tenant law, a form of nonfreehold estate characterized by a fixed beginning and ending date.

estate from period to period (periodic tenancy) in landlord-tenant law, a form of nonfreehold estate characterized by its continuance for successive periods until notice of termination is given by either party.

estate (tenancy) at will in landlord-tenant law, an estate (a nonfreehold estate) that may be terminated at the will of either party.

estoppel the legal principle by which a person is prevented (estopped) from asserting a position that is inconsistent with his or her prior conduct, if injustice would thereby result to a person who has changed position in justifiable reliance upon that conduct.

estray statute a statute that provides procedures by which a finder attempts to restore lost property to its true owner. These statutes commonly provide for advertising the goods followed by a stated period after which the finder acquires title to all or part of the property.

Ethics in Government Act federal statute that restricts some former government officials from lobbying their former agencies after leaving office.

eviction physical removal of a tenant from all or part of the leased premises by the landlord or person acting under the landlord's authority, or by a person having title to the property superior to the landlord. See *constructive eviction*.

evidence legally admissible testimony of witnesses, and documents or other pertinent items offered to prove the facts alleged in a case.

exclusionary rule rule stating that evidence obtained in violation of the Fourth, Fifth, and Sixth Amendments must be excluded in a criminal prosecution of the person whose rights were violated.

exclusive dealing contract contract in which a buyer agrees to deal only with a particular seller, or not to deal in the goods of the seller's competitors.

exculpatory clause contract term that exempts a person from liability for his or her own torts.

executed contract a promise or contract that has been completed or performed.

execution judicial process by which a judgment is enforced, involving seizure of the debtor's assets, their public sale, and application of the proceeds to the unpaid judgment.

execution sale public sale of a debtor's real and personal property to satisfy a judgment.

executor (executrix) the person appointed or authorized by a probate court to discover, collect, and distribute a decedent's assets and pay lawful claims and taxes against the estate.

executory contract a promise or contract that is yet to be performed.

executory interest (executory limitation) a future interest that exists in property when the property is conveyed in fee simple subject to an executory limitation. See *future interest*.

exemption statute a statute or constitutional provision that exempts certain property of a debtor from creditors' claims.

exhibits tangible items that have been established as part of the evidence in a lawsuit.

exoneration in suretyship law, the surety's right, before paying the creditor, to compel the principal to perform.

expectation interest the interest of the injured promisee most commonly protected by both legal and equitable contract remedies, designed to give the promisee the benefit of the bargain; that is, the court protects the injured party's expectation that the contract will be performed, not breached. See *benefit of the bargain*.

Expedited Funds Availability Act federal statute enacted in 1987, designed to ensure that checking account customers have prompt access to funds they deposit, and to expedite the return of dishonored checks. *See Regulation CC*.

express authority in agency law, authority based on explicit oral or written statements of the principal defining the agent's power. See *authority*.

express condition a condition provided for in the language (oral or written) of a promise or agreement. See *condition*.

express contract a contract that arises from the language, either oral or written, of the parties.

express trust trust that arises as a result of the settlor's language indicating his or her intent to create it.

express warranty in a sales contract, any affirmation of fact or promise made by the sellor to the buyer that relates to the goods and becomes part of the basis of the bargain, creates an express warranty that the goods will conform to the affirmation or promise. See UCC §2-313.

expropriation nationalization in accordance with international law. See *nationalization, confiscation*.

extension an agreement between a debtor and at least two creditors that extends the time for payment. See *composition*.

extension clause clause extending the maturity of an instrument (generally a note) from its original due date to a future time specified in the instrument.

extraction process by which a debtor uses the proceeds of the sale of inventory to pay his or her salary, overhead, and other fixed expenses.

extradition the surrender by one state (or country) of an individual accused of a crime to another state or country having jurisdiction to try the offender.

F.A.S. term a delivery term used in a sales contract requiring the seller to deliver goods (at the seller's expense and risk) alongside a named freighter, tanker, or other vessel and obtain and tender to the buyer a receipt for the goods. See UCC §2-319.

F.O.B. term a delivery term in a sales contract requiring or authorizing the seller to ship the goods to the buyer. If the term is F.O.B. place of shipment, the seller bears the expense and risk of putting the goods in the carrier's possession. If the term is F.O.B. destination, the seller bears the expense and risk of transporting the goods to the named destination and there tendering delivery to the buyer. See UCC §2-319.

factor (commission merchant) agent entrusted with possession and control of the principal's goods for purposes of sale, compensated by a commission or "factorage."

failure of consideration in contract law, the failure of the other contracting party to perform his or her promise; failure of a constructive condition of exchange. See *constructive condition of exchange*.

Fair Credit Billing Act federal statute that regulates billing practices and disputes for open-end credit accounts.

Fair Credit Reporting Act (FCRA) federal statute protecting consumers from inaccurate and obsolete information in reports by consumer reporting agencies.

Fair Debt Collection Practices Act (FDCPA) federal statute imposing restrictions and obligations upon all third persons (such as collection agencies) who are engaged in the business of collecting debts for others.

Fair Labor Standards Act (FLSA) federal statute, enacted in 1938, that regulates minimum wages, hours of employment, and child labor.

fair market value in real property law, the amount of money that a willing purchaser would pay to a willing property owner considering all uses for which the land is suited or might be applied.

false imprisonment (false arrest) an intentional tort in which liability is imposed upon a person who intentionally confines another within fixed boundaries.

farm products crops or livestock, products of crops or livestock in the unmanufactured state, and supplies used or produced in farming operations. See UCC §9-109(3).

Federal Insecticide, Fungicide, and Rodenticide Act (FIFRA) federal statute requiring manufacturers of pesticides to register their products with the EPA and to meet labeling requirements on proper use and safety precautions.

federal question jurisdiction one type of subject matter jurisdiction possessed by federal courts. It empowers federal courts to hear cases in which the Constitution or a federal statute or treaty is at issue.

Federal Trade Commission administrative agency established in 1914 by the Federal Trade Commission Act empowered to enforce both the Clayton and Federal Trade Commission Acts, but not the Sherman Act. See also *Federal Trade Commission Act, Sherman Antitrust Act, Clayton Act.*

Federal Trade Commission Act federal statute enacted in 1914 which created the Federal Trade Commission, and authorizes the FTC to issue cease and desist orders prohibiting unfair methods of competition and unfair or deceptive trade practices.

fee simple absolute all the rights a person may possess in real property; the largest quantity of ownership interest in land recognized by the law.

fee simple determinable a defeasible fee simple interest in land that is automatically terminated (with the property reverting to the grantor) upon occurrence or nonoccurrence of an event stated in the instrument creating the interest. See *possibility of reverter.*

fee simple subject to a condition subsequent a defeasible fee simple interest in land that terminates upon occurrence or nonoccurrence of an event stated in the instrument, provided that the grantor takes some affirmative step to terminate the estate. See *power of termination.*

fee simple subject to an executory limitation a defeasible fee simple interest in land that passes to a third party (other than the grantor or his or her heirs) upon occurrence or nonoccurrence of an event stated in the instrument creating the interest. See *executory interest.*

felonies serious crimes, generally those punishable by death or imprisonment in the penitentiary. See *misdemeanor, offense.*

fellow servant doctrine common law defense to employer liability under which an employer is not liable for negligent injury to an employee caused by the conduct of a fellow employee.

fidelity bond a suretyship contract that secures an employer against embezzlement or defalcation by an employee.

fiduciary relationship relationship in which one person is under a duty to act solely for the benefit of another concerning matters within the scope of the relation. See *duty of loyalty.*

field warehousing a security device commonly used in inventory financing in which a warehouse is created on the debtor's premises. Inventory is then stored in the warehouse in exchange for warehouse receipts that are used by the debtor as collateral on a loan.

finance charge under the federal Truth-in-Lending Act, the cost of consumer credit expressed in a dollar amount.

financing statement statement filed by a secured party

in an appropriate public office to perfect a security interest in personal property or fixtures. See *perfection.*

finder a person who discovers lost property and reduces it to possession.

firm offer rule rule of sales law stating that a written, signed offer to buy or sell goods made by a merchant stating that it will be held open is binding without consideration for the period stated, not exceeding three months. See UCC §2-205.

fitness for a particular purpose an implied warranty arising under UCC Article 2 providing that goods will be fit for the buyer's particular purpose when the seller has reason to know of a particular purpose for which the buyer requires goods and when the buyer relies on the seller's skill or judgment to select suitable goods. See UCC §2-315.

fixture an item of personal property that, by virtue of its attachment to, or close association with, land, is regarded as part of the land.

fixture filing in secured transactions law, a type of public filing used when the collateral is fixtures. It requires filing a financing statement covering the goods that are or are to become fixtures in the office where a mortgage on the underlying real estate would be recorded. See UCC §9-313(1)(b).

floating lien (floating charge) lien created by an after-acquired property clause that ''floats'' over the debtor's ever-changing property (usually inventory) and covers whatever property is found there. See *after-acquired property clause.*

floor planning inventory financing secured by after-acquired inventory. See *floating lien.*

foreclosure 1. in morgage law, the method by which mortgaged property, or proceeds of its sale, is applied in satisfaction of the debt secured by the mortgage. 2. in antitrust law, an anticompetitive consequence of vertical merger referring to the reduced ability of former suppliers or customers to sell to or buy from the merged firm.

foreign corporation a corporation organized under the laws of a given state that does business in another state is a ''foreign'' corporation in the latter state. See also *corporation, domestic corporation.*

Foreign Corrupt Practices Act federal statute enacted in 1977 that imposes substantial internal control requirements upon companies reporting under the Securities Exchange Act of 1934 and makes it a crime for United States companies and individuals to bribe foreign officials for certain corrupt purposes.

forfeiture in contract law, the denial of compensation that results when the promisee loses the right to the agreed exchange after relying substantially, through preparation or performance, on the expectation of that exchange.

forgery under the UCC, one form of ''unauthorized signature''—a signature or indoresement made without actual, implied, or apparent authority. See UCC §1-201(43).

formal contracts contracts governed by special rules that result from the contract's formal characteristics. Contrast *simple contract*.

four unities traditional formalities that must be present to create a joint tenancy: the unities of time, title, interest, and possession.

franchise a license from the owner of a trademark or trade name (the franchisor) permitting another (the franchisee) to sell a product or service under that name or mark.

fraud (deceit) an intentional tort under which the plaintiff may recover by proving that the defendant made a fraudulent misrepresentation of material existing fact with the intent to induce the plaintiff to rely upon it, and that the plaintiff justifiably relied upon the misrepresentation to his injury. See *fraudulent misrepresentation, misrepresentation*.

fraud in the essence see *fraud in the execution*.

fraud in the execution type of fraud that occurs when a misrepresentation induces a party to sign an instrument with neither knowledge nor reasonable opportunity to obtain knowledge of its character or its essential terms. See UCC §3-305(2)(c).

fraud in the factum see *fraud in the execution*.

fraudulent conveyance the conveyance of property by a debtor to a third party with intent to hinder, delay, or defraud creditors.

fraudulent misrepresentation a misrepresentation made with knowledge of its untrue character or in reckless disregard of the truth. See *misrepresentation, scienter*.

Freedom of Information Act (FOIA) federal statute, which is part of the Administrative Procedure Act, that requires federal agencies to make most agency records available for examination or copying to any person who requests the records. See *Administrative Procedure Act*.

freedom of speech freedom of expression guaranteed by the First Amendment to the Constitution including oral and written communications and nonverbal actions with symbolic value.

freehold estate an estate in land that is characterized by its uncertain or potentially unlimited duration, including the fee simple absolute, the defeasible fees, and the life estate.

freight forwarder a person in the business of consolidating less than carload shipments to obtain the benefit of lower rail and truck rates.

frolic servant's departure from the scope of employment which relieves the master of liability for the servant's torts. See *scope of employment, respondeat superior doctrine*.

frustration of purpose contract doctrine developed to relieve a contracting party of his or her duty to perform when the underlying purpose of the contract is defeated.

Full Faith and Credit Clause clause of the Constitution that provides that full faith and credit shall be given in each state to the judicial proceedings of every other state. The clause prevents relitigation of cases previously decided in other states, and enables a plaintiff to obtain enforcement of a judgment in other states.

full warranty under the Magnuson-Moss Warranty Act, a written warranty covering consumer goods that meets the federal minimum standards for warranty.

fungible goods goods, such as grain, any unit or part of which is undistinguishable from another.

future goods in sales law, goods not both existing and identified. See UCC §2-105(2).

future interest an interest in property which takes effect in possession and enjoyment, if at all, at some future time.

gap fillers term used to describe provisions of Article 2 of the UCC which supply missing terms in the parties' agreement.

garnishment a debt collection remedy directed to a third party who holds property of, or is indebted to, the debtor.

general agent agent authorized to conduct a series of transactions involving continuity of service.

general creditor a creditor who has neither a lien upon the debtor's assets nor a priority in distribution of the debtor's assets.

general devise a transfer by will payable out of the general assets of a testator's estate.

general guaranty (offer for) an offer for a suretyship contract which may be accepted by any person to whom the principal communicates the offer and who accepts it by extending the credit contemplated by the offer.

general intangibles any personal property other than goods, accounts, chattel paper, documents, instruments, and money. See UCC §9-106.

general partner partner who is personally liable to partnership creditors for the full amount of all debts and obligations incurred by the partnership.

Generally Accepted Accounting Principles (GAAP) principles which determine how accounting information is presented in financial statements.

Generally Accepted Auditing Standards (GAAS) standards which determine how the work of a particular audit is performed.

gift a voluntary transfer of an interest in property by the owner (the donor) to another (the donee) without consideration or compensation.

gift causa mortis a gift made in anticipation or contemplation of the donor's imminent death.

good faith honesty in fact in the conduct or transaction concerned. In the case of a merchant, it also includes observance of reasonable commercial standards of fair dealing in the trade. See UCC §§1-201(19), 2-103(1)(b).

goods in general, all things, including specially manufactured goods, which are movable at the time of identification to the contract for sale; tangible personal property. See UC §§2-105(1), 2-107.

grand jury a group of citizens whose function is to consider evidence of criminal conduct presented by the prosecutor and to determine whether the accused should be required to stand trial for a criminal offense.

grantee the person to whom an interest in real property is transferred by deed.

grantor the person transferring interest in real property by deed.

group boycott (concerted refusal to deal) a horizontal combination intended to eliminate (or prevent the entry of) a competitor of the parties to the combination. See *horizontal restraint*.

guaranty in suretyship law, a contract that creates a secondary obligation; that is, the promisor (guarantor) undertakes to perform only if another person fails to perform.

guaranty of collection (conditional guaranty, guaranty of collectibility) type of guaranty in which the creditor must put the principal in default and also exhaust all legal remedies against the principal before suing the guarantor.

guardian a person appointed by a court to manage, subject to court supervision, the affairs and properties of a person (ward) considered incapable of administering his or her own affairs.

heirs people who are entitled to the decedent's property if he or she dies intestate. See *intestate*.

Herfindahl-Hirschman Index (HHI) an aid to interpreting market concentration data that is computed by summing the squares of the individual market shares of all firms included in the market.

holder a person who is in possession of a document of title, or an instrument, or a certificated investment security drawn, issued, or indorsed to him or to his order or to bearer or in blank. See UCC §1-201(20).

holder in due course holder of commercial paper who takes an instrument for value, in good faith, and without notice (1) that the instrument is overdue, (2) that the instrument has been dishonored, or (3) of any defense against or claim to it on the part of any person. See UCC §3-302.

holder in due course doctrine doctrine of commercial paper law stating that if a negotiable instrument is negotiated to a holder in due course, the holder in due course takes free of all claims and most defenses to the instrument.

holding rule of law used to resolve the issues in a court case.

holding company a company that confines its activities to owning stock in, and supervising management of, other companies.

holographic will generally, a will entirely in the handwriting of the testator.

honorary trust term used to describe a transfer of property in trust for the erection or maintenance of monuments, the care of graves, or the care of specific animals. Such an arrangement is not a trust under the definition of trust because it lacks a beneficiary. See *trust*.

horizontal merger a merger between former competitors.

horizontal restraint of trade a restraint of trade involving an agreement among competitors—persons at the same functional level. See *restraint of trade, vertical restraint of trade*.

hot cargo clause a provision in a collective bargaining agreement by which an employer voluntarily agrees not to do business with a nonunion company or a company involved in a labor dispute.

identification of goods the process by which the particular existing goods referred to in a contract for sale are designated and specified.

illegal bargain traditional term used to describe a contract that is unenforceable because it violates an applicable criminal or civil statute, constitutes the commission of or inducement to commit a tort, or is otherwise contrary to public policy.

illusory promise promissory language in a contract that makes one party's performance entirely optional. An illusory promise is not a promise at all and therefore does not furnish consideration for a return promise. See *promise*.

immunity a person's freedom against having a given legal relation altered by the act or omission of another. The person who has no ability to alter the given legal relation is operating under a disability.

implied authority in agency law, authority which is implied from a general express grant of authority; that is, it flows as a natural and logical consequence of the express authority granted and cannot contradict that authority. See *authority*.

implied in fact contract a promise or contract that is inferred from conduct other than language.

implied trust trust that arises by operation of law, not by the express language of the settlor. Implied trusts include resulting trusts and constructive trusts.

implied warranty a warranty that arises by operation of the law under Article 2 of the Uniform Commercial Code, including the warranty of merchantability and fitness for a particular purpose. See UCC §§2-314, 2-315.

implied warranty of authority principle of agency law by which a person who purports to make a contract for a principal impliedly represents that he or she has the power to bind the principal.

implied warranty of habitability warranty applicable

primarily to residential leases imposing an implied covenant in the lease that the premises will meet certain minimum standards of habitability, and making the landlord-tenant relation governed by contract rather than property principles.

import-export clause clause of the Constitution that prohibits a state from imposing a direct tax on imports or exports solely because the goods have been received from or are bound for a foreign country.

impracticability (impossibility) a contract doctrine relieving a contracting party from a duty to perform if performance as agreed has been made impracticable by the occurrence of a contingency, the nonoccurrence of which was a basic assumption on which the contract was made. See UCC §2-615.

inchoate crimes crimes that are designed to culminate in the commission of another crime but fail to do so.

incidental beneificiary in contract law, a beneficiary who is not an intended beneficiary. See *beneficiary, intended beneficiary*.

incidental damages damages recoverable by an injured buyer or seller for breach of a sales contract in addition to the basic measure of damages, designed to provide reimbursement for reasonable expenses incurred by the injured party as a result of the breach. For specific examples, see UCC §§2-710, 2-715(1).

incomplete instrument an instrument, ultimately intended to be negotiable, which is signed by the maker or drawer but which omits some term or terms necessary to complete the instrument. See UCC §3-115.

incontestable clause clause in a life insurance policy that prevents the insurer from asserting a misrepresentation or breach of warranty as a basis for avoiding the contract after the policy has been in effect for a given period, such as one or two years.

incorporation by reference a legal doctrine under which the terms of one identifiable writing are made part of another writing by referring to, identifying, and adopting the former as part of the latter.

indemnity contract contract in which the promisor (indemnitor) agrees to save the promisee (indemnitee) harmless from (indemnify or reimburse him for) the legal consequences of the promisee's conduct or that of some other person.

indenture 1. trust agreement between a corporation issuing bonds or debentures and a trustee, usually a financial institution, under which the securities are issued and administered. 2. deed signed by both grantor and grantee.

independent contractor a person who contracts to do something for another but whose physical conduct in the performance of the undertaking is not subject to the other's control or right of control. An independent contractor may or may not be an agent.

independent promises a term traditionally used to describe promises in leases and other conveyances of land, meaning that nonperformance of one promise by one party does not excuse further performance of another promise by the other.

indictment a written accusation issued by a grand jury setting forth the facts and charging the accused with violation of specific criminal statutes. See *grand jury*.

indorsement in negotiable instruments, terms referring to the payee's or other holder's signature (and in some cases additional language) appearing on the instrument. An indorsement usually appears on the back of the instrument.

informal (simple) contracts contracts that are enforceable without regard to form; basically, any contract other than a contract under seal, a recognizance, or a negotiable contract.

information a written accusation prepared by the prosecutor that sets forth the facts and charges the accused of violating criminal statutes. An alternative to grand jury indictment as a means of initiating criminal prosecution.

infringement unauthorized use of intellectual property.

initial transaction statement (ITS) statement of the transfer of an uncertificated security issued to the new registered owner, which is signed by the issuer and contains a description of the issue of which the security is a part, the number of shares or units transferred, and the date the transfer was registered. See UCC §8-408.

injunction an equitable judicial remedy involving an order directed to a defendant by a court to do (mandatory injunction) or to refrain from doing (prohibitory or negative injunction) an act.

injunction against breach an equitable contract remedy closely related to specific performance involving a court order not to breach a contract. See *specific performance*.

insider in bankruptcy law, a creditor, such as a relative of an individual debtor, who has a particularly close relationship to the debtor.

insider trading buying or selling securities based upon access to confidential or proprietary information not available to the public.

Insider Trading Sanctions Act of 1984 federal statute permitting the SEC to file suit against persons violating the Securities Exchange Act of 1934 or rules by purchasing or selling a security while in possession of material nonpublic information. The SEC may recover a civil penalty from the violator not exceeding three times the profit gained or loss avoided as a result of the unlawful purchase or sale.

insolvency state of the debtor who has insufficient assets to meet his or her total obligations (balance sheet insolvency) or who is unable to pay debts as they come due (equity insolvency).

installment contract in sales law, a contract requiring or authorizing the seller to deliver the goods in separate lots to be separately accepted by the buyer. See UCC §2-612(1).

installment sales contract (contract for deed) real estate contract in which the seller finances the buyer who takes possession of the property and makes periodic installment payments against the price. The seller retains title as security for performance of the contract and delivers the deed only after the purchase price is paid.

instrument 1. in general, term referring to any written document, particularly legal documents such as contracts, wills, and deeds. 2. under UCC Article 3, a negotiable instrument as defined in §3-104 (see §3-102(1)(e)). 3. under UCC Article 9, commercial paper, such as notes, checks, and other drafts; certificated securities such as stocks and bonds; and any other writing that evidences a right to the payment of money and is not itself a security agreement or lease. See UCC §9-105(1)(i).

insurable interest the legal principles designed to prevent net profit from occurrence of insured events; that is, to prevent use of an insurance policy as a gambling device and to minimize any inducement to cause the event insured against, the person who recovers under the policy must have an insurable interest in the property or person insured.

insurance a contractual arrangement used to transfer and distribute risk.

integrated agreement in contract law, a writing that constitutes the final written expression of one or more terms of an agreement, either complete (exclusive statement of all terms of the agreement) or partial (conclusive on some but not all issues).

intellectual property the bundle of property rights associated with ideas and creative thoughts.

intended beneficiary if a contractual promise is made with intent to benefit a beneficiary, that person is an intended beneficiary. See *beneficiary*.

intent in tort law, a person's conduct is intentional if she desires to cause the consequences of her act, or believes that the consequences are substantially certain to result from it.

inter alia among other things.

inter vivos trust trust created during the settlor's lifetime.

intermediary bank in bank deposits and collections, any bank to which a check is transferred in the course of collection other than the depositary or payor bank. See UCC §4-105(c).

international law (public international law, law of nations) system of law that governs relationships among states.

interpleader a legal proceeding used when one person possesses property or a fund in which he claims no interest, but which is claimed by two or more other persons. In this case, the stakeholder may file an equitable interpleader action, requiring the rival claimants to litigate their claims to the property with each other rather than the stakeholder. The interpleader therefore relieves the stakeholder from potential liability for paying the wrong claimant.

interpretation the process by which a court ascertains the meaning of a contract or contract term.

intestate a person who (1) fails to leave a will; (2) fails to leave a valid will; or (3) leaves a valid will that does not dispose of all of his or her property.

intestate succession statutes state statutes governing the distribution of property of a person who dies without a will, without a valid will, or with a will that does not dispose of the decedent's entire estate. See *heirs*.

intrastate offering exemption exemption from registration under the Securities Act of 1933 for securities offered and sold only to persons within a single state by a corporation incorporated by and doing business within the state.

inventory goods that are held primarily for immediate or ultimate resale in the ordinary course of the seller's business. See UCC §9-109(4).

inverse condemnation a condemnation action initiated by a property owner to recover compensation for property taken by the government for public use, used when the government takes private property for public use, but does so without a formal condemnation procedure and without compensation. See *condemnation, eminent domain*.

Investment Advisors Act of 1940 federal statute regulating persons who are in the business of rendering investment advice but are not securities brokers or dealers.

invitee a person invited to enter or remain on the land of another for purposes connected with business dealings (a business invitee) or for a purpose for which the land is held open to the public (a public invitee).

involuntary (constructive) (quasi) bailment bailment in which a person obtains possession of another's goods without either the latter's knowledge or consent.

involuntary case bankruptcy case in which the creditor attempts to force the debtor into bankruptcy.

irregular (anomalous) indorsement an indorsement that is not in the chain of title (not necessary to negotiate the instrument). Such an indorsement gives notice to later holders of the indorser's accommodation status. See UCC §3-415(4).

issue 1. in commercial paper law, the first delivery of an instrument to a holder or a remitter. See UCC §3-102(1)(a). (See *delivery, remitter*.) 2. in the law of decedent's estates, lineal descendants.

joint and several promises promises of the same performance made by two or more parties in which the promisors bind themselves jointly as one party and also severally as separate parties. See *joint liability, several liability*.

joint liability term describing contract liability when two or more promisors undertake the duty to render the same performance. In joint liability, all co-promisors are liable for the entire performance. Thus, a joint promisor is liable for the performance of each co-promisor. See *joint and several promises, several liability*.

joint tenancy   form of coownership characterized by the right of survivorship; for example, if one of two joint tenants dies, the deceased's share is owned by the other, who becomes sole owner.

joint venture   an association of two or more persons to carry out one enterprise, a specific transaction, or one series of transactions for profit. See *partnership*.

judgment creditor   a person who has obtained a judgment against another, the judgment debtor, which has not been satisfied.

judgment debtor   a person against whom a judgment has been recovered, which the debtor has not satisfied.

judgment lien   generally, a lien upon the judgment debtor's real property. See *lien*.

judgment notwithstanding the verdict (judgment *non obstante veredicto*, or judgment *n.o.v.*), motion for   motion filed by a party against whom the jury has decided a case which requests the court to find as a matter of law that the jury's verdict was incorrect and to enter judgment in favor of the moving party.

judgment rate   term referring to the rate of interest required by state law to be paid on money judgments.

judicial lien   lien created by judicial action, including judgment, levy, garnishment, or other legal or equitable process or proceeding.

jurisdiction   the power and authority of a court to render a binding decision of law.

jury instructions or charges   instructions by the court to the jury which explain the rules of law pertinent to a case.

jus tertii defense   in commercial paper law, a defense based on a claim of a third party to the instrument.

knowledge   a person's subjective conscious belief in the truth of a fact or condition.

Labor-Management Relations Act (Taft-Hartley Act)   federal statute that amended the National Labor Relations Act in 1947, making illegal certain unfair labor practices committed by unions.

Labor Management Reporting and Disclosure Act (Landrum-Griffin Act)   federal statute that amended the National Labor Relations Act in 1959 and which regulates internal union activities.

landlord's lien   statutory lien that secures payment of rent by giving the landlord a lien upon the tenant's personal property located on the premises.

landlord-tenant relationship   legal relationship created by the transfer of the right of possession of real property from its owner (the landlord) to another (the tenant) in consideration of rent.

lapse   in decedents' estates law, an event occurring if a beneficiary under a will predeceases the testator.

last clear chance doctrine   doctrine of negligence law that allows a plaintiff to recover despite his or her own contributory negligence, if the defendant had the "last clear chance" to avoid the accident and negligently failed to do so.

law   the body of rules and principles of conduct that are enforceable through sanctions.

law merchant   term referring to the system of routine rules, customs, or practices used in the business community to regulate transactions and solve controversies.

lease   an agreement that creates a landlord-tenant relationship. See *landlord-tenant relationship*.

legacy   a gift of money by will.

legal detriment   an element of consideration requiring that the promisee of a contractual promise either (1) refrain (or promise to refrain) from doing something that he or she has a legal right to do, or (2) do (or promise to do) something that he or she is not legally obligated to do, in exchange for the promise.

legal system   institutions and processes for enforcing the law.

letter of credit   an engagement by a bank or other person made at the request of a customer that the issuer will honor drafts or other demands for payment upon compliance with the conditions specified in the credit. See UCC §5-103(1)(a). See *standby letter of credit*.

levy   a sheriff's act in taking custody of a debtor's property pursuant to creditors' remedies available under state law.

liability   see *power*.

libel   the publication of a defamatory statement by written or printed words, by its embodiment in other physical form, or by radio or television communication. See *defamation*. Contrast *slander*.

license   a revocable privilege to enter upon or perform acts on another's land.

licensee   a person privileged to enter or remain upon another's land only by virtue of the possessor's consent.

lien   an interest in property designed to secure the payment or other performance of an obligation.

lien creditor   in secured transactions law, a creditor who has acquired a lien upon the property involved by attachment, levy, or other judicial process, and includes an assignee for the benefit of creditors, a trustee in bankruptcy, and a receiver in equity. See UCC §9-301(3).

life estate   an interest in property limited in duration to the life or lives of one or more persons.

life insurance   a contract to make designated payments upon the death of the person whose life is insured.

life tenant   the owner of a life estate.

limited partner   partner whose liability to creditors of the partnership is limited to the amount of capital he or she has contributed to the partnership.

limited partnership   a partnership formed by two or more persons under a limited-partnership statute having as members one or more general partners and one or more limited partners. See *general partners, limited partners*. See ULPA §1, RULPA §101(7).

limited warranty under the Magnuson-Moss Warranty Act, a written warranty covering consumer goods which does not meet the federal minimum standards for warranty.

liquidated claim a claim that is fixed in amount.

liquidated damages clause a contract term specifying the amount of damages to be awarded in the event of a breach.

liquidation (straight bankruptcy) case bankruptcy case under Chapter 7 of the Bankruptcy Code in which the debtor surrenders all nonexempt assets to a trustee in bankruptcy, who converts the assets to cash and distributes the proceeds to creditors who have filed claims against the estate, according to priorities prescribed by law. The debtor is then generally discharged from liability on most debts remaining unpaid.

litigation contesting a disputed claim in court.

lockout temporary closing of all or part of a business by refusal to allow employees to work.

long arm statutes state statutes codifying the minimum contacts that subject a nonresident defendant to a state court's jurisdiction in a civil case.

lost property status of property when its owner has casually and involuntarily parted with it without recalling either the circumstances or the place of the loss.

lost-volume seller in sales law, a seller injured by a buyer's breach of contract who sells a standardized product or one in unlimited supply. Specifically, a lost volume seller is one who, but for the buyer's breach, would have had the benefit of both the original contract and the resale contract. See UCC §2-708(2).

lot a parcel or single article that is the subject matter of a separate sale or delivery, whether or not it is sufficient to perform the contract. See UCC §2-105(5).

Magnuson-Moss Warranty Act a federal statute regulating written warranties that accompany the sale of consumer goods.

mailbox acceptance rule (deposited acceptance rule) rule of contract law stating that an acceptance is normally effective when sent or dispatched—that is, when the offeree relinquishes control over his or her acceptance.

main-purpose (leading-object) rule exception to the Statute of Frauds writing requirement for suretyship promises which provides that a surety's oral promise is enforceable if it is made to benefit the surety's personal economic interest, rather than to aid the debtor.

majority the age at which a person attains full contractual capacity.

maker in commercial paper law, the person who makes or executes a note and promises to pay money. See *note*.

malicious prosecution an intentional tort imposing liability for the initiation of a criminal case by a private person against another for any purpose other than to bring an offender to justice, if the case is initiated without cause to believe that the accused has committed a crime, and the case is terminated in favor of the accused.

mandatory injunction See *injunction*.

market concentration a function of the number of firms in a market and their respective market shares.

market extension merger a merger that joins firms selling the same product, but operating in different geographic markets.

marketable title a title to real property that a reasonably prudent and legally well-informed buyer is willing to take and pay for; that is, title is marketable if no reasonable doubt exists concerning its validity and it is unlikely that the buyer will be exposed to a lawsuit in order to defend it.

Marketable Title Acts in real property law, state statutes that reduce the period of title search by extinguishing all claims and title defects automatically after a fixed period, unless preserved by filing a statutory notice.

master a principal who has control of, or the right to control, an agent's physical conduct.

master of the offer rule principle of contract law allowing the offeror to dictate the terms under which the offer may be accepted, including the time, place, and manner of acceptance. See *offer*.

material alteration in commercial paper law, an alteration that changes the contract of any party to the instrument in any respect. See UCC §3-407(1). In contract law generally, an alteration of a writing which varies the legal relations of any party with the maker of the alteration or with third parties.

material breach in contract law, a breach of contract that causes the nonoccurrence of a constructive condition of exchange to the other party's duty (thereby discharging that duty). See *substantial performance doctrine*.

material misrepresentation a misrepresentation is material if either (1) a reasonable person would attach importance to the existence or nonexistence of the fact represented, or (2) the person making the misrepresentation knows or should know that the other person is likely to regard the fact as important.

mechanic's lien statutory lien given to persons who supply services, labor, or material in the construction or improvement of real property.

mediation tactic used to aid in resolving disputes in which an unbiased third party assists in negotiations and recommends a solution that the parties are free to accept or reject.

merchant in sales law, a person who deals in goods of the kind or who otherwise by her occupation holds herself out as having knowledge or skill peculiar to the business practices or goods involved in a particular transaction. See UCC §2-104(1).

merchantability   an implied warranty under Article 2 of the UCC generally requiring that goods sold by a merchant dealing in goods of the kind be fit for the ordinary purposes for which such goods are used. See UCC §2-314.

merger (integration) clause   a clause contained in a written contract expressly stating that the writing is the entire agreement of the parties, and that there are no understandings, promises, or representations except those contained therein.

merger guidelines   guidelines issued by the Justice Department detailing the general principles and specific standards used to determine which mergers are likely to be challenged by the government under §7 of the Clayton Act.

midnight deadline   term used in commercial paper and bank deposits and collections meaning with respect to a bank midnight of the next banking day following dishonor or receipt of notice of dishonor. See UCC §4-104(1)(h).

minor (infant)   a person who has not yet reached the age of contractual capacity.

mirror-image rule   principle of contract law stating that to create a contract the acceptance must exactly conform to (be the "mirror image" of) the terms of the offer.

misdemeanors   crimes less serious than felonies, usually crimes punishable by fine or imprisonment in a local jail or for a term of less than one year.

mislaid (misplaced) property   property that is intentionally and voluntarily placed in a given location by its owner and subsequently left behind when the owner departs, forgetting to take the property.

misrepresentation   an assertion that is not in accord with existing facts.

mistake   a belief that does not accord with existing facts.

misuse   in product liability cases, the use of a product by the plaintiff for purposes neither intended nor foreseeable by the defendant seller.

mitigation of damages   steps taken by an injured party to keep damages to a minimum.

model   in sales contracts, goods exhibited by the seller to the buyer for inspection during precontract negotiation to describe goods to be sold when the goods themselves are not at hand. See UCC §2-313(1)(c).

model acts   statutes that serve as guidelines to state legislatures in drafting legislation, such as the Model Business Corporation Act or the Model Penal Code.

Model Business Corporation Act (MBCA)   model statute drafted by a committee of the American Bar Association which is the basis of incorporation statutes in many states.

money   a medium of exchange authorized or adopted by a domestic or foreign government as a part of its currency. See UCC §1-201(24).

moral consideration   a common form of past consideration resting at most upon a moral but not legal obligation. See *past consideration*.

mortgage   an interest in real property that is created to secure performance of an obligation, normally repayment of a debt.

mortgagee   the person receiving the benefit of the security afforded by a mortgage; the grantee of the mortgage deed.

mortgagor   the person creating a mortgage and giving the security to a mortgagee; the grantor of the mortgage deed.

motion   an application to the court to issue an order on a matter of law.

motion for directed verdict   motion requesting the court to direct a verdict in favor of the moving party, because for example, the other party has not presented a prima facie case.

motion for summary judgment   motion made during the discovery stage of a civil case alleging that no relevant facts are in dispute, thereby allowing the judge to decide the case as a matter of law.

motion to dismiss the complaint   motion filed by a defendant in a civil case, usually in lieu of answering the complaint, asking the court to dismiss the lawsuit for lack of jurisdiction, or because the complaint fails to state a claim on which judicial relief can be granted.

motion for judgment on the pleadings   motion in a civil case made after all pleadings have been filed which allows the court to rule as a matter of law that one of the parties in a lawsuit is entitled to judgment.

multiparty credit card   credit card issued by a bank which enlists both cardholders and merchants who honor its cards. Unlike a dual-party card, however, merchants honor cards issued by any participating bank. See *dual-party credit card*.

mutual mistake   as used in contract law, mistake occurring when both parties, at the time of the contract, are mistaken about a basic assumption upon which the contract was made. See *mistake*.

mutuality of consideration   requirement for enforceability of contracts that both parties to the contract must provide consideration. See *consideration*.

naked restraints   promises in restraint of trade that have no purpose other than to suppress or eliminate competition. See *restraint of trade*.

National Ambient Air Quality Standards (NAAQS)   air quality standards adopted by the EPA under the Clean Air Act for various identified pollutants.

National Environmental Policy Act (NEPA)   federal statute that imposes a duty on federal agencies to consider environmental matters in administering their programs. See *Environmental Impact Statement*.

National Labor Relations Act (NRLA, Wagner Act) federal statute enacted in 1935, establishing employees' basic rights to engage in collective action and defining various unfair labor practices by employers.

National Labor Relations Board federal agency responsible for administering the NLRA and issuing rules and regulations.

National Pollutant Discharge Elimination System (NPDES) system created by the Clean Water Act for controlling "point-source" pollution, which consists of discharges into a body of water through a confined and discrete conveyance such as a pipe, ditch, or conduit.

nationalization forced taking of foreign assets by a host government. See *expropriation, confiscation*.

natural persons human beings.

necessaries in the context of minors' contracts, such articles of property and such services as are reasonably necessary to enable a minor to earn the money required to provide the necessities of life for herself and those who are legally dependent upon her.

negative (restrictive) covenant in real property law, a covenant restricting or limiting the permissible uses of the land or the acts that may be performed upon it.

negative (prohibitory) injunction See *injunction*.

negligence conduct that falls below the standard established by law for the protection of others against unreasonable risk of harm. Generally, the standard to which a person must conform to avoid being negligent is that of a reasonable person under like circumstances. See *reasonable person*.

negotiable document of title a document of title is negotiable if by its terms the goods are to be delivered to bearer or to the order of a named person; or, where recognized in overseas trade, it runs to a named person or assigns. See UCC §7-104(1). See *document of title*.

negotiability a legal concept characteristic of commercial paper, documents of title, and certificated investment securities which is designed to promote the free transferability of the paper from one owner to the next and to enhance its marketability, by permitting transfer free of claims and defenses.

negotiation 1. process of dispute resolution by which parties with differing demands reach an agreement through compromise and concession. 2. in the law of commercial paper, the transfer of an instrument in such form that the transferee becomes a holder. See UCC §3-202(1). See *holder*.

nolo contendere a form of plea in a criminal case. By pleading nolo contendere (no contest), the defendant may be sentenced as if he or she had been found guilty. The plea may not, however, be used as an admission of guilt in other court proceedings.

nominal consideration (recited consideration) a statement in a contract that property or services are to be exchanged for "$1.00 and other valuable consideration," or similar language.

nominal damages minimal damages awarded to acknowledge the existence of a contract breach or other injury when the plaintiff cannot prove or does not incur loss or injury.

nonconforming use in the law of zoning, a property which does not conform to a new restriction on a zoned area, but which lawfully existed when the zoning ordinance went into effect, and has continued in existence since that time.

noncumulative dividend preferences dividend preference in which preferred dividends not paid in prior years do not accumulate and need not be satisfied before dividends are subsequently paid to shareholders with subordinate dividend rights. That is, only the current year's preference need be satisfied before dividends are paid on shares with subordinate dividend rights.

nonfreehold estate an estate in land that has a fixed or determinate duration.

nonparticipating shares preferred shares that are entitled to receive the amount of the stated dividend preference and no more.

nonpossessory security interest a security interest in personal property in which the debtor retains possession of the collateral that is subject to the security interest.

nonprofit corporation corporation organized for religious, educational, or philanthropic purposes whose income is applied to the specific purpose for which the organization is created rather than the personal enrichment of the persons who own or operate it. See *corporation, business corporation*.

nonrestrictive indorsement in commercial paper, an indorsement that transfers the holder's entire interest in the instrument. See *restrictive indorsement*.

Norris-LaGuardia Act federal statute enacted in 1932 that restricts the federal courts' power to issue injunctions in labor disputes.

note a writing signed by the maker containing an unconditional promise by the maker to pay a sum certain in money to the order of the payee or to bearer on demand or at a definite time. See UCC §§3-104(1), 3-104(2)(d).

notice a person has notice of a fact when he or she has actual knowledge of the fact; receives notification of the fact; or when surrounding facts give the person reason to know that it exists. See *knowledge, notification*.

notice by publication notice accomplished by advertising or publicizing a fact in a newspaper or other publication. See *notification*.

notice of dishonor in commercial paper, notice required to be given to secondary parties liable on an instrument that the instrument has been dishonored, as a condition precedent to secondary liability. See UCC §3-508.

notification formal act intended to affect legal relations between the notifier and the person notified. See *knowledge*. How a person "notifies" or "gives" a notice or notification to another, and when a person "receives" a notice or notification are outlined in UCC §1-201(26).

novation a special form of substituted contract that adds a new party to a contract, who was not a party to the original duty. See *substituted contract*.

Nuclear Regulatory Commission (NRC) (formerly Atomic Energy Commission) federal agency responsible for civilian nuclear regulation.

Nuclear Waste Policy Act federal statute, enacted in 1982, that requires the federal government to select and develop a site for permanent disposal of high level radioactive waste.

nuisance human activity conducted on land or physical condition of land that is harmful or annoying to neighboring landowners or members of the public generally.

nuncupative will an oral will dictated by a testator during his or her last illness before a sufficient number of witnesses and later reduced to writing.

objective theory of contract principle of contract law designed to protect the stability of contractual relationships, which provides that a contracting party is generally held to the impression his conduct or communication creates in a reasonable person in the position of the other party, and may not later assert that his subjective intention differs from his outward manifestation.

obligee the person entitled to receive a performance under a contract; promisee. See *obligor*.

obligor a person required to render a performance under a contract; promisor. See *obligee*.

Occupational Safety and Health Act (OSHA) federal statute enacted in 1970 which generally requires employers to provide safe and healthful working conditions free from recognized hazards likely to cause death or serious physical harm to employees.

Occupational Safety and Health Administration division of the Department of Labor which has primary responsibility for the administration and enforcement of the Occupational Safety and Health Act.

offenses general term for crimes, including felonies and misdemeanors. See *crime*.

offer a conditional promise made by the offeror to the offeree, giving the offeree the power of acceptance, or the power to create a contract. As defined in the *Restatement (Second) of Contracts*, "A manifestation of willingness to enter into a bargain so made as to justify another person in understanding that his assent to that bargain is invited and will conclude it." See *bargain*.

offeree person to whom an offer is directed who has power to create a contract by acceptance.

offeror person making an offer.

omnibus clause in an insurance contract, a clause defining additional insureds as a class bearing a specified relationship to the named insured.

on us check a check that is deposited in a bank that is also the payor bank. Contrast *transit check*.

open-end credit credit extended on an account in which the debtor will incur obligations in a series of transactions. Contrast *closed-end credit*.

operation of law general legal concept used to describe the manner in which a party's rights or duties are determined automatically by the application of a rule of law to a given set of facts, without the act or cooperation of the party.

option contract a contract to keep an offer open for a specified time.

order in commercial paper, a direction to pay, but more than an authorization or request. See UCC §3-102(1)(b).

order paper in commercial paper, an instrument payable to the order or assigns of any person therein specified with reasonable certainty. See UCC §3-110(1). Also includes an instrument bearing a special indorsement. Contrast *bearer paper*.

original acquisition method of acquiring title to unowned goods, such as wild animals and abandoned property, by reducing them to possession.

original jurisdiction term referring to the jurisdiction of a court that has the power to render the initial decision in a case.

ostensible ownership doctrine of sales law applied when a seller retains sold goods. It provides that the sale is void against the seller's creditors if the seller's retention is fraudulent under any rule of law of the state where the goods are situated. See UCC §2-402.

output contract a sales contract in which a seller agrees to sell his or her entire output of goods to the buyer. Contrast *requirments contract*.

ownership the entire bundle of rights recognized in property possessed by a person or persons called the owner; title.

parol evidence as used in applying the parol evidence rule, parol evidence includes oral or written evidence of prior or contemporaneous agreements or negotiations and more generally anything not contained in the integrated writing. See *parol evidence rule*.

parol evidence rule principle of contract law stating that if parties to a contract adopt a writing intended to be a final expression of some or all terms of the agreement, then all prior or contemporaneous, oral or written, agreements are discharged to the extent that they are within the scope of, or are inconsistent with, the writing. Because, under the rule, the writing effectively *becomes* the agreement, parol evidence is inadmissible in court to vary or contradict the terms of the writing. See *integration, parol evidence*.

part performance doctrine an exception to the Statute of Frauds writing requirement for land sale contracts recognized when the party seeking enforcement has changed position in reasonable reliance upon the oral contract.

partial integration see *integrated agreement*.

partial breach breach of contract occurring when a party renders substantial but not full performance. The injured promisee achieves the benefit of the bargain partially through an award of damages and partially through the promisor's substantial performance. See *substantial performance doctrine, total breach, material breach*.

partially disclosed principal in agency law, a principal whose existence, but not identity, is known by the third party.

participating shares type of preferred shares that are entitled to share in dividends with other classes of shares in addition to the dividend preference. Contrast *nonparticipating shares*.

parties in contract law, the promisors and promisees of the various contractual promises; the persons who have engaged in a transaction or made an agreement. See UCC §1-201(29); the plaintiffs and defendants in a lawsuit.

partition method of terminating co-ownership by which the property is divided into distinct portions, resulting in individual ownership by the former cotenants of each portion. See *co-ownership*.

partnership an association of two or more persons to carry on as co-owners a business for profit. See UPA §6(1).

partnership agreement (articles of partnership) contract governing the rights and obligations of the various partners and the internal structure of the partnership. See *partnership*.

partnership by estoppel principle of partnership law under which basic equitable estoppel principles are used to impose partnership liability upon a person who is not, in fact, a partner.

partnership interest a partner's share of the profits and surplus of the partnership. See UPA §26. See *partnership*.

party wall in real property, a wall built next to, or astride, a boundary line designed to serve simultaneously as a common wall of two adjoining structures.

par value as applied to shares of stock, the amount designated as par value for the shares in the articles of incorporation.

past consideration a promise made or performance rendered before a return promise is made. The return promise is not binding upon the promisor because it has not been bargained for. See *moral consideration*.

patent a grant of the exclusive right to make, use, and sell an invention for a term of years.

payee specified person to whom or to whose order an instrument, such as a note or draft, is made payable.

payment guaranteed words of guaranty added to a signature on commercial paper meaning that the signer promises that if the instrument is not paid when due,

the signer will pay it without resort by the holder to any other party. See UCC §3-416(1).

payor bank the bank by which a check is payable as drawn or accepted. See UCC §4-105(b).

per capita distribution distribution of a decedent's estate under which the estate is divided by the number of surviving descendants, regardless of degree. See *per stirpes distribution*.

per stirpes distribution (taking by representation) distribution of a decedent's estate under which the lineal descendant's or "issue" of a deceased heir or devisee inherit the share of an estate that their immediate ancestor would have inherited had he survived (outlived) the intestate or testator.

perfect-tender rule principle of sales law requiring the seller, in order to recover, to tender goods conforming in every respect to the terms of the contract. See UCC §2-601.

perfection in secured transactions, the process by which a secured party achieves protection against third-party claimants to the collateral, including the debtor's other creditors, buyers of the collateral from the debtor, and other persons holding a security interest in the same collateral.

performance bond a suretyship contract that secures an owner (commonly a governmental body) for the proper performance of a building-construction contract by a contractor.

per se violation violations of §1 of the Sherman Act that are so inherently destructive of competition that they are conclusively presumed to be unreasonable and therefore illegal without elaborate inquiry concerning the precise harm they have caused or the business excuse for their use.

personal defenses in commercial paper law, offenses that are defeated by a holder in due course. They include any defense to a simple contract (including fraud and misrepresentation), unauthorized completion, and just tertii defenses. See UCC §§3-305, 3-306.

personal jurisdiction a court's power and authority to issue a judgment that is binding on the parties.

personal property all things capable of ownership except real property. Contrast *real property*.

petit jury body of disinterested persons selected to determine all issues of fact in a court case.

plaintiff party who initiates a civil or criminal case seeking some form of judicial relief from another, the defendant.

plant patent a patent that may be issued to anyone who invents or discovers and asexually reproduces any distinct and new variety of plant.

pleadings written documents that summarize the facts and establish the legal issues of a civil lawsuit.

pledge in secured transactions, a method of perfection established by the creditor's taking possession of the collateral; a possessory security interest.

police power a state's inherent authority to establish

laws protecting the health, safety, morals, and general welfare of its citizens.

positive law law that is specifically enacted or adopted by an authority such as the government or the monarch.

possession physical control of a tangible thing, coupled with an intent to exert control.

possessory security interest (pledge) type of security interest in which the debtor delivers possession of the collateral to the secured party, who retains the property until the debt is paid. Contrast *nonpossessory security interest.*

possibility of reverter a future interest in property existing in the grantor or his successors in interest after creation of a fee simple determinable.

post-obituary note instrument payable upon receipt of an inheritance or future interest.

potential competition doctrine antitrust doctrine used to challenge market extension and product extension mergers under §7 of the Clayton Act which have the effect of eliminating a potential competitor (the acquiring firm) from the market in which the acquired firm operates.

pour-over trust an intervivos trust to which property is added by testamentary disposition; that is, on death, property is "poured over" or into the trust created during life.

power the ability on the part of a person to produce a change in a given legal relation by doing or failing to do a given act. The person whose legal relation is liable to be changed through exercise of another's power is subject to a liability.

power given as security (agency coupled with an interest) a power to affect another's legal relations, created in the form of an agency authority, but for the benefit of the power holder or a third person, and given to secure performance of a duty or to protect a title, such power being given when the duty or title is created or given for consideration. See *Restatement (Second) of Agency* §138.

power of attorney a written instrument by which one person authorizes another to act as his or her agent.

power of termination (right of entry for condition broken) future interest existing in property in the grantor or his successors in interest after creation of a fee simple subject to a condition subsequent.

power to tax an inherent power of the states giving them the authority to require financial contributions to state government.

prayer for relief statement in the complaint in a civil suit in which the plaintiff requests that the court provide a remedy for the alleged wrong, usually an award of damages.

precedent the holding of a prior case that serves as authority for resolution of the issues of subsequent cases that involve the same or similar facts.

preemptive right in corporation law, the right of an existing shareholder to purchase a new issue of shares, in proportion to his or her present interest in the corporation, before the shares are sold to others.

preexisting duty rule common law contract principle stating that a promise to perform (or the performance of) a preexisting legal or public duty does not furnish consideration to support a return promise.

preference in bankruptcy law, a transfer of property by an insolvent debtor to a creditor shortly before bankruptcy on account of an antecedent debt, by means of which the creditor receives more than he or she would have received in the bankruptcy proceeding if the transfer had not been made. See *antecedent debt.*

preferred shares in corporation law, class of shares of stock that have preference over other classes in the payment of dividends or in the assets of the corporation upon liquidation, or both.

Pregnancy Discrimination Act federal statute enacted in 1978 prohibiting employment discrimination based on pregnancy.

preliminary hearing in criminal prosecutions, a proceeding held before the magistrate to protect an accused individual from unwarranted prosecution, and in which the prosecution must establish that probable cause exists to believe that a crime has been committed and that the accused committed it.

prescription a method of obtaining an easement by the adverse use of another's land, if the use is hostile, open and notorious, and is continuous and uninterrupted for the period of the statute of limitations. See *easement.*

present possessory estate an estate in property in which the owner has the present right to possession of the property. Contrast *future interest.*

presenting bank any bank presenting a check except a payor bank. See UCC §4-105(e).

presentment in commercial paper, a demand for payment or acceptance of an instrument made by the holder upon the maker, acceptor, or drawee. See UCC §3-504(1).

presentment warranties in commercial paper, warranties regarding forgery and alteration given to the party who is to pay or accept an instrument by any person presenting the instrument for payment or acceptance and any prior transferor of the instrument. See UCC §§3-417, 4-207.

prevention and hindrance term sometimes used to describe a breach of the duty to act in good faith in contract performance.

price discrimination practice by a seller of charging one buyer more than another for the same commodity.

price fixing cooperative setting of price levels or ranges by competing firms. Includes generally any agreement between competitors which affects or is intended to affect price, however accomplished.

prima facie case in a civil case, some evidence supporting each allegation of the complaint that, unless contradicted or rebutted by other evidence, entitles the plaintiff to recover. That is, the defendant automatically prevails without producing any evidence unless the plaintiff proves a prima facie case.

primary contract liability in commercial paper, the form of contract liability undertaken by the maker of a note and the acceptor of a draft. It involves an absolute obligation to pay an instrument. See *secondary contract liability*.

primary line competitive injury in price discrimination cases, injury occurring at the same functional level as the discriminating seller; that is, competitors of the discriminating seller are injured. Contrast *secondary line competitive injury*.

primary picketing in labor law, picketing the business with which the union has a genuine dispute.

principal in suretyship law, the person for whose debt or default the surety is liable. See also *agency*.

principal and income allocation the process of apportioning receipts and expenditures in the administration of a trust between the income beneficiary and the remainderman.

priorities rules of law, usually created by statute such as federal bankruptcy law, granting a creditor who does not possess a lien upon a debtor's property a priority in distribution of the debtor's assets over certain other creditors.

private corporation corporation formed by private individuals for private purposes and including, generally, nonprofit and business corporations. Contrast *public corporation*.

private international law a branch of conflicts of law that determines when a domestic court should exercise jurisdiction over a case involving foreign persons or territories, when foreign rather than domestic law should apply to a case, and when judgments rendered by foreign courts should be recognized and enforced in a domestic court.

private law rules and principles that involve persons (whether artificial or natural) as private individuals.

private nuisance an intential tort providing a remedy for invasions of the private interest in the use and enjoyment of land.

private trust an express trust in which the trust property is devoted to the use of specified persons designated as beneficiaries. See *express trust;* contrast *charitable trust*.

privilege the legal freedom on the part of one person as against another to do or refrain from doing an act. There is no right on the part of the person against whom the privilege exists that the person possessing the privilege should not engage in the particular course of action or nonaction in question.

Privileges and Immunities Clause provision of the Constitution which prohibits states from unreasonably

discriminating against out-of-state citizens, including out-of-state businesses.

privity of contract term used to refer to the relationship among persons who have entered into a contractual relationship.

probable cause in criminal law, facts and circumstances that would lead a reasonable person to believe: (1) for an arrest or indictment—that an offense has been committed and that the accused committed it, (2) for a search warrant—that the items are located in the place to be searched and that the items are connected with illegal activities.

probate any matter or proceeding pertaining to the administration of a decedent's estate.

probate court a state court having jurisdiction over the administration of a decedent's estate.

procedural law law that establishes the mechanisms with which to enforce the rights and duties created by substantive law.

procedural unconscionability a form of unconscionability occurring when a person signs a standardized-form contract containing a provision, commonly in fine print, which substantially alters his or her reasonable expectations under the agreement; unfair surprise. See *unconscionability*.

proceeds in secured transactions, whatever is received upon the sale, exchange, collection, or other disposition of collateral or proceeds. See UCC §9-306(1).

process of posting the usual internal procedure used by the payor bank to determine whether to pay a check and to record the payment. See UCC §4-109.

product extension merger merger that combines firms producing related though not identical products.

products liability the area of law imposing liability upon manufacturers and other suppliers of goods for personal injury and property damage caused by the products they sell.

professional corporation a closely held corporation formed by professionals such as doctors, lawyers, accountants, and engineers. See *closely-held corporation, corporation*.

profit (profit à prendre) a right of use in another's property that involves the right to remove part of the land or products of the land. See *easement*.

promise 1. in general, a commitment or undertaking that something will or will not happen in the future. 2. in commercial paper, an undertaking to pay that must more than merely acknowledge the existence of an obligation. See UCC §3-102(1)(c).

promisee person to whom a promise is made.

promisor person making a promise.

promissory estoppel doctrine of contract law making otherwise unenforceable promises enforceable if relied upon. Specifically, a promise which the promisor should reasonably expect to induce action or forbearance on the part of the promisee or a third person and which does induce such action or forbearance is binding if unjustice can be avoided only by enforcement of the promise. See *estoppel.*

promoters   persons organizing and planning a corporation. See *corporation.*

promulgate   to publish; to announce officially.

property   sum of the various legal relationships between identifiable persons with respect to a thing, tangible or intangible.

proprietorship (sole proprietorship)   a business owned and controlled exclusively by one person.

prosecution   a legal proceeding in which a person is charged with a crime and guilt or innocence is determined.

prospectus   the first part of a registration statement filed under the Securities Act of 1933 which must be delivered to persons to whom a security is offered or sold. See *registration statement.*

protest   in commercial paper, a certificate of dishonor signed and sealed by a United States consul or vice consul, a notary public, or any other person authorized by local law to certify dishonor. See UCC §3-509(1).

proviso   clause or part of a clause contained in a statute which either excepts something from the enacting clause, qualifies, modifies, or restrains its generality, or excludes some possible ground of misinterpretation concerning its extent. Provisos usually are preceded by the words ''provided,'' ''provided that,'' or ''provided, however.''

proximate cause   in negligence law, the various legal issues that collectively limit the defendant's liability for the consequences of his or her negligent acts. Generally, to recover the plaintiff must prove that the defendant's negligent conduct was a substantial factor in producing the plaintiff's injury (causation in fact), and that the defendant owed a duty to the particular injured plaintiff to protect him or her against the event that in fact caused the injury (foreseeability of harm).

proxy   grant of authority by a shareholder to another to vote his or her shares.

prudent-person rule   principle governing trust investments under which the trustee owes a duty to the beneficiary to make only those investments of trust property which a prudent person would make of her or his own property, taking into consideration both the preservation of the estate and the amount and regularity of the income to be generated.

public corporation (municipal, political corporation)   corporation created by the government for political purposes to administer civil government, often vested with local legislative powers. See *corporation, private corporation.*

public invitee   a member of the public invited to enter or remain upon another's land for a purpose for which the land is held open to the public.

public law   principles and rules that involve the government in its capacity of representing society.

publicly-held corporation   corporation whose shares are owned by many people, such as a corporation that has shares traded on a securities exchange, or for which public share price quotations exist. See *corporation.*

public nuisance   criminal offense proscribing various activities or physical conditions as offensive to the public health, safety, morals, peace, or comfort.

Public Utility Holding Company Act of 1935   federal statute designed to correct abuses in the financing and operation of electric and gas utilities owned by holding companies.

punitive (exemplary) damages   damages that are designed to punish the conduct of the defendant and to deter similar future conduct by the defendant or others. See *damages.*

purchase money mortgage   traditionally, a mortgage taken by a seller of real property to secure payment of its purchase price. Now generally used to describe any mortgage given on real property to secure its purchase price no matter who provides financing. See *mortgage.*

purchase money security interest   a security interest that is taken or retained by a seller of the collateral to secure all or part of its price, or taken by a person who makes an advance or incurs an obligation that enables the debtor to acquire rights in collateral. See UCC §9-107.

purchaser   person who takes property by sale, discount, negotiation, mortgage, pledge, lien, issue or reissue, gift, or any other voluntary transaction creating an interest in property. See UCC §§1-201(32), (33).

pure notice recording statute   recording statute under which a subsequent purchaser who takes without actual knowledge of a prior unrecorded conveyance prevails, regardless of who later records first. See *recording statute.*

pure race recording statute   statute under which the first purchaser to record an interest in property prevails even if he or she takes with actual knowledge of a prior unrecorded conveyance. See *recording statute.*

qualified indoresement   in commercial paper, an indorsement that contains the words ''without recourse'' added to the signature. A qualified indorsement negates secondary contract liability. See *unqualified indorsement.*

quasi-contract (implied-in-law contract)   a form of restitution designed to provide a remedy when a benefit is conferred by one party upon another, who retains the benefit. If necessary to prevent unjust enrichment of the benefited party, the law implies or imposes a promise (the quasi-contract) to pay the reasonable value of the benefit conferred. See *restitution, constructive trust.*

quitclaim deed   deed that conveys whatever interest the grantor has in property, but makes no warranties or promises regarding title to the grantee. See *deed, warranty deed.*

race-notice recording statute recording statute under which a subsequent puchaser prevails over a prior unrecorded conveyance if he or she both (1) takes without actual knowledge of the prior conveyance, and (2) records first. See *recording statute*.

ratification 1. in contracts generally, an election to be bound upon a previously voidable obligation. See *voidable contract*. 2. in agency law, an indication by the principal through words or conduct of an intent to be bound upon (to treat as authorized) a previously unauthorized contract made on his or her behalf.

reaffirmation agreement an agreement in which a debtor promises to pay a debt discharged in bankruptcy.

real defenses in commercial paper, defenses that may be successfully asserted against a holder in due course, including forgery; material alteration; infancy, other incapacity, duress and illegality; fraud in the execution; discharge in bankruptcy; and any other discharge known to the holder when he or she takes the instrument. See UCC §§3-305, 3-306.

Real Estate Settlement Procedures Act (RESPA) federal statute requiring advance itemized disclosure of real estate closing costs to the buyer.

real fraud see *fraud in the execution*.

real property property interests recognized in land and structures, objects, or other interests attached to or closely associated with land. See *property, personal property*.

reasonable (ordinary) care the amount of care a reasonably careful and prudent person would use under similar circumstances.

reasonable grounds for insecurity see *adequate assurance of due performance*. See UCC §2-609.

reasonable person a hypothetical, fictitious person who possesses the characteristics attentiveness, knowledge, intelligence, and judgment required by society for the protection of others. See *negligence, reasonable care*.

receiver a person appointed by a court to take possession of and administer, preserve, or manage a debtor's property under court direction.

reciprocal dealing anticompetitive arrangement that arises when two parties are related as buyer to seller in one or more markets and seller to buyer in another or others. One party then agrees to buy from the other in one market, if the other agrees to buy from it in another market.

recorder of deeds office public office in which documents evidencing an interest in real property are recorded.

recording statutes state statutes designed to provide reliable public information on the status of real estate titles. Recording statutes protect purchasers and mortgagees by allowing them to defeat prior unrecorded recordable interests in property.

recoupment in general, action by which a defendant reduces an amount owing to the plaintiff by asserting claims or defenses arising out of the same contract or transaction on which the plaintiff's action is founded; action by which the obligor of an assigned right asserts against the assignee defenses that he or she has against the assignor arising out of the contract creating the assigned right. Contrast *set-off*.

recoupment cycle in secured transactions involving inventory, the process of converting the proceeds of the sale of inventory to cash, which is then used to purchase more inventory.

reformation an equitable remedy used to rewrite or reform a written contract which, because of a mistake by both parties regarding the content or effect of the writing, fails to correctly state the parties' agreement.

registration statement statement that must be filed with the SEC before securities are offered or sold to the public.

Regulation A SEC regulation governing limited offerings under the Securities Act of 1933, providing a simplified form of registration for small issues (not more than $1.5 million). Securities Act Rules 251–264.

Regulation B regulation issued by the Federal Reserve Board to implement the Equal Credit Opportunity Act.

Regulation D SEC regulation governing limited offerings under the Securities Act of 1933, which simplifies and coordinates the various limited offering exemptions. Securities Act Rules 501–506.

Regulation Z regulation issued by the Federal Reserve Board to implement the Truth-in-Lending Act.

Regulation CC regulation issued by the Federal Reserve Board to implement the Expedited Funds Availability Act.

rehabilitation case bankruptcy case in which the debtor retains his or her assets and pays creditors out of future earnings pursuant to a plan filed with and approved by the court. Contrast *liquidation case*.

reimbursement in suretyship law, the surety's right to be reimbursed by the principal after paying or otherwise performing the principal obligation.

rejection 1. in contract formation, the offeree's statement or other conduct indicating an intention not to accept an offer. 2. in sales law, an action taken by the buyer after delivery of nonconforming goods, indicating an intention to reject and return (rather than retain) the goods. Contrast *acceptance*.

reliance interest an interest of an injured promisee that may be protected by contract remedies, designed to reimburse the promisee for expenses incurred in reliance upon the contract.

remand action of an appellate court that sends the case back to a lower court.

remedy at law dollar damages. Contrast *equitable remedy*.

remainder a future interest arising in a third party (someone other than the grantor), which takes effect in possession and enjoyment on the natural termination of the preceding estate.

remittance chain   the chain of banks in the check collection process which become accountable for the amount of a check, beginning with the payor bank and ultimately ending with the depositary bank's liability to pay its customer, the depositor of the check.

remitter   a person, not a party to the instrument, who purchases an instrument in order to pay his or her own debt to the payee named in the instrument.

reorganization plan   in a bankruptcy case, a rehabilitation plan filed with and approved by the court which divides creditors and shareholders into classes, and then designates how claimants within each class are to be treated.

replevin   a statutory prejudgment creditor's remedy enabling the plaintiff to recover possession of specific goods wrongfully taken or detained.

repudiation   in contract law, words or conduct of one contracting party that unequivocally indicate her inability or unwillingness to perform without breach.

requirements contract   a sales contract in which a buyer promises to purchase his requirements of a given commodity from a seller.

res ipsa loquitur   doctrine of negligence law under which it may be inferred that the plaintiff's harm was caused by the defendant's negligence if (1) the event is one that does not ordinarily occur in the absence of negligence, (2) other responsible causes are eliminated by the evidence, and (3) the indicated negligence is within the scope of the defendant's duty to the plaintiff.

res judicata   doctrine providing that final judgment by a court of competent jurisdiction is conclusive on the parties and prevents relitigation of the cause of action.

resale price maintenance   an agreement between a seller and a buyer fixing the price at which the buyer may resell the goods purchased.

rescission   a contract remedy in which the contract is avoided, and each party receives restitution for the value of any benefit conferred on the other, thereby restoring both parties to the position they occupied before the contract was made.

respondeat superior doctrine   doctrine of agency law imposing liability without fault upon masters for the torts of servants committed while acting within the scope of their employment. See *master, servant*.

Resource Conservation and Recovery Act (RCRA)   federal statute that established a plan for transporting and disposing of hazardous waste.

Restatement of the Law   major civil law treatise published by the American Law Institute (ALI), the stated purpose of which is to define the principles of the common law as they would be decided today by the great majority of the courts.

restitution   generally, the act of restoring something to its rightful owner, commonly to make good for some loss, damage, or injury. As a judicial remedy, a person who has been unjustly enriched at the expense of another is required to make restitution to the other for the value of the benefit conferred. See *unjust enrichment, quasi-contract, constructive trust*.

restitution interest   an interest of a promisee that may be protected by contract remedies. The interest is measured by the value of the benefit conferred by the promisee on the other party.

restraint of trade   a promise is in restraint of trade if its performance limits competition in any business or restricts the promisor in the exercise of any gainful occupation.

restrictive indorsement   an indorsement limiting or restricting in some way the rights acquired by the indorsee. See *nonrestrictive indorsement*.

resulting trust   in implied trust arising when a person makes a disposition of property under circumstances indicating that he or she does intend that the person taking or holding the property should have a beneficial interest in it. See *implied trust*.

reverse   action of an appellate court which sets aside the judgment entered by a lower court.

reverse discrimination   employment discrimination in favor of minorities and women.

reversion   a future interest remaining in a grantor of property who transfers away less than his or her entire interest in the property.

Revised Model Business Corporation Act (RMBCA)   Model Business Corporation Act, as revised and renumbered in 1984. It is reprinted in Appendix F.

Revised Uniform Limited Partnership Act (RULPA)   revision of the Uniform Limited Partnership Act promulgated by the National Conference of Commissioners on Uniform State Laws in 1976, and amended in 1985. It is reprinted in Appendix E. See *limited partnership, Uniform Limited Partnership Act*.

revocation   in contract formation, the offeror's statement or other conduct after the offer is made, indicating that he or she no longer intends to enter into the proposed contract.

revocation of acceptance   in sales law, action taken by a buyer to revoke a previous acceptance of goods in limited circumstances in which the nonconformity of goods substantially impairs their value to the buyer. See *acceptance*. See UCC §2-608.

rezoning   an amendment to a zoning ordinance that reclassifies property into a new zone.

right   a legally enforceable claim of one person against another, that the other shall do or not do a given act. The person against whom the right exists has a "duty"; that is, he or she is under a legally enforceable obligation to do or refrain from doing an act.

right of foreclosure   the right of a secured creditor to take possession of and sell the collateral to satisfy a debt.

right of survivorship   characteristic of the joint tenancy and tenancy by the entirety form of co-ownership. Under the right of survivorship if one of the joint tenants or tenants by the entirety dies, the deceased's share is owned by the other, who becomes the sole owner. If the property is owned by more than two joint tenants, the deceased's shared belongs to the survivors jointly. See *joint tenancy, tenancy by the entirety, co-ownership*.

right to privacy the right to be left alone. Interference with this right is compensable in a tort action.

right-to-work laws state laws that prohibit union and agency shops. See *union shop, agency shop*.

risk of loss contract rules determining the rights of the parties if the property to be sold under the contract (such as goods) is lost, destroyed, or stolen. Risk of loss rules define when the risk of such casualties passes from the seller to the buyer.

Robinson-Patman Act amendment to §2 of the Clayton Act, enacted in 1936 to reach secondary line anticompetitive effects of price discrimination and to outlaw some of the more flagrant devices used to exact price concessions.

rule of privilege rule of law that enables a person to prevent certain information from being introduced into evidence in court.

rule of reason basic standard by which violations of §1 of the Sherman Act are measured. Under the rule of reason, the Sherman Act does not condemn all restraints of trade, but only those restraints the character or effect of which is unreasonably anticompetitive. See *Sherman Antitrust Act*.

runaway shop unfair labor practice in which an employer closes a facility or moves its operation to another facility to avoid having to bargain with a union.

sale the passing of title to goods from the seller to the buyer for a price. See UCC §2-106(1).

sale on approval sale in which goods are delivered to a consumer primarily for use and may be returned by the buyer even though they conform to the contract. See UCC §§2-326, 2-327.

sale or return sale in which goods are delivered to a merchant for resale and may be returned even though they conform to the contract. See UCC §§2-326, 2-327.

sale with reserve auction sale in which the auctioneer (seller) may withdraw the goods at any time prior to announcing completion of the sale. See UCC §2-328.

sample in sales contracts, goods drawn from the bulk of goods involved in the sale and exhibited by the seller to the buyer for inspection during precontract negotiation to describe goods to be sold. See UCC §2-313(1)(c). Contrast *model*.

scienter in fraud cases, a term used by the courts to refer to a defendant's knowledge of falsity of his misrepresentation. See *fraudulent misrepresentation*.

scope of employment conduct of a servant of the kind he or she is employed to perform that occurs substantially within authorized time and space limitations, and is motivated, at least in part, by a purpose to serve the master. See *respondeat superior doctrine, vicarious liability*.

scrip a certificate representing the right to receive a portion of a share used as an alternative to fractional shares in distributing share dividends.

search warrant a document issued by a judge or magistrate, upon a showing of probable cause, authorizing governmental officials to search a specific place and seize specific items connected with illegal activities.

secondary boycott an unfair labor practice by a union in a labor dispute involving pressuring the primary employer by striking, picketing, or otherwise boycotting a business with which the primary employer does business.

secondary contract liability in commercial paper, the form of contract liability undertaken by the drawer of a draft and the indorser of any instrument. It includes an obligation to pay the instrument only if the primary party does not and certain conditions are met. See *primary contract liability*. See UCC §§3-413, 3-414.

secondary line competitive injury in price discrimination cases, injury that occurs among buyers from the discriminating seller who later compete in the resale of the goods. That is, injury occurs at a functional level below (or vertical to) the discriminating seller. If the buyer receiving the discrimination itself resells, competition may be affected two functional levels below the discriminating seller. Injury at this level (among competitors of the buyer's customers) is "third line" or "tertiary line" injury. Contrast *primary line competitive injury*.

secret limitation in agency law, a limitation placed by the principal upon the normal incidents of an agent's authority and which is not known to third parties dealing with the agent.

secured creditor generally, a creditor who has a contractually created lien in a debtor's property.

secured party in a secured transaction, the lender, seller, or other party in whose favor a security interest exists. See UCC §9-105(1)(m).

secured transaction a transaction in which a borrower or buyer gives a lender or seller an interest in personal property or fixtures to secure performance of an obligation. Contrast *mortgage*.

Securities Act of 1933 federal statute governing the public distribution of securities. With certain exceptions it prohibits the offer or sale of securities to the public unless the offering is properly registered. The Act requires broad disclosure of relevant corporate information to prospective investors, provides civil remedies for violations, and prohibits fraudulent or deceptive practices in the sale of securities.

Securities and Exchange Commission federal administrative agency established by the Securities Exchange Act of 1934 to administer federal securities law.

Securities Exchange Act of 1934   federal statute that created the Securities and Exchange Commission and regulates secondary trading in securities, the securities markets, and persons conducting securities transactions. The Act imposes registration and reporting requirements on many issuers and others, and regulates proxy solicitation, tender offers, insider trading, and fraud and manipulative practices in securities trading.

security   1. under securities law, a wide variety of investment instruments such as stocks, bonds, and investment contracts. 2. under UCC Article 8, a share, participation, or other interest in the property of the issuing corporation, or an obligation of the issuer. See UCC §8-102. 3. in debtor-creditor law, devices used by creditors to protect themselves against other creditors in the event of the debtor's bankruptcy and to provide for expeditious collection upon default. Usually provided by a contractually created lien in the debtor's real or personal property (a mortgage or secured transaction), or the promise of a surety to pay the debt if the debtor does not.

security agreement   in a secured transaction, the contract creating or providing for a security interest. See UCC §9-105(1)(l).

security interest   in a secured transaction, an interest in personal property or fixtures that secures payment or performance of an obligation. See UCC §1-201(37).

self-help   secured creditors' remedy under which, upon default by the debtor, the creditor simply repossesses the collateral without resort to judicial process.

servant   agent whose physical conduct in the performance of his or her duties is subject to the control or right of control of the principal (master).

service mark   any word, name, symbol, or device used to identify and distinguish a particular service for sales and advertising purposes. See *trademark*.

service of process   formal delivery of a complaint and a summons to the defendant.

set-off   in general, action by which a defendant subtracts (sets off) against amounts owing to the plaintiff, amounts owed by the plaintiff to the defendant arising out of a contract or transaction other than the one upon which the plaintiff's claim is based; action by which the obligor of an assigned right asserts against the assignee defenses that she has against the assignor arising independently of the contract creating the assigned right. Contrast *recoupment*.

settlement   as used in bank deposits and collections, a term referring to payment of an item in cash, through adjustment and offsetting balances through clearing houses, debit or credit entries in accounts between banks, or the forwarding of various types of remittance instruments.

settlor (trustor)   person who creates a trust. See *trust*.

several liability   in contract law, term describing liability of copromisors if each promises a separate performance to be rendered respectively by each of them, or each makes a separate promise that the same performance will be rendered. See *joint and several promises, joint liability*.

shareholder derivative suit   lawsuit in which shareholders sue not in their individual capacities, but as representatives of the corporation, in order to enforce a corporate cause of action.

shelter (umbrella) rule   in commercial paper, doctrine providing that the transfer of an instrument by a holder in due course vests in the transferee the rights of a holder in due course even if the transferee cannot himself qualify under UCC §3-302. See UCC §3-201(1).

Sherman Antitrust Act   federal statute, enacted in 1890, which makes illegal contracts, combinations, or conspiracies in restraint of trade and monopolization, attempts to monopolize, and conspiracies to monopolize.

shipment contract   sales contract in which the seller is authorized or required to ship goods to the buyer, but is not required to deliver them at any particular destination. See *destination contract*.

shipment under reservation (documentary sale)   sales contract in which the seller draws a draft against the buyer for the purchase price and forwards it, together with a bill of lading covering the goods, to the buyer's bank with instructions not to surrender the bill of lading to the buyer until the buyer accepts or pays the draft.

sight draft   a demand draft.

signature   any symbol adopted or executed by a party with present intention to authenticate a writing. See UCC §1-201(39).

single-party credit card   credit card issued by a business to sell goods or services on credit to its customers, the cardholders. That is, a single-party card is a simple credit sale with the card used to identify persons to whom credit should be extended.

slander   communication of a defamatory statement by spoken words or gestures. See *defamation*. Contrast *libel*.

Social Security Act   federal statute enacted in 1935 to provide income to retired workers and later amended to include benefits to disabled workers and to dependents of deceased workers.

solicitation   an inchoate crime committed when a person, with intent that a crime be committed, asks, orders, or otherwise encourages another to commit that crime.

sovereign immunity   a doctrine of international law under which domestic courts, in certain circumstances, will not exercise jurisdiction over a foreign state or its instrumentalities.

special agent   agent who conducts a transaction or series of transactions not involving continuity of service. Contrast *general agent*.

special guaranty (offer for)   an offer for a suretyship contract made to a particular creditor that can only be accepted by that creditor. Contrast *general guaranty*.

special indorsee the person to whom a specially indorsed instrument becomes payable. The instrument may be further negotiated only the the special indorsee's indorsement. See *special indorsement*.

special indorsement in commercial paper, an indorsement that specifies the person to whom or to whose order the instrument is further payable. Contrast *blank indorsement*.

special permit an administrative remedy provided for in zoning ordinances that allows a landowner to use his or her land in a manner expressly permitted by the ordinance, provided conditions and standards set forth in the zoning regulations are met.

specially manufactured goods goods which are to be manufactured or acquired for a particular buyer, and which are not suitable for sale to others in the ordinary course of the seller's business.

specific devise a devise of particularly designated property. See *devise*.

specific performance an equitable contract remedy requiring that the breaching party actually perform the contract as agreed. See *injunction against breach*.

spendthrift trust trust in which the beneficiary may not voluntarily transfer the interest, and creditors of the beneficiary may not reach it to satisfy their claims.

spot zoning a zoning amendment classifying a property or group of properties within a district to a use that is inconsistent with the general zoning pattern of the surrounding area, and is designed primarily for the economic benefit of the owner.

stale check a check that is more than six months old.

standard mortgage clause clause usually found in fire insurance or homeowner's policies that is designed to protect the lender holding a mortgage on the insured property. Under the clause, the mortgagee becomes an insured, and any loss is payable to the mortgagor and mortgagee as their interests appear. In addition, the clause provides that the mortgagee may collect for losses under the policy even if the mortgagor would be denied recovery.

Standard State Zoning Enabling Act statute drafted in 1924 that is the basis of many state statutes authorizing local governments to enact zoning ordinances.

standby letter of credit a letter of credit that represents an obligation to the beneficiary on the part of the issuer (i) to repay money borrowed by or advanced to or for the account of the customer, or (ii) to make payment on account of any evidence of indebtedness undertaken by the customer, or (iii) to make payment on account of any default by the customer in the performance of an obligation. See *letter of credit*.

stare decisis doctrine forming the basis of the common law which provides that courts will adhere to and apply basic principles of law decided in prior cases to later cases involving substantially the same or similar facts and issues.

state implementation plan (SIP) under the Clean Air Act, state plan designed to attain the air quality established by the National Ambient Air Quality Standards (NAAQS).

Statute of Elizabeth English statute, enacted in 1570, providing that any transfer of property made with the end purpose and intent of delaying, hindering, or defrauding creditors is void. The Statute of Elizabeth is the basis of modern fraudulent conveyances law.

Statute of Frauds English statute, enacted in 1677, requiring that certain types of contracts be evidenced by a writing to be enforceable; more generally, the term refers to any statute requiring that a contract be evidenced by a writing to be enforceable. See, for example, UCC §§2-201, 8-319, 1-206, 9-203(1)(a).

statute of limitations statute that requires the plaintiff to file a lawsuit within a specified period of time after a cause of action arises, or be barred from recovery. See, for example, UCC §§2-725, 6-111.

statutes written laws enacted by the legislature.

statutory lien a lien imposed or authorized solely by statute, which arises by operation of law when specified circumstances or conditions occur.

stock subscription an offer or agreement by a subscriber to purchase and pay for a specified number of previously unissued shares of the corporation.

stop-payment order oral or written order directed by the drawer to the drawee bank to countermand, or stop, an order to pay contained in a check.

straight voting method of shareholder voting in which each share is entitled to one vote on each matter, including one vote for each vacant directorship. Contrast *cumulative voting*.

strict foreclosure method of foreclosure in secured transactions in which, after default and repossession, the secured party merely retains the collateral in full satisfaction of the debt. It is used as an alternative to selling the collateral and applying the proceeds to the unpaid obligation.

strict liability liability that is imposed without fault; liability that is imposed upon a defendant in the absence of both negligence and an intent to interfere with the plaintiff's legally protected interests.

strict liability in tort theory of recovery in products liability under which the plaintiff recovers by proving that an injury resulted from a condition of a product, that the condition was an unreasonably dangerous one (that is, the product was defective), and that the condition existed when the product left the seller's control. See *defective product*.

strike a concerted work stoppage by the employees.

substantial performance doctrine a doctrine of contract law under which a person is entitled to recover under a contract despite immaterial defects in performance. Because such "substantial performance" is not full performance, however, the other contracting party may recover damages for partial breach. See *partial breach, material breach, total breach.*

subject-matter jurisdiction   the types or categories of cases that a court is empowered to hear. See *jurisdiction.* Contrast *personal jurisdiction.*

sublease   in landlord-tenant law, transfer by the tenant of all or part of his or her interest in the property for a period less than the entire term; or a transfer, originally for the entire term, if the tenant may reacquire the right to possession upon occurrence of an event.

subrogation   an equitable remedy involving an equitable assignment grounded in restitution and designed to prevent unjust enrichment. In suretyship law, it refers to the surety's right to succeed to the position of the creditor, once the surety has satisfied the principal obligation, for purposes of proceeding against the principal. In insurance law, it refers to the insurance company's right, after paying the insured, to succeed the insured's rights in contract or tort against any third party causing the loss.

substituted contract   a contract accepted by a contracting party in full satisfaction of a duty owed, which immediately discharges the original duty.

subpoena   a legal process commanding a witness to appear and give testimony.

substantive criminal law   the law defining which acts or omissions are crimes and describing the punishment to be imposed for that conduct. See *crime.* Contrast *criminal procedure.*

substantive law   law defining the rights to which a person is entitled and the duties a person is obligated to perform. Contrast *procedural law.*

substantive unconscionability   unconscionability involving contractual oppression, occurring when a contract or provision is unreasonably harsh or unfair, generally exacted by a party with vastly superior bargaining power. See *unconscionability.*

sum certain   requirement in commercial paper to aid in valuation of the instrument, that the sum of money payable be certain. Generally, the sum payable is certain if, at any time of payment, the holder can determine the amount then payable from the instrument with any necessary computation. See UCC §3-106.

summons   in a civil case, document delivered to the defendant with the complaint ordering the defendant to appear in court on a certain date or to answer the complaint within a specified number of days.

supervening event   in contract law, an extraordinary event occurring after a contract is made but before performance.

supplementary proceedings   proceedings provided as part of a creditor's lawsuit that may be used to discover assets in the debtor's hands, and provide for injunctions against transfers and appointment of receivers.

Supremacy Clause   constitutional provision stating that the federal Constitution, federal statutes, and federal treaties are the supreme law of the land.

surety   in suretyship, the person liable on the debt or obligation of another, the principal.

suretyship   legal relationship existing when two parties (principal and surety) are liable for the same performance to a creditor who is entitled to but one satisfaction, and as between the two who are liable, the principal rather than the surety should perform.

surrender   in landlord-tenant law, a contract involving either the transfer of the landlord's reversion to the tenant or of the tenant's nonfreehold estate to the landlord.

symbolic delivery   method of delivery of a gift that involves the delivery of another object in place of the actual subject matter. Contrast *constructive delivery.*

tariff   1. a schedule, scheme, or system of duties imposed by a government on imported or exported goods. 2. a public document filed by a common carrier setting forth its rates and services, and the rules, regulations, and procedures relating to those services.

tax lien   statutory lien held by the state or federal government or a government subdivision to secure payment of delinquent taxes. See *lien, statutory lien.*

tenancy by the entirety   a specialized form of joint tenancy with right of survivorship existing between co-tenants who are husband and wife. See *co-ownership, joint tenancy.*

tenancy in common   form of co-ownership having no right of survivorship; on death of a tenant in common, the deceased tenant's interest passes to the tenant's estate, rather than to the surviving co-tenants. See *right of survivorship, joint tenancy, tenancy by the entirety, co-ownership.*

tenancy in partnership   special form of co-ownership with right of survivorship by which partners hold title to specific partnership property.

tenant (lessee)   one to whom the right of possession of real property is transferred in a landlord-tenant relationship.

tender of performance   in contract law, actual performance of the contract or an offer of performance coupled with the manifested present ability to do so.

termination   1. in partnership law, an event occurring upon completion of the winding up or liquidation process. See also *winding up (liquidation).* 2. in sales contracts, an event occurring when either party pursuant to a power created by agreement or law puts an end to the contract otherwise than for its breach. See UCC §2-106(3).

termination statement   in secured transactions, a statement filed in an appropriate public office indicating that a financing arrangement has been terminated.

testamentary disposition a transfer of property through a will.

testamentary trust trust created in the settlor's will.

testate a person who dies leaving a valid will directing the disposition of his or her property is said to die "testate." Contrast *intestate*.

testator a person making a will.

third line (tertiary line) competitive injury See *secondary line competitive injury*.

third party in contract law, anyone other than the contracting parties who may be affected by or have rights under the contract; generally, anyone other than the parties. See *party*.

time draft a draft that is payable at some fixed or determinable future time. Contrast *demand draft*.

third-party complaint in a civil case, pleading filed by a defendant to sue other persons not named as parties in the original suit.

through bill of lading a bill of lading issued by the first of two or more carriers when the carriage is to be performed in part by connecting carriers other than the issuer.

time instrument in commercial paper, an instrument calling for future (other than demand) payment. See *instrument*.

time of the essence clause a contract term making time of performance a condition to the promisor's duty.

title ownership.

title closing (settlement) performance of a real estate contract in which the seller of property conveys the property by delivering a deed to the buyer and the buyer pays the purchase price.

title insurance a form of real estate title protection under which a title insurance company agrees to indemnify or reimburse the insured property owner or lender against losses resulting from certain specified defects in the title to the covered property.

title search systematic examination of the chronological public record of transactions concerning a particular tract of real property.

Title VII of the Civil Rights Act of 1964 federal statute amended by the Equal Employment Opportunity Act of 1972, which prohibits employment discrimination based on race, color, national origin, religion, and sex.

Torrens system a method of assuring real estate titles that involves registration of title to property, instead of recording evidence of that title.

tort a private or civil wrong or injury, other than breach of contract, for which the court will provide a remedy in the form of an action for damages.

tort-feasor person who commits a tort.

total breach breach of contract involving a material defect in performance. In this case, the constructive condition to the other party's duty does not occur and his duty to perform does not arise. The injured party is then entitled to damages for total breach—damages

based upon all of his right to performance. See *substantial performance doctrine, partial breach, material breach*.

Toxic Substances Control Act (TSCA) federal statute that provides comprehensive regulation of toxic substances.

trade acceptance draft drawn by a seller of goods on credit against his or her buyer.

trade fixtures chattels that are attached for use in a tenant's trade or business (for example, counters, machinery, shelves, or light fixtures).

trademark any word, name, symbol, or device adopted and used by a manufacturer or merchant to identify and distinguish his or her goods from those manufactured or sold by others.

trade secret any formula, pattern, device, or compilation of information which is used in one's business, and which gives the user an advantage over competitors who do not know or use it.

trading partnership a commercial or merchandising business, involved in maintaining an inventory and buying and selling it for profit. See *partnership*.

transfer warranties in commercial paper, warranties regarding forgery and alteration that run to the various holders or other transferees of an instrument and that are given by any person who transfers an instrument for consideration. See UCC §§3-417, 4-207.

transit check in bank deposits and collections, a check deposited in one bank but payable by another. Contrast *on us check*.

treason an attempt by overt acts to overthrow the government of the sovereign to which the offender owes allegiance, or to betray the sovereign into the hands of a foreign power.

treaty an agreement or contract between two or more nations or sovereigns, formally signed by an authorized representative, and ratified by the sovereign or supreme power of each state.

trespass intentional interference with another's right to exclusive possession of real property, for which the trespasser may be held liable in tort to the property owner.

trespass to chattels intentional interference with possession or use of another's personal property, or impairment of its physical condition, value, or quality, under circumstances not constituting an outright conversion of the property, but for which tort liability may be imposed. Contrast *conversion*.

trespasser a person who enters or remains upon another's land without a privilege to do so created by the possessor's consent or otherwise.

trial formal proceeding in court in which the issues of fact of a lawsuit are determined and the pertinent law is applied to the facts to resolve the dispute or criminal proceeding.

true consignment type of consignment in which the

consignee acts as the consignor's agent for the purpose of selling goods to a third party. Title remains in the consignor but the consignee does not undertake an absolute obligation to pay for the goods. See *consignment, consignment intended as security*.

trust   method of transferring property that splits title to property between the trustee, who holds legal title, and the beneficiary or beneficiaries, who hold beneficial or equitable title. The trustee is subject to a fiduciary duty to deal with the property for the benefit of the beneficiaries.

Trust Indenture Act of 1939   federal statute that protects bondholders by regulating the terms of bond indentures under which large issues of corporate debt securities are administered.

trust property (res, corpus)   the property held by the trustee in trust.

trustee   see trust.

trustee in bankruptcy   the trustee of a debtor's property in a bankruptcy liquidation who locates and collects the debtor's property, converts the assets to cash, and distributes the proceeds to creditors who have filed claims against the estate. The trustee represents the debtor's general unsecured creditors.

Truth-in-Lending Act (TILA)   federal statute that requires creditors to disclose to consumers specified contractual terms of credit transactions.

turntable doctrine   rule of tort law stating the conditions under which a possessor of land is liable for injury to trespassing children. See also *attractive nuisance doctrine*.

tying contract   contract in which a seller agrees to sell one product (the so-called tying product) only if the buyer also purchases a second product (the tied product) from the seller.

ultra vires acts   acts beyond the scope of a corporation's powers or stated purposes.

unauthorized completion   in commercial paper, term describing completion of an instrument on which the signature of the maker or drawer is genuine or authorized, but on which other essential terms, such as the payee and amount, are completed in an unauthorized manner. See UCC §3-115, 3-407(3).

unauthorized signature   a signature made without actual, implied, or apparent authority and includes a forgery. See UCC §1-201(43).

uncertificated securities   securities not represented by an instrument. See UCC §8-102(1)(b).

unconscionability   doctrine of contract law allowing a court to refuse to enforce unconscionable contracts or terms. Unconscionability is generally recognized to include an absence of meaningful choice on the part of one of the parties, together with contract terms that are unreasonably favorable to the other party. See UCC §2-302.

underwriter   person who purchases securities from an issuer with a view toward distribution to the public, and any person who participates in the underwriting effort.

undisclosed principal   in agency law, a principal whose existence and identity are unknown to the third party.

undivided property interest   characteristic of co-ownership arrangements such as joint tenancy and tenancy in common meaning that each co-tenant has a simultaneous, proportionate share of the entire property, but no separate interest in any particular or identifiable portion of it.

undue influence   facts or circumstances rendering a contract voidable because of unfair persuasion in the bargaining process.

unenforceable contract   a contract for breach of which a court will not award a contract remedy (either damages or specific performance). Contrast *voidable contract*.

unfair labor practices   conduct by employers and unions that is illegal under federal labor law.

unfair labor practice strike   strike caused in whole or in part by the employer's commission of an unfair labor practice.

uniform codes, acts, or laws   legislation drafted by the National Conference of Commissioners on Uniform State Laws for areas of the law requiring uniformity among the states. After a uniform act is drafted, it is submitted to the various state legislatures, which consider it for enactment like other legislative bills.

Uniform Commercial Code (UCC)   uniform state law enacted in virtually all states governing a wide variety of commercial transactions including sales of goods, commercial paper, bank deposits and collections, letters of credit, bulk transfers, documents of title, investment securities, secured transactions, and sales of accounts and chattel paper. It is reprinted in Appendix B.

Uniform Consumer Credit Code (UCCC)   uniform state law designed to replace piecemeal state consumer credit laws with one comprehensive code.

Uniform Fraudulent Conveyance Act (UFCA)   uniform state law drafted in 1918 to provide uniformity in state fraudulent conveyance law and to reach transfers made without actual intent to defraud. See *fraudulent conveyance, Statute of Elizabeth*.

Uniform Fraudulent Transfer Act   revision of Uniform Fraudulent Conveyance Act, drafted in 1984, and designed to integrate fraudulent conveyance law with the Uniform Commercial Code and the federal Bankruptcy Code.

Uniform Limited Partnership Act (ULPA)   uniform state law adopted in 1916 to govern limited partnership. It is reprinted in Appendix D.

Uniform Partnership Act (UPA)   uniform state law governing partnership, adopted in 1914 and subsequently enacted in virtually all states. It is reprinted in Appendix C.

Uniform Principal and Income Act uniform state law adopted in 1931 and revised in 1962 that resolves in the absence of express provision, how various receipts and expenditures are to be allocated in a trust between the income beneficiary and the remainderman.

Uniform Probate Code uniform state law adopted in 1969 designed to modernize probate law and provide greater uniformity among the states.

Uniform Relocation Assistance and Real Property Acquisition Policies Act federal statute passed in 1970 to provide for uniform and equitable treatment of persons displaced from their homes, businesses, and farms by federal and federally assisted programs, and to establish uniform and equitable land-acquisition policies for these programs.

Uniform Residential Landlord Tenant Act (URLTA) uniform state law drafted to govern the residential landlord-tenant relationship.

Uniform Simultaneous Death Act uniform state law adopted in most states that determines how property is distributed when persons whose rights depend upon survivorship (for example, joint tenants) die in a common disaster.

Uniform Testamentary Additions to Trusts Act uniform state law stating requirements under which property may be transferred by will to a trust created during the testator's life. See *pour over trust*.

Uniform Vendor and Purchaser Risk Act uniform state law governing risk of loss in land sale contracts.

unilateral contract a contract involving a promise in exchange for performance of an act. Contrast *bilateral contract*.

unilateral mistake in contract law, a situation in which one but not both parties are mistaken about a basic assumption upon which the contract is made. See *mistake*.

union shop agreement between an employer and a union requiring newly hired employees to join the union within a specified period after beginning employment.

United States Code (U.S.C.) compilation or codification of all federal statutes.

unjust enrichment a person is unjustly enriched if he has received a benefit from another, and it would be unjust to allow retention of the benefit without paying for it.

unqualified indorsement in commercial paper, an indorsement under which the indorser undertakes secondary contract liability. See *indorsement*. Contrast *qualified indorsement*.

usage of trade any regularly observed practice or method of dealing in a trade, place, or location. See UCC §1-205(2).

usurious contract contract in which interest rates greater than the maximum legal rate are charged.

usury the act of charging an interest rate in excess of that allowed by state law.

utility patent a patent granted to a person who invents or discovers any new and useful process, machine, manufacture, or composition of matter, or any new and useful improvement thereof.

value generally, any consideration sufficient to support a simple contract, including satisfaction of or security for an antecedent debt. See UCC §1-201(44). For commercial paper, however, see UCC §3-303.

variances administrative relief provided for in zoning ordinances that permits either a different use of land than that provided for in the ordinance, or modification of area, setback, or similar restrictions.

venue place of trial; the particular court, among those having subject matter and personal jurisdiction, which should hear a case.

verdict a formal decision on the issues of a case.

vertical merger a merger between firms standing in a buyer-seller or supplier-supplied relation.

vertical restraint a restraint of trade between persons standing in a buyer-seller or supplier-supplied relationship. See *restraint of trade*. Contrast *horizontal restraint*.

vesting event occurring when the employees' rights to their interests in a pension plan cannot be forfeited or taken away.

vicarious liability term describing liability of the master for the servant's tortious conduct without regard to the negligence or other fault of the master. See also *respondeat superior doctrine*.

void promise a promise that is totally without legal force or effect.

voidable contract contract in which one or more parties have the power, by electing to do so, to avoid the legal relations created by the contract, or by ratification of the contract to extinguish the power of avoidance. Contrast *unenforceable contract*.

voidable title rule rule of sales law that allows a person with voidable title to transfer a good title to a good-faith purchaser for value. See UCC §2-403(1).

voir dire examination a procedure by which potential jurors are questioned under oath to determine their suitability to serve on a jury for a particular case.

voluntary case bankruptcy case in which the debtor files a petition with the court requesting the relief afforded by the Bankruptcy Code. Contrast *involuntary case*.

voting (pooling) agreement a contract between two or more shareholders stating how their shares will be voted on certain matters, usually the election of directors.

voting trust a trust created when a group of shareholders transfer legal title to their shares to a trustee in exchange for ''voting trust certificates.'' The trustee then votes the shares subject to any limitations in the trust agreement.

waiver the voluntary surrender or relinquishment of a known right, usually unaccompanied by consideration.

waiver-of-defense clause contractual term indicating that a buyer or lessee will not assert against a subsequent assignee any claim or defense he or she may have against the seller or lender.

ward see *guardian*.

warehouseman a person engaged in the business of storing goods for hire. See UCC §7-102(1)(h).

warehouse receipt a receipt issued by a person engaged in the business of storing goods for hire. See UCC §1-201(45).

warranty generally, a statement or other representation made by a seller of goods about the quality, character, or capabilities of the good sold. See *express warranty, implied warranty*.

warranty against infringement warranty made by merchant seller that goods will be delivered free of any third-party claim of patent or trademark infringement. See UCC §2-312(3).

warranty deed type of deed containing a number of promises or warranties, known as covenants of title, concerning the status of the grantor's title.

warranty disclaimer contract term that limits, modifies, or excludes warranty liability.

warranty of title sales warranty that the title conveyed will be good and its transfer rightful, and that the goods will be delivered free of security interests or other liens, except those known to the buyer. See UCC §2-312(1).

waste conduct of a life tenant resulting in a substantial and unreasonable reduction in the value of the property passing to the following estates.

watered shares shares issued without consideration, or for cash, property, or services worth less than the required consideration.

wildcat strike strike by a minority of employees without authorization by the union.

will a formal instrument by which a person makes a disposition of his or her property to take effect after death.

winding up (liquidation) the series of transactions necessary to settle partnership affairs after dissolution.

It includes completing unfinished transactions, converting assets to cash, paying debts, and distributing any excess to partners. See also *dissolution*.

workers' compensation statute state statute providing compensation for an injured employee if the injury was accidental and arose out of and in the course of employment.

writ of attachment writ issued under the prejudgment creditor's remedy of attachment directing a sheriff to take custody of a debtor's personal or real property and hold it during the trial of the case to assure its availability if and when a creditor obtains a judgment. See *attachment*.

writ of certiorari writ issued by the Supreme Court granting a petitioning party the right to Supreme Court review.

writ of execution writ issued pursuant to the judicial process of execution, which directs the sheriff to levy upon the debtor's real and personal property, sell the property at public sale, and apply the proceeds to the unpaid judgment. See *execution*.

writ of habeas corpus a post-conviction remedy in criminal cases involving a judicial order to a government official (such as a warden) requiring him or her to produce the prisoner in order to test the legality of the imprisonment.

writing printing, typewriting, or any other intentional reduction to tangible form. See UCC §1-201(46).

yellow dog contract illegal agreement by which an employee, as a condition of employment, agrees not to join or retain membership in a union.

zoning the process by which a municipality regulates the use that may be made of property and the physical configuration of the development of land within its jurisdiction.

The Constitution of the United States

Preamble

We the People of the United States, in Order to form a more perfect Union, establish Justice, insure domestic Tranquility, provide for the common defence, promote the general Welfare, and secure the Blessings of Liberty to ourselves and our Posterity, do ordain and establish this Constitution for the United States of America.

Article I

Section 1. All legislative Powers herein granted shall be vested in a Congress of the United States, which shall consist of a Senate and a House of Representatives.

Section 2. [1] The House of Representatives shall be composed of Members chosen every second Year by the People of the several States, and the Electors in each State shall have the Qualifications requisite for Electors of the most numerous Branch of the State Legislature.

[2] No Person shall be a Representative who shall not have attained to the Age of twenty five Years, and been seven Years a Citizen of the United States, and who shall not, when elected, be an Inhabitant of that State in which he shall be chosen.

[3] Representatives and direct Taxes shall be apportioned among the several States which may be included within this Union, according to their respective Numbers, which shall be determined by adding to the whole Number of free Persons, including those bound to Service for a Term of Years, and excluding Indians not taxed, three fifths of all other Persons. The actual Enumeration shall be made within three Years after the first Meeting of the Congress of the United States, and within every subsequent Term of ten Years, in such Manner as they shall by Law direct. The Number of Representatives shall not exceed one for every thirty Thousand, but each State shall have at Least one Representative; and until such enumeration shall be made, the State of New Hampshire shall be entitled to chuse three, Massachusetts eight, Rhode Island and Providence Plantations one, Connecticut five, New York six, New Jersey four, Pennsylvania eight, Delaware one, Maryland six, Virginia ten, North Carolina five, South Carolina five, and Georgia three.

[4] When vacancies happen in the Representation from any State, the Executive Authority thereof shall issue Writs of Election to fill such Vacancies.

[5] The House of Representatives shall chuse their Speaker and other Officers and shall have the sole Power of Impeachment.

Section 3. [1] The Senate of the United States shall be composed of two Senators from each State, chosen by the Legislature thereof, for six Years; and each Senator shall have one vote.

[2] Immediately after they shall be assembled in Consequence of the first Election, they shall be divided as equally as may be into three Classes. The Seats of the Senators of the first Class shall be vacated at the Expiration of the Second Year, of the second Class at the Expiration of the fourth Year, and of the third Class at the Expiration of the sixth Year, so that one third may be chosen every second Year, and if Vacancies happen by Resignation, or otherwise, during the Recess of the Legislature of any State, the Executive thereof may make temporary Appointments until the next Meeting of the Legislature, which shall then fill such Vacancies.

[3] No Person shall be a Senator who shall not have attained to the Age of thirty Years, and been nine Years a Citizen of the United States, and who shall not, when elected, be an Inhabitant of that State for which he shall be chosen.

[4] The Vice President of the United States shall be President of the Senate, but shall have no Vote, unless they be equally divided.

[5] The Senate shall chuse their other Officers, and also a President pro tempore, in the Absence of the Vice President, or when he shall exercise the Office of President of the United States.

[6] The Senate shall have the sole Power to try all Impeachments. When sitting for that Purpose, they shall be on Oath or Affirmation. When the President of the United States is tried, the Chief Justice shall preside: And no Person shall be convicted without the Concurrence of two thirds of the Members present.

[7] Judgment in Cases of Impeachment shall not extend further than to removal from Office, and disqualification to hold and enjoy any Office of honor, Trust, or Profit under the United States: but the Party convicted shall nevertheless be liable and subject to Indictment, Trial, Judgment, and Punishment, according to Law.

Section 4. [1] The Times, Places and Manner of holding Elections for Senators and Representatives, shall be prescribed in each State by the Legislature thereof; but the Congress may at any time by Law make or alter such Regulations, except as to the Places of chusing Senators.

[2] The Congress shall assemble at least once in every Year, and such Meeting shall be on the first Monday in December, unless they shall by Law appoint a different Day.

Section 5. [1] Each House shall be the Judge of the Elections, Returns, and Qualifications of its own Members, and a Majority of each shall constitute a Quorum to do Business, but a smaller Number may adjourn from day to day, and may be authorized to compel the Attendance of absent Members, in such Manner, and under such Penalties as each House may provide.

[2] Each House may determine the Rules of its Proceedings, punish its Members for Disorderly Behavior, and, with the Concurrence of two thirds, expel a Member.

[3] Each House shall keep a Journal of its Proceedings, and from time to time publish the same, excepting such Parts as may in their Judgment require Secrecy; and the Yeas and Nays of the Members of either House on any question shall, at the Desire of one fifth of those Present, be entered on the Journal.

[4] Neither House, during the Session of Congress, shall, without the Consent of the other, adjourn for more than three days, nor to any other Place than that in which the two Houses shall be sitting.

Section 6. [1] The Senators and Representatives shall receive a Compensation for their Services, to be ascertained by Law, and paid out of the Treasury of the United States. They shall in all Cases, except Treason, Felony and Breach of the Peace, be privileged from Arrest during their Attendance at the Session of their respective Houses, and in going to and returning from the same; and for any speech or Debate in either House, they shall not be questioned in any other Place.

[2] No Senator or Representative shall, during the Time for which he was elected, be appointed to any civil Office under the Authority of the United States, which shall have been created, or the Emoluments whereof shall have been increased during such time and no Person holding any Office under the United States, shall be a Member of either House during his Continuance in Office.

Section 7. [1] All Bills for raising Revenue shall originate in the House of Representatives; but the Senate may propose or concur with Amendments as on other Bills.

[2] Every Bill which shall have passed the House of Representatives and the Senate, shall, before it become a Law, be presented to the President of the United States; If he approve he shall sign it, but if not he shall return it, with his Objections to the House in which it shall have originated, who shall enter the Objections at large on their Journal, and proceed to reconsider it. If after such Reconsideration two thirds of that House shall agree to pass the Bill, it shall be sent together with the Objections, to the other House, by which it shall likewise be reconsidered, and if approved by two thirds of that House, it shall become a Law. But in all such Cases the Votes of both Houses shall be determined by Yeas and Nays, and the Names of the Persons voting for and against the Bill shall be entered on the Journal of each House respectively. If any Bill shall not be returned by the President within ten Days (Sundays excepted) after it shall have been presented to him, the Same shall be a Law, in like Manner as if he had signed it, unless the Congress by their Adjournment prevent its Return in which Case it shall not be a Law.

[3] Every Order, Resolution, or Vote, to Which the Concurrence of the Senate and House of Representatives may be necessary (except on a question of Adjournment) shall be presented to the President of the United States; and before the Same shall take Effect, shall be approved by him, or being disapproved by him, shall be repassed by two thirds of the Senate and House of Representatives, according to the Rules and Limitations prescribed in the Case of a Bill.

Section 8. [1] The Congress shall have Power To lay and collect Taxes, Duties, Imposts and Excises, to pay the Debts and provide for the common Defence and general Welfare of the United States; but all Duties, Imposts and Excises shall be uniform throughout the United States;

[2] To borrow money on the credit of the United States;

[3] To regulate Commerce with foreign Nations, and among the several States, and with the Indian Tribes;

[4] To establish an uniform Rule of Naturalization,

and uniform Laws on the subject of Bankruptcies throughout the United States;

[5] To coin Money, regulate the Value thereof, and of foreign Coin, and fix the Standard of Weights and Measures;

[6] To provide for the Punishment of counterfeiting the Securities and current Coin of the United States;

[7] To Establish Post Offices and Post Roads;

[8] To promote the Progress of Science and useful Arts, by securing for limited Times to Authors and Inventors the exclusive Right to their respective Writings and Discoveries;

[9] To constitute Tribunals inferior to the supreme Court;

[10] To define and punish Piracies and Felonies committed on the high Seas, and Offenses against the Law of Nations;

[11] To declare War, grant Letters of Marque and Reprisal, and make Rules concerning Captures on Land and Water;

[12] To raise and support Armies, but no Appropriation of Money to that Use shall be for a longer Term than two Years;

[13] To provide and maintain a Navy;

[14] To make Rules for the Government and Regulation of the land and naval Forces;

[15] To provide for calling forth the Militia to execute the Laws of the Union, suppress Insurrections and repel Invasions;

[16] To provide for organizing, arming, and disciplining, the Militia, and for governing such Part of them as may be employed in the Service of the United States, reserving to the States respectively, the Appointment of the Officers, and the Authority of training the Militia according to the discipline prescribed by Congress;

[17] To exercise exclusive Legislation in all Cases whatsoever, over such District (not exceeding ten Miles square) as may, by Cession of particular States, and the Acceptance of Congress, become the Seat of the Government of the United States, and to exercise like Authority over all Places purchased by the consent of the Legislature of the State in which the Same shall be, for the Erection of Forts, Magazines, Arsenals, dock-Yards, and other needful Buildings;—And

[18] To make all Laws which shall be necessary and proper for carrying into Execution the foregoing Powers, and all other Powers vested by this Constitution in the Government of the United States, or in any department or Officer thereof.

Section 9. [1] The Migration or Importation of Such Persons as any of the States now existing shall think proper to admit, shall not be prohibited by the Congress prior to the Year one thousand eight hundred and eight, but a Tax or duty may be imposed on such Importation, not exceeding ten dollars for each Person.

[2] The privilege of the Writ of Habeas Corpus shall not be suspended, unless when in Cases of Rebellion or Invasion the public Safety may require it.

[3] No Bill of Attainder or ex post facto law shall be passed.

[4] No Capitation, or other direct, Tax shall be laid, unless in Proportion to the Census or Enumeration herein before directed to be taken.

[5] No Tax or Duty shall be laid on articles exported from any State.

[6] No Preference shall be given by any Regulation of Commerce or Revenue to the Ports of one State over those of another: nor shall Vessels bound to, or from, one State be obliged to enter, clear, or pay Duties in another.

[7] No money shall be drawn from the Treasury, but in Consequence of Appropriations made by Law; and a regular Statement and Account of the Receipts and Expenditures of all public Money shall be published from time to time.

[8] No Title of Nobility shall be granted by the United States: And no Person holding any Office of Profit or Trust under them, shall, without the Consent of the Congress, accept of any present, Emolument, Office, or Title, of any kind whatever, from any King, Prince, or foreign State.

Section 10. [1] No State shall enter into any Treaty, Alliance, or Confederation; grant Letters of Marque and Reprisal; coin Money; emit Bills of Credit; make any Thing but gold and silver Coin a Tender in Payment of Debts; pass any Bill of Attainder, ex post facto Law, or Law impairing the Obligation of Contracts, or grant any Title of Nobility.

[2] No State shall, without the Consent of the Congress, lay any Imposts or Duties on Imports or Exports, except what may be absolutely necessary for executing its inspection Laws: and the net Produce of all Duties and Imposts, laid by any States on Imports or Exports, shall be for the Use of the Treasury of the United States; and all such Laws shall be subject to the Revision and Controul of the Congress.

[3] No State shall, without the Consent of Congress, lay any Duty of Tonnage, keep Troops, or Ships of War in time of Peace, enter into any Agreement or Compact with another State, or with a foreign Power, or engage in War, unless actually invaded, or in such imminent Danger as will not admit of delay.

Article II

Section 1. [1] The executive Power shall be vested in a President of the United States of America. He shall hold his Office during the Term of four Years, and, together with the Vice President, chosen for the same Term, be elected, as follows:

[2] Each State shall appoint, in such Manner as the Legislature thereof may direct, a Number of Electors,

equal to the whole Number of Senators and Representatives to which the State may be entitled in the Congress; but no Senator or Representative, or Person holding an Office of Trust or Profit under the United States, shall be appointed as Elector.

[3] The Electors shall meet in their respective States, and vote by Ballot for two Persons, of whom one at least shall not be an Inhabitant of the same State with themselves. And they shall make a List of all the Persons voted for, and of the Number of Votes for each; which List they shall sign and certify, and transmit sealed to the Seat of the Government of the United States, directed to the President of the Senate. The President of the Senate shall, in the Presence of the Senate and House of Representatives, open all the Certificates, and the Votes shall then be counted. The Person having the greatest Number of Votes shall be the President, if such Number be a Majority of the whole Number of Electors appointed; and if there be more than one who have such Majority, and have an equal Number of Votes, then the House of Representatives shall immediately chuse by Ballot one of them for President; and if no Person have a Majority, then from the five highest on the List the said House shall in like Manner chuse the President. But in chusing the President, the Votes shall be taken by States the Representation from each State having one Vote; A quorum for this Purpose shall consist of a Member or Members from two thirds of the States, and a Majority of all the States shall be necessary to a Choice. In every Case, after the Choice of the President, the Person having the greater Number of Votes of the Electors shall be the Vice President. But if there should remain two or more who have equal Votes, the Senate shall chuse from them by Ballot the Vice President.

[4] The Congress may determine the Time of chusing the Electors, and the Day on which they shall give their Votes; which Day shall be the same throughout the United States.

[5] No person except a natural born Citizen, or a Citizen of the United States, at the time of the Adoption of this constitution, shall be eligible to the Office of President; neither shall any Person be eligible to that Office who shall not have attained to the Age of thirty five Years, and been fourteen Years a Resident within the United States.

[6] In case of the removal of the President from Office, or of his Death, Resignation or Inability to discharge the Powers and Duties of the said Office, the Same shall devolve on the Vice President, and the Congress may by Law provide for the Case of Removal, Death, Resignation or Inability, both of the President and Vice President, declaring what Officer shall then act as President, and such Officer shall act accordingly, until the disability be removed, or a President shall be elected.

[7] The President shall, at stated Times, receive for his Services, a Compensation, which shall neither be increased nor diminished during the Period for which he shall have been elected, and he shall not receive within that Period any other Emolument from the United States, or any of them.

[8] Before he enter on the Execution of his Office, he shall take the following Oath or Affirmation: ''I do solemnly swear (or affirm) that I will faithfully execute the Office of President of the United States, and will to the best of my Ability, preserve, protect and defend the Constitution of the United States.''

Section 2. [1] The President shall be Commander in Chief of the Army and Navy of the United States, and of the militia of the several States, when called into the actual Service of the United States; he may require the Opinion, in writing, of the principal Officer in each of the Executive Departments, upon any Subject relating to the Duties of their respective Offices, and he shall have Power to grant Reprieves and Pardons for Offenses against the United States, except in Cases of Impeachment.

[2] He shall have Power, by and with the Advice and Consent of the Senate to make Treaties, provided two thirds of the Senators present concur, and he shall nominate, and by and with the Advice and Consent of the Senate, shall appoint Ambassadors, other public Ministers and Consuls, Judges of the supreme Court, and all other Officers of the United States, whose Appointments are not herein otherwise provided for, and which shall be established by Law; but the Congress may by Law vest the Appointment of such inferior Officers, as they think proper, in the President alone, in the Courts of Law, or in the Heads of Departments.

[3] The President shall have Power to fill up all Vacancies that may happen during the Recess of the Senate, by granting Commissions which shall expire at the End of their next Session.

Section 3. He shall from time to time give to the Congress Information of the State of the Union, and recommend to their Consideration such Measures as he shall judge necessary and expedient; he may, on extraordinary Occasions, convene both Houses, or either of them, and in Case of Disagreement between them, with Respect to the Time of Adjournment, he may adjourn them to such Time as he shall think proper; he shall receive Ambassadors and other public Ministers; he shall take Care that the Laws be faithfully executed, and shall Commission all the Officers of the United States.

Section 4. The President, Vice President and all civil Officers of the United States shall be removed from Office on Impeachment for, and Conviction of, Treason, Bribery, or other high Crimes and Misdemeanors.

Article III

Section 1. The judicial Power of the United States, shall be vested in one supreme Court, and in such inferior Courts as the Congress may from time to time ordain and establish. The Judges, both of the supreme and inferior Courts, shall hold their Offices during good Behaviour, and shall, at stated Times, receive for their Services a Compensation, which shall not be diminished during their Continuance in Office.

Section 2. [1] The judicial Power shall extend to all Cases, in Law and Equity, arising under this Constitution, the Laws of the United States, and Treaties made, or which shall be made, under their Authority;—to all Cases affecting Ambassadors, other public Ministers and Consuls;—to all Cases of admiralty and maritime Jurisdiction;—to Controversies to which the United States shall be a Party;—to Controversies between two or more States;—between a State and Citizens of another State;—between Citizens of different States;—between Citizens of the same State claiming Lands under the Grants of different States, and between a State, or the Citizens thereof, and foreign States, Citizens or Subjects.

[2] In all Cases affecting Ambassadors, other public Ministers and Consuls, and those in which a State shall be a Party, the supreme Court shall have original Jurisdiction. In all the other Cases before mentioned, the supreme Court shall have appellate Jurisdiction, both as to Law and Fact, with such Exceptions, and under such Regulations as the Congress shall make.

[3] The trial of all Crimes, except in Cases of Impeachment, shall be by Jury; and such Trial shall be held in the State where the said Crimes shall have been committed; but when not committed within any State, the Trial shall be at such Place or Places as the Congress may by Law have directed.

Section 3. [1] Treason against the United States, shall consist only in levying War against them, or, in adhering to their Enemies, giving them Aid and Comfort. No Person shall be convicted of Treason unless on the Testimony of two Witnesses to the same overt Act, or on Confession in open Court.

[2] The Congress shall have Power to declare the Punishment of Treason, but no Attainder of Treason shall work Corruption of Blood, or Forfeiture except during the Life of the Person attainted.

Article IV

Section 1. Full Faith and Credit shall be given in each State to the public Acts, Records, and judicial Proceedings of every other State. And the Congress may by general Laws prescribe the Manner in which such Acts, Records and Proceedings shall be proved, and the Effect thereof.

Section 2. [1] The Citizens of each State shall be entitled to all Privileges and Immunities of Citizens in the Several States.

[2] A Person charged in any State with Treason, Felony, or other Crime, who shall flee from Justice, and be found in another State, shall on demand of the executive Authority of the State from which he fled, be delivered up, to be removed to the State having Jurisdiction of the Crime.

[3] No Person held to Service or Labour in one State, under the Laws thereof, escaping into another, shall, in Consequence of any Law or Regulation therein, be discharged from such Service or Labour, but shall be delivered up on Claim of the Party to whom such Service or Labour may be due.

Section 3. [1] New States may be admitted by the Congress into this Union; but no new State shall be formed or erected within the Jurisdiction of any other State; nor any State be formed by the Junction of two or more States, or Parts of States, without the Consent of the Legislatures of the States concerned as well as of the Congress.

[2] The Congress shall have Power to dispose of and make all needful Rules and Regulations respecting the Territory or other Property belonging to the United States; and nothing in this Constitution shall be so construed as to Prejudice any Claims of the United States, or of any particular State.

Section 4. The United States shall guarantee to every State in this Union a Republican Form of Government, and shall protect each of them against Invasion; and on Application of the Legislature, or of the Executive (when the Legislature cannot be convened) against domestic Violence.

Article V

The Congress, whenever two thirds of both Houses shall deem it necessary, shall propose Amendments to this Constitution, or, on the Application of the Legislatures of two thirds of the several States, shall call a Convention for proposing Amendments, which, in either Case, shall be valid to all Intents and Purposes, as part of this Constitution, when ratified by the Legislatures of three fourths of the several States, or by Conventions in three fourths thereof, as the one or the other Mode of Ratification may be proposed by the Congress; Provided that no Amendment which may be made prior to the Year One thousand eight hundred and eight shall in any Manner affect the first and fourth Clauses in the Ninth Section of the first Article; and that no State, without its Consent, shall be deprived of its equal Suffrage in the Senate.

Article VI

[1] All Debts contracted and Engagements entered into, before the Adoption of this Constitution shall be as valid against the United States under this Constitution, as under the Confederation.

[2] This Constitution, and the Laws of the United States which shall be made in Pursuance thereof; and all Treaties made, or which shall be made, under the Au-

thority of the United States, shall be the supreme Law of the Land; and the Judges in every State shall be bound thereby, any Thing in the Constitution or Laws of any State to the Contrary notwithstanding.

[3] The Senators and Representatives before mentioned, and the Members of the several State Legislatures, and all executive and judicial Officers, both of the United States and of the several States, shall be bound by Oath or Affirmation, to support this Constitution; but no religious Test shall ever be required as a Qualification to any Office or public Trust under the United States.

Article VII

The Ratification of the conventions of nine States shall be sufficient for the Establishment of this Constitution between the States so ratifying the Same.

ARTICLES IN ADDITION TO, AND AMENDMENT OF, THE CONSTITUTION OF THE UNITED STATES OF AMERICA, PROPOSED BY CONGRESS, AND RATIFIED BY THE LEGISLATURES OF THE SEVERAL STATES PURSUANT TO THE FIFTH ARTICLE OF THE ORIGINAL CONSTITUTION.

Amendment I [1791]

Congress shall make no law respecting an establishment of religion, or prohibiting the free exercise thereof; or abridging the freedom of speech, or of the press; or the right of the people peaceably to assemble, and to petition the Government for a redress of grievances.

Amendment II [1791]

A well regulated Militia, being necessary to the security of a free State, the right of the people to keep and bear Arms, shall not be infringed.

Amendment III [1791]

No Soldier shall, in time of peace be quartered in any house, without the consent of the Owner, nor in time of war, but in a manner to be prescribed by law.

Amendment IV [1791]

The right of the people to be secure in their persons, houses, papers, and effects, against unreasonable searches and seizures, shall not be violated, and no Warrants shall issue, but upon probable cause, supported by Oath or affirmation, and particularly describing the place to be searched, and the persons or things to be seized.

Amendment V [1791]

No person shall be held to answer for a capital, or otherwise infamous crime, unless on a presentment or indictment of a Grand Jury, except in cases arising in the land or naval forces, or in the Militia, when in actual service in time of War or public danger; nor shall any person be subject for the same offence to be twice put in jeopardy of life or limb; nor shall be compelled in any criminal case to be a witness against himself, nor be deprived of life, liberty, or property, without due process of law; nor shall private property be taken for public use, without just compensation.

Amendment VI [1791]

In all criminal prosecutions, the accused shall enjoy the right to a speedy and public trial, by an impartial jury of the State and district wherein the crime shall have been committed, which district shall have been previously ascertained by law, and to be informed of the nature and cause of the accusation; to be confronted with the witnesses against him; to have compulsory process for obtaining witnesses in his favor, and to have the Assistance of Counsel for his defence.

Amendment VII [1791]

In Suits at common law, where the value in controversy shall exceed twenty dollars, the right of trial by jury shall be preserved, and no fact tried by jury, shall be otherwise re-examined in any Court of the United States, than according to the rules of the common law.

Amendment VIII [1791]

Excessive bail shall not be required, nor excessive fines imposed, nor cruel and unusual punishments inflicted.

Amendment IX [1791]

The enumeration in the Constitution, of certain rights, shall not be construed to deny or disparage others retained by the people.

Amendment X [1791]

The powers not delegated to the United States by the Constitution, nor prohibited by it to the States, are reserved to the States respectively, or to the people.

Amendment XI [1798]

The Judicial power of the Untied States shall not be construed to extend to any suit in law or equity, commenced or prosecuted against one of the Untied States by Citizens of another State, or by Citizens or Subjects of any Foreign State.

Amendment XII [1804]

The Electors shall meet in their respective states and vote by ballot for President and Vice-President, one of whom, at least, shall not be an inhabitant of the same state with themselves; they shall name in their ballots the person voted for as President, and in distinct ballots the person voted for as Vice-President, and they shall make distinct lists of all persons voted for as President, and of all persons voted for as Vice-President, and of the number of votes for each, which lists they shall sign and certify, and transmit sealed to the seat of the government of the United States, directed to the President of the Senate;— The President of the Senate shall, in the presence of the Senate and House of Representatives, open all the certificates and the votes shall then be counted;—The person having the greatest number of votes for President, shall be the President, if such number be a majority of the whole number of Electors appointed; and if no person have such majority, then from the persons having the highest numbers not exceeding three on the list of those voted for as President, the House of Representatives shall choose immediately, by ballot, the President. But in choosing the President, the votes shall be taken by states, the representation from each state having one vote; a quorum for this purpose shall consist of a member or members from two-thirds of the states, and a majority of all the states shall be necessary to a choice. And if the House of Representatives shall not choose a President whenever the right of choice shall devolve upon them before the fourth day of March next following, then the Vice-President shall act as President, as in the case of the death or other constitutional disability of the President.—The person having the greatest number of votes as Vice-President, shall be the Vice-President, if such number be a majority of the whole number of Electors appointed, and if no person have a majority, then from the two highest numbers on the list, the Senate shall choose the Vice-President; a quorum for the purpose shall consist of two-thirds of the whole number of Senators, and a majority of the whole number shall be necessary to a choice. But no person constitutionally ineligible to the office of President shall be eligible to that of Vice-President of the United States.

Amendment XIII [1865]

Section 1. Neither slavery nor involuntary servitude, except as a punishment for crime whereof the party shall have been duly convicted, shall exist within the United States, or any place subject to their jurisdiction.

Section 2. Congress shall have power to enforce this article by appropriate legislation.

Amendment XIV [1868]

Section 1. All persons born or naturalized in the United States, and subject to the jurisdiction thereof, are citizens of the United States and of the State wherein they reside. No State shall make or enforce any law which shall abridge the privileges or immunities of citizens of the United States; nor shall any State deprive any person of life, liberty, or property, without due process of law; nor deny to any person within its jurisdiction the equal protection of the laws.

Section 2. Representatives shall be apportioned among the several States according to their respective numbers, counting the whole number of persons in each State excluding Indians not taxed. But when the right to vote at any election for the choice of electors for President and Vice President of the United States, Representatives in Congress, the Executive and Judicial officers of a State, or the members of the Legislature thereof, is denied to any of the male inhabitants of such State, being twenty-one years of age, and citizens of the United States, or in any way abridged, except for participation in rebellion, or other crime, the basis of representation therein shall be reduced in the proportion which the number of such male citizens shall bear to the whole number of male citizens twenty-one years of age in such State.

Section 3. No person shall be a Senator or Representative in Congress, or elector of President and Vice President, or hold any office, civil or military, under the United States, as a member of any State, who having previously taken an oath, as a member of Congress, or as an officer of the United States, or as a member of any State legislature, or as an executive or judicial officer of any State, to support the Constitution of the United States, shall have engaged in insurrection or rebellion against the same, or given aid or comfort to the enemies thereof. But Congress may by a vote of two-thirds of each House, remove such disability.

Section 4. The validity of the public debt of the United States, authorized by law, including debts incurred for payment of pensions and bounties for services in suppressing insurrection or rebellion, shall not be questioned. But neither the United States nor any State shall assume or pay any debt or obligation incurred in aid of insurrection or rebellion against the United States, or any claim for the loss or emancipation of any slave; but all such debts, obligations and claims shall be held illegal and void.

Section 5. The Congress shall have power to enforce, by appropriate legislation, the provisions of this article.

Amendment XV [1870]

Section 1. The right of citizens of the United States to vote shall not be denied or abridged by the United States or by any State on account of race, color, or previous condition of servitude.

Section 2. The Congress shall have power to enforce this article by appropriate legislation.

Amendment XVI [1913]

The Congress shall have power to lay and collect taxes on incomes, from whatever source derived, without apportionment among the several States, and without regard to any census or enumeration.

Amendment XVII [1913]

[1] The Senate of the United States shall be composed of two Senators from each State, elected by the people thereof, for six years; and each Senator shall have one vote. The electors in each State shall have the qualifications requisite for electors of the most numerous branch of the State legislatures.

[2] When vacancies happen in the representation of any State in the Senate, the executive authority of such State shall issue writs of election to fill such vacancies: *Provided,* That the legislature of any State may empower the executive thereof to make temporary appointments until the people fill the vacancies by election as the legislature may direct.

[3] This amendment shall not be so construed as to affect the election or term of any Senator chosen before it becomes valid as part of the Constitution.

Amendment XVIII [1919]

Section 1. After one year from the ratification of this article the manufacture, sale, or transportation of intoxicating liquors within, the importation thereof into, or the exportation thereof from the United States and all territory subject to the jurisdiction thereof for beverage purposes is hereby prohibited.

Section 2. The Congress and the several States shall have concurrent power to enforce this article by appropriate legislation.

Section 3. This article shall be inoperative unless it shall have been ratified as an amendment to the Constitution by the legislatures of the several States, as provided in the Constitution, within seven years from the date of the submission hereof to the States by the Congress.

Amendment XIX [1920]

[1] The right of citizens of the United States to vote shall not be denied or abridged by the United States or by any State on account of sex.

[2] Congress shall have power to enforce this article by appropriate legislation.

Amendment XX [1933]

Section 1. The terms of the President and Vice President shall end at noon on the 20th day of January, and the terms of Senators and Representatives at noon on the 3d day of January, of the years in which such terms would have ended if this article had not been ratified; and the terms of their successors shall then begin.

Section 2. The Congress shall assemble at least once in every year, and such meeting shall begin at noon on the 3d day of January, unless they shall by law appoint a different day.

Section 3. If, at the time fixed for the beginning of the term of the President, the President elect shall have died, the Vice President elect shall become President. If the President shall not have been chosen before the time fixed for the beginning of his term, or if the President elect shall have failed to qualify, then the Vice President elect shall act as President until a President shall have qualified; and the Congress may by law provide for the case wherein neither a President elect nor a Vice President elect shall have qualified, declaring who shall then act as President, or the manner in which one who is to act shall be selected, and such person shall act accordingly until a President or Vice President shall have qualified.

Section 4. The Congress may by law provide for the case of the death of any of the persons from whom the House of Representatives may choose a President whenever the right choice shall have devolved upon them, and for the case of the death of any of the persons from whom the Senate may choose a Vice President whenever the right of choice shall have devolved upon them.

Section 5. Sections 1 and 2 shall take effect on the 15th day of October following the ratification of this article.

Section 6. This article shall be inoperative unless it shall have been ratified as an amendment to the Constitution by the legislatures of three-fourths of the several States within seven years from the date of its submission.

Amendment XXI [1933]

Section 1. The eighteenth article of amendment to the Constitution of the United States is hereby repealed.

Section 2. The transportation or importation into any State, Territory, or possession of the United States for delivery or use therein of intoxicating liquors, in violation of the laws thereof, is hereby prohibited.

Section 3. This article shall be inoperative unless it shall have been ratified as an amendment to the Constitution by conventions in the several States, as provided in the Constitution, within seven years from the date of the submission hereof to the States by the Congress.

Amendment XXII [1951]

Section 1. No person shall be elected to the office of the President more than twice, and no person who has held the office of President, or acted as President, for more than two years of a term to which some other person was elected President shall be elected to the office of President more than once. But this Article shall not apply to any person holding the office of President when this Article was proposed by the Congress, and shall not prevent any person who may be holding the office of President, or acting as President, during the term within which this Article becomes operative from holding the office of President or acting as President during the remainder of such term.

Section 2. This article shall be inoperative unless it shall have been ratified as an amendment to the Constitution by the legislatures of three-fourths of the several States within seven years from the date of its submission to the States by the Congress.

Amendment XXIII [1961]

Section 1. The District constituting the seat of Government of the United States shall appoint in such manner as the Congress may direct:

A number of electors of President and Vice President equal to the whole number of Senators and Representatives in Congress to which the District would be entitled if it were a State, but in no event more than the least populous state; they shall be in addition to those appointed by the states, but they shall be considered, for the purposes of the election of President and Vice President, to be electors appointed by a state; and they shall meet in the District and perform such duties as provided by the twelfth article of amendment.

Section 2. The Congress shall have power to enforce this article by appropriate legislation.

Amendment XXIV [1964]

Section 1. The right of citizens of the United States to vote in any primary or other election for President or Vice President, for electors for President or Vice President, or for Senator or Representative in Congress, shall not be denied or abridged by the United States, or any State by reason of failure to pay any poll tax or other tax.

Section 2. The Congress shall have power to enforce this article by appropriate legislation.

Amendment XXV [1967]

Section 1. In case of the removal of the President from office or of his death or resignation, the Vice President shall become President.

Section 2. Whenever there is a vacancy in the office of the Vice President, the President shall nominate a Vice President who shall take office upon confirmation by a majority vote of both Houses of Congress.

Section 3. Whenever the President transmits to the President pro tempore of the Senate and the Speaker of the House of Representatives his written declaration that he is unable to discharge the powers and duties of his office, and until he transmits to them a written declaration to the contrary, such powers and duties shall be discharged by the Vice President as Acting President.

Section 4. Whenever the Vice President and a majority of either the principal officers of the executive departments or of such other body as Congress may by law provide, transmit to the President pro tempore of the Senate and the Speaker of the House of Representatives their written declaration that the President is unable to discharge the powers and duties of his office, the Vice President shall immediately assume the powers and duties of the office as Acting President.

Thereafter, when the President transmits to the President pro tempore of the Senate and the Speaker of the House of Representatives his written declaration that no inability exists, he shall resume the powers and duties of his office unless the Vice President and a majority of either the principal officers of the executive department or of such other body as Congress may by law provide, transmit within four days to the President pro tempore of the Senate and the Speaker of the House of Representatives their written declaration and the President is unable to discharge the powers and duties of his office. Thereupon Congress shall decide the issue, assembling within forty-eight hours for that purpose if not in session. If the Congress, within twenty-one days after receipt of the latter written declaration, or, if Congress is not in session, within twenty-one days after Congress is required to assemble, determines by two-thirds vote of both Houses that the President is unable to discharge the power and duties of his office, the Vice President shall continue to discharge the same as Acting President; otherwise, the President shall resume the powers and duties of his office.

Amendment XXVI [1971]

Section 1. The right of citizens of the United States, who are eighteen years of age or older, to vote shall not be denied or abridged by the United States or by any State on account of age.

Section 2. The Congress shall have power to enforce this article by appropriate legislation.

Appendix B

Uniform Commercial Code (1987 Official Text)

Table of Sections

ARTICLE 2A. Leases

PART 1. General Provisions

PART 2. Formation and Construction of Lease Contract

PART 3. Effect of Lease Contract

PART 4. Performance of Lease Contract: Repudiated, Substituted and Excused

ARTICLE 1. General Provisions

PART 1. *Short Title, Construction, Application and Subject Matter of the Act.*

§ 1—101. Short Title.

This Act shall be known and may be cited as Uniform Commercial Code.

§ 1—102. Purposes; Rules of Construction; Variation by Agreement.

(1) This Act shall be liberally construed and applied to promote its underlying purposes and policies.

(2) Underlying purposes and policies of this Act are

    (a) to simplify, clarify and modernize the law governing commercial transactions;

    (b) to permit the continued expansion of commercial practices through custom, usage and agreement of the parties;

    (c) to make uniform the law among the various jurisdictions.

(3) The effect of provisions of this Act may be varied by agreement, except as otherwise provided in this Act and except that the obligations of good faith, diligence, reasonableness and care prescribed by this Act may not be disclaimed by agreement but the parties may by agreement determine the standards by which the performance of such obligations is to be measured if such standards are not manifestly unreasonable.

(4) The presence in certain provisions of this Act of the words "unless otherwise agreed" or words of similar import does not imply that the effect of other provisions may not be varied by agreement under subsection (3).

(5) In this Act unless the context otherwise requires

    (a) words in the singular number include the plural, and in the plural include the singular;

    (b) words of the masculine gender include the feminine and the neuter, and when the sense so indicates words of the neuter gender may refer to any gender.

§ 1—103. Supplementary General Principles of Law Applicable.

Unless displaced by the particular provisions of this Act, the principles of law and equity, including the law merchant and the law relative to capacity to contract, principal and agent, estoppel, fraud, misrepresentation, duress, coercion, mistake, bankruptcy, or other validating or invalidating cause shall supplement its provisions.

§ 1—104. Construction Against Implicit Repeal.

This Act being a general act intended as a unified coverage of its subject matter, no part of it shall be deemed to be impliedly repealed by subsequent legislation if such construction can reasonably be avoided.

§ 1—105. Territorial Application of the Act; Parties' Power to Choose Applicable Law.

(1) Except as provided hereafter in this section, when a transaction bears a reasonable relation to this state and also to another state or nation the parties may agree that the law either of this state or of such other state or nation shall govern their rights and duties. Failing such agreement this Act applies to transactions bearing an appropriate relation to this state.

(2) Where one of the following provisions of this Act specifies the applicable law, that provision governs and a contrary agreement is effective only to the extent permitted by the law (including the conflict of laws rules) so specified:

> Rights of creditors against sold goods. Section 2—402.
> Applicability of the Article on Leases. Sections 2A—105, 2A—106.
> Applicability of the Article on Bank Deposits and Collections. Section 4—102.
> Bulk transfers subject to the Article on Bulk Transfers. Section 6—102.
> Applicability of the Article on Investment Securities. Section 8—106.*
> Perfection provisions of the Article on Secured Transactions. Section 9—103.
> As amended in 1972 and 1987.

§ 1—106. Remedies to Be Liberally Administered.

(1) The remedies provided by this Act shall be liberally administered to the end that the aggrieved party may be put in as good a position as if the other party had fully performed but neither consequential or special nor penal damages may be had except as specifically provided in this Act or by other rule of law.

(2) Any right or obligation declared by this Act is enforceable by action unless the provision declaring it specifies a different and limited effect.

§ 1—107. Waiver or Renunciation of Claim or Right After Breach.

Any claim or right arising out of an alleged breach can be discharged in whole or in part without consideration by a written waiver or renunciation signed and delivered by the aggrieved party.

§ 1—108. Severability.

If any provision or clause of this Act or application thereof to any person or circumstances is held invalid, such invalidity shall not affect other provisions or applications of the Act which can be given effect without the invalid provision or application, and to this end the provisions of this Act are declared to be severable.

§ 1—109. Section Captions.

Section captions are parts of this Act.

PART 2. *General Definitions and Principles of Interpretation*

§ 1—201. General Definitions.

Subject to additional definitions contained in the subsequent Articles of this Act which are applicable to specific Articles or Parts thereof, and unless the context otherwise requires, in this Act:

(1) "Action" in the sense of a judicial proceeding includes recoupment, counterclaim, set-off, suit in equity and any other proceedings in which rights are determined.

(2) "Aggrieved party" means a party entitled to resort to a remedy.

(3) "Agreement" means the bargain of the parties in fact as found in their language or by implication from other circumstances including course of dealing or usage of trade or course of performance as provided in this Act (Sections 1—205 and 2—208). Whether an agreement has legal consequences is determined by the provisions of this Act, if applicable; otherwise by the law of contracts (Section 1—103). (Compare "Contract".)

(4) "Bank" means any person engaged in the business of banking.

(5) "Bearer" means the person in possession of an instrument, document of title, or certificated security payable to bearer or indorsed in blank.

(6) "Bill of lading" means a document evidencing the receipt of goods for shipment issued by a person engaged in the business of transporting or forwarding goods, and includes an airbill. "Airbill" means a document serving for air transportation as a bill of lading does for marine or rail transportation, and includes an air consignment note or air waybill.

(7) "Branch" includes a separately incorporated foreign branch of a bank.

(8) "Burden of establishing" a fact means the burden of persuading the triers of fact that the existence of the fact is more probable than its non-existence.

(9) "Buyer in ordinary course of business" means a person who in good faith and without knowledge that the sale to him is in violation of the ownership rights or security interest of a third party in the goods buys in ordinary course from a person in the business of selling goods of that kind but does not include a pawnbroker. All persons who sell minerals or the like (including oil and gas) at wellhead or minehead shall be deemed to be persons in the business of selling goods of that kind. "Buying" may be for cash or by exchange of other property or on secured or unsecured credit and includes

---

*This provision should be added to § 1—105 in jurisdictions enacting UCC Article 2A—Leases.

receiving goods or documents of title under a pre-existing contract for sale but does not include a transfer in bulk or as security for or in total or partial satisfaction of a money debt.

(10) "Conspicuous": A term or clause is conspicuous when it is so written that a reasonable person against whom it is to operate ought to have noticed it. A printed heading in capitals (as: NON-NEGOTIABLE BILL OF LADING) is conspicuous. Language in the body of a form is "conspicuous" if it is in larger or other contrasting type or color. But in a telegram any stated term is "conspicuous". Whether a term or clause is "conspicuous" or not is for decision by the court.

(11) "Contract" means the total legal obligation which results from the parties' agreement as affected by this Act and any other applicable rules of law. (Compare "Agreement".)

(12) "Creditor" includes a general creditor, a secured creditor, a lien creditor and any representative of creditors, including an assignee for the benefit of creditors, a trustee in bankruptcy, a receiver in equity and an executor or administrator of an insolvent debtor's or assignor's estate.

(13) "Defendant" includes a person in the position of defendant in a cross-action or counterclaim.

(14) "Delivery" with respect to instruments, documents of title, chattel paper, or certified securities means voluntary transfer of possession.

(15) "Document of title" includes bill of lading, dock warrant, dock receipt, warehouse receipt or order for the delivery of goods, and also any other document which in the regular course of business or financing is treated as adequately evidencing that the person in possession of it is entitled to receive, hold and dispose of the document and the goods it covers. To be a document of title a document must purport to be issued by or addressed to a bailee and purport to cover goods in the bailee's possession which are either identified or are fungible portions of an identified mass.

(16) "Fault" means wrongful act, omission or breach.

(17) "Fungible" with respect to goods or securities means goods or securities of which any unit is, by nature or usage of trade, the equivalent of any other like unit. Goods which are not fungible shall be deemed fungible for the purposes of this Act to the extent that under a particular agreement or document unlike units are treated as equivalents.

(18) "Genuine" means free of forgery or counterfeiting.

(19) "Good faith" means honesty in fact in the conduct or transaction concerned.

(20) "Holder" means a person who is in possession of a document of title or an instrument or a certificated investment security drawn, issued, or indorsed to him or his order or to bearer or in blank.

(21) To "honor" is to pay or to accept and pay, or where a credit so engages to purchase or discount a draft complying with the terms of the credit.

(22) "Insolvency proceedings" includes any assignment for the benefit of creditors or other proceedings intended to liquidate or rehabilitate the estate of the person involved.

(23) A person is "insolvent" who either has ceased to pay his debts in the ordinary course of business or cannot pay his debts as they become due or is insolvent within the meaning of the federal bankruptcy law.

(24) "Money" means a medium of exchange authorized or adopted by a domestic or foreign government as a part of its currency.

(25) A person has "notice" of a fact when
    (a) he has actual knowledge of it; or
    (b) he has received a notice or notification of it; or
    (c) from all the facts and circumstances known to him at the time in question he has reason to know that it exists.
A person "knows" or has "knowledge" of a fact when he has actual knowledge of it. "Discover" or "learn" or a word or phrase of similar import refers to knowledge rather than to reason to know. The time and circumstances under which a notice or notification may cease to be effective are not determined by this Act.

(26) A person "notifies" or "gives" a notice or notification to another by taking such steps as may be reasonably required to inform the other in ordinary course whether or not such other actually comes to know of it. A person "receives" a notice or notification when
    (a) it comes to his attention; or
    (b) it is duly delivered at the place of business through which the contract was made or at any other place held out by him as the place for receipt of such communications.

(27) Notice, knowledge or a notice or notification received by an organization is effective for a particular transaction from the time when it is brought to the attention of the individual conducting that transaction, and in any event from the time when it would have been brought to his attention if the organization had exercised due diligence. An organization exercises due diligence if it maintains reaasonable routines for communicating significant information to the person conducting the transaction and there is reasonable compliance with the routines. Due diligence does not require an individual acting for the organization to communicate information unless such communication is part of his regular duties or unless he has reason to know of the transaction and that the transaction would be materially affected by the information.

(28) "Organization" includes a corporation, government or govermental subdivision or agency, business

trust, estate, trust, partnership or association, two or more persons having a joint or common interest, or any other legal or commercial entity.

(29) "Party", as distinct from "third party", means a person who has engaged in a transaction or made an agreement within this Act.

(30) "Person" includes an individual or an organization (See Section 1—102).

(31) "Presumption" or "presumed" means that the trier of fact must find the existence of the fact presumed unless and until evidence is introduced which would support a finding of its non-existence.

(32) "Purchase" includes taking by sale, discount, negotiation, mortgage, pledge, lien, issue or re-issue, gift or any other voluntary transaction creating an interest in property.

(33) "Purchaser" means a person who takes by purchase.

(34) "Remedy" means any remedial right to which an aggrieved party is entitled with or without resort to a tribunal.

(35) "Representative" includes an agent, an officer of a corporation or association, and a trustee, executor or administrator of an estate, or any other person empowered to act for another.

(36) "Rights" includes remedies.

(37) "Security interest" means an interest in personal property or fixtures which secures payment or performance of an obligation. The retention or reservation of title by a seller of goods notwithstanding shipment or delivery to the buyer (Section 2—401) is limited in effect to a reservation of a "security interest". The term also includes any interest of a buyer of accounts or chattel paper which is subject to Article 9. The special property interest of a buyer of goods on identification of such goods to a contract for sale under Section 2—401 is not a "security interest", but a buyer may also acquire a "security interest" by complying with Article 9. Unless a lease or consignment is intended as security, reservation of title thereunder is not a "security interest" but a consignment is in any event subject to the provisions on consignment sales (Section 2—326). Whether a lease is intended as security is to be determined by the facts of each case; however, (a) the inclusion of an option to purchase does not of itself make the lease one intended for security, and (b) an agreement that upon compliance with the terms of the lease the lessee shall become or has the option to become the owner of the property for no additional consideration or for a nominal consideration does make the lease one intended for security.

[(37) "Security interest"* means an interest in personal property or fixtures which secures payment or performance of an obligation. The retention or reservation of title by a seller of goods notwithstanding shipment or delivery to the buyer (Section 2—401) is limited in effect to a reservation of a "security interest". The term also includes any interest of a buyer of accounts or chattel paper which is subject to Article 9. The special property interest of a buyer of goods on identification of those goods to a contract for sale under Section 2—401 is not a "security interest", but a buyer may also acquire a "security interest" by complyng with Article 9. Unless a consignment is intended as security, reservation of title thereunder is not a "security interest", but a consignment in any event is subject to the provisions on consignment sales (Section 2—326).

Whether a transaction creates a lease or security interest is determined by the facts of each case; however, a transaction creates a security interest if the consideration the lessee is to pay the lessor for the right to possession and use of the goods is an obligation for the term of the lease not subject to termination by the lessee, and

(a) the original term of the lease is equal to or greater than the remaining economic life of the goods,

(b) the lessee is bound to renew the lease for the remaining economic life of the goods or is bound to become the owner of the goods,

(c) the lessee has an option to renew the lease for the remaining economic life of the goods for no additional consideration or nominal additional consideration upon compliance with the lease agreement, or

(d) the lessee has an option to become the owner of the goods for no additional consideration or nominal additional consideration upon compliance with the lease agreement.

A transaction does not create a security interest merely because it provides that

(a) the present value of the consideration the lessee is obligated to pay the lessor for the right to possession and use of the goods is substantially equal to or is greater than the fair market value of the goods at the time the lease is entered into,

(b) the lessee assumes risk of loss of the goods, or agrees to pay taxes, insurance, filing, recording, or registration fees, or service or maintenance costs with respect to the goods,

(c) the lessee has an option to renew the lease or to become the owner of the goods,

---

*This revised version of § 1—201(37) was promulaged in conjunction with the promulgation in 1987 of UCC Article 2A—Leases.

(d) the lessee has an option to renew the lease for a fixed rent that is equal to or greater than the reasonably predictable fair market rent for the use of the goods for the term of the renewal at the time the option is to be performed, or

(e) the lessee has an option to become the owner of the goods for a fixed price that is equal to or greater than the reasonably predictable fair market value of goods at the time the option is to be performed.

For purposes of this subsection (37):

(x) Additional consideration is not nominal if (i) when the option to renew the lease is granted to the lessee the rent is stated to be the fair market rent for the use of the goods for the term of the renewal determined at the time the option is to be performed, or (ii) when the option to become the owner of the goods is granted to the lessee the price is stated to be the fair market value of the goods determined at the time the option is to be performed. Additional consideration is nominal if it is less than the lessee's reasonably predictable cost of performing under the lease agreement if the option is not exercised;

(y) "Reasonably predictable" and "remaining economic life of the goods" are to be determined with reference to the facts and circumstances at the time the transaction is entered into; and

(z) "Present value" means the amount as of a date certain of one or more sums payable in the future, discounted to the date certain. The discount is determined by the interest rate specified by the parties if the rate is not manifestly unreasonable at the time the transaction is entered into; otherwise, the discount is determined by a commercially reasonable rate that takes into account the facts and circumstances of each case at the time the transaction was entered into.]

(38) "Send" in connection with any writing or notice means to deposit in the mail or deliver for transmission by any other usual means of communication with postage or cost of transmission provided for and properly addressed and in the case of an instrument to an address specified thereon or otherwise agreed, or if there be none to any address reasonable under the circumstances. The receipt of any writing or notice within the time at which it would have arrived if properly sent has the effect of a proper sending.

(39) "Signed" includes any symbol executed or adopted by a party with present intention to authenticate a writing.

(40) "Surety" includes guarantor.

(41) "Telegram" includes a message transmitted by radio, teletype, cable, any mechanical method of transmission, or the like.

(42) "Term" means that portion of an agreement which relates to a particular matter.

(43) "Unauthorized" signature or indorsement means one made without actual, implied or apparent authority and includes a forgery.

(44) "Value". Except as otherwise provided with respect to negotiable instruments and bank collections (Sections 3—303, 4—208 and 4—209) a person gives "value" for rights if he acquires them

(a) in return for a binding commitment to extend credit or for the extension of immediately available credit whether or not drawn upon and whether or not a charge-back is provided for in the event of difficulties in collection; or

(b) as security for or in total or partial satisfaction of a pre-existing claim; or

(c) by accepting delivery pursuant to a pre-existing contract for purchase; or

(d) generally, in return for any consideration sufficient to support a simple contract.

(45) "Warehouse receipt" means a receipt issued by a person engaged in the business of storing goods for hire.

(46) "Written" or "writing" includes printing, typewriting or any other intentional reduction to tangible form. As amended in 1962, 1972, 1977, 1987.

§ 1—202. Prima Facie Evidence by Third Party Documents.

A document in due form purporting to be a bill of lading, policy or certificate of insurance, official weigher's or inspector's certificate, consular invoice, or any other document authorized or required by the contract to be issued by a third party shall be prima facie evidence of its own authenticity and genuineness and of the facts stated in the document by the third party.

§ 1—203. Obligation of Good Faith.

Every contract or duty within this Act imposes an obligation of good faith in its performance or enforcement.

§ 1—204. Time; Reasonable Time; "Seasonably".

(1) Whenever this Act requires any action to be taken within a reasonable time, any time which is not manifestly unreasonable may be fixed by agreement.

(2) What is a reasonable time for taking any action depends on the nature, purpose and circumstances of such action.

(3) An action is taken "seasonably" when it is taken at or within the time agreed or if no time is agreed at or within a reasonable time.

§ 1—205. Course of Dealing and Usage of Trade.

(1) A course of dealing is a sequence of previous conduct between the parties to a particular transaction which is fairly to be regarded as establishing a common basis of understanding for interpreting their expressions and other conduct.

(2) A usage of trade is any practice or method of dealing having such regularity of observance in a place, vocation or trade as to justify an expectation that it will be observed with respect to the transaction in question. The existence and scope of such a usage are to be proved as facts. If it is established that such a usage is embodied in a written trade code or similar writing the interpretation of the writing is for the court.

(3) A course of dealing between parties and any usage of trade in the vocation or trade in which they are engaged or of which they are or should be aware give particular meaning to and supplement or qualify terms of an agreement.

(4) The express terms of an agreement and an applicable course of dealing or usage of trade shall be construed wherever reasonable as consistent with each other; but when such construction is unreasonable express terms control both course of dealing and usage of trade and course of dealing controls usage of trade.

(5) An applicable usage of trade in the place where any part of performance is to occur shall be used in interpreting the agreement as to that part of the performance.

(6) Evidence of a relevant usage of trade offered by one party is not admissible unless and until he has given the other party such notice as the court finds sufficient to prevent unfair surprise to the latter.

§ 1—206. Statute of Frauds for Kinds of Personal Property Not Otherwise Covered.

(1) Except in the cases described in subsection (2) of this section a contract for the sale of personal property is not enforceable by way of action or defense beyond five thousand dollars in amount or value of remedy unless there is some writing which indicates that a contract for sale has been made between the parties at a defined or stated price, reasonably indentifies the subject matter, and is signed by the party against whom enforcement is sought or by his authorized agent.

(2) Subsection (1) of this section does not apply to contracts for the sale of goods (Section 2—201) nor of securities (Section 8—319) nor to security agreements (Section 9—203).

§ 1—207. Performance or Acceptance Under Reservation of Rights.

A party who with explicit reservation of rights performs or promises performance or assents to performance in a manner demanded or offered by the other party does not thereby prejudice the rights reserved. Such words as "without prejudice", "under protest" or the like are sufficient.

§ 1—208. Option to Accelerate at Will.

A term providing that one party or his successor in interest may accelerate payment or performance or require collateral or additional collateral "at will" or "when he deems himself insecure" or in words of similar import shall be construed to mean that he shall have power to do so only if he in good faith believes that the prospect of payment or performance is impaired. The burden of establishing lack of good faith is on the party against whom the power has been exercised.

§ 1—209. Subordinated Obligations.

An obligation may be issued as subordinated to payment of another obligation of the person obligated, or a creditor may subordinate his right to payment of an obligation by agreement with either the person obligated or another creditor of the person obligated. Such a subordination does not create a security interest as against either the common debtor or a subordinated creditor. This section shall be construed as declaring the law as it existed prior to the enactment of this section and not as modifying it. Added 1966.

> **Note:** This new section is proposed as an optional provision to make it clear that a subordination agreement does not create a security interest unless so intended.

ARTICLE 2. Sales

PART 1. *Short Title, General Construction and Subject Matter.*

§ 2—101. Short Title.

This Article shall be known and may be cited as Uniform Commercial Code—Sales.

§ 2—102. Scope; Certain Security and Other Transactions Excluded From This Article.

Unless the context otherwise requires, this Article applies to transactions in goods; it does not apply to any transaction which although in the form of an unconditional contract to sell or present sale is intended to operate only as a security transaction nor does this Article impair or repeal any statute regulating sales to consumers, farmers or other specified classes of buyers.

§ 2—103. Definitions and Index of Definitions.

(1) In this Article unless the context otherwise requires

    (a) "Buyer" means a person who buys or contracts to buy goods.

(b) "Good faith" in the case of a merchant means honesty in fact and the observance of reasonable commercial standards of fair dealing in the trade.

(c) "Receipt" of goods means taking physical possession of them.

(d) "Seller" means a person who sells or contracts to sell goods.

(2) Other definitions applying to this Article or to specified Parts thereof, and the sections in which they appear are:

"Acceptance". Section 2—606.
"Banker's credit". Section 2—325.
"Between merchants". Section 2—104.
"Cancellation". Section 2—106(4).
"Commercial unit". Section 2—105.
"Confirmed credit". Section 2—325.
"Conforming to contract". Section 2—106.
"Contract for sale". Section 2—106.
"Cover". Section 2—712.
"Entrusting". Section 2—403.
"Financing agency". Section 2—104.
"Future goods". Section 2—105.
"Goods". Section 2—105.
"Identification". Section 2—501.
"Installment contract". Section 2—612.
"Letter of Credit". Section 2—325.
"Lot". Section 2—105.
"Merchant". Section 2—104.
"Overseas". Section 2—323.
"Person in position of seller". Section 2—707.
"Present sale". Section 2—106.
"Sale". Section 2—106.
"Sale on approval". Section 2—326.
"Sale or return". Section 2—326.
"Termination". Section 2—106.

(3) The following definitions in other Articles apply to this Article:

"Check". Section 3—104.
"Consignee". Section 7—102.
"Consignor". Section 7—102.
"Consumer goods". Section 9—109.
"Dishonor". Section 3—507.
"Draft". Section 3—104.

(4) In addition Article 1 contains general definitions and principles of construction and interpretation applicable throughout this Article.

§ 2—104. Definitions: "Merchant"; "Between Merchants"; "Financing Agency".

(1) "Merchant" means a person who deals in goods of the kind or otherwise by his occupation holds himself out as having knowledge or skill peculiar to the practices or goods involved in the transaction or to whom such knowledge or skill may be attributed by his employment

of an agent or broker or other intermediary who by his occupation holds himself out as having such knowledge or skill.

(2) "Financing agency" means a bank, finance company or other person who in the ordinary course of business makes advances against goods or documents of title or who by arrangement with either the seller or the buyer intervenes in ordinary course to make or collect payment due or claimed under the contract for sale, as by purchasing or paying the seller's draft or making advances against it or by merely taking it for collection whether or not the documents of title accompany the draft. "Financing agency" includes also a bank or other person who similarly intervenes between persons who are in the position of seller and buyer in respect to the goods (Section 2—707).

(3) "Between merchants" means in any transaction with respect to which both parties are chargeable with the knowledge or skill of merchants.

§ 2—105. Definitions: Transferability; "Goods"; "Future" Goods; "Lot"; "Commercial Unit".

(1) "Goods" means all things (including specially manufactured goods) which are movable at the time of identification to the contract for sale other than the money in which the price is to be paid, investment securities (Article 8) and things in action. "Goods" also includes the unborn young of animals and growing crops and other identified things attached to realty as described in the section on goods to be severed from realty (Section 2—107).

(2) Goods must be both existing and identified before any interest in them can pass. Goods which are not both existing and identified are "future" goods. A purported present sale of future goods or of any interest therein operates as a contract to sell.

(3) There may be a sale of a part interest in existing identified goods.

(4) An undivided share in an identified bulk of fungible goods is sufficiently identified to be sold although the quantity of the bulk is not determined. Any agreed proportion of such a bulk or any quantity thereof agreed upon by number, weight or other measure may to the extent of the seller's interest in the bulk be sold to the buyer who then becomes an owner in common.

(5) "Lot" means a parcel or a single article which is the subject matter of a separate sale or delivery, whether or not it is sufficient to perform the contract.

(6) "Commercial unit" means such a unit of goods as by commercial usage is a single whole for purposes of sale and division of which materially impairs its character or value on the market or in use. A commercial unit may be a single article (as a machine) or a set of articles (as a suite of furniture or an assortment of sizes) or a quantity (as a bale, gross, or carload) or any other unit

treated in use or in the relevant market as a single whole.

§ 2—106. Definitions: "Contract"; "Agreement"; "Contract for Sale"; "Sale"; "Present Sale"; "Conforming" to Contract; "Termination"; "Cancellation".

(1) In this Article unless the context otherwise requires "contract" and "agreement" are limited to those relating to the present or future sale of goods. "Contract for sale" includes both a present sale of goods and a contract to sell goods at a future time. A "sale" consists in the passing of title from the seller to the buyer for a price (Section 2—401). A "present sale" means a sale which is accomplished by the making of the contract.

(2) Goods or conduct including any part of a performance are "conforming" or conform to the contract when they are in accordance with the obligations under the contract.

(3) "Termination" occurs when either party pursuant to a power created by agreement or law puts an end to the contract otherwise than for its breach. On "termination" all obligations which are still executory on both sides are discharged but any right based on prior breach or performance survives.

(4) "Cancellation" occurs when either party puts an end to the contract for breach by the other and its effect is the same as that of "termination" except that the cancelling party also retains any remedy for breach of the whole contract or any unperformed balance.

§ 2—107. Goods to Be Severed From Realty: Recording.

(1) A contract for the sale of minerals or the like (including oil and gas) or a structure or its materials to be removed from realty is a contract for the sale of goods within this Article if they are to be severed by the seller but until severance a purported present sale thereof which is not effective as a transfer of an interest in land is effective only as a contract to sell.

(2) A contract for the sale apart from the land of growing crops or other things attached to realty and capable of severance without material harm thereto but not described in subsection (1) or of timber to be cut is a contract for the sale of goods within this Article whether the subject matter is to be severed by the buyer or by the seller even though it forms part of the realty at the time of contracting, and the parties can by identification effect a present sale before severance.

(3) The provisions of this section are subject to any third party rights provided by the law relating to realty records, and the contract for sale may be executed and recorded as a document transferring an interest in land and shall then constitute notice to third parties of the

buyer's right under the contract for sale. As amended 1972.

PART 2. *Form, Formation and Readjustment of Contract.*

§ 2—201. Formal Requirements; Statute of Frauds.

(1) Except as otherwise provided in this section a contract for the sale of goods for the price of $500 or more is not enforceable by way of action or defense unless there is some writing sufficient to indicate that a contract for sale has been made between the parties and signed by the party against whom enforcement is sought or by his authorized agent or broker. A writing is not insufficient because it omits or incorrectly states a term agreed upon but the contract is not enforceable under this paragraph beyond the quantity of goods shown in such writing.

(2) Between merchants if within a reasonable time a writing in confirmation of the contract and sufficient against the sender is received and the party receiving it has reason to know its contents, it satisfies the requirements of subsection (1) against such party unless written notice of objection to its contents is given within 10 days after it is received.

(3) A contract which does not satisfy the requirements of subsection (1) but which is valid in other respects is enforceable

(a) if the goods are to be specially manufactured for the buyer and are not suitable for sale to others in the ordinary course of the seller's business and the seller, before notice of repudiation is received and under circumstances which reasonably indicate that the goods are for the buyer, has made either a substantial beginning of their manufacture or commitments for their procurement; or

(b) if the party against whom enforcement is sought admits in his pleading, testimony or otherwise in court that a contract for sale was made, but the contract is not enforceable under this provision beyond the quantity of goods admitted; or

(c) with respect to goods for which payment has been made and accepted or which have been received and accepted (Section 2—606).

§ 2—202. Final Written Expression: Parol or Extrinsic Evidence.

Terms with respect to which the confirmatory memoranda of the parties agree or which are otherwise set forth in a writing intended by the parties as a final expression of their agreement with respect to such terms as are included therin may not be contradicted by evidence of any prior agreement or of a contemporaneous oral agreement but may be explained or supplemented

(a) by course and dealing or usage of trade (Section 1—205) or by course of performance (Section 2—208); and

(b) by evidence of consistent additional terms unless the court finds the writing to have been intended also as a complete and exclusive statement of the terms of the agreement.

§ 2—203. Seals Inoperative.

The affixing of a seal to a writing evidencing a contract for sale or an offer to buy or sell goods does not constitute the writing a sealed instrument and the law with respect to sealed instruments does not apply to such a contract or offer.

§ 2—204. Formation in General.

(1) A contract for sale of goods may be made in any manner sufficient to show agreement, including conduct by both parties which recognizes the existence of such a contract.

(2) An agreement sufficient to constitute a contract for sale may be found even though the moment of its making is undetermined.

(3) Even though one or more terms are left open a contract for sale does not fail for indefiniteness if the parties have intended to make a contract and there is a reasonably certain basis for giving an appropriate remedy.

§ 2—205. Firm Offers.

An offer by a merchant to buy or sell goods in a signed writing which by its terms gives assurance that it will be held open is not revocable, for lack of consideration, during the time stated or if no time is stated for a reasonable time, but in no event may such period of irrevocability exceed three months; but any such term of assurance on a form supplied by the offeree must be separately signed by the offeror.

§ 2—206. Offer and Acceptance in Formation of Contract.

(1) Unless otherwise unambiguously indicated by the language or circumstances

(a) an offer to make a contract shall be construed as inviting acceptance in any manner and by any medium reasonable in the circumstances;

(b) an order or other offer to buy goods for prompt or current shipment shall be construed as inviting acceptance either by a prompt promise to ship or by the prompt or current shipment of conforming or non-conforming goods, but such a shipment of non-conforming goods does not constitute an acceptance if the seller seasonably notifies the buyer that the shipment is offered only as an accommodation to the buyer.

(2) Where the beginning of a requested performance is a reasonable mode of acceptance an offeror who is not notified of acceptance within a reasonable time may treat the offer as having lapsed before acceptance.

§ 2—207. Additional Terms in Acceptance or Confirmation.

(1) A definite and seasonable expression of acceptance or a written confirmation which is sent within a reasonable time operates as an acceptance even though it states terms additional to or different from those offered or agreed upon, unless acceptance is expressly made conditional on assent to the additional or different terms.

(2) The additional terms are to be construed as proposals for addition to the contract. Between merchants such terms become part of the contract unless:

(a) the offer expressly limits acceptance to the terms of the offer;

(b) they materially alter it; or

(c) notification of objection to them has already been given or is given within a reasonable time after notice of them is received.

(3) Conduct by both parties which recognizes the existence of a contract is sufficient to establish a contract for sale although the writings of the parties do not otherwise establish a contract. In such case the terms of the particular contract consist of those terms on which the writings of the parties agree, together with any supplementary terms incorporated under any other provisions of this Act.

§ 2—208. Course of Performance or Practical Construction.

(1) Where the contract for sale involves repeated occasions for performance by either party with knowledge of the nature of the performance and opportunity for objection to it by the other, any course of performance accepted or acquiesced in without objection shall be relevant to determine the meaning of the agreement.

(2) The express terms of the agreement and any such course of performance, as well as any course of dealing and usage of trade, shall be construed whenever reasonable as consistent with each other; but when such construction is unreasonable, express terms shall control course of performance and course of performance shall control both course of dealing and usage of trade (Section 1—205).

(3) Subject to the provisions of the next section on modification and waiver, such course of performance shall be relevant to show a waiver or modification of any term inconsistent with such course of performance.

§ 2—209. Modification, Rescission and Waiver.

(1) An agreement modifying a contract within this Article needs no consideration to be binding.

(2) A signed agreement which excludes modification or rescission except by a signed writing cannot be otherwise modified or rescinded, but except as between merchants such a requirement on a form supplied by the merchant must be separately signed by the other party.

(3) The requirements of the statute of frauds section of this Article (Section 2—201) must be satisfied if the contract as modified is within its provisions.

(4) Although an attempt at modification or rescission does not satisfy the requirements of subsection (2) or (3) it can operate as a waiver.

(5) A party who has made a waiver affecting an executory portion of the contract may retract the waiver by reasonable notification received by the other party that strict performance will be required of any term waived, unless the retraction would be unjust in view of a material change of position in reliance on the waiver.

§ 2—210. Delegation of Performance; Assignment of Rights.

(1) A party may perform his duty through a delegate unless otherwise agreed or unless the other party has a substantial interest in having his original promisor perform or control the acts required by the contract. No delegation of performance relieves the party delegating of any duty to perform or any liability for breach.

(2) Unless otherwise agreed all rights of either seller or buyer can be assigned except where the assignment would materially change the duty of the other party, or increase materially the burden or risk imposed on him by his contract, or impair materially his chance of obtaining return performance. A right to damages for breach of the whole contract or a right arising out of the assignor's due performance of his entire obligation can be assigned despite agreement otherwise.

(3) Unless the circumstances indicate the contrary a prohibition of assignment of "the contract" is to be construed as barring only the delegation to the assignee of the assignor's performance.

(4) An assignment of "the contract" or of "all my rights under the contract" or an assignment in similar general terms is an assignment of rights and unless the language or the circumstances (as in an assignment for security) indicate the contrary, it is a delegation of performance of the duties of the assignor and its acceptance by the assignee constitutes a promise by him to perform those duties. This promise is enforceable by either the assignor or the other party to the original contract.

(5) The other party may treat any assignment which delegates performance as creating reasonable grounds for insecurity and may without prejudice to his rights against the assignor demand assurances from the assignee (Section 2—609).

PART 3. *General Obligation and Construction of Contract.*

§ 2—301. General Obligations of Parties.

The obligation of the seller is to transfer and deliver and that of the buyer is to accept and pay in accordance with the contract.

§ 2—302. Unconscionable Contract or Clause.

(1) If the court as a matter of law finds the contract or any clause of the contract to have been unconscionable at the time it was made the court may refuse to enforce the contract, or it may enforce the remainder of the contract without the unconscionable clause, or it may so limit the application of any unconscionable clause as to avoid any unconscionable result.

(2) When it is claimed or appears to the court that the contract or any clause thereof may be unconscionable the parties shall be afforded a reasonable opportunity to present evidence as to its commercial setting, purpose and effect to aid the court in making the determination.

§ 2—303. Allocation or Division of Risks.

Where this Article allocates a risk or a burden as between the parties "unless otherwise agreed", the agreement may not only shift the allocation but may also divide the risk or burden.

§ 2—304. Price Payable in Money, Goods, Realty, or Otherwise.

(1) The price can be made payable in money or otherwise. If it is payable in whole or in part in goods each party is a seller of the goods which he is to transfer.

(2) Even though all or part of the price is payable in an interest in realty the transfer of the goods and the seller's obligations with reference to them are subject to this Article, but not the transfer of the interest in realty or the transferor's obligations in connection therewith.

§ 2—305. Open Price Term.

(1) The parties if they so intend can conclude a contract for sale even though the price is not settled. In such a case the price is a reasonable price at the time for delivery if

    (a) nothing is said as to price; or

    (b) the price is left to be agreed by the parties and they fail to agree; or

    (c) the price is to be fixed in terms of some agreed market or other standard as set or recorded by a third person or agency and it is not so set or recorded.

(2) A price to be fixed by the seller or by the buyer means a price for him to fix in good faith.

(3) When a price left to be fixed otherwise than by agreement of the parties fails to be fixed through fault of

one party the other may at his option treat the contract as cancelled or himself fix a reasonable price.

(4) Where, however, the parties intend not to be bound unless the price be fixed or agreed and it is not fixed or agreed there is no contract. In such a case the buyer must return any goods already received or if unable so to do must pay their reasonable value at the time of delivery and the seller must return any portion of the price paid on account.

§ 2—306.   Output, Requirements and Exclusive Dealings.

(1) A term which measures the quantity by the output of the seller or the requirements of the buyer means such actual output or requirements as may occur in good faith, except that no quantity unreasonably disproportionate to any stated estimate or in the absence of a stated estimate to any normal or otherwise comparable prior output or requirements may be tendered or demanded.

(2) A lawful agreement by either the seller or the buyer for exclusive dealing in the kind of goods concerned imposes unless otherwise agreed an obligation by the seller to use best efforts to supply the goods and by the buyer to use best efforts to promote their sale.

§ 2—307.   Delivery in Single Lot or Several Lots.

Unless otherwise agreed all goods called for by a contract for sale must be tendered in a single delivery and payment is due only on such tender but where the circumstances give either party the right to make or demand delivery in lots the price if it can be apportioned may be demanded for each lot.

§ 2—308.   Absence of Specified Place for Delivery.

Unless otherwise agreed

(a) the place for delivery of goods is the seller's place of business or if he has none his residence; but

(b) in a contract for sale of identified goods which to the knowledge of the parties at the time of contracting are in some other place, that place is the place for their delivery; and

(c) documents of title may be delivered through customary banking channels.

§ 2—309.   Absence of Specific Time Provisions; Notice of Termination.

(1) The time for shipment or delivery or any other action under a contract if not provided in this Article or agreed upon shall be a reasonable time.

(2) Where the contract provides for successive performance but is indefinite in duration it is valid for a reasonable time but unless otherwise agreed may be terminated at any time by either party.

(3) Termination of a contract by one party except on the happening of an agreed event requires that reasonable notification be received by the other party and an agreement dispensing with notification is invalid if its operation would be unconscionable.

§ 2—310.   Open Time for Payment or Running of Credit; Authority to Ship Under Reservation.

Unless otherwise agreed

(a) payment is due at the time and place at which the buyer is to receive the goods even though the place of shipment is the place of delivery; and

(b) if the seller is authorized to send the goods he may ship them under reservation, and may tender the documents of title, but the buyer may inspect the goods after their arrival before payment is due unless such inspection is inconsistent with the terms of the contract (Section 2—513); and

(c) if delivery is authorized and made by way of documents of title otherwise than by subsection (b) then payment is due at the time and place at which the buyer is to receive the documents regardless of where the goods are to be received; and

(d) where the seller is required or authorized to ship the goods on credit the credit period runs from the time of shipment but post-dating the invoice or delaying its dispatch will correspondingly delay the starting of the credit period.

§ 2—311.   Options and Cooperation Respecting Performance.

(1) An agreement for sale which is otherwise sufficiently definite (subsection (3) of Section 2—204) to be a contract is not made invalid by the fact that it leaves particulars of performance to be specified by one of the parties. Any such specification must be made in good faith and within limits set by commercial reasonableness.

(2) Unless otherwise agreed specifications relating to assortment of the goods are at the buyer's option and except as otherwise provided in subsections (1) (c) and (3) of Section 2—319 specifications or arrangements relating to shipment are at the seller's option.

(3) Where such specification would materially affect the other party's performance but is not seasonably made or where one party's cooperation is necessary to the agreed performance of the other but is not seasonably forthcoming, the other party in addition to all other remedies

(a) is excused for any resulting delay in his own performance; and

(b) may also either proceed to perform in any reasonable manner or after the time for a material part of his own performance treat the failure to specify or to cooperate as a breach by failure to deliver or accept the goods.

§ 2—312. Warranty of Title and Against Infringement; Buyer's Obligation Against Infringement.

(1) Subject to subsection (2) there is in a contract for sale a warranty by the seller that

   (a) the title conveyed shall be good, and its transfer rightful; and

   (b) the goods shall be delivered free from any security interest or other lien or encumbrance of which the buyer at the time of contracting has no knowledge.

(2) A warranty under subsection (1) will be excluded or modified only by specific language or by circumstances which give the buyer reason to know that the person selling does not claim title in himself or that he is purporting to sell only such right or title as he or a third person may have.

(3) Unless otherwise agreed a seller who is a merchant regularly dealing in goods of the kind warrants that the goods shall be delivered free of the rightful claim of any third person by way of infringement or the like but a buyer who furnishes specifications to the seller must hold the seller harmless against any such claim which arises out of compliance with the specifications.

§ 2—313. Express Warranties by Affirmation, Promise, Description, Sample.

(1) Express warranties by the seller are created as follows:

   (a) Any affirmation of fact or promise made by the seller to the buyer which relates to the goods and becomes part of the basis of the bargain creates an express warranty that the goods shall conform to the affirmation or promise.

   (b) Any description of the goods which is made part of the basis of the bargain creates an express warranty that the goods shall conform to the description.

   (c) Any sample or model which is made part of the basis of the bargain creates an express warranty that the whole of the goods shall conform to the sample or model.

(2) It is not necessary to the creation of an express warranty that the seller use formal words such as "warrant" or "guarantee" or that he have a specific intention to make a warranty, but an affirmation merely of the value of the goods or a statement purporting to be merely the seller's opinion or commendation of the goods does not create a warranty.

§ 2—314. Implied Warranty: Merchantability; Usage of Trade.

(1) Unless excluded or modified (Section 2—316), a warranty that the goods shall be merchantable is implied in a contract for their sale if the seller is a merchant with respect to goods of that kind. Under this section the serving for value of food or drink to be consumed either on the premises or elsewhere is a sale.

(2) Goods to be merchantable must be at least such as

   (a) pass without objection in the trade under the contract description; and

   (b) in the case of fungible goods, are of fair average quality within the description; and

   (c) are fit for the ordinary purposes for which such goods are used; and

   (d) run, within the variations permitted by the agreement, of even kind, quality and quantity within each unit and among all units involved; and

   (e) are adequately contained, packaged, and labeled as the agreement may require; and

   (f) conform to the promises or affirmations of fact made on the container or label if any.

(3) Unless excluded or modified (Section 2—316) other implied warranties may arise from course of dealing or usage of trade.

§ 2—315. Implied Warranty: Fitness for Particular Purpose.

Where the seller at the time of contracting has reason to know any particular purpose for which the goods are required and that the buyer is relying on the seller's skill or judgment to select or furnish suitable goods, there is unless excluded or modified under the next section an implied warranty that the goods shall be fit for such purpose.

§ 2—316. Exclusion or Modification of Warranties.

(1) Words or conduct relevant to the creation of an express warranty and words or conduct tending to negate or limit warranty shall be construed wherever reasonable as consistent with each other; but subject to the provisions of this Article on parol or extrinsic evidence (Section 2—202) negation or limitation is inoperative to the extent that such construction is unreasonable.

(2) Subject to subsection (3), to exclude or modify the implied warranty of merchantability or any part of it the language must mention merchantability and in case of a writing must be conspicuous, and to exclude or modify any implied warranty of fitness the exclusion must be by a writing and conspicuous. Language to exclude all implied warranties of fitness is sufficient if it states, for example, that "There are no warranties which extend beyond the description on the face hereof."

(3) Notwithstanding subsection (2)

(a) unless the circumstances indicate otherwise, all implied warranties are excluded by expressions like "as is", "with all faults" or other language which in common understanding calls the buyer's attention to the exclusion of warranties and makes plain that there is no implied warranty; and

(b) when the buyer before entering into the contract has examined the goods or the sample or model as fully as he desired or has refused to examine the goods there is no implied warranty with regard to defects which an examination ought in the circumstances to have revealed to him; and

(c) an implied warranty can also be excluded or modified by course of dealing or course of performance or usage of trade.

(4) Remedies for breach of warranty can be limited in accordance with the provisions of this Article on liquidation or limitation of damages and on contractual modification of remedy (Sections 2—718 and 2—719).

§ 2—317. Cumulation and Conflict of Warranties Express or Implied.

Warranties whether express or implied shall be construed as consistent with each other and as cumulative, but if such construction is unreasonable the intention of the parties shall determine which warranty is dominant. In ascertaining that intention the following rules apply:

(a) Exact or technical specifications displace an inconsistent sample or model or general language of description.

(b) A sample from an existing bulk displaces inconsistent general language of description.

(c) Express warranties displace inconsistent implied warranties other than an implied warranty of fitness for a particular purpose.

§ 2—318. Third Party Beneficiaries of Warranties Express or Implied.

Note: If this Act is introduced in the Congress of the United States this section should be omitted. (States to select one alternative.)

Alternative A. A seller's warranty whether express or implied extends to any natural person who is in the family or household of his buyer or who is a guest in his home if it is reasonable to expect that such person may use, consume or be affected by the goods and who is injured in person by breach of the warranty. A seller may not exclude or limit the operation of this section.

Alternative B. A seller's warranty whether express or implied extends to any natural person who may reasonably be expected to use, consume or be affected by the goods and who is injured in person by breach of the warranty. A seller may not exclude or limit the operation of this section.

Alternative C. A seller's warranty whether express or implied extends to any person who may reasonably be expected to use, consume or be affected by the goods and who is injured by breach of the warranty. A seller may not exclude or limit the operation of this section with respect to injury to the person of an individual to whom the warranty extends. As amended 1966.

§ 2—319. F.O.B. and F.A.S. Terms.

(1) Unless otherwise agreed the term F.O.B. (which means "free on board") at a named place, even though used only in connection with the stated price, is a delivery term under which

(a) when the term is F.O.B. the place of shipment, the seller must at that place ship the goods in the manner provided in this Article (Section 2—504) and bear the expense and risk of putting them into the possession of the carrier; or

(b) when the term is F.O.B. the place of destination, the seller must at his own expense and risk transport the goods to that place and there tender delivery of them in the manner provided in this Article (Section 2—503);

(c) when under either (a) or (b) the term is also F.O.B. vessel, car or other vehicle, the seller must in addition at his own expense and risk load the goods on board. If the term is F.O.B. vessel the buyer must name the vessel and in an appropriate case the seller must comply with the provisions of this Article on the form of bill of lading (Section 2—323).

(2) Unless otherwise agreed the term F.A.S. vessel (which means "free alongside") at a named port, even though used only in connection with the stated price, is a delivery term under which the seller must

(a) at his own expense and risk deliver the goods alongside the vessel in the manner usual in that port or on a dock designated and provided by the buyer; and

(b) obtain and tender a receipt for the goods in exchange for which the carrier is under a duty to issue a bill of lading.

(3) Unless otherwise agreed in any case falling within subsection (1)(a) or (c) or subsection (2) the buyer must seasonably give any needed instructions for making delivery, including when the term is F.A.S. or F.O.B. the loading berth of the vessel and in an appropriate case its name and sailing date. The seller may treat the failure of

needed instructions as a failure of cooperation under this Article (Section 2—311). He may also at his option move the goods in any reasonable manner preparatory to delivery or shipment.

(4) Under the term F.O.B. vessel or F.A.S. unless otherwise agreed the buyer must make payment against tender of the required documents and the seller may not tender nor the buyer demand delivery of the goods in substitution for the documents.

§ 2—320. C.I.F. and C. & F. Terms.

(1) The term C.I.F. means that the price includes in a lump sum the cost of the goods and the insurance and freight to the named destination. The term C. & F. or C.F. means that the price so includes cost and freight to the named destination.

(2) Unless otherwise agreed and even though used only in connection with the stated price and destination, the term C.I.F. destination or its equivalent requires the seller at his own expense and risk to

  (a) put the goods into the possession of a carrier at the port for shipment and obtain a negotiable bill or bills of lading covering the entire transportation to the named destination; and

  (b) load the goods and obtain a receipt from the carrier (which may be contained in the bill of lading) showing that the freight has been paid or provided for; and

  (c) obtain a policy or certificate of insurance, including any war risk insurance, of a kind and on terms then current at the port of shipment in the usual amount, in the currency of the contract, shown to cover the same goods covered by the bill of lading and providing for payment of loss to the order of the buyer or for the account of whom it may concern; but the seller may add to the price the amount of the premium for any such war risk insurance; and

  (d) prepare an invoice of the goods and procure any other documents required to effect shipment or to comply with the contract; and

  (e) forward and tender with commercial promptness all the documents in due form and with any indorsement necessary to perfect the buyer's rights.

(3) Unless otherwise agreed the term C. & F. or its equivalent has the same effect and imposes upon the seller the same obligations and risks as a C.I.F. term except the obligation as to insurance.

(4) Under the term C.I.F. or C. & F. unless otherwise agreed the buyer must make payment against tender of the required documents and the seller may not tender nor the buyer demand delivery of the goods in substitution for the documents.

§ 2—321. C.I.F. or C. & F.: "Net Landed Weights"; "Payment on Arrival"; Warranty of Condition on Arrival.

Under a contract containing a term C.I.F. or C. & F.

(1) Where the price is based on or is to be adjusted according to "net landed weights", "delivered weights", "out turn" quantity or quality or the like, unless otherwise agreed the seller must reasonably estimate the price. The payment due on tender of the documents called for by the contract is the amount so estimated, but after final adjustment of the price a settlement must be made with commercial promptness.

(2) An agreement described in subsection (1) or any warranty of quality or condition of the goods on arrival places upon the seller the risk of ordinary deterioration, shrinkage and the like in transportation but has no effect on the place or time of identification to the contract for sale or delivery or on the passing of the risk of loss.

(3) Unless otherwise agreed where the contract provides for payment on or after arrival of the goods the seller must before payment allow such preliminary inspection as is feasible; but if the goods are lost delivery of the documents and payment are due when the goods should have arrived.

§ 2—322. Delivery "Ex-Ship".

(1) Unless otherwise agreed a term for delivery of goods "ex-ship" (which means from the carrying vessel) or in equivalent language is not restricted to a particular ship and requires delivery from a ship which has reached a place at the named port of destination where goods of the kind are usually discharged.

(2) Under such a term unless otherwise agreed

  (a) the seller must discharge all liens arising out of the carriage and furnish the buyer with a direction which puts the carrier under a duty to deliver the goods; and

  (b) the risk of loss does not pass to the buyer until the goods leave the ship's tackle or are otherwise properly unloaded.

§ 2—323. Form of Bill of Lading Required in Overseas Shipment; "Overseas".

(1) Where the contract contemplates overseas shipment and contains a term C.I.F. or C. & F. or F.O.B. vessel, the seller unless otherwise agreed must obtain a negotiable bill of lading stating that the goods have been loaded on board or, in the case of a term C.I.F. or C. & F., received for shipment.

(2) Where in a case within subsection (1) a bill of lading has been issued in a set of parts, unless otherwise agreed if the documents are not to be sent from abroad the buyer may demand tender of the full set; otherwise only one part of the bill of lading need be tendered. Even if the agreement expressly requires a full set

(a) due tender of a single part is acceptable within the provisions of this Article on cure of improper delivery (subsection (1) of Section 2—508); and

(b) even though the full set is demanded, if the documents are sent from abroad the person tendering an incomplete set may nevertheless require payment upon furnishing an indemnity which the buyer in good faith deems adequate.

(3) A shipment by water or by air or a contract contemplating such shipment is "overseas" insofar as by usage of trade or agreement it is subject to the commercial, financing or shipping practices characteristic of international deep water commerce.

§ 2—324. "No Arrival, No Sale" Term.

Under a term "no arrival, no sale" or terms of like meaning, unless otherwise agreed,

(a) the seller must properly ship conforming goods and if they arrive by any means he must tender them on arrival but he assumes no obligation that the goods will arrive unless he has caused the non-arrival; and

(b) where without fault of the seller the goods are in part lost or have so deteriorated as no longer to conform to the contract or arrive after the contract time, the buyer may proceed as if there had been casualty to identified goods (Section 2—613).

§ 2—325. "Letter of Credit" Term; "Confirmed Credit".

(1) Failure of the buyer seasonably to furnish an agreed letter of credit is a breach of the contract for sale.

(2) The delivery to seller of a proper letter of credit suspends the buyer's obligation to pay. If the letter of credit is dishonored, the seller may on seasonable notification to the buyer require payment directly from him.

(3) Unless otherwise agreed the term "letter of credit" or "banker's credit" in a contract for sale means an irrevocable credit issued by a financing agency of good repute and, where the shipment is overseas, of good international repute. The term "confirmed credit" means that the credit must also carry the direct obligation of such an agency which does business in the seller's financial market.

§ 2—326. Sale on Approval and Sale or Return; Consignment Sales and Rights of Creditors.

(1) Unless otherwise agreed, if delivered goods may be returned by the buyer even though they conform to the contract, the transaction is

(a) a "sale on approval" if the goods are delivered primarily for use, and

(b) a "sale or return" if the goods are delivered primarily for resale.

(2) Except as provided in subsection (3), goods held on approval are not subject to the claims of the buyer's creditors until acceptance; goods held on sale or return are subject to such claims while in the buyer's possession.

(3) Where goods are delivered to a person for sale and such person maintains a place of business at which he deals in goods of the kind involved, under a name other than the name of the person making delivery, then with respect to claims of creditors of the person conducting the business the goods are deemed to be on sale or return. The provisions of this subsection are applicable even though an agreement purports to reserve title to the person making delivery until payment or resale or uses such words as "on consignment" or "on memorandum". However, this subsection is not applicable if the person making delivery

(a) complies with an applicable law providing for a consignor's interest or the like to be evidenced by a sign, or

(b) establishes that the person conducting the business is generally known by his creditors to be substantially engaged in selling the goods of others, or

(c) complies with the filing provisions of the Article on Secured Transactions (Article 9).

(4) Any "or return" term of a contract for sale is to be treated as a separate contract for sale within the statute of frauds section of this Article (Section 2—201) and as contradicting the sale aspect of the contract within the provisions of this Article on parol or extrinsic evidence (Section 2—202).

§ 2—327. Special Incidents of Sale on Approval and Sale or Return.

(1) Under a sale on approval unless otherwise agreed

(a) although the goods are identified to the contract the risk of loss and the title do not pass to the buyer until acceptance; and

(b) use of the goods consistent with the purpose of trial is not acceptance but failure seasonably to notify the seller of election to return the goods is acceptance, and if the goods conform to the contract acceptance of any part is acceptance of the whole; and

(c) after due notification of election to return, the return is at the seller's risk and expense but a merchant buyer must follow any reasonable instructions.

(2) Under a sale or return unless otherwise agreed

(a) the option to return extends to the whole or any commercial unit of the goods while in substantially their original condition, but must be exercised seasonally; and

(b) the return is at the buyer's risk and expense.

§ 2—328. Sale by Auction.

(1) In a sale by auction if goods are put up in lots each lot is the subject of a separate sale.

(2) A sale by auction is complete when the auctioneer so announces by the fall of the hammer or in other customary manner. Where a bid is made while the hammer is falling in acceptance of a prior bid the auctioneer may in his discretion reopen the bidding or declare the goods sold under the bid on which the hammer was falling.

(3) Such a sale is with reserve unless the goods are in explicit terms put up without reserve. In an auction with reserve the auctioneer may withdraw the goods at any time until he announces completion of the sale. In an auction without reserve, after the auctioneer calls for bids on an article or lot, that article or lot cannot be withdrawn unless no bid is made within a reasonable time. In either case a bidder may retract his bid until the auctioneer's announcement of completion of the sale, but a bidder's retraction does not revive any previous bid.

(4) If the auctioneer knowingly receives a bid on the seller's behalf or the seller makes or procures such a bid, and notice has not been given that liberty for such bidding is reserved, the buyer may at his option avoid the sale or take the goods at the price of the last good faith bid prior to the completion of the sale. This subsection shall not apply to any bid at a forced sale.

PART 4. *Title, Creditors and Good Faith Purchasers.*

§ 2—401. Passing of Title; Reservation for Security; Limited Application of This Section.

Each provision of this Article with regard to the rights, obligations and remedies of the seller, the buyer, purchasers or other third parties applies irrespective of title to the goods except where the provision refers to such title. Insofar as situations are not covered by the other provisions of this Article and matters concerning title become material the following rules apply:

(1) Title to goods cannot pass under a contract for sale prior to their identification to the contract (Section 2—501), and unless otherwise explicitly agreed the buyer acquires by their identification a special property as limited by this Act. Any retention or reservation by the seller of the title (property) in goods shipped or delivered to the buyer is limited in effect to a reservation of a security interest. Subject to these provisions and to the provisions of the Article on Secured Transactions (Article 9), title to goods passes from the seller to the buyer in any manner and on any conditions explicitly agreed on by the parties.

(2) Unless otherwise explicitly agreed title passes to the buyer at the time and place at which the seller completes his performance with reference to the physical delivery of the goods, despite any reservation of a security interest and even though a document of title is to be delivered at a different time or place; and in particular and despite any reservation of a security interest by the bill of lading

(a) if the contract requires or authorizes the seller to send the goods to the buyer but does not require him to deliver them at destination, title passes to the buyer at the time and place of shipment; but

(b) if the contract requires delivery at destination, title passes on tender there.

(3) Unless otherwise explicitly agreed where delivery is to be made without moving the goods,

(a) if the seller is to deliver a document of title, title passes at the time when and the place where he delivers such documents; or

(b) if the goods are at the time of contracting already identified and no documents are to be delivered, title passes at the time and place of contracting.

(4) A rejection or other refusal by the buyer to receive or retain the goods, whether or not justified, or a justified revocation of acceptance revests title to the goods in the seller. Such revesting occurs by operation of law and is not a "sale".

§ 2—402. Rights of Seller's Creditors Against Sold Goods.

(1) Except as provided in subsections (2) and (3), rights of unsecured creditors of the seller with respect to goods which have been identified to a contract for sale are subject to the buyer's rights to recover the goods under this Article (Sections 2—502 and 2—716).

(2) A creditor of the seller may treat a sale or an identification of goods to a contract for sale as void if as against him a retention of possession by the seller is fraudulent under any rule of law of the state where the goods are situated, except that retention of possession in good faith and current course of trade by a merchant-seller for a commercially reasonable time after a sale or identification is not fraudulent.

(3) Nothing in this Article shall be deemed to impair the rights of creditors of the seller

(a) under the provisions of the Article on Secured Transactions (Article 9); or

(b) where identification to the contract or delivery is made not in current course of trade but in satisfaction of or as security for a pre-existing claim for money, security or the like and is made under circumstances which under any rule of law of the state where the goods are situated would apart from this Article constitute the transaction a fraudulent transfer or voidable preference.

§ 2—403. Power to Transfer; Good Faith Purchase of Goods; "Entrusting".

(1) A purchaser of goods acquires all title which his transferor had or had power to transfer except that a purchaser of a limited interest acquires rights only to the extent of the interest purchased. A person with voidable title has power to transfer a good title to a good faith purchaser for value. When goods have been delivered under a transaction of purchase the purchaser has such power even though

(a) the transferor was deceived as to the identity of the purchaser, or

(b) the delivery was in exchange for a check which is later dishonored, or

(c) it was agreed that the transaction was to be a "cash sale", or

(d) the delivery was procured through fraud punishable as larcenous under the criminal law.

(2) Any entrusting of possession of goods to a merchant who deals in goods of that kind gives him power to transfer all rights of the entruster to a buyer in ordinary course of business.

(3) "Entrusting" includes any delivery and any acquiescence in retention of possession regardless of any condition expressed between the parties to the delivery or acquiescence and regardless of whether the procurement of the entrusting or the possessor's disposition of the goods have been such as to be larcenous under the criminal law.

(4) The rights of other purchasers of goods and of lien creditors are governed by the Articles on Secured Transactions (Article 9), Bulk Transfers (Article 6) and Documents of Title (Article 7).

PART 5. *Performance.*

§ 2—501. Insurable Interest in Goods; Manner of Identification of Goods.

(1) The buyer obtains a special property and an insurable interest in goods by identification of existing goods as goods to which the contract refers even though the goods so identified are non-conforming and he has an option to return or reject them. Such identification can be made at any time and in any manner explicitly agreed to by the parties. In the absence of explicit agreement identification occurs

(a) when the contract is made if it is for the sale of goods already existing and identified;

(b) if the contract is for the sale of future goods other than those described in paragraph (c), when goods are shipped, marked or otherwise designated by the seller as goods to which the contract refers;

(c) when the crops are planted or otherwise become growing crops or the young are conceived if the contract is for the sale of unborn young to be born within twelve months after contracting or for the sale of crops to be harvested within twelve months or the next normal harvest season after contracting, whichever is longer.

(2) The seller retains an insurable interest in goods so long as title to or any security interest in the goods remains in him and where the identification is by the seller alone he may until default or insolvency or notification to the buyer that the identification is final substitute other goods for those identified.

(3) Nothing in this section impairs any insurable interest recognized under any other statute or rule of law.

§ 2—502. Buyer's Right to Goods on Seller's Insolvency.

(1) Subject to subsection (2) and even though the goods have not been shipped a buyer who has paid a part or all of the price of goods in which he has a special property under the provisions of the immediately preceding section may on making and keeping good a tender of any unpaid portion of their price recover them from the seller if the seller becomes insolvent within ten days after receipt of the first installment on their price.

(2) If the identification creating his special property has been made by the buyer he acquires the right to recover the goods only if they conform to the contract for sale.

§ 2—503. Manner of Seller's Tender of Delivery.

(1) Tender of delivery requires that the seller put and hold conforming goods at the buyer's disposition and give the buyer any notification reasonably necessary to enable him to take delivery. The manner, time and place for tender are determined by the agreement and this Article, and in particular

(a) tender must be at a reasonable hour, and if it is of goods they must be kept available for the period reasonably necessary to enable the buyer to take possession; but

(b) unless otherwise agreed the buyer must furnish facilities reasonably suited to the receipt of the goods.

(2) Where the case is within the next section respecting shipment tender requires that the seller comply with its provisions.

(3) Where the seller is required to deliver at a particular destination tender requires that he comply with subsection (1) and also in any appropriate case tender documents as described in subsections (4) and (5) of this section.

(4) Where goods are in the possession of a bailee and are to be delivered without being moved

(a) tender requires that the seller either tender a negotiable document of title covering such goods or procure acknowledgment by the bailee of the buyer's right to possession of the goods; but

(b) tender to the buyer of a non-negotiable document of title or of a written direction to the bailee to deliver is sufficient tender unless the buyer seasonably objects, and receipt by the bailee of notification of the buyer's rights fixes those rights as against the bailee and all third persons; but risk of loss of the goods and of any failure by the bailee to honor the non-negotiable document of title or to obey the direction remains on the seller until the buyer has had a reasonable time to present the document or direction, and a refusal by the bailee to honor the document or to obey the direction defeats the tender.

(5) Where the contract requires the seller to deliver documents

(a) he must tender all such documents in correct form, except as provided in this Article with respect to bills of lading in a set (subsection (2) of Section 2—323); and

(b) tender through customary banking channels is sufficient and dishonor of a draft accompanying the documents constitutes non-acceptance or rejection.

§ 2—504. Shipment by Seller.

Where the seller is required or authorized to send the goods to the buyer and the contract does not require him to deliver them at a particular destination, then unless otherwise agreed he must

(a) put the goods in the possession of such a carrier and make such a contract for their transportation as may be reasonable having regard to the nature of the goods and other circumstances of the case; and

(b) obtain and promptly deliver or tender in due form any document necessary to enable the buyer to obtain possession of the goods or otherwise required by the agreement or by usage of trade; and

(c) promptly notify the buyer of the shipment.

Failure to notify the buyer under paragraph (c) or to make a proper contract under paragraph (a) is a ground for rejection only if material delay or loss ensues.

§ 2—505. Seller's Shipment Under Reservation.

(1) Where the seller has identified goods to the contract by or before shipment:

(a) his procurement of a negotiable bill of lading to his own order or otherwise reserves in him a security interest in the goods. His procure-

ment of the bill to the order of a financing agency or of the buyer indicates in addition only the seller's expectation of transferring that interest to the person named.

(b) a non-negotiable bill of lading to himself or his nominee reserves possession of the goods as security but except in a case of conditional delivery (subsection (2) of Section 2—507) a non-negotiable bill of lading naming the buyer as consignee reserves no security interest even though the seller retains possession of the bill of lading.

(2) When shipment by the seller with reservation of a security interest is in violation of the contract for sale it constitutes an improper contract for transportation within the preceding section but impairs neither the rights given to the buyer by shipment and identification of the goods to the contract nor the seller's powers as a holder of a negotiable document.

§ 2—506. Rights of Financing Agency.

(1) A financing agency by paying or purchasing for value a draft which relates to a shipment of goods acquires to the extent of the payment or purchase and in addition to its own rights under the draft and any document of title securing it any rights of the shipper in the goods including the right to stop delivery and the shipper's right to have the draft honored by the buyer.

(2) The right to reimbursement of a financing agency which has in good faith honored or purchased the draft under commitment to or authority from the buyer is not impaired by subsequent discovery of defects with reference to any relevant document which was apparently regular on its face.

§ 2—507. Effect of Seller's Tender; Delivery on Condition.

(1) Tender of delivery is a condition to the buyer's duty to accept the goods and, unless otherwise agreed, to his duty to pay for them. Tender entitles the seller to acceptance of the goods and to payment according to the contract.

(2) Where payment is due and demanded on the delivery to the buyer of goods or documents of title, his right as against the seller to retain or dispose of them is conditional upon his making the payment due.

§ 2—508. Cure by Seller of Improper Tender or Delivery; Replacement.

(1) Where any tender or delivery by the seller is rejected because non-conforming and the time for performance has not yet expired, the seller may seasonably notify the buyer of his intention to cure and may then within the contract time make a conforming delivery.

(2) Where the buyer rejects a non-conforming tender which the seller had reasonable grounds to believe would be acceptable with or without money allowance the seller may if he seasonably notifies the buyer have a further reasonable time to substitute a conforming tender.

§ 2—509. Risk of Loss in the Absence of Breach.

(1) Where the contract requires or authorizes the seller to ship the goods by carrier

  (a) if it does not require him to deliver them at a particular destination, the risk of loss passes to the buyer when the goods are duly delivered to the carrier even though the shipment is under reservation (Section 2—505); but

  (b) if it does require him to deliver them at a particular destination and the goods are there duly tendered while in the possession of the carrier, the risk of loss passes to the buyer when the goods are there duly so tendered as to enable the buyer to take delivery.

(2) Where the goods are held by a bailee to be delivered without being moved, the risk of loss passes to the buyer

  (a) on his receipt of a negotiable document of title covering the goods; or

  (b) on acknowledgment by the bailee of the buyer's right to possession of the goods; or

  (c) after his receipt of a non-negotiable document of title or other written direction to deliver, as provided in subsection (4)(b) of Section 2—503.

(3) In any case not within subsection (1) or (2), the risk of loss passes to the buyer on his receipt of the goods if the seller is a merchant; otherwise the risk passes to the buyer on tender of delivery.

(4) The provisions of this section are subject to contrary agreement of the parties and to the provisions of this Article on sale on approval (Section 2—327) and on effect of breach on risk of loss (Section 2—510).

§ 2—510. Effect of Breach on Risk of Loss.

(1) Where a tender or delivery of goods so fails to conform to the contract as to give a right of rejection the risk of their loss remains on the seller until cure or acceptance.

(2) Where the buyer rightfully revokes acceptance he may to the extent of any deficiency in his effective insurance coverage treat the risk of loss as having rested on the seller from the beginning.

(3) Where the buyer as to conforming goods already identified to the contract for sale repudiates or is otherwise in breach before risk of their loss has passed to him, the seller may to the extent of any deficiency in his effective insurance coverage treat the risk of loss as resting on the buyer for a commercially reasonable time.

§ 2—511. Tender of Payment by Buyer; Payment by Check.

(1) Unless otherwise agreed tender of payment is a condition to the seller's duty to tender and complete any delivery.

(2) Tender of payment is sufficient when made by any means or in any manner current in the ordinary course of business unless the seller demands payment in legal tender and gives any extension of time reasonably necessary to procure it.

(3) Subject to the provisions of this Act on the effect of an instrument on an obligation (Section 3—802), payment by check is conditional and is defeated as between the parties by dishonor of the check on due presentment.

§ 2—512. Payment by Buyer Before Inspection.

(1) Where the contract requires payment before inspection non-conformity of the goods does not excuse the buyer from so making payment unless

  (a) the non-conformity appears without inspection; or

  (b) despite tender of the required documents the circumstances would justify injunction against honor under the provisions of this Act (Section 5—114.)

(2) Payment pursuant to subsection (1) does not constitute an acceptance of goods or impair the buyer's right to inspect or any of his remedies.

§ 2—513. Buyer's Right to Inspection of Goods.

(1) Unless otherwise agreed and subject to subsection (3), where goods are tendered or delivered or identified to the contract for sale, the buyer has a right before payment or acceptance to inspect them at any reasonable place and time and in any reasonable manner. When the seller is required or authorized to send the goods to the buyer, the inspection may be after their arrival.

(2) Expenses of inspection must be borne by the buyer but may be recovered from the seller if the goods do not conform and are rejected.

(3) Unless otherwise agreed and subject to the provisions of this Article on C.I.F. contracts (subsection (3) of Section 2—321), the buyer is not entitled to inspect the goods before payment of the price when the contract provides

  (a) for delivery "C.O.D." or on other like terms; or

  (b) for payment against documents of title, except where such payment is due only after the goods are to become available for inspection.

(4) A place or method of inspection fixed by the parties is presumed to be exclusive but unless otherwise expressly agreed it does not postpone identification or shift the place for delivery or for passing the risk of loss. If

compliance becomes impossible, inspection shall be as provided in this section unless the place or method fixed was clearly intended as an indispensable condition failure of which avoids the contract.

§ 2—514. When Documents Deliverable on Acceptance; When on Payment.

Unless otherwise agreed documents against which a draft is drawn are to be delivered to the drawee on acceptance of the draft if it is payable more than three days after presentment; otherwise, only on payment.

§ 2—515. Preserving Evidence of Goods in Dispute.

In furtherance of the adjustment of any claim or dispute

    (a) either party on reasonable notification to the other and for the purpose of ascertaining the facts and preserving evidence has the right to inspect, test and sample the goods including such of them as may be in the possession or control of the other; and

    (b) the parties may agree to a third party inspection or survey to determine the conformity or condition of the goods and may agree that the findings shall be binding upon them in any subsequent litigation or adjustment.

PART 6. *Breach, Repudiation and Excuse.*

§ 2—601. Buyer's Rights on Improper Delivery.

Subject to the provisions of this Article on breach in installment contracts (Section 2—612) and unless otherwise agreed under the sections on contractual limitations of remedy (Sections 2—718 and 2—719), if the goods or the tender of delivery fail in any respect to conform to the contract, the buyer may

    (a) reject the whole; or

    (b) accept the whole; or

    (c) accept any commercial unit or units and reject the rest.

§ 2—602. Manner and Effect of Rightful Rejection.

(1) Rejection of goods must be within a reasonable time after their delivery or tender. It is ineffective unless the buyer seasonably notifies the seller.

(2) Subject to the provisions of the two following sections on rejected goods (Sections 2—603 and 2—604),

    (a) after rejection any exercise of ownership by the buyer with respect to any commercial unit is wrongful as against the seller; and

    (b) if the buyer has before rejection taken physical possession of goods in which he does not have a security interest under the provisions of this Article (subsection (3) of Section 2—711), he is under a duty after rejection to hold them with reasonable care at the seller's disposition for a time sufficient to permit the seller to remove them; but

    (c) the buyer has no further obligations with regard to goods rightfully rejected.

(3) The seller's rights with respect to goods wrongfully rejected are governed by the provisions of this Article on Seller's remedies in general (Section 2—703).

§ 2—603. Merchant Buyer's Duties as to Rightfully Rejected Goods.

(1) Subject to any security interest in the buyer (subsection (3) of Section 2—711), when the seller has no agent or place of business at the market of rejection a merchant buyer is under a duty after rejection of goods in his possession or control to follow any reasonable instructions received from the seller with respect to the goods and in the absence of such instructions to make reasonable efforts to sell them for the seller's account if they are perishable or threaten to decline in value speedily. Instructions are not reasonable if on demand indemnity for expenses is not forthcoming.

(2) When the buyer sells goods under subsection (1), he is entitled to reimbursement from the seller or out of the proceeds for reasonable expenses of caring for and selling them, and if the expenses include no selling commission then to such commission as is usual in the trade or if there is none to a reasonable sum not exceeding ten percent on the gross proceeds.

(3) In complying with this section the buyer is held only to good faith and good faith conduct hereunder is neither acceptance nor conversion nor the basis of an action for damages.

§ 2—604. Buyer's Options as to Salvage of Rightfully Rejected Goods.

Subject to the provisions of the immediately preceding section on perishables if the seller gives no instructions within a reasonable time after notification of rejection the buyer may store the rejected goods for the seller's account or reship them to him or resell them for the seller's account with reimbursement as provided in the preceding section. Such action is not acceptance or conversion.

§ 2—605. Waiver of Buyer's Objections by Failure to Particularize.

(1) The buyer's failure to state in connection with rejection a particular defect which is ascertainable by reasonable inspection precludes him from relying on the unstated defect to justify rejection or to establish breach

    (a) where the seller could have cured it if stated seasonably; or

    (b) between merchants when the seller has after rejection made a request in writing for a full and final written statement of all defects on which the buyer proposes to rely.

(2) Payment against documents made without reservation of rights precludes recovery of the payment for defects apparent on the face of the documents.

§ 2—606. What Constitutes Acceptance of Goods.

(1) Acceptance of goods occurs when the buyer

(a) after a reasonable opportunity to inspect the goods signifies to the seller that the goods are conforming or that he will take or retain them in spite of their non-conformity; or

(b) fails to make an effective rejection (subsection (1) of Section 2—602), but such acceptance does not occur until the buyer has had a reasonable opportunity to inspect them; or

(c) does any act inconsistent with the seller's ownership; but if such act is wrongful as against the seller it is an acceptance only if ratified by him.

(2) Acceptance of a part of any commercial unit is acceptance of that entire unit.

§ 2—607. Effect of Acceptance; Notice of Breach; Burden of Establishing Breach After Acceptance; Notice of Claim or Litigation to Person Answerable Over.

(1) The buyer must pay at the contract rate for any goods accepted.

(2) Acceptance of goods by the buyer precludes rejection of the goods accepted and if made with knowledge of a non-conformity cannot be revoked because of it unless the acceptance was on the reasonable assumption that the non-conformity would be seasonably cured but acceptance does not of itself impair any other remedy provided by this Article for non-conformity.

(3) Where a tender has been accepted

(a) the buyer must within a reasonable time after he discovers or should have discovered any breach notify the seller of breach or be barred from any remedy; and

(b) if the claim is one for infringement or the like (subsection (3) of Section 2—312) and the buyer is sued as a result of such a breach he must so notify the seller within a reasonable time after he receives notice of the litigation or be barred from any remedy over for liability established by the litigation.

(4) The burden is on the buyer to establish any breach with respect to the goods accepted.

(5) Where the buyer is sued for breach of a warranty or other obligation for which his seller is answerable over

(a) he may give his seller written notice of the litigation. If the notice states that the seller may come in and defend and that if the seller does not do so he will be bound in any action against him by his buyer by any determination of fact common to the two litigations, then un-

less the seller after seasonable receipt of the notice does come in and defend he is so bound.

(b) if the claim is one for infringement or the like (subsection (3) of Section 2—312) the original seller may demand in writing that his buyer turn over to him control of the litigation including settlement or else be barred from any remedy over and if he also agrees to bear all expense and to satisfy any adverse judgment, then unless the buyer after seasonable receipt of the demand does turn over control the buyer is so barred.

(6) The provisions of subsection (3), (4) and (5) apply to any obligation of a buyer to hold the seller harmless against infringement or the like (subsection (3) of Section 2—312).

§ 2—608. Revocation of Acceptance in Whole or in Part.

(1) The buyer may revoke his acceptance of a lot or commercial unit whose non-conformity substantially impairs its value to him if he has accepted it

(a) on the reasonable assumption that its non-conformity would be cured and it has not been seasonably cured; or

(b) without discovery of such non-conformity if his acceptance was reasonably induced either by the difficulty of discovery before acceptance or by the seller's assurances.

(2) Revocation of acceptance must occur within a reasonable time after the buyer discovers or should have discovered the ground for it and before any substantial change in condition of the goods which is not caused by their own defects. It is not effective until the buyer notifies the seller of it.

(3) A buyer who so revokes has the same rights and duties with regard to the goods involved as if he had rejected them.

§ 2—609. Right to Adequate Assurance of Performance.

(1) A contract for sale imposes an obligation on each party that the other's expectation of receiving due performance will not be impaired. When reasonable grounds for insecurity arise with respect to the performance of either party the other may in writing demand adequate assurance of due performance and until he receives such assurance may if commercially reasonable suspend any performance for which he has not already received the agreed return.

(2) Between merchants the reasonableness of grounds for insecurity and the adequacy of any assurance offered shall be determined according to commercial standards.

(3) Acceptance of any improper delivery or payment

does not prejudice the aggrieved party's right to demand adequate assurance of future performance.

(4) After receipt of a justified demand failure to provide within a reasonable time not exceeding thirty days such assurance of due performance as is adequate under the circumstances of the particular case is a repudiation of the contract.

§ 2—610. Anticipatory Repudiation.

When either party repudiates the contract with respect to a performance not yet due the loss of which will substantially impair the value of the contract to the other, the aggrieved party may

- (a) for a commercially reasonable time await performance by the repudiating party; or
- (b) resort to any remedy for breach (Section 2—703 or Section 2—711), even though he has notified the repudiating party that he would await the latter's performance and has urged retraction; and
- (c) in either case suspend his own performance or proceed in accordance with the provisions of this Article on the seller's right to identify goods to the contract notwithstanding breach or to salvage unfinished goods (Section 2—704).

§ 2—611. Retraction of Anticipatory Repudiation.

(1) Until the repudiating party's next performance is due he can retract his repudiation unless the aggrieved party has since the repudiation cancelled or materially changed his position or otherwise indicated that he considers the repudiation final.

(2) Retraction may be by any method which clearly indicates to the aggrieved party that the repudiating party intends to perform, but must include any assurance justifiably demanded under the provisions of this Article (Section 2—609).

(3) Retraction reinstates the repudiating party's rights under the contract with due excuse and allowance to the aggrieved party for any delay occasioned by the repudiation.

§ 2—612. "Installment Contract"; Breach.

(1) An "installment contract" is one which requires or authorizes the delivery of goods in separate lots to be separately accepted, even though the contract contains a clause "each delivery is a separate contract" or its equivalent.

(2) The buyer may reject any installment which is non-conforming if the non-conformity substantially impairs the value of that installment and cannot be cured or if the non-conformity is a defect in the required documents; but if the non-conformity does not fall within subsection (3) and the seller gives adequate assurance of its cure the buyer must accept that installment.

(3) Whenever non-conformity or default with respect to one or more installments substantially impairs the value of the whole contract there is a breach of the whole. But the aggrieved party reinstates the contract if he accepts a non-conforming installment without seasonably notifying of cancellation or if he brings an action with respect only to past installments or demands performance as to future installments.

§ 2—613. Casualty to Identified Goods.

Where the contract requires for its performance goods identified when the contract is made, and the goods suffer casualty without fault of either party before the risk of loss passes to the buyer, or in a proper case under a "no arrival, no sale" term (Section 2—324) then

- (a) if the loss is total the contract is avoided; and
- (b) if the loss is partial or the goods have so deteriorated as no longer to conform to the contract the buyer may nevertheless demand inspection and at his option either treat the contract as avoided or accept the goods with due allowance from the contract price for the deterioration or the deficiency in quantity but without further right against the seller.

§ 2—614. Substituted Performance.

(1) Where without fault of either party the agreed berthing, loading, or unloading facilities fail or an agreed type of carrier becomes unavailable or the agreed manner of delivery otherwise becomes commercially impracticable but a commercially reasonable substitute is available, such substitute performance must be tendered and accepted.

(2) If the agreed means or manner of payment fails because of domestic or foreign governmental regulation, the seller may withhold or stop delivery unless the buyer provides a means or manner of payment which is commercially a substantial equivalent. If delivery has already been taken, payment by the means or in the manner provided by the regulation discharges the buyers obligation unless the regulation is discriminatory, oppressive or predatory.

§ 2—615. Excuse by Failure of Presupposed Conditions.

Except so far as a seller may have assumed a greater obligation and subject to the preceding section on substituted performance:

- (a) Delay in delivery or non-delivery in whole or in part by a seller who complies with paragraphs (b) and (c) is not a breach of his duty under a contract for sale if performance as agreed has been made impracticable by the occurrence of a contingency the non-occurrence of which was a basic assumption on which the contract was made or by compliance in good faith with any applicable foreign or domestic governmental regulation or order whether or not it later proves to be invalid.

(b) Where the causes mentioned in paragraph (a) affect only a part of the seller's capacity to perform, he must allocate production and deliveries among his customers but may at his option include regular customers not then under contract as well as his own requirements for further manufacture. He may so allocate in any manner which is fair and reasonable.

(c) The seller must notify the buyer seasonably that there will be delay or non-delivery and, when allocation is required under paragraph (b), of the estimated quota thus made available for the buyer.

§ 2—616. Procedure on Notice Claiming Excuse.

(1) Where the buyer receives notification of a material or indefinite delay or an allocation justified under the preceding section he may by written notification to the seller as to any delivery concerned, and where the prospective deficiency substantially impairs the value of the whole contract under the provisions of this Article relating to breach of installment contracts (Section 2—612), then also as to the whole,

(a) terminate and thereby discharge any unexecuted portion of the contract; or

(b) modify the contract by agreeing to take his available quota in substitution.

(2) If after receipt of such notification from the seller the buyer fails so to modify the contract within a reasonable time not exceeding thirty days the contract lapses with respect to any deliveries affected.

(3) The provisions of this section may not be negated by agreement except in so far as the seller has assumed a greater obligation under the preceding section.

PART 7. Remedies.

§ 2—701. Remedies for Breach of Collateral Contracts Not Impaired.

Remedies for breach of any obligation or promise collateral or ancillary to a contract for sale or not impaired by the provisions of this Article.

§ 2—702. Seller's Remedies on Discovery of Buyer's Insolvency.

(1) Where the seller discovers the buyer to be insolvent he may refuse delivery except for cash including payment for all goods theretofore delivered under the contract, and stop delivery under this Article (Section 2—705).

(2) Where the seller discovers that the buyer has received goods on credit while insolvent he may reclaim the goods upon demand made within ten days after the receipt, but if misrepresentation of solvency has been made to the particular seller in writing within three months before delivery the ten day limitation does not apply. Except as provided in this subsection the seller may not base a right to reclaim goods on the buyer's fraudulent or innocent misrepresentation of solvency or of intent to pay.

(3) The seller's right to reclaim under subsection (2) is subject to the rights of a buyer in ordinary course or other good faith purchaser under this Article (Section 2—403). Successful reclamation of goods excludes all other remedies with respect to them. As amended 1966.

§ 2—703. Seller's Remedies in General.

Where the buyer wrongfully rejects or revokes acceptance of goods or fails to make a payment due on or before delivery or repudiates with respect to a part or the whole, then with respect to any goods directly affected and, if the breach is of the whole contract (Section 2—612), then also with respect to the whole undelivered balance, the aggrieved seller may

(a) withhold delivery of such goods;

(b) stop delivery by any bailee as hereafter provided (Section 2—705);

(c) proceed under the next section respecting goods still unidentified to the contract;

(d) resell and recover damages as hereafter provided (Section 2—706);

(e) recover damages for non-acceptance (Section 2—708) or in a proper case the price (Section 2—709);

(f) cancel.

§ 2—704. Seller's Right to Identify Goods to the Contract Notwithstanding Breach or to Salvage Unfinished Goods.

(1) An aggrieved seller under the preceding section may

(a) identify to the contract conforming goods not already identified if at the time he learned of the breach they are in his possession or control;

(b) treat as the subject of resale goods which have demonstrably been intended for the particular contract even though those goods are unfinished.

(2) Where the goods are unfinished an aggrieved seller may in the exercise of reasonable commercial judgment for the purposes of avoiding loss and of effective realization either complete the manufacture and wholly identify the goods to the contract or cease manufacture and resell for scrap or salvage value or proceed in any other reasonable manner.

§ 2—705. Seller's Stoppage of Delivery in Transit or Otherwise.

(1) The seller may stop delivery of goods in the possession of a carrier or other bailee when he discovers the buyer to be insolvent (Section 2—702) and may stop delivery of carload, truckload, planeload or larger shipments of express or freight when the buyer repudiates or fails to make a payment due before delivery or if for any other reason the seller has a right to withhold or reclaim the goods.

(2) As against such buyer the seller may stop delivery until

   (a) receipt of the goods by the buyer; or

   (b) acknowledgment to the buyer by any bailee of the goods except a carrier that the bailee holds the goods for the buyer; or

   (c) such acknowledgment to the buyer by a carrier by reshipment or as warehouseman; or

   (d) negotiation to the buyer of any negotiable document of title covering the goods.

(3) (a) To stop delivery the seller must so notify as to enable the bailee by reasonable diligence to prevent delivery of the goods.

   (b) After such notification the bailee must hold and deliver the goods according to the directions of the seller but the seller is liable to the bailee for any ensuing charges or damages.

   (c) If a negotiable document of title has been issued for goods the bailee is not obliged to obey a notification to stop until surrender of the document.

   (d) A carrier who has issued a non-negotiable bill of lading is not obliged to obey a notification to stop received from a person other than the consignor.

§ 2—706. Seller's Resale Including Contract for Resale.

(1) Under the conditions stated in Section 2—703 on seller's remedies, the seller may resell the goods concerned or the undelivered balance thereof. Where the resale is made in good faith and in a commercially reasonable manner the seller may recover the difference between the resale price and the contract price together with any incidental damages allowed under the provisions of this Article (Section 2—710), but less expenses saved in consequence of the buyer's breach.

(2) Except as otherwise provided in subsection (3) or unless otherwise agreed resale may be at public or private sale including sale by way of one or more contracts to sell or of identification to an existing contract of the seller. Sale may be as a unit or in parcels and at any time and place and on any terms but every aspect of the sale including the method, manner, time, place and terms must be commercially reasonable. The resale must be

reasonably identified as referring to the broken contract, but it is not necessary that the goods be in existence or that any or all of them have been identified to the contract before the breach.

(3) Where the resale is at private sale the seller must give the buyer reasonable notification of his intention to resell.

(4) Where the resale is at public sale

   (a) only identified goods can be sold except where there is a recognized market for a public sale of futures in goods of the kind; and

   (b) it must be made at a usual place or market for public sale if one is reasonably available and except in the case of goods which are perishable or threaten to decline in value speedily the seller must give the buyer reasonable notice of the time and place of the resale; and

   (c) if the goods are not to be within the view of those attending the sale the notification of sale must state the place where the goods are located and provide for their reasonable inspection by prospective bidders; and

   (d) the seller may buy.

(5) A purchaser who buys in good faith at a resale takes the goods free of any rights of the original buyer even though the seller fails to comply with one or more of the requirements of this section.

(6) The seller is not accountable to the buyer for any profit made on any resale. A person in the position of a seller (Section 2—707) or a buyer who has rightfully rejected or justifiably revoked acceptance must account for any excess over the amount of his security interest, as hereinafter defined (subsection (3) of Section 2—711).

§ 2—707. "Person in the Position of a Seller".

(1) A "person in the position of a seller" includes as against a principal an agent who has paid or become responsible for the price of goods on behalf of his principal or anyone who otherwise holds a security interest or other right in goods similar to that of a seller.

(2) A person in the position of a seller may as provided in this Article withhold or stop delivery (Section 2—705) and resell (Section 2—706) and recover incidental damages (Section 2—710).

§ 2—708. Seller's Damages for Non-Acceptance or Repudiation.

(1) Subject to subsection (2) and to the provisions of this Article with respect to proof of market price (Section 2—723), the measure of damages for non-acceptance or repudiation by the buyer is the difference between the market price at the time and place for tender and the unpaid contract price together with any incidental dam-

ages provided in this Article (Section 2—710), but less expenses saved in consequence of the buyer's breach.

(2) If the measure of damages provided in subsection (1) is inadequate to put the seller in as good a position as performance would have done then the measure of damages is the profit (including reasonable overhead) which the seller would have made from full performance by the buyer, together with any incidental damages provided in this Article (Section 2—710), due allowance for costs reasonably incurred and due credit for payments or proceeds of resale.

§ 2—709. Action for the Price.

(1) When the buyer fails to pay the price as it becomes due the seller may recover, together with any incidental damages under the next section, the price

(a) of goods accepted or of conforming goods lost or damaged within a commercially reasonable time after risk of their loss has passed to the buyer; and

(b) of goods identified to the contract if the seller is unable after reasonable effort to resell them at a reasonable price or the circumstances reasonably indicate that such effort will be unavailing.

(2) Where the seller sues for the price he must hold for the buyer any goods which have been identified to the contract and are still in his control except that if resale becomes possible he may resell them at any time prior to the collection of the judgment. The net proceeds of any such resale must be credited to the buyer and payment of the judgment entitles him to any goods not resold.

(3) After the buyer has wrongfully rejected or revoked acceptance of the goods or has failed to make a payment due or has repudiated (Section 2—610), a seller who is held not entitled to the price under this section shall nevertheless be awarded damages for non-acceptance under the preceding section.

§ 2—710. Seller's Incidental Damages.

Incidental damages to an aggrieved seller include any commercially reasonable charges, expenses or commissions incurred in stopping delivery, in the transportation, care and custody of goods after the buyer's breach, in connection with return or resale of the goods or otherwise resulting from the breach.

§ 2—711. Buyer's Remedies in General; Buyer's Security Interest in Rejected Goods.

(1) Where the seller fails to make delivery or repudiates or the buyer rightfully rejects or justifiably revokes acceptance then with respect to any goods involved, and with respect to the whole if the breach goes to the whole contract (Section 2—612), the buyer may cancel and

whether or not he has done so may in addition to recovering so much of the price as has been paid

(a) "cover" and have damages under the next section as to all the goods affected whether or not they have been identified to the contract; or

(b) recover damages for non-delivery as provided in this Article (Section 2—713).

(2) Where the seller fails to deliver or repudiates the buyer may also

(a) if the goods have been identified recover them as provided in this Article (Section 2—502); or

(b) in a proper case obtain specific performance or replevy the goods as provided in this Article (Section 2—716).

(3) On rightful rejection of justifiable revocation of acceptance a buyer has a security interest in goods in his possession or control for any payments made on their price and any expenses reasonably incurred in their inspection, receipt, transportation, care and custody and may hold such goods and resell them in like manner as an aggrieved seller (Section 2—706).

§ 2—712. "Cover"; Buyer's Procurement of Substitute Goods.

(1) After a breach within the preceding section the buyer may "cover" by making in good faith and without unreasonable delay any reasonable purchase of or contract to purchase goods in substitution for those due from the seller.

(2) The buyer may recover from the seller as damages the difference between the cost of cover and the contract price together with any incidental or consequential damages as hereinafter defined (Section 2—715), but less expenses saved in consequence of the seller's breach.

(3) Failure of the buyer to effect cover within this section does not bar him from any other remedy.

§ 2—713. Buyer's Damages for Non-Delivery or Repudiation.

(1) Subject to the provisions of this Article with respect to proof of market price (Section 2—723), the measure of damages for non-delivery or repudiation by the seller is the difference between the market price at the time when the buyer learned of the breach and the contract price together with any incidental and consequential damages provided in this Article (Section 2—715), but less expenses saved in consequence of the seller's breach.

(2) Market price is to be determined as of the place for tender or, in cases of rejection after arrival or revocation of acceptance, as of the place of arrival.

§ 2—714. Buyer's Damages for Breach in Regard to Accepted Goods.

(1) Where the buyer has accepted goods and given notification (subsection (3) of Section 2—607) he may recover as damages for any non-conformity of tender the loss resulting in the ordinary course of events from the seller's breach as determined in any manner which is reasonable.

(2) The measure of damages for breach of warranty is the difference at the time and place of acceptance between the value of the goods accepted and the value they would have had if they had been as warranted, unless special circumstances show proximate damages of a different amount.

(3) In a proper case any incidental and consequential damages under the next section may also be recovered.

§ 2—715. Buyer's Incidental and Consequential Damages.

(1) Incidental damages resulting from the seller's breach include expenses reasonably incurred in inspection, receipt, transportation and care and custody of goods rightfully rejected, any commercially reasonable charges, expenses or commissions in connection with effecting cover and any other reasonable expense incident to the delay or other breach.

(2) Consequential damages resulting from the seller's breach include

(a) any loss resulting from general or particular requirements and needs of which the seller at the time of contracting had reason to know and which could not reasonably be prevented by cover or otherwise; and

(b) injury to person or property proximately resulting from any breach of warranty.

§ 2—716. Buyer's Right to Specific Performance or Replevin.

(1) Specific performance may be decreed where the goods are unique or in other proper circumstances.

(2) The decree for specific performance may include such terms and conditions as to payment of the price, damages, or other relief as the court may deem just.

(3) The buyer has a right of replevin for goods identified to the contract if after reasonable effort he is unable to effect cover for such goods or the circumstances reasonably indicate that such effort will be unavailing or if the goods have been shipped under reservation and satisfaction of the security interest in them has been made or tendered.

§ 2—717. Deduction of Damages From the Price.

The buyer on notifying the seller of his intention to do so may deduct all or any part of the damages resulting from any breach of the contract from any part of the price still due under the same contract.

§ 2—718. Liquidation or Limitation of Damages; Deposits.

(1) Damages for breach by either party may be liquidated in the agreement but only at an amount which is reasonable in the light of the anticipated or actual harm caused by the breach, the difficulties of proof of loss, and the inconvenience of nonfeasibility of otherwise obtaining an adequate remedy. A term fixing unreasonably large liquidated damages is void as a penalty.

(2) Where the seller justifiably withholds delivery of goods because of the buyer's breach, the buyer is entitled to restitution of any amount by which the sum of his payments exceeds

(a) the amount to which the seller is entitled by virtue of terms liquidating the seller's damages in accordance with subsection (1), or

(b) in the absence of such terms, twenty percent of the value of the total performance for which the buyer is obligated under the contract or $500, whichever is smaller.

(3) The buyer's right to restitution under subsection (2) is subject to offset to the extent that the seller establishes

(a) a right to recover damages under the provisions of this Article other than subsection (1), and

(b) the amount or value of any benefits received by the buyer directly or indirectly by reason of the contract.

(4) Where a seller has received payment in goods their reasonable value or the proceeds of their resale shall be treated as payments for the purposes of subsection (2); but if the seller has notice of the buyer's breach before reselling goods received in part performance, his resale is subject to the conditions laid down in this Article on resale by an aggrieved seller (Section 2—706).

§ 2—719. Contractual Modification or Limitation of Remedy.

(1) Subject to the provisions of subsections (2) and (3) of this section and of the preceding section on liquidation and limitation of damages,

(a) the agreement may provide for remedies in addition to or in substitution for those provided in this Article and may limit or alter the measure of damages recoverable under this Article, as by limiting the buyer's remedies to return of the goods and repayment of the price or to repair and replacement of non-conforming goods or parts; and

(b) resort to a remedy as provided is optional unless the remedy is expressly agreed to be exclusive, in which case it is the sole remedy.

(2) Where circumstances cause an exclusive or limited remedy to fail of its essential purpose, remedy may be had as provided in this Act.

(3) Consequential damages may be limited or excluded unless the limitation or exclusion is unconscionable. Limitation of consequential damages for injury to the person in the case of consumer goods is prima facie unconscionable but limitation of damages where the loss is commercial is not.

§ 2—720. Effect of "Cancellation" or "Rescission" on Claims for Antecedent Breach.

Unless the contrary intention clearly appears, expressions of "cancellation" or "rescission" of the contract or the like shall not be construed as a renunciation or discharge of any claim in damages for an antecedent breach.

§ 2—721. Remedies for Fraud.

Remedies for material misrepresentation or fraud include all remedies available under this Article for non-fraudulent breach. Neither rescission or a claim for rescission of the contract for sale nor rejection or return of the goods shall bar or be deemed inconsistent with a claim for damages or other remedy.

§ 2—722. Who Can Sue Third Parties for Injury to Goods.

Where a third party so deals with goods which have been identified to a contract for sale as to cause actionable injury to a party to that contract

(a) a right of action against the third party is in either party to the contract for sale who has title to or a security interest or a special property or an insurable interest in the goods; and if the goods have been destroyed or converted a right of action is also in the party who either bore the risk of loss under the contract for sale or has since the injury assumed that risk as against the other;

(b) if at the time of the injury the party plaintiff did not bear the risk of loss as against the other party to the contract for sale and there is no arrangement between them for disposition of the recovery, his suit or settlement is, subject to his own interest, as a fiduciary for the other party to the contract;

(c) either party may with the consent of the other sue for the benefit of whom it may concern.

§ 2—723. Proof of Market Price: Time and Place.

(1) If an action based on anticipatory repudiation comes to trial before the time for performance with respect to some or all of the goods, any damages based on market price (Section 2—708 or Section 2—713) shall be determined according to the price of such goods prevailing at the time when the aggrieved party learned of the repudiation.

(2) If evidence of a price prevailing at the times or places described in this Article is not readily available the price prevailing within any reasonable time before or after the time described or at any other place which in commercial judgment or under usage of trade would serve as a reasonable substitute for the one described may be used, making any proper allowance for the cost of transporting the goods to or from such other place.

(3) Evidence of a relevant price prevailing at a time or place other than the one described in this Article offered by one party is not admissible unless and until he has given the other party such notice as the court finds sufficient to prevent unfair surprise.

§ 2—724. Admissibility of Market Quotations.

Whenever the prevailing price or value of any goods regularly bought and sold in any established commodity market is in issue, reports in official publications or trade journals or in newspapers or periodicals of general circulation published as the reports of such market shall be admissible in evidence. The circumstances of the preparation of such a report may be shown to affect its weight but not its admissibility.

§ 2—725. Statute of Limitations in Contracts for Sale.

(1) An action for breach of any contract for sale must be commenced within four years after the cause of action has accrued. By the original agreement the parties may reduce the period of limitation to not less than one year but may not extend it.

(2) A cause of action accrues when the breach occurs, regardless of the aggrieved party's lack of knowledge of the breach. A breach of warranty occurs when tender of delivery is made, except that where a warranty explicitly extends to future performance of the goods and discovery of the breach must await the time of such performance the cause of action accrues when the breach is or should have been discovered.

(3) Where an action commenced within the time limited by subsection (1) is so terminated as to leave available a remedy by another action for the same breach such other action may be commenced after the expiration of the time limited and within six months after the termination of the first action unless the termination resulted from voluntary discontinuance or from dismissal for failure or neglect to prosecute.

(4) This section does not alter the law on tolling of the statute of limitations nor does it apply to causes of action which have accrued before this Act becomes effective.

ARTICLE 2A. Leases*

PART 1. General Provisions.

§ 2A—101. Short Title.
This Article shall be known and may be cited as the Uniform Commercial Code—Leases.

§ 2A—102. Scope.
This Article applies to any transaction, regardless of form, that creates a lease.

§ 2A—103. Definitions and Index of Definitions.
(1) In This Article unless the context otherwise requires:

(a) "Buyer in ordinary course of business" means a person who in good faith and without knowledge that the sale to him [or her] is in violation of the ownership rights or security interest or leasehold interest of a third party in the goods buys in ordinary course from a person in the business of selling goods of that kind but does not include a pawnbroker. "Buying" may be for cash or by exchange of other property under a pre-existing contract for sale but does not include a transfer in bulk or as security for or in total or partial satisfaction of a money debt.

(b) "Cancellation" occurs when either party puts an end to the lease contract for default by the other party.

(c) "Commercial unit" means such a unit of goods as by commercial usage is a single whole for purposes of lease and division of which materially impairs its character or value on the market or in use. A commercial unit may be a single article, as a machine, or a set of articles, as a suite of furniture or a line of machinery, or a quantity, as a gross or carload, or any other unit treated in use or in the relevant market as a single whole.

(d) "Conforming" goods or performance under a lease contract means goods or performance that are in accordance with the obligations under the lease contract.

(e) "Consumer lease" means a lease that a lessor regularly engaged in the business of leasing or selling makes to a lessee, except an organization, who takes under the lease primarily for a personal, family, or household purpose, if the total payments to be made under the lease contract, excluding payments for options to renew or buy, do not exceed $25,000.

(f) "Fault" means wrongful act, omission, breach, or default.

(g) "Finance lease" means a lease in which (i) the lessor does not select, manufacture or supply the goods, (ii) the lessor acquires the goods or the right to possession and use of the goods in connection with the lease, and (iii) either the lessee receives a copy of the contract evidencing the lessor's purchase of the goods on or before signing the lease contract, or the lessee's approval of the contract evidencing the lessor's purchase of the goods is a condition to effectiveness of the lease contract.

(h) "Goods" means all things that are movable at the time of identification to the lease contract, or are fixtures (Section 2A—309), but the term does not include money, documents, instruments, accounts, chattel paper, general intangibles, or minerals or the like, including oil and gas, before extraction. The term also includes the unborn young of animals.

(i) "Installment lease contract" means a lease contract that authorizes or requires the delivery of goods in separate lots to be separately accepted, even though the lease contract contains a clause "each delivery is a separate lease" or its equivalent.

(j) "Lease" means a transfer of the right to possession and use of goods for a term in return for consideration, but a sale, including a sale on approval or a sale or return, or retention or creation of a security interest is not a lease. Unless the context clearly indicates otherwise, the term includes a sublease.

(k) "Lease agreement" means the bargain, with respect to the lease, of the lessor and the lessee in fact as found in their language or by implication from other circumstances including course of dealing or usage of trade or course of performance as provided in this Article. Unless the context clearly indicates otherwise, the term includes a sublease agreement.

(l) "Lease contract" means the total legal obligation that results from the lease agreement as affected by this Article and any other applicable rules of law. Unless the context clearly indicates otherwise, the term includes a sublease contract.

*Note that conforming amendments to §§ 1—105, 1—201(37), and 9—113 were promulgated in 1987 in conjunction with promulgation of Article 2A. These amendments appear in brackets ([ ]) in the text of these sections.

(m) "Leasehold interest" means the interest of the lessor or the lessee under a lease contract.

(n) "Lessee" means a person who acquires the right to possession and use of goods under a lease. Unless the context clearly indicates otherwise, the term includes a sublessee.

(o) "Lessee in ordinary course of business" means a person who in good faith and without knowledge that the lease to him [or her] is in violation of the ownership rights or security interest or leasehold interest of a third party in the goods leases in ordinary course from a person in the business of selling or leasing goods of that kind but does not include a pawnbroker. "Leasing" may be for cash or by exchange of other property or on secured or unsecured credit and includes receiving goods or documents of title under a pre-existing lease contract but does not include a transfer in bulk or as security for or in total or partial satisfaction of a money debt.

(p) "Lessor" means a person who transfers the right to possession and use of goods under a lease. Unless the context clearly indicates otherwise, the term includes a sublessor.

(q) "Lessor's residual interest" means the lessor's interest in the goods after expiration, termination, or cancellation of the lease contract.

(r) "Lien" means a charge against or interest in goods to secure payment of a debt or performance of an obligation, but the term does not include a security interest.

(s) "Lot" means a parcel or a single article that is the subject matter of a separate lease or delivery, whether or not it is sufficient to perform the lease contract.

(t) "Merchant lessee" means a lessee that is a merchant with respect to goods of the kind subject to the lease.

(u) "Present value" means the amount as of a date certain of one or more sums payable in the future, discounted to the date certain. The discount is determined by the interest rate specified by the parties if the rate was not manifestly unreasonable at the time the transaction was entered into; otherwise, the discount is determined by a commercially reasonable rate that takes into account the facts and circumstances of each case at the time the transaction was entered into.

(v) "Purchase" includes taking by sale, lease, mortgage, security interest, pledge, gift, or any other voluntary transaction creating an interest in goods.

(w) "Sublease" means a lease of goods the right to possession and use of which was acquired by the lessor as a lessee under an existing lease.

(x) "Supplier" means a person from whom a lessor buys or leases goods to be leased under a finance lease.

(y) "Supply contract" means a contract under which a lessor buys or leases goods to be leased.

(z) "Termination" occurs when either party pursuant to a power created by agreement or law puts an end to the lease contract otherwise than for default.

(2) Other definitions applying to this Article and the sections in which they appear are:

"Accessions". Section 2A—310(1).
"Construction mortgage". Section 2A—309(1)(d).
"Encumbrance". Section 2A—309(1)(e).
"Fixtures". Section 2A—309(1)(a).
"Fixture filing". Section 2A—309(1)(b).
"Purchase money lease". Section 2A—309(1)(c).

(3) The following definitions in other Articles apply to this Article:

"Accounts". Section 9—106.
"Between merchants". Section 2—104(3).
"Buyer". Section 2—103(1)(a).
"Chattel paper". Section 9—105(1)(b).
"Consumer goods". Section 9—109(1).
"Documents". Section 9—105(1)(f).
"Entrusting". Section 2—403(3).
"General intangibles". Section 9—106.
"Good faith". Section 2—103(1)(b).
"Instruments". Section 9—105(1)(i).
"Merchant". Section 2—104(1).
"Mortgage". Section 9—105(1)(j).
"Pursuant to commitment". Section 9—105(1)(k).
"Receipt". Section 2—103(1)(c).
"Sale". Section 2—106(1).
"Sale on Approval". Section 2—326.
"Sale or Return". Section 2—326.
"Seller". Section 2—103(1)(d).

(4) In addition Article 1 contains general definitions and principles of construction and interpretation applicable throughout this Article.

§ 2A—104. Leases Subject to Other Statutes.

(1) A lease, although subject to this Article, is also subject to any applicable:

(a) statute of the United States;

(b) certificate of title statute of this State: (list any certificate of title statutes covering automobiles, trailers, mobile homes, boats, farm tractors, and the like);

(c) certificate of title statute of another jurisdiction (Section 2A—105); or

(d) consumer protection statute of this State.

(2) In case of conflict between the provisions of this Article, other than Sections 2A—105, 2A—304(3) and 2A—305(3), and any statute referred to in subsection (1), the provisions of that statute control.

(3) Failure to comply with any applicable statute has only the effect specified therein.

§ 2A—105. Territorial Application of Article to Goods Covered by Certificate of Title.

Subject to the provisions of Sections 2A—304(3) and 2A—305(3), with respect to goods covered by a certificate of title issued under a statute of this State or of another jurisdiction, compliance and the effect of compliance or noncompliance with a certificate of title statute are governed by the law (including the conflict of laws rules) of the jurisdiction issuing the certificate until the earlier of (a) surrender of the certificate, or (b) four months after the goods are removed from that jurisdiction and thereafter until a new certificate of title is issued by another jurisdiction.

§ 2A—106. Limitation on Power of Parties to Consumer Lease to Choose Applicable Law and Judicial Forum.

(1) If the law chosen by the parties to a consumer lease is that of a jurisdiction other than a jurisdiction in which the lessee resides at the time the lease agreement becomes enforceable or within thirty days thereafter or in which the goods are to be used, the choice is not enforceable.

(2) If the judicial forum chosen by the parties to a consumer lease is a forum that would not otherwise have jurisdiction over the lessee, the choice is not enforceable.

§ 2A—107. Waiver or Renunciation of Claim or Right After Default.

Any claim or right arising out of an alleged default or breach of warranty may be discharged in whole or in part without consideration by a written waiver or renunciation signed and delivered by the aggrieved party.

§ 2A—108. Unconscionability.

(1) If the court as a matter of law finds a lease contract or any clause of a lease contract to have been unconscionable at the time it was made the court may refuse to enforce the lease contract, or it may enforce the remainder of the lease contract without the unconscionable clause, or it may so limit the application of any unconscionable clause as to avoid any unconscionable result.

(2) With respect to a consumer lease, if the court as a matter of law finds that a lease contract or any clause of a lease contract has been induced by unconscionable conduct or that unconscionable conduct has occurred in the collection of a claim arising from a lease contract, the court may grant appropriate relief.

(3) Before making a finding of unconscionability under subsection (1) or (2), the court, on its own motion or that of a party, shall afford the parties a reasonable opportunity to present evidence as to the setting, purpose, and effect of the lease contract or clause thereof, or of the conduct.

(4) In an action in which the lessee claims unconscionability with respect to a consumer lease:

(a) If the court finds unconscionability under subsection (1) or (2), the court shall award reasonable attorney's fees to the lessee.

(b) If the court does not find unconscionability and the lessee claiming unconscionability has brought or maintained an action he [or she] knew to be groundless, the court shall award reasonable attorney's fees to the party against whom the claim is made.

(c) In determining attorney's fees, the amount of the recovery on behalf of the claimant under subsections (1) and (2) is not controlling.

§ 2A—109. Option to Accelerate At Will.

(1) A term providing that one party or his [or her] successor in interest may accelerate payment of performance or require collateral or additional collateral "at will" or "when he [or she] deems himself [or herself] insecure" or in words of similar import must be construed to mean that he [or she] has power to do so only if he [or she] in good faith believes that the prospect of payment of performance is impaired.

(2) With respect to a consumer lease, the burden of establishing good faith under subsection (1) is on the party who exercised the power; otherwise the burden of establishing lack of good faith is on the party against whom the power has been exercised.

PART 2. Formation and Construction of Lease Contract.

§ 2A—201. Statute of Frauds.

(1) A lease contract is not enforceable by way of action or defense unless:

(a) the total payments to be made under the lease contract, excluding payments for options to renew or buy, are less than $1,000; or

(b) there is a writing, signed by the party against whom enforcement is sought or by that party's authorized agent, sufficient to indicate that a lease contract has been made between the parties and to describe the goods leased and the lease term.

(2) Any description of leased goods or of the lease term is sufficient and satisfies subsection (1)(b), whether or not it is specific, if it reasonably identifies what is described.

(3) A writing is not insufficient because it omits or incorrectly states a term agreed upon, but the lease con-

tract is not enforceable under subsection (1)(b) beyond the lease term and the quantity of goods shown in the writing.

(4) A lease contract that does not satisfy the requirements of subsection (1), but which is valid in other respects, is enforceable:

(a) if the goods are to be specially manufactured or obtained for the lessee and are not suitable for lease or sale to others in the ordinary course of the lessor's business, and the lessor, before notice of repudiation is received and under circumstances that reasonably indicate that the goods are for the lessee, has made either a substantial beginning of their manufacture or commitments for their procurement;

(b) if the party against whom enforcement is sought admits in that party's pleading, testimony or otherwise in court that a lease contract was made, but the lease contract is not enforceable under this provision beyond the quantity of goods admitted; or

(c) with respect to goods that have been received and accepted by the lessee.

(5) The lease term under a lease contract referred to in subsection (4) is:

(a) if there is a writing signed by the party against whom enforcement is sought or by that party's authorized agent specifying the lease term, the term so specified;

(b) if the party against whom enforcement is sought admits in that party's pleading, testimony, or otherwise in court a lease term, the term so admitted; or

(c) a reasonable lease term.

§ 2A—202. Final Written Expression: Parol or Extrinsic Evidence.

Terms with respect to which the confirmatory memoranda of the parties agree or which are otherwise set forth in a writing intended by the parties as a final expression of their agreement with respect to such terms as are included therein may not be contradicted by evidence of any prior agreement or of a contemporaneous oral agreement but may be explained or supplemented:

(a) by course of dealing or usage of trade or by course of performance; and

(b) by evidence of consistent additional terms unless the court finds the writing to have been intended also as a complete and exclusive statement of the terms of the agreement.

§ 2A—203. Seals Inoperative.

The affixing of a seal to a writing evidencing a lease contract or an offer to enter into a lease contract does not render the writing a sealed instrument and the law with respect to sealed instruments does not apply to the lease contract or offer.

§ 2A—204. Formation in General.

(1) A lease contract may be made in any manner sufficient to show agreement, including conduct by both parties which recognizes the existence of a lease contract.

(2) An agreement sufficient to constitute a lease contract may be found although the moment of its making is undetermined.

(3) Although one or more terms are left open, a lease contract does not fail for indefiniteness if the parties have intended to make a lease contract and there is a reasonably certain basis for giving an appropriate remedy.

§ 2A—205. Firm Offers.

An offer by a merchant to lease goods to or from another person in a signed writing that by its terms gives assurance it will be held open is not revocable, for lack of consideration, during the time stated or, if no time is stated, for a reasonable time, but in no event may the period of irrevocability exceed three months. Any such term of assurance on a form supplied by the offeree must be separately signed by the offeror.

§ 2A—206. Offer and Acceptance in Formation of Lease Contract.

(1) Unless otherwise unambiguously indicated by the language or circumstances, an offer to make a lease contract must be construed as inviting acceptance in any manner and by any medium reasonable in the circumstances.

(2) If the beginning of a requested performance is a reasonable mode of acceptance, an offeror who is not notified of acceptance within a reasonable time may treat the offer as having lapsed before acceptance.

§ 2A—207. Course of Performance or Practical Construction.

(1) If a lease contract involves repeated occasions for performance by either party with knowledge of the nature of the performance and opportunity for objection to it by the other, any course of performance accepted or acquiesced in without objection is relevant to determine the meaning of the lease agreement.

(2) The express terms of a lease agreement and any course of performance, as well as any course of dealing and usage of trade, must be construed whenever reasonable as consistent with each other; but if that construction is unreasonable, express terms control course of performance, course of performance controls both course of dealing and usage of trade, and course of dealing controls usage of trade.

(3) Subject to the provisions of Section 2A—208 on

modification and waiver, course of performance is relevant to show a waiver or modification of any term inconsistent with the course of performance.

§ 2A—208. Modification, Rescission and Waiver.

(1) An agreement modifying a lease contract needs no consideration to be binding.

(2) A signed lease agreement that excludes modification or rescission except by a signed writing may not be otherwise modified or rescinded, but, except as between merchants, such a requirement on a form supplied by a merchant must be separately signed by the other party.

(3) Although an attempt at modification or rescission does not satisfy the requirements of subsection (2), it may operate as a waiver.

(4) A party who has made a waiver affecting an executory portion of a lease contract may retract the waiver by reasonable notification received by the other party that strict performance will be required of any term waived, unless the retraction would be unjust in view of a material change of position in reliance on the waiver.

§ 2A—209. Lessee Under Finance Lease as Beneficiary of Supply Contract.

(1) The benefit of the supplier's promises to the lessor under the supply contract and of all warranties, whether express or implied, under the supply contract, extends to the lessee to the extent of the lessee's leasehold interest under a finance lease related to the supply contract, but subject to the terms of the supply contract and all of the supplier's defenses or claims arising therefrom.

(2) The extension of the benefit of the supplier's promises and warranties to the lessee (Section 2A—209(1)) does not: (a) modify the rights and obligations of the parties to the supply contract, whether arising therefrom or otherwise, or (b) impose any duty or liability under the supply contract on the lessee.

(3) Any modification or rescission of the supply contract by the supplier and the lessor is effective against the lessee unless, prior to the modification or rescission, the supplier has received notice that the lessee has entered into a finance lease related to the supply contract. If the supply contract is modified or rescinded after the lessee enters the finance lease, the lessee has a cause of action against the lessor, and against the supplier if the supplier has notice of the lessee's entering the finance lease when the supply contract is modified or rescinded. The lessee's recovery from such action shall put the lessee in as good a position as if the modification or rescission had not occurred.

§ 2A—210. Express Warranties.

(1) Express warranties by the lessor are created as follows:

(a) Any affirmation of fact or promise made by the lessor to the lessee which relates to the goods and becomes part of the basis of the bargain creates an express warranty that the goods will conform to the affirmation or promise.

(b) Any description of the goods which is made part of the basis of the bargain creates an express warranty that the goods will conform to the description.

(c) Any sample or model that is made part of the basis of the bargain creates an express warranty that the whole of the goods will conform to the sample or model.

(2) It is not necessary to the creation of an express warranty that the lessor use formal words, such as "warrant" or "guarantee," or that the lessor have a specific intention to make a warranty, but an affirmation merely of the value of the goods or a statement purporting to be merely the lessor's opinion or commendation of the goods does not create a warranty.

§ 2A—211. Warranties Against Interference and Against Infringement; Lessee's Obligation Against Infringement.

(1) There is in a lease contract a warranty that for the lease term no person holds a claim to or interest in the goods that arose from an act or omission of the lessor, other than a claim by way of infringement or the like, which will interfere with the lessee's enjoyment of its leasehold interest.

(2) Except in a finance lease there is in a lease contract by a lessor who is a merchant regularly dealing in goods of the kind a warranty that the goods are delivered free of the rightful claim of any person by way of infringement or the like.

(3) A lessee who furnishes specifications to a lessor or a supplier shall hold the lessor and the supplier harmless against any claim by way of infringement or the like that arises out of compliance with the specifications.

§ 2A—212. Implied Warranty of Merchantability.

(1) Except in a finance lease, a warranty that the goods will be merchantable is implied in a lease contract if the lessor is a merchant with respect to goods of that kind.

(2) Goods to be merchantable must be at least such as

(a) pass without objection in the trade under the description in the lease agreement;

(b) in the case of fungible goods, are of fair average quality within the description;

(c) are fit for the ordinary purposes for which goods of that type are used;

(d) run, within the variation permitted by the lease agreement, of even kind, quality, and quantity within each unit and among all units involved;

(e) are adequately contained, packaged, and labeled as the lease agreement may require; and

(f) conform to any promises or affirmations of fact made on the container or label.

(3) Other implied warranties may arise from course of dealing or usage of trade.

§ 2A—213. Implied Warranty of Fitness for Particular Purpose.

Except in a finance lease, if the lessor at the time the lease contract is made has reason to know of any particular purpose for which the goods are required and that the lessee is relying on the lessor's skill or judgment to select or furnish suitable goods, there is in the lease contract an implied warranty that the goods will be fit for that purpose.

§ 2A—214. Exclusion or Modification of Warranties.

(1) Words or conduct relevant to the creation of an express warranty and words or conduct tending to negate or limit a warranty must be construed wherever reasonable as consistent with each other; but, subject to the provisions of Section 2A—202 on parol or extrinsic evidence, negation or limitation is inoperative to the extent that the construction is unreasonable.

(2) Subject to subsection (3), to exclude or modify the implied warranty of merchantability or any part of it the language must mention "merchantability", be by a writing, and be conspicuous. Subject to subsection (3), to exclude or modify any implied warranty of fitness the exclusion must be by a writing and be conspicuous. Language to exclude all implied warranties of fitness is sufficient if it is in writing, is conspicuous and states, for example, "There is no warranty that the goods will be fit for a particular purpose".

(3) Notwithstanding subsection (2), but subject to subsection (4),

    (a) unless the circumstances indicate otherwise, all implied warranties are excluded by expressions like "as is," or "with all faults," or by other language that in common understanding calls the lessee's attention to the exclusion of warranties and makes plain that there is no implied warranty, if in writing and conspicuous;

    (b) if the lessee before entering into the lease contract has examined the goods or the sample or model as fully as desired or has refused to examine the goods, there is no implied warranty with regard to defects that an examination ought in the circumstances to have revealed; and

    (c) an implied warranty may also be excluded or modified by course of dealing, course of performance, or usage of trade.

(4) To exclude or modify a warranty against interference or against infringement (Section 2A—211) or any part of it, the language must be specific, be by a writing,

and be conspicuous, unless the circumstances, including course of performance, course of dealing, or usage of trade, give the lessee reason to know that the goods are being leased subject to a claim or interest of any person.

§ 2A—215. Cumulation and Conflict of Warranties Express or Implied.

Warranties, whether express or implied, must be construed as consistent with each other and as cumulative, but if that construction is unreasonable, the intention of the parties determines which warranty is dominant. In ascertaining that intention the following rules apply:

    (a) Exact or technical specifications displace an inconsistent sample or model or general language of description.

    (b) A sample from an existing bulk displaces inconsistent general language of description.

    (c) Express warranties displace inconsistent implied warranties other than an implied warranty of fitness for a particular purpose.

§ 2A—216. Third-Party Beneficiaries of Express and Implied Warranties.

Alternative A. A warranty to or for the benefit of a lessee under this Article, whether express or implied, extends to any natural person who is in the family or household of the lessee or who is a guest in the lessee's home if it is reasonable to expect that such person may use, consume, or be affected by the goods and who is injured in person by breach of the warranty. This section does not displace principles of law and equity that extend a warranty to or for the benefit of a lessee to other persons. The operation of this section may not be excluded, modified, or limited, but an exclusion, modification, or limitation of the warranty, including any with respect to rights and remedies, effective against the lessee is also effective against any beneficiary designated under this section.

Alternative B. A warranty to or for the benefit of a lessee under this Article, whether express or implied, extends to any natural person who may reasonably be expected to use, consume, or be affected by the goods and who is injured in person by breach of the warranty. This section does not displace principles of law and equity that extend a warranty to or for the benefit of a lessee to other persons. The operation of this section may not be excluded, modified, or limited, but an exclusion, modification, or limitation of the warranty, including any with respect to rights and remedies, effective against the lessee is also effective against the beneficiary designated under this section.

Alternative C. A warranty to or for the benefit of a lessee under this Article, whether express or implied, extends to any person who may reasonably be expected to use, consume, or be affected by the goods and who is injured by breach of the warranty. The operation of this section may not be excluded, modified, or limited with respect to injury to the person of an individual to whom the warranty extends, but an exclusion, modification, or limitation of the warranty, including any with respect to rights and remedies, effective against the lessee is also effective against the beneficiary designated under this section.

§ 2A—217.   Identification.

Identification of goods as goods to which a lease contract refers may be made at any time and in any manner explicitly agreed to by the parties. In the absence of explicit agreement, identification occurs:

(a) when the lease contract is made if the lease contract is for a lease of goods that are existing and identified;

(b) when the goods are shipped, marked, or otherwise designated by the lessor as goods to which the lease contract refers, if the lease contract is for a lease of goods that are not existing and identified; or

(c) when the young are conceived, if the lease contract is for a lease of unborn young of animals.

§ 2A—218.   Insurance and Proceeds.

(1) A lessee obtains an insurable interest when existing goods are identified to the lease contract even though the goods identified are non-conforming and the lessee has an option to reject them.

(2) If a lessee has an insurable interest only by reason of the lessor's identification of the goods, the lessor, until default or insolvency or notification to the lessee that identification is final, may substitute other goods for those identified.

(3) Notwithstanding a lessee's insurable interest under subsections (1) and (2), the lessor retains an insurable interest until an option to buy has been exercised by the lessee and risk of loss has passed to the lessee.

(4) Nothing in this section impairs any insurable interest recognized under any other statute or rule of law.

(5) The parties by agreement may determine that one or more parties have an obligation to obtain and pay for insurance covering the goods and by agreement may determine the beneficiary of the proceeds of the insurance.

§ 2A—219.   Risk of Loss.

(1) Except in the case of a finance lease, risk of loss is retained by the lessor and does not pass to the lessee. In the case of a finance lease, risk of loss passes to the lessee.

(2) Subject to the provisions of this Article on the effect of default on risk of loss (Section 2A—220), if risk

of loss is to pass to the lessee and the time of passage is not stated, the following rules apply:

(a) If the lease contract requires or authorizes the goods to be shipped by carrier

(i) and it does not require delivery at a particular destination, the risk of loss passes to the lessee when the goods are duly delivered to the carrier; but

(ii) if it does require delivery at a particular destination and the goods are there duly tendered while in the possession of the carrier, the risk of loss passes to the lessee when the goods are there duly so tendered as to enable the lessee to take delivery.

(b) If the goods are held by a bailee to be delivered without being moved, the risk of loss passes to the lessee on acknowledgment by the bailee of the lessee's right to possession of the goods.

(c) In any case not within subsection (a) or (b), the risk of loss passses to the lessee on the lessee's receipt of the goods if the lessor, or, in the case of a finance lease, the supplier, is a merchant; otherwise the risk passes to the lessee on tender of delivery.

§ 2A—220.   Effect of Default on Risk of Loss.

(1) Where risk of loss is to pass to the lessee and the time of passage is not stated:

(a) If a tender or delivery of goods so fails to conform to the lease contract as to give a right of rejection, the risk of their loss remains with the lessor, or, in the case of a finance lease, the supplier, until cure or acceptance.

(b) If the lessee rightfully revokes acceptance, he [or she], to the extent of any deficiency in his [or her] effective insurance coverage, may treat the risk of loss as having remained with the lessor from the beginning.

(2) Whether or not risk of loss is to pass to the lessee, if the lessee as to conforming goods already identified to a lease contract repudiates or is otherwise in default under the lease contract, the lessor, or, in the case of a finance lease, the supplier, to the extent of any deficiency in his [or her] effective insurance coverage may treat the risk of loss as resting on the lessee for a commercially reasonable time.

§ 2A—221.   Casualty to Identified Goods.

If a lease contract requires goods identified when the lease contract is made, and the goods suffer casualty without fault of the lessee, the lessor or the supplier before delivery, or the goods suffer casualty before risk of loss passes to the lessee pursuant to the lease agreement or Section 2A—219, then:

    (a) if the loss is total, the lease contract is avoided; and

    (b) if the loss is partial or the goods have so deteriorated as to no longer conform to the lease contract, the lessee may nevertheless demand inspection and at his [or her] option either treat the lease contract as avoided or, except in a finance lease that is not a consumer lease, accept the goods with due allowance from the rent payable for the balance of the lease term for the deterioration or the deficiency in quantity but without further right against the lessor.

PART 3. *Effect of Lease Contract.*

§ 2A–301. **Enforceability of Lease Contract.**

Except as otherwise provided in this Article, a lease contract is effective and enforceable according to its terms between the parties, against purchasers of the goods, and against creditors of the parties.

§ 2A—302. **Title to and Possession of Goods.**

Except as otherwise provided in this Article, each provision of this Article applies whether the lessor or a third party has title to the goods, and whether the lessor, the lessee, or a third party has possession of the goods, notwithstanding any statute or rule of law that possession or the absence of possession is fraudulent.

§ 2A—303. **Alienability of Party's Interest Under Lease Contract or of Lessor's Residual Interest in Goods; Delegation of Performance; Assignment of Rights.**

(1) Any interest of a party under a lease contract and the lessor's residual interest in the goods may be transferred unless

    (a) the transfer is voluntary and the lease contract prohibits the transfer; or

    (b) the transfer materially changes the duty of or materially increases the burden or risk imposed on the other party to the lease contract, and within a reasonable time after notice of the transfer the other party demands that the transferee comply with subsection (2) and the transferee fails to comply.

(2) Within a reasonable time after demand pursuant to subsection (1)(b), the transferee shall:

    (a) cure or provide adequate assurance that he [or she] will promptly cure any default other than one arising from the transfer;

    (b) compensate or provide adequate assurance that he [or she] will promptly compensate the other party to the lease contract and any other person holding an interest in the lease contract, except the party whose interest is being transferred, for any loss to that party resulting from the transfer;

    (c) provide adequate assurance of future due performance under the lease contract; and

    (d) assume the lease contract.

(3) Demand pursuant to subsection (1)(b) is without prejudice to the other party's rights against the transferee and the party whose interest is transferred.

(4) An assignment of "the lease" or of "all my rights under the lease" or an assignment in similar general terms is a transfer of rights, and unless the language or the circumstances, as in an assignment for security, indicate the contrary, the assignment constitutes a promise by him [or her] to perform those duties. This promise is enforceable by either the assignor or the other party to the lease contract.

(5) Unless otherwise agreed by the lessor and the lessee, no delegation of performance relieves the assignor as against the other party of any duty to perform or any liability for default.

(6) A right to damages for default with respect to the whole lease contract or a right arising out of the assignor's due performance of his [or her] entire obligation can be assigned despite agreement otherwise.

(7) To prohibit the transfer of an interest of a party under a lease contract, the language of prohibition must be specific, by a writing, and conspicuous.

§ 2A—304. **Subsequent Lease of Goods by Lessor.**

(1) Subject to the provisions of Section 2A—303, a subsequent lessee from a lessor of goods under an existing lease contract obtains, to the extent of the leasehold interest transferred, the leasehold interest in the goods that the lessor had or had power to transfer, and except as provided in subsection (2) and Section 2A—527(4), takes subject to the existing lease contract. A lessor with voidable title has power to transfer a good leasehold interest to a good faith subsequent lessee for value, but only to the extent set forth in the preceding sentence. When goods have been delivered under a transaction of purchase the lessor has that power even though:

    (a) the lessor's transferor was deceived as to the identity of the lessor;

    (b) the delivery was in exchange for a check which is later dishonored;

    (c) it was agreed that the transaction was to be a "cash sale"; or

    (d) the delivery was procured through fraud punishable as larcenous under the criminal law.

(2) A subsequent lessee in the ordinary course of business from a lessor who is a merchant dealing in goods of that kind to whom the goods were entrusted by the existing lessee before the interest of the subsequent lessee became enforceable against the lessor obtains, to the extent of the leasehold interest transferred, all of the lessor's

and the existing lessee's rights to the goods, and takes free of the existing lease contract.

(3) A subsequent lessee from the lessor of goods that are subject to an existing lease contract and are covered by a certificate of title issued under a statute of this State or of another jurisdiction takes no greater rights than those provided both by this section and by the certificate of title statute.

§ 2A—305. Sale or Sublease of Goods by Lessee.

(1) Subject to the provisions of Section 2A—303, a buyer or sublessee from the lessee of goods under an existing lease contract obtains, to the extent of the interest transferred, the leasehold interest in the goods that the lessee had or had power to transfer, and except as provided in subsection (2) and Section 2A—511(4), takes subject to the existing lease contract. A lessee with a voidable leasehold interest has power to transfer a good leasehold interest to a good faith buyer for value or a good faith sublessee for value, but only to the extent set forth in the preceding sentence. When goods have been delivered under a transaction of lease the lessee has that power even though:

(a) the lessor was deceived as to the identity of the lessee;
(b) the delivery was in exchange for a check which is later dishonored; or
(c) the delivery was procured through fraud punishable as larcenous under the criminal law.

(2) A buyer in the ordinary course of business or a sublessee in the ordinary course of business from a lessee who is a merchant dealing in goods of that kind to whom the goods were entrusted by the lessor obtains, to the extent of the interest transferred, all of the lessor's and lessee's rights to the goods, and takes free of the existing lease contract.

(3) A buyer or sublessee from the lessee of goods that are subject to an existing lease contract and are covered by a certificate of title issued under a statute of this State or of another jurisdiction takes no greater rights than those provided both by this section and by the certificate of title statute.

§ 2A—306. Priority of Certain Liens Arising by Operation of Law.

If a person in the ordinary course of his [or her] business furnishes services or materials with respect to goods subject to a lease contract, a lien upon those goods in the possession of that person given by statute or rule of law for those materials or services takes priority over any interest of the lessor or lessee under the lease contract or this Article unless the lien is created by statute and the statute provides otherwise or unless the lien is created by rule of law and the rule of law provides otherwise.

§ 2A—307. Priority of Liens Arising by Attachment or Levy on, Security Interests in, and Other Claims to Goods.

(1) Except as otherwise provided in Section 2A—306, a creditor of a lessee takes subject to the lease contract.

(2) Except as otherwise provided in subsections (3) and (4) of this section and in Sections 2A—306 and 2A—308, a creditor of a lessor takes subject to the lease contract:

(a) unless the creditor holds a lien that attached to the goods before the lease contract became enforceable, or
(b) unless the creditor holds a security interest in the goods that under the Article on Secured Transactions (Article 9) would have priority over any other security interest in the goods perfected by a filing covering the goods and made at the time the lease contract became enforceable, whether or not any other security interest existed.

(3) A lessee in the ordinary course of business takes the leasehold interest free of a security interest in the goods created by the lessor even though the security interest is perfected and the lessee knows of its existence.

(4) A lessee other than a lessee in the ordinary course of business takes the leasehold interest free of a security interest to the extent that it secures future advances made after the secured party acquires knowledge of the lease or more than 45 days after the lease contract becomes enforceable, whichever first occurs, unless the future advances are made pursuant to a commitment entered into without knowledge of the lease and before the expiration of the 45-day period.

§ 2A—308. Special Rights of Creditors.

(1) A creditor of a lessor in possession of goods subject to a lease contract may treat the lease contract as void if as against the creditor retention of possession by the lessor is fraudulent under any statute or rule of law, but retention of possession in good faith and current course of trade by the lessor for a commercially reasonable time after the lease contract becomes enforceable is not fraudulent.

(2) Nothing in this Article impairs the rights of creditors of a lessor if the lease contract (a) becomes enforceable, not in current course of trade but in satisfaction of or as security for a pre-existing claim for money, security, or the like, and (b) is made under circumstances which under any statute or rule of law apart from this Article would constitute the transaction a fraudulent transfer or voidable preference.

(3) A creditor of a seller may treat a sale or an identification of goods to a contract for sale as void if as against the creditor retention of possession by the seller is fraudulent under any statute or rule of law, but retention of possession of the goods pursuant to a lease con-

tract entered into by the seller as lessee and the buyer as lessor in connection with the sale or identification of the goods is not fraudulent if the buyer bought for value and in good faith.

§ 2A—309. Lessor's and Lessee's Rights When Goods Become Fixtures.

(1) In this section:

    (a) goods are "fixtures" when they become so related to particular real estate that an interest in them arises under real estate law;

    (b) a "fixture filing" is the filing, in the office where a mortgage on the real estate would be recorded or registered, of a financing statement concerning goods that are or are to become fixtures and conforming to the requirements of subsection (5) of Section 9—402;

    (c) a lease is a "purchase money lease" unless the lessee has possession or use of the goods or the right to possession or use of the goods before the lease agreement is enforceable;

    (d) a mortgage is a "construction mortgage" to the extent it secures an obligation incurred for the construction of an improvement on land including the acquisition cost of the land, if the recorded writing so indicates; and

    (e) "encumbrance" includes real estate mortgages and other liens on real estate and all other rights in real estate that are not ownership interests.

(2) Under this Article a lease may be of goods that are fixtures or may continue in goods that become fixtures, but no lease exists under this Article of ordinary building materials incorporated into an improvement on land.

(3) This Article does not prevent creation of a lease of fixtures pursuant to real estate law.

(4) The perfected interest of a lessor of fixtures has priority over a conflicting interest of an encumbrancer or owner of the real estate if:

    (a) the lease is a purchase money lease, the conflicting interest of the encumbrancer or owner arises before the goods become fixtures, the interest of the lessor is perfected by a fixture filing before the goods become fixtures or within ten days thereafter, and the lessee has an interest of record in the real estate or is in possession of the real estate; or

    (b) the interest of the lessor is perfected by a fixture filing before the interest of the encumbrancer or owner is of record, the lessor's interest has priority over any conflicting interest of a predecessor in title of the encumbrancer or owner, and the lessee has an interest of record in the real estate or is in possession of the real estate.

(5) The interest of a lessor of fixtures, whether or not perfected, has priority over the conflicting interest of an encumbrancer or owner of the real estate if:

    (a) the fixtures are readily removable factory or office machines, readily removable equipment that is not primarily used or leased for use in the operation of the real estate, or readily removable replacements of domestic appliances that are goods subject to a consumer lease, and before the goods become fixtures the lease contract is enforceable; or

    (b) the conflicting interest is a lien on the real estate obtained by legal or equitable proceedings after the lease contract is enforceable; or

    (c) the encumbrancer or owner has consented in writing to the lease or has disclaimed an interest in the goods as fixtures; or

    (d) the lessee has a right to remove the goods as against the encumbrancer or owner. If the lessee's right to remove terminates, the priority of the interest of the lessor continues for a reasonable time.

(6) Notwithstanding paragraph (a) of subsection (4) but otherwise subject to subsections (4) and (5), the interest of a lessor of fixtures is subordinate to the conflicting interest of an encumbrancer of the real estate under a construction mortgage recorded before the goods become fixtures if the goods become fixtures before the completion of the construction. To the extent given to refinance a construction mortgage, the conflicting interest of an encumbrancer of the real estate under a mortgage has this priority to the same extent as the encumbrancer of the real estate under the construction mortgage.

(7) In cases not within the preceding subsections, priority between the interest of a lessor of fixtures and the conflicting interest of an encumbrancer or owner of the real estate who is not the lessee is determined by the priority rules governing conflicting interests in real estate.

(8) If the interest of a lessor has priority over all conflicting interests of all owners and encumbrancers of the real estate, the lessor or the lessee may (a) on default, expiration, termination, or cancellation of the lease agreement by the other party but subject to the provisions of the lease agreement and this Article, or (b) if necessary to enforce his [or her] other rights and remedies under this Article, remove the goods from the real estate, free and clear of all conflicting interests of all owners and encumbrancers of the real estate, but he [or she] must reimburse any encumbrancer or owner of the real estate who is not the lessee and who has not otherwise agreed for the cost of repair of any physical injury, but not for any diminution in value of the real estate caused by the absence of the goods removed or by any necessity of replacing them. A person entitled to reimbursement may

refuse permission to remove until the party seeking removal gives adequate security for the performance of this obligation.

(9) Even though the lease agreement does not create a security interest, the interest of a lessor of fixtures is perfected by filing a financing statement as a fixture filing for leased goods that are or are to become fixtures in accordance with the relevant provisions of the Article on Secured Transactions (Article 9).

§ 2A—310.   Lessor's and Lessee's Rights When Goods Become Accessions.

(1) Goods are "accessions" when they are installed in or affixed to other goods.

(2) The interest of a lessor or a lessee under a lease contract entered into before the goods became accessions is superior to all interests in the whole except as stated in subsection (4).

(3) The interest of a lessor or a lessee under a lease contract entered into at the time or after the goods became accessions is superior to all subsequently acquired interests in the whole except as stated in subsection (4) but is subordinate to interests in the whole existing at the time the lease contract was made unless the holders of such interests in the whole have in writing consented to the lease or disclaimed an interest in the goods as part of the whole.

(4) The interest of a lessor or a lessee under a lease contract described in subsection (2) or (3) is subordinate to the interest of

    (a) a buyer in the ordinary course of business or a lessee in the ordinary course of business of any interest in the whole acquired after the goods became accessions; or

    (b) a creditor with a security interest in the whole perfected before the lease contract was made to the extent that the creditor makes subsequent advances without knowledge of the lease contract.

(5) When under subsections (2) or (3) and (4) a lessor or a lessee of accessions holds an interest that is superior to all interests in the whole, the lessor or the lessee may (a) on default, expiration, termination, or cancellation of the lease contract by the other party but subject to the provisions of the lease contract and this Article, or (b) if necessary to enforce his [or her] other rights and remedies under this Article, remove the goods from the whole, free and clear of all interests in the whole, but he [or she] must reimburse any holder of an interest in the whole who is not the lessee and who has not otherwise agreed for the cost of repair of any physical injury but not for any diminution in value of the whole caused by the absence of the goods removed or by any necessity for replacing them. A person entitled to reimbursement may refuse permission to remove until the party seeking re-

moval gives adequate security for the performance of this obligation.

PART 4.   *Performance of Lease Contract: Repudiated, Substituted and Excused.*

§ 2A—401.   Insecurity: Adequate Assurance of Performance.

(1) A lease contract imposes an obligation on each party that the other's expectation of receiving due performance will not be impaired.

(2) If reasonable grounds for insecurity arise with respect to the performance of either party, the insecure party may demand in writing adequate assurance of due performance. Until the insecure party receives that assurance, if commercially reasonable the insecure party may suspend any performance for which he [or she] has not already received the agreed return.

(3) A repudiation of the lease contract occurs if assurance of due performance adequate under the circumstances of the particular case is not provided to the insecure party within a reasonable time, not to exceed 30 days after receipt of a demand by the other party.

(4) Between merchants, the reasonableness of grounds for insecurity and the adequacy of any assurance offered must be determined according to commercial standards.

(5) Acceptance of any non-conforming delivery or payment does not prejudice the aggrieved party's right to demand adequate assurance of future performance.

§ 2A—402.   Anticipatory Repudiation.

If either party repudiates a lease contract with respect to a performance not yet due under the lease contract, the loss of which performance will substantially impair the value of the lease contract to the other, the aggrieved party may:

    (a) for a commercially reasonable time, await retraction of repudiation and performance by the repudiating party;

    (b) make demand pursuant to Section 2A—401 and await assurance of future performance adequate under the circumstances of the particular case; or

    (c) resort to any right or remedy upon default under the lease contract or this Article, even though the aggrieved party has notified the repudiating party that the aggrieved party would await the repudiating party's performance and assurance and has urged retraction. In addition, whether or not the aggrieved party is pursuing one of the foregoing remedies, the aggrieved party may suspend performance or, if the aggrieved party is the lessor, proceed in accordance with the provisions of this Article on the lessor's right to identify goods to the lease contract notwithstanding default or to salvage unfinished goods (Section 2A—524).

§ 2A—403. Retraction of Anticipatory Repudiation.

(1) Until the repudiating party's next performance is due, the repudiating party can retract the repudiation unless, since the repudiation, the aggrieved party has cancelled the lease contract or materially changed the aggrieved party's position or otherwise indicated that the aggrieved party considers the repudiation final.

(2) Retraction may be by any method that clearly indicates to the aggrieved party that the repudiating party intends to perform under the lease contract and includes any assurance demanded under Section 2A—401.

(3) Retraction reinstates a repudiating party's rights under a lease contract with due excuse and allowance to the aggrieved party for any delay occasioned by the repudiation.

§ 2A—404. Substituted Performance.

(1) If without fault of the lessee, the lessor and the supplier, the agreed berthing, loading, or unloading facilities fail or the agreed type of carrier becomes unavailable or the agreed manner of delivery otherwise becomes commercially impracticable, but a commercially reasonable substitute is available, the substitute performance must be tendered and accepted.

(2) If the agreed means or manner of payment fails because of domestic or foreign governmental regulation:

    (a) the lessor may withhold or stop delivery or cause the supplier to withhold or stop delivery unless the lessee provides a means or manner of payment that is commercially a substantial equivalent; and

    (b) if delivery has already been taken, payment by the means or in the manner provided by the regulation discharges the lessee's obligation unless the regulation is discriminatory, oppressive, or predatory.

§ 2A—405. Excused Performance.

Subject to Section 2A—404 on substituted performance, the following rules apply:

    (a) Delay in delivery or non-delivery in whole or in part by a lessor or a supplier who complies with paragraphs (b) and (c) is not a default under the lease contract if performance as agreed has been made impracticable by the occurrence of a contingency the nonoccurrence of which was a basic assumption on which the lease contract was made or by compliance in good faith with any applicable foreign or domestic governmental regulation or order, whether or not the regulation or order later proves to be invalid.

    (b) If the causes mentioned in paragraph (a) affect only part of the lessor's or the supplier's capacity to perform, he [or she] shall allocate production and deliveries among his [or her] customers but at his [or her] option may include regular customers not then under contract for sale or lease as well as his [or her] own requirements for further manufacture. He [or she] may so allocate in any manner that is fair and reasonable.

    (c) The lessor seasonably shall notify the lessee and in the case of a finance lease the supplier seasonably shall notify the lessor and the lessee, if known, that there will be delay or non-delivery and, if allocation is required under paragraph (b), of the estimated quota thus made available for the lessee.

§ 2A—406. Procedure on Excused Performance.

(1) If the lessee receives notification of a material or indefinite delay or an allocation justified under Section 2A—405, the lessee may by written notification to the lessor as to any goods involved, and with respect to all of the goods if under an installment lease contract the value of the whole lease contract is substantially impaired (Section 2A—510):

    (a) terminate the lease contract (Section 2A—505(2)); or

    (b) except in a finance lease that is not a consumer lease, modify the lease contract by accepting the available quota in substitution, with due allowance from the rent payable for the balance of the lease term for the deficiency but without further right against the lessor.

(2) If, after receipt of a notification from the lessor under Section 2A—405, the lessee fails so to modify the lease agreement within a reasonable time not exceeding 30 days, the lease contract lapses with respect to any deliveries affected.

§ 2A—407. Irrevocable Promises: Finance Leases.

(1) In the case of a finance lease that is not a consumer lease the lessee's promises under the lease contract become irrevocable and independent upon the lessee's acceptance of the goods.

(2) A promise that has become irrevocable and independent under subsection (1):

    (a) is effective and enforceable between the parties, and by or against third parties including assignees of the parties, and

    (b) is not subject to cancellation, termination, modification, repudiation, excuse, or substitution without the consent of the party to whom the promise runs.

PART 5.   Default.

A. In General

§ 2A—501.   Default: Procedure.

(1) Whether the lessor or the lessee is in default under a lease contract is determined by the lease agreement and this Article.

(2) If the lessor or the lessee is in default under the lease contract, the party seeking enforcement has rights and remedies as provided in this Article and, except as limited by this Article, as provided in the lease agreement.

(3) If the lessor or the lessee is in default under the lease contract, the party seeking enforcement may reduce the party's claim to judgment, or otherwise enforce the lease contract by self-help or any available judicial procedure or nonjudicial procedure, including administrative proceeding, arbitration, or the like, in accordance with this Article.

(4) Except as otherwise provided in this Article or the lease agreement, the rights and remedies referred to in subsection (2) and (3) are cumulative.

(5) If the lease agreement covers both real property and goods, the party seeking enforcement may proceed under this Part as to the goods, or under other applicable law as to both the real property and the goods in accordance with his [or her] rights and remedies in respect of the real property, in which case this Part does not apply.

§ 2A—502.   Notice After Default.

Except as otherwise provided in this Article or the lease agreement, the lessor or lessee in default under the lease contract is not entitled to notice of default or notice of enforcement from the other party to the lease agreement.

§ 2A—503.   Modification or Impairment of Rights and Remedies.

(1) Except as otherwise provided in this Article, the lease agreement may include rights and remedies for default in addition to or in substitution for those provided in this Article and may limit or alter the measure of damages recoverable under this Article.

(2) Resort to a remedy provided under this Article or in the lease agreement is optional unless the remedy is expressly agreed to be exclusive. If circumstances cause an exclusive or limited remedy to fail of its essential purpose, or provision for an exclusive remedy is unconscionable, remedy may be had as provided in this Article.

(3) Consequential damages may be liquidated under Section 2A—504, or may otherwise be limited, altered, or excluded unless the limitation, alteration, or exclusion is unconscionable. Limitation of consequential damages for injury to the person in the case of consumer goods is prima facie unconscionable but limitation of damages where the loss is commercial is not.

(4) Rights and remedies on default by the lessor or the lessee with respect to any obligation or promise collateral or ancillary to the lease contract are not impaired by this Article.

§ 2A—504.   Liquidation of Damages.

(1) Damages payable by either party for default, or any other act or omission, including indemnity for loss or diminution of anticipated tax benefits or loss or damage to lessor's residual interest, may be liquidated in the lease agreement but only at an amount or by a formula that is reasonable in light of the then anticipated harm caused by the default or other act or omission.

(2) If the lease agreement provides for liquidation of damages, and such provision does not comply with subsection (1), or such provision is an exclusive or limited remedy that circumstances cause to fail of its essential purpose, remedy may be had as provided in this Article.

(3) If the lessor justifiably withholds or stops delivery of goods because of the lessee's default or insolvency (Section 2A—525 or 2A—526), the lessee is entitled to restitution of any amount by which the sum of his [or her] payments exceeds:

> (a) the amount to which the lessor is entitled by virtue of terms liquidating the lessor's damages in accordance with subsection (1); or
>
> (b) in the absence of those terms, 20 percent of the then present value of the total rent the lessee was obligated to pay for the balance of the lease term, or, in the case of a consumer lease, the lesser of such amount or $500.

(4) A lessee's right to restitution under subsection (3) is subject to offset to the extent the lessor establishes:

> (a) a right to recover damages under the provisions of this Article other than subsection (1); and
>
> (b) the amount or value of any benefits received by the lessee directly or indirectly by reason of the lease contract.

§ 2A—505.   Cancellation and Termination and Effect of Cancellation, Termination, Rescission, or Fraud on Rights and Remedies.

(1) On cancellation of the lease contract, all obligations that are still executory on both sides are discharged, but any right based on prior default or performance survives, and the cancelling party also retains any remedy for default of the whole lease contract or any unperformed balance.

(2) On termination of the lease contract, all obligations that are still executory on both sides are discharged but any right based on prior default or performance survives.

(3) Unless the contrary intention clearly appears, expressions of "cancellation," "rescission," or the like of the lease contract may not be construed as a renuncia-

tion or discharge of any claim in damages for an antecedent default.

(4) Rights and remedies for material misrepresentation or fraud include all rights and remedies available under this Article for default.

(5) Neither rescission nor a claim for rescission of the lease contract nor rejection or return of the goods may bar or be deemed inconsistent with a claim for damages or other right or remedy.

§ 2A—506.   Statute of Limitations.

(1) An action for default under a lease contract, including breach of warranty or indemnity, must be commenced within 4 years after the cause of action accrued. By the original lease contract the parties may reduce the period of limitation to not less than one year.

(2) A cause of action for default accrues when the act or omission on which the default or breach of warranty is based is or should have been discovered by the aggrieved party, or when the default occurs, whichever is later. A cause of action for indemnity accrues when the act or omission on which the claim for indemnity is based is or should have been discovered by the indemnified party, whichever is later.

(3) If an action commenced within the time limited by subsection (1) is so terminated as to leave available a remedy by another action for the same default or breach of warranty or indemnity, the other action may be commenced after the expiration of the time limited and within 6 months after the termination of the first action unless the termination resulted from voluntary discontinuance or from dismissal for failure or neglect to prosecute.

(4) This section does not alter the law on tolling of the statute of limitations nor does it apply to causes of action that have accrued before this Article becomes effective.

§ 2A—507.   Proof of Market Rent: Time and Place.

(1) Damages based on market rent (Section 2A–519 or 2A–528) are determined according to the rent for the use of the goods concerned for a lease term identical to the remaining lease term of the original lease agreement and prevailing at the time of the default.

(2) If evidence of rent for the use of the goods concerned for a lease term identical to the remaining lease term of the original lease agreement and prevailing at the times or places described in this Article is not readily available, the rent prevailing within any reasonable time before or after the time described or at any other place or for a different lease term which in commercial judgment or under usage of trade would serve as a reasonable substitute for the one described may be used, making any proper allowance for the difference, including the cost of transporting the goods to or from the other place.

(3) Evidence of a relevant rent prevailing at a time or place or for a lease term other than the one described in this Article offered by one party is not admissible unless and until he [or she] has given the other party notice the court finds sufficient to prevent unfair surprise.

(4) If the prevailing rent or value of any goods regularly leased in any established market is in issue, reports in official publications or trade journals or in newspapers or periodicals of general circulation published as the reports of that market are admissible in evidence. The circumstances of the preparation of the report may be shown to affect its weight but not its admissibility.

B. Default by Lessor

§ 2A—508.   Lessee's Remedies.

(1) If a lessor fails to deliver the goods in conformity to the lease contract (Section 2A—509) or repudiates the lease contract (Section 2A—402), or a lessee rightfully rejects the goods (Section 2A—509) or justifiably revokes acceptance of the goods (Section 2A—517), then with respect to any goods involved, and with respect to all of the goods if under an installment lease contract the value of the whole lease contract is substantially impaired (Section 2A–510), the lessor is in default under the lease contract and the lessee may:

   (a) cancel the lease contract (Section 2A—505(1));

   (b) recover so much of the rent and security as has been paid, but in the case of an installment lease contract the recovery is that which is just under the circumstances;

   (c) cover and recover damages as to all goods affected whether or not they have been identified to the lease contract (Sections 2A—518 and 2A—520), or recover damages for non-delivery (Sections 2A—519 and 2A—520).

(2) If a lessor fails to deliver the goods in conformity to the lease contract or repudiates the lease contract, the lessee may also:

   (a) if the goods have been identified, recover them (Section 2A—522); or

   (b) in a proper case, obtain specific performance or replevy the goods (Section 2A—521).

(3) If a lessor is otherwise in default under a lease contract, the lessee may exercise the rights and remedies provided in the lease contract and this Article.

(4) If a lessor has breached a warranty, whether express or implied, the lessee may recover damages (Section 2A—519(4)).

(5) On rightful rejection or justifiable revocation of acceptance, a lessee has a security interest in goods in the lessee's possession or control for any rent and security that has been paid and any expenses reasonably incurred in their inspection, receipt, transportation, and

care and custody and may hold those goods and dispose of them in good faith and in a commercially reasonable manner, subject to the provisions of Section 2A—527(5).

(6) Subject to the provisions of Section 2A—407, a lessee, on notifying the lessor of the lessee's intention to do so, may deduct all or any part of the damages resulting from any default under the lease contract from any part of the rent still due under the same lease contract.

§ 2A—509. Lessee's Rights on Improper Delivery; Rightful Rejection.

(1) Subject to the provisions of Section 2A—510 on default in installment lease contracts, if the goods or the tender or delivery fail in any respect to conform to the lease contract, the lessee may reject or accept the goods or accept any commercial unit or units and reject the rest of the goods.

(2) Rejection of goods is ineffective unless it is within a reasonable time after tender or delivery of the goods and the lessee seasonably notifies the lessor.

§ 2A—510. Installment Lease Contracts: Rejection and Default.

(1) Under an installment lease contract a lessee may reject any delivery that is nonconforming if the nonconformity substantially impairs the value of that delivery and cannot be cured or the nonconformity is a defect in the required documents; but if the nonconformity does not fall within subsection (2) and the lessor or the supplier gives adequate assurance of its cure, the lessee must accept that delivery.

(2) Whenever nonconformity or default with respect to one or more deliveries substantially impairs the value of the installment lease contract as a whole there is a default with respect to the whole. But, the aggrieved party reinstates the installment lease contract as a whole if the aggrieved party accepts a nonconforming delivery without seasonably notifying of cancellation or brings an action with respect only to past deliveries or demands performance as to future deliveries.

§ 2A—511. Merchant Lessee's Duties as to Rightfully Rejected Goods.

(1) Subject to any security interest of a lessee (Section 2A—508(5)), if a lessor or a supplier has no agent or place of business at the market of rejection, a merchant lessee, after rejection of goods in his [or her] possession or control, shall follow any reasonable instructions received from the lessor or the supplier with respect to the goods. In the absence of those instructions a merchant lessee shall make reasonable efforts to sell, lease, or otherwise dispose of the goods for the lessor's account if they threaten to decline in value speedily. Instructions

are not reasonable if on demand indemnity for expenses is not forthcoming.

(2) If a merchant lessee (subsection (1)) or any other lessee (Section 2A—512) disposes of goods, he [or she] is entitled to reimbursement either from the lessor or the supplier or out of the proceeds for reasonable expenses of caring for and disposing of the goods and, if the expenses include no disposition commission, to such commission as is usual in the trade, or if there is none, to a reasonable sum not exceeding 10 percent of the gross proceeds.

(3) In complying with this section or Section 2A—512, the lessee is held only to good faith. Good faith conduct hereunder is neither acceptance or conversion nor the basis of an action for damages.

(4) A purchaser who purchases in good faith from a lessee pursuant to this section or Section 2A—512 takes the goods free of any rights of the lessor and the supplier even though the lessee fails to comply with one or more of the requirements of this Article.

§ 2A—512. Lessee's Duties as to Rightfully Rejected Goods.

(1) Except as otherwise provided with respect to goods that threaten to decline in value speedily (Section 2A—511) and subject to any security interest of a lessee (Section 2A—508(5)):

    (a) the lessee, after rejection of goods in the lessee's possession, shall hold them with reasonable care at the lessor's or supplier's disposition for a reasonable time after the lessee's seasonable notification of rejection;

    (b) if the lessor or the supplier gives no instructions within a reasonable time after notification of rejection, the lessee may store the rejected goods for the lessor's or the supplier's account or ship them to the lessor or the supplier or dispose of them for the lessor's or the supplier's account with reimbursement in the manner provided in Section 2A—511; but

    (c) the lessee has no further obligations with regard to goods rightfully rejected.

(2) Action by the lessee pursuant to subsection (1) is not acceptance or conversion.

§ 2A—513. Cure by Lessor of Improper Tender or Delivery; Replacement.

(1) If any tender or delivery by the lessor or the supplier is rejected because nonconforming and the time for performance has not yet expired, the lessor or the supplier may seasonably notify the lessee of the lessor's or the supplier's intention to cure and may then make a conforming delivery within the time provided in the lease contract.

(2) If the lessee rejects a nonconforming tender that the lessor or the supplier had reasonable grounds to believe would be acceptable with or without money allowance, the lessor or the supplier may have a further reasonable time to substitute a conforming tender if he [or she] seasonably notifies the lessee.

§ 2A—514. Waiver of Lessee's Objections.

(1) In rejecting goods, a lessee's failure to state a particular defect that is ascertainable by reasonable inspection precludes the lessee from relying on the defect to justify rejection or to establish default:

    (a) if, states seasonably, the lessor or the supplier could have cured it (Section 2A—513);

    (b) between merchants if the lessor or the supplier after rejection has made a request in writing for a full and final written statement of all defects on which the lessee proposes to rely.

(2) A lessee's failure to reserve rights when paying rent or other consideration against documents precludes recovery of the payment for defects apparent on the face of the documents.

§ 2A—515. Acceptance of Goods.

(1) Acceptance of goods occurs after the lessee has had a reasonable opportunity to inspect the goods and

    (a) the lessee signifies or acts with respect to the goods in a manner that signifies to the lessor or the supplier that the goods are conforming or that the lessee will take or retain them in spite of their nonconformity; or

    (b) the lessee fails to make an effective rejection of the goods (Section 2A—509(2)).

(2) Acceptance of a part of any commercial unit is acceptance of that entire unit.

§ 2A—516. Effect of Acceptance of Goods; Notice of Default; Burden of Establishing Default After Acceptance; Notice of Claim or Litigation to Person Answerable Over.

(1) A lessee must pay rent for any goods accepted in accordance with the lease contract, with due allowance for goods rightfully rejected or not delivered.

(2) A lessee's acceptance of goods precludes rejection of the goods accepted. In the case of a finance lease, if made with knowledge of a nonconformity, acceptance cannot be revoked because of it. In any other case, if made with knowledge of a nonconformity, acceptance cannot be revoked because of it unless the acceptance was on the reasonable assumption that the nonconformity would be seasonably cured. Acceptance does not of itself impair any other remedy provided by this Article or the lease agreement for nonconformity.

(3) If a tender has been accepted:

    (a) within a reasonable time after the lessee discovers or should have discovered any default,

the lessee shall notify the lessor and the supplier, or be barred from any remedy;

    (b) except in the case of a consumer lease, within a reasonable time after the lessee receives notice of litigation for infringement or the like (Section 2A–211) the lessee shall notify the lessor or be barred from any remedy over for liability established by the litigation; and

    (c) the burden is on the lessee to establish any default.

(4) If a lessee is sued for breach of a warranty or other obligation for which a lessor or a supplier is answerable over:

    (a) The lessee may give the lessor or the supplier written notice of the litigation. If the notice states that the lessor or the supplier may come in and defend and that if the lessor or the supplier does not do so he [or she] will be bound in any action against him [or her] by the lessee by any determination of fact common to the two litigations, then unless the lessor or the supplier after seasonable receipt of the notice does come in and defend he [or she] is so bound.

    (b) The lessor or the supplier may demand in writing that the lessee turn over control of the litigation including settlement if the claim is one for infringement or the like (Section 2A–211) or else be barred from any remedy over. If the demand states that the lessor or the supplier agrees to bear all expenses and to satisfy and adverse judgment, then unless the lessee after seasonable receipt of the demand does turn over control the lessee is so barred.

(5) The provisions of subsections (3) and (4) apply to any obligation of a lessee to hold the lessor or the supplier harmless against infringement or the like (Section 2A–211).

§ 2A—517. Revocation of Acceptance of Goods.

(1) A lessee may revoke acceptance of a lot or commercial unit whose nonconformity substantially impairs its value to the lessee if he [or she] has accepted it:

    (a) except in the case of a finance lease, on the reasonable assumption that its nonconformity would be cured and it has not been seasonably cured; or

    (b) without discovery of the nonconformity if the lessee's acceptance was reasonably induced either by the lessor's assurances or, except in the case of a finance lease, by the difficulty of discovery before acceptance.

(2) Revocation of acceptance must occur within a reasonable time after the lessee discovers or should have discovered the ground for it and before any substantial change in condition of the goods which is not caused by

the nonconformity. Revocation is not effective until the lessee notifies the lessor.

(3) A lessee who so revokes has the same rights and duties with regard to the goods involved as if the lessee had rejected them.

§ 2A—518. Cover; Substitute Goods.

(1) After default by a lessor under the lease contract (Section 2A—508(1)), the lessee may cover by making any purchase or lease of or contract to purchase or lease goods in substitution for those due from the lessor.

(2) Except as otherwise provided with respect to damages liquidated in the lease agreement (Section 2A—504) or determined by agreement of the parties (Section 1—102(3)), if a lessee's cover is by lease agreement substantially similar to the original lease agreement and the lease agreement is made in good faith and in a commercially reasonable manner, the lessee may recover from the lessor as damages (a) the present value, as of the date of default, of the difference between the total rent for the lease term of the new lease agreement and the total rent for the remaining lease term of the original lease agreement and (b) any incidental or consequential damages less expenses saved in consequence of the lessor's default.

(3) If a lessee's cover is by lease agreement that for any reason does not qualify for treatment under subsection (2), or is by purchase or otherwise, the lessee may recover from the lessor as if the lessee had elected not to cover and Section 2A—519 governs.

§ 2A—519. Lessee's Damages for Nondelivery, Repudiation, Default and Breach of Warranty in Regard to Accepted Goods.

(1) Except as otherwise provided with respect to damages liquidated in the lease agreement (Section 2A—504) or determined by agreement of the parties (Section 1—102(3)), if a lessee elects not to cover or a lessee elects to cover and the cover is by lease agreement that for any reason does not qualify for treatment under Section 2A—518(2), or is by purchase or otherwise, the measure of damages for nondelivery or repudiation by the lessor or for rejection or revocation of acceptance by the lessee is the present value as of the date of the default of the difference between the then market rent and the original rent, computed for the remaining lease term of the original lease agreement together with incidental and consequential damages, less expenses saved in consequence of the lessor's default.

(2) Market rent is to be determined as of the place for tender or, in cases of rejection after arrival or revocation of acceptance, as of the place of arrival.

(3) If the lessee has accepted goods and given notification (Section 2A—516(3)), the measure of damages for non-conforming tender or delivery by a lessor is the loss resulting in the ordinary course of events from the lessor's default as determined in any manner that is reasonable together with incidental and consequential damages, less expenses saved in consequence of the lessor's default.

(4) The measure of damages for breach of warranty is the present value at the time and place of acceptance of the difference between the value of the use of the goods accepted and the value if they had been as warranted for the lease term, unless special circumstances show proximate damages of a different amount, together with incidental and consequential damages, less expenses saved in consequence of the lessor's default or breach of warranty.

§ 2A—520. Lessee's Incidental and Consequential Damages.

(1) Incidental damages resulting from a lessor's default include expenses reasonably incurred in inspection, receipt, transportation, and care and custody of goods rightfully rejected or goods the acceptance of which is justifiably revoked, any commercially reasonable charges, expenses or commissions in connection with effecting cover, and any other reasonable expense incident to the default.

(2) Consequential damages resulting from a lessor's default include:

(a) any loss resulting from general or particular requirements and needs of which the lessor at the time of contracting had reason to know and which could not reasonably be prevented by cover or otherwise; and

(b) injury to person or property proximately resulting from any breach of warranty.

§ 2A—521. Lessee's Right to Specific Performance or Replevin.

(1) Specific performance may be decreed if the goods are unique or in other proper circumstances.

(2) A decree for specific performance may include any terms and conditions as to payment of the rent, damages, or other relief that the court deems just.

(3) A lessee has a right of replevin, detinue, sequestration, claim and delivery, or the like for goods identified to the lease contract if after reasonable effort the lessee is unable to effect cover for those goods or the circumstances reasonably indicate that the effort will be unavailing.

§ 2A—522. Lessee's Right to Goods on Lessor's Insolvency.

(1) Subject to subsection (2) and even though the goods have not been shipped, a lessee who has paid a part or all of the rent and security for goods identified to a lease contract (Section 2A—217) on making and keeping good a tender of any unpaid portion of the rent and security due under the lease contract may recover the

goods identified from the lessor if the lessor becomes insolvent within 10 days after receipt of the first install-ment of rent and security.

(2) A lessee acquires the right to recover goods iden-tified to a lease contract only if they conform to the lease contract.

C. Default by Lessee

§ 2A—523. Lessor's Remedies.

(1) If a lessee wrongfully rejects or revokes accep-tance of goods or fails to make a payment when due or repudiates with respect to a part or the whole, then, with respect to any goods involved, and with respect to all the goods if under an installment lease contract the value of the whole lease contract is substantially impaired (Sec-tion 2A—510), the lessee is in default under the lease contract and the lessor may:

  (a) cancel the lease contract (Section 2A—505(1));

  (b) proceed respecting goods not identified to the lease contract (Section 2A—524);

  (c) withhold delivery of the goods and take pos-session of goods previously delivered (Section 2A—525);

  (d) stop delivery of the goods by any bailee (Sec-tion 2A—526);

  (e) dispose of the goods and recover damages (Section 2A—527), or retain the goods and recover damages (Section 2A—528), or in a proper case recover rent (Section 2A—529).

(2) If a lessee is otherwise in default under a lease contract, the lessor may exercise the rights and remedies provided in the lease contract and this Article.

§ 2A—524. Lessor's Right to Identify Goods to Lease Contract.

(1) A lessor aggrieved under Section 2A—523(1) may:

  (a) identify to the lease contract conforming goods not already identified if at the time the lessor learned of the default they were in the lessor's or the supplier's possession or control; and

  (b) dispose of goods (Section 2A—527(1)) that demonstrably have been intended for the par-ticular lease contract even though those goods are unfinished.

(2) If the goods are unfinished, in the exercise of rea-sonable commercial judgment for the purposes of avoid-ing loss and of effective realization, an aggrieved lessor or the supplier may either complete manufacture and wholly identify the goods to the lease contract or cease manufacture and lease, sell, or otherwise dispose of the goods for scrap or salvage value or proceed in any other reasonable manner.

§ 2A—525. Lessor's Right to Possession of Goods.

(1) If a lessor discovers the lessee to be insolvent, the lessor may refuse to deliver the goods.

(2) The lessor has on default by the lessee under the lease contract the right to take possession of the goods. If the lease contract so provides, the lessor may require the lessee to assemble the goods and make them avail-able to the lessor at a place to be designated by the lessor which is reasonably convenient to both parties. Without removal, the lessor may render unusable any goods em-ployed in trade or business, and may dispose of goods on the lessee's premises (Section 2A—527).

(3) The lessor may proceed under subsection (2) with-out judicial process if that can be done without breach of the peace or the lessor may proceed by action.

§ 2A—526. Lessor's Stoppage of Delivery in Transit or Otherwise.

(1) A lessor may stop delivery of goods in the posses-sion of a carrier or other bailee if the lessor discovers the lessee to be insolvent and may stop delivery of carload, truckload, planeload, or larger shipments of express or freight if the lessee repudiates or fails to make a payment due before delivery, whether for rent, security or other-wise under the lease contract, or for any other reason the lessor has a right to withhold or take possession of the goods.

(2) In pursuing its remedies under subsection (1), the lessor may stop delivery until

  (a) receipt of the goods by the lessee;

  (b) acknowledgment to the lessee by any bailee of the goods, except a carrier, that the bailee holds the goods for the lessee; or

  (c) such an acknowledgment to the lessee by a carrier via reshipment or as warehouseman.

(3) (a) To stop delivery, a lessor shall so notify as to enable the bailee by reasonable diligence to prevent delivery of the goods.

  (b) After notification, the bailee shall hold and de-liver the goods according to the directions of the lessor, but the lessor is liable to the bailee for any ensuing charges or damages.

  (c) A carrier who has issued a nonnegotiable bill of lading is not obliged to obey a notification to stop received from a person other than the consignor.

§ 2A—527. Lessor's Rights to Dispose of Goods.

(1) After a default by a lessee under the lease contract (Section 2A—523(1)) or after the lessor refuses to de-liver or takes possession of goods (Section 2A—525 or 2A—526), the lessor may dispose of the goods con-cerned or the undelivered balance thereof by lease, sale or otherwise.

(2) Except as otherwise provided with respect to dam-ages liquidated in the lease agreement (Section 2A—

504) or determined by agreement of the parties (Section 1—102(3)), if the disposition is by lease agreement substantially similar to the original lease agreement and the lease agreement is made in good faith and in a commercially reasonable manner, the lessor may recover from the lessee as damages (a) accrued and unpaid rent as of the date of default, (b) the present value as of the date of default of the difference between the total rent for the remaining lease term of the original lease agreement and the total rent for the lease term of the new lease agreement, and (c) any incidental damages allowed under Section 2A—530, less expenses saved in consequence of the lessee's default.

(3) If the lessor's disposition is by lease agreement that for any reason does not qualify for treatment under subsection (2), or is by sale or otherwise, the lessor may recover from the lessee as if the lessor had elected not to dispose of the goods and Section 2A—528 governs.

(4) A subsequent buyer or lessee who buys or leases from the lessor in good faith for value as a result of a disposition under this section takes the goods free of the original lease contract and any rights of the original lessee even though the lessor fails to comply with one or more of the requirements of this Article.

(5) The lessor is not accountable to the lessee for any profit made on any disposition. A lessee who has rightfully rejected or justifiably revoked acceptance shall account to the lessor for any excess over the amount of the lessee's security interest (Section 2A—508(5)).

§ 2A—528. Lessor's Damages for Non-Acceptance or Repudiation.

(1) Except as otherwise provided with respect to damages liquidated in the lease agreement (Section 2A—504) or determined by agreement of the parties (Section 1—102(3)), if a lessor elects to retain the goods or a lessor elects to dispose of the goods and disposition is by lease agreement that for any reason does not qualify for treatment under Section 2A—527(2), or is by sale or otherwise, the lessor may recover from the lessee as damages for non-acceptance or repudiation by the lessee (a) accrued and unpaid rent as of the date of default, (b) the present value as of the date of default of the difference between the total rent for the remaining lease term of the original lease agreement and the market rent at the time and place for tender computed for the same lease term, and (c) any incidental damages allowed under Section 2A—530, less expenses saved in consequence of the lessee's default.

(2) If the measure of damages provided in subsection (1) is inadequate to put a lessor in as good a position as performance would have, the measure of damages is the profit, including reasonable overhead, the lessor would have made from full performance by the lessee, together with any incidental damages allowed under Section 2A—

530, due allowance for costs reasonably incurred and due credit for payments or proceeds of disposition.

§ 2A—529. Lessor's Action for the Rent.

(1) After default by the lessee under the lease contract (Section 2A—523(1)), if the lessor complies with subsection (2), the lessor may recover from the lessee as damages:

  (a) for goods accepted by the lessee and for conforming goods lost or damaged within a commercially reasonable time after risk of loss passes to the lessee (Section 2A—219), (i) accrued and unpaid rent as of the date of default, (ii) the present value as of the date of default of the rent for the remaining lease term of the lease agreement, and (iii) any incidental damages allowed under Section 2A—530, less expenses saved in consequence of the lessee's default; and

  (b) for goods identified to the lease contract if the lessor is unable after reasonable effort to dispose of them at a reasonable price or the circumstances reasonably indicate that effort will be unavailing, (i) accrued and unpaid rent as of the date of default, (ii) the present value as of the date of default of the rent for the remaining lease term of the lease agreement, and (iii) any incidental damages allowed under Section 2A—530, less expenses saved in consequence of the lessee's default.

(2) Except as provided in subsection (3), the lessor shall hold for the lessee for the remaining lease term of the lease agreement any goods that have been identified to the lease contract and are in the lessor's control.

(3) The lessor may dispose of the goods at any time before collection of the judgment for damages obtained pursuant to subsection (1). If the disposition is before the end of the remaining lease term of the lease agreement, the lessor's recovery against the lessee for damages will be governed by Section 2A—527 or Section 2A—528.

(4) Payment of the judgment for damages obtained pursuant to subsection (1) entitles the lessee to use and possession of the goods not then disposed of for the remaining lease term of the lease agreement.

(5) After a lessee has wrongfully rejected or revoked acceptance of goods, has failed to pay rent then due, or has repudiated (Section 2A—402), a lessor who is held not entitled to rent under this section must nevertheless be awarded damages for non-acceptance under Sections 2A—527 and 2A—528.

§ 2A—530. Lessor's Incidental Damages.

Incidental damages to an aggrieved lessor include any commercially reasonable charges, expenses, or commissions incurred in stopping delivery, in the transportation, care and custody of goods after the lessee's default, in connection with return or disposition of the goods, or otherwise resulting from the default.

§ 2A—531. Standing to Sue Third Parties for Injury to Goods.

(1) If a third party so deals with goods that have been identified to a lease contract as to cause actionable injury to a party to the lease contract (a) the lessor has a right of action against the third party, and (b) the lessee also has a right of action against the third party if the lessee:

> (i) has a security interest in the goods;
>
> (ii) has an insurable interest in the goods; or
>
> (iii) bears the risk of loss under the lease contract or has since the injury assumed that risk as against the lessor and the goods have been converted or destroyed.

(2) If at the time of the injury the party plaintiff did not bear the risk of loss as against the other party to the lease contract and there is no arrangement between them for disposition of the recovery, his [or her] suit or settlement, subject to his [or her] own interest, is as a fiduciary for the other party to the lease contract.

(3) Either party with the consent of the other may sue for the benefit of whom it may concern.

ARTICLE 3. Commercial Paper

PART 1. Short Title, Form and Interpretation.

§ 3—101. Short Title.

This Article shall be known and may be cited as Uniform Commercial Code—Commercial Paper.

§ 3—102. Definitions and Index of Definitions.

(1) In this Article unless the context otherwise requires

> (a) "Issue" means the first delivery of an instrument to a holder or a remitter.
>
> (b) An "order" is a direction to pay and must be more than an authorization or request. It must identify the person to pay with reasonable certainty. It may be addressed to one or more such persons jointly or in the alternative but not in succession.
>
> (c) A "promise" is an undertaking to pay and must be more than an acknowledgment of an obligation.
>
> (d) "Secondary party" means a drawer or endorser.
>
> (e) "Instrument" means a negotiable instrument.

(2) Other definitions applying to this Article and the sections in which they appear are:

"Acceptance". Section 3—410.
"Accommodation party". Section 3—415.
"Alteration". Section 3—407.
"Certificate of deposit". Section 3—104.
"Certification". Section 3—411.

"Check". Section 3—104.
"Definite time". Section 3—109.
"Dishonor". Section 3—507.
"Draft". Section 3—104.
"Holder in due course". Section 3—302.
"Negotiation". Section 3—202.
"Note". Section 3—104.
"Notice of dishonor". Section 3—508.
"On demand". Section 3—108.
"Presentment". Section 3—504.
"Protest". Section 3—509.
"Restrictive Indorsement". Section 3—205.
"Signature". Section 3—401.

(3) The following definitions in other Articles apply to this Article:

"Account". Section 4—104.
"Banking day". Section 4—104.
"Clearing house". Section 4—104.
"Collecting bank". Section 4—105.
"Customer". Section 4—104.
"Depositary bank". Section 4—105.
"Documentary draft". Section 4—104.
"Intermediary bank". Section 4—105.
"Item". Section 4—104.
"Midnight deadline". Section 4—104.
"Payor bank". Section 4—105.

(4) In addition Article 1 contains general definitions and principles of construction and interpretation applicable throughout this Article.

§ 3—103. Limitations on Scope of Article.

(1) This Article does not apply to money, documents of title or investment securities.

(2) The provisions of this Article are subject to the provisions of the Article on Bank Deposits and Collections (Article 4) and Secured Transactions (Article 9).

§ 3—104. Form of Negotiable Instruments; "Draft"; "Check"; "Certificate of Deposit"; "Note".

(1) Subject to the provisions of Section 2A—303, a subsequent lessee from a lessor of goods under an existing lease contract obtains, to the extent of the leasehold interest transferred, the leasehold interest in the goods that the lessor had or had power to transfer, and except as provided in subsection (2) and Section 2A—527(4), takes subject to the existing lease contract. A lessor with voidable title has power to transfer a good leasehold interest to a good faith subsequent lessee for value, but only to the extent set forth in the preceding sentence. When goods have been delivered under a transaction of purchase the lessor has that power even though:

> (a) the lessor's transferor was deceived as to the identity of the lessor;
>
> (b) the delivery was in exchange for a check which is later dishonored;

(c) it was agreed that the transaction was to be a "cash sale"; or

(d) the delivery was procured through fraud punishable as larcenous under the criminal law.

(2) A writing which complies with the requirements of this section is

(a) a "draft" ("bill of exchange") if it is an order;

(b) a "check" if it is a draft drawn on a bank and payable on demand;

(c) a "certificate of deposit" if it is an acknowledgment by a bank of receipt of money with an engagement to repay it;

(d) a "note" if it is a promise other than a certificate of deposit.

(3) As used in other Articles of this Act, and as the context may require, the terms "draft", "check", "certificate of deposit" and "note" may refer to instruments which are not negotiable within this Article as well as to instruments which are so negotiable.

§ 3—105. When Promise or Order Unconditional.

(1) A promise or order otherwise unconditional is not made conditional by the fact that the instrument

(a) is subject to implied or constructive conditions; or

(b) states its consideration, whether performed or promised, or the transaction which gave rise to the instrument, or that the promise or order is made or the instrument matures in accordance with or "as per" such transaction; or

(c) refers to or states that it arises out of a separate agreement or refers to a separate agreement for rights as to prepayment or acceleration; or

(d) states that it is drawn under a letter of credit; or

(e) states that it is secured, whether by mortgage, reservation of title or otherwise; or

(f) indicates a particular account to be debited or any other fund or source from which reimbursement is expected; or

(g) is limited to payment out of a particular fund or the proceeds of a particular source, if the instrument is issued by a government or governmental agency or unit; or

(h) is limited to payment out of the entire assets of a partnership, unincorporated association, trust or estate by or on behalf of which the instrument is issued.

(2) A promise or order is not unconditional if the instrument

(a) states that it is subject to or governed by any other agreement; or

(b) states that it is to be paid only out of a particular fund or source except as provided in this section. As amended 1962.

§ 3—106. Sum Certain.

(1) The sum payable is a sum certain even though it is to be paid

(a) with stated interest or by stated installments; or

(b) with stated different rates of interest before and after default or a specified date; or

(c) with a stated discount or addition if paid before or after the date fixed for payment; or

(d) with exchange or less exchange, whether at a fixed rate or at the current rate; or

(e) with costs of collection or an attorney's fee or both upon default.

(2) Nothing in this section shall validate any term which is otherwise illegal.

§ 3—107. Money.

(1) An instrument is payable in money if the medium of exchange in which it is payable is money at the time the instrument is made. An instrument payable in "currency" or "current funds" is payable in money.

(2) A promise or order to pay a sum stated in a foreign currency is for a sum certain in money and, unless a different medium of payment is specified in the instrument, may be satisfied by payment of that number of dollars which the stated foreign currency will purchase at the buying sight rate for that currency on the day on which the instrument is payable or, if payable on demand, on the day of demand. If such an instrument specifies a foreign currency as the medium of payment the instrument is payable in that currency.

§ 3—108. Payable on Demand.

Instruments payable on demand include those payable at sight or on presentation and those in which no time for payment is stated.

§ 3—109. Definite Time.

(1) An instrument is payable at a definite time if by its terms it is payable

(a) on or before a stated date or at a fixed period after a stated date; or

(b) at a fixed period after sight; or

(c) at a definite time subject to any acceleration; or

(d) at a definite time subject to extension at the option of the holder, or to extension to a further definite time at the option of the maker or acceptor or automatically upon or after a specified act or event.

(2) An instrument which by its terms is otherwise payable only upon an act or event uncertain as to time of occurrence is not payable at a definite time even though the act or event has occurred.

§ 3—110. Payable to Order.

(1) An instrument is payable to order when by its

terms it is payable to the order or assigns of any person therein specified with reasonable certainty, or to him or his order, or when it is conspicuously designated on its face as "exchange" or the like and names a payee. It may be payable to the order of

(a) the maker or drawer; or

(b) the drawee; or

(c) a payee who is not maker, drawer or drawee; or

(d) two or more payees together or in the alternative; or

(e) an estate, trust or fund, in which case it is payable to the order of the representative of such estate, trust or fund or his successors; or

(f) an office, or an officer by his title as such in which case it is payable to the principal but the incumbent of the office or his successors may act as if he or they were the holder; or

(g) a partnership or unincorporated association, in which case it is payable to the partnership or association and may be indorsed or transferred by any person thereto authorized.

(2) An instrument not payable to order is not made so payable by such words as "payable upon return of this instrument properly indorsed."

(3) An instrument made payable both to order and to bearer is payable to order unless the bearer words are handwritten or typewritten.

§ 3—111.   Payable to Bearer.

An instrument is payable to bearer when by its terms it is payable to

(a) bearer or the order of bearer; or

(b) a specified person or bearer; or

(c) "cash" or the order of "cash", or any other indication which does not purport to designate a specific payee.

§ 3—112.   Terms and Omissions Not Affecting Negotiability.

(1) The negotiability of an instrument is not affected by

(a) the omission of a statement of any consideration or of the place where the instrument is drawn or payable; or

(b) a statement that collateral has been given to secure obligations either on the instrument or otherwise of an obligor on the instrument or that in case of default on those obligations the holder may realize on or dispose of the collateral; or

(c) a promise or power to maintain or protect collateral or to give additional collateral; or

(d) a term authorizing a confession of judgment on the instrument if it is not paid when due; or

(e) a term purporting to waive the benefit of any

law intended for the advantage or protection of any obligor; or

(f) a term in a draft providing that the payee by indorsing or cashing it acknowledges full satisfaction of an obligation of the drawer; or

(g) a statement in a draft drawn in a set of parts (Section 3—801) to the effect that the order is effective only if no other part has been honored.

(2) Nothing in this section shall validate any term which is otherwise illegal. As amended 1962.

§ 3—113.   Seal.

An instrument otherwise negotiable is within this Article even though it is under a seal.

§ 3—114.   Date, Antedating, Postdating.

(1) The negotiability of an instrument is not affected by the fact that it is undated, antedated or postdated.

(2) Where an instrument is antedated or postdated the time when it is payable is determined by the stated date if the instrument is payable on demand or at a fixed period after date.

(3) Where the instrument or any signature thereon is dated, the date is presumed to be correct.

§ 3—115.   Incomplete Instruments.

(1) When a paper whose contents at the time of signing show that it is intended to become an instrument is signed while still incomplete in any necessary respect it cannot be enforced until completed, but when it is completed in accordance with authority given it is effective as completed.

(2) If the completion is unauthorized the rules as to material alteration apply (Section 3—407), even though the paper was not delivered by the maker or drawer; but the burden of establishing that any completion is unauthorized is on the party so asserting.

§ 3—116.   Instruments Payable to Two or More Persons.

An instrument payable to the order of two or more persons

(a) if in the alternative payable to any one of them and may be negotiated, discharged or enforced by any of them who has possession of it;

(b) if not in the alternative is payable to all of them and may be negotiated, discharged or enforced only by all of them.

§ 3—117.   Instruments Payable With Words of Description.

An instrument made payable to a named person with the addition of words describing him

(a) as agent or officer of a specified person is payable to his principal but the agent or officer may act as if he were the holder;

(b) as any other fiduciary for a specified person or purpose is payable to the payee and may be negotiated, discharged or enforced by him;

(c) in any other manner is payable to the payee unconditionally and the additional words are without effect on subsequent parties.

§ 3—118. Ambiguous Terms and Rules of Construction.

The following rules apply to every instrument:

(a) Where there is doubt whether the instrument is a draft or a note the holder may treat it as either. A draft drawn on the drawer is effective as a note.

(b) Handwritten terms control typewritten and printed terms, and typewritten control printed.

(c) Words control figures except that if the words are ambiguous figures control.

(d) Unless otherwise specified a provision for interest means interest at the judgment rate at the place of payment from the date of the instrument, or if it is undated from the date of issue.

(e) Unless the instrument otherwise specifies two or more persons who sign as maker, acceptor or drawer or indorser and as a part of the same transaction are jointly and severally liable even though the instrument contains such words as "I promise to pay."

(f) Unless otherwise specified consent to extension authorizes a single extension for not longer than the original period. A consent to extension, expressed in the instrument, is binding on secondary parties and accommodation makers. A holder may not exercise his option to extend an instrument over the objection of a maker or acceptor or other party who in accordance with Section 3—604 tenders full payment when the instrument is due.

§ 3—119. Other Writings Affecting Instrument.

(1) As between the obligor and his immediate obligee or any transferee the terms of an instrument may be modified or affected by any other written agreement executed as a part of the same transaction, except that a holder in due course is not affected by any limitation of his rights arising out of the separate written agreement if he had no notice of the limitation when he took the instrument.

(2) A separate agreement does not affect the negotiability of an instrument.

§ 3—120. Instruments "Payable Through" Bank.

An instrument which states that it is "payable through" a bank or the like designates that bank as a collecting bank to make presentment but does not of itself authorize the bank to pay the instrument.

§ 3—121. Intruments Payable at Bank.

Note: If this Act is introduced in the Congress of the United States this section should be omitted. (States to select either alternative)

Alternative A. A note or acceptance which states that it is payable at a bank is the equivalent of a draft drawn on the bank payable when it falls due out of any funds of the maker or acceptor in current account or otherwise available for such payment.

Alternative B. A note or acceptance which states that it is payable at a bank is not of itself an order or authorization to the bank to pay it.

§ 3—122. Accrual or Cause of Action.

(1) A cause of action against a maker or an acceptor accrues

(a) in the case of a time instrument on the day after maturity;

(b) in the case of a demand instrument upon its date or, if no date is stated, on the date of issue.

(2) A cause of action against the obligor of a demand or time certificate of deposit accrues upon demand, but demand on a time certificate may not be made until on or after the date of maturity.

(3) A cause of action against a drawer of a draft or an indorser of any instrument accrues upon demand following dishonor of the instrument. Notice of dishonor is a demand.

(4) Unless an instrument provides otherwise, interest runs at the rate provided by law for a judgment

(a) in the case of a maker, acceptor or other primary obligor of a demand instrument, from the date of demand;

(b) in all other cases from the date of accrual of the cause of action. As amended 1962.

PART 2. *Transfer and Negotiation.*

§ 3—201. Transfer: Right to Indorsement.

(1) Transfer of an instrument vests in the transferee such rights as the transferor has therein, except that a transferee who has himself been a party to any fraud or illegality affecting the instrument or who as a prior holder had notice of a defense or claim against it cannot improve his position by taking from a later holder in due course.

(2) A transfer of a security interest in an instrument vests the foregoing rights in the transferee to the extent of the interest transferred.

(3) Unless otherwise agreed any transfer for value of an instrument not then payable to bearer gives the transferee the specifically enforceable right to have the unqualified indorsement of the transferor. Negotiation takes effect only when the indorsement is made and until that time there is no presumption that the transferee is the owner.

§ 3—202. Negotiation.

(1) Negotiation is the transfer of an instrument in such form that the transferee becomes a holder. If the instrument is payable to order it is negotiated by delivery with any necessary indorsement; if payable to bearer it is negotiated by delivery.

(2) An indorsement must be written by or on behalf of the holder and on the instrument or on a paper so firmly affixed thereto as to become a part thereof.

(3) An indorsement is effective for negotiation only when it conveys the entire instrument or any unpaid residue. If it purports to be of less it operates only as a partial assignment.

(4) Words of assignment, condition, waiver, guaranty, limitation or disclaimer of liability and the like accompanying an indorsement do not affect its character as an indorsement.

§ 3—203. Wrong or Misspelled Name.

Where an instrument is made payable to a person under a misspelled name or one other than his own he may indorse in that name or his own or both; but signature in both names may be required by a person paying or giving value for the instrument.

§ 3—204. Special Indorsement; Blank Indorsement.

(1) A special indorsement specifies the person to whom or to whose order it makes the instrument payable. Any instrument specially indorsed becomes payable to the order of the special indorsee and may be further negotiated only by his indorsement.

(2) An indorsement in blank specifies no particular indorsee and may consist of a mere signature. An instrument payable to order and indorsed in blank becomes payable to bearer and may be negotiated by delivery alone until specially indorsed.

(3) The holder may convert a blank indorsement into a special indorsement by writing over the signature of the indorser in blank any contract consistent with the character of the indorsement.

§ § 3—205. Restrictive Indorsements.

An indorsement is restrictive which either

    (a) is conditional; or

    (b) purports to prohibit further transfer of the instrument; or

    (c) includes the words "for collection", "for deposit", "pay any bank", or like terms signifying a purpose of deposit or collection; or

    (d) otherwise states that it is for the benefit or use of the indorser or of another person.

§ 3—206. Effect of Restrictive Indorsement.

(1) No restrictive indorsement prevents further transfer or negotiation of the instrument.

(2) An intermediary bank, or a payor bank which is not the depositary bank, is neither given notice nor otherwise affected by a restrictive indorsement of any person except the bank's immediate transferor or the person presenting for payment.

(3) Except for an intermediary bank, any transferee under an indorsement which is conditional or includes the words "for collection", "for deposit", "pay any bank", or like terms (subparagraphs (a) and (c) of Section 3—205) must pay or apply any value given by him for or on the security of the instrument consistently with the indorsement and to the extent that he does so he becomes a holder for value. In addition such transferee is a holder in due course if he otherwise complies with the requirements of Section 3—302 on what constitutes a holder in due course.

(4) The first taker under an indorsement for the benefit of the indorser or another person (subparagraph (d) of Section 3—205) must pay or apply any value given by him for or on the security of the instrument consistently with the indorsement and to the extent that he does so he becomes a holder for value. In addition such taker is a holder in due course if he otherwise complies with the requirements of Section 3—302 on what constitutes a holder in due course. A later holder for value is neither given notice nor otherwise affected by such restrictive indorsement unless he has knowledge that a fiduciary or other person has negotiated the instrument in any transaction for his own benefit or otherwise in breach of duty (subsection (2) of Section 3—304).

§ 3—207. Negotiation Effective Although It May Be Rescinded.

(1) Negotiation is effective to transfer the instrument although the negotiation is

    (a) made by an infant, a corporation exceeding its powers, or any other person without capacity; or

    (b) obtained by fraud, duress or mistake of any kind; or

    (c) part of an illegal transaction; or

    (d) made in breach of duty.

(2) Except as against a subsequent holder in due course such negotiation is in an appropriate case subject to rescission, the declaration of a constructive trust or any other remedy permitted by law.

§ 3—208. Reacquisition.

Where an instrument is returned to or reacquired by a prior party he may cancel any indorsement which is not necessary to his title and reissue or further negotiate the instrument, but any intervening party is discharged as against the reacquiring party and subsequent holders not in due course and if his indorsement has been cancelled is discharged as against subsequent holders in due course as well.

PART 3.   Rights of a Holder.

§ 3—301. Rights of a Holder.

The holder of an instrument whether or not he is the owner may transfer or negotiate it and, expect as otherwise provided in Section 3—603 on payment or satisfaction, discharge it or enforce payment in his own name.

§ 3—302. Holder in Due Course.

(1) A holder in due course is a holder who takes the instrument

    (a) for value; and

    (b) in good faith; and

    (c) without notice that it is overdue or has been dishonored or of any defense against or claim to it on the part of any person.

(2) A payee may be a holder in due course.

(3) A holder does not become a holder in due course of an instrument:

    (a) by purchase of it at judicial sale or by taking it under legal process; or

    (b) by acquiring it in taking over an estate; or

    (c) by purchasing it as part of a bulk transaction not in regular course of business of the transferor.

(4) A purchaser of a limited interest can be a holder in due course only to the extent of the interest purchased.

§ 3—303. Taking for Value.

A holder takes the instrument for value

    (a) to the extent that the agreed consideration has been performed or that he acquires a security interest in or a lien on the instrument otherwise than by legal process; or

    (b) when he takes the instrument in payment of or as security for an antecedent claim against any person whether or not the claim is due; or

    (c) when he gives a negotiable instrument for it or makes an irrevocable commitment to a third person.

§ 3—304. Notice a Purchaser.

(1) The purchaser has notice of a claim or defense if

    (a) the instrument is so incomplete, bears such visible evidence of forgery or alteration, or is otherwise so irregular as to call into question its validity, terms or ownership or to create an ambiguity as to the party to pay; or

    (b) the purchaser has notice that the obligation of any party is voidable in whole or in part, or that all parties have been discharged.

(2) The purchaser has notice of a claim against the instrument when he has knowledge that a fiduciary has negotiated the instrument in payment of or as security for his own debt or in any transaction for his own benefit or otherwise in breach of duty.

(3) The purchaser has notice that an instrument is overdue if he has reason to know

    (a) that any part of the principal amount is overdue or that there is an uncured default in payment of another instrument of the same series; or

    (b) that acceleration of the instrument has been made; or

    (c) that he is taking a demand instrument after demand has been made or more than a reasonable length of time after its issue. A reasonable time for a check drawn and payable within the states and territories of the United States and the District of Columbia is presumed to be thirty days.

(4) Knowledge of the following facts does not of itself give the purchaser notice of a defense or claim

    (a) that the instrument is antedated or postdated;

    (b) that it was issued or negotiated in return for an executory promise or accompanied by a separate agreement, unless the purchaser has notice that a defense or claim has arisen from the terms thereof;

    (c) that any party has signed for accommodation;

    (d) that an incomplete instrument has been completed, unless the purchase has notice of any improper completion;

    (e) that any person negotiating the instrument is or was a fiduciary;

    (f) that there has been default in payment of interest on the instrument or in payment of any other instrument, except one of the same series.

(5) The filing or recording of a document does not of itself constitute notice within the provisions of this Article to a person who would otherwise be a holder in due course.

(6) To be effective notice must be received at such time and in such manner as to give a reasonable opportunity to act on it.

§ 3—305. Rights of a Holder in Due Course.

To the extent that a holder is a holder in due course he takes the instrument free from

    (1) all claims to it on the part of any person; and

    (2) all defenses of any party to the instrument with whom the holder has not dealt except

(a) infancy, to the extent that it is a defense to a simple contract; and

(b) such other incapacity, or duress, or illegality of the transaction, as renders the obligation of the party a nullity; and

(c) such misrepresentation as has induced the party to sign the instrument with neither knowledge nor reasonable opportunity to obtain knowledge of its character or its essential terms; and

(d) discharge in insolvency proceedings; and

(e) any other discharge of which the holder has notice when he takes the instrument.

§ 3—306. Rights of One Not Holder in Due Course.

Unless he has the rights of a holder in due course any person takes the instrument subject to

(a) all valid claims to it on the part of any person; and

(b) all defenses of any party which would be available in an action on a simple contract; and

(c) the defenses of want or failure of consideration, non-performance of any condition precedent, non-delivery, or delivery for a special purpose (Section 3—408); and

(d) the defense that he or a person through whom he holds the instrument acquired it by theft, or that payment or satisfaction to such holder would be inconsistent with the terms of a restrictive indorsement. The claim of any third person to the instrument is not otherwise available as a defense to any party liable thereon unless the third person himself defends the action for such party.

§ 3—307. Burden of Establishing Signatures, Defenses and Due Course.

(1) Unless specifically denied in the pleadings each signature on an instrument is admitted. When the effectiveness of a signature is put in issue

(a) The burden of establishing it is on the party claiming under the signature; but

(b) the signature is presumed to be genuine or authorized except where the action is to enforce the obligation of a purported signer who has died or become incompetent before proof is required.

(2) When signatures are admitted or established, production of the instrument entitles a holder to recover on it unless the defendant establishes a defense.

(3) After it is shown that a defense exists a person claiming the rights of a holder in due course has the burden of establishing that he or some person under whom he claims is in all respects a holder in due course.

PART 4. Liability of Parties.

§ 3—401. Signature.

(1) No person is liable on an instrument unless his signature appears thereon.

(2) A signature is made by use of any name, including any trade or assumed name, upon an instrument, or by any word or mark used in lieu of a written signature.

§ 3—402. Signature in Ambiguous Capacity.

Unless the instrument clearly indicates that a signature is made in some other capacity it is an indorsement.

§ 3—403. Signature by Authorized Representative.

(1) A signature may be made by an agent or other representative, and his authority to make it may be established as in other cases of representation. No particular form of appointment is necessary to establish such authority.

(2) An authorized representative who signs his own name to an instrument

(a) is personally obligated if the instrument neither names the person represented nor shows that the representative signed in a representative capacity;

(b) except as otherwise established between the immediate parties, is personally obligated if the instrument names the person represented but does not show that the representative signed in a representative capacity, or if the instrument does not name the person represented but does show that the representative signed in a representative capacity.

(3) Except as otherwise established the name of an organization preceded or followed by the name and office of an authorized individual is a signature made in a representative capacity.

§ 3—404. Unauthorized Signatures.

(1) Any unauthorized signature is wholly inoperative as that of the person whose name is signed unless he ratifies it or is precluded from denying it; but it operates as the signature of the unauthorized signer in favor of any person who in good faith pays the instrument or takes it for value.

(2) Any unauthorized signature may be ratified for all purposes of this Article. Such ratification does not of itself affect any rights of the person ratifying against the actual signer.

§ 3—405. Impostors; Signature in Name of Payee.

(1) An indorsement by any person in the name of a named payee is effective if

(a) an impostor by use of mails or otherwise has induced the maker or drawer to issue the instrument to him or his confederate in the name of the payee; or

(b) a person signing as or on behalf of a maker or drawer intends the payee to have no interest in the instrument; or

(c) an agent or employee of the maker or drawer has supplied him with the name of the payee intending the latter to have no such interest.

(2) Nothing in this section shall affect the criminal or civil liability of the person so indorsing.

§ 3—406. Negligence Contributing to Alteration or Unauthorized Signature.

Any person who by his negligence substantially contributes to a material alteration of the instrument or to the making of an unauthorized signature is precluded from asserting the alteration or lack of authority against a holder in due course or against a drawee or other payor who pays the instrument in good faith and in accordance with the reasonable commercial standards of the drawee's or payor's business.

§ 3—407. Alteration.

(1) Any alteration of an instrument is material which changes the contract of any party thereto in any respect, including any such change in

(a) the number or relations of the parties; or

(b) an incomplete instrument, by completing it otherwise than as authorized; or

(c) the writing as signed, by adding to it or by removing any part of it.

(2) As against any person other than a subsequent holder in due course,

(a) alteration by the holder which is both fraudulent and material discharges any party whose contract is thereby changed unless that party assents or is precluded from asserting the defense;

(b) no other alteration discharges any party and the instrument may be enforced according to its original tenor, or as to incomplete instruments according to the authority given.

(3) A subsequent holder in due course may in all cases enforce the instrument according to its original tenor, and when an incomplete instrument has been completed, he may enforce it as completed.

§ 3—408. Consideration.

Want or failure of consideration is a defense as against any person not having the rights of a holder in due course (Section 3—305), except that no consideration is necessary for an instrument or obligation thereon given in payment of or as security for an antecedent obligation of any kind. Nothing in this section shall be taken to displace any statute outside this Act under which a promise is enforceable notwithstanding lack or failure of considera-

tion. Partial failure of consideration is a defense pro tanto whether or not the failure is in an ascertained or liquidated amount.

§ 3—409. Draft Not an Assignment.

(1) A check or other draft does not of itself operate as an assignment of any funds in the hands of the drawee available for its payment, and the drawee is not liable on the instrument until he accepts it.

(2) Nothing in this section shall affect any liability in contract, tort or otherwise arising from any letter of credit or other obligation or representation which is not an acceptance.

§ 3—410. Definition and Operation of Acceptance.

(1) Acceptance is the drawee's signed engagement to honor the draft as presented. It must be written on the draft, and may consist of his signature alone. It becomes operative when completed by delivery or notification.

(2) A draft may be accepted although it has not been signed by the drawer or is otherwise incomplete or is overdue or has been dishonored.

(3) Where the draft is payable at a fixed period after sight and the acceptor fails to date his acceptance the holder may complete it by supplying a date in good faith.

§ 3—411. Certification of a Check.

(1) Certification of a check is acceptance. Where a holder procures certification the drawer and all prior indorsers are discharged.

(2) Unless otherwise agreed a bank has no obligation to certify a check.

(3) A bank may certify a check before returning it for lack of proper indorsement. If it does so the drawer is discharged.

§ 3—412. Acceptance Varying Draft.

(1) Where the drawee's proffered acceptance in any manner varies the draft as presented the holder may refuse the acceptance and treat the draft as dishonored in which case the drawee is entitled to have this acceptance cancelled.

(2) The terms of the draft are not varied by an acceptance to pay at any particular bank or place in the United States, unless the acceptance states that the draft is to be paid only at such bank or place.

(3) Where the holder assents to an acceptance varying the terms of the draft each drawer and indorser who does not affirmatively assent is discharged. As amended 1962.

§ 3—413. Contract of Maker, Drawer and Acceptor.

(1) The maker or acceptor engages that he will pay the instrument according to its tenor at the time of his engagement or as completed pursuant to Section 3—115 on incomplete instruments.

(2) The drawer engages that upon dishonor of the draft and any necessary notice of dishonor or protest he will pay the amount of the draft to the holder or to any indorser who takes it up. The drawer may disclaim this liability by drawing without recourse.

(3) By making, drawing or accepting the party admits as against all subsequent parties including the drawee the existence of the payee and his then capacity to indorse.

§ 3—414. Contract of Indorser; Order of Liability.

(1) Unless the indorsement otherwise specifies (as by such words as "without recourse") every indorser engages that upon dishonor and any necessary notice of dishonor and protest he will pay the instrument according to its tenor at the time of his indorsement to the holder or to any subsequent indorser who takes it up, even though the indorser who takes it up was not obligated to do so.

(2) Unless they otherwise agree indorsers are liable to one another in the order in which they indorse, which is presumed to be the order in which their signatures appear on the instrument.

§ 3—415. Contract of Accommodation Party.

(1) An accommodation party is one who signs the instrument in any capacity for the purpose of lending his name to another party to it.

(2) When the instrument has been taken for value before it is due the accommodation party is liable in the capacity in which he has signed even though the taker knows of the accommodation.

(3) As against a holder in due course and without notice of the accommodation oral proof of the accommodation is not admissible to give the accommodation party the benefit of discharges dependent on his character as such. In other cases the accommodation character may be shown by oral proof.

(4) An indorsement which shows that it is not in the chain of title is notice of its accommodation character.

(5) An accommodation party is not liable to the party accommodated, and if he pays the instrument has a right of recourse on the instrument against such party.

§ 3—416. Contract of Guarantor.

(1) "Payment guaranteed" or equivalent words added to a signature mean that the signer engages that if the instrument is not paid when due he will pay it according to its tenor without resort by the holder to any other party.

(2) "Collection guaranteed" or equivalent words added to a signature mean that the signer engages that if the instrument is not paid when due he will pay it according to its tenor, but only after the holder has reduced his claim against the maker or acceptor to judgment and execution has been returned unsatisfied, or after the

maker or acceptor has become insolvent or it is otherwise apparent that it is useless to proceed against him.

(3) Words of guaranty which do not otherwise specify guarantee payment.

(4) No words of guaranty added to the signature of a sole maker or acceptor affect his liability on the instrument. Such words added to the signature of one of two or more makers or acceptors create a presumption that the signature is for the accommodation of the others.

(5) When words of guaranty are used presentment, notice of dishonor and protest are not necessary to charge the user.

(6) Any guaranty written on the instrument is enforceable notwithstanding any statute of frauds.

§ 3—417. Warranties on Presentment and Transfer.

(1) Any person who obtains payment or acceptance and any prior transferor warrants to a person who in good faith pays or accepts that

    (a) he has a good title to the instrument or is authorized to obtain payment or acceptance on behalf of one who has a good title; and

    (b) he has no knowledge that the signature of the maker or drawer is unauthorized, except that this warranty is not given by a holder in due course acting in good faith

        (i) to a maker with respect to the maker's own signature; or

        (ii) to a drawer with respect to the drawer's own signature, whether or not the drawer is also the drawee; or

        (iii) to an acceptor of a draft if the holder in due course took the draft after the acceptance or obtained the acceptance without knowledge that the drawer's signature was unauthorized; and

    (c) the instrument has not been materially altered, except that this warranty is not given by a holder in due course acting in good faith

        (i) to the maker of a note; or

        (ii) to the drawer of a draft whether or not the drawer is also the drawee; or

        (iii) to the acceptor of a draft with respect to an alteration made prior to the acceptance if the holder in due course took the draft after the acceptance, even though the acceptance provided "payable as originally drawn" or equivalent terms; or

        (iv) to the acceptor of a draft with respect to an alteration made after the acceptance.

(2) Any person who transfers an instrument and receives consideration warrants to his transferee and if the transfer is by indorsement to any subsequent holder who takes the instrument in good faith that

    (a) he has a good title to the instrument or is authorized to obtain payment or acceptance on behalf of one who has a good title and the transfer is otherwise rightful; and

(b) all signatures are genuine or authorized; and

(c) the instrument has not been materially altered; and

(d) no defense of any party is good against him; and

(e) he has no knowledge of any insolvency proceeding instituted with respect to the maker or acceptor or the drawer of an unaccepted instrument.

(3) By transferring ''without recourse'' the transferor limits the obligation stated in subsection (2)(d) to a warranty that he has no knowledge of such a defense.

(4) A selling agent or broker who does not disclose the fact that he is acting only as such gives the warranties provided in this section, but if he makes such disclosure warrants only his good faith and authority.

§ 3—418. Finality of Payment or Acceptance.

Except for recovery of bank payments as provided in the Article on Bank Deposits and Collections (Article 4) and except for liability for breach of warranty on presentment under the preceding section, payment or acceptance of any instrument is final in favor of a holder in due course, or a person who has in good faith changed his position in reliance on the payment.

§ 3—419. Conversion of Instrument; Innocent Representative.

(1) An instrument is converted when

(a) a drawee to whom it is delivered for acceptance refuses to return it on demand; or

(b) any person to whom it is delivered for payment refuses on demand either to pay or to return it; or

(c) it is paid on a forged indorsement.

(2) In an action against a drawee under subsection (1) the measure of the drawee's liability is the face amount of the instrument. In any other action under subsection (1) the measure of liability is presumed to be the face amount of the instrument.

(3) Subject to the provisions of this Act concerning restrictive indorsements a representative, including a depositary or collecting bank, who has in good faith and in accordance with the reasonable commercial standards applicable to the business of such representative dealt with an instrument or its proceeds on behalf of one who was not the true owner is not liable in conversion or otherwise to the true owner beyond the amount of any proceeds remaining in his hands.

(4) An intermediary bank or payor bank which is not a depositary bank is not liable in conversion solely by reason of the fact that proceeds of an item indorsed restrictively (Sections 3—205 and 3—206) are not paid or

applied consistently with the restrictive indorsement of an indorser other than its immediate transferor.

PART 5. *Presentment, Notice of Dishonor and Protest.*

§ 3—501. When Presentment, Notice of Dishonor, and Protest Necessary or Permissible.

(1) Unless excused (Section 3—511) presentment is necessary to charge secondary parties as follows:

(a) presentment for acceptance is necessary to charge the drawer and indorsers of a draft where the draft so provides, or is payable elsewhere than at the residence or place of business of the drawee, or its date of payment depends upon such presentment. The holder may at his option present for acceptance any other draft payable at a stated date;

(b) presentment for payment is necessary to charge any indorser;

(c) in the case of any drawer, the acceptor of a draft payable at a bank or the maker of a note payable at a bank, presentment for payment is necessary, but failure to make presentment discharges such drawer, acceptor or maker only as stated in Section 3—502(1)(b).

(2) Unless excused (Section 3—511)

(a) notice of any dishonor is necessary to charge any indorser;

(b) in the case of any drawer, the acceptor of a draft payable at a bank or the maker of a note payable at a bank, notice of any dishonor is necessary, but failure to give such notice discharges such drawer, acceptor or maker only as stated in Section 3—502(1)(b).

(3) Unless excused (Section 3—511) protest of any dishonor is necessary to charge the drawer and indorsers of any draft which on its face appears to be drawn or payable outside of the states, territories, dependencies and possessions of the United States, the District of Columbia and the Commonwealth of Puerto Rico. The holder may at his option make protest of any dishonor of any other instrument and in the case of a foreign draft may on insolvency of the acceptor before maturity make protest for better security.

(4) Notwithstanding any provision of this section, neither presentment nor notice of dishonor nor protest is necessary to charge an indorser who has indorsed an instrument after maturity. As amended 1966.

§ 3—502. Unexcused Delay; Discharge.

(1) Where without excuse any necessary presentment or notice of dishonor is delayed beyond the time when it is due

(a) any indorser is discharged; and

(b) any drawer or the acceptor of a draft payable at a bank or the maker of a note payable at a bank who because the drawee or payor bank becomes insolvent during the delay is deprived of funds maintained with the drawee or payor bank to cover the instrument may discharge his liability by written assignment to the holder of his rights against the drawee or payor bank in respect of such funds, but such drawer, acceptor or maker is not otherwise discharged.

(2) Where without excuse a necessary protest is delayed beyond the time when it is due any drawer or indorser is discharged.

§ 3—503. Time of Presentment.

(1) Unless a different time is expressed in the instrument the time for any presentment is determined as follows:

    (a) where an instrument is payable at or a fixed period after a stated date any presentment for acceptance must be made on or before the date it is payable;

    (b) where an instrument is payable after sight it must either be presented for acceptance or negotiated within a reasonable time after date or issue, whichever is later;

    (c) where an instrument shows the date on which it is payable presentment for payment is due on that date;

    (d) where an instrument is accelerated presentment for payment is due within a reasonable time after the acceleration;

    (e) with respect to the liability of any secondary party presentment for acceptance or payment of any other instrument is due within a reasonable time after such party becomes liable thereon.

(2) A reasonable time for presentment is determined by the nature of the instrument, any usage of banking or trade and the facts of the particular case. In the case of an uncertified check which is drawn and payable within the United States and which is not a draft drawn by a bank the following are presumed to be reasonable periods within which to present for payment or to initiate bank collection:

    (a) with respect to the liability of the drawer, thirty days after date or issue, whichever is later; and

    (b) with respect to the liability of an indorser, seven days after his indorsement.

(3) Where any presentment is due on a day which is not a full business day for either the person making presentment or the party to pay or accept, presentment is due on the next following day which is a full business day for both parties.

(4) Presentment to be sufficient must be made at a reasonable hour, and if at a bank during its banking day.

§ 3—504. How Presentment Is Made.

(1) Presentment is a demand for acceptance or payment made upon the maker, acceptor, drawee or other payor by or on behalf of the holder.

(2) Presentment may be made

    (a) by mail, in which event the time of presentment is determined by the time of receipt of the mail; or

    (b) through a clearing house; or

    (c) at the place of acceptance or payment specified in the instrument or if there be none at the place of business or residence of the party to accept or pay. If neither the party to accept or pay nor anyone authorized to act for him is present or accessible at such place presentment is excused.

(3) It may be made

    (a) to any one of two or more makers, acceptors, drawees or other payors; or

    (b) to any person who has authority to make or refuse the acceptance or payment.

(4) A draft accepted or a note made payable at a bank in the United States must be presented at such bank.

(5) In the cases described in Section 4—210 presentment may be made in the manner and with the result stated in that section. As amended 1962.

§ 3—505. Rights of Party to Whom Presentment Is Made.

(1) The party to whom presentment is made may without dishonor require

    (a) exhibition of the instrument; and

    (b) reasonable identification of the person making presentment and evidence of his authority to make it if made for another; and

    (c) that the instrument be produced for acceptance or payment at a place specified in it, or if there be none at any place reasonable in the circumstances; and

    (d) a signed receipt on the instrument for any partial or full payment and its surrender upon full payment.

(2) Failure to comply with any such requirement invalidates the presentment but the person presenting has a reasonable time in which to comply and the time for acceptance or payment runs from the time of compliance.

§ 3—506. Time Allowed for Acceptance or Payment.

(1) Acceptance may be deferred without dishonor until the close of the next business day following presentment. The holder may also in a good faith effort to obtain acceptance and without either dishonor of the instrument or discharge of secondary parties allow postponement of acceptance for an additional business day.

(2) Except as a longer time is allowed in the case of

documentary drafts drawn under a letter of credit, and unless an earlier time is agreed to by the party to pay, payment of an instrument may be deferred without dishonor pending reasonable examination to determine whether it is properly payable, but payment must be made in any event before the close of business on the day of presentment.

§ 3—507. Dishonor; Holder's Right of Recourse; Term Allowing Re-Presentment.

(1) An instrument is dishonored when

    (a) a necessary or optional presentment is duly made and due acceptance or payment is refused or cannot be obtained within the prescribed time or in case of bank collections the instrument is seasonably returned by the midnight deadline (Section 4—301); or

    (b) presentment is excused and the instrument is not duly accepted or paid.

(2) Subject to any necessary notice of dishonor and protest, the holder has upon dishonor an immediate right of recourse against the drawers and indorsers.

(3) Return of an instrument for lack of proper indorsement is not dishonor.

(4) A term in a draft or an indorsement thereof allowing a stated time for re-presentment in the event of any dishonor of the draft by nonacceptance if a time draft or by nonpayment if a sight draft gives the holder as against any secondary party bound by the term an option to waive the dishonor without affecting the liability of the secondary party and he may present again up to the end of the stated time.

§ 3—508. Notice of Dishonor.

(1) Notice of dishonor may be given to any person who may be liable on the instrument by or on behalf of the holder or any party who has himself received notice, or any other party who can be compelled to pay the instrument. In addition an agent or bank in whose hands the instrument is dishonored may give notice to his principal or customer or to another agent or bank from which the instrument was received.

(2) Any necessary notice must be given by a bank before its midnight deadline and by any other person before midnight of the third business day after dishonor or receipt of notice of dishonor.

(3) Notice may be given in any reasonable manner. It may be oral or written and in any terms which identify the instrument and state that it has been dishonored. A misdescription which does not mislead the party notified does not vitiate the notice. Sending the instrument bearing a stamp, ticket or writing stating that acceptance or payment has been refused or sending a notice of debit with respect to the instrument is sufficient.

(4) Written notice is given when sent although it is not received.

(5) Notice to one partner is notice to each although the firm has been dissolved.

(6) When any party is in insolvency proceedings instituted after the issue of the instrument notice may be given either to the party or to the representative of his estate.

(7) When any party is dead or incompetent notice may be sent to his last known address or given to his personal representative.

(8) Notice operates for the benefit of all parties who have rights on the instrument against the party notified.

§ 3—509. Protest; Noting for Protest.

(1) A protest is a certificate of dishonor made under the hand and seal of a United States consul or vice consul or a notary public or other person authorized to certify dishonor by the law of the place where dishonor occurs. It may be made upon information satisfactory to such person.

(2) The protest must identify the instrument and certify either that due presentment has been made or the reason why it is excused and that the instrument has been dishonored by nonacceptance or nonpayment.

(3) The protest may also certify that notice of dishonor has been given to all parties or to specified parties.

(4) Subject to subsection (5) any necessary protest is due by the time that notice of dishonor is due.

(5) If, before protest is due, an instrument has been noted for protest by the officer to make protest, the protest may be made at any time thereafter as of the date of the noting.

§ 3—510. Evidence of Dishonor and Notice of Dishonor.

The following are admissible as evidence and create a presumption of dishonor and of any notice of dishonor therein shown:

    (a) a document regular in form as provided in the preceding section which purports to be a protest;

    (b) the purported stamp or writing of the drawee, payor bank or presenting bank on the instrument or accompanying it stating that acceptance or payment has been refused for reasons consistent with dishonor;

    (c) any book or record of the drawee, payor bank, or any collecting bank kept in the usual course of business which shows dishonor, even though there is no evidence of who made the entry.

§ 3—511. Waived or Excused Presentment, Protest or Notice of Dishonor or Delay Therein.

(1) Delay in presentment, protest or notice of dishonor is excused when the party is without notice that it is due or when the delay is caused by circumstances beyond his

control and he exercises reasonable diligence after the cause of the delay ceases to operate.

(2) Presentment or notice or protest as the case may be is entirely excused when

    (a) the party to be charged has waived it expressly or by implication either before or after it is due; or

    (b) such party has himself dishonored the instrument or has countermanded payment or otherwise has no reason to expect or right to require that the instrument be accepted or paid; or

    (c) by reasonable diligence the presentment or protest cannot be made or the notice given.

(3) Presentment is also entirely excused when

    (a) the maker, acceptor or drawee of any instrument except a documentary draft is dead or in insolvency proceedings instituted after the issue of the instrument; or

    (b) acceptance or payment is refused but not for want of proper presentment.

(4) Where a draft has been dishonored by nonacceptance a later presentment for payment and any notice of dishonor and protest for nonpayment are excused unless in the meantime the instrument has been accepted.

(5) A waiver of protest is also a waiver of presentment and of notice of dishonor even though protest is not required.

(6) Where a waiver of presentment or notice or protest is embodied in the instrument itself it is binding upon all parties; but where it is written above the signature of an indorser it binds him only.

PART 6.   *Discharge.*

§ 3—601.   Discharge of Parties.

(1) The extent of the discharge of any party from liability on an instrument is governed by the sections on

    (a) payment or satisfaction (Section 3—603); or

    (b) tender of payment (Section 3—604); or

    (c) cancellation or renunciation (Section 3—605); or

    (d) impairment of right of recourse or of collateral (Section 3—606); or

    (e) reacquisition of the instrument by a prior party (Section 3—208); or

    (f) fraudulent and material alteration (Section 3—407); or

    (g) certification of a check (Section 3—411); or

    (h) acceptance varying a draft (Section 3—412); or

    (i) unexcused delay in presentment or notice of dishonor or protest (Section 3—502).

(2) Any party is also discharged from his liability on an instrument to another party by any other act or agreement with such party which would discharge his simple contract for the payment of money.

(3) The liability of all parties is discharged when any party who has himself no right of action or recourse on the instrument

    (a) reacquires the instrument in his own right; or

    (b) is discharged under any provision of this Article, except as otherwise provided with respect to discharge for impairment of recourse or of collateral (Section 3—606).

§ 3—602.   Effect of Discharge Against Holder in Due Course.

No discharge of any party provided by this Article is effective against a subsequent holder in due course unless he has notice thereof when he takes the instrument.

§ 3—603.   Payment or Satisfaction.

(1) The liability of any party is discharged to the extent of his payment or satisfaction to the holder even though it is made with knowledge of a claim of another person to the instrument unless prior to such payment or satisfaction the person making the claim either supplies indemnity deemed adequate by the party seeking the discharge or enjoins payment or satisfaction by order of a court of competent jurisdiction in an action in which the adverse claimant and the holder are parties. This subsection does not, however, result in the discharge of the liability

    (a) of a party who in bad faith pays or satisfies a holder who acquired the instrument by theft or who (unless having the rights of a holder in due course) holds through one who so acquired it; or

    (b) of a party (other than an intermediary bank or a payor bank which is not a depositary bank) who pays or satisfies the holder of an instrument which has been restrictively indorsed in a manner not consistent with the terms of such restrictive indorsement.

(2) Payment or satisfaction may be made with the consent of the holder by any person including a stranger to the instrument. Surrender of the instrument to such a person gives him the rights of a transferee (Section 3—201).

§ 3—604.   Tender of Payment.

(1) Any party making tender of full payment to a holder when or after it is due is discharged to the extent of all subsequent liability for interest, costs and attorney's fees.

(2) The holder's refusal of such tender wholly discharges any party who has a right of recourse against the party making the tender.

(3) Where the maker or acceptor of an instrument payable otherwise than on demand is able and ready to pay at every place of payment specified in the instrument when it is due, it is equivalent to tender.

§ 3—605. Cancellation and Renunciation.

(1) The holder of an instrument may even without consideration discharge any party

    (a) in any manner apparent on the face of the instrument or the indorsement, as by intentionally cancelling the instrument or the party's signature by destruction or mutilation, or by striking out the party's signature; or

    (b) by renouncing his rights by a writing signed and delivered or by surrender of the instrument to the party to be discharged.

(2) Neither cancellation nor renunciation without surrender of the instrument affects the title thereto.

§ 3—606. Impairment of Recourse or of Collateral.

(1) The holder discharges any party to the instrument to the extent that without such party's consent the holder

    (a) without express reservation of rights releases or agrees not to sue any person against whom the party has to the knowledge of the holder a right of recourse or agrees to suspend the right to enforce against such person the instrument or collateral or otherwise discharges such person, except that failure or delay in effecting any required presentment, protest or notice of dishonor with respect to any such person does not discharge any party as to whom presentment, protest or notice of dishonor is effective or unnecessary; or

    (b) unjustifiably impairs any collateral for the instrument given by or on behalf of the party or any person against whom he has a right of recourse.

(2) By express reservation of rights against a party with a right of recourse the holder preserves

    (a) all his rights against such party as of the time when the instrument was originally due; and

    (b) the right of the party to pay the instrument as of that time; and

    (c) all rights of such party to recourse against others.

PART 7. *Advice of International Sight Draft.*

§ 3—701. Letter of Advice of International Sight Draft.

(1) A "letter of advice" is a drawer's communication to the drawee that a described draft has been drawn.

(2) Unless otherwise agreed when a bank receives from another bank a letter of advice of an international sight draft the drawee bank may immediately debit the drawer's account and stop the running of interest pro tanto. Such a debit and any resulting credit to any account covering outstanding drafts leaves in the drawer full power to stop payment or otherwise dispose of the amount and creates no trust or interest in favor of the holder

(3) Unless otherwise agreed and except where a draft is drawn under a credit issued by the drawee, the drawee of an international sight draft owes the drawer no duty to pay an unadvised draft but if it does so and the draft is genuine, may appropriately debit the drawer's account.

PART 8. *Miscellaneous.*

§ 3—801. Drafts in a Set.

(1) Where a draft is drawn in a set of parts, each of which is numbered and expressed to be an order only if no other part has been honored, the whole of the parts constitutes one draft but a taker of any part may become a holder in due course of the draft.

(2) Any person who negotiates, indorses or accepts a single part of a draft drawn in a set thereby becomes liable to any holder in due course of that part as if it were the whole set, but as between different holders in due course to whom different parts have been negotiated the holder whose title first accrues has all rights to the draft and its proceeds.

(3) As against the drawee that first presented part of a draft drawn in a set is the part entitled to payment, or if a time draft to acceptance and payment. Acceptance of any subsequently presented part renders the drawee liable thereon under subsection (2). With respect both to a holder and to the drawer payment of a subsequently presented part of a draft payable at sight has the same effect as payment of a check notwithstanding an effective stop order (Section 4—407).

(4) Except as otherwise provided in this section, where any part of a draft in a set is discharged by payment or otherwise the whole draft is discharged.

§ 3—802. Effect of Instrument on Obligation for Which It Is Given.

(1) Unless otherwise agreed where an instrument is taken for an underlying obligation

    (a) the obligation is pro tanto discharged if a bank is drawer, maker or acceptor of the instrument and there is no recourse on the instrument against the underlying obligor; and

    (b) in any other case the obligation is suspended pro tanto until the instrument is due or if it is payable on demand until its presentment. If the instrument is dishonored action may be maintained on either the instrument or the obligation; discharge of the underlying obligor on the instrument also discharges him on the obligation.

(2) The taking in good faith of a check which is not postdated does not of itself so extend the time on the original obligation as to discharge a surety.

§ 3—803. Notice to Third Party.

Where a defendant is sued for breach of an obligation for which a third person is answerable over under this Article he may give the third person written notice of the litigation, and the person notified may then give similar notice to any other person who is answerable over to him under this Article. If the notice states that the person notified may come in and defend and that if the person notified does not do so he will in any action against him by the person giving the notice be bound by any determination of fact common to the two litigations, then unless after seasonable receipt of the notice the person notified does come in and defend he is so bound.

§ 3—804.   Lost, Destroyed or Stolen Instruments.

The owner of an instrument which is lost, whether by destruction, theft or otherwise, may maintain an action in his own name and recover from any party liable thereon upon due proof of his ownership, the facts which prevent his production of the instrument and its terms. The court may require security indemnifying the defendant against loss by reason of further claims on the instrument.

§ 3—805.   Instruments Not Payable to Order or to Bearer.

This Article applies to any instrument whose terms do not preclude transfer and which is otherwise negotiable within this Article but which is not payable to order or to bearer, except that there can be no holder in due course of such an instrument.

ARTICLE 4.   Bank Deposits and Collections

PART 1.   *General Provisions and Definitions.*

§ 4—101.   Short Title.

This Article shall be known and may be cited as Uniform Commercial Code—Bank Deposits and Collections.

§ 4—102.   Applicability.

(1) To the extent that items within this Article are also within the scope of Articles 3 and 8, they are subject to the provisions of those Articles. In the event of conflict the provisions of this Article govern those of Article 3 but the provisions of Article 8 govern those of this Article.

(2) The liability of a bank for action or non-action with respect to any item handled by it for purposes of presentment, payment or collection is governed by the law of the place where the bank is located. In the case of action or non-action by or at a branch or separate office of a bank, its liability is governed by the law of the place where the branch or separate office is located.

§ 4—103.   Variation by Agreement; Measure of Damages; Certain Action Constituting Ordinary Care.

(1) The effect of the provisions of this Article may be varied by agreement except that no agreement can dis-

claim a bank's responsibility for its own lack of good faith or failure to exercise ordinary care or can limit the measure of damages for such lack or failure; but the parties may by agreement determine the standards by which such responsibility is to be measured if such standards are not manifestly unreasonable.

(2) Federal Reserve regulations and operating letters, clearinghouse rules, and the like, have the effect of agreement under subsection (1), whether or not specifically assented to by all parties interested in items handled.

(3) Action or non-action approved by this Article or pursuant to Federal Reserve regulations or operating letters constitutes the exercise of ordinary care and, in the absence of special instructions, action or non-action consistent with clearinghouse rules and the like or with a general banking usage not disapproved by this Article, prima facie constitutes the exercise of ordinary care.

(4) The specification or apprval of certain procedures by the Article does not constitute disapproval of other procedures which may be reasonable under the circumstances.

(5) The measure of damages for failure to exercise ordinary care in handling an item is the amount of the item reduced by an amount which could not have been realized by the use of ordinary care, and where there is bad faith it includes other damages, if any, suffered by the party as a proximate consequence.

§ 4—104.   Definition and Index of Definitions.

(1) In this Article unless the context otherwise requires

(a) "Account" means any account with a bank and includes a checking, time, interest or savings account;

(b) "Afternoon" means the period of a day between noon and midnight;

(c) "Banking day" means that part of any day on which a bank is open to the public for carrying on substantially all of its banking functions;

(d) "Clearinghouse" means any association of banks or other payors regularly clearing items;

(e) "Customer" means any person having an account with a bank or for whom a bank has agreed to collect items and includes a bank carrying an account with another bank;

(f) "Documentary draft" means any negotiable or non-negotiable draft with accompanying documents, securities or other papers to be delivered against honor of the draft;

(g) "Item" means any instrument for the payment of money even though it is not negotiable but does not include money;

(h) "Midnight deadline" with respect to a bank is midnight on its next banking day following the banking day on which it receives the relevant item or notice or from which the time for taking action commences to run, whichever is later;

(i) "Properly payable" includes the availability of funds for payment at the time of decision to pay or dishonor;

(j) "Settle" means to pay in cash, by clearing house settlement, in a charge or credit or by remittance, or otherwise as instructed. A settlement may be either provisional or final;

(k) "Suspends payments" with respect to a bank means that it has been closed by order of the supervisory authorities, that a public officer has been appointed to take it over or that it ceases or refuses to make payments in the ordinary course of business.

(2) Other definitions applying to this Article and the sections in which they appear are:

"Collecting bank"	Section 4—105.
"Depositary bank"	Section 4—105.
"Intermediary bank"	Section 4—105.
"Payor bank"	Section 4—105.
"Presenting bank"	Section 4—105.
"Remitting bank"	Section 4—105.

(3) The following definitions in other Articles apply to this Article:

"Acceptance"	Section 3—410.
"Certificate of deposit"	Section 3—104.
"Certification"	Section 3—411.
"Check"	Section 3—104.
"Draft"	Section 3—104.
"Holder in due course"	Section 3—302.
"Notice of dishonor"	Section 3—508.
"Presentment"	Section 3—504.
"Protest"	Section 3—509.
"Secondary party"	Section 3—102.

(4) In addition Article 1 contains general definitions and principles of construction and interpretation applicable throughout this Article.

§ 4—105. "Depositary Bank"; "Intermediary Bank"; "Collecting Bank"; "Payor Bank"; "Presenting Bank"; "Remitting Bank".

In this Article unless the context otherwise requires:

(a) "Depositary bank" means the first bank to which an item is transferred for collection even though it is also the payor bank;

(b) "Payor bank" means a bank by which an item is payable as drawn or accepted;

(c) "Intermediary bank" means any bank to which an item is transferred in course of collection except the depositary or payor bank;

(d) "Collecting bank" means any bank handling the item for collection except the payor bank;

(e) "Presenting bank" means any bank presenting an item except a payor bank;

(f) "Remitting bank" means any payor or intermediary bank remitting for an item.

§ 4—106. Separate Office of a Bank.

A branch or separate office of a bank [maintaining its own deposit ledgers] is a separate bank for the purpose of computing the time within which and determining the place at or to which action may be taken or notices or orders shall be given under this Article and under Article 3. As amended 1962.

> **Note:** The brackets are to make it optional with the several states whether to require a branch to maintain its own deposit ledgers in order to be considered to be a separate bank for certain purposes under Article 4. In some states "maintaining its own deposit ledgers" is a satisfactory test. In others branch banking practices are such that this test would not be suitable.

§ 4—107. Time of Receipt of Items.

(1) For the purpose of allowing time to process items, prove balances and make the necessary entries on its books to determine its position for the day, a bank may fix an afternoon hour of 2 P.M. or later as a cut-off hour for the handling of money and items and the making of entries on its books.

(2) Any item or deposit of money received on any day after a cut-off hour so fixed or after the close of the banking day may be treated as being received at the opening of the next banking day.

§ 4—108. Delays.

(1) Unless otherwise instructed, a collecting bank in a good faith effort to secure payment may, in the case of specific items and with or without the approval of any person involved, waive, modify or extend time limits imposed or permitted by this Act for a period not in excess of an additional banking day without discharge of secondary parties and without liability to its transferor or any prior party.

(2) Delay by a collecting bank or payor bank beyond time limits prescribed or permitted by this Act or by instructions is excused if caused by interruption of communication facilities, suspension of payments by another bank, war, emergency conditions or other circumstances beyond the control of the bank provided it exercises such diligence as the circumstances require.

§ 4—109 Process of Posting.

The "process of posting" means the usual procedure followed by a payor bank in determining to pay an item and in recording the payment including one or more of the following or other steps as determined by the bank:

(a) verification of any signature;

(b) ascertaining that sufficient funds are available;

(c) affixing a "paid" or other stamp;

(d) entering a charge or entry to a customer's account;

(e) correcting or reversing an entry or erroneous action with respect to the item. Added 1962.

PART 2. Collection of Items: Depositary and Collecting Banks.

§ 4—201. Presumption and Duration of Agency Status of Collecting Banks and Provisional Status of Credits; Applicability of Article; Item Indorsed "Pay Any Bank".

(1) Unless a contrary intent clearly appears and prior to the time that a settlement given by a collecting bank for an item is or becomes final (subsection (3) of Section 4—211 and Sections 4—212 and 4—213) the bank is an agent or sub-agent of the owner of the item and any settlement given for the item is provisional. This provision applies regardless of the form of indorsement or lack of indorsement and even though credit given for the item is subject to immediate withdrawal as of right or is in fact withdrawn; but the continuance of ownership of an item by its owner and any rights of the owner to proceeds of the item are subject to rights of a collecting bank such as those resulting from outstanding advances on the item and valid rights of setoff. When an item is handled by banks for purposes of presentment, payment and collection, the relevant provisions of this Article apply even though action of parties clearly establishes that a particular bank has purchased the item and is the owner of it.

(2) After an item has been indorsed with the words "pay any bank" or the like, only a bank may acquire the rights of a holder

(a) until the item has been returned to the customer initiating collection; or

(b) until the item has been specially indorsed by a bank to a person who is not a bank.

§ 4—202. Responsibility for Collection; When Action Seasonable.

(1) A collecting bank must use ordinary care in

(a) presenting an item or sending it for presentment; and

(b) sending notice of dishonor or non-payment or returning an item other than a documentary draft to the bank's transferor [or directly to the depositary bank under subsection (2) of Section 4—212] *(see note to Section 4—212)* after learning that the item has not been paid or accepted, as the case may be; and

(c) settling for an item when the bank receives final settlement; and

(d) making or providing for any necessary protest; and

(e) notifying its transferor of any loss or delay in transit within a reasonable time after discovery thereof.

(2) A collecting bank taking proper action before its midnight deadline following receipt of an item, notice or payment acts seasonably; taking proper action within a reasonably longer time may be seasonable but the bank has the burden of so establishing.

(3) Subject to subsection (1) (a), a bank is not liable for the insolvency, neglect, misconduct, mistake or default of another bank or person or for loss or destruction of an item in transit or in the possession of others.

§ 4—203. Effect of Instructions.

Subject to the provisions of Article 3 concerning conversion of instruments (Section 3—419) and the provisions of both Article 3 and this Article concerning restrictive indorsements only a collecting bank's transferor can give instructions which affect the bank or constitute notice to it and a collecting bank is not liable to prior parties for any action taken pursuant to such instructions or in accordance with any agreement with its transferor.

§ 4—204. Methods of Sending and Presenting; Sending Direct to Payor Bank.

(1) A collecting bank must send items by reasonably prompt method taking into consideration any relevant instructions, the nature of the item, the number of such items on hand, and the cost of collection involved and the method generally used by it or others to present such items.

(2) A collecting bank may send

(a) any item direct to the payor bank;

(b) any item to any non-bank payor if authorized by its transferor; and

(c) any item other than documentary drafts to any non-bank payor, if authorized by Federal Reserve regulation or operating letter, clearinghouse rule or the like.

(3) Presentment may be made by a presenting bank at a place where the payor bank has requested that presentment be made. As amended 1962.

§ 4—205. Supplying Missing Indorsement; No Notice from Prior Indorsement.

(1) A depositary bank which has taken an item for collection may supply any indorsement of the customer which is necessary to title unless the item contains the words "payee's indorsement required" or the like. In the absence of such a requirement a statement placed on the item by the depositary bank to the effect that the item was deposited by a customer or credited to his account is effective as the customer's indorsement.

(2) An intermediary bank, or payor bank which is not a depositary bank, is neither given notice nor otherwise affected by a restrictive indorsement of any person except the bank's immediate transferor.

§ 4—206. Transfer Between Banks.

Any agreed method which identifies the transferor bank is sufficient for the item's further transfer to another bank.

§ 4—207. Warranties of Customer and Collecting Bank on Transfer or Presentment of Items; Time for Claims.

(1) Each customer or collecting bank who obtains payment or acceptance of an item and each prior customer and collecting bank warrants to the payor bank or other payor who in good faith pays or accepts the item that

    (a) he has a good title to the item or is authorized to obtain payment or acceptance on behalf of one who has a good title; and

    (b) he has no knowledge that the signature of the maker or drawer is unauthorized, except that this warranty is not given by any customer or collecting bank that is a holder in due course and acts in good faith

        (i) to a maker with respect to the maker's own signature; or

        (ii) to a drawer with respect to the drawer's own signature, whether or not the drawer is also the drawee; or

        (iii) to an acceptor of an item if the holder in due course took the item after the acceptance or obtained the acceptance without knowledge that the drawer's signature was unauthorized; and

    (c) the item has not been materially altered, except that this warranty is not given by any customer or collecting bank that is a holder in due course and acts in good faith

        (i) to the maker of a note; or

        (ii) to the drawer of a draft whether or not the drawer is also the drawee; or

        (iii) to the acceptor of an item with respect to an alteration made prior to the acceptance if the holder in due course took the item after the acceptance, even though the acceptance provided "payable as originally drawn" or equivalent terms; or

        (iv) to the acceptor of an item with respect to an alteration made after the acceptance.

(2) Each customer and collecting bank who transfers an item and receives a settlement or other consideration for it warrants to his transferee and to any subsequent collecting bank who takes the item in good faith that

    (a) he has a good title to the item or is authorized to obtain payment or acceptance on behalf of one who has a good title and the transfer is otherwise rightful; and

    (b) all signatures are genuine or authorized; and

    (c) the item has not been materially altered; and

    (d) no defense of any party is good against him; and

    (e) he has no knowledge of any insolvency proceeding instituted with respect to the maker or acceptor or the drawer of an unaccepted item.

In addition each customer and collecting bank so transferring an item and receiving a settlement or other consideration engages that upon dishonor and any necessary notice of dishonor and protest he will take up the item.

(3) The warranties and the engagement to honor set forth in the two preceding subsections arise notwithstanding the absence of indorsement or words of guaranty or warranty in the transfer or presentment and a collecting bank remains liable for their breach despite remittance to its transferor. Damages for breach of such warranties or engagement to honor shall not exceed the consideration received by the customer or collecting bank responsible plus finance charges and expenses related to the item, if any.

(4) Unless a claim for breach of warranty under this section is made within a reasonable time after the person claiming learns of the breach, the person liable is discharged to the extent of any loss caused by the delay in making claim.

§ 4—208. Security Interest of Collecting Bank in Items, Accompanying Documents and Proceeds.

(1) A bank has a security interest in an item and any accompanying documents or the proceeds of either

    (a) in case of an item deposited in an account to the extent to which credit given for the item has been withdrawn or applied;

    (b) in case of an item for which it has given credit available for withdrawal as of right, to the extent of the credit given whether or not the credit is drawn upon and whether or not there is a right of charge-back; or

    (c) if it makes an advance on or against the item.

(2) When credit which has been given for several items received at one time or pursuant to a single agreement is withdrawn or applied in part the security interest remains upon all the items, any accompanying documents or the proceeds of either. For the purpose of this section, credits first given are first withdrawn.

(3) Receipt by a collecting bank of a final settlement for an item is a realization on its security interest in the item, accompanying documents and proceeds. To the extent and so long as the bank does not receive final settlement for the item or give up possession of the item or accompanying documents for purposes other than collection, the security interest continues and is subject to the provisions of Article 9 except that

    (a) no security agreement is necessary to make the security interest enforceable (subsection (1)(a) of Section 9–203); and

(b) no filing is required to perfect the security interest; and

(c) the security interest has priority over conflicting perfected security interests in the item, accompanying documents or proceeds.

§ 4—209. When Bank Gives Value for Purposes of Holder in Due Course.

For purposes of determining its status as a holder in due course, the bank has given value to the extent that it has a security interest in an item provided that the bank otherwise complies with the requirements of Section 3—302 on what constitutes a holder in due course.

§ 4—210. Presentment by Notice of Item Not Payable by, Through or at a Bank; Liability of Secondary Parties.

(1) Unless otherwise instructed, a collecting bank may present an item not payable by, through or at a bank by sending to the party to accept or pay a written notice that the bank holds the item for acceptance or payment. The notice must be sent in time to be received on or before the day when presentment is due and the bank must meet any requirement of the party to accept or pay under Section 3—505 by the close of the bank's next banking day after it knows of the requirement.

(2) Where presentment is made by notice and neither honor nor request for compliance with a requirement under Section 3—505 is received by the close of business on the day after maturity or in the case of demand items by the close of business on the third banking day after notice was sent, the presenting bank may treat the item as dishonored and charge any secondary party by sending him notice of the facts.

§ 4—211. Media of Remittance; Provisional and Final Settlement in Remittance Cases.

(1) A collecting bank may take in settlement of an item

(a) a check of the remitting bank or of another bank on any bank except the remitting bank; or

(b) a cashier's check or similar primary obligation of a remitting bank which is a member of or clears through a member of the same clearinghouse or group as the collecting bank; or

(c) appropriate authority to charge an account of the remitting bank or of another bank with the collecting bank; or

(d) if the item is drawn upon or payable by a person other than a bank, a cashier's check, certified check or other bank check or obligation.

(2) If before its midnight deadline the collecting bank properly dishonors a remittance check or authorization to charge on itself or presents or forwards for collection a remittance instrument of or on another bank which is of a kind approved by subsection (1) or has not been authorized by it, the collecting bank is not liable to prior parties in the event of the dishonor of such check, instrument or authorization.

(3) A settlement for an item by means of a remittance instrument or authorization to charge is or becomes final a settlement as to both the person making and the person receiving the settlement

(a) if the remittance instrument or authorization to charge is of a kind approved by subsection (1) or has not been authorized by the person receiving the settlement and in either case the person receiving the settlement acts seasonably before its midnight deadline in presenting, forwarding for collection or paying the instrument or authorization,—at the time the remittance instrument or authorization is finally paid by the payor by which it is payable;

(b) if the person receiving the settlement has authorized remittance by a non-bank check or obligation or by a cashier's check or similar primary obligation of or a check upon the payor or other remitting bank which is not of a kind approved by subsection (1) (b),—at the time of the receipt of such remittance check or obligation; or

(c) if in a case not covered by subparagraphs (a) or (b) the person receiving the settlement fails to seasonably present, forward for collection, pay or return a remittance instrument or authorization to it to charge before its midnight deadline,—at such midnight deadline.

§ 4—212. Right of Charge-Back or Refund.

(1) If a collecting bank has made provisional settlement with its customer for an item and itself fails by reason of dishonor, suspension of payments by a bank or otherwise to receive a settlement for the item which is or becomes final, the bank may revoke the settlement given by it, charge back the amount of any credit given for the item to its customer's account or obtain refund from its customer whether or not it is able to return the items if by its midnight deadline or within a longer reasonable time after it learns the facts it returns the item or sends notification of the facts. These rights to revoke, charge-back and obtain refund terminate if and when a settlement for the item received by the bank is or becomes final (subsection (3) of Section 4—211 and subsections (2) and (3) of Section 4—213).

[(2) Within the time and manner prescribed by this section and Section 4—301, an intermediary or payor bank, as the case may be, may return an unpaid item directly to the depositary bank and may send for collection a draft on the depositary bank and obtain reimbursement. In such case, if the depositary bank has received provisional settlement for the item, it must reimburse the bank drawing the draft and any provisional credits for the item between banks shall become and remain final.]

> **Note:** Direct returns is recognized as an innovation that is not yet established bank practice, and therefore, Paragraph 2 has been bracketed. Some lawyers have doubts whether it should be included in legislation or left to development by agreement.

(3) A depositary bank which is also the payor may charge-back the amount of an item to its customer's account or obtain refund in accordance with the section governing return of an item received by a payor bank for credit on its books. (Section 4—301).

(4) The right to charge-back is not affected by

    (a) prior use of the credit given for the item; or

    (b) failure by any bank to exercise ordinary care with respect to the item but any bank so failing remains liable.

(5) A failure to charge-back or claim refund does not affect other rights of the bank against the customer or any other party.

(6) If credit is given in dollars as the equivalent of the value of an item payable in a foreign currency the dollar amount of any charge-back or refund shall be calculated on the basis of the buying sight rate for the foreign currency prevailing on the day when the person entitled to the charge-back or refund learns that it will not receive payment in ordinary course.

§ 4—213. Final Payment of Item by Payor Bank; When Provisional Debits and Credits Become Final; When Certain Credits Become Available for Withdrawal.

(1) An item is finally paid by a payor bank when the bank has done any of the following, whichever happens first:

    (a) paid the item in cash; or

    (b) settled for the item without reserving a right to revoke the settlement and without having such right under statute, clearing house rule or agreement; or

    (c) completed the process of posting the item to the indicated account of the drawer, maker or other person to be charged therewith; or

    (d) made a provisional settlement for the item and failed to revoke the settlement in the time and manner permitted by statute, clearing house rule or agreement.

Upon a final payment under subparagraphs (b), (c) or (d) the payor bank shall be accountable for the amount of the item.

(2) If provisional settlement for an item between the presenting and payor banks is made through a clearing house or by debits or credits in an account between them, then to the extent that provisional debits or credits for the item are entered in accounts between the presenting and payor banks or between the presenting and successive prior collecting banks seriatim, they become final upon final payment of the item by the payor bank.

(3) If a collecting bank receives a settlement for an item which is or becomes final (subsection (3) of Section 4—211, subsection (2) of Section 4—213) the bank is accountable to its customer for the amount of the item and any provisional credit given for the item in an account with its customer becomes final.

(4) Subject to any right of the bank to apply the credit to an obligation of the customer, credit given by a bank for an item in an account with its customer becomes available for withdrawal as of right

    (a) in any case where the bank has received a provisional settlement for the item,—when such settlement becomes final and the bank has had a reasonable time to learn that the settlement is final;

    (b) in any case where the bank is both a depositary bank and a payor bank and the item is finally paid,—at the opening of the bank's second banking day following receipt of the item.

(5) A deposit of money in a bank is final when made but, subject to any right of the bank to apply the deposit to an obligation of the customer, the deposit becomes available for withdrawal as of right at the opening of the bank's next banking day following receipt of the deposit.

§ 4—214. Insolvency and Preference.

(1) Any item in or coming into the possession of a payor or collecting bank which suspends payment and which item is not finally paid shall be returned by the receiver, trustee or agent in charge of the closed bank to the presenting bank or the closed bank's customer.

(2) If a payor bank finally pays an item and suspends payments without making a settlement for the item with its customer or the presenting bank which settlement is or becomes final, the owner of the item has a preferred claim against the payor bank.

(3) If a payor bank gives or a collecting bank gives or receives a provisional settlement for an item and thereafter suspends payments, the suspension does not prevent or interfere with the settlement becoming final if such finality occurs automatically upon the lapse of certain time or the happening of certain events (subsection (3) of Section 4—211, subsections (1) (d), (2) and (3) of Section 4—213).

(4) If a collecting bank receives from subsequent parties settlement for an item which settlement is or becomes final and suspends payments without making a

settlement for the item with its customer which is or becomes final, the owner of the item has a preferred claim against such collecting bank.

PART 3. Collection of Items: Payor Banks.

§ 4—301. Deferred Posting; Recovery of Payment by Return of Items; Time of Dishonor.

(1) Where an authorized settlement for a demand item (other than a documentary draft) received by a payor bank otherwise than for immediate payment over the counter has been made before midnight of the banking day of receipt the payor bank may revoke the settlement and recover any payment if before it has made final payment (subsection (1) of Section 4—213) and before its midnight deadline it

   (a) returns the item; or
   (b) sends written notice of dishonor or nonpayment if the item is held for protest or is otherwise unavailable for return.

(2) If a demand item is received by a payor bank for credit on its books it may return such item or send notice of dishonor and may revoke any credit given or recover the amount thereof withdrawn by its customer, if it acts within the time limit and in the manner specified in the preceding subsection.

(3) Unless previous notice of dishonor has been sent an item is dishonored at the time when for purposes of dishonor it is returned or notice sent in accordance with this section.

(4) An item is returned:

   (a) as to an item received through a clearing house, when it is delivered to the presenting or last collecting bank or to the clearing house or is sent or delivered in accordance with its rules; or
   (b) in all other cases, when it is sent or delivered to the bank's customer or transferor or pursuant to his instructions.

§ 4—302. Payor Bank's Responsibility for Late Return of Item.

In the absence of a valid defense such as breach of a presentment warranty (subsection (1) of Section 4—207), settlement effected or the like, if an item is presented on and received by a payor bank the bank is accountable for the amount of

   (a) a demand item other than a documentary draft whether properly payable or not if the bank, in any case where it is not also the depositary bank, retains the item beyond midnight of the banking day of receipt without settling for it or, regardless of whether it is also the depositary bank, does not pay or return the item or send notice of dishonor until after its midnight deadline; or
   (b) any other properly payable item unless within the time allowed for acceptance or payment of that item the bank either accepts or pays the item or returns it and accompanying documents.

§ 4—303. When Items Subject to Notice, Stop-Order, Legal Process or Setoff; Order in Which Items May Be Charged or Certified.

(1) Any knowledge, notice or stop-order received by, legal process served upon or setoff exercised by a payor bank, whether or not effective under other rules of law to terminate, suspend or modify the bank's right or duty to pay an item or to charge its customer's account for the item, comes too late to so terminate, suspend or modify such right or duty if the knowledge, notice, stop-order or legal process is received or served and a reasonable time for the bank to act thereon expires or the setoff is exercised after the bank has done any of the following:

   (a) accepted or certified the item;
   (b) paid the item in cash;
   (c) settled for the item without reserving a right to revoke the settlement and without having such right under statute, clearinghouse rule or agreement;
   (d) completed the process of posting the item to the indicated account of the drawer, maker or other person to be charged therewith or otherwise has evidenced by examination of such indicated account and by action its decision to pay the item; or
   (e) become accountable for the amount of the item under subsection (1) (d) of Section 4—213 and Section 4—302 dealing with the payor bank's responsibility for late return of items.

(2) Subject to the provisions of subsection (1) items may be accepted, paid, certified or charged to the indicated account of its customer in any order convenient to the bank.

PART 4. Relationship Between Payor Bank and Its Customer.

§ 4—401. When Bank May Charge Customer's Account.

(1) As against its customer, a bank may charge against his account any item which is otherwise properly payable from that account even though the charge creates an overdraft.

(2) A bank which in good faith makes payment to a holder may charge the indicated account of its customer according to

   (a) the original tenor of his altered item; or
   (b) the tenor of his completed item, even though the bank knows the item has been completed unless the bank has notice that the completion was improper.

§ 4—402. Bank's Liability to Customer for Wrongful Dishonor.

A payor bank is liable to its customer for damages proximately caused by the wrongful dishonor of an item. When the dishonor occurs through mistake liability is limited to actual damages proved. If so proximately caused and proved damages may include damages for an arrest or prosecution of the customer or other consequential damages. Whether any consequential damages are proximately caused by the wrongful dishonor is a question of fact to be determined in each case.

§ 4—403. Customer's Right to Stop Payment; Burden of Proof of Loss.

(1) A customer may by order to his bank stop payment of any item payable for his account but the order must be received at such time and in such manner as to afford the bank a reasonable opportunity to act on it prior to any action by the bank with respect to the item described in Section 4—303.

(2) An oral order is binding upon the bank only for fourteen calendar days unless confirmed in writing within that period. A written order is effective for only six months unless renewed in writing.

(3) The burden of establishing the fact and amount of loss resulting from the payment of an item contrary to a binding stop payment order is on the customer.

§ 4—404. Bank Not Obligated to Pay Check More Than Six Months Old.

A bank is under no obligation to a customer having a checking account to pay a check, other than a certified check, which is presented more than six months after its date, but it may charge its customer's account for a payment made thereafter in good faith.

§ 4—405. Death or Incompetence of Customer.

(1) A payor or collecting bank's authority to accept, pay or collect an item or to account for proceeds of its collection if otherwise effective is not rendered ineffective by incompetence of a customer of either bank existing at the time the item is issued or its collection is undertaken if the bank does not know of an adjudication of incompetence. Neither death nor incompetence of a customer revokes such authority to accept, pay, collect or account until the bank knows of the fact of death or of an adjudication of incompetence and has reasonable opportunity to act on it.

(2) Even with knowledge a bank may for ten days after the date of death pay or certify checks drawn on or prior to that date unless ordered to stop payment by a person claiming an interest in the account.

§ 4—406. Customer's Duty to Discover and Report Unauthorized Signature or Alteration.

(1) When a bank sends to its customer a statement of account accompanied by items paid in good faith in support of the debit entries or holds the statement and items pursuant to a request for instructions of its customer or otherwise in a reasonable manner makes the statement and items available to the customer, the customer must exercise reasonable care and promptness to examine the statement and items to discover his unauthorized signature or any alteration on an item and must notify the bank promptly after discovery thereof.

(2) If the bank establishes that the customer failed with respect to an item to comply with the duties imposed on the customer by subsection (1) the customer is precluded from asserting against the bank

(a) his unauthorized signature or any alteration on the item if the bank also establishes that it suffered a loss by reason of such failure; and

(b) an unauthorized signature or alteration by the same wrongdoer on any other item paid in good faith by the bank after the first item and statement was available to the customer for a reasonable period not exceeding fourteen calendar days and before the bank receives notification from the customer of any such unauthorized signature or alteration.

(3) The preclusion under subsection (2) does not apply if the customer establishes lack of ordinary care on the part of the bank in paying the item(s).

(4) Without regard to care or lack of care of either the customer or the bank a customer who does not within one year from the time the statement and items are made available to the customer (subsection (1)) discover and report his unauthorized signature or any alteration on the face or back of the item or does not within three years from that time discover and report any unauthorized indorsement is precluded from asserting against the bank such unauthorized signature or indorsement or such alteration.

(5) If under this section a payor bank has a valid defense against a claim of a customer upon or resulting from payment of an item and waives or fails upon request to assert the defense the bank may not assert against any collecting bank or other prior party presenting or transferring the item a claim based upon the unauthorized signature or alteration giving rise to the customer's claim.

§ 4—407. Payor Bank's Right to Subrogation on Improper Payment.

If a payor bank has paid an item over the stop payment order of the drawer or maker or otherwise under circumstances giving a basis for objection by the drawer or maker, to prevent unjust enrichment and only to the extent necessary to prevent loss to the bank by reason of its payment of the item, the payor bank shall be subrogated to the rights

(a) of any holder in due course on the item against the drawer or maker; and

(b) of the payee or any other holder of the item against the drawer or maker either on the item or under the transaction out of which the item arose; and

(c) of the drawer or maker against the payee or any other holder of the item with respect to the transaction out of which the item arose.

PART 5. *Collection of Documentary Drafts.*

§ 4—501. Handling of Documentary Drafts; Duty to Send for Presentment and to Notify Customer of Dishonor.

A bank which takes a documentary draft for collection must present or send the draft and accompanying documents for presentment and upon learning that the draft has not been paid or accepted in due course must seasonably notify its customer of such fact even though it may have discounted or bought the draft or extended credit available for withdrawal as of right.

§ 4—502. Presentment of "On Arrival" Draft.

When a draft or the relevant instructions require presentment "on arrival", "when goods arrive" or the like, the collecting bank need not present until in its judgment a reasonable time for arrival of the goods has expired. Refusal to pay or accept because the goods have not arrived is not dishonor; the bank must notify its transferor of such refusal but need not present the draft again until it is instructed to do so or learns of the arrival of the goods.

§ 4—503. Responsibility of Presenting Bank for Documents and Goods; Report of Reasons for Dishonor; Referee in Case of Need.

Unless otherwise instructed and except as provided in Article 5 a bank presenting a documentary draft

(a) must deliver the documents to the drawee on acceptance of the draft if it is payable more than three days after presentment; otherwise, only on payment; and

(b) upon dishonor, either in the case of presentment for acceptance or presentment for payment, may seek and follow instructions from any referee in case of need designated in the draft or if the presenting bank does not choose to utilize his services it must use diligence and good faith to ascertain the reason for dishonor, must notify its transferor of the dishonor and of the results of its effort to ascertain the reasons therefor and must request instructions.

But the presenting bank is under no obligation with respect to goods represented by the documents except to follow any reasonable instructions seasonably received; it has a right to reimbursement for any expense incurred in following instructions and to prepayment of or indemnity for such expenses.

§ 4—504. Privilege of Presenting Bank to Deal With Goods; Security Interest for Expenses.

(1) A presenting bank which, following the dishonor of a documentary draft, has seasonably requested instructions but does not receive them within a reasonable time may store, sell, or otherwise deal with the goods in any reasonable manner.

(2) For its reasonable expenses incurred by action under subsection (1) the presenting bank has a lien upon the goods or their proceeds, which may be foreclosed in the same manner as an unpaid seller's lien.

ARTICLE 5. Letters of Credit

§ 5—101. Short Title.

This Article shall be known and may be cited as Uniform Commercial Code—Letters of Credit.

§ 5—102. Scope.

(1) This Article applies

(a) to a credit issued by a bank if the credit requires a documentary draft or a documentary demand for payment; and

(b) to a credit issued by a person other than a bank if the credit requires that the draft or demand for payment be accompanied by a document of title; and

(c) to a credit issued by a bank or other person if the credit is not within subparagraphs (a) or (b) but conspicuously state that it is a letter of credit or is conspicuously so entitled.

(2) Unless the engagement meets the requirements of subsection (1), this Article does not apply to engagements to make advances or to honor drafts or demands for payment, to authorities to pay or purchase, to guarantees or to general agreements.

(3) This Article deals with some but not all of the rules and concepts of letters of credit as such rules or concepts have developed prior to this act or may hereafter develop. The fact that this Article states a rule does not by itself require, imply or negate application of the same or a converse rule to a situation not provided for or to a person not specified by this Article.

§ 5—103. Definitions.

(1) In this Article unless the context otherwise requires

(a) "Credit" or "letter of credit" means an engagement by a bank or other person made at the request of a customer and of a kind within the scope of this Article (Section 5—102) that the issuer will honor drafts or other demands for payment upon compliance with the conditions specified in the credit. A credit may be either revocable or irrevocable. The engagement may be either an agreement to honor or a statement that the bank or other person is authorized to honor.

(b) A "documentary draft" or a "documentary demand for payment" is one honor of which is conditioned upon the presentation of a document or documents. "Document" means any paper including document of title, security, invoice, certificate, notice of default and the like.

(c) An "issuer" is a bank or other person issuing a credit.

(d) A "beneficiary" of a credit is a person who is entitled under its terms to draw or demand payment.

(e) An "advising bank" is a bank which gives notification of the issuance of a credit by another bank.

(f) A "confirming bank" is a bank which engages either that it will itself honor a credit already issued by another bank or that such a credit will be honored by the issuer or a third bank.

(g) A "customer" is a buyer or other person who causes an issuer to issue a credit. The term also includes a bank which procures issuance or confirmation on behalf of that bank's customer.

(2) Other definitions applying to this Article and the sections in which they appear are:

"Notation of Credit".	Section 5—108.
"Presenter".	Section 5—112(3).

(3) Definitions in other Articles applying to this Article and the sections in which they appear are:

"Accept" or "Acceptance".	Section 3—410.
"Contract for sale".	Section 2—106.
"Draft".	Section 3—104.
"Holder in due course".	Section 3—302.
"Midnight deadline".	Section 4—104.
"Security".	Section 8—102.

(4) In addition, Article 1 contains general definitions and principles of construction and interpretation applicable throughout this Article.

§ 5—104. Formal Requirements; Signing.

(1) Except as otherwise required in subsection (1) (c) of Section 5—102 on scope, no particular form of phrasing is required for a credit. A credit must be in writing and signed by the issuer and a confirmation must be in writing and signed by the confirming bank. A modification of the terms of a credit or confirmation must be signed by the issuer or confirming bank.

(2) A telegram may be a sufficient signed writing if it identifies its sender by an authorized authentication. The authentication may be in code and the authorized naming of the issuer in an advice of credit is a sufficient signing.

§ 5—105. Consideration.

No consideration is necessary to establish a credit or to enlarge or otherwise modify its terms.

§ 5—106. Time and Effect of Establishment of Credit.

(1) Unless otherwise agreed a credit is established

(a) as regards the customer as soon as a letter of credit is sent to him or the letter of credit or an authorized written advice of its issuance is sent to the beneficiary; and

(b) as regards the beneficiary when he receives a letter of credit or an authorized written advice of its issuance.

(2) Unless otherwise agreed once an irrevocable credit is established as regards the customer it can be modified or revoked only with the consent of the customer and once it is established as regards the beneficiary it can be modified or revoked only with his consent.

(3) Unless otherwise agreed after a revocable credit is established it may be modified or revoked by the issuer without notice to or consent from the customer or beneficiary.

(4) Notwithstanding any modification or revocation of a revocable credit any person authorized to honor or negotiate under the terms of the original credit is entitled to reimbursement for or honor of any draft or demand for payment duly honored or negotiated before receipt of notice of the modification or revocation and the issuer in turn is entitled to reimbursement from its customer.

§ 5—107. Advice of Credit; Confirmation; Error in Statement of Terms.

(1) Unless otherwise specified an advising bank by advising a credit issued by another bank does not assume any obligation to honor drafts drawn or demands for payment made under the credit but it does assume obligation for the accuracy of its own statement.

(2) A confirming bank by confirming a credit becomes directly obligated on the credit to the extent of its confirmation as though it were its issuer and acquires the rights of an issuer.

(3) Even though an advising bank incorrectly advises the terms of a credit it has been authorized to advise the credit is established as against the issuer to the extent of its original terms.

(4) Unless otherwise specified the customer bears as against the issuer all risks of transmission and reasonable translation or interpretation of any message relating to a credit.

§ 5—108. "Notation Credit"; Exhaustion of Credit.

(1) A credit which specifies that any person purchasing or paying drafts drawn or demands for payment made under it must note the amount of the draft or demand on the letter or advice of credit is a "notation credit".

(2) Under a notation credit

    (a) a person paying the beneficiary or purchasing a draft or demand for payment from him acquires a right to honor only if the appropriate notation is made and by transferring or forwarding for honor the documents under the credit such a person warrants to the issuer that the notation has been made; and

    (b) unless the credit or a signed statement that an appropriate notation has been made accompanies the draft or demand for payment the issuer may delay honor until evidence of notation has been procured which is satisfactory to it but its obligation and that of its customer continue for a reasonable time not exceeding thirty days to obtain such evidence.

(3) If the credit is not a notation credit

    (a) the issuer may honor complying drafts or demands for payment presented to it in the order in which they are presented and is discharged pro tanto by honor of any such draft or demand;

    (b) as between competing good faith purchasers of complying drafts or demands the person first purchasing has priority over a subsequent purchaser even though the later purchased draft or demand has been first honored.

§ 5—109.   Issuer's Obligation to Its Customer.

(1) An issuer's obligation to its customer includes good faith and observance of any general banking usage but unless otherwise agreed does not include liability or responsibility

    (a) for performance of the underlying contract for sale or other transaction between the customer and the beneficiary; or

    (b) for any act or omission of any person other than itself or its own branch or for loss or destruction of a draft, demand or document in transit or in the possession of others; or

    (c) based on knowledge or lack of knowledge of any usage of any particular trade.

(2) An issuer must examine documents with care so as to ascertain that on their face they appear to comply with the terms of the credit but unless otherwise agreed assumes no liability or responsibility for the genuineness, falsification or effect of any document which appears on such examination to be regular on its face.

(3) A non-bank issuer is not bound by any banking usage of which it has no knowledge.

§ 5—110.   Availability of Credit in Portions; Presenter's Reservation of Lien or Claim.

(1) Unless otherwise specified a credit may be used in portions in the discretion of the beneficiary.

(2) Unless otherwise specified a person by presenting a documentary draft or demand for payment under a credit relinquishes upon its honor all claims to the documents and a person by transferring such draft or demand or causing such presentment authorizes such relinquishment. An explicit reservation of claim makes the draft or demand noncomplying.

§ 5—111.   Warranties on Transfer and Presentment.

(1) Unless otherwise agreed the beneficiary by transferring or presenting a documentary draft or demand for payment warrants to all interested parties that the necessary conditions of the credit have been complied with. This is in addition to any warranties arising under Articles 3, 4, 7 and 8.

(2) Unless otherwise agreed a negotiating, advising, confirming, collecting or issuing bank presenting or transferring a draft or demand for payment under a credit warrants only the matters warranted by a collecting bank under Article 4 and any such bank transferring a document warrants only the matters warranted by an intermediary under Articles 7 and 8.

§ 5—112.   Time Allowed for Honor or Rejection; Withholding Honor or Rejection by Consent; "Presenter".

(1) A bank to which a documentary draft or demand for payment is presented under a credit may without dishonor of the draft, demand or credit

    (a) defer honor until the close of the third banking day following receipt of the documents; and

    (b) further defer honor if the presenter has expressly or impliedly consented thereto.

Failure to honor within the time here specified constitutes dishonor of the draft or demand and of the credit [except as otherwise provided in subsection (4) of Section 5—114 on conditional payment].

> **Note:** The bracketed language in the last sentence of subsection (1) should be included only if the optional provisions of Section 5—114(4) and (5) are included.

(2) Upon dishonor the bank may unless otherwise instructed fulfill its duty to return the draft or demand and the documents by holding them at the disposal of the presenter and sending him an advice to that effect.

(3) "Presenter" means any person presenting a draft or demand for payment for honor under a credit even though that person is a confirming bank or other correspondent which is acting under an issuer's authorization.

§ 5—113.   Indemnities.

(1) A bank seeking to obtain (whether for itself or another) honor, negotiation or reimbursement under a credit may give an indemnity to induce such honor, negotiation or reimbursement.

(2) An indemnity agreement inducing honor, negotiation or reimbursement

(a) unless otherwise explicitly agreed applies to defects in the documents but not in the goods; and

(b) unless a longer time is explicitly agreed expires at the end of ten business days following receipt of the documents by the ultimate customer unless notice of objection is sent before such expiration date. The ultimate customer may send notice of objection to the person from whom he received the documents and any bank receiving such notice is under a duty to send notice to its transferor before its midnight deadline.

§ 5—114. Issuer's Duty and Privilege to Honor; Right to Reimbursement.

(1) An issuer must honor a draft or demand for payment which complies with the terms of the relevant credit regardless of whether the goods or documents conform to the underlying contract for sale or other contract between the customer and the beneficiary. The issuer is not excused from honor of such a draft or demand by reason of an additional general term that all documents must be satisfactory to the issuer, but an issuer may require that specified documents must be satisfactory to it.

(2) Unless otherwise agreed when documents appear on their face to comply with the terms of a credit but a required document does not in fact conform to the warranties made on negotiation or transfer of a document of title (Section 7—507) or of a certificated security (Section 8—306) or is forged or fraudulent or there is fraud in the transaction:

(a) the issuer must honor the draft or demand for payment if honor is demanded by a negotiating bank or other holder of the draft or demand which has taken the draft or demand under the credit and under circumstances which would make it a holder in due course (Section 3—302) and in an appropriate case would make it a person to whom a document of title has been duly negotiated (Section 7—502) or a bona fide purchaser of a certificated security (Section 8—302); and

(b) in all other cases as against its customer, an issuer acting in good faith may honor the draft or demand for payment despite notification from the customer of fraud, forgery or other defect not apparent on the face of the documents but a court of appropriate jurisdiction may enjoin such honor.

(3) Unless otherwise agreed an issuer which has duly honored a draft or demand for payment is entitled to immediate reimbursement of any payment made under the credit and to be put in effectively available funds not later than the day before maturity of any acceptance made under the credit.

[(4) When a credit provides for payment by the issuer on receipt of notice that the required documents are in the possession of a correspondent or other agent of the issuer

(a) any payment made on receipt of such notice is conditional; and

(b) the issuer may reject documents which do not comply with the credit if it does so within three banking days following its receipt of the documents; and

(c) in the event of such rejection, the issuer is entitled by charge back or otherwise to return of the payment made.]

[(5) In the case covered by subsection (4) failure to reject documents within the time specified in subparagraph (b) constitutes acceptance of the documents and makes the payment final in favor of the beneficiary.] Amended in 1977.

> **Note:** Subsections (4) and (5) are bracketed as optional. If they are included the bracketed language in the last sentence of Section 5—112(1) should also be included.

§ 5—115. Remedy for Improper Dishonor or Anticipatory Repudiation.

(1) When an issuer wrongfully dishonors a draft or demand for payment presented under a credit the person entitled to honor has with respect to any documents the rights of a person in the position of a seller (Section 2—707) and may recover from the issuer the face amount of the draft or demand together with incidental damages under Section 2—710 on seller's incidental damages and interest but less any amount realized by resale or other use or disposition of the subject matter of the transaction. In the event no resale or other utilization is made the documents, goods or other subject matter involved in the transaction must be turned over to the issuer on payment of judgment.

(2) When an issuer wrongfully cancels or otherwise repudiates a credit before presentment of a draft or demand for payment drawn under it the beneficiary has the rights of a seller after anticipatory repudiation by the buyer under Section 2—610 if he learns of the repudiation in time reasonably to avoid procurement of the required documents. Otherwise the beneficiary has an immediate right of action for wrongful dishonor.

§ 5—116. Transfer and Assignment.

(1) The right to draw under a credit can be transferred or assigned only when the credit is expressly designated as transferable or assignable.

(2) Even though the credit specifically states that it is nontransferable or nonassignable the beneficiary may be-

fore performance of the conditions of the credit assign his right to proceeds. Such an assignment is an assignment of an account under Article 9 on Secured Transactions and is governed by that Article except that

    (a) the assignment is ineffective until the letter of credit or advice of credit is delivered to the assignee which delivery constitutes perfection of the security interest under Article 9; and

    (b) the issuer may honor drafts or demands for payment drawn under the credit until it receives a notification of the assignment signed by the beneficiary which reasonably identifies the credit involved in the assignment and contains a request to pay the assignee; and

    (c) after what reasonably appears to be such a notification has been received the issuer may without dishonor refuse to accept or pay even to a person otherwise entitled to honor until the letter of credit or advice of credit is exhibited to the issuer.

(3) Except where the beneficiary has effectively assigned his right to draw or his right to proceeds, nothing in this section limits his right to transfer or negotiate drafts or demands drawn under the credit. Amended in 1972.

§ 5—117. Insolvency of Bank Holding Funds for Documentary Credit.

(1) Where an issuer or an advising or confirming bank or a bank which has for a customer procured issuance of a credit by another bank becomes insolvent before final payment under the credit and the credit is one to which this Article is made applicable by paragraphs (a) or (b) of Section 5—102(1) on scope, the receipt or allocation of funds or collateral to secure or meet obligations under the credit shall have the following results:

    (a) to the extent of any funds or collateral turned over after or before the insolvency as indemnity against or specifically for the purpose of payment of drafts or demands for payment drawn under the designated credit, the drafts or demands for payment drawn under the designated credit, the drafts or demands are entitled to payment in preference over depositors or other general creditors of the issuer or bank; and

    (b) on expiration of the credit or surrender of the beneficiary's rights under it unused any person who has given such funds or collateral is similarly entitled to return thereof; and

    (c) a charge to a general or current account with a bank if specifically consented to for the purpose of indemnity against or payment of drafts or demands for payment drawn under the designated credit falls under the same rules as if the funds had been drawn out in cash and then turned over with specific instructions.

(2) After honor or reimbursement under this section the customer or other person for whose account the insolvent bank has acted is entitled to receive the documents involved.

ARTICLE 6. Bulk Transfers

§ 6—101. Short Title.
This Article shall be known and may be cited as Uniform Commercial Code—Bulk Transfers.

§ 6—102. "Bulk Transfers"; Transfers of Equipment; Enterprises Subject to This Article; Bulk Transfers Subject to This Article.

(1) A "bulk transfer" is any transfer in bulk and not in the ordinary course of the transferor's business of a major part of the materials, supplies, merchandise or other inventory (Section 9—109) of an enterprise subject to this Article.

(2) A transfer of a substantial part of the equipment (Section 9—109) of such an enterprise is a bulk transfer if it is made in connection with a bulk transfer of inventory, but not otherwise.

(3) The enterprises subject to this Article are all those whose principal business is the sale of merchandise from stock, including those who manufacture what they sell.

(4) Except as limited by the following section all bulk transfers of goods located within this state are subject to this Article.

§ 6—103. Transfers Excepted From This Article.
The following transfers are not subject to this Article:

(1) Those made to give security for the performance of an obligation;

(2) General assignments for the benefit of all the creditors of the transferor, and subsequent transfers by the assignee thereunder;

(3) Transfers in settlement or realization of a lien or other security interests;

(4) Sales by executors, administrators, receivers, trustees in bankruptcy, or any public officer under judicial process;

(5) Sales made in the course of judicial or administrative proceedings for the dissolution or reorganization of a corporation and of which notice is sent to the creditors of the corporation pursuant to order of the court or administrative agency;

(6) Transfers to a person maintaining a known place of business in this State who becomes bound to pay the debts of the transferor in full and gives public notice of that fact, and who is solvent after becoming so bound;

(7) A transfer to a new business enterprise organized to take over and continue the business, if public notice of the transaction is given and the new enterprise assumes the debts of the transferor and he receives nothing from the transaction except an interest in the new enterprise junior to the claims of creditors;

(8) Transfers of property which is exempt from execution.

Public notice under subsection (6) or subsection (7) may be given by publishing once a week for two consecutive weeks in a newspaper of general circulation where the transferor had its principal place of business in this state an advertisement including the names and addresses of the transferor and transferee and the effective date of the transfer. As amended 1962.

§ 6—104. Schedule of Property, List of Creditors.

(1) Except as provided with respect to auction sales (Section 6—108), a bulk transfer subject to this Article is ineffective against any creditor of the transferor unless:

  (a) The transferee requires the transferor to furnish a list of his existing creditors prepared as stated in this section; and

  (b) The parties prepare a schedule of the property transferred sufficient to identify it; and

  (c) The transferee preserves the list and schedule for six months next following the transfer and permits inspection of either or both and copying therefrom at all reasonable hours by any creditor of the transferor, or files the list and schedule in (a public office to be here identified).

(2) The list of creditors must be signed and sworn to or affirmed by the transferor or his agent. It must contain the names and business addresses of all creditors of the transferor, with the amounts when known, and also the names of all persons who are known to the transferor to assert claims against him even though such claims are disputed. If the transferor is the obligor of an outstanding issue of bonds, debentures or the like as to which there is an indenture trustee, the list of creditors need include only the name and address of the indenture trustee and the aggregate outstanding principal amount of the issue.

(3) Responsibility for the completeness and accuracy of the list of creditors rests on the transferor, and the transfer is not rendered ineffective by errors or ommissions therein unless the transferee is shown to have had knowledge. As amended 1962.

§ 6—105. Notice to Creditors.

In addition to the requirements of the preceding section, any bulk transfer subject to this Article except one made by auction sale (Section 6—108) is ineffective against any creditor of the tranferor unless at least ten days before he takes possession of the goods or pays for them, whichever happens first, the transferee gives notice of the transfer in the manner and to the persons hereafter provided (Section 6—107).

[§ 6—106. Applications of the Proceeds.

In addition to the requirements of the two preceding sections:

(1) Upon every bulk transfer subject to this Article for which new consideration becomes payable except those made by sale at auction it is the duty of the transferee to assure that such consideration is applied so far as necessary to pay those debts of the transferor which are either shown on the list furnished by the transferor (Section 6—104) or filed in writing in the place stated in the notice (Section 6—107) within thirty days after the mailing of such notice. This duty of the transferee runs to all the holders of such debts, and may be enforced by any of them for the benefit of all.

(2) If any of said debts are in dispute the necessary sum may be withheld from distribution until the dispute is settled or adjudicated.

(3) If the consideration payable is not enough to pay all of the said debts in full distribution shall be made pro rata.]

> **Note:** This section is bracketed to indicate division of opinion as to whether or not it is a wise provision, and to suggest that this is a point on which State enactments may differ without serious damage to the principle of uniformity.
>
> In any State where this section is omitted, the following parts of sections, also bracketed in the text, should also be omitted, namely:
>
> > Section 6—107(2) (e).
> >   6—108(3) (c).
> >   6—109(2).
>
> In any State where this section is enacted, these other provisions should be also.

OPTIONAL SUBSECTION (4). [(4) The transferee may within ten days after he takes possession of the goods pay the consideration into the (specify court) in the county where the transferor had its principal place of business in this state and thereafter may discharge his duty under this section by giving notice by registered or certified mail to all the persons to whom the duty runs that the consideration has been paid into that court and that they should file their claims there. On motion of any interested party, the court may order the distribution of the consideration to the persons entitled to it.] As amended 1962.

> **Note:** Optional subsection (4) is recommended for those states which do not have a general statute providing for payment of money into court.

§ 6—107. The Notice.

(1) The notice to creditors (Section 6—105) shall state:

  (a) that a bulk transfer is about to be made; and

  (b) the names and business addresses of the transferor and transferee, and all other business names and addresses used by the transferor within three years last past so far as known to the transferee; and

(c) whether or not all the debts of the transferor are to be paid in full as they fall due as a result of the transaction, and if so, the address to which creditors should send their bills.

(2) If the debts of the transferor are not to be paid in full as they fall due or if the transferee is in doubt on that point then the notice shall state further:

(a) the location and general description of the property to be transferred and the estimated total of the transferor's debts:

(b) the address where the schedule of property and list of creditors (Section 6—104) may be inspected;

(c) whether the transfer is to pay existing debts and if so the amount of such debts and to whom owing;

(d) whether the transfer is for new consideration and if so the amount of such consideration and the time and place of payment; [and]

[(e) if for new consideration the time and place where creditors of the transferor are to file their claims.]

(3) The notice in any case shall be delivered personally or sent by registered or certified mail to all the persons shown on the list of creditors furnished against the transferor. As amended 1962.

Note: The words in brackets are optional. See Note under §6—106.]

§ 6—108. Auction Sales; "Auctioneer".

(1) A bulk transfer is subject to this Article even though it is by sale at auction, but only in the manner and with the results stated in this section.

(2) The transferor shall furnish a list of his creditors and assist in the preparation of a schedule of the property to be sold, both prepared as before stated (Section 6—104).

(3) The person or persons other than the transferor who direct, control or are responsible for the auction are collectively called the "auctioneer". The auctioneer shall:

(a) receive and retain the list of creditors and prepare and retain the schedule of property for the period stated in this Article (Section 6—104);

(b) give notice of the auction personally or by registered or certified mail at least ten days before it occurs to all persons shown on the list of creditors and to all other persons who are known to him to hold or assert claims against the transferor; [and]

[(c) assure that the net proceeds of the auction are applied as provided in this Article (Section 6—106).]

(4) Failure of the auctioneer to perform any of these duties does not affect the validity of the sale or the title

of the purchasers, but if the auctioneer knows that the auction constitutes a bulk transfer such failure renders the auctioneer liable to the creditors of the transferor as a class for the sums owing to them from the transferor up to but not exceeding the net proceeds of the auction. If the auctioneer consists of several persons their liability is joint and several. As amended 1962.

Note: The words in brackets are optional. See Note under § 6—106.

§ 6—109. What Creditors Protected; [Credit for Payment to Particular Creditors].

(1) The creditors of the transferor mentioned in this Article are those holding claims based on transactions or events occurring before the bulk transfer, but creditors who become such after notice to creditors is given (Sections 6—105 and 6—107) are not entitled to notice.

[(2) Against the aggregate obligation imposed by the provisions of this Article concerning the application of the proceeds (Section 6—106 and subsection (3) (c) of 6—108) the transferee or auctioneer is entitled to credit for sums paid to particular creditors of the transferor, not exceeding the sums believed in good faith at the time of the payment to be properly payable to such creditors.]

Note: The words in brackets are optional. See Note under § 6—106.

§ 6—110. Subsequent Transfers.

When the title of a transferee to property is subject to a defect by reason of his non-compliance with the requirements of this Article, then:

(1) a purchaser of any of such property from such transferee who pays no value or who takes with notice of such non-compliance takes subject to such defect, but

(2) a purchaser for value in good faith and without such notice takes free of such defect.

§ 6—111. Limitation of Actions and Levies.

No action under this Article shall be brought nor levy made more than six months after the date on which the transferee took possession of the goods unless the transfer has been concealed. If the transfer has been concealed, actions may be brought or levies made within six months after its discovery.

ARTICLE 7. Warehouse Receipts, Bills of Lading and Other Documents of Title

PART 1. General.

§ 7—101. Short Title.

This Article shall be known and may be cited as Uniform Commercial Code—Documents of Title.

§ 7—102. Definitions and Index of Definitions.

(1) In this Article, unless the context otherwise requires:

(a) "Bailee" means the person who by a warehouse receipt, bill of lading or other document of title acknowledges possession of goods and contracts to deliver them.

(b) "Consignee" means the person named in a bill to whom or to whose order the bill promises delivery.

(c) "Consignor" means the person named in a bill as the person from whom the goods have been received for shipment.

(d) "Delivery order" means a written order to deliver goods directed to a warehouseman, carrier or other person who in the ordinary course of business issues warehouse receipts or bills of lading.

(e) "Document" means document of title as defined in the general definitions in Article 1 (Section 1—201),

(f) "Goods" means all things which are treated as movable for the purposes of a contract of storage or transportation.

(g) "Issuer" means a bailee who issues a document except that in relation to an unaccepted delivery order it means the person who orders the possessor of goods to deliver. Issuer includes any person for whom an agent or employee purports to act in issuing a document if the agent or employee has real or apparent authority to issue documents, notwithstanding that the issuer received no goods or that the goods were misdescribed or that in any other respect the agent or employee violated his instructions.

(h) "Warehouseman" is a person engaged in the business of storing goods for hire.

(2) Other definitions applying to this Article or to specified Parts thereof, and the sections in which they appear are:

"Duly negotiate".   Section 7—501.
"Person entitled under the
document".   Section 7—403(4).

(3) Definitions in other Articles applying to this Article and the sections in which they appear are:

"Contract for sale".   Section 2—106.
"Overseas".   Section 2—323.
"Receipt" of goods.   Section 2—103.

(4) In addition Article 1 contains general definitions and principles of construction and interpretation applicable throughout this Article.

§ 7—103. Relation of Article to Treaty, Statute, Tariff, Classification or Regulation.

To the extent that any treaty or statute of the United States, regulatory statute of this State or tariff, classification or regulation filed or issued pursuant thereto is applicable, the provisions of this Article are subject thereto.

§ 7—104. Negotiable and Non-Negotiable Warehouse Receipt, Bill of Lading or Other Document of Title.

(1) A warehouse receipt, bill of lading or other document of title is negotiable

(a) if by its terms the goods are to be delivered to bearer or to the order of a named person; or

(b) where recognized in overseas trade, if it runs to a named person or assigns.

(2) Any other document is non-negotiable. A bill of lading in which it is stated that the goods are consigned to a named person is not made negotiable by a provision that the goods are to be delivered only against a written order signed by the same or another named person.

PART 2. *Warehouse Receipts: Special Provisions.*

§ 7—201. Who May Issue a Warehouse Receipt; Storage Under Government Bond.

(1) A warehouse receipt may be issued by any warehouseman.

(2) Where goods including distilled spirits and agricultural commodities are stored under a statute requiring a bond against withdrawal or a license for the issuance of receipts in the nature of warehouse receipts, a receipt issued for the goods has like effect as a warehouse receipt even though issued by a person who is not the owner of the goods and is not a warehouseman.

§ 7—202. Form of Warehouse Receipt; Essential Terms; Optional Terms.

(1) A warehouse receipt need not be in any particular form.

(2) Unless a warehouse receipt embodies within its written or printed terms each of the following, the warehouseman is liable for damages caused by the omission to a person injured thereby:

(a) the location of the warehouse where the goods are stored;

(b) the date of issue of the receipt;

(c) the consecutive number of the receipt;

(d) a statement whether the goods received will be delivered to the bearer, to a specified person, or to a specified person or his order;

(e) the rate of storage and handling charges, except that where goods are stored under a field warehousing arrangement a statement of that fact is sufficient on a non-negotiable receipt;

(f) a description of the goods or of the packages containing them;

(g) the signature of the warehouseman, which may be made by his authorized agent;

(h) if the receipt is issued for goods of which the warehouseman is owner, either solely or jointly or in common with others, the fact of such ownership; and

(i) a statement of the amount of advances made and of liabilities incurred for which the warehouseman claims a lien or security interest (Section 7—209). If the precise amount of such advances made or of such liabilities incurred is, at the time of the issue of the receipt, unknown to the warehouseman or to his agent who issues it, a statement of the fact that advances have been made or liabilities incurred and the purpose thereof is sufficient.

(3) A warehouseman may insert in his receipt any other terms which are not contrary to the provisions of this Act and do not impair his obligation of delivery (Section 7—403) or his duty of care (Section 7—204). Any contrary provisions shall be ineffective.

§ 7—203. Liability for Non-Receipt or Misdescription.

A party to or purchaser for value in good faith of a document of title other than a bill of lading relying in either case upon the description therein of the goods may recover from the issuer damages caused by the non-receipt or misdescription of the goods, except to the extent that the document conspicuously indicates that the issuer does not know whether any part of all of the goods in fact were received or conform to the description, as where the description is in terms of marks or labels or kind, quantity or condition, or the receipt or description is qualified by "contents, condition and quality unknown", "said to contain" or the like, if such indication be true, or the party or purchaser otherwise has notice.

§ 7—204. Duty of Care; Contractual Limitation of Warehouseman's Liability.

(1) A warehouseman is liable for damages for loss of or injury to the goods caused by his failure to exercise such care in regard to them as a reasonably careful man would exercise under like circumstances but unless otherwise agreed he is not liable for damages which could not have been avoided by the exercise of such care.

(2) Damages may be limited by a term in the warehouse receipt or storage agreement limiting the amount of liability in case of loss or damage, and setting forth a specific liability per article or item, or value per unit of weight, beyond which the warehouseman shall not be liable; provided, however, that such liability may on written request of the bailor at the time of signing such storage agreement or within a reasonable time after receipt of the warehouse receipt be increased on part or all of the goods thereunder, in which event increased rates may be charged based on such increased valuation, but that no such increase shall be permitted contrary to a lawful limitation of liability contained in the warehouseman's tariff, if any. No such limitation is effective with respect to the warehouseman's liability for conversion to his own use.

(3) Reasonable provisions as to the time and manner of presenting claims and instituting actions based on the bailment may be included in the warehouse receipt or tariff.

(4) This section does not impair or repeal. . .

> **Note:** Insert in subsection (4) a reference to any statute which imposes a higher responsibility upon the warehouseman or invalidates contractual limitations which would be permissible under this Article.

§ 7—205. Title Under Warehouse Receipt Defeated in Certain Cases.

A buyer in the ordinary course of business of fungible goods sold and delivered by a warehouseman who is also in the business of buying and selling such goods takes free of any claim under a warehouse receipt even though it has been duly negotiated.

§ 7—206. Termination of Storage at Warehouseman's Option.

(1) A warehouseman may on notifying the person on whose account the goods are held and any other person known to claim an interest in the goods require payment of any charges and removal of the goods from the warehouse at the termination of the period of storage fixed by the document, or, if no period is fixed, within a stated period not less than thirty days after the notification. If the goods are not removed before the date specified in the notification, the warehouseman may sell them in accordance with the provisions of the section on enforcement of a warehouseman's lien (Section 7—210).

(2) If a warehouseman in good faith believes that the goods are about to deteriorate or decline in value to less than the amount of his lien within the time prescribed in subsection (1) for notification, advertisement and sale, the warehouseman may specify in the notification any reasonable shorter time for removal of the goods and in case the goods are not removed, may sell them at public sale held not less than one week after a single advertisement or posting.

(3) If as a result of a quality or condition of the goods of which the warehouseman had no notice at the time of deposit the goods are a hazard to other property or to the warehouse or to persons, the warehouseman may sell the goods at public or private sale without advertisement on reasonable notification to all persons known to claim an interest in the goods. If the warehouseman after a reason-

able effort is unable to sell the goods he may dispose of them in any lawful manner and shall incur no liability by reason of such disposition.

(4) The warehouseman must deliver the goods to any person entitled to them this Article upon due demand made at any time prior to sale or other disposition under this section.

(5) The warehouseman may satisfy his lien from the proceeds of any sale or disposition under this section but must hold the balance for delivery on the demand of any person to whom he would have been bound to deliver the goods.

§ 7—207. Goods Must Be Kept Separate; Fungible Goods.

(1) Unless the warehouse receipt otherwise provides, a warehouseman must keep separate the goods covered by each receipt so as to permit at all times identification and delivery of those goods except that different lots of fungible goods may be commingled.

(2) Fungible goods so commingled are owned in common by the persons entitled thereto and the warehouseman is severally liable to each owner for that owner's share. Where because of overissue a mass of fungible goods is insufficient to meet all the receipts which the warehouseman has issued against it, the persons entitled include all holders to whom overissued receipts have been duly negotiated.

§ 7—208. Altered Warehouse Receipts.

Where a blank in a negotiable warehouse receipt has been filled in without authority, a purchaser for value and without notice of the want of authority may treat the insertion as authorized. Any other unauthorized alteration leaves any receipt enforceable against the issuer according to its original tenor.

§ 7—209. Lien of Warehouseman.

(1) A warehouseman has a lien against the bailor on the goods covered by a warehouse receipt or on the proceeds thereof in his possession for charges for storage or transportation (including demurrage and terminal charges), insurance, labor, or charges present or future in relation to the goods, and for expenses necessary for preservation of the goods or reasonably incurred in their sale pursuant to law. If the person on whose account the goods are held is liable for like charges or expenses in relation to other goods whenever deposited and it is stated in the receipt that a lien is claimed for charges or expenses in relation to other goods, the warehouseman also has a lien against him for such charges and expenses whether or not the other goods have been delivered by the warehouseman. But against a person to whom a negotiable warehouse receipt is duly negotiated a warehouseman's lien is limited to charges in an amount or at

a rate specified on the receipt or if no charges are so specified then to a reasonable charge for storage of the goods covered by the receipt subsequent to the date of the receipt.

(2) The warehouseman may also reserve a security interest against the bailor for a maximum amount specified on the receipt for charges other than those specified in subsection (1), such as for money advanced and interest. Such a security interest is governed by the Article on Secured Transactions (Article 9).

(3) (a) A warehouseman's lien for charges and expenses under subsection (1) or a security interest under subsection (2) is also effective against any person who so entrusted the bailor with possession of the goods that a pledge of them by him to a good faith purchaser for value would have been valid but is not effective against a person as to whom the document confers no right in the goods covered by it under Section 7—503.

(b) A warehouseman's lien on household goods for charges and expenses in relation to the goods under subsection (1) is also effective against all persons if the depositor was the legal possessor of the goods at the time of deposit. "Household goods" means furniture, furnishings and personal effects used by the depositor in a dwelling.

(4) A warehouseman loses his lien on any goods which he voluntarily delivers or which he unjustifiably refuses to deliver. As amended in 1966.

§ 7—210. Enforcement of Warehouseman's Lien.

(1) Except as provided in subsection (2), a warehouseman's lien may be enforced by public or private sale of the goods in block or in parcels, at any time or place and on any terms which are commercially reasonable, after notifying all persons known to claim an interest in the goods. Such notification must include a statement of the amount due, the nature of the proposed sale and the time and place of any public sale. The fact that a better price could have been obtained by a sale at a different time or in a different method from that selected by the warehouseman is not of itself sufficient to establish that the sale was not made in a commercially reasonable manner. If the warehouseman either sells the goods in the usual manner in any recognized market therefor, or if he sells at the price current in such market at the time of his sale, of if he has otherwise sold in conformity with commercially reasonable practices among dealers in the type of goods sold, he has sold in a commercially reasonable manner. A sale of more goods than apparently necessary to be offered to insure satisfaction of the obligation is not commercially reasonable except in cases covered by the preceding sentence.

(2) A warehouseman's lien on goods other than goods

stored by a merchant in the course of his business may be enforced only as follows:

    (a) All persons known to claim an interest in the goods must be notified.

    (b) The notification must be delivered in person or sent by registered or certified letter to the last known address of any person to be notified.

    (c) The notification must include an itemized statement of the claim, a description of the goods subject to the lien, a demand for payment within a specified time not less than ten days after receipt of the notification, and a conspicuous statement that unless the claim is paid within that time the goods will be advertised for sale and sold by auction at a specified time and place.

    (d) The sale must conform to the terms of the notification.

    (e) The sale must be held at the nearest suitable place to that where the goods are held or stored.

    (f) After the expiration of the time given in the notification, an advertisement of the sale must be published once a week for two weeks consecutively in a newspaper of general circulation where the sale is to be held. The advertisement must include a description of the goods, the name of the person on whose account they are being held, and the time and place of the sale. The sale must take place at least fifteen days after the first publication. If there is no newspaper of general circulation where the sale is to be held, the advertisement must be posted at least ten days before the sale in not less than six conspicuous places in the neighborhood of the proposed sale.

(3) Before any sale pursuant to this section any person claiming a right in the goods may pay the amount necessary to satisfy the lien and the reasonable expenses incurred under this section. In that event the goods must not be sold, but must be retained by the warehouseman subject to the terms of the receipt and this Article.

(4) The warehouseman may buy at any public sale pursuant to this section.

(5) A purchaser in good faith of goods sold to enforce a warehouseman's lien takes the goods free of any rights of persons against whom the lien was valid, despite noncompliance by the warehouseman with the requirements of this section.

(6) The warehouseman may satisfy his lien from the proceeds of any sale pursuant to this section but must hold the balance, if any, for delivery on demand to any person to whom he would have been bound to deliver the goods.

(7) The rights provided by this section shall be in addition to all other rights allowed by law to a creditor against his debtor.

(8) Where a lien is on goods stored by a merchant in the course of his business the lien may be enforced in accordance with either subsection (1) or (2).

(9) The warehouseman is liable for damages caused by failure to comply with the requirements for sale under this section and in case of willful violation is liable for conversion. As amended in 1962.

PART 3. Bills of Lading: Special Provisions.

§ 7—301. Liability for Non-Receipt or Misdescription; "Said to Contain"; "Shipper's Load and Count"; Improper Handling.

(1) A consignee of a non-negotiable bill who has given value in good faith or a holder to whom a negotiable bill has been duly negotiated relying in either case upon the description therein of the goods, or upon the date therein shown, may recover from the issuer damages caused by the misdating of the bill or the nonreceipt or misdescription of the goods, except to the extent that the document indicates that the issuer does not know whether any part or all of the goods in fact were received or conform to the description, as where the description is in terms of marks or labels or kind, quantity, or condition or the receipt or description is qualified by "contents or condition of contents of packages unknown", "said to contain", "shipper's weight, load and count" or the like, if such indication be true.

(2) When goods are loaded by an issuer who is a common carrier, the issuer must count the packages of goods if package freight and ascertain the kind and quantity if bulk freight. In such cases "shipper's weight, load and count" or other words indicating that the description was made by the shipper are ineffective except as to freight concealed by packages.

(3) When bulk freight is loaded by a shipper who makes available to the issuer adequate facilities for weighing such freight, an issuer who is a common carrier must ascertain the kind and quantity within a reasonable time after receiving the written request for the shipper to do so. In such cases "shipper's weight" or other words of like purport are ineffective.

(4) The issuer may by inserting in the bill the words "shipper's weight, load and count" or other words of like purport indicate that the goods were loaded by the shipper; and if such statement be true the issuer shall not be liable for damages caused by the improper loading. But their omission does not imply liability for such damages.

(5) The shipper shall be deemed to have guaranteed to the issuer the accuracy at the time of shipment of the description, marks, labels, number, kind, quantity, condition and weight, as furnished by him; and the shipper shall indemnify the issuer against damage caused by inaccuracies in such particulars. The right of the issuer to such indemnity shall in no way limit his responsibility

and liability under the contract of carriage to any person other than the shipper.

§ 7—302. Through Bills of Lading and Similar Documents.

(1) The issuer of a through bill of lading or other document embodying an undertaking to be performed in part by persons acting as its agents or by connecting carriers is liable to anyone entitled to recover on the document for any breach by such other persons or by a connecting carrier of its obligation under the document but to the extent that the bill covers an undertaking to be performed overseas or in territory not contiguous to the continental United States or an undertaking including matters other than transportation this liability may be varied by agreement of the parties.

(2) Where goods covered by a through bill of lading or other document embodying an undertaking to be performed in part by persons other than the issuer are received by any such person, he is subject with respect to his own performance while the goods are in his possession to the obligation of the issuer. His obligation is discharged by delivery of the goods to another such person pursuant to the document, and does not include liability for breach by any other such persons or by the issuer.

(3) The issuer of such through bill of lading or other document shall be entitled to recover from the connecting carrier or such other person in possession of the goods when the breach of the obligation under the document occurred, the amount it may be required to pay to anyone entitled to recover on the document therefor, as may be evidenced by any receipt, judgment, or transcript thereof, and the amount of any expense reasonably incurred by it in defending any action brought by anyone entitled to recover on the document therefor.

§ 7—303. Diversion; Reconsignment; Change of Instructions.

(1) Unless the bill of lading otherwise provides, the carrier may deliver the goods to a person or destination other than that stated in the bill or may otherwise dispose of the goods on instructions from

    (a) the holder of a negotiable bill; or

    (b) the consignor on a non-negotiable bill notwithstanding contrary instructions from the consignee; or

    (c) the consignee on a non-negotiable bill in the absence of contrary instructions from the consignor, if the goods have arrived at the billed destination or if the consignee is in possession of the bill; or

    (d) the consignee on a non-negotiable bill if he is entitled as against the consignor to dispose of them.

(2) Unless such instructions are noted on a negotiable bill of lading, a person to whom the bill is duly negotiated can hold the bailee according to the original terms.

§ 7—304. Bills of Lading in a Set.

(1) Except where customary in overseas transportation, a bill of lading must not be issued in a set of parts. The issuer is liable for damages caused by violation of this subsection.

(2) Where a bill of lading is lawfully drawn in a set of parts, each of which is numbered and expressed to be valid only if the goods have not been delivered against any other part, the whole of the parts constitute one bill.

(3) Where a bill of lading is lawfully issued in a set of parts and different parts are negotiated to different persons, the title of the holder to whom the first due negotiation is made prevails as to both the document and the goods even though any later holder may have received the goods from the carrier in good faith and discharged the carrier's obligation by surrender of his part.

(4) Any person who negotiates or transfers a single part of a bill of lading drawn in a set is liable to holders of that part as if it were the whole set.

(5) The bailee is obliged to deliver in accordance with Part 4 of this Article against the first presented part of a bill of lading lawfully drawn in a set. Such delivery discharges the bailee's obligation on the whole bill.

§ 7—305. Destination Bills.

(1) Instead of issuing a bill of lading to the consignor at the place of shipment a carrier may at the request of the consignor procure the bill to be issued at destination or at any other place designated in the request.

(2) Upon request of anyone entitled as against the carrier to control the goods while in transit and on surrender of any outstanding bill of lading or the receipt covering such goods, the issuer may procure a substitute bill to be issued at any place designated in the request.

§ 7—306. Altered Bills of Lading.

An unauthorized alteration or filling in of a blank in a bill of lading leaves the bill enforceable according to its original tenor.

§ 7—307. Lien of Carrier.

(1) A carrier has a lien on the goods covered by a bill of lading for charges subsequent to the date of its receipt of the goods for storage or transportation (including demurrage and terminal charges) and for expenses necessary for preservation of the goods incident to their transportation or reasonably incurred in their sale pursuant to law. But against a purchaser for value of a negotiable bill of lading a carrier's lien is limited to charges stated in the bill or the applicable tariffs, or if no charges are stated then to a reasonable charge.

(2) A lien for charges and expenses under subsection (1) on goods which the carrier was required by law to receive for transportation is effective against the consignor or any person entitled to the goods unless the carrier had notice that the consignor lacked authority to subject the goods to such charges and expenses. Any other lien

under subsection (1) is effective against the consignor and any person who permitted the bailor to have control or possession of the goods unless the carrier had notice that the bailor lacked such authority.

(3) A carrier loses his lien on any goods which he voluntarily delivers or which he unjustifiably refuses to deliver.

§ 7—308. Enforcement of Carrier's Lien.

(1) A carrier's lien may be enforced by public or private sale of the goods, in block or in parcels, at any time or place and on any terms which are commercially reasonable, after notifying all persons known to claim an interest in the goods. Such notification must include a statement of the amount due, the nature of the proposed sale and the time and place of any public sale. The fact that a better price could have been obtained by a sale at a different time or in a different method from that selected by the carrier is not of itself sufficient to establish that the sale was not made in a commercially reasonable manner. If the carrier either sells the goods in the usual manner in any recognized market therefor or if he sells at the price current in such market at the time of his sale or if he has otherwise sold in conformity with commercially reasonable practices among dealers in the type of goods sold he has sold in a commercially reasonable manner. A sale of more goods than apparently necessary to be offered to ensure satisfaction of the obligation is not commercially reasonable except in cases covered by the preceding sentence.

(2) Before any sale pursuant to this section any person claiming a right in the goods may pay the amount necessary to satisfy the lien and the reasonable expenses incurred under this section. In that event the goods must not be sold, but must be retained by the carrier subject to the terms of the bill and this Article.

(3) The carrier may buy at any public sale pursuant to this section.

(4) A purchaser in good faith of goods sold to enforce a carrier's lien takes good sold free of any rights of persons against whom the lien was valid, despite noncompliance by the carrier with the requirements of this section.

(5) The carrier may satisfy his lien from the proceeds of any sale pursuant to this section but must hold the balance, if any, for delivery on demand to any person to whom he would have been bound to deliver the goods.

(6) The rights provided by this section shall be in addition to all other rights allowed by law to a creditor against his debtor.

(7) A carrier's lien may be enforced in accordance with either subsection (1) or the procedure set forth in subsection (2) of Section 7—210.

(8) The carrier is liable for damages caused by failure to comply with the requirements for sale under this section and in case of willful violation is liable for conversion.

§ 7—309. Duty of Care; Contractual Limitation of Carrier's Liability.

(1) A carrier who issues a bill of lading whether negotiable or non-negotiable must exercise the degree of care in relation to the goods which a reasonably careful man would exercise under like circumstances. This subsection does not repeal or change any law or rule of law which imposes liability upon a common carrier for damages not caused by its negligence.

(2) Damages may be limited by a provision that the carrier's liability shall not exceed a value stated in the document if the carrier's rates are dependent upon value and the consignor by the carrier's tariff is afforded an opportunity to declare a higher value or a value as lawfully provided in the tariff, or where no tariff is filed he is otherwise advised of such opportunity; but no such limitation is effective with respect to the carrier's liability for conversion to its own use.

(3) Reasonable provisions as to the time and manner of presenting claims and instituting actions based on the shipment may be included in a bill of lading or tariff.

PART 4. *Warehouse Receipts and Bills of Lading: General Obligations.*

§ 7—401. Irregularities in Issue of Receipt or Bill or Conduct of Issuer.

The obligations imposed by this Article on an issuer apply to a document of title regardless of the fact that

    (a) the document may not comply with the requirements of this Article or of any other law or regulation regarding its issue, form or content; or

    (b) the issuer may have violated laws regulating the conduct of his business; or

    (c) the goods covered by the document were owned by the bailee at the time the document was issued; or

    (d) the person issuing the document does not come within the definition of warehouseman if it purports to be a warehouse receipt.

§ 7—402. Duplicate Receipt or Bill; Overissue.

Neither a duplicate nor any other document of title purporting to cover goods already represented by an outstanding document of the same issuer confers any right in the goods, except as provided in the case of bills in a set, overissue of documents for fungible goods and substitutes for lost, stolen or destroyed documents. But the issuer is liable for damages caused by his overissue or failure to identify a duplicate document as such by conspicuous notation on its face.

§ 7—403. Obligation of Warehouseman or Carrier to Deliver; Excuse.

(1) The bailee must deliver the goods to a person entitled under the document who complies with subsections

(2) and (3), unless and to the extent that the bailee establishes any of the following:

(a) delivery of the goods to a person whose receipt was rightful as against the claimant;

(b) damage to or delay, loss or destruction of the goods for which the bailee is not liable[, but the burden of establishing negligence in such cases is on the person entitled under the document];

Note: The brackets in (1) (b) indicate that State enactments may differ on this point without serious damage to the principle of uniformity.

(c) previous sale or other disposition of the goods in lawful enforcement of a lien or on warehouseman's lawful termination of storage;

(d) the exercise by a seller of his right to stop delivery pursuant to the provisions of the Article on Sales (Section 2—705);

(e) a diversion, reconsignment or other disposition pursuant to the provisions of this Article (Section 7—303) or tariff regulating such right;

(f) release, satisfaction or any other fact affording a personal defense against the claimant;

(g) any other lawful excuse.

(2) A person claiming goods covered by a document of title must satisfy the bailee's lien where the bailee so requests or where the bailee is prohibited by law from delivering the goods until the charges are paid.

(3) Unless the person claiming is one against whom the document confers no right under Sec. 7—503(1), he must surrender for cancellation or notation of partial deliveries any outstanding negotiable document covering the goods, and the bailee must cancel the document or conspicuously note the partial delivery thereon or be liable to any person to whom the document is duly negotiated.

(4) "Person entitled under the document" means holder in the case of a negotiable document, or the person to whom delivery is to be made by the terms of or pursuant to written instructions under a non-negotiable document.

§ 7—404. No Liability for Good Faith Delivery Pursuant to Receipt or Bill.

A bailee who in good faith including observance of reasonable commercial standards has received goods and delivered or otherwise disposed of them according to the terms of the document of title or pursuant to this Article is not liable therefor. This rule applies even though the person from whom he received the goods had no authority to procure the document or to dispose of the goods and even though the person to whom he delivered the goods had no authority to receive them.

PART 5. Warehouse Receipts and Bills of Lading: Negotiation and Transfer.

§ 7—501. Form of Negotiation and Requirements of "Due Negotiation".

(1) A negotiable document of title running to the order of a named person is negotiated by his indorsement and delivery. After his indorsement in blank or to bearer any person can negotiate it by delivery alone.

(2) (a) A negotiable document of title is also negotiated by delivery alone when by its original terms it runs to bearer.

(b) When a document running to the order of a named person is delivered to him the effect is the same as if the document had been negotiated.

(3) Negotiation of a negotiable document of title after it has been indorsed to a specified person requires indorsement by the special indorsee as well as delivery.

(4) A negotiable document of title is "duly negotiated" when it is negotiated in the manner stated in this section to a holder who purchases it in good faith without notice of any defense against or claim to it on the part of any person and for value, unless it is established that the negotiation is not in the regular course of business or financing or involves receiving the document in settlement or payment of a money obligation.

(5) Indorsement of a non-negotiable document neither makes it negotiable nor adds to the transferee's rights.

(6) The naming in a negotiable bill of a person to be notified of the arrival of the goods does not limit the negotiability of the bill nor constitute notice to a purchaser thereof of any interest of such person in the goods.

§ 7—502. Rights Acquired by Due Negotiation.

(1) Subject to the following section and to the provisions of Section 7—205 on fungible goods, a holder to whom a negotiable document of title has been duly negotiated acquires thereby:

(a) title to the document;

(b) title to the goods;

(c) all rights accruing under the law of agency or estoppel, including rights to goods delivered to the bailee after the document was issued; and

(d) the direct obligation of the issuer to hold or deliver the goods according to the terms of the document free of any defense or claim by him except those arising under the terms of the document or under this Article. In the case of a delivery order the bailee's obligation accrues only upon acceptance and the obligation acquired by the holder is that the issuer and any indorser will procure the acceptance of the bailee.

(2) Subject to the following section, title and rights so acquired are not defeated by any stoppage of the goods represented by the document or by surrender of such goods by the bailee, and are not impaired even though the negotiation or any prior negotiation constituted a breach of duty or even though any person has been deprived of possession of the document by misrepresentation, fraud, accident, mistake, duress, loss, theft or conversion, or even though a previous sale or other transfer of the goods or document has been made to a third person.

§ 7—503. Document of Title to Goods Defeated in Certain Cases.

(1) A document of title confers no right in goods against a person who before issuance of the document had a legal interest or a perfected security interest in them and who neither

    (a) delivered or entrusted them or any document of title covering them to the bailor or his nominee with actual or apparent authority to ship, store or sell or with power to obtain delivery under this Article (Section 7—403) or with power of disposition under this Act (Section 2—403 and 9—307) or other statute or rule of law; nor

    (b) acquiesced in the procurement by the bailor or his nominee of any document of title.

(2) Title to goods based upon an unaccepted delivery order is subject to the rights of anyone to whom a negotiable warehouse receipt or bill of lading covering the goods has been duly negotiated. Such a title may be defeated under the next section to the same extent as the rights of the issuer or a transferee from the issuer.

(3) Title to goods based upon a bill of lading issued to a freight forwarder is subject to the rights of anyone to whom a bill issued by the freight forwarder is duly negotiated; but delivery by the carrier in accordance with Part 4 of this Article pursuant to its own bill of lading discharges the carrier's obligation to deliverer.

§ 7—504. Rights Acquired in the Absence of Due Negotiation; Effect of Diversion; Seller's Stoppage of Delivery.

(1) A transferee of a document, whether negotiable or non-negotiable, to whom the document has been delivered but not duly negotiated, acquires the title and rights which his transferor had or had actual authority to convey.

(2) In the case of a non-negotiable document, until but not after the bailee receives notification of the transfer, the rights of the transferee may be defeated

    (a) by those creditors of the transferor who could treat the sale as void under Section 2—402; or

    (b) by a buyer from the transferor in ordinary course of business if the bailee has delivered the goods to the buyer or received notification of his rights; or

    (c) as against the bailee by good faith dealings of the bailee with the transferor.

(3) A diversion or other change of shipping instructions by the consignor in a non-negotiable bill of lading which causes the bailee not to deliver to the consignee defeats the consignee's title to the goods if they have been delivered to a buyer in ordinary course of business and in any event defeats the consignee's rights against the bailee.

(4) Delivery pursuant to a non-negotiable document may be stopped by a seller under Section 2—705, and subject to the requirement of due notification there provided. A bailee honoring the seller's instructions is entitled to be indemnified by the seller against any resulting loss or expense.

§ 7—505. Indorser Not a Guarantor for Other Parties.

The indorsement of a document of title issued by a bailee does not make the indorser liable for any default by the bailee or by previous indorsers.

§ 7—506. Delivery Without Indorsement: Rights to Compel Indorsement.

The transferee of a negotiable document of title has a specifically enforceable right to have his transferor supply any necessary indorsement but the transfer becomes a negotiation only as of the time the indorsement is supplied.

§ 7—507. Warranties on Negotiation or Transfer of Receipt or Bill.

Where a person negotiates or transfers a document of title for value otherwise than as a mere intermediary under the next following section, then unless otherwise agreed he warrants to his immediate purchaser only in addition to any warranty made in selling the goods

    (a) that the document is genuine; and

    (b) that he has no knowledge of any fact which would impair its validity or worth; and

    (c) that his negotiation or transfer is rightful and fully effective with respect to the title to the document and the goods it represents.

§ 7—508. Warranties of Collecting Bank as to Documents.

A collecting bank or other intermediary known to be entrusted with documents on behalf of another or with collection of a draft or other claim against delivery of documents warrants by such delivery of the documents only its own good faith and authority. This rule applies even though the intermediary has purchased or made advances against the claim or draft to be collected.

§ 7—509. Receipt or Bill: When Adequate Compliance With Commercial Contract.

The question whether a document is adequate to fulfill the obligations of a contract for sale or the conditions of a credit is governed by the Articles on Sales (Article 2) and on Letters of Credit (Article 5).

PART 6. Warehouse Receipts and Bills of Lading: Miscellaneous Provisions.

§ 7—601. Lost and Missing Documents.

(1) If a document has been lost, stolen or destroyed, a court may order delivery of the goods or issuance of a substitute document and the bailee may without liability to any person comply with such order. If the document was negotiable the claimant must post security approved by the court to indemnify any person who may suffer loss as a result of non-surrender of the document. If the document was not negotiable, such security may be required at the discretion of the court. The court may also in its discretion order payment of the bailee's reasonable costs and counsel fees.

(2) A bailee who without court order delivers goods to a person claiming under a missing negotiable document is liable to any person injured thereby, and if the delivery is not in good faith becomes liable for conversion. Delivery in good faith is not conversion if made in accordance with a filed classification or tariff or, where no classification or tariff is filed, if the claimant posts security with the bailee in an amount at least double the value of the goods at the time of posting to indemnify any person injured by the delivery who files a notice of claim within one year after the delivery.

§ 7—602. Attachment of Goods Covered by a Negotiable Document.

Except where the document was originally issued upon delivery of the goods by a person who had no power to dispose of them, no lien attaches by virtue of any judicial process to goods in the possession of a bailee for which a negotiable document of title is outstanding unless the document be first surrendered to the bailee or its negotiation enjoined, and the bailee shall not be compelled to deliver the goods pursuant to process until the document is surrendered to him or impounded by the court. One who purchases the document for value without notice of the process or injunction takes free of the lien imposed by judicial process.

§ 7—603. Conflicting Claims; Interpleader.

If more than one person claims title or possession of the goods, the bailee is excused from delivery until he has had a reasonable time to ascertain the validity of the adverse claims or to bring an action to compel all claimants to interplead and may compel such interpleader, either in defending an action for non-delivery of the goods, or by original action, whichever is appropriate.

ARTICLE 8. Investment Securities

PART 1. Short Title and General Matters.

§ 8—101. Short Title.

This Article shall be known and may be cited as Uniform Commercial Code—Investment Securities.

§ 8—102. Definitions and Index of Definitions.

(1) In this Article, unless the context otherwise requires:

(a) A ''certificated security'' is a share, participation, or other interest in property of or an enterprise of the issuer or an obligation of the issuer which is

(i) represented by an instrument issued in bearer or registered form;

(ii) of a type commonly dealt in on securities exchanges or markets or commonly recognized in any area in which it is issued or dealt in as a medium for investment; and

(iii) either one of a class or series or by its terms divisible into a class or series of shares, participations, interests, or obligations.

(b) An ''uncertificated security'' is a share, participation, or other interest in property or an enterprise of the issuer or an obligation of the issuer which is

(i) not represented by an instrument and the transfer of which is registered upon books maintained for that purpose by or on behalf of the issuer;

(ii) of a type commonly dealt in on securities exchanges or markets; and

(iii) either one of a class or series or by its terms divisible into a class or series of shares, participations, interests, or obligations.

(c) A ''security'' is either a certificated or an uncertificated security. If a security is certificated, the terms ''security'' and ''certificated security'' may mean either the intangible interest, the instrument representing that interest, or both, as the context requires. A writing that is a certificated security is governed by this Article and not by Article 3, even though it also meets the requirements of that Article. This Article does not apply to money. If a certificated security has been retained by or surrendered to the issuer or its transfer agent for reasons other than registration of transfer, other temporary purpose, payment, exchange, or acquisition by the issuer, that security shall be treated as an uncertificated security for purposes of this Article.

(d) A certificated security is in "registered form" if

    (i) it specifies a person entitled to the security or the rights it represents; and

    (ii) its transfer may be registered upon books maintained for that purpose by or on behalf of the issuer, or the security so states.

(e) A certificated security is in "bearer form" if it runs to bearer according to its terms and not by reason of any indorsement.

(2) A "subsequent purchaser" is a person who takes other than by original issue.

(3) A "clearing corporation" is a corporation registered as a "clearing agency" under the federal securities laws or a corporation:

(a) at least 90 percent of whose capital stock is held by or for one or more organizations, none of which, other than a national securities exchange or association, holds in excess of 20 percent of the capital stock of the corporation, and each of which is

    (i) subject to supervision or regulation pursuant to the provisions of federal or state banking laws or state insurance laws.

    (ii) a broker or dealer or investment company registered under the federal securities laws, or

    (iii) a national securities exchange or association registered under the federal securities laws; and

(b) any remaining capital stock of which is held by individuals who have purchased it at or prior to the time of their taking office as directors of the corporation and who have purchased only so much of the capital stock as is necessary to permit them to qualify as directors.

(4) A "custodian bank" is a bank or trust company that is supervised and examined by state or federal authority having supervision over banks and is acting as custodian for a clearing corporation.

(5) Other definitions applying to this Article or to specified Parts thereof and the sections in which they appear are:

"Adverse claim".	Section 8—302.
"Bona fide purchase".	Section 8—302.
"Broker".	Section 8—303.
"Debtor".	Section 9—105.
"Financial intermediary".	Section 8—313.
"Guarantee of the signature".	Section 8—402.
"Initial transaction statement".	Section 8—408.
"Instruction".	Section 8—308.
"Intermediary bank".	Section 4—105.
"Issuer".	Section 8—201.
"Overissue".	Section 8—104.
"Secured Party".	Section 9—105.
"Security Agreement".	Section 9—105.

(6) In addition, Article 1 contains general definitions and principles of construction and interpretation applicable throughout this Article. Amended in 1962, 1973 and 1977.

§ 8—103. Issuer's Lien.

A lien upon a security in favor of an issuer thereof is valid against a purchaser only if:

(a) the security is certificated and the right of the issuer to the lien is noted conspicuously thereon; or

(b) the security is uncertificated and a notation of the right of the issuer to the lien is contained in the initial transaction statement sent to the purchaser or, if his interest is transferred to him other than by registration of transfer, pledge, or release, the initial transaction statement sent to the registered owner or the registered pledgee. Amended in 1977.

§ 8—104. Effect of Overissue; "Overissue".

(1) The provision of this Article which validate a security or compel its issue or reissue do not apply to the extent that validation, issue, or reissue would result in overissue; but if:

(a) an identical security which does not constitute an overissue is reasonably available for purchase, the person entitled to issue or validation may compel the issuer to purchase the security for him and either to deliver a certificated security or to register the transfer of an uncertificated security to him, against surrender of any certificated security he holds; or

(b) a security is not so available for purchase, the person entitled to issue or validation may recover from the issuer the price he or the last purchaser for value paid for it with interest from the date of his demand.

(2) "Overissue" means the issue of securities in excess of the amount the issuer has corporate power to issue. Amended in 1977.

§ 8—105. Certificated Securities Negotiable; Statements and Instructions Not Negotiable; Presumptions.

(1) Certificated securities governed by this Article are negotiable instruments.

(2) Statements (Section 8—408), notices, or the like, sent by the issuer of uncertificated securities and instruc-

tions (Section 8—308) are neither negotiable instruments nor certificated securities.

(3) In any action on a security:

(a) unless specifically denied in the pleadings, each signature on a certificated security, in a necessary indorsement, on an initial transaction statement, or on an instruction, is admitted;

(b) if the effectiveness of a signature is put in issue, the burden of establishing it is on the party claiming under the signature, but the signature is presumed to be genuine or authorized;

(c) if signature on the certificated security are admitted or established, production of the security entitles a holder to recover on it unless the defendant establishes a defense or a defect going to the validity of the security;

(d) if signatures on an initial transaction statement are admitted or established, the facts stated in the statement are presumed to be true as of the time of its issuance; and

(e) after it is shown that a defense or defect exists, the plaintiff has the burden of establishing that he or some person under whom he claims is a person against whom the defense or defect is ineffective (Section 8—202). Amended in 1977.

§ 8—106. Applicability.

The law (including the conflict of laws rules) of the jurisdiction of organization of the issuer governs the validity of a security, the effectiveness of registration by the issuer, and the rights and duties of the issuer with respect to:

(a) registration of transfer of a certificated security;

(b) registration of transfer, pledge, or release of an uncertificated security; and

(c) sending of statements of uncertificated securities. Amended in 1977.

§ 8—107. Securities Transferable; Action for Price.

(1) Unless otherwise agreed and subject to any applicable law or regulation respecting short sales, a person obligated to transfer securities may transfer any certificated security of the specified issue in bearer form or registered in the name of the transferee, or indorsed to him or in blank, or he may transfer an equivalent uncertificated security to the transferee or a person designated by the transferee.

(2) If the buyer fails to pay the price as it come due under a contract of sale, the seller may recover the price of:

(a) certificated securities accepted by the buyer;

(b) uncertificated securities that have been trans-

ferred to the buyer or a person designated by the buyer; and

(c) other securities if efforts at their resale would be unduly burdensome or if there is no readily available market for their resale. Amended in 1977.

§ 8—108. Registration of Pledge and Release of Uncertificated Securities.

A security interest in an uncertificated security may be evidenced by the registration of pledge to the secured party or a person designated by him. There can be no more than one registered owner of an uncertificated security at any time. The registered owner of an uncertificated security is the person in whose name the security is registered, even if the security is subject to a registered pledge. The rights of a registered pledgee of an uncertificated security under this Article are terminated by the registration of release. Added in 1977.

PART 2. Issue—Issuer.

§ 8—201. "Issuer".

(1) With respect to obligations on or defenses to a security, "issuer" includes a person who:

(a) places or authorizes the placing of his name on a certificated security (otherwise than as authenticating trustee, registrar, transfer agent, or the like) to evidence that it represents a share, participation, or other interest in his property or in an enterprise, or to evidence his duty to perform an obligation represented by the certificated security;

(b) creates shares, participations, or other interests in his property or in an enterprise or undertakes obligations, which shares, participations, interests, or obligations are uncertificated securities;

(c) directly or indirectly creates fractional interests in his rights or property, which fractional interests are represented by certificated securities; or

(d) becomes responsible for or in place of any other person described as an issuer in this section.

(2) With respect to obligations on or defenses to a security, a guarantor is an issuer to the extent of his guaranty, whether or not his obligation is noted on a certificated security or on statements of uncertificated securities sent pursuant to Section 8—408.

(3) With respect to registration of transfer, pledge, or release (Part 4 of this Article), "issuer" means a person on whose behalf transfer books are maintained. Amended in 1977.

§ 8—202. Issuer's Responsibility and Defenses; Notice of Defect or Defense.

(1) Even against a purchaser for value and without notice, the terms of a security include:

   (a) if the security is certificated, those stated on the security;

   (b) if the security is uncertificated, those contained in the initial transaction statement sent to such purchaser or, if his interest is transferred to him other than by registration of transfer, pledge, or release, the initial transaction statement sent to the registered owner or registered pledgee; and

   (c) those made part of the security by reference, on the certificated security or in the initial transaction statement, to another instrument, indenture, or document or to a constitution, statute, ordinance, rule, regulation, order or the like, to the extent that the terms referred to do not conflict with the terms stated on the certificated security or contained in the statement. A reference under this paragraph does not of itself charge a purchaser for value with notice of a defect going to the validity of the security, even though the certificated security or statement expressly states that a person accepting it admits notice.

(2) A certificated security in the hands of a purchaser for value or an uncertificated security as to which an initial transaction statement has been sent to a purchaser for value, other than a security issued by a government or governmental agency or unit, even though issued with a defect going to its validity, is valid with respect to the purchaser if he is without notice of the particular defect unless the defect involves a violation of constitutional provisions, in which case the security is valid with respect to a subsequent purchaser for value and without notice of the defect. This subsection applies to an issuer that is a government or governmental agency or unit only if either there has been substantial compliance with the legal requirements governing the issue or the issuer has received a substantial consideration for the issue as a whole or for the particular security and a stated purpose of the issue is one for which the issuer has power to borrow money or issue the security.

(3) Except as provided in the case of certain unauthorized signatures (Section 8—205), lack of genuineness of a certificated security or an initial transaction statement is a complete defense, even against a purchaser for value and without notice.

(4) All other defenses of the issuer of a certificated or uncertificated security, including nondelivery and conditional delivery of a certificated security, are ineffective against a purchaser for value who has taken without notice of the particular defense.

(5) Nothing in this section shall be construed to affect the right of a party to a "when, as and if issued" or a "when distributed" contract to cancel the contract in the event of a material change in the character of the security that is the subject of the contract or in the plan or arrangement pursuant to which the security is to be issued or distributed. Amended in 1977.

§ 8—203. Staleness as Notice of Defects or Defenses.

(1) After an act or event creating a right to immediate performance of the principal obligation represented by a certificated security or that sets a date on or after which the security is to be presented or surrendered for redemption or exchange, a purchaser is charged with notice of any defect in its issue or defense of the issuer if:

   (a) the act or event is one requiring the payment of money, the delivery of certificated securities, the registration of transfer of uncertificated securities, or any of these on presentation or surrender of the certificated security, the funds or securities are available on the date set for payment or exchange, and he takes the security more than one year after that date; and

   (b) the act or event is not covered by paragraph (a) and he takes the security more than two years after the date set for surrender or presentation or the date on which performance became due.

(2) A call that has been revoked is not within subsection (1). Amended in 1977.

§ 8—204. Effect of Issuer's Restrictions on Transfer.

A restriction on transfer of a security imposed by the issuer, even if otherwise lawful, is ineffective against any person without actual knowledge of it unless:

   (a) the security is certificated and the restriction is noted conspicuously thereon; or

   (b) the security is uncertificated and a notation of the restriction is contained in the initial transaction statement sent to the person or, if his interest is transferred to him other than by registration of transfer, pledge, or release, the initial transaction statement sent to the registered owner or the registered pledgee. Amended in 1977.

§ 8—205. Effect of Unauthorized Signature on Certificated Security or Initial Transaction Statement.

An unauthorized signature placed on a certificated security prior to or in the course of issue or placed on an initial transaction statement is ineffective, but the signature is effective in favor of a purchaser for value of the certificated security or a purchaser for value of the certificated security or a purchaser for value of an uncertificated security to whom the initial transaction statement has been sent, if the purchaser is without notice of the lack of authority and the signing has been done by:

(a) an authenticating trustee, registrar, transfer agent, or other person entrusted by the issuer with the signing of the security, of similar securities, or of initial transaction statements or the immediate preparation for signing of any of them; or

(b) an employee of the issuer, or of any of the foregoing, entrusted with responsible handling of the security or initial transaction statement. Amended in 1977.

§ 8—206. Completion or Alteration of Certificated Security or Initial Transaction Statement.

(1) If a certificated security contains the signatures necessary to its issue or transfer but is incomplete in any other respect:

(a) any person may complete it by filling in the blanks as authorized; and

(b) even though the blanks are incorrectly filled in, the security as completed is enforceable by a purchaser who took it for value and without notice of the incorrectness.

(2) A complete certificated security that has been improperly altered, even though fraudulently, remains enforceable, but only according to its original terms.

(3) If an initial transaction statement contains the signatures necessary to its validity, but is incomplete in any other respect:

(a) any person may complete it by filling in the blanks as authorized; and

(b) even though the blanks are incorrectly filled in, the statement as completed is effective in favor of the person to whom it is sent if he purchased the security referred to therein for value and without notice of the incorrectness.

(4) A complete initial transaction statement that has been improperly altered, even though fraudulently, is effective in favor of a purchaser to whom it has been sent, but only according to its original terms. Amended in 1977.

§ 8—207. Rights and Duties of Issuer With Respect to Registered Owners and Registered Pledgees.

(1) Prior to due presentment for registration of transfer of a certificated security in registered form, the issuer or indenture trustee may treat the registered owner as the person exclusively entitled to vote, to receive notifications, and otherwise to exercise all the rights and powers of an owner.

(2) Subject to the provisions of subsections (3), (4), and (6), the issuer or indenture trustee may treat the registered owner of an uncertificated security as the person exclusively entitled to vote, to receive notifications, and otherwise to exercise all the rights and powers of an owner.

(3) The registered owner of an uncertificated security that is subject to a registered pledge is not entitled to registration of transfer prior to the due presentment to the issuer of a release instruction. The exercise of conversion rights with respect to a convertible uncertificated security is a transfer within the meaning of this section.

(4) Upon due presentment of a transfer instruction from the registered pledgee of an uncertificated security, the issuer shall:

(a) register the transfer of the security to the new owner free of pledge, if the instruction specifies a new owner (who may be the registered pledgee) and does not specify a pledgee;

(b) register the transfer of the security to the new owner subject to the interest of the existing pledgee, if the instruction specifies a new owner and the existing pledgee; or

(c) register the release of the security from the existing pledge and register the pledge of the security to the other pledgee, if the instruction specifies the existing owner and another pledgee.

(5) Continuity of perfection of a security interest is not broken by registration of transfer under subsection (4)(b) or by registration of release and pledge under subsection (4)(c), if the security interest is assigned.

(6) If an uncertificated security is subject to a registered pledge:

(a) any uncertificated securities issued in exchange for or distributed with respect to the pledged security shall be registered subject to the pledge;

(b) any certificated securities issued in exchange for or distributed with respect to the pledged security shall be delivered to the registered pledgee; and

(c) any money paid in exchange for or in redemption of part or all of the security shall be paid to the registered pledgee.

(7) Nothing in this Article shall be construed to affect the liability of the registered owner of a security for calls, assessments, or the like. Amended in 1977.

§ 8—208. Effect of Signature of Authenticating Trustee, Registrar, or Transfer Agent.

(1) A person placing his signature upon a certificated security or an initial transaction statement as authenticating trustee, registrar, transfer agent, or the like, warrants to a purchaser for value of the certificated security or a purchaser for value of an uncertificated security to whom the initial transaction statement has been sent, if the purchaser is without notice of the particular defect, that:

(a) the certificated security or initial transaction statement is genuine;

(b) his own participation in the issue or registration of the transfer, pledge, or release of the security is within his capacity and within the scope of the authority received by him from the issuer; and

(c) he has reasonable grounds to believe the security is in the form and within the amount the issuer is authorized to issue.

(2) Unless otherwise agreed, a person by so placing his signature does not assume responsibility for the validity of the security in other respects. Amended in 1962 and 1977.

PART 3.   Transfer.

§ 8—301.   Rights Acquired by Purchaser.

(1) Upon transfer of a security to a purchaser (Section 8—313), the purchaser acquires the rights in the security which his transferor had or had actual authority to convey unless the purchaser's rights are limited by Section 8—302(4).

(2) A transferee of a limited interest acquires rights only to the extent of the interest transferred. The creation or release of a security interest in a security is the transfer of a limited interest in that security. Amended in 1977.

§ 8—302.   "Bona Fide Purchaser"; "Adverse Claim"; Title Acquired by Bona Fide Purchaser.

(1) A "bona fide purchaser" is a purchaser for value in good faith and without notice of any adverse claim:
   (a) who takes delivery of a certificated security in bearer form or in registered form, issued or indorsed to him or in blank;
   (b) to whom the transfer, pledge, or release of an uncertificated security is registered on the books of the issuer; or
   (c) to whom a security is transferred under the provisions of paragraph (c), (d)(i), or (g) of Section 8—313(1).

(2) "Adverse claim" includes a claim that a transfer was or would be wrongful and that a particular adverse person is the owner of or has an interest in the security.

(3) A bona fide purchaser in addition to acquiring the rights of a purchaser (Section 8—301) also acquires his interest in the security free of any adverse claim.

(4) Notwithstanding Section 8—301(1), the transferee of a particular certificated security who has been a party to any fraud or illegality affecting the security, or who as a prior holder of that certificated security had notice of an adverse claim, cannot improve his position by taking from a bona fide purchaser. Amended in 1977.

§ 8—303.   "Broker".

"Broker" means a person engaged for all or part of his time in the business of buying and selling securities, who in the transaction concerned acts for, buys a security from, or sells a security to, a customer. Nothing in this Article determines the capacity in which a person acts for purposes of any other statute or rule to which the person is subject.

§ 8—304.   Notice to Purchaser of Adverse Claims.

(1) A purchaser (including a broker for the seller or buyer, but excluding an intermediary bank) of a certificated security is charged with notice of adverse claims if:
   (a) the security, whether in bearer or registered form, has been indorsed "for collection" or "for surrender" or for some other purpose not involving transfer; or
   (b) the security is in bearer form and has on it an unambiguous statement that it is the property of a person other than the transferor. The mere writing of a name on a security is not such a statement.

(2) A purchaser (including a broker for the seller or buyer, but excluding an intermediary bank) to whom the transfer, pledge, or release of an uncertificated security is registered is charged with notice of adverse claims as to which the issuer has a duty under Section 8—403(4) at the time of registration and which are noted in the initial transaction statement sent to the purchaser or, if his interest is transferred to him other than by registration of transfer, pledge, or release, the initial transaction statement sent to the registered owner or the registered pledgee.

(3) The fact that the purchaser (including a broker for the seller or buyer) of a certificated or uncertificated security has notice that the security is held for a third person or is registered in the name of or indorsed by a fiduciary does not create a duty of inquiry into the rightfulness of the transfer or constitute constructive notice of adverse claims. However, if the purchase (excluding an intermediary bank) has knowledge that the proceeds are being used or that the transaction is for the individual benefit of the fiduciary or otherwise in breach of duty, the purchaser is charged with notice of adverse claims. Amended in 1977.

§ 8—305.   Staleness as Notice of Adverse Claims.

An act or event that creates a right to immediate performance of the principal obligation represented by a certificated security or sets a date on or after which a certificated security is to be presented or surrendered for redemption or exchange does not itself constitute any notice of adverse claims except in the case of a transfer:
   (a) after one year from any date set for presentment or surrender for redemption or exchange; or
   (b) after six months from any date set for payment of money against presentation or surrender of the security if funds are available for payment on that date. Amended in 1977.

§ 8—306. Warranties on Presentment and Transfer of Certificated Securities; Warranties of Originators of Instructions.

(1) A person who presents a certificated security for registration of transfer or for payment or exchange warrants to the issuer that he is entitled to the registration, payment, or exchange. But, a purchaser for value and without notice of adverse claims who receives a new, reissued, or reregistered certificated security on registration of transfer or receives an initial transaction statement confirming the registration of transfer of an equivalent uncertificated security to him warrants only that he has no knowledge of any unauthorized signature (Section 8—311) in a necessary indorsement.

(2) A person by transferring a certificated security to a purchaser for value warrants only that:

(a) his transfer is effective and rightful;

(b) the security is genuine and has not been materially altered; and

(c) he knows of no fact which might impair the validity of the security.

(3) If a certificated security is delivered by an intermediary known to be entrusted with delivery of the security on behalf of another or with collection of a draft or other claim against delivery, the intermediary by delivery warrants only his own good faith and authority, even though he has purchased or made advances against the claim to be collected against the delivery.

(4) A pledgee or other holder for security who redelivers a certificated security received, or after payment and on order of the debtor delivers that security to a third person, makes only the warranties of an intermediary under subsection (3).

(5) A person who originates an instruction warrants to the issuer that:

(a) he is an appropriate person to originate the instruction; and

(b) at the time the instruction is presented to the issuer he will be entitled to the registration of transfer, pledge, or release.

(6) A person who originates an instruction warrants to any person specially guaranteeing his signature (subsection 8—312 (3)) that:

(a) he is an appropriate person to originate the instruction; and

(b) at the time the instruction is presented to the issuer

(i) he will be entitled to the registration of transfer, pledge, or release; and

(ii) the transfer, pledge, or release requested in the instruction will be registered by the issuer free from all liens, security interests, restrictions, and claims other than those specified in the instructions.

(7) A person who originates an instruction warrants to a purchaser for value and to any person guaranteeing the instruction (Section 8—312(6)) that:

(a) he is an appropriate person to originate the instruction;

(b) the uncertificated security referred to therein is valid; and

(c) at the time the instruction is presented to the issuer

(i) the transferor will be entitled to the registration of transfer, pledge, or release;

(ii) the transfer, pledge, or release requested in the instruction will be registered by the issuer free from all liens, security interests, restrictions, and claims other than those specified in the instruction; and

(iii) the requested transfer, pledge, or release will be rightful.

(8) If a secured party is the registered pledgee or the registered owner of an uncertificated security, a person who originates an instruction of release or transfer to the debtor or, after payment and on order of the debtor, a transfer instruction to a third person, warrants to the debtor or the third person only that he is an appropriate person to originate the instruction and, at the time the instruction is presented to the issuer, the transferor will be entitled to the registration of release or transfer. If a transfer instruction to a third person who is a purchaser for value is originated on order of the debtor, the debtor makes to the purchaser the warranties of paragraphs (b), (c)(ii) and (c)(iii) of subsection (7).

(9) A person who transfers an uncertificated security to a purchaser for value and does not originate an instruction in connection with the transfer warrants only that:

(a) his transfer is effective and rightful; and

(b) the uncertificated security is valid.

(10) A broker gives to his customer and to the issuer and a purchaser the applicable warranties provided in this section and has the rights and privileges of a purchaser under this section. The warranties of and in favor of the broker, acting as an agent are in addition to applicable warranties given by and in favor of his customer. Amended in 1962 and 1977.

§ 8—307. Effect of Delivery Without Indorsement; Right to Compel Indorsement.

If a certificated security in registered form has been delivered to a purchaser without a necessary indorsement he may become a bona fide purchaser only as of the time the indorsement is supplied; but against the transferor, the transfer is complete upon delivery and the purchaser has a specifically enforceable right to have any necessary indorsement supplied. Amended in 1977.

§ 8—308. Indorsements; Instructions.

(1) An indorsement of a certificated security in registered form is made when an appropriate person signs on it or on a separate document an assignment or transfer of the security or a power to assign or transfer it or his

signature is written without more upon the back of the security.

(2) An indorsement may be in blank or special. An indorsement in blank includes an indorsement to bearer. A special indorsement specifies to whom the security is to be transferred, or who has power to transfer it. A holder may convert a blank indorsement into a special indorsement.

(3) An indorsement purporting to be only of part of a certificated security representing units intended by the issuer to be separately transferable is effective to the extent of the indorsement.

(4) An "instruction" is an order to the issuer of an uncertificated security requesting that the transfer, pledge, or release from pledge of the uncertificated security specified therein be registered.

(5) An instruction originated by an appropriate person is:

(a) a writing signed by an appropriate person; or

(b) a communication to the issuer in any form agreed upon in a writing signed by the issuer and an appropriate person.

If an instruction has been originated by an appropriate person but is incomplete in any other respect, any person may complete it as authorized and the issuer may rely on it as completed even though it has been completed incorrectly.

(6) "An appropriate person" in subsection (1) means the person specified by the certificated security or by special indorsement to be entitled to the security.

(7) "An appropriate person" in subsection (5) means:

(a) for an instruction to transfer or pledge an uncertificated security which is then not subject to a registered pledge, the registered owner; or

(b) for an instruction to transfer or release an uncertificated security which is then subject to a registered pledge, the registered pledgee.

(8) In addition to the persons designated in subsections (6) and (7), "an appropriate person" in subsections (1) and (5) includes:

(a) if the person designated is described as a fiduciary but is no longer serving in the described capacity, either that person or his successor;

(b) if the persons designated are described as more than one person as fiduciaries and one or more are no longer serving in the described capacity, the remaining fiduciary or fiduciaries, whether or not a successor has been appointed or qualified;

(c) if the person designated is an individual and is without capacity to act by virtue of death, incompetence, infancy, or otherwise, his executor, administrator, guardian, or like fiduciary;

(d) if the persons designated are described as more than one person as tenants by the en-

tirety or with right of survivorship and by reason of death all cannot sign, the survivor or survivors;

(e) a person having power to sign under applicable law or controlling instrument; and

(f) to the extent that the person designated or any of the foregoing persons may act through an agent, his authorized agent.

(9) Unless otherwise agreed, the indorser of a certificated security by his indorsement or the originator of an instruction by his origination assumes no obligation that the security will be honored by the issuer but only the obligations provided in Section 8—306.

(10) Whether the person signing is appropriate is determined as of the date of signing and an indorsement made by or an instruction originated by him does not become unauthorized for the purposes of this Article by virtue of any subsequent change of circumstances.

(11) Failure of fiduciary to comply with a controlling instrument or with the law of the state having jurisdiction of the fiduciary relationship, including any law requiring the fiduciary to obtain court approval of the transfer, pledge, or release, does not render his indorsement or an instruction originated by him unauthorized for the purposes of this Article. Amended in 1962 and 1977.

§ 8—309. Effect of Indorsement Without Delivery.

An indorsement of a certificated security, whether special of in blank, does not constitute a transfer until delivery of the certificated security on which it appears or, if the indorsement is on a separate document, until delivery of both the document and the certificated security. Amended in 1977.

§ 8—310. Indorsement of Certificated Security in Bearer Form.

An indorsement of a certificated security in bearer form may give notice of adverse claims (Section 8—304) but does not otherwise affect any right to registration the holder possesses. Amended in 1977.

§ 8—311. Effect of Unauthorized Indorsement or Instruction.

Unless the owner or pledgee has ratified an authorization indorsement or instruction or is otherwise precluded from asserting its ineffectiveness:

(a) he may assert its ineffectiveness against the issuer or any purchaser, other than a purchaser for value and without notice of adverse claims, who has in good faith received a new, reissued, or reregistered certificated security on registration of transfer or received an initial transaction statement confirming the registration of transfer, pledge, or release of an equivalent uncertificated security to him; and

(b) an issuer who registers the transfer of a certificated security upon the unauthorized indorsement or who registers the transfer, pledge, or release of an uncertificated security upon the unauthorized instruction is subject to liability for improper registration (Section 8—404). Amended in 1977.

§ 8—312. Effect of Guaranteeing Signature, Indorsement or Instruction.

(1) Any person guaranteeing a signature of an indorser of a certificated security warrants that at the time of signing:

(a) the signature was genuine;

(b) the signer was an appropriate person to indorse (Section 8—308); and

(c) the signer had legal capacity to sign.

(2) Any person guaranteeing a signature of the originator of an instruction warrants that at the time of signing:

(a) the signature was genuine;

(b) the signer was an appropriate person to originate the instruction (Section 8—308) if the person specified in the instruction as the registered owner or registered pledgee of the uncertificated security was, in fact, the registered owner or registered pledgee of the security, as to which fact the signature guarantor makes no warranty;

(c) the signer had legal capacity to sign; and

(d) the taxpayer identification number, if any, appearing on the instruction as that of the registered owner or registered pledgee was the taxpayer identification number of the signer or of the owner or pledgee for whom the signer was acting.

(3) Any person specially guaranteeing the signature of the originator of an instruction makes not only the warranties of a signature guarantor (subsection (2)) but also warrants that at the time the instruction is presented to the issuer:

(a) the person specified in the instruction as the registered owner or registered pledgee of the uncertificated security will be the registered owner or registered pledgee; and

(b) the transfer, pledge, or release of the uncertificated security requested in the instruction will be registered by the issuer free from all liens, security interests, restrictions, and claims other than those specified in the instruction.

(4) The guarantor under subsections (1) and (2) or the special guarantor under subsection (3) does not otherwise warrant the rightfulness of the particular transfer, pledge, or release.

(5) Any person guaranteeing an indorsement of a certificated security makes not only the warranties of a signature guarantor under subsection (1) but also warrants the rightfulness of the particular transfer in all respects.

(6) Any person guaranteeing an instruction requesting the transfer, pledge, or release of an uncertificated security makes not only the warranties of a special signature guarantor under subsection (3) but also warrants the rightfulness of the particular transfer, pledge, or release in all respects.

(7) No issuer may require a special guarantee of signature (subsection (3)), a guarantee of indorsement (subsection (5)), or a guarantee of instruction (subsection (6)) as a condition to registration of transfer, pledge, or release.

(8) The foregoing warranties are made to any person taking or dealing with the security in reliance on the guarantee, and the guarantor is liable to the person for any loss resulting from breach of the warranties. Amended in 1977.

§ 8—313. When Transfer to Purchaser Occurs; Financial Intermediary as Bona Fide Purchaser; "Financial Intermediary".

(1) Transfer of a security or a limited interest (including a security interest) therein to a purchaser occurs only:

(a) at the time he or a person designated by him acquires possession of a certificated security;

(b) at the time the transfer, pledge, or release of an uncertificated security is registered to him or a person designated by him;

(c) at the time his financial intermediary acquires possession of a certificated security specially indorsed to or issued in the name of the purchaser;

(d) at the time a financial intermediary, not a clearing corporation, sends him confirmation of the purchase and also by book entry or otherwise identifies as belonging to the purchaser

(i) a specific certificated security in the financial intermediary's possession;

(ii) a quantity of securities that constitute or are part of a fungible bulk of certificated securities in the financial intermediary's possession or of uncertificated securities registered in the name of the financial intermediary; or

(iii) a quantity of securities that constitute or are part of a fungible bulk of securities shown on the account of the financial intermediary on the books of another financial intermediary;

(e) with respect to an identified certificated security to be delivered while still in the possession of a third person, not a financial intermediary, at the time that person acknowledges that he holds for the purchaser;

(f) with respect to a specific uncertificated security the pledge or transfer of which has been registered to a third person, not a financial intermediary, at the time that person acknowledges that he holds for the purchaser;

(g) at the time appropriate entries to the account of the purchaser or a person designated by him on the books of a clearing corporation are made under Section 8—320;

(h) with respect to the transfer of a security interest where the debtor has signed a security agreement containing a description of the security, at the time a written notification, which, in the case of the creation of the security interest, is signed by the debtor (which may be a copy of the security agreement) or which, in the case of the release or assignment of the security interest created pursuant to this paragraph, is signed by the secured party, is received by

(i) a financial intermediary on whose books the interest of the transferor in the security appears;

(ii) a third person, not a financial intermediary, in possession of the security, if it is certificated;

(iii) a third person, not a financial intermediary, who is the registered owner of the security, if it is uncertificated and not subject to a registered pledge; or

(iv) a third person, not a financial intermediary, who is the registered pledgee of the security if it is uncertificated and subject to a registration pledge;

(i) with respect to the transfer of a security interest where the transferor has signed a security agreement containing a description of the security, at the time new value is given by the secured party; or

(j) with respect to the transfer of a security interest where the secured party is a financial intermediary and the security has already been transferred to the financial intermediary under paragraphs (a), (b), (c), (d), or (g), at the time the transferor has signed a security agreement containing a description of the security and value is given by the secured party.

(2) The purchaser is the owner of a security held for him by a financial intermediary, but cannot be a bona fide purchaser of a security so held except in the circumstances specified in paragraphs (c), (d)(i), and (g) of subsection (1). If a security so held is part of a fungible bulk, as in the circumstances specified in paragraphs (d)(ii) and (d)(iii) of subsection (1), the purchaser is the owner of a proportionate property interest in the fungible bulk.

(3) Notice of an adverse claim received by the financial intermediary or by the purchaser after the financial intermediary takes delivery of a certificated security as a holder for value or after the transfer, pledge, or release of an uncertificated security has been registered free of the claim to a financial intermediary who has given value is not effective either as to the financial intermediary or as to the purchaser. However, as between the financial intermediary and the purchaser the purchaser may demand transfer of an equivalent security as to which no notice of adverse claim has been received.

(4) A "financial intermediary" is a bank, broker, clearing corporation, or other person (or the nominee of any of them) which in the ordinary course of its business maintains security accounts for its customers and is acting in that capacity. A financial intermediary may have a security interest in securities held in account for its customer. Amended in 1962 and 1977.

§ 8—314. Duty to Transfer, When Completed.

(1) Unless otherwise agreed, if a sale of a security is made on an exchange or otherwise through brokers:

(a) the selling customer fulfills his duty to transfer at the time he:

(i) places a certificated security in the possession of the selling broker or a person designated by the broker;

(ii) causes an uncertificated security to be registered in the name of the selling broker or a person designated by the broker;

(iii) if requested, causes an acknowledgment to be made to the selling broker that a certificated or uncertificated security is held for the broker; or

(iv) places in the possession of the selling broker or of a person designated by the broker a transfer instruction for an uncertificated security, providing the issuer does not refuse to register the requested transfer if the instruction is presented to the issuer for registration within thirty days thereafter; and

(b) the selling broker, including a correspondent broker acting for a selling customer, fulfills his duty to transfer at the time he:

(i) places a certificated security in the possession of the buying broker or a person designated by the buying broker;

(ii) causes an uncertificated security to be registered in the name of the buying broker or a person designated by the buying broker;

(iii) places in the possession of the buying broker or of a person designated by the buying broker a transfer instruction for an uncertificated security, providing the issuer does not refuse to register the requested transfer if the instruction is presented to the issuer for registration within thirty days thereafter; or

(iv) effects clearance of the sale in accordance with the rules if the exchange on which the transaction took place.

(2) Except as provided in this section or unless otherwise agreed, a transferor's duty to transfer a security under a contract of purchase is not fulfilled until he:

(a) places a certificated security in form to be negotiated by the purchaser in the possession of the purchaser or of a person designated by the purchaser;

(b) causes an uncertificated security to be registered in the name of the purchaser or a person designated by the purchaser; or

(c) if the purchaser requests, causes an acknowledgment to be made to the purchaser that a certificated or uncertificated security is held for the purchaser.

(3) Unless made on an exchange, a sale to a broker purchasing for his own account is within subsection (2) and not within subsection (1). Amended in 1977.

§ 8—315. Action Against Transferee Based Upon Wrongful Transfer.

(1) Any person against whom the transfer of a security is wrongful for any reason, including his incapacity , as against anyone except a bona fide purchaser, may:

(a) reclaim possession of the certificated security wrongfully transferred;

(b) obtain possession of any new certificated security representing all or part of the same rights;

(c) compel the origination of an instruction to transfer to him or a person designated by him an uncertificated security constituting all or part of the same rights; or

(d) have damages.

(2) If the transfer is wrongful because of an unauthorized indorsement of a certificated security, the owner may also reclaim or obtain possession of the security or a new certificated security, even from a bona fide purchaser, if the ineffectiveness of the purported indorsement can be asserted against him under the provisions of this Article on unauthorized indorsements (Section 8—311).

(3) The right to obtain or reclaim possession of a certificated security or to compel the origination of a transfer instruction may be specifically enforced and the transfer of a certificated or uncertificated security enjoined and a certificated security impounded pending the litigation. Amended in 1977.

§ 8—316. Purchaser's Right to Requisites for Registration of Transfer, Pledge, or Release on Books.

Unless otherwise agreed, the transferor of a certificated security or the transferor, pledgor, or pledgee of an uncertificated security on due demand must supply his purchaser with any proof of his authority to transfer, pledge, or release or with any other requisite necessary to obtain registration of the transfer, pledge, or release of the security; but if the transfer, pledge or release is not for value, a transferor, pledger, or pledgee need not do so unless the purchaser furnishes the necessary expenses. Failure within a reasonable time to comply with demand made gives the purchaser the right to reject or rescind the transfer, pledge, or release. Amended in 1977.

§ 8—317. Creditor's Rights.

(1) Subject to the exceptions in subsections (3) and (4), no attachment or levy upon a certificated security or any share or other interest represented thereby which is outstanding is valid until the security is actually seized by the officer making the attachment or levy, but a certificated security which has been surrendered to the issuer may be reached by a creditor by legal process at the issuer's chief executive office in the United States.

(2) An uncertificated security registered in the name of the debtor may not be reached by a creditor except by legal process at the issuer's chief executive office in the United States.

(3) The interest of a debtor in a certificated security that is in the possession of a secured party not a financial intermediary or in an uncertificated security registered in the name of a secured party not a financial intermediary (or in the name of a nominee if the secured party) may be reached by a creditor by legal process upon the secured party.

(4) The interest of a debtor in a certificated security that is in the possession of or registered in the name of a financial intermediary or in an uncertificated security registered in the name of a financial intermediary may be reached by a creditor by legal process upon the financial intermediary on whose books the interest of the debtor appears.

(5) Unless otherwise provided by law, a creditor's lien upon the interest of a debtor in a security obtained pursuant to subsection (3) or (4) is not a restraint on the transfer of the security, free of the lien, to a third party for new value; but in the event of a transfer, the lien applies to the proceeds of the transfer in the hands of the secured party or financial intermediary, subject to any claims having priority.

(6) A creditor whose debtor is the owner of a security is entitled to aid from courts of appropriate jurisdiction, by injunction or otherwise, in reaching the security or in satisfying the claim by means allowed at law or in equity in regard to property that cannot readily be reached by ordinary legal process. Amended in 1977.

§ 8—318. No Conversion by Good Faith Conduct.

An agent or bailee who in good faith (including observance of reasonable commercial standards if he is in the business of buying, selling, or otherwise dealing with securities) has received certificated securities and sold, pledged, or delivered them or has sold or caused the transfer or pledge of uncertificated securities over which he had control according to the instructions of his principal, is not liable for conversion or for participation in breach of fiduciary duty although the principal had no right so to deal with the securities. Amended in 1977.

§ 8—319. Statute of Frauds.

A contract for the sale of securities is not enforceable by way of action or defense unless:

(a) there is some writing signed by the party against whom enforcement is sought or by his authorized agent or broker, sufficient to indicate that a contract has been made for sale of a stated quantity of described securities at a defined or stated price;

(b) delivery of a certificated security or transfer instruction has been accepted, or transfer of an uncertificated security has been registered and the transferee has failed to send written objection to the issuer within ten days after receipt of the initial transaction statement confirming the registration, or payment has been made, but the contract is enforceable under this provision only to the extent of the delivery, registration, or payment;

(c) within a reasonable time a writing in confirmation of the sale or purchase and sufficient against the sender under paragraph (a) has been received by the party against whom enforcement is sought and he has failed to send written objection to its contents within ten days after its receipt; or

(d) the party against whom enforcement is sought admits in his pleading, testimony, or otherwise in court that a contract was made for the sale of a stated quantity of described securities at a defined or stated price. Amended in 1977.

§ 8—320. Transfer or Pledge Within Central Depository System.

(1) In addition to other methods, a transfer, pledge, or release of a security or any interest therein may be effected by the making of appropriate entries on the books of a clearing corporation reducing the account of the transferor, pledgor, or pledgee and increasing the account of the transferee, pledgee, or pledgor by the amount of the obligation or the number of shares or rights transferred, pledged, or released, if the security is shown on the account of a transferor, pledgor, or pledgee on the books of the clearing corporation; is subject to the control of the clearing corporation; and

(a) if certificated,

(i) is in the custody of the clearing corporation, another clearing corporation, a custodian bank, or a nominee of any of them; and

(ii) is in bearer form or indorsed in blank by an appropriate person or registered in the name of the clearing corporation, a custodian bank, or a nominee of any of them; or

(b) if uncertificated, is registered in the name of the clearing corporation, another clearing corporation, a custodian bank, or a nominee of any of them.

(2) Under this section entries may be made with respect to like securities or interests therein as a part of a fungible bulk and may refer merely to a quantity of a particular security without reference to the name of the registered owner, certificate or bond number, or the like, and, in appropriate cases, may be on a net basis taking into account other transfers, pledges, or releases of the same security.

(3) A transfer under this section is effective (Section 8—313) and the purchaser acquires the rights of the transferor (Section 8—301). A pledge or release under this section is the transfer of a limited interest. If a pledge or the creation of a security interest is intended, the security interest is perfected at the time when both value is given by the pledgee and the appropriate entries are made (Section 8—321). A transferee or pledgee under this section may be a bona fide purchaser (Section 8—302).

(4) A transfer or pledge under this section is not a registration of transfer under Part 4.

(5) That entries made on the books of the clearing corporation as provided in subsection (1) are not appropriate does not affect the validity or effect of the entries or the liabilities or obligations of the clearing corporation to any person adversely affected thereby. Added in 1962 and amended in 1977.

§ 8—321. Enforceability, Attachment, Perfection and Termination of Security Interests.

(1) A security interest in a security is enforceable and can attach only if it is transferred to the secured party or a person designated by him pursuant to a provision of Section 8—313(1).

(2) A security interest so transferred pursuant to agreement by a transferor who has rights in the security to a transferee who has given value is a perfected security interest, but a security interest that has been transferred solely under paragraph (i) of Section 8—313(1) becomes unperfected after 21 days unless, within that

time, the requirements for transfer under any other provision of Section 8—313(1) are satisfied.

(3) A security interest in a security is subject to the provisions of Article 9, but:

    (a) no filing is required to perfect the security interest; and

    (b) no written security agreement signed by the debtor is necessary to make the security interest enforceable, except as provided in paragraph (h), (i), or (j) of Section 8—313(1). The secured party has the rights and duties provided under Section 9—207, to the extent they are applicable, whether or not the security is certificated, and, if certificated, whether or not it is in his possession.

(4) Unless otherwise agreed, a security interest in a security is terminated by transfer to the debtor or a person designated by him pursuant to a provision of Section 8—313(1). If a security is thus transferred, the security interest, if not terminated, becomes unperfected unless the security is certificated and is delivered to the debtor for the purpose of ultimate sale or exchange or presentation, collection, renewal, or registration of transfer. In that case, the security interest becomes unperfected after 21 days unless, within that time, the security (or securities for which it has been exchanged) is transferred to the secured party or a person designated by him pursuant to a provision of Section 8—313(1). Added in 1977.

PART 4. *Registration.*

§ 8—401. Duty of Issuer to Register Transfer, Pledge, or Release.

(1) If a certificated security in registered form is presented to the issuer with a request to register transfer or an instruction is presented to the issuer with a request to register transfer, pledge, or release, the issuer shall register the transfer, pledge, or release as requested if:

    (a) the security is indorsed or the instruction was originated by the appropriate person or persons (Section 8—308);

    (b) reasonable assurance is given that those indorsements or instructions are genuine and effective (Section 8—402);

    (c) the issuer has no duty as to adverse claims or has discharged the duty (Section 8—403);

    (d) any applicable law relating to the collection of taxes has been complied with; and

    (e) the transfer, pledge, or release is in fact rightful or is to a bona fide purchaser.

(2) If an issuer is under a duty to register a transfer, pledge, or release of a security, the issuer is also liable to the person presenting a certificated security or an instruction for registration or his principal for loss resulting

from any unreasonable delay in registration or from failure or refusal to register the transfer, pledge, or release. Amended in 1977.

§ 8—402. Assurance that Indorsements and Instructions Are Effective.

(1) The issuer may require the following assurance that each necessary indorsement of a certificated security or each instruction (Section 8—308) is genuine and effective:

    (a) in all cases, a guarantee of the signature (Section 8—312(1) or (2)) of the person indorsing a certificated security or originating an instruction including, in the case of an instruction, a warranty of the taxpayer identification number or, in the absence thereof, other reasonable assurance of identity;

    (b) if the indorsement is made or the instruction is originated by an agent, appropriate assurance of authority to sign;

    (c) if the indorsement is made or the instruction is originated by a fiduciary, appropriate evidence of appointment or incumbency;

    (d) if there is more than one fiduciary, reasonable assurance that all who are required to sign have done so; and

    (e) if the indorsement is made or the instruction is originated by a person not covered by any of the foregoing, assurance appropriate to the case corresponding as nearly as may be to the foregoing.

(2) A ''guarantee of the signature'' in subsection (1) means a guarantee signed by or on behalf of a person reasonably believed by the issuer to be responsible. The issuer may adopt standards with respect to responsibility if they are not manifestly unreasonable.

(3) ''Appropriate evidence of appointment of incumbency'' in subsection (1) means:

    (a) in the case of a fiduciary appointed or qualified by a court, a certificate issued by or under the direction or supervision of that court or an officer thereof and dated within sixty days before the date of presentation for transfer, pledge, or release; or

    (b) in any other case, a copy of a document showing the appointment or a certificate issued by or on behalf of a person reasonably believed by the issuer to be responsible or, in the absence of that document or certificate, other evidence reasonably deemed by the issuer to be appropriate. The issuer may adopt standards with respect to the evidence if they are not manifestly unreasonable. The issuer is not charged with notice of the contents of any document obtained pursuant to this paragraph

(b) except to the extent that the contents relate directly to the appointment or incumbency.

(4) The issuer may elect to require reasonable assurance beyond that specified in this section, but if it does so and, for a purpose other than that specified in subsection (3) (b), both requires and obtains a copy of a will, trust, indenture, articles of co-partnership, by-laws, or other controlling instrument, it is charged with notice of all matters contained therein affecting the transfer, pledge, or release. Amended in 1977.

§ 8—403. Issuer's Duty as to Adverse Claims.

(1) An issuer to whom a certificated security is presented for registration shall inquire into adverse claims if:

(a) a written notification of an adverse claim is received at a time and in a manner affording the issuer a reasonable opportunity to act on it prior to the issuance of a new, reissued, or reregistered certificated security, and the notification identifies the claimant, the registered owner, and the issuer of which the security is a part, and provides an address for communications directed to the claimant; or

(b) the issuer is charged with notice of an adverse claim from a controlling instrument it has elected to require under Section 8—402(4).

(2) The issuer may discharge any duty of inquiry by any reasonable means, including notifying an adverse claimant by registered or certified mail at the address furnished by him or, if there be no such address, at his residence or regular place of business that the certificated security has been presented for registration of transfer by a named person, and that the transfer will be registered unless within thirty days from the date of mailing the notification, either:

(a) an appropriate restraining order, injunction, or other process issues from a court of competent jurisdiction; or

(b) there is filed with the issuer an indemnity bond, sufficient in the issuer's judgment to protect the issuer and any transfer agent, registrar, or other agent of the issuer involved from any loss it or they may suffer by complying with the adverse claim.

(3) Unless an issuer is charged with notice of an adverse claim from a controlling instrument which it has elected to require under Section 8—402(4) or receives notification of an adverse claim under subsection (1), if a certificated security presented for registration is indorsed by the appropriate person or persons the issuer is under no duty to inquire into adverse claims. In particular:

(a) an issuer registering a certificated security in the name of a person who is a fiduciary or who is described as a fiduciary is not bound to inquire into the existence, extent, or correct description of the fiduciary relationship; and thereafter the issuer may assume without inquiry that the newly registered owner continues to be the fiduciary until the issuer receives written notice that the fiduciary is no longer acting as such with respect to the particular security;

(b) an issuer registering transfer on an indorsement by a fiduciary is not bound to inquire whether the transfer is made in compliance with a controlling instrument or with the law of the state having jurisdiction of the fiduciary relationship, including any law requiring the fiduciary to obtain court approval of the transfer; and

(c) the issuer is not charged with notice of the contents of any court record or file or other recorded or unrecorded document even though the document is in its possession and even though the transfer is made on the indorsement of a fiduciary to the fiduciary himself or to his nominee.

(4) An issuer is under no duty as to adverse claims with respect to an uncertificated security except:

(a) claims embodied in a restraining order, injunction, or other legal process served upon the issuer if the process was served at a time and in a manner affording the issuer a reasonable opportunity to act on it in accordance with the requirements of subsection (5);

(b) claims of which the issuer has received a written notification from the registered owner or the registered pledgee if the notification was received at a time and in a manner affording the issuer a reasonable opportunity to act on it in accordance with the requirements of subsection (5);

(c) claims (including restrictions on transfer not imposed by the issuer) to which the registration of transfer to the present registered owner was subject and were so noted in the initial transaction statement sent to him; and

(d) claims as to which an issuer is charged with notice from a controlling instrument it has elected to require under Section 8—402(4).

(5) If the issuer of an uncertificated security is under a duty as to an adverse claim, he discharges that duty by:

(a) including a notation of the claim in any statements sent with respect to the security under Sections 8—408 (3), (6), and (7); and

(b) refusing to register the transfer or pledge of the security unless the nature of the claim does not preclude transfer or pledge subject thereto.

(6) If the transfer or pledge of the security is registered subject to an adverse claim, a notation of the claim must be included in the initial transaction statement and

all subsequent statements sent to the transferee and pledgee under Section 8—408.

(7) Notwithstanding subsections (4) and (5), if an uncertificated security was subject to a registered pledge at the time the issuer first came under a duty as to a particular adverse claim, the issuer has no duty as to that claim if transfer of the security is requested by the registered pledgee or an appropriate person acting for the registered pledgee unless:

    (a) the claim was embodied in legal process which expressly provides otherwise;

    (b) the claim was asserted in a written notification from the registered pledgee;

    (c) the claim was one as to which the issuer was charged with notice from a controlling instrument it required under Section 8—402(4) in connection with the pledgee's request for transfer; or

    (d) the transfer requested is to the registered owner. Amended in 1977.

§ 8—404. Liability and Non-Liability for Registration.

(1) Except as provided in any law relating to the collection of taxes, the issuer is not liable to the owner, pledgee, or any other person suffering loss as a result of the registration of a transfer, pledge, or release of a security if:

    (a) there were on or with a certificated security the necessary indorsements or the issuer had received an instruction originated by an appropriate person (Section 8—308); and

    (b) the issuer had no duty as to adverse claims or has discharged the duty (Section 8—403).

(2) If an issuer has registered a transfer of a certificated security to a person not entitled to it, the issuer on demand shall deliver a like security to the true owner unless:

    (a) the registration was pursuant to subsection (1);

    (b) the owner is precluded from asserting any claim for registering the transfer under Section 8—405(1); or

    (c) the delivery would result in overissue, in which case the issuer's liability is governed by Section 8—104.

(3) If an issuer has improperly registered a transfer, pledge, or release of an uncertificated security, the issuer on demand from the injured party shall restore the records as to the injured party to the condition that would have obtained if the improper registration had not been made unless:

    (a) the registration was pursuant to subsection (1); or

    (b) the registration would result in overissue, in which case the issuer's liability is governed by Section 8—104. Amended in 1977.

§ 8—405. Lost, Destroyed, and Stolen Certificated Securities.

(1) If a certificated security has been lost, apparently destroyed, or wrongfully taken, and the owner fails to notify the issuer of that fact within a reasonable time after he has notice of it and the issuer registers a transfer of the security before receiving notification, the owner is precluded from asserting against the issuer any claim for registering the transfer under Section 8—404 or any claim to a new security under this section.

(2) If the owner of a certificated security claims that the security has been lost, destroyed, or wrongfully taken, the issuer shall issue a new certificated security or, at the option of the issuer, an equivalent uncertificated security in place of the original security if the owner:

    (a) so requests before the issuer has notice that the security has been acquired by a bona fide purchaser;

    (b) files with the issuer a sufficient indemnity bond; and

    (c) satisfies any other reasonable requirements imposed by the issuer.

(3) If, after the issue of a new certificated or uncertificated security, a bona fide purchaser of the original certificated security presents it for registration of transfer, the issuer shall register the transfer unless registration would result in overissue, in which event the issuer's liability is governed by Section 8—104. In addition to any rights on the indemnity bond, the issuer may recover the new certificated security from the person to whom it was issued or any person taking under him except a bona fide purchaser or may cancel the uncertificated security unless a bona fide purchaser or any person taking under a bona fide purchaser is then the registered owner or registered pledgee thereof. Amended in 1977.

§ 8—406. Duty of Authenticating Trustee, Transfer Agent, or Registrar.

(1) If a person acts as authenticating trustee, transfer agent, registrar, or other agent for an issuer in the registration of transfers of its certificated securities or in the registration of transfers, pledges, and releases of its uncertificated securities, in the issue of new securities, or in the cancellation of surrendered securities:

    (a) he is under a duty to the issuer to exercise good faith and due diligence in performing his functions; and

    (b) with regard to the particular functions he performs, he has the same obligation to the holder or owner of a certificated security or to the owner or pledgee of an uncertificated security and has the same rights and privileges as the issuer has in regard to those functions.

(2) Notice to an authenticating trustee, transfer agent, registrar or other agent is notice to the issuer with respect

to the functions performed by the agent. Amended in 1977.

§ 8—407. Exchangeability of Securities.

(1) No issuer is subject to the requirements of this section unless it regularly maintains a system for issuing the class of securities involved under which both certificated and uncertificated securities are regularly issued to the category of owners, which includes the person in whose name the new security is to be registered.

(2) Upon surrender of a certificated security with all necessary indorsements and presentation of a written request by the person surrendering the security, the issuer, if he has no duty as to adverse claims or has discharged the duty (Section 8—403), shall issue to the person or a person designated by him an equivalent uncertificated security subject to all liens, restrictions, and claims that were noted on the certificated security.

(3) Upon receipt of a transfer instruction originated by an appropriate person who so requests, the issuer of an uncertificated security shall cancel the uncertificated security and issue an equivalent certificated security on which must be noted conspicuously any liens and restrictions of the issuer and any adverse claims (as to which the issuer has a duty under Section 8—403(4)) to which the uncertificated security was subject. The certificated security shall be registered in the name of and delivered to:

    (a) the registered owner, if the uncertificated security was not subject to a registered pledge; or

    (b) the registered pledgee, if the uncertificated security was subject to a registered pledge. Added in 1977.

§ 8—408. Statements of Uncertificated Securities.

(1) Within two business days after the transfer of an uncertificated security has been registered, the issuer shall send the new registered owner and, if the security has been transferred subject to a registered pledge, to the registered pledgee a written statement containing:

    (a) a description of the issue of which the uncertificated security is a part;

    (b) the number of shares or units transferred;

    (c) the name and address and any taxpayer identification number of the new registered owner and, if the security has been transferred subject to a registered pledge, the name and address and any taxpayer identification number of the registered pledgee;

    (d) a notation of any liens and restrictions of the issuer and any adverse claims (as to which the issuer has a duty under Section 8—403(4)) to which the uncertificated security is or may be subject at the time of registration or a state-

ment that there are none of those liens, restrictions, or adverse claims; and

    (e) the date the transfer was registered.

(2) Within two business days after the pledge of an uncertificated security has been registered, the issuer shall send to the registered owner and the registered pledgee a written statement containing:

    (a) a description of the issue of which the uncertificated security is a part;

    (b) the number of shares or units pledged;

    (c) the name and address and any taxpayer identification number of the registered owner and the registered pledgee;

    (d) a notation of any liens and restrictions of the issuer and any adverse claims (as to which the issuer has a duty under Section 8—403(4)) to which the uncertificated security is or may be subject at the time of registration or a statement that there are none of those liens, restrictions, or adverse claims; and

    (e) the date the pledge was registered.

(3) Within two business days after the release from pledge of an uncertificated security has been registered, the issuer shall send to the registered owner and the pledgee whose interest was released a written statement containing:

    (a) a description of the issue of which the uncertificated security is a part;

    (b) the number of shares or units released from pledge;

    (c) the name and address and any taxpayer identification number of the registered owner and the pledgee whose interests was released;

    (d) a notation of any liens and restrictions of the issuer and any adverse claims (as to which the issuer has a duty under Section 8—403(4)) to which the uncertificated security is or may be subject at the time of registration or a statement that there are none of those liens, restrictions, or adverse claims; and

    (e) the date the release was registered.

(4) An "initial transaction statement" is the statement sent to:

    (a) the new registered owner and, if applicable, to the registered pledgee pursuant to subsection (1);

    (b) the registered pledgee pursuant to subsection (2); or

    (c) the registered owner pursuant to subsection (3).

Each initial transaction statement shall be signed by or on behalf of the issuer and must be identified as "Initial Transaction Statement".

(5) Within two business days after the transfer of an uncertificated security has been registered, the issuer

shall send to the former registered owner and the former registered pledgee, if any, a written statement containing:

    (a) a description of the issue of which the uncertificated security is a part;

    (b) the number of shares or units transferred;

    (c) the name and address and any taxpayer identification number of the former registered owner and of any former registered pledgee; and

    (d) the date the transfer was registered.

(6) At periodic intervals no less frequent than annually and at any time upon the reasonable written request of the registered owner, the issuer shall send to the registered owner of each uncertificated security a dated written statement containing:

    (a) a description of the issue of which the uncertificated security is a part;

    (b) the name and address and any taxpayer identification number of the registered owner;

    (c) the number of shares or units of the uncerfiticated security registered in the name of the registered owner on the date of the statement;

    (d) the name and address and any taxpayer identification number of any registered pledgee and the number of shares or units subject to the pledge; and

    (e) a notation of any liens and restrictions of the issuer and any adverse claims (as to which the issuer has a duty under Section 8—403(4)) to which the uncertificated security is or may be subject or a statement that there are none of those liens, restrictions, or adverse claims.

(7) At periodic intervals no less frequent than annually and at any time upon the reasonable written request of the registered pledgee, the issuer shall send to the registered pledgee of each uncertificated security a dated written statement containing:

    (a) a description of the issue of which the uncertificated security is a part;

    (b) the name and address and any taxpayer identification number of the registered owner;

    (c) the name and address and any taxpayer identification number of the registered pledgee;

    (d) the number of shares or units subject to the pledge; and

    (e) a notation of any liens and restrictions of the issuer and any adverse claims (as to which the issuer has a duty under Section 8—403(4)) to which the uncertificated security is or may be subject or a statement that there are none of those liens, restrictions, or adverse claims.

(8) If the issuer sends the statements described in subsections (6) and (7) at periodic intervals no less frequent than quarterly, the issuer is not obliged to send additional statements upon request unless the owner or pledgee requesting them pays to the issuer the reasonable cost of furnishing them.

(9) Each statement sent pursuant to this section must bear a conspicuous legend reading substantially as follows: "This statement is merely a record of the rights of the addressee as of the time of its issuance. Delivery of this statement, of itself, confers no rights on the recipient. This statement is neither a negotiable instrument nor a security." Added in 1977.

ARTICLE 9. Secured Transactions; Sales of Accounts and Chattel Paper

PART 1. Short Title, Applicability and Definitions.

§ 9—101. Short Title.

This Article shall be known and may be cited as Uniform Commercial Code—Secured Transactions.

§ 9—102. Policy and Subject Matter of Article.

(1) Except as otherwise provided in Section 9—104 on excluded transactions, this Article applies

    (a) to any transaction (regardless of its form) which is intended to create a security interest in personal property or fixtures including goods, documents, instruments, general intangibles, chattel paper or accounts; and also

    (b) to any sale of accounts or chattel paper.

(2) This Article applies to security interests created by contract including pledge, assignment, chattel mortgage, chattel trust, trust deed, factor's lien, equipment trust, conditional sale, trust receipt, other lien or title retention contract and lease or consignment intended as security. This Article does not apply to statutory liens except as provided in Section 9—310.

(3) The application of this Article to a security interest in a secured obligation is not affected by the fact that the obligation is itself secured by a transaction or interest to which this Article does not apply. Amended in 1972.

> **Note:** The adoption of this Article should be accompanied by the repeal of existing statutes dealing with conditional sales, trust receipts, factors liens where the factor is given a non-possessory lien, chattel mortgages, crop mortgages, mortgages on railroad equipment, assignment of accounts and generally statutes regulating security interests in personal property.
>
> Where the state has a retail installment selling act or small loan act, that legislation should be carefully examined to determine what changes in those acts are needed to conform them to this Article. This Article primarily sets out rules defining rights of a secured party against persons dealing with the debtor; it does not prescribe regulations

and controls which may be necessary to curb abuses arising in the small loan business or in the financing of consumer purchases on credit. Accordingly there is no intention to repeal existing regulatory acts in those fields by enactment or re-enactment of Article 9. See Section 9—203(4) and the Note thereto.

§ 9—103. Perfection of Security Interest in Multiple State Transactions.

(1) Documents, instruments and ordinary goods.

   (a) This subsection applies to documents and instruments and to goods other than those covered by a certificate of title described in subsection (2), mobile goods described in subsection (3), and minerals described in subsection (5).

   (b) Except as otherwise provided in this subsection, perfection and the effect of perfection or nonperfection of a security interest in collateral are governed by the law of the jurisdiction where the collateral is when the last event occurs on which is based the assertion that the security interest is perfected or unperfected.

   (c) If the parties to a transaction creating a purchase money security interest in goods in one jurisdiction understand at the time that the security interest attaches that the goods will be kept in another jurisdiction, then the law of the other jurisdiction governs the perfection and the effect of perfection or non-perfection of the security interest from the time it attaches until thirty days after the debtor receives possession of the goods and thereafter if the goods are taken to the other jurisdiction before the end of the thirty-day period.

   (d) When collateral is brought into and kept in this state while subject to a security interest perfected under the law of the jurisdiction from which the collateral was removed, the security interest remains perfected, but if action is required by Part 3 of this Article to perfect the security interest,

     (i) if the action is not taken before the expiration of the period of perfection in the other jurisdiction or the end of four months after the collateral is brought into this state, whichever period first expires, the security interest becomes unperfected at the end of that period and is thereafter deemed to have been unperfected as against a person who became a purchaser after removal;

     (ii) if the action is taken before the expiration of the period specified in subparagraph

(i), the security interest continues perfected thereafter;

     (iii) for the purpose of priority over a buyer of consumer goods (subsection (2) of Section 9—307), the period of the effectiveness of a filing in the jurisdiction from which the collateral is removed is governed by the rules with respect to perfection in subparagraphs (i) and (ii).

(2) Certificate of title.

   (a) This subsection applies to goods covered by a certificate of title issued under a statute of this state or of another jurisdiction under the law of which indication of a security interest on the certificate is required as a condition of perfection.

   (b) Except as otherwise provided in this subsection, perfection and the effect of perfection or nonperfection of the security interest are governed by the law (including the conflict of laws rules) of the jurisdiction issuing the certificate until four months after the goods are removed from that jurisdiction and thereafter until the goods are registered in another jurisdiction, but in any event not beyond surrender of the certificate. After the expiration of that period, the goods are not covered by the certificate of title within the meaning of this section.

   (c) Except with respect to the rights of a buyer described in the next paragraph, a security interest, perfected in another jurisdiction otherwise than by notation on a certificate of title, in goods brought into this state and thereafter covered by a certificate of title issued by this state is subject to the rules stated in paragraph (d) of subsection (1).

(d) If goods are brought into this state while a security interest therein is perfected in any manner under the law of the jurisdiction from which the goods are removed and a certificate of title is issued by this state and the certificate does not show that the goods are subject to the security interest or that they may be subject to security interests not shown on the certificate, the security interest is subordinate to the rights of a buyer of the goods who is not in the business of selling goods of that kind to the extent that he gives value and receives delivery of the goods after issuance of the certificate and without knowledge of the security interest.

(3) Accounts, general intangibles and mobile goods.

   (a) This subsection applies to accounts (other than an account described in subsection (5) on minerals) and general intangibles (other than uncertificated securities) and to goods which are mobile and which are of a type normally used in more than one jurisdiction, such as motor vehicles, trailers, rolling stock, airplanes, shipping containers, road building and construction machinery and commercial harvesting machinery and the like, if the goods are equipment or are inventory leased or held for lease by the debtor to others, and are not covered by a certificate of title described in subsection (2).

(b) The law (including the conflict of laws rules) of the jurisdiction in which the debtor is located governs the perfection and the effect of perfection or non-perfection of the security interest.

(c) If, however, the debtor is located in a jurisdiction which is not a part of the United States, and which does not provide for perfection of the security interest by filing or recording in that jurisdiction, the law of the jurisdiction in the United States in which the debtor has its major executive office in the United States governs the perfection and the effect of perfection or non-perfection of the security interest through filing. In the alternative, if the debtor is located in a jurisdiction which is not a part of the United States or Canada and the collateral is accounts or general intangibles for money due or to become due, the security interest may be perfected by notification to the account debtor. As used in this paragraph, "United States" includes its territories and possessions and the Commonwealth of Puerto Rico.

(d) A debtor shall be deemed located at his place of business if he has one, at his chief executive office if he has more than one place of business, otherwise at his residence. If, however, the debtor is a foreign air carrier under the Federal Aviation Act of 1958, as amended, it shall be deemed located at the designated office of the agent upon whom service of process may be made on behalf of the foreign air carrier.

(e) A security interest perfected under the law of the jurisdiction of the location of the debtor is perfected until the expiration of four months after a change of the debtor's location to another jurisdiction, or until perfection would have ceased by the law of the first jurisdiction, whichever period first expires. Unless perfected in the new jurisdiction before the end of that period, it becomes unperfected thereafter and is deemed to have been unperfected as against a person who became a purchaser after the change.

(4) Chattel paper.

The rules stated for goods in subsection (1) apply to a possessory security interest in chattel paper. The rules stated for accounts in subsection (3) apply to a nonpossessory security interest in chattel paper, but the security interest may not be perfected by notification to the account debtor.

(5) Minerals.

Perfection and the effect of perfection or non-perfection of a security interest which is created by a debtor who has an interest in minerals or the like (including oil and gas) before extraction and which attaches thereto as extracted, or which attaches to an account resulting from the sale thereof at the wellhead or minehead are governed by the law (including the conflict of laws rules) of the jurisdiction wherein the wellhead or minehead is located.

(6) Uncertificated securities.

The law (including the conflict of laws rules) of the jurisdiction of organization of the issuer governs the perfection and the effect of perfection or non-perfection of a security interest in uncertificated securities. Amended in 1972 and 1977.

§ 9—104. Transactions Excluded From Article.

This Article does not apply

(a) to a security interest subject to any statute of the United States, to the extent that such statute governs the rights of parties to the third parties affected by transactions in particular types of property; or

(b) to a landlord's lien; or

(c) to a lien given by statute or other rule of law for services or materials except as provided in Section 9—301 on priority of such liens; of

(d) to a transfer of a claim for wages, salary or other compensation of an employee; or

(e) to a transfer by a governmental subdivision or agency; or

(f) to a sale of accounts or chattel paper as part of a sale of the business out of which they arose, or an assignment of accounts or chattel paper which is for the purpose of collection only, or a transfer of a right to payment under a contract to an assignee who is also to do the performance under the contract or a transfer of a single account to an assignee in whole or partial satisfaction of a pre-existing indebtedness; or

(g) to a transfer of an interest in or claim in or under any policy of insurance, except as provided with respect to proceeds (Section 9—306) and priorities in proceeds (Section 9—312); or

(h) to a right represented by a judgment (other than a judgment taken on a right to payment which was collateral); or

(i) to any right of set-off; or

(j) except to the extent that provision is made for fixtures in Section 9—313, to the creation or transfer of an interest in or lien on real estate, including a lease or rents thereunder; or

(k) to a transfer in whole or in part of any claim arising out of tort; or

(l) to a transfer of an interest in any deposit account (subsection (1) of Section 9—105), except as provided with respect to proceeds (Section 9—306) and priorities in proceeds (Section 9—312). Amended in 1972.

§ 9—105.   Definitions and Index of Definitions.

(1) In this Article unless the context otherwise requires:

(a) "Account debtor" means the person who is obligated on an account, chattel paper or general intangible;

(b) "Chattel paper" means a writing or writings which evidence both a monetary obligation and a security interest in or a lease of specific goods, but a charter or other contract involving the use or hire of a vessel is not chattel paper. When a transaction is evidenced both by such a security agreement or a lease and by an instrument or a series of instruments, the group of writings taken together constitutes chattel paper;

(c) "Collateral" means the property subject to a security interest, and includes accounts and chattel paper which have been sold;

(d) "Debtor" means the person who owes payment or other performance of the obligation secured, whether or not he owns or has rights in the collateral, and includes the seller of accounts or chattel paper. Where the debtor and the owner of the collateral are not the same person, the term "debtor" means the owner of the collateral in any provision of the Article dealing with the collateral, the obligor in any provision dealing with the obligation, and may include both where the context so requires;

(e) "Deposit account" means a demand, time, savings, passbook or like account maintained with a bank, savings and loan association, credit union or like organization, other than an account evidenced by a certificate of deposit;

(f) "Document" means document of title as defined in the general definitions of Article 1 (Section 1—201), and a receipt of the kind described in subsection (2) of Section 7—201;

(g) "Encumbrance" includes real estate mortgages and other liens on real estate and all other rights in real estate that are not ownership interests;

(h) "Goods" includes all things which are movable at the time the security interest attaches or which are fixtures (Section 9—313), but does not include money, documents, instruments, accounts, chattel paper, general intangibles, or minerals or the like (including oil and gas) before extraction. "Goods" also includes standing timber which is to be cut and removed under a conveyance or contract for sale, the unborn young of animals, and growing crops;

(i) "Instrument" means a negotiable instrument (defined in Section 3—104), or a certificated security (defined in Section 8—102) or any other writing which evidences a right to the payment of money and is not itself a security agreement or lease and is of a type which is in ordinary course of business transferred by delivery with any necessary indorsement or assignment;

(j) "Mortgage" means a consensual interest created by a real estate mortgage, a trust deed on real estate, or the like;

(k) An advance is made "pursuant to commitment" if the secured party has bound himself to make it, whether or not a subsequent event of default or other event not within his control has relieved or may relieve him from his obligation;

(l) "Security agreement" means an agreement which creates or provides for a security interest;

(m) "Secured party" means a lender, seller or other person in whose favor there is a security interest, including a person to whom accounts or chattel paper have been sold. When the holders of obligations issued under an indenture of trust, equipment trust agreement or the like are represented by a trustee or other person, the representative is the secured party;

(n) "Transmitting utility" means any person primarily engaged in the railroad, street railway or trolley bus business, the electric or electronics communications transmission business, the transmission of goods by pipeline, or the transmission or the production and transmission of electricity, steam, gas or water, or the provision of sewer service.

(2) Other definitions applying to the Article and the sections in which they appear are:

"Account".	Section 9—106.
"Attach".	Section 9—203.
"Construction mortgage".	Section 9—313(1).
"Consumer goods".	Section 9—109(1).

"Equipment".   Section 9—109(2).
"Farm products".   Section 9—109(3).
"Fixture".   Section 9—313(1).
"Fixture filing".   Section 9—313(1).
"General intangibles".   Section 9—106.
"Inventory".   Section 9—109(4).
"Lien creditor".   Section 9—301(3).
"Proceeds".   Section 9—306(1).
"Purchase money security
  interest".   Section 9—107.
"United States".   Section 9—103.

(3) The following definitions in other Articles apply to this Article:

"Check".   Section 3—104.
"Contract for sale".   Section 2—106.
"Holder in due course".   Section 3—302.
"Note".   Section 3—104.
"Sale".   Section 2—106.

(4) In addition Article 1 contains general definitions and principles of construction and interpretation applicable throughout this Article. Amended in 1966, 1972 and 1977.

§ 9—106. Definitions: "Account"; "General Intangibles".

"Account" means any right to payment for goods sold or leased or for services rendered which is not evidenced by an instrument or chattel paper, whether or not it has been earned by performance. "General intangibles" means any personal property (including things in action) other than goods, accounts, chattel paper, documents, instruments, and money. All rights to payment earned or unearned under a charter or other contract involving the use or hire of a vessel and all rights incident to the charter or contract are accounts. Amended in 1966, 1972.

§ 9—107. Definitions: "Purchase Money Security Interest".

A security interest is a "purchase money security interest" to the extent that it is

    (a) taken or retained by the seller of the collateral to secure all or part of its price; or

    (b) taken by a person who by making advances or incurring an obligation gives value to enable the debtor to acquire rights in or the use of collateral if such value is in fact so used.

§ 9—108. When After-Acquired Collateral Not Security for Antecedent Debt.

Where a secured party makes an advance, incurs an obligation, releases a perfected security interest, or otherwise gives new value which is to be secured in whole or in part by after-acquired property his security interest in the after-acquired collateral shall be deemed to be taken for new value and not as security for an antecedent debt

if the debtor acquires his rights in such collateral either in the ordinary course of his business or under a contract of purchase made pursuant to the security agreement within a reasonable time after new value is given.

§ 9—109. Classification of Goods; "Consumer Goods"; "Equipment"; "Farm Products"; "Inventory".

Goods are

    (1) "consumer goods" if they are used or bought for use primarily for personal, family or household purposes;

    (2) "equipment" if they are used or bought for use primarily in business (including farming or a profession) or by a debtor who is a non-profit organization or a governmental subdivision or agency or if the goods are not included in the definitions of inventory, farm products or consumer goods;

    (3) "farm products" if they are crops or livestock or supplies used or produced in farming operations or if they are products of crops or livestock in their unmanufactured states (such as ginned cotton, wool-clip, maple syrup, milk and eggs), and if they are in the possession of a debtor engaged in raising, fattening, grazing or other farming operations. If goods are farm products they are neither equipment nor inventory;

    (4) "inventory" if they are held by a person who holds them for sale or lease or to be furnished under contracts of service or if he has so furnished them, or if they are raw materials, work in process or materials used or consumed in a business. Inventory of a person is not to be classified as his equipment.

§ 9—110. Sufficiency of Description.

For the purposes of this Article any description of personal property or real estate is sufficient whether or not it is specific if it reasonably identifies what is described.

§ 9—111. Applicability of Bulk Transfer Laws.

The creation of a security interest is not a bulk transfer under Article 6 (see Section 6—103).

§ 9—112. Where Collateral Is Not Owed by Debtor.

Unless otherwise agreed, when a secured party knows that collateral is owned by a person who is not the debtor, the owner of the collateral is entitled to receive from the secured party any surplus under Section 9—502(2) or under Section 9—504(1), and is not liable for the debt or for any deficiency after resale, and he has the same right as the debtor

    (a) to receive statements under Section 9—208;

    (b) to receive notice of and to object to a secured party's proposal to retain the collateral in satisfaction of the indebtedness under Section 9—505;

    (c) to redeem the collateral under Section 9—506;

(d) to obtain injunctive or other relief under Section 9—507(1); and

(e) to recover losses caused to him under Section 9—208(2).

§ 9—113.   Security Interests Arising Under Article on Sales.

A security interest arising solely under the Article on Sales (Article 2) is subject to the provisions of this Article except that to the extent that and so long as the debtor does not have or does not lawfully obtain possession of the goods

(a) no security agreement is necessary to make the security interest enforceable; and

(b) no filing is required to perfect the security interest; and

(c) the rights of the secured party on default by the debtor are governed by the Article on Sales (Article 2).

[§ 9—113.   Security Interests Arising Under Article on Sales or Under Article on Leases.

A security interest arising solely under the Article on Sales (Article 2) or the Article on Leases (Article 2A) is subject to the provisions of this Article except that to the extent that and so long as the debtor does not have or does not lawfully obtain possession of the goods

(a) no security agreement is necessary to make the security interest enforceable; and

(b) no filing is required to perfect the security interest; and

(c) the rights of the secured party on default by the debtor are governed (i) by the Article on Sales (Article 2) in the case of a security interest arising solely under such Article or (ii) by the Article on Leases (Article 2A) in the case of a security interest arising solely under such Article.*]

§ 9—114.   Consignment.

(1) A person who delivers goods under a consignment which is not a security interest and who would be required to file under this Article by paragraph (3) (c) of Section 2—326 has priority over a secured party who is or becomes a creditor of the consignee and who would have a perfected security interest in the goods if they were the property of the consignee, and also has priority with respect to identifiable cash proceeds received on or before delivery of the goods to a buyer, if

(a) the consignor complies with the filing provision of the Article on Sales with respect to

consignments (paragraph (3) (c) of Section 2—326) before the consignee receives possession of the goods; and

(b) the consignor gives notification in writing to the holder of the security interest if the holder has filed a financing statement covering the same types of goods before the date of the filing made by the consignor; and

(c) the holder of the security interest receives the notification within five years before the consignee receives possession of the goods; and

(d) the notification states that the consignor expects to deliver goods on consignment to the consignee, describing the goods by item or type.

(2) In the case of a consignment which is not a security interest and in which the requirements of the preceding subsection have not been met, a person who delivers goods to another is subordinate to a person who would have a perfected security interest in the goods if they were the property of the debtor. Added in 1972.

PART 2.   Validity of Security Agreement and Rights of Parties Thereto.

§ 9—201.   General Validity of Security Agreement.

Except as otherwise provided by this Act a security agreement is effective according to its terms between the parties, against purchasers of the collateral and against creditors. Nothing in this Article validates any charge or practice illegal under any statute or regulation thereunder governing usury, small loans, retail installment sales, or the like, or extends the application of any such statute or regulation to any transaction not otherwise subject thereto.

§ 9—202.   Title to Collateral Immaterial.

Each provision of this Article with regard to rights, obligations and remedies applies whether title to collateral is in the secured party or in the debtor.

§ 9—203.   Attachment and Enforceability of Security Interest; Proceeds; Formal Requisites.

(1) Subject to the provisions of Section 4—208 on the security interest of a collecting bank, Section 8—321 on security interests in securities and Section 9—113 on a security interest arising under the Article on Sales, a security interest is not enforceable against the debtor or third parties with respect to the collateral and does not attach unless:

(a) the collateral is in the possession of the secured party pursuant to agreement, or the debtor has signed a security agreement which contains a description of the collateral and in addition, when the security interest covers

---

*This version of § 9—113 should be adopted in jurisdictions enacting UCC Article 2A—Leases.

crops growing or to be grown or timber to be cut, a description of the land concerned;

(b) value has been given; and

(c) the debtor has rights in the collateral.

(2) A security interest attaches when it becomes enforceable against the debtor with respect to the collateral. Attachment occurs as soon as all of the events specified in subsection (1) have taken place unless explicit agreement postpones the time of attaching.

(3) Unless otherwise agreed a security agreement gives the secured party the rights to proceeds provided by Section 9—306.

(4) A transaction, although subject to this Article, is also subject to . . . .*, and in the case of conflict between the provisions of this Article and any such statute, the provisions of such statute control. Failure to comply with any applicable statute has only the effect which is specified therein. Amended in 1972 and 1977.

Note: At* in subsection (4) insert reference to any local statute regulating small loans, retail installment sales and the like.

The foregoing subsection (4) is designed to make it clear that certain transactions, although subject to this Article, must also comply with other applicable legislation.

This Article is designed to regulate all the "security" aspects of transactions within its scope. There is, however, much regulatory legislation, particularly in the consumer field, which supplements this Article and should not be repealed by its enactment. Examples are small loan acts, retail installment selling acts and the like. Such acts may provide for licensing and rate regulation and may prescribe particular forms of contract. Such provisions should remain in force despite the enactment of this Article. On the other hand if a retail installment selling act contains provisions on filing, rights on default, etc., such provisions should be repealed as inconsistent with this Article except that inconsistent provisions as to deficiencies, penalties, etc., in the Uniform Consumer Credit Code and other recent related legislation should remain because those statutes were drafted after the substantial enactment of the Article and with the intention of modifying certain provisions of this Article as to consumer credit.

§ 9—204. After-Acquired Property; Future Advances.

(1) Except as provided in subsection (2), a security agreement may provide that any or all obligations covered by the security agreement are to be secured by after-acquired collateral.

(2) No security interest attaches under an after-acquired property clause to consumer goods other than accessions (Section 9—314) when given as additional security unless the debtor acquires rights in them within ten days after the secured party gives value.

(3) Obligations covered by a security agreement may include future advances or other value whether or not the advances or value are given pursuant to commitment (subsection (1) of Section 9—105). Amended in 1972.

§ 9—205. Use or Disposition of Collateral Without Accounting Permissible.

A security interest is not invalid or fraudulent against creditors by reason of liberty in the debtor to use, commingle or dispose of all or part of the collateral (including returned or repossessed goods) or to collect or compromise accounts or chattel paper, or to accept the return of goods or make repossessions, or to use, commingle or dispose of proceeds, or by reason of the failure of the secured party to require the debtor to account for proceeds or replace collateral. This section does not relax the requirements of possession where perfection of a security interest depends upon possession of the collateral by the secured party or by a bailee. Amended in 1972.

§ 9—206. Agreement Not to Assert Defenses Against Assignee; Modification of Sales Warranties Where Security Agreement Exists.

(1) Subject to any statute or decision which establishes a different rule for buyers or lessees of consumer goods, an agreement by a buyer or lessee that he will not assert against an assignee any claim or defense which he may have against the seller or lessor is enforceable by an assignee who takes his assignment for value, in good faith and without notice of a claim or defense, except as to defenses of a type which may be asserted against a holder in due course of a negotiable instrument under the Article on Commercial Paper (Article 3). A buyer who as part of one transaction signs both a negotiable instrument and a security agreement makes such an agreement.

(2) When a seller retains a purchase money security interest in goods the Article on Sales (Article 2) governs the sale and any disclaimer, limitation or modification of the seller's warranties. Amended in 1962.

§ 9—207. Rights and Duties When Collateral Is in Secured Party's Possession.

(1) A secured party must use reasonable care in the custody and preservation of collateral in his possession. In the case of an instrument or chattel paper reasonable care includes taking necessary steps to preserve rights against prior parties unless otherwise agreed.

(2) Unless otherwise agreed, when collateral is in the secured party's possession

(a) reasonable expenses (including the cost of any insurance and payment of taxes or other charges) incurred in the custody, preservation, use or operation of the collateral are chargeable to the debtor and are secured by the collateral;

(b) the risk of accidental loss or damage is on the debtor to the extent of any deficiency in any effective insurance coverage;

(c) the secured party may hold as additional security any increase or profits (except money) received from the collateral, but money so received, unless remitted to the debtor, shall be applied in reduction of the secured obligation;

(d) the secured party must keep the collateral identifiable but fungible collateral may be commingled;

(e) the secured party may repledge the collateral upon terms which do not impair the debtor's right to redeem it.

(3) A secured party is liable for any loss caused by his failure to meet any obligation imposed by the preceding subsections but does not lose his security interest.

(4) A secured party may use or operate the collateral for the purpose of preserving the collateral or its value or pursuant to the order of a court of appropriate jurisdiction or, except in the case of consumer goods, in the manner and to the extent provided in the security agreement.

§ 9—208. Request for Statement of Account or List of Collateral.

(1) A debtor may sign a statement indicating what he believes to be the aggregate amount of unpaid indebtedness as of a specified date and may send it to the secured party with a request that the statement be approved or corrected and returned to the debtor. When the security agreement or any other record kept by the secured party identifies the collateral a debtor may similarly request the secured party to approve or correct a list of the collateral.

(2) The secured party must comply with such a request within two weeks after receipt by sending a written correction or approval. If the secured party claims a security interest in all of a particular type of collateral owned by the debtor he may indicate that fact in his reply and need not approve or correct an itemized list of such collateral. If the secured party without reasonable excuse fails to comply he is liable for any loss caused to the debtor thereby; and if the debtor has properly included in his request a good faith statement of the obligation or a list of the collateral or both the secured party may claim a security interest only as shown in the statement against persons misled by his failure to comply. If he no longer has an interest in the obligation or collateral at the time the request is received he must disclose the name and address of any successor in interest known to him and he is liable for any loss caused to the debtor as a result of failure to disclose. A successor in interest is not subject to this section until a request is received by him.

(3) A debtor is entitled to such a statement once every six months without charge. The secured party may require payment of a charge not exceeding $10 for each additional statement furnished.

PART 3. Rights of Third Parties; Perfected and Unperfected Security Interests; Rules of Priority.

§ 9—301. Persons Who Take Priority Over Unperfected Security Interests; Rights of "Lien Creditor".

(1) Except as otherwise provided in subsection (2), an unperfected security interest is subordinate to the rights of

(a) persons entitled to priority under Section 9—312;

(b) a person who becomes a lien creditor before the security interest is perfected;

(c) in the case of goods, instruments, documents, and chattel paper, a person who is not a secured party and who is a transferee in bulk or other buyer not in ordinary course of business or is a buyer of farm products in ordinary course of business, to the extent that he gives value and receives delivery of the collateral without knowledge of the security interest and before it is perfected.

(d) in the case of accounts and general intangibles, a person who is not a secured party and who is a transferee to the extent that he gives value without knowledge of the security interest and before it is perfected

(2) If the secured party files with respect to a purchase money security interest before or within ten days after the debtor receives possession of the collateral, he takes priority over the rights of a transferee in bulk or of a lien creditor which arise between the time the security interest attaches and the time of filing.

(3) A "lien creditor" means a creditor who has acquired a lien on the property involved by attachment, levy or the like and includes an assignee for benefit of creditors from the time of assignment, and a trustee in bankruptcy from the date of the filing of the petition or a receiver in equity from the time of appointment.

(4) A person who becomes a lien creditor while a security interest is perfected takes subject to the security interest only to the extent that it secures advances made before he becomes a lien creditor or within 45 days thereafter or made without knowledge of the lien or pursuant to a commitment entered into without knowledge of the lien. Amended in 1972.

§ 9—302. When Filing Is Required to Perfect Security Interest; Security Interests to Which Filing Provisions of This Article Do Not Apply.

(1) A financing statement must be filed to perfect all security interests except the following:

(a) a security interest in collateral in possession of the secured party under Section 9—305;

(b) a security interest temporarily perfected in instruments or documents without delivery under Section 9—304 or in proceeds for a ten-day period under Section 9—306;

(c) a security interest created by an assignment of a beneficial interest in a trust or a decedent's estate;

(d) a purchase money security interest in consumer goods; but filing is required for a motor vehicle required to be registered; and fixture filing is required for priority over conflicting interests in fixtures to the extent provided in Section 9—313;

(e) an assignment of accounts which does not alone or in conjunction with other assignments to the same assignee transfer a significant part of the outstanding accounts of the assignor;

(f) a security interest of a collecting bank (Section 4—208) or in securities (Section 8—321) or arising under Article on Sales (see Section 9—113) or covered in subsection (3) of this section;

(g) an assignment for the benefit of all the creditors of the transferor, and subsequent transfers by the assignee thereunder.

(2) If a secured party assigns a perfected security interest, no filing under this Article is required in order to continue the perfected status of the security interest against creditors of and transferees from the original debtor.

(3) The filing of a financing statement otherwise required by this Article is not necessary or effective to perfect a security interest in property subject to

(a) a statute or treaty of the United States which provides for a national or international registration or a national or international certificate of title or which specifies a place of filing different from that specified in this Article for filing of the security interest; or

(b) the following statutes of this state; [list any certificate of title statute covering automobiles, trailers, mobile homes, boats, farm tractors, or the like, and any central filing statute*.]; but during any period in which collateral is inventory held for sale by a person who is in the business of selling goods of that kind, the filing provisions of this Article (Part 4) apply to a security interest in that collateral created by him as debtor; or

(c) a certificate of title statute of another jurisdiction under the law of which indication of a security interest on the certificate is required as a condition of perfection (subsection (2) of Section 9—103).

(4) Compliance with a statute or treaty described in subsection (3) is equivalent to the filing of a financing statement under this Article, and a security interest in property subject to the statute or treaty can be perfected only by compliance therewith except as provided in Section 9—103 on multiple state transactions. Duration and renewal of perfection of a security interest perfected by compliance with the statute or treaty are governed by the provisions of the statute or treaty; in other respects the security interest is subject to this Article. Amended in 1972 and 1977.

>***Note:** It is recommended that the provisions of certificate of title acts for perfection of security interests by notation on the certificates should be amended to exclude coverage of inventory held for sale.

§ 9—303. When Security Interest Is Perfected; Continuity of Perfection.

(1) A security interest is perfected when it has attached and when all of the applicable steps required for perfection have been taken. Such steps are specified in Sections 9—302, 9—304, 9—305 and 9—306. If such steps are taken before the security interest attaches, it is perfected at the time when it attaches.

(2) If a security interest is originally perfected in any way permitted under this Article and is subsequently perfected in some other way under this Article, without an intermediate period when it was unperfected, the security interest shall be deemed to be perfected continuously for the purposes of this Article.

§ 9—304. Perfection of Security Interest in Instruments, Documents, and Goods Covered by Documents; Perfection by Permissive Filing; Temporary Perfection Without Filing or Transfer of Possession.

(1) A security interest in chattel paper or negotiable documents may be perfected by filing. A security interest in money or instruments (other than certificated securities or instruments which constitute part of chattel paper can be perfected only by the secured party's taking possession, except as provided in subsections (4) and (5) of this section and subsections (2) and (3) of Section 9—306 on proceeds.

(2) During the period that goods are in the possession of the issuer of a negotiable document therefor, a security interest in the goods is perfected by perfecting a security interest in the document, and any security interest in the goods otherwise perfected during such period is subject thereto.

(3) A security interest in goods in the possession of a bailee other than one who has issued a negotiable document therefor is perfected by issuance of a document in the name of the secured party or by the bailee's receipt of notification of the secured party's interest or by filing as to the goods.

(4) A security interest in instruments (other than certificated securities) or negotiable documents is perfected without filing or the taking of possession for a period of 21 days from the time it attaches to the extent that it arises for new value given under a written security agreement.

(5) A security interest remains perfected for a period of 21 days without filing where a secured party having a perfected security interest in an instrument (other than a certificated security), a negotiable document or goods in possession of bailee other than one who has issued a negotiable document therefor

    (a) makes available to the debtor the goods or documents representing the goods for the purpose of ultimate sale or exchange or for the purpose of loading, unloading, storing, shipping, transshipping, manufacturing, processing or otherwise dealing with them in a manner preliminary to their sale or exchange, but priority between conflicting security interests in the goods is subject to subsection (3) of Section 9—312; or

    (b) delivers the instrument to the debtor for the purpose of ultimate sale or exchange or of presentation, collection, renewal or registration of transfer.

(6) After the 21-day period in subsections (4) and (5) perfection depends upon compliance with applicable provisions of this Article. Amended in 1972 and 1977.

§ 9—305. When Possession by Secured Party Perfects Security Interest Without Filing.

A security interest in letters of credit and advices of credit (subsection (2)(a) of Section 5—116) goods instruments (other than certificated securities), money negotiable documents, or chattel paper may be perfected by the secured party's taking possession of the collateral. If such collateral other than goods covered by a negotiable document is held by a bailee, the secured party is deemed to have possession from the time the bailee receives notification of the secured party's interest. A security interest is perfected by possession from the time possession is taken without relation back and continues only so long as possession is retained, unless otherwise specified in this Article. The security interest may be otherwise perfected as provided in this Article before or after the period of possession by the secured party. Amended in 1972 and 1977.

§ 9—306. "Proceeds"; Secured Party's Rights on Disposition of Collateral.

(1) "Proceeds" includes whatever is received upon the sale, exchange, collection or other disposition of collateral or proceeds. Insurance payable by reason of loss or damage to the collateral is proceeds, except to the extent that it is payable to a person other than a party to

the security agreement. Money, checks, deposit accounts, and the like are "cash proceeds". All other proceeds are "non-cash proceeds".

(2) Except where this Article otherwise provides, a security interest continues in collateral notwithstanding sale, exchange or other disposition thereof unless the disposition was authorized by the secured party in the security agreement or otherwise, and also continues in any identifiable proceeds including collections received by the debtor.

(3) The security interest in proceeds is a continuously perfected security interest if the interest in the original collateral was perfected but it ceases to be a perfected security interest and becomes unperfected ten days after receipt of the proceeds by the debtor unless

    (a) a filed financing statement covers the original collateral and the proceeds are collateral in which a security interest may be perfected by filing in the office or offices where the financing statement has been filed and, if the proceeds are acquired with cash proceeds, the description of collateral in the financing statement indicates the types of property constituting the proceeds; or

    (b) a filed financing statement covers the original collateral and the proceeds are identifiable cash proceeds; or

    (c) the security interest in the proceeds is perfected before the expiration of the ten-day period.

Except as provided in this section, a security interest in proceeds can be perfected only by the methods or under the circumstances permitted in this Article for original collateral of the same type.

(4) In the event of insolvency proceedings instituted by or against a debtor, a secured party with a perfected security interest in proceeds has a perfected security interest only in the following proceeds:

    (a) in identifiable non-cash proceeds and in separate deposit accounts containing only proceeds;

    (b) in identifiable cash proceeds in the form of money which is neither commingled with other money nor deposited in a deposit account prior to the insolvency proceedings;

    (c) in identifiable cash proceeds in the form of checks and the like which are not deposited in a deposit account prior to the insolvency proceedings; and

    (d) in all cash and deposit accounts of the debtor in which proceeds have been commingled with other funds, but the perfected security interest under this paragraph (d) is

      (i) subject to any right to set-off; and

      (ii) limited to an amount not greater than the amount of any cash proceeds received by the debtor within ten days before the institution of the insolvency proceedings less the sum of (I) the payments to the secured party on account of cash proceeds received by the debtor during such period and (II) the cash proceeds received by the debtor during such period to which the secured party is entitled under paragraphs (a) through (c) of this subsection (4).

(5) If a sale of goods results in an account or chattel paper which is transferred by the seller to a secured party, and if the goods are returned to or are repossessed by the seller or the secured party, the following rules determine priorities:

(a) If the goods were collateral at the time of sale, for an indebtedness of the seller which is still unpaid, the original security interest attaches again to the goods and continues as a perfected security interest if it was perfected at the time when the goods were sold. If the security interest was originally perfected by a filing which is still effective, nothing further is required to continue the perfected status; in any other case, the secured party must take possession of the returned or repossessed goods or must file.

(b) An unpaid transferee of the chattel paper has a security interest in the goods against the transferor. Such security interest is prior to a security interest asserted under paragraph (a) to the extent that the transferee of the chattel paper was entitled to priority under Section 9—308.

(c) An unpaid transferee of the account has a security interest in the goods against the transferor. Such security interest is subordinate to a security interest asserted under paragraph (a).

(d) A security interest of an unpaid transferee asserted under paragraph (b) and (c) must be perfected for protection against creditors of the transferor and purchasers of the returned or repossessed goods. Amended in 1972.

§ 9—307.   Protection of Buyers of Goods.

(1) A buyer in ordinary course of business (subsection (9) of Section 1—201) other than a person buying farm products from a person engaged in farming operations takes free of a security interest created by his seller even though the security interest is perfected and even though the buyer knows of its existence.

(2) In the case of consumer goods, a buyer takes free of a security interest even though perfected if he buys without knowledge of the security interest, for value and for his own personal, family or household purposes unless prior to the purchase the secured party has filed in financing statement covering such goods.

(3) A buyer other than a buyer in ordinary course of business (subsection (1) of this section) takes free of a security interest to the extent that it secures future advances made after the secured party acquires knowledge of the purchase, or more than 45 days after the purchase, whichever first occurs, unless made pursuant to a commitment entered into without knowledge of the purchase and before the expiration of the 45-day period. Amended in 1972.

§ 9—308.   Purchase of Chattel Paper and Instruments.

A purchaser of chattel paper or an instrument who gives new value and takes possession of it in the ordinary course of his business has priority over a security interest in the chattel paper or instrument

(a) which is perfected under Section 9—304 (permissive filing and temporary perfection) or under Section 9—306 (perfection as to proceeds) if he acts without knowledge that the specific paper or instrument is subject to a security interest; or

(b) which is claimed merely as proceeds of inventory subject to a security interest (Section 9—306) even though he knows that the specific paper or instrument is subject to the security interest. Amended in 1972.

§ 9—309.   Protection of Purchasers of Instruments, Documents and Securities.

Nothing in this Article limits the rights of a holder in due course of a negotiable instrument (Section 3—302) or a holder to whom a negotiable document of title has been duly negotiated (Section 7—501) or a bona fide purchaser of a security (Section 8—302) and such holders or purchasers take priority over an earlier security interest even though perfected. Filing under this Article does not constitute notice of the security interest to such holders or purchasers. Amended in 1977.

§ 9—310.   Priority of Certain Liens Arising by Operation of Law.

When a person in the ordinary course of his business furnishes services or materials with respect to goods subject to a security interest, a lien upon goods in the possession of such person given by statute or rule of law for such materials or services takes priority over a perfected security interest unless the lien is statutory and the statute expressly provides otherwise.

§ 9—311.   Alienability of Debtor's Rights: Judicial Process.

The debtor's rights in collateral may be voluntarily or involuntarily transferred (by way of sale, creation of a security interest, attachment, levy, garnishment or other judicial process) notwithstanding a provision in the security agreement prohibiting any transfer or making the transfer constitute a default.

§ 9—312. Priorities Among Conflicting Security Interests in the Same Collateral.

(1) The rules of priority stated in other sections of this Part and in the following sections shall govern when applicable: Section 4—208 with respect to the security interests of collecting banks in items being collected, accompanying documents and proceeds; Section 9—103 on security interests related to other jurisdictions; Section 9—114 on consignments.

(2) A perfected security interest in crops for new value given to enable the debtor to produce the crops during the production season and given not more than three months before the crops become growing crops by planting or otherwise takes priority over an earlier perfected security interest to the extent that such earlier interest secures obligations due more than six months before the crops become growing crops by planting or otherwise, even though the person giving new value had knowledge of the earlier security interest.

(3) A perfected purchase money security interest in inventory has priority over a conflicting security interest in the same inventory and also has priority in identifiable cash proceeds received on or before the delivery of the inventory to a buyer if

  (a) the purchase money security interest is perfected at the time the debtor receives possession of the inventory; and

  (b) the purchase money secured party gives notification in writing to the holder of the conflicting security interest if the holder had filed a financing statement covering the same types of inventory (i) before the date of the filing made by the purchase money secured party, or (ii) before the beginning of the 21-day period where the purchase money security interest is temporarily perfected without filing or possession (subsection (5) of Section 9—304); and

  (c) the holder of the conflicting security interest receives the notification within five years before the debtor receives possession of the inventory; and

  (d) the notification states that the person giving the notice has or expects to acquire a purchase money security interest in inventory of the debtor, describing such inventory by item or type.

(4) A purchase money security interest in collateral other than inventory has priority over a conflicting security interest in the same collateral or its proceeds if the purchase money security interest is perfected at the time the debtor receives possession of the collateral or within ten days thereafter.

(5) In all cases not governed by other rules stated in this section (including cases of purchase money security interests which do not qualify for the special priorities set forth in subsections (3) and (4) of this section), priority between conflicting security interests in the same collateral shall be determined according to the following rules:

  (a) Conflicting security interests rank according to priority in time of filing or perfection. Priority dates from the time a filing is first made covering the collateral or the time the security interest is first perfected, whichever is earlier, provided that there is no period thereafter when there is neither filing nor perfection.

  (b) So long as conflicting security interests are unperfected, the first to attach has priority.

(6) For the purposes of subsection (5) a date of filing or perfection as to collateral is also a date of filing or perfection as to proceeds.

(7) If future advances are made while a security interest is perfected by filing, the taking of possession, or under Section 8—321 on securities, the security interest has the same priority for the purposes of subsection (5) with respect to the future advances as it does with respect to the first advance. If a commitment is made before or while the security interest is so perfected, the security interest has the same priority with respect to advances made pursuant thereto. In other cases a perfected security interest has priority from the date the advance is made. Amended in 1972 and 1977.

§ 9—313. Priority of Security Interests in Fixtures.

(1) In this section and in the provisions of Part 4 of this Article referring to fixture filing, unless the context otherwise requires

  (a) goods are "fixtures" when they become so related to particular real estate that an interest in them arises under real estate law

  (b) a "fixture filing" is the filing in the office where a mortgage on the real estate would be filed or recorded of a financing statement covering goods which are or are to become fixtures and conforming to the requirements of subsection (5) of Section 9—402

  (c) a mortgage is a "construction mortgage" to the extent that it secures an obligation incurred for the construction of an improvement on land including the acquisition cost of the land, if the recorded writing so indicates.

(2) A security interest under this Article may be created in goods which are fixtures or may continue in goods which become fixtures, but no security interest ex-

ists under this Article in ordinary building materials incorporated into an improvement on land.

(3) This Article does not prevent creation of an encumbrance upon fixtures pursuant to real estate law.

(4) A perfected security interest in fixtures has priority over the conflicting interest of an encumbrancer or owner of the real estate where

(a) the security interest is a purchase money security interest, the interest of the encumbrancer or owner arises before the goods become fixtures, the security interest is perfected by a fixture filing before the goods become fixtures or within ten days thereafter, and the debtor has an interest of record in the real estate or is in possession of the real estate; or

(b) the security interest is perfected by a fixture filing before the interest of the encumbrancer or owner is of record, the security interest has priority over any conflicting interest of a predecessor in title of the encumbrancer or owner, and the debtor has an interest of record in the real estate or is in possession of the real estate; or

(c) the fixtures are readily removable factory or office machines or readily removable replacements of domestic appliances which are consumer goods, and before the goods become fixtures the security interest is perfected by any method permitted by this Article; or

(d) the conflicting interest is a lien on the real estate obtained by legal or equitable proceedings after the security interest was perfected by any method permitted by this Article.

(5) A security interest in fixtures, whether or not perfected, has priority over the conflicting interest of an encumbrancer or owner of the real estate where

(a) the encumbrancer or owner has consented in writing to the security interest or has disclaimed an interest in the goods as fixtures; or

(b) the debtor has a right to remove the goods as against the encumbrancer or owner. If the debtor's right terminates, the priority of the security interest continues for a reasonable time.

(6) Notwithstanding paragraph (a) of subsection (4) but otherwise subject to subsections (4) and (5), a security interest in fixtures is subordinate to a construction mortgage recorded before the goods become fixtures if the goods become fixtures before the completion of the construction. To the extent that it is given to refinance a construction mortgage, a mortgage has this priority to the same extent as the construction mortgage.

(7) In cases not within the preceding subsections, a security interest in fixtures is subordinate to the conflicting interest of an encumbrancer or owner of the related real estate who is not the debtor.

(8) When the secured party has priority over all owners and encumbrancers of the real estate, he may, on default, subject to the provisions of Part 5, remove his collateral from the real estate but he must reimburse any encumbrancer or owner of the real estate who is not the debtor and who has not otherwise agreed for the cost of repair of any physical injury, but not for any diminution in value of the real estate caused by the absence of the goods removed or by any necessity of replacing them. A person entitled to reimbursement may refuse permission to remove until the secured party gives adequate security for the performance of this obligation. Amended in 1972.

§ 9—314. Accessions.

(1) A security interest in goods which attaches before they are installed in or affixed to other goods takes priority as to the goods installed or affixed (called in this section "accessions") over the claims of all persons to the whole except as stated in subsection (3) and subject to Section 9—315(1).

(2) A security interest which attaches to goods after they become part of a whole is valid against all persons subsequently acquiring interests in the whole except as stated in subsection (3) but is invalid against any person with an interest in the whole at the time the security interest attaches to the goods who has not in writing consented to the security interest or disclaimed an interest in the goods as part of the whole.

(3) The security interests described in subsections (1) and (2) do not take priority over

(a) a subsequent purchaser for value of any interest in the whole; or

(b) a creditor with a lien on the whole subsequently obtained by judicial proceedings; or

(c) a creditor with a prior perfected security interest in the whole to the extent that he makes subsequent advances

if the subsequent purchase is made, the lien by judicial proceedings obtained or the subsequent advance under the prior perfected security interest is made or contracted for without knowledge of the security interest and before it is perfected. A purchaser of the whole at a foreclosure sale other than the holder of a perfected security interest purchasing at his own foreclosure sale is a subsequent purchaser within this section.

(4) When under subsections (1) or (2) and (3) a secured party has an interest in accessions which has priority over the claims of all persons who have interests in the whole, he may on default subject to the provisions of Part 5 remove his collateral from the whole but he must reimburse any encumbrancer or owner of the whole who is not the debtor and who has not otherwise agreed for the cost of repair of any physical injury but not for any diminution in value of the whole caused by the absence of the goods removed or by any necessity for replacing

them. A person entitled to reimbursement may refuse permission to remove until the secured party gives adequate security for the performance of this obligation.

§ 9—315.   Priority When Goods Are Commingled or Processed.

(1) If a security interest in goods was perfected and subsequently the goods or a part thereof have become part of a product or mass, the security interest continues in the product or mass if

(a) the goods are so manufactured, processed, assembled or commingled that their identity is lost in the product or mass; or

(b) a financing statement covering the original goods also covers the product into which the goods have been manufactured, processed or assembled.

In a case to which paragraph (b) applies, no separate security interest in that part of the original goods which has been manufactured, processed or assembled into the product may be claimed under Section 9—314.

(2) When under subsection (1) more than one security interest attaches to the product or mass, they rank equally according to the ratio that the cost of the goods to which each interest originally attached bears to the cost of the total product or mass.

§ 9—316.   Priority Subject to Subordination.

Nothing in this Article prevents subordination by agreement by any person entitled to priority.

§ 9—317.   Secured Party Not Obligated on Contract of Debtor.

The mere existence of a security interest or authority given to the debtor to dispose of or use collateral does not impose contract or tort liability upon the secured party for the debtor's acts or omissions.

§ 9—318.   Defenses Against Assignee; Modification of Contract After Notification of Assignment; Term Prohibiting Assignment Ineffective; Identification and Proof of Assignment.

(1) Unless an account debtor has made an enforceable agreement not to assert defenses or claims arising out of a sale as provided in Section 9—206 the rights of an assignee are subject to

(a) all the terms of the contract between the account debtor and assignor and any defense or claim arising therefrom; and

(b) any other defense or claim of the account debtor against the assignor which accrues before the account debtor receives notification of the assignment.

(2) So far as the right to payment or a part thereof under an assigned contract has not been fully earned by performance, and notwithstanding notification of the as-

signment, any modification of or substitution for the contract made in good faith and in accordance with reasonable commercial standards is effective against an assignee unless the account debtor has otherwise agreed but the assignee acquires corresponding rights under the modified or substituted contract. The assignment may provide that such modification or substitution is a breach by the assignor.

(3) The account debtor is authorized to pay the assignor until the account debtor receives notification that the amount due or to become due has been assigned and that payment is to be made to the assignee. A notification which does not reasonably identify the rights assigned is ineffective. If requested by the account debtor, the assignee must seasonably furnish reasonable proof that the assignment has been made and unless he does so the account debtor may pay the assignor.

(4) A term in any contract between an account debtor and an assignor is ineffective if it prohibits assignment of an account or prohibits creation of a security interest in a general intangible for money due or to become due or requires the account debtor's consent to such assignment or security interest. Amended in 1972.

PART 4.   Filing.

§ 9—401.   Place of Filing; Erroneous Filing; Removal of Collateral.

First Alternative Subsection (1). (1) The proper place to file in order to perfect a security interest is as follows:

(a) when the collateral is timber to be cut or is minerals or the like (including oil and gas) or accounts subject to subsection (5) of Section 9—103, or when the financing statement is filed as a fixture filing (Section 9—313) and the collateral is goods which are or are to become fixtures, then in the office where a mortgage on the real estate would be filed or recorded;

(b) in all other cases, in the office of the [Secretary of State].

Second Alternative Subsection (1). (1) The proper place to file in order to perfect a security interest is as follows;

(a) when the collateral is equipment used in farming operations, or farm products, or accounts or general intangibles arising from or relating to the sale of farm products by a farmer, or consumer goods, then in the office of the . . . . . in the county of the debtor's residence or if the debtor is not a resident of this state then in the office of the . . . . . in the county where the goods are kept, and in addition when the collateral is crops growing or to be grown in the office of the . . . . . in the county where the land is located;

(b) when the collateral is timber to be cut or is minerals or the like (including oil and gas) or accounts subject to subsection (5) of Section 9—103, or when the financing statement is filed as a fixture filing (Section 9—313) and the collateral is goods which are or are to become fixtures, then in the office where a mortgage on the real estate would be filed or recorded;

(c) in all other cases, in the office of the [Secretary of State].

Third Alternative Subsection (1). (1) The proper place to file in order to perfect a security interest is as follows:

(a) when the collateral is equipment used in farming operations, or farm products, or accounts or general intangibles arising from or relating to the sale of farm products by a farmer, or consumer goods, then in the office of the . . . . . in the county of the debtor's residence or if the debtor is not a resident of this state then in the office of the . . . . . in the county where the goods are kept, and in addition when the collateral is crops growing or to be grown in the office of the . . . . . in the county where the land is located;

(b) when the collateral is timber to be cut or is minerals or the like (including oil and gas) or accounts subject to subsection (5) of Section 9—103, or when the financing statement is filed as a fixture filing (Section 9—313) and the collateral is goods which are or are to become fixtures, then in the office where a mortgage on the real estate would be filed or recorded;

(c) in all other cases, in the office of the [Secretary of State] and in addition, if the debtor has a place of business in only one county of this state, also in the office of . . . . . of such county, or, if the debtor has no place of business in this state, but resides in the state, also in the office of . . . . . of the county in which he resides.

Note: One of the three alternatives should be selected as subsection (1).

(2) A filing which is made in good faith in an improper place or not in all of the places required by this section is nevertheless effective with regard to any collateral as to which the filing complied with the requirements of this Article and is also effective with regard to collateral covered by the financing statement against any person who has knowledge of the contents of such financing statement.

(3) A filing which is made in the proper place in this state continues effective even though the debtor's residence or place of business or the location of the collateral or its use, whichever controlled the original filing, is thereafter changed.

Alternative Subsection (3).

[(3) A filing which is made in the proper county continues effective for four months after a change to another county of the debtor's residence or place of business or the location of the collateral, whichever controlled the original filing. It becomes ineffective thereafter unless a copy of the financing statement signed by the secured party is filed in the new county within said period. The security interest may also be perfected in the new county after the expiration of the four-month period; in such case perfection dates from the time of perfection in the new county. A change in the use of the collateral does not impair the effectiveness of the original filing.]

(4) The rules stated in Section 9—103 determine whether filing is necessary in this state.

(5) Notwithstanding the preceding subsections, and subject to subsection (3) or section 9—302, the proper place to file in order to perfect a security interest in collateral, including fixtures, of a transmitting utility is the office of the [Secretary of State]. This filing constitutes a fixture filing (Section 9—313) as to the collateral described therein which is or is to become fixtures.

(6) For the purposes of this section, the residence of an organization is its place of business if it has one or its chief executive office if it has more than one place of business. Amended in 1962 and 1972.

> **Note:** Subsection (6) should be used only if the state chooses the Second or Third Alternative Subsection (1).

§ 9—402. Formal Requisites of Financing Statement; Amendments; Mortgage as Financing Statement.

(1) A financing statement is sufficient if it gives the names of the debtor and the secured party, is signed by the debtor, gives an address of the secured party from which information concerning the security interest may be obtained, gives a mailing address of the debtor and contains a statement indicating the types, or describing the items, of collateral. A financing statement may be filed before a security agreement is made or a security interest otherwise attaches. When the financing statement covers crops growing or to be grown, the statement must also contain a description of the real estate concerned. When the financing statement covers timber to be cut or

covers minerals or the like (including oil and gas) or accounts subject to subsection (5) of Section 9—103, or when the financing statement is filed as a fixture filing (Section 9—313) and the collateral is goods which are or are to become fixtures, the statement must also comply with subsection (5). A copy of the security agreement is sufficient as a financing statement if it contains the above information and is signed by the debtor. A carbon, photographic or other reproduction of a security agreement or a financing statement is sufficient as a financing statement if the security agreement so provides or if the original has been filed in this state.

(2) A financing statement which otherwise complies with subsection (1) is sufficient when it is signed by the secured party instead of the debtor if it is filed to perfect a security interest in

(a) collateral already subject to a security interest in another jurisdiction when it is brought into this state, or when the debtor's location is changed to this state. Such a financing statement must state that the collateral was brought into this state or that the debtor's location was changed to this state under such circumstances; or

(b) proceeds under Section 9—306 if the security interest in the original collateral was perfected. Such a financing statement must describe the original collateral; or

(c) collateral as to which the filing has lapsed; or

(d) collateral acquired after a change of name, identity or corporate structure of the debtor (subsection (7)).

(3) A form substantially as follows is sufficient to comply with subsection (1):

Name of debtor (or assignor) . . . .
Address . . . .
Name of secured party (or assignee) . . . .
Address . . . .

1. This financing statement covers the following types (or items) of property:
  (Describe) . . . .
2. (If collateral is crops) The above described crops are growing or are to be grown on:
  (Describe Real Estate) . . . .
3. (If applicable) The above goods are to become fixtures on *
  (Describe Real Estate) . . . . and
  this financing statement is to be filed [for rec-

ord] in the real estate records. (If the debtor does not have an interest of record) The name of a record owner is . . . .

4. (If products of collateral are claimed) Products of the collateral are also covered.

(use . . . .
whichever { Signature of Debtor (or Assig-
is   nor)
applicable) . . . .
            Signature of Secured Party (or Assignee)

(4) A financing statement may be amended by filing a writing signed by both the debtor and the secured party. An amendment does not extend the period of effectiveness of a financing statement. If any amendment adds collateral, it is effective as to the added collateral only from the filing date of the amendment. In this Article, unless the context otherwise requires, the term "financing statement" means the original financing statement and any amendments.

(5) A financing statement covering timber to be cut or covering minerals or the like (including oil and gas) or accounts subject to subsection (5) of Section 9—103, or a financing statement filed as a fixture filing (Section 9—313) where the debtor is not a transmitting utility, must show that it covers this type of collateral, must recite that it is to be filed [for record] in the real estate records, and the financing statement must contain a description of the real estate [sufficient if it were contained in a mortgage of the real estate to give constructive notice of the mortgage under the law of this state]. If the debtor does not have an interest or record in the real estate, the financing statement must show the name of a record owner.

(6) A mortgage is effective as a financing statement filed as a fixture filing from the date of its recording if

(a) the goods are described in the mortgage by item or type; and

(b) the goods are or are to become fixtures related to the real estate described in the mortgage; and

(c) the mortgage complies with the requirements for a financing statement in this section other than a recital that it is to be filed in the real estate records; and

(d) the mortgage is duly recorded.

No fee with reference to the financing statement is required other than the regular recording and satisfaction fees with respect to the mortgage.

(7) A financing statement sufficiently shows the name of the debtor if it gives the individual, partnership or corporate name of the debtor, whether or not it adds other trade names or names of partners. Where the debtor so changes his name or in the case of an organization its name, identity or corporate structure that a filed financing statement becomes seriously misleading, the filing is not

---

*Where appropriate substitute either "The above timber is standing on . . . ." or "The above minerals or the like (including oil and gas) or accounts will be financed at the wellhead or minehead of the well or mine located on . . . ."

effective to perfect a security interest in collateral acquired by the debtor more than four months after the change, unless a new appropriate financing statement is filed before the expiration of that time. A filed financing statement remains effective with respect to collateral transferred by the debtor even though the secured party knows of or consents to the transfer.

(8) A financing statement substantially complying with the requirements of this section is effective even though it contains minor errors which are not seriously misleading. Amended in 1972.

Note: Language in brackets is optional.

Note: Where the state has any special recording system for real estate other than the usual grantor-grantee index (as, for instance, a tract system or a title registration or Torrens system) local adaptations of subsection (5) and Section 9—403(7) may be necessary. See Mass. Gen. Laws Chapter 106, Section 9—409.

§ 9—403. What Constitutes Filing; Duration of Filing; Effect of Lapsed Filing; Duties of Filing Officer.

(1) Presentation for filing of a financing statement and tender of the filing fee or acceptance of the statement by the filing officer constitutes filing under this Article.

(2) Except as provided in subsection (6) a filed financing statement is effective for a period of five years from the date of filing. The effectiveness of a filed financing statement lapses on the expiration of the five year period unless a continuation statement is filed prior to the lapse. If a security interest perfected by filing exists at the time insolvency proceedings are commenced by or against the debtor, the security interest remains perfected until termination of the insolvency proceedings and thereafter for a period of sixty days or until expiration of the five year period, whichever occurs later. Upon lapse the security interest becomes unperfected, unless it is perfected without filing. If the security interest becomes unperfected upon lapse, it is deemed to have been unperfected as against a person who became a purchaser or lien creditor before lapse.

(3) A continuation statement may be filed by the secured party within six months prior to the expiration of the five-year period specified in subsection (2). Any such continuation statement must be signed by the secured party, identify the original statement by file number and state that the original statement is still effective. A continuation statement signed by a person other than the secured party of record must be accompanied by a separate written statement of assignment signed by the secured party of record and complying with subsection (2) of Section 9—405, including payment of the required fee. Upon timely filing of the continuation statement, the effectiveness of the original statement is continued for five years after the last date to which the filing was effective

whereupon it lapses in the same manner as provided in subsection (2) unless another continuation statement is filed prior to such lapse. Succeeding continuation statements may be filed in the same manner to continue the effectiveness of the original statement. Unless a statute on disposition of public records provides otherwise, the filing officer may remove a lapsed statement from the files and destroy it immediately if he has retained a microfilm or other photographic record, or in other cases after one year after the lapse. The filing officer shall so arrange matters by physical annexation of financing statements to continuation statements or other related filings, or by other means, that if he physically destroys the financing statements of a period more than five years past, those which have been continued by a continuation statement or which are still effective under subsection (6) shall be retained.

(4) Except as provided in subsection (7) a filing officer shall mark each statement with a file number and with the date and hour of filing and shall hold the statement or a microfilm or other photographic copy thereof for public inspection. In addition the filing officer shall index the statement according to the name of the debtor and shall note in the index the file number and the address of the debtor given in the statement.

(5) The uniform fee for filing and indexing and for stamping a copy furnished by the secured party to show the date and place of filing for an original financing statement or for a continuation statement shall be $. . . . . if the statement is in the standard form prescribed by the [Secretary of State] and otherwise shall be $. . . . ., plus in each case, if the financing statement is subject to subsection (5) of Section 9—402, $. . . . . The uniform fee for each name more than one required to be indexed shall be $. . . . . The secured party may at his option show a trade name for any person and an extra uniform indexing fee of $. . . . . shall be paid with respect thereto.

(6) If the debtor is a transmitting utility (subsection (5) of Section 9—401) and a filed financing statement so states, it is effective until a termination statement is filed. A real estate mortgage which is effective as a fixture filing under subsection (6) of Section 9—402 remains effective as a fixture filing until the mortgage is released or satisfied of record or its effectiveness otherwise terminates as to the real estate.

(7) When a financing statement covers timber to be cut or covers minerals or the like (including oil and gas) or accounts subject to subsection (5) of Section 9—103, or is filed as a fixture filing, [it shall be filed for record and] the filing officer shall index it under the names of the debtor and any owner of record shown on the financing statement in the same fashion as if they were the mortgagors in a mortgage of the real estate described, and, to the extent that the law of this state provides for

indexing of mortgages under the name of the mortgagee, under the name of the secured party as if he were the mortgagee thereunder, or where indexing is by description in the same fashion as if the financing statement were a mortgage of the real estate described. Amended in 1972.

> **Note:** In states in which writings will not appear in the real estate records and indices unless actually recorded the bracketed language in subsection (7) should be used.

§ 9—404.   Termination Statement.

(1) If a financing statement covering consumer goods is filed on or after . . . . , then within one month or within ten days following written demand by the debtor after there is no outstanding secured obligation and no commitment to make advances, incur obligations or otherwise give value, the secured party must file with each filing officer with whom the financing statement was filed, a termination statement to the effect that he no longer claims a security interest under the financing statement, which shall be identified by file number. In other cases whenever there is no outstanding secured obligation and no commitment to make advances, incur obligations or otherwise give value, the secured party must on written demand by the debtor send the debtor, for each filing officer with whom the financing statement was filed, a termination statement to the effect that he no longer claims a security interest under the financing statement, which shall be identified by file number. A termination statement signed by a person other than the secured party of record must be accompanied by a separate written statement of assignment signed by the secured party of record complying with subsection (2) of Section 9—405, including payment of the required fee. If the affected secured party fails to file such a termination statement as required by this subsection, or to send such a termination statement within ten days after proper demand therefor, he shall be liable to the debtor for one hundred dollars, and in addition for any loss caused to the debtor by such failure.

(2) On presentation to the filing officer of such a termination statement he must note it in the index. If he has received the termination statement in duplicate, he shall return one copy of the termination statement to the secured party stamped to show the time of receipt thereof. If the filing officer has a microfilm or other photographic record of the financing statement, and of any related continuation statement, statement of assignment and statement of release, he may remove the originals from the files at any time after receipt of the termination statement, or if he has no such record, he may remove them from the files at any time after one year after receipt of the termination statement.

(3) If the termination statement is in the standard form prescribed by the [Secretary of State], the uniform fee for filing and indexing the termination statement shall be $. . . . . , and otherwise shall be $. . . . . , plus in each case an additional fee of $. . . . . , for each name more than one against which the termination statement is required to be indexed. Amended in 1972.

> **Note:** The date to be inserted should be the effective date of the revised Article 9.

§ 9—405.   Assignment of Security Interest; Duties of Filing Officer; Fees.

(1) A financing statement may disclose an assignment of a security interest in the collateral described in the financing statement by indication in the financing statement of the name and address of the assignee or by an assignment itself or a copy thereof on the face or back of the statement. On presentation to the filing officer of such a financing statement the filing officer shall mark the same as provided in Section 9—403(4). The uniform fee for filing, indexing and furnishing filing data for a financing statement so indicating an assignment shall be $. . . . . if the statement is in the standard form prescribed by the [Secretary of State] and otherwise shall be $. . . . . , plus in each case an additional fee of $. . . . . , for each name more than one against which the financing statement is required to be indexed.

(2) A secured party may assign or record all or part of his rights under a financing statement by the filing in the place where the original financing statement was filed of a separate written statement of assignment signed by the secured party of record and setting forth the name of the secured party of record and the debtor, the file number and the date of filing of the financing statement and the name and address of the assignee and containing a description of the collateral assigned. A copy of the assignment is sufficient as a separate statement if it complies with the preceding sentence. On presentation to the filing officer of such a separate statement, the filing officer shall mark such separate statement with the date and hour of the filing. He shall note the assignment on the index of the financing statement, or in the case of a fixture filing, or a filing covering timber to be cut, or covering minerals or the like (including oil and gas) or accounts subject to subsection (5) of Section 9—103, he shall index the assignment under the name of the assignor as grantor and, to the extent that the law of this state provides for indexing the assignment of a mortgage under the name of the assignee, he shall index the assignment of the financing statement under the name of the assignee. The uniform fee for filing, indexing and furnishing filing data about such a separate statement of assignment shall be $. . . . . if the statement is in the standard form prescribed by the [Secretary of State] and otherwise shall be $. . . . . , plus in each case an additional fee of $. . . . . for each name more than one against which the statement of assignment is required to be indexed. Notwithstanding the provisions of this

subsection, an assignment of record of a security interest in a fixture contained in a mortgage effective as a fixture filing (subsection (6) of Section 9—402) may be made only by an assignment of the mortgage in the manner provided by the law of this state other than this Act.

(3) After the disclosure or filing of an assignment under this section, the assignee is the secured party of record. Amended in 1972.

§ 9—406. Release of Collateral; Duties of Filing Officer; Fees.

A secured party of record may by this signed statement release all or a part of any collateral described in a filed financing statement. The statement of release is sufficient if it contains a description of the collateral being released, the name and address of the debtor, the name and address of the secured party, and the file number of the financing statement. A statement of release signed by a person other than the secured party of record must be accompanied by a separate written statement of assignment signed by the secured party of record and complying with subsection (2) of Section 9—405, including payment of the required fee. Upon presentation of such a statement of release to the filing officer he shall mark the statement with the hour and date of filing and shall note the same upon the margin of the index of the filing of the financing statement. The uniform fee for filing and noting such a statement of release shall be $. . . . . if the statement is in the standard form prescribed by the [Secretary of State] and otherwise shall be $. . . . . plus in each case an additional fee of $. . . . . for each name more than one against which the statement of release is required to be indexed. Amended in 1972.

[§ 9—407. Information From Filing Officer].

[(1) If the person filing any financing statement, termination statement, statement or assignment, or statement of release, furnishes the filing officer a copy thereof, the filing officer shall upon request note upon the copy the file number and date and hour of the filing of the original and deliver or send the copy to such person.]

[(2) Upon request of any person, the filing officer shall issue his certificate showing whether there is on file on the date and hour stated therein, any presently effective financing statement naming a particular debtor and any statement of assignment thereof and if there is, giving the date and hour of filing of each such statement and the names and addresses of each secured party therein. The uniform fee for such a certificate shall be $. . . . . if the request for the certificate is in the standard form prescribed by the [Secretary of State] and otherwise shall be $. . . . . Upon request the filing officer shall furnish a copy of any filed financing statement or statement of assignment for a uniform fee of $. . . . . per page.] Amended in 1972.

Note: This section is proposed as an optional provision to require filing officers to furnish certificates. Local law and practices should be consulted with regard to the advisability of adoption.

§ 9—408. Financing Statements Covering Consigned or Leased Goods.

A consignor or lessor of goods may file a financing statement using the terms "consignee," "lessor," "lessee" or the like instead of the terms specified in Section 9—402. The provisions of this Part shall apply as appropriate to such a financing statement but its filing shall not of itself be a factor in determining whether or not the consignment or lease is intended as security (Section 1—201(37)). However, if it is determined for other reasons that the consignment or lease is so intended, a security interest of the consignor or lessor which attaches to the consigned or leased goods is perfected by such filing. Added in 1972.

PART 5. *Default.*

§ 9—501. Default; Procedure When Security Agreement Covers Both Real and Personal Property.

(1) When a debtor is in default under a security agreement, a secured party has the rights and remedies provided in this Part and except as limited by subsection (3) those provided in the security agreement. He may reduce his claim to judgment, foreclose or otherwise enforce the security interest by any available judicial procedure. If the collateral is documents the secured party may proceed either as to the documents or as to the goods covered thereby. A secured party in possession has the rights, remedies and duties provided in Section 9—207. The rights and remedies referred to in this subsection are cumulative.

(2) After default, the debtor has the rights and remedies provided in this Part, those provided in the security agreement and those provided in Section 9—207.

(3) To the extent that they give rights to the debtor and impose duties on the secured party, the rules stated in the subsections referred to below may not be waived or varied except as provided with respect to compulsory disposition of collateral (subsection (3) of Section 9—504 and Section 9—505) and with respect to redemption of collateral (Section 9—506) but the parties may by agreement determine the standards by which the fulfillment of these rights and duties is to be measured if such standards are not manifestly unreasonable:

    (a) subsection (2) of Section 9—502 and subsection (2) of Section 9—504 insofar as they require accounting for surplus proceeds of collateral;

(b) subsection (3) of Section 9—504 and subsection (1) of Section 9—505 which deal with disposition of collateral;

(c) subsection (2) of Section 9—505 which deals with acceptance of collateral as discharge of obligation;

(d) Section 9—506 which deals with redemption of collateral; and

(e) subsection (1) of Section 9—507 which deals with the secured party's liability for failure to comply with this Part.

(4) If the security agreement covers both real and personal property, the secured party may proceed under this Part as to the personal property or he may proceed as to both the real and the personal property in accordance with his rights and remedies in respect of the real property in which case the provisions of this Part do not apply.

(5) When a secured party has reduced his claim to judgment the lien of any levy which may be made upon his collateral by virtue of any execution based upon the judgment shall relate back to the date of the perfection of the security interest in such collateral. A judicial sale, pursuant to such execution, is a foreclosure of the security interest by judicial procedure within the meaning of this section, and the secured party may purchase at the sale and thereafter hold the collateral free of any other requirements of this Article. Amended in 1972.

§ 9—502. Collection Rights of Secured Party.

(1) When so agreed and in any event on default the secured party is entitled to notify an account debtor or the obligor on an instrument to make payment to him whether or not the assignor was theretofore making collections on the collateral, and also to take control of any proceeds to which he is entitled under Section 9—306.

(2) A secured party who by agreement is entitled to charge back uncollected collateral or otherwise to full or limited recourse against the debtor and who undertakes to collect from the account debtors or obligors must proceed in a commercially reasonable manner and may deduct his reasonable expenses of realization from the collections. If the security agreement secures an indebtedness, the secured party must account to the debtor for any surplus, and unless otherwise agreed, the debtor is liable for any deficiency. But, if the underlying transaction was a sale of accounts or chattel paper, the debtor is entitled to any surplus or is liable for any deficiency only if the security agreement so provides. Amended in 1972.

§ 9—503. Secured Party's Right to Take Possession After Default.

Unless otherwise agreed a secured party has on default the right to take possession of the collateral. In taking possession a secured party may proceed without judicial process if this can be done without breach of the peace or may proceed by action. If the security agreement so provides the secured party may require the debtor to assemble the collateral and make it available to the secured party at a place to be designated by the secured party which is reasonably convenient to both parties. Without removal a secured party may render equipment unusable, and may dispose of collateral on the debtor's premises under Section 9—504.

§ 9—504. Secured Party's Right to Dispose of Collateral After Default; Effect of Disposition.

(1) A secured party after default may sell, lease or otherwise dispose of any or all of the collateral in its then condition or following any commercially reasonable preparation or processing. Any sale of goods is subject to the Article on Sales (Article 2). The proceeds of disposition shall be applied in the order following to

(a) the reasonable expenses of retaking, holding, preparing for sale or lease, selling, leasing and the like and, to the extent provided for in the agreement and not prohibited by law, the reasonable attorney's fees and legal expenses incurred by the secured party;

(b) the satisfaction of indebtedness secured by the security interest under which the disposition is made;

(c) the satisfaction of indebtedness secured by any subordinate security interest in the collateral if written notification of demand therefor is received before distribution of the proceeds is completed. If requested by the secured party, the holder of a subordinate security interest must seasonably furnish reasonable proof of his interest, and unless he does so, the secured party need not comply with his demand.

(2) If the security interest secures an indebtedness, the secured party must account to the debtor for any surplus, and, unless otherwise agreed, the debtor is liable for any deficiency. But if the underlying transaction was a sale of accounts or chattel paper, the debtor is entitled to any surplus or is liable for any deficiency only if the security agreement so provides.

(3) Disposition of the collateral may be by public or private proceedings and may be made by way of one or more contracts. Sale or other disposition may be as a unit or in parcels and at any time and place and on any terms but every aspect of the disposition including the method, manner, time, place and terms must be commercially reasonable. Unless collateral is perishable or threatens to decline speedily in value or is of a type customarily sold on a recognized market, reasonable notification of the time and place of any public sale or reasonable notification of the time after which any private sale or other intended disposition is to be made shall be sent by the secured party to the debtor, if he has not signed after

default a statement renouncing or modifying his right to notification of sale. In the case of consumer goods no other notification need be sent. In other cases notification shall be sent to any other secured party from whom the secured party has received (before sending his notification to the debtor or before the debtor's renunciation of his rights) written notice of a claim of an interest in the collateral. The secured party may buy at any public sale and if the collateral is of a type customarily sold in a recognized market or is of a type which is the subject of widely distributed standard price quotations he may buy at private sale.

(4) When collateral is disposed of by a secured party after default, the disposition transfers to a purchaser for value all of the debtor's rights therein, discharges the security interest under which it is made and any security interest or lien subordinate thereto. The purchaser takes free of all such rights and interests even though the secured party fails to comply with the requirements of this Part or of any judicial proceedings

> (a) in the case of a public sale, if the purchaser has no knowledge of any defects in the sale and if he does not buy in collusion with the secured party, other bidders or the person conducting the sale; or
>
> (b) in any other case, if the purchaser acts in good faith.

(5) A person who is liable to a secured party under a guaranty, indorsement, repurchase agreement or the like and who receives a transfer of collateral from the secured party or is subrogated to his rights has thereafter the rights and duties of the secured party. Such a transfer of collateral is not a sale or disposition of the collateral under this Article. Amended in 1972.

§ 9—505. Compulsory Disposition of Collateral; Acceptance of the Collateral as Discharge of Obligation.

(1) If the debtor has paid sixty percent of the cash price in the case of a purchase money security interest in consumer goods or sixty percent of the loan in the case of another security interest in consumer goods, and has not signed after default a statement renouncing or modifying his rights under this Part a secured party who has taken possession of collateral must dispose of it under Section 9—504 and if he fails to do so within ninety days after he takes possession the debtor at his option may recover in conversion or under Section 9—507(1) on secured party's liability.

(2) In any other case involving consumer goods or any other collateral a secured party in possession may, after default, propose to retain the collateral in satisfaction of the obligation. Written notice of such proposal shall be sent to the debtor is he has not signed after default a statement renouncing or modifying his rights under this subsection. In the case of consumer goods no other no-

tice need be given. In other cases notice shall be sent to any other secured party from whom the secured party has received (before sending his notice to the debtor or before the debtor's renunciation of his rights) written notice of a claim of an interest in the collateral. If the secured party receives objection in writing from a person entitled to receive notification within twenty-one days after the notice was sent, the secured party must dispose of the collateral under Section 9—504. In the absence of such written objection the secured party may retain the collateral in satisfaction of the debtor's obligation. Amended in 1972.

§ 9—506. Debtor's Right to Redeem Collateral.

At any time before the secured party has disposed of collateral or entered into a contract for its disposition under Section 9—504 or before the obligation has been discharged under Section 9—505(2) the debtor or any other secured party may unless otherwise agreed in writing after default redeem the collateral by tendering fulfillment of all obligations secured by the collateral as well as the expenses reasonably incurred by the secured party in retaking, holding and preparing the collateral for disposition, in arranging for the sale, and to the extent provided in the agreement and not prohibited by law, his reasonably attorneys' fees and legal expenses.

§ 9—507. Secured Party's Liability for Failure to Comply With This Part.

(1) If it is established that the secured party is not proceeding in accordance with the provisions of this Part disposition may be ordered or restrained on appropriate terms and conditions. If the disposition has occurred the debtor or any person entitled to notification or whose security interest has been made known to the secured party prior to the disposition has a right to recover from the secured party any loss caused by a failure to comply with the provisions of this Part. If the collateral is consumer goods, the debtor has a right to recover in any event an amount not less than the credit service charge plus ten percent of the principal amount of the debtor or the time price differential plus 10 percent of the cash price.

(2) The fact that a better price could have been obtained by a sale at a different time or in a different method from that selected by the secured party is not of itself sufficient to establish that the sale was not made in a commercially reasonable manner. If the secured party either sells the collateral in the usual manner in any recognized market therefor or if he sells at the price current in such market at the time of his sale or if he has otherwise sold in conformity with reasonable commercial practices among dealers in the type of property sold he has sold in a commercially reasonable manner. The principles stated in the two preceding sentences with respect to sales also apply as may be appropriate to other types

of disposition. A disposition which has been approved in any judicial proceeding or by any bona fide creditors' committee or representative of creditors shall conclusively be deemed to be commercially reasonable, but this sentence does not indicate that any such approval must be obtained in any case nor does it indicate that any disposition not so approved is not commercially reasonable.

ARTICLE 10.   Effective Date and Repealer

[Text omitted.]

ARTICLE 11.   Effective Date and Transition Provisions

[Text omitted.]

Table of Sections

PART I. Preliminary Provisions

§ 1. Name of Act.
This act may be cited as Uniform Partnership Act.

§ 2. Definition of Terms.
In this act, "Court" includes every court and judge having jurisdiction in the case.

"Business" includes every trade, occupation, or profession.

"Person" includes individuals, partnerships, corporations, and other associations.

"Bankrupt" includes bankrupt under the Federal Bankruptcy Act or insolvent under any state insolvent act.

"Conveyance" includes every assignment, lease, mortgage, or encumbrance.

"Real property" includes land and any interest or estate in land.

§ 3. Interpretation of Knowledge and Notice.
(1) A person has "knowledge" of a fact within the meaning of this act not only when he has actual knowledge thereof, but also when he has knowledge of such other facts as in the circumstances shows bad faith.

(2) A person has "notice" of a fact within the meaning of this act when the person who claims the benefit of the notice:

   (a) States the fact to such person, or

   (b) Delivers through the mail, or by other means of communication, a written statement of the fact to such person or to a proper person at his place of business or residence.

§ 4. Rules of Construction.
(1) The rule that statutes in derogation of the common law are to be strictly construed shall have no application to this act.

(2) The law of estoppel shall apply under this act.

(3) The law of agency shall apply under this act.

(4) This act shall be so interpreted and construed as to effect its general purpose to make uniform the law of those states which enact it.

(5) This act shall not be construed so as to impair the obligations of any contract existing when the act goes into effect, nor to affect any action or proceedings begun or right accrued before this act takes effect.

§ 5. Rules for Cases Not Provided for in This Act.
In any case not provided for in this act the rules of law and equity, including the law merchant, shall govern.

PART II. Nature of a Partnership

§ 6. Partnership Defined.
(1) A partnership is an association of two or more persons to carry on as co-owners a business for profit.

(2) But any association formed under any other statute of this state, or any statute adopted by authority, other than the authority of this state, is not a partnership under this act, unless such association would have been a partnership in this state prior to the adoption of this act; but this act shall apply to limited partnerships except in so far as the statutes relating to such partnerships are inconsistent herewith.

§ 7. Rules for Determining the Existence of a Partnership.
In determining whether a partnership exists, these rules shall apply:

(1) Except as provided by Section 16 persons who are not partners as to each other are not partners as to third persons.

(2) Joint tenancy, tenancy in common, tenancy by the entireties, joint property, common property, or part ownership does not of itself establish a partnership, whether such co-owners do or do not share any profits made by the use of the property.

(3) The sharing of gross returns does not of itself establish a partnership, whether or not the persons sharing them have a joint or common right or interest in any property from which the returns are derived.

(4) The receipt by a person of a share of the profits of a business is prima facie evidence that he is a partner in the business, but no such inference shall be drawn if such profits were received in payment:

   (a) As a debt by installments or otherwise,

   (b) As wages of an employee or rent to a landlord,

   (c) As an annuity to a widow or representative of a deceased partner,

   (d) As interest on a loan, though the amount of payment vary with the profits of the business,

   (e) As the consideration for the sale of a goodwill of a business or other property by installments or otherwise.

§ 8. Partnership Property.
(1) All property originally brought into the partnership stock or subsequently acquired by purchase or otherwise, on account of the partnership, is partnership property.

(2) Unless the contrary intention appears, property acquired with partnership funds is partnership property.

(3) Any estate in real property may be acquired in the partnership name. Title so acquired can be conveyed only in the partnership name.

(4) A conveyance to a partnership in the partnership name, though without words of inheritance, passes the entire estate of the grantor unless a contrary intent appears.

PART III. Relations of Partners to Persons Dealing With the Partnership

§ 9. Partner Agent of Partnership as to Partnership Business.

(1) Every partner is an agent of the partnership for the purpose of its business, and the act of every partner, including the execution in the partnership name of any instrument, for apparently carrying on in the usual way the business of the partnership of which he is a member binds the partnership, unless the partner so acting has in fact no authority to act for the partnership in the particular matter, and the person with whom he is dealing has knowledge of the fact that he has no such authority.

(2) An act of a partner which is not apparently for the carrying on of the business of the partnership in the usual way does not bind the partnership unless authorized by the other partners.

(3) Unless authorized by the other partners or unless they have abandoned the business, one or more but less than all the partners have no authority to:

(a) Assign the partnership property in trust for creditors or on the assignee's promise to pay the debts of the partnership,

(b) Dispose of the good-will of the business,

(c) Do any other act which would make it impossible to carry on the ordinary business of a partnership,

(d) Confess a judgment,

(e) Submit a partnership claim or liability to arbitration or reference.

(4) No act of a partner in contravention of a restriction on authority shall bind the partnership to persons having knowledge of the restriction.

§ 10. Conveyance of Real Property of the Partnership.

(1) Where title to real property is in the partnership name, any partner may convey title to such property by a conveyance executed in the partnership name; but the partnership may recover such property unless the partner's act binds the partnership under the provisions of paragraph (1) of Section 9, or unless such property has been conveyed by the grantee or a person claiming through such grantee to a holder for value without knowledge that the partner, in making the conveyance, has exceeded his authority.

(2) Where title to real property is in the name of the partnership, a conveyance executed by a partner, in his own name, passes the equitable interest of the partnership, provided the act is one within the authority of the partner under the provisions of paragraph (1) of Section 9.

(3) Where title to real property is in the name of one or more but not all the partners, and the record does not disclose the right of the partnership, the partners in whose name the title stands may convey title to such property, but the partnership may recover such property if the partners' act does not bind the partnership under the provisions of paragraph (1) of Section 9, unless the purchaser or his assignee, is a holder of value, without knowledge.

(4) Where the title to real property is in the name of one or more or all the partners, or in a third person in trust for the partnership, a conveyance executed by a partner in the partnership name, or in his own name, passes the equitable interest of the partnership, provided the act is one within the authority of the partner under the provisions of paragraph (1) of Section 9.

(5) Where the title to real property is in the names of all the partners a conveyance executed by all the partners passes all their rights in such property.

§ 11. Partnership Bound by Admission of Partner.

An admission or representation made by any partner concerning partnership affairs within the scope of his authority as conferred by this act is evidence against the partnership.

§ 12. Partnership Charged with Knowledge of or Notice to Partner.

Notice to any partner of any matter relating to partnership affairs, and the knowledge of the partner acting in the particular matter, acquired while a partner or then present to his mind, and the knowledge of any other partner who reasonably could and should have communicated it to the acting partner, operate as notice to or knowledge of the partnership, except in the case of a fraud on the partnership committed by or with the consent of that partner.

§ 13. Partnership Bound by Partner's Wrongful Act.

Where, by any wrongful act or omission of any partner acting in the ordinary course of the business of the partnership or with the authority of his co-partners, loss or injury is caused to any person, not being a partner in the partnership, or any penalty is incurred, the partnership is liable therefor to the same extent as the partner so acting or omitting to act.

§ 14. Partnership Bound by Partner's Breach of Trust.

The partnership is bound to make good the loss:

(a) Where one partner acting within the scope of his apparent authority receives money or property of a third person and misapplies it; and

(b) Where the partnership in the course of its business receives money or property of a third person and the money or property so received is misapplied by any partner while it is in the custody of the partnership.

§ 15. Nature of Partner's Liability.
All partners are liable
- (a) Jointly and severally for everything chargeable to the partnership under Sections 13 and 14.
- (b) Jointly for all other debts and obligations of the partnership; but any partner may enter into a separate obligation to perform a partnership contract.

§ 16. Partner by Estoppel.
(1) When a person, by words spoken or written or by conduct, represents himself, or consents to another representing him to anyone, as a partner in an existing partnership or with one or more persons not actual partners, he is liable to any such person to whom such representation has been made, who has, on the faith of such representation, given credit to the actual or apparent partnership, and if he has made such representation or consented to its being made in a public manner he is liable to such person, whether the representation has or has not been made or communicated to such person so giving credit by or with the knowledge of the apparent partner making the representation or consenting to its being made.
- (a) When a partnership liability results, he is liable as though he were an actual member of the partnership.
- (b) When no partnership liability results, he is liable jointly with the other persons, if any, so consenting to the contract or representation as to incur liability, otherwise separately.

(2) When a person has been thus represented to be a partner in an existing partnership, or with one or more persons not actual partners, he is an agent of the persons consenting to such representation to bind them to the same extent and in the same manner as though he were a partner in fact, with respect to persons who rely upon the representation. Where all the members of the existing partnership consent to the representation, a partnership act or obligation results; but in all other cases it is the joint act or obligation of the person acting and the persons consenting to the representation.

§ 17. Liability of Incoming Partner.
A person admitted as a partner into an existing partnership is liable for all the obligations of the partnership arising before his admission as though he had been a partner when such obligations were incurred, except that this liability shall be satisfied only out of partnership property.

PART IV. Relations of Partners to One Another

§ 18. Rules Determining Rights and Duties of Partners.
The rights and duties of the partners in relation to the partnership shall be determined, subject to any agreement between them, by the following rules:
- (a) Each partner shall be repaid his contributions, whether by way of capital or advances to the partnership property and share equally in the profits and surplus remaining after all liabilities, including those to partners, are satisfied; and must contribute toward the losses, whether of capital or otherwise, sustained by the partnership according to his share in the profits.
- (b) The partnership must indemnify every partner in respect of payments made and personal liabilities reasonably incurred by him in the ordinary and proper conduct of its business, or for the preservation of its business or property.
- (c) A partner, who in aid of the partnership makes any payment or advance beyond the amount of capital which he agreed to contribute, shall be paid interest from the date of the payment or advance.
- (d) A partner shall receive interest on the capital contributed by him only from the date when repayment should be made.
- (e) All partners have equal rights in the management and conduct of the partnership business.
- (f) No partner is entitled to remuneration for acting in the partnership business, except that a surviving partner is entitled to reasonable compensation for his services in winding up the partnership affairs.
- (g) No person can become a member of a partnership without the consent of all the partners.
- (h) Any difference arising as to ordinary matters connected with the partnership business may be decided by a majority of the partners; but no act in contravention of any agreement between the partners may be done rightfully without the consent of all the partners.

§ 19. Partnership Books.
The partnership books shall be kept, subject to any agreement between the partners, at the principal place of business of the partnership, and every partner shall at all times have access to and may inspect and copy any of them.

§ 20. Duty of Partners to Render Information.
Partners shall render on demand true and full information of all things affecting the partnership to any partner or

the legal representative of any deceased partner or partner under legal disability.

§ 21. Partner Accountable as a Fiduciary.

(1) Every partner must account to the partnership for any benefit, and hold as trustee for it any profits derived by him without the consent of the other partners from any transaction connected with the formation, conduct, or liquidation of the partnership or from any use by him of its property.

(2) This section applies also to the representatives of a deceased partner engaged in the liquidation of the affairs of the partnership as the personal representatives of the last surviving partner.

§ 22. Right to an Account.

Any partner shall have the right to a formal account as to partnership affairs:

(a) If he is wrongfully excluded from the partnership business or possession of its property by his co-partners,

(b) If the right exists under the terms of any agreement,

(c) As provided by Section 21,

(d) Whenever other circumstances render it just and reasonable.

§ 23. Continuation of Partnership Beyond Fixed Term.

(1) When a partnership for a fixed term or particular undertaking is continued after the termination of such term or particular undertaking without any express agreement, the rights and duties of the partners remain the same as they were at such termination, so far as is consistent with a partnership at will.

(2) A continuation of the business by the partners or such of them as habitually acted therein during the term, without any settlement or liquidation of the partnership affairs, is prima facie evidence of a continuation of the partnership.

PART V. *Property Rights of a Partner*

§ 24. Extent of Property Rights of a Partner.

The property rights of a partner are (1) his rights in specific partnership property, (2) his interest in the partnership, and (3) his right to participate in the management.

§ 25. Nature of a Partner's Right in Specific Partnership Property.

(1) A partner is co-owner with his partners of specific partnership property holding as a tenant in partnership.

(2) The incidents of this tenancy are such that:

(a) A partner, subject to the provisions of this act and to any agreement between the partners, has an equal right with his partners to possess specific partnership property for partnership purposes; but he has no right to possess such property for any other purpose without the consent of his partners.

(b) A partner's right in specific partnership property is not assignable except in connection with the assignment of rights of all the partners in the same property.

(c) A partner's right in specific partnership property is not subject to attachment or execution, except on a claim against the partnership. When partnership property is attached for a partnership debt the partners, or any of them, or the representatives of a deceased partner, cannot claim any right under the homestead or exemption laws.

(d) On the death of a partner his right in specific partnership property vests in the surviving partner or partners, except where the deceased was the last surviving partner, when his right in such property vests in his legal representative. Such surviving partner or partners, or the legal representative of the last surviving partner, has no right to possess the partnership property for any but a partnership purpose.

(e) A partner's right in specific partnership property is not subject to dower, curtesy, or allowances to widows, heirs, or next of kin.

§ 26. Nature of Partner's Interest in the Partnership.

A partner's interest in the partnership is his share of the profits and surplus, and the same is personal property.

§ 27. Assignment of Partner's Interest.

(1) A conveyance by a partner of his interest in the partnership does not of itself dissolve the partnership, nor, as against the other partners in the absence of agreement, entitle the assignee, during the continuance of the partnership, to interfere in the management or administration of the partnership business or affairs, or to require any information or account of partnership transactions, or to inspect the partnership books; but it merely entitles the assignee to receive in accordance with his contract the profits to which the assigning partner would otherwise be entitled.

(2) In case of a dissolution of the partnership, the assignee is entitled to receive his assignor's interest and may require an account from the date only of the last account agreed to by all the partners.

§ 28. Partner's Interest Subject to Charging Order.

(1) On due application to a competent court by any judgment creditor of a partner, the court which entered the judgment, order, or decree, or any other court, may charge the interest of the debtor partner with payment of

the unsatisfied amount of such judgment debt with interest thereon; and may then or later appoint a receiver of his share of the profits, and of any other money due or to fall due to him in respect of the partnership, and make all other orders, directions, accounts and inquiries which the debtor partner might have made, or which the circumstances of the case may require.

(2) The interest charged may be redeemed at any time before foreclosure, or in case of a sale being directed by the court may be purchased without thereby causing a dissolution:

    (a) With separate property, by any one or more of the partners, or

    (b) With partnership property, by any one or more of the partners with the consent of all the partners whose interests are not so charged or sold.

(3) Nothing in this act shall be held to deprive a partner of his right, if any, under the exemption laws, as regards his interest in the partnership.

PART VI. Dissolution and Winding Up

§ 29. Dissolution Defined.
The dissolution of a partnership is the change in the relation of the partners caused by any partner ceasing to be associated in the carrying on as distinguished from the winding up of the business.

§ 30. Partnership Not Terminated by Dissolution.
On dissolution the partnership is not terminated, but continues until the winding up of partnership affairs is completed.

§ 31. Causes of Dissolution.
Dissolution is caused:

(1) Without violation of the agreement between the partners,

    (a) By the termination of the definite term or particular undertaking specified in the agreement,

    (b) By the express will of any partner when no definite term or particular undertaking is specified,

    (c) By the express will of all the partners who have not assigned their interests or suffered them to be charged for their separate debts, either before or after the termination of any specified term or particular undertaking,

    (d) By the expulsion of any partner from the business bona fide in accordance with such a power conferred by the agreement between the partners;

(2) In contravention of the agreement between the partners, where the circumstances do not permit a dissolution under any other provision of this section, by the express will of any partner at any time;

(3) By any event which makes it unlawful for the business of the partnership to be carried on or for the members to carry it on in partnership;

(4) By the death of any partner;

(5) By the bankruptcy of any partner or partnership;

(6) By the decree of court under Section 32.

§ 32. Dissolution by Decree of Court.
(1) On application by or for a partner the court shall decree a dissolution whenever:

    (a) A partner has been declared a lunatic in any judicial proceeding or is shown to be of unsound mind,

    (b) A partner becomes in any other way incapable of performing his part of the partnership contract,

    (c) A partner has been guilty of such conduct as tends to affect prejudicially the carrying on of the business,

    (d) A partner willfully or persistently commits a breach of the partnership agreement, or otherwise so conducts himself in matters relating to the partnership business that it is not reasonably practicable to carry on the business in partnership with him,

    (e) The business of the partnership can only be carried on at a loss,

    (f) Other circumstances render a dissolution equitable.

(2) On the application of the purchaser of a partner's interest under Sections 27 and 28:

    (a) After the termination of the specified term or particular undertaking,

    (b) At any time if the partnership was a partnership at will when the interest was assigned or when the charging order was issued.

§ 33. General Effect of Dissolution on Authority of Partner.
Except so far as may be necessary to wind up partnership affairs or to complete transactions begun but not then finished, dissolution terminates all authority of any partner to act for the partnership.

(1) With respect to the partners,

    (a) When the dissolution is not by the act, bankruptcy or death of a partner; or

    (b) When the dissolution is by such act, bankruptcy or death of a partner, in cases where Section 34 so requires.

(2) With respect to persons not partners, as declared in Section 35.

§ 34. Right of Partner to Contribution From Co-partners After Dissolution.
Where the dissolution is caused by the act, death or bankruptcy of a partner, each partner is liable to his co-

partners for his share of any liability created by any partner acting for the partnership as if the partnership had not been dissolved unless

    (a) The dissolution being by act of any partner, the partner acting for the partnership had knowledge of the dissolution, or

    (b) The dissolution being by the death or bankruptcy of a partner, the partner acting for the partnership had knowledge or notice of the death or bankruptcy.

§ 35. Power of Partner to Bind Partnership to Third Persons After Dissolution.

(1) After dissolution a partner can bind the partnership except as provided in Paragraph (3)

    (a) By any act appropriate for winding up partnership affairs or completing transactions unfinished at dissolution;

    (b) By any transaction which would bind the partnership if dissolution had not taken place, provided the other party to the transaction

        (I) Had extended credit to the partnership prior to dissolution and had no knowledge or notice of the dissolution; or

        (II) Though he had not so extended credit, had nevertheless known of the partnership prior to dissolution, and, having no knowledge or notice of dissolution, the fact of dissolution had not been advertised in a newspaper of general circulation in the place (or in each place if more than one) at which the partnership business was regularly carried on.

(2) The liability of a partner under Paragraph (1b) shall be satisfied out of partnership assets alone when such partner had been prior to dissolution

    (a) Unknown as a partner to the person with whom the contract is made; and

    (b) So far unknown and inactive in partnership affairs that the business reputation of the partnership could not be said to have been in any degree due to his connection with it.

(3) The partnership is in no case bound by any act of a partner after dissolution

    (a) Where the partnership is dissolved because it is unlawful to carry on the business, unless the act is appropriate for winding up partnership affairs; or

    (b) Where the partner has become bankrupt; or

    (c) Where the partner has no authority to wind up partnership affairs; except by a transaction with one who

        (I) Had extended credit to the partnership prior to dissolution and had no knowledge or notice of his want of authority; or

        (II) Had not extended credit to the partnership prior to dissolution, and, having no knowledge or notice of his want of authority, the fact of his want of authority has not been advertised in the manner provided for advertising the fact of dissolution in Paragraph (1bII).

(4) Nothing in this section shall affect the liability under Section 16 of any person who after dissolution represents himself or consents to another representing him as a partner in a partnership engaged in carrying on business.

§ 36. Effect of Dissolution on Partner's Existing Liability.

(1) The dissolution of the partnership does not of itself discharge the existing liability of any partner.

(2) A partner is discharged from any existing liability upon dissolution of the partnership by an agreement to that effect between himself, the partnership creditor and the person or partnership continuing the business; and such agreement may be inferred from the course of dealing between the creditor having knowledge of the dissolution and the person or partnership continuing the business.

(3) Where a person agrees to assume the existing obligations of a dissolved partnership, the partners whose obligations have been assumed shall be discharged from any liability to any creditor of the partnership who, knowing of the agreement, consents to a material alteration in the nature or time of payment of such obligations.

(4) The individual property of a deceased partner shall be liable for all obligations of the partnership incurred while he was a partner but subject to the prior payment of his separate debts.

§ 37. Right to Wind Up.

Unless otherwise agreed the partners who have not wrongfully dissolved the partnership or the legal representative of the last surviving partner, not bankrupt, has the right to wind up the partnership affairs; provided, however, that any partner, his legal representative or his assignee, upon cause shown, may obtain winding up by the court.

§ 38. Rights of Partners to Application of Partnership Property.

(1) When dissolution is caused in any way, except in contravention of the partnership agreement, each partner, as against his co-partners and all persons claiming through them in respect of their interests in the partnership, unless otherwise agreed, may have the partnership property applied to discharge its liabilities, and the surplus applied to pay in cash the net amount owing to the respective partners. But if dissolution is caused by expulsion of a partner, bona fide under the partnership agreement and if the expelled partner is discharged from all partnership liabilities, either by payment or agreement

under Section 36 (2), he shall receive in cash only the net amount due him from the partnership.

(2) When dissolution is caused in contravention of the partnership agreement the rights of the partners shall be as follows:

 (a) Each partner who has not caused dissolution wrongfully shall have,

  (I) All the rights specified in Paragraph (1) of this section, and

  (II) The right, as against each partner who has caused the dissolution wrongfully, to damages for breach of the agreement.

 (b) The partners who have not caused the dissolution wrongfully, if they all desire to continue the business in the same name, either by themselves or jointly with others, may do so, during the agreed term for the partnership and for that purpose may possess the partnership property, provided they secure the payment by bond approved by the court, or pay to any partner who has caused the dissolution wrongfully, the value of his interest in the partnership at the dissolution, less any damages recoverable under clause (2aII) of this section, and in like manner indemnify him against all present or future partnership liabilities.

 (c) A partner who has caused the dissolution wrongfully shall have:

  (I) If the business is not continued under the provisions of Paragraph (2b) all the rights of a partner under Paragraph (1), subject to clause (2aII), of this section,

  (II) If the business is continued under Paragraph (2b) of this section the right as against his co-partners and all claiming through them in respect of their interests in the partnership, to have the value of his interest in the partnership, less any damages caused to his co-partners by the dissolution, ascertained and paid to him in cash, or the payment secured by bond approved by the court, and to be released from all existing liabilities of the partnership; but in ascertaining the value of the partner's interest the value of the goodwill of the business shall not be considered.

§ 39. Rights Where Partnership Is Dissolved for Fraud or Misrepresentation.

Where a partnership contract is rescinded on the ground of the fraud or misrepresentation of one of the parties thereto, the party entitled to rescind is, without prejudice to any other right, entitled,

 (a) To a lien on, or right of retention of, the surplus of the partnership property after satisfying the partnership liabilities to third persons for any sum of money paid by him for the purchase of an interest in the partnership and for any capital or advances contributed by him; and

 (b) To stand, after all liabilities to third persons have been satisfied, in the place of the creditors of the partnership for any payments made by him in respect of the partnership liabilities; and

 (c) To be indemnified by the person guilty of the fraud or making the representation against all debts and liabilities of the partnership.

§ 40. Rules for Distribution.

In settling accounts between the partners after dissolution, the following rules shall be observed, subject to any agreement to the contrary:

 (a) The assets of the partnership are;

  (I) The partnership property,

  (II) The contributions of the partners necessary for the payment of all the liabilities specified in clause (b) of this paragraph.

 (b) The liabilities of the partnership shall rank in order of payment, as follows:

  (I) Those owing to creditors other than partners,

  (II) Those owing to partners other than for capital and profits,

  (III) Those owing to partners in respect of capital,

  (IV) Those owing to partners in respect of profits.

 (c) The assets shall be applied in the order of their declaration in clause (a) of this paragraph to the satisfaction of the liabilities.

 (d) The partners shall contribute, as provided by Section 18 (a) the amount necessary to satisfy the liabilities; but if any, but not all, of the partners are insolvent, or, not being subject to process, refuse to contribute, the other partners shall contribute their share of the liabilities, and, in the relative proportions in which they share the profits, the additional amount necessary to pay the liabilities.

 (e) An assignee for the benefit of creditors or any person appointed by the court shall have the right to enforce the contributions specified in clause (d) of this paragraph.

 (f) Any partner or his legal representative shall have the right to enforce the contributions specified in clause (d) of this paragraph, to the extent of the amount which he has paid in excess of his share of the liability.

 (g) The individual property of a deceased partner shall be liable for the contributions specified in clause (d) of this paragraph.

 (h) When partnership property and the individual properties of the partners are in possession of a court for distribution, partnership creditors shall have priority partnership property and separate creditors on individual property, saving the rights of lien or secured creditors as heretofore.

(i) Where a partner has become bankrupt or his estate is insolvent the claims against his separate property shall rank in the following order:

    (I) Those owing to separate creditors,

    (II) Those owing to partnership creditors,

    (III) Those owing to partners by way of contribution.

§ 41. Liability of Persons Continuing the Business in Certain Cases.

(1) When any new partner is admitted into an existing partnership, or when any partner retires and assigns (or the representative of the deceased partner assigns) his rights in partnership property to two or more of the partners, or to one or more of the partners and one or more third persons, if the business is continued without liquidation of the partnership affairs, creditors of the first or dissolved partnership are also creditors of the partnership so continuing the business.

(2) When all but one partner retire and assign (or the representative of a deceased partner assigns) their rights in partnership property to the remaining partner, who continues the business without liquidation of partnership affairs, either alone or with others, creditors of the dissolved partnership are also creditors of the person or partnership so continuing the business.

(3) When any partner retires or dies and the business of the dissolved partnership is continued as set forth in paragraphs (1) and (2) of this section, with the consent of the retired partners or the representative of the deceased partner, but without any assignment of his right in partnership property, rights of creditors of the dissolved partnership and of the creditors of the person or partnership continuing the business shall be as if such assignment had been made.

(4) When all partners or their representatives assign their rights in partnership property to one or more third persons who promise to pay the debts and who continue the business of the dissolved partnership, creditors of the dissolved partnership are also creditors of the person or partnership continuing the business.

(5) When any partner wrongfully causes a dissolution and the remaining partners continue the business under the provisions of Section 38 (2b), either alone or with others, and without liquidation of the partnership affairs, creditors of the dissolved partnership are also creditors of the person or partnership continuing the business.

(6) When a partner is expelled and the remaining partners continue the business either alone or with others, without liquidation of the partnership affairs, creditors of the dissolved partnership are also creditors of the person or partnership continuing the business.

(7) The liability of a third person becoming a partner in the partnership continuing the business, under this section, to the creditors of the dissolved partnership shall be satisfied out of partnership property only.

(8) When the business of a partnership after dissolution is continued under any conditions set forth in this section the creditors of the dissolved partnership, as against the separate creditors of the retiring or deceased partner or the representative of the deceased partner, have a prior right to any claim of the retired partner or the representative of the deceased partner against the person or partnership continuing the business, on account of the retired or deceased partner's interest in the dissolved partnership or on account of any consideration promised for such interest or for his right in partnership property.

(9) Nothing in this section shall be held to modify any right of creditors to set aside any assignment on the ground of fraud.

(10) The use by the person or partnership continuing the business of the partnership name, or the name of a deceased partner as part thereof, shall not of itself make the individual property of the deceased partner liable for any debts contracted by such person or partnership.

§ 42. Rights of Retiring or Estate of Deceased Partner When the Business is Continued.

When any partner retires or dies, and the business is continued under any of the conditions set forth in Section 41 (1, 2, 3, 5, 6), or Section 38 (2b), without any settlement of accounts as between him or his estate and the person or partnership continuing the business, unless otherwise agreed, he or his legal representative as against such persons or partnership may have the value of his interest at the date of dissolution ascertained, and shall receive as an ordinary creditor an amount equal to the value of his interest in the dissolved partnership with interest, or, at his option or at the option of his legal representative, in lieu of interest, the profits attributable to the use of his right in the property of the dissolved partnership; provided that the creditors of the dissolved partnership as against the separate creditors, or the representative of the retired or deceased partner, shall have priority on any claim arising under this section, as provided by Section 41(8) of this act.

§ 43. Accrual of Actions.

The right to an account of his interest shall accrue to any partner, or his legal representative, as against the winding up partners or the surviving partners or the person or partnership continuing the business, at the date of dissolution, in the absence of any agreement to the contrary.

PART VII. *Miscellaneous Provisions*

§ 44. When Act Takes Effect.

This act shall take effect on the . . . . day of . . . . one thousand nine hundred and . . . .

§ 45. Legislation Repealed.

All acts or parts of acts inconsistent with this act are hereby repealed.

Appendix D

Uniform Limited Partnership Act (1916)

Table of Sections

§ 1. Limited Partnership Defined.

A limited partnership is a partnership formed by two or more persons under the provisions of Section 2, having as members one or more general partners and one or more limited partners. The limited partners as such shall not be bound by the obligations of the partnership.

§ 2. Formation.

(1) Two or more persons desiring to form a limited partnership shall

    (a) Sign and swear to a certificate, which shall state

        I. The name of the partnership,

        II. The character of the business,

        III. The location of the principal place of business,

        IV. The name and place of residence of each member; general and limited partners being respectively designated,

        V. The term for which the partnership is to exist,

        VI. The amount of cash and a description of and the agreed value of the other property contributed by each limited partner,

        VII. The additional contributions, if any, agreed to be made by each limited partner and the times at which or events on the happening of which they shall be made,

VIII. The time, if agreed upon, when the contribution of each limited partner is to be returned,

IX. The share of the profits or the other compensation by way of income which each limited partner shall receive by reason of his contribution,

X. The right, if given, of a limited partner to substitute an assignee as contributor in his place, and the terms and conditions of the substitution,

XI. The right, if given, of the partners to admit additional limited partners,

XII. The right, if given, of one or more of the limited partners to priority over other limited partners, as to contributions or as to compensation by way of income, and the nature of such priority,

XIII. The right, if given, of the remaining general partner or partners to continue the business on the death, retirement or insanity of a general partner, and

XIV. The right, if given, of a limited partner to demand and receive property other than cash in return for his contribution.

(b) File for record the certificate in the office of [here designate the proper office].

(2) A limited partnership is formed if there has been substantial compliance in good faith with the requirements of paragraph (1).

§ 3. Business Which May Be Carried on.

A limited partnership may carry on any business which a partnership without limited partners may carry on, excepts [here designate the business to be prohibited].

§ 4. Character of Limited Partner's Contribution.

The contributions of a limited partner may be cash or other property, but not services.

§ 5. A Name Not to Contain Surname of Limited Partner; Exceptions.

(1) The surname of a limited partner shall not appear in the partnership name, unless

(a) It is also the surname of a general partner, or

(b) Prior to the time when the limited partner became such the business had been carried on under a name in which his surname appeared.

(2) A limited partner whose name appears in a partnership name contrary to the provisions of paragraph (1) is liable as a general partner to partnership creditors who extend credit to the partnership without actual knowledge that he is not a general partner.

§ 6. Liability for False Statements in Certificate.

If the certificate contains a false statement, one who suffers loss by reliance on such statement may hold liable any party to the certificate who knew the statement to be false.

(a) At the time he signed the certificate, or

(b) Subsequently, but within a sufficient time before the statement was relied upon to enable him to cancel or amend the certificate, or to file a petition for its cancellation or amendment as provided in Section 25(3).

§ 7. Limited Partner Not Liable to Creditors.

A limited partner shall not become liable as a general partner unless, in addition to the exercise of his rights and powers as a limited partner, he takes part in the control of the business.

§ 8. Admission of Additional Limited Partners.

After the formation of a limited partnership, additional limited partners may be admitted upon filing an amendment to the original certificate in accordance with the requirements of Section 25.

§ 9. Rights, Powers and Liabilities of a General Partner.

(1) A general partner shall have all the rights and powers and be subject to all the restrictions and liabilities of a partner in a partnership without limited partners, except that without the written consent or ratification of the specific act by all the limited partners, a general partner or all of the general partners have no authority to

(a) Do any act in contravention of the certificate,

(b) Do any act which would make it impossible to carry on the ordinary business of the partnership,

(c) Confess a judgment against the partnership,

(d) Possess partnership property, or assign their rights in specific partnership property, for other than a partnership purpose,

(e) Admit a person as a general partner,

(f) Admit a person as a limited partner, unless the right so to do is given in the certificate,

(g) Continue the business with partnership property on the death, retirement or insanity of a general partner, unless the right so to do is given in the certificate.

§ 10. Rights of a Limited Partner.

(1) A limited partner shall have the same rights as a general partner to

(a) Have the partnership books kept at the principal place of business of the partnership, and at all times to inspect and copy any of them.

(b) Have on demand true and full information of all things affecting the partnership, and a formal account of partnership affairs whenever circumstances render it just and reasonable, and

(c) Have dissolution and winding up by decree of court.

(2) A limited partner shall have the right to receive a share of the profits or other compensation by way of income, and to the return of his contribution as provided in Sections 15 and 16.

§ 11. Status of Person Erroneously Believing Himself a Limited Partner.

A person who has contributed to the capital of a business conducted by a person or partnership erroneously believing that he has become a limited partner in a limited partnership, is not, by reason of his exercise of the rights of a limited partner, a general partner with the person or in the partnership carrying on the business, or bound by the obligations of such person or partnership; provided that on ascertaining the mistake he promptly renounces his interest in the profits of the business, or other compensation by way of income.

§ 12. One Person Both General and Limited Partner.

(1) A person may be a general partner and a limited partner in the same partnership at the same time.

(2) A person who is a general, and also at the same time a limited partner, shall have all the rights and powers and be subject to all the restrictions of a general partner; except that, in respect to his contribution, he shall have the rights against the other members which he would have had if he were not also a general partner.

§ 13. Loans and Other Business Transactions with Limited Partner.

(1) A limited partner also may loan money to and transact other business with the partnership, and, unless he is also a general partner, receive on account of resulting claims against the partnership, with general creditors, a pro rata share of the assets. No limited partner shall in respect to any such claim

(a) Receive or hold as collateral security any partnership property, or

(b) Receive from a general partner or the partnership any payment, conveyance, or release from liability, if at the time the assets of the partnership are not sufficient to discharge partnership liabilities to persons not claiming as general or limited partners,

(2) The receiving of collateral security, or a payment, conveyance, or release in violation of the provisions of paragraph (1) is a fraud on the creditors of the partnership.

§ 14. Relation of Limited Partners Inter Se.

Where there are several limited partners the members may agree that one or more of the limited partners shall have a priority over other limited partners as to the return of their contributions, as to their compensation by way of income, or as to any other matter. If such an agreement is made it shall be stated in the certificate, and in the absence of such a statement all the limited partners shall stand upon equal footing.

§ 15. Compensation of Limited Partner.

A limited partner may receive from the partnership the share of the profits or the compensation by way of income stipulated for in the certificate; provided, that after such payment is made, whether from the property of the partnership or that of a general partner, the partnership assets are in excess of all liabilities of the partnership except liabilities to limited partners on account of their contributions and to general partners.

§ 16. Withdrawal or Reduction of Limited Partner's Contribution.

(1) A limited partner shall not receive from a general partner or out of partnership property any part of his contribution until

(a) All liabilities of the partnership, except liabilities to general partners and to limited partners on account of their contributions, have been paid or there remains property of the partnership sufficient to pay them,

(b) The consent of all members is had, unless the return of the contribution may be rightfully demanded under the provisions of paragraph (2), and

(c) The certificate is cancelled or so amended as to set forth the withdrawal or reduction.

(2) Subject to the provisions of paragraph (1) a limited partner may rightfully demand the return of his contribution

(a) On the dissolution of a partnership, or

(b) When the date specified in the certificate for its return has arrived, or

(c) After he has given six months' notice in writing to all other members, if no time is specified in the certificate either for the return of the contribution or for the dissolution of the partnership.

(3) In the absence of any statement in the certificate to the contrary or the consent of all members, a limited partner, irrespective of the nature of his contribution, has only the right to demand and receive cash in return for his contribution.

(4) A limited partner may have the partnership dissolved and its affairs wound up when

(a) He rightfully but unsuccessfully demands the return of his contribution, or

(b) The other liabilities of the partnership have not been paid, or the partnership property is insufficient for their payment as required by paragraph (la) and the limited partner would otherwise be entitled to the return of his contribution.

§ 17. Liability of Limited Partner to Partnership.

(1) A limited partner is liable to the partnership
  (a) For the difference between his contribution as actually made and that stated in the certificate as having been made, and
  (b) For any unpaid contribution which he agreed in the certificate to make in the future at the time and on the conditions stated in the certificate.

(2) A limited partner holds as trustee for the partnership
  (a) Specific property stated in the certificate as contributed by him, but which was not contributed or which has been wrongfully returned, and
  (b) Money or other property wrongfully paid or conveyed to him on account of his contribution.

(3) The liabilities of a limited partner as set forth in this section can be waived or compromised only by the consent of all members; but a waiver or compromise shall not affect the right of a creditor of a partnership who extended credit or whose claim arose after the filing and before a cancellation or amendment of the certificate, to enforce such liabilities.

(4) When a contributor has rightfully received the return in whole or in part of the capital of his contribution, he is nevertheless liable to the partnership for any sum, not in excess of such return with interest, necessary to discharge its liabilities to all creditors who extended credit or whose claims arose before such return.

§ 18. Nature of Limited Partner's Interest in Partnership.

A limited partner's interest in the partnership is personal property.

§ 19. Assignment of Limited Partner's Interest.

(1) A limited partner's interest is assignable.

(2) A substituted limited partner is a person admitted to all the rights of a limited partner who has died or has assigned his interest in a partnership.

(3) An assignee, who does not become a substituted limited partner, has no right to require any information or account of the partnership transactions or to inspect the partnership books; he is only entitled to receive the share of the profits or other compensation by way of income, or the return of his contribution, to which his assignor would otherwise be entitled.

(4) An assignee shall have the right to become a substituted limited partner if all the members (except the assignor) consent thereto or if the assignor, being thereunto empowered by the certificate, gives the assignee that right.

(5) An assignee becomes a substituted limited partner when the certificate is appropriately amended in accordance with Section 25.

(6) The substituted limited partner has all the rights and powers, and is subject to all the restrictions and liabilities of his assignor, except those liabilities of which he was ignorant at the time he became a limited partner and which could not be ascertained from the certificate.

(7) The substitution of the assignee as a limited partner does not release the assignor from liability to the partnership under Sections 6 and 17.

§ 20. Effect of Retirement, Death or Insanity of a General Partner.

The retirement, death or insanity of a general partner dissolves the partnership, unless the business is continued by the remaining general partners
  (a) Under a right so to do stated in the certificate, or
  (b) With the consent of all members.

§ 21. Death of a Limited Partner.

(1) On the death of a limited partner his executor or administrator shall have all the rights of a limited partner for the purpose of settling his estate, and such power as the deceased had to constitute his assignee a substituted limited partner.

(2) The estate of a deceased limited partner shall be liable for all his liabilities as a limited partner.

§ 22. Rights of Creditors of Limited Partner.

(1) On due application to a court of competent jurisdiction by any judgment creditor of a limited partner, the court may charge the interest of the indebted limited partner with payment of the unsatisfied amount of the judgment debt; and may appoint a receiver, and make all other orders, directions, and inquiries which the circumstances of the case may require.

(2) The interest may be redeemed with the separate property of any general partner, but may not be redeemed with partnership property.

(3) The remedies conferred by paragraph (1) shall not be deemed exclusive of others which may exist.

(4) Nothing in this act shall be held to deprive a limited partner of his statutory exemption.

§ 23. Distribution of Assets.

(1) In settling accounts after dissolution the liabilities of the partnership shall be entitled to payment in the following order:
  (a) Those to creditors, in the order of priority as provided by law, except those to limited partners on account of their contributions, and to general partners,
  (b) Those to limited partners in respect to their share of the profits and other compensation by way of income and on their contributions,

(c) Those to limited partners in respect to the capital of their contributions,

(d) Those to general partners other than for capital and profits,

(e) Those to general partners in respect to profits,

(f) Those to general partners in respect to capital.

(2) Subject to any statement in the certificate or to subsequent agreement, limited partners share in the partnership assets in respect to their claims for capital, and in respect to their claims for profits or for compensation by way of income on their contributions respectively, in proportion to the respective amounts of such claims.

§ 24. When Certificate Shall Be Cancelled or Amended.

(1) The certificate shall be cancelled when the partnership is dissolved or all limited partners cease to be such.

(2) A certificate shall be amended when

(a) There is a change in the name of the partnership or in the amount or character of the contribution of any limited partner,

(b) A person is substituted as a limited partner,

(c) An additional limited partner is admitted,

(d) A person is admitted as a general partner,

(e) A general partner retires, dies or becomes insane, and the business in continued under Section 20,

(f) There is a change in the character of the business of the partnership,

(g) There is a false or erroneous statement in the certificate,

(h) There is a change in the time as stated in the certificate for the dissolution of the partnership or for the return of a contribution,

(i) A time is fixed for the dissolution of the partnership, or the return of a contribution, no time having been specified in the certificate, or

(j) The members desire to make a change on any other statement in the certificate in order that it shall accurately represent the agreement between them.

§ 25. Requirements for Amendment and for Cancellation of Certificate.

(1) The writing to amend a certificate shall

(a) Conform to the requirements of Section 2(1a) as far as necessary to set forth clearly the change in the certificate which it is desire to make, and

(b) Be signed and sworn to by all members, and an amendment substituting a limited partner or adding a limited or general partner shall be signed also by the member to be substituted or added, and when a limited partner is to be substituted, the amendment shall also be signed by the assigning limited partner.

(2) The writing to cancel a certificate shall be signed by all members.

(3) A person desiring the cancellation or amendment of a certificate, if any person designated in paragraphs (1) and (2) as a person who must execute the writing refuses to do so, may petition the [here designate the proper court] to direct a cancellation or amendment thereof.

(4) If the court finds that the petitioner has a right to have the writing executed by a person who refuses to do so, it shall order the [here designate the responsible official in the office designated in Section 2] in the office where the certificate is recorded to record the cancellation or amendment of the certificate; and where the certificate is to be amended, the court shall also cause to be filed for record in said office a certified copy of its decree setting forth the amendment.

(5) A certificate is amended or cancelled when there is filed for record in the office [here designate the office designated in Section 2] where the certificate is recorded

(a) A writing in accordance with the provisions of paragraph (1), or (2) or

(b) A certified copy of the order of court in accordance with the provisions of paragraph (4).

(6) After the certificate is duly amended in accordance with this section, the amended certificate shall thereafter be for all purposes the certificate provided for by this act.

§ 26. Parties to Actions.

A contributor, unless he is a general partner, is not a proper party to proceedings by or against a partnership, except where the object is to enforce a limited partner's right against or liability to the partnership.

§ 27. Name of Act.

This act may be cited as The Uniform Limited Partnership Act.

§ 28. Rules of Construction.

(1) The rule that statutes in derogation of the common law are to be strictly construed shall have no application to this act.

(2) This act shall be so interpreted and construed as to effect its general purpose to make uniform the law of those states which enact it.

(3) This act shall not be so construed as to impair the obligations of any contract existing when the act goes into effect, nor to affect any action or proceedings begun or right accrued before this act takes effect.

§ 29. Rules for Cases not Provided for in This Act.

In any case not provided for in this act the rules of law and equity, including the law merchant, shall govern.

§ 30. Provisions for Existing Limited Partnerships.

(1) A limited partnership formed under any statute of this state prior to the adoption of this act, may become a limited partnership under this act by complying with the provisions of Section 2; provided the certificate sets forth

(a) The amount of the original contribution of each limited partner, and the time when the contribution was made, and

(b) That the property of the partnership exceeds the amount sufficient to discharge its liabilities to persons not claiming as general or limited partners by an amount greater than the sum of the contributions of its limited partners.

(2) A limited partnership formed under any statute of this state prior to the adoption of this act, until or unless it becomes a limited partnership under this act, shall continue to be governed by the provisions of [here insert proper reference to the existing limited partnership act or acts], except that such partnership shall not be renewed unless so provided in the original agreement.

§ 31. Act (Acts) Repealed.

Excepts as affecting existing limited partnerships to the extent set forth in Section 30, the act (acts) of [here designate the existing limited partnership act or acts] is (are) hereby repealed.

Appendix E

Revised Uniform Limited Partnership Act (1976) with 1985 Amendments

Table of Sections

ARTICLE 9.   Foreign Limited Partnerships

901. Law Governing.
902. Registration.
903. Issuance of Registration.
904. Name.
905. Changes and Amendments.
906. Cancellation of Registration.
907. Transaction of Business Without Registration.
908. Action by [Appropriate Official].

ARTICLE 10.   Derivative Actions

1001. Right of Action.
1002. Proper Plaintiff.
1003. Pleading.
1004. Expenses.

ARTICLE 11.   Miscellaneous

1101. Construction and Application.
1102. Short Title.
1103. Severability.
1104. Effective Date, Extended Effective Date and Repeal.
1105. Rules for Cases Not Provided for in This Act.
1106. Savings Clause.

ARTICLE 1.   General Provisions

§ 101.   Definitions.

As used in this [Act], unless the context otherwise requires:

(1) "Certificate of limited partnership" means the certificate referred to in Section 201, and the certificate as amended or restated.

(2) "Contribution" means any cash, property, services rendered, or a promissory note or other binding obligation to contribute cash or property or to perform services, which a partner contributes to a limited partnership in his capacity as a partner.

(3) "Event of withdrawal of a general partner" means an event that causes a person to cease to be a general partner as provided in Section 402.

(4) "Foreign limited partnership" means a partnership formed under the laws of any state other than this State and having as partners one or more general partners and one or more limited partners.

(5) "General partner" means a person who has been admitted to a limited partnership as a general partner in accordance with the partnership agreement and named in the certificate of limited partnership as a general partner.

(6) "Limited partner" means a person who has been admitted to a limited partnership as a limited partner in accordance with the partnership agreement.

(7) "Limited partnership" and "domestic limited partnership" mean a partnership formed by two or more persons under the laws of this State and having one or more general partners and one or more limited partners.

(8) "Partner" means a limited of general partner.

(9) "Partnership agreement" means any valid agreement, written or oral, of the partners as to the affairs of a limited partnership and the conduct of its business.

(10) "Partnership interest" means a partner's share of the profits and losses of a limited partnership and the right to receive distributions of partnership assets.

(11) "Person" means a natural person, partnership, limited partnership (domestic or foreign), trust, estate, association, or corporation.

(12) "State" means a state, territory, or possession of the United States, the District of Columbia, or the Commonwealth of Puerto Rico.

§ 102.   Name.

The name of each limited partnership as set forth in its certificate of limited partnership:

(1) shall contain without abbreviation the words "limited partnership";

(2) may not contain the name of a limited partner unless (i) it is also the name of a general partner or the corporate name of a corporate general partner, or (ii) the business of the limited partnership had been carried on under that name before the admission of that limited partner;

(3) may not be the same as, or deceptively similar to, the name of any corporation or limited partnership organized under the laws of this State or licensed or registered as a foreign corporation or limited partnership in this State; and

(4) may not contain the following words [here insert prohibited words].

§ 103.   Reservation of Name.

(a) The exclusive right to the use of a name may be reserved by:

(1) any person intending to organize a limited partnership under this [Act] and to adopt that name;

(2) any domestic limited partnership or any foreign limited partnership registered in this State which, in either case, intends to adopt that name;

(3) any foreign limited partnership intending to register in this State and adopt that name; and

(4) any person intending to organize a foreign limited partnership and intending to have it register in this State and adopt that name.

(b) The reservation shall be made by filing with the Secretary of State an application, executed by the applicant, to reserve a specified name. If the Secretary of State finds that the name is available for use by a domestic or foreign limited partnership, he [or she] shall reserve the name for the exclusive use of the applicant for a period of 120 days. Once having so reserved a name, the same applicant may not again reserve the same name until more than 60 days after the expiration of the last 120-day period for which that applicant reserved that name. The right to the exclusive use of a reserved name may be transferred to any other person by filing in the office of the Secretary of State a notice of the transfer, executed by the applicant for whom the name was reserved and specifying the name and address of the transferee.

§ 104.   Specified Office and Agent.

Each Limited Partnership shall continuously maintain in this State:

(1) an office, which may but need not be a place of its business in this State, at which shall be kept the records required by Section 105 to be maintained; and

(2) an agent for service of process on the limited partnership, which agent must be an individual resident of this State, a domestic corporation, or a foreign corporation authorized to do business in this State.

§ 105.   Records to Be Kept.

(a) Each limited partnership shall keep at the office referred to in Section 104(1) the following:

(1) a current list of the full name and last known business address of each partner, separately identifying the general partners (in alphabetical order) and the limited partners (in alphabetical order);

(2) a copy of the certificate of limited partnership and all certificates of amendment thereto, together with executed copies of any powers of attorney pursuant to which any certificate has been executed;

(3) copies of the limited partnership's federal, state and local income tax returns and reports, if any, for the three most recent years;

(4) copies of any then effective written partnership agreements and of any financial statements of the limited partnership for the three most recent years; and

(5) unless contained in a written partnership agreement, a writing setting out:

(i) the amount of cash and a description and statement of the agreed value of the other property or services contributed by each partner and which each partner has agreed to contribute;

(ii) the times at which or events on the happening of which any additional contributions agreed to be made by each partner are to be made;

(iii) any right of a partner to receive, or of a general partner to make, distributions to

a partner which include a return of all or any part of the partner's contribution; and

(iv) any events upon the happening of which the limited partnership is to be dissolved and its affairs wound up.

(b) Records kept under this section are subject to inspection and copying at the reasonable request and at the expense of any partner during ordinary business hours.

§ 106.   Nature of Business.

A limited partnership may carry on any business that a partnership without limited partners may carry on except [here designate prohibited activities].

§ 107.   Business Transactions of Partner with Partnership.

Except as provided in the partnership agreement, a partner may lend money to and transact other business with the limited partnership and, subject to other applicable law, has the same rights and obligations with respect thereto as a person who is not a partner.

ARTICLE 2.   Formation; Certificate of Limited Partnership

§ 201.   Certificate of Limited Partnership.

(a) In order to form a limited partnership, a certificate of limited partnership must be executed and filed in the office of the Secretary of State. The certificate shall set forth:

(1) the name of the limited partnership;

(2) the address of the office and the name and address of the agent for service of process required to be maintained by Section 104;

(3) the name and the business address of each general partner;

(4) the latest date upon which the limited partnership is to dissolve; and

(5) any other matters the general partners determine to include therein.

(b) A limited partnership is formed at the time of the filing of the certificate of limited partnership in the office of the Secretary of State or at any later time specified in the certificate of limited partnership if, in either case, there has been substantial compliance with the requirements of this section.

§ 202.   Amendment to Certificate.

(a) A certificate of limited partnership is amended by filing a certificate of amendment thereto in the office of the Secretary of State. The certificate shall set forth:

(1) the name of the limited partnership;

(2) the date of filing the certificate; and

(3) the amendment to the certificate.

(b) Within 30 days after the happening of any of the following events, an amendment to a certificate of limited partnership reflecting the occurrence of the event or events shall be filed:

    (1) the admission of a new general partner;

    (2) the withdrawal of a general partner; or

    (3) the continuation of the business under Section 801 after an event of withdrawal of a general partner.

(c) A general partner who becomes aware that any statement in a certificate of limited partnership was false when made or that any arrangements or other facts described have changed, making the certificate inaccurate in any respect, shall promptly amend the certificate.

(d) A certificate of limited partnership may be amended at any time for any other proper purpose the general partners determine.

(e) No person has any liability because an amendment to a certificate of limited partnership has not been filed to reflect the occurrence of any event referred to in subsection (b) of this section if the amendment is filed within the 30-day period specified in subsection (b).

(f) A restated certificate of limited partnership may be executed and filed in the same manner as a certificate of amendment.

§ 203. Cancellation of Certificate.

A certificate of limited partnership shall be cancelled upon the dissolution and the commencement of winding up of the partnership or at any other time there are no limited partners. A certificate of cancellation shall be filed in the office of the Secretary of State and set forth:

    (1) the name of the limited partnership;

    (2) the date of filing of its certificate of limited partnership;

    (3) the reason for filing the certificate of cancellation;

    (4) the effective date (which shall be a date certain) of cancellation if it is not to be effective upon the filing of the certificate; and

    (5) any other information the general partners filing the certificate determine.

§ 204. Execution of Certificates.

(a) Each certificate required by this Article to be filed in the office of the Secretary of State shall be executed in the following manner:

    (1) An original certificate of limited partnership must be signed by all general partners;

    (2) a certificate of amendment must be signed by at least one general partner and by each other general partner designated in the certificate as a new general partner; and

    (3) a certificate of cancellation must be signed by all general partners.

(b) Any person may sign a certificate by an attorney-in-fact, but a power of attorney to sign a certificate relating to the admission of a general partner must specifically describe the admission.

(c) The execution of a certificate by a general partner constitutes an affirmation under the penalties of perjury that the facts stated therein are true.

§ 205. Execution by Judicial Act.

If a person required by Section 204 to execute any certificate fails or refuses to do so, any other person who is adversely affected by the failure or refusal may petition the [designate the appropriate court] to direct the execution of the certificate. If the court finds that it is proper for the certificate to be executed and that any person so designated has failed or refused to execute the certificate, it shall order the Secretary of State to record an appropriate certificate.

§ 206. Filing in Office of Secretary of State.

(a) Two signed copies of the certificate of limited partnership and of any certificates of amendment or cancellation (or of any judicial decree of amendment or cancellation) shall be delivered to the Secretary of State. A person who executes a certificate as an agent or fiduciary need not exhibit evidence of his [or her] authority as a prerequisite to filing. Unless the Secretary of State finds that any certificate does not conform to law, upon receipt of all filing fees required by law he [or she] shall:

    (1) endorse on each duplicate original the word "Filed" and the day, month, and year of the filing thereof;

    (2) file one duplicate original in his [or her] office; and

    (3) return the other duplicate original to the person who filed it or his [or her] representative.

(b) Upon the filing of a certificate of amendment (or judicial decree of amendment) in the office of the Secretary of State, the certificate of limited partnership shall be amended as set forth therein, and upon the effective date of a certificate of cancellation (or a judicial decree thereof), the certificate of limited partnership is cancelled.

§ 207. Liability for False Statement in Certificate.

If any certificate of limited partnership or certificate of amendment or cancellation contains a false statement, one who suffers loss by reliance on the statement may recover damages for the loss from:

    (1) any person who executes the certificate, or causes another to execute it on his behalf, and knew, and any general partner who knew or should have known, the statement to be false at the time the certificate was executed; and

    (2) any general partner who thereafter knows or should have known that any arrangement or other fact

described in the certificate has changed, making the statement inaccurate in any respect within a sufficient time before the statement was relied upon reasonably to have enabled that general partner to cancel or amend the certificate, or to file a petition for its cancellation or amendment under Section 205.

§ 208. Scope of Notice.

The fact that a certificate of limited partnership is on file in the office of the Secretary of State is notice that the partnership is a limited partnership and the persons designated therein as general partners are general partners, but it is not notice of any other fact.

§ 209. Delivery of Certificates to Limited Partners.

Upon the return by the Secretary of State pursuant to Section 206 of a certificate marked ''Filed'', the general partners shall promptly deliver or mail a copy of the certificate of limited partnership and each certificate of amendment or cancellation to each limited partner unless the partnership agreement provides otherwise.

ARTICLE 3. Limited Partners

§ 301. Admission of Limited Partners.

(a) A person becomes a limited partner:
- (1) at the time the limited partnership is formed; or
- (2) at any later time specified in the records of the limited partnership for becoming a limited partner.

(b) After the filing of a limited partnership's original certificate of limited partnership, a person may be admitted as an additional limited partner:
- (1) in the case of a person acquiring a partnership interest directly from the limited partnership, upon compliance with the partnership agreement or, if the partnership agreement does not so provide, upon the written consent of all partners; and
- (2) in the case of an assignee of a partnership interest of a partner who has the power, as provided in Section 704, to grant the assignee the right to become a limited partner, upon the exercise of that power and compliance with any conditions limiting the grant or exercise of the power.

§ 302. Voting.

Subject to Section 303, the partnership agreement may grant to all or a specified group of the limited partners the right to vote (on a per capita or other basis) upon any matter.

§ 303. Liability to Third Parties.

(a) Except as provided in subsection (d), a limited partner is not liable for the obligations of a limited part-

nership unless he [or she] is also a general partner or, in addition to the exercise of his [or her] rights and powers as a limited partner, he [or she] participates in the control of the business. However, if the limited partner participates in the control of the business, he [or she] is liable only to persons who transact business with the limited partnership reasonably believing, based upon the limited partner's conduct, that the limited partner is a general partner.

(b) A limited partner does not participate in the control of the business within the meaning of subsection (a) solely by doing one or more of the following:
- (1) being a contractor for an agent or employee of the limited partnership or of a general partner or being an officer, director, or shareholder of a general partner that is a corporation;
- (2) consulting with and advising a general partner with respect to the business of the limited partnership;
- (3) acting as surety for the limited partnership or guaranteeing or assuming one or more specific obligations of the limited partnership;
- (4) taking any action required or permitted by law to bring or pursue a derivative action in the right of the limited partnership;
- (5) requesting or attending a meeting of partners;
- (6) proposing, approving, or disapproving, by voting or otherwise, one or more of the following matters:
  - (i) the dissolution and winding up of the limited partnership;
  - (ii) the sale, exchange, lease, mortgage, pledge, or other transfer of all or substantially all of the assets of the limited partnership;
  - (iii) the incurrence of indebtedness by the limited partnership other than in the ordinary course of its business;
  - (iv) a change in the nature of the business;
  - (v) the admission or removal of a general partner;
  - (vi) the admission or removal of a limited partner;
  - (vii) a transaction involving an actual or potential conflict of interest between a general partner and the limited partnership or the limited partners;
  - (viii) an amendment to the partnership agreement or certificate of limited partnership; or
  - (ix) matters related to the business of the limited partnership not otherwise enumerated in this subsection (b), which the partnership agreement states in writing may be subject to the approval or disapproval of limited partners;

(7) winding up the limited partnership pursuant to Section 803; or

(8) exercising any right or power permitted to limited partners under this [Act] and not specifically enumerated in this subsection (b).

(c) The enumeration in subsection (b) does not mean that the possession or exercise of any other powers by a limited partner constitutes participation by him [or her] in the business of the limited partnership.

(d) A limited partner who knowingly permits his [or her] name to be used in the name of the limited partnership, except under circumstances permitted by Section 102(2), is liable to creditors who extend credit to the limited partnership without actual knowledge that the limited partner is not a general partner.

§ 304. Person Erroneously Believing Himself [or Herself] Limited Partner.

(a) Except as provided in subsection (b), a person who makes a contribution to a business enterprise and erroneously but in good faith believes that he [or she] has become a limited partner in the enterprise is not a general partner in the enterprise and is not bound by its obligations by reason of making the contribution, receiving distributions from the enterprise, or exercising any rights of a limited partner, if, on ascertaining the mistake, he [or she]:

(1) causes an appropriate certificate of limited partnership or a certificate of amendment to be executed and filed; or

(2) withdraws from future equity participation in the enterprise by executing and filing in the office of the Secretary of State a certificate declaring withdrawal under this section.

(b) A person who makes a contribution of the kind described in subsection (a) is liable as a general partner to any third party who transacts business with the enterprise (i) before the person withdraws and an appropriate certificate is filed to show withdrawal, or (ii) before an appropriate certificate is filed to show that he [or she] is not a general partner, but in either case only if the third party actually believed in good faith that the person was a general partner at the time of the transaction.

§ 305. Information.

Each limited partner has the right to:

(1) inspect and copy any of the partnership records required to be maintained by Section 105; and

(2) obtain from the general partners from time to time upon reasonable demand (i) true and full information regarding the state of the business and financial condition of the limited partnership, (ii) promptly after becoming available, a copy of the limited partnership's federal, state, and local income tax returns for each year, and (iii) other information regarding the affairs of the limited partnership as is just and reasonable.

ARTICLE 4.   General Partners

§ 401.   Admission of Additional General Partners.

After the filing of a limited partnership's original certificate of limited partnership, additional general partners may be admitted as provided in writing in the partnership agreement or, if the partnership agreement does not provide in writing for the admission of additional general partners, with the written consent of all partners.

§ 402.   Events of Withdrawal.

Except as approved by the specific written consent of all partners at the time, a person ceases to be a general partner of a limited partnership upon the happening of any of the following events:

(1) the general partner withdraws from the limited partnership as provided in Section 602;

(2) the general partner ceases to be a member of the limited partnership as provided in Section 702;

(3) the general partner is removed as a general partner is accordance with the partnership agreement;

(4) unless otherwise provided in writing in the partnership agreement, the general partner: (i) makes an assignment for the benefit of creditors; (ii) files a voluntary petition in bankruptcy; (iii) is adjudicated a bankrupt or insolvent; (iv) files a petition or answer seeking for himself [or herself] any reorganization, arrangement, composition, readjustment, liquidation, dissolution or similar relief under any statute, law, or regulation; (v) files an answer or other pleading admitting or failing to contest the material allegations of a petition filed against him [or her] in any proceeding of this nature; or (vi) seeks, consents to, or acquiesces in the appointment of a trustee, receiver, or liquidator of the general partner or of all or any substantial part of his [or her] properties;

(5) unless otherwise provided in writing in the partnership agreement, [120] days after the commencement of any proceeding against the general partner seeking reorganization, arrangement, composition, readjustment, liquidation, dissolution or similar relief under any statute, law, or regulation, the proceeding has not been dismissed, or if within [90] days after the appointment without his [or her] consent or acquiescence of a trustee, receiver, or liquidator of the general partner or of all or any substantial part of his [or her] properties, the appointment is not vacated or stayed or within [90] days after the expiration of any such stay, the appointment is not vacated;

(6) in the case of a general partner who is a natural person,

(i) his [or her] death; or

(ii) the entry of an order by a court of competent jurisdiction adjudicating him [or her] incompetent to manage his [or her] person or his [or her] estate;

(7) in the case of a general partner who is acting as a general partner by virtue of being a trustee of a trust, the termination of the trust (but not merely the substitution of a new trustee);

(8) in the case of a general partner that is a separate partnership, the dissolution and commencement of winding up of the separate partnership;

(9) in the case of a general partner that is a corporation, the filing of a certificate of dissolution, or its equivalent, for the corporation or the revocation of its charter; or

(10) in the case of an estate, the distribution by the fiduciary of the estate's entire interest in the partnership.

§ 403. General Powers and Liabilities.

(a) Except as provided in this [Act] or in the partnership agreement, a general partner of a limited partnership has the rights and powers and is subject to the restrictions of a partner in a partnership without limited partners.

(b) Except as provided in this [Act], a general partner of a limited partnership has the liabilities of a partner in a partnership without limited partners to persons other than the partnership and the other partners. Except as provided in this [Act] or in the partnership agreement, a general partner of a limited partnership has the liabilities of a partner in a partnership without limited partners to the partnership and to the other partners.

§ 404. Contributions by General Partner.

A general partner of a limited partnership may make contributions to the partnership and share in the profits and losses of, and in distributions from, the limited partnership as a general partner. A general partner also may make contributions to and share in profits, losses, and distributions as a limited partner. A person who is both a general partner and a limited partner has the rights and powers, and is subject to the restrictions and liabilities, of a general partner and, except as provided in the partnership agreement, also has the powers, and is subject to the restrictions, of a limited partner to the extent of his [or her] participation in the partnership as a limited partner.

§ 405. Voting.

The partnership agreement may grant to all or certain identified general partners the right to vote (on a per capita or any other basis), separately or with all or any class of the limited partners, on any matter.

ARTICLE 5. Finance

§ 501. Form of Contribution.

The contribution of a partner may be in cash, property, or services rendered, or a promissory note or other obligation to contribute cash or property or to perform services.

§ 502. Liability for Contribution.

(a) A promise by a limited partner to contribute to the limited partnership is not enforceable unless set out in a writing signed by the limited partner.

(b) Except as provided in the partnership agreement, a partner is obligated to the limited partnership to perform any enforceable promise to contribute cash or property or to perform services, even if he [or she] is unable to perform because of death, disability, or any other reason. If a partner does not make the required contribution of property or services, he [or she] is obligated at the option of the limited partnership to contribute cash equal to that portion of the value, as stated in the partnership records required to be kept pursuant to Section 105, of the stated contribution which has not been made.

(c) Unless otherwise provided in the partnership agreement, the obligation of a partner to make a contribution or return money or other property paid or distributed in violation of this [Act] may be compromised only by consent of all partners. Notwithstanding the compromise, a creditor of a limited partnership who extends credit or otherwise acts in reliance on that obligation after the partner signs a writing which reflects the obligation and before the amendment or cancellation thereof to reflect the compromise may enforce the original obligation.

§ 503. Sharing of Profits and Losses.

The profits and losses of a limited partnership shall be allocated among the partners, and among classes of partners, in the manner provided in writing in the partnership agreement. If the partnership agreement does not so provide in writing, profits and losses shall be allocated on the basis of the value, as stated in the partnership records required to be kept pursuant to Section 105, of the contributions made by each partner to the extent they have been received by the partnership and have not been returned.

§ 504. Sharing of Distributions.

Distributions of cash or other assets of a limited partnership shall be allocated among the partners and among classes of partners in the manner provided in writing in the partnership agreement. If the partnership agreement does not so provide in writing, distributions shall be made on the basis of the value, as stated in the partnership records required to be kept pursuant to Section 105, of the contributions made by each partner to the extent they have been received by the partnership and have not been returned.

ARTICLE 6. Distributions and Withdrawal

§ 601. Interim Distributions.

Except as provided in this Article, a partner is entitled to receive distributions from a limited partnership before his [or her] withdrawal from the limited partnership and before the dissolution and winding up thereof to the extent and at the times or upon the happening of the events specified in the partnership agreement.

§ 602. Withdrawal of General Partner.

A general partner may withdraw from a limited partnership at any time by giving written notice to the other partners, but if the withdrawal violates the partnership agreement, the limited partnership may recover from the withdrawing general partner damages for breach of the partnership agreement and offset the damages against the amount otherwise distributable to him [or her].

§ 603. Withdrawal of Limited Partner.

A limited partner may withdraw from a limited partnership at the time or upon the happening of events specified in writing in the partnership agreement. If the agreement does not specify in writing the time or the events upon the happening of which a limited partner may withdraw or a definite time for the dissolution and winding up of the limited partnership, a limited partner may withdraw upon not less than six months' prior written notice to each general partner at his [or her] address on the books of the limited partnership at its office in this State.

§ 604. Distribution Upon Withdrawal.

Except as provided in this Article, upon withdrawal any withdrawing partner is entitled to receive any distribution to which he [or she] is entitled under the partnership agreement and, if not otherwise provided in the agreement, he [or she] is entitled to receive, within a reasonable time after withdrawal, the fair value of his [or her] interest in the limited partnership as of the date of withdrawal based upon his [or her] right to share in distributions from the limited partnership.

§ 605. Distribution in Kind.

Except as provided in writing in the partnership agreement, a partner, regardless of the nature of his [or her] contribution, has no right to demand and receive any distribution from a limited partnership in any form other than cash. Except as provided in writing in the partnership agreement, a partner may not be compelled to accept a distribution of any asset in kind from a limited partnership to the extent that the percentage of the asset distributed to him [or her] exceeds a percentage of that asset which is equal to the percentage in which he [or she] shares in distributions from the limited partnership.

§ 606. Right to Distribution.

At the time a partner becomes entitled to receive a distribution, he [or she] has the status of, and is entitled to all remedies available to, a creditor of the limited partnership with respect to the distribution.

§ 607. Limitations on Distribution.

A partner may not receive a distribution from a limited partnership to the extent that, after giving effect to the distribution, all liabilities of the limited partnership, other than liabilities to partners on account of their partnership interests, exceed the fair value of the partnership assets.

§ 608. Liability Upon Return of Contribution.

(a) If a partner has received the return of any part of his [or her] contribution without violation of the partnership agreement or this [Act], he [or she] is liable to the limited partnership for a period of one year thereafter for the amount of the returned contribution, but only to the extent necessary to discharge the limited partnership's liabilities to creditors who extended credit to the limited partnership during the period the contribution was held by the partnership.

(b) If a partner has received the return of any part of his [or her] contribution in violation of the partnership agreement or this [Act], he [or she] is liable to the limited partnership for a period of six years thereafter for the amount of the contribution wrongfully returned.

(c) A partner receives a return of his [or her] contribution to the extent that a distribution to him [or her] reduces his [or her] share of the fair value of the net assets of the limited partnership below the value, as set forth in the partnership records required to be kept pursuant to Section 105, of his contribution which has not been distributed to him [or her].

ARTICLE 7. Assignment of Partnership Interests

§ 701. Nature of Partnership Interest.

A partnership interest is personal property.

§ 702. Assignment of Partnership Interest.

Except as provided in the partnership agreement, a partnership interest is assignable in whole or in part. An assignment of a partnership interest does not dissolve a limited partnership or entitle the assignee to become or to exercise any rights of a partner. An interest assignment entitles the assignee to receive, to the extent assigned, only the distribution to which the assignor would be entitled. Except as provided in the partnership agreement, a partner ceases to be a partner upon assignment of all his [or her] partnership interest.

§ 703. Rights of Creditor.

On application to a court of competent jurisdiction by any judgment creditor of a partner, the court may charge the partnership interest of the partner with payment of the unsatisfied amount of the judgment with interest. To the extent so charged, the judgment creditor has only the rights of an assignee of the partnership interest. This

[Act] does not deprive any partner of the benefit of any exemption laws applicable to his [or her] partnership interest.

§ 704. Right of Assignee to Become Limited Partner.

(a) An assignee of a partnership interest, including an assignee of a general partner, may become a limited partner if and to the extent that (i) the assignor gives the assignee that right in accordance with authority described in the partnership agreement, or (ii) all other partners consent.

(b) An assignee who has become a limited partner has, to the extent assigned, the rights and powers, and is subject to the restrictions and liabilities, of a limited partner under the partnership agreement and this [Act]. An assignee who becomes a limited partner also is liable for the obligations of his [or her] assignor to make and return contributions as provided in Articles 5 and 6. However, the assignee is not obligated for liabilities unknown to the assignee at the time he [or she] became a limited partner.

(c) If an assignee of a partnership interest becomes a limited partner, the assignor is not released from his [or her] liability to the limited partnership under Sections 207 and 502.

§ 705. Power of Estate of Deceased or Incompetent Partner.

If a partner who is an individual dies or a court of competent jurisdiction adjudges him [or her] to be incompetent to manage his [or her] person or his [or her] property, the partner's executor, administrator, guardian, conservator, or other legal representative may exercise all the partner's rights for the purpose of settling his [or her] estate or administering his [or her] property, including any power the partner had to give an assignee the right to become a limited partner. If a partner is a corporation, trust, or other entity and is dissolved or terminated, the powers of that partner may be exercised by its legal representative or successor.

ARTICLE 8. Dissolution

§ 801. Nonjudicial Dissolution.

A limited partnership is dissolved and its affairs shall be wound up upon the happening of the first to occur of the following:

(1) at the time specified in the certificate of limited partnership;

(2) upon the happening of events specified in writing in the partnership agreement;

(3) written consent of all partners;

(4) an event of withdrawal of a general partner unless at the time there is at least one other general partner and the written provisions of the partnership agreement permit the business of the limited partnership to be carried on by the remaining general partner and that partner does so, but the limited partnership is not dissolved and is not required to be wound up by reason of any event of withdrawal, if, within 90 days after the withdrawal, all partners agree in writing to continue the business of the limited partnership and to the appointment of one or more additional general partners if necessary or desired; or

(5) entry of a decree of judicial dissolution under Section 802.

§ 802. Judicial Dissolution.

On application by or for a partner the [designate the appropriate court] court may decree dissolution of a limited partnership whenever it is not reasonably practicable to carry on the business in conformity with the partnership agreement.

§ 803. Winding Up.

Except as provided in the partnership agreement, the general partners who have not wrongfully dissolved a limited partnership or, if none, the limited partners, may wind up the limited partnership's affairs; but the [designate the appropriate court] court may wind up the limited partnership's affairs upon application of any partner, his [or her] legal representative, or assignee.

§ 804. Distribution of Assets.

Upon the winding up of a limited partnership, the assets shall be distributed as follows:

(1) to creditors, including partners who are creditors, to the extent permitted by law, in satisfaction of liabilities of the limited partnership other than liabilities for distributions to partners under Section 601 or 604;

(2) except as provided in the partnership agreement, to partners and former partners in satisfaction of liabilities for distributions under Section 601 or 604; and

(3) except as provided in the partnership agreement, to partners first for the return of their contributions and secondly respecting their partnership interests, in the proportions in which the partners share in distributions.

ARTICLE 9. Foreign Limited Partnerships

§ 901. Law Governing.

Subject to the Constitution of this State, (i) the laws of the state under which a foreign limited partnership is organized govern its organization and internal affairs and the liability of its limited partners, and (ii) a foreign limited partnership may not be denied registration by reason of any difference between those laws and the laws of this State.

§ 902. Registration.

Before transacting business in this State, a foreign limited partnership shall register with the Secretary of State.

In order to register, a foreign limited partnership shall submit to the Secretary of State, in duplicate, an application for registration as a foreign limited partnership, signed and sworn to by a general partner and setting forth:

(1) the name of the foreign limited partnership and, if different, the name under which it proposes to register and transact business in this State;

(2) the State and date of its formation;

(3) the name and address of any agent for service of process on the foreign limited partnership whom the foreign limited partnership elects to appoint; the agent must be an individual resident of this State, a domestic corporation, or a foreign corporation having a place of business in, and authorized to do business in, this State;

(4) a statement that the Secretary of State is appointed the agent of the foreign limited partnership for service of process if no agent has been appointed under paragraph (3) or, if appointed, the agent's authority has been revoked or if the agent cannot be found or served with the exercise of reasonable diligence;

(5) the address of the office required to be maintained in the state of its organization by the laws of that state or, if not so required, of the principal office of the foreign limited partnership;

(6) the name and business address of each general partner; and

(7) the address of the office at which is kept a list of the names and addresses of the limited partners and their capital contributions, together with an undertaking by the foreign limited partnership to keep those records until the foreign limited partnership's registration in this State is cancelled or withdrawn.

§ 903. Issuance of Registration.

(a) If the Secretary finds that an application for registration conforms to law and all requisite fees have been paid, he [or she] shall:

(1) endorse on the application the word "Filed," and the month, day and year of the filing thereof;

(2) file in his [or her] office a duplicate original of the application; and

(3) issue a certificate of registration to transact business in this State.

(b) The certificate of registration, together with a duplicate original of the application, shall be returned to the person who filed the application or his [or her] representative.

§ 904. Name.

A foreign limited partnership may register with the Secretary of State under any name, whether or not it is the name under which it is registered in its state of organization, that includes without abbreviation the words "limited partnership" and that could be registered by a domestic limited partnership.

§ 905. Changes and Amendments.

If any statement in the application for registration of a foreign limited partnership was false when made or any arrangements or other facts described have changed, making the application inaccurate in any respect, the foreign limited partnership shall promptly file in the office if the Secretary of State a certificate, signed and sworn to by a general partner, correcting such statement.

§ 906. Cancellation of Registration.

A foreign limited partnership may cancel its registration by filing with the Secretary of State a certificate of cancellation signed and sworn to by a general partner. A cancellation does not terminate the authority of the Secretary of State to accept service of process on the foreign limited partnership with respect to [claims for relief] [causes of action] arising out of the transactions of business in this State.

§ 907. Transaction of Business Without Registration.

(a) A foreign limited partnership transacting business in this State may not maintain any action, suit, or proceeding in any court of this State until it has registered in this State.

(b) The failure of a foreign limited partnership to register in this State does not impair the validity of any contract or act of the foreign limited partnership or prevent the foreign limited partnership from defending any action, suit, or proceeding in any court of this State.

(c) A limited partner of a foreign limited partnership is not liable as a general partner of the foreign limited partnership solely by reason of having transacted business in this State without registration.

(d) A foreign limited partnership, by transacting business in this State without registration, appoints the Secretary of State as its agent for service of process with respect to [claims for relief] [causes of action] arising out of the transaction of business in this State.

§ 908. Action by [Appropriate Official].

The [designate the appropriate official] may bring an action to restrain a foreign limited partnership from transacting business in this State in violation of this Article.

ARTICLE 10.   Derivative Actions

§ 1001. Right of Action.

A limited partner may bring an action in the right of a limited partnership to recover a judgment in its favor if general partners with authority to do so have refused to bring the action or if an effort to cause those general partners to bring the action is not likely to succeed.

§ 1002. Proper Plaintiff.

In a derivative action, the plaintiff must be a partner at the time of bringing the action and (i) must have been a partner at the time of the transaction of which he [or she] complains or (ii) his [or her] status as a partner must have devolved upon him [or her] by operation of law or pursuant to the terms of the partnership agreement from a person who was a partner at the time of the transaction.

§ 1003. Pleading.

In a derivative action, the complaint shall set forth with particularity the effort of the plaintiff to secure initiation of the action by a general partner or the reasons for not making the effort.

§ 1004. Expenses.

If a derivative action is successful, in whole or in part, or if anything is received by the plaintiff as a result of a judgment, compromise or settlement of an action or claim, the court may award the plaintiff reasonable expenses, including reasonable attorney's fees, and shall direct him [or her] to remit to the limited partnership the remainder of those proceeds received by him [or her].

ARTICLE 11.   Miscellaneous

§ 1101. Construction and Application.

This [Act] shall also be applied and construed to effectuate its general purpose to make uniform the law with respect to the subject of this [Act] among states enacting it.

§ 1102. Short Title.

This [Act] may be cited as the Uniform Limited Partnership Act.

§ 1103. Severability.

If any provision of this [Act] or its application to any person or circumstance is held invalid, the invalidity does not affect other provisions or applications of the [Act] which can be given effect without the invalid provision or application, and to this end the provisions of this [Act] are severable.

§ 1104. Effective Date, Extended Effective Date and Repeal.

Except as set forth below, the effective date of this [Act] is _____ and the following acts [list existing limited partnership acts] are hereby repealed:

(1) The existing provisions for execution and filing of certificates of limited partnerships and amendments thereunder and cancellations thereof continue in effect until [specify time required to create central filing system], the extended effective date, and Sections 102, 103, 104, 105, 201, 202, 203, 204 and 206 are not effective until the extended effective date.

(2) Section 402, specifying the conditions under which a general partner ceases to be a member of a limited partnership, is not effective until the extended effective date, and the applicable provisions of existing law continue to govern until the extended effective date.

(3) Sections 501, 502 and 608 apply only to contributions and distributions made after the effective date of this [Act].

(4) Section 704 applies only to assignments made after the effective date of this [Act].

(5) Article 9, dealing with registration of foreign limited partnerships, is not effective until the extended effective date.

(6) Unless otherwise agreed by the partners, the applicable provisions of existing law governing allocation of profits and losses (rather than the provisions of Section 503), distributions to a withdrawing partner (rather than the provisions of Section 604), and distribution of assets upon the winding up of a limited partnership (rather than the provisions of Section 804) govern limited partnerships formed before the effective date of this [Act].

§ 1105. Rules for Cases Not Provided for in This [Act].

In any case not provided for in this [Act] the provisions of the Uniform Partnership Act govern.

§ 1106. Savings Clause.

The repeal of any statutory provision by this [Act] does not impair, or otherwise affect, the organization or the continued existence of a limited partnership existing at the effective date of this [Act], nor does the repeal of any existing statutory provision by this [Act] impair any contract or affect any right accrued before the effective date of this [Act].

Appendix F

Revised Model Business Corporation Act (1984) (as amended through 1988)

Table of Sections

CHAPTER 16.   Records and Reports

Subchapter A.   Records

16.01 Corporate Records.
16.02 Inspection of Records by Shareholders.
16.03 Scope of Inspection Right.
16.04 Court-Ordered Inspection.

Subchapter B.   Reports

16.20 Financial Statements for Shareholders.
16.21 Other Reports to Shareholders.
16.22 Annual Report for Secretary of State.

CHAPTER 17.   Transition Provisions

17.01 Application to Existing Domestic Corporations.
17.02 Application to Qualified Foreign Corporations.
17.03 Saving Provisions.
17.04 Severability.
17.05 Repeal.
17.06 Effective Date.

CHAPTER 1.   General Provisions

Subchapter A.   Short Title and Reservation of Power

§ 1.01   Short Title.

This Act shall be known and may be cited as the "[name of state] Business Corporation Act."

§ 1.02   Reservation of Power to Amend or Repeal.

The [name of state legislature] has power to amend or repeal all or part of this Act at any time and all domestic and foreign corporations subject to this Act are governed by the amendment or repeal.

Subchapter B.   Filing Documents

§ 1.20   Filing Requirements.

(a) A document must satisfy the requirements of this section, and of any other section that adds to or varies these requirements, to be entitled to filing by the secretary of state.

(b) This Act must require or permit filing the document in the office of the secretary of state.

(c) The document must contain the information required by this Act. It may contain other information as well.

(d) The document must be typewritten or printed.

(e) The document must be in the English language. A corporate name need not be in English if written in English letters or Arabic or Roman numerals, and the certificate of existence required of foreign corporations need not be in English if accompanied by a reasonably authenticated English translation.

(f) The document must be executed:

(1) by the chairman of the board of directors of a domestic or foreign corporation, by its president, or by another of its officers;

(2) if directors have not been selected or the corporation has not been formed, by an incorporator; or

(3) if the corporation is in the hands of a receiver, trustee, or other court-appointed fiduciary, by that fiduciary.

(g) The person executing the document shall sign it and state beneath or opposite his signature his name and the capacity in which he signs. The document may but need not contain: (1) the corporate seal, (2) an attestation by the secretary or an assistant secretary, and (3) an acknowledgment, verification, or proof.

(h) If the secretary of state has prescribed a mandatory form for the document under Section 1.21, the document must be in or on the prescribed form.

(i) The document must be delivered to the office of the secretary of state for filing and must be accompanied by one exact or conformed copy (except as provided in Sections 5.03 and 15.09), the correct filing fee, and any franchise tax, license fee, or penalty required by this Act or other law.

§ 1.21   Forms.

(a) The secretary of state may prescribe and furnish on request forms for: (1) an application for a certificate of existence, (2) a foreign corporation's application for a certificate of authority to transact business in this state, (3) a foreign corporation's application for a certificate of withdrawal, and (4) the annual report. If the secretary of state so requires, use of these forms is mandatory.

(b) The secretary of state may prescribe and furnish on request forms for other documents required or permitted to be filed by this Act but their use is not mandatory.

§ 1.22   Filing, Service and Copying Fees.

(a) The secretary of state shall collect the following fees when the documents described in this subsection are delivered to him for filing:

	Document	Fee
(1)	Articles of incorporation	$_____.
(2)	Application for use of indistinguishable name	$_____.
(3)	Application for reserved name	$_____.
(4)	Notice of transfer of reserved name	$_____.
(5)	Application for registered name	$_____.
(6)	Application for renewal of registered name	$_____.

(7) Corporation's statement of change of registered agent or registered office or both $_____.

(8) Agent's statement of change of registered office for each affected corporation $_____.
   not to exceed a total of $_____.

(9) Agent's statement of resignation No Fee.

(10) Amendment of articles of incorporation $_____.

(11) Restatement of articles of incorporation $_____.
   with amendment of articles $_____.

(12) Articles of merger or share exchange $_____.

(13) Articles of dissolution $_____.

(14) Articles of revocation of dissolution $_____.

(15) Certificate of administrative dissolution No fee.

(16) Application for reinstatement following administrative dissolution $_____.

(17) Certificate of reinstatement No fee.

(18) Certificate of judicial dissolution No fee.

(19) Application for certificate of authority $_____.

(20) Application for amended certificate of authority $_____.

(21) Application for certificate of withdrawal $_____.

(22) Certificate of revocation of authority to transact business No fee.

(23) Annual report $_____.

(24) Articles of correction $_____.

(25) Application for certificate of existence or authorization $_____.

(26) Any other document required or permitted to be filed by this Act. $_____

(b) The secretary of state shall collect a fee of $_____ each time process is served on him under this Act. The party to a proceeding causing service of process is entitled to recover this fee as costs if he prevails in the proceeding.

(c) The secretary of state shall collect the following fees for copying and certifying the copy of any filed document relating to a domestic or foreign corporation:

   (1) $ _____ a page for copying; and

   (2) $ _____ for the certificate.

§ 1.23 Effective Time and Date of Document.

(a) Except as provided in subsection (b) and Section 1.24(c), a document accepted for filing is effective:

   (1) at the time of filing on the date it is filed, as evidenced by the secretary of state's date and time endorsement on the original document; or

   (2) at the time specified in the document as its effective time on the date it is filed.

(b) A document may specify a delayed effective time and date, and if it does so the document becomes effective at the time and date specified. If a delayed effective date but no time is specified, the document is effective at the close of business on that date. A delayed effective date for a document may not be later than the 90th day after the date it is filed.

§ 1.24 Correcting Filed Document.

(a) A domestic or foreign corporation may correct a document filed by the secretary of state if the document (1) contains an incorrect statement or (2) was defectively executed, attested, sealed, verified, or acknowledged.

(b) A document is corrected:

   (1) by preparing articles of correction that (i) describe the document (including its filing date) or attach a copy of it to the articles, (ii) specify the incorrect statement and the reason it is incorrect or the manner in which the execution was defective, and (iii) correct the incorrect statement or defective execution; and

   (2) by delivering the articles to the secretary of state for filing.

(c) Articles of correction are effective on the effective date of the document they correct except as to persons relying on the uncorrected document and adversely affected by the correction. As to those persons, articles of correction are effective when filed.

§ 1.25 Filing Duty of Secretary of State.

(a) If a document delivered to the office of the secretary of state for filing satisfies the requirements of Section 1.20, the secretary of state shall file it.

(b) The secretary of state files a document by stamping or otherwise endorsing "Filed," together with his name and official title and the date and time of receipt, on both the original and the document copy and on the receipt for the filing fee. After filing a document, except as provided in Sections 5.03 and 15.10, the secretary of state shall deliver the document copy, with the filing fee receipt (or acknowledgment of receipt if no fee is required) attached, to the domestic or foreign corporation or its representative.

(c) If the secretary of state refuses to file a document, he shall return it to the domestic or foreign corporation or its representative within five days after the document was delivered, together with a brief, written explanation of the reason for his refusal.

(d) The secretary of state's duty to file documents under this section is ministerial. His filing or refusing to file a document does not:

(1) affect the validity or invalidity of the document in whole or part;

(2) relate to the correctness or incorrectness of information contained in the document;

(3) create a presumption that the document is valid or invalid or that information contained in the document is correct or incorrect.

§ 1.26 Appeal From Secretary of State's Refusal to File Document.

(a) If the secretary of state refuses to file a document delivered to his office for filing, the domestic or foreign corporation may appeal the refusal to the [name or describe] court [of the county where the corporations's principal office (or, if none in this state, its registered office) is or will be located] [of $_____ county]. The appeal is commenced by petitioning the court to compel filing the document and by attaching to the petition the document and the secretary of state's explanation of his refusal to file.

(b) The court may summarily order the secretary of state to file the document or take other action the court considers appropriate.

(c) The court's final decision may be appealed as in other civil proceedings.

§ 1.27 Evidentiary Effect of Copy of Filed Document.

A certificate attached to a copy of the document filed by the secretary of state, bearing his signature (which may be in facsimile) and the seal of this state, is conclusive evidence that the original document is on file with the secretary of state.

§ 1.28 Certificate of Existence.

(a) Anyone may apply to the secretary of state to furnish a certificate of existence for a domestic corporation or a certificate of authorization for a foreign corporation.

(b) A certificate of existence or authorization sets forth:

(1) the domestic corporation's corporate name or the foreign corporation's corporate name used in this state;

(2) that (i) the domestic corporation is duly incorporated under the law of this state, the date of its incorporation, and the period of its duration if less than perpetual; or (ii) that the foreign corporation is authorized to transact business in this state;

(3) that all fees, taxes, and penalties owed to this state have been paid, if (i) payment is reflected in the records of the secretary of state and (ii) nonpayment affects the existence or authorization of the domestic or foreign corporation;

(4) that its most recent annual report required by section 16.22 has been delivered to the secretary of state;

(5) that articles of dissolution have not been filed; and

(6) other facts of record in the office of the secretary of state that may be requested by the applicant.

(c) Subject to any qualification stated in the certificate, a certificate of existence or authorization issued by the secretary of state may be relied upon as conclusive evidence that the domestic or foreign corporation is in existence or is authorized to transact business in this state.

§ 1.29 Penalty for Signing False Document.

(a) A person commits an offense if he signs a document he knows is false in any material respect with intent that the document be delivered to the secretary of state for filing.

(b) An offense under this section is a [_____] misdemeanor [punishable by a fine of not to exceed $_____].

Subchapter C. Secretary of State

§ 1.30 Powers.

The secretary of state has the power reasonably necessary to perform the duties required of him by this Act.

Subchapter D. Definitions

§ 1.40 Act Definitions.

In this Act:

(1) "Articles of incorporation" include amended and restated articles of incorporation and articles of merger.

(2) "Authorized shares" means the shares of all classes a domestic or foreign corporation is authorized to issue.

(3) "Conspicuous" means so written that a reasonable person against whom the writing is to operate should have noticed it. For example, printing in italics or boldface or contrasting color, or typing in capitals or underlined, is conspicuous.

(4) "Corporation" or "domestic corporation" means a corporation for profit, which is not a foreign corporation, incorporated under or subject to the provisions of this Act.

(5) "Deliver" includes mail.

(6) "Distribution" means a direct or indirect transfer of money or other property (except its own shares) or incurrence of indebtedness by a corporation to or for the benefit of its shareholders in respect of any of its shares. A distribution may be in the form of a declaration or payment of a dividend; a purchase, redemption, or other

acquisition of shares; a distribution of indebtedness; or otherwise.

(7) "Effective date of notice" is defined in Section 1.41.

(8) "Employee" includes an officer but not a director. A director may accept duties that make him also an employee.

(9) "Entity" includes corporation and foreign corporation; not-for-profit corporation; profit and not-for profit unincorporated association; business trust, estate, partnership, trust, and two or more persons having a joint or common economic interest; and state, United States, and foreign government.

(10) "Foreign corporation" means a corporation for profit incorporated under a law other than the law of this state.

(11) "Governmental subdivision" includes authority, county, district, and municipality.

(12) "Includes" denotes a partial definition.

(13) "Individual" includes the estate of an incompetent or deceased individual.

(14) "Means" denotes an exhaustive definition.

(15) "Notice" is defined in section 1.41.

(16) "Person" includes individual and entity.

(17) "Principal office" means the office (in or out of this state) so designated in the annual report where the principal executive offices of a domestic or foreign corporation are located.

(18) "Proceeding" includes civil suit and criminal, administrative, and investigatory action.

(19) "Record date" means the date established under Chapter 6 or 7 on which a corporation determines the identity of its shareholders and their shareholdings for purposes of this Act. The determinations shall be made as of the close of business on the record date unless another time for doing so is specified when the record date is fixed.

(20) "Secretary" means the corporate officer to whom the board of directors has delegated responsibility under Section 8.40(c) for custody of the minutes of the meetings of the board of directors and of the shareholders and for authenticating records of the corporation.

(21) "Shares" mean the unit into which the proprietary interests in a corporation are divided.

(22) "Shareholder" means the person in whose name shares are registered in the records of a corporation or the beneficial owner of shares to the extent of the rights granted by a nominee certificate on file with a corporation.

(23) "State," when referring to a part of the United States, includes a state and commonwealth (and their agencies and governmental subdivisions) and a territory, and insular possession (and their agencies and governmental subdivisions) of the United States.

(24) "Subscriber" means a person who subscribes for shares in a corporation, whether before or after incorporation.

(25) "United States" includes district, authority, bureau, commission, department, and any other agency of the United States.

(26) "Voting group" means all shares of one or more classes or series that under the articles of incorporation or this Act are entitled to vote and be counted together collectively on a matter at a meeting of shareholders. All shares entitled by the articles of incorporation or this Act to vote generally on the matter are for that purpose a single voting group.

§ 1.41 Notice.

(a) Notice under this Act shall be in writing unless oral notice is reasonable under the circumstances.

(b) Notice may be communicated in person; by telephone, telegraph, teletype, or other form of wire or wireless communication; or by mail or private carrier. If these forms of personal notice are impracticable, notice may be communicated by a newspaper of general circulation in the area where published; or by radio, television, or other form of public broadcast communication.

(c) Written notice by a domestic or foreign corporation to its shareholder, if in a comprehensible form, is effective when mailed, if mailed postpaid and correctly addressed to the shareholder's address shown in the corporation's current record of shareholders.

(d) Written notice to a domestic or foreign corporation (authorized to transact business in this state) may be addressed to its registered agent at its registered office or to the corporation or its secretary at its principal office shown in its most recent annual report or, in the case of a foreign corporation that has not yet delivered an annual report, in its application for a certificate of authority.

(e) Except as provided in subsections (c) and (d), written notice, if in a comprehensible form, is effective at the earliest of the following:

(1) when received;

(2) five days after its deposit in the United States Mail, as evidenced by the postmark, if mailed postpaid and correctly addressed;

(3) on the date shown on the return receipt, if sent by registered or certified mail, return receipt requested, and the receipt is signed by or on behalf of the addressee.

(f) Oral notice is effective when communicated if communicated in a comprehensible manner.

(g) If this Act prescribes notice requirements for particular circumstances, those requirements govern. If articles of incorporation or bylaws prescribe notice requirements, not inconsistent with this section or other provisions of this Act, those requirements govern.

§ 1.42 Number of Shareholders.

(a) For purposes of this Act, the following identified as a shareholder in a corporation's current record of shareholders constitutes one shareholder:

(1) three or fewer co-owners;

(2) a corporation, partnership, trust, estate, or other entity;

(3) the trustees, guardians, custodians, or other fiduciaries of a single trust, estate, or account.

(b) For purposes of this Act, shareholdings registered in substantially similar names constitute one shareholder if it is reasonable to believe that the names represent the same person.

CHAPTER 2. Incorporation

§ 2.01 Incorporators.

One or more persons may act as the incorporator or incorporators of a corporation by delivering articles of incorporation to the secretary of state for filing.

§ 2.02 Articles of Incorporation.

(a) The articles of incorporation must set forth:

(1) a corporate name for the corporation that satisfies the requirements of section 4.01;

(2) the number of shares the corporation is authorized to issue;

(3) the street address of the corporation's initial registered office and the name of its initial registered agent at the office; and

(4) the name and address of each incorporator.

(b) The articles of incorporation may set forth:

(1) the names and addresses of the individuals who are to serve as the initial directors;

(2) provisions not inconsistent with law regarding:

(i) the purpose or purposes for which the corporation is organized;

(ii) managing the business and regulating the affairs of the corporation;

(iii) defining, limiting, and regulating the powers of the corporation, its board of directors, and shareholders;

(iv) a par value for authorized shares or classes of shares;

(v) the imposition of personal liability on shareholders for the debts of the corporation to a specified extent and upon specified conditions; and

(3) any provision that under this Act is required or permitted to be set forth in the bylaws.

(c) The articles of incorporation need not set forth any of the corporate powers enumerated in this Act.

§ 2.03 Incorporation.

(a) Unless a delayed effective date is specified, the corporate existence begins when the articles of incorporation are filed.

(b) The secretary of state's filing of the articles of incorporation is conclusive proof that the incorporators satisfied all conditions precedent to incorporation except in a proceeding by the state to cancel or revoke the incorporation or involuntarily dissolve the corporation.

§ 2.04 Liability for Preincorporation Transactions.

All persons purporting to act as or on behalf of a corporation, knowing there was no incorporation under this Act, are jointly and severally liable for all liabilities created while so acting.

§ 2.05 Organization of Corporation.

(a) After incorporation:

(1) if initial directors are named in the articles of incorporation, the initial directors shall hold an organizational meeting, at the call of a majority of the directors, to complete the organization of the corporation by appointing officers, adopting bylaws, and carrying on any other business brought before the meeting;

(2) if initial directors are not named in the articles, the incorporator or incorporators shall hold an organizational meeting at the call of a majority of the incorporators:

(i) to elect directors and complete the organization of the corporation; or

(ii) to elect a board of directors who shall complete the organization of the corporation.

(b) Action required or permitted by this Act to be taken by incorporators at an organizational meeting may be taken without a meeting if the action taken is evidenced by one or more written consents describing the action taken and signed by each incorporator.

(c) An organizational meeting may be held in or out of this state.

§ 2.06 Bylaws.

(a) The incorporators or board of directors of a corporation shall adopt initial bylaws for the corporation.

(b) The bylaws of a corporation may contain any provision for managing the business and regulating the affairs of the corporation that is not inconsistent with law or the articles of incorporation.

§ 2.07 Emergency Bylaws.

(a) Unless the articles of incorporation provide otherwise, the board of directors of a corporation may adopt bylaws to be effective only in an emergency defined in subsection (d). The emergency bylaws, which are subject to amendment or repeal by the shareholders, may make all provisions necessary for managing the corporation during the emergency, including:

(1) procedures for calling a meeting of the board of directors;

(2) quorum requirements for the meeting; and

(3) designation of additional or substitute directors.

(b) All provisions of the regular bylaws consistent with the emergency bylaws remain effective during the emergency. The emergency bylaws are not effective after the emergency ends.

(c) Corporate action taken in good faith in accordance with the emergency bylaws:

(1) binds the corporation; and

(2) may not be used to impose liability on a corporation director, officer, employee, or agent.

(d) An emergency exists for purposes of this section if a quorum of the corporation's directors cannot readily be assembled because of some catastrophic event.

CHAPTER 3. Purposes and Powers

§ 3.01 Purposes.

(a) Every corporation incorporated under this Act has the purpose of engaging in any lawful business unless a more limited purpose is set forth in the articles of incorporation.

(b) A corporation engaging in a business that is subject to regulation under statute of this state may incorporate under this Act only of permitted by, and subject to all limitations of, the other statute.

§ 3.02 General Powers.

Unless its articles of incorporation provide otherwise, every corporation has perpetual duration and succession in its corporate name and has the same powers as an individual to do all things necessary or convenient to carry out its business and affairs, including without limitation power:

(1) to sue and be sued, complain and defend in its corporate name;

(2) to have a corporate seal, which may be altered at will, and use it, or a fascimile of it, by impressing or affixing it or in any other manner reproducing it;

(3) to make and amend bylaws, not inconsistent with its articles of incorporation or with the laws of this state, for managing the business and regulating the affairs of the corporation;

(4) to purchase, receive, lease, or otherwise acquire, and own, hold, improve, use, and otherwise deal with, real or personal property, or any legal or equitable interest in property, wherever located;

(5) to sell, convey, mortgage, pledge, lease, exchange, and otherwise dispose of all or any part of its property;

(6) to purchase, receive, subscribe for, or otherwise acquire; own, hold, vote, use, sell, mortgage, lend, pledge, or otherwise dispose of; and deal in and with shares or other interests in, or obligations of, any other entity;

(7) to make contracts and guarantees, incur liabilities, borrow money, issue its notes, bonds, and other obligations, (which may be convertible into or include the option to purchase other securites of the corporation), and secure any of its obligations by mortgage or pledge of any of its property, franchise, or income;

(8) to lend money, invest and reinvest its funds, and receive and hold real and personal property as security for repayment;

(9) to be a promoter, partner, member, associate, or manager of any partnership, joint venture, trust, or other entity;

(10) to conduct its business, locate offices, and exercise the powers granted by this Act within or without this state;

(11) to elect directors and appoint officers, employees, and agents of the corporation, define their duties, fix their compensation, and lend them money and credit;

(12) to pay pensions and establish pension plans, pension trusts, profit sharing plans, share bonus plans, share option plans, and benefit or incentive plans for any or all of its current or former directors, officers, employees, and agents;

(13) to make donations for the public welfare or for charitable, scientific, or educational purposes;

(14) to transact any lawful business that will aid governmental policy;

(15) to make payments or donations, or do any other act, not inconsistent with law, that furthers the business and affairs of the corporation.

§ 3.03 Emergency Powers.

(a) In anticipation of or during an emergency defined in subsection (d), the board of directors of a corporation may:

(1) modify lines of succession to accommodate the incapacity of any director, officer, employee, or agent; and

(2) relocate the principal office, designate alternative principal offices or regional offices, or authorize the officers to do so.

(b) During an emergency defined in subsection (d), unless emergency bylaws provide otherwise:

(1) notice of a meeting of the board of directors need be given only to those directors whom it is practicable to reach and may be given in any practicable manner, including by publication and radio; and

(2) one or more officers of the corporation present at a meeting of the board of directors may be deemed to be directors for the meeting, in order of rank and within the same rank in order of seniority, as necessary to achieve a quorum.

(c) Corporate action taken in good faith during an emergency under this section to further the ordinary business affairs of the corporation:

(1) binds the corporation; and

(2) may not be used to impose liability on a corporate director, officer, employee, or agent.

(d) An emergency exists for purposes of this section if a quorum of the corporation's directors cannot readily be assembled because of some catastrophic event.

§ 3.04 Ultra Vires.

(a) Except as provided in subsection (b), the validity of corporate action may not be challenged on the ground that the corporation lacks or lacked power to act.

(b) A corporation's power to act may be challenged:

(1) in a proceeding by a shareholder against the corporation to enjoin the act;

(2) in a proceeding by the corporation, directly, derivatively, or through a receiver, trustee, or other legal representative, against an incumbent or former director, officer, employee, or agent of the corporation; or

(3) in a proceeding by the Attorney General under section 14.30.

(c) In a shareholder's proceeding under subsection (b)(1) to enjoin an unauthorized corporate act, the court may enjoin or set aside the act, if equitable and if all affected persons are parties to the proceeding, and may award damages for loss (other than anticipated profits) suffered by the corporation or another party because of enjoining the unauthorized act.

CHAPTER 4. Name

§ 4.01 Corporate Name.

(a) A corporate name:

(1) must contain the word "corporation," "incorporated," "company," or "limited," or the abbreviation "corp.," "inc.," "co.," or "ltd.", or words or abbreviations of like import in another language: and

(2) may not contain language stating or implying that the corporation is organized for a purpose other than that permitted by Section 3.01 and its articles of incorporation.

(b) Except as authorized by subsections (c) and (d), a corporate name must be distinguishable upon the records of the secretary of state from:

(1) the corporate name of a corporation incorporated or authorized to transact business in this state;

(2) a corporate name reserved or registered under Section 4.02 or 4.03;

(3) the fictitious name adopted by a foreign corporation authorized to transact business in this state because its real name is unavailable; and

(4) the corporate name of a not-for-profit corporation incorporated or authorized to transact business in this state.

(c) A corporation may apply to the secretary of state for authorization to use a name that is not distinguishable upon his records from one or more of the names described in subsection (b). The secretary of state shall authorize use of the name applied for if:

(1) the other corporation consents to the use in writing and submits an undertaking in form satisfactory to the secretary of state to change its name to a name that is distinguishable upon the records of the secretary of state from the name of the applying corporation; or

(2) the applicant delivers to the secretary of state a certified copy of the final judgment of a court of competent jurisdiction establishing the applicant's right to use the name applied for in this state.

(d) A corporation may use the name (including the fictitious name) of another domestic or foreign corporation that is used in this state if the other corporation is incorporated or authorized to transact business in this state and the proposed user corporation:

(1) has merged with the other corporation;

(2) has been formed by reorganization of the other corporation; or

(3) has acquired all or substantially all of the assets, including the corporate name, of the other corporation.

(e) This Act does not control the use of fictitious names.

§ 4.02 Reserved Name.

(a) A person may reserve the exclusive use of a corporate name, including a fictitious name for a foreign corporation whose corporate name is not available, by delivering an application to the secretary of state for filing. The application must set forth the name and address of the applicant and the name proposed to be reserved. If the secretary of state finds that the corporate name applied for is available, he shall reserve the name for the applicant's exclusive use for a nonrenewable 120-day period.

(b) The owner of a reserved corporate name may transfer the reservation to another person by delivering to the secretary of state a signed notice of the transfer that states the name and address of the transferee.

§ 4.03 Registered Name.

(a) A foreign corporation may register its corporate name, or its corporate name with any addition required by section 15.06, if the name is distinguishable upon the records of the secretary of state from the corporate names that are not available under Section 4.01(b)(3).

(b) A foreign corporation registers its corporate name, or its corporate name with any addition required by Section 15.06, by delivering to the secretary of state for filing an application:

    (1) setting forth its corporate name, or its corporate name with any addition required by Section 15.06, the state or country and date of its incorporation, and a brief description of the nature of the business in which it is engaged; and

    (2) accompanied by a certificate of existence (or a document of similar import) from the state or country of incorporation.

(c) The name is registered for the applicant's exclusive use upon the effective date of the application.

(d) A foreign corporation whose registration is effective may renew it for successive years by delivering to the secretary of state for filing a renewal application, which complies with the requirements of subsection (b), between October 1 and December 31 of the preceding year. The renewal application renews the registration for the following calendar year.

(e) A foreign corporation whose registration is effective may thereafter qualify as a foreign corporation under that name or consent in writing to the use of that name by a corporation thereafter incorporated under this Act or by another foreign corporation thereafter authorized to transact business in this state. The registration terminates when the domestic corporation is incorporated or the foreign corporation qualifies or consents to the qualification of another foreign corporation under the registered name.

CHAPTER 5. Office and Agent

§ 5.01 Registered Office and Registered Agent.

Each corporation must continuously maintain in this state:

    (1) a registered office that may be the same as any of its places of business; and

    (2) a registered agent, who may be:

        (i) an individual who resides in this state and whose business office is identical with the registered office;

        (ii) a domestic corporation or not-for-profit domestic corporation whose business office is identical with the registered office; or

        (iii) a foreign corporation or not-for-profit foreign corporation authorized to transact business in this state whose business office is identical with the registered office.

§ 5.02 Change of Registered Office or Registered Agent.

(a) A corporation may change its registered office or registered agent by delivering to the secretary of state for filing a statement of change that sets forth:

    (1) the name of the corporation;

    (2) the street address of its current registered office;

    (3) if the current registered office is to be changed, the street address of the new registered office;

    (4) the name of its current registered agent;

    (5) if the current registered agent is to be changed, the name of the new registered agent and the new agent's written consent (either on the statement or attached to it) to the appointment; and

    (6) that after the change or changes are made, the street addresses of its registered office and the business office of its registered agent will be identical.

(b) If a registered agent changes the street address of his business office, he may change the street address of the registered office of any corporation for which he is the registered agent by notifying the corporation in writing of the change and signing (either manually or in facsimile) and delivering to the secretary of state for filing a statement that complies with the requirements of subsection (a) and recites that the corporation has been notified of the change.

§ 5.03 Resignation of Registered Agent.

(a) A registered agent may resign his agency appointment by signing and delivering to the secretary of state for filing the signed original and two exact or conformed copies of a statement of resignation. The statement may include a statement that the registered office is also discontinued.

(b) After filing the statement the secretary of state shall mail one copy to the registered office (if not discontinued) and the other copy to the corporation at its principal office.

(c) The agency appointment is terminated, and the registered office discontinued if so provided, on the 31st day after the date on which the statement was filed.

§ 5.04 Service on Corporation.

(a) A corporation's registered agent is the corporation's agent for service of process, notice, or demand required or permitted by law to be served on the corporation.

(b) If a corporation has no registered agent, or the agent cannot with reasonable diligence be served, the corporation may be served by registered or certified mail, return receipt requested, addressed to the secretary of the corporation at its principal office. Service is perfected under this subsection at the earliest of:

    (1) the date the corporation receives the mail;

    (2) the date shown on the return receipt, if signed on behalf of the corporation; or

(3) five days after its deposit in the United States Mail, if mailed postpaid and correctly addressed.

(c) This section does not prescribe the only means, or necessarily the required means, of serving a corporation.

CHAPTER 6. Shares and Distributions

Subchapter A. Shares

§ 6.01 Authorized Shares.

(a) The articles of incorporation must prescribe the classes of shares and the number of shares of each class that the corporation is authorized to issue. If more than one class of shares is authorized, the articles of incorporation must prescribe a distinguishing designation for each class, and prior to the issuance of shares of a class the preferences, limitations, and relative rights of that class must be described in the articles of incorporation. All shares of a class must have preferences, limitations, and relative rights identical with those of other shares of the same class except to the extent otherwise permitted by Section 6.02.

(b) The articles of incorporation must authorize (1) one or more classes of shares that together have unlimited voting rights, and (2) one or more classes of shares (which may be the same class or classes as those with voting rights) that together are entitled to receive the net assets of the corporation upon dissolution.

(c) The articles of incorporation may authorize one or more classes of shares that:

(1) have special, conditional, or limited voting rights, or no right to vote, except to the extent prohibited by this Act;

(2) are redeemable or convertible as specified in the articles of incorporation (i) at the option of the corporation, the shareholder, or another person or upon the occurrence or a designated event; (ii) for cash, indebtedness, securities, or other property; (iii) in a designated amount or in an amount determined in accordance with a designated formula or by reference to extrinsic data or events;

(3) entitle the holders to distributions calculated in any manner, including dividends that may be cumulative, noncumulative, or partially cumulative;

(4) have preference over any other class of shares with respect to distributions, including dividends and distributions upon the dissolution of the corporation.

(d) The description of the designations, preferences, limitations, and relative rights of share classes in subsection (c) is not exhaustive.

§ 6.02 Terms of Class or Series Determined by Board of Directors.

(a) If the articles of incorporation so provide, the board of directors may determine, in whole or in part, the preferences, limitations, and relative rights (within the limits set forth in Section 6.01) of (1) any class of shares before the issuance of any shares of that class or (2) one or more series within a class before the issuance of any shares of that series.

(b) Each series of a class must be given a distinguishing designation.

(c) All shares of a series must have preferences, limitations, and relative rights identical with those of other shares of the same series and, except to the extent otherwise provided in the description of the series, of those of other series of the same class.

(d) Before issuing any shares of a class or series created under this section, the corporation must deliver to the secretary of state for filing articles of amendment, which are effective without shareholder action, that set forth:

(1) the name of the corporation;

(2) the text of the amendment determining the terms of the class or series of shares;

(3) the date it was adopted; and

(4) a statement that the amendment was duly adopted by the board of directors.

§ 6.03 Issued and Outstanding Shares.

(a) A corporation may issue the number of shares of each class or series authorized by the articles of incorporation. Shares that are issued are outstanding shares until they are reacquired, redeemed, converted, or cancelled.

(b) The reacquisition, redemption, or conversion of outstanding shares is subject to the limitations of subsection (c) of this section and to Section 6.40.

(c) At all times that shares of the corporation are outstanding, one or more shares that together have unlimited voting rights and one or more shares that together are entitled to receive the net assets of the corporation upon dissolution must be outstanding.

§ 6.04 Fractional Shares.

(a) A corporation may:

(1) issue fractions of a share or pay in money the value of fractions of a share;

(2) arrange for disposition of fractional shares by the shareholders;

(3) issue scrip in registered or bearer form entitling the holder to receive a full share upon surrendering enough scrip to equal a full share.

(b) Each certificate representing scrip must be conspicuously labeled "scrip" and must contain the information required by Section 6.25(b).

(c) The holder of a fractional share is entitled to exercise the rights of a shareholder, including the right to vote, to receive dividends, and to participate in the assets of the corporation upon liquidation. The holder of scrip is not entitled to any of these rights unless the scrip provides for them.

(d) The board of directors may authorize the issuance of scrip subject to any condition considered desirable, including:

(1) that the scrip will become void if not exchanged for full shares before a specified date; and

(2) that the shares for which the scrip is exchangeable may be sold and the proceeds paid to the scripholders.

Subchapter B. Issuance of Shares

§ 6.20 Subscription for Shares Before Incorporation.

(a) A subscription for shares entered into before incorporation is irrevocable for six months unless the subscription agreement provides a longer or shorter period or all the subscribers agree to revocation.

(b) The board of directors may determine the payment terms of subscriptions for shares that were entered into before incorporation, unless the subscription agreement specifies them. A call for payment by the board of directors must be uniform so far as practicable as to all shares of the same class or series, unless the subscription agreement specifies otherwise.

(c) Shares issued pursuant to subscriptions entered into before incorporation are fully paid and nonassessable when the corporation receives the consideration specified in the subscription agreement.

(d) If a subscriber defaults in payment of money or property under a subscription agreement entered into before incorporation, the corporation may collect the amount owed as any other debt. Alternatively, unless the subscription agreement provides otherwise, the corporation may rescind the agreement and may sell the shares if the debt remains unpaid more than 20 days after the corporation sends written demand for payment to the subscriber.

(e) A subscription agreement entered into after incorporation is a contract between the subscriber and the corporation subject to Section 6.21.

§ 6.21 Issuance of Shares.

(a) The powers granted in this section to the board of directors may be reserved to the shareholders by the articles of incorporation.

(b) The board of directors may authorize shares to be issued for consideration consisting of any tangible or intangible property or benefit to the corporation, including cash, promissory notes, services performed, contracts for services to be performed, or other securities of the corporation.

(c) Before the corporation issues shares, the board of directors must determine that the consideration received or to be received for shares to be issued is adequate. That determination by the board of directors is conclusive insofar as the adequacy of consideration for the issuance of shares relates to whether the shares are validly issued, fully paid, and nonassessable.

(d) When the corporation receives the consideration for which the board of directors authorized the issuance of shares, the shares issued therefor are fully paid and nonassessable.

(e) The corporation may place in escrow shares issued for a contract for future services or benefits or a promissory note, or make other arrangements to restrict the transfer of the shares, and may credit distributions in respect of the shares against their purchase price, until the services are performed, the note is paid, or the benefits received. If the services are not performed, the note is not paid, or the benefits are not received, the shares escrowed or restricted and the distributions credited may be cancelled in whole or part.

§ 6.22 Liability of Shareholders.

(a) A purchaser from a corporation of its own shares is not liable to the corporation or its creditors with respect to the shares except to pay the consideration for which the shares were authorized to be issued (Section 6.21) or specified in the subscription agreement (Section 6.20).

(b) Unless otherwise provided in the articles of incorporation, a shareholder of a corporation is not personally liable for the acts or debts of the corporation except that he may become personally liable by reason of his own acts or conduct.

§ 6.23 Share Dividends.

(a) Unless the articles of incorporation provide otherwise, shares may be issued pro rata and without consideration to the corporation's shareholders or to the shareholders of one or more classes or series. An issuance of shares under this subsection is a share dividend.

(b) Shares of one class or series may not be issued as a share dividend in respect of shares of another class or series unless (1) the articles of incorporation so authorize, (2) a majority of the votes entitled to be cast by the class or series to be issued approve the issue, or (3) there are no outstanding shares of the class or series to be issued.

(c) If the board of directors does not fix the record date for determining shareholders entitled to a share dividend, it is the date the board of directors authorizes the share dividend.

§ 6.24   Share Options.

A corporation may issue rights, options, or warrants for the purchase of shares of the corporation. The board of directors shall determine the terms upon which the rights, options, or warrants are issued, their form and content, and the consideration for which the shares are to be issued.

§ 6.25   Form and Content of Certificates.

(a) Shares may but need not be represented by certificates. Unless this Act or another statute expressly provides otherwise, the rights and obligations of shareholders are identical whether or not their shares are represented by certificates.

(b) At a minimum each share certificate must state on its face:

(1) the name of the issuing corporation and that it is organized under the law of this state;

(2) the name of the person to whom issued; and

(3) the number and class of shares and the designation of the series, if any, the certificate represents.

(c) If the issuing corporation is authorized to issue different classes of shares or different series within a class, the designations, relative rights, preferences, and limitations applicable to each class and the variations in rights, preferences, and limitations determined for each series (and the authority of the board of directors to determine variations for future series) must be summarized on the front or back of each certificate. Alternatively, each certificate may state conspicuously on its front or back that the corporation will furnish the shareholder this information on request in writing and without charge.

(d) Each share certificate (1) must be signed (either manually or in facsimile) by two officers designated in the bylaws or by the board of directors and (2) may bear the corporate seal or its facsimile.

(e) If the person who signed (either manually or in facsimile) a share certificate no longer holds office when the certificate is issued, the certificate is nevertheless valid.

§ 6.26   Shares Without Certificates.

(a) Unless the articles of incorporation or bylaws provide otherwise, the board of directors of a corporation may authorize the issue of some or all of the shares of any or all of its classes or series without certificates. The authorization does not affect shares already represented by certificates until they are surrendered to the corporation.

(b) Within a reasonable time after the issue or transfer of shares without certificates, the corporation shall send the shareholder a written statement of the information required on certificates by Section 6.25(b) and (c), and, if applicable, Section 6.27.

§ 6.27   Restriction on Transfer of Shares and Other Securities.

(a) The articles of incorporation, bylaws, an agreement among shareholders, or an agreement between shareholders and the corporation may impose restrictions on the transfer or registration of transfer of shares of the corporation. A restriction does not affect shares issued before the restriction was adopted unless the holders of the shares are parties to the restriction agreement or voted in favor of the restriction.

(b) A restriction on the transfer or registration of transfer of shares is valid and enforceable against the holder or a transferee of the holder if the restriction is authorized by this section and its existence is noted conspicuously on the front or back of the certificate or is contained in the information statement required by Section 6.26(b). Unless so noted, a restriction is not enforceable against a person without knowledge of the restriction.

(c) A restriction on the transfer or registration of transfer of shares is authorized:

(1) to maintain the corporation's status when it is dependent on the number or identity of its shareholders;

(2) to preserve exemptions under federal or state securities law;

(3) for any other reasonable purpose.

(d) A restriction on the transfer or registration of transfer of shares may:

(1) obligate the shareholder first to offer the corporation or other persons (separately, consecutively, or simultaneously) an opportunity to acquire the restricted shares;

(2) obligate the corporation or other persons (separately, consecutively, or simultaneously) to acquire the restricted shares;

(3) require the corporation, the holders of any class of its shares, or another person to approve the transfer of the restricted shares, if the requirement is not manifestly unreasonable;

(4) prohibit the transfer of the restricted shares to designated persons or classes of persons, if the prohibition is not manifestly unreasonable.

(e) For purposes of this section, "shares" includes a security convertible into or carrying a right to subscribe for or acquire shares.

§ 6.28   Expense of Issue.

A corporation may pay the expenses of selling or underwriting its shares, and of organizing or reorganizing the corporation, from the consideration received for shares.

Subchapter C. Subsequent Acquisition of Shares by Shareholders and Corporation

§ 6.30 Shareholders' Preemptive Rights.

(a) The shareholders of a corporation do not have a preemptive right to acquire the corporation's unissued shares except to the extent the articles of incorporation so provide.

(b) A statement included in the articles of incorporation that "the corporation elects to have preemptive rights" (or words of similar import) means that the following principles apply except to the extent the articles of incorporation expressly provide otherwise:

(1) The shareholders of the corporation have a preemptive right, granted on uniform terms and conditions prescribed by the board of directors to provide a fair and reasonable opportunity to exercise the right, to acquire proportional amounts of the corporation's unissued shares upon the decision of the board of directors to issue them.

(2) A shareholder may waive his preemptive right. A waiver evidenced by a writing is irrevocable even though it is not supported by consideration.

(3) There is no preemptive right with respect to:

(i) shares issued as compensation to directors, officers, agents, or employees of the corporation, its subsidiaries or affiliates;

(ii) shares issued to satisfy conversion or option rights created to provide compensation to directors, officers, agents, or employees of the corporation, its subsidiaries or affiliates;

(iii) shares authorized in articles of incorporation that are issued within six months from the effective date of incorporation;

(iv) shares sold otherwise than for money.

(4) Holders of shares of any class without general voting rights but with preferential rights to distributions or assets have no preemptive rights with respect to shares of any class.

(5) Holders of shares of any class with general voting rights but without preferential rights to distributions or assets have no preemptive rights with respect to shares of any class with preferential rights to distributions or assets unless the shares with preferential rights are convertible into or carry a right to subscribe for or acquire shares without preferential rights.

(6) Shares subject to preemptive rights that are not acquired by shareholders may be issued to any person for a period of one year after being offered to shareholders at a consideration set by the board of directors that is not lower than the consideration set for the exercise of preemptive rights. An offer at a lower consideration or after the expiration of one year is subject to the shareholders' preemptive rights.

(c) For purposes of this section, "shares" includes a security convertible into or carrying a right to subscribe for or acquire shares.

§ 6.31 Corporation's Acquisition of Its Own Shares.

(a) A corporation may acquire its own shares and shares so acquired constitute authorized but unissued shares.

(b) If the articles of incorporation prohibit the reissue of acquired shares, the number of authorized shares is reduced by the number of shares acquired, effective upon amendment of the articles of incorporation.

(c) Articles of amendment may be adopted by the board of directors without shareholder action, shall be delivered to the secretary of state for filing, and shall set forth:

(1) the name of the corporation;

(2) the reduction in the number of authorized shares, itemized by class and series; and

(3) the total number of authorized shares, itemized by class and series, remaining after reduction of the shares.

Subchapter D. Distributions

§ 6.40 Distributions to Shareholders.

(a) A board of directors may authorize and the corporation may make distributions to its shareholders subject to restriction by the articles of incorporation and the limitation in subsection (c).

(b) If the board of directors does not fix the record date for determining shareholders entitled to a distribution (other than one involving a purchase, redemption, or other acquisition of the corporation's shares), it is the date the board of directors authorizes the distribution.

(c) No distribution may be made if, after giving it effect:

(1) the corporation would not be able to pay its debts as they become due in the usual course of business; or

(2) the corporation's total assets would be less than the sum of its total liabilities plus (unless the articles of incorporation permit otherwise) the amount that would be needed, if the corporation were to be dissolved at the time of the distribution, to satisfy the preferential rights upon dissolution of shareholders whose preferential rights are superior to those receiving the distribution.

(d) The board of directors may base a determination that a distribution is not prohibited under subsection (c) either on financial statements prepared on the basis of accounting practices and principles that are reasonable in the circumstances or on a fair valuation or other method that is reasonable in the circumstances.

(e) Except as provided in subsection (g), the effect of a distribution under subsection (c) is measured:

(1) in the case of distribution by purchase, redemption, or other acquisition of the corporation's shares, as of the earlier of (i) the date money or other property is transferred or debt incurred by the corporation or (ii) the date the shareholder ceases to be a shareholder with respect to the acquired shares;

(2) in the case of any other distribution of indebtedness, as of the date the indebtedness is distributed; and

(3) in all other cases, as of (i) the date the distribution is authorized if the payment occurs within 120 days after the date of authorization or (ii) the date the payment is made if it occurs more than 120 days after the date of authorization.

(f) A corporation's indebtedness to a shareholder incurred by reason of a distribution made in accordance with this section is at parity with the corporation's indebtedness to its general, unsecured creditors except to the extent subordinated by agreement.

(g) Indebtedness of a corporation, including indebtedness issued as a distribution, is not considered a liability for purposes of determinations under subsection (c) if its terms provide that payment of principal and interest are made only if and to the extent that payment of a distribution to shareholders could then be made under this section. If the indebtedness is issued as a distribution, each payment of principal or interest is treated as a distribution, the effect of which is measured on the date the payment is actually made.

CHAPTER 7. Shareholders

Subchapter A. Meetings

§ 7.01 Annual Meeting.

(a) A corporation shall hold annually at a time stated in or fixed in accordance with the bylaws a meeting of shareholders.

(b) Annual shareholders' meetings may be held in or out of this state at the place stated in or fixed in accordance with the bylaws. If no place is stated in or fixed in accordance with the bylaws, annual meetings shall be held at the corporation's principal office.

(c) The failure to hold an annual meeting at the time stated in or fixed in accordance with a corporation's bylaws does not affect the validity of any corporate action.

§ 7.02 Special Meeting.

(a) A corporation shall hold a special meeting of shareholders:

(1) on call of its board of directors or the person or persons authorized to do so by the articles of incorporation or bylaws; or

(2) if the holders of at least 10 percent of all the votes entitled to be cast on any issue proposed to be considered at the proposed special meeting sign, date, and deliver to the corporation's secretary one or more written demands for the meeting describing the purpose or purposes for which it is to be held.

(b) If not otherwise fixed under sections 7.03 or 7.07, the record date for determining shareholders entitled to demand a special meeting is the date the first shareholder signs the demand.

(c) Special shareholders' meetings may be held in or out of this state at the place stated in or fixed in accordance with the bylaws. If no place is stated or fixed in accordance with the bylaws, special meetings shall be held at the corporation's principal office.

(d) Only business within the purpose or purposes described in the meeting notice required by Section 7.05(c) may be conducted at a special shareholders' meeting.

§ 7.03 Court-Ordered Meeting.

(a) The [name or describe] court of the county where a corporation's principal office (or, if none in this state, its registered office) is located may summarily order a meeting to be held:

(1) on application of any shareholder of the corporation entitled to participate in an annual meeting if an annual meeting was not held within the earlier of 6 months after the end of the corporation's fiscal year or 15 months after its last annual meeting; or

(2) on application of a shareholder who signed a demand for a special meeting valid under Section 7.02 if:

(i) notice of the special meeting was not given within 30 days after the date the demand was delivered to the corporation's secretary; or

(ii) the special meeting was not held in accordance with the notice.

(b) The court may fix the time and place of the meeting, determine the shares entitled to participate in the meeting, specify a record date for determining shareholders entitled to notice of and to vote at the meeting, prescribe the form and content of the meeting notice, fix the quorum required for specific matters to be considered at the meeting (or direct that the votes represented at the meeting constitute a quorum for action on those matters), and enter other orders necessary to accomplish the purpose or purposes of the meeting.

§ 7.04 Action Without Meeting.

(a) Action required or permitted by this Act to be taken at a shareholders' meeting may be taken without a meeting if the action is taken by all the shareholders entitled to vote on the action. The action must be evidenced by one or more written consents describing the action taken, signed by all the shareholders entitled to vote on the action, and delivered to the corporation for inclusion in the minutes or filing with the corporate records.

(b) If not otherwise determined under Sections 7.03 or 7.07, the record date for determining shareholders entitled to take action without a meeting is the date the first shareholder signs the consent under subsection (a).

(c) A consent signed under this section has the effect of a meeting vote and may be described as such in any document.

(d) If this Act requires that notice of proposed action be given to nonvoting shareholders and the action is to be taken by unanimous consent of the voting shareholders, the corporation must give its nonvoting shareholders written notice of the proposed action at least 10 days before the action is taken. The notice must contain or be accompanied by the same material that, under this Act, would have been required to be sent to nonvoting shareholders in a notice of meeting at which the proposed action would have been submitted to the shareholders for action.

§ 7.05 Notice of Meeting.

(a) A corporation shall notify shareholders of the date, time, and place of each annual and special shareholders' meeting no fewer than 10 nor more than 60 days before the meeting date. Unless this Act or the articles of incorporation require otherwise, the corporation is required to give notice only to the shareholders entitled to vote at the meeting.

(b) Unless this Act or the articles of incorporation require otherwise, notice of an annual meeting need not include a description of the purpose or purposes for which the meeting is called.

(c) Notice of a special meeting must include a description of the purpose or purposes for which the meeting is called.

(d) If not otherwise fixed under Section 7.03 or 7.07, the record date for determining shareholders entitled to notice of and to vote at an annual or special shareholders' meeting is the day before the first notice is delivered to shareholders.

(e) Unless the bylaws require otherwise, if an annual or special shareholders' meeting is adjourned to a different date, time, or place, notice need not be given of the new date, time, or place if the new date, time, or place is announced at the meeting before adjournment. If a new record date for the adjourned meeting is or must be fixed under Section 7.07, however, notice of the adjourned meeting must be given under this section to persons who are shareholders as of the new record date.

§ 7.06 Waiver of Notice.

(a) A shareholder may waive any notice required by this Act, the articles of incorporation, or bylaws before or after the date and time stated in the notice. The waiver must be in writing, be signed by the shareholder entitled to the notice, and be delivered to the corporation for inclusion in the minutes or filing with the corporate records.

(b) A shareholder's attendance at a meeting:

(1) waives objection to lack of notice or defective notice of the meeting, unless the shareholder at the beginning of the meeting objects to holding the meeting or transacting business at the meeting;

(2) waives objection to consideration of a particular matter at the meeting that is not within the purpose or purposes described in the meeting notice, unless the shareholder objects to to considering the matter when it is presented.

§ 7.07 Record Date.

(a) The bylaws may fix or provide the manner of fixing the record date for one or more voting groups in order to determine the shareholders entitled to notice of a shareholders' meeting, to demand a special meeting, to vote, or to take any other action. If the bylaws do not fix or provide for fixing a record date, the board of directors of the corporation may fix a future date as the record date.

(b) A record date fixed under this section may not be more than 70 days before the meeting or action requiring a determination of shareholders.

(c) A determination of shareholders entitled to notice of or to vote at a shareholders' meeting is effective for any adjournment of the meeting unless the board of directors fixes a new record date, which it must do if the meeting is adjourned to a date more than 120 days after the date fixed for the original meeting.

(d) If a court orders a meeting adjourned to a date more than 120 days after the date fixed for the original meeting, it may provide that the original record date continues in effect or it may fix a new record date.

Subchapter B. Voting

§ 7.20 Shareholders' List for Meeting.

(a) After fixing a record date for a meeting, a corporation shall prepare an alphabetical list of the names of all its shareholders who are entitled to notice of a shareholders' meeting. The list must be arranged by voting group (and within each voting group by class or series of shares) and show the address of and number of shares held by each shareholder.

(b) The shareholders' list must be available for inspection by any shareholder, beginning two business days after notice of the meeting is given for which the list was prepared and continuing through the meeting, at the corporation's principal office or at a place identified in the meeting notice in the city where the meeting will be held. A shareholder, his agent, or attorney is entitled on written demand to inspect and, subject to the requirements of Section 16.02(c), to copy the list, during regular business hours and at his expense, during the period it is available for inspection.

(c) The corporation shall make the shareholders' list available at the meeting, and any shareholder, his agent, or attorney is entitled to inspect the list at any time during the meeting or any adjournment.

(d) If the corporation refuses to allow a shareholder, his agent, or attorney to inspect the shareholders' list before or at the meeting (or copy the list as permitted by subsection (b)), the [name or describe] court of the county where a corporation's principal office (or, if none in this state, its registered office) is located, on application of the shareholder, may summarily order the inspection or copying at the corporation's expense and may postpone the meeting for which the list was prepared until the inspection or copying is complete.

(e) Refusal or failure to prepare or make available the shareholders' list does not affect the validity of action taken at the meeting.

§ 7.21 Voting Entitlement of Shares.

(a) Except as provided in subsections (b) and (c) or unless the articles of incorporation provide otherwise, each outstanding share, regardless of class, is entitled to one vote on each matter voted on at a shareholders' meeting. Only shares are entitled to vote.

(b) Absent special circumstances, the shares of a corporation are not entitled to vote if they are owned, directly or indirectly, by a second corporation, domestic or foreign, and the first corporation owns, directly or indirectly, a majority of the shares entitled to vote for directors of the second corporation.

(c) Subsection (b) does not limit the power of a corporation to vote any shares, including its own shares, held by it in a fiduciary capacity.

(d) Redeemable shares are not entitled to vote after notice of redemption is mailed to the holders and a sum sufficient to redeem the shares has been deposited with a bank, trust company, or other financial institution under an irrevocable obligation to pay the holders the redemption price on surrender of the shares.

§ 7.22 Proxies.

(a) A shareholder may vote his shares in person or by proxy.

(b) A shareholder may appoint a proxy to vote or otherwise act for him by signing an appointment form, either personally or by his attorney-in-fact.

(c) An appointment of a proxy is effective when received by the secretary or other officer or agent authorized to tabulate votes. An appointment is valid for 11 months unless a longer period is expressly provided in the appointment form.

(d) An appointment of a proxy is revocable by the shareholder unless the appointment form conspicuously states that it is irrevocable and the appointment is coupled with an interest. Appointments coupled with an interest include the appointment of:

   (1) a pledgee;

   (2) a person who purchased or agreed to purchase the shares;

   (3) a creditor of the corporation who extended it credit under terms requiring the appointment;

   (4) an employee of the corporation whose employment contract requires the appointment; or

   (5) a party to a voting agreement created under Section 7.31.

(e) The death or incapacity of the shareholder appointing a proxy does not affect the right of the corporation to accept the proxy's authority unless notice of the death or incapacity is received by the secretary or other officer or agent authorized to tabulate votes before the proxy exercises his authority under the appointment.

(f) An appointment made irrevocable under subsection (d) is revoked when the interest with which it is coupled is extinguished.

(g) A transferee for value of shares subject to an irrevocable appointment may revoke the appointment if he did not know of its existence when he acquired the shares and the existence of the irrevocable appointment was not noted conspicuously on the certificate representing the shares or on the information statement for shares without certificates.

(h) Subject to Section 7.24 and to any express limitation on the proxy's authority appearing on the face of the appointment form, a corporation is entitled to accept the proxy's vote or other action as that of the shareholder making the appointment.

§ 7.23 Shares Held by Nominees.

(a) A corporation may establish a procedure by which the beneficial owner of shares that are registered in the name of a nominee is recognized by the corporation as the shareholder. The extent of this recognition may be determined in the procedure.

(b) The procedure may set forth:

   (1) the types of nominees to which it applies;

   (2) the rights or privileges that the corporation recognizes in a beneficial owner;

   (3) the manner in which the procedure is selected by the nominee;

(4) the information that must be provided when the procedure is selected;

(5) the period for which selection of the procedure is effective; and

(6) other aspects of the rights and duties created.

§ 7.24 Corporation's Acceptance of Votes.

(a) If the name signed on a vote, consent, waiver, or proxy appointment corresponds to the name of a shareholder, the corporation if acting in good faith is entitled to accept the vote, consent, waiver, or proxy appointment and give it effect as the act of the shareholder.

(b) If the name signed on a vote, consent, waiver, or proxy appointment does not correspond to the name of its shareholder, the corporation if acting in good faith is nevertheless entitled to accept the vote, consent, waiver, or proxy appointment and give it effect as the act of the shareholder if:

(1) the shareholder is an entity and the name signed purports to be that of an officer or agent of the entity;

(2) the name signed purports to be that of an administrator, executor, guardian, or conservator representing the shareholder and, if the corporation requests, evidence of fiduciary status acceptable to the corporation has been presented with respect to the vote, consent, waiver, or proxy appointment;

(3) the name signed purports to be that of a receiver or trustee in bankruptcy of the shareholder and, if the corporation requests, evidence of this status acceptable to the corporation has been presented with respect to the vote, consent, waiver, or proxy appointment;

(4) the name signed purports to be that of a pledgee, beneficial owner, or attorney-in-fact of the shareholder and, if the corporation requests, evidence acceptable to the corporation of the signatory's authority to sign for the shareholder has been presented with respect to the vote, consent, waiver, or proxy appointment;

(5) two or more persons are the shareholder as cotenants or fiduciaries and the name signed purports to be the name of at least one of the coowners and the person signing appears to be acting on behalf of all the coowners.

(c) The corporation is entitled to reject a vote, consent, waiver, or proxy appointment if the secretary or other officer or agent authorized to tabulate votes, acting in good faith, has reasonable basis for doubt about the validity of the signature on it or about the signatory's authority to sign for the shareholder.

(d) The corporation and its officer or agent who accepts or rejects a vote, consent, waiver, or proxy appointment in good faith and in accordance with the standards of this section are not liable in damages to the shareholder for the consequences of the acceptance or rejection.

(e) Corporate action based on the acceptance or rejection of a vote, consent, waiver, or proxy appointment under this section is valid unless a court of competent jurisdiction determines otherwise.

§ 7.25 Quorum and Voting Requirements for Voting Groups.

(a) Shares entitled to vote as a separate voting group may take action on a matter at a meeting only if a quorum of those shares exists with respect to that matter. Unless the articles of incorporation or this Act provide otherwise, a majority of the votes entitled to be cast on the matter by the voting group constitutes a quorum of that voting group for action on that matter.

(b) Once a share is represented for any purpose at a meeting, it is deemed present for quorum purposes for the remainder of the meeting and for any adjournment of that meeting unless a new record date is or must be set for that adjourned meeting.

(c) If a quorum exists, action on a matter (other than the election of directors) by a voting group is approved if the votes cast within the voting group favoring the action exceed the votes cast opposing the action, unless the articles of incorporation or this Act require a greater number of affirmative votes.

(d) An amendment of articles of incorporation adding, changing, or deleting a quorum or voting requirement for a voting group greater than specified in subsection (b) or (c) is governed by Section 7.27.

(e) The election of directors is governed by Section 7.28.

§ 7.26 Action by Single and Multiple Voting Groups.

(a) If the articles of incorporation or this Act provide for voting by a single voting group on a matter, action on that matter is taken when voted upon by that voting group as provided in Section 7.25.

(b) If the articles of incorporation or this Act provide for voting by two or more voting groups on a matter, action on that matter is taken only when voted upon by each of those voting groups counted separately as provided in Section 7.25. Action may be taken by one voting group on a matter even though no action is taken by another voting group entitled to vote on the matter.

§ 7.27 Greater Quorum or Voting Requirements.

(a) The articles of incorporation may provide for a greater quorum or voting requirement for shareholders (or voting groups of shareholders) than is provided for by this Act.

(b) An amendment to the articles of incorporation that adds, changes, or deletes a greater quorum or voting requirement must meet the same quorum requirement and be adopted by the same vote and voting groups required to take action under the quorum and voting requirements then in effect or proposed to be adopted, whichever is greater.

§ 7.28 Voting for Directors; Cumulative Voting.

(a) Unless otherwise provided in the articles of incorporation, directors are elected by a plurality of the votes cast by the shares entitled to vote in the election at a meeting at which a quorum is present.

(b) Shareholders do not have a right to cumulate their votes for directors unless the articles of incorporation so provide.

(c) A statement included in the articles of incorporation that ''[all] [a designated voting group of] shareholders are entitled to cumulate their votes for directors'' (or words of similar import) means that the shareholders designated are entitled to multiply the number of votes they are entitled to cast by the number of directors for whom they are entitled to vote and cast the product for a single candidate or distribute the product among two or more candidates.

(d) Shares otherwise entitled to vote cumulatively may not be voted cumulatively at a particular meeting unless:

(1) the meeting notice or proxy statement accompanying the notice states conspicuously that cumulative voting is authorized; or

(2) a shareholder who has the right to cumulate his votes gives notice to the corporation not less than 48 hours before the time set for the meeting of his intent to cumulate his votes during the meeting, and if one shareholder gives this notice all other shareholders in the same voting group participating in the election are entitled to cumulate their votes without giving further notice.

Subchapter C. Voting Trusts and Agreements

§ 7.30 Voting Trusts.

(a) One or more shareholders may create a voting trust, conferring on a trustee the right to vote or otherwise act for them, by signing an agreement setting out the provisions of the trust (which may include anything consistent with its purpose) and transferring their shares to the trustee. When a voting trust agreement is signed, the trustee shall prepare a list of the names and addresses of all owners of beneficial interests in the trust, together with the number and class of shares each transferred to the trust, and deliver copies of the list and agreement to the corporation's principal office.

(b) A voting trust becomes effective on the date the first shares subject to the trust are registered in the trustee's name. A voting trust is valid for not more than 10

years after its effective date unless extended under subsection (c).

(c) All or some of the parties to a voting trust may extend it for additional terms of not more than 10 years each by signing an extension agreement and obtaining the voting trustee's written consent to the extension. An extension is valid for 10 years from the date the first shareholder signs the extension agreement. The voting trustee must deliver copies of the extension agreement and list of beneficial owners to the corporation's principal office. An extension agreement binds only those parties signing it.

§ 7.31 Voting Agreements.

(a) Two or more shareholders may provide for the manner in which they will vote their shares by signing an agreement for that purpose. A voting agreement created under this section is not subject to the provisions of section 7.30.

(b) A voting agreement created under this section is specifically enforceable.

Subchapter D. Derivative Proceedings

§ 7.40 Procedure in Derivative Proceedings.

(a) A person may not commence a proceeding in the right of a domestic or foreign corporation unless he was a shareholder of the corporation when the transaction complained of occurred or unless he became a shareholder through transfer by operation of law from one who was a shareholder at that time.

(b) A complaint in a proceeding brought in the right of a corporation must be verified and allege with particularity the demand made, if any, to obtain action by the board of directors and either that the demand was refused or ignored or why he did not make the demand. Whether or not a demand for action was made, if the corporation commences an investigation of the changes made in the demand or complaint, the court may stay any proceeding until the investigation is completed.

(c) A proceeding commenced under this section may not be discontinued or settled without the court's approval. If the court determines that a proposed discontinuance or settlement will substantially affect the interest of the corporation's shareholders or a class of shareholders, the court shall direct that notice be given the shareholders affected.

(d) On termination of the proceeding the court may require the plaintiff to pay any defendant's reasonable expenses (including counsel fees) incurred in defending the proceeding if it finds that the proceeding was commenced without reasonable cause.

(e) For purposes of this section, ''shareholder'' includes a beneficial owner whose shares are held in a voting trust or held by a nominee on his behalf.

CHAPTER 8. Directors and Officers

Subchapter A. Board of Directors

§ 8.01 Requirement for and Duties of Board of Directors.

(a) Except as provided in subsection (c), each corporation must have a board of directors.

(b) All corporate powers shall be exercised by or under the authority of, and the business and affairs of the corporation managed under the direction of, its board of directors, subject to any limitation set forth in the articles of incorporation.

(c) A corporation having 50 or fewer shareholders may dispense with or limit the authority of a board of directors by describing in its articles of incorporation who will perform some or all of the duties of a board of directors.

§ 8.02 Qualifications of Directors.

The articles of incorporation or bylaws may prescribe qualifications for directors. A director need not be a resident of this state or a shareholder of the corporation unless the articles of incorporation or bylaws so prescribe.

§ 8.03 Number and Election of Directors.

(a) A board of directors must consist of one or more individuals, with the number specified in or fixed in accordance with the articles of incorporation or bylaws.

(b) If a board of directors has power to fix or change the number of directors, the board may increase or decrease by 30 percent or less the number of directors last approved by the shareholders, but only the shareholders may increase or decrease by more than 30 percent the number of directors last approved by the shareholders.

(c) The articles of incorporation or bylaws may establish a variable range for the size of the board of directors by fixing a minimum and maximum number of directors. If a variable range is established, the number of directors may be fixed or changed from time to time, within the minimum and maximum, by the shareholders or the board of directors. After shares are issued, only the shareholders may change the range for the size of the board or change from a fixed to a variable-range size board or vice versa.

(d) Directors are elected at the first annual shareholders' meeting and at each annual meeting thereafter unless their terms are staggered under section 8.06.

§ 8.04 Election of Directors by Certain Classes of Shareholders.

If the articles of incorporation authorize dividing the shares into classes, the articles may also authorize the election of all or a specified number of directors by the holders of one or more authorized classes of shares. Each class (or classes) of shares entitled to elect one or more directors is a separate voting group for purposes of the election of directors.

§ 8.05 Terms of Directors Generally.

(a) The terms of the initial directors of a corporation expire at the first shareholders' meeting at which directors are elected.

(b) The terms of all other directors expire at the next annual shareholders' meeting following their election unless their terms are staggered under Section 8.06.

(c) A decrease in the number of directors does not shorten an incumbent director's term.

(d) The term of a director elected to fill a vacancy expires at the next shareholders' meeting at which directors are elected.

(e) Despite the expiration of a director's term, he continues to serve until his successor is elected and qualifies or until there is a decrease in the number of directors.

§ 8.06 Staggered Terms for Directors.

If there are nine or more directors, the articles of incorporation may provide for staggering their terms by dividing the total number of directors into two or three groups, with each group containing one-half or one-third of the total, as near as may be. In that event, the terms of directors in the first group expire at the first annual shareholders' meeting after their election, the terms of the second group expire at the second annual shareholders' meeting after their election, and the terms of the third group, if any, expire at the third annual shareholders' meeting after their election. At each annual shareholders' meeting held thereafter, directors shall be chosen for a term of two years or three years, as the case may be, to succeed those whose terms expire.

§ 8.07 Resignation of Directors.

(a) A director may resign at any time by delivering written notice to the board of directors, its chairman, or to the corporation.

(b) A resignation is effective when the notice is delivered unless the notice specifies a later effective date.

§ 8.08 Removal of Directors by Shareholders.

(a) The shareholders may remove one or more directors with or without cause unless the articles of incorporation provide that directors may be removed only for cause.

(b) If a director is elected by a voting group of shareholders, only the shareholders of that voting group may participate in the vote to remove him.

(c) If cumulative voting is authorized, a director may not be removed if the number of votes sufficient to elect him under cumulative voting is voted against his removal. If cumulative voting is not authorized, a director may be removed only if the number of votes cast to remove him exceeds the number of votes cast not to remove him.

(d) A director may be removed by the shareholders only at a meeting called for the purpose of removing him and the meeting notice must state that the purpose, or one of the purposes, of the meeting is removal of the director.

§ 8.09 Removal of Directors by Judicial Proceeding.

(a) The [name or describe] court of the county where a corporation's principal office (or, if none in this state, its registered office) is located may remove a director of the corporation from office in a proceeding commenced either by the corporation or by its shareholders holding at least 10 percent of the outstanding shares of any class if the court finds that (1) the director engaged in fraudulent or dishonest conduct, or gross abuse of authority or discretion, with respect to the corporation and (2) removal is in the best interest of the corporation.

(b) The court that removes a director may bar the director from reelection for a period prescribed by the court.

(c) If shareholders commence a proceeding under subsection (a), they shall make the corporation a party defendant.

§ 8.10 Vacancy on Board.

(a) Unless the articles of incorporation provide otherwise, if a vacancy occurs on a board of directors, including a vacancy resulting from an increase in the number of directors:

(1) the shareholders may fill the vacancy;

(2) the board of directors may fill the vacancy; or

(3) if the directors remaining in office constitute fewer than a quorum of the board, they may fill the vacancy by the affirmative vote of a majority of all the directors remaining in office.

(b) If the vacant office was held by a director elected by a voting group of shareholders, only the holders of shares of that voting group are entitled to vote to fill the vacancy if it is filled by the shareholders.

(c) A vacancy that will occur at a specific later date (by reason of a resignation effective at a later date under Section 8.07(b) or otherwise) may be filled before the vacancy occurs but the new director may not take office until the vacancy occurs.

§ 8.11 Compensation of Directors.

Unless the articles of incorporation or bylaws provide otherwise, the board of directors may fix the compensation of directors.

Subchapter B. Meetings and Action of the Board

§ 8.20 Meetings.

(a) The board of directors may hold irregular or special meetings in or out of this state.

(b) Unless the articles of incorporation or bylaws provide otherwise, the board of directors may permit any or all directors to participate in a regular or special meeting by, or conduct the meeting through the use of, any means of communication by which all directors participating may simultaneously hear each other during the meeting. A director participating in a meeting by this means is deemed to be present in person at the meeting.

§ 8.21 Action Without Meeting.

(a) Unless the articles of incorporation or bylaws provide otherwise, action required or permitted by this Act to be taken at a board of directors' meeting may be taken without a meeting if the action is taken by all members of the board. The action must be evidenced by one or more written consents describing the action taken, signed by each director, and included in the minutes or filed with the corporate records reflecting the action taken.

(b) Action taken under this section is effective when the last director signs the consent, unless the consent specifies a different effective date.

(c) A consent signed under this section has the effect of a meeting vote and may be described as such in any document.

§ 8.22 Notice of Meeting.

(a) Unless the articles of incorporation or bylaws provide otherwise, regular meetings of the board of directors may be held without notice of the date, time, place, or purpose of the meeting.

(b) Unless the article of incorporation or bylaws provide for a longer or shorter period, special meetings of the board of directors must be preceded by at least two days' notice of the date, time, and place of the meeting. The notice need not describe the purpose of the special meeting unless required by the articles of incorporation or bylaws.

§ 8.23 Waiver of Notice.

(a) A director may waive any notice required by this Act, the articles of incorporation, or bylaws before or after the date and time stated in the notice. Except as provided by subsection (b), the wavier must be in writing, signed by the director entitled to the notice, and filed with the minutes or corporate records.

(b) A director's attendance at or participation in a meeting waives any required notice to him of the meeting unless the director at the beginning of the meeting (or promptly upon his arrival) objects to holding the meeting or transacting business at the meeting and does not thereafter vote for or assent to action taken at the meeting.

§ 8.24 Quorum and Voting.

(a) Unless the articles of incorporation or bylaws require a greater number, a quorum of a board of directors consists of:

    (1) a majority of the fixed number of directors if the corporation has a fixed board size; or

    (2) a majority of the number of directors prescribed, or if no number is prescribed the number in office immediately before the meeting begins, if the corporation has a variable-range size board.

(b) The articles of incorporation or bylaws may authorize a quorum of a board of directors to consist of no fewer than one-third of the fixed or prescribed number of directors determined under subsection (a).

(c) If a quorum is present when a vote is taken, the affirmative vote of a majority of directors present is the act of the board of directors unless the articles of incorporation or bylaws require the vote of a greater number of directors.

(d) A director who is present at a meeting of the board of directors or a committee of the board of directors when corporate action is taken is deemed to have assented to the action taken unless: (1) he objects at the beginning of the meeting (or promptly upon his arrival) to holding it or transacting business at the meeting; (2) his dissent or abstention from the action taken is entered in the minutes of the meeting; or (3) he delivers written notice of his dissent or abstention to the presiding officer of the meeting before its adjournment or to the corporation immediately after adjournment of the meeting. The right of dissent or abstention is not available to a director who votes in favor of the action taken.

§ 8.25 Committees.

(a) Unless the articles of incorporation or bylaws provide otherwise, a board of directors may create one or more committees and appoint members of the board of directors to serve on them. Each committee must have two or more members, who serve at the pleasure of the board of directors.

(b) The creation of a committee and appointment of members to it must be approved by the greater of (1) a majority of all the directors in office when the action is taken or (2) the number of directors required by the articles of incorporation or bylaws to take action under Section 8.24.

(c) Sections 8.20 through 8.24, which govern meetings, action without meetings, notice and wavier of notice, and quorum and voting requirements of the board of directors, apply to committees and their members as well.

(d) To the extent specified by the board of directors or in the articles of incorporation or bylaws, each committee may exercise the authority of the board of directors under Section 8.01.

(e) A committee may not, however:

    (1) authorize distributions;

    (2) approve or propose to shareholders action that this Act requires to be approved by shareholders;

    (3) fill vacancies on the board of directors or on any of its committees;

    (4) amend articles of incorporation pursuant to Section 10.02;

    (5) adopt, amend, or repeal bylaws;

    (6) approve a plan of merger not requiring shareholder approval;

    (7) authorize or approve reacquisition of shares, except according to a formula or method prescribed by the board of directors; or

    (8) authorize or approve the issuance or sale or contract for sale of shares, or determine the designation and relative rights, preferences, and limitations of a class or series of shares, except that the board of directors may authorize a committee (or a senior executive officer of the corporation) to do so within limits specifically prescribed by the board of directors.

(f) The creation of, delegation of authority to, or action by a committee does not alone constitute compliance by a director with the standards of conduct described in Section 8.30.

Subchapter C. Standards of Conduct

§ 8.30 General Standards for Directors.

(a) A director shall discharge his duties as a director, including his duties as a member of a committee:

    (1) in good faith;

    (2) with the care an ordinarily prudent person in a like position would exercise under similar circumstances; and

    (3) in a manner he reasonably believes to be in the best interests of the corporation.

(b) In discharging his duties a director is entitled to rely on information, opinions, reports, or statements, including financial statements and other financial data, if prepared or presented by:

    (1) one or more officers or employees of the corporation whom the director reasonably believes to be reliable and competent in the matters presented;

    (2) legal counsel, public accountants, or other persons as to matters the director reasonably believes are within the person's professional or expert competence; or

(3) a committee of the board of directors of which he is not a member if the director reasonably believes the committee merits confidence.

(c) A director is not acting in good faith if he has knowledge concerning the matter in question that makes reliance otherwise permitted by subsection (b) unwarranted.

(d) A director is not liable for any action taken as a director, or any failure to take any action, if he performed the duties of his office in compliance with this section.

§ 8.31 Director Conflict of Interest. [Repealed]

§ 8.32 Loans to Directors.

(a) Except as provided by subsection (c), a corporation may not lend money to or guarantee the obligation of a director of the corporation unless:

(1) the particular loan or guarantee is approved by a majority of the votes represented by the outstanding voting shares of all classes, voting as a single voting group, except the votes of shares owned by or voted under the control of the benefited director; or

(2) the corporation's board of directors determines that the loan or guarantee benefits the corporation and either approves the specific loan or guarantee or a general plan authorizing loans and guarantees.

(b) The fact that a loan or guarantee is made in violation of this section does not affect the borrower's liability on the loan.

(c) This section does not apply to loans and guarantees authorized by statute regulating any special class of corporations.

§ 8.33 Liability for Unlawful Distributions.

(a) A director who votes for or assents to a distribution made in violation of Section 6.40 or the articles of incorporation is personally liable to the corporation for the amount of the distribution that exceeds what could have been distributed without violating Section 6.40 or the articles of incorporation if it is established that he did not perform his duties in compliance with Section 8.30. In any proceeding commenced under this section, a director has all of the defenses ordinarily available to a director.

(b) A director held liable under subsection (a) for an unlawful distribution is entitled to contribution:

(1) from every other director who could be held liable under subsection (a) for the unlawful distribution; and

(2) from each shareholder for the amount the shareholder accepted knowing the distribution was made in violation of Section 6.40 or the articles of incorporation.

(c) A proceeding under this section is barred unless it is commenced within two years after the date on which the effect of the distribution was measured under Section 6.40(e) or (g).

Subchapter D. Officers

§ 8.40 Required Officers.

(a) A corporation has the officers described in its bylaws or appointed by the board of directors in accordance with the bylaws.

(b) A duly appointed officer may appoint one or more officers or assistant officers if authorized by the bylaws or the board of directors.

(c) The bylaws or the board of directors shall delegate to one of the officers responsibility for preparing minutes of the directors' and shareholders' meetings and for authenticating records of the corporation.

(d) The same individual may simultaneously hold more than one office in a corporation.

§ 8.41 Duties of Officers.

Each officer has the authority and shall perform the duties set forth in the bylaws or, to the extent consistent with the bylaws, the duties prescribed by the board of directors or by direction of an officer authorized by the board of directors to prescribe the duties of other officers.

§ 8.42 Standards of Conduct for Officers.

(a) An officer with discretionary authority shall discharge his duties under that authority:

(1) in good faith;

(2) with the care an ordinarily prudent person in a like position would exercise under similar circumstances; and

(3) in a manner he reasonably believes to be in the best interests of the corporation.

(b) In discharging his duties an officer is entitled to rely on information, opinions, reports, or statements, including financial statements and other financial data, if prepared or presented by:

(1) one or more officers or employees of the corporation whom the officer reasonably believes to be reliable and competent in the matters presented; or

(2) legal counsel, public accountants, or other persons as to matters the officer reasonably believes are within the person's professional or expert competence.

(c) An officer is not acting in good faith if he has knowledge concerning the matter in question that makes reliance otherwise permitted by subsection (b) unwarranted.

(d) An officer is not liable for any action taken as an officer, or any failure to take any action, if he performed the duties of his office in compliance with this section.

§ 8.43 Resignation and Removal of Officers.

(a) An officer may resign at any time by delivering notice to the corporation. A resignation is effective when the notice is delivered unless the notice specifies a later effective date. If a resignation is made effective at a later date and the corporation accepts the future effective date, its board of directors may fill the pending vacancy before the effective date if the board of directors provides that the successor does not take office until the effective date.

(b) A board of directors may remove any officer at any time with or without cause.

§ 8.44 Contract Rights of Officers.

(a) The appointment of an officer does not itself create contract rights.

(b) An officer's removal does not affect the officer's contract rights, if any, with the corporation. An officer's resignation does not affect the corporation's contract rights, if any, with the officer.

Subchapter E. Indemnification

§ 8.50 Subchapter Definitions.

In this subchapter:

(1) "Corporation" includes any domestic or foreign predecessor entity of a corporation in a merger or other transaction in which the predecessor's existence ceased upon consummation of the transaction.

(2) "Director" means an individual who is or was a director of a corporation or an individual who, while a director or a corporation, is or was serving at the corporation's request as a director, officer, partner, trustee, employee, or agent of another foreign or domestic corporation, partnership, joint venture, trust, employee benefit plan, or other enterprise. A director is considered to be serving an employee benefit plan at the corporation's request if his duties to the corporation also impose duties on, or otherwise involve services by, him to the plan or to participants in or beneficiaries of the plan. "Director" includes, unless the context requires otherwise, the estate or personal representative of a director.

(3) "Expenses" include counsel fees.

(4) "Liability" means the obligation to pay a judgment, settlement, penalty, fine (including an excise tax assessed with respect to an employee benefit plan), or reasonable expenses incurred with respect to a proceeding.

(5) "Official capacity" means: (i) when used with respect to a director, the office of director in a corporation; and (ii) when used with respect to an individual other than a director, as contemplated in Section 8.56, the office in a corporation held by the officer or the employment or agency relationship undertaken by the employee or agent on behalf of the corporation. "Official capacity" does not include service for any other foreign or domestic corporation or any partnership, joint venture, trust, employee benefit plan, or other enterprise.

(6) "Party" includes an individual who was, is, or is threatened to be made a named defendant or respondent in a proceeding.

(7) "Proceeding" means any threatened, pending, or completed action, suit, or proceeding, whether civil, criminal, administrative, or investigative and whether formal or informal.

§ 8.51 Authority to Indemnify.

(a) Except as provided in subsection (d), a corporation may idemnify an individual made a party to a proceeding because he is or was a director against liability incurred in the proceeding if:

(1) he conducted himself in good faith; and

(2) he reasonably believed:

    (i) in the case of conduct in his official capacity with the corporation, that his conduct was in its best interests; and

    (ii) in all other cases, that his conduct was at least not opposed to its best interests; and

(3) in the case of any criminal proceeding, he had no reasonable cause to believe his conduct was unlawful.

(b) A director's conduct with respect to an employee benefit plan for a purpose he reasonably believed to be in the interests of the participants in and beneficiaries of the plan is conduct that satisfies the requirement of subsection (a)(2)(ii).

(c) The termination of a proceeding by judgment, order, settlement, conviction, or upon a plea of nolo contendere or its equivalent is not, of itself, determinative that the director did not meet the standard of conduct described in this section.

(d) A corporation may not idemnify a director under this section:

(1) in connection with a proceeding by or in the right of the corporation in which the director was adjudged liable to the corporation; or

(2) in connection with any other proceeding charging improper personal benefit to him, whether or not involving action in his official capacity, in which he was adjudged liable on the basis that personal benefit was improperly received by him.

(e) Idemnification permitted under this section in connection with a proceeding by or in the right of the corporation is limited to reasonable expenses incurred in connection with the proceeding.

§ 8.52   Mandatory Indemnification.

Unless limited by its articles of incorporation, a corporation shall idemnify a director who was wholly successful, on the merits or otherwise, in the defense of any proceeding to which he was a party because he is or was a director of the corporation against reasonable expenses incurred by him in connection with the proceeding.

§ 8.53   Advance for Expenses.

(a) A corporation may pay for or reimburse the reasonable expenses incurred by a director who is a party to a proceeding in advance of final disposition of the proceeding if:

(1) the director furnishes the corporation a written affirmation of his good faith belief that he has met the standard of conduct described in Section 8.51;

(2) the director furnishes the corporation a written undertaking, executed personally or on his behalf, to repay the advance if it is ultimately determined that he did not meet the standard of conduct; and

(3) a determination is made that the facts then known to those making the determination would not preclude indemnification under this subchapter.

(b) The undertaking required by subsection (a)(2) must be an unlimited general obligation of the director but need not be secured and may be accepted without reference to financial ability to make repayment.

(c) Determinations and authorizations of payments under this section shall be made in the manner specified in Section 8.55.

§ 8.54   Court-Ordered Indemnification.

Unless a corporation's articles of incorporation provide otherwise, a director of the corporation who is a party to a proceeding may apply for indemnification to the court conducting the proceeding or to another court of competent jurisdiction. On receipt of an application, the court after giving any notice the court considers necessary may order indemnification if it determines:

(1) the director is entitled to mandatory indemnification under Section 8.52, in which case the court shall also order the corporation to pay the director's reasonable expenses incurred to obtain court-ordered indemnification; or

(2) the director is fairly and reasonably entitled to indemnification in view of all the relevant circumstances whether or not he met the standard of conduct set forth in Section 8.51 or was adjudged liable as described in Section 8.51(d), but if he was adjudged so liable his indemnification is limited to reasonable expenses incurred.

§ 8.55   Determination and Authorization of Indemnification.

(a) A corporation may not indemnify a director under section 8.51 unless authorized in the specific case after a determination has been made that idemnification of the director is permissible in the circumstances because he has met the standard of conduct set forth in section 8.51.

(b) The determination shall be made:

(1) by the board of directors by majority vote of a quorum consisting of directors not at the time parties to the proceeding;

(2) if a quorum cannot be obtained under subdivision (1), by majority vote of a committee duly designated by the board of directors (in which designation directors who are parties may participate), consisting solely of two or more directors not at the time parties to the proceeding;

(3) by special legal counsel:

(i) selected by the board of directors or its committee in the manner prescribed in subdivision (1) or (2); or

(ii) if a quorum of the board of directors cannot be obtained under subdivision (1) and a committee cannot be designated under subdivision (2), selected by majority vote of the full board of directors (in which selection directors who are parties may participate); or

(4) by the shareholders, but shares owned by or voted under the control of directors who are at the time parties to the proceeding may not be voted on the determination.

(c) Authorization of indemnification and evaluation as to reasonableness of expenses shall be made in the same manner as the determination that indemnification is permissible, except that if the determination is made by special legal counsel, authorization of indemnification and evaluation as to reasonableness of expenses shall be made by those entitled under subsection (b)(3) to select counsel.

§ 8.56   Indemnification of Officers, Employees, and Agents.

Unless a corporation's articles of incorporation provide otherwise:

(1) an officer of the corporation who is not a director is entitled to mandatory indemnification under Section 8.52, and is entitled to apply for court-ordered indemnification under Section 8.54, in each case to the same extent as a director;

(2) the corporation may indemnify and advance expenses under this subchapter to an officer, employee, or agent of the corporation who is not a director to the same extent as to a director; and

(3) a corporation may also indemnify and advance expenses to an officer, employee, or agent who is not a director to the extent, consistent with public policy, that may be provided by its articles of incorporation, bylaws, general or specific action of its board of directors, or contract.

§ 8.57 Insurance.

A corporation may purchase and maintain insurance on behalf of an individual who is or was a director, officer, employee, or agent of the corporation, or who, while a director, officer, employee, or agent of the corporation, is or was serving at the request of the corporation as a director, officer, partner, trustee, employee, or agent of another foreign or domestic corporation, partnership, joint venture, trust, employee benefit plan, or other enterprise, against liability asserted against or incurred by him in that capacity or arising from his status as a director, officer, employee, or agent, whether or not the corporation would have power to indemnify him against the same liability under Section 8.51 or 8.52.

§ 8.58 Application of Subchapter.

(a) A provision treating a corporation's indemnification of or advance for expenses to directors that is contained in its articles of incorporation, bylaws, a resolution of its shareholders or board of directors, or in a contract or otherwise, is valid only if and to the extent the provision is consistent with this subchapter. If articles of incorporation limit indemnification or advance for expenses, indemnification and advance for expenses are valid only to the extent consistent with the articles.

(b) This subchapter does not limit a corporation's power to pay or reimburse expenses incurred by a director in connection with his appearance as a witness in a proceeding at a time when he has not been made a named defendant or respondent to the proceeding.

Subchapter F. Directors' Conflicting Interest Transactions

§ 8.60. Subchapter Definitions.

In this subchapter:

(1) "Conflicting interest" with respect to a corporation means the interest a director of the corporation has respecting a transaction effected or proposed to be effected by the corporation (or by a subsidiary of the corporation or any other entity in which the corporation has a controlling interest) if:

    (i) whether or not the transaction is brought before the board of directors of the corporation for action, the director knows at the time of commitment that he or a related person is a party to the transaction or has a beneficial financial interest in or so closely linked to the transaction and of such financial significance to the director or a related person that the interest would reasonably be expected to exert an influence on the director's judgment if he were called upon to vote on the transaction; or

    (ii) the transaction is brought (or is of such character and significance to the corporation that it would in the normal course be brought) before the board of directors of the corporation for action, and the director knows at the time of commitment that any of the following persons is either a party to the transaction or has a beneficial financial interest in or so closely linked to the transaction and of such financial significance to the person that the interest would reasonably be expected to exert an influence on the director's judgment if he were called upon to vote on the transaction: (A) an entity (other than the corporation) of which the director is a director, general partner, agent, or employee; (B) an entity that controls, is controlled by, or is under common control with one or more of the entities specified in subclause (A); or (C) an individual who is a general partner, principal, or employer of the director.

(2) "Director's conflicting interest transaction" with respect to a corporation means a transaction effected or proposed to be effected by the corporation (or by a subsidiary of the corporation or any other entity in which the corporation has a controlling interest) respecting which a director of the corporation has a conflicting interest.

(3) "Related person" of a director means (i) a child, grandchild, sibling, parent, or spouse of, or an individual occupying the same household as, the director, or a trust or estate of which an individual specified in this clause (i) is a substantial beneficiary; or (ii) a trust, estate, incompetent, conservatee, or minor of which the director is a fiduciary.

(4) "Required disclosure" means disclosure by the director who has a conflicting interest of (i) the existence and nature of his conflicting interest, and (ii) all facts known to him respecting the subject matter of the transaction that an ordinarily prudent person would reasonably believe to be material to a judgment about whether or not to proceed with the transaction.

(5) "Time of commitment" respecting a transaction means the time when the transaction is consummated or, if made pursuant to contract, the time when the corporation (or its subsidiary or the entity in which it has a controlling interest) becomes contractually obligated so that its unilateral withdrawal from the transaction would entail significant loss, liability, or other damage.

§ 8.61. Judicial Action.

(a) A transaction effected or proposed to be effected by a corporation (or by a subsidiary of the corporation or any other entity in which the corporation has a controlling interest) that is not a director's conflicting interest transaction may not be enjoined, set aside, or give rise to an award of damages or other sanctions, in a proceeding by a shareholder or by or in the right of the corporation, because a director of the corporation, or any person with whom or which he has a personal, economic, or other association, has an interest in the transaction.

(b) A director's conflicting interest transaction may not be enjoined, set aside, or give rise to an award of damages or other sanctions, in a proceeding by a shareholder or by or in the right of the corporation, because the director, or any person with whom or which he has a personal, economic, or other association, has an interest in the transaction, if:

(1) directors' action respecting the transaction was at any time taken in compliance with Section 8.62;

(2) shareholders' action respecting the transaction was at any time taken in compliance with Section 8.63;

(3) the transaction, judged according to the circumstances at the time of commitment, is established to have been fair to the corporation; or

(4) the transaction pertained to the compensation, or the reimbursement of expenses, of one or more directors unless the transaction, judged according to the circumstances at the time of commitment, is established to have been unfair to the corporation.

§ 8.62. Directors' Action.

(a) Directors' action respecting a transaction is effective for purposes of Section 8.61(b)(1) if the transaction received the affirmative vote of a majority (but no fewer than two) of those qualified directors on the board of directors or on a duly empowered committee of the board who voted on the transaction after either required disclosure to them (to the extent the information was not known by them) or compliance with subsection (b).

(b) If a director has a conflicting interest respecting a transaction, but neither he nor a related person of the director specified in section 8.60(3)(i) is a party to the transaction, and if the director has a duty under law or professional canon, or a duty of confidentiality to another person, respecting information relating to the transaction such that the director may not make the disclosure described in Section 8.60(4)(ii), then disclosure is sufficient for purposes of subsection (a) if the director (1) discloses to the directors voting on the transaction the existence and nature of his conflicting interest and informs them of the character and limitations imposed by that duty before

their vote on the transaction, and (2) plays no part, directly or indirectly, in their deliberations or vote.

(c) A majority (but no fewer than two) of all the qualified directors on the board of directors, or on the committee, constitutes a quorum for purposes of action that complies with this section. Directors' action that otherwise complies with this section is not affected by the presence or vote of a director who is not a qualified director.

(d) For purposes of this section, "qualified director" means, with respect to a director's conflicting interest transaction, any director who does not have either (1) a conflicting interest respecting the transaction, or (2) a familial, financial, professional, or employment relationship with a second director who does have a conflicting interest respecting the transaction, which relationship would, in the circumstances, reasonably be expected to exert an influence on the first director's judgment when voting on the transaction.

§ 8.63. Shareholders' Action.

(a) Shareholders' action respecting a transaction is effective for purposes of Section 8.61(b)(2) if a majority of the votes entitled to be cast by the holders of all qualified shares were cast in favor of the transaction after (1) notice to shareholders describing the director's conflicting interest transaction, (2) provision of the information referred to in subsection (d), and (3) required disclosure to the shareholders who voted on the transaction (to the extent the information was not known by them).

(b) For purposes of this section, "qualified shares" means any shares entitled to vote with respect to the director's conflicting interest transaction except shares that, to the knowledge, before the vote, of the secretary (or other officer or agent of the corporation authorized to tabulate votes), are beneficially owned (or the voting of which is controlled) by a director who has a conflicting interest respecting the transaction or by a related person of the director, or both.

(c) A majority of the votes entitled to be cast by the holders of all qualified shares constitutes a quorum for purposes of action that complies with this section. Subject to the provisions of subsections (d) and (e), shareholders' action that otherwise complies with this section is not affected by the presence of holders, or the voting, of shares that are not qualified shares.

(d) For purposes of compliance with subsection (a), a director who has a conflicting interest respecting the transaction shall, before the shareholders' vote, inform the secretary (or other officer or agent of the corporation authorized to tabulate votes) of the number, and the identity of persons holding or controlling the vote, of all shares that the director knows are beneficially owned (or the voting of which is controlled) by the director or by a related person of the director, or both.

(e) If a shareholders' vote does not comply with subsection (a) solely because of a failure of a director to comply with subsection (d), and if the director establishes that his failure did not determine and was not intended by him to influence the outcome of the vote, the court may, with or without further proceedings respecting Section 8.61(b)(3), take such action respecting the transaction and the director, and give such effect, if any, to the shareholders' vote, as it considers appropriate in the circumstances.

CHAPTER 9. [Reserved]

CHAPTER 10. Amendment of Articles of Incorporation and Bylaws

Subchapter A. Amendment of Articles of Incorporation

§ 10.01 Authority to Amend.

(a) A corporation may amend its articles of incorporation at any time to add or change a provision that is required or permitted in the articles of incorporation or to delete a provision not required in the articles of incorporation. Whether a provision is required or permitted in the articles of incorporation is determined as of the effective date of the amendment.

(b) A shareholder of the corporation does not have a vested property right resulting from any provision in the articles of incorporation, including provisions relating to management, control, capital structure, dividend entitlement, or purpose or duration of the corporation.

§ 10.02 Amendment by Board of Directors.

Unless the articles of incorporation provide otherwise, a corporation's board of directors may adopt one or more amendments to the corporation's articles of incorporation without shareholder action:

(1) to extend the duration of the corporation if it was incorporated at a time when limited duration was required by law;

(2) to delete the names and addresses of the initial directors:

(3) to delete the name and address of the initial registered agent or registered office, if a statement of change is on file with the secretary of state;

(4) to change each issued and unissued authorized share of an outstanding class into a greater number of whole shares if the corporation has only shares of that class outstanding;

(5) to change the corporate name by substituting the word "corporation," "incorporated," "company," "limited," or the abbreviation "corp.," "inc.," "co.," or "ltd.," for a similar word or abbreviation in the name, or by adding, deleting, or changing a geographical attribution for the name; or

(6) to make any other change expressly permitted by this Act to be made without shareholder action.

§ 10.03 Amendment by Board of Directors and Shareholders.

(a) A corporation's board of directors may propose one or more amendments to the articles of incorporation for submission to the shareholders.

(b) For the amendment to be adopted:

(1) the board of directors must recommend the amendment to the shareholders unless the board of directors determines that because of conflict of interest or other special circumstances it should make no recommendation and communicates the basis for its determination to the shareholders with the amendment; and

(2) the shareholders entitled to vote on the amendment must approve the amendment as provided in subsection (e).

(c) The board of directors may condition its submission of the proposed amendment on any basis.

(d) The corporation shall notify each shareholder, whether or not entitled to vote, of the proposed shareholders' meeting in accordance with section 7.05. The notice of meeting must also state that the purpose, or one of the purposes, of the meeting is to consider the proposed amendment and contain or be accompanied by a copy or summary of the amendment.

(e) Unless this Act, the articles of incorporation, or the board of directors (acting pursuant to subsection (c)) require a greater vote or a vote by voting groups, the amendment to be adopted must be approved by:

(1) a majority of the votes entitled to be cast on the amendment by any voting group with respect to which the amendment would create dissenters' rights; and

(2) the votes required by Sections 7.25 and 7.26 by every other voting group entitled to vote on the amendment.

§ 10.04 Voting on Amendments by Voting Groups.

(a) The holders of the outstanding shares of a class are entitled to vote as a separate voting group (if shareholder voting is otherwise required by this Act) on a proposed amendment if the amendment would:

(1) increase or decrease the aggregate number of authorized shares of the class;

(2) effect an exchange or reclassification of all or part of the shares of the class into shares of another class;

(3) effect an exchange or reclassification, or create the right of exchange, of all or part of the shares of another class into shares of the class;

(4) change the designation, rights, preferences, or limitations of all or part of the shares of the class;

(5) change the shares of all or part of the class into a different number of shares of the same class;

(6) create a new class of shares having rights or preferences with respect to distributions or to dissolution that are prior, superior, or substantially equal to the shares of the class;

(7) increase the rights, preferences, or number of authorized shares of any class that, after giving effect to the amendment, have rights or preferences with respect to distributions or to dissolution that are prior, superior, or substantially equal to the shares of the class;

(8) limit or deny an existing preemptive right of all or part of the shares of the class; or

(9) cancel or otherwise affect rights to distributions or dividends that have accumulated but not yet been declared on all or part of the shares of the class.

(b) If a proposed amendment would affect a series of a class of shares in one or more of the ways described in subsection (a), the shares of that series are entitled to vote as a separate voting group on the proposed amendment.

(c) If a proposed amendment that entitles two or more series of shares to vote as separate voting groups under this section would affect those two or more series in the same or a substantially similar way, the shares of all the series so affected must vote together as a single voting group on the proposed amendment.

(d) A class or series of shares is entitled to the voting rights granted by this section although the articles of incorporation provide that the shares are nonvoting shares.

§ 10.05   Amendment Before Issuance of Shares.

If a corporation has not yet issued shares, its incorporators or board of directors may adopt one or more amendments to the corporation's articles of incorporation.

§ 10.06   Articles of Amendment.

A corporation amending its articles of incorporation shall deliver to the secretary of state for filing articles of amendment setting forth:

(1) the name of the corporation;

(2) the text of each amendment adopted;

(3) if an amendment provides for an exchange, reclassification, or cancellation of issued shares, provisions for implementing the amendment if not contained in the amendment itself;

(4) the date of each amendment's adoption;

(5) if an amendment was adopted by the incorporators or board of directors without shareholder action, a statement to that effect and that shareholder action was not required;

(6) if an amendment was approved by the shareholders:

(i) the designation, number of outstanding shares, number of votes entitled to be cast by each voting group entitled to vote separately on the amendment, and number of votes of each voting group indisputably represented at the meeting;

(ii) either the total number of votes cast for and against the amendment by each voting group entitled to vote separately on the amendment or the total number of undisputed votes cast for the amendment by each voting group and a statement that the number cast for the amendment by each voting group was sufficient for approval by that voting group.

§ 10.07   Restated Articles of Incorporation.

(a) A corporation's board of directors may restate its articles of incorporation at any time with or without shareholder action.

(b) The restatement may include one or more amendments to the articles. If the restatement includes an amendment requiring shareholder approval, it must be adopted as provided in section 10.03.

(c) If the board of directors submits a restatement for shareholder action, the corporation shall notify each shareholder, whether or not entitled to vote, of the proposed shareholders' meeting in accordance with Section 7.05. The notice must also state that the purpose, or one of the purposes, of the meeting is to consider the proposed restatement and contain or be accompanied by a copy of the restatement that identifies any amendment or other change it would make in the articles.

(d) A corporation restating its articles of incorporation shall deliver to the secretary of state for filing articles of restatement setting forth the name of the corporation and the text of the restated articles of incorporation together with a certificate setting forth:

(1) whether the restatement contains an amendment to the articles requiring shareholder approval and, if it does not, that the board of directors adopted the restatement; or

(2) if the restatement contains an amendment to the articles requiring shareholder approval, the information required by Section 10.06.

(e) Duly adopted restated articles of incorporation supersede the original articles of incorporation and all amendments to them.

(f) The secretary of state may certify restated articles of incorporation, as the articles of incorporation currently in effect, without including the certificate information required by subsection (d).

§ 10.08 Amendment Pursuant to Reorganization.

(a) A corporation's articles of incorporation may be amended without action by the board of directors or shareholders to carry out a plan of reorganization ordered or decreed by a court of competent jurisdiction under federal statute if the articles of incorporation after amendment contain only provisions required or permitted by Section 2.02.

(b) The individual or individuals designated by the court shall deliver to the secretary of state for filing articles of amendment setting forth:

    (1) the name of the corporation;

    (2) the text of each amendment approved by the court;

    (3) the date of the court's order or decree approving the articles of amendment;

    (4) the title of the reorganization proceeding in which the order or decree was entered; and

    (5) a statement that the court had jurisdiction of the proceeding under federal statute.

(c) Shareholders of a corporation undergoing reorganization do not have dissenters' rights except as and to the extent provided in the reorganization plan.

(d) This section does not apply after entry of a final decree in the reorganization proceeding even though the court retains jurisdiction of the proceeding for limited purposes unrelated to consummation of the reorganization plan.

§ 10.09 Effect of Amendment.

An amendment to articles of incorporation does not affect a cause of action existing against or in favor of the corporation, a proceeding to which the corporation is a party, or the existing rights of persons other than shareholders of the corporation. An amendment changing a corporation's name does not abate a proceeding brought by or against the corporation in its former name.

Subchapter B.   Amendment of Bylaws

§ 10.20 Amendment by Board of Directors or Shareholders.

(a) A corporation's board of directors may amend or repeal the corporation's bylaws unless:

    (1) the articles of incorporation or this Act reserve this power exclusively to the shareholders in whole or part; or

    (2) the shareholders in amending or repealing a particular bylaw provide expressly that the board of directors may not amend or repeal that bylaw.

(b) A corporation's shareholders may amend or repeal the corporation's bylaws even though the bylaws may also be amended or repealed by its board of directors.

§ 10.21 Bylaw Increasing Quorum or Voting Requirement for Shareholders.

(a) If expressly authorized by the articles of incorporation, the shareholders may adopt or amend a bylaw that fixes a greater quorum or voting requirement for shareholders (or voting groups of shareholders) than is required by this Act. The adoption or amendment of a bylaw that adds, changes, or deletes a greater quorum or voting requirement for shareholders must meet the same quorum requirement and be adopted by the same vote and voting groups required to take action under the quorum and voting requirement then in effect or proposed to be adopted, whichever is greater.

(b) A bylaw that fixes a greater quorum or voting requirement for shareholders under subsection (a) may not be adopted, amended, or repealed by the board of directors.

§ 10.22 Bylaw Increasing Quorum or Voting Requirement for Directors.

(a) A bylaw that fixes a greater quorum or voting requirement for the board of directors may be amended or repealed:

    (1) if originally adopted by the shareholders, only by the shareholders;

    (2) if originally adopted by the board of directors, either by the shareholders or by the board of directors.

(b) A bylaw adopted or amended by the shareholders that fixes a greater quorum or voting requirement for the board of directors may provide that it may be amended or repealed only by a specified vote of either the shareholders or the board of directors.

(c) Action by the board of directors under subsection (a)(2) to adopt or amend by a bylaw that changes the quorum or voting requirement for the board of directors must meet the same quorum requirement and be adopted by the same vote required to take action under the quorum and voting requirement then in effect or proposed to be adopted, whichever is greater.

CHAPTER 11.   Merger and Share Exchange

§ 11.01 Merger.

(a) One or more corporations may merge into another corporation if the board of directors of each corporation adopts and its shareholders (if required by section 11.03) approve a plan of merger.

(b) The plan of merger must set forth:

    (1) the name of each corporation planning to merge and the name of the surviving corpora-

tion into which each other corporation plans to merge;

(2) the terms and conditions of the merger; and

(3) the manner and basis of converting the shares of each corporation into shares, obligations, or other securities of the surviving or any other corporation or into cash or other property in whole or part.

(c) The plan of merger may set forth:

(1) amendments to the articles of incorporation of the surviving corporation; and

(2) other provisions relating to the merger.

§ 11.02 Share Exchange.

(a) A corporation may acquire all of the outstanding shares of one or more classes or series of another corporation if the board of directors of each corporation adopts and its shareholders (if required by section 11.03) approve the exchange.

(b) The plan of exchange must set forth:

(1) the name of the corporation whose shares will be acquired and the name of the acquiring corporation;

(2) the terms and conditions of the exchange;

(3) the manner and basis of exchanging the shares to be acquired for shares, obligations, or other securities of the acquiring or any other corporation or for cash or other property in whole or part.

(c) The plan of exchange may set forth other provisions relating to the exchange.

(d) This section does not limit the power of a corporation to acquire all or part of the shares of one or more classes or series of another corporation through a voluntary exchange or otherwise.

§ 11.03 Action on Plan.

(a) After adopting a plan of merger or share exchange, the board of directors of each corporation party to the merger, and the board of directors of the corporation whose shares will be acquired in the share exchange, shall submit the plan of merger (except as provided in subsection (g)) or share exchange for approval by its shareholders.

(b) For a plan of merger or share exchange to be approved:

(1) the board of directors must recommend the plan of merger or share exchange to the shareholders, unless the board of directors determines that because of conflict of interest or other special circumstances it should make no recommendation and communicates the basis for its determination to the shareholders with the plan; and

(2) the shareholders entitled to vote must approve the plan.

(c) The board of directors may condition its submission of the proposed merger or share exchange on any basis.

(d) The corporation shall notify each shareholder, whether or not entitled to vote, of the proposed shareholders' meeting in accordance with Section 7.05. The notice must also state that the purpose, or one of the purposes, of the meeting is to consider the plan of merger or share exchange and contain or be accompanied by a copy or summary of the plan.

(e) Unless this Act, the articles of incorporation, or the board of directors (acting pursuant to subsection (c)) require a greater vote or a vote by voting groups, the plan of merger or share exchange to be authorized must be approved by each voting group entitled to vote separately on the plan by a majority of all the votes entitled to be cast on the plan by that voting group.

(f) Separate voting by voting groups is required:

(1) on a plan of merger if the plan contains a provision that, if contained in proposed amendment to articles of incorporation, would require action by one or more separate voting groups on the proposed amendment under Section 10.04;

(2) on a plan of share exchange by each class or series of shares included in the exchange, with each class or series constituting a separate voting group.

(g) Action by the shareholders of the surviving corporation on a plan of merger is not required if:

(1) the articles of incorporation of the surviving corporation will not differ (except for amendments enumerated in Section 10.02) from its articles before the merger;

(2) each shareholder of the surviving corporation whose shares were outstanding immediately before the effective date of the merger will hold the same number of shares, with identical designations, preferences, limitations, and relative rights, immediately after;

(3) the number of voting shares outstanding immediately after the merger, plus the number of voting shares issuable as a result of the merger (either by the conversion of securities issued pursuant to the merger or the exercise of rights and warrants issued pursuant to the merger), will not exceed by more than 20 percent the total number of voting shares of the surviving corporation outstanding immediately before the merger; and

(4) the number of participating shares outstanding immediately after the merger, plus the number of participating shares issuable as a result of the merger (either by the conversion of securities issued pursuant to the merger or the exercise of rights and warrants issued pursuant

to the merger), will not exceed by more than 20 percent the total number of participating shares outstanding immediately before the merger.

(h) As used in subsection (g):

(1) "Participating shares" means shares that entitle their holders to participate without limitation in distributions.

(2) "Voting shares" means shares that entitle their holders to vote unconditionally in elections of directors.

(i) After a merger or share exchange is authorized, and at any time before articles of merger or share exchange are filed, the planned merger or share exchange may be abandoned (subject to any contractual rights), without further shareholder action, in accordance with the procedure set forth in the plan of merger or share exchange or, if none is set forth, in the manner determined by the board of directors.

§ 11.04 Merger of Subsidiary.

(a) A parent corporation owning at least 90 percent of the outstanding shares of each class of a subsidiary corporation may merge the subsidiary into itself without approval of the shareholders of the parent or subsidiary.

(b) The board of directors of the parent shall adopt a plan of merger that sets forth:

(1) the names of the parent and subsidiary; and

(2) the manner and basis of converting the shares of the subsidiary into shares, obligations, or other securities of the parent or any other corporation or into cash or other property in whole or part.

(c) The parent shall mail a copy or summary of the plan of merger to each shareholder of the subsidiary who does not waive the mailing requirement in writing.

(d) The parent may not deliver articles of merger to the secretary of state for filing until at least 30 days after the date it mailed a copy of the plan of merger to each shareholder of the subsidiary who did not waive the mailing requirement.

(e) Articles of merger under this section may not contain amendments to the articles of incorporation of the parent corporation (except for amendments enumerated in section 10.02).

§ 11.05 Articles of Merger or Share Exchange.

(a) After a plan of merger or share exchange is approved by the shareholders, or adopted by the board of directors if shareholder approval is not required, the surviving or acquiring corporation shall deliver to the secretary of state for filing articles of merger or share exchange setting forth:

(1) the plan of merger or share exchange;

(2) if shareholder approval was not required, a statement to that effect;

(3) if approval of the shareholders of one or more corporations party to the merger or share exchange was required:

(i) the designation, number of outstanding shares, and number of votes entitled to be cast by each voting group entitled to vote separately on the plan as to each corporation; and

(ii) either the total number of votes cast for and against the plan by each voting group entitled to vote separately on the plan or the total number of undisputed votes cast for the plan separately by each voting group and a statement that the number cast for the plan by each voting group was sufficient for approval by that voting group.

(b) Unless a delayed effective date is specified, a merger or share exchange takes effect when the articles of merger or share exchange are filed.

§ 11.06 Effect of Merger or Share Exchange.

(a) When a merger takes effect:

(1) every other corporation party to the merger merges into the surviving corporation and the separate existence of every corporation except the surviving corporation ceases;

(2) the title to all real estate and other property owned by each corporation party to the merger is vested in the surviving corporation without reversion or impairment;

(3) the surviving corporation has all liabilities of each corporation party to the merger;

(4) a proceeding pending against any corporation party to the merger may be continued as if the merger did not occur or the surviving corporation may be substituted in the proceeding for the corporation whose existence ceased;

(5) the articles of incorporation of the surviving corporation are amended to the extent provided in the plan of merger; and

(6) the shares of each corporation party to the merger that are to be converted into shares, obligations, or other securities of the surviving or any other corporation or into cash or other property are converted and the former holders of the shares are entitled only to the rights provided in the articles of merger or to their rights under Chapter 13.

(b) When a share exchange takes effect, the shares of each acquired corporation are exchanged as provided in the plan, and the former holders of the shares are entitled only to the exchange rights provided in the articles of share exchange or to their rights under Chapter 13.

§ 11.07 Merger or Share Exchange With Foreign Corporation.

(a) One or more foreign corporations may merge or enter into a share exchange with one or more domestic corporations if:

(1) in a merger, the merger is permitted by the law of the state or country under whose law each foreign corporation is incorporated and each foreign corporation complies with that law in effecting the merger;

(2) in a share exchange, the corporation whose shares will be acquired is a domestic corporation, whether or not a share exchange is permitted by the law of the state or country under whose law the acquiring corporation is incorporated;

(3) the foreign corporation complies with Section 11.05 if it is the surviving corporation of the merger or acquiring corporation of the share exchange; and

(4) each domestic corporation complies with the applicable provisions of Sections 11.01 through 11.04 and, if it is the surviving corporation of the merger or acquiring corporation of the share exchange, with Section 11.05.

(b) Upon the merger or share exchange taking effect, the surviving foreign corporation of a merger and the acquiring foreign corporation of a share exchange is deemed:

(1) to appoint the secretary of state as its agent for service of process in a proceeding to enforce any obligation or the rights of dissenting shareholders of each domestic corporation party to the merger or share exchange; and

(2) to agree that it will promptly pay to the dissenting shareholders of each domestic corporation party to the merger or share exchange the amount, if any, to which they are entitled under Chapter 13.

(c) This section does not limit the power of a foreign corporation to acquire all or part of the shares of one or more classes or series of a domestic corporation through a voluntary exchange or otherwise.

CHAPTER 12.   Sale of Assets

§ 12.01 Sale of Assets in Regular Course of Business and Mortgage of Assets.

(a) A corporation may, on the terms and conditions and for the consideration determined by the board of directors:

(1) sell, lease, exchange, or otherwise dispose of all, or substantially all, of its property in the usual and regular course of business,

(2) mortgage, pledge, dedicate to the repayment of indebtedness (whether with or without recourse), or otherwise encumber any or all of its property whether or not in the usual and regular course of business, or

(3) transfer any or all of its property to a corporation all the shares of which are owned by the corporation.

(b) Unless the articles of incorporation require it, approval by the shareholders of a transaction described in subsection (a) is not required.

§ 12.02 Sale of Assets Other Than in Regular Course of Business.

(a) A corporation may sell, lease, exchange, or otherwise dispose of all, or substantially all, of its property (with or without the good will), otherwise than in the usual and regular course of business, on the terms and conditions and for the consideration determined by the corporation's board of directors, if the board of directors proposes and its shareholders approve the proposed transaction.

(b) For a transaction to be authorized:

(1) the board of directors must recommend the proposed transaction to the shareholders unless the board of directors determines that because of conflict of interest or other special circumstances it should make no recommendation and communicates the basis for its determination to the shareholders with the submission of the proposed transaction; and

(2) the shareholders entitled to vote must approve the transaction.

(c) The board of directors may condition its submission of the proposed transaction on any basis.

(d) The corporation shall notify each shareholder, whether or not entitled to vote, of the proposed shareholders' meeting in accordance with section 7.05. The notice must also state that the purpose, or one of the purposes, of the meeting is to consider the sale, lease, exchange, or other disposition of all, or substantially all, the property of the corporation and contain or be accompanied by a description of the transaction.

(e) Unless the articles of incorporation or the board of directors (acting pursuant to subsection (c)) require a greater vote or a vote by voting groups, the transaction to be authorized must be approved by a majority of all the votes entitled to be cast on the transaction.

(f) After a sale, lease, exchange, or other disposition of property is authorized, the transaction may be abandoned (subject to any contractual rights) without further shareholder action.

(g) A transaction that constitutes a distribution is governed by section 6.40 and not by this section.

CHAPTER 13. Dissenters' Rights

Subchapter A. *Right to Dissent and Obtain Payment for Shares*

§ 13.01 Definitions.

In this chapter:

(1) "Corporation" means the issuer of the shares held by a dissenter before the corporate action, or the surviving or acquiring corporation by merger or share exchange of that issuer.

(2) "Dissenter" means a shareholder who is entitled to dissent from corporate action under Section 13.02 and who exercises that right when and in the manner required by Sections 13.20 through 13.28.

(3) "Fair value," with respect to a dissenter's shares, means the value of the shares immediately before the effectuation of the corporate action to which the dissenter objects, excluding any appreciation or depreciation in anticipation of the corporate action unless exclusion would be inequitable.

(4) "Interest" means interest from the effective date of the corporate action until the date of payment, at the average rate currently paid by the corporation on its principal bank loans or, if none, at a rate that is fair and equitable under all the circumstances.

(5) "Record shareholder" means the person in whose name shares are registered in the records of a corporation or the beneficial owner of shares to the extent of the rights granted by a nominee certificate on file with a corporation.

(6) "Beneficial shareholder" means the person who is a beneficial owner of shares held in a voting trust or by a nominee as the record shareholder.

(7) "Shareholder" means the record shareholder or the beneficial shareholder.

§ 13.02 Right to Dissent.

(a) A shareholder is entitled to dissent from, and obtain payment of the fair value of his shares in the event of, any of the following corporate actions:

(1) consummation of a plan of merger to which the corporation is a party (i) if shareholder approval is required for the merger by section 11.03 or the articles of incorporation and the shareholder is entitled to vote on the merger or (ii) if the corporation is a subsidiary that is merged with its parent under section 11.04;

(2) consummation of a plan of share exchange to which the corporation is a party as the corpo-

ration whose shares will be acquired, if the shareholder is entitled to vote on the plan;

(3) consummation of a sale or exchange of all, or substantially all, of the property of the corporation other than in the usual and regular course of business, if the shareholder is entitled to vote on the sale or exchange, including a sale in dissolution, but not including a sale pursuant to court order or a sale for cash pursuant to a plan by which all or substantially all of the net proceeds of the sale will be distributed to the shareholders within one year after the date of the sale;

(4) an amendment of the articles of incorporation that materially and adversely affects rights in respect of a dissenter's shares because it:

 (i) alters or abolishes a preferential right of the shares;

 (ii) creates, alters, or abolishes a right in respect of redemption, including a provision respecting a sinking fund for the redemption or repurchase, of the shares;

 (iii) alters or abolishes a preemptive right of the holder of the shares to acquire shares or other securities;

 (iv) excludes or limits the right of the shares to vote on any matter, or to cumulate votes, other than a limitation by dilution through issuance of shares or other securities with similar voting rights; or

 (v) reduces the number of shares owned by the shareholder to a fraction of a share if the fractional share so created is to be acquired for cash under section 6.04; or

(5) any corporate action taken pursuant to a shareholder vote to the extent the articles of incorporation, bylaws, or a resolution of the board of directors provides that voting or nonvoting shareholders are entitled to dissent and obtain payment for their shares.

(b) A shareholder entitled to dissent and obtain payment for his shares under this chapter may not challenge the corporate action creating his entitlement unless the action is unlawful or fraudulent with respect to the shareholder or the corporation.

§ 13.03 Dissent by Nominees and Beneficial Owners.

(a) A record shareholder may assert dissenters' rights as to fewer than all the shares registered in his name only if he dissents with respect to all shares beneficially owned by any one person and notifies the corporation in writing of the name and address of each person on whose behalf he asserts dissenters' rights. The rights of a partial dissenter under this subsection are determined as if the shares as to which he dissents and his other shares were registered in the names of different shareholders.

(b) A beneficial shareholder may assert dissenters' rights as to shares held on his behalf only if:

(1) he submits to the corporation the record shareholder's written consent to the dissent not later than the time the beneficial shareholder asserts dissenters' rights; and

(2) he does so with respect to all shares of which he is the beneficial shareholder or over which he has power to direct the vote.

Subchapter B. Procedure for Exercise of Dissenters' Rights

§ 13.20   Notice of Dissenters' Rights.

(a) If proposed corporate action creating dissenters' rights under section 13.02 is submitted to a vote at a shareholders' meeting, the meeting notice must state that shareholders are or may be entitled to assert dissenters' rights under this chapter and be accompanied by a copy of this chapter.

(b) If corporate action creating dissenters' rights under section 13.02 is taken without a vote of shareholders, the corporation shall notify in writing all shareholders entitled to assert dissenters' rights that the action was taken and send them the dissenters' notice described in section 13.22.

§ 13.21   Notice of Intent to Demand Payment.

(a) If proposed corporate action creating dissenters' rights under section 13.02 is submitted to a vote at a shareholders' meeting, a shareholder who wishes to assert dissenters' rights (1) must deliver to the corporation before the vote is taken written notice of his intent to demand payment for his shares if the proposed action is effectuated and (2) must not vote his shares in favor of the proposed action.

(b) A shareholder who does not satisfy the requirements of subsection (a) is not entitled to payment for his shares under this chapter.

§ 13.22   Dissenters' Notice.

(a) If proposed corporate action creating dissenters' rights under section 13.02 is authorized at a shareholders' meeting, the corporation shall deliver a written dissenters' notice to all shareholders who satisfied the requirements of section 13.21.

(b) The dissenters' notice must be sent no later than 10 days after the corporate action was taken, and must:

(1) state where the payment demand must be sent and where and when certificates for certificated shares must be deposited;

(2) inform holders of uncertificated shares to what extent transfer of the shares will be restricted after the payment demand is received;

(3) supply a form for demanding payment that includes the date of the first announcement to news media or to shareholders of the terms of the proposed corporate action and requires that the person asserting dissenters' rights certify whether or not he acquired beneficial ownership of the shares before that date;

(4) set a date by which the corporation must receive the payment demand, which date may not be fewer than 30 nor more than 60 days after the date the subsection (a) notice is delivered; and

(5) be accompanied by a copy of this chapter.

§ 13.23   Duty to Demand Payment.

(a) A shareholder sent a dissenters' notice described in section 13.22 must demand payment, certify whether he acquired beneficial ownership of the shares before the date required to be set forth in the dissenter's notice pursuant to section 13.22(b)(3), and deposit his certificates in accordance with the terms of the notice.

(b) The shareholder who demands payment and deposits his shares under section (a) retains all other rights of a shareholder until these rights are cancelled or modified by the taking of the proposed corporate action.

(c) A shareholder who does not demand payment or deposit his share certificates where required, each by the date set in the dissenters' notice, is not entitled to payment for his shares under this chapter.

§ 13.24   Share Restrictions.

(a) The corporation may restrict the transfer of uncertificated shares from the date the demand for their payment is received until the proposed corporate action is taken or the restrictions released under section 13.26.

(b) The person for whom dissenters' rights are asserted as to uncertificated shares retains all other rights of a shareholder until these rights are cancelled or modified by the taking of the proposed corporation action.

§ 13.25   Payment.

(a) Except as provided in section 13.27, as soon as the proposed corporate action is taken, or upon receipt of a payment demand, the corporation shall pay each dissenter who complied with section 13.23 the amount the corporation estimates to be the fair value of his shares, plus accrued interest.

(b) The payment must be accompanied by:

(1) the corporation's balance sheet as of the end of a fiscal year ending not more than 16 months before the date of payment, an income statement for that year, a statement of changes in shareholders' equity for that year, and the

latest available interim financial statements, if any;

(2) a statement of the corporation's estimate of the fair value of the shares;

(3) an explanation of how the interest was calculated;

(4) a statement of the dissenter's right to demand payment under section 13.28; and

(5) a copy of this chapter.

§ 13.26 Failure to Take Action.

(a) If the corporation does not take the proposed action within 60 days after the date set for demanding payment and depositing share certificates, the corporation shall return the deposited certificates and release the transfer restrictions imposed on uncertificated shares.

(b) If after returning deposited certificates and releasing transfer restrictions, the corporation takes the proposed action, it must send the new dissenters' notice under section 13.22 and repeat the payment demand procedure.

§ 13.27 After-Acquired Shares.

(a) A corporation may elect to withhold payment required by section 13.25 from a dissenter unless he was the beneficial owner of the shares before the date set forth in the dissenters' notice as the date of the first announcement to news media or to shareholders of the terms of the proposed corporate action.

(b) To the extent the corporation elects to withhold payment under subsection (a), after taking the proposed corporate action, it shall estimate the fair value of the shares, plus accrued interest, and shall pay this amount to each dissenter who agrees to accept it in full satisfaction of his demand. The corporation shall send with its offer a statement of its estimate of the fair value of the shares, an explanation of how the interest was calculated, and a statement of the dissenter's right to demand payment under section 13.28.

§ 13.28 Procedure if Shareholder Dissatisfied With Payment or Offer.

(a) A dissenter may notify the corporation in writing of his own estimate of the fair value of his shares and amount of interest due, and demand payment of his estimate (less any payment under section 13.25), or reject the corporation's offer under section 13.27 and demand payment of the fair value of his shares and interest due, if:

(1) the dissenter believes that the amount paid under section 13.25 or offered under section 13.27 is less than the fair value of his shares or that the interest due is incorrectly calculated;

(2) the corporation fails to make payment under section 13.25 within 60 days after the date set for demanding payment; or

(3) the corporation, having failed to take the proposed action, does not return the deposited certificates or release the transfer restrictions imposed on uncertificated shares within 60 days after the date set for demanding payment.

(b) A dissenter waives his right to demand payment under this section unless he notifies the corporation of his demand in writing under subsection (a) within 30 days after the corporation made or offered payment for his shares.

Subchapter C.   Judicial Appraisal of Shares

§ 13.30 Court Action.

(a) If a demand for payment under section 13.28 remains unsettled, the corporation shall commence a proceeding within 60 days after receiving the payment demand and petition the court to determine the fair value of the shares and accrued interest. If the corporation does not commence the proceeding within the 60-day period, it shall pay each dissenter whose demand remains unsettled the amount demanded.

(b) The corporation shall commence the proceeding in the [name or describe] court of the county where a corporation's principal office (or, if none in this state, its registered office) is located. If the corporation is a foreign corporation without a registered office in this state, it shall commence the proceeding in the county in this state where the registered office of the domestic corporation merged with or whose shares were acquired by the foreign corporation was located.

(c) The corporation shall make all dissenters (whether or not residents of this state) whose demands remain unsettled parties to the proceeding as in an action against their shares and all parties must be served with a copy of the petition. Nonresidents may be served by registered or certified mail or by publication as provided by law.

(d) The jurisdiction of the court in which the proceeding is commenced under subsection (b) is plenary and exclusive. The court may appoint one or more persons as appraisers to receive evidence and recommend decision on the question of fair value. The appraisers have the powers described in the order appointing them, or in any amendment to it. The dissenters are entitled to the same discovery rights as parties in other civil proceedings.

(e) Each dissenter made a party to the proceeding is entitled to judgment (1) for the amount, if any, by which the court finds the fair value of his shares, plus interest, exceeds the amount paid by the corporation or (2) for the fair value, plus accrued interest, of his after-acquired shares for which the corporation elected to withhold payment under section 13.27.

§ 13.31   Court Costs and Counsel Fees.

(a) The court in an appraisal proceeding commenced under section 13.30 shall determine all costs of the proceeding, including the reasonable compensation and expenses of appraisers appointed by the court. The court shall assess the costs against the corporation, except that the court may assess costs against all or some of the dissenters, in amounts the court finds equitable, to the extent the court finds the dissenters acted arbitrarily vexatiously, or not in good faith in demanding payment under section 13.28.

(b) The court may also assess the fees and expenses of counsel and experts for the respective parties, in amounts the court finds equitable:

(1) against the corporation and in favor of any or all dissenters if the court finds the corporation did not substantially comply with the requirements of sections 13.20 through 13.28; or

(2) against either the corporation or a dissenter, in favor of any other party, if the court finds that the party against whom the fees and expenses are assessed acted arbitrarily, vexatiously, or not in good faith with respect to the rights provided by this chapter.

(c) If the court finds that the services of counsel for any dissenter were of substantial benefit to other dissenters similarly situated, and that the fees for those services should not be assessed against the corporation, the court may award to these counsel reasonable fees to be paid out of the amounts awarded the dissenters who were benefited.

CHAPTER 14.   Dissolution

Subchapter A.   Voluntary Dissolution

§ 14.01   Dissolution by Incorporators or Initial Directors.

A majority of the incorporators or initial directors of a corporation that has not issued shares or has not commenced business may dissolve the corporation by delivering to the secretary of state for filing articles of dissolution that set forth:

(1) the name of the corporation;

(2) the date of its incorporation;

(3) either (i) that none of the corporation's shares has been issued or (ii) that the corporation has not commenced business;

(4) that no debt of the corporation remains unpaid;

(5) that the net assets of the corporation remaining after winding up have been distributed to the shareholders, if shares were issued; and

(6) that a majority of the incorporators or initial directors authorized the dissolution.

§ 14.02   Dissolution by Board of Directors and Shareholders.

(a) A corporation's board of directors may propose dissolution for submission to the shareholders.

(b) For a proposal to dissolve to be adopted:

(1) the board of directors must recommend dissolution to the shareholders unless the board of directors determines that because of conflict of interest or other special circumstances it should make no recommendation and communicates the basis for its determination to the shareholders; and

(2) the shareholders entitled to vote must approve the proposal to dissolve as provided in subsection (e).

(c) The board of directors may condition its submission of the proposal for dissolution on any basis.

(d) The corporation shall notify each shareholder, whether or not entitled to vote, of the proposed shareholders' meeting in accordance with section 7.05. The notice must also state that the purpose, or one of the purposes, of the meeting is to consider dissolving the corporation.

(e) Unless the articles of incorporation or the board of directors (acting pursuant to subsection (c)) require a greater vote or a vote by voting groups, the proposal to dissolve to be adopted must be approved by a majority of all the votes entitled to be cast on that proposal.

§ 14.03   Articles of Dissolution.

(a) At any time after dissolution is authorized, the corporation may dissolve by delivering to the secretary of state for filing articles of dissolution setting forth:

(1) the name of the corporation;

(2) the date dissolution was authorized;

(3) if dissolution was approved by the shareholders:

(i) the number of votes entitled to be cast on the proposal to dissolve; and

(ii) either the total number of votes cast for and against dissolution or the total number of undisputed votes cast for dissolution and a statement that the number cast for dissolution was sufficient for approval.

(4) If voting by voting groups is required, the information required by subparagraph (3) shall be separately provided for each voting group entitled to vote separately on the plan to dissolve.

(b) A corporation is dissolved upon the effective date of its articles of dissolution.

§ 14.04   Revocation of Dissolution.

(a) A corporation may revoke its dissolution within 120 days of its effective date.

(b) Revocation of dissolution must be authorized in the same manner as the dissolution was authorized unless that authorization permitted revocation by action by the board of directors alone, in which event the board of directors may revoke the dissolution without shareholder action.

(c) After the revocation of dissolution is authorized, the corporation may revoke the dissolution by delivering to the secretary of state for filing articles of revocation of dissolution, together with a copy of its articles of dissolution, that set forth:

(1) the name of the corporation;

(2) the effective date of the dissolution that was revoked;

(3) the date that the revocation of dissolution was authorized;

(4) if the corporation's board of directors (or incorporators) revoked the dissolution, a statement to that effect;

(5) if the corporation's board of directors revoked a dissolution authorized by the shareholders, a statement that revocation was permitted by action by the board of directors alone pursuant to that authorization; and

(6) if shareholder action was required to revoke the dissolution, the information required by section 14.03(3) or (4).

(d) Unless a delayed effective date is specified, revocation of dissolution is effective when articles of revocation of dissolution are filed.

(e) When the revocation of dissolution is effective, it relates back to and takes effect as of the effective date of the dissolution and the corporation resumes carrying on its business as if dissolution had never occurred.

§ 14.05 Effect of Dissolution.

(a) A dissolved corporation continues its corporate existence but may not carry on any business except that appropriate to wind up and liquidate its business and affairs, including:

(1) collecting its assets;

(2) disposing of its properties that will not be distributed in kind to its shareholders;

(3) discharging or making provision for discharging its liabilities;

(4) distributing its remaining property among its shareholders according to their interests; and

(5) doing every other act necessary to wind up and liquidate its business and affairs.

(b) Dissolution of a corporation does not:

(1) transfer title to the corporation's property;

(2) prevent transfer of its shares or securities, although the authorization to dissolve may provide for closing the corporation's share transfer records;

(3) subject its directors or officers to standards of conduct different from those prescribed in chapter 8;

(4) change quorum or voting requirements for its board of directors or shareholders; change provisions for selection, resignation, or removal of its directors or officers or both; or change provisions for amending its bylaws;

(5) prevent commencement of a proceedings by or against the corporation in its corporate name;

(6) abate or suspend a proceeding pending by or against the corporation on the effective date of dissolution; or

(7) terminate the authority of the registered agent of the corporation.

§ 14.06 Known Claims Against Dissolved Corporation.

(a) A dissolved corporation may dispose of the known claims against it by following the procedure described in this section.

(b) The dissolved corporation shall notify its known claimants in writing of the dissolution at any time after its effective date. The written notice must:

(1) describe information that must be included in a claim;

(2) provide a mailing address where a claim may be sent;

(3) state the deadline, which may not be fewer than 120 days from the effective date of the written notice, by which the dissolved corporation must receive the claim; and

(4) state that the claim will be barred if not received by the deadline.

(c) A claim against the dissolved corporation is barred:

(1) if a claimant who was given written notice under subsection (b) does not deliver the claim to the dissolved corporation by the deadline;

(2) if a claimant whose claim was rejected by the dissolved corporation does not commence a proceeding to enforce the claim within 90 days from the effective date of the rejection notice.

(d) For purposes of this section, "claim" does not include a contingent liability or a claim based on an event occurring after the effective date of dissolution.

§ 14.07 Unknown Claims Against Dissolved Corporation.

(a) A dissolved corporation may also publish notice of its dissolution and request that persons with claims against the corporation present them in accordance with the notice.

(b) The notice must:

(1) be published one time in a newspaper of general circulation in the county where the dis-

solved corporation's principal office (or, if none in this state, its registered office) is or was last located;

(2) describe the information that must be included in a claim and provide a mailing address where the claim may be sent; and

(3) state that a claim against the corporation will be barred unless a proceeding to enforce the claim is commenced within five years after the publication of the notice.

(c) If the dissolved corporation publishes a newspaper notice in accordance with subsection (b), the claim of each of the following claimants is barred unless the claimant commences a proceeding to enforce the claim against the dissolved corporation within five years after the publication date of the newspaper notice:

(1) a claimant who did not receive written notice under section 14.06;

(2) a claimant whose claim was timely sent to the dissolved corporation but not acted on;

(3) a claimant shoe claim is contingent or based on an event occurring after the effective date of dissolution.

(d) A claim may be enforced under this section:

(1) against the dissolved corporation, to the extent of its undistributed assets; or

(2) if the assets have been distributed in liquidation, against a shareholder of the dissolved corporation to the extent of his pro rata share of the claim or the corporate assets distributed to him in liquidation, whichever is less, but a shareholder's total liability for all claims under this section may not exceed the total amount of assets distributed to him.

Subchapter B. Administrative Dissolution

§ 14.20 Grounds for Administrative Dissolution.

The secretary of state may commence a proceeding under section 14.21 to administratively dissolve a corporation if:

(1) the corporation does not pay within 60 days after they are due any franchise taxes or penalties imposed by this Act or other law;

(2) the corporation does not deliver its annual report to the secretary of state within 60 days after it is due;

(3) the corporation is without a registered agent or registered office in this state for 60 days or more;

(4) the corporation does not notify the secretary of state within 60 days that its registered agent or registered office has been changed, that its registered agent has resigned, or that its registered office has been discontinued; or

(5) the corporation's period of duration stated in its articles of incorporation expires.

§ 14.21 Procedure for and Effect of Administrative Dissolution.

(a) If the secretary of state determines that one or more grounds exist under section 14.20 for dissolving a corporation, he shall serve the corporation with written notice of his determination under section 5.04.

(b) If the corporation does not correct each ground for dissolution or demonstrate to the reasonable satisfaction of the secretary of state that each ground determined by the secretary of state does not exist within 60 days after service of the notice is perfected under section 5.04, the secretary of state shall administratively dissolve the corporation by signing a certificate of dissolution that recites the ground or grounds for dissolution and its effective date. The secretary of state shall file the original of the certificate and serve a copy on the corporation under section 5.04.

(c) A corporation administratively dissolved continues its corporate existence but may not carry on any business except that necessary to wind up and liquidate its business and affairs under section 14.05 and notify claimants under sections 14.06 and 14.07.

(d) The administrative dissolution of a corporation does not terminate the authority of its registered agent.

§ 14.22 Reinstatement Following Administrative Dissolution.

(a) A corporation administratively dissolved under section 14.21 may apply to the secretary of state for reinstatement within two years after the effective date of dissolution. The application must:

(1) recite the name of the corporation and the effective date of its administrative dissolution;

(2) state that the ground or grounds for dissolution either did not exist or have been eliminated;

(3) state that the corporation's name satisfies the requirements of section 4.01; and

(4) contain a certificate from the [taxing authority] reciting that all taxes owed by the corporation have been paid.

(b) If the secretary of state determines that the application contains the information required by subsection (a) and that the information is correct, he shall cancel the certificate of dissolution and prepare a certificate of reinstatement that recites his determination and the effective date of reinstatement, file the original of the certificate, and serve a copy on the corporation under section 5.04.

(c) When the reinstatement is effective, it relates back to and takes effect as of the effective date of the administrative dissolution and the corporation resumes carrying on its business as if the administrative dissolution had never occurred.

§ 14.23 Appeal From Denial of Reinstatement.

(a) If the secretary of state denies a corporation's application for reinstatement following administrative dissolution, he shall serve the corporation under section 5.04 with a written notice that explains the reason or reasons for denial.

(b) The corporation may appeal the denial of reinstatement to the [name or describe] court within 30 days after service of the notice of denial is perfected. The corporation appeals by petitioning the court to set aside the dissolution and attaching to the petition copies of the secretary of state's certificate of dissolution, the corporation's application for reinstatement, and the secretary of state's notice of denial.

(c) The court may summarily order the secretary of state to reinstate the dissolved corporation or may take other action the court considers appropriate.

(d) The court's final decision may be appealed as in other civil proceedings.

Subchapter C. Judicial Dissolution

§ 14.30 Grounds for Judicial Dissolution.

The [name or describe court or courts] may dissolve a corporation:

(1) in a proceeding by the attorney general if it is established that:

(i) the corporation obtained its articles of incorporation through fraud; or

(ii) the corporation has continued to exceed or abuse the authority conferred upon it by law;

(2) in a proceeding by a shareholder if it is established that:

(i) the directors are deadlocked in the management of the corporate affairs, the shareholders are unable to break the deadlock, and irreparable injury to the corporation is threatened or being suffered, or the business and affairs of the corporation can no longer be conducted to the advantage of the shareholders generally, because of the deadlock;

(ii) the directors or those in control of the corporation have acted, are acting, or will act in a manner that is illegal, oppressive, or fraudulent;

(iii) the shareholders are deadlocked in voting power and have failed, for a period that includes at least two consecutive annual meeting dates, to elect successors to directors whose terms have expired; or

(iv) the corporate assets are being misapplied or wasted;

(3) in a proceeding by a creditor if it is established that:

(i) the creditor's claim has been reduced to judgment, the execution on the judgment returned unsatisfied, and the corporation is insolvent;

(ii) the corporation has admitted in writing that the creditor's claim is due and owing and the corporation is insolvent; or

(4) in a proceeding by the corporation to have its voluntary dissolution continued under court supervision.

§ 14.31 Procedure for Judicial Dissolution.

(a) Venue for a proceeding by the attorney general to dissolve a corporation lies in [name the county or counties]. Venue for a proceeding brought by any other party named in section 14.30 lies in the county where a corporation's principal office (or, if none in this state, its registered office) is or was last located.

(b) It is not necessary to make shareholders parties to a proceeding to dissolve a corporation unless relief is sought against them individually.

(c) A court in a proceeding brought to dissolve a corporation may issue injunctions, appoint a receiver or custodian pendente lite with all powers and duties the court directs, take other action required to preserve the corporate assets wherever located, and carry on the business of the corporation until a full hearing can be held.

§ 14.32 Receivership or Custodianship.

(a) A court in a judicial proceeding brought to dissolve a corporation may appoint one or more receivers to wind up and liquidate, or one or more custodians to manage, the business and affairs of the corporation. The court shall hold a hearing, after notifying all parties to the proceeding and any interested persons designated by the court, before appointing a receiver or custodian. The court appointing a receiver or custodian has exclusive jurisdiction over the corporation and all its property wherever located.

(b) The court may appoint an individual or a domestic or foreign corporation (authorized to transact business in this state) as a receiver or custodian. The court may require the receiver or custodian to post bond, with or without sureties, in an amount the court directs.

(c) The court shall describe the powers and duties of the receiver or custodian in its appointing order, which may be amended from time to time. Among other powers:

(1) the receiver (i) may dispose of all or any part of the assets of the corporation wherever located, at a public or private sale, if authorized by the court; and (ii) may sue and defend in his own name as receiver of the corporation in all courts of this state;

(2) the custodian may exercise all of the powers of the corporation, through or in place of its board of directors or officer, to the extent necessary to manage the affairs of the corporation in the best interests of its shareholders and creditors.

(d) The court during a receivership may redesignate the receiver a custodian, and during a custodianship may redesignate the custodian a receiver, if doing so is in the best interests of the corporation, its shareholders, and creditors.

(e) The court from time to time during the receivership or custodianship may order compensation paid and expense disbursements or reimbursements made to the receiver or custodian and his counsel from the assets of the corporation or proceeds from the sale of the assets.

§ 14.33 Decree of Dissolution.

(a) If after a hearing the court determines that one or more grounds for judicial dissolution described in section 14.30 exist, it may enter a decree dissolving the corporation and specifying the effective date of the dissolution, and the clerk of the court shall deliver a certified copy of the decree to the secretary of state, who shall file it.

(b) After entering the decree of dissolution, the court shall direct the winding up and liquidation of the corporation's business and affairs in accordance with section 14.05 and the notification of claimants in accordance with sections 14.06 and 14.07.

Subchapter D. Miscellaneous

§ 14.40 Deposit With State Treasurer.

Assets of a dissolved corporation that should be transferred to a creditor, claimant, or shareholder of the corporation who cannot be found or who is not competent to receive them shall be reduced to cash and deposited with the state treasurer or other appropriate state official for safekeeping. When the creditor, claimant, or shareholder furnishes satisfactory proof of entitlement to the amount deposited, the state treasurer or other appropriate state official shall pay him or his representative that amount.

CHAPTER 15. Foreign Corporations

Subchapter A. Certificate of Authority

§ 15.01 Authority to Transact Business Required.

(a) A foreign corporation may not transact business in this state until it obtains a certificate of authority from the secretary of state.

(b) The following activities, among others, do not constitute transacting business within the meaning of subsection (a):

(1) maintaining, defending, or settling any proceeding;

(2) holding meetings of the board of directors or shareholders or carrying on other activities concerning internal corporate affairs;

(3) maintaining bank accounts;

(4) maintaining offices or agencies for the transfer, exchange, and registration of the corporation's own securities or maintaining trust-

ees or depositaries with respect to those securities;

(5) selling through independent contractors;

(6) soliciting or obtaining orders, whether by mail or through employees or agents or otherwise, if the orders require acceptance outside this state before they become contracts;

(7) creating or acquiring indebtedness, mortgages, and security interests in real or personal property;

(8) securing or collecting debts or enforcing mortgages and security interests in property securing the debts;

(9) owning, without more, real or personal property;

(10) conducting an isolated transaction that is completed within 30 days and that is not one in the course of repeated transactions of a like nature;

(11) transacting business in interstate commerce.

(c) The list of activities in subsection (b) is not exhaustive.

§ 15.02 Consequences of Transacting Business Without Authority.

(a) A foreign corporation transacting business in this state without a certificate of authority may not maintain a proceeding in any court in this state until it obtains a certificate of authority.

(b) The successor to a foreign corporation that transacted business in this state without a certificate of authority and the assignee of a cause of action arising out of that business may not maintain a proceeding based on that cause of action in any court in this state until the foreign corporation or its successor obtains a certificate of authority.

(c) A court may stay a proceeding commenced by a foreign corporation, its successor, or assignee until it determines whether the foreign corporation or its successor requires a certificate of authority. If it so determines the court may further stay the proceeding until the foreign corporation or its successor obtains the certificate.

(d) A foreign corporation is liable for a civil penalty of $_____ for each day, but not to exceed a total of $___ for each year, it transacts business in this state without a certificate of authority. The attorney general may collect all penalties due under this subsection.

(e) Notwithstanding subsections (a) and (b), the failure of a foreign corporation to obtain a certificate of authority does not impair the validity of its corporate acts or prevent it from defending any proceeding in this state.

§ 15.03 Application for Certificate of Authority.

(a) A foreign corporation may apply for a certificate of authority to transact business in this state by delivering an application to the secretary of state for filing. The application must set forth:

(1) the name of the foreign corporation or, if its name is unavailable for use in this state, a corporate name that satisfies the requirements of section 15.06;

(2) the name of the state or country under whose law it is incorporated;

(3) its date of incorporation and period of duration;

(4) the street address of its principal office;

(5) the address of its registered office in this state and the name of its registered agent at that office; and

(6) the names and usual business addresses of its current directors and officer.

(b) The foreign corporation shall deliver with the completed application a certificate of existence (or a document of similar import) duly authenticated by the secretary of state or other official having custody of corporate records in the state or country under whose law it is incorporated.

§ 15.04 Amended Certificate of Authority.

(a) A foreign corporation authorized to transact business in this state must obtain an amended certificate of authority from the secretary of state if it changes:

(1) its corporate name;

(2) the period of its duration; or

(3) the state or country of its incorporation.

(b) The requirements of section 15.03 for obtaining an original certificate of authority apply to obtaining an amended certificate under this section.

§ 15.05 Effect of Certificate of Authority.

(a) A certificate of authority authorizes the foreign corporation to which it is issued to transact business in this state subject, however, to the right of the state to revoke the certificate as provided in this Act.

(b) A foreign corporation with a valid certificate of authority has the same but no greater rights and has the same but no greater privileges as, and except as otherwise provided by this Act is subject to the same duties, restrictions, penalties, and liabilities now or later imposed on, a domestic corporation of like character.

(c) This Act does not authorize this state to regulate the organization or internal affairs of a foreign corporation authorized to transact business in this state.

§ 15.06 Corporate Name of Foreign Corporation.

(a) If the corporate name of a foreign corporation does not satisfy the requirements of section 4.01, the foreign corporation to obtain or maintain a certificate of authority to transact business in this state:

(1) may add the word "corporation," "incorporated," "company," or "limited," or the ab-breviation "corp.," "inc.," "co.," or "ltd.," to its corporate name for use in this state; or

(2) may use a fictitious name to transact business in this state if its real name is unavailable and it delivers to the secretary of state for filing a copy of the resolution of its board of directors, certified by its secretary, adopting the fictitious name.

(b) Except as authorized by subsections (c) and (d), the corporate name (including a fictitious name) of a foreign corporation must be distinguishable upon the records of the secretary of state from:

(1) the corporate name of a corporation incorporated or authorized to transact business in this state;

(2) a corporate name reserved or registered under section 4.02 or 4.03;

(3) the fictitious name of another foreign corporation authorized to transact business in this state; and

(4) the corporate name of a not-for-profit corporation incorporated or authorized to transact business in this state.

(c) A foreign corporation may apply to the secretary of state for authorization to use in this state the name of another corporation (incorporated or authorized to transact business in this state) that is not distinguishable upon his records from the name applied for. The secretary of state shall authorize use of the name applied for if:

(1) the other corporation consents to the use in writing and submits an undertaking in form satisfactory to the secretary of state to change its name to a name that is distinguishable upon the records of the secretary of state from the name of the applying corporation; or

(2) the applicant delivers to the secretary of state a certified copy of a final judgment of a court of competent jurisdiction establishing the applicant's right to use the name applied for in this state.

(d) A foreign corporation may use in this state the name (including the fictitious name) of another domestic or foreign corporation that is used in this state if the other corporation is incorporated or authorized to transact business in this state and the foreign corporation;

(1) has merged with the other corporation;

(2) has been formed by reorganization of the other corporation; or

(3) has acquired all or substantially all of the assets, including the corporate name, of the other corporation.

(e) If a foreign corporation authorized to transact business in this state changes its corporate name to one that does not satisfy the requirements of section 4.01, it may not transact business in this state under the changed name until it adopts a name satisfying the requirements of section 4.01 and obtains an amended certificate of authority under section 15.04.

§ 15.07 Registered Office and Registered Agent of Foreign Corporation.

Each foreign corporation authorized to transact business in this state must continuously maintain in this state:

(1) a registered office that may be the same as any of its places of business; and

(2) a registered agent, who may be:

(i) an individual who resides in this state and whose business office is identical with the registered office;

(ii) a domestic corporation or not-for-profit domestic corporation whose business office is identical with the registered office; or

(iii) a foreign corporation or foreign not-for-profit corporation authorized to transact business in this state whose business office is identical with the registered office.

§ 15.08 Change of Registered Office or Registered Agent of Foreign Corporation.

(a) A foreign corporation authorized to transact business in this state may change its registered office or registered agent by delivering to the secretary of state for filing a statement of change that sets forth:

(1) its name;

(2) the street address of its current registered office;

(3) if the current registered office is to be changed, the street address of its new registered office;

(4) the name of its current registered agent;

(5) if the current registered agent is to be changed, the name of its new registered agent and the new agent's written consent (either on the statement or attached to it) to the appointment; and

(6) that after the change or changes are made, the street addresses of its registered office and the business office of its registered agent will be identical.

(b) If a registered agent changes the street address of his business office, he may change the street address of the registered office of any foreign corporation for which he is the registered agent by notifying the corporation in writing of the change and signing (either manually or in facsimile) and delivering to the secretary of state for filing a statement of change that complies with the requirements of subsection (a) and recites that the corporation has been notified of the change.

§ 15.09 Resignation of Registered Agent of Foreign Corporation.

(a) The registered agent of a foreign corporation may resign his agency appointment by signing and delivering to the secretary of state for filing the original and two exact or conformed copies of a statement of resignation. The statement of resignation may include a statement that the registered office is also discontinued.

(b) After filing the statement, the secretary of state shall attach the filing receipt to one copy and mail the copy and receipt to the registered office if not discontinued. The secretary of state shall mail the other copy to the foreign corporation at its principal office address shown in its most recent annual report.

(c) The agency appointment is terminated, and the registered office discontinued if so provided, on the 31st day after the date on which the statement was filed.

§ 15.10 Service on Foreign Corporation.

(a) The registered agent of a foreign corporation authorized to transact business in this state is the corporation's agent for service of process, notice, or demand required or permitted by law to be served on the foreign corporation.

(b) A foreign corporation may be served by registered or certified mail, return receipt requested, addressed to the secretary of the foreign corporation at its principal office shown in its application for a certificate of authority or in its most recent annual report if the foreign corporation:

(1) has no registered agent or its registered agent cannot with reasonable diligence be served;

(2) has withdrawn from transacting business in this state under section 15.20; or

(3) has had its certificate of authority revoked under section 15.31.

(c) Service is perfected under subsection (b) at the earliest of:

(1) the date the foreign corporation receives the mail;

(2) the date shown on the return receipt, if signed on behalf of the foreign corporation; or

(3) five days after its deposit in the United States Mail, if mailed postpaid and correctly addressed.

(d) This section does not prescribe the only means, or necessarily the required means, of serving a foreign corporation.

Subchapter B. Withdrawal

§ 15.20 Withdrawal of Foreign Corporation.

(a) A foreign corporation authorized to transact business in this state may not withdraw from this state until it obtains a certificate of withdrawal from the secretary of state.

(b) A foreign corporation authorized to transact business in this state may apply for a certificate of withdrawal by delivering an application to the secretary of state for filing. The application must set forth:

(1) the name of the foreign corporation and the name of the state or country under whose law it is incorporated;

(2) that it is not transacting business in this state and that it surrenders its authority to transact business in this state;

(3) that it revokes the authority of its registered agent to accept service on its behalf and appoints the secretary of state as its agent for service of process in any proceeding based on a cause of action arising during the time it was authorized to transact business in this state;

(4) a mailing address to which the secretary of state may mail a copy of any process served on him under subdivision (3); and

(5) a commitment to notify the secretary of state in the future of any change in its mailing address.

(c) After the withdrawal of the corporation is effective, service of process on the secretary of state under this section is service on the foreign corporation. Upon receipt of process, the secretary of state shall mail a copy of the process to the foreign corporation at the mailing address set forth in its application for withdrawal.

Subchapter C. Revocation of Certificate of Authority

§ 15.30 Grounds for Revocation.

The secretary of state may commence a proceeding under section 15.31 to revoke the certificate of authority of a foreign corporation authorized to transact business in this state if:

(1) the foreign corporation does not deliver its annual report to the secretary of state within 60 days after it is due;

(2) the foreign corporation does not pay within 60 days after they are due any franchise taxes or penalties imposed by this Act or other law;

(3) the foreign corporation is without a registered agent or registered office in this state for 60 days or more;

(4) the foreign corporation does not inform the secretary of state under section 15.08 or 15.09 that its registered agent or registered office has changed, that its registered agent has resigned, or that its registered office has been discontinued within 60 days of the change, resignation, or discontinuance;

(5) an incorporator, director, officer, or agent of the foreign corporation signed a document he knew was false in any material respect with intent that the document be delivered to the secretary of state for filing;

(6) the secretary of state receives a duly authenticated certificate from the secretary of state or other official having custody of corporate records in the state or country under whose law the foreign corporation is incorporated stating that it has been dissolved or disappeared as the result of a merger.

§ 15.31 Procedure for and Effect of Revocation.

(a) If the secretary of state determines that one or more grounds exist under section 15.30 for revocation of a certificate of authority, he shall serve the foreign corporation with written notice of his determination under section 15.10.

(b) If the foreign corporation does not correct each ground for revocation or demonstrate to the reasonable satisfaction of the secretary of state that each ground determined by the secretary of state does not exist within 60 days after service of the notice is perfected under section 15.10, the secretary of state may revoke the foreign corporation's certificate of authority by signing a certificate of revocation that recites the ground or grounds for revocation and its effective date. The secretary of state shall file the original of the certificate and serve a copy on the foreign corporation under section 15.10.

(c) The authority of a foreign corporation to transact business in this state ceases on the date shown on the certificate revoking its certificate of authority.

(d) The secretary of state's revocation of a foreign corporation's certificate of authority appoints the secretary of state the foreign corporation's agent for service of process in any proceeding based on a cause of action which arose during the time the foreign corporation was authorized to transact business in this state. Service of process on the secretary of state under this subsection is service on the foreign corporation. Upon receipt of process, the secretary of state shall mail a copy of the process to the secretary of the foreign corporation at its principal office shown in its most recent annual report or in any subsequent communication received from the corporation stating the current mailing address of its principal office, or, if none are on file, in its application for a certificate of authority.

(e) Revocation of a foreign corporation's certificate of authority does not terminate the authority of the registered agent of the corporation.

§ 15.32 Appeal From Revocation.

(a) A foreign corporation may appeal the secretary of state's revocation of its certificate of authority to the [name or describe] court within 30 days after service of the certificate of revocation is perfected under section 15.10. The foreign corporation appeals by petitioning the court to set aside the revocation and attaching to the petition copies of its cerificate of authority and the secretary of state's certificate of revocation.

(b) The court may summarily order the secretary of state to reinstate the certificate of authority or may take any other action the court considers appropriate.

(c) The court's final decision may be appealed as in other civil proceedings.

CHAPTER 16. Records and Reports

Subchapter A. Records

§ 16.01 Corporate Records.

(a) A corporation shall keep as permanent records minutes of all meetings of its shareholders and board of directors, a record of all actions taken by the shareholders or board of directors without a meeting, and a record of all actions taken by a committee of the board of directors in actions taken by a committee of the board of directors in place of the board of directors on behalf of the corporation.

(b) A corporation shall maintain appropriate accounting records.

(c) A corporation or its agent shall maintain a record of its shareholders, in a form that permits preparation of a list of the names and addresses of all shareholders, in alphabetical order by class of shares showing the number and class of shares held by each.

(d) A corporation shall maintain its records in written form or in another form capable of conversion into written form within a reasonable time.

(e) A corporation shall keep a copy of the following records at its principal office:

    (1) its articles or restated articles of incorporation and all amendments to them currently in effect;

    (2) its bylaws or restated bylaws and all amendment to them currently in effect;

    (3) resolution adopted by its board of directors creating one or more classes or series of shares, and fixing their relative rights, preferences, and limitations, if shares issued pursuant to those resolutions are outstanding;

    (4) the minutes of all shareholders' meetings, and records of all action taken by shareholders without a meeting, for the past three years;

    (5) all written communications to shareholders generally within the past three years, including the financial statements furnished for the past three years under section 16.20;

    (6) a list of the names and business addresses of its current directors and officers; and

    (7) its most recent annual report delivered to the secretary of state under section 16.22.

§ 16.02 Inspection of Records by Shareholders.

(a) Subject to section 16.03(c), a shareholder of a corporation is entitled to inspect and copy, during regular business hours at the corporation's principal office, any of the records of the corporation described in section 16.01(e) if he gives the corporation written notice of his demand at least five business days before the date on which he wishes to inspect and copy.

(b) A shareholder of a corporation is entitled to inspect and copy, during regular business hours at a reasonable location specified by the corporation, any of the following records of the corporation if the shareholder meets the requirements of subsection (c) and gives the corporation written notice of his demand at least five business days before the date on which he wishes to inspect and copy:

    (1) excerpts from minutes of any meeting of the board of directors, records of any action of a committee of the board of directors while acting in place of the board of directors on behalf of the corporation, minutes of any meeting of the shareholders, and records of action taken by the shareholders or board of directors without a meeting, to the extent not subject to inspection under section 16.02(a);

    (2) accounting records of the corporation; and

    (3) the record of shareholders.

(c) A shareholder may inspect and copy the records identified in subsection (b) only if:

    (1) his demand is made in good faith and for a proper purpose;

    (2) he describes with reasonable particularity his purpose and the records he desires to inspect; and

    (3) the records are directly connected with his purpose.

(d) The right of inspection granted by this section may not be abolished or limited by a corporation's articles of incorporation or bylaws.

(e) This section does not affect:

    (1) the right of a shareholder to inspect records under section 7.20 or, if the shareholder is in litigation with the corporation, to the same extent as any other litigant

    (2) the power of a court, independently of this Act, to compel the production of corporate records for examination.

(f) For purposes of this section, "shareholder" includes a beneficial owner whose shares are held in a voting trust or by a nominee on his behalf.

§ 16.03 Scope of Inspection Right.

(a) A shareholder's agent or attorney has the same inspection and copying rights as the shareholder he represents.

(b) The right to copy records under section 16.02 includes, if reasonable, the right to receive copies made by photographic, xerographic, or other means.

(c) The corporation may impose a reasonable charge, covering the costs of labor and material, for copies of any documents provided to the shareholder. The charge may not exceed the estimated cost of production or reproduction of the records.

(d) The corporation may comply with a shareholder's demand to inspect the record of shareholders under section 16.02(b)(3) by providing him with a list of its shareholders that was compiled no earlier than the date of the shareholder's demand.

§ 16.04 Court-Ordered Inspection.

(a) If a corporation does not allow a shareholder who complies with section 16.02(a) to inspect and copy any records required by that subsection to be available for inspection, the [name or describe court] of the county where the corporation's principal office (or, if none in this state, its registered office) is located may summarily order inspection and copying of the records demanded at the corporation's expense upon application of the shareholder.

(b) If a corporation does not within a reasonable time allow a shareholder to inspect and copy any other record, the shareholder who complies with section 16.02(b) and (c) may apply to the [name or describe court] in the county where the corporation's principal office (or, if none in this state, its registered office) is located for an order to permit inspection and copying of the records demanded. The court shall dispose of an application under this subsection on an expedited basis.

(c) If the court orders inspection and copying of the records demanded, it shall also order the corporation to pay the shareholder's costs (including reasonable counsel fees) incurred to obtain the order unless the corporation proves that it refused inspection in good faith because it had a reasonable basis for doubt about the right of the shareholder to inspect the records demanded.

(d) If the court orders inspection and copying of the records demanded, it may impose reasonable restrictions on the use or distribution of the records by the demanding shareholder.

Subchapter B. Reports

§ 16.20 Financial Statements for Shareholders.

(a) A corporation shall furnish its shareholders annual financial statements, which may be consolidated or combined statements of the corporation and one or more of its subsidiaries, as appropriate, that include a balance sheet as of the end of the fiscal year, an income statement for that year, and a statement of changes in shareholders' equity for the year unless that information appears elsewhere in the financial statements. If financial statements are prepared for the corporation on the basis of generally accepted accounting principles, the annual financial statements must also be prepared on that basis.

(b) If the annual financial statements are reported upon by a public accountant, his report must accompany them. If not, the statements must be accompanied by a statement of the president or the person responsible for the corporation's accounting records:

    (1) stating his reasonable belief whether the statements were prepared on the basis of generally accepted accounting principles and, if not, describing the basis of preparation; and

    (2) describing any respects in which the statements were not prepared on a basis of accounting consistent with the statements prepared for the preceding year.

(c) A corporation shall mail the annual financial statements to each shareholder within 120 days after the close of each fiscal year. Thereafter, on written request from a shareholder who was not mailed the statements, the corporation shall mail him the latest financial statements.

§ 16.21 Other Reports to Shareholders.

(a) If a corporation indemnifies or advances expenses to a director under section 8.51, 8.52, 8.53, or 8.54 in connection with a proceeding by or in the right of the corporation, the corporation shall report the indemnification or advance in writing to the shareholders' meeting.

(b) If a corporation issues or authorizes the issuance of shares for promissory notes or for promises to render services in the future, the corporation shall report in writing to the shareholders the number of shares authorized or issued, and the consideration received by the corporation, with or before the notice of the next shareholders' meeting.

§ 16.22 Annual Report for Secretary of State.

(a) Each domestic corporation, and each foreign corporation authorized to transact business in this state, shall deliver to the secretary of state for filing an annual report that sets forth:

    (1) the name of the corporation and the state or country under whose law it is incorporated;

    (2) the address of its registered office and the name of its registered agent at that office in this state;

    (3) the address of its principal office;

(4) the names and business addresses of its directors and principal officers;

(5) a brief description of the nature of its business;

(6) the total number of authorized shares, itemized by class and series, if any, within each class; and

(7) the total number of issued and outstanding shares itemized by class and series, if any, within each class.

(b) Information in the annual report must be current as of the date the annual report is executed on behalf of the corporation.

(c) The first annual report must be delivered to the secretary of state between January 1 and April 1 of the year following the calendar year in which a domestic corporation was incorporated or a foreign corporation was authorized to transact business. Subsequent annual reports must be delivered to the secretary of state between January 1 and April 1 of the following calendar years.

(d) If an annual report does not contain the information required by this section, the secretary of state shall promptly notify the reporting domestic or foreign corporation in writing and return the report to it for correction. If the report is corrected to contain the information required by this section and delivered to the secretary of state within 30 days after the effective date of notice, it is deemed to be timely filed.

CHAPTER 17.   Transition Provisions

§ 17.01   Application to Existing Domestic Corporations.

This Act applies to all domestic corporations in existence on its effective date that were incorporated under any general statute of this state providing for incorporation of corporations for profit if power to amend or repeal the statute under which the corporation was incorporated was reserved.

§ 17.02   Applications to Qualified Foreign Corporations.

A foreign corporation authorized to transact business in this state on the effective date of this Act is subject to this Act but is not required to obtain a new certificate of authority to transact business under this Act.

§ 17.03   Saving Provisions.

(a) Except as provided in subsection(b), the repeal of a statute by this Act does not affect:

(1) the operation of the statute or any action taken under it before its repeal;

(2) any ratification, right, remedy, privilege, obligation, or liability acquired, accrued, or incurred under the statute before its repeal;

(3) any violation of the statute, or any penalty, forfeiture, or punishment incurred because of the violation, before its repeal;

(4) any proceeding, reorganization, or dissolution commenced under the statute before its repeal, and the proceeding, reorganization, or dissolution may be completed in accordance with the statute as if it had not been repealed.

(b) If a penalty or punishment imposed for violation of a statute repealed by this Act is reduced by this Act, the penalty or punishment if not already imposed shall be imposed in accordance with this Act.

§ 17.04   Severability.

If any provision of this Act or its application to any person or circumstance is held invalid by a court of competent jurisdiction, the invalidity does not affect other provisions or applications of the Act that can be given effect without the invalid provision or application, and to this end the provisions of the Act are severable.

§ 17.05   Repeal.

The following laws and parts of laws are repealed: [to be inserted].

§ 17.06   Effective Date.

This Act takes effect _____ .

Supplement to Appendix F   Cross-Reference Tables

1969 Model Business Corporation Act as amended to 1984 Revised Model Business Corporation Act as amended

1969	1984	1969	1984	1969	1984	1969	1984
§ 1	§ 1.01	§ 38	§ 8.05, 8.10	§ 77	§ 11.07	§ 114	§ 15.08, 15.09
2	1.40	39	8.08	78	12.01	115	15.10
3	3.01	40	8.24	79	12.02	116	None
4	3.02	41	8.60-8.63	80	13.02, 13.03	117	None
5	8.50-8.58	42	8.25	81	13.02,	118	15.04
6	6.31	43	8.20, 8.22,		13.20–13.31	119	15.20
7	3.04		8.23	82	14.01	120	Ch. 1
8	4.01	44	8.21	83	None	121	15.30, 15.31
9	4.02	45	6.40	84	14.02	122	15.31
10	4.03	46	None	85	None	123	17.02
11	403	47	8.32	86	None	124	15.02
12	5.01	48	8.33	87	None, see	125	16.22
13	5.02, 5.03	49	7.40		14.05, 14.06	126	16.22
14	5.04	50	8.40, 8.41	88	None, see	127	None
15	6.01, 6.03	51	8.43, 8.44		14.04	128	1.22
16	6.02	52	16.01–16.04	89	None, see	129	1.22
17	6.20	53	2.01		14.04	130	None
18	6.03, 6.21	54	2.02	90	Ch. 1	131	None
19	6.21	55	Ch. 1	91	None, see	132	None
20	6.24	56	2.03		14.04	133	None
21	Repealed	57	2.05	92	14.03	134	None
22	6.28	58	10.01	93	Ch. 1	135	None
23	6.25, 6.26	59	10.02, 10.03,	94	14.30, 14.31	136	1.29
24	6.04		10.05, 10.07	95	14.20	137	None
25	6.22	60	7.26, 10.04	96	14.31	138	None
26	6.30	61	10.06	97	14.30, 14.31	139	1.30
26A	6.30	62	10.06	98	14.30, 14.31	140	1.26
27	2.06, 10.20,	63	1.23, 10.09	99	14.31, 14.32	141	1.27
	10.22	64	10.07	100	14.33	142	1.21
27A	2.07, 3.03	65	10.08	101	14.32	143	7.27, 10.21
28	7.01, 7.02	66	None	102	14.33	144	7.06, 8.23
29	7.05	67	Repealed	103	14.33	145	7.04
30	7.07	68	Repealed	104	14.40	146	2.04
31	7.20	69	Repealed	105	14.06, 14.07	147	17.01
32	7.25, 7.26,	70	Repealed	106	15.01	148	None
	10.21	71	11.01	107	15.05	149	1.02
33	7.21, 7.24, 7.28	72	None	108	15.06	150	17.03
34	7.30, 7.31	72A	11.02	109	15.06	151	17.04
35	8.01, 8.11,	73	11.03	110	15.03	152	17.05
	8.30	74	11.05	111	Ch. 1		
36	8.03, 8.05	75	11.04	112	15.05		
37	8.06	76	11.06	113	15.07		

1984 Revised Model Business Corporation Act as amended to 1969 Model Business Corporation Act as amended

1984	1969	1984	1969	1984	1969	1984	1969
§ 1.01	§ 1	§ 6.40	§ 45	§ 8.51	§ 5(b), (c), (h) part	§14.02	§ 84(a)–(c)
1.02	149	7.01	28 ¶¶ 1,2	8.52	5(d)(1)	14.03	83 ¶ 2, 84(d), 92, 93
1.20	New	7.02	28 ¶ 3	8.53	5(f)	14.04	88–91
1.21	142	7.03	New	8.54	5(d)(2)	14.05	87 ¶ 6
1.22	128, 129	7.04	145	8.55	5(e)	14.06	87(a)
1.23	New	7.05	29	8.56	5(i)	14.07	105
1.24	New	7.06	144	8.57	5(k)	14.20	95
1.25	New	7.07	30	8.58	5(g)	14.21	New
1.26	140	7.20	31	8.60–8.63	41	14.22	New
1.27	141	7.21	33 ¶¶ 1,2,9	10.01	58	14.23	New
1.28	New	7.22	33 ¶ 3	10.02	59(a) sent. 3	14.30	94(b), (c), 97(a)–(d)
1.29	136	7.23	2(f)	10.03	59(a) sent. 1, (b), (c)	14.31	96 sent. 1, 97 ¶¶ 2, 3, 98 ¶ 1
1.30	139	7.24	33 ¶¶ 5–8	10.04	60		
1.40	2	7.25	32	10.05	59(a) sent. 2	14.32	98 ¶¶ 2–4, 99, 101
1.41	New	7.26	New	10.06	61, 62		
1.42	New	7.27	143	10.07	64	14.33	100, 102, 153
2.01	53	7.28	33 ¶ 4	10.08	65	14.40	104
2.02	54	7.30	34 ¶ 1	10.09	63	15.01	106
2.03	55, 56	7.31	34 ¶ 2	10.20	27 sent. 2	15.02	124
2.04	146	7.40	49	10.21	New	15.03	110,111
2.05	57	8.01	35 ¶ 1 part	10.22	New	15.04	118
2.06	27 sents. 1, 3	8.02	35 ¶ 1 part	11.01	71	15.05	107, 112
2.07	27A part	8.03	36 part	11.02	72A	15.06	107, 112
3.01	3	8.04	New	11.03	73	15.07	113
3.02	4	8.05	36 part, 38 part	11.04	75 ¶¶ 1, 2	15.08	114 ¶¶ 1, 2, 4
3.03	27A part	8.06	37	11.05	74, 75 ¶¶ 3–5	15.09	114 ¶ 3
3.04	7	8.07	New	11.06	76	15.10	115
4.01	8	8.08	39	11.07	77	15.20	119, 120
4.02	9	8.09	New	12.01	78	15.30	121 ¶ 1
4.03	10, 11	8.10	38 part	12.02	79	15.31	121 ¶ 2, 122
5.01	12	8.11	35 ¶ 1 part	13.01	81(a)	15.32	140, ¶ 2
5.02	13 part	8.20	43 ¶ ¶ 1,3	13.02	80(a), (c), (d)	16.01	52 ¶ 1
5.03	13 part	8.21	44	13.03	80(b)	16.02	52 ¶ 2
5.04	14	8.22	43 ¶ 2 part	13.20	81(b), (d) sent. 2	16.03	New
6.01	15	8.23	144, 43 ¶ 2 part	13.21	81(c)	16.04	52 ¶ 3
6.02	16	8.24	40	13.22	81(d) sents. 1, 3, 4	16.20	52 ¶ 4
6.03	New	8.25	42	13.23	81(e) sent. 1	16.21	New
6.04	24	8.30	35 ¶ 2	13.24	81(e) sents. 2, 3	16.22	125, 126
6.20	17	8.32	47	13.25	81(f)(3)	17.01	147
6.21	18(a), 19	8.33	48	13.26	81(f)(1), (2)	17.02	123
6.22	25	8.40	50 ¶ 1	13.27	81(j)(1)	17.03	150
6.23	18(b)	8.41	50 ¶ 2	13.28	81(g), (j)(2)	17.04	151
6.24	20	8.42	New	13.30	81(j)(3), (h)	17.05	153
6.25	23¶¶ 1–3	8.43	51 part	13.31	81(i)	17.06	New
6.26	23 ¶ 5	8.44	51 part	14.01	82		
6.27	New	8.50	5(a), (b)(3), (h)				
6.28	22						
6.30	26, 26A						
6.31	6						

Table of Cases

Table of Statutes

Index